PRAISE FOR *The Bedford Anthology of American Literature*

"In a number of respects, this anthology is exceptional. *The Bedford Anthology* has two major advantages: a realistic balance of texts that acknowledges the frequent practice of assigning novels and autobiographies in full, and an incredibly fruitful, focused approach guided by questions of print culture and its attendant questions of authorship, circulation, and reception of literary texts."

– Matt Cohen
Duke University

"Unlike many other anthologies, I can see myself teaching almost everything included here. Not only is the anthology representative, but it also serves to focus on some of the chief issues in American studies today."

– Rosemary Fithian Guruswamy
Radford University

"Susan Belasco and Linck Johnson have done a fine job conceptualizing a kind of American literature anthology not currently available. Their focused attention to reading, writing, and print culture will remind students (and all of us) of the significance of literature as a way of knowing. As I read I also considered whether the introductory American survey I teach would need significant revision if I were to use an anthology like this one. I found I could teach *my* course with *their* book."

– Pattie Cowell
Colorado State University

"I admire this anthology a great deal. But what recommends it, finally, is not simply its economies but the acuity of its choices, the unobtrusive depth of its learning, and its pedagogical and historical imaginativeness."

– Richard Millington
Smith College

"My overall reaction to this anthology is that it is one of the most thoughtfully organized and written anthologies of American literature that I have seen in recent years. Rich in visual materials, which are especially effective for an undergraduate audience, it is equally fulfilling in the content and choice of selections."

– Sharon M. Harris
University of Connecticut

"In sum, this text offers the best view of the cultural mosaic that is 'American Literature' that I have ever seen. I love the clear organization, and the various helpful apparati, especially the historical contextualizations of a work's particular 'place and time.'"

– Thomas Gannon
University of Nebraska

"Its selections are judiciously made, its introductions sound and focused on the real-world concerns of authorship in American history, its contextual material diverse, enriching, and to-the-point. I think that instructors who want for their undergraduate students a manageable anthology with an essential and diverse selection of texts, engaging biographical introductions, and contexts that ground the literature practically in the world of reading, publishing, and authorship will find *The Bedford Anthology of American Literature* a very attractive choice."

– Robert D. Habich
Ball State University

"The strongest part of this anthology is its obvious desire to be a teaching tool with a more contemporary edge. Anything that offers these primary texts with a more modern gloss such as the sections entitled 'Through a Modern Lens' is terrific."

– Paul Gutjahr
Indiana University

"The introductions are acute and generous without being overwhelming; they suggest depth without going into detail that might be stultifying to the new student of American literature."

– Daneen Wardrop
Western Michigan State University

The Bedford Anthology of American Literature

VOLUME ONE
Beginnings to 1865

The Bedford Anthology of American Literature

VOLUME ONE
Beginnings to 1865

Susan Belasco
University of Nebraska, Lincoln

Linck Johnson
Colgate University

Bedford / St. Martin's
BOSTON · NEW YORK

For Bedford / St. Martin's
EXECUTIVE EDITOR: Stephen A. Scipione
SENIOR DEVELOPMENTAL EDITOR: Maura Shea
SENIOR PRODUCTION EDITOR: Lori Chong Roncka
PRODUCTION SUPERVISOR: Jennifer L. Wetzel
EXECUTIVE MARKETING MANAGER: Jenna Bookin Barry
MARKETING MANAGER: Adrienne Petsick
ASSOCIATE DEVELOPMENTAL EDITOR: Kaitlin Hannon
EDITORIAL ASSISTANT: Abby Bielagus
PRODUCTION ASSISTANTS: Kristen Merrill and Amy Derjue
COPYEDITOR: Mary Lou Wilshaw-Watts
TEXT DESIGN: Judith Arisman, Arisman Design Studio
COVER DESIGN: Donna Lee Dennison
COVER ART: Cator Print 178. *View of Baltimore, from Federal Hill (1850).* Artist: Lane, Fitz Hugh, 1804-1865. Other Contributor: Sarony & Major. Pict 27. 14" × 18.10". Courtesy of the Enoch Pratt Free Library, Central Library/State Library Resource Center, Baltimore, MD.
COMPOSITION: Stratford Publishing Services, Inc.
PRINTING AND BINDING: Quebecor World Taunton

PRESIDENT: Joan E. Feinberg
EDITORIAL DIRECTOR: Denise B. Wydra
EDITOR IN CHIEF: Karen S. Henry
DIRECTOR OF MARKETING: Karen Melton Soeltz
DIRECTOR OF EDITING, DESIGN, AND PRODUCTION: Marcia Cohen
MANAGING EDITOR: Elizabeth M. Schaaf

Library of Congress Control Number: 2006921308

Manufactured in the United States of America.

1 0 9 8 7 6
f e d c b a

For information, write: Bedford / St. Martin's, 75 Arlington Street, Boston, MA 02116 (617-399-4000)

ISBN-10: 0-312-41207-X
ISBN-13: 978-0-312-41207-4

Acknowledgments and copyrights are continued at the back of the book on pages 1390–95, which constitute an extension of the copyright page. It is a violation of the law to reproduce these selections by any means whatsoever without the written permission of the copyright holder.

For Max Johnson and Stephen Jenkins

Preface

The Bedford Anthology of American Literature is designed to meet the challenge of teaching courses that cover American literature from its beginnings to the present day. That challenge has grown even more daunting during the last three decades, as the canon has expanded dramatically. We have been studying, teaching, and writing about American literature for over thirty years, yet like all teachers we grapple with questions about the selection, organization, and presentation of material, especially in relation to a changing student population. Indeed, even as instructors have recognized the claims of a growing number of writers and kinds of writings for a place on our syllabi, college students have become increasingly diverse in their backgrounds, experiences, and preparation for literary study. At the same time, rapid changes in technology have profoundly shaped students' understanding of language and communication, as well as their responses to both texts and textbooks.

The Bedford Anthology of American Literature takes a new approach to anthologizing American literature. The editors of any anthology inevitably build upon the work of earlier editors, and we have learned much from our predecessors and colleagues. Seeing anthologies of American literature become thicker and heavier, or expand into multiple volumes, however, we are concerned by the impact of that development on instructors and students alike. How, in the limited span of a semester or a quarter, can an instructor hope to cover the ever-growing list of writers and works or assign more than a relatively small number of the selections in most anthologies? And how do students respond when they find themselves skipping over large portions of an expensive anthology? Moreover, although we are deeply committed to anthologies as the most effective medium for representing the full range of American literature, we know from direct experience and the comments of other instructors that students find it awkward and unappealing to read certain kinds of works, especially novels and other extended prose narratives, in the somewhat cumbersome format of an anthology.

The Bedford Anthology of American Literature represents an effort to preserve the strengths of traditional anthologies while responding to changes in both the canon and in teaching methods that have emerged during the last thirty years. At every stage of our work on this anthology, we have been guided by the needs of instructors and their students. We have drawn on our extensive experiences at a wide range of institutions, and we have communicated with hundreds of instructors in colleges and universities across the country about how a new anthology might best meet their needs and the needs of contemporary college students. While the texts, notes, and introductions are based on current scholarship in the field, to which we are deeply indebted, *The Bedford Anthology of American Literature* is a tool for teaching and learning, and it aims at broad representation rather than comprehensive coverage. It consequently provides a rich but not unlimited range of choices to instructors facing the daunting task of creating syllabi and reading assignments of representative works from every period of American literature.

Two of the major pedagogical challenges facing teachers of the American literature survey course are engaging students in the readings and helping them understand history and context. We have, therefore, sought to bring together in an attractive format texts chosen on the basis of their literary or historical importance, their inherent interest, and their proven effectiveness in the classroom, either when studied on their own or in relation to other texts in the anthology. In addition to a core of commonly taught texts that instructors rely on, we have included rarely anthologized texts that have proven to be very successful in the classroom. We have also given some prominence to various kinds of life writings, which we view as a vital element in American literature and which we have found to be particularly attractive to students. In a further effort to stimulate student interest in and understanding of literary texts, as well as of their vital social, political, and cultural contexts, we have also incorporated features, including illustrations, that show the changing material conditions in which literary works were produced. We have thus sought to offer in reasonably compact volumes a foundation of essential texts that instructors need with a substantial amount of additional material to help them construct their own surveys of American literature. For students, our anthology offers a variety of ways to read and think about American literature and, we hope, fosters a greater understanding and appreciation of it.

Features of *The Bedford Anthology of American Literature*, Volumes One and Two

A Teachable Collection of Literary Works. The selection of writers and works has been shaped by the new understandings of and approaches to American literature that have emerged during the last three decades. The selections consequently reflect the rich diversity of American literature, especially in terms of gender, race, and ethnicity. At the same time, the selection of writers and texts has been guided by what is actually taught in survey courses of American literature, based on extensive analysis of syllabi and reviews by over five hundred instructors nationwide.

An Apparatus Designed and Written for Students. We have sought to make the introductory materials in the anthology lively and readable, while providing other features designed to engage the interest of students and enhance their appreciation and understanding of the texts. Biographical introductions highlight important aspects of the authors' backgrounds and experiences, while charting the course of their careers as writers. Marginal quotations, most often an appreciative observation by another writer, call attention to the characteristics or value of the author's work, and Web site references point to further information. Individual prose works and groups of poems are separately introduced in a selection headnote that provides information about the writing and publication of the works, as well as brief comments on their distinctive features or literary and historical significance. Explanatory notes are provided for each text and are designed to foster reading comprehension and assist students in understanding a work, not to provide critical commentary on the text. Indeed, we have consistently sought to provide contexts for reading texts and to raise questions designed to stimulate discussion rather than to offer interpretations of the texts.

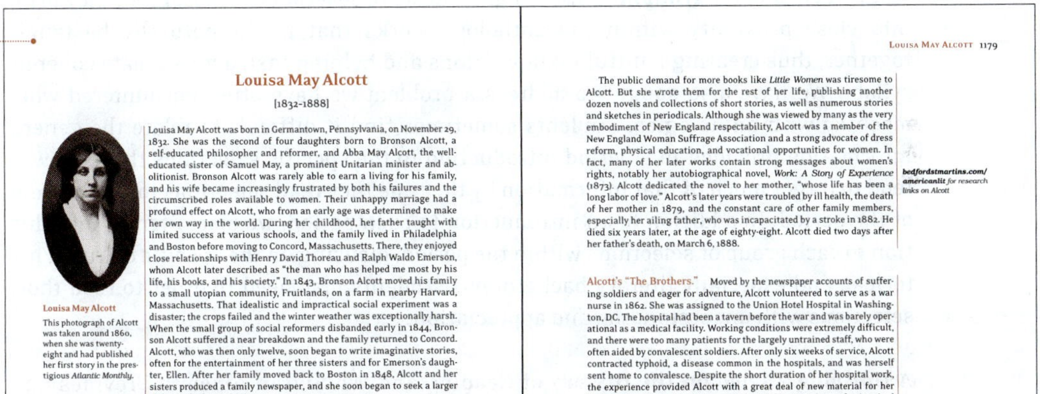

Louisa May Alcott

[1832-1888]

Louisa May Alcott was born in Germantown, Pennsylvania, on November 29, 1832. She was the second of four daughters born to Bronson Alcott, a self-educated philosopher and reformer, and Abba May Alcott, the well-educated sister of Samuel May, a prominent Unitarian minister and abolitionist. Bronson Alcott was rarely able to earn a living for his family, and his wife became increasingly frustrated by both his failures and the circumscribed roles available to women. Their unhappy marriage had a profound effect on Alcott, who from an early age was determined to make her own way in the world. During her childhood, her father taught with limited success at various schools, and the family lived in Philadelphia and Boston before moving to Concord, Massachusetts. There, they enjoyed close relationships with Henry David Thoreau and Ralph Waldo Emerson, whom Alcott later described as "the man who has helped me most by his life, his books, and his society." In 1843, Bronson Alcott moved his family to a small utopian community, Fruitlands, on a farm in nearby Harvard, Massachusetts. That idealistic and impractical social experiment was a disaster; the crops failed and the winter weather was exceptionally harsh. When the small group of social reformers disbanded early in 1844, Bronson Alcott suffered a near breakdown and the family returned to Concord. Alcott, who was then only twelve, soon began to write imaginative stories, often for the entertainment of her three sisters and for Emerson's daughter, Ellen. After her family moved back to Boston in 1848, Alcott and her sisters produced a family newspaper, and she soon began to seek a larger audience for her writings.

Louisa May Alcott
This photograph of Alcott was taken around 1860, when she was twenty-eight and had published her first story in the prestigious *Atlantic Monthly*.

Throughout her literary career, Alcott struggled with the conflict between her literary aspirations and the pressures of the marketplace. A story she had written in Concord, "The Rival Painters, a Tale of Rome," was published in a Boston family newspaper, the *Olive Branch*, in 1852. From that point on, Alcott wrote constantly, publishing a collection of fairy tales, *Flower Fables* (1854), and stories in various periodicals, including the prestigious *Atlantic Monthly*. As scholars have recently discovered, Alcott also wrote dozens of fantasies and sensational thrillers, often publishing them anonymously or under the pseudonym A. M. Barnard. Alcott's first major literary success was *Hospital Sketches* (1863), based on the letters she wrote to her family while serving as a volunteer nurse in an army hospital in Washington, D.C. Her first novel, *Moods* (1864), was an adult romance steeped in the transcendentalism of her friends in Concord, such as Emerson. Thomas Niles, a literary representative for the publishing company of Roberts Brothers, was eager to tap into the lucrative market for children's literature, and he suggested that Alcott write a book for children. *Little Women*, Alcott's most famous work, appeared in two volumes, the first in 1868 and the second in 1869. Based loosely on her family life, the book made Alcott a celebrity; it also gained her a steady income, vitally important since she was now her family's primary breadwinner.

She is a natural source of stories.
–Ralph Waldo Emerson

1178

LOUISA MAY ALCOTT 1179

The public demand for more books like *Little Women* was tiresome to Alcott. But she wrote them for the rest of her life, publishing another dozen novels and collections of short stories, as well as numerous stories and sketches in periodicals. Although she was viewed by many as the very embodiment of New England respectability, Alcott was a member of the New England Woman Suffrage Association and a strong advocate of dress reform, physical education, and vocational opportunities for women. In fact, many of her later works contain strong messages about women's rights, notably her autobiographical novel, *Work: A Story of Experience* (1873). Alcott dedicated the novel to her mother, "whose life has been a long labor of love." Alcott's later years were troubled by ill health, the death of her mother in 1879, and the constant care of other family members, especially her ailing father, who was incapacitated by a stroke in 1882. He died six years later, at the age of eighty-eight. Alcott died two days after her father's death, on March 6, 1888.

bedfordstmartins.com/americanlit *for research links on Alcott*

Alcott's "The Brothers." Moved by the newspaper accounts of suffering soldiers and eager for adventure, Alcott volunteered to serve as a war nurse in 1862. She was assigned to the Union Hotel Hospital in Washington, DC. The hospital had been a tavern before the war and was barely operational as a medical facility. Working conditions were extremely difficult, and there were too many patients for the largely untrained staff, who were often aided by convalescent soldiers. After only six weeks of service, Alcott contracted typhoid, a disease common in the hospitals, and was herself sent home to convalesce. Despite the short duration of her hospital work, the experience provided Alcott with a great deal of new material for her writing, including *Hospital Sketches* (1863). Her experience also inspired

Hospital Nursing
This photograph of a nurse and her patients was taken at a Union hospital in Nashville, Tennessee. Most of the thousands of Union and Confederate women who served as nurses during the Civil War were unpaid volunteers who also spent time cleaning and cooking for their patients.

An Emphasis on Complete Works. In choosing selections for the anthology, we have sought to include complete texts – rather than excerpts – whenever possible. In Volume One, we have included portions of extended works of nonfiction that can be effectively excerpted, including William Bradford's *Of Plimoth Plantation*, Benjamin Franklin's *Autobiography*, and Henry David Thoreau's *Walden*. But all poems are printed in their entirety, and we have selected sketches, stories, or novellas rather than excerpts from novels. Lengthy works of fiction, which we believe students find far more comfortable to read as separate texts, are not included in the anthology. While we hope that many instructors will find the selections from key writers fully adequate for their purposes, we understand that other instructors may well wish to supplement the anthology with longer works of fiction. In order to make such works available for packaging with the anthology or for independent purchase, Bedford / St. Martin's has published the Bedford College Editions, attractive (and very competitively priced) reprints of five of the most frequently taught American novels: Nathaniel Hawthorne's *The Scarlet Letter*, Harriet Beecher Stowe's *Uncle Tom's Cabin*, Herman Melville's *Benito Cereno*, Mark Twain's *Adventures of Huckleberry Finn*, and Kate Chopin's *The Awakening*.

An Organization Designed for Greater Coherence and Comprehension. The overall organization of the anthology is chronological. Volume One begins with Native American origin tales and concludes with the Civil War. Volume Two covers writers from 1865 to the present. Each volume, in turn, is divided into three **literary periods**. Within each of those periods, we have divided selections into related groups of authors or kinds of texts. Such **chapter groupings** are designed to serve several purposes. First, they bring into close proximity within the anthology works that might naturally be taught together, thus creating fruitful juxtapositions and helping instructors create coherent syllabi. We have also sought to address a problem we have often encountered when teaching with anthologies. Students sometimes find it difficult to relate the general information provided in a period introduction to the specific selections that follow or tend to forget much of that information by the time they read selections toward the end of the period. In addition to an introduction to each period, we also offer an introduction to each group of selections within the period, focusing on the specific cultural, historical, and especially literary backgrounds students may need in order to read those selections with understanding and appreciation.

A Unifying Theme on the History of Reading and Writing in America Provides Contexts for the Literature. A thematic thread – the history of reading and writing in America – is woven throughout both volumes to assist students in understanding the context of the works and to emphasize the role literature has played in the unfolding story of culture and history in what became the United States. In the period introductions, as well as in the introductions to groups of authors and texts within each period, we emphasize developments such as the growth of literacy, the expansion of the educational system, changes in the production and distribution of books, and the emergence and increasing importance of periodicals in the literary culture of the United States. We further develop that theme in our introductions to authors, in which we indicate the ways such developments shaped their writings and literary careers, as well as in our

Writing Colonial Lives

WHEN BENJAMIN FRANKLIN began writing his celebrated "autobiography" in 1771, that term was not used to identify such first-person narratives. The term was not commonly used until the early decades of the nineteenth century, and *The Autobiography of Benjamin Franklin* was not published under that title until 1868. Nonetheless, autobiography has a long history in Western culture, most often traced back to the *Confessions* of St. Augustine (354–430), the Roman Catholic bishop of Hippo in North Africa.

◄ Benjamin Franklin

The author of the *Autobiography of Benjamin Franklin*, probably the most famous self-portrait in American literature, was also frequently the subject of portraiture. This painting by George Dunlop Leslie, after the original painted in London by Mason Chamberlain in 1762, depicts Franklin as a writer and scientist. The thunderstorm raging outside the window is an allusion to his celebrated experiments with electricity. (The bells behind him are rigged to ring when lightning strikes outside.) But the books visible at the extreme left, behind the bells, and especially the manuscript and the quill pen Franklin holds were equally central to both his sense of identity and his growing fame.

335

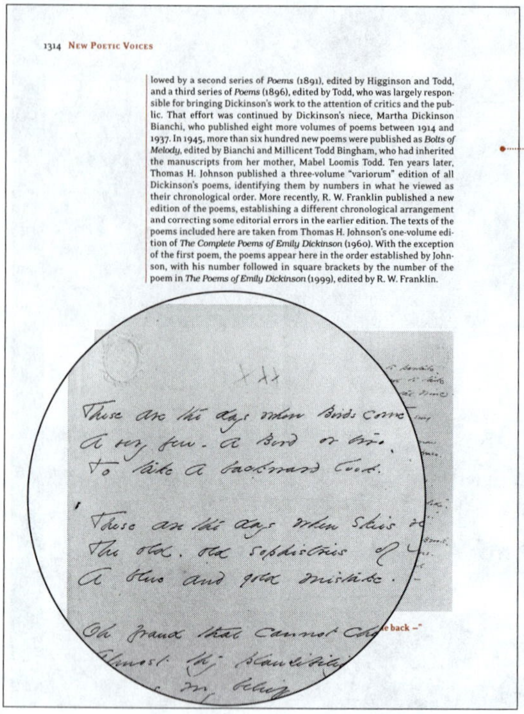
1314 New Poetic Voices

lowed by a second series of *Poems* (1891), edited by Higginson and Todd, and a third series of *Poems* (1896), edited by Todd, who was largely responsible for bringing Dickinson's work to the attention of critics and the public. That effort was continued by Dickinson's niece, Martha Dickinson Bianchi, who published eight more volumes of poems between 1914 and 1937. In 1945, more than six hundred new poems were published as *Bolts of Melody*, edited by Bianchi and Millicent Todd Bingham, who had inherited the manuscripts from her mother, Mabel Loomis Todd. Ten years later, Thomas H. Johnson published a three-volume "variorum" edition of all Dickinson's poems, identifying them by numbers in what he viewed as their chronological order. More recently, R. W. Franklin published a new edition of the poems, establishing a different chronological arrangement and correcting some editorial errors in the earlier edition. The texts of the poems included here are taken from Thomas H. Johnson's one-volume edition of *The Complete Poems of Emily Dickinson* (1960). With the exception of the first poem, the poems appear here in the order established by Johnson, with his number followed in square brackets by the number of the poem in *The Poems of Emily Dickinson* (1999), edited by R. W. Franklin.

headnotes to selections, in which we discuss the writing and initial publication of the works. The history of reading and writing is further delineated in illustrations ranging from **manuscript pages**, including the opening of Bradford's *Of Plimoth Plantation* and a poem by Emily Dickinson, through a wide array of printed materials beginning with Columbus's 1493 letter describing the results of his first voyage to what came to be called *America.*

"American Contexts" Highlight a Wide Range of Writings under Compelling Topics. In addition to the works of the individual authors included in the anthology, briefer selections from many other writers are gathered together in clusters of related works called "**American Contexts.**" Those sections focus on topics ranging from "Colonial Diaries and Journals" to "'Mine Eyes Have Seen the Glory': The Meanings of the Civil War" in Volume One and, in Volume Two, from "'The America of the Mind': Critics, Writers, and the Representation of Reality" to "'Inventing the Truth': The Contemporary Memoir." Such clusters are designed to extend the range and resonance of the anthology by introducing additional voices and other kinds of writing, from diaries, journals, and memoirs to editorials, critical essays, political speeches, and social criticism. Although individual selections within those clusters could of course be assigned separately, the "American Contexts" are designed as coherent units, most often intended to be taught as either an introduction or a coda to a larger period or grouping in the anthology. Some clusters invite discussion of distinctive genres, while others allow an opportunity to explore contested ideological issues, critical controversies, cultural developments, and responses to events like the Civil War.

"Through a Modern Lens" Helps Students Make Connections between Writers from the Past and the Present. In order to bring later perspectives to bear on some of the writers and texts in Volume One, we have included brief sections throughout the volume under the general rubric "**Through a Modern Lens.**" These include but are not limited to N. Scott Momaday's recent celebration of Native American origin and creation stories, Robert Lowell's exploration of one of the most prominent eighteenth-century writers in "Mr. Edwards and the Spider," and a tribute by the contemporary African American poet Kevin Young to Phillis Wheatley. In addition to revealing connections across time and space, the "Through a Modern Lens" feature offers rich opportunities for discussion of a number of connected issues: the imaginative effort required to understand the attitudes, conditions, and modes of expression of earlier periods; the sometimes tense rela-

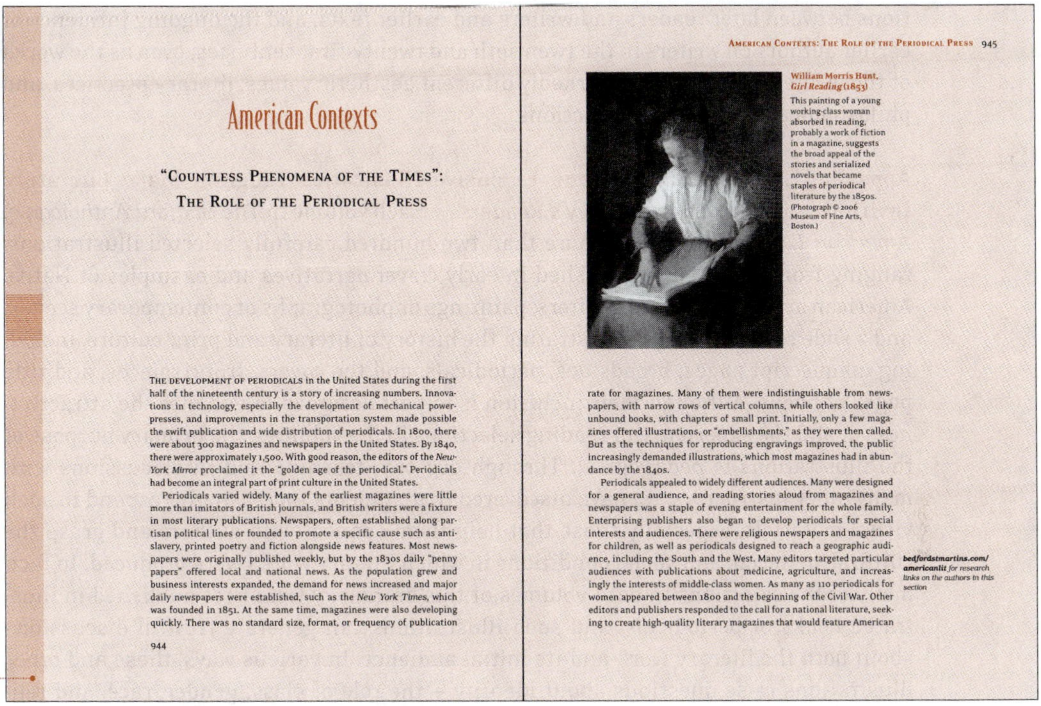

American Contexts

"Countless Phenomena of the Times": The Role of the Periodical Press

THE DEVELOPMENT OF PERIODICALS in the United States during the first half of the nineteenth century is a story of increasing numbers. Innovations in technology, especially the development of mechanical power-presses, and improvements in the transportation system made possible the swift publication and wide distribution of periodicals. In 1800, there were about 300 magazines and newspapers in the United States. By 1840, there were approximately 1,500. With good reason, the editors of the *New-York Mirror* proclaimed it the "golden age of the periodical." Periodicals had become an integral part of print culture in the United States.

Periodicals varied widely. Many of the earliest magazines were little more than imitators of British journals, and British writers were a fixture in most literary publications. Newspapers, often established along partisan political lines or founded to promote a specific cause such as antislavery, printed poetry and fiction alongside news features. Most newspapers were originally published weekly, but by the 1830s daily "penny papers" offered local and national news. As the population grew and business interests expanded, the demand for news increased and major daily newspapers were established, such as the *New York Times*, which was founded in 1851. At the same time, magazines were also developing quickly. There was no standard size, format, or frequency of publication

944

AMERICAN CONTEXTS: THE ROLE OF THE PERIODICAL PRESS 945

William Morris Hunt, *Girl Reading* (1853)

This painting of a young working-class woman absorbed in reading, probably a work of fiction in a magazine, suggests the broad appeal of the stories and serialized novels that became staples of periodical literature by the 1850s. (Photograph © 2006 Museum of Fine Arts, Boston.)

rate for magazines. Many of them were indistinguishable from newspapers, with narrow rows of vertical columns, while others looked like unbound books, with chapters of small print. Initially, only a few magazines offered illustrations, or "embellishments," as they were then called. But as the techniques for reproducing engravings improved, the public increasingly demanded illustrations, which most magazines had in abundance by the 1840s.

Periodicals appealed to widely different audiences. Many were designed for a general audience, and reading stories aloud from magazines and newspapers was a staple of evening entertainment for the whole family. Enterprising publishers also began to develop periodicals for special interests and audiences. There were religious newspapers and magazines for children, as well as periodicals designed to reach a geographic audience, including the South and the West. Many editors targeted particular audiences with publications about medicine, agriculture, and increasingly the interests of middle-class women. As many as 110 periodicals for women appeared between 1800 and the beginning of the Civil War. Other editors and publishers responded to the call for a national literature, seeking to create high-quality literary magazines that would feature American

bedfordstmartins.com/americanlit *for research links on the authors in this section*

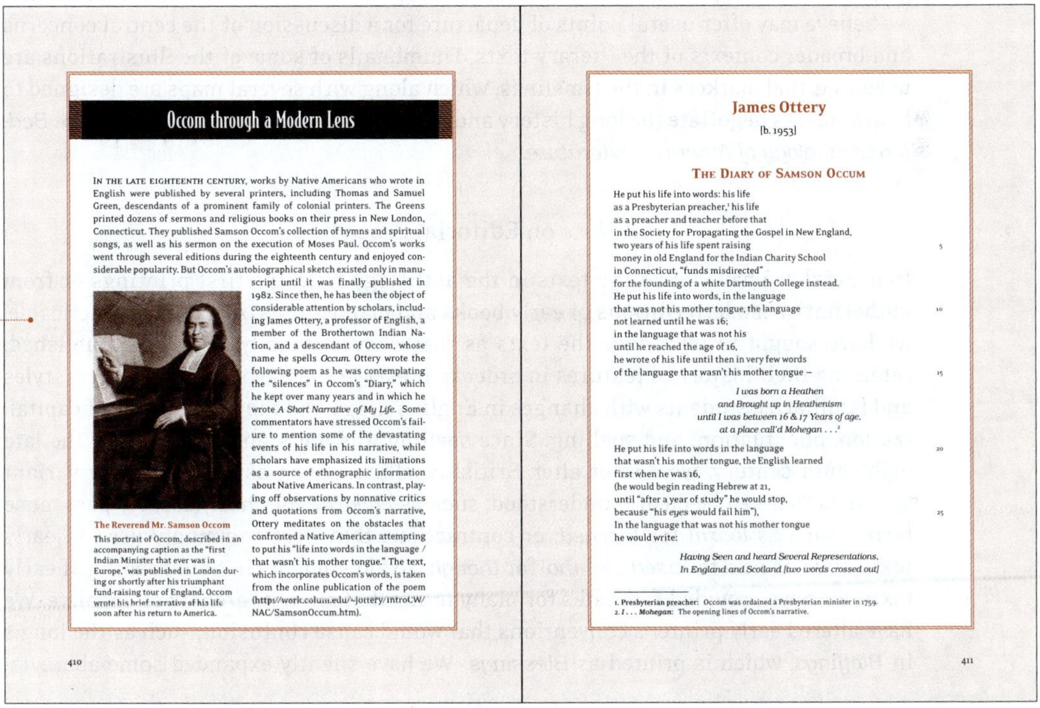

Occom through a Modern Lens

IN THE LATE EIGHTEENTH CENTURY, works by Native Americans who wrote in English were published by several printers, including Thomas and Samuel Green, descendants of a prominent family of colonial printers. The Greens printed dozens of sermons and religious books on their press in New London, Connecticut. They published Samson Occom's collection of hymns and spiritual songs, as well as his sermon on the execution of Moses Paul. Occom's works went through several editions during the eighteenth century and enjoyed considerable popularity. But Occom's autobiographical sketch existed only in manuscript until it was finally published in 1982. Since then, he has been the object of considerable attention by scholars, including James Ottery, a professor of English, a member of the Brothertown Indian Nation, and a descendant of Occom, whose name he spells *Occum*. Ottery wrote the following poem as he was contemplating the "silences" in Occom's "Diary," which he kept over many years and in which he wrote *A Short Narrative of My Life*. Some commentators have stressed Occom's failure to mention some of the devastating events of his life in his narrative, while scholars have emphasized its limitations as a source of ethnographic information about Native Americans. In contrast, playing off observations by nonnative critics and quotations from Occom's narrative, Ottery meditates on the obstacles that confronted a Native American attempting to put his "life into words in the language / that wasn't his mother tongue." The text, which incorporates Occom's words, is taken from the online publication of the poem (http://work.colum.edu/~jottery/IntroCW/NAC/SamsonOccum.htm).

The Reverend Mr. Samson Occom

This portrait of Occom, described in an accompanying caption as the "first Indian Minister that ever was in Europe," was published in London during or shortly after his triumphant fund-raising tour of England. Occom wrote his brief narrative of his life soon after his return to America.

410

James Ottery

[b. 1953]

The Diary of Samson Occum

He put his life into words: his life
as a Presbyterian preacher,[1] his life
as a preacher and teacher before that
in the Society for Propagating the Gospel in New England,
two years of his life spent raising
money in old England for the Indian Charity School
in Connecticut, "funds misdirected"
for the founding of a white Dartmouth College instead.
He put his life into words, in the language
that was not his mother tongue, the language
not learned until he was 16;
in the language that was not his
until he reached the age of 16,
he wrote of his life until then in very few words
of the language that wasn't his mother tongue –

I was born a Heathen
and Brought up in Heathenism
until I was between 16 & 17 Years of age.
at a place call'd Mohegan . . .[2]

He put his life into words in the language
that wasn't his mother tongue, the English learned
first when he was 16,
(he would begin reading Hebrew at 21,
until "after a year of study" he would stop,
because "his *eyes* would fail him"),
In the language that was not his mother tongue
he would write:

Having Seen and heard Several Representations,
In England and Scotland [two words crossed out]

1. **Presbyterian preacher:** Occom was ordained a Presbyterian minister in 1759.
2. ***I . . . Mohegan:*** The opening lines of Occom's narrative.

411

tions between later readers and writers and earlier texts; and the ongoing influence of earlier authors on writers in the twentieth and twenty-first centuries, even as the works of those later writers reveal markedly different aesthetic values, literary practices, and philosophical or religious convictions.

Appealing Two-Color Design and Extensive Illustration Program Make Literature Inviting and Accessible for Today's Readers. Each volume in *The Bedford Anthology of American Literature* includes more than two hundred carefully selected illustrations, ranging from engravings published in early travel narratives and examples of Native American arts to portraits of writers, paintings or photographs of contemporary scenes, and a wide range of images illustrating the history of literary and print culture, including manuscript pages, broadsides, periodicals, and the covers, frontispieces, and title pages of books. Although their inclusion is in part designed to enhance the attractiveness of and the experience of reading selections in the volumes, the primary purpose of the illustrations is pedagogical. Through our own teaching and in discussions with many other instructors, we have discovered that students increasingly respond to such visual materials, especially those that help them connect with authors and grasp the cultural, material, and social conditions in which literary works were produced. In fact, many of the selections in both volumes of this anthology were first published in illustrated books or periodicals, and such illustrations can generate fruitful discussions about both the literary work and its initial audience. In various ways, those and other illustrations raise questions about identity – the role of class, gender, race, and religion – and about self-representation and the representation of reality, questions that we believe may offer useful points of departure for a discussion of the central concerns and broader contexts of the literary texts. Thumbnails of some of the illustrations are used as visual markers in the timelines, which along with several maps are designed to help students negotiate the long history and the complex geography covered in *The Bedford Anthology of American Literature.*

A Note on Editorial Procedures

In general, we have taken the texts in the anthology from the first printings or from authoritative modern editions of early books and manuscripts. As far as is practicable, we have sought to reproduce the texts as they were originally written or published, retaining their historical features in order to preserve the flavor of the authors' styles and familiarize students with changes in English usage and the conventions of capitalization, punctuation, and spelling. Since spelling was not standardized until the late eighteenth century, we do not alter British spellings, such as *humour*; early variant spellings that can be clearly understood, such as *chearful* for *cheerful*; early past tense forms, such as *learnt* for *learned*; or contractions that were commonly used in early texts, such as *us'd* for *used* and *tho'* for *though.* To aid students in their reading of early texts, we have provided footnotes for many terms that are now archaic or obsolete. We have altered early printer's conventions that would cause confusion, such as the long s in *Bleffings*, which is printed as *Blessings*. We have silently expanded some abbrevia-

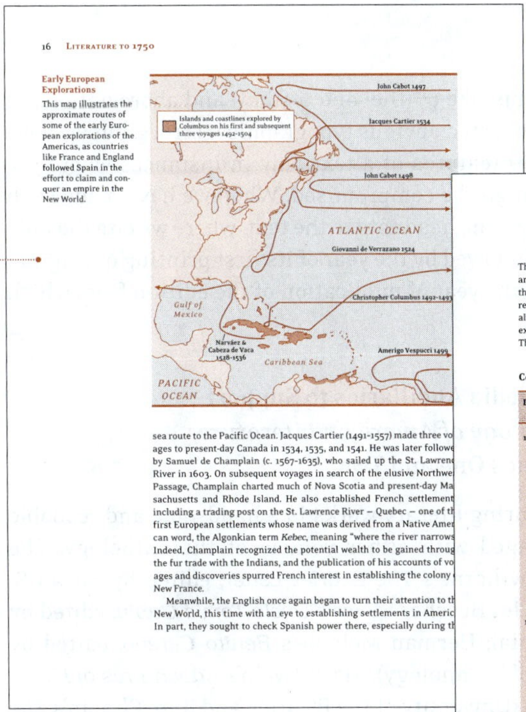

Early European Explorations

This map illustrates the approximate routes of some of the early European explorations of the Americas, as countries like France and England followed Spain in the effort to claim and conquer an empire in the New World.

sea route to the Pacific Ocean. Jacques Cartier (1491-1557) made three vo
ages to present-day Canada in 1534, 1535, and 1541. He was later followe
by Samuel de Champlain (c. 1567-1635), who sailed up the St. Lawren
River in 1603. On subsequent voyages in search of the elusive Northwe
Passage, Champlain charted much of Nova Scotia and present-day Ma
sachusetts and Rhode Island. He also established French settlement
including a trading post on the St. Lawrence River – Quebec – one of th
first European settlements whose name was derived from a Native Amer
can word, the Algonkian term *Kebec*, meaning "where the river narrows
Indeed, Champlain recognized the potential wealth to be gained throug
the fur trade with the Indians, and the publication of his accounts of vo
ages and discoveries spurred French interest in establishing the colony
New France.

Meanwhile, the English once again began to turn their attention to th
New World, this time with an eye to establishing settlements in Americ
In part, they sought to check Spanish power there, especially during th

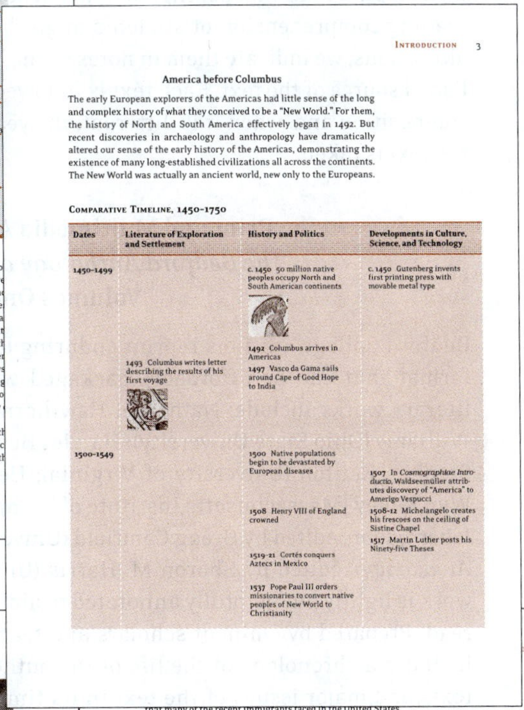

America before Columbus

The early European explorers of the Americas had little sense of the long and complex history of what they conceived to be a "New World." For them, the history of North and South America effectively began in 1492. But recent discoveries in archaeology and anthropology have dramatically altered our sense of the early history of the Americas, demonstrating the existence of many long-established civilizations all across the continents. The New World was actually an ancient world, new only to the Europeans.

COMPARATIVE TIMELINE, 1450–1750

Dates	Literature of Exploration and Settlement	History and Politics	Developments in Culture, Science, and Technology
1450–1499	1493 Columbus writes letter describing the results of his first voyage	c. 1450 50 million native peoples occupy North and South American continents 1492 Columbus arrives in Americas 1497 Vasco da Gama sails around Cape of Good Hope to India	c. 1450 Gutenberg invents first printing press with movable metal type
1500–1549		1500 Native populations begin to be devastated by European diseases 1508 Henry VIII of England crowned 1519–21 Cortés conquers Aztecs in Mexico 1537 Pope Paul III orders missionaries to convert native peoples of New World to Christianity	1507 In *Cosmographiae Introductio*, Waldseemüller attributes discovery of "America" to Amerigo Vespucci 1508–12 Michelangelo creates his frescoes on the ceiling of Sistine Chapel 1517 Martin Luther posts his Ninety-five Theses

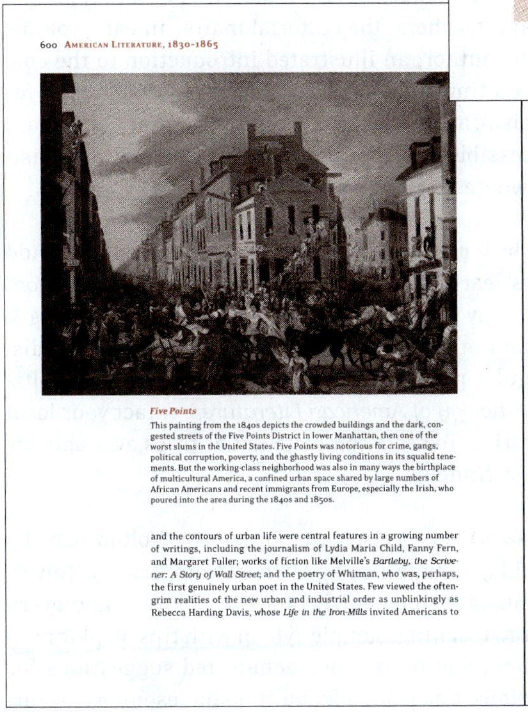

Five Points

This painting from the 1840s depicts the crowded buildings and the dark, congested streets of the Five Points District in lower Manhattan, then one of the worst slums in the United States. Five Points was notorious for crime, gangs, political corruption, poverty, and the ghastly living conditions in its squalid tenements. But the working-class neighborhood was also in many ways the birthplace of multicultural America, a confined urban space shared by large numbers of African Americans and recent immigrants from Europe, especially the Irish, who poured into the area during the 1840s and 1850s.

and the contours of urban life were central features in a growing number of writings, including the journalism of Lydia Maria Child, Fanny Fern, and Margaret Fuller; works of fiction like Melville's *Bartleby, the Scrivener: A Story of Wall Street*; and the poetry of Whitman, who was, perhaps, the first genuinely urban poet in the United States. Few viewed the often-grim realities of the new urban and industrial order as unblinkingly as Rebecca Harding Davis, whose *Life in the Iron-Mills* invited Americans to

that many of the recent immigrants faced in the United States.

The nation's burgeoning population, which grew from under thirteen million in 1830 to over thirty-one million in 1860, also generated a growing hunger for land and increasing pressures for territorial expansion. From the time of the first arrival of European settlers, Native Americans had been forced from their lands and relentlessly driven westward, a process that culminated when Congress passed the Indian Removal Act in 1830. The law authorized the exchange of land west of the Mississippi for Indian holdings in the East, especially the rich agricultural lands of the "Five Civilized Tribes" – the Cherokee, Choctaw, Creek, Chickasaw, and Seminole Indians – in Mississippi, Alabama, Georgia, and Florida. Although some writers and reformers protested the brutal policy, the

Crossing the Platte on the Oregon Trail

Before the completion of the transcontinental railroad in 1869, the only overland route to the new lands in the West was the Oregon Trail, which generally followed the Platte River to its headwaters, crossed the Rocky Mountains, and then split into trails leading to California or the Oregon Territory. Beginning with what was called "the great migration" of 1843, when a wagon train of one thousand settlers set off from Independence, Missouri, half a million people followed the trail, either on foot or in covered wagons. As this 1859 watercolor suggests, Indian attacks were not the major threat to the settlers. They died in far greater numbers – as many as one in ten – from injuries, disease, exhaustion, and malnutrition during the arduous, four- to six-month journey.

tions, including early abbreviated forms like y^e (the) and y^t (that) and abbreviations of the books of the Bible. We have also corrected obvious typographical errors, but we have altered punctuation, spelling, or other features of a text only in instances where the reading comprehension of students might be compromised. When we have made such alterations, we indicate them in notes or the headnote to the text, where we cite the published source of the text. Each text is followed by the year of its first printing or original composition and, when it is different, the year of publication of the edition from which the text is taken.

Print and Multimedia Ancillaries to Support *The Bedford Anthology of American Literature*, Volumes One and Two

Bedford College Editions reprint enduring literary works in a handsome and readable format that can be affordably packaged with either volume of the anthology. The literary works include: Nathaniel Hawthorne's *The Scarlet Letter*, edited by Susan S. Williams (Ohio State University); Harriet Beecher Stowe's *Uncle Tom's Cabin*, edited by Stephen Railton (University of Virginia); Herman Melville's *Benito Cereno*, edited by Wyn Kelley (Massachusetts Institute of Technology); Mark Twain's *Adventures of Huckleberry Finn*, edited by Gregg Camfield (University of the Pacific); and Kate Chopin's *The Awakening*, edited by Sharon M. Harris (University of Connecticut). The text of each work is lightly but helpfully annotated to aid readers without dictating how they should read. Prepared by eminent scholars and teachers, the editorial matter in each volume includes a chronology of the life of the author; an illustrated introduction to the contexts and major issues of the text in its time and ours; an annotated bibliography for further reading in backgrounds, criticism, and online; and a concise glossary of literary terms. The text of the work is also accessible online at an accompanying Web site (visit **bedfordstmartins.com/americanlit**), where it can be searched electronically.

Award-Winning Trade Titles Available for Packaging at Significant Savings. Add more value and choice to your students' learning experiences by packaging *The Bedford Anthology of American Literature* with any of a thousand titles from Farrar, Straus & Giroux, Picador, St. Martin's Press, and other Holtzbrinck trade publishers – at discounts of up to 50 percent off the regular price. To learn more, or to package a Holtzbrinck trade book with *The Bedford Anthology of American Literature*, contact your local Bedford / St. Martin's sales representative. To see a complete list of titles available for packaging, go to **bedfordstmartins.com/tradeup**.

Resources for Teaching The Bedford Anthology of American Literature, Volume One by Lisa Logan, University of Central Florida; Volume Two by Michael Soto, Trinity University. These extensive instructor's manuals include entries for every author and every thematic cluster and offer approaches to teaching; sample syllabi with tips on planning the course; connections to other authors and texts; classroom-tested suggestions for discussion, writing, and oral presentations; and print and multimedia resources for fur-

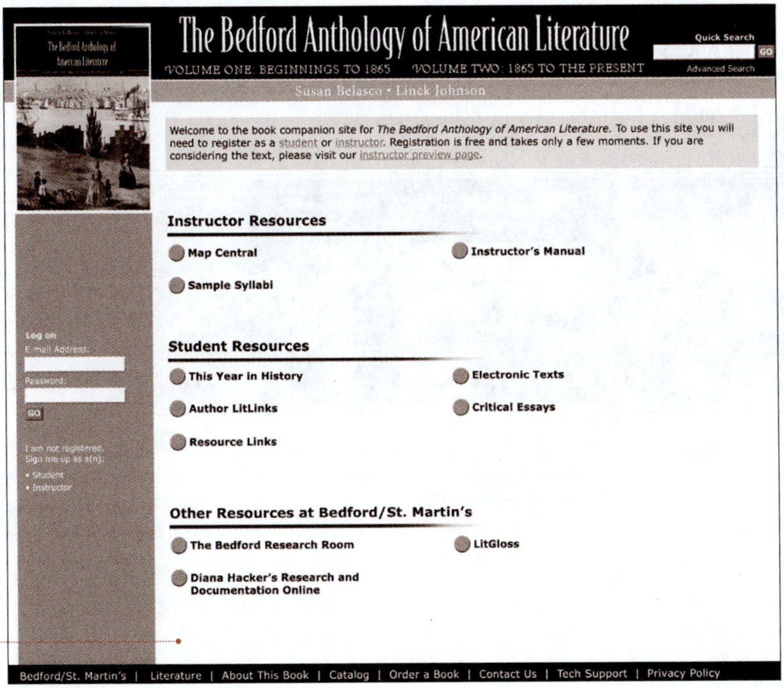

ther research. The instructor's manuals are available in print – Volume One and a combined volume – or as downloadable files from the companion Web site.

Background Readings for Teachers of American Literature, compiled by Venetria Patton, Purdue University. This collection of critical essays for instructors provides an overview of recent changes in the field of American literary studies. The twenty-three readings include important scholarship, newer critical approaches, and practical ideas from experienced teachers. Organized by various approaches ranging from historical context to race and ethnicity and gender and sexuality, this professional resource is relevant to a wide range of courses in American literature, from surveys to graduate seminars.

Companion Web Site at bedfordstmartins.com/americanlit. This site is equipped with student and instructor resources that include annotated research links (LitLinks) for almost every author in the anthology, as well as for broader topics in American literature; maps, including all of the maps in the book plus access to many more at Map Central; This Year in History, which offers snapshots of important literary, historical, and cultural moments; additional critical essays directly related to several selections in the anthology; the instructor's manual (downloadable); and sample syllabi.

Instructor DVD, *Archive America*. This DVD is designed for instructors to use in classroom presentations to help contextualize literary works in a manner that captures students' attention. The focus is on major themes in American literary history, which are brought to life through a rich collection of material that includes art, contextual documents, maps, audio recordings, and video clips.

Acknowledgments

The Bedford Anthology of American Literature is the product of the most challenging, enjoyable, and rewarding work the editors have ever undertaken. We have taken equal pleasure and satisfaction in working with and learning from others who share our deep commitment to teaching American literature. This anthology is the result of a truly collaborative effort, not only between the editors, but also among the hundreds of dedicated people who have helped shape the contents, design, and features of the anthology, including our colleagues, the staff at Bedford / St. Martin's, the authors and editors of the companion and ancillary texts, the members of our Editorial Advisory Board, and the hundreds of reviewers and survey respondents whose thoughtful comments have so enriched our understanding of the needs of instructors and their students at a wide range of institutions all across the United States.

We are delighted to thank all of those who have contributed to our work on this anthology, both directly and indirectly. From graduate school onward, we have learned from our teachers, students in our classes, and our colleagues. We would especially like to remember the late E. Hudson Long of Baylor University and the late Joseph L. Slater of Colgate University, two remarkable individuals with distinguished careers in the study and teaching of American literature. For their support and stimulating conversation, we want to thank our valued colleagues at Colgate University and the University of Nebraska, Lincoln: Peter Balakian, Sarah Bay-Cheng, Michael Coyle, George Hudson, Neill Joy, Jane Pinchin, Phillip Richards, and Sarah Wider; and Grace Bauer, Stephen Behrendt, Robert Bergstrom, Franz Blaha, Kwakiutl Dreher, Kalenda Eaton, Thomas C. Gannon, Melissa Homestead, Maureen Honey, Tom Lynch, Amelia Montes, Marshall Olds, Linda Pratt, Kenneth Price, Guy Reynolds, Joy Ritchie, Gregory Rutledge, Gerry Shapiro, Judy Slater, and Nick Spencer. We are also deeply and directly indebted to the authors of the two-volume *Resources for Teaching* THE BEDFORD ANTHOLOGY OF AMERICAN LITERATURE for their many excellent suggestions: Lisa Logan, University of Central Florida, and Michael Soto, Trinity University. The editors of the companion volumes also provided many ideas and shared a variety of important insights. Venetria Patton, Purdue University, editor of *Background Readings for Teachers of American Literature*, offered us several excellent ideas as she compiled the essays for that volume. For their excellent contributions to *Archive America*, the Instructor DVD, we would like to thank: Amanda Gailey, University of Nebraska, Lincoln; Vicky Gailey; Andrew Jewell, University of Nebraska, Lincoln; John David Miles, Duke University; Darcie Rives, University of Nebraska, Lincoln; Jefferson Slagle, Ohio State University; Laura Tohe, Arizona State University; Stefanie Wortman, University of Missouri, Columbia. The editors of the novels in the Bedford College Editions series also made numerous suggestions: Gregg Camfield, University of the Pacific; Sharon M. Harris, University of Connecticut; Wyn Kelley, Massachusetts Institute of Technology; Stephen Railton, University of Virginia; and Susan S. Williams, Ohio State University. Members of our Editorial Advisory Board have provided detailed reviews, sound advice, and helpful support on Volume One: David J. Carlson, California State University, San Bernardino; Matt Cohen, Duke University; Pattie Cowell, Colorado State University; Paul Crumbley, Utah State University; William Merrill Decker, Oklahoma State University; Thomas C. Gannon, University of Nebraska, Lincoln; Sharon M. Harris, University of Connecticut; Lisa Logan, University of Central Florida; Richard Millington, Smith College; Barbara Packer, University of California, Los Angeles; Venetria Patton, Purdue University; Sarah Robbins, Kennesaw State University; Michael Soto, Trinity University; Zabelle Stodola, University of Arkansas at Little Rock; Susan S. Williams, Ohio State University.

Throughout the years that we have been working on *The Bedford Anthology of American Literature*, we have been helped and guided by a large number of instructors at a variety of institutions. For their suggestions on Volume One, we are thankful to Stacy Alaimo, University of Texas at Arlington; James Albrecht, Pacific Lutheran University; Joseph Alkana, University of Miami; Scott Ash, Nassau Community College; Dorothy Baker, University of Houston at University Park; Matthew Bell, Emerson College; Peter Bellis, University of Miami; Alfred Bendixen, California State University at Los Angeles; Tyler Blake, Mid-America Nazarene University; Cheryl Bohde, McLennan Community College; Ashlee Brand, South Texas Community College; Virginia Brooks, Palm Beach Community College, North; Matthew Brown, California State University at Chico;

Donna Burney, Howard Payne University; Tracy Butts, California State University at Chico; Donna Campbell, Washington State University; Kevin Coots, Ashland Community College; Deborah Core, Eastern Kentucky University; Robert Cummings, University of Georgia; Jennifer Daniels, Northern Virginia Community College at Annandale; Jean Darcy, Queensborough Community College; Christine Doyle, Central Connecticut State University; James Egan, Brown University; Gregory Eiselein, Kansas State University; Karen English, San Jose State University; John Ernest, University of New Hampshire; Patricia Flanary, Lexington Community College; Annamaria Formichella-Elsden, Buena Vista University; Theresa Gaul, Texas Christian University; Rosemary Guruswamy, Radford University; Paul Gutjahr, Indiana University; Robert D. Habich, Ball State University; Carol Henderson, University of Delaware; Desiree Henderson, University of Texas at El Paso; Laura Henigman, James Madison University; William Hug, Jacksonville State University; Jocelyn Adkins Irby, Tennessee State University; Miranda Johnson-Parries, Old Dominion University; Patricia Kalayjian, California State University at Dominguez Hills; Valerie Karno, University of Rhode Island; Jimmie Killingsworth, Texas A&M University; Mark Knockemus, Northeastern Technical College; Cecilia Koncharr-Farr, College of Saint Catherine; Erika Kreger, San Jose State University; Peggy Kulesz, University of Texas at Arlington; Linda Leavell, Oklahoma State University; Jian-Zhong Lin, Eastern Connecticut State University; Lisa MacFarlane, University of New Hampshire; Stephen J. Martelli, Massasoit Community College; Stephen Mathis, Northern Essex Community College; David Mazel, Adams State College; Anthony Michel, California State University at Fresno; Bruce Michelson, University of Illinois; Quentin Miller, Suffolk University; Sally Mitchell, Temple University; Randall Moon, Hazard Community College; Wesley Mott, Worcester Polytechnic Institute; James Nagel, University of Georgia; Randy Nelson, Davidson College; Lisa Norwood, Drake University; Sandra Oh, University of Miami; Patricia Okker, University of Missouri at Columbia; B. Parris, University of Washington; David Payne, University of Georgia; Nancy Penney, Lord Fairfax Community College; Jeff Perkins, Somerset Community College; Leland Person, University of Cincinnati; John Pleimann, Jefferson College; Sharon Reedy, Pellissippi State Technological Community College; Donna Reiss, Tidewater Community College at Virginia Beach; Connie Richards, Salisbury State University; David M. Robinson, Oregon State University; Lois Rudnick, University of Massachusetts at Boston; Dorothy Seyler, Northern Virginia Community College at Annandale; Alan Silva, Hamline University; Jack Summers, Central Piedmont Community College; Timothy Sweet, West Virginia University; James Tanner, University of North Texas; Robert Tilton, University of Connecticut; Herbert Tucker, University of Virginia; Joseph Urgo, University of Mississippi; Edward Vega, Palm Beach Community College; Beverly Voloshin, San Francisco State University; Daneen Wardrop, Western Michigan University; Steven Ware, Puget Sound Christian College; Eric Weil, Shaw University; Ellen Weinauer, University of South Mississippi; Cindy Weinstein, California Institute of Technology; Carol Westcamp, University of Arkansas at Fort Smith; Warren Westcott, Tennessee State University; Gary Williams, University of Idaho; Michael Ziser, University of California at Davis.

Staff members of the University of Nebraska, Lincoln, and Colgate University libraries have helped us locate texts and solve bibliographic problems; we are especially appreciative of Kathy Johnson and Carl Peterson. We have also benefited from the several students who served so ably as research assistants for this project: Soojin Ahn, Jaclyn Cruikshank, Amanda Gailey, Ramon Guerra, Elizabeth Lorang, Janel Simons, and Stephanie Veverka. We are also grateful to the many students in our classes in American literature who have provided ideas and inspiration throughout our teaching careers at several colleges and universities.

Working with the extraordinarily talented staff members of Bedford / St. Martin's has been an enriching educational experience as well as a constant pleasure. The first member of the editorial staff we met at Bedford / St. Martin's was executive editor Steve Scipione, and we have come to depend on his expert professional opinions and high good humor. Our untiring editor, Maura Shea, provided strong support and wise counsel on an almost daily basis for nearly four years. In her absence during a brief leave, we greatly valued the help and good cheer of Laura Arcari. Joan Feinberg, president of Bedford / St. Martin's, imaginatively guided a long series of stimulating discussions about American literature in general and our anthology in particular. Karen Henry, executive editor, has been a constant source of sound advice and soothing reassurance. Other members of the editorial staff – Denise Wydra, Anne Noyes, Stefanie Wortman, Kaitlin Hannon, Abby Bielagus – have also helped in many ways, large and small. We also want to thank the members of the new media staff who have taught us much about the technical possibilities of Web sites and DVDs: Harriet Wald, Kim Hampton, and Coleen O'Hanley. Lori Chong Roncka and the other members of the production staff, Marcia Cohen, Elizabeth Schaaf, Pat Ollague, Kristen Merrill, and Amy Derjue, patiently made hundreds – perhaps thousands – of invaluable suggestions. We greatly respect and admire the members of the art and design staff: Donna Dennison, Anna Palchik, Judith Arisman, Tom Macy, Rose Corbett Gordon, and Martha Friedman. We also thank Virginia Creeden for her work on permissions and Jenna Bookin Barry and Adrienne Petsick for teaching us about marketing plans.

Finally, our wonderful family members and good friends have offered enthusiastic encouragement and happy diversions: Peggy Belasco; Bill Belasco and Teresa Morales; Janet and Steve Jenkins; Lance Johnson; Roslyn and Vincent Reilly; Reagan Sides and Kirby Gosnell; and Pamela Stockton.

We lovingly dedicate *The Bedford Anthology of American Literature* to Max Johnson and Stephen Jenkins, our familial connections to the next generation of college students.

Susan Belasco
Linck Johnson

About the Editors

Susan Belasco (B.A., Baylor University; Ph.D., Texas A&M University), professor of English and women's studies at the University of Nebraska, Lincoln, has taught courses in writing and American literature at several institutions since 1974, including McLennan Community College; Allegheny College; California State University, Los Angeles; and the University of Tulsa. The editor of Margaret Fuller's *Summer on the Lakes* and Fanny Fern's *Ruth Hall*, she is also the coeditor of three collections of essays: *Approaches to Teaching Stowe's "Uncle Tom's Cabin," Periodical Literature in Nineteenth-Century America*, and *Leaves of Grass: The Sesquicentennial Essays*. The editor of "Walt Whitman's Periodical Poetry" for the *Walt Whitman Archive* (**whitmanarchive.org**), she is the current president of the Research Society for American Periodicals.

Linck Johnson (B.A., Cornell University; Ph.D., Princeton University), the Charles A. Dana Professor of English at Colgate University, has taught courses in writing and American literature and culture since 1974. He is the author of *Thoreau's Complex Weave: The Writing of "A Week on the Concord and Merrimack Rivers," with the Text of the First Draft*; the Historical Introduction to *A Week* in the Princeton University Press edition of the *Writings of Henry D. Thoreau*; and numerous articles and contributions to books. The recipient of a National Endowment for the Humanities Fellowship at the American Antiquarian Society, he is a member of the Editorial Board of the *Collected Works of Ralph Waldo Emerson* and *ESQ: A Journal of the American Renaissance*.

Contents

≡ LITERATURE TO 1750 ≡

Native American Origin and Creation Stories

Explorations and Early Encounters

Colonial Settlements

AMERICAN LITERATURE, 1750-1830

Writing Colonial Lives

AMERICAN CONTEXTS
"TO BEGIN THE WORLD OVER AGAIN": THE EMERGING IDEA OF "AMERICA"

Literature for a New Nation

AMERICAN CONTEXTS

"WHO READS AN AMERICAN BOOK?": CALLS FOR A NATIONAL LITERATURE

AMERICAN LITERATURE, 1830–1865

The Era of Reform

American Facts and American Fiction

AMERICAN CONTEXTS
"COUNTLESS PHENOMENA OF THE TIMES": THE ROLE OF THE PERIODICAL PRESS

American Contexts

"Mine Eyes Have Seen the Glory": The Meanings of the Civil War

Literature to 1750

EARLY IN 1493, less than fifty years after the invention of the printing press by Johannes Gutenberg in Germany, an untitled letter addressed to Luis de Santángel, secretary of the royal court of Spain, was published in Barcelona. Written in Spanish by an Italian navigator Christopher Columbus, the letter was soon translated into Latin and other languages and disseminated throughout Europe. By the end of 1493, eleven editions of the letter had been printed, making it one of the early "bestsellers" in European publishing. The popularity of the letter is understandable since it was the first public account of the discoveries Columbus had made during his voyage in 1492, from Spain westward to what he called "the Indies." Although he was clearly disappointed that he had not reached his ultimate goal, the fabled province of Cathay on the mainland of Asia, Columbus excitedly described the lands he had touched upon and immediately claimed for the sponsors of his expedition, King Ferdinand and Queen Isabel of Spain: "There I found very many islands, filled with people innumerable, and of them all I have taken possession for their highnesses, by proclamation and with the royal standard unfurled, and no opposition was offered to me."

Those "people innumerable" were the Arawak, some of whom – the Taino – were the indigenous inhabitants of what are now the Bahamas, Cuba, and Hispaniola (Haiti and the Dominican Republic). Thinking he had reached the East Indies, however, Columbus called the inhabitants of the islands *los indios*, "the Indians," a name that would thereafter be applied indiscriminately to all of the indigenous peoples of the Western Hemisphere. Those peoples were first represented to Europe by the natives Columbus described in his letter: a simple, timid, unlettered people who went naked and lived an Eden-like existence amid the beauty and bounty of the islands. For Columbus, those people were part of the bounty of the islands, at once a source of potential converts to Christianity and a boundless source of slaves. As he departed the first island, Columbus thus took several captives to provide information and evidence of his discoveries, an act that anticipated the carnage and devastation that Europeans following his lead would bring to the indigenous peoples of what soon came to be called "America."

◀ (OVERLEAF)

The American Colonies

This engraving by George Bickham appeared in *A Short Description of the American Colonies*, published in London in 1750. In addition to representing the racial diversity of the colonies, the three figures offer a kind of allegorical history of Virginia, where the English settlers had driven Native Americans from their land and imported slaves from Africa to cultivate tobacco, represented here by the pipes being offered by the slave to the wealthy planter on the right.

America before Columbus

The early European explorers of the Americas had little sense of the long and complex history of what they conceived to be a "New World." For them, the history of North and South America effectively began in 1492. But recent discoveries in archaeology and anthropology have dramatically altered our sense of the early history of the Americas, demonstrating the existence of many long-established civilizations all across the continents. The New World was actually an ancient world, new only to the Europeans.

COMPARATIVE TIMELINE, 1450–1750

Dates	Literature of Exploration and Settlement	History and Politics	Developments in Culture, Science, and Technology
1450–1499	1493 Columbus writes letter describing the results of his first voyage 	c. 1450 50 million native peoples occupy North and South American continents  1492 Columbus arrives in Americas; 1497 Vasco da Gama sails around Cape of Good Hope to India	c. 1450 Gutenberg invents first printing press with movable metal type
1500–1549		1500 Native populations begin to be devastated by European diseases; 1508 Henry VIII of England crowned; 1519–21 Cortés conquers Aztecs in Mexico; 1537 Pope Paul III orders missionaries to convert native peoples of New World to Christianity	1507 In *Cosmographiae Introductio*, Waldseemüller attributes discovery of "America" to Amerigo Vespucci; 1508–12 Michelangelo creates his frescoes on the ceiling of Sistine Chapel; 1517 Martin Luther posts his Ninety-five Theses

Many scholars now believe that the earliest inhabitants of North America began migrating from Siberia about fifteen thousand years ago, though recent archaeological finds suggest an even earlier date. As global climate changes ended the Ice Age and altered the position of glaciers in the Bering Strait, it became possible for populations to cross over from Asia to North America. Waves of migration took place, and groups of people subsequently pushed eastward to present-day Canada and southward along the Pacific coast to what are now the southwestern United States and Mexico. These earliest settlers of North America, called Paleo-

Dates	Literature of Exploration and Settlement	History and Politics	Developments in Culture, Science, and Technology
1500–1549 (cont.)	 1542 *The Narrative of Cabeza de Vaca*	1539 de Soto invades present-day Florida	1539 First printing press in Americas arrives in Mexico City 1543 Copernicus argues in *On the Revolutions of the Heavenly Spheres* that the sun is center of universe
1550–1599	1552 Las Casas, *The Brief Relation of the Devastation of the Indies*  1588 Hariot, *A Briefe and True Report of the New Found Land of Virginia* 1589 Hakluyt's *Navigations*	1558–1603 Protestant Elizabeth I reigns in England 1585 Raleigh reaches Roanoke Island, in what English called "Virginia" 1585–1604 Anglo-Spanish War	 1590 Compound microscope invented
1600–1609		 1603–13 Champlain explores St. Lawrence River and eventually founds Quebec 1607 Jamestown established in present-day Virginia 1609 John Smyth founds Baptist Church	1600 British East India Company founded 1603 Shakespeare's *Hamlet* first appears in print 1609 Galileo demonstrates his first telescope

Indians by anthropologists, were nomadic tribes who hunted large animals and gathered edible plants, berries, and nuts. When food supplies ran short, they moved on to new areas. Although population estimates vary, historians believe that roughly 100,000 people inhabited North America at the end of the Paleolithic era, between about 8000 and 6000 BCE.

Gradual alterations in climate and the extinction of many of the large animals caused changes in the living patterns of the human inhabitants. About five thousand years ago, they began to live in larger territorial groups and learned to cultivate crops for food. These Archaic Indians, as they are

Dates	Literature of Exploration and Settlement	History and Politics	Developments in Culture, Science, and Technology
1610–1619	1613 *Les Voyages du Sieur de Champlain* published in France	 1614 Pocahontas marries John Rolfe 1616–19 "Great Dying" – believed to be a combination of the plague, smallpox, cholera, measles, hepatitis, and whooping cough transmitted by Europeans – decimates Native American population 1619 Virginia's House of Burgesses, first European representative body in Americas, convenes	1611 King James Bible published in England
1620–1629	1622 Bradford and Winslow's *Mourt's Relation*  1624 John Smith, *Generall Historie of Virginia, New-England, and the Summer Isles*	1620 *Mayflower* reaches Plymouth in present-day Massachusetts	 1621 First Thanksgiving celebrated at Plymouth 1625 Bacon, *Complete Essays*

now usually called by anthropologists, probably grew to a population of about one million people, dispersed across the continent. As they adapted to their local environments, they began to develop distinct languages, rituals, stories, kinship systems, and trade networks. By 1500 BCE, agriculture was becoming established in the Americas. Maize or Indian corn was a staple, and two other important crops, squash and beans, were grown in abundance. As the native populations continued to expand across North and South America, the age of the Archaic Indian gave way to new phases in the history of the indigenous people. The sophisticated Mayan civiliza-

Dates	Literature of Exploration and Settlement	History and Politics	Developments in Culture, Science, and Technology
1630–1639	1630 Winthrop delivers address "A Modell of Christian Charity"; Bradford begins writing *Of Plimoth Plantation* 	1630 Great Migration begins; American colonial population: 4,600 1634 Settlers arrive in Maryland, led by Lord Baltimore 1636 After being banned from Massachusetts Bay Colony as a dissident, Roger Williams founds Rhode Island 1637 Pequot War	1638 First printing press in colonial America arrives in Boston
1640–1649	1640 *Bay Psalm Book*	1640 American colonial population: 26,600 1642 Civil war breaks out in England	1642 Puritans close all theaters in England 1644 Descartes, *Principles of Philosophy*
1650–1659	1650 Bradstreet, *The Tenth Muse* 	1650 American colonial population: 50,400 1653 Oliver Cromwell becomes lord protector of England	

tion flourished in Mexico while the Hohokam and Anasazi cultures emerged with highly developed towns and irrigation systems in the American Southwest. In the center of the continent, the Mississippi River valley became a densely settled area of towns and villages. In the Northeast and Southeast, an extensive network of native tribes lived in villages near rivers, lakes, and the ocean, where they could fish and hunt. By the time of Columbus's first voyage in 1492, the North and South American continents were populated by approximately 50 million people, an estimated five million of whom lived in what is today the continental United States.

Dates	Literature of Exploration and Settlement	History and Politics	Developments in Culture, Science, and Technology
1660–1669	1662 Wigglesworth, *The Day of Doom*	1660 American colonial population: 75,100 1661 Charles II restored to throne of England 1664 Colony of New Jersey founded 1664–65 "Great Plague" sweeps England	1662 Church of England publishes new edition of *Book of Common Prayer* 1663 John Eliot publishes an Algonkian translation of the Bible 1665 Newton develops law of universal gravitation 1667 Milton, *Paradise Lost*
1670–1679	1673 Sewall begins writing *Diary*	1670 American colonial population: 111,900 1675–76 King Philip's War	1678 Bunyan, *The Pilgrim's Progress*
1680–1689		1680 American colonial population: 151,500 1681 Pennsylvania founded by William Penn	

From its earliest history, the complex society that developed in North America was multilingual and culturally diverse. The population was divided into roughly three hundred distinct cultural groups. Those groups spoke about two hundred languages, plus many different dialects of those languages, and embraced a wide variety of customs and systems of belief. They also developed distinctive cultural traditions, creating masterpieces of arts and crafts in a wide range of media, including stone, ceramics, wood, shell, and copper. Some groups employed petroglyphs and pictographs, images carved in or painted on rock, while others developed dif-

Dates	Literature of Exploration and Settlement	History and Politics	Developments in Culture, Science, and Technology
1680–1689 (cont.)	1682 Rowlandson, *The Sovereignty and Goodness of God* 1682–1725 Edward Taylor writes *Preparatory Meditations*	 Soveraignty & Goodness OF GOD NARRATIVE 1685 James Stuart becomes King James II of England 1689 At end of Glorious Revolution, William and Mary are proclaimed rulers of England, Scotland, and Ireland	1687 Newton publishes his law of gravity
1690–1699	c. 1690 *New England Primer* 	1690 American colonial population: 210,400 1692 Salem witch trials	1690 Locke, *Two Treatises of Civil Government*
1700–1709	1700 Pastorius, *Circumstantial Geographical Description of the Lately Discovered Province of Pennsylvania* 1702 Mather, *Magnalia Christi Americana*  1704–05 Sarah Kemble Knight travels from Boston to New York 1709–12 Byrd writes diary of daily life in Virginia	1700 American colonial population: 250,900 1702 Anne Stuart takes throne of England, Scotland, and Ireland 1707 Act of Union establishes Great Britain from separate kingdoms of England, Scotland, and Ireland	1701 Pylarini gives first smallpox inoculations 1709 First pianoforte built in Florence

ferent methods of recording important historical and political events, exemplified by the wampum belts of the Iroquois Confederation. In the absence of written languages, however, a crucial means of cultural transmission was the spoken word, as tribal customs, history, and traditions were passed down generation to generation through poems, songs, and stories. At the same time, the cultural differences and competition among the various groups frequently led to violent clashes and tribal wars. Larger villages also dealt with a variety of internal problems. These included environmental challenges, like overcultivation of the land, overhunting, and

Dates	Literature of Exploration and Settlement	History and Politics	Developments in Culture, Science, and Technology
1710–1719		1710 American colonial population: 331,700 1718 New Orleans founded by French	1719 Defoe, *Robinson Crusoe*
1720–1729	1728 Byrd, *History of the Dividing Line*	1720 American colonial population: 466,200	1721 Bach composes *Brandenburg* Concertos 1726 Swift, *Gulliver's Travels*
1730–1739		1730 American colonial population: 629,400 1732 James Oglethorpe obtains charter for Georgia	1730–50 First Great Awakening  1739 Hume, *A Treatise of Human Nature*
1740–1750	c. 1740 Jonathan Edwards writes *Personal Narrative* 1741 Jonathan Edwards, "Sinners in the Hands of an Angry God"	1740 American colonial population: 905,600 1741 Bering explores Alaska	1741 *American Magazine* founded by Andrew Bradford 1742 First performance of Handel's *Messiah* 1744 Benjamin Franklin publishes first novel in colonial America, Samuel Richardson's *Pamela*

Native American Peoples, 1492

At the time of Columbus's first voyage in 1492, the entire Western Hemisphere was populated by diverse groups of Native Americans. This map illustrates the approximate locations of some of the larger groups in North and Central America. The linguistic and cultural diversity of Native American peoples, as well as local conflicts among different tribes, made it difficult to organize united resistance to European invaders.

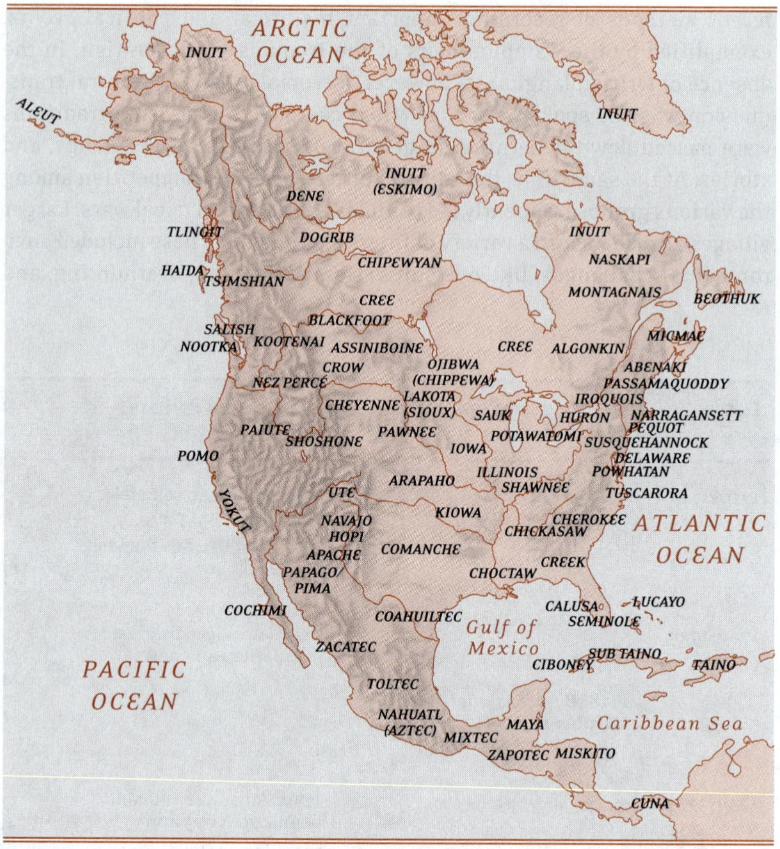

waste disposal, as well as social issues, such as the maintenance of law and order. Indeed, the native populations that the earliest European explorers variously viewed as primitive, savage, or simple were actually composed of widely varying groups of people dealing with complex problems in a world of almost dizzying complexity and diversity.

Christianity, Islam, and the Lure of Asia

European exploration of that world did not begin in earnest until the end of the fifteenth century. Much earlier, around 1000, the Vikings made a series of exploratory voyages from their colony in Greenland. Traveling in their longboats to the eastern shore of Canada, the Vikings apparently undertook fairly extensive explorations but made no significant effort to establish permanent colonies. During the following centuries, much of the attention of Europe was focused on the Middle East and Asia, not on the unknown continents to the west. Those centuries were marked by a grow-

Dry Fork Canyon Petroglyphs

These life-sized effigies were carved into a stone wall at a site in present-day Utah about 1,000 years ago by members of the Fremont culture, a northern branch of the Anasazi. The meaning of such petroglyphs remains mysterious to archaeologists and historians alike.

ing struggle for global domination and control among competing cultures, especially between the Christian countries of Europe and the Islamic nations of Africa and the Middle East. Islam had become the most dynamic and powerful culture in the world, united by a common language, Arabic, and far outstripping Europe in technology, science, and warfare. By the twelfth century, Islam dominated the Iberian Peninsula, comprising Spain and Portugal, all of North Africa, and much of what was known as Asia Minor. Between the eleventh and fourteenth centuries, Europe undertook a series of religious crusades in an effort to oust the Muslims from the Holy Land, but those wars ended in failure. In the thirteenth century, the Mongol Empire, under the leadership of Genghis Khan, conquered much of China and pressed into both Europe and the Islamic world. In the fourteenth century, a powerful group of Muslims, the Ottoman Turks, fought back against the Mongols and came to dominate the crucial trade routes to Asia in the eastern Mediterranean. As a consequence, Muslim merchants along those trade routes made lucrative profits and swelled their own economies at the expense of Europe.

For Europeans, the allure of Asia was intensified by a type of travel writing known as the "Wonders of the East." That genre included two of the most popular books of the Middle Ages: *The Travels of Marco Polo*, written at the end of the thirteenth century, and *Mandeville's Travels*, also known as *The Book of Sir John Mandeville*, written in the middle of the fourteenth century. There was apparently no such person as "Sir John Mandeville," whose account was equally fictitious. But it was evidently accepted as a

Niccolò and Maffeo Polo with Caravan

In his famous journey to the Far East in 1271, the Venetian merchant and writer Marco Polo joined his father (Niccolò) and his uncle (Maffeo), who in this illustration from a Catalonian map are shown traveling in a caravan on the overland trade route to China.

factual narrative by most medieval readers, who were treated to descriptions of wonders like the riches of the great khan of Cathay, whose palace, "the most passing fair in all the world," was graced by "twenty-four pillars of gold" and whose throne "was all wrought of gold and of precious stones and great pearls." Marco Polo described similar splendors in his account of his journey along what was later called the "Silk Road," actually a series of overland trade routes from Turkey to China, and the seventeen years he claimed to have spent in the kingdom of Kublai Khan. Although his book was widely known as *Il Milione*, shorthand for "The Million Lies," it captured the imagination of Europeans. Manuscript editions in various languages ran into the hundreds, and the book became a bestseller when a printed edition appeared late in the fifteenth century, after the invention of the printing press in 1450.

At the same time that they were being dazzled by the *Travels* of Mandeville and Marco Polo, Europeans were paying exorbitant prices for silks, spices, gold, and ivory from Asia. Since the Turks continued to dominate the overland trade routes, European nations increasingly turned west in an effort to gain easier access to the riches of the East. For many Christians in Europe, especially in Spain and Portugal, the desire to discover sea routes to the East and thus to overcome the commercial advantages enjoyed by Muslims was heightened by centuries of fighting for control of the Iberian Peninsula. In fact, *conquistadores*, or "conquerors," the term used to refer to the Spanish explorers and soldiers on expeditions to the New World, derived from *reconquista*, the effort to reconquer the Iberian Peninsula from the Muslim Moors from North Africa. Significantly, after almost six centuries of conflict, the Spanish Christians finally expelled the Moors in 1492, the year Columbus made his first voyage across the Atlantic.

Conquest and Colonization in the New World

Columbus's voyages were part of a broader European movement, especially by Portugal and Spain, to explore and exploit new territories. Portuguese navigators were among the first to use advances in maritime technology in order to undertake increasingly extended voyages. Bartholomeu Dias (1450-1500) rounded the tip of Africa in 1487, and Vasco da Gama (1469-1524) sailed around the Cape of Good Hope to India in 1497. While the Portuguese generally pursued southern and eastern routes, especially along the African coast, the Spanish began to push west across the Atlantic. During his four voyages from 1492 to 1504, Columbus landed on most of the major islands of the Caribbean, as well as parts of the coasts of South and Central America. He continued to believe that he had reached Asia, but Columbus recognized that the lands he encountered constituted a "New World" to Europeans. Although many of those places were densely populated by peoples with their own languages and names, Columbus renamed the inhabitants and their lands, in effect claiming both for Spain. When he landed on the first of the islands that he encountered during his first voyage in 1492, an island its Taino inhabitants called *Guanahani*, Columbus renamed it *San Salvador*, in turn naming the other islands he landed upon *Santa Maria de la Concepción*, *Fernandina*, *Isabella*, *Juana* (after Prince Don Juan, son of King Ferdinand and Queen Isabel), and finally *Española*, derived from *España*, or "Spain."

Ironically, given his zeal for naming, the lands Columbus discovered were later named for another Italian navigator working for Spain, Amerigo Vespucci (1451-1512). A merchant in Seville who sold pickles, which were eaten by mariners to prevent scurvy during extended voyages, Vespucci claimed to have made as many as five trips to the northern parts of the New World beginning in 1497. Although it is not clear that he ever set foot in North America, accounts of Vespucci's voyages were published in *Cosmographiae Introductio* (1507), a manual of geography by the German cartographer Martin Waldseemüller. Believing that Amerigo Vespucci was the discoverer of the previously unknown landmass between Europe and Asia, Waldseemüller called it "America," which swiftly became the popular name for the New World. During the following centuries, questions about the suitability of that name persisted, especially in what came to be called the United States of America, which many believed should have been named *Columbia* in honor of Columbus. In his book *English Traits* (1856), Ralph Waldo Emerson emphasized the incongruity of the fact that "broad America must wear the name of a thief," Amerigo Vespucci, "the pickle-dealer at Seville, who . . . managed in this lying world to supplant Columbus, and baptize half the earth with his own dishonest name."

Although his name was not applied to the lands Columbus explored, his voyages led to Spain's domination over much of the New World. The brutal process of conquest and colonization initiated in the islands of the Caribbean swiftly spread to large portions of the Americas. Within forty years of Columbus's first voyage, Hernán Cortés (1485-1547) had conquered the Aztec and Mayan Empires of Mexico and Central America, while Francisco Pizarro (1475-1541) had conquered the Inca of Peru. Inspired by reports of gold and other riches in areas to the north, Hernando de Soto (c. 1496-1542) and Francisco Vásquez de Coronado (c. 1510-1554) explored and claimed lands from Florida all across the southern parts of the present United States. By the middle of the sixteenth century, the Spanish had gained an extensive and fabulously rich empire, won at an enormous cost to the indigenous inhabitants of the Americas. Through the introduction of diseases for which they had no immunity, as well as by the enslavement or slaughter of large numbers of those inhabitants, the size of the native population decreased dramatically, leaving in some places only a handful of survivors of tribes whose history, names, and ancient cultures were virtually erased. Within a few years of Columbus's landing on Hispaniola, for example, its enslaved Taino population had declined so precipitously that the Spaniards began to import slaves, first from other islands and then from Africa.

The brutality of Spanish policies was exposed and publicized by a Dominican missionary, Bartolomé de Las Casas. Initially, he sought reform through oral arguments and letters to Holy Roman Emperor Charles V of Spain. Determined to exploit the power of the printed word, however, Las Casas ignored the requirement that he receive royal permission to publish a powerful exposé of Spanish policies, *The Brief Relation of the Devastation of the Indies* (1552). In that horrifying account of the atrocities committed by the Spanish, Las Casas observed that nearly two million

Bartolomé de Las Casas, *Narratio regionum indicarum per Hispanos* (1598)

This was one of several engravings by the ardent Protestant Theodor de Bry in a Latin translation of the *Brevissima relacion* he published in Frankfurt. Along with Las Casas's grim account, which was also translated into other European languages, such stark images helped spread the "Black Legend" of Spanish atrocities against the native peoples of the Americas.

people had been taken captive and brought from other islands to work as slaves in the gold mines of Hispaniola and San Juan (now Puerto Rico), adding, "And it is a great sorrow and heartbreak to see this coastal land which was so flourishing, now a depopulated desert." Translated into French in 1579 and into English in 1583, Las Casas's account caused a sensation throughout Europe. It also helped give rise to what came to be called the "Black Legend," the stereotype of helpless and innocent natives slaughtered by cruel and bloodthirsty Spaniards. Indeed, both the French and English later seized upon the account to justify their efforts to supplant Spain in the Americas.

"And it is a great sorrow and heartbreak to see this coastal land which was so flourishing, now a depopulated desert."

Inspired by Spanish gains there, other European countries began to explore the Americas in the ongoing effort to find new and shorter trade routes to Asia. When he learned of Columbus's success, John Cabot (born Giovanni Caboto in Italy about 1451) went to England and received a grant for a voyage from King Henry VII. Believing that shorter routes to Asia were possible by taking a more northerly direction, Cabot crossed the Atlantic twice, in 1497 and 1498, eventually exploring the coastline from Newfoundland and Labrador as far south as the Chesapeake Bay. The English discontinued their explorations after Cabot failed to find what was called a "Northwest Passage" to Asia, but the French continued the quest for such a northern

Early European Explorations

This map illustrates the approximate routes of some of the early European explorations of the Americas, as countries like France and England followed Spain in the effort to claim and conquer an empire in the New World.

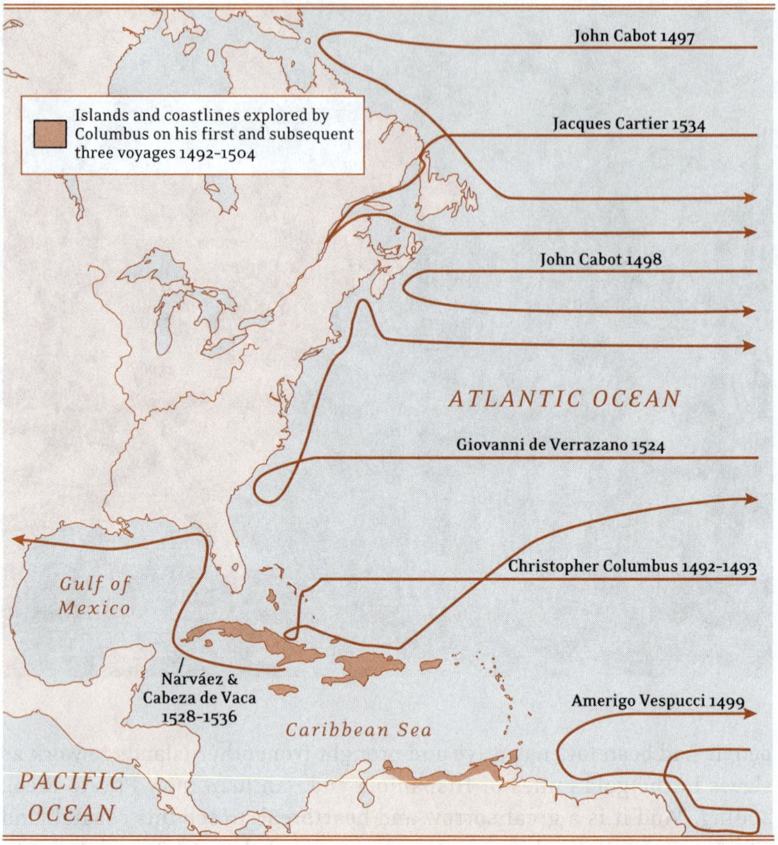

sea route to the Pacific Ocean. Jacques Cartier (1491–1557) made three voyages to present-day Canada in 1534, 1535, and 1541. He was later followed by Samuel de Champlain (c. 1567–1635), who sailed up the St. Lawrence River in 1603. On subsequent voyages in search of the elusive Northwest Passage, Champlain charted much of Nova Scotia and present-day Massachusetts and Rhode Island. He also established French settlements, including a trading post on the St. Lawrence River – Quebec – one of the first European settlements whose name was derived from a Native American word, the Algonkian term *Kebec*, meaning "where the river narrows." Indeed, Champlain recognized the potential wealth to be gained through the fur trade with the Indians, and the publication of his accounts of voyages and discoveries spurred French interest in establishing the colony of New France.

Meanwhile, the English once again began to turn their attention to the New World, this time with an eye to establishing settlements in America. In part, they sought to check Spanish power there, especially during the

Anglo-Spanish War (1585-1604). Even before the formal outbreak of hostilities, the English navigator Sir Francis Drake (1540?-1596) had circumnavigated the globe in 1577-80, plundering Spanish ships and settlements in the Americas. The destruction of the Spanish Armada in 1588 led to the ascendancy of English sea power, fueling the country's desire for an empire in the New World. That desire was also heightened by the printing and popularity of accounts of the explorations of that world, for example Richard Hakluyt's *Divers Voyages Touching the Discoverie of America and the Ilands Adjacent unto the Same* (1582). In what is now usually called *Discourse Concerning Western Planting*, written two years later, Hakluyt

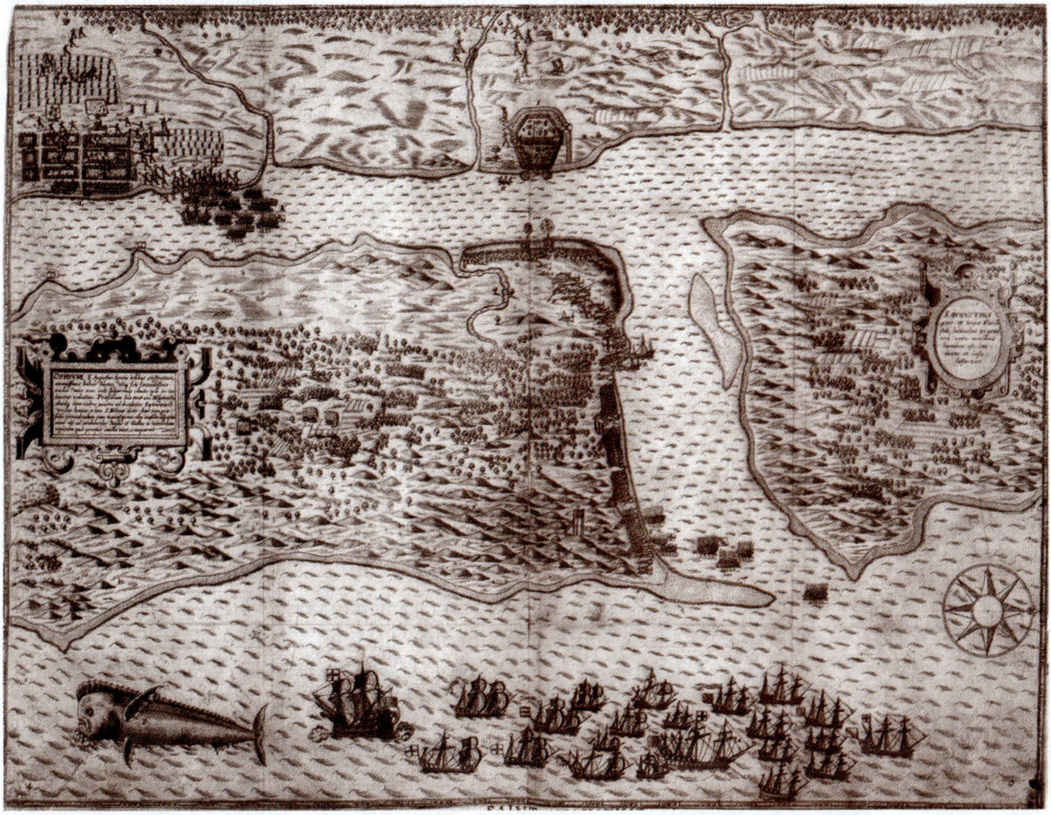

Baptista Boazio, *Augustine par Floridae* (1589)

In an early demonstration of the growing ascendancy of English sea power, Sir Francis Drake attacked the Spanish settlement at St. Augustine, Florida, in 1586, as illustrated by this map published in London. After looting and burning the settlement, Drake sailed north, stopping at the ill-fated English colony at Roanoke Island before returning to England.

outlined a new approach to colonization, proposing that the poor and discontented in the mother country should be resettled in new lands in North America, where they could gather and export the raw materials that would sustain the growing manufacturing capability of England. Under the direction of Sir Walter Raleigh, the English in 1585 attempted to establish a colony in Virginia, an area named after their "virgin" queen Elizabeth I. The colony at Roanoke Island, off the coast of present-day North Carolina, was abandoned after only ten months, and a second group of more than one hundred settlers who arrived there in 1587 disappeared, leaving hardly a trace and giving rise to the mystery of the so-called Lost Colony.

Despite the disastrous end of the colony at Roanoke Island, the English pursued their efforts to explore and colonize North America. Its beauty and seemingly limitless potential were promoted by the English historian and naturalist Thomas Hariot in his *Briefe and True Report of the New Found Land of Virginia* (1588), which is generally considered to be the first original book about North America published in English. After cataloging the animals, plants, and other natural resources that had been discovered in the relatively small area that he and others had explored during their stay at Roanoke Island in 1585, Hariot asked, "Why may wee not then looke for in good hope from the inner parts of more and greater plentie, as well as of other things, as of those which wee have alreadie discovered?" In 1607, the English finally established a permanent colony in Virginia, Jamestown, named after Queen Elizabeth's successor, King James I. A key figure in the early survival of the colony, which was undermined by organizational problems, rampant disease, and conflicts with the tribes of the Powhatan Confederacy, was Captain John Smith. An adventurer, explorer, and a professional soldier, Smith was also a brilliant publicist who tirelessly promoted colonization in widely distributed works like *A Map of Virginia: With a Description of the Countrey* (1612). He also reconnoitered and named an area that became the next dramatic stage for English colonization, which Smith urged in yet another of his best-selling works, *A Description of New England* (1616).

"Why may wee not then looke for in good hope from the inner parts of more and greater plentie, as well as of other things, as of those which wee have alreadie discovered?"

The Protestant Reformation and the Puritan "Errand into the Wilderness"

In addition to commercial interests and the nationalistic desire to dispossess the Spanish, English colonization was driven by religious forces unleashed by the Protestant Reformation. Throughout the Middle Ages, Roman Catholicism was the sole Christian religion of Europe. During the early Renaissance, however, advancements in science and technology, the rise of the middle class, and an increasingly literate population brought significant challenges to the power and authority of the Catholic Church. In the view of growing numbers of people, the church, with its extensive hierarchy and vast wealth, had moved away from the simplicity and spirituality of the religion practiced by Christ and his disciples. Efforts to reform the church began as early as the 1380s. A central figure of that movement in England was John Wycliffe, who has been described as the "Morning Star of the Reformation." The official Bible of the Catholic Church was the Latin Vulgate (meaning common or vulgar tongue), a fourth-century translation by St. Jerome. Over the centuries, however, Latin became the language of the highly educated, so common people could not understand church liturgy or read the Bible. Strongly believing that all Christians should be able to read the Bible, Wycliffe translated it from Latin into English and recruited itinerant preachers, called Lollards, to spread the scriptures in English.

Although the movement he inspired was short-lived, Wycliffe anticipated the efforts of later reformers, who also emphasized the importance of individual reading and interpretation of the Bible. Their efforts to make it available in translation to large numbers of people were powerfully aided by the development of the printing press. Martin Luther, the leader of the Protestant Reformation in Germany, hurried his translation of the New Testament through the press in 1522 and then published parts of the Old Testament as he completed them, finally printing the whole Bible in 1534. After seizing control of the holdings of the Catholic Church and establishing the Church of England, Henry VIII ordered the preparation and publication of the Great Bible (1537), the first authorized Bible in English. The Reformation in England was briefly checked when the Catholic queen, Mary Tudor, ascended the throne in 1553. The widespread religious persecutions during her five-year reign drove many Protestant clergymen to Geneva, Switzerland, where with the support of the radical reformers John Calvin and John Knox the English exiles produced the Geneva Bible (1560). The first Bible in English to add numbers to chapters and verses for easy reference, as well as interpretive marginal notes, the Geneva Bible was so popular that nearly 150 editions were published between 1560 and 1644.

During those decades, Protestantism became firmly established in England. But more radical religious reformers faced growing pressure to conform to the practices and teachings of the Church of England. Elizabeth I, who assumed the throne after the death of Queen Mary in 1558, had little sympathy for the "Puritans," those who sought further to "purify" the Church of England of the vestiges of Roman Catholicism. Her successor, James I, who ruled England from 1603 to 1625, was even more disdainful of the Puritans. In an effort to supplant the strongly anti-Catholic Geneva Bible, the favored Bible of the Puritans, James sponsored a new translation, the King James Version, which became the official Bible of the

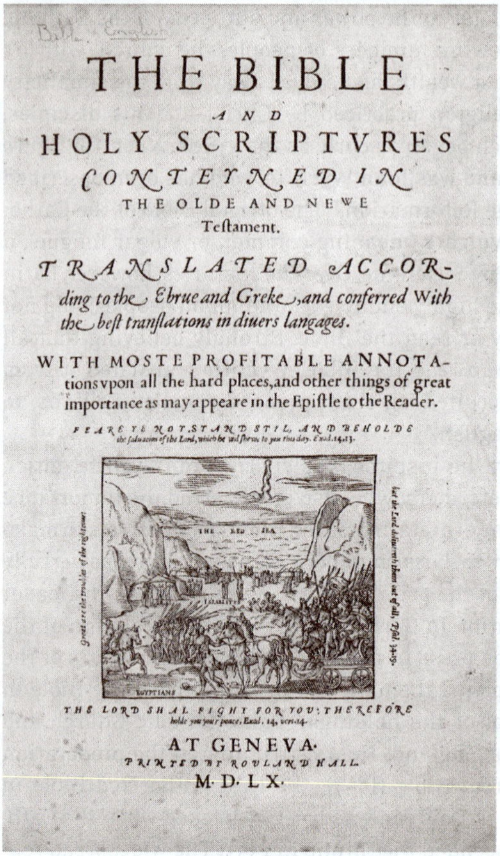

THE BIBLE
AND
HOLY SCRIPTVRES
CONTEYNED IN
THE OLDE AND NEWE
Testament.
TRANSLATED ACCORding to the Ebrue and Greke, and conferred With the best translations in diuers langages.
WITH MOSTE PROFITABLE ANNOTAtions vpon all the hard places, and other things of great importance as may appeare in the Epistle to the Reader.
FEARE YE NOT, STAND STIL, AND BEHOLDE the saluacion of the Lord, which he wil shewe to you this day. Exod. 14, 13.
THE LORD SHAL FIGHT FOR YOU: THEREFORE holde you your peace, Exod. 14, vers. 14.
AT GENEVA.
PRINTED BY ROVLAND HALL.
M. D. LX.

Geneva Bible

The title page from the 1560 edition of the Geneva Bible depicts the Egyptians pursuing the Hebrews as they near the Red Sea. This Bible was used by both the Pilgrims and the Puritans, who conceived of themselves as the new Israelites journeying out of spiritual bondage to the promised land.

Church of England. Nonetheless, most Puritans remained committed to the established church, which they sought to reform from within. But some Puritans formally separated themselves from the Church of England. Following the model established by John Calvin in Geneva, such "Separatists" formed independent churches, each based on a formal covenant, or binding agreement, freely entered into by all members of the church. That drastic step was an act of treason, and King James described a Separatist as "a rat to be trapped and tossed away." Facing growing persecution in England, a small group of Separatists that called themselves "Pilgrims" fled the country in 1608.

After living in the Netherlands for more than a decade, the Pilgrims sailed to New England on the *Mayflower* in 1620. In a moving description of their arrival on the shores of Cape Cod in November, William Bradford in his history *Of Plimoth Plantation* declared, "Besides, what could they see but a hideous and desolate wilderness, full of wild beasts and wild men."

But the survival of the Pilgrims would be due in large part to the aid and security provided by those "wild men." The Pilgrims established their colony on the south shore of Massachusetts Bay, on the grounds of what they thought was an abandoned Indian village but was actually the summer home of a local tribe, the Wampanoag. After a difficult winter, during which about half of the ninety-nine "first comers" who had arrived at Plymouth aboard the *Mayflower* died of disease and malnutrition, the forlorn Pilgrims were visited by Squanto. A Patuxet Indian who had been captured as a young man and taken to England, where he learned to speak English, Squanto assisted the Pilgrims by showing them how to hunt and fish as well as how to plant crops that would grow in New England. In 1621, the colony at Plymouth signed a peace treaty with Massasoit, the chief of the Wampanoag, with whom the Pilgrims lived in peace for several decades. With the settlement on an increasingly secure footing, Bradford and Edward Winslow sent an account of its first year to England, where it was published as *A Relation or Journal of the Beginning and Proceedings of the English Plantation Settled at Plimoth in New England* (1622), commonly known as *Mourt's Relation*. Largely ignoring the hardships of the first winter, the book instead focused on the rich natural resources of New England. It consequently helped attract additional colonists to Plymouth and the surrounding area, where the population rapidly increased from the fifty survivors of the first winter to as many as 3,000 by 1640.

"Besides, what could they see but a hideous and desolate wilderness, full of wild beasts and wild men."

Despite its success, Plymouth was soon overshadowed by another colony established by religious dissidents from England. Following the death of King James in 1625, the throne passed to his son, Charles I, who was even more hostile to those who sought to purify the Church of England. Despairing of conditions in England, some of the beleaguered Puritans began to consider the possibility of immigrating to New England, where they might establish a truly reformed church, without the hierarchy and stripped of what they viewed as the noxious ceremonies, rituals, and trappings held over from the Catholic Church in the Church of England. The Massachusetts Bay Company, formed by a group of wealthy Puritans in London, obtained a royal charter, or grant, to establish a colony in New England. In 1630, what came to be called the Great Migration began, as a group of more than seven hundred people led by John Winthrop sailed on a fleet of ships from England to an area north of Plymouth, around present-day Boston. Unlike the Pilgrims, who were forced by circumstances to leave first England and then Holland, the Puritans embarked on what the minister Samuel Danforth later described as an "errand into the wilderness," a journey as fraught with significance as the analogous journey of the ancient Israelites out of bondage in Egypt to the promised land. Indeed, the Puritans viewed themselves as God's new chosen people, whose holy task was to establish a church and community based strictly on the revealed word of God in the Bible. As many historians have emphasized, however, the Puritans were also strongly entrepreneurial and eager to capitalize on the plentiful land and rich opportunities available in the New World. Although the early years of the Massachusetts Bay Colony were difficult, the settlements grew and expanded from the coastal regions into the interior of New England. Over time, additional colonies were established, including new ones in present-day Rhode Island, Connecticut, and New Hampshire. By 1660, some 33,000 colonists were living in New England.

The growth and expansion of the colonies generated increasing conflicts with the indigenous population. The seal of the Massachusetts Bay Colony, which depicts an Indian saying, "Come Over and Help Us," suggests that a major impulse for colonization was to bring civilization and Christianity to the native peoples of New England. But their populations were increasingly decimated by the new diseases that the colonists brought with them, as well as by the Europeans' relentless incursions into tribal lands. In 1637, in the first of the many wars fought between the English settlers in New England and an Indian people, a military force from the Massachusetts Bay Colony attacked and burned a Pequot fort in what is now southeastern Connecticut. Between four hundred and seven hundred men, women, and children were killed, and most of the surviving

Seal of the Massachusetts Bay Colony

Designed in 1629, the seal depicts an Indian attired only in a girdle of leaves speaking the words "Come Over and Help Us," a plea for the gift of civilization and Christianity. In fact, most Indians neither wanted nor needed the help of the English settlers, who finally drove all but a few remnants of the native tribes out of New England.

Pequot were captured and divided as slaves or tributaries among the English and their Indian allies, the Mohegan and Narragansett. The Pequot War checked further Indian resistance in New England for nearly forty years. As disagreements about land boundaries increased and antagonism escalated, however, Massasoit's son Metacom led a coalition of tribes to war against the colonists in 1675. Called King Philip's War because the colonists considered Metacom as arrogant and proud as the hated King Philip of Spain, the war was devastating for both the colonists and the Indians. By the time it ended with Metacom's death in 1676, the war had claimed large numbers of casualties on both sides and caused the widespread destruction of property. Most crucially, in the aftermath of the war the power of the New England tribes was broken and the remaining native peoples were pushed farther and farther into the interior.

Literature and Cultural Diversity in Colonial America

As they expanded and solidified their hold on territory, the Puritans also established a vital literary culture in New England. Better educated than most other colonists, the Puritans and their New England neighbors were not simply people of the Bible. They also loved books of many kinds, which they imported and produced in growing profusion. Just as printing had earlier given enormous impetus to the early exploration and colonization of America, as well as to the Protestant Reformation, print culture played an important role in the Puritan settlement of New England. Two years after the first printing press in the colonies was brought to Boston in 1638, the publication of what is commonly known as the *Bay Psalm Book* marked the beginning of the American printing industry. In the following decades, it produced Bibles, religious tracts and sermons, histories, and reprints of English books like John Bunyan's *The Pilgrim's Progress*, among the most popular of all books written in English. Books written in New England also gained popularity. Anne Bradstreet's *The Tenth Muse* (1650), the first volume of poetry published by an English colonist, was printed in London. But in 1678, a second edition was published in Boston, where two of the best-selling books in colonial America were also published: Michael Wigglesworth's *The Day of Doom* (1662) and Mary Rowlandson's *The Sovereignty and Goodness of God* (1682). The first printing of Wigglesworth's long narrative poem about Judgment Day sold out within a year and was reprinted dozens of times, while Rowlandson's account of her captivity among the Indians during King Philip's War was one of the most popular of all prose works published during the seventeenth century, especially in America. By 1700, the publication of books and pamphlets was a growing business, serving more than 91,000 people in New England.

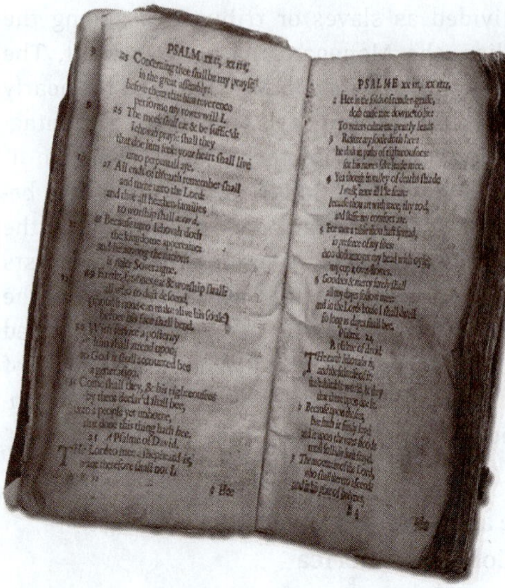

The Bay Psalm Book
The first book printed in what became the United States was *The Whole Book of Psalmes Faithfully Translated into English Metre*, published in 1640 for use in churches in New England. The Puritans prohibited the use of musical instruments and other distractions from the holy scriptures, but congregations sang the psalms in a chorus of praise for God. Psalm 23 begins at the bottom of the left page, where its familiar opening verse is translated: "The Lord to me a shepheard is, / want therefore shall not I."

But the rapid growth of the New England colonies also led to the decline of Puritanism. Its original sense of mission and community was undermined by a variety of factors, including changing patterns of immigration and the growth of commerce and cities. In 1700, Boston was an increasingly diverse city of 7,000 inhabitants, surpassing all other settlements in the English colonies, and its population grew to 17,000 by 1750. Even as Puritanism began to wane, however, it produced what are widely regarded as two of the most significant writers in colonial American literature, Edward Taylor and Jonathan Edwards. During his long career as a minister, which lasted from the 1670s until his death in 1729, Taylor wrote hundreds of sermons and over four hundred manuscript pages of verse. Although he modestly declined to publish any of his work, the power of the printed word was exploited by other Puritan ministers, including

Edwards. An influential preacher and theologian, Edwards was also one of the leaders of the "Great Awakening," an effort to revive the spirit of Puritanism in New England that lasted from roughly 1730 to 1750. Although that far-reaching religious revival was spread by itinerant preachers throughout the colonies, the Great Awakening is now perhaps best known through a single sermon, Edwards's "Sinners in the Hands of an Angry God," which was published soon after he delivered the sermon in 1741.

The emphasis on and pervasive influence of print culture in New England helps account for the central place Puritanism has assumed in the early history of American literature. Certainly, the achievements of Puritan writers have tended to overshadow other writings of the period before 1750. Nonetheless, a diverse array of histories, letters, poems, promotional tracts, and travel narratives were also produced throughout the colonies controlled by Great Britain. Partly because the printing business developed more slowly in the colonies outside of New England, most of the works in English published by settlers in or by visitors to the middle and southern colonies were printed in London. Many other works were circulated in manuscript form. The latter method was preferred by writers among the colonial gentry in southern colonies like Virginia, where the pattern of development differed radically from that followed in New England. Although the Jamestown Colony nearly succumbed to hardship, disease, and conflicts with the native peoples of the area, the successful introduction of tobacco and the cultivation of other crops spurred the development of a rapidly expanding system of slave labor and the emergence of a wealthy planter elite composed of men like William Byrd II. Educated in London, Byrd collected one of the largest and most diverse libraries in the colonies at Westover, his plantation on the James River. He also wrote a wide range of works, notably a remarkable private diary and *History of the Dividing Line*, an account of a survey conducted in 1728 of the disputed border between Virginia and North Carolina.

At the opening of that work, Byrd traces the overall development of the British colonies in North America, from the time when all English territory went under the "General Name of Virginia" to 1728, by which time that territory had been divided into twelve colonies extending from New Hampshire in the north as far south as the Carolinas. (The last of the original thirteen British colonies, Georgia, was founded in 1732 by the philanthropist James Oglethorpe as a penal colony for the resettlement of people confined in debtor prisons in England.) In contrast to most historians in New England, who piously celebrated the achievements of founders like William Bradford and John Winthrop, Byrd satirically observes that when the first "adventurers" in Virginia finally established themselves at Jamestown "they built a church that cost no more than fifty pounds and a tavern that cost five hundred." Byrd, a firm supporter of the Church of

England, was equally irreverent about the "swarm of dissenters" that had fled to Plymouth and the "Puritanical sect" that had founded the Massachusetts Bay Colony. At the same time, he acknowledges the achievements of those "frugal and industrious" settlers. Byrd also emphasizes the vital role religion played in the establishment of the British colonies – not only in New England, but also in Maryland, established in 1634 by Sir George Calvert, "a zealous Catholic," and in Pennsylvania, founded in 1681 as a place of religious freedom by the English Quaker William Penn. "The Quakers flocked over to this country in shoals," Byrd sardonically observes, "being averse to go to Heaven the same way with the bishops [of the Church of England]."

As Byrd and many others recognized, the colonies were less a single, unified entity than a group of diverse, loosely associated provinces under the general dominion of the king of Great Britain. Moreover, those colonies together constituted only part of the rich and complex tapestry

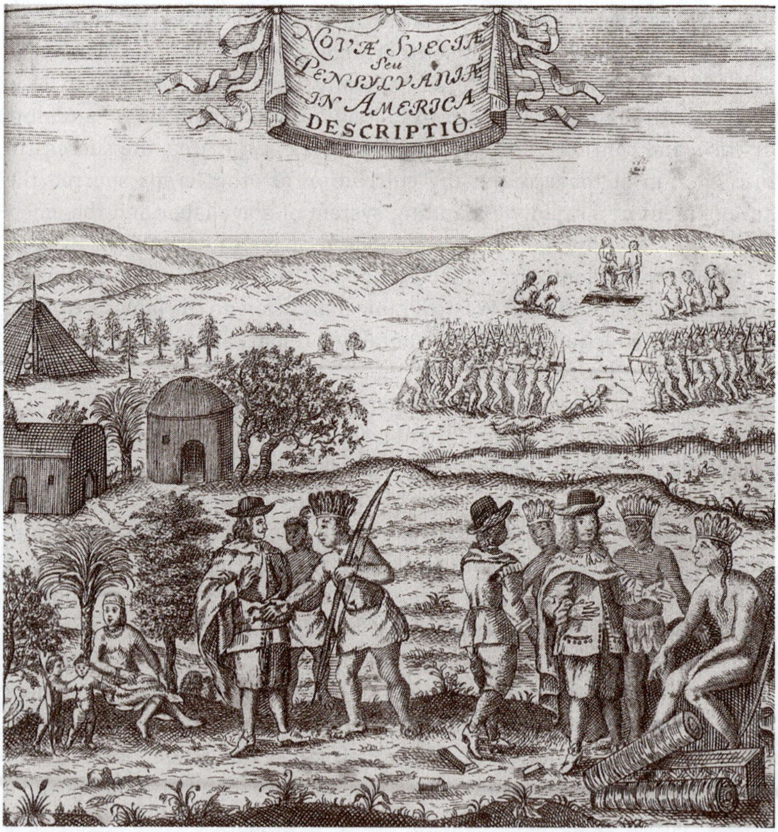

Novae Sveciae seu Pensylvania in America

This engraving from a Swedish book published in Stockholm in 1702 is thought to show William Penn negotiating with the Indians, while a Native American mother watches over her children in the foreground and two groups of Native Americans battle in the background. Penn's land grant included a portion of what had originally been New Sweden, and Pennsylvania attracted settlers from throughout Europe.

formed by the colonial experience in North America. At roughly the same time the Pilgrims and Puritans were establishing their colonies in New England, the Dutch established New Amsterdam on Manhattan Island in 1625, while in 1638 the settlements constituting New Sweden were founded farther south, primarily in the present state of Delaware. Those settlements ultimately came under control of the British, whose colonies also became increasingly less English as large numbers of immigrants were drawn from other European countries and growing numbers of slaves were forcibly transported to North America. By 1750, the thirteen British colonies had a population of nearly 1.2 million people, including large numbers of immigrants from Germany, Scotland, Ireland, and Holland, as well as nearly half a million enslaved people from Africa. But those thirteen colonies occupied only a small portion of the continent of North America, vast areas of which were controlled by the French and the Spanish, as well as by Native American peoples. Although much of the diversity of the world Columbus discovered had been destroyed since his first landing in the West Indies little more than 250 years earlier, North America remained a complex, multilingual, and culturally diverse place in 1750.

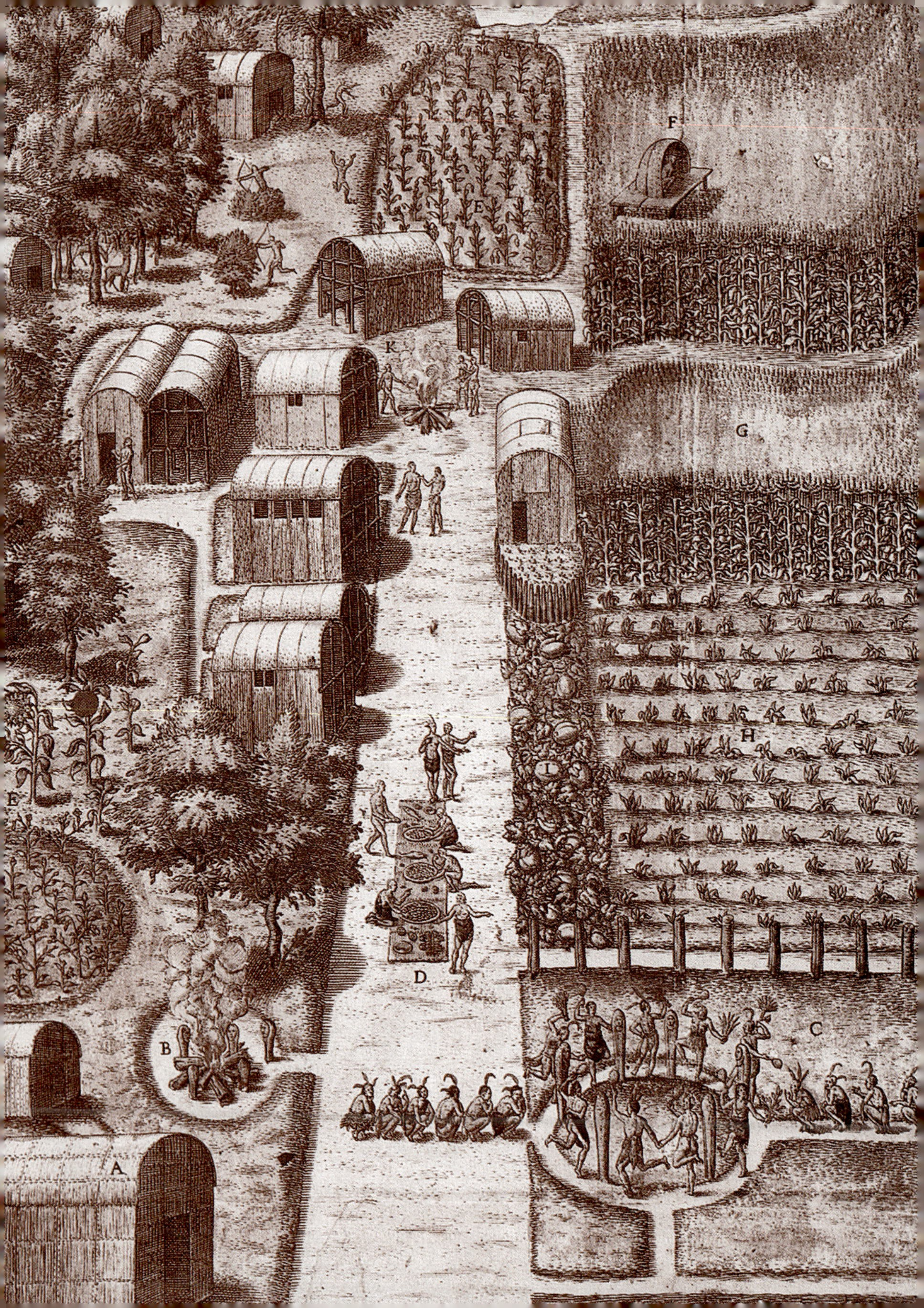

F
E
K
G
H
I
E
D
B
C
A

Native American Origin and Creation Stories

THE ORAL LITERATURE OF Native Americans includes poems, songs, and stories, many of which existed centuries before the arrival of the earliest European explorers in the late-fifteenth and sixteenth centuries. Although the Europeans could not comprehend it, the Native American societies they encountered had long, dynamic, and complex histories. There were multiple civilizations in existence throughout the Americas. Even within

◀ **Secotan Village**

This engraving by Theodor de Bry was copied from a drawing by John White, an English artist who visited the village of Secotan on the coast of present-day North Carolina in 1585. White notes on the original that the building marked *A* at the lower left was a tomb where the bodies of important leaders were kept, while the fire burning at *B* was "the place of solemn prayer." In addition to the dwellings lining the central space, where men and women ate, the drawing illustrates the careful management and use of land. Men hunt deer on the outskirts of the village, whose crops include tobacco, pumpkins, and sunflowers, as well as corn in three stages of growth. White's idealized drawing reveals a world of natural abundance and social harmony, religion and peace, a world that would soon be disrupted by invaders from England.

the more limited boundaries of what is today the continental United States, there was enormous diversity. Native American peoples ranged from the Iroquois Confederacy of tribes in the Northeast to the Cherokee in the Southeast, from the Akimel O'odham (Pima) in the Southwest to ancient tribes like the Hupa on the West coast and several groups that came to be called the Sioux in the upper Mississippi valley and on the Great Plains. Native American peoples were divided among many tribes and clans, spoke literally hundreds of mutually unintelligible languages, and lived under a wide variety of political and social organizations. Some subsisted by hunting, fishing, and gathering nuts, seeds, and berries, while many others were farmers living in villages and towns, especially in the Northeast and Southeast. Still others lived in urban centers in the middle of the continent, where the great Mississippian culture lasted for nearly nine hundred years, as well as in the Southwest, where many tribes built complex cities and developed extensive irrigation systems for their crops.

Native American peoples were also culturally diverse in ways that were difficult for European explorers to understand or value. In contrast to Christianized Europe, there were a wide variety of religious and mythological beliefs throughout the Americas. Although there were no written languages that Europeans could fully comprehend, Native Americans had developed various forms of writing, including Incan *quipus* (knotted cords), Mayan hieroglyphics, and the wampum belts used by the Iroquois.

Iroquois Wampum Belt

Wampum belts, made of beads acquired through trade with coastal tribes in New England, were used by the Iroquois to commemorate events, record beliefs, and seal agreements. This belt symbolizes the formation of the Haudenosaunee, which later became known by the French as the Iroquois Confederacy. The pine tree in the center represents the Onondaga Nation. The rectangles represent the other four nations of the Haudenosaunee: the Mohawk, Oneida, Seneca, and Cayuga.

But the primary vehicle for the preservation of culture was spoken language, through which poems, songs, and stories were passed down from generation to generation. Storytelling was a central feature of communal life, a principal way in which Native American peoples provided entertainment, educated their young, and transmitted their traditions. European explorers and missionaries, who were emissaries of an increasingly pervasive print culture, consequently tended to view Native American societies and religions as simple and unsophisticated. They also misunderstood the names of and distinctions among various tribes and groups. For example, when the Spanish missionaries encountered tribes in the southern part of present-day Arizona, they named them the "Pima," a corruption of the tribe's word for "no," which the missionaries mistook for a proper noun. Later, the French used the word *Sioux*, their rendering of an Ojibwa word meaning enemies or "treacherous snakes," as the collective name for three large nations with different cultures and dialects. The large, loosely constructed group that came to be known as the Sioux called themselves names that signified allies or an alliance of friends: the Dakota, the Lakota, and the Nakota.

At the same time, some of the early explorers attempted to learn Native American languages and record the stories they heard. One of the first was Gabriel Sagard, a French missionary and early ethnographer who visited New France, as the French colony in present-day eastern Canada was called, in 1623-24. Sagard studied the Huron language and even prepared a dictionary for missionaries to use. He also transcribed and translated a version of a creation story that he learned from the Hurons, which Sagard published in an account of his journey, *Le Grand Voyage du Pays des Hurons* (1632). Sagard's book anticipated the way in which much Native American lore would be preserved. Because the societies themselves were being systematically destroyed, the primary means of preserving vestiges of their oral heritages was through transcription and translation into European languages.

In what became the United States, however, the effort at preservation did not begin in earnest until the nineteenth century, when Native Americans and their rich cultures were being erased from the landscape and memory of the nation. The texts of many ancient narratives were consequently first published at a comparatively late date, and translations of such works continue to appear in print. Both Native Americans and European Americans have participated in the effort to record the history, mythology, and narrative traditions of the Indians. Among the first Native Americans who sought to preserve oral culture in print was David Cusick, a Tuscarora who published *Sketches of the Ancient History of the Six Nations* in 1827. Another important figure who spurred the emerging interest in Native American culture and history was Henry Rowe Schoolcraft (1793-1864), a federal agent of Indian affairs for the Great Lakes region who married the half-Ojibwa daughter of a fur trader and learned both the

Gabriel Sagard, *Le Grand Voyage du Pays des Hurons* (1632)
As the title page of his book indicates, Sagard offers an overview of Huron culture and a review of missionary efforts in New France. The book includes one of the earliest translations of a Native American oral story, as well as a dictionary of the Huron language.

language and much of the lore of her tribe. His wife, Jane Johnston Schoolcraft (1800-1841), was one of the first Native Americans to write short stories based on Indian lore, while Schoolcraft himself published over twenty books about Indian history, customs, and language, notably his *Historical and Statistical Information Respecting . . . the Indian Tribes of the United States* (6 vol., 1851-57).

Throughout the late-nineteenth and twentieth centuries, hundreds of other anthropologists and historians also attempted to preserve the oral traditions of Native Americans. Versions of the same story often differed dramatically. By its very nature, an oral tradition is evolutionary and adaptive, so stories inevitably change from generation to generation. Moreover, different tellers shaped stories in various ways, while different interpreters imposed their own cultural beliefs on the stories they transcribed and translated. Differences in language presented additional obstacles to these early interpreters, since there was no English equivalent for many of the concepts and words in Native American languages. In the Lakota story included here, "*Wohpe* and the Gift of the Pipe," for example, the term *wakan* has often been translated as "holy," especially by missionaries eager to put a Christian spin on a narrative. But the term actually has a much more complicated meaning, blending the concepts of both mystery and power. Finally, the force and meaning of many Native American poems, songs, and stories depends on oral performance, which is difficult to capture on the printed page, especially in translation. Indeed, crucial elements of oral performance – the expressions and gestures of the speaker, the rhythms and sounds of the original language, and both the physical and cultural context in which the story is told – are quite literally lost in translation into English and onto the printed page.

When making the effort to study and understand Native American oral literature, we consequently must accept the fact that the record is fragmentary and often problematic. The stories gathered in the following section are intended as examples from several geographical locations of the kinds of indigenous origin and creation stories that were a part of the multiple cultures in existence at the time of the first explorations of what Europeans thought of as a "new" world. The narratives presented here include accounts of the beginning of the world, the creation of natural phenomena, the history of ritual objects, and the origin of ceremonies and cultural traditions, each offering at least a glimpse of the richness and complexity of the earliest literature of North America.

Iroquois Confederacy

The people known as the Iroquois originally lived in a large area of present-day New York State, east of the Hudson River and south of the St. Lawrence River. At the time of the first European explorations of the area around 1600, there were approximately 20,000 people in the political union of the five tribes of the Iroquois Confederacy: the Cayuga, Mohawk, Seneca, Oneida, and Onondaga. The Tuscarora were incorporated into the league in 1722, and the confederacy became known as the Six Indian Nations or Six Nations Confederacy. The various tribes spoke dialects of what is called the Iroquoian-Northern language. The Iroquois were farmers and hunters who lived in small villages, a distinctive feature of which was the "longhouse," a large multifamily dwelling that often housed an entire clan. In fact, the Iroquois called themselves *Haudenosaunee*, or "the people of the longhouse." Their social structure was matrilineal, and when a couple married the man moved into the woman's longhouse. In addition

You don't have anything if you don't have the stories.
-Leslie Marmon Silko

to determining kinship and making many family decisions, women also owned property.

Known for their military prowess, the Iroquois were powerful and savvy warriors who used their strong political organization to their advantage. Despite their relatively small numbers, the Iroquois successfully resisted the incursions of European settlers until the Revolutionary War, when they sided with the British. American troops invaded their homeland in 1779, driving many of the Iroquois into southern Canada. In the decades following the war, they lost much of their land through deceptive treaties. Many of the Iroquois were removed to reservations in New York, from which some tribes were later relocated to Wisconsin, now the home of most of the Oneida, and to the Indian Territory, now Oklahoma, home of the modern-day Seneca-Cayuga tribe.

***bedfordstmartins.com/ americanlit** for research links on Native American tales and stories*

"Origin of Folk Stories" (Seneca). The most populous of the original five tribes of the Iroquois Nation, the Seneca occupied an area between the Genesee River and Seneca Lake in the Finger Lakes region of present-day New York State. Like the other Iroquois tribes, the Seneca lived in villages with longhouses – dwellings for extended families – and were primarily agricultural, raising corn, squash, and beans. They also followed the political organization of the larger Iroquois Nation, holding elections to remove leaders who were proven to be corrupt or incompetent. The Seneca were fiercely protective of their homes and were skilled in warfare. One of their most famous leaders was Red Jacket (1750-1830), known for his skill as an orator, his political leadership, and his valiant efforts to maintain tribal lands and culture in the face of constant incursions by white settlers. In a speech attributed to him in 1805, Red Jacket is recorded as saying, "The Great Spirit . . . has made a great difference between his white and red children; we do not wish to destroy your religion or take it from you. We only want to enjoy our own." The oral cultures of Native American tribes depended on the telling of stories to preserve their history, religion, and traditions. There was, consequently, considerable interest in how stories originated. In the following Seneca story, which is variously known as the "Origin of Folk Stories" and "The Story-Telling Stone," an outcast orphan becomes a hero through his knowledge of the source, or origin, of stories. The text is taken from *Seneca Myths and Folk Tales* (1923), collected by Arthur C. Parker, a Seneca.

ORIGIN OF FOLK STORIES

There was once a boy who had no home. His parents were dead and his uncles would not care for him. In order to live this boy, whose name was Gaqka, or Crow, made a bower of branches for an abiding place and hunted birds and squirrels for food.

He had almost no clothing but was very ragged and dirty. When the people from the village saw him they called him Filth-Covered-One, and laughed as they passed by, holding their noses. No one thought he would ever amount to anything, which made him feel heavy-hearted. He resolved to go away from his tormentors and become a great hunter.

One night Gaqka found a canoe. He had never seen this canoe before, so he took it. Stepping in he grasped the paddle, when the canoe immediately shot into the air, and he paddled above the clouds and under the moon. For a long time he went always southward. Finally the canoe dropped into a river and then Gaqka paddled for shore.

On the other side of the river was a great cliff that had a face that looked like a man. It was at the forks of the river where this cliff stood. The boy resolved to make his home on the top of the cliff and so climbed it and built a bark cabin.

The first night he sat on the edge of the cliff he heard a voice saying, "Give me some tobacco." Looking around the boy, seeing no one, replied, "Why should I give tobacco?"

There was no answer and the boy began to fix his arrows for the next day's hunt. After a while the voice spoke again, "Give me some tobacco."

Gaqka now took out some tobacco and threw it over the cliff. The voice spoke again: "Now I will tell you a story."

Feeling greatly awed the boy listened to a story that seemed to come directly out of the rock upon which he was sitting. Finally the voice paused, for the story had ended. Then it spoke again saying, "It shall be the custom hereafter to present me with a small gift for my stories." So the boy gave the rock a few bone beads. Then the rock said, "Hereafter when I speak, announcing that I shall tell a story you must say, 'Nio,' and as I speak you must say 'Hĕⁿ´,' that I may know that you are listening. You must never fall asleep but continue to listen until I say 'Dā´neho nigagā´is.' (So thus finished is the length of my story). Then you shall give me presents and I shall be satisfied."

The next day the boy hunted and killed a great many birds. These he made into soup and roasts. He skinned the birds and saved the skins, keeping them in a bag.

That evening the boy sat on the rock again and looked westward at the sinking sun. He wondered if his friend would speak again. While waiting he chipped some new arrow-points, and made them very small so that he could use them in a blow gun. Suddenly, as he worked, he heard the voice again. "Give me some tobacco to smoke," it said. Gaqka threw a pinch of tobacco over the cliff and the voice said, "Hau'nio'´," and commenced a story. Long into the night one wonderful tale after another flowed from the rock, until it called out, "So thus finished is the length of my story." Gaqka was sorry to have the stories ended but he gave the rock an awl made from a bird's leg and a pinch of tobacco.

The next day the boy hunted far to the east and there found a village. Nobody knew who he was but he soon found many friends. There were some hunters who offered to teach him how to kill big game, and these went with him to his own camp on the high rock. At night he allowed them to listen to the stories that came forth from the rock, but it would speak only when Gaqka was present. He therefore had many friends with whom to hunt.

Now after a time Gaqka made a new suit of clothing from deer skin and desired to obtain a decorated pouch. He, therefore, went to the village and found one house where there were two daughters living with an old mother. He asked that a pouch be made and the youngest daughter spoke up and said, "It is now finished. I have been waiting for you to come for it." So she gave him a handsome pouch.

Then the old mother spoke, saying, "I now perceive that my future son-in-law has passed through the door and is here." Soon thereafter, the younger woman brought Gaqka a basket of bread and said, "My mother greatly desires that you should marry me." Gaqka looked at the girl and was satisfied, and ate the bread. The older daughter was greatly displeased and frowned in an evil manner.

That night the bride said to her husband, "We must now go away. My older sister will kill you for she is jealous." So Gaqka arose and took his bride to his own lodge. Soon the rock spoke and began to relate wonder stories of things that happened in the old days. The bride was not surprised, but said, "This standing rock, indeed, is my grandfather. I will now present you with a pouch into which you must put a trophy[1] for every tale related."

All winter long the young couple stayed in the lodge on the great rock and heard all the wonder tales of the old days. Gaqka's bag was full of stories and he knew all the lore of former times.

As springtime came the bride said, "We must now go north to your own people and you shall become a great man." But Gaqka was sad and said, "Alas, in my own country I am an outcast and called by an unpleasant name."

The bride only laughed, saying, "Nevertheless we shall go north."

Taking their pelts and birdskins, the young couple descended the cliff and seated themselves in the canoe. "This is my canoe," said the bride. "I sent it through the air to you."

The bride seated herself in the bow of the canoe and Gaqka in the stern. Grasping a paddle he swept it through the water, but soon the canoe arose and went through the air. Meanwhile the bride was singing all kinds of songs, which Gaqka learned as he paddled.

When they reached the north, the bride said, "Now I shall remove your clothing and take all the scars from your face and body." She then caused him to pass through a hollow log, and when Gaqka emerged from the other end he was dressed in the finest clothing and was a handsome man.

Together the two walked to the village where the people came out to see them. After a while Gaqka said, "I am the boy whom you once were accustomed to call 'Cia''dōdă'. I have now returned." That night the people of the village gathered around and listened to the tales he told, and he instructed them to give him small presents and tobacco. He would plunge his hand in his pouch and take out a trophy, saying, "Ho ho'! So here is another one!" and then looking at his trophy would relate an ancient tale.

Everybody now thought Gaqka a great man and listened to his stories. He was the first man to find out all about the adventures of the old-time people. That is why there are so many legends now.

[1923]

---

1. **trophy:** A token or an object used as an aid to the memory of an occasion or event.

"A Tale of the Foundation of the Great Island, Now North America" (Tuscarora). The rich oral cultures of virtually all Native American tribes include stories that account for the creation of the world. One type of account that recurs in several cultures is called the earth-diver story, which generally follows a standard narrative line in which a flood covers the earth until an animal dives into the waters and retrieves enough mud and soil to begin the creation of a new earth. The following version of the Iroquois creation story was the first translated and published by David Cusick, a Tuscarora. Thought to have been born at the end of the eighteenth century in Oneida Territory in present-day Madison County, New York, Cusick was evidently educated at a Christian mission school in Niagara County, New York. In the preface to his *Sketches of Ancient History of the Six Nations*, which was first published in Lewiston, New York, in 1827, Cusick explains that he wanted "to throw some light on the history of the original population of the country" by recording and translating the stories and traditional lore of the Iroquois. Although he was dedicated to preserving those accounts, many Seneca scholars today suggest that Cusick's religious training shaped his versions of native stories. Certainly, his version of the Iroquois creation story bears some striking similarities to Christian creation stories. In Cusick's version, a woman who is a part of the newly formed earth bears twins, one good and one evil, who ultimately battle for supremacy. In the end, the evil twin becomes a kind of devil. The text is taken from the second edition of *David Cusick's Sketches of Ancient History of the Six Nations* (1828).

A TALE OF THE FOUNDATION OF THE GREAT ISLAND, NOW NORTH AMERICA – THE TWO INFANTS BORN, AND THE CREATION OF THE UNIVERSE

Among the ancients there were two worlds in existence. The lower world was in a great darkness; the possession of the great monsters; but the upper world was inhabited by mankind;[1] and there was a woman conceived and would have the twin born. When her travail[2] drew near, and her situation seemed to produce a great distress on her mind, and she was induced by some of her relations to lay herself on a mattrass which was prepared, so as to gain refreshments to her wearied body; but while she was asleep the very place sunk down towards the dark world. The monsters of the great water were alarmed at her appearance of descending to the lower world; in consequence all the species of the creatures were immediately collected into where it was expected she would fall. When the monsters were assembled, and they made consultation, one of them was appointed

1. **mankind:** Human beings occupied the upper world while mysterious, nonhuman creatures occupied the lower world.
2. **travail:** Labor pains.

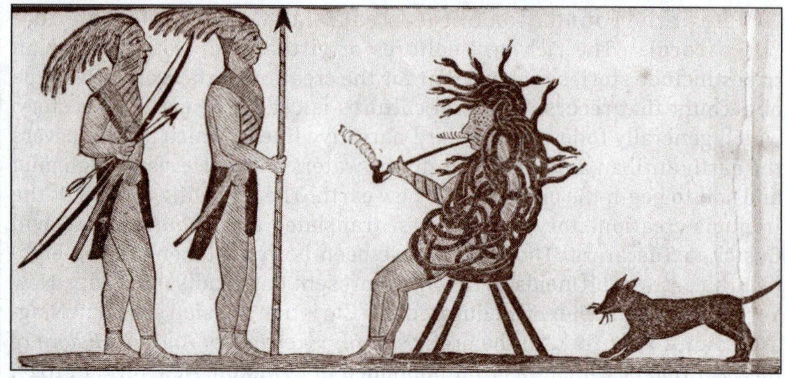

Atotarho, a Famous War Chief, Resided at Onondaga

This was one of several illustrations, probably based on those made by the author or his brother Dennis, that appeared in *David Cusick's Sketches of the Ancient History of the Six Nations* (1828).

in haste to search the great deep, in order to procure some earth, if it could be obtained; accordingly the monster descends, which succeeds, and returns to the place. Another requisition was presented, who would be capable to secure the woman from the terrors of the great water, but none was able to comply except a large turtle came forward and made proposal to them to endure her lasting weight, which was accepted. The woman was yet descending from a great distance. The turtle executes upon the spot, and a small quantity of earth was varnished on the back part of the turtle. The woman alights on the seat prepared, and she receives a satisfaction.[3] While holding her, the turtle increased every moment and became a considerable island of earth, and apparently covered with small bushes. The woman remained in a state of unlimited darkness, and she was overtaken by her travail to which she was subject. While she was in the limits of distress one of the infants in her womb was moved by an evil opinion and he was determined to pass out under the side of the parent's arm, and the other infant in vain endeavoured to prevent his design. The woman was in a painful condition during the time of their disputes, and the infants entered the dark world by compulsion, and their parent expired in a few moments. They had the power of sustenance without a nurse, and remained in the dark regions. After a time the turtle increased to a great Island and the infants were grown up, and one of them possessed with a gentle disposition, and named ENIGORIO, i. e. the good mind. The other youth possessed an insolence of character, and was named ENIGONHAHETGEA, i. e. the bad mind. The good mind was not contented to remain in a dark situation, and he was anxious to create a great light in the dark world; but the bad mind was desirous that the world should remain in a natural state. The good mind determines to prosecute his designs, and therefore commences the work of creation. At first he took the parent's head, (the deceased) of which he created an orb, and established it in the centre of the firmament, and it became of a very superiour nature to bestow light to the new world, (now the sun) and again he took the remnant of the body and formed another orb, which was inferiour to the light (now moon). In the orb a cloud of legs appeared to prove it was the body of the good mind, (parent) The former was to give

3. **she receives a satisfaction:** That is, the woman has a safe landing on the seat.

light to the day and the latter to the night; and he also created numerous spots of light, (now stars): these were to regulate the days, nights, seasons, years, &c. Whenever the light extended to the dark world the monsters were displeased and immediately concealed themselves in the deep places, lest they should be discovered by some human beings. The good mind continued the works of creation, and he formed numerous creeks and rivers on the Great Island, and then created numerous species of animals of the smallest and greatest, to inhabit the forests, and fishes of all kinds to inhabit the waters. When he had made the universe he was in doubt respecting some beings to possess the Great Island; and he formed two images of the dust of the ground in his own likeness, male and female, and by his breathing into their noistrils he gave them the living souls, and named them EA-GWE-HOWE, i. e. a real people;[4] and he gave the Great Island all the animals of game for their maintenance; and he appointed thunder to water the earth by frequent rains, agreeable to the nature of the system; after this the Island became fruitful and vegetation afforded the animals subsistence. The bad mind, while his brother was making the universe, went throughout the Island and made numerous high mountains and falls of water, and great steeps, and also creates various reptiles which would be injurious to mankind; but the good mind restored the Island to its former condition. The bad mind proceeded further in his motives and he made two images of clay in the form of mankind; but while he was giving them existence they became apes; and when he had not the power to create mankind he was envious against his brother; and again he made two of clay. The good mind discovered his brothers contrivances, and aided in giving them living souls,[5] (it is said these had the most knowledge of good and evil.) The good mind now accomplishes the works of creation, notwithstanding the imaginations of the bad mind were continually evil; and he attempted to enclose all the animals of game in the earth, so as to deprive them from mankind; but the good mind released them from confinement, (the animals were dispersed, and traces of them were made on the rocks near the cave where it was closed). The good mind experiences that his brother was at variance with the works of creation, and feels not disposed to favour any of his proceedings, but gives admonitions of his future state. Afterwards the good mind requested his brother to accompany him, as he was proposed to inspect the game, &c. but when a short distance from their nominal residence, the bad mind became so unmanly that he could not conduct his brother any more. The bad mind offered a challenge to his brother and resolved that who gains the victory should govern the universe; and appointed a day to meet the contest. The good mind was willing to submit to the offer, and he enters the reconciliation with his brother; which he falsely mentions that by whipping with flags would destroy his temporal life; and he earnestly solicits his brother also to notice the instrument of death, which he manifestly relates by the use of deer horns, beating his body he would expire. On the day appointed the engagement commenced, which lasted for two days: after

4. **EA-GWE-HOWE, i. e. a real people:** Iroquois name for human beings.
5. **giving them living souls:** "It appears by the fictitious accounts that the said beings became civilized people, and made their residence in the southern parts of the Island; but afterwards they were destroyed by the barbarous nations, and their fortifications were ruined unto this day." [Cusick's note.]

pulling up the trees and mountains as the track of a terrible whirlwind, at last the good mind gained the victory by using the horns, as mentioned the instrument of death, which he succeeded in deceiving his brother and he crushed him in the earth; and the last words uttered from the bad mind were, that he would have equal power over the souls of mankind after death; and he sinks down to eternal doom, and became the Evil Spirit. After this tumult the good mind repaired to the battle ground, and then visited the people and retires from the earth.

[1827, 1828]

Cherokee

The Cherokee originally occupied a large area of the Southeast, including parts of present-day North and South Carolina, Georgia, Alabama, Virginia, Tennessee, Kentucky, and Alabama. When they were encountered by the Spanish explorer Hernando de Soto in the mid-sixteenth century, the Cherokee were a large and complex nation made up of many smaller tribal units. Only rough estimates of the combined population of these units are possible, but it is thought that there were about 50,000 Cherokee in 1670. A series of smallpox epidemics introduced by European explorers de-

Sequoyah

This portrait of Sequoyah holding a copy of his alphabet of the Cherokee language, which he spent over a decade developing, appeared in *Indian Tribes of North America* (1836–44), by Thomas McKenney and James Hall.

creased the Cherokee population by as much as 50 percent by the mid-1700s. The well-organized Cherokee were an agricultural people who lived in small villages with a central council house devoted to meetings and religious ceremonies. Although the social structure was matrilineal, women did not have as much power as they did in the tribes of the Iroquois Confederacy.

The Cherokee spoke several dialects of Iroquoian. They were an oral culture until 1821, when a written alphabet of the Cherokee language was developed by one of their leaders, Sequoyah (1776-1843). By making literacy available to the Cherokee in their own language, Sequoyah sought to combat their growing assimilation into the dominant, English-speaking culture of the United States. In 1828, the *Cherokee Phoenix* became the first newspaper in the United States published in a Native American language and English. Like other eastern tribes throughout the early history of the colonies and the United States, the Cherokee were pressed to give up lands to white settlers. In 1830, Congress passed the Indian Removal Act, which authorized the president to exchange lands west of the Mississippi for the lands held by eastern tribes, including the Cherokee. The Cherokee, who included a population of over 17,000 in Georgia, resisted by filing a lawsuit against the state of Georgia. The Supreme Court refused to hear the case, ruling that the Cherokee had no legal standing and therefore could not sue the state. Eight years later, thousands of native peoples were forcibly removed from their lands and made to march over one thousand miles to "Indian Territory," present-day Oklahoma, a trek the Cherokee call the "Trail of Tears." Over 4,000 Cherokee died during the arduous removal. In the new territory, the Cherokee rebuilt their nation and developed a constitution, well before Oklahoma became a state in 1907.

bedfordstmartins.com/ americanlit *for research links on Native American tales and stories*

"How the World Was Made" (Cherokee). The rich oral culture of the Cherokee includes a wide variety of legends, myths, and stories. The following is an account of how the natural world was made and how it might be destroyed. Unlike many other Native American creation stories, the Cherokee account does not provide explanations for the origins of animals and humans. This story was transcribed and translated by the anthropologist James Mooney (1861-1921). The text is taken from the nineteenth annual *Report of the Bureau of American Ethnology to the Secretary of the Smithsonian Institution* (1900).

HOW THE WORLD WAS MADE

The earth is a great island floating in a sea of water, and suspended at each of the four cardinal points by a cord hanging down from the sky vault, which is of solid rock. When the world grows old and worn out, the people will die and the cords will break and let the earth sink down into the ocean, and all will be water again. The Indians are afraid of this.

When all was water, the animals were above in Gălûñ´lătĭ,[1] beyond the arch; but it was very much crowded, and they were wanting more room. They wondered what was below the water, and at last Dâyuni´sĭ, "Beaver's Grandchild," the little Water-beetle, offered to go and see if it could learn. It darted in every direction over the surface of the water, but could find no firm place to rest. Then it dived to the bottom and came up with some soft mud, which began to grow and spread on every side until it became the island which we call the earth. It was afterward fastened to the sky with four cords, but no one remembers who did this.

At first the earth was flat and very soft and wet. The animals were anxious to get down, and sent out different birds to see if it was yet dry, but they found no place to alight and came back again to Gălûñ´lătĭ. At last it seemed to be time, and they sent out the Buzzard and told him to go and make ready for them. This was the Great Buzzard, the father of all the buzzards we see now. He flew all over the earth, low down near the ground, and it was still soft. When he reached the Cherokee country, he was very tired, and his wings began to flap and strike the ground, and wherever they struck the earth there was a valley, and where they turned up again there was a mountain. When the animals above saw this, they were afraid that the whole world would be mountains, so they called him back, but the Cherokee country remains full of mountains to this day.[2]

When the earth was dry and the animals came down, it was still dark, so they got the sun and set it in a track to go every day across the island from east to west, just overhead. It was too hot this way, and Tsiska´gĭlĭ´, the Red Crawfish, had his shell scorched a bright red, so that his meat was spoiled; and the Cherokee do not eat it. The conjurers put the sun another handbreadth higher in the air, but it was still too hot. They raised it another time, and another, until it was seven handbreadths high and just under the sky arch. Then it was right, and they left it so. This is why the conjurers call the highest place Gûlkwâ´gine Di´gălûñ´lătiyûñ´, "the seventh height," because it is seven handbreadths above the earth. Every day the sun goes along under this arch, and returns at night on the upper side to the starting place.

There is another world under this, and it is like ours in everything – animals, plants, and people – save that the seasons are different. The streams that come down from the mountains are the trails by which we reach this underworld, and the springs at their heads are the doorways by which we enter it, but to do this one must fast and go to water and have one of the underground people for a guide. We know that the seasons in the underworld are different from ours, because the water in the springs is always warmer in winter and cooler in summer than the outer air.

When the animals and plants were first made – we do not know by whom – they were told to watch and keep awake for seven nights, just as young men now fast and keep awake when they pray to their medicine. They tried to do this, and nearly all were awake through the first night, but the next night several dropped off to sleep, and the third night others were asleep, and then others, until, on the seventh night, of all the

---

1. **Gălûñ´lătĭ:** The Cherokee otherworld, where at one time all of the animals lived.
2. **full of mountains to this day:** The Cherokee originally occupied a large area of the southern Appalachian Mountains.

animals only the owl, the panther, and one or two more were still awake. To these were given the power to see and to go about in the dark, and to make prey of the birds and animals which must sleep at night. Of the trees only the cedar, the pine, the spruce, the holly, and the laurel were awake to the end, and to them it was given to be always green and to be greatest for medicine, but to the others it was said: "Because you have not endured to the end you shall lose your hair every winter."

Men came after the animals and plants. At first there were only a brother and sister until he struck her with a fish and told her to multiply, and so it was. In seven days a child was born to her, and thereafter every seven days another, and they increased very fast until there was danger that the world could not keep them. Then it was made that a woman should have only one child in a year, and it has been so ever since.

[1900]

Akimel O'odham (Pima)

The Akimel O'odham, commonly known as the Pima, are among the oldest residents of the Southwest. They are descendants of the ancient Hohokam, who as early as the second century BCE began to develop a large and complex civilization in what is now southern Arizona, New Mexico, and northern Mexico. Culturally similar to the natives of central Mexico, the Hohokam lived in large adobe towns, which the Spanish would call "pueblos," and built an extensive system of canals to irrigate their arid farmlands. Following a series of droughts, however, the Hohokam abandoned their majestic pueblos and moved into smaller villages along the Salt and the Gila rivers. They were an agricultural people, who developed prosperous farms and villages. When Spanish explorers encountered these dispersed peoples in the early 1600s, they renamed them the Pima and the Papago. In the eighteenth century, the Spanish were allied with the Pima against the incursions of the Apache. In the nineteenth century, Pima villages became trading posts, selling animals and food to settlers bound for southern California and those participating in the California gold rush of the late 1840s. As part of the Gadsden Purchase of 1853, however, the Pima lands in Mexico became part of the United States. The prosperity of the Pima farmers and traders ended, and the tribe was soon consigned to the Gila River Reservation, established in 1859. Today, the Pima and Papago tribes have reclaimed their original names, the Akimel O'odham (River People) and the Tohono O'odham (Desert People).

bedfordstmartins.com/ americanlit *for research links on Native American tales and stories*

"The Story of the Creation" (Pima). The Pima did not have a written language, and much of the record of their complex culture is lost. But some of their stories were preserved orally in tribal culture and finally transcribed by J. William Lloyd, a physician and writer. At the Pan-American Fair in Buffalo, New York, in 1901, Lloyd met Edward H. Wood, a Pima

Casa Grande

This is a drawing by J. Ross Browne of the Casa Grande, or the "Big House," an imposing four-story structure built in the fourteenth century by the Hohokam, ancestors of the Akimel O'odham (Pima). The drawing of the ruins, which in 1892 became the first archaeological site in the United States to be protected as a national monument, appeared as an illustration in Browne's *Adventures in Apache Country* (1869).

whose uncle, Thin Leather, knew many of the Pima stories and legends. Together Lloyd and Wood worked with Thin Leather in Arizona to collect and record Pima narratives. The following story begins in a way similar to that of the book of Genesis, but this Pima creation myth draws on many elements of the natural landscape of the Southwest. The text is taken from the collection put together by Lloyd and Thin Leather, *Aw-Aw-Tam Indian Nights, Being the Myths and Legends of the Pimas of Arizona* (1911).

THE STORY OF THE CREATION

In the beginning there was no earth, no water – nothing. There was only a Person, *Juh-wert-a-Mah-kai (The Doctor of the Earth).*

He just floated, for there was no place for him to stand upon. There was no sun, no light, and he just floated about in the darkness, which was Darkness itself.

He wandered around in the nowhere till he thought he had wandered enough. Then he rubbed on his breast and rubbed out *moah-haht-tack*, that is perspiration, or greasy earth. This he rubbed out on the palm of his hand and held out. It tipped over three times, but the fourth time it stood straight in the middle of the air and there it remains now as the world.

The first bush he created was the greasewood bush.

And he made ants, little tiny ants, to live on that bush, on its gum which comes out of its stem.

But these little ants did not do any good, so he created white ants, and these worked and enlarged the earth; and they kept on increasing it, larger and larger, until at last it was big enough for himself to rest on.

Then he created a Person. He made him out of his eye, out of the shadow of his eyes, to assist him, to be like him, and to help him in creating trees and human beings and everything that was to be on the earth.

The name of this being was *Noo-ee* (the Buzzard).

Nooee was given all power, but he did not do the work he was created for. He did not care to help Juhwertamahkai, but let him go by himself.

And so the Doctor of the Earth himself created the mountains and everything that has seed and is good to eat. For if he had created human beings first they would have had nothing to live on.

But after making Nooee and before making the mountains and seed for food, Juhwertamahkai made the sun.

In order to make the sun he first made water, and this he placed in a hollow vessel, like an earthen dish *(hwas-hah-ah)* to harden into something like ice. And this hardened ball he placed in the sky. First he placed it in the North, but it did not work; then he placed it in the West, but it did not work; then he placed it in the South, but it did not work; then he placed it in the East and there it worked as he wanted it to.

And the moon he made in the same way and tried in the same places, with the same results.

But when he made the stars he took the water in his mouth and spurted it up into the sky. But the first night his stars did not give light enough. So he took the Doctor-stone (diamond),[1] the *tone-dum-haw-teh*, and smashed it up, and took the pieces and threw them into the sky to mix with the water in the stars, and then there was light enough.

And now Juhwertamahkai, rubbed again on his breast, and from the substance he obtained there made two little dolls, and these he laid on the earth. And they were human beings, man and woman.

And now for a time the people increased till they filled the earth. For the first parents were perfect, and there was no sickness and no death. But when the earth was full, then there was nothing to eat, so they killed and ate each other.

But Juhwertamahkai did not like the way his people acted, to kill and eat each other, and so he let the sky fall to kill them. But when the sky dropped he, himself, took a staff and broke a hole thru, thru which he and Nooee emerged and escaped, leaving behind them all the people dead.

And Juhwertamahkai, being now on the top of this fallen sky, again made a man and a woman, in the same way as before. But this man and woman became grey when old, and their children became grey still younger, and their children became grey younger still, and so on till the babies were gray in their cradles.

---

1. **diamond:** Probably a quartz crystal, which is prevalent in the Southwest.

And Juhwertamahkai, who had made a new earth and sky, just as there had been before, did not like his people becoming grey in their cradles, so he let the sky fall on them again, and again made a hole and escaped, with Nooee, as before.

And Juhwertamahkai, on top of this second sky, again made a new heaven and a new earth, just as he had done before, and new people.

But these new people made a vice of smoking. Before human beings had never smoked till they were old, but now they smoked younger, and each generation still younger, till the infants wanted to smoke in their cradles.

And Juhwertamahkai did not like this, and let the sky fall again, and created everything new again in the same way, and this time he created the earth as it is now.

But at first the whole slope of the world was westward, and tho there were peaks rising from this slope there were no true valleys, and all the water that fell ran away and there was no water for the people to drink. So Juhwertamahkai sent Nooee to fly around among the mountains, and over the earth, to cut valleys with his wings, so that the water could be caught and distributed and there might be enough for the people to drink.

Now the sun was male and the moon was female and they met once a month. And the moon became a mother and went to a mountain called *Tahs-my-et-tahn Toe-ahk* (sun striking mountain) and there was born her baby. But she had duties to attend to, to turn around and give light, so she made a place for the child by tramping down the weedy bushes and there left it. And the child, having no milk, was nourished on the earth.

And this child was the coyote, and as he grew he went out to walk and in his walk came to the house of Juhwertamahkai and Nooee, where they lived.

And when he came there Juhwertamahkai knew him and called him *Toe-hahvs*, because he was laid on the weedy bushes of that name.

But now out of the North came another powerful personage, who has two names, *See-ur-huh* and *Ee-ee-toy.*

Now Seeurhuh means older brother, and when this personage came to Juhwertamahkai, Nooee and Toehahvs he called them his younger brothers. But they claimed to have been here first, and to be older than he, and there was a dispute between them. But finally, because he insisted so strongly, and just to please him, they let him be called older brother.

[1911]

Lakota

The Lakota are part of what became known as the Sioux Nation, a confederation of three large groups of native peoples of the same linguistic stock – the Dakota (Santee or Eastern Sioux), Lakota (Teton Sioux), and Nakota (Yankton Sioux). Those peoples are further divided into smaller tribal groups, such as the Oglala of the Lakota. When the French encountered these peoples, whose own names mean allies or friends, they called them collectively the "Sioux." They originally lived south of Lake Superior in present-day northern Wisconsin and eastern Minnesota, but conflicts with the neighboring Ojibwa forced the Sioux westward during the seventeenth century. The Dakota settled in what is now southern and western Minnesota, where they retained their agricultural way of life. But the Lakota and the Nakota moved farther north and west into present-day North and South Dakota, western Nebraska, and eastern Wyoming, where they became nomadic hunters of buffalo and other large game. By 1750, there were probably 30,000 Sioux, half of them Lakota. Allies of the British in both the Revolutionary War and the War of 1812, the Sioux in 1825 signed a treaty with the United States under the terms of which they were granted possession of the "Great Sioux Reservation," a vast territory including much of present-day Minnesota, North and South Dakota, Wisconsin, Iowa, Missouri, and Wyoming.

Under the terms of a series of later treaties, however, the Sioux were steadily forced to sell or yield their lands to the federal government. They were further displaced by the Homestead Act of 1862, which offered white settlers free title to 160 acres of "public domain" land in the West. During

Sitting Bull

This autographed photo of the Lakota chief holding a pipe, the sacred emblem of the Great Sioux Nation, was taken in 1884, five years before their once-vast lands were reduced to a handful of reservations with defined boundaries by an act of Congress.

the next thirty years, as hundreds of thousands of farms were established on the Great Plains, the Lakota struggled to survive and maintain their way of life in the Black Hills, a section of South Dakota west of the Missouri River, which they were granted in perpetuity by the Fort Laramie Treaty of 1868. That treaty was violated when gold was discovered in the Black Hills in the 1870s, attracting thousands of white prospectors and triggering a war between the Sioux and the U.S. Army. Despite the leadership of Sitting Bull (1831-1890), a Lakota chief and medicine man, and the defeat of General George Custer at the battle of Little Bighorn in 1876, the Sioux finally bowed to the military forces of the United States and to the federal government's determination to open their lands to white settlers. As Sitting Bull said of those settlers in a speech delivered in 1877, "They claim this mother of ours, the earth, for their own and fence their neighbors away; they deface her with their buildings and their refuse. That nation is like a spring freshet that overruns its banks and destroys all who are in its path. We cannot dwell side by side." Finally, in 1889, Congress reduced the Great Sioux Reservation, which had earlier occupied much of the area of seven states, into five scattered reservations, the largest of which was and remains the Pine Ridge Reservation in South Dakota.

bedfordstmartins.com/ americanlit *for research links on Native American tales and stories*

"*Wohpe* and the Gift of the Pipe" (Lakota). The following Lakota story, as it was told by Finger, a holy man of the Oglala Sioux, was recorded by James R. Walker, a physician at the Pine Ridge Reservation from 1896 to 1914. Other versions of this tale exist, including a later one collected in John G. Neihardt's *Black Elk Speaks* (1932), based on recordings of conversations Neihardt had in 1930 with Black Elk, an Oglala Sioux then living at Pine Ridge. A central tale to the Lakota, "*Wohpe* and the Gift of the Pipe" explains the origin and importance of what is commonly known as the peace pipe, which figured prominently in Lakota culture. Sharing the long, elaborately decorated pipe was a ritual among Lakota leaders, as well as a ceremonial way of endorsing agreements between individuals and groups. The text of the story, which was told to Walker by Finger on March 25, 1914, is taken from James R. Walker, *Lakota Belief and Ritual*, edited by Raymond J. DeMallie and Elaine A. Jahner (1980).

WOHPE AND THE GIFT OF THE PIPE

Question: You say that when *Wohpe*[1] gave the pipe to the Lakotas she was in their camp for many days. Was it she that gave the first pipe to the Lakotas?

Answer: Yes.

Question: Can you tell me how she did this?

---

1. ***Wohpe***: Falling Star, the mythological White Buffalo (Calf) Woman who brings the sacred pipe to the Lakota.

Answer: Yes, but it is a long story.

Question: Will you tell it?

Answer: (The legend of the giving of the pipe to the Lakotas)

In the long ago the Lakotas were in camp and two young men lay upon a hill watching for signs. They saw a long way in the distance a lone person coming, and they ran further toward it and lay on another hill hidden so that if it were an enemy they would be able to intercept it or signal to the camp. When the person came close, they saw that it was a woman and when she came nearer that she was without clothing of any kind except that her hair was very long and fell over her body like a robe. One young man said to the other that he would go and meet the woman and embrace her and if he found her good, he would hold her in his tipi.[2] His companion cautioned him to be careful for this might be a buffalo woman who could enchant him and take him with her to her people and hold him there forever. But the young man would not be persuaded and met the woman on the hill next to where they had watched her. His companion saw him attempt to embrace her and there was a cloud closed about them so that he could not see what happened. In a short time the cloud disappeared and the woman was alone. She beckoned to the other young man and told him to come there and assured him that he would not be harmed. As she spoke in the Lakota language the young man thought she belonged to his people and went to where she stood.

When he got there, she showed him the bare bones of his companion and told him that the Crazy Buffalo had caused his companion to try to do her harm and that she had destroyed him and picked his bones bare. The young man was very much afraid and drew his bow and arrow to shoot the woman, but she told him that if he would do as she directed, no harm would come to him and he should get any girl he wished for his woman, for she was *wakan*[3] and he could not hurt her with his arrows. But if he refused to do as she should direct, or attempt to shoot her, he would be destroyed as his companion had been. Then the young man promised to do as she should bid him.

She then directed him to return to the camp and call all the council together and tell them that in a short time they would see four puffs of smoke[4] under the sun at midday. When they saw this sign they should prepare a feast, and all sit in the customary circle to have the feast served when she would enter the camp, but the men must all sit with their head bowed and look at the ground until she was in their midst. Then she would serve the feast to them and after they had feasted she would tell them what to do: that they must obey her in everything; that if they obeyed her in everything they would have their prayers to the *Wakan Tanka*[5] answered and be prosperous and happy; but that if they disobeyed her or attempted to do her any harm, they would be neglected by *Wakan Tanka* and be punished as the young man who had attempted to embrace her had been.

---

2. **tipi**: Often spelled *tepee*, a portable, conical house used by the Plains Indians, usually constructed of cottonwood poles and buffalo hides or canvas.
3. ***wakan***: Powerful and spiritually mysterious.
4. **four puffs of smoke**: Four is a sacred number to the Lakota, and many other tribes, as evidenced in the four directions and the four winds.
5. ***Wakan Tanka***: The Lakota "Great Spirit," or literally "Big Power."

Then she disappeared as a mist disappears so that the young man knew that she was *wakan*. He returned to the camp and told these things to the people and the council decided to do as she had instructed the young man. They made preparations for the feast and in a few days they saw four puffs of black smoke under the sun at midday, so they prepared for a feast and all dressed in their best clothing and sat in the circle ready to be served and every man bowed his head and looked toward the ground. Suddenly the women began uttering low exclamations of admiration, but all the men steadily kept their eyes toward the ground except one young man and he looked toward the entrance of the camp. He saw a puff of black smoke which blew into his eyes and a voice said, "You have disobeyed me and there will be smoke in your eyes as long as you live." From that time, that young man had very sore eyes and all the time they were as if biting smoke was in them.

Then the woman entered the circle and took the food and served it, first to the little children and then to the women and then she bade the men to look up. They did so and saw a very beautiful woman dressed in the softest deer skin which was ornamented with fringes and colors more beautiful than any woman of the Lakota had ever worked. Then she served the men with food, and when they had feasted she told them that she wished to serve them always; that they had first seen her as smoke and that they should always see her as smoke. Then she took from her pouch a pipe and willow bark and Lakota tobacco and filled the pipe with the bark and tobacco and lighted it with a coal of fire.

She smoked a few whiffs and handed the pipe to the chief and told him to smoke and hand it to another. Thus the pipe was passed until all had smoked. She then instructed the council how to gather the bark and the tobacco and prepare it, and gave the pipe into their keeping, telling them that as long as they preserved this pipe she would serve them. But she would serve them in this way. When the smoke came from the pipe she would be present and hear their prayers and take them to the *Wakan Tanka* and plead for them that their prayers should be answered.

After this she remained in this camp for many days and all the time she was there everyone was happy for she went from tipi to tipi with good words for all. When the time came for her to go, she called all the people together and bade the women to build a great fire of dried cottonwood, which they did. Then she directed all to sit in a circle about the fire and the shaman[6] to have an abundance of sweetgrass. She stood in the midst of the circle and when the fire had burned to coals she directed the shaman to place on it the sweetgrass. This made a cloud of smoke and the woman entered the smoke and disappeared. Then the shamans knew that it was *Wohpe* who had given the pipe and they appointed a custodian for it with instructions that it was to be kept sacred and used only on the most solemn and important occasions. With due ceremony they made wrappers for the pipe so that it is *wakan*. The shamans instructed the people that they could make other pipes and use them and that *Wohpe* would be in the smoke of any such pipe if smoked with proper solemnity and form.

Thus it was that the Beautiful Woman brought the pipe to the Lakotas.

[1980]

---

6. **shaman:** *Shaman* is actually a term for an East Asian medicine man. Walker may have misunderstood or mistranslated the Lakota term *wicasa wakan*, a man who acquires power through a "vision quest," a process of deep understanding of the world of the spirits.

Hupa

The Hupa (or Hoopa, as the name is sometimes spelled today) and their neighbors the Yurok and the Karuk are aboriginal peoples that long ago established themselves in what is now northwestern California. (Tests have determined that a fire pit on the Hupa lands dates to more than seven thousand years ago.) The Hupa lived in small villages of cedar-plank houses with small round doorways on the banks of the Trinity River. They fished for the plentiful salmon in the river, gathered acorns and berries, and hunted small game. They were also skilled at crafts. Men practiced woodworking, while women fashioned distinctive bowl-shaped hats and baskets. For centuries, the Hupa were largely unknown to European explorers and settlers. Following the discovery of gold in California in 1848, however, miners and settlers moved onto Hupa lands, causing serious disruption to their way of life. In 1864, they were resettled on the Hoopa Valley Reservation, which included a large portion of their original tribal lands. The Hupa speak a dialect of the Athabaskan language, which was also spoken by several Native American peoples of the Southwest and the Great Plains. The Hupa language has been extensively studied by linguists, and many of their oral narratives and stories have been transcribed and translated into English.

bedfordstmartins.com/ americanlit *for research links on Native American tales and stories*

"The Boy Who Grew Up at Ta'k'imiłding" (Hupa). This story accounts for the origin of the World Renewal Dances, sacred ceremonies that are unique to the traditional cultures of the Yurok, Karuk, and Hupa.

Hupa Jump Dancers
This photograph of the Hupa in the ceremonial garb worn for the Jump Dance was taken by A. W. Ericson in the 1890s. Even at a time when the policy of the Federal government was to eradicate the indigenous cultures of Native American peoples, the Hupa maintained a strong sense of their cultural identity, which they have preserved to the present day.

The dances take two forms. The purpose of the White Deerskin Dance, *xonsit ch'idilye* or Summer World Renewal, is to inspire life and vitality for the coming year. The purpose of the Jump Dance, *xay ch'idilye* or Winter World Renewal, is to protect against disease and natural disasters. Both dances are intended to celebrate the *k'ixinay*, supernatural beings who dwell in the "Heaven" of the story and who influence the human world below. The young boy who lives in the principal village of the Hupa, *Ta'k'imiłding*, has been chosen by the *k'ixinay* for the vital role of initiating the ceremonial dances, which are still performed in the Hoopa Valley. This version of the story is a translation by Victor Golla of a recording made in 1963 of an oral narration by Minnie Reeves (1880-1972). "Minnie Reeves's telling of this sacred story was appropriately solemn and serious," Golla observes. "Although her version was abbreviated and broken here and there by a hesitation and a groping for words, it was clear that she was reciting well-known lines and phrases – a sacred text in the most real sense." The text is taken from *Surviving through the Days: A California Indian Reader*, edited by Herbert W. Luthin (2002).

THE BOY WHO GREW UP AT TA'K'IMIŁDING

There once was a boy who grew up at Ta'k'imiłding – born into the Big House there.

He did nothing but sing all the time. He would always be singing. He was a good boy and did what he was told, but he would stay there in the Big House at Ta'k'imiłding, singing all day long.

One day his mother went down to the river to fetch water, leaving the boy singing in the house. She dipped up some water, and was on her way back up to the house when a sound stopped her. It sounded like someone was singing inside a cloud that hovered over her house. She put her water basket down and listened. She could hear it clearly: Someone was singing there inside the hovering cloud. After a while the cloud lifted up into the air. She could still hear the singing. Eventually it vanished into the sky.

She went on back to the house. When she went inside, the boy was gone. It was clear that he had gone off inside the hovering cloud.

When her husband returned from hunting she told him what had happened. They had loved him very much, and they cried and cried.

A long time passed and there was no sign of the boy. Then, one day, many years later, the man went up the hill to hunt. After hunting for a while he got tired and decided to rest under a big tan oak. As he sat there smoking his pipe he was suddenly aware of a young man walking toward him out of the forest. Looking more closely he saw that it was the boy, now grown up. He leapt to his feet and ran to embrace his son.

"Stop there, Father! Don't come toward me," the young man said. "Don't try to touch me. I can't bear the scent of human beings anymore."

Then he continued, "The only reason I have come back is to tell people the way things should be done in the future. When I went off to Heaven in that cloud, I found them dancing there, dancing without ever stopping, dancing the whole day long.

"And that is why I have returned — why you see me now. I have come to tell you about the dances. I am here to tell you the ways they should be danced, and the places where they should happen.

"You will dance downstream through Hoopa Valley, you will finish the dance over there on Bald Hill: That is where the White Deerskin Dance is to be danced.

"Ten days after the White Deerskin Dance is finished, you will dance the Jump Dance for another ten days. There behind the Jump Dance fence I will always be looking on. I will always come back for the Jump Dance, although you won't ever see me. Because I will be looking on from there, invisible though I am, don't let anyone go back of the fence, don't even let a dog go back there.

"I will always be watching."

That is the end of the story.

[2002]

Native American Stories through a Modern Lens

As Native Americans have sought to regain their lands and to reaffirm their identities, especially during the last fifty years, their rich oral traditions have become increasingly important to writers who draw on tribal lore and memories. Indeed, some scholars have referred to the late twentieth century as the "Renaissance" of Native American literature. The writers who have participated in that rebirth are as varied as the tribes that once inhabited North America, but few figures have been as influential in the emergence of Native American literature as N. Scott Momaday. Of Kiowa, English, and Cherokee descent, Momaday was born in 1934 in Oklahoma and spent most of his childhood on Indian reservations in Arizona and New Mexico, where his parents were teachers, and where he was exposed to the culture and traditions of the Navajo, Apache, and Pueblo. Momaday was the first Native American to win the Pulitzer Prize for Fiction, awarded for his novel *House Made of Dawn* (1969). He has also written widely about the rituals and oral traditions of Native Americans. In the following essay, Momaday sketches a portrait of the native peoples of America before the arrival of Christopher Columbus in 1492. As he emphasizes, the "New World" that Columbus believed he had encountered was actually an ancient world, one filled with an astonishing variety of peoples and societies. But a common feature of many of those diverse cultures was and remains storytelling. Momaday explains that Native Americans "tell stories in order to affirm our being and our place in the scheme of things," demonstrating the vital importance of orality in understanding Native American cultures and literature. The text is taken from *America in 1492*, edited by Alvin M. Josephy Jr. (1993).

Effigy Pot

What is now known as the Mississippian culture thrived from 900 CE to shortly after the mid-sixteenth-century arrival of Hernando de Soto and his Spanish conquistadores, who spread disease and destruction during their long march across what is now the southeast United States. Along with the great mounds built by the Mississippian Indians, some artifacts like this haunting effigy, or head, pot have survived, but their exact meaning has been lost.

N. Scott Momaday

[b. 1934]

The Becoming of the Native: Man in America before Columbus

THURSDAY, 11 OCTOBER 1492
The moon, in its third quarter, rose in the east shortly before midnight. I estimate that we were making about 9 knots and had gone some 67½ miles between the beginning of night and 2 o'clock in the morning. Then, at two hours after midnight, the *Pinta* fired a cannon, my prearranged signal for the sighting of land.

FRIDAY, 12 OCTOBER 1492
At dawn we saw naked people. . . .

–The Log of Christopher Columbus

It was not until 1498, when he explored what is now Venezuela, that Columbus realized he had touched upon a continent. On his last voyage, in 1502, he reached Central America. It is almost certain that he never knew of the great landmass to the north, an expanse that reached almost to Asia and to the top of the world, or that he had found a great chain of land that linked two of the earth's seven continents. In the little time that remained to him (he died in 1506) the enormity of his discovery was virtually unknown and unimagined. Christopher Columbus, the Admiral of the Ocean Sea, went to his grave believing he had reached Asia. But his accomplishment was even greater than he dreamed. He had in fact sailed beyond the *orbis*, the circle believed to describe the limits of the earth, and beyond medieval geography. His voyage to the New World was a navigation in time; it was a passage from the Middle Ages to the Renaissance.

There are moments in history to which one can point and say, "At this hour, on this day, the history of the world was changed forever." Such a moment occurred at two o'clock on the morning of October 12, 1492, when a cannon, fired from the Spanish caravel *Pinta*, announced the sighting of land. The land sighted was probably Samana Cay in the Bahamas. It was the New World.

It is this term, "New World," with which I should like to begin this discussion, not only because it is everywhere a common designation of the Americas but also because it represents one of the great anomalies of history. The British writer J. B. Priestley,[1] after visiting the United States, commented that "New World" is a misnomer. The American Southwest seemed to him the oldest

1. J. B. Priestley: (1894–1984) British novelist, playwright, and essayist.

landscape he had ever seen. Indeed, the New World is ancient. Here is a quintessential irony.

For Americans in general, a real part of the irony consists of their Eurocentric understanding of history. Columbus and his Old World contemporaries knew a good deal about the past, the past that was peculiarly theirs, for it had been recorded in writing. It was informed by a continuity that could be traced back to the story of Creation in the Old Testament. Most Americans have inherited that same understanding of the past. American history, therefore, as distinct from other histories, begins in the popular mind with the European intercession in the "New World." Relatively little is known of the Americas and their peoples before Columbus, although we are learning more all the time. On the far side of 1492 in the Americas there is a prehistoric darkness in which are mysteries as profound and provocative as are those of Stonehenge and Lascaux and Afrasiab.[2]

Who were the "naked people" Columbus and his men observed at dawn on that autumn day five hundred years ago? Columbus, the first ethnographer in the New World, tells us a few things about them. They were broad in the forehead, straight and well-proportioned. They were friendly and bore gifts to their visitors. They were skilled boat-builders and boatmen. They painted their faces and their bodies. They made clothes and hammocks out of cotton. They lived in sturdy houses. They had dogs. And they too lived their daily lives in the element of language; they traded in words and names. We do not know what name or names they conferred upon their seafaring guests, but on October 17, on the sixth day of his sojourn among them, Columbus referred to them in his log as "Indios."

In 1492 the "Indians" were widespread in North, Central, and South America. They were the only human occupants of a third of the earth's land surface. And by the year 1492 they had been in the New World for untold thousands of years.

The "Paleo-Indians," as they are known, the ancestors of modern American Indians, came from Asia and entered upon the continent of North America by means of the Bering land bridge, a wide corridor of land, now submerged, connecting Siberia and Alaska. During the last glaciation (20,000 to 14,000 years ago) the top of the world was dominated by ice. Even so, most of Asia and most of Beringia were unglaciated. From Alaska to the Great Plains of the present United States ran a kind of corridor between the Cordilleran and Laurentide ice sheets, a thoroughfare for the migration of hunters and the animals they hunted. It is known that human bands had reached the Lena River drainage in northeastern Siberia at least 18,000 years ago. Over the next 7,000 years these nomads crossed the Bering bridge and dispersed widely throughout the Americas.

This dispersal is one of the great chapters in the story of mankind. It was an

---

2. **Stonehenge and Lascaux and Afrasiab:** Stonehenge, a group of prehistoric stone megaliths near Wiltshire, England, dates from c. 2950 BCE. Lascaux, a cave in Dordogne, France, is decorated with Paleolithic wall paintings of animals. Afrasiab, a fortress on several hills near the ancient city of Samarkand in Uzbekistan, dates from the sixth century BCE.

explosion, a revolution on a scale scarcely to be imagined. By 1492 there were untold numbers of indigenous human societies in the New World, untold numbers of languages and dialects, architecture to rival any monument of the Old World, astronomical observatories and solar calendars, a profound knowledge of natural medicine and the healing arts, very highly developed oral traditions, dramas, ceremonies, and – above all – a spiritual comprehension of the universe, a sense of the natural and supernatural, a sense of the sacred. Here was every evidence of man's long, inexorable ascendancy to civilization.

It is appropriate that I interject here my particular point of view. I am an American Indian, and I believe that I can therefore speak to the question of America before Columbus with a certain advantage of ancestral experience, a cultural continuity that reaches far back in time. My forebears have been in North America for many thousands of years. In my blood I have a real sense of that occupation. It is worth something to me, as indeed that long, unbroken tenure is worth something to every Native American.

I am Kiowa. The Kiowas are a Plains Indian people who reside now in Oklahoma. But they are newcomers to the Southern Plains, not having ventured below the Arkansas River until the eighteenth century. In 1492 they were near the headwaters of the Yellowstone River, in what is now western Montana. Their migration to the Southern Plains is the most recent migration of all those which have described the great dispersal of native peoples, and their Plains culture is the last culture to evolve in North America.

According to their origin myth, the Kiowas entered the world through a hollow log.[3] Where was the log, I wonder. And what was at the other end? When I imagine my blood back through generations to the earliest man in America, I see in my mind's eye a procession of shamanistic figures,[4] like those strange anthropomorphic forms painted on the cliffs of Barrier Canyon, Utah, emerging from the mists. They proceed, it seems, from the source of geology itself, from timelessness into time.

When man set foot on the continent of North America he was surely an endangered species. His resources were few, as we think of them from our vantage point in the twentieth century. He was almost wholly at the mercy of the elements, and the world he inhabited was hard and unforgiving. The simple accomplishment of survival must have demanded all of his strength. But he had certain indispensable resources. He knew how to hunt. He possessed tools and weapons, however crude. He could make fire. He probably had dogs and travois, perhaps sleds. He had some sense of society, of community, of cooperation. And,

---

3. **hollow log:** This is a common image in Native American narratives. For example, in "Origin of Folk Stories," the Seneca story printed on page 34, Gaqka passes through a hollow log at the urging of his wife and he is healed.

4. **shamanistic figures:** According to some worldviews, shamans are persons with special access to good and evil spirits and who have special powers of healing.

alone among the creatures of the earth, he could think and speak. He had a human sense of morality, an irresistible craving for order, beauty, appropriate behavior. He was intensely spiritual.

The Kiowas provide us with a fortunate example of migration and dispersal, I believe. Although their migration from the Yellowstone to the Wichita Mountains is recent (nonetheless prehistoric in the main), it was surely preceded by countless migrations of the same kind in the same landscape, generally speaking, over a period of some thousands of years. The experience of the Kiowas, then, from earliest evidence to the present, may serve to indicate in a general way the experience of other tribes and other cultures. It may allow us to understand something about the American Indian and about the condition of his presence in America in 1492.

The hollow log of the Kiowa origin myth is a not uncommon image in comparative mythology. The story of the tree of life is found throughout the world, and in most instances it is symbolic of passage, origination, evolution. It is tempting to associate the hollow log with the passage to America, the peopling of the Americas, to find in it a metaphorical reflection of the land bridge.

We tell stories in order to affirm our being and our place in the scheme of things. When the Kiowas entered upon the Great Plains they had to tell new stories of themselves, stories that would enable them to appropriate an unknown and intimidating landscape to their experience. They were peculiarly vulnerable in that landscape, and they told a story of dissension, finally of a schism in the tribe, brought about by a quarrel between two great chiefs. They encountered awesome forces and features in nature, and they explained them in story too. And so they told the story of Man-Ka-Ih, the storm spirit, which speaks the Kiowa language and does the Kiowas no harm, and they told of the tree that bore the seven sisters into the sky, where they became the stars of the Big Dipper. In so doing they not only accounted for the great monolith that is Devils Tower, Wyoming (in Kiowa, Tsoai, "rock tree"), but related themselves to the stars in the process. When they came upon the Plains they were befriended by the Crows, who gave them the sun-dance fetish Tai-Me, which was from that time on their most powerful medicine, and they told a story of the coming of Tai-Me in their hour of need. Language was their element. Words, spoken words, were the manifestations of their deepest belief, of their deepest feelings, of their deepest life. When Europeans first came to America, having had writing for hundreds of years and lately the printing press, they could not conceive of the spoken word as sacred, could not understand the American Indian's profound belief in the efficacy of language.

I have told the story of the arrowmaker many times. When I was a child I heard it told more times than I can say. It was at the center of my oral tradition long before I knew what that tradition was, and that is as it should be. The story had never been written down. It had existed, perhaps hundreds of years, at the level of the human voice.

If an arrow is well made, it will have tooth marks upon it. That is how you know. The Kiowas made fine arrows and straightened them in their teeth. Then they drew them to the bow to see that they were straight. Once there was a man and his wife. They were alone at night in their tipi. By the light of a fire the man was making arrows. After a while he caught sight of something. There was a small opening in the tipi where two hides were sewn together. Someone was there on the outside, looking in. The man went on with his work, but he said to his wife, "Someone is standing outside. Do not be afraid. Let us talk easily, as of ordinary things." He took up an arrow and straightened it in his teeth; then, as it was right for him to do, he drew it to the bow and took aim, first in this direction and then in that. And all the while he was talking, as if to his wife. But this is how he spoke: "I know that you are there on the outside, for I can feel your eyes upon me. If you are a Kiowa, you will understand what I am saying, and you will speak your name." But there was no answer, and the man went on in the same way, pointing the arrow all around. At last his aim fell upon the place where his enemy stood, and he let go of the string. The arrow went straight to the enemy's heart.

Only after I had lived with the story for many years did I understand that it is about language. The storyteller is anonymous and illiterate, but he exists in his words, and he has survived for untold generations. The arrowmaker is a man made of words, and he too is a storyteller. He achieves victory over his enemy by exerting the force of language upon the unknown. What he does is far less important than what he says. His arrows are words. His enemy (and the presence outside *is* an enemy, for the storyteller tells us so) is vanquished by the word. The story is concise, beautiful, and alive. I know of nothing in literature that is more intensely alive.

Concurrent with the evolution of an oral tradition is the rise of ceremony. The sun dance was the preeminent expression of the spiritual life of the Plains culture. And it was a whole and intricate and profound expression.

And within the symmetry of this design of language and religion there came art. Universal in the world of the American Indian is a profound aesthetic sense. From ancient rock paintings to contemporary theater, through such forms as beadwork, featherwork, leathercraft, wood carving, ceramics, ledger-book drawing, music, and dance, American Indian art has rivaled other great art of the world. In museums and galleries around the globe are treasures of that art that are scarcely to be imagined.

These various expressions of the human spirit, emblematic of the American Indian today and five hundred years ago and long before that, are informed by an equation of man and the landscape that has had to be perceived, if neither appreciated nor acknowledged, by every society that has made contact with it. The naked people Columbus saw in 1492 were the members of a society altogether worthy and well made, a people of the everlasting earth, possessed of honor and dignity and a generosity of spirit unsurpassed.

[1993]

ORBIS TYPVS VNIVERSALIS IVXTA
OCEANVS OCCIDENTALIS
GRONLAND
Norwegia
Dacia
Liuonia
Littouia
Prussia
Polonia
Tartaria
Colchis
albania
Marehircanū
Mare maiore
Asia minor
Armenia maior
Hircania
Parthia
Gallia
Hispania
Italia
Mediterraneū
Egiptus
Mesopotamia
arabia deserta
Caldea
Persia
Rudiana
Arabia felix
Mare Rubrū
Libia in terior
Ethiopia
AFRICA
Fortunate
Brasil
America
Caput s.crucis
Allepago de s.pauli
Equinoctialis circulus
Tropicus capricorni
Mons Lune
Melinda
monsanbiqui
bona spe ranza
Madaga scar

Explorations and Early Encounters

THE EXPLORATION AND COLONIZATION of the Americas was spurred and widely publicized by the emerging print culture of Europe. Between the time that Johannes Gutenberg invented the printing press in 1450 and Columbus's first voyage in 1492, printing was introduced throughout Europe. Printed books consequently became familiar objects to most people, especially to the growing literate population. Although exact numbers are difficult to determine, some historians believe that there were as many as thirty thousand different editions of books printed in Europe before 1500. At least half of those books were religious in nature – church histories, collections of sermons, biblical commentaries, and, of course,

◀ **Orbis Typus Universalis**

This map, one of the first to use the name *America*, was drawn by the German cartographer Martin Waldseemüller in 1507. Fifteen years after Columbus's first voyage, Europeans still had no idea of the shape or extent of the Americas, which are here represented only by part of present-day Brazil and a few islands in the Caribbean.

the Latin Bible, the first book published by Gutenberg. But many secular works were also published, ranging from books on farming and home remedies to treatises on science, especially astrology and alchemy, to editions of the Greek and Latin classics. The printing press also made books that had been popular in manuscript editions available to a far wider audience. Among the most sought after of these early printed books was *The Travels of Marco Polo*, the tales of a famous Venetian traveler who in 1298-99 had written an account of the riches and wonders of China. First published in a French translation, the book was subsequently translated into several more languages and printed in many editions, including one owned and pored over by Christopher Columbus.

Like most of those who followed his lead, Columbus exploited the power of the printed word to "discover," or bring to prominence, his "discoveries" in the New World. Accounts of the exploration of that world served a variety of purposes for both the authors and their audiences in Europe. Navigators and explorers were eager to report their findings to the rulers or companies that sponsored them, heralding the success or (in rare cases) explaining the failure of their expeditions. Sponsors expected a good return on their investments. In many cases, they also wanted to

Adam and Eve in America

This celebrated engraving is the opening image in the first volume of *America*, a series of lavishly illustrated travel narratives Theodor de Bry began to publish in Frankfurt, Germany, in 1590. The engraving depicts Adam and Eve at the moment prior to the Fall, the consequences of which are illustrated by the laborers in the background. At the same time, America is symbolically represented as the Garden of Eden, an unspoiled world of peace and plenty that captured the imagination of Europeans.

establish an unassailable claim on new lands. Printed accounts of explorations and discoveries consequently became a kind of official patent, a way of taking possession of territory in the New World. On his return voyage to Spain in 1493, Columbus wrote a letter to the sovereigns of Spain, describing the inhabitants, natural beauty, and unrivaled riches of the islands he had explored off what he mistakenly thought to be the mainland of Asia. As he doubtless anticipated, the letter was swiftly published in Spain, and translations were soon printed throughout Europe. After that, a chronicle of virtually every major voyage to and investigation of the New World quickly appeared in print in Europe, where the literature of exploration became a fixed and fascinating fact of life.

During the sixteenth century, Spain remained the dominant power in the New World. It eventually claimed territory in North, Central, and South America more than ten times the size of the Iberian Peninsula shared by Portugal and Spain. One of its few failures was an expedition in 1527 to establish a colony in present-day Florida. As a result, a leader and a survivor of this disastrous expedition, Álvar Núñez Cabeza de Vaca, spent eight years first as a captive and then as a wanderer among the Indian tribes in what is now the southwest part of the United States. Although he developed a growing respect for the indigenous populations and pleaded for more humane policies toward them, the adventures described in *The Narrative of Cabeza de Vaca* (1542) fueled the flames of Spanish conquest in the Americas.

Other nations also explored and began to colonize the New World. Since they did not have the means to combat the Spanish in the extensive areas under their control, the French and the English concentrated their efforts along the eastern coast of North America. Although hopes were fading of finding a Northwest Passage that would lead through the continent to China and India, the French began to recognize the natural resources and potential of trade with the native peoples of North America. Under the sponsorship of Henry IV of France, Samuel de Champlain founded Quebec in 1608, the year after the English established their first permanent settlement, Jamestown, in what they called Virginia. Champlain also tirelessly promoted the vast potential of North America in a series of accounts of his adventures and explorations, including *Les Voyages du Sieur de Champlain* (1613). His books were widely read in France, generating growing enthusiasm for an empire in the New World. Indeed, by virtue of his explorations and writings, Champlain has been called "the Father of New France," a vast territory that ultimately extended from Newfoundland to Lake Superior and from Hudson Bay to the Gulf of Mexico.

In a dedicatory letter written to Marie de Médicis, the queen regent of France and widow of King Henry IV, Champlain in his *Voyages*

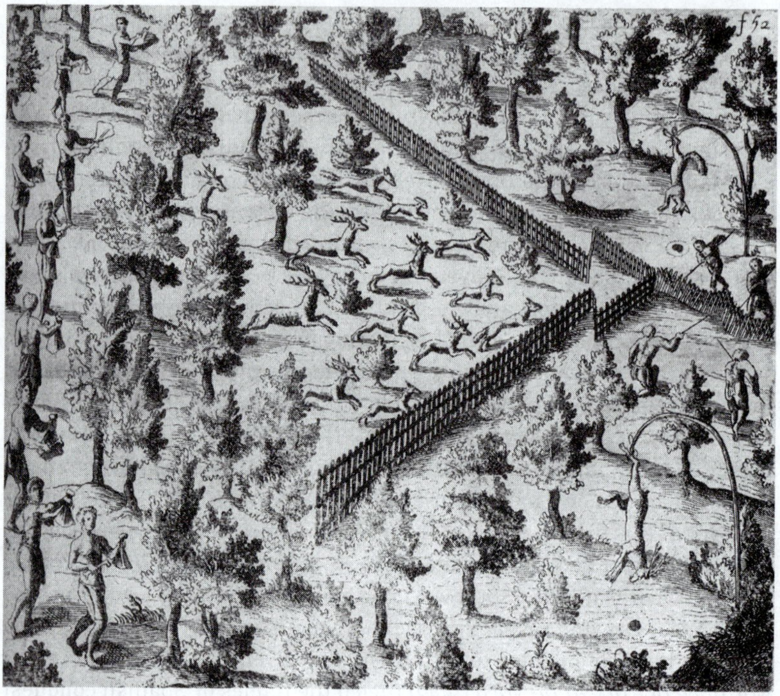

Les Voyages du Sieur de Champlain

This engraving from the 1619 edition of Champlain's *Voyages* shows a deer trap used by Algonkin and Montagnais tribes near the French settlement at Quebec. In contrast to many European explorers, Champlain carefully observed and described the practices of native peoples, though the stylized figures and landscape depicted here more closely resemble those in a European hunting picture than a scene from eastern Canada.

emphasizes the importance of navigation to his country's aspirations in North America:

By this art we obtain a knowledge of different countries, regions, and realms. By it we attract and bring to our own land all kinds of riches; by it the idolatry of paganism is overthrown and Christianity proclaimed throughout all the regions of the earth.

> Of all the most useful and excellent arts, that of navigation has always seemed to me to occupy the first place. For the more hazardous it is, and the more numerous the perils and losses by which it is attended, so much the more is it esteemed and exalted above all others, being wholly unsuited to the timid and irresolute. By this art we obtain a knowledge of different countries, regions, and realms. By it we attract and bring to our own land all kinds of riches; by it the idolatry of paganism is overthrown and Christianity proclaimed throughout all the regions of the earth. This is the art which won my love in my early years, and induced me to expose myself almost all my life to the impetuous waves of the ocean, and led me to explore the coasts of a part of America, especially of New France.

Champlain's letter reveals a good deal about both the early European explorers and the literature of exploration of America. Like Champlain, the early explorers prided themselves on their courage in going where no European had gone before and gaining the first glimpse of what for them and their audience was an unknown world. Certain of their cultural superiority, they wished to enrich their own countries and to promote Christianity. Many of the early narratives of exploration were essentially imperial apologias, justifications of incursions into the Americas by soldiers and settlers carrying the flags of European nations and bearing the banner of Christianity. For the most part, European explorers were also supremely confident that they could completely understand and communicate what they heard and saw in ancient lands they persisted in calling a New World. Even as they carefully mapped and charted that world, many of the explorers offered detailed descriptions of the plants, animals, and practices of the native peoples of the Americas.

But narratives that often appear to be simply factual, firsthand accounts of what the European explorers observed and experienced were complicated by a number of factors. Lacking a vocabulary adequate to describe the unique particulars of the New World, early explorers often identified what they saw or heard in terms of what they had previously known in the Old World. In his description of Hispaniola in his 1493 letter, for example, Columbus noted that he heard the song of the nightingale, or European thrush, which did not exist in the Western Hemisphere. Moreover, although European navigators and explorers cast themselves as reporters rather than writers, their accounts were influenced by literary texts ranging from ancient epics and medieval romances to popular books like *Mandeville's Travels*, with its imaginary descriptions of the wonders of the East. In fact, the descriptions of European explorers were shaped by both what they actually encountered and the wonders they expected to find. Recalling Mandeville's descriptions of the fantastic creatures in the unknown lands of the East, Columbus in his letter confidently reported that "men are born with tails" in one of the provinces he had not explored on the island he renamed Juana, now Cuba. Indeed, as the following selections from the writings of Columbus, Cabeza de Vaca, and Champlain illustrate, in the European literature of exploration "America" was poised between imagination and reality, theory and fact. Certainly these texts reveal some of the complex ways in which such navigators and explorers sought at once to comprehend and to make explicable to their audiences the actualities of a heavily populated world equal in landmass to the "world" known to Europeans before Columbus's first voyage in 1492.

Christopher Columbus

[1451–1506]

Born in the Italian seaport of Genoa in 1451, Christopher Columbus was the son of Domenico Columbo, a wool merchant, and Suzanna Fontanarossa, the daughter of a wool merchant. Columbus evidently had no formal education, and he apparently learned to read and write only as an adult. He was trained in the wool trade and may also have studied mapmaking with his brother, Bartolomeo. His first experience at sea was in 1474, when he spent a year on a ship bound for Khios, an island in the Aegean Sea. Two years later, Columbus was a member of the crew of a commercial ship that was attacked by French privateers. Few other details are known about his life until 1477, when Columbus was living in Lisbon, Portugal, where his brother was working as a mapmaker. That year, he became a merchant sailor with the Portuguese fleet and sailed to Ireland and possibly Iceland. Other voyages took him to the coast of West Africa.

Columbus was poised for a career as an explorer. In the fifteenth century, the expansion of the Muslim Ottoman Empire began to disrupt the lucrative overland trade routes from Christian Europe to India and China. Europeans were consequently determined to discover another trade route to the East. Inspired by his earlier voyages, his commitment to spreading Christianity, and a favorite book, *The Travels of Marco Polo*, with its accounts of the riches of the East, Columbus sought support for a voyage that would find a way there by sailing west across the Atlantic Ocean. By the fifteenth century, most Europeans no longer believed that the world was flat, but there was widespread disagreement about the size of the circumference of the earth. Columbus first offered his services to the rulers of Portugal. But they believed that his calculations were wrong, and their interests were, at least for the moment, focused on West Africa. Columbus then approached the courts of France and England, both of which also rejected his plan. Finally, he turned to the new monarchs of a united Spain, King Ferdinand and Queen Isabel, who granted him permission and funding for a voyage to begin in 1492. On August 3, Columbus set sail from Palos, Spain, with three ships, the *Santa María*, the *Niña*, and the *Pinta*. He reached what are now called the West Indies on October 12, 1492. Believing he had reached the East Indies, Columbus renamed each island he encountered, claiming for Spain both the lands and their natives, whom he collectively called "*los indios*," or the Indians. He also started a colony by leaving thirty-nine crew members on the island he named Hispaniola, where he assumed they would begin to Christianize the natives and establish plantations that would bring economic benefits to Spain.

bedfordstmartins.com/ americanlit *for research links on Columbus*

Returning to Spain in 1493, Columbus reported his "discoveries" and proclaimed the great riches of the "New World." During the following five years, he undertook three additional voyages, further exploring the islands of the Caribbean as well as stretches of the coasts of Central and South America. Columbus never set foot on North America, and until the

The Columbus Letter

The Latin translation of Columbus's letter published in Basel in 1494 contains the first portrait of the peoples he encountered, represented by two groups of naked "Indians." The scene focuses on the imminent exchange of gifts between the figure on the shore and the two Europeans landing on the island. Like the ship in the foreground, which bears little resemblance to the light, three-masted caravels used for exploration during the fifteenth century, the peaceful scene bears little relation to the brutal Spanish conquest of the Americas that swiftly followed Columbus's first voyage in 1492.

end of his life believed that the lands he explored were close to the mainland of Asia. Although he did not achieve his ultimate goal of finding a new trade route to China, Columbus gained riches for himself and paved the way for the expansion of European commerce and Christianity into these new territories for the next three hundred years.

What was a boon for Spain and later for other European nations, however, was a catastrophe for the indigenous inhabitants of the lands Columbus opened up to colonization. Ancient religious practices and cultural traditions were destroyed by colonists determined to impose European culture and spread Catholicism. In addition to being exposed to diseases to which they had no immunity, the native populations were frequently subjected to enslavement or slaughter. On the island of Hispaniola, for example, the native Taino population was reduced from as many as one million in 1492 to roughly thirty thousand in 1510, only four years after Columbus died and was buried in Spain. At the request of his widow, however, his remains were later moved to Hispaniola, where they were buried by the side of the altar in the cathedral of Santa Domingo.

Columbus's "Letter." Onboard the *Niña* on his homeward passage to Spain in 1493, and in the midst of a hurricane, Columbus wrote a formal letter to Luís de Santangel, secretary to the royal court of Spain, which had supported his project to find a new trade route to China. Columbus clearly intended his letter to be read by the sovereigns who sponsored his voyage, the Spanish monarchs King Ferdinand and Queen Isabel. Although he drew heavily on the detailed journal he kept during his eight-month voyage, Columbus sought to heighten interest in his discoveries by exaggerating some of his findings, especially the "gold incalculable" to be found on the islands he had explored. Columbus also designed the letter as a public report of his voyage, discoveries, and formal claim of new territories for Spain. The letter was consequently printed in Barcelona in late March or early April 1493. A brief pamphlet printed on two leaves of folio-sized paper, the letter is considered by many scholars to be the single most important printed document in the history of the early exploration of the Americas. Copies of the pamphlet were distributed throughout Spain, and soon there were nearly two dozen editions of the letter in several European languages, some of them accompanied by fanciful illustrations of the natives Columbus had encountered. For the first time, an account of the "New World" was available for large numbers to read, and Columbus's letter fired the imaginations of Europeans and spurred further exploration of what later came to be called America. The text is taken from *The Voyages of Christopher Columbus*, edited and translated from the Spanish by Cecil Jane (1930).

LETTER OF COLUMBUS, DESCRIBING THE RESULTS OF HIS FIRST VOYAGE

Sir:

Since I know that you will be pleased at the great victory with which Our Lord has crowned my voyage, I write this to you, from which you will learn how in thirty-three days I passed from the Canary Islands to the Indies, with the fleet which the most illustrious king and queen, our sovereigns, gave to me. There I found very many islands, filled with people innumerable, and of them all I have taken possession for their highnesses, by proclamation made and with the royal standard unfurled, and no opposition was offered to me.

To the first island which I found I gave the name "San Salvador," in remembrance of the Divine Majesty, Who had marvellously bestowed all this; the Indians call it "Guanahani." To the second, I gave the name the island of "Santa Maria de Concepcion," to the third, "Fernandina," to the fourth, "Isabella," to the fifth island, "Juana," and so each received from me a new name.[1]

---

1. **To the first island . . . a new name:** The islands Columbus named have not been positively identified, except for *Juana*, his name for what is now Cuba.

When I came to Juana, I followed its coast to the westward, and I found it to be so extensive that I thought that it must be the mainland, the province of Cathay.[2] And since there were neither towns nor villages on the seashore, but small hamlets only, with the people of which I could not have speech, because they all fled immediately, I went forward on the same course, thinking that I could not fail to find great cities and towns. At the end of many leagues, seeing that there was no change and that the coast was bearing me northwards, which I wished to avoid, since winter was already approaching and I proposed to make from it to the south, and as, moreover, the wind was carrying me forward, I determined not to wait for a change in the weather and retraced my path as far as a remarkable harbour known to me. From that point, I sent two men inland to learn if there were a king or great cities. They travelled three days' journey, finding an infinity of small hamlets and people without number, but nothing of importance. For this reason, they returned.

I understood sufficiently from other Indians, whom I had already taken, that this land was nothing but an island, and I therefore followed its coast eastward for one hundred and seven leagues to the point where it ended. From that point, I saw another island, distant about eighteen leagues from the first, to the east, and to it I at once gave the name "Española."[3] I went there and followed its northern coast, as I had followed that of Juana, to the eastward for one hundred and eighty-eight great leagues in a straight line. This island and all the others are very fertile to a limitless degree, and this island is extremely so. In it there are many harbours on the coast of the sea, beyond comparison with others that I know in Christendom, and many rivers, good and large, which is marvellous. Its lands are high; there are in it many sierras and very lofty mountains, beyond comparison with that of Teneriffe.[4] All are most beautiful, of a thousand shapes; all are accessible and are filled with trees of a thousand kinds and tall, so that they seem to touch the sky. I am told that they never lose their foliage, and this I can believe, for I saw them as green and lovely as they are in Spain in May, and some of them were flowering, some bearing fruit, and some on another stage, according to their nature. The nightingale was singing[5] and other birds of a thousand kinds, in the month of November, there where I went. There are six or eight kinds of palm, which are a wonder to behold on account of their beautiful variety, but so are the other trees and fruits and plants. In it are marvellous pine groves; there are very wide and smiling plains, and there is honey; and there are birds of many kinds and fruits in great diversity. In the interior, there are mines of metals, and the population is without number. Española is a marvel.

The sierras and the mountains, the plains, the arable and pasture lands, are so lovely and so rich for planting and sowing, for breeding cattle of every kind, for building towns and villages. The harbours of the sea here are such as cannot be believed to exist unless they have been seen, and so with the rivers, many and great, and of good water, the

---

2. **Cathay:** A province of China, which Columbus initially thought he had reached.
3. **"Española":** Today, the island of Hispaniola includes the countries of Haiti and the Dominican Republic.
4. **Teneriffe:** One of the Canary Islands, an archipelago off the coast of northwestern Africa.
5. **The nightingale was singing:** Columbus was mistaken, since the nightingale, or European thrush, was not native to the West Indies.

majority of which contain gold. In the trees, fruits and plants, there is a great difference from those of Juana. In this island, there are many spices and great mines of gold and of other metals.

The people of this island and of all the other islands which I have found and of which I have information, all go naked, men and women, as their mothers bore them, although some of the women cover a single place with the leaf of a plant or with a net of cotton which they make for the purpose. They have no iron or steel or weapons, nor are they fitted to use them. This is not because they are not well built and of handsome stature, but because they are very marvellously timorous. They have no other arms than spears made of canes, cut in seeding time, to the ends of which they fix a small sharpened stick. Of these they do not dare to make use, for many times it has happened that I have sent ashore two or three men to some town to have speech with them, and countless people have come out to them, and as soon as they have seen my men approaching, they have fled, a father even not waiting for his son. This is not because ill has been done to any one of them; on the contrary, at every place where I have been and have been able to have speech with them, I have given to them of that which I had, such as cloth and many other things, receiving nothing in exchange. But so they are, incurably timid. It is true that, after they have been reassured and have lost this fear, they are so guileless and so generous with all that they possess, that no one would believe it who has not seen it. They refuse nothing that they possess, if it be asked of them; on the contrary, they invite any one to share it and display as much love as if they would give their hearts. They are content with whatever trifle of whatever kind it may be that is given to them, whether it be of value or valueless. I forbade that they should be given things so worthless as fragments of broken crockery, scraps of broken glass and ends of straps, although when they were able to get them, they fancied that they possessed the best jewel in the world. So it was found that for a strap a sailor received gold to the weight of two and a half castellanos,[6] and others received much more for other things which were worth less. As for new blancas,[7] for them they would give everything which they had, although it might be two or three castellanos' weight of gold or an arroba[8] or two of spun cotton. They took even the pieces of the broken hoops of the wine barrels and, like savages, gave what they had, so that it seemed to me to be wrong and I forbade it. I gave them a thousand handsome good things, which I had brought, in order that they might conceive affection for us and, more than that, might become Christians and be inclined to the love and service of your highnesses and of the whole Castilian nation,[9] and strive to aid us and to give us of the things which they have in abundance and which are necessary to us.

They do not hold any creed nor are they idolaters; only they all believe that power and good are in the heavens and are very firmly convinced that I, with these ships and men, came from the heavens, and in this belief they everywhere received me after they had mastered their fear. This belief is not the result of ignorance, for they are, on the contrary, of a very acute intelligence and they are men who navigate all those seas, so that it

6. **castellanos:** Gold coins.
7. **blancas:** Small coins worth less than a cent.
8. **arroba:** Roll of cloth.
9. **Castilian nation:** Spain.

is amazing how good an account they give of everything. It is because they have never seen people clothed or ships of such a kind.

As soon as I arrived in the Indies, in the first island which I found, I took by force some of the natives,[10] in order that they might learn and might give me information of that which there is in these parts. And so it was that they soon understood us, and we them, either by speech or signs, and they have been very serviceable. I still carry them with me, and they are always assured that I come from Heaven, for all the intercourse which they have had with me. They were the first to announce this wherever I went, and the others went running from house to house, and to the neighbouring towns, with loud cries of, "Come! Come! See the men from Heaven!" So all, men and women alike, when their minds are set at rest concerning us, came, not one, small or great, remaining behind, and they all brought something to eat and drink, which they gave with extraordinary affection.

In all the islands, they have very many canoes, which are like rowing fustas, some larger and some smaller; some are greater than a fusta of eighteen benches.[11] They are not so broad, because they are made of a single log of wood, but a fusta would not keep up with them in rowing, since their speed is a thing incredible. In these they navigate among all those islands, which are innumerable, and carry their goods. One of these canoes I have seen with seventy and eighty men in it, each one with his oar.

In all these islands, I saw no great diversity in the appearance of the people or in their manners and language. On the contrary, they all understand one another, which is a very curious thing, on account of which I hope that their highnesses will determine upon their conversion to our holy faith, towards which they are very inclined.

I have already said how I went one hundred and seven leagues in a straight line from west to east along the seashore of the island of Juana, and as a result of this voyage I can say that this island is larger than England and Scotland together, for, beyond these one hundred and seven leagues, there remain to the westward two provinces to which I have not gone. One of these provinces they call "Avan," and there people are born with tails. These provinces cannot have a length of less than fifty or sixty leagues, as I could understand from those Indians whom I have and who know all the islands.

The other island, Española, has a circumference greater than all Spain from Collioure by the seacoast to Fuenterabia in Vizcaya, for I voyaged along one side for one hundred and eighty-eight great leagues in a straight line from west to east.[12] It is a land to be desired and, when seen, never to be left. I have taken possession of all for their highnesses, and all are more richly endowed than I know how or am able to say, and I hold all for their highnesses, so that they may dispose of them as they do of the kingdoms of Castile and as absolutely. But especially, in this Española, in the situation most convenient and in the best position for the mines of gold and for all trade as well with

10. **took by force some of the natives:** Columbus enslaved some natives, whom he taught Spanish so that they could serve as translators.

11. **a fusta of eighteen benches:** To facilitate trade among the islands, the natives built large canoes made of a single log, with benches for rowers and space at either end for passengers and cargo.

12. **from west to east:** In equating the circuit of the island to the distance around the Spanish peninsula from Collioure on the Gulf of Lyons to Fuenterabia on the Bay of Biscay, Columbus greatly exaggerated the size of Hispaniola.

the mainland here as with that there, belonging to the Grand Khan,[13] where will be great trade and profit, I have taken possession of a large town, to which I gave the name "Villa de Navidad," and in it I have made fortifications and a fort, which will now by this time be entirely completed. In it I have left enough men for such a purpose with arms and artillery and provisions for more than a year, and a fusta, and one, a master of all seacraft, to build others, and I have established great friendship with the king of that land, so much so, that he was proud to call me "brother" and to treat me as such. And even were he to change his attitude to one of hostility towards these men, he and his do not know what arms are. They go naked, as I have already said, and they are the most timorous people in the world, so that the men whom I have left there alone would suffice to destroy all that land, and the island is without danger for their persons, if they know how to govern themselves.

In all these islands, it seems to me that all men are content with one woman, and to their chief or king they give as many as twenty. It appears to me that the women work more than do the men. I have not been able to learn if they hold private property; it seemed to me to be that all took a share in that which any one had, especially of eatable things.

In these islands I have so far found no human monstrosities, as many expected, but on the contrary the whole population is very well formed, nor are they negroes as in Guinea, but their hair is flowing and they are not born where there is intense force in the rays of the sun. It is true that the sun has there great power, although it is distant from the equinoctial line twenty-six degrees. In these islands, where there are high mountains, the cold was severe this winter, but they endure it, being used to it and with the help of meats which they consume with many and extremely hot spices. As I have found no monsters, so I have had no report of any, except in an island "Quaris," which is the second at the coming into the Indies,[14] and which is inhabited by a people who are regarded in all the islands as very fierce and who eat human flesh. They have many canoes with which they range through all the islands of India and pillage and take whatever they can. They are no more malformed than are the others, except that they have the custom of wearing their hair long like women, and they use bows and arrows of the same cane stems, with a small piece of wood at the end, owing to their lack of iron which they do not possess. They are ferocious among these other people who are cowardly to an excessive degree, but I make no more account of them than of the rest. These are they who have intercourse with the women of "Martinio,"[15] which is the first island met on the way from Spain to the Indies, in which there is not a man. These women engage in no feminine occupation, but use bows and arrows of cane, like those already mentioned, and they arm and protect themselves with plates of copper, of which they have much.

In another island, which they assure me is larger than Española, the people have no hair. In it there is gold incalculable, and from it and from the other islands I bring with me Indians as evidence.

---

13. **Grand Khan:** The name given to the leader of the Mongolian Empire in China.
14. **an island "Quaris" . . . at the coming into the Indies:** The captive natives evidently indicated the position of this island, which they called "Quaris." Columbus landed on the island, which he renamed Dominica, during his second voyage in 1494.
15. **"Martinio":** Martinique, as the island was later named by the French.

In conclusion, to speak only of that which has been accomplished on this voyage, which was so hasty, their highnesses can see that I will give them as much gold as they may need, if their highnesses will render me very slight assistance; moreover, I will give them spices and cotton, as much as their highnesses shall command; and mastic, as much as they shall order to be shipped and which, up to now, has been found only in Greece, in the island of Chios, and the Seignory[16] sells it for what it pleases; and aloe, as much as they shall order to be shipped; and slaves, as many as they shall order to be shipped and who will be from the idolaters.[17] I believe also that I have found rhubarb and cinnamon, and I shall find a thousand other things of value, which the people whom I have left there will have discovered, for I have not delayed at any point, so far as the wind allowed me to sail, except in the town of Navidad, in order to leave it secured and well established, and in truth I should have done much more if the ships had served me as reason demanded.[18]

This is enough. And the eternal God, Our Lord, Who gives to all those who walk in His way, triumph over things which appear to be impossible, and this was notably one. For, although men have talked or have written of these lands, all was conjectural, without suggestion of ocular evidence, but amounted only to this, that those who heard for the most part listened and judged rather by hearsay than from even a small something tangible. So that, since Our Redeemer has given the victory to our most illustrious king and queen, and to their renowned kingdoms, in so great a matter, for this all Christendom ought to feel delight and make great feasts and give solemn thanks to the Holy Trinity, with many solemn prayers for the great exaltation which they shall have in the turning of so many peoples to our holy faith, and afterwards for the temporal benefits, because not only Spain but all Christendom will have hence refreshment and gain.

This in accordance with that which has been accomplished, thus briefly.

Done in the caravel, off the Canary Islands, on the fifteenth of February, in the year one thousand four hundred and ninety-three.

At your orders.

THE ADMIRAL

After having written this,[19] and being in the sea of Castile, there came upon me so great a south-south-west wind that I was obliged to lighten ship. But I ran here to-day into this port of Lisbon, which was the greatest marvel in the world, whence I decided to write to their highnesses. In all the Indies, I have always found weather like May. There I went in thirty-three days and I should have returned in twenty-eight, save for these storms which have detained me for fourteen days, beating about in this sea. Here all the sailors say that never has there been so bad a winter nor so many ships lost.

Done on the fourth day of March.

[1493, 1930]

---

16. **Seignory:** The system of government in Genoa, Italy, where Columbus was born.
17. **idolaters:** Non-Christians. Columbus includes the discovery of a new source of slaves as one of the important outcomes of his voyage.
18. **ships . . . demanded:** The *Santa María*, Columbus's flagship, was grounded on a reef near Hispaniola and sank on December 25, 1492. His other ships, the *Pinta* and the *Niña*, were caravels, smaller vessels designed for speed and maneuverability in difficult waters.
19. **After having written this:** This note was wrapped around the letter and sealed.

Álvar Núñez Cabeza de Vaca

[c. 1490–c. 1557]

Álvar Núñez Cabeza de Vaca was born in Jerez, Spain, around 1490. His aristocratic family had been given the title Cabeza de Vaca, or "Head of a Cow," in honor of an ancestor who had helped the Spanish Christians gain an important victory over the Moors by marking an unguarded mountain pass with the skull of a cow. Very little is known about Cabeza de Vaca's life before he was appointed to serve as treasurer and second in command of a royal expedition led by Pánfilo de Narváez. The expedition of five ships and six hundred men left Spain on June 17, 1527, to establish a Spanish colony in Florida. By the time the expedition finally arrived in April 1528 in what is today known as Tampa Bay, the number of men had been reduced to three hundred by death and desertion. The conquistadores wandered for nearly six months north through Florida, where many of the men became sick with malaria and dysentery. They also encountered fierce opposition from the Apalachee Indians, who tenaciously defended their lands against the invaders. Narváez consequently decided to retreat by

La relacion y comentarios del gouernador Aluar nuñez cabeça de vaca

The frontispiece of the second edition of Cabeza de Vaca's report to the Spanish crown, published in Spain in 1555, bears the coat of arms of the Holy Roman Emperor Charles V (Charles I of Spain) held by the double-headed eagle of the House of Hapsburg.

building makeshift barges and sailing to Spanish settlements in Mexico. Separated from Narváez, whose barge was apparently lost at sea, Cabeza de Vaca and eighty men on two of the other barges were shipwrecked on what he later described as the "Isle of Misfortune," probably Galveston Island off the coast of present-day Texas, in November 1528.

During the next eight years, Cabeza de Vaca underwent one of the most remarkable and transformative experiences in the early annals of European exploration of the Americas. By the end of the first winter, all but a handful of the Spaniards had died of disease, exposure, or starvation. In a twist of fate, the surviving conquistadores, the would-be conquerors, were taken captive by the Karankawa Indians. Cabeza de Vaca was a slave for two years, after which he managed to escape to the mainland, where he lived for five years among a seminomadic tribe, the Coahuiltecans. He worked as a trader, bartering coral and seashells with the native inhabitants, from whom he eventually learned that three other survivors of the Spanish expedition were living on the coast. With them, Cabeza de Vaca decided to make his way to Mexico, embarking in 1535 upon what proved to be a two-thousand-mile journey on foot through territory that had never before been seen by Europeans. As the four men made their way across what is now the southwestern United States and northern Mexico, they gained a growing reputation as healers, finding a warm welcome and a growing following among the numerous tribes they encountered.

During these years of living among native peoples, Cabeza de Vaca experienced considerable change in his worldview. In his later account of the final approach to the Spanish settlements in Mexico, for example, he grimly described the devastating effects that had already been wrought by his countrymen, especially the Spanish slave hunters who captured slaves to work on the ranches, sugar plantations, and in the gold mines: "It made us extremely sad to see how fertile the land was, and very beautiful, and very full of springs and rivers, and to see every place deserted and burned, and the people so thin and ill, all of them fled and hidden." As they neared the end of their long journey, the ragged survivors of the Narváez expedition encountered a group of slave hunters, who to Cabeza de Vaca's horror sought to seize the hundreds of Pima Indians accompanying the revered healers into Mexico. After insisting that the Indians remain free, Cabeza de Vaca and his three companions went on to the nearest Spanish settlement, from which they were escorted to Mexico City in July 1536.

bedfordstmartins.com/ americanlit *for research links on Cabeza de Vaca*

When he returned to Spain later that year, Cabeza de Vaca was a far different man than the zealous conquistador who had left the country nine years earlier. He soon began to write an account of his experiences in the New World, *La relacion que dio Aluar nuñez cabeça de vaca* (1542). Still deeply committed to the Catholic faith and Spanish culture, he sought to encourage further expeditions to America. But he also urged the adoption of more benign and just policies toward the native populations of the New World. Cabeza de Vaca later returned there as the governor of an expedition to present-day Paraguay, where he came into conflict with Spanish colonists who were primarily interested in exploiting the lands they settled and the native peoples of the country. Accused of corruption, Cabeza de

Vaca was arrested and returned in chains to Spain in 1545. When the dispute was finally settled in 1551, he was exiled to North Africa and forbidden ever to return to the New World. While in exile, he wrote an account of his experiences in South America, *La relacion y comentarios del gouernador Aluar nuñez cabeza de vaca* (1555). The account was published after he was allowed to return to Spain, where he died about 1557.

Cabeza de Vaca's *Narrative.* Begun as a formal report to Emperor Charles V of Spain on the disastrous royal expedition led by Pánfilo de Narváez, *La relacion que dio Aluar nuñez cabeça de vaca* was published in 1542. A second edition was published in 1555, and the book was subsequently translated into many languages. The first English translation was a partial version published in an early collection of travel literature compiled by Samuel Purchas in 1625. A complete English translation was not published until 1851.

Few accounts of the early explorations of the Americas equal the historical, anthropological, and literary significance of Cabeza de Vaca's *Narrative.* Even before the formal account was published, his reports of a vast area that no European had set foot on inspired Spanish expeditions into North America, notably the brutal march led by Francisco Vásquez de Coronado across the Southwest to the Great Plains. Although Cabeza de Vaca sought to inspire more humane treatment of the indigenous peoples, his account led directly to their further devastation by Spanish conquistadores. At the same time, his account contains the richest and most detailed descriptions of those indigenous peoples and their cultural traditions. Cabeza de Vaca's *Narrative* was also the first captivity narrative, a story of a European's forced immersion into and subsequent effort to come to terms with an alien culture. The following selections include the proem, or preface, addressed to Emperor Charles V, as well as chapters in which Cabeza de Vaca describes the experiences of the few Spanish survivors of the expedition after they were shipwrecked on an island off the coast of present-day Texas. The text is taken from *Spanish Explorers in the Southern United States, 1528-1543*, edited by Frederick W. Hodge (1907).

From THE NARRATIVE OF CABEZA DE VACA

Proem

Sacred Caesarian Catholic Majesty:

Among the many who have held sway, I think no prince can be found whose service has been attended with the ardor and emulation shown for that of your Highness[1] at this time. The inducement is evident and powerful: men do not pursue together the same

1. **your Highness:** Emperor Charles V (1500-1558), grandson of and successor to Ferdinand and Isabel, monarchs of Spain.

career without motive, and strangers are observed to strive with those who are equally impelled by religion and loyalty.

Although ambition and love of action are common to all, as to the advantages that each may gain, there are great inequalities of fortune, the result not of conduct, but only accident, nor caused by the fault of any one, but coming in the providence of God and solely by His will. Hence to one arises deeds more signal than he thought to achieve; to another the opposite in every way occurs, so that he can show no higher proof of purpose than his effort, and at times even this is so concealed that it cannot of itself appear.

As for me, I can say in undertaking the march I made on the main by the royal authority, I firmly trusted that my conduct and services would be as evident and distinguished as were those of my ancestors and that I should not have to speak in order to be reckoned among those who for diligence and fidelity in affairs your Majesty honors. Yet, as neither my counsel nor my constancy availed to gain aught for which we set out, agreeably to your interests, for our sins, no one of the many armaments that have gone into those parts has been permitted to find itself in straits great like ours, or come to an end alike forlorn and fatal. To me, one only duty remains, to present a relation of what was seen and heard in the ten years I wandered lost and in privation through many and remote lands. Not merely a statement of positions and distances, animals and vegetation, but of the diverse customs of the many and very barbarous people with whom I talked and dwelt, as well as all other matters I could hear of and discern, that in some way I may avail your Highness. My hope of going out from among those nations was always small, still my care and diligence were none the less to keep in particular remembrance everything, that if at any time God our Lord should will to bring me where I now am, it might testify to my exertion in the royal behalf.

As the narrative is in my opinion of no trivial value to those who in your name go to subdue those countries and bring them to a knowledge of the true faith and true Lord, and under the imperial dominion, I have written this with much exactness; and although in it may be read things very novel and for some persons difficult to believe, nevertheless they may without hesitation credit me as strictly faithful. Better than to exaggerate, I have lessened in all things, and it is sufficient to say the relation is offered to your Majesty for truth. I beg it may be received in the name of homage, since it is the most that one could bring who returned thence naked.

Chapter 14
The departure of four Christians[2]

The four Christians being gone, after a few days such cold and tempestuous weather succeeded that the Indians could not pull up roots, the cane weirs[3] in which they took fish no longer yielded any thing, and the houses being very open, our people began to

2. **The departure of four Christians:** After their barges were driven ashore on an island off the coast of present-day Texas, the surviving members of the expedition sent four of their men in search of a Spanish settlement on the gulf coast of Mexico, which they mistakenly believed was nearby. Throughout his account, Cabeza de Vaca refers to the Spanish conquistadores as "Christians."
3. **cane weirs:** Traps made of cane poles set in a stream to catch fish.

die. Five Christians, of a mess [quartered] on the coast, came to such extremity that they ate their dead; the body of the last one only as found unconsumed. Their names were Sierra, Diego Lopez, Corral, Palacios and Gonçalo Ruiz. This produced great commotion among the Indians giving rise to so much censure that had they known it in season to have done so, doubtless they would have destroyed any survivor, and we should have found ourselves in the utmost perplexity. Finally, of eighty men who arrived in the two instances, fifteen only remained alive.

After this, the natives were visited by a disease of the bowels, of which half their number died. They conceived that we had destroyed them,[4] and believing it firmly, they concerted among themselves to dispatch those of us who survived. When they were about to execute their purpose, an Indian who had charge of me, told them not to believe we were the cause of those deaths, since if we had such power we should also have averted the fatality from so many of our people, whom they had seen die without our being able to minister relief, already very few of us remaining, and none doing hurt or wrong, and that it would be better to leave us unharmed. God our Lord willed that the others should heed this opinion and counsel, and be hindered in their design.

To this island we gave the name Malhado.[5] The people[6] we found there are large and well formed; they have no other arms than bows and arrows, in the use of which they are very dexterous. The men have one of their nipples bored from side to side, and some have both, wearing a cane in each, the length of two palms and a half, and the thickness of two fingers. They have the under lip also bored, and wear in it a piece of cane the breadth of half a finger. Their women are accustomed to great toil. The stay they make on the island is from October to the end of February. Their subsistence then is the root I have spoken of, got from under the water in November and December. They have weirs of cane and take fish only in this season; afterwards they live on the roots. At the end of February, they go into other parts to seek food; for then the root is beginning to grow and is not food.

Those people love their offspring the most of any in the world, and treat them with the greatest mildness. When it occurs that a son dies, the parents and kindred weep as does everybody; the wailing continuing for him a whole year. They begin before dawn every day, the parents first and after them the whole town. They do the same at noon and at sunset. After a year of mourning has passed, the rites of the dead are performed; then they wash and purify themselves from the stain of smoke. They lament all the deceased in this manner, except the aged, for whom they show no regret, as they say that their season has passed, they having no enjoyment, and that living they would occupy the earth and take aliment from the young. Their custom is to bury the dead, unless it be those among them who have been physicians. These they burn. While the fire kindles they are all dancing and making high festivity, until the bones become powder. After the

4. **They conceived that we had destroyed them:** The Indians believed that Cabeza de Vaca and his men were sorcerers, capable of putting spells on them.

5. **Malhado:** "Misfortune" was the name Cabeza de Vaca gave to Galveston Island, where the remnants of the expedition landed after a hurricane in the Gulf of Mexico.

6. **The people:** The Capoques and Hans, coastal tribes of present-day Texas.

lapse of a year the funeral honors are celebrated, every one taking part in them, when that dust is presented in water for the relatives to drink.

Every man has an acknowledged wife. The physicians are allowed more freedom: they may have two or three wives, among whom exist the greatest friendship and harmony. From the time a daughter marries, all that he who takes her to wife kills in hunting or catches in fishing, the woman brings to the house of her father, without daring to eat or take any part of it, and thence victuals[7] are taken to the husband. From that time neither her father nor mother enters his house, nor can he enter theirs, nor the houses of their children; and if by chance they are in the direction of meeting, they turn aside, and pass the distance of a crossbow shot from each other, carrying the head low the while, the eyes cast on the ground; for they hold it improper to see or to speak to each other. But the woman has liberty to converse and communicate with the parents and relatives of her husband. The custom exists from this island the distance of more than fifty leagues[8] inland.

There is another custom, which is, when a son or brother dies, at the house where the death takes place they do not go after food for three months, but sooner famish, their relatives and neighbors providing what they eat. As in the time we were there a great number of the natives died, in most houses there was very great hunger, because of the keeping of this their custom and observance; for although they who sought after food worked hard, yet from the severity of the season they could get but little; in consequence, the Indians who kept me, left the island, and passed over in canoes to the main, into some bays where are many oysters. For three months in the year they eat nothing besides these, and drink very bad water. There is great want of wood: mosquitos are in great plenty. The houses are of mats, set up on masses of oyster shells, which they sleep upon, and in skins, should they accidentally possess them. In this way we lived until April [1529], when we went to the seashore, where we ate blackberries all the month, during which time the Indians did not omit to observe their *areitos*[9] and festivities.

Chapter 15
What befell us among the people of Malhado

On an island of which I have spoken, they wished to make us physicians without examination or inquiring for diplomas. They cure by blowing upon the sick, and with that breath and the imposing of hands they cast out infirmity. They ordered that we also should do this, and be of use to them in some way. We laughed at what they did, telling them it was folly, that we knew not how to heal. In consequence, they withheld food from us until we should practise what they required. Seeing our persistence, an Indian told me I knew not what I uttered, in saying that what he knew availed nothing; for stones

7. **victuals:** Food or provisions.
8. **fifty leagues:** A league was a measure of distance, equivalent to about three miles.
9. ***areitos*:** The term originally referred to the dance ceremonies of the Arawak Indians of the West Indies, the first native people that Columbus encountered in his explorations; here, Cabeza de Vaca uses the term more generally, to refer to all native dance ceremonies.

and other matters growing about in the fields have virtue, and that passing a pebble along the stomach would take away pain and restore health, and certainly then we who were extraordinary men must possess power and efficacy over all other things. At last, finding ourselves in great want we were constrained to obey; but without fear lest we should be blamed for any failure or success.

Their custom is, on finding themselves sick to send for a physician, and after he has applied the cure, they give him not only all they have, but seek among their relatives for more to give. The practitioner scarifies over the seat of pain, and then sucks about the wound. They make cauteries with fire, a remedy among them in high repute, which I have tried on myself and found benefit from it. They afterwards blow on the spot, and having finished, the patient considers that he is relieved.

Our method was to bless the sick, breathing upon them, and recite a Pater-noster and an Ave-Maria,[10] praying with all earnestness to God our Lord that he would give health and influence them to make us some good return. In his clemency he willed that all those for whom we supplicated, should tell the others that they were sound and in health, directly after we made the sign of the blessed cross over them. For this the Indians treated us kindly; they deprived themselves of food that they might give to us, and presented us with skins and some trifles.

So protracted was the hunger we there experienced, that many times I was three days without eating. The natives also endured as much; and it appeared to me a thing impossible that life could be so prolonged, although afterwards I found myself in greater hunger and necessity, which I shall speak of farther on.

The Indians who had Alonzo del Castillo, Andrés Dorantes, and the others that remained alive, were of a different tongue and ancestry from these, and went to the opposite shore of the main to eat oysters, where they staid until the first day of April, when they returned. The distance is two leagues in the widest part. The island is half a league in breadth and five leagues in length.

The inhabitants of all this region go naked. The women alone have any part of their persons covered, and it is with a wool that grows on trees.[11] The damsels dress themselves in deer-skin. The people are generous to each other of what they possess. They have no chief. All that are of a lineage keep together. They speak two languages; those of one are called Capoques, those of the other, Han. They have a custom when they meet, or from time to time when they visit, of remaining half an hour before they speak, weeping; and, this over, he that is visited first rises and gives the other all he has, which is received, and after a little while he carries it away, and often goes without saying a word. They have other strange customs; but I have told the principal of them, and the most remarkable, that I may pass on and further relate what befell us.

---

10. **Pater-noster and an Ave-Maria:** The recitation of two prayers important in the Catholic religion, the Lord's Prayer and the Hail Mary.
11. **a wool that grows on trees:** Spanish moss.

Chapter 16

The Christians leave the island of Malhado

After Dorantes and Castillo returned to the island, they brought together the Christians, who were somewhat separated, and found them in all to be fourteen. As I have said, I was opposite on the main, where my Indians had taken me, and where so great sickness had come upon me, that if anything before had given me hopes of life, this were enough to have entirely bereft me of them.

When the Christians heard of my condition, they gave an Indian the cloak of marten skins we had taken from the cacique,[12] as before related, to pass them over to where I was that they might visit me. Twelve of them crossed; for two were so feeble that their comrades could not venture to bring them. The names of those who came were Alonzo del Castillo, Andrés Dorantes, Diego Dorantes, Valdevieso, Estrada, Tostado, Chaves, Gutierrez, Asturiano a clergyman, Diego de Huelva, Estevanico the black, and Benitez; and when they reached the main land, they found another, who was one of our company, named Francisco de Leon. The thirteen together followed along the coast. So soon as they had come over, my Indians informed me of it, and that Hieronymo de Alvaniz and Lope de Oviedo remained on the island. But sickness prevented me from going with my companions or even seeing them.

I was obliged to remain with the people belonging to the island more than a year, and because of the hard work they put upon me and the harsh treatment, I resolved to flee from them and go to those of Charruco, who inhabit the forests and country of the main, the life I led being insupportable. Besides much other labor, I had to get out roots from below the water, and from among the cane where they grew in the ground. From this employment I had my fingers so worn that did a straw but touch them they would bleed. Many of the canes are broken, so they often tore my flesh, and I had to go in the midst of them with only the clothing on I have mentioned.

Accordingly, I put myself to contriving how I might get over to the other Indians, among whom matters turned somewhat more favorably for me. I set to trafficking, and strove to make my employment profitable in the ways I could best contrive, and by that means I got food and good treatment. The Indians would beg me to go from one quarter to another for things of which they have need; for in consequence of incessant hostilities, they cannot traverse the country, nor make many exchanges. With my merchandise and trade I went into the interior as far as I pleased, and travelled along the coast forty or fifty leagues. The principal wares were cones and other pieces of sea-snail, conchs used for cutting, and fruit like a bean of the highest value among them, which they use as a medicine and employ in their dances and festivities. Among other matters were sea-beads. Such were what I carried into the interior; and in barter I got and brought back skins, ochre with which they rub and color the face, hard canes of which to make arrows, sinews, cement and flint for the heads, and tassels of the hair of deer that by dyeing they

12. **cacique:** A native chief.

make red. This occupation suited me well; for the travel allowed me liberty to go where I wished, I was not obliged to work, and was not a slave. Wherever I went I received fair treatment, and the Indians gave me to eat out of regard to my commodities. My leading object, while journeying in this business, was to find out the way by which I should go forward, and I became well known. The inhabitants were pleased when they saw me, and I had brought them what they wanted; and those who did not know me sought and desired the acquaintance, for my reputation. The hardships that I underwent in this were long to tell, as well of peril and privation as of storms and cold. Oftentimes they overtook me alone and in the wilderness; but I came forth from them all by the great mercy of God our Lord. Because of them I avoided pursuing the business in winter, a season in which the natives themselves retire to their huts and ranches, torpid and incapable of exertion.

I was in this country nearly six years, alone among the Indians, and naked like them. The reason why I remained so long, was that I might take with me the Christian, Lope de Oviedo, from the island; Alaniz, his companion, who had been left with him by Alonzo del Castillo, and by Andrés Dorantes, and the rest, died soon after their departure; and to get the survivor out from there, I went over to the island every year, and entreated him that we should go, in the best way we could contrive, in quest of Christians. He put me off every year, saying in the next coming we would start. At last I got him off, crossing him over the bay, and over four rivers in the coast, as he could not swim. In this way we went on with some Indians, until coming to a bay a league in width, and everywhere deep. From the appearance we supposed it to be that which is called Espiritu Sancto. We met some Indians on the other side of it, coming to visit ours, who told us that beyond them were three men like us, and gave their names. We asked for the others, and were told that they were all dead of cold and hunger; that the Indians farther on, of whom they were, for their diversion had killed Diego Dorantes, Valdevieso, and Diego de Huelva, because they left one house for another; and that other Indians, their neighbors with whom Captain Dorantes now was, had in consequence of a dream, killed Esquivel and Mendez. We asked how the living were situated, and they answered that they were very ill used, the boys and some of the Indian men being very idle, out of cruelty gave them many kicks, cuffs, and blows with sticks; that such was the life they led.

We desired to be informed of the country ahead, and of the subsistence: they said there was nothing to eat, and that it was thin of people, who suffered of cold, having no skins or other things to cover them. They told us also if we wished to see those three Christians, two days from that time the Indians who had them would come to eat walnuts a league from there on the margin of that river; and that we might know what they told us of the ill usage to be true, they slapped my companion and beat him with a stick, and I was not left without my portion. Many times they threw lumps of mud at us, and every day they put their arrows to our hearts, saying that they were inclined to kill us in the way that they had destroyed our friends. Lope Oviedo, my comrade, in fear said that he wished to go back with the women of those who had crossed the bay with us, the men having remained some distance behind. I contended strongly against his returning, and urged my objections; but in no way could I keep him. So he went back, and I remained alone with those savages. They are called Quevenes, and those with whom he returned, Deaguanes.

Chapter 19
Our separation by the Indians

When the six months were over, I had to spend with the Christians to put in execution the plan we had concerted, the Indians went after prickly pears, the place at which they grew being thirty leagues off; and when we approached the point of flight, those among whom we were, quarrelled about a woman. After striking with fists, beating with sticks and bruising heads in great anger, each took his lodge and went his way, whence it became necessary that the Christians should also separate, and in no way could we come together until another year.

In this time I passed a hard life, caused as much by hunger as ill usage. Three times I was obliged to run from my masters, and each time they went in pursuit and endeavored to slay me; but God our Lord in his mercy chose to protect and preserve me; and when the season of prickly pears returned, we again came together in the same place. After we had arranged our escape, and appointed a time, that very day the Indians separated and all went back. I told my comrades I would wait for them among the prickly-pear plants until the moon should be full. This day was the first of September, and the first of the moon; and I said that if in this time they did not come as we had agreed, I would leave and go alone. So we parted, each going with his Indians. I remained with mine until the thirteenth day of the moon, having determined to flee to others when it should be full.

At this time Andrés Dorantes arrived with Estevanico and informed me that they had left Castillo with other Indians near by, called Lanegados; that they had encountered great obstacles and wandered about lost; that the next day the Indians, among whom we were, would move to where Castillo was, and were going to unite with those who held him and become friends, having been at war until then, and that in this way we should recover Castillo.

We had thirst all the time we ate the pears, which we quenched with their juice. We caught it in a hole made in the earth, and when it was full we drank until satisfied. It is sweet, and the color of must. In this manner they collect it for lack of vessels. There are many kinds of prickly pears, among them some very good, although they all appeared to me to be so, hunger never having given me leisure to choose, nor to reflect upon which were the best.

Nearly all these people drink rain-water, which lies about in spots. Although there are rivers, as the Indians never have fixed habitations, there are no familiar or known places for getting water. Throughout the country are extensive and beautiful plains with good pasturage; and I think it would be a very fruitful region were it worked and inhabited by civilized men. We nowhere saw mountains.

These Indians told us that there was another people next in advance of us, called Camones, living towards the coast, and that they had killed the people who came in the boat of Peñalosa and Tellez, who arrived so feeble that even while being slain they could offer no resistance, and were all destroyed. We were shown their clothes and arms, and were told that the boat lay there stranded. This, the fifth boat, had remained till then unaccounted for. We have already stated how the boat of the Governor had been carried out to sea, and that of the comptroller and the friars had been cast away on the coast, of which Esquevel narrated the fate of the men. We have once told how the two boats in which Castillo, I, and Dorantes came, foundered near the Island of Malhado.

Chapter 20
Of our escape

The second day after we had moved, we commended ourselves to God and set forth with speed, trusting, for all the lateness of the season and that the prickly pears were about ending, with the mast which remained in the woods [field], we might still be enabled to travel over a large territory. Hurrying on that day in great dread lest the Indians should overtake us, we saw some smokes, and going in the direction of them we arrived there after vespers, and found an Indian. He ran as he discovered us coming, not being willing to wait for us. We sent the negro[13] after him, when he stopped, seeing him alone. The negro told him we were seeking the people who made those fires. He answered that their houses were near by, and he would guide us to them. So we followed him. He ran to make known our approach, and at sunset we saw the houses. Before our arrival, at the distance of two crossbow shots from them, we found four Indians, who waited for us and received us well. We said in the language of the Mariames, that we were coming to look for them. They were evidently pleased with our company, and took us to their dwellings. Dorantes and the negro were lodged in the house of a physician,[14] Castillo and myself in that of another.

These people speak a different language, and are called Avavares. They are the same that carried bows to those with whom we formerly lived, going to traffic with them, and although they are of a different nation and tongue, they understand the other language. They arrived that day with their lodges, at the place where we found them. The community directly brought us a great many prickly pears, having heard of us before, of our cures, and of the wonders our Lord worked by us, which, although there had been no others, were adequate to open ways for us through a country poor like this, to afford us people where oftentimes there are none, and to lead us through immediate dangers, not permitting us to be killed, sustaining us under great want, and putting into those nations the heart of kindness, as we shall relate hereafter.

Chapter 21
Our cure of some of the afflicted

That same night of our arrival, some Indians came to Castillo and told him that they had great pain in the head, begging him to cure them. After he made over them the sign of the cross, and commended them to God, they instantly said that all the pain had left, and went to their houses bringing us prickly pears, with a piece of venison, a thing to us little known. As the report of Castillo's performances spread, many came to us that

---

13. **the negro:** Estevánico, the Moorish slave of one of the other Spanish survivors Andrés Dorantes.
14. **physician:** Medicine man.

night sick, that we should heal them, each bringing a piece of venison, until the quantity became so great we knew not where to dispose of it. We gave many thanks to God, for every day went on increasing his compassion and his gifts. After the sick were attended to, they began to dance and sing, making themselves festive, until sunrise; and because of our arrival, the rejoicing was continued for three days.

When these were ended, we asked the Indians about the country farther on, the people we should find in it, and of the subsistence there. They answered us, that throughout all the region prickly-pear plants abounded; but the fruit was now gathered and all the people had gone back to their houses. They said the country was very cold, and there were few skins. Reflecting on this, and that it was already winter, we resolved to pass the season with these Indians.

Five days after our arrival, all the Indians went off, taking us with them to gather more prickly pears, where there were other peoples speaking different tongues. After walking five days in great hunger, since on the way was no manner of fruit, we came to a river and put up our houses. We then went to seek the product of certain trees, which is like peas. As there are no paths in the country, I was detained some time. The others returned, and coming to look for them in the dark I got lost. Thank God I found a burning tree, and in the warmth of it I passed the cold of that night. In the morning, loading myself with sticks, and taking two brands with me, I returned to seek them. In this manner I wandered five days, ever with my fire and load; for if the wood had failed me where none could be found, as many parts are without any, though I might have sought sticks elsewhere, there would have been no fire to kindle them. This was all the protection I had against cold, while walking naked as I was born. Going to the low woods near the rivers, I prepared myself for the night, stopping in them before sunset. I made a hole in the ground and threw in fuel which the trees abundantly afforded, collected in good quantity from those that were fallen and dry. About the whole I made four fires, in the form of a cross, which I watched and made up from time to time. I also gathered some bundles of the coarse straw that there abounds, with which I covered myself in the hole. In this way I was sheltered at night from cold. On one occasion while I slept, the fire fell upon the straw, when it began to blaze so rapidly that notwithstanding the haste I made to get out of it, I carried some marks on my hair of the danger to which I was exposed. All this while I tasted not a mouthful, nor did I find anything I could eat. My feet were bare and bled a good deal. Through the mercy of God, the wind did not blow from the north in all this time, otherwise I should have died.

At the end of the fifth day I arrived on the margin of a river, where I found the Indians, who with the Christians, had considered me dead, supposing that I had been stung by a viper. All were rejoiced to see me, and most so were my companions. They said that up to that time they had struggled with great hunger, which was the cause of their not having sought me. At night, all gave me of their prickly pears, and the next morning we set out for a place where they were in large quantity, with which we satisfied our great craving, the Christians rendering thanks to our Lord that He had ever given us His aid.

[1542/1555, 1907]

Samuel de Champlain

[c. 1570–1635]

The son of ship captain Antoine de Champlain and his wife, Marguerite Le Roy, Samuel de Champlain was born in Brouage, then a seaport and center of the salt industry in southwestern France. Little is known about Champlain's early life except that he was raised a Catholic and probably educated by a parish priest. Historians are not even certain of the year of his birth, which is variously given as 1567 or 1570. When he was about twenty, Champlain joined the army and fought in France's ongoing foreign wars with Spain and domestic conflicts with the Protestant French Huguenots. When the Peace of Vervins was signed between France and Spain in 1598, Champlain left the army and began to pursue navigation and exploration as a career.

Champlain's opportunity came in 1599, when he undertook the first of a series of voyages with an uncle who was the captain of the *Saint-Julian.* The ship was chartered by the Spanish government for transporting troops and supplies to its colonies in the New World, from which it brought back treasures to Spain. During these early voyages, Champlain traveled first to Spain, where he learned to speak Spanish, and then to the West Indies and Central America. As he would throughout his life, Champlain kept a detailed journal of his observations and experiences during these voyages. When he returned to France, he wrote his first travel account, *Bref Discourse des Choses plus Remarquables que Sammeul Champlain de Brouage*, which he presented in manuscript to Henry IV, the king of France. Illustrated with sixty maps and pictures that Champlain drew, the book provided a detailed description of the lands and native peoples of the New World. Although the manuscript was evidently circulated at court, it was not published until 1858, when an English translation appeared as *Narrative of a Voyage to the West Indies and Mexico in the years 1599–1602*.

Samuel de Champlain

The only authentic portrait of Champlain is this detail from an etching based on his own drawing of the 1609 battle between French soldiers, their Algonkin and Montagnais allies, and the Mohawk on the shore of Lake Champlain. The etching was published in the 1613 edition of Champlain's *Voyages*.

In 1603, Champlain sailed again, this time to North America, where he became a leader in the establishment of New France. For the next thirty years, Champlain made nearly a dozen voyages across the Atlantic, charting the coast of New England, exploring the possibility of a Northwest Passage, mapping thousands of miles of territory, claiming lands for France, and establishing its first permanent settlement, Quebec. According to his biographers, Champlain was successful for several reasons. He learned from the mistakes of earlier French explorers, refusing, for example, to waste time searching for gold and other treasure. Committed to Christianizing the native peoples, he encouraged many Catholic missionaries to come to Canada. The resourceful Champlain was also adept at forging alliances with various native tribes, alliances that provided security for French business ventures and settlements. Finally, Champlain adapted to the cold climate of the northern parts of North America, where the French based their colonial economy on agriculture, fishing, and the fur trade.

Champlain, the first governor of Canada, . . . had already gone to war against the Iroquois in their forest forts, and penetrated to the Great Lakes and wintered there, before a Pilgrim had heard of New England.
–Henry David Thoreau

Throughout his years of shuttling back and forth across the Atlantic, Champlain publicized himself and New France by writing several books that were widely read in France. He published *Des Sauvages, ou, Voyage de Samuel Champlain, de Brouage, fait en la France nouvell*, in Paris in 1603. During a visit to France in 1610, two years after he founded Quebec, Champlain married the twelve-year-old Hélène Boullé. Because of her young age, she remained with her parents until 1620, when she came to live with Champlain in Quebec. Lonely and ill-suited to colonial life, she returned permanently to France in 1624. Champlain, however, vigorously promoted colonization, notably in *Les Voyages du Sieur de Champlain*, which detailed accounts of his experiences and observations in New France. The first volume was published in 1613, a second volume appeared in 1619, and the final volume of the *Voyages* was published in 1632. Appropriately, the final volume included an appendix, *Traitté de la Marine, et du Devoir d'un bon Marinier*, in which Champlain described the qualities and characteristics of a good mariner. He died in Quebec on December 25, 1635.

bedfordstmartins.com/americanlit *for research links on Champlain*

Champlain's *Voyages*. Although he described himself simply as a mariner or a navigator, Champlain was also a draftsman and a skilled writer. His books are filled with navigational charts, maps, and illustrations of native peoples and their practices, along with Champlain's descriptions of the landscape, flora, and fauna of North America, as well as of his exploits in what became New France. Seeking to contrast the actions of the French to the brutal policies of the Spanish in the Americas, Champlain placed particular emphasis on the friendly relations he established with some of the native tribes in the areas along the St. Lawrence River. During 1608-09, Champlain formed an alliance with the Algonkin, Montagnais, and Huron against the Mohawk, the keepers of the eastern door of the powerful Iroquois Confederacy. In exchange for access to remote regions and assistance with the fur trade, the three tribes asked for French help in their ongoing conflicts with the Mohawk. In the following selection, Champlain describes the first battle between the French soldiers, their Indian allies, and the Mohawk on the shore of what he named Lake Champlain. Some historians have questioned the accuracy of Champlain's account of the nature of Iroquois warfare, but the outcome and consequences of the battle are not in dispute. The Mohawk were defeated, and the French-Indian alliance provided Champlain time to develop and secure a small settlement, Quebec, effectively the beginning of New France. But the Iroquois consequently allied themselves with the Dutch and later with the English, first disrupting French trade and finally helping to bring an end to French dominion in North America. The text is taken from Charles P. Otis's translation of *Les Voyages du Sieur de Champlain* (1613), in *Voyages of Samuel de Champlain, 1604-1618*, edited by W. L. Grant (1907).

From THE VOYAGES OF SAMUEL DE CHAMPLAIN

We set out on the next day, continuing our course in the river as far as the entrance of the lake.[1] There are many pretty islands here, low, and containing very fine woods and meadows, with abundance of fowl and such animals of the chase as stags, fallow-deer, fawns, roe-bucks, bears, and others, which go from the main land to these islands. We captured a large number of these animals. There are also many beavers, not only in this river, but also in numerous other little ones that flow into it. These regions, although they are pleasant, are not inhabited by any savages, on account of their wars; but they withdraw as far as possible from the rivers into the interior, in order not to be suddenly surprised.

The next day we entered the lake, which is of great extent, say eighty or a hundred leagues long,[2] where I saw four fine islands, ten, twelve, and fifteen leagues long, which were formerly inhabited by the savages, like the River of the Iroquois; but they have been abandoned since the wars of the savages with one another prevail. There are also many rivers falling into the lake, bordered by many fine trees of the same kinds as those we have in France, with many vines finer than any I have seen in any other place; also many chestnut-trees on the border of this lake, which I had not seen before. There is also a great abundance of fish, of many varieties; among others, one called by the savages of the country *Chaousarou*,[3] which varies in length, the largest being, as the people told me, eight or ten feet long. I saw some five feet long, which were as large as my thigh; the head being as big as my two fists, with a snout two feet and a half long, and a double row of very sharp and dangerous teeth. Its body is, in shape, much like that of a pike; but it is armed with scales so strong that a poniard[4] could not pierce them. Its color is silver-gray. The extremity of its snout is like that of swine. This fish makes war upon all others in the lakes and rivers. It also possesses remarkable dexterity, as these people informed me, which is exhibited in the following manner. When it wants to capture birds, it swims in among the rushes, or reeds, which are found on the banks of the lake in several

---

1. **We set out . . . entrance of the lake:** They entered the lake from what Champlain called "the River of the Iroquois," now the Richelieu River, which flows northward out of Lake Champlain and empties into the St. Lawrence River near Montreal.
2. **eighty or a hundred leagues long:** That is, 240 to 300 miles long. Lake Champlain is actually about 110 miles long and 12 miles across at its widest point.
3. ***Chaousarou*:** The word is not French but probably an Algonkian term for a long-nose gar, a large fish that even today can reach a length of six feet and weigh fifty pounds.
4. **poniard:** A small, slim dagger.

places, where it puts its snout out of water and keeps perfectly still: so that, when the birds come and light on its snout, supposing it to be only the stump of a tree, it adroitly closes it, which it had kept ajar, and pulls the birds by the feet down under water. The savages gave me the head of one of them, of which they make great account, saying that, when they have the headache, they bleed themselves with the teeth of this fish on the spot where they suffer pain, when it suddenly passes away.

Continuing our course over this lake on the western side, I noticed, while observing the country, some very high mountains on the eastern side,[5] on the top of which there was snow. I made inquiry of the savages whether these localities were inhabited, when they told me that the Iroquois dwelt there, and that there were beautiful valleys in these places, with plains productive in grain, such as I had eaten in this country, together with many kinds of fruit without limit. They said also that the lake extended near mountains, some twenty-five leagues distant from us, as I judge. I saw, on the south, other mountains, no less high than the first, but without any snow. The savages told me that these mountains were thickly settled, and that it was there we were to find their enemies; but that it was necessary to pass a fall in order to go there (which I afterwards saw), when we should enter another lake,[6] nine or ten leagues long. After reaching the end of the lake, we should have to go, they said, two leagues by land, and pass through a river flowing into the sea on the Norumbegue coast, near that of Florida,[7] whither it took them only two days to go by canoe, as I have since ascertained from some prisoners we captured, who gave me minute information in regard to all they had personal knowledge of, through some Algonquin interpreters, who understood the Iroquois language.

Now, as we began to approach within two or three days' journey of the abode of their enemies, we advanced only at night, resting during the day. But they did not fail to practise constantly their accustomed superstitions, in order to ascertain what was to be the result of their undertaking; and they often asked me if I had had a dream, and seen their enemies, to which I replied in the negative. Yet I did not cease to encourage them, and inspire in them hope. When night came, we set out on the journey until the next day, when we withdrew into the interior of the forest, and spent the rest of the day there. About ten or eleven o'clock, after taking a little walk about our encampment, I retired. While sleeping, I dreamed that I saw our enemies, the Iroquois, drowning in the lake near a mountain, within sight. When I expressed a wish to help them, our allies, the savages, told me we must let them all die, and that they were of no importance. When I awoke, they did not fail to ask me, as usual, if I had had a dream. I told them that I had, in

---

5. **mountains on the eastern side:** The mountains to the east of Lake Champlain are known today as the Green Mountains of Vermont; the mountains to the south and west of the lake are the Adirondack Mountains of New York.

6. **pass a fall . . . another lake:** The waterfall is at present-day Ticonderoga. Lake George is on the other side of the falls, directly south of Lake Champlain.

7. **river . . . Florida:** In this garbled geographical account, probably the result of his inability fully to understand his Indian guides, Champlain refers to "Norumbegue," the Algonkian name for the coastal area where the Penobscot River flows into the Atlantic Ocean in present-day Maine, far to the north of Florida. The river he describes, separated by less than two leagues, or six miles, from Lake George, is actually the Hudson River, which flows south and empties into the Atlantic Ocean between Manhattan Island and New Jersey.

fact, had a dream. This, upon being related, gave them so much confidence that they did not doubt any longer that good was to happen to them.

When it was evening, we embarked in our canoes to continue our course; and, as we advanced very quietly and without making any noise, we met on the 29th of the month the Iroquois, about ten o'clock at evening, at the extremity of a cape which extends into the lake on the western bank.[8] They had come to fight. We both began to utter loud cries, all getting their arms in readiness. We withdrew out on the water, and the Iroquois went on shore, where they drew up all their canoes close to each other and began to fell trees with poor axes, which they acquire in war sometimes, using also others of stone. Thus they barricaded themselves very well.

Our forces also passed the entire night, their canoes being drawn up close to each other, and fastened to poles, so that they might not get separated, and that they might be all in readiness to fight, if occasion required. We were out upon the water, within arrow range of their barricades. When they were armed and in array, they despatched two canoes by themselves to the enemy to inquire if they wished to fight, to which the latter replied that they wanted nothing else: but they said that, at present, there was not much light, and that it would be necessary to wait for daylight, so as to be able to recognize each other; and that, as soon as the sun rose, they would offer us battle. This was agreed to by our side. Meanwhile, the entire night was spent in dancing and singing, on both sides, with endless insults and other talk; as, how little courage we had, how feeble a resistance we should make against their arms, and that, when day came, we should realize it to our ruin. Ours also were not slow in retorting, telling them they would see such execution of arms as never before, together with an abundance of such talk as is not unusual in the siege of a town. After this singing, dancing, and bandying words on both sides to the fill, when day came, my companions and myself continued under cover, for fear that the enemy would see us. We arranged our arms in the best manner possible, being, however, separated, each in one of the canoes of the savage Montagnais.[9] After arming ourselves with light armor, we each took an arquebuse,[10] and went on shore. I saw the enemy go out of their barricade, nearly two hundred in number, stout and rugged in appearance. They came at a slow pace towards us, with a dignity and assurance which greatly amused me, having three chiefs at their head. Our men also advanced in the same order, telling me that those who had three large plumes were the chiefs, and that they had only these three, and that they could be distinguished by these plumes, which were much larger than those of their companions, and that I should do

8. **cape . . . on the western bank:** Crown Point, on what is today the New York side of southern Lake Champlain, where the French later built an important fortress, Fort St. Frédéric. It was captured by the British during the French and Indian War, also known as the Seven Years' War (1756-63), which ended French dominion in North America.

9. **Montagnais:** "Mountain people," the French name for the Algonkian-speaking peoples who lived in the rugged terrain along the gulf of the Saint Lawrence River near present-day Labrador, Canada.

10. **arquebuse:** An early firearm developed by the Spanish conquistadores in the mid-fifteenth century. It was loaded through the long muzzle and fired by a slow-burning fuse, lit in advance of a battle from a spark made by rubbing together flint and steel. When ready to fire, the shooter would blow on the fuse and pull a trigger, which ignited the gunpowder in the base of the barrel of the gun.

what I could to kill them. I promised to do all in my power, and said that I was very sorry they could not understand me, so that I might give order and shape to their mode of attacking their enemies, and then we should, without doubt, defeat them all; but that this could not now be obviated, and that I should be very glad to show them my courage and good-will when we should engage in the fight.

As soon as we had landed, they began to run for some two hundred paces towards their enemies, who stood firmly, not having as yet noticed my companions, who went into the woods with some savages. Our men began to call me with loud cries; and, in order to give me a passage-way, they opened in two parts, and put me at their head, where I marched some twenty paces in advance of the rest, until I was within about thirty paces of the enemy, who at once noticed me, and, halting, gazed at me, as I did also at them. When I saw them making a move to fire at us, I rested my musket against my cheek, and aimed directly at one of the three chiefs. With the same shot, two fell to the ground; and one of their men was so wounded that he died some time after. I had loaded my musket with four balls. When our side saw this shot so favorable for them, they began to raise such loud cries that one could not have heard it thunder. Meanwhile, the arrows flew on both sides. The Iroquois were greatly astonished that two men had been so quickly killed, although they were equipped with armor woven from cotton thread, and with wood which was proof against their arrows. This caused great alarm among them. As I was loading again, one of my companions fired a shot from the woods, which astonished them anew to such a degree that, seeing their chiefs dead, they lost courage, and took to flight, abandoning their camp and fort, and fleeing into the woods, whither I pursued them, killing still more of them. Our savages also killed several of them, and took ten or twelve prisoners. The remainder escaped with the wounded. Fifteen or sixteen were wounded on our side with arrow-shots; but they were soon healed.

After gaining the victory, our men amused themselves by taking a great quantity of Indian corn and some meal from their enemies, also their armor, which they had left behind that they might run better. After feasting sumptuously, dancing and singing, we returned three hours after, with the prisoners. The spot where this attack took place is in latitude 43° and some minutes, and the lake was called Lake Champlain.

[1613, 1907]

1620

Colonial Settlements

In the United States, the settlement of America has most often been represented by a single scene, the landing of the Pilgrims at Plymouth Rock. Images of the peaceful gathering of the Pilgrims and their Wampanoag neighbors at the "First Thanksgiving" the following year have tended to mask a more complex and darker reality. Indeed, the settlement of North America was characterized by ongoing conflict, not only between European settlers and Native American peoples, but also among

◀ **Enrico Causini, *Landing of the Pilgrims, 1620* (1825)**

This sandstone relief in the rotunda of the U.S. Capitol, the meeting place of the Senate and House of Representatives, suggests the central place the Pilgrims later assumed in American history. As the Pilgrim father steps ashore at Plymouth Rock, he is greeted by an Indian offering an ear of corn, the staple crop of Native American societies throughout North America. In fact, the Pilgrims settled on the grounds of a village used in the summer by a group of Wampanoag, a tribe whose aid was crucial to the survival of Plymouth Plantation. But the wave of English immigration that followed the settlement ultimately led to the dispossession or destruction of Indian peoples throughout New England.

European countries, especially Spain, France, and England. Seeking to break Spain's monopoly in America, a group of French Huguenots (Protestant Lutherans) sought to establish a settlement in Florida as early as 1562. But the effort ended when the settlers at the colony on St. John's River and the survivors of a French fleet sent to aid them were massacred by Spanish forces in 1564. To safeguard Florida, Spain established a fort at Saint Augustine, the first permanent European settlement in what is now the United States. The French consequently turned their attention northward, to Canada, where they established a settlement at Port Royal, in present-day Nova Scotia, in 1605, and a fur-trading post at Quebec in 1608. In an effort to compete with France and Spain by exploiting the resources of the New World, the English concentrated their efforts in the area between Canada and Florida, an extensive territory they called "Virginia."

Despite the failure of their first settlements at Roanoke Island, off the coast of present-day North Carolina, English efforts at colonization were sustained by glowing printed accounts of the beauty and potential of the

The Arrival of the Englishmen in Virginia

Based on a watercolor by the English artist John White, this engraving by Theodor de Bry appears in his edition of Thomas Hariot's *A Briefe and True Report of the New Found Land of Virginia*, published in Frankfurt in 1590. The map of the coast of present-day North Carolina, where the English sought to establish a settlement at Roanoke Island, provides the Algonkian names for villages and shows Native Americans involved in fishing, hunting, and agriculture. It also shows the wrecks of previous European ships along the Outer Banks.

New World. Thomas Hariot's *A Briefe and True Report of the New Found Land of Virginia*, first published as a pamphlet in 1588, was swiftly reprinted by Richard Hakluyt in his popular compilation *The Principall Navigations, Voiages and Discoveries of the English Nation* (1589) and then circulated throughout Europe in lavishly illustrated editions in English and three other languages, published in 1590 by Theodor de Bry in Frankfurt, Germany. Another avid proponent of colonization who recognized the power of print was Captain John Smith. Smith was one of the leaders and the most vigorous promoter of the first permanent English colony in North America, at Jamestown, Virginia, which he helped establish in 1607. Knowing that advertisements were crucial to the success of the colony, Smith wrote a series of books designed to encourage the English colonization of North America, including his *A Map of Virginia: With a Description of the Countrey* (1612) and *A Description of New England* (1616). But his most famous work was *The Generall Historie of Virginia, New-England, and the Summer Isles* (1624), in which Smith at once promoted colonization and laid the foundations for one of the most enduring myths of America, his dramatic rescue by the Indian "princess" Pocahontas.

That famous and possibly fictional event has also tended to mask a darker reality. Smith's heroic adventures and the rosy pictures painted in promotional tracts and travel narratives bore little relation to actualities in the Jamestown Colony. During the early decades of the colony, life there was made almost unendurable by rampant disease, the shortage of food and other supplies, and the tense relations between the colonists and the native peoples of the powerful Powhatan Confederacy. Although the successful cultivation of tobacco established the economic viability of the colony, the consequent expansion into native lands triggered a devastating attack on the scattered English settlements in 1622. The cultivation of tobacco also demanded massive amounts of physical labor, which was initially provided by indentured servants from England. The grim conditions under which they lived and worked were vividly described by a young man named Richard Frethorne, who arrived in Virginia as an indentured servant in 1623. In a series of letters he sent to his parents in England, Frethorne described his lack of clothing, desperate hunger, and constant fear that he would die of disease or be killed by the Indians. Listing the names of twenty people who had already perished at his small settlement, where there were only "32 to fight against 3000 if they should come," Frethorne pleaded with his parents to send aid so that he might "be redeemed out of Egypt."

Even as Jamestown struggled for survival, other English settlers established colonies in what came to be called New England. In contrast to Frethorne, the earliest settlers of New England conceived of their flight from England as a reenactment of the biblical Exodus, a journey out of spiritual bondage to the promised land of the New World. Whereas the

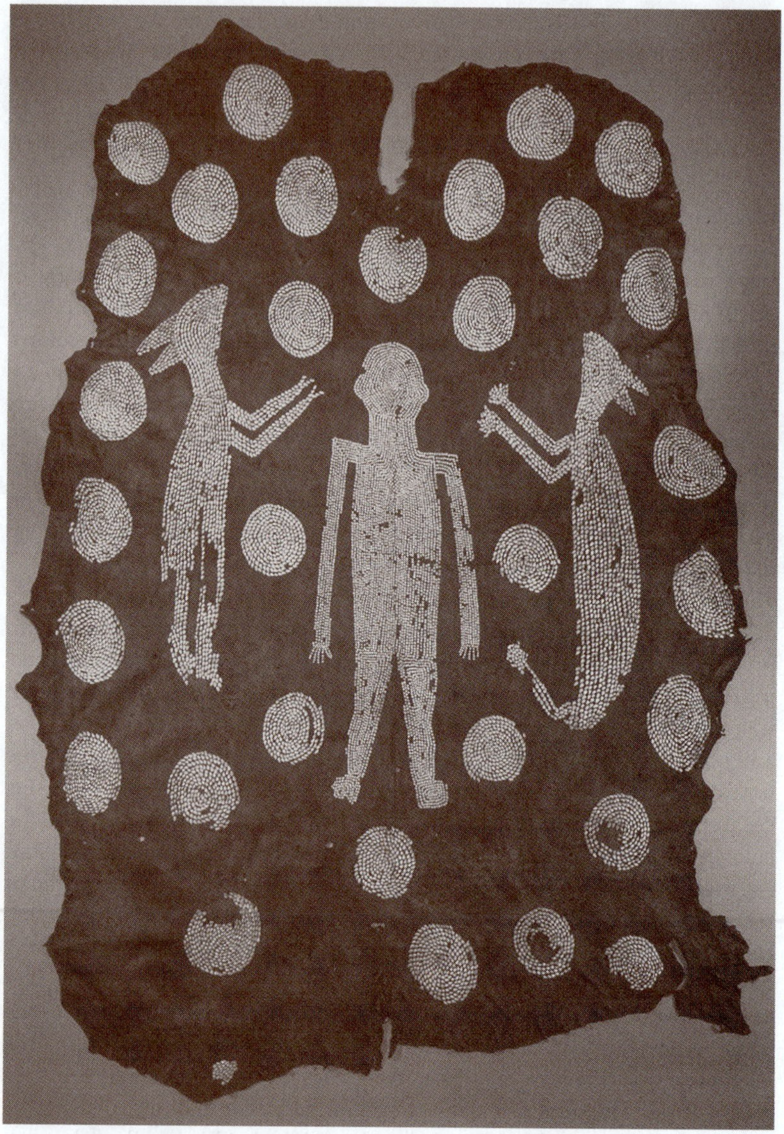

Powhatan's Mantle

This seven-foot-long ceremonial mantle of Wahunsonacock, chief of the Powhatan Confederacy and called Powhatan by the English, was made from the hides of seven deer and decorated with a design created from thousands of shells gathered by the Algonkin nations living in the rich area around the Chesapeake Bay.

settlement at Jamestown was primarily a commercial venture, religion played a central role in the founding of New England, which was a direct outgrowth of the Protestant Reformation. In an effort to restore what they viewed as the ancient purity and simplicity of the church as established by Christ and his disciples in the first century, reformers sought further to "purify" the religious practices and rituals of the Church of England, which they believed had not gone far enough in ridding itself of the vestiges of Roman Catholicism. The Puritans, as they came to be called, sought reform from within the Church of England. The Pilgrims were Separatists, the name for Puritans who formally separated themselves from the established church in order to form their own independent church, an act of treason in England. They consequently left the country, settling for a time in Holland before deciding to try their fortunes in North America, where 102 colonists landed on present-day Cape Cod, Massachusetts, in November 1620. During the following decade, Puritans faced mounting intolerance in England. The idea of the Great Migration, the resettlement of large numbers of Puritan immigrants from the Old to the New World, was born in 1629, when a wealthy group of men organized the Massachusetts Bay Company and obtained a royal charter to establish a colony in New England. The following year, seven hundred adults and children led by John Winthrop embarked from England on a fleet of ships that arrived at present-day Salem, Massachusetts, in July 1630.

Believing they had been assigned a special place in God's plan of human history, both the Pilgrims and the Puritans kept detailed records of the founding of New England. The earliest history of Plymouth was based on journals kept by two of the leaders of the colony, William Bradford and Edward Winslow, whose accounts were published as *A Relation or Journal of the Beginning and Proceeding of the English Plantation Settled at Plimoth in New England* (1622). Usually called *Mourt's Relation* because the preface was signed by "G. Mourt," the book was designed to promote the settlement at Plymouth. Drawing on his journal and his contributions to *Mourt's Relation*, Bradford in 1630 began to write *Of Plimoth Plantation*, a formal history of the Pilgrims from the establishment of their Separatist Church through their years in Holland to their arrival and the early years of their settlement at Plymouth. Bradford's book was not published until the nineteenth century, but many historians were familiar with the manuscript, which became an important source for early accounts of the founding of New England.

The Puritans were equally eager to promote their colony and to preserve its history in writing. In March of 1631, Thomas Dudley (1574-1653), then the deputy governor and later the governor of the Massachusetts Bay Colony, wrote to an English friend from his new home in Boston:

> For the satisfaction of your Honor, and some friends, and for the use of such as shall hereafter intend to increase our plantation in New England, I have in the throng of domestic, and not altogether free from public business, thought fit to commit to memory our present condition, and what hath befallen us since our arrival here; which I will do shortly, after my usual manner, and must do rudely, having yet no table, nor other room to write in, than by the fireside upon my knee, in this sharp winter; to which my family must have leave to resort, though they break good manners, and make me sometimes forget what I would say, and say what I would not.

Even as he sought to persuade others in England to come to the new colony by offering an account of his experiences, Dudley was beset by many of the practical problems of writing in the primitive settlement of Boston. Regardless of such obstacles, however, writing was an integral part of the settlement of New England. At about the same time Bradford began to write his history of Plymouth in 1630, for example, John Winthrop began a journal in which he carefully recorded the history of the Massachusetts Bay Colony. Published posthumously as *A Journal of the Transactions and Occurrences in the settlement of Massachusetts and the Other New-England Colonies, from the year 1630 to 1644* (1790), Winthrop's account later appeared and is now best known as *The History of New England.*

In contrast to Bradford's small band of Pilgrims, the larger and more affluent group of Puritans had substantial resources for establishing a colony. Among the provisions they transported to the New World were books, which were vital elements of the cultural and religious life of colonists in New England. The key book was the Bible, which the Puritans viewed as the revealed word of God and consequently as the ultimate source of authority in all human affairs, from domestic arrangements to the structure of civil and religious institutions. In "A Modell of Christian Charity," an address he delivered either on the eve of or during the voyage to New England, Winthrop described the venture as an effort to establish "a Citty upon a hill," a model Christian community based on the letter and the spirit of the Bible. The Puritans also brought along books offering practical aid in building the new colony, including handbooks on law and medicine, as well as technical books on carpentry and farming. Finally, just as they constructed their dwellings and laid out their fields along English lines, the Puritans transplanted European culture to the New World, bringing with them dictionaries, encyclopedias, books on logic and rhetoric, and the works of Greek and Latin writers. Indeed, the Puritans were shaped not only by the Protestant Reformation but also by the humanistic values of the Renaissance.

Although they initially depended on books brought or imported from England, the Puritans soon began to publish their own. In 1638, the first printing press arrived in the Massachusetts Bay Colony and Stephen Daye established the Glover Press in Cambridge. The first book printed in the English colonies was *The Whole Book of Psalmes Faithfully Translated into English Metre* (1640), popularly called *The Bay Psalm Book.* Of the more than two hundred books, pamphlets, and broadsides published in Massachusetts Bay Colony during the following sixty years, one of the most unusual was John Eliot's translation of the Bible into an Algonkian language, published in 1663 as part of a broader missionary effort to Christianize the Indians. But the most familiar product of the Puritan press was the *New England Primer,* first published around 1690. During the follow-

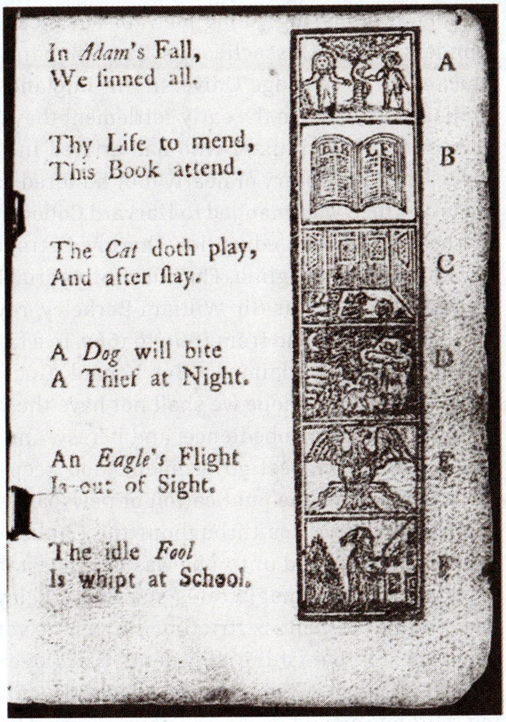
In *Adam's* Fall,
We finned all.
A

Thy Life to mend,
This Book attend.
B

The *Cat* doth play,
And after flay.
C

A *Dog* will bite
A Thief at Night.
D

An *Eagle's* Flight
Is out of Sight.
E

The idle *Fool*
Is whipt at School.
F

New England Primer

First published in Boston around 1690, the *New England Primer* was probably the single most successful production of the press in colonial America. As this copy printed in 1750 indicates, the book continued to instruct children in reading, writing, and religion even after Puritanism began to wane in New England.

ing 150 years, more than three million copies were printed for use at home and in schools, where the so-called Little Bible of New England was used to teach spelling and reading, as well as to instill moral and religious values.

Education was a central concern of the Puritans. Like other Protestants, they placed great emphasis on the ability of individuals to read and interpret the Bible. Literacy rates had consequently been relatively high among the Puritans in England, even for women and girls, and the rates remained high among those who came to New England. Girls were generally taught to read and write at "dame schools," often run by women in private homes. The colonists also began to establish schools modeled on the grammar schools in England, in which the curriculum for young boys included religious training, instruction in mathematics and rhetoric, and the study of Latin and Greek. Gradually, laws were passed requiring the education of all children. In 1647, for example, the General Court, or legislature, of the Massachusetts Bay Colony passed an act designed to promote universal literacy and thus prevent "that old deluder Satan" from keeping "men from the knowledge of the Scriptures." Under the act, every town of fifty householders had to hire a schoolmaster, and towns of more than one hundred householders were required to establish a Latin grammar school capable of preparing young men for advanced study at a university. The founders of the Massachusetts Bay Company, many of whom had been educated at Cambridge University in England, were eager to establish a similar institution in the early settlement they named Cambridge. In 1638, John Harvard, a minister who had arrived in the colony the year before, bequeathed his library of nearly four hundred volumes to New College, the name of which was changed to Harvard College.

The emphasis on education sharply distinguished the Massachusetts Bay Colony from Virginia. The most influential figure in the early development of Virginia was Sir William Berkeley, royal governor of the colony from 1642 to 1652 and from 1660 to 1667. In a famous diatribe, the authoritarian Berkeley exclaimed: "But I thank God, there are no free schools nor printing, and I hope we shall not have these hundred years; for learning has brought disobedience, and heresy, and sects into this world, and libels against the best government. God keep us from both!" Insofar as "printing" meant the publication of newspapers, Berkeley's hostility was shared by authorities throughout the English colonies, where no newspaper was permitted until one was briefly established in Boston in 1690. Certainly, Puritan magistrates shared Berkeley's intolerance of political and religious dissent, restricting the right to vote to men who were church members and banishing dissidents like Roger Williams. In contrast to Berkeley, however, the Puritans viewed education as a means of promoting religious orthodoxy and social stability. They also believed that literature could serve similar ends. Although Harvard College was established to train men for the ministry, it also emphasized a broad education in the arts and sciences, including languages and literature. In a sermon delivered in 1677, the influential Puritan minister Increase Mather thus told the legislators of the Massachusetts Bay Colony that they must support schools and the college to insure that there would be "able instruments raised up for the propagating of Truth in succeeding Generations," adding, "And some have well and truly observed, that the Interest of Religion and good Literature, have risen and fallen together."

"And some have well and truly observed, that the Interest of Religion and good Literature, have risen and fallen together."

The premium placed on both literacy and literature in New England helps account for the prominence of Puritan writers in the early literary history of what became the United States. Poetry was especially valued by the Puritans, who avidly read English religious poets like George Herbert and who also wrote a large amount of poetry. The first bestseller published in the colonies was a long narrative poem by a Puritan minister, Michael Wigglesworth's *The Day of Doom*, "A Poetical Account of the Great and Last Judgment" (1662). The 224 ballad stanzas of the poem were read, recited, and frequently memorized by children and adults alike, revealing the powerful intersection of literature and religion among the Puritans. Although Wigglesworth has now fallen into obscurity, two other Puritan poets have assumed central places in early American literature. The first is Anne Bradstreet, who came to New England in 1630 along with her father and husband, both of whom later served as governors of the Massachusetts Bay Colony. A collection of Bradstreet's poems, *The Tenth Muse Lately Sprung up in America*, was published in London in 1650, and a second edition was later published in Boston. Her poetry was also widely read and admired at the time, in sharp contrast to the work of the other most important Puritan poet, Edward Taylor. A minister living in the isolated frontier community of Westfield, Massachusetts, Taylor wrote a staggering amount of poetry, including funeral elegies, religious meditations, and a history of Christianity. But almost none of his work was published or even circulated beyond a small group of family and friends. In fact, Taylor's work was unknown until the 1930s, when his manuscripts were discovered and some of his poems were finally published, revealing him as one of the preeminent writers among the Puritans of New England.

The habits of personal reflection and spiritual meditation that found expression in the poetry of Bradstreet and Taylor also generated significant works in prose. Those who believed they had experienced God's grace and were consequently among the elect were required to give a public account of their conversion experience. Many also recorded those experiences in diaries or wrote more formal spiritual autobiographies. The conditions and conflicts arising from the settlement of New England spawned another kind of life writing, the captivity narrative. Despite their professed intention of spreading the light of the Gospels in what they viewed

Anonymous, *Ninigret, Sachem of the Niantic* (c. 1681)

This is the only surviving seventeenth-century portrait of a New England sachem, a chief or political leader of tribes such as the Niantic. Like other tribes living in and around the areas where the English settled, the Niantic population was steadily reduced by disease and war, and the remnants of the tribe finally joined with the Narragansett around 1700.

as the "wilderness" of the New World, the Puritans and other European settlers more often spread disease and destruction among the native inhabitants of New England. The growing number of English settlers and their inexorable expansion into tribal lands resulted in a series of wars with the Indians. During one of the earliest and bloodiest of those conflicts, King Philip's War of 1675-76, Mary Rowlandson was taken prisoner during an attack by Narragansett, Nipmuc, and Wampanoag Indians on her settlement in Lancaster, Massachusetts. Following her release, she wrote *The Sovereignty and Goodness of God . . . Being a Narrative of the Captivity and Restoration of Mrs. Mary Rowlandson*, which was published in both Boston and London in 1682. The widespread popularity of the book, which was a major bestseller, led to the publication of many similar narratives during the following decades, as the wars between the New England colonists and the Indians became part of the larger struggle between England and France for control of North America. Indeed, the captivity narrative became one of the most popular of all literary genres in colonial America.

The sense of vulnerability produced by ongoing conflicts with the Indians contributed to fears of and a series of narratives about witchcraft in New England. During the seventeenth century, accusations of witchcraft were far more common in England, France, and Germany than in New England. But the most famous of all witchcraft trials took place at Salem in 1692-93. Beginning with reports of the erratic behavior of two young girls, and the charge of witchcraft made by an enslaved girl from the West Indies, the accusations spread, fueled by fear, class divisions, and religious differences. In the view of some historians, the accusations also revealed anxieties about the increasing power of women, especially wealthy widows, in the colony. Eventually, 160 people (most of them women) were accused and many of those were incarcerated. Five people died in jail, while twenty others – thirteen women and seven men – were executed. Less than five years later, a day of repentance for the trials was observed throughout the Massachusetts Bay Colony. Nonetheless, the trials gained lasting notoriety, partly as a result of narratives like *The Wonders of the Invisible World* (1692), in which the prominent Puritan minister Cotton Mather described a "horrible plot against the country by witchcraft," culminating in Satan's unleashing of an "army of devils" upon Salem.

Even as the Puritans were undergoing the convulsions of the witch trials, another group of religious dissidents, the Society of Friends (Quakers), was seeking refuge in North America. Like the Puritans, the Quakers sought to return to what they viewed as the simplicity of early Christianity. But the Quakers rejected the Puritan doctrines of original sin, predestination, and election, the salvation of only a few chosen by God. Instead, the Quakers believed that every individual was imbued by God with an "Inner Light" of spiritual understanding and was therefore potentially

William Penn, *The Benefit of Plantations, or Colonies* (1735)

Penn's promotional tracts were translated into Dutch and German and frequently reprinted even after his death in 1718. The promise of freedom and prosperity in Pennsylvania drew large numbers of emigrants from throughout Europe, dramatically increasing the ethnic, linguistic, and religious diversity of the English colonies in North America.

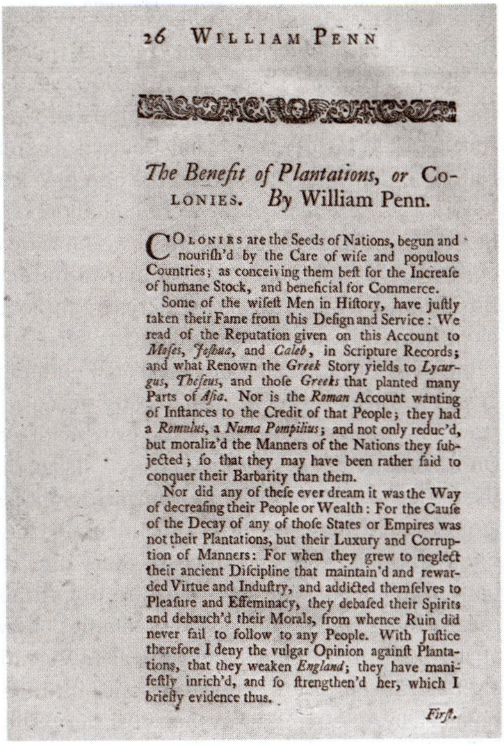

26 WILLIAM PENN

The Benefit of Plantations, or COLONIES. *By* William Penn.

COLONIES are the Seeds of Nations, begun and nouriſh'd by the Care of wiſe and populous Countries; as conceiving them beſt for the Increaſe of humane Stock, and beneficial for Commerce.

Some of the wiſeſt Men in Hiſtory, have juſtly taken their Fame from this Deſign and Service: We read of the Reputation given on this Account to *Moſes*, *Joſhua*, and *Caleb*, in Scripture Records; and what Renown the *Greek* Story yields to *Lycurgus*, *Theſeus*, and thoſe *Greeks* that planted many Parts of *Aſia*. Nor is the *Roman* Account wanting of Inſtances to the Credit of that People; they had a *Romulus*, a *Numa Pompilius*; and not only reduc'd, but moraliz'd the Manners of the Nations they ſubjected; ſo that they may have been rather ſaid to conquer their Barbarity than them.

Nor did any of theſe ever dream it was the Way of decreaſing their People or Wealth: For the Cauſe of the Decay of any of thoſe States or Empires was not their Plantations, but their Luxury and Corruption of Manners: For when they grew to neglect their ancient Diſcipline that maintain'd and rewarded Virtue and Induſtry, and addicted themſelves to Pleaſure and Effeminacy, they debaſed their Spirits and debauch'd their Morals, from whence Ruin did never fail to follow to any People. With Juſtice therefore I deny the vulgar Opinion againſt Plantations, that they weaken *England*; they have manifeſtly inrich'd, and ſo ſtrengthen'd her, which I briefly evidence thus.

Firſt.

among the saved. Pacifists who refused to serve in the army or to pay taxes in support of the Anglican Church, the Quakers were widely persecuted in England. In 1680, however, a wealthy convert to the Society of Friends, William Penn, received a huge land grant in North America to pay off a debt owed to his late father by the king of England. Just as John Winthrop had earlier described the Puritan commonwealth as a "Citty upon a hill," Penn called his new colony of Pennsylvania a "holy experiment" and an "example to all Nations." In an effort to establish his experiment in religious and political freedom upon a just and secure foundation, Penn established friendly relations with the native population of the area by making a treaty of friendship with the Delaware Confederation in 1682. Penn also tirelessly promoted his colony, publishing tracts in English, Dutch, and German. Pennsylvania immediately began to attract thousands of Quakers from England and equal numbers of Protestants of various sects from other European countries, especially Germany. Like earlier settlers from the Netherlands and Sweden, whose colonies in North America had come under English rule, the new settlers contributed to the growing body of colonial literature written in languages other than English. For example, the leader of the first wave of German immigrants, Francis

Daniel Pastorious, soon wrote *Positive Information from America* (1684), the first of a series of works he sent to Germany for publication.

The settlement of Pennsylvania added yet another element to the growing diversity, both ethnic and religious, of the English colonies in North America. As diaries and journals written around the turn of the eighteenth century illustrate, the experiences and physical circumstances of people living in different colonies were equally diverse. The diaries of Samuel Sewell and Cotton Mather, both of whom were associated with the witchcraft trials at Salem, reveal strikingly different aspects of Puritan life in Boston, which by 1700 was an increasingly commercial and cosmopolitan city of seven thousand. Written at the same time, Sarah Kemble Knight's celebrated journal of her journey from Boston through Connecticut to New York in 1704-05 offers a fascinating account of the hardships of early travel and the social mores of the provincial world of rural New England. Only a small number of the numerous slaves that had been imported into the region worked on the family farms that predominated in New England, and farmers there had little in common with wealthy southern planters like William Byrd II. Certainly, his diary illustrates the radically different path development had taken in Virginia. Although there were class and racial divisions throughout the colonies, nowhere else was the social structure as hierarchical and rigid as in Virginia, where by the end of the eighteenth century the initial reliance on indentured servants had been replaced by an expanding system of slavery. The exploitation of slave labor led to the emergence of a small gentry class with the kind of privileged and increasingly opulent lifestyle described by Byrd, who ultimately owned a vast estate of nearly 180,000 acres in Virginia.

A century after the establishment of the first permanent English settlement at Jamestown, the various colonies had thus developed distinctly different cultural institutions, social structures, and systems of government. There were, consequently, few widely shared colonial experiences, even within the relatively narrow boundaries of the English colonies in North America. A major exception was the Great Awakening, a religious revival that swept through the colonies from the 1730s to roughly 1750. Beginning among Presbyterians in Pennsylvania and New Jersey, the revival spread among various sects, first in the North and later to the South. The Great Awakening was closely associated with developments in England, especially the rise of Methodism within the Church of England. A major figure in the North American revival was George Whitefield, an itinerant Methodist preacher from England who toured the colonies during 1739-42. Exploiting his formidable oratorical abilities and the growing resources of print culture, including handbills and newspaper advertising, Whitefield drew huge crowds. His mesmerizing sermons on the terrors of hell and the pressing need for conversion also sparked local revivals, first in the middle colonies and then in New England.

John Collet, *George Whitefield Preaching*

Painted by a British artist in the 1760s, this work represents Whitefield's preaching during his earlier tour of the English colonies in North America. The painting captures the dramatic, extemporaneous style of Whitefield's sermons, as well as the fact that he often preached to large outdoor assemblies of men and women from every class and background.

There, the groundwork had already been laid by another famous revivalist, Jonathan Edwards. In fact, Whitefield's evangelical style had originally been inspired by reading Edwards's vivid account of revivals that spread through the Connecticut Valley during the 1730s, *A Faithful Narrative of the Surprising Work of God*, which was first published in London in 1737 and then in Boston in 1738. The foremost theologian of the colonial period, Edwards also wrote a series of massive religious treatises, as well as the most famous of all Puritan spiritual autobiographies, his *Personal Narrative.* But he gained renown and is now probably best known for his sermons, especially "Sinners in the Hands of an Angry God," delivered during the height of the Great Awakening in 1741. Although many Puritan ministers opposed the movement, which they viewed as a dangerous manifestation of religious "enthusiasm," or irrational emotionalism, Edwards and other young ministers viewed the Great Awakening as a vital means of reviving the spiritual piety of the founders of the Massachusetts Bay Colony and restoring the central role the church had assumed in early New England.

In fact, as Edwards and many others recognized, the changing economy, growth of cities, and increasingly diverse population of New England had already loosened the grip of Puritanism, which continued to wane in the decades between the Great Awakening and the Revolution. Nonetheless, it remained a vital force. In reaction to what they viewed as a rising tide of rationalism and secularism, during the 1790s theological descendants of Jonathan Edwards launched a powerful counterattack, now known as the Second Great Awakening. That long-lasting revival sharply altered the course of society and culture in what by then had become the United States. Puritanism also continued to exert a strong pull, not only on those who affirmed its fundamental beliefs but also on those who questioned or rejected its religious doctrines, including philosophers, theologians, and writers as diverse as Ralph Waldo Emerson, Emily Dickinson, and Nathaniel Hawthorne. Indeed, of all the *-isms* that have shaped American culture and society, Puritanism in its varied manifestations has been among the most enduring, at once deeply coloring the American mind and profoundly shaping the contours of life in the United States.

Captain John Smith

[1580-1631]

This bushy-bearded, high-foreheaded, trusting man,
Who could turn his hand to anything at a pinch,
Bragging, canny, impatient, durable
And fallen in love with the country at first sight.
For that is something which happens or does not.
It did to him.
-Stephen Vincent Benét

The legendary Captain John Smith was born in Willoughby, England, in 1580. The son of a successful farmer, Smith apparently attended schools in neighboring towns until he was fifteen. Although his father wanted him to return to the farm, Smith longed for a life of adventure. In what was apparently something of a compromise between father and son, Smith was apprenticed to a merchant. When his father died in 1596, however, Smith left his apprenticeship and began a career as a soldier, going first to the Netherlands, which Protestant England was supporting in its fight for independence from Catholic Spain. For the next several years, Smith traveled widely as a soldier of fortune, visiting France, Scotland, Italy, and Greece. Eventually, he joined the Imperial Army of Austria, which was at war with the Turks. After being promoted to the rank of captain, Smith was wounded in a battle and captured by the Turks in 1602. In a later account of his adventures, Smith claimed that he was consequently sold as a slave and sent to Constantinople, where he managed to kill his master and make a daring escape. He then traveled extensively throughout Europe and finally arrived in northern Africa. A distinguished and decorated soldier, Smith returned to England in 1605.

Still eager for new adventures, Smith worked with the Virginia Company, chartered by James I of England and formed by a group of investors seeking to establish a new colony in North America. Smith invested some of his own money in the venture and joined a company of one hundred colonists that embarked on three ships in December 1606. When the group reached Virginia in April 1607, Smith learned that he had been selected by the company to serve as one of its seven council members of the new colony at Jamestown. That fall, he was also appointed supply officer and set about procuring food from the native population, a confederation of tribes led by the emperor Powhatan. But the powerful chief was determined to stop the encroachment of the English settlers. In an ambush on a small party of colonists late in 1607, Smith's companions were killed and he was captured and brought before Powhatan. According to the memorable story Smith told later in his life, he was ordered to be executed but saved at the last minute by Powhatan's daughter Pocahontas. But he did not mention Pocahontas in an account of his experiences Smith wrote soon after his safe return to the colony, a letter published in London as *A True Relation of Such Occurrences and Accidents of Note as Hath Happened in Virginia* (1608). Smith also sent off to London a map of the area and information he had gathered from other colonists, which were later published as *A Map of Virginia: With a Description of the Countrey* (1612). In the meantime, conditions were becoming increasingly difficult at Jamestown, where Smith was elected president of the governing council in 1608. Many of the colonists were unprepared for either the hard work of settlement or the hostility of the native population, and disease and the lack of food contributed to their low morale. As a result of the strict discipline and labor policies instituted by Smith, the situation in the colony began to improve. But he became increasingly unpopular. After he was badly burned in a gunpowder explosion, Smith was forced to sail to England for treatment in 1609.

Although he wanted to return, reports of Smith's unpopular leadership made it impossible, and he never again set foot in Virginia. He consequently

Simon de Passe, *Captain John Smith* (1616)

This portrait of Smith in his armor, hand on his sword, portrays him as the very image of the Renaissance soldier, explorer, and adventurer. It was engraved after his final return to England, where he spent the rest of his life writing about his experiences in the New World.

bedfordstmartins.com/americanlit *for research links on Smith* turned his attention elsewhere: to New England. In 1614, Smith sailed there in order to conduct a survey for the establishment of a new colony. On his return voyage in 1615, he was captured by pirates. During his captivity, he wrote *A Description of New England* (1616). This book encouraged others to establish settlements there, notably the Pilgrims, to whom Smith offered his services as a guide on their voyage in 1620. But the Pilgrims did not consider Smith to be sufficiently religious, and he never again participated in a colonial settlement. Instead, the former soldier, explorer, and adventurer spent his remaining years in England, devoting himself to writing. During the final decade of his life, he published *New England's Trials* (1620, 1622), his *Generall Historie of Virginia, New-England, and the Summer Isles* (1624), and an autobiography, *The True Travels, Adventures, and Observations of Captaine John Smith, In Europe, Asia, Africa, and America* (1630). Smith did not live to complete his final work. *Advertisements for the Unexperienced Planters in New England, or Anywhere,* another attempt to promote successful colonial settlement in the New World, was published shortly after his death in 1631.

Smith's *Generall Historie of Virginia.* The most famous of Smith's books, *The Generall Historie of Virginia, New-England, and the Summer Isles*, is among the first histories of the English colonies in America. In April 1621, members of the Virginia Company in London proposed publishing a history of its colony in Jamestown that would generate interest among English readers and consequently encourage additional settlers to emigrate to the New World. At the time, Jamestown was beginning to thrive, largely because of the export of tobacco, which had turned the struggling colony into an increasingly profitable venture. In the following year, the always uneasy relations between the colony and the native population once again broke down, and nearly four hundred colonists were killed in an attack on Jamestown. Although Smith wanted to return to Virginia to assist in the preservation of the colony, his request was turned down by the Virginia Company. Nor is it clear that the company had Smith in mind as the author of its history of Virginia. In an effort to gain support for his return to the colony, however, Smith completed much of the first book of his *Generall Historie* by September 1622, when he published a prospectus in order to raise funds for its publication. The Duchess of Richmond and Lenox agreed to serve as his patron, and Smith dedicated the book to her when *The Generall Historie* was first published in 1624. Six more editions appeared between 1626 and 1632.

The Generall Historie is divided into six books, which include a detailed account of the Virginia Colony, as well as briefer histories of the exploration and English settlement of New England and the Summer Isles, also known as the Bermuda Islands. The main character in the book is Smith, who refers to himself in the third person throughout *The Generall Historie*. Much of this lengthy account was based on his experiences and observations, but Smith also made liberal use of published sources, including

Captain John Smith, *The Generall Historie of Virginia* (1624)

The title page of Smith's history was illustrated by engravings of several of his exploits and adventures, including his rescue by Pocahontas. The caption reads: "King Powhatan commands C. Smith to be slayne, his daughter Pokahantas beggs his life [.] his thankfulness and how he subjected 39 of their kings. reade ye history."

C:S
King Powhatan comands C:Smith to be slayne, his
daughter Pokahontas beggs his life his thankfullness
and how he subiected 39 of their kings. reade ye histor
printed by James Reve

material he had earlier gathered together in his *A Map of Virginia: With a Description of the Countrey* (1612). In fact, Smith probably viewed himself, and is viewed by most scholars, as the compiler or editor rather than the sole author of *The Generall Historie*. Certainly, the book is a miscellany, combining personal history, accounts written by others, editorial commentary on actions and events, adventure stories, digressions on the flora and fauna, and descriptions of the native peoples of North America. Smith's most original contribution is the third book of *The Generall Historie*, in which he narrates the events in Virginia from 1607 through 1609, especially his account of the strained relations between the English colonists and the confederacy of Indian tribes ruled by Powhatan. That part of *The Generall Historie* is, in turn, probably most famous for Smith's account of being saved from execution by Powhatan's daughter, Pocahontas. Whether the incident actually took place and, if so, whether Smith either exaggerated its significance or simply misunderstood its meaning have been matters of dispute ever since he published his history and gave rise to one of the most enduring myths of early America. The text of the following selections from *The Generall Historie* is taken from *The Complete Works of Captain John Smith*, edited by Philip L. Barbour (1986).

From THE GENERALL HISTORIE OF VIRGINIA, NEW-ENGLAND, AND THE SUMMER ISLES

From The Third Book

CHAPTER II

WHAT HAPPENED TILL THE FIRST SUPPLY

Being thus left to our fortunes, it fortuned that within ten dayes scarce ten amongst us could either goe, or well stand, such extreame weaknes and sicknes oppressed us. And thereat none need marvaile, if they consider the cause and reason, which was this; whilest the ships stayed, our allowance was somewhat bettered, by a daily proportion of Bisket, which the sailers would pilfer to sell, give, or exchange with us, for money, Saxefras,[1] furres, or love. But when they departed, there remained neither taverne, beere-house, nor place of reliefe, but the common Kettell.[2] Had we beene as free from all sinnes as gluttony, and drunkennesse, we might have beene canonized for Saints; But our President would never have beene admitted, for ingrossing to his private,[3] Oatmeale, Sacke, Oyle, Aquavitae,[4] Beefe, Egges, or what not, but the Kettell; that indeed he allowed equally to be distributed, and that was halfe a pint of wheat, and as much barley boyled with water for a man a day, and this having fryed some 26. weekes in the ships hold, contained as many wormes as graines; so that we might truely call it rather so much bran then corne,[5] our drinke was water, our lodgings Castles in the ayre: with this lodging and dyet, our extreame toile in bearing and planting Pallisadoes,[6] so strained and bruised us, and our continuall labour in the extremitie of the heat had so weakened us, as were cause sufficient to have made us as miserable in our native Countrey, or any other place in the world. From May, to September, those that escaped, lived upon Sturgeon, and Sea-crabs, fiftie in this time we buried, the rest seeing the Presidents projects to escape these miseries in our Pinnace[7] by flight (who all this time had neither felt want nor sicknes) so moved our dead spirits, as we deposed him; and established Ratcliffe in his place, (Gosnoll being dead) Kendall deposed, Smith newly recovered, Martin and Ratcliffe was by his care preserved and relieved, and the most of the souldiers recovered, with the skilfull diligence of Master Thomas Wotton our Chirurgian[8] generall. But now was all our provision spent, the Sturgeon gone, all helps abandoned, each houre expecting the fury of the Salvages;[9] when God the patron of all good indevours, in that

---

1. **Saxefras:** Leaves from the sassafras tree were used to make tea and medicines.
2. **common Kettell:** Shared resources.
3. **ingrossing to his private:** The president of the colony, Edward Maria Wingfield (c. 1560–1613), took many of the common supplies for his own use.
4. **Aquavitae:** Brandy.
5. **corne:** Grain.
6. **Pallisadoes:** Rows of fences made of wooden stakes, used for defense.
7. **Pinnace:** A small sailboat.
8. **Chirurgian:** Surgeon.
9. **Salvages:** Savages, the name given to Indians.

desperate extremitie so changed the hearts of the Salvages, that they brought such plenty of their fruits, and provision, as no man wanted.

And now where some affirmed it was ill done of the Councell to send forth men so badly provided, this incontradictable reason will shew them plainely they are too ill advised to nourish such ill conceits; first, the fault of our going was our owne, what could be thought fitting or necessary we had, but what we should find, or want, or where we should be, we were all ignorant, and supposing to make our passage in two moneths, with victuall[10] to live, and the advantage of the spring to worke; we were at Sea five moneths, where we both spent our victuall and lost the opportunitie of the time, and season to plant, by the unskilfull presumption of our ignorant transporters, that understood not at all, what they undertooke.

Such actions have ever since the worlds beginning beene subject to such accidents, and every thing of worth is found full of difficulties, but nothing so difficult as to establish a Common-wealth so farre remote from men and meanes, and where mens mindes are so untoward as neither doe well themselves, nor suffer others. But to proceed.

The new President and Martin, being little beloved, of weake judgement in dangers, and lesse industrie in peace, committed the managing of all things abroad to Captaine Smith: who by his owne example, good words, and faire promises, set some to mow, others to binde thatch, some to build houses, others to thatch them, himselfe alwayes bearing the greatest taske for his owne share, so that in short time, he provided most of them lodgings, neglecting any for himselfe. This done, seeing the Salvages superfluitie beginne to decrease (with some of his workemen) shipped himselfe in the Shallop[11] to search the Country for trade. The want of the language, knowledge to mannage his boat without sailes, the want of a sufficient power, (knowing the multitude of the Salvages) apparell for his men, and other necessaries, were infinite impediments, yet no discouragement. Being but six or seaven in company he went downe the river to Kecoughtan,[12] where at first they scorned him, as a famished man, and would in derision offer him a handfull of Corne, a peece of bread, for their swords and muskets, and such like proportions also for their apparell. But seeing by trade and courtesie there was nothing to be had, he made bold to try such conclusions as necessitie inforced, though contrary to his Commission: Let fly his muskets, ran his boat on shore, whereat they all fled into the woods. So marching towards their houses, they might see great heapes of corne: much adoe he had to restraine his hungry souldiers from present taking of it, expecting as it hapned that the Salvages would assault them, as not long after they did with a most hydeous noyse. Sixtie or seaventie of them, some blacke, some red, some white, some party-coloured, came in a square order,[13] singing and dauncing out of the woods, with their *Okee* (which was an Idoll made of skinnes, stuffed with mosse, all painted and

10. **victuall:** Food or provisions.
11. **Shallop:** A light sailboat primarily used for fishing.
12. **Kecoughtan:** Tribal village near the mouth of the James River.
13. **square order:** In a military formation.

hung with chaines and copper) borne before them: and in this manner being well armed, with Clubs, Targets, Bowes and Arrowes, they charged the English, that so kindly received them with their muskets loaden with Pistoll shot, that downe fell their God, and divers[14] lay sprauling on the ground; the rest fled againe to the woods, and ere long sent one of their *Quiyoughkasoucks*[15] to offer peace, and redeeme their *Okee.* Smith told them, if onely six of them would come unarmed and loade his boat, he would not only be their friend, but restore them their *Okee*, and give them Beads, Copper, and Hatchets besides: which on both sides was to their contents performed: and then they brought him Venison, Turkies, wild foule, bread, and what they had, singing and dauncing in signe of friendship till they departed. In his returne he discovered the Towne and Country of Warraskoyack.[16]

Thus God unboundlesse by his power,
Made them thus kind, would us devour.

Smith perceiving (notwithstanding their late miserie) not any regarded but from hand to mouth (the company being well recovered) caused the Pinnace to be provided with things fitting to get provision for the yeare following; but in the interim he made 3. or 4. journies and discovered the people of Chickahamania:[17] yet what he carefully provided the rest carelesly spent. Wingfield and Kendall living in disgrace, seeing all things at randome in the absence of Smith, the companies dislike of their Presidents weaknes, and their small love to Martins never mending sicknes, strengthened themselves with the sailers, and other confederates to regaine their former credit and authority, or at least such meanes abord the Pinnace, (being fitted to saile as Smith had appointed for trade) to alter her course and to goe for England. Smith unexpectedly returning had the plot discovered to him, much trouble he had to prevent it, till with store of sakre[18] and musket shot he forced them stay or sinke in the river, which action cost the life of captaine Kendall. These brawles are so disgustfull, as some will say they were better forgotten, yet all men of good judgement will conclude, it were better their basenes should be manifest to the world, then the busines beare the scorne and shame of their excused disorders. The President and captaine Archer not long after intended also to have abandoned the country, which project also was curbed, and suppressed by Smith. The Spaniard never more greedily desired gold then he victuall, nor his souldiers more to abandon the Country, then he to keepe it. But finding plentie of Corne in the river of Chickahamania where hundreds of Salvages in divers places stood with baskets expecting his comming. And now the winter approaching, the rivers became so covered with swans, geese, duckes, and cranes, that we daily feasted with good bread, Virginia

---

14. **divers:** Several or many.
15. ***Quiyoughkasoucks*:** Priests or gods.
16. **Warraskoyack:** Tribal village on the Pagan River.
17. **the people of Chickahamania:** The Chickahominy tribe lived in villages along the Chickahominy River, near Jamestown.
18. **sakre:** Shot for a small cannon.

pease, pumpions, and putchamins,[19] fish, fowle, and diverse sorts of wild beasts as fat as we could eate them: so that none of our Tuftaffaty humorists[20] desired to goe for England. But our Comaedies never endured long without a Tragedie; some idle exceptions being muttered against Captaine Smith, for not discovering the head of Chickahamania river, and taxed by the Councell, to be too slow in so worthy an attempt. The next voyage hee proceeded so farre that with much labour by cutting of trees in sunder he made his passage, but when his Barge could passe no farther, he left her in a broad bay out of danger of shot, commanding none should goe a shore till his returne: himselfe with two English and two Salvages went up higher in a Canowe, but hee was not long absent, but his men went a shore, whose want of government, gave both occasion and opportunity to the Salvages to surprise one George Cassen, whom they slew, and much failed not to have cut of the boat and all the rest. Smith little dreaming of that accident, being got to the marshes at the rivers head, twentie myles in the desert, had his two men slaine (as is supposed) sleeping by the Canowe, whilst himselfe by fowling sought them victuall, who finding he was beset with 200. Salvages, two of them hee slew, still defending himselfe with the ayd of a Salvage his guid, whom he bound to his arme with his garters, and used him as a buckler,[21] yet he was shot in his thigh a little, and had many arrowes that stucke in his cloathes but no great hurt, till at last they tooke him prisoner. When this newes came to James towne, much was their sorrow for his losse, fewe expecting what ensued. Sixe or seven weekes those Barbarians kept him prisoner, many strange triumphes and conjurations they made of him, yet hee so demeaned himselfe amongst them, as he not onely diverted them from surprising the Fort, but procured his owne libertie, and got himselfe and his company such estimation amongst them, that those Salvages admired him more then their owne *Quiyouckosucks*.[22] The manner how they used and delivered him, is as followeth.

The Salvages having drawne from George Cassen whether Captaine Smith was gone, prosecuting that oportunity they followed him with 300. bowmen, conducted by the King of Pamaunkee,[23] who in divisions searching the turnings of the river, found Robinson and Emry by the fire side, those they shot full of arrowes and slew. Then finding the Captaine, as is said, that used the Salvage that was his guide as his sheld (three of them being slaine and divers other so gauld[24]) all the rest would not come neere him. Thinking thus to have returned to his boat, regarding them, as he marched, more then his way, slipped up to the middle in an oasie[25] creeke and his Salvage with him, yet durst they not come to him till being neere dead with cold, he threw away his armes. Then according to their composition[26] they drew him forth and led him to the fire, where his men were

19. **putchamins:** Persimmons.
20. **Tuftaffaty humorists:** Obstinate colonists, dressed in inappropriately ornate clothes.
21. **buckler:** A shield.
22. ***Quiyouckosucks*:** Alternate spelling for the term for priests or gods. See note 15.
23. **King of Pamaunkee:** Powhatan's half-brother, Opechancanough.
24. **gauld:** Galled or harassed in warfare, especially by arrows or shot.
25. **oasie:** Boggy.
26. **composition:** Early term for an agreement or prior arrangement.

slaine. Diligently they chafed his benummed limbs. He demanding for their Captaine, they shewed him Opechankanough, King of Pamaunkee, to whom he gave a round Ivory double compass Dyall.[27] Much they marvailed at the playing of the Fly and Needle, which they could see so plainely, and yet not touch it, because of the glasse that covered them. But when he demonstrated by that Globe-like Jewell, the roundnesse of the earth, and skies, the spheare of the Sunne, Moone, and Starres, and how the Sunne did chase the night round about the world continually; the greatnesse of the Land and Sea, the diversitie of Nations, varietie of complexions, and how we were to them Antipodes, and many other such like matters, they all stood as amazed with admiration. Notwithstanding, within an houre after they tyed him to a tree, and as many as could stand about him prepared to shoot him, but the King holding up the Compass in his hand, they all laid downe their Bowes and Arrowes, and in a triumphant manner led him to Orapaks,[28] where he was after their manner kindly feasted, and well used.

Their order in conducting him was thus; Drawing themselves all in fyle,[29] the King in the middest had all their Peeces and Swords borne before him. Captaine Smith was led after him by three great Salvages, holding him fast by each arme: and on each side six went in fyle with their Arrowes nocked. But arriving at the Towne (which was but onely thirtie or fortie hunting houses made of Mats, which they remove as they please, as we our tents) all the women and children staring to behold him, the souldiers first all in fyle performed the forme of a Bissone[30] so well as could be; and on each flanke, officers as Serjeants to see them keepe their order. A good time they continued this exercise, and then cast themselves in a ring, dauncing in such severall Postures, and singing and yelling out such hellish notes and screeches; being strangely painted, every one his quiver of Arrowes, and at his backe a club; on his arme a Fox or an Otters skinne, or some such matter for his vambrace;[31] their heads and shoulders painted red, with Oyle and *Pocones*[32] mingled together, which Scarlet-like colour made an exceeding handsome shew; his Bow in his hand, and the skinne of a Bird with her wings abroad dryed, tyed on his head, a peece of copper, a white shell, a long feather, with a small rattle growing at the tayles of their snakes tyed to it, or some such like toy. All this while Smith and the King stood in the middest guarded, as before is said, and after three dances they all departed. Smith they conducted to a long house, where thirtie or fortie tall fellowes did guard him, and ere long more bread and venison was brought him then would have served twentie men, I thinke his stomacke at that time was not very good; what he left they put in baskets and tyed over his head. About midnight they set the meate againe before him, all this time not one of them would eate a bit with him, till the next morning they brought him as much more, and then did they eate all the old, and reserved the new as they had done the other, which made him thinke they would fat him to eat him. Yet in

27. **Dyall:** Dial.
28. **Orapaks:** A temporary hunting village.
29. **fyle:** File.
30. **Bissone:** Alternate spelling for *besom*, a broomlike shape.
31. **vambrace:** A piece of armor for the forearm.
32. **Oyle and *Pocones*:** Red dye made from a vegetable root, mixed with oil.

this desperate estate to defend him from the cold, one Maocassater brought him his gowne, in requitall of some beads and toyes Smith had given him at his first arrivall in Virginia.

Two dayes after a man would have slaine him (but that the guard prevented it) for the death of his sonne, to whom they conducted him to recover[33] the poore man then breathing his last. Smith told them that at James towne he had a water would doe it, if they would let him fetch it, but they would not permit that; but made all the preparations they could to assault James towne, craving his advice, and for recompence he should have life, libertie, land, and women. In part of a Table booke[34] he writ his minde to them at the Fort, what was intended, how they should follow that direction to affright the messengers, and without fayle send him such things as he writ for. And an Inventory with them. The difficultie and danger, he told the Salvages, of the Mines, great gunnes, and other Engins exceedingly affrighted them, yet according to his request they went to James towne, in as bitter weather as could be of frost and snow, and within three dayes returned with an answer.

But when they came to James towne, seeing men sally out as he had told them they would, they fled; yet in the night they came againe to the same place where he had told them they should receive an answer, and such things as he had promised them, which they found accordingly, and with which they returned with no small expedition, to the wonder of them all that heard it, that he could either divine, or the paper could speake: then they led him to the Youghtanunds, the Mattapanients, the Payankatanks, the Nantaughtacunds, and Onawmanients[35] upon the rivers of Rapahanock, and Patawomek, over all those rivers, and backe againe by divers other severall Nations, to the Kings habitation at Pamaunkee, where they entertained him with most strange and fearefull Conjurations;[36]

> As if neare led to hell,
> Amongst the Devils to dwell.

Not long after, early in a morning a great fire was made in a long house,[37] and a mat spread on the one side, as on the other, on the one they caused him to sit, and all the guard went out of the house, and presently came skipping in a great grim fellow, all painted over with coale, mingled with oyle; and many Snakes and Wesels skins stuffed with mosse, and all their tayles tyed together, so as they met on the crowne of his head in a tassell; and round about the tassell was as a Coronet of feathers, the skins hanging round about his head, backe, and shoulders, and in a manner covered his face; with a hellish voyce and a rattle in his hand. With most strange gestures and passions he

---

33. **recover:** Revive or restore to life.
34. **Table booke:** A small notebook.
35. **Youghtanunds . . . Onawmanients:** Several tribes in the confederation ruled by Powhatan.
36. **Conjurations:** Invoking of spirits. The following lines are from Martin Fotherby's *Atheomastix* (1622), a collection of translations of ancient writers such as Seneca, Solon, Lucretius, and Euripides. Smith frequently quotes from Fotherby (1549?-1619) in *The Generall Historie.*
37. **long house:** Communal dwelling house.

began his invocation, and environed the fire with a circle of meale; which done, three more such like devils came rushing in with the like antique[38] tricks, painted halfe blacke, halfe red: but all their eyes were painted white, and some red stroakes like Mutchato's,[39] along their cheekes: round about him those fiends daunced a pretty while, and then came in three more as ugly as the rest; with red eyes, and white stroakes over their blacke faces, at last they all sat downe right against him; three of them on the one hand of the chiefe Priest, and three on the other. Then all with their rattles began a song, which ended, the chiefe Priest layd downe five wheat cornes: then strayning his armes and hands with such violence that he sweat, and his veynes swelled, he began a short Oration: at the conclusion they all gave a short groane; and then layd down three graines more. After that, began their song againe, and then another Oration, ever laying downe so many cornes as before, till they had twice incirculed the fire; that done, they tooke a bunch of little stickes prepared for that purpose, continuing still their devotion, and at the end of every song and Oration, they layd downe a sticke betwixt the divisions of Corne. Till night, neither he nor they did either eate or drinke, and then they feasted merrily, with the best provisions they could make. Three dayes they used this Ceremony; the meaning whereof they told him, was to know if he intended them well or no. The circle of meale signified their Country, the circles of corne the bounds of the Sea, and the stickes his Country. They imagined the world to be flat and round, like a trencher,[40] and they in the middest. After this they brought him a bagge of gunpowder, which they carefully preserved till the next spring, to plant as they did their corne; because they would be acquainted with the nature of that seede. Opitchapam[41] the Kings brother invited him to his house, where, with as many platters of bread, foule, and wild beasts, as did environ him, he bid him wellcome; but not any of them would eate a bit with him, but put up all the remainder in Baskets. At his returne to Opechancanoughs, all the Kings women, and their children, flocked about him for their parts, as a due by Custome, to be merry with such fragments.

> But his waking mind in hydeous dreames did oft see wondrous shapes,
> Of bodies strange, and huge in growth, and of stupendious makes.[42]

At last they brought him to Meronocomoco,[43] where was Powhatan their Emperor. Here more then two hundred of those grim Courtiers stood wondering at him, as he had beene a monster; till Powhatan and his trayne had put themselves in their greatest braveries.[44] Before a fire upon a seat like a bedsted, he sat covered with a great robe, made of Rarowcun[45] skinnes, and all the tayles hanging by. On either hand did sit a young wench of 16 or 18 yeares, and along on each side the house, two rowes of men, and

---

38. **antique:** Variant spelling for *antic*, or grotesque.
39. **Mutchato's:** Moustaches.
40. **trencher:** A wooden plate or platter.
41. **Opitchapam:** Powhatan's half-brother. See note 23.
42. **But . . . makes:** Lines from *Atheomastix*; see note 36.
43. **Meronocomoco:** Powhatan's village, north of Jamestown.
44. **braveries:** Finery or fine clothes.
45. **Rarowcun:** Early spelling for *raccoon*.

behind them as many women, with all their heads and shoulders painted red; many of their heads bedecked with the white downe of Birds; but every one with something: and a great chayne of white beads about their necks. At his entrance before the King, all the people gave a great shout. The Queene of Appamatuck[46] was appointed to bring him water to wash his hands, and another brought him a bunch of feathers, in stead of a Towell to dry them: having feasted him after their best barbarous manner they could, a long consultation was held, but the conclusion was, two great stones were brought before Powhatan: then as many as could layd hands on him, dragged him to them, and thereon laid his head, and being ready with their clubs, to beate out his braines, Pocahontas the Kings dearest daughter, when no intreaty could prevaile, got his head in her armes, and laid her owne upon his to save him from death: whereat the Emperour was contented he should live to make him hatchets, and her bells, beads, and copper; for they thought him as well of all occupations as themselves. For the King himselfe will make his owne robes, shooes, bowes, arrowes, pots; plant, hunt, or doe any thing so well as the rest.

> They say he bore a pleasant shew,
> But sure his heart was sad.
> For who can pleasant be, and rest,
> That lives in feare and dread:
> And having life suspected, doth
> It still suspected lead.[47]

Two dayes after, Powhatan having disguised himselfe in the most fearefullest manner he could, caused Captaine Smith to be brought forth to a great house in the woods, and there upon a mat by the fire to be left alone. Not long after from behinde a mat that divided the house, was made the most dolefullest noyse he ever heard; then Powhatan more like a devill then a man with some two hundred more as blacke as himselfe, came unto him and told him now they were friends, and presently he should goe to James towne, to send him two great gunnes, and a gryndstone, for which he would give him the Country of Capahowosick, and for ever esteeme him as his sonne Nantaquoud. So to James towne with 12 guides Powhatan sent him. That night they quarterd in the woods, he still expecting (as he had done all this long time of his imprisonment) every houre to be put to one death or other: for all their feasting. But almightie God (by his divine providence) had mollified the hearts of those sterne Barbarians with compassion. The next morning betimes they came to the Fort, where Smith having used the Salvages with what kindnesse he could, he shewed Rawhunt, Powhatans trusty servant two demi-Culverings[48] and a millstone to carry Powhatan: they found them somewhat too heavie; but when they did see him discharge them, being loaded with stones, among the boughs of a great tree loaded with Isickles, the yce and branches came so tumbling downe, that the poore Salvages ran away halfe dead with feare. But at last we regained some

---

46. **Queen of Appamatuck:** Opossunoquonuske was the leader of the Appamatuck, who lived in a small village west of Jamestown.
47. **They . . . lead:** Lines from *Atheomastix*; see note 36.
48. **demi-Culverings:** Small cannons.

conference with them, and gave them such toyes, and sent to Powhatan, his women, and children such presents, as gave them in generall full content. Now in James Towne they were all in combustion, the strongest preparing once more to run away with the Pinnace; which with the hazzard of his life, with Sakre falcon[49] and musket shot, Smith forced now the third time to stay or sinke. Some no better then they should be, had plotted with the President, the next day to have put him to death by the Leviticall law, for the lives of Robinson and Emry, pretending the fault was his that had led them to their ends: but he quickly tooke such order with such Lawyers, that he layd them by the heeles till he sent some of them prisoners for England. Now ever once in foure or five dayes, Pocahontas with her attendants, brought him so much provision, that saved many of their lives, that els for all this had starved with hunger.

> Thus from numbe death our good God sent reliefe,
> The sweete asswager of all other griefe.[50]

His relation of the plenty he had seene, especially at Werawocomoco, and of the state and bountie of Powhatan, (which till that time was unknowne) so revived their dead spirits (especially the love of Pocahontas) as all mens feare was abandoned. Thus you may see what difficulties still crossed any good indevour: and the good successe of the businesse being thus oft brought to the very period of destruction; yet you see by what strange means God hath still delivered it. As for the insufficiency of them admitted in Commission, that error could not be prevented by the Electors; there being no other choise, and all strangers to each others education, qualities, or disposition. And if any deeme it a shame to our Nation to have any mention made of those inormities, let them peruse the Histories of the Spanyards Discoveries and Plantations, where they may see how many mutinies, disorders, and dissentions have accompanied them, and crossed their attempts: which being knowne to be particular mens offences; doth take away the generall scorne and contempt, which malice, presumption, covetousnesse, or ignorance might produce; to the scandall and reproach of those, whose actions and valiant resolutions deserve a more worthy respect.

Now whether it had beene better for Captaine Smith, to have concluded with any of those severall projects, to have abandoned the Countrey, with some ten or twelve of them, who were called the better sort, and have left Master Hunt our Preacher, Master Anthony Gosnoll, a most honest, worthy, and industrious Gentleman, Master Thomas Wotton, and some 27 others of his Countrymen to the fury of the Salvages, famine, and all manner of mischiefes, and inconveniences, (for they were but fortie in all to keepe possession of this large Country;) or starve himselfe with them for company, for want of lodging: or but adventuring abroad to make them provision, or by his opposition to preserve the action, and save all their lives; I leave to the censure of all honest men to consider. But

49. **Sakre falcon:** A small cannon, named after the saker falcon, a Middle Eastern bird of prey.
50. **Thus . . . griefe:** The first line is Smith's, while the second is from *Atheomastix*; see note 36.

We men imagine in our Jolitie,
That 'tis all one, or good or bad to be.
But then anone wee alter this againe,
If happily wee feele the sence of paine;
For then we're turn'd into a mourning vaine.[51]

Written by Thomas Studley, the first Cape Merchant in Virginia,
Robert Fenton, Edward Harrington, and J. S.[52]
[1624, 1986]

51. **We . . . vaine:** Lines from *Atheomastix*; see note 36.
52. **Written by . . . and J. S.:** *J. S.* is John Smith, but little is known about the other authors or their possible contributions to this portion of *The Generall Historie*. They may have provided notes to Smith, or he may have invoked their names in order to affirm the authenticity of his account.

Jamestown through a Modern Lens

The story of Pocahontas was first recounted by John Smith in his *Generall Historie of Virginia, New-England, and the Summer Isles* (1624). Since he had not mentioned the incident in an earlier account, *A True Relation of . . . Virginia* (1608), and since Smith told the story in various ways in later accounts, many historians consider it an exaggeration or a fiction. Others suggest that the event Smith described was a staged ritual symbolizing his death as a foreigner and rebirth as a member of the Powhatan Confederacy. Nonetheless, the romantic story of the love-struck Pocahontas became an American legend, the subject of numerous plays and poems during the nineteenth and twentieth centuries. In 1995, the story was also the basis for a popular movie, which generated strong protests by several Native American groups critical of the distorted version of history portrayed in the animated film produced by Disney Studios.

Certainly, the legend of Pocahontas has veiled her historical reality, as well as the brutal reality of Indian-European relations in colonial America. Pocahontas, which means "playful one," was the nickname of Matoaka, a daughter of

Pocahontas in England

The only portrait of Pocahontas made during her lifetime, and the only creditable image of her, this engraving was made by Simon de Passe in 1616 and later published in Captain John Smith's *The Generall Historie of Virginia* (1624). A caption below the portrait, which casts her as a symbol of assimilation to English culture, read in part: "Matoaka als [alias] Rebecca, daughter to the mighty Prince Powhatan . . . converted and baptized in the Christian faith, and wife to the worthy Mr. John Rolff [*sic*]."

Powhatan, chief of a powerful confederation of about thirty Algonkian-speaking tribes settled in the coastal areas around the Chesapeake Bay. She was apparently born in 1595 or 1596, so Pocahontas would still have been a young girl in 1607, when Smith claimed that she had saved him from execution. Whatever happened on that occasion, and whatever friendship Smith may have thereafter felt for Pocahontas, the colonists continued to encroach on native lands in the area around Jamestown. After Smith returned to England and in the midst of continued hostilities between the Indians and the colonists, the English captured Pocahontas in 1613. In an effort to force Powhatan to agree to their demands for land and right of way, they held her hostage in Jamestown. While in captivity, Pocahontas was converted to Christianity and married a colonist, John Rolfe, in 1614. Tired of the constant skirmishes with the colonists, Powhatan made an uneasy peace with the English. In 1616, Rolfe took his wife, now named Rebecca Rolfe, and their infant son, Thomas, to England. Unable to withstand the many new diseases she encountered, Pocahontas died there in March 1617. Powhatan died in 1618. Rolfe returned to Virginia, where he died in 1622, possibly in an attack led by Powhatan's half-brother, Opechancanough, who sought to wipe out the entire settlement at Jamestown. In response, the Virginia Company vowed to exterminate the Powhatan, whose once-powerful confederacy was destroyed by the 1640s.

Among those who have sought to alter our understanding of Indian-European relations in early Virginia and to rescue Pocahontas from American legend, few have been as forceful or as influential as Paula Gunn Allen. Of Laguna Pueblo, Lakota, and Lebanese ancestry, Allen grew up in Laguna Pueblo in New Mexico. She is the author of several volumes of poems and stories, as well as a novel, and frequently draws on both her own complex sense of identity and her experiences as a Native American. A major force in the emergence of Native American studies, Allen has also written numerous critical and scholarly works, including *Pocahontas: Medicine Woman, Spy, Entrepreneur, Diplomat* (2003). Fifteen years earlier, Allen wrote the following poem, in which she assumes the voice of Pocahontas and vividly imagines the young girl's complex understanding of the conditions of her life, especially her marriage to John Rolfe. The text of the poem is taken from Paula Gunn Allen, *Life Is a Fatal Disease, Collected Poems 1962-1995* (1997).

Paula Gunn Allen

[b. 1939]

Pocahontas to Her English Husband, John Rolfe

In a way, then, Pocahontas was a kind of traitor to her people. . . . Perhaps I am being a little too hard on her. The crucial point, it seems to me, is to remember that Pocahontas was a hostage. Would she have converted freely to Christianity if she had not been in captivity? There is no easy answer to this question other than to note that once she was free to do what she wanted, she avoided her own people like the plague. . . .

Pocahontas was a white dream – a dream of cultural superiority.

– Charles Larson
American Indian Fiction

Had I not cradled you in my arms,
oh beloved perfidious[1] one,
you would have died.
And how many times did I pluck you
from certain death in the wilderness –
my world through which you stumbled
as though blind?
Had I not set you tasks,
your masters far across the sea
would have abandoned you –
did abandon you, as many times
they left you
to reap the harvest of their lies.
Still you survived, oh my fair husband,
and brought them gold
wrung from a harvest I taught you
to plant. Tobacco.[2]
It is not without irony that by this crop

---

1. **perfidious:** Deceitful and untrustworthy.
2. **Tobacco:** John Rolfe led the way in establishing tobacco as a major cash crop in Virginia, where it was first planted by the English colonists in 1616. By 1638, the Chesapeake Bay area had become the principal supplier of tobacco to Europe, exporting three million pounds a year.

your descendants die, for other
powers than you know
take part in this as in all things.
And indeed I did rescue you –
not once but a thousand thousand times
and in my arms you slept, a foolish child,
and under my protecting gaze you played,
chattering nonsense about a God
you had not wit to name. I'm sure
you wondered at my silence, saying I was
a simple wanton, a savage maid,
dusky daughter of heathen sires
who cartwheeled naked through the muddy towns
learning the ways of grace only
by your firm guidance, through
your husbandly rule:
no doubt, no doubt.
I spoke little, you said.
And you listened less,
but played with your gaudy dreams
and sent ponderous missives to the throne
striving thereby to curry favor
with your king.
I saw you well. I
understood your ploys and still
protected you, going so far as to die
in your keeping – a wasting,
putrefying Christian death[3] – and you,
deceiver, whiteman, father of my son,
survived, reaping wealth greater
than any you had ever dreamed
from what I taught you
and from the wasting of my bones.

[1988, 1997]

3. **death:** Pocahontas died in England in March 1617, just as the Rolfes were about to return to Virginia.

William Bradford

[1590–1657]

William Bradford was born in March 1590 in Austerfield, a town in Yorkshire, northern England. His parents, William and Alice Hanson Bradford, were prosperous farmers. When Bradford was only a year old, his father died, and his mother soon remarried. Raised by his grandfather and uncles, Bradford was educated at a local grammar school and trained to be a farmer. When he was twelve or thirteen, however, he became absorbed in reading the Bible and was deeply moved by the preaching of Richard Clyfton, an Anglican priest in a nearby parish who was seeking to reform, or "purify," the Church of England. Finally deciding that such efforts were futile, Clyfton organized a Separatist congregation that met at the home of William Brewster in Scrooby, a town in Nottinghamshire. The formation of such an independent church constituted a formal secession from the Church of England, a treasonous act according to the laws of England. Nonetheless, over the strenuous opposition of his family, Bradford in 1616 left home to join the church in Scrooby.

William Bradford Statue

No likeness of Bradford was made during his lifetime, but he and the Pilgrims were later the subject of numerous works in every medium, including this statue Cyrus E. Dallin was commissioned to design as part of Plymouth's tercentenary celebration in 1921.

From then until his death forty-one years later, Bradford devoted himself to the interests and welfare of the "Pilgrims," as he called members of the devout group of Separatists. But their pilgrimage was not simply spiritual; it also became an arduous physical journey in quest of a place where they could establish a church and worship God according to what Bradford later described as "the simplicity of the gospel." As the new congregation grew to be more openly defiant of the laws of church and state, the Scrooby group determined that they could avoid persecution and survive only if they left England. They consequently fled to the Netherlands, where Bradford joined them in 1609. The only occupations open to English immigrants there were handicrafts, so Bradford learned the weaving trade. In 1611, when he was twenty-one, Bradford came into an inheritance of land in England, but he did not return home. Instead, he immediately sold the property, using the proceeds to buy a loom and a house, as well as to make a contribution toward the purchase of a church building for the Separatists. Two years later, he married Dorothy May, the daughter of an English Separatist; the couple's only child, John, was born in 1618. By then, the Pilgrims were already planning yet another removal, this time from Europe to the New World. Leaving behind their young son, whom they never saw again, Bradford and his wife embarked aboard the *Mayflower* for the voyage to the northern part of the Virginia Territory, near the mouth of the Hudson River, where the Separatists had obtained a land grant from the English government. But high seas prevented the ship from reaching its destination and after a sixty-five-day voyage it anchored instead off Cape Cod, in November 1620. While Bradford and others were exploring the coastline, Dorothy Bradford either fell or jumped overboard and drowned in Provincetown Harbor. Despite the tragic loss and possible suicide of his "dearest consort," the first of many Pilgrims who perished that winter, Bradford and the other Separatists determined to settle on the mainland at a place called "Plimoth" (later spelled *Plymouth*), the name the harbor had been given by Captain John Smith on a map included in his *Description of New England* (1616).

Bradford swiftly became the central figure in the new colony, both as its civic leader and as the primary author of its fame. Along with forty others, he signed the Mayflower Compact, establishing the basis for government in Plymouth. In 1621, he was elected governor, an office in which Bradford served for all but five of the remaining years of his life. He married a widow, Alice Carpenter, in 1623; the couple had three children. In an effort to preserve the security of the colony by establishing peaceful relations with the Indians, Bradford negotiated a long-lasting treaty with Massasoit, the chief of the Wampanoag. Bradford also became the major historian of and spokesperson for the colony. His first publication, a compilation of passages from his diary and that of Edward Winslow, was *A Relation or Journal of the Beginning and Proceedings of the English Plantation Settled at Plimoth in New England* (1622), commonly known as *Mourt's Relation*. Bradford began to write his most famous work, *Of Plimoth Plantation*, in 1630, later adding sections that carried the history of the colony up to 1647. During the last ten years of his life, the largely self-educated first historian of New England also wrote poetry, letters, and a series of five *Dialogues* designed to provide guidance for the second generation of Pilgrims, who were increasingly straying from the mission of the original settlers of Plymouth.

bedfordstmartins.com/ americanlit *for research links on Bradford*

Shortly before his death, Bradford wrote a poem in which he movingly and with characteristic modesty offered an assessment of his life:

From my years young in days of youth,
God did make known to me this truth,
And call'd me from my native place
For to enjoy the means of grace.
In wilderness he did me guide,
And in strange lands for me provide,

In fears and wants, through weal and woe,
A Pilgrim passed I to and fro.

Bradford, the simple Pilgrim who in American history and myth would later take his place as the most revered of the "Pilgrim Fathers," died at his home in Plymouth on May 9, 1657.

Bradford's *Of Plimoth Plantation.* Bradford wrote his famous history over a period of twenty years. He wrote the first ten chapters in 1630, at the beginning of the Great Migration, during which thousands of Puritans emigrated to New England. Concerned that his own small colony would be overshadowed by the larger and more powerful group in the Massachusetts Bay Colony, Bradford clearly sought to affirm the vital role of the Pilgrims in both the English Reformation and the settlement of New England. Just as he and other Protestant reformers sought to simplify forms of worship and strip churches of ornamentation, Bradford in a prefatory note observed that he would offer his account "in a plain style, with singular regard unto the simple truth in all things." For him, that regard for "simple truth" meant accurately recording and seeking to interpret the meaning of events dictated by God, the true author of all history. Beginning with an account of the origin of the Pilgrim Church during the Reformation in England, Bradford in 1630 described the persecutions the Separatists endured, their consequent departure to and difficult years in Holland, their decision to remove to New England, and their voyage aboard the *Mayflower*, ending with their arrival at Cape Cod and their choice of a place of settlement at Plymouth. According to a note he added in 1646, Bradford wrote most of the remainder of the book intermittently during the intervening years; he added a few sections as late as 1650.

Bradford did not prepare his account for publication; indeed, the book existed only in manuscript for two hundred years. But portions of his account were known to readers of other early histories. Nathaniel Morton paraphrased much of it in *New England's Memoriall* (1669), and the manuscript was also consulted by historians like William Hubbard, who made substantial use of it in his *History of New England*, written in 1683, and Cotton Mather, who depended on it for his *Magnalia Christi Americana* (1702). In the eighteenth century, the manuscript passed through many hands before it was mysteriously lost during the American Revolution. It later emerged in England, in the library of the Bishop of London. *Of Plimoth Plantation* was published in its entirety in 1856 under the direction of Charles Deane, an editor of publications for the Massachusetts Historical Society. Regarded as one of the most important and valuable documents in early American history, the manuscript was finally returned to the United States in 1897, following forty years of negotiations involving a complex cast of characters, including American historians, politicians, and ambassadors, as well as British bishops, prime ministers, and even Queen Victoria. On May 26, 1897, the manuscript was placed in the state house of Massachusetts, an occasion marked by elaborate ceremonies in

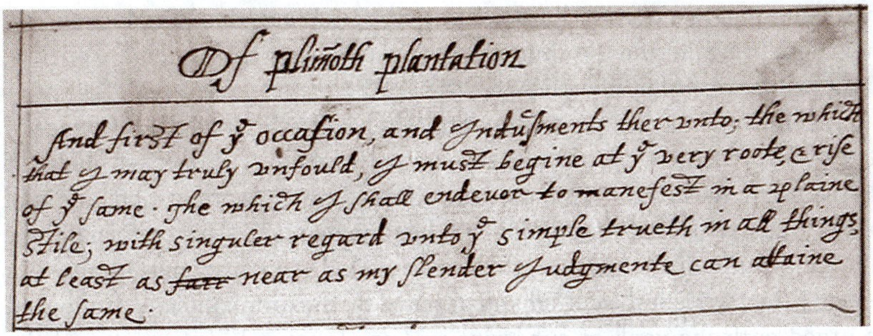
Of plimoth plantation

And first of ye occasion, and Indusments ther unto; the which
that I may truly unfould, I must begine at ye very roote & rise
of ye same. The which I shall endevor to manefest in a plaine
Stile; with singuler regard unto ye simple trueth in all things,
at least as ~~farr~~ near as my slender Judgmente can attaine
the same.

Bradford's Manuscript

As the precise layout and careful handwriting of this detail from the first page of Bradford's manuscript suggest, he evidently began to write his history with an eye to publication. But he continued to add to it for nearly twenty years, and the complete manuscript was not published until the mid-nineteenth century.

Boston and extensively reported in newspapers throughout the United States. The text of the following selections is taken from *Of Plimoth Plantation*, an exact transcription of the manuscript published in Boston by order of the Commonwealth of Massachusetts in 1900. We have retained Bradford's original capitalization, punctuation, paragraphing, and spelling, except in a few instances where a now-archaic spelling obscures the meaning of a passage. But we have regularized his inconsistent chapter headings and expanded his abbreviations, including y^e (*the*) and y^t (*that*), which Bradford used throughout his manuscript.

From Of Plimoth Plantation

[*From* Book 1]

And first of the occasion and indūsments ther unto; the which that I may truly unfould, I must begine at the very roote & rise of the same. The which I shall endevor to manefest in a plaine stile, with singuler regard unto the simple trueth in all things, at least as near as my slender judgmente can attaine the same.

From *Chapter 1*

It is well knowne unto the godly and judicious, how ever since the first breaking out of the lighte of the gospell in our Honourable Nation of England, (which was the first of nations whom the Lord adorned ther with, affter that grosse darknes of popery which had covered & overspred the Christian worled,) what warrs & opposissions ever since, Satan hath raised, maintained, and continued against the Saincts, from time to time, in one sorte or other. Some times by bloody death and cruell torments; other whiles imprisonments, banishments, & other hard usages; as being loath his kingdom should goe downe, the trueth prevaile, and the churches of God reverte to their anciente puritie, and recover their primative order, libertie, & bewtie. [. . .]

But that I may come more near my intendmente; when as by the travell & diligence of some godly & zealous preachers, & Gods blessing on their labours, as in other places of the land, so in the North parts,[1] many became inlightened by the word of God, and had their ignorance & sins discovered unto them, and begane by his grace to reforme their lives, and make conscience of their wayes, the worke of God was no sooner manifest in them, but presently they were both scoffed and scorned by the prophane multitude, and the ministers urged with the yoak of subscription,[2] or els must be silenced; and the poore people were so vexed with apparators, & pursuants, & the comissarie courts,[3] as truly their affliction was not smale; which, notwithstanding, they bore sundrie years with much patience, till they were occasioned (by the continuance & encrease of these troubls, and other means which the Lord raised up in those days) to see further into things by the light of the word of God. How not only these base and beggerly ceremonies were unlawfull, but also that the lordly & tiranous power of the prelats ought not to be submitted unto; which thus, contrary to the freedome of the gospell, would load & burden mens consciences, and by their compulsive power make a prophane mixture of persons & things in the worship of God. [. . .]

So many therfore of these proffessors as saw the evill of these things, in thes parts, and whose harts the Lord had touched with heavenly zeale for his trueth, they shooke of this yoake of antichristian bondage, and as the Lords free people, joyned them selves (by a covenant of the Lord[4]) into a church estate, in the felowship of the gospell, to walke in all his wayes, made known, or to be made known unto them, according to their best endeavours, whatsoever it should cost them, the Lord assisting them. And that it cost them something this ensewing historie will declare. [. . .]

But after these things they could not long continue in any peaceable condition, but were hunted & persecuted on every side, so as their former afflictions were but as fleabitings in comparison of these which now came upon them. For some were taken & clapt up in prison, others had their houses besett & watcht night and day, & hardly escaped their hands; and the most were faine to flie & leave their howses & habitations, and the means of their livelehood. Yet these & many other sharper things which affterward befell them, were no other then they looked for, and therfore were the better prepared to bear them by the assistance of Gods grace & spirite. Yet seeing them selves thus molested, and that ther was no hope of their continuance ther, by a joynte consente they resolved to goe into the Low-Countries, wher they heard was freedome of Religion for all

1. **North parts:** Northern England and Scotland.
2. **yoak of subscription:** Compelled to subscribe to the laws of the Church of England.
3. **apparators, & pursuants, & the comissarie courts:** The various offices and officials of the Church of England.
4. **a covenant of the Lord:** An agreement entered into by all members of a congregation to act in accordance with the laws of the church.

men; as also how sundrie from London, & other parts of the land, had been exiled and persecuted for the same cause, & were gone thither, and lived at Amsterdam, & in other places of the land. So affter they had continued togeither aboute a year, and kept their meetings every Saboth in one place or other, exercising the worship of God amongst them selves, notwithstanding all the dilligence & malice of their adverssaries, they seeing they could no longer continue in that condition, they resolved to get over into Hollād as they could; which was in the year 1607. & 1608. [. . .]

CHAPTER 4
SHOWING THE REASONS & CAUSES OF THEIR REMOOVALL

After they had lived in this citie[5] about some 11. or 12. years, (which is the more observable being the whole time of that famose truce between that state & the Spaniards,) and sundrie of them were taken away by death, & many others begane to be well striken in years, the grave mistris Experience haveing taught them many things, those prudent governours with sundrie of the sagest members begane both deeply to apprehend their present dangers, & wisely to foresee the future, & thinke of timly remedy. In the agitation of their thoughts, and much discours of things hear aboute, at length they began to incline to this conclusion, of remoovall to some other place. Not out of any newfanglednes, or other such like giddie humor, by which men are oftentimes transported to their great hurt & danger, but for sundrie weightie & solid reasons; some of the cheefe of which I will hear breefly touch. And first, they saw & found by experience the hardnes of the place & countrie to be such, as few in comparison would come to them, and fewer that would bide it out, and continew with them. For many that came to them, and many more that desired to be with them, could not endure that great labor and hard fare, with other inconveniences which they underwent & were contented with. But though they loved their persons, approved their cause, and honoured their sufferings, yet they left them as it weer weeping, as Orpah did her mother in law Naomie, or as those Romans did Cato in Utica, who desired to be excused & borne with, though they could not all be Catoes.[6] For many, though they desird to injoye the ordinances of God in their puritie, and the libertie of the gospell with them, yet, alass, they admitted of bondage, with danger of conscience, rather then to indure these hardships; yea, some preferred & chose the prisons in England, rather then this libertie in Holland, with these afflictions. But it was thought that if a better and easier place of living could be had, it would draw many,

5. **citie:** After leaving England, the Separatists settled in the city of Leyden in the Netherlands. They lived there until 1620, near the end of a twelve-year truce (begun in March 1609) in the Netherlands's long war of independence from Spain.
6. **Orpah . . . Catoes:** In the Old Testament, Orpah and Ruth were the daughters-in-law of Naomi; after their husbands died, Naomi wanted the two women to return to their own people. Orpah wept and left, but Ruth remained with Naomi (Ruth 1: 1-20). Cato the Younger (95 BCE-46 BCE), a Roman statesman, was intensely devoted to the Republic and opposed to Julius Caesar, who was gaining unprecedented power in Rome. Cato committed suicide after forces led by Scipio, another defender of the Republic, were defeated by Caesar.

& take away these discouragments. Yea, their pastor would often say, that many of those who both wrate & preached now against them, if they were in a place wher they might have libertie and live comfortably, they would then practise as they did.

Secondly. They saw that though the people generally bore all these difficulties very cherfully, & with a resolute courage, being in the best & strength of their years, yet old age began to steale on many of them, (and their great & continuall labours, with other crosses and sorrows, hastened it before the time,) so as it was not only probably thought, but apparently seen, that within a few years more they would be in danger to scatter, by necessities pressing them, or sinke under their burdens, or both. And therfore according to the devine proverb, that a wise man seeth the plague when it cometh, & hideth him selfe, Pro. 22. 3., so they like skillfull & beaten souldiers were fearfull either to be intrapped or surrounded by their enimies, so as they should neither be able to fight nor flie; and therfor thought it better to dislodge betimes to some place of better advantage & less danger, if any such could be found. Thirdly; as necessitie was a taskmaster over them, so they were forced to be such, not only to their servants, but in a sorte, to their dearest chilldren; the which as it did not a litle wound the tender harts of many a loving father & mother, so it produced likwise sundrie sad & sorowful effects. For many of their children, that were of best dispositions and gracious inclinations, haveing lernde to bear the yoake in their youth,[7] and willing to bear parte of their parents burden, were, often times, so oppressed with their hevie labours, that though their minds were free and willing, yet their bodies bowed under the weight of the same, and became decreped in their early youth; the vigor of nature being consumed in the very budd as it were. But that which was more lamentable, and of all sorowes most heavie to be borne, was that many of their children, by these occasions, and the great licentiousnes of youth in that countrie,[8] and the manifold temptations of the place, were drawne away by evill examples into extravagante & dangerous courses, getting the raines off their neks, & departing from their parents. Some became souldiers, others tooke upon them farr viages by sea, and other some worse courses, tending to dissolutnes & the danger of their soules, to the great greefe of their parents and dishonour of God. So that they saw their posteritie would be in danger to degenerate & be corrupted.

Lastly, (and which was not least,) a great hope & inward zeall they had of laying some good foundation, or at least to make some way therunto, for the propagating & advancing the gospell of the kingdom of Christ in those remote parts of the world; yea, though they should be but even as stepping-stones unto others for the perfornning of so great a work.

These, & some other like reasons, moved them to undertake this resolution of their removall; the which they afterward prosecuted with so great difficulties, as by the sequell will appeare.

---

7. **to bear . . . youth:** See Lamentations 3:27: "It is good for a man that he bear the yoke of his youth."
8. **great licentiousness of youth in that countrie:** To the horror of the Separatists, who devoted the Sabbath entirely to religion and worship, after attending church Dutch children spent the rest of the day feasting and playing games.

The place they had thoughts on was some of those vast & unpeopled countries of America, which are frutfull & fitt for habitation, being devoyd of all civill inhabitants, wher ther are only salvage & brutish men, which range up and downe, litle otherwise then the wild beasts of the same. This proposition being made publike and coming to the scaning of all, it raised many variable opinions amongst men, and caused many fears & doubts amongst them selves. Some, from their reasons & hops conceived, laboured to stirr up & incourage the rest to undertake & prosecute the same; others, againe, out of their fears, objected against it, & sought to diverte from it, aledging many things, and those neither unreasonable nor unprobable; as that it was a great designe, and subjecte to many unconceivable perills & dangers; as, besids the casulties of the seas (which none can be freed from) the length of the vioage was such, as the weake bodys of women and other persons worne out with age & traville (as many of them were) could never be able to endure. And yet if they should, the miseries of the land which they should be exposed unto, would be to hard to be borne; and lickly, some or all of them togeither, to consume & utterly to ruinate them. For ther they should be liable, to famine, and nakednes, & the wante, in a maner, of all things. The chang of aire, diate, & drinking of water, would infecte their bodies with sore sicknesеs, and greevous diseases. And also those which should escape or overcome these difficulties, should yett be in continuall danger of the salvage people, who are cruell, barbarous, & most trecherous, being most furious in their rage, and merciles wher they overcome; not being contente only to kill, & take away life, but delight to tormente men in the most bloodie mañer that may be; fleaing some alive with the shells of fishes, cutting of the members & joynts of others by peesmeale, and broiling on the coles, eate the collops[9] of their flesh in their sight whilst they live; with other cruelties horrible to be related. And surely it could not be thought but the very hearing of these things could not but move the very bowels of men to grate within them, and make the weake to quake & tremble. It was furder objected, that it would require greater sum̃es of money to furnish such a voiage, and to fitt them with necessaries, then their consumed estats would amounte too; and yett they must as well looke to be seconded with supplies, as presently to be trãsported. Also many presidents of ill success, & lamentable misseries befalne others in the like designes, were easie to be found, and not forgotten to be aledged; besids their owne experience, in their former troubles & hardships in their removall into Holand, and how hard a thing it was for them to live in that strange place, though it was a neighbour countrie, & a civill and rich comone wealth.

It was answered, that all great & honourable actions are accompanied with great difficulties, and must be both enterprised and overcome with answerable courages. It was granted the dangers were great, but not desperate; the difficulties were many, but not invincible. For though their were many of them likly, yet they were not cartaine; it might be sundrie of the things feared might never befale; others by providente care & the use of good means, might in a great measure be prevented; and all of them, through the help of God, by fortitude and patience, might either be borne, or overcome. True it was, that

9. **collops:** Cooking term for slices of meat.

such atempts were not to be made and undertaken without good ground & reason; not rashly or lightly as many have done for curiositie or hope of gaina, &c. But their condition was not ordinarie; their ends were good & honourable; their calling lawfull, & urgente; and therfore they might expecte the blessing of God in their proceding. Yea, though they should loose their lives in this action, yet might they have comforte in the same, and their endeavors would be honourable. They lived hear but as men in exile, & in a poore condition; and as great miseries might possibly befale them in this place, for the 12. years of truce were now out, & ther was nothing but beating of drumes, and preparing for warr, the events wherof are allway uncertaine. The Spaniard might prove as cruell as the salvages of America, and the famine and pestelence as sore hear as ther, & their libertie less to looke out for remedie. After many other perticuler things answered & aledged on both sids, it was fully concluded by the major parte, to put this designe in execution, and to prosecute it by the best means they could.

CHAPTER 9
OF THEIR VIOAGE, & HOW THEY PASSED THE SEA, AND OF THEIR SAFE ARRIVALL AT CAPE CODD

September 6. These troubls being blowne over, and now all being compacte togeather in one shipe,[10] they put to sea againe with a prosperus winde, which continued diverce days together, which was some incouragmente unto them; yet according to the usuall maner many were afflicted with sea-sicknes. And I may not omite hear a spetiall worke of Gods providence. Ther was a proud & very profane yonge man, one of the sea-men, of a lustie,[11] able body, which made him the more hauty; he would allway be contemning the poore people in their sicknes, & cursing them dayly with greēous execrations, and did not let[12] to tell them, that he hoped to help to cast halfe of them over board before they came to their jurneys end, and to make mery with what they had; and if he were by any gently reproved, he would curse and swear most bitterly. But it plased God before they came halfe seas over, to smite this yong man with a greeveous disease, of which he dyed in a desperate maner, and so was him selfe the first that was throwne overbord. Thus his curses light on his owne head; and it was an astonishmente to all his fellows, for they noted it to be the just hand of God upon him.

After they had injoyed faire winds and weather for a season, they were incountred many times with crosse winds, and mette with many feirce stormes, with which the shipe was shroudly[13] shaken, and her upper works made very leakie; and one of the maine beames in the midd ships was bowed & craked, which put them in some fear that

---

10. **togeather in one shipe:** The original plan called for two ships to sail from England, the *Speedwell* and the *Mayflower.* The *Speedwell,* a smaller boat that brought Bradford and the other members of the Separatist community from Holland to England, proved to be unseaworthy. During the delay, some members of the Holland group decided not to go to the New World; 102 people eventually sailed on the *Mayflower.*

11. **lustie:** Healthy and strong.

12. **let:** Hesitate.

13. **shroudly:** Early form of *shrewdly,* meaning wickedly.

the shipe could not be able to performe the vioage. So some of the cheefe of the company, perceiveing the mariners to feare the suffisiencie of the shipe, as appeared by their mutterings, they entred into serious consulltation with the mr.[14] & other officers of the ship, to consider in time of the danger; and rather to returne then to cast them selves into a desperate & inevitable perill. And truly ther was great distraction & differance of opinion amongst the mariners them selves; faine[15] would they doe what could be done for their wages sake, (being now halfe the seas over,) and on the other hand they were loath to hazard their lives too desperatly. But in examening of all opinions, the mr. & others affirmed they knew the ship to be stronge & firme under water; and for the buckling of the maine beame, ther was a great iron scrue the passengers brought out of Holland, which would raise the beame into his place; the which being done, the carpenter & mr. affirmed that with a post put under it, set firme in the lower deck, & otherways bounde, he would make it sufficiente. And as for the decks & uper workes they would calke them as well as they could, and though with the workeing of the ship they would not longe keepe stanch,[16] yet ther would otherwise be no great danger, if they did not overpress her with sails. So they comited them selves to the will of God, & resolved to proseede. In sundrie of these stormes the winds were so feirce, & the seas so high, as they could not beare a knote of saile, but were forced to hull,[17] for diverce days togither. And in one of them, as they thus lay at hull, in a mighty storme, a lustie yonge man (called John Howland) coming upon some occasion above the grattings, was, with a seele[18] of the shipe throwne into [the] sea; but it pleased God that he caught hould of the top-saile halliards, which hunge over board, & rane out at length; yet he held his hould (though he was sundrie fadomes under water) till he was hald up by the same rope to the brime of the water, and then with a boat hooke & other means got into the shipe againe, & his life saved; and though he was something ill with it, yet he lived many years after, and became a profitable member both in church & comone wealthe. In all this viage ther died but one of the passengers, which was William Butten, a youth, servant to Samuell Fuller, when they drew near the coast. But to omite other things, (that I may be breefe,) after longe beating at sea they fell with that land which is called Cape Cod; the which being made & certainly knowne to be it, they were not a litle joyfull. After some deliberation had amongst them selves & with the mr. of the ship, they tacked aboute and resolved to stande for the southward (the wind & weather being faire) to finde some place aboute Hudsons river for their habitation. But after they had sailed that course aboute halfe the day, they fell amongst deangerous shoulds and roring breakers, and they were so farr intangled ther with as they conceived them selves in great danger; & the wind shrinking upon them withall, they resolved to bear up againe for the Cape, and thought them selves hapy to gett out of those dangers before night overtooke them, as by Gods providence they did. And the next day they gott into the Cape-harbor wher they ridd in

14. **mr.:** Abbreviation for master, the captain of a merchant ship.
15. **faine:** Willingly.
16. **stanch:** Watertight.
17. **hull:** Drift with the direction of the wind using short sails.
18. **seele:** Roll or pitch.

saftie.[19] A word or too by the way of this cape; it was thus first named by Capten Gosnole & his company,[20] Anno:[21] 1602, and after by Capten Smith was caled Cape James; but it retains the former name amongst seamen. Also that pointe which first shewed those dangerous shoulds unto them, they called Pointe Care, & Tuckers Terrour; but the French & Dutch to this day call it Malabarr, by reason of those perilous shoulds, and the losses they have suffered their.[22]

Being thus arived in a good harbor and brought safe to land, they fell upon their knees & blessed the God of heaven, who had brought them over the vast & furious ocean, and delivered them from all the periles & miseries therof, againe to set their feete on the firme and stable earth, their proper elemente. And no marvell if they were thus joyefull, seeing wise Seneca was so affected with sailing a few miles on the coast of his owne Italy; as he affirmed, that he had rather remaine twentie years on his way by land, then pass by sea to any place in a short time; so tedious & dreadfull was the same unto him.[23]

But hear I cannot but stay and make a pause, and stand half amased at this poore peoples presente condition; and so I thinke will the reader too, when he well considers the same. Being thus passed the vast ocean, and a sea of troubles before in their preparation (as may be remembred by that which wente before), they had now no freinds to wellcome them, nor inns to entertaine or refresh their weatherbeaten bodys, no houses or much less townes to repaire too, to seeke for succoure. It is recorded in scripture as a mercie to the apostle & his shipwraked company, that the barbarians shewed them no smale kindnes[24] in refreshing them, but these savage barbarians, when they mette with them (as after will appeare) were readier to fill their sids full of arrows then otherwise. And for the season it was winter, and they that know the winters of that cuntrie know them to be sharp & violent, & subjecte to cruell & feirce stormes, deangerous to travill to known places, much more to serch an unknown coast. Besids, what could they see but a hidious & desolate wildernes, full of wild beasts & willd men? and what multituds ther might be of them they knew not. Nether could they, as it were, goe up to the tope of Pisgah,[25] to vew from this wildernes a more goodly cuntrie to feed their hops; for which way soever they turnd their eys (save upward to the heavens) they could have litle solace

19. **And the next day . . . saftie:** According to the Julian, or Old Style, calendar, they anchored in what is now Provincetown Harbor on November 11, 1620. In the Gregorian, or New Style, calendar – which was not adopted in England until 1752 – the date was November 21, 1620.

20. **named by Capten Gosnole & his company:** Because they took much of that fish there. [Bradford's note.]

21. **Anno:** In the year of (Latin).

22. **Malabarr . . . suffered their:** The Malabar Coast of southwest India was then well known for intense monsoon storms and perilous sandbars, as well as for conflicts among competing Europeans for access to the fertile rice lands.

23. **wise Seneca . . . unto him:** Epistle 53. [Bradford's note.] Bradford is loosely quoting from the *Moral Epistles to Lucilius*, a central ethical work of the ancient world, by the Roman philosopher Seneca (4? BCE–65 CE).

24. **kindnes:** Acts 28. [Bradford's note.] Bradford contrasts the experiences of the Pilgrims with those of the apostle Paul and his men, who were shipwrecked on the island of Malta: "And the barbarous people showed us no little kindness: for they kindled a fire, and received us every one, because of the present rain, and because of the cold" (Acts 28:2).

25. **Pisgah:** The mountain from which God showed Moses the promised land (Deuteronomy 34:1–4).

or content in respecte of any outward objects. For sum̃er being done, all things stand upon them with a wetherbeaten face; and the whole countrie, full of woods & thickets, represented a wild & savage heiw. If they looked behind them, ther was the mighty ocean which they had passed, and was now as a maine barr & goulfe to seperate them from all the civill parts of the world. If it be said they had a ship to sucour them, it is trew; but what heard they daly from the mr. & company? but that with speede they should looke out a place with their shallop,[26] wher they would be at some near distance; for the season was shuch as he would not stirr from thence till a safe harbor was discovered by them wher they would be, and he might goe without danger; and that victells[27] consumed apace, but he must & would keepe sufficient for them selves & their returne. Yea, it was muttered by some, that if they gott not a place in time, they would turne them & their goods ashore & leave them. Let it also be considred what weake hopes of supply & succoure they left behinde them, that might bear up their minds in this sade condition and trialls they were under; and they could not but be very smale. It is true, indeed, the affections & love of their brethren at Leyden was cordiall & entire towards them, but they had litle power to help them, or them selves; and how the case stode betweene them & the marchants at their coming away, hath allready been declared. What could now sustaine them but the spirite of God & his grace? May not & ought not the children of these fathers rightly say: *Our faithers were Englishmen which came over this great ocean, and were ready to perish in this willderness; but they cried unto the Lord, and he heard their voyce, and looked on their adversitie, &c.*[28] *Let them therfore praise the Lord, because he is good, & his mercies endure for ever. Yea, let them which have been redeemed of the Lord, shew how he hath delivered them from the hand of the oppressour. When they wandered in the deserte willdernes out of the way, and found no citie to dwell in, both hungrie, & thirstie, ther sowle was overwhelmed in them. Let them confess before the Lord his loving kindnes, and his wonderfull works before the sons of men.*[29]

CHAPTER 10

SHOWING HOW THEY SOUGHT OUT A PLACE OF HABITATION, AND WHAT BEFELL THEM THERABOUTE

Being thus arrived at Cap-Cod the 11. of November, and necessitie calling them to looke out a place for habitation, (as well as the maisters & mariners importunitie,) they having brought a large shalop with them out of England, stowed in quarters in the ship, they now gott her out & sett their carpenters to worke to trime her up; but being much brused

26. **shallop:** Light sailboat used primarily for coastal fishing.
27. **victells:** Food (victuals).
28. ***Our fathers . . . adversitie, &c.:*** Deuteronomy 26:5, 7. [Bradford's note.] Bradford refers to the plight of the Israelites before Moses led them to the promised land: "And the Egyptians evil entreated us, and afflicted us, and laid upon us hard bondage: And when we cried unto the LORD God of our fathers, the LORD heard our voice, and looked on our affliction, and our labor, and our oppression: And the LORD brought us forth out of Egypt with a mighty hand, and with an outstretched arm, and with great terribleness, and with signs, and with wonders" (Deuteronomy 26:6-8).
29. ***Yea, let them . . . sons of men:*** Psalms 107:1-5, 8. [Bradford's note.]

& shatered in the shipe with foule weather, they saw she would be longe in mending. Wherupon a few of them tendered them selves to goe by land and discovere those nearest places, whilst the shallop was in mending; and the rather because as they wente into that harbor ther seemed to be an opening some 2. or 3 leagues of, which the maister judged to be a river. It was conceived ther might be some danger in the attempte, yet seeing them resolute, they were permited to goe, being 16. of them well armed, under the conduct of Captain Standish,[30] having shuch instructions given them as was thought meete. They sett forth the 15. of November: and when they had marched aboute the space of a mile by the sea side, they espied 5. or 6. persons with a dogg coming towards them, who were salvages; but they fled from them, & rañe up into the woods, and the English followed them, partly to see if they could speake with them, and partly to discover if ther might not be more of them lying in ambush. But the Indeans seeing them selves thus followed, they againe forsooke the woods, & rane away on the sands as hard as they could, so as they could not come near them, but followed them by the tracte of their feet sundrie miles, and saw that they had come the same way. So, night coming on, they made their randevous & set out their sentinels, and rested in quiete *that night*, and the next morning followed their tracte till they had headed a great creake, & so left the sands, & turned an other way into the woods. But they still followed them by geuss, hopeing to find their dwellings; but they soone lost both them & them selves, falling into shuch thickets as were ready to tear their cloaths & armore in peeces, but were most distresed for wante of drinke. But at length they found water & refreshed them selves, being the first New-England water they drunke of, and was now in thir great thirste as pleasante unto them as wine or bear had been in for-times. Afterwards they directed their course to come to the other shore, for they knew it was a necke of land they were to crosse over, and so at length gott to the sea-side, and marched to this supposed river, & by the way found a pond[31] of clear fresh water, and shortly after a good quantitie of clear ground wher the Indeans had formerly set corne, and some of their graves. And proceeding furder they saw new-stuble wher corne had been set the same year, also they found wher latly a house had been, wher some planks and a great ketle was remaining, and heaps of sand newly padled with their hands, which they, digging up, found in them diverce faire Indean baskets filled with corne, and some in eares, faire and good, of diverce collours, which seemed to them a very goodly sight, (haveing never seen any shuch before). This was near the place of that supposed river they came to seeck; unto which they wente and found it to open it selfe into 2. armes with a high cliffe of sand in the enterance,[32] but more like to be crikes of salte water then any fresh, for ought they saw; and that ther was good harborige for their shalope; leaving it further to be discovered by their shalop when she was ready. So their time limeted them being expired, they

---

30. **Captain Standish:** Miles Standish (1584?–1656), an English soldier who had fought in the Netherlands, was engaged to handle military affairs for the colonists.
31. **pond:** The spring-fed pond is in present-day Truro, Massachusetts.
32. **enterance:** The Pamet River is a narrow saltwater river or creek that runs across Cape Cod, nearly dividing the peninsula.

returned to the ship, least they should be in fear of their saftie; and tooke with them parte of the corne, and buried up the rest, and so like the men from Eshcoll carried with them of the fruits of the land, & showed their breethren;[33] of which, & their returne, they were marvelusly glad, and their harts incouraged.

After this, the shalop being got ready, they set out again for the better discovery of this place, & the mr. of the ship desired to goe him selfe, so ther went some 30. men, but found it to be no harbor for ships but only for boats; ther was allso found 2. of their houses covered with matts, & sundrie of their implements in them, but the people were rune away & could not be seen; also ther was found more of their corne, & of their beans of various collours. The corne & beans they brought away, purposing to give them full satisfaction when they should meete with any of them (as about some 6. months afterward they did, to their good contente). And here is to be noted a spetiall providence of God, and a great mercie to this poore people, that hear they gott seed to plant them corne the next year, or els they might have starved, for they had none, nor any liklyhood to get any till the season had beene past (as the sequell did manyfest). Neither is it lickly they had had this, if the first viage had not been made, for the ground was now all covered with snow, & hard frozen. But the Lord is never wanting unto his in their greatest needs; let his holy name have all the praise.

The month of November being spente in these affairs, & much foule weather falling in, the 6. *of December*: they sente out their shallop againe with 10. of their principall men, & some sea men, upon further discovery, intending to circulate that deepe bay of Cap-codd. The weather was very could, & it frose so hard as the sprea of the sea lighting on their coats, they were as if they had been glased; yet *that night* betimes they gott downe into the botome of the bay, and as they drue nere the shore they saw some 10. or 12. Indeans very busie aboute some thing. They landed aboute a league or 2. from them, and had much a doe to put a shore any wher, it lay so full of flats.[34] Being landed, it grew late, and they made them selves a barricade with loggs & bowes as well as they could in the time, & set out their sentenill & betooke them to rest, and saw the smoake of the fire the savages made that night. When *morning* was come they devided their company, some to coaste along the shore in the boate, and the rest marched throw the woods to see the land, if any fit place might be for their dwelling. They came allso to the place wher they saw the Indans the night before, & found they had been cuting up a great fish like a grampus,[35] being some 2. inches thike of fate like a hogg, some peeces wher of they had left by the way; and the shallop found 2. more of these fishes dead on the sands, a thing usuall after storms in that place, by reason of the great flats of sand that lye of. So they ranged up and doune all that day, but found no people, nor any place they liked. When the sune grue low, they hasted out of the woods to meete with their shallop, to whom

---

33. **men from Eshcoll . . . breethren:** In the Old Testament account, Moses sent a group of men to investigate the promised land, where they found grapes, pomegranates, and figs near a brook, called Eshcol (Numbers 13:23-7).

34. **flats:** Expanse of low, level ground; they landed on a beach near present-day Eastham, Massachusetts.

35. **grampus:** A large fish the size of a dolphin (*Grampus griseus*).

they made signes to come to them into a *creeke*[36] hardby, the which they did at high-water; of which they were very glad, for they had not seen each other all that day, since the morning. So they made them a barricado (as usually they did every night) with loggs, staks, & thike pine bowes, the height of a man, leaving it open to leeward, partly to shelter them from the could & wind (making their fire in the midle, & lying round aboute it), and partly to defend them from any sudden assaults of the savags, if they should surround them. So being very weary, they betooke them to rest. But aboute *midnight*, they heard a hideous & great crie, and their sentinell caled, "Arme, arme"; so they bestired them & stood to their armes, & shote of a cupple of moskets, and then the noys seased. They concluded it was a companie of wolves, or such like willd beasts; for one of the sea men tould them he had often heard shuch a noyse in New-found land. So they rested till about 5. of the clock in the *morning*; for the tide, & ther purposs to goe from thence, made them be stiring betimes. So after praier they prepared for breakfast, and it being day dawning, it was thought best to be carring things downe to the boate. But some said it was not best to carrie the armes downe, others said they would be the readier, for they had laped them up in their coats from the dew. But some 3. or 4. would not cary theirs till they wente them selves, yet as it fell out, the water being not high enough, they layed them downe on the banke side, & came up to breakfast. But presently, all on the sudain, they heard a great & strange crie, which they knew to be the same voyces they heard in the night, though they varied their notes, & one of their company being abroad came runing in, & cried, "Men, Indeans, Indeans"; and withall, their arowes came flying amongst them. Their men rane with all speed to recover their armes, as by the good providence of God they did. In the mean time, of those that were ther ready, tow muskets were discharged at them, & 2. more stood ready in the enterance of ther randevoue, but were comanded not to shoote till they could take full aime at them; & the other 2. charged againe with all speed, for ther were only 4. had armes ther, & defended the baricado which was first assalted. The crie of the Indeans was dreadfull, espetially when they saw ther men rune out of the randevoue towourds the shallop, to recover their armes, the Indeans wheeling aboute upon them. But some ruñing out with coats of malle[37] on, & cutlasses in their hands, they soone got their armes, & let flye amongs them, and quickly stopped their violence. Yet ther was a lustie man, and no less valiante, stood behind a tree within halfe a musket shot, and let his arrows flie at them. He was seen shoot 3. arrowes, which were all avoyded. He stood 3. shot of a musket, till one taking full aime at him, and made the barke or splinters of the tree fly about his ears, after which he gave an extraordinary shrike, and away they wente all of them. They left some to keep the shalop, and followed them aboute a quarter of a mille, and shouted once or twise, and shot of 2. or 3. peces, & so returned. This they did, that they might conceive that they were not affrade of them or any way discouraged. Thus it pleased God to vanquish their enimies, and give them deliverance; and by his spetiall providence so to dispose that not any one of them were either hurte, or hitt, though their arrows came close

36. ***creeke***: The Herring River in present-day Eastham, Massachusetts.

37. **coats of malle**: Coats of mail, flexible armor made of metal rings or plates.

by them, & on every side them, and sundry of their coats, which hunge up in the barricado, were shot throw & throw. Aterwards they gave God sollamne thanks & praise for their deliverance, & gathered up a bundle of their arrows, & sente them into England afterward by the mr. of the ship, and called that place the first encounter. From hence they departed, & costed all along, but discerned no place likly for harbor; & therfore hasted to a place that their pillote, (one Mr. Coppin who had bine in the cuntrie before) did assure them was a good harbor, which he had been in, and they might fetch it before night; of which they were glad, for it begane to be foule weather. After some houres sailing, it begane to snow & raine, & about the midle of the afternoone, the wind increased, & the sea became very rough, and they broake their rudder, & it was as much as 2. men could doe to steere her with a cupple of oares. But their pillott bad them be of good cheere, for he saw the harbor; but the storme increasing, & night drawing on, they bore what saile they could to gett in, while they could see. But herwith they broake their mast in 3. peeces, & their saill fell over bord, in a very grown sea, so as they had like to have been cast away; yet by Gods mercie they recovered them selves, & having the floud[38] with them, struck into the harbore. But when it came too, the pillott was deceived in the place, and said, the Lord be mercifull unto them, for his eys never saw that place before; & he & the mr. mate would have rune her ashore, in a cove full of breakers, before the winde. But a lusty seaman which steered, bad those which rowed, if they were men, about with her, or ells they were all cast away; the which they did with speed. So he bid them be of good cheere & row lustly, for ther was a faire sound before them, & he doubted not but they should find one place or other wher they might ride in saftie. And though it was *very darke*, and rained sore, yet in the end they gott under the lee[39] of a smalle iland, and remained ther all that night in saftie. But they knew not this to be an iland till morning, but were devided in their minds; some would keepe the boate for fear they might be amongst the Indians; others were so weake and could, they could not endure, but got a shore, & with much adoe got fire, (all things being so wett,) and the rest were glad to come to them; for after midnight the wind shifted to the north-west, & it frose hard. But though this had been a day & night of much trouble & danger unto them, yet God gave them a *morning* of comforte & refreshing (as usually he doth to his children), for the next day was a faire sunshinig day, and they found them sellvs to be on an iland secure from the Indeans, wher they might drie their stufe, fixe their peeces,[40] & rest them selves, and gave God thanks for his mercies, in their manifould deliverances. And this being the *last day of the weeke*, they prepared ther to keepe the *Sabath*. On *Munday* they sounded the harbor, and founde it fitt for shipping; and marched into the land, & found diverse cornfeilds, & litle runing brooks, a place (as they supposed) fitt for situation;[41] at least it was the best they could find, and the season, & their presente

38. **floud:** Short for flood tide, a powerful, incoming tide.
39. **lee:** Sheltered side, away from the wind.
40. **peeces:** Firearms.
41. **a place . . . fitt for situation:** Near Plymouth, Massachusetts, where the Pilgrims landed on November 11/21, 1620. See note 19.

necessitie, made them glad to accepte of it. So they returned to their shipp againe with this news to the rest of their people, which did much comforte their harts.

On the 15. of *December*: they wayed anchor to goe to the place they had discovered, & came within 2. leagues of it, but were faine[42] to bear up againe; but the 16. *day* the winde came faire, and they arrived safe in this harbor. And after wards tooke better view of the place, and resolved wher to pitch their dwelling; and the 25. *day* begane to erecte the first house for comone use to receive them and their goods.

From Booke 2

The rest of this History (if God give me life, & opportunitie) I shall, for brevitis sake, handle by way of *annalls*, noteing only the heads of principall things, and passages as they fell in order of time, and may seeme to be profitable to know, or to make use of. And this may be as the 2. Booke.

The remainder of Anno: 1620

I shall a litle returne backe and begine with a combination[43] made by them before they came ashore, being the first foundation of their govermente in this place; occasioned partly by the discontented & mutinous speeches that some of the strangers[44] amongst them had let fall from them in the ship – That when they came a shore they would use their owne libertie; for none had power to comand them, the patente they had being for Virginia, and not for New-england, which belonged to an other Goverment, with which the Virginia Company had nothing to doe. And partly that shuch an acte by them done (this their condition considered) might be as firme as any patent, and in some respects more sure.

The forme was as followeth.[45]

> In the name of God, Amen. We whose names are underwriten, the loyall subjects of our dread soveraigne Lord, King James, by the grace of God, of Great Britaine, Franc, & Ireland king, defender of the faith, &c., haveing undertaken, for the glorie of God, and advancemente of the Christian faith, and honour of our king & countrie, a voyage to plant the first colonie in the Northerne parts of Virginia, doe by these presents solemnly & mutualy in the presence of God, and one of another, covenant & combine our selves togeather into a civill body politick, for our better ordering & preservation & furtherance of the ends aforesaid; and by vertue hearof to enacte, constitute, and frame such just & equall lawes, ordinances, acts, constitutions, & offices, from time to time, as shall be thought most meete & convenient for the generall good of the Colonie, unto which we promise all due submission and

42. **faine:** Obliged or compelled.
43. **combination:** An agreement for union or joining together.
44. **strangers:** Those who did not follow the religious beliefs of the Pilgrims.
45. **The forme was as followeth:** The original document of the Mayflower Compact is lost. Bradford clearly used the first printing of the compact (which was published in 1622), copying it into his manuscript with a few minor alterations.

obedience. In witnes wherof we have hereunder subscribed our names at Cap-Codd the 11. of November, in the year of the raigne of our soveraigne lord, King James, of England, France, & Ireland the eighteenth, and of Scotland the fiftie fourth. Anno Domini[46] 1620.

After this they chose, or rather confirmed, Mr. John Carver[47] (a man godly & well approved amongst them) their Governour for that year. And after they had provided a place for their goods, or comone store, (which were long in unlading for want of boats, foulnes of winter weather, and sicknes of diverce,) and begune some small cottages for their habitation, as time would admitte, they mette and consulted of lawes & orders, both for their civill & military Govermente, as the necessitie of their condition did require, still adding therunto as urgent occasion in severall times, and as cases did require.

In these hard & difficulte beginings they found some discontents & murmurings arise amongst some, and mutinous speeches & carriags in other; but they were soone quelled & overcome by the wisdome, patience, and just & equall carrage of things by the Govr and better part, which clave[48] faithfully togeather in the maine. But that which was most sadd & lamentable was, that in 2. or 3. moneths time halfe of their company dyed, espetialy in Jan: & February, being the depth of winter, and wanting houses & other comforts; being infected with the scurvie & other diseases, which this long vioage & their inacomodate condition had brought upon them; so as ther dyed some times 2. or 3. of a day, in the foresaid time; that of 100. & odd persons, scarce 50. remained. And of these in the time of most distres, ther was but 6. or 7. sound persons, who, to their great comendations be it spoken, spared no pains, night nor day, but with abundance of toyle and hazard of their owne health, fetched them woode, made them fires, drest them meat, made their beads, washed their lothsome cloaths, cloathed & uncloathed them; in a word, did all the homly & necessarie offices for them which dainty & quesie stomacks cannot endure to hear named; and all this willingly & cherfully, without any grudging in the least, shewing herein their true love unto their freinds & bretheren. A rare example & worthy to be remembred. Tow of these 7. were Mr. William Brewster, ther reverend Elder, & Myles Standish, ther Captein & military comander, unto whom my selfe, & many others, were much beholden in our low & sicke condition. And yet the Lord so upheld these persons, as in this generall calamity they were not at all infected either with sicknes, or lamnes. And what I have said of these, I may say of many others who dyed in this generall vissitation, & others yet living, that whilst they had health, yea, or any strength continuing, they were not wanting to any that had need of them. And I doute not but their recompence is with the Lord.

But I may not hear pass by an other remarkable passage not to be forgotten. As this calamitie fell among the passengers that were to be left here to plant, and were hasted a

46. **Anno Domini:** Full form of AD, literally "in the year of the Lord" (Latin).
47. **Carver:** John Carver (1575?–1621). Along with Bradford and William Brewster (1567–1644), Carver proposed the immigration to America. He served as governor of the colony until his death, five months after the landing at Plymouth.
48. **clave:** Past tense of *cleave*, to become strongly attached to others.

shore and made to drinke water, that the sea-men might have the more bear, and one[49] in his sicknes desiring but a small cann of beere, it was answered, that if he were their owne father he should have none, the disease begane to fall amongst them also, so as allmost halfe of their company dyed before they went away, and many of their officers and lustyest men, as the boatson,[50] gunner, 3. quarter-maisters,[51] the cooke, & others. At which the mr. was something strucken and sent to the sick a shore and tould the Govr he should send for beer for them that had need of it, though he drunke water homward bound. But now amongst his company ther was farr another kind of carriage in this miserie then amongst the passengers; for they that before had been boone companions in drinking & joyllity in the time of their health & wellfare, begane now to deserte one another in this calamitie, saing they would not hasard ther lives for them, they should be infected by coming to help them in their cabins, and so, after they came to dye by it, would doe litle or nothing for them, but if they dyed let them dye. But shuch of the passengers as were yet abord shewed them what mercy they could, which made some of their harts relente, as the boatson (& some others), who was a prowd yonge man, and would often curse & scofe at the passengers; but when he grew weak, they had compassion on him and helped him; then he confessed he did not deserve it at their hands, he had abused them in word & deed. O! saith he, you, I now see, shew your love like Christians indeed one to another, but we let one another lye & dye like doggs. Another lay cursing his wife, saing if it had not ben for her he had never come this unlucky viage, and anone cursing his felows, saing he had done this & that, for some of them, he had spente so much, & so much, amongst them, and they were now weary of him, and did not help him, having need. Another gave his companion all he had, if he died, to help him in his weaknes; he went and got a litle spise & made him a mess of meat once or twise, and because he dyed not so soone as he expected, he went amongst his fellows, & swore the rogue would cousen[52] him, he would see him choaked before he made him any more meate; and yet the pore fellow dyed before morning.

All this while the Indians came skulking about them, and would sometimes show them selves aloofe of, but when any aproached near them, they would rune away. And once they stoale away their tools wher they had been at worke, & were gone to diner. But about the 16. *of March* a certaine Indian came bouldly amongst them, and spoke to them in broken English, which they could well understand, but marvelled at it. At length they understood by discourse with him, that he was not of these parts, but belonged to the eastrene parts, wher some English-ships came to fhish, with whom he was aquainted, & could name sundrie of them by their names, amongst whom he had gott his language. He became proftable to them in aquainting them with many things concerning the state of the cuntry in the east-parts wher he lived, which was afterwards profitable unto them;

---

49. **one:** Which was this author him selfe. [Bradford's note.]
50. **boatson:** Ship's officer (a boatswain) in charge of equipment and the crew.
51. **quarter-maisters:** Ship's officers (quartermasters) responsible for providing quarters, rations, and other supplies.
52. **cousen:** An alternative spelling for *cozen*, meaning to cheat or defraud.

as also of the people hear, of their names, number, & strength; of their situation & distance from this place, and who was cheefe amongst them. His name was *Samaset*;[53] he tould them also of another Indian whos name was *Squanto*,[54] a native of this place, who had been in England & could speake better English then him selfe. Being, after some time of entertainmente & gifts, dismist, a while after he came againe, & 5. more with him, & they brought againe all the tooles that were stolen away before, and made way for the coming of their great Sachem, called *Massasoyt*;[55] who, about 4. *or* 5. *days after*, came with the cheefe of his freinds & other attendance, with the aforesaid *Squanto*. With whom, after frendly entertainment, & some gifts given him, they made a peace with him (which hath now continued this 24. years) in these terms.

1. That neither he nor any of his, should injurie or doe hurte to any of their peopl.

2. That if any of his did any hurte to any of theirs, he should send the offender, that they might punish him.

3. That if any thing were taken away from any of theirs, he should cause it to be restored; and they should doe the like to his.

4. If any did unjustly warr against him, they would aide him; if any did warr against them, he should aide them.

5. He should send to his neighbours confederats, to certifie them of this, that they might not wrong them, but might be likewise comprised in the conditions of peace.

6. That when ther men came to them, they should leave their bows & arrows behind them.

After these things he returned to his place caled *Sowams*, some 40. mile from this place, but *Squanto* contiũed with them, and was their interpreter, and was a spetiall instrument sent of God for their good beyond their expectation. He directed them how to set their corne, wher to take fish, and to procure other comodities, and was also their pilott to bring them to unknowne places for their profitt, and never left them till he dyed. He was a *native of this place*, & scarce any left alive besids him selfe. He was caried away with diverce others by one *Hunt*, a mr. of a ship, who thought to sell them for slaves in Spaine; but he got away for England, and was entertained by a marchante in London, & imployed to New-foundland & other parts, & lastly brought hither into these parts by one Mr. *Dermer*, a gentle-man imployed by Sr. Ferdinando Gorges & others, for discovery, & other designes in these parts. Of whom I shall say some thing, because it is mentioned in a booke set forth Anno: 1622. by the Presidente & Counsell for New-England,[56]

---

53. ***Samaset***: A member of the Abenaki tribe of southeastern Maine, Samaset or Samoset (d. 1653?) had learned English from fishermen. He was the first Indian to make contact with the Pilgrims.

54. ***Squanto***: A Patuxet who traveled to England with Captain John Smith (1580–1631), Squanto was later kidnapped and nearly sold as a slave. During his years away, his entire tribe died of disease; the Pilgrims settled on land the tribe had once occupied.

55. ***Massasoyt***: A chief of the Wampanoag tribe, Massasoyt or Massasoit (1590?–1661) signed a peace treaty with the Pilgrims on March 22, 1621. The treaty was kept until the 1660s, when tensions between the colonists and the Indians erupted into a series of conflicts that culminated in King Philip's War (1675–76).

56. **in a booke . . . New-England**: Page 17. [Bradford's note.] Bradford refers to *A Briefe Relation of the Discovery and Plantation of New England* (1622), published by Sir Fernando Gorges (1566?–1647?), an English promoter of exploration and colonization.

that he made the peace betweene the salvages of these parts & the English; of which this plantation, as it is intimated, had the benefite. But what a peace it was, may apeare by what befell him & his men.

This Mr. Dermer was hear the same year that these people came, as apears by a relation written by him, & given me by a freind, bearing date June 30. Anno: 1620. And they came in November: following, so ther was but 4. months differance. In which relation to his honored freind, he hath these passages of this very place.

> I will first begine (saith he) with that place from whence *Squanto* or *Tisquantem*, was taken away; which in Cap: *Smiths mape*[57] is called *Plimoth*: and I would that Plimoth had the like comodities. I would that the first plantation might hear be seated, if ther come to the number of 50. persons, or upward. Otherwise at Charlton,[58] because ther the savages are lese to be feared. The *Pocanawkits*,[59] which live to the *west* of *Plimoth*, bear an inveterate malice to the English, and are of more streingth then all the savags from thence to Penobscote. Their desire of revenge was occasioned by an English man, who having many of them on bord, made a great slaughter with their murderers[60] & smale shot, when as (they say) they offered no injurie on their parts. Whether they were English or no, it may be douted; yet they beleeve they were, for the Frenche have so possest them; for which cause *Squanto* cañot deney but they would have kiled me when I was at *Namasket*, had he not entreated hard for me. The soyle of the borders of this great bay, may be compared to most of the plantations which I have seene in Virginia. The land is of diverce sorts; for *Patuxite* is a hardy but strong soyle, *Nawsel* & *Saughtughtett* are for the most part a blakish & deep mould, much like that wher groweth the best Tobaco in Virginia. In the botume of that great bay is store of Codd & basse, or mulett, etc.

But above all he comends *Pacanawkite* for the richest soyle, and much open ground fitt for English graine, &c.

> *Massachussets* is about 9. leagues[61] from *Plimoth*, & situate in the mids betweene both, is full of ilands & peninsules very fertill for the most parte.

With sundrie shuch relations which I forbear to transcribe, being now better knowne then they were to him.

He was taken prisoner by the Indeans at *Manamoiak* (a place not farr from hence, now well knowne). He gave them what they demanded for his liberty, but when they had gott what they desired, they kept him still & indevored to kill his men; but he was freed by seasing on some of them, and kept them bound till they gave him a cannows load of corne. Of which, see Purch: lib. 9. fol. 1778.[62] But this was Anno: 1619.

---

57. Cap: ***Smiths mape***: Smith included a map in his *A Description of New England* (1616).
58. **Charlton**: The name on Smith's map of a place near the mouth of the Charles River, in present-day Boston.
59. ***Pocanawkits***: Another name for the Wampanoag.
60. **murderers**: Ship's guns.
61. **leagues**: A league, an early measure of distance, was about three miles.
62. **see Purch . . . 1778**: Samuel Purchas (1577?-1626), an English clergyman, was the author of a four-volume compilation of travel literature, *Haklutus Posthumus, or Purchas His Pilgrims* (1625). Using Latin abbreviations, Bradford refers to volume four, chapter nine, page 1778.

After the writing of the former relation he came to the Ile of *Capawack*[63] (which lyes south of this place in the way to Virginia), and the foresaid *Squanto* with him, wher he going a shore amongst the Indans to trad, as he used to doe, was betrayed & assaulted by them, & *all his men slaine, but one that kept the boat*; but him selfe gott abord very sore wounded, & they had cut of his head upon the cudy[64] of his boat, had not the man reskued him with a sword. And so they got away, & made shift to gett into Virginia, wher he dyed; whether of his wounds or the diseases of the cuntrie, or both togeather, is uncertaine. By all which it may appeare how farr these people were from peace, and with what danger this plantation was begune, save as the powerfull hand of the Lord did protect them. These things were partly the reason why they kept aloofe & were so long before they came to the English. An other reason (as after them selvs made knōw) was how aboute 3. *years before*, a French-ship was cast away at *Cap-Codd*, but the men gott ahore, & saved their lives, and much of their victails, & other goods; but after the Indeans heard of it, they geathered togeather from these parts, and never left watching & dogging them till they got advantage, and *kild them all but* 3. *or* 4. which they kept, & sent from one Sachem to another, to make sporte with, and used them worse then slaves; (of which the foresaid Mr. Dermer redeemed 2. of them;) and they conceived this ship was now come to revenge it.

Also, (as after was made knowne,) before they came to the English to make freindship, they gott all the *Powachs*[65] of the cuntrie, for 3. days togeather, in a horid and divellish maner to curse & execrate them with their cunjurations, which asembly & service they held in a darke & dismale swampe.

But to returne. The spring now approaching, it pleased God the mortalitie begane to cease amongst them, and the sick and lame recovered apace, which put as it were new life into them; though they had borne their sadd affliction with much patience & contentednes, as I thinke any people could doe. But it was the Lord which upheld them, and had beforehand prepared them; many having long borne the yoake, yea from their youth.[66] Many other smaler maters I omite, sundrie of them having been allready published in a Jurnall made by one of the company; and some other passages of jurneys and relations allredy published, to which I referr those that are willing to know them more perticulerly. And being now come to the 25. of March I shall begine the year 1621.

From *Anno: 1621*

They begane now to gather in the small harvest they had, and to fitte up their houses and dwellings against winter, being all well recovered in health & strenght, and had all things in good plenty; for as some were thus imployed in affairs abroad, others were excersised in fishing, aboute codd, & bass, & other fish, of which they tooke good store, of which every family had their portion. All the sōmer ther was no wante. And now begane to come in store of foule, as winter aproached, of which this place did abound

63. **Ile of *Capawack*:** Now called Martha's Vineyard.
64. **cudy:** Now spelled *cuddy*, a small room or compartment on a boat.
65. ***Powachs*:** Medicine men.
66. **borne the yoake . . . youth:** See note 7.

when they came first (but afterward decreased by degrees). And besids water foule, ther was great store of wild Turkies, of which they tooke many, besids venison, &c. Besids they had aboute a peck a meale a weeke to a person, or now since harvest, Indean corne to that proportion. Which made many afterwards write so largly of their plenty hear to their freinds in England, which were not fained, but true reports.

From *Anno Domini: 1632*

Also the people of the plantation begane to grow in their owtward estats, by reason of the flowing of many people into the cuntrie, espetially into the Bay of the Massachusets; by which means corne & catle rose to a great prise, by which many were much inriched, and co͞modities grue plentifull; and yet in other regards this benefite turned to their hurte, and this accession of strength to their weaknes. For now as their stocks increased, and the increse vendible,[67] ther was no longer any holding them togeather, but now they must of necessitie goe to their great lots; they could not other wise keep their katle; and having oxen growne, they must have land for plowing & tillage. And no man now thought he could live, except he had catle and a great deale of ground to keep them; all striving to increase their stocks. By which means they were scatered all over the bay, quickly, and the towne, in which they lived compactly till now, was left very thine, and in a short time allmost desolate. And if this had been all, it had been less, thoug to much; but the church must also be devided, and those that had lived so long togeather in Christian & comfortable fellowship must now part and suffer many divissions. First, those that lived on their lots on the other side of the bay (called Duxberie) they could not long bring their wives & children to the publick worship & church meetings here, but with such burthen, as, growing to some competente number, they sued to be dismissed and become a body of them selves; and so they were dismiste (about this time), though very unwillingly. But to touch this sadd matter, and handle things together that fell out afterward. To prevent any further scatering from this place, and weakning of the same, it was thought best to give out some good farms to spetiall persons, that would promise to live at Plimoth, and lickly to be helpfull to the church or comonewelth, and so tye the lands to Plimoth as farmes for the same; and ther they might keepe their catle & tillage by some servants, and retaine their dwellings here. And so some spetiall lands were granted at a place generall, called Greens Harbor, wher no allotments had been in the former divission, a plase very weell meadowed, and fitt to keep & rear catle, good store. But alass! this remedy proved worse then the disease; for within a few yers those that had thus gott footing ther rente them selves away, partly by force, and partly wearing the rest with importunitie and pleas of necessitie, so as they must either suffer them to goe, or live in continuall opposition and contention. And others still, as they conceived them selves straitened, or to want acco͞modation, break away under one pretence or other, thinking their owne conceived necessitie, and the example of others, a warrente sufficente for them. And this, I fear, will be the ruine of New-England, at least of the churches of God ther, & will provock the Lords displeasure against them.

[1630-50, 1900]

---

67. **vendible:** Saleable.

Plymouth Plantation through a Modern Lens

WHEN WILLIAM BRADFORD and his fellow Pilgrims landed in Plymouth in 1620, they encountered not an uninhabited wilderness but a native population of Wampanoag Indians with long-established communities and culture. In 1600, the estimated population of the Wampanoag in present-day Massachusetts and Rhode Island was twelve thousand. Living in about forty villages on the mainland

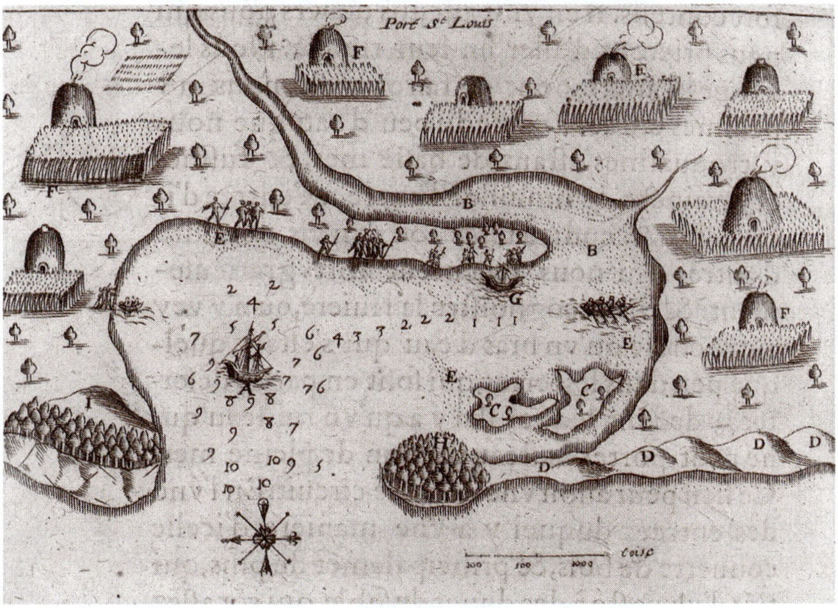

Plymouth before the Pilgrims

Based on a sketch made when Samuel de Champlain visited what he named Port St. Louis in 1605, this engraving was published in his *Voyages* in 1613, three years before Captain John Smith published a map in which he named the harbor and surrounding area Plymouth. As Champlain's sketch reveals, the location was the home of a group of Wampanoag, or "Eastern People," who cultivated corn and other crops and lived in beehive-shaped "wigwams." The Pilgrims adopted their agricultural practices and initially built similar dwellings, but they soon began to construct "proper" English houses.

and coastal islands, the Wampanoag were hunters and farmers who maintained small but highly productive fields in which they cultivated maize, squash, pumpkins, and beans. By 1620, the population of the tribe had been reduced by nearly one-half by a series of epidemic diseases spread from white hunters and fur traders from Canada. The arrival of the Pilgrims meant exposure to new diseases and further encroachment on native lands; in recent years, historians have provided much more accurate accounts of the ways in which European settlers appropriated food and land from the Indians with little or no regard for the civilizations they displaced.

The holiday of Thanksgiving has received particular attention from Native Americans seeking to provide other perspectives on the European settlement of North America. In 1970, when the state of Massachusetts made plans for a celebration of the 350th anniversary of the Pilgrims' landing at Plymouth, a Wampanoag elder named Wamsutta (Frank B.) James was invited to give one of the speeches. After reading the speech in advance, state officials refused to allow James to present it. Native American activists responded by making Thanksgiving a national day of mourning. Every year since then, Native Americans have consequently gathered at Plymouth Rock on Thanksgiving Day to protest the genocide of the native peoples of North America. In November 2004, Moonanum James, the son of Wamsutta James and co-leader of the United American Indians of New England, explained in an interview: "We are not anti-Thanksgiving. Every day is a day of thanksgiving for our people. We give thanks that we are still living on the land that was stolen from us. But we are against the myths and romanticized notions of Thanksgiving."

Wamsutta (Frank B.) James

[1923–2001]

Suppressed Speech on the 350th Anniversary of the Pilgrims' Landing at Plymouth Rock, September 10, 1970

I speak to you as a man – a Wampanoag Man.[1] I am a proud man, proud of my ancestry, my accomplishments won by a strict parental direction ("You must succeed – your face is a different color in this small Cape Cod community!"). I am a product of poverty and discrimination from these two social and economic diseases. I, and my brothers and sisters, have painfully overcome, and to some extent we have earned the respect of our community. We are Indians first – but we are termed "good citizens." Sometimes we are arrogant but only because society has pressured us to be so.

It is with mixed emotion that I stand here to share my thoughts. This is a time of celebration for you – celebrating an anniversary of a beginning for the white man in America. A time of looking back, of reflection. It is with a heavy heart that I look back upon what happened to my People.

Even before the Pilgrims landed it was common practice for explorers to capture Indians, take them to Europe and sell them as slaves for 220 shillings[2] apiece. The Pilgrims had hardly explored the shores of Cape Cod for four days before they had robbed the graves of my ancestors and stolen their corn and beans. *Mourt's Relation*[3] describes a searching party of sixteen men. Mourt goes on to say that this party took as much of the Indians' winter provisions as they were able to carry.

Massasoit, the great Sachem of the Wampanoag, knew these facts, yet he and his People welcomed and befriended the settlers of the Plymouth Plantation. Perhaps he did this because his Tribe had been depleted by an epidemic. Or his

1. **Wampanoag Man:** A descendant of the tribe that occupied a large section of what is now southeastern Massachusetts and southern Rhode Island, including the coastal islands, at the time of the Pilgrims' landing in 1620.
2. **shillings:** Formerly British coins, each worth one-twentieth of the British pound sterling.
3. ***Mourt's Relation*:** Common name for *A Relation or Journall . . . of the English Plantation Settled at Plimoth in New England*, an account of the first year of the colony published in England in 1622.

knowledge of the harsh oncoming winter was the reason for his peaceful acceptance of these acts. This action by Massasoit was perhaps our biggest mistake. We, the Wampanoag, welcomed you, the white man, with open arms, little knowing that it was the beginning of the end; that before fifty years were to pass, the Wampanoag would no longer be a free people.

What happened in those short fifty years? What has happened in the last three hundred years? History gives us facts and there were atrocities; there were broken promises – and most of these centered around land ownership. Among ourselves we understood that there were boundaries, but never before had we had to deal with fences and stone walls. But the white man had a need to prove his worth by the amount of land that he owned. Only ten years later, when the Puritans came, they treated the Wampanoag with even less kindness in converting the souls of the so-called "savages." Although the Puritans were harsh to members of their own society, the Indian was pressed between stone slabs and hanged as quickly as any other "witch."

And so down through the years there is record after record of Indian lands taken and, in token, reservations set up for him upon which to live. The Indian, having been stripped of his power, could only stand by and watch while the white man took his land and used it for his personal gain. This the Indian could not understand; for to him, land was survival, to farm, to hunt, to be enjoyed. It was not to be abused. We see incident after incident, where the white man sought to tame the "savage" and convert him to the Christian ways of life. The early Pilgrim settlers led the Indian to believe that if he did not behave, they would dig up the ground and unleash the great epidemic again.

The white man used the Indian's nautical skills and abilities. They let him be only a seaman – but never a captain. Time and time again, in the white man's society, we Indians have been termed "low man on the totem pole."

Has the Wampanoag really disappeared? There is still an aura of mystery. We know there was an epidemic that took many Indian lives – some Wampanoags moved west and joined the Cherokee and Cheyenne. They were forced to move. Some even went north to Canada! Many Wampanoag put aside their Indian heritage and accepted the white man's way for their own survival. There are some Wampanoag who do not wish it known they are Indian for social or economic reasons.

What happened to those Wampanoags who chose to remain and live among the early settlers? What kind of existence did they live as "civilized" people? True, living was not as complex as life today, but they dealt with the confusion and the change. Honesty, trust, concern, pride, and politics wove themselves in and out of their daily living. Hence, he was termed crafty, cunning, rapacious, and dirty.

History wants us to believe that the Indian was a savage, illiterate, uncivilized animal. A history that was written by an organized, disciplined people, to expose us as an unorganized and undisciplined entity. Two distinctly different cultures met. One thought they must control life; the other believed life was to be enjoyed, because nature decreed it. Let us remember, the Indian is and was just as human as the white man. The Indian feels pain, gets hurt, and becomes defensive, has dreams, bears tragedy and failure, suffers from loneliness, needs to cry as well as laugh. He, too, is often misunderstood.

The white man in the presence of the Indian is still mystified by his uncanny ability to make him feel uncomfortable. This may be the image the white man has created of the Indian; his "savageness" has boomeranged and isn't a mystery; it is fear; fear of the Indian's temperament!

High on a hill, overlooking the famed Plymouth Rock, stands the statue of our great Sachem, Massasoit. Massasoit has stood there many years in silence. We the descendants of this great Sachem have been a silent people. The necessity of making a living in this materialistic society of the white man caused us to be silent. Today, I and many of my people are choosing to face the truth. We are Indians!

Although time has drained our culture, and our language is almost extinct, we the Wampanoags still walk the lands of Massachusetts. We may be fragmented, we may be confused. Many years have passed since we have been a people together. Our lands were invaded. We fought as hard to keep our land as you the whites did to take our land away from us. We were conquered, we became the American prisoners of war in many cases, and wards of the United States Government, until only recently.

Our spirit refuses to die. Yesterday we walked the woodland paths and sandy trails. Today we must walk the macadam[4] highways and roads. We are uniting. We're standing not in our wigwams but in your concrete tent. We stand tall and proud, and before too many moons pass we'll right the wrongs we have allowed to happen to us.

We forfeited our country. Our lands have fallen into the hands of the aggressor. We have allowed the white man to keep us on our knees. What has happened

---

4. **macadam:** Broken stone bound with tar and compacted in order to form a smooth road surface.

cannot be changed, but today we must work towards a more humane America, a more Indian America, where men and nature once again are important; where the Indian values of honor, truth, and brotherhood prevail.

You the white man are celebrating an anniversary. We the Wampanoags will help you celebrate in the concept of a beginning. It was the beginning of a new life for the Pilgrims. Now, 350 years later it is a beginning of a new determination for the original American: the American Indian.

There are some factors concerning the Wampanoags and other Indians across this vast nation. We now have 350 years of experience living amongst the white man. We can now speak his language. We can now think as a white man thinks. We can now compete with him for the top jobs. We're being heard; we are now being listened to. The important point is that along with these necessities of everyday living, we still have the spirit, we still have the unique culture, we still have the will and, most important of all, the determination to remain as Indians. We are determined, and our presence here this evening is living testimony that this is only the beginning of the American Indian, particularly the Wampanoag, to regain the position in this country that is rightfully ours.

[1970]

John Winthrop

[1588-1649]

John Winthrop was born on January 22, 1588, to Adam and Anne Browne Winthrop, wealthy landowners near Groton, in Suffolk County, England. The only son in a privileged, upper-class family, Winthrop was well educated by private tutors and spent two years at Cambridge University. But he was unhappy and unpopular there, partly because his piety and newly formed Puritan beliefs alienated him from other students. Returning to Groton before receiving a degree, Winthrop in 1605 married Mary Forth, with whom he had six children. After she died in 1615, Winthrop married Thomasine Clopton, who died in childbirth before they had been married a year. In 1618, he married his third wife, Margaret Tyndal, by all accounts a remarkable woman to whom Winthrop was deeply devoted and happily married until her death in 1647. In addition to becoming the stepmother to his surviving children, she bore eight children, four of whom survived infancy. From the time he left Cambridge, Winthrop was trained to take over management of the family's ancestral estate. He also studied law to gain skills that would aid him after he succeeded his father as lord of the manor at Groton. During the 1620s, however, Puritans faced growing pressure and persecution in England. Despairing of the future there, Winthrop believed that "God will bring some heavye Affliction upon this lande," as he warned in "Arguments for the Plantation of New England," a tract published in 1629. Winthrop therefore joined with other like-minded investors to form the Massachusetts Bay Company, a trading company designed to establish a colony in New England based on Puritan religious principles.

Anonymous, *John Winthrop* (c. 1640)

This anonymous portrait, painted around 1640, suggests Winthrop's dignity and authority. The fact that his portrait was painted, as well as his elaborate neck ruff, also indicate the wealth and social status of the first governor of the Massachusetts Bay Colony.

Winthrop devoted the remaining twenty years of his life to the interests and welfare of the Massachusetts Bay Colony. Elected as governor in October 1629, Winthrop, his wife and children, and seven hundred other colonists sailed for New England in a fleet of eleven ships in the spring and summer of 1630. Either immediately before or during the voyage, he wrote and delivered "A Modell of Christian Charity," an address in which Winthrop affirmed the religious principles and social ideals of the new colony. He also began a journal that he would keep for the rest of his life, a crucial account of the founding of the colony later published and now best known as *The History of New England from 1630 to 1649*. Certainly, he was in a strong position to provide that account, since Winthrop was elected more than a dozen times as governor or deputy governor of the Massachusetts Bay Colony. He was consequently also at the center of debates over the proper balance between the authority of the governors and the liberties of the governed. Winthrop was firmly committed to the concept of centralized authority, both civil and religious, which he believed was established by the will of God, and he was sometimes accused of overstepping the bounds of his own authority. At the same time, Winthrop remained equally committed to the vision of a harmonious, selfless community he had envisaged in "A Modell of Christian Charity." Indeed, his social idealism and skillful political leadership were crucial to the initial survival and early success of the Massachusetts Bay Colony. Winthrop died in Boston, the city he helped found, on March 26, 1649.

bedfordstmartins.com/ americanlit *for research links on Winthrop*

Winthrop's "A Modell of Christian Charity." It was long thought that Winthrop delivered his famous address to the assembled passengers aboard the *Arabella*, the flagship of the fleet that sailed to North America in 1630 to found the Massachusetts Bay Colony. But recent scholarship indicates that he may have delivered it in the port of Southampton on the eve of the Puritans' departure from England. As governor of their new colony, Winthrop carefully laid out the religious and social principles that would form the foundation of the Puritan commonwealth, which would be based on the letter and spirit of the Bible. He thus offered an outline of the "covenant," or agreement, the Puritans had entered into with their God, who they believed had given them a divine commission to establish a colony dedicated to his worship and governed by his word. Indeed, the contractual language and precise style of the address clearly reveal Winthrop's training as a lawyer. But the address served other ends as well. Speaking to those who were leaving the comforts and security of their homes in England for the hardships and uncertainty of life in New England, Winthrop sought to articulate the larger meaning and broader significance of their errand into the "wilderness" of the New World. Woven throughout his address are frequent allusions to the Bible, especially to the Old Testament accounts of the journey of the Israelites out of bondage in Egypt to the promised land, a drama that was being reenacted by God's new chosen people, the Puritans. The original manuscript of "A Modell of Christian Charity" is lost, but a copy of the address was discovered among Winthrop's papers by one of his descendants and first published by the Massachusetts Historical Society in 1838. The following text of the address, which retains the original capitalization, punctuation, and spelling, is taken from the standard edition published in *Old South Leaflets*, Number 217, edited by Samuel E. Morison (1916).

A MODELL OF CHRISTIAN CHARITY

Christian Charitie

I.

A MODELL HEREOF

God Almightie in his most holy and wise providence, hath soe disposed of the Condition of mankinde, as in all times some must be rich, some poore, some highe and eminent in power and dignitie; others meane and in subjection.

THE REASON HEREOF

First, to hold conformity with the rest of his workes, being delighted to shewe forthe the glory of his wisdome in the variety and difference of the Creatures; and the glory of his power, in ordering all these differences for the preservation and good of the whole; and the glory of his greatnes, that as it is the glory of princes to have many officers, soe this great King will have many Stewards, counting himselfe more honoured in dispenceing his guifts to man by man, then if hee did it by his owne immediate hands.

Secondly, That he might have the more occasion to manifest the work of his Spirit: first upon the wicked in moderateing and restraineing them, soe that the riche and mighty should not eate upp the poore, nor the poore and dispised rise upp against their superiours and shake off theire yoake; 2ly in the regenerate, in exerciseing his graces in them, as in the greate ones, theire love, mercy, gentlenes, temperance etc.; in the poore and inferior sorte, theire faithe patience, obedience etc.

Thirdly, that every man might have need of other, and from hence they might be all knitt more nearly together in the Bonds of brotherly affection. From hence it appeares plainely that noe man is made more honourable than another or more wealthy etc., out of any perticuler and singuler respect to himselfe, but for the glory of his Creator and the common good of the Creature, Man. Therefore God still reserves the propperty of these gifts to himself as [in] Ezekiel: 16. 17. He there calls wealthe his gold and his silver.[1] [In] Proverbs: 3. 9. he claims theire service as his due, honor the Lord with thy riches etc.[2] All men being thus (by divine providence) ranked into two sortes, riche and poore;

---

1. **He there calls . . . silver:** "Thou hast also taken thy fair jewels of my gold and of my silver, which I had given thee, and madest to thyself images of men, and didst commit whoredom with them" (Ezekiel 16:17). Winthrop probably used the Geneva Bible, a translation by William Whittingham, the brother-in-law of John Calvin, which went through over 140 editions between 1566 and 1640. This English translation was popular with the Puritans for what many saw as its Calvinist leanings and anti-Catholic stance, especially in the marginal notes that accompanied many texts. James I, king of England, disapproved of the Geneva Bible and commissioned the King James Version of the Bible, published in 1611. With the exception of the marginal notes, however, the two versions were very similar. Biblical quotations in the notes here are taken from the King James Version, which eventually superseded the Geneva Bible.

2. **he claims . . . with thy riches etc.:** "Honour the LORD with thy substance, and with the first fruits of all thine increase: So shall thy barns be filled with plenty, and thy presses shall burst out with new wine" (Proverbs 3:9-10).

under the first are comprehended all such as are able to live comfortably by theire owne meanes duely improved; and all others are poore according to the former distribution.

There are two rules whereby wee are to walke one towards another: JUSTICE and MERCY. These are allwayes distinguished in theire Act and in their object, yet may they both concurre in the same subject in eache respect; as sometimes there may be an occasion of shewing mercy to a rich man in some sudden danger of distresse, and alsoe doeing of meere justice to a poor man in regard of some perticuler contract, etc.

There is likewise a double Lawe by which wee are regulated in our conversation one towardes another in both the former respects: the lawe of nature and the lawe of grace, or the morrall lawe or the lawe of the gospell, to omitt the rule of justice as not propperly belonging to this purpose otherwise then it may fall into consideration in some perticuler Cases. By the first of these lawes man as he was enabled soe withall [is] commanded to love his neighbour as himself.[3] Upon this ground stands all the precepts of the morrall lawe, which concernes our dealings with men. To apply this to the works of mercy, this lawe requires two things. First, that every man afford his help to another in every want or distresse. Secondly, that hee performed this out of the same affection which makes him carefull of his owne goods, according to that of our Savior. Matthew: "Whatsoever ye would that men should doe to you."[4] This was practised by Abraham and Lott in entertaining the Angells and the old man of Gibea.[5]

The lawe of Grace or the Gospell hath some differance from the former, as in these respects. First the lawe of nature was given to man in the estate of innocency; this of the gospell in the estate of regeneracy.[6] 2ly, the former propounds one man to another, as the same flesh and image of god; this as a brother in Christ allsoe, and in the Communion of the same spirit and soe teacheth us to put a difference betweene Christians and others. *Doe good to all, especially to the houshold of faith;* upon this ground the Israelites were to putt a difference betweene the brethren of such as were strangers though not of Canaanites.[7] 3ly. The Lawe of nature could give noe rules for dealing with enemies, for all are to be considered as friends in the state of innocency, but the Gospell commands love to an enemy. Proofe. If thine Enemie hunger, feed him; Love your Enemies, doe good to them that hate you. Matthew: 5. 44.

This lawe of the Gospell propoundes likewise a difference of seasons and occasions. There is a time when a christian must sell all and give to the poore, as they did in the

3. **commanded . . . as himself:** "Thou shalt love thy neighbour as thyself" (Matthew 19:19).
4. **"Whatsoever . . . you":** "Therefore all things whatsoever ye would that men should do to you, do ye even so to them: for this is the law and the prophets" (Matthew 7:12).
5. **This was practised . . . Gibea:** Winthrop's examples of selfless help to others include Abraham's welcome of three angels (Genesis 18:1–2); Abraham's nephew Lot's defense of two angels against a mob (Genesis 19:1–14); and an old man of Gibea who offered shelter to a stranger (Judges 19:16–21).
6. **in the estate of regeneracy:** Winthrop develops a central set of Puritan beliefs: that human beings were innocent when they were first created and living in the Garden of Eden; that after Adam and Eve sinned they were cast out of the garden and human beings thereafter lived in an unregenerate state; and that the sacrifice of Jesus Christ offered the possibility of regeneracy and salvation to those who believe.
7. **Canaanites:** Canaan was the promised land of the Israelites.

Apostles times.[8] There is a time allsoe when a christian (though they give not all yet) must give beyond their abillity, as they of Macedonia, Corinthians: 2, 6. Likewise community of perills calls for extraordinary liberality, and soe doth community in some speciall service for the Churche. Lastly, when there is noe other meanes whereby our Christian brother may be relieved in his distresse, wee must help him beyond our ability, rather then tempt God in putting him upon help by miraculous or extraordinary meanes.

This duty of mercy is exercised in the kinds, *Giveing, lending* and *forgiving.* –

Quest. What rule shall a man observe in giveing in respect of the measure?

Ans. If the time and occasion be ordinary he is to give out of his abundance. Let him lay aside as God hath blessed him. If the time and occasion be extraordinary, he must be ruled by them; taking this withall, that then a man cannot likely doe too much, especially if he may leave himselfe and his family under probable meanes of comfortable subsistence.

Objection. A man must lay upp for posterity, the fathers lay upp for posterity and children and he "is worse than an infidell" that "provideth not for his owne."

Ans. For the first, it is plaine that it being spoken by way of Comparison, it must be meant of the ordinary and usuall course of fathers and cannot extend to times and occasions extraordinary. For the other place, the Apostle speakes against such as walked inordinately, and it is without question, that he is worse then an Infidell who throughe his owne sloathe and voluptuousnes shall neglect to provide for his family.

Objection. "The wise mans Eies are in his head" saith Salomon, "and foreseeth the plague;"[9] therefore wee must forecast and lay upp against evill times when hee or his may stand in need of all he can gather.

Ans. This very Argument Salomon useth to persuade to liberallity, Ecclesiastes: "Cast thy bread upon the waters," and "for thou knowest not what evill may come upon the land."[10] Luke 16: "Make you friends of the riches of iniquity;"[11] you will ask how this shall be? very well. For first he that gives to the poore, lends to the lord and he will repay him even in this life an hundred fold to him or his – The righteous is ever mercifull and lendeth and his seed enjoyeth the blessing; and besides wee know what advantage

8. **Apostles times**: "Now when Jesus heard these things, he said unto him, 'Yet lackest thou one thing: sell all that thou hast, and distribute unto the poor, and thou shalt have treasure in heaven: and come, follow me'" (Luke 18:22).

9. **"The wise . . . plague"**: "The wise man's eyes are in his head; but the fool walketh in darkness" (Ecclesiastes 2:14). Salomon, a variant of Solomon, (c. 970–930 BCE) was the son of David and king of Israel, renowned for his wisdom.

10. **"Cast . . . land"**: "Cast thy bread upon the waters: for thou shalt find it after many days. Give a portion to seven, and also to eight; for thou knowest not what evil shall be upon the earth" (Ecclesiastes 11:1–2).

11. **"Make . . . iniquity"**: In Luke's account, Christ gives numerous examples of the responsibilities of discipleship, including his parable of the dishonest steward who reduces by half the bills of debtors to his master so that the steward will be welcome in their homes: "'And I say unto you, Make to yourselves friends of the mammon of unrighteousness; that, when ye fail, they may receive you into everlasting habitations'" (Luke 16:9).

it will be to us in the day of account when many such witnesses shall stand forth for Us to witnesse the improvement of our Tallent.[12] And I would knowe of those whoe pleade soe much for laying up for time to come, whether they hold that to be Gospell, Matthew 6. 19. "Lay not upp for yourselves Treasures upon Earth," etc.[13] If they acknowledge it, what extent will they allowe it? if onely to those primitive times, lett them consider the reason whereopon our Saviour groundes it. The first is that they are subject to the moathe, the rust, the Theife. Secondly, They will steale away the hearte; where the treasure is there will the heart be allsoe. The reasons are of like force at all times. Therefore the exhortation must be generall and perpetuall, with allwayes in respect of the love and affection to riches and in regard of the things themselves when any speciall service for the churche or perticuler Distresse of our brother Doe call for the use of them; otherwise it is not onely lawfull but necessary to lay upp as Joseph did[14] to have ready uppon such occasions, as the Lord (whose stewards wee are of them) shall call for them from us. Christ gives us an Instance of the first, when hee sent his disciples for the Ass, and bidds them answer the owner thus, the Lord hath need of him.[15] Soe when the Tabernacle was to be builte he sends to his people to call for their silver and gold, etc.; and yeildes them noe other reason but that it was for his worke. When Elisha comes to the widow of Sareptah and findes her prepareing to make ready her pittance for herselfe and family, he bids her first provide for him, he challengeth first god's parte which shee must first give before shee must serve her owne family.[16] All these teache us that the Lord lookes that when hee is pleased to call for his right in any thing wee have, our owne Interest wee have must stand aside till his turne be served. For the other, wee need looke noe further then to that of John I: "He whoe hath this worlds goodes and seeth his brother to neede and shutts upp his compassion from him, how dwelleth the love of God in him," which comes punctually to this Conclusion: if thy brother be in want and thou canst help him, thou needst not make doubt, what thou shouldst doe, if thou lovest God thou must help him.

Quest. What rule must wee observe in lending?

Ans. Thou must observe whether thy brother hath present or probable, or possible means of repayeing thee, if ther be none of these, thou must give him according to his necessity, rather then lend him as he requires. If he hath present meanes of repayeing thee, thou art to looke at him not as an Act of mercy, but by way of Commerce, wherein thou arte to walk by the rule of Justice; but if his meanes of repayeing thee be onely probable or possible, then is hee an object of thy mercy, thou must lend him, though there be danger of loseing it, Deuteronomy: 15. 7. "If any of thy brethren be poore," etc., "thou

12. **Tallent:** A talent was a unit of currency used by the ancient Greeks and Romans.
13. **"Lay not . . . etc.:** "'Lay not up for yourselves treasures upon earth, where moth and rust doth corrupt, and where thieves break through and steal: But lay up for yourselves treasures in heaven, where neither moth nor rust doth corrupt, and where thieves do not break through nor steal: For where your treasure is, there will your heart be also'" (Matthew 6:19–21).
14. **lay upp as Joseph did:** The son of Jacob and Rachel, Joseph stored food for seven years to prepare for a famine (Genesis 41:46–57).
15. **Christ . . . need of him:** The story is in Matthew 21:1–7.
16. **When Elisha . . . family:** 1 Kings 17:10–24.

shalt lend him sufficient."[17] That men might not shift off this duty by the apparant hazzard, he tells them that though the yeare of Jubile[18] were at hand (when he must remitt it, if hee were not able to repay it before) yet he must lend him and that chearefully: "It may not greive thee to give him" saith hee; and because some might object, "why soe I should soone impovishe myself and my family," he adds "with all thy Worke,"[19] etc; for our Saviour, Matthew: 5. 42. "From him that would borrow of thee turne not away."

Quest. What rule must we observe in forgiveing?

Ans. Whether thou didst lend by way of Commerce or in mercy, if he have noething to pay thee, must forgive, (except in cause where thou hast a surety or a lawfull pleadge) Deuteronomy 15. 2. Every seaventh yeare the Creditor was to quitt that which he lent to his brother if he were poore as appears – ver[se]: 8: "Save when there shall be no poore with thee." In all these and like Cases, Christ was a generall rule, Matthew 7. 22. "Whatsoever ye would that men should doe to you, doe yee the same to them allsoe."

Quest. What rule must wee observe and walke by in cause of Community of perill?

Ans. The same as before, but with more enlargement towards others and lesse respect towards our selves and our owne right. Hence it was that in the primitive Churche they sold all, had all things in Common, neither did any man say that which he possessed was his owne. Likewise in theire returne out of the Captivity, because the worke was greate for the restoreing of the church and the danger of enemies was Common to all, Nehemiah exhortes the Jews to liberallity and readiness in remitting theire debts to theire brethren, and disposing liberally of his owne to such as wanted, and stande not upon his owne due, which hee might have demanded of them.[20] Thus did some of our forefathers in times of persecution in England, and soe did many of the faithful of other Churches, whereof wee keepe an honorable remembrance of them; and it is to be observed that both in Scriptures and latter stories of the churches that such as have beene most bountifull to the poore saintes, especially in these extraordinary times and occasions, God hath left them highly commended to posterity, as Zacheus, Cornelius, Dorcas, Bishop Hooper, the Cuttler of Brussells and divers others.[21] Observe againe that the Scripture gives noe causion to restraine any from being over liberall this way; but all men to the liberall and cherefull practise hereof by the sweetest promises;

---

17. **"If any . . . sufficient":** "'If there be among you a poor man of one of thy brethren within any of thy gates in thy land, which the Lord thy God giveth thee, thou shalt not harden thine heart, nor shut thine hand from thy poor brother: But thou shalt open thine hand wide unto him, and shalt surely lend him sufficient for his need, *in that* which he wanteth'" (Deuteronomy 15:7–8).

18. **yeare of Jubile:** According to Judaic law, every seventh year is a sabbatical year, a period of time devoted wholly to religion, with no work. The Jubilee year is celebrated once every fifty years, at the conclusion of seven sabbatical-year sequences.

19. **"It may not grieve . . . Worke":** "'Beware that there be not a thought in thy wicked heart, saying, "The seventh year, the year of release, is at hand"; and thine eye be evil against thy poor brother, and thou givest him nought; and he cry unto the LORD against thee, and it be sin unto thee. Thou shalt surely give him, and thine heart shall not be grieved when thou givest unto him: because that for this thing the LORD thy God shall bless thee in all thy works, and in all that thou puttest thine hand unto'" (Deuteronomy 15:9–10).

20. **Nehemiah . . . demanded of them:** The Old Testament book of Nehemiah tells the story of the Hebrew leader who introduced religious reforms and supervised the rebuilding of the walls of Jerusalem (c. 444 BCE).

21. **as Zacheus . . . and divers others:** A list of Christian martyrs.

as to instance one for many, Isaiah 58. 6: "Is not this the fast I have chosen to loose the bonds of wickednes, to take off the heavy burdens, to lett the oppressed goe free and to breake every yoake, to deale thy bread to the hungry and to bring the poore that wander into thy house, when thou seest the naked to cover them. And then shall thy light breake forth as the morneing, and thy healthe shall growe speedily, thy righteousness shall goe before god, and the glory of the Lord shall embrace thee; then thou shalt call and the Lord shall Answer thee" etc. [Verse] 10: "If thou power out thy soule to the hungry, then shall thy light spring out in darknes, and the lord shall guide thee continually, and satisfie thy soule in draught, and make fatt thy bones, thou shalt be like a watered Garden, and they shalt be of thee that shall build the old wast places" etc. On the contrary, most heavy cursses are layed upon such as are straightened towards the Lord and his people, Judges 5. [23]: "Cursse ye Meroshe because ye came not to help the Lord," etc. Proverbs [21. 13] "Hee whoe shutteth his eares from hearing the cry of the poore, he shall cry and shall not be heard." Matthew 25: "Goe ye carssed into everlasting fire" etc. "I was hungry and ye fedd mee not." 2 Corinthians 9. 6: "He that soweth spareingly shall reape spareingly."

Haveing already sett forth the practice of mercy according to the rule of god's lawe, it will be usefull to lay open the groundes of it allsoe, being the other parte of the Commandment, and that is the affection from which this exercise of mercy must arise. The Apostle tells us that this love is the fullfilling of the lawe,[22] not that it is enough to love our brother and soe noe further; but in regard of the excellency of his partes giveing any motion to the other as the Soule to the body and the power it hath to sett all the faculties on worke in the outward exercise of this duty. As when wee bid one make the clocke strike, he doth not lay hand on the hammer, which is the immediate instrument of the sound, but setts on worke the first mover or maine wheele, knoweing that will certainely produce the sound which hee intends. Soe the way to drawe men to workes of mercy, is not by force of Argument from the goodnes or necessity of the worke; for though this course may enforce a rationall minde to some present Act of mercy, as is frequent in experience, yet it cannot worke such a habit in a soule, as shall make it prompt upon all occasions to produce the same effect, but by frameing these affections of love in the hearte which will as natively bring forthe the other, as any cause doth produce effect.

The deffinition which the Scripture gives us of love is this: "Love is the bond of perfection."[23] First, it is a bond or ligament. 2ly it makes the worke perfect. There is noe body but consists of partes and that which knitts these partes together, gives the body its perfection, because it makes eache parte soe contiguous to others as thereby they doe mutually participate with each other, both in strengthe and infirmity, in pleasure and paine. To instance in the most perfect of all bodies: Christ and his church make one body. The severall partes of this body, considered aparte before they were united, were

---

22. **The Apostle . . . lawe:** The Apostle Paul wrote, "Love worketh no ill to his neighbour: therefore love is the fulfilling of the law" (Romans 13:10).

23. **"Love is the bond of perfection":** See Colossians 3:14: "And above all these things *put on* charity, which is the bond of perfectness."

as disproportionate and as much disordering as soe many contrary qualities or elements, but when christ comes and by his spirit and love knitts all these partes to himselfe and each to other, it is become the most perfect and best proportioned body in the world. Ephesians 4. 16: "Christ, by whome all the body being knitt together by every joint for the furniture thereof, according to the effectuall power which is in the measure of every perfection of partes," "a glorious body without spott or wrinkle," the ligaments hereof being Christ, or his love, for Christ is love (1 John 4. 8). Soe this definition is right: "Love is the bond of perfection."

From hence we may frame these conclusions. 1. First of all, true Christians are of one body in Christ, 1 Corinthians 12. 12, 27: "Ye are the body of Christ and members of their parte." 2ly. The ligaments of this body which knitt together are love. 3ly. Noe body can be perfect which wants its propper ligament. 4ly. All the partes of this body being thus united are made soe contiguous in a speciall relation as they must needes partake of each other's strength and infirmity; joy and sorrowe, weale and woe. 1 Corinthians: 12. 26: "If one member suffers, all suffer with it, if one be in honor, all rejoyce with it." 5ly. This sensibleness and sympathy of each other's conditions will necessarily infuse into each parte a native desire and endeavour to strengthen, defend, preserve and comfort the other.

To insist a little on this Conclusion being the product of all the former, the truthe hereof will appeare both by precept and patterne. 1 John 3. 10: "Yee ought to lay downe your lives for the brethren." Galatians 6. 2: "beare ye one another's burthens and soe fulfill the lawe of Christ." For patterns wee have that first of our Saviour whoe out of his good will in obedience to his father, becomeing a parte of this body, and being knitt with it in the bond of love, found such a native sensiblenes of our infirmities and sorrowes as hee willingly yielded himselfe to deathe to ease the infirmities of the rest of his body, and soe heald theire sorrowes. From the like sympathy of partes did the Apostles and many thousands of the Saintes lay downe theire lives for Christ. Againe, the like wee may see in the members of this body among themselves. Romans 9. Paule could have beene contented to have beene separated from Christ, that the Jewes might not be cutt off from the body. It is very observable what hee professeth of his affectionate partaking with every member: "whoe is weake" saith hee "and I am not weake? whoe is offended and I burne not;"[24] and againe, 2 Corinthians: 7. 13. "therefore wee are comforted because yee were comforted." Of Epaphroditus he speaketh, Philippians 2. 30. that he regarded not his owne life to do him service.[25] Soe Phebe and others are called the servants of the churche.[26] Now it is apparent that they served not for wages, or by constrainte, but out of love. The like wee shall finde in the histories of the churche in all ages, the sweete svmpathie of affections which was in the members of this body one towardes another, theire chearfullness in serveing and suffering together, how liberall

24. **"whoe is weake . . . and I burne not"**: 2 Corinthians 11:19.
25. **Of Epaphroditus . . . service**: In his letter to the Philippians, written from a Roman prison, Paul tells them that he is sending Epaphroditus to serve as their minister in his absence (Philippians 2:25-30).
26. **Soe Phebe . . . churche**: "I commend unto you Phebe our sister, which is a servant of the church which is at Cenchrea" (Romans 16:1).

they were without repineing; harbourers without grudgeing and helpfull without reproaching; and all from hence, because they had fervent love amongst them, which onely make the practise of mercy constant and easie.

The next consideration is how this love comes to be wrought. Adam in his first estate was a perfect modell of mankinde in all their generations, and in him this love was perfected in regard of the habit. But Adam rent himselfe from his Creator, rent all his posterity allsoe one from another; whence it comes that every man is borne with this principle in him, to love and seeke himselfe onely, and thus a man continueth till Christ comes and takes possession of the soule and infuseth another principle, love to God and our brother. And this latter haveing continuall supply from Christ, as the head and roote by which he is united, gets the predomineing in the soule, soe by little and little expells the former. 1 John 4. 7. "love cometh of god and every one that loveth is borne of god," soe that this love is the fruite of the new birthe, and none can have it but the new Creature. Now when this quallity is thus formed in the soules of men, it workes like the Spirit upon the drie bones. Ezekiel 37: "bone came to bone." It gathers together the scattered bones, or perfect old man Adam, and knitts them into one body againe in Christ, whereby a man is become againe a living soule.

The third Consideration is concerning the exercise of this love which is twofold, inward or outward. The outward hath beene handled in the former preface of this discourse. For unfolding the other wee must take in our way that maxime of philosophy *Simile simili gaudet*, or like will to like; for as it is things which are turned with disaffection to eache other, the ground of it is from a dissimilitude ariseing from the contrary or different nature of the things themselves; for the ground of love is an apprehension of some resemblance in things loved to that which affects it. This is the cause why the Lord loves the creature, soe farre as it hathe any of his Image in it; he loves his elect because they are like himselfe, he beholds them in his beloved sonne. Soe a mother loves her childe, because shee throughly conceives a resemblance of herselfe in it. Thus it is betweene the members of Christ. Eache discernes, by the worke of the Spirit, his owne Image and resemblance in another, and therefore cannot but love him as he loves himself. Now when the soule, which is of a sociable nature, findes any thing like to it selfe, it is like Adam when Eve was brought to him. She must have it one with herselfe. This is flesh of my flesh (saith the soule) and bone of my bone. Shee conceives a greate delighte in it, therefore shee desires neareness and familiarity with it. Shee hath a greate propensity to doe it good and receives such content in it, as fearing the miscarriage of her beloved, shee bestowes it in the inmost closett of her heart. Shee will not endure that it shall want any good which shee can give it. If by occasion shee be withdrawne from the company of it, shee is still looking towardes the place where shee left her beloved. If shee hearde it groane, shee is with it presently. If shee finde it sadd and disconsolate, shee sighes and moanes with it. Shee hath noe such joy as to see her beloved merry and thriving. If shee see it wronged, shee canot heare it without passion. Shee setts noe boundes to her affections, nor hath any thought of reward. Shee findes recompense enough in the exercise of her love towardes it. Wee may see this Acted to life in Jonathan and David.[27] Jonathan a valiant man endued with the spirit of Christ, soe

27. **Jonathan and David:** The account is in 1 Samuel 19-20.

soone as he discovers the same spirit in David had presently his hearte knitt to him by this linement of love, soe that it is said he loved him as his owne soule. He takes soe great pleasure in him, that hee stripps himselfe to adorne his beloved. His fathers kingdome was not soe precious to him as his beloved David. David shall have it with all his hearte, himself desires noe more but that hee may be neare to him to rejoyce in his good. Hee chooseth to converse with him in the wildernesse even to the hazzard of his owne life, rather then with the greate Courtiers in his fathers Pallace. When hee sees danger towards him, hee spares neither rare paines nor perill to direct it. When Injury was offered his beloved David, hee would not beare it, though from his owne father; and when they must parte for a season onely, they thought theire heartes would have broake for sorrowe, had not theire affections found vent by aboundance of teares. Other instances might be brought to showe the nature of this affection, as of Ruthe and Naomi,[28] and many others; but this truthe is cleared enough.

If any shall object that it is not possible that love should be bred or upheld without hope of requitall, it is graunted; but that is not our cause; for this love is allwayes under reward. It never gives, but it allwayes receives with advantage; first, in regard that among the members of the same body, love and affection are reciprocall in a most equall and sweete kinde of Commerce. 2ly, in regard of the pleasure and content that the exercise of love carries with it, as wee may see in the naturall body. The mouth is at all the paines to receive and mince the foode which serves for the nourishment of all the other partes of the body, yet it hath noe cause to complaine; for first the other partes send backe by severall passages a due proportion of the same nourishment, in a better forme for the strengthening and comforting the mouthe. 2ly the labour of the mouthe is accompanied vith such pleasure and content as farre exceedes the paines it takes. Soe is it in all the labour of love among christians. The partie loving, reapes love againe, as was showed before, which the soule covetts more then all the wealthe in the world. 3ly. Nothing yeildes more pleasure and content to the soule then when it findes that which it may love fervently, for to love and live beloved is the soules paradise, both here and in heaven. In the State of Wedlock there be many comfortes to beare out the troubles of that Condition; but let such as have tryed the most, say if there be any sweetnes in that Condition comparable to the exercise of mutuall love.

From former Considerations arise these Conclusions.

1. First, This love among Christians is a reall thing, not Imaginarie.

2ly. This love is as absolutely necessary to the being of the body of Christ, as the sinews and other ligaments of a naturall body are to the being of that body.

3ly. This love is a divine, spirituall nature free, active, strong, couragious, permanent; under valueing all things beneathe its propper object; and of all the graces, this makes us nearer to resemble the virtues of our heavenly father.

---

28. **Ruthe and Naomi:** After the death of her husband and her two sons, Ruth entreats her daughters-in-law, Orpah and Naomi, to return to their own people, where they will be better off, and to their own gods. Orpah reluctantly does so, but Naomi insists on staying with Ruth, saying: "'whither thou goest, I will go; and where thou lodgest, I will lodge: thy people *shall* be my people, and thy God my God'" (Ruth 1:1-22).

4thly It rests in the love and welfare of its beloved. For the full and certaine knowledge of these truthes concerning the nature, use, and excellency of this grace, that which the holy ghost hath left recorded, 1 Corinthians 13, may give full satisfaction, which is needful for every true member of this lovely body of the Lord Jesus, to worke upon theire heartes by prayer, meditation, continuall exercise at least of the speciall [influence] of this grace, till Christ be formed in them and they in him, all in eache other, knitt together by this bond of love.

II.

It rests now to make some application of this discourse by the present designe, which gave the occasion of writeing of it. Herein are 4 things to be propounded: first the persons, 2ly the worke, 3ly the end, 4thly the meanes.

1. For the persons. Wee are a Company professing our selves fellow members of Christ, in which respect onely though wee were absent from each other many miles, and had our imployments as farre distant, yet wee ought to account ourselves knitt together by this bond of love, and live in the excercise of it, if wee would have comforte of our being in Christ. This was notorious in the practise of the Christians in former times; as is testified of the Waldenses,[29] from the mouth of one of the adversaries *Æneas sylvius*[30] "mutuo [ament] penè antequam norunt," they use to love any of theire owne religion even before they were acquainted with them.

2nly for the worke wee have in hand. It is by a mutuall consent, through a speciall overvaluing providence and a more then an ordinary approbation of the Churches of Christ, to seeke out a place of Cohabitation and Consorteshipp under a due forme of Government both civill and ecclesiasticall. In such cases as this, the care of the publique must oversway all private respects, by which, not only conscience, but meare civill pollicy, dothe binde us. For it is a true rule that particular Estates cannott subsist in the ruine of the publique.

3ly The end is to improve our lives to doe more service to the Lord; the comforte and encrease of the body of Christe whereof wee are members; that ourselves and posterity may be the better preserved from the Common corruptions of this evill world, to serve the Lord and worke out our Salvation under the power and purity of his holy ordinances.

4ly for the meanes whereby this must bee effected. They are 2fold, a Conformity with the worke and end wee aime at. These wee see are extraordinary, therefore wee must not content our selves with usuall ordinary meanes. Whatsoever wee did or ought to have done when wee lived in England, the same must wee doe, and more allsoe, where wee goe. That which the most in theire Churches mainetaine as a truthe in profession onely, wee must bring into familiar and constant practise, as in this duty of love. Wee must love brotherly without dissimulation; wee must love one another with a pure hearte fervently. Wee must beare one anothers burthens. We must not looke onely on our owne

---

29. **Waldenses:** Members of a twelfth-century Protestant group organized by a French religious reformer, Peter Valdes.

30. ***Æneas Sylvius:*** Aeneas Sylvius Piccolomini (1405–1464) became Pope Pius II in 1458.

things, but allsoe on the things of our brethren, neither must wee thinke that the lord will beare with such faileings at our hands as hee dothe from those among whome wee have lived; and that for 3 Reasons.

1. In regard of the more neare bond of marriage betweene him and us, wherein hee hath taken us to be his after a most strickt and peculiar manner, which will make him the more Jealous of our love and obedience. Soe he tells the people of Israell, you onely have I knowne of all the families of the Earthe, therefore will I punishe you for your Transgressions. 2ly, because the lord will be sanctified in them that come neare him. Wee know that there were many that corrupted the service of the Lord, some setting upp Altars before his owne, others offering both strange fire and strange Sacrifices allsoe; yet there came noe fire from heaven or other sudden judgement upon them, as did upon Nadab and Abihu,[31] whoe yet wee may thinke did not sinne presumptuously. 3ly When God gives a speciall commission he lookes to have it strickly observed in every Article. When hee gave Saule a Commission to destroy Amaleck, Hee indented with him upon certaine Articles, and because hee failed in one of the least, and that upon a faire pretence, it lost him the kingdome which should have beene his reward if hee had observed his Commission.[32]

Thus stands the cause betweene God and us. We are entered into Covenant with him for this worke.[33] Wee have taken out a Commission, the Lord hath given us leave to drawe our own Articles. Wee have professed to enterprise these Actions, upon these and those ends, wee have hereupon besought him of favour and blessing. Now if the Lord shall please to heare us, and bring us in peace to the place wee desire, then hath hee ratified this Covenant and sealed our Commission, [and] will expect a strict performance of the Articles contained in it; but if wee shall neglect the observation of these Articles which are the ends wee have propounded, and, dissembling with our God, shall fall to embrace this present world and prosecute our carnall intentions, seekeing greate things for our selves and our posterity, the Lord will surely breake out in wrathe against us; be revenged of such a perjured people and make us knowe the price of the breache of such a covenant.

Now the onely way to avoyde this shipwracke, and to provide for our posterity, is to followe the counsell of Micah,[34] to doe justly, to love mercy, to walke humbly with our

---

31. **Nadab and Abihu:** See Leviticus 10:1–2: "And Nadab and Abihu, the sons of Aaron, took either of them his censer, and put fire therein, and put incense thereon, and offered strange fire before the Lord, which he commanded them not. And there went out fire from the Lord, and devoured them, and they died before the Lord."

32. **When hee gave Saule . . . Commission:** The story of Saul's failure to follow God's command is found in 1 Samuel 15:1–34.

33. **Covenant with him for this worke:** A covenant is a legal agreement or contract. The Puritans believed that the covenant promises of the Old Testament did not simply apply to ancient Israel but to any society that followed God's laws and commands.

34. **counsell of Micah:** The Old Testament prophet Micah called upon Israel to repent its sins, warning of the wrath of God and the destruction of Jerusalem. But he also prophesied the glorious future of the city as the center of pure worship: "And many nations shall come, and say, 'Come, and let us go up to the mountain of the LORD, and to the house of the God of Jacob; and he will teach us his ways, and we will walk in his paths': for the law shall go forth of Zion, and the word of God from Jerusalem" (Micah 4:2).

God. For this end, wee must be knitt together in this work as one man. Wee must entertaine each other in brotherly Affection, wee must be willing to abridge our selves of our superfluities, for the supply of others necessities. Wee must uphold a familiar Commerce together in all meekenes, gentlenes, patience and liberality. Wee must delight in eache other, make other's conditions our owne, rejoyce together, mourne together, labour and suffer together, allwayes haveing before our eyes our Commission and Community in the worke, our Community as members of the same body. Soe shall wee keepe the unitie of the spirit in the bond of peace. The Lord will be our God, and delight to dwell among Us as his owne people, and will command a blessing upon us in all our wayes, soe that wee shall see much more of his wisdome, power, goodnes and truthe, then formerly wee have been acquainted with. Wee shall finde that the God of Israell is among us, when tenn of us shall be able to resist a thousand of our enemies; when hee shall make us a prayse and glory that men shall say of succeeding plantations, "the lord make it like that of NEW ENGLAND." For wee must Consider that wee shall be as a Citty upon a hill.[35] The eies of all people are uppon Us, soe that if wee shall deale falsely with our god in this worke wee have undertaken, and soe cause him to withdrawe his present help from us, wee shall be made a story and a by-word through the world. Wee shall open the mouthes of enemies to speake evill of the wayes of god, and all professours for God's sake. Wee shall shame the faces of many of god's worthy servants, and cause theire prayers to be turned into Cursses upon us till wee be consumed out of the good land whither wee are a goeing.

And to shutt upp this discourse with that exhortation of Moses, that faithfull servant of the Lord, in his last farewell to Israell, Deuteronomy 30. Beloved, there is now sett before us life and good, Death and evill, in that wee are Commanded this day to love the Lord our God, and to love one another, to walke in his wayes and to keepe his Commandements and his Ordinance and his lawes, and the articles of our Covenant with him, that wee may live and be multiplied, and that the Lord our God may blesse us in the land whither wee goe to possesse it. But if our heartes shall turne away, soe that wee will not obey, but shall be seduced, and worshipp other Gods, our pleasures and proffitts, and serve them; it is propounded unto us this day, wee shall surely perishe out of the good Land whither wee passe over this vast sea to possesse it.

> Therefore lett us choose life,
> that wee and our seede
> may live by obeyeing his
> voyce and cleaveing to him,
> for hee is our life and
> our prosperity.

[1630, 1916]

---

35. **a Citty upon a hill:** See Matthew 5:14: "'Ye are the light of the world. A city that is set on an hill cannot be hid.'"

Anne Bradstreet

[c. 1612-1672]

Anne Bradstreet was born in Northampton, England, probably in 1612, the second child of Dorothy Yorke and Thomas Dudley, an estate manager of a wealthy Puritan landowner, the Earl of Lincoln. Given access to the earl's extensive library, Bradstreet was encouraged to read and write by her father, who occasionally wrote poetry. Bradstreet also received an education beyond that of most young girls of her day. Although little is known about the details of her training, the numerous allusions in her later poems indicate that she had read widely – not simply in the Bible and religious works, but also in history, literature, and natural science. In 1628, when she was about sixteen, she married Simon Bradstreet (1603-1697), a Puritan associate of her father and a graduate of Cambridge University. After Simon Bradstreet and her father became involved with the Massachusetts Bay Company, the young couple and her parents sailed to North America in 1630 aboard the *Arabella*, the flagship of the Puritan migration led by John Winthrop.

To have written poems, the first good poems in America, while rearing eight children, lying frequently sick, keeping house at the edge of wilderness, was to have managed a poet's range and extension within confines as severe as any American poet has confronted.

-Adrienne Rich

The stormy seventy-six-day voyage and the primitive conditions in New England took a physical and psychological toll on the emigrants, many of whom had lived a life of comfort and relative luxury in England. Lady Arabella Johnson, after whom the *Arabella* was named, died a few weeks after their arrival; her husband, Isaac Johnson, the wealthiest and one of the most revered of the Puritans, succumbed to disease only a few months later, before he was thirty years old. Although she was frail and often ill, Bradstreet survived the initial hardships, as well as the births of eight children, a frequent cause of death for women in the seventeenth century. Her life in the colony was made all the more difficult by the family's frequent moves – from the first primitive settlement in Charlestown to Cambridge to the more distant Ipswich and finally, in 1647, to the even more isolated village of Andover – as well as by the public duties of her beloved husband, Simon. An able and highly regarded administrator, Simon Bradstreet was often away from home on the business of the colony, for which he served as a magistrate and later as governor.

Although little is known about why or exactly when Bradstreet began to write poetry, many scholars believe that she initially composed her poems primarily as a diversion from the rigors and tedium of colonial life. Bradstreet apparently had no idea of publishing her poems, which were written for her own enjoyment and circulated only among her admiring family and friends. Probably without her knowledge, her brother-in-law, the Reverend John Woodbridge, took Bradstreet's manuscript with him to England, where it was published in 1650 as *The Tenth Muse Lately Sprung up in America*. Bradstreet's name did not appear on the title page of the volume, whose author was simply identified as "a Gentlewoman in those parts." In fact, it was the first book of poetry published by any person – man or woman – living in the English colonies in North America. When Bradstreet learned of its publication, she began to work on a second edition, in which she planned to correct errors, revise earlier poems, and add some of her later work. Publication of that volume was evidently considered in 1666, when Bradstreet is thought to have written a poetic prologue to the new edition, "The Author to Her Book." But the volume was not published, and Bradstreet continued to write poems, including some verses on the devastating fire that destroyed her house in Andover in 1666. Having spent most of her sixty years struggling to make a home for herself and her family in the "wilderness" of New England, Bradstreet died six years later, in 1672.

By then, she had produced one of the most important bodies of poetry written by a colonist in seventeenth-century America. Although writing was not considered an appropriate activity for a woman in colonial America, Bradstreet was well known as a poet in her own day and her fellow colonists were clearly proud of her achievement. A second edition of her poetry was published in Boston as *Several Poems Compiled with Great*

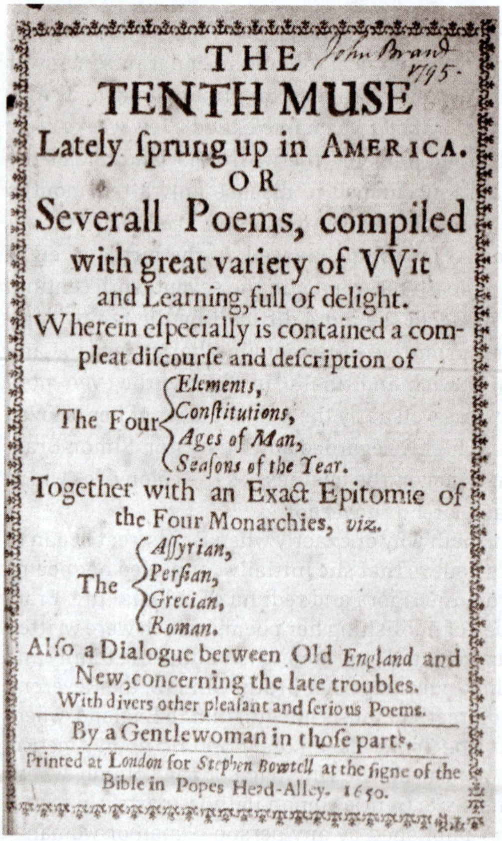
THE TENTH MUSE
Lately ſprung up in AMERICA.
OR
Severall Poems, compiled with great variety of VVit and Learning, full of delight.
Wherein eſpecially is contained a compleat diſcourſe and deſcription of
The Four { *Elements, Conſtitutions, Ages of Man, Seaſons of the Year.*
Together with an Exact Epitomie of the Four Monarchies, *viz.*
The { *Aſſyrian, Perſian, Grecian, Roman.*
Alſo a Dialogue between Old *England* and New, concerning the late troubles.
With divers other pleaſant and ſerious Poems.
By a Gentlewoman in thoſe parts.
Printed at *London* for *Stephen Bowtell* at the ſigne of the Bible in Popes Head-Alley. 1650.

Title Page of Anne Bradstreet's *The Tenth Muse* (1650)

Variety of Wit and Learning in 1678. In his *Magnalia Christi Americana* (1702), the Puritan clergyman and historian Cotton Mather commemorated her as "Ann Bradstreet, the Daughter of our Governour Dudley, and the Consort of our Governour Bradstreet, whose Poems, divers times Printed, have afforded a grateful Entertainment unto the Ingenious, and a Monument for her Memory beyond the Stateliest *Marbles*."

bedfordstmartins.com/ americanlit *for research links on Bradstreet*

Bradstreet's Poetry. When he oversaw the publication in London of *The Tenth Muse Lately Sprung up in America* (1650), Bradstreet's brother-in-law John Woodbridge wrote a preface to the volume in which he anticipated that some readers might

> question whether it be a woman's work, and ask, is it possible? If any do, take this as an answer from him that dares avow it; it is the work of a woman, honored, and esteemed where she lives, for her gracious demeanor, her eminent parts, her pious conversation, her courteous disposition, her exact diligence in her place, and discreet managing of her family occasions, and more than so, these poems are the fruit but of some few hours, curtailed from her sleep and other refreshments.

As Woodbridge's testimonial indicates, and as many scholars have observed, early women writers confronted formidable obstacles. In addition to skepticism about the authenticity of their work, women faced questions about the propriety of writing at a time when both literature and learning were widely believed to be the provinces of men. Bradstreet was a particularly striking exception to that rule, since *The Tenth Muse* was dominated by a series of ambitious meditative and philosophical poems that revealed not only her artistry but also her wide reading and detailed knowledge of world history, natural science, mythology, and the Bible. The volume also included a number of poems in which Bradstreet implicitly commented on the capacity and role of women, including an epitaph to her mother, Dorothy Dudley, and especially her formal elegy to Elizabeth I, the celebrated queen of England who had died in 1603. Bradstreet's contemporaries highly valued the relatively conventional poems of *The Tenth Muse.* Most modern readers are more drawn to her later work, especially the personal poems in which Bradstreet poignantly describes the difficulties of colonial life for a woman, writing about subjects like her fears of childbirth, the many absences of her husband, and the burning of the Bradstreet home in 1666. Eighteen of her later poems, along with the poetry from *The Tenth Muse,* were published posthumously in Bradstreet's *Several Poems* (1678). But a complete edition of her poetry and prose was not published until 1867, almost two centuries after her death in 1672. The texts of the following poems, which are here arranged according to the dates of their original publication, are taken from *The Works of Anne Bradstreet,* edited by Jeannine Hensley (1967).

THE PROLOGUE

1

To sing of wars, of captains, and of kings,
Of cities founded, commonwealths begun,
For my mean[1] pen are too superior things:
Or how they all, or each their dates have run
Let poets and historians set these forth,
My obscure lines shall not so dim their worth.

2

But when my wond'ring eyes and envious heart
Great Bartas' sugared lines[2] do but read o'er,
Fool I do grudge the Muses[3] did not part
'Twixt him and me that overfluent store;
A Bartas can do what a Bartas will
But simple I according to my skill.

3

From schoolboy's tongue no rhet'ric we expect,
Nor yet a sweet consort[4] from broken strings,
Nor perfect beauty where's a main defect:
My foolish, broken, blemished Muse so sings,
And this to mend, alas, no art is able,
'Cause nature made it so irreparable.

4

Nor can I, like that fluent sweet tongued Greek,[5]
Who lisped at first, in future times speak plain.
By art he gladly found what he did seek,
A full requital of his striving pain.

1. **mean:** Humble or lowly.
2. **Great Bartas' sugared lines:** Guillaume du Bartas (1544–1590), French poet whose epic poems based on the Bible were translated into ornate heroic couplets by the English poet Joshua Sylvester (1563–1618) as *The Divine Weeks of the World's Birth* (1604).
3. **Muses:** The nine goddesses who preside over the arts and sciences in Greek mythology.
4. **consort:** Harmony.
5. **sweet tongued Greek:** Demosthenes, an Athenian orator known for putting stones in his mouth in order to practice precise enunciation.

Art can do much, but this maxim's most sure:
A weak or wounded brain admits no cure.

5

I am obnoxious to each carping tongue
Who says my hand a needle better fits,
A poet's pen all scorn I should thus wrong,
For such despite they cast on female wits:
If what I do prove well, it won't advance,
They'll say it's stol'n, or else it was by chance.

6

But sure the antique Greeks were far more mild
Else of our sex, why feignèd they those nine
And poesy made Calliope's own child;[6]
So 'mongst the rest they placed the arts divine:
But this weak knot they will full soon untie,
The Greeks did nought, but play the fools and lie.

7

Let Greeks be Greeks, and women what they are
Men have precedency and still excel,
It is but vain unjustly to wage war;
Men can do best, and women know it well.
Preeminence in all and each is yours;
Yet grant some small acknowledgement of ours.

8

And oh ye high flown quills[7] that soar the skies,
And ever with your prey still catch your praise,
If e'er you deign these lowly lines your eyes,
Give thyme or parsley wreath, I ask no bays;[8]
This mean and unrefinèd ore of mine
Will make your glist'ring gold but more to shine.

[1650, 1967]

6. **Calliope's own child:** In Greek mythology, Calliope was the Muse of epic poetry.
7. **quills:** Figuratively poets, who wrote with quill pens made from feathers.
8. **bays:** In ancient times, bay or laurel leaves were used to make triumphal crowns for victors.

In Honour of That High and Mighty Princess Queen Elizabeth of Happy Memory[1]

The Proem[2]

Although, great Queen, thou now in silence lie
Yet thy loud herald Fame doth to the sky
Thy wondrous worth proclaim in every clime,
And so hath vowed while there is world or time.
So great's thy glory and thine excellence,
The sound thereof rapts[3] every human sense,
That men account it no impiety,
To say thou wert a fleshly deity.
Thousands bring offerings (though out of date)
Thy world of honours to accumulate;
'Mongst hundred hecatombs[4] of roaring verse,
Mine bleating stands before thy royal herse.
Thou never didst nor canst thou now disdain
T' accept the tribute of a loyal brain.
Thy clemency did erst esteem as much
The acclamations of the poor as rich,
Which makes me deem my rudeness is no wrong,
Though I resound thy praises 'mongst the throng.

The Poem

No Phoenix pen,[5] nor Spenser's poetry,[6]
No Speed's[7] nor Camden's learned history,[8]
Eliza's works wars, praise, can e'er compact,
The world's the theatre where she did act.

---

1. **Queen Elizabeth of Happy Memory:** Elizabeth I was queen of England from 1588 until her death in 1603.
2. **Proem:** Preface or preamble.
3. **rapts:** Enraptures or gives intense pleasure.
4. **hecatombs:** A great number of persons, animals, or things given in sacrifice, taken from the ritual sacrifices of a hundred oxen in ancient Greece and Rome.
5. **Phoenix pen:** *The Phoenix Next* (1593) was a collection of poetry by several writers, probably published in honor of the English poet Sir Philip Sidney (1554–1586), a favorite of Elizabeth I.
6. **Spenser's poetry:** Edmund Spenser (c. 1552–1599) was the author of *The Faerie Queene* (1590, 1596), an allegorical celebration of Elizabeth I and the English people.
7. **Speed's:** John Speed (c. 1552–1629), a historian and mapmaker, published *Historie of Great Britain* (1611) and an atlas, *The Theatre of the Empire of Great Britaine* (1612).
8. **Camden's learned history:** William Camden (1551–1623) wrote *Rerum Anglicarum et Hibernicarum Annales, regnante Elizabetha*, a history of the life of Elizabeth I. An English translation, *The True and Royall History of the famous Empresse Elizabeth, Queene of England France and Ireland & c. True Faith's defendresse of Divine renowne and happy Memory*, appeared in 1625.

No memories nor volumes can contain
The 'leven Olympiads[9] of her happy reign.
Who was so good, so just, so learn'd, so wise,
From all the kings on earth she won the prize.
Nor say I more than duly is her due,
Millions will testify that this is true.
She hath wiped off th' aspersion of her sex,
That women wisdom lack to play the rex.[10]
Spain's monarch, says not so, nor yet his host;
She taught them better manners, to their cost.[11]
The Salic law,[12] in force now had not been,
If France had ever hoped for such a queen.
But can you, doctors, now this point dispute,
She's argument enough to make you mute.
Since first the Sun did run his ne'er run race,
And earth had, once a year, a new old face,
Since time was time, and man unmanly man,
Come show me such a Phoenix if you can.
Was ever people better ruled than hers?
Was ever land more happy freed from stirs?
Did ever wealth in England more abound?
Her victories in foreign coasts resound;
Ships more invincible than Spain's, her foe,
She wracked, she sacked, she sunk his Armado;
Her stately troops advanced to Lisbon's wall,[13]
Don Anthony in's right there to install.
She frankly helped Frank's brave distressed king;
The states united now her fame do sing.
She their protectrix was; they well do know
Unto our dread virago,[14] what they owe.
Her nobles sacrificed their noble blood,
Nor men nor coin she spared to do them good.

9. **The 'leven Olympiads:** In ancient Greece, the Olympics occurred every four years; the reign of Elizabeth I was roughly forty-four years.
10. **rex:** King (Latin).
11. **to their cost:** In one of the military triumphs of Elizabeth I's reign, the English defeated the armada, assembled by Philip II of Spain, in 1588.
12. **Salic law:** A medieval law written by the Salian Franks which prohibited women from succession to the crown.
13. **Lisbon's wall:** Elizabeth I sent Sir Francis Drake (c. 1540-1596) to Lisbon on a failed mission to establish Don Antonio of Crato (1531-1595) as king of Portugal.
14. **virago:** Although the current meaning of the word has the negative connotations of an ill-tempered woman, an early meaning was a woman of strength and spirit, or a warrior.

The rude untamed Irish, she did quell,
Before her picture the proud Tyrone fell.[15]
Had ever prince such counsellors as she?
Herself Minerva caused them so to be.
Such captains and such soldiers never seen,
As were the subjects of our Pallas queen.[16]
Her seamen through all straits the world did round;
Terra incognita[17] might know the sound.
Her Drake came laden home with Spanish gold;[18]
Her Essex took Cadiz, their Herculean hold.[19]
But time would fail me, so my tongue would too,
To tell of half she did, or she could do.
Semiramis[20] to her is but obscure,
More infamy than fame she did procure.
She built her glory but on Babel's walls,[21]
World's wonder for a while, but yet it falls.
Fierce Tomris[22] (Cyrus' headsman) Scythians' queen,
Had put her harness off, had she but seen
Our Amazon in th' Camp of Tilbury,[23]
Judging all valour and all majesty
Within that princess to have residence,
And prostrate yielded to her excellence.

---

15. **the proud Tyrone fell:** The Irish leader Hugh O'Neill, the second Earl of Tyrone (c. 1540–1616), led a failed uprising against the English from 1595 to 1603.
16. **Herself Minerva . . . our Pallas queen:** Pallas, the Greek goddess of wisdom and war, was called Minerva by the Romans.
17. ***Terra incognita*:** Unknown or unexplored land (Latin).
18. **Her Drake . . . Spanish gold:** Sir Francis Drake (c. 1540–1596), an explorer who circumnavigated the globe and brought back a cargo of spices and gold captured from Spanish ships and ports. He was knighted by Elizabeth I upon his return in 1581.
19. **Her Essex . . . their Herculean hold:** An early favorite of Elizabeth I, Robert Devereux, the second Earl of Essex (1566–1601), captured Cádiz, a "Herculean hold" or strongly fortified port in southern Spain in 1596.
20. **Semiramis:** Queen of ancient Assyria who built Babylon and was famed for her beauty, wisdom, and power.
21. **Babel's walls:** In Genesis 11:1–9, the townspeople of Babel attempt to build a tower to reach heaven. God thwarts the plan by causing the languages of the builders to be mutually incomprehensible.
22. **Fierce Tomris:** The queen of the Massagetae, a Sythian tribe, who defeated the forces of Cyrus the Great of Persia in 529 BCE.
23. **Camp of Tilbury:** Before the battle with the Spanish Armada in 1588, Elizabeth I addressed the English troops at their camp at Tilbury, a port in southeastern England. In that famous speech, Elizabeth I told her troops: "I know I have the body of a weak and feeble woman, but I have the heart and stomach of a king, and a king of England too, and think foul scorn that Parma or Spain, or any prince of Europe should dare to invade the borders of my realm; the which, rather than any dishonour shall grow by me, I myself will take up arms, I myself will be your general, judge, and rewarder of every one of your virtues in the field."

Dido,[24] first foundress of proud Carthage walls
(Who living consummates her funerals),
A great Eliza, but compared with ours,
How vanisheth her glory, wealth, and powers.
Profuse, proud Cleopatra, whose wrong name,
Instead of glory, proved her country's shame,[25]
Of her what worth in stories to be seen,
But that she was a rich Egyptian queen.
Zenobya, potent empress of the East,
And of all these without compare the best,
Whom none but great Aurelius could quell;[26]
Yet for our Queen is no fit parallel.
She was a Phoenix queen,[27] so shall she be,
Her ashes not revived, more Phoenix she.
Her personal perfections, who would tell
Must dip his pen in th' Heleconian well,[28]
Which I may not, my pride doth but aspire
To read what others write and so admire.
Now say, have women worth? or have they none?
Or had they some, but with our Queen is't gone?
Nay masculines, you have thus taxed us long,
But she, though dead, will vindicate our wrong.
Let such as say our sex is void of reason,
Know 'tis a slander now but once was treason.
But happy England which had such a queen;
Yea happy, happy, had those days still been.
But happiness lies in a higher sphere,
Then wonder not Eliza moves not here.
Full fraught with honour, riches and with days
She set, she set, like Titan[29] in his rays.

24. **Dido:** The founder and queen of Carthage whose story is told in the *Aeneid*, by the Roman poet Virgil (70–19 BCE). After she is abandoned by Aeneas, Dido commits suicide upon a funeral pyre.

25. **Cleopatra, whose wrong name . . . her country's shame:** *Cleopatra*, the name of the famous queen of Egypt (69–30 BCE), means "glory to the father." Bradstreet suggests that the name is "wrong" because Cleopatra actually brought shame upon her country or fatherland.

26. **Zenobya . . . Aurelius could quell:** Zenobia was a third-century queen of Palmyra, a city on the edge of the Syrian Desert, who led her people in a war against Rome. She was defeated by the emperor Aurelian in 273.

27. **Phoenix queen:** The Phoenix is a mythical bird that burns itself on a funeral pyre and then rises from its own ashes to begin another life cycle.

28. **Heleconian well:** In Greek mythology, the source of poetic inspiration was a spring on Mount Helicon.

29. **Titan in his rays:** Some Roman poets called the sun god *Titan*, derived from the Titans of Greek mythology, divine beings associated with natural phenomena who were defeated by the younger gods led by Zeus.

No more shall rise or set so glorious sun
Until the heaven's great revolution;
If then new things their old forms shall retain,
Eliza shall rule Albion[30] once again.

Her Epitaph

Here sleeps the queen, this is the royal bed
Of th' damask rose, sprung from the white and red,
Whose sweet perfume fills the all-filling air.
This rose is withered, once so lovely fair.
On neither tree did grow such rose before,
The greater was our gain, our loss the more.

Another

Here lies the pride of queens, pattern of kings,
So blaze it, Fame, here's feathers for thy wings.
Here lies the envied, yet unparalleled prince,
Whose living virtues speak (though dead long since).
If many worlds, as that fantastic framed,
In every one be her great glory famed.

[1650, 1967]

30. **Albion:** England (Latin).

AN EPITAPH ON MY DEAR AND EVER-HONOURED MOTHER MRS. DOROTHY DUDLEY, WHO DECEASED DECEMBER 27, 1643, AND OF HER AGE, 61

Here lies,
A worthy matron of unspotted life,
A loving mother and obedient wife,
A friendly neighbor, pitiful to poor,
Whom oft she fed and clothed with her store;
To servants wisely awful,[1] but yet kind,

1. **awful:** Early term for inspiring reverence, wonder, or fear.

And as they did, so they reward did find.
A true instructor of her family,
The which she ordered with dexterity.
The public meetings ever did frequent,
And in her closet[2] constant hours she spent;
Religious in all her words and ways,
Preparing still for death, till end of days:
Of all her children, children lived to see,
Then dying, left a blessed memory.

[1650, 1967]

2. **closet:** Early term for a small, private room used for study or prayer.

TO HER FATHER WITH SOME VERSES

Most truly honoured, and as truly dear,
If worth in me or ought I do appear,
Who can of right better demand the same
Than may your worthy self from whom it came?
The principal[1] might yield a greater sum,
Yet handled ill, amounts but to this crumb;
My stock's[2] so small I know not how to pay,
My bond[3] remains in force unto this day;
Yet for part payment take this simple mite,
Where nothing's to be had, kings loose their right.
Such is my debt I may not say forgive,
But as I can, I'll pay it while I live;
Such is my bond, none can discharge but I,
Yet paying is not paid until I die.

[1678, 1967]

1. **principal:** A sum of money on which interest is paid.
2. **stock's:** *Stock* here refers to money or capital.
3. **bond:** A certificate promising to repay borrowed money at a fixed rate of interest and at a certain time.

The Flesh and the Spirit

In secret place where once I stood
Close by the banks of Lacrim flood,[1]
I heard two sisters reason on
Things that are past and things to come;
One flesh was called, who had her eye
On worldly wealth and vanity;
The other Spirit, who did rear
Her thoughts unto a higher sphere:
Sister, quoth Flesh, what liv'st thou on,
Nothing but meditation?
Doth contemplation feed thee so
Regardlessly to let earth go?
Can speculation satisfy
Notion[2] without reality?
Dost dream of things beyond the moon,
And dost thou hope to dwell there soon?
Hast treasures there laid up in store
That all in th' world thou count'st but poor?
Art fancy sick, or turned a sot[3]
To catch at shadows which are not?
Come, come, I'll show unto thy sense,
Industry hath its recompense.
What canst desire, but thou may'st see
True substance in variety?
Dost honour like? Acquire the same,
As some to their immortal fame,
And trophies[4] to thy name erect
Which wearing time shall ne'er deject.
For riches doth thou long full sore?
Behold enough of precious store.
Earth hath more silver, pearls, and gold,
Than eyes can see or hands can hold.
Affect's thou pleasure Take thy fill,
Earth hath enough of what you will.

---

1. **Lacrim flood:** In Latin, *lacrima* means tear; *lacrimo* means to weep or shed tears.
2. **Notion:** Conception or belief.
3. **sot:** Foolish person.
4. **trophies:** In ancient Greece and Rome, trophies – weapons and other spoils of war – were often arranged for display.

Then let not go, what thou may'st find
For things unknown, only in mind.

Spirit: Be still thou unregenerate part,
Disturb no more my settled heart,
For I have vowed (and so will do)
Thee as a foe still to pursue.
And combat with thee will and must,
Until I see thee laid in th' dust.
Sisters we are, yea, twins we be,
Yet deadly feud 'twixt thee and me;
For from one father are we not,
Thou by old Adam wast begot,
But my arise is from above,
Whence my dear Father I do love.
Thou speak'st me fair, but hat'st me sore,
Thy flatt'ring shows I'll trust no more.
How oft thy slave, hast thou me made,
When I believed what thou hast said,
And never had more cause of woe
Than when I did what thou bad'st do.
I'll stop mine ears at these thy charms,
And count them for my deadly harms.
Thy sinful pleasures I do hate,
Thy riches are to me no bait,
Thine honours do, nor will I love;
For my ambition lies above.
My greatest honour it shall be
When I am victor over thee,
And triumph shall with laurel head,[5]
When thou my captive shalt be led,
How I do live, thou need'st not scoff,
For I have meat thou know'st not of;
The hidden manna[6] I do eat,
The word of life it is my meat.
My thoughts do yield me more content
Than can thy hours in pleasure spent.
Nor are they shadows which I catch,

---

5. **laurel head:** In ancient times, bay or laurel leaves were used to make triumphal crowns for victors.
6. **manna:** The food that was miraculously supplied to the Israelites in the wilderness (Exodus 16:15-16).

Nor fancies vain at which I snatch,
But reach at things that are so high,
Beyond thy dull capacity;
Eternal substance I do see,
With which enriched I would be.
Mine eye doth pierce the heavens and see
What is invisible to thee.
My garments are not silk nor gold,
Nor such like trash which earth doth hold,
But royal robes I shall have on,
More glorious than the glist'ring sun;
My crown not diamonds, pearls, and gold,
But such as angels' heads enfold.
The city[7] where I hope to dwell,
There's none on earth can parallel;
The stately walls both high and strong,
Are made of precious jasper stone;
The gates of pearl, both rich and clear,
And angels are for porters there;
The streets thereof transparent gold,
Such as no eye did e'er behold;
A crystal river there doth run,
Which doth proceed from the Lamb's throne.
Of life, there are the waters sure,
Which shall remain forever pure,
Nor sun, nor moon, they have no need,
For glory doth from God proceed.
No candle there, nor yet torchlight,
For there shall be no darksome night.
From sickness and infirmity
For evermore they shall be free;
Nor withering age shall e'er come there,
But beauty shall be bright and clear;
This city pure is not for thee,
For things unclean there shall not be.
If I of heaven may have my fill,
Take thou the world and all that will.

[1678, 1967]

---

7. **city:** Bradstreet echoes the description of the new Jerusalem in Revelation, chapters 21-22.

THE AUTHOR TO HER BOOK

Thou ill-formed offspring[1] of my feeble brain,
Who after birth didst by my side remain,
Till snatched from thence by friends, less wise than true,
Who thee abroad, exposed to public view,
Made thee in rags, halting to th' press to trudge,
Where errors were not lessened (all may judge).
At thy return my blushing was not small,
My rambling brat (in print) should mother call,
I cast thee by as one unfit for light,
Thy visage was so irksome in my sight;
Yet being mine own, at length affection would
Thy blemishes amend, if so I could:
I washed thy face, but more defects I saw,
And rubbing off a spot still made a flaw.
I stretched thy joints to make thee even feet,[2]
Yet still thou run'st more hobbling than is meet;
In better dress to trim thee was my mind,
But nought save homespun cloth i' th' house I find.
In this array 'mongst vulgars[3] mayst thou roam.
In critic's hands beware thou dost not come,
And take thy way where yet thou art not known;
If for thy father asked, say thou hadst none;
And for thy mother, she alas is poor,
Which caused her thus to send thee out of door.

[1678, 1967]

1. **offspring:** Her poems. Probably without her knowledge, Bradstreet's brother-in-law had arranged for the publication of a volume of her poems as *The Tenth Muse* (1650). She may have written this poem in 1666, when the publication of a second edition of her book was a possibility.
2. **feet:** In prosody, a poetic foot is a group of syllables forming a metrical unit.
3. **vulgars:** Common or ordinary people.

BEFORE THE BIRTH OF ONE OF HER CHILDREN

All things within this fading world hath end,
Adversity doth still our joys attend;
No ties so strong, no friends so dear and sweet,
But with death's parting blow is sure to meet.
The sentence past is most irrevocable,
A common thing, yet oh, inevitable.
How soon, my Dear, death may my steps attend,

How soon't may be thy lot to lose thy friend,
We both are ignorant, yet love bids me
These farewell lines to recommend to thee,
That when that knot's untied that made us one,
I may seem thine, who in effect am none.
And if I see not half my days that's due,
What nature would, God grant to yours and you;
The many faults that well you know I have
Let be interred in my oblivious grave;
If any worth or virtue were in me,
Let that live freshly in thy memory
And when thou feel'st no grief, as I no harms,
Yet love thy dead, who long lay in thine arms.
And when thy loss shall be repaid with gains
Look to my little babes, my dear remains.
And if thou love thyself, or loved'st me,
These O protect from step-dame's injury.[1]
And if chance to thine eyes shall bring this verse,
With some sad sighs honour my absent hearse;
And kiss this paper for thy love's dear sake,
Who with salt tears this last farewell did take.

[1678, 1967]

1. **step-dame's injury:** A stepmother's unkind action.

TO MY DEAR AND LOVING HUSBAND

If ever two were one, then surely we.
If ever man were loved by wife, then thee;
If ever wife was happy in a man,
Compare with me, ye women, if you can.
I prize thy love more than whole mines of gold
Or all the riches that the East doth hold.
My love is such that rivers cannot quench,
Nor ought but love from thee, give recompense.
Thy love is such I can no way repay,
The heavens reward thee manifold,[1] I pray.
Then while we live, in love let's so persevere
That when we live no more, we may live ever.

[1678, 1967]

1. **manifold:** In many and various ways.

A LETTER TO HER HUSBAND, ABSENT UPON PUBLIC EMPLOYMENT

My head, my heart, mine eyes, my life, nay, more,
My joy, my magazine[1] of earthly store,
If two be one, as surely thou and I,
How stayest thou there, whilst I at Ipswich[2] lie?
So many steps, head from the heart to sever,
If but a neck, soon should we be together.
I, like the Earth this season, mourn in black,
My Sun is gone so far in's zodiac,[3]
Whom whilst I 'joyed, nor storms, nor frost I felt,
His warmth such frigid colds did cause to melt.
My chilled limbs now numbed lie forlorn;
Return, return, sweet Sol, from Capricorn;[4]
In this dead time, alas, what can I more
Than view those fruits which through thy heat I bore?
Which sweet contentment yield me for a space,
True living pictures of their father's face.
O strange effect! now thou art southward gone,
I weary grow the tedious day so long;
But when thou northward to me shalt return,
I wish my Sun may never set, but burn
Within the Cancer[5] of my glowing breast,
The welcome house of him my dearest guest.
Where ever, ever stay, and go not thence,
Till nature's sad decree shall call thee hence;
Flesh of thy flesh, bone of thy bone,[6]
I here, thou there, yet both but one.

[1678, 1967]

1. **magazine:** An early term for a storehouse.
2. **Ipswich:** A town north of Boston, Massachusetts, where the Bradstreets lived from 1647 until her death in 1672.
3. **zodiac:** Circuit or circle. In astrology, a belt of the heavens on either side of the path of the sun, which includes all the positions of the sun, moon, and principal planets, divided into twelve equal divisions or signs (Aries, Taurus, etc.).
4. **Return . . . from Capricorn:** *Sol* is the sun, which enters Capricorn, the tenth sign of the zodiac, near the end of December.
5. **Cancer:** The fourth sign of the zodiac, entered by the sun near the end of June.
6. **bone:** See Genesis 2:23: "And Adam said, 'This *is* now bone of my bones, and flesh of my flesh: she shall be called Woman, because she was taken out of Man.'"

Here Follows Some Verses upon the Burning of Our House July 10th, 1666. Copied Out of a Loose Paper

In silent night when rest I took
For sorrow near I did not look
I wakened was with thund'ring noise
And piteous shrieks of dreadful voice.
That fearful sound of "Fire!" and "Fire!"
Let no man know is my desire.
I, starting up, the light did spy,
And to my God my heart did cry
To strengthen me in my distress
And not to leave me succorless.
Then, coming out, beheld a space
The flame consume my dwelling place.
And when I could no longer look,
I blest His name that gave and took,[1]
That laid my goods now in the dust.
Yea, so it was, and so 'twas just.
It was His own, it was not mine,
Far be it that I should repine;
He might of all justly bereft
But yet sufficient for us left.
When by the ruins oft I past
My sorrowing eyes aside did cast,
And here and there the places spy
Where oft I sat and long did lie:
Here stood that trunk, and there that chest,
There lay that store I counted best.
My pleasant things in ashes lie,
And them behold no more shall I.
Under thy roof no guest shall sit,
Nor at thy table eat a bit.
No pleasant tale shall e'er be told,
Nor things recounted done of old.
No candle e'er shall shine in thee,
Nor bridegroom's voice e'er heard shall be.
In silence ever shall thou lie,

1. **that gave and took:** See Job 1:21: "Naked came I out of my mother's womb, and naked shall I return thither; the Lord gave, and the Lord hath taken away; blessed be the name of the Lord."

Adieu, Adieu, all's vanity.[2]
Then straight I 'gin my heart to chide,
And did thy wealth on earth abide?
Didst fix thy hope on mold'ring dust?
The arm of flesh didst make thy trust?
Raise up thy thoughts above the sky
That dunghill mists away may fly.
Thou hast an house on high erect,
Framed by that mighty Architect,
With glory richly furnished,
Stands permanent though this be fled.
It's purchased and paid for too
By Him who hath enough to do.
A price so vast as is unknown
Yet by His gift is made thine own;
There's wealth enough, I need no more,
Farewell, my pelf,[3] farewell my store.
The world no longer let me love,
My hope and treasure lies above.

[1867, 1972]

2. **all's vanity:** Worthless or futile; see Ecclesiastes 1:2: "Vanity of vanities, saith the Preacher, vanity of vanities; all *is* vanity."
3. **pelf:** Property that is gained in a dishonorable way.

AS WEARY PILGRIM

As weary pilgrim, now at rest,
    Hugs with delight his silent nest,
His wasted limbs now lie full soft
    That mirey[1] steps have trodden oft,
Blesses himself to think upon
    His dangers past, and travails done.
The burning sun no more shall heat,
    Nor stormy rains on him shall beat.
The briars and thorns no more shall scratch,
    Nor hungry wolves at him shall catch.
He erring paths no more shall tread,
    Nor wild fruits eat instead of bread.

1. **mirey:** Bogged down or involved in difficulties.

For waters cold he doth not long
    For thirst no more shall parch his tongue.
No rugged stones his feet shall gall,[2]
    Nor stumps nor rocks cause him to fall.
All cares and fears he bids farewell
    And means in safety now to dwell.
A pilgrim I, on earth perplexed
    With sins, with cares and sorrows vext,
By age and pains brought to decay,
    And my clay house[3] mold'ring away.
Oh, how I long to be at rest
    And soar on high among the blest.
This body shall in silence sleep,
    Mine eyes no more shall ever weep,
No fainting fits shall me assail,
    Nor grinding pains my body frail,
With cares and fears ne'er cumb'red be
    Nor losses know, nor sorrows see.
What though my flesh shall there consume,
    It is the bed Christ did perfume,
And when a few years shall be gone,
    This mortal shall be clothed upon.
A corrupt carcass down it lays,
    A glorious body it shall rise.
In weakness and dishonour sown,
    In power 'tis raised by Christ alone.
Then soul and body shall unite
    And of their Maker have the sight.
Such lasting joys shall there behold
    As ear ne'er heard nor tongue e'er told.
Lord make me ready for that day,
    Then come, dear Bridegroom,[4] come away.

Aug. 31, 1669

[1867, 1967]

2. **gall:** Make sore by rubbing.
3. **clay house:** Poetic term for the human body.
4. **Bridegroom:** Christ, figuratively the soul's bridegroom in its final spiritual union in heaven. See also Matthew 25:6: "And at midnight there was a cry made, Behold, the bridegroom cometh; go ye out to meet him."

Bradstreet through a Modern Lens

ANNE BRADSTREET'S POETRY has been read and admired for three and a half centuries. The seventeenth-century poets Nathaniel Ward, John Rogers, and John Norton all wrote poems in tribute to Bradstreet. Rogers probably compiled the second edition of her work, *Select Poems* (1676), published six years after her death and later reprinted in 1758. Nineteenth-century readers were also familiar with Bradstreet. In his introduction to *The Works of Anne Bradstreet* (1867), John

Anne Bradstreet

Relatively few portraits of women were painted in the colonies during the seventeenth century, and no likeness of Bradstreet was made during her lifetime. Here, she is imagined by the contemporary artist Ladonna Gulley Warwick in her painting *Anne Bradstreet, The Tenth Muse Lately Sprung Up in America.* The artist and her grandson, depicted in the lower right-hand corner of the painting, are descendants of Bradstreet's sister, Mercy.

Harvard Ellis described her poems as "quaint and curious," adding that "they constitute a singular and valuable relic of the earliest literature of the country." Twentieth-century admirers have discovered a far wider range of value and resonance in Bradstreet's life and writings. In the most sustained poetic tribute, *Homage to Mistress Bradstreet* (1948), John Berryman imagined her life as a series of rebellions, initially against the grim conditions in the New World and finally against illness, personal loss, and the onset of old age. Feminist critics have discovered in Bradstreet's poetry a different pattern of resistance, one aligned against the patriarchal structures of Puritan society. Certainly, her work has assumed a central place in the tradition of women's literature, in which Bradstreet is sometimes compared to Emily Dickinson, another poet determined to make time for her work amidst the demands of everyday life. In the following poem, written when she was a college student, Rose Murray imagines the conditions of that life and suggests what writing poetry may have meant to Bradstreet. The text of the poem is taken from the online anthology *The Best Fiction and Poetry from California State University, Northridge*, where Murray published under the name Rose Shade.

Rose Murray

Puritan Woman

I am obnoxious to each carping tongue
Who says my hand a needle better fits.[1]
Anne Bradstreet

There in Massachusetts
We built our "city upon a hill"[2]

---

1. **I am . . . fits:** The epigraph is from stanza five of Bradstreet's "The Prologue," reprinted on page 170.
2. **"city . . . hill":** Along with her parents and her husband, Bradstreet sailed to New England in 1630 aboard the *Arabella*, the flagship of the Puritan migration led by John Winthrop. Either on the eve of its departure from England or during the voyage, Winthrop delivered his address "A Modell of Christian Charity," reprinted on page 155. In it, Winthrop famously declares that the Puritan settlement would "be as a Citty upon a hill," a reference to Matthew 5:14: " 'Ye are the light of the world. A city that is set on an hill cannot be hid.' "

For all the world to see
And find example in –
But that first winter
There was just the land,
Lying before us
Like a vast unfinished garment –
And my cold hands holding needle
Were only female
And busy with the work of babes.
The men would slash and shape the earth,
And style to God's design
The stuff of law and state;
I had small garments of my own
To fashion. So in the chill
Of winter nights by candle –
When the children were in bed –
Why did my hand, shaped only
For the shaft of spinning wheel
Or bar of cradle,
Dare to grasp a pen?
Perhaps it was the bare house,
The wolf's howl, the Indians,
The memory of those months of shifting sea[3] –
And Simon gone away for days;[4]
Perhaps the words, dancing into shape
In neat and airy couplets,[5]
Imposed design on savage vastness
And hemmed up the ragged edge of newness
With thread from across the seas.
So between the cradle
And the oven, with fresh brown
Bread baking and infants babbling,
I wrote, and Simon understood.

[1971]

3. **months of shifting sea:** The stormy voyage of the *Arabella* lasted two and a half months.
4. **Simon gone away for days:** Bradstreet's husband, Simon, was frequently away from home on public business.
5. **couplets:** Many of Bradstreet's poems were written in couplets, units of two rhymed lines of verse.

Mary Rowlandson

[1636?–1711]

Mary Rowlandson was born about 1636 in England, the fifth child of John and Joan White, devout Puritans who moved their family to Massachusetts in 1639. Granted a sixty-acre tract of land near Salem, John White steadily increased his holdings there before seeking additional land by moving his family to Lancaster, about thirty miles west of Boston. In 1656, Mary married the town's minister, Joseph Rowlandson, with whom she had four children, one of whom died in infancy.

Mary Rowlandson would have died in the almost total obscurity reserved for most women of her time had it not been for King Philip's War, the most traumatic event in her life and in the early life of the English colonies in New England. In *Of Plimoth Plantation*, William Bradford describes the peace treaty entered into between the Pilgrims and Massasoit, the great leader of the Wampanoag people. That treaty lasted for more than fifty years, but relations between the Indians and the colonists became increasingly strained. Even as the Indian population declined, primarily as a result of European diseases, immigration into New England steadily increased until 1649, when the triumph of parliamentary forces in the English civil war led to the establishment of a Puritan commonwealth in England. After the collapse of the commonwealth and the restoration of Charles II to the throne in 1660, Anglicanism once again became the official Church of England. As a result, large numbers of Puritans were once again prompted to leave the country to seek greater religious freedom and economic opportunity in New England. During the decade 1660–70, the combined population of Plymouth and the Massachusetts Bay Colony rose from roughly 20,000 to 35,000, and it continued to increase dramatically. Colonial authorities consequently sought to assert greater authority over the Indians, pressuring them to cede increasingly large tracts of land. In a desperate effort to stem the rising tide of English expansion, Massasoit's son, Metacomet – called King Philip by the colonists – finally led a coalition of tribes to war in 1675. The year-long war was fought with unprecedented ferocity on both sides. About 5,000 Indians and as many as half that number of English colonists were killed during the bitter conflict. In terms of the number of casualties relative to the total populations of the combatants, it was the bloodiest war in American history, claiming the lives of roughly 40 percent of the Indians and more than 5 percent of the colonists.

bedfordstmartins.com/ americanlit *for research links on Rowlandson*

Many of the colonists were killed during raids on frontier towns in Massachusetts, as Metacomet sought to reverse the westward advance of the English. In February 1676, a combined force of Narragansett, Nipmuc, and Wampanoag Indians attacked Lancaster, where Mary Rowlandson and her three children were taken captive. Her youngest child soon died, and she was separated from her other children during most of the three months she lived among the Indians. She was finally ransomed and reunited with her husband and children in Boston, from where the family moved to Weathersfield, Connecticut, in 1677. Rowlandson apparently wrote the account of her captivity before her husband died in 1678, but it was not published until 1682. By then, she had married Captain Samuel Talcott of Weathersfield, where Rowlandson lived until her death in 1711, thirty-five years after the events recorded in *The Sovereignty and Goodness of God.*

Rowlandson's *The Sovereignty and Goodness of God.* No copy of the first edition of Rowlandson's narrative has survived, but three additional editions were published in 1682, two of them in Boston and another in London. As the title page of the "corrected and amended" second edition indicates, the full title of the narrative was *The Sovereignty and Goodness of God, Together with the Faithfulness of His Promises Displayed: Being a Narrative of the Captivity and Restoration of Mrs. Mary Rowlandson.* (The London edition, designed to appeal to a more diverse and cosmopolitan

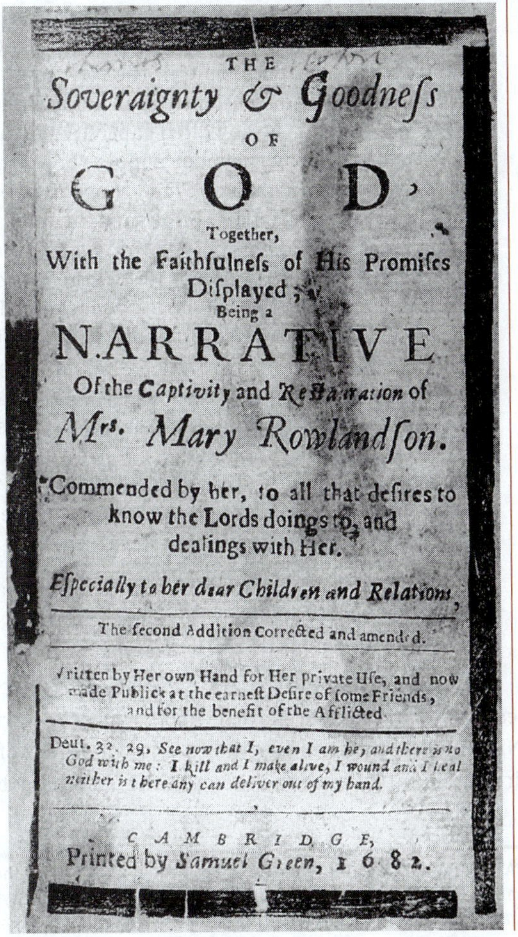
THE
Soveraignty & Goodneſs
OF
GOD,
Together,
With the Faithfulneſs of His Promiſes
Diſplayed;
Being a
NARRATIVE
Of the *Captivity* and *Reſtauration* of
Mrs. Mary Rowlandſon.
Commended by her, to all that deſires to
know the Lords doings to, and
dealings with Her.
Eſpecially to her dear Children and Relations.
The ſecond Addition Corrected and amended.
Written by Her own Hand for Her private Uſe, and now
made Publick at the earneſt Deſire of ſome Friends,
and for the benefit of the Afflicted.
Deut. 32. 29. *See now that I, even I am he, and there is no God with me: I kill and I make alive, I wound and I heal neither is there any can deliver out of my hand.*
CAMBRIDGE,
Printed by *Samuel Green,* 1682.

Frontispiece of the Second Edition of *The Sovereignty and Goodness of God* (1682)

audience, was simply entitled *A True History of the Captivity and Restoration of Mary Rowlandson, A Minister's Wife in New England.*) With the sole exception of Anne Bradstreet's *The Tenth Muse*, which was published in London eighteen years before a second edition of her poetry appeared in Boston in 1678, Rowlandson's account was the first book written by a woman to be published in the English colonies in North America. In an effort to justify what many in New England might have viewed as her immodest usurpation of male prerogative, a note on the title page explains that Rowlandson wrote the account for her "private Use," allowing it to be "made public at the earnest Desire of some Friends, and for the Benefit of the afflicted." Moreover, all of the 1682 editions included an anonymous preface, probably written by the distinguished Puritan minister Increase Mather, which also emphasizes that friends had pressed Rowlandson to allow the work to come into "public view," since it was unfitting that "such works of God should be hid from present and future generations."

Certainly, the narrative proved to have a powerful appeal for both Rowlandson's contemporaries and later generations of readers. The 1682 edition published in Boston sold more than a thousand copies, or roughly one for every hundred people in the New England colonies, where it was both widely read and frequently read aloud. Indeed, as one of the first and most compelling of the so-called captivity narratives, *The Sovereignty and Goodness of God* was the most popular book published in North America in the seventeenth century. Since those first editions of the book, more than forty others have been published, usually as either *A True History of the Captivity and Restoration of Mrs. Mary Rowlandson* or *A Narrative of the Captivity and Restoration of Mrs. Mary Rowlandson.* Although its popularity has waned during the last few decades, Rowlandson's account has become the subject of serious scholarly study. It also continues to engage the attention of readers drawn to the text for other reasons. For example, a new edition recently published as *The Captive* offers Rowlandson's story as an example of faith and endurance "to Christians of the present age." The text printed below is taken from *Narratives of the Indian Wars*, edited by Charles H. Lincoln (1913), which follows the text of the second edition published in 1682, including "The Preface to the Reader."

THE SOVEREIGNTY AND GOODNESS OF GOD

The Preface to the Reader

It was on Tuesday, Feb. 1, 1675,[1] in the afternoon, when the Narrhagansets quarters (in or toward the Nipmug Country, whither they are now retyred for fear of the English Army lying in their own Country) were the second time beaten up, by the Forces of the united

1. **Feb. 1, 1675:** According to the Julian – or Old Style – calendar, in which the year begins on March 25 instead of January 1. Ten days were also added in the Gregorian – or New Style – calendar, which was not adopted in England until 1752, and by which the date was February 11, 1676.

Colonies,[2] who thereupon soon betook themselves to flight, and were all the next day pursued by the English, some overtaken and destroyed. But on Thursday, Feb. 3d, The English having now been six dayes on their march, from their head quarters, at Wickford, in the Narrhaganset Country, toward, and after the Enemy, and provision grown exceeding short, insomuch that they were fain to kill some Horses for the supply, especially of their Indian friends, they were necessitated to consider what was best to be done. And about noon (having hitherto followed the chase as hard as they might) a Councill was called, and though some few were of another mind, yet it was concluded by far the greater part of the Councill of War, that the Army should desist the pursuit, and retire: the Forces of Plimouth and the Bay[3] to the next Town of the Bay, and Connecticut Forces to their own next Towns; which determination was immediately put in execution. The consequent whereof, as it was not difficult to be foreseen by those that knew the causless enmity of these Barbarians, against the English, and the malicious and revengefull spirit of these Heathen: so it soon Proved dismall.

The Narrhagansets were now driven quite from their own Country, and all their provisions there hoarded up, to which they durst not at present return, and being so numerous as they were, soon devoured those to whom they went,[4] whereby both the one and other were now reduced to extream straits, and so necessitated to take the first and best opportunity for supply, and very glad, no doubt, of such an opportunity as this, to provide for themselves, and make spoil of the English at once; and seeing themselves thus discharged of their pursuers, and a little refreshed after their flight, the very next week on Thursday, Feb. 10, they fell with mighty force and fury upon Lancaster: which small Town, remote from aid of others, and not being Garisoned as it might, the Army being now come in, and as the time indeed required (the design of the Indians against that place being known to the English some time before) was not able to make effectual resistance: but notwithstanding utmost endeavour of the Inhabitants, most of the buildings were turned into ashes; many People (Men, Women and Children) slain, and others captivated. The most solemn and remarkable part of this Trajedy, may that justly be reputed, which fell upon the Family of that reverend Servant of God, Mr. Joseph Rolandson, the faithfull Pastor of Christ in that place, who being gone down to the Councill of the Massachusets to seek aid for the defence of the place, at his return found the Town in flames, or smoke, his own house being set on fire by the Enemy, through the disadvantage of a defective Fortification, and all in it consumed: his precious yokefellow, and dear Children, wounded and captivated (as the issue evidenced, and following Narrative declares) by these cruel and barbarous Salvages. A sad Catestrophe! Thus all things come alike to all: None knows either love or hatred by all that is before him. It is no new thing for Gods precious ones to drink as deep as others, of the Cup of common

---

2. **Forces of the united Colonies:** In 1643, the United Colonies of New England were formed to coordinate defense and settle boundary disputes. The league, which included Massachusetts Bay, Plymouth, Connecticut, and New Haven, excluded Maine and Narragansett Bay (Rhode Island) for political and religious reasons.

3. **the Bay:** Short for the Massachusetts Bay Colony.

4. **devoured those to whom they went:** That is, depleted the food supply of the neighboring tribes.

Calamity: Take just Lot[5] (yet captivated) for instance beside others. But it is not my business to dilate on these things, but only in few words introductively to preface to the following script, which is a Narrative of the wonderfully awfull, wise, holy, powerfull, and gracious providence of God, towards that worthy and precious Gentlewoman, the dear Consort of the said Reverend Mr. Rowlandson, and her Children with her, as in casting of her into such a waterless pit, so in preserving, supporting, and carrying thorow so many such extream hazards, unspeakable difficulties and disconsolateness, and at last delivering her out of them all, and her surviving Children also. It was a strange and amazing dispensation, that the Lord should so afflict his precious Servant, and Hand maid. It was as strange, if not more, that he should so bear up the spirits of his Servant under such bereavments and of his handmaid under such captivity, travels and hardships (much too hard for flesh and blood) as he did, and at length deliver and restore. But he was their Saviour, who hath said, *When thou passest through the Waters, I will be with thee, and thorough the Rivers, they shall not overflow thee: When thou walkest through the fire, thou shall not be burnt, nor shall the flame kindle upon thee,* Isaiah 43. ver. 2. and again, *He woundeth and his hands make whole. He shall deliver thee in six troubles, yea in seven there shall no evil touch thee. In Famine he shall redeem thee from Death, and in War from the power of the sword.* Job 5: 18, 19, 20. Methinks this dispensation doth bear some resemblance to those of Joseph, David and Daniel; yea, and of the three Children too,[6] the stories whereof do represent us with the excellent textures of divine Providence, curious pieces of divine work: and truly so doth this, and therefore not to be forgotten, but worthy to be exhibited to, and viewed, and pondered by all, that disdain not to consider the operation of his hands.

The works of the Lord (not only of Creation, but of Providence also, especially those that do more peculiarly concern his dear ones, that are as the Apple of his Eye, as the Signet upon His Hand, the Delight of his Eyes, and the Object of his tenderest Care) [are] great, sought out of all those that have pleasure therein. And of these verily this is none of the least.

This Narrative was penned by the Gentlewoman her self, to be to her a memorandum of Gods dealing with her, that she might never forget, but remember the same, and the severall circumstances thereof, all the dayes of her life. A pious scope which deserves both commendation and imitation. Some friends having obtained a sight of it, could not but be so much affected with the many passages of working providence discovered therein, as to judge it worthy of publick view, and altogether unmeet that such works of God should be hid from present and future Generations: And therefore though this Gentlewomans modesty would not thrust it into the Press, yet her gratitude unto God made her not hardly perswadable to let it pass, that God might have his due glory, and others benefit by it as well as her self. I hope by this time none will cast any reflection upon this Gentlewoman, on the score of this publication of her affliction and deliverance. If any

5. **Take just Lot:** A reference to the account of Lot's captivity in Genesis 14:12-16.
6. **Joseph . . . and of the three Children too:** The heroic stories are in Daniel, chapters 1-6.

should, doubtless they may be reckoned with the nine lepers, of whom it is said, *Were there not ten cleansed, where are the nine?* but one returning to give God thanks.[7] Let such further know that this was a dispensation of publick note, and of universall concernment, and so much the more, by how much the nearer this Gentlewoman stood related to that faithfull Servant of God, whose capacity and employment was publick in the house of God, and his name on that account of a very sweet savour in the Churches of Christ, who is there of a true Christian spirit, that did not look upon himself much concerned in this bereavment, this Captivity in the time thereof, and in his [this] deliverance when it came, yea more then in many others; and how many are there, to whom so concerned, it will doubtless be a very acceptable thing to see the way of God with this Gentlewoman in the aforesaid dispensation, thus laid out and pourtrayed before their eyes.

To conclude: whatever any coy phantasies may deem, yet it highly concerns those that have so deeply tasted, how good the Lord is, to enquire with David, *What shall I render to the Lord for all his benefits to me.* Psalms 116.12. He thinks nothing too great; yea, being sensible of his own disproportion to the due praises of God he calls in help. *Oh, magnifie the Lord with me, let us exalt his Name together,* Psalms 34. 3. And it is but reason, that our praises should hold proportion with our prayers: and that as many hath helped together by prayer for the obtaining of his Mercy, so praises should be returned by many on this behalf; And forasmuch as not the generall but particular knowledge of things makes deepest impression upon the affections, this Narrative particularizing the several passages of this providence will not a little conduce thereunto. And therefore holy David in order to the attainment of that end, accounts himself concerned to declare what God had done for his soul, Psalms 66. 16. *Come and hear, all ye that fear God, and I will declare what God hath done for my soul, i. e.* for his life, see v. 9, 10. *He holdeth our soul in life, and suffers not our feet to be moved, for thou our God hast proved us, thou hast tryed us, as silver is tryed.* Life-mercies, are heart-affecting mercies, of great impression and force, to enlarge pious hearts, in the praises of God, so that such know not how but to talk of Gods acts, and to speak of and publish his wonderfull works. Deep troubles, when the waters come in unto thy soul, are wont to produce vowes: vowes must be paid. It is better not vow, than vow and not to pay.[8] I may say, that as none knows what it is to fight and pursue such an enemy as this, but they that have fought and pursued them: so none can imagine what it is to be captivated, and enslaved to such atheisticall, proud, wild, cruel, barbarous, bruitish (in one word) diabolicall creatures as these, the worst of the heathen; nor what difficulties, hardships, hazards, sorrows, anxieties and perplexities do unavoidably wait upon such a condition, but those that have tryed it. No serious spirit then (especially knowing any thing of this Gentlewomans piety) can imagine but that the vows of God are upon her. Excuse her then if she come thus into publick, to pay those vows, come and hear what she hath to say.

7. **but one returning to give God thanks:** See Luke 17:18–19.

8. **It is better . . . and not to pay:** Ecclesiastes 5:5.

I am confident that no Friend of divine Providence will ever repent his time and pains spent in reading over these sheets, but will judg them worth perusing again and again.

Hear Reader, you may see an instance of the Soveraignty of God, who doth what he will with his own as well as others; and who may say to him, What doest thou?[9] Here you may see an instance of the faith and patience of the Saints, under the most heart-sinking tryals; here you may see, the promises are breasts full of consolation, when all the world besides is empty, and gives nothing but sorrow. That God is indeed the supream Lord of the world, ruling the most unruly, weakening the most cruel and salvage, granting his People mercy in the sight of the unmercifull, curbing the lusts of the most filthy, holding the hands of the violent, delivering the prey from the mighty, and gathering together the out casts of Israel. Once and again you have heard, but hear you may see, that power belongeth unto god; that our God is the God of Salvation, and to him belong the issues from Death. That our God is in the Heavens, and doth whatever pleases him. Here you have Sampson Riddle examplified, and that great promise, Romans 8. 28,[10] verified, *Out of the Eater comes forth meat, and sweetness out of the strong*; The worst of evils working together for the best good. How evident is it that the Lord hath made this Gentlewoman a gainer by all this affliction, that she can say, 'tis good for her yea better that she hath been, then that she should not have been thus afflicted.

Oh how doth God shine forth in such things as these!

Reader, if thou gettest no good by such a Declaration as this, the fault must needs be thine own. Read therefore, Peruse, Ponder, and from hence lay by something from the experience of another against thine own turn comes, that so thou also through patience and consolation of the Scripture mayest have hope.

TER AMICAM[11]

On the tenth of February 1675, Came the Indians with great numbers upon Lancaster:[12] Their first coming was about Sun-rising; hearing the noise of some Guns, we looked out; several Houses were burning, and the Smoke ascending to Heaven. There were five persons taken in one house, the Father, and the Mother and a sucking Child, they knockt on the head; the other two they took and carried away alive. Their were two others, who being out of their Garison upon some occasion were set upon; one was knockt on the head, the other escaped: Another their was who running along was shot and wounded,

9. **What dost thou?**: See Job 9:12.
10. **Sampson Riddle . . . Romans 8. 28**: Samson, who kills a lion and later finds a swarm of bees and honey in the carcass, poses the following riddle to the Philistines: "Out of the eater came forth meat, and out of the strong came forth sweetness" (Judges 14:14). The author of the preface also alludes to the "great promise" conveyed by the apostle Paul in chapter eight of his Epistle to the Romans, "And we know that all things work together for good to them that love God, to them who are called according to *his* purpose."
11. **TER AMICAM**: "Thy three-fold friend" (Latin). This may have been a misprint for *Per Amicum*, "by a friend" (Latin).
12. **On the tenth of February . . . Lancaster**: February 20, 1676; Lancaster, Massachusetts, was then an isolated frontier settlement about thirty miles west of Boston.

and fell down; he begged of them his life, promising them Money (as they told me) but they would not hearken to him but knockt him in head, and stript him naked, and split open his Bowels. Another seeing many of the Indians about his Barn, ventured and went out, but was quickly shot down. There were three others belonging to the same Garison[13] who were killed; the Indians getting up upon the roof of the Barn, had advantage to shoot down upon them over their Fortification. Thus these murtherous wretches went on, burning, and destroying before them.

At length they came and beset our own house, and quickly it was the dolefullest day that ever mine eyes saw. The House stood upon the edg of a hill; some of the Indians got behind the hill, others into the Barn, and others behind any thing that could shelter them; from all which places they shot against the House, so that the Bullets seemed to fly like hail; and quickly they wounded one man among us, then another, and then a third, About two hours (according to my observation, in that amazing time) they had been about the house before they prevailed to fire it (which they did with Flax and Hemp, which they brought out of the Barn, and there being no defence about the House, only two Flankers[14] at two opposite corners and one of them not finished) they fired it once and one ventured out and quenched it, but they quickly fired it again, and that took. Now is the dreadfull hour come, that I have often heard of (in time of War, as it was the case of others) but now mine eyes see it. Some in our house were fighting for their lives, others wallowing in their blood, the House on fire over our heads, and the bloody Heathen ready to knock us on the head, if we stirred out. Now might we hear Mothers and Children crying out for themselves, and one another, Lord, What shall we do? Then I took my Children (and one of my sisters, hers) to go forth and leave the house: but as soon as we came to the dore and appeared, the Indians shot so thick that the bulletts rattled against the House, as if one had taken an handfull of stones and threw them, so that we were fain to give back. We had six stout Dogs belonging to our Garrison, but none of them would stir, though another time, if any Indian had come to the door, they were ready to fly upon him and tear him down. The Lord hereby would make us the more to acknowledge his hand, and to see that our help is always in him. But out we must go, the fire increasing, and coming along behind us, roaring, and the Indians gaping before us with their Guns, Spears and Hatchets to devour us. No sooner were we out of the House, but my Brother in Law (being before wounded, in defending the house, in or near the throat) fell down dead, wherat the Indians scornfully shouted, and hallowed, and were presently upon him, stripping off his cloaths, the bulletts flying thick, one went through my side, and the same (as would seem) through the bowels and hand of my dear Child in my arms. One of my elder Sisters Children, named William, had then his Leg broken, which the Indians perceiving, they knockt him on head. Thus were we butchered by those merciless Heathen, standing amazed, with the blood running down to our heels. My eldest Sister being yet in the House, and seeing those wofull sights, the Infidels haling Mothers one way, and Children another, and some wallowing in their blood: and her elder Son telling her that her Son William was dead, and my self was

13. **Garison:** Building erected for the defense of the settlement.
14. **Flankers:** Projecting fortifications designed to guard a position.

wounded, she said, And, Lord, let me dy with them; which was no sooner said, but she was struck with a Bullet, and fell down dead over the threshold. I hope she is reaping the fruit of her good labours, being faithfull to the service of God in her place. In her younger years she lay under much trouble upon spiritual accounts, till it pleased God to make that precious Scripture take hold of her heart, 2 Corinthians 12. 9. *And he said unto me, my Grace is sufficient for thee.* More then twenty years after I have heard her tell how sweet and comfortable that place was to her. But to return: The Indians laid hold of us, pulling me one way, and the Children another, and said, Come go along with us; I told them they would kill me: they answered, If I were willing to go along with them, they would not hurt me.

Oh the dolefull sight that now was to behold at this House! *Come, behold the works of the Lord, what dissolations he has made in the Earth.*[15] Of thirty seven persons who were in this one House, none escaped either present death, or a bitter captivity, save only one, who might say as he, Job 1. 15, *And I only am escaped alone to tell the News.* There were twelve killed, some shot, some stab'd with their Spears, some knock'd down with their Hatchets. When we are in prosperity, Oh the little that we think of such dreadfull sights, and to see our dear Friends, and Relations ly bleeding out their heart-blood upon the ground. There was one who was chopt into the head with a Hatchet, and stript naked, and yet was crawling up and down. It is a solemn sight to see so many Christians lying in their blood, some here, and some there, like a company of Sheep torn by Wolves, All of them stript naked by a company of hell-hounds, roaring, singing, ranting and insulting, as if they would have torn our very hearts out; yet the Lord by his Almighty power preserved a number of us from death, for there were twenty-four of us taken alive and carried Captive.

I had often before this said, that if the Indians should come, I should chuse rather to be killed by them then taken alive but when it came to the tryal my mind changed; their glittering weapons so daunted my spirit, that I chose rather to go along with those (as I may say) ravenous Beasts, then that moment to end my dayes; and that I may the better declare what happened to me during that grievous Captivity, I shall particularly speak of the severall Removes[16] we had up and down the Wilderness.

The first Remove

Now away we must go with those Barbarous Creatures, with our bodies wounded and bleeding, and our hearts no less than our bodies. About a mile we went that night, up upon a hill within sight of the Town, where they intended to lodge. There was hard by a vacant house (deserted by the English before, for fear of the Indians). I asked them whither I might not lodge in the house that night to which they answered, what will you love English men still? this was the dolefullest night that ever my eyes saw. Oh the roaring, and singing and danceing, and yelling of those black creatures in the night, which

15. ***Come, behold . . . in the Earth***: Psalms 46:8.
16. **Removes**: Changes in location.

made the place a lively resemblance of hell. And as miserable was the wast that was there made, of Horses, Cattle, Sheep, Swine, Calves, Lambs, Roasting Pigs, and Fowl (which they had plundered in the Town) some roasting, some lying and burning, and some boyling to feed our merciless Enemies; who were joyful enough though we were disconsolate. To add to the dolefulness of the former day, and the dismalness of the present night: my thoughts ran upon my losses and sad bereaved condition. All was gone, my Husband gone (at least separated from me, he being in the Bay; and to add to my grief, the Indians told me they would kill him as he came homeward) my Children gone, my Relations and Friends gone, our House and home and all our comforts within door, and without, all was gone, (except my life) and I knew not but the next moment that might go too. There remained nothing to me but one poor wounded Babe, and it seemed at present worse than death that it was in such a pitiful condition, bespeaking Compassion, and I had no refreshing for it, nor suitable things to revive it. Little do many think what is the savageness and bruitishness of this barbarous Enemy, I[17] even those that seem to profess more than others among them, when the English have fallen into their hands.

Those seven that were killed at Lancaster the summer before upon a Sabbath day, and the one that was afterward killed upon a week day, were slain and mangled in a barbarous manner, by one-ey'd John, and Marlborough's Praying Indians,[18] which Capt. Mosely brought to Boston, as the Indians told me.

The second Remove

But now, the next morning, I must turn my back upon the Town, and travel with them into the vast and desolate Wilderness, I knew not whither. It is not my tongue, or pen can express the sorrows of my heart, and bitterness of my spirit, that I had at this departure: but God was with me, in a wonderfull manner, carrying me along, and bearing up my spirit, that it did not quite fail. One of the Indians carried my poor wounded Babe upon a horse, it went moaning all along, I shall dy, I shall dy. I went on foot after it, with sorrow that cannot be exprest. At length I took it off the horse, and carried it in my armes till my strength failed, and I fell down with it: Then they set me upon a horse with my wounded Child in my lap, and there being no furniture upon the horse back, as we were going down a steep hill, we both fell over the horses head, at which they like inhumane creatures laught, and rejoyced to see it, though I thought we should there have ended our dayes, as overcome with so many difficulties. But the Lord renewed my strength still, and carried me along, that I might see more of his Power; yea, so much that I could never have thought of, had I not experienced it.

After this it quickly began to snow, and when night came on, they stopt: and now down I must sit in the snow, by a little fire, and a few boughs behind me, with my sick

17. **I:** Early form of *ay* or *aye*, meaning yes.
18. **Marlborough's Praying Indians:** A group of Christianized Indians who lived in a settlement in Marlborough, Massachusetts, was accused of involvement in the attack on Lancaster, but the charges were disproved in court.

Child in my lap; and calling much for water, being now (through the wound) fallen into a violent Fever. My own wound also growing so stiff, that I could scarce sit down or rise up; yet so it must be, that I must sit all this cold winter night upon the cold snowy ground, with my sick Child in my armes, looking that every hour would be the last of its life; and having no Christian friend near me, either to comfort or help me. Oh, I may see the wonderfull power of God, that my Spirit did not utterly sink under my affliction: still the Lord upheld me with his gracious and mercifull Spirit, and we were both alive to see the light of the next morning.

The third Remove

The morning being come, they prepared to go on their way. One of the Indians got up upon a horse, and they set me up behind him, with my poor sick Babe in my lap. A very wearisome and tedious day I had of it; what with my own wound, and my Childs being so exceeding sick, and in a lamentable condition with her wound. It may be easily judged what a poor feeble condition we were in, there being not the least crumb of refreshing that came within either of our mouths, from Wednesday night to Saturday night, except only a little cold water. This day in the afternoon, about an hour by Sun, we came to the place where they intended, *viz.* an Indian Town, called Wenimesset, Norward of Quabaug. When we were come, Oh the number of Pagans (now merciless enemies) that there came about me, that I may say as David, Psalms 27. 13, *I had fainted, unless I had believed*, etc. The next day was the Sabbath: I then remembered how careless I had been of Gods holy time, how many Sabbaths I had lost and mispent, and how evily I had walked in Gods sight; which lay so close unto my spirit, that it was easie for me to see how righteous it was with God to cut off the thread of my life, and cast me out of his presence for ever. Yet the Lord still shewed mercy to me, and upheld me; and as he wounded me with one hand, so he healed me with the other. This day there came to me one Robbert Pepper (a man belonging to Roxbury) who was taken in Captain Beers his Fight,[19] and had been now a considerable time with the Indians; and up with them almost as far as Albany, to see king Philip, as he told me, and was now very lately come into these parts. Hearing, I say, that I was in this Indian Town, he obtained leave to come and see me. He told me, he himself was wounded in the leg at Captain Beers his Fight; and was not able some time to go, but as they carried him, and as he took Oaken leaves and laid to his wound, and through the blessing of God he was able to travel again. Then I took Oaken leaves and laid to my side, and with the blessing of God it cured me also; yet before the cure was wrought, I may say, as it is in Psalms 38. 5, 6. *My wounds stink and are corrupt, I am troubled, I am bowed down greatly, I go mourning all the day long.* I sat much alone with a poor wounded Child in my lap, which moaned night and day, having nothing to revive the body, or cheer the spirits of her, but in stead of that, sometimes one Indian would come and tell me one hour, that your Master will knock your Child in

---

19. **taken in Captain Beers his Fight:** Captain Beers was killed, along with most of his men, at a battle in Northfield, Massachusetts, in September 1675. Those who were not killed were held in captivity.

the head, and then a second, and then a third, your Master will quickly knock your Child in the head.

This was the comfort I had from them, miserable comforters are ye all, as he said.[20] Thus nine dayes I sat upon my knees, with my Babe in my lap, till my flesh was raw again; my Child being even ready to depart this sorrowfull world, they bade me carry it out to another Wigwam (I suppose because they would not be troubled with such spectacles) Whither I went with a very heavy heart, and down I sat with the picture of death in my lap. About two houres in the night, my sweet Babe like a Lambe departed this life, on Feb. 18, 1675. It being about six yeares, and five months old. It was nine dayes from the first wounding, in this miserable condition, without any refreshing of one nature or other, except a little cold water. I cannot, but take notice, how at another time I could not bear to be in the room where any dead person was, but now the case is changed; I must and could ly down by my dead Babe, side by side all the night after. I have thought since of the wonderfull goodness of God to me, in preserving me in the use of my reason and senses, in that distressed time, that I did not use wicked and violent means to end my own miserable life. In the morning, when they understood that my child was dead they sent for me home to my Masters Wigwam: (by my Master in this writing, must be understood Quanopin, who was a Saggamore, and married King Phillips wives Sister;[21] not that he first took me, but I was sold to him by another Narrhaganset Indian, who took me when first I came out of the Garison). I went to take up my dead child in my arms to carry it with me, but they bid me let it alone: there was no resisting, but goe I must and leave it. When I had been at my masters wigwam, I took the first opportunity I could get, to go look after my dead child: when I came I askt them what they had done with it? then they told me it was upon the hill: then they went and shewed me where it was, where I saw the ground was newly digged, and there they told me they had buried it: There I left that Child in the Wilderness, and must commit it, and my self also in this Wilderness-condition, to him who is above all. God having taken away this dear Child, I went to see my daughter Mary, who was at this same Indian Town, at a Wigwam not very far off, though we had little liberty or opportunity to see one another. She was about ten years old, and taken from the door at first by a Praying Ind and afterward sold for a gun. When I came in sight, she would fall a weeping; at which they were provoked, and would not let me come near her, but bade me be gone; which was a heart-cutting word to me. I had one Child dead, another in the Wilderness, I knew not where, the third they would not let me come near to: *Me* (as he said) *have ye bereaved of my Children, Joseph is not, and Simeon is not, and ye will take Benjamin also, all these things are against me.*[22] I could not sit still in this condition, but kept walking from one place to another. And as I

---

20. **miserable comforters . . . he said:** Job 16:2.

21. **Quanopin . . . married King Phillips wives Sister:** Rowlandson became the servant of Quinnapin's wife Weetamoo, the older daughter of Corbitant, the sachem, or chief, of the Pocasset. Trained to succeed her father as sachem, Weetamoo was an accomplished hunter and a skilled diplomat who first married the sachem of the Wampanoag and, after he died, later married Quinnapin, the sachem of the Narragansett.

22. ***Me . . . against me*:** Jacobs's lamentation for his children is in Genesis 42:16.

was going along, my heart was even overwhelm'd with the thoughts of my condition, and that I should have Children, and a Nation which I knew not ruled over them. Whereupon I earnestly entreated the Lord, that he would consider my low estate, and shew me a token for good, and if it were his blessed will, some sign and hope of some relief. And indeed quickly the Lord answered, in some measure, my poor prayers: for as I was going up and down mourning and lamenting my condition, my Son came to me, and asked me how I did; I had not seen him before, since the destruction of the Town, and I knew not where he was, till I was informed by himself, that he was amongst a smaller percel of Indians, whose place was about six miles off; with tears in his eyes, he asked me whether his Sister Sarah was dead; and told me he had seen his Sister Mary; and prayed me, that I would not be troubled in reference to himself. The occasion of his coming to see me at this time, was this: There was, as I said, about six miles from us, a smal Plantation of Indians, where it seems he had been during his Captivity: and at this time, there were some Forces of the Ind. gathered out of our company, and some also from them (among whom was my Sons master) to go to assault and burn Medfield: In this time of the absence of his master, his dame brought him to see me. I took this to be some gracious answer to my earnest and unfeigned desire. The next day, *viz.* to this, the Indians returned from Medfield,[23] all the company, for those that belonged to the other smal company, came thorough the Town that now we were at. But before they came to us, Oh! the outragious roaring and hooping that there was: They began their din about a mile before they came to us. By their noise and hooping they signified how many they had destroyed (which was at that time twenty three.) Those that were with us at home, were gathered together as soon as they heard the hooping, and every time that the other went over their number, these at home gave a shout, that the very Earth rung again: And thus they continued till those that had been upon the expedition were come up to the Sagamores Wigwam; and then, Oh, the hideous insulting and triumphing that there was over some Englishmens scalps that they had taken (as their manner is) and brought with them. I cannot but take notice of the wonderfull mercy of God to me in those afflictions, in sending me a Bible. One of the Indians that came from Medfield fight, had brought some plunder, came to me, and asked me, if I would have a Bible, he had got one in his Basket. I was glad of it, and asked him, whether he thought the Indians would let me read? he answered, yes: So I took the Bible, and in that melancholy time, it came into my mind to read first the 28. Chap. of Deuteronomy, which I did, and when I had read it, my dark heart wrought on this manner, That there was no mercy for me, that the blessings were gone, and the curses come in their room, and that I had lost my opportunity. But the Lord helped me still to go on reading till I came to Chap. 30 the seven first verses, where I found, There was mercy promised again, if we would return to him by repentance; and though we were scatered from one end of the Earth to the other, yet the Lord would gather us together, and turn all those curses upon our Enemies. I do not desire to live to forget this Scripture, and what comfort it was to me.

---

23. **Medfield:** The attack on Medfield, where fifty houses were burned, took place on February 21, 1675 (March 3, 1676), eleven days after the attack on Lancaster.

Now the Ind. began to talk of removing from this place, some one way, and some another. There were now besides my self nine English Captives in this place (all of them Children, except one Woman). I got an opportunity to go and take my leave of them; they being to go one way, and I another, I asked them whether they were earnest with God for deliverance, they told me, they did as they were able, and it was some comfort to me, that the Lord stirred up Children to look to him. The Woman *viz.* Goodwife Joslin[24] told me, she should never see me again, and that she could find in her heart to run away; I wisht her not to run away by any means, for we were near thirty miles from any English Town, and she very big with Child, and had but one week to reckon; and another Child in her Arms, two years old, and bad Rivers there were to go over, and we were feeble, with our poor and course entertainment. I had my Bible with me, I pulled it out, and asked her whether she would read; we opened the Bible and lighted on Psalms 27, in which Psalm we especially took notice of that, *ver. ult.*,[25] *Wait on the Lord, Be of good courage, and he shall strengthen thine Heart, wait I say on the Lord.*

The fourth Remove

And now I must part with that little Company I had. Here I parted from my Daughter Mary, (whom I never saw again till I saw her in Dorchester, returned from Captivity), and from four little Cousins and Neighbours, some of which I never saw afterward: the Lord only knows the end of them. Amongst them also was that poor Woman before mentioned, who came to a sad end, as some of the company told me in my travel: She having much grief upon her Spirit, about her miserable condition, being so near her time, she would be often asking the Indians to let her go home; they not being willing to that, and yet vexed with her importunity, gathered a great company together about her, and stript her naked, and set her in the midst of them; and when they had sung and danced about her (in their hellish manner) as long as they pleased, they knockt her on head, and the child in her arms with her: when they had done that, they made a fire and put them both into it, and told the other Children that were with them, that if they attempted to go home, they would serve them in like manner: The Children said, she did not shed one tear, but prayed all the while. But to return to my own Journey; we travelled about half a day or little more, and came to a desolate place in the Wilderness, where there were no Wigwams or Inhabitants before; we came about the middle of the afternoon to this place, cold and wet, and snowy, and hungry, and weary, and no refreshing, for man, but the cold ground to sit on, and our poor Indian cheer.

Heart-aking thoughts here I had about my poor Children, who were scattered up and down among the wild beasts of the forrest: My head was light and dissey (either through hunger or hard lodging, or trouble or altogether) my knees feeble, my body raw by sitting double night and day, that I cannot express to man the affliction that lay upon my Spirit,

---

24. ***viz.* Goodwife Joslin:** Abbreviation for *videlicit* (Latin), "in other words"; a goodwife was the mistress of the house.
25. ***ver. ult.*:** Abbreviation for "last verse" (Latin), that is, Psalms 27:14.

but the Lord helped me at that time to express it to himself. I opened my Bible to read, and the Lord brought that precious Scripture to me, Jeremiah 31. 16. *Thus saith the Lord, refrain thy voice from weeping, and thine eyes from tears, for thy work shall be rewarded, and they shall come again from the land of the Enemy.* This was a sweet Cordial to me, when I was ready to faint, many and many a time have I sat down, and weept sweetly over this Scripture. At this place we continued about four dayes.

The fifth Remove

The occasion (as I thought) of their moving at this time, was, the English Army, it being near and following them: For they went, as if they had gone for their lives, for some considerable way, and then they made a stop, and chose some of their stoutest men, and sent them back to hold the English Army in play whilst the rest escaped: And then, like Jehu,[26] they marched on furiously, with their old, and with their young: some carried their old decrepit mothers, some carried one, and some another. Four of them carried a great Indian upon a Bier; but going through a thick Wood with him, they were hindered, and could make no hast; whereupon they took him upon their backs, and carried him, one at a time, till they came to Bacquaug River. Upon a Friday, a little after noon we came to this River. When all the company was come up, and were gathered together, I thought to count the number of them, but they were so many, and being somewhat in motion, it was beyond my skil. In this travel, because of my wound, I was somewhat favoured in my load; I carried only my knitting work and two quarts of parched meal: Being very faint I asked my mistriss to give me one spoonfull of the meal, but she would not give me a taste. They quickly fell to cutting dry trees, to make Rafts to carry them over the river: and soon my turn came to go over: By the advantage of some brush which they had laid upon the Raft to sit upon, I did not wet my foot (which many of themselves at the other end were mid-leg deep) which cannot but be acknowledged as a favour of God to my weakned body, it being a very cold time. I was not before acquainted with such kind of doings or dangers. *When thou passeth through the waters I will be with thee, and through the Rivers they shall not overflow thee,* Isaiah 43. 2. A certain number of us got over the River that night, but it was the night after the Sabbath before all the company was got over. On the Saturday they boyled an old Horses leg which they had got, and so we drank of the broth, as soon as they thought it was ready, and when it was almost all gone, they filled it up again.

The first week of my being among them, I hardly ate any thing; the second week, I found my stomach grow very faint for want of something; and yet it was very hard to get down their filthy trash: but the third week, though I could think how formerly my stomach would turn against this or that, and I could starve and dy before I could eat such things, yet they were sweet and savoury to my taste. I was at this time knitting a pair of white cotton stockins for my mistriss; and had not yet wrought upon a Sabbath day; when the Sabbath came they bade me go to work; I told them it was the Sabbath-day, and

---

26. **Jehu:** King of Israel from 843-816 BCE, whose bloody reign is described in 2 Kings, chapters 9-10.

desired them to let me rest, and told them I would do as much more to morrow; to which they answered me, they would break my face. And here I cannot but take notice of the strange providence of God in preserving the heathen: They were many hundreds, old and young, some sick, and some lame, many had Papooses at their backs, the greatest number at this time with us, were Squaws, and they travelled with all they had, bag and baggage, and yet they got over this River aforesaid; and on Munday they set their Wigwams on fire, and away they went: On that very day came the English Army after them to this River, and saw the smoak of their Wigwams, and yet this River put a stop to them. God did not give them courage or activity to go over after us; we were not ready for so great a mercy as victory and deliverance; if we had been, God would have found out a way for the English to have passed this River, as well as for the Indians with their Squaws and Children, and all their Luggage. *Oh that my People had hearkened to me, and Israel had walked in my ways, I should soon have subdued their Enemies, and turned my hand against their Adversaries*, Psalms 81: 13. 14.

The sixth Remove

On Munday (as I said) they set their Wigwams on fire, and went away. It was a cold morning, and before us there was a great Brook with ice on it; some waded through it, up to the knees and higher, but others went till they came to a Beaver-dam, and I amongst them, where through the good providence of God, I did not wet my foot. I went along that day mourning and lamenting, leaving farther my own Country, and travelling into the vast and howling Wilderness, and I understood something of Lot's Wife's Temptation,[27] when she looked back: we came that day to a great Swamp, by the side of which we took up our lodging that night. When I came to the brow of the hil, that looked toward the Swamp, I thought we had been come to a great Indian Town (though there were none but our own Company). The Indians were as thick as the trees: it seemed as if there had been a thousand Hatchets going at once: if one looked before one, there was nothing but Indians, and behind one, nothing but Indians, and so on either hand, I my self in the midst, and no Christian soul near me, and yet how hath the Lord preserved me in safety? Oh the experience that I have had of the goodness of God, to me and mine!

The seventh Remove

After a restless and hungry night there, we had a wearisome time of it the next day. The Swamp by which we lay, was, as it were, a deep Dungeon, and an exceeding high and steep hill before it. Before I got to the top of the hill, I thought my heart and legs, and all would have broken, and failed me. What through faintness, and soreness of body, it was a grievous day of travel to me. As we went along, I saw a place where English Cattle had been: that was comfort to me, such as it was: quickly after that we came to an English

---

27. **Lot's Wife's Temptation:** Despite warnings, as she was leaving her home Lot's wife turned back to look at the city of Sodom and for that was turned into a pillar of salt; see Genesis 19:26.

Path, which so took with me, that I thought I could have freely lyen down and dyed. That day, a little after noon, we came to Squaukheag, where the Indians quickly spread themselves over the deserted English Fields, gleaning what they could find; some pickt up ears of Wheat that were crickled down, some found ears of Indian Corn, some found Ground-nuts, and others sheaves of Wheat that were frozen together in the shock, and went to threshing of them out. My self got two ears of Indian Corn, and whilst I did but turn my back, one of them was stolen from me, which much troubled me. There came an Indian to them at that time, with a basket of Horse-liver. I asked him to give me a piece: What, sayes he, can you eat Horse-liver? I told him, I would try, if he would give a piece, which he did, and I laid it on the coals to rost; but before it was half ready they got half of it away from me, so that I was fain to take the rest and eat it as it was, with the blood about my mouth, and yet a savoury bit it was to me: *For to the hungry Soul every bitter thing is sweet.*[28] A solemn sight methought it was, to see Fields of wheat and Indian Corn forsaken and spoiled: and the remainders of them to be food for our merciless Enemies. That night we had a mess of wheat for our Supper.

The eighth Remove

On the morrow morning we must go over the River, *i. e.* Connecticot, to meet with King Philip; two Cannoos full, they had carried over, the next Turn I my self was to go; but as my foot was upon the Cannoo to step in, there was a sudden out-cry among them, and I must step back; and instead of going over the River, I must go four or five miles up the River farther Northward. Some of the Indians ran one way, and some another. The cause of this rout was, as I thought, their espying some English Scouts, who were thereabout. In this travel up the River, about noon the Company made a stop, and sate down; some to eat, and others to rest them. As I sate amongst them, musing of things past, my Son Joseph unexpectedly came to me: we asked of each others welfare, bemoaning our dolefull condition, and the change that had come upon uss. We had Husband and Father, and Children, and Sisters, and Friends, and Relations, and House, and Home, and many Comforts of this Life: but now we may say, as Job, *Naked came I out of my Mothers Womb, and naked shall I return: The Lord gave, and the Lord hath taken away, Blessed be the Name of the Lord.*[29] I asked him whither he would read; he told me, he earnestly desired it, I gave him my Bible, and he lighted upon that comfortable Scripture, Psalms 118. 17, 18. *I shall not dy but live, and declare the works of the Lord: the Lord hath chastened me sore, yet he hath not given me over to death.* Look here, Mother (sayes he) did you read this? And here I may take occasion to mention one principall ground of my setting forth these Lines: even as the Psalmist sayes, To declare the Works of the Lord, and his wonderfull Power in carrying us along, preserving us in the Wilderness, while under the

28. ***For to the hungry . . . sweet:*** Proverbs 27:7.
29. ***Naked . . . Name of the Lord:*** Job 1:21.

Enemies hand, and returning of us in safety again, And His goodness in bringing to my hand so many comfortable and suitable Scriptures in my distress. But to Return, We travelled on till night; and in the morning, we must go over the River to Philip's Crew. When I was in the Cannoo, I could not but be amazed at the numerous crew of Pagans that were on the Bank on the other side. When I came ashore, they gathered all about me, I sitting alone in the midst: I observed they asked one another questions, and laughed, and rejoyced over their Gains and Victories. Then my heart began to fail: and I fell a weeping which was the first time to my remembrance, that I wept before them. Although I had met with so much Affliction, and my heart was many times ready to break, yet could I not shed one tear in their sight: but rather had been all this while in a maze, and like one astonished: but now I may say as, Psalms 137. 1. *By the Rivers of Babylon, there we sate down: yea, we wept when we remembered Zion.* There one of them asked me, why I wept, I could hardly tell what to say: yet I answered, they would kill me: No, said he, none will hurt you. Then came one of them and gave me two spoonfulls of Meal to comfort me, and another gave me half a pint of Pease; which was more worth than many Bushels at another time. Then I went to see King Philip, he bade me come in and sit down, and asked me whether I woold smoke it (a usual Complement nowadayes amongst Saints and Sinners) but this no way suited me. For though I had formerly used Tobacco, yet I had left it ever since I was first taken. It seems to be a Bait, the Devil layes to make men loose their precious time: I remember with shame, how formerly, when I had taken two or three pipes, I was presently ready for another, such a bewitching thing it is: But I thank God, he has now given me power over it; surely there are many who may be better imployed than to ly sucking a stinking Tobacco-pipe.

Now the Indians gather their Forces to go against North-Hampton:[30] over-night one went about yelling and hooting to give notice of the design. Whereupon they fell to boyling of Ground-nuts, and parching of Corn (as many as had it) for their Provision: and in the morning away they went. During my abode in this place, Philip spake to me to make a shirt for his boy, which I did, for which he gave me a shilling: I offered the mony to my master, but he bade me keep it: and with it I bought a piece of Horse flesh. Afterwards he asked me to make a Cap for his boy, for which he invited me to Dinner. I went, and he gave me a Pancake, about as big as two fingers; it was made of parched wheat, beaten, and fryed in Bears grease, but I thought I never tasted pleasanter meat in my life. There was a Squaw who spake to me to make a shirt for her *Sannup*,[31] for which she gave me a piece of Bear. Another asked me to knit a pair of Stockins, for which she gave me a quart of Pease: I boyled my Pease and Bear together, and invited my master and mistriss to dinner, but the proud Gossip,[32] because I served them both in one Dish, would eat nothing, except one bit that he gave her upon the point of his knife. Hearing

30. **to go against North-Hampton**: The attack on Northampton, Massachusetts, where the Indians were repulsed, took place on March 14, 1675 (March 24, 1676).
31. ***Sannup***: Husband.
32. **Gossip**: Apparently used here in the sense of a person of light and trifling character.

that my son was come to this place, I went to see him, and found him lying flat upon the ground: I asked him how he could sleep so? he answered me, That he was not asleep, but at Prayer; and lay so, that they might not observe what he was doing. I pray God he may remember these things now he is returned in safey. At this Place (the Sun now getting higher) what with the beams and heat of the Sun, and the smoak of the Wigwams, I thought I should have been blind. I could scarce discern one Wigwam from another. There was here one Mary Thurston of Medfield, who seeing how it was with me, lent me a Hat to wear: but as soon as I was gone, the Squaw (who owned that Mary Thurston) came running after me, and got it away again. Here was the Squaw that gave me one spoonfull of Meal. I put it in my Pocket to keep it safe: yet notwithstanding some body stole it, but put five Indian Corns in the room of it: which Corns were the greatest Provisions I had in my travel for one day.

The Indians returning from North-Hampton, brought with them some Horses, and Sheep, and other things which they had taken: I desired them, that they would carry me to Albany, upon one of those Horses, and sell me for Powder: for so they had sometimes discoursed. I was utterly hopless of getting home on foot, the way that I came. I could hardly bear to think of the many weary steps I had taken, to come to this place.

The ninth Remove

But in stead of going either to Albany or homeward, we must go five miles up the River, and then go over it. Here we abode a while. Here lived a sorry Indian, who spoke to me to make him a shirt. When I had done it, he would pay me nothing. But he living by the River side, where I often went to fetch water, I would often be putting of him in mind, and calling for my pay: at last he told me if I would make another shirt, for a Papoos not yet born, he would give me a knife, which he did when I had done it. I carried the knife in, and my master asked me to give it him, and I was not a little glad that I had any thing that they would accept of, and be pleased with. When we were at this place, my Masters maid came home, she had been gone three weeks into the Narrhaganset Country, to fetch Corn, where they had stored up some in the ground: she brought home about a peck and half of Corn. This was about the time that their great Captain, Naananto, was killed in the Narrhaganset Countrey. My Son being now about a mile from me, I asked liberty to go and see him, they bade me go, and away I went: but quickly lost my self, travelling over Hills and thorough Swamps, and could not find the way to him. And I cannot but admire at the wonderfull power and goodness of God to me, in that, though I was gone from home, and met with all sorts of Indians, and those I had no knowledge of, and there being no Christian soul near me; yet not one of them offered the least imaginable miscarriage to me. I turned homeward again, and met with my master, he shewed me the way to my Son: When I came to him I found him not well: and withall he had a boyl on his side, which much troubled him: We bemoaned one another awhile, as the Lord helped us, and then I returned again. When I was returned, I found my self as unsatisfied as I was before. I went up and down mourning and lamenting: and my spirit was ready to sink, with the thoughts of my poor Children: my Son was ill, and I could not but think of his mournfull looks, and no Christian Friend was near him, to do any office of love for him, either for Soul or Body. And my poor Girl, I knew not where she was, nor whither she was sick, or well, or alive, or dead. I repaired under these thoughts to my Bible (my great comfort in that time) and that Scripture came to my hand, *Cast thy burden upon the Lord, and He shall sustain thee,* Psalms 55. 22.

But I was fain to go and look after something to satisfie my hunger, and going among the Wigwams, I went into one, and there found a Squaw who shewed her self very kind to me, and gave me a piece of Bear. I put it into my pocket, and came home, but could not find an opportunity to broil it, for fear they would get it from me, and there it lay all that day and night in my stinking pocket. In the morning I went to the same Squaw, who had a Kettle of Ground nuts boyling; I asked her to let me boyle my piece of Bear in her Kettle, which she did, and gave me some Ground-nuts to eat with it: and I cannot but think how pleasant it was to me. I have sometime seen Bear baked very handsomly among the English, and some like it, but the thoughts that it was Bear, made me tremble: but now that was savoury to me that one would think was enough to turn the stomach of a bruit Creature.

One bitter cold day, I could find no room to sit down before the fire: I went out, and could not tell what to do, but I went in to another Wigwam, where they were also sitting round the fire, but the Squaw laid a skin for me, and bid me sit down, and gave me some Ground-nuts, and bade me come again: and told me they would buy me, if they were able, and yet these were strangers to me that I never saw before.

The tenth Remove

That day a small part of the Company removed about three quarters of a mile, intending further the next day. When they came to the place where they intended to lodge, and had pitched their wigwams, being hungry I went again back to the place we were before at, to get something to eat: being encouraged by the Squaws kindness, who bade me come again; when I was there, there came an Indian to look after me, who when he had found me, kickt me all along: I went home and found Venison roasting that night, but they would not give me one bit of it. Sometimes I met with favour, and sometimes with nothing but frowns.

The eleventh Remove

The next day in the morning they took their Travel, intending a dayes journey up the River, I took my load at my back, and quickly we came to wade over the River: and passed over tiresome and wearisome hills. One hill was so steep that I was fain to creep up upon my knees, and to hold by the twiggs and bushes to keep my self from falling backward. My head also was so light, that I usually reeled as I went; but I hope all these wearisome steps that I have taken, are but a forewarning to me of the heavenly rest. *I know, O Lord, that thy Judgements are right, and that thou in faithfulness hast afflicted me,* Psalms 119. 75.

The twelfth Remove

It was upon a Sabbath-day-morning, that they prepared for their Travel. This morning I asked my master whither he would sell me to my Husband; he answered me *Nux*,[33] which did much rejoyce my spirit. My mistriss, before we went, was gone to the burial of a Papoos, and returning, she found me sitting and reading in my Bible; she snatched it hastily out of my hand, and threw it out of doors; I ran out and catcht it up, and put it into my pocket, and never let her see it afterward. Then they packed up their things to be gone, and gave me my load: I complained it was too heavy, whereupon she gave me a slap in the face, and bade me go; I lifted up my heart to God, hoping the Redemption was not far off: and the rather because their insolency grew worse and worse.

But the thoughts of my going homeward (for so we bent our course) much cheared my Spirit, and made my burden seem light, and almost nothing at all. But (to my amazment and great perplexity) the scale was soon turned: for when we had gone a little way, on a sudden my mistriss gives out, she would go no further, but turn back again, and said, I must go back again with her, and she called her *Sannup*, and would have had him gone back also, but he would not, but said, He would go on, and come to us again in three dayes. My Spirit was upon this, I confess, very impatient, and almost outragious. I thought I could as well have dyed as went back: I cannot declare the trouble that I was in about it; but yet back again I must go. As soon as I had an opportunity, I took my Bible to read, and that quieting Scripture came to my hand, Psalms 46. 10. *Be still, and know that I am God.* Which stilled my spirit for the present: But a sore time of tryal, I concluded, I had to go through, My master being gone, who seemed to me the best friend that I had of an Indian, both in cold and hunger, and quickly so it proved. Down I sat, with my heart as full as it could hold, and yet so hungry that I could not sit neither: but going out to see what I could find, and walking among the Trees, I found six Acorns, and two Ches-nuts, which were some refreshment to me. Towards Night I gathered me some sticks for my own comfort, that I might not ly a-cold: but when we came to ly down they bade me go out, and ly some-where-else, for they had company (they said) come in more than their own: I told them, I could not tell where to go, they bade me go look; I told them, if I went to another Wigwam they would be angry, and send me home again. Then one of the Company drew his sword, and told me he would run me thorough if I did not go presently. Then was I fain to stoop to this rude fellow, and to go out in the night, I knew not whither. Mine eyes have seen that fellow afterwards walking up and down Boston, under the appearance of a Friend-Indian, and severall others of the like Cut. I went to one Wigwam, and they told me they had no room. Then I went to another, and they said the same; at last an old Indian bade me come to him, and his Squaw gave me some Ground-nuts; she gave me also something to lay under my head, and a good fire we had: and through the good providence of God, I had a comfortable lodging that night. In the morning, another Indian bade me come at night, and he would give me six Ground-nuts, which I did. We were at this place and time about two miles from Connecticut

---

33. ***Nux***: Yes.

River. We went in the morning to gather Ground-nuts, to the River, and went back again that night. I went with a good load at my back (for they when they went, though but a little way, would carry all their trumpery with them) I told them the skin was off my back, but I had no other comforting answer from them than this, That it would be no matter if my head were off too.

The thirteenth Remove

Instead of going toward the Bay, which was that I desired, I must go with them five or six miles down the River into a mighty Thicket of Brush: where we abode almost a fortnight. Here one asked me to make a shirt for her Papoos, for which she gave me a mess of Broth, which was thickened with meal made of the Bark of a Tree, and to make it the better, she had put into it about a handfull of Pease, and a few roasted Ground-nuts. I had not seen my son a pritty while, and here was an Indian of whom I made inquiry after him, and asked him when he saw him: he answered me, that such a time his master roasted him, and that himself did eat a piece of him, as big as his two fingers, and that he was very good meat: But the Lord upheld my Spirit, under this discouragement; and I considered their horrible addictedness to lying, and that there is not one of them that makes the least conscience of speaking of truth. In this place, on a cold night, as I lay by the fire, I removed a stick that kept the heat from me, a Squaw moved it down again, at which I lookt up, and she threw a handfull of ashes in mine eyes; I thought I should have been quite blinded, and have never seen more: but lying down, the water run out of my eyes, and carried the dirt with it, that by the morning, I recovered my sight again. Yet upon this, and the like occasions, I hope it is not too much to say with Job, *Have pitty upon me, have pitty upon me, O ye my Frends, for the Hand of the Lord has touched me.*[34] And here I cannot but remember how many times sitting in their Wigwams, and musing on things past, I should suddenly leap up and run out, as if I had been at home, forgetting where I was, and what my condition was: But when I was without, and saw nothing but Wilderness, and Woods, and a company of barbarous heathens, my mind quickly returned to me, which made me think of that, spoken concerning Sampson, who said, *I will go out and shake my self as at other times, but he wist not that the Lord was departed from him.*[35] About this time I began to think that all my hopes of Restoration would come to nothing. I thought of the English Army, and hoped for their coming, and being taken by them, but that failed. I hoped to be carried to Albany, as the Indians had discoursed before, but that failed also. I thought of being sold to my Husband, as my master spake, but in stead of that, my master himself was gone, and I left behind, so that my Spirit was now quite ready to sink. I asked them to let me go out and pick up some sticks, that I might get alone, And poure out my heart unto the Lord. Then also I took my Bible to read, but I found no comfort here neither, which many times I was wont to find: So easie a thing it is with God to dry up the Streames of Scripture-comfort from us. Yet I

34. ***Have pity . . . has touched me***: Job 19:21.
35. ***I will go . . . departed from him***: Judges 16:20.

can say, that in all my sorrows and afflictions, God did not leave me to have my impatience work towards himself, as if his wayes were unrighteous. But I knew that he laid upon me less then I deserved. Afterward, before this dolefull time ended with me, I was turning the leaves of my Bible, and the Lord brought to me some Scriptures, which did a little revive me, as that Isaiah 55. 8, *For my thoughts are not your thoughts, neither are your wayes my ways, saith the Lord.* And also that, Psalms 37. 5, *Commit thy way unto the Lord, trust also in him, and he shal bring it to pass.* About this time they came yelping from Hadly, where they had killed three English men, and brought one Captive with them, *viz.* Thomas Read. They all gathered about the poor Man, asking him many Questions. I desired also to go and see him; and when I came, he was crying bitterly, supposing they would quickly kill him. Whereupon I asked one of them, whether they intended to kill him; he answered me, they would not: He being a little cheared with that, I asked him about the wel-fare of my Husband, he told me he saw him such a time in the Bay, and he was well, but very melancholly. By which I certainly understood (though I suspected it before) that whatsoever the Indians told me respecting him was vanity and lies. Some of them told me, he was dead, and they had killed him: some said he was Married again, and that the Governour wished him to Marry; and told him he should have his choice, and that all perswaded I was dead. So like were these barbarous creatures to him who was a lyer from the beginning.[36]

As I was sitting once in the Wigwam here, Phillips Maid came in with the Child in her arms, and asked me to give her a piece of my Apron, to make a flap for it, I told her I would not: then my Mistriss bad me give it, but still I said no: the maid told me if I would not give her a piece, she would tear a piece off it: I told her I would tear her Coat then, with that my Mistriss rises up, and takes up a stick big enough to have killed me, and struck at me with it, but I stept out, and she struck the stick into the Mat of the Wigwam. But while she was pulling of it out, I ran to the Maid and gave her all my Apron, and so that storm went over.

Hearing that my Son was come to this place, I went to see him, and told him his Father was well, but very melancholly: he told me he was as much grieved for his Father as for himself; I wondered at his speech, for I thought I had enough upon my spirit in reference to my self, to make me mindless of my Husband and every one else: they being safe among their Friends. He told me also, that a while before, his Master (together with other Indians) were going to the French for Powder; but by the way the Mohawks met with them, and killed four of their Company which made the rest turn back again, for which I desire that my self and he may bless the Lord; for it might have been worse with him, had he been sold to the French, than it proved to be in his remaining with the Indians.

I went to see an English Youth in this place, one John Gilberd of Springfield. I found him lying without dores, upon the ground; I asked him how he did? he told me he was very sick of a flux,[37] with eating so much blood: They had turned him out of the Wigwam, and with him an Indian Papoos, almost dead, (whose Parents had been killed) in a bitter

---

36. **who was a lyer from the beginning:** Satan was such a liar.
37. **flux:** Early term for dysentery.

cold day, without fire or clothes: the young man himself had nothing on, but his shirt and wastcoat. This sight was enough to melt a heart of flint. There they lay quivering in the Cold, the youth round like a dog; the Papoos stretcht out, with his eyes and nose and mouth full of dirt, and yet alive, and groaning. I advised John to go and get to some fire: he told me he could not stand, but I perswaded him still, lest he should ly there and die: and with much adoe I got him to a fire, and went my self home. As soon as I was got home, his Masters Daughter came after me, to know what I had done with the English man, I told her I had got him to a fire in such a place. Now had I need to pray Pauls Prayer, 2 Thessalonians 3. 2. *That we may be delivered from unreasonable and wicked men.* For her satisfactlon I went along with her, and brought her to him; but before I got home again, it was noised about, that I was running away and getting the English youth, along with me; that as soon as I came in, they began to rant and domineer: asking me Where I had been, and what I had been doing? and saying they would knock him on the head: I told them, I had been seeing the English Youth, and that I would not run away, they told me I lyed, and taking up a Hatchet, they came to me, and said they would knock me down if I stirred out again; and so confined me to the Wigwam. Now may I say with David, 2 Samuel 24. 14. *I am in a great strait.* If I keep in, I must dy with hunger, and if I go out, I must be knockt in head. This distressed condition held that day, and half the next; And then the Lord remembred me, whose mercyes are great. Then came an Indian to me with a pair of stockings that were too big for him, and he would have me ravel them out, and knit them fit for him. I shewed my self willing, and bid him ask my mistriss if I might go along with him a little way; she said yes, I might, but I was not a little refresht with that news, that I had my liberty again. Then I went along with him, and he gave me some roasted Ground-nuts, which did again revive my feeble stomach.

Being got out of her sight, I had time and liberty again to look into my Bible: Which was my Guid by day, and my Pillow by night. Now that comfortable Scripture presented it self to me, Isaiah 54. 7. *For a smal moment have I forsaken thee, but with great mercies will I gather thee.* Thus the Lord carried me along from one time to another, and made good to me this precious promise, and many others. Then my Son came to see me, and I asked his master to let him stay a while with me, that I might comb his head, and look over him, for he was almost overcome with lice. He told me, when I had done, that he was very hungry, but I had nothing to relieve him; but bid him go into the Wigwams as he went along, and see if he could get any thing among them. Which he did, and it seemes tarried a little too long; for his Master was angry with him, and beat him, and then sold him. Then he came running to tell me he had a new Master, and that he had given him some Groundnuts already. Then I went along with him to his new Master who told me he loved him: and he should not want. So his Master carried him away, and I never saw him afterward, till I saw him at Pascataqua in Portsmouth.

That night they bade me go out of the Wigwam again: my Mistrisses Papoos was sick, and it died that night, and there was one benefit in it, that there was more room. I went to a Wigwam, and they bade me come in, and gave me a skin to ly upon, and a mess of Venson and Ground-nuts, which was a choice Dish among them. On the morrow they buried the Papoos, and afterward, both morning and evening, there came a company to mourn and howle with her: though I confess, I could not much condole with them. Many sorrowfull dayes I had in this place: often getting alone; *like a Crane, or a Swallow, so did I chatter: I did mourn as a Dove, mine eyes ail with looking upward. Oh, Lord, I am oppressed; undertake for me,* Isaiah 38. 14. I could tell the Lord as Hezeckiah, ver. 3, *Remember now O Lord, I beseech thee, how I have walked before thee in truth.*[38] Now had I time to examine all my wayes: my Conscience did not accuse me of un-righteousness toward one or other: yet I saw how in my walk with God, I had been a careless creature. As David said, *Against thee, thee only have I sinned:*[39] and I might say with the poor Publican, *God be merciful unto me a sinner.*[40] On the Sabbath-dayes, I could look upon the Sun and think how People were going to the house of God, to have their Souls refresht; and then home, and their bodies also: but I was destitute of both; and might say as the poor Prodigal, *he would fain have filled his belly with the husks that the Swine did eat, and no man gave unto him,* Luke 15. 16. For I must say with him, *Father I have sinned against Heaven, and in thy sight.*[41] I remembred how on the night before and after the Sabbath, when my Family was about me, and Relations and Neighbours with us, we could pray and sing, and then refresh our bodies with the good creatures of God; and then have a comfortable Bed to ly down on: but in stead of all this, I had only a little Swill for the body, and then like a Swine, must ly down on the ground. I cannot express to man the sorrow that lay upon my Spirit, the Lord knows it. Yet that comfortable Scripture would often come to my mind, *For a small moment have I forsaken thee, but with great mercies will I gather thee.*[42]

The fourteenth Remove

Now must we pack up and be gone from this Thicket, bending our course toward the Bay-towns, I haveing nothing to eat by the way this day, but a few crumbs of Cake, that an Indian gave my girle the same day we were taken. She gave it me, and I put it in my pocket: there it lay, till it was so mouldy (for want of good baking) that one could not tell what it was made of; it fell all to crumbs, and grew so dry and hard, that it was like little flints; and this refreshed me many times, when I was ready to faint. It was in my thoughts when I put it into my mouth, that if ever I returned, I would tell the World what a blessing the Lord gave to such mean food. As we went along, they killed a Deer, with a young one in her, they gave me a piece of the Fawn, and it was so young and tender, that one might eat the bones as well as the flesh, and yet I thought it very good. When night came on we sate down; it rained, but they quickly got up a Bark Wigwam, where I lay dry that night. I looked out in the morning, and many of them had line in the rain all night, I saw by their Reaking.[43] Thus the Lord dealt mercifully with me many times. and I fared better than many of them. In the morning they took the blood of the Deer, and put it into

38. ***Remember . . . in truth***: Isaiah 38:3.
39. ***Against thee . . . have I sinned***: Psalms 51:4.
40. ***God . . . unto me a sinner***: Luke 18:13.
41. ***Father . . . in thy sight***: Luke 15:21.
42. ***For a small moment . . . will I gather thee***: Isaiah 54:7.
43. **Reaking**: Early term for giving off smoke or fumes.

the Paunch, and so boyled it; I could eat nothing of that, though they ate it sweetly. And yet they were so nice[44] in other things, that when I had fetcht water, and had put the Dish I dipt the water with, into the Kettle of water which I brought, they would say, they would knock me down; for they said, it was a sluttish[45] trick.

The fifteenth Remove

We went on our Travel. I having got one handfull of Ground-nuts, for my support that day, they gave me my load, and I went on cheerfully (with the thoughts of going homeward) haveing my burden more on my back than my spirit: we came to Baquaug River again that day, near which we abode a few dayes. Sometimes one of them would give me a Pipe, another a little Tobacco, another a little Salt: which I would change for a little Victuals. I cannot but think what a Wolvish appetite persons have in a starving condition: for many times when they gave me that which was hot, I was so greedy, that I should burn my mouth, that it would trouble me hours after, and yet I should quickly do the same again. And after I was thoroughly hungry, I was never again satisfied. For though sometimes it fell out, that I got enough, and did eat till I could eat no more, yet I was as unsatisfied as I was when I began. And now could I see that Scripture verified (there being many Scriptures which we do not take notice of, or understand till we are afflicted) Micah 6. 14. *Thou shalt eat and not be satisfied.* Now might I see more than ever before, the miseries that sin hath brought upon us: Many times I should be ready to run out against the Heathen, but the Scripture would quiet me again, Amos 3. 6, *Shal there be evil in the City, and the Lord hath not done it?* The Lord help me to make a right improvment of His Word, and that I might learn that great lesson, Micah 6. 8, 9. *He hath shewed thee (Oh Man) what is good, and what doth the Lord require of thee, but to do justly, and love mercy, and walk humbly with thy God? Hear ye the rod, and who hath appointed it.*

The sixteenth Remove

We began this Remove with wading over Baquag River: the water was up to the knees, and the stream very swift, and so cold that I thought it would have cut me in sunder. I was so weak and feeble, that I reeled as I went along, and thought there I must end my dayes at last, after my bearing and getting thorough so many difficulties; the Indians stood laughing to see me staggering along: but in my distress the Lord gave me experience of the truth, and goodness of that promise, Isaiah 43. 2. *When thou passest thorough the Waters, I will be with thee, and through the Rivers, they shall not overflow thee.* Then I sat down to put on my stockins and shoos, with the teares running down mine eyes, and many sorrowfull thoughts in my heart, but I gat up to go along with them. Quickly there came up to us an Indian, who informed them, that I must go to Wachusit

---

44. **nice:** Early term for fastidious or scrupulous.
45. **sluttish:** Slovenly.

to my master, for there was a Letter come from the Council to the Saggamores, about redeeming the Captives, and that there would be another in fourteen dayes, and that I must be there ready. My heart was so heavy before that I could scarce speak or go in the path; and yet now so light, that I could run. My strength seemed to come again, and recruit my feeble knees, and aking heart: yet it pleased them to go but one mile that night, and there we stayed two dayes. In that time came a company of Indians to us, near thirty, all on horseback. My heart skipt within me, thinking they had been English-men at the first sight of them, for they were dressed in English Apparel, with Hats, white Neckcloths, and Sashes about their wasts, and Ribbonds upon their shoulders: but when they came near, their was a vast difference between the lovely faces of Christians, and the foul looks of those Heathens, which much damped my spirit again.

The seventeenth Remove

A comfortable Remove it was to me, because of my hopes. They gave me a pack, and along we went chearfully; but quickly my will proved more than my strength; having little or no refreshing my strength failed me, and my spirit were almost quite gone. Now may I say with David, Psalms 119. 22, 23, 24. *I am poor and needy, and my heart is wounded within me. I am gone like the shadow when it declineth: I am tossed up and down like the locust; my knees are weak through fasting, and my flesh faileth of fatness.* At night we came to an Indian Town, and the Indians sate down by a Wigwam discoursing, but I was almost spent, and could scarce speak. I laid down my load, and went into the Wigwam, and there sat an Indian boyling of Horses feet (they being wont to eat the flesh first, and when the feet were old and dried, and they had nothing else, they would cut off the feet and use them). I asked him to give me a little of his Broth, or Water they were boiling in; he took a dish, and gave me one spoonfull of Samp,[46] and bid me take as much of the Broth as I would. Then I put some of the hot water to the Samp, and drank it up, and my spirit came again. He gave me also a piece of the Ruff or Ridding[47] of the small Guts, and I broiled it on the coals; and now may I say with Jonathan, *See, I pray you how mine eyes have been enlightened, because I tasted a little of this honey,* 1 Samuel 14. 29. Now is my Spirit revived again; though means be never so inconsiderable, yet if the Lord bestow his blessing upon them, they shall refresh both Soul and Body.

The eighteenth Remove

We took up our packs and along we went, but a wearisome day I had of it. As we went along I saw an English-man stript naked, and lying dead upon the ground, but knew not who it was. Then we came to another Indian Town, where we stayed all night. In this Town there were four English Children, Captives; and one of them my own Sisters. I

46. **Samp:** Porridge made from coarsely ground corn.

47. **a piece of the Ruff or Ridding:** That is, a part that was rough (difficult to eat) or an inedible part that was usually discarded.

went to see how she did, and she was well, considering her Captive-condition. I would have tarried that night with her, but they that owned her would not suffer it. Then I went into another Wigwam, where they were boyling Corn and Beans, which was a lovely sight to see, but I could not get a taste thereof. Then I went to another Wigwam, where there were two of the English Children; the Squaw was boyling Horses feet, then she cut me off a little piece, and gave one of the English Children a piece also. Being very hungry I had quickly eat up mine, but the Child could not bite it, it was so tough and sinewy, but lay sucking, gnawing, chewing and slabbering of it in the mouth and hand, then I took it of the Child, and eat it my self, and savoury it was to my taste. Then I may say as Job, Chap. 6. 7. *The things that my soul refused to touch, are as my sorrowfull meat.* Thus the Lord made that pleasant refreshing, which another time would have been an abomination. Then I went home to my mistresses Wigwam; and they told me I disgraced my master with begging, and if I did so any more, they would knock me in head: I told them, they had as good knock me in head as starve me to death.

The nineteeth Remove

They said, when we went out, that we must travel to Wachuset this day. But a bitter weary day I had of it, travelling now three dayes together, without resting any day between. At last, after many weary steps, I saw Wachuset hills, but many miles off. Then we came to a great Swamp, through which we travelled, up to the knees in mud and water, which was heavy going to one tyred before. Being almost spent, I thought I should have sunk down at last, and never gat out; but I may say, as in Psalms 94. 18, *When my foot slipped, thy mercy, O Lord, held me up.* Going along, having indeed my life, but little spirit, Philip, who was in the Company, came up and took me by the hand, and said, Two weeks more and you shal be Mistress again. I asked him, if he spake true? he answered, Yes, and quickly you shal come to your master again; who had been gone from us three weeks. After many weary steps we came to Wachuset, where he was: and glad I was to see him. He asked me, When I washt me? I told him not this month, then he fetcht me some water himself, and bid me wash, and gave me the Glass to see how I lookt; and bid his Squaw give me something to eat: so she gave me a mess of Beans and meat, and a little Ground-nut Cake. I was wonderfully revived with this favour shewed me, Psalms 106. 46, *He made them also to be pittied, of all those that carried them Captives.*

My master had three Squaws, living sometimes with one, and sometimes with another one, this old Squaw, at whose Wigwam I was, and with whom my Master had been those three weeks. Another was Wattimore,[48] with whom I had lived and served all this while: A severe and proud Dame she was, bestowing every day in dressing her self neat as much time as any of the Gentry of the land: powdering her hair, and painting her face, going with Neck-laces, with Jewels in her ears, and Bracelets upon her hands: When she had dressed her self, her work was to make Girdles of Wampom and Beads. The third Squaw was a younger one, by whom he had two Papooses. By that time I was

---

48. **Wattimore:** Her name is usually given as Weetamoo; see note 20.

refresht by the old Squaw, with whom my master was, Wettimores Maid came to call me home, at which I fell a weeping. Then the old Squaw told me, to encourage me, that if I wanted victuals, I should come to her, and that I should ly there in her Wigwam. Then I went with the maid, and quickly came again and lodged there. The Squaw laid a Mat under me, and a good Rugg over me; the first time I had any such kindness shewed me. I understood that Wettimore thought, that if she should let me go and serve with the old Squaw, she would be in danger to loose, not only my service, but the redemption-pay also. And I was not a little glad to hear this; being by it raised in my hopes, that in Gods due time there would be an end of this sorrowfull hour. Then came an Indian, and asked me to knit him three pair of Stockins, for which I had a Hat, and a silk Handkerchief. Then another asked me to make her a shift, for which she gave me an Apron.

Then came Tom and Peter, with the second Letter from the Council, about the Captives. Though they were Indians, I gat them by the hand, and burst out into tears; my heart was so full that I could not speak to them; but recovering my self, I asked them how my husband did, and all my friends and acquaintance? they said, They are all very well but melancholy. They brought me two Biskets, and a pound of Tobacco. The Tobacco I quickly gave away; when it was all gone, one asked me to give him a pipe of Tobacco, I told him it was all gone; then began he to rant and threaten. I told him when my Husband came I would give him some: Hang him Rogue (sayes he) I will knock out his brains, if he comes here. And then again, in the same breath they would say, That if there should come an hundred without Guns, they would do them no hurt. So unstable and like mad men they were. So that fearing the worst, I durst not send to my Husband, though there were some thoughts of his coming to Redeem and fetch me, not knowing what might follow. For there was little more trust to them then to the master they served. When the Letter was come, the Saggamores met to consult about the Captives, and called me to them to enquire how much my husband would give to redeem me, when I came I sate down among them, as I was wont to do, as their manner is: Then they bade me stand up, and said, they were the General Court.[49] They bid me speak what I thought he would give. Now knowing that all we had was destroyed by the Indians, I was in a great strait: I thought if I should speak of but a little, it would be slighted, and hinder the matter; if of a great sum, I knew not where it would be procured: yet at a venture, I said Twenty pounds, yet desired them to take less; but they would not hear of that, but sent that message to Boston, that for Twenty pounds I should be redeemed. It was a Praying-Indian that wrote their Letter for them. There was another Praying Indian, who told me, that he had a brother, that would not eat Horse; his conscience was so tender and scrupulous (though as large as hell, for the destruction of poor Christians). Then he said, he read that Scripture to him, 2 Kings, 6. 25. *There was a famine in Samaria, and behold they besieged it, untill an Asses head was sold for fourscore pieces of silver, and the fourth part of a Kab*[50] *of Doves dung, for five pieces of silver.* He expounded this place to his brother, and shewed him that it was lawfull to eat that in a Famine which is not at

---

49. **General Court:** The legislature of the Massachusetts Bay Colony.

50. ***Kab*:** A unit of dry measure (Hebrew).

another time. And now, sayes he, he will eat Horse with any Indian of them all. There was another Praying-Indian, who when he had done all the mischief that he could, betrayed his own Father into the English hands, thereby to purchase his own life. Another Praying-Indian was at Sudbury-fight,[51] though, as he deserved, he was afterward hanged for it. There was another Praying Indian, so wicked and cruel, as to wear a string about his neck, strung with Christians fingers. Another Praying-Indian, when they went to Sudbury-fight, went with them, and his Squaw also with him, with her Papoos at her back: Before they went to that fight, they got a company together to *Powaw*;[52] the manner was as followeth. There was one that kneeled upon a Deerskin, with the company round him in a ring who kneeled, and striking upon the ground with their hands, and with sticks, and muttering or humming with their mouths; besides him who kneeled in the ring, there also stood one with a Gun in his hand: Then he on the Deer-skin made a speech, and all manifested assent to it: and so they did many times together. Then they bade him with the Gun go out of the ring, which he did, but when he was out, they called him in again; but he seemed to make a stand, then they called the more earnestly, till he returned again: Then they all sang. Then they gave him two Guns, in either hand one: And so he on the Deer-skin began again; and at the end of every sentence in his speaking, they all assented, humming or muttering with their mouthes, and striking upon the ground with their hands. Then they bade him with the two Guns go out of the ring again; which he did, a little way. Then they called him in again, but he made a stand; so they called him with greater earnestness; but he stood reeling and wavering as if he knew not whither he should stand or fall, or which way to go. Then they called him with exceeding great vehemency, all of them, one and another: after a little while he turned in, staggering as he went, with his Armes stretched out, in either hand a Gun. As soon as he came in, they all sang and rejoyced exceedingly a while. And then he upon the Deer-skin, made another speech unto which they all assented in a rejoicing manner: and so they ended their business, and forthwith went to Sudbury-fight. To my thinking they went without any scruple, but that they should prosper, and gain the victory. And they went out not so rejoycing, but they came home with as great a Victory. For they said they had killed two Captains, and almost an hundred men. One English-man they brought along with them: and he said, it was too true, for they had made sad work at Sudbury, as indeed it proved. Yet they came home without that rejoycing and triumphing over their victory, which they were wont to shew at other times, but rather like Dogs (as they say) which have lost their ears. Yet I could not perceive that it was for their own loss of men: They said, they had not lost above five or six: and I missed none, except in one Wigwam. When they went, they acted as if the Devil had told them that they should gain the victory: and now they acted, as if the Devil had told them they should have a fall. Whither it were so or no, I cannot tell, but so it proved, for quickly they began to fall, and so held on that Summer, till they came to utter ruine. They came home on a Sabbath day, and the *Powaw* that kneeled upon the Deer-skin came home (I may say, without abuse) as black as the Devil.

---

51. **Sudbury-fight:** The attack at Sudbury, Massachusetts, occurred on April 18/28, 1676.
52. ***Powaw*:** A ceremony conducted by a spiritual healer or leader, often spelled *pow-wow*.

When my master came home, he came to me and bid me make a shirt for his Papoos, of a holland-laced Pillowbeer.[53] About that time there came an Indian to me and bid me come to his Wigwam, at night, and he would give me some Pork and Ground-nuts. Which I did, and as I was eating, another Indian said to me, he seems to be your good Friend, but he killed two Englishmen at Sudbury, and there ly their Cloaths behind you: I looked behind me, and there I saw bloody Cloaths, with Bullet-holes in them; yet the Lord suffered not this wretch to do me any hurt; Yea, instead of that, he many times refresht me: five or six times did he and his Squaw refresh my feeble carcass. If I went to their Wigwam at any time, they would alwayes give me something, and yet they were strangers that I never saw before. Another Squaw gave me a piece of fresh Pork, and a little Salt with it, and lent me her Pan to Fry it in; and I cannot but remember what a sweet pleasant and delightfull relish that bit had to me, to this day. So little do we prize common mercies when we have them to the full.

The twentieth Remove

It was their usual manner to remove, when they had done any mischief, lest they should be found out: and so they did at this time. We went about three or four miles, and there they built a great Wigwam, big enough to hold an hundred Indians, which they did in preparation to a great day of Dancing. They would say now amongst themselves, that the Governour would be so angry for his loss at Sudbury, that he would send no more about the Captives, which made me grieve and tremble. My Sister being not far from the place where we now were, and hearing that I was here, desired her master to let her come and see me, and he was willing to it, and would go with her: but she being ready before him, told him she would go before, and was come within a Mile or two of the place; Then he overtook her, and began to rant as if he had been mad; and made her go back again in the Rain; so that I never saw her till I saw her in Charlestown. But the Lord requited many of their ill doings, for this Indian her Master, was hanged afterward at Boston. The Indians now began to come from all quarters, against their merry dancing day. Among some of them came one Goodwife Kettle: I told her my heart was so heavy that it was ready to break: so is mine too said she, but yet said, I hope we shall hear some good news shortly. I could hear how earnestly my Sister desired to see me, and I as earnestly desired to see her: and yet neither of us could get an opportunity. My Daughter was also now about a mile off, and I had not seen her in nine or ten weeks, as I had not seen my Sister since our first taking. I earnestly desired them to let me go and see them: yea, I intreated, begged, and perswaded them, but to let me see my Daughter; and yet so hard hearted were they, that they would not suffer it. They made use of their tyrannical power whilst they had it: but through the Lords wonderfull mercy, their time was now but short.

On a Sabbath day, the Sun being about an hour high in the afternoon, came Mr. John Hoar[54] (the Council permitting him, and his own foreward spirit inclining him) together

53. **Pillowbeer:** A pillow covering made of linen.
54. **Mr. John Hoar:** John Hoar (c. 1616–1704), a lawyer from Concord, Massachusetts, represented Rowlandson's husband at the council of the Sagamore Indians.

with the two forementioned Indians, Tom and Peter, with their third Letter from the Council. When they came near, I was abroad: though I saw them not, they presently called me in, and bade me sit down and not stir. Then they catched up their Guns, and away they ran, as if an Enemy had been at hand; and the Guns went off apace. I manifested some great trouble, and they asked me what was the matter? I told them, I thought they had killed the English-man (for they had in the mean time informed me that an English-man was come) they said, No; They shot over his Horse and under, and before his Horse; and they pusht him this way and that way, at their pleasure: shewing what they could do: Then they let them come to their Wigwams. I begged of them to let me see the English-man, but they would not. But there was I fain to sit their pleasure. When they had talked their fill with him, they suffered me to go to him. We asked each other of our welfare, and how my Husband did, and all my Friends? He told me they were all well, and would be glad to see me. Amongst other things which my Husband sent me, there came a pound of Tobacco: which I sold for nine shillings in Money: for many of the Indians for want of Tobacco, smoaked Hemlock, and Ground-Ivy. It was a great mistake in any, who thought I sent for Tobacco: for through the favour of God, that desire was overcome. I now asked them, whither I should go home with Mr. Hoar? They answered No, one and another of them: and it being night, we lay down with that answer; in the morning, Mr Hoar invited the Saggamores to Dinner; but when we went to get it ready, we found that they had stollen the greatest part of the Provision Mr. Hoar had brought, out of his Bags, in the night. And we may see the wonderfull power of God, in that one passage, in that when there was such a great number of the Indians together, and so greedy of a little good food; and no English there, but Mr. Hoar and my self: that there they did not knock us in the head, and take what we had: there being not only some Provision, but also Tradingcloth, a part of the twenty pounds agreed upon: But instead of doing us any mischief, they seemed to be ashamed of the fact, and said, it were some Matchit Indian[55] that did it. Oh, that we could believe that there is no thing too hard for God! God shewed his Power over the Heathen in this, as he did over the hungry Lyons when Daniel was cast into the Den.[56] Mr. Hoar called them betime to Dinner, but they ate very little, they being so busie in dressing themselves, and getting ready for their Dance: which was carried on by eight of them, four Men and four Squaws: My master and mistress being two. He was dressed in his Holland shirt, with great Laces sewed at the tail of it, he had his silver Buttons, his white Stockins, his Garters were hung round with Shillings, and he had Girdles of Wampom upon his head and shoulders. She had a Kersey Coat,[57] and covered with Girdles of Wampom from the Loins upward: her armes from her elbows to her hands were covered with Bracelets; there were handfulls of Necklaces about her neck, and severall sorts of Jewels in her ears. She had fine red Stokins, and white Shoos, her hair powdered and face painted Red, that was alwayes before Black. And all the Dancers were after the same manner. There were two other singing

---

55. **Matchit Indian:** That is, a bad Indian.
56. **when Daniel was cast into the Den:** God sent an angel to deliver the prophet Daniel from harm when he was cast into the lion's den (Daniel 6:1–29).
57. **Kersey Coat:** A coat of coarse, ribbed wool.

and knocking on a Kettle for their musick. They keept hopping up and down one after another, with a Kettle of water in the midst, standing warm upon some Embers, to drink of when they were dry. They held on till it was almost night, throwing out Wampom to the standers by. At night I asked them again, if I should go home? They all as one said No, except my Husband would come for me. When we were lain down, my Master went out of the Wigwam, and by and by sent in an Indian called James the Printer, who told Mr. Hoar, that my Master would let me go home to morrow, if he would let him have one pint of Liquors. Then Mr. Hoar called his own Indians, Tom and Peter, and bid them go and see whither he would promise it before them three: and if he would, he should have it; which he did, and he had it. Then Philip smeling the business cal'd me to him, and asked me what I would give him, to tell me some good news, and speak a good word for me. I told him, I could not tell what to give him, I would any thing I had, and asked him what he would have? He said, two Coats and twenty shillings in Mony, and half a bushel of seed Corn, and some Tobacco. I thanked him for his love: but I knew the good news as well as the crafty Fox. My Master after he had had his drink, quickly came ranting into the Wigwam again, and called for Mr. Hoar, drinking to him, and saying, He was a good man: and then again he would say, Hang him Rogue: Being almost drunk, he would drink to him, and yet presently say he should be hanged. Then he called for me. I trembled to hear him, yet I was fain to go to him, and he drank to me, shewing no incivility. He was the first Indian I saw drunk all the while that I was amongst them. At last his Squaw ran out, and he after her, round the Wigwam, with his mony jingling at his knees: But she escaped him: But having an old Squaw he ran to her: and so through the Lords mercy, we were no more troubled that night. Yet I had not a comfortable nights rest: for I think I can say, I did not sleep for three nights together. The night before the Letter came from the Council, I could not rest, I was so full of feares and troubles, God many times leaving us most in the dark, when deliverance is nearest: yea, at this time I could not rest night nor day. The next night I was overjoyed, Mr. Hoar being come, and that with such good tidings. The third night I was even swallowed up with the thoughts of things, *viz.* that ever I should go home again; and that I must go, leaving my Children behind me in the Wilderness; so that sleep was now almost departed from mine eyes.

On Tuesday morning they called their General Court (as they call it) to consult and determine, whether I should go home or no: And they all as one man did seemingly consent to it, that I should go home; except Philip, who would not come among them.

But before I go any further, I would take leave to mention a few remarkable passages of providence, which I took special notice of in my afflicted time.

1. Of the fair opportunity lost in the long March, a little after the Fort-fight, when our English Army was so numerous, and in pursuit of the Enemy, and so near as to take several and destroy them: and the Enemy in such distress for food, that our men might track them by their rooting in the earth for Ground-nuts, whilest they were flying for their lives. I say, that then our Army should want Provision, and be forced to leave their pursuit and return homeward: and the very next week the Enemy came upon our Town, like Bears bereft of their whelps, or so many ravenous Wolves, rending us and our Lambs to death. But what shall I say? God seemed to leave his People to themselves,

and order all things for his own holy ends. *Shal there be evil in the City and the Lord hath not done it? They are not grieved for the affliction of Joseph, therefore shal they go Captive, with the first that go Captive.*[58] It is the Lords doing, and it should be marvelous in our eyes.

2. I cannot but remember how the Indians derided the slowness, and dulness of the English Army, in its setting out. For after the desolations at Lancaster and Medfield, as I went along with them, they asked me when I thought the English Army would come after them? I told them I could not tell: It may be they will come in May, said they. Thus did they scoffe at us, as if the English would be a quarter of a year getting ready.

3. Which also I have hinted before, when the English Army with new supplies were sent forth to pursue after the enemy, and they understanding it, fled before them till they came to Baquaug River, where they forthwith went over safely: that that River should be impassable to the English. I can but admire to see the wonderfull providence of God in preserving the heathen for farther affliction to our poor Countrey. They could go in great numbers over, but the English must stop: God had an over-ruling hand in all those things.

4. It was thought, if their Corn were cut down, they would starve and dy with hunger: and all their Corn that could be found, was destroyed, and they driven from that little they had in store, into the Woods in the midst of Winter; and yet how to admiration did the Lord preserve them for his holy ends, and the destruction of many still amongst the English! strangely did the Lord provide for them; that I did not see (all the time I was among them) one Man, Woman, or Child, die with hunger.

Though many times they would eat that, that a Hog or a Dog would hardly touch; yet by that God strengthned them to be a scourge to his People.

The chief and commonest food was Ground-nuts: They eat also Nuts and Acorns, Harty-choaks,[59] Lilly roots, Ground-beans, and several other weeds and roots, that I know not.

They would pick up old bones, and cut them to pieces at the joynts, and if they were full of wormes and magots, they would scald them over the fire to make the vermine come out, and then boile them, and drink up the Liquor, and then beat the great ends of them in a Morter, and so eat them. They would eat Horses guts, and ears, and all sorts of wild Birds which they could catch: also Bear, Vennison, Beaver, Tortois, Frogs, Squirrels, Dogs, Skunks, Rattle-snakes; yea, the very Bark of Trees; besides all sorts of creatures, and provision which they plundered from the English. I can but stand in admiration to see the wonderful power of God, in providing for such a vast number of our Enemies in the Wilderness, where there was nothing to be seen, but from hand to mouth. Many times in a morning, the generality of them would eat up all they had, and yet have some forther supply against they wanted. It is said, Psalms 81. 13, 14. *Oh, that my People had hearkned to me, and Israel had walked in my wayes, I should soon have subdued their Enemies, and turned my hand against their Adversaries.* But now

58. ***Shal there be evil . . . Captive***: Amos 3:6 and 6:6–7.
59. **Harty-choaks**: Artichokes.

our perverse and evil carriages in the sight of the Lord, have so offended him, that instead of turning his hand against them, the Lord feeds and nourishes them up to be a scourge to the whole Land.

5. Another thing that I would observe is, the strange providence of God, in turning things about when the Indians was at the highest, and the English at the lowest. I was with the Enemy eleven weeks and five dayes, and not one Week passed without the fury of the Enemy, and some desolation by fire and sword upon one place or other. They mourned (with their black faces) for their own lossess, yet triumphed and rejoyced in their inhumane, and many times devilish cruelty to the English. They would boast much of their Victories; saying, that in two hours time they had destroyed such a Captain, and his Company at such a place; and such a Captain and his Company in such a place; and such a Captain and his Company in such a place: and boast how many Towns they had destroyed, and then scoffe, and say, They had done them a good turn, to send them to Heaven so soon. Again, they would say, This Summer that they would knock all the Rogues in the head, or drive them into the Sea, or make them flie the Countrey: thinking surely, Agag-like, *The bitterness of Death is past.*[60] Now the Heathen begins to think all is their own, and the poor Christians hopes to fail (as to man) and now their eyes are more to God, and their hearts sigh heaven-ward: and to say in good earnest, *Help Lord, or we perish*: When the Lord had brought his people to this, that they saw no help in any thing but himself: then he takes the quarrel into his own hand: and though they had made a pit, in their own imaginations, as deep as hell for the Christians that Summer, yet the Lord hurll'd them selves into it. And the Lord had not so many wayes before to preserve them, but now he hath as many to destroy them.

But to return again to my going home, where we may see a remarkable change of Providence: At first they were all against it, except my Husband would come for me; but afterwards they assented to it, and seemed much to rejoyce in it; some askt me to send them some Bread, others some Tobacco, others shaking me by the hand, offering me a Hood and Scarfe to ride in; not one moving hand or tongue against it. Thus hath the Lord answered my poor desire, and the many earnest requests of others put up unto God for me. In my travels an Indian came to me, and told me, if I were willing, he and his Squaw would run away, and go home along with me: I told him No: I was not willing to run away, but desired to wait Gods time, that I might go home quietly, and without fear. And now God hath granted me my desire. O the wonderfull power of God that I have seen, and the experience that I have had: I have been in the midst of those roaring Lyons, and Salvage Bears, that feared neither God, nor Man, nor the Devil, by night and day, alone and in company: sleeping all sorts together, and yet not one of them ever offered me the least abuse of unchastity to me, in word or action. Though some are ready to say, I speak it for my own credit; But I speak it in the presence of God, and to his Glory. Gods Power is as great now, and as sufficient to save, as when he preserved Daniel in the Lions Den; or

---

60. ***The bitterness of Death is past***: 1 Samuel 15:32. Agag, the king of Amalek, was defeated by Saul and later slain by Samuel.

the three Children in the fiery Furnace.[61] I may well say as his Psalms 107. 12, *Oh give thanks unto the Lord for he is good, for his mercy endureth for ever.* Let the Redeemed of the Lord say so, whom he hath redeemed from the hand of the Enemy, especially that I should come away in the midst of so many hundreds of Enemies quietly and peacably, and not a Dog moving his tongue. So I took my leave of them, and in coming along my heart melted into tears, more then all the while I was with them, and I was almost swallowed up with the thoughts that ever I should go home again. About the Sun going down, Mr. Hoar, and my self, and the two Indians came to Lancaster, and a solemn sight it was to me. There had I lived many comfortable years amongst my Relations and Neighbours, and now not one Christian to be seen, nor one house left standing. We went on to a Farm house that was yet standing, where we lay all night: and a comfortable lodging we had, though nothing but straw to ly on. The Lord preserved us in safety that night, and raised us up again in the morning, and carried us along, that before noon, we came to Concord. Now was I full of joy, and yet not without sorrow: joy to see such a lovely sight, so many Christians together, and some of them my Neighbors: There I met with my Brother, and my Brother in Law, who asked me, if I knew where his Wife was? Poor heart! he had helped to bury her, and knew it not; she being shot down by the house was partly burnt: so that those who were at Boston at the desolation of the Town, and came back afterward, and buried the dead, did not know her. Yet I was not without sorrow, to think how many were looking and longing, and my own Children amongst the rest, to enjoy that deliverance that I had now received, and I did not know whither ever I should see them again. Being recruited with food and raiment[62] we went to Boston that day, where I met with my dear Husband, but the thoughts of our dear Children, one being dead, and the other we could not tell where, abated our comfort each to other. I was not before so much hem'd in with the merciless and cruel Heathen, but now as much with pittiful, tender-hearted and compassionate Christians. In that poor, and destressed, and beggerly condition I was received in, I was kindly entertained in severall Houses: so much love I received from several (some of whom I knew, and others I knew not) that I am not capable to declare it. But the Lord knows them all by name: The Lord reward them seven fold into their bosoms of his spirituals, for their temporals.[63] The twenty pounds the price of my redemption was raised by some Boston Gentlemen, and Mrs. Usher, whose bounty and religious charity, I would not forget to make mention of. Then Mr. Thomas Shepard of Charlstown received us into his House, where we continued eleven weeks; and a Father and Mother they were to us. And many more tender-hearted Friends we met with in that place. We were now in the midst of love, yet not without much and frequent heaviness of heart for our poor Children, and other Relations, who were still in affliction. The week following, after my coming in, the Governour and Council sent forth to

61. **the three Children in the fiery Furnace:** Daniel's friends Shadrach, Meshach, and Abednego, who were cast into a fiery furnace for refusing to worship false gods, were delivered from death by God (Daniel 3:13–30).
62. **recruited with food and raiment:** That is, refreshed with food and clothing.
63. **temporals:** Worldly possessions.

the Indians again; and that not without success; for they brought in my Sister, and Good-wife Kettle: Their not knowing where our Children were, was a sore tryal to us still, and yet we were not without secret hopes that we should see them again. That which was dead lay heavier upon my spirit, than those which were alive and amongst the Heathen; thinking how it suffered with its wounds, and I was no way able to relieve it; and how it was buried by the Heathen in the Wilderness from among all Christians. We were hurried up and down in our thoughts, sometime we should hear a report that they were gone this way, and sometimes that; and that they were come in, in this place or that: We kept enquiring and listning to hear concerning them, but no certain news as yet. About this time the Council had ordered a day of publick Thanks-giving: though I thought I had still cause of mourning, and being unsettled in our minds, we thought we would ride toward the Eastward, to see if we could hear any thing concerning our Children. And as we were riding along (God is the wise disposer of all things) between Ipswich and Rowly we met with Mr. William Hubbard, who told us that our Son Joseph was come in to Major Waldrens, and another with him, which was my Sisters Son. I asked him how he knew it? He said, the Major himself told him so. So along we went till we came to Newbury; and their Minister being absent, they desired my Husband to Preach the Thanks giving for them; but he was not willing to stay there that night, but would go over to Salisbury, to hear further, and come again in the morning; which he did, and Preached there that day. At night, when he had done, one came and told him that his Daughter was come in at Providence: Here was mercy on both hands: Now hath God fulfiled that precious Scripture which was such a comfort to me in my distressed condition. When my heart was ready to sink into the Earth (my Children being gone I could not tell whither) and my knees trembled under me, And I was walking through the valley of the shadow of Death: Then the Lord brought, and now has fulfilled that reviving word unto me: *Thus saith the Lord, Refrain thy voice from weeping, and thine eyes from tears, for thy Work shall be rewarded, saith the Lord, and they shall come again from the Land of the Enemy.*[64] Now we were between them, the one on the East, and the other on the West: Our Son being nearest, we went to him first, to Portsmouth, where we met with him, and with the Major also: who told us he had done what he could, but could not redeem him under seven pounds; which the good People thereabouts were pleased to pay. The Lord reward the Major, and all the rest, though unknown to me, for their labour of Love. My Sisters Son was redeemed for four pounds, which the Council gave order for the payment of. Having now received one of our Children, we hastened toward the other; going back through Newbury, my Husband preached there on the Sabbath-day: for which they rewarded him many fold.

On Munday we came to Charlstown, where we heard that the Governour of Road-Island had sent over for our Daughter, to take care of her, being now within his Jurisdiction: which should not pass without our acknowledgments. But she being nearer Rehoboth than Road-Island, Mr. Newman went over, and took care of her, and brought her to his own House. And the goodness of God was admirable to us in our low estate, in

64. ***Thus . . . the Land of the Enemy***: Jeremiah 31:16.

that he raised up passionate[65] Friends on every side to us, when we had nothing to recompance any for their love. The Indians were now gone that way, that it was apprehended dangerous to go to her: But the Carts which carried Provision to the English Army, being guarded, brought her with them to Dorchester, where we received her safe: blessed be the Lord for it, For great is his Power, and he can do whatsoever seemeth him good. Her coming in was after this manner: She was travelling one day with the Indians, with her basket at her back; the company of Indians were got before her, and gone out of sight, all except one Squaw; she followed the Squaw till night, and then both of them lay down, having nothing over them but the heavens, and under them but the earth. Thus she travelled three dayes together, not knowing whither she was going: having nothing to eat or drink but water, and green Hirtle-berries. At last they came into Providence, where she was kindly entertained by several of that Town. The Indians often said, that I should never have her under twenty pounds: But now the Lord hath brought her in upon free-cost, and given her to me the second time. The Lord make us a blessing indeed, each to others. Now have I seen that Scripture also fulfilled, Deuteronomy 30: 4, 7. *If any of thine be driven out to the outmost parts of heaven, from thence will the Lord thy God gather thee, and from thence will he fetch thee. And the Lord thy God will put all these curses upon thine enemies, and on them which hate thee, which persecuted thee.* Thus hath the Lord brought me and mine out of that horrible pit, and hath set us in the midst of tender-hearted and compassionate Christians. It is the desire of my soul, that we may walk worthy of the mercies received, and which we are receiving.

Our Family being now gathered together (those of us that were living) the South Church in Boston hired an House for us: Then we removed from Mr. Shepards, those cordial Friends, and went to Boston, where we continued about three quarters of a year: Still the Lord went along with us, and provided graciously for us. I thought it somewhat strange to set up House-keeping with bare walls; but as Solomon sayes, *Mony answers all things*;[66] and that we had through the benevolence of Christian-friends, some in this Town, and some in that, and others: And some from England, that in a little time we might look, and see the House furnished with love. The Lord hath been exceeding good to us in our low estate, in that when we had neither house nor home, nor other necessaries; the Lord so moved the hearts of these and those towards us, that we wanted neither food, nor raiment for our selves or ours, Proverbs 18. 24. *There is a Friend which sticketh closer than a Brother.* And how many such Friends have we found, and now living amongst? And truly such a Friend have we found him to be unto us, in whose house we lived, *viz.* Mr. James Whitcomb, a Friend unto us near hand, and afar off.

I can remember the time, when I used to sleep quietly without workings in my thoughts, whole nights together, but now it is other wayes with me. When all are fast about me, and no eye open, but his who ever waketh, my thoughts are upon things past, upon the awfull dispensation of the Lord towards us; upon his wonderfull power and might, in carrying of us through so many difficulties, in returning us in safety, and suffering

65. **passionate:** Compassionate.
66. ***Mony answers all things*:** Ecclesiastes 10:19.

none to hurt us. I remember in the night season, how the other day I was in the midst of thousands of enemies, and nothing but death before me: It is then hard work to perswade my self, that ever I should be satisfied with bread again. But now we are fed with the finest of the Wheat, and, as I may say, With honey out of the rock: In stead of the Husk, we have the fatted Calf: The thoughts of these things in the particulars of them, and of the love and goodness of God towards us, make it true of me, what David said of himself, Psalms 6. 6. *I watered my Couch with my tears.* Oh! the wonderfull power of God that mine eyes have seen, affording matter enough for my thoughts to run in, that when others are sleeping mine eyes are weeping.

I have seen the extrem vanity of this World: One hour I have been in health, and wealth, wanting nothing: But the next hour in sickness and wounds, and death, having nothing but sorrow and affliction.

Before I knew what affliction meant, I was ready sometimes to wish for it. When I lived in prosperity, having the comforts of the World about me, my relations by me, my Heart chearfull, and taking little care for any thing; and yet seeing many, whom I preferred before my self, under many tryals and afflictions, in sickness, weakness, poverty, losses, crosses, and cares of the World, I should be sometimes jealous least I should have my portion in this life, and that Scripture would come to my mind, Hebrews 12. 6. *For whom the Lord loveth he chasteneth and scourgeth every Son whom he receiveth.* But now I see the Lord had his time to scourge and chasten me. The portion of some is to have their afflictions by drops, now one drop and then another; but the dregs of the Cup, the Wine of astonishment, like a sweeping rain that leaveth no food, did the Lord prepare to be my portion. Affliction I wanted, and affliction I had, full measure (I thought) pressed down and running over; yet I see, when God calls a Person to any thing, and through never so many difficulties, yet he is fully able to carry them through and make them see, and say they have been gainers thereby. And I hope I can say in some measure, As David did, *It is good for me that I have been afflicted.* The Lord hath shewed me the vanity of these outward things. That they are the Vanity of vanities, and vexation of spirit; that they are but a shadow, a blast, a bubble, and things of no continuance. That we must rely on God himself, and our whole dependance must be upon him. If trouble from smaller matters begin to arise in me, I have something at hand to check my self with, and say, why am I troubled? It was but the other day that if I had had the world, I would have given it for my freedom, or to have been a Servant to a Christian. I have learned to look beyond present and smaller troubles, and to be quieted under them, as Moses said, Exodus 14. 13. *Stand still and see the salvation the Lord.*

[1682, 1913]

Edward Taylor

[c. 1642–1729]

Edward Taylor was born into a Puritan family in Leicestershire, England, probably in 1642, the year in which a civil war erupted that culminated in the execution of King Charles I and the establishment of a Puritan commonwealth in that country in 1650. Very little is known about Taylor's childhood and early education, but he clearly studied languages and the Bible. Some historians believe that he may also have received formal training in those subjects at Cambridge University. After the restoration of King Charles II to the throne of England in 1660, however, conditions there became increasingly dangerous and difficult for Puritans like Taylor. Parliament swiftly passed the Act of Uniformity (1662), which required all teachers and ministers to sign an oath of allegiance to the Church of England. When he refused to sign the oath, Taylor lost his teaching position. Along with a growing number of other religious dissidents in England, he consequently decided to immigrate to New England.

Gravestone of Edward Taylor

No likeness of Taylor was made during his lifetime, much of which he spent in the small community of Westfield, Massachusetts, where he was the minister for nearly sixty years and where he was buried in 1729. His elaborately carved gravestone, which is typical of those erected by the Puritans throughout New England, is crowned by the representation of a winged figure, a hopeful symbol of resurrection.

There, Taylor fulfilled his cherished desire to become a Puritan minister. Arriving in Boston in 1668, at the age of twenty-six, he carried letters of introduction to such important men as the eminent Puritan minister Increase Mather; he was soon admitted as an advanced student to Harvard College. Although he wrote some elegies and other poems as a student, he devoted himself to his studies, which included Hebrew, Latin, and Greek, as well as logic and church history. After his graduation in 1671, Taylor accepted a position as minister of a congregation in Westfield, Massachusetts, then a frontier town a hundred miles west of Boston. His ministry was successful, and Taylor was encouraged by the small congregation to organize it into a formal church. About this time, he met Elizabeth Fitch, with whom he began a courtship that involved the exchange of poems; they were married in early November 1674. The couple had eight children, five of whom died in childhood, before Elizabeth died in 1689. Three years later, Taylor married Ruth Wyllys, with whom he had six additional children. Taylor died on June 24, 1729, having devoted nearly sixty years of his long life to the spiritual and temporal needs of his small congregation in Westfield.

Although he felt intellectually isolated there, Taylor read widely and created an impressive body of work. Immediately after settling in Westfield, he began to gather a library, often laboriously copying out by hand books he could not obtain by other means. In addition to his pastoral duties, he also wrote constantly. Scholars estimate that he preached about three thousand sermons, usually two a week, of which fewer than one hundred have survived. He also kept a journal and composed more than forty thousand lines of verse, poems ranging from private meditations and funeral elegies to a history of Christianity. For Taylor, writing poetry was at once a creative and a religious act, an integral part of his devotional life. For the most part, he imitated the poetic style of George Herbert, John Donne, and other seventeenth-century British writers called the "metaphysical poets." Like their work, Taylor's poems are often complex and ornate, characterized by verbal dexterity, elaborate imagery, and extended metaphors. Family members were probably familiar with some of Taylor's poems, a few of which he also sent to friends in Boston. Aside from parts of those poems, however, none of Taylor's poetry was published during his lifetime. Moreover, at the time of his death in 1729, Taylor specifically requested that descendants keep his manuscripts private. His work consequently languished in obscurity until the manuscripts were discovered in an archive at Yale University by the scholar Thomas H. Johnson, who published the first edition of Taylor's poems in 1939. Since then, he has come to be recognized as a major colonial poet, one whose work illuminates both the intellectual and spiritual passion of Puritanism in New England.

bedfordstmartins.com/ americanlit *for research links on Taylor*

Taylor's *Preparatory Meditations*. This is perhaps the single most celebrated and important group of Taylor's poems, the full title of which is *Preparatory Meditations before my Approach to the Lord's Supper. Chiefly upon the Doctrine preached on the Day of Administration.* As that title indicates, Taylor wrote each of the poems in preparation for administering Communion, or the Lord's Supper. Taylor administered Communion roughly once a month, and 217 of his *Preparatory Meditations* survive, dating from 1682 to 1725. Although they rejected the Catholic doctrine of transubstantiation, or the transformation of the bread and wine into the body and blood of Christ, Puritans believed that God's elect experienced a spiritual union with Christ at the Lord's Supper. As Taylor put it in one of a series of sermons on the Lord's Supper, the sacrament of Communion was "the marriage feast of the King's son," in which God "celebrates the espousals made between His own and only begotten Son, and heir of all things, and the souls of His elect." The sacrament, consequently, required from the elect devout preparation, including prayer, meditation, and self-examination. In contrast to his Communion-day sermon, which Taylor usually delivered upon the same biblical text, his poetic meditation on that text, or doctrine, was thus a private act of devotion addressed directly to God. The texts of the following selections from the *Preparatory Meditations* are taken from *The Poems of Edward Taylor*, edited by Donald E. Stanford (1960).

PROLOGUE

Lord, Can a Crumb of Dust the Earth outweigh,
Outmatch all mountains, nay the Chrystall Sky?
Imbosom in't designs that shall Display
And trace into the Boundless Deity?
Yea hand a Pen whose moysture doth guild ore
Eternall Glory with a glorious glore.[1]

If it its Pen had of an Angels Quill,[2]
And Sharpend on a Pretious Stone ground tite,
And dipt in Liquid Gold, and mov'de by Skill
In Christall leaves should golden Letters write
It would but blot and blur yea jag, and jar
Unless thou mak'st the Pen, and Scribener.

I am this Crumb of Dust which is design'd
To make my Pen unto thy Praise alone,
And my dull Phancy[3] I would gladly grinde
Unto an Edge on Zions Pretious Stone.[4]
And Write in Liquid Gold upon thy Name
My Letters till thy glory forth doth flame.

Let not th'attempts breake down my Dust I pray
Nor laugh thou them to scorn but pardon give.
Inspire this Crumb of Dust till it display
Thy Glory through't: and then thy dust shall live.
Its failings then thou'lt overlook I trust,
They being Slips slipt from thy Crumb of Dust.

Thy Crumb of Dust breaths two words from its breast,
That thou wilt guide its pen to write aright
To Prove thou art, and that thou art the best
And shew thy Properties to shine most bright.
And then thy Works will shine as flowers on Stems
Or as in Jewellary Shops, do jems.

[c. 1682, 1960]

---

1. **glore:** Scottish dialect spelling of *glory*.
2. **Quill:** A writing instrument made by slitting the end of the shaft of a wing or tail feather of a large bird. The end is then dipped into ink and used as a pen.
3. **Phancy:** Fancy, the term frequently used in the seventeenth century for the imagination.
4. **Zions Pretious Stone:** In Christian thought, Zion is the heavenly city, the streets of which are paved with precious stones: "And the foundations of the wall of the city were garnished with all manner of precious stones. The first foundation was jasper; the second, sapphire; the third, a chalcedony; the fourth, an emerald" (Revelations 21:19).

Meditation 8 (First Series)
John 6:51 I am the Living Bread[1]

I kening through Astronomy Divine
The Worlds bright Battlement, wherein I spy
A Golden Path my Pensill cannot line,
From that bright Throne unto my Threshold ly.
And while my puzzled thoughts about it pore
I finde the Bread of Life in't at my doore.

When that this Bird of Paradise[2] put in
This Wicker Cage (my Corps) to tweedle praise
Had peckt the Fruite forbad: and so did fling
Away its Food; and lost its golden dayes;
It fell into Celestiall Famine sore:
And never could attain a morsell more.

Alas! alas! Poore Bird, what wilt thou doe?
The Creatures field no food for Souls e're gave.
And if thou knock at Angells dores they show
An Empty Barrell: they no soul bread have.
Alas! Poore Bird, the Worlds White Loafe is done.
And cannot yield thee here the smallest Crumb.

In this sad state, Gods Tender Bowells[3] run
Out streams of Grace: And he to end all strife
The Purest Wheate in Heaven, his deare-dear Son
Grinds, and kneads up into this Bread of Life.
Which Bread of Life from Heaven down came and stands
Disht on thy Table up by Angells Hands.

Did God mould up this Bread in Heaven, and bake,
Which from his Table came, and to thine goeth?
Doth he bespeake thee thus, This Soule Bread take.
Come Eate thy fill of this thy Gods White Loafe?
Its Food too fine for Angells, yet come, take
And Eate thy fill. Its Heavens Sugar Cake.

1. **I am the Living Bread:** The text for this meditation is from John 6:22–59, which includes the account of Jesus Christ establishing the ritual of the Lord's Supper, the sacrament of Communion: "'I am the living bread which came down from heaven: if any man eat of this bread, he shall live for ever: and the bread that I will give is my flesh, which I will give for the life of the world'" (John 6:51).
2. **Bird of Paradise:** A beautiful tropical bird, here representing the soul encaged within the body.
3. **Bowells:** The deep interior of the body, including the heart, considered the seat of tender and compassionate emotions.

What Grace is this knead in this Loafe? This thing
　　Souls are but petty things it to admire.
Yee Angells, help: This fill would to the brim
　　Heav'ns whelm'd-down[4] Chrystall meele Bowle, yea and higher.
　　This Bread of Life dropt in thy mouth, doth Cry.
　　Eate, Eate me, Soul, and thou shalt never dy.

[June 8, 1684, 1960]

---

4. **welm'd-down:** Turned upside down.

MEDITATION 38 (FIRST SERIES)
1 JOHN 2:1 AN ADVOCATE WITH THE FATHER[1]

Oh! What a thing is Man? Lord, Who am I?
　　That thou shouldst give him Law[2] (Oh! golden Line)
To regulate his Thoughts, Words, Life thereby.
　　And judge him Wilt thereby too in thy time.
　　A Court of Justice thou in heaven holdst
　　To try his Case while he's here housd on mould.[3]

How do thy Angells lay before thine eye
　　My Deeds both White, and Black I dayly doe?
How doth thy Court thou Pannellst[4] there them try?
　　But flesh complains. What right for this? let's know.
　　For right, or wrong I can't appeare unto't.
　　And shall a sentence Pass on such a suite?

Soft; blemish not this golden Bench, or place.
　　Here is no Bribe, nor Colourings[5] to hide
Nor Pettifogger[6] to befog the Case
　　But Justice hath her Glory here well tri'de.
　　Her spotless Law all spotted Cases tends.
　　Without Respect or Disrespect them ends.

---

1. **An Advocate . . . Father:** The text for this meditation is from 1 John 2:1–2: "My little children, these things write I unto you, that ye sin not. And if any man sin, we have an advocate with the Father, Jesus Christ the righteous: And he is the propitiation for our sins: and not for our's only, but also for *the sins of* the whole world."
2. **Law:** The Ten Commandments.
3. **mould:** The body, which decays.
4. **Pannellst:** To impanel, as on a jury.
5. **Colourings:** Pervading character or tone.
6. **Pettifogger:** An early term for one who deals with petty cases or employs dubious legal practices.

God's Judge himselfe: and Christ Atturny is,
The Holy Ghost Regesterer[7] is founde.
Angells the sergeants[8] are, all Creatures kiss
The booke, and doe as Evidences[9] abounde.
All Cases pass according to pure Law
And in the sentence is no Fret,[10] nor flaw.

What saist, my soule? Here all thy Deeds are tri'de.
Is Christ thy Advocate to pleade thy Cause?
Art thou his Client? Such shall never slide.
He never lost his Case: he pleads such Laws
As Carry do the same, nor doth refuse
The Vilest sinners Case that doth him Choose.

This is his Honour, not Dishonour: nay
No Habeas-Corpus[11] gainst his Clients came
For all their Fines his Purse doth make down pay.
He Non-Suites Satan's Suite or Casts the Same.[12]
He'l plead thy Case, and not accept a Fee.
He'l plead Sub Forma Pauperis[13] for thee.

My Case is bad. Lord, be my Advocate.
My sin is red: I'me under Gods Arrest.
Thou hast the Hint of Pleading; plead my State.
Although it's bad thy Plea will make it best.
If thou wilt plead my Case before the King:
I'le Waggon Loads of Love, and Glory bring.

[July 6, 1690, 1960]

---

7. **Regesterer:** Keeper of records.
8. **sergeants:** Those who keep order in a court.
9. **Evidences:** Witnesses.
10. **Fret:** Anxiety or distress.
11. **Habeas-Corpus:** Literally, "you shall have the body in court" (Latin). A law requiring a person under arrest to be brought before a judge or court in a timely manner. In this context, Christ's clients are brought to trial immediately because Christ has already offered himself for their sins.
12. **He Non-Suites . . . or Casts the Same:** That is, Christ nullifies or dismisses the "suite," or lawsuit, brought by Satan.
13. **Sub Forma Pauperis:** Literally, "in the rank or form of a pauper" (Latin). It refers to someone who is without the funds to pursue a lawsuit or the costs of a criminal defense. If the court grants this status, the person is entitled to a waiver of the legal expenses or an appointment of counsel.

Taylor's *God's Determinations*. The full title of this poetic sequence is *God's determinations touching upon his Elect: and the Elect's combat in their conversion, and coming up to God in Christ, together with the comfortable effects thereof.* The ambitious series of poems covers the whole of spiritual history, from the creation of the world and the fall of man through Christ's crucifixion and the redemption of God's elect to the final, joyous ascent of their souls to heaven. The texts of the following two poems, the first and final poems in the sequence, are taken from *The Poems of Edward Taylor*, edited by Donald E. Stanford (1960).

THE PREFACE

Infinity, when all things it beheld
In Nothing, and of Nothing all did build,
Upon what Base was fixt the Lath, wherein
He turn'd this Globe, and riggalld[1] it so trim?
Who blew the Bellows of his Furnace Vast?
Or held the Mould wherein the world was Cast?
Who laid its Corner Stone?[2] Or whose Command?
Where stand the Pillars upon which it stands?
Who Lac'de and Fillitted[3] the earth so fine,
With Rivers like green Ribbons Smaragdine[4]?
Who made the Sea's its Selvedge,[5] and it locks
Like a Quilt Ball[6] within a Silver Box?
Who Spread its Canopy? Or Curtains Spun?
Who in this Bowling Alley bowld the Sun?
Who made it always when it rises set
To go at once both down, and up to get?
Who th'Curtain rods made for this Tapistry?
Who hung the twinckling Lanthorns in the Sky?
Who? who did this? or who is he? Why, know
Its Onely Might Almighty this did doe.
His hand hath made this noble worke which Stands

1. **riggalld:** Grooved.
2. **Corner Stone:** See Job 38:1-7: "Then the LORD answered Job out of the whirlwind, and said, 'Who is this that darkeneth counsel by words without knowledge? Gird up now thy loins like a man; for I will demand of thee, and answer thou me. Where wast thou when I laid the foundations of the earth? declare, if thou hast understanding. Who hath laid the measures thereof, if thou knowest? or who hath stretched the line upon it? Whereupon are the foundations thereof fastened? or who laid the corner stone thereof?' "
3. **Lac'de and Fillitted:** That is, bound up with fine cords or ribbons.
4. **Smaragdine:** Emerald green.
5. **Selvedge:** Edge of woven fabric finished to prevent unraveling.
6. **Quilt Ball:** Ball made of worsted thread.

His Glorious Handywork not made by hands.
Who spake all things from nothing; and with ease
Can speake all things to nothing, if he please.
Whose Little finger at his pleasure Can
Out mete[7] ten thousand worlds with halfe a Span:
Whose Might Almighty can by half a looks
Root up the rocks and rock the hills by th'roots.
Can take this mighty World up in his hande,
And shake it like a Squitchen[8] or a Wand.
Whose single Frown will make the Heavens shake
Like as an aspen leafe the Winde makes quake.
Oh! what a might is this Whose single frown
Doth shake the world as it would shake it down?
Which All from Nothing fet,[9] from Nothing, All:
Hath All on Nothing set, lets Nothing fall.
Gave All to nothing Man indeed, whereby
Through nothing man all might him Glorify.
In Nothing then imbosst the brightest Gem
More pretious than all pretiousness in them.
But Nothing man did throw down all by Sin:
And darkened that lightsom Gem in him.
  That now his Brightest Diamond is grown
  Darker by far than any Coalpit Stone.

[c. 1685, 1960]

7. **Out mete:** Out measure.
8. **Squitchen:** A switch.
9. **fet:** Fetched or obtained.

THE JOY OF CHURCH FELLOWSHIP RIGHTLY ATTENDED

In Heaven soaring up, I dropt an Eare
  On Earth: and oh! sweet Melody:
And listening, found it was the Saints[1] who were
  Encoacht for Heaven that sang for Joy.
  For in Christs Coach they sweetly sing;
  As they to Glory ride therein.

1. **Saints:** To the Puritans, saints were the elect, those chosen for salvation by God.

Oh! joyous hearts! Enfir'de with holy Flame!
Is speech thus tassled[2] with praise?
Will not your inward fire of Joy contain;
That it in open flames doth blaze?
For in Christ's Coach Saints sweetly sing,
As they to Glory ride therein.

And if a string do slip, by Chance, they soon
Do screw it up again: whereby
They set it in a more melodious Tune
And a Diviner Harmony.
For in Christs Coach they sweetly sing
As they to Glory ride therein.

In all their Acts, publick, and private, nay
And secret too, they praise impart.
But in their Acts Divine and Worship, they
With Hymns do offer up their Heart.
Thus in Christs Coach they sweetly sing
As they to Glory ride therein.

Some few not in;[3] and some whose Time, and Place
Block up this Coaches way do goe
As Travellers afoot, and so do trace
The Road that gives them right thereto
While in this Coach these sweetly sing
As they to Glory ride therein.

[c. 1685, 1960]

---

2. **tassled:** Embellished.
3. **Some few not in:** That is, those who were outside the "Coach," or the church.

Taylor's Miscellaneous Poems. From the time he was in college to the end of his life, Taylor wrote a wide range of miscellaneous poems. Some of them were occasioned by specific events, including the deaths of his first wife and several of his children, while others were more abstract meditations on religious issues like the struggle between the terrors of death and the triumphant faith in Resurrection. Still other poems reveal Taylor's richly imaginative response to the mundane particulars of his immediate material world, which he uses to develop sustained and often surprising analogies or parallels to spiritual mysteries, like the operation of God's saving grace on the souls of the elect. In such poems, Taylor reveals his mastery of a device earlier exploited by English poets like John Donne and George Herbert, the "metaphysical conceit," which the English critic Dr.

Samuel Johnson famously defined as "a combination of dissimilar images, or the discovery of occult resemblances in things apparently unlike." The texts of the following poems are taken from *Poems of Edward Taylor*, edited by Donald E. Stanford (1960).

UPON WEDLOCK, AND DEATH OF CHILDREN

A Curious Knot[1] God made in Paradise,
And drew it out inamled[2] neatly Fresh.
It was the True-Love Knot, more sweet than spice
And set with all the flowres of Graces dress.
Its Weddens Knot,[3] that ne're can be unti'de.
No Alexanders Sword[4] can it divide.

The slips[5] here planted, gay and glorious grow:
Unless an Hellish breath do sindge their Plumes.
Here Primrose, Cowslips, Roses, Lilies blow
With Violets and Pinkes that voide perfumes.
Whose beautious leaves ore laid with Hony Dew.
And Chanting birds Cherp out sweet Musick true.

When in this Knot I planted was, my Stock
Soon knotted, and a manly flower out brake.[6]
And after it my branch again did knot
Brought out another Flowre[7] its sweet breathd mate.
One knot gave one tother the tothers place.
Whence Checkling smiles fought in each others face.

But oh! a glorious hand from glory came
Guarded with Angells, soon did Crop this flowre
Which almost tore the root up of the same
At that unlookt for, Dolesome, darksome houre.

1. **Knot:** A flower bed, sometimes called a flower-knot, laid out in an intricate design.
2. **inamled:** Enameled, or polished.
3. **Weddens Knot:** The wedding ceremony in which a couple is joined in matrimony.
4. **Alexanders Sword:** Ancient legends said that whoever could untie the Gordian knot, a complicated knot tied by Gordius, father of King Midas, would rule Asia. Alexander the Great (356-323 BCE) simply cut the knot in two with his sword and then conquered much of the ancient world.
5. **slips:** Cuttings taken from a plant for planting or grafting.
6. **a manly flower out brake:** Samuel Taylor, his first son, born on August 27, 1675.
7. **another Flowre:** A daughter, Elizabeth Taylor, was born on December 27, 1677; but she died a year later (see line 20).

In Pray're to Christ perfum'de it did ascend,
And Angells bright did it to heaven tend.

But pausing on't, this sweet perfum'd my thought,
Christ would in Glory have a Flowre, Choice, Prime,
And having Choice, chose this my branch forth brought.
Lord take't. I thanke thee, thou takst ought of mine,
It is my pledg in glory, part of mee
Is now in it, Lord, glorifi'de with thee.

But praying ore my branch, my branch did sprout
And bore another manly flower,[8] and gay
And after that another, sweet brake out,
The which the former hand soon got away.[9]
But oh! the tortures, Vomit, screechings, groans,
And six weeks Fever would pierce hearts like stones.

Griefe o're doth flow: and nature fault would finde
Were not thy Will, my Spell Charm, Joy, and Gem:
That as I said, I say, take, Lord, they're thine.
I piecemeale pass to Glory bright in them.
I joy, may I sweet Flowers for Glory breed,
Whether thou getst them green, or lets them seed.

[c. 1682, 1960]

8. **bore another manly flower:** Another son, James Taylor, was born on October 12, 1678.
9. **And after that another . . . got away:** A second daughter, Abigail Taylor, was born on August 6, 1681; like the first daughter, she died a year later.

UPON A SPIDER CATCHING A FLY

Thou sorrow, venom Elfe.
Is this thy play,
To spin a web out of thyselfe
To Catch a Fly?
For Why?

I saw a pettish[1] wasp
Fall foule therein.
Whom yet thy Whorle pins[2] did not clasp
Lest he should fiing
His sting.

1. **pettish:** Peevish or ill-humored.
2. **Whorle pins:** Small flywheels fixed on the side of a spinning wheel to regulate speed.

But as affraid, remote
Didst stand hereat
And with thy little fingers stroke
And gently tap
His back.

Thus gently him didst treate
Lest he should pet,
And in a froppish,[3] waspish heate
Should greatly fret
Thy net.

Whereas the silly Fly,
Caught by its leg
Thou by the throate tookst hastily
And 'hinde the head
Bite Dead.

This goes to pot, that not
Nature doth call.[4]
Strive not above what strength hath got
Lest in the brawle
Thou fall.

This Frey[5] seems thus to us.
Hells Spider gets
His intrails spun to whip Cords thus
And wove to nets
And sets.

To tangle Adams race
In's stratigems
To their Destructions, spoil'd, made base
By venom things
Damn'd Sins.

But mighty, Gracious Lord
Communicate
Thy Grace to breake the Cord, afford
Us Glorys Gate
And State.

3. **froppish:** Fretful or peevish.
4. **This goes to pot, that not / Nature doth call:** That is, those who do not call upon "Nature," or natural reason, "go to pot."
5. **Frey:** Fray, a battle or fight.

We'l Nightingaile sing like
  When pearcht on high
In Glories Cage, thy glory, bright,
  And thankfully,
    For joy.

[?, 1960]

HUSWIFERY[1]

Make me, O Lord, thy Spining Wheele compleate.[2]
  Thy Holy Worde my Distaff make for mee.
Make mine Affections thy Swift Flyers neate
 And make my Soule thy holy Spoole to bee.
 My Conversation make to be thy Reele
 And reele the yarn thereon spun of thy Wheele.

Make me thy Loome then, knit therein this Twine:
 And make thy Holy Spirit, Lord, winde quills:[3]
Then weave the Web thyselfe. The yarn is fine.
 Thine Ordinances make my Fulling Mills.[4]
 Then dy the same in Heavenly Colours Choice,
 All pinkt with Varnisht Flowers of Paradise.

Then cloath therewith mine Understanding, Will,
 Affections, Judgment, Conscience, Memory
My Words, and Actions, that their shine may fill
 My wayes with glory and thee glorify.
 Then mine apparell shall display before yee
 That I am Cloathd in Holy robes for glory.

[?, 1960]

1. **Huswifery:** A collective term for household duties, usually performed by the wife, or housewife. In this poem, the emphasis is on the process of making cloth, in preparation for making clothes.
2. **Spining Wheele compleate:** The spinning wheel, which produces thread from raw wool or flax, operates by using a distaff, which holds the flax or wool in place; flyers, which regulate the spinning; a spool, which captures and twists the yarn; and a reel, upon which the thread is wound.
3. **quills:** Spindles or bobbins on which thread is wound.
4. **Fulling Mills:** A mill in which cloth is "fulled," or cleaned, by being beaten with wooden mallets and cleansed with soap or fuller's earth, an absorbent, claylike substance.

A FIG[1] FOR THEE OH! DEATH

Thou King of Terrours with thy Gastly Eyes
With Butter[2] teeth, bare bones Grim looks likewise.
And Grizzly Hide, and clawing Tallons, fell,
Opning to Sinners Vile, Trap Door of Hell,
That on in Sin impenitently trip
The Downfall art of the infernall Pit,
Thou struckst thy teeth deep in my Lord's blest Side:
Who dasht it out, and all its venom 'stroyde
That now thy Poundrill[3] shall onely dash
My Flesh and bones to bits, and Cask shall clash.[4]
Thou'rt not so frightfull now to me, thy knocks
Do crack my shell. Its Heavenly kernells box
Abides most safe. Thy blows do break its shell,
Thy Teeth its Nut. Cracks are that on it fell.
Thence out its kirnell fair and nut, by worms
Once Viciated out, new formd forth turns
And on the wings of some bright Angell flies
Out to bright glory of Gods blissfull joyes.
Hence thou to mee with all thy Gastly face
Art not so dreadfull unto mee through Grace.
I am resolvde to fight thee, and ne'er yield,
Blood up to th'Ears; and in the battle field
Chasing thee hence: But not for this my flesh,
My Body, my vile harlot, its thy Mess,[5]
Labouring to drown me into Sin, disguise
By Eating and by drinking such evill joyes
Though Grace preserv'd mee that I nere have
Surprised been nor tumbled in such grave.[6]
Hence for my strumpet I'le ne'er draw my Sword
Nor thee restrain at all by Iron Curb
Nor for her safty will I 'gainst thee strive

1. **Fig:** Something that is small, valueless, or contemptible.
2. **Butter:** Yellow in color.
3. **Poundrill:** A pestle, used for crushing substances in a bowl.
4. **Cask shall clash:** That is, his body will reverberate with the blow.
5. **Mess:** Serving of food; a meal.
6. **My Body . . . in such grave:** Taylor wrote two versions of this poem. The first was in his manuscript book; the second version, reprinted here, was included in his manuscript collection of finished poems, *Poetical Works.* Lines 24–28 in the first version are somewhat clearer: "My harlot body, make thou it, thy Mess, / That oft ensnared mee with its Strumpets guide / Of Meats and drinks dainty Sensualities. / Yet Grace ne'er suffer me to turn aside/ As Sinners oft fall in & do abide."

But let thy frozen gripes take her Captive
And her imprison in thy dungeon Cave
And grinde to powder in thy Mill the grave,
Which powder in thy Van[7] thou'st safely keep
Till she hath slept out quite her fatall Sleep.
When the last Cock shall Crow the last day in
And the Arch Angells Trumpets sound shall ring[8]
Then th'Eye Omniscient seek shall all there round
Each dust death's mill had very finely ground,
Which in death's smoky furnace well refinde
And Each to'ts fellow hath exactly joyn't,
Is raised up anew and made all bright
And Christalized; all top full of delight.
And entertains its Soule again in bliss
And Holy Angells waiting all on this,
The Soule and Body now, as two true Lovers
Ery night how do they hug and kiss each other.
And going hand in hand thus through the skies
Up to Eternall glory glorious rise.
Is this the Worst thy terrours then canst, why
Then should this grimace at me terrify?
Why camst thou then so slowly? Mend thy pace.
Thy Slowness me detains from Christ's bright face.
Although thy terrours rise to th'highst degree,
I still am where I was, a Fig for thee.

[?, 1960]

7. **Van:** A winnowing basket, used to separate grain from the chaff.
8. **the last day . . . Trumpets sound shall ring:** Judgment Day, announced by the trumpets of seven angels, as described in Revelations, chapters 8–11.

Francis Daniel Pastorius

[1651–c. 1719]

The only child of a distinguished lawyer, Melchoir Adam Pastorius, and his wife, Magdalena, Francis Pastorius was born on September 16, 1651, in Sommerhausen, then a part of the German duchy of Franconia. At about the age of seventeen, Pastorius entered the University of Altorf, where he was educated in classical and modern languages, science, and theology. Pastorius then studied law, earning a degree at the University of Nuremberg in 1676, and taught for a brief period in Frankfurt. There, he became acquainted with Philip Jacob Spener (1635-1705), a minister and theologian who advanced a reform movement within the Lutheran Church known as Pietism. Believing that the church Martin Luther had established was becoming remote from the daily lives of individuals, Spener sought to revitalize the original Lutheran doctrine of a priesthood of believers, emphasizing the importance of Bible study, daily devotion, and prayer. He organized small groups for such purposes and attracted a number of intellectuals to Frankfurt, including the English Quaker William Penn (1644-1718), who visited the city in 1677.

After Penn founded the new colony of Pennsylvania in 1681, a group formed the Frankfurt Land Company and arranged to buy a tract of land near Philadelphia. Pastorius, who agreed to serve as the agent for the company, consequently immigrated to Pennsylvania in 1683. When he arrived, Pastorius immediately confronted problems about the land purchase, which had been concluded without Penn's knowledge. But Pastorius was tenacious, and Penn soon agreed to the sale with the provision that the company settle thirty families on the tract within a year. In an effort to attract colonists to Germantown, which he immediately began to lay out, Pastorius published a pamphlet, the title of which is translated as *Positive Information from America, concerning the Country of Pennsylvania, from a German who has migrated thither, dated Philadelphia, March 7, 1684.* Observing that his sole purpose was to "set forth faithfully both the inconveniences of the journey and the defects of this province, as well as that plentifulness of the same which has been praised by others almost to excess," Pastorius affirmed: "For I desire nothing more in my little corner of the earth than to walk in the footsteps of Him who is the way, and to follow His holy teachings, because He is the Truth, in order that I may forever enjoy with Him eternal life." Committing himself to the new settlement, Patorius soon married another German immigrant, Anneke Klosterman, a widow with two children who arrived in 1684.

bedfordstmartins.com/ americanlit *for research links on Pastorius*

Pastorius became one of the ablest leaders of both the settlement at Germantown and the colony of Pennsylvania. Although he united with the Quakers, Pastorius encouraged settlers from all religious faiths, not simply those belonging to the Society of Friends. Deeply concerned with human freedom, Pastorius in 1688 wrote what is widely regarded to be the first formal protest of a religious group against the institution of slavery.

In it, Pastorius asks, "Have not these negroes as much right to fight for their freedom as you have to keep them slaves?" The protest, which was sent by the Germantown Friends to the yearly meeting of the Society in Philadelphia, was instrumental in the eventual abolition of slavery in the German settlements in the English colonies. Pastorius's little-known role in the history of the antislavery movement was later commemorated in a long narrative poem, *The Pennsylvania Pilgrim* (1872), by the Quaker poet and abolitionist John Greenleaf Whittier. Even as he sought freedom for the slaves, Pastorius followed Penn's example of maintaining friendly relationships with the Indians, ironically observing of the native and immigrant populations of Pennsylvania that, "if I were to call the former savages and the latter Christians, I should do great injustice to many of both varieties."

Pastorius was also deeply engaged in the cultural life of the settlement at Germantown. He owned the largest library, a collection of about 250 books in several languages, and he wrote constantly. Another version of his first tract on Pennsylvania was edited by his father and published in 1692, followed by an even fuller version of the work in 1700. His various manuscript volumes included collections of sayings, descriptions of nature, and philosophical speculations, as well as exercises designed to maintain his knowledge of languages. Sensitive to the language barriers between English colonists and the growing German population of Pennsylvania, Pastorius wrote a textbook designed for use in the schools, *A New Primmer or Methodical Directions to attain the True Spelling, Reading & Writing of English* (1698). He also wrote poetry, some of it in English. In a poem apparently written toward the end of his life, Pastorius hailed "the young generations yet to be," urging them to look with pity upon the trials and with toleration upon the failings of the first of those who had left their "sacred hearths and homes" in Germany for

> New forest-homes beyond the mighty sea,
> There undisturbed and free
> To live as brothers of one family.

Pastorius, who had done so much to lay the foundations of community, freedom, and brotherhood at Germantown, died there in late 1719 or early 1720.

Pastorius's Letter from Philadelphia. In 1700, an expanded version of Pastorius's earlier tracts on Pennsylvania was published in Leipzig, Germany. The bulk of the book, the title of which is translated as *Circumstantial Geographical Description of the Lately Discovered Province of Pennsylvania*, was devoted to a survey of the development of Germantown and the larger colony of Pennsylvania. In a kind of appendix, the volume also included a collection of letters written by Pastorius, his father, his brothers, and even some by William Penn. In the following letter, Pastorius candidly responds to a series of questions that his father has evidently raised about the government of the colony, its native peoples, the conduct of religious life there, and the character of William Penn. The text of the letter, translated from the German by Gertrude S. Kimball, is taken from *Narratives of Early Pennsylvania, West New Jersey, and Delaware, 1630-1707*, edited by Albert C. Myers (1912).

LETTER SENT FROM PHILADELPHIA MAY 30, 1698

I received in proper condition, on April 25, 1698, my honored father's latest, of August 15, and I was greatly rejoiced by the sight of his dear handwriting. But to answer his questions submitted, I would wish that my pen could reach down to the uttermost depth of my soul, for so should I do the same with more satisfaction than is the case now. Nevertheless I do not doubt that my honored father will supply by his keen apprehension that which is not perfectly expressed on this paper:

1. *Now as to the first question, concerning the ordering of the civil government.*

William Penn is and remains lord of the proprietary and sanctioned prince over Pennsylvania, and although he has not been here with us for some years,[1] nevertheless he has done us more service in England through his presence there, than probably might have been the case if he had remained here all the time. The estimable man has very many enemies on account of his religion, who however rather overdo matters, since they, for their part, are not surely informed, much less can they see into another's heart. We expect his arrival in this country without fail, this summer, or next autumn, if no ill-health or other hindrance occurs.

So far as relates to the form of the civil government here at Philadelphia, as the capital city, I state briefly that each year certain persons are elected from the whole people, who make the necessary laws and ordinances for that year according to the condition of the time and the people, and thereby prevent encroaching vices and moreover, throughout the whole year, in all circumstances, they help to care for the common weal, by and with the governor of the province. At the same time the aforesaid proprietary, William Penn, ordains a certain twelve, from among those thus elected, to be justices, who decide all disputes occurring according to the laws thus made, after the facts have been investigated by twelve neighbors. And all this is done in open court, so that everyone, great and small, may enter and listen.

In my German city, Germanton, there is an entirely different condition of things. For,

1. **William Penn . . . some years:** William Penn (1644-1718) was the Quaker founder of the Pennsylvania Colony, which was established by a charter obtained from Charles II of England in 1681. Penn, the proprietor of the colony, returned to England in 1684 and did not return to Pennsylvania again until 1699.

by virtue of the franchise obtained from William Penn, this town has its own court, its own burgomaster and council, together with the necessary officials, and well-regulated town laws, council regulations, and a town seal.

The inhabitants of this city are for the most part tradespeople, such as cloth, fustian,[2] and linen weavers, tailors, shoemakers, locksmiths, carpenters, who however at the same time are also occupied with the cultivation of the soil and the raising of cattle.

This region would be sufficient to maintain twice as many inhabitants as are now actually there.

This town lies two hours' distance from Philadelphia, and includes not only six thousand acres (*morgen*)[3] by the survey, but twelve thousand *morgen* of land have also been assigned to us by William Penn for the establishing of some villages. As to the taxation and tribute of the subjects, in this country, it is treated as it is with the English nation, where neither the king himself nor his envoys, bailiffs, nor governors may lay any kind of burden or tax upon the subjects, unless those subjects themselves have first voluntarily resolved and consented to give a specified amount, and, according to their fundamental laws, no tax may remain in force for longer than a single year.

2. *To come to my honored father's second question.*

What form of government have the so-called savages and half-naked people? Whether they become citizens and intermarry with the Christians? Again, whether their children also associate with the Christian children and they play with one another, etc.?

It may be stated in reply, that, so far as I have yet gone about among them, I have found them reasonable people and capable of understanding good teaching and manners, who give evidence of an inward devotion to God, and in fact show themselves much more desirous of a knowledge of God than are many with you who teach Christianity by words from the pulpit, but belie the same through their ungodly lives, and therefore, in yonder great Day of Judgment, will be put to shame by these heathen.

We Christians in Germanton and Philadelphia have no longer the opportunity to associate with them, in view of the fact that their savage kings have accepted a sum of money from William Penn, and, together with their people, have withdrawn very far away from us, into the wild forest, where, after their hereditary custom, they support themselves by the chase, shooting birds and game, and also by catching fish, and dwell only in huts made of bushes and trees drawn together. They carry on no cattle-breeding whatever, and cultivate no field or garden; accordingly they bring very little else to the Christians to market than the pelts, the skins of animals, and the birds which they have shot, and fishes, nor do they associate much with the Christians; and certainly no mutual marriage-contract between us and them has yet taken place. They exchange their elk and deer-skins, beaver, marten, and turkeys, ordinarily, for powder, lead, blankets, and brandy, together with other sweet drinks.

2. **fustian:** Thick, durable cloth, more frequently used for coverings than for clothing.
3. ***morgen*:** German measure of land equal to about two-thirds of an acre.

In the business of our German Company, however, we now use in trade Spanish and English coins, as also the Dutch thalers;[4] with this difference only, that that which is worth four shillings on the other side of the sea, passes for five here.

3. *Concerning the third question: How our divine worship is regulated and constituted in this place?*

The answer is that, as experience testifies that by the coercion of conscience nothing else than hypocrites and word-Christians are made, of whom almost the entire world is now full, we have therefore found it desirable to grant freedom of conscience, so that each serves God according to his best understanding, and may believe whatever he is able to believe.

It is certain, once for all, that there is only one single undoubted Truth. Sects however are very numerous, and each sectarian presumes to know the nearest and most direct way to Heaven, and to be able to point it out to others, though nevertheless there is surely no more than a single One Who on the basis of truth has said: I am the Way, the Truth and the Life.

Although now each sect, with us, is accustomed to hold undisturbed its assembly on the seventh day of the week, it is nevertheless proved by experience and trial, that the most part serve a God unknown to them out of mere habit, concerning Whom they have heard other people speak. But they will neither feel nor listen to God Himself, nor taste His goodness; they are without spiritual apprehension, and their fleshly senses do not comprehend what the Spirit of God is, the verbal or historical narrative to which they listen does not reach the heart, and therefore does not edify them; so soon as the church-meeting is over, all is again forgotten; if the intention of their hearts is set upon usury, finance, deceit, and luxury before the service, it is still set thereon. Not once is amendment of life kept in mind, or how one shall put on Christ, or how Christ the Lord shall impress his image on them.

Such societies and sects one should reasonably avoid, and on the other hand seek his companions among those holy ones in the light of truth, who love the great goodness and truth of God with all their heart, trust His holy providence and highly extol His power, whose souls are in God and God is in them, of whose souls the Holy Ghost bears witness that they are the children of God.

We should follow yonder One our Master, Who has given us those words which His Heavenly Father gave to Him.

His true disciples abide by this His Word, and He gives His Spirit to these disciples, which the world neither perceives nor is able to receive, which also could not be purchased by Simon Magus[5] for any money, but he who desires to have the same must turn

---

4. **thalers:** Silver coins.

5. **Simon Magus:** First-century Samaritan thought to be the first Gnostic, an adherent of what many early Christians perceived as a heretical movement designed to corrupt the early Christian church by introducing alternative rites, beliefs, and myths. Simon is mentioned briefly in the Bible as a magician who offered the apostles money for access to the Holy Spirit (Acts 8:9–11, 18–20).

from the old path of sin, renounce the world, cast himself into the father-heart of God, and resign himself entirely to the dear Lord, and beseech Him humbly, that He may draw him to Himself, for the Lord Christ says: No man can come to me except the Father which hath sent me draw him. John vi., and Ephesians i.[6] It all depends on the mercy of God, and not at all on any man's wish or deed.

I must acknowledge that our age and the religious disputes are beyond my comprehension and understanding, and that with all the individual churches there is wanting the life of the inner man, and the life at one at Christ. Molinas and his sect of the Quietists[7] have much alarmed the Papal See, in that he pointed out the way to Heaven through the inward faith of the heart and love to God and our neighbor, and not through works, pilgrimages, and penance. And because similar teachings will be also urged at the present time here and there among the Evangelical churches, by the Pietists,[8] therefore, many of them, both clergy and laymen, men devoted to a luxurious life and to ease, are much alarmed, saying that man can not be without sin, that there must be bad and good men together, that it may certainly be permitted to have a little Jesuitical drinking-bout in good fraternal spirit.[9]

I for my part hold this as my entire secure hope, that I look up to God alone, and with my whole heart cling to and trust Him, under Whose protection alone is safety, and without Him there is neither safety nor Truth nor faith. He alone can illumine the hearts of men, He can destroy the living, and bring the dead to life again, and knows how to protect His own in the midst of the fiery furnace.

But they that are joined unto the Lord are one Spirit with him. I Corinthians vi. 17. They may become partakers of the divine nature. II Peter i. 4. And hereby know we that we dwell in him and he in us, because he hath given us of his Spirit. John iv. 13. We behold as in a mirror the glory of the Lord. II Corinthians iii. 18.

And Luther,[10] in vol. VI., Altenberg, fol. 625, says clearly: "Thou shalt therefore so hold by the faith that thou shalt become by the same one with Christ, that out of thee and Him shall be, as it were, one person, Who will never permit them to separate or part from one another." And in the *Kirchen-Postill*, fol. 243. "We should become filled with the Spirit of God, so that, as respects the inner man, we may be entirely consecrated and sanctified."

---

6. **John vi., and Ephesians i:** The verses are taken from John 6:44 and Ephesians 1:4-6.
7. **Molinas . . . Quietists:** Miguel de Molinos (1640-1696) of Spain was the founder of Quietism, a form of religious mysticism that involves devotional contemplation and abandonment of the individual will. Pope Innocent XI condemned Molinos as a heretic in 1687.
8. **Pietists:** In the seventeenth century, the reaction of many Lutherans against what they viewed as the increasing dogmatism of their church led to the movement known as Pietism, which called for the revival of devotion and practical Christianity.
9. **Jesuitical drinking-bout . . . fraternal spirit:** The Jesuits were the Society of Jesus, a Roman Catholic order founded in 1534, specifically to promote missionary work in non-Christian countries. They were strong opponents of the Protestant Reformation, committed to education, and well known for their willingness to engage in dialogue with others, which is apparently the sense of this passage.
10. **Luther:** The works of Martin Luther (1483-1546), a leader of the Protestant Reformation, were widely read, especially in Germany. Pastorius refers by volume and page to an edition published in Altenberg, Germany, and to a standard collection of Luther's church sermons, the *Kirchen-Postill*.

The holy name of this great God should be at all times held in high esteem by us all, in the new as in the old world, and kept holy above all else. And it is well with him, yes forever well with all those who desire the speedy coming of Jesus, and have oil in their lamps, and are ready to go in with the blessed Bridegroom to His eternal wedding-feast.[11]

4. *Concerning the fourth question: How our German Company and Brotherhood is at present constituted.*

It should be stated that this same company was started by some pious and God-fearing persons, not so much for the sake of worldly gain, but rather to have a Pella[12] or place of refuge for themselves and other upright people of their country, when the just God should pour out His cup of wrath over sinful Europe.

With this intention they arranged to purchase from the proprietor, through me, about thirty thousand acres of land in this country, of which the third part is now cultivated, but two-thirds still lie waste.

The principal members are, by name: Doctor Jacob Schütz, Jacobus von de Walle, Doctor Weilich, Daniel Behagel, Johann Lebrunn, Doctor Gerhard von Maastrich, the Syndic of Bremen, Doctor Johann Willhelm Peters of near Magdeburg, Balthasar Jabert of Lübeck, and Joannes Kembler, a preacher at the same place. Of these partners some were to have come over here to me and helped to bring the undertaking to the desired result, but up to this time that has not happened, because they fear the solitude and tediousness, to all of which I, thank God! am now well accustomed, and shall so remain accustomed until my happy end.

However, that the merciful God has so graciously preserved my honored father together with his dear ones in this recent devastation of the French war,[13] gives me occasion to extol His everlasting goodness and fervently to beseech Him to protect you still further, with gentle fatherly care, from all chances of misfortune, but especially that He will bring us ever more and more into His holy fear and obedience, so that we may feel abhorrence to offend Him, and, on the contrary, may strive to fulfil His holy will with happy hearts.

In the meantime, my honored father's calm resolve to live his own life and to serve God, has much pleased and rejoiced me. A blessed foretaste of those things whereof we are to expect the fullness in eternity after laying aside this earthly tabernacle!

---

11. **Bridegroom . . . wedding-feast:** The parable is told in Matthew 25:1-13.
12. **Pella:** The ancient capital of Macedonia, Pella remained a center of Greek culture even after it came under Roman rule. During the revolt of the Jews and the Roman siege of Jerusalem in 66 CE, the city offered a safe refuge to the small Christian community of Mount Zion.
13. **French war:** The Nine Years' War (also known as the War of the Grand Alliance) was fought in Europe and America from 1688 to 1697. In Europe, a coalition of European countries fought French expansion along the Rhine River. In America, what was called King William's War – the first of the French and Indian Wars – was fought between French and English colonists over control of the settlements in Canada.

O blessed leading of the Holy Ghost! for what else should it be, or what could it be called, save the holy grace of God, that has also at last made my honored father (after he has become gray in the service of many offices at Windsheimb)[14] so white in soul and temper that he has recognised the overwhelming wickedness of mankind, and on that account has gone out from Babel.[15] May the Heavenly Father of all Light preserve this gift of the Holy Spirit in my honored father's heart until his departure from this life and entering into eternity.

5. *Concerning the fifth question: Whether William Penn, the proprietor of this country, is easy of access, and if one might address some lines of compliment to him.*

It may be stated, that this worthy man is a good Christian, and consequently entirely averse to the idle compliments of the world. But he who wishes to exchange sensible and truthful words with him, either by mouth or by letter, will find him not only easy of access, but also prompt in reply, since he is, from his heart, sweet-natured, humble, and eager to serve all men.

Furthermore, my two sons greet my honored father affectionately, and daily pray for his temporal and eternal well-being, wishing ardently either to see him once in person, or at least to obtain some information respecting the course of his life and the occupations conducted by him.

Finally, that my honored father has had troublesome dreams concerning me, and at the same time has regarded it as a bad omen that my little tree, planted in his garden before my departure, has withered, is truly not without [meaning], for I, my wife and youngest son have gone through severe illness, yet, praise be to God, are fully restored again. But such things are a reminder of our mortality. All must have an end, and therefore this letter also, in closing which I greet my honored father a thousand times, and kiss him (through the air) with the heart of a child, perhaps for the last time, and most trustingly commend you with us, and us with you, to the beneficent protecting and guiding hand of God; and I remain

My honored father's

Truly dutiful son,

Philadelphia F. D. P.

30 May 1698

[1700, 1912]

---

14. **Windsheimb:** By the time of this letter, Pastorius's father had retired from the Bavarian town of Windsheim to Nuremberg.

15. **Babel:** In Genesis 11:1-9, the townspeople of Babel attempt to build a tower to reach heaven. God thwarts the plan by causing the languages of the builders to be mutually incomprehensible.

American Contexts

Colonial Diaries and Journals

"About ten o'clock in the morning, made this book, and put these papers in it," the influential Puritan minister Jonathan Edwards noted on January 22, 1742. His book was made up of sheets of paper on which Edwards had been writing daily notes and meditations. Most colonial writers referred to such a book as a diary or journal, though the latter term was more often used to refer more specifically to an itinerary or record of travel. In creating a personal record of his spiritual growth and experiences, Edwards was following a long tradition. Such private writings were given impetus by the Protestant Reformation, with its strong emphasis on the role of reflection and self-examination in the spiritual lives of individuals. From the arrival of the first English settlers, keeping a diary was, consequently, a common activity in the colonies, especially among the Puritans in New England.

But diaries were not simply used for spiritual purposes. As the large numbers of published and unpublished diaries that survive from the colonial period indicate, men and women kept them for many reasons. The variety of purposes they served are illustrated by the diaries and journals represented in this section. The Boston merchant and public servant Samuel Sewall kept a detailed record of his activities in the bustling city and outlying towns in Massachusetts, while his contemporary and frequent associate the Puritan minister Cotton Mather turned inward to his emotional and spiritual struggles. Based on a diary she kept during the trip, Sarah Kemble Knight's *Journal* is a lively account of her five-month journey from Boston through what she viewed as the crude and provincial towns of Connecticut to New York. At about the same time she took that trip in 1704-05, William Byrd returned from England, where he had been educated, to take charge of Westover, the extensive tobacco plantation he had inherited in Virginia. There, a world away from Boston and New York, he recorded the daily activities and routines of an elegant country gentleman, even as he offered glimpses of the dark realities of slavery and indentured servitude upon which the plantation system depended. Indeed, Knight's *Journal* and the diaries of Sewall, Mather, and Byrd do not simply reveal the attitudes, characters, and experiences of their authors. The selections that follow, all written in the twenty-year period between 1692 and 1712, also illustrate some of the conflicts, divisions, and diversity of life in the colonies during a period of increasing commerce and urbanization in the North and the rapid expansion and consolidation of the slave-labor system in the South.

bedfordstmartins.com/ americanlit *for research links on the authors in this section*

Samuel Sewall

[1652-1730]

Born into a prominent Puritan merchant family in England, Samuel Sewall was brought by his parents to the Massachusetts Bay Colony in 1661. An industrious young man with a quick intelligence, Sewall earned two degrees from Harvard College. Late in his career there, at the end of 1673, he began a diary that he kept with rare interruptions until a few months before his death in 1730. Although he was a devout Puritan, Sewall's diary devotes less attention to his private spiritual life than to his activities as a businessman and public servant of the Massachusetts Bay Colony. From 1691 to 1725, Sewall served as a member of the Governor's Council, and he played a prominent role in the witch trials at Salem. On May 27, 1692, Sewall was appointed to the Commission of Oyer and Terminer, a special judicial group assigned "to enquire of, hear and determine all manner of crimes and offenses" involving witchcraft at Salem. The trials, which resulted in the executions of twenty people, cast a shadow over Sewall's reputation. But he later publicly recanted his part in the witch trials. He also argued for more humane treatment of the Indians and wrote an early antislavery tract, *The Selling of Joseph* (1700). Sewall was unconventional in other ways as well, famously refusing to follow the emerging fashion for men of his class to wear wigs. Indeed, his diary offers a rich portrait of life in Massachusetts during a period of rapid change and

John Smithbert, *Judge Samuel Sewall* (1729)

The Scottish-born Smithbert, who had studied art in England and Italy before setting up shop in Boston, painted this portrait the year before Sewall's death in 1730. As the portrait reveals, to the very end of his life Sewall resisted the then-current fashion for men to shave their heads and wear elaborate powdered wigs. (Photograph © 2006 Museum of Fine Arts, Boston.)

transition, describing domestic scenes, religious services, social gatherings, and public spectacles like the execution of seven pirates in Boston. The text of the following selections from the diary, which was first published between 1878 and 1882, is taken from *The Diary of Samuel Sewall*, edited by M. Halsey Thomas (1973).

From THE DIARY OF SAMUEL SEWALL

April 11th 1692. Went to Salem, where, in the Meeting-house, the persons accused of Witchcraft were examined;[1] was a very great Assembly; 'twas awfull to see how the afflicted persons were agitated. Mr. Noyes pray'd at the beginning, and Mr. Higginson concluded. [*In the margin*], Vae, Vae, Vae,[2] Witchcraft.

---

1. **Went to Salem . . . examined:** This is Sewall's first reference to the trials at Salem, where in 1692 nineteen men and women were accused and convicted of practicing witchcraft and sentenced to death by hanging. A twentieth man was pressed to death with heavy stones for refusing to stand trial on similar charges. Sewall was one of seven men appointed to the Commission of Oyer and Terminer (a special court authorized to judge criminal cases) to hear the witchcraft cases.
2. **Vae, Vae, Vae:** Woe, Woe, Woe (Latin).

* * * * * * *

July 20th 1692. Fast at the house of Capt. Alden, upon his account.[3] Mr. Willard pray'd. I read a Sermon out of Dr. Preston, 1st and 2d Uses of God's Alsufficiency. Capt. Scottow pray'd, Mr. Allen came in and pray'd, Mr. Cotton Mather, then Capt. Hill. Sung the first part 103. Psalms,[4] concluded about 5. aclock. Brave Shower of Rain while Capt. Scottow was praying, after much Drought. Cous. Daniel Gookin sups with us, and bespeaks my marrying of him to morrow.

July 27, 1692. A plentifull Rain falls after great Drought.

July 30, 1692. Mrs. Cary[5] makes her escape out of Cambridge-Prison, who was Committed for Witchcraft.

Thorsday, Augt. 4. At Salem, Mr. Waterhouse brings the news of the desolation at Jamaica, June 7th. 1700 persons kill'd, besides the Loss of Houses and Goods by the Earthquake.[6]

* * * * * * *

Augt. 19th 1692. This day [*in the margin*, Dolefull! Witchcraft] George Burrough, John Willard, John Procter, Martha Carrier and George Jacobs were executed at Salem, a very great number of Spectators being present. Mr. Cotton Mather was there, Mr. Sims, Hale, Noyes, Chiever, &c. All of them said they were innocent, Carrier and all. Mr. Mather says they all died by a Righteous Sentence. Mr. Burrough by his Speech, Prayer, protestation of his Innocence, did much move unthinking persons, which occasions their speaking hardly concerning his being executed.

Augt. 25. Fast at the old [*First*] Church, respecting the Witchcraft, Drought, &c.

* * * * * * *

3. **Fast . . . Capt. Alden:** Sewall took part in a fast, a ritual abstention from food and drink, at the home of Captain John Alden (c. 1626–1701/2), the son of Priscilla and John Alden of Plymouth. Alden was accused of witchcraft, imprisoned for fifteen weeks, and later escaped with the help of friends.
4. **103. Psalms:** Psalms 103, which begins: "Bless the Lord, O my soul; and all that is within me, *bless* his holy name."
5. **Mrs. Cary:** Elizabeth Cary was tried for witchcraft, committed to prison in Cambridge, and escaped to New York.
6. ***Thorsday* . . . Earthquake:** *Thursday* is derived from the Old English *Thu(n)resdoeg*, "day of Thunor or Thor," the Scandinavian god of thunder, whose weapon was a hammer. A powerful earthquake completely destroyed Port Royal, the main port of Jamaica, on June 7, 1692.

Monday, Sept. 19, 1692. About noon, at Salem, Giles Corey[7] was press'd to death for standing Mute; much pains was used with him two days, one after another, by the Court and Capt. Gardner of Nantucket who had been of his acquaintance: but all in vain.

Sept. 20. Now I hear from Salem that about 18 years agoe, he was suspected to have stampd and press'd a man to death, but was cleared. Twas not remembred till Anne Putnam was told of it by said Corey's Spectre the Sabbath-day night before Execution.

Sept. 20, 1692. The Swan brings in a rich French Prize[8] of about 300 Tuns, laden with Claret, White Wine, Brandy, Salt, Linnen Paper, &c.

Sept. 21. A petition is sent to Town in behalf of Dorcas Hoar, who now confesses: Accordingly an order is sent to the Sherriff to forbear her Execution, notwithstanding her being in the Warran to die to morrow. This is the first condemned person who has confess'd.[9]

* * * * * * *

Thorsday, Sept. 22, 1692. William Stoughton, Esqr., John Hathorne, Esqr., Mr. Cotton Mather, and Capt. John Higginson, with my Brother St., were at our house, speaking about publishing some Trials of the Witches.[10]

* * * * * * *

Nov. 6 [1692]. Joseph threw a knop of Brass and hit his Sister Betty on the forhead so as to make it bleed and swell; upon which, and for his playing at Prayer-time, and eating when Return Thanks, I whipd him pretty smartly. When I first went in (call'd by his Grandmother) he sought to shadow and hide himself from me behind the head of the Cradle: which gave me the sorrowfull remembrance of Adam's carriage.[11]

* * * * * * *

7. **Giles Corey:** While the others accused of witchcraft submitted to trials, Giles Corey refused and faced the penalty for such an action: being pressed to death by heavy stones.
8. **French Prize:** The ship was taken during King William's War (1690-97), the first of a long series of wars between England and France for supremacy in North America.
9. **confess'd:** Under the terms of the court at Salem, confession of witchcraft insured immunity from execution.
10. **Trials of the Witches:** *The Wonders of the Invisible World* (1693), Cotton Mather's defense of the trials, which was rushed into print in Boston in October 1692.
11. **Adam's carriage:** After Adam and Eve ate the forbidden fruit, they "hid themselves from the presence of the Lord God amongst the trees of the garden" (Genesis 3:8).

Nov. 22, 1692. I prayd that God would pardon all my Sinfull Wanderings, and direct me for the future. That God would bless the Assembly in their debates, and that would chuse and assist our Judges, &c., and save New England as to Enemies and Witchcrafts, and vindicate the late Judges, consisting with his Justice and Holiness, &c., with Fasting. [. . .]

* * * * * * *

Jany. 15. [1697]. [. . .] Copy of the Bill I put up on the Fast day;[12] giving it to Mr. Willard as he pass'd by, and standing up at the reading of it, and bowing when finished; in the Afternoon.

Samuel Sewall, sensible of the reiterated strokes of God upon himself and family; and being sensible, that as to the Guilt contracted, upon the opening of the late Commission of Oyer and Terminer at Salem (to which the order for this Day relates) he is, upon many accounts, more concerned than any that he knows of, Desires to take the Blame and Shame of it, Asking pardon of Men, And especially desiring prayers that God, who has an Unlimited Authority, would pardon that Sin and all other his Sins; personal and Relative: And according to his infinite Benignity, and Soveraignty, Not Visit the Sin of him, or of any other, upon himself or any of his, nor upon the Land: But that He would powerfully defend him against all Temptations to Sin, for the future; and vouchsafe him the Efficacious, Saving Conduct of his Word and Spirit.

* * * * * * *

Fourth-day, June, 19. 1700. [. . .] Having been long and much dissatisfied with the Trade of fetching Negros from Guinea; at last I had a strong Inclination to Write something about it; but it wore off. At last reading Bayne, Ephesians[13] about servants, who mentions Blackamoors; I began to be uneasy that I had so long neglected doing any thing. When I was thus thinking, in came Brother Belknap to shew me a Petition he intended to present to the General Court for the freeing a Negro and his wife, who were unjustly held in Bondage. And there is a Motion by a Boston Committee to get a Law that all Importers of Negros shall pay 40 s[14] *per* head, to discourage the bringing of them. And Mr. C. Mather resolves to publish a sheet to exhort Masters to labour their Conversion.

12. **Copy of the Bill . . . Fast Day:** Sewall publicly recanted his role in the witch trials and had this confession of his sins read aloud at church on the day set aside by the colony for fasting and repentance for the trials at Salem.
13. **Bayne, Ephesians:** Paul Baynes, *A Commentarie on the First Chapter of the Epistle of Saint Paul, Written to the Ephesians* (1618).
14. **40 s:** In the currency system, 40 shillings equaled 2 pounds.

Which makes me hope that I was call'd of God to Write this Apology for them;[15] Let his Blessing accompany the same.

* * * * * * *

Tuesday, June, 10th [1701]. Having last night heard that Josiah Willard had cut off his hair (a very full head of hair) and put on a Wigg,[16] I went to him this morning. Told his Mother what I came about, and she call'd him. I enquired of him what Extremity had forced him to put off his own hair, and put on a Wigg? He answered, none at all. But said that his Hair was streight, and that it parted behinde. Seem'd to argue that men might as well shave their hair off their head, as off their face. I answered men were men before they had hair on their faces, (half of mankind have never any). God seems to have ordain'd our Hair as a Test, to see whether we can bring our minds to be content to be at his finding: or whether we would be our own Carvers, Lords, and come no more at Him. If disliked our Skin, or Nails; 'tis no Thanks to us, that for all that, we cut them not off: Pain and danger restrain us. Your Calling is to teach men self Denial. Twill be displeasing and burdensom to good men: And they that care not what men think of them care not what God thinks of them. Father, Brother Simon, Mr. Pemberton, Mr. Wigglesworth, Oakes, Noyes (Oliver), Brattle of Cambridge their example. Allow me to be so far a *Censor Morum*[17] for this end of the Town. Pray'd him to read the Tenth Chapter of the Third book of Calvins Institutions.[18] I read it this morning in course, not of choice. Told him that it was condemn'd by a Meeting of Ministers at Northampton in Mr. Stoddards house, when the said Josiah was there. Told him of the Solemnity of the Covenant which he and I had lately enter'd into, which put me upon discoursing to him. He seem'd to say would leave off his Wigg when his hair was grown. I spake to his Father of it a day or two after: He thank'd me that had discoursed his Son, and told me that when his hair was grown to cover his ears, he promis'd to leave off his Wigg. If he had known of it, would have forbidden him. His Mother heard him talk of it; but was afraid positively to forbid him; lest he should do it, and so be more faulty.

* * * * * * *

15. **this Apology for them:** Sewall's *The Selling of Joseph*, published on June 24, 1700, is generally regarded as the first antislavery tract printed in the American colonies. As he later recorded, for publishing the tract Sewall was subjected to "frowns and harsh words" in Boston, where many wealthy people owned slaves.
16. **Wigg:** Fashionable men in Boston began to shave their heads and wear elaborate wigs in the early eighteenth century. Josiah Willard was the son of Sewall's minister.
17. ***Censor Morum*:** Judge of morals (Latin).
18. **Calvins Institutions:** John Calvin's *Institutes of the Christian Religion*, first published in 1536, outlines the central principles of Calvinist theology.

Sabbath, Novr 30. [. . .] I spent this Sabbath at Mr. Colman's, partly out of dislike to Mr. Josiah Willard's cutting off his Hair, and wearing a Wigg: He preach'd for Mr. Pemberton in the morning; He that contemns the Law of Nature, is not fit to be a publisher of the Law of Grace.

* * * * * * *

Feria Sexta, Junij,[19] *30, 1704.* As the Governour sat at the Council-Table twas told him, Madam Paige was dead; He clap'd his hands, and quickly went out, and return'd not to the Chamber again; but ordered Mr. Secretary to prorogue the Court till the 16th of August, which Mr. Secretary did by going into the House of Deputies. After Dinner, about 3. p.m. I went to see the Execution.[20] By the way (cous. Ephr. Savage with me) James Hawkins certifies us of Madam Paiges death; he was to make a Tomb. Many were the people that saw upon Broughton's Hill. But when I came to see how the River was cover'd with People, I was amazed: Some say there were 100 Boats. 150 boats and Canoes, saith Cousin Moody of York. He told them. Mr. Cotton Mather came with Capt Quelch and six others for Execution from the Prison to Scarlet's Wharf, and from thence in the Boat to the place of Execution about the midway between Hudson's point and Broughton's Warehouse. Mr. Bridge was there also. When the scaffold was hoisted to a due height, the seven Malefactors went up; Mr. Mather pray'd for them standing upon the Boat. Ropes were all fasten'd to the Gallows (save King, who was Repriev'd). When the Scaffold was let sink, there was such a Screech of the Women that my wife heard it sitting in our Entry next the Orchard, and was much surprised at it; yet the wind was sou-west. Our house is a full mile from the place.

[1692-1704, 1973]

---

19. ***Feria Sexta, Junij***: Friday, June (Latin).
20. **Execution**: Seven convicted pirates were publicly executed in Boston on June 30, 1704.

Cotton Mather

[1663-1728]

The eldest son of the eminent Puritan minister Increase Mather, Cotton Mather became one of the most active and influential religious figures of his day. As a minister of the Second Church in Boston and in his hundreds of published writings, Mather sought to revive the spirit of the early founders and to preserve the Puritan theocracy of the Massachusetts Bay Colony. Like the founders of the colony, Mather viewed the Puritans as analogous to the ancient Israelites, whose mission was to establish proper worship in a new land promised them by God. Mather celebrated the process by which the "wilderness" of New England was transformed into an ideal Christian society in his most important book, *Magnalia Christi Americana* (1702). The title may be translated as "A history of the wonderful works of Christ in America," but in the minds of many Mather is most closely associated with the most notorious episode in the history of New England, the witch trials at Salem. Although he did not participate directly in the trials, Mather contributed to the hysteria over witchcraft in his sermons and works like *The Wonders of the Invisible World*, a defense of the trials published in 1692. Keenly aware of his own shortcomings, Mather recorded what he viewed as his many failures in a diary in which he meditated at length on his religious work and spiritual condition. Although it is clear that Mather kept his diary throughout his life, much of it was lost or destroyed. What remains is the diary he kept from 1681 through 1708. The following entries were written during a time of great personal trial for Mather. His first wife, Abigail, died on December 5, 1702. Mather's complex responses to the romantic attentions he received during the following months from an attractive young woman reveal some of the private struggles of a very prominent man and Puritan minister in Boston. The text is taken from *The Diary of Cotton Mather*, edited by Worthington C. Ford (1911-12).

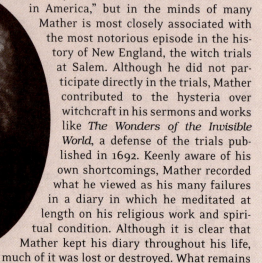

Peter Pelham, *Cottonus Matherus* (1728)

Mather's renown was so great that the *Boston Gazette* began running announcements of the forthcoming publication of this print portrait only six days after his death in 1728.

From THE DIARY OF COTTON MATHER

February begins with a very astonishing Trial.

There is a young Gentlewoman[1] of incomparable Accomplishments. No Gentlewoman in the English *America* has had a more polite Education. She is one of rare Witt and Sense; and of a comely Aspect; and extremely Winning in her Conversation, and she has a Mother of an extraordinary Character for her Piety.

This young Gentlewoman first Addresses me with diverse Letters, and then makes me a Visit at my House; wherein she gives me to understand, that she has long had a

1. **Gentlewoman:** Although Mather never names the woman, scholars have identified her as Katherine Maccarty, the daughter of a Boston merchant.

more than ordinary Value for my Ministry; and that since my present Condition has given her more of Liberty to think of me, she must confess herself charmed with my Person, to such a Degree, that she could not but break in upon me, with her most importunate Requests, that I would make her mine; and that the highest Consideration she had in it, was her eternal Salvation, for if she were mine, she could not but hope the Effect of it would be, that she should also be Christ's.

I endeavoured faithfully to sett before her, all the discouraging Circumstances attending me, that I could think of. She told me, that she had weigh'd all those Discouragements, but was fortified and resolved with a strong Faith in the mighty God, for to encounter them all. And whereas I had mention'd my way of living, in continual Prayers, Tears, Fasts, and macerating Devotions and Reservations, to divert her from her Proposal, she told me, that this very Consideration was that which animated her; for she desired nothing so much as a Share in my way of Living.

I was in a great Strait, how to treat so polite a Gentlewoman, thus applying herself unto me. I plainly told her, that I feared, whether her Proposal would not meet with unsurmountable Oppositions from those who had a great Interest in disposing of me. However I desired, that there might be Time taken, to see what would be the wisest and fittest Resolution.

In the mean Time, if I could not make her my own, I should be glad of being any way Instrumental, to make her the Lord's.

I turned my Discourse, and my Design into that Channel; and with as exquisite Artifice as I could use, I made my Essayes[2] to engage her young Soul into Piety.

She is not much more than twenty years old. I know she has been a very aiery Person.[3] Her Reputation has been under some Disadvantage.

What Snares may be laying for me, I know not. Much Prayer with Fasting and Patience, must be my way to encounter them.

I think, how would my Lord Jesus Christ Himself treat a returning Sinner.

I shall shortly see more into the Meaning of this odd Matter.

12 d. 12 m. [*February.*] *1702.*[4] *Friday.* Being this Day, forty Years old; (How solemn a Word!) I sett apart the Day, for the Duties of a *secret Fast*,[5] before the Lord.

In the Devotions of this Day, my Spirit felt several Irradiations from Heaven; but among my Dissolutions into Tears, there was none more sensible, than in this Thought:

Oh! the wondrous and glorious Vertue, in the Blood of my Lord Jesus Christ! That all the Sins committed in forty Years together, are now pardoned, thro' the atoning Vertue of that Blood! Oh! what a Blessed Thing is the Righteousness of my Lord Jesus Christ; that a Man who has been horribly sinning for forty Years together, may stand in that Righteousness

---

2. **Essayes**: Efforts.
3. **aiery Person**: Someone who is light or insubstantial.
4. **1702**: In the Julian, or Old Style, calendar, the year began on March 25 instead of January 1. The year was, therefore, 1703 in the Gregorian – or New Style – calendar, which was not adopted in England until 1752.
5. ***Fast***: Ritual abstinence from food and drink.

before God, and be treated and loved, as if he had been all this while in the exactest Manner glorifying of the Lord.

My sore Distresses and Temptations, I this day carried unto the Lord; with Hope of His Compassions, to his tempted Servant.

The cheef of them lies in this. The well accomplished Gentlewoman, mention'd, (tho' not by Name,) in the Close of the former Year; one whome every body does with Admiration confess to be, for her charming Accomplishments, an incomparable Person; addressing me to make her mine; and professing a Disposition unto the most Holy Flights of Religion to ly at the Bottom of her Addresses: I am in the greatest Straits imaginable, what Course to steer. Nature itself causes in me, a mighty Tenderness for a person so very amiable. Breeding requires me to treat her with Honour and Respect, and very much of Deference, to all that she shall at any time ask of me. But Religion, above all, obliges me, instead of a rash rejecting her Conversation, to contrive rather, how I may imitate the Goodness of the Lord Jesus Christ, in His Dealing with such as are upon a Conversion unto Him.

On the other side; I cannot but fear a fearful Snare, and that I may soon fall into some Error in my Conversation, if the Point proposed unto me, be found, after all, unattaineable, thro' the violent Storm of Opposition, which I cannot but foresee and suspect will be made unto it.

The dreadful Confusions, which I behold Heaven, even *devising* for me, do exceedingly break and wast my spirit. I should recover a wondrous Degree of Health, if I were not broken by these Distresses, and grievous Temptations. But these things cause me to spend more Time than ordinary for the most part every Day, in Prayers and in Tears, prostrate on my Study-floor before the Lord. Yea, and they cause me by Night also sometimes to hold my *Vigils*, in which I cry to God, until, and after, the Middle of the Night, that He would look down upon me, and help me, and save me, and not cast me off.

18 d. 12 m. Thursday. This Day was kept as a Fast, thro' the Province. I enjoy'd great Assistences, in the services of the Day.

As for my special soul-harassing Point; I did some Dayes ago, under my Hand, vehemently beg, as for my Life, that it might be desisted from, and that I might not be kill'd by hearing any more of it. Yett such was my flexible Tenderness, as to be conquered by the Importunities of several, to allow some further Interviewes. But I resolved, that I would make them turn chiefly upon the most glorious Design in the World. I did, accordingly; and once especially, I did, with all the Charms I could imagine, draw that witty Gentlewoman unto tearful Expressions of her Consent, unto all the Articles in the Covenant of Grace, the Articles of her Marriage and Union with the Great L[ord] Redeemer. I had Abundance of Satisfaction in this Action; whatever may be the Issue of our Conversation.

20 d. 12 m. Satureday. My grievous Distresses, (occasion'd especially by the late Addresses made unto me, by the person formerly mentioned, and the Opposition of her Enemies,) cause me to fall down before the Lord, with Prayers and with Tears continually. And because my Heart is sore pained within me, to think, what I shall do, or what will be the Issue of my distressing Affayr, I think it proper to multiply my *Vigils* before the Lord. One of them I kept this Night; and as it grew towards the Morning, after I had cried unto the Lord, for my Releef and Succour, under the Temptations now harassing of me, I did again throw myself prostrate in the Dust, before the Lord; beseeching of Him, that if He would not hear my cries for myself, He would yett hear my cries for my Flock; and hereupon I wrestled with the Lord for my great Congregation, that the Interests of Religion might prevail mightily among them, and especially in the young People of my Congregation.

It was a Consolation unto me, to think, that when my People were all asleep in their Beds, their poor Pastor should be watching, and praying and weeping for them.

The Lord, in His holy Sovereignity orders it, that I am left unto great Vexations from Satan, about this Time; who fills me with fears, that I am a man rejected and abhorred of God, and given up to the worst of Delusions; and that the Lord will make no more use of me to glorify Him. I am scarce able to live under these doleful Disconsolations.

And that I may be left utterly destitute of all humane Support, my Relatives, thro' their extreme Distaste at the Talk of my Respects for the Person, above mentioned; and fear lest I should over-value her; do treat me with unsupportable Strangeness and Harshness.

Lord, I am oppressed; undertake for me!

5 d. 4 m. [*June.*] *Satureday.* I sett apart this Day, for Prayer with Fasting in my Study, to justify and glorify the Lord, under all His holy Frowns upon me, and obtain Grace to carry it well in my present Condition, and to resign myself, and all my Concerns into His glorious Hands.

12 d. 4 m. Satureday. I attended the like Duties again.

The Holy Justice and Wisdome of God, shines forth, in His awful Dispensations towards me.

A lying Spirit is gone forth, and the People of the Town, are strangely under the Influences of it.

I have the Inconvenience of being a Person, whom the Eye and the Talk of the People is very much upon. My present Circumstances give them Opportunities to invent and report Abundance of disadvantageous Falsehoods, of my being engaged in such and such Courtships, wherein I am really unconcerned. But the Addresses which I have had from the young Gentlewoman so often mentioned in these Papers, and the Discourses thereby raised among the dissatisfied People, afford the greatest Theme for their mischievous and malicious Lying to turn upon. When all Assaults upon me from that Quarter, have been hitherto unsuccessful, at last, I am unhappily persecuted with Insinuations, that I had proceeded so far in Countenancing that matter, I could not with Honour and Justice now steer clear of it, as I have done. God strangely appears for me, in this Point also, by disposing the young Gentlewoman, with her Mother, to furnish me with their Assertions, *That I have never done any unworthy Thing; but acted most honourably and righteously towards them, and as became a Christian, and a Minister; and they will give all the World leave to censure them after the hardest Manner in the World, if ever they should speak the Contrary;* Yea, they have proceeded so far beyond all Bounds in my Vindication, as to say, *They verily look upon* Mr M——r *to be as great a Saint of God, as any upon Earth.* Nevertheless, the Divel owes me a Spite, and he inspires his People in this Town, to whisper impertinent Stories, which have a Tendency to make me Contemptible, and hurt my Serviceableness, and strike at, yea, strike out the Apple of my Eye. My Spirit is on this Occasion too much disturbed. I am encountring an *Hour and Power of Darkness.* My Temptations from the Clamour of many People, among whom I hear the Defaming of many; the desolate Condition of my Family, not likely to be provided for; and the Desertions which my Soul suffers, while I behold the dreadful Frown of God upon my Prayers, my Fasts, my Fears, my Resignations, and all my Endeavours to glorify Him: these things do exceedingly unhinge me; and cause me sometimes to *speak unadvisedly with my Lips.* Tis well, if they do not perfectly kill me.

17 d. 5 m. Satureday. I sett apart this Day, for Prayer with Fasting, in my Study, to obtain a good Progress and Success of the affayr, which I am now managing; and a Deliverance from any further Vexation, Temptation, or Encumbrance by the young Gentlewoman, that has vexed me with so many of her Wiles, and by such exquisite Methods been trying to ensnare or trouble me.

The Rage of that young Gentlewoman, whom out of obedience to God, I have rejected, (and never more pleased God than in rejecting of her Addresses to me,) is transporting her, to threaten that she will be a Thorn in my Side, and contrive all possible Wayes to vex me, affront me, disgrace me, in my Attempting a Return to the married State with another Gentlewoman. Instead of using other Contrivances, to quell the Rage of a Person, who is of so rare a Witt, but so little Grace, that I may expect unknown Damages from her, I carried her to the Lord Jesus Christ. I pleaded, that my Lord Jesus Christ is able to do every thing; that He can restrain Satan, and all Satanic Influences at His Pleasure; that my Temptations had already proceeded a great Way; and His Name would suffer, and His poor Servant would sink, if He should permitt them to proceed any further; and that I had out of Obedience unto Him, exposed myself unto the Rage, by which I was now likely to be incommoded. And I concluded still, with a triumphant Faith in my Lord Jesus Christ, for my Victory over the Mischiefs which threatned me.

Behold, within a few Dayes, the Gentlewoman without my seeking it, sent me a Letter, with a Promise under her Hand, that she would offer me none of those Disquietments, which in her Passion she had threatned. I was astonished at this work of Heaven; and with the Tears of a raptured Soul, I offered up a Sacrifice of Love and Praise unto the Lord.

My Conversation with the lovely Person,[6] to whom Heaven has directed me, goes on, with pure, chast, noble Strokes, and the Smiles of God upon it.

And the Universal Satisfaction which it has given to the People of God, thro' town and Countrey, proclames itself, to a Degree which perfectly amazes me.

[1703, 1911-12]

---

6. **lovely Person:** In August 1703, Mather married a widow, Elizabeth Hubbard, who, unlike Katherine Maccarty, was greatly admired by his family and friends.

Sarah Kemble Knight

[1666–1727]

The daughter of a successful merchant, Thomas Kemble, and his wife, Elizabeth Trerice, Sarah Kemble Knight received early lessons in independence. She worked in her father's business and was later a teacher of handwriting, a copier of legal documents, and a shop manager. In 1689, Knight married Richard Knight, a sea captain, who died while on business in London. A widow with financial means and practical abilities, Knight continued her own business success and left a large estate to her daughter when she died in 1727. Knight, however, is now best known for her account of a journey she took more than twenty years earlier. After the death of her cousin, Caleb Trowbridge, Knight was determined to help settle his estate in favor of his young widow. Knight consequently decided to travel to Trowbridge's home in New Haven, Connecticut. On October 2, 1704, she began what proved to be a five-month journey, going first to New Haven, then to New York, and finally returning to Boston on March 3, 1705. It was unusual for a woman of her time to undertake such an arduous trip on horseback, especially since most of Knight's traveling companions were strangers. Used by mail carriers, the route she took was frequently traveled, but roads in the early eighteenth century were rough, unmarked, and dangerous. Knight kept notes in a diary and wrote her journal after she returned to Boston. Instead of writing about the business of her trip, she devoted her lively narrative to her itinerary, describing the inns where she stayed and the food she ate. She also offered blunt opinions about the people she met, the incidents she observed, and the stories she heard. Certainly, Knight revealed attitudes common in her time and place, especially among members of her class, including her support of slavery and her disdain for Native Americans. Her journal, found among family papers, was first edited and published by Timothy Dwight as *The Private Journal Kept by Madam Knight, On a Journey From Boston to New York, In the Year 1704* (1825). The text of the following selections is taken from *The Journal of Madam Knight*, edited by George P. Winship (1920).

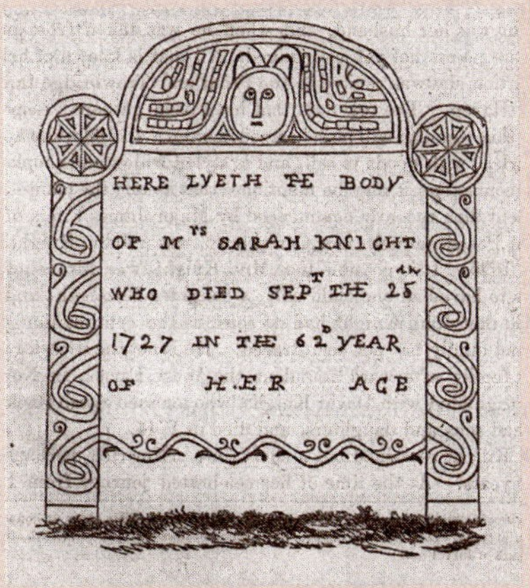

Gravestone of Madam Knight

No likeness of Knight was made in her lifetime, during most of which she lived in Boston. She spent the last years of her life in Connecticut, where she ran an inn and successfully invested in property. This drawing of her gravestone was published by Frances Manwaring Caulkins in an 1860 edition of her *History of New London*.

From The Private Journal of a Journey from Boston to New York

Friday, October 6th

I got up very early, in Order to hire somebody to go with mee to New Haven,[1] being in Great parplexity at the thoughts of proceeding alone; which my most hospitable entertainer observing, himselfe went, and soon return'd with a young Gentleman of the town, who he could confide in to Go with mee; and about eight this morning, with Mr. Joshua Wheeler my new Guide, takeing leave of this worthy Gentleman, Wee advanced on towards Seabrook. The Rodes all along this way are very bad, Incumbred with Rocks and mountainos passages, which were very disagreeable to my tired carcass; but we went on with a moderate pace which made the Journy more pleasent. But after about eight miles Rideing, in going over a Bridge under which the River Run very swift, my hors stumbled, and very narrowly 'scaped falling over into the water; which extreemly frightened mee. But through God's Goodness I met with no harm, and mounting agen, in about half a miles Rideing, come to an ordinary,[2] were well entertained by a woman of about seventy and vantage, but of as Sound Intellectuals as one of seventeen. Shee entertain'd Mr. Wheeler with some passages of a Wedding awhile ago at a place hard by, the Brides-Groom being about her Age or something above, Saying his Children was dredfully against their fathers marrying, which she condemned them extreemly for.

From hence wee went pretty briskly forward, and arriv'd at Saybrook ferry about two of the Clock afternoon; and crossing it, wee call'd at an Inn to Bait, (foreseeing we should not have such another Opportunity till we come to Killingsworth.) Landlady come in, with her hair about her ears, and hands at full pay scratching. Shee told us shee had some mutton which shee would broil, which I was glad to hear; But I supose forgot to wash her scratchers; in a little time shee brot it in; but it being pickled, and my Guide said it smelt strong of head sause,[3] we left it, and paid sixpence a piece for our Dinners, which was only smell.

So wee putt forward with all speed, and about seven at night come to Killingsworth, and were tollerably well with Travillers fare, and Lodgd there that night.

Saturday, Oct. 7th

[W]e sett out early in the Morning, and being something unaquainted with the way, having ask't it of some wee mett, they told us wee must Ride a mile or two and turne down a Lane on the Right hand; and by their Direction wee Rode on but not Yet comeing to the turning, we mett a Young fellow and ask't him how farr it was to the Lane which turn'd

---

1. **New Haven:** New Haven, in southern Connecticut, is about two hundred miles south and west of Boston.
2. **ordinary:** An early term for an inn that provided meals, usually at fixed times and prices.
3. **head sause:** Probably a reference to what was sometimes called head cheese, a mix of chopped and boiled parts of the sheep's head, feet, tongue, and heart.

down towards Guilford. Hee said wee must Ride a little further, and turn down by the Corner of uncle Sams Lott. My Guide vented his Spleen at the Lubber;[4] and we soon after came into the Rhode, and keeping still on, without any thing further Remarkabell, about two a clock afternoon we arrived at New Haven, where I was received with all Posible Respects and civility. Here I discharged Mr. Wheeler with a reward to his satisfaction, and took some time to rest after so long and toilsome a Journey; and Inform'd myselfe of the manners and customs of the place, and at the same time employed myselfe in the afair I went there upon.

They are Govern'd by the same Laws as wee in Boston, (or little differing,) thr'out this whole Colony of Connecticot, And much the same way of Church Government, and many of them good, Sociable people, and I hope Religious too: but a little too much Independant in their principalls, and, as I have been told, were formerly in their Zeal very Riggid in their Administrations towards such as their Lawes made Offenders, even to a harmless Kiss or Innocent merriment among Young people. Whipping being a frequent and counted an easy Punishment, about which as other Crimes, the Judges were absolute in their Sentances. They told mee a pleasant story about a pair of Justices in those parts, which I may not omit the relation of.

A negro Slave belonging to a man in the Town, stole a hogs head from his master, and gave or sold it to an Indian, native of the place. The Indian sold it in the neighbourhood, and so the theft was found out. Thereupon the Heathen was Seized, and carried to the Justices House to be Examined. But his worship (it seems) was gone into the feild, with a Brother in office, to gather in his Pompions.[5] Whither the malefactor is hurried, And Complaint made, and satisfaction in the name of Justice demanded. Their Worships cann't proceed in form without a Bench: whereupon they Order one to be Imediately erected, which, for want of fitter materials, they made with pompions – which being finished, down setts their Worships, and the Malefactor call'd, and by the Senior Justice Interrogated after the following manner. You Indian why did You steal from this man? You sho'dn't do so – it's a Grandy wicked thing to steal. Hol't Hol't cryes Justice Junior Brother, You speak negro to him. I'le ask him. You sirrah, why did You steal this man's Hoggshead? Hoggshead? (replys the Indian,) me no stomany. No? says his Worship; and pulling off his hatt, Patted his own head with his hand, sais, Tatapa – You, Tatapa – you; all one this. Hoggshead all one this. Hah! says Netop, now me stomany that. Whereupon the Company fell into a great fitt of Laughter, even to Roreing. Silence is comanded, but to no effect: for they continued perfectly Shouting. Nay, sais his worship, in an angry tone, if it be so, *take mee off the Bench.*

Their Diversions in this part of the Country are on Lecture days and Training days[6] mostly: on the former there is Riding from town to town.

And on training dayes The Youth divert themselves by Shooting at the Target, as they

4. **Lubber:** Early term for a large, clumsy person.
5. **Pompions:** Pumpkins.
6. **Lecture days and Training days:** Sermons or lectures were given at weekly religious services on Thursdays. Training days were set aside for training members of the militia.

call it, (but it very much resembles a pillory,) where hee that hitts neerest the white has some yards of Red Ribbin presented him which being tied to his hattband, the two ends streeming down his back, he is Led away in Triumph, with great applause, as the winners of the Olympiack Games. They generally marry very young: the males oftener as I am told under twentie than above; they generally make public wedings, and have a way something singular (as they say) in some of them, *viz.*[7] Just before Joyning hands the Bridegroom quitts the place, who is soon followed by the Bridesmen, and as it were, dragg'd back to duty – being the reverse to the former practice among us, to steal man's Pride.

There are great plenty of Oysters all along by the sea side, as farr as I Rode in the Colony, and those very good. And they Generally lived very well and comfortably in their famelies. But too Indulgent (especially the farmers) to their slaves: sufering too great familiarity from them, permitting them to sit at Table and eat with them, (as they say to save time,) and into the dish goes the black hoof as freely as the white hand. They told me that there was a farmer lived nere the Town where I lodgd who had some difference with his slave, concerning something the master had promised him and did not punctualy perform; which caused some hard words between them; But at length they put the matter to Arbitration and Bound themselves to stand to the award of such as they named – which done, the Arbitrators Having heard the Allegations of both parties, Order the master to pay 40 s[8] to black face, and acknowledge his fault. And so the matter ended: the poor master very honestly standing to the award.

There are every where in the Towns as I passed, a Number of Indians the Natives of the Country, and are the most salvage[9] of all the salvages of that kind that I had ever Seen: little or no care taken (as I heard upon enquiry) to make them otherwise. They have in some places Landes of their owne, and Govern'd by Law's of their own making; they marry many wives and at pleasure put them away, and on the least dislike or fickle humour, on either side, saying *stand away* to one another is a sufficient Divorce. And indeed those uncomely *Stand aways* are too much in Vougue among the English in this (Indulgent Colony) as their Records plentifully prove, and that on very trivial matters, of which some have been told me, but are not proper to be Related by a Female pen, tho some of that foolish sex have had too large a share in the story.

If the natives committ any crime on their own precincts among themselves, the English takes no Cognezens of. But if on the English ground, they are punishable by our Laws. They mourn for their Dead by blacking their faces, and cutting their hair, after an Awkerd and frightfull manner; But can't bear You should mention the names of their dead Relations to them: they trade most for Rum, for which they'd hazzard their very lives; and the English fit them Generally as well, by seasoning it plentifully with water.

They give the title of merchant to every trader; who Rate their Goods according to the time and spetia they pay in: *viz.* Pay, mony, Pay as mony, and trusting. *Pay* is Grain, Pork,

---

7. **viz.:** Abbreviation for *videlicet* (Latin), meaning namely or in other words.
8. **40 s:** In the currency system, 40 shillings equaled 2 pounds.
9. **salvage:** Early spelling of *savage.*

Beef, &c. at the prices sett by the General Court that Year; *mony* is pieces of Eight, Ryalls, or Boston or Bay shillings (as they call them,) or Good hard money, as sometimes silver coin is termed by them; also Wampom, *vizt.* Indian beads which serves for change. *Pay as mony* is provisions, as afores'd one Third cheaper then as the Assembly or Gene'l Court sets it; and *Trust* as they and the merch't agree for time.

Now, when the buyer comes to ask for a comodity, sometimes before the merchant answers that he has it, he sais, *is Your pay redy?* Perhaps the Chap Reply's Yes: what do You pay in? say's the merchant. The buyer having answered, then the price is set; as suppose he wants a sixpenny knife, in pay it is 12d – in pay as money eight pence, and hard money its own price, *viz.* 6d. It seems a very Intricate way of trade and what *Lex Mercatoria*[10] had not thought of.

Being at a merchants house, in comes a tall country fellow, with his alfogeos[11] full of Tobacco; for they seldom Loose their Cudd, but keep Chewing and Spitting as long as they'r eyes are open, he advanc't to the midle of the Room, makes an Awkward Nodd, and spitting a Large deal of Aromatick Tincture, he gave a scrape with his shovel like shoo, leaving a small shovel full of dirt on the floor, made a full stop, Hugging his own pretty Body with his hands under his arms, Stood staring rown'd him, like a Catt let out of a Baskett. At last, like the creature Balaam Rode on,[12] he opened his mouth and said: have You any Ribinen for Hatbands to sell I pray? The Questions and Answers about the pay being past, the Ribin is bro't and opened. Bumpkin Simpers, cryes its confounded Gay I vow; and beckning to the door, in comes Jone Tawdry, dropping about 50 curtsees, and stands by him: hee shows her the Ribin. *Law You,* sais shee, *its right Gent,*[13] do You, take it, *tis dreadfull pretty.* Then she enquires, *have You any hood silk I pray?* which being brought and bought, Have You any *thred silk to sew it with* says shee, which being accomodated with they Departed. They Generaly stand after they come in a great while speachless, and sometimes dont say a word till they are askt what they want, which I Impute to the Awe they stand in of the merchants, who they are constantly almost Indebted too; and must take what they bring without Liberty to choose for themselves; but they serve them as well, making the merchants stay long enough for their pay.

We may Observe here the great necessity and bennifitt both of Education and Conversation; for these people have as Large a portion of mother witt, and sometimes a Larger, than those who have bin brought up in Citties; But for want of emprovements, Render themselves almost Ridiculos, as above. I should be glad if they would leave such follies, and am sure all that Love Clean Houses (at least) would be glad on't too.

They are generaly very plain in their dress, throuout all the Colony, as I saw, and follow one another in their modes; that You may know where they belong, especially the women, meet them where you will.

---

10. ***Lex Mercatoria***: The law of the merchants (Latin).
11. **alfogeos**: Early term for the pouchlike cheeks of a baboon.
12. **the creature Balaam Rode on**: In the Old Testament, an ass rebukes his master, Balaam, who was hired to curse the Israelites (Numbers 22-24).
13. ***Gent***: Genteel.

Their Cheif Red Letter day is St. Election,[14] which is annualy Observed according to Charter, to choose their Govenor: a blessing they can never be thankfull enough for, as they will find, if ever it be their hard fortune to loose it. The present Govenor in Conecticott is the Honourable John Winthrop Esq.[15] A Gentleman of an Ancient and Honourable Family, whose Father was Govenor here sometime before, and his Grand father had bin Governor of the Massachusetts. This gentleman is a very curteous and afable person, much Given to Hospitality, and has by his Good services Gain'd the affection of the people as much as any who had bin before him in that post.

[1705, 1920]

14. **St. Election:** Knight satirically refers to the annual Election Day as a holiday of religious importance.
15. **John Winthrop Esq.:** Fitz-John Winthrop (1638-1707) served as governor of Connecticut from 1698 to 1707. He was the eldest son of John Winthrop, one of the founders and the first governor of the Massachusetts Bay Colony.

William Byrd

[1674-1744]

The son of one of the most prominent families in colonial Virginia, William Byrd was born there and educated in England. When his father died in 1704, Byrd inherited a large fortune and extensive landholdings, including several tobacco plantations and Westover, his home on the James River. Fluent in several languages, Byrd collected an extensive library of over 3,000 volumes at Westover. In size and diversity, it was one of the finest libraries in the American colonies. Active in politics, Byrd was a member of the Virginia House of Burgesses (the first representative government in the colonies) and served on a commission to establish the boundary between North Carolina and Virginia. Byrd describes that surveying expedition in the most famous of several travel narratives he wrote, *History of the Dividing Line* (1728). With the exception of a pamphlet he published on the medicinal qualities of tobacco, however, all of Byrd's writings were circulated in manuscript among his family and friends and not published until the nineteenth century. Most of those writings were based on Byrd's diaries, which he kept throughout his life. Byrd wrote the diaries in shorthand, a system of rapid writing used primarily by secretaries. (Scholars have determined that Byrd's shorthand notations were based on a method developed by William Mason, a London secretary, in 1672.) In his diaries, Byrd candidly records details about his public and especially his private life, ranging from his daily schedule and reading to arguments with his wife and his sexual activities. When the diaries were finally transcribed and published in the twentieth century, they were also recognized

William Byrd

This anonymous portrait was painted sometime between 1715 and 1725, when Byrd was in his forties. In the portrait, he assumes the pose of and is portrayed as the very embodiment of the colonial English gentleman, gesturing toward a natural background that may have been intended to represent Westover, his extensive plantation in Virginia.

as a major source of information about plantation life and the extensive slave system that emerged in colonial Virginia. The text of the following selections of entries written during 1712 is taken from *The Secret Diary of William Byrd of Westover, 1709-1712*, edited by Louis B. Wright and Marion Tinling (1941).

From THE SECRET DIARY OF WILLIAM BYRD OF WESTOVER

January, 1712

1. I lay abed till 9 o'clock this morning to bring my wife into temper again and rogered her[1] by way of reconciliation. I read nothing because Mr. Mumford was here, nor did I say my prayers, for the same reason. However I ate boiled milk for breakfast, and after my wife tempted me to eat some pancakes with her. Mr. Mumford and I went to shoot with our bows and arrows but shot nothing, and afterwards we played at billiards till dinner, and when we came we found Ben Harrison there, who dined with us. I ate

1. **rogered her:** That is, had sexual intercourse with her. As his diary illustrates, Byrd had a tempestuous relationship with his first wife, Lucy Parke (d. 1719), who later died of smallpox when Byrd was working as a colonial agent in London.

some partridge for dinner. In the afternoon we played at billiards again and I won two bits. I had a letter from Colonel Duke by H-l[2] the bricklayer who came to offer his services to work for me. Mr. Mumford went away in the evening and John Bannister with him to see his mother. I took a walk about the plantation and at night we drank some mead of my wife's making which was very good. I gave the people some cider and a dram to the negroes. I read some Latin in Terence[3] and had good health, good thoughts, and good humor, thank God Almighty. I said my prayers.

16. I rose about 7 o'clock and read a chapter in Hebrew and some Greek in Lucian.[4] I said my prayers and ate boiled milk for breakfast. I danced my dance.[5] My wife was something better and rode out because it was very fine weather and not cold. We killed a beef this morning that came yesterday from Burkland where they were all well, thank God. I settled some accounts till dinner and then I ate some hash of beef. In the afternoon my wife shaved me and then I walked out to see my people plant trees and I was angry with John for mistaking Mr. G-r-l's directions. Then I showed him again and helped him plant several trees. Then I took a walk till night. When I came in my [wife] persuaded me me [*sic*] to eat skim milk for supper. Then I read some Latin in Terence. I said my prayers and had good thoughts, good humor, and good health, thank God Almighty. I dreamed a coffin was brought into my house and thrown into the hall.

18. I rose about 7 o'clock and read a chapter in Hebrew and some Greek in Lucian. I said my prayers and ate boiled milk for breakfast. I danced my dance. The weather was clear and cold but the wind was northeast. I settled several accounts and then read some Latin in Terence till dinner, and then I ate some boiled beef but I was displeased with my wife for giving the child marrow against my opinion. In the afternoon I read a little more Latin and then went to see my people plant peach trees and afterwards took a great walk about the plantation and found everything in order, for which I praised God. I was entertained with seeing a hawk which had taken a small bird pursued by another hawk, so that he was forced to let go his prey. My walk lasted till the evening and at night I read some Latin in Terence. I said my prayers and had good health, good thoughts, and good humor, thank God Almighty. . . .

February, 1712

5. I rose about 8 o'clock, my wife kept me so long in bed where I rogered her. I read nothing because I put my matters in order. I neglected to say my prayers but ate boiled milk for breakfast. My wife caused several of the people[6] to be whipped for their lazi-

---

2. **H-l:** Because Byrd wrote his diary in shorthand, he often did not include vowels in names, making them difficult or impossible to transcribe.
3. **Latin in Terence:** African-born Roman writer (185–159 BCE) of comedies, which Byrd was reading in Latin.
4. **some Greek in Lucian:** A Greek satirist (c. 120–180) famous for his parodies of ancient myths.
5. **I danced my dance:** Most scholars believe that Byrd refers to performing exercises or calisthenics.
6. **people:** Although many of the Byrds' servants were slaves brought from Africa, some were white indentured servants from Europe who also labored under difficult and often inhumane conditions.

ness. I settled accounts and put several matters in order till dinner. I ate some boiled beef. In the afternoon I ordered my sloop to go to Colonel Eppes' for some poplar trees for the Governor and then I went to visit Mrs. Harrison that I found in a small way. She entertained me with apples and bad wine and I stayed with her till evening and then I took a walk about my plantation. When I returned I learned Peter Poythress had been here. At night I read some Latin. I said my prayers and had good health, good thoughts, and good humor, thank God Almighty. I rogered my wife again.

March, 1712

2. I rose about 7 o'clock and read a chapter in Hebrew but no Greek because Mr. G-r-l was here and I wished to talk with him. I ate boiled milk for breakfast and danced my dance. I reprimanded him for drawing so many notes on me. However I told him if he would let me know his debts I would pay them provided he would let a mulatto of mine that is his apprentice come to work at Falling Creek the last two years of his service, which he agreed. I had a terrible quarrel with my wife concerning Jenny that I took away from her when she was beating her with the tongs. She lifted up her hands to strike me but forbore to do it. She gave me abundance of bad words and endeavored to strangle herself, but I believe in jest only. However after acting a mad woman a long time she was passive again. I ate some roast beef for dinner. In the afternoon Mr. G-r-l went away and I took a walk about the plantation. At night we drank some cider by way of reconciliation and I read nothing. I said my prayers and had good health, good thoughts, and good humor, thank God Almighty. I sent Tom to Williamsburg with some fish to the Governor and my sister Custis. My daughter was indisposed with a small fever.

23. I rose about 6 o'clock and read two chapters in Hebrew and some Greek in the Greek Testament.[7] I said my prayers and ate boiled milk for breakfast. I danced my dance. The sloop came from Appomattox with 60 hogsheads of tobacco. Shockoe Billy came from the Falls and bore a letter from Tom Turpin which let me know all was well there. He desired me to provide myself with another overseer because I found fault with some of his management and I wrote him word I would do as he desired. I ate some roast shoat for dinner. My wife had a little fever this morning but it soon went off again. About 2 o'clock Tom Randolph came and was wet with a gust that happened about that time and soon after came Tom from Williamsburg and told me the Doctor was gone to Rappahannock with Mrs. Russell and would not be home before this night. Mr. Randolph and I took a walk about the plantation. At night came G-r-l and told me all was well at Falling Creek. We drank a bottle of cider. I said a short prayer and had good health, good thoughts, and good humor, thank God Almighty. It thundered and rained this evening. My wife [took] another dose of bark.[8]

---

7. **Greek Testament:** The New Testament of the Bible, published in Greek.
8. **bark:** Quinine, made from the bark of the cinchona tree ground into powder, was taken as a medicine to reduce fever.

April, 1712

4. I rose about 7 o'clock and read a chapter in Hebrew and some Greek in Lucian. I said my prayers and ate boiled milk for breakfast. I wrote two letters to the quarters and one to Williamsburg and sent the last by my sister Custis who would go, notwithstanding it was like to rain. About 11 o'clock Mr. Salle went away likewise. I settled several accounts and wrote in my journal till dinner and then I ate some fish. In the afternoon I rogered my wife again. The weather was very bad and it rained almost all day so that my poor sister was terribly wet except she called at some house. My wife and I took a nap after dinner and after our roger. I settled several accounts and read some news. It rained till night so that I could not walk. At night came the master of a ship lately come from Lisbon. We gave him some supper and I ate some broiled turkey with him. He told me he would let me have eight dozen of bottles of Lisbon wine. I said my prayers and had good health, good thoughts, and good humor, thank God Almighty.

May, 1712

22. I rose about 6 o'clock and read two chapters in Hebrew and some Greek in Lucian. I said my prayers and ate boiled milk for breakfast. I danced my dance. It rained a little this morning. My wife caused Prue[9] to be whipped violently notwithstanding I desired not, which provoked me to have Anaka[10] whipped likewise who had deserved it much more, on which my wife flew into such a passion that she hoped she would be revenged of me. I was moved very much at this but only thanked her for the present lest I should say things foolish in my passion. I wrote more accounts to go to England. My wife was sorry for what she had said and came to ask my pardon and I forgave her in my heart but seemed to resent, that she might be the more sorry for her folly. She ate no dinner nor appeared the whole day. I ate some bacon for dinner. In the afternoon I wrote two more accounts till the evening and then took a walk in the garden. I said my prayers and was reconciled to my wife and gave her a flourish in token of it. I had good health, good thoughts, but was a little out of humor, for which God forgive me.

25. I rose about 8 o'clock and read two chapters in Hebrew and no Greek. I said my prayers and ate boiled milk for breakfast. I danced my dance. The weather was very clear and cold. About 11 o'clock we went to church where Mr. Anderson gave us a good sermon. The two Mrs. Thomsons were come up to see Mrs. Eppes and I invited them to come and see us. I took three of the masters of ships home with us to dinner and I ate some dried beef. In the afternoon the masters went away very early and we went to take a walk in the evening. At night we drank a bottle and the women went upstairs by themselves. I said my prayers and was out of humor that my wife did not come to bed soon. I had good health, good humor, and good health [*sic*], thank God Almighty.

---

9. **Prue:** A servant; her race and status are not known.
10. **Anaka:** An enslaved African woman.

27. I rose about 5 o'clock and read a chapter in Hebrew and some Greek. I said my prayers and ate milk and hominy for breakfast. I danced my dance. The weather was cloudy and hot. My wife was pretty well, thank God. About 9 o'clock Mr. Mumford and Tom Randolph went away. I read some English and then a sermon in Tillotson till dinner and then I ate some roast mutton for dinner. In the afternoon I took a nap and then read some news. My wife and Mrs. Dunn went out in the coach and I read some Latin till the evening and then I took a walk about the plantation and in the orchard where there was abundance of fruit. I said my prayers and had good health, good thoughts, and good humor, thank God Almighty. Negro Sue was brought to bed of a boy.

September, 1712

29. I rose about 7 o'clock and went again into the river against my ague.[11] I read a chapter in Hebrew and some Greek in Lucian. I said my prayers and ate boiled milk for breakfast. I danced my dance. I continued very well, thank God. The weather was cold, the wind northeast. My wife was pretty well. About 11 o'clock I was a little fevered and my head ached a little; however I would not give way to it. I had not much stomach to dinner; however I ate some broiled beef. In the afternoon I put several things in order in the library and at night Mr. Catesby came and told me he had seen a bear. I took Tom L-s-n and went with a gun and Mr. Catesby shot him. It was only a cub and he sat on a tree to eat grapes. I was better with this diversion and we were merry in the evening. I said my prayers and had good health, good thoughts, and good humor, thank God Almighty.

[1712, 1941]

---

11. **ague**: A bout of fever and shivering, often associated with malaria, which was then common in the southern colonies.

Jonathan Edwards

[1703-1758]

Jonathan Edwards was born in East Windsor, Connecticut, on October 5, 1703. He was one of eleven children but the only son of Esther Stoddard, the daughter of an influential minister, and Timothy Edwards, the minister of the congregation of East Windsor. Edwards was tutored at home by his father and mother, learning Latin, Greek, and Hebrew. At age thirteen, he went to the Yale Collegiate School at Wethersfield, about ten miles from his home. He was a good student who clearly flourished at the school. At the same time, Edwards was deeply religious and pursued many solitary interests, including a fascination with nature. In his *Personal Narrative* – which along with some letters to his father constitute most of the information available about his early life – Edwards describes an illness at college and his ongoing concern with the state of his soul: "[God] brought me nigh to the grave, and shook me over the pit of hell." In the aftermath of his illness, Edwards eventually found a new inner peace and what he describes in his *Narrative* as a "delightful" conviction of the absolute sovereignty of God, a conviction which he held throughout his life.

Joseph Badger, *Jonathan Edwards* (1720)

Painted when he was only seventeen and in his final year at Yale College, this portrait reveals the gravity that Edwards would later display as one of the greatest preachers in the history of New England.

Given his background, education, and profound piety, Edwards was virtually destined to become a famous Puritan minister. From an early age, he was also distinguished by his remarkable intellect and wide-ranging interests. He spent his final year of college at Yale in New Haven, where in addition to pursuing his theological studies Edwards wrote "Of Insects," one of the earliest of a series of essays that included "Of Atoms," "Of Light Rays," and "Of the Rainbow." Like his other scientific and philosophical writings, those essays revealed his abiding interest in natural phenomena and his rigorous study of the "new" sciences, especially the optical and astronomical theories of Isaac Newton. After he graduated first in his class in 1720, Edwards remained at Yale in order to prepare for the ministry. Licensed to preach in 1722, he accepted a position in a small Presbyterian church in New York City, where Edwards continued his habits of meditation and solitary reflection during long walks on the banks of the Hudson River. In a diary he kept during those years, Edwards prays: "Lord, grant that I may hence learn to withdraw my thoughts, affections, desires and expectations, entirely from the world, and may fix them on the

Next after the Bible, read and study Edwards.
-Lyman Beecher

heavenly state, where reigns heavenly, sweet, calm and delightful love without alloy."

Edwards, however, became deeply involved in the religious affairs and theological conflicts of this world. In May of 1724, Yale offered him the position of tutor, which meant that he was, in effect, the president of the college. Edwards remained there until he was ordained as a minister in 1727. He then became an assistant pastor in the church led by his grandfather Solomon Stoddard, sometimes called "Pope" Stoddard in derisive recognition of the influence he wielded from his powerful pulpit in the affluent commercial town of Northampton, Massachusetts. That year, Edwards also married Sarah Pierpont, with whom he eventually had eleven children. After his grandfather's death in 1729, Edwards succeeded him as pastor of the church in Northampton, from which his renown soon spread throughout New England. A sermon he delivered in Boston, "God Glorified," was published amid great acclaim in 1731; Edwards began to publish his sermons regularly, a collection of which appeared as *Discourses on Various Important Subjects* in 1738. Edwards was quickly becoming a foremost Puritan writer. But he gained his greatest fame as one of the leaders of the Great Awakening, a religious revival that flared up locally in 1734-35 and then swept across the colonies in the early 1740s. Answering critics who viewed the first revival as an uncontrolled manifestation of religious "enthusiasm," or mere emotionalism, Edwards published *A Faithful Narrative of the Surprising Works of God in the Conversion of Many Hundred Souls in Northampton and Neighboring Towns* (1736). During the second and far-more-intense wave of revivals, Edwards delivered his most famous sermon, "Sinners in the Hands of an Angry God," which was published soon after he delivered it in 1741. Two years later, he published his fullest defense of the Great Awakening, *Some Thoughts Concerning the Present Revival of Religion in New-England, and the Way in Which It Ought to Be Acknowledged and Prompted* (1743).

bedfordstmartins.com/americanlit *for research links on Edwards*

In the aftermath of the Great Awakening, Edwards was increasingly at odds with his congregation in Northampton. Although there were numerous sources of tension, the major point of contention was the requirement for participation in the sacrament of Communion, or the Lord's Supper. In an earlier period, Communion was administered only to full church members – that is, those who had experienced and given a public account of their conversion. As the number of full church members declined, however, the strict requirement was relaxed by ministers like Solomon Stoddard, who argued that Communion should be open to all members of the congregation, whether or not they had given evidence of their conversion. Edwards initially followed that practice, but in his *Treatise Concerning Religious Affections* (1746) he argues for a return to the earlier requirement. His effort to impose that rule ultimately led to his dismissal from his church in Northampton, where Edwards vigorously defended his position in his "Farewell Sermon," delivered in June 1750. Undaunted by "the People's Publick Rejection of their Minister," as he describes it in the full title of the published version of the sermon, Edwards became a missionary to the Housatonic River Indians in Stockbridge, Massachusetts. There, he composed a number of works, including two of his most important theological treatises, *Freedom of Will* (1754) and *The Great Christian Doctrine of Original Sin Defended* (1758). In 1757, he was appointed president of Princeton College, but he died a few months after his induction, on February 16, 1758.

Edwards's "On Sarah Pierpont." The subject of this untitled tribute to "a young lady" is assumed to be Sarah Pierpont, whom Edwards married in 1727. Certainly, the passage reveals the deep admiration and regard Edwards has for the woman he calls his "dearest companion." Although the original has not survived, Edwards is thought to have written the passage on the blank endpaper of a book he presented to Sarah Pierpont in 1723, when she was thirteen and he was twenty. The young minister's graceful tribute has been hailed as a striking example of the Puritan plain style and of Edwards's early artistry, a simple yet lyrical work that may be read as a kind of prose poem. The text is taken from the Yale University Press *Works of Jonathan Edwards*, Vol. 16, edited by George S. Claghorn (1998).

On Sarah Pierpont

They say there is a young lady in [New Haven] who is beloved of that almighty Being, who made and rules the world, and that there are certain seasons in which this great Being, in some way or other invisible, comes to her and fills her mind with exceeding sweet delight, and that she hardly cares for anything, except to meditate on him – that she expects after a while to be received up where he is, to be raised out of the world and caught up into heaven; being assured that he loves her too well to let her remain at a distance from him always. There she is to dwell with him, and to be ravished with his love, favor and delight, forever. Therefore, if you present all the world before her, with the richest of its treasures, she disregards it and cares not for it, and is unmindful of any pain or affliction. She has a strange sweetness in her mind, and sweetness of temper, uncommon purity in her affections; is most just and praiseworthy in all her actions; and you could not persuade her to do anything thought wrong or sinful, if you would give her all the world, lest she should offend this great Being. She is of a wonderful sweetness, calmness and universal benevolence of mind; especially after those times in which this great God has manifested himself to her mind. She will sometimes go about, singing sweetly, from place to [place]; and seems to be always full of joy and pleasure; and no one knows for what. She loves to be alone, and to wander in the fields and on the mountains, and seems to have someone invisible always conversing with her.

[c. 1723, 1998]

Edwards's *Personal Narrative.* In his autobiography, Edwards offers few details concerning the outward aspects of his life or his personal relationships. Instead, it is a spiritual autobiography, designed as a record of his religious doubts, struggles, and triumphs. Since the latest date he refers to in the narrative is 1739, Edwards evidently wrote it later, probably around 1740. Although we do not know why he wrote the account, it may well have been inspired by his involvement in the wave of religious revivals known collectively as the Great Awakening. Even though he was a strong supporter of the movement, Edwards was concerned about the possibility that some of those who were swept up in the spirit of the revivals might confuse mere emotional excess as a sign of a true conversion experience. Edwards may consequently have written his dispassionate account as a kind of spiritual guide for others, an effort to help them distinguish between false or misleading signs and true evidences of the operation of God's grace within their souls. The narrative apparently circulated in manuscript, but it did not appear in print until seven years after his death, when Samuel Hopkins published it as "An Account of His Conversion, Experiences, and Religious Exercises" in *The Life and Character of the Late Rev. Mr. Jonathan Edwards* (1765). The following text is taken from the Yale University Press *Works of Jonathan Edwards*, Vol. 16, edited by George S. Claghorn (1998).

PERSONAL NARRATIVE

I had a variety of concerns and exercises about my soul from my childhood; but had two more remarkable seasons of awakening,[1] before I met with that change, by which I was brought to those new dispositions, and that new sense of things, that I have since had. The first time was when I was a boy, some years before I went to college, at a time of remarkable awakening in my father's congregation. I was then very much affected for many months, and concerned about the things of religion, and my soul's salvation; and was abundant in duties. I used to pray five times a day in secret, and to spend much time in religious talk with other boys; and used to meet with them to pray together. I experienced I know not what kind of delight in religion. My mind was much engaged in it, and had much self-righteous pleasure; and it was my delight to abound in religious duties. I, with some of my schoolmates joined together, and built a booth in a swamp, in a very secret and retired place, for a place of prayer. And besides, I had particular secret places of my own in the woods, where I used to retire by myself; and used to be from time to time much affected. My affections seemed to be lively and easily moved, and I seemed to be in my element, when engaged in religious duties. And I am ready to think, many are deceived with such affections, and such a kind of delight, as I then had in religion, and mistake it for grace.

But in process of time, my convictions and affections wore off; and I entirely lost all

1. **awakening:** Spiritual awakening.

those affections and delights, and left off secret prayer, at least as to any constant performance of it; and returned like a dog to his vomit,[2] and went on in ways of sin.

Indeed, I was at some times very uneasy, especially towards the latter part of the time of my being at college. Till it pleased God, in my last year at college, at a time when I was in the midst of many uneasy thoughts about the state of my soul, to seize me with a pleurisy;[3] in which he brought me nigh to the grave, and shook me over the pit of hell.

But yet, it was not long after my recovery, before I fell again into my old ways of sin. But God would not suffer me to go on with any quietness; but I had great and violent inward struggles: till after many conflicts with wicked inclinations, and repeated resolutions, and bonds that I laid myself under by a kind of vows to God, I was brought wholly to break off all former wicked ways, and all ways of known outward sin; and to apply myself to seek my salvation, and practice the duties of religion: but without that kind of affection and delight, that I had formerly experienced. My concern now wrought more by inward struggles and conflicts, and self-reflections. I made seeking my salvation the main business of my life. But yet it seems to me, I sought after a miserable manner: which has made me sometimes since to question, whether ever it issued in that which was saving; being ready to doubt, whether such miserable seeking was ever succeeded. But yet I was brought to seek salvation, in a manner that I never was before. I felt a spirit to part with all things in the world, for an interest in Christ. My concern continued and prevailed, with many exercising things and inward struggles; but yet it never seemed to be proper to express my concern that I had, by the name of terror.

From my childhood up, my mind had been wont to be full of objections against the doctrine of God's sovereignty, in choosing whom he would to eternal life, and rejecting whom he pleased; leaving them eternally to perish, and be everlastingly tormented in hell. It used to appear like a horrible doctrine to me. But I remember the time very well, when I seemed to be convinced, and fully satisfied, as to this sovereignty of God, and his justice in thus eternally disposing of men, according to his sovereign pleasure. But never could give an account, how, or by what means, I was thus convinced; not in the least imagining, in the time of it, nor a long time after, that there was any extraordinary influence of God's Spirit in it: but only that now I saw further, and my reason apprehended the justice and reasonableness of it. However, my mind rested in it; and it put an end to all those cavils and objections, that had till then abode with me, all the preceding part of my life. And there has been a wonderful alteration in my mind, with respect to the doctrine of God's sovereignty, from that day to this; so that I scarce ever have found so much as the rising of an objection against God's sovereignty, in the most absolute sense, in showing mercy on whom he will show mercy, and hardening and eternally damning whom he will.[4] God's absolute sovereignty, and justice, with respect to salvation and damnation, is what my mind seems to rest assured of, as much as of anything

---

2. **returned like a dog to his vomit:** See Proverbs 26:11: "As a dog returneth to his vomit, so a fool returneth to his folly."

3. **pleurisy:** An upper-respiratory illness that makes it difficult and painful to breathe.

4. **in showing mercy . . . and eternally damning whom he will:** See Romans 9:18: "Therefore hath he mercy on whom he will *have mercy*, and whom he will he hardeneth."

that I see with my eyes; at least it is so at times. But I have oftentimes since that first conviction, had quite another kind of sense of God's sovereignty, than I had then. I have often since, not only had a conviction, but a *delightful* conviction. The doctrine of God's sovereignty has very often appeared, an exceeding pleasant, bright and sweet doctrine to me: and absolute sovereignty is what I love to ascribe to God. But my first conviction was not with this.

The first that I remember that ever I found anything of that sort of inward, sweet delight in God and divine things, that I have lived much in since, was on reading those words, I Timothy 1:17, "Now unto the King eternal, immortal, invisible, the only wise God, be honor and glory forever and ever, Amen." As I read the words, there came into my soul, and was as it were diffused through it, a sense of the glory of the divine being; a new sense, quite different from anything I ever experienced before. Never any words of Scripture seemed to me as these words did. I thought with myself, how excellent a Being that was; and how happy I should be, if I might enjoy that God, and be wrapt up to God in heaven, and be as it were swallowed up in him. I kept saying, and as it were singing over these words of Scripture to myself; and went to prayer, to pray to God that I might enjoy him; and prayed in a manner quite different from what I used to do; with a new sort of affection. But it never came into my thought, that there was anything spiritual, or of a saving nature in this.

From about that time, I began to have a new kind of apprehensions and ideas of Christ, and the work of redemption, and the glorious way of salvation by him. I had an inward, sweet sense of these things, that at times came into my heart; and my soul was led away in pleasant views and contemplations of them. And my mind was greatly engaged, to spend my time in reading and meditating on Christ; and the beauty and excellency of his person, and the lovely way of salvation, by free grace in him. I found no books so delightful to me, as those that treated of these subjects. Those words (Canticles 2:1)[5] used to be abundantly with me: "I am the rose of Sharon, the lily of the valleys." The words seemed to me, sweetly to represent, the loveliness and beauty of Jesus Christ. And the whole book of Canticles used to be pleasant to me; and I used to be much in reading it, about that time. And found, from time to time, an inward sweetness, that used, as it were, to carry me away in my contemplations; in what I know not how to express otherwise, than by a calm, sweet abstraction of soul from all the concerns o[f] this world; and a kind of vision, or fixed ideas and imaginations, of being alone in the mountains, or some solitary wilderness, far from all mankind, sweetly conversing with Christ, and wrapt and swallowed up in God. The sense I had of divine things, would often of a sudden as it were, kindle up a sweet burning in my heart; an ardor of my soul, that I know not how to express.

Not long after I first began to experience these things, I gave an account to my father, of some things that had passed in my mind. I was pretty much affected by the discourse

5. **Canticles 2:1:** Canticles is another name for the Song of Solomon, a collection of love poems in the Old Testament. In the Christian tradition, it has been interpreted as an allegory of the love of Christ for his bride the church, or of the individual's experience of divine love.

we had together. And when the discourse was ended, I walked abroad alone, in a solitary place in my father's pasture, for contemplation. And as I was walking there, and looked up on the sky and clouds; there came into my mind, a sweet sense of the glorious majesty and grace of God, that I know not how to express. I seemed to see them both in a sweet conjunction: majesty and meekness joined together: it was a sweet and gentle, and holy majesty; and also a majestic meekness; an awful sweetness; a high, and great, and holy gentleness.

After this my sense of divine things gradually increased, and became more and more lively, and had more of that inward sweetness. The appearance of everything was altered: there seemed to be, as it were, a calm, sweet cast, or appearance of divine glory, in almost everything. God's excellency, his wisdom, his purity and love, seemed to appear in everything; in the sun, moon and stars; in the clouds, and blue sky; in the grass, flowers, trees; in the water, and all nature; which used greatly to fix my mind. I often used to sit and view the moon, for a long time; and so in the daytime, spent much time in viewing the clouds and sky, to behold the sweet glory of God in these things: in the meantime, singing forth with a low voice, my contemplations of the Creator and Redeemer. And scarce anything, among all the works of nature, was so sweet to me as thunder and lightning. Formerly, nothing had been so terrible to me. I used to be a person uncommonly terrified with thunder: and it used to strike me with terror, when I saw a thunderstorm rising. But now, on the contrary, it rejoiced me. I felt God at the first appearance of a thunderstorm. And used to take the opportunity at such times, to fix myself to view the clouds, and see the lightnings play, and hear the majestic and awful voice of God's thunder: which often times was exceeding entertaining, leading me to sweet contemplations of my great and glorious God. And while I viewed, used to spend my time, as it always seemed natural to me, to sing or chant forth my meditations; to speak my thoughts in soliloquies, and speak with a singing voice.

I felt then a great satisfaction as to my good estate.[6] But that did not content me. I had vehement longings of soul after God and Christ, and after more holiness; wherewith my heart seemed to be full, and ready to break: which often brought to my mind, the words of the Psalmist, Psalms 119:28, "My soul breaketh for the longing it hath." I often felt a mourning and lamenting in my heart, that I had not turned to God sooner, that I might have had more time to grow in grace. My mind was greatly fixed on divine things; I was almost perpetually in the contemplation of them. Spent most of my time in thinking of divine things, year after year. And used to spend abundance of my time, in walking alone in the woods, and solitary places, for meditation, soliloquy and prayer, and converse with God. And it was always my manner, at such times, to sing forth my contemplations. And was almost constantly in ejaculatory prayer, wherever I was. Prayer seemed to be natural to me; as the breath, by which the inward burnings of my heart had vent.

The delights which I now felt in things of religion, were of an exceeding different kind, from those forementioned, that I had when I was a boy. They were totally of

6. **estate:** Condition of life or spiritual condition.

another kind; and what I then had no more notion or idea of, than one born blind has of pleasant and beautiful colors. They were of a more inward, pure, soul-animating and refreshing nature. Those former delights, never reached the heart; and did not arise from any sight of the divine excellency of the things of God; or any taste of the soul-satisfying, and life-giving good, there is in them.

My sense of divine things seemed gradually to increase, till I went to preach at New York;[7] which was about a year and a half after they began. While I was there, I felt them, very sensibly, in a much higher degree, than I had done before. My longings after God and holiness, were much increased. Pure and humble, holy and heavenly Christianity, appeared exceeding amiable to me. I felt in me a burning desire to be in everything a complete Christian; and conformed to the blessed image of Christ: and that I might live in all things, according to the pure, sweet and blessed rules of the gospel. I had an eager thirsting after progress in these things. My longings after it, put me upon pursuing and pressing after them. It was my continual strife day and night, and constant inquiry, how I should be more holy, and live more holily, and more becoming a child of God, and disciple of Christ. I sought an increase of grace and holiness, and that I might live an holy life, with vastly more earnestness, than ever I sought grace, before I had it. I used to be continually examining myself, and studying and contriving for likely ways and means, how I should live holily, with far greater diligence and earnestness, than ever I pursued anything in my life: but with too great a dependence on my own strength; which afterwards proved a great damage to me. My experience had not then taught me, as it has done since, my extreme feebleness and impotence, every manner of way; and the innumerable and bottomless depths of secret corruption and deceit, that there was in my heart. However, I went on with my eager pursuit after more holiness; and sweet conformity to Christ.

The heaven I desired was a heaven of holiness; to be with God, and to spend my eternity in divine love, and holy communion with Christ. My mind was very much taken up with contemplations on heaven, and the enjoyments of those there; and living there in perfect holiness, humility and love. And it used at that time to appear a great part of the happiness of heaven, that there the saints could express their love to Christ. It appeared to me a great clog and hindrance and burden to me, that what I felt within, I could not express to God, and give vent to, as I desired. The inward ardor of my soul, seemed to be hindered and pent up, and could not freely flame out as it would. I used often to think, how in heaven, this sweet principle should freely and fully vent and express itself. Heaven appeared to me exceeding delightful as a world of love. It appeared to me, that all happiness consisted in living in pure, humble, heavenly, divine love.

I remember the thoughts I used then to have of holiness. I remember I then said sometimes to myself, I do certainly know that I love holiness, such as the gospel prescribes. It appeared to me, there was nothing in it but what was ravishingly lovely. It appeared to me, to be the highest beauty and amiableness, above all other beauties: that

---

7. **till I went to preach at New York:** Edwards was an assistant minister in a Presbyterian church in New York City from August 1722 through April 1723.

it was a divine beauty; far purer than anything here upon earth; and that everything else, was like mire, filth and defilement, in comparison of it.

Holiness, as I then wrote down some of my contemplations on it, appeared to me to be of a sweet, pleasant, charming, serene, calm nature. It seemed to me, it brought an inexpressible purity, brightness, peacefulness and ravishment to the soul: and that it made the soul like a field or garden of God, with all manner of pleasant flowers; that is all pleasant, delightful and undisturbed; enjoying a sweet calm, and the gently vivifying beams of the sun. The soul of a true Christian, as I then wrote my meditations, appeared like such a little white flower, as we see in the spring of the year; low and humble on the ground, opening its bosom, to receive the pleasant beams of the sun's glory; rejoicing as it were, in a calm rapture; diffusing around a sweet fragrancy; standing peacefully and lovingly, in the midst of other flowers round about; all in like manner opening their bosoms, to drink in the light of the sun.

There was no part of creature-holiness, that I then, and at other times, had so great a sense of the loveliness of, as humility, brokenness of heart and poverty of spirit: and there was nothing that I had such a spirit to long for. My heart as it were panted after this, to lie low before GOD, and in the dust; that I might be nothing, and that God might be all; that I might become as a little child.[8]

While I was there at New York, I sometimes was much affected with reflections on my past life, considering how late it was, before I began to be truly religious; and how wickedly I had lived till then: and once so as to weep abundantly, and for a considerable time together.

On January 12, 1722/3,[9] I made a solemn dedication of myself to God, and wrote it down; giving up myself, and all that I had to God; to be for the future in no respect my own; to act as one that had no right to himself, in any respect. And solemnly vowed to take God for my whole portion and felicity; looking on nothing else as any part of my happiness, nor acting as if it were: and his law for the constant rule of my obedience; engaging to fight with all my might, against the world, the flesh and the devil, to the end of my life. But have reason to be infinitely humbled, when I consider, how much I have failed of answering my obligation.

I had then abundance of sweet religious conversation in the family where I lived, with Mr. John Smith, and his pious mother. My heart was knit in affection to those, in whom were appearances of true piety; and I could bear the thoughts of no other companions, but such as were holy, and the disciples of the blessed Jesus.

I had great longings for the advancement of Christ's kingdom in the world. My secret prayer used to be in great part taken up in praying for it. If I heard the least hint of anything that happened in any part of the world, that appeared to me, in some respect or

---

8. **that I might become as a little child:** See Mark 10:15: "'Verily I say unto you, Whosoever shall not receive the kingdom of God as a little child, he shall not enter therein.'"

9. **January 12, 1722/3:** The year was 1722 in the Julian – or Old Style – calendar, in which the year begins on March 25 instead of January 1, and 1723 in the Gregorian – or New Style – calendar, which was not adopted in England until 1752.

other, to have a favorable aspect on the interest of Christ's kingdom, my soul eagerly catched at it; and it would much animate and refresh me. I used to be earnest to read public news-letters, mainly for that end; to see if I could not find some news favorable to the interest of religion in the world.

I very frequently used to retire into a solitary place, on the banks of Hudson's River, at some distance from the city, for contemplation on divine things, and secret converse with God; and had many sweet hours there. Sometimes Mr. Smith and I walked there together, to converse of the things of God; and our conversation used much to turn on the advancement of Christ's kingdom in the world, and the glorious things that God would accomplish for his church in the latter days.

I had then, and at other times, the greatest delight in the holy Scriptures, of any book whatsoever. Oftentimes in reading it, every word seemed to touch my heart. I felt an harmony between something in my heart, and those sweet and powerful words. I seemed often to see so much light, exhibited by every sentence, and such a refreshing ravishing food communicated, that I could not get along in reading. Used oftentimes to dwell long on one sentence, to see the wonders contained in it; and yet almost every sentence seemed to be full of wonders.

I came away from New York in the month of April 1723, and had a most bitter parting with Madam Smith and her son. My heart seemed to sink within me, at leaving the family and city, where I had enjoyed so many sweet and pleasant days. I went from New York to Wethersfield by water.[10] As I sailed away, I kept sight of the city as long as I could; and when I was out of sight of it, it would affect me much to look that way, with a kind of melancholy mixed with sweetness. However, that night after this sorrowful parting, I was greatly comforted in God at Westchester, where we went ashore to lodge: and had a pleasant time of it all the voyage to Saybrook. It was sweet to me to think of meeting dear Christians in heaven, where we should never part more. At Saybrook we went ashore to lodge on Saturday, and there kept sabbath; where I had a sweet and refreshing season, walking alone in the fields.

After I came home to Windsor, remained much in a like frame of my mind, as I had been in at New York; but only sometimes felt my heart ready to sink, with the thoughts of my friends at New York. And my refuge and support was in contemplations on the heavenly state; as I find in my diary of May 1, 1723. It was my comfort to think of that state, where there is fullness of joy; where reigns heavenly, sweet, calm and delightful love, without alloy; where there are continually the dearest expressions of this love; where is the enjoyment of the persons loved, without ever parting; where these persons that appear so lovely in this world, will really be inexpressibly more lovely, and full of love to us. And how sweetly will the mutual lovers join together to sing the praises of God and the Lamb! How full will it fill us with joy, to think, that this enjoyment, these sweet exercises will never cease or come to an end; but will last to all eternity!

Continued much in the same frame in the general, that I had been in at New York, till

---

10. **from New York . . . by water:** Edwards sailed home on the Long Island Sound and the Connecticut River, stopping along the way at Westchester, New York, and Saybrook, Connecticut.

I went to New Haven, to live there as Tutor of the College; having one special season of uncommon sweetness: particularly once at Bolton, in a journey from Boston, walking out alone in the fields. After I went to New Haven, I sunk in religion; my mind being diverted from my eager and violent pursuits after holiness, by some affairs that greatly perplexed and distracted my mind.

In September 1725, was taken ill at New Haven; and endeavoring to go home to Windsor, was so ill at the North Village, that I could go no further: where I lay sick for about a quarter of a year. And in this sickness, God was pleased to visit me again with the sweet influences of his spirit. My mind was greatly engaged there on divine, pleasant contemplations, and longings of soul. I observed that those who watched with me, would often be looking out for the morning, and seemed to wish for it. Which brought to my mind those words of the Psalmist, which my soul with sweetness made its own language, "My soul waiteth for the Lord more than they that watch for the morning: I say, more than they that watch for the morning" [Psalms 130:6]. And when the light of the morning came, and the beams of the sun came in at the windows, it refreshed my soul from one morning to another. It seemed to me to be some image of the sweet light of God's glory.

I remember, about that time, I used greatly to long for the conversion of some that I was concerned with. It seemed to me, I could gladly honor them, and with delight be a servant to them, and lie at their feet, if they were but truly holy.

But sometime after this, I was again greatly diverted in my mind, with some temporal concerns, that exceedingly took up my thoughts, greatly to the wounding of my soul: and went on through various exercises, that it would be tedious to relate, that gave me much more experience of my own heart, than ever I had before.

Since I came to this town,[11] I have often had sweet complacency in God in views of his glorious perfections, and the excellency of Jesus Christ. God has appeared to me, a glorious and lovely being, chiefly on the account of his holiness. The holiness of God has always appeared to me the most lovely of all his attributes. The doctrines of God's absolute sovereignty, and free grace, in showing mercy to whom he would show mercy; and man's absolute dependence on the operations of God's Holy Spirit, have very often appeared to me as sweet and glorious doctrines. These doctrines have been much my delight. God's sovereignty has ever appeared to me, as great part of his glory. It has often been sweet to me to go to God, and adore him as a sovereign God, and ask sovereign mercy of him.

I have loved the doctrines of the gospel: they have been to my soul like green pastures. The gospel has seemed to me to be the richest treasure; the treasure that I have most desired, and longed that it might dwell richly in me. The way of salvation by Christ, has appeared in a general way, glorious and excellent, and most pleasant and beautiful. It has often seemed to me, that it would in a great measure spoil heaven, to receive it in any other way. That text has often been affecting and delightful to me, Isaiah 32:2, "A man shall be an hiding place from the wind, and a covert from the tempest," etc.

---

11. **Since I came to this town:** Northampton, Massachusetts, where Edwards took a position as assistant pastor in 1727.

It has often appeared sweet to me, to be united to Christ; to have him for my head, and to be a member of his body: and also to have Christ for my teacher and prophet. I very often think with sweetness and longings and pantings of soul, of being a little child, taking hold of Christ, to be led by him through the wilderness of this world. That text, Matthew 18 at the beginning, has often been sweet to me, "Except ye be converted, and become as little children" etc. I love to think of coming to Christ, to receive salvation of him, poor in spirit, and quite empty of self; humbly exalting him alone; cut entirely off from my own root, and to grow into, and out of Christ: to have God in Christ to be all in all; and to live by faith on the Son of God, a life of humble, unfeigned confidence in him. That Scripture has often been sweet to me, Psalms 115:1, "Not unto us, O Lord, not unto us, but unto thy name give glory, for thy mercy, and for thy truth's sake." And those words of Christ, Luke 10:21, "In that hour Jesus rejoiced in spirit, and said, I thank thee, O Father, Lord of heaven and earth, that thou hast hid these things from the wise and prudent, and hast revealed them unto babes: even so Father, for so it seemed good in thy sight." That sovereignty of God that Christ rejoiced in, seemed to me to be worthy to be rejoiced in; and that rejoicing of Christ, seemed to me to show the excellency of Christ, and the spirit that he was of.

Sometimes only mentioning a single word, causes my heart to burn within me: or only seeing the name of Christ, or the name of some attribute of God. And God has appeared glorious to me, on account of the Trinity. It has made me have exalting thoughts of God, that he subsists in three persons; Father, Son, and Holy Ghost.

The sweetest joys and delights I have experienced, have not been those that have arisen from a hope of my own good estate; but in a direct view of the glorious things of the gospel. When I enjoy this sweetness, it seems to carry me above the thoughts of my own safe estate. It seems at such times a loss that I cannot bear, to take off my eye from the glorious, pleasant object I behold without me, to turn my eye in upon myself, and my own good estate.

My heart has been much on the advancement of Christ's kingdom in the world. The histories of the past advancement of Christ's kingdom, have been sweet to me. When I have read histories of past ages, the pleasantest thing in all my reading has been, to read of the kingdom of Christ being promoted. And when I have expected in my reading, to come to any such thing, I have lotted[12] upon it all the way as I read. And my mind has been much entertained and delighted, with the Scripture promises and prophecies, of the future glorious advancement of Christ's kingdom on earth.

I have sometimes had a sense of the excellent fullness of Christ, and his meetness and suitableness as a savior; whereby he has appeared to me, far above all, the chief of ten thousands.[13] And his blood and atonement has appeared sweet, and his righteousness sweet; which is always accompanied with an ardency of spirit, and inward

12. **lotted:** Relied.
13. **the chief of ten thousands:** See the Song of Solomon 5:10: "My beloved is white and ruddy, the chiefest among ten thousand."

strugglings and breathings and groanings, that cannot be uttered, to be emptied of myself, and swallowed up in Christ.

Once, as I rid out into the woods for my health, *anno*[14] 1737; and having lit from my horse in a retired place, as my manner commonly has been, to walk for divine contemplation and prayer; I had a view, that for me was extraordinary, of the glory of the Son of God; as mediator between God and man; and his wonderful, great, full, pure and sweet grace and love, and meek and gentle condescension. This grace, that appeared to me so calm and sweet, appeared great above the heavens. The person of Christ appeared ineffably excellent, with an excellency great enough to swallow up all thought and conception. Which continued, as near as I can judge, about an hour; which kept me, the bigger part of the time, in a flood of tears, and weeping aloud. I felt withal, an ardency of soul to be, what I know not otherwise how to express, than to be emptied and annihilated; to lie in the dust, and to be full of Christ alone; to love him with a holy and pure love; to trust in him; to live upon him; to serve and follow him, and to be totally wrapt up in the fullness of Christ; and to be perfectly sanctified and made pure, with a divine and heavenly purity. I have several other times, had views very much of the same nature, and that have had the same effects.

I have many times had a sense of the glory of the third person in the Trinity, in his office of Sanctifier; in his holy operations communicating divine light and life to the soul. God in the communications of his Holy Spirit, has appeared as an infinite fountain of divine glory and sweetness; being full and sufficient to fill and satisfy the soul: pouring forth itself in sweet communications, like the sun in its glory, sweetly and pleasantly diffusing light and life.

I have sometimes had an affecting sense of the excellency of the word of God, as a word of life; as the light of life; a sweet, excellent, life-giving word: accompanied with a thirsting after that word, that it might dwell richly in my heart.

I have often since I lived in this town, had very affecting views of my own sinfulness and vileness; very frequently so as to hold me in a kind of loud weeping, sometimes for a considerable time together: so that I have often been forced to shut myself up. I have had a vastly greater sense of my own wickedness, and the badness of my heart, since my conversion, than ever I had before. It has often appeared to me, that if God should mark iniquity against me, I should appear the very worst of all mankind; of all that have been since the beginning of the world to this time: and that I should have by far the lowest place in hell. When others that have come to talk with me about their soul concerns, have expressed the sense they have had of their own wickedness, by saying that it seemed to them, that they were as bad as the devil himself; I thought their expressions seemed exceeding faint and feeble, to represent my wickedness. I thought I should wonder, that they should content themselves with such expressions as these, if I had any

---

14. ***anno***: In the year of (Latin).

reason to imagine, that their sin bore any proportion to mine. It seemed to me, I should wonder at myself, if I should express my wickedness in such feeble terms as they did.

My wickedness, as I am in myself, has long appeared to me perfectly ineffable, and infinitely swallowing up all thought and imagination; like an infinite deluge, or infinite mountains over my head. I know not how to express better, what my sins appear to me to be, than by heaping infinite upon infinite, and multiplying infinite by infinite. I go about very often, for this many years, with these expressions in my mind, and in my mouth, "Infinite upon infinite. Infinite upon infinite!" When I look into my heart, and take a view of my wickedness, it looks like an abyss infinitely deeper than hell. And it appears to me, that were it not for free grace, exalted and raised up to the infinite height of all the fullness and glory of the great Jehovah,[15] and the arm of his power and grace stretched forth, in all the majesty of his power, and in all the glory of his sovereignty; I should appear sunk down in my sins infinitely below hell itself, far beyond sight of everything, but the piercing eye of God's grace, that can pierce even down to such a depth, and to the bottom of such an abyss.

And yet, I ben't in the least inclined to think, that I have a greater conviction of sin than ordinary. It seems to me, my conviction of sin is exceeding small, and faint. It appears to me enough to amaze me, that I have no more sense of my sin. I know certainly, that I have very little sense of my sinfulness. That my sins appear to me so great, don't seem to me to be, because I have so much more conviction of sin than other Christians, but because I am so much worse, and have so much more wickedness to be convinced of. When I have had these turns of weeping and crying for my sins, I thought I knew in the time of it, that my repentance was nothing to my sin.

I have greatly longed of late, for a broken heart, and to lie low before God. And when I ask for humility of God, I can't bear the thoughts of being no more humble, than other Christians. It seems to me, that though their degrees of humility may be suitable for them; yet it would be a vile self-exaltation in me, not to be the lowest in humility of all mankind. Others speak of their longing to be humbled to the dust. Though that may be a proper expression for them, I always think for myself, that I ought to be humbled down below hell. 'Tis an expression that it has long been natural for me to use in prayer to God. I ought to lie infinitely low before God.

It is affecting to me to think, how ignorant I was, when I was a young Christian, of the bottomless, infinite depths of wickedness, pride, hypocrisy and deceit left in my heart.

I have vastly a greater sense, of my universal, exceeding dependence on God's grace and strength, and mere good pleasure, of late, than I used formerly to have; and have experienced more of an abhorrence of my own righteousness. The thought of any comfort or joy, arising in me, on any consideration, or reflection on my own amiableness, or any of my performances or experiences, or any goodness of heart or life, is nauseous and detestable to me. And yet I am greatly afflicted with a proud and self-righteous

---

15. **Jehovah:** A form of the Hebrew name for God.

spirit; much more sensibly, than I used to be formerly. I see that serpent rising and putting forth its head, continually, everywhere, all around me.

Though it seems to me, that in some respects I was a far better Christian, for two or three years after my first conversion, than I am now; and lived in a more constant delight and pleasure: yet of late years, I have had a more full and constant sense of the absolute sovereignty of God, and a delight in that sovereignty; and have had more of a sense of the glory of Christ, as a mediator, as revealed in the gospel. On one Saturday night in particular, had a particular discovery of the excellency of the gospel of Christ, above all other doctrines; so that I could not but say to myself; "This is my chosen light, my chosen doctrine": and of Christ, "This is my chosen prophet." It appeared to me to be sweet beyond all expression, to follow Christ, and to be taught and enlightened and instructed by him; to learn of him; and live to him.

Another Saturday night, January 1738/9,[16] had such a sense, how sweet and blessed a thing it was, to walk in the way of duty, to do that which was right and meet to be done, and agreeable to the holy mind of God; that it caused me to break forth into a kind of a loud weeping, which held me some time; so that I was forced to shut myself up, and fasten the doors. I could not but as it were cry out, "How happy are they which do that which is right in the sight of God! They are blessed indeed, they are the happy ones!" I had at the same time, a very affecting sense, how meet and suitable it was that God should govern the world, and order all things according to his own pleasure; and I rejoiced in it, that God reigned, and that his will was done.

[c. after 1739, 1998]

16. January 1738/9: See note 9.

Edwards's *Sinners in the Hands of an Angry God.* Edwards delivered this sermon in Enfield, Connecticut, on Sunday, July 8, 1741. Perhaps his most famous – or infamous – work, it has tended to cast Edwards as a preacher of "fire and brimstone," a phrase used in the sermon. According to one of his early biographers, however, Edwards delivered the sermon in a quiet, unexpressive voice, reading slowly from his prepared text. As he read the sermon, many in the crowd began to moan and cry. One member of the audience, the Reverend Stephen William, recorded in his diary that "the shrieks & crys were piercing & Amazing." The sermon was swiftly published in Boston, giving added impetus to what Edwards in an earlier work had called the "Surprising Work of God," now known as the Great Awakening, the religious revivals that spread throughout the American colonies during the 1730s and 1740s. The text is taken from the Yale University Press *Works of Jonathan Edwards*, Vol. 22, edited by Harry S. Stout and Nathan O. Hatch (2003).

First Printing of Edwards's Most Famous Sermon

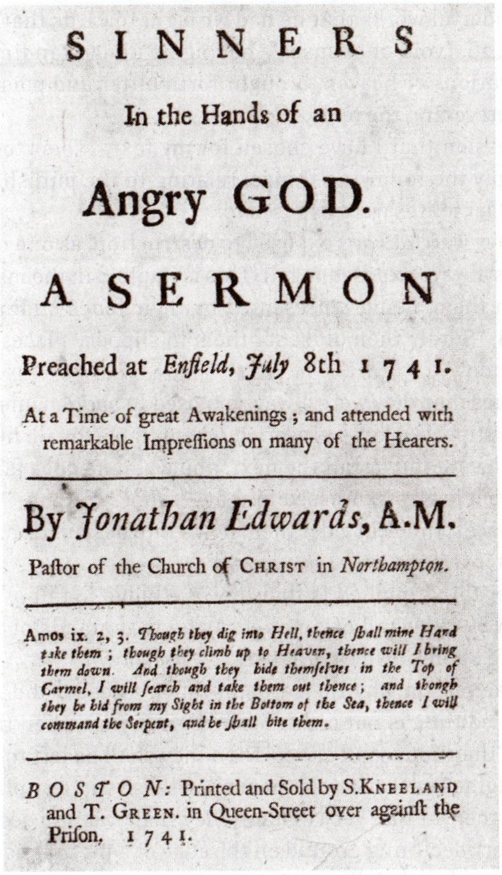

SINNERS
In the Hands of an
Angry GOD.
A SERMON
Preached at *Enfield, July* 8th 1741.
At a Time of great Awakenings; and attended with remarkable Impreſſions on many of the Hearers.

By *Jonathan Edwards*, A.M.
Paſtor of the Church of CHRIST in *Northampton.*

Amos ix. 2, 3. *Though they dig into Hell, thence ſhall mine Hand take them; though they climb up to Heaven, thence will I bring them down. And though they hide themſelves in the Top of Carmel, I will ſearch and take them out thence; and though they be hid from my Sight in the Bottom of the Sea, thence I will command the Serpent, and he ſhall bite them.*

BOSTON: Printed and Sold by S. KNEELAND and T. GREEN. in Queen-Street over againſt the Priſon, 1741.

Sinners in the Hands of an Angry God

DEUTERONOMY 32:35.

Their foot shall slide in due time.[1]

In this verse is threatened the vengeance of God on the wicked unbelieving Israelites, that were God's visible people, and lived under means of grace;[2] and that, notwithstanding

1. ***Their foot . . . in due time***: The complete verse from Deuteronomy reads: "To me *belongeth* vengeance, and recompence; their foot shall slide in *due* time: for the day of their calamity *is* at hand, and the things that shall come upon them make haste."
2. **means of grace**: For the Israelites, the "means of grace" were the Ten Commandments, given to them by God. For the Puritans, the principal statement of Protestant beliefs and practices was the Westminster Confession of Faith, a creed completed in 1646 by an assembly of ministers, delegates of Parliament, and representatives of Scotland. In the Westminster Confession, "God's covenant with man" is outlined in chapter 7 as "the preaching of the Word, and the administration of the sacraments of Baptism and the Lord's Supper."

all God's wonderful works that he had wrought towards that people, yet remained, as is expressed, v. 28, "void of counsel,"[3] having no understanding in them; and that, under all the cultivations of heaven, brought forth bitter and poisonous fruit;[4] as in the two verses next preceding the text.

The expression that I have chosen for my text, "Their foot shall slide in due time," seems to imply the following things, relating to the punishment and destruction that these wicked Israelites were exposed to.

1. That they were *always* exposed to destruction, as one that stands or walks in slippery places is always exposed to fall. This is implied in the manner of their destruction's coming upon them, being represented by their foot's sliding. The same is expressed, Psalms 73:18, "Surely thou didst set them in slippery places: thou castedst them down into destruction."

2. It implies that they were always exposed to *sudden* unexpected destruction. As he that walks in slippery places is every moment liable to fall; he can't foresee one moment whether he shall stand or fall the next; and when he does fall, he falls at once, without warning. Which is also expressed in that, Psalms 73:18-19, "Surely thou didst set them in slippery places: thou castedst them down into destruction. How are they brought into desolation as in a moment!"

3. Another thing implied is that they are liable to fall *of themselves*, without being thrown down by the hand of another. As he that stands or walks on slippery ground, needs nothing but his own weight to throw him down.

4. That the reason why they are not fallen already, and don't fall now, is only that God's appointed time is not come. For it is said, that when that due time, or appointed time comes, "their foot shall slide." Then they shall be left to fall as they are inclined by their own weight. God won't hold them up in these slippery places any longer, but will let them go; and then, at that very instant, they shall fall into destruction; as he that stands in such slippery declining ground on the edge of a pit that he can't stand alone, when he is let go he immediately falls and is lost.

The observation from the words that I would now insist upon is this:

[Doctrine]

THERE IS NOTHING THAT KEEPS WICKED MEN, AT ANY ONE MOMENT, OUT OF HELL, BUT THE MERE PLEASURE OF GOD.

By "the mere pleasure of God," I mean his sovereign pleasure, his arbitrary will, restrained by no obligation, hindered by no manner of difficulty, any more than if nothing

3. **"void of counsel"**: "For they are a nation void of counsel, neither is there any understanding in them" (Deuteronomy 32:28).

4. **poisonous fruit**: "For their vine is of the vine of Sodom, and of the fields of Gomorrah: their grapes are grapes of gall, their clusters are bitter: Their wine is the poison of dragons, and the cruel venom of asps" (Deuteronomy 32:32-33). For the evil and immoral behavior of their citizens, the cities of Sodom and Gomorrah were destroyed by God (Genesis 19:24-26).

else but God's mere will had in the least degree, or in any respect whatsoever, any hand in the preservation of wicked men one moment.

The truth of this observation may appear by the following considerations.

I. There is no want of *power* in God to cast wicked men into hell at any moment. Men's hands can't be strong when God rises up: the strongest have no power to resist him, nor can any deliver out of his hands.

He is not only able to cast wicked men into hell, but he can most *easily* do it. Sometimes an earthly prince meets with a great deal of difficulty to subdue a rebel, that has found means to fortify himself, and has made himself strong by the numbers of his followers. But it is not so with God. There is no fortress that is any defense from the power of God. Though hand join in hand, and vast multitudes of God's enemies combine and associate themselves, they are easily broken in pieces: they are as great heaps of light chaff[5] before the whirlwind; or large quantities of dry stubble before devouring flames. We find it easy to tread on and crush a worm that we see crawling on the earth; so 'tis easy for us to cut or singe a slender thread that anything hangs by; thus easy is it for God when he pleases to cast his enemies down to hell. What are we, that we should think to stand before him, at whose rebuke the earth trembles, and before whom the rocks are thrown down?

II. They *deserve* to be cast into hell; so that divine justice never stands in the way, it makes no objection against God's using his power at any moment to destroy them. Yea, on the contrary, justice calls aloud for an infinite punishment of their sins. Divine justice says of the tree that brings forth such grapes of Sodom, "Cut it down; why cumbreth[6] it the ground" (Luke 13:7). The sword of divine justice is every moment brandished over their heads, and 'tis nothing but the hand of arbitrary mercy, and God's mere will, that holds it back.

III. They are *already* under a sentence of condemnation to hell. They don't only justly deserve to be cast down thither; but the sentence of the law of God, that eternal and immutable rule of righteousness that God has fixed between him and mankind, is gone out against them, and stands against them; so that they are bound over already to hell. John 3:18, "He that believeth not is condemned already." So that every unconverted man properly belongs to hell; that is his place; from thence he is. John 8:23, "Ye are from beneath." And thither he is bound; 'tis the place that justice, and God's Word, and the sentence of his unchangeable law assigns to him.

IV. They are now the objects of that very *same* anger and wrath of God that is expressed in the torments of hell: and the reason why they don't go down to hell at each moment, is not because God, in whose power they are, is not then very angry with them; as angry as he is with many of those miserable creatures that he is now tormenting in hell, and do there feel and bear the fierceness of his wrath. Yea, God is a great deal more angry with great numbers that are now on earth, yea, doubtless with many that are now

5. **chaff:** Husks of corn or other grains, separated by winnowing or threshing.
6. **cumbreth:** Obstruct.

in this congregation, that it may be are at ease and quiet, than he is with many of those that are now in the flames of hell.

So that it is not because God is unmindful of their wickedness, and don't resent it, that he don't let loose his hand and cut them off. God is not altogether such an one as themselves, though they may imagine him to be so. The wrath of God burns against them, their damnation don't slumber, the pit is prepared, the fire is made ready, the furnace is now hot, ready to receive them, the flames do now rage and glow. The glittering sword is whet, and held over them, and the pit hath opened her mouth under them.

V. The *devil* stands ready to fall upon them and seize them as his own, at what moment God shall permit him. They belong to him; he has their souls in his possession, and under his dominion. The Scripture represents them as his "goods" (Luke 11:21). The devils watch them; they are ever by them, at their right hand; they stand waiting for them, like greedy hungry lions that see their prey, and expect to have it, but are for the present kept back; if God should withdraw his hand, by which they are restrained, they would in one moment fly upon their poor souls. The old serpent is gaping for them; hell opens its mouth wide to receive them; and if God should permit it, they would be hastily swallowed up and lost.

VI. There are in the souls of wicked men those hellish *principles* reigning, that would presently kindle and flame out into hell fire, if it were not for God's restraints. There is laid in the very nature of carnal men a foundation for the torments of hell: there are those corrupt principles, in reigning power in them, and in full possession of them, that are seeds of hell fire. These principles are active and powerful, and exceeding violent in their nature, and if it were not for the restraining hand of God upon them, they would soon break out, they would flame out after the same manner as the same corruptions, the same enmity does in the hearts of damned souls, and would beget the same torments in 'em as they do in them. The souls of the wicked are in Scripture compared to the troubled sea (Isaiah 57:20). For the present God restrains their wickedness by his mighty power, as he does the raging waves of the troubled sea, saying, "Hitherto shalt thou come, and no further" [Job 38:11]; but if God should withdraw that restraining power, it would soon carry all afore it. Sin is the ruin and misery of the soul; it is destructive in its nature; and if God should leave it without restraint, there would need nothing else to make the soul perfectly miserable. The corruption of the heart of man is a thing that is immoderate and boundless in its fury; and while wicked men live here, it is like fire pent up by God's restraints, whenas if it were let loose it would set on fire the course of nature; and as the heart is now a sink of sin, so, if sin was not restrained, it would immediately turn the soul into a fiery oven, or a furnace of fire and brimstone.

VII. It is no security to wicked men for one moment, that there are no *visible means of death* at hand. 'Tis no security to a natural man,[7] that he is now in health, and that he don't see which way he should now immediately go out of the world by any accident, and that there is no visible danger in any respect in his circumstances. The manifold and

---

7. **a natural man:** That is, an unredeemed person living in a state of nature rather than in a state of grace.

continual experience of the world in all ages, shows that this is no evidence that a man is not on the very brink of eternity, and that the next step won't be into another world. The unseen, unthought of ways and means of persons going suddenly out of the world are innumerable and inconceivable. Unconverted men walk over the pit of hell on a rotten covering, and there are innumerable places in this covering so weak that they won't bear their weight, and these places are not seen. The arrows of death fly unseen at noonday;[8] the sharpest sight can't discern them. God has so many different unsearchable ways of taking wicked men out of the world and sending 'em to hell, that there is nothing to make it appear that God had need to be at the expense of a miracle, or go out of the ordinary course of his providence, to destroy any wicked man, at any moment. All the means that there are of sinners going out of the world, are so in God's hands, and so universally absolutely subject to his power and determination, that it don't depend at all less on the mere will of God, whether sinners shall at any moment go to hell, than if means were never made use of, or at all concerned in the case.

VIII. Natural men's *prudence* and *care* to preserve their own *lives*, or the care of others to preserve them, don't secure 'em a moment. This divine providence and universal experience does also bear testimony to. There is this clear evidence that men's own wisdom is no security to them from death: that if it were otherwise we should see some difference between the wise and politic men of the world, and others, with regard to their liableness to early and unexpected death; but how is it in fact? Ecclesiastes 2:16, "How dieth the wise man? as the fool."

IX. All wicked men's *pains* and *contrivance* they use to escape *hell*, while they continue to reject Christ, and so remain wicked men, don't secure 'em from hell one moment. Almost every natural man that hears of hell, flatters himself that he shall escape it; he depends upon himself for his own security; he flatters himself in what he has done, in what he is now doing, or what he intends to do; everyone lays out matters in his own mind how he shall avoid damnation, and flatters himself that he contrives well for himself, and that his schemes won't fail. They hear indeed that there are but few saved, and that the bigger part of men that have died heretofore are gone to hell; but each one imagines that he lays out matters better for his own escape than others have done: he don't intend to come to that place of torment; he says within himself, that he intends to take care that shall be effectual, and to order matters so for himself as not to fail.

But the foolish children of men do miserably delude themselves in their own schemes, and in their confidence in their own strength and wisdom; they trust to nothing but a shadow. The bigger part of those that heretofore have lived under the same means of grace, and are now dead, are undoubtedly gone to hell: and it was not because they were not as wise as those that are now alive; it was not because they did not lay out matters as well for themselves to secure their own escape. If it were so, that we could come to speak with them, and could inquire of them, one by one, whether they expected when alive, and

8. **The arrows . . . noonday:** See Psalms 91:5-6: "Thou shalt not be afraid for the terror by night; nor for the arrow that flieth by day; / Nor for the pestilence that walketh in darkness; nor for the destruction that wasteth at noonday."

when they used to hear about hell, ever to be the subjects of that misery, we doubtless should hear one and another reply, "No, I never intended to come here; I had laid out matters otherwise in my mind; I thought I should contrive well for myself; I thought my scheme good; I intended to take effectual care; but it came upon me unexpected; I did not look for it at that time, and in that manner; it came as a thief; death outwitted me; God's wrath was too quick for me; O my cursed foolishness! I was flattering myself, and pleasing myself with vain dreams of what I would do hereafter, and when I was saying, 'Peace and safety,' then sudden destruction came upon me" [I Thessalonians 5:3].

X. God has laid himself under *no obligation* by any promise to keep any natural man out of hell one moment. God certainly has made no promises either of eternal life, or of any deliverance or preservation from eternal death, but what are contained in the covenant of grace,[9] the promises that are given in Christ, in whom all the promises are yea and amen. But surely they have no interest in the promises of the covenant of grace that are not the children of the covenant, and that don't believe in any of the promises of the covenant, and have no interest in the *Mediator*[10] of the covenant.

So that whatever some have imagined and pretended about promises made to natural men's earnest seeking and knocking, 'tis plain and manifest that whatever pains a natural man takes in religion, whatever prayers he makes, till he believes in Christ, God is under no manner of obligation to keep him a *moment* from eternal destruction.

So that thus it is, that natural men are held in the hand of God over the pit of hell; they have deserved the fiery pit, and are already sentenced to it; and God is dreadfully provoked, his anger is as great towards them as to those that are actually suffering the executions of the fierceness of his wrath in hell, and they have done nothing in the least to appease or abate that anger, neither is God in the least bound by any promise to hold 'em up one moment; the devil is waiting for them, hell is gaping for them, the flames gather and flash about them, and would fain lay hold on them, and swallow them up; the fire pent up in their own hearts is struggling to break out; and they have no interest in any mediator, there are no means within reach that can be any security to them. In short, they have no refuge, nothing to take hold of, all that preserves them every moment is the mere arbitrary will, and uncovenanted unobliged forbearance of an incensed God.

Application

The *Use* may be of *Awakening* to unconverted persons in this congregation. This that you have heard is the case of everyone of you that are out of Christ. That world of misery, that lake of burning brimstone is extended abroad under you. *There* is the dreadful pit of the glowing flames of the wrath of God; there is hell's wide gaping mouth open; and you

---

9. **covenant of grace**: In Christian theology, God created a new covenant by sending his son, Jesus Christ, to intercede for fallen humankind. In this covenant of grace, those who believe in Jesus may be saved.
10. ***Mediator***: In the covenant of grace, Jesus Christ is the mediator between God and human beings.

have nothing to stand upon, nor anything to take hold of: there is nothing between you and hell but the air; 'tis only the power and mere pleasure of God that holds you up.

You probably are not sensible of this; you find you are kept out of hell, but don't see the hand of God in it, but look at other things, as the good state of your bodily constitution, your care of your own life, and the means you use for your own preservation. But indeed these things are nothing; if God should withdraw his hand, they would avail no more to keep you from falling, than the thin air to hold up a person that is suspended in it.

Your wickedness makes you as it were heavy as lead, and to tend downwards with great weight and pressure towards hell; and if God should let you go, you would immediately sink and swiftly descend and plunge into the bottomless gulf, and your healthy constitution, and your own care and prudence, and best contrivance, and all your righteousness, would have no more influence to uphold you and keep you out of hell, than a spider's web would have to stop a falling rock. Were it not that so is the sovereign pleasure of God, the earth would not bear you one moment; for you are a burden to it; the creation groans with you; the creature is made subject to the bondage of your corruption, not willingly; the sun don't willingly shine upon you to give you light to serve sin and Satan; the earth don't willingly yield her increase to satisfy your lusts; nor is it willingly a stage for your wickedness to be acted upon; the air don't willingly serve you for breath to maintain the flame of life in your vitals, while you spend your life in the service of God's enemies. God's creatures are good, and were made for men to serve God with, and don't willingly subserve to any other purpose, and groan when they are abused to purposes so directly contrary to their nature and end. And the world would spew you out, were it not for the sovereign hand of him who hath subjected it in hope. There are the black clouds of God's wrath now hanging directly over your heads, full of the dreadful storm, and big with thunder; and were it not for the restraining hand of God it would immediately burst forth upon you. The sovereign pleasure of God for the present stays his rough wind; otherwise it would come with fury, and your destruction would come like a whirlwind, and you would be like the chaff of the summer threshing floor.

The wrath of God is like great waters that are dammed for the present; they increase more and more, and rise higher and higher, till an outlet is given, and the longer the stream is stopped, the more rapid and mighty is its course, when once it is let loose. 'Tis true, that judgment against your evil works has not been executed hitherto; the floods of God's vengeance have been withheld; but your guilt in the meantime is constantly increasing, and you are every day treasuring up more wrath; the waters are continually rising and waxing more and more mighty; and there is nothing but the mere pleasure of God that holds the waters back that are unwilling to be stopped, and press hard to go forward; if God should only withdraw his hand from the floodgate, it would immediately fly open, and the fiery floods of the fierceness and wrath of God would rush forth with inconceivable fury, and would come upon you with omnipotent power; and if your strength were ten thousand times greater than it is, yea, ten thousand times greater than the strength of the stoutest, sturdiest devil in hell, it would be nothing to withstand or endure it.

The bow of God's wrath is bent, and the arrow made ready on the string, and Justice bends the arrow at your heart, and strains the bow, and it is nothing but the mere pleasure of God, and that of an angry God, without any promise or obligation at all, that keeps the arrow one moment from being made drunk with your blood.

Thus are all you that never passed under a great change of heart, by the mighty power of the Spirit of God upon your souls; all that were never born again, and made new creatures, and raised from being dead in sin, to a state of new, and before altogether unexperienced light and life (however you may have reformed your life in many things, and may have had religious affections, and may keep up a form of religion in your families and closets,[11] and in the house of God, and may be strict in it), you are thus in the hands of an angry God; 'tis nothing but his mere pleasure that keeps you from being this moment swallowed up in everlasting destruction.

However unconvinced you may now be of the truth of what you hear, by and by you will be fully convinced of it. Those that are gone from being in the like circumstances with you, see that it was so with them; for destruction came suddenly upon most of them, when they expected nothing of it, and while they were saying, "Peace and safety": now they see, that those things that they depended on for peace and safety, were nothing but thin air and empty shadows.

The God that holds you over the pit of hell, much as one holds a spider, or some loathsome insect, over the fire, abhors you, and is dreadfully provoked; his wrath towards you burns like fire; he looks upon you as worthy of nothing else, but to be cast into the fire; he is of purer eyes than to bear to have you in his sight; you are ten thousand times so abominable in his eyes as the most hateful venomous serpent is in ours. You have offended him infinitely more than ever a stubborn rebel did his prince: and yet 'tis nothing but his hand that holds you from falling into the fire every moment; 'tis to be ascribed to nothing else, that you did not go to hell the last night; that you was suffered to awake again in this world, after you closed your eyes to sleep: and there is no other reason to be given why you have not dropped into hell since you arose in the morning, but that God's hand has held you up; there is no other reason to be given why you han't gone to hell since you have sat here in the house of God, provoking his pure eyes by your sinful wicked manner of attending his solemn worship: yea, there is nothing else that is to be given as a reason why you don't this very moment drop down into hell.

O sinner! Consider the fearful danger you are in: 'tis a great furnace of wrath, a wide and bottomless pit, full of the fire of wrath, that you are held over in the hand of that God, whose wrath is provoked and incensed as much against you as against many of the damned in hell; you hang by a slender thread, with the flames of divine wrath flashing about it, and ready every moment to singe it, and burn it asunder; and you have no interest in any mediator, and nothing to lay hold of to save yourself, nothing to keep off the flames of wrath, nothing of your own, nothing that you ever have done, nothing that you can do, to induce God to spare you one moment.

---

11. **closets:** Private rooms used for study or prayer.

And consider here more particularly several things concerning that wrath that you are in such danger of.

First. Whose wrath it is: it is the wrath of the infinite God. If it were only the wrath of man, though it were of the most potent prince, it would be comparatively little to be regarded. The wrath of kings is very much dreaded, especially of absolute monarchs, that have the possessions and lives of their subjects wholly in their power, to be disposed of at their mere will. Proverbs 20:2, "The fear of a king is as the roaring of a lion: whoso provoketh him to anger, sinneth against his own soul." The subject that very much enrages an arbitrary prince, is liable to suffer the most extreme torments, that human art can invent or human power can inflict. But the greatest earthly potentates, in their greatest majesty and strength, and when clothed in their greatest terrors, are but feeble despicable worms of the dust, in comparison of the great and almighty Creator and King of heaven and earth: it is but little that they can do, when most enraged, and when they have exerted the utmost of their fury. All the kings of the earth before God are as grasshoppers, they are nothing and less than nothing: both their love and their hatred is to be despised. The wrath of the great King of kings is as much more terrible than their's, as his majesty is greater. Luke 12:4-5, "And I say unto you my friends, Be not afraid of them that kill the body, and after that have no more that they can do. But I will forewarn you whom ye shall fear: Fear him which after he hath killed hath power to cast into hell; yea, I say unto you, fear him."

Second. 'Tis the *fierceness* of his wrath that you are exposed to. We often read of the *fury* of God; as in Isaiah 59:18, "According to their deeds, accordingly he will repay fury to his adversaries." So Isaiah 66:15, "For, behold, the Lord will come with fire, and with chariots like a whirlwind, to render his anger with fury, and his rebukes with flames of fire." And so in many other places. So we read of God's *fierceness*. Revelations 19:15, there we read of "the winepress of the fierceness and wrath of almighty God." The words are exceeding terrible: if it had only been said, "the wrath of God," the words would have implied that which is infinitely dreadful; but 'tis not only said so, but "the fierceness and wrath of God": the fury of God! the fierceness of Jehovah![12] Oh how dreadful must that be! Who can utter or conceive what such expressions carry in them! But it is not only said so, but "the fierceness and wrath of *almighty God*." As though there would be a very great manifestation of his almighty power, in what the fierceness of his wrath should inflict, as though omnipotence should be as it were enraged, and exerted, as men are wont to exert their strength in the fierceness of their wrath. Oh! then what will be consequence! What will become of the poor worm that shall suffer it! Whose hands can be strong? and whose heart endure? To what a dreadful, inexpressible, inconceivable depth of misery must the poor creature be sunk, who shall be the subject of this!

Consider this, you that are here present, that yet remain in an unregenerate state. That God will execute the fierceness of his anger, implies that he will inflict wrath without any pity: when God beholds the ineffable extremity of your case, and sees your torment to be so vastly disproportioned to your strength, and sees how your poor soul is

---

12. **Jehovah:** A form of the Hebrew name for God.

crushed and sinks down, as it were into an infinite gloom, he will have no compassion upon you, he will not forbear the executions of his wrath, or in the least lighten his hand; there shall be no moderation or mercy, nor will God then at all stay his rough wind; he will have no regard to your welfare, nor be at all careful lest you should suffer too much, in any other sense than only that you shall not suffer beyond what strict justice requires: nothing shall be withheld, because it's so hard for you to bear. Ezekiel 8:18, "Therefore will I also deal in fury: mine eye shall not spare, neither will I have pity; and though they cry in mine ears with a loud voice, yet I will not hear them." Now God stands ready to pity you; this is a day of mercy; you may cry now with some encouragement of obtaining mercy: but when once the day of mercy is past, your most lamentable and dolorous cries and shrieks will be in vain; you will be wholly lost and thrown away of God as to any regard to your welfare; God will have no other use to put you to but only to suffer misery; you shall be continued in being to no other end; for you will be a vessel of wrath fitted to destruction; and there will be no other use of this vessel but only to be filled full of wrath: God will be so far from pitying you when you cry to him, that 'tis said he will only laugh and mock (Proverbs 1:25-32).

How awful are those words, Isaiah 63:3, which are the words of the great God, "I will tread them in mine anger, and will trample them in my fury, and their blood shall be sprinkled upon my garments, and I will stain all my raiment." 'Tis perhaps impossible to conceive of words that carry in them greater manifestations of these three things, viz.[13] contempt, and hatred, and fierceness of indignation. If you cry to God to pity you, he will be so far from pitying you in your doleful case, or showing you the least regard or favor, that instead of that he'll only tread you under foot: and though he will know that you can't bear the weight of omnipotence treading upon you, yet he won't regard that, but he will crush you under his feet without mercy; he'll crush out your blood, and make it fly, and it shall be sprinkled on his garments, so as to stain all his raiment. He will not only hate you, but he will have you in the utmost contempt; no place shall be thought fit for you, but under his feet, to be trodden down as the mire of the streets.

Third. The misery you are exposed to is that which God will inflict to that end, that he might *show* what that *wrath* of Jehovah is. God hath had it on his heart to show to angels and men, both how excellent his love is, and also how terrible his wrath is. Sometimes earthly kings have a mind to show how terrible *their* wrath is, by the extreme punishments they would execute on those that provoke 'em. Nebuchadnezzar, that mighty and haughty monarch of the Chaldean empire, was willing to show *his* wrath, when enraged with Shadrach, Meshach, and Abednego;[14] and accordingly gave order that the burning fiery furnace should be het seven times hotter than it was before; doubtless it was raised to the utmost degree of fierceness that human art could raise it: but the great God is also willing to show *his wrath*, and magnify his awful majesty and mighty power in the extreme sufferings of his enemies. Romans 9:22, "What if God, willing to show *his*

---

13. **viz.:** In other words (abbreviation of the Latin word *videlicet*).
14. **Shadrach, Meshach, and Abednego:** The story of their deliverance from the fiery furnace is recounted in Daniel 3:1-30.

wrath, and to make his power known, endured with much longsuffering the vessels of wrath fitted to destruction?" And seeing this is his design, and what he has determined, to show how terrible the unmixed, unrestrained wrath, the fury and fierceness of Jehovah is, he will do it to effect. There will be something accomplished and brought to pass, that will be dreadful with a witness. When the great and angry God hath risen up and executed his awful vengeance on the poor sinner; and the wretch is actually suffering the infinite weight and power of his indignation, then will God call upon the whole universe to behold that awful majesty, and mighty power that is to be seen in it. Isaiah 33:12-14. "And the people shall be as the burning of lime: as thorns cut up shall they be burnt in the fire. Hear, ye that are far off, what I have done; and ye that are near, acknowledge my might. The sinners in Zion are afraid; fearfulness hath surprised the hypocrites. Who among us shall dwell with the devouring fire? who among us shall dwell with everlasting burnings?"

Thus it will be with you that are in an unconverted state, if you continue in it; the infinite might, and majesty and terribleness of the omnipotent God shall be magnified upon you, in the ineffable strength of your torments: you shall be tormented in the presence of the holy angels, and in the presence of the Lamb; and when you shall be in this state of suffering, the glorious inhabitants of heaven shall go forth and look on the awful spectacle, that they may see what the wrath and fierceness of the Almighty is, and when they have seen it, they will fall down and adore that great power and majesty. Isaiah 66:23-24, "And it shall come to pass, that from one new moon to another, and from one sabbath to another, shall all flesh come to worship before me, saith the Lord. And they shall go forth, and look upon the carcasses of the men that have transgressed against me: for their worm shall not die, neither shall their fire be quenched; and they shall be an abhorring unto all flesh."

Fourth. 'Tis *everlasting* wrath. It would be dreadful to suffer this fierceness and wrath of almighty God one moment; but you must suffer it to all eternity: there will be no end to this exquisite horrible misery. When you look forward, you shall see a long forever, a boundless duration before you, which will swallow up your thoughts, and amaze your soul; and you will absolutely despair of ever having any deliverance, any end, any mitigation, any rest at all; you will know certainly that you must wear out long ages, millions of millions of ages, in wrestling and conflicting with this almighty merciless vengeance; and then when you have so done, when so many ages have actually been spent by you in this manner, you will know that all is but a point to what remains. So that your punishment will indeed be infinite. Oh who can express what the state of a soul in such circumstances is! All that we can possibly say about it, gives but a very feeble faint representation of it; 'tis inexpressible and inconceivable: for "who knows the power of God's anger?" [Psalms 90:11].

How dreadful is the state of those that are daily and hourly in danger of this great wrath, and infinite misery! But this is the dismal case of every soul in this congregation, that has not been born again, however moral and strict, sober and religious they may otherwise be. Oh that you would consider it, whether you be young or old. There is reason to think, that there are many in this congregation now hearing this discourse, that will actually be the subjects of this very misery to all eternity. We know not who they are, or in what seats they sit, or what thoughts they now have: it may be they are now at ease, and hear all these things without much disturbance, and are now flattering themselves that they are not the persons, promising themselves that they shall escape. If we knew that there was one person, and but one, in the whole congregation that was to be the subject of this misery, what an awful thing would it be to think of! If we knew who it was, what an awful sight would it be to see such a person! How might all the rest of the congregation lift up a lamentable and bitter cry over him! But alas! instead of one, how many is it likely will remember this discourse in hell? And it would be a wonder if some that are now present, should not be in hell in a very short time, before this year is out. And it would be no wonder if some person that now sits here in some seat of this meeting house in health, and quiet and secure, should be there before tomorrow morning. Those of you that finally continue in a natural condition, that shall keep out of hell longest, will be there in a little time! your damnation don't slumber; it will come swiftly, and in all probability very suddenly upon many of you. You have reason to wonder, that you are not already in hell. 'Tis doubtless the case of some that heretofore you have seen and known, that never deserved hell more than you, and that heretofore appeared as likely to have been now alive as you: their case is past all hope; they are crying in extreme misery and perfect despair; but here you are in the land of the living, and in the house of God, and have an opportunity to obtain salvation. What would not those poor damned, hopeless souls give for one day's such opportunity as you now enjoy!

And now you have an extraordinary opportunity, a day wherein Christ has flung the door of mercy wide open, and stands in the door calling and crying with a loud voice to poor sinners; a day wherein many are flocking to him, and pressing into the kingdom of God; many are daily coming from the east, west, north and south; many that were very lately in the same miserable condition that you are in, are in now an happy state, with their hearts filled with love to him that has loved them and washed them from their sins in his own blood, and rejoicing in hope of the glory of God. How awful is it to be left behind at such a day! To see so many others feasting, while you are pining and perishing! To see so many rejoicing and singing for joy of heart, while you have cause to mourn for sorrow of heart, and howl for vexation of spirit! How can you rest one moment in such a condition? Are not your souls as precious as the souls of the people at Suffield,[15] where they are flocking from day to day to Christ?

Are there not many here that have lived *long* in the world, that are not to this day born again, and so are aliens from the commonwealth of Israel, and have done nothing ever since they have lived, but treasure up wrath against the day of wrath? Oh sirs, your case in an especial manner is extremely dangerous; your guilt and hardness of heart is extremely great. Don't you see how generally persons of your years are passed over and left, in the present remarkable and wonderful dispensation of God's mercy? You had need to consider yourselves, and wake thoroughly out of sleep; you cannot bear the fierceness and wrath of the infinite God.

And you that are *young men*, and *young women*, will you neglect this precious season

15. **Suffield:** The next neighbor town. [Edwards's note.]

that you now enjoy, when so many others of your age are renouncing all youthful vanities, and flocking to Christ? You especially have now an extraordinary opportunity; but if you neglect it, it will soon be with you as it is with those persons that spent away all the precious days of youth in sin, and are now come to such a dreadful pass in blindness and hardness.

And you *children* that are unconverted, don't you know that you are going down to hell, to bear the dreadful wrath of that God that is now angry with you every day, and every night? Will you be content to be the children of the devil, when so many other children in the land are converted, and are become the holy and happy children of the King of kings?

And let everyone that is yet out of Christ, and hanging over the pit of hell, whether they be old men and women, or middle aged, or young people, or little children, now hearken to the loud calls of God's Word and providence. This acceptable year of the Lord, that is a day of such great favor to some, will doubtless be a day of as remarkable vengeance to others. Men's hearts harden, and their guilt increases apace at such a day as this, if they neglect their souls: and never was there so great danger of such persons being given up to hardness of heart, and blindness of mind. God seems now to be hastily gathering in his elect in all parts of the land; and probably the bigger part of adult persons that ever shall be saved, will be brought in now in a little time, and that it will be as it was on that great outpouring of the Spirit upon the Jews in the apostles' days, the election will obtain, and the rest will be blinded. If this should be the case with you, you will eternally curse this day, and will curse the day that ever you was born, to see such a season of the pouring out of God's Spirit; and will wish that you had died and gone to hell before you had seen it. Now undoubtedly it is, as it was in the days of John the Baptist, the ax is in an extraordinary manner laid at the root of the trees, that every tree that brings not forth good fruit, may be hewn down, and cast into the fire.

Therefore let everyone that is out of Christ, now awake and fly from the wrath to come. The wrath of almighty God is now undoubtedly hanging over great part of this congregation: let everyone fly out of Sodom. Haste and escape for your lives, look not behind you, escape to the mountain, lest you be consumed [Genesis 19:17].

[1741, 2003]

Edwards's *Images or Shadows of Divine Things*. Throughout his adult life, Edwards jotted down entries in which he developed his ideas about the connections or correspondence between natural phenomena and spiritual laws. Edwards stitched together 212 numbered entries to form a handmade book, which he variously entitled *The Images of Divine Things*; *The Shadows of Divine Things*; *The Book of Nature and Common Providence*; and *The Language and Lessons of Nature*. As those titles suggest, his ultimate purpose was to establish the unity between the natural world and the supernatural realm of which it was the image or shadow. Emphasizing the remarkable analogies among all of God's works in the created world, Edwards asks: "Why is it not rational to suppose that the corporeal and visible world should be designedly made and constituted in analogy to the more spiritual, noble, and real world?" (see below, entry 59). Edwards never completed his ambitious project, and his manuscript was not published until 1948. The text of the following selections is taken from the Yale University Press *Works of Jonathan Edwards*, Vol. 11, edited by Wallace E. Anderson, Mason I. Lowance, and David Watters (1993).

From Images or Shadows of Divine Things

3. Roses grow upon briars, which is to signify that all temporal sweets are mixt with bitter. But what seems more especially to be meant by it is that pure happiness, the crown of glory, is to be come at in no other way than by bearing Christ's cross, by a life of mortification, self-denial, and labour, and bearing all things for Christ. The rose, that is chief of all flowers, is the last thing that comes out. The briary, prickly bush grows before that; the end and crown of all is the beautifull and fragrant rose.

4. The heavens' being filled with glorious, luminous bodies is to signify the glory and happiness of the heavenly inhabitants, and amongst these the sun signifies Christ and the moon the church.

8. Again it is apparent and allowed that there is a great and remarkeable analogy in God's works. There is a wonderfull resemblance in the effects which God produces, and consentaneity[1] in His manner of working in one thing and another throughout all nature. It is very observable in the visible world; therefore it is allowed that God does purposely make and order one thing to be in agreeableness and harmony with another. And if so, why should not we suppose that He makes the inferiour in imitation of the superiour, the material of the spiritual, on purpose to have a resemblance and shadow of them? We see that even in the material world, God makes one part of it strangely to agree with another, and why is it not reasonable to suppose He makes the whole as a shadow of the spiritual world? (Vid.[2] Image 59.)

59. (Add this to Image 8.) If there be such an admirable analogy observed by the creatour in His works through the whole system of the natural world, so that one thing seems to be made in imitation of another, and especially the less perfect to be made in imitation of the more perfect, so that the less perfect is as it were a figure or image of the more perfect, so beasts are made in imitation of men, plants are [a] kind of types of animals, minerals are in many things in imitation of plants. Why is it not rational to suppose that the corporeal and visible world should be designedly made and constituted in analogy to the more spiritual, noble, and real world? It is certainly agreeable to what is apparently the method of God's working.

60. That of so vast and innumerable a multitude of blossoms that appear on a tree, so few come to ripe fruit, and that so few of so vast a multitude of seeds as are yearly pro-

1. **consentaneity:** The quality of being accordant, agreeable, or suited.
2. **Vid.:** Abbreviation of *vide* (Latin), meaning see or consult. In this case, Image 59, which follows.

duced, so few come to be a plant, and that there is so great a waste of the seed of both plants and animals, but one in a great multitude ever bringing forth anything, seem to be lively types how few are saved out of the mass of mankind, and particuarly how few are sincere, of professing Christians, that never wither away but endure to the end, and how of the many that are called few are chosen.

64. Hills and mountains are types of heaven, and often made use of as such in Scripture. These are difficultly ascended. To ascend them, one must go against the natural tendency of the flesh; this must be contradicted in all the ascent, in every step of it, and the ascent is attended with labour, sweat and hardship. There are commonly many hideous rocks in the way. It is a great deal easier descending into valleys. This is a representation of the difficulty, labour, and self-denial of the way to heaven, and how agreeable it is, to the inclination of the flesh, to descend into hell. At the bottom of valleys, especially deep valleys, there is water, with a lake or other waters, but water, as has been shown elsewhere in notes on Scripture, commonly signifies misery, especially that which is occasioned by the wrath of God. So in hell is a lake or gulf of misery and wrath.

79. The whole material universe is preserved by gravity or attraction, or the mutual tendency of all bodies to each other. One part of the universe is hereby made beneficial to another; the beauty, harmony, and order, regular progress, life, and motion, and in short all the well-being of the whole frame depends on it. This is a type of love or charity in the spiritual world.

123. The glory of the face of the earth is the grass and green leaves and flowers. These fade away, they last but a little while and then are gone. After the spring and summer, a winter comes that wholly defaces and destroys all, and that which is most taking and pleasant, and as it were the crown of its glory, viz.,[3] the flower of the trees and the field, fades soonest. The glory of the heavens consists in its brightness, its shining lights which continue the same through winter and summer, age after age. This represents the great difference between earthly glory, riches, and pleasures, which fades as the leaves and as the grass and flower of the field, and the glory and happiness of heaven, which fadeth not away, which is agreeable to many representations in the Scripture.

146. The late invention of telescopes, whereby heavenly objects are brought so much nearer and made so much plainer to sight and such wonderfull discoveries have been made in the heavens, is a type and forerunner of the great increase in the knowledge of heavenly things that shall be in the approaching glorious times of the Christian church.

147. The changing of the course of trade and the supplying of the world with its treasures from America is a type and forerunner of what is approaching in spiritual things, when the world shall be supplied with spiritual treasures from America.

[?, 1993]

3. **viz.:** In other words (abbreviation of the Latin *videlicet*).

Edwards through a Modern Lens

JONATHAN EDWARDS exerted a powerful influence on his contemporaries, directly through his preaching and indirectly through his published sermons and other writings, which were widely read by ministers and laypersons in the colonies and Great Britain. After his death in 1758, Edwards retained a central place in American culture, especially among philosophers and theologians, but also among writers. Indeed, he has influenced writers as diverse as the evangelical Harriet Beecher Stowe, who responds to what she describes as the "refined poetry of torture" of Edwards's sermons in her historical novel *The Minister's Wooing* (1859), and the far-more-questioning and skeptical poet Emily Dickinson. But few American writers have confronted Edwards as directly and persistently as the poet Robert Lowell (1917–1977). A descendant on his mother's side of

Jonathan Edwards

The only portrait of Edwards painted during his lifetime was the likeness done in 1720 by Joseph Badger, reprinted on page 276. In it, the unsmiling Edwards appears aloof and severe, an image that many of his later admirers sought to adjust, as illustrated by this 1877 lithograph by John Ferguson Weir. Weir softened Edwards's features and expression, further altering the Badger portrait by positioning Edwards at his desk, a book in one hand and a pen in the other, signs of his status as one of the major intellects and writers of colonial America.

Edward Winslow, who came to America on the *Mayflower* in 1620, Lowell was also the great-grandnephew of James Russell Lowell, a poet and the first editor of the *Atlantic Monthly*. Lowell was consequently deeply rooted in New England history and literature, which he read widely and on which many of his poems are based. Having spent much of his childhood in East Windsor, Connecticut, the birthplace of Jonathan Edwards, Lowell felt a special interest in the Puritan minister's life and work. Of his several poems on the subject, the most famous is "Mr. Edwards and the Spider." In it, Lowell reveals his familiarity with three of Edwards's works: "Of Insects," an early scientific essay in which he explains the "mystery" of how spiders seemed to fly, and two sermons, "Sinners in the Hands of an Angry God" and "The Future Punishment of the Wicked, Unavoidable and Intolerable." The text is taken from Lowell's first collection of poetry, *Lord Weary's Castle* (1946).

Robert Lowell

[1917–1977]

Mr. Edwards and the Spider

I saw the spiders marching through the air,
Swimming from tree to tree that mildewed day
In latter August when the hay
Came creaking to the barn. But where
The wind is westerly,
Where gnarled November makes the spiders fly
Into the apparitions of the sky,
They purpose nothing but their ease and die
Urgently beating east to sunrise and the sea;[1]

1. **I saw . . . the sea:** In the opening stanza, Lowell draws directly on Edwards's observations in "Of Insects," in which he describes spiders "marching through the air, from tree to tree," and one spider in particular "swimming in the air" at the end of a long web glistening with dew. Edwards adds that spiders "never fly except when the wind is westerly, and I never saw them fly but when they were hastening to the sea," in fair weather from late August to the middle of October, "flying for nothing but their ease and comfort."

What are we in the hands of the great God?[2]
It was in vain you set up thorn and briar
In battle array against the fire
And treason crackling in your blood;
For the wild thorns grow tame
And will do nothing to oppose the flame;
Your lacerations tell the losing game
You play against a sickness past your cure.
How will the hands be strong? How will the heart endure?[3]

A very little thing, a little worm,
Or hourglass-blazoned spider,[4] it is said,
Can kill a tiger. Will the dead
Hold up his mirror and affirm
To the four winds the smell
And flash of his authority? It's well
If God who holds you to the pit of hell,
Much as one holds a spider, will destroy,
Baffle and dissipate your soul. As a small boy

On Windsor Marsh,[5] I saw the spider die
When thrown into the bowels of fierce fire:
There's no long struggle, no desire
To get up on its feet and fly –
It stretches out its feet
And dies. This is the sinner's last retreat;
Yes, and no strength exerted on the heat
Then sinews the abolished will, when sick
And full of burning, it will whistle on a brick.

---

2. **What are we . . . the great God?:** In his 1741 sermon "The Future Punishment of the Wicked, Unavoidable, and Intolerable" Edwards asks: "What art thou in the hands of the great God, who made heaven and earth by speaking a word? . . . and, when fixed time shall come, will shake all to pieces?"
3. **How will . . . endure?:** Edwards delivered "The Future Punishment of the Wicked, Unavoidable, and Intolerable" on the biblical text Ezekiel 22:14: "Can thine heart endure, or can thine hands be strong, in the days that I shall deal with thee?"
4. **hourglass-blazoned spider:** A black widow is a highly poisonous spider with red markings in the shape of an hourglass on a black body.
5. **Windsor Marsh:** On the bank of the Connecticut River near East Windsor, Connecticut, where Edwards was born.

But who can plumb the sinking of that soul?
Josiah Hawley,[6] picture yourself cast
Into a brick-kiln where the blast
Fans your quick vitals to a coal –
If measured by a glass,
How long would it seem burning! Let there pass
A minute, ten, ten trillion; but the blaze
Is infinite, eternal: this is death,
To die and know it. This is the Black Widow, death.

[1946]

6. **Josiah Hawley:** Edwards's uncle Josiah Hawley (1682–1735), a leading businessman in the Connecticut River valley, committed suicide by cutting his throat on a Sunday morning, evidently in despair over the state of his soul during an intense religious revival led by Edwards during 1734–35. In a letter to Benjamin Colman, the pastor of Brattle Street Church in Boston, Edwards describes Hawley's death as part of Satan's desperate counterattack against the revival, "this Extraordinary breaking forth of the work of God."

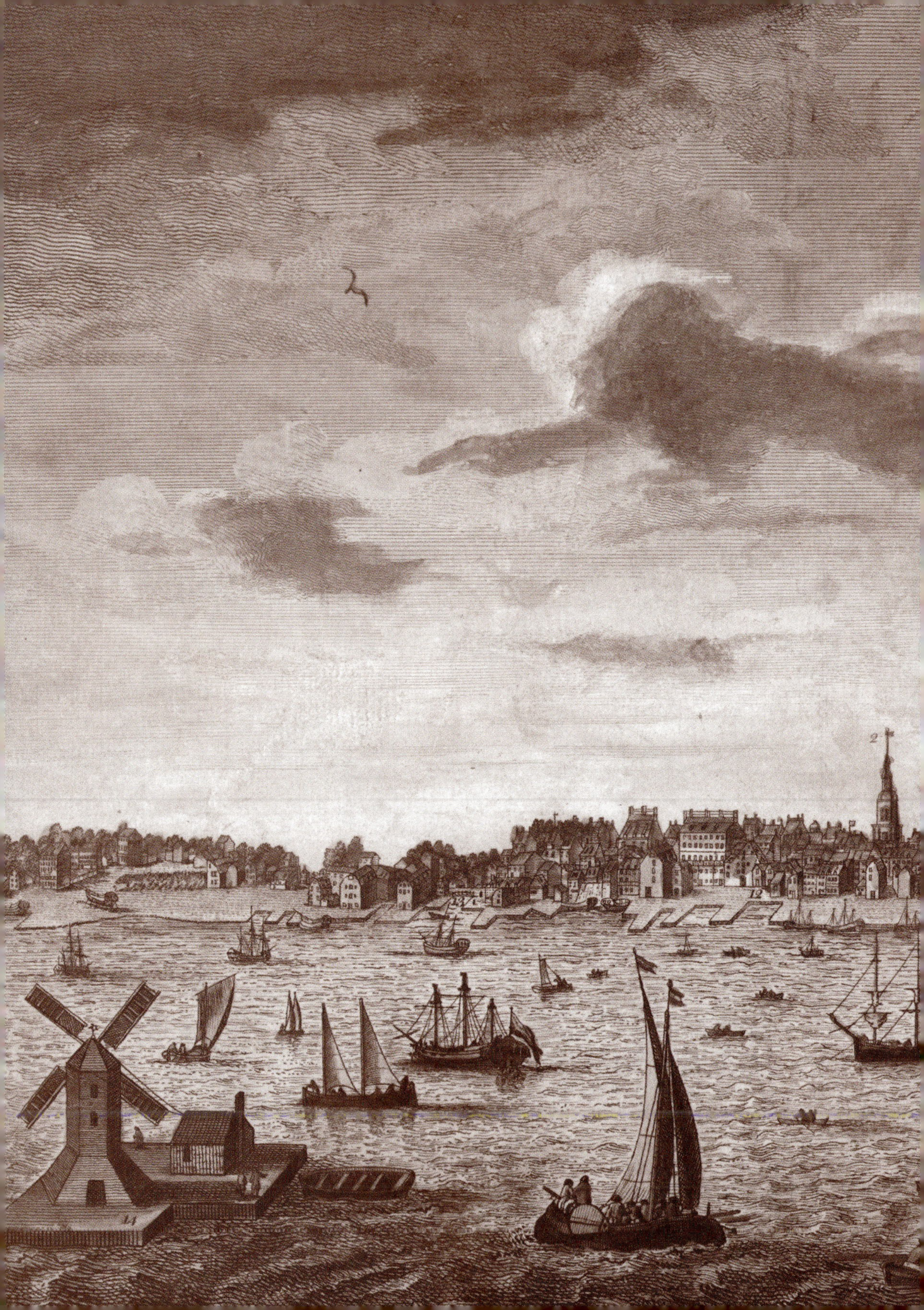

American Literature

1750–1830

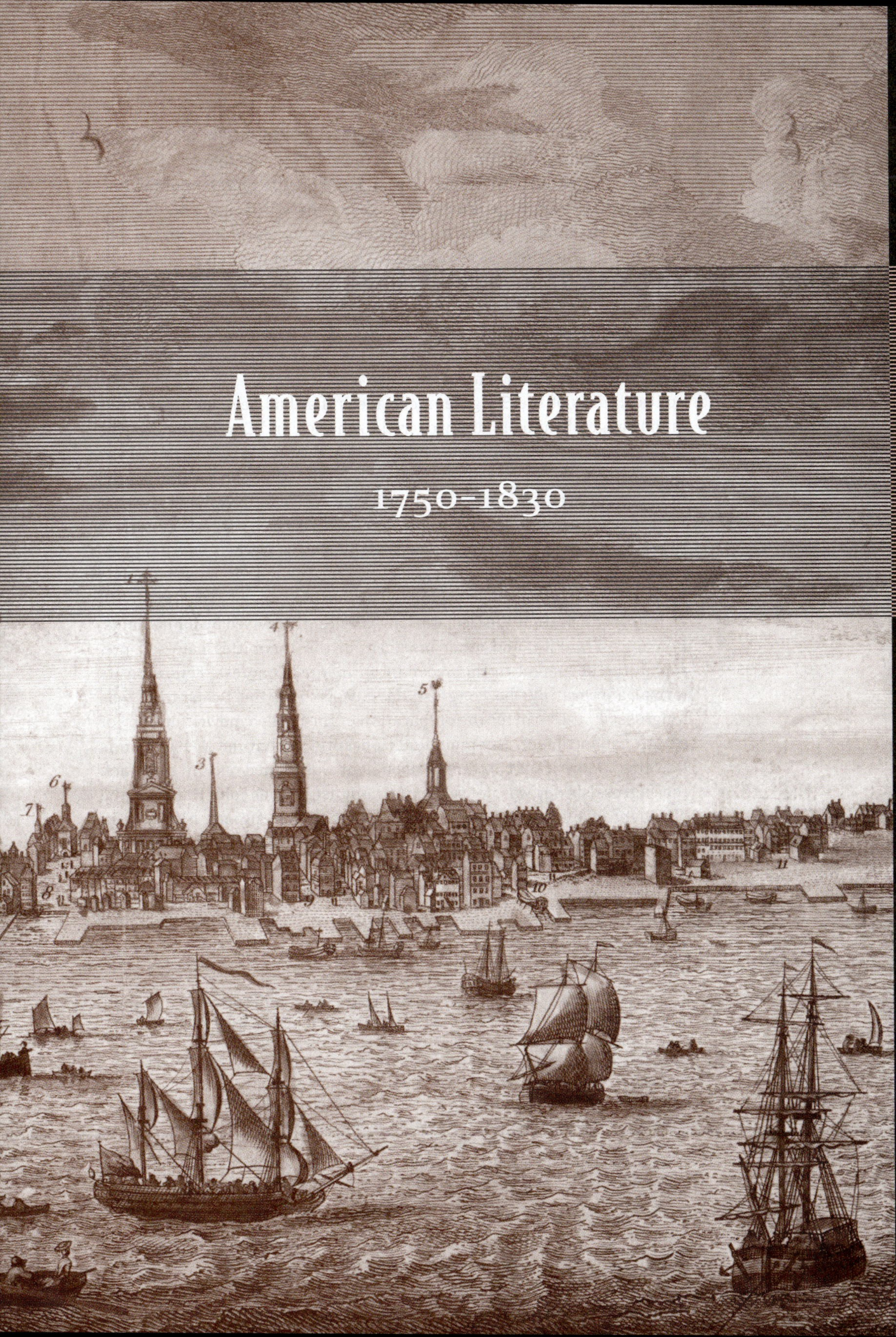

PERHAPS THE MOST FAMILIAR and celebrated event of the period 1750-1830 is the signing of the Declaration of Independence. As symbolically charged as that occasion was, the story of the Declaration also reveals the crucial roles that writing, reading, and printing played in the colonies and later in the new nation. Early in 1776, the Second Continental Congress appointed a committee of five delegates to draft a declaration. The committee, in turn, assigned the task to its youngest member, Thomas Jefferson, already renowned for his powerful writing style. Jefferson later stated that he "used neither book nor pamphlet" as he wrote the Declaration, which he intended "to be an expression of the American mind." But the document was also a concentrated expression of the political ideas of the Enlightenment, ideas that had been developed by a broad range of thinkers and writers in America and Europe. Indeed, the justification for declaring independence was firmly based on some of the fundamental tenets of Enlightenment thought: that the natural world, human nature, and social institutions are governed by universal laws; that all men are created equal and are endowed with certain natural rights; and that governments exist only by the consent of the governed, who are justified in rebelling if their natural rights are violated, as most colonists believed their rights had been violated by Parliament and King George III.

Jefferson's draft of the Declaration was slightly revised by John Adams, Benjamin Franklin, and other members of the committee before it presented the document to the Second Continental Congress. Following its formal approval by the congress on July 4, 1776, the Declaration was "engrossed," the term for the preparation of the final, handwritten copy of an official document. A common misconception about the Declaration is that the handwritten parchment document was signed on July 4. In fact, the engrossed copy was not ready until August 2, when John Hancock, the president of the congress, led the way by famously signing his name in very large handwriting. Fifty-six representatives eventually signed the document, though not all of them were present at the ceremony on August 2,

◀ (OVERLEAF)

City of Philadelphia

This view of Philadelphia around 1750 illustrates the growth and vitality of cities along the seaboard of the English colonies in North America, from Portsmouth, New Hampshire, and Boston in the north as far south as Savannah, Georgia. By then, few cities in the British Empire surpassed those in America, where later in the century a proud citizen boldly predicted, "Europe shall mourn her ancient fame declined / And Philadelphia be the Athens of mankind." With its depiction of the bustling port and the church spires dominating the skyline, this view of Philadelphia captured the distinctive combination of commerce and religion in colonial cities. They were also vital cultural centers, as well as the centers of the political ferment that led to the Declaration of Independence.

and some of them signed it much later. When the Declaration was originally approved on July 4, however, a copy was simply delivered to a Philadelphia printer, John Dunlap. He immediately prepared a "broadside," a single printed sheet that was sent to the British government and distributed throughout the thirteen colonies. During the following week, the Declaration was read to enthusiastic crowds in Philadelphia and Boston, as well as to General George Washington's troops in New York. But most colonists read the text, which was printed in twenty-four newspapers, beginning on July 6 with the *Pennsylvania Evening Post.* The Declaration was also printed in German, in the Philadelphia *Pennsylvanischer Staatsbote.* The printed version – published and widely distributed well before the official handwritten document was signed – was the means by which

COMPARATIVE TIMELINE, 1750–1830

Dates	American Literature	History and Politics	Developments in Culture, Science, and Technology
1750–1759	1751 Jonathan Edwards's "Farewell Sermon Preached at the First Precinct in Northampton" is published	1750 Population of thirteen colonies: 1,170,800 1756–63 French and Indian Wars (Seven Years' War)	1750 English astronomer Thomas Wright first proposes existence of Milky Way galaxy  1752 Franklin's famous kite experiment proves lightning is electricity 1754 New York Society Library offers books on loan for annual membership fee 1755 Samuel Johnson publishes first English dictionary 1755 "Yankee Doodle" is a popular song 1759 British Museum opens in London
1760–1769	1765 John Dickinson, *Declaration of Rights and Grievances*	1760 Population of thirteen colonies: 1,593,600 1765 Stamp Act imposes special tax on all publications and legal documents in American colonies	1763 All thirteen colonies have printing presses

both the colonists and the British government learned that the American Revolution was at hand.

Print Culture and the Road to Revolution

Colonial printers and newspapers did not simply spread the news of separation from Great Britain. They were also deeply involved in the political events leading up to the Declaration of Independence. Changes in print culture between 1750 and 1776 were crucial to the development of both colonial unity and a growing sense of national identity that culminated in the American Revolution. In the middle of the eighteenth century, there was little unity or unanimity among the colonies, each of which had developed its own assemblies and forms of government. When in 1754 Franklin

Dates	American Literature	History and Politics	Developments in Culture, Science, and Technology
1760–1769 (cont.)	 1768 Occom, *A Short Narrative of My Life* 1768 John Dickinson, "The Liberty Song"		
1770–1779	1771 Franklin begins writing his *Autobiography* 1773 Wheatley, *Poems on Various Subjects, Religious and Moral* 1774 *Journal of John Woolman* 1774 *Some Account . . . of the Life of Elizabeth Ashbridge* 1776 Paine, *Common Sense*	1770 Population of thirteen colonies: 2,148,100  1775 Battles of Lexington, Concord, and Bunker Hill 1776 Declaration of Independence is ratified by Second Continental Congress 1776–83 American Revolutionary War	1779 *United States Magazine* is founded in Philadelphia

offered his "plan of union" (the Albany Plan), under which all of the colonies would have been united for defense against Indian attacks, it was rejected by both the British government and the individual colonies. They were further divided by differing economies and patterns of immigration. Although English settlers lived throughout the colonies, even that group was divided by religious differences among the Congregationalists of Puritan descent in New England, Anglicans (Church of England) and Quakers, primarily in the middle colonies or the South, and Catholics in Maryland. At the same time, there were large numbers of settlers from other countries: Scotch-Irish Presbyterians, who spoke English but were hostile to English settlers and especially to the British government that had forced them out of northern Ireland; people of Dutch descent, primarily in or near New York City; and immigrants from Germany, the majority

Dates	American Literature	History and Politics	Developments in Culture, Science, and Technology
1780–1789	1782 Crèvecoeur, *Letters from an American Farmer*  1787 Royall Tyler, *The Contrast* 1787 Barlow, *The Vision of Columbus* 1788 *The Federalist Papers*, Hamilton, Jay, and Madison's writings in favor of ratifying the Constitution, are published 1789 Brown, *The Power of Sympathy* 1789 Equiano, *The Interesting Narrative of the Life of Olaudah Equiano, or Gustavus Vassa* 	1780 U.S. population: 2,780,400 1784 Methodist Church organized in United States 1788 U.S. Constitution ratified 1789 Washington elected as first president of United States 1789–99 French Revolution	1783 *Philadelphia Evening Post* becomes America's first daily newspaper 1783 Webster publishes first volume of *Grammatical Institute of the English Language*, the *Speller* 1786 *Columbian Magazine* is founded 1786 Young Ladies' Academy of Philadelphia is established as first institution to offer formal education for women in America 1787 *American Magazine* is founded 1788 Wedgwood creates his famous medallion showing the figure of a supplicant slave, which is eventually adopted as symbol of abolitionist movement

of them in Pennsylvania. Most of the Indians had been driven out of the thirteen colonies, but there were still remnants of the Iroquois Confederacy in western New York and Pennsylvania, as well as significant numbers of Cherokee, Creek, Choctaw, and Chickasaw on the frontiers of Georgia and North Carolina. There were also more than half a million people from Africa in the colonies, 90 percent of them slaves in the South.

Such ethnic, racial, religious, and linguistic diversity led to deep divisions within and among the colonies, which were connected by rudimentary postal services and transportation systems. Such conditions also posed formidable obstacles to the development of print culture in colonial America. There was a thriving manuscript culture, especially but not exclusively among women writers, who circulated poems and stories in letters and kept handwritten commonplace books. But the publishing trade

Dates	American Literature	History and Politics	Developments in Culture, Science, and Technology
1790–1799		1790 U.S. population: 3,929,214; first official U.S. Census	1790 Beginning of "Second Great Awakening," evangelical religious revival in America
	1791 Rowson, *Charlotte Temple*		
	1792 Murray begins "The Gleaner" in the *Massachusetts Magazine*	1792 Washington reelected president	1792 Wollstonecraft's *Vindication of the Rights of Woman* stirs debate on women's education 
			1792 *Lady's Magazine and Repository of Useful Knowledge*, America's first literary journal for women, is published
			1793 Invention of cotton gin
	1794 Dwight, *Greenfield Hill* 1794 Radcliffe, *The Mysteries of Udolpho*		1794 Philadelphia's American Philosophical Society provides space for paintings and natural history specimens for public display
		1796 Adams elected president 	1796 Washington's famous Farewell Address is printed in *Claypoole's American Daily Advertiser*
	1797 Foster, *The Coquette*		
	1798 Brown, *Wieland*		1798 Coleridge and Wordsworth publish *Lyrical Ballads* in Britain
	1799 Brown, *Edgar Huntly*		

was still in its infancy in the colonies. The technology of printing had not developed significantly since the perfection of moveable type in the middle of the fifteenth century, and presses were little different from the first one introduced into Massachusetts Bay Colony in 1639. Colonial print shops were small operations, generally consisting of a single room with a hand-cranked press on which printers and their apprentices could produce only about 800 to 1,000 finished sheets in a day. While most of the colonies had weekly newspapers, they were designed to serve a particular region. Of the twenty or so newspapers in the colonies in 1750, four were in Boston; three were in New York City; and three were in Philadelphia, one of which was published in German. The magazine developed only gradually in the eighteenth century, and few American magazines were successful until after the Revolutionary War. While many printers also had book

Dates	American Literature	History and Politics	Developments in Culture, Science, and Technology
1800–1809	1800 Weems, *The Life and Memorable Actions of George Washington* 1801 Tenney, *Female Quixotism*	1800 U.S. population: 5,308,483 1800 Jefferson elected president 1801 Haitian slaves, led by L'Ouverture, seize power from the French and establish first black republic 1803 Louisiana Purchase 1804 Jefferson reelected president  1807 Slave trade is abolished in Great Britain 1808 Madison elected president	1800 U.S. Library of Congress founded 1801 *Port Folio*, a popular magazine of the era, is founded 1802 World's first successful steamship, the *Charlotte Dundas*, built in England 1805 Lewis and Clark expedition reaches Pacific Ocean  1808 Scott, *Marmion*
1810–1819		1810 U.S. population: 7,239,881 1812 Madison reelected president 1812–15 War of 1812	1810 Scott, *The Lady of the Lake* 1811 First steam-powered ferry begins operation between New York City and Hoboken, New Jersey 1812–15 Byron, *Childe Harold*

shops and newspapers advertised a variety of titles, books were expensive and were regarded as a luxury by most colonists. Moreover, only those living in cities along the coast had ready access to significant numbers of books, most of which were imported from England.

Nonetheless, by 1750 a more vital and widespread print culture began to emerge in the colonies. Few figures were as central to that process as Benjamin Franklin, who in writing his own epitaph called himself simply "B. Franklin Printer." In fact, as some of his biographers have suggested, Franklin's printing business was the first media conglomerate. After establishing his business in Philadelphia, Franklin acquired the *Pennsylvania Gazette*, which he transformed into one of the most successful newspapers in the colonies. In addition to his own popular annual, *Poor Richard's Almanack*, his publishing house produced a steady stream of

Dates	American Literature	History and Politics	Developments in Culture, Science, and Technology
1810–1819 (cont.)	**1815** Freneau, *A Collection of Poems* **1819–20** Irving, *The Sketch Book of Geoffrey Crayon, Gent.*	**1816** Monroe elected president **1819** United States acquires Florida from Spain	**1813** Stereotype printing revolutionizes production of multiple copies of a text **1814** Scott, *Waverly* **1815** *North American Review* founded in Boston **1816** *Boston Recorder*, first religious newspaper, founded
1820–1830	**1821** Cooper, *The Spy* **1821** Bryant, *Poems*  **1822** Sedgwick, *A New-England Tale*	**1820** U.S. population: 9,638,453 **1820** Monroe reelected president **1820** The Missouri Compromise excludes slavery from Louisiana Purchase territory to north and west of Missouri	**1821** *Saturday Evening Post* begins publication in United States

pamphlets, broadsides, and books, including Bibles. Most of the books that Franklin printed were British, including his edition of Samuel Richardson's *Pamela* (1744), the first novel published in colonial America. But novels were widely viewed with suspicion in the colonies, where the few who wrote books generally devoted themselves to religious themes and experiences. Among the most notable examples of such works were Phillis Wheatley's *Poems on Various Subjects, Religious and Moral* (1773), the first book of poetry published by an African American; Quaker spiritual autobiographies like *Some Account of the Fore Part of the Life of Elizabeth Ashbridge*, probably written in the 1750s and published in England in 1774; and *The Journal of John Woolman*, published the same year in Philadelphia. In 1771, Franklin himself began to write a very different kind of personal narrative, his *Autobiography*. But he did not return to work on the

Dates	American Literature	History and Politics	Developments in Culture, Science and Technology
1820–1830 (cont.)	1823 Cooper, *The Pioneers*	1824 John Quincy Adams elected president	1824 Debut of Beethoven's Symphony no. 9 1825 Erie Canal opens, providing passage from Albany, New York, to Lake Erie
	 1826 Cooper, *Last of the Mohicans* 1827 Sedgwick, *Hope Leslie*	1828 Jackson elected president	1825–1880s Cole and other Hudson River school artists depict romanticized American landscapes 1826 Morey patents internal combustion engine 1827 *Freedom's Journal*, first African American periodical, is founded 1828 Webster publishes *An American Dictionary of the English Language* 1828 *Cherokee Phoenix*, first Native American newspaper, is founded
	1830 Longstreet begins to write sketches of *Georgia Scenes*		

The Declaration of Independence Read to a Crowd

Printed copies of the Declaration were distributed throughout the colonies, where they were published in newspapers and read aloud in public spaces. This illustration from an early history of England shows a man on horseback reading the Declaration to a cheering crowd. The notice posted on the wall reads "America Independant, 1776."

book until 1784, explaining that the "Affairs of the Revolution occasion'd the Interruption."

Indeed, from the early 1760s through the Revolutionary War, editors, printers, and most writers were increasingly preoccupied by political issues, especially the growing conflicts between the colonies and the government of Great Britain. Under the terms of the treaty that ended the French and Indian War, also known as the Seven Years' War (1756-63), France ceded to Great Britain its claim to all territories in Canada and east of the Mississippi River. Seeking ways to pay its large postwar debt, as well as to support its army in North America, the British Parliament in 1764 passed the American Revenue Act, the first of a series of bills designed to raise money in the colonies. The acts generated heated opposition among colonists, who denounced them as "taxation without representation." Resistance grew even stronger following the passage in 1765 of the Stamp Act, which imposed a special tax on broadsides, pamphlets, books, newspapers, and legal documents of all types. The passage of the act was a galvanizing event for American printers, who along with other influential

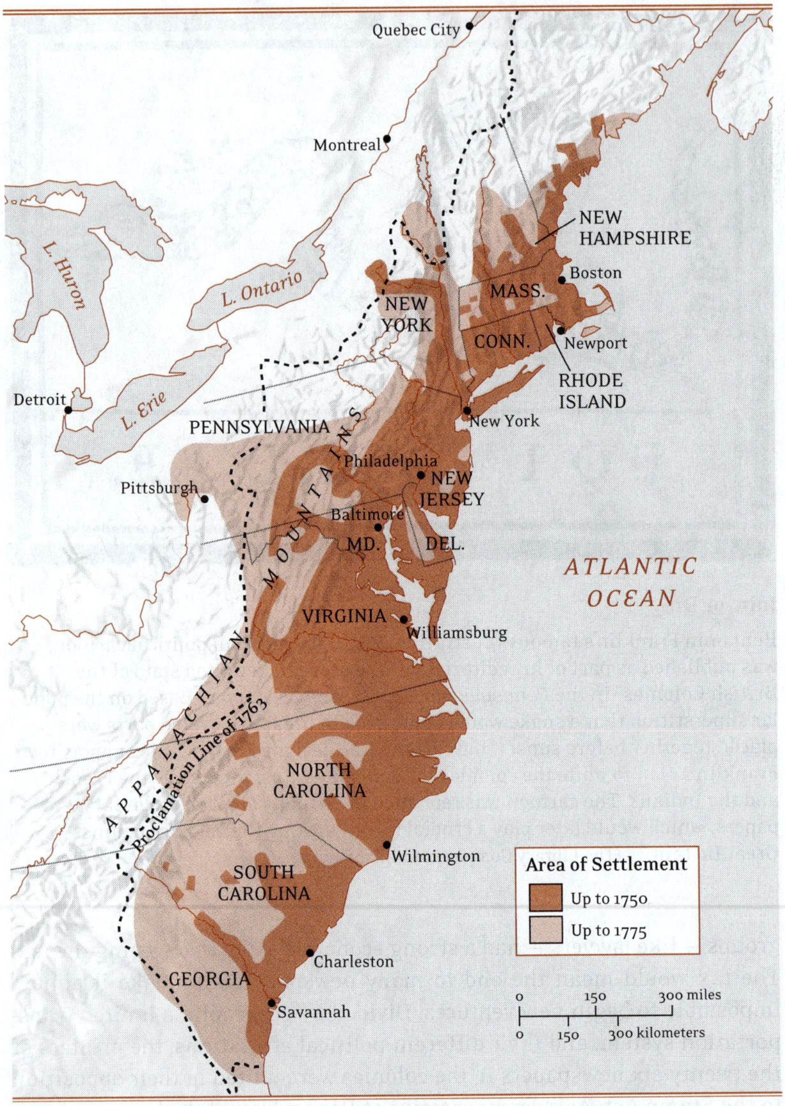

The Thirteen Colonies in 1775

This map of the colonies on the eve of independence includes the "proclamation line" of 1763, a royal decree prohibiting settlement in lands west of the Appalachian Mountains, which were reserved as the hunting grounds for the Indians. By 1775, American settlers had already expanded into the prohibited area. As a result of the treaty that ended the Revolutionary War in 1783, the Louisiana Purchase of 1803, and a treaty with Spain in 1819, within fifty years the boundaries of the United States extended from Canada to the tip of Florida and from the Atlantic coast to the Rocky Mountains.

Join, or Die

Benjamin Franklin's famous illustration, the first American political cartoon, was published as part of his editorial on "the present disunited state of the British Colonies" in the *Pennsylvania Gazette* on May 9, 1754. Based on the popular superstition that a snake would come back to life if its severed parts were placed together before sunset, the cartoon was designed to generate support for Franklin's plan to unite the colonies for defense against attacks by the French and the Indians. The cartoon was reprinted in virtually all of the colonial newspapers, which would later play a crucial role in uniting the colonies against Great Britain. (The Library Company of Philadelphia.)

groups – like lawyers – had a strong economic stake in opposing the tax. The tax would mean the end to many newspapers and make it almost impossible to begin new ventures. Divided by geography, a limited transportation system, and their different political affiliations, the printers of the twenty-six newspapers in the colonies were united in their opposition to the Stamp Act. As a representative of Pennsylvania, the former printer Benjamin Franklin testified against the act before Parliament. Its repeal in 1766 demonstrated the growing power of the colonial press.

During the turbulent decade that followed, the press assumed an increasingly central role in the political life of the colonies. Many intellectuals absorbed Enlightenment political ideas directly through books imported from Europe, notably works by the English philosopher John Locke, whose *Treatises of Civil Government* strongly shaped the ideas to which Jefferson finally gave such eloquent expression in the Declaration of Independence. Long before that document was written, however,

The TIMES are Dreadful, Diſmal Doleful Dolorous, and DOLLAR-LESS.

An Emblem of the Effects of the STAMP

O! the fatal Stamp

Thurſday, October 31, 1765. NUMB. 1195.

THE

PENNSYLVANIA JOURNAL;

AND

WEEKLY ADVERTISER.

EXPIRING: In Hopes of a Reſurrection to LIFE again.

I AM ſorry to be obliged to acquaint my Readers, that as The STAMP-ACT, is fear'd to be obligatory upon us after the *Firſt of November* enſuing, (the *fatal To morrow*) the Publiſher of this Paper unable to bear the Burthen, has thought it expedient TO STOP awhile, in order to deliberate, whether any Methods can be found to elude the Chains forged for us, and eſcape the inſupportable Slavery, which it is hoped, from the laſt Repreſentations now made againſt that Act, may be effected. Mean while, I muſt earneſtly Requeſt every Individual of my Subſcribers many of whom have been long behind Hand, that they would immediately Diſcharge their reſpective Arrears that I may be able, not only to ſupport myſelf during the Interval, but be better prepared to proceed again with this Paper, whenever an opening for that Purpoſe appears, which I hope will be ſoon.

WILLIAM BRADFORD

Colonial Response to the Stamp Act

The Stamp Act generated strong opposition, especially in colonial newspapers, as illustrated by this response in William Bradford's "expiring" *Pennsylvania Gazette* on October 31, 1765. The skull and crossbones served as "An Emblem of the Effects of the Stamp," both for individual newspapers and "Liberty of the Press."

Locke's ideas were widely disseminated in almanacs, newspapers, and pamphlets. The importance colonial Americans placed on rudimentary education and the ability to read created a growing audience for such works, which made information about social and political developments available even to common people living on isolated farms or in villages distant from urban centers. Almanacs, which one printer claimed were "read by Multitudes who read nothing else," were especially influential. So were the growing number of newspapers, which helped generate unity among the colonies through news sharing and copying, unquestioned parts of periodical publication in the era before copyright laws.

The text that most powerfully strengthened that unity, as well as the resolve of the colonies to declare their independence from Great Britain, was also written by a newspaper editor, Thomas Paine, whose pamphlet *Common Sense* appeared in January 1776. At a time when few copies of individual books were printed – usually no more than two thousand – Paine's pamphlet sold half a million copies, becoming the first bestseller written in colonial America. A few months before it appeared, Benjamin Franklin said that he had never heard an expression in support of independence "from any person, drunk or sober." Following the publication of *Common Sense*, the logic of separation from Great Britain seemed irresistibly clear to most colonists, including the delegates to the Second Continental Congress, who voted in favor of independence six months later, on July 2. If the Declaration of

> *"The Revolution was in the Minds of the People."*

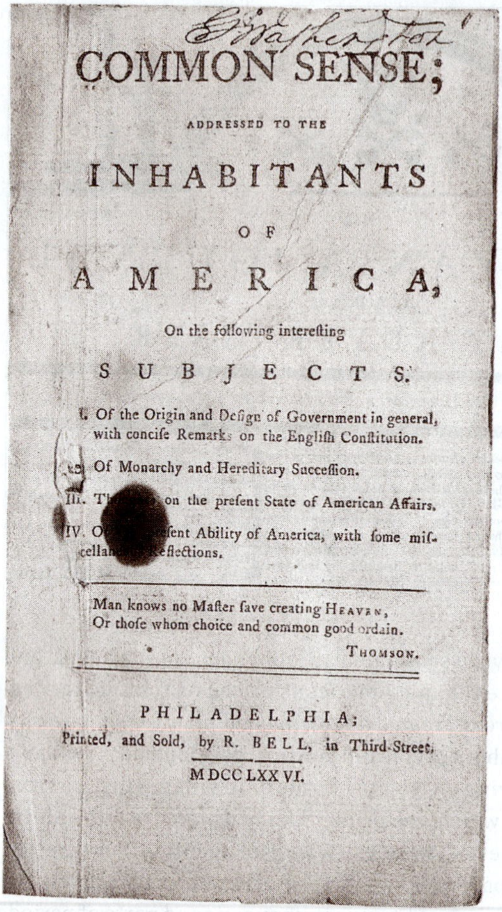
G° Washington

COMMON SENSE;

ADDRESSED TO THE

INHABITANTS

OF

AMERICA,

On the following interefting

SUBJECTS.

I. Of the Origin and Defign of Government in general, with concife Remarks on the Englifh Conftitution.

II. Of Monarchy and Hereditary Succeffion.

III. Th[...] on the prefent State of American Affairs.

IV. O[...]fent Ability of America, with fome mifcella[...]eflections.

Man knows no Mafter fave creating Heaven,
Or thofe whom choice and common good ordain.

Thomson.

PHILADELPHIA;
Printed, and Sold, by R. BELL, in Third-Street.
MDCCLXXVI.

Washington's Inscribed Copy of *Common Sense*

Even after he accepted command of the Continental army in June 1775, George Washington firmly declared that he would not prosecute the war in order to gain independence. Two weeks after Thomas Paine's incendiary pamphlet was published in January 1776, however, Washington observed that "the sound doctrine and unanswerable reasoning contained in the pamphlet 'Common Sense' will not leave numbers at a loss to decide upon the propriety of separation" from Great Britain.

Independence, approved two days afterward, laid the foundation for the United States, the site had first been cleared and prepared by a decade of agitation in colonial newspapers, as well as in anti-British broadsides and political tracts culminating in *Common Sense.* As John Adams later recalled in a letter to Thomas Jefferson, "the Revolution was in the Minds of the People" before the first shots were fired.

Society and Culture in the New Nation

The Declaration of Independence and the long war that ensued established an independent country. But the new nation was forged and the foundations of a national culture were laid during the period of consolidation and rapid expansion in the decades following the Revolution. In 1775, there were roughly 2.5 million inhabitants of the thirteen colonies, who were squeezed into a relatively narrow corridor of land between the Atlantic Ocean and the Appalachian Mountains. As part of the peace treaty that formally ended the Revolutionary War in 1783, Britain granted to the United States all of the land east of the Mississippi River between Canada and the Spanish claim in Florida. In 1790, the year of the first census, the population of the country was nearly 4 million. Although Indians were not counted in the census, it nonetheless revealed the remarkable diversity of the new nation. Only 48 percent of its inhabitants were of English descent. People of African descent, the overwhelming majority of them slaves, constituted the second largest group (19 percent); a provision in the Constitution provided that the importation of slaves could not be prohibited until 1808. The next largest groups were Scots or Scotch-Irish (12 percent) and Germans (10 percent), followed by smaller numbers of the French, Irish, Welsh, Dutch, and Swedes.

Between 1790 and 1830, both the population and the size of the country grew dramatically. In 1803, a vast territory was acquired through the

Captains Lewis and Clark Holding a Council with the Indians

This illustration appeared in Patrick Gass's *Journal of Voyages and Travels of Corps of Discovery* (1807), the first full and authentic account of the famous expedition that explored a vast territory from the Mississippi River to the shore of the Pacific Ocean.

Louisiana Purchase, which extended the nation's boundaries to the Rocky Mountains. From 1804 to 1806, an expedition led by Meriwether Lewis and William Clark explored the territory along the Missouri River and across the Rocky Mountains to the mouth of the Columbia River in present-day Washington. Although the journals of Lewis and Clark were not published until 1814, government documents, newspaper reports, and an account written by a member of the expedition – Patrick Gass's *Journal* (1807) – offered the American public their first glimpses of the vast potential of the immense area west of the Mississippi River. In 1807, Thomas Jefferson prophetically referred to "our country, from the Mississippi to the Pacific." By 1810, its population exceeded 7 million people, an increasing number of whom were pressing westward, driving the Indians before them.

During the following decade, the expanding country survived two crises. The seizure of ships and the impressments of thousands of American sailors by the British navy culminated in the War of 1812. The three-year war ended in a stalemate. Nonetheless, it drew Americans together and fueled nationalism – indeed, it served as a kind of second American Revolution. In an 1819 treaty, Spain ceded Florida and its claim to territory in the northwest to the United States. But growing divisions over slavery generated a bitter sectional crisis that was resolved in 1820 by the Missouri Compromise, under the terms of which Missouri entered the Union as a slave state but slavery was excluded from all the Louisiana Purchase territory to the north and west of it. By 1830, there were twenty-four states (twelve free and twelve slave) with a total population approaching 13 million, including nearly 2 million slaves in the South.

Most slaves were prohibited by law or other restrictions from learning to read and write, but the burgeoning white population was increasingly literate. At the time of the Revolution, adult literacy rates for men and women were generally higher in the colonies than in western Europe, ranging from 50 to 60 percent in the southern colonies to as high as 90 percent in New England. But the rates for recent immigrants from Scotland, Ireland, and other European countries were much lower. Literacy rates also varied widely according to class, religion, and locale, since they were higher in urban than in rural areas. Following the Revolution, however, the belief that the survival of republican values and institutions depended on an informed citizenry led most states to mandate publicly funded education. That nationalistic educational philosophy also promoted the growth of libraries, providing at least some Americans with increased access to books and periodicals. Two kinds of libraries existed: social or membership libraries, established by specific groups or organizations, and commercial circulating libraries, which charged fees for the loan of books. The number of books available for loan in either kind of library was generally small (three thousand was the median number in

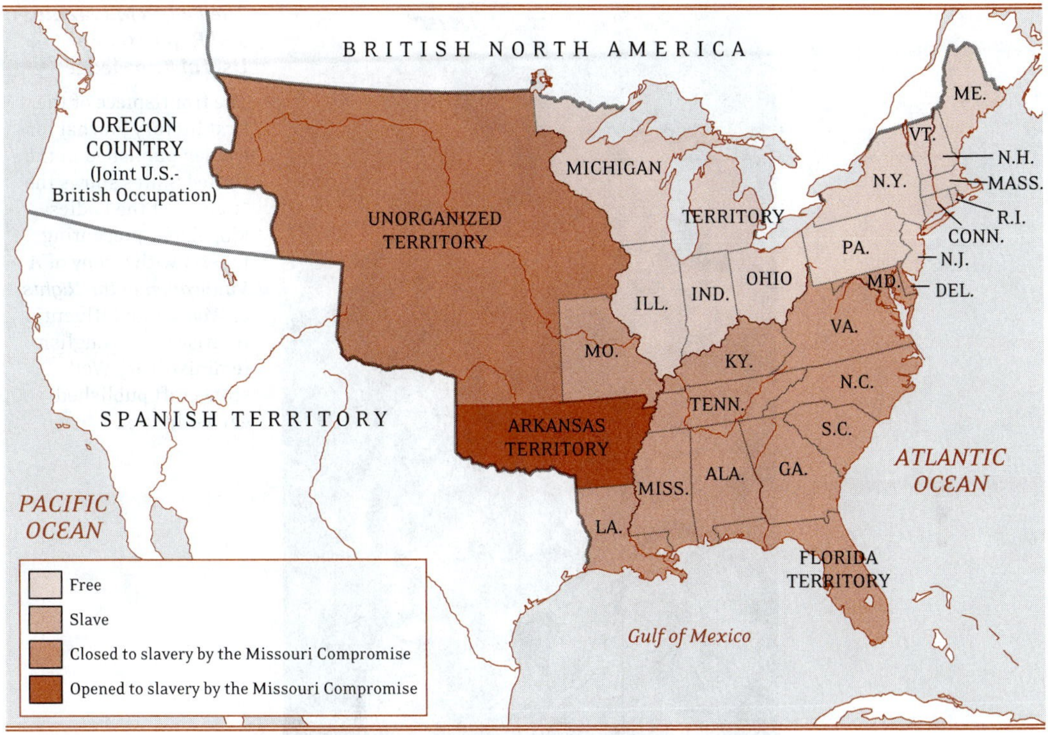

The Missouri Compromise

This map reveals the remarkable expansion of the nation between the end of the Revolution and the Missouri Compromise in 1820. Under the terms of the Compromise, Maine was admitted as a free state and Missouri as a slave state, thus retaining the precarious balance between free and slave states.

the first decade of the nineteenth century) and access to them was often limited to white men. At the same time, there was a growing emphasis on the need to educate women. Despite their important role in the war effort, women made few political gains during the Revolution. In the following years, however, the emerging ideal of "republican mothers," who would nurture and help instill civic virtues in the rising generation of Americans, led to the establishment of institutions like the Young Ladies' Academy, founded in 1786. "I expect to see our young women forming a new era in female history," Judith Sargent Murray proclaimed in 1798. Her vision proved to be far too optimistic, but the modest educational and social advances women made helped prepare the way for their increasing participation in the cultural life of the new nation.

"I expect to see our young women forming a new era in female history."

The most immediate beneficiaries of rising literacy rates and the

The Lady's Magazine, and Repository of Useful Knowledge

The frontispiece of the first literary journal for women published in the United States shows the "Genius of the Ladies Magazine" presenting Liberty with a copy of *A Vindication of the Rights of Woman*, an influential treatise by the English feminist Mary Wollstonecraft published earlier in 1792.

expanding population were newspapers. Following the Revolutionary War, during which the printing business was severely disrupted by shortages of paper and other basic supplies, newspapers swiftly rebounded. The newspaper in which the Declaration of Independence was first printed, the weekly *Philadelphia Evening Post*, became the first daily in the United States on May 30, 1783. As in the decade before the war, politics remained a central preoccupation of newspapers in the years leading up to the ratification of the Constitution in 1788 and the election of George Washington as the first president in 1789. The debate over the Constitution was largely conducted in print, notably in the letters to newspapers Alexander

Hamilton, John Jay, and James Madison wrote in favor of ratification, which were collected and published as *The Federalist* (1788), better known as the *Federalist Papers*. Despite the title of Washington's famous Farewell Address – issued on the occasion of his retirement from the presidency – it was not delivered as a speech but was instead printed in *Claypoole's American Daily Advertiser* on September 17, 1796. That year, newspapers also played a central role in the country's first contested presidential election, in which John Adams narrowly defeated Thomas Jefferson. Certainly, newspapers revealed the growing political divisions in the United States. By 1800, there were more than two hundred newspapers in the country, almost all of them firmly allied with either the Federalists, who favored a strong federal government and advocated the development of industries and trade, or the Jeffersonian Republicans, who opposed centralized government and advocated a primarily agrarian society.

Although book production lagged behind the strong growth of newspapers, it slowly increased during the decades following the Revolution. The war and its heroes provided ready materials for American writers like Mercy Otis Warren, a poet and dramatist who published a three-volume history of the American Revolution in 1805, and Mason Weems, whose two enormously popular biographies of George Washington (1800 and 1806) included the famous and undoubtedly fictitious account of his refusal to lie about chopping down a cherry tree. American publishers also reprinted books by two of the "Founding Fathers," Jefferson's *Notes on the State of Virginia* and an early edition of Franklin's *Autobiography*, both of which had originally been published in Paris and London.

But the books read by many common people were often limited to almanacs and the Bible, still found in most homes in America. The fervor generated by the series of religious revivals known as the Great Awakening of 1720-50 waned during the second half of the eighteenth century. Beginning in the 1790s, however, there was a resurgence of evangelical activity known as the "Second Great Awakening." The movement was in large part a reaction against Deism, the "rational" religion of the Enlightenment that rejected orthodox Christian doctrines such as miracles, revelation, and the divinity of Jesus. The Second Great Awakening had a profound impact on all aspects of life in the new nation, including its print culture, as the evangelicals began to spread their message not only through preaching but also by distributing Christian books designed to offer moral and religious instruction to the American masses.

At the same time, the emphasis on secular instruction created a strong market for basic schoolbooks. Noah Webster published the first volume of his *Grammatical Institute of the English Language*, the *Speller* (later called *The American Spelling Book*) in 1783. Since there was then no federal copyright law, which was not passed by Congress until 1790, under the new

"... the continued increase of the wealth, the learning, the moral and religious elevation of character, and the glory of my country."

Constitution, Webster was obliged to travel around the country to secure a copyright for the book in each of the states. The first American "speller," the book was reprinted throughout the nineteenth century and ultimately sold an estimated 100 million copies. The royalties on such books allowed him to work on his most cherished project, *An American Dictionary of the English Language* (1828), which the patriotic Webster in his preface hoped would result in "the continued increase of the wealth, the learning, the moral and religious elevation of character, and the glory of my country."

The Emergence of an American Literature

The patriotism that inspired Webster's lexical work also spurred the development of imaginative literature, including drama. George Washington's name appeared first on the list of subscribers supporting the publication of Royall Tyler's *The Contrast* (1787), the first play written by an American to be performed by a professional acting company in the United States. Although the stage was dominated by English actors and plays, especially those of Shakespeare, there were numerous efforts to introduce drama written by and for Americans. The journalist Judith Sargent Murray also wrote plays, including *The Medium, or Virtue Triumphant* (1795), the first play written by an American to be performed at the Federal Street Theatre in Boston. A plea for women's rights, the play was not well received, so Murray followed it with *The Traveller Returned* (1796), a comedy set during the American Revolution. Other episodes in the nation's history also provided material for playwrights. The first of the so-called Indian plays, which became enormously popular in the following decades, was apparently *The Indian Princess*, a retelling of the Pocahontas story staged in New York in 1808.

Poets also explored American history, even as they predicted a bright future for the new nation. In one of her final works, Phillis Wheatley hailed the end of the Revolutionary War with "Liberty and Peace," a celebration of the glorious destiny of America. Other poets also wrote in support of the cause, including Phillip Freneau, often called "the poet of the American Revolution." The growing political divisions in the country were mirrored by its poets, especially by the deep divide between Freneau, who was accused of being Jefferson's Antifederalist mouthpiece, and Federalist poets like Joel Barlow, Timothy Dwight, and other members of a literary group at Yale College known as the "Connecticut Wits." Like the radical Freneau, however, the conservative group patriotically championed a literature based on American scenes and themes, as exemplified by Barlow's massive epic *The Vision of Columbus* (1787) and Dwight's *Greenfield Hill*

(1794), a long pastoral poem celebrating an idealized Connecticut as a utopian model for economic and social development in the United States.

As the novel became an increasingly popular form, writers also sought to produce "American" novels, though they were closely modeled on works imported from England. Taking their cue from earlier English novels like Samuel Richardson's *Pamela*, which Franklin had reprinted fifty years earlier, in the 1790s American writers like William Hill Brown, Susanna Rowson, and Hannah Webster Foster wrote novels with strong instructive lessons for women. Ironically, one of those lessons was the danger of taking ideas about life and love from novels, as the heroine does in Tabitha Gilman Tenney's *Female Quixotism* (1801). Nonetheless, in yet another reaction against eighteenth-century rationalism, such works revealed the growing emphasis on emotion and sentiment in American literature. Even more heightened emotions and far more extreme psychological states were staples of the so-called gothic romances, sensational tales of horror and the supernatural like Ann Radcliffe's *The Mysteries of Udolpho* (1794) and Matthew Gregory Lewis's *The Monk* (1796), two bestsellers imported from England. With their heavy doses of doom, gloom, magic, and mystery, such works strongly influenced American writers like Charles Brockden Brown. But he and other native novelists faced an uphill battle in their struggle against foreign competition, since the copyright law of 1790 accorded protection only to books published in the United States, not to those that were first published elsewhere. As Brown bitterly complained, cheap, pirated editions of English novels consequently swamped the limited literary marketplace in the United States.

The growth of periodical publishing provided somewhat brighter prospects for American writers. None of the magazines established before or during the Revolutionary War survived the conflict. By 1800, however, many new magazines appeared, frequently with patriotic titles like the *American Magazine*, the *Columbian Magazine*, the *National Magazine*, and the *United States Magazine*. "Those institutions are the most effectual guard to public liberty which diffuse the rudiments of literature among a people," the editors of one magazine declared in 1790. Others viewed magazines and other periodicals as vital, not only to the preservation of liberty, but also to the development of American literature. Washington Irving, who would later become the first American to earn his living as a professional writer, began his career by contributing essays on New York culture and society to his brother's newspaper, the *Morning Courier*. In 1807, he and his brother started a satirical magazine, *Salmagundi*, and during the War of 1812 Irving edited yet another periodical, the *Analectic Magazine*. The resurgent nationalism of the postwar period led to the establishment of many more magazines, notably the *North American Review*,

"Those institutions are the most effectual guard to public liberty which diffuse the rudiments of literature among a people."

Alexander Anderson, *Evening Amusements*

This woodcut, produced around 1820, illustrates the growing popularity of reading in American homes as books became cheaper and more widely available. Although most of the books read were English, during the following decade American authors would claim an increasing share of the literary marketplace in the United States.

a distinguished literary journal founded in Boston in 1815. A new term, *magazinist*, began to be used for those who wrote for magazines, more than one hundred of which were in circulation in 1825.

During the 1820s, conditions for American writers and for the creation of a national literature improved dramatically. The publication of *The Sketch Book of Geoffrey Crayon, Gent.* (1819–20) gained Irving international attention, which had never before been accorded to a writer from the United States. It was swiftly followed by William Cullen Bryant's celebrated first book, *Poems*, and James Fenimore Cooper's first significant novel, *The Spy*, both published in 1821. The commercial success of Cooper's novels illustrated the impact of both cultural changes and changes in the production of books, the costs of which were decreased by new methods of papermaking and typesetting, as well as the use of cloth rather than leather bindings. The small first printing of *The Spy* was quickly followed by additional printings of three thousand and then five thousand copies. Cooper's subsequent novels sold even more briskly. When *The Pioneers* was published in 1823, for example, people waited in line in New York City to buy the book, and the first edition of thirty-five hundred copies sold out by noon on the day it appeared in bookstores. Where Charles Brockden Brown had earlier complained about pirated editions of English novels in the United States, Cooper complained that his popular novels were being published in pirated editions in England.

The literary marketplace was still dominated by English works, but the critical and commercial success of writers like Irving and Cooper inspired other would-be authors in the United States. An increasing number of them were women, including Catharine Maria Sedgwick, whose first novel appeared in 1822. She also contributed numerous sketches and stories to periodicals, including annual gift books, the popularity of which provided yet another outlet for American writers. Boston, New York, and Philadelphia remained the centers of American publishing, but periodicals were also established to serve distant population centers in the Ohio Valley, especially Cincinnati, other parts of the Midwest, and the South. As the Indians were pushed further and further west, a written Native American literature began to emerge in works like those of Jane Johnston Schoolcraft (Bame-wa-wa-ge-zhik-a-quay, or Woman of the Stars Rushing through the Sky). Schoolcraft's acclaimed stories based on the legends and tales of her mother's tribe, the Ojibwa, appeared in a manuscript magazine she and her husband, Henry Rowe Schoolcraft, hand copied and circulated from their remote home in the Michigan Territory to cities in the Midwest and Northeast. At about the same time, Augustus Baldwin Longstreet established the tradition of American frontier humor in a series of sketches he first published in obscure Southern newspapers and later collected as *Georgia Scenes.* Like so many other writers of the period, Longstreet looked back to an earlier time, in his case the first decades of the Republic. By the time he began to write those sketches in 1830, however, life on the former frontier was not the only thing that had changed – so had American literature. A distinctly national literature was no longer simply a patriotic hope or the distant possibility envisaged by early critics. It was increasingly a reality for publishers, readers, and writers in the United States.

Writing Colonial Lives

WHEN BENJAMIN FRANKLIN began writing his celebrated "autobiography" in 1771, that term was not used to identify such first-person narratives. The term was not commonly used until the early decades of the nineteenth century, and *The Autobiography of Benjamin Franklin* was not published under that title until 1868. Nonetheless, autobiography has a long history in Western culture, most often traced back to the *Confessions* of St. Augustine (354-430), the Roman Catholic bishop of Hippo in North Africa.

◄ **Benjamin Franklin**

The author of the *Autobiography of Benjamin Franklin*, probably the most famous self-portrait in American literature, was also frequently the subject of portraiture. This painting by George Dunlop Leslie, after the original painted in London by Mason Chamberlain in 1762, depicts Franklin as a writer and scientist. The thunderstorm raging outside the window is an allusion to his celebrated experiments with electricity. (The bells behind him are rigged to ring when lightning strikes outside.) But the books visible at the extreme left, behind the bells, and especially the manuscript and the quill pen Franklin holds were equally central to both his sense of identity and his growing fame.

As that genealogy suggests, one important source of autobiography was the Christian emphasis on self-examination, a characteristic that assumed even greater importance during the Protestant Reformation of the sixteenth and seventeenth centuries. Since for most Protestants the sole promise of salvation was the operation of God's grace within the soul, individuals were encouraged to turn inward to discover signs of their ultimate spiritual destiny. The settlement of New England was powerfully fueled by the Reformation, and the Puritans produced large numbers of autobiographical writings, including journals, captivity narratives, and more formal spiritual autobiographies like Jonathan Edwards's *Personal Narrative.*

Franklin, who was born and raised in Puritan Boston, also emphasized the need for self-examination. But his narrative is anything but a spiritual autobiography. Despite his professed belief in God and Providence, Franklin displayed little interest in the spiritual life. In what he called a "History of my Life," Franklin turned not inward to the soul but outward to the world of men (which virtually all of the major characters in his narrative are) and events. Indeed, the *Autobiography* was very much a product of the Enlightenment. Like many Enlightenment thinkers, who viewed themselves as the "party of humanity," Franklin placed less emphasis on salvation or the need to prepare for the next world than on the pursuit of happiness and the need to improve conditions in this world. With his satirical wit, his distaste for religious orthodoxy and social pretense, and his emphasis on reason and tolerance, Franklin displayed an especially strong kinship with Voltaire and other Enlightenment writers in France. He was even more directly influenced by the major philosophers of the Enlightenment in Great Britain. Just as the Declaration revealed the impact of the political philosophy of John Locke's *Treatises of Government,* the *Autobiography* displays the impact of the empirical philosophy of works like Locke's *Essay Concerning Human Understanding.* Affirming the natural goodness of human beings, Locke denied that there were innate ideas. Instead, he argued that the human mind was a tabula rasa, a blank slate inscribed by sense experience alone. Locke's views were further developed by one of the friends Franklin made in England, the Scottish philosopher David Hume. The skeptical and utilitarian Hume emphasized the limitations of human knowledge, which in his view did not extend beyond what we can observe, and the primary task of which was to provide us with a practical guide to life. A similar understanding of human nature and individual understanding is revealed in the *Autobiography,* in which Franklin charts his intellectual growth through observation and education, especially his voracious reading.

In fact, Franklin's account was probably inspired by a number of the books he mentions in his *Autobiography.* For example, he refers to *Plutarch's Lives,* which was widely available in English translations in the

Printed for Nat: Ponder in the Poultry.
THE
Pilgrim's Progreſs
FROM
THIS WORLD,
TO
That which is to come
Delivered under the Similitude of a
DREAM
Wherein is Diſcovered,
The Manner of his ſetting out,
His Dangerous JOURNEY,
AND
Safe Arrival at the Deſired Countrey.
By JOHN BUNYAN.
The Third Edition, with Additions.
I have uſed Similitudes, Hoſea, 12. 10.
Licenſed and Entred according to Order.
LONDON,
Printed for Nath. Ponder, at the Peacock
in the Poultrey near Cornhil, 1679.

John Bunyan, *The Pilgrim's Progress*

The frontispiece from this early edition shows the author asleep, as in his dream the character Christian – with his guidebook, the Bible, in hand – begins his journey from the City of Destruction to the Celestial City. Bunyan's allegory, which has been more widely read than any book in English except the Bible, remained enormously popular in America for at least two hundred years after it was first published in 1678.

eighteenth century. Those brief biographies of eminent Greek and Roman statesmen were very popular reading, especially in schools. By the time he began his autobiography, Franklin surely had a sense of his own growing importance as a historical figure as well as his role in the emerging effort to establish a new republic in America. Franklin also alludes to an even more popular book in colonial America: John Bunyan's *The Pilgrim's Progress* (1678), an allegorical account of the adventures of Christian, a young man who journeys from the City of Destruction to salvation in the Celestial City. In fact, Franklin's story may be read as a kind of secularized version of *The Pilgrim's Progress*, which was second only to the Bible among the books read in many homes in colonial America. Certainly, it provided a compelling narrative model to Franklin, though, as one of his recent biographers has observed, his "was the story of a very real pilgrim . . . in a very real world."

His "was the story of a very real pilgrim . . . in a very real world."

In offering an account of his triumphant progress through that world, Franklin cast himself as an exemplary figure, at once a distinct individual and a representative American. At the very time when many people in the colonies first began to think of themselves as Americans, Franklin was one of the first to develop an idea of what it meant to be one. He began his

Autobiography shortly before the Revolution, while he was in England seeking to gain greater economic and political autonomy for the American colonies. Franklin wrote the later sections of the *Autobiography* after America had gained its independence from England. The triumphant story of his own rise in the world was thus also the story of the rise of his country. Franklin had broken away from his older brother, to whom he had been indentured at an early age, and gone on to gain international fame as a scientist and statesman. At the same time, America finally broke away from its mother country, England, afterwards assuming an increasingly important place in the affairs of the world.

Although it has overshadowed virtually all other American autobiographies, Franklin's was not the only one written in the colonies during the last half of the eighteenth century. Nor did Franklin tell the whole story of life in colonial America. In contrast to his *Autobiography*, the narratives by two other authors represented in this section, the Quakers Elizabeth Ashbridge and John Woolman, followed the long tradition of the spiritual autobiography. In fact, like other autobiographies written by Quakers, or members of the Society of Friends, their narratives were published posthumously only after a committee had determined that the works were of sufficient didactic and spiritual value to merit publication. Ashbridge told the story of her difficult life and struggles, from her early days in England – when she wept because she was not born a boy and therefore could not become an Anglican priest – to the spiritual crisis that finally led her to become an active member and teacher among the Quakers in America. Through her involvement in the Society of Friends, Ashbridge gained what few women had in colonial America: the right to speak publicly and to write her own story. But perhaps the most famous of all Quaker spiritual autobiographies is *The Journal of John Woolman*. Raised in a Quaker colony near Philadelphia, Woolman traced his journey from a spiritually troubled youth to a successful businessman to his final transformation into a tireless missionary and preacher, seeking to convert others and to promote antislavery among members of the Society of Friends.

Other significant autobiographies of the period also contained pleas on behalf of oppressed groups. Samson Occom, a Mohegan who converted to Christianity and became a missionary among the Indians, bitterly described their harsh treatment by the European colonists of New England. Occom was thus among the first Native American writers in English to use his adopted language to expose the plight of the Indians. Another convert to Christianity, Olaudah Equiano, used an account of his torturous experiences to reveal the horrors of slavery and the slave trade. His celebrated account also helped establish a new and vital genre, the slave narrative. Describing such works as the print origins (as distinguished from oral sources) of black literature in the United States, the eminent African

American novelist Toni Morrison has observed that slave narratives also "gave fuel to the fires that abolitionists were setting everywhere." Indeed, just as Equiano's narrative was instrumental in abolishing the Atlantic slave trade, other writers would later develop the slave narrative into one of the most powerful of all of the weapons employed in the antislavery crusade during the decades before the Civil War.

Slave narratives also "gave fuel to the fires that abolitionists were setting everywhere."

Even as they pursued very different ends, Ashbridge, Woolman, Occom, and Equiano offered a profoundly different image of what Franklin described as life in colonial America. Partly in an effort to attract immigrants, as well as to establish the sharp differences between his country and the countries of Europe, Franklin for the most part described a fluid, egalitarian society in which even a poor boy from a humble family could rise to fame and fortune. The other writers placed far greater emphasis on the obstacles to freedom and opportunity in colonial America. Ashbridge arrived in the colonies in 1732 and later made her way to Pennsylvania, where the young Franklin was already well advanced on what he later described as his smooth road to success in his adopted city of Philadelphia. Ashbridge described a different and far darker reality, a world of

The Potter Family

This mid-eighteenth-century painting at once reveals the affluence and confirms the status of the Potter family of Matunuck, Rhode Island. The young boy serving tea is either a servant or a slave, a reminder that slavery and indentured servitude were widespread in the North as well as in the South.

indentured servitude, social stratification, and religious intolerance. She also emphasized the subservient role of women, while Woolman, Occom, and Equiano exposed the bigotry and brutality faced by Native Americans and African Americans, especially the growing number of slaves in the colonies. Five years after he began his autobiography, Franklin helped prepare the Declaration of Independence, which affirmed that "all men are created equal," and that they are endowed with certain inalienable rights, including "life, liberty, and the pursuit of happiness." As the colonists set out on their path toward independence from England, however, the kind of autonomy and freedom they sought were far from the reality of many of those born in or brought to America.

Benjamin Franklin

[1706–1790]

[Franklin's Autobiography *is] a fond look back upon an earlier self, giving an intensely ambitious young man the benefit of the older man's relaxation.*
– John Updike

Benjamin Franklin was born in Boston on January 17, 1706, to Josiah and Abiah Folger Franklin. Josiah Franklin, a soap maker, had come to America with his first wife, who died in childbirth. In addition to the five surviving children of his first marriage, Josiah and Abiah had ten children, of which Franklin was the eighth and the youngest son. His father initially intended him to become a minister, so Franklin was sent to the Boston Latin School in preparation for study at Harvard College. For reasons that are not clear – perhaps because Franklin did not seem suited for the ministry – his father withdrew him from the Latin School and enrolled him in an academy for the practical study of writing and arithmetic. After only two years of schooling, Franklin went to work in his father's business. Later, at the age of twelve, he was apprenticed to his half-brother, James Franklin, who ran a printing shop. Franklin initially resisted the apprenticeship, which was a lengthy one of nine years instead of the usual seven. James Franklin was also a hard taskmaster, and he and the young Franklin were frequently at odds. In 1721, James Franklin started the *New England Courant*, one of the first newspapers established in Boston. Bored with typesetting, Franklin spent all of his spare time reading. He also began to submit anonymous columns to the newspaper, adopting the persona of "Silence Dogood," the independent-minded widow of a country minister. James Franklin, who had no idea of the identity of the author of the popular "Dogood Papers," was furious when he learned that they were written by his young apprentice. From that point, the always difficult relationship between the half-brothers deteriorated, and Franklin decided to run away in the fall of 1723. Using the cover story that he had "got a naughty Girl with Child," Franklin booked passage on a ship to New York City and proceeded from there to Philadelphia.

During the following twenty-five years, Franklin became one of the most prominent and successful citizens of his adopted city. The year after he arrived in Philadelphia, where he found work in a printing shop, he was encouraged to start his own business by the colonial governor of Pennsylvania, Sir William Keith. Promising letters of credit, Governor Keith urged Franklin to go to England to buy equipment. When he landed there, Franklin learned that no letters had been sent. He consequently found work in a printing shop in London, where the publishing trade was far more advanced than it was in the colonies. Returning to Philadelphia two years later, in 1726, the twenty-year-old Franklin had already gained considerable experience in printing. He soon established his own business and, in 1729, he also took over a struggling newspaper. Franklin shortened its title to the *Pennsylvania Gazette* and established a lively weekly that soon became one of the most distinguished newspapers in the colonies and one of the earliest financial successes in the history of American periodicals. Building on its success, Franklin introduced his phenomenally popular annual, *Poor Richard's Almanack* (1733-58), famous for its maxims about the value of frugality and hard work. He later established the second monthly magazine in America, the *General Magazine* (1741), and published several pamphlets, including his *Proposal for Promoting Useful Knowledge* (1743). In 1730, Franklin married Deborah Read. The couple had two children, and they took in his illegitimate son, William, later the royal governor of New Jersey. Franklin also became increasingly involved in civic affairs – he founded the first American subscription library, helped establish an academy that became the University of Pennsylvania, and laid the foundation for the American Philosophical Society, formed in 1743 to support "all philosophical Experiments that let Light into the Nature of Things, tend to increase the Power of Man over Matter, and multiply the Conveniencies or Pleasures of Life."

In 1748, Franklin essentially retired from business, selling the *Pennsylvania Gazette* for a considerable profit and embarking on a second career devoted to scientific investigation and public service. The publication of his *Experiments and Observations on Electricity* (1751-54) brought him international recognition, but Franklin gained even greater fame as a diplomat and statesman. As Pennsylvania's representative to the Albany Congress in the summer of 1754, his "plan of union" was among the first proposals for uniting all of the colonies under a general government. During much of the time between 1757 and 1775, Franklin was in England, serving as a colonial agent – first for Pennsylvania, and later for Georgia, New Jersey, and Massachusetts. Franklin tried to persuade the British government to allow more self-rule in the colonies, and he testified before the House of Commons for the repeal of the detested Stamp Act, one of a series of taxation measures that generated violent opposition. When Franklin returned to America in 1775, he was chosen as a delegate to the Second Continental Congress, in which he served with John Adams and Thomas Jefferson on the committee assigned to write the Declaration of Independence. The following year, he was appointed commissioner to the court of France, where Franklin helped negotiate and signed the peace treaty with

bedfordstmartins.com/ americanlit *for research links on Franklin*

Great Britain that ended the Revolutionary War in 1783. After his return to Philadelphia two years later, the tireless Franklin was elected president of the Pennsylvania Society for the Promotion of the Abolition of Slavery. He was later appointed as a delegate to the convention that framed the federal Constitution, which he signed on September 17, 1787. Throughout his four decades of public service, Franklin continued to write articles for periodicals and publish pamphlets. He also worked intermittently on his autobiography, though he was not able to complete it before his death. Franklin's last publication was an ironic letter to the *Federal Gazette*, "On the Slave Trade," published a month before he died on April 17, 1790. Nearly twenty thousand people lined the streets for his funeral procession in Philadelphia, where he was buried next to his wife in the Christ Church Burial Ground.

Franklin's *Autobiography*. What is now known as *The Autobiography of Benjamin Franklin* had a long and complex compositional history. The first part of what Franklin variously referred to as his "memoirs" and "the History of my Life" was written in the summer of 1771, while he was staying in southern England at Twyford, the summer home of his friend Jonathan Shipley (1714-1788), then the Anglican bishop of St. Asaph's in Wales. Franklin addressed this part of the narrative to his older son, William Franklin (1731-1813), who had been appointed the royal governor of New Jersey in 1762. (Sadly, there is no evidence that it was ever read by William, who was later estranged from his father when he supported the British government during the Revolution.) The second part of the manuscript was written thirteen years later, in 1784, while Franklin was living in France. The final two parts were written after his return to America, in August 1788 and in the winter of 1789-90. The four parts of the manuscript cover his life only up until 1758, well before his greatest achievements as a diplomat and statesman. Franklin, who spent most of his early life as a printer, died before he completed or had an opportunity to prepare the manuscript for publication. His account is further complicated by the fact that Franklin did not always have copies of what he had written earlier when he returned to work on the *Autobiography*. Moreover, he made outlines of topics he wanted to cover in the work and jotted down pages of notes without clearly indicating whether he intended to use all of those materials in the final version.

The publication history of the *Autobiography* is equally complex. At various times, Franklin shared the manuscript with friends, including his neighbor in Paris, Louis Guillaume Le Veillard. In one of the many ironies of the history of the text, what became the most famous of all American life writings was first published in Paris in Le Veillard's French translation of part one, *Memoires de la Vie Privée de Benjamin Franklin* (1791). In a further irony, the first edition of the autobiography published in English was actually a translation of the French edition, *The Private Life of the Late*

The Private Life of the Late Benjamin Franklin

The first English edition of Franklin's *Autobiography* was a translation of the original 1791 French edition, published in Paris a year after his death.
(The Library Company of Philadelphia.)

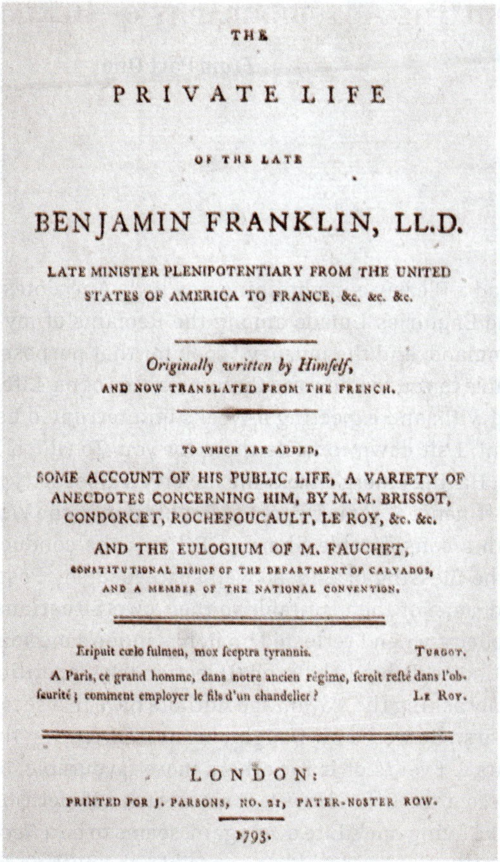

THE
PRIVATE LIFE
OF THE LATE
BENJAMIN FRANKLIN, LL.D.
LATE MINISTER PLENIPOTENTIARY FROM THE UNITED STATES OF AMERICA TO FRANCE, &c. &c. &c.

Originally written by Himſelf,
AND NOW TRANSLATED FROM THE FRENCH.

TO WHICH ARE ADDED,
SOME ACCOUNT OF HIS PUBLIC LIFE, A VARIETY OF ANECDOTES CONCERNING HIM, BY M. M. BRISSOT, CONDORCET, ROCHEFOUCAULT, LE ROY, &c. &c.

AND THE EULOGIUM OF M. FAUCHET,
CONSTITUTIONAL BISHOP OF THE DEPARTMENT OF CALVADOS, AND A MEMBER OF THE NATIONAL CONVENTION.

Eripuit cœlo fulmen, mox ſceptra tyrannis. TURGOT.
A Paris, ce grand homme, dans notre ancien régime, ſeroit reſté dans l'obſcurité; comment employer le fils d'un chandelier? LE ROY.

LONDON:
PRINTED FOR J. PARSONS, NO. 21, PATER-NOSTER ROW.
1793.

Benjamin Franklin, LL.D., which was published in London in 1793. Several American editions of *The Life of Dr. Benjamin Franklin* followed before his grandson and literary executor, William Temple Franklin, published a version that included the first three parts of the text in his edition of *Memoirs of the Life and Writings of Benjamin Franklin* (1818). But it was not until John Bigelow's 1868 edition of what he was the first to call *The Autobiography of Benjamin Franklin* that all four parts of the work appeared in English. The text of the following selections from parts one and two is based on the authoritative text established by J. A. Leo Lemay and P. M. Zall, editors of *The Autobiography of Benjamin Franklin: A Genetic Text* (1981). We have silently expanded some abbreviations and slightly adjusted punctuation to facilitate reading of the text. In a few instances, we have also altered Franklin's spellings, though we have retained early variant spellings of familiar words, for example *chearfully* and *Wharff.*

From THE AUTOBIOGRAPHY OF BENJAMIN FRANKLIN

From Part One

Twyford, at the Bishop
of St Asaph's
1771.

Dear Son,

I have ever had a Pleasure in obtaining any little Anecdotes of my Ancestors. You may remember the Enquiries I made among the Remains of my Relations[1] when you were with me in England; and the Journey I took for that purpose. Now imagining it may be equally agreable to you to know the Circumstances of *my* Life, many of which you are yet unacquainted with; and expecting a Weeks uninterrupted Leisure in my present Country Retirement, I sit down to write them for you. To which I have besides some other Inducements. Having emerg'd from the Poverty & Obscurity in which I was born & bred, to a State of Affluence & some Degree of Reputation in the World, and having gone so far thro' Life with a considerable Share of Felicity, the conducing Means I made use of, which, with the Blessing of God, so well succeeded, my Posterity may like to know, as they may find some of them suitable to their own Situations, & therefore fit to be imitated. That Felicity, when I reflected on it, has induc'd me sometimes to say, that were it offer'd to my Choice, I should have no Objection to a Repetition of the same Life from its Beginning, only asking the Advantage Authors have in a second Edition to correct some Faults of the first. So would I if I might, besides correcting the Faults, change some sinister Accidents & Events of it for others more favourable, but tho' this were deny'd, I should still accept the Offer. However, since such a Repetition is not to be expected, the Thing most like living one's Life over again, seems to be a *Recollection* of that Life; and to make that Recollection as durable as possible, the putting it down in Writing. Hereby, too, I shall indulge the Inclination so natural in old Men, to be talking of themselves and their own past Actions, and I shall indulge it, without being troublesome to others who thro' respect to Age might think themselves oblig'd to give me a Hearing, since this may be read or not as any one pleases. And lastly, (I may as well confess it, since my Denial of it will be believ'd by no body) perhaps I shall a good deal gratify my own *Vanity*. Indeed I scarce ever heard or saw the introductory Words, *Without Vanity I may say*, &c. but some vain thing immediately follow'd. Most People dislike Vanity in others whatever Share they have of it themselves, but I give it fair Quarter wherever I meet with it, being persuaded that it is often productive of Good to the Possessor & to others that are within his Sphere of Action: And therefore in many Cases it would not be quite absurd if a Man were to thank God for his Vanity among the other Comforts of Life.

And now I speak of thanking God, I desire with all Humility to acknowledge, that I owe the mention'd Happiness of my past Life to his kind Providence, which led me to the

---

1. **Remains of my Relations:** Franklin and his son, William, visited surviving relatives in 1758.

Means I us'd & gave them Success. My Belief of This, induces me to *hope*, tho' I must not *presume*, that the same Goodness will still be exercis'd towards me in continuing that Happiness, or in enabling me to bear a fatal Reverso,[2] which I may experience as others have done, the Complexion of my future Fortune being known to him only: and in whose Power it is to bless to us even our Afflictions.

The Notes one of my Uncles (who had the same kind of Curiosity in collecting Family Anecdotes) once put into my Hands, furnish'd me with several Particulars, relating to our Ancestors. From those Notes I learnt that the Family had liv'd in the same Village, Ecton in Northamptonshire, for 300 Years, & how much longer he knew not, (perhaps from the Time when the Name *Franklin* that before was the Name of an Order of People, was assum'd by them for a Surname, when others took Surnames all over the Kingdom.)[3] on a Freehold of about 30 Acres, aided by the Smith's Business which had continued in the Family till his Time, the eldest Son being always bred to that Business. A Custom which he & my Father both followed as to their eldest Sons. When I search'd the Register at Ecton, I found an Account of their Births, Marriages and Burials, from the Year 1555 only, there being no Register kept in that Parish at any time preceding. By that Register I perceiv'd that I was the youngest Son of the youngest Son for 5 Generations back. My Grandfather Thomas, who was born in 1598, lived at Ecton till he grew too old to follow Business longer, when he went to live with his Son John, a Dyer at Banbury in Oxfordshire, with whom my Father serv'd an Apprenticeship. There my Grandfather died and lies buried. We saw his Gravestone in 1758. His eldest Son Thomas liv'd in the House at Ecton, and left it with the Land to his only Child, a Daughter, who with her Husband, one Fisher of Wellingborough sold it to Mr Isted, now Lord of the Manor there. My Grandfather had 4 Sons that grew up, viz.[4] Thomas, John, Benjamin and Josiah. I will give you what Account I can of them at this distance from my Papers, and if those are not lost in my Absence, you will among them find many more Particulars. Thomas was bred a Smith under his Father, but being ingenious, and encourag'd in Learning (as all his Brothers like wise werre,) by an Esquire Palmer then the principal Gentleman in that Parish, he qualify'd himself for the Business of Scrivener,[5] became a considerable Man in the County Affairs, was a chief Mover of all publick Spirited Undertakings, for the County or Town of Northampton & his own Village, of which many Instances were told us at Ecton and he was much taken Notice of and patroniz'd by the then Lord Halifax. He died in 1702 Jan. 6. old Stile,[6] just 4 Years to a Day before I was born. The Account we receiv'd of his Life & Character from some old People at Ecton, I remember struck you as

---

2. **Reverso:** A backhanded stroke (a dueling term).
3. **the Name *Franklin* . . . Kingdom:** A franklin was a landowner of free but not noble birth in Medieval England. Franklin evidently intended to insert a more detailed note at this point in the text about the origin of his surname. In the 1791 French edition, Louis Guillaume Le Veillard included a translation of a note Franklin had written on a separate sheet of paper.
4. **viz.:** Abbreviation for *videlicet* (Latin), meaning "namely" or "in other words."
5. **Scrivener:** A professional transcriber of documents.
6. **old Stile:** The Julian ("Old Style") calendar, in which the year began on March 25, did not include leap years. In 1752, England adopted the use of the Gregorian ("New Style") calendar, a more accurate astronomical calendar, which began the new year on January 1 and included an extra day every four years.

something extraordinary from its Similarity to what you knew of mine. Had he died on the same Day, you said one might have suppos'd a Transmigration. John was bred a Dyer, I believe of Woollens. Benjamin, was bred a Silk Dyer, serving an Apprenticeship at London. He was an ingenious Man, I remember him well, for when I was a Boy he came over to my Father in Boston, and lived in the House with us some Years. He lived to a great Age. His Grandson Samuel Franklin now lives in Boston. He left behind him two Quarto Volumes, M.S.[7] of his own Poetry, consisting of little occasional Pieces address'd to his Friends and Relations, of which the following sent to me, is a Specimen.

Sent to My Name upon a Report
of his Inclination to Martial affaires
7 July 1710

Beleeve me Ben. It is a Dangerous Trade
The Sword has Many Marr'd as well as Made
By it doe many fall Not Many Rise
Makes Many poor few Rich and fewer Wise
Fills Towns with Ruin, fields with blood beside
Tis Sloths Maintainer, And the Shield of pride
Fair Citties Rich to Day, in plenty flow
War fills with want, Tomorrow, & with woe
Ruin'd Estates, The Nurse of Vice, broke limbs & scarss
Are the Effects of Desolating Warrs

Sent to B. F. in N. E.
15 July 1710

B e to thy parents an Obedient Son
E ach Day let Duty constantly be Done
N ever give Way to sloth or lust or pride
I f free you'd be from Thousand Ills beside
A bove all Ills be sure Avoide the shelfe
M ans Danger lyes in Satan sin and selfe
I n vertue Learning Wisdome progress Make
N ere shrink at Suffering for thy saviours sake
F raud and all Falshood in thy Dealings Flee
R eligious Always in thy station be
A dore the Maker of thy Inward part
N ow's the Accepted time, Give him thy Heart
K eep a Good Consceince 'tis a constant Frind
L ike Judge and Witness This Thy Acts Attend
I n Heart with bended knee Alone Adore
N one but the Three in One Forevermore.

7. Quarto Volumes, M.S.: *M.S.* (or *ms.*) is the abbreviation for manuscript. Folio, quarto, and octavo were standard sizes of books: in a folio, the whole sheet of paper was folded once, forming two leaves; in a quarto, it was folded twice, forming four leaves; in an octavo, it was folded three times, forming eight leaves.

He had form'd a Shorthand of his own, which he taught me, but never practicing it I have now forgot it. I was nam'd after this Uncle, there being a particular Affection between him and my Father. He was very pious, a great Attender of Sermons of the best Preachers, which he took down in his Shorthand and had with him many Volumes of them. He was also much of a Politician, too much perhaps for his Station. There fell lately into my Hands in London a Collection he had made of all the principal Pamphlets relating to Publick Affairs from 1641 to 1717. Many of the Volumes are wanting, as appears by the Numbering, but there still remains 8 Vols. Folio, and 24 in 4to & 8vo.[8] A Dealer in old Books met with them, and knowing me by my sometimes buying of him, he brought them to me. It seems my Uncle must have left them here when he went to America, which was above 50 Years since. There are many of his Notes in the Margins.

This obscure Family of ours was early in the Reformation, and continu'd Protestants thro' the Reign of Queen Mary,[9] when they were sometimes in Danger of Trouble on Account of their Zeal against Popery. They had got an English Bible,[10] & to conceal & secure it, it was fast'ned open with Tapes under & within the Frame of a joint Stool.[11] When my Great Great Grandfather read in it to his Family, he turn'd up the Joint Stool upon his Knees, turning over the Leaves[12] then under the Tapes. One of the Children stood at the Door to give Notice if he saw the Apparitor coming, who was an Officer of the Spiritual Court.[13] In that Case the Stool was turn'd down again upon its feet, when the Bible remain'd conceal'd under it as before. This Anecdote I had from my Uncle Benjamin. The Family continu'd all of the Church of England till about the End of Charles the Second's Reign, when some of the Ministers that had been outed for Nonconformity, holding Conventicles in Northamptonshire, Benjamin & Josiah adher'd to them, and so continu'd all their Lives.[14] The rest of the Family remain'd with the Episcopal Church.

Josiah, my Father, married young, and carried his Wife with three Children unto New England, about 1682. The Conventicles having been forbidden by Law, & frequently disturbed, induced some considerable Men of his Acquaintance to remove to that Country, and he was prevail'd with to accompany them thither, where they expected to enjoy their Mode of Religion with Freedom. By the same Wife he had 4 Children more born there, and by a second Wife ten more, in all 17, of which I remember 13 sitting at one time at his

---

8. **4to & 8vo:** Quarto and octavo; see note 7.
9. **Queen Mary:** The daughter of Henry VIII and Catherine of Aragon, Queen Mary ruled England from 1553 to 1558. She wished to reinstate Roman Catholicism in the country and persecuted Protestants. Her reign was characterized by religious dissent, economic turmoil, and the loss of a war with France.
10. **English Bible:** The Geneva Bible (1560), first printed in England in 1575, was embraced by the Puritans, who brought it with them to the New World. It was eventually banned by the Church of England in favor of the King James Version.
11. **Joint Stool:** A low, backless and armless square seat with four legs, common in the seventeenth century.
12. **Leaves:** The pages of the Bible.
13. **Apparitor . . . Spiritual Court:** An officer charged with carrying out the orders of the ecclesiastical courts in England.
14. **Charles the Second's Reign . . . all their Lives:** Charles II (1630-1685) was the English king from 1660 to 1685. During his reign, Nonconformists, those who refused to acknowledge the Church of England, held secret meetings, or "Conventicles," before they were outlawed in 1664.

Table, who all grew up to be Men & Women, and married; I was the youngest Son and the youngest Child but two, & was born in Boston, N. England.

My Mother the second Wife was Abiah Folger, a Daughter of Peter Folger, one of the first Settlers of New England, of whom honourable mention is made by Cotton Mather,[15] in his Church History of that Country, (entitled Magnalia Christi Americana) as a *godly learned Englishman*, if I remember the Words rightly. I have heard that he wrote sundry small occasional Pieces, but only one of them was printed which I saw now many Years since. It was written in 1675, in the homespun Verse of that Time & People, and address'd to those then concern'd in the Government there. It was in favour of Liberty of Conscience, & in behalf of the Baptists, Quakers, & other Sectaries,[16] that had been under Persecution; ascribing the Indian Wars & other Distresses, that had befallen the Country to that Persecution, as so many Judgments of God, to punish so heinous an Offence; and exhorting a Repeal of those uncharitable Laws. The whole appear'd to me as written with a good deal of Decent Plainness & manly Freedom. The six last concluding Lines I remember, tho' I have forgotten the two first of the Stanza, but the Purport of them was that his Censures proceeded from *Goodwill*, & therefore he would be known as the Author,

> because to be a Libeller, (says he)
>   I hate it with my Heart.
> From Sherburne Town[17] where now I dwell,
>   My Name I do put here,
> Without Offence, your real Friend,
>   It is Peter Folgier.

My elder Brothers were all put Apprentices to different Trades. I was put to the Grammar School at Eight Years of Age, my Father intending to devote me as the Tithe of his Sons to the Service of the Church.[18] My early Readiness in learning to read (which must have been very early, as I do not remember when I could not read) and the Opinion of all his Friends that I should certainly make a good Scholar, encourag'd him in this Purpose of his. My Uncle Benjamin too approv'd of it, and propos'd to give me all his Shorthand Volumes of Sermons I suppose as a Stock to set up with, if I would learn his Character.[19] I continu'd however at the Grammar School not quite one Year, tho' in that time I had risen gradually from the Middle of the Class of that Year to be the Head of it, and farther was remov'd into the next Class above it, in order to go with that into the third at the End of the Year. But my Father in the mean time, from a View of the Expence of a College Education which, having so large a Family, he could not well afford, and the mean Living

---

15. **Cotton Mather:** (1663-1728) Puritan theologian and author of *Magnalia Christi Americana*, or "The Great Work of Christ in America" (1702); he actually described Folger as "an Able Godly Englishman."
16. **Sectaries:** Members of a religious or political sect.
17. **Sherburne Town:** In the Island of Nantucket. [Franklin's note.]
18. **Tithe . . . Service of the Church:** One-tenth of one's annual income was considered the appropriate donation for the support of the church and clergy. Franklin was the tenth son, so his father intended to train him for the church.
19. **Character:** Individual shorthand notation.

many so educated were afterwards able to obtain, Reasons that he gave to his Friends in my Hearing, altered his first Intention, took me from the Grammar School, and sent me to a School for Writing & Arithmetic kept by a then famous Man, Mr George Brownell, very successful in his Profession generally, and that by mild encouraging Methods. Under him I acquired fair Writing pretty soon, but I fail'd in the Arithmetic, & made no Progress in it. At Ten Years old, I was taken home to assist my Father in his Business, which was that of a Tallow Chandler and Sope-Boiler.[20] A Business he was not bred to, but had assumed on his Arrival in New England & on finding his Dying Trade[21] would not maintain his Family, being in little Request. Accordingly I was employed in cutting Wick for the Candles, filling the Dipping Mold, & the Molds for cast Candles, attending the Shop, going of Errands, &c. I dislik'd the Trade and had a strong Inclination for the Sea; but my Father declar'd against it; however, living near the Water, I was much in and about it, learnt early to swim well, & to manage Boats, and when in a Boat or Canoe with other Boys I was commonly allow'd to govern, especially in any case of Difficulty; and upon other Occasions I was generally a Leader among the Boys, and sometimes led them into Scrapes, of which I will mention one Instance, as it shows an early projecting public Spirit, tho' not then justly conducted. There was a Salt Marsh that bounded part of the Mill Pond, on the Edge of which at Highwater, we us'd to stand to fish for Minews. By much Trampling, we had made it a mere Quagmire. My Proposal was to build a Wharf there fit for us to stand upon, and I show'd my Comrades a large Heap of Stones which were intended for a new House near the Marsh, and which would very well suit our Purpose. Accordingly in the Evening when the Workmen were gone, I assembled a Number of my Playfellows, and working with them diligently like so many Emmets,[22] sometimes two or three to a Stone, we brought them all away and built our little Wharff. The next Morning the Workmen were surpriz'd at Missing the Stones; which were found in our Wharff; Enquiry was made after the Removers; we were discovered & complain'd of; several of us were corrected by our Fathers; and tho' I pleaded the Usefulness of the Work, mine convinc'd me that nothing was useful which was not honest.

I think you may like to know something of his Person & Character. He had an excellent Constitution of Body, was of middle Stature, but well set and very strong. He was ingenious, could draw prettily, was skill'd a little in Music and had a clear pleasing Voice, so that when he play'd Psalm Tunes on his Violin & sung withal as he some times did in an Evening after the Business of the Day was over, it was extreamly agreable to hear. He had a mechanical Genius too, and on occasion was very handy in the Use of other Tradesmen's Tools. But his great Excellence lay in a sound Understanding, and solid Judgment in prudential Matters, both in private & publick Affairs. In the latter indeed he was never employed, the numerous Family he had to educate & the Straitness of his Circumstances, keeping him close to his Trade, but I remember well his being frequently visited by leading People, who consulted him for his Opinion on Affairs of the

---

20. **Tallow Chandler and Sope-Boiler:** Producer of candles and soaps (*sope* was an early spelling of *soap*).
21. **Dying Trade:** The business of dying cloth and other material.
22. **Emmets:** An early term for ants.

Town or of the Church he belong'd to & show'd a good deal of Respect for his Judgment and Advice. He was also much consulted by private Persons about their Affairs when any Difficulty occur'd, & frequently chosen an Arbitrator between contending Parties. At his Table he lik'd to have as often as he could, some sensible Friend or Neighbour, to converse with, and always took care to start some ingenious or useful Topic for Discourse, which might tend to improve the Minds of his Children. By this means he turn'd our Attention to what was good, just, & prudent in the Conduct of Life; and little or no Notice was ever taken of what related to the Victuals on the Table, whether it was well or ill drest, in or out of season, of good or bad flavour, preferable or inferior to this or that other thing of the kind; so that I was bro't up in such a perfect Inattention to those Matters as to be quite Indifferent what kind of Food was set before me; and so unobservant of it, that to this Day, if I am ask'd I can scarce tell, a few Hours after Dinner, what I din'd upon. This has been a Convenience to me in travelling, where my Companions have been sometimes very unhappy for want of a suitable Gratification of their more delicate because better instructed Tastes and Appetites.

My Mother had likewise an excellent Constitution. She suckled all her 10 Children. I never knew either my Father or Mother to have any Sickness but that of which they dy'd, he at 89 & she at 85 Years of age. They lie buried together at Boston, where I some Years since plac'd a Marble stone over their Grave with this Inscription

Josiah Franklin
And Abiah his Wife
Lie here interred.
They lived lovingly together in Wedlock
Fifty-five Years. –
Without an Estate or any gainful Employment,
By constant Labour and Industry,
With God's Blessing,
They maintained a large Family
Comfortably;
And brought up thirteen Children,
And seven Grandchildren
Reputably.
From this Instance, Reader,
Be encouraged to Diligence in thy Calling,
And distrust not Providence.
He was a pious & prudent Man,
She a discreet and virtuous Woman.
Their youngest Son,
In filial Regard to their Memory,
Places this Stone.
J. F. born 1655 – Died 1744. Ætat[23] 89
A. F. born 1667 – died 1752 — 85

23. Ætat: Aged (Latin).

By my rambling Digressions I perceive my self to be grown old. I us'd to write more methodically. But one does not dress for private Company as for a publick Ball. 'Tis perhaps only Negligence.

To return. I continu'd thus employ'd in my Father's Business for two Years, that is till I was 12 Years old; and my Brother John, who was bred to that Business having left my Father, married and set up for himself at Rhodeisland, there was all Appearance that I was destin'd to supply his Place and be a Tallow Chandler. But my Dislike to the Trade continuing, my Father was under Apprehensions that if he did not find one for me more agreable, I should break away and get to Sea, as his Son Josiah had done to his great Vexation. He therefore sometimes took me to walk with him, and see Joiners, Bricklayers, Turners, Braziers,[24] &c. at their Work, that he might observe my Inclination, & endeavour to fix it on some Trade or other on Land. It has ever since been a Pleasure to me to see good Workmen handle their Tools; and it has been useful to me, having learnt so much by it, as to be able to do little jobs my self in my House, when a Workman could not readily be got; & to construct little Machines for my Experiments while the Intention of making the Experiment was fresh & warm in my Mind. My Father at last fix'd upon the Cutler's Trade,[25] and my Uncle Benjamin's Son Samuel who was bred to that Business in London being about that time establish'd in Boston, I was sent to be with him some time on liking. But his Expectations of a Fee with me displeasing my Father, I was taken home again.

From a Child I was fond of Reading, and all the little Money that came into my Hands was ever laid out in Books. Pleas'd with the Pilgrim's Progress,[26] my first Collection was of John Bunyan's Works, in separate little Volumes. I afterwards sold them to enable me to buy R. Burton's Historical Collections; they were small Chapmen's Books and cheap, 40 or 50 in all. My Father's little Library consisted chiefly of Books in polemic Divinity, most of which I read, and have since often regretted, that at a time when I had such a Thirst for Knowledge, more proper Books had not fallen in my Way, since it was now resolv'd I should not be a Clergyman. Plutarch's Lives[27] there was, in which I read abundantly, and I still think that time spent to great Advantage. There was also a Book of Defoe's called an Essay on Projects and another of Dr Mather's[28] call'd Essays to do Good, which perhaps gave me a Turn of Thinking that had an Influence on some of the principal future Events of my Life.

This Bookish Inclination at length determin'd my Father to make me a Printer, tho' he had already one Son, (James) of that Profession. In 1717 my Brother James return'd

---

24. **Joiners . . . Braziers:** A list of common trades: woodworkers, bricklayers, lathe workers, and workers in brass.

25. **Cutler's Trade:** The business of making and selling utensils for eating and serving food.

26. **Pilgrim's Progress:** A tremendously popular book by the English author John Bunyan (1628-1688), *The Pilgrim's Progress* is an allegory chronicling the journey of a man named Christian from the City of Destruction to the Celestial City.

27. **Plutarch's Lives:** Plutarch (c. 46-120), Greek biographer and author of *Parallel Lives* of the noble Greeks and Romans.

28. **Book of Defoe's . . . another of Dr. Mather's:** *An Essay on Projects* (1697), by the English author Daniel Defoe (1660-1731); and Cotton Mather's *Bonifacius: An Essay upon the Good* (1710).

from England with a Press & Letters to set up his Business in Boston. I lik'd it much better than that of my Father, but still had a Hankering for the Sea. To prevent the apprehended Effect of such an Inclination, my Father was impatient to have me bound to my Brother. I stood out some time, but at last was persuaded and signed the Indentures,[29] when I was yet but 12 Years old. I was to serve as an Apprentice till I was 21 Years of Age, only I was to be allow'd Journeyman's Wages[30] during the last Year. In a little time I made great Proficiency in the Business, and became a useful Hand to my Brother. I now had Access to better Books. An Acquaintance with the Apprentices of Booksellers, enabled me sometimes to borrow a small one, which I was careful to return soon & clean. Often I sat up in my Room reading the greatest Part of the Night, when the Book was borrow'd in the Evening & to be return'd early in the Morning lest it should be miss'd or wanted. And after some time an ingenious Tradesman[31] who had a pretty Collection of Books, & who frequented our Printing House, took Notice of me, invited me to his Library, & very kindly lent me such Books as I chose to read. I now took a Fancy to Poetry, and made some little Pieces. My Brother, thinking it might turn to account encourag'd me, & put me on composing two occasional Ballads. One was called the *Light House Tragedy*, & contain'd an Account of the drowning of Capt. Worthilake with his Two Daughters; the other was a Sailor Song on the Taking of *Teach* or Blackbeard the Pirate. They were wretched Stuff, in the Grubstreet Ballad Stile,[32] and when they were printed he sent me about the Town to sell them. The first sold wonderfully, the Event being recent, having made a great Noise. This flatter'd my Vanity. But my Father discourag'd me, by ridiculing my Performances, and telling me Verse-makers were generally Beggars; so I escap'd being a Poet, most probably a very bad one. But as Prose Writing has been a great Use to me in the Course of my Life, and was a principal Means of my Advancement, I shall tell you how in such a Situation I acquir'd what little Ability I have in that Way.

There was another Bookish Lad in the Town, John Collins by Name, with whom I was intimately acquainted. We sometimes disputed, and very fond we were of Argument, & very desirous of confuting one another. Which disputacious Turn, by the way, is apt to become a very bad Habit, making People often extreamly disagreable in Company, by the Contradiction that is necessary to bring it into Practice, & thence, besides souring & spoiling the Conversation, is productive of Disgusts & perhaps Enmities where you may have occasion for Friendship. I had caught it by reading my Father's Books of Dispute about Religion. Persons of good Sense, I have since observ'd, seldom fall into it, except Lawyers, University Men, and Men of all Sorts that have been bred at Edinborough. A Question was once some how or other started between Collins & me, of the Propriety of educating the Female Sex in Learning, & their Abilities for Study. He was of Opinion that it was improper; & that they were naturally unequal to it. I took the contrary Side,

29. **Indentures:** Agreements binding an apprentice to a master.
30. **Journeyman's Wages:** A journeyman was no longer bound by indentures and was paid by the day.
31. **Tradesman:** Mr. Matthew Adams. [Franklin's note.]
32. **Grubstreet Ballad Stile:** In the style of sensational ballads and poems written for quick profits by poor writers, many of whom lived in Grub Street in London during the eighteenth century. The ballads Franklin mentions have not been found.

perhaps a little for Dispute sake. He was naturally more eloquent, had a ready Plenty of Words, and sometimes as I thought bore me down more by his Fluency than by the Strength of his Reasons. As we parted without settling the Point, & were not to see one another again for some time, I sat down to put my Arguments in Writing, which I copied fair & sent to him. He answer'd & I reply'd. Three or four Letters of a Side had pass'd, when my Father happen'd to find my Papers, and read them. Without entring into the Discussion, he took occasion to talk to me about the Manner of my Writing, observ'd that tho' I had the Advantage of my Antagonist in correct Spelling & pointing[33] (which I ow'd to the Printing House) I fell far short in elegance of Expression, in Method and in Perspicuity, of which he convinc'd me by several Instances. I saw the Justice of his Remarks, & thence grew more attentive to the *Manner* in Writing, and determin'd to endeavour at Improvement.

About this time I met with an odd Volume of the Spectator.[34] I had never before seen any of them. I bought it, read it over and over, and was much delighted with it. I thought the Writing excellent, & wish'd if possible to imitate it. With that View, I took some of the Papers, & making short Hints of the Sentiment in each Sentence, laid them by a few Days, and then without looking at the Book, try'd to compleat the Papers again, by expressing each hinted Sentiment at length & as fully as it had been express'd before, in any suitable Words that should come to hand.

Then I compar'd my Spectator with the Original, discover'd some of my Faults & corrected them. But I found I wanted a Stock of Words or a Readiness in recollecting & using them, which I thought I should have acquir'd before that time, if I had gone on making Verses, since the continual Occasion for Words of the same Import but of different Length, to suit the Measure, or of different Sound for the Rhyme, would have laid me under a constant Necessity of searching for Variety, and also have tended to fix that Variety in my Mind, & make me Master of it. Therefore I took some of the Tales & turn'd them into Verse: And after a time, when I had pretty well forgotten the Prose, turn'd them back again. I also sometimes jumbled my Collections of Hints into Confusion, and after some Weeks, endeavour'd to reduce them into the best Order, before I began to form the full Sentences & compleat the Paper. This was to teach me Method in the Arrangement of Thoughts. By comparing my Work afterwards with the original, I discover'd many faults and amended them; but I sometimes had the Pleasure of Fancying that in certain Particulars of small Import, I had been lucky enough to improve the Method or the Language and this encourag'd me to think I might possibly in time come to be a tolerable English Writer, of which I was extreamly ambitious.

My Time for these Exercises & for Reading, was at Night after Work, or before Work began in the Morning; or on Sundays, when I contrived to be in the Printing House alone, evading as much as I could the common Attendance on publick Worship, which

---

33. **pointing:** Punctuation.
34. **Spectator:** A highly regarded London magazine that was concerned with reforming the manners of its readers; published between 1710 and 1712, it featured essays by Joseph Addison (1672–1719) and Richard Steele (1672–1729).

my Father used to exact of me when I was under his Care: – And which indeed I still thought a Duty; tho' I could not, as it seemed to me, afford the Time to practise it.

When about 16 Years of Age, I happen'd to meet with a Book written by one Tryon,[35] recommending a Vegetable Diet. I determined to go into it. My Brother being yet unmarried, did not keep House, but boarded himself & his Apprentices in another Family. My refusing to eat Flesh occasioned an Inconveniency, and I was frequently chid for my singularity. I made my self acquainted with Tryon's Manner of preparing some of his Dishes, such as Boiling Potatoes, or Rice, making Hasty Pudding, & a few others, and then propos'd to my Brother, that if he would give me Weekly half the Money he paid for my Board, I would board my self. He instantly agreed to it, and I presently found that I could save half what he paid me. This was an additional Fund for buying Books: But I had another Advantage in it. My Brother and the rest going from the Printing House to their Meals, I remain'd there alone, and dispatching presently my light Repast, (which often was no more than a Bisket or a Slice of Bread, a Handful of Raisins or a Tart from the Pastry Cook's, and a Glass of Water) had the rest of the Time till their Return, for Study, in which I made the greater Progress from that greater Clearness of Head & quicker Apprehension which usually attend Temperance in Eating & Drinking. And now it was that being on some Occasion made asham'd of my Ignorance in Figures, which I had twice fail'd in learning when at School, I took Cocker's Book of Arithmetick,[36] & went thro' the whole by my self with great Ease. I also read Seller's & Sturmy's Books of Navigation, & became acquainted with the little Geometry they contain, but never proceeded far in that Science. And I read about this Time Locke on Human Understanding and the Art of Thinking by Messrs du Port Royal.[37]

While I was intent on improving my Language, I met with an English Grammar (I think it was Greenwood's)[38] at the End of which there were two little Sketches of the Arts of Rhetoric and Logic, the latter finishing with a Specimen of a Dispute in the Socratic Method. And soon after I procur'd Xenophon's Memorable Things of Socrates,[39] wherein there are many Instances of the same Method. I was charm'd with it, adopted it, dropt my abrupt Contradiction, and positive Argumentation, and put on the humble Enquirer & Doubter. And being then, from reading Shaftsbury & Collins,[40] become a real Doubter

---

35. **Tryon:** Thomas Tryon (1634-1703), the author of *The Way to Health* (1691), which advocated a vegetarian diet and abstinence from tobacco and alcohol.
36. **Cocker's Book of Arithmetick:** Edward Cocker (1631-1676), an English engraver and author of *Arithmetick.* Published the year of his death, the book went through over one hundred editions during the next century.
37. **I also read . . . Messrs du Port Royal:** *An Epitome of the Art of Navigation* (1681), by John Seller (1630-1697); *The Mariner's Magazine: Or Sturmy's Mathematical and Practical Arts* (1699), by Samuel Sturmy (1633-1669); *An Essay Concerning Human Understanding* (1690), by the English philosopher John Locke (1632-1704); and *Logic: Or the Art of Thinking* (1687), by Pierre Nichol (1625?-1695) of Port Royal, a celebrated Benedictine abbey in France.
38. **Greenwood's:** *An Essay towards a Practical English Grammar* (1711), by James Greenwood (d. 1737).
39. **Xenophon's . . . Socrates:** The Greek historian Xenophon (434?-355 BCE) wrote a life of Socrates, which was translated by Edward Bysshe as *The Memorable Things of Socrates* (1712).
40. **Shaftsbury & Collins:** The English philosopher Anthony Ashley Cooper, third Earl of Shaftesbury (1671-1713), was the author of *Characteristics of Men, Manners, Opinons, Times* (1711); Anthony Collins (1676-1729), an English Deist, wrote *A Discourse of Free Thinking* (1713).

in many Points of our Religious Doctrine, I found this Method safest for my self & very embarassing to those against whom I used it, therefore I took a Delight in it, practis'd it continually & grew very artful & expert in drawing People even of superior Knowledge into Concessions the Consequences of which they did not foresee, entangling them in Difficulties out of which they could not extricate themselves, and so obtaining Victories that neither my self nor my Cause always deserved. I continu'd this Method some few Years, but gradually left it, retaining only the Habit of expressing my self in Terms of modest Diffidence, never using when I advance any thing that may possibly be disputed, the Words, *Certainly, undoubtedly,* or any others that give the Air of Positiveness to an Opinion; but rather say, *I conceive,* or *I apprehend* a Thing to be so or so, *It appears to me,* or *I should think it so or so for such & such Reasons,* or *I imagine* it to be so, or *it is so* if *I am not mistaken.* This Habit I believe has been of great Advantage to me, when I have had occasion to inculcate my Opinions & persuade Men into Measures that I have been from time to time engag'd in promoting. And as the chief Ends of Conversation are to *inform,* or to be *informed,* to *please* or to *persuade,* I wish well meaning sensible Men would not lessen their Power of doing Good by a Positive assuming Manner that seldom fails to disgust, tends to create Opposition, and to defeat every one of those Purposes for which Speech was given us, to wit, giving or receiving Information, or Pleasure: For If you would *inform,* a positive dogmatical Manner in advancing your Sentiments, may provoke Contradiction & prevent a candid Attention. If you wish Information & Improvement from the Knowledge of others and yet at the same time express your self as firmly fix'd in your present Opinions, modest sensible Men, who do not love Disputation, will probably leave you undisturb'd in the Possession of your Error; and by such a Manner you can seldom hope to recommend your self in *pleasing* your Hearers, or to persuade those whose Concurrence you desire. Pope says, judiciously,

> *Men should be taught as if you taught them not,*
> *And things unknown propos'd as things forgot,* —

farther recommending it to us,

> *To speak tho' sure, with seeming Diffidence.*[41]

And he might have couple'd with this Line that which he has coupled with another, I think less properly,

> *For want of Modesty is want of Sense.*

If you ask why *less properly,* I must repeat the Lines;

> "Immodest Words admit of *no* Defence;
> "*For* Want of Modesty is Want of Sense."

Now is not *Want of Sense,* (where a Man is so unfortunate as to want it) some Apology for his *Want of Modesty?* and would not the Lines stand more justly thus?

---

41. ***Men . . . Diffidence***: Franklin is loosely quoting from *An Essay on Criticism* (1711), by the English poet Alexander Pope (1688-1744). In the original, the lines read: "Men must be taught as if you taught them not; / And Things unknown propos'd as Things forgot;" and "And speak, tho' sure, with seeming Diffidence."

Immodest Words admit *but this* Defence,
That Want of Modesty is Want of Sense.[42]

This however I should submit to better Judgments.

My Brother had in 1720 or 21, begun to print a Newspaper. It was the second that appear'd in America, & was called *The New England Courant.* The only one before it, was *the Boston News Letter.* I remember his being dissuaded by some of his Friends from the Undertaking, as not likely to succeed, one Newspaper being in their Judgment enough for America. At this time 1771 there are not less than five & twenty. He went on however with the Undertaking, and after having work'd in composing the Types & printing off the Sheets I was employ'd to carry the Papers thro' the Streets to the Customers. He had some ingenious Men among his Friends who amus'd themselves by writing little Pieces for this Paper, which gain'd it Credit, & made it more in Demand; and these Gentlemen often visited us. Hearing their Conversations, and their Accounts of the Approbation their Papers were receiv'd with, I was excited to try my Hand among them. But being still a Boy, & suspecting that my Brother would object to printing any Thing of mine in his Paper if he knew it to be mine, I contriv'd to disguise my Hand, & writing an anonymous Paper I put it in at Night under the Door of the Printing House. It was found in the Morning & communicated to his Writing Friends when they call'd in as Usual. They read it, commented on it in my Hearing, and I had the exquisite Pleasure, of finding it met with their Approbation, and that in their different Guesses at the Author none were named but Men of some Character among us for Learning & Ingenuity. I suppose now that I was rather lucky in my Judges: And that perhaps they were not really so very good ones as I then esteem'd them. Encourag'd however by this, I wrote and convey'd in the same Way to the Press several more Papers, which were equally approv'd, and I kept my Secret till my small Fund of Sense for such Performances was pretty well exhausted, & then I discovered it;[43] when I began to be considered a little more by my Brother's Acquaintance, and in a manner that did not quite please him, as he thought, probably with reason, that it tended to make me too vain. And perhaps this might be one Occasion of the Differences that we began to have about this Time. Tho' a Brother, he considered himself as my Master, & me as his Apprentice; and accordingly expected the same Services from me as he would from another; while I thought he demean'd me too much in some he requir'd of me, who from a Brother expected more Indulgence. Our Disputes were often brought before our Father, and I fancy I was either generally in the right, or else a better Pleader, because the judgment was generally in my favour: But my Brother was passionate & had often beaten me, which I took extreamly amiss;[44] and thinking my Apprenticeship very tedious, I was continually wishing for some Opportunity of shortening it, which at length offered in a manner unexpected.

---

42. **Immodest . . . Sense:** Franklin is quoting not Pope but Wentworth Dillon, Earl of Roscommon (1633?-1685), the author of *Essay on Translated Verse*: "Immodest words admit of no defence, / For want of decency is want of sense."

43. **discovered it:** Early usage for divulged or disclosed it.

44. **amiss:** I fancy his harsh and tyrannical Treatment of me, might be a means of impressing me with that Aversion to arbitrary Power that has stuck to me thro' my whole Life. [Franklin's note.]

One of the Pieces in our News-Paper, on some political Point which I have now forgotten, gave Offence to the Assembly. He was taken up, censur'd and imprison'd for a Month by the Speaker's Warrant, I suppose because he would not discover his Author. I too was taken up & examin'd before the Council; but tho' I did not give them any Satisfaction, they contented themselves with admonishing me, and dismiss'd me; considering me perhaps as an Apprentice who was bound to keep his Master's Secrets. During my Brother's Confinement, which I resented a good deal, notwithstanding our private Differences, I had the Management of the Paper, and I made bold to give our Rulers some Rubs in it, which my Brother took very kindly, while others began to consider me in an unfavourable Light, as a young Genius that had a Turn for Libelling & Satyr. My Brother's Discharge was accompany'd with an Order of the House, (a very odd one) *that James Franklin should no longer print the Paper called the New England Courant.* There was a Consultation held in our Printing House among his Friends what he should do in this Case. Some propos'd to evade the Order by changing the Name of the Paper; but my Brother seeing Inconveniences in that, it was finally concluded on as a better Way, to let it be printed for the future under the Name of *Benjamin Franklin.* And to avoid the Censure of the Assembly that might fall on him, as still printing it by his Apprentice, the Contrivance was, that my old Indenture should be return'd to me with a full Discharge on the Back of it, to be shown on Occasion; but to secure to him the Benefit of my Service I was to sign new Indentures for the Remainder of the Term, which were to be kept private. A very flimsy Scheme it was, but however it was immediately executed, and the Paper went on accordingly under my Name for several Months. At length a fresh Difference arising between my Brother and me, I took upon me to assert my Freedom, presuming that he would not venture to produce the new Indentures. It was not fair in me to take this Advantage, and this I therefore reckon one of the first Errata[45] of my Life: But the Unfairness of it weigh'd little with me, when under the Impressions of Resentment, for the Blows his Passion too often urg'd him to bestow upon me. Tho' He was otherwise not an ill-natur'd Man: Perhaps I was too saucy & provoking.

When he found I would leave him, he took care to prevent my getting Employment in any other Printing-House of the Town, by going round & speaking to every Master, who accordingly refus'd to give me Work. I then thought of going to New York as the nearest Place where there was a Printer: and I was the rather inclin'd to leave Boston, when I reflected that I had already made my self a little obnoxious, to the governing Party; & from the arbitrary Proceedings of the Assembly in my Brother's Case it was likely I might if I stay'd soon bring my self into Scrapes; and farther that my indiscrete Disputations about Religion began to make me pointed at with Horror by good People, as an Infidel or Atheist; I determin'd on the Point: but my Father now siding with my Brother, I was sensible that if I attempted to go openly, Means would be used to prevent me. My Friend Collins therefore undertook to manage a little for me. He agreed with the Captain of a New York Sloop for my Passage, under the Notion of my being a young Acquaintance of his that had got a naughty Girl with Child, whose Friends would compel me to marry

45. **Errata:** A printer's term for typographical errors (Latin).

her, and therefore I could not appear or come away publickly. So I sold some of my Books to raise a little Money, Was taken on board privately, and as we had a fair Wind, in three Days I found my self in New York near 300 Miles from home, a Boy of but 17, without the least Recommendation to or Knowledge of any Person in the Place, and with very little Money in my Pocket.

My Inclinations for the Sea, were by this time worne out, or I might now have gratify'd them. But having a Trade, & supposing my self a pretty good Workman, I offer'd my Service to the Printer of the Place, old Mr. W^{m}. Bradford. He could give me no Employment, having little to do, and Help enough already: But, says he, my Son at Philadelphia has lately lost his principal Hand, Aquila Rose, by Death. If you go thither I believe he may employ you. Philadelphia was 100 Miles farther. I set out, however, in a Boat for Amboy;[46] leaving my Chest and Things to follow me round by Sea. In crossing the Bay we met with a Squall that tore our rotten Sails to pieces, prevented our getting into the Kill, and drove us upon Long Island. In our Way a drunken Dutchman, who was a Passenger too, fell over board; when he was sinking I reach'd thro' the Water to his shock Pate[47] & drew him up so that we got him in again. His Ducking sober'd him a little, & he went to sleep, taking first out of his Pocket a Book which he desir'd I would dry for him. It prov'd to be my old favourite Author Bunyan's Pilgrim's Progress in Dutch, finely printed on good Paper with copper Cuts,[48] a Dress better than I had ever seen it wear in its own Language. I have since Found that it has been translated into most of the Languages of Europe, and suppose it has been more generally read than any other Book except perhaps the Bible. Honest John was the first that I know of who mix'd Narration & Dialogue, a Method of Writing very engaging to the Reader, who in the most interesting Parts finds himself as it were brought into the Company, & present at the Discourse. De foe in his Cruso,[49] his Moll Flanders, Religious Courtship, Family Instructor, & other Pieces, has imitated it with Success. And Richardson has done the same in his Pamela, &c.[50]

When we drew near the Island we found it was at a Place where there could be no Landing, there being a great Surff on the stony Beach. So we dropt Anchor & swung round towards the Shore. Some People came down to the Water Edge & hallow'd to us, as we did to them. But the Wind was so high & the Surff so loud, that we could not hear so as to understand each other. There were Canoes on the Shore, & we made Signs & hallow'd that they should fetch us, but they either did not understand us, or thought it impracticable. So they went away, and Night coming on, we had no Remedy but to wait till the Wind should abate, and in the mean time the Boatman & I concluded to sleep if we could, and so crouded into the Scuttle with the Dutchman who was still wet, and the Spray beating over the Head of our Boat, leak'd thro' to us, so that we were soon almost

46. **Amboy:** Perth Amboy, on the coast of New Jersey.
47. **shock Pate:** A thick head of hair.
48. **copper Cuts:** Engraved illustrations.
49. **De foe in his Cruso** *Robinson Crusoe* (1719), the most famous of the works Franklin mentions by Daniel Defoe (1660-1731).
50. **Richardson . . . in his Pamela, &c.:** *Pamela; or, Virtue Rewarded* (1740), one of a number of popular works by the English novelist Samuel Richardson (1689-1761).

as wet as he. In this Manner we lay all Night with very little Rest. But the Wind abating the next Day, we made a Shift to reach Amboy before Night, having been 30 Hours on the Water without Victuals, or any Drink but a Bottle of filthy Rum: – The Water we sail'd on being salt.

In the Evening I found my self very feverish, & went ill to Bed. But having read somewhere that cold Water drank plentifully was good for a Fever, I follow'd the Prescription, sweat plentifully most of the Night, my Fever left me, and in the Morning crossing the Ferry, proceeded on my journey, on foot, having 50 Miles to Burlington,[51] where I was told I should find Boats that would carry me the rest of the Way to Philadelphia.

It rain'd very hard all the Day, I was thoroughly soak'd, and by Noon a good deal tir'd, so I stopt at a poor Inn, where I staid all Night, beginning now to wish I had never left home. I cut so miserable a Figure too, that I found by the Questions ask'd me I was suspected to be some runaway Servant, and in danger of being taken up on that Suspicion. However I proceeded the next Day, and got in the Evening to an Inn within 8 or 10 Miles of Burlington, kept by one Dr Brown.

He entred into Conversation with me while I took some Refreshment, and finding I had read a little, became very sociable and friendly. Our Acquaintance continu'd as long as he liv'd. He had been, I imagine, an itinerant Doctor, for there was no Town in England, or Country in Europe, of which he could not give a very particular Account. He had some Letters, & was ingenious, but much of an Unbeliever, & wickedly undertook some Years after to travesty the Bible in doggrel Verse as Cotton had done Virgil.[52] By this means he set many of the Facts in a very ridiculous Light, & might have hurt weak minds if his Work had been publish'd: – but it never was. At his House I lay that Night, and the next Morning reach'd Burlington. But had the Mortification to find that the regular Boats were gone, a little before my coming, and no other expected to go till Tuesday, this being Saturday. Wherefore I return'd to an old Woman in the Town of whom I had bought Gingerbread to eat on the Water, & ask'd her Advice; she invited me to lodge at her House till a Passage by Water should offer; & being tired with my foot Travelling, I accepted the Invitation. She understanding I was a Printer, would have had me stay at that Town & follow my Business, being ignorant of the Stock necessary to begin with. She was very hospitable, gave me a Dinner of Ox Cheek with great Goodwill, accepting only of a Pot of Ale in return. And I tho't my self fix'd till Tuesday should come. However walking in the Evening by the Side of the River a Boat came by, which I found was going towards Philadelphia, with several People in her. They took me in, and as there was no Wind, we row'd all the Way; and about Midnight not having yet seen the City, some of the Company were confident we must have pass'd it, and would row no farther, the others knew not where we were, so we put towards the Shore, got into a Creek, landed near an old Fence with the Rails of which we made a Fire, the Night being cold, in October, and there we remain'd till Daylight. Then one of the Company knew the Place to be Cooper's

---

51. **Burlington:** Burlington, New Jersey, northeast of Philadelphia.
52. **as Cotton had done Virgil:** The English poet Charles Cotton (1630-1687) published parodies of the Roman poets Virgil and Lucian.

Creek a little above Philadelphia, which we saw as soon as we got out of the Creek, and arriv'd there about 8 or 9 a Clock, on the Sunday morning, and landed at the Market street Wharff.

I have been the more particular in this Description of my Journey, & shall be so of my first Entry into that City, that you may in your Mind compare such unlikely Beginning with the Figure I have since made there. I was in my working Dress, my best Cloaths being to come round by Sea. I was dirty from my Journey; my Pockets were stuff'd out with Shirts & Stockings; I knew no Soul, nor where to look for Lodging. I was fatigu'd with Travelling, Rowing & Want of Rest. I was very hungry, and my whole Stock of Cash consisted of a Dutch Dollar and about a Shilling in Copper. The latter I gave the People of the Boat for my Passage, who at first refus'd it on Account of my Rowing; but I insisted on their taking it, a Man being sometimes more generous when he has but a little Money than when he has plenty, perhaps thro' Fear of being thought to have but little. Then I walk'd up the Street, gazing about, till near the Market House I met a Boy with Bread. I had made many a Meal on Bread, & inquiring where he got it, I went immediately to the Baker's he directed me to in second Street; and ask'd for Bisket, intending such as we had in Boston, but they it seems were not made in Philadelphia, then I ask'd for a threepenny Loaf, and was told they had none such: so not considering or knowing the Difference of Money & the greater Cheapness nor the Names of his Bread, I bad him give me three pennyworth of any sort. He gave me accordingly three great Puffy Rolls. I was surpriz'd at the Quantity, but took it, and having no Room in my Pockets, walk'd off, with a Roll under each Arm, & eating the other. Thus I went up Market Street as far as fourth Street, passing by the Door of Mr Read, my future Wife's Father, when she standing at the Door saw me, & thought I made as I certainly did a most awkward ridiculous Appearance. Then I turn'd and went down Chestnut Street and part of Walnut Street, eating my Roll all the Way, and coming round found my self again at Market street Wharff, near the Boat I came in, to which I went for a Draught of the River Water, and being fill'd with one of my Rolls, gave the other two to a Woman & her Child that came down the River in the Boat with us and were waiting to go farther. Thus refresh'd I walk'd again up the Street, which by this time had many clean dress'd People in it who were all walking the same Way; I join'd them, and thereby was led into the great Meeting House of the Quakers near the Market. I sat down among them, and after looking round a while & hearing nothing said, being very drowzy thro' Labour & want of Rest the preceding Night, I fell fast asleep, and continu'd so till the Meeting broke up, when one was kind enough to rouse me. This was therefore the first House I was in or slept in, in Philadelphia.[53]

[1771, 1981]

---

53. **Philadelphia:** In the final portion of part one, Franklin describes his early experiences in the city, where he worked in a printing shop; the two years he spent in London; and his return to Philadelphia, where he began his own printing business and married Deborah Read in 1730. Appropriately, given the importance of books in his own life and education, Franklin ends part one with a brief description of his "first Project of a public Nature, that for a Subscription Library."

From Part Two

At the time I establish'd my self in Pensylvania, there was not a good Bookseller's Shop in any of the Colonies to the Southward of Boston. In New-York & Philadelphia the Printers were indeed Stationers, they sold only Paper, &c. Almanacks, Ballads, and a few common School Books. Those who lov'd Reading were oblig'd to send for their Books from England. The Members of the Junto had each a few. We had left the Alehouse where we first met, and hired a Room to hold our Club in. I propos'd that we should all of us bring our Books to that Room, where they would not only be ready to consult in our Conferences, but become a common Benefit, each of us being at Liberty to borrow such as he wish'd to read at home. This was accordingly done, and for some time contented us. Finding the Advantage of this little Collection, I propos'd to render the Benefit from Books more common by commencing a Public Subscription Library. I drew a Sketch of the Plan and Rules that would be necessary, and got a skilful Conveyancer Mr Charles Brockden[1] to put the whole in Form of Articles of Agreement to be subscribed, by which each Subscriber engag'd to pay a certain Sum down for the first Purchase of Books and an annual Contribution for encreasing them. So few were the Readers at that time in Philadelphia, and the Majority of us so poor, that I was not able with great Industry to find more than Fifty Persons, mostly young Tradesmen, willing to pay down for this purpose Forty shillings each, & Ten Shillings per Annum. On this little Fund we began. The Books were imported. The Library was open one Day in the Week for lending them to the Subscribers, on their Promisory Notes to pay Double the Value if not duly returned. The Institution soon manifested its Utility, was imitated by other Towns and in other Provinces, the Librarys were augmented by Donations, Reading became fashionable, and our People having no publick Amusements to divert their Attention from Study became better acquainted with Books, and in a few Years were observ'd by Strangers to be better instructed & more intelligent than People of the same Rank generally are in other Countries.

When we were about to sign the above-mentioned Articles, which were to be binding on us, our Heirs, &c. for fifty Years, Mr Brockden, the Scrivener, said to us, "You are young Men, but it is scarce probable that any of you will live to see the Expiration of the Term fix'd in this Instrument." A Number of us, however, are yet living: But the Instrument was after a few Years rendered null by a Charter that incorporated & gave Perpetuity to the Company.

The Objections, & Reluctances I met with in Soliciting the Subscriptions, made me soon feel the Impropriety of presenting one's self as the Proposer of any useful Project that might be suppos'd to raise one's Reputation in the smallest degree above that of one's Neighbours, when one has need of their Assistance to accomplish that Project. I therefore put my self as much as I could out of sight, and stated it as a Scheme of *a Number of Friends*, who had requested me to go about and propose it to such as they thought Lovers of Reading. In this way my Affair went on more smoothly, and I ever after practis'd it on such Occasions; and from my frequent Successes, can heartily recommend it.

1. **Mr. Charles Brockden:** (1683–1769) Lawyer who drafted legal documents for the transfer of property.

The present little Sacrifice of your Vanity will afterwards be amply repaid. If it remains a while uncertain to whom the Merit belongs, some one more vain than yourself will be encourag'd to claim it, and then even Envy will be dispos'd to do you justice, by plucking those assum'd Feathers, & restoring them to their right Owner.

This Library afforded me the Means of Improvement by constant Study, for which I set apart an Hour or two each Day; and thus repair'd in some Degree the Loss of the Learned Education my Father once intended for me. Reading was the only Amusement I allow'd my self. I spent no time in Taverns, Games, or Frolicks of any kind. And my Industry in my Business continu'd as indefatigable as it was necessary. I was in debt for my Printinghouse, I had a young Family coming on to be educated, and I had to contend with for Business two Printers who were establish'd in the Place before me. My Circumstances however grew daily easier: my original Habits of Frugality continuing. And My Father having among his Instructions to me when a Boy, frequently repeated a Proverb of Solomon, *"Seest thou a Man diligent in his Calling, he shall stand before Kings, he shall not stand before mean Men."*[2] I from thence consider'd Industry as a Means of obtaining Wealth and Distinction, which encourag'd me; tho' I did not think that I should ever literally stand before Kings, which however has since happened. – for I have stood before five, & even had the honour of sitting down with one, the King of Denmark, to Dinner.

We have an English Proverb that says,

> He that would thrive
> Must ask his Wife;

it was lucky for me that I had one as much dispos'd to Industry & Frugality as my self. She assisted me chearfully in my Business, folding & stitching Pamphlets, tending Shop, purchasing old Linen Rags for the Paper-makers, &c &c. We kept no idle Servants, our Table was plain & simple, our Furniture of the cheapest. For instance my Breakfast was a long time Bread & Milk, (no Tea,) and I ate it out of a twopenny earthen Porringer[3] with a Pewter Spoon. But mark how Luxury will enter Families, and make a Progress, in Spite of Principle. Being Call'd one Morning to Breakfast, I found it in a China Bowl with a Spoon of Silver. They had been bought for me without my Knowledge by my Wife, and had cost her the enormous Sum of three and twenty Shillings, for which she had no other Excuse or Apology to make, but that she thought *her* Husband deserv'd a Silver Spoon & China Bowl as well as any of his Neighbours. This was the first Appearance of Plate & China in our House, which afterwards in a Course of Years as our Wealth encreas'd, augmented gradually to several Hundred Pounds in Value.

I had been religiously educated as a Presbyterian; and tho' some of the Dogmas of that Persuasion, such as the Eternal Decrees of God, Election, Reprobation,[4] &c.

---

2. ***"Seest . . . Men"***: Proverbs 22:29.
3. **Porringer:** Early term for a basin used for soup or porridge.
4. **Reprobation:** Early term for predestined to damnation.

appear'd to me unintelligible, others doubtful, & I early absented myself from the Public Assemblies of the Sect, Sunday being my Studying-Day, I never was without some religious Principles; I never doubted, for instance, the Existance of the Deity, that he made the World, & govern'd it by his Providence; that the most acceptable Service of God was the doing Good to Man; that our Souls are immortal; and that all Crime will be punished & Virtue rewarded either here or hereafter; these I esteem'd the Essentials of every Religion, and being to be found in all the Religions we had in our Country I respected them all, tho' with different degrees of Respect as I found them more or less mix'd with other Articles which without any Tendency to inspire, promote or confirm Morality, serv'd principally to divide us & make us unfriendly to one another. This Respect to all, with an Opinion that the worst had some good Effects, induc'd me to avoid all Discourse that might tend to lessen the good Opinion another might have of his own Religion; and as our Province increas'd in People and new Places of worship were continually wanted, & generally erected by voluntary Contribution, my Mite for such purpose, whatever might be the Sect, was never refused.

Tho' I seldom attended any Public Worship, I had still an Opinion of its Propriety, and of its Utility when rightly conducted, and I regularly paid my annual Subscription for the Support of the only Presbyterian Minister or Meeting we had in Philadelphia. He us'd to visit me sometimes as a Friend, and admonish me to attend his Administrations, and I was now and then prevail'd on to do so, once for five Sundays successively. Had he been, *in my Opinion*, a good Preacher perhaps I might have continued, notwithstanding the occasion I had for the Sunday's Leisure in my Course of Study: But his Discourses were chiefly either polemic Arguments, or Explications of the peculiar Doctrines of our Sect, and were all to me very dry, uninteresting and unedifying, since not a single moral Principle was inculcated or enforc'd, their Aim seeming to be rather to make us Presbyterians than good Citizens. At length he took for his Text that Verse of the 4th Chapter of Philippians, *Finally, Brethren, Whatsoever Things are true, honest, just, pure, lovely, or of good report, if there be any virtue, or any praise, think on these Things;*[5] & I imagin'd in a Sermon on such a Text, we could not miss of having some Morality: But he confin'd himself to five Points only as meant by the Apostle, viz. 1. Keeping holy the Sabbath Day. 2. Being diligent in Reading the Holy Scriptures. 3. Attending duly the Publick Worship. 4. Partaking of the Sacrament. 5. Paying a due Respect to God's Ministers. These might be all good Things, but as they were not the kind of good Things that I expected from that Text, I despaired of ever meeting with them from any other, was disgusted, and attended his Preaching no more. I had some Years before compos'd a little Liturgy or Form of Prayer for my own private Use, viz, in 1728. entitled, *Articles of Belief & Acts of Religion.* I return'd to the Use of this, and went no more to the public Assemblies. My Conduct might be blameable, but I leave it without attempting farther to excuse it, my present purpose being to relate Facts, and not to make Apologies for them.

---

5. ***"Finally . . . Things"***: Franklin loosely quotes Philippians 4:8.

It was about this time[6] that I conceiv'd the bold and arduous Project of arriving at moral Perfection. I wish'd to live without committing any Fault at any time; I would conquer all that either Natural Inclination, Custom, or Company might lead me into. As I knew, or thought I knew, what was right and wrong, I did not see why I might not *always* do the one and avoid the other. But I soon found I had undertaken a Task of more Difficulty than I had imagined: While my Care was employ'd in guarding against one Fault, I was often surpriz'd by another. Habit took the Advantage of Inattention. Inclination was sometimes too strong for Reason. I concluded at length, that the mere speculative Conviction that it was our Interest to be compleatly virtuous, was not sufficient to prevent our Slipping, and that the contrary Habits must be broken and good Ones acquired and established, before we can have any Dependance on a steady uniform Rectitude of Conduct. For this purpose I therefore contriv'd the following Method.

In the various Enumerations of the moral Virtues I had met with in my Reading, I found the Catalogue more or less numerous, as different Writers included more or fewer Ideas under the same Name. Temperance, for Example, was by some confin'd to Eating & Drinking, while by others it was extended to mean the moderating every other Pleasure, Appetite, Inclination or Passion, bodily or mental, even to our Avarice & Ambition. I propos'd to myself, for the sake of Clearness, to use rather more Names with fewer Ideas annex'd to each, than a few Names with more Ideas; and I included under Thirteen Names of Virtues all that at that time occurr'd to me as necessary or desirable, and annex'd to each a short Precept, which fully express'd the Extent I gave to its Meaning.

These Names of Virtues with their Precepts were

1. TEMPERANCE.

Eat not to Dulness

Drink not to Elevation.

2. SILENCE.

Speak not but what may benefit others or your self. Avoid trifling Conversation.

3. ORDER.

Let all your Things have their Places. Let each Part of your Business have its Time.

4. RESOLUTION.

Resolve to perform what you ought. Perform without fail what you resolve.

5. FRUGALITY.

Make no Expence but to do good to others or yourself: i.e. Waste nothing.

6. INDUSTRY.

Lose no Time. Be always employ'd in something useful. Cut off all unnecessary Actions.

7. SINCERITY.

Use no hurtful Deceit.

Think innocently and justly; and, if you speak; speak accordingly.

---

6. **It was about this time:** Around 1730, the year Franklin began his own business and married Deborah Read.

8. JUSTICE.

Wrong none, by doing Injuries or omitting the Benefits that are your Duty.

9. MODERATION.

Avoid Extreams. Forbear resenting Injuries so much as you think they deserve.

10. CLEANLINESS.

Tolerate no Uncleanness in Body, Cloaths or Habitation.

11. TRANQUILITY.

Be not disturbed at Trifles, or at Accidents common or unavoidable.

12. CHASTITY.

Rarely use Venery but for Health or Offspring; Never to Dulness, Weakness, or the Injury of your own or another's Peace or Reputation.

13. HUMILITY.

Imitate Jesus and Socrates.

My intention being to acquire the *Habitude*[7] of all these Virtues, I judg'd it would be well not to distract my Attention by attempting the whole at once, but to fix it on one of them at a time, and when I should be Master of that, then to proceed to another, and so on till I should have gone thro' the thirteen. And as the previous Acquisition of some might facilitate the Acquisition of certain others, I arrang'd them with that View as they stand above. *Temperance* first, as it tends to procure that Coolness & Clearness of Head, which is so necessary where constant Vigilance was to be kept up, and Guard maintained, against the unremitting Attraction of ancient Habits, and the Force of perpetual Temptations. This being acquir'd & establish'd, *Silence* would be more easy, and my Desire being to gain Knowledge at the same time that I improv'd in Virtue, and considering that in Conversation it was obtain'd rather by the Use of the Ears than of the Tongue, & therefore wishing to break a Habit I was getting into of Prattling, Punning & Joking, which only made me acceptable to trifling Company, I gave *Silence* the second Place. This, and the next, *Order*, I expected would allow me more Time for attending to my Project and my Studies; RESOLUTION once become habitual, would keep me firm in my Endeavours to obtain all the subsequent Virtues; *Frugality* & *Industry*, by freeing me from my remaining Debt, & producing Affluence & Independance would make more easy the Practice of *Sincerity* and *Justice*, &c. &c.. Conceiving then that agreeable to the Advice of Pythagoras in his Golden Verses,[8] daily Examination would be necessary, I contriv'd the following Method for conducting that Examination.

I made a little Book in which I allotted a Page for each of the Virtues. I rul'd each Page with red Ink so as to have seven Columns, one for each Day of the Week, marking each

---

7. ***Habitude***: Habitual tendency or way of behaving.

8. **Advice of Pythagoras in his Golden Verses:** Nicholas Rowe (1674–1718) translated *The Golden Verses of Pythagoras* (1732), a Greek philosopher of the sixth century BCE. Franklin indicated that the lines directing such daily self-examination should be inserted in a note; he evidently wished to include at least part of a passage beginning: "Let not the stealing God of Sleep surprize, / Nor creep in Slumbers on thy weary Eyes, / Ere ev'ry Action of the former Day, / Strictly thou dost, and righteously survey."

Column with a Letter for the Day. I cross'd these Columns with thirteen red Lines, marking the Beginning of each Line with the first Letter of one of the Virtues, on which Line & in its proper Column I might mark by a little black Spot every Fault I found upon Examination, to have been committed respecting that Virtue upon that Day.

FORM OF THE PAGES

TEMPERANCE							
Eat not to Dulness. *Drink not to Elevation.*							
	S	M	T	W	T	F	S
T							
S	••	•		•		•	
O	•	•	•		•	•	•
R			•			•	
F		•			•		
I			•				
S							
J							
M							
Cl.							
T							
Ch							
H							

I determined to give a Week's strict Attention to each of the Virtues successively. Thus in the first Week my great Guard was to avoid every the least Offence against Temperance, leaving the other Virtues to their ordinary Chance, only marking every Evening the Faults of the Day. Thus if in the first Week I could keep my first Line marked T clear of Spots, I suppos'd the Habit of that Virtue so much strengthen'd and its opposite weaken'd, that I might venture extending my Attention to include the next, and for the following Week keep both Lines clear of Spots. Proceeding thus to the last, I could go thro' a Course compleat in Thirteen Weeks, and four Courses in a Year. And like him who having a Garden to weed, does not attempt to eradicate all the bad Herbs at once, which would exceed his Reach and his Strength, but works on one of the Beds at a time, & having accomplish'd the first proceeds to a second; so I should have, (I hoped) the encouraging Pleasure of seeing on my Pages the Progress I made in Virtue, by clearing successively my Lines of their Spots, till in the End by a Number of Courses, I should be happy in viewing a clean Book after a thirteen Weeks daily Examination.

This my little Book had for its Motto these Lines from *Addison's Cato*;[9]

Here will I hold: If there is a Pow'r above us,
(And that there is, all Nature cries aloud
Thro' all her Works) he must delight in Virtue,
And that which he delights in must be happy.

Another from *Cicero.*[10]

O Vitae Philosophia Dux! O Virtutum indagatrix, expultrixque vitiorum! Unus dies bene, & ex preceptis tuis actus, peccanti immortalitati est anteponendus.

Another from the Proverbs of Solomon speaking of Wisdom or Virtue;

Length of Days is in her right hand, and in her Left Hand Riches and Honours; Her Ways are Ways of Pleasantness, and all her Paths are Peace. III, 16, 17.

And conceiving God to be the Fountain of Wisdom, I thought it right and necessary to solicit his Assistance for obtaining it; to this End I form'd the following little Prayer, which was prefix'd to my Tables of Examination; for daily Use.

O Powerful Goodness! bountiful Father! merciful Guide! Increase in me that Wisdom which discovers my truest Interests; Strengthen my Resolutions to perform what that Wisdom dictates, Accept my kind Offices to thy other Children, as the only Return in my Power for thy continual Favours to me.

I us'd also sometimes a little Prayer which I took from *Thomson's* Poems.[11] viz

Father of Light and Life, thou Good supreme,
O teach me what is good, teach me thy self!
Save me from Folly, Vanity and Vice,
From every low Pursuit, and fill my Soul
With Knowledge, conscious Peace, & Virtue pure,
Sacred, substantial, neverfading Bliss!

---

9. ***Addison's Cato***: English author and essayist Joseph Addison (1672–1719), from his *Cato: A Tragedy* (1713), 5.1.15–18.
10. ***Cicero***: Roman philosopher and orator Marcus Tullius Cicero (106–43 BCE), from his *Tusculan Disputations.* Franklin omitted several lines from the passage; the lines he quotes are translated: "O Philosophy, leader of life! O seeker of virtue, and critic of vice! From your teachings, a single day of good is preferred to an eternity of sin."
11. ***Thomson's* Poems**: English poet James Thomson (1700–1748); the quotation is from "Winter," lines 218–23, in *The Seasons* (1726).

The Precept of *Order* requiring that *every Part of my Business should have its allotted Time*, one Page in my little Book contain'd the following Scheme of Employment for the Twenty-four Hours of a natural Day,

The Morning Question, What Good Shall I do this Day?	5	Rise, wash, and address *Powerful Goodness*; contrive Day's Business and take the Resolution of the day; prosecute the present Study: and breakfast?
	6	
	7	
	8	Work.
	9	
	10	
	11	
	12	Read, or overlook my Accounts, and dine.
	1	
	2	Work.
	3	
	4	
	5	
Evening Question, What Good have I done to day?	6	Put Things in Their Places, Supper, Musick, or Diversion, or Conversation, Examination of the Day.
	7	
	8	
	9	
	10	Sleep –
	11	
	12	
	1	
	2	
	3	
	4	

I enter'd upon the Execution of this Plan for Self Examination, and continu'd it with occasional Intermissions for some time. I was surpriz'd to find myself so much fuller of Faults than I had imagined, but I had the Satisfaction of seeing them diminish. To avoid the Trouble of renewing now & then my little Book, which by scraping out the Marks on the Paper of old Faults to make room for new Ones in a new Course, became full of Holes: I transferr'd my Tables & Precepts to the Ivory Leaves of a Memorandum Book, on which the Lines were drawn with red Ink that made a durable Stain, and on those Lines I mark'd my Faults with a black Lead Pencil, which Marks I could easily wipe out with a wet Sponge. After a while I went thro' one Course only in a Year, and afterwards only one in several Years; till at length I omitted them entirely, being employ'd in Voyages & Business abroad with a Multiplicity of Affairs, that interfered. But I always carried my little Book with me. My Scheme of ORDER, gave me the most Trouble, and I found, that tho' it might be practicable where a Man's Business was such as to leave him the Disposition of his Time, that of a Journey-man Printer for instance, it was not possible to be exactly observ'd by a Master, who must mix with the World, and often receive People of Business at their own Hours. *Order* too, with regard to Places for Things, Papers, &c. I found extreamly difficult to acquire. I had not been early accustomed to it, & having an exceeding good Memory, I was not so sensible of the Inconvenience attending Want of Method. This Article therefore cost me so much painful Attention & my Faults in it vex'd me so much, and I made so little Progress in Amendment, & had such frequent Relapses, that I was almost ready to give up the Attempt, and content my self with a faulty Character in that respect. Like the Man who in buying an Ax of a Smith my Neighbour, desired to have the whole of its Surface as bright as the Edge; the Smith consented to grind it bright for him if he would turn the Wheel. He turn'd while the Smith press'd the broad Face of the Ax hard & heavily on the Stone, which made the Turning of it very fatiguing. The Man came every now & then from the Wheel to see how the Work went on; and at length would take his Ax as it was without farther Grinding. No, says the Smith, Turn on, turn on; we shall have it bright by and by; as yet 'tis only speckled. Yes, says the Man; but – *I think I like a speckled Ax best.* And I believe this may have been the Case with many who having for want of some such Means as I employ'd found the Difficulty of obtaining good, & breaking bad Habits, in other Points of Vice & Virtue, have given up the Struggle, & concluded that *a speckled Ax was best.* For something that pretended to be Reason was every now and then suggesting to me, that such extream Nicety as I exacted of my self might be a kind of Foppery in Morals, which if it were known would make me ridiculous; that a perfect Character might be attended with the Inconvenience of being envied and hated; and that a benevolent Man should allow a few Faults in himself, to keep his Friends in Countenance. In Truth I found myself incorrigible with respect to *Order*; and now I am grown old, and my Memory bad, I feel very sensibly the want of it. But on the whole, tho' I never arrived at the Perfection I had been so ambitious of obtaining, but fell far short of it, yet I was by the Endeavour made a better and a happier Man than I otherwise should have been, if I had not attempted it; As those who aim at perfect Writing by imitating the engraved Copies, tho' they never reach the wish'd for Excellence of those Copies, their Hand is mended by the Endeavour, and is tolerable while it continues fair & legible.

And it may be well my Posterity should be informed, that to this little Artifice, with the Blessing of God, their Ancestor ow'd the constant Felicity of his Life down to his 79th Year in which this is written. What Reverses may attend the Remainder is in the Hand of Providence: But if they arrive the Reflection on past Happiness enjoy'd ought to help his Bearing them with more Resignation. To *Temperance* he ascribes his long-continu'd Health, & what is still left to him of a good Constitution. To *Industry* and *Frugality* the early Easiness of his Circumstances, & Acquisition of his Fortune, with all that Knowledge which enabled him to be an useful Citizen, and obtain'd for him some Degree of Reputation among the Learned. To *Sincerity & Justice* the Confidence of his Country, and the honourable Employs it conferr'd upon him. And to the joint Influence of the whole Mass of the Virtues, even in their imperfect State he was able to acquire them, all that Evenness of Temper, & that Chearfulness in Conversation which makes his Company still sought for, & agreable even to his younger Acquaintance. I hope therefore that some of my Descendants may follow the Example & reap the Benefit.

It will be remark'd that, tho' my Scheme was not wholly without Religion there was in it no mark of any of the distinguishing Tenets of any particular Sect. I had purposely avoided them; for being fully persuaded of the Utility and Excellency of my Method, and that it might be serviceable to People in all Religions, and intending some time or other to publish it, I would not have any thing in it that should prejudice any one of any Sect against it. I purposed writing a little Comment on each Virtue, in which I would have shown the Advantages of possessing it, & the Mischiefs attending its opposite Vice; and I should have called my Book the ART *of Virtue*, because it would have shown the *Means & Manner* of obtaining Virtue; which would have distinguish'd it from the mere Exhortation to be good, that does not instruct & indicate the Means; but is like the Apostle's Man of verbal Charity, who only, without showing to the Naked & the Hungry *how* or where they might get Cloaths or Victuals, exhorted them to be fed & clothed. *James* II, 15, 16.[12]

But it so happened that my Intention of writing & publishing this Comment was never fulfilled. I did indeed, from time to time put down short Hints of the Sentiments, Reasonings, &c. to be made use of in it; some of which I have still by me: But the necessary close Attention to private Business in the earlier part of Life, and public Business since, have occasioned my postponing it. For it being connected in my Mind with a *great and extensive Project* that required the whole Man to execute, and which an unforeseen Succession of Employs prevented my attending to, it has hitherto remain'd unfinish'd.

In this Piece it was my Design to explain and enforce this Doctrine, that vicious Actions are not hurtful because they are forbidden, but forbidden because they are hurtful, the Nature of Man alone consider'd: That it was therefore every ones Interest to be virtuous, who wish'd to be happy even in this World. And I should from this Circumstance, there being always in the World a Number of rich Merchants, Nobility, States and Princes, who have need of honest Instruments for the Management of their Affairs, and such being so rare, have endeavoured to convince young Persons, that no Qualities were so likely to make a poor Man's Fortune as those of Probity & Integrity.

My List of Virtues contain'd at first but twelve: But a Quaker Friend having kindly inform'd me that I was generally thought proud; that my Pride show'd itself frequently in Conversation; that I was not content with being in the right when discussing any Point, but was overbearing & rather insolent; of which he convinc'd me by mentioning several Instances; – I determined endeavouring to cure myself if I could of this Vice or Folly among the rest, and I added *Humility* to my List, giving an extensive Meaning to

---

12. ***James* II, 15, 16:** The passage in James 2:15–16 reads: "If a brother or sister be naked, and destitute of daily food, And one of you say unto them, Depart in peace, be ye warmed and filled; notwithstanding ye give them not those things which are needful to the body; what doth it profit?"

the Word. I cannot boast of much Success in acquiring the *Reality* of this Virtue; but I had a good deal with regard to the *Appearance* of it. I made it a Rule to forbear all direct Contradiction to the Sentiments of others, and all positive Assertion of my own. I even forbid myself agreable to the old Laws of our Junto, the Use of every Word or Expression in the Language that imported a fix'd Opinion; such as *certainly, undoubtedly,* &c. and I adopted instead of them, *I conceive, I apprehend,* or *I imagine* a thing to be so or so, or it so appears to me at present. When another asserted something that I thought an Error, I deny'd my self the Pleasure of contradicting him abruptly, and of showing immediately some Absurdity in his Proposition; and in answering I began by observing that in certain Cases or Circumstances his Opinion would be right, but that in the present case there *appear'd* or *seem'd* to me some Difference, &c. I soon found the Advantage of this Change in my Manners. The Conversations I engag'd in went on more pleasantly. The modest way in which I propos'd my Opinions, procur'd them a readier Reception and less Contradiction; I had less Mortification when I was found to be in the wrong, and I more easily prevail'd with others to give up their Mistakes & join with me when I happen'd to be in the right. And this Mode, which I at first put on, with some violence to natural Inclination, became at length so easy & so habitual to me, that perhaps for these Fifty Years past no one has ever heard a dogmatical Expression escape me. And to this Habit (after my Character of Integrity) I think it principally owing, that I had early so much Weight with my Fellow Citizens, when I proposed new Institutions, or Alterations in the old; and so much Influence in public Councils when I became a Member. For I was but a bad Speaker, never eloquent, subject to much Hesitation in my choice of Words, hardly correct in Language, and yet I generally carried my Points.

In reality there is perhaps no one of our natural Passions so hard to subdue as *Pride.* Disguise it, struggle with it, beat it down, stifle it, mortify it as much as one pleases, it is still alive, and will every now and then peep out and show itself. You will see it perhaps often in this History. For even if I could conceive that I had compleatly overcome it, I should probably be proud of my Humility.

Thus far written at Passy 1784

[1784, 1981]

Franklin through a Modern Lens

BENJAMIN FRANKLIN is a national icon, one of the most familiar figures in the history and literature of the United States. Images of Franklin also abound in American mythology and popular culture, from the man of science trailing his famous kite to the most fatherly of the Founding Fathers – the elderly statesman featured on the hundred dollar bill, the largest denomination in circulation in the United States. Indeed, although he retired from business to devote the last half of his long life to public service, Franklin's *Autobiography* stands as the classic "rags-to-riches" story, seemingly the very embodiment of the American dream. Appropriately, the publication in 1868 of the first complete edition of the *Autobiography* caught the attention of another national icon and American success story, Mark Twain. Like Franklin, Twain began his career as a printer and journalist, and like Franklin – though not all readers recognized such elements in his *Autobiography* – Twain was a consummate humorist, ironist, and satirist. Certainly, those qualities were evident in the columns, or "Memoranda," Twain wrote for a successful monthly magazine, the *Galaxy*, between May 1870 and April 1871. The popular columns included humorous anecdotes, satirical commentaries on culture and society, and short reviews like "The Late Benjamin Franklin." Twain's complex response to Franklin's example, maxims, and life story may be compared with that of the editor of the 1868 edition, John Bigelow,

Portrait of Franklin on the Hundred Dollar Bill

This engraving was first used on the hundred dollar bill in 1918. The back of the bill features Independence Hall, where Franklin participated in the creation of both the Declaration of Independence and the Constitution of the United States.

who urged "the rising generation of Americans" to "study the lessons of humility, economy, industry, toleration, charity, and patriotism which are made so captivating in this 'Autobiography.'" The text of "The Late Benjamin Franklin" is taken from its first printing in the *Galaxy*, July 1870.

Mark Twain

[1835-1910]

The Late Benjamin Franklin

[Never put off till to-morrow what you can do day after to-morrow just as well.[1]
– B. F.]

This party was one of those persons whom they call Philosophers. He was twins, being born simultaneously in two different houses in the city of Boston. These houses remain unto this day, and have signs upon them worded in accordance with the facts. The signs are considered well enough to have, though not necessary, because the inhabitants points out the two birth-places to the stranger anyhow, and sometimes as often as several times in the same day. The subject of this memoir was of a vicious disposition, and early prostituted his talents to the invention of maxims and aphorisms calculated to inflict suffering upon the rising generation of all subsequent ages. His simplest acts, also, were contrived with a view to their being held up for the emulation of boys forever – boys who might otherwise have been happy. It was in this spirit that he became the son of a soap-boiler; and probably for no other reason than that the efforts of all future boys who tried to be anything might be looked upon with suspicion unless they were the sons of soap-boilers. With a malevolence which is without parallel in history, he would work all day and then sit up nights and let on to be studying algebra by the light of a smouldering fire, so that all other boys might have to do that also or else have Benjamin Franklin thrown up to them. Not satisfied with these proceedings, he had a fashion of living wholly on bread and water, and studying astronomy at meal time – a thing which has brought affliction to millions of boys since, whose fathers had read Franklin's pernicious biography.

---

1. **Never . . . well:** Ironic rewording of a common English proverb, "Never put off till tomorrow what you can do today."

His maxims were full of animosity toward boys. Nowadays a boy cannot follow out a single natural instinct without tumbling over some of those everlasting aphorisms and hearing from Franklin on the spot. If he buys two cents' worth of peanuts, his father says, "Remember what Franklin has said, my son – 'A groat a day's a penny a year;' " and the comfort is all gone out of those peanuts. If he wants to spin his top when he is done work, his father quotes, "Procrastination is the thief of time." If he does a virtuous action, he never gets anything for it, because "Virtue is its own reward." And that boy is hounded to death and robbed of his natural rest, because Franklin said once in one of his inspired flights of malignity –

> Early to bed and early to rise
> Make a man healthy and wealthy and wise.

As if it were any object to a boy to be healthy and wealthy and wise on such terms. The sorrow that that maxim has cost me through my parents' experimenting on me with it, tongue cannot tell. The legitimate result is my present state of general debility, indigence, and mental aberration. My parents used to have me up before nine o'clock in the morning, sometimes, when I was a boy. If they had let me take my natural rest, where would I have been now? Keeping store, no doubt, and respected by all.

And what an adroit old adventurer the subject of this memoir was! In order to get a chance to fly his kite on Sunday, he used to hang a key on the string and let on to be fishing for lightning. And a guileless public would go home chirping about the "wisdom" and the "genius" of the hoary Sabbath-breaker. If anybody caught him playing "mumble-peg"[2] by himself, after the age of sixty, he would immediately appear to be ciphering out how the grass grew – as if it was any of his business. My grandfather knew him well, and he says Franklin was always fixed – always ready. If a body, during his old age, happened on him unexpectedly when he was catching flies, or making mud pies, or sliding on a cellar-door, he would immediately look wise, and rip out a maxim, and walk off with his nose in the air and his cap turned wrong side before, trying to appear absent-minded and eccentric. He was a hard lot.

He invented a stove[3] that would smoke your head off in four hours by the clock. One can see the almost devilish satisfaction he took in it, by his giving it his name.

---

2. **"mumble-peg":** A boy's game in which the players throw or flip a jackknife in various ways so that it sticks in the ground. The winner drives a peg into the ground, which the loser must root out using only his teeth.

3. **stove:** The Franklin stove, a free-standing, cast-iron fireplace. Franklin originally designed it so that the smoke came out the bottom, believing it would therefore produce more heat. Instead, the smoke frequently smothered the fire and filled the room.

He was always proud of telling how he entered Philadelphia, for the first time, with nothing in the world but two shillings in his pocket and four rolls of bread under his arm. But really, when you come to examine it critically, it was nothing. Anybody could have done it.

To the subject of this memoir belongs the honor of recommending the army to go back to bows and arrows in place of bayonets and muskets. He observed, with his customary force, that the bayonet was very well, under some circumstances, but that he doubted whether it could be used with accuracy at long range.

Benjamin Franklin did a great many notable things for his country, and made her young name to be honored in many lands as the mother of such a son. It is not the idea of this memoir to ignore that or cover it up. No; the simple idea of it is to snub those pretentious maxims of his, which he worked up with a great show of originality out of truisms that had become wearisome platitudes as early as the dispersion from Babel;[4] and also to snub his stove, and his military inspirations, his unseemly endeavor to make himself conspicuous when he entered Philadelphia, and his flying his kite and fooling away his time in all sorts of such ways, when he ought to have been foraging for soap-fat, or constructing candles. I merely desired to do away with somewhat of the prevalent calamitous idea among heads of families that Franklin *acquired* his great genius by working for nothing, studying by moonlight, and getting up in the night instead of waiting till morning like a Christian, and that this programme, rigidly inflicted, will make a Franklin of every father's fool. It is time these gentlemen were finding out that these execrable eccentricities of instinct and conduct are only the *evidences* of genius, not the *creators* of it. I wish I had been the father of my parents long enough to make them comprehend this truth, and thus prepare them to let their son have an easier time of it. When I was a child I had to boil soap, notwithstanding my father was wealthy, and I had to get up early and study geometry at breakfast, and peddle my own poetry, and do everything just as Franklin did, in the solemn hope that I would be a Franklin some day. And here I am.

[1870]

4. **Babel:** In Genesis 11:1–9, the townspeople of Babel attempt to build a tower to reach heaven. God thwarts the plan by causing the languages of the builders to be mutually incomprehensible.

Elizabeth Ashbridge

[1713-1755]

Elizabeth Ashbridge was born Elizabeth Sampson in Middlewich, in the county of Cheshire, England, in 1713. Most of what is known about her life is contained in her autobiography. She was raised in the Anglican Church by her parents, Thomas and Mary Sampson. Her father, a ship's surgeon, was frequently away from home, and Ashbridge was educated primarily by her devout mother. "In my very Infancy, I had an awful regard for religion & a great love for religious people, particularly the Ministers," Ashbridge later recalled, "and sometimes wept with Sorrow, that I was not a boy that I might have been one." At the age of fourteen and to the distress of her parents, she eloped with an impoverished weaver who died five months later. Thomas Sampson refused to allow his daughter to return to the family home, so Ashbridge went to live with a Quaker relative in Dublin.

Ashbridge ultimately discovered her own calling as a Quaker minister and preacher in America. Agreeing to terms of indentured servitude in order to pay for her passage, she arrived in New York City in 1732. According to her later account, Ashbridge initially endured great hardship at the hands of a cruel master. But she managed to save enough money to buy herself out of her indenture and began to earn a living as a seamstress. She then entered into what Ashbridge described as yet another "cruel Servitude," her marriage to a man she identified only as Sullivan, who "fell in Love with me for my Dancing." After several years of spiritual struggle in her unhappy marriage, Ashbridge abandoned the Anglican Church and

bedfordstmartins.com/ americanlit *for research links on Ashbridge*

Quaker Meeting in Philadelphia

This undated wood engraving illustrates one of the reasons other Protestant denominations were so hostile to the Quakers – their emphasis on the equality of women, including the right of women like Elizabeth Ashbridge not only to speak in meetings but also to preach the Gospel.

became increasingly devoted to the religion of the Quakers, or the Society of Friends. Despite her husband's violent objections, she became a Quaker minister in 1738. Sullivan deserted her and joined the military. He died two years later, after writing her that he had also become a Quaker. Free of her unhappy marriage, Ashbridge maintained herself by keeping a school, even as she began to earn a reputation as a Quaker preacher. In 1746, she married Aaron Ashbridge (1712-1776), a fellow Quaker, and they evidently enjoyed a happy relationship based on their mutual interests and Aaron's support of Ashbridge's calling as a preacher. While on a missionary tour of England and Ireland, she died in County Carlow, Ireland, in 1755.

Some Account of the Fore Part of the Life of Elizabeth Ashbridge. Ashbridge's vivid account of her eventful life and religious experiences is among the earliest autobiographies written by a woman. Just as her involvement in the Society of Friends allowed her to become a preacher, a role denied to women in virtually all other Christian denominations, the notoriety of her preaching evidently encouraged Ashbridge to write and ultimately led to the publication of her spiritual autobiography, a genre traditionally associated with men. In describing the hardships and spiritual struggles that culminated in her surrender to God and entry into the Quaker community, Ashbridge implicitly challenged both male authority and traditional conceptions of proper female behavior. At the opening of the work, she explains:

> My Life being attended with many uncommon Occurences, some of which I thought disobedience brought upon myself, and others I believe were for my Good, I therefore thought proper to make some remarks on the Dealings of Divine Goodness to me, and have often had cause with David to say, it was good for me that I have been afflicted &c. and most earnestly I desire that whosover reads the following lines may take warning and shun the Evils that I have thro' the Deceitfulness of Satan been drawn into.

The "uncommon Occurences" included her early first marriage and almost immediate widowhood, a harsh term of indentured servitude in colonial America, and the difficulties of her second marriage to a man who was unsympathetic to her efforts to find spiritual fulfillment. The autobiography ends with his death in 1740, though it is not clear when Ashbridge wrote her account. In 1774, nearly twenty years after her death, her third husband, Aaron Ashbridge, arranged for the publication of the work in England, where it appeared under the full title *Some Account of the Fore Part of the Life of Elizabeth Ashbridge, who died in Truth's service at the house of Robert Lecky at Kilnock in the County of Carlow Ireland; the 16th of 5th mo. 1755. Written by her own Hand many years ago.* The account subsequently went through several editions in the eighteenth and nineteenth centuries and was widely read by Quakers in England and the United States, where it was published in 1807. The following selection begins shortly after her second marriage, as Ashbridge begins a journey from New Jersey to visit relatives in Pennsylvania. The selection is taken from Daniel B. Shea's authoritative edition, based on early copies of Ashbridge's manuscript, which was published in *Journeys in New Worlds: Early American Women's Narratives*, edited by William L. Andrews (1990).

From SOME ACCOUNT OF THE FORE PART OF THE LIFE OF ELIZABETH ASHBRIDGE

I now began to think of my Relations in Pennsylvania whom I had not yet seen; and having a great Desire that way, Got Leave of my Husband to go & also a Certificate from the Priest on Long Island in order that if I made any stay, I might be receiv'd as a Member wherever I came; Then Setting out, my husband bore me Company to the Blazing Star Ferry, saw me Safe over & then returned. On the way near a place called Maidenhead [New Jersey] I fell from my horse & I was Disabled from Traveling for some time: In the interval I abode at the house of an Honest Like Dutchman, who with his wife were very kind to me, & tho' they had much trouble going to the Doctor and waiting upon me, (for I was Several Days unable to help my self) yet would have nothing for it (which I thought Exceeding kind) but Charged me if ever I came that way again to call and Lodge there. I mention this because by and by I shall have occasion to remark this Place again.

Hence I came to Trenton [New Jersey] Ferry, where I met with no small Mortification upon hearing that my Relations were Quakers, & what was the worst of all my Aunt a Preacher. I was Sorry to hear it, for I was Exceedingly prejudiced against these People & have often wondered with what face they Could Call them Selves Christians. I Repented my Coming and had a mind to have turned back. At Last I Concluded to go & see them since I was so far on my journey, but Expected little Comfort from my Visit. But see how God brings unforeseen things to Pass, for by my going there I was brought to my Knowledge of his Truth. I went from Trenton to Philadelphia by Water, thence to my Uncle's on Horseback, where I met with very kind reception; for tho' my Uncle was dead and my Aunt married again, yet both her husband and She received me in a very kind manner.

I had not been there three Hours before I met with a Shock, & my opinion began to alter with respect to these People. For seeing a Book lying on the Table (& being much for reading) I took it up: My Aunt Observing said, "Cousin that is a Quakers' Book," for Perceiving I was not a Quaker, I suppose she thought I would not like it: I made her no answer but revolving in my mind, "what can these People write about, for I have heard that they Deny the Scriptures & have no other bible but George Fox's Journal,[1] & Deny all

1. George Fox's Journal: Fox (1624–1691) was an English religious leader who founded the Society of Friends, known as the Quakers. His *Journal* (1694) recounted his spiritual experiences and became a guidebook and source of inspiration for Quakers.

the holy Ordinances?" So resolved to read, but had not read two Pages before my very heart burned within me and Tears Issued from my Eyes, which I was Afraid would be seen; therefore with the Book (Saml. Crisp's Two Letters[2]) I walked into the garden, sat Down, and the piece being Small, read it through before I went in; but Some Times was forced to Stop to Vent my Tears, my heart as it were uttering these involuntary Expressions; "my God must I (if ever I come to the true knowledge of thy Truth) be of this man's Opinion, who has sought thee as I have done & join with these People that a few hours ago I preferred the Papists before? O thou, the God of my Salvation & of my Life, who hast in an abundant manner manifested thy Long Suffering & tender Mercy, Redeeming me as from the Lowest Hell, a Monument of thy grace: Lord, my soul beseecheth thee to Direct me in the right way & keep me from Error, & then According to thy Covenant, I'll think nothing too near to Part with for thy name's Sake. If these things be so, Oh! happy People thus beloved of God."

After I came a little to my Self again I washed my face least any in the House should perceive I had been weeping. But this night got but Little Sleep, for the old Enemy began to Suggest that I was one of those that wavered & was not Steadfast in the faith, advancing several Texts of Scripture against me & them, as, in the Latter Days there should be those that would deceive the very Elect: & these were they, & that I was in danger of being deluded. Here the Subtile Serpent transformed himself so hiddenly that I verily believed this to be a timely Caution from a good Angel – so resolved to beware of the Deceiver, & for Some weeks Did not touch any of their Books.

The next Day being the first of the week I wanted to have gone to Church, which was Distant about four Miles, but being a Stranger and having nobody to go along with me, was forced to Give it out, & as most of the Family was going to Meeting, I went with them, but with a resolution not to like them, & so it was fully Suffered: for as they sat in silence I looked over the Meeting, thinking with my self, "how like fools these People sit, how much better would it be to stay at home & read the Bible or some good Book, than to come here and go to Sleep." For my Part I was very Sleepy & thought they were no better than my Self. Indeed at Length I fell a sleep, and had like to fallen Down, but this was the last time I ever fell asleep in a Meeting, Tho' often Assaulted with it.

Now I began to be lifted up with Spiritual Pride & thought my Self better than they, but thro' Mercy this did not Last Long, for in a Little time I was brought Low & saw that these were the People to whom I must join. It may seem strange that I who had Lived so long with one of this Society in Dublin, should yet be so great a Stranger to them. In answer let it be Considered that During the time I was there I never read one of their Books nor went to one Meeting, & besides I had heard such ridiculous stories of them as made me Esteem them the worst of any Society of People; but God that knew the Sincerity of my heart looked with Pity on my Weakness & soon Let me see my Error.

---

2. **Saml. Crisp's Two Letters:** The book Ashbridge takes up was a famous Quaker conversion narrative, *Two Letters Written by Samuel Crisp . . . Upon his Change from a Chaplain of the Church of England, to Join with the People Called Quakers*, first published in 1722.

In a few weeks there was an afternoon's Meeting held at my Uncle's to which came that Servant of the Lord Wm. Hammans who was made then Instrumental to the Convincing me of the truth more Perfectly, & helping me over Some great Doubts: tho' I believe no one did ever sit in Greater opposition than I did when he first stood up; but I was soon brought Down for he preached the Gospel with such Power I was forced to give up & Confess it was the truth. As soon as meeting Ended I Endeavoured to get alone, for I was not fit to be seen, I being So broken; yet afterward the Restless adversary assaulted me again, on this wise. In the morning before this meeting, I had been Disputing with my Uncle about Baptism, which was the subject this good Man Dwelt upon, which was handled so Clearly as to answer all my Scruples beyond all objection: yet the Crooked Serpent alleged that the Sermon that I had heard did not proceed from divine Revelation but that my Uncle and Aunt had acquainted the Friend of me; which being Strongly Suggested, I fell to Accusing them with it, of which they both cleared themselves, saying they had not seen him Since my Coming into these Parts until he came into the meeting. I then Concluded he was a messenger sent of God to me, & with fervent Cryes Desired I might be Directed a right and now Laid aside all Prejudice & set my heart open to receive the truth in the Love of it. And the Lord in his own good time revealed to my Soul not only the Beauty there is in truth, & how those should shine that continue faithful to it, but also the Emptiness of all shadows, which in the day were Gloryous, but now he the Son of Glory was come to put an end to them all, & to Establish Everlasting Righteousness in the room thereof, which is a work in the Soul. He likewise let me see that all I had gone through was to prepare me for this Day & that the time was near that he would require me to go forth & declare to others what he the God of Mercy had done for my Soul; at which I was Surprized & begged to be Excused for fear I should bring dishonour to the truth, and cause his Holy name to be Evil spoken of.

All the while, I never Let any know the Condition I was in, nor did I appear like a Friend, & fear'd a Discovery I now began to think of returning to my husband but found a restraint to stay where I was. I then Hired to keep School & hearing of a place for him, wrote desiring him to come to me, but Let him know nothing how it was with me. I loved to go to meetings, but did not like to be seen to go on week days, & therefore to Shun it used to go from my school through the Woods, but notwithstanding all my care the Neighbours that were not friends began to revile me, calling me Quaker, saying they supposed I intended to be a fool and turn Preacher; I then receiv'd the same censure that I (a little above a year before) had Passed on one of the handmaids of the Lord at Boston, & so weak was I, alas! I could not bear the reproach, & in order to Change their Opinions got into greater Excess in Apparel than I had freedom to Wear for some time before I came Acquainted with Friends.

In this Condition I continued till my Husband came, & then began the Tryal of my Faith. Before he reached me he heard I was turned Quaker, at which he stampt, saying, "I'd rather heard She had been dead as well as I Love her, for if so, all my comfort is gone." He then came to me & had not seen me before for four Months. I got up & met him saying, "My Dear, I am glad to see thee," at which he flew in a Passion of anger & said, "the Divel thee thee, don't thee me."[3] I used all the mild means I could to pacify him, & at Length got him fit to go & Speak to my Relations, but he was Alarmed, and as soon as we got alone said, "so I see your Quaker relations have made you one." I told him they had not, which was true, nor had I ever told him how it was with me: But he would have it that I was one, & therefore would not let me stay among them; & having found a place to his mind, hired and came Directly back to fetch me hence, & in one afternoon walked near thirty Miles to keep me from Meeting, the next Day being first Day;[4] & on the Morrow took me to the Afforesaid Place & hired Lodgings at a churchman's house; who was one of the Wardens, & a bitter Enemy to Friends & used to Do all he could to irritate my Husband against them, & would tell me abundance of Ridiculous Stuff; but my Judgement was too Clearly convinced to believe it.

I still did not appear like a Friend, but they all believed I was one. When my Husband and he Used to be making their Diversion & reviling, I used to sit in Silence, but now and then an involuntary Sigh would break from me: at which he would tell my husband: "there, did not I tell you that your wife was a Quaker; & She will be a preacher." Upon which My Husband once in a Great rage came up to me, & Shaking his hand over me, said, "you had better be hanged in that Day." I then, Peter like, in a panick denied my being a Quaker, at which great horror seized upon me, which Continued near three Months: so that I again feared that by Denying the Lord that Bought me, the heavens were Shut against me; for great Darkness Surrounded, & I was again plunged into Despair. I used to Walk much alone in the Wood, where no Eye saw nor Ear heard, & there Lament my miserable Condition, & have often gone from Morning till Night and have not broke my Fast.

Thus I was brought so Low that my Life was a burden to me; the Devil seem'd to Vaunt that tho' the Sins of my youth were forgiven, yet now he was sure of Me, for that I had Committed the unpardonable Sin & Hell inevitable would be my portion, & my Torment would be greater than if I had hanged my Self at first. In this Doleful State I had none to bewail my Doleful Condition; & Even in the Night when I Could not Sleep under the painful Distress of mind, if my husband perceived me weeping he would revile me for it. At Length when he and his Friends thought themselves too weak to over Set me (tho' I feared it was all ready done) he went to the Priest at Chester [Pennsylvania] to Advise what to Do with me. This man knew I was a member of the Church, for I had Shewn him my Certificate: his advice was to take me out of Pennsylvania, and find some place where there was no Quakers; and then it would wear off. To this my Husband Agreed saying he did not Care where he went, if he Could but restore me to that Livelyness of

---

3. **"The Divel thee . . . don't thee me":** Ashbridge's language is evidence to her husband that she is following the practices and plain speech of the Quakers, who continued to use the informal *thee* and *thou* long after those terms were displaced by *you*, originally a plural pronoun that was used in the singular to signify politeness or respect.

4. **first Day:** To avoid references to pagan deities, Quakers referred to days of the week and the months by number; first day was Sunday.

Temper I was naturally of, & to that Church of which I was a member. I on my Part had no Spirit to oppose the Proposal, neither much cared where I was, For I seemed to have nothing to hope for, but Dayly Expected to be made a Spectacle of Divine Wrath, & was Possessed with a Thought that it would be by Thunder ere long.

The time of Removal came, & I must go. I was not Suffered to go to bid my Relations farewell; my husband was Poor & kept no horse, so I must travel on foot; we came to Wilmington [Delaware] (fifteen Miles) thence to Philadelphia by Water; here he took me to a Tavern where I soon became the Spectacle & discourse of the Company. My Husband told them, "my wife is a Quaker," & that he Designed if Possible to find out some Place where there was none. "O," thought I, "I was once in a Condition deserving that name, but now it is over with me. O! that I might from a true hope once more have an Opportunity to Confess to the truth;" tho' I was Sure of Suffering all manner of Crueltys, I would not Regard it.

These were my Concerns while he was Entertaining the Company with my Story, in which he told them that I had been a good Dancer, but now he Could get me neither to Dance nor Sing, upon which one of the Company stands up saying, "I'll go fetch my Fiddle, & we'll have a Dance," at which my husband was much pleased. The fiddle came, the sight of which put me in a sad Condition for fear if I Refused my husband would be in a great Passion: however I took up this resolution, not to Comply whatever be the Consequence. He comes to me, takes me by the hand saying, "come my Dear, shake off that Gloom, & let's have a civil Dance; you would now and then when you was a good Churchwoman, & that's better than a Stiff Quaker." I trembling desired to be Excused; but he Insisted on it, and knowing his Temper to be exceeding Cholerick, durst not say much, yet did not Consent. He then pluck'd me round the Room till Tears affected my Eyes, at Sight whereof the Musician Stopt and said, "I'll play no more, Let your wife alone," of which I was Glad.

There was also a man in Company who came from Freehold in East Jersey: he said, "I see your Wife is a Quaker, but if you will take my advice you need not go so far (for my husband's design was for Staten Island); come & live amongst us, we'll soon cure her of her Quakerism, for we want a School Master & Mistress Too" (I followed the Same Business); to which he agreed, & a happy turn it was for me, as will be seen by and by: and the Wonderfull turn of Providence, who had not yet Abandoned me, but raised a glimmering hope, affording the Answer of peace in refusing to Dance, for which I was more rejoyced than to be made Mistress of much Riches; & in floods of Tears said, "Lord, I dread to ask and yet without thy gracious Pardon I'm Miserable; I therefore fall Down before thy Throne, imploring Mercy at thine hand. O Lord once more I beseech thee, try my Obedience, & then what soever thou Commands, I will Obey, & not fear to Confess thee before men."

Thus was my Soul Engaged before God in Sincerity & he in tender Mercy heard my cries, & in me has Shewn that he Delights not in the Death of a Sinner, for he again set my mind at Liberty to praise him & I longed for an Opportunity to Confess to his Truth, which he shewed me should come, but in what manner I did not see, but believed the word that I had heard, which in a little time was fulfilled to me. My Husband as aforesaid agreed to go to Freehold, & in our way thither we came to Maidenhead, where I went to see the kind Dutchman before mentioned, who made us welcome & Invited us to stay a day or Two.

While we were here, there was held a great Meeting of the Presbyterians, not only for Worship but Business also: for one of their preachers being Charged with Drunkenness, was this day to have his Trial before a great number of their Priests, &c. We went to it, of which I was afterwards glad. Here I perceived great Divisions among the People about who Should be their Shepherd: I greatly Pitied their Condition, for I now saw beyond the Men made Ministers, & What they Preached for: and which those at this Meeting might have done had not the prejudice of Education, which is very prevalent, blinded their Eyes. Some Insisted to have the old Offender restored, some to have a young man they had upon trial some weeks, a third Party was for sending for one from New England. At length stood up one & Directing himself to the Chief Speaker said "Sir, when we have been at the Expence (which will be no Small Matter) of fetching this Gentleman from New England, may be he'll not stay with us." *Answer*, "don't you know how to make him stay?" *Reply*, "no Sir." "I'll tell you then," said he (to which I gave good attention), "give him a good Salary & I'll Engage he'll Stay." "O" thought I, "these Mercenary creatures: they are all Actuated by one & the same thing, even the Love of Money, & not the regard of Souls." This (Called Reverend) Gentleman, whom these People almost adored, to my knowledge had left his flock on Long Island & moved to Philadelphia where he could get more money. I my self have heard some of them on the Island say that they almost Impoverished themselves to keep him, but not being able to Equal Philadelphia's Invitation he left them without a Shepherd. This man therefore, knowing their Ministry all proceeded from one Cause, might be purchased with the Same thing; surely these and Such like are the Shepherd that regards the fleece more than the flock, in whose mouths are Lies; saying the Lord had sent them, & that they were Christ's Ambassadors, whose Command to those he sent was, "Freely ye have receiv'd, freely give; & Blessed be his holy Name;"[5] so they do to this day.

I durst not say any Thing to my Husband of the Remarks I had made, but laid them up in my heart, & they Served to Strengthen me in my Resolution. Hence we set forward to Freehold, & Coming through Stony Brook [New Jersey] my Husband turned towards me tauntingly & Said, "Here's one of Satan's Synagogues, don't you want to be in it? O I hope to See you Cured of this New Religion." I made no answer but went on, and in a little time, we came to a large run of Water over which was no Bridge, & being Strangers knew no way to escape it, but thro' we must go: he Carried over our Clothes, which we had in Bundles. I took off my Shoes and waded over in my Stockings, which Served some what to prevent the Chill of the Water, being Very Cold & a fall of Snow in the 12 Mo.[6] My heart was Concerned in Prayer that the Lord would Sanctify all my Afflictions to me & give me Patience to bear whatsoever should be suffered to come upon me. We Walked the most

5. **"Freely . . . Name"**: Matthew 10:8.
6. **12 Mo.**: Twelfth month, or December. See note 4.

part of a mile before we came to the first house, which was a sort of a Tavern. My husband Called for Some Spiritous Liquors, but I got some weakened Cider Mull'd, which when I had Drank of (the Cold being struck to my heart) made me Extremely sick, in so much that when we were a Little past the house I expected I should have Fainted, & not being able to stand, fell Down under a Fence. My husband Observing, tauntingly said, "What's the Matter now; what, are you Drunk; where is your Religion now?" He knew better & at that time I believe he Pitied me, yet was Suffered grievously to Afflict me. In a Little time I grew Better, & going on We came to another Tavern, where we Lodged: the next Day I was Indifferent well, so proceeded, and as we Journeyed a young man Driving an Empty Cart overtook us. I desired my husband to ask the young man to Let us Ride; he did, twas readily granted.

I now thought my Self well off, & took it as a great favour, for my Proud heart was humbled, & I did not regard the Looks of it, tho' the time had been that I would not have been seen in one; this Cart belonged to a man at Shrewsbury [New Jersey] & was to go thro' the place we Designed for, so we rode on (but soon had the Care of the team to our Selves from a failure in the Driver) to the place where I was Intended to be made a prey of; but see how unforeseen things are brought to Pass, by a Providential hand. Tis said and answered, "shall we do Evil that good may Come?" God forbid, yet hence good came to me. Here my husband would have had me Stay while we went to see the Team Safe at home: I Told him, no, since he had led me thro' the Country like a Vagabond, I would not stay behind him, so went on, & Lodged that Night at the man's house who owned the Team. Next morning in our Return to Freehold, we met a man riding on full Speed, who Stopping said to my Husband, "Sir, are you a School Master?" *Answer*, "Yes." "I came to tell you," replied the Stranger, "of Two new School Houses, & want a Master in Each, & are two miles apart." How this Stranger came to hear of us, who Came but the night before, I never knew, but I was glad he was not one Called a Quaker, Least my husband might have thought it had been a Plot; and then turning to my husband I said, "my Dear, look on me with Pity; if thou has any Affections left for me, which I hope thou hast, for I am not Conscious of having Done anything to Alienate them; here is (continued I) an Opportunity to Settle us both, for I am willing to do all in my Power towards getting an Honest Livelihood."

My Expressions took place, & after a Little Pause he consented, took the young man's Directions, & made towards the place, & in our way came to the house of a Worthy Friend, Whose wife was a Preacher, tho' we did not know it. I was Surprized to see the People so kind to us that were Strangers; we had not been long in the house till we were Invited to Lodge there that night, being the Last in the Week. I said nothing but waited to hear my Master Speak; he soon Consented saying, "My wife has had a Tedious Travel & I pity her"; at which kind Expression I was Affected, for they Were now very Seldom Used to me. The friends' kindness could not proceed from my appearing in the Garb of a Quaker, for I had not yet altered my dress: The Woman of the house, after we had Concluded to Stay, fixed her Eyes upon me & Said, "I believe thou hast met with a deal of Trouble," to which I made but Little Answer. My husband, Observing they were of that sort of people he had so much Endeavoured to shun, would give us no Opportunity for any discourse that night, but the next morning I let the friend know a Little how it was with me. Meeting time came, to which I longed to go, but durst not ask my husband leave for fear of Disturbing him, till we were Settled, & then thought I, "if ever I am favoured to be in this Place, come Life or Death, I'll fight through, for my Salvation is at Stake." The Friend getting ready for Meeting, asked my husband if he would go, saying they knew who were to be his Employers, & if they were at Meeting would Speak to them. He then consented to go; then said the Woman Friend, "& wilt thou Let thy Wife go?," which he denied, making Several Objections, all which She answered so prudently that he Could not be angry, & at Last Consented; & with Joy I went, for I had not been at one for near four Months, & an Heavenly Meeting This was: I now renewed my Covenant & Saw the Word of the Lord made Good, that I should have another Opportunity to Confess his Name, for which my Spirit did rejoice in the God of my Salvation, who had brought Strange things to Pass: May I ever be preserved in Humility, never forgetting his tender Mercies to me.

Here According to my Desire we Settled; my husband got one School & I the Other, & took a Room at a Friend's house a Mile from Each School and Eight Miles from the Meeting House: before next first day we were got to our new Settlement: & now Concluded to Let my husband to see I was determined to joyn with friends. When first day Came I directed my Self to him in this manner, "My Dear, art thou willing to let me go to a Meeting?," at which he flew into a rage, saying, "No you shan't." I then Drew up my resolution & told him as a Dutyfull Wife ought, So I was ready to obey all his Lawfull Commands, but where they Imposed upon my Conscience, I no longer Durst: For I had already done it too Long, & wronged my Self by it, & tho' he was near & I loved him as a Wife ought, yet God was nearer than all the World to me, & had made me sensible this was the way I ought to go, the which I Assured him was no Small Cross to my own will, yet had Given up My heart, & hoped that he that Called for it would Enable me the residue of my Life to keep it steadyly devoted to him, whatever I Suffered for it, adding I hoped not to make him any the worse Wife for it. But all I could Say was in vain; he was Inflexible & Would not Consent.

I had now put my hand to the Plough, & resolved not to Look back, so went without Leave; but Expected to be immediately followed & forced back, but he did not: I went to one of the neighbours & got a Girl to Show me the way, then went on rejoicing & Praising God in my heart, who had thus far given me Power & another Opportunity to Confess to his Truth. Thus for some time I had to go Eight Miles on foot to Meetings, which I never thought hard; My Husband soon bought a Horse, but would not Let me ride him, neither when my Shoes were worn out would he Let me have a new Pair, thinking by that means to keep me from going to meetings, but this did not hinder me, for I have taken Strings & tyed round to keep them on.

He finding no hard Usage could alter my resolution, neither threatening to beat me, nor doing it, for he several times Struck me with sore Blows, which I Endeavoured to bear with Patience, believing the time would Come when he would see I was in the right (which he Accordingly Did), he once came up to me & took out his pen knife saying, "if you offer to go to Meeting tomorrow, with this knife I'll cripple you, for you shall not be a Quaker." I made him no Answer, but when Morning came, set out as Usual & he was not Suffered to hurt me. In Despair of recovering me himself, he now flew to the Priest for help and told him I had been a very Religious Woman in the way of the Church of England, was a member of it, & had a good Certificate from Long Island, but now was bewitched and turn'd Quaker, which almost broke his heart. He therefore Desired as he was one who had the Care of souls, he would Come and pay me a Visit and use his Endeavours to reclaim me & hoped by the Blessing of God it would be done. The Priest Consented to Come, the time was Set, which was to be that Day two Weeks, for he said he could not come Sooner. My Husband Came home extremely Pleased, & told me of it, at which I smiled Saying, "I hope to be Enabled to give him a reason for the hope that is in me," at the same time believing the Priest would never Trouble me (nor ever did).

Before his Appointed time came it was required of me in a more Publick manner to Confess to the world what I was and to give up in Prayer in a Meeting, the sight of which & the power that attended it made me Tremble, & I could not hold my Self still. I now again desired Death & would have freely given up my Natural Life a Ransom; & what made it harder to me I was not yet taken under the care of Friends, & what kept me from requesting it was for fear I might be overcome & bring a Scandal on the Society. I begged to be Excused till I was joyned to Friends & then I would give up freely, to which I receiv'd this Answer, as tho' I had heard a Distinct Voice: "I am a Covenant keeping God, and the word that I spoke to thee when I found thee In Distress, even that I would never leave thee nor forsake thee If thou would be obedient to what I should make known to thee, I will Assuredly make good: but if thou refuse, my Spirit shall not always strive; fear not, I will make way for thee through all thy difficulties, which shall be many for my name's Sake, but be thou faithfull & I will give thee a Crown of Life." I being then Sure it was God that Spoke said, "thy will O God, be done, I am in thy hand; do with me according to thy Word," & gave up. But after it was over the Enemy came in like a flood, telling me I had done what I ought not, & Should now bring Dishonour to this People. This gave me a Little Shock, but it did not at this time Last Long.

This Day as Usual I had gone on foot. My Husband (as he afterwards told me) lying on the Bed at home, these Words ran thro' him, "Lord where shall I fly to shun thee &C.,"[7] upon which he arose and seeing it Rain got his horse and Came to fetch me; and Coming just as the Meeting broke up, I got on horseback as quick as possible, least he Should hear what had happened. Nevertheless he heard of it, and as soon as we were got into the woods he began, saying, "What do you mean thus to make my Life unhappy? What, could you not be a Quaker without turning fool after this manner?" I Answered in Tears saying, "my Dear, look on me with Pity, if thou hast any. Canst thou think, that I in the Bloom of my Days, would bear all that thou knowest of & a great deal more that thou knowest not of if I did not believe it to be my Duty?" This took hold of him, & taking my hand he said, "Well, I'll E'en give you up, for I see it don't avail to Strive. If it be of God I can't over throw it, & if it be of your self it will soon fall." I saw tears stand in his Eyes, at which my heart was overcome with Joy, and I would not have Changed Conditions with a Queen.

---

7. **"Lord . . . etc."**: See Psalms 139:7: "Whither shall I go from thy spirit? or whither shall I flee from thy presence?"

I already began to reap the fruits of my Obedience, but my Tryal Ended not here, the time being up that the Priest was to come; but no Priest Appeared. My Husband went to fetch him, but he would not come, saying he was busy; which so Displeased my husband, that he'd never go to hear him more, & for Some time went to no place of Worship. Now the Unwearied adversary found out another Scheme, and with it wrought so Strong that I thought all I had gone through but a little to this: It came upon me in such an unexpected manner, in hearing a Woman relate a book she had read in which it was Asserted that Christ was not the son of God. As soon as She had Spoke these words, if a man had spoke I could not have more distinctly heard these words, "no more he is, it's all a fancy & the Contrivance of men," & an horrour of Great Darkness fell upon me, which Continued for three weeks.

The Exercise I was under I am not Able to Express, neither durst I let any know how it was with me. I again sought Desolate Places where I might make my moan, & have Lain whole nights, & don't know that my Eyes were Shut to Sleep. I again thought my self alone, but would not let go my Faith in him, often saying in my heart, "I'll believe till I Die," & kept a hope that he that had Delivered me out of the Paw of the Bear & out of the jaws of the Devouring Lion, would in his own time Deliver me out of his temptation also; which he in Mercy Did, and let me see that this was for my good, in order to Prepare me for future Service which he had for me to Do & that it was Necessary his Ministers should be dipt into all States, that thereby they might be able to Speak to all Conditions, for which my Soul was thankfull to him, the God of Mercies, who had at Several times redeemed me from great distress, & I found the truth of his Words, that all things should work together for good to those that Loved & feared him, which I did with my whole heart & hope ever shall while I have a being. This happened just after my first appearance, & Friends had not been to talk with me, nor did they know well what to do till I had appeared again, which was not for some time, when the Monthly Meeting appointed four Friends to give me a Visit, which I was Glad of; and gave them Such Satisfaction, that they left me well Satisfy'd. I then Joyned with Friends.

My Husband still went to no place of Worship. One day he said, "I'd go to Meeting, only I am afraid I shall hear you Clack, which I cannot bear." I used no persuasions, yet when Meeting time Came, he got the horse, took me behind him & went to Meeting: but for several months if he saw me offer to rise, he would go out, till once I got up before he was aware and then (as he afterwards said) he was ashamed to go, & from that time never did, nor hindered me from going to Meetings. And tho' he (poor man) did not take up the Cross, yet his judgement was Convinced: & sometimes in a flood of tears would say, "My Dear, I have seen the Beauty there is in the Truth, & that thou art in the Right, and I Pray God Preserve thee in it. But as for me the Cross is too heavy, I cannot Bear it." I told him, I hoped he that had given me strength Would also favour him: "O!" said he, "I can't bear the Reproach thou Doest, to be Called turncoat & to become a Laughing Stock to the World; but I'll no Longer hinder thee," which I looked on as a great favour, that my way was thus far made easy, and a little hope remained that my Prayers would be heard on his account.

In this Place he had got linked in with some, that he was afraid would make game of him, which Indeed they already Did, asking him when he Designed to Commence Preacher, for that they saw he Intended to turn Quaker, & seemed to Love his Wife better since she did than before (we were now got to a little house by our Selves which tho' Mean, & little to put in it, our Bed no better than Chaff, yet I was truly Content & did not Envy the Rich their Riches; the only Desire I had now was my own preservation, & to be Bless'd with the Reformation of my husband). These men used to Come to our house & there Provoke my husband to Sit up and Drink, some times till near day, while I have been sorrowing in a Stable. As I once sat in this Condition I heard my husband say to his Company, "I can't bear any Longer to Afflict my Poor Wife in this manner, for whatever you may think of her, I do believe she is a good Woman," upon which he came to me and said, "Come in, my Dear; God has Given thee a Deal of Patience. I'll put an End to this Practice;" and so he did, for this was the Last time they sat up at Night.

My Husband now thought that if he was in any Place where it was not known that he'd been so bitter against Friends, he Could do better than here. But I was much against his Moving; fearing it would tend to his hurt, having been for some months much Altered for the Better, & would often in a broken and Affectionate Manner condemn his bad Usage to me: I told him I hoped it had been for my Good, even to the Better Establishing me in the Truth, & therefore would not have him to be Afflicted about it, & According to the Measure of Grace received did what I could both by Example and advice for his good: & my Advice was for him to fight thro' here, fearing he would Grow Weaker and the Enemy Gain advantage over him, if he thus fled: but All I could say did not prevail against his Moving; & hearing of a place at Bordentown [New Jersey] went there, but that did not suit; he then Moved to Mount Holly [New Jersey] & there we Settled. He got a good School & So Did I.

Here we might have Done very well; we soon got our house Prettily furnished for Poor folks; I now began to think I wanted but one thing to complete my Happiness, Viz. the Reformation of my husband, which Alas! I had too much reason to Doubt; for it fell out according to my Fears, & he grew worse here, & took much to Drinking, so that it Seem'd as if my Life was to be a Continual scene of Sorrows & most Earnestly I Pray'd to Almighty God to Endue me with Patience to bear my Afflictions & submit to his Providence, which I can say in Truth I did without murmuring or ever uttering an unsavoury expression to the Best of my Knowledge; except once, my husband Coming home a little in drink (in which frame he was very fractious) & finding me at Work by a Candle, came to me, put it out & fetching me a box on the Ear said, "you don't Earn your light;" on which unkind Usage (for he had not struck me for Two Years so it went hard with me) I utter'd these Rash Expressions, "thou art a Vile Man," & was a little angry, but soon recovered & was Sorry for it; he struck me again, which I received without so much as a word in return, & that likewise Displeased him: so he went on in a Distracted like manner uttering Several Expressions that bespoke Despair, as that he now believed that he was predestinated to damnation, & he did not care how soon God would Strike him Dead, & the like. I durst say but Little; at Length in the Bitterness of my Soul, I Broke out in these Words, "Lord look Down on mine Afflictions and deliver me by some means or Other." I was answered, I Should Soon be, & so I was, but in such a manner, as I Verily thought It would have killed me. In a little time he went to Burlington where he got in Drink, & Enlisted him Self to go a Common soldier to Cuba anno 1740.

I had drank many bitter Cups – but this Seemed to Exceed them all for indeed my very Senses Seemed Shaken; I now a Thousand times blamed my Self for making Such an unadvised request, fearing I had Displeased God in it, & tho' he had Granted it, it was in Displeasure, & Suffered to be in this manner to Punish me; Tho' I can truly say I never Desired his Death, no more than my own, nay not so much. I have since had cause to believe his mind was benefitted by the Undertaking, (which hope makes up for all I have Suffered from him) being Informed he did in the army what he Could not Do at home (Viz) Suffered for the Testimony of Truth. When they Came to prepare for an Engagement, he refused to fight; for which he was whipt and brought before the General, who asked him why he Enlisted if he would not fight; "I did it," said he, "in a drunken frolick, when the Divel had the Better of me, but my judgment is convinced that I ought not, neither will I whatever I Suffer; I have but one Life, & you may take that if you Please, but I'll never take up Arms."[8] They used him with much Cruelty to make him yield but Could not, by means whereof he was So Disabled that the General sent him to the Hospital at Chelsea, where in Nine Months time he Died & I hope made a Good End, for which I prayed both night & Day, till I heard of his Death.

Thus I thought it my duty to say what I could in his Favour, as I have been obliged to say so much of his hard usage to me, all which I hope Did me good, & altho' he was so bad, yet had Several Good Properties, & I never thought him the Worst of Men. He was one I Lov'd & had he let Religion have its Perfect work, I should have thought my Self Happy in the Lowest State of Life; & I've Cause to bless God, who Enabled me in the Station of a Wife to Do my Duty & now a Widow to Submit to his Will, always believing everything he doeth to be right. May he in all Stations of Life so Preserve me by the arm of Divine Power, that I may never forget his tender mercies to me, the Rememberance whereof doth often Bow my Soul, in Humility before his Throne, saying, "Lord, what was I; that thou should have reveal'd to me the Knowledge of thy Truth, & do so much for me, who Deserved thy Displeasure rather, But in me hast thou shewn thy Long Suffering & tender Mercy; may thou O God be Glorifyed and I abased for it is thy own Works that praise thee, and of a Truth to the humble Soul thou Makest every bitter thing Sweet. The End.

[1774, 1990]

---

8. **"I'll never take up Arms"**: Quakers are pacifists who reject the use of force to settle personal or national disputes.

John Woolman

[1720-1772]

John Woolman

The only known portrait of Woolman, this sketch was apparently drawn from memory by his friend Robert Smith III, of Burlington, New Jersey.

bedfordstmartins.com/ americanlit *for research links on Woolman*

John Woolman was born in Burlington County, New Jersey, on October 19, 1720, the fourth of thirteen children of Samuel and Elizabeth Burr Woolman. His parents, successful farmers, were part of a colony of Quakers who had settled in the counties near Philadelphia. Woolman was sent to a village school and, with the encouragement of his parents, developed lifelong habits of reading and study. He worked on the family farm until he was twenty-one, when he left to work as a tailor's apprentice in a retail store in nearby Mount Holly. There, he gained his first direct experience of slavery, which was widespread in eighteenth-century New Jersey. When he was asked to draw up a bill of sale for a woman owned by his employer, Woolman reluctantly agreed. Afterward, however, he told his employer that he believed "slave-holding to be a practice inconsistent with the Christian religion," as Woolman later wrote in his journal. In his late twenties, Woolman opened his own store. He also studied law so that he could prepare deeds and wills.

As his retail business grew, Woolman became increasingly concerned about the conflict between material success and the simple, spiritual life advocated by the Quakers. He consequently began to curtail his business and devote more time to the activities of the Society of Friends. After he became a Quaker minister, Woolman traveled frequently to meetings, speaking against the preoccupation with luxury and wealth, the use of force, and war. He also sought to convince his fellow Quakers to abandon slave-holding, which was then a common and accepted practice among members of the Society of Friends. Both publicly and privately, Woolman lived by his convictions, refusing to wear dyed clothes because of the poor conditions for workers in dye factories and giving up the use of sugar because of the exploitation of slave labor on sugar plantations in the West Indies. In 1749, he married a longtime friend and fellow Quaker, Sarah Ellis. He later gave up his retail business altogether and supported his family by working as a tailor, occasionally as a teacher, and as a farmer. In 1752, Woolman began his journal, which would become his most important and influential work, though he also wrote numerous letters as well as essays on the slave trade and on topics such as the importance of silent worship. But he spent most of his time speaking and serving as a Quaker missionary, participating in over thirty missions throughout the colonies, including the South. While on a trip to England to participate in Quaker meetings, Woolman contracted smallpox and died in London on October 7, 1772.

Woolman's *Journal*. Inspired by the spiritual autobiography of George Fox (1624-1691), the founder of the Society of Friends whose *Journal* was published in 1694, many Quakers wrote similar accounts of their experiences. Woolman began his journal in 1752 and continued to write it until shortly before his death in 1772. Like Fox and other Quakers, Woolman provided few details of his daily life or personal relationships. Instead, he focused on his spiritual development, tracing his progress from early doubts and struggles through the growing religious convictions that culminated in his work as a minister and missionary. The journal was first published in Philadelphia in 1774 as *A Journal of the Life, Gospel Labours, and Christian Experiences of That Faithful Minister of Jesus Christ, John Woolman, Late of Mount-Holly, in the Province of New-Jersey.* Since then, it has never been out of print, and it has been read and valued by generations of Americans for its luminous account of the development of the inner life of an individual. Its admirers have included writers such as Ralph Waldo Emerson, Walt Whitman, and the Quaker poet John Greenleaf Whittier, who published an edition of the journal in 1871. In his preface to that edition, Whittier explained that the *Journal* "has a sweetness as of violets," symbols of devotion whose purity and simplicity are mirrored in Woolman's life and writings. The text of the following selections is taken from *The Journal and Major Essays of John Woolman*, edited by Phillips P. Moulton (1971).

[Woolman's journal is] beyond comparison the sweetest and purest autobiography in the language.

– William Ellery Channing

From THE JOURNAL OF JOHN WOOLMAN

Chapter I

1720–1742

I have often felt a motion of love to leave some hints in writing of my experience of the goodness of God, and now, in the thirty-sixth year of my age, I begin this work. I was born in Northampton, in Burlington County in West Jersey, A.D. 1720, and before I was seven years old I began to be acquainted with the operations of divine love. Through the care of my parents, I was taught to read near as soon as I was capable of it, and as I went from school one Seventh Day,[1] I remember, while my companions went to play by the way, I went forward out of sight; and sitting down, I read the twenty-second chapter of the Revelations: "He showed me a river of water, clear as crystal, proceeding out of the throne of God and the Lamb, etc." And in reading it my mind was drawn to seek after that pure habitation which I then believed God had prepared for his servants. The place where I sat and the sweetness that attended my mind remains fresh in my memory.

This and the like gracious visitations had that effect upon me, that when boys used ill language it troubled me, and through the continued mercies of God I was preserved from it. The pious instructions of my parents were often fresh in my mind when I happened amongst wicked children, and was of use to me. My parents, having a large family

1. **Seventh Day:** Saturday. To avoid references to pagan deities, Quakers referred to the days of the week and the months by number.

of children, used frequently on First Days after meeting[2] to put us to read in the Holy Scriptures or some religious books, one after another, the rest sitting by without much conversation, which I have since often thought was a good practice. From what I had read and heard, I believed there had been in past ages people who walked in uprightness before God in a degree exceeding any that I knew, or heard of, now living; and the apprehension of there being less steadiness and firmness amongst people in this age than in past ages often troubled me while I was a child.

I had a dream about the ninth year of my age as follows: I saw the moon rise near the west and run a regular course eastward, so swift that in about a quarter of an hour she reached our meridian, when there descended from her a small cloud on a direct line to the earth, which lighted on a pleasant green about twenty yards from the door of my father's house (in which I thought I stood) and was immediately turned into a beautiful green tree. The moon appeared to run on with equal swiftness and soon set in the east, at which time the sun arose at the place where it commonly does in the summer, and shining with full radiance in a serene air, it appeared as pleasant a morning as ever I saw.

All this time I stood still in the door in an awful[3] frame of mind, and I observed that as heat increased by the rising sun, it wrought so powerfully on the little green tree that the leaves gradually withered; and before noon it appeared dry and dead. There then appeared a being, small of size, full of strength and resolution, moving swift from the north, southward, called a sun worm.[4]

Another thing remarkable in my childhood was that once, going to a neighbour's house, I saw on the way a robin sitting on her nest; and as I came near she went off, but having young ones, flew about and with many cries expressed her concern for them. I stood and threw stones at her, till one striking her, she fell down dead. At first I was pleased with the exploit, but after a few minutes was seized with horror, as having in a sportive way killed an innocent creature while she was careful for her young. I beheld her lying dead and thought those young ones for which she was so careful must now perish for want of their dam to nourish them; and after some painful considerations on the subject, I climbed up the tree, took all the young birds and killed them, supposing that better than to leave them to pine away and die miserably, and believed in this case that Scripture proverb was fulfilled, "The tender mercies of the wicked are cruel."[5] I then went on my errand, but for some hours could think of little else but the cruelties I had committed, and was much troubled.

Thus he whose tender mercies are over all his works hath placed a principle in the human mind which incites to exercise goodness toward every living creature; and this

2. **meeting:** Quakers referred to their worship services as meetings or assemblies; these were held on the first day of the week (Sunday).

3. **awful:** Inspiring reverential wonder.

4. **sun worm:** *Worm* was an early term for a dragon or snake, which in Woolman's dream is generated by the intense light of the midday sun.

5. **"The . . . cruel":** Proverbs 12:10.

being singly attended to, people become tender-hearted and sympathizing, but being frequently and totally rejected, the mind shuts itself up in a contrary disposition.

About the twelfth year of my age, my father being abroad, my mother reproved me for some misconduct, to which I made an undutiful reply; and the next First Day as I was with my father returning from meeting, he told me he understood I had behaved amiss to my mother and advised me to be more careful in future. I knew myself blameable, and in shame and confusion remained silent. Being thus awakened to a sense of my wickedness, I felt remorse in my mind, and getting home I retired and prayed to the Lord to forgive me, and do not remember that I ever after that spoke unhandsomely to either of my parents, however foolish in other things.

Having attained the age of sixteen years, I began to love wanton company, and though I was preserved from profane language or scandalous conduct, still I perceived a plant in me which produced much wild grapes. Yet my merciful Father forsook me not utterly, but at times through his grace I was brought seriously to consider my ways, and the sight of my backsliding affected me with sorrow. But for want of rightly attending to the reproofs of instruction, vanity was added to vanity, and repentance to repentance; upon the whole my mind was more and more alienated from the Truth, and I hastened toward destruction.[6] While I meditate on the gulf toward which I travelled and reflect on my youthful disobedience, for these things I weep; mine eye runneth down with water.

Advancing in age the number of my acquaintance increased, and thereby my way grew more difficult. Though I had heretofore found comfort in reading the Holy Scriptures and thinking on heavenly things, I was now estranged therefrom. I knew I was going from the flock of Christ and had no resolution to return; hence serious reflections were uneasy to me and youthful vanities and diversions my greatest pleasure. Running in this road I found many like myself, and we associated in that which is reverse to true friendship.

But in this swift race it pleased God to visit me with sickness, so that I doubted of recovering. And then did darkness, horror, and amazement with full force seize me, even when my pain and distress of body was very great. I thought it would have been better for me never to have had a being than to see the day which I now saw. I was filled with confusion, and in great affliction both of mind and body I lay and bewailed myself. I had not confidence to lift up my cries to God, whom I had thus offended, but in a deep sense of my great folly I was humbled before him, and at length that Word which is as a fire and a hammer broke and dissolved my rebellious heart. And then my cries were put up in contrition, and in the multitude of his mercies I found inward relief, and felt a close engagement that if he was pleased to restore my health, I might walk humbly before him.

After my recovery this exercise remained with me a considerable time; but by degrees giving way to youthful vanities, they gained strength, and getting with wanton young people I lost ground. The Lord had been very gracious and spoke peace to me in

6. **destruction:** A sinful life.

the time of my distress, and I now most ungratefully turned again to folly, on which account at times I felt sharp reproof but did not get low enough to cry for help. I was not so hardy as to commit things scandalous, but to exceed in vanity and promote mirth was my chief study. Still I retained a love and esteem for pious people, and their company brought an awe upon me.

My dear parents several times admonished me in the fear of the Lord, and their admonition entered into my heart and had a good effect for a season, but not getting deep enough to pray rightly, the tempter when he came found entrance. I remember once, having spent a part of the day in wantonness, as I went to bed at night there lay in a window near my bed a Bible, which I opened, and first cast my eye on the text, "We lie down in our shame, and our confusion covers us."[7] This I knew to be my case, and meeting with so unexpected a reproof, I was somewhat affected with it and went to bed under remorse of conscience, which I soon cast off again.

Thus time passed on; my heart was replenished with mirth and wantonness, while pleasing scenes of vanity were presented to my imagination till I attained the age of eighteen years, near which time I felt the judgments of God in my soul like a consuming fire, and looking over my past life the prospect was moving. I was often sad and longed to be delivered from those vanities; then again my heart was strongly inclined to them, and there was in me a sore conflict. At times I turned to folly, and then again sorrow and confusion took hold of me. In a while I resolved totally to leave off some of my vanities, but there was a secret reserve in my heart of the more refined part of them, and I was not low enough to find true peace. Thus for some months I had great trouble, there remaining in me an unsubjected will which rendered my labours fruitless, till at length through the merciful continuance of heavenly visitations I was made to bow down in spirit before the Lord.

I remember one evening I had spent some time in reading a pious author, and walking out alone I humbly prayed to the Lord for his help, that I might be delivered from all those vanities which so ensnared me. Thus being brought low, he helped me; and as I learned to bear the cross I felt refreshment to come from his presence; but not keeping in that strength which gave victory, I lost ground again, the sense of which greatly affected me; and I sought deserts and lonely places and there with tears did confess my sins to God and humbly craved help of him. And I may say with reverence he was near to me in my troubles, and in those times of humiliation opened my ear to discipline.

I was now led to look seriously at the means by which I was drawn from the pure Truth, and learned this: that if I would live in the life which the faithful servants of God lived in, I must not go into company as heretofore in my own will, but all the cravings of sense must be governed by a divine principle. In times of sorrow and abasement these instructions were sealed upon me, and I felt the power of Christ prevail over selfish desires, so that I was preserved in a good degree of steadiness. And being young and believing at that time that a single life was best for me, I was strengthened to keep from such company as had often been a snare to me.

7. "We . . . us": Jeremiah 3:25.

I kept steady to meetings, spent First Days after noon chiefly in reading the Scriptures and other good books, and was early convinced in my mind that true religion consisted in an inward life, wherein the heart doth love and reverence God the Creator and learn to exercise true justice and goodness, not only toward all men but also toward the brute creatures; that as the mind was moved on an inward principle to love God as an invisible, incomprehensible being, on the same principle it was moved to love him in all his manifestations in the visible world; that as by his breath the flame of life was kindled in all animal and sensitive creatures, to say we love God as unseen and at the same time exercise cruelty toward the least creature moving by his life, or by life derived from him, was a contradiction in itself.

I found no narrowness respecting sects and opinions, but believed that sincere, upright-hearted people in every Society who truly loved God were accepted of him.

As I lived under the cross[8] and simply followed the openings of Truth,[9] my mind from day to day was more enlightened; my former acquaintance was left to judge of me as they would, for I found it safest for me to live in private and keep these things sealed up in my own breast.

While I silently ponder on that change wrought in me, I find no language equal to it nor any means to convey to another a clear idea of it. I looked upon the works of God in this visible creation and an awfulness covered me; my heart was tender and often contrite, and a universal love to my fellow creatures increased in me. This will be understood by such who have trodden in the same path. Some glances of real beauty may be seen in their faces who dwell in true meekness. There is a harmony in the sound of that voice to which divine love gives utterance, and some appearance of right order in their temper and conduct whose passions are fully regulated. Yet all these do not fully show forth that inward life to such who have not felt it, but this white stone and new name is known rightly to such only who have it.[10]

Now though I had been thus strengthened to bear the cross, I still found myself in great danger, having many weaknesses attending me and strong temptations to wrestle with, in the feeling whereof I frequently withdrew into private places and often with tears besought the Lord to help me, whose gracious ear was open to my cry.

All this time I lived with my parents and wrought on the plantation,[11] and having had schooling pretty well for a planter, I used to improve in winter evenings and other leisure times. And being now in the twenty-first year of my age, a man in much business shopkeeping and baking asked me if I would hire with him to tend shop and keep books. I acquainted my father with the proposal, and after some deliberation it was agreed for me to go.

---

8. **under the cross:** In accordance with the teachings of Christ.

9. **openings of Truth:** Quakers believe that, if they wait silently, God may speak directly to the faithful in moments of revelation called "openings."

10. **white stone . . . who have it:** See Revelations 2:17: "He that hath an ear, let him hear what the Spirit saith unto the churches; To him that overcometh will I give to eat of the hidden manna, and will give him a white stone, and in the stone a new name written, which no man knoweth saving he that receiveth it."

11. **wrought on the plantation:** Worked on the family farm.

At home I had lived retired, and now having a prospect of being much in the way of company, I felt frequent and fervent cries in my heart to God, the Father of Mercies, that he would preserve me from all taint and corruption, that in this more public employ I might serve him, my gracious Redeemer, in that humility and self-denial with which I had been in a small degree exercised in a very private life.

The man who employed me furnished a shop in Mount Holly, about five miles from my father's house and six from his own, and there I lived alone and tended his shop. Shortly after my settlement here I was visited by several young people, my former acquaintance, who knew not but vanities would be as agreeable to me now as ever; and at these times I cried to the Lord in secret for wisdom and strength, for I felt myself encompassed with difficulties and had fresh occasion to bewail the follies of time past in contracting a familiarity with a libertine people. And as I had now left my father's house outwardly, I found my Heavenly Father to be merciful to me beyond what I can express.

By day I was much amongst people and had many trials to go through, but in evenings I was mostly alone and may with thankfulness acknowledge that in those times the spirit of supplication was often poured upon me, under which I was frequently exercised and felt my strength renewed.

In a few months after I came here, my master bought several Scotch menservants[12] from on board a vessel and brought them to Mount Holly to sell, one of which was taken sick and died. The latter part of his sickness he, being delirious, used to curse and swear most sorrowfully, and after he was buried I was left to sleep alone the next night in the same chamber where he died. I perceived in me a timorousness. I knew, however, I had not injured the man but assisted in taking care of him according to my capacity, and was not free to ask anyone on that occasion to sleep with me. Nature was feeble, but every trial was a fresh incitement to give myself up wholly to the service of God, for I found no helper like him in times of trouble.

After a while my former acquaintance gave over expecting me as one of their company, and I began to be known to some whose conversation was helpful to me. And now, as I had experienced the love of God through Jesus Christ to redeem me from many pollutions and to be a succour to me through a sea of conflicts, with which no person was fully acquainted, and as my heart was often enlarged in this heavenly principle, I felt a tender compassion for the youth who remained entangled in snares like those which had entangled me. From one month to another this love and tenderness increased, and my mind was more strongly engaged for the good of my fellow creatures.

I went to meetings in an awful frame of mind and endeavoured to be inwardly acquainted with the language of the True Shepherd. And one day being under a strong exercise of spirit, I stood up and said some words in a meeting, but not keeping close to the divine opening,[13] I said more than was required of me; and being soon sensible of my

---

12. **menservants:** Woolman's master had bought the contracts of men whose travel expenses to the colonies had been paid in exchange for a contracted number of years of work as indentured servants.
13. **not keeping . . . opening:** When Quakers speak at meetings, they are expected to focus on the revelation from God and not comment on worldly matters.

error, I was afflicted in mind some weeks without any light or comfort, even to that degree that I could take satisfaction in nothing. I remembered God and was troubled, and in the depth of my distress he had pity upon me and sent the Comforter. I then felt forgiveness for my offense, and my mind became calm and quiet, being truly thankful to my gracious Redeemer for his mercies. And after this, feeling the spring of divine love opened and a concern to speak, I said a few words in a meeting, in which I found peace. This I believe was about six weeks from the first time, and as I was thus humbled and disciplined under the cross, my understanding became more strengthened to distinguish the language of the pure Spirit which inwardly moves upon the heart and taught [me] to wait in silence sometimes many weeks together, until I felt that rise which prepares the creature to stand like a trumpet through which the Lord speaks to his flock.

From an inward purifying, and steadfast abiding under it, springs a lively operative desire for the good of others. All faithful people are not called to the public ministry, but whoever are, are called to minister of that which they have tasted and handled spiritually. The outward modes of worship are various, but wherever men are true ministers of Jesus Christ it is from the operation of his spirit upon their hearts, first purifying them and thus giving them a feeling sense of the conditions of others. This truth was early fixed in my mind, and I was taught to watch the pure opening and to take heed lest while I was standing to speak, my own will should get uppermost and cause me to utter words from worldly wisdom and depart from the channel of the true gospel ministry.

In the management of my outward affairs I may say with thankfulness I found Truth to be my support and I was respected in my master's family, who came to live in Mount Holly within two year after my going there.

About the twenty-third year of my age, I had many fresh and heavenly openings in respect to the care and providence of the Almighty over his creatures in general, and over man as the most noble amongst those which are visible. And being clearly convinced in my judgment that to place my whole trust in God was best for me, I felt renewed engagements that in all things I might act on an inward principle of virtue and pursue worldly business no further than as Truth opened my way therein.

About the time called Christmas I observed many people from the country and dwellers in town who, resorting to the public houses, spent their time in drinking and vain sports, tending to corrupt one another, on which account I was much troubled. At one house in particular there was much disorder, and I believed it was a duty laid on me to go and speak to the master of that house. I considered I was young and that several elderly Friends in town had opportunity to see these things, and though I would gladly have been excused, yet I could not feel my mind clear.

The exercise was heavy, and as I was reading what the Almighty said to Ezekiel,[14] respecting his duty as a watchman, the matter was set home more clearly; and then with prayer and tears I besought the Lord for his assistance, who in loving-kindness gave me a resigned heart. Then at a suitable opportunity I went to the public house, and seeing

---

14. **Ezekiel:** An Old Testament prophet and author of the Book of Ezekiel.

the man amongst a company, I went to him and told him I wanted to speak with him; so we went aside, and there in the fear and dread of the Almighty I expressed to him what rested on my mind, which he took kindly, and afterward showed more regard to me than before. In a few years after, he died middle-aged, and I often thought that had I neglected my duty in that case it would have given me great trouble, and I was humbly thankful to my gracious Father, who had supported me herein.

My employer, having a Negro woman, sold her and directed me to write a bill of sale, the man being waiting who bought her. The thing was sudden, and though the thoughts of writing an instrument of slavery for one of my fellow creatures felt uneasy,[15] yet I remembered I was hired by the year, that it was my master who directed me to do it, and that it was an elderly man, a member of our Society, who bought her; so through weakness I gave way and wrote it, but at the executing it, I was so afflicted in my mind that I said before my master and the Friend that I believed slavekeeping to be a practice inconsistent with the Christian religion. This in some degree abated my uneasiness, yet as often as I reflected seriously upon it I thought I should have been clearer if I had desired to be excused from it as a thing against my conscience, for such it was. And some time after this a young man of our Society spake to me to write an instrument of slavery, he having lately taken a Negro into his house. I told him I was not easy to write it, for though many kept slaves in our Society, as in others, I still believed the practice was not right, and desired to be excused from writing [it]. I spoke to him in good will, and he told me that keeping slaves was not altogether agreeable to his mind, but that the slave being a gift made to his wife, he had accepted of her.

From Chapter III

1749–1756

Scrupling to do writings relative to keeping slaves having been a means of sundry small trials to me, in which I have so evidently felt my own will set aside that I think it good to mention a few of them. Tradesmen and retailers of goods, who depend on their business for a living, are naturally inclined to keep the good will of their customers; nor is it a pleasant thing for young men to be under a necessity to question the judgment or honesty of elderly men, and more especially of such who have a fair reputation. Deep-rooted customs, though wrong, are not easily altered, but it is the duty of everyone to be firm in that which they certainly know is right for them. A charitable, benevolent man, well acquainted with a Negro, may, I believe, under some certain circumstances keep him in his family as a servant on no other motives than the Negro's good; but man, as man, knows not what shall be after him, nor hath he any assurance that his children will attain to that perfection in wisdom and goodness necessary in every absolute governor.

15. **felt uneasy:** Woolman's conscience was not comfortable with writing the bill of sale for a person.

Hence it is clear to me that I ought not to be the scribe where wills are drawn in which some children are made absolute masters over others during life.

About this time an ancient man of good esteem in the neighbourhood came to my house to get his will wrote. He had young Negroes, and I asking him privately how he purposed to dispose of them, he told me. I then said, "I cannot write thy will without breaking my own peace," and respectfully gave him my reasons for it. He signified that he had a choice that I should have wrote it, but as I could not consistent with my conscience, he did not desire it and so he got it wrote by some other person. And a few years after, there being great alterations in his family, he came again to get me to write his will. His Negroes were yet young, and his son, to whom he intended to give them, was since he first spoke to me, from a libertine become a sober young man; and he supposed that I would have been free on that account to write it. We had much friendly talk on the subject and then deferred it, and a few days after, he came again and directed their freedom, and so I wrote his will.

Near the time the last-mentioned friend first spoke to me, a neighbour received a bad bruise in his body and sent for me to bleed him, which being done he desired me to write his will. I took notes, and amongst other things he told me to which of his children he gave his young Negro. I considered the pain and distress he was in and knew not how it would end, so I wrote his will, save only that part concerning his slave, and carrying it to his bedside read it to him and then told him in a friendly way that I could not write any instruments by which my fellow creatures were made slaves, without bringing trouble on my own mind. I let him know that I charged nothing for what I had done and desired to be excused from doing the other part in the way he proposed. Then we had a serious conference on the subject, and at length, he agreeing to set her free, I finished his will.

Having found drawings in my mind to visit Friends on Long Island, and having got a certificate from our Monthly Meeting, I set off 12th day, 5th month, 1756. When I reached the island I lodged the first night at the house of my dear friend Richard Hallett. The next day being the first of the week, I was at their meeting, in which we had experience of the renewed manifestations of the love of Jesus Christ, to the comfort of the honest-hearted. I went that night to Flushing, and the next day in company with my beloved friend Matthew Franklin we crossed the ferry at White Stone, were at three meetings on that side the water, and then came on to the island, where I spent the remainder of the week in visiting meetings. The Lord I believe hath a people in those parts who are honestly concerned to serve him, but many I fear are too much clogged with the things of this life and do not come forward bearing the cross in such faithfulness as the Almighty calls for.

My mind was deeply engaged in this visit, both in public and private; and at several places where I was, on observing that they had slaves, I found myself under a necessity in a friendly way to labour with them on that subject, expressing as way opened the inconsistency of that practice with the purity of the Christian religion and the ill effects of it manifested amongst us.

The latter end of the week their Yearly Meeting began, at which were our Friends

John Scarborough, Jane Hoskins, and Susanna Brown from Pennsylvania. The public meetings were large and measurably favoured with divine goodness.

The exercise of my mind at this meeting was chiefly on account of those who were considered as the foremost rank in the Society, and in a meeting of ministers and elders, way opened that I expressed in some measure what lay upon me; and at a time when Friends were met for transacting public business, we sitting a while silent, I felt a weight on my mind and stood up; and through the gracious regard of our Heavenly Father, strength was given fully to clear my mind of a burden which for some days had been increasing upon me.

Through the humbling dispensations of divine providence men are sometimes fitted for his service. The messages of the prophet Jeremiah were so disagreeable to the people and so reverse to the spirit they lived in that he became the object of their reproach and in the weakness of nature thought to desist from his prophetic office, but saith he: "His word was in my heart as a burning fire shut up in my bones, and I was weary with forebearing and could not stay."[16] I saw at this time that if I was honest to declare that which Truth opened in me, I could not please all men, and laboured to be content in the way of my duty, however disagreeable to my own inclination. After this I went homeward, taking Woodbridge and Plainfield in my way, in both which meetings the pure influence of divine love was manifested, in a humbling sense whereof I went home, having been out about 24 days and rode about 316 miles.

While I was out on this journey my heart was much affected with a sense of the state of the churches in our southern provinces, and believing the Lord was calling me to some further labour amongst them, I was bowed in reverence before him, with fervent desires that I might find strength to resign myself up to his heavenly will.

Until the year 1756 I continued to retail goods, besides following my trade as a tailor, about which time I grew uneasy on account of my business growing too cumbersome. I began with selling trimmings for garments and from thence proceeded to sell clothes and linens, and at length having got a considerable shop of goods, my trade increased every year and the road to large business appeared open; but I felt a stop in my mind.

Through the mercies of the Almighty I had in a good degree learned to be content with a plain way of living. I had but a small family, that on serious consideration I believed Truth did not require me to engage in much cumbrous affairs. It had been my general practice to buy and sell things really useful. Things that served chiefly to please the vain mind in people I was not easy to trade in, seldom did it, and whenever I did I found it weaken me as a Christian.

The increase of business became my burden, for though my natural inclination was toward merchandise, yet I believed Truth required me to live more free from outward cumbers, and there was now a strife in my mind between the two; and in this exercise my prayers were put up to the Lord, who graciously heard me and gave me a heart resigned to his holy will. Then I lessened my outward business, and as I had opportunity

---

16. "His . . . stay": Jeremiah 20:9.

told my customers of my intentions that they might consider what shop to turn to, and so in a while wholly laid down merchandise, following my trade as a tailor, myself only, having no apprentice. I also had a nursery of apple trees, in which I employed some of my time – hoeing, grafting, trimming, and inoculating.

In merchandise it is the custom where I lived to sell chiefly on credit, and poor people often get in debt, and when payment is expected, not having wherewith to pay, their creditors often sue for it at law. Having often observed occurrences of this kind, I found it good for me to advise poor people to take such goods as were most useful and not costly.

In the time of trading, I had an opportunity of seeing that too liberal a use of spirituous liquors and the custom of wearing too costly apparel lead some people into great inconveniences, and these two things appear to be often connected one with the other. For by not attending to that use of things which is consistent with universal righteousness, there is an increase of labour which extends beyond what our Heavenly Father intends for us. And by great labour, and often by much sweating in the heat, there is even amongst such who are not drunkards a craving of some liquors to revive the spirits: that partly by the wanton, luxurious drinking of some, and partly by the drinkings of others led to it through immoderate labour, very great quantities of rum are every year expended in our colonies, the greater part of which we should have no need did we steadily attend to pure wisdom.

Where men take pleasure in feeling their minds elevated with strong drink and so indulge their appetite as to disorder their understandings, neglect their duty as members in a family or civil society, and cast off all pretense to religion, their case is much to be pitied. And where such whose lives are for the most part regular, and whose examples have a strong influence on the minds of others, adhere to some customs which strongly draw toward the use of more strong liquor than pure wisdom directs to the use of, this also, as it hinders the spreading of the spirit of meekness and strengthens the hands of the more excessive drinkers, is a case to be lamented.

As the least degree of luxury hath some connection with evil, for those who profess to be disciples of Christ and are looked upon as leaders of the people, to have that mind in them which was also in him, and so stand separate from every wrong way, is a means of help to the weaker. As I have sometimes been much spent in the heat and taken spirits to revive me, I have found by experience that in such circumstance the mind is not so calm nor I so fitly disposed for divine meditation as when all such extremes are avoided, and have felt an increasing care to attend to that Holy Spirit which sets right bounds to our desires and leads those who faithfully follow it to apply all the gifts of divine providence to the purposes for which they were intended. Did such who have the care of great estates attend with singleness of heart to this Heavenly Instructor, which so opens and enlarges the mind that men love their neighbours as themselves, they would have wisdom given them to manage without finding occasion to employ some people in the luxuries of life or to make it necessary for others to labour too hard. But for want of steadily regarding this principle of divine love, a selfish spirit takes place in the minds of people, which is attended with darkness and manifold confusions in the world.

[1774, 1971]

Samson Occom

[1723–1792]

Samson Occom was born in 1723 near New London, Connecticut. In his autobiography, Occom later described the "wandering life" of his parents, members of the Mohegan tribe, who raised him in "Heathenism." Although they were allies of the English, by the time of Occom's birth the Mohegans were struggling with the constant encroachment of the colonists as well as the devastating effects of diseases such as smallpox and measles. During Occom's childhood, the population of the tribe dwindled to a few hundred people. At the age of sixteen, Occom heard some of the itinerant evangelists associated with the religious revival known as the Great Awakening (1735–45). These "Extraordinary Ministers," as he called them, included Eleazer Wheelock, George Whitefield, and James Davenport, who traveled throughout New England seeking to revive piety and religious fervor among the Congregationalist Churches. The young Occom was deeply moved and converted to Christianity. He also began to teach himself to read and write. Eager to learn more, Occom became the first student at a college-prepatory school Wheelock established in Lebanon, Connecticut. In only four years at the school, 1743–47, Occom swiftly gained fluency in English and proficiency in Latin, Greek, and Hebrew.

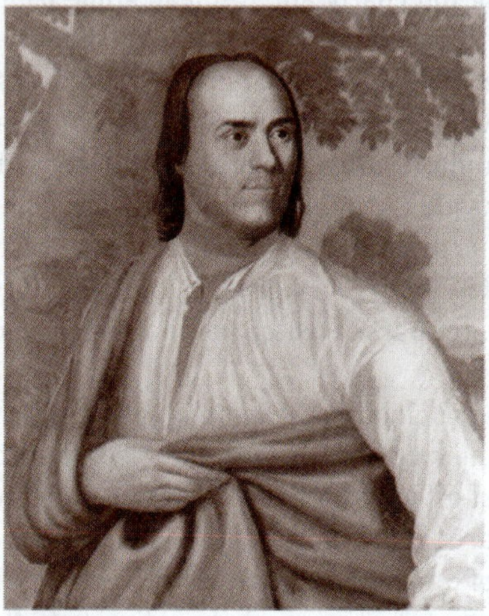

Nathaniel Smibert, *An Indian Priest*

Only recently identified as Samson Occom, this portrait was painted by Smibert sometime in the period 1751–56, when Occom was a schoolmaster and preacher among the Montauk tribe on Long Island.

Although his poor health and failing eyesight prevented him from continuing his studies, Occom became a noted minister and advocate for the Indians. In 1749, he moved to eastern Long Island to become the schoolmaster of the Montauk tribe, among whom Occom taught and preached for the following decade. He married a Montauk woman, Mary Fowler, with whom he had ten children. In 1759, Occom was ordained as a minister by the Presbytery of Long Island. He then became an itinerant minister in southern New England and, in 1761, a missionary to the Oneida Indians in central New York. By 1764, Occom and his family were living in Connecticut, assisting in raising money for Moor's Indian Charity School, which Wheelock had established in 1753 to train Indian missionaries for work among their own people. At Wheelock's request, Occom undertook a successful fund-raising campaign in England, where he preached over three hundred sermons. Then at the height of his fame, Occom modestly hoped that he would be rewarded with a ministry among the Mohegans. But he was not offered any position, and his bitterness was reflected in his autobiography, written shortly after his return to America in 1768. To his fur-

I have this day received your obliging kind epistle, and am greatly satisfied with your reasons respecting negroes, and think highly reasonable what you offer in vindication of their natural rights.

– Phillis Wheatley

ther dismay, Wheelock decided to move his school to Hanover, New Hampshire, where he used the funds Occom had raised to establish Dartmouth College.

Concerned that his people would not benefit from the new college, Occom ended his relationship with Wheelock and pursued his own plans to improve the lives of the Indians. He continued to preach, and he published *A Sermon Preached at the Execution of Moses Paul* (1772), a fellow Christian Mohegan who murdered a man while drunk. The execution sermon, designed to condemn the person who was about to die and to serve as a cautionary tale for the audience, was a common and popular form. Occom's emphasis in the sermon on the need for temperance also mirrored a common concern of civil and religious leaders, who feared that excessive drinking among both Native Americans and European settlers posed a threat to the social stability of colonial America. The sermon went through nineteen editions, and Occom also published *A Choice Collection of Spiritual Hymns* (1774). But he devoted most of his energies to a plan to establish a new settlement of Christian Indians on the lands of the Oneida tribe in central New York. The plan was finally realized in 1785, and Occom became the teacher in the new community, called Brothertown. Two years later, when the community established the first Presbyterian church organized solely by Indians, Occom became its minister. He continued to serve Brothertown and other Indian communities until his death in 1792. He is thought to be buried in an unmarked grave in an abandoned Indian cemetery in the hills above present-day Deansboro, New York.

bedfordstmartins.com/ americanlit *for research links on Occom*

Occom's *A Short Narrative of My Life.* Occom wrote his brief autobiography, one of the first works in English written by a Native American, shortly after he returned from a fund-raising campaign in England. He had spent three years there, working to raise money for Eleazar Wheelock, who intended to establish an Indian charity school but instead established Dartmouth College with the substantial funds Occom brought back from England. In part, Occom wrote his autobiography to dispel rumors spread by disgruntled fellow missionaries that he was not a Mohegan. Some also alleged that Occom had converted to Christianity solely to raise money for a school for Indians. Occom dispelled both charges in his narrative, which he wrote in a diary he kept from the 1750s to 1790. In an entry prefacing the narrative, dated September 17, 1768, he alluded to "gross Mistakes" in accounts being circulated about him, adding: "That it is against my mind to give a History of my self whilst I am alive, yet to do justice to myself and to those who may desire to know some thing concerning me, – and for the Honor of Religion I will venture to give a Short Narrative of my Life." Emphasizing his conversion to Christianity, his subsequent hunger for education, and his later work as a preacher and a teacher, Occom implicitly offers his own life as both an example of the capacity of Native Americans and an illustration of the discrimination Indian missionaries and their people suffered in colonial America. His account was possibly read by a few people at the time, but it was not published in its entirety until 1982. The text is taken from the unedited transcription of the manuscript at Dartmouth College, which was published in *The Elders Wrote: An Anthology of Early Prose by North American Indians, 1768–1931*, edited by Bernd Peyer (1982). Occom evidently wrote the account in some haste, and we have slightly adjusted his punctuation. For example, we have omitted dashes between sentences and inserted apostrophes in some contractions (*Liv'd* for *Livd*).

A SHORT NARRATIVE OF MY LIFE

From my Birth till I received the Christian Religion

I was Born a Heathen and Brought up In Heathenism, till I was between 16 & 17 years of age, at a Place Call'd Mohegan, in New London, Connecticut, in New England. My Parents Liv'd a wandering life, for did all the Indians at Mohegan, they Chiefly Depended upon Hunting, Fishing, & Fowling for their Living and had no Connection with the English, excepting to Traffic[1] with them in their small Trifles; and they Strictly maintained and followed their Heathenish Ways, Customs & Religion, though there was Some Preaching among them. Once a Fortnight, in ye Summer Season, a Minister from New London used to come up, and the Indians to attend; not that they regarded the Christian Religion, but they had Blankets given to them every Fall of the Year and for these things they would attend and there was a Sort of School kept, when I was quite young, but I believe there never was one that ever Learnt to read any thing, – and when I was about 10 Years of age there was a man who went about among the Indian Wigwams, and wherever he Could find the Indian Children, would make them read; but the Children Used to take Care to keep out of his way; – and he used to Catch me Some times and make me Say over my Letters; and I believe I learnt Some of them. But this was Soon over too; and all this Time there was not one amongst us, that made a Profession of Christianity. Neither did we Cultivate our Land, nor kept any Sort of Creatures except Dogs, which we used in Hunting; and we Dwelt in Wigwams. These are a Sort of Tents, Covered with Matts, made of Flags.[2] And to this Time we were unaquainted with the English Tongue in general though there were a few, who understood a little of it.

From the Time of our Reformation till I left Mr. Wheelocks

When I was 16 years of age, we heard a Strange Rumor among the English, that there were Extraordinary Ministers Preaching from Place to Place and a Strange Concern among the White People. This was in the Spring of the Year. But we Saw nothing of these

1. Traffic: Early term for trade.
2. Flags: Long, stiff, sword-shaped leaves.

things, till Some Time in the Summer, when Some Ministers began to visit us and Preach the Word of God; and the Common People all Came frequently and exhorted us to the things of God, which it pleased the Lord, as I humbly hope, to Bless and accompany with Divine Influence to the Conviction and Saving Conversion of a Number of us; amongst whom I was one that was Imprest with the things we had heard. These Preachers did not only come to us, but we frequently went to their meetings and Churches. After I was awakened[3] & converted, I went to all the meetings, I could come at; & Continued under Trouble of Mind about 6 months; at which time I began to Learn the English Letters; got me a Primer,[4] and used to go to my English Neighbours frequently for Assistance in Reading, but went to no School. And when I was 17 years of age, I had, as I trust, a Discovery of the way of Salvation through Jesus Christ, and was enabl'd to put my trust in him alone for Life & Salvation. From this Time the Distress and Burden of my mind was removed, and I found Serenity and Pleasure of Soul, in Serving God. By this time I just began to Read in the New Testament without Spelling, – and I had a Stronger Desire Still to Learn to read the Word of God, and at the Same Time had an uncommon Pity and Compassion to my Poor Brethren According to the Flesh. I used to wish I was capable of Instructing my poor Kindred. I used to think, if I Could once Learn to Read I would Instruct the poor Children in Reading, – and used frequently to talk with our Indians Concerning Religion. This continued till I was in my 19th year: by this Time I Could Read a little in the Bible. At this Time my Poor Mother was going to Lebanon, and having had Some Knowledge of Mr. Wheelock[5] and hearing he had a Number of English youth under his Tuition,[6] I had a great Inclination to go to him and be with him a week or a Fortnight, and Desired my Mother to Ask Mr. Wheelock whether he would take me a little while to Instruct me in Reading. Mother did so; and when She Came Back, She Said Mr. Wheelock wanted to See me as Soon as possible. So I went up, thinking I Should be back again in a few Days; when I got up there, he received me With kindness and Compassion and in Stead of Staying a Forthnight or 3 Weeks, I Spent 4 Years with him. After I had been with him Some Time, he began to acquaint his Friends of my being with him, and of his Intentions of Educating me, and my Circumstances. And the good People began to give Some Assistance to Mr. Wheelock, and gave me Some old and Some New Clothes. Then he represented the Case to the Honorable Commissioners at Boston, who were Commission'd by the Honorable Society in London for Propagating the gospel among the Indians in New England and parts adjacent, and they allowed him 60 £ in old Tender, which was about

3. **awakened:** To be made aware of or stirred by Christianity.
4. **Primer:** Textbook used to teach children to read.
5. **Mr. Wheelock:** Eleazer Wheelock (1711-1779), a teacher and Congregationalist minister; he later founded the Moor's Indian Charity School (1753) and Dartmouth College, established in 1769 "for the education and instruction of youth of the Indian tribes in this land in reading, writing, and all parts of learning which shall appear necessary and expedient for civilizing and Christianizing children of pagans, as well as in all liberal arts and sciences, and also of English youth and any others."
6. **Tuition:** Supervision for purposes of instruction.

6 £ Sterling,[7] and they Continu'd it 2 or 3 years, I can't tell exactly. While I was at Mr. Wheelock's, I was very weakly and my Health much impaired, and at the End of 4 Years, I over Strained my Eyes to such a Degree, I Could not persue my Studies any Longer; and out of these 4 years I Lost Just about one year; – And was obliged to quit my Studies.

From the Time I left Mr. Wheelock till I went to Europe

As soon as I left Mr. Wheelock, I endeavored to find Some Employ among the Indians; went to Nahantuck, thinking they may want a School Master, but they had one; then went to Narraganset, and they were Indifferent about a School, and went back to Mohegan, and heard a number of our Indians were going to Montauk, on Long Island, and I went with them, and the Indians there were very desirous to have me keep a School amongst them, and I Consented, and went back a while to Mohegan and Some time in November I went on the Island, I think it is 17 years ago last November. I agreed to keep School with them Half a Year, and left it with them to give me what they Pleased; and they took turns to Provide Food for me. I had near 30 Scholars this winter; I had an evening School too for those that could not attend the Day School – and began to Carry on their meetings, they had a Minister, one Mr. Horton, the Scotch Society's Missionary; but he Spent, I think two thirds of his Time at Sheenecock, 30 Miles from Montauk. We met together 3 times for Divine Worship every Sabbath and once on every Wednesday evening. I (used) to read the Scriptures to them and used to expound upon Some particular Passages in my own Tongue. Visited the Sick and attended their Burials. When the half year expired, they Desired me to Continue with them, which I complied with, for another half year, when I had fulfilled that, they were urgent to have me Stay Longer, So I continued amongst them till I was Married, which was about 2 years after I went there. And Continued to Instruct them in the Same manner as I did before. After I was married a while, I found there was need of a Support more than I needed while I was Single, – and made my Case Known to Mr. Buell[8] and to Mr. Wheelock, and also the Needy Circumstances and the Desires of these Indians of my Continuing amongst them, and the Commissioners were so good as to grant £ 15 a year Sterling – And I kept on in my Service as usual, yea I had additional Service; I kept School as I did before and Carried on the Religious Meetings as often as ever, and attended the Sick and their Funerals, and did what Writings they wanted, and often Sat as a Judge to reconcile and Decide their Matters Between them, and had visitors of Indians from all Quarters; and, as our Custom is, we freely Entertain all Visitors. And was fetched often from my Tribe and from others to see into their Affairs Both Religious, Temporal, – Besides my Domestic Concerns. And it Pleased the Lord to Increase my Family fast – and Soon after I was

7. **60 £ in old Tender . . . 6 £ Sterling:** Several different currencies, including "Old Tender," were circulated in the colonies, where the English pound sterling (£) was also widely used. Although the dollar was not introduced until after the Revolution, scholars estimate that during the period 1766–72 the value of the English pound sterling was about $4.50, or what today would be roughly equivalent to $75.

8. **Mr. Buell:** Samuel Buell (1716–1798), Presbyterian minister of the church in East Hampton, Long Island, New York. Buell preached Occom's ordination sermon in 1759.

Married, Mr. Horton left these Indians and the Shenecock & after this I was (alone) and then I had the whole care of these Indians at Montauk, and visited the Shenecock Indians often. Used to set out Saturdays towards Night and come back again Mondays. I have been obliged to Set out from Home after Sun Set, and Ride 30 Miles in the Night, to Preach to these Indians. And Some Indians at Shenecock Sent their Children to my School at Montauk, I kept one of them Some Time, and had a Young Man a half year from Mohegan, a Lad from Nahantuck, who was with me almost a year; and had little or nothing for keeping them.

My Method in the School was, as Soon as the Children got together, and took their proper Seats, I Prayed with them, then began to hear them. I generally began (after some of them Could Spell and Read,) With those that were yet in their Alphabets, So around, as they were properly Seated till I got through and I obliged them to Study their Books, and to help one another. When they could not make out a hard word they Brought it to me – and I usually heard them, in the Summer Season 8 Times a Day 4 in the morning, and in ye after Noon. In the Winter Season 6 Times a Day, As Soon as they could Spell, they were obliged to Spell when ever they wanted to go out. I concluded with Prayer; I generally heard my Evening Scholars 3 Times Round, And as they go out the School, every one, that Can Spell, is obliged to Spell a Word, and to go out Leisurely one after another. I Catechised 3 or 4 Times a Week according to the Assembly's Shout or Catechism, and many Times Proposed Questions of my own, and in my own Tongue. I found Difficulty with Some Children, who were Some what Dull, most of these can soon learn to Say over their Letters, they Distinguish the Sounds by the Ear, but their Eyes can't Distinguish the Letters, and the way I took to cure them was by making an Alphabet on Small bits of paper, and glued them on Small Chips of Cedar after this manner A B & C. I put these on Letters in order on a Bench then point to one Letter and bid a Child to take notice of it, and then I order the Child to fetch me the Letter from the Bench; if he Brings the Letter, it is well, if not he must go again and again till he brings ye right Letter. When they can bring any Letters this way, then I just Jumble them together, and bid them to set them in Alphabetical order, and it is a Pleasure to them; and they soon Learn their Letters this way. I frequently Discussed or Exhorted my Scholars, in Religious matters. My Method in our Religious Meetings was this; Sabbath Morning we Assemble together about 10 o'C and begin with Singing; we generally Sung Dr. Watt's Psalms or Hymns. I distinctly read the Psalm or Hymn first, and then gave the meaning of it to them, after that Sing, then Pray, and Sing again after Prayer. Then proceed to Read from Suitable portion of Scripture, and so Just give the plain Sense of it in Familiar Discourse and apply it to them. So continued with Prayer and Singing. In the after Noon and Evening we Proceed in the Same Manner, and so in Wednesday Evening. Some Time after Mr. Horton left these Indians, there was a remarkable revival of religion among these Indians and many were hopefully converted to the Saving knowledge of God in Jesus. It is to be observed before Mr. Horton left these Indians they had Some Prejudices infused in their minds, by Some Enthusiastical Exhorters from New England, against Mr. Horton, and many of them had left him; by this means he was Discouraged, and was disposed from these Indians. And being acquainted with the Enthusiasts in New England & the make and the Disposition of the Indians I took a mild way to reclaim them. I opposed them not openly but let them go on in their way, and whenever I had an opportunity, I would read Such pages of the Scriptures, and I thought would confound their Notions, and I would come to them with all Authority, Saying "these Saith the Lord"; and by this means, the Lord was pleased to Bless my poor Endeavours, and they were reclaimed, and Brought to hear almost any of the ministers.

I am now to give an Account of my Circumstances and manner of Living. I Dwelt in a Wigwam, a Small Hut with Small Poles and Covered with Matts made of Flags, and I was oblig'd to remove twice a Year, about 2 miles Distance, by reason of the Scarcity of wood, for in one Neck of Land they Planted their Corn, and in another, they had their wood, and I was oblig'd to have my Corn carted and my Hay also, – and I got my Ground Plow'd every year, which Cost me about 12 shillings an acre; and I kept a Cow and a Horse, for which I paid 21 shillings every year York currency,[9] and went 18 miles to Mill for every Dust of meal we used in my family. I Hired or Joined with my Neighbours to go to Mill, with a Horse or ox Cart, or on Horse Back, and Some time went myself. My Family Increasing fast, and my Visitors also. I was oblig'd to contrive every way to Support my Family; I took all opportunities, to get Some thing to feed my Family Daily. I Planted my own Corn, Potatoes, and Beans; I used to be out hoeing my Corn Some times before Sun Rise and after my School is Dismist, and by this means I was able to raise my own Pork, for I was allowed to keep 5 Swine. Some mornings & Evenings I would be out with my Hook and Line to Catch fish, and in the Fall of Year and in the Spring, I used my gun, and fed my Family with Fowls. I Could more than pay for my Powder & Shot with Feathers. At other Times I Bound old Books for Easthampton People, made wooden Spoons and Ladles, Stocked Guns, & worked on Cedar to make Pails, (Piggins),[10] and Churns & C. Besides all these Difficulties I met with advers Providence, I bought a Mare, had it but a little while, and she fell into the Quick Sand and Died, After a while Bought another, I kept her about half year, and she was gone, and I never have heard of nor Seen her from that Day to this; it was Supposed Some Rogue Stole her. I got another and Died with a Distemper, and last of all I Bought a Young Mare, and kept her till She had one Colt, and She broke her Leg and Died, and Presently after the Colt[11] Died also. In the whole I Lost 5 Horse Kind; all these Losses helped to pull me down; and by this Time I got greatly in Debt, and acquainted my Circumstances to Some of my Friends, and they Represented my Case to the Commissioners of Boston, and Interceded with them for me, and they were pleased to vote 15 £ for my Help, and Soon after Sent a Letter to my good Friend at New London, acquainting him that they had Superseded their Vote; and my Friends were so good as to represent my Needy Circumstances Still to them, and they were so good at Last, as to Vote £ 15 and Sent it, for which I am very thankful; and the Reverend Mr. Buell was so kind as to write in my behalf to the gentlemen of Boston; and he told me

---

9. **York currency:** In the currency issued in New York, twenty shillings also equaled a pound (£), but it was less valuable than the English £ sterling. The combined annual costs of having the ground plowed and keeping the animals was about $4.20, or what today would be roughly equivalent to $70. See note 7.
10. **Piggins:** A piggin, a small wooden pail with an upright stave for a handle, was often used as a dipper.
11. **Colt:** The manuscript reads "Cold."

they were much Displeased with him, and heard also once again that they blamed me for being Extravagant; I Can't Conceive how these gentlemen would have me Live. I am ready to (forgive) their Ignorance, and I would wish they had Changed Circumstances with me but one month, that they may know, by experience what my Case really was; but I am now fully convinced, that it was not Ignorance, For I believe it can be proved to the world that these Same Gentlemen gave a young Missionary a Single man, *one Hundred Pounds* for one year, and fifty Pounds for an Interpreter, and thirty Pounds for an Introducer; so it Cost them one Hundred & Eighty Pounds in one Single Year, and they Sent too where there was no Need of a Missionary.

Now you See what difference they made between me and other missionaries; they gave me 180 Pounds for 12 years Service, which they gave for one years Services in another Mission. In my Service (I speak like a fool, but I am Constrained) I was my own Interpreter. I was both a School master and Minister to the Indians, yea I was their Ear, Eye & Hand, as Well as Mouth. I leave it with the World, as wicked as it is, to Judge, whether I ought not to have had half as much, they gave a young man Just mentioned which would have been but £ 50 a year; and if they ought to have given me that, I am not under obligations to them, I owe them nothing at all; what can be the Reason that they used me after this manner? I can't think of any thing, but this as a Poor Indian Boy Said, Who was Bound out to an English Family, and he used to Drive Plow for a young man, and he whipt and Beat him allmost every Day, and the young man found fault with him, and Complained of him to his master and the poor Boy was Called to answer for himself before his master, and he was asked, what it was he did, that he was So Complained of and beat almost every Day. He Said, he did not know, but he Supposed it was because he could not drive any better; but says he, I Drive as well as I know how; and at other Times he Beats me, because he is of a mind to beat me; but says he believes he Beats me for the most of the Time "because I am an Indian".

So I am *ready* to Say, they have used me thus, because I Can't Influence the Indians so well as other missionaries; but I can assure them I have endeavoured to teach them as well as I know how; – but I *must Say*, "I believe it is because I am a poor Indian". I Can't help that God has made me So; I did not make my self so.

[1768, 1982]

Occom through a Modern Lens

IN THE LATE EIGHTEENTH CENTURY, works by Native Americans who wrote in English were published by several printers, including Thomas and Samuel Green, descendants of a prominent family of colonial printers. The Greens printed dozens of sermons and religious books on their press in New London, Connecticut. They published Samson Occom's collection of hymns and spiritual songs, as well as his sermon on the execution of Moses Paul. Occom's works went through several editions during the eighteenth century and enjoyed considerable popularity. But Occom's autobiographical sketch existed only in manuscript until it was finally published in 1982. Since then, he has been the object of considerable attention by scholars, including James Ottery, a professor of English, a member of the Brothertown Indian Nation, and a descendant of Occom, whose name he spells *Occum.* Ottery wrote the following poem as he was contemplating the "silences" in Occom's "Diary," which he kept over many years and in which he wrote *A Short Narrative of My Life.* Some commentators have stressed Occom's failure to mention some of the devastating events of his life in his narrative, while scholars have emphasized its limitations as a source of ethnographic information about Native Americans. In contrast, playing off observations by nonnative critics and quotations from Occom's narrative, Ottery meditates on the obstacles that confronted a Native American attempting to put his "life into words in the language / that wasn't his mother tongue." The text, which incorporates Occom's words, is taken from the online publication of the poem (http://work.colum.edu/~jottery/IntroCW/NAC/SamsonOccum.htm).

The Reverend Mr. Samson Occom

This portrait of Occom, described in an accompanying caption as the "first Indian Minister that ever was in Europe," was published in London during or shortly after his triumphant fund-raising tour of England. Occom wrote his brief narrative of his life soon after his return to America.

James Ottery

[b. 1953]

The Diary of Samson Occum

He put his life into words: his life
as a Presbyterian preacher,[1] his life
as a preacher and teacher before that
in the Society for Propagating the Gospel in New England,
two years of his life spent raising
money in old England for the Indian Charity School
in Connecticut, "funds misdirected"
for the founding of a white Dartmouth College instead.
He put his life into words, in the language
that was not his mother tongue, the language
not learned until he was 16;
in the language that was not his
until he reached the age of 16,
he wrote of his life until then in very few words
of the language that wasn't his mother tongue –

I was born a Heathen
and Brought up in Heathenism
until I was between 16 & 17 Years of age,
at a place call'd Mohegan . . .[2]

He put his life into words in the language
that wasn't his mother tongue, the English learned
first when he was 16,
(he would begin reading Hebrew at 21,
until "after a year of study" he would stop,
because "his *eyes* would fail him"),
In the language that was not his mother tongue
he would write:

Having Seen and heard Several Representations,
In England and Scotland [two words crossed out]

1. **Presbyterian preacher:** Occom was ordained a Presbyterian minister in 1759.
2. ***I . . . Mohegan:*** The opening lines of Occom's narrative.

by . . . Some gentlemen in America, Concerning me,
and finding many [crossed out: misrepresentations]
gross Mistakes in their account, — I
I thought it my Duty to Give
a Short, Plain, and Honest Account of my Self
whilst I am still alive, yet to doe Justice
to myself and to those
who may desire [two words crossed out]
to know something concerning [word crossed out] me . . .[3]

He put his life into words and we read it
in the words of another who read enough of his life
to write of Mohegan "at the center of the most fervent
religious awakening in New England,"[4] and how two converted
were "Sarah Occum" and Samson her son,
how Sarah convinced a good reverend
(who would years later "misdirect" the Indian Charity School funds)
to teach her son the white man's language,
how she had no money to pay his lessons,
how she "probably contributed some labor" to the Rev. Wheelock
and perhaps other members of his family.

Samson Occum put his life into the words
of the white man because he "believed
the Indian had to conform to white ways"
in order to be saved,
conform to the ways of the white man
who slaughtered his mother's people at Mystic River,[5]
conform to the ways of the white man
who would crowd out the Mohegans and the rest
of the New England tribes,
conform to ways of the white man
who brought "intemperance, licentiousness and disease,"

---

3. ***Having . . . me***: The quotation is from a transcription of Occom's heavily revised introduction to his account, which is not included in the published version of *A Short Narrative of My Life*.
4. **"religious awakening in New England"**: The Great Awakening, the religious revival that swept across New England during the 1730s and 1740s.
5. **slaughtered . . . at Mystic River**: In 1637, seven hundred Pequot women, children, and elderly people were killed in Mystic, Connecticut, when their fort was set ablaze by colonial troops under the command of Captain John Mason. Following the massacre, the surviving members of the tribe were sold as slaves or put under the power of other tribes, such as the Mohegans.

conform to the ways of the white man
because his ways, Samson Occum could see,
were to be the way of the New World,
conform to the ways of the white man and hope
that white men someday would be
better men for it.

Samson Occum put his life into the words of the white man
because he believed it was what he had to do.
But not his whole life.

In the language that's not his mother tongue:
he does not write much of his wife,
he does not write much of daughters and sons
he does not write much of his personal "life" –
how poverty and depression may have led to alcohol.
He does not write of these things in the white man's words:

Sometimes there are not words for life
in a language that is not your mother tongue.

[2001]

Olaudah Equiano

[1745?-1797]

Olaudah Equiano

In this engraving, which appeared on the title page of the first edition of *The Interesting Narrative of the Life of Olaudah Equiano*, the author holds a Bible open to chapters 4-5 of Acts.

With typically eighteenth-century reticence he records his singular and representative life for one purpose: to change things.

– Toni Morrison

Little is known for certain about the early life of Olaudah Equiano. Recent biographical investigations indicate that he may have been born in South Carolina in 1747 and that he was later purchased by Michael Henry Pascal, an officer in the British navy, who took him to England as early as 1754. Equiano, however, tells a different story in his autobiography. According to him, he was born in an Ibo village near the Niger River in West Africa around 1745. His parents expected him to become a chief or an elder of the village, but when he was about ten years old Equiano and his sister were kidnapped by slave traders. After being separated from her, he was sold to British traders and placed aboard a slave ship bound for the Americas. Equiano was first transported to Barbados and then to Virginia, where he was purchased by a local planter in 1756. The planter soon sold Equiano to Pascal, who took him to England in 1757.

From that point on, Equiano's account is fully corroborated by historical evidence. Pascal renamed him Gustavus Vassa – after the nobleman who led the Swedish people in their struggle for independence from Denmark and later became the first Swedish king – and sent him to school in London, where Equiano learned to read and write and where he was baptized in 1759. Along with Pascal, Equiano also served in the British navy and saw action in both Canada and the Mediterranean during the Seven Years' War (also known as the French and Indian War) between England and France (1756-63). But he was denied the prize money that was usually distributed to all sailors aboard a naval ship, as well as the freedom he had been promised by Pascal, who in 1762 sold Equiano back into slavery in the West Indies. There, he was purchased by Robert King, a Quaker merchant from Philadelphia. As the assistant to King, whose trade frequently included slaves, Equiano gained first-hand experience of slavery in both the American colonies and the West Indies. But he was also permitted to engage in his own modest trading business, and Equiano finally earned enough to purchase his freedom from King for £40 – roughly $175, or more than $3,000 in today's currency – on July 11, 1766.

During the final three decades of his life, Equiano worked at various trades even as he increasingly devoted himself to efforts to end slavery and the slave trade. He lived mostly in London, where he sometimes worked as a hairdresser or a servant. But the curious and restless Equiano joined expeditions to the Arctic and Central America, and he made several voyages to North America. In what he viewed as a crucial turning point of his life, Equiano converted to Christianity, which further fueled his humanitarian efforts. By 1777, he was writing hostile newspaper reviews of proslavery books, and during the following decade he helped form the Sons of Africa, a group of black men who campaigned against slavery and the slave trade. As part of that campaign, Equiano wrote *The Interesting Narrative of the Life of Olaudah Equiano* (1789), which was published by subscription, and whose list of influential subscribers included the Prince of

Wales. Following its publication, Equiano frequently spoke at antislavery meetings and wrote numerous letters to newspapers in response to racist articles. As the editor of a London newspaper observed of one of those responses, "We cannot but think the letter a good argument in favour of the natural Abilities, as well as good feelings, of the Negro Race, and a solid answer in their favour." Equiano, who also spoke in favor of racial intermarriage, married an Englishwoman, Susan Cullen, in 1792. The couple had two daughters before Equiano died in London on April 31, 1797.

bedfordstmartins.com/americanlit *for research links on Equiano*

Equiano's *Narrative*. Equiano's famous narrative, one of the earliest autobiographical accounts written by a black person in the Anglo-American world, was first published in London in 1789. The book sold extremely well in England, Ireland, and the United States, where it was published in 1791. In the early nineteenth century, it became an international bestseller, with numerous new editions in English, Dutch, French, and Russian. Addressing members of Parliament, Equiano clearly stated his purpose in the preface to the first edition:

> My Lords and Gentlemen, Permit me, with the greatest deference and respect, to lay at your feet the following genuine narrative; the chief design of which is to excite in your august assemblies a sense of compassion for the miseries which the Slave-Trade has entailed on my unfortunate countrymen. By the horrors of that trade I was first torn away from all the tender connections that were naturally dear to my heart; but these, through the mysterious ways of Providence, I ought to regard as infinitely more than

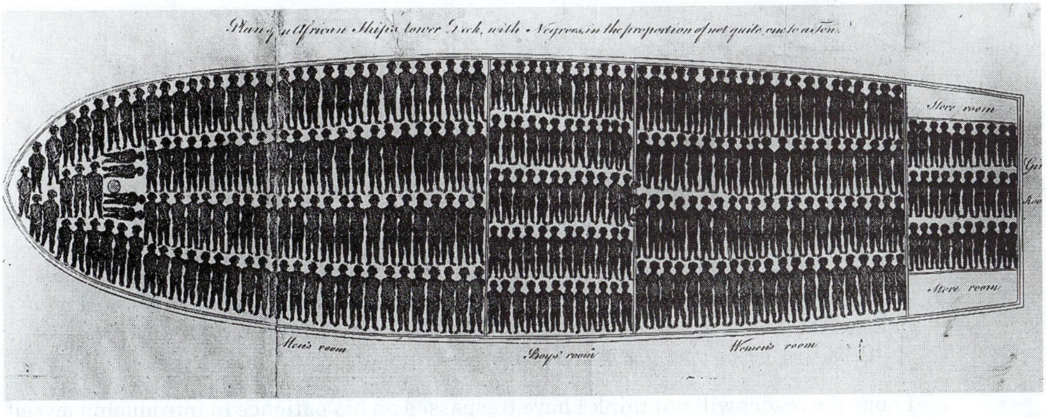

Plan of a Slave Ship

This engraving, published in 1789 by the Society for Effecting the Abolition of the Slave Trade to illustrate the brutal conditions aboard slave ships, was accompanied by the caption: "Plan of an African Ship's Lower Deck with Negroes in the Proportion of Only One to Ten."

compensated by the introduction I have thence obtained to the knowledge of the Christian religion, and of a nation which, by its liberal sentiments, its humanity, the glorious freedom of its government, and its proficiency in arts and sciences, has exalted the dignity of human nature.

Questions have recently been raised about Equiano's claim that he was born in Africa, since both his baptismal record and a Royal Navy muster roll indicate that he was born in South Carolina. If he was born in the American colonies – and the evidence is not conclusive – Equiano must have based his initial account of his early life in Africa on what he had read in books and stories he had heard from other slaves. Indeed, Equiano may well have intended his account to represent the experience of the more than one million Africans who were captured and transported as slaves to the New World from 1741 to 1760. At the same time, by claiming to have been one of them, Equiano could directly and authoritatively testify to the horrors of what was called the "Middle Passage" – the second leg of triangular voyages in which ships from Europe carried manufactured goods – like brandy, cloth, iron, guns, and gunpowder – to Africa, traded them there for human cargoes bound for the Americas, and finally exchanged the slaves for sugar, tobacco, and other products that were shipped back to Europe. Whether it was based on his own early memories or on his later experiences of slavery and the communal memories of other slaves, the following chapter from *The Interesting Narrative of the Life of Olaudah Equiano* stands as one of the most powerful of all indictments of the international slave trade, which was finally abolished by Great Britain and the United States in 1807. The text is taken from the first American printing of the *Narrative*, published in two volumes in New York City (1791). The lengthy paragraphs of that edition have been divided into shorter units to facilitate reading.

From The Interesting Narrative of the Life of Olaudah Equiano, or Gustavus Vassa, the African, Written by Himself

Chapter 2

The author's birth and parentage — His being kidnapped with his sister — Their separation — Surprise at meeting again — Are finally separated — Account of the different places and incidents the author met with till his arrival on the coast — The effect the sight of a slave-ship had on him — He sails for the West Indies — Horrors of a slave-ship — Arrives at Barbadoes, where the cargo is sold and dispersed.

I hope the reader will not think I have trespassed on his patience in introducing myself to him with some account of the manners and customs of my country.[1] They had been

1. **my country:** In the first chapter, Equiano says he was born in the Ibo village of Essaka in western Africa.

implanted in me with great care, and made an impression on my mind, which time could not erase, and which all the adversity and variety of fortune I have since experienced, served only to rivet and record: for, whether the love of one's country be real or imaginary, or a lesson of reason, or an instinct of nature, I still look back with pleasure on the first scenes of my life, though that pleasure has been for the most part mingled with sorrow.

I have already acquainted the reader with the time and place of my birth. My father, besides many slaves, had a numerous family, of which seven lived to grow up, including myself and sister, who was the only daughter. As I was the youngest of the sons, I became, of course, the greatest favorite with my mother, and was always with her; and she used to take particular pains to form my mind. I was trained up from my earliest years in the art of war: my daily exercise was shooting and throwing javelins, and my mother adorned me with emblems, after the manner of our greatest warriors. In this way I grew up till I had turned the age of eleven, when an end was put to my happiness in the following manner: Generally, when the grown people in the neighborhood were gone far in the fields to labor, the children assembled together in some of the neighboring premises to play; and commonly some of us used to get up a tree to look out for any assailant, or kidnapper, that might come upon us – for they sometimes took those opportunities of our parents' absence, to attack and carry off as many as they could seize. One day as I was watching at the top of a tree in our yard, I saw one of those people come into the yard of our next neighbor but one, to kidnap, there being many stout[2] young people in it. Immediately on this I gave the alarm of the rogue, and he was surrounded by the stoutest of them, who entangled him with cords, so that he could not escape, till some of the grown people came and secured him. But, alas! ere long it was my fate to be thus attacked, and to be carried off, when none of the grown people were nigh.

One day, when all our people were gone out to their works as usual, and only I and my dear sister were left to mind the house, two men and a woman got over our walls, and in a moment seized us both, and, without giving us time to cry out, or make resistance, they stopped our mouths, and ran off with us into the nearest wood. Here they tied our hands, and continued to carry us as far as they could, till night came on, when we reached a small house, where the robbers halted for refreshment, and spent the night. We were then unbound, but were unable to take any food; and, being quite overpowered by fatigue and grief, our only relief was some sleep, which allayed our misfortune for a short time. The next morning we left the house, and continued travelling all the day. For a long time we had kept the woods, but at last we came into a road which I believed I knew. I had now some hopes of being delivered; for we had advanced but a little way before I discovered some people at a distance, on which I began to cry out for their assistance; but my cries had no other effect than to make them tie me faster and stop my mouth, and then they put me into a large sack. They also stopped my sister's mouth, and tied her hands; and in this manner we proceeded till we were out of sight of these people. When we went to rest the following night, they offered us some victuals, but we refused

2. **stout:** Large and strong.

it; and the only comfort we had was in being in one another's arms all that night, and bathing each other with our tears. But alas! we were soon deprived of even the small comfort of weeping together.

The next day proved a day of greater sorrow than I had yet experienced; for my sister and I were then separated, while we lay clasped in each other's arms. It was in vain that we besought them not to part us; she was torn from me, and immediately carried away, while I was left in a state of distraction not to be described. I cried and grieved continually; and for several days did not eat anything but what they forced into my mouth. At length, after many days' travelling, during which I had often changed masters, I got into the hands of a chieftain, in a very pleasant country. This man had two wives and some children, and they all used me extremely well, and did all they could do to comfort me; particularly the first wife, who was something like my mother. Although I was a great many days' journey from my father's house, yet these people spoke exactly the same language with us. This first master of mine, as I may call him, was a smith,[3] and my principal employment was working his bellows, which were the same kind as I had seen in my vicinity. They were in some respects not unlike the stoves here in gentlemen's kitchens, and were covered over with leather; and in the middle of that leather a stick was fixed, and a person stood up, and worked it in the same manner as is done to pump water out of a cask with a hand pump. I believe it was gold he worked, for it was of a lovely bright yellow color, and was worn by the women on their wrists and ankles.

I was there I suppose about a month, and they at last used to trust me some little distance from the house. This liberty I used in embracing every opportunity to inquire the way to my own home; and I also sometimes, for the same purpose, went with the maidens, in the cool of the evenings, to bring pitchers of water from the springs for the use of the house. I had also remarked where the sun rose in the morning, and set in the evening, as I had travelled along; and I had observed that my father's house was towards the rising of the sun. I therefore determined to seize the first opportunity of making my escape, and to shape my course for that quarter; for I was quite oppressed and weighed down by grief after my mother and friends; and my love of liberty, ever great, was strengthened by the mortifying circumstance of not daring to eat with the free-born children, although I was mostly their companion.

While I was projecting my escape, one day an unlucky event happened, which quite disconcerted my plan, and put an end to my hopes. I used to be sometimes employed in assisting an elderly slave to cook and take care of the poultry; and one morning, while I was feeding some chickens, I happened to toss a small pebble at one of them, which hit it on the middle, and directly killed it. The old slave, having soon after missed the chicken, inquired after it; and on my relating the accident (for I told her the truth, for my mother would never suffer me to tell a lie), she flew into a violent passion, and threatened that I should suffer for it; and, my master being out, she immediately went and told her mistress what I had done. This alarmed me very much, and I expected an instant flogging, which to me was uncommonly dreadful, for I had seldom been beaten at home.

3. **smith:** A metalworker; short for blacksmith.

I therefore resolved to fly; and accordingly I ran into a thicket that was hard by, and hid myself in the bushes. Soon afterwards my mistress and the slave returned, and, not seeing me, they searched all the house, but not finding me, and I not making answer when they called to me, they thought I had run away, and the whole neighborhood was raised in the pursuit of me.

In that part of the country, as in ours, the houses and villages were skirted with woods, or shrubberies, and the bushes were so thick that a man could readily conceal himself in them, so as to elude the strictest search. The neighbors continued the whole day looking for me, and several times many of them came within a few yards of the place where I lay hid. I expected every moment, when I heard a rustling among the trees, to be found out, and punished by my master; but they never discovered me, though they were often so near that I even heard their conjectures as they were looking about for me; and I now learned from them that any attempts to return home would be hopeless. Most of them supposed I had fled towards home; but the distance was so great, and the way so intricate, that they thought I could never reach it, and that I should be lost in the woods. When I heard this I was seized with a violent panic, and abandoned myself to despair. Night, too, began to approach, and aggravated all my fears. I had before entertained hopes of getting home, and had determined when it should be dark to make the attempt; but I was now convinced it was fruitless, and began to consider that, if possibly I could escape all other animals, I could not those of the human kind; and that, not knowing the way, I must perish in the woods. Thus was I like the hunted deer –

> — Every leaf and every whisp'ring breath,
> Convey'd a foe, and every foe a death.[4]

I heard frequent rustlings among the leaves, and being pretty sure they were snakes, I expected every instant to be stung by them. This increased my anguish, and the horror of my situation became now quite insupportable. I at length quitted the thicket, very faint and hungry, for I had not eaten or drank anything all the day, and crept to my master's kitchen, from whence I set out at first, which was an open shed, and laid myself down in the ashes with an anxious wish for death, to relieve me from all my pains. I was scarcely awake in the morning, when the old woman slave, who was the first up, came to light the fire, and saw me in the fireplace. She was very much surprised to see me, and could scarcely believe her own eyes. She now promised to intercede for me, and went for her master, who soon after came, and, having slightly reprimanded me, ordered me to be taken care of, and not ill treated.

Soon after this, my master's only daughter, and child by his first wife, sickened and died, which affected him so much that for sometime he was almost frantic, and really would have killed himself, had he not been watched and prevented. However, in a short time afterwards he recovered, and I was again sold. I was now carried to the left of the sun's rising, through many dreary wastes and dismal woods, amidst the hideous roarings of wild beasts. The people I was sold to used to carry me very often, when I was

---

4. **Every . . . death:** The lines are unidentified; Equiano probably composed them himself.

tired, either on their shoulders or on their backs. I saw many convenient well-built sheds along the road, at proper distances, to accommodate the merchants and travellers, who lay in those buildings along with their wives, who often accompany them; and they always go well armed.

From the time I left my own nation, I always found somebody that understood me till I came to the sea coast. The languages of different nations did not totally differ, nor were they so copious as those of the Europeans, particularly the English. They were therefore easily learned; and, while I was journeying thus through Africa, I acquired two or three different tongues. In this manner I had been travelling for a considerable time, when, one evening, to my great surprise, whom should I see brought to the house where I was but my dear sister! As soon as she saw me, she gave a loud shriek, and ran into my arms – I was quite overpowered; neither of us could speak, but, for a considerable time, clung to each other in mutual embraces, unable to do anything but weep. Our meeting affected all who saw us; and, indeed, I must acknowledge, in honor of those sable destroyers of human rights, that I never met with any ill treatment, or saw any offered to their slaves, except tying them, when necessary, to keep them from running away.

When these people knew we were brother and sister, they indulged us to be together; and the man, to whom I supposed we belonged, lay with us, he in the middle, while she and I held one another by the hands across his breast all night; and thus for a while we forgot our misfortunes, in the joy of being together; but even this small comfort was soon to have an end; for scarcely had the fatal morning appeared when she was again torn from me forever! I was now more miserable, if possible, than before. The small relief which her presence gave me from pain, was gone, and the wretchedness of my situation was redoubled by my anxiety after her fate, and my apprehensions lest her sufferings should be greater than mine, when I could not be with her to alleviate them. Yes, thou dear partner of all my childish sports! thou sharer of my joys and sorrows! happy should I have ever esteemed myself to encounter every misery for you and to procure your freedom by the sacrifice of my own. Though you were early forced from my arms, your image has been always riveted in my heart, from which neither time nor fortune have been able to remove it; so that, while the thoughts of your sufferings have damped my prosperity, they have mingled with adversity and increased its bitterness. To that Heaven which protects the weak from the strong, I commit the care of your innocence and virtues, if they have not already received their full reward, and if your youth and delicacy have not long since fallen victims to the violence of the African trader, the pestilential stench of a Guinea ship, the seasoning in the European colonies, or the lash and lust of a brutal and unrelenting overseer.

I did not long remain after my sister. I was again sold, and carried through a number of places, till after travelling a considerable time, I came to a town called Tinmah, in the most beautiful country I had yet seen in Africa. It was extremely rich, and there were many rivulets which flowed through it, and supplied a large pond in the centre of the town, where the people washed. Here I saw for the first time cocoanuts, which I thought superior to any nuts I had ever tasted before; and the trees, which were loaded, were also interspersed among the houses, which had commodious shades adjoining, and were in the same manner as ours, the insides being neatly plastered and whitewashed. Here I also saw and tasted for the first time, sugar-cane. Their money consisted of little white shells, the size of the finger nail. I was sold here for one hundred and seventy-two of them, by a merchant who lived and brought me there.

I had been about two or three days at his house, when a wealthy widow, a neighbor of his, came there one evening, and brought with her an only son, a young gentleman about my own age and size. Here they saw me; and, having taken a fancy to me, I was bought of the merchant, and went home with them. Her house and premises were situated close to one of those rivulets I have mentioned, and were the finest I ever saw in Africa: they were very extensive, and she had a number of slaves to attend her. The next day I was washed and perfumed, and when meal time came, I was led into the presence of my mistress, and ate and drank before her with her son. This filled me with astonishment; and I could scarce help expressing my surprise that the young gentleman should suffer me, who was bound, to eat with him who was free; and not only so, but that he would not at any time either eat or drink till I had taken first, because I was the eldest, which was agreeable to our custom. Indeed, every thing here, and all their treatment of me, made me forget that I was a slave. The language of these people resembled ours so nearly, that we understood each other perfectly. They had also the very same customs as we. There were likewise slaves daily to attend us, while my young master and I, with other boys, sported with our darts and bows and arrows, as I had been used to do at home. In this resemblance to my former happy state, I passed about two months; and I now began to think I was to be adopted into the family, and was beginning to be reconciled to my situation, and to forget by degrees my misfortunes, when all at once the delusion vanished; for, without the least previous knowledge, one morning early, while my dear master and companion was still asleep, I was awakened out of my reverie to fresh sorrow, and hurried away even amongst the uncircumcised.

Thus, at the very moment I dreamed of the greatest happiness, I found myself most miserable; and it seemed as if fortune wished to give me this taste of joy only to render the reverse more poignant. The change I now experienced was as painful as it was sudden and unexpected. It was a change indeed, from a state of bliss to a scene which is inexpressible by me, as it discovered to me an element I had never before beheld, and till then had no idea of, and wherein such instances of hardship and cruelty continually occurred, as I can never reflect on but with horror.

All the nations and people I had hitherto passed through, resembled our own in their manners, customs, and language; but I came at length to a country, the inhabitants of which differed from us in all those particulars. I was very much struck with this difference, especially when I came among a people who did not circumcise, and ate without washing their hands. They cooked also in iron pots, and had European cutlasses and cross bows, which were unknown to us, and fought with their fists among themselves. Their women were not so modest as ours, for they ate, and drank, and slept with their men. But above all, I was amazed to see no sacrifices or offerings among them. In some of those places the people ornamented themselves with scars, and likewise filed their teeth very sharp. They wanted sometimes to ornament me in the same manner, but I would not suffer them; hoping that I might some time be among a people who did not thus disfigure themselves, as I thought they did. At last I came to the banks of a large river which was covered with canoes, in which the people appeared to live with their household utensils, and provisions of all kinds. I was beyond measure astonished at this, as I had never before seen any water larger than a pond or a rivulet; and my surprise was mingled with no small fear when I was put into one of these canoes, and we began to paddle and move along the river. We continued going on thus till night, and when we came to land, and made fires on the banks, each family by themselves; some dragged their canoes on shore, others stayed and cooked in theirs, and laid in them all night. Those on the land had mats, of which they made tents, some in the shape of little houses; in these we slept; and after the morning meal, we embarked again and proceeded as before. I was often very much astonished to see some of the women, as well as the men, jump into the water, dive to the bottom, come up again, and swim about.

Thus I continued to travel, sometimes by land, sometimes by water, through different countries and various nations, till, at the end of six or seven months after I had been kidnapped, I arrived at the sea coast. It would be tedious and uninteresting to relate all the incidents which befell me during this journey, and which I have not yet forgotten; of the various hands I passed through, and the manners and customs of all the different people among whom I lived – I shall therefore only observe, that in all the places where I was, the soil was exceedingly rich; the pumpkins, eadas,[5] plantains, yams, &c. &c., were in great abundance, and of incredible size. There were also vast quantities of different gums, though not used for any purpose, and everywhere a great deal of tobacco. The cotton even grew quite wild, and there was plenty of red-wood. I saw no mechanics[6] whatever in all the way, except such as I have mentioned. The chief employment in all these countries was agriculture, and both the males and females, as with us, were brought up to it, and trained in the arts of war.

The first object which saluted my eyes when I arrived on the coast, was the sea, and a slave ship, which was then riding at anchor, and waiting for its cargo. These filled me with astonishment, which was soon converted into terror, when I was carried on board. I was immediately handled, and tossed up to see if I were sound, by some of the crew; and I was now persuaded that I had gotten into a world of bad spirits, and that they were going to kill me. Their complexions, too, differing so much from ours, their long hair, and the language they spoke (which was very different from any I had ever heard), united to confirm me in this belief. Indeed, such were the horrors of my views and fears at the moment, that, if ten thousand worlds had been my own, I would have freely parted with them all to have exchanged my condition with that of the meanest slave in my own country. When I looked round the ship too, and saw a large furnance of copper boiling, and a multitude of black people of every description chained together, every one of their countenances expressing dejection and sorrow, I no longer doubted of my fate; and, quite overpowered with horror and anguish, I fell motionless on the deck and fainted. When I recovered a little, I found some black people about me, who I believed were some of those who had brought me on board, and had been receiving their pay; they talked to

---

5. **eadas:** Also spelled *eddoes*, meaning edible roots.
6. **mechanics:** Early term for manual laborers or artisans.

me in order to cheer me, but all in vain. I asked them if we were not to be eaten by those white men with horrible looks, red faces, and long hair. They told me I was not, and one of the crew brought me a small portion of spirituous liquor in a wine glass; but being afraid of him, I would not take it out of his hand. One of the blacks therefore took it from him and gave it to me, and I took a little down my palate, which, instead of reviving me, as they thought it would, threw me into the greatest consternation at the strange feeling it produced, having never tasted any such liquor before. Soon after this, the blacks who brought me on board went off, and left me abandoned to despair.

I now saw myself deprived of all chance of returning to my native country, or even the least glimpse of hope of gaining the shore, which I now considered as friendly; and I even wished for my former slavery in preference to my present situation, which was filled with horrors of every kind, still heightened by my ignorance of what I was to undergo. I was not long suffered to indulge my grief; I was soon put down under the decks, and there I received such a salutation in my nostrils as I had never experienced in my life: so that, with the loathsomeness of the stench, and crying together, I became so sick and low that I was not able to eat, nor had I the least desire to taste anything. I now wished for the last friend, death, to relieve me; but soon, to my grief, two of the white men offered me eatables; and, on my refusing to eat, one of them held me fast by the hands, and laid me across, I think, the windlass, and tied my feet, while the other flogged me severely. I had never experienced anything of this kind before, and, although not being used to the water, I naturally feared that element the first time I saw it, yet, nevertheless, could I have got over the nettings, I would have jumped over the side, but I could not; and besides, the crew used to watch us very closely who were not chained down to the decks, lest we should leap into the water; and I have seen some of these poor African prisoners most severely cut, for attempting to do so, and hourly whipped for not eating. This indeed was often the case with myself.

In a little time after, amongst the poor chained men, I found some of my own nation, which in a small degree gave ease to my mind. I inquired of these what was to be done with us? They gave me to understand, we were to be carried to these white people's country to work for them. I then was a little revived, and thought, if it were no worse than working, my situation was not so desperate; but still I feared I should be put to death, the white people looked and acted, as I thought, in so savage a manner; for I had never seen among any people such instances of brutal cruelty; and this not only shown towards us blacks, but also to some of the whites themselves. One white man in particular I saw, when we were permitted to be on deck, flogged so unmercifully with a large rope near the foremast, that he died in consequence of it; and they tossed him over the side as they would have done a brute. This made me fear these people the more; and I expected nothing less than to be treated in the same manner. I could not help expressing my fears and apprehensions to some of my countrymen; I asked them if these people had no country, but lived in this hollow place (the ship)? They told me they did not, but came from a distant one. "Then," said I, "how comes it in all our country we never heard of them?" They told me because they lived so very far off. I then asked where were their women? had they any like themselves? I was told they had. "And why," said I, "do we not see them?" They answered, because they were left behind. I asked how the vessel could go? They told me they could not tell; but that there was cloth put upon the masts by the help of the ropes I saw, and then the vessel went on; and the white men had some spell or magic they put in the water when they liked, in order to stop the vessel. I was exceedingly amazed at this account, and really thought they were spirits. I therefore wished much to be from amongst them, for I expected they would sacrifice me; but my wishes were vain – for we were so quartered that it was impossible for any of us to make our escape.

While we stayed on the coast I was mostly on deck; and one day, to my great astonishment, I saw one of these vessels coming in with the sails up. As soon as the whites saw it, they gave a great shout, at which we were amazed; and the more so, as the vessel appeared larger by approaching nearer. At last, she came to an anchor in my sight, and when the anchor was let go, I and my countrymen who saw it, were lost in astonishment to observe the vessel stop – and were now convinced it was done by magic. Soon after this the other ship got her boats out, and they came on board of us, and the people of both ships seemed very glad to see each other. Several of the strangers also shook hands with us black people, and made motions with their hands, signifying I suppose, we were to go to their country, but we did not understand them.

At last, when the ship we were in, had got in all her cargo, they made ready with many fearful noises, and we were all put under deck, so that we could not see how they managed the vessel. But this disappointment was the least of my sorrow. The stench of the hold while we were on the coast was so intolerably loathsome, that it was dangerous to remain there for any time, and some of us had been permitted to stay on the deck for the fresh air; but now that the whole ship's cargo were confined together, it became absolutely pestilential. The closeness of the place, and the heat of the climate, added to the number in the ship, which was so crowded that each had scarcely room to turn himself, almost suffocated us. This produced copious perspirations, so that the air soon became unfit for respiration, from a variety of loathsome smells, and brought on a sickness among the slaves, of which many died – thus falling victims to the improvident avarice, as I may call it, of their purchasers. This wretched situation was again aggravated by the galling of the chains, now became insupportable, and the filth of the necessary tubs,[7] into which the children often fell, and were almost suffocated. The shrieks of the women, and the groans of the dying, rendered the whole a scene of horror almost inconceivable. Happily perhaps, for myself, I was soon reduced so low here that it was thought necessary to keep me almost always on deck; and from my extreme youth I was not put in fetters. In this situation I expected every hour to share the fate of my companions, some of whom were almost daily brought upon deck at the point of death, which I began to hope would soon put an end to my miseries. Often did I think many of the inhabitants of the deep much more happy than myself. I envied them the freedom they enjoyed, and as often wished I could change my condition for theirs. Every circumstance I met with, served only to render my state more painful, and heightened my apprehensions, and my opinion of the cruelty of the whites.

---

7. **tubs:** Latrines.

One day they had taken a number of fishes; and when they had killed and satisfied themselves with as many as they thought fit, to our astonishment who were on deck, rather than give any of them to us to eat, as we expected, they tossed the remaining fish into the sea again, although we begged and prayed for some as well as we could, but in vain; and some of my countrymen, being pressed by hunger, took an opportunity, when they thought no one saw them, of trying to get a little privately; but they were discovered, and the attempt procured them some very severe floggings.

One day, when we had a smooth sea and moderate wind, two of my wearied countrymen who were chained together (I was near them at the time), preferring death to such a life of misery, somehow made through the nettings and jumped into the sea; immediately, another quite dejected fellow, who, on account of his illness, was suffered to be out of irons, also followed their example; and I believe many more would very soon have done the same, if they had not been prevented by the ship's crew, who were instantly alarmed. Those of us that were the most active, were in a moment put down under the deck; and there was such a noise and confusion amongst the people of the ship as I never heard before, to stop her, and get the boat out to go after the slaves. However, two of the wretches were drowned, but they got the other, and afterwards flogged him unmercifully, for thus attempting to prefer death to slavery. In this manner we continued to undergo more hardships than I can now relate, hardships which are inseparable from this accursed trade. Many a time we were near suffocation from the want of fresh air, which we were often without for whole days together. This, and the stench of the necessary tubs, carried off many.

During our passage, I first saw flying fishes, which surprised me very much; they used frequently to fly across the ship, and many of them fell on the deck. I also now first saw the use of the quadrant; I had often with astonishment seen the mariners make observations with it, and I could not think what it meant. They at last took notice of my surprise; and one of them, willing to increase it, as well as to gratify my curiosity, made me one day look through it. The clouds appeared to me to be land, which disappeared as they passed along. This heightened my wonder; and I was now more persuaded than ever, that I was in another world, and that every thing about me was magic.

At last we came in sight of the island of Barbadoes, at which the whites on board gave a great shout, and made many signs of joy to us. We did not know what to think of this; but as the vessel drew nearer, we plainly saw the harbor, and other ships of different kinds and sizes, and we soon anchored amongst them, off Bridgetown. Many merchants and planters now came on board, though it was in the evening. They put us in separate parcels,[8] and examined us attentively. They also made us jump, and pointed to the land, signifying we were to go there. We thought by this, we should be eaten by these ugly men, as they appeared to us; and, when soon after we were all put down under the deck again, there was much dread and trembling among us, and nothing but bitter cries to be heard all the night from these apprehensions, insomuch, that at last the white people got some old slaves from the land to pacify us. They told us we were not to be eaten, but

---

8. **parcels:** Divisions or groups.

to work, and were soon to go on land, where we should see many of our country people. This report eased us much. And sure enough, soon after we were landed, there came to us Africans of all languages.

We were conducted immediately to the merchant's yard, where we were all pent up together, like so many sheep in a fold, without regard to sex or age. As every object was new to me, everything I saw filled me with surprise. What struck me first, was, that the houses were built with bricks and stories, and in every other respect different from those I had seen in Africa; but I was still more astonished on seeing people on horseback. I did not know what this could mean; and, indeed, I thought these people were full of nothing but magical arts. While I was in this astonishment, one of my fellow prisoners spoke to a countryman of his, about the horses, who said they were the same kind they had in their country. I understood them, though they were from a distant part of Africa; and I thought it odd I had not seen any horses there; but afterwards, when I came to converse with different Africans, I found they had many horses amongst them, and much larger than those I then saw.

We were not many days in the merchant's custody, before we were sold after their usual manner, which is this: On a signal given (as the beat of a drum), the buyers rush at once into the yard where the slaves are confined, and make choice of that parcel they like best. The noise and clamor with which this is attended, and the eagerness visible in the countenances of the buyers, serve not a little to increase the apprehension of terrified Africans, who may well be supposed to consider them as the ministers of that destruction to which they think themselves devoted. In this manner, without scruple, are relations and friends separated, most of them never to see each other again.

I remember, in the vessel in which I was brought over, in the men's apartment, there were several brothers, who, in the sale, were sold in different lots; and it was very moving on this occasion, to see and hear their cries at parting. O, ye nominal Christians! might not an African ask you – Learned you this from your God, who says unto you, Do unto all men as you would men should do unto you? Is it not enough that we are torn from our country and friends, to toil for your luxury and lust of gain? Must every tender feeling be likewise sacrificed to your avarice? Are the dearest friends and relations, now rendered more dear by their separation from their kindred, still to be parted from each other, and thus prevented from cheering the gloom of slavery, with the small comfort of being together, and mingling their sufferings and sorrows? Why are parents to lose their children, brothers their sisters, or husbands their wives? Surely, this is a new refinement in cruelty, which, while it has no advantage to atone for it, thus aggravates distress, and adds fresh horrors even to the wretchedness of slavery.

[1789, 1791]

American Contexts

"To Begin the World Over Again": The Emerging Idea of "America"

The disaffection with British policies that led to the American Revolution developed for more than a decade before what Ralph Waldo Emerson later called "the shot heard round the world" was fired at the battles of Concord and Lexington in April 1775. Following the French and Indian War, also known as the Seven Years' War (1756-63), which ended France's empire in North America, the colonists viewed themselves as British patriots who had fought to preserve liberty and individual rights, including the right to property. Rather than being recognized for their sacrifices during the war, they were treated as subjects by Parliament. During the following twelve years, deep divisions arose between Britain and the American colonies, especially over issues of taxation. Many of those living in the colonies consequently began to think of themselves as "Americans," a people with a distinct identity whose liberty and property were threatened by a series of repressive laws passed by Parliament. Although as many as a third of the colonists actively opposed or were hostile to the Revolution, by 1775 thousands of others were so determined to defend their rights that they were ready to take up arms against the British army. The aspirations and hopes of those colonists were perhaps most eloquently expressed by Thomas Paine, an Englishman who had only recently emigrated to America. Two years after he arrived in Philadelphia in 1774, Paine published

bedfordstmartins.com/ americanlit *for research links on the authors in this section*

Common Sense (1776), a fifty-page pamphlet in which he powerfully affirmed the necessity for American independence from Britain. In the conclusion of his best-selling pamphlet, Paine reminds the colonists of the extraordinary moment in which they live: "We have it in our power to begin the world over again. A situation, similar to the present, hath not happened since the days of Noah until now. The birthday of a new world is at hand, and a race of men perhaps as numerous as all Europe contains, are to receive their portion of freedom from the event of a few months."

Paine was echoing a common sentiment in the colonies. In fact, from the beginning of English colonization of North America, the New World was viewed by many as a place for new beginnings, new opportunities, and new experiments of all kinds – political, religious, social, and cultural. The selection from *Common Sense* and the other documents in the following section reveal the ways in which a wide variety of speakers and writers conceived of "America" in the years before and after the Revolution. In various ways, they also addressed the famous question raised in the first of these documents, a selection from *Letters from an American Farmer*, in

Frontispiece of the *Massachusetts Magazine* (1790)

This allegorical engraving celebrated the triumph of the Enlightenment ideals of liberty and equality in America. Two female figures radiating light, one of them holding a staff with a liberty cap, stand next to a globe on a pedestal. The items at their feet include keys, discarded shackles, and a book open to "The Rights of Men." In the background, a man in armor and a haggard woman, representing war and discord, flee into the darkness.

which J. Hector St. John de Crèvecoeur asks: "What then is the American, this new man?" Responses to that question, and to broader questions about the country's emerging political and social values, range from patriotic verses to writings by three of the so-called Founding Fathers, John Adams, Thomas Jefferson, and George Washington. The selections also include appeals by those who sought to extend individual rights and liberty to marginalized or oppressed groups in the new country. Writing to her husband, John Adams – who was then serving on the committee to draft the Declaration of Independence – Abigail Adams urged him to "Remember the Ladies, and be more generous and favourable to them than your ancestors." In a petition to the president and Congress, the former slave Absalom Jones asks that the rights guaranteed by the Declaration of Independence and the Bill of Rights be extended to black men. At the same time, the Shawnee warrior Tecumseh strongly protested the forced sale of tribal lands and the brutal treatment of the Indians by the government, asking the territorial governor and future president William Henry Harrison: "How can we have confidence in the white people?" Indeed, the questions that emerged as the new nation formed were far-reaching. How would the country govern and protect itself? How could the existing colonies become a single entity, the United States of America? What were the rights of citizenship? To whom would those rights be extended? How would those who had refused to be what they described as "slaves" to Great Britain deal with the institution of slavery in their own country? And how would they deal with the native inhabitants of that country? What, finally, did "America" mean; what did it mean to be an "American"?

J. Hector St. John de Crèvecoeur

[1735-1813]

Born in France in 1735, Michel Guillaume Jean de Crèvecoeur left his native country when he was nineteen, moving to England, then to Canada, and finally to New York in 1759. He changed his name to J. Hector St. John de Crèvecoeur and traveled widely in the colonies as a surveyor and trader until 1769, when the newly married Crèvecoeur bought a farm in Orange County, New York. He lived there until the beginning of the Revolution, when his staunch support of British rule in the colonies forced him to leave his family and sail for England. In the preface to the first edition of *Letters from an American Farmer* (1782), which he had begun to write in New Jersey and sold to the English bookseller Thomas Davies, Crèvecoeur explains: "The following Letters are the genuine production of the American Farmer whose name they bear. They were privately written to gratify

J. Hector St. John de Crèvecoeur

The portrait is an anonymous copy of a miniature painted by the French artist Joseph Vallière in 1786, when Crèvecoeur was back in France. Attired in a powdered wig and the formal clothing of a French diplomat, Crèvecoeur bears little resemblance to the image he projects in his celebrated book, *Letters from an American Farmer.*

the curiosity of a friend; and are made public, because they contain much authentic information, little known on this side the Atlantic: they cannot therefore fail of being highly interesting to the people of England, at a time when everybody's attention is directed toward the affairs of America." Appearing near the end of the Revolutionary War, the book was an immediate success; so was the expanded edition Crèvecoeur translated and published in France in 1783 (dated 1784). That year, Crèvecoeur returned as a French diplomat to the United States, where he discovered that his wife was dead and their farm in ruins. He later returned for good to France, where in 1787 Crèvecoeur published yet another expanded edition of his famous book, which for many in the Old World of Europe served as a major source of both information about and imaginary visions of the New World of America. The text of the following selection is taken from a reprint published in 1904 of the first London edition, which appeared under the full title *Letters from an American Farmer; Describing Certain Provincial Situations, Manners, and Customs, Not Generally Known; and Conveying Some Idea of the Late and Present Circumstances of the British Colonies in North America* (1782).

LETTERS FROM AN AMERICAN FARMER

From Letter III. What Is an American

I wish I could be acquainted with the feelings and thoughts which must agitate the heart and present themselves to the mind of an enlightened Englishman, when he first lands on this continent. He must greatly rejoice that he lived at a time to see this fair country discovered and settled; he must necessarily feel a share of national pride, when he views the chain of settlements which embellishes these extended shores. When he says to himself, this is the work of my countrymen, who, when convulsed by factions, afflicted by a variety of miseries and wants, restless and impatient, took refuge here. They brought along with them their national genius, to which they principally owe what liberty they enjoy, and what substance they possess. Here he sees the industry of his native country displayed in a new manner, and traces in their works the embrios of all the arts, sciences, and ingenuity which flourish in Europe. Here he beholds fair cities, substantial villages, extensive fields, an immense country filled with decent houses, good roads, orchards, meadows, and bridges, where an hundred years ago all was wild, woody and uncultivated! What a train of pleasing ideas this fair spectacle must suggest; it is a prospect which must inspire a good citizen with the most heartfelt pleasure. The difficulty consists in the manner of viewing so extensive a scene. He is arrived on a new continent; a modern society offers itself to his contemplation, different from what he had hitherto seen. It is not composed, as in Europe, of great lords who possess every thing, and of a herd of people who have nothing. Here are no aristocratical families, no courts, no kings, no bishops, no ecclesiastical dominion, no invisible power giving to a few a very visible one; no great manufacturers employing thousands, no great refinements of luxury. The rich and the poor are not so far removed from each other as they are in Europe. Some few towns excepted, we are all tillers of the earth, from Nova Scotia to West Florida. We are a people of cultivators, scattered over an immense territory, communicating with each other by means of good roads, and navigable rivers, united by the silken bands of mild government, all respecting the laws, without dreading their power, because they are equitable. We are all animated with the spirit of an industry which is unfettered and unrestrained, because each person works for himself. If he travels through our rural districts he views not the hostile castle, and the haughty mansion, contrasted with the clay-built hut and miserable cabbin, where cattle and men help to keep each other warm, and dwell in meanness, smoke, and indigence. A pleasing uniformity of decent competence appears throughout our habitations. The meanest of our log-houses is a dry and comfortable habitation. Lawyer or merchant are the fairest titles our towns afford; that of a farmer is the only appellation of the rural inhabitants of our country. It must take some time ere he can reconcile himself to our dictionary, which is but short in words of dignity, and names of honour. There, on a Sunday, he sees a congregation of respectable farmers and their wives, all clad in neat homespun, well mounted, or riding in their own humble waggons. There is not among them an esquire, saving the unlettered magistrate. There he sees a parson as simple as his flock, a farmer who does not riot[1] on the labour of others. We have no princes, for whom we toil, starve, and bleed: we are the most perfect society now existing in the world. Here man is free as he ought to be; nor is this pleasing equality so transitory as many others are. Many ages will not see the shores of our great lakes replenished with inland nations, nor the unknown bounds of North America entirely peopled. Who can tell how far it extends? Who can tell the millions of men whom it will feed and contain? for no European foot has as yet travelled half the extent of this mighty continent!

The next wish of this traveller will be to know whence came all these people? they are a mixture of English, Scotch, Irish, French, Dutch, Germans, and Swedes. From this promiscuous breed, that race now called Americans have arisen. The eastern provinces[2] must indeed be excepted, as being the unmixed descendents of Englishmen. I have heard many wish that they had been more intermixed also: for my part, I am no wisher, and think it much better as it has happened. They exhibit a most conspicuous figure in this great and variegated picture; they too enter for a great share in the pleasing perspective displayed in these thirteen provinces. I know it is fashionable to reflect on them, but I respect them for what they have done; for the accuracy and wisdom with which they have settled their territory; for the decency of their manners; for their early love of letters; their ancient college,[3] the first in this hemisphere; for their industry; which to me who am but a farmer, is the criterion of everything. There never was a

---

1. **riot:** To indulge in feasting, drinking, or other sensual excesses.
2. **eastern provinces:** New England.
3. **college:** Harvard College, founded in 1636.

people, situated as they are, who with so ungratful a soil have done more in so short a time. Do you think that the monarchical ingredients which are more prevalent in other governments, have purged them from all foul stains? Their histories assert the contrary.

In this great American asylum,[4] the poor of Europe have by some means met together, and in consequence of various causes; to what purpose should they ask one another what countrymen they are? Alas, two thirds of them had no country. Can a wretch who wanders about, who works and starves, whose life is a continual scene of sore affliction or pinching penury; can that man call England or any other kingdom his country? A country that had no bread for him, whose fields procured him no harvest, who met with nothing but the frowns of the rich, the severity of the laws, with jails and punishments; who owned not a single foot of the extensive surface of this planet? No! urged by a variety of motives, here they came. Every thing has tended to regenerate them; new laws, a new mode of living, a new social system; here they are become men: in Europe they were as so many useless plants, wanting vegitative mould, and refreshing showers; they withered, and were mowed down by want, hunger, and war; but now by the power of transplantation, like all other plants they have taken root and flourished! Formerly they were not numbered in any civil lists[5] of their country, except in those of the poor; here they rank as citizens. By what invisible power has this surprising metamorphosis been performed? By that of the laws and that of their industry. The laws, the indulgent laws, protect them as they arrive, stamping on them the symbol of adoption; they receive ample rewards for their labours; these accumulated rewards procure them lands; those lands confer on them the title of freemen, and to that title every benefit is affixed which men can possibly require. This is the great operation daily performed by our laws. From whence proceed these laws? From our government. Whence the government? It is derived from the original genius and strong desire of the people ratified and confirmed by the crown.[6] This is the great chain which links us all, this is the picture which every province exhibits, Nova Scotia excepted.[7] There the crown has done all; either there were no people who had genius, or it was not much attended to: the consequence is, that the province is very thinly inhabited indeed; the power of the crown in conjunction with the musketos has prevented men from settling there. Yet some parts of it flourished once, and it contained a mild harmless set of people. But for the fault of a few leaders, the whole were banished. The greatest political error the crown ever committed in America, was to cut off men from a country which wanted nothing but men!

What attachment can a poor European emigrant have for a country where he had nothing? The knowledge of the language, the love of a few kindred as poor as himself, were the only cords that tied him: his country is now that which gives him land, bread,

---

4. **asylum:** Place of refuge, security, and shelter.
5. **civil lists:** Rosters of individuals employed by a government.
6. **It is derived . . . confirmed by the crown:** Crèvecoeur stresses the important role of British rule in the successful government of the colonies.
7. **Novia Scotia excepted:** A reference to the Great Expulsion of 1755, when the French Acadians in Nova Scotia were rounded up by British soldiers, put on ships, and forced to leave the colony.

protection, and consequence: *Ubi panis ibi patria*,[8] is the motto of all emigrants. What then is the American, this new man? He is either an European, or the descendant of an European, hence that strange mixture of blood, which you will find in no other country. I could point out to you a family whose grandfather was an Englishman, whose wife was Dutch, whose son married a French woman, and whose present four sons have now four wives of different nations. *He* is an American, who leaving behind him all his ancient prejudices and manners, receives new ones from the new mode of life he has embraced, the new government he obeys, and the new rank he holds. He becomes an American by being received in the broad lap of our great *Alma Mater*.[9] Here individuals of all nations are melted into a new race of men, whose labours and posterity will one day cause great changes in the world. Americans are the western pilgrims, who are carrying along with them that great mass of arts, sciences, vigour, and industry which began long since in the east; they will finish the great circle. The Americans were once scattered all over Europe; here they are incorporated into one of the finest systems of population which has ever appeared, and which will hereafter become distinct by the power of the different climates they inhabit. The American ought therefore to love this country much better than that wherein either he or his forefathers were born. Here the rewards of his industry follow with equal steps the progress of his labour; his labour is founded on the basis of nature, *self-interest*; can it want a stronger allurement? Wives and children, who before in vain demanded of him a morsel of bread, now, fat and frolicsome, gladly help their father to clear those fields whence exuberant crops are to arise to feed and to clothe them all; without any part being claimed, either by a despotic prince, a rich abbot, or a mighty lord. Here religion demands but little of him; a small voluntary salary to the minister, and gratitude to God; can he refuse these? The American is a new man, who acts upon new principles; he must therefore entertain new ideas, and form new opinions. From involuntary idleness, servile dependence, penury, and useless labour, he has passed to toils of a very different nature, rewarded by ample subsistence. – This is an American.

[1782, 1904]

---

8. ***Ubi panis ibi patria***: Where there is bread, there is my country (Latin).
9. ***Alma Mater***: Bounteous mother (Latin).

John Dickinson

[1732-1808]

John Dickinson was a Philadelphia lawyer and the author of the influential *Letters from a Farmer in Pennsylvania to the Inhabitants of the British Colonies* (1768), in which he argued that parliamentary taxes were invasions of the rights of the colonists. As a member of the Second Continental Congress, Dickinson later declined to sign the Declaration of Independence because he hoped for reconciliation with the British. But he remained active in the American cause, serving as a member of the Continental Congress during the Revolutionary War. Later, he drafted the Articles of Confederation and helped to secure ratification of the Constitution in 1788. Twenty years earlier, Dickinson wrote "The Liberty Song," occasioned by the British seizure of John Hancock's ship, the *Liberty*, in Boston Harbor. When the ship was impounded on suspicion of carrying contraband, a riot took place on the dock, private citizens tried to take over the customs post, and the British officers took refuge on another ship in the harbor. Ironically, the lyrics of "The Liberty Song," which commemorate colonial resistance and is often considered the first patriotic song in American history, were written to the tune of "Hearts of Oak," the anthem of the British Royal Navy. Another irony of the song is that Dickinson in the refrain urges Americans to live "not as SLAVES, but as FREEMEN." In fact, slave labor was important to the economy of the colonies, as well as to Dickinson, a Quaker. Although he had inherited slaves and had bought more, he was increasingly uneasy with the contradiction between working for freedom while holding slaves. When the Quakers decided in 1776 that slaveholding would no longer be permitted among members of the Society of Friends, Dickinson began to free his slaves. The text is taken from the first printing of "The Liberty Song" in the *Boston Chronicle*, July 18, 1768.

The Liberty Song

Come join hand in hand brave AMERICANS all,
And rouse your bold hearts at fair LIBERTY'S call;
No tyrannous acts shall suppress your just claim,
Or stain with dishonour AMERICA'S name
In FREEDOM we're born *and in FREEDOM we'll* live,
Our purses are ready,
Steady, Friends, steady,
Not as SLAVES, but as FREEMEN our Money we'll give.

Our worthy Forefathers – Let's give them a cheer —
To Climates unknown did courageously steer;
Thro' Oceans, to Deserts, for FREEDOM they came,
And dying bequeath'd us their FREEDOM and Fame.
In FREEDOM we're born, *&c.*

Their generous bosoms all dangers despis'd,
So highly, so wisely, their *Birthrights* they priz'd;
We'll keep what they gave, we will piously keep,
Nor frustrate their toils on the land and the deep –
In FREEDOM we're born *&c.*

The Tree their own Hands had to LIBERTY rear'd;
They liv'd to behold growing strong and rever'd;
With Transport they cry'd, "Now our wishes we gain,

For our children shall gather the fruits of our pain" –
In freedom *we're* born *&c.*

Swarms of Placemen and Pensioners[1] soon will appear
Like Locusts deforming the Charms of the Year;
Suns vainly will rise, Showers vainly descend,
If we are to drudge for what others shall spend.
In freedom *we're* born, *&c.*

Then join Hand in Hand brave AMERICANS all,
By uniting we stand, by dividing we fall;
IN SO RIGHTEOUS a Cause let us hope to succeed,
For Heaven approves of each generous Deed.
In freedom *we're* born, *&c.*

All Ages shall speak with Amaze and Applause,
Of the Courage we'll shew in support of our LAWS;
To die we can bear – but to serve we disdain.
For Shame is to FREEDOM more dreadful than pain.
In freedom *we're* born, *&c.*

This Bumper[2] I crown for our Sovereign's Health,
And this for Britannia's Glory and wealth;
That Wealth and that glory immortal may be,
If She is but JUST — and if we are but FREE.
In freedom *we're* born, *and in* freedom *we'll* live
Our purses are ready,
Steady, Friends, Steady,
Not as slaves *but as* freemen *our Money we'll give.*

[1768]

1. **Placemen and Pensioners:** In early usage, *placemen* was a derogatory term for those who held offices in a sovereign government, and *pensioners* were hired soldiers or mercenaries, often with base motives.
2. **Bumper:** Early term for a generous glass of alcohol, used for a toast.

Hannah Griffitts

[1727–1817]

Hannah Griffitts was a devout Quaker who devoted her long life to writing poetry and to serving the Society of Friends. Her poem "The Female Patriots" appeared anonymously in the *Pennsylvania Chronicle* (1767–74). Founded by William Goddard, an acquaintance of Benjamin Franklin, the weekly newspaper published anonymously numerous political articles written by Samuel and John Adams and Thomas Paine. Known for its strong antitaxation stance, the paper also published John Dickinson's series of *Letters from a Farmer in Pennsylvania to the Inhabitants of the British Colonies* (1768). "The Female Patriots," published six months after Dickinson's "The Liberty Song," was among the earliest protests by a colonial woman against taxation by the British government. Along with many other works by colonial women writers, the poem was copied into a manuscript commonplace book by one of Griffitts's friends and fellow poets, Milcah Martha Moore (1740-1829). Moore identified the author of "The Female Patriots" as Fidelia, the pseudonym Griffitts adopted in most of her publications and in the poems she circulated in letters to friends and relatives. The text of the poem is taken from its first printing in the *Pennsylvania Chronicle*, December 18-25, 1768.

THE FEMALE PATRIOTS

GENTLEMEN,

I send you the inclosed female Performance for a Place in your Paper, if you think it may contribute any Thing to the Entertainment or Reformation of your Male Readers, and am, Your's, &c.

Q. R.[1]

The FEMALE PATRIOTS
Addressed to the Daughters of Liberty in America, 1768

Since the Men, from a Party or Fear of a Frown.
Are kept by a *Sugar plumb* quietly down,
Supinely asleep – and depriv'd of their Sight,
Are stripp'd of their Freedom, and robb'd of their Right;
If the Sons, so degenerate! the Blessings despite,
Let the *Daughters* of Liberty nobly arise;
And tho' we've no Voice but a Negative here,
The Use of the *Taxables*,[2] let us forbear: –
(Then Merchants import till your Stores are all full,
May the Buyers be few, and your Traffick be dull!)
Stand firmly resolv'd, and bid *Grenville*[3] to see,

1. Q. R.: The anonymous poem was printed with this introduction.
2. *Taxables*: Tea, Paper, Glass, and Paints. [Griffitts's note.]
3. *Grenville*: George Grenville (1712-1770), the prime minister of Great Britain from 1763-1765, supported numerous taxation measures, including the Sugar Act (1764) and the Stamp Act (1765).

That rather than Freedom we part with our *Tea*,
And well as we love the dear Draught when a-dry
As American Patriots our Taste we deny –
Pennsylvania's gay Meadows can richly afford,
To pamper our Fancy or furnish our Board;
And Paper sufficient at *Home* still we have,
To assure the *Wiseacre*, we will not sign *Slave*;
When this *Homespun*[4] shall fail, to remonstrate our Grief,
We can speak viva Voce,[5] or scratch on a Leaf;
Refuse all their Colours, tho' richest of Dye,
When the Juice of a Berry our Paint can supply,
To humour our Fancy – and as for our Houses,
They'll do without Painting as well as our Spouses;
While to keep out the Cold of a keen Winter Morn,
We can screen the North-west with a well polished Horn;
And trust me a *Woman*, by honest Invention,
Might give this *State-Doctor* a Dose of Prevention.
  Join mutual in this – and but small as it seems,
We may jostle a *Grenville*, and puzzle his Schemes;
But a Motive more worthy our *Patriot-Pen*,
Thus acting – we point out their Duty to *Men*;
And should the *Bound-Pensioners*[6] tell us to hush,
We can throw back the Satire, by bidding them blush.

A FEMALE

[1768]

4. ***Homespun***: Simple, coarse cloth made at home.
5. **viva Voce**: Oral rather than written communication (Latin).
6. ***Bound-Pensioners***: In early usage, *pensioners* were hired soldiers or mercenaries, often with base motives. The phrase suggests that the pensioners were bound together by mutual self-interest.

Thomas Paine

[1737-1809]

Born into a poor family in England and largely self-educated, Thomas Paine emigrated to the colonies after meeting Benjamin Franklin in London in 1774. As the coeditor of the *Pennsylvania Magazine*, Paine became deeply involved in political activities that would lead to the American Revolution. Following the battles of Concord and Lexington and the occupation of Boston by the British army, he wrote the first pamphlet to advocate immediate independence from England, *Common Sense*, which was published anonymously "By an Englishman" on January 10, 1776. In his introduction, Paine affirms,

> The cause of America is in a great measure the cause of all mankind. Many circumstances have, and will arise, which are not local, but universal, and through which the principles of all Lovers of Mankind are affected, and in the Event of which, their Affections are interested. The laying of a Country desolate with Fire and Sword, declaring War against the natural rights of all Mankind, and extirpating the Defenders thereof from the Face of the Earth, is the Concern of every Man to whom Nature hath given the Power of feeling; of which Class, regardless of Party Censure, is the AUTHOR.

Paine's simple style – designed, as he put it, "to make those who can scarcely read understand" – contributed to the phenomenal success of *Common Sense*. Published first in English and then in a German translation, the pamphlet sold an estimated 150,000 copies in three months, and its total sales ultimately reached half a million copies, plus extracts published in newspapers. The *Connecticut Gazette* described it as "a landflood that sweeps all before it." Certainly, Paine's words swept aside much of the lingering allegiance to King George III, paving the way for the Declaration of Independence, which was signed in Philadelphia six months after *Common Sense* was published in the same city. The text of the following selection is taken from volume one of *The Writings of Thomas Paine*, edited by Moncure Daniel Conway (1894-1896).

From COMMON SENSE

As much hath been said of the advantages of reconciliation, which, like an agreeable dream, hath passed away and left us as we were, it is but right that we should examine the contrary side of the argument, and enquire into some of the many material injuries which these Colonies sustain, and always will sustain, by being connected with and dependant on Great-Britain. To examine that connection and dependance, on the principles of nature and common sense, to see what we have to trust to, if separated, and what we are to expect, if dependant.

I have heard it asserted by some, that as America has flourished under her former connection with Great-Britain, the same connection is necessary towards her future happiness, and will always have the same effect. Nothing can be more fallacious than this kind of argument. We may as well assert that because a child has thrived upon milk, that it is never to have meat, or that the first twenty years of our lives is to become a precedent for the next twenty. But even this is admitting more than is true; for I answer roundly, that America would have flourished as much, and probably much more, had no European power taken any notice of her. The commerce by which she hath enriched herself are the necessaries of life, and will always have a market while eating is the custom of Europe.

But she has protected us, say some. That she hath engrossed us is true, and defended the Continent at our expense as well as her own, is admitted; and she would have defended Turkey from the same motive, *viz.* for the sake of trade and dominion.

Alas! we have been long led away by ancient prejudices and made large sacrifices to superstition. We have boasted the protection of Great Britain, without considering, that her motive was *interest* not *attachment*; and that she did not protect us from *our enemies* on *our account*; but from *her enemies* on *her own account*, from those who had no quarrel with us on any *other account*, and who will always be our enemies on the *same account*. Let Britain waive her pretensions to the Continent, or the Continent throw off the dependance, and we should be at peace with France and Spain, were they at war with Britain. The miseries of Hanover's last war[1] ought to warn us against connections.

It hath lately been asserted in parliament, that the Colonies have no relation to each other but through the Parent Country, *i. e.* that Pennsylvania and the Jerseys,[2] and so on for the rest, are sister Colonies by the way of England; this is certainly a very roundabout way of proving relationship, but it is the nearest and only true way of proving enmity (or enemyship, if I may so call it.) France and Spain never were, nor perhaps ever will be, our enemies as *Americans*, but as our being the *subjects of Great Britain*.

But Britain is the parent country, say some. Then the more shame upon her conduct. Even brutes do not devour their young, nor savages make war upon their families; Wherefore, the assertion, if true, turns to her reproach; but it happens not to be true, or only partly so, and the phrase *parent* or *mother country* hath been jesuitically[3] adopted by the King and his parasites, with a low papistical design of gaining an unfair bias on the credulous weakness of our minds. Europe, and not England, is the parent country of America. This new World hath been the asylum for the persecuted lovers of civil and religious liberty from *every part* of Europe. Hither have they fled, not from the tender embraces of the mother, but from the cruelty of the monster; and it is so far true of England, that the same tyranny which drove the first emigrants from home, pursues their descendants still.

In this extensive quarter of the globe, we forget the narrow limits of three hundred and sixty miles (the extent of England) and carry our friendship on a larger scale; we claim brotherhood with every European Christian, and triumph in the generosity of the sentiment.

It is pleasant to observe by what regular gradations we surmount the force of local prejudices, as we enlarge our acquaintance with the World. A man born in any town in England divided into parishes, will naturally associate most with his fellow parishioners (because their interests in many cases will be common) and distinguish him by

---

1. **Hanover's last war:** The French and Indian War, also known as the Seven Years' War (1756–63), was a result of the colonial rivalry between Great Britain and France as well as internal power struggles in Germany between the kingdoms of Prussia and Hanover. (King George III of Great Britain was a descendant of the House of Hanover.) At the conclusion of the war, which eventually involved several European countries, Great Britain emerged as the dominant colonial power in North America.
2. **Jerseys:** At the time, the colony was divided into East and West Jersey.
3. **jesuitically:** Cleverly, in the manner of the Jesuits, a Roman Catholic order of priests.

the name of *neighbour*; if he meet him but a few miles from home, he drops the narrow idea of a street, and salutes him by the name of *townsman*; if he travel out of the county and meet him in any other, he forgets the minor divisions of street and town, and calls him *countryman, i. e. countyman*: but if in their foreign excursions they should associate in France, or any other part of *Europe*, their local remembrance would be enlarged into that of *Englishmen*. And by a just parity of reasoning, all Europeans meeting in America, or any other quarter of the globe, are *countrymen*; for England, Holland, Germany, or Sweden, when compared with the whole, stand in the same places on the larger scale, which the divisions of street, town, and county do on the smaller ones; Distinctions too limited for Continental minds. Not one third of the inhabitants, even of this province,[4] are of English descent. Wherefore, I reprobate the phrase of Parent or Mother Country applied to England only, as being false, selfish, narrow and ungenerous.

But, admitting that we were all of English descent, what does it amount to? Nothing. Britain, being now an open enemy, extinguishes every other name and title: and to say that reconciliation is our duty, is truly farcical. The first king of England, of the present line (William the Conqueror) was a Frenchman, and half the peers of England are descendants from the same country; wherefore, by the same method of reasoning, England ought to be governed by France.

Much hath been said of the united strength of Britain and the Colonies, that in conjunction they might bid defiance to the world: But this is mere presumption; the fate of war is uncertain, neither do the expressions mean any thing; for this continent would never suffer itself to be drained of inhabitants, to support the British arms in either Asia, Africa, or Europe.

Besides, what have we to do with setting the world at defiance? Our plan is commerce, and that, well attended to, will secure us the peace and friendship of all Europe; because it is the interest of all Europe to have America a free port. Her trade will always be a protection, and her barrenness of gold and silver secure her from invaders.

I challenge the warmest advocate for reconciliation to show a single advantage that this continent can reap by being connected with Great Britain. I repeat the challenge; not a single advantage is derived. Our corn[5] will fetch its price in any market in Europe, and our imported goods must be paid for buy them where we will.

But the injuries and disadvantages which we sustain by that connection, are without number; and our duty to mankind at large, as well as to ourselves, instruct us to renounce the alliance: because, any submission to, or dependance on, Great Britain, tends directly to involve this Continent in European wars and quarrels, and set us at variance with nations who would otherwise seek our friendship, and against whom we have neither anger nor complaint. As Europe is our market for trade, we ought to form no partial connection with any part of it. It is the true interest of America to steer clear of European contentions, which she never can do, while, by her dependance on Britain, she is made the makeweight in the scale of British politics.

---

4. **this province:** Pennsylvania.
5. **corn:** Early term for any cereal grain.

Europe is too thickly planted with Kingdoms to be long at peace, and whenever a war breaks out between England and any foreign power, the trade of America goes to ruin, *because of her connection with Britain.* The next war may not turn out like the last,[6] and should it not, the advocates for reconciliation now will be wishing for separation then, because neutrality in that case would be a safer convoy than a man of war. Every thing that is right or reasonable pleads for separation. The blood of the slain, the weeping voice of nature cries, 'TIS TIME TO PART. Even the distance at which the Almighty hath placed England and America is a strong and natural proof that the authority of the one over the other, was never the design of Heaven. The time likewise at which the Continent was discovered, adds weight to the argument, and the manner in which it was peopled, encreases the force of it. The Reformation was preceded by the discovery of America: As if the Almighty graciously meant to open a sanctuary to the persecuted in future years, when home should afford neither friendship nor safety. . . .

Ye that tell us of harmony and reconciliation, can ye restore to us the time that is past? Can ye give to prostitution its former innocence? neither can ye reconcile Britain and America. The last cord now is broken, the people of England are presenting addresses against us. There are injuries which nature cannot forgive; she would cease to be nature if she did. As well can the lover forgive the ravisher of his mistress, as the Continent forgive the murders of Britain. The Almighty hath implanted in us these unextinguishable feelings for good and wise purposes. They are the Guardians of his Image in our hearts. They distinguish us from the herd of common animals. The social compact would dissolve, and justice be extirpated from the earth, or have only a casual existence were we callous to the touches of affection. The robber and the murderer would often escape unpunished, did not the injuries which our tempers sustain, provoke us into justice.

O! ye that love mankind! Ye that dare oppose not only the tyranny but the tyrant, stand forth! Every spot of the old world is overrun with oppression. Freedom hath been hunted round the Globe. Asia and Africa have long expelled her. Europe regards her like a stranger, and England hath given her warning to depart. O! receive the fugitive, and prepare in time an asylum for mankind.

[1776, 1894]

6. **last:** The French and Indian War; see note 1.

John Adams

[1735-1826]

and

Abigail Adams

[1744-1818]

John Adams, a Boston lawyer, married Abigail Smith in 1764, ten years before he was elected as a delegate from Massachusetts to the First Continental Congress. From the beginning of their courtship throughout his long years of public service, culminating in his term as the second president (1797-1801), the couple exchanged over eleven hundred letters, which provide fascinating insights into the emergence and early development of the United States. The couple wrote frankly to each another, debating controversial issues like the role of women in society, the subject of one of the following exchanges. The other letters reprinted here were exchanged shortly before Adams and other representatives to the Second Continental Congress voted in favor of the Declaration of Independence and reveal their anxieties about the coming revolution, as well as their excitement

Benjamin Blyth, *Portraits of Abigail and John Adams* (1766)

These paired portraits were painted by Benjamin Blyth in 1766, two years after the couple's marriage and at the beginning of a decade in which they became increasingly involved in the movement toward independence, culminating in John Adams's role in the preparation of the Declaration of Independence in 1776.

about building a new nation. The texts of the following selections from their letters are taken from *The Adams Family: An Electronic Archive*, "The Correspondence Between John and Abigail Adams," the Massachusetts Historical Society (http://www.masshist.org/digitaladams/aea/letter/).

LETTER FROM ABIGAIL ADAMS TO JOHN ADAMS, MARCH 31, 1776

I feel very differently at the approach of spring to what I did a month ago.[1] We knew not then whether we could plant or sow with safety, whether when we had toil'd we could reap the fruits of our own industery, whether we could rest in our own Cottages, or whether we should not be driven from the sea coasts to seek shelter in the wilderness, but now we feel as if we might sit under our own vine[2] and eat the good of the land.

I feel a gaieti de Coar[3] to which before I was a stranger. I think the Sun looks brighter, the Birds sing more melodiously, and Nature puts on a more chearfull countanance. We feel a temporary peace, and the poor fugitives are returning to their deserted habitations.

Tho we felicitate ourselves, we sympathize with those who are trembling least the Lot of Boston should be theirs. But they cannot be in similar circumstances unless pusilanimity and cowardise should take possession of them. They have time and warning given them to see the Evil and shun it. – I long to hear that you have declared an independency – and by the way in the new Code of Laws which I suppose it will be necessary for you to make I desire you would Remember the Ladies, and be more generous and favourable to them than your ancestors. Do not put such unlimited power into the hands of the Husbands. Remember all Men would be tyrants if they could. If perticuliar care and attention is not paid to the Laidies we are determined to foment a Rebelion, and will not hold ourselves bound by any Laws in which we have no voice, or Representation.

That your Sex are Naturally Tyrannical is a Truth so thoroughly established as to admit of no dispute, but such of you as wish to be happy willingly give up the harsh title of Master for the more tender and endearing one of Friend. Why then, not put it out of the power of the vicious and the Lawless to use us with cruelty and indignity with impunity. Men of Sense in all Ages abhor those customs which treat us only as the vassals[4] of your Sex. Regard us then as Beings placed by providence under your protection and in immitation of the Supreem Being make use of that power only for our happiness.

1. **a month ago:** During the previous month, American forces had seized Dorchester Heights, from which most of Boston was within range of their artillery. The occupying British army (along with one thousand Loyalists) consequently evacuated the city by sea on March 26, 1776.
2. **sit under our own vine:** See Micah 4:4: "But they shall sit every man under his vine and under his fig tree; and none shall make them afraid: for the mouth of the LORD of hosts hath spoken it."
3. **gaieti de Coar:** Properly *gaité de Coeur* (French), meaning cheerfulness or lightness of heart.
4. **vassals:** Persons in subordinate positions.

Letter from John Adams to Abigail Adams, April 14, 1776

Your Description of your own Gaiety de Coeur, charms me. Thanks be to God you have just Cause to rejoice – and may the bright Prospect be obscured by no Cloud.

As to Declarations of Independency, be patient. Read our Privateering Laws, and our Commercial Laws.[1] What signifies a Word.

As to your extraordinary Code of Laws, I cannot but laugh. We have been told that our Struggle has loosened the bands of Government every where. That Children and Apprentices were disobedient – that schools and Colledges were grown turbulent – that Indians slighted their Guardians and Negroes grew insolent to their Masters.

But your Letter was the first Intimation that another Tribe more numerous and powerfull than all the rest were grown discontented. – This is rather too coarse a Compliment but you are so saucy, I wont blot it out.

Depend upon it, We know better than to repeal our Masculine systems. Altho they are in full Force, you know they are little more than Theory. We dare not exert our Power in its full Latitude. We are obliged to go fair, and softly, and in Practice you know We are the subjects. We have only the Name of Masters, and rather than give up this, which would compleatly subject Us to the Despotism of the Peticoat, I hope General Washington, and all our brave Heroes would fight. I am sure every good Politician would plot, as long as he would against Despotism, Empire, Monarchy, Aristocracy, Oligarchy, or Ochlocracy.[2] – A fine Story indeed. I begin to think the Ministry as deep as they are wicked. After stirring up Tories, Landjobbers, Trimmers,[3] Bigots, Canadians, Indians, Negroes, Hanoverians, Hessians, Russians, Irish Roman Catholicks, Scotch Renegades, at last they have stimulated the [ladies][4] to demand new Priviledges and threaten to rebell.

---

1. **Read . . . Commercial Laws:** Although the Second Continental Congress had not yet voted in favor of independence, it had already assumed executive and legislative powers previously exercised by King George III and the British Parliament.

2. **Despotism . . . Ochlocracy:** Governmental structures that provide ruling powers by a tyrant (despotism), an emperor (empire), a king or queen (monarchy), members of the nobility (aristocracy), a small elite group (oligarchy), or a mob (ochlocracy).

3. **Tories, Landjobbers, Trimmers:** American colonists who supported the British (Tories); persons who buy and sell land on speculation (landjobbers); and persons who change political positions as their personal interests change (trimmers).

4. **[ladies]:** Adams left a blank space at this point in his letter, possibly as a kind of visual joke to indicate that he was not sure that "ladies," the term Abigail had used in her letter, was the appropriate word to describe those who were suddenly demanding new privileges and threatening to rebel, as he put it with comic exaggeration.

LETTERS FROM JOHN ADAMS TO ABIGAIL ADAMS, JULY 3, 1776[1]

[1]

Yesterday the greatest Question was decided, which ever was debated in America, and a greater perhaps, never was or will be decided among Men. A Resolution was passed without one dissenting Colony "that these United Colonies, are, and of right ought to be free and independent States, and as such, they have, and of Right ought to have full Power to make War, conclude Peace, establish Commerce, and to do all the other Acts and Things, which other States may rightfully do." You will see in a few days a Declaration setting forth the Causes, which have impell'd Us to this mighty Revolution, and the Reasons which will justify it, in the Sight of God and Man. A Plan of Confederation will be taken up in a few days.

When I look back to the Year 1761, and recollect the Argument concerning Writs of Assistance, in the Superiour Court, which I have hitherto considered as the Commencement of the Controversy, between Great Britain and America, and run through the whole Period from that Time to this, and recollect the series of political Events, the Chain of Causes and Effects, I am surprized at the Suddenness, as well as Greatness of this Revolution. Britain has been fill'd with Folly, and America with Wisdom, at least this is my judgment. – Time must determine. It is the Will of Heaven, that the two Countries should be sundered forever. It may be the Will of Heaven that America shall suffer Calamities still more wasting and Distresses yet more dreadfull. If this is to be the Case, it will have this good Effect, at least: it will inspire Us with many Virtues, which We have not, and correct many Errors, Follies, and Vices, which threaten to disturb, dishonour, and destroy Us. – The Furnace of Affliction produces Refinement, in States as well as Individuals. And the new Governments we are assuming, in every Part, will require a Purification from our Vices, and an Augmentation of our Virtues or they will be no Blessings. The People will have unbounded Power. And the People are extreamly addicted to Corruption and Venality, as well as the Great. I am not without Apprehensions from this Quarter. – But I must submit all my Hopes and Fears, to an overruling Providence, in which, unfashionable [as] the Faith may be, I firmly believe.

[2]

Had a Declaration of Independency been made seven Months ago, it would have been attended with many great and glorious Effects. . . . We might before this Hour, have formed Alliances with foreign States. – We should have mastered Quebec and been in Possession of Canada. . . .

1. **July 3, 1776:** Adams wrote two letters to his wife on that day; the following selections from the letters are therefore labeled [1] and [2].

But on the other Hand, the Delay of this Declaration to this Time, has many great Advantages attending it. – The Hopes of Reconciliation, which were fondly entertained by Multitudes of honest and well meaning tho weak and mistaken People, have been gradually and at last totally extinguished. – Time has been given for the whole People, maturely to consider the great Question of Independence and to ripen their judgments, dissipate their Fears, and allure their Hopes, by discussing it in News Papers and Pamphletts, by debating it, in Assemblies, Conventions, Committees of Safety and Inspection, in Town and County Meetings, as well as in private Conversations, so that the whole People in every Colony of the 13, have now adopted it, as their own Act. – This will cement the Union, and avoid those Heats and perhaps Convulsions which might have been occasioned, by such a Declaration Six Months ago.

But the Day is past. The Second Day of July 1776,[2] will be the most memorable Epocha, in the History of America. I am apt to believe that it will be celebrated, by succeeding Generations, as the great anniversary Festival. It ought to be commemorated, as the Day of Deliverance by solemn Acts of Devotion to God Almighty. It ought to be solemnized with Pomp and Parade, with Shews, Games, Sports, Guns, Bells, Bonfires and Illuminations from one End of this Continent to the other from this Time forward forever more.

You will think me transported with Enthusiasm but I am not. – I am well aware of the Toil and Blood and Treasure, that it will cost Us to maintain this Declaration, and support and defend these States. – Yet through all the Gloom I can see the Rays of ravishing Light and Glory. I can see that the End is more than worth all the Means. And that Posterity will tryumph in that Days Transaction, even altho We should rue it, which I trust in God We shall not.

[1776]

---

2. July 1776: On July 2, 1776, the Second Continental Congress voted in favor of a resolution declaring independence from Great Britain. On July 4, 1776, the delegates formally approved an official document, the Declaration of Independence, making the Fourth of July the day celebrated as the inception of the United States.

Thomas Jefferson

[1743-1826]

Thomas Jefferson, the third president of the United States, was born on April 13, 1743, into a wealthy family that owned a large plantation in central Virginia. His political career began in 1769 when he was elected to the Virginia House of Burgesses, where he served for six years. In 1774, Jefferson published *A Summary View of the Rights of British America*, a pamphlet in which he argues that colonial allegiance to the British monarch was strictly voluntary. The pamphlet earned him attention beyond Virginia and propelled him into an increasingly prominent role in the movement toward independence from Great Britain. At age thirty-three,

Jefferson was elected to the Second Continental Congress, which appointed him to the committee charged with drafting the declaration of independence. He later served as the wartime governor of Virginia, as a member of Congress, as the minister to France, and as secretary of state in the first administration of George Washington. Jefferson ran for president in 1796 but lost to John Adams, becoming vice president under the system then in place. In 1800, Jefferson was elected president and served for two terms, after which he retired to his home in Monticello, Virginia.

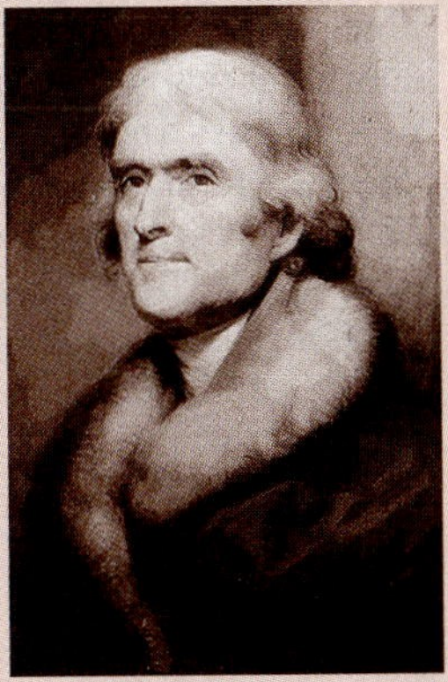

Thomas Jefferson

This copy of an 1805 portrait by the Philadelphia painter Rembrandt Peale shows Jefferson at the beginning of his second term as president of the United States. Peale and his famous father, Charles Willson Peale, went to Washington to paint celebrities' portraits to hang in their museum in Philadelphia.

Jefferson's Draft of the Declaration of Independence. On June 7, 1776, Richard Henry Lee, a delegate from Virginia to the Second Continental Congress, offered a resolution that began: "Resolved: That these United Colonies are, and of right ought to be, free and independent States, that they are absolved from all allegiance to the British Crown, and that all political connection between them and the State of Great Britain is, and ought to be, totally dissolved." Although no vote was taken on Lee's resolution, a committee of five delegates – John Adams of Massachusetts, Roger Sherman of Connecticut, Benjamin Franklin of Pennsylvania, Robert R. Livingston of New York, and Thomas Jefferson of Virginia – was charged with the preparation of a formal declaration. Jefferson wrote the first draft of the document and showed it to Adams and Franklin, who made some

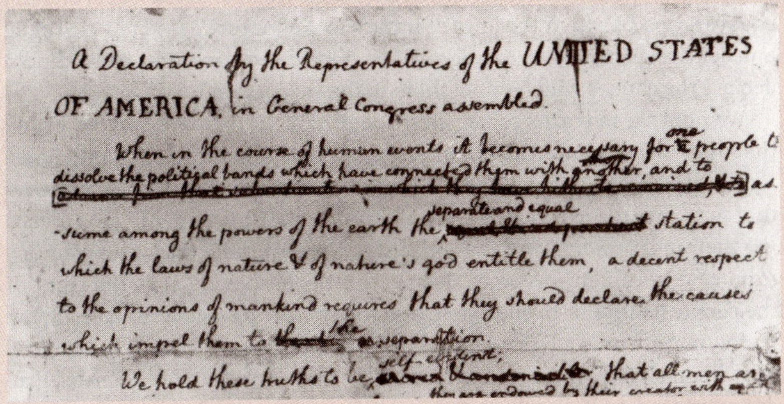

A Declaration by the Representatives of the UNITED STATES OF AMERICA, in General Congress assembled.

When in the course of human events it becomes necessary for one people to dissolve the political bands which have connected them with another, and to assume among the powers of the earth the separate and equal station to which the laws of nature & of nature's god entitle them, a decent respect to the opinions of mankind requires that they should declare the causes which impel them to the separation.

We hold these truths to be self-evident; that all men are ... they are endowed by their creator with ...

Opening of Jefferson's Draft of the Declaration of Independence

Jefferson carefully preserved his original draft of the Declaration, indicating the minor revisions made by other members of the committee assigned the task of preparing the document, as well as the numerous changes made by the Second Continental Congress before it approved the amended version on July 4, 1776.

minor changes. The committee as a whole apparently made only a few additional changes before it reported the document to Congress. On July 1, the Congress reconvened to debate Lee's resolution, which it voted to adopt the following day, July 2, 1776. The delegates then began to debate the draft of the Declaration of Independence, which was further revised and amended before it was formally approved on July 4. Jefferson believed that Congress had mangled his draft, copies of which he sent to friends. He also carefully preserved the original document, indicating all of the changes that had been made in his draft, which Jefferson included in a brief account of his life begun in 1821 and published after his death as his *Autobiography* (1829). "As the sentiments of men are known not only by what they receive, but what they reject also, I will state the form of the Declaration as originally reported," Jefferson observed. "The parts struck out by Congress shall be distinguished by a black line drawn under them; and those inserted by them shall be placed in the margin, or in a concurrent column." The following text of Jefferson's draft, printed here according to his instructions, is taken from volume one of *The Writings of Thomas Jefferson*, edited by Andrew A. Lipscomb and Albert Ellery Bergh (1903).

Draft of the Declaration of Independence

A Declaration by the Representatives of the United States of America, in *General* Congress assembled.

When, in the course of human events, it becomes necessary for one people to dissolve the political bands which have connected them with another, and to assume among the powers of the earth the separate and equal station to which the laws of nature and of nature's God entitle them, a decent respect to the opinions of mankind requires that they should declare the causes which impel them to the separation.

certain

We hold these truths to be self evident: that all men are created equal; that they are endowed by their Creator with inherent and inalienable rights; that among these are life, liberty, and the pursuit of happiness;[1] that to secure these rights, governments are instituted among men, deriving their just powers from the consent of the governed; that whenever any form of government becomes destructive of these ends, it is the right of the people to alter or to abolish it, and to institute new government, laying its foundation on such principles, and organizing its powers in such form, as to them shall seem most likely to effect their safety and happiness. Prudence, indeed, will dictate that governments long established should not

1. **pursuit of happiness:** In his *Second Treatise of Government* (1690), the English philosopher John Locke (1632–1704) had originally defined the natural rights of individuals as life, liberty, and estate (that is, private property).

be changed for light and transient causes; and accordingly all experience
hath shown that mankind are more disposed to suffer while evils are sufferable, than to right themselves by abolishing the forms to which they are
accustomed. But when a long train of abuses and usurpations, begun at a
distinguished period and pursuing invariably the same object, evinces a
design to reduce them under absolute despotism, it is their right, it is their
duty to throw off such government, and to provide new guards for their
future security. Such as been the patient sufferance of these colonies; and
such is now the necessity which constrains them to expunge their former alter
systems of government. The history of the present king of Great Britain[2] is
a history of unremitting injuries and usurpations, among which appears repeated
no solitary fact to contradict the uniform tenor of the rest, but all have in all having
direct object the establishment of an absolute tyranny over these states.
To prove this, let facts be submitted to a candid world for the truth of
which we pledge a faith yet unsullied by falsehood.

He has refused his assent to laws the most wholesome and necessary for the public good.

He has forbidden his governors to pass laws of immediate and pressing importance, unless suspended in their operation till his assent should be obtained; and, when so suspended, he has utterly neglected to attend to them.

He has refused to pass other laws for the accommodation of large districts of people, unless those people would relinquish the right of representation in the legislature, a right inestimable to them, and formidable to tyrants only.

He has called together legislative bodies at places unusual, uncomfortable, and distant from the depository of their public records, for the sole purpose of fatiguing them into compliance with his measures.

He has dissolved representative houses repeatedly and continually for opposing with manly firmness his invasions on the rights of the people.

He has refused for a long time after such dissolutions to cause others to be elected, whereby the legislative powers, incapable of annihilation, have returned to the people at large for their exercise, the state remaining, in the meantime, exposed to all the dangers of invasion from without and convulsions within.

He has endeavored to prevent the population of these states; for that purpose obstructing the laws for naturalization of foreigners, refusing to pass others to encourage their migrations hither, and raising the conditions of new appropriations of lands.

He has suffered the administration of justice totally to cease in some of obstructed
these states refusing his assent to laws for establishing judiciary powers. by

2. **the present king of Great Britain:** George III reigned from 1760 to 1820.

He has made our judges dependent on his will alone for the tenure of their offices, and the amount and payment of their salaries.

He has erected a multitude of new offices, by a self-assumed power and sent hither swarms of new officers to harass our people and eat out their substance.

He has kept among us in times of peace standing armies and ships of war without the consent of our legislatures.

He has affected to render the military independent of, and superior to, the civil power.

He has combined with others to subject us to a jurisdiction foreign to our constitutions and unacknowledged by our laws, giving his assent to their acts of pretended legislation for quartering large bodies of armed troops among us; for protecting them by a mock trial from punishment for any murders which they should commit on the inhabitants of these states; for cutting off our trade with all parts of the world; for imposing taxes on us without our consent; for depriving us _ of the benefits of trial by jury; for transporting us beyond seas to be tried for pretended offences; for abolishing the free system of English laws in a neighboring province,[3] establishing therein an arbitrary government, and enlarging its boundaries, so as to render it at once an example and fit instrument for introducing the same absolute rule into these states; for taking away our charters, abolishing our most valuable laws, and altering fundamentally the forms of our governments; for suspending our own legislatures, and declaring themselves invested with power to legislate for us in all cases whatsoever.

in many cases

colonies

He has abdicated government here withdrawing his governors, and declaring us out of his allegiance and protection.

by declaring us out of his protection, and waging war against us.

He has plundered our seas, ravaged our coasts, burnt our towns, and destroyed the lives of our people.

He is at this time transporting large armies of foreign mercenaries[4] to complete the works of death, desolation and tyranny already begun with circumstances of cruelty and perfidy _ unworthy the head of a civilized nation.

scarcely paralleled in the most barbarous ages, and totally

He has constrained our fellow citizens taken captive on the high seas, to bear arms against their country, to become the executioners of their friends and brethren, or to fall themselves by their hands.

He has _ endeavored to bring on the inhabitants of our frontiers, the merciless Indian savages, whose known rule of warfare is an undistinguished destruction of all ages, sexes and conditions of existence.

excited domestic insurrection among us, and has

---

3. **a neighboring province:** The Quebec Act of 1774, unpopular in England and especially in the American colonies, provided special concessions to the British province of Quebec, expanding its borders, retaining the use of French civil law, and guaranteeing French Canadians the right to practice Roman Catholicism.

4. **foreign mercenaries:** George III hired troops, mainly from the Hesse-Cassel state in Germany, to help suppress the growing rebellion in the American colonies.

He has incited treasonable insurrections of our fellow citizens, with the allurements of forfeiture and confiscation of our property.

He has waged cruel war against human nature itself, violating its most sacred rights of life and liberty in the persons of a distant people who never offended him, captivating and carrying them into slavery in another hemisphere, or to incur miserable death in their transportation thither. This piratical warfare, the opprobium of INFIDEL powers, is the warfare of the CHRISTIAN king of Great Britain. Determined to keep open a market where MEN should be bought and sold, he has prostituted his negative for suppressing every legislative attempt to prohibit or to restrain this execrable commerce. And that this assemblage of horrors might want no fact of distinguished die, he is now exciting those very people to rise in arms among us, and to purchase that liberty of which he has deprived them, by murdering the people on whom he also obtruded them: thus paying off former crimes committed against the LIBERTIES of one people, with crimes which he urges them to commit against the LIVES of another.

In every stage of these oppressions we have petitioned for redress in the most humble terms: our repeated petitions have been answered only by repeated injuries.

A prince whose character is thus marked by every act which may define a tyrant is unfit to be the ruler of a _ people who mean to be free. Future ages will scarcely believe that the hardiness of one man adventured, within the short compass of twelve years only, to lay a foundation so broad and so undisguised for tyranny over a people fostered and fixed in principles of freedom.

free

Nor have we been wanting in attentions to our British brethren. We have warned them from time to time of attempts by their legislature to extend a jurisdiction over these our states. We have reminded them of the circumstances of our emigration and settlement here, no one of which could warrant so strange a pretension: that these were effected at the expense of our own blood and treasure, unassisted by the wealth or the strength of Great Britain: that in constituting indeed our several forms of government, we had adopted one common king, thereby laying a foundation for perpetual league and amity with them: but that submission to their parliament was no part of our constitution, nor ever in idea, if history may be credited: and, we _ appealed to their native justice and magnanimity as well as to the ties of our common kindred to disavow these usurpations which were likely to interrupt our connection and correspondence. They too have been deaf to the voice of justice and of consanguinity, and when occasions have been given them, by the regular course of their laws, of removing from their councils the disturbers of our harmony, they have, by their free election, re-established them in power. At this very time too, they are permitting their chief magistrate to send over not only soldiers of our common blood, but Scotch and foreign mercenaries to invade and destroy us. These facts have given the last stab to agonizing affection,

an unwarrantable; us

have

and we have conjured them by

would inevitably

and manly spirit bids us to renounce forever these unfeeling brethren. We must endeavor to forget our former love for them, and hold them as we hold the rest of mankind, enemies in war, in peace friends. We might have been a free and a great people together; but a communication of grandeur and of freedom, it seems, is below their dignity. Be it so, since they will have it. The road to happiness and to glory is open to us, too. We will tread it apart from them, and acquiesce in the necessity which denounces our eternal separation _!

We must therefore

and hold them as we hold the rest of mankind, enemies in war, in peace friends.

We, therefore, the representatives of the United States of America in General Congress assembled, appealing to the supreme judge of the world for the rectitude of our intentions, do in the name, and by the authority of the good people of these colonies, solemnly publish and declare, that these united colonies are, and of right ought to be free and independent states; that they are absolved from all allegiance to the British crown, and that all political connection between them and the state of Great Britain is, and ought to be, totally dissolved; and that as free and independent states, they have full power to levy war, conclude peace, contract alliances, establish commerce, and to do all other acts and things which independent states may of right do.

And for the support of this declaration, with a firm reliance on the protection of divine providence, we mutually pledge to each other our lives, our fortunes, and our sacred honor.

We therefore the representatives of the United States of America in General Congress assembled, do in the name, and by the authority of the good people of these states reject and renounce all allegiance and subjection to the kings of Great Britain and all others who may hereafter claim by, through or under them; we utterly dissolve all political connection which may heretofore have subsisted between us and the people or parliament of Great Britain: and finally we do assert and declare these colonies to be free and independent states, and that as free and independent states, they have full power to levy war, conclude peace, contract alliances, establish commerce, and to do all other acts and things which independent states may of right do.

And for the support of this declaration we mutually pledge to each other our lives, our fortunes, and our sacred honor.

[1776, 1829, 1903]

Jefferson's *Notes on the State of Virginia*. Jefferson's only full-length book was written in response to a series of questions he received from François Barbé-Marbois (1745–1837), then the secretary to the French legation in the newly formed United States. *Notes on the State of Virginia* includes twenty-three sections, each a response to a specific "query" raised by Barbé-Marbois. In his responses, Jefferson provides detailed observations on climate, geography, population, culture, and politics, adding his views about the future development of both the state and the United States. *Notes on the State of Virginia* was privately printed in France in 1784. Concerned that an unauthorized French translation would appear, Jefferson published the book in London in 1787; four editions were published in the United States in 1788. The sections included here, "Religion" and "Manners" – a commentary on the effects of slavery – reflect Jefferson's ongoing concern with issues of freedom and natural rights. In Virginia, Jefferson had introduced a bill in the assembly providing for complete religious freedom for all inhabitants of the state, regardless of their beliefs. As a slaveholder, however, Jefferson's views on race and slavery were far more complex and often conflicting. Suggesting that blacks "are inferior to whites in endowments of both body and mind," Jefferson elsewhere in *Notes on the State of Virginia* observes: "This unfortunate difference of colour, and perhaps of faculty, is a powerful obstacle to the emancipation of these people." At the same time, in "Manners" Jefferson emphasizes the corrosive effects of slavery on both the master and the slave, insisting that the institution posed one of the greatest threats to the stability and welfare of the United States. The text of the two sections is taken from the first London edition of *Notes on the State of Virginia* (1787), as reprinted in the Library of America edition of *Thomas Jefferson: Writings* (1984).

From NOTES ON THE STATE OF VIRGINIA

Query XVII

THE DIFFERENT RELIGIONS RECEIVED INTO THAT STATE?

The first settlers in this country were emigrants from England, of the English church, just at a point of time when it was flushed with complete victory over the religious of all other persuasions. Possessed, as they became, of the powers of making, administering, and executing the laws, they shewed equal intolerance in this country with their Presbyterian brethren, who had emigrated to the northern government. The poor Quakers were flying from persecution in England. They cast their eyes on these new countries as asylums of civil and religious freedom; but they found them free only for the reigning sect. Several acts of the Virginia assembly of 1659, 1662, and 1693, had made it penal in parents to refuse to have their children baptized; had prohibited the unlawful assembling of Quakers; had made it penal for any master of a vessel to bring a Quaker into the state; had ordered those already here, and such as should come thereafter, to be imprisoned till they should abjure the country; provided a milder punishment for their first and second return, but death for their third; had inhibited all persons from suffering their meetings in or near their houses, entertaining them individually, or disposing of books which supported their tenets. If no capital execution took place here, as did in New-England, it was not owing to the moderation of the church, or spirit of the legislature, as may be inferred from the law itself; but to historical circumstances which have not been handed down to us. The Anglicans retained full possession of the country about a century. Other opinions began then to creep in, and the great care of the government to support their own church, having begotten an equal degree of indolence in its clergy, two-thirds of the people had become dissenters at the commencement of the present revolution. The laws indeed were still oppressive on them, but the spirit of the one party had subsided into moderation, and of the other had risen to a degree of determination which commanded respect.

The present state of our laws on the subject of religion is this. The convention of May 1776, in their declaration of rights, declared it to be a truth, and a natural right, that the exercise of religion should be free; but when they proceeded to form on that declaration the ordinance of government, instead of taking up every principle declared in the bill of rights, and guarding it by legislative sanction, they passed over that which asserted our religious rights, leaving them as they found them.[1] The same convention, however, when they met as a member of the general assembly in October 1776, repealed all *acts of parliament* which had rendered criminal the maintaining any opinions in matters of religion, the forbearing to repair to church, and the exercising any mode of worship; and suspended the laws giving salaries to the clergy, which suspension was made perpetual in October 1779. Statutory oppressions in religion being thus wiped away, we remain at present under those only imposed by the common law, or by our own acts of assembly. At the common law, *heresy* was a capital offence, punishable by burning. Its definition was left to the ecclesiastical judges, before whom the conviction was, till the statute of the 1 El. c. 1.[2] circumscribed it, by declaring, that nothing should be deemed heresy, but what had been so determined by authority of the canonical scriptures, or by one of the four first general councils, or by some other council having for the grounds of their declaration the express and plain words of the scriptures. Heresy, thus circumscribed, being an offence at the common law, our act of assembly of October 1777, c. 17. gives cognizance of it to the general court, by declaring, that the jurisdiction of that court shall be general in all matters at the common law. The execution is by the writ *De haeretico comburendo.*[3] By our own act of assembly of 1705, c. 30, if a person brought up in the Christian religion denies the being of a God, or the Trinity, or asserts there are more Gods than one, or denies the Christian religion to be true, or the scriptures to be of divine authority, he is punishable on the first offence by incapacity to hold any office or employment ecclesiastical, civil, or military; on the second by disability to sue, to take any gift or legacy, to be guardian, executor, or administrator, and by three years imprisonment, without bail.

---

1. **religious rights . . . as they found them**: The Virginia Declaration of Rights, passed on May 15, 1776, includes section 16, which provides: "That religion, or the duty which we owe to our Creator, and the manner of discharging it, can be directed only by reason and conviction, not by force or violence; and therefore all men are equally entitled to the free exercise of religion, according to the dictates of conscience; and that it is the mutual duty of all to practice Christian forbearance, love, and charity toward each other."
2. **1 El. c. 1.**: During the first two years of her reign in England (1558-60), Elizabeth I, a Protestant, reinstated the Acts of Supremacy, which stipulated the primacy of the ecclesiastical laws of the Church of England (the Anglicans) and maintained the monarch as the head of the Church.
3. ***De haeretico comburendo***: "On the burning of a heretic" (Latin).

A father's right to the custody of his own children being founded in law on his right of guardianship, this being taken away, they may of course be severed from him, and put, by the authority of a court, into more orthodox hands. This is a summary view of that religious slavery, under which a people have been willing to remain, who have lavished their lives and fortunes for the establishment of their civil freedom.[4] The error seems not sufficiently eradicated, that the operations of the mind, as well as the acts of the body, are subject to the coercion of the laws. But our rulers can have authority over such natural rights only as we have submitted to them. The rights of conscience we never submitted, we could not submit. We are answerable for them to our God. The legitimate powers of government extend to such acts only as are injurious to others. But it does me no injury for my neighbour to say there are twenty gods, or no god. It neither picks my pocket nor breaks my leg. If it be said, his testimony in a court of justice cannot be relied on, reject it then, and be the stigma on him. Constraint may make him worse by making him a hypocrite, but it will never make him a truer man. It may fix him obstinately in his errors, but will not cure them. Reason and free enquiry are the only effectual agents against error. Give a loose to them, they will support the true religion, by bringing every false one to their tribunal, to the test of their investigation. They are the natural enemies of error, and of error only. Had not the Roman government permitted free enquiry, Christianity could never have been introduced. Had not free enquiry been indulged, at the aera of the reformation, the corruptions of Christianity could not have been purged away. If it be restrained now, the present corruptions will be protected, and new ones encouraged. Was the government to prescribe to us our medicine and diet, our bodies would be in such keeping as our souls are now. Thus in France the emetic was once forbidden as a medicine, and the potatoe as an article of food. Government is just as infallible too when it fixes systems in physics. Galileo was sent to the inquisition for affirming that the earth was a sphere: the government had declared it to be as flat as a trencher, and Galileo was obliged to abjure his error.[5] This error however at length prevailed, the earth became a globe, and Descartes[6] declared it was whirled round its axis by a vortex. The government in which he lived was wise enough to see that this was no question of civil jurisdiction, or we should all have been involved by authority in vortices. In fact, the vortices have been exploded, and the Newtonian principle of gravitation is now more firmly established, on the basis of reason, than it would be were the government to step in, and to make it an article of necessary faith. Reason and experiment have been indulged, and error has fled before them. It is error alone which needs the support of government. Truth can stand by itself. Subject opinion to coercion: whom will you make your inquisitors? Fallible men; men governed by bad passions, by private

---

4. **freedom:** Furneaux passim. [Jefferson's note.] In *Letters to the Honorable Mr. Justice Blackstone* (1770), the English minister Philip Furneaux (1726-1783) argues that religious views should not incur civil penalties.
5. **Galileo . . . error:** Galileo Galilei (1564-1642), an Italian scientist, was forced by the Inquisition to retract his belief in the Copernican theory that Earth is round and rotates around the sun.
6. **Descartes:** René Descartes (1596-1650), French philosopher and mathematician.

as well as public reasons. And why subject it to coercion? To produce uniformity. But is uniformity of opinion desireable? No more than of face and stature. Introduce the bed of Procrustes[7] then, and as there is danger that the large men may beat the small, make us all of a size, by lopping the former and stretching the latter. Difference of opinion is advantageous in religion. The several sects perform the office of a Censor morum[8] over each other. Is uniformity attainable? Millions of innocent men, women, and children, since the introduction of Christianity, have been burnt, tortured, fined, imprisoned; yet we have not advanced one inch towards uniformity. What has been the effect of coercion? To make one half the world fools, and the other half hypocrites. To support roguery[9] and error all over the earth. Let us reflect that it is inhabited by a thousand millions of people. That these profess probably a thousand different systems of religion. That ours is but one of that thousand. That if there be but one right, and ours that one, we should wish to see the 999 wandering sects gathered into the fold of truth. But against such a majority we cannot effect this by force. Reason and persuasion are the only practicable instruments. To make way for these, free enquiry must be indulged; and how can we wish others to indulge it while we refuse it ourselves. But every state, says an inquisitor, has established some religion. No two, say I, have established the same. Is this a proof of the infallibility of establishments? Our sister states of Pennsylvania and New York, however, have long subsisted without any establishment at all. The experiment was new and doubtful when they made it. It has answered beyond conception. They flourish infinitely. Religion is well supported; of various kinds, indeed, but all good enough; all sufficient to preserve peace and order: or if a sect arises, whose tenets would subvert morals, good sense has fair play, and reasons and laughs it out of doors, without suffering the state to be troubled with it. They do not hang more malefactors than we do. They are not more disturbed with religious dissensions. On the contrary, their harmony is unparalleled, and can be ascribed to nothing but their unbounded tolerance, because there is no other circumstance in which they differ from every nation on earth. They have made the happy discovery, that the way to silence religious disputes, is to take no notice of them. Let us too give this experiment fair play, and get rid, while we may, of those tyrannical laws. It is true, we are as yet secured against them by the spirit of the times. I doubt whether the people of this country would suffer an execution for heresy, or a three years imprisonment for not comprehending the mysteries of the Trinity. But is the spirit of the people an infallible, a permanent reliance? Is it government? Is this the kind of protection we receive in return for the rights we give up? Besides, the spirit of the times may alter, will alter. Our rulers will become corrupt, our people careless. A single zealot may commence persecutor, and better men be his victims. It can never be too often repeated, that the time for fixing every essential right on a legal basis is while our rulers are honest, and ourselves united. From the conclusion of this war we shall be going down hill. It will not then be necessary to resort every moment to the people for support. They will be forgotten, therefore, and their rights dis-

---

7. **bed of Procrustes:** In Greek mythology, Procrustes was a host who stretched or cut off part of the legs of his guests to make them fit his bed.
8. **Censor morum:** A critic of morals (Latin).
9. **roguery:** Dishonest acts.

regarded. They will forget themselves, but in the sole faculty of making money, and will never think of uniting to effect a due respect for their rights. The shackles, therefore, which shall not be knocked off at the conclusion of this war, will remain on us long, will be made heavier and heavier, till our rights shall revive or expire in a convulsion.

Query XVIII

THE PARTICULAR *CUSTOMS AND MANNERS THAT MAY HAPPEN TO BE RECEIVED IN THAT STATE?*

It is difficult to determine on the standard by which the manners of a nation may be tried, whether *catholic*,[10] or *particular*. It is more difficult for a native to bring to that standard the manners of his own nation, familiarized to him by habit. There must doubtless be an unhappy influence on the manners of our people produced by the existence of slavery among us. The whole commerce between master and slave is a perpetual exercise of the most boisterous passions, the most unremitting despotism on the one part, and degrading submissions on the other. Our children see this, and learn to imitate it; for man is an imitative animal. This quality is the germ of all education in him. From his cradle to his grave he is learning to do what he sees others do. If a parent could find no motive either in his philanthropy or his self-love, for restraining the intemperance of passion towards his slave, it should always be a sufficient one that his child is present. But generally it is not sufficient. The parent storms, the child looks on, catches the lineaments of wrath, puts on the same airs in the circle of smaller slaves, gives a loose to his worst of passions, and thus nursed, educated, and daily exercised in tyranny, cannot but be stamped by it with odious peculiarities. The man must be a prodigy who can retain his manners and morals undepraved by such circumstances. And with what execration should the statesman be loaded, who permitting one half the citizens thus to trample on the rights of the other, transforms those into despots, and these into enemies, destroys the morals of the one part, and the amor patriae[11] of the other. For if a slave can have a country in this world, it must be any other in preference to that in which he is born to live and labour for another: in which he must lock up the faculties of his nature, contribute as far as depends on his individual endeavours to the evanishment of the human race, or entail his own miserable condition on the endless generations proceeding from him. With the morals of the people, their industry also is destroyed. For in a warm climate, no man will labour for himself who can make another labour for him. This is so true, that of the proprietors of slaves a very small proportion indeed are ever seen to labour. And can the liberties of a nation be thought secure when we have removed their only firm basis, a conviction in the minds of the people that these liberties are of the gift of God? That they are not to be violated but with his wrath? Indeed I tremble for my country when I reflect that God is just: that his justice cannot sleep for ever: that considering numbers, nature and natural means only, a revolution of the wheel of fortune, an exchange of situation, is among possible events: that it may

---

10. **catholic:** Liberal or all-embracing.
11. **amor patriae:** Love of one's country (Latin).

become probable by supernatural interference! The Almighty has no attribute which can take side with us in such a contest. But it is impossible to be temperate and to pursue this subject through the various considerations of policy, of morals, of history natural and civil. We must be contented to hope they will force their way into every one's mind. I think a change already perceptible, since the origin of the present revolution. The spirit of the master is abating, that of the slave rising from the dust, his condition mollifying, the way I hope preparing, under the auspices of heaven, for a total emancipation, and that this is disposed, in the order of events, to be with the consent of the masters, rather than by their extirpation.

[1787, 1984]

George Washington

[1732-1799]

The son of a Virginia planter and his wife, George Washington began his military career at age twenty-two when he served as a lieutenant colonel in the French and Indian War. After the war, Washington returned to his Virginia plantation and became increasingly resistant to British interference in colonial affairs. Serving as a delegate to the Second Continental Congress in May 1775, Washington was appointed commander in chief of the Continental army, which he led for the next six years. In 1781, with the aid of French allies, Washington oversaw the surrender of the British at Yorktown, Virginia, the battle that effectively ended the Revolutionary War. When the Constitution was ratified in 1788, Washington was unanimously elected the first president of the United States and took the oath of office on April 30, 1789. As a part of a tour that he and Thomas Jefferson took to campaign for the passage of the first ten amendments to the Constitution, usually called the Bill of Rights, President Washington visited Newport, Rhode Island, on August 18, 1790. Moses Seixas (1744-1809), the warden of the Hebrew Congregation at Newport, presented Washington with a letter congratulating him on his presidency, reminding him of Jewish persecution, and urging the ongoing commitment of the new nation to religious freedom. In his letter, Seixas writes,

> Deprived as we heretofore have been of the invaluable rights of free citizens, we now (with a deep sense of gratitude to the Almighty disposer of all events) behold a government erected by the Majesty of the People – a Government which to bigotry gives no sanction, to persecution no assistance, but generously affording to All liberty of conscience and immunities of Citizenship, deeming every one, of whatever Nation, tongue, or language, equal parts of the great governmental machine.

In response, Washington wrote a letter in which he echoes Seixas's moving words and affirms the freedom of all Americans to worship as they

Touro Synagogue

Dedicated in 1763, the Jeshuat Israel Synagogue in Rhode Island (later renamed the Touro Synagogue) is the sole surviving synagogue built in colonial America. The neoclassical building was designed by Peter Harrison, the foremost architect in colonial America. A designer of churches, Harrison initially refused to work on the synagogue. But he finally agreed, and Harrison became so engaged in what he described as "a labor of love" that he charged no fee for his services.

choose. The letter was frequently reprinted and became one of the most influential statements in favor of religious toleration. On the occasion of the designation of the Touro Synagogue as a "National Historic Site" in 1946, President Harry S Truman recalled Washington's letter by writing: "The setting apart of this historic shrine as a national monument is symbolic of our national tradition of freedom, which has inspired men and women of every creed, race, and ancestry to contribute their highest gifts to the development of our national culture." The text of the letter is taken from the transcription of the original, now on display at the B'nai B'rith Klutznick National Jewish Museum, in Washington, D.C.

LETTER TO THE TOURO SYNAGOGUE

To the Hebrew Congregation in Newport Rhode Island
Gentlemen:

While I receive with much satisfaction, your Address replete with expressions of affection and esteem, I rejoice in the opportunity of answering you, that I shall always retain, a grateful remembrance of the cordial welcome I experienced in my visit to Newport, from all classes of Citizens.

The reflection on the days of difficulty and danger which are past, is rendered the more sweet, from a consciousness that they are succeeded by days of uncommon prosperity and security. If we have wisdom to make the best use of the advantages with which we are now favored, we cannot fail, under the just administration of a good Government, to become a great and a happy people.

The Citizens of the United States of America have a right to applaud themselves for having given to mankind examples of an enlarged and liberal policy: a policy worthy of imitation. All possess alike liberty of conscience and immunities of citizenship. It is now no more that toleration is spoken of, as if it was by the indulgence of one class of people, that another enjoyed the exercise of their inherent natural rights. For happily the Government of the United States, which gives to bigotry no sanction, to persecution no assistance, requires only that they who live under its protection, should demean themselves[1] as good citizens, in giving it on all occasions their effectual support. It would be inconsistent with the frankness of my character not to avow that I am pleased with your favorable opinion of my administration, and fervent wishes for my felicity. May the Children of the Stock of Abraham, who dwell in this land, continue to merit and enjoy the good will of the other inhabitants, while every one shall sit in safety under his own vine and fig tree, and there shall be none to make him afraid.[2] May the father of all mercies scatter light and not darkness in our paths, and make us all in our several vocations useful here, and in his own due time and way everlastingly happy.

George Washington
[1790]

---

1. **demean themselves:** Conduct themselves.
2. **Children of the Stock of Abraham . . . none to make him afraid:** Abraham was the Hebrew patriarch from whom all Jews trace their descent, as described in the Old Testament (Genesis 11:27-25:10). See also Micah 4:4: "But they shall sit every man under his vine and under his fig tree; and none shall make them afraid: for the mouth of the LORD of hosts hath spoken it."

Absalom Jones

[1746-1818]

Born into slavery, Absalom Jones was eventually able to buy his freedom in 1784. Having taught himself to read with a copy of the New Testament, he became the first African American priest in the Episcopal Church, then joined the Methodist Church, and finally helped form the African Methodist Episcopal Church. Actively involved in the movement to abolish the slave trade, Jones constantly underscored the contradictions between the institution of slavery and the freedoms guaranteed by the Declaration of Independence and the Bill of Rights. Jones redoubled his efforts to

Absalom Jones (detail)

This portrait of Jones, prominently holding a large Bible, was painted in 1810 by Raphaelle Peale, son of the celebrated Philadelphia painter Charles Willson Peale. The fact that the portrait was painted indicates the status of the sitter, a former slave who became an influential religious figure and a leader of the African American community in Philadelphia.

protest the injustice after Congress passed the Fugitive Slave Act of 1793, which provided that runaway slaves could be arrested or seized in any state or territory and returned to their masters. In the following petition, signed by Jones and seventy-three others in 1799, he appeals to the president and members of Congress to consider the place of "People of Color" in the United States. In 1808, Jones also published a *Thanksgiving Sermon* to commemorate the official end of the African slave trade, which a provision in the Constitution had allowed to continue for twenty years after the document was ratified in 1788. But the fugitive slave law was never rescinded. In fact, it was significantly strengthened by a second and far more rigorous law passed as part of the Compromise of 1850, more than fifty years after Jones's "Petition." The text is taken from the publication of the "Petition" in the appendix to *Remarks on the Slavery of Black People, Particularly To Those Who are in Legislative or Executive Stations in the General or State Governments; and also To Such Individuals as Hold Them in Bondage*, by John Parrish (Philadelphia, 1806).

PETITION OF THE PEOPLE OF COLOUR

To the President, Senate, and House of Representatives.

The Petition of the People of Colour, free men, within the City and Suburbs of Philadelphia, humbly sheweth,

That, thankful to God, our Creator, and to the Government under which we live, for the blessings and benefits granted to us in the enjoyment of our natural right to liberty, and the protection of our persons and property, from the oppression and violence which so great a number of like colour and national descent are subject to, we feel ourselves bound, from a sense of these blessings, to continue in our respective allotments, and to lead honest and peaceable lives, rendering due submission unto the laws, and exciting and encouraging each other thereto, agreeable to the uniform advice of our friends, of every denomination; yet while we feel impressed with grateful sensations for the Providential favour we ourselves enjoy, we cannot be insensible of the condition of our afflicted brethren, suffering under various circumstances, in different parts of these states; but deeply sympathizing with them, are incited by a sense of social duty, and humbly conceive ourselves authorized to address and petition you on their behalf, believing them to be objects of your representation in your public councils, in common with ourselves and every other class of citizens within the jurisdiction of the United States, according to the design of the present Constitution, formed by the General Convention, and ratified in the different states, as set forth in the preamble thereto in the following words, viz.[1] "We, the people of the United States, in order to form a more perfect union, establish justice, insure domestic tranquillity, provide for the common defence, and to secure the blessings of liberty to ourselves and posterity, do ordain, &c." We apprehend this solemn compact is violated, by a trade carried on in a clandestine manner, to the coast of Guinea,[2] and another equally wicked, practised openly by citizens of some of the southern states, upon the waters of Maryland and Delaware; men sufficiently callous to qualify them for the brutal purpose, are employed in kidnapping those of our brethren that are free, and purchasing others of such as claim a property in them: thus, those poor helpless victims, like droves of cattle, are seized, fettered, and hurried into places provided for this most horrid traffic, such as dark cellars and garrets, as is notorious at Northwest-fork, Chestertown, Eastown,[3] and divers other places. After a sufficient number is obtained, they are forced on board vessels, crouded under hatches, without the least commiseration, left to deplore the sad separation of the dearest ties in nature, husband from wife, and parents from children; thus packed together, they are transported to Georgia and other places, and there inhumanly exposed to sale. Can any commerce, trade, or transaction, so detestably shock the feeling of man, or degrade the dignity of his nature equal to this? And how increasingly is the evil aggra-

1. **viz.:** Abbreviation for *videlicit* (Latin), meaning namely or in other words.
2. **the coast of Guinea:** The major part of the transatlantic slave trade was conducted in the area of western Africa referred to as Guinea, which stretched from present-day Senegal to Angola.
3. **Northwest-fork, Chestertown, Eastown:** Towns on the eastern shore of Delaware and Maryland that were centers for the slave trade.

vated, when practised in a land high in profession of the benign doctrines of our Blessed Lord, who taught his followers to do unto others as they would they should do unto them. Your petitioners desire not to enlarge, though volumes might be filled with the sufferings of this grossly abused part of the human species, seven hundred thousand of whom, it is said, are now in unconditional bondage in these states: but conscious of the rectitude of our motives in a concern so nearly affecting us, and so effectually interesting to the welfare of this country, we cannot but address you as guardians of our rights, and patrons of equal and national liberties, hoping you will view the subject in an impartial, unprejudiced light. We do not ask for an immediate emancipation of all, knowing that the degraded state of many, and their want of education, would greatly disqualify for such a change; yet, humbly desire you may exert every means in your power to undo the heavy burdens, and prepare the way for the oppressed to go free, that every yoke may be broken. The law not long since enacted by Congress, called the Fugitive Bill,[4] is in its execution found to be attended with circumstances peculiarly hard and distressing; for many of our afflicted brethren, in order to avoid the barbarities wantonly exercised upon them, or through fear of being carried off by those men-stealers, being forced to seek refuge by flight, they are then, by armed men, under colour of this law, cruelly treated, or brought back in chains to those that have no claim upon them. In the Constitution and the Fugitive Bill, no mention is made of black people, or slaves; therefore, if the Bill of Rights, or the Declaration of Congress are of any validity, we beseech, that as we are men, we may be admitted to partake of the liberties and unalienable rights therein held forth; firmly believing that the extending of justice and equity to all classes, would be a means of drawing down the blessing of Heaven upon this land, for the peace and prosperity of which, and the real happiness of every member of the community, we fervently pray. Philadelphia, 30th of December, 1799.

Absalom Jones and others, 73 subscribers.

[1799, 1806]

---

4. **Fugitive Bill:** The Fugitive Slave Act of 1793. The legislation authorized slave owners or their agents to apprehend fugitives in any state or territory, and it permitted slave hunters to give oral testimony before a judge in order to gain a certificate to take custody of runaways. As a consequence, many free blacks were enslaved without any possibility of appeal.

Tecumseh

[1768-1813]

Tecumseh, a Shawnee military leader, learned from an early age about the encroachment of white settlers. His father was killed in the Battle of Point Pleasant, following which the Shawnees were pushed farther away from their lands in southern Ohio. In the early 1800s, Tecumseh decided that uniting several tribes was the only way to gain enough power and influence to persuade the new American government to deal fairly with Indians. In

Tecumseh

This engraving, probably the most authentic portrait of Tecumseh, was based on a sketch made by a French artist in a live sitting with the Indian leader. He is depicted in a British army uniform, indicating that he fought on the British side in the War of 1812, but his head covering marks his Indian identity.

1808, he and other tribal leaders established the capital of an Indian confederacy at a site near Tippecanoe in central Indiana. Meanwhile, the United States was buying Indian lands through treaties with various tribes. William Henry Harrison (1773-1841), then governor of the Indiana Territory and later the ninth president, had specific orders from the federal government to defend existing settlements and to gain the titles to more Indian lands to enable additional settlements. Tecumseh and Harrison were on a collision course in Indiana. Through the Treaty of Fort Wayne, negotiated first in 1803 and then revised in 1809, the Indians lost nearly three million acres of land. In speeches delivered to Harrison in 1810, Tecumseh strongly objected to the treaties and protested the brutal treatment of Indians by the Americans. Oratory had a long tradition in Native American culture, and Tecumseh was, by all accounts, a powerful speaker. But the governor was unmoved by the eloquent appeals. While Tecumseh was away in the summer of 1811, recruiting more tribes to join his confederation, Harrison determined to destroy Tippecanoe. After provoking an attack by the Indians, led by Tecumseh's younger brother Tenskwatawa (the Prophet), Harrison's forces defeated them and burned Tippecanoe to the ground on November 8, 1811. During the War of 1812, Tecumseh allied himself with the British. He was killed at the Battle of the Thames River in Canada, where his forces, along with British troops, were defeated by an American army commanded by Harrison. There are many versions based on rough transcriptions of the original translations of the speeches Tecumseh delivered to Harrison in August 1810. The text of the following passages from his second speech is taken from Edward Eggleston and Lillie Eggleston Seelye, *Tecumseh and the Shawnee Prophet* (1878).

SPEECH OF TECUMSEH TO GOVERNOR HARRISON

"Brother: I wish you to listen to me well. As I think you do not clearly understand what I before said to you, I will explain it again. . . .

"Brother, since the peace was made, you have killed some of the Shawnees, Winnebagoes, Delawares, and Miamis, and you have taken our land from us, and I do not see how we can remain at peace if you continue to do so. You try to force the red people to do some injury. It is you that are pushing them on to do mischief. You endeavor to make distinctions. You wish to prevent the Indians doing as we wish them – to unite, and let them consider their lands as the common property of the whole; you take tribes aside and advise them not to come into this measure; and until our design is accomplished we do not wish to accept of your invitation to go and see the President. The reason I tell you this, you want, by your distinctions of Indian tribes in allotting to each a particular tract of land, to make them to war with each other. You never see an Indian come and endeavor to make the white people do so. You are continually driving the red people; when, at last, you will drive them into the Great Lake, where they can't either stand or walk.

"Brother, you ought to know what you are doing with the Indians. Perhaps it is by direction of the President to make those distinctions. It is a very bad thing, and we do not like it. Since my residence at Tippecanoe we have endeavored to level all distinctions – to destroy village chiefs, by whom all mischief is done. It is they who sell our lands to the Americans. Our object is to let our affairs be transacted by warriors.[1]

"Brother, this land that was sold and the goods that were given for it were only done by a few. The treaty was afterwards brought here, and the Weas were induced to give their consent because of their small numbers. The treaty at Fort Wayne was made through the threats of Winnemac; but in future we are prepared to punish those chiefs who may come forward to propose to sell the land. If you continue to purchase of them it will produce war among the different tribes, and at last, I do not know what will be the consequence to the white people.

"Brother, I was glad to hear your speech. You said that if we could show that the land was sold by people that had no right to sell, you would restore it. Those that did sell did not own it. It was me. These tribes set up a claim, but the tribes with me will not agree with their claim. If the land is not restored to us you will see, when we return to our homes, how it will be settled. We shall have a great council, at which all the tribes will be present, when we shall show to those who sold that they had no right to the claim that they set up; and we will see what will be done to those chiefs that did sell the land to you. I am not alone in this determination; it is the determination of all the warriors and red people that listen to me. I now wish you to listen to me. If you do not, it will appear as if you wished me to kill all the chiefs that sold you the land. I tell you so because I am authorized by all the tribes to do so. I am the head of them all; I am a warrior, and all the warriors will meet together in two or three moons from this; then I will call for those chiefs that sold you the land and shall know what to do with them. If you do not restore the land, you will have a hand in killing them.

"Brother, do not believe that I came here to get presents from you. If you offer us any, we will not take. By taking goods from you, you will hereafter say that with them you purchased another piece of land from us. . . . It has been the object of both myself and brother to prevent the lands being sold. Should you not return the land, it will occasion us to call a great council that will meet at the Huron village, where the council-fire has already been lighted, at which those who sold the lands shall be called, and shall suffer for their conduct.

"Brother, I wish you would take pity on the red people and do what I have requested. If you will not give up the land and do cross the boundary of your present settlement, it will be very hard, and produce great troubles among us. How can we have confidence in the white people? When Jesus Christ came on earth, you killed him and nailed him on a cross. You thought he was dead, but you were mistaken. You have Shakers among you, and you laugh and make light of their worship.[2] Everything I have said to you is the truth. The Great Spirit has inspired me, and I speak nothing but the truth to you. . . ."

[1810, 1878]

---

1. **warriors:** Among the Shawnee and other tribes, civil chiefs were hereditary positions that were held for life, while war chiefs were chosen on the basis of their merit and skill.
2. **Shakers . . . worship:** Shakers were members of a religious movement brought to America in 1774 by the English prophet Ann Lee (1736-1784), who had a revelation that she was the Second Coming of Christ, the vital female principle in God the Father-Mother. The group, formally known as "The United Society of Believers," established communal settlements from Maine to Indiana. Their radical religious beliefs, including the requirement of celibacy, as well as the impassioned shaking that took place during their services, generated a good deal of derision and hostility among members of more orthodox Protestant sects.

Literature for a New Nation

FOLLOWING THE TRIUMPHANT CONCLUSION of the American Revolution in 1783, Americans faced the daunting task of establishing a new nation. The most immediate and pressing problems were political – the challenges of creating a new system of government, first under the Articles of Confederation and then under the Constitution, ratified by the states in 1788. The related effort to define and establish the nation's cultural identity

◀ **Asher Durand, *Kindred Spirits***

The emergence of American literature in the 1820s coincided with the establishment of the first coherent school of American painting, the Hudson River school, a group led by Thomas Cole and Asher Durand. Like the writers Washington Irving, James Fenimore Cooper, and William Cullen Bryant, the painters associated with the school celebrated the beauty of nature and the majesty of the American landscape, especially the scenery of the Hudson River valley and the Catskill Mountains. *Kindred Spirits* (1849), painted as a memorial to Cole shortly after his premature death in 1848, depicts him and his close friend Bryant, who has taken off his hat, probably as a gesture of reverence to the spiritual power of the unspoiled natural scene. Cole directs his (and our) attention to the most famous sites in the Catskill Mountains: Kaaterskill Cove, the dramatic gorge below the spectacular waterfall in the distance, the 260-foot Kaaterskill Falls.

was equally daunting and considerably more prolonged. As many scholars have noted, the culture of the new nation was at once provincial and post-colonial, still dominated by the literature and arts of Great Britain. The position of writers was particularly complex and conflicted. Their literary models were primarily British, especially earlier eighteenth-century poets like Alexander Pope, novelists like Samuel Richardson, and essayists like Joseph Addison and Richard Steele, who wrote for the influential periodical the *Spectator.* Given the standards of taste shaped by their works and shared by audiences on both sides of the Atlantic, American writers felt a strong need to maintain ties with England, to which many of them still looked for acceptance and approval. At the same time, they felt an increasingly strong pull toward literary independence and the establishment of new modes of expression more appropriate to the material conditions, social values, and political institutions of the United States. The position of American writers was further complicated by a lingering assumption that culture was the province of the elite and the educated, an assumption that threatened to put literature and the arts in conflict with the values of the emerging social and political order in the new nation, based on the republican principles of liberty and equality.

The characteristics of "American" culture and the role of the literature and the arts in the new nation were consequently subjects of ongoing controversy during the decades of the early national period. A major forum for such discussion and debate was the periodical press, which was growing quickly and which itself became an increasingly important element of American culture. Like newspapers, many magazines were primarily vehicles for the discussion of contemporary politics. But they revealed cultural as well as growing political divisions in the United States. One of the more successful and long-lived magazines of the period was the weekly *Port Folio* (1801-27), whose editor, John Dennie, wrote a column under the name "Oliver Oldschool." Dennie's conservatism was reflected in both his literary taste and his views on language. Noah Webster, who later compiled the first *American Dictionary of the English Language* (1828), had proclaimed in 1789: "As an independent nation, our honor requires us to have a system of our own, in language as well as government." In contrast, Dennie regularly featured articles critical of "Americanisms" in language. Similarly, although he published works by a few American writers, Dennie devoted much more space to British literature in *Port Folio.* The editors of the *North American Review* were far more interested in the development of a distinctly American literature. Its first issue in 1815 opened with what became a regular feature of the magazine, a catalog and description of "books relating to America." Later that year, in an "Essay on American Language and Literature," a contributor to the *Review* complained about the "barrenness of American literature," urging writers to cultivate a national language and exploit the "native peculiarities" of the United States.

"As an independent nation, our honor requires us to have a system of our own, in language as well as government."

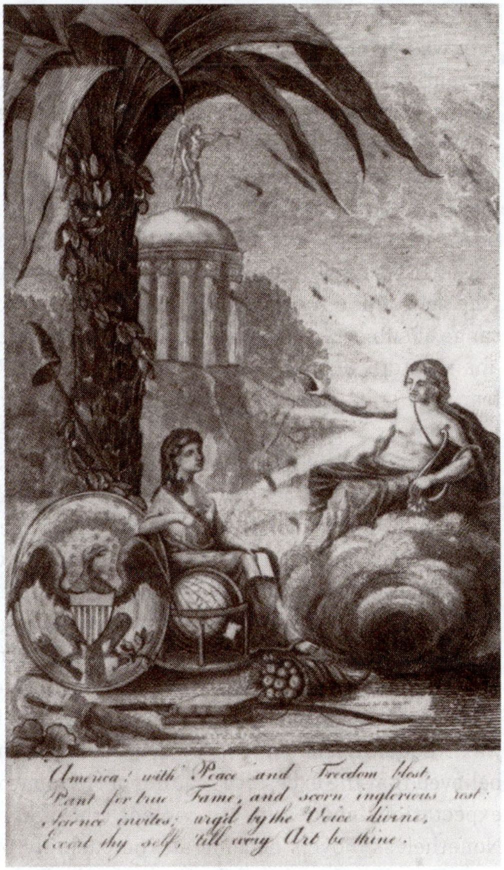
America! with Peace and Freedom blest,
Pant for true Fame, and scorn inglorious rest:
Science invites; urg'd by the Voice divine,
Exert thy self, 'till every Art be thine.

Frontispiece of the *Columbian Magazine*, 1789

In this allegorical illustration of the country following the Revolutionary War, America is depicted as a seated young woman who has put aside her shield to enjoy the benefits of peace and prosperity, represented by the horn of plenty at her feet. Her liberty pole and cap rest against the tree behind her. But the focus here is on education and the arts, as she holds a book in her hand and listens as Apollo, with a lyre, points to the Temple of Fame and sings: "America! with Peace and Freedom blest, / Pant for true Fame, and scorn inglorious rest: / Science invites; urg'd by the Voice divine, / Exert thy self, 'till every Art be thine."

Since poetry was still considered the highest literary form, those who were eager to develop a national literature were consequently ever alert to the emergence of significant poetic voices in the United States. Before the Revolution, there was an active manuscript culture in the colonies, where poems were often circulated in letters and commonplace books. Some poems also appeared in early periodicals, and a few books of poetry were published, including *The Patriot Muse* (1764), a series of poems on the French and Indian War by the New York physician Benjamin Youngs Prime. Prime wrote some popular political songs during the Revolution, which he later reviewed in a long narrative poem with the telltale title *Columbia's Glory; or, British Pride Humbled* (1791). Along with much of the other patriotic verse of the period, Prime's work has fallen into obscurity, in contrast to the poetry of Phillis Wheatley, a slave who was brought to the colonies in 1761. Educated and encouraged by her masters, Wheatley was heavily influenced by Alexander Pope and the other eighteenth-century English poets she read and studied. Her *Poems on Various Subjects, Religious and Moral* (1773), the first book of poetry published by an African American, was printed in England. During the Revolution, however, Wheatley fervently embraced the American cause and wrote a number of patriotic poems, like "To His Excellency General Washington" (1776).

Wheatley died soon after the war ended, so it is not possible to guess what direction her poetry might have taken or what role she might have played in efforts to create a distinctly American literature. She almost certainly would have confronted the difficulties all poets faced in the new nation, as exemplified by the career of Philip Freneau. Primarily known as "the poet of the American Revolution," Freneau actually wrote on a wide range of subjects – the American scene, slavery, and the condition of Indians – before, during, and especially after the Revolution. But he quickly learned that poetry was not going to provide him with a living. Although newspapers and magazines regularly published poetry, much of it was copied from British periodicals. By far the most popular books of poetry in early nineteenth-century America were written by poets like Sir Walter Scott and another wildly popular English poet Lord Byron. Like many other American writers of his day, Freneau supported himself and his work as a poet by earning money in other ways – in his case, by editing periodicals or serving as the master of sailing ships. Although he managed to publish several books of poetry, including a two-volume edition of his collected poems in 1815, Freneau died in poverty and obscurity in 1832.

Some early American novelists fared better than poets. The novel itself was frequently condemned by critics in the United States, where many believed that the excessive reading of fiction would encourage unrealistic expectations about life, stir violent emotions, and undermine morality. Nonetheless, novels became an increasingly popular form of entertainment. In 1789, the year of the first presidential election under the recently ratified Constitution, newspapers in Massachusetts proudly announced the publication of "THE FIRST AMERICAN NOVEL," William Hill Brown's *The Power of Sympathy*. Brown sought to disarm moralistic critics by dedicating the work to "The Young Ladies" of the United States, offering them a story intended to "expose the fatal Consequences of Seduction." Although that novel soon fell into obscurity, two other didactic and sentimental stories of the seduction, betrayal, and consequent death of a young woman became the first best-selling American novels: Susanna Rowson's *Charlotte: A Tale of Truth* (1791), first published in England and better known as *Charlotte Temple*, which went through 150 editions in the nineteenth century; and *The Coquette; or, The History of Eliza Wharton* (1797), published anonymously by "A Lady of Massachusetts," later identified as Hannah Webster Foster, the wife of a Massachusetts clergyman. Another significant figure in the emergence of the American novel was Charles Brockden Brown, who between 1798 and 1800 published his four major works, including *Wieland* (1798) and *Edgar Huntly* (1799). Although he essentially

Title Page of the First American Edition of *Charlotte Temple*
Published in England in 1791 and the United States in 1794, Rowson's enduringly popular novel went through roughly 150 editions during the following century.

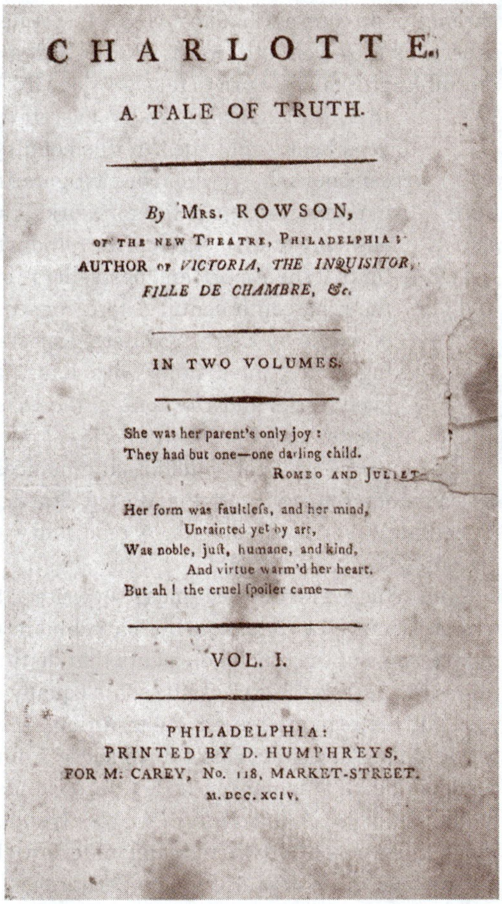
CHARLOTTE.

A TALE OF TRUTH.

By MRS. ROWSON,
OF THE NEW THEATRE, PHILADELPHIA;
AUTHOR OF *VICTORIA, THE INQUISITOR, FILLE DE CHAMBRE, &c.*

IN TWO VOLUMES.

She was her parent's only joy:
They had but one—one darling child.
ROMEO AND JULIET.

Her form was faultlefs, and her mind,
Untainted yet by art,
Was noble, juft, humane, and kind,
And virtue warm'd her heart.
But ah! the cruel fpoiler came—

VOL. I.

PHILADELPHIA:
PRINTED BY D. HUMPHREYS,
FOR M. CAREY, No. 118, MARKET-STREET.
M.DCC.XCIV.

followed the current fashion for gothic romances, tales of mystery and psychological terror that originated in England, Brown claimed originality in his use of an American setting and indigenous material. As he observed in his preface to *Edgar Huntly*, instead of relying upon the "Gothic castles and chimeras" of English novels, Brown sought to engage the emotions and sympathies of his readers by drawing upon "incidents of Indian hostility, and the perils of the western wilderness," which he asserted were far more suitable "for a native American."

Despite such early efforts and occasional successes, American novels did not gain a wide readership until the 1820s. Only about one hundred novels by American writers were published between 1789 and 1820. One reason was the American book trade, which was still in its infancy and plagued by problems of production and distribution. Moreover, in the absence of an international copyright law, American publishers (or booksellers, as they were still most often called) were usually more eager to reprint English books than to take a risk on an American writer. As late as 1821, the critic Alexander Everett attributed "the paucity of good books published in this country" to the failure of American booksellers, whom he castigated for "investing their capital in republications of foreign works" rather than offering "generous encouragement for the production of original compositions." The American "bestsellers" of the first two decades of the nineteenth century were consequently almost all reprints of works by English writers, especially Sir Walter Scott. Having first gained fame with long narrative poems like *Marmion* (1808) and *The Lady of the Lake* (1810), Scott scored even greater successes with a series of novels beginning with *Waverley* (1814). Scott's historical romances were an astounding success in both England and the United States, where all of them were immediately reprinted, voraciously read, and widely reviewed in American periodicals.

As late as 1821, the critic Alexander Everett attributed "the paucity of good books published in this country" to the failure of American booksellers, whom he castigated for "investing their capital in republications of foreign works."

Even as he overshadowed American writers, Scott offered them crucial lessons about how to exploit the native materials of their own country. In fact, some of the crucial elements that distinguished his historical fiction – his powerful sense of place, his equally commanding sense of the past, and his keen interest in oral traditions – strongly influenced a number of American writers who gained success during the 1820s. Taking his cue from Scott, Washington Irving pursued his own interest in the past in his first book, *A History of New York* (1809), a popular comic work in which he satirized both history and historians. During a trip to England a decade later, he visited Scott, who encouraged Irving to explore German Romantic literature, especially the legends and tales that had been generated by the growing interest in folk culture. As a result, Irving wrote the two most famous stories in his popular collection *The Sketch Book of Geoffrey Crayon, Gent.* (1819-20): "Rip Van Winkle" and "The Legend of Sleepy Hollow," in which he essentially naturalized German folktales and displayed his own strong sense of an American place, the Catskill Mountains of New York. Scott's historical romances exerted an even stronger influence on James Fenimore Cooper, who also capitalized on American settings and sources, especially in his historical novels *The Pioneers* (1823), *The Last of the Mohicans* (1826), and *The Prairie* (1827), the first three of his "Leather-Stocking Tales." Although he published many other works of fiction and nonfiction, that series of novels about the life and adventures of the frontiersman Natty Bumppo, or Leather-Stocking, earned Cooper international fame as "the American Scott."

Prose writers also began to explore other locales and different periods of American history. Inspired by Scott, Catharine Maria Sedgwick sought

Christian Schussele, *Washington Irving and His Literary Friends at Sunnyside* (1863)

Painted after Irving's death in 1859, this group portrait celebrates his central role in the creation of American literature by placing him at the center of a gathering of writers who gained prominence between the 1820s and the Civil War. From left to right, they are Henry Tuckerman, Oliver Wendell Holmes, William Gilmore Simms, Fitz-Greene Halleck, Nathaniel Hawthorne, Henry Wadsworth Longfellow, Nathaniel Parker Willis, William H. Prescott, Washington Irving, James K. Paulding, Ralph Waldo Emerson, William Cullen Bryant, John Pendleton Kennedy, James Fenimore Cooper, and George Bancroft. This gathering never took place, but many of the writers represented had visited Irving at Sunnyside, his country home on the Hudson River.

(Gift of John D. Rockefeller Jr. Historic Hudson Valley. Tarrytown, New York.)

to expand what she described as "the scanty stock of native American literature" by writing novels like *A New-England Tale* (1822), *Redwood* (1824), and *Hope Leslie* (1827), a historical romance set at the time of the Pequot War in seventeenth-century Connecticut. A writer for the *North American Review*, which for more than a decade had been exhorting American writers to explore "native" scenes and themes, especially commended Sedgwick for her depiction of the characters, history, and landscape of

New England. At the same time Cooper and Sedgwick were publishing their acclaimed novels about the early conflicts between European settlers and the Indians, Jane Johnston Schoolcraft, whose Native American name was Bame-wa-wa-ge-zhik-a-quay (Woman of the Stars Rushing through the Sky), was writing stories in which she sought to preserve in English the legends and tales of her mother's tribe, the Ojibwa. Among the earliest written works of Native American literature, Schoolcraft's stories spurred interest in both Indian lore and the remote region around the Great Lakes inhabited by the Ojibwa. Indeed, regionalism became an increasingly important element in American novels, stories, and sketches, from Sedgwick's New England to Schoolcraft's "wilderness" to the southern frontier humorously depicted by Augustus Baldwin Longstreet in *Georgia Scenes*, a popular collection of sketches he began to write in 1830.

By then, the foundations of a literary culture had finally been laid in the United States. Americans even had a poet they could point to with pride, William Cullen Bryant. Just as many American prose writers followed the example of Sir Walter Scott, Bryant was strongly influenced by British Romantic poets, especially William Wordsworth. With its emphasis on the dignity of the individual, the literary value of common speech, and the vital role of nature in human life, Romanticism exerted an increasingly strong pull on American writers, whose new, democratic country was far more noted for the grandeur of its natural scenery than for the richness of its cultural traditions. At the same time, Bryant was hailed for his mastery of traditional English poetics. When his poem "Thanatopsis" was submitted to the *North American Review* in 1817, one of its editors reportedly exclaimed, "No one, on this side of the Atlantic is capable of writing such verses!" The following year, Bryant wrote an extended essay for an influential British journal, the *Edinburgh Review,* in which he surveyed American poetry and assessed the literary situation in the United States. "The fondness for literature is fast increasing in our country," he confidently observed. "The popular English works of the day are reprinted in our country – they are dispersed all over the union – they are to be found in every body's hands – they are made the subject of every body's conversation. What should hinder our native works, if they are of equal merit, from meeting an equally favorable reception?"

"The fondness for literature is fast increasing in our country."

Certainly, the warm reception of Bryant's first book, *Poems* (1821) – as well as of the prose works by Irving, Cooper, Sedgwick, Schoolcraft, and Longstreet – indicated that there was a growing audience for such "native works" in the United States. Like earlier poets, Bryant could not earn a living as a poet. He supported himself first as a lawyer and later as the editor of the New York *Evening Post*, one of the large-circulation newspapers that were fast becoming a major force in the nation's print culture. Nonetheless, literature was also gaining a foothold in that print culture, and both

Cooper and Irving demonstrated that it was possible to be professional writers in the United States. At the same time, the prose writers who emerged in the 1820s experimented with genres that later assumed a prominent place in American literature, including the sketch and short story, the potential of which would be more fully developed by writers like Nathaniel Hawthorne and Edgar Allan Poe. In retrospect, literature from the Revolution to 1830 may appear to be simply a prelude to the "American Renaissance," the term frequently used to describe the period from 1830 to 1865. But the remarkable achievements of that period would not have been possible without the earlier efforts of those who first struggled to create an American literature and an audience for that literature in the United States.

American Contexts

"Who Reads an American Book?": Calls for a National Literature

"The Americans have no national literature, and no learned men," a writer for the *British Critic* asserted in 1818. In a book review published in the prestigious *Edinburgh Review* two years later, the eminent English essayist Sydney Smith went further, offering a sweeping critique of American culture that ignited a firestorm of protest in the United States. "Americans are a brave, industrious, and acute people," Smith observed, "but they have hitherto given no indications of genius, and made no approaches to the heroic, either in their morality or character." He then asked a famous series of questions:

> In the four quarters of the globe, who reads an American book? or goes to an American play? or looks at an American picture or statue? What does the world yet owe to American physicians or surgeons? What new substances have their chemists discovered? or what old ones have they analyzed? What new constellations have been discovered by the telescopes of Americans? – what have they done in the mathematics? Who drinks out of American glasses? or eats from American plates? or wears American coats or gowns? or sleeps in American blankets? – Finally, under which of the old tyrannical governments of Europe is every sixth man a slave, whom his fellow creatures may buy and sell and torture?

Americans quickly rallied to answer Smith's dismissive questions, which intensified anxieties and widespread concerns about cultural, scientific, and social advances in the United States. For many, developing a national literature was one of the most crucial means of rebutting critics like Smith and putting America on an equal footing with the nations of Europe, especially Great Britain. In his "Remarks on National Literature" (1823), delivered three years after Smith's article appeared, the Unitarian minister William Ellery Channing thus defined *national literature* in terms that underscored its vital importance to the United States. "We mean the thoughts of profound and original minds, elaborated by the toil of composition, and fixed and made immortal in books," Channing explained. "We mean the manifestation of a nation's intellect in the only forms by which it can multiply itself at home, and send itself abroad. We mean that a nation shall take a place, by its authors, among the lights of the world."

The following texts illustrate the increasingly urgent calls for a national literature from the end of the American Revolution through the 1820s. As the texts also reveal, such appeals raised fundamental questions about what conditions were necessary for the development of a national literature, what indigenous materials native writers might employ, and what characteristics their productions would embody. One of the earliest calls for American literary independence was issued in the prologue to *The Contrast* (1787), a play in which Royall Tyler claimed originality for employing American characters, scenes, and themes. A decade later, Judith Sargent Murray attributed the scarcity of successful plays and other works by American authors to the lack of a supportive audience in their native country. From time to time, the performance of plays had been banned in the colonies, mainly because of the objections of various religious groups, especially the Puritans and the Quakers. Tyler, Murray, and other playwrights like Mercy Otis Warren were therefore particularly notable for their efforts to establish the viability of theater in America.

bedfordstmartins.com/ americanlit *for research links on the authors in this section*

At the turn of the nineteenth century, the novelist Charles Brockden Brown also emphasized the importance of developing a national culture that would nourish the arts and literature in the United States. Brown placed particular emphasis on the potential role of periodicals, which would at once help develop an audience for American writers at home and display the results of their efforts to critics abroad. Several of those magazines were established specifically to foster and support work by American writers, notably the *North American Review*, founded in Boston in 1815. The pages of the *Review* were filled with advice and exhortations to American writers by critics like William Tudor, who cataloged the rich literary resources available to them, and Edward Tyrell Channing, who emphasized the need for freedom and originality in the emerging literature of the United States.

Despite such expressions of literary nationalism, some of the major obstacles to the development of a national literature were not overcome until the 1820s. Before that, the emerging publishing industry in the United States was limited by primitive methods of both production and distribution. American printers or booksellers published small numbers of books and periodicals, usually for a local audience. Moreover, in the absence of an international copyright law, booksellers could reprint the works of popular English authors without paying them any royalties. Most American periodicals were consequently filled with articles, reviews, and stories from British journals, while the limited marketplace for books was dominated by popular British writers like Sir Walter Scott. Scott's popular historical romances offered a powerful model for writers like James Fenimore Cooper, one of a number of American novelists who began to exploit incidents from the early history of the United States. In *Notions of the Americans* (1828), a response to European critics, Cooper described the improving economic conditions for writers in his native country, where literature had finally begun to be profitable. By 1825, about one hundred magazines were in regular circulation in the United States. Advances in technology and transportation also spurred the production of books, a growing number of which were written by Americans. In fact, during the decade following the publication of Smith's critique of American culture, successful writers like Cooper, Washington Irving, and Catharine Maria Sedgwick produced an answer to one of his questions: If by 1830 the country had not yet developed a distinctly national literature, it could at least proudly reply that American books were being read in growing numbers in both the United States and in Europe.

Royall Tyler

[1757-1826]

Born into a wealthy family in Boston, Royall Tyler graduated from Harvard College and served with distinction during the American Revolution. Before settling on a career in law, he wrote several plays, though at the time theater was still viewed with suspicion by many people in the United States. Of those plays, the most famous was and is *The Contrast*. The first American play produced by a professional theatrical company, *The Contrast* was performed at the John Street Theater in New York City in April 1787. Following its success there, it was also performed in Philadelphia, Baltimore, and Boston. Adopting the story line of a famous British play by Richard Brinsley Sheridan, *The School for Scandal* (1777), Tyler shifted the action to New York City and introduced some memorable American types,

Frontispiece of *The Contrast*

This engraving, from the published edition of Royall Tyler's play, includes likenesses of some of the original cast members, including Thomas Signell as Jonathan (center).

especially Jonathan, the comic, resourceful Yankee. In the poetic prologue, Tyler challenged his audience to embrace the "native themes" he showcased in his play. The text of the prologue is taken from the first published edition of *The Contrast* (1790).

PROLOGUE TO *THE CONTRAST*

Written by a YOUNG GENTLEMAN *of New-York,*
and Spoken by MR. WIGNELL[1]

Exult each patriot heart! – this night is shewn
A piece, which we may fairly call our own;
Where the proud titles of "My Lord! Your Grace!"
To humble Mr. and plain Sir give place.
Our Author pictures not from foreign climes
The fashions, or the follies of the times;
But has confin'd the subject of his work
To the gay scenes – the circles of New-York.
On native themes his Muse displays her pow'rs;
If ours the faults, the virtues too are ours.
Why should our thoughts to distant countries roam,
When each refinement may be found at home?
Who travels now to ape the rich or great,
To deck an equipage[2] and roll in state;
To court the graces,[3] or to dance with ease,
Or by hypocrisy to strive to please?
Our free-born ancestors such arts despis'd;
Genuine sincerity alone they priz'd;
Their minds, with honest emulation fir'd.
To solid good – not ornament – aspir'd;
Or, if ambition rous'd a bolder flame,
Stern virtue throve, where indolence was shame.

But modern youths, with imitative sense,
Deem taste in dress the proof of excellence;
And spurn the meanness of your homespun arts,
Since homespun habits would obscure their parts;
Whilst all, which aims at splendour and parade,

---

1. **Mr. Wignell:** Thomas Wignell (1753-1803), a popular comic actor, played the part of Jonathan in the New York production in 1787 and published *The Contrast* in 1790.
2. **equipage:** A carriage with horses and attendants.
3. **graces:** The three daughters of Zeus in Greek mythology, the Graces were personifications of beauty and gracefulness.

Must come from Europe, and be ready made.
Strange! we should thus our native worth disclaim,
And check the progress of our rising fame.
Yet one, whilst imitation bears the sway,
Aspires to nobler heights, and points the way.
Be rous'd, my friends! his bold example view;
Let your own Bards be proud to copy you!
Should rigid critics reprobate our play,
At least the patriotic heart will say,
"Glorious our fall, since in a noble cause.
"The bold attempt alone demands applause."
Still may the wisdom of the Comic Muse
Exalt your merits, or your faults accuse.
But think not, tis her aim to be severe; –
We all are mortals, and as mortals err.
If candour pleases, we are truly blest;
Vice trembles, when compell'd to stand confess'd.
Let not light Censure on your faults offend,
Which aims not to expose them, but amend.
Thus does our Author to your candour trust;
Conscious, the free are generous, as just.

[1787, 1790]

Judith Sargent Murray

[1751-1820]

Born into a prominent family in Gloucester, Massachusetts, Judith Sargent Murray was an early champion of women's education and rights. A prolific author of essays, poetry, plays, and a novel, she commented on almost every facet of life in the new nation – culture, politics, religion, and society. Murray published articles under pseudonyms in various magazines, beginning with the *Gentleman and Lady's Town and Country Magazine*. Her articles signed "Constantia" earned Murray a reputation, and she began

Judith Sargent Murray

This portrait of "Mrs. John Stevens," as Murray was known during her marriage to her first husband, was painted when she was eighteen or nineteen years old by John Singleton Copley, the foremost artist in colonial America, who gained fame for his innovative portraits of prominent people in New England.

to write regularly for the *Massachusetts Magazine*. Between February 1792 and the end of 1794, Murray wrote a series of one hundred essays on contemporary culture for the magazine, in which she took on a masculine persona of "The Gleaner." She later collected these essays into a three-volume book dedicated to President John Adams. As a playwright, Murray was especially eager for American plays with native scenes and themes to assume a secure place in the new national culture. The text of the following selection from sketch number 96 is taken from volume three of *The Gleaner* (1798).

From The Gleaner, *Number 96*

Were I at liberty my plans to choose,
My politics, my fashions, and my muse
Should be American – Columbia's fame
Hath to Columbia's meed a righteous claim:
Her laws, her magistrates I would revere,
Holding this younger world supremely dear.[1]

Hardly a day passes that does not furnish some new instance of the paucity of national attachment in our country. We regret much the frequent occasions which impel us to reiterate expressions of concern, on account of an evil so truly alarming. The real patriot must necessarily lament the present aspect of affairs. French men and measures – English men and measures.[2] These do in fact divide the majority of the people; while those who rally round the standard of America are reduced to a very inconsiderable party.

We are far removed from the elder world; the wide Atlantic is our barrier. Persons of information affirm, that we possess within ourselves the sources of independence; and it is certainly true, that the interior of our country, reduced to a state of cultivation, would become amply productive, largely supplying every *essential article of life*. Necessity is pronounced the mother of invention – Improvement follows; and those elegancies, or superfluities, to which we are attached, would, by a natural process, become the growth of America. Why then do we not *radically throw off every foreign yoke* – assert ourselves, and no longer delay to fill our rank as free sovereign, and independent States?

While I am writing, a circle of ladies in the next room are discussing this very subject, and a respectable female, in an elevated tone of voice, declares, she had rather take the fashion of her garments from an American presidentress, than from any princess in Europe. We wish this idea was adopted, from the State of New-Hampshire, to those far

---

1. **Were . . . dear:** The epigraph was written by Murray, who was also a poet. *Columbia* was a popular name for the United States.
2. **French . . . measures:** Americans were then divided over loyalties to the French and English, who were at war following the French Revolution.

distant and extensive banks, whose verdant borders are washed by the waters of the Ohio; and that American habiliments,[3] politics, and sentiments of every description, might henceforward receive an American stamp.

Perhaps our deficiency in national partiality is in nothing more apparent than in the little taste we discover for American literature. Indigenous productions are received with cold neglect, if not contempt, or they are condemned to an ordeal, the severity of which is sufficient to terrify the most daring adventurer. Mortifying indifference, or invidious criticism – these, in their respective operations, chill the opening bud, or blast its expansive leaves, and the apathy with which we regard the toils of intellect, is truly astonishing. An original genius hath produced a sentiment of the following nature: *If the first rate abilities, cloathed in the habiliments of mortality, were passing through the streets of our metropolis, they would be elbowed by the crowd, knocked down by a truckman, or rode over by a hackney coach.*[4] And we add – better so, than if they were consigned to the lingering tortures of the rack,[5] or condemned to suffer death under the axe of a mangling and barbarous executioner.

We do not say that the office of a *candid critic* is not beneficial, and even *essential*: But when an author, or his productions, are to be dissected, in the name of every principle of humanity let *a man of feeling preside* – let the operation be conducted by an artist, who, possessing the abilities to discriminate, will be governed by the admonitions of decency. An informed, judicious, and well disposed critic, will not wholly reject the influence of sympathy; and his feelings will induce him, when culling into view a glaring absurdity, to produce, if possible, some pleasing selection, which may soothe the bosom he is thus necessitated to lacerate. When a work is to be analyzed, if the plot is deficient in conception, and in adjustment – if the ideas are extravagant, the events tragical, and the catastrophe improbable – the critic, if he is not a *usurper*,[6] if he is legally invested with the robes of office, will, however, find something to admire in the style; and if it abounds with just sentiments, and classical allusions, he will produce them, not only with marks of decided approbation, but with triumph.

The stage is undoubtedly a very powerful engine in forming the opinions and manners of a people. Is it not then of importance to supply the American stage with American scenes? I am aware that very few productions in this line have appeared, and I think the reason is obvious. Writers, especially dramatic writers, are not properly encouraged. Applause, that powerful spring of action, (if we except the ebullitions of the moment) is withheld, or sparingly administered. No incentives are furnished, and indignant genius, conscious of its own resources, retires to the intellectual banquet, disdaining to spread the feast for malevolence and ingratitude.

If productions, *confessedly indifferent*, were, from the ascendency of local preferences, *endured in their turn, and received with manifest partiality*, it would, perhaps, stimulate

3. **habiliments:** Early term for clothing.
4. **truckman . . . hackney coach:** A truckman was a person who did business by barter or exchange, often carrying goods in a wheeled vehicle; a hackney coach was a horse-drawn vehicle for hire.
5. **rack:** An instrument of torture on which a victim was tied and stretched.
6. ***usurper*:** A person who has encroached or infringed on someone's rights.

to more polished efforts, and the Columbian Drama[7] might at length boast the most finished productions. But so far are we from evincing this predilection that even performances, decidedly meritorious, are almost forgotten. Tyler's plays are strangely neglected; and the finished scenes of the correct and elegant Mrs. Warren, have never yet passed in review before an American audience.[8] Was the American taste decidedly in favour of native worth, the superintendants of the Drama would find it for their interest to cherish indigenous abilities, and the influence of patronage would invigorate and rear to maturity the now drooping plant.

[1795, 1798]

7. **Columbian Drama:** American drama.
8. **Tyler's plays . . . Mrs. Warren:** Royall Tyler (1757-1820) was among the first American playwrights. The prologue to his best-known play, *The Contrast*, is printed on page 480. Mercy Otis Warren (1728-1814) was the author of patriotic pamphlets, poems, and plays. She later published a three-volume history of the American Revolution (1805).

Charles Brockden Brown

[1771-1810]

Charles Brockden Brown

This undated portrait of Brown was painted by James Sharpless, an Englishman who came to the United States and settled in New York City around 1798.

Born in Philadelphia and trained as a lawyer, Charles Brockden Brown was one of the first significant novelists in the United States. Between 1797 and 1801, Brown published six novels of gothic romance, including *Wieland*, *Ormond*, *Edgar Huntly*, and *Arthur Mervyn*. He was also the founder and editor of a number of literary journals, beginning with the *Monthly Magazine and American Review*, established in 1799. He continued to contribute to the magazine after it changed its title to the *American Review, and Literary Journal*. In his early articles, Brown pressed his readers to help in the formation of an American literature, expressing pride in "contemplating the bold, enterprising, and independent spirit of my contemporaries," and offering his magazine as a vehicle for "the literary harvest of America." The text of the following selection is taken from the preface to volume one of the *American Review, and Literary Journal, for the Year 1801*.

From THE PREFACE TO *THE AMERICAN REVIEW, AND LITERARY JOURNAL*

The people of the United States are, perhaps, more distinguished than those of Europe as a people of business; and by an universal attention to the active and lucrative pursuits of life. This habit has grown out of the necessities of their situation, while engaged in the settlement of a new country, in the means of self-preservation, in defending their possessions, in removing the obstacles and embarrassments arising from their colonial condition, and in forming and establishing independent systems of government. When, now, that our population is increased, our national independence secured, and our governments established, and we are relieved from the necessities of colonists and emigrants, there is reason to expect more attention to polite literature and science.

Nothing, it is thought, will tend more to excite this attention, and to render the pursuits of knowledge more compatible with those of business, than those periodical publications which impart information in small portions; by which, men engaged in active occupations, may gradually acquire a degree of intellectual cultivation and improvement, without any infringement of the time allotted to their customary and necessary concerns.

Much has been said about the claims which the natives of America may urge to the praise of genius and learning. Some European critics hold our pretensions in contempt; and many among ourselves seem inclined to degrade our countrymen below the common level. Their judgment has been formed from very imperfect evidence, and very narrow views; though it must be admitted that we have not contributed our share to the great fund of knowledge and science which is continually receiving such vast accessions from every part of Europe.

Genius in composition, like genius in every other art, must be aided by culture, nourished by patronage,[1] and supplied with leisure and materials. The genius of the poet, orator, and historian, cannot be exercised with vigour and effect, without suitable encouragement, any more than that of the artist and mechanic. Neither the one or the other is beyond the sphere of social affections, and domestic duties and wants; neither can be expected to produce works of ingenuity and labour without such a recompense as the natural ambition of man, and the necessities of his nature and situation demand.

No one is so absurd as to suppose that the natives of America are unfitted, by any radical defect of understanding, for vieing with the artizans of Europe, in all those useful and elegant fabrics which are daily purchased by us. Similar and suitable circumstances would show Americans equally qualified to excel in arts and literature, as the natives of the other continent. But a people much engaged in the labours of agriculture, in a country rude and untouched by the hand of refinement, cannot, with any tolerable facility or success, carry on, at the same time, the operations of imagination, and indulge in the speculations of Raphael, Newton, or Pope.[2]

---

1. **patronage:** Financial support given by a person or an organization.
2. **Raphael . . . Pope:** Brown refers to three major figures in the arts and sciences: Raphael (1483–1520), an Italian painter and architect; Sir Isaac Newton (1642–1727), an English mathematician and physicist; and Alexander Pope (1688–1744), an English poet.

The causes, indeed, why the intellectual soil of America is so comparatively sterile, are obvious. We do not cultivate it; nor, while we can resort to foreign fields, from whence all our wants are so easily and readily supplied, and which have been cultivated for ages, do we find sufficient inducement to labour in our own. We are united by language, manners, and taste, by the bonds of peace and commercial intercourse, with an enlightened nation, the centre of whose arts and population may be considered as much *our* centre, as much the fountain whence *we* draw light and knowledge, through books, as that of the inhabitants of Wales and Cumberland. In relation to the British capital, as the centre of English literature, arts, and science, the situation of *New* and *Old-York* may be regarded as the same. It is only the gradual influence of time, that by increasing our numbers, and furnishing a ready market for the works of domestic hands and heads, that will, at length, generate and continue a race of artists and authors purely indigenous, and who may vie with those of Europe.

[1801]

William Tudor

[1779-1830]

William Tudor was a merchant, politician, and author of half a dozen books and printed lectures. A prominent Bostonian, Tudor was deeply engaged in building national cultural institutions. In 1807, he helped found the Boston Athenaeum, one of the first major libraries in the United States. He also served as the first editor of the *North American Review*, the most prestigious and well-funded American magazine of the period. The backers of the *Review* regarded it as their mission to encourage American writers and to foster a distinctly national literature. In an address delivered to the Phi Beta Kappa Society at Harvard College in 1815, Tudor thus emphasized the rich materials available to would-be writers in the United States, whom he especially encouraged to exploit the unique resource of the magnificent American landscape. The text of the following selection is taken from the printed version of the address in the *North American Review*, November 1815.

From AN ESSAY ON AMERICAN SCENERY

The early history of illustrious nations, has been the source of the great master pieces of poetry: the fabulous ages of Greece are the foundation of the Illiad and Odyssey, and the same period gave Virgil his hero for the Aeneid. Many modern epicks have taken the heroes of the earlier periods, and revolutions of modern times. The American Revolution may some centuries hence, become a fit and fruitful subject for an heroick poem;

when ages will have consecrated its principles, and all remembrance of party feuds and passions, shall have been obliterated – when the inferiour actors and events will have been levelled by time, and a few memorable actions and immortal names shall remain, the only monuments, to engage and concentrate the admiration of a remote posterity.

From the close of the 16th to the middle of the 18th century many most interesting events took place on this continent, and circumstances have concurred with time in casting a shade of obscurity resembling that of antiquity, over the transactions of that period; while, by the great revolutions which have since happened, the connexion between those days and our own is interrupted, and they are so disconnected with the present era, that no passionate feeling is blended with their consideration; they are now exclusively the domain of history and poetry. All the communities then standing have passed away, or exist under new relations. The remarkable Confederacy of Indian tribes under the name of the five nations is extinct.[1] The foundations of the French Empire in America have been torn up, the possessions that were once French are now held by the British, and the English colonies have become an independent nation. All these changes have insulated this portion of history, and divested it of the irritation attendant on recent political affairs.

The region in which these occurrences took place, abounds with grand and beautiful scenery, possessing some peculiar features. The numerous waterfalls, the enchanting beauty of Lake George and its pellucid flood, of Lake Champlain,[2] and the lesser lakes, afford many objects of the most picturesque character; while the inland seas from Superiour to Ontario, and that astounding cataract, whose roar would hardly be increased by the united murmurs of all the cascades of Europe, are calculated to inspire vast and sublime conceptions. The effects too of our climate composed of a Siberian winter and an Italian summer, furnish peculiar and new objects for description. The circumstances of remote regions are here blended, and strikingly opposite appearances witnessed in the same spot, at different seasons of the year – In our winters, we have the sun at the same altitude as in Italy, shining on an unlimited surface of snow, which can only be found in the higher latitudes of Europe, where the sun in the winter rises little above the horizon. The dazzling brilliance of a winter's day, and a moon-light night, when the utmost splendour of the sky is reflected from a surface of spotless white, attended with the most excessive cold, is peculiar to the northern part of the United States. What too can surpass the celestial purity and transparency of the atmosphere in a fine autumnal day, when our vision and our thoughts seem carried 'to the third heaven;' the gorgeous magnificence of their close, when the sun sinks from our view, surrounded with varied

---

1. **The remarkable Confederacy . . . extinct:** The Iroquois Confederacy was a sophisticated democratic governance and social system of Indian nations located in present-day New York State. The confederacy originally included the Mohawk, Onondaga, Seneca, Oneida, and Cayuga; a sixth nation, the Tuscarora, joined in the eighteenth century (see p. 33). The confederacy was largely destroyed by settlement and the land policies of the colonial and then the federal governments.

2. **Lake George . . . Lake Champlain:** Lake George, known for its clear waters, is in northeastern New York. Lake Champlain forms the border between New York and Vermont. Both lakes were theaters of battle in the French and Indian War and in the Revolutionary War.

masses of clouds, fringed with gold and purple, and reflecting in evanescent tints, all the hues of the rainbow.

A most remarkable feature in the landscape at this same season, and which those who see it for the first time must behold with astonishment, is the singular appearance of the woods; where all the hues of the most lively flowers, the vivid colours of tulips, are given to the trees of the forest, and nature appears in a moment of capricious gayety to have attired the groves in the gaudiest and most fantastick livery. Nothing comparable to this effect can be seen in any part of Europe.

Many other beauties of inanimate nature might be enumerated, and these just mentioned are only cited, as being in a degree peculiar. These extensive and variegated forests afford shelter to a variety of animals, beautiful in form and curious in their habits, such among others, are the beaver and the deer; and to birds of most exquisite plumage. The graceful shape and various species of some of the diminutive quadrupeds, the very abundance of some of these animals, and of certain kinds of birds, which almost darken the air in their flight, serve to enrich and animate the scenery. Prominent among objects of this class, is the king of birds, Jove's own imperial Eagle,[3] the sacred emblem of our country:

> Formed by nature for braving the severest cold, feeding equally on the produce of the sea and of the land, possessing powers of flight capable of outstripping even the tempests themselves; unawed by any but men; and from the etherial heights to which he soars, looking abroad at one glance to an immeasurable expanse of forests, fields, lakes and ocean deep below him, he appears indifferent to the little localities of change of seasons; as in a few minutes he can pass from summer to winter, from the lower to the higher regions of the atmosphere, the abode of eternal cold, and from thence descend at will to the torrid and arctick zones of the earth.[4]

In the same territories are found those enormous bones of animals now extinct, that have generated so many fables among the savages, and speculations among philosophers; and those extensive fortifications so buried in obscurity, that even tradition is silent respecting them; – objects which lead to that musing on former times most propitious to poetry.

Such are some of the subordinate subjects that would be fruitful of allusion, and fertile in description to the poet. The human actors on this theatre are still more striking, and their history replete with interest and romantick adventure. The English and French were founding extensive empires here, and their contiguous possessions produced a century of conflicts, which terminated at last, in the exclusive power of the former. European affairs were more than once affected by the disputes of these two nations in the regions of Canada, and the decision of the most important contests on the Old

---

3. **Jove's own imperial Eagle:** Jove (or Jupiter) was the Roman name for Zeus, god of the sky, whose thunderbolts were borne by an eagle. The eagle also symbolized the power of imperial Rome.
4. **earth:** Wilson's Ornithology. [Tudor's note.] The reference is to the first natural history of American birds, *American Ornithology* (1808–14), by Alexander Wilson (1766–1813).

Continent has been produced by the issue of operations in the remote wilds of North America. The period also was one of great interest in European annals; France and England were rivals in glory, both in arts and arms.

Between these powers were interposed the Aborigines,[5] who became the allies of these nations and the most efficient part of their force. Before speaking more particularly of them, it will be necessary to deprecate the prejudices naturally entertained on the subject, from what we now see. The degenerate, miserable remains of the Indian nations, which have dwindled into insignificance and lingered among us, as the tide of civilization has flowed, mere floating deformities on its surface, poor, squalid and enervated with intoxicating liquors, should no more be taken for the representatives of their ancestors, who first met the Europeans on the edge of their boundless forests, severe and untamed as the regions they tenanted, than the Greek slaves, who now tremble at the frown of a petty Turkish tyrant, can be considered the likeness of their immortal progenitors, of those immoveable bands, before whom at Platoea, Thermopylae and Marathon, the whole Persian empire[6] broke and subsided like the waves of the sea, against the rocks they defended. To form an idea of what they once were, to see them in the energy and originality of their primitive condition, we must now journey a thousand miles. They possessed so many traits in common with some of the nations of antiquity, that they perhaps exhibit the counterpart of what the Greeks were in the heroick ages, and particularly the Spartans during the vigour of their institutions. Their origin has been the source of many theories and conjectures, few of which are more reasonable, than the suggestion of Spencer in his Fairy Queen;[7] that they are the descendants of the man whom Prometheus animated by stealing fire from Heaven.[8] Whether this race of men could like the Greeks have gradually acquired civilization, or whether they are a distinct species incapable of being tamed, may be uncertain: sudden civilization at least, has been shewn to be impossible; they diminish and waste before its progress, like snow before the vernal influence. The sublime allegorical painting of Guido,[9] in which Apollo encircled by the hours, is chasing night and her shadows over the surface of the globe, might almost represent the extinction of our savage precursors before the dawn of science and cultivation. The history of these people then is not less interesting, since in a short period they will exist no where else, and even in the next century, the Indian warriour and hunter will perhaps only be found on the shores of the Pacifick ocean.

[1815]

---

5. **Aborigines:** The original inhabitants of North America, or the Indians.
6. **Persian empire:** Tudor compares the situation of the Indians to that of the Greeks, who were crushed and oppressed after the fall of Constantinople in 1453 by the Ottoman Turks. Like the demoralized Indians, these Greeks, Tudor suggests, should not be mistaken for their proud ancestors, who had defeated the Persians at Platoea, Thermopylae, and Marathon during the Persian Wars (492–449 BCE).
7. **Fairy Queen:** *The Faerie Queene* (1590, 1596), a long narrative poem by the English poet Edmund Spenser (1552–1599).
8. **Prometheus . . . fire from Heaven:** In Greek mythology, Prometheus stole fire from Zeus and returned it to the earth. As a punishment, Zeus chained Prometheus to a rock where an eagle fed on his liver each day.
9. **painting of Guido:** In the Rospigliosi Place at Rome. [Tudor's note.] The painting is *Aurora*, by Guido Reni (1575–1642).

Edward Tyrell Channing

[1790–1856]

Edward Tyrell Channing, one of the founders of the prestigious *North American Review*, became its third editor in 1818. The following year, he resigned to become the Boylston Professor of Rhetoric and Oratory at Harvard College, where for nearly twenty-five years he taught some of the men who would become distinguished American writers, including Ralph Waldo Emerson and Henry David Thoreau. Channing, who was deeply interested in the creation of a national literature, emphasized the importance of originality and the danger of imitating classical and European literary models. The text of the following selection from his essay "On Models in Literature" is taken from the *North American Review* (July 1816).

From On Models in Literature

Let us just look at one or two ways, in which freedom and originality of mind are assailed or endangered. The first is by inculcating an excessive fondness for the ancient classicks, and asserting their supremacy in literature. By some means or other, the ancients have exerted an enormous influence among literary men, and in nations too, that have had hardly any thing of real congeniality with them. And many a lover of his own home, of the domestick fame and character of his country, has, in his fits of vexation, been tempted to wish that the Barbarians[1] had either done their work more faithfully among the fair fabricks of Greece and Rome, or else left those illustrious nations to live, and provoke the rest of the world to independent greatness, instead of being their school or nurse. As it now is, the old nations survive, in a sort of mixed state of grandeur and desolation. We grow tender among ruins and fragments. We love to soften down the errours and grossness of the fallen, and to extol and venerate the remains of their greatness, without making a very scrupulous estimate of its real worth. The grave-yard is common ground, where the living from every land may come together. There is no rancour nor heartburning there. We can all give praise with generous complacency, when no pretensions are set up. The Romans worshipped Greece, after they had conquered her.

Besides, the earliest nations in letters have a sort of patriarchal claim to the reverence of those who come after. Nothing remains of them but their finished and best works. We have no records of their early attempts and failures – nothing to inspire pity, to lessen admiration, or to encourage us when we fail. They seem to have started up at once, as if by an "over-night creation," into elegance and beauty, full of the ease, delight,

1. **Barbarians:** General term for people of northern Europe who invaded both Greece and Rome, which was sacked by the Vandals in 455.

and earnestness of men who draw directly from nature. They are set off from the earlier world, and connected with every after age, by appearing to be the very beginners of literature. They become the lights and helps of other nations, who are slower and later in attention to the mind – And even when their followers have surpassed their guides, and become quite equal to looking about, and making a fortune for themselves, it is still hard to throw off the veneration and deference which all have felt, and which gives them something common in their taste, pride, and obligations.

The boy at school (in the best, but most complying hours of his life) is set to work upon the ancient classicks.[2] He hears and reads of the god-like people, who began and finished the world's literature. This is taken in with his rudiments, and along with it, indifference towards his own language, which he acquired as unconsciously as he grew, and thinks too familiar for study or respect, while every thing ancient is brought home to him in solemnity and wonders, and fastens itself upon him more closely than his prayers.

The effect of this is, in many cases, to make what is foreign, artificial, and uncongenial, the foundation of a man's literary habits, ambition, and prejudices. It is hardly possible that a man, thus trained and dependent, should not lose self respect, and come to think every thing vulgar at home.

But it ought to be remembered, that the question is not upon the merits of the ancients, or any models whatever. Men will always settle this matter for themselves, according to their own taste and feelings. What we contend for is, that the literature of a country is just as domestick and individual, as its character or political institutions. Its charm is its nativeness. It is made for home, to be the luxury of those who have the feeling and love of home, and whose characters and taste have been formed there. No matter for rudeness, or want of systems and schools. It is enough that all is our own, and just such as we were made to have and relish. A country then must be the former and finisher of its own genius. It has, or should have, nothing to do with strangers. They are not expected to feel the beauty of your old poetical language, depending as it does on early and tender associations; connecting the softer and ruder ages of the country, and inspiring an inward and inexplicable joy, like a tale of childhood. The stranger perhaps is only alarmed or disgusted by the hoarse and wild musick of your forests, or sea-shore, by the frantick superstition of your fathers, or the lovely fairy scenes, that lie far back in the mists of your fable. He cannot feel your pride in the splendid barbarism of your country, when the mind was in health and free, and the foundations of your character and greatness laid for ever. All these things are for the native. They help to give a character to his country and her literature, and he loves them too well, to be concerned at the world's admiration or contempt.

So long then as a country is proud of itself, it will repel every encroachment upon its native literature. Improvements will offer themselves under a thousand forms. Intimacy with other nations, especially if they are polished, and the leaders of fashion, will

---

2. **classicks:** Greek and Roman classics were dominant subjects in nineteenth-century school curricula.

tempt men to imitate them in every thing. But a nation should keep itself at home, and value the things of its own household. It will have but feeble claims to excellence and distinction, when it stoops to put on foreign ornament and manner, and to adopt from other nations, images, allusions, and a metaphorical language, which are perfectly unmeaning and sickly, out of their own birth-place. The most polished will be the dreariest ages of its literature. Its writers will be afraid to speak the language that God has given them, till they have mingled the rough torrent with the allaying streams of a softer region. A strange idiom will be introduced into style. And the whole literature of a country will be mere gaudy patchwork, borrowed from every region that has any beauty to lend.

It may be well too just to hint, that it is not foreign models alone which are to be feared. We must also be shy of ourselves. For men of real genius and independence will sometimes introduce dangerous novelties, and make errours and corruptions popular and contagious, however short-lived they may prove. And besides this, there is good reason to fear that every country, as it falls into luxury and refinement, will be doomed to have an Augustan age,[3] a classical era of its own, when fine writers will determine, what shall be correct taste, pure language, and legitimate poetry. A domestick master may not be as alarming as a foreigner, and long before a man has ceased to study and love the early literature of his country, he may expect to hear that the old language is barbarous and obsolete, and rejected by all chaste authors, who wish to keep the national literature uniform and pure. As to all this, a man must judge for himself. And one would think, that if there must be models, a writer would do well to go as near to the original as possible, even to the very fathers of poetry. If there is luxury for him in such society, and if his books can find readers, in spite of the old cast about them, let him turn to the rougher and more intrepid ages of his country, before men troubled themselves about elegance or plan, and wrote right on as they felt, even though they were uttering a thought for the first time, feeling probably very little concern whether a softer age laughed at or worshipped them – whether they were to be ranked among the classicks, or barbarians of poetry, whether theirs was to be called an Augustan era, or merely the plain old English days of Elizabeth.[4]

[1816]

---

3. **Augustan age:** The period in English literature from roughly 1690 to 1744, during which poets, such as Alexander Pope and John Dryden, and prose writers, such as Jonathan Swift and Joseph Addison, promoted harmony and precision as the hallmarks of good writing and strove to imitate Horace, Ovid, Virgil, and other writers of the Augustan Age in Rome.
4. **Elizabeth:** Elizabeth I (1533-1603), queen of England.

James Fenimore Cooper

[1789–1851]

James Fenimore Cooper, the son of a wealthy New York landowner and congressman, did not begin his literary career until the age of thirty. After attending Yale College, from which he was expelled because of a series of pranks, Cooper first served as a midshipman in the navy and then settled into a career as a gentleman farmer. While reading an English novel aloud to his wife, he told her that he could write a better one, and she challenged him to do so. The result was his first novel, *Precaution* (1820), which he immediately followed with *The Spy* (1821). In 1823, he published *The Pioneers*, one of the first bestsellers in the United States, and the first of a famous five-novel sequence called the Leather-Stocking Tales. Late in the 1820s, Cooper traveled through Europe and collected the material for *Notions of the Americans: Picked up by a Travelling Bachelor* (1828), his response to the many English criticisms of America and Americans that were being published in periodicals and in books written by visitors to the United States. Cooper developed *Notions of the Americans* as a series of letters written by the "travelling bachelor" to a variety of European "gentlemen" who had asked about particular American customs and institutions. The gentlemen recipients – none of them an actual person – include various members of the nobility as well as religious leaders. The following selection is from letter 24, "To the Abbate Giromachi," in which Cooper discusses the status of literature and the arts in the United States. The text is taken from the first edition of *Notions of the Americans* (1828).

James Fenimore Cooper

This portrait of Cooper was painted in 1822 by John Wesley Jarvis, one of the foremost portrait painters in New York City.

From Notions of the Americans

The purely intellectual day of America is yet in its dawn. But its sun will not arise from darkness, like those of nations with whose experience we are familiar; nor is the approach of its meridian to be calculated by the known progress of any other people. The learned professions are now full to overflowing, not so much with learning as with incumbents, certainly, but so much so, as to begin to give a new direction to education and talents. Writers are already getting to be numerous, for literature is beginning to be profitable. Those authors who are successful, receive prices for their labours, which exceed those paid to the authors of any country, England alone excepted; and which exceed even the prices paid to the most distinguished authors of the mother country, if the difference in the relative value of money in the two countries, and in the luxury of the press, be computed. The same work which is sold in England for six dollars, is sold in the United States for two. The profit to the publisher is obtained out of a common rate of per centage. Now, as thirty-three and a third per cent. on six thousand dollars, is two thousand,[1] and on two thousand dollars, only six hundred and sixty-six, it is quite evident, that if both parties sell one thousand copies of a work, the English publisher pockets three times the most profit. And yet, with one or two exceptions, and notwithstanding the great difference in the population of the two countries, the English bookseller rarely sells more, if he does as many, copies of a book, than the American. It is the extraordinary demand which enables the American publisher to pay so well, and which, provided there was no English competition, would enable him to pay still better, or rather still more generally, than he does at present.

The literature of the United States is a subject of the highest interest to the civilized world; for when it does begin to be felt, it will be felt with a force, a directness, and a common sense in its application, that has never yet been known. If there were no other points of difference between this country and other nations, those of its political and religious freedom, alone, would give a colour of the highest importance to the writings of a people so thoroughly imbued with their distinctive principles, and so keenly alive to their advantages. The example of America has been silently operating on Europe for half a century; but its doctrines and its experience, exhibited with the understanding of those familiar with both, have never yet been pressed on our attention. I think the time for the experiment is getting near.

[1828]

1. **two thousand:** This calculation supposes one-third of the price to go to the trade in discount, one-third to the expenses, and the other third to constitute the joint profit of the author and publisher. [Cooper's note.]

Philip Freneau

[1752–1832]

Philip Freneau was born in New York City on January 2, 1752, to Pierre and Agnes Watson Fresneau (the original spelling of the family name, later changed by Philip to *Freneau*). His father was descended from French Protestants, called Huguenots, thousands of whom fled religious persecution in their native country and came to the American colonies. There, the Fresneaus established a successful family business in the wine trade. Freneau's mother was a member of an affluent New Jersey family, and together the couple made their home first in New York and then on a thousand-acre estate, named Mount Pleasant, near Monmouth County, New Jersey. Educated by tutors and then at a preparatory school, Freneau was admitted as a sophomore to the College of New Jersey (now Princeton University). His college friends included the future president James Madison and Hugh Henry Brackenridge, who became one of the first successful novelists in the new nation.

. . . a man of genius . . .
– Thomas Jefferson

After college, Freneau taught school for a time in Maryland but appears to have had some difficulty in deciding on a direction for his life. He published a collection of his poems, *The American Village*, in 1772. But finding that it was impossible to make a living as a poet, he took a position as a secretary to a wealthy planter in the West Indies and sailed there in 1776. Although Freneau is often thought of as "the poet of the American Revolution," he spent the early years of the war in the West Indies. On a voyage home in 1778, his ship was captured by the British. After his release, he enlisted on a blockade runner and was captured again. This time, he was imprisoned aboard a British ship anchored in New York harbor, a brutal experience that inspired his poem "The British Prison Ship," published in 1781. For the next three years, Freneau lived in Philadelphia, where he wrote a series of poems in support of the American cause for the *Freeman's Journal*. Now earning a reputation as both a poet and a journalist, Freneau published a long narrative poem, *A Journey from Philadelphia to New York* (1787), as well as collections of his shorter poems in 1787 and 1788.

During the 1790s, Freneau spent most of his time working for the periodical press. In 1790, he joined the staff of a New York newspaper, the *Daily Advertiser*. The following year, he established his own newspaper, the *National Gazette*, in Philadelphia. Firmly connected to the Jeffersonian Republicans and bitterly opposed to Federalists such as Alexander Hamilton, Freneau was called a "rascal" by George Washington. Freneau strongly supported the French Revolution and other democratic causes, writing frequently about them for his newspaper. The *Gazette* failed in 1793, after which Freneau tried his hand at running a printing business from his home and then editing the New York *Time Piece and Literary Companion*. After 1799, Freneau retired to a farm he had inherited from his

bedfordstmartins.com/ americanlit *for research links on Freneau* father, where he continued to publish essays and poems but lived in increasing poverty and obscurity. He died on December 18, 1832.

Freneau's Poems. Freneau began to write poetry in college, where he joined literary clubs and participated, along with many other students, in the growing movement in favor of independence for the American colonies. With his friend Hugh Henry Brackenridge, Freneau wrote his best-known college poem, "The Rising Glory of America," which Brackenridge read at their graduation in 1771. Beginning with *The American Village* (1772), Freneau published several books of poetry, including a two-volume edition of his *Poems* (1809). But many of his verses first appeared in periodicals like the New York *Daily Advertiser*, where "To Sir Toby" was published as "The Island Field Negro" in 1791. Like that antislavery poem and earlier verses like "On the Emigration to America and the Peopling of the Western Country" (1785), much of the poetry Freneau wrote after the Revolution was devoted to social and political commentary. Even as he participated in the increasingly heated debates between the Jeffersonian Republicans and the Federalists, however, Freneau also actively sought to establish foundations for a national literature, exploring American scenes

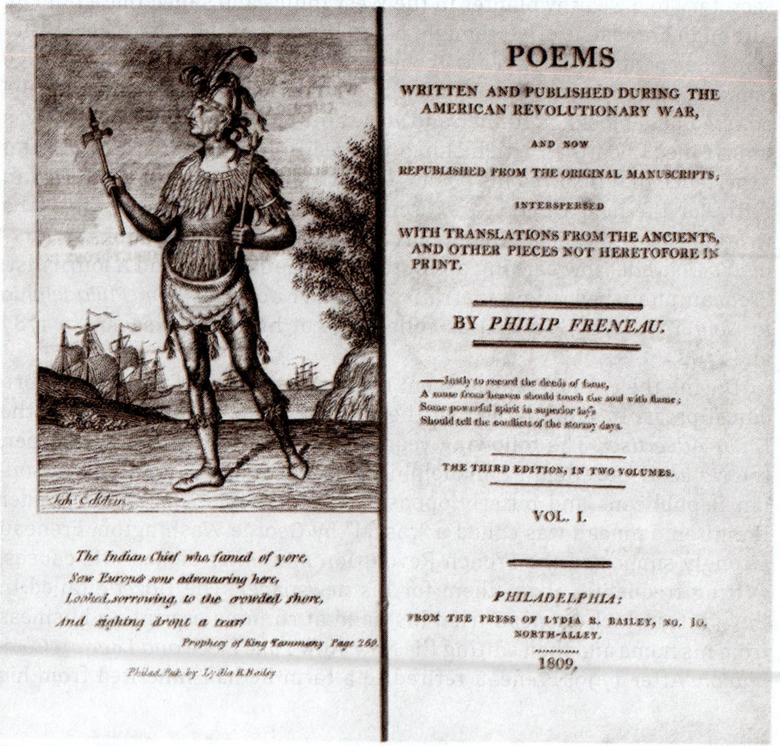

The Indian Chief who famed of yore,
Saw Europe's sons adventuring here,
Looked, sorrowing, to the crowded shore,
And sighing dropt a tear!
Prophecy of King Tammany Page 269.
POEMS
WRITTEN AND PUBLISHED DURING THE AMERICAN REVOLUTIONARY WAR,
AND NOW
REPUBLISHED FROM THE ORIGINAL MANUSCRIPTS;
INTERSPERSED
WITH TRANSLATIONS FROM THE ANCIENTS, AND OTHER PIECES NOT HERETOFORE IN PRINT.
BY PHILIP FRENEAU.
——Justly to record the deeds of fame,
A muse from heaven should touch the soul with flame;
Some powerful spirit in superior lay's
Should tell the conflicts of the stormy days.
THE THIRD EDITION, IN TWO VOLUMES.
VOL. I.
PHILADELPHIA:
FROM THE PRESS OF LYDIA R. BAILEY, NO. 10, NORTH-ALLEY.
1809.

Philip Freneau, *Poems* (1809)

The frontispiece and title page of this two-volume edition of Freneau's poetry emphasizes his use of American themes and his patriotic involvement in the American Revolution. From the time of the earliest European maps and settlements, the image of an Indian was frequently used as a symbol of America.

and themes in poems like "The Wild Honey Suckle" and "The Indian Burying Ground." In fact, "the poet of the American Revolution" is perhaps better understood as a post-Revolutionary or postcolonial poet who sought to free the new nation from the lingering cultural, political, and social influences of Great Britain. The texts of the following poems are taken from volume 2 of *The Poems of Philip Freneau* (1903), edited by F. L. Pattee.

TO SIR TOBY[1]

A Sugar Planter in the interior parts of Jamaica, near the City of San Jago de la Vega, (Spanish Town) 1784

"The motions of his spirit are black as night,
And his affections dark as Erebus."
- Shakespeare[2]

If there exists a hell – the case is clear –
Sir Toby's slaves enjoy that portion here:
Here are no blazing brimstone lakes – 'tis true;
But kindled Rum too often burns as blue;
In which some fiend, whom nature must detest,
Steeps Toby's brand, and marks poor Cudjoe's breast.[3]
Here whips on whips excite perpetual fears,
And mingled howlings vibrate on my ears:
Here nature's plagues abound, to fret and teaze,
Snakes, scorpions, despots, lizards, centipees –
No art, no care escapes the busy lash;
All have their dues – and all are paid in cash –
The eternal driver keeps a steady eye
On a black herd, who would his vengeance fly,
But chained, imprisoned, on a burning soil,
For the mean avarice of a tyrant, toil!
The lengthy cart-whip guards this monster's reign –
And cracks, like pistols, from the fields of cane.
Ye powers! who formed these wretched tribes, relate,
What had they done, to merit such a fate!

1. **"To Sir Toby":** Written in 1784, the poem was first published under the title "The Island Field Negro" in the New York *Daily Advertiser*, in February 1791.
2. **Shakespeare:** The epigraph is from *The Merchant of Venice*, 5.1.79. In Greek mythology, Erebus was a dark region in the underworld.
3. **Cudjoe's breast:** "This passage has a reference to the West India custom (sanctioned by law) of branding a newly imported slave on the breast, with a red hot iron, as an evidence of the purchaser's property." [Freneau's note.] *Cudjoe* was a name frequently given to a male slave.

Why were they brought from Eboe's[4] sultry waste,
To see that plenty which they must not taste –
Food, which they cannot buy, and dare not steal;
Yams and potatoes – many a scanty meal! –
One, with a gibbet[5] wakes his negro's fears,
One to the windmill nails him by the ears;
One keeps his slave in darkened dens, unfed,
One puts the wretch in pickle ere he's dead:
This, from a tree suspends him by the thumbs,
That, from his table grudges even the crumbs!
O'er yond' rough hills a tribe of females go,
Each with her gourd,[6] her infant, and her hoe;
Scorched by a sun that has no mercy here,
Driven by a devil, whom men call overseer –
In chains, twelve wretches to their labours haste;
Twice twelve I saw, with iron collars graced! –
Are such the fruits that spring from vast domains?
Is wealth, thus got, Sir Toby, worth your pains! –
Who would your wealth on terms, like these, possess,
Where all we see is pregnant with distress –
Angola's natives[7] scourged by ruffian hands,
And toil's hard product shipp'd to foreign lands.
Talk not of blossoms, and your endless spring;
What joy, what smile, can scenes of misery bring? –
Though Nature, here, has every blessing spread,
Poor is the labourer – and how meanly fed! –
Here Stygian[8] paintings light and shade renew,
Pictures of hell, that Virgil's[9] pencil drew:
Here, surly Charons[10] make their annual trip,
And ghosts arrive in every Guinea ship,[11]

---

4. **Eboe's:** "A small negro kingdom near the river Senegal." [Freneau's note.]
5. **gibbet:** A gallows.
6. **gourd:** Drinking container made from the dried skin of a large, fleshy fruit.
7. **Angola's natives:** A Portuguese possession from the end of the sixteenth century until 1975, Angola is on the western coast of southern Africa.
8. **Stygian:** In Greek mythology, the souls of the dead are ferried across the river Styx to the underworld; as an adjective, the word means very dark.
9. **Virgil's:** "See Eneid, Book 6th. – and Fenelon's Telemachus, Book 18." [Freneau's note.] Aeneas visits the underworld in the sixth book of the *Aeneid* by the Roman poet Virgil (70–19 BCE). François de Salignac de la Mothe-Fénelon (1651–1715) was the author of *Aventures de Télémaque* (1699), a retelling of Greek myths concerning Telemachus, the son of Ulysses.
10. **Charons:** In Greek mythology, Charon was the pilot of the ferry that carried the souls of the dead across the river Styx to the underworld.
11. **Guinea ship:** A slave ship from Guinea, West Africa, though the term came to refer to a slave ship from any African country.

To find what beasts these western isles afford,
Plutonian[12] scourges, and despotic lords: –
    Here, they, of stuff determined to be free,
Must climb the rude cliffs of the Liguanee;[13]
Beyond the clouds, in sculking haste repair,
And hardly safe from brother traitors there. – [14]

[1791, 1903]

---

12. **Plutonian:** Of or associated with the underworld of Greek mythology.
13. **Liguanee:** "The mountains northward of Kingston." [Freneau's note.] The Blue Mountains are north of Kingston, on the coast of southeastern Jamaica.
14. **there:** "Alluding to the *Independent* negroes in the blue mountains, who for a stipulated reward, deliver up every fugitive that falls into their hands, to the English government." [Freneau's note.]

ON THE EMIGRATION TO AMERICA

And Peopling the Western Country

To western woods, and lonely plains,
Palemon[1] from the crowd departs,
Where Nature's wildest genius reigns,
To tame the soil, and plant the arts –
What wonders there shall freedom show,
What mighty states successive grow!

From Europe's proud, despotic shores
Hither the stranger takes his way,
And in our new found world explores
A happier soil, a milder sway,
Where no proud despot holds him down,
No slaves insult him with a crown.

What charming scenes attract the eye,
On wild Ohio's savage stream!
There Nature reigns, whose works outvie
The boldest pattern art can frame;
There ages past have rolled away,
And forests bloomed but to decay.

From these fair plains, these rural seats,
So long concealed, so lately known,

---

1. **Palemon:** The name of several literary characters that set out on journeys, such as Palamoun in "The Knight's Tale," by Geoffrey Chaucer (c. 1342-1400), and Palemon in "Autumn" of *The Seasons*, by the English poet James Thomson (1700-1748).

The unsocial Indian far retreats,
To make some other clime his own,
When other streams, less pleasing, flow,
And darker forests round him grow.

Great Sire[2] of floods! whose varied wave
Through climes and countries takes its way,
To whom creating Nature gave
Ten thousand streams to swell thy sway!
No longer shall they useless prove,
Nor idly through the forests rove;

Nor longer shall your princely flood
From distant lakes be swelled in vain,
Nor longer through a darksome wood
Advance, unnoticed, to the main,[3]
Far other ends, the heavens decree –
And commerce plans new freights for thee.

While virtue warms the generous breast,
There heaven-born freedom shall reside,
Nor shall the voice of war molest,
Nor Europe's all-aspiring pride –
There Reason shall new laws devise,
And order from confusion rise.

Forsaking kings and regal state,
With all their pomp and fancied bliss,
The traveller owns,[4] convinced though late,
No realm so free, so blest as this –
The east is half to slaves consigned,
Where kings and priests enchain the mind.

O come the time, and haste the day,
When man shall man no longer crush,
When Reason shall enforce her sway,
Nor these fair regions raise our blush,
Where still the African complains,
And mourns his yet unbroken chains.

---

2. **Great Sire:** "Mississippi." [Freneau's note.]
3. **main:** Sea or ocean.
4. **owns:** Admits or acknowledges.

Far brighter scenes a future age,
The muse predicts, these States will hail,
Whose genius may the world engage,
Whose deeds may over death prevail,
And happier systems bring to view,
Than all the eastern sages knew.

[1785, 1903]

THE WILD HONEY SUCKLE

Fair flower, that dost so comely grow,
Hid in this silent, dull retreat,
Untouched thy honied blossoms blow,[1]
Unseen thy little branches greet:
No roving foot shall crush thee here,
No busy hand provoke a tear.

By Nature's self in white arrayed,
She bade thee shun the vulgar[2] eye,
And planted here the guardian shade,
And sent soft waters murmuring by;
Thus quietly thy summer goes,
Thy days declining to repose.

Smit with those charms, that must decay,
I grieve to see your future doom;
They died – nor were those flowers more gay,
The flowers that did in Eden bloom;
Unpitying frosts, and Autumn's power
Shall leave no vestige of this flower.

From morning suns and evening dews
At first thy little being came:
If nothing once, you nothing lose,
For when you die you are the same;
The space between, is but an hour,
The trail duration of a flower.

[1786, 1903]

1. **blow:** An early term for bloom.
2. **vulgar:** An early meaning was common or ordinary.

THE INDIAN BURYING GROUND

In spite of all the learned have said,
  I still my old opinion keep;
The posture, that we give the dead,
  Points out the soul's eternal sleep.

Not so the ancients of these lands –
  The Indian, when from life released,
Again is seated with his friends,
  And shares again the joyous feast.[1]

His imaged birds, and painted bowl,
  And venison, for a journey dressed,
Bespeak the nature of the soul,
  Activity, that knows no rest.

His bow, for action ready bent,
  And arrows, with a head of stone,
Can only mean that life is spent,
  And not the old ideas gone.

Thou, stranger, that shalt come this way,
  No fraud upon the dead commit –
Observe the swelling turf, and say
  They do not lie, but here they sit.

Here still a lofty rock remains,
  On which the curious eye may trace
(Now wasted, half, by wearing rains)
  The fancies of a ruder race.

Here still an aged elm aspires,
  Beneath whose far-projecting shade
And which the shepherd still admires)
  The children of the forest played!

There oft a restless Indian queen
  (Pale Shebah,[2] with her braided hair)

---

1. feast: "The North American Indians bury their dead in a sitting posture; decorating the corpse with wampum, the images of birds, quadrupeds, &c: And (if that of a warrior) with bows, arrows, tomhawks, and other military weapons." [Freneau's note.]
2. Shebah: *Sheba* is the biblical name of Saba in southwestern Arabia. In an Old Testament story, the queen of Sheba visited King Solomon in Jerusalem (1 Kings 10:1-13).

And many a barbarous form is seen
   To chide the man that lingers there.

By midnight moons, o'er moistening dews;
   In habit for the chase arrayed,
The hunter still the deer pursues,
   The hunter and the deer, a shade!

And long shall timorous fancy see
   The painted chief, and pointed spear,
And Reason's self shall bow the knee
   To shadows and delusions here.

[1788, 1903]

Phillis Wheatley

[c. 1753-1784]

Born on the west coast of Africa, Phillis Wheatley was captured by slave traders and transported on the schooner *Phillis* to Boston, where she arrived in 1761, when she was seven or eight years old. She was purchased by John Wheatley to serve as a companion for his wife, Susanna. The Wheatleys were prosperous people with a wide circle of friends and were active members of the New South Congregational Church. Their household included the Wheatley twins, Mary and Nathaniel, who were then eighteen, as well as several slaves. Although Phillis was in poor health and very young to be trained as a domestic servant, Susanna Wheatley evidently chose her because of her quick intelligence. Mary Wheatley soon began teaching her to read and write and also gave her instructions in religion and the Bible. Phillis remained legally a slave throughout her childhood, but she lived mostly as a member of the family and had considerable freedom to study. She advanced quickly, learning Latin, history, and geography, and received a good education, especially for a young girl of the time.

. . . the first decidedly American poet on this continent, Black or white, male or female.
– June Jordan

At about age twelve, Phillis began to write poetry, efforts that were strongly encouraged by the Wheatleys. Throughout her adolescence she wrote poems, and a few appeared in newspapers. Her first published poem was "On Messrs. Hussey and Coffin," based on the true story of the narrow escape of two men whose ship was wrecked during a storm. The poem appeared in the Rhode Island *Newport Mercury* on December 21, 1767. Wheatley began to keep "proposals," notes about poems she had written or that she wanted to write. Scholars have been able to piece together a publication history of her work mainly through her notes and surviving letters. In 1770, she wrote "On the Death of the Rev. Mr. George Whitefield," a me-

bedfordstmartins.com/americanlit *for research links on Wheatley*

Phillis Wheatley, *Poems on Various Subjects* (1773)

The portrait of Wheatley on the frontispiece of her book was done by Scipio Moorhead, the artist she hailed in her poem "To S. M. a Young *African* Painter, on Seeing His Works."

morial to a prominent British Evangelical that gained Wheatley her first important public notice. The poem was published as a broadside (a large, single sheet of paper) in Boston in 1770 and was subsequently reprinted at the end of a published sermon on the death of Whitefield by Ebenezer Pemberton, a well-known Boston clergyman. Although the publication of this broadside made her famous in New England, Wheatley was unsuccessful at publishing a collection of her poems in America. Taking her manuscript with her, Wheatley accompanied Nathaniel Wheatley on a trip to London, where her *Poems on Various Subjects, Religious and Moral* appeared in 1773. In England, she was not subject to the race prejudice that existed in America, and she was widely acclaimed for her work, meeting a variety of people, both English and American, living in London, including Benjamin Franklin.

When she returned from London, Wheatley was emancipated by John Wheatley. But the final decade of her short life was difficult. Susanna Wheatley died in 1774, and both John and Mary Wheatley died in 1778. That year, Phillis married John Peters. Little is known about him or their marriage, apart from the fact that the couple faced both financial and personal hardships, including the early death of their first two children. Wheatley's aspirations as a poet were also frequently frustrated, partly by the disruptions caused by the Revolutionary War. During the following years, there were proposals to publish a second volume of her poetry. Nothing came of those efforts, however, and Wheatley published only a few additional poems, including *Liberty and Peace*, a pamphlet that appeared shortly before her death on December 5, 1784. Her final surviving child died a short time later, and the two were buried together in a now-unknown grave in Boston.

Wheatley's Poems and Letters. Phillis Wheatley was an anomaly in the eighteenth century: a slave who had been well educated and encouraged to write. When her *Poems on Various Subjects, Religious and Moral* was published in London in 1773, the publisher offered a conventional disclaimer in a preface, explaining that the thirty-nine poems "were written for the Amusement of the Author, as they were the Products of her leisure Moments," and that she had published them only at the urging "of many of her best, and most generous Friends." In order to counter suspicions that she was not the author of the poems, however, the volume included a letter to the publisher from John Wheatley, who testified to Phillis's swift attainment of "the English language, to which she was an utter Stranger" before her arrival in Boston. The publisher also printed an "attestation" signed by eighteen influential men of the city, including the royal governor of Massachusetts, Thomas Hutchinson, who affirmed that Wheatley had "been examined by some of the best judges, and is thought qualified to write [the poems]."

From her earliest efforts to her final poems, Wheatley wrote in the style of eighteenth-century English poets who were popular on both sides of the Atlantic, especially Alexander Pope. Nonetheless, while she closely followed the poetic conventions of the period, Wheatley was also an innovator. As many scholars have noted, she was the founder not only of the African American literary tradition but also of the tradition of black women's writing in America. In both her poems and her letters to famous people, Wheatley's major themes are religion, politics, and the tyranny of slavery. Even before the formal Declaration of Independence, Wheatley was a fervent supporter of the American cause, which she celebrates in poems like "To His Excellency General Washington." At the same time, Wheatley recognized the contradiction between the institution of slavery in the American colonies and their struggle for "liberty," a struggle she implicitly sought to align with the cause of freedom for the slaves. The texts of the following poems and letters are taken from *The Poems of Phillis Wheatley: Revised and Enlarged Edition* (1989), edited by Julian D. Mason Jr.

ON BEING BROUGHT FROM AFRICA TO AMERICA

'Twas mercy brought me from my *Pagan* land,
Taught my benighted soul to understand
That there's a God, that there's a *Saviour* too:
Once I redemption neither sought nor knew.

Some view our sable[1] race with scornful eye,
"Their colour is a diabolic die."
Remember, *Christians*, *Negros*, black as *Cain*,[2]
May be refin'd, and join th' angelic train.

[1773, 1989]

---

1. **sable:** Dark brown or black.
2. **black as *Cain*:** The eldest son of Adam and Eve, Cain murdered his brother Abel and was consequently cursed by God. To prevent others from killing him, "the Lord set a mark upon Cain" (Genesis 4:15), a mark that some readers of the Bible associated with blackness.

To the University of Cambridge,[1] in New-England

While an intrinsic ardor prompts to write,
The muses promise to assist my pen;
'Twas not long since I left my native shore
The land of errors, and *Egyptian* gloom:[2]
Father of mercy, 'twas thy gracious hand
Brought me in safety from those dark abodes.

Students, to you 'tis giv'n to scan the heights
Above, to traverse the ethereal space,
And mark the systems of revolving worlds.
Still more, ye sons of science ye receive
The blissful news by messengers from heav'n,
How *Jesus'* blood for your redemption flows.
See him with hands out-stretcht upon the cross;
Immense compassion in his bosom glows;
He hears revilers, nor resents their scorn:
What matchless mercy in the Son of God!
When the whole human race by sin had fall'n,
He deign'd to die that they might rise again,
And share with him in the sublimest skies,
Life without death, and glory without end.

Improve your privileges while they stay,
Ye pupils, and each hour redeem, that bears

---

1. **University of Cambridge:** Harvard College.
2. ***Egyptian* gloom:** A reference to the Christian belief that the unconverted live in error or wrong. Egypt (i.e., Africa) is therefore in a state of gloom, or darkness, because it has not been illuminated by the light of the Gospels.

Or good or bad report of you to heav'n.
Let sin, that baneful evil to the soul,
By you be shunn'd, nor once remit your guard;
Suppress the deadly serpent in its egg.
Ye blooming plants of human race devine,
An *Ethiop*[3] tells you 'tis your greatest foe;
Its transient sweetness turns to endless pain,
And in immense perdition sinks the soul.

[1773, 1989]

3. ***Ethiop***: A common term in Wheatley's day for anyone from Africa.

TO THE RIGHT HONOURABLE WILLIAM, EARL OF DARTMOUTH, HIS MAJESTY'S PRINCIPAL SECRETARY OF STATE FOR NORTH-AMERICA, &C[1]

Hail, happy days, when, smiling like the morn,
Fair *Freedom* rose *New-England* to adorn:
The northern clime beneath her genial ray,
Dartmouth, congratulates thy blissful sway:
Elate with hope her race no longer mourns,
Each soul expands, each grateful bosom burns,
While in thine hand with pleasure we behold
The silken reins, and *Freedom's* charms unfold.
Long lost to realms beneath the northern skies
She shines supreme, while hated *faction* dies:
Soon as appear'd the *Goddess* long desir'd,
Sick at the view, she lanquish'd and expir'd;
Thus from the splendors of the morning light
The owl in sadness seeks the caves of night.

No more, *America*, in mournful strain
Of wrongs, and grievance unredress'd complain,
No longer shalt thou dread the iron chain,
Which wanton *Tyranny* with lawless hand
Had made, and with it meant t' enslave the land.

1. **Earl of Dartmouth**: William Legge (1731–1801), the second Earl of Dartmouth, was appointed secretary to the American colonies in 1772. Like many others, Wheatley hoped that he would be sympathetic to colonial concerns and grievances.

Should you, my lord, while you peruse my song,
Wonder from whence my love of *Freedom* sprung,
Whence flow these wishes for the common good,
By feeling hearts alone best understood,
I, young in life, by seeming cruel fate
Was snatch'd from *Afric's* fancy'd happy seat:
What pangs excruciating must molest,
What sorrows labour in my parent's breast?
Steel'd was that soul and by no misery mov'd
That from a father seiz'd his babe belov'd:
Such, such my case. And can I then but pray
Others may never feel tyrannic sway?

For favours past, great Sir, our thanks are due,
And thee we ask thy favours to renew,
Since in thy pow'r, as in thy will before,
To sooth the griefs, which thou did'st once deplore.
May heav'nly grace the sacred sanction give
To all thy works, and thou for ever live
Not only on the wings of fleeting *Fame*,
Though praise immortal crowns the patriot's name,
But to conduct to heav'ns refulgent fane,[2]
May fiery coursers sweep th' ethereal plain,
And bear thee upwards to that blest abode,
Where, like the prophet, thou shalt find thy God.

[1773, 1989]

2. fane: Early term for a temple or shrine.

TO S. M.[1] A YOUNG *AFRICAN* PAINTER, ON SEEING HIS WORKS

To show the lab'ring bosom's deep intent,
And thought in living characters to paint,
When first thy pencil did those beauties give,
And breathing figures learnt from thee to live,

1. S. M.: Scipio Moorhead (c. 1750) was a painter tutored by Sarah Moorhead, an art teacher and the wife of his master, Reverend John Moorhead. He engraved the portrait of Wheatley that appeared opposite the title page of her *Poems on Various Subjects* (1773).

How did those prospects give my soul delight,
A new creation rushing on my sight?
Still, wond'rous youth! each noble path pursue,
On deathless glories fix thine ardent view:
Still may the painter's and the poet's fire
To aid thy pencil, and thy verse conspire!
And may the charms of each seraphic[2] theme
Conduct thy footsteps to immortal fame!
High to the blissful wonders of the skies
Elate thy soul, and raise thy wishful eyes.
Thrice happy, when exalted to survey
That splendid city, crown'd with endless day,
Whose twice six gates[3] on radiant hinges ring:
Celestial *Salem*[4] blooms in endless spring.

Calm and serene thy moments glide along,
And may the muse inspire each future song!
Still, with the sweets of contemplation bless'd,
May peace with balmy wings your soul invest!
But when these shades of time are chas'd away,
And darkness ends in everlasting day,
On what seraphic pinions[5] shall we move,
And view the landscapes in the realms above?
There shall thy tongue in heav'nly murmurs flow,
And there my muse with heav'nly transport glow:
No more to tell of *Damon's*[6] tender sighs,
Or rising radiance of *Aurora's*[7] eyes,
For nobler themes demand a nobler strain,
And purer language on th' ethereal plain.
Cease, gentle muse! the solemn gloom of night
Now seals the fair creation from my sight.

[1773, 1989]

---

2. **seraphic:** Angelic.
3. **twice six gates:** Many early descriptions of heaven reflected the idea that it has twelve gates, corresponding to the twelve tribes of Israel.
4. ***Salem*:** Short for Jerusalem.
5. **seraphic pinions:** Angel wings.
6. ***Damon's*:** In Greek mythology, Damon offered himself as bail for his friend Pythias, who had been sentenced to death by King Dionysius I of Syracuse. When Pythias returned just in time to take his own place for execution, the king was so moved by their loyalty to each other that he released both youths.
7. ***Aurora's*:** In Roman mythology, Aurora is the goddess of the dawn.

A FAREWELL TO AMERICA. TO MRS. S.W.[1]

I

Adieu, *New-England's* smiling meads,
Adieu, the flow'ry plain:
I leave thine op'ning charms, O spring,
And tempt the roaring main.

II

In vain for me the flow'rets rise,
And boast their gaudy pride,
While here beneath the northern skies
I mourn for *health* deny'd.

III

Celestial maid of rosy hue,
O let me feel thy reign!
I languish till thy face I view,
Thy vanish'd joys regain.

IV

Susannah mourns, nor can I bear
To see the crystal show'r,
Or mark the tender falling tear
At sad departure's hour;

V

Not unregarding can I see
Her soul with grief opprest:
But let no sighs, no groans for me,
Steal from her pensive breast.

VI

In vain the feather'd warblers sing,
In vain the garden blooms,

1. **Mrs. S.W.:** Susanna Wheatley (1709–1774), Phillis Wheatley's mistress; the poem was written on the occasion of her voyage to England.

And on the bosom of the spring
  Breathes out her sweet perfumes,

VII

While for *Britannia's* distant shore
  We sweep the liquid plain,
And with astonish'd eyes explore
  The wide-extended main.

VIII

Lo! *Health* appears! celestial dame!
  Complacent and serene,
With *Hebe's*[2] mantle o'er her Frame,
  With soul-delighting mein.

IX

To mark the vale where *London* lies
  With misty vapours crown'd,
Which cloud *Aurora's*[3] thousand dyes,
  And veil her charms around,

X

Why, *Phoebus*,[4] moves thy car so slow?
  So slow thy rising ray?
Give us the famous town to view
  Thou glorious king of day!

XI

For thee, *Britannia*, I resign
  New-England's smiling fields;
To view again her charms divine,
  What joy the prospect yields!

---

2. ***Hebe's***: In Greek mythology, Hebe, the daughter of Hera and Zeus, was the goddess of youth and cup-bearer of the gods.
3. ***Aurora's***: In Roman mythology, Aurora was the goddess of the dawn.
4. ***Phoebus***: In Greek mythology, another name for Apollo, the god of the sun.

XII

But thou! Temptation hence away,
With all thy fatal train
Nor once seduce my soul away,
By thine enchanting strain.

XIII

Thrice happy they, whose heav'nly shield
Secures their souls from harms,
And fell *Temptation* on the field
Of all its pow'r disarms!

[Boston, May 7, 1773; 1989]

TO HIS EXCELLENCY GENERAL WASHINGTON[1]

The following LETTER *and* VERSES, *were written by the famous* Phillis Wheatley, *the African Poetess, and presented to his Excellency Gen.* Washington.

Sir,

I have taken the freedom to address your Excellency in the enclosed poem, and entreat your acceptance, though I am not insensible of its inaccuracies. Your being appointed by the Grand Continental Congress to be Generalissimo of the armies of North America, together with the fame of your virtues, excite sensations not easy to suppress. Your generosity, therefore, I presume, will pardon the attempt. Wishing your Excellency all possible success in the great cause you are so generously engaged in. I am,

Your Excellency's most obedient humble servant,
PHILLIS WHEATLEY

Providence, Oct. 26, 1775.
His Excellency Gen. Washington.

Celestial choir! enthron'd in realms of light,
Columbia's[2] scenes of glorious toils I write.
While freedom's cause her anxious breast alarms,
She flashes dreadful in refulgent arms.
See mother earth her offspring's fate bemoan,

1. **General Washington:** George Washington had been appointed commander in chief of the Continental army in June 1775. Early in 1776, Washington wrote to thank Wheatley for her letter and the poem, which were published in the *Virginia Gazette* (March 1776) and the *Pennsylvania Magazine* (April 1776).
2. **Columbia's:** America was often referred to as the land Columbus founded, or simply as *Columbia.*

And nations gaze at scenes before unknown!
See the bright beams of heaven's revolving light
Involved in sorrows and the veil of night!
    The goddess comes, she moves divinely fair,
Olive and laurel binds her golden hair:
Wherever shines this native of the skies,
Unnumber'd charms and recent graces rise.
    Muse! bow propitious while my pen relates
How pour her armies through a thousand gates:
As when Eolus[3] heaven's fair face deforms,
Enwrapp'd in tempest and a night of storms;
Astonish'd ocean feels the wild uproar,
The refluent surges beat the sounding shore;
Or thick as leaves in Autumn's golden reign,
Such, and so many, moves the warrior's train.
In bright array they seek the work of war,
Where high unfurl'd the ensign[4] waves in air.
Shall I to Washington their praise recite?
Enough thou know'st them in the fields of fight.
Thee, first in place and honours, – we demand
The grace and glory of thy martial band.
Fam'd for thy valour, for thy virtues more,
Hear every tongue thy guardian aid implore!
    One century scarce perform'd its destin'd round,
When Gallic powers[5] Columbia's fury found;
And so may you, whoever dares disgrace
The land of freedom's heaven-defended race!
Fix'd are the eyes of nations on the scales,
For in their hopes Columbia's arm prevails.
Anon Britannia droops the pensive head,
While round increase the rising hills of dead.
Ah! cruel blindness to Columbia's state!
Lament thy thirst of boundless power too late.
    Proceed, great chief, with virtue on thy side,
Thy ev'ry action let the goddess guide.
A crown, a mansion, and a throne that shine,
With gold unfading, WASHINGTON! be thine.

[1776, 1989]

3. **Eolus:** In Greek mythology, Eolus was the keeper of the winds.
4. **ensign:** A flag or standard.
5. **Gallic powers:** The French colonial empire in America ended with the conclusion of the French and Indian War (1754-1763).

Liberty and Peace, A Poem

Lo! Freedom comes. Th' prescient Muse foretold,
All Eyes th' accomplish'd Prophecy behold:
Her Port describ'd, "*She moves divinely fair,*
"*Olive and Laurel bind her golden Hair.*"
She, the bright Progeny of Heaven, descends,
And every Grace her sovereign Step attends;
For now kind Heaven, indulgent to our Prayer,
In smiling *Peace* resolves the Din of *War.*
Fix'd in *Columbia*[1] her illustrious Line,
And bids in thee her future Councils shine.
To every Realm her Portals open'd wide,
Receives from each the full commercial Tide.
Each Art and Science now with rising Charms
Th' expanding Heart with Emulation warms.
E'en great *Britannia* sees with dread Surprize,
And from the dazzl'ing Splendors turns her Eyes!
Britain, whose Navies swept th' *Atlantic* o'er,
And Thunder sent to every distant Shore:
E'en thou, in Manners cruel as thou art,
The Sword resign'd, resume the friendly Part!
For *Galia's* Power espous'd *Columbia's* Cause,[2]
And new-born *Rome* shall give *Britannia* Law,
Nor unremember'd in the grateful Strain,
Shall princely *Louis'* friendly Deeds remain;
The generous Prince[3] th' impending Vengeance eye's,
Sees the fierce Wrong, and to the rescue flies.
Perish that Thirst of boundless Power, that drew
On *Albion's*[4] Head the Curse to Tyrants due.
But thou appeas'd submit to Heaven's decree,
That bids this Realm of Freedom rival thee!
Now sheathe the Sword that bade the Brave attone
With guiltless Blood for Madness not their own.
Sent from th' Enjoyment of their native Shore

1. ***Columbia*:** America was often referred to as the land Columbus founded, or simply as *Columbia.*
2. ***Galia's* Power espous'd *Columbia's* Cause:** The French had supported the colonies during the American Revolution.
3. **Prince:** Louis XVI (1754–1793), king of France from 1774 to 1792.
4. ***Albion's*:** Poetic name for England.

Ill-fated – never to behold her more!
From every Kingdom on *Europa's* Coast
Throng'd various Troops, their Glory, Strength and Boast.
With heart-felt pity fair *Hibernia*[5] saw
Columbia menac'd by the Tyrant's Law:
On hostile Fields fraternal Arms engage,
And mutual Deaths, all dealt with mutual Rage;
The Muse's Ear hears mother Earth deplore
Her ample Surface smoak with kindred Gore:
The hostile Field destroys the social Ties,
And ever-lasting Slumber seals their Eyes.
Columbia mourns, the haughty Foes deride,
Her Treasures plunder'd, and her Towns destroy'd:
Witness how *Charlestown's* curling Smoaks[6] arise,
In sable Columns to the clouded Skies!
The ample Dome, high-wrought with curious Toil,
In one sad Hour the savage Troops despoil.
Descending *Peace* the Power of War confounds;
From every Tongue celestial *Peace* resounds:
As from the East th' illustrious King of Day,
With rising Radiance drives the Shades away,
So Freedom comes array'd with Charms divine,
And in her Train Commerce and Plenty shine.
Britannia owns her Independent Reign,
Hibernia, Scotia, and the Realms of *Spain*;
And great *Germania's* ample Coast admires
The generous Spirit that *Columbia* fires.
Auspicious Heaven shall fill with fav'ring Gales,
Where e'er *Columbia* spreads her swelling Sails:
To every Realm shall *Peace* her Charms display,
And Heavenly *Freedom* spread her golden Ray.

[1784, 1989]

5. ***Hibernia***: Poetic name for Ireland.
6. **Smoaks**: After the battle of Bunker Hill on June 17, 1775 – the first battle of the American Revolution – the British burned Charlestown, which was clearly visible from Boston.

LETTER TO SAMSON OCCOM[1]

The following is an extract of a Letter from Phillis, a Negro Girl of Mr. Wheatley's, in Boston, to the Rev. Samson Occom, which we are desired to insert as a Specimen of her Ingenuity.—It is dated 11th Feb., 1774.

Rev'd and honor'd Sir,

I have this Day received your obliging kind Epistle, and am greatly satisfied with your Reasons respecting the Negroes, and think highly reasonable what you offer in Vindication of their natural Rights: Those that invade them cannot be insensible that the divine Light is chasing away the thick Darkness which broods over the Land of Africa; and the Chaos which has reign'd so long, is converting into beautiful Order, and [r]eveals more and more clearly, the glorious Dispensation of civil and religious Liberty, which are so inseparably united, that there is little or no Enjoyment of one without the other: Otherwise, perhaps, the Israelites had been less solicitous for their Freedom from Egyptian slavery; I do not say they would have been contented without it, by no means, for in every human Breast, God has implanted a Principle, which we call Love of Freedom; it is impatient of Oppression, and pants for Deliverance; and by the Leave of our modern Egyptians I will assert, that the same Principle lives in us. God grant Deliverance in his own Way and Time, and get him honour upon all those whose Avarice impels them to countenance and help forward the Calamities of their fellow Creatures. This I desire not for their Hurt, but to convince them of the strange Absurdity of their Conduct whose Words and Actions are so diametrically opposite. How well the Cry for Liberty, and the reverse Disposition for the exercise of oppressive Power over others agree, – I humbly think it does not require the Penetration of a Philosopher to determine.

[1774, 1989]

1. Samson Occom: (1723-1792) Mohegan Indian minister and a longtime friend of Wheatley's (see p. 402). This letter was published in the *Connecticut Gazette; and the Universal Intelligencer* on March 11, 1774.

Wheatley through a Modern Lens

ALTHOUGH SHE WAS NOT THE FIRST African American to appear in print, Phillis Wheatley was apparently the first to publish a book. Certainly, she was the first to publish a book of poetry. The scholar Henry Louis Gates Jr. has affirmed that the "birth of the African American tradition occurred in 1773," when Wheatley's *Poems on Various Subjects, Religious and Moral* was published in London. Not surprisingly, the earliest notices revealed less interest in the poetry than in the fact that it had been written by "a young untutored African," as one English reviewer described Wheatley. In his *Notes on the State of Virginia*, Thomas Jefferson dismissed Wheatley's poetry, observing that "Religion indeed has produced a Phyllis Wheately [*sic*]; but it could not produce a poet. The compositions published under her name are below the dignity of criticism." Following her death in 1784, the year Jefferson's critique first appeared, Wheatley fell into obscurity until her poetry was rediscovered by abolitionists in the 1830s. Since then, her achievement has remained a source of pride and inspiration for a wide range of African American writers, including Countee Cullen, Gwendolyn Brooks, and Margaret Walker, who in 1973 organized a poetry festival to commemorate the two hundredth anniversary of the publication of Wheatley's book. The festival featured readings by eleven black women poets, several of whom read poems they had written about Wheatley. As the following poem by the award-winning poet Kevin Young illustrates, she remains a vital presence; appropriately, his "Homage to Phillis Wheatley" appeared as the final work in an anthology edited by Young, *Giant Steps: The New Generation of African American Writers* (2000).

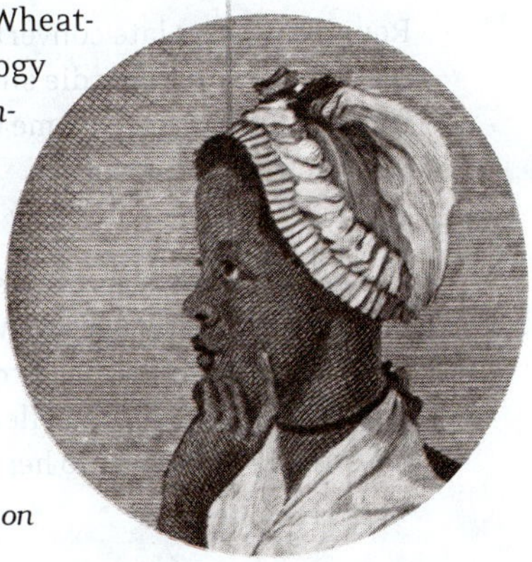

Phillis Wheatley

A detail from Scipio Moorhead's portrait of Wheatley, used as the frontispiece of her *Poems on Various Subjects* (1773).

Kevin Young

[b. 1970]

Homage to Phillis Wheatley

Poet & Servant to Mr. Wheatley of Boston, on her Maiden Voyage to Britain

There are days I can understand
why you would want to board
broad back of some ship
and sail: venture, not homeward
but toward Civilization's

Cold seat, – having from wild
been stolen, and sent into more wild
of Columbia,[1] our exiles
and Christians clamoring upon
the cobblestones of Bostontown –
Sail across an Atlantic (this time) mild,
the ship's polite and consumptive
passengers proud. Your sickness
quit soon as you disembarked in mist
of England – free, finally, of our Republic's

Rough clime, its late converts who thought
they would not die, or die simply
in struggle, martyr to some God, –
you know of gods there
are many, who is really only

One – and that sleep, restless fever
would take most you loved. Why
fate fight? Death, dark mistress,
would come a-heralding silent
the streets, – no door to her closed,

1. **Columbia:** Wheatley frequently referred to America as *Columbia.*

No stair (servant or front) too steep.
Gen. Washington, whom you praise,
victorious, knows this – will even admit
you to his parlor.[2] Who could resist a Negress
who can recite Latin and speak the Queen's?[3]

Docked among the fog and slight sun
of London, you know who you are not
but that is little new. Native
of nowhere, – you'll stay a spell, return,
write, grow still. I wake with you

In my mind, leaning, learning
to write – your slight profile
that long pull of lower lip, its pout
proving you rescued by
some sadness too large to name.

My Most Excellence, my quill
and ink lady, you spill such script
no translation it needs –
your need is what's missing, unwritten
wish to cross back but not back

Into that land (for you) of the dead –
you want to see from above
deck the sea, to pluck from wind
a sense no Land can
give: drifting, looking not

For Leviathan's breath,[4] nor waves
made of tea, nor for mermen half-
out of water (as you) – down
in the deep is not the narwhal[5] enough real?
Beneath our wind-whipt banner you smile

At Sea which owns no country.

[2000]

---

2. **Gen. Washington . . . his parlor:** See Wheatley's "To His Excellency General Washington" on page 512. In his reply, Washington praised Wheatley for her "great poetical Talents" and invited her to meet him.
3. **Queen's:** Short for "Queen's [or proper] English."
4. **Leviathan's breath:** A sea monster, usually a whale.
5. **narwhal:** A small Arctic whale.

Washington Irving

[1783-1859]

Washington Irving was born in New York City on April 3, 1783, the youngest of eleven children of Sarah and William Irving. Irving's English-born mother was the granddaughter of a clergyman, and William Irving was an affluent merchant who strongly supported the cause of American independence. Born the same year that the Treaty of Paris ended the Revolution, Irving was named after its hero George Washington. As a child, Irving was part of a supportive family that would remain important to him throughout his life. He attended private schools but was not a strong student, displaying more interest in art, music, and especially English literature than in the Greek and Latin that was a staple of education for boys at the time. Since William Irving expected all of his sons to support themselves, Irving was sent to study law in 1801. The following year, his brother Peter established a newspaper, the *Morning Chronicle*, to which Irving contributed satirical pieces on New York culture and society called the "Letters of Jonathan Oldstyle, Gent.," the first of a series of pseudonyms he would adopt in his writings. Worried about his health, Irving's brothers sent him to Europe for recreation and further education in 1804, when he was twenty-one.

Washington Irving

This portrait of Irving was painted in 1820, shortly after he gained international fame by publishing *The Sketch Book.* The painting is attributed to Charles Robert Leslie, an English artist famous for his portraits of other artists and literary figures, including Irving's friend and mentor Sir Walter Scott.

Returning to the United States after two years of extensive travel, Irving completed his legal studies and was admitted to the bar. But he was far more drawn to literature than to law. Along with his brother William and the writer James Kirke Paulding, Irving established a new magazine, *Salmagundi*, contributing the kind of satirical pieces in which he delighted and for which he was increasingly known. After the short-lived magazine failed in 1808, Irving wrote *A History of New York* (1809), a satire of both pedantic histories and current events, in which he adopted the persona of an elderly Dutch American antiquarian, Diedrich Knickerbocker. The book was hailed as a great comic work in both the United States and England, where its admirers included the influential writer Sir Walter Scott. Just before it was published, however, Irving suffered a devastating personal loss, the death from tuberculosis of his eighteen-year-old fiancée, Matilda Hoffman. The grief-stricken Irving would never marry. During the following years, he wrote little imaginative literature, devoting himself instead to his brothers' businesses and to editing the *Analectic Magazine.* The magazine primarily published articles and stories from foreign periodicals, but it also ran biographies of the American heroes of the War of 1812. Perhaps as a result, Irving in 1814 resigned the editorship and briefly served as a colonel in the New York State militia.

Irving? Thrice welcome, warm heart and fine brain . . .
– James Russell Lowell

When the war ended in 1815, Irving once again went to Europe, where he lived for the next seventeen years. Initially, he worked with his brother

Peter in the overseas branch of the family import business in Liverpool, England. In 1818, the business failed, taking with it much of the Irving family fortune. To earn money, Irving wrote reviews for British periodicals and served for a time as a book agent for the American bookseller Moses Thomas. He also began *The Sketch Book of Geoffrey Crayon, Gent.*, a collection of travel sketches of England in which Irving also included what would become his two most famous stories set in America, "Rip Van Winkle" and "The Legend of Sleepy Hollow." Published in installments in New York in 1819 and in book form both there and in London the following year, *The Sketch Book* was enormously popular on both sides of the Atlantic. Irving swiftly followed it with *Bracebridge Hall* (1822), another well-received collection of sketches about English country life written under the name of his persona Geoffrey Crayon. But his next book, *Tales of a Traveller* (1824), was a commercial and critical failure. Seeking both a change of scene and a new direction for his literary career, Irving accepted an invitation to become an attaché to the American legation in Madrid. There, he turned to biography and history, publishing *The Life and Voyages of Christopher Columbus* (1828) and *A Chronicle of the Conquest of Granada* (1829). Even after he returned to London as secretary of the American legation in 1829, he continued to draw upon his vivid impressions of Spain, notably in his collection of Romantic sketches and tales, *The Alhambra* (1832).

After Irving returned to the United States in 1832, he primarily devoted himself to American scenes and subjects. Like many Americans at the time, he was especially fascinated by the West, which Irving explored in works like *A Tour on the Prairies* (1835), a narrative of his journey through what is now Arkansas and Oklahoma; *Astoria* (1836), a history of John Jacob Astor's fur-trading company in the Oregon Territory; and *The Rocky Mountains; or, Scenes, Incidents, and Adventures in the Far West* (1837). Having become the country's most celebrated author – and its first to make a living exclusively from writing – Irving in 1835 bought a country home, Sunnyside, on the banks of the Hudson River near Tarrytown, New York. With the exception of the years 1842-45, when he served with distinction as the ambassador to Spain, Irving lived for the rest of his life at Sunnyside, where he enjoyed the company of his many friends and family members. Although the pace of his writing slowed, he published several additional books, including *A Book of the Hudson* (1849), and he prepared a fifteen-volume "Author's Revised Edition" of his *Works*. During the 1850s, he devoted his energies to a five-volume biography of his namesake, George Washington, which Irving completed shortly before his death at Sunnyside on November 28, 1859.

bedfordstmartins.com/ americanlit *for research links on Irving*

Irving's *Sketch Book*. While living in England in 1818, Irving began writing the essays, sketches, and tales for the book that gained him an international reputation, *The Sketch Book of Geoffrey Crayon, Gent.* Irving was encouraged by the popular English writer Sir Walter Scott, who also advised Irving to read German folktales, the primary source of his most

John Quidor, *The Return of Rip Van Winkle* (1849)

Quidor, a struggling artist who had to earn his living by painting signs, was fascinated by "Rip Van Winkle." In his dynamic rendering of the climax of the story, Quidor accurately depicts key details of the setting, especially the Dutch houses of the village against the background of the Catskill Mountains.

famous story, "Rip Van Winkle." That story, ostensibly found among the papers of the antiquarian Diedrich Knickerbocker, was not typical of most of the sketches in the volume, which record the impressions and observations of Irving's other persona, Geoffrey Crayon, an American traveler in England. Irving, however, clearly recognized the appeal of "Rip Van Winkle," a humorous and satirical yet deeply resonant story set in a richly evocative American setting, the Catskill Mountains of New York State. Preceded and implicitly paired with "The Wife," a sentimental story strikingly different in tone and setting, "Rip Van Winkle" was included in the first of six installments of *The Sketch Book* published in New York between May 1819 and February 1820.

In the prospectus, printed at the beginning of the first installment, Irving explained:

> The following writings are published on experiment; should they please, they may be followed by others. The writer will have to contend with some disadvantages. He is unsettled in his abode, subject to interruptions, and has his share of cares and vicissitudes. He cannot, therefore, promise a regular plan, nor regular periods of publication. Should he be encouraged to proceed, much time may elapse between the appearance of his numbers; and their size must depend on the materials he has on hand. His writings will partake of the fluctuations of his own thoughts and feelings; sometimes treating of scenes before him, sometimes of others purely imaginary, and sometimes wandering back with his recollections to his native country. He

> will not be able to give them that tranquil attention necessary to finished composition; and as they must be transmitted across the Atlantic for publication, he must trust to others to correct the frequent errors of the press. Should his writings, however, with all their imperfections, be well received, he cannot conceal that it would be a source of the purist gratification; for though he does not aspire to those high honours that are the rewards of loftier intellects; yet it is the dearest wish of his heart to have a secure and cherished, though humble, corner in the good opinions and kind feelings of his countrymen.

As that passage suggests, Irving carefully crafted the persona of Geoffrey Crayon. By casting himself as an amateur, an idle gentleman traveler who did not take himself or his writings too seriously, Irving sought at once to disarm and appeal to an American audience still skeptical about both the claims of merely imaginative literature and the status of writing as a profession. Certainly, his "experiment" proved to be a huge success, both among Irving's "countrymen" and in England, where a full version of *The Sketch Book* was published in 1820.

The texts of the following works – three of the five Irving included in the first installment of *The Sketch Book* — are taken from the initial American publication of that installment in May 1819.

THE AUTHOR'S ACCOUNT OF HIMSELF

> "I am of this mind with Homer, that as the snaile that crept out of her shel was turned eftsoones into a toad, and thereby was forced to make a stoole to sit on; so the traveller that stragleth from his owne country is in a short time transformed into so monstrous a shape, that he is faine to alter his mansion with his manners, and to live where he can, not where he would."
>
> - *Lyly's Euphues.*[1]

I was always fond of visiting new scenes, and observing strange characters and manners. Even when a mere child I began my travels, and made many tours of discovery into foreign parts and unknown regions of my native city, to the frequent alarm of my parents, and the emolument of the town-crier. As I grew into boyhood, I extended the range of my observations. My holiday afternoons were spent in rambles about the surrounding country. I made myself familiar with all its places famous in history or fable. I knew every spot where a murder or robbery had been committed, or a ghost been seen. I visited the neighbouring villages, and added greatly to my stock of knowledge, by noting their habits and customs, and conversing with their sages and great men. I even journeyed one long summer's day to the summit of the most distant hill, from whence I

---

1. ***Lyly's Euphues***: The epigraph is from *Euphues and His England* (1580) by John Lyly (1554-1606), an English writer who developed euphuism, an elaborate prose style marked by repetition, rhetorical questions, and classical allusions.

stretched my eye over many a mile of terra incognita, and was astonished to find how vast a globe I inhabited.

This rambling propensity strengthened with my years. Books of voyages and travels became my passion, and in devouring their contents, I neglected the regular exercises of the school. How wistfully would I wander about the pier heads in fine weather, and watch the parting ships, bound to distant climes – with what longing eyes would I gaze after their lessening sails, and waft myself in imagination to the ends of the earth.

Farther reading and thinking, though they brought this vague inclination into more reasonable bounds, only served to make it more decided. I visited various parts of my own country; and had I been merely a lover of fine scenery, I should have felt little desire to seek elsewhere for its gratification: for on no country have the charms of nature been more prodigally lavished. Her mighty lakes, like oceans of liquid silver; her mountains, with their bright aerial tints; her valleys, teeming with wild fertility; her tremendous cataracts, thundering in their solitudes; her boundless plains, waving with spontaneous verdure; her broad deep rivers, rolling in solemn silence to the ocean; her trackless forests, where vegetation puts forth all its magnificence; her skies, kindling with the magic of summer clouds and glorious sunshine: – no, never need an American look beyond his own country for the sublime and beautiful of natural scenery.

But Europe held forth all the charms of storied and poetical association. There were to be seen the masterpieces of art, the refinements of highly cultivated society, the quaint peculiarities of ancient and local custom. My native country was full of youthful promise; Europe was rich in the accumulated treasures of age. Her very ruins told the history of times gone by, and every mouldering stone was a chronicle. I longed to wander over the scenes of renowned achievement – to tread, as it were, in the footsteps of antiquity – to loiter about the ruined castle – to meditate on the falling tower – to escape, in short, from the commonplace realities of the present, and lose myself among the shadowy grandeurs of the past.

I had, beside all this, an earnest desire to see the great men of the earth. We have, it is true, our great men in America: not a city but has an ample share of them. I have mingled among them in my time, and been almost withered by the shade into which they cast me; for there is nothing so baleful to a small man as the shade of a great one, particularly the great man of a city. But I was anxious to see the great men of Europe; for I had read in the works of various philosophers, that all animals degenerated in America, and man among the number.[2] A great man of Europe, therefore, thought I, must be as superior to a great man of America, as a peak of the Alps to a highland of the Hudson; and in this idea I was confirmed, by observing the comparative importance and swelling magnitude of many English travellers among us; who, I was assured, were very little people

2. **man among the number:** Comte George-Louis Leclerc de Buffon (1707-1788), an influential French naturalist and scientist, had argued that people in North America would degenerate because its cold and damp climate was not conducive to physical development. Thomas Jefferson vigorously refuted Buffon, as well as critics who argued that the American environment also stunted intellectual growth, in his *Notes on the State of Virginia*, which was privately printed in Paris in 1784 and later published in London and Philadelphia.

in their own country. I will visit this land of wonders, therefore, thought I, and see the gigantic race from which I am degenerated.

It has been either my good or evil lot to have my roving passion gratified. I have wandered through different countries, and witnessed many of the shifting scenes of life. I cannot say that I have studied them with the eye of a philosopher, but rather with the sauntering gaze with which humble lovers of the picturesque stroll from the window of one print shop to another; caught sometimes by the delineations of beauty, sometimes by the distortions of caricature, and sometimes by the loveliness of landscape. As it is the fashion for modern tourists to travel pencil in hand, and bring home their port folios filled with sketches, I am disposed to get up a few for the entertainment of my friends. When I look over, however, the hints and memorandums I have taken down for the purpose, my heart almost fails me to find how my idle humour has led me aside from the great objects studied by every regular traveller who would make a book. I fear I shall give equal disappointment with an unlucky landscape painter, who had travelled on the continent, but following the bent of his vagrant inclination, had sketched in nooks, and corners, and by-places. His sketch book was accordingly crowded with cottages, and landscapes, and obscure ruins; but he had neglected to paint St. Peter's, or the Coliseum; the cascade of Terni, or the bay of Naples;[3] and had not a single glacier or volcano in his whole collection.

[1819]

3. **St. Peter's . . . Naples:** Irving refers to several favorite tourist destinations: St. Peter's Basilica in Rome, built in the sixteenth century; the Colosseum (as it is usually spelled), a vast amphitheater in Rome built in 75 CE; the man-made falls or cascade at Terni in Italy, built in 272 BCE; and the bay of Naples in southern Italy, upon which is located the volcano, Mount Vesuvius, and the ruins of Pompeii.

THE WIFE

The treasures of the deep are not so precious
As are the concealed comforts of a man
Lock'd up in woman's love. I scent the air
Of blessings, when I come but near the house.
What a delicious breath marriage sends forth –
The violet bed's not sweeter!

Middleton[1]

I have often had occasion to remark the fortitude with which women sustain the most overwhelming reverses of fortune. Those disasters which break down the spirit of a man, and prostrate him in the dust, seem to call forth all the energies of the softer sex, and give such intrepidity and elevation to their character, that at times it approaches to

1. **Middleton:** The epigraph is from *Women Beware Women*, 3.1, a tragedy by the English dramatist Thomas Middleton (1570–1627).

sublimity. Nothing can be more touching than to behold a soft and tender female, who had been all weakness and dependence, and alive to every trivial roughness while treading the prosperous paths of life, suddenly rising in mental force, to be the comforter and supporter of her husband, under misfortune, and abiding, with unshrinking firmness, the bitterest blasts of adversity.

As the vine which has long twined its graceful foliage around the oak, and been lifted by it into sunshine, will, when the hardy plant is rifted by the thunderbolt, cling round it with its caressing tendrils, and bind up its shattered boughs; so is it beautifully ordered by Providence, that woman, who is the mere dependant and ornament of man in his happier hours, should be his stay and solace when smitten with sudden calamity, winding herself into the rugged recesses of his nature, tenderly supporting the drooping head, and binding up the broken heart.

I was once congratulating a friend, who had around him a blooming family, knit together in the strongest affection. "I can wish you no better lot," said he, with enthusiasm, "than to have a wife and children – if you are prosperous, there they are to share your prosperity; if otherwise, there they are to comfort you." And, indeed, I have observed that married men falling into misfortune, are more apt to retrieve their situation in the world than single men; partly because they are more stimulated to exertion by the necessities of the helpless and beloved beings who depend upon them for subsistence; but chiefly because their spirits are soothed and relieved by domestic endearments, and their self respect kept alive by finding, that though all abroad is darkness and humiliation, yet there is still a little world of love, of which they are monarchs. Whereas a single man is apt to run to waste and self neglect; to fancy himself lonely and abandoned, and his heart to fall to ruin like some deserted mansion, for want of an inhabitant.

These observations call to mind a little domestic story, of which I was once a witness. My intimate friend, Leslie, had married a beautiful and accomplished girl, who had been brought up in the midst of fashionable life. She had, it is true, no fortune, but that of my friend was ample; and he delighted in the anticipation of indulging her in every elegant pursuit and administering to those delicate tastes and fancies, that spread a kind of witchery about the sex. "Her life," said he, "shall be like a fairy tale."

The very difference in their characters produced an harmonious combination: he was of a romantic, and somewhat serious, cast; she was all life and gladness. I have often noticed the mute rapture with which he would gaze upon her in company, of which her sprightly powers made her the delight; and how, in the midst of applause, her eye would still turn to him, as if there alone she sought favour and acceptance. When leaning on his arm, her slender form contrasted finely with his tall, manly person. The fond confiding air with which she looked up to him, seemed to call forth a flush of triumphant pride and cherishing tenderness, as if he doated on his lovely burthen for its very helplessness. Never did a couple set forward on the flowery path of early and well-suited marriage with a fairer prospect of felicity.

It was the mishap of my friend, however, to have embarked his fortune in large speculations; and he had not been married many months, when, by a succession of sudden disasters, it was swept from him, and he found himself reduced almost to penury. For a time he kept his situation to himself, and went about with a haggard countenance, and a breaking heart. His life was but a protracted agony; and what rendered it more insupportable, was the necessity of keeping up a smile in the presence of his wife; for he could not bring himself to overwhelm her with the news. She saw, however, with the quick eyes of affection, that all was not well with him. She marked his altered looks and stifled sighs, and was not to be deceived by his sickly and vapid attempts at cheerfulness. She tasked all her sprightly powers and tender blandishments to win him back to happiness; but she only drove the arrow deeper into his soul. The more he saw cause to love her, the more torturing was the thought that he was soon to make her wretched. A little while, thought he, and the smile will vanish from that cheek – the song will die away from those lips – the lustre of those eyes will be quenched with sorrow; and the happy heart which now beats lightly in that bosom, will be weighed down, like mine, by the cares and miseries of the world.

At length he came to me one day, and related his whole situation in a tone of the deepest despair. When I had heard him through, I inquired, "does your wife know all this?" At the question he burst into an agony of tears. "For God's sake!" cried he, "if you have any pity on me, don't mention my wife; it is the thought of her that drives me almost to madness!"

"And why not?" said I. "She must know it sooner or later: you cannot keep it long from her, and the intelligence may break upon her in a more startling manner, than if imparted by yourself; for the accents of those we love soften the harshest tidings. Besides, you are depriving yourself of the comforts of her sympathy; and not merely that, but also endangering the only bond that can keep hearts together – an unreserved community of thought and feeling. She will soon perceive that something is secretly preying upon your mind; and true love will not brook reserve, but feels undervalued and outraged, when even the sorrows of those it loves are concealed from it."

"Oh, but, my friend! to think what a blow I am to give to all her future prospects – how I am to strike her very soul to the earth, by telling her that her husband is a beggar! – that she is to forego all the elegancies of life – all the pleasures of society – to shrink with me into indigence and obscurity! To tell her that I have dragged her down from the sphere in which she might have continued to move in constant brightness – the light of every eye – the admiration of every heart! How can she bear poverty? she has been brought up in all the refinements of opulence. How can she bear neglect? she has been the idol of society. Oh, it will break her heart, it will break her heart! –"

I saw his grief was eloquent, and I let it have its flow; for sorrow relieves itself by words. When his paroxysm had subsided, and he had relapsed into moody silence, I resumed the subject gently, and urged him to break his situation at once to his wife. He shook his head mournfully, but positively.

"But how are you to keep it from her? It is necessary she should know it, that you may take the steps proper to the alteration of your circumstances. You must change your style of living — nay," observing a pang to pass across his countenance, "don't let that afflict you. I am sure you have never placed your happiness in outward show – you have yet friends, warm friends, who will not think the worse of you for being less splendidly lodged: and surely it does not require a palace to be happy with Mary –"

"I could be happy with her," cried he convulsively, "in a hovel! I could go down with her into poverty and the dust! I could – I could — God bless her! God bless her!" cried he, bursting into a transport of grief and tenderness.

"And believe me, my friend," said I, stepping up, and grasping him warmly by the hand, "believe me, she can be the same with you. Aye, more: it will be a source of pride and triumph to her – it will call forth all the latent energies and fervent sympathies of her nature; for she will rejoice to prove that she loves you for yourself. There is in every true woman's heart a spark of heavenly fire, which lies dormant in the broad daylight of prosperity; but which kindles up, and beams and blazes in the dark hour of adversity. No man knows what the wife of his bosom is – no man knows what a ministering angel she is – until he has gone with her through the fiery trials of this world."

There was something in the earnestness of my manner, and the figurative style of my language, that caught the excited imagination of Leslie. I knew the auditor I had to deal with; and following up the impression I had made, I finished by persuading him to go home and unburden his sad heart to his wife.

I must confess, notwithstanding all I had said, I felt some little solicitude for the result. Who can calculate on the fortitude of one whose whole life has been a round of pleasures? Her gay spirits might revolt at the dark, downward path of low humility, suddenly pointed out before her, and might cling to the sunny regions in which they had hitherto revelled. Besides, ruin in fashionable life is accompanied by so many galling mortifications, to which, in other ranks, it is a stranger. In short, I could not meet Leslie, the next morning, without trepidation. He had made the disclosure.

"And how did she bear it?"

"Like an angel! It seemed rather to be a relief to her mind, for she threw her arms around my neck, and asked if this was all that had lately made me unhappy – but, poor girl," added he, "she cannot realize the change we must undergo. She has no idea of poverty but in the abstract: she has only read of it in poetry, where it is allied to love. She feels as yet no privation: she experiences no want of accustomed conveniences or elegancies. When we come practically to experience its sordid cares, its paltry wants, its petty humiliations – then will be the real trial."

"But," said I, "now that you have got over the severest task, that of breaking it to her, the sooner you let the world into the secret the better. The disclosure may be mortifying; but then it is a single misery, and soon over; whereas you otherwise suffer it, in anticipation, every hour in the day. It is not poverty, so much as pretence, that harasses a ruined man – the struggle between a proud mind and an empty purse – the keeping up a hollow show that must soon come to an end. Have the courage to appear poor, and you disarm poverty of its sharpest sting." On this point I found Leslie perfectly prepared. He had no false pride himself, and as to his wife, she was only anxious to conform to their altered fortunes.

Some days afterwards he called upon me in the evening. He had disposed of his dwelling house, and taken a small cottage in the country, a few miles from town. He had been busied all day in sending out furniture. The new establishment required few articles, and those of the simplest kind. All the splendid furniture of his late residence had been sold, excepting his wife's harp. That, he said, was too closely associated with the idea of herself; it belonged to the little story of their loves; for some of the sweetest moments of their courtship were those when he had leaned over that instrument, and listened to the melting tones of her voice. I could not but smile at this instance of romantic gallantry in a doating husband.

He was now going out to the cottage, where his wife had been all day, superintending its arrangement. My feelings had become strongly interested in the progress of this family story, and as it was a fine evening, I offered to accompany him.

He was wearied with the fatigues of the day, and as we walked out, fell into a fit of gloomy musing.

"Poor Mary!" at length broke, with a heavy sigh, from his lips.

"And what of her," asked I, "has any thing happened to her?"

"What," said he, darting an impatient glance, "is it nothing to be reduced to this paltry situation – to be caged in a miserable cottage – to be obliged to toil almost in the menial concerns of her wretched habitation?"

"Has she then repined at the change?"

"Repined! she has been nothing but sweetness and good humour. Indeed, she seems in better spirits than I have ever known her; she has been to me all love, and tenderness, and comfort!"

"Admirable girl!" exclaimed I. "You call yourself poor, my friend; you never were so rich – you never knew the boundless treasures of excellence you possessed in that woman."

"Oh, but my friend, if this first meeting at the cottage were over, I think I could then be comfortable. But this is her first day of real experience: She has been introduced into a humble dwelling – she has been employed all day in arranging its miserable equipments – she has for the first time known the fatigues of domestic employment – she has for the first time looked around her on a home destitute of every thing elegant, and almost convenient; and may now be sitting down, exhausted and spiritless, brooding over a prospect of future poverty."

There was a degree of probability in this picture that I could not gainsay, so we walked on in silence.

After turning from the main road, up a narrow lane, so thickly shaded by forest trees, as to give it a complete air of seclusion, we came in sight of the cottage. It was humble enough in its appearance for the most pastoral poet: and yet it had a pleasing rural look. A wild vine had overrun one end with a profusion of foliage; a few trees threw their branches gracefully over it; and I observed several pots of flowers tastefully disposed about the door, and on the grass plot in front. A small wicket gate opened upon a footpath that wound through some shrubbery to the door. Just as we approached, we heard the sound of music – Leslie grasped my arm; we paused and listened. It was Mary's voice, in a style of the most touching simplicity, singing a little air of which her husband was peculiarly fond.

I felt Leslie's hand tremble on my arm. He stepped forward, to hear more distinctly. His step made a noise on the gravel walk. A bright beautiful face glanced out at the window, and vanished – a light footstep was heard – and Mary came tripping forth to meet us. She was in a pretty rural dress of white; a few wild flowers were twisted in her fine hair; a fresh bloom was on her cheek; her whole countenance beamed with smiles — I had never seen her look so lovely.

"My dear George," cried she, "I am so glad you are come; I've been watching and watching for you; and running down the lane, and looking out for you. I've set out a table under a beautiful tree behind the cottage; and I've been gathering some of the most delicious strawberries, for I know you are fond of them – and we have such excellent cream – and every thing is so sweet and still here – Oh!" said she, putting her arm within his, and looking up brightly in his face, "Oh, we shall be so snug!"

Poor Leslie was overcome. He caught her to his bosom – he folded his arms around her – he kissed her again and again – he could not speak, but the tears gushed into his eyes. And he has often assured me, that though the world has since gone prosperously with him, and his life has been a happy one, yet never has he experienced a moment of such unutterable felicity.

[1819]

RIP VAN WINKLE

[The following Tale was found among the papers of the late Diedrich Knickerbocker, an old gentleman of New-York, who was very curious in the Dutch history of the province, and the manners of the descendants from its primitive settlers. His historical researches, however, did not lay so much among books, as among men; for the former are lamentably scanty on his favourite topics; whereas he found the old burghers, and still more, their wives, rich in that legendary lore, so invaluable to true history. Whenever, therefore, he happened upon a genuine Dutch family, snugly shut up in its low-roofed farm house, under a spreading sycamore, he looked upon it as a little clasped volume of black-letter,[1] and studied it with the zeal of a bookworm.

The result of all these researches was a history of the province, during the reign of the Dutch governors, which he published some years since. There have been various opinions as to the literary character of his work, and, to tell the truth, it is not a whit better than it should be. Its chief merit is its scrupulous accuracy, which, indeed, was a little questioned, on its first appearance, but has since been completely established; and it is now admitted into all historical collections, as a book of unquestionable authority.[2]

The old gentleman died shortly after the publication of his work, and now, that he is dead and gone, it cannot do much harm to his memory, to say, that his time might have been much better employed in weightier labours. He, however, was apt to ride his hobby his own way; and though it did now and then kick up the dust a little in the eyes of his

1. **clasped volume of black-letter:** In addition to using a type of font that resembled a medieval manuscript, many early printed books were fitted with clasp closures.
2. **book of unquestionable authority:** Irving's popular *A History of New York* (1809), written under the pseudonym Diedrich Knickerbocker, was a hilariously inaccurate spoof of the early history of New York, as his readers would surely have remembered.

neighbours, and grieve the spirit of some friends, for whom he felt the truest deference and affection; yet his errors and follies are remembered "more in sorrow than in anger,"[3] and it begins to be suspected, that he never intended to injure or offend. But however his memory may be appreciated by critics, it is still held dear among many folk, whose good opinion is well worth having; particularly certain biscuit bakers, who have gone so far as to imprint his likeness on their new year cakes, and have thus given him a chance for immortality, almost equal to being stamped on a Waterloo medal, or a Queen Anne's farthing.[4]]

Rip Van Winkle

A Posthumous Writing of Diedrich Knickerbocker

By Woden, God of Saxons,
From whence comes Wensday, that is Wodensday,
Truth is a thing that ever I will keep
Unto thylke day in which I creep into
My sepulchre —

Cartwright[5]

Whoever has made a voyage up the Hudson, must remember the Kaatskill mountains.[6] They are a dismembered branch of the great Appalachian family, and are seen away to the west of the river, swelling up to a noble height, and lording it over the surrounding country. Every change of season, every change of weather, indeed, every hour of the day, produces some change in the magical hues and shapes of these mountains, and they are regarded by all the good wives, far and near, as perfect barometers. When the weather is fair and settled, they are clothed in blue and purple, and print their bold outlines on the clear evening sky; but some times, when the rest of the landscape is cloudless, they will gather a hood of gray vapours about their summits, which, in the last rays of the setting sun, will glow and light up like a crown of glory.

At the foot of these fairy mountains, the voyager may have descried the light smoke curling up from a village, whose shingle roofs gleam among the trees, just where the blue tints of the upland melt away into the fresh green of the nearer landscape. It is a little village of great antiquity, having been founded by some of the Dutch colonists, in

3. **"more . . . anger":** The quotation is from Shakespeare's *Hamlet*, 1.1.231-32. In the original text, Irving added this note: "Vide the excellent discourse of G. C. Verplanck, Esq. before the New-York Historical Society." *Vide* (Latin) means see; Verplanck (1786-1870) was a well-known politician and one of Irving's friends in New York.

4. **Waterloo medal, or a Queen Anne's farthing:** Medals were given to British soldiers who had taken part in the series of battles leading up to the battle of Waterloo, where Napoleon was defeated on June 18, 1805. Queen Anne's farthings, only a small number of which were minted in 1713, were also in considerable demand by collectors in the early nineteenth century.

5. **Cartwright:** The lines are spoken by Moth, a pedantic antiquarian, in *The Ordinary*, 3.1.1050-54, by the English playwright William Cartwright (1611-1643).

6. **Kaatskill mountains:** The Catskill Mountains, an extension of the Appalachian Mountains, are located in eastern New York.

the early times of the province, just about the beginning of the government of the good Peter Stuyvesant,[7] (may he rest in peace!) and there were some of the houses of the original settlers standing within a few years, with lattice windows, gable fronts surmounted with weathercocks, and built of small yellow bricks brought from Holland.

In that same village, and in one of these very houses, (which, to tell the precise truth, was sadly time worn and weather beaten,) there lived many years since, while the country was yet a province of Great Britain, a simple good natured fellow, of the name of Rip Van Winkle. He was a descendant of the Van Winkles who figured so gallantly in the chivalrous days of Peter Stuyvesant, and accompanied him to the siege of Fort Christina.[8] He inherited, however, but little of the martial character of his ancestors. I have observed that he was a simple good natured man; he was moreover a kind neighbour, and an obedient, henpecked husband. Indeed, to the latter circumstance might be owing that meekness of spirit which gained him such universal popularity; for those men are most apt to be obsequious and conciliating abroad, who are under the discipline of shrews at home. Their tempers, doubtless, are rendered pliant and malleable in the fiery furnace of domestic tribulation, and a curtain lecture[9] is worth all the sermons in the world for teaching the virtues of patience and long suffering. A termagant wife may, therefore, in some respects, be considered a tolerable blessing; and if so, Rip Van Winkle was thrice blessed.

Certain it is, that he was a great favourite among all the good wives of the village, who, as usual with the amiable sex, took his part in all family squabbles, and never failed, whenever they talked those matters over in their evening gossippings, to lay all the blame on Dame Van Winkle. The children of the village, too, would shout with joy whenever he approached. He assisted at their sports, made their playthings, taught them to fly kites and shoot marbles, and told them long stories of ghosts, witches, and Indians. Whenever he went dodging about the village, he was surrounded by a troop of them, hanging on his skirts, clambering on his back, and playing a thousand tricks on him with impunity; and not a dog would bark at him throughout the neighbourhood.

The great error in Rip's composition was an insuperable aversion to all kinds of profitable labour. It could not be for the want of assiduity or perseverance; for he would sit on a wet rock, with a rod as long and heavy as a Tartar's lance, and fish all day without a murmur, even though he should not be encouraged by a single nibble. He would carry a fowling piece on his shoulder, for hours together, trudging through woods and swamps, and up hill and down dale, to shoot a few squirrels or wild pigeons. He would never even refuse to assist a neighbour in the roughest toil, and was a foremost man at all country frolicks for husking Indian corn, or building stone fences; the women of the village, too,

---

7. **Peter Stuyvesant:** (1592–1672) Last governor of the Dutch province of New Netherland; he was frequently satirized by Irving in his *History of New York.*

8. **Fort Christina:** The first Swedish settlement in North America was established in 1638 at Fort Christina, near present-day Wilmington, Delaware. In 1655, the Dutch under Peter Stuyvesant took control of the fort and the land became part of New Netherland.

9. **curtain lecture:** Archaic term for a reprimand given by a wife to her husband behind lowered curtains, typically used on a four-poster bed in the seventeenth and eighteenth centuries.

used to employ him to run their errands, and to do such little odd jobs as their less obliging husbands would not do for them; – in a word, Rip was ready to attend to any body's business but his own; but as to doing family duty, and keeping his farm in order, it was impossible.

In fact, he declared it was no use to work on his farm; it was the most pestilent little piece of ground in the whole country; every thing about it went wrong, and would go wrong, in spite of him. His fences were continually falling to pieces; his cow would either go astray, or get among the cabbages; weeds were sure to grow quicker in his fields than any where else; the rain always made a point of setting in just as he had some out-door work to do. So that though his patrimonial estate had dwindled away under his management, acre by acre, until there was little more left than a mere patch of Indian corn and potatoes, yet it was the worst conditioned farm in the neighbourhood.

His children, too, were as ragged and wild as if they belonged to nobody. His son Rip, an urchin begotten in his own likeness, promised to inherit the habits, with the old clothes of his father. He was generally seen trooping like a colt at his mother's heels, equipped in a pair of his father's cast-off galligaskins,[10] which he had much ado to hold up with one hand, as a fine lady does her train in bad weather.

Rip Van Winkle, however, was one of those happy mortals, of foolish, well-oiled dispositions, who take the world easy, eat white bread or brown, which ever can be got with least thought or trouble, and would rather starve on a penny than work for a pound. If left to himself, he would have whistled life away, in perfect contentment; but his wife kept continually dinning in his ears about his idleness, his carelessness, and the ruin he was bringing on his family. Morning, noon, and night, her tongue was incessantly going, and every thing he said or did was sure to produce a torrent of household eloquence. Rip had but one way of replying to all lectures of the kind, and that, by frequent use, had grown into a habit. He shrugged his shoulders, shook his head, cast up his eyes, but said nothing. This, however, always provoked a fresh volley from his wife, so that he was fain to draw off his forces, and take to the outside of the house – the only side which, in truth, belongs to a henpecked husband.

Rip's sole domestic adherent was his dog Wolf, who was as much henpecked as his master; for Dame Van Winkle regarded them as companions in idleness, and even looked upon Wolf with an evil eye, as the cause of his master's so often going astray. True it is, in all points of spirit befitting an honourable dog, he was as courageous an animal as ever scoured the woods – but what courage can withstand the ever-during and all-besetting terrors of a woman's tongue? The moment Wolf entered the house, his crest fell, his tail drooped to the ground, or curled between his legs, he sneaked about with a gallows air, casting many a sidelong glance at Dame Van Winkle, and at the least flourish of a broomstick or ladle, would fly to the door with yelping precipitation.

Times grew worse and worse with Rip Van Winkle as years of matrimony rolled on; a tart temper never mellows with age, and a sharp tongue is the only edge tool that grows keener by constant use. For a long while he used to console himself, when driven from

---

10. **galligaskins:** British name for loose-fitting trousers.

home, by frequenting a kind of perpetual club of the sages, philosophers, and other idle personages of the village, that held its sessions on a bench before a small inn, designated by a rubicund portrait of his majesty George the Third. Here they used to sit in the shade, of a long lazy summer's day, talk listlessly over village gossip, or tell endless sleepy stories about nothing. But it would have been worth any statesman's money to have heard the profound discussions that sometimes took place, when by chance an old newspaper fell into their hands, from some passing traveller. How solemnly they would listen to the contents, as drawled out by Derrick Van Bummel, the schoolmaster, a dapper learned little man, who was not to be daunted by the most gigantic word in the dictionary; and how sagely they would deliberate upon public events some months after they had taken place.

The opinions of this junto were completely controlled by Nicholas Vedder, a patriarch of the village, and landlord of the inn, at the door of which he took his seat from morning till night, just moving sufficiently to avoid the sun, and keep in the shade of a large tree; so that the neighbours could tell the hour by his movements as accurately as by a sun dial. It is true, he was rarely heard to speak, but smoked his pipe incessantly. His adherents, however, (for every great man has his adherents,) perfectly understood him, and knew how to gather his opinions. When any thing that was read or related displeased him, he was observed to smoke his pipe vehemently, and send forth short, frequent, and angry puffs; but when pleased, he would inhale the smoke slowly and tranquilly, and emit it in light and placid clouds, and sometimes taking the pipe from his mouth, and letting the fragrant vapour curl about his nose, would gravely nod his head in token of perfect approbation.

From even this strong hold the unlucky Rip was at length routed by his termagant wife, who would suddenly break in upon the tranquillity of the assemblage, call the members all to nought, nor was that august personage, Nicholas Vedder himself, sacred from the daring tongue of this terrible virago, who charged him outright with encouraging her husband in habits of idleness.

Poor Rip was at last reduced almost to despair; and his only alternative to escape from the labour of the farm and the clamour of his wife, was to take gun in hand, and stroll away into the woods. Here he would sometimes seat himself at the foot of a tree, and share the contents of his wallet[11] with Wolf, with whom he sympathised as a fellow sufferer in persecution. "Poor Wolf," he would say, "thy mistress leads thee a dogs' life of it; but never mind, my lad, while I live thou shalt never want a friend to stand by thee!" Wolf would wag his tail, look wistfully in his master's face, and if dogs can feel pity, I verily believe he reciprocated the sentiment with all his heart.

In a long ramble of the kind on a fine autumnal day, Rip had unconsciously scrambled to one of the highest parts of the Kaatskill mountains. He was after his favourite sport of squirrel shooting, and the still solitudes had echoed and re-echoed with the reports of his gun. Panting and fatigued, he threw himself, late in the afternoon, on a green knoll, covered with mountain herbage, that crowned the brow of a precipice. From an opening

11. **wallet:** Early term for a bag used by a traveler for holding provisions.

between the trees, he could overlook all the lower country for many a mile of rich woodland. He saw at a distance the lordly Hudson, far, far below him, moving on its silent but majestic course, the reflection of a purple cloud, or the sail of a lagging bark, here and there sleeping on its glassy bosom, and at last losing itself in the blue highlands.

On the other side he looked down into a deep mountain glen, wild, lonely, and shagged, the bottom filled with fragments from the impending cliffs, and scarcely lighted by the reflected rays of the setting sun. For some time Rip lay musing on this scene, evening was gradually advancing, the mountains began to throw their long blue shadows over the valleys, he saw that it would be dark long before he could reach the village, and he heaved a heavy sigh when he thought of encountering the terrors of Dame Van Winkle.

As he was about to descend, he heard a voice from a distance, hallooing, "Rip Van Winkle! Rip Van Winkle!" He looked around, but could see nothing but a crow winging its solitary flight across the mountain. He thought his fancy must have deceived him, and turned again to descend, when he heard the same cry ring through the still evening air; "Rip Van Winkle! Rip Van Winkle!" – at the same time Wolf bristled up his back, and giving a low growl, skulked to his master's side, looking fearfully down into the glen. Rip now felt a vague apprehension stealing over him; he looked anxiously in the same direction, and perceived a strange figure slowly toiling up the rocks, and bending under the weight of something he carried on his back. He was surprised to see any human being in this lonely and unfrequented place, but supposing it to be some one of the neighbourhood in need of his assistance, he hastened down to yield it.

On nearer approach, he was still more surprised at the singularity of the stranger's appearance. He was a short square built old fellow, with thick bushy hair, and a grizzled beard. His dress was of the antique Dutch fashion – a cloth jerkin[12] strapped round the waist – several pair of breeches, the outer one of ample volume, decorated with rows of buttons down the sides, and bunches at the knees. He bore on his shoulder a stout keg, that seemed full of liquor, and made signs for Rip to approach and assist him with the load. Though rather shy and distrustful of this new acquaintance, Rip complied with his usual alacrity, and mutually relieving each other, they clambered up a narrow gully, apparently the dry bed of a mountain torrent. As they ascended, Rip every now and then heard long rolling peals, like distant thunder, that seemed to issue out of a deep ravine, or rather cleft between lofty rocks, toward which their rugged path conducted. He paused for an instant, but supposing it to be the muttering of one of those transient thunder showers which often take place in mountain heights, he proceeded. Passing through the ravine, they came to a hollow, like a small amphitheatre, surrounded by perpendicular precipices, over the brinks of which impending trees shot their branches, so that you only caught glimpses of the azure sky, and the bright evening cloud. During the whole time, Rip and his companion had laboured on in silence; for though the former marvelled greatly what could be the object of carrying a keg of liquor up this wild mountain,

---

12. **jerkin:** A man's close-fitting jacket, usually made of leather.

yet there was something strange and incomprehensible about the unknown, that inspired awe, and checked familiarity.

On entering the amphitheatre, new objects of wonder presented themselves. On a level spot in the centre was a company of odd-looking personages playing at nine-pins. They were dressed in a quaint, outlandish fashion: some wore short doublets,[13] others jerkins, with long knives in their belts, and most had enormous breeches, of similar style with that of the guide's. Their visages, too, were peculiar: one had a large head, broad face, and small piggish eyes; the face of another seemed to consist entirely of nose, and was surmounted by a white sugarloaf hat, set off with a little red cockstail. They all had beards, of various shapes and colours. There was one who seemed to be the commander. He was a stout old gentleman, with a weather-beaten countenance; he wore a laced doublet, broad belt and hanger,[14] high crowned hat and feather, red stockings, and high heeled shoes, with roses in them. The whole group reminded Rip of the figures in an old Flemish painting, in the parlour of Dominie[15] Van Schaick, the village parson, and which had been brought over from Holland at the time of the settlement.

What seemed particularly odd to Rip, was, that though these folks were evidently amusing themselves, yet they maintained the gravest faces, the most mysterious silence, and were, withal, the most melancholy party of pleasure he had ever witnessed. Nothing interrupted the stillness of the scene, but the noise of the balls, which, whenever they were rolled, echoed along the mountains like rumbling peals of thunder.

As Rip and his companion approached them, they suddenly desisted from their play, and stared at him with such fixed statue-like gaze, and such strange, uncouth, lack lustre countenances, that his heart turned within him, and his knees smote together. His companion now emptied the contents of the keg into large flagons, and made signs to him to wait upon the company. He obeyed with fear and trembling; they quaffed the liquor in profound silence, and then returned to their game.

By degrees, Rip's awe and apprehension subsided. He even ventured, when no eye was fixed upon him, to taste the beverage, which he found had much of the flavour of excellent Hollands.[16] He was naturally a thirsty soul, and was soon tempted to repeat the draught. One taste provoked another, and he reiterated his visits to the flagon so often, that at length his senses were overpowered, his eyes swam in his head, his head gradually declined, and he fell into a deep sleep.

On awaking, he found himself on the green knoll from whence he had first seen the old man of the glen. He rubbed his eyes – it was a bright sunny morning. The birds were hopping and twittering among the bushes, and the eagle was wheeling aloft, and breasting the pure mountain breeze. "Surely," thought Rip, "I have not slept here all night." He recalled the occurrences before he fell asleep. The strange man with the keg of liquor –

13. **doublets:** Padded jackets, commonly worn by men from the fourteenth through the seventeenth centuries.
14. **hanger:** A short sword.
15. **Dominie:** A title for a pastor or clergyman.
16. **Hollands:** Dutch gin.

the mountain ravine – the wild retreat among the rocks – the wo-begone party at nine-pins – the flagon – "Oh! that flagon! that wicked flagon!" thought Rip – "what excuse shall I make to Dame Van Winkle?"

He looked round for his gun, but in place of the clean well-oiled fowling-piece, he found an old firelock lying by him, the barrel encrusted with rust, the lock falling off, and the stock worm-eaten. He now suspected that the grave roysters of the mountain had put a trick upon him, and having dosed him with liquor, had robbed him of his gun. Wolf, too, had disappeared, but he might have strayed away after a squirrel or partridge. He whistled after him, shouted his name, but all in vain; the echoes repeated his whistle and shout, but no dog was to be seen.

He determined to revisit the scene of the last evening's gambol, and if he met with any of the party, to demand his dog and gun. As he arose to walk he found himself stiff in the joints, and wanting in his usual activity. "These mountain beds do not agree with me," thought Rip, "and if this frolick should lay me up with a fit of the rheumatism, I shall have a blessed time with Dame Van Winkle." With some difficulty he got down into the glen: he found the gully up which he and his companion had ascended the preceding evening, but to his astonishment a mountain stream was now foaming down it, leaping from rock to rock, and filling the glen with babbling murmurs. He, however, made shift to scramble up its sides, working his toilsome way through thickets of birch, sassafras, and witch hazle, and sometimes tripped up or entangled by the wild grape vines that twisted their coils and tendrils from tree to tree, and spread a kind of network in his path.

At length he reached to where the ravine had opened through the cliffs, to the amphitheatre; but no traces of such opening remained. The rocks presented a high impenetrable wall, over which the torrent came tumbling in a sheet of feathery foam, and fell into a broad deep basin, black from the shadows of the surrounding forest. Here, then, poor Rip was brought to a stand. He again called and whistled after his dog; he was only answered by the cawing of a flock of idle crows, sporting high in air about a dry tree that overhung a sunny precipice; and who, secure in their elevation, seemed to look down and scoff at the poor man's perplexities. What was to be done? the morning was passing away, and Rip felt famished for his breakfast. He grieved to give up his dog and gun; he dreaded to meet his wife; but it would not do to starve among the mountains. He shook his head, shouldered the rusty firelock, and, with a heart full of trouble and anxiety, turned his steps homeward.

As he approached the village, he met a number of people, but none that he knew, which somewhat surprised him, for he had thought himself acquainted with every one in the country round. Their dress, too, was of a different fashion from that to which he was accustomed. They all stared at him with equal marks of surprise, and whenever they cast eyes upon him, invariably stroked their chins. The constant recurrence of this gesture, induced Rip, involuntarily, to do the same, when, to his astonishment, he found his beard had grown a foot long!

He had now entered the skirts of the village. A troop of strange children ran at his heels, hooting after him, and pointing at his gray beard. The dogs, too, not one of which he recognized for his old acquaintances, barked at him as he passed. The very village seemed altered: it was larger and more populous. There were rows of houses which he had never seen before, and those which had been his familiar haunts had disappeared. Strange names were over the doors – strange faces at the windows – every thing was strange. His mind now began to misgive him, that both he and the world around him were bewitched. Surely this was his native village, which he had left but the day before. There stood the Kaatskill mountains – there ran the silver Hudson at a distance – there was every hill and dale precisely as it had always been – Rip was sorely perplexed – "That flagon last night," thought he, "has addled my poor head sadly!"

It was with some difficulty he found the way to his own house, which he approached with silent awe, expecting every moment to hear the shrill voice of Dame Van Winkle. He found the house gone to decay – the roof fallen in, the windows shattered, and the doors off the hinges. A half starved dog, that looked like Wolf, was skulking about it. Rip called him by name, but the cur snarled, showed his teeth, and passed on. This was an unkind cut indeed – "My very dog," sighed poor Rip, "has forgotten me!"

He entered the house, which, to tell the truth, Dame Van Winkle had always kept in neat order. It was empty, forlorn, and apparently abandoned. This desolateness overcame all his connubial fears – he called loudly for his wife and children – the lonely chambers rung for a moment with his voice, and then all again was silence.

He now hurried forth, and hastened to his old resort, the little village inn – but it too was gone. A large ricketty wooden building stood in its place, with great gaping windows, some of them broken, and mended with old hats and petticoats, and over the door was painted, "The Union Hotel, by Jonathan Doolittle." Instead of the great tree that used to shelter the quiet little Dutch inn of yore, there now was reared a tall naked pole, with something on top that looked like a red night cap,[17] and from it was fluttering a flag, on which was a singular assemblage of stars and stripes – all this was strange and incomprehensible. He recognised on the sign, however, the ruby face of King George, under which he had smoked so many a peaceful pipe, but even this was singularly metamorphosed. The red coat was changed for one of blue and buff,[18] a sword was stuck in the hand instead of a sceptre, the head was decorated with a cocked hat, and underneath was painted in large characters, GENERAL WASHINGTON.

There was, as usual, a crowd of folk about the door, but none that Rip recollected. The very character of the people seemed changed. There was a busy, bustling, disputatious tone about it, instead of the accustomed phlegm and drowsy tranquillity. He looked in vain for the sage Nicholas Vedder, with his broad face, double chin, and fair long pipe, uttering clouds of tobacco smoke instead of idle speeches; or Van Bummel, the schoolmaster, doling forth the contents of an ancient newspaper. In place of these, a lean bilious looking fellow, with his pockets full of handbills, was haranguing vehemently about rights of citizens – election – members of congress – liberty – Bunker's hill –

---

17. **red night cap:** A soft hat used as a republican symbol, often displayed on the top of a pole to signify liberty.
18. **blue and buff:** Colors of the uniforms of American soldiers in the Revolutionary War.

heroes of seventy-six – and other words, that were a perfect Babylonish jargon[19] to the bewildered Van Winkle.

The appearance of Rip, with his long grizzled beard, his rusty fowling piece, his uncouth dress, and the army of women and children that had gathered at his heels, soon attracted the attention of the tavern politicians. They crowded around him, eyeing him from head to foot, with great curiosity. The orator bustled up to him, and drawing him partly aside, inquired "which side he voted?" Rip stared in vacant stupidity. Another short but busy little fellow pulled him by the arm, and raising on tiptoe, inquired in his ear, "whether he was Federal or Democrat."[20] Rip was equally at a loss to comprehend the question; when a knowing, self-important old gentleman, in a sharp cocked hat, made his way through the crowd, putting them to the right and left with his elbows as he passed, and planting himself before Van Winkle, with one arm akimbo, the other resting on his cane, his keen eyes and sharp hat penetrating, as it were, into his very soul, demanded, in an austere tone, "what brought him to the election with a gun on his shoulder, and a mob at his heels, and whether he meant to breed a riot in the village?" "Alas! gentlemen," cried Rip, somewhat dismayed, "I am a poor quiet man, a native of the place, and a loyal subject of the King, God bless him!"

Here a general shout burst from the bystanders – "A tory! a tory! a spy! a refugee! hustle him! away with him!" It was with great difficulty that the self-important man in the cocked hat restored order; and having assumed a tenfold austerity of brow, demanded again of the unknown culprit, what he came there for, and whom he was seeking. The poor man humbly assured them that he meant no harm; but merely came there in search of some of his neighbours, who used to keep about the tavern.

"Well – who are they? – name them."

Rip bethought himself a moment, and inquired, "where's Nicholas Vedder?"

There was a silence for a little while, when an old man replied, in a thin piping voice, "Nicholas Vedder? why he is dead and gone these eighteen years! There was a wooden tombstone in the church yard that used to tell all about him, but that's rotted and gone too."

"Where's Brom Dutcher?"

"Oh he went off to the army in the beginning of the war; some say he was killed at the battle of Stoney-Point – others say he was drowned in a squall, at the foot of Antony's Nose.[21] I don't know – he never came back again."

"Where's Van Bummel, the schoolmaster?"

"He went off to the wars too, was a great militia general, and is now in Congress."

Rip's heart died away, at hearing of these sad changes in his home and friends, and finding himself thus alone in the world. Every answer puzzled him, too, by treating of

---

19. **Babylonish jargon:** Unintelligible language.

20. **Federal or Democrat:** The political parties during Washington's administrations were the Federalists, led by Alexander Hamilton, and the Democratic Republicans, led by Thomas Jefferson.

21. **Stoney-Point . . . Antony's Nose:** Stoney Point, a mountain on the Hudson River, was captured by American troops under the command of General Anthony Wayne during the Revolution. Early in the war, the Americans built Fort Independence just south of Antony's Nose, a mountain overlooking a narrow point of the Hudson River.

such enormous lapses of time, and of matters which he could not understand: war – congress – Stoney-Point; – he had no courage to ask after any more friends, but cried out in despair, "does nobody here know Rip Van Winkle?"

"Oh, Rip Van Winkle!" exclaimed two or three, "Oh, to be sure! that's Rip Van Winkle yonder, leaning against the tree."

Rip looked, and beheld a precise counterpart of himself, as he went up the mountain: apparently as lazy, and certainly as ragged. The poor fellow was now completely confounded. He doubted his own identity, and whether he was himself or another man. In the midst of his bewilderment, the man in the cocked hat demanded who he was, and what was his name?

"God knows," exclaimed he, at his wit's end; "I'm not myself – I'm somebody else – that's me yonder – no – that's somebody else, got into my shoes – I was myself last night, but I fell asleep on the mountain, and they've changed my gun, and every thing's changed, and I'm changed, and I can't tell what's my name, or who I am!"

The bystanders began now to look at each other, nod, wink significantly, and tap their fingers against their foreheads. There was a whisper, also, about securing the gun, and keeping the old fellow from doing mischief. At the very suggestion of which, the self-important man in the cocked hat retired with some precipitation. At this critical moment a fresh likely woman pressed through the throng to get a peep at the gray-bearded man. She had a chubby child in her arms, which, frightened at his looks, began to cry. "Hush, Rip," cried she, "hush, you little fool, the old man won't hurt you." The name of the child, the air of the mother, the tone of her voice, all awakened a train of recollections in his mind. "What is your name, my good woman?" asked he.

"Judith Gardenier."

"And your father's name?"

"Ah, poor man, his name was Rip Van Winkle; it's twenty years since he went away from home with his gun, and never has been heard of since – his dog came home without him; but whether he shot himself, or was carried away by the Indians, nobody can tell. I was then but a little girl."

Rip had but one question more to ask; but he put it with a faltering voice:

"Where's your mother?"

Oh, she too had died but a short time since; she broke a blood vessel in a fit of passion at a New-England pedlar.

There was a drop of comfort, at least, in this intelligence. The honest man could contain himself no longer. He caught his daughter and her child in his arms. "I am your father!" cried he – "Young Rip Van Winkle once – old Rip Van Winkle now! – Does nobody know poor Rip Van Winkle!"

All stood amazed, until an old woman, tottering out from among the crowd, put her hand to her brow, and peering under it in his face for a moment, exclaimed, "Sure enough! it is Rip Van Winkle – it is himself. Welcome home again, old neighbour – Why, where have you been these twenty long years?"

Rip's story was soon told, for the whole twenty years had been to him but as one night. The neighbours stared when they heard it; some were seen to wink at each other, and put their tongues in their cheeks; and the self-important man in the cocked hat, who, when the alarm was over, had returned to the field, screwed down the corners of his mouth, and shook his head – upon which there was a general shaking of the head throughout the assemblage.

It was determined, however, to take the opinion of old Peter Vanderdonk, who was seen slowly advancing up the road. He was a descendant of the historian of that name, who wrote one of the earliest accounts of the province.[22] Peter was the most ancient inhabitant of the village, and well versed in all the wonderful events and traditions of the neighbourhood. He recollected Rip at once, and corroborated his story in the most satisfactory manner. He assured the company that it was a fact, handed down from his ancestor the historian, that the Kaatskill mountains had always been haunted by strange beings. That it was affirmed that the great Hendrick Hudson,[23] the first discoverer of the river and country, kept a kind of vigil there every twenty years, with his crew of the Half-moon, being permitted in this way to revisit the scenes of his enterprize, and keep a guardian eye upon the river, and the great city called by his name. That his father had once seen them in their old Dutch dresses playing at nine pins in a hollow of the mountain; and that he himself had heard, one summer afternoon, the sound of their balls, like long peals of thunder.

To make a long story short, the company broke up, and returned to the more important concerns of the election. Rip's daughter took him home to live with her; she had a snug, well-furnished house, and a stout cheery farmer for a husband, whom Rip recollected for one of the urchins that used to climb upon his back. As to Rip's son and heir, who was the ditto of himself, seen leaning against the tree, he was employed to work on the farm; but evinced an hereditary disposition to attend to any thing else but his business.

Rip now resumed his old walks and habits; he soon found many of his former cronies, though all rather the worse for the wear and tear of time; and preferred making friends among the rising generation, with whom he soon grew into great favour.

Having nothing to do at home, and being arrived at that happy age when a man can do nothing with impunity, he took his place once more on the bench, at the inn door, and was reverenced as one of the patriarchs of the village, and a chronicle of the old times "before the war." It was some time before he could get into the regular track of gossip, or could be made to comprehend the strange events that had taken place during his torpor. How that there had been a revolutionary war – that the country had thrown off the yoke of old England – and that, instead of being a subject of his Majesty George the Third, he was now a free citizen of the United States. Rip, in fact, was no politician; the changes of states and empires made but little impression on him. But there was one species of despotism under which he had long groaned, and that was – petticoat government. Happily, that was at an end; he had got his neck out of the yoke of matrimony, and could go

22. **historian . . . province:** Adriaen van der Donk (1620-1655?), author of *Description of New Netherland* (1655).

23. **Hendrick Hudson:** Henry Hudson (1565-1611), English navigator who explored northeastern North America for the Dutch.

in and out whenever he pleased, without dreading the tyranny of Dame Van Winkle. Whenever her name was mentioned, however, he shook his head, shrugged his shoulders, and cast up his eyes; which might pass either for an expression of resignation to his fate, or joy at his deliverance.

He used to tell his story to every stranger that arrived at Mr. Doolittle's hotel. He was observed, at first, to vary on some points every time he told it, which was, doubtless, owing to his having so recently awaked. It at last settled down precisely to the tale I have related, and not a man, woman, or child in the neighbourhood, but knew it by heart. Some always pretended to doubt the reality of it, and insisted that Rip had been out of his head, and that this was one point on which he always remained flighty. The old Dutch inhabitants, however, almost universally gave it full credit. Even to this day they never hear a thunder storm of a summer afternoon, about the Kaatskill, but they say Hendrick Hudson and his crew are at their game of nine pins; and it is a common wish of all henpecked husbands in the neighbourhood, when life hangs heavy on their hands, that they might have a quieting draught out of Rip Van Winkle's flagon.

Note

The foregoing tale, one would suspect, had been suggested to Mr. Knickerbocker by a little German superstition about Charles V.[24] and the Kypphauser mountain; the subjoined note, however, which he had appended to the tale, shows that it is an absolute fact, narrated with his usual fidelity:

"The story of Rip Van Winkle may seem incredible to many, but nevertheless I give it my full belief, for I know the vicinity of our old Dutch settlements to have been very subject to marvellous events and appearances. Indeed, I have heard many stranger stories than this, in the villages along the Hudson; all of which were too well authenticated to admit of a doubt. I have even talked with Rip Van Winkle myself, who, when last I saw him, was a very venerable old man, and so perfectly rational and consistent on every other point, that I think no conscientious person could refuse to take this into the bargain; nay, I have seen a certificate on the subject taken before a country justice, and signed with a cross, in the justice's own hand writing. The story, therefore, is beyond the possibility of doubt.

D. K."

[1819]

---

24. **German superstition about Charles V.:** Irving later altered this to "The Emperor Frederick *der Rothbart*," the Holy Roman Emperor Frederick Barbarossa (1152–1190), who in legend was said to be sleeping in a mountain cave awaiting his country's rise to its former glory. Irving thus hinted at his indebtedness to German folklore but concealed his primary source for "Rip Van Winkle," the story of Peter Klaus in a collection of tales by J. C. C. N. Otmar.

Catharine Maria Sedgwick

[1789-1867]

Catharine Maria Sedgwick was born in Stockbridge, Massachusetts, on December 28, 1789, the sixth of seven surviving children of Theodore and Pamela Dwight Sedgwick. Her mother was descended from a distinguished Connecticut family, and her father rose from a modest background to considerable political prominence. A staunch Federalist, he served in the state legislature, as a member of Congress and the Speaker of the House of Representatives, and on the Massachusetts Supreme Court. Sedgwick received little education at home and only an adequate formal education, first at a grammar school and then a finishing school in Boston. But she was an avid reader, mostly of novels, and her father was fond of reading aloud to the family in the evening, so Sedgwick was also exposed to passages from Shakespeare's plays and other standard works of English and Continental literature. As early as 1805, Sedgwick began to divide her time between Stockbridge and the homes of her married siblings in Albany, New York, and New York City, where she spent an increasing amount of time after the death of her mother in 1807 and her father in 1813. Her substantial inheritances freed Sedgwick to travel, to read and study, and ultimately to pursue her interest in writing, which at the time promised few financial rewards.

Catharine Maria Sedgwick

This engraving was based on a portrait painted by Charles C. Ingham around 1830, by which time Sedgwick was one of the most popular and respected authors in the United States. The Irish-born Ingham moved to New York in 1816 and soon became known as the city's foremost "ladies' painter," partly because men were thought to be too busy to submit to the numerous sittings that his painstaking technique required.

Sedgwick's early works were inspired by both nationalistic sentiments and religious values. In 1821, she left the Calvinistic Congregational Church, in which she was raised, to join the liberal Unitarian Meeting House in New York City. Soon after that, she wrote "Mary Hollis," a tract denouncing religious intolerance that Sedgwick swiftly expanded into her first novel, *A New-England Tale* (1822). The novel was also a direct response to calls for a native American literature; in a lengthy review, James Fenimore Cooper praised Sedgwick for her realistic depiction "of the multitude of local peculiarities, which form our distinctive features." Similar qualities distinguished her second novel, *Redwood* (1824), which Sedgwick dedicated to William Cullen Bryant. The popularity of that novel created strong demand for her work among the editors of periodicals and annuals like *The Atlantic Souvenir*, where the first of her more than one hundred sketches and stories appeared in 1826. Always interested in American history, which was viewed by many critics as a major resource for native writers, Sedgwick set her next and most famous novel, *Hope Leslie* (1827), in seventeenth century New England. In it, Sedgwick sharply revised conventional histories by calling into question the Puritans' harsh treatment of the Indians. She explored a more inspiring period of American history in *The Linwoods* (1835), a novel set during the Revolutionary War in which Sedgwick mingled fictional characters and historical figures like General Lafayette and George Washington. Turning from American history to the more immediate religious and social concerns of her middle-class audience, Sedgwick then wrote a series of domestic fictions

bedfordstmartins.com/americanlit *for research links on Sedgwick* that were among the most widely read of all her many books: *Home: Scenes and Character Illustrating Christian Truth* (1835), *The Poor Rich Man and the Rich Poor Man* (1836), and *Live and Let Live; or, Domestic Service Illustrated* (1837).

During the final three decades of her life, Sedgwick increasingly devoted herself to charitable work and teaching, both in various Sunday schools and in her sister-in-law's Young Ladies' School. Nonetheless, she remained a literary celebrity, whose earlier works were often reprinted. She continued to write, especially works for children, but also dozens of articles, sketches, and stories for a diverse group of periodicals, from *Godey's Lady's Book* to the *United States Magazine and Democratic Review.* Although she was less engaged in reform issues than some other women writers of the period, Sedgwick was deeply involved in improving prison conditions and sympathetic to causes like abolition and women's rights. In her final novel, *Married or Single?* (1857), Sedgwick thus supported what was then the unconventional and even radical idea that not all women must be wives and mothers. Sedgwick, who never married, at once relished her own autonomy and enjoyed a rich domestic life at the center of her siblings' growing families. She spent the last years of her life living with a niece in Boston, where Sedgwick died on July 31, 1867.

. . . in a kind and playful humour she has penetrated into all the hiding places of the heart; and she has brought them before us in pictures as simply beautiful as nature himself.
– Lydia Maria Child

Sedgwick's "Cacoethes Scribendi." This story was first published in *The Atlantic Souvenir*, an annual gift book established in 1826. Such annuals, designed to be given as holiday gifts, had been popular in Europe since early in the nineteenth century, but the *Souvenir* was the first to be published in the United States. In the preface to the 1826 edition, its editor explained:

> The publishers of the present volume, present to the public a work, which although on a plan by no means novel in other countries, has never yet been introduced among us. Nothing would seem more naturally to suggest itself, as one of those marks of remembrance and affection, which old custom has associated with the gaiety of Christmas, than a little volume of lighter literature, adorned with beautiful specimens of art.

By the time "Cacoethes Scribendi" appeared in the 1830 edition, the *Souvenir* had become an elaborate production, with twelve illustrations accompanying more than 350 pages of poems, sketches, and stories. Although most of the works were published anonymously, those by particularly notable writers were signed or otherwise identified. Sedgwick's story was identified as "By the Author of Hope Leslie," the title of the popular novel she had published in 1827. "Cacoethes Scribendi," a Latin phrase meaning the incurable disease of writing, suggests the satiric intent of the story, written at a time when few women wrote satire. Although by 1830 the prolific Sedgwick had become one of the most popular writers in the country, much of the satire in her story seems directed at women writers and their productions. Indeed, despite their increasing success in the literary marketplace, many women writers of the period either felt ambivalent about writing as a profession or simply felt obliged to affirm more traditional female roles, as Sedgwick may seem to do in "Cacoethes Scribendi." The text is taken from its first printing in *The Atlantic Souvenir* (1830).

CACOETHES SCRIBENDI[1]

Glory and gain the industrious tribe provoke.
Pope[2]

The little secluded and quiet village of H. lies at no great distance from our 'literary emporium.'[3] It was never remarked or remarkable for any thing, save one mournful pre-eminence, to those who sojourned within its borders – it was duller even than common villages. The young men of the better class all emigrated.[4] The most daring spirits adventured on the sea. Some went to Boston; some to the south; and some to the west; and left a community of women who lived like nuns, with the advantage of more liberty and fresh air, but without the consolation and excitement of a religious vow. Literally, there was not a single young gentleman in the village – nothing in manly shape to which these desperate circumstances could give the form and quality and use of a beau.[5] Some dashing city blades, who once strayed from the turnpike to this sequestered spot, averred that the girls stared at them as if, like Miranda, they would have exclaimed –

'What is't? a spirit?
Lord, how it looks about! Believe me, sir,
It carries a brave form: – But 'tis a spirit.'[6]

A peculiar fatality hung over this devoted place. If death seized on either head of a family, he was sure to take the husband; every woman in H. was a widow or maiden; and it is a sad fact, that when the holiest office of the church was celebrated, they were compelled to borrow deacons from an adjacent village. But, incredible as it may be, there was no great diminution of happiness in consequences of the absence of the nobler sex. Mothers were occupied with their children and housewifery, and the young ladies read their books with as much interest as if they had lovers to discuss them with, and worked

1. **Cacoethes Scribendi:** A familiar Latin phrase variously translated as the incurable disease of writing, the incurable passion for writing, or an incurable itch to write. The phrase was used by several Roman authors, notably the satirist Juvenal (60-140), who famously observed: *Tenet insanabile multos scribendi cacoethes et aegro in corde senescit* (Many suffer from the incurable disease of writing, and it wastes their hearts).
2. **Glory . . . provoke:** From *The Dunciad*, 2.29, a mock epic about writers and the business of writing, by the English poet Alexander Pope (1688-1744).
3. **literary emporium:** Until the 1840s, Boston was the literary center of the United States.
4. **emigrated:** Common usage for people who left their birthplaces to seek fortunes elsewhere, as many of the young men in New England villages did during the early decades of the nineteenth century.
5. **beau:** Early term for a male admirer.
6. **What . . . spirit:** Shakespeare's *The Tempest*, 1.2.411-13. The lines are spoken by Miranda, the daughter of Prospero, who has never seen any man other than her father and his servant, Caliban.

their frills and capes as diligently, and wore them as complacently, as if they were to be seen by manly eyes. Never were there pleasanter gatherings or parties (for that was the word even in their nomenclature) than those of the young girls of H. There was no mincing – no affectation – no hope of passing for what they were not – no envy of the pretty and fortunate – no insolent triumph over the plain and demure and neglected, – but all was good will and good humour. They were a pretty circle of girls – a garland of bright fresh flowers. Never were there more sparkling glances, – never sweeter smiles – nor more of them. Their present was all health and cheerfulness; and their future, not the gloomy perspective of dreary singleness, for somewhere in the passage of life they were sure to be mated. Most of the young men who had abandoned their native soil, as soon as they found themselves *getting along*, loyally returned to lay their fortunes at the feet of the companions of their childhood.

The girls made occasional visits to Boston, and occasional journeys to various parts of the country, for they were all enterprising and independent, and had the characteristic New England avidity for seizing a 'privilege;' and in these various ways, to borrow a phrase of their good grandames, 'a door was opened for them,' and in due time they fulfilled the destiny of women.

We spoke strictly, and à la lettre,[7] when we said that in the village of H. there was not a single *beau*. But on the outskirts of the town, at a pleasant farm, embracing hill and valley, upland and meadow land; in a neat house, looking to the south, with true economy of sunshine and comfort, and overlooking the prettiest winding stream that ever sent up its sparkling beauty to the eye, and flanked on the north by a rich maple grove, beautiful in spring and summer, and glorious in autumn, and the kindest defence in winter; – on this farm and in this house dwelt a youth, to fame unknown,[8] but known and loved by every inhabitant of H., old and young, grave and gay, lively and severe. Ralph Hepburn was one of nature's favourites. He had a figure that would have adorned courts and cities; and a face that adorned human nature, for it was full of good humour, kindheartedness, spirit, and intelligence; and driving the plough or wielding the scythe, his cheek flushed with manly and profitable exercise, he looked as if he had been moulded in a poet's fancy – as farmers look in Georgics and Pastorals.[9] His gifts were by no means all external. He wrote verses in every album in the village, and very pretty album verses they were, and numerous too – for the number of albums was equivalent to the whole female population. He was admirable at pencil sketches; and once with a little paint, the refuse of a house painting, he achieved an admirable portrait of his grandmother and her cat. There was, to be sure, a striking likeness between the two figures, but he was limited to the same colours for both; and besides, it was not out of

7. **à la lettre:** Literally (French).
8. **a youth, to fame unknown:** A reference to the opening lines of the epitaph at the end of "Elegy Written in a Country Churchyard" by the English poet Thomas Gray (1716–1771): "Here rests his head upon the lap of Earth / A youth to Fortune and to Fame unknown" (ll. 117–18).
9. **Georgics and Pastorals:** Poems celebrating rural life, notably those of the Roman poet Virgil (70–19 BCE), whose pastoral *Eclogues* and *Georgics* were widely available in popular translations in the eighteenth and nineteenth century.

nature, for the old lady and her cat had purred together in the chimney corner, till their physiognomies bore an obvious resemblance to each other. Ralph had a talent for music too. His voice was the sweetest of all the Sunday choir, and one would have fancied, from the bright eyes that were turned on him from the long line and double lines of treble and counter singers, that Ralph Hepburn was a note book,[10] or that the girls listened with their eyes as well as their ears. Ralph did not restrict himself to psalmody.[11] He had an ear so exquisitely susceptible to the 'touches of sweet harmony,' that he discovered, by the stroke of his axe, the musical capacities of certain species of wood, and he made himself a violin of chesnut, and drew strains from it, that if they could not create a soul under the ribs of death,[12] could make the prettiest feet and the lightest hearts dance, an achievement far more to Ralph's taste than the aforesaid miracle. In short, it seemed as if nature, in her love of compensation, had showered on Ralph all the gifts that are usually diffused through a community of beaux. Yet Ralph was no prodigy; none of his talents were in excess, but all in moderate degree. No genius was ever so good humoured, so useful, so practical; and though, in his small and modest way, a Crichton,[13] he was not, like most universal geniuses, good for nothing for any particular office in life. His farm was not a pattern farm – a prize farm for an agricultural society, but in wonderful order considering – his miscellaneous pursuits. He was the delight of his grandfather for his sagacity in hunting bees – the old man's favourite, in truth his only pursuit. He was so skilled in woodcraft that the report of his gun was as certain a signal of death as the tolling of a church bell. The fish always caught as his bait. He manufactured half his farming utensils, improved upon old inventions, and struck out some new ones; tamed partridges – the most untameable of all the feathered tribe; domesticated squirrels; rivalled Scheherazade[14] herself in telling stories, strange and long – the latter quality being essential at a country fireside; and, in short, Ralph made a perpetual holiday of a life of labour.

Every girl in the village street knew when Ralph's wagon or sleigh traversed it; indeed, there was scarcely a house to which the horses did not, as if by instinct, turn up while their master greeted its fair tenants. This state of affairs had continued for two winters and two summers since Ralph came to his majority and, by the death of his father, to the sole proprietorship of the 'Hepburn farm,' – the name his patrimonial acres had obtained from the singular circumstance (in our *moving* country) of their having remained in the same family for four generations. Never was the matrimonial destiny of a young lord, or heir just come to his estate, more thoroughly canvassed than young Hepburn's by mothers, aunts, daughters, and nieces. But Ralph, perhaps from

10. **note book:** A book of music printed with large notes, designed to be shared by several singers.
11. **psalmody:** The singing of psalms and other sacred works.
12. **create a soul under the ribs of death:** A reference to *Comus* by the English poet John Milton (1608-1674): "I was all ear, / And took in strains that might create a soul / Under the ribs of Death" (ll. 560-62).
13. **Crichton:** Born in Scotland, James Crichton (c. 1560-1582) went to St. Andrews University at the age of ten and was universally recognized as a genius.
14. **Scheherazade:** The storyteller in *The Thousand and One Nights*, anonymous Arabic tales first translated into English in the eighteenth century.

sheer good heartedness, seemed reluctant to give to one the heart that diffused rays of sunshine through the whole village.

With all decent people he eschewed the doctrines of a certain erratic female lecturer on the odious monopoly of marriage,[15] yet Ralph, like a tender hearted judge, hesitated to place on a single brow the crown matrimonial which so many deserved, and which, though Ralph was far enough from a coxcomb,[16] he could not but see so many coveted.

Whether our hero perceived that his mind was becoming elated or distracted with this general favour, or that he observed a dawning of rivalry among the fair competitors, or whatever was the cause, the fact was, that he by degrees circumscribed his visits, and finally concentrated them in the family of his aunt Courland.

Mrs. Courland was a widow, and Ralph was the kindest of nephews to her, and the kindest of cousins to her children. To their mother he seemed their guardian angel. That the five lawless, daring little urchins did not drown themselves when they were swimming, nor shoot themselves when they were shooting, was, in her eyes, Ralph's merit; and then 'he was so attentive to Alice, her only daughter – a brother could not be kinder.' But who would not be kind to Alice? she was a sweet girl of seventeen, not beautiful, not handsome perhaps, – but pretty enough – with soft hazel eyes, a profusion of light brown hair, always in the neatest trim, and a mouth that could not but be lovely and loveable, for all kind and tender affections were playing about it. Though Alice was the only daughter of a doting mother, the only sister of five loving boys, the only niece of three single, fond aunts, and, last and greatest, the only cousin of our only beau, Ralph Hepburn, no girl of seventeen was ever more disinterested, unassuming, unostentatious, and unspoiled. Ralph and Alice had always lived on terms of cousinly affection – an affection of a neutral tint that they never thought of being shaded into the deep dye of a more tender passion. Ralph rendered her all cousinly offices. If he had twenty damsels to escort, not an uncommon case, he never forgot Alice. When he returned from any little excursion, he always brought some graceful offering to Alice.

He had lately paid a visit to Boston. It was at the season of the periodical inundation of annuals.[17] He brought two of the prettiest to Alice. Ah! little did she think they were to prove Pandora's box to her. Poor simple girl! she sat down to read them, as if an annual were meant to be read, and she was honestly interested and charmed. Her mother observed her delight. "What have you there, Alice?" she asked. "Oh the prettiest story, mamma! – two such tried faithful lovers, and married at last! It ends beautifully: I hate love stories that don't end in marriage."

"And so do I, Alice," exclaimed Ralph, who entered at the moment, and for the first time Alice felt her cheeks tingle at his approach. He had brought a basket, containing a

---

15. **doctrines . . . of marriage:** In a series of lectures delivered in the late 1820s, the Scottish-born reformer Frances Wright (1795–1852) scandalized American audiences by advocating abolition, atheism, sexual freedom, and women's rights.
16. **coxcomb:** Early term for a vain or conceited man.
17. **periodical inundation of annuals:** Like the volume in which Sedgwick's story appeared, annuals were handsomely bound and illustrated collections of poetry, sketches, and stories published at the end of the year and designed to be given as holiday gifts.

choice plant he had obtained for her, and she laid down the annual and went with him to the garden to see it set by his own hand.

Mrs. Courland seized upon the annual with avidity. She had imbibed a literary taste in Boston, where the best and happiest years of her life were passed. She had some literary ambition too. She read the North American Review[18] from beginning to end, and she fancied no conversation could be sensible or improving that was not about books. But she had been effectually prevented, by the necessities of a narrow income, and by the unceasing wants of five teasing boys, from indulging her literary inclinations; for Mrs. Courland, like all New England women, had been taught to consider domestic duties as the first temporal duties of her sex. She had recently seen some of the native productions with which the press is daily teeming, and which certainly have a tendency to dispel our early illusions about the craft of authorship. She had even felt some obscure intimations, within her secret soul, that she might herself become an author. The annual was destined to fix her fate. She opened it – the publisher had written the names of the authors of the anonymous pieces against their productions. Among them she found some of the familiar friends of her childhood and youth.

If, by a sudden gift of second sight, she had seen them enthroned as kings and queens, she would not have been more astonished. She turned to their pieces, and read them, as perchance no one else ever did, from beginning to end – faithfully. Not a sentence – a sentence! not a word was skipped. She paused to consider commas, colons, and dashes. All the art and magic of authorship were made level to her comprehension, and when she closed the book, she *felt a call* to become an author, and before she retired to bed she obeyed the call, as if it had been, in truth, a divinity stirring within her. In the morning she presented an article to *her* public, consisting of her own family and a few select friends. All applauded, and every voice, save one, was unanimous for publication – that one was Alice. She was a modest, prudent girl; she feared failure, and feared notoriety still more. Her mother laughed at her childish scruples. The piece was sent off, and in due time graced the pages of an annual. Mrs. Courland's fate was now decided. She had, to use her own phrase, started in the career of letters, and she was no Atalanta[19] to be seduced from her straight onward way. She was a social, sympathetic, good hearted creature too, and she could not bear to go forth in the golden field to reap alone.

She was, besides, a prudent woman, as most of her countrywomen are, and the little pecuniary equivalent for this delightful exercise of talents was not overlooked. Mrs. Courland, as we have somewhere said, had three single sisters – worthy women they were – but nobody ever dreamed of their taking to authorship. She, however, held them all in sisterly estimation. Their talents were magnified as the talents of persons who live in a circumscribed sphere are apt to be, particularly if seen through the dilating medium of affection.

---

18. **North American Review:** Established in Boston in 1815, this influential journal included reviews of current European and American literature as well as articles on politics, economics, and religion.
19. **Atalanta:** A huntress in Greek mythology who vowed to marry only the man who could beat her in a footrace. Hippomenes won the race by dropping three golden apples, which Atalanta stopped to retrieve.

Miss Anne, the oldest, was fond of flowers, a successful cultivator, and a diligent student of the science of botany. All this taste and knowledge, Mrs. Courland thought, might be turned to excellent account; and she persuaded Miss Anne to write a little book entitled 'Familiar Dialogues on Botany.' The second sister, Miss Ruth, had a turn for education ('bachelor's wives and maid's children are always well taught'), and Miss Ruth undertook a popular treatise on that subject. Miss Sally, the youngest, was the saint of the family, and she doubted about the propriety of a literary occupation, till her scruples were overcome by the fortunate suggestion that her coup d'essai[20] should be a Saturday night book entitled 'Solemn Hours,' – and solemn hours they were to their unhappy readers. Mrs. Courland next besieged her old mother. "You know, mamma," she said, "you have such a precious fund of anecdotes of the revolution and the French war, and you talk just like the 'Annals of the Parish,'[21] and I am certain you can write a book fully as good."

"My child, you are distracted! I write a dreadful poor hand, and I never learned to spell – no girls did in my time."

"Spell! that is not of the least consequence – the printers correct the spelling."

But the honest old lady would not be tempted on the crusade, and her daughter consoled herself with the reflection that if she would not write, she was an admirable subject to be written about, and her diligent fingers worked off three distinct stories in which the old lady figured.

Mrs. Courland's ambition, of course, embraced within its widening circle her favourite nephew Ralph. She had always thought him a genius, and genius in her estimation was the philosopher's stone.[22] In his youth she had laboured to persuade his father to send him to Cambridge,[23] but the old man uniformly replied that Ralph 'was a smart lad on the farm, and steady, and by that he knew he was no genius.' As Ralph's character was developed, and talent after talent broke forth, his aunt renewed her lamentations over his ignoble destiny. That Ralph was useful, good, and happy – the most difficult and rare results achieved in life – was nothing, so long as he was but a farmer in H. Once she did half persuade him to turn painter, but his good sense and filial duty triumphed over her eloquence, and suppressed the hankerings after distinction that are innate in every human breast, from the little ragged chimneysweep that hopes to be a *boss*,[24] to the political aspirant whose bright goal is the presidential chair.

Now Mrs. Courland fancied Ralph might climb the steep of fame without quitting his farm; occasional authorship was compatible with his vocation. But alas! she could not persuade Ralph to pluck the laurels that she saw ready grown to his hand. She was not

---

20. **coup d'essai**: A first attempt (French).
21. **'Annals of the Parish'**: A common title for books that chronicled local events during the term of a pastor or parish priest. All of the titles suggested in this passage were common topics of books published in the early nineteenth century.
22. **philosopher's stone**: In the medieval science of alchemy, the elusive philosopher's stone was thought to be the substance that could turn metal into gold.
23. **Cambridge**: Harvard College in Cambridge, Massachusetts.
24. ***boss***: Derived from the Dutch word *baas*, meaning "master," the term *boss* had only recently begun to be used for the person in charge of workers or an organization.

offended, for she was the best natured woman in the world, but she heartily pitied him, and seldom mentioned his name without repeating that stanza of Gray's, inspired for the consolation of hopeless obscurity:

> 'Full many a gem of purest ray serene,' &c.[25]

Poor Alice's sorrows we have reserved to the last, for they were heaviest. 'Alice,' her mother said, 'was gifted; she was well educated, well informed; she was every thing necessary to be an author.' But Alice resisted; and, though the gentlest, most complying of all good daughters, she would have resisted to the death – she would as soon have stood in a pillory as appeared in print. Her mother, Mrs. Courland, was not an obstinate woman, and gave up in despair. But still our poor heroine was destined to be the victim of this *cacoethes scribendi*; for Mrs. Courland divided the world into two classes, or rather parts – authors and subjects for authors; the one active, the other passive. At first blush one would have thought the village of H. rather a barren field for such a reaper as Mrs. Courland, but her zeal and indefatigableness worked wonders. She converted the stern scholastic divine of H. into as much of a La Roche[26] as she could describe; a tall wrinkled bony old woman, who reminded her of Meg Merrilies,[27] sat for a witch; the school master for an Ichabod Crane;[28] a poor half witted boy was made to utter as much pathos and sentiment and wit as she could put into his lips; and a crazy vagrant was a God-send to her. Then every 'wide spreading elm,' 'blasted pine,' or 'gnarled oak,'[29] flourished on her pages. The village church and school house stood there according to their actual dimensions. One old *pilgrim* house was as prolific as haunted tower or ruined abbey. It was surveyed outside, ransacked inside, and again made habitable for the reimbodied spirits of its founders.

The most kind hearted of women, Mrs. Courland's interests came to be so at variance with the prosperity of the little community of H., that a sudden calamity, a death, a funeral, were fortunate events to her. To do her justice she felt them in a twofold capacity. She wept as a woman, and exulted as an author. The days of the calamities of authors have passed by. We have all wept over Otway and shivered at the thought of Tasso.[30] But times are changed. The lean sheaf is devouring the full one.[31] A new class of

---

25. **'Full . . . serene,' &c.:** From Gray's "Elegy Written in a Country Churchyard" (see note 8).
26. **La Roche:** Protestant clergyman in a story of that title by the Scottish writer Henry MacKenzie (1745–1831).
27. **Meg Merrilies:** A gypsy nurse in the popular novel *Guy Mannering* by the Scottish writer Sir Walter Scott (1771–1832).
28. **Ichabod Crane:** The hapless schoolteacher in "The Legend of Sleepy Hollow," by Washington Irving (1783–1859).
29. **wide spreading elm . . . gnarled oak:** Examples of overused phrases in the popular literature of the period.
30. **Otway . . . Tasso:** Never able to earn a living from his writing, the English dramatist Thomas Otway (1652–1685) lived in extreme poverty and died at the age of thirty-four. The Italian poet Torquato Tasso (1544–1595) also lived a difficult life of poverty and illness.
31. **The lean sheaf . . . full one:** In Genesis 41:6–7, the Pharaoh has a dream that is interpreted by Jacob to mean that seven years of plenty in Egypt will be followed by seven years of famine: "And, behold, seven thin ears and blasted with the east wind sprung up after them. And the seven thin ears devoured the seven rank and full ears."

sufferers has arisen, and there is nothing more touching in all the memoirs Mr. D'Israeli[32] has collected, than the trials of poor Alice, tragi-comic though they were. Mrs. Courland's new passion ran most naturally in the worn channel of maternal affection. Her boys were too purely boys for her art – but Alice, her sweet Alice, was preeminently lovely in the new light in which she now placed every object. Not an incident of her life but was inscribed on her mother's memory, and thence transferred to her pages, by way of precept, or example, or pathetic or ludicrous circumstance. She regretted now, for the first time, that Alice had no lover whom she might introduce among her dramatis personae.[33] Once her thoughts did glance on Ralph, but she had not quite merged the woman in the author; she knew instinctively that Alice would be particularly offended at being thus paired with Ralph. But Alice's *public life* was not limited to her mother's productions. She was the darling niece of her three aunts. She had studied botany with the eldest, and Miss Anne had recorded in her private diary all her favourite's clever remarks during their progress in the science. This diary was now a mine of gold to her, and faithfully worked up for a circulating medium. But, most trying of all to poor Alice, was the attitude in which she appeared in her aunt Sally's 'solemn hours.' Every aspiration of piety to which her young lips had given utterance was there *printed*. She felt as if she were condemned to say her prayers in the market place. Every act of kindness, every deed of charity, she had ever performed, were produced to the public. Alice would have been consoled if she had known how small that public was; but, as it was, she felt like a modest country girl when she first enters an apartment hung on every side with mirrors, when, shrinking from observation, she sees in every direction her image multiplied and often distorted; for, notwithstanding Alice's dutiful respect for her good aunts, and her consciousness of their affectionate intentions, she could not but perceive that they were unskilled painters. She grew afraid to speak or to act, and from being the most artless, frank, and, at home, social little creature in the world, she became as silent and as stiff as a statue. And, in the circle of her young associates, her natural gaiety was constantly checked by their winks and smiles, and broader allusions to her multiplied portraits; for they had instantly recognized them through the thin veil of feigned names of persons and places. They called her a blue stocking[34] too; for they had the vulgar notion that every body must be tinged that lived under the same roof with an author. Our poor victim was afraid to speak of a book – worse than that, she was afraid to touch one, and the last Waverley novel[35] actually lay in the house a month before she opened it. She avoided wearing even a blue ribbon, as fearfully as a forsaken damsel shuns the colour of green.

---

32. **Mr. D'Israeli:** Isaac D'Israeli (1766–1848), English author of popular collections of anecdotes about writers, like *Curiosities of Literature* (1849) and *Calamities and Quarrels of Authors* (1859).
33. **dramatis personae:** Cast of characters (Latin).
34. **blue stocking:** A denigrating term commonly used in the nineteenth century to describe a woman with literary or intellectual interests.
35. **Waverley novel:** *Waverley* (1814) was the first novel by the Scottish writer Sir Walter Scott (1771–1832). The enormously popular novels he subsequently published were frequently identified as "By the Author of Waverley" and often referred to collectively as Waverley novels.

It was during the height of this literary fever in the Courland family, that Ralph Hepburn, as has been mentioned, concentrated all his visiting there. He was of a compassionate disposition, and he knew Alice was, unless relieved by him, in solitary possession of their once social parlour, while her mother and aunts were driving their quills in their several apartments.

Oh! what a changed place was that parlour! Not the tower of Babel,[36] after the builders had forsaken it, exhibited a sadder reverse; not a Lancaster school,[37] when the boys have left it, a more striking contrast. Mrs. Courland and her sisters were all 'talking women,' and too generous to encroach on one another's rights and happiness. They had acquired the power to hear and speak simultaneously. Their parlour was the general gathering place, a sort of village exchange, where all the innocent gossips, old and young, met together. 'There are tongues in trees,'[38] and surely there seemed to be tongues in the very walls of that vocal parlour. Every thing there had a social aspect. There was something agreeable and conversable in the litter of netting and knitting work, of sewing implements, and all the signs and shows of happy female occupation.

Now, all was as orderly as a town drawing room in company hours. Not a sound was heard there save Ralph's and Alice's voices, mingling in soft and suppressed murmurs, as if afraid of breaking the chain of their aunt's ideas, or, perchance, of too rudely jarring a tenderer chain. One evening, after tea, Mrs. Courland remained with her daughter, instead of retiring, as usual, to her writing desk. "Alice, my dear," said the good mother, "I have noticed for a few days past that you look out of spirits. You will listen to nothing I say on that subject; but if you would try it, my dear, if you would only try it, you would find there is nothing so tranquillizing as the occupation of writing."

"I shall never try it, mamma."

"You are afraid of being called a blue stocking. Ah! Ralph, how are you?" Ralph entered at this moment. "Ralph, tell me honestly, do you not think it a weakness in Alice to be so afraid of blue stockings?"

"It would be a pity, aunt, to put blue stockings on such pretty feet as Alice's."

Alice blushed and smiled, and her mother said – "Nonsense, Ralph; you should bear in mind the celebrated saying of the Edinburgh wit[39] – 'no matter how blue the stockings are, if the petticoats are long enough to hide them.'"

"Hide Alice's feet! Oh aunt, worse and worse!"

"Better hide her feet, Ralph, than her talents – that is a sin for which both she and you will have to answer. Oh! you and Alice need not exchange such significant glances! You are doing yourselves and the public injustice, and you have no idea how easy writing is."

---

36. **tower of Babel:** In Genesis 11:1-9, the townspeople of Babel attempt to build a tower to reach heaven. God thwarts the plan by causing the languages of the builders to be mutually incomprehensible.
37. **Lancaster school:** Joseph Lancaster (1778-1838), an English educator, established schools in which older students under adult supervision were responsible for monitoring and teaching the younger students. The system was widely adopted in common schools in the United States.
38. **There . . . trees:** From Shakespeare's *As You Like It*, 2.1.15-17: "And this our life exempt from public haunt / Finds tongues in trees, books in the running brooks, / Sermons in stones, and good in every thing."
39. **Edinburgh wit:** The English writer Sydney Smith (1771-1845), the first editor and a frequent contributor to the *Edinburgh Review*, was renowned for his aphorisms and wit.

"Easy writing, but hard reading, aunt."

"That's false modesty, Ralph. If I had but your opportunities to collect materials" – Mrs. Courland did not know that in literature, as in some species of manufacture, the most exquisite productions are wrought from the smallest quantity of raw material – "There's your journey to New York, Ralph," she continued, "you might have made three capital articles out of that. The revolutionary officer would have worked up for the 'Legendary;' the mysterious lady for the 'Token;' and the man in black for the 'Remember Me;' – all founded on fact, all romantic and pathetic."[40]

"But mamma," said Alice, expressing in words what Ralph's arch smile expressed almost as plainly, "you know the officer drank too much; and the mysterious lady turned out to be a runaway milliner; and the man in black – oh! what a theme for a pathetic story! – the man in black was a widower, on his way to Newhaven, where he was to select his third wife from three *recommended* candidates."

"Pshaw! Alice: do you suppose it is necessary to tell things precisely as they are?"

"Alice is wrong, aunt, and you are right; and if she will open her writing desk for me, I will sit down this moment, and write a story – a true story – true from beginning to end; and if it moves you, my dear aunt, if it meets your approbation, my destiny is decided."

Mrs. Courland was delighted; she had slain the giant, and she saw fame and fortune smiling on her favourite. She arranged the desk for him herself; she prepared a folio sheet of paper, folded the ominous margins; and was so absorbed in her bright visions, that she did not hear a little by-talk between Ralph and Alice, nor see the tell-tale flush on their cheeks, nor notice the perturbation with which Alice walked first to one window and then to another, and finally settled herself to that best of all sedatives – hemming a ruffle. Ralph chewed off the end of his quill, mended his pen twice, though his aunt assured him 'printers did not mind the penmanship,' and had achieved a single line when Mrs. Courland's vigilant eye was averted by the entrance of her servant girl, who put a packet into her hands. She looked at the direction, cut the string, broke the seals, and took out a periodical fresh from the publisher. She opened at the first article – a strangely mingled current of maternal pride and literary triumph rushed through her heart and brightened her face. She whispered to the servant a summons to all her sisters to the parlour, and an intimation, sufficiently intelligible to them, of her joyful reason for interrupting them.

Our readers will sympathize with her, and with Alice too, when we disclose to them the secret of her joy. The article in question was a clever composition written by our devoted Alice when she was at school. One of her fond aunts had preserved it; and aunts and mother had combined in the pious fraud of giving it to the public, unknown to Alice. They were perfectly aware of her determination never to be an author. But they fancied it was the mere timidity of an unfledged bird; and that when, by their innocent artifice, she found that her pinions could soar in a literary atmosphere, she would realize the

---

40. **"The revolutionary officer . . . all romantic and pathetic":** Although *The Token* was the title of an actual annual, the passage spoofs the titles and contents of the increasingly popular literary annuals.

sweet fluttering sensations they had experienced at their first flight. The good souls all hurried to the parlour, eager to witness the coup de théatre.[41] Miss Sally's pen stood emblematically erect in her turban; Miss Ruth, in her haste, had overset her inkstand, and the drops were trickling down her white dressing, or, as she now called it, writing gown; and Miss Anne had a wild flower in her hand, as she hoped, of an undescribed species, which, in her joyful agitation, she most unluckily picked to pieces. All bit their lips to keep impatient congratulation from bursting forth. Ralph was so intent on his writing, and Alice on her hemming, that neither noticed the irruption; and Mrs. Courland was obliged twice to speak to her daughter before she could draw her attention.

"Alice, look here – Alice, my dear."

"What is it, mamma? something new of yours?"

"No; guess again, Alice."

"Of one of my aunts, of course?"

"Neither, dear, neither. Come and look for yourself, and see if you can then tell whose it is."

Alice dutifully laid aside her work, approached and took the book. The moment her eye glanced on the fatal page, all her apathy vanished – deep crimson overspread her cheeks, brow, and neck. She burst into tears of irrepressible vexation, and threw the book into the blazing fire.

The gentle Alice! Never had she been guilty of such an ebullition of temper. Her poor dismayed aunts retreated; her mother looked at her in mute astonishment; and Ralph, struck with her emotion, started from the desk, and would have asked an explanation, but Alice exclaimed – "Don't say any thing about it, mamma – I cannot bear it now."

Mrs. Courland knew instinctively that Ralph would sympathize entirely with Alice, and quite willing to avoid an éclaircissement,[42] she said – "Some other time, Ralph, I'll tell you the whole. Show me now what you have written. How have you begun?"

Ralph handed her the paper with a novice's trembling hand.

"Oh! how very little! and so scratched and interlined! but never mind – 'c'est le premier pas qui coute.'"[43]

While making these general observations, the good mother was getting out and fixing her spectacles, and Alice and Ralph had retreated behind her. Alice rested her head on his shoulder, and Ralph's lips were not far from her ear. Whether he was soothing her ruffled spirit, or what he was doing, is not recorded. Mrs. Courland read and re-read the sentence. She dropped a tear on it. She forgot her literary aspirations for Ralph and Alice – forgot she was herself an author – forgot every thing but the mother; and rising, embraced them both as her dear children, and expressed, in her raised and moistened eye, consent to their union, which Ralph had dutifully and prettily asked in that short and true story of his love for his sweet cousin Alice.

---

41. **coup de théatre:** A dramatic or sensational turn of events, especially in a play (French).
42. **éclaircissement:** An enlightening explanation of something that has previously been obscure or inexplicable, typically someone's conduct (French).
43. **'c'est le premier pas qui coute':** It is the first step which counts (French).

In due time the village of H. was animated with the celebration of Alice's nuptials: and when her mother and aunts saw her the happy mistress of the Hepburn farm, and the happiest of wives, they relinquished, without a sigh, the hope of ever seeing her an AUTHOR.

[1830]

Augustus Baldwin Longstreet

[1790-1870]

... a clever fellow, imbued with a spirit of the truest humor, and endowed, moreover, with an exquisitely discriminative and penetrating understanding of character *in general, and of Southern character in particular.*

– Edgar Allan Poe

Augustus Baldwin Longstreet was born in Augusta, Georgia, on September 22, 1790, to William and Hannah Randolph Longstreet, who had moved there from New Jersey in 1784. Longstreet was sent to a private school in South Carolina and then to Yale, where he graduated in just two years. After studying law in Connecticut, Longstreet returned to Georgia and began a career as a lawyer. He married Frances Eliza Parke in 1817 and settled in Greensboro, Georgia. In the early 1820s, Longstreet seemed destined for a career in politics. He was elected to the state assembly in 1821 and then to a judgeship in 1822. But the sudden deaths of his son and his mother-in-law caused Longstreet to drop out of a congressional race in 1824. Religion became an increasingly important source of comfort to him, and two years later Longstreet and his wife joined the Methodist Church. In 1827, they bought a plantation outside Augusta, where Longstreet entered into an active law partnership and also began informal preaching and lecturing on behalf of the temperance movement, to which he had become deeply committed.

Drawing upon the memories of his youth and his experiences as a circuit-riding lawyer and judge, Longstreet in 1830 began to write a series of sketches about life on the Georgia frontier during an earlier era. Several of his sketches were published anonymously in the weekly *Southern Recorder* of Milledgeville, Georgia, during 1833-34. Longstreet then bought a weekly newspaper, the *States Rights Sentinel*, in which he printed additional sketches, signed either "Baldwin" or "Hall," as well as opinion pieces on politics and morals signed "Bob Short." At the end of 1835, Longstreet used the printing press of his newspaper to publish a collection of the sketches as *Georgia Scenes*. The book proved to be very popular and received important critical attention, notably from Edgar Allan Poe, who reviewed it in the *Southern Literary Messenger*. Responding to ongoing demand for the book, the major New York publishing firm of Harper & Brothers published a "second edition" of *Georgia Scenes* under Longstreet's name in 1840, establishing him as a southern writer with a national reputation.

bedfordstmartins.com/americanlit *for research links on Longstreet*

After having created and established the humorous frontier sketch as a new genre in American literature, the restless Longstreet moved into yet another career path. Turning from the law and literature, in 1838 he decided to become a minister and was ordained in the Methodist Church. After a brief stint as the pastor of a church in Augusta, in 1839 Longstreet was invited to become the president of Emory College in Atlanta, Georgia, where he served until 1849. He was briefly the president of Centenary College in Louisiana before being elected president of the University of Mississippi (1849-56). He then served as the president of the University of South Carolina until 1861, when the whole student body left to serve in the Civil War. During those years, Longstreet devoted his pen to religious issues and political causes, especially the defense of slavery, the subject of works like *A Voice from the South* (1847). Inspired by what he described as an effort to induce youths in college "to improve the opportunities which these institutions afforded them of becoming useful and distinguished men," Longstreet also wrote *Master William Mitten; or, A Youth of Brilliant Talents Who Was Ruined by Bad Luck*, a didactic novel published serially in the *Southern Magazine* in 1859 and as a book in 1864. He died at his home in Oxford, Mississippi, on July 9, 1870.

Longstreet's *Georgia Scenes*. "The Dance" was the first of eight sketches by Longstreet contributed to the *Southern Recorder* of Milledgeville, Georgia, in 1833-34. Longstreet reprinted those sketches and published eleven more (including "Georgia Theatrics") in his own newspaper, the *States Rights Sentinel*, from the office of which he published a collection of the sketches in 1835 under the full title *Georgia Scenes, Characters, Incidents, &c., in the first Half Century of the Republic. By a Native Georgian.* The first sketch in the collection was "Georgia Theatrics," signed *Hall*, followed by "The Dance," signed *Baldwin*. In his preface, Longstreet explained that "*Hall* is the writer of those sketches in which men appear as the principal actors, and *Baldwin* of those in which women are the prominent figures." Writing for the *Southern Literary Messenger* in March 1836, Edgar Allan Poe highly praised the collection. Poe observed that, although he was not of a "merry" disposition, he had laughed out loud throughout the book. During the three years following the publication of *Georgia Scenes*, Longstreet wrote a few additional sketches for the *Augusta Mirror*, but none of those sketches appeared in the "second edition" of the book published by Harper & Brothers in 1840. In a note, the publishers explained that the new edition had been "printed verbatim from the original edition," since they had "been unable to prevail upon the author to revise the work." They also expressed the hope that Longstreet would revise and expand the book "before another edition shall be required," but he never did so. To meet the ongoing demand for *Georgia Scenes*, Harper & Brothers therefore simply reprinted the second edition, first in 1850 and again in 1855, the edition from which the texts of the following two sketches are taken.

Georgia Scenes

An illustration of the sketch "Georgia Theatrics," from *Georgia Scenes* (1835). (Documenting the American South [http://docsouth.unc.edu], The University of North Carolina at Chapel Hill Libraries.)

GEORGIA THEATRICS

If my memory fail me not, the 10th of June, 1809 found me, at about 11 o'clock in the forenoon, ascending a long and gentle slope in what was called "The Dark Corner" of Lincoln.[1] I believe it took its name from the moral darkness which reigned over that portion of the county at the time of which I am speaking. If in this point of view it was but a shade darker than the rest of the county, it was inconceivably dark. If any man can name a trick or sin which had not been committed at the time of which I am speaking, in the very focus of all the county's illumination (Lincolnton), he must himself be the most inventive of the tricky, and the very Judas of sinners. Since that time, however (all humour aside), Lincoln has become a living proof "that light shineth in darkness." Could I venture to mingle the solemn with the ludicrous, even for the purposes of honourable contrast, I could adduce from this county instances of the most numerous and wonderful transitions, from vice and folly to virtue and holiness, which have ever, perhaps, been witnessed since the days of the apostolic ministry. So much, lest it should be thought by some that what I am about to relate is characteristic of the county in which it occurred.

Whatever may be said of the *moral* condition of the Dark Corner at the time just mentioned, its *natural* condition was anything but dark. It smiled in all the charms of spring; and spring borrowed a new charm from its undulating grounds, its luxuriant woodlands, its sportive streams, its vocal birds, and its blushing flowers.

Rapt with the enchantment of the season and the scenery around me, I was slowly rising the slope, when I was startled by loud, profane, and boisterous voices, which seemed to proceed from a thick covert of undergrowth about two hundred yards in the advance of me, and about one hundred to the right of my road.

---

1. **Lincoln:** Lincoln County is located in the northeastern part of Georgia; the county seat is Lincolnton.

"You kin, kin you?"

"Yes, I kin, and am able to do it! Boo-oo-oo. Oh, wake snakes, and walk your chalks! Brimstone and — fire! Don't hold me, Nick Stoval! The fight's made up, and let's go at it. — my soul if I don't jump down his throat, and gallop every chitterling out of him before you can say 'quit!'"

"Now, Nick, don't hold him! Jist let the wild-cat come, and I'll tame him. Ned'll see me a fair fight won't you, Ned?"

"Oh, yes; I'll see you a fair fight, blast my old shoes if I don't."

"That's sufficient, as Tom Haynes said when he saw the elephant. Now let him come."

Thus they went on, with countless oaths interspersed, which I dare not even hint at, and with much that I could not distinctly hear.

In Mercy's name! thought I, what band of ruffians has selected this holy season and this heavenly retreat for such Pandaemonian riots![2] I quickened my gait, and had come nearly opposite to the thick grove whence the noise proceeded, when my eye caught indistinctly, and at intervals, through the foliage of the dwarf-oaks and hickories which intervened, glimpses of a man or men, who seemed to be in a violent struggle; and I could occasionally catch those deep-drawn, emphatic oaths which men in conflict utter when they deal blows. I dismounted, and hurried to the spot with all speed. I had overcome about half the space which separated it from me, when I saw the combatants come to the ground, and, after a short struggle, I saw the uppermost one (for I could not see the other) make a heavy plunge with both his thumbs, and at the same instant I heard a cry in the accent of keenest torture, "Enough! My eye's out!"

I was so completely horrorstruck, that I stood transfixed for a moment to the spot where the cry met me. The accomplices in the hellish deed which had been perpetrated had all fled at my approach; at least I supposed so, for they were not to be seen.

"Now, blast your corn-shucking soul," said the victor (a youth about eighteen years old) as he rose from the ground, "come cutt'n your shines 'bout me agin, next time I come to the Courthouse, will you! Get your owl-eye in agin if you can!"

At this moment he saw me for the first time. He looked excessively embarrassed, and was moving off, when I called to him, in a tone imboldened by the sacredness of my office and the iniquity of his crime, "Come back, you brute! and assist me in relieving your fellow mortal, whom you have ruined for ever!"

My rudeness subdued his embarrassment in an instant; and, with a taunting curl of the nose, he replied, "You needn't kick before you're spurr'd. There a'nt nobody there, nor ha'nt been nother. I was jist seein' how I could 'a' *fout*." So saying, he bounded to his plough, which stood in the corner of the fence about fifty yards beyond the battle ground.

And, would you believe it, gentle reader! his report was true. All that I had heard and seen was nothing more nor less than a Lincoln rehearsal; in which the youth who had just left me had played all the parts of all the characters in a Courthouse fight.

---

2. **Pandaemonian riots:** In *Paradise Lost*, the epic poem by John Milton (1608–1674), Pandemonium is the home of all the devils and lost souls, a place of wild and noisy confusion and constant uproar.

I went to the ground from which he had risen, and there were the prints of his two thumbs, plunged up to the balls in the mellow earth, about the distance of a man's eyes apart; and the ground around was broken up as if two stags had been engaged upon it.

HALL

[1834/1835, 1855]

THE DANCE

A Personal Adventure of the Author

Some years ago I was called by business to one of the frontier counties, then but recently settled. It became necessary for me, while there, to enlist the services of Thomas Gibson, Esq., one of the magistrates of the county, who resided about a mile and a half from my lodgings; and to this circumstance was I indebted for my introduction to him. I had made the intended disposition of my business, and was on the eve of my departure for the city of my residence, when I was induced to remain a day longer by an invitation from the squire to attend a dance at his house on the following day. Having learned from my landlord that I would probably "be expected at the frolic" about the hour of 10 in the forenoon, and being desirous of seeing all that passed upon the occasion, I went over about an hour before the time.

The squire's dwelling consisted of but one room, which answered the threefold purpose of dining-room, bedroom, and kitchen. The house was constructed of logs, and the floor was of *puncheons*; a term which, in Georgia, means split logs, with their faces a little smoothed with the axe or hatchet. To gratify his daughters, Polly and Silvy, the old gentleman and his lady had consented to *camp out* for a day, and to surrender the habitation to the girls and their young friends.

When I reached there I found all things in readiness for the promised amusement. The girls, as the old gentleman informed me, had compelled the family to breakfast under the trees, for they had completely stripped the house of its furniture before the sun rose. They were already attired for the dance, in neat but plain habiliments[1] of their own manufacture. "What!" says some weakly, sickly, delicate, useless, affected, "charming creature" of the city, "dressed for a ball at 9 in the morning!" Even so, my delectable Miss Octavia Matilda Juliana Claudia Ipecacuanha: and what have you to say against it? If people must dance, is it not much more rational to employ the hour allotted to exercise in that amusement, than the hours sacred to repose and meditation? And which is entitled to the most credit; the young lady who rises with the dawn, and puts herself and whole house in order for a ball four hours before it begins, or the one who requires a fortnight to get herself dressed for it?

The squire and I employed the interval in conversation about the first settlement of the country, in the course of which I picked up some useful and much interesting infor-

1. **habiliments:** Early term for clothing or outfits.

mation. We were at length interrupted, however, by the sound of a violin, which proceeded from a thick wood at my left. The performer soon after made his appearance, and proved to be no other than Billy Porter, a negro fellow of much harmless wit and humour, who was well known throughout the state. Poor Billy! "his harp is now hung upon the willow;"[2] and I would not blush to offer a tear to his memory, for his name is associated with some of the happiest scenes of my life, and he sleeps with many a dear friend, who used to join me in provoking his wit and in laughing at his eccentricities; but I am leading my reader to the grave instead of the dance, which I promised. If, however, his memory reaches twelve years back, he will excuse this short tribute of respect to BILLY PORTER.

Billy, to give his own account of himself, "had been taking a turn with the brethren (the Bar); and, hearing the ladies wanted to see *pretty Billy*, had come to give them a benefit." The squire had not seen him before; and it is no disrespect to his understanding or politeness to say, that he found it impossible to give me his attention for half an hour after Billy arrived. I had nothing to do, therefore, while the young people were assembling, but to improve my knowledge of Billy's character, to the squire's amusement. I had been thus engaged about thirty minutes, when I saw several fine, bouncing, ruddy-cheeked girls descending a hill about the eighth of a mile off. They, too, were attired in manufactures of their own hands. The refinements of the present day in female dress[3] had not even reached our republican *cities* at this time; and, of course, the *country girls* were wholly ignorant of them. They carried no more cloth upon their arms or straw upon their heads than was necessary to cover them. They used no artificial means of spreading their frock tails to an interesting extent from their ankles. They had no boards laced to their breasts, nor any corsets laced to their sides; consequently, they looked, for all the world, like human beings, and could be distinctly recognised as such at the distance of two hundred paces. Their movements were as free and active as nature would permit them to be. Let me not be understood as interposing the least objection to any lady in this land of liberty dressing just as she pleases. If she choose to lay her neck and shoulders bare, what right have I to look at them? much less to find fault with them. If she choose to put three yards of muslin in a frock sleeve, what right have I to ask why a little strip of it was not put in the body? If she like the pattern of a hoisted umbrella for a frock, and the shape of a cheese-cask for her body, what is all that to me? But to return.

The girls were met by Polly and Silvy Gibson at some distance from the house, who welcomed them – "with a kiss, of course" – oh, no; but with something much less equivocal: a hearty shake of the hand and smiling countenances, which had some meaning.

[*Note.* – The custom of kissing, as practised in these days by the *amiables*, is borrowed from the French, and by them from Judas.][4]

---

2. **"his harp . . . willow":** A rephrasing of a line from Psalms 137:1-3: "By the rivers of Babylon, there we sat down, yea, we wept, when we remembered Zion. We hanged our harps upon the willows in the midst thereof."
3. **present day in female dress:** Fashions for American women – which then included elaborate bonnets, corsets and stays, and wide hoopskirts – were a frequent subject of critical and satirical commentary.
4. ***amiables* . . . from Judas:** The custom of kissing among fashionable people is here ironically associated with the kiss of Judas, given after he betrayed Christ (Luke 22:46-48).

The young ladies had generally collected before any of the young men appeared. It was not long, however, before a large number of both sexes were assembled, and they adjourned to the *ballroom*.

But for the snapping of a fiddle-string, the young people would have been engaged in the amusement of the day in less than three minutes from the time they entered the house. Here were no formal introductions to be given, no drawing for places or partners, no parade of managers, no ceremonies. It was perfectly understood that all were invited *to dance*, and that none were invited who were unworthy to be danced with; consequently, no gentleman hesitated to ask any lady present to dance with him, and no lady refused to dance with a gentleman merely because she had not been made acquainted with him.

In a short time the string was repaired, and off went the party to a good old republican six reel.[5] I had been thrown among *fashionables* so long that I had almost forgotten my native dance. But it revived rapidly as they wheeled through its mazes, and with it returned many long-forgotten, pleasing recollections. Not only did the reel return to me, but the very persons who used to figure in it with me, in the heyday of youth.

Here was my old sweetheart, Polly Jackson, identically personified in Polly Gibson; and here was Jim Johnson's, in Silvy; and Bill Martin's, in Nancy Ware. Polly Gibson had my old flame's very steps as well as her looks. "Ah!" said I, "squire, this puts me in mind of old times. I have not seen a six reel for five-and-twenty years. It recalls to my mind many a happy hour, and many a jovial friend who used to enliven it with me. Your Polly looks so much like my old sweetheart, Polly Jackson, that, were I young again, I certainly should fall in love with her."

"That was the name of her mother," said the squire.

"Where did you marry her?" inquired I.

"In Wilkes," said he; "she was the daughter of old Nathan Jackson, of that county."

"It isn't possible!" returned I. "Then it is the very girl of whom I am speaking. Where is she?"

"She's out," said the squire, "preparing dinner for the young people; but she'll be in towards the close of the day. But come along, and I'll make you acquainted with her at once, if you'll promise not to run away with her, for I tell you what it is, she's the likeliest *gal* in all these parts yet."

"Well," said I, "I'll promise not to run away with her, but you must not let her know who I am. I wish to make myself known to her; and, for fear of the worst, you shall witness the introduction. But don't get jealous, squire, if she seems a little too glad to see me; for, I assure you, we had a strong notion of each other when we were young."

"No danger," replied the squire; "she hadn't seen *me* then, or she never could have loved such a hard favoured[6] man as you are."

---

5. **reel:** The Virginia reel was a popular lively country dance performed by several couples facing each other in parallel lines. There were many variations in the form of the reel, but, in general, the steps in the dance involve the couples moving back and forth, from side to side, and in circles. In addition, the couples exchange places, moving from the front of the line to the end.

6. **hard favoured:** Tough or severe in looks.

In the mean time the dance went on, and I employed myself in selecting from the party the best examples of the dancers of my day and Mrs. Gibson's for her entertainment. In this I had not the least difficulty; for the dancers before me and those of my day were in all respects identical.

Jim Johnson kept up the double shuffle from the beginning to the end of the reel: and here was Jim over again in Sammy Tant. Bill Martin always set to his partner with the same step; and a very curious step it was. He brought his right foot close behind his left, and with it performed precisely the motion of the thumb in cracking that insect which Burns has immortalized;[7] then moved his right back, threw his weight upon it, brought his left behind it, and *cracked* with that as before; and so on alternately. Just so did Bill Kemp, to a nail. Bob Simons danced for all the world like a "Suple Jack" (or, as we commonly call it, a "*Suple* Sawney"), when the string is pulled with varied force, at intervals of seconds: and so did *Jake* Slack. Davy Moore went like a suit of clothes upon a clothing line on a windy day: and here was his antitype in Ned Clark. Rhoda Nobles swam through the reel like a cork on wavy waters; always giving two or three pretty little perchbite *diddles*[8] as she rose from a coupee:[9] Nancy Ware was her very self. Becky Lewis made a business of dancing; she disposed of her part as quick as possible, stopped dead short as soon as she got through, and looked as sober as a judge all the time; even so did Chloe Dawson. I used to tell Polly Jackson, that Becky's countenance, when she closed a dance, always seemed to say, "Now, if you want any more dancing, you may do it yourself."

The dance grew merrier as it progressed; the young people became more easy in each other's company, and often enlivened the scene with most humorous remarks. Occasionally some sharp cuts passed between the boys, such as would have produced half a dozen duels at a city ball; but here they were taken as they were meant, in good humour. Jim Johnson being a little tardy in meeting his partner at a turn of the reel, "I *ax* pardon, Miss Chloe," said he, "Jake Slack went to make a crosshop[10] just now, and tied his legs in a hard knot, and I stop'd to help him untie them." A little after, Jake hung his toe in a crack of the floor, and nearly fell; "Ding my buttons," said he, "if I didn't know I should stumble over Jim Johnson's foot at last; Jim, draw your foot up to your own end of the reel." (Jim was at the other end of the reel, and had, in truth, a prodigious foot.)

Towards the middle of the day, many of the neighbouring farmers dropped in, and joined the squire and myself in talking of old times. At length dinner was announced. It consisted of plain *fare*, but there was a profusion of it. Rough planks, supported by stakes driven in the ground, served for a table; at which the old and young of both sexes seated themselves at the same time. I soon recognised Mrs. Gibson from all the matrons

---

7. **immortalized:** A reference to "To a Louse," by the Scottish poet Robert Burns (1759–1796). The dancer's step is compared to the way the body louse, a common insect, was caught and cracked between the thumb and forefinger.
8. **perchbite *diddles*:** Short, rapid fishlike motions.
9. **coupee:** A step in which one leg is bent and held above the ground while the dancer leans or motions forward on the other leg, making a kind of bow or salutation.
10. **crosshop:** A slight jump, another dance step in the reel.

present. Thirty years had wrought great changes in her appearance, but they had left some of her features entirely unimpaired. Her eye beamed with all its youthful fire; and, to my astonishment, her mouth was still beautified with a full set of teeth, unblemished by time. The rose on her cheek had rather freshened than faded and her smile was the very same that first subdued my heart; but her fine form was wholly lost, and, with it, all the grace of her movements. Pleasing but melancholy reflections occupied my mind as I gazed on her dispensing her cheerful hospitalities. I thought of the sad history of many of her companions and mine, who used to carry light hearts through the merry dance. I compared my after life with the cloudless days of my attachment to Polly. Then I was light hearted, gay, contented, and happy. I aspired to nothing but a good name, a good wife, and an easy competence. The first and last were mine already; and Polly had given me too many little tokens of her favour to leave a doubt now that the second was at my command. But I was foolishly told that my talents were of too high an order to be employed in the drudgeries of a farm, and I more foolishly believed it. I forsook the pleasures which I had tried and proved, and went in pursuit of those imaginary joys which seemed to encircle the seat of Fame. From that moment to the present, my life had been little else than one unbroken scene of disaster, disappointment, vexation, and toil. And now, when I was too old to enjoy the pleasures which I had discarded, I found that my aim was absolutely hopeless; and that my pursuits had only served to unfit me for the humbler walks of life, and to exclude me from the higher. The gloom of these reflections was, however, lightened in a measure by the promises of the coming hour, when I was to live over again with Mrs. Gibson some of the happiest moments of my life.

After a hasty repast the young people returned to their amusement, followed by myself, with several of the elders of the company. An hour had scarcely elapsed before Mrs. Gibson entered, accompanied by a goodly number of matrons of her own age. This accession to the company produced its usual effects. It raised the tone of conversation a full octave, and gave it a triple time movement; added new life to the wit and limbs of the young folks, and set the old men to cracking jokes.

At length the time arrived for me to surprise and delight Mrs. Gibson. The young people insisted upon the old folks taking a reel; and this was just what I had been waiting for; for, after many plans for making the discovery, I had finally concluded upon that which I thought would make *her* joy general among the company: and that was, to announce myself, just before leading her to the dance, in a voice audible to most of the assembly. I therefore readily assented to the proposition of the young folks, as did two others of my age, and we made to the ladies for our partners. I, of course, offered my hand to Mrs. Gibson.

"Come," said I, "Mrs. Gibson, let us see if we can't out-dance these young people."

"Dear me, sir," said she, "I haven't danced a step these twenty years."

"Neither have I; but I've resolved to try once more, if you will join me, just for old time's sake."

"I really cannot think of dancing," said she.

"Well," continued I (raising my voice to a pretty high pitch, on purpose to be heard, while my countenance kindled with exultation at the astonishment and delight which I was about to produce), "you surely will dance with an old friend and sweetheart, who used to dance with you when a girl!"

At this disclosure her features assumed a vast variety of expressions; but none of them responded precisely to my expectation: indeed, some of them were of such an equivocal and alarming character, that I deemed it advisable not to prolong her suspense. I therefore proceeded:

"Have you forgot your old sweetheart, Abram Baldwin?"

"What!" said she, looking more astonished and confused than ever. "Abram Baldwin! Abram Baldwin! I don't think I ever heard the name before."

"Do you remember Jim Johnson?" said I.

"Oh, yes," said she, "mighty well," her countenance brightening with a smile.

"And Bill Martin?"

"Yes, perfectly well; why, *who* are you?"

Here we were interrupted by one of the gentlemen, who had led his partner to the floor, with, "Come, stranger, we're getting mighty tired o' standing. It won't do for old people that's going to dance to take up much time in standing; they'll lose all their *spryness.* Don't stand begging Polly Gibson, she never dances; but take my Sal there, next to her; she'll run a reel with you, to old Nick's house[11] and back *agin.*"

No alternative was left me, and therefore I offered my hand to Mrs. Sally – I didn't know who.

"Well," thought I, as I moved to my place, "the squire is pretty secure from jealousy; but Polly will soon remember me when she sees my steps in the reel. I will dance precisely as I used to in my youth, if it tire me to death." There was one step that was almost exclusively my own, for few of the dancers of my day could perform it at all, and none with the grace and ease that I did. "She'll remember Abram Baldwin," thought I, "as soon as she sees the *double cross-hop.*" It was performed by rising and crossing the legs twice or thrice before lighting, and I used to carry it to the third cross with considerable ease. It was a step solely adapted to setting or balancing, as all will perceive; but I thought the occasion would justify a little perversion of it, and therefore resolved to lead off with it, that Polly might be at once relieved from suspense. Just, however, as I reached my place, Mrs. Gibson's youngest son, a boy about eight years old, ran in and cried out, "Mammy, old Boler's jump'd upon the planks, and dragg'd off a great hunk o' meat as big as your head, and broke a dish and two plates all to darn smashes!" Away went Mrs. Gibson, and off went the music. Still I hoped that matters would be adjusted in time for Polly to return and see the double cross-hop; and I felt the mortification which my delay in getting a partner had occasioned somewhat solaced by the reflection that it had thrown me at the foot of the reel.

The first and second couples had nearly completed their performances, and Polly had not returned. I began to grow uneasy, and to interpose as many delays as I could without attracting notice.

---

11. **old Nick's house:** The house of the devil or Satan.

The six reel is closed by the foot couple balancing at the head of the set, then in the middle, then at the foot, again in the middle, meeting at the head, and leading down.

My partner and I had commenced balancing at the head, and Polly had not returned. I balanced until my partner forced me on. I now deemed it advisable to give myself up wholly to the double cross-hop; so that, if Polly should return in time to see any step, it should be this, though I was already nearly exhausted. Accordingly, I made the attempt to introduce it in the turns of the reel; but the first experiment convinced me of three things at once: 1st. That I could not have used the step in this way in my best days; 2d. That my strength would not more than support it in its proper place for the remainder of the reel; and, 3d. If I tried it again in this way, I should knock my brains out against the puncheons; for my partner, who seemed determined to confirm her husband's report of her, evinced no disposition to wait upon experiments; but, fetching me a jerk while I was up and my legs crossed, had wellnigh sent me head foremost to Old Nick's house, sure enough.

We met in the middle, my back to the door, and from the silence that prevailed in the yard, I flattered myself that Polly might be even now catching the first glimpse of the favourite step, when I heard her voice at some distance from the house: "Get you gone! G-e-e-t you gone! G-e-e-e-e-t you gone!" Matters out doors were now clearly explained. There had been a struggle to get the meat from Boler; Boler had triumphed, and retreated to the woods with his booty, and Mrs. Gibson was heaping indignities upon him in the last resort.

The three "*Get-you-gones*" met me precisely at the three closing balances; and the last brought my moral energies to a perfect level with my physical.

Mrs. Gibson returned, however, in a few minutes after, in a good humour; for she possessed a lovely disposition, which even marriage could not spoil. As soon as I could collect breath enough for regular conversation (for, to speak in my native dialect, I was "*mortal tired*"), I took a seat by her, resolved not to quit the house without making myself known to her, if possible.

"How much," said I, "your Polly looks and dances like you used to, at her age."

"I've told my old man so a hundred times," said she. "Why, who upon earth are you!"

"Did you ever see two persons dance more alike than Jim Johnson and Sammy Tant?"

"Never. Why, who can you be!"

"You remember Becky Lewis?"

"Yes!"

"Well, look at Chloe Dawson, and you'll see her ever again."

"Well, law me! Now I know I must have seen you somewhere; but, to save my life, I can't tell where. Where did your father live?"

"He died when I was small."

"And where did you use to see me?"

"At your father's, and old Mr. Dawson's, and at Mrs. Barnes's, and at Squire Noble's, and many other places."

"Well, goodness me! it's mighty strange I can't call you to mind."

I now began to get petulant, and thought it best to leave her.

The dance wound up with the old merry jig, and the company dispersed.

The next day I set out for my residence. I had been at home rather more than two months, when I received the following letter from Squire Gibson:

"DEAR SIR: I send you the money collected on the notes[12] you left with me. Since you left here, Polly has been thinking about old times, and she says, to save her life, she can't recollect you."

BALDWIN

[1833/1835, 1855]

12. notes: A shortened form of *promissory notes.* Although the business that the narrator conducts is vaguely described, it apparently involves the magistrate's assistance in obtaining the payment of money owed to him or a client.

William Cullen Bryant

[1794–1878]

William Cullen Bryant

The eminent artist Samuel F. B. Morse, a fervent cultural nationalist, painted this portrait of America's most celebrated poet in 1825, shortly after Bryant closed his law practice and moved his family to New York City.

William Cullen Bryant was born on November 3, 1794, to Peter Bryant, a physician, and Sarah Snell Bryant in Cummington, Massachusetts. The family owned a large library, and Bryant was educated at home, at district schools, and later at Williams College. A precocious child, Bryant was taught to write poetry by his father. In 1807, some of his early works – imitations of the poems he read and translated from Greek and Latin – were published in a local newspaper, the Hampshire *Gazette.* The following year, the thirteen-year-old Bryant became absorbed in national politics. He wrote and (with the help of his Federalist father) published *The Embargo; or, Sketches of the Times; A Satire*, in which Bryant attacked and called for the resignation of President Thomas Jefferson. After just one year at Williams College, Bryant began to study law and was admitted to the bar in 1815. He spent the next decade working as an attorney and serving as a justice of the peace in Great Barrington, Massachusetts.

Bryant, however, was less drawn to the law than he was to literature. He began to publish poems and essays in periodicals, as well as his first book in 1821. Despite the distinction of his work, Bryant knew that he could not support himself or a family by writing poetry. Following his marriage in 1821, Bryant continued to practice law until 1825, when he moved his family to New York City. Still seeking a career in literature, he assumed the editorship of the *New York Review and Atheneum Magazine.* Although the magazine failed by the end of the year, Bryant remained in New York and joined the editorial staff of the *Evening Post.* He worked on the newspaper for the rest of his life, first as an associate editor and later as its part owner and editor in chief. Under his leadership, the *Evening Post* became one of the most respected newspapers in the country; his frequent editorials exerted considerable political influence. Having moved well away from the conservative politics of his youth, Bryant was a strong supporter of liberal causes and initially of the Democratic Party. But his growing opposition to slavery finally prompted Bryant to help form the Republican Party, in which he was an enthusiastic supporter of Abraham Lincoln and the Union cause in the Civil War.

. . . a poet who, to our mind, stands among the first in the world . . .
– Walt Whitman

During his years as an editor, Bryant continued to publish poetry and became one of the most popular American poets of the first half of the nineteenth century. A second volume of his *Poems* appeared in 1832, followed by *The Fountain and Other Poems* (1842), *The White-Footed Deer and Other Poems* (1846), *Poems, by William Cullen Bryant* (1853), and *Thirty Poems* (1864). Drawing on his early training in Latin, Bryant published popular translations of the *Iliad* (1870) and the *Odyssey* (1872). He also published prose works, including two series of *Letters of a Traveller* (1850, 1859); a notable volume of literary criticism, *Poets and Poetry of the English Language* (1871); and a collection of his *Orations and Addresses* (1873). When he died on June 12, 1878, Bryant was widely hailed in obituaries as one of the most respected editors and revered literary figures in the United States.

bedfordstmartins.com/americanlit *for research links on Bryant*

Bryant's Poems. Influenced by his reading of William Wordsworth and other English Romantic poets, Bryant wrote what would become some of his best-known poems in 1814-15, including an early version of "Thanatopsis," a stoical meditation on death in which he celebrated the grandeur and endurance of nature. His father found the poem in a desk drawer, copied it, and sent it without Bryant's knowledge to the prestigious magazine of literature and politics, the *North American Review*. The publication of "Thanatopsis" in September 1817, when he was twenty-three years old, earned Bryant his first important recognition. He consequently began to contribute poems and essays on poetry to the *Review* and other periodicals in both the United States and Great Britain. In 1821, Bryant published his first book, *Poems*, which included a revised version of "Thanatopsis" and sensitive poems like "The Yellow Violet" and "To a Waterfowl," in which he found in nature both moral lessons about temporal life and reassuring signs of the presence and power of a divine being. "To Cole, the Painter, Departing for Europe" (1829), is a sonnet addressed to Bryant's close friend Thomas Cole, an important early American landscape painter and the founder of the Hudson River school of art. Bryant wrote the final poem in this section, "The Prairies" (1834), after visiting his brothers in what was then the western frontier in Illinois. Riding through a vast, seemingly uninhabited landscape that was once the home of the Mound Builders, an ancient "race" now "vanished from the earth," Bryant meditates on the rise and fall of civilizations even as he foresees the time when the prairies will be filled by the "advancing multitudes" of American settlers pressing ever westward across the United States. The texts of the following poems are taken from *Poems, by William Cullen Bryant. Collected and Arranged by the Author* (1853).

THANATOPSIS[1]

To him who in the love of Nature holds
Communion with her visible forms, she speaks
A various language; for his gayer hours
She has a voice of gladness, and a smile
And eloquence of beauty, and she glides
Into his darker musings, with a mild
And healing sympathy, that steals away
Their sharpness, ere he is aware. When thoughts
Of the last bitter hour come like a blight
Over thy spirit, and sad images
Of the stern agony, and shroud, and pall,
And breathless darkness, and the narrow house,
Make thee to shudder, and grow sick at heart; –
Go forth, under the open sky, and list
To Nature's teachings, while from all around –
Earth and her waters, and the depths of air, –
Comes a still voice – Yet a few days, and thee
The all-beholding sun shall see no more
In all his course; nor yet in the cold ground,
Where thy pale form was laid, with many tears,
Nor in the embrace of ocean, shall exist
Thy image. Earth, that nourished thee, shall claim
Thy growth, to be resolved to earth again,
And, lost each human trace, surrendering up
Thine individual being, shalt thou go
To mix for ever with the elements,
To be a brother to the insensible rock
And to the sluggish clod, which the rude swain[2]

1. **Thanatopsis:** A meditation on death (Greek).
2. **swain:** A poetic term for a country youth.

Turns with his share,[3] and treads upon. The oak
Shall send his roots abroad, and pierce thy mould.

Yet not to thine eternal resting-place
Shalt thou retire alone – nor couldst thou wish
Couch more magnificent. Thou shalt lie down
With patriarchs of the infant world – with kings,
The powerful of the earth – the wise, the good,
Fair forms, and hoary seers of ages past,
All in one mighty sepulchre. – The hills
Rock-ribbed and ancient as the sun, – the vales
Stretching in pensive quietness between;
The venerable woods – rivers that move
In majesty, and the complaining brooks
That make the meadows green; and, poured round all,
Old ocean's gray and melancholy waste, –
Are but the solemn decorations all
Of the great tomb of man. The golden sun,
The planets, all the infinite host of heaven,
Are shining on the sad abodes of death,
Through the still lapse of ages. All that tread
The globe are but a handful to the tribes
That slumber in its bosom. – Take the wings
Of morning – and the Barcan desert[4] pierce,
Or lose thyself in the continuous woods
Where rolls the Oregan,[5] and hears no sound,
Save his own dashings – yet – the dead are there:
And millions in those solitudes, since first
The flight of years began, have laid them down
In their last sleep – the dead reign there alone.
So shalt thou rest – and what if thou withdraw
Unheeded by the living, and no friend
Take note of thy departure? All that breathe
Will share thy destiny. The gay will laugh
When thou art gone, the solemn brood of care
Plod on, and each one as before will chase
His favourite phantom; yet all these shall leave
Their mirth and their employments, and shall come,

3. **share:** Short for plowshare, the main cutting blade of a plow.
4. **Barcan desert:** Ancient section of the Sahara Desert, south of the Mediterranean Sea in northern Africa.
5. **Oregan:** Indian name for the Columbia River.

And make their bed with thee.[6] As the long train
Of ages glide away, the sons of men,
The youth in life's green spring, and he who goes
In the full strength of years, matron, and maid,
And the sweet babe, and the gray-headed man,
Shall one by one be gathered to thy side,
By those, who in their turn shall follow them.

So live, that when thy summons comes to join
The innumerable caravan,[7] that moves
To that mysterious realm, where each shall take
His chamber in the silent halls of death,
Thou go not like the quarry-slave at night,
Scourged to his dungeon, but, sustained and soothed
By an unfaltering trust, approach thy grave,
Like one who wraps the drapery of his couch[8]
About him, and lies down to pleasant dreams.

[1817, 1853]

---

6. **And make their bed with thee:** The first version of the poem, published in the *North American Review* in 1817, ended here. In *Poems* (1821), Bryant added the concluding passage, which he slightly revised in later editions of his work.
7. **caravan:** Historical term for a group of people, usually pilgrims, traveling together across a desert in Asia or North Africa.
8. **couch:** Early term for a bed.

THE YELLOW VIOLET

When beechen buds begin to swell,
And woods the blue-bird's warble know,
The yellow violet's modest bell
Peeps from the last year's leaves below.

Ere russet fields their green resume,
Sweet flower, I love, in forest bare,
To meet thee, when thy faint perfume
Alone is in the virgin air.

Of all her train, the hands of Spring
First plant thee in the watery mould,
And I have seen thee blossoming
Beside the snow-bank's edges cold.

Thy parent sun, who bade thee view
Pale skies, and chilling moisture sip,

Has bathed thee in his own bright hue,
And streaked with jet thy glowing lip.

Yet slight thy form, and low thy seat,
And earthward bent thy gentle eye,
Unapt the passing view to meet,
When loftier flowers are flaunting nigh.

Oft, in the sunless April day,
Thy early smile has stayed my walk;
But midst the gorgeous blooms of May,
I passed thee on thy humble stalk.

So they, who climb to wealth, forget
The friends in darker fortunes tried.
I copied them – but I regret
That I should ape the ways of pride.

And when again the genial hour
Awakes the painted tribes of light,
I'll not o'erlook the modest flower
That made the woods of April bright.

[1821, 1853]

TO A WATERFOWL

Whither, midst falling dew,
While glow the heavens with the last steps of day,
Far, through their rosy depths, dost thou pursue
Thy solitary way?

Vainly the fowler's eye
Might mark thy distant flight to do thee wrong,
As, darkly painted on the crimson sky,
Thy figure floats along.

Seek'st thou the plashy[1] brink
Of weedy lake, or marge of river wide,
Or where the rocking billows rise and sink
On the chafed ocean side?

There is a Power whose care
Teaches thy way along that pathless coast, –

1. **plashy:** A plash is a pool or a puddle.

The desert and illimitable air, –
 Lone wandering, but not lost.

 All day thy wings have fanned,
At that far height, the cold, thin atmosphere,
Yet stoop not, weary, to the welcome land,
 Though the dark night is near.

 And soon that toil shall end;
Soon shalt thou find a summer home, and rest,
And scream among thy fellows; reeds shall bend,
 Soon, o'er thy sheltered nest.

 Thou'rt gone, the abyss of heaven
Hath swallowed up thy form; yet, on my heart
Deeply hath sunk the lesson thou hast given,
 And shall not soon depart.

 He who, from zone to zone,
Guides through the boundless sky thy certain flight,
In the long way that I must tread alone,
 Will lead my steps aright.

[1818, 1853]

TO COLE,[1] THE PAINTER, DEPARTING FOR EUROPE

A Sonnet

Thine eyes shall see the light of distant skies:
 Yet, COLE! thy heart shall bear to Europe's strand
 A living image of thy native land,
Such as on thine own glorious canvas lies;
Lone lakes – savannas[2] where the bison roves –
 Rocks rich with summer garlands – solemn streams –
 Skies, where the desert eagle wheels and screams –
Spring bloom and autumn blaze of boundless groves.
Fair scenes shall greet thee where thou goest – fair,
 But different – everywhere the trace of men,
 Paths, homes, graves, ruins, from the lowest glen

1. Cole: Bryant's close friend Thomas Cole (1801–1848), the founder of the Hudson River school of art, pioneered early landscape painting in America. He traveled abroad from 1829–32. After Cole's death at age forty-seven, Bryant presented a funeral oration at the National Academy of Design in New York, in which he called Cole "not only a great artist but a great teacher; the contemplation of his works made men better."
2. savannas: Grassy plains.

To where life shrinks from the fierce Alpine air,
Gaze on them, till the tears shall dim thy sight,
But keep that earlier, wilder image bright.

[1829, 1853]

THE PRAIRIES

These are the gardens of the Desert,[1] these
The unshorn fields, boundless and beautiful,
For which the speech of England has no name[2] –
The Prairies. I behold them for the first,
And my heart swells, while the dilated sight
Takes in the encircling vastness. Lo! they stretch
In airy undulations, far away,
As if the ocean, in his gentlest swell,
Stood still, with all his rounded billows fixed,
And motionless for ever. – Motionless? –
No – they are all unchained again. The clouds
Sweep over with their shadows, and, beneath,
The surface rolls and fluctuates to the eye;
Dark hollows seem to glide along and chase
The sunny ridges. Breezes of the South!
Who toss the golden and the flame-like flowers,
And pass the prairie-hawk that, poised on high,
Flaps his broad wings, yet moves not – ye have played
Among the palms of Mexico and vines
Of Texas, and have crisped the limpid brooks
That from the fountains of Sonora[3] glide
Into the calm Pacific – have ye fanned
A nobler or a lovelier scene than this?
Man hath no part in all this glorious work:
The hand that built the firmament hath heaved
And smoothed these verdant swells, and sown their slopes
With herbage, planted them with island groves,
And hedged them round with forests. Fitting floor
For this magnificent temple of the sky –

---

1. **Desert:** Here used in an earlier sense of an uninhabited tract of land or a wilderness.
2. **For which . . . no name:** The word *prairies* was adopted from the French, the first European explorers of the upper Midwest. In the earliest version of the poem, published in 1833, the line read: "And fresh as the young earth, ere man had sinned," that is, before the Fall of Adam and Eve in the Garden of Eden.
3. **Sonora:** A river in northwestern Mexico that runs into the Gulf of California.

With flowers whose glory and whose multitude
Rival the constellations! The great heavens
Seem to stoop down upon the scene in love, –
A nearer vault, and of a tenderer blue,
Than that which bends above the eastern hills.

As o'er the verdant waste I guide my steed,
Among the high rank grass that sweeps his sides
The hollow beating of his footstep seems
A sacrilegious sound. I think of those
Upon whose rest he tramples. Are they here –
The dead of other days? – and did the dust
Of these fair solitudes once stir with life
And burn with passion? Let the mighty mounds[4]
That overlook the rivers, or that rise
In the dim forest crowded with old oaks,
Answer. A race, that long has passed away,
Built them; – a disciplined and populous race
Heaped, with long toil, the earth, while yet the Greek
Was hewing the Pentelicus[5] to forms
Of symmetry, and rearing on its rock
The glittering Parthenon. These ample fields
Nourished their harvests, here their herds were fed,
When haply by their stalls the bison lowed,
And bowed his maned shoulder to the yoke.
All day this desert murmured with their toils,
Till twilight blushed, and lovers walked, and wooed
In a forgotten language, and old tunes,
From instruments of unremembered form,
Gave the soft winds a voice. The red man came –
The roaming hunter tribes, warlike and fierce,
And the mound-builders vanished from the earth.
The solitude of centuries untold
Has settled where they dwelt. The prairie-wolf
Hunts in their meadows, and his fresh-dug den
Yawns by my path. The gopher mines the ground
Where stood their swarming cities. All is gone –

4. **mighty mounds:** Large earthen mounds were built in major urban centers throughout the Midwest by the Mississippians, a Native American group whose culture emerged around 700 CE and lasted almost nine hundred years. Bryant followed a contemporary theory that the mounds were built by an ancient culture that predated the American Indians.

5. **Pentelicus:** Mountain in Greece where marble was quarried for the Parthenon, the ancient Greek temple built in 447–432 BCE.

All – save the piles of earth that hold their bones –
The platforms where they worshipped unknown gods –
The barriers which they builded from the soil
To keep the foe at bay – till o'er the walls
The wild beleaguerers broke, and, one by one,
The strongholds of the plain were forced, and heaped
With corpses. The brown vultures of the wood
Flocked to those vast uncovered sepulchres,
And sat, unscared and silent, at their feast.
Haply some solitary fugitive,
Lurking in marsh and forest, till the sense
Of desolation and of fear became
Bitterer than death, yielded himself to die.
Man's better nature triumphed then. Kind words
Welcomed and soothed him; the rude conquerors
Seated the captive with their chiefs; he chose
A bride among their maidens, and at length
Seemed to forget, – yet ne'er forgot, – the wife
Of his first love, and her sweet little ones,
Butchered, amid their shrieks, with all his race.

Thus change the forms of being. Thus arise
Races of living things, glorious in strength,
And perish, as the quickening breath of God
Fills them, or is withdrawn. The red man, too,
Has left the blooming wilds he ranged so long,
And, nearer to the Rocky Mountains, sought
A wilder hunting-ground. The beaver builds
No longer by these streams, but far away,
On waters whose blue surface ne'er gave back
The white man's face – among Missouri's springs,
And pools whose issues swell the Oregan,[6]
He rears his little Venice. In these plains
The bison feeds no more. Twice twenty leagues
Beyond remotest smoke of hunter's camp,
Roams the majestic brute, in herds that shake
The earth with thundering steps – yet here I meet
His ancient footprints stamped beside the pool.

Still this great solitude is quick with life.
Myriads of insects, gaudy as the flowers

6. **Missouri's springs . . . Oregan:** The Missouri River flows from the confluence of three rivers in Montana; *Oregan* was the Indian name for the Columbia River.

They flutter over, gentle quadrupeds,
And birds, that scarce have learned the fear of man,
Are here, and sliding reptiles of the ground,
Startlingly beautiful. The graceful deer
Bounds to the wood at my approach. The bee,
A more adventurous colonist than man,
With whom he came across the eastern deep,[7]
Fills the savannas with his murmurings,
And hides his sweets, as in the golden age,
Within the hollow oak. I listen long
To his domestic hum, and think I hear
The sound of that advancing multitude
Which soon shall fill these deserts. From the ground
Comes up the laugh of children, the soft voice
Of maidens, and the sweet and solemn hymn
Of Sabbath worshippers. The low of herds
Blends with the rustling of the heavy grain
Over the dark-brown furrows. All at once
A fresher wind sweeps by, and breaks my dream,
And I am in the wilderness alone.

[1833, 1834/1853]

---

7. **bee . . . across the eastern deep:** Honeybees originated in Africa and spread to India, China, and Europe, from whence they were brought by early colonists across the Atlantic to the Americas.

Jane Johnston Schoolcraft

[1800-1841]

Jane Johnston Schoolcraft, whose Native American name is Bame-wa-wa-ge-zhik-a-quay (Woman of the Stars Rushing through the Sky), was born near the Canadian border in present-day Sault Ste. Marie, Michigan. She was the third of eight children and the eldest daughter of an Irish fur trader, John Johnston, and Ozha-guscoday-way-quay (Woman of the Green Valley), an Ojibwa chief's daughter, who took the English name *Susan* when she married Johnston. At the time of Schoolcraft's birth in 1800, the Ojibwa (also anglicized as *Chippewa, Ojibwe*, and *Ojibway*) were one of the most populous and widely distributed Indian groups in North America, inhabiting a vast area around the Great Lakes in southern Canada and the northern parts of the United States. Like her siblings, Schoolcraft learned to speak both Ojibwa and English. During her childhood, she traveled with her father to Detroit, Montreal, Quebec City, and, in 1809, to Great Britain,

***bedfordstmartins.com/ americanlit** for research links on Schoolcraft*

Jane Johnston Schoolcraft

This is an anonymous and undated sketch of Schoolcraft as a young woman. As her attire indicates, Schoolcraft was raised and educated in the white community, but she also learned the language and lore of her mother's tribe, the Ojibwa.

where he attended to the affairs of his estate in Ireland and to other business affairs in London. Schoolcraft may have attended a school during that trip and for short periods after her return in 1810, but she received most of her education at home. She was instructed by her mother in the legends and traditions of the Ojibwa, while her book-loving father taught her the classics of European literature, as well as the Bible.

In 1822, Schoolcraft met her future husband and literary collaborator, Henry Rowe Schoolcraft, a United States Indian agent who lodged with the Johnston family after he arrived in Sault Ste. Marie. A geologist who had earlier participated in and published an account of a major expedition to discover the source of the Mississippi River, Henry soon began to develop a deep interest in North American Indians. Schoolcraft taught him to speak Ojibwa and assisted him in an effort to establish a written vocabulary of the language, known to its own speakers as Anishinabe or Anishinaabemowin. After they married in 1823, the couple collaborated on a compilation of Ojibwa legends and tales. They later created a magazine to feature work on the language and lore of the tribe, the *Literary Voyager or Muzzeniegun*, an Ojibwa word for a written or printed document. Schoolcraft contributed numerous poems, in both English and Ojibwa, as well as stories based on the legends she and her husband had begun to collect. Acclaimed as the "northern Pocahontas," she was visited in her remote home by literary admirers of her work, which was used by Chandler R. Gilman in *Legends of a Log Cabin* (1835) and *Life on the Lakes* (1836). Working with her mother, Schoolcraft also gathered and authenticated much of the material her husband published in his *Algic Researches* (1839).

That book, which appeared two years before Schoolcraft's sudden death in 1841, was part of her lasting legacy. Just as she drew upon Ojibwa lore in her own stories, the legends published in *Algic Researches* inspired one of the most popular of all nineteenth-century American poems and probably the most familiar poem on Native American subjects, Henry Wadsworth Longfellow's *The Song of Hiawatha* (1856). In a graceful letter of acknowledgment written to Henry Rowe Schoolcraft, Longfellow observed, "without your books I could not have written mine." But it was equally true that *Algic Researches* and the other books on Indian history and tribal lore by Henry Rowe Schoolcraft could not have been written without the inspiration and collaboration of Jane Johnston Schoolcraft.

Schoolcraft's "Mishosha, or the Magician and His Daughters." During the winter of 1826-27, Schoolcraft and her husband Henry Rowe Schoolcraft produced the *Literary Voyager or Muzzeniegun*. Rather than a printed periodical, it was a weekly "manuscript magazine," handwritten copies of which were distributed to students of Indian history and culture throughout Michigan and in cities in the East, including New York City. The magazine included lists of Ojibwa words and notes on the language, as well as essays, poems, and stories. Schoolcraft wrote and published many of her pieces under her Native American name, Bame-wa-wa-ge-zhik-a-quay, or other pen names like Rosa and Leelinau. Her versions of Ojibwa legends proved to be especially attractive to readers and other writers, as a result of both the narrative appeal of the stories and the insights they offered into Native American culture. For the most part, Schoolcraft adopted the language of contemporary English and American writers, but her subject matter was strikingly original. In fact, she was among the first Native American writers to use the literary conventions of the increasingly dominant culture to demonstrate and preserve the rich oral and cultural traditions of the native tribes of the United States. By birth and education, Schoolcraft was a product of two cultures, European and Native American, and her writings represented an early effort to bring together those frequently conflicting cultures. She consequently assumed a pioneering role in the establishment of a written Native American literature, as illustrated by the following story, based on the Ojibwa legend of two orphaned boys who are saved from an evil magician by the combined efforts of his two resourceful daughters, the elder orphan, and the powers of Nature. The first installment of the story appeared in the January 1827 issue of the *Literary Voyager.* Although production of the short-lived magazine ceased before the second installment could appear, Henry Rowe Schoolcraft published both parts in his *Algic Researches* (1839). Philip P. Mason also included both parts in his edition of *The Literary Voyager or Muzzeniegun* (1962), from which the following text of the entire story is taken.

MISHOSHA, OR THE MAGICIAN AND HIS DAUGHTERS

A Chippewa Tale or Legend

In an early age of the world, when there were fewer inhabitants in the earth than there now are, there lived an Indian, who had a wife and two children, in a remote situation. Buried in the solitude of the forest, it was not often that he saw any one, out of the circle of his own family. Such a situation seemed favorable for his pursuits; and his life passed on in uninterrupted happiness, till he discovered a wanton disposition in his wife.

This woman secretly cherished a passion for a young man whom she accidentally met in the woods, and she lost no opportunity of courting his approaches. She even planned the death of her husband, who, she justly concluded, would put her to death, should he discover her infidelity. But this design was frustrated by the alertness of the husband, who having cause to suspect her, determined to watch narrowly, to ascertain the truth, before he should come to a determination how to act. He followed her silently one day, at a distance, and hid himself behind a tree. He soon beheld a tall, handsome man approach his wife, and lead her away.

He was now convinced of her crime, and thought of killing her, the moment she returned. In the meantime he went home, and pondered on his situation. At last he came to the determination of leaving her forever, thinking that her own conscience would in the end, punish her sufficiently; and relying on her maternal feelings, to take care of the two boys, whom he determined to leave behind.

When the wife returned, she was disappointed in not finding her husband, having concerted a plan to dispatch him. When she saw that day after day passed, and he did not return she at last guessed the true cause of his absence. She then returned to her paramour, leaving the two helpless boys behind, telling them that she was going a short distance, and would return; but determined never to see them more.

The children thus abandoned, soon made way with the food that was left in the lodge, and were compelled to quit it, in search of more. The eldest boy possessed much intrepidity, as well as great tenderness for his little brother, frequently carrying him when he became weary, and gathering all the wild fruit he saw. Thus they went deeper into the forest, soon losing all traces of their former habitation, till they were completely lost in the labyrinths of the wilderness.

The elder boy fortunately had a knife, with which he made a bow and arrows, and was thus enabled to kill a few birds for himself and brother. In this way they lived some time, still pressing on, they knew not whither. At last they saw an opening through the woods, and were shortly after delighted to find themselves on the borders of a broad lake. Here the elder boy busied himself in picking the seed pods of the wild rose. In the meanwhile the younger, amused himself by shooting some arrows into the sand, one of which, happened to fall into the lake. The elder brother, not willing to lose his time in making another, waded into the water to reach it. Just as he was about to grasp the arrow, a canoe passed by him with the rapidity of lightning. An old man, sitting in the centre, seized the affrighted youth, and placed him in the canoe. In vain the boy addressed him. "My grandfather" (a term of respect for old people) "pray take my little brother also. Alone, I cannot go with you; he will starve if I leave him." The old magician (for such was his real character) laughed at him. Then giving his canoe a slap, and commanding it to go, it glided through the water with inconceivable swiftness. In a few minutes they reached the habitation of Mishosha, standing on an island in the centre of the lake. Here he lived, with his two daughters, the terror of all the surrounding country.

Leading the young man up to the lodge "Here my eldest daughter," said he, "I have brought a young man who shall become your husband." The youth saw surprize depicted in the countenance of the daughter, but she made no reply, seeming thereby to acquiesce in the commands of her father. In the evening he overheard the daughters in conversation. "There again!" said the elder daughter, "our father has brought another victim, under the pretence of giving me a husband. When will his enmity to the human race cease; or when shall we be spared witnessing such scenes of vice and wickedness, as we are daily compelled to behold."

When the old magician was asleep, the youth told the elder daughter, how he had been carried off, and compelled to leave his helpless brother on the shore. She told him to get up and take her father's canoe, and using the charm he had observed, it would carry him quickly to his brother. That he could carry him food, prepare a lodge for him, and return by morning. He did in every thing as he had been directed, and after providing for the subsistence of his brother, told him that in a short time he should come for him. Then returning to the enchanted island, resumed his place in the lodge before the magician awoke. Once during the night Mishosha awoke, and not seeing his son in law, asked his eldest daughter what had become of him. She replied that he had merely stepped out, and would be back soon. This satisfied him. In the morning, finding the young man in the lodge, his suspicions were completely lulled. "I see, my daughter, you have told me the truth."

As soon as the sun rose, Mishosha thus addressed the young man. "Come, my son, I have a mind to gather gulls eggs. I am acquainted with an island where there are great quantities; and I wish your aid in gathering them." The young man, saw no reasonable excuse, and getting into the canoe, the magician gave it a slap, and bidding it go, in an instant they were at the island. They found the shore covered with gulls eggs, and the island surrounded with birds of this kind. "Go, my son," said the old man, "and gather them, while I remain in the canoe." But the young man was no sooner ashore than Mishosha pushed his canoe a little from land and exclaimed: "Listen ye gulls! you have long expected something from me. I now give you an offering. Fly down, and devour him." Then striking his canoe, left the young man to his fate.

The birds immediately came in clouds around their victim, darkening all the air with their numbers. But the youth, seizing the first that came near him, and drawing his knife, cut off its head, and immediately skinning the bird, hung the feathers as a trophy on his breast. "Thus," he exclaimed, "will I treat every one of you who approaches me. Forbear, therefore, and listen to my words. It is not for you to eat human food. You have been given by the Great Spirit as food for man. Neither is it in the power of that old magician to do you any good. Take me on your beaks and carry me to his lodge, and you shall see that I am not ungrateful."

The gulls obeyed, collecting in a cloud for him to rest upon, and quickly flew to the lodge, where they arrived before the magician. The daughters were surprized at his return, but Mishosha conducted as if nothing extraordinary had taken place.

On the following day he again addressed the youth. "Come, my son," said he, "I will take you to an island covered with the most beautiful pebbles, looking like silver. I wish you to assist me in gathering some of them. They will make handsome ornaments, and are possessed of great virtues." Entering the canoe, the magician made use of his charm, and they were carried, in a few moments, to a solitary bay in an island, where there was a smooth sandy beach. The young man went ashore as usual. "A little further, a little further," cried the old man, "upon that rock you will get some finer ones." Then pushing his canoe from land, "Come thou great king of fishes," cried he, "you have long expected an offering from me. Come, and eat the stranger I have put ashore on your island." So saying, he commanded his canoe to return, and was soon out of sight. Immediately a monstrous fish shoved his long snout from the water, moving partially on the beach, and opening wide his jaws to receive his victim.

"When" exclaimed the young man, drawing his knife, and placing himself in a threatening attitude, "when did you ever taste human food. Have a care of yourself. You were given by the Great Spirit to man, and if you, or any of your tribes, taste human flesh, you will fall sick and die. Listen not to the words of that wicked old man, but carry me back to his island, in return for which, I shall present you a piece of red cloth."

The fish complied, raising his back out of water to allow the young man to get on. Then taking his way through the lake, landed his charge safely at the island, before the return of the magician.

The daughters were still more surprized to see him thus escaped a second time, from the arts of their father. But the old man maintained his taciturnity. He could not, however, help saying to himself, "What manner of boy is this, who ever escapes from my power. His spirit shall not however save him. I will entrap him tomorrow. Ha! ha! ha!"[1]

Next day the magician addressed the young man as follows: "Come, my son," said he, "you must go with me to procure some young eagles. I wish to tame them. I have discovered an island where they are in great abundance." When they had reached the island, Mishosha led him inland until they came to the foot of a tall pine, upon which the nests were. "Now, my son," said he, "climb up this tree and bring down the birds." The young man obeyed. When he had with great difficulty got near the nest, "Now," exclaimed the magician, addressing the tree, "stretch yourself up and be very tall." The tree rose up at the command. "Listen, ye eagles," continued the old man, "you have long expected a gift from me. I now present you this boy, who has had the presumption to molest your young. Stretch forth your claws and seize him." So saying he left the young man to his fate, and returned.

But the intrepid youth drawing his knife, and cutting off the head of the first eagle that menaced him, raised his voice and exclaimed, "Thus will I deal with all who come near me. What right have you, ye ravenous birds, who were made to feed on beasts, to eat human flesh? Is it because that cowardly old canoe-man has bid you do so? He is an old woman. He can neither do you good nor harm. See, I have already slain one of your number. Respect my bravery, and carry me back that I may show you how I shall treat you."

The eagles, pleased with his spirit, assented, and clustering thick around him formed a seat with their backs, and flew toward the enchanted island. As they crossed the water they passed over the magician, lying half asleep in his canoe.

The return of the young man was hailed with joy by the daughters, who now plainly saw that he was under the guidance of a strong spirit. But the ire of the old man was excited, although he kept his temper under subjection. He taxed his wits for some new mode of ridding himself of the youth, who had so successfully baffled his skill. He next invited him to go a hunting.

Taking his canoe, they proceeded to an island and built a lodge to shelter themselves during the night. In the mean while the magician caused a deep fall of snow, with a storm of wind and severe cold. According to custom, the young man pulled off his moccasins and leggings and hung them before the fire to dry. After he had gone to sleep the magician, watching his opportunity, got up, and taking one moccasin and one legging,

---

1. Ha! ha! ha!: The first installment of the story in the *Literary Voyager* ended at this point.

threw them into the fire. He then went to sleep. In the morning, stretching himself as he arose and uttering an exclamation of surprise, "My son," said he, "what has become of your moccasin and legging? I believe this is the moon in which fire attracts, and I fear they have been drawn in." The young man suspected the true cause of his loss, and rightly attributed it to a design of the magician to freeze him to death on the march. But he maintained the strictest silence, and drawing his conaus[2] over his head thus communed with himself: "I have full faith in the Manito[3] who has preserved me thus far, I do not fear that he will forsake me in this cruel emergency. Great is his power, and I invoke it now that he may enable me to prevail over this wicked enemy of mankind."

He then drew on the remaining moccasin and legging, and taking a dead coal from the fireplace, invoked his spirit to give it efficacy, and blackened his foot and leg as far as the lost garment usually reached. He then got up and announced himself ready for the march. In vain Mishosha led him through snows and over morasses, hoping to see the lad sink at every moment. But in this he was disappointed, and for the first time they returned home together.

Taking courage from this success, the young man now determined to try his own power, having previously consulted with the daughters. They all agreed that the life the old man led was detestable, and that whoever would rid the world of him, would entitle himself to the thanks of the human race.

On the following day the young man thus addressed his hoary captor. "My grandfather, I have often gone with you on perilous excursions and never murmured. I must now request that you will accompany me. I wish to visit my little brother, and to bring him home with me." They accordingly went on a visit to the main land, and found the little lad in the spot where he had been left. After taking him into the canoe, the young man again addressed the magician: "My grandfather, will you go and cut me a few of those red willows on the bank, I wish to prepare some smoking mixture." "Certainly, my son," replied the old man, "what you wish is not very hard. Ha, ha, ha! do you think me too old to get up there?" No sooner was Mishosha ashore, than the young man, placing himself in the proper position struck the canoe with his hand, and pronouncing the charm, N'CHIMAUN POLL, the canoe immediately flew through the water on its return to the island. It was evening when the two brothers arrived, and carried the canoe ashore. But the elder daughter informed the young man that unless he sat up and watched the canoe, and kept his hand upon it, such was the power of their father, it would slip off and return to him. Panigwun watched faithfully till near the dawn of day, when he could no longer resist the drowsiness which oppressed him, and fell into a short doze. In the meantime the canoe slipped off and sought its master, who soon returned in high glee. "Ha, ha, ha! my son," said he; "you thought to play me a trick. It was very clever. But you see I am too old for you."

---

2. **conaus:** This unknown word was possibly a misreading of Schoolcraft's original manuscript. The context suggests that she meant a blanketlike covering or rough cape.
3. **Manito:** Spirit of Nature.

A short time after, the young[4] again addressed the magician. "My grandfather, I wish to try my skill in hunting. It is said there is plenty of game on an island not far off, and I have to request that you will take me there in your canoe." They accordingly went to the island and spent the day in hunting. Night coming on they put up a temporary lodge. When the magician had sunk into a profound sleep, the young man got up, and taking one of Mishosha's leggings and moccasins from the place where they hung, threw them into the fire, thus retaliating the artifice before played upon himself. He had discovered that the foot and leg were the only vulnerable parts on the magician's body. Having committed these articles to the fire, he besought his Manito that he would raise a great storm of snow, wind, and hail, and then laid himself down beside the old man. Consternation was depicted on the countenance of the latter, when he awoke in the morning and found his moccasin and legging missing. "I believe, my grandfather," said the young man, "that this is the moon in which fire attracts, and I fear your foot and leg garments have been drawn in." Then rising and bidding the old man follow him, he began the morning's hunt, frequently turning to see how Mishosha kept up. He saw him faltering at every step, and almost benumbed with cold, but encouraged him to follow, saying, we shall soon get through and reach the shore; although he took pains, at the same time, to lead him in round-about ways, so as to let the frost take complete effect. At length the old man reached the brink of the island where the woods are succeeded by a border of smooth sand. But he could go no farther; his legs became stiff and refused motion, and he found himself fixed to the spot. But he still kept stretching out his arms and swinging his body to and fro. Every moment he found the numbness creeping higher. He felt his legs growing downward like roots, the feathers of his head turned to leaves, and in a few seconds he stood a tall and stiff sycamore, leaning toward the water.

Panigwun leaped into the canoe, and pronounced the charm, was soon transported to the island, where he related his victory to the daughters. They applauded the deed, agreed to put on mortal shapes, become wives to the two young men, and for ever quit the enchanted island. And passing immediately over to the main land, they lived lives of happiness and peace.

Bame-wa-wa-ge-zhik-a-quay

[1827, 1839, 1962]

---

4. **the young:** The word *man* was probably omitted in the manuscript.

American Literature

1830–1865

"WE HAVE LISTENED TOO LONG to the courtly muses of Europe," Ralph Waldo Emerson proclaimed in "The American Scholar," an address he delivered at Harvard College in 1837. Emerson developed an old and familiar theme, calling on writers to assert their literary independence from Europe, just as more than sixty years earlier Americans had declared their political independence from England. For him, the challenge remained what it had been since the Revolution: American writers needed to develop new literary forms and modes of expression in response to the democratic institutions, material realities, and social dynamics of life in the United States. Despite the earlier efforts of revered authors like William Cullen Bryant and Washington Irving, many critics shared Emerson's belief that American writers had not yet created a truly indigenous or "native" literature. At the opening of "American Literature," an essay published in 1846, Emerson's friend Margaret Fuller thus observed:

> Some thinkers may object to this essay, that we are about to write of that which has, as yet, no existence. For it does not follow because many books are written by persons born in America that there exists here an American literature. Books which imitate or represent the thoughts and life of Europe do not constitute an American literature. Before such can exist, an original idea must animate this nation and fresh currents of life must call into life fresh thoughts along its shores.

As difficult as it was to recognize in 1846, however, a distinctly American literature had already begun to emerge. Although nagging questions remained about what constituted a native literature, some major works published during the previous decade illustrated the variety and increasing vitality of American writing. Those works also illustrated the ways in

◀ (OVERLEAF)

George Caleb Bingham, *Stump Speaking* (1853–54)

Bingham, a professional painter widely known for his depictions of people and frontier life in Missouri, was also an active politician. In *Stump Speaking*, one of the paintings collectively known as his "election series," he portrayed a distinctive part of American electioneering, the "stump speech," so called because political candidates in frontier areas frequently stood upon the stumps of trees to address voters. Here, the speech is delivered from a makeshift platform by a politician gesturing to the crowd of men while some boys play in the foreground. In the antebellum period, the electoral franchise was extended to nearly all adult white males, who dominated the political process in the United States. But the value placed upon oratory and the numerous reform societies that sprang up during the period offered an opportunity for women, African Americans, and members of other minority groups to speak out publicly on a wide range of political and social issues during the turbulent decades before the Civil War.

which European Romanticism, which exerted such a powerful force on American writers, was adapted by them to their own ends and purposes. The natural world, a major focus of many Romantic writers, took on a special, spiritual significance in Emerson's first book, *Nature* (1836). He also extended the Romantic emphasis on the importance of the individual to democratic, egalitarian ends in "Self-Reliance" and other essays in what many readers view as his two most important books, *Essays* (1841) and *Essays: Second Series* (1844). The radical and revolutionary implications

COMPARATIVE TIMELINE, 1830–1865

Dates	American Literature	History and Politics	Developments in Culture, Science, and Technology
1830–1839	1830 Second edition of David Walker's *Appeal* (1829)	1830 U.S. population: 12,866,020	1828–30 Steam locomotives developed; 35,000 miles of railroad track laid in the United States
		1830 Mormon Church organized and publication of the *Book of Mormon* 1830 Indian Removal Act allocates money to relocate tribes to west of Mississippi River 1830 Revolutions in France, Belgium, Poland	1830 *Godey's Lady's Book* founded 
	1831 Poe, *Poems* 	1831 Turner's slave rebellion in Virginia 1832 Jackson reelected president 1832 Black Hawk War	1831 Garrison founds the *Liberator*, an abolitionist newspaper
	1833 Apess, "An Indian's Looking-Glass for the White Man" 1833 Child, *Appeal on Behalf of That Class of Americans Called Africans*	1833 Abolition of slavery in British colonies; American Anti-Slavery Society founded	1833 *Knickerbocker* founded in New York City 1833 First penny-press newspaper, *New York Sun*, established 1833 First tax-supported public library (New Hampshire) 1833 Large-scale manufacturing of eyeglasses begins
	1834 Sigourney, *Sketches and Poems*		1834 *Southern Literary Messenger* founded 1835 Colt invents revolver

of Romanticism were developed by Margaret Fuller, notably in *Woman in the Nineteenth Century*, a groundbreaking feminist analysis published in 1845. The Romantic concern for human rights and dignity gained additional resonance in works like the *Narrative of the Life of Frederick Douglass* (1845), one of the numerous slave narratives that so enriched the literature of the United States. The nation's literature also revealed a Romantic emphasis on imagination and individual psychology, as well as on the importance of history and locale, which American writers explored in a wide range of works. One of the most popular forms was the short story, usually called the sketch or tale, which strongly appealed to the

Dates	American Literature	History and Politics	Developments in Culture, Science, and Technology
1830-1839 (cont.)	1836 Emerson, *Nature* 1836 Holmes, *Poems* 1837 Hawthorne, *Twice-Told Tales* 1837 Whittier, *Poems Written during the Progress of the Abolition Question*	1836 Van Buren elected president 1836 Battle of the Alamo and establishment of Republic of Texas 1837 Economic panic, severe downturn in American economy 1837-1901 Victoria becomes queen of Great Britain 1838-39 "Trail of Tears": Cherokee forced from their lands by federal troops	 1837 Invention of steam-driven flatbed press for printing books 1837 *United States Magazine and Democratic Review* founded 1837 Deere patents steel plow 1838 Daguerre develops daguerreotype photographic process
1840-1849	1840 Poe, *Tales of the Grotesque and Arabesque* 1840 Brownson, *The Laboring Classes* 1841 Catherine Beecher, *Treatise on Domestic Economy* 1841 Emerson, *Essays* 	1840 U.S. population: 17,069,453 1840 Harrison elected president 1841 First wagon trains travel west on Oregon Trail 1841 Tyler becomes president after death of Harrison	1840 *Dial* established as journal of the transcendentalists 1841 *New-York Tribune* founded by Greeley 1841 *Graham's Lady's and Gentleman's Magazine* founded 1841 Barnum opens his American Museum in New York City 1841 Development of electroplate process in printing

growing number of readers in the United States and which American writers brought to a new level of originality and distinction. Indeed, the short story was a primary source of the growing force and interest of American literature, as exemplified by such diverse collections as Edgar Allan Poe's *Tales of the Grotesque and Arabesque* (1840), Harriet Beecher Stowe's *The Mayflower, or Sketches of Scenes and Characters among the Descendents of the Pilgrims* (1843), and Nathaniel Hawthorne's *Twice-Told Tales* (1837) and *Mosses from an Old Manse* (1846).

The spirit of innovation that characterized many of the works published by the time Fuller's essay "American Literature" appeared in 1846

Dates	American Literature	History and Politics	Developments in Culture, Science, and Technology
1840–1849 (cont.)	1842 Griswold, *The Poets and Poetry of America*		1842 Dickens's American tour
	1843 Smith, *The Sinless Child and Other Poems*		1843 Invention of typewriter
	1844 Emerson, *Essays; Second Series*	1844 Polk elected president	1844 Morse invents telegraph 1844 *New York Ledger* founded
	1845 Poe, *The Raven and Other Poems* 1845 Fuller, *Woman in the Nineteenth Century* 1845 Douglass, *Narrative of the Life of Frederick Douglass*	1845–60 Roughly two million people, mostly from northern Europe (especially Ireland), immigrate to the United States 1845 United States annexes Texas, which enters Union as slave state	
	1846 Hawthorne, *Mosses from an Old Manse*	1846–48 United States wages war against Mexico; treaty cedes entire Southwest to United States 1846 United States acquires large portion of Oregon Country through treaty with Great Britain	1846 Howe invents sewing machine 
		1847 Brigham Young leads group of Mormons to Utah	1847 *North Star* founded by Douglass
		1848 Taylor elected president 1848 Revolutions in France, the Austrian Empire, the German states, and Italian states 1848 First women's rights convention in United States held in Seneca Falls, New York	1848 Marx and Engels, *The Communist Manifesto*
	1849 Thoreau, "Resistance to Civil Government"	1848–49 California gold rush	

was even more apparent in the work of American writers during the following decade. Herman Melville published his first novel in 1846, and within a few years three of the most celebrated American novels appeared: Hawthorne's *The Scarlet Letter* (1850), Melville's *Moby-Dick* (1851), and Stowe's *Uncle Tom's Cabin* (1851-52). In various ways, all of those books pressed against the formal boundaries and accepted subjects of novels. They were followed in short order by other books that challenged both literary and social conventions. One was Henry Thoreau's *Walden* (1854), an experimental prose work that blended elements from a wide range of genres, including autobiography, nature writing, social criticism, and utopian

Dates	American Literature	History and Politics	Developments in Culture, Science, and Technology
1850–1865	1850 *Narrative of Sojourner Truth* 	1850 U.S. population: 23,191,876 1850 Compromise of 1850 admits California to Union as a free state and enacts strict fugitive slave law 	1850 *Harper's New Monthly Magazine* founded 1850 Jenny Lind, "the Swedish Nightingale," begins American tour
	1850 Hawthorne, *The Scarlet Letter* 1850 Marvel, *Reveries of a Bachelor*	1850 Fillmore becomes president after death of Taylor	
	1851 Melville, *Moby-Dick* 1851 Smith, *Woman and Her Needs* 1851–52 Stowe, *Uncle Tom's Cabin*		1851 *New York Times* is founded 1851 Powers, *The Greek Slave* (sculpture)
		1852 Pierce elected president	
	1853 Fern, *Fern Leaves*		1853 *Putnam's Monthly Magazine* founded
	1854 Harper, *Poems on Miscellaneous Subjects* 1854 Thoreau, *Walden*	1854 Kansas-Nebraska Act incorporates doctrine of popular sovereignty to decide issue of slavery; beginning of Republican Party	
	1855 Longfellow, *The Song of Hiawatha* 1855 Whitman, *Leaves of Grass* 1855 Melville, *Benito Cereno*		

tracts. Another was Walt Whitman's *Leaves of Grass* (1855), which represented a radical and self-conscious attempt to break with traditional poetic practices. Certainly he refused to listen to "the courtly muses of Europe," whose influence on American writers Emerson had deplored in "The American Scholar." At about the same time Whitman's volume was published, the equally innovative American poet Emily Dickinson began her own remarkable career. In fact, so much important writing was produced during the early 1850s that those years have been described as the "American Renaissance," a term that with almost equal justification may be applied to the whole period from 1830 through the Civil War.

Dates	American Literature	History and Politics	Developments in Culture, Science, and Technology
1850–1865 (cont.)	1856 Melville, *Piazza Tales* 	1856 Civil war breaks out between proslavery elements and free-soil settlers in Kansas	1856 Bessemer invents process for manufacturing steel
		1856 Buchanan elected president	
		1857 *Dred Scott* decision declares that African Americans have no constitutional rights	1857 *Atlantic Monthly* founded by Emerson, Longfellow, and others
		1857 Economic panic, another severe downturn in American economy	1857 *Harper's Weekly*, New York news and literary magazine, founded
			1858 First transatlantic telegraph sent successfully via submarine cable
		1859 John Brown attempts to lead slave insurrection at Harpers Ferry, Virginia	1859 Darwin, *Origin of Species*
	1860–65 Dickinson writes several hundred poems	1860 U.S. population: 31,443,321	1859 *Anglo-African Magazine* founded
	1861 Jacobs, *Incidents in the Life of a Slave Girl*	1860 Lincoln elected president by carrying all eighteen free states	
	1861 Cooke, *Poems*		
	1861 Davis, *Life in the Iron-Mills*	1861 Representatives of southern states form Confederate States of America	
	1862 Stoddard, *The Morgesons*	1861 Confederate troops fire on Fort Sumter in Charleston harbor, starting Civil War	
	1863 Alcott, *Hospital Sketches*	1863 Emancipation Proclamation	
		1864 Lincoln reelected president	1864 Pasteur invents pasteurization
	1865 Whitman, *Drum-Taps*	1865 Lee surrenders at Appomattox, ending Civil War; Lincoln assassinated	1865 Mendel discovers genetics

Technology, Transportation, and the Growth of the Literary Marketplace

The literary achievements of the period were spurred by a wide range of factors, from intense nationalism to major changes in the book trade in the United States. "God has predestined, mankind expects, great things from our race; and great things we feel in our souls," Melville affirmed in 1850. "We are the pioneers of the world; the advance-guard sent in through the wilderness of untried things, to break a new path in the New World that is ours." Such expansive and optimistic visions were in part a product of the nation's rapid economic growth. Although there were two severe depressions during the boom-and-bust period – in 1837 and again in 1857 – the growing prosperity of many Americans generated enormous self-confidence in themselves and their country. A major engine of economic growth was technology, as new inventions transformed both agriculture and industry.

"We are the pioneers of the world; the advance-guard sent in through the wilderness of untried things, to break a new path in the New World that is ours."

The production of printed materials was also radically altered by new technologies, including the introduction of cheap, machine-made paper. The development of mechanical power-presses and the lower costs of printing made it possible for an ever-larger percentage of the expanding population to afford books and periodicals. The number of readers steadily increased as a result of rising literacy rates and the significant growth in the number of schools, which were major consumers of books – as many as 40 percent of those published during the period were textbooks. Even as reading became an increasingly popular form of entertainment at home and during travel, it served as an important means of instruction and self-improvement outside the classroom, especially for groups whose educational opportunities were limited. The first four women to receive college degrees in the United States graduated from Oberlin in 1841, and only a few other colleges were open to women until after the Civil War. Economic pressures limited the formal education of most working-class Americans, including writers like Melville and Whitman, both of whom left school to find jobs before they were twelve years old. Like many others – including former slaves such as Frederick Douglass and Harriet Jacobs, who had been denied any formal education – Melville and Whitman largely educated themselves by reading works they either purchased or withdrew from the expanding system of local libraries, yet another major market for books and periodicals in the United States.

The expansion of every part of the literary marketplace encouraged many aspiring writers to seek to make a career of authorship, something only a handful of American writers had managed to do before 1830.

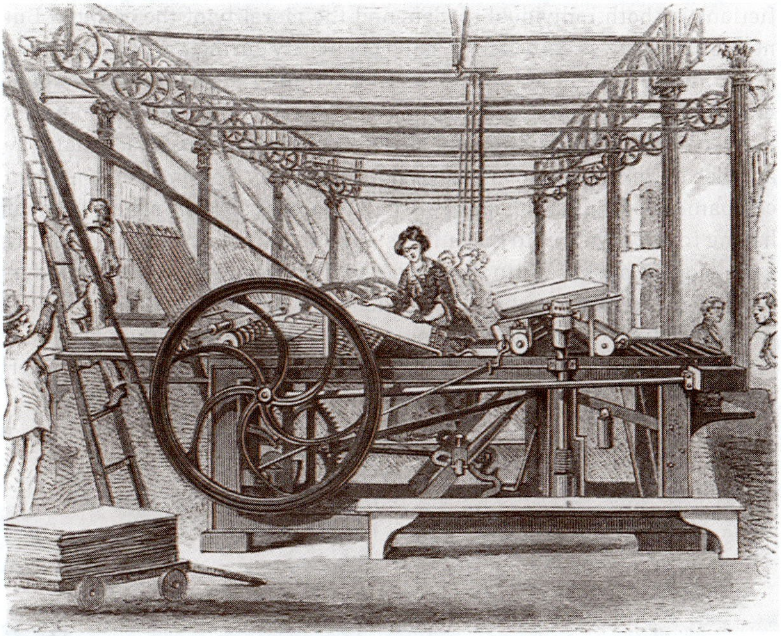

The Power-Press

An illustration from Jacob Abbott's *The Harper Establishment; Or, How the Story Books Are Made* (1855). At the time, Harper & Brothers was the largest publisher in the United States, printing a million books a year at its plant in New York City. The great pressroom contained nearly thirty power-presses, each attended by a young woman, called "the feeder." Her only job was to place fresh sheets of paper on the inclined surface in front of her, called the "apron" of the press, which mechanically printed and moved each sheet to the completed stack to her right. The sheets were then gathered, folded, placed in proper order, and stitched together to make a pamphlet or book.

Although making a living through authorship was still a precarious pursuit, many writers were determined to try. By the mid-1830s, Nathaniel Hawthorne and Edgar Allan Poe were regularly contributing stories and sketches to magazines, and the growing number of periodicals during the following decade spurred the efforts of other writers. Many of them were women, who claimed an increasingly large share of the market for periodical literature. After publishing a textbook in 1833, for example, Harriet Beecher Stowe soon began to write sketches and stories for religious newspapers and magazines like *Godey's Lady's Book*.

There was also a growing market for books of all kinds, including poetry and increasingly novels. Novels were still viewed with suspicion by many clerical critics, who worried about the impact of romantic, unrealistic fictions on both individual readers and the morality of the country. But novels nonetheless gained increasing popularity during the period, emerging in the 1850s as the best-sellers in the United States. With the aid of new methods of production and promotion, such books sold in numbers that would have been unimaginable only decades earlier. In addition, the absence of an international copyright law made it possible for American companies to produce cheap reprints of popular British novels without having to pay royalties to the authors. Proudly describing the astonishing growth of the book trade in the two decades between 1835 and 1855 – during which the number of books published in the United States "had advanced ten times as fast as the population" – the publisher George Palmer Putnam triumphantly added: "If we compare the *numbers* printed of each edition, the growth is still greater; for, twenty years ago who *imagined* edi-

Leila T. Bauman, *Geese in Flight*

As its title suggests, one theme of this naive American painting is natural movement, variously illustrated by the galloping horse, the currents of wind and water, and the chevron of migrating geese. But its central story is the development of human modes of transportation, from the pedestrians, carriage, and railroad train in the foreground to the skiff, sailing ships, and steamboat in the background. In the painting, the natural and the man made are harmoniously balanced. By the time it was painted in the 1850s, however, technological advances had already begun radically to transform life in many parts of the United States.

tions of 300,000, or 75,000, or 30,000, or even the now common number of 10,000?"

The widespread distribution of books and periodicals was made possible by the establishment of a national postal system and a revolution in transportation, which profoundly altered virtually every aspect of life in the United States. By 1830, steamboats plied all of the major rivers in the country, as well as the Great Lakes, and railroad tracks soon began to spread out in a vast network across the nation. From 1828, when the first steam locomotive was built in America, to 1860, almost 35,000 miles of track were laid in the United States. That expanding system made it possible to transport cheaply both people and goods, including printed material, to even the most distant markets. It consequently led to the emergence of mass-circulation newspapers like the *New-York Tribune*, which by the 1850s was distributed throughout the country, and the establishment of magazines targeted at a national audience, including *Putnam's Monthly Magazine* and the *Atlantic Monthly*. Both of those magazines featured the work of American writers, though at the time that essentially meant writers from New England and New York. The centers of publishing in Boston, Philadelphia, and increasingly New York City became the major exporters of literary culture to the rest of the country, which was supplied with books, periodicals, and even lecturers from the East. Certainly the transportation revolution had a direct impact on writers like Emerson, whose extensive lecture tours took him from cities on the East Coast to towns beyond the Mississippi River. As he observed in one of his lectures, Emerson also viewed advances in transportation as a crucial means of binding together the vast and increasingly diverse country into a single, unified nation:

> Not only is distance annihilated, but when, as now, the locomotive and the steamboat, like enormous shuttles, shoot every day across the thousand various threads of national descent and employment and bind them fast in one web, an hourly assimilation goes forward, and there is no danger that local peculiarities and hostilities should be preserved.

Religion, Immigration, and Territorial Expansion

Another force that helped bind the country together was religion. Despite theological disputes among the proliferating sects of the country, most of them could gather together under the broad umbrella of Protestantism. Catholics, who founded Maryland in 1634, and Jews had a long history in the English colonies that became the United States. But the vast majority of Americans during the first half of the nineteenth century were Protestants. Protestantism was further strengthened by the upsurge of evangelical activity in the decades before the Civil War, a period known as the Second

The Camp Meeting at Sing Sing, New York

An illustration from *Harper's Weekly* of one of the many camp meetings held throughout rural America in the decades before the Civil War. At this gathering, which began on Monday and ended on Saturday, three sermons were delivered each day: at ten in the morning, two in the afternoon, and six in the evening, after which there were "prayer meetings, experience meetings, and exhortations, until ten at night." As many as fifty ministers preached at the largest of the camp meetings, some of which attracted congregations of more than twenty thousand people.

Great Awakening, when widespread revivals led to a tremendous rise in church membership and religious sentiment in the United States. The trademark of the revivals was evangelical preaching at "camp meetings," outdoor religious gatherings that frequently drew thousands of people. But the Great Awakening was sustained by the printed as well as the spoken word. Evangelicals emphasized the importance of reading the Bible and religious tracts. Large numbers of Protestant books were published by the American Sunday-School Union and the American Tract Society, which were among the largest publishing firms in the United States. Millions of copies of their publications were distributed by members of "conversion societies," individuals or families who passed out tracts in towns and cities, and by traveling booksellers, who carried their religious wares into even the remotest rural areas, often to people who otherwise had little or no access to books. Indeed, in both their preaching and publications, the Evangelicals communicated in a language common people could readily understand. The rhetoric, symbolism, and religious themes of much of the literature of the period also revealed the impact of the Great Awakening, even on writers who questioned or subverted some of the fundamental beliefs of their more orthodox readers.

By the middle of the century, however, Protestantism faced growing challenges from both within and without. Its institutional authority was undermined by various "come-outers," religious dissenters and reformers who seceded from the Protestant churches, as well as by radical abolitionists, who insisted that the support of slavery within many of those churches violated the true spirit of Christianity. In *Narrative of the Life of Frederick Douglass*, Douglass concluded with a vigorous critique of "the *slaveholding religion* of this land," increasingly dominated by evangelical sects composed of both slaveholders in the South and those who shared their religious beliefs in the North. Conservative clergymen frequently clashed with both abolitionists and supporters of women's rights, who also appealed to the authority of Christ and the New Testament in rejecting the social dictates of American Protestantism. The rising tide of immigration posed a different kind of challenge to the religious practices, social values, and national self-image shaped by the pervasive Protestant culture of the United States. Although most of the new immigrants were farmers and skilled laborers from Protestant countries in Europe, the single largest group – roughly two million people between 1845 and 1860 – was composed of desperately poor Catholic immigrants driven to seek refuge in America by catastrophic crop failures and famine in Ireland.

The surge of immigration helped generate unprecedented urban and industrial growth. Viewed with distrust by American Protestants, Catholic immigrants confronted considerable hostility and various forms of discrimination. Most of the Irish immigrants were consequently crowded into slums in Boston, New York, Philadelphia, and Baltimore. Many found work in the textile mills that had sprouted up in New England cities like Lowell, Massachusetts; still more, along with many other immigrants, moved on to industrial cities like Pittsburgh or the new cities of what was then the West. Between 1830 and 1850, for example, the population of Chicago grew from fifty people to more than 100,000. By the eve of the Civil War, there were fifteen cities with populations above 50,000, and more than a million people lived in the congested metropolis of New York City. Most workers still labored on the land, and many writers of the period continued to focus their attention on nature and rural life, the realms explored in works like Thoreau's *Walden; or, Life in the Woods*. But the city

***The Tract Primer* (c. 1848)**

As the cover of this religious tract demonstrates, the home was widely viewed as the primary setting for the intellectual and moral instruction of children, with the mother as teacher.

Five Points

This painting from the 1840s depicts the crowded buildings and the dark, congested streets of the Five Points District in lower Manhattan, then one of the worst slums in the United States. Five Points was notorious for crime, gangs, political corruption, poverty, and the ghastly living conditions in its squalid tenements. But the working-class neighborhood was also in many ways the birthplace of multicultural America, a confined urban space shared by large numbers of African Americans and recent immigrants from Europe, especially the Irish, who poured into the area during the 1840s and 1850s.

and the contours of urban life were central features in a growing number of writings, including the journalism of Lydia Maria Child, Fanny Fern, and Margaret Fuller; works of fiction like Melville's *Bartleby, the Scrivener: A Story of Wall Street*; and the poetry of Whitman, who was, perhaps, the first genuinely urban poet in the United States. Few viewed the often-grim realities of the new urban and industrial order as unblinkingly as Rebecca Harding Davis, whose *Life in the Iron-Mills* invited Americans to confront realities they often sought to evade: the growing gap between wealth and poverty, as well as the appalling living and working conditions that many of the recent immigrants faced in the United States.

The nation's burgeoning population, which grew from under thirteen million in 1830 to over thirty-one million in 1860, also generated a growing hunger for land and increasing pressures for territorial expansion. From the time of the first arrival of European settlers, Native Americans had been forced from their lands and relentlessly driven westward, a process that culminated when Congress passed the Indian Removal Act in 1830. The law authorized the exchange of land west of the Mississippi for Indian holdings in the East, especially the rich agricultural lands of the "Five Civilized Tribes" – the Cherokee, Choctaw, Creek, Chickasaw, and Seminole Indians – in Mississippi, Alabama, Georgia, and Florida. Although some writers and reformers protested the brutal policy, the

Crossing the Platte on the Oregon Trail

Before the completion of the transcontinental railroad in 1869, the only overland route to the new lands in the West was the Oregon Trail, which generally followed the Platte River to its headwaters, crossed the Rocky Mountains, and then split into trails leading to California or the Oregon Territory. Beginning with what was called "the great migration" of 1843, when a wagon train of one thousand settlers set off from Independence, Missouri, half a million people followed the trail, either on foot or in covered wagons. As this 1859 watercolor suggests, Indian attacks were not the major threat to the settlers. They died in far greater numbers – as many as one in ten – from injuries, disease, exhaustion, and malnutrition during the arduous, four- to six-month journey.

"our manifest destiny to over spread and to possess the whole of the continent which Providence has given us for the development of the great experiment of liberty and . . . self-government entrusted to us."

forced removal of the Indians was supported by most white Americans.

But Americans were increasingly divided about the extension of slave territory. Over the protests of abolitionists and the opposition of antislavery politicians, Congress in 1844 approved the annexation of the slave state of Texas, which had been an independent republic since Anglo-American settlers had rebelled against Mexican rule in 1836. Border skirmishes along the Rio Grande in the spring of 1846 offered a pretext for the United States to declare war on Mexico. In the treaty that ended the war in 1848, Mexico relinquished all claims to Texas and ceded a vast territory to the United States. Combined with Texas, the new territory added more than a million square miles to the national domain; by then, it had also been greatly expanded by the formal acquisition of a large portion of Oregon Country through an 1846 treaty with Great Britain. Even as European immigrants began to flood into eastern cities, thousands of settlers joined the great migration described in works like Francis Parkman's *The Oregon Trail* (1849), a celebration of the frontier spirit and America's westward expansion. Within a few short years, the nation had thus fulfilled what John L. O'Sullivan, the influential editor of the *United States Magazine and Democratic Review*, described in 1845 as "our manifest destiny to over spread and to possess the whole of the continent which Providence has given us for the development of the great experiment of liberty and . . . self-government entrusted to us."

Sectionalism and the Coming of the Civil War

Ironically, what many Americans viewed as the triumphant fulfillment of their "manifest destiny" – a phrase newspapers picked up and made familiar throughout the United States – helped sow the seeds of the Civil War. The need to organize the territories gained from Mexico, which was made all the more pressing by the massive increase in westward migration triggered by the discovery of gold in California, once again raised the issue of the extension of slavery. In an effort to settle the issue once and for all, Congress forged the Compromise of 1850. Among the key provisions of the compromise, which included the admission of California as a free state but made no restriction on slavery in the other new territories, was a far-more-stringent fugitive slave law. Under the revised law, a person suspected of being a runaway slave could be arrested without warrant and was denied trial by jury or the right to testify on his or her own behalf, while any person aiding a runaway was subject to a $1,000 fine and six months' imprisonment. Moreover, special commissioners were authorized to call upon the aid of all citizens to assist in the capture of runaways – in the view of many Northerners, making them complicit in slavery, which most had previously viewed as "the peculiar institution" of the South. The passage of the law generated widespread protests in the North, where opposition was sometimes violent. Sectional divisions were deepened by the passage in 1854 of the Kansas-Nebraska Act, which incorporated the doctrine of "squatter" or "popular sovereignty" – that is, the right of the people of the territories to decide whether slavery would be prohibited – in an area where slavery had previously been excluded by the Missouri Compromise of 1820.

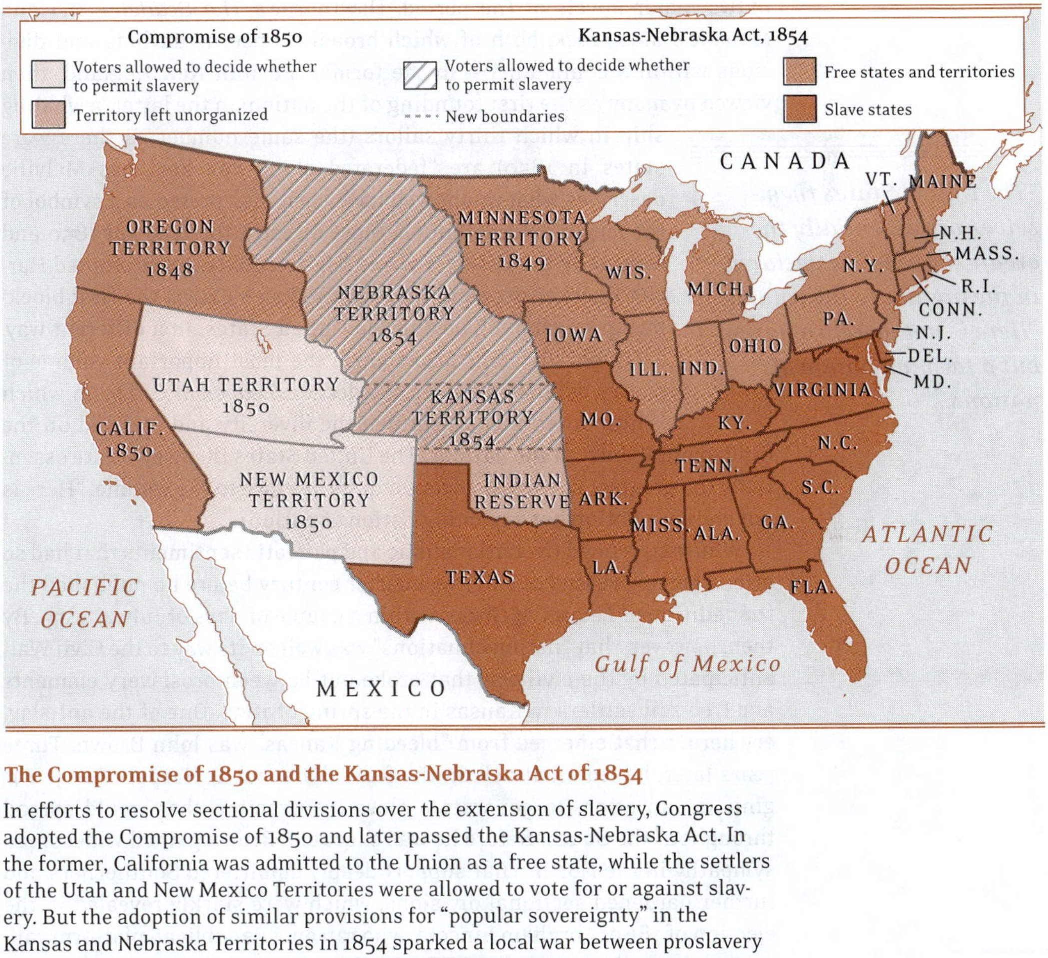

The Compromise of 1850 and the Kansas-Nebraska Act of 1854

In efforts to resolve sectional divisions over the extension of slavery, Congress adopted the Compromise of 1850 and later passed the Kansas-Nebraska Act. In the former, California was admitted to the Union as a free state, while the settlers of the Utah and New Mexico Territories were allowed to vote for or against slavery. But the adoption of similar provisions for "popular sovereignty" in the Kansas and Nebraska Territories in 1854 sparked a local war between proslavery and antislavery settlers that deepened sectional divisions and served as a prelude to the Civil War.

The Compromise of 1850 and the Kansas-Nebraska Act bitterly divided the North and South. Certainly many works of the 1850s, frequently cited as one of the richest decades in American literary history, were shadowed by the deep divisions in the United States. That is not to say that all or even most of the writings of the period mirrored such divisions. The most popular book published in 1850 was Ik Marvel's *Reveries of a Bachelor*, in which the narrator's main concern is whether he will marry. Many of the other popular works published during the decade were novels like Susan Warner's *The Wide, Wide World* and Maria Susanna Cummins's *The Lamplighter*, domestic fictions in which larger social and political issues generally played a minor role. But those issues were at least obliquely treated in two major novels of the period, Hawthorne's *The Scarlet Letter* and Melville's *Moby-Dick*, both of which broadly concern conflicts and divisions within a community – in the former, Puritan New England, then viewed by many as the first founding of the nation; in the latter, a whaling ship in which thirty sailors (the same number as there were states in 1850) are "federated along one keel," as Melville describes what might well have been interpreted as a symbol of the larger political union. More directly, the crisis of 1850 and especially the passage of the Fugitive Slave Act prompted Harriet Beecher Stowe to write *Uncle Tom's Cabin*, the first blockbuster novel published in the United States. In a different way, sectional divisions also shaped the most important volume of poetry published during the decade, *Leaves of Grass*, in which Whitman at once celebrated the diversity and insisted on the fundamental unity of the nation. "The United States themselves are essentially the greatest poem," he declared in the preface to the volume. "Here is not merely a nation but a teeming nation of nations."

"The United States themselves are essentially the greatest poem," he declared in the preface to the volume. "Here is not merely a nation but a teeming nation of nations."

Whitman echoed the nationalistic and patriotic sentiments that had so often been expressed during the quarter century before he published the first edition of *Leaves of Grass*, within a couple of days of July 4, 1855. By then, however, that "nation of nations" was well on its way to the Civil War, anticipated by the civil war that broke out between proslavery elements and free-soil settlers in Kansas in the spring of 1856. One of the antislavery heroes that emerged from "bleeding Kansas" was John Brown. Three years later, he led an attack on the federal arsenal at Harpers Ferry, Virginia, in an effort to generate a slave insurrection that would spread throughout the South. Before he was executed, Brown gained widespread sympathy in the North. That support deeply embittered Southerners and further hardened sectional divisions, which were starkly revealed in the election of 1860. Abraham Lincoln, who ran on a Republican platform calling for the exclusion of slavery from all new territories, carried the eighteen free states but did not gain a single electoral vote in any of the fourteen slave states. Within three months of his election, eleven Southern states seceded; on April 12, 1861, Confederate troops fired on Fort Sumter in Charleston Harbor and the war began. The American Renaissance did not abruptly end with the outbreak of the Civil War. Younger writers like Louisa May Alcott and Elizabeth Barstow Stoddard published stories and novels during the war. It also inspired some of the finest poems written by Whitman and Dickinson, as well as a remarkable volume of verse by Melville, *Battle-Pieces and Aspects of the War* (1866). But the elegiac themes of their poetry, as well as the muted tone and realistic details of much of the other work written during the years 1861-65, marked a significant shift in both the national mood and the consciousness of writers seeking to come to terms with the devastating toll exacted by the Civil War.

The Era of Reform

THE PERIOD OFTEN CALLED THE "AMERICAN RENAISSANCE," a tribute to the extraordinary richness and range of literary achievement during the decades before the Civil War, was also one of the most active periods of reform in American history. Spurred by the rapid social change and cultural ferment of the period, reformers turned their attention to virtually every aspect of life in the United States. Some focused their attention on dietary concerns and domestic relations, others worked to end injustices

◀ **Fugitive Slave Law Convention**

This daguerreotype was taken at a Fugitive Slave Law convention in Cazenovia, New York, in August 1850. Frederick Douglass is pictured seated at the edge of the table on the right. Standing behind him is Gerrit Smith, a wealthy landowner who later helped finance John Brown's attack on Harpers Ferry. On either side of Smith, in matching attire, are the teenaged Edmonston sisters, Mary and Emily, former slaves in the District of Columbia. Two years earlier, they had been captured while attempting to escape and put up for sale at the slave pens in Alexandria, Virginia. After they were purchased for $2,250 by an agent of the New York Anti-Slavery Society, they were brought north to show the kind of people victimized by the slave trade.

like slavery, and still others sought to reform the institutions of the church and the state, including insane asylums, prisons, and schools. As diverse as the proliferating causes were, however, there were close connections among various reforms and reformers. Most activists were involved in a number of different causes, and the reformers were also united by several common assumptions and beliefs. Most were devout Protestants, who viewed social reform as a religious calling or duty. Most believed in the perfectibility – or at least the possibility of the radical improvement – of the individual and society. And virtually all reformers affirmed the power of the word, whether spoken or written.

The ability of reformers to spread that word was made possible by some of the same developments that encouraged literary production during the period. The increasing power of the periodical press led to the establishment of numerous magazines and newspapers sponsored by reform societies or devoted to a single cause. A notable example was temperance, which drew more supporters than any other reform and which enlisted scores of magazines and newspapers in its crusade against alcohol. Like many literary works of the period, the work of reform was also shaped by the popularity of lectures and the consequent development of the lyceum system, a network of local educational institutions that sponsored lecture series in which many writers and reformers found a hospitable welcome, or at least a public forum. At a time when eloquence was held in high esteem, even reformers espousing unpopular causes could hope to gain an audience through the power of their oratory, which was displayed in meetings of reform societies and in countless lectures, both at large halls in cities and in the lyceums that sprouted up in small towns and villages throughout the country. By exploiting the potent combination of print and public lectures – many of which were either reported on or printed in newspapers – reformers appealed at once to the individual consciences of their auditors and the conscience of the nation to address the many injustices of nineteenth-century America.

Among the injustices that began to stir the conscience of some Americans was the treatment of Native Americans. "I ask you, shall the red man live, or shall he be swept from the earth?" the Cherokee leader Elias Boudinot asked in *An Appeal to Whites*, published in 1826. "They hang upon your mercy as to a garment. Will you push them from you, or will you save them?" While such questions had been raised as early as the administration of President Thomas Jefferson (1800-08), they gained added urgency during the congressional debate over bills for the removal of the Cherokee people from their lands in Georgia to territory west of the Mississippi River. Many of the Cherokee people were literate in English, and in 1828 Boudinot founded the *Cherokee Phoenix*, from which editorials opposing the legislation were reprinted in urban newspapers around the country. The Cherokee people also appealed directly to Congress in a series of "memorials," or petitions, now known as the *Cherokee Memorials*. After passage of the Indian Removal Act in 1830, most of the Cherokee people continued to resist the policy, both in the courts of law and the court of public opinion, until they were forcibly driven from their lands during the winter of 1838-39. During almost exactly the same period, the losing battle for Native American rights was carried forward in New England by William Apess, a Pequot of mixed Indian and Caucasian heritage. For Apess, an ordained Methodist minister, race prejudice was at odds with the preaching of Christ and the very spirit of Christianity. He also exposed the brutal treatment of Native Americans by their ostensibly "Christian" conquerors, notably in his "Eulogy on King Philip," a lecture read in Boston in 1836.

Robert Lindneux, *Trail of Tears*

After a decade-long struggle to retain their tribal lands in Georgia, in the winter of 1838-39 the Cherokee people were forcibly rounded up by federal soldiers for removal to lands west of the Mississippi. This 1942 painting portrays their long trek to "Indian Territory," present-day Oklahoma. The torturous journey, which reduced the Cherokee population by over 30 percent, came to be known as "The Path Where They Cried," or "The Trail of Tears."

Apess's brief career as a preacher and writer ended with the publication of that work, after which he was soon forgotten. In sharp contrast, another work published in Boston in 1836 marked the beginning of the long literary career of one of the most influential writers in American literary history, Ralph Waldo Emerson. *Nature*, his first book, became a kind of manifesto for the transcendentalists, a loosely connected group of writers and intellectuals in and around Boston. Transcendentalism was an offshoot of Unitarianism, which by the 1820s became the dominant religion of eastern Massachusetts. The Unitarians rejected as "irrational" the doctrine of the Trinity – the union in one God of the Father, Son, and Holy Ghost – as well as such Puritan doctrines as predestination and the innate depravity of human beings. Instead, the Unitarians emphasized the individual's freedom of choice and capacity for good. In one of his most famous sermons, for example, the Unitarian minister William Ellery Channing celebrated what he described as the human potential to achieve "likeness to God." That conception of human capacity strongly influenced the "transcendentalists," a term that was sometimes used in derision of their belief in the power of human intuition, or "inward beholding," to apprehend a "transcendent" reality that was essentially mental or spiritual in nature. Although many of them were trained as Unitarian ministers, the transcendentalists revolted against what they viewed as the cold rationality and materialism of Unitarianism. Some of them remained Unitarian ministers, seeking to infuse the church with a new spirit and to transform it into a vehicle for social reform. Others abandoned the ministry, including Emerson, who resigned from his church in Boston in 1832. Nonetheless, he remained a kind of secular minister or preacher, who once described the lyceum as his "pulpit." From that pulpit, Emerson delivered hundreds of lectures throughout the North, preaching the gospel of "self-culture," the full development of the intellectual, moral, and spiritual nature of each individual.

Although Emerson was the most prominent of the transcendentalists, the group encompassed diverse individuals and a wide range of views, especially concerning social reform. Emerson's belief that the reformation of society would ultimately be achieved only through the spiritual transformation of its individual members was shared by his young friend Henry David Thoreau. Like Emerson, Thoreau spoke out strongly against injustices like slavery and the Mexican War, notably in his famous essay "Resistance to Civil Government," now better known as "Civil Disobedience." But he rejected the associations and methods of organized reformers, suggesting that their focus on social ills blinded them to the rich resources of nature and the self. In fact, Thoreau's masterpiece, *Walden* (1854), may at least in part be understood as a kind of manual of self-reform and a challenge to those who sought to change the world through different means.

He and Emerson were consequently often at odds with some of the other transcendentalists, who insisted that individual moral reform must go hand-in-hand with organized efforts to reform society. One of the earliest, most militant, and most tenacious crusaders against slavery among the transcendentalists was Theodore Parker, who attacked a wide range of social abuses from the pulpit of his church in Boston. Other members of the group turned their attention to the plight of exploited laborers in the North. In 1840, Emerson's friend George Ripley thus resigned from the Unitarian ministry to establish the Brook Farm Institute of Agriculture and Education, one of the many utopian communities founded during that decade. Such experiments in communal living or "association" varied widely, but virtually all of them sought to offer models of social reorganization, harmonious communities in which individuals could escape the corrosive influences and competitive pressures of an increasingly urban and industrial society. Another of Emerson's closest friends was Margaret

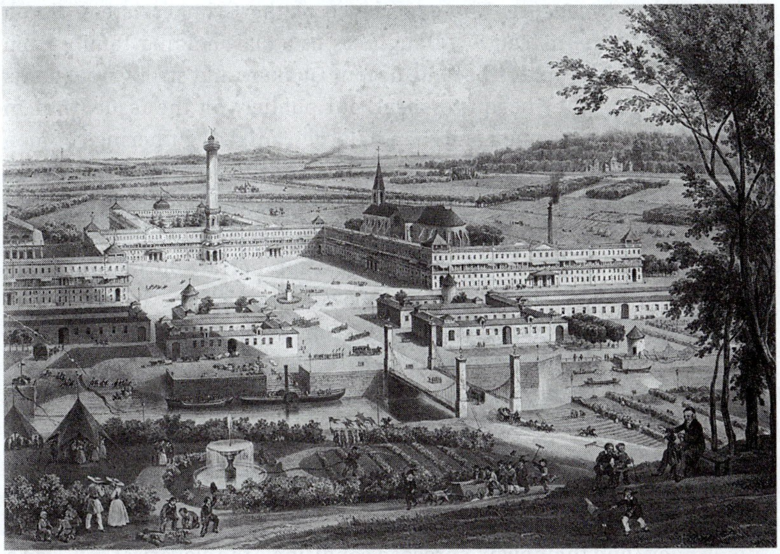

Charles Dubigny, *View of a Phalanx* (c. 1848)

The writings of the French utopian theorist Charles Fourier (1772-1837) had a strong impact on a number of American communities, including Brook Farm, which adopted his ideas of social organization in 1844. But the reality of Brook Farm and other communities differed radically from this imaginary (and never-built) rendering of an ideal Fourierist "phalanx," an economic unit composed of 1,620 people whose members would live in the "phalanstery," or community building, and in which work would be divided among people according to their natural inclinations.

Fuller, a sympathetic observer of and visitor to Brook Farm. Her career illustrated the growing trend toward social activism within transcendentalism, as she became increasingly engaged in various reforms, including "woman's rights," as the feminist movement was then known. In *Woman in the Nineteenth Century* (1845), Fuller affirmed that women must develop their personal natures and their public roles, an argument that influenced many of those who emerged as leaders of the feminist movement, including Elizabeth Cady Stanton and Susan B. Anthony.

The crusaders for women's rights faced formidable obstacles. One was the domestic ideology of the period, often called "the cult of domesticity." On the one hand, that pervasive ideology emphasized the crucial role of women, who were widely viewed as more virtuous than men and consequently as the primary nurturers of moral values from their central position in the domestic sphere. On the other hand, the belief that women's proper place was in the home effectively barred them from careers and direct involvement in public issues. Although some women challenged such a narrow definition of their role, they encountered firm opposition and often harsh censure. The experience of the Grimké sisters, Sarah and Angelina, was instructive. Daughters of a slaveholding family from South Carolina, the sisters became devout Quakers and strong opponents of slavery. When they began to speak out publicly on the issue, first in small gatherings of women and then in larger "mixed" gatherings of men and women, the sisters were chastised both in the press and the pulpit. In a "Pastoral Letter" read from every Congregational pulpit in the state in 1837, the Congregationalist Clergy of Massachusetts called attention to what the New Testament defined as "the appropriate duties and influence of women." Asserting that the "power of woman is in her dependence," the clergy added: "When she assumes the place and tone of a man as a public reformer . . . her character becomes unnatural." Despite such opposition, the Grimkés continued to speak out against slavery and increasingly on behalf of women's rights. As Angelina Grimké observed in 1837, "The investigation of the rights of the slave has led me to a better understanding of my own." That understanding of the connections between slavery and their own oppressed condition, "the slavery of sex," led a growing number of women into the feminist crusade. Their efforts to generate public discussion of the issue culminated in July 1848, when a convention was held in Seneca Falls, New York, to consider the "the condition and rights of woman." That was a signal event in the history of women in the United States, largely because of the "Declaration of Sentiments" adopted at the end of the convention. At once an indictment of the "repeated injuries and usurpations on the part of man toward woman" and a call for women's full equality, that radical document gained national atten-

"The investigation of the rights of the slave has led me to a better understanding of my own."

tion and generated strong momentum for the feminist movement during the following decade.

After 1850, however, women's rights and all other reforms were overshadowed by the antislavery movement. That movement had a long history in America, especially among the Quakers, who in the late eighteenth century became the first religious sect to bar slaveholders from their "Society." Beginning in the 1820s, the gentle persuasion of the Quakers began to be superseded by far more militant demands for the end of slavery, as exemplified by *An Appeal to the Colored Citizens of the World* (1829), a fierce assault on slavery and American racism by David Walker, a free black who grew up in the South before settling in Boston. Like many other writings of the period, Walker's book revealed an important influence on antebellum reform, the religious revivalism that was such a powerful force within American Protestantism during the first half of the nineteenth century. Walker insisted that slavery must end, if necessary by a slave revolt, an affirmation of violent means that distinguished him from the most prominent of the radical abolitionists, the pacifist William Lloyd Garrison, founder and editor of the Boston *Liberator* (1831–65). That was the first newspaper to call for the immediate end of slavery, without compensation to slaveholders, and Garrison was viewed as a dangerous radical by many Americans. In fact, his views were so unpopular that Garrison was

A Printing Press Demolished at Slavery's Bidding

The caption of this widely distributed illustration read: "The people of the free states have attacked 'the tyrant's foe, and the people's friend,' – Oct. 1835, at Utica, July 1836, at Cincinnati, O., Aug. 1837 at Alton, Ill. and finally shot E. P. Lovejoy, because he would not basely surrender 'THE LIBERTY OF THE PRESS, THE PALLADIUM OF ALL OUR LIBERTIES.'"

attacked by a mob in Boston in 1836, part of a wave of violence against antislavery lecturers, meetings of antislavery societies, and those seeking to distribute antislavery literature. Antislavery newspapers were also the target of violence during the decade. The first great martyr of the abolitionist movement was the Reverend Elijah P. Lovejoy, editor of the *Observer* in Alton, Illinois, where he was killed while defending his press from a proslavery mob in 1837. In response to such attacks, the abolitionists sought to link their cause with the rights of freedom of the press and freedom of speech, articles of faith among most Americans. The antislavery appeal slowly began to shape public opinion, especially after 1850, when the message began to be amplified and spread in mass-market urban dailies like Horace Greeley's *New-York Tribune*, the most influential newspaper in the United States.

As crucial as they were, newspapers were not the only means by which abolitionists exploited the growing power of the printing press. As David Walker demonstrated, books could also be used to carry the antislavery message to ever-larger numbers of people. One writer who was determined to do so was Lydia Maria Child, who risked her reputation as one of Boston's most respected authors by publishing *An Appeal on Behalf of That Class of Americans Called Africans* (1833), the first book to call for the immediate emancipation of the slaves and the end of all forms of discrimination against people of color in the United States. Among the most moving appeals for an end to slavery and racism were the so-called slave narratives, autobiographical accounts written by former slaves. "The fugitive slave literature is destined to be a powerful lever," an anonymous reviewer observed in 1849. "We see in it the easy and infallible means of abolitionizing the free States. Argument provokes argument, reason is met by sophistry. But narratives of slaves go right to the hearts of men." Of the hundreds of slave narratives published in the United States between the Revolution and the Civil War, few went so deeply into the hearts of readers in the North as *Narrative of the Life of Frederick Douglass, an American Slave, Written by Himself* (1845). The phenomenal success of his book inspired a vivid succession of similar accounts during the following few years, including *Narrative of the Life of William Wells Brown* (1848) and *Life and Adventures of Henry Bibb, Written by Himself* (1849). Such narratives also provided inspiration and material for fictional treatments of slavery, especially Harriet Beecher Stowe's *Uncle Tom's Cabin*, a best-selling novel that more than any other single work helped to generate antislavery sentiment in the North. The impact of the novel was so great that, when he met Stowe during the Civil War, Abraham Lincoln reportedly greeted her with the words, "So you're the little lady who made this big war."

"The fugitive slave literature is destined to be a powerful lever. . . . We see in it the easy and infallible means of abolitionizing the free States. Argument provokes argument, reason is met by sophistry. But narratives of slaves go right to the hearts of men."

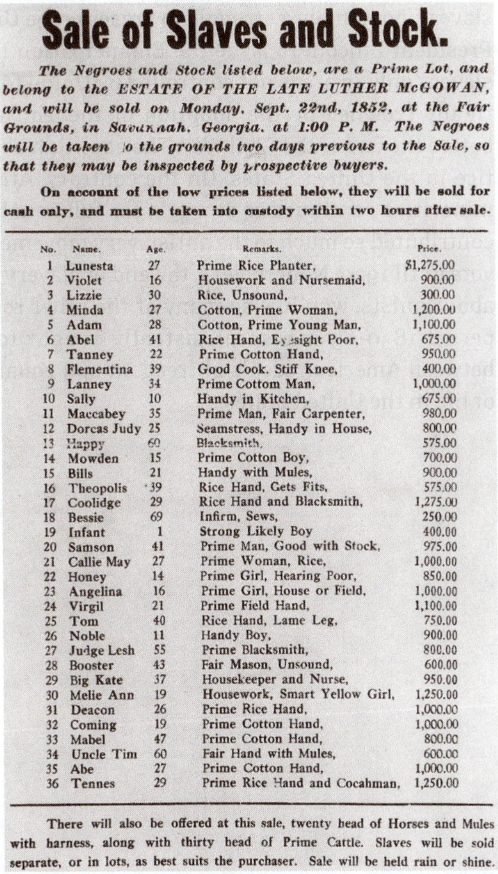

Sale of Slaves and Stock.

The Negroes and Stock listed below, are a Prime Lot, and belong to the ESTATE OF THE LATE LUTHER McGOWAN, and will be sold on Monday, Sept. 22nd, 1852, at the Fair Grounds, in Savannah. Georgia. at 1:00 P. M. The Negroes will be taken to the grounds two days previous to the Sale, so that they may be inspected by prospective buyers.

On account of the low prices listed below, they will be sold for cash only, and must be taken into custody within two hours after sale.

No.	Name.	Age.	Remarks.	Price.
1	Lunesta	27	Prime Rice Planter,	$1,275.00
2	Violet	16	Housework and Nursemaid,	900.00
3	Lizzie	30	Rice, Unsound,	300.00
4	Minda	27	Cotton, Prime Woman,	1,200.00
5	Adam	28	Cotton, Prime Young Man,	1,100.00
6	Abel	41	Rice Hand, Eyesight Poor,	675.00
7	Tanney	22	Prime Cotton Hand,	950.00
8	Flementina	39	Good Cook. Stiff Knee,	400.00
9	Lanney	34	Prime Cottom Man,	1,000.00
10	Sally	10	Handy in Kitchen,	675.00
11	Maccabey	35	Prime Man, Fair Carpenter,	980.00
12	Dorcas Judy	25	Seamstress, Handy in House,	800.00
13	Happy	60	Blacksmith,	575.00
14	Mowden	15	Prime Cotton Boy,	700.00
15	Bills	21	Handy with Mules,	900.00
16	Theopolis	39	Rice Hand, Gets Fits,	575.00
17	Coolidge	29	Rice Hand and Blacksmith,	1,275.00
18	Bessie	69	Infirm, Sews,	250.00
19	Infant	1	Strong Likely Boy	400.00
20	Samson	41	Prime Man, Good with Stock,	975.00
21	Callie May	27	Prime Woman, Rice,	1,000.00
22	Honey	14	Prime Girl, Hearing Poor,	850.00
23	Angelina	16	Prime Girl, House or Field,	1,000.00
24	Virgil	21	Prime Field Hand,	1,100.00
25	Tom	40	Rice Hand, Lame Leg,	750.00
26	Noble	11	Handy Boy,	900.00
27	Judge Lesh	55	Prime Blacksmith,	800.00
28	Booster	43	Fair Mason, Unsound,	600.00
29	Big Kate	37	Housekeeper and Nurse,	950.00
30	Melie Ann	19	Housework, Smart Yellow Girl,	1,250.00
31	Deacon	26	Prime Rice Hand,	1,000.00
32	Coming	19	Prime Cotton Hand,	1,000.00
33	Mabel	47	Prime Cotton Hand,	800.00
34	Uncle Tim	60	Fair Hand with Mules,	600.00
35	Abe	27	Prime Cotton Hand,	1,000.00
36	Tennes	29	Prime Rice Hand and Cocahman,	1,250.00

There will also be offered at this sale, twenty head of Horses and Mules with harness, along with thirty head of Prime Cattle. Slaves will be sold separate, or in lots, as best suits the purchaser. Sale will be held rain or shine.

Slave Sale Broadside, 1852

The abolitionists often cited the selling of slaves and the consequent breaking up of their families as a vivid illustration of the inhumanity of a system that mistreated and sought to transform human beings into brutes. (As the note at the bottom of this duotoned reproduction of the broadside indicates, "Slaves will be sold separate, or in lots, as best suits the purchaser.") The struggle against such dehumanization was a major theme in many of the slave narratives and much of the antislavery fiction of the period. (Chicago Historical Society [ICHi-22003].)

Certainly, the long war of words between the abolitionists and proslavery apologists was a major source of the sectional divisions that culminated in the Civil War. On the eve of that war, Harriet Jacobs – who adopted the pseudonym "Linda Brent" – added yet another powerful appeal to Northern readers with *Incidents in the Life of a Slave Girl*, the first full-length narrative written by a former female slave in America. In a letter to the *Liberator*, the black abolitionist William C. Nell expressed the hope that Jacobs's account would "find its way into every family, where all, especially mothers and daughters, may learn yet about the barbarism of American slavery and the character of its victims." In fact, few read the book, which appeared only three months before the outbreak of the war in April 1861. But the abolitionists continued their crusade during the four long years of the conflict, which they sought to transform into a war to end slavery, not simply a struggle to preserve the Union. They helped convince President Lincoln to issue the Emancipation Proclamation, which ended slavery only in areas not controlled by Union forces, and their efforts were finally crowned by the adoption of the Thirteenth Amendment shortly before the end of the Civil War. The abolition of slavery hardly ended injustice in the United States. On the contrary, African Americans and other minorities continued to struggle for full equality, while women, who had contributed so much to the antislavery movement, did not gain the right to vote until 1920. Nonetheless, the end of slavery was a major victory for the abolitionists, who like so many of the other reformers and writers of the period 1830-65 had so persistently sought to expose the yawning gap between American ideals of freedom and equality and the harsh realities of life in the United States.

American Contexts

"I Will Be Heard": The Rhetoric of Antebellum Reform

In a letter in 1840, Ralph Waldo Emerson wrote his friend the English author Thomas Carlyle that "We are a little wild here with numberless projects of social reform." As Emerson indicated, reform movements swept the nation in the decades before the Civil War. Responding to the swiftly changing social, political, and economic conditions, reformers sought and called for change by exploiting every rhetorical form available to them, from speeches to newspaper articles, pamphlets, and books.

One of the major concerns was the exploitation of laborers, both in the institution of slavery in the South and the factory system in the North. The emergence of radical abolitionism was fueled by evangelical intensity, as both black and white Americans took up the cause. David Walker's *An Appeal to the Colored Citizens of the World* (1829) was one of the most militant attacks on the "inhuman system of slavery" by an African American man in the United States. "I will be heard," thundered William Lloyd Garrison in his fiery editorial of the first issue of his weekly antislavery newspaper, the *Liberator*, founded in 1831. Abolitionism ultimately became the dominant cause of the antebellum period, but some reformers believed that concern for the plight of slaves in the South blinded people to the condition of laborers in the North. One of the first voices raised on their

bedfordstmartins.com/ americanlit *for research links on the authors in this section*

behalf was that of the transcendentalist and reformer Orestes A. Brownson. Like the writings of Walker and Garrison, though for different reasons, Brownson's controversial article *The Laboring Classes* (1840) was viewed by many as a serious threat to the social order. The abolitionists were accused of fomenting slave insurrections and sectional divisions that threatened the Union. Brownson was charged with fomenting class divisions that would lead to war between the rich and the poor. Certainly, he offered one of the most radical and sweeping critiques of the "*Christian* community" in New England, which tolerated a system of labor in the mills and factories that Brownson viewed as even more oppressive than chattel slavery in the South.

Women, who played an important role in the antislavery crusade, also began to press for what was called "woman's rights." But women were by no means united in their approaches to social reform. In a popular and influential book of the period, *A Treatise on Domestic Economy* (1841), Catherine Beecher argued that the division of the sexes into separate spheres of influence was crucial to both the elevation of women and the perfection of the American social experiment, which she viewed as nothing less than the ultimate stage in "the regeneration of the Earth." Others insisted that separate spheres were inherently unequal, since such a division of labor effectively denied women the right to earn a living, as well as their rights as citizens. That position was developed fully in the "Declaration of Sentiments," drafted by Elizabeth Cady Stanton for the first "Woman's Rights Convention," as it was called, at Seneca Falls, New York, in 1848. Partly in response to what she described as the "grand jubilee of ridicule" generated by the Seneca Falls Convention and other women's rights conventions that followed, Elizabeth Oakes Smith wrote *Woman and Her Needs* (1851). Smith, too, strongly challenged the ideology of domesticity, affirming that women had "a right to be heard and felt in human affairs." Among the women who claimed that right, one of the most remarkable was an illiterate former slave and itinerant preacher named Sojourner Truth, who delivered a memorable speech at a woman's rights convention in Ohio in the early summer of 1851. In her vigorous defense of the feminists from theological attacks by a group of ministers, Truth demonstrated the power of her own preaching, even as the report of her speech in an antislavery newspaper illustrated the crucial role of the press in disseminating the words of such eloquent reformers.

David Walker

[1785-1830]

David Walker was born in North Carolina, the son of an enslaved father and a free mother. Sometime in the 1820s, he settled in Boston, where Walker opened a shop near the wharves and became increasingly involved in the early abolitionist movement. In addition to delivering antislavery lectures, Walker began writing articles for *Freedom's Journal*, the first African American newspaper published in the United States. Seeking to reach a larger audience, he also wrote *An Appeal to the Colored Citizens of the World*, which Walker printed at his own expense in 1829. With the help of black sailors frequenting his shop who smuggled the book into Southern ports, the *Appeal* was widely distributed, and it forever changed the antislavery movement by introducing a new urgency and militancy. The text of the following selection, the opening paragraphs of the preamble, is taken from *David Walker's Appeal in Four Articles; Together with a Preamble, to the Colored Citizens of the World, but in Particular and Very Expressly, to Those of the United States of America* (rev. ed., 1830).

From An Appeal to the Colored Citizens of the World

My dearly beloved Brethren and Fellow Citizens.

Having travelled over a considerable portion of these United States, and having, in the course of my travels, taken the most accurate observations of things as they exist – the result of my observations has warranted the full and unshaken conviction, that we, (coloured people of these United States,) are the most degraded, wretched, and abject set of beings that ever lived since the world began; and I pray God that none like us ever may live again until time shall be no more. They tell us of the Israelites in Egypt, the Helots in Sparta, and of the Roman Slaves,[1] which last were made up from almost every nation under heaven, whose sufferings under those ancient and heathen nations, were, in comparison with ours, under this enlightened and Christian nation, no more than a cypher – or, in other words, those heathen nations of antiquity, had but little more among them than the name and form of slavery; while wretchedness and endless miseries were reserved, apparently in a phial, to be poured out upon our fathers, ourselves and our children, by *Christian* Americans!

These positions I shall endeavour, by the help of the Lord, to demonstrate in the course of this *Appeal*, to the satisfaction of the most incredulous mind – and may God

1. **Israelites . . . Slaves:** Walker refers to ancient examples of slavery, including the serfs in Sparta who were technically free but had no legal or civil rights.

Almighty, who is the Father of our Lord Jesus Christ, open your hearts to understand and believe the truth.

The *causes*, my brethren, which produce our wretchedness and miseries, are so very numerous and aggravating, that I believe the pen only of a Josephus or a Plutarch,[2] can well enumerate and explain them. Upon subjects, then, of such incomprehensible magnitude, so impenetrable, and so notorious, I shall be obliged to omit a large class of, and content myself with giving you an exposition of a few of those, which do indeed rage to such an alarming pitch, that they cannot but be a perpetual source of terror and dismay to every reflecting mind.

I am fully aware, in making this appeal to my much afflicted and suffering brethren, that I shall not only be assailed by those whose greatest earthly desires are, to keep us in abject ignorance and wretchedness, and who are of the firm conviction that Heaven has designed us and our children to be slaves and *beasts of burden* to them and their children. I say, I do not only expect to be held up to the public as an ignorant, impudent and restless disturber of the public peace, by such avaricious creatures, as well as a mover of insubordination – and perhaps put in prison or to death, for giving a superficial exposition of our miseries, and exposing tyrants. But I am persuaded, that many of my brethren, particularly those who are ignorantly in league with slaveholders or tyrants, who acquire their daily bread by the blood and sweat of their more ignorant brethren – and not a few of those too, who are too ignorant to see an inch beyond their noses, will rise up and call me cursed – Yea, the jealous ones among us will perhaps use more abject subtlety, by affirming that this work is not worth perusing, that we are well situated, and there is no use in trying to better our condition, for we cannot. I will ask one question here. – Can our condition be any worse? – Can it be more mean and abject? If there are any changes, will they not be for the better though they may appear for the worst at first? Can they get us any lower? Where can they get us? They are afraid to treat us worse, for they know well, the day they do it they are gone. But against all accusations which may or can be preferred against me, I appeal to Heaven for my motive in writing – who knows what my object is, if possible, to awaken in the breasts of my afflicted, degraded and slumbering brethren, a spirit of inquiry and investigation respecting our miseries and wretchedness in this *Republican Land of Liberty!!!!!!*

The sources from which our miseries are derived, and on which I shall comment, I shall not combine in one, but shall put them under distinct heads and expose them in their turn; in doing which, keeping truth on my side, and not departing from the strictest rules of morality, I shall endeavour to penetrate, search out, and lay them open for your inspection. If you cannot or will not profit by them, I shall have done *my* duty to you, my country and my God.

And as the inhuman system of *slavery*, is the *source* from which most of our miseries proceed, I shall begin with that *curse to nations*, which has spread terror and devastation through so many nations of antiquity, and which is raging to such a pitch at the

---

2. **Josephus . . . Plutarch:** Flavius Josephus (c. 37?–100?), a Jewish priest, soldier, and historian who lived during the Roman occupation of ancient Judea (present-day Israel); Plutarch (46?–120?), Greek biographer famed for his *Parallel Lives of Illustrious Greeks and Romans*.

present day in Spain and in Portugal. It had one tug in England, in France, and in the United States of America; yet the inhabitants thereof, do not learn wisdom, and erase it entirely from their dwellings and from all with whom they have to do. The fact is, the labour of slaves comes so cheap to the avaricious usurpers, and is (as they think) of such great utility to the country where it exists, that those who are actuated by sordid avarice only, overlook the evils, which will as sure as the Lord lives, follow after the good. In fact, they are so happy to keep in ignorance and degradation, and to receive the homage and the labour of the slaves, they forget that God rules in the armies of heaven and among the inhabitants of the earth, having his ears continually open to the cries, tears and groans of his oppressed people; and being a just and holy Being will at one day appear fully in behalf of the oppressed, and arrest the progress of the avaricious oppressors; for although the destruction of the oppressors God may not effect by the oppressed, yet the Lord our God will bring other destructions upon them – for not unfrequently will he cause them to rise up one against another, to be split and divided, and to oppress each other, and sometimes to open hostilities with sword in hand. Some may ask, what is the matter with this united and happy people? – Some say it is the cause of political usurpers, tyrants, oppressors, But has not the Lord an oppressed and suffering people among them? Does the Lord condescend to hear their cries and see their tears in consequence of oppression? Will he let the oppressors rest comfortably and happy always? Will he not cause the very children of the oppressors to rise up against them, and oftimes put them to death? "God works in many ways his wonders to perform."

[1829, 1830]

William Lloyd Garrison

[1805-1879]

William Lloyd Garrison was born in Newburyport, Massachusetts, into a poor, working-class family. At the age of thirteen, he was apprenticed to the editor of a local newspaper and became increasingly absorbed in politics. His career as an abolitionist began in 1828, when he met Benjamin Lundy (1789-1839), the editor of the *Genius of Universal Emancipation.* Lundy, a Quaker and an early pioneer in the abolition movement, established his antislavery newspaper in Mt. Pleasant, Ohio, but later moved it to Baltimore, Maryland, and then to Washington, D.C. In 1829, Garrison became Lundy's associate editor and delivered his first antislavery speech, in a Boston church. Thereafter, he lectured constantly and wrote increasingly militant antislavery articles for newspapers. With the financial support of reform-minded individuals as well as many free blacks in the North, Garrison established his own antislavery newspaper, the *Liberator,* which he edited from 1831 to 1865. "To the Public," in which Garrison outlines his antislavery position and the purpose of his newspaper, appeared in the first issue of the *Liberator,* on January 1, 1831.

The Masthead of the *Liberator*

Many abolitionists recalled that, as children, they were first introduced to antislavery ideas by such pictorial headings. This one, from 1838, underscores the sharp division between Southern slavery and Northern freedom: on the left, an auction with the announcement SLAVES HORSES AND OTHER CATTLE TO BE SOLD; on the right, the banner EMANCIPATION and a scene of free labor under the rising sun of liberty.

To the Public

In the month of August, I issued proposals for publishing "THE LIBERATOR" in Washington city; but the enterprise, though hailed in different sections of the country, was palsied by public indifference. Since that time, the removal of the Genius of Universal Emancipation to the Seat of Government has rendered less imperious the establishment of a similar periodical in that quarter.

During my recent tour for the purpose of exciting the minds of the people by a series of discourses on the subject of slavery, every place that I visited gave fresh evidence of the fact, that a greater revolution in public sentiment was to be effected in the free states – *and particularly in New-England* – than at the south. I found contempt more bitter, opposition more active, detraction more relentless, prejudice more stubborn, and apathy more frozen, than among slave owners themselves. Of course, there were individual exceptions to the contrary. This state of things afflicted, but did not dishearten me. I determined, at every hazard, to lift up the standard of emancipation in the eyes of the nation, *within sight of Bunker Hill and in the birth place of liberty.* That standard is now unfurled; and long may it float, unhurt by the spoliations of time or the missiles of a desperate foe – yea, till every chain be broken, and every bondman set free! Let southern oppressors tremble – let their secret abettors tremble – let their northern apologists tremble – let all the enemies of the persecuted blacks tremble.

I deem the publication of my original Prospectus unnecessary, as it has obtained a wide circulation. The principles therein inculcated will be steadily pursued in this paper, excepting that I shall not array myself as the political partisan of any man. In defending the great cause of human rights, I wish to derive the assistance of all religions and of all parties.

Assenting to the "self-evident truth" maintained in the American Declaration of

Independence, "that all men are created equal, and endowed by their Creator with certain inalienable rights – among which are life, liberty and the pursuit of happiness," I shall strenuously contend for the immediate enfranchisement of our slave population. In Parkstreet Church, on the Fourth of July, 1829, in an address on slavery, I unreflectingly assented to the popular but pernicious doctrine of gradual abolition. I seize this opportunity to make a full and unequivocal recantation, and thus publicly to ask pardon of my God, of my country, and of my brethren the poor slaves, for having uttered a sentiment so full of timidity, injustice and absurdity. A similar recantation, from my pen, was published in the Genius of Universal Emancipation at Baltimore, in September, 1829. My conscience is now satisfied.

I am aware, that many object to the severity of my language; but is there not cause for severity? I *will* be as harsh as truth, and as uncompromising as justice. On this subject, I do not wish to think, or speak, or write, with moderation. No! no! Tell a man whose house is on fire, to give a moderate alarm; tell him to moderately rescue his wife from the hand of the ravisher; tell the mother to gradually extricate her babe from the fire into which it has fallen; – but urge me not to use moderation in a cause like the present. I am in earnest – I will not equivocate – I will not excuse – I will not retreat a single inch – AND I WILL BE HEARD. The apathy of the people is enough to make every statue leap from its pedestal, and to hasten the resurrection of the dead.

It is pretended, that I am retarding the cause of emancipation by the coarseness of my invective, and the precipitancy of my measures. The *charge is not true.* On this question my influence, – humble as it is, – is felt at this moment to a considerable extent, and shall be felt in coming years – not perniciously, but beneficially – not as a curse, but as a blessing; and posterity will bear testimony that I was right. I desire to thank God, that he enables me to disregard "the fear of man which bringeth a snare," and to speak his truth in its simplicity and power. And here I close with this fresh dedication:

Oppression! I have seen thee, face to face,
And met thy cruel eye and cloudy brow;
But thy soul-withering glance I fear not now –
For dread to prouder feelings doth give place
Of deep abhorrence! Scorning the disgrace
Of slavish knees that at thy footstool bow,
I also kneel – but with far other vow
Do hail thee and thy hord of hirelings base: –
I swear, while life-blood warms my throbbing veins,
Still to oppose and thwart, with heart and hand,
Thy brutalising sway – till Afric's chains
Are burst, and Freedom rules the rescued land, –
Trampling Oppression and his iron rod:
Such is the vow I take – SO HELP ME GOD![1]

[1831]

1. **Oppression! . . . SO HELP ME GOD!**: A sonnet by the Scottish poet William Pringle (1789–1834), who had been secretary of Britain's Society for the Abolition of Slavery.

Orestes A. Brownson

[1803-1876]

Born in Stockbridge, Vermont, Orestes Augustus Brownson was raised as a Congregationalist and remained deeply religious. Turning first to Presbyterianism, he later became a Unitarian minister and an important figure in the early period of the transcendentalist movement. Increasingly uncomfortable with many Protestant beliefs, Brownson converted to Roman Catholicism in 1844, after which he rejected many of his earlier associations and beliefs. During the previous decade, however, he was one of the most radical religious and social critics among the transcendentalists. From 1838 to 1842, Brownson edited the *Boston Quarterly Review*. Of all of the extended essays and reviews he wrote for the journal, none was as controversial as "The Laboring Classes," which created a furor when it was published in 1840. Indeed, Brownson offered an early analysis of capitalism and the class system that anticipated the work of the German socialist, Karl Marx (1818-1883). The text of the following selection is taken from *The Laboring Classes, An Article from the Boston Quarterly Review*, which was published as a pamphlet in 1840.

New England Textile Mill

The first factory workforce in the United States was primarily made up of New England farm daughters, who were recruited to work in textile mills like those in Lowell, Massachusetts. The young women in this factory, with their male supervisor sitting on the right, paused from their work – roughly twelve hours a day, six days a week – to pose for this daguerreotype, made around 1850.
(Courtesy George Eastman House.)

From The Laboring Classes

In regard to labor two systems obtain; one that of slave labor, the other that of free labor. Of the two, the first is, in our judgement, except so far as the feelings are concerned, decidedly the least oppressive. If the slave has never been a free man, we think, as a general rule, his sufferings are less than those of the free laborer at wages. As to actual freedom one has just about as much as the other. The laborer at wages has all the disadvantages of freedom and none of its blessings, while the slave, if denied the blessings, is freed from the disadvantages. We are no advocates of slavery, we are as heartily opposed to it as any modern abolitionist can be; but we say frankly that, if there must always be a laboring population distinct from proprietors and employers, we regard the slave system as decidedly preferable to the system at wages. It is no pleasant thing to go days without food, to lie idle for weeks, seeking work and finding none, to rise in the morning with a wife and children you love, and know not where to procure them a breakfast, and to see constantly before you no brighter prospect than the almshouse. Yet these are no unfrequent incidents in the lives of our laboring population. Even in seasons of general prosperity, when there was only the ordinary cry of "hard times," we have seen hundreds of people in a not very populous village, in a wealthy portion of our common country, suffering for the want of the necessaries of life, willing to work, and yet finding no work to do. Many and many is the application of a poor man for work, merely for his food, we have seen rejected. These things are little thought of, for the applicants are poor; they fill no conspicuous place in society, and they have no biographers. But their wrongs are chronicled in heaven. It is said there is no want in this country. There may be less than in some other countries. But death by actual starvation in this country is we apprehend no uncommon occurrence. The sufferings of a quiet, unassuming but useful class of females in our cities, in general sempstresses, too proud to beg or to apply to the almshouse, are not easily told. They are industrious; they do all that they can find to do; but yet the little there is for them to do, and the miserable pittance they receive for it, is hardly sufficient to keep soul and body together. And yet there is a man who employs them to make shirts, trousers, &c., and grows rich on their labors. He is one of our respectable citizens, perhaps is praised in the newspapers for his liberal donations to some charitable institution. He passes among us as a pattern of morality, and is honored as a worthy Christian. And why should he not be, since our *Christian* community is made up of such as he, and since our clergy would not dare question his piety, lest they should incur the reproach of infidelity, and lose their standing, and their salaries? Nay, since our clergy are raised up, educated, fashioned, and sustained by such as he? Not a few of our churches rest on Mammon for their foundation. The basement is a trader's shop.

We pass through our manufacturing villages; most of them appear neat and flourishing. The operatives are well dressed, and we are told, well paid. They are said to be healthy, contented, and happy. This is the fair side of the picture; the side exhibited to distinguished visitors. There is a dark side, moral as well as physical. Of the common operatives, few, if any, by their wages, acquire a competence. A few of what

Carlyle[1] terms not inaptly the *body-servants* are well paid, and now and then an agent or an overseer rides in his coach. But the great mass wear out their health, spirits, and morals, without becoming one whit better off than when they commenced labor. The bills of mortality in these factory villages are not striking, we admit, for the poor girls when they can toil no longer go home to die. The average life, working life we mean, of the girls that come to Lowell,[2] for instance, from Maine, New Hampshire, and Vermont, we have been assured, is only about three years. What becomes of them then? Few of them ever marry; fewer still ever return to their native places with reputations unimpaired. "She has worked in a Factory," is almost enough to damn to infamy the most worthy and virtuous girl. We know no sadder sight on earth than one of our factory villages presents, when the bell at break of day, or at the hour of breakfast, or dinner, calls out its hundreds or thousands of operatives. We stand and look at these hard working men and women hurrying in all directions, and ask ourselves, where go the proceeds of their labors? The man who employs them, and for whom they are toiling as so many slaves, is one of our city nabobs, revelling in luxury; or he is a member of our legislature, enacting laws to put money in his own pocket; or he is a member of Congress, contending for a high Tariff to tax the poor for the benefit of the rich; or in these times he is shedding crocodile tears over the deplorable condition of the poor laborer, while he docks his wages twenty-five per cent.; building miniature log cabins, shouting Harrison and "hard cider."[3] And this man too would fain pass for a Christian and a republican. He shouts for liberty, stickles for equality, and is horrified at a Southern planter who keeps slaves.

One thing is certain; that of the amount actually produced by the operative, he retains a less proportion than it costs the master to feed, clothe, and lodge his slave. Wages is a cunning device of the devil, for the benefit of tender consciences, who would retain all the advantages of the slave system, without the expense, trouble, and odium of being slave-holders.

[1840]

---

1. **Carlyle:** Brownson's article was a review of *Chartism* (1839), by the British historian and social critic Thomas Carlyle (1795-1881). Carlyle argued that the working class was worse off in England than elsewhere in Europe because of the rise of the manufacturing system that exploited and oppressed laborers.
2. **Lowell:** The Boott Cotton Mills began to operate in Lowell, Massachusetts, in the 1830s. Factory "girls" who worked in the mills lived in adjacent housing.
3. **Harrison and "hard cider":** In the presidential campaign of 1840, William Henry Harrison's campaign staff offered free cider (the most popular alcoholic beverage in nineteenth-century America) to supporters of the Whig ticket of Harrison and John Tyler.

Catherine E. Beecher

[1800-1878]

Catherine E. Beecher was born in East Hampton, New York. Other prominent members of her family included her father, Lyman Beecher, a noted Calvinist minister; her brother Henry Ward Beecher, one of the most famous preachers of the nineteenth century; and her sister Harriet Beecher Stowe, the author of *Uncle Tom's Cabin.* A pioneer in education for women, Catherine Beecher established the Hartford Female Seminary in 1823. She was also a prolific writer, publishing dozens of articles and books. Her most famous and influential work was *A Treatise on Domestic Economy*, first published in 1841 and reprinted nearly every year until 1856. Believing that domestic life was central to the moral and spiritual good of the nation, Beecher argued that the role of the American woman was to maintain an orderly home, a refuge from the chaotic public sphere. The text of the following selection is taken from the introductory chapter of the first edition of *A Treatise on Domestic Economy, for the Use of Young Ladies at Home, and at School* (1841).

From A Treatise on Domestic Economy

It thus appears, that the sublime and elevating anticipations which have filled the mind and heart of the religious world, have become so far developed, that philosophers and statesmen perceive the signs of its approach and are predicting the same grand consummation. There is a day advancing, "by seers predicted, and by poets sung," when the curse of selfishness shall be removed; when "scenes surpassing fable, and yet true,"[1] shall be realized; when all nations shall rejoice and be made blessed, under those benevolent influences which the Messiah came to establish on earth.

And this is the nation, which the Disposer of events designs shall go forth as the cynosure of nations, to guide them to the light and blessedness of that day. To us is committed the grand, the responsible privilege, of exhibiting to the world, the beneficent influences of Christianity, when carried into every social, civil, and political institution, and though we have, as yet, made such imperfect advances, already the light is streaming into the dark prison-house of despotic lands, while startled kings and sages, philosophers and statesmen, are watching us with that interest which a career so illustrious, and so involving their own destiny, is calculated to excite. They are studying our institutions, scrutinizing our experience, and watching for our mistakes, that they may learn whether "a social revolution, so irresistible, be advantageous or prejudicial to mankind."

1. **"by seers . . . and yet true":** The quotations are from a vision of the restoration of God's glory to the earth in book 6 of *The Task* (1785), a popular poem by the British poet William Cowper (1731-1800).

There are persons, who regard these interesting truths merely as food for national vanity; but every reflecting and Christian mind, must consider it as an occasion for solemn and anxious reflection. Are we, then, a spectacle to the world? Has the Eternal Lawgiver appointed us to work out a problem involving the destiny of the whole earth? Are such momentous interests to be advanced or retarded, just in proportion as we are faithful to our high trust? "What manner of persons, then, ought we to be," in attempting to sustain so solemn, so glorious a responsibility?

But the part to be enacted by American women, in this great moral enterprise, is the point to which special attention should here be directed.

The success of democratic institutions, as is conceded by all, depends upon the intellectual and moral character of the mass of the people. If they are intelligent and virtuous, democracy is a blessing; but if they are ignorant and wicked, it is only a curse, and is much more dreadful than any other form of civil government, as a thousand tyrants are more to be dreaded than one. It is equally conceded, that the formation of the moral and intellectual character of the young is committed mainly to the female hand. The mother writes the character of the future man; the sister bends the fibres that hereafter are the forest tree; the wife sways the heart, whose energies may turn for good or for evil the destinies of a nation. Let the women of a country be made virtuous and intelligent, and the men will certainly be the same. The proper education of a man decides the welfare of an individual; but educate a woman, and the interests of a whole family are secured.

If this be so, as none will deny, then to American women, more than to any others on earth, is committed the exalted privilege of extending over the world those blessed influences, that are to renovate degraded man, and "clothe all climes with beauty."[2]

No American woman, then, has any occasion for feeling that hers is an humble or insignificant lot. The value of what an individual accomplishes, is to be estimated by the importance of the enterprise achieved, and not by the particular position of the laborer. The drops of heaven that freshen the earth are each of equal value, whether they fall in the lowland meadow, or the princely parterre.[3] The builders of a temple are of equal importance, whether they labor on the foundations, or toil upon the dome.

Thus, also, with those labors that are to be made effectual in the regeneration of the Earth. The woman who is rearing a family of children; the woman who labors in the schoolroom; the woman who, in her retired chamber, earns, with her needle, the mite to contribute for the intellectual and moral elevation of her country; even the humble domestic, whose example and influence may be moulding and forming young minds, while her faithful services sustain a prosperous domestic state; – each and all may be cheered by the consciousness, that they are agents in accomplishing the greatest work that ever was committed to human responsibility. It is the building of a glorious temple, whose base shall be coextensive with the bounds of the earth, whose summit shall pierce the skies, whose splendor shall beam on all lands, and those who hew the lowliest

2. **"clothe . . . beauty":** See note 1.

3. **parterre:** An ornamental garden, composed of flower beds and paths arranged in a distinct pattern or design.

stone, as much as those who carve the highest capital, will be equally honored when its top-stone shall be laid, with new rejoicings of the morning stars, and shoutings of the sons of God.[4]

[1841]

---

4. **morning stars . . . God:** See Job 38:7: "When the morning stars sang together, and all the sons of God shouted for joy."

Seneca Falls Woman's Convention

[July 19-20, 1848]

On July 19-20, 1848, the first women's rights convention was held at Seneca Falls, New York. Attended by one hundred people on the first day and three hundred on the second, the convention marked the beginning of a seventy-year campaign that ended when women were finally accorded the right to vote by the passage of the Nineteenth Amendment to the Constitution in 1920. The Seneca Falls Woman's Convention was the idea of Elizabeth Cady Stanton – an abolitionist and feminist who had moved with her husband and their children from Boston to Seneca Falls – and her close friend from Philadelphia, the Quaker reformer Lucretia Mott. Stanton, who drafted the "Declaration of Sentiments," modeled it on the Declaration of Independence. She read the "Declaration of Sentiments" on the first day of the convention and led a section-by-section debate, finally winning approval at the end of the day, when it was signed by sixty-eight women and thirty-two men, including Frederick Douglass. But their radical demand for women's full equality generated such controversy and derision that some of those who supported the "Declaration of Sentiments" later withdrew their signatures. The text is taken from *History of Woman Suffrage* (1881), edited by Elizabeth Cady Stanton, Susan B. Anthony, and Matilda Joslyn Gage.

Declaration of Sentiments

When, in the course of human events it becomes necessary for one portion of the family of man to assume among the people of the earth a position different from that which they have hitherto occupied, but one to which the laws of nature and of nature's God entitle them, a decent respect to the opinions of mankind requires that they should declare the causes that impel them to such a course.

We hold these truths to be self-evident: that all men and women are created equal; that they are endowed by their Creator with certain inalienable rights; that among these are life, liberty, and the pursuit of happiness; that to secure these rights governments

Yᴱ MAY SESSION OF Yᴱ WOMAN'S RIGHTS CONVENTION—Yᴱ ORATOR OF Yᴱ DAY DENOUNCING Yᴱ LORDS OF CREATION.

A Satirical Depiction of a Woman's Rights Convention

Printed in *Harper's Weekly* in 1859, this caricature reveals that feminists were often treated with derision or hostility, especially in the popular press. Their meetings were also frequently disrupted by hecklers, like the jeering men crowded into the balconies of this hall. Despite such strong resistance, the movement gained the support of some men and a growing number of women, who as this illustration also reveals were the primary organizers of and speakers at the numerous meetings and conventions held in the wake of the 1848 convention at Seneca Falls.

are instituted, deriving their just powers from the consent of the governed. Whenever any form of government becomes destructive of these ends, it is the right of those who suffer from it to refuse allegiance to it, and to insist upon the institution of a new government, laying its foundation on such principles, and organizing its powers in such form, as to them shall seem most likely to effect their safety and happiness. Prudence indeed, will dictate that governments long established should not be changed for light and transient causes; and accordingly all experience hath shown that mankind are more disposed to suffer, while evils are sufferable, than to right themselves by abolishing the forms to which they were accustomed. But when a long train of abuses and usurpations, pursuing invariably the same object evinces a design to reduce them under absolute despotism, it is their duty to throw off such government, and to provide new guards for their future security. Such has been the patient sufferance of the women under this government, and such is now the necessity which constrains them to demand the equal station to which they are entitled.

The history of mankind is a history of repeated injuries and usurpations on the part of man toward woman, having in direct object the establishment of an absolute tyranny over her. To prove this, let facts be submitted to a candid world.

He has never permitted her to exercise her inalienable right to the elective franchise.

He has compelled her to submit to laws, in the formation of which she had no voice.

He has withheld from her rights which are given to the most ignorant and degraded men – both natives and foreigners.

Having deprived her of this first right of a citizen, the elective franchise, thereby leaving her without representation in the halls of legislation, he has oppressed her on all sides.

He has made her, if married, in the eye of the law, civilly dead.

He has taken from her all right in property, even to the wages she earns.

He has made her, morally, an irresponsible being, as she can commit many crimes with impunity, provided they be done in the presence of her husband. In the covenant of marriage, she is compelled to promise obedience to her husband, he becoming, to all intents and purposes, her master – the law giving him power to deprive her of her liberty, and to administer chastisement.

He has so framed the laws of divorce, as to what shall be the proper causes, and in case of separation, to whom the guardianship of the children shall be given, as to be wholly regardless of the happiness of women – the law, in all cases, going upon a false supposition of the supremacy of man, and giving all power into his hands.

After depriving her of all rights as a married woman, if single, and the owner of property, he has taxed her to support a government which recognizes her only when her property can be made profitable to it.

He has monopolized nearly all the profitable employments, and from those she is permitted to follow, she receives but a scanty remuneration. He closes against her all the avenues to wealth and distinction which he considers most honorable to himself. As a teacher of theology, medicine, or law, she is not known.

He has denied her the facilities for obtaining a thorough education, all colleges being closed against her.

He allows her in Church, as well as State, but a subordinate position, claiming Apostolic authority for her exclusion from the ministry, and, with some exceptions, from any public participation in the affairs of the Church.

He has created a false public sentiment by giving to the world a different code of morals for men and women, by which moral delinquencies which exclude women from society, are not only tolerated, but deemed of little account in man.

He has usurped the prerogative of Jehovah himself, claiming it as his right to assign for her a sphere of action, when that belongs to her conscience and to her God.

He has endeavored, in every way that he could, to destroy her confidence in her own powers, to lessen her self-respect, and to make her willing to lead a dependent and abject life.

Now, in view of this entire disfranchisement of one-half the people of this country, their social and religious degradation – in view of the unjust laws above mentioned, and because women do feel themselves aggrieved, oppressed, and fraudulently deprived of their most sacred rights, we insist that they have immediate admission to all the rights and privileges which belong to them as citizens of the United States.

In entering upon the great work before us, we anticipate no small amount of misconception, misrepresentation, and ridicule; but we shall use every instrumentality within our power to effect our object. We shall employ agents, circulate tracts, petition the State and National legislatures, and endeavor to enlist the pulpit and the press in our behalf. We hope this Convention will be followed by a series of Conventions embracing every part of the country.

[1848, 1881]

Elizabeth Oakes Smith

[1806-1893]

Elizabeth Oakes Smith, whose life and work are described in more detail on page 1210 of this volume, was best known for her poetry and her popular reform novel, *The Newsboy* (1854), about the plight of homeless boys living on the streets of New York City. Smith was also deeply concerned with women's rights, and she spent much of her career lecturing and writing about issues like the reform of marriage laws and women's suffrage. *Woman and Her Needs* was first published as a series of ten articles in the *New-York Tribune* (November 1850-June 1851) and then as a pamphlet. The text of the following selection is the opening chapter of that pamphlet (1851).

From WOMAN AND HER NEEDS

They who seek nothing but their own just liberty, *have always right to win it and to keep it,* whenever they have power, be the voices never so numerous that oppose it.

-MILTON[1]

From the moment that an individual or a class of individuals, in any community, have become conscious of a series of grievances demanding redress, from that moment they

1. **Milton:** John Milton (1608-1674), poet and propagandist for the republican Commonwealth, established after the Civil War in England culminated in the defeat and execution of King Charles I. The quotation is from *The Ready and Easy Way to Establish a Free Commonwealth* (1660), in which Milton argued that its supporters had the right to defend their freedom and "liberty" even if a greater number called for the restoration of the monarchy in England.

are morally bound to make that conviction vital in action, and to do what in them lies to correct such abuse. Our nature is not such a tissue of lies, our intuitions are not so deceptive, that we need distrust the truth thus forced upon the life. Wherever the pang is felt, a wrong exists – the groan goes not forth from a glad heart, and he or she who has felt the iron of social wrong piercing into the soul, is the one to cast about and demand relief. The saintly patience so often preached is but another mode of protracting the world's misery; we wrong ourselves, and we roll onward the Juggernautic car that is to crush those who succeed us, when we supinely endure those evils which a strong purpose, an energetic will, and an unfaltering trust in the good might help us to redress.

Whatever difference of opinion may exist amongst us as to the *propriety* of the recent Conventions held in our Country, called "Woman's Rights," the fact stands by itself, a handwriting on the wall, proclaiming a sense of wrong, a sense of something demanding redress, and this is fact enough to *justify the movement* to all candid eyes. Indeed enough to render it praiseworthy. For one, I am glad to see that our Republic has produced a class of women, who, feeling the Need of a larger sphere and a better recognition, have that clearness of intellect and strength of purpose by which they go to work resolutely to solve the difficulty. They might stay at home and fret and dawdle; be miserable themselves and make all within their sphere miserable likewise; but instead of this, they meet and talk the matter over, devise plans, explain difficulties, rehearse social oppressions and political disabilities, in the hope of evolving something permanently good.

All this is well, and grows naturally from the progress of institutions like our own, in which opinions are fearlessly discussed, and all thought traced home to its source. It isn't in the nature of things that any class in our midst should be long indifferent to topics of general interest; far less that such should feel the pressure of evils without inquiring into the best means of abatement. When our Fathers planted themselves upon the firm base of human freedom, claimed the inalienable rights of life, liberty, and the pursuit of happiness, they might have foreseen that at some day their daughters would sift thoroughly their opinions and their consequences, and daringly challenge the same rights.

For myself, I may not sympathize with a Convention – I may not feel *that* the best mode of arriving at truth to my own mind – I may feel that its singleness of import would be lost to me while standing in the solid phalanx of associated inquiry; but these objections do not apply to the majority of minds, and I reverence their search in their own way, the many converging lights of many minds all bent upon the same point, even although I myself peer about with my solitary lantern.

These Conventions have called forth from the Press one grand jubilee of ridicule "from Dan even unto Beersheba,"[2] as if it were the funniest thing in the world for human beings to feel the evils oppressing themselves or others, and to look round for redress. It would seem as if Inquiry must always come under beaver and broadcloth – it must be mustachioed and bearded – and yet the graceful Greek made the quality feminine.

---

2. **"from Dan even unto Beersheba"**: See 1 Kings 4:25; the phrase was a way of designating the length and breadth of a country, since Dan was the northernmost and Beersheba the southernmost cities in ancient Israel.

Truth, too, is feminine, but then she must have a masculine exponent to the modern ear, or she becomes absurd. I do not exactly see how she should be so changed when needed for our sex, from what she is when performing good offices for the other. But enough of trifling. The state of things thus appearing in our own day is just the state we might have prophesied would take place at some time. We must meet it, recognize it, and help to direct it wisely. It argues great things for Woman, and through her for the world. We have *Needs* becoming more and more tangible and urgent, and now is the time to consider what they are.

There is a large class of our sex so well cared for, "whom the winds of heaven are not allowed to visit too roughly," who are hemmed in by conventional forms, and by the appliances of wealth, till they can form no estimate of the sufferings of their less fortunate sisters. Perhaps I do wrong to say less fortunate, for suffering to a woman occupies the place of labor to a man, giving a breadth, depth, and fullness, not otherwise attained. Therefore let her who is called to suffer beware how she despises the cross which it implies; rather let her glory that she is accounted worthy to receive this testimony to the capabilities of her soul.

But there is, as I have said, a class unconscious of this bearing; delicate, amiable, lovely even; but limited and superficial. These follow the bent of their masculine friends and admirers, and lisp pretty ridicule about the folly of "Woman's Rights" and "Woman's Movements." These see no need of reform or change of any kind; indeed they are denied that comprehensiveness of thought by which they could hold the several parts of a subject in the mind, and see its bearings. Society is a sort of grown-up mystery which they pretend not to comprehend, supposing it to have gradually developed to its present size and shape from Adam and Eve, by natural gradation, like Church Bishops.

Then there is another class doomed to debasement, vice, labor of body and soul, in all their terrible manifestations. Daughters of suffering without its ennobling influence; too weak in thought, it may be, to discern the best good; or it may be too strong in passion to resist the allurements of the immediate; or it may be ignorant only, they wake to the sad realities of life too late to find redress for its evils. These are the kind over whom infinite Pity would weep as it were drops of blood. These may scoff at reform, but it is the scoffing of a lost spirit, or that of despair. It is the blind utterance of regions denied the light of infinite love, and condemned to the Fata Morganas[3] of depraved vision.

Then come the class of our sex capable of thought, of impulse, of responsibility – the worthy to be called Woman. Not free from faults any more than the strong of the other sex, but of that full humanity which may sometimes err, but yet which loves and seeks for the true and the good. These include all who are identified with suffering, in whatever shape, and from whatever cause; for these, when suffering proceeds from their own acts even, have that fund of greatness or goodness left that they perceive and acknowledge the opposite of what they are. These are the ones who are victims to the falseness of society, and who see and feel that something may and will be done to redeem it. They

---

3. **Fata Morganas:** The Italian version of the name of Morgan Le Fay, the adversarial half-sister of King Arthur, whose plots against Arthur are told in Thomas Malory's *Morte d'Arthur*.

are not content to be the creatures of luxury, the toys of the drawing-room, however well they may grace it – they are too true, too earnest in life, to trifle with its realities. They are capable of thinking, it may be far more capable of it than those of their own household who help to sway the destinies of the country through the ballot-box. They are capable of feeling, and analyzing too, the evils that surround themselves and others – they have individuality, resource, and that antagonism which weak men ridicule, because it shames their own imbecility; which makes them obnoxious to those of less earnestness of character, and helps them to an eclectic power, at once their crown of glory.

To say that such beings have no right to a hearing in a world whose destinies they effect, is to reproach the First Cause for having imparted to his creatures a superfluous intelligence – to say they have no interest in the nature of legislation, when its terrible penalties hang like the hair-suspended sword of Damocles[4] over their heads, is a contradiction as weak as it is selfish and cruel.

Heretofore, women have acted singly – they have been content with individual influence, however exercised, and it has often been of the very worst kind; but now, in our country at least, they seem disposed to associate as do our compeers of the other sex, for the purpose of evolving better views, and of confirming some degree of power. There is no reason why they should not do this. They are the mothers and wives and sisters of the Republic, and their interests cannot be separated from those of the fathers and husbands and brothers of the Republic. It is folly to meet them with contempt and ridicule, for the period for such weapons is passing away.

Their movements as yet may not be altogether the best or the wisest – all is as yet new; but their movements truly and solemnly point to a step higher in the scale of influence. There is a holy significance in them – a prophetic power that speaks well for themselves, and, as I before said, well for the world. It cannot be, from the nature of things, that so much of human intelligence can be brought into vivid action without some great and good result. It has always been so in all subjects that have enlisted thought – men have come from the turmoil of mental action, with new and broader perceptions, a higher and freer humanity, a better identification of the individual with his species, and why should not Woman the same?

I know it is women who sneer most at these movements of each other, and that women oftenest turn their backs upon the sufferings of each other. I do not mean the griefs or physical pains of those in their own rank and circle; far from it; their hearts are rarely at fault there; but to the cry of those ready to perish, to the needs of the erring, the despised, and neglected of their sex, they are deaf and blind. To the long, torturing discords of ill-assorted marriages, to the oppressions of the family circle, the evasions of property and the lengthening catalogue of domestic discomforts growing out of the evils of society, they are *cruel, selfishly indifferent, or remorselessly severe* upon each other.

---

4. **sword of Damocles:** In Greek legend, Damocles was a courtier who took the place of Dionysius, a king, for a day, in order to have the experience of power and good fortune. During a banquet, Damocles noticed that a sword was hanging by a horsehair directly over the throne on which he was seated, indicating how quickly power and good fortune can end. The phrase is used to indicate this moral lesson.

It is true they have not condemned such to the stake literally; have not roasted them alive; hung, quartered, tortured with thumb-screws, impaled on hooks, confined in dungeons and beheaded on blocks, as men have done, the good, the great, the heroic, "of whom the world is not worthy," of their own sex: for they have been denied the power – men choosing to hold the prerogative of externally inflicted cruelty in their own hands; but they have condemned their suffering sisters to the intangible and manifold tortures which can fall only upon the spirit, and which are ten-fold more cruel than any external wrong, without once attempting to move tongue or finger in their behalf. Indeed, I have sometimes thought that women instinctively avoid each other when suffering from social ills, as if that kind of misery had something allied to a stain attached to it; and so it has in fact; the human instinct is not at fault; a *misplaced* individual is humiliated; he or she feels it in the very soul, and all that is within recoils at the wrong. *Appositeness, freedom, joy, are a part of the beautiful,* and where any or all of these are wanting, harmony is wanting, and dignity also, unless the character be allied to the sublime.

Much of this great movement of our sex argues a better and nobler sympathy for each other, the growth of a loyalty full of promise. We think we see a broader and better spirit awakening within us, a nearer and more wholesome humanity – ill-directed it may be as yet, groping after a hidden, unrevealed good, yet the search has opened, and the good will be grasped.

The world needs the action of Woman thought in its destinies. The indefinite influence springing from the private circle is not enough; this is shaded away into the graceful lights of feminine subserviency and household endearment; blessing the individual husband, or ennobling the one group at the family altar, but the world goes on with its manifold wrongs, and woman has nothing but tears to bestow – the outrages that may wring either her own heart or that of others, are perpetrated before her eyes, and she can only wring helpless hands, or plead with idle remonstrance, while her lord and master tells her these things are quite beyond her comprehension; she cannot see how unavoidable it is, but it is not the less unavoidable, and she must shut her eyes and ears, and "mind her spinning." Or, if blessed with a large share of manly arrogance, he will tell her, as did the captain of a militia company of a country town, who, in practising in the court of his house those martial evolutions that were to electrify the village upon parade, accidentally stepped down the trap-door of the cellar. His wife rushed out to succor her liege lord, when she was met with, "Go in, woman; what do you know about war?"

Sure enough, what does she? But this directness of sympathy, this promptitude to relieve, makes her fruitful in resource in small matters, and why should it not in large? If an evil come under her own inspection, she at once casts about for redress, and good comes of it. There is no reason why she should not enlarge her sphere in this way, and no fear of her being the less feminine or endearing by the process.

The majority of women in society are suffering in the absence of wholesome, earnest, invigorating subjects of thought; expending themselves upon trifles, and fretting themselves and others for lack of employment. The routine of housekeeping, the study of the arts, or the management of children, is no more enough to fill their whole lives, than these things to the merchant, the artist, the professional man, who, over and above his business, whatever it may be, finds time to give the more earnest part of his nature "an airing." As occasion comes, he is a man for the ballot-box, the navy, or the public parade.

I have not, and do not say yet, that women should go to these; I have not reached that part of the subject; I only pray that she may be recognized as an intelligence, and not be compelled to dwarf herself lest she should be thought unfeminine.

I wish to show that while she has been created as one part of human intelligence, she has not only a right to be heard and felt in human affairs, not by tolerance merely, but as a welcome and needed element of human thought; and that, when she is thus recognized, the world will be the better for it, and go onward with new power in the progress of disenthrallment.

There is a woman view, which women must learn to take; as yet they have made no demonstration that looks like a defined, appropriate perception. The key-note has been struck by the other sex, and women have responded; this response has been strong and significant, but it will evolve nothing, because it indicates no urgent need. It has done good in one respect – it has raised the cry of contempt, the scoffings of ridicule, and this antagonism is needed to make us look deeper into the soul of things. We shall learn to search and see whether we are capable of bringing anything to the stock of human thought worthy of acceptance. If we can, let us bring it; if not, we will learn to hold our peace.

[1851]

Sojourner Truth

[1797-1883]

Sojourner Truth, born a slave in New York, was emancipated in 1827. Illiterate throughout her remarkable life, Truth was an ardent Christian and abolitionist. She was among the first black women to speak publicly in the United States. To a friend, Truth dictated the story of her life, which was published as *The Narrative of Sojourner Truth* in 1850. Truth sold the slim book to audiences wherever her itinerant lecturing and preaching took her. The following extemporaneous address, one of her most characteristic and famous speeches, was delivered at a women's rights convention in Akron, Ohio. The text is taken from the report of her speech in *The Anti-Slavery Bugle*, June 21, 1851.

I SELL THE SHADOW TO SUPPORT THE SUBSTANCE.
SOJOURNER TRUTH.

Sojourner Truth

A former slave in New York State, Sojourner Truth published a narrative of her life in 1850. In her bag, she often carried copies of the book to sell at her lectures. She apparently also sold visiting cards like this one, which bears the inscription: "I SELL THE SHADOW TO SUPPORT THE SUBSTANCE."

Speech to a Women's Rights Convention

One of the most unique and interesting speeches of the Convention was made by Sojourner Truth, an emancipated slave. It is impossible to transfer it to paper, or convey any adequate idea of the effect it produced upon the audience. Those only can appreciate it who saw her powerful form, her whole-souled earnest gestures, and listened to her strong and truthful tones. She came forward to the platform and addressing the President said with great simplicity:

May I say a few words? Receiving an affirmative answer, she proceeded; I want to say a few words about this matter. I am a woman's rights. I have as much muscle as any man, and can do as much work as any man. I have plowed and reaped and husked and chopped and mowed, and can any man do more than that? I have heard much about the sexes being equal; I can carry as much as any man, and can eat as much too, if I can get it. I am as strong as any man that is now. As for intellect, all I can say is, if woman have a pint and man a quart – why can't she have her little pint full? You need not be afraid to give us our rights for fear we will take too much, – for we can't take more than our pint'll hold. The poor men seem to be all in confusion, and don't know what to do. Why children, if you have woman's rights give it to her and you will feel better. You will have your own rights, and they won't be so much trouble. I can't read, but I can hear. I have heard the bible and have learned that Eve caused man to sin. Well if woman upset the world, do give her a chance to set it right side up again. The Lady has spoken about Jesus, how he never spurned woman from him, and she was right. When Lazarus died, Mary and Martha came to him with faith and love and besought him to raise their brother. And Jesus wept – and Lazarus came forth.[1] And how came Jesus into the world? Through God who created him and woman who bore him. Man, where is your part? But the women are coming up blessed be God and a few of the men are coming up with them. But man is in a tight place, the poor slave is on him, woman is coming on him, and he is surely between a hawk and a buzzard.

[1851]

1. **Lazarus came forth:** Two sisters, Mary and Martha, asked Jesus to raise their brother, Lazarus, from the dead. The account of the miracle is in John 1:1-44.

William Apess

[1798–1839]

William Apess

This portrait of Apess was used as the frontispiece in the second edition of his *A Son of the Forest* (1831), the first full-length autobiography to be published by a Native American.

William Apess was born in Colrain, Massachusetts. According to his account in *A Son of the Forest* (1829), the first full-length autobiography published by a Native American, his paternal grandfather was a white man who married the granddaughter of King Philip, the Wampanoag tribal leader who in the seventeenth century had led a losing battle against the English settlers during King Philip's War. Apess's father married an Indian woman after joining the remnants of the once-powerful Pequot tribe, which by the end of the eighteenth century was greatly diminished by disease, warfare, and ill-treatment at the hands of the English settlers and then of the government of the United States. When Apess was very young, about four, his parents separated. He was then sent to live briefly with his maternal grandparents, whom he remembered as frequently intoxicated and abusive. At about the age of five, he was put to work as an indentured servant with a series of white families. At fourteen, he escaped, joined the army, and fought in the War of 1812.

Although Apess was not raised in his native Pequot culture, he was deeply interested in the history and rights of Native Americans. An ardent Christian, Apess became a Methodist minister and in 1833 went to preach at Mashpee, Massachusetts, the only Indian settlement remaining in that state. There, he became involved in the settlement's struggle to retain its independence, which Apess vigorously supported in his book *Indian Nullification of the Unconstitutional Laws of Massachusetts, Relative to the Marshpee* [sic] *Tribe* (1835). Although the book was not published until after the state legislature granted the tribe's right to self-government, Apess's efforts were influential in helping the Indians to assert their rights and retain their autonomy. At a time when the Native American presence was being all but erased from the official history of the country, Apess also exhorted his white audiences to confront the brutal narrative of the conquest and displacement of the Indians by the European settlers of America. That tragic history was the central theme of his final work, *Eulogy on King Philip*, a lecture Apess read and published in Boston in 1836. Little is known of the remaining years of his life, which ended in 1839 when he died in New York City.

bedfordstmartins.com/americanlit *for research links on Apess*

Apess's *An Indian's Looking-Glass for the White Man.* *The Experiences of Five Christian Indians of the Pequo'd Tribe* (1833), Apess's second book, is a collection of the accounts of five Pequots who were converted to Christianity. Although little is known about the composition of the book, one of the narratives was written by his wife and another by his aunt. The first and final chapters were written and signed by Apess. In the first chapter, Apess describes his early life and conversion to Christianity. In the final chapter, reprinted here, Apess's training as a minister and preacher is evident, as he adopts a firmly Christian perspective to develop a sustained critique of the pervasive race prejudice of the period. The text is from *On Our Own Ground: The Complete Writings of William Apess, a Pequot*, edited by Barry O'Connell (1992).

An Indian's Looking-Glass for the White Man

Having a desire to place a few things before my fellow creatures who are traveling with me to the grave, and to that God who is the maker and preserver both of the white man and the Indian, whose abilities are the same and who are to be judged by one God, who will show no favor to outward appearances but will judge righteousness. Now I ask if degradation has not been heaped long enough upon the Indians? And if so, can there not be a compromise? Is it right to hold and promote prejudices? If not, why not put them all away? I mean here, among those who are civilized. It may be that many are ignorant of the situation of many of my brethren within the limits of New England. Let me for a few moments turn your attention to the reservations in the different states of New England, and, with but few exceptions, we shall find them as follows: the most mean, abject, miserable race of beings in the world – a complete place of prodigality and prostitution.

Let a gentleman and lady of integrity and respectability visit these places, and they would be surprised; as they wandered from one hut to the other they would view, with the females who are left alone, children half-starved and some almost as naked as they came into the world. And it is a fact that I have seen them as much so – while the females are left without protection, and are seduced by white men, and are finally left to be common prostitutes for them and to be destroyed by that burning, fiery curse, that has swept millions, both of red and white men, into the grave with sorrow and disgrace – rum. One reason why they are left so is because their most sensible and active men are absent at sea. Another reason is because they are made to believe they are minors and have not the abilities given them from God to take care of themselves, without it is to see to a few little articles, such as baskets and brooms. Their land is in common stock, and they have nothing to make them enterprising.

Another reason is because those men who are Agents,[1] many of them are unfaithful

1. **Agents:** The state of Massachusetts had appointed agents to oversee the Indians of Mashpee, thus denying them the right to self-government.

and care not whether the Indians live or die; they are much imposed upon by their neighbors, who have no principle. They would think it no crime to go upon Indian lands and cut and carry off their most valuable timber, or anything else they chose; and I doubt not but they think it clear gain. Another reason is because they have no education to take care of themselves; if they had, I would risk them to take care of their own property.

Now I will ask if the Indians are not called the most ingenious people among us. And are they not said to be men of talents? And I would ask: Could there be a more efficient way to distress and murder them by inches than the way they have taken? And there is no people in the world but who may be destroyed in the same way. Now, if these people are what they are held up in our view to be, I would take the liberty to ask why they are not brought forward and pains taken to educate them, to give them all a common education, and those of the brightest and first-rate talents put forward and held up to office. Perhaps some unholy, unprincipled men would cry out, "The skin was not good enough"; but stop, friends – I am not talking about the skin but about principles. I would ask if there cannot be as good feelings and principles under a red skin as there can be under a white. And let me ask: Is it not on the account of a bad principle that we who are red children have had to suffer so much as we have? And let me ask: Did not this bad principle proceed from the whites or their forefathers? And I would ask: Is it worthwhile to nourish it any longer? If not, then let us have a change, although some men no doubt will spout their corrupt principles against it, that are in the halls of legislation and elsewhere. But I presume this kind of talk will seem surprising and horrible. I do not see why it should so long as they (the whites) say that they think as much of us as they do of themselves.

This I have heard repeatedly, from the most respectable gentlemen and ladies – and having heard so much precept, I should now wish to see the example. And I would ask who has a better right to look for these things than the naturalist himself – the candid man would say none.

I know that many say that they are willing, perhaps the majority of the people, that we should enjoy our rights and privileges as they do. If so, I would ask, Why are not we protected in our persons and property throughout the Union? Is it not because there reigns in the breast of many who are leaders a most unrighteous, unbecoming, and impure black principle, and as corrupt and unholy as it can be – while these very same unfeeling, self-esteemed characters pretend to take the skin as a pretext to keep us from our unalienable and lawful rights? I would ask you if you would like to be disfranchised from all your rights, merely because your skin is white, and for no other crime. I'll venture to say, these very characters who hold the skin to be such a barrier in the way would be the first to cry out, "Injustice! awful injustice!"

But, reader, I acknowledge that this is a confused world, and I am not seeking for office, but merely placing before you the black inconsistency that you place before me – which is ten times blacker than any skin that you will find in the universe. And now let me exhort you to do away that principle, as it appears ten times worse in the sight of God and candid men than skins of color – more disgraceful than all the skins that Jehovah ever made. If black or red skins or any other skin of color is disgraceful to God, it appears that he has disgraced himself a great deal – for he has made fifteen colored people to one white and placed them here upon this earth.

Now let me ask you, white man, if it is a disgrace for to eat, drink, and sleep with the image of God, or sit, or walk and talk with them. Or have you the folly to think that the white man, being one in fifteen or sixteen, are the only beloved images of God? Assemble all nations together in your imagination, and then let the whites be seated among them, and then let us look for the whites, and I doubt not it would be hard finding them; for to the rest of the nations, they are still but a handful. Now suppose these skins were put together, and each skin had its national crimes written upon it – which skin do you think would have the greatest? I will ask one question more. Can you charge the Indians with robbing a nation almost of their whole continent, and murdering their women and children, and then depriving the remainder of their lawful rights, that nature and God require them to have? And to cap the climax, rob another nation to till their grounds and welter out their days under the lash with hunger and fatigue under the scorching rays of a burning sun? I should look at all the skins, and I know that when I cast my eye upon that white skin, and if I saw those crimes written upon it, I should enter my protest against it immediately and cleave to that which is more honorable. And I can tell you that I am satisfied with the manner of my creation, fully – whether others are or not.

But we will strive to penetrate more fully into the conduct of those who profess to have pure principles and who tell us to follow Jesus Christ and imitate him and have his Spirit. Let us see if they come anywhere near him and his ancient disciples. The first thing we are to look at are his precepts, of which we will mention a few. "Thou shalt love the Lord thy God with all thy heart, with all thy soul, with all thy mind, and with all thy strength. The second is like unto it. Thou shalt love thy neighbor as thyself. On these two precepts hang all the law and the prophets" (Matthew 22:37, 38, 39, 40). "By this shall all men know that they are my disciples, if ye have love one to another" (John 13:35). Our Lord left this special command with his followers, that they should love one another.

Again, John in his Epistles says, "He who loveth God loveth his brother also" (1 John 4:21). "Let us not love in word but in deed" (1 John 3:18). "Let your love be without dissimulation. See that ye love one another with a pure heart fervently" (1 Peter 1:22). "If any man say, I love God, and hateth his brother, he is a liar" (1 John 4:20). "Whosoever hateth his brother is a murderer, and no murderer hath eternal life abiding in him" [1 John 3:15]. The first thing that takes our attention is the saying of Jesus, "Thou shalt love," etc. The first question I would ask my brethren in the ministry, as well as that of the membership: What is love, or its effects? Now, if they who teach are not essentially affected with pure love, the love of God, how can they teach as they ought? Again, the holy teachers of old said, "Now if any man have not the spirit of Christ, he is none of his" (Romans 8:9). Now, my brethren in the ministry, let me ask you a few sincere questions. Did you ever hear or read of Christ teaching his disciples that they ought to despise one because his skin was different from theirs? Jesus Christ being a Jew, and those of his Apostles certainly were not whites – and did not he who completed the plan of salvation complete it for the whites as well as for the Jews, and others? And were not the whites the most degraded people on the earth at that time? And none were more so, for they sacrificed their children to dumb idols! And did not St. Paul labor more abundantly for building up a Christian nation among you than any of the Apostles? And you know as well as I that you are not indebted to a principle beneath a white skin for your religious services but to a colored one.

What then is the matter now? Is not religion the same now under a colored skin as it ever was? If so, I would ask, why is not a man of color respected? You may say, as many say, we have white men enough. But was this the spirit of Christ and his Apostles? If it had been, there would not have been one white preacher in the world – for Jesus Christ never would have imparted his grace or word to them, for he could forever have withheld it from them. But we find that Jesus Christ and his Apostles never looked at the outward appearances. Jesus in particular looked at the hearts, and his Apostles through him, being discerners of the spirit, looked at their fruit without any regard to the skin, color, or nation; as St. Paul himself speaks, "Where there is neither Greek nor Jew, circumcision nor uncircumcision, Barbarian nor Scythian, bond nor free – but Christ is all, and in all" [Colossians 3:11]. If you can find a spirit like Jesus Christ and his Apostles prevailing now in any of the white congregations, I should like to know it. I ask: Is it not the case that everybody that is not white is treated with contempt and counted as barbarians? And I ask if the word of God justifies the white man in so doing. When the prophets prophesied, of whom did they speak? When they spoke of heathens, was it not the whites and others who were counted Gentiles? And I ask if all nations with the exception of the Jews were not counted heathens. And according to the writings of some, it could not mean the Indians, for they are counted Jews.[2] And now I would ask: Why is all this distinction made among these Christian societies? I would ask: What is all this ado about missionary societies, if it be not to Christianize those who are not Christians? And what is it for? To degrade them worse, to bring them into society where they must welter out their days in disgrace merely because their skin is of a different complexion. What folly it is to try to make the state of human society worse than it is. How astonished some may be at this – but let me ask: Is it not so? Let me refer you to the churches only. And, my brethren, is there any agreement? Do brethren and sisters love one another? Do they not rather hate one another? Outward forms and ceremonies, the lusts of the flesh, the lusts of the eye, and pride of life is of more value to many professors than the love of God shed abroad in their hearts, or an attachment to his altar, to his ordinances, or to his children. But you may ask: Who are the children of God? Perhaps you may say, none but white. If so, the word of the Lord is not true.

I will refer you to St. Peter's precepts (Acts 10): "God is no respecter of persons," etc. Now if this is the case, my white brother, what better are you than God? And if no better, why do you, who profess his Gospel and to have his spirit, act so contrary to it? Let me ask why the men of a different skin are so despised. Why are not they educated and placed in your pulpits? I ask if his services well performed are not as good as if a white man performed them. I ask if a marriage or a funeral ceremony or the ordinance of the

---

2. **counted Jews:** Apess refers to several prevalent racial theories of the nineteenth century, among them the idea that Native Americans were descended from the ancient tribes of Israel.

Lord's house would not be as acceptable in the sight of God as though he was white. And if so, why is it not to you? I ask again: Why is it not as acceptable to have men to exercise their office in one place as well as in another? Perhaps you will say that if we admit you to all of these privileges you will want more. I expect that I can guess what that is – Why, say you, there would be intermarriages. How that would be I am not able to say – and if it should be, it would be nothing strange or new to me; for I can assure you that I know a great many that have intermarried, both of the whites and the Indians – and many are their sons and daughters and people, too, of the first respectability. And I could point to some in the famous city of Boston and elsewhere. You may look now at the disgraceful act in the statute law passed by the legislature of Massachusetts, and behold the fifty-pound fine levied upon any clergyman or justice of the peace that dare to encourage the laws of God and nature by a legitimate union in holy wedlock between the Indians and whites. I would ask how this looks to your lawmakers. I would ask if this corresponds with your sayings – that you think as much of the Indians as you do of the whites. I do not wonder that you blush, many of you, while you read; for many have broken the ill-fated laws made by man to hedge up the laws of God and nature. I would ask if they who have made the law have not broken it – but there is no other state in New England that has this law but Massachusetts; and I think, as many of you do not, that you have done yourselves no credit.

But as I am not looking for a wife, having one of the finest cast, as you no doubt would understand while you read her experience and travail of soul in the way to heaven, you will see that it is not my object. And if I had none, I should not want anyone to take my right from me and choose a wife for me; for I think that I or any of my brethren have a right to choose a wife for themselves as well as the whites – and as the whites have taken the liberty to choose my brethren, the Indians, hundreds and thousands of them, as partners in life, I believe the Indians have as much right to choose their partners among the whites if they wish. I would ask you if you can see anything inconsistent in your conduct and talk about the Indians. And if you do, I hope you will try to become more consistent. Now, if the Lord Jesus Christ, who is counted by all to be a Jew – and it is well known that the Jews are a colored people,[3] especially those living in the East, where Christ was born – and if he should appear among us, would he not be shut out of doors by many, very quickly? And by those too who profess religion?

By what you read, you may learn how deep your principles are. I should say they were skin-deep. I should not wonder if some of the most selfish and ignorant would spout a charge of their principles now and then at me. But I would ask: How are you to love your neighbors as yourself? Is it to cheat them? Is it to wrong them in anything? Now, to cheat them out of any of their rights is robbery. And I ask: Can you deny that you are not robbing the Indians daily, and many others? But at last you may think I am what is called a hard and uncharitable man. But not so. I believe there are many who would not hesitate to advocate our cause; and those too who are men of fame and respectability – as well

---

3. **colored people:** Another common nineteenth-century idea was that the ancient Hebrews were people of color.

as ladies of honor and virtue. There is a Webster, an Everett, and a Wirt,[4] and many others who are distinguished characters – besides a host of my fellow citizens, who advocate our cause daily. And how I congratulate such noble spirits – how they are to be prized and valued; for they are well calculated to promote the happiness of mankind. They well know that man was made for society, and not for hissing-stocks[5] and outcasts. And when such a principle as this lies within the hearts of men, how much it is like its God – and how it honors its Maker – and how it imitates the feelings of the Good Samaritan, that had his wounds bound up, who had been among thieves and robbers.

Do not get tired, ye noble-hearted – only think how many poor Indians want their wounds done up daily; the Lord will reward you, and pray you stop not till this tree of distinction shall be leveled to the earth, and the mantle of prejudice torn from every American heart – then shall peace pervade the Union.

[1833, 1992]

4. **a Webster, an Everett, and a Wirt:** Daniel Webster (1782-1852), a famous orator and senator from Massachusetts; Edward Everett (1794-1865), a professor of Greek at Harvard and a governor of Massachusetts; and William Wirt (1772-1834), a lawyer and politician who was once nominated for president of the United States.

5. **hissing-stocks:** An early term for "laughing-stocks," persons subjected to mockery or ridicule.

Lydia Maria Child

[1802-1880]

Lydia Maria Francis Child was born in Medford, Massachusetts, in 1802, the youngest of five surviving children born to Convers Francis and Susannah Rand Francis. After her mother's death, Child was sent to live first with a married sister in Maine and later with her brother Convers Francis Jr., a Harvard-trained Unitarian minister in Watertown, Massachusetts. Throughout a childhood during which Child felt envious of the formal education her brother received, she read widely in literature and history. Drawing on her reading and her observations of the Abenaki and Penobscot Indians in Maine, Child published her first novel, *Hobomok, A Tale of Early Times,* in 1824. A second historical novel, *The Rebels; or, Boston before the Revolution,* followed in 1825. Two years later, Child established the first magazine for children, *Juvenile Miscellany,* a successful venture that gained her considerable financial rewards. In 1828, she married David Lee Child, a lawyer, abolitionist, and editor of the *Massachusetts Journal.* Child helped to edit the newspaper, for which she also wrote dozens of anonymous articles and stories. At the same time, Child was also writing works for women. *The American Frugal Housewife,* first published in 1829, went through thirty-three editions; Child followed up on its success with *The Mother's Book,* the first book on child rearing in the

bedfordstmartins.com/ americanlit *for research links on Child*

United States, published in 1831. As an acknowledgment of her increasing reputation, she was granted permission to use the library of the Boston Athenaeum, founded in 1807 to serve the city as a center for intellectual activities. Child was only the second woman to be given the honor of using a library established to serve an exclusively male membership.

By 1833, Child was being hailed by the prestigious *North American Review* as the nation's foremost woman writer. That same year, Child sealed her reputation as a committed abolitionist with the publication of *An Appeal in Favor of That Class of Americans Called Africans*, the first full-scale analysis of slavery in historical, legal, economic, political, and moral terms. With its call for immediate emancipation, the book was hailed by radical abolitionists, like her friend William Lloyd Garrison, editor of the *Liberator*. But it was sharply criticized by the conservative elite in Boston. In fact, publication of the book cost Child her editorship of the *Juvenile Miscellany* as well as her privileges at the Boston Athenaeum. Undeterred, she wrote numerous articles and a landmark feminist study, *The History of the Condition of Women, in Various Ages and Nations* (1835). In 1841, Child moved with her husband to New York City, where she became the editor of the *National Anti-Slavery Standard*. After resigning in 1843 because of factionalism in the New York Anti-Slavery Society and dissension about editorial policies, Child ended much of her direct involvement in antislavery societies. But she continued to support abolitionism in her essays and fiction, and she assisted Harriet Jacobs in preparing her narrative, *Incidents in the Life of a Slave Girl*, for publication in 1861. After the Civil War, Child published a novel, *A Romance of the Republic* (1867), and in 1868, *An Appeal for the Indians*, whose cause she and other abolitionists had long championed. Her last publication was a tribute to William Lloyd Garrison, which appeared in the *Atlantic Monthly* shortly after his death in 1879. By the time she died the following year, Child had published more than thirty books and pamphlets and over 250 articles, many of them written to promote the wide range of reforms to which she had devoted so much of her long and productive life.

Child's "Letter from New-York [The Trial of Amelia Norman]." Child began to write a weekly column in the *National Anti-Slavery Standard* in 1841, when she became the editor of the newspaper. Her "Letter from New-York" series, which often expanded on the editorial column she also wrote each week, became very popular with readers for its personal tone and informal style. Connecting a variety of reform issues, Child frankly discussed social problems like prostitution, prison conditions, alcoholism, prejudice, capital punishment, poverty in the cities, and the oppression of minorities and women. The following "Letter" puts a human face on a sensational trial in which a woman was tried and acquitted for the attempted murder of a man who had seduced her. First published in the *Boston Courier* on February 6, 1844, the "Letter" was reprinted on February 22, 1844, in the *National Anti-Slavery Standard*, from which the text is taken.

LETTER FROM NEW-YORK [THE TRIAL OF AMELIA NORMAN]

Unusual excitement has prevailed in this city for a fortnight past, concerning the trial of Amelia Norman for an assault on Henry S. Ballard, with intent to kill. That the prosecutor is a Bostonian by birth, is a fact I would gladly suppress, for the credit of my native city, and for the sake of his worthy and highly respectable parents.

There was a host of witnesses, many of them of the highest respectability, ready to prove that this was a case of deliberate seduction and base desertion. That the poor girl had been subjected to wrongs and insults, enough to drive her mad. At the period of her arrest, she was living at the house of a respectable and kind-hearted German, by the name of Behren. He supposed her to be a widow, and hired her to iron shirts for his clothing-store; an employment she would not have been likely to seek, if she had been the abandoned creature Ballard chooses to represent her. The German testified that for several days previous to her arrest, he and his family considered her insane; that she acted in the wildest way, and was evidently quite unconscious what she was doing; that at times, her anguish seemed intolerable, and vented itself in sobs and tears; then she would laugh, by the half hour together, with a mad laughter. Whether she was an accountable being at the moment she committed the desperate deed, and how far she was in a state to be capable of deliberate intent, passes the wisdom of mortals to decide. She herself says: "God alone can judge me, for he alone knows to what a dreadful state of agony and desperation I was driven."

In prison, her despair was most painful to witness. The physician, as he passed and repassed her cell, in the course of his professional duties, often saw her for hours together, lying on the stone floor, sobbing and groaning in mortal agony. I shall never forget her pale and haggard looks, and the utter hopelessness of her tones, when I first saw her in that tomblike apartment. May I be forgiven, if, at times, I hated law, so unequal in its operation, so crushing in its power. The kind-hearted physician made the most touching representations concerning the state of her health, and his continual fear of suicide. The bail demanded for her temporary release, was $5,000. Efforts were made to reduce this sum; but Ballard's counsel, aware that her situation excited commiseration, spared no pains to prevent it. Exertions were made to obtain affidavits that she still continued to say she would kill her seducer, if ever she could get at him. But the sympathies of all who approached her were excited in her favor, and the worst thing they could report of her was, that in one of her bitter moods, she said, "she sometimes thought turn about was fair play." Two-thirds of the community, nurtured and trained as they are in the law of violence, needed to summon all *their* respect for law and order, to keep from openly expressing sympathy with this opinion. Let them ask themselves what they would have said and done, if they had been situated like her; with all those terrible wrongs eating into her heart and brain, like fire. May this consideration lead no one to excuse or palliate the dreadful crime of murder, but may it teach them to reflect well on the false structure of society,

William Thom, the Beggar Poet of England,[1] says, with impetuous eloquence:

> Here let me speak out – and be heard, too, while I tell it – that the world does not at all times know how unsafely it sits; when Despair has loosed honor's last hold upon the heart – when transcendent wretchedness lays weeping Reason in the dust – when every unsympathizing on looker is deemed an enemy – who *then* can limit the consequences? For my own part, I confess that, ever since that dreadful night, I can never hear of an extraordinary criminal, without the wish to pierce through the mere judicial views of his career, under which, I am persuaded, there would often be found to exist an unseen impulse – a chain with one end fixed in nature's holiest ground, that drew him on to his destiny.

The trial was to have commenced on Monday, the 15th. On the preceding Saturday afternoon, the prisoner's counsel announced the necessity of withdrawing his services, in order to attend to another important case, which came on the same day. The idea of transferring her case to a stranger, without time to examine into its merits, proved the drop too much for a spirit that had so long been under the pressure of extreme despondency. The unfortunate girl made preparations for suicide, by braiding a rope from her bedclothes. In twenty minutes more, she would have passed beyond the power of human tribunals; but the keeper chanced at that moment to enter her gallery, to summon another prisoner, and discovered her preparations.

Ballard's counsel was extremely desirous to push the case through on Monday. He seemed to calculate that it would be an easy matter to thrust aside this "vile prostitute," as he termed her, and by adroit management of legal technicalities, screen his client from public exposure. But, thank God, human sympathies are warm and active, even amid the malaria of cities. The young friend[2] to whom I dedicated my volume of New-York Letters, whose kindness of heart is only equalled by his energy of purpose, gained the ear of the judges, and earnestly entreated for postponement. He took upon himself the expenses of the trial, trusting Providence for aid. A noble-souled, warm-hearted stranger, a Mr. Carney, of Boston, though a man of limited means, offered fifty dollars, and went with him to procure the services of David Graham, esq. one of the ablest lawyers in our criminal courts. The sum was of course much smaller than his usual fee, but he was influenced by higher motives than pecuniary recompense. When he entered upon the case, he was surprised at the amount of respectable testimony in favor of the girl's character, previous to her acquaintance with Ballard. His heart was touched by the story of her wrongs, confirmed as it was by a multitude of witnesses. On the second day of the trial, he wrote me a noble letter, returning the money, for the prisoner's benefit, declaring that this trial involved considerations higher and holier than the relations of lawyer and client. The blessing of God be with him! During four weary days, he exerted

1. **Beggar Poet of England:** William Thom (1798-1848), a Scottish poet and weaver.
2. **young friend:** John Hopper (1815-1864), a Quaker lawyer.

himself with watchful vigilance and untiring zeal. His appeal in behalf of outraged womanhood, was a noble burst of heartfelt eloquence, which I shall forever remember with gratitude and admiration.

The case was likewise conducted with great ability on the part of Mr. Sandford, counsel for the prosecution, and a personal friend of Ballard's; but it was a kind of ability from which my open-hearted nature shrinks, as it would from the cunning of the fox, and the subtlety of the serpent. He could not have managed the case as he did, if he had ever had a sister or daughter thus betrayed. This consideration abated the indignation which sometimes kindled in my soul, at witnessing so much power exerted against a poor human being, already so crushed and desolate. Moreover, I pitied him for obvious ill-health, for having the management of so bad a cause, and for the almost total want of sympathy to sustain him in his trying position.

In opening the case, he assured the jury that Amelia Norman was a woman of the town, before Ballard became acquainted with her; that she had decoyed him to her lodgings, and had followed him up with a series of annoying persecutions, to obtain money, according to the custom of prostitutes with their poor victims. That on one occasion, she had even gone to his store with an infamous companion, and beat him with their parasols. He did not, however, mention that this companion was another victim of his treacherous client. Having thus blackened the character of the unfortunate prisoner, he contended that no evidence concerning her character or Ballard's should be admitted; that the testimony must be strictly confined to the evening when the stabbing took place. The judge sustained him; and for two days, there was a perpetual fighting with witnesses, to keep the truth out of court. Sandford contended that the jury were to decide solely upon the fact whether the woman assaulted Ballard with intent to kill; and that they had nothing to do with the prior or subsequent history of either of the parties. Graham, on the other hand, urged that it was necessary to prove the wrongs she had suffered, and her consequent state of mind and health, in order to decide upon her intent. There was keen sparring between the lawyers, and the witnesses were sometimes bewildered which to answer. This suppression of evidence, after defaming the character of the girl in such wholesale terms, doubtless produced its effect on the mind of the jury, and somewhat influenced their verdict.

But though Mr. Sandford sprung every way, to stop up any crevice through which the impertinent light might enter, enough did get before the jury, to satisfy them that Amelia Norman had been a virtuous, discreet, amiable, and quiet girl, before her acquaintance with Ballard; and that the history of her wrongs was no fiction of romance.

The counsel for the prisoner, on his part, described her seducer's character and conduct in terms that must have been anything but soothing or agreeable to his ear.[3]

---

3. **agreeable to his ear:** He stated that a deliberate plan of seduction had been laid, that Ballard had lived with the prisoner at various respectable boardinghouses, calling her his wife, assuming the name of Mr. and Mrs. Brown, Mr. and Mrs. Williams, &c. That he had afterward left her at a house of prostitution, pretending it was a respectable boardinghouse, and had gone to Europe without her knowledge, leaving her without money. That she left the house as soon as she discovered its character, and strove to earn her living by honest industry. That when he returned from Europe, she remonstrated with him for deserting her, and he answered, "Damn you, go and get your living, as other prostitutes do." [Child's note]

Mr. Sandford reminded the jury that one lawyer's word was just as much to be believed as another; that it was their duty to be guided only by the evidence. Mr. Graham retorted "But where is *your* evidence? There stand *our* thirty witnesses, ready to prove every word we have stated, and a good deal more, if the court will only allow them to be heard." And then he distinctly named the witnesses, their occupations, places of residence, &c. with what they *would* testify if opportunity were given.

It was an adroit game; as exciting to watch, as a skillful game of chess. I never before felt so much intellectual respect, and so much moral aversion, for the legal profession.

Mr. Sandford's Biblical arguments evinced much less acuteness than his legal distinctions. While portraying the horrors of murder, he urged the usual plea, that the Divine abhorrence of it was evinced by the requisition of "blood for blood," and he sustained this position, by the mark which God set upon Cain. He apparently forgot that the mark was set upon Cain in order that men should *not* slay him. Unfortunately for the advocates of capital punishment, this is the only case on record, where the direct agency of God was interposed in a case of murder.

Mr. Sandford likewise found the first seducer in the Bible, in the person of our mother Eve, and said the serpent had been busy with the sex ever since. He drew a lively picture of poor innocent men tempted, betrayed, and persecuted by women. This was putting the saddle on the wrong horse, with a vengeance! And he himself afterward implied as much; for he reminded the jury that there were twelve thousand prostitutes in New-York, supported by money that came from our citizens; and added, that *all these prostitutes had the same wrongs to revenge upon somebody.* He asked the jury whether it would be worse to have the virtue of their daughters ruined, or their young and generous sons brought home stabbed by the hands of prostitutes. If this precedent were established, he feared that strangers visiting New-York would stumble over the dead bodies of citizens, at the very thresholds of their own doors.

I had no doubt that if all deeply injured women were to undertake to redress their wrongs in this bad way, there would be a huge pile of dead citizens. (I even thought it not impossible that some of the honorable court themselves might be among the missing.) I was aware that ribs all around the room felt unsafe in view of the picture the pleader had drawn. It unquestionably was an argument that came home to men's business and bosoms. Yet I felt no very active pity for their terror. I indignantly asked what had been done to the twelve thousand men, who made these poor creatures prostitutes? I remembered that strangers visiting our city continually stumbled upon something worse than dead bodies, viz: degraded, ruined souls, in the forms of those twelve thousand prostitutes: and I asked, what do "law and order" do for *them*? Mr. Sandford declared that women could take care of themselves as well as men. Perhaps so; but his twelve thousand facts show that women do *not* take care of themselves; and he urged that "generous youths" were continually led astray by this band of prostitutes, though of course, the temptation must be merely animal, unmingled with the seductive influence of the affections, which so often leads woman to ruin, through the agency of her best impulses.

But to return to the trial; Mr. Graham dwelt strongly on the point that unless the jury deemed there was sufficient evidence of deliberate intent, to constitute murder in case the man had died, they were bound to acquit. The jury were doubtless in a state to go through any legal loophole, that might be opened. The frantic state of the prisoner's mind, so clearly shown in the evidence, seemed to them too nearly akin to insanity to be easily distinguished. The inequality of the laws roused their sense of justice, and probably made them feel that a verdict of guilty would be like tying down the stones and letting the mad dogs loose. They felt little anxiety to protect Ballard, by sending his victim to Sing Sing, that he might feel safe to prowl about after other daughters and sisters of honest families. The popular indignation, which was with difficulty suppressed by a strong constabulary force, showed plainly enough that the public would like to say to them –

"I beseech you,
Wrest once the law to your authority;
To do a great right do a little wrong;
And curb this cruel devil of his will."[4]

I believe they strove to resist this magnetic influence, and to return such a verdict as they honestly believed the testimony in the case rendered lawful. When the foreman pronounced the words "Not Guilty!" the building shook with such a thunder of applause as I never before heard. Some of the very officers appointed to keep order, involuntarily let their tip-staffs fall on the floor, and clapped with the multitude. It was the surging of long repressed sympathies coming in like a roaring sea.

I am by no means deaf to the plea for the preservation of law and order. My compassion for the prisoner's wrongs has never for a moment blinded me to the guilt of revenge. But legislators may rest assured that law will yield, like a rope of sand before the influence of humane sentiments, in cases of this kind, until the laws are better regulated. Seduction is going on by wholesale, with a systematic arrangement, and a number and variety of agents, which would astonish those who have never looked beneath the hypocritical surface of things. In our cities, almost every girl, in the humbler classes of life, walks among snares and pitfalls at every step, unconscious of their presence, until she finds herself fallen, and entangled in a frightful net-work, from which she sees no escape. Life and property are protected, but what protection is there for pure hearts, confiding souls, and youthful innocence?

During the first two days of the trial, Ballard was brought into court, by subpoena from the prisoner's counsel, and they took mischievous satisfaction in calling him forward when the court opened. But forward he would *not* come. He hid behind stove pipes, and skulked in corners. This was, perhaps, a prudent measure, for the populace were in that excited state, that it might have been unsafe for him to have been generally recognized. As he passed out of court, the citizens around the door would call out, "Don't come too near us! It is as much as we can do to keep our canes and umbrellas off your shoulders." The expressions were rude, but the sentiment which dictated them was noble. I hope I have not spoken too harshly of this individual. I certainly wish him nothing worse than he has brought upon himself. What can be more pitiful than the old age of a seducer, going unmourned to his grave, with the remembered curses of his victims?

4. "I . . . will": Shakespeare, *The Merchant of Venice*, 4.1.214–17.

What more painful than the consciousness of such a return to all a mother's love, and a mother's prayers? What penalty more severe than the loss of those pure domestic affections, which he has so wantonly desecrated? What punishment equal to the recollections of his dying bed? God pity him! For him, too, there is a return path to our Father's mansion; would that he might be persuaded to enter it.

The conduct of the prisoner, during the trial, was marked by a beautiful propriety. Sad and subdued, she made no artificial appeals to sympathy, and showed no disposition to consider herself a heroine of romance. When the verdict was given, she became very faint and dizzy, and for some time after, seemed stunned and bewildered. Her health is much shattered by physical suffering and mental excitement; but her constitution is naturally good, and under the influence of care and kindness, the process of renovation goes rapidly on. She is evidently a girl of strong feelings, but quiet, reserved, and docile to the influence of those she loves. A proper education would have made of her a noble woman. I sometimes fear that, like poor Fleur de Marie,[5] she will never be able to wash from her mind the "stern inexorable past." I shall never forget the mournful smile with which she said, "I don't know as it is worth while to try to make anything of me. I am nothing but a wreck." "Nay, Amelia," replied I, "noble vessels may be built from the timbers of a wreck."

The public sympathy manifested in this case, has cheered my hopes, and increased my respect for human nature. When the poor girl returned to her cell, after her acquittal, some of the judges, several of the jury, her lawyers, and the officers of the prison, all gathered round her to express congratulation and sympathy. There was something beautiful in the compassionate respect with which they treated this erring sister, because she was unfortunate and wretched. I trust that no changes of politics will ever dismiss Dr. Macready, the physician of the Tombs,[6] or Mr. Fallon, the keeper. I shall always bless them; not merely for their kindness to this poor girl, but for the tenderness of heart, which leads them to treat all the prisoners under their care with as much gentleness as possible. May the foul, moral atmosphere of the place never stifle their kind impulses.

The hours I spent in that hateful building, awaiting the opening of this case, were very sad to me. It was exceedingly painful to see poor ragged beggars summarily dismissed to the penitentiary, for petty larcenies; having the strong conviction, ever present in my mind, that all society is carrying on a great system of fraud and theft, and that these poor wretches merely lacked the knowledge and cunning necessary to keep theirs under legal protection.

The Egyptian architecture, with its monotonous recurrence of the straight line and the square, its heavy pillars, its cavernous dome of massive rings, its general expression of overpowering strength, is well suited to a building for such a purpose. But the graceful palm leaves, intertwined with lotus blossoms, spoke soothingly to me of the occasional triumph of the moral sentiments over legal technicalities, and of beautiful bursts

---

5. **Fleur de Marie:** The Parisian prostitute who is the heroine of *Les Mystères de Paris* (1842-43) by Eugène Sue (1804-1857), a popular French novelist.

6. **the Tombs:** Informal name for the Halls of Justice and House of Detention, a prison built in New York City in 1840. The massive structure was designed to look like an ancient Egyptian tomb.

of eloquence from the heart. Moreover, I remembered that time had wrought such changes in opinion, that thousands of convents had been converted into manufactories and primary schools; and I joyfully prophesied the day when regenerated society would have no more need of prisons. The Tombs, with its style of architecture too subterranean for picture galleries or concert rooms, may then be reserved for fossil remains and mineralogical cabinets.

[1844]

Ralph Waldo Emerson

[1803-1882]

Ralph Waldo Emerson was born in Boston, Massachusetts, on May 25, 1803. For generations, the men in the Emerson family had served as clergymen, and his father was the pastor of the First Church of Boston. When he died in 1811, the family was nearly destitute, but Emerson's mother was determined that her sons would be educated. At the age of fourteen, Emerson enrolled in Harvard College. An undistinguished student, he graduated in 1821 and taught at a school for young women until 1825. He then entered Harvard Divinity School and was ordained as a minister in 1829. Soon after that, he became the pastor of the prominent Second Church of Boston. With such a background, and with his gift for preaching, a distinguished clerical career seemed the likely path for Emerson. But his religious convictions were deeply influenced by works of German philosophy and theology, which were becoming available to American readers in translations and as filtered through English writers like Samuel Taylor Coleridge. Inspired by such Romantic idealism, Emerson increasingly came to value the moral instincts of the individual over the tenets of organized religion. His skepticism about orthodox Christianity grew, and in 1832 he resigned from his position at Second Church.

Ralph Waldo Emerson

This daguerreotype, made in 1857, shows Emerson in the formal clothing he customarily wore for lectures, a primary source of his income and the source material for nearly all of the books he published between 1840 and 1870.

Emerson then embarked on an extended tour of Europe, determined to chart a new course for his life. While there, he met a number of well-known English writers, including Coleridge, William Wordsworth, and most importantly Thomas Carlyle, with whom he would enjoy a lifelong correspondence. When Emerson returned to the United States in 1834, he settled in Concord, Massachusetts. Unlike many of his contemporaries who had to balance the need to earn a living with their intellectual pursuits, Emerson had an independent income. In 1829, the year of his ordination, he had married Ellen Tucker, a young woman from an affluent family in New Hampshire. The shock of her death from tuberculosis sixteen months later probably contributed to Emerson's decision to leave the ministry. The settlement of her estate also left him with a legacy of $1,200 per year – at that time an income sufficient for a comfortable, though not a lavish, lifestyle. Although he apparently never got over her death, in 1835 Emerson married Lydia Jackson, an accomplished and by all accounts a remarkable person with whom he shared religious convictions, as well as a wide range of literary and philosophical interests. The couple settled into "Coolidge House," a comfortable home Emerson purchased on the outskirts of Concord, Massachusetts. By then, all of the elements were in place for the independent scholarly life Emerson had in mind for himself. That life included reading and study, occasional preaching, and especially writing – daily entries in the journals and notebooks he would keep throughout his life, letters to an increasingly large number of correspondents in the United States and Europe, and his first book, *Nature* (1836).

Although it was published anonymously, the author of that little book was an open secret, and Emerson soon found himself at the center of a small circle of intellectuals who met regularly in Boston or Concord. Called the transcendentalists because of their embrace of idealistic or "transcendental" philosophy, the group was initially composed of Unitarian ministers but ultimately came to include writers as diverse as Emerson's friends Henry David Thoreau and Margaret Fuller. It was not, however, the publication of his first book that gained Emerson prominence. Two lectures, both delivered at Harvard, marked the beginning of his engagement with a larger audience: "The American Scholar" (1837), which Oliver Wendell Holmes called an "intellectual Declaration of Independence" and his address to the Harvard Divinity School in 1838. That address, in which Emerson vigorously exposed what he viewed as the defects in orthodox Christianity and in the training of Unitarian ministers, generated a furious controversy in Boston. In fact, some of the conservative Unitarian clergy were so outraged that Emerson was not invited back to speak at Harvard for thirty years. But he continued to preach occasionally, and Emerson also began to exploit a new form of communicating with audiences, both in and far beyond the confines of Boston. "A lecture is a new literature," he buoyantly observed in his journal in 1839, "which leaves aside all tradition, time, place, circumstance, & addresses an assembly as mere human beings, – no more."

I was simmering, simmering, simmering; Emerson brought me to a boil.
-Walt Whitman

The hundreds of lectures Emerson delivered during the following decades were the primary source of both his income and his books. *Essays* (1841) was derived from his lectures, as was *Essays: Second Series* (1844). During the period in which he wrote and published those celebrated volumes, Emerson also helped to establish and edit the *Dial*, the unofficial journal of the Transcendental Club. He also wrote a good deal of poetry, which he gathered together in his *Poems*, published in 1847. From 1845 to 1846, he delivered a lecture series he would later revise and publish as *Representative Men* (1850), a collection of biographical studies of individual greatness as represented by figures ranging from Plato through Shakespeare to modern figures like Goethe and Napoleon. Outraged by the passage of the Fugitive Slave Act in 1850, Emerson became increasingly involved in the antislavery crusade during that decade. But he continued to spend most of his time riding what he called "the lyceum express," a reference to his tours to lyceums and lecture halls throughout the North. During those extended tours, he first delivered the lectures revised for *English Traits* (1856), based on his second trip to Europe in 1847-48, and

Conduct of Life (1860). In the view of most scholars, those were the last of his major works, though Emerson published a collection of late essays as *Society and Solitude* in 1870. By then, however, both his health and memory had begun to fail, and Emerson wrote little more before he died on April 27, 1882.

bedfordstmartins.com/ americanlit *for research links on Emerson*

Emerson's *Nature*. Emerson's first book, which he published anonymously in 1836, was a slim volume of ninety-five pages divided into nine sections – "Introduction," "Nature," "Commodity," "Beauty," "Language," "Discipline," "Idealism," "Spirit," and "Prospects." Part philosophy, part sermon, and part poetry, the book was Emerson's fullest statement concerning the relationship between man and the natural world, as well as the relationship between matter and spirit. Written during a period of rapid economic growth and the emergence of an increasingly strong market economy in the United States, the book reveals Emerson's deep concern about the role of nature, both in individual lives and in American life. The book also reveals the impact of Emerson's reading, especially of *Aids to Reflection*, by the British writer Samuel Taylor Coleridge. Influenced by the German philosopher Immanuel Kant, Coleridge distinguished between the "Understanding," a rational faculty of the mind dependent on sense experience, and "Reason," an "inward beholding" or intuitive apprehension of spiritual truth. Emerson adopted that crucial distinction in *Nature*. Emerson's nature is thus comprised of a series of "signs," which for those who develop the ability to read them ultimately lead to the recognition of a spiritual reality that transcends nature. With its emphasis on the power of human intuition and the inexhaustible significance of nature, Emerson's little book became a central document for the group of writers and thinkers known as the transcendentalists. The text of the following selections is taken from the first edition of *Nature* (1836).

From NATURE

Introduction

Our age is retrospective. It builds the sepulchres of the fathers. It writes biographies, histories, and criticism. The foregoing generations beheld God and nature face to face; we, through their eyes. Why should not we also enjoy an original relation to the universe? Why should not we have a poetry and philosophy of insight and not of tradition, and a religion by revelation to us, and not the history of theirs? Embosomed for a season in nature, whose floods of life stream around and through us, and invite us by the powers they supply, to action proportioned to nature, why should we grope among the dry bones of the past, or put the living generation into masquerade out of its faded wardrobe? The sun shines to-day also. There is more wool and flax in the fields. There are new lands, new men, new thoughts. Let us demand our own works and laws and worship.

Undoubtedly we have no questions to ask which are unanswerable. We must trust the perfection of the creation so far, as to believe that whatever curiosity the order of things has awakened in our minds, the order of things can satisfy. Every man's condition is a solution in hieroglyphic to those inquiries he would put. He acts it as life, before he apprehends it as truth. In like manner, nature is already, in its forms and tendencies, describing its own design. Let us interrogate the great apparition, that shines so peacefully around us. Let us inquire, to what end is nature?

All science has one aim, namely, to find a theory of nature. We have theories of races and of functions, but scarcely yet a remote approximation to an idea of creation. We are now so far from the road to truth, that religious teachers dispute and hate each other, and speculative men are esteemed unsound and frivolous. But to a sound judgment, the most abstract truth is the most practical. Whenever a true theory appears, it will be its own evidence. Its test is, that it will explain all phenomena. Now many are thought not only unexplained but inexplicable; as language, sleep, dreams, beasts, sex.

Philosophically considered, the universe is composed of Nature and the Soul. Strictly speaking, therefore, all that is separate from us, all which Philosophy distinguishes as the NOT ME,[1] that is, both nature and art, all other men and my own body, must be ranked under this name, NATURE. In enumerating the values of nature and casting up their sum, I shall use the word in both senses; – in its common and in its philosophical import. In inquiries so general as our present one, the inaccuracy is not material; no confusion of thought will occur. *Nature*, in the common sense, refers to essences unchanged by man; space, the air, the river, the leaf. *Art* is applied to the mixture of his will with the same things, as in a house, a canal, a statue, a picture. But his operations taken together are so insignificant, a little chipping, baking, patching, and washing, that in an impression so grand as that of the world on the human mind, they do not vary the result.

Chapter I. Nature

To go into solitude, a man needs to retire as much from his chamber as from society. I am not solitary whilst I read and write, though nobody is with me. But if a man would be alone, let him look at the stars. The rays that come from those heavenly worlds, will separate between him and vulgar things. One might think the atmosphere was made transparent with this design, to give man, in the heavenly bodies, the perpetual presence of the sublime. Seen in the streets of cities, how great they are! If the stars should appear one night in a thousand years, how would men believe and adore; and preserve for many generations the remembrance of the city of God which had been shown! But every night come out these preachers of beauty, and light the universe with their admonishing smile.

The stars awaken a certain reverence, because though always present, they are always inaccessible; but all natural objects make a kindred impression, when the mind

1. NOT ME: Emerson alludes to *Sartor Resartus* (1833-34), in which the British writer Thomas Carlyle used the German philosophical distinction between the ME (the self) and the NOT ME, everything else, including the body.

is open to their influence. Nature never wears a mean appearance. Neither does the wisest man extort all her secret, and lose his curiosity by finding out all her perfection. Nature never became a toy to a wise spirit. The flowers, the animals, the mountains, reflected all the wisdom of his best hour, as much as they had delighted the simplicity of his childhood.

When we speak of nature in this manner, we have a distinct but most poetical sense in the mind. We mean the integrity of impression made by manifold natural objects. It is this which distinguishes the stick of timber of the wood-cutter, from the tree of the poet. The charming landscape which I saw this morning, is indubitably made up of some twenty or thirty farms. Miller owns this field, Locke that, and Manning the woodland beyond. But none of them owns the landscape. There is a property in the horizon which no man has but he whose eye can integrate all the parts, that is, the poet. This is the best part of these men's farms, yet to this their land-deeds give them no title.

To speak truly, few adult persons can see nature. Most persons do not see the sun. At least they have a very superficial seeing. The sun illuminates only the eye of the man, but shines into the eye and the heart of the child. The lover of nature is he whose inward and outward senses are still truly adjusted to each other; who has retained the spirit of infancy even into the era of manhood. His intercourse with heaven and earth, becomes part of his daily food. In the presence of nature, a wild delight runs through the man, in spite of real sorrows. Nature says, – he is my creature, and maugre[2] all his impertinent griefs, he shall be glad with me. Not the sun or the summer alone, but every hour and season yields its tribute of delight; for every hour and change corresponds to and authorizes a different state of the mind, from breathless noon to grimmest midnight. Nature is a setting that fits equally well a comic or a mourning piece. In good health, the air is a cordial of incredible virtue. Crossing a bare common, in snow puddles, at twilight, under a clouded sky, without having in my thoughts any occurrence of special good fortune, I have enjoyed a perfect exhilaration. Almost I fear to think how glad I am. In the woods too, a man casts off his years, as the snake his slough, and at what period soever of life, is always a child. In the woods, is perpetual youth. Within these plantations of God, a decorum and sanctity reign, a perennial festival is dressed, and the guest sees not how he should tire of them in a thousand years. In the woods, we return to reason and faith. There I feel that nothing can befal me in life, – no disgrace, no calamity, (leaving me my eyes,) which nature cannot repair. Standing on the bare ground, – my head bathed by the blithe air, and uplifted into infinite space, – all mean egotism vanishes. I become a transparent eye-ball.[3] I am nothing. I see all. The currents of the Universal Being circulate through me; I am part or particle of God. The name of the nearest friend sounds then foreign and accidental. To be brothers, to be acquaintances, – master or servant, is then a trifle and a disturbance. I am the lover of uncontained and immortal beauty. In the wilderness, I find something more dear and connate than in

2. **maugre:** An early term meaning "in spite of."
3. **transparent eye-ball:** Emerson is describing a mystical experience in which he has the sense of seeing both inward and outward, but this complex phrase has prompted many interpretations by generations of readers and scholars.

streets or villages. In the tranquil landscape, and especially in the distant line of the horizon, man beholds somewhat as beautiful as his own nature.

The greatest delight which the fields and woods minister, is the suggestion of an occult relation between man and the vegetable. I am not alone and unacknowledged. They nod to me and I to them. The waving of the boughs in the storm, is new to me and old. It takes me by surprise, and yet is not unknown. Its effect is like that of a higher thought or a better emotion coming over me, when I deemed I was thinking justly or doing right.

Yet it is certain that the power to produce this delight, does not reside in nature, but in man, or in a harmony of both. It is necessary to use these pleasures with great temperance. For, nature is not always tricked in holiday attire, but the same scene which yesterday breathed perfume and glittered as for the frolic of the nymphs, is overspread with melancholy today. Nature always wears the colors of the spirit. To a man laboring under calamity, the heat of his own fire hath sadness in it. Then, there is a kind of contempt of the landscape felt by him who has just lost by death a dear friend. The sky is less grand as it shuts down over less worth in the population.

Chapter III. Beauty

A nobler want of man is served by nature, namely, the love of Beauty.

The ancient Greeks called the world χοσμος,[4] beauty. Such is the constitution of all things, or such the plastic power of the human eye, that the primary forms, as the sky, the mountain, the tree, the animal, give us a delight *in and for themselves*; a pleasure arising from outline, color, motion, and grouping. This seems partly owing to the eye itself. The eye is the best of artists. By the mutual action of its structure and of the laws of light, perspective is produced, which integrates every mass of objects, of what character soever, into a well colored and shaded globe, so that where the particular objects are mean and unaffecting, the landscape which they compose, is round and symmetrical. And as the eye is the best composer, so light is the first of painters. There is no object so foul that intense light will not make beautiful. And the stimulus it affords to the sense, and a sort of infinitude which it hath, like space and time, make all matter gay. Even the corpse hath its own beauty. But beside this general grace diffused over nature, almost all the individual forms are agreeable to the eye, as is proved by our endless imitations of some of them, as the acorn, the grape, the pine-cone, the wheat-ear, the egg, the wings and forms of most birds, the lion's claw, the serpent, the butterfly, sea-shells, flames, clouds; buds, leaves, and the forms of many trees, as the palm.

For better consideration, we may distribute the aspects of Beauty in a threefold manner.

1. First, the simple perception of natural forms is a delight. The influence of the forms and actions in nature, is so needful to man, that, in its lowest functions, it seems to lie on the confines of commodity and beauty. To the body and mind which have been cramped by noxious work or company, nature is medicinal and restores their tone. The

---

4. **χοσμος**: Cosmos.

tradesman, the attorney comes out of the din and craft of the street, and sees the sky and the woods, and is a man again. In their eternal calm, he finds himself. The health of the eye seems to demand a horizon. We are never tired, so long as we can see far enough.

But in other hours, Nature satisfies the soul purely by its loveliness, and without any mixture of corporeal benefit. I have seen the spectacle of morning from the hill-top over against my house, from day-break to sun-rise, with emotions which an angel might share. The long slender bars of cloud float like fishes in the sea of crimson light. From the earth, as a shore, I look out into that silent sea. I seem to partake its rapid transformations: the active enchantment reaches my dust, and I dilate and conspire with the morning wind. How does Nature deify us with a few and cheap elements! Give me health and a day, and I will make the pomp of emperors ridiculous. The dawn is my Assyria; the sun-set and moon-rise my Paphos, and unimaginable realms of faerie; broad noon shall be my England of the senses and the understanding; the night shall be my Germany of mystic philosophy and dreams.[5]

Not less excellent, except for our less susceptibility in the afternoon, was the charm, last evening, of a January sunset. The western clouds divided and subdivided themselves into pink flakes modulated with tints of unspeakable softness; and the air had so much life and sweetness, that it was a pain to come within doors. What was it that nature would say? Was there no meaning in the live repose of the valley behind the mill, and which Homer or Shakspeare could not re-form for me in words? The leafless trees become spires of flame in the sunset, with the blue east for their background, and the stars of the dead calices of flowers, and every withered stem and stubble rimed with frost, contribute something to the mute music.

The inhabitants of cities suppose that the country landscape is pleasant only half the year. I please myself with observing the graces of the winter scenery, and believe that we are as much touched by it as by the genial influences of summer. To the attentive eye, each moment of the year has its own beauty, and in the same field, it beholds, every hour, a picture which was never seen before, and which shall never be seen again. The heavens change every moment, and reflect their glory or gloom on the plains beneath. The state of the crop in the surrounding farms alters the expression of the earth from week to week. The succession of native plants in the pastures and road-sides, which make the silent clock by which time tells the summer hours, will make even the divisions of the day sensible to a keen observer. The tribes of birds and insects, like the plants punctual to their time, follow each other, and the year has room for all. By water-courses, the variety is greater. In July, the blue pontederia or pickerel-weed blooms in large beds in the shallow parts of our pleasant river,[6] and swarms with yellow butterflies in continual

5. **The dawn . . . dreams:** Emerson traces a series of contrasting worldviews. One of the earliest Christian civilizations of the Middle East, Assyria was an ancient empire in the upper valley of the Tigris. Paphos was an ancient city in Cyprus where an elaborate sanctuary was built to honor Aphrodite, the goddess of love, beauty, and sexual fulfillment. John Locke's empirical philosophy (the "England of the senses") is in direct contrast with the German romantic philosophies.

6. **our pleasant river:** The Concord River, which flows through the town where Emerson lived and wrote, Concord, Massachusetts.

motion. Art cannot rival this pomp of purple and gold. Indeed the river is a perpetual gala, and boasts each month a new ornament.

But this beauty of Nature which is seen and felt as beauty, is the least part. The shows of day, the dewy morning, the rainbow, mountains, orchards in blossom, stars, moonlight, shadows in still water, and the like, if too eagerly hunted, become shows merely, and mock us with their unreality. Go out of the house to see the moon, and 't is mere tinsel; it will not please as when its light shines upon your necessary journey. The beauty that shimmers in the yellow afternoons of October, who ever could clutch it? Go forth to find it, and it is gone: 't is only a mirage as you look from the windows of diligence.

2. The presence of a higher, namely, of the spiritual element is essential to its perfection. The high and divine beauty which can be loved without effeminacy, is that which is found in combination with the human will, and never separate. Beauty is the mark God sets upon virtue. Every natural action is graceful. Every heroic act is also decent, and causes the place and the bystanders to shine. We are taught by great actions that the universe is the property of every individual in it. Every rational creature has all nature for his dowry and estate. It is his, if he will. He may divest himself of it; he may creep into a corner, and abdicate his kingdom, as most men do, but he is entitled to the world by his constitution. In proportion to the energy of his thought and will, he takes up the world into himself. "All those things for which men plough, build, or sail, obey virtue;" said an ancient historian.[7] "The winds and waves," said Gibbon,[8] "are always on the side of the ablest navigators." So are the sun and moon and all the stars of heaven. When a noble act is done,[9] – perchance in a scene of great natural beauty; when Leonidas and his three hundred martyrs consume one day in dying, and the sun and moon come each and look at them once in the steep defile of Thermopylae; when Arnold Winkelried, in the high Alps, under the shadow of the avalanche, gathers in his side a sheaf of Austrian spears to break the line for his comrades; are not these heroes entitled to add the beauty of the scene to the beauty of the deed? When the bark of Columbus nears the shore of America; – before it, the beach lined with savages, fleeing out of all their huts of cane; the sea behind; and the purple mountains of the Indian Archipelago around, can we separate the man from the living picture? Does not the New World clothe his form with her palm-groves and savannahs as fit drapery? Ever does natural beauty steal in like air, and envelope great actions. When Sir Harry Vane was dragged up the Tower-hill, sitting on a sled, to suffer death, as the champion of the English laws, one of the multitude cried out to him, "You never sate on so glorious a seat." Charles II., to intimidate the citizens of London, caused the patriot Lord Russel to be drawn in an open coach, through the principal streets of the city, on his way to the scaffold. "But," to use the simple narrative of his biographer, "the multitude imagined they saw liberty and

7. **an ancient historian:** From "The Conspiracy of Cataline" by Sallust, a first-century BCE Roman historian.
8. **"The winds . . . navigators":** From *The Decline and Fall of the Roman Empire* by the British historian Edward Gibbon (1737–1794).
9. **When a noble act is done:** In the following passage, Emerson cites the heroism of several historical figures from European, British, and American history.

virtue sitting by his side." In private places, among sordid objects, an act of truth or heroism seems at once to draw to itself the sky as its temple, the sun as its candle. Nature stretcheth out her arms to embrace man, only let his thoughts be of equal greatness. Willingly does she follow his steps with the rose and the violet, and bend her lines of grandeur and grace to the decoration of her darling child. Only let his thoughts be of equal scope, and the frame will suit the picture. A virtuous man, is in unison with her works, and makes the central figure of the visible sphere. Homer, Pindar, Socrates, Phocion,[10] associate themselves fitly in our memory with the whole geography and climate of Greece. The visible heavens and earth sympathize with Jesus. And in common life, whosoever has seen a person of powerful character and happy genius, will have remarked how easily he took all things along with him, – the persons, the opinions, and the day, and nature became ancillary to a man.

3. There is still another aspect under which the beauty of the world may be viewed, namely, as it becomes an object of the intellect. Beside the relation of things to virtue, they have a relation to thought. The intellect searches out the absolute order of things as they stand in the mind of God, and without the colors of affection. The intellectual and the active powers seem to succeed each other in man, and the exclusive activity of the one, generates the exclusive activity of the other. There is something unfriendly in each to the other, but they are like the alternate periods of feeding and working in animals; each prepares and certainly will be followed by the other. Therefore does beauty, which, in relation to actions, as we have seen comes unsought, and comes because it is unsought, remain for the apprehension and pursuit of the intellect; and then again, in its turn, of the active power. Nothing divine dies. All good is eternally reproductive. The beauty of nature reforms itself in the mind, and not for barren contemplation, but for new creation.

All men are in some degree impressed by the face of the world. Some men even to delight. This love of beauty is Taste. Others have the same love in such excess, that, not content with admiring, they seek to embody it in new forms. The creation of beauty is Art.

The production of a work of art throws a light upon the mystery of humanity. A work of art is an abstract or epitome of the world. It is the result or expression of nature, in miniature. For although the works of nature are innumerable and all different, the result or the expression of them all is similar and single. Nature is a sea of forms radically alike and even unique. A leaf, a sun-beam, a landscape, the ocean, make an analogous impression on the mind. What is common to them all, – that perfectness and harmony, is beauty. Therefore the standard of beauty, is the entire circuit of natural forms, – the totality of nature; which the Italians expressed by defining beauty *"il piu nell' uno."*[11] Nothing is quite beautiful alone: nothing but is beautiful in the whole. A single object is only so far beautiful as it suggests this universal grace. The poet, the

10. **Homer . . . Phocion:** The ancient Greek poets Homer and Pindar; the philosopher Socrates; and Phocion, an eloquent Athenian politican.

11. ***"il piu nell' uno"*:** The many in one (Italian).

painter, the sculptor, the musician, the architect seek each to concentrate this radiance of the world on one point, and each in his several work to satisfy the love of beauty which stimulates him to produce. Thus is Art, a nature passed through the alembic[12] of man. Thus in art, does nature work through the will of a man filled with the beauty of her first works.

The world thus exists to the soul to satisfy the desire of beauty. Extend this element to the uttermost, and I call it an ultimate end. No reason can be asked or given why the soul seeks beauty. Beauty, in its largest and profoundest sense, is one expression for the universe. God is the all-fair. Truth, and goodness, and beauty, are but different faces of the same All. But beauty in nature is not ultimate. It is the herald of inward and eternal beauty, and is not alone a solid and satisfactory good. It must therefore stand as a part and not as yet the last or highest expression of the final cause of Nature.

Chapter IV. Language

A third use which Nature subserves to man is that of Language. Nature is the vehicle of thought, and in a simple, double, and threefold degree.

1. Words are signs of natural facts.
2. Particular natural facts are symbols of particular facts.
3. Nature is the symbol of spirits.

1. Words are signs of natural facts. The use of natural history is to give us aid in supernatural history. The use of the outer creation is to give us language for the beings and changes of the inward creation. Every word which is used to express a moral or intellectual fact, if traced to its root, is found to be borrowed from some material appearance. *Right* originally means *straight*; *wrong* means *twisted*. *Spirit* primarily means *wind*; *transgression*, the crossing of a *line*; *supercilious*, the *raising of the eye-brow*. We say the *heart* to express emotion, the *head* to denote thought; and *thought* and *emotion* are, in their turn, words borrowed from sensible things, and now appropriated to spiritual nature. Most of the process by which this transformation is made, is hidden from us in the remote time when language was framed; but the same tendency may be daily observed in children. Children and savages use only nouns or names of things, which they continually convert into verbs, and apply to analogous mental acts.

2. But this origin of all words that convey a spiritual import, – so conspicuous a fact in the history of language, – is our least debt to nature. It is not words only that are emblematic; it is things which are emblematic. Every natural fact is a symbol of some spiritual fact. Every appearance in nature corresponds to some state of the mind, and that state of the mind can only be described by presenting that natural appearance as its picture. An enraged man is a lion, a cunning man is a fox, a firm man is a rock, a learned man is a torch. A lamb is innocence; a snake is subtle spite; flowers express to

12. **alembic:** An early term for a distilling apparatus.

us the delicate affections. Light and darkness are our familiar expression for knowledge and ignorance; and heat for love. Visible distance behind and before us, is respectively our image of memory and hope.

Who looks upon a river in a meditative hour, and is not reminded of the flux of all things? Throw a stone into the stream, and the circles that propagate themselves are the beautiful type of all influence. Man is conscious of a universal soul within or behind his individual life, wherein, as in a firmament, the natures of Justice, Truth, Love, Freedom, arise and shine. This universal soul, he calls Reason: it is not mine or thine or his, but we are its; we are its property and men. And the blue sky in which the private earth is buried, the sky with its eternal calm, and full of everlasting orbs, is the type of Reason. That which, intellectually considered, we call Reason, considered in relation to nature, we call Spirit. Spirit is the Creator. Spirit hath life in itself. And man in all ages and countries, embodies it in his language, as the FATHER.

It is easily seen that there is nothing lucky or capricious in these analogies, but that they are constant, and pervade nature. These are not the dreams of a few poets, here and there, but man is an analogist, and studies relations in all objects. He is placed in the centre of beings, and a ray of relation passes from every other being to him. And neither can man be understood without these objects, nor these objects without man. All the facts in natural history taken by themselves, have no value, but are barren like a single sex. But marry it to human history, and it is full of life. Whole Floras, all Linnaeus' and Buffon's volumes,[13] are but dry catalogues of facts; but the most trivial of these facts, the habit of a plant, the organs, or work, or noise of an insect, applied to the illustration of a fact in intellectual philosophy, or, in any way associated to human nature, affects us in the most lively and agreeable manner. The seed of a plant, – to what affecting analogies in the nature of man, is that little fruit made use of, in all discourse, up to the voice of Paul, who calls the human corpse a seed, – "It is sown a natural body; it is raised a spiritual body."[14] The motion of the earth round its axis, and round the sun, makes the day, and the year. These are certain amounts of brute light and heat. But is there no intent of an analogy between man's life and the seasons? And do the seasons gain no grandeur or pathos from that analogy? The instincts of the ant are very unimportant considered as the ant's; but the moment a ray of relation is seen to extend from it to man, and the little drudge is seen to be a monitor, a little body with a mighty heart, then all its habits, even that said to be recently observed, that it never sleeps, become sublime.

Because of this radical correspondence between visible things and human thoughts, savages, who have only what is necessary, converse in figures. As we go back in history, language becomes more picturesque, until its infancy, when it is all poetry; or, all spiritual facts are represented by natural symbols. The same symbols are found to make the

13. **Linnaeus' and Buffon's volumes:** The French naturalist Georges-Louis Leclerc, Comte de Buffon (1707–1788) wrote *Historie Nautrelle* (1780), a forty-four-volume encyclopedia of everything known about the natural world; the Swedish botanist Carl von Linné (Linnaeus) (1707-1778) was the author of a number of books of plant classifications.

14. **"It . . . body":** 1 Corinthians 15:44.

original elements of all languages. It has moreover been observed, that the idioms of all languages approach each other in passages of the greatest eloquence and power. And as this is the first language, so is it the last. This immediate dependence of language upon nature, this conversion of an outward phenomenon into a type of somewhat in human life, never loses its power to affect us. It is this which gives that piquancy to the conversation of a strong-natured farmer or back-woodsman, which all men relish.

Thus is nature an interpreter, by whose means man converses with his fellow men. A man's power to connect his thought with its proper symbol, and so utter it, depends on the simplicity of his character, that is, upon his love of truth and his desire to communicate it without loss. The corruption of man is followed by the corruption of language. When simplicity of character and the sovereignty of ideas is broken up by the prevalence of secondary desires, the desire of riches, the desire of pleasure, the desire of power, the desire of praise, – and duplicity and falsehood take place of simplicity and truth, the power over nature as an interpreter of the will, is in a degree lost; new imagery ceases to be created, and old words are perverted to stand for things which are not; a paper currency is employed when there is no bullion in the vaults. In due time, the fraud is manifest, and words lose all power to stimulate the understanding or the affections. Hundreds of writers may be found in every long-civilized nation, who for a short time believe, and make others believe, that they see and utter truths, who do not of themselves clothe one thought in its natural garment, but who feed unconsciously upon the language created by the primary writers of the country, those, namely, who hold primarily on nature.

But wise men pierce this rotten diction and fasten words again to visible things; so that picturesque language is at once a commanding certificate that he who employs it, is a man in alliance with truth and God. The moment our discourse rises above the ground line of familiar facts, and is inflamed with passion or exalted by thought, it clothes itself in images. A man conversing in earnest, if he watch his intellectual processes, will find that always a material image, more or less luminous, arises in his mind, contemporaneous with every thought, which furnishes the vestment of the thought. Hence, good writing and brilliant discourse are perpetual allegories. This imagery is spontaneous. It is the blending of experience with the present action of the mind. It is proper creation. It is the working of the Original Cause through the instruments he has already made.

These facts may suggest the advantage which the country-life possesses for a powerful mind, over the artificial and curtailed life of cities. We know more from nature than we can at will communicate. Its light flows into the mind evermore, and we forget its presence. The poet, the orator, bred in the woods, whose senses have been nourished by their fair and appeasing changes, year after year, without design and without heed, – shall not lose their lesson altogether, in the roar of cities or broil of politics. Long hereafter, amidst agitation and terror in national councils, – in the hour of revolution, – these solemn images shall reappear in their morning lustre, as fit symbols and words of the thoughts which the passing events shall awaken. At the call of a noble sentiment, again the woods wave, the pines murmur, the river rolls and shines, and the cattle low upon the mountains, as he saw and heard them in his infancy. And with these forms, the spells of persuasion, the keys of power are put into his hands.

3. We are thus assisted by natural objects in the expression of particular meanings. But how great a language to convey such peppercorn informations! Did it need such noble races of creatures, this profusion of forms, this host of orbs in heaven, to furnish man with the dictionary and grammar of his municipal speech? Whilst we use this grand cipher to expedite the affairs of our pot and kettle, we feel that we have not yet put it to its use, neither are able. We are like travellers using the cinders of a volcano to roast their eggs. Whilst we see that it always stands ready to clothe what we would say, we cannot avoid the question, whether the characters are not significant of themselves. Have mountains, and waves, and skies, no significance but what we consciously give them, when we employ them as emblems of our thoughts? The world is emblematic. Parts of speech are metaphors because the whole of nature is a metaphor of the human mind. The laws of moral nature answer to those of matter as face to face in a glass. "The visible world and the relation of its parts, is the dial plate of the invisible." The axioms of physics translate the laws of ethics. Thus, "the whole is greater than its part;" "reaction is equal to action;" "the smallest weight may be made to lift the greatest, the difference of weight being compensated by time;" and many the like propositions, which have an ethical as well as physical sense. These propositions[15] have a much more extensive and universal sense when applied to human life, than when confined to technical use.

In like manner, the memorable words of history, and the proverbs of nations, consist usually of a natural fact, selected as a picture or parable of a moral truth. Thus; A rolling stone gathers no moss; A bird in the hand is worth two in the bush; A cripple in the right way, will beat a racer in the wrong; Make hay whilst the sun shines; 'T is hard to carry a full cup even; Vinegar is the son of wine; The last ounce broke the camel's back; Long-lived trees make roots first; – and the like. In their primary sense these are trivial facts, but we repeat them for the value of their analogical import. What is true of proverbs, is true of all fables, parables, and allegories.

This relation between the mind and matter is not fancied by some poet, but stands in the will of God, and so is free to be known by all men. It appears to men, or it does not appear. When in fortunate hours we ponder this miracle, the wise man doubts, if, at all other times, he is not blind and deaf;

> — "Can these things be,
> And overcome us like a summer's cloud,
> Without our special wonder?"

for the universe becomes transparent, and the light of higher laws than its own, shines through it. It is the standing problem which has exercised the wonder and the study of every fine genius since the world began; from the era of the Egyptians and the Brahmins, to that of Pythagoras, of Plato, of Bacon, of Leibnitz, of Swedenborg. There sits the Sphinx at the road-side, and from age to age, as each prophet comes by, he tries his fortune at reading her riddle. There seems to be a necessity in spirit to manifest itself in

---

15. **propositions:** Throughout this section, Emerson uses a number of quotations and paraphrases, many of which his contemporary readers would have recognized without a specific citation. The citations range from the Swedish philosopher Emanuel Swedenborg to Shakespeare to the Bible, Plato, and the German philosopher Goethe.

material forms; and day and night, river and storm, beast and bird, acid and alkali, pre-exist in necessary Ideas in the mind of God, and are what they are by virtue of preceding affections, in the world of spirit. A Fact is the end or last issue of spirit. The visible creation is the terminus or the circumference of the invisible world. "Material objects," said a French philosopher,[16] "are necessarily kinds of *scoriae*[17] of the substantial thoughts of the Creator, which must always preserve an exact relation to their first origin; in other words, visible nature must have a spiritual and moral side."

This doctrine is abstruse, and though the images of "garment," "scoriae," "mirror," &c., may stimulate the fancy, we must summon the aid of subtler and more vital expositors to make it plain. "Every scripture is to be interpreted by the same spirit which gave it forth," – is the fundamental law of criticism. A life in harmony with nature, the love of truth and of virtue, will purge the eyes to understand her text. By degrees we may come to know the primitive sense of the permanent objects of nature, so that the world shall be to us an open book, and every form significant of its hidden life and final cause.

A new interest surprises us, whilst, under the view now suggested, we contemplate the fearful extent and multitude of objects; since "every object rightly seen, unlocks a new faculty of the soul." That which was unconscious truth, becomes, when interpreted and defined in an object, a part of the domain of knowledge, – a new amount to the magazine of power.

Chapter VII. Spirit

It is essential to a true theory of nature and of man, that it should contain somewhat progressive. Uses that are exhausted or that may be, and facts that end in the statement, cannot be all that is true of this brave lodging wherein man is harbored, and wherein all his faculties find appropriate and endless exercise. And all the uses of nature admit of being summed in one, which yields the activity of man an infinite scope. Through all its kingdoms, to the suburbs and outskirts of things, it is faithful to the cause whence it had its origin. It always speaks of Spirit. It suggests the absolute. It is a perpetual effect. It is a great shadow pointing always to the sun behind us.

The aspect of nature is devout. Like the figure of Jesus, she stands with bended head, and hands folded upon the breast. The happiest man is he who learns from nature the lesson of worship.

Of that ineffable essence which we call Spirit, he that thinks most, will say least. We can foresee God in the coarse and, as it were, distant phenomena of matter; but when we try to define and describe himself, both language and thought desert us, and we are as helpless as fools and savages. That essence refuses to be recorded in propositions, but when man has worshipped him intellectually, the noblest ministry of nature is to stand as the apparition of God. It is the great organ through which the universal spirit speaks to the individual, and strives to lead back the individual to it.

---

16. **French philosopher:** In 1835, Emerson read an English translation of the first sixty pages of *Le Vrai Messie*, or *The True Messiah* (1829) by Guillaume Caspar Lencroy Oegger (1790?–1853?).
17. ***scoriae*:** Slag separated from molten metal during the smelting process.

When we consider Spirit, we see that the views already presented do not include the whole circumference of man. We must add some related thoughts.

Three problems are put by nature to the mind; What is matter? Whence is it? and Whereto? The first of these questions only, the ideal theory answers. Idealism saith: matter is a phenomenon, not a substance. Idealism acquaints us with the total disparity between the evidence of our own being, and the evidence of the world's being. The one is perfect; the other, incapable of any assurance; the mind is a part of the nature of things; the world is a divine dream, from which we may presently awake to the glories and certainties of day. Idealism is a hypothesis to account for nature by other principles than those of carpentry and chemistry. Yet, if it only deny the existence of matter, it does not satisfy the demands of the spirit. It leaves God out of me. It leaves me in the splendid labyrinth of my perceptions, to wander without end. Then the heart resists it, because it baulks the affections in denying substantive being to men and women. Nature is so pervaded with human life, that there is something of humanity in all, and in every particular. But this theory makes nature foreign to me, and does not account for that consanguinity which we acknowledge to it.

Let it stand then, in the present state of our knowledge, merely as a useful introductory hypothesis, serving to apprize us of the eternal distinction between the soul and the world.

But when, following the invisible steps of thought, we come to inquire, Whence is matter? and Whereto? many truths arise to us out of the recesses of consciousness. We learn that the highest is present to the soul of man, that the dread universal essence, which is not wisdom, or love, or beauty, or power, but all in one, and each entirely, is that for which all things exist, and that by which they are; that spirit creates; that behind nature, throughout nature, spirit is present; that spirit is one and not compound; that spirit does not act upon us from without, that is, in space and time, but spiritually, or through ourselves. Therefore, that spirit, that is, the Supreme Being, does not build up nature around us, but puts it forth through us, as the life of the tree puts forth new branches and leaves through the pores of the old. As a plant upon the earth, so a man rests upon the bosom of God; he is nourished by unfailing fountains, and draws, at his need, inexhaustible power. Who can set bounds to the possibilities of man? Once inspire the infinite, by being admitted to behold the absolute natures of justice and truth, and we learn that man has access to the entire mind of the Creator, is himself the creator in the finite. This view, which admonishes me where the sources of wisdom and power lie, and points to virtue as to

> "The golden key
> Which opes the palace of eternity,"[18]

carries upon its face the highest certificate of truth, because it animates me to create my own world through the purification of my soul.

18. "The . . . eternity": John Milton, *Comus*, lines 13-14.

The world proceeds from the same spirit as the body of man. It is a remoter and inferior incarnation of God, a projection of God in the unconscious. But it differs from the body in one important respect. It is not, like that, now subjected to the human will. Its serene order is inviolable by us. It is therefore, to us, the present expositor of the divine mind. It is a fixed point whereby we may measure our departure. As we degenerate, the contrast between us and our house is more evident. We are as much strangers in nature, as we are aliens from God. We do not understand the notes of birds. The fox and the deer run away from us; the bear and tiger rend us. We do not know the uses of more than a few plants, as corn and the apple, the potato and the vine. Is not the landscape, every glimpse of which hath a grandeur, a face of him? Yet this may show us what discord is between man and nature, for you cannot freely admire a noble landscape, if laborers are digging in the field hard by. The poet finds something ridiculous in his delight, until he is out of the sight of men.

From Chapter VIII. Prospects

In inquiries respecting the laws of the world and the frame of things, the highest reason is always the truest. That which seems faintly possible – it is so refined, is often faint and dim because it is deepest seated in the mind among the eternal verities. Empirical science is apt to cloud the sight, and, by the very knowledge of functions and processes, to bereave the student of the manly contemplation of the whole. The savant becomes unpoetic. But the best read naturalist who lends an entire and devout attention to truth, will see that there remains much to learn of his relation to the world, and that it is not to be learned by any addition or subtraction or other comparison of known quantities, but is arrived at by untaught sallies of the spirit, by a continual self-recovery, and by entire humility. He will perceive that there are far more excellent qualities in the student than preciseness and infallibility; that a guess is often more fruitful than all indisputable affirmation, and that a dream may let us deeper into the secret of nature than a hundred concerted experiments.

• • •

At present, man applies to nature but half his force. He works on the world with his understanding alone. He lives in it, and masters it by a penny-wisdom; and he that works most in it, is but a half-man, and whilst his arms are strong and his digestion good, his mind is imbruted and he is a selfish savage. His relation to nature, his power over it, is through the understanding; as by manure; the economic use of fire, wind, water, and the mariner's needle; steam, coal, chemical agriculture; the repairs of the human body by the dentist and the surgeon. This is such a resumption of power, as if a banished king should buy his territories inch by inch, instead of vaulting at once into his throne. Meantime, in the thick darkness, there are not wanting gleams of a better light, – occasional examples of the action of man upon nature with his entire force, – with reason as well as understanding. Such examples are; the traditions of miracles in the earliest antiquity of all nations; the history of Jesus Christ; the achievements of a principle, as in religious and political revolutions, and in the abolition of the Slave-trade; the miracles of enthusiasm, as those reported of Swedenborg, Hohenlohe, and the

Shakers;[19] many obscure and yet contested facts, now arranged under the name of Animal Magnetism;[20] prayer; eloquence; self-healing; and the wisdom of children. These are examples of Reason's momentary grasp of the sceptre; the exertions of a power which exists not in time or space, but an instantaneous in-streaming causing power. The difference between the actual and the ideal force of man is happily figured by the schoolmen, in saying, that the knowledge of man is an evening knowledge, *vespertina cognitio*, but that of God is a morning knowledge, *matutina cognitio*.

The problem of restoring to the world original and eternal beauty, is solved by the redemption of the soul. The ruin or the blank, that we see when we look at nature, is in our own eye. The axis of vision is not coincident with the axis of things, and so they appear not transparent but opake. The reason why the world lacks unity, and lies broken and in heaps, is, because man is disunited with himself. He cannot be a naturalist, until he satisfies all the demands of the spirit. Love is as much its demand, as perception. Indeed, neither can be perfect without the other. In the uttermost meaning of the words, thought is devout, and devotion is thought. Deep calls unto deep.[21] But in actual life, the marriage is not celebrated. There are innocent men who worship God after the tradition of their fathers, but their sense of duty has not yet extended to the use of all their faculties. And there are patient naturalists, but they freeze their subject under the wintry light of the understanding. Is not prayer also a study of truth, – a sally of the soul into the unfound infinite? No man ever prayed heartily, without learning something. But when a faithful thinker, resolute to detach every object from personal relations, and see it in the light of thought, shall, at the same time, kindle science with the fire of the holiest affections, then will God go forth anew into the creation.

It will not need, when the mind is prepared for study, to search for objects. The invariable mark of wisdom is to see the miraculous in the common. What is a day? What is a year? What is summer? What is woman? What is a child? What is sleep? To our blindness, these things seem unaffecting. We make fables to hide the baldness of the fact and conform it, as we say, to the higher law of the mind. But when the fact is seen under the light of an idea, the gaudy fable fades and shrivels. We behold the real higher law. To the wise, therefore, a fact is true poetry, and the most beautiful of fables. These wonders are brought to our own door. You also are a man. Man and woman, and their social life, poverty, labor, sleep, fear, fortune, are known to you. Learn that none of these things is superficial, but that each phenomenon hath its roots in the faculties and affections of the mind. Whilst the abstract question occupies your intellect, nature brings it in the

19. **Swedenborg, Hohenlohe, and the Shakers:** Emanuel Swedenborg (1688-1772) was a Swedish philosopher whose spiritual beliefs blended Christianity, mysticism, and pantheism. Leopold Franz Emmerich, prince of the German province of Hohenlohe (1794-1849), was reputed to have the miraculous power to heal people. The Shakers were members of a religious movement brought to America in 1774 by the English prophetess Ann Lee, who was believed to work miracles by members of the sect, formally known as the United Society of Believers in Christ's Second Coming.

20. **Animal Magnetism:** An early term for hypnotism.

21. **Deep calls unto deep:** See Psalms 42:7: "Deep calleth unto deep at the noise of thy waterspouts: all thy waves and thy billows are gone over me."

concrete to be solved by your hands. It were a wise inquiry for the closest, to compare, point by point, especially at remarkable crises in life, our daily history, with the rise and progress of ideas in the mind.

So shall we come to look at the world with new eyes. It shall answer the endless inquiry of the intellect, – What is truth? and of the affections, – What is good? by yielding itself passive to the educated Will. Then shall come to pass what my poet said; 'Nature is not fixed but fluid. Spirit alters, moulds, makes it. The immobility or bruteness of nature, is the absence of spirit; to pure spirit, it is fluid, it is volatile, it is obedient. Every spirit builds itself a house; and beyond its house, a world; and beyond its world, a heaven. Know then, that the world exists for you. For you is the phenomenon perfect. What we are, that only can we see. All that Adam had, all that Caesar could, you have and can do. Adam called his house, heaven and earth; Caesar called his house, Rome; you perhaps call yours, a cobbler's trade; a hundred acres of ploughed land; or a scholar's garret. Yet line for line and point for point, your dominion is as great as theirs, though without fine names. Build, therefore, your own world. As fast as you conform your life to the pure idea in your mind, that will unfold its great proportions. A correspondent revolution in things will attend the influx of the spirit. So fast will disagreeable appearances, swine, spiders, snakes, pests, mad-houses, prisons, enemies, vanish; they are temporary and shall be no more seen. The sordor and filths of nature, the sun shall dry up, and the wind exhale. As when the summer comes from the south, the snow-banks melt, and the face of the earth becomes green before it, so shall the advancing spirit create its ornaments along its path, and carry with it the beauty it visits, and the song which enchants it; it shall draw beautiful faces, and warm hearts, and wise discourse, and heroic acts, around its way, until evil is no more seen. The kingdom of man over nature, which cometh not with observation,[22] – a dominion such as now is beyond his dream of God, – he shall enter without more wonder than the blind man feels who is gradually restored to perfect sight.'

[1836]

22. **"The kingdom . . . observation"**: See Christ's words in Luke 17:20: "And when he was demanded of the Pharisees, when the kingdom of God should come, he answered them and said, 'The kingdom of God cometh not with observation.'"

Emerson's "The American Scholar." Delivered at the annual meeting of the Phi Beta Kappa Society at Harvard, "The American Scholar" is probably Emerson's most famous address. It was originally published as a pamphlet entitled *An Oration, Delivered before the Phi Beta Kappa Society at Cambridge, August 31, 1837*, but Emerson later altered the title to "The American Scholar" in his collection *Nature; Addresses, and Lectures* (1849). The address initially follows a popular theme of the day, developed by many previous speakers at Harvard: It was time for the new country to cast off the influence of European models and develop its own ideas and culture. But the address also offered Emerson an occasion to celebrate individualism and to challenge the institutional structures that limit the development of the individual. His conception of the scholar as "Man

Thinking," his advice about the use of books and reading, and his emphasis on the importance of "self-trust" to the individual remain among Emerson's celebrated contributions to American thought. The text is taken from the first edition of *An Oration, Delivered before the Phi Beta Kappa Society at Cambridge, August 31, 1837* (1837).

THE AMERICAN SCHOLAR

MR. PRESIDENT, AND GENTLEMEN,

I greet you on the re-commencement of our literary year. Our anniversary is one of hope, and, perhaps, not enough of labor. We do not meet for games of strength or skill, for the recitation of histories, tragedies and odes, like the ancient Greeks; for parliaments of love and poesy, like the Troubadours; nor for the advancement of science, like our contemporaries in the British and European capitals. Thus far, our holiday has been simply a friendly sign of the survival of the love of letters amongst a people too busy to give to letters any more. As such, it is precious as the sign of an indestructible instinct. Perhaps the time is already come, when it ought to be, and will be something else; when the sluggard intellect of this continent will look from under its iron lids and fill the postponed expectation of the world with something better than the exertions of mechanical skill. Our day of dependence, our long apprenticeship to the learning of other lands, draws to a close. The millions that around us are rushing into life, cannot always be fed on the sere remains of foreign harvests. Events, actions arise, that must be sung, that will sing themselves. Who can doubt that poetry will revive and lead in a new age, as the star in the constellation Harp which now flames in our zenith, astronomers announce, shall one day be the pole-star for a thousand years.

In the light of this hope, I accept the topic which not only usage, but the nature of our association, seem to prescribe to this day, – the AMERICAN SCHOLAR. Year by year, we come up hither to read one more chapter of his biography. Let us inquire what new lights, new events and more days have thrown on his character, his duties and his hopes.

It is one of those fables, which out of an unknown antiquity, convey an unlooked for wisdom, that the gods, in the beginning, divided Man into men, that he might be more helpful to himself; just as the hand was divided into fingers, the better to answer its end.

The old fable covers a doctrine ever new and sublime; that there is One Man, – present to all particular men only partially, or through one faculty; and that you must take the whole society to find the whole man. Man is not a farmer, or a professor, or an engineer, but he is all. Man is priest, and scholar, and statesman, and producer, and soldier. In the *divided* or social state, these functions are parcelled out to individuals, each of whom aims to do his stint of the joint work, whilst each other performs his. The fable implies that the individual to possess himself, must sometimes return from his own labor to embrace all the other laborers. But unfortunately, this original unit, this fountain of power, has been so distributed to multitudes, has been so minutely subdivided and peddled out, that it is spilled into drops, and cannot be gathered. The state of society is one in which the members have suffered amputation from the trunk, and strut about so many walking monsters, – a good finger, a neck, a stomach, an elbow, but never a man.

Man is thus metamorphosed into a thing, into many things. The planter, who is Man sent out into the field to gather food, is seldom cheered by any idea of the true dignity of his ministry. He sees his bushel and his cart, and nothing beyond, and sinks into the farmer, instead of Man on the farm. The tradesman scarcely ever gives an ideal worth to his work, but is ridden by the routine of his craft, and the soul is subject to dollars. The priest becomes a form; the attorney, a statute-book; the mechanic, a machine; the sailor, a rope of a ship.

In this distribution of functions, the scholar is the delegated intellect. In the right state, he is, *Man Thinking*. In the degenerate state, when the victim of society, he tends to become a mere thinker, or, still worse, the parrot of other men's thinking.

In this view of him, as Man Thinking, the whole theory of his office is contained. Him nature solicits, with all her placid, all her monitory pictures. Him the past instructs. Him the future invites. Is not, indeed, every man a student, and do not all things exist for the student's behoof? And, finally, is not the true scholar the only true master? But, as the old oracle said, "All things have two handles. Beware of the wrong one."[1] In life, too often, the scholar errs with mankind and forfeits his privilege. Let us see him in his school, and consider him in reference to the main influences he receives.

I. The first in time and the first in importance of the influences upon the mind is that of nature. Every day, the sun; and, after sunset, night and her stars. Ever the winds blow; ever the grass grows. Every day, men and women, conversing, beholding and beholden. The scholar must needs stand wistful and admiring before this great spectacle. He must settle its value in his mind. What is nature to him? There is never a beginning, there is never an end to the inexplicable continuity of this web of God, but always circular power returning into itself. Therein it resembles his own spirit, whose beginning, whose ending he never can find – so entire, so boundless. Far, too, as her splendors shine, system on system shooting like rays, upward, downward, without centre, without circumference, – in the mass and in the particle nature hastens to render account of herself to the mind. Classification begins. To the young mind, every thing is individual, stands by itself. By and by, it finds how to join two things, and see in them one nature; then three, then three thousand; and so, tyrannized over by its own unifying instinct, it goes on tying things together, diminishing anomalies, discovering roots running under ground, whereby contrary and remote things cohere, and flower out from one stem. It presently learns, that, since the dawn of history, there has been a constant accumulation and classifying of facts. But what is classification but the perceiving that these objects are not chaotic, and are not foreign, but have a law which is also a law of the human mind? The astronomer discovers that geometry, a pure abstraction of the human mind, is the measure of planetary motion. The chemist finds proportions and intelligible method throughout matter: and science is nothing but the finding of analogy, identity in the most remote parts. The ambitious soul sits down before each refrac-

1. "All . . . wrong one": From the writing of the Roman philosopher Epictetus (c. 55–c. 135).

tory fact; one after another, reduces all strange constitutions, all new powers, to their class and their law, and goes on forever to animate the last fibre of organization, the outskirts of nature, by insight.

Thus to him, to this school-boy under the bending dome of day, is suggested, that he and it proceed from one root; one is leaf and one is flower; relation, sympathy, stirring in every vein. And what is that Root? Is not that the soul of his soul? – A thought too bold – a dream too wild. Yet when this spiritual light shall have revealed the law of more earthly natures, – when he has learned to worship the soul, and to see that the natural philosophy that now is, is only the first gropings of its gigantic hand, he shall look forward to an ever expanding knowledge as to a becoming creator. He shall see that nature is the opposite of the soul, answering to it part for part. One is seal, and one is print. Its beauty is the beauty of his own mind. Its laws are the laws of his own mind. Nature then becomes to him the measure of his attainments. So much of nature as he is ignorant of, so much of his own mind does he not yet possess. And, in fine, the ancient precept, "Know thyself," and the modern precept, "Study nature," become at last one maxim.

II. The next great influence into the spirit of the scholar, is, the mind of the Past, – in whatever form, whether of literature, of art, of institutions, that mind is inscribed. Books are the best type of the influence of the past, and perhaps we shall get at the truth – learn the amount of this influence more conveniently – by considering their value alone.

The theory of books is noble. The scholar of the first age received into him the world around; brooded thereon; gave it the new arrangement of his own mind, and uttered it again. It came into him – life; it went out from him – truth. It came to him – short-lived actions; it went out from him – immortal thoughts. It came to him – business; it went from him – poetry. It was – dead fact; now, it is quick thought. It can stand, and it can go. It now endures, it now flies, it now inspires. Precisely in proportion to the depth of mind from which it issued, so high does it soar, so long does it sing.

Or, I might say, it depends on how far the process had gone, of transmuting life into truth. In proportion to the completeness of the distillation, so will the purity and imperishableness of the product be. But none is quite perfect. As no air-pump can by any means make a perfect vacuum, so neither can any artist entirely exclude the conventional, the local, the perishable from his book, or write a book of pure thought that shall be as efficient, in all respects, to a remote posterity, as to cotemporaries, or rather to the second age. Each age, it is found, must write its own books; or rather, each generation for the next succeeding. The books of an older period will not fit this.

Yet hence arises a grave mischief. The sacredness which attaches to the act of creation, – the act of thought, – is instantly transferred to the record. The poet chanting, was felt to be a divine man. Henceforth the chant is divine also. The writer was a just and wise spirit. Henceforward it is settled, the book is perfect; as love of the hero corrupts into worship of his statue. Instantly, the book becomes noxious. The guide is a tyrant. We sought a brother, and lo, a governor. The sluggish and perverted mind of the multitude, always slow to open to the incursions of Reason, having once so opened, having once received this book, stands upon it, and makes an outcry, if it is disparaged. Colleges are built on it. Books are written on it by thinkers, not by Man Thinking; by men of talent, that is, who start wrong, who set out from accepted dogmas, not from their own sight of principles. Meek young men grow up in libraries, believing it their duty to accept the views which Cicero, which Locke, which Bacon have given, forgetful that Cicero, Locke and Bacon[2] were only young men in libraries when they wrote these books.

Hence, instead of Man Thinking, we have the bookworm. Hence, the book-learned class, who value books, as such; not as related to nature and the human constitution, but as making a sort of Third Estate[3] with the world and the soul. Hence, the restorers of readings, the emendators, the bibliomaniacs of all degrees.

This is bad; this is worse than it seems. Books are the best of things, well used; abused, among the worst. What is the right use? What is the one end which all means go to effect? They are for nothing but to inspire. I had better never see a book than to be warped by its attraction clean out of my own orbit, and made a satellite instead of a system. The one thing in the world of value, is, the active soul, – the soul, free, sovereign, active. This every man is entitled to; this every man contains within him, although in almost all men, obstructed, and as yet unborn. The soul active sees absolute truth; and utters truth, or creates. In this action, it is genius; not the privilege of here and there a favorite, but the sound estate of every man. In its essence, it is progressive. The book, the college, the school of art, the institution of any kind, stop with some past utterance of genius. This is good, say they – let us hold by this. They pin me down. They look backward and not forward. But genius always looks forward. The eyes of man are set in his forehead, not in his hindhead. Man hopes. Genius creates. To create, – to create, – is the proof of divine presence. Whatever talents may be, if the man create not, the pure efflux of the Deity is not his: – cinders and smoke, there may be, but not yet flame. There are creative manners, there are creative actions, and creative words; manners, actions, words, that is, indicative of no custom or authority, but springing spontaneous from the mind's own sense of good and fair.

On the other part, instead of being its own seer, let it receive always from another mind its truth, though it were in torrents of light, without periods of solitude, inquest and self-recovery, and a fatal disservice is done. Genius is always sufficiently the enemy of genius by over-influence. The literature of every nation bear me witness. The English dramatic poets have Shakspearized now for two hundred years.

Undoubtedly there is a right way of reading, – so it be sternly subordinated. Man Thinking must not be subdued by his instruments. Books are for the scholar's idle times. When he can read God directly, the hour is too precious to be wasted in other mens' transcripts of their readings. But when the intervals of darkness come, as come they must, – when the soul seeth not, when the sun is hid, and the stars withdraw their shining, – we repair to the lamps which were kindled by their ray to guide our steps to the East again, where the dawn is. We hear that we may speak. The Arabian proverb says, "A fig tree looking on a fig tree, becometh fruitful."

2. **Cicero, Locke, and Bacon:** Marcus Tullius Cicero (106–43 BCE), a renowned Roman orator; the English philosophers John Locke (1632–1704) and Sir Francis Bacon (1561–1626).

3. **Third Estate:** Before the French Revolution in 1789, this term was used in France to describe the common people; the First Estate was the clergy, and the Second Estate was the nobility.

It is remarkable, the character of the pleasure we derive from the best books. They impress us ever with the conviction that one nature wrote and the same reads. We read the verses of one of the great English poets, of Chaucer, of Marvell, of Dryden, with the most modern joy, – with a pleasure, I mean, which is in great part caused by the abstraction of all *time* from their verses. There is some awe mixed with the joy of our surprise, when this poet, who lived in some past world, two or three hundred years ago, says that which lies close to my own soul, that which I also had well nigh thought and said. But for the evidence thence afforded to the philosophical doctrine of the identity of all minds, we should suppose some pre-established harmony, some foresight of souls that were to be, and some preparation of stores for their future wants, like the fact observed in insects, who lay up food before death for the young grub they shall never see.

I would not be hurried by any love of system, by any exaggeration of instincts, to underrate the Book. We all know, that as the human body can be nourished on any food, though it were boiled grass and the broth of shoes, so the human mind can be fed by any knowledge. And great and heroic men have existed, who had almost no other information than by the printed page. I only would say, that it needs a strong head to bear that diet. One must be an inventor to read well. As the proverb says, "He that would bring home the wealth of the Indies, must carry out the wealth of the Indies." There is then creative reading, as well as creative writing. When the mind is braced by labor and invention, the page of whatever book we read becomes luminous with manifold allusion. Every sentence is doubly significant, and the sense of our author is as broad as the world. We then see, what is always true, that as the seer's hour of vision is short and rare among heavy days and months, so is its record, perchance, the least part of his volume. The discerning will read in his Plato or Shakspeare, only that least part, – only the authentic utterances of the oracle, – and all the rest he rejects, were it never so many times Plato's and Shakspeare's.

Of course, there is a portion of reading quite indispensable to a wise man. History and exact science he must learn by laborious reading. Colleges, in like manner, have their indispensable office, – to teach elements. But they can only highly serve us, when they aim not to drill, but to create; when they gather from far every ray of various genius to their hospitable halls, and, by the concentrated fires, set the hearts of their youth on flame. Thought and knowledge are natures in which apparatus and pretension avail nothing. Gowns, and pecuniary foundations, though of towns of gold, can never countervail the least sentence or syllable of wit. Forget this, and our American colleges will recede in their public importance whilst they grow richer every year.

III. There goes in the world a notion that the scholar should be a recluse, a valetudinarian, – as unfit for any handiwork or public labor, as a penknife for an axe. The so-called "practical men" sneer at speculative men, as if, because they speculate or *see*, they could do nothing. I have heard it said that the clergy, – who are always more universally than any other class, the scholars of their day, – are addressed as women: that the rough, spontaneous conversation of men they do not hear, but only a mincing and diluted speech. They are often virtually disfranchised; and, indeed, there are advocates for their celibacy. As far as this is true of the studious classes, it is not just and wise. Action is with the scholar subordinate, but it is essential. Without it, he is not yet man.

Without it, thought can never ripen into truth. Whilst the world hangs before the eye as a cloud of beauty, we cannot even see its beauty. Inaction is cowardice, but there can be no scholar without the heroic mind. The preamble of thought, the transition through which it passes from the unconscious to the conscious, is action. Only so much do I know, as I have lived. Instantly we know whose words are loaded with life, and whose not.

The world, – this shadow of the soul, or *other me*, lies wide around. Its attractions are the keys which unlock my thoughts and make me acquainted with myself. I launch eagerly into this resounding tumult. I grasp the hands of those next me, and take my place in the ring to suffer and to work, taught by an instinct that so shall the dumb abyss be vocal with speech. I pierce its order; I dissipate its fear; I dispose of it within the circuit of my expanding life. So much only of life as I know by experience, so much of the wilderness have I vanquished and planted, or so far have I extended my being, my dominion. I do not see how any man can afford, for the sake of his nerves and his nap, to spare any action in which he can partake. It is pearls and rubies to his discourse. Drudgery, calamity, exasperation, want, are instructors in eloquence and wisdom. The true scholar grudges every opportunity of action past by, as a loss of power.

It is the raw material out of which the intellect moulds her splendid products. A strange process too, this, by which experience is converted into thought, as a mulberry leaf is converted into satin. The manufacture goes forward at all hours.

The actions and events of our childhood and youth are now matters of calmest observation. They lie like fair pictures in the air. Not so with our recent actions, – with the business which we now have in hand. On this we are quite unable to speculate. Our affections as yet circulate through it. We no more feel or know it, than we feel the feet, or the hand, or the brain of our body. The new deed is yet a part of life, – remains for a time immersed in our unconscious life. In some contemplative hour, it detaches itself from the life like a ripe fruit, to become a thought of the mind. Instantly, it is raised, transfigured; the corruptible has put on incorruption. Always now it is an object of beauty, however base its origin and neighborhood. Observe, too, the impossibility of antedating this act. In its grub state, it cannot fly, it cannot shine, – it is a dull grub. But suddenly, without observation, the selfsame thing unfurls beautiful wings, and is an angel of wisdom. So is there no fact, no event, in our private history, which shall not, sooner or later, lose its adhesive inert form, and astonish us by soaring from our body into the empyrean. Cradle and infancy, school and playground, the fear of boys, and dogs, and ferules, the love of little maids and berries, and many another fact that once filled the whole sky, are gone already; friend and relative, profession and party, town and country, nation and world, must also soar and sing.

Of course, he who has put forth his total strength in fit actions, has the richest return of wisdom. I will not shut myself out of this globe of action and transplant an oak into a flower pot, there to hunger and pine; nor trust the revenue of some single faculty, and exhaust one vein of thought, much like those Savoyards,[4] who, getting their livelihood

4. Savoyards: Savoy is located in the French Alps.

by carving shepherds, shepherdesses, and smoking Dutchmen, for all Europe, went out one day to the mountain to find stock, and discovered that they had whittled up the last of their pine trees. Authors we have in numbers, who have written out their vein, and who, moved by a commendable prudence, sail for Greece or Palestine, follow the trapper into the prairie, or ramble round Algiers to replenish their merchantable stock.

If it were only for a vocabulary the scholar would be covetous of action. Life is our dictionary. Years are well spent in country labors; in town – in the insight into trades and manufactures; in frank intercourse with many men and women; in science; in art; to the one end of mastering in all their facts a language, by which to illustrate and embody our perceptions. I learn immediately from any speaker how much he has already lived, through the poverty or the splendor of his speech. Life lies behind us as the quarry from whence we get tiles and copestones for the masonry of to-day. This is the way to learn grammar. Colleges and books only copy the language which the field and the workyard made.

But the final value of action, like that of books, and better than books, is, that it is a resource. That great principle of Undulation in nature, that shows itself in the inspiring and expiring of the breath; in desire and satiety; in the ebb and flow of the sea, in day and night, in heat and cold, and as yet more deeply ingrained in every atom and every fluid, is known to us under the name of Polarity, – these "fits of easy transmission and reflection," as Newton called them, are the law of nature because they are the law of spirit.

The mind now thinks; now acts; and each fit reproduces the other. When the artist has exhausted his materials, when the fancy no longer paints, when thoughts are no longer apprehended, and books are a weariness, – he has always the resource *to live.* Character is higher than intellect. Thinking is the function. Living is the functionary. The stream retreats to its source. A great soul will be strong to live, as well as strong to think. Does he lack organ or medium to impart his truths? He can still fall back on this elemental force of living them. This is a total act. Thinking is a partial act. Let the grandeur of justice shine in his affairs. Let the beauty of affection cheer his lowly roof. Those "far from fame" who dwell and act with him, will feel the force of his constitution in the doings and passages of the day better than it can be measured by any public and designed display. Time shall teach him that the scholar loses no hour which the man lives. Herein he unfolds the sacred germ of his instinct screened from influence. What is lost in seemliness is gained in strength. Not out of those on whom systems of education have exhausted their culture, comes the helpful giant to destroy the old or to build the new, but out of unhandselled savage nature, out of terrible Druids and Berserkirs, come at last Alfred and Shakspear.[5]

I hear therefore with joy whatever is beginning to be said of the dignity and necessity of labor to every citizen. There is virtue yet in the hoe and the spade, for learned as well as for unlearned hands. And labor is every where welcome; always we are invited to work; only be this limitation observed, that a man shall not for the sake of wider activity sacrifice any opinion to the popular judgments and modes of action.

5. **Druids . . . Shakspear:** Emerson refers to the Celts and Anglo-Saxons, the early conquerors of England; King Alfred the Great (849-899) was the king of the West Saxons.

I have now spoken of the education of the scholar by nature, by books, and by action. It remains to say somewhat of his duties.

They are such as become Man Thinking. They may all be comprised in self-trust. The office of the scholar is to cheer, to raise, and to guide men by showing them facts amidst appearances. He plies the slow, unhonored, and unpaid task of observation. Flamsteed and Herschel,[6] in their glazed observatory, may catalogue the stars with the praise of all men, and, the results being splendid and useful, honor is sure. But he, in his private observatory, cataloguing obscure and nebulous stars of the human mind, which as yet no man has thought of as such, – watching days and months, sometimes, for a few facts; correcting still his old records; – must relinquish display and immediate fame. In the long period of his preparation, he must betray often an ignorance and shiftlessness in popular arts, incurring the disdain of the able who shoulder him aside. Long he must stammer in his speech; often forego the living for the dead. Worse yet, he must accept – how often! poverty and solitude. For the ease and pleasure of treading the old road, accepting the fashions, the education, the region of society, he takes the cross of making his own, and, of course, the self accusation, the faint heart, the frequent uncertainty and loss of time which are the nettles and tangling vines in the way of the self-relying and self-directed; and the state of virtual hostility in which he seems to stand to society, and especially to educated society. For all this loss and scorn, what offset? He is to find consolation in exercising the highest functions of human nature. He is one who raises himself from private considerations, and breathes and lives on public and illustrious thoughts. He is the world's eye. He is the world's heart. He is to resist the vulgar prosperity that retrogrades ever to barbarism, by preserving and communicating heroic sentiments, noble biographies, melodious verse, and the conclusions of history. Whatsoever oracles the human heart in all emergencies, in all solemn hours has uttered as its commentary on the world of actions, – these he shall receive and impart. And whatsoever new verdict Reason from her inviolable seat pronounces on the passing men and events of to-day, – this he shall hear and promulgate.

These being his functions, it becomes him to feel all confidence in himself, and to defer never to the popular cry. He and he only knows the world. The world of any moment is the merest appearance. Some great decorum, some fetish of a government, some ephemeral trade, or war, or man, is cried up by half mankind and cried down by the other half, as if all depended on this particular up or down. The odds are that the whole question is not worth the poorest thought which the scholar has lost in listening to the controversy. Let him not quit his belief that a popgun is a popgun, though the ancient and honorable of the earth affirm it to be the crack of doom. In silence, in steadiness, in severe abstraction, let him hold by himself; add observation to observation; patient of neglect, patient of reproach, and bide his own time, – happy enough if he can satisfy himself alone that this day he has seen something truly. Success treads on every right step. For the instinct is sure that prompts him to tell his brother what he thinks. He then learns that in going down into the secrets of his own mind, he has descended into the secrets of all minds. He learns that he who has mastered any law in his private thoughts,

---

6. **Flamsteed and Herschel:** The astronomers John Flamsteed (1646–1719) and William Herschel (1738–1822), who discovered the planet Uranus.

is master to that extent of all men whose language he speaks, and of all into whose language his own can be translated. The poet in utter solitude remembering his spontaneous thoughts and recording them, is found to have recorded that which men in "cities vast" find true for them also. The orator distrusts at first the fitness of his frank confessions, – his want of knowledge of the persons he addresses, – until he finds that he is the complement of his hearers; – that they drink his words because he fulfils for them their own nature; the deeper he dives into his privatest secretest presentiment, – to his wonder he finds, this is the most acceptable, most public, and universally true. The people delight in it; the better part of every man feels, This is my music: this is myself.

In self-trust, all the virtues are comprehended. Free should the scholar be, – free and brave. Free even to the definition of freedom, "without any hindrance that does not arise out of his own constitution." Brave; for fear is a thing which a scholar by his very function puts behind him. Fear always springs from ignorance. It is a shame to him if his tranquillity, amid dangerous times, arise from the presumption that like children and women, his is a protected class; or if he seek a temporary peace by the diversion of his thoughts from politics or vexed questions, hiding his head like an ostrich in the flowering bushes, peeping into microscopes, and turning rhymes, as a boy whistles to keep his courage up. So is the danger a danger still: so is the fear worse. Manlike let him turn and face it. Let him look into its eye and search its nature, inspect its origin – see the whelping of this lion, – which lies no great way back; he will then find in himself a perfect comprehension of its nature and extent; he will have made his hands meet on the other side, and can henceforth defy it, and pass on superior. The world is his who can see through its pretension. What deafness, what stone-blind custom, what overgrown error you behold, is there only by sufferance, – by your sufferance. See it to be a lie, and you have already dealt it its mortal blow.

Yes, we are the cowed, – we the trustless. It is a mischievous notion that we are come late into nature; that the world was finished a long time ago. As the world was plastic and fluid in the hands of God, so it is ever to so much of his attributes as we bring to it. To ignorance and sin, it is flint. They adapt themselves to it as they may; but in proportion as a man has anything in him divine, the firmament flows before him, and takes his signet and form. Not he is great who can alter matter, but he who can alter my state of mind. They are the kings of the world who give the color of their present thought to all nature and all art, and persuade men by the cheerful serenity of their carrying the matter, that this thing which they do, is the apple which the ages have desired to pluck, now at last ripe, and inviting nations to the harvest. The great man makes the great thing. Wherever Macdonald sits, there is the head of the table.[7] Linnaeus makes botany the most alluring of studies and wins it from the farmer and the herb-woman. Davy, chemistry: and Cuvier,[8] fossils. The day is always his, who works in it with serenity and great

---

7. **table:** Emerson substitutes another name in an old Scottish proverb, "Where Macgregor sits, there is the head of the table."

8. **Linnaeus . . . Davy . . . Cuvier:** Carl Linnaeus or Carl von Linné (1707-1778) was the Swedish developer of taxonomy, the naming and classifying of organisms. Sir Humphry Davy (1778-1829) was an English chemist who studied the chemical effects of electricity. Georges Cuvier (1769-1832), an eminent French paleontologist, was among the most influential scientists of the early nineteenth century.

aims. The unstable estimates of men crowd to him whose mind is filled with a truth, as the heaped waves of the Atlantic follow the moon.

For this self-trust, the reason is deeper than can be fathomed, – darker than can be enlightened. I might not carry with me the feeling of my audience in stating my own belief. But I have already shown the ground of my hope, in adverting to the doctrine that man is one. I believe man has been wronged: he has wronged himself. He has almost lost the light that can lead him back to his prerogatives. Men are become of no account. Men in history, men in the world of to-day are bugs, are spawn, and are called "the mass" and "the herd." In a century, in a millenium, one or two men; that is to say – one or two approximations to the right state of every man. All the rest behold in the hero or the poet their own green and crude being – ripened; yes, and are content to be less, so *that* may attain to its full stature. What a testimony – full of grandeur, full of pity, is borne to the demands of his own nature, by the poor clansman, the poor partisan, who rejoices in the glory of his chief. The poor and the low find some amends to their immense moral capacity, for their acquiescence in a political and social inferiority. They are content to be brushed like flies from the path of a great person, so that justice shall be done by him to that common nature which it is the dearest desire of all to see enlarged and glorified. They sun themselves in the great man's light, and feel it to be their own element. They cast the dignity of man from their downtrod selves upon the shoulders of a hero, and will perish to add one drop of blood to make that great heart beat, those giant sinews combat and conquer. He lives for us, and we live in him.

Men such as they are, very naturally seek money or power; and power because it is as good as money, – the "spoils," so called, "of office." And why not? for they aspire to the highest, and this, in their sleep-walking, they dream is highest. Wake them, and they shall quit the false good and leap to the true, and leave governments to clerks and desks. This revolution is to be wrought by the gradual domestication of the idea of Culture. The main enterprise of the world for splendor, for extent, is the upbuilding of a man. Here are the materials strown along the ground. The private life of one man shall be a more illustrious monarchy, – more formidable to its enemy, more sweet and serene in its influence to its friend, than any kingdom in history. For a man, rightly viewed, comprehendeth the particular natures of all men. Each philosopher, each bard, each actor, has only done for me, as by a delegate, what one day I can do for myself. The books which once we valued more than the apple of the eye, we have quite exhausted. What is that but saying that we have come up with the point of view which the universal mind took through the eyes of that one scribe; we have been that man, and have passed on. First, one; then, another; we drain all cisterns, and waxing greater by all these supplies, we crave a better and more abundant food. The man has never lived that can feed us ever. The human mind cannot be enshrined in a person who shall set a barrier on any one side to this unbounded, unboundable empire. It is one central fire which flaming now out of the lips of Etna, lightens the capes of Sicily; and now out of the throat of Vesuvius, illuminates the towers and vineyards of Naples. It is one light which beams out of a thousand stars. It is one soul which animates all men.

But I have dwelt perhaps tediously upon this abstraction of the Scholar. I ought not to delay longer to add what I have to say, of nearer reference to the time and to this country.

Historically, there is thought to be a difference in the ideas which predominate over successive epochs, and there are data for marking the genius of the Classic, of the Romantic, and now of the Reflective or Philosophical age. With the views I have intimated of the oneness or the identity of the mind through all individuals, I do not much dwell on these differences. In fact, I believe each individual passes through all three. The boy is a Greek; the youth, romantic; the adult, reflective. I deny not, however, that a revolution in the leading idea may be distinctly enough traced.

Our age is bewailed as the age of Introversion. Must that needs be evil? We, it seems, are critical. We are embarrassed with second thoughts. We cannot enjoy any thing for hankering to know whereof the pleasure consists. We are lined with eyes. We see with our feet. The time is infected with Hamlet's unhappiness, –

> "Sicklied o'er with the pale cast of thought."[9]

Is it so bad then? Sight is the last thing to be pitied. Would we be blind? Do we fear lest we should outsee nature and God, and drink truth dry? I look upon the discontent of the literary class as a mere announcement of the fact that they find themselves not in the state of mind of their fathers, and regret the coming state as untried; as a boy dreads the water before he has learned that he can swim. If there is any period one would desire to be born in, – is it not the age of Revolution; when the old and the new stand side by side, and admit of being compared; when the energies of all men are searched by fear and by hope; when the historic glories of the old, can be compensated by the rich possibilities of the new era? This time, like all times, is a very good one, if we but know what to do with it.

I read with joy some of the auspicious signs of the coming days as they glimmer already through poetry and art, through philosophy and science, through church and state.

One of these signs is the fact that the same movement which effected the elevation of what was called the lowest class in the state, assumed in literature a very marked and as benign an aspect. Instead of the sublime and beautiful, the near, the low, the common, was explored and poetised. That which had been negligently trodden under foot by those who were harnessing and provisioning themselves for long journeys into far countries, is suddenly found to be richer than all foreign parts. The literature of the poor, the feelings of the child, the philosophy of the street, the meaning of household life, are the topics of the time. It is a great stride. It is a sign – is it not? of new vigor, when the extremities are made active, when currents of warm life run into the hands and the feet. I ask not for the great, the remote, the romantic; what is doing in Italy or Arabia; what is Greek art, or Provençal Minstrelsy; I embrace the common, I explore and sit at the feet of the familiar, the low. Give me insight into to-day, and you may have the antique and future worlds. What would we really know the meaning of? The meal in the firkin; the milk in the pan; the ballad in the street; the news of the boat; the glance of the eye; the form and the gait of the body; – show me the ultimate reason of these matters; – show

9. **"Sicklied . . . thought"**: Shakespeare, *Hamlet*, 3.1.85.

me the sublime presence of the highest spiritual cause lurking, as always it does lurk, in these suburbs and extremities of nature; let me see every trifle bristling with the polarity that ranges it instantly on an eternal law; and the shop, the plough, and the ledger, referred to the like cause by which light undulates and poets sing; – and the world lies no longer a dull miscellany and lumber room, but has form and order; there is no trifle; there is no puzzle; but one design unites and animates the farthest pinnacle and the lowest trench.

This idea has inspired the genius of Goldsmith, Burns, Cowper, and, in a newer time, of Goethe, Wordsworth, and Carlyle. This idea they have differently followed and with various success. In contrast with their writing, the style of Pope, of Johnson, of Gibbon, looks cold and pedantic. This writing is blood-warm. Man is surprised to find that things near are not less beautiful and wondrous than things remote. The near explains the far. The drop is a small ocean. A man is related to all nature. This perception of the worth of the vulgar, is fruitful in discoveries. Goethe, in this very thing the most modern of the moderns, has shown us, as none ever did, the genius of the ancients.

There is one man of genius who has done much for this philosophy of life, whose literary value has never yet been rightly estimated; – I mean Emanuel Swedenborg. The most imaginative of men, yet writing with the precision of a mathematician, he endeavored to engraft a purely philosophical Ethics on the popular Christianity of his time. Such an attempt, of course, must have difficulty which no genius could surmount. But he saw and showed the connexion between nature and the affections of the soul. He pierced the emblematic or spiritual character of the visible, audible, tangible world. Especially did his shade-loving muse hover over and interpret the lower parts of nature; he showed the mysterious bond that allies moral evil to the foul material forms, and has given in epical parables a theory of insanity, of beasts, of unclean and fearful things.

Another sign of our times, also marked by an analogous political movement is, the new importance given to the single person. Every thing that tends to insulate the individual, – to surround him with barriers of natural respect, so that each man shall feel the world is his, and man shall treat with man as a sovereign state with a sovereign state; – tends to true union as well as greatness. "I learned," said the melancholy Pestalozzi,[10] "that no man in God's wide earth is either willing or able to help any other man." Help must come from the bosom alone. The scholar is that man who must take up into himself all the ability of the time, all the contributions of the past, all the hopes of the future. He must be an university of knowledges. If there be one lesson more than another which should pierce his ear, it is, The world is nothing, the man is all; in yourself is the law of all nature, and you know not yet how a globule of sap ascends; in yourself slumbers the whole of Reason; it is for you to know all, it is for you to dare all. Mr. President and Gentlemen, this confidence in the unsearched might of man, belongs by

---

10. **Pestalozzi:** Johann Heinrich Pestalozzi (1746–1827) was a Swiss educator whose ideas influenced several of the transcendentalists.

all motives, by all prophecy, by all preparation, to the American Scholar. We have listened too long to the courtly muses of Europe. The spirit of the American freeman is already suspected to be timid, imitative, tame. Public and private avarice make the air we breathe thick and fat. The scholar is decent, indolent, complaisant. See already the tragic consequence. The mind of this country taught to aim at low objects, eats upon itself. There is no work for any but the decorous and the complaisant. Young men of the fairest promise, who begin life upon our shores, inflated by the mountain winds, shined upon by all the stars of God, find the earth below not in unison with these, – but are hindered from action by the disgust which the principles on which business is managed inspire, and turn drudges, or die of disgust, – some of them suicides. What is the remedy? They did not yet see, and thousands of young men as hopeful now crowding to the barriers for the career, do not yet see, that if the single man plant himself indomitably on his instincts, and there abide, the huge world will come round to him. Patience – patience; – with the shades of all the good and great for company; and for solace, the perspective of your own infinite life; and for work, the study, and the communication of principles, the making those instincts prevalent, the conversion of the world. Is it not the chief disgrace in the world, not to be an unit; – not to be reckoned one character; – not to yield that peculiar fruit which each man was created to bear, but to be reckoned in the gross, in the hundred, or the thousand, of the party, the section, to which we belong; and our opinion predicted geographically, as the north, or the south. Not so, brothers and friends, – please God, ours shall not be so. We will walk on our own feet; we will work with our own hands; we will speak our own minds. Then shall man be no longer a name for pity, for doubt, and for sensual indulgence. The dread of man and the love of man shall be a wall of defence and a wreath of love around all. A nation of men will for the first time exist, because each believes himself inspired by the Divine Soul which also inspires all men.

[1837]

Emerson's "Self-Reliance." The second "chapter" of *Essays* (1841), "Self-Reliance" is Emerson's most confident and aggressive affirmation of the importance of self-culture to the intellectual and moral development of the individual. Written during the controversy over his 1838 address at the Harvard Divinity School, which had outraged conservatives, and at a time when Emerson was facing growing pressures to participate in various organized reforms, the essay is also his most sustained defense of individualism. "Trust thyself: every heart beats to that iron string," "Whoso would be a man must be a nonconformist," and "A foolish consistency is the hobgoblin of little minds" are just a few of the often-quoted assertions in his essay, admired by generations of readers and writers. The text is taken from the first edition of *Essays* (1841).

SELF-RELIANCE

Ne te quaesiveris extra.[1]

"Man is his own star, and the soul that can
Render an honest and a perfect man,
Command all light, all influence, all fate,
Nothing to him falls early or too late.
Our acts our angels are, or good or ill,
Our fatal shadows that walk by us still."
-Epilogue to Beaumont and Fletcher's
Honest Man's Fortune[2]

Cast the bantling on the rocks,
Suckle him with the she-wolf's teat:
Wintered with the hawk and fox,
Power and speed be hands and feet.[3]

I read the other day some verses written by an eminent painter[4] which were original and not conventional. Always the soul hears an admonition in such lines, let the subject be what it may. The sentiment they instil is of more value than any thought they may contain. To believe your own thought, to believe that what is true for you in your private heart, is true for all men, – that is genius. Speak your latent conviction and it shall be the universal sense; for always the inmost becomes the outmost, – and our first thought is rendered back to us by the trumpets of the Last Judgment. Familiar as the voice of the mind is to each, the highest merit we ascribe to Moses, Plato, and Milton, is that they set at naught books and traditions, and spoke not what men but what they thought. A man should learn to detect and watch that gleam of light which flashes across his mind from within, more than the lustre of the firmament of bards and sages. Yet he dismisses without notice his thought, because it is his. In every work of genius we recognise our own rejected thoughts: they come back to us with a certain alienated majesty. Great works of art have no more affecting lesson for us than this. They teach us to abide by our spontaneous impression with good humored inflexibility then most when the whole cry of voices is on the other side. Else, to-morrow a stranger will say with masterly good sense precisely what we have thought and felt all the time, and we shall be forced to take with shame our own opinion from another.

There is a time in every man's education when he arrives at the conviction that envy is ignorance; that imitation is suicide; that he must take himself for better, for worse, as his portion; that though the wide universe is full of good, no kernel of nourishing corn can come to him but through his toil bestowed on that plot of ground which is given to him to till. The power which resides in him is new in nature, and none but he knows

---

1. ***Ne . . . extra***: From *Satire* 1.7 by Persius (34-62), a Roman satirist. "Don't seek the self outside the self."
2. ***Honest Man's Fortune***: A play by the English dramatists Francis Beaumont (1586-1616) and John Fletcher (1579-1625).
3. **Cast . . . feet**: The lines were written by Emerson.
4. **eminent painter**: Washington Allston (1779-1843), who was also regarded by many of his contemporaries as an innovative poet.

what that is which he can do, nor does he know until he has tried. Not for nothing one face, one character, one fact makes much impression on him, and another none. It is not without preestablished harmony, this sculpture in the memory. The eye was placed where one ray should fall, that it might testify of that particular ray. Bravely let him speak the utmost syllable of his confession. We but half express ourselves, and are ashamed of that divine idea which each of us represents. It may be safely trusted as proportionate and of good issues, so it be faithfully imparted, but God will not have his work made manifest by cowards. It needs a divine man to exhibit any thing divine. A man is relieved and gay when he has put his heart into his work and done his best; but what he has said or done otherwise, shall give him no peace. It is a deliverance which does not deliver. In the attempt his genius deserts him; no muse befriends; no invention, no hope.

Trust thyself: every heart vibrates to that iron string. Accept the place the divine Providence has found for you; the society of your contemporaries, the connexion of events. Great men have always done so and confided themselves childlike to the genius of their age, betraying their perception that the Eternal was stirring at their heart, working through their hands, predominating in all their being. And we are now men, and must accept in the highest mind the same transcendent destiny; and not pinched in a corner, not cowards fleeing before a revolution, but redeemers and benefactors, pious aspirants to be noble clay plastic under the Almighty effort, let us advance and advance on Chaos and the Dark.

What pretty oracles nature yields us on this text in the face and behavior of children, babes and even brutes. That divided and rebel mind, that distrust of a sentiment because our arithmetic has computed the strength and means opposed to our purpose, these have not. Their mind being whole, their eye is as yet unconquered, and when we look in their faces, we are disconcerted. Infancy conforms to nobody: all conform to it, so that one babe commonly makes four or five out of the adults who prattle and play to it. So God has armed youth and puberty and manhood no less with its own piquancy and charm, and made it enviable and gracious and its claims not to be put by, if it will stand by itself. Do not think the youth has no force because he cannot speak to you and me. Hark! in the next room, who spoke so clear and emphatic? Good Heaven! it is he! it is that very lump of bashfulness and phlegm which for weeks has done nothing but eat when you were by, that now rolls out these words like bell-strokes. It seems he knows how to speak to his contemporaries. Bashful or bold, then, he will know how to make us seniors very unnecessary.

The nonchalance of boys who are sure of a dinner, and would disdain as much as a lord to do or say aught to conciliate one, is the healthy attitude of human nature. How is a boy the master of society; independent, irresponsible, looking out from his corner on such people and facts as pass by, he tries and sentences them on their merits, in the swift summary way of boys, as good, bad, interesting, silly, eloquent, troublesome. He cumbers himself never about consequences, about interests: he gives an independent, genuine verdict. You must court him: he does not court you. But the man is, as it were, clapped into jail by his consciousness. As soon as he has once acted or spoken with éclat, he is a committed person, watched by the sympathy or the hatred of hundreds whose affections must now enter into his account. There is no Lethe for this. Ah, that he could pass again into his neutral, godlike independence! Who can thus lose all pledge, and having observed, observe again from the same unaffected, unbiased, unbribable, unaffrighted innocence, must always be formidable, must always engage the poet's and the man's regards. Of such an immortal youth the force would be felt. He would utter opinions on all passing affairs, which being seen to be not private but necessary, would sink like darts into the ear of men, and put them in fear.

These are the voices which we hear in solitude, but they grow faint and inaudible as we enter into the world. Society everywhere is in conspiracy against the manhood of every one of its members. Society is a joint-stock company in which the members agree for the better securing of his bread to each shareholder, to surrender the liberty and culture of the eater. The virtue in most request is conformity. Self-reliance is its aversion. It loves not realities and creators, but names and customs.

Whoso would be a man must be a nonconformist. He who would gather immortal palms must not be hindered by the name of goodness, but must explore if it be goodness. Nothing is at last sacred but the integrity of our own mind. Absolve you to yourself, and you shall have the suffrage of the world. I remember an answer which when quite young I was prompted to make to a valued adviser who was wont to importune me with the dear old doctrines of the church. On my saying, What have I to do with the sacredness of traditions, if I live wholly from within? my friend suggested – "But these impulses may be from below, not from above." I replied, 'They do not seem to me to be such; but if I am the devil's child, I will live then from the devil.' No law can be sacred to me but that of my nature. Good and bad are but names very readily transferable to that or this; the only right is what is after my constitution, the only wrong what is against it. A man is to carry himself in the presence of all opposition as if every thing were titular and ephemeral but he. I am ashamed to think how easily we capitulate to badges and names, to large societies and dead institutions. Every decent and well-spoken individual affects and sways me more than is right. I ought to go upright and vital, and speak the rude truth in all ways. If malice and vanity wear the coat of philanthropy, shall that pass? If an angry bigot assumes this bountiful cause of Abolition, and comes to me with his last news from Barbadoes,[5] why should I not say to him, 'Go love thy infant; love thy wood-chopper: be good-natured and modest: have that grace; and never varnish your hard, uncharitable ambition with this incredible tenderness for black folk a thousand miles off. Thy love afar is spite at home.' Rough and graceless would be such greeting, but truth is handsomer than the affectation of love. Your goodness must have some edge to it – else it is none. The doctrine of hatred must be preached as the counteraction of the doctrine of love when that pules and whines. I shun father and mother and wife and brother, when my genius calls me. I would write on the lintels of the door-post, *Whim*. I hope it is somewhat better than whim at last, but we cannot spend the day in explanation. Expect me not to show cause why I seek or why I exclude company. Then, again, do not tell me, as a good man did to-day, of my obligation to put all poor men in good situations. Are they *my* poor? I tell thee, thou foolish philanthropist, that I grudge the dollar, the dime, the cent I give to such men as do not belong to me and to whom I do not belong.

5. **Barbadoes:** Caribbean island of Barbados where slavery was abolished in 1834.

There is a class of persons to whom by all spiritual affinity I am bought and sold; for them I will go to prison, if need be; but your miscellaneous popular charities; the education at college of fools; the building of meeting-houses to the vain end to which many now stand; alms to sots; and the thousandfold Relief Societies; – though I confess with shame I sometimes succumb and give the dollar, it is a wicked dollar which by-and-by I shall have the manhood to withhold.

Virtues are in the popular estimate rather the exception than the rule. There is the man *and* his virtues. Men do what is called a good action, as some piece of courage or charity, much as they would pay a fine in expiation of daily non-appearance on parade. Their works are done as an apology or extenuation of their living in the world, – as invalids and the insane pay a high board. Their virtues are penances. I do not wish to expiate, but to live. My life is not an apology, but a life. It is for itself and not for a spectacle. I much prefer that it should be of a lower strain, so it be genuine and equal, than that it should be glittering and unsteady. I wish it to be sound and sweet, and not to need diet and bleeding.[6] My life should be unique; it should be an alms, a battle, a conquest, a medicine. I ask primary evidence that you are a man, and refuse this appeal from the man to his actions. I know that for myself it makes no difference whether I do or forbear those actions which are reckoned excellent. I cannot consent to pay for a privilege where I have intrinsic right. Few and mean as my gifts may be, I actually am, and do not need for my own assurance or the assurance of my fellows any secondary testimony.

What I must do, is all that concerns me, not what the people think. This rule, equally arduous in actual and in intellectual life, may serve for the whole distinction between greatness and meanness. It is the harder, because you will always find those who think they know what is your duty better than you know it. It is easy in the world to live after the world's opinion; it is easy in solitude to live after our own; but the great man is he who in the midst of the crowd keeps with perfect sweetness the independence of solitude.

The objection to conforming to usages that have become dead to you, is, that it scatters your force. It loses your time and blurs the impression of your character. If you maintain a dead church, contribute to a dead Bible-Society, vote with a great party either for the Government or against it, spread your table like base housekeepers, – under all these screens, I have difficulty to detect the precise man you are. And, of course, so much force is withdrawn from your proper life. But do your thing, and I shall know you. Do your work, and you shall reinforce yourself. A man must consider what a blind-man's-buff is this game of conformity. If I know your sect, I anticipate your argument. I hear a preacher announce for his text and topic the expediency of one of the institutions of his church. Do I not know beforehand that not possibly can he say a new and spontaneous word? Do I not know that with all this ostentation of examining the grounds of the institution, he will do no such thing? Do I not know that he is pledged to himself not to look but at one side; the permitted side, not as a man, but as a parish minister? He is a retained attorney, and these airs of the bench are the emptiest affectation. Well, most men have bound their eyes with one or another handkerchief, and attached

6. **diet and bleeding:** Bleeding was an old medical practice in which patients were "bled" in order to cleanse the body.

themselves to some one of these communities of opinion. This conformity makes them not false in a few particulars, authors of a few lies, but false in all particulars. Their every truth is not quite true. Their two is not the real two, their four not the real four: so that every word they say chagrins us, and we know not where to begin to set them right. Meantime nature is not slow to equip us in the prison-uniform of the party to which we adhere. We come to wear one cut of face and figure, and acquire by degrees the gentlest asinine expression. There is a mortifying experience in particular which does not fail to wreak itself also in the general history; I mean, "the foolish face of praise,"[7] the forced smile which we put on in company where we do not feel at ease in answer to conversation which does not interest us. The muscles, not spontaneously moved, but moved by a low usurping wilfulness, grow tight about the outline of the face and make the most disagreeable sensation, a sensation of rebuke and warning which no brave young man will suffer twice.

For non-conformity the world whips you with its displeasure. And therefore a man must know how to estimate a sour face. The bystanders look askance on him in the public street or in the friend's parlor. If this aversation had its origin in contempt and resistance like his own, he might well go home with a sad countenance; but the sour faces of the multitude, like their sweet faces, have no deep cause, – disguise no god, but are put on and off as the wind blows, and a newspaper directs. Yet is the discontent of the multitude more formidable than that of the senate and the college. It is easy enough for a firm man who knows the world to brook the rage of the cultivated classes. Their rage is decorous and prudent, for they are timid as being very vulnerable themselves. But when to their feminine rage the indignation of the people is added, when the ignorant and the poor are aroused, when the unintelligent brute force that lies at the bottom of society is made to growl and mow, it needs the habit of magnanimity and religion to treat it godlike as a trifle of no concernment.

The other terror that scares us from self-trust is our consistency; a reverence for our past act or word, because the eyes of others have no other data for computing our orbit than our past acts, and we are loath to disappoint them.

But why should you keep your head over your shoulder? Why drag about this monstrous corpse of your memory, lest you contradict somewhat you have stated in this or that public place? Suppose you should contradict yourself; what then? It seems to be a rule of wisdom never to rely on your memory alone, scarcely even in acts of pure memory, but bring the past for judgment into the thousand-eyed present, and live ever in a new day. Trust your emotion. In your metaphysics you have denied personality to the Deity: yet when the devout motions of the soul come, yield to them heart and life, though they should clothe God with shape and color. Leave your theory as Joseph his coat in the hand of the harlot, and flee.[8]

---

7. **"the . . . praise":** Alexander Pope (1688-1744), "Epistle to Dr. Arbuthnot," line 212.
8. **harlot, and flee:** In the Old Testament account, Joseph is sold into slavery by his brothers and becomes the servant of Potiphar, the captain of the guard for the Pharaoh of Egypt. Potiphar's wife tempted Joseph and grabbed his cloak. In his haste to get away from her, he left his cloak in her hands and fled (Genesis 39).

A foolish consistency is the hobgoblin of little minds, adored by little statesmen and philosophers and divines. With consistency a great soul has simply nothing to do. He may as well concern himself with his shadow on the wall. Out upon your guarded lips! Sew them up with packthread, do. Else, if you would be a man, speak what you think to-day in words as hard as cannon balls, and to-morrow speak what to-morrow thinks in hard words again, though it contradict every thing you said to-day. Ah, then, exclaim the aged ladies, you shall be sure to be misunderstood. Misunderstood! It is a right fool's word. Is it so bad then to be misunderstood? Pythagoras was misunderstood, and Socrates, and Jesus, and Luther, and Copernicus, and Galileo, and Newton, and every pure and wise spirit that ever took flesh. To be great is to be misunderstood.

I suppose no man can violate his nature. All the sallies of his will are rounded in by the law of his being as the inequalities of Andes and Himalayas are insignificant in the curve of the sphere. Nor does it matter how you gauge and try him. A character is like an acrostic or Alexandrian stanza; – read it forward, backward, or across, it still spells the same thing. In this pleasing contrite wood-life which God allows me, let me record day by day my honest thought without prospect or retrospect, and, I cannot doubt, it will be found symmetrical, though I mean it not, and see it not. My book should smell of pines and resound with the hum of insects. The swallow over my window should interweave that thread or straw he carries in his bill into my web also. We pass for what we are. Character teaches above our wills. Men imagine that they communicate their virtue or vice only by overt actions and do not see that virtue or vice emit a breath every moment.

Fear never but you shall be consistent in whatever variety of actions, so they be each honest and natural in their hour. For of one will, the actions will be harmonious, however unlike they seem. These varieties are lost sight of when seen at a little distance, at a little height of thought. One tendency unites them all. The voyage of the best ship is a zigzag line of a hundred tacks. This is only microscopic criticism. See the line from a sufficient distance, and it straightens itself to the average tendency. Your genuine action will explain itself and will explain your other genuine actions. Your conformity explains nothing. Act singly, and what you have already done singly, will justify you now. Greatness always appeals to the future. If I can be great enough now to do right and scorn eyes, I must have done so much right before, as to defend me now. Be it how it will, do right now. Always scorn appearances, and you always may. The force of character is cumulative. All the foregone days of virtue work their health into this. What makes the majesty of the heroes of the senate and the field, which so fills the imagination? The consciousness of a train of great days and victories behind. There they all stand and shed an united light on the advancing actor. He is attended as by a visible escort of angels to every man's eye. That is it which throws thunder into Chatham's voice, and dignity into Washington's port, and America into Adams's eye.[9] Honor is venerable to us because it is no ephemeris. It is always ancient virtue. We worship it to-day, because it is

9. **Chatham's voice . . . Adams's eye:** The English politician William Pitt, Earl of Chatham (1708-1778); the American presidents George Washington (1732-1799) and either John Adams (1735-1826) or John Quincy Adams (1767-1848).

not of to-day. We love it and pay it homage, because it is not a trap for our love and homage, but is self-dependent, self-derived, and therefore of an old immaculate pedigree, even if shown in a young person.

I hope in these days we have heard the last of conformity and consistency. Let the words be gazetted and ridiculous henceforward. Instead of the gong for dinner, let us hear a whistle from the Spartan fife. Let us bow and apologize never more. A great man is coming to eat at my house. I do not wish to please him: I wish that he should wish to please me. I will stand here for humanity, and though I would make it kind, I would made it true. Let us affront and reprimand the smooth mediocrity and squalid contentment of the times, and hurl in the face of custom, and trade, and office, the fact which is the upshot of all history, that there is a great responsible Thinker and Actor moving wherever moves a man; that a true man belongs to no other time or place, but is the centre of things. Where he is, there is nature. He measures you, and all men, and all events. You are constrained to accept his standard. Ordinarily every body in society reminds us of somewhat else or of some other person. Character, reality, reminds you of nothing else. It takes place of the whole creation. The man must be so much that he must make all circumstances indifferent, – put all means into the shade. This all great men are and do. Every true man is a cause, a country, and an age; requires infinite spaces and numbers and time fully to accomplish his thought; – and posterity seem to follow his steps as a procession. A man Caesar is born, and for ages after, we have a Roman Empire. Christ is born, and millions of minds so grow and cleave to his genius, that he is confounded with virtue and the possible of man. An institution is the lengthened shadow of one man; as, the Reformation, of Luther; Quakerism, of Fox; Methodism, of Wesley; Abolition, of Clarkson. Scipio,[10] Milton called “the height of Rome;” and all history resolves itself very easily into the biography of a few stout and earnest persons.

Let a man then know his worth, and keep things under his feet. Let him not peep or steal, or skulk up and down with the air of a charity-boy, a bastard, or an interloper, in the world which exists for him. But the man in the street finding no worth in himself which corresponds to the force which built a tower or sculptured a marble god, feels poor when he looks on these. To him a palace, a statue, or a costly book have an alien and forbidding air, much like a gay equipage, and seem to say like that, ‘Who are you, sir?’ Yet they all are his, suitors for his notice, petitioners to his faculties that they will come out and take possession. The picture waits for my verdict: it is not to command me, but I am to settle its claims to praise. That popular fable of the sot who was picked up dead drunk in the street, carried to the duke’s house, washed and dressed and laid in the duke’s bed, and, on his waking, treated with all obsequious ceremony like the duke, and assured that he had been insane, – owes its popularity to the fact, that it symbolizes so well the state of man, who is in the world a sort of sot, but now and then wakes up, exercises his reason, and finds himself a true prince.

Our reading is mendicant and sycophantic. In history, our imagination makes fools

10. **Scipio:** Scipio Africanus (237–183 BCE), Roman general who conquered Carthage.

of us, plays us false. Kingdom and lordship, power and estate are a gaudier vocabulary than private John and Edward in a small house and common day's work: but the things of life are the same to both: the sum total of both is the same. Why all this deference to Alfred, and Scanderbeg, and Gustavus?[11] Suppose they were virtuous: did they wear out virtue? As great a stake depends on your private act to-day, as followed their public and renowned steps. When private men shall act with vast views, the lustre will be transferred from the actions of kings to those of gentlemen.

The world has indeed been instructed by its kings, who have so magnetized the eyes of nations. It has been taught by this colossal symbol the mutual reverence that is due from man to man. The joyful loyalty with which men have every where suffered the king, the noble, or the great proprietor to walk among them by a law of his own, make his own scale of men and things, and reverse theirs, pay for benefits not with money but with honor, and represent the Law in his person, was the hieroglyphic by which they obscurely signified their consciousness of their own right and comeliness, the right of every man.

The magnetism which all original action exerts is explained when we inquire the reason of self-trust. Who is the Trustee? What is the aboriginal Self on which a universal reliance may be grounded? What is the nature and power of that science-baffling star, without parallax, without calculable elements, which shoots a ray of beauty even into trivial and impure actions, if the least mark of independence appear? The inquiry leads us to that source, at once the essence of genius, the essence of virtue, and the essence of life, which we call Spontaneity or Instinct. We denote this primary wisdom as Intuition, whilst all later teachings are tuitions. In that deep force, the last fact behind which analysis cannot go, all things find their common origin. For the sense of being which in calm hours rises, we know not how, in the soul, is not diverse from things, from space, from light, from time, from man, but one with them, and proceedeth obviously from the same source whence their life and being also proceedeth. We first share the life by which things exist, and afterwards see them as appearances in nature, and forget that we have shared their cause. Here is the fountain of action and the fountain of thought. Here are the lungs of that inspiration which giveth man wisdom, of that inspiration of man which cannot be denied without impiety and atheism. We lie in the lap of immense intelligence, which makes us organs of its activity and receivers of its truth. When we discern justice, when we discern truth, we do nothing of ourselves, but allow a passage to its beams. If we ask whence this comes, if we seek to pry into the soul that causes, — all metaphysics, all philosophy is at fault. Its presence or its absence is all we can affirm. Every man discerns between the voluntary acts of his mind, and his involuntary perceptions. And to his involuntary perceptions, he knows a perfect respect is due. He may err in the expression of them, but he knows that these things are so, like day and

---

11. **Alfred . . . Gustavus:** Emerson refers to the national heroes of three countries: Alfred the Great (849–899) of England, Scanderbeg (1404–1468) of Albania, and Gustavus (1594–1632) of Sweden.

night, not to be disputed. All my wilful actions and acquisitions are but roving; – the most trivial reverie, the faintest native emotion are domestic and divine. Thoughtless people contradict as readily the statement of perceptions as of opinions, or rather much more readily; for, they do not distinguish between perception and notion. They fancy that I choose to see this or that thing. But perception is not whimsical, but fatal. If I see a trait, my children will see it after me, and in course of time, all mankind, – although it may chance that no one has seen it before me. For my perception of it is as much a fact as the sun.

The relations of the soul to the divine spirit are so pure that it is profane to seek to interpose helps. It must be that when God speaketh, he should communicate not one thing, but all things; should fill the world with his voice; should scatter forth light, nature, time, souls, from the centre of the present thought; and new date and new create the whole. Whenever a mind is simple, and receives a divine wisdom, then old things pass away, – means, teachers, texts, temples fall; it lives now and absorbs past and future into the present hour. All things are made sacred by relation to it, – one thing as much as another. All things are dissolved to their centre by their cause, and in the universal miracle petty and particular miracles disappear. This is and must be. If, therefore, a man claims to know and speak of God, and carries you backward to the phraseology of some old mouldered nation in another country, in another world, believe him not. Is the acorn better than the oak which is its fulness and completion? Is the parent better than the child into whom he has cast his ripened being? Whence then this worship of the past? The centuries are conspirators against the sanity and majesty of the soul. Time and space are but physiological colors which the eye maketh, but the soul is light; where it is, is day; where it was, is night; and history is an impertinence and an injury, if it be anything more than a cheerful apologue or parable of my being and becoming.

Man is timid and apologetic. He is no longer upright. He dares not say 'I think,' 'I am,' but quotes some saint or sage. He is ashamed before the blade of grass or the blowing rose. These roses under my window make no reference to former roses or to better ones; they are for what they are; they exist with God to-day. There is no time to them. There is simply the rose; it is perfect in every moment of its existence. Before a leaf-bud has burst, its whole life acts; in the full-blown flower, there is no more; in the leafless root, there is no less. Its nature is satisfied, and it satisfies nature, in all moments alike. There is no time to it. But man postpones or remembers; he does not live in the present, but with reverted eye laments the past, or, heedless of the riches that surround him, stands on tiptoe to foresee the future. He cannot be happy and strong until he too lives with nature in the present, above time.

This should be plain enough. Yet see what strong intellects dare not yet hear God himself, unless he speak the phraseology of I know not what David, or Jeremiah, or Paul. We shall not always set so great a price on a few texts, on a few lives. We are like children who repeat by rote the sentences of grandames and tutors, and, as they grow older, of the men of talents and character they chance to see, – painfully recollecting the exact words they spoke; afterwards, when they come into the point of view which those had who uttered these sayings, they understand them, and are willing to let the words go;

for, at any time, they can use words as good, when occasion comes. So was it with us, so will it be, if we proceed. If we live truly, we shall see truly. It is as easy for the strong man to be strong, as it is for the weak to be weak. When we have new perception, we shall gladly disburthen the memory of its hoarded treasures as old rubbish. When a man lives with God, his voice shall be as sweet as the murmur of the brook and the rustle of the corn.

And now at last the highest truth on this subject remains unsaid; probably, cannot be said; for all that we say is the far off remembering of the intuition. That thought, by what I can now nearest approach to say it, is this. When good is near you, when you have life in yourself, – it is not by any known or appointed way; you shall not discern the footprints of any other; you shall not see the face of man; you shall not hear any name; – the way, the thought, the good shall be wholly strange and new. It shall exclude all other being. You take the way from man not to man. All persons that ever existed are its fugitive ministers. There shall be no fear in it. Fear and hope are alike beneath it. It asks nothing. There is somewhat low even in hope. We are then in vision. There is nothing that can be called gratitude nor properly joy. The soul is raised over passion. It seeth identity and eternal causation. It is a perceiving that Truth and Right are. Hence it becomes a Tranquillity out of the knowing that all things go well. Vast spaces of nature; the Atlantic Ocean, the South Sea; vast intervals of time, years, centuries, are of no account. This which I think and feel, underlay that former state of life and circumstances, as it does underlie my present, and will always all circumstance, and what is called life, and what is called death.

Life only avails, not the having lived. Power ceases in the instant of repose; it resides in the moment of transition from a past to a new state; in the shooting of the gulf; in the darting to an aim. This one fact the world hates, that the soul *becomes*; for, that forever degrades the past; turns all riches to poverty; all reputation to a shame; confounds the saint with the rogue; shoves Jesus and Judas equally aside. Why then do we prate of self-reliance? Inasmuch as the soul is present, there will be power not confident but agent. To talk of reliance, is a poor external way of speaking. Speak rather of that which relies, because it works and is. Who has more soul than I, masters me, though he should not raise his finger. Round him I must revolve by the gravitation of spirits; who has less, I rule with like facility. We fancy it rhetoric when we speak of eminent virtue. We do not yet see that virtue is Height, and that a man or a company of men plastic and permeable to principles, by the law of nature must overpower and ride all cities, nations, kings, rich men, poets, who are not.

This is the ultimate fact which we so quickly reach on this as on every topic, the resolution of all into the ever blessed ONE. Virtue is the governor, the creator, the reality. All things real are so by so much of virtue as they contain. Hardship, husbandry, hunting, whaling, war, eloquence, personal weight, are somewhat, and engage my respect as examples of the soul's presence and impure action. I see the same law working in nature for conservation and growth. The poise of a planet, the bended tree recovering itself from the strong wind, the vital resources of every vegetable and animal, are also demonstrations of the self-sufficing, and therefore self-relying soul. All history from its highest to its trivial passages is the various record of this power.

Thus all concentrates; let us not rove; let us sit at home with the cause. Let us stun and astonish the intruding rabble of men and books and institutions by a simple declaration of the divine fact. Bid them take the shoes from off their feet,[12] for God is here within. Let our simplicity judge them, and our docility to our own law demonstrate the poverty of nature and fortune beside our native riches.

But now we are a mob. Man does not stand in awe of man, nor is the soul admonished to stay at home, to put itself in communication with the internal ocean, but it goes abroad to beg a cup of water of the urns of men. We must go alone. Isolation must precede true society. I like the silent church before the service begins, better than any preaching. How far off, how cool, how chaste the persons look, begirt each one with a precinct or sanctuary. So let us always sit. Why should we assume the faults of our friend, or wife, or father, or child, because they sit around our hearth, or are said to have the same blood? All men have my blood, and I have all men's. Not for that will I adopt their petulance or folly, even to the extent of being ashamed of it. But your isolation must not be mechanical, but spiritual, that is, must be elevation. At times the whole world seems to be in conspiracy to importune you with emphatic trifles. Friend, client, child, sickness, fear, want, charity, all knock at once at thy closet door and say, 'Come out unto us.' – Do not spill thy soul; do not all descend; keep thy state; stay at home in thine own heaven; come not for a moment into their facts, into their hubbub of conflicting appearances, but let in the light of thy law on their confusion. The power men possess to annoy me, I give them by a weak curiosity. No man can come near me but through my act. "What we love that we have, but by desire we bereave ourselves of the love."

If we cannot at once rise to the sanctities of obedience and faith, let us at least resist our temptations, let us enter into the state of war, and wake Thor and Woden,[13] courage and constancy in our Saxon breasts. This is to be done in our smooth times by speaking the truth. Check this lying hospitality and lying affection. Live no longer to the expectation of these deceived and deceiving people with whom we converse. Say to them, O father, O mother, O wife, O brother, O friend, I have lived with you after appearances hitherto. Henceforward I am the truth's. Be it known unto you that henceforward I obey no law less than the eternal law. I will have no covenants but proximities. I shall endeavor to nourish my parents, to support my family, to be the chaste husband of one wife, – but these relations I must fill after a new and unprecedented way. I appeal from your customs. I must be myself. I cannot break myself any longer for you, or you. If you can love me for what I am, we shall be the happier. If you cannot, I will still seek to deserve that you should. I must be myself. I will not hide my tastes or aversions. I will so trust that what is deep is holy, that I will do strongly before the sun and moon whatever inly rejoices me, and the heart appoints. If you are noble, I will love you; if you are not, I will not hurt you and myself by hypocritical attentions. If you are true, but not in the same truth with me, cleave to your companions; I will seek my own. I do this not selfishly but humbly and truly. It is alike your interest and mine and all men's, however long we have dwelt in lies, to live in truth. Does this sound harsh to-day? You will soon love what is dictated by your nature as well as mine, and if we follow the truth, it will bring us

12. **Bid . . . feet:** See Exodus 3.5.
13. **Thor and Woden:** Norse gods of thunder and war.

out safe at last. – But so you may give these friends pain. Yes, but I cannot sell my liberty and my power, to save their sensibility. Besides, all persons have their moments of reason when they look out into the region of absolute truth; then will they justify me and do the same thing.

The populace think that your rejection of popular standards is a rejection of all standard, and mere antinomianism; and the bold sensualist will use the name of philosophy to gild his crimes. But the law of consciousness abides. There are two confessionals, in one or the other of which we must be shriven. You may fulfil your round of duties by clearing yourself in the *direct*, or, in the *reflex* way. Consider whether you have satisfied your relations to father, mother, cousin, neighbor, town, cat, and dog; whether any of these can upbraid you. But I may also neglect this reflex standard, and absolve me to myself. I have my own stern claims and perfect circle. It denies the name of duty to many offices that are called duties. But if I can discharge its debts, it enables me to dispense with the popular code. If any one imagines that this law is lax, let him keep its commandment one day.

And truly it demands something godlike in him who has cast off the common motives of humanity, and has ventured to trust himself for a task-master. High be his heart, faithful his will, clear his sight, that he may in good earnest be doctrine, society, law to himself, that a simple purpose may be to him as strong as iron necessity is to others.

If any man consider the present aspects of what is called by distinction *society*, he will see the need of these ethics. The sinew and heart of man seem to be drawn out, and we are become timorous desponding whimperers. We are afraid of truth, afraid of fortune, afraid of death, and afraid of each other. Our age yields no great and perfect persons. We want men and women who shall renovate life and our social state, but we see that most natures are insolvent; cannot satisfy their own wants, have an ambition out of all proportion to their practical force, and so do lean and beg day and night continually. Our housekeeping is mendicant, our arts, our occupations, our marriages, our religion we have not chosen, but society has chosen for us. We are parlor soldiers. The rugged battle of fate, where strength is born, we shun.

If our young men miscarry in their first enterprizes, they lose all heart. If the young merchant fails, men say he is *ruined*. If the finest genius studies at one of our colleges, and is not installed in an office within one year afterwards in the cities or suburbs of Boston or New York, it seems to his friends and to himself that he is right in being disheartened and in complaining the rest of his life. A sturdy lad from New Hampshire or Vermont, who in turn tries all the professions, who *teams it, farms it, peddles*, keeps a school, preaches, edits a newspaper, goes to Congress, buys a township, and so forth, in successive years, and always, like a cat, falls on his feet, is worth a hundred of these city dolls. He walks abreast with his days, and feels no shame in not 'studying a profession,' for he does not postpone his life, but lives already. He has not one chance, but a hundred chances. Let a stoic[14] arise who shall reveal the resources of man, and tell men they are

---

14. **stoic:** Adherent of Greek school of philosophy that encouraged being attuned with one's inner self and being content with one's present state of being.

not leaning willows, but can and must detach themselves; that with the exercise of self-trust, new powers shall appear; that a man is the word made flesh, born to shed healing to the nations, that he should be ashamed of our compassion, and that the moment he acts from himself, tossing the laws, the books, idolatries, and customs out of the window, – we pity him no more but thank and revere him, – and that teacher shall restore the life of man to splendor, and make his name dear to all History.

It is easy to see that a greater self-reliance, – a new respect for the divinity in man, – must work a revolution in all the offices and relations of men; in their religion; in their education; in their pursuits; their modes of living; their association; in their property; in their speculative views.

1. In what prayers do men allow themselves! That which they call a holy office, is not so much as brave and manly. Prayer looks abroad and asks for some foreign addition to come through some foreign virtue, and loses itself in endless mazes of natural and supernatural, and mediatorial and miraculous. Prayer that craves a particular commodity – any thing less than all good, is vicious. Prayer is the contemplation of the facts of life from the highest point of view. It is the soliloquy of a beholding and jubilant soul. It is the spirit of God pronouncing his works good. But prayer as a means to effect a private end, is theft and meanness. It supposes dualism and not unity in nature and consciousness. As soon as the man is at one with God, he will not beg. He will then see prayer in all action. The prayer of the farmer kneeling in his field to weed it, the prayer of the rower kneeling with the stroke of his oar, are true prayers heard throughout nature, though for cheap ends. Caratach, in Fletcher's *Bonduca*, when admonished to inquire the mind of the god Audate, replies,

> "His hidden meaning lie in our endeavors,
> Our valors are our best gods."[15]

Another sort of false prayers are our regrets. Discontent is the want of self-reliance: it is infirmity of will. Regret calamities, if you can thereby help the sufferer; if not, attend your own work, and already the evil begins to be repaired. Our sympathy is just as base. We come to them who weep foolishly, and sit down and cry for company, instead of imparting to them truth and health in rough electric shocks, putting them once more in communication with the soul. The secret of fortune is joy in our hands. Welcome evermore to gods and men is the self-helping man. For him all doors are flung wide. Him all tongues greet, all honors crown, all eyes follow with desire. Our love goes out to him and embraces him, because he did not need it. We solicitously and apologetically caress and celebrate him, because he held on his way and scorned our disapprobation. The gods love him because men hated him. "To the persevering mortal," said Zoroaster,[16] "the blessed Immortals are swift."

As men's prayers are a disease of the will, so are their creeds a disease of the intellect. They say with those foolish Israelites, 'Let not God speak to us, lest we die. Speak thou, speak any man with us, and we will obey.' Everywhere I am bereaved of meeting God in

15. "His . . . gods": Beaumont and Fletcher's *Bonduca*, lines 1294–95.
16. Zoroaster: Persian philosopher of the sixth century BCE.

my brother, because he has shut his own temple doors, and recites fables merely of his brother's, or his brother's brother's God. Every new mind is a new classification. If it prove a mind of uncommon activity and power, a Locke, a Lavoisier, a Hutton, a Bentham, a Spurzheim,[17] it imposes its classification on other men, and lo! a new system. In proportion always to the depth of the thought, and so to the number of the objects it touches and brings within reach of the pupil, is his complacency. But chiefly is this apparent in creeds and churches, which are also classifications of some powerful mind acting on the great elemental thought of Duty, and man's relation to the Highest. Such is Calvinism, Quakerism, Swedenborgianism. The pupil takes the same delight in subordinating every thing to the new terminology that a girl does who has just learned botany, in seeing a new earth and new seasons thereby. It will happen for a time, that the pupil will feel a real debt to the teacher, – will find his intellectual power has grown by the study of his writings. This will continue until he has exhausted his master's mind. But in all unbalanced minds, the classification is idolized, passes for the end, and not for a speedily exhaustible means, so that the walls of the system blend to their eye in the remote horizon with the walls of the universe; the luminaries of heaven seem to them hung on the arch their master built. They cannot imagine how you aliens have any right to see, – how you can see; 'It must be somehow that you stole the light from us.' They do not yet perceive, that, light unsystematic, indomitable, will break into any cabin, even into theirs. Let them chirp awhile and call it their own. If they are honest and do well, presently their neat new pinfold will be too strait and low, will crack, will lean, will rot and vanish, and the immortal light, all young and joyful, million-orbed, million-colored, will beam over the universe as on the first morning.

2. It is for want of self-culture that the idol of Travelling, the idol of Italy, of England, of Egypt, remains for all educated Americans. They who made England, Italy, or Greece venerable in the imagination, did so not by rambling round creation as a moth round a lamp, but by sticking fast where they were, like an axis of the earth. In manly hours, we feel that duty is our place, and that the merrymen of circumstance should follow as they may. The soul is no traveller: the wise man stays at home with the soul, and when his necessities, his duties, on any occasion call him from his house, or into foreign lands, he is at home still, and is not gadding abroad from himself, and shall make men sensible by the expression of his countenance, that he goes the missionary of wisdom and virtue, and visits cities and men like a sovereign, and not like an interloper or a valet.

I have no churlish objection to the circumnavigation of the globe, for the purposes of art, of study, and benevolence, so that the man is first domesticated, or does not go abroad with the hope of finding somewhat greater than he knows. He who travels to be amused, or to get somewhat which he does not carry, travels away from himself, and grows old even in youth among old things. In Thebes, in Palmyra,[18] his will and mind have become old and dilapidated as they. He carries ruins to ruins.

---

17. **Locke . . . Spurzheim:** Emerson refers to several scientists and philosophers known for their development of systems of thinking: John Locke (1632-1704), Antoine Lavoisier (1743-1794), Charles Hutton (1737-1823), Jeremy Bentham (1748-1832), and Johann Kaspar Spurzheim (1776-1832).

18. **Thebes . . . Palmyra:** Thebes, the capital city of ancient Egypt; Palmyra, an oasis in the Syrian desert that was a cultural center of the Greco-Roman world.

Travelling is a fool's paradise. We owe to our first journeys the discovery that place is nothing. At home I dream that at Naples, at Rome, I can be intoxicated with beauty, and lose my sadness. I pack my trunk, embrace my friends, embark on the sea, and at last wake up in Naples, and there beside me is the stern Fact, the sad self, unrelenting, identical, that I fled from. I seek the Vatican, and the palaces. I affect to be intoxicated with sights and suggestions, but I am not intoxicated. My giant goes with me wherever I go.

3. But the rage of travelling is itself only a symptom of a deeper unsoundness affecting the whole intellectual action. The intellect is vagabond, and the universal system of education fosters restlessness. Our minds travel when our bodies are forced to stay at home. We imitate; and what is imitation but the travelling of the mind? Our houses are built with foreign taste; our shelves are garnished with foreign ornaments; our opinions, our tastes, our whole minds lean, and follow the Past and the Distant, as the eyes of a maid follow her mistress. The soul created the arts wherever they have flourished. It was in his own mind that the artist sought his model. It was an application of his own thought to the thing to be done and the conditions to be observed. And why need we copy the Doric or the Gothic model? Beauty, convenience, grandeur of thought, and quaint expression are as near to us as to any, and if the American artist will study with hope and love the precise thing to be done by him, considering the climate, the soil, the length of the day, the wants of the people, the habit and form of the government, he will create a house in which all these will find themselves fitted, and taste and sentiment will be satisfied also.

Insist on yourself; never imitate. Your own gift you can present every moment with the cumulative force of a whole life's cultivation; but of the adopted talent of another, you have only an extemporaneous, half possession. That which each can do best, none but his Maker can teach him. No man yet knows what it is, nor can, till that person has exhibited it. Where is the master who could have taught Shakspeare? Where is the master who could have instructed Franklin, or Washington, or Bacon, or Newton? Every great man is an unique. The Scipionism of Scipio is precisely that part he could not borrow. If any body will tell me whom the great man imitates in the original crisis when he performs a great act, I will tell him who else than himself can teach him. Shakspeare will never be made by the study of Shakspeare. Do that which is assigned thee, and thou canst not hope too much or dare too much. There is at this moment, there is for me an utterance bare and grand as that of the colossal chisel of Phidias,[19] or trowel of the Egyptians, or the pen of Moses, or Dante, but different from all these. Not possibly will the soul all rich, all eloquent, with thousand-cloven tongue, deign to repeat itself; but if I can hear what these patriarchs say, surely I can reply to them in the same pitch of voice: for the ear and the tongue are two organs of one nature. Dwell up there in the simple and noble regions of thy life, obey thy heart, and thou shalt reproduce the Foreworld again.

4. As our Religion, our Education, our Art look abroad, so does our spirit of society. All men plume themselves on the improvement of society, and no man improves.

Society never advances. It recedes as fast on one side as it gains on the other. Its prog-

19. **Phidias:** Greek sculptor, sixth century BCE.

ress is only apparent, like the workers of a treadmill. It undergoes continual changes: it is barbarous, it is civilized, it is christianized, it is rich, it is scientific; but this change is not amelioration. For every thing that is given, something is taken. Society acquires new arts and loses old instincts. What a contrast between the well-clad, reading, writing, thinking American, with a watch, a pencil, and a bill of exchange in his pocket, and the naked New Zealander, whose property is a club, a spear, a mat, and an undivided twentieth of a shed to sleep under. But compare the health of the two men, and you shall see that his aboriginal strength the white man has lost. If the traveller tell us truly, strike the savage with a broad axe, and in a day or two the flesh shall unite and heal as if you struck the blow into soft pitch, and the same blow shall send the white to his grave.

The civilized man has built a coach, but has lost the use of his feet. He is supported on crutches, but loses so much support of muscle. He has got a fine Geneva watch, but he has lost the skill to tell the hour by the sun. A Greenwich nautical almanac he has, and so being sure of the information when he wants it, the man in the street does not know a star in the sky. The solstice he does not observe; the equinox he knows as little; and the whole bright calendar of the year is without a dial in his mind. His notebooks impair his memory; his libraries overload his wit; the insurance office increases the number of accidents; and it may be a question whether machinery does not encumber; whether we have not lost by refinement some energy, by a christianity entrenched in establishments and forms, some vigor of wild virtue. For every stoic was a stoic; but in Christendom where is the Christian?

There is no more deviation in the moral standard than in the standard of height or bulk. No greater men are now than ever were. A singular equality may be observed between the great men of the first and of the last ages; nor can all the science, art, religion and philosophy of the nineteenth century avail to educate greater men than Plutarch's heroes, three or four and twenty centuries ago. Not in time is the race progressive. Phocion, Socrates, Anaxagoras, Diogenes,[20] are great men, but they leave no class. He who is really of their class will not be called by their name, but be wholly his own man, and, in his turn the founder of a sect. The arts and inventions of each period are only its costume, and do not invigorate men. The harm of the improved machinery may compensate its good. Hudson and Behring[21] accomplished so much in their fishing-boats, as to astonish Parry and Franklin,[22] whose equipment exhausted the resources of science and art. Galileo, with an opera-glass, discovered a more splendid series of facts than any one since. Columbus found the New World in an undecked boat. It is curious to see the periodical disuse and perishing of means and machinery which were introduced with loud laudation, a few years or centuries before. The great genius returns to essential man. We reckoned the improvements of the art of war among the triumphs of science, and yet Napoleon conquered Europe by the Bivouac, which consisted of falling back on naked valor, and disencumbering it of all aids. The Emperor held it impossible

20. **Phocion . . . Diogenes:** Ancient Greek philosophers.
21. **Hudson and Behring:** Navigators Henry Hudson (d. 1611) and Vitus Jonassen Bering (1680–1741).
22. **Parry and Franklin:** Arctic explorers Sir William Edward Perry (1790–1855) and Sir John Franklin (1786–1847).

to make a perfect army, says Las Cases,[23] "without abolishing our arms, magazines, commissaries, and carriages, until in imitation of the Roman custom, the soldier should receive his supply of corn, grind it in his hand-mill, and bake his bread himself."

Society is a wave. The wave moves onward, but the water of which it is composed, does not. The same particle does not rise from the valley to the ridge. Its unity is only phenomenal. The persons who make up a nation to-day, next year die, and their experience with them.

And so the reliance on Property, including the reliance on governments which protect it, is the want of self-reliance. Men have looked away from themselves and at things so long, that they have come to esteem what they call the soul's progress, namely, the religious, learned, and civil institutions, as guards of property, and they deprecate assaults on these, because they feel them to be assaults on property. They measure their esteem of each other, by what each has, and not by what each is. But a cultivated man becomes ashamed of his property, ashamed of what he has, out of new respect for his being. Especially he hates what he has, if he see that it is accidental, – came to him by inheritance, or gift, or crime; then he feels that it is not having; it does not belong to him, has no root in him, and merely lies there, because no revolution or no robber takes it away. But that which a man is, does always by necessity acquire, and what the man acquires is permanent and living property, which does not wait the beck of rulers, or mobs, or revolutions, or fire, or storm, or bankruptcies, but perpetually renews itself wherever the man is put. "Thy lot or portion of life," said the Caliph Ali,[24] "is seeking after thee; therefore be at rest from seeking after it." Our dependence on these foreign goods leads us to our slavish respect for numbers. The political parties meet in numerous conventions; the greater the concourse, and with each new uproar of announcement, The delegation from Essex! The Democrats from New Hampshire! The Whigs of Maine! the young patriot feels himself stronger than before by a new thousand of eyes and arms. In like manner the reformers summon conventions, and vote and resolve in multitude. But not so, O friends! will the God deign to enter and inhabit you, but by a method precisely the reverse. It is only as a man puts off from himself all external support, and stands alone, that I see him to be strong and to prevail. He is weaker by every recruit to his banner. Is not a man better than a town? Ask nothing of men, and in the endless mutation, thou only firm column must presently appear the upholder of all that surrounds thee. He who knows that power is in the soul, that he is weak only because he has looked for good out of him and elsewhere, and so perceiving, throws himself unhesitatingly on his thought, instantly rights himself, stands in the erect position, commands his limbs, works miracles; just as a man who stands on his feet is stronger than a man who stands on his head.

So use all that is called Fortune. Most men gamble with her, and gain all, and lose all, as her wheel rolls. But do thou leave as unlawful these winnings, and deal with Cause and Effect, the chancellors of God. In the Will work and acquire, and thou hast chained

23. **Las Cases:** Comte Emmanuel de Las Cases (1766–1842) wrote an eight-volume biography of Napoleon, *Mémorial de Sainte-Hélène* (1823).

24. **Caliph Ali:** Caliph Ali (602?–661) was the first leader of the Shiite branch of Islam.

the wheel of Chance, and shalt always drag her after thee. A political victory, a rise of rents, the recovery of your sick, or the return of your absent friend, or some other quite external event, raises your spirits, and you think good days are preparing for you. Do not believe it. It can never be so. Nothing can bring you peace but yourself. Nothing can bring you peace but the triumph of principles.

[1841]

Emerson's "Circles." Published in *Essays* (1841), "Circles" is one of Emerson's most challenging explorations of the individual's relationship to nature and the spiritual world. In it, he develops the idea that the concentric circles that permeate nature and experience are metaphors for the boundlessness of life. That ancient idea had particular resonance for Americans, who were caught up in the notion of the boundless potential of their new country. But where most Americans thought in terms of material growth and territorial expansion, Emerson in "Circles" celebrates the spiritual expansion of individuals moving ever outward from their center, or soul, toward an ever-receding horizon, a sign of their infinite or divine potential. The essay is also an affirmation of the creative potential of individuals, one in which Emerson offers a strong hint about his intentions and methods as a writer. He thus describes himself as "only an experimenter," whose design was not to settle but rather "to unsettle all things." The text is taken from the first edition of *Essays* (1841).

CIRCLES

The eye is the first circle; the horizon which it forms is the second; and throughout nature this primary figure is repeated without end. It is the highest emblem in the cipher of the world. St. Augustine[1] described the nature of God as a circle whose centre was everywhere, and its circumference nowhere. We are all our lifetime reading the copious sense of this first of forms. One moral we have already deduced in considering the circular or compensatory character of every human action. Another analogy we shall now trace; that every action admits of being outdone. Our life is an apprenticeship to the truth that around every circle another can be drawn; that there is no end in nature, but every end is a beginning; that there is always another dawn risen on mid-noon, and under every deep a lower deep opens.

This fact, as far as it symbolizes the moral fact of the Unattainable, the flying Perfect, around which the hands of man can never meet, at once the inspirer and the condemner of every success, may conveniently serve us to connect many illustrations of human power in every department.

There are no fixtures in nature. The universe is fluid and volatile. Permanence is but a word of degrees. Our globe seen by God, is a transparent law, not a mass of facts. The law dissolves the fact and holds it fluid. Our culture is the predominance of an idea

1. **St. Augustine:** St. Augustine (354-430), Roman Catholic bishop and theologian.

which draws after it all this train of cities and institutions. Let us rise into another idea: they will disappear. The Greek sculpture is all melted away, as if it had been statues of ice: here and there a solitary figure or fragment remaining, as we see flecks and scraps of snow left in cold dells and mountain clefts, in June and July. For, the genius that created it, creates now somewhat else. The Greek letters last a little longer, but are already passing under the same sentence, and tumbling into the inevitable pit which the creation of new thought opens for all that is old. The new continents are built out of the ruins of an old planet: the new races fed out of the decomposition of the foregoing. New arts destroy the old. See the investment of capital in aqueducts, made useless by hydraulics; fortifications, by gunpowder; roads and canals, by railways; sails, by steam; steam by electricity.

You admire this tower of granite, weathering the hurts of so many ages. Yet a little waving hand built this huge wall, and that which builds, is better than that which is built. The hand that built, can topple it down much faster. Better than the hand, and nimbler, was the invisible thought which wrought through it, and thus ever behind the coarse effect, is a fine cause, which, being narrowly seen, is itself the effect of a finer cause. Every thing looks permanent until its secret is known. A rich estate appears to women and children, a firm and lasting fact; to a merchant, one easily created out of any materials, and easily lost. An orchard, good tillage, good grounds, seem a fixture, like a gold mine, or a river, to a citizen, but to a large farmer, not much more fixed than the state of the crop. Nature looks provokingly stable and secular, but it has a cause like all the rest; and when once I comprehend that, will these fields stretch so immovably wide, these leaves hang so individually considerable? Permanence is a word of degrees. Every thing is medial. Moons are no more bounds to spiritual power than bat-balls.

The key to every man is his thought. Sturdy and defying though he look, he has a helm which he obeys, which is, the idea after which all his facts are classified. He can only be reformed by showing him a new idea which commands his own. The life of man is a self-evolving circle, which, from a ring imperceptibly small, rushes on all sides outwards to new and larger circles, and that without end. The extent to which this generation of circles, wheel without wheel will go, depends on the force or truth of the individual soul. For, it is the inert effort of each thought having formed itself into a circular wave of circumstance, as, for instance, an empire, rules of an art, a local usage, a religious rite, to heap itself on that ridge, and to solidify, and hem in the life. But if the soul is quick and strong, it bursts over that boundary on all sides, and expands another orbit on the great deep, which also runs up into a high wave, with attempt again to stop and to bind. But the heart refuses to be imprisoned; in its first and narrowest pulses, it already tends outward with a vast force, and to immense and innumerable expansions.

Every ultimate fact is only the first of a new series. Every general law only a particular fact of some more general law presently to disclose itself. There is no outside, no enclosing wall, no circumference to us. The man finishes his story, – how good! how final! how it puts a new face on all things! He fills the sky. Lo, on the other side, rises also a man, and draws a circle around the circle we had just pronounced the outline of the sphere. Then already is our first speaker, not man, but only a first speaker. His only redress is forthwith to draw a circle outside of his antagonist. And so men do by themselves. The result of to-day which haunts the mind and cannot be escaped, will presently be abridged into a word, and the principle that seemed to explain nature, will itself be included as one example of a bolder generalization. In the thought of tomorrow there is a power to upheave all thy creed, all the creeds, all the literatures of the nations, and marshal thee to a heaven which no epic dream has yet depicted. Every man is not so much a workman in the world, as he is a suggestion of that he should be. Men walk as prophecies of the next age.

Step by step we scale this mysterious ladder: the steps are actions; the new prospect is power. Every several result is threatened and judged by that which follows. Every one seems to be contradicted by the new; it is only limited by the new. The new statement is always hated by the old, and, to those dwelling in the old, comes like an abyss of skepticism. But the eye soon gets wonted to it, for the eye and it are effects of one cause; then its innocency and benefit appear, and, presently, all its energy spent, it pales and dwindles before the revelation of the new hour.

Fear not the new generalization. Does the fact look crass and material, threatening to degrade thy theory of spirit? Resist it not; it goes to refine and raise thy theory of matter just as much.

There are no fixtures to men, if we appeal to consciousness. Every man supposes himself not to be fully understood; and if there is any truth in him, if he rests at last on the divine soul, I see not how it can be otherwise. The last chamber, the last closet, he must feel, was never opened; there is always a residuum unknown, unanalyzable. That is, every man believes that he has a greater possibility.

Our moods do not believe in each other. To-day, I am full of thoughts, and can write what I please. I see no reason why I should not have the same thought, the same power of expression to-morrow. What I write, whilst I write it, seems the most natural thing in the world: but, yesterday, I saw a dreary vacuity in this direction in which now I see so much; and a month hence, I doubt not, I shall wonder who he was that wrote so many continuous pages. Alas for this infirm faith, this will not strenuous, this vast ebb of a vast flow! I am God in nature; I am a weed by the wall.

The continual effort to raise himself above himself, to work a pitch above his last height, betrays itself in a man's relations. We thirst for approbation, yet cannot forgive the approver. The sweet of nature is love; yet if I have a friend, I am tormented by my imperfections. The love of me accuses the other party. If he were high enough to slight me, then could I love him, and rise by my affection to new heights. A man's growth is seen in the successive choirs of his friends. For every friend whom he loses for truth, he gains a better. I thought, as I walked in the woods and mused on my friends, why should I play with them this game of idolatry? I know and see too well, when not voluntarily blind, the speedy limits of persons called high and worthy. Rich, noble, and great they are by the liberality of our speech, but truth is sad. O blessed Spirit, whom I forsake for these, they are not thee! Every personal consideration that we allow, costs us heavenly state. We sell the thrones of angels for a short and turbulent pleasure.

How often must we learn this lesson? Men cease to interest us when we find their limitations. The only sin is limitation. As soon as you once come up with a man's limitations, it is all over with him. Has he talents? has he enterprises? has he knowledge? it boots not. Infinitely alluring and attractive was he to you yesterday, a great hope, a sea to swim in; now, you have found his shores, found it a pond, and you care not if you never see it again.

Each new step we take in thought reconciles twenty seemingly discordant facts, as expressions of one law. Aristotle and Plato[2] are reckoned the respective heads of two schools. A wise man will see that Aristotle Platonizes. By going one step farther back in thought, discordant opinions are reconciled, by being seen to be two extremes of one principle, and we can never go so far back as to preclude a still higher vision.

Beware when the great God lets loose a thinker on this planet. Then all things are at risk. It is as when a conflagration has broken out in a great city, and no man knows what is safe, or where it will end. There is not a piece of science, but its flank may be turned to-morrow; there is not any literary reputation, not the so-called eternal names of fame, that may not be revised and condemned. The very hopes of man, the thoughts of his heart, the religion of nations, the manners and morals of mankind, are all at the mercy of a new generalization. Generalization is always a new influx of the divinity into the mind. Hence the thrill that attends it.

Valor consists in the power of self-recovery, so that a man cannot have his flank turned, cannot be out-generaled, but put him where you will, he stands. This can only be by his preferring truth to his past apprehension of truth; and his alert acceptance of it from whatever quarter; the intrepid conviction that his laws, his relations to society, his christianity, his world, may at any time be superseded and decease.

There are degrees in idealism. We learn first to play with it academically, as the magnet was once a toy. Then we see in the heyday of youth and poetry that it may be true, that it is true in gleams and fragments. Then, its countenance waxes stern and grand, and we see that it must be true. It now shows itself ethical and practical. We learn that God IS; that he is in me; and that all things are shadows of him. The idealism of Berkeley[3] is only a crude statement of the idealism of Jesus, and that, again, is a crude statement of the fact that all nature is the rapid efflux of goodness executing and organizing itself. Much more obviously is history and the state of the world at any one time, directly dependent on the intellectual classification then existing in the minds of men. The things which are dear to men at this hour, are so on account of the ideas which have emerged on their mental horizon, and which cause the present order of things as a tree bears its apples. A new degree of culture would instantly revolutionize the entire system of human pursuits.

Conversation is a game of circles. In conversation we pluck up the *termini*[4] which bound the common of silence on every side. The parties are not to be judged by the spirit they partake and even express under this Pentecost.[5] To-morrow they will have receded from this high-water mark. To-morrow you shall find them stooping under the old pack-

---

2. **Aristotle and Plato:** Aristotle (384–322 BCE) and Plato (427?–347 BCE), leaders of opposing schools of Greek philosophy.
3. **Berkeley:** George Berkeley (1685–1753), English philosopher.
4. ***termini*:** Limits or ends (Latin).
5. **Pentecost:** Christian festival celebrating the descent of the Holy Ghost upon Christ's disciples.

saddles. Yet let us enjoy the cloven flame whilst it glows on our walls. When each new speaker strikes a new light, emancipates us from the oppression of the last speaker, to oppress us with the greatness and exclusiveness of his own thought, then yields us to another redeemer, we seem to recover our rights, to become men. O what truths profound and executable only in ages and orbs, are supposed in the announcement of every truth! In common hours, society sits cold and statuesque. We all stand waiting, empty, – knowing, possibly, that we can be full, surrounded by mighty symbols which are not symbols to us, but prose and trivial toys. Then cometh the god, and converts the statues into fiery men, and by a flash of his eye burns up the veil which shrouded all things, and the meaning of the very furniture, of cup and saucer, of chair and clock and tester, is manifest. The facts which loomed so large in the fogs of yesterday, – property, climate, breeding, personal beauty, and the like, have strangely changed their proportions. All that we reckoned settled, shakes now and rattles; and literatures, cities, climates, religions, leave their foundations, and dance before our eyes. And yet here again see the swift circumscription. Good as is discourse, silence is better, and shames it. The length of the discourse indicates the distance of thought betwixt the speaker and the hearer. If they were at a perfect understanding in any part, no words would be necessary thereon. If at one in all parts, no words would be suffered.

Literature is a point outside of our hodiernal[6] circle, through which a new one may be described. The use of literature is to afford us a platform whence we may command a view of our present life, a purchase by which we may move it. We fill ourselves with ancient learning; install ourselves the best we can in Greek, in Punic, in Roman houses, only that we may wiselier see French, English, and American houses and modes of living. In like manner, we see literature best from the midst of wild nature, or from the din of affairs, or from a high religion. The field cannot be well seen from within the field. The astronomer must have his diameter of the earth's orbit as a base to find the parallax of any star.

Therefore, we value the poet. All the argument, and all the wisdom, is not in the encyclopedia, or the treatise on metaphysics, or the Body of Divinity, but in the sonnet or the play. In my daily work I incline to repeat my old steps, and do not believe in remedial force, in the power of change and reform. But some Petrarch or Ariosto,[7] filled with the new wine of his imagination, writes me an ode, or a brisk romance, full of daring thought and action. He smites and arouses me with his shrill tones, breaks up my whole chain of habits, and I open my eye on my own possibilities. He claps wings to the sides of all the solid old lumber of the world, and I am capable once more of choosing a straight path in theory and practice.

We have the same need to command a view of the religion of the world. We can never see christianity from the catechism: – from the pastures, from a boat in the pond, from amidst the songs of wood-birds, we possibly may. Cleansed by the elemental light and wind, steeped in the sea of beautiful forms which the field offers us we may chance

6. **hodiernal:** Pertaining to today.
7. **Petrarch or Ariosto:** The Italian poets Francesco Petrarch (1304–1374) and Lodovico Ariosto (1474–1533).

to cast a right glance back upon biography. Christianity is rightly dear to the best of mankind; yet was there never a young philosopher whose breeding had fallen into the christian church, by whom that brave text of Paul's, was not specially prized, "Then shall also the Son be subject unto Him who put all things under him, that God may be all in all."[8] Let the claims and virtues of persons be never so great and welcome, the instinct of man presses eagerly onward to the impersonal and illimitable, and gladly arms itself against the dogmatism of bigots with this generous word, out of the book itself.

The natural world may be conceived of as a system of concentric circles, and we now and then detect in nature slight dislocations, which apprize us that this surface on which we now stand, is not fixed, but sliding. These manifold tenacious qualities, this chemistry and vegetation, these metals and animals, which seem to stand there for their own sake, are means and methods only, are words of God, and as fugitive as other words. Has the naturalist or chemist learned his craft, who has explored the gravity of atoms and the elective affinities, who has not yet discerned the deeper law whereof this is only a partial or approximate statement, namely, that like draws to like; and that the goods which belong to you, gravitate to you, and need not be pursued with pains and cost? Yet is that statement approximate also, and not final. Omnipresence is a higher fact. Not through subtle, subterranean channels, need friend and fact be drawn to their counterpart, but, rightly considered, these things proceed from the eternal generation of the soul. Cause and effect are two sides of one fact.

The same law of eternal procession ranges all that we call the virtues, and extinguishes each in the light of a better. The great man will not be prudent in the popular sense; all his prudence will be so much deduction from his grandeur. But it behoves each to see when he sacrifices prudence, to what god he devotes it; if to ease and pleasure, he had better be prudent still: if to a great trust, he can well spare his mule and panniers, who has a winged chariot instead. Geoffrey draws on his boots to go through the woods, that his feet may be safer from the bite of snakes; Aaron never thinks of such a peril. In many years, neither is harmed by such an accident. Yet it seems to me that with every precaution you take against such an evil, you put yourself into the power of the evil. I suppose that the highest prudence is the lowest prudence. Is this too sudden a rushing from the centre to the verge of our orbit? Think how many times we shall fall back into pitiful calculations, before we take up our rest in the great sentiment, or make the verge of to-day the new centre. Besides, your bravest sentiment is familiar to the humblest men. The poor and the low have their way of expressing the last facts of philosophy as well as you. "Blessed be nothing," and "the worse things are, the better they are," are proverbs which express the transcendentalism of common life.

One man's justice is another's injustice; one man's beauty, another's ugliness; one man's wisdom, another's folly, as one beholds the same objects from a higher point of view. One man thinks justice consists in paying debts, and has no measure in his abhorrence of another who is very remiss in this duty, and makes the creditor wait tediously.

---

8. "Then . . . all": 1 Corinthians 15:28.

But that second man has his own way of looking at things; asks himself, which debt must I pay first, the debt to the rich, or the debt to the poor? the debt of money, or the debt of thought to mankind, of genius to nature? For you, O broker, there is no other principle but arithmetic. For me, commerce is of trivial import; love, faith, truth of character, the aspiration of man, these are sacred: nor can I detach one duty, like you, from all other duties, and concentrate my forces mechanically on the payment of moneys. Let me live onward: you shall find that, though slower, the progress of my character will liquidate all these debts without injustice to higher claims. If a man should dedicate himself to the payment of notes, would not this be injustice? Owes he no debt but money? And are all claims on him to be postponed to a landlord's or a banker's?

There is no virtue which is final; all are initial. The virtues of society are vices of the saint. The terror of reform is the discovery that we must cast away our virtues, or what we have always esteemed such, into the same pit that has consumed our grosser vices.

> "Forgive his crimes, forgive his virtues too,
> Those smaller faults, half converts to the right."[9]

It is the highest power of divine moments that they abolish our contritions also. I accuse myself of sloth and unprofitableness, day by day; but when these waves of God flow into me, I no longer reckon lost time. I no longer poorly compute my possible achievement by what remains to me of the month or the year; for these moments confer a sort of omnipresence and omnipotence, which asks nothing of duration, but sees that the energy of the mind is commensurate with the work to be done, without time.

And thus, O circular philosopher, I hear some reader exclaim, you have arrived at a fine pyrrhonism,[10] at an equivalence and indifferency of all actions, and would fain teach us, that, *if we are true*, forsooth, our crimes may be lively stones out of which we shall construct the temple of the true God.

I am not careful to justify myself. I own I am gladdened by seeing the predominance of the saccharine principle throughout vegetable nature, and not less by beholding in morals that unrestrained inundation of the principle of good into every chink and hole that selfishness has left open, yea, into selfishness and sin itself; so that no evil is pure; nor hell itself without its extreme satisfactions. But lest I should mislead any when I have my own head, and obey my whims, let me remind the reader that I am only an experimenter. Do not set the least value on what I do, or the least discredit on what I do not, as if I pretended to settle anything as true or false. I unsettle all things. No facts are to me sacred; none are profane; I simply experiment, an endless seeker, with no Past at my back.

Yet this incessant movement and progression, which all things partake, could never become sensible to us, but by contrast to some principle of fixture or stability in the soul. Whilst the eternal generation of circles proceeds, the eternal generator abides.

9. **Forgive . . . right:** The slightly misquoted lines are from a popular poem *The Complaint; or, Night Thoughts* (1742–45), by the English poet Edward Young (1683–1765).
10. **pyrrhonism:** The Greek philosopher Pyrrho (c. 365–c. 270 BCE) developed the philosophy of skepticism, based on his sense that certainty of knowledge is impossible.

That central life is somewhat superior to creation, superior to knowledge and thought, and contains all its circles. Forever it labors to create a life and thought as large and excellent as itself; but in vain; for that which is made, instructs how to make a better.

Thus there is no sleep, no pause, no preservation, but all things renew, germinate, and spring. Why should we import rags and relics into the new hour? Nature abhors the old, and old age seems the only disease: all others run into this one. We call it by many names, fever, intemperance, insanity, stupidity, and crime: they are all forms of old age: they are rest, conservatism, appropriation, inertia, not newness, not the way onward. We grizzle every day. I see no need of it. Whilst we converse with what is above us, we do not grow old, but grow young. Infancy, youth, receptive, aspiring, with religious eye looking upward, counts itself nothing, and abandons itself to the instruction flowing from all sides. But the man and woman of seventy, assume to know all; throw up their hope; renounce aspiration; accept the actual for the necessary; and talk down to the young. Let them then become organs of the Holy Ghost; let them be lovers; let them behold truth; and their eyes are uplifted, their wrinkles smoothed, they are perfumed again with hope and power. This old age ought not to creep on a human mind. In nature, every moment is new; the past is always swallowed and forgotten; the coming only is sacred. Nothing is secure but life, transition, the energizing spirit. No love can be bound by oath or covenant to secure it against a higher love. No truth so sublime but it may be trivial tomorrow in the light of new thoughts. People wish to be settled: only as far as they are unsettled, is there any hope for them.

Life is a series of surprises. We do not guess to-day the mood, the pleasure, the power of to-morrow, when we are building up our being. Of lower states, – of acts of routine and sense, we can tell somewhat, but the masterpieces of God, the total growths, and universal movements of the soul, he hideth; they are incalculable. I can know that truth is divine and helpful, but how it shall help me, I can have no guess, for, *so to be* is the sole inlet of *so to know*. The new position of the advancing man has all the powers of the old, yet has them all new. It carries in its bosom all the energies of the past, yet is itself an exhalation of the morning. I cast away in this new moment all my once hoarded knowledge, as vacant and vain. Now, for the first time, seem I to know any thing rightly. The simplest words, – we do not know what they mean, except when we love and aspire.

The difference between talents and character is adroitness to keep the old and trodden round, and power and courage to make a new road to new and better goals. Character makes an overpowering present, a cheerful, determined hour, which fortifies all the company, by making them see that much is possible and excellent, that was not thought of. Character dulls the impression of particular events. When we see the conqueror, we do not think much of any one battle or success. We see that we had exaggerated the difficulty. It was easy to him. The great man is not convulsible or tormentable. He is so much, that events pass over him without much impression. People say sometimes, 'See what I have overcome; see how cheerful I am; see how completely I have triumphed over these black events.' Not if they still remind me of the black event, – they have not yet conquered. Is it conquest to be a gay and decorated sepulchre, or a half-crazed widow hysterically laughing? True conquest is the causing the black event to fade and disappear as an early cloud of insignificant result in a history so large and advancing.

The one thing which we seek with insatiable desire, is to forget ourselves, to be surprised out of our propriety, to lose our sempiternal memory, and to do something without knowing how or why; in short, to draw a new circle. Nothing great was ever achieved without enthusiasm. The way of life is wonderful. It is by abandonment. The great moments of history are the facilities of performance through the strength of ideas, as the works of genius and religion. "A man," said Oliver Cromwell,[11] "never rises so high as when he knows not whither he is going." Dream and drunkenness, the use of opium and alcohol are the semblance and counterfeit of this oracular genius, and hence their dangerous attraction for men. For the like reason, they ask the aid of wild passions, as in gaming and war, to ape in some manner these flames and generosities of the heart.

---

11. **Oliver Cromwell:** (1599–1658) military and political leader of the Puritan Revolution in England.

Emerson's "Experience." This essay appeared in Emerson's third book, *Essays: Second Series*, published in 1844. In a review of the volume in the *New-York Tribune*, Margaret Fuller observed,

> If only as a representative of the claims of individual culture in a nation which tends to lay such stress on artificial organization and external results, Mr. Emerson would be invaluable here. History will inscribe his name as a father of the country, for he is one who pleads her cause against herself.

Certainly, the essays in the volume were part of Emerson's ongoing critique of American culture and society. "Experience," however, was also inspired by deeply private concerns, especially Emerson's grief over the death of his beloved son Waldo at the age of five in 1842. In a striking departure from his usual practice of excluding details of his personal life from his essays, Emerson describes that loss early in "Experience." But the essay is less an autobiography than a philosophy of life or living – a kind of guide to what Emerson elsewhere called "the conduct of life." Opening with images of darkness and disorientation, he embarks on a sustained meditation on the gap between actual and ideal experience. "I know that the world I converse with in the city and in the farms is not the world I *think*," he observes in "Experience." In fact, most of the essay is devoted to a somber exploration of the experience of living in what Emerson characterizes as the *unreality* of the actual world. For him, that experience is illuminated and is made meaningful only by moments of "sanity and revelations," as he puts it in a final counter to the darkness and shadows evoked at the opening of the essay. However rare and fleeting, such moments opened up the ultimate possibility of "the transformation of genius into practical power," Emerson's final, affirmative words in "Experience." The text is taken from the first edition of *Essays: Second Series* (1844).

Experience

The lords of life, the lords of life, –
I saw them pass,
In their own guise,
Like and unlike,
Portly and grim,
Use and Surprise,
Surface and Dream,
Succession swift, and spectral Wrong,
Temperament without a tongue,
And the inventor of the game
Omnipresent without name; –
Some to see, some to be guessed,
They marched from east to west:
Little man, least of all,
Among the legs of his guardians tall,
Walked about with puzzled look: –
Him by the hand dear nature took;
Dearest nature, strong and kind,
Whispered, 'Darling, never mind!
Tomorrow they will wear another face,
The founder thou! these are thy race!'[1]

Where do we find ourselves? In a series of which we do not know the extremes, and believe that it has none. We wake and find ourselves on a stair; there are stairs below us, which we seem to have ascended; there are stairs above us, many a one, which go upward and out of sight. But the Genius which, according to the old belief, stands at the door by which we enter, and gives us the lethe to drink,[2] that we may tell no tales, mixed the cup too strongly, and we cannot shake off the lethargy now at noonday. Sleep lingers all our lifetime about our eyes, as night hovers all day in the boughs of the fir-tree. All things swim and glitter. Our life is not so much threatened as our perception. Ghostlike we glide through nature, and should not know our place again. Did our birth fall in some fit of indigence and frugality in nature, that she was so sparing of her fire and so liberal of her earth, that it appears to us that we lack the affirmative principle, and though we have health and reason, yet we have no superfluity of spirit for new creation? We have enough to live and bring the year about, but not an ounce to impart or to invest. Ah that our Genius were a little more of a genius! We are like millers on the lower levels of a stream, when the factories above them have exhausted the water. We too fancy that the upper people must have raised their dams.

If any of us knew what we were doing, or where we are going, then when we think we best know! We do not know today whether we are busy or idle. In times when we thought ourselves indolent, we have afterwards discovered, that much was accomplished, and

1. **The lords . . . thy race!":** The poem was written by Emerson.
2. **lethe to drink:** Drinking from the Lethe, a river in Greek mythology, induces forgetfulness.

much was begun in us. All our days are so unprofitable while they pass, that 'tis wonderful where or when we ever got anything of this which we call wisdom, poetry, virtue. We never got it on any dated calendar day. Some heavenly days must have been intercalated somewhere, like those that Hermes won with dice of the Moon, that Osiris might be born.[3] It is said, all martyrdoms looked mean when they were suffered. Every ship is a romantic object, except that we sail in. Embark, and the romance quits our vessel, and hangs on every other sail in the horizon. Our life looks trivial, and we shun to record it. Men seem to have learned of the horizon the art of perpetual retreating and reference. 'Yonder uplands are rich pasturage, and my neighbor has fertile meadow, but my field,' says the querulous farmer, 'only holds the world together.' I quote another man's saying; unluckily, that other withdraws himself in the same way, and quotes me. 'Tis the trick of nature thus to degrade today; a good deal of buzz, and somewhere a result slipped magically in. Every roof is agreeable to the eye, until it is lifted; then we find tragedy and moaning women, and hard-eyed husbands, and deluges of lethe, and the men ask, 'What's the news?' as if the old were so bad. How many individuals can we count in society? how many actions? how many opinions? So much of our time is preparation, so much is routine, and so much retrospect, that the pith of each man's genius contracts itself to a very few hours. The history of literature – take the net result of Tiraboschi, Warton, or Schlegel,[4] – is a sum of very few ideas, and of very few original tales, – all the rest being variation of these. So in this great society wide lying around us, a critical analysis would find very few spontaneous actions. It is almost all custom and gross sense. There are even few opinions, and these seem organic in the speakers, and do not disturb the universal necessity.

What opium is instilled into all disaster! It shows formidable as we approach it, but there is at last no rough rasping friction, but the most slippery sliding surfaces. We fall soft on a thought. *Ate Dea* is gentle,

> "Over men's heads walking aloft,
> With tender feet treading so soft."[5]

People give and bemoan themselves, but it is not half so bad with them as they say. There are moods in which we court suffering, in the hope that here, at least, we shall find reality, sharp peaks and edges of truth. But it turns out to be scene-painting and counterfeit. The only thing grief has taught me, is to know how shallow it is. That, like all the rest, plays about the surface, and never introduces me into the reality, for contact with which, we would even pay the costly price of sons and lovers. Was it Boscovich[6] who found out that bodies never come in contact? Well, souls never touch their objects. An

---

3. **Hermes . . . born:** In *Morals*, Plutarch tells the Egyptian story of how the goddess Hermes overturned her husband's ruling that she could not bear children on any day of the year by winning five new days in the calendar from the Moon. Osiris was born on one of those days.

4. **Tiraboschi . . . Schlegel:** Literary histories by the Italian writer Girolamo Tiraboschi (1731-1794), the British writer Thomas Warton (1728-1790), and the German writer Friedrich von Schlegel (1772-1829).

5. ***Ate Dea* . . . treading so soft:** Roman goddess of evil, infatuation, and mischief; Homer's *The Iliad*, Book 19.

6. **Boscovich:** Ruggiero Giuseppe Boscovich (1711-1787), an Italian physicist.

innavigable sea washes with silent waves between us and the things we aim at and converse with. Grief too will make us idealists. In the death of my son, now more than two years ago, I seem to have lost a beautiful estate, – no more. I cannot get it nearer to me. If tomorrow I should be informed of the bankruptcy of my principal debtors, the loss of my property would be a great inconvenience to me, perhaps, for many years; but it would leave me as it found me, – neither better nor worse. So is it with this calamity: it does not touch me: some thing which I fancied was a part of me, which could not be torn away without tearing me, nor enlarged without enriching me, falls off from me, and leaves no scar. It was caducous. I grieve that grief can teach me nothing, nor carry me one step into real nature. The Indian who was laid under a curse, that the wind should not blow on him, nor water flow to him, nor fire burn him, is a type of us all. The dearest events are summer-rain, and we the Para coats[7] that shed every drop. Nothing is left us now but death. We look to that with a grim satisfaction, saying, there at least is reality that will not dodge us.

I take this evanescence and lubricity of all objects, which lets them slip through our fingers then when we clutch hardest, to be the most unhandsome part of our condition. Nature does not like to be observed, and likes that we should be her fools and playmates. We may have the sphere for our cricket-ball, but not a berry for our philosophy. Direct strokes she never gave us power to make; all our blows glance, all our hits are accidents. Our relations to each other are oblique and casual.

Dream delivers us to dream, and there is no end to illusion. Life is a train of moods like a string of beads, and, as we pass through them, they prove to be many-colored lenses which paint the world their own hue, and each shows only what lies in its focus. From the mountain you see the mountain. We animate what we can, and we see only what we animate. Nature and books belong to the eyes that see them. It depends on the mood of the man, whether he shall see the sunset or the fine poem. There are always sunsets, and there is always genius; but only a few hours so serene that we can relish nature or criticism. The more or less depends on structure or temperament. Temperament is the iron wire on which the beads are strung. Of what use is fortune or talent to a cold and defective nature? Who cares what sensibility or discrimination a man has at some time shown, if he falls asleep in his chair? or if he laugh and giggle? or if he apologize? or is affected with egotism? or thinks of his dollar? or cannot go by food? or has gotten a child in his boyhood? Of what use is genius, if the organ is too convex or too concave, and cannot find a focal distance within the actual horizon of human life? Of what use, if the brain is too cold or too hot, and the man does not care enough for results, to stimulate him to experiment, and hold him up in it? or if the web is too finely woven, too irritable by pleasure and pain, so that life stagnates from too much reception, without due outlet? Of what use to make heroic vows of amendment, if the same old lawbreaker is to keep them? What cheer can the religious sentiment yield, when that is suspected to be secretly dependent on the seasons of the year, and the state of the blood? I knew a witty physician who found theology in the biliary duct, and used to affirm that

7. **Para coats:** Rubber raincoats.

if there was disease in the liver, the man became a Calvinist, and if that organ was sound, he became a Unitarian. Very mortifying is the reluctant experience that some unfriendly excess or imbecility neutralizes the promise of genius. We see young men who owe us a new world, so readily and lavishly they promise, but they never acquit the debt; they die young and dodge the account: or if they live, they lose themselves in the crowd.

Temperament also enters fully into the system of illusions, and shuts us in a prison of glass which we cannot see. There is an optical illusion about every person we meet. In truth, they are all creatures of given temperament, which will appear in a given character, whose boundaries they will never pass: but we look at them, they seem alive, and we presume there is impulse in them. In the moment it seems impulse; in the year, in the lifetime, it turns out to be a certain uniform tune which the revolving barrel of the music-box must play. Men resist the conclusion in the morning, but adopt it as the evening wears on, that temper prevails over everything of time, place, and condition, and is inconsumable in the flames of religion. Some modifications the moral sentiment avails to impose, but the individual texture holds its dominion, if not to bias the moral judgments, yet to fix the measure of activity and of enjoyment.

I thus express the law as it is read from the platform of ordinary life, but must not leave it without noticing the capital exception. For temperament is a power which no man willingly hears any one praise but himself. On the platform of physics, we cannot resist the contracting influences of so-called science. Temperament puts all divinity to rout. I know the mental proclivity of physicians. I hear the chuckle of the phrenologists. Theoretic kidnappers and slave-drivers, they esteem each man the victim of another, who winds him round his finger by knowing the law of his being, and by such cheap signboards as the color of his beard, or the slope of his occiput, reads the inventory of his fortunes and character. The grossest ignorance does not disgust like this impudent knowingness. The physicians say, they are not materialists; but they are: – Spirit is matter reduced to an extreme thinness: O *so* thin! – But the definition of *spiritual* should be, *that which is its own evidence*. What notions do they attach to love! what to religion! One would not willingly pronounce these words in their hearing, and give them the occasion to profane them. I saw a gracious gentleman who adapts his conversation to the form of the head of the man he talks with! I had fancied that the value of life lay in its inscrutable possibilities; in the fact that I never know, in addressing myself to a new individual, what may befall me. I carry the keys of my castle in my hand, ready to throw them at the feet of my lord, whenever and in what disguise so ever he shall appear. I know he is in the neighborhood hidden among vagabonds. Shall I preclude my future, by taking a high seat, and kindly adapting my conversation to the shape of heads? When I come to that, the doctors shall buy me for a cent. — "But, sir, medical history; the report to the Institute; the proven facts!' – I distrust the facts and the inferences. Temperament is the veto or limitation-power in the constitution, very justly applied to restrain an opposite excess in the constitution, but absurdly offered as a bar to original equity. When virtue is in presence, all subordinate powers sleep. On its own level, or in view of nature, temperament is final. I see not, if one be once caught in this trap of so-called sciences, any escape for the man from the links of the chain of physical necessity.

Given such an embryo, such a history must follow. On this platform, one lives in a sty of sensualism, and would soon come to suicide. But it is impossible that the creative power should exclude itself. Into every intelligence there is a door which is never closed, through which the creator passes. The intellect, seeker of absolute truth, or the heart, lover of absolute good, intervenes for our succor, and at one whisper of these high powers, we awake from ineffectual struggles with this nightmare. We hurl it into its own hell, and cannot again contract ourselves to so base a state.

The secret of the illusoriness is in the necessity of a succession of moods or objects. Gladly we would anchor, but the anchorage is quicksand. This onward trick of nature is too strong for us: *Pero si muove.*[8] When, at night, I look at the moon and stars, I seem stationary, and they to hurry. Our love of the real draws us to permanence, but health of body consists in circulation, and sanity of mind in variety or facility of association. We need change of objects. Dedication to one thought is quickly odious. We house with the insane, and must humor them; then conversation dies out. Once I took such delight in Montaigne, that I thought I should not need any other book; before that, in Shakspeare; then in Plutarch; then in Plotinus; at one time in Bacon; afterwards in Goethe; even in Bettine;[9] but now I turn the pages of either of them languidly, whilst I still cherish their genius. So with pictures; each will bear an emphasis of attention once, which it cannot retain, though we fain would continue to be pleased in that manner. How strongly I have felt of pictures, that when you have seen one well, you must take your leave of it; you shall never see it again. I have had good lessons from pictures, which I have since seen without emotion or remark. A deduction must be made from the opinion, which even the wise express of a new book or occurrence. Their opinion gives me tidings of their mood, and some vague guess at the new fact, but is nowise to be trusted as the lasting relation between that intellect and that thing. The child asks, 'Mamma, why don't I like the story as well as when you told it me yesterday?' Alas, child, it is even so with the oldest cherubim of knowledge. But will it answer thy question to say, Because thou wert born to a whole, and this story is a particular? The reason of the pain this discovery causes us (and we make it late in respect to works of art and intellect), is the plaint of tragedy which murmurs from it in regard to persons, to friendship and love.

That immobility and absence of elasticity which we find in the arts, we find with more pain in the artist. There is no power of expansion in men. Our friends early appear to us as representatives of certain ideas, which they never pass or exceed. They stand on the brink of the ocean of thought and power, but they never take the single step that would bring them there. A man is like a bit of Labrador spar,[10] which has no lustre as you turn it in your hand, until you come to a particular angle; then it shows deep and beautiful colors. There is no adaptation or universal applicability in men, but each has his spe-

---

8. ***Pero si muove*:** "Nevertheless, it moves" (Italian); what Galileo reportedly said after he was forced by the Roman Catholic Church to deny his theory that the earth revolves around the sun.
9. **Bettine:** Elizabeth Brentano von Arnim (1785–1859) wrote *Goethe's Correspondence with a Child* (1835), a book admired by Emerson.
10. **Labrador spar:** Brilliantly colored rock solidified from lava.

cial talent, and the mastery of successful men consists in adroitly keeping themselves where and when that turn shall be oftenest to be practised. We do what we must, and call it by the best names we can, and would fain have the praise of having intended the result which ensues. I cannot recall any form of man who is not superfluous sometimes. But is not this pitiful? Life is not worth the taking, to do tricks in.

Of course, it needs the whole society, to give the symmetry we seek. The parti-colored wheel must revolve very fast to appear white. Something is learned too by conversing with so much folly and defect. In fine, whoever loses, we are always of the gaining party. Divinity is behind our failures and follies also. The plays of children are nonsense, but very educative nonsense. So it is with the largest and solemnest things, with commerce, government, church, marriage, and so with the history of every man's bread, and the ways by which he is to come by it. Like a bird which alights nowhere, but hops perpetually from bough to bough, is the Power which abides in no man and in no woman, but for a moment speaks from this one, and for another moment from that one.

But what help from these fineries or pedantries? What help from thought? Life is not dialectics. We, I think, in these times, have had lessons enough of the futility of criticism. Our young people have thought and written much on labor and reform, and for all that they have written, neither the world nor themselves have got on a step. Intellectual tasting of life will not supersede muscular activity. If a man should consider the nicety of the passage of a piece of bread down his throat, he would starve. At Education-Farm,[11] the noblest theory of life sat on the noblest figures of young men and maidens, quite powerless and melancholy. It would not rake or pitch a ton of hay; it would not rub down a horse; and the men and maidens it left pale and hungry. A political orator wittily compared our party promises to western roads, which opened stately enough, with planted trees on either side, to tempt the traveller, but soon became narrow and narrower, and ended in a squirrel-track, and ran up a tree. So does culture with us; it ends in head-ache. Unspeakably sad and barren does life look to those, who a few months ago were dazzled with the splendor of the promise of the times. "There is now no longer any right course of action, nor any self-devotion left among the Iranis."[12] Objections and criticism we have had our fill of. There are objections to every course of life and action, and the practical wisdom infers an indifferency, from the omnipresence of objection. The whole frame of things preaches indifferency. Do not craze yourself with thinking, but go about your business anywhere. Life is not intellectual or critical, but sturdy. Its chief good is for well-mixed people who can enjoy what they find, without question. Nature hates peeping, and our mothers speak her very sense when they say, "Children; eat your victuals, and say no more of it." To fill the hour, – that is happiness; to fill the hour, and leave no crevice for a repentance or an approval. We live amid surfaces, and the true art of life is to skate well on them. Under the oldest mouldiest conventions, a man of native

---

11. **Education-Farm:** Brook Farm (1841–1847), the utopian community in West Roxbury, Massachusetts.
12. **"There . . . Iranis":** From a collection of Persian prophetic works translated into English, *The Desatir, or Sacred Writings of the Ancient Persian Prophets* (1818).

force prospers just as well as in the newest world, and that by skill of handling and treatment. He can take hold anywhere. Life itself is a mixture of power and form, and will not bear the least excess of either. To finish the moment, to find the journey's end in every step of the road, to live the greatest number of good hours, is wisdom. It is not the part of men, but of fanatics, or of mathematicians, if you will, to say, that, the shortness of life considered, it is not worth caring whether for so short a duration we were sprawling in want, or sitting high. Since our office is with moments, let us husband them. Five minutes of today are worth as much to me, as five minutes in the next millennium. Let us be poised, and wise, and our own, today. Let us treat the men and women well: treat them as if they were real: perhaps they are. Men live in their fancy, like drunkards whose hands are too soft and tremulous for successful labor. It is a tempest of fancies, and the only ballast I know, is a respect to the present hour. Without any shadow of doubt, amidst this vertigo of shows and politics, I settle myself ever the firmer in the creed, that we should not postpone and refer and wish, but do broad justice where we are, by whomsoever we deal with, accepting our actual companions and circumstances, however humble or odious, as the mystic officials to whom the universe has delegated its whole pleasure for us. If these are mean and malignant, their contentment, which is the last victory of justice, is a more satisfying echo to the heart, than the voice of poets and the casual sympathy of admirable persons. I think that however a thoughtful man may suffer from the defects and absurdities of his company, he cannot without affectation deny to any set of men and women, a sensibility to extraordinary merit. The coarse and frivolous have an instinct of superiority, if they have not a sympathy, and honor it in their blind capricious way with sincere homage.

The fine young people despise life, but in me, and in such as with me are free from dyspepsia, and to whom a day is a sound and solid good, it is a great excess of politeness to look scornful and to cry for company. I am grown by sympathy a little eager and sentimental, but leave me alone, and I should relish every hour and what it brought me, the pot-luck of the day, as heartily as the oldest gossip in the bar-room. I am thankful for small mercies. I compared notes with one of my friends who expects everything of the universe, and is disappointed when anything is less than the best, and I found that I begin at the other extreme, expecting nothing, and am always full of thanks for moderate goods. I accept the clangor and jangle of contrary tendencies. I find my account in sots and bores also. They give a reality to the circumjacent picture, which such a vanishing meteorous appearance can ill spare. In the morning I awake, and find the old world, wife, babes, and mother, Concord and Boston, the dear old spiritual world, and even the dear old devil not far off. If we will take the good we find, asking no questions, we shall have heaping measures. The great gifts are not got by analysis. Everything good is on the highway. The middle region of our being is the temperate zone. We may climb into the thin and cold realm of pure geometry and lifeless science, or sink into that of sensation. Between these extremes is the equator of life, of thought, of spirit, of poetry, – a narrow belt. Moreover, in popular experience, everything good is on the highway. A collector peeps into all the picture-shops of Europe, for a landscape of Poussin, a crayon-sketch of Salvator; but the Transfiguration, the Last Judgment, the

Communion of St. Jerome,[13] and what are as transcendent as these, are on the walls of the Vatican, the Uffizii, or the Louvre, where every footman may see them; to say nothing of nature's pictures in every street, of sunsets and sunrises every day, and the sculpture of the human body never absent. A collector recently bought at public auction, in London, for one hundred and fifty-seven guineas, an autograph of Shakspeare: but for nothing a school-boy can read Hamlet, and can detect secrets of highest concernment yet unpublished therein. I think I will never read any but the commonest books, – the Bible, Homer, Dante, Shakspeare, and Milton. Then we are impatient of so public a life and planet, and run hither and thither for nooks and secrets. The imagination delights in the wood-craft of Indians, trappers, and bee-hunters. We fancy that we are strangers, and not so intimately domesticated in the planet as the wild man, and the wild beast and bird. But the exclusion reaches them also; reaches the climbing, flying, gliding, feathered and four-footed man. Fox and woodchuck, hawk and snipe, and bittern, when nearly seen, have no more root in the deep world than man, and are just such superficial tenants of the globe. Then the new molecular philosophy shows astronomical interspaces betwixt atom and atom, shows that the world is all outside: it has no inside.

The mid-world is best. Nature, as we know her, is no saint. The lights of the church, the ascetics, Gentoos and Grahamites,[14] she does not distinguish by any favor. She comes eating and drinking and sinning. Her darlings, the great, the strong, the beautiful, are not children of our law, do not come out of the Sunday School, nor weigh their food, nor punctually keep the commandments. If we will be strong with her strength, we must not harbor such disconsolate consciences, borrowed too from the consciences of other nations. We must set up the strong present tense against all the rumors of wrath, past or to come. So many things are unsettled which it is of the first importance to settle, – and, pending their settlement, we will do as we do. Whilst the debate goes forward on the equity of commerce, and will not be closed for a century or two, New and Old England may keep shop. Law of copyright and international copyright is to be discussed, and, in the interim, we will sell our books for the most we can. Expediency of literature, reason of literature, lawfulness of writing down a thought, is questioned; much is to say on both sides, and, while the fight waxes hot, thou, dearest scholar, stick to thy foolish task, add a line every hour, and between whiles add a line. Right to hold land, right of property, is disputed, and the conventions convene, and before the vote is taken, dig away in your garden, and spend your earnings as a waif or godsend to all serene and beautiful purposes. Life itself is a bubble and a skepticism, and a sleep within a sleep. Grant it, and as much more as they will, – but thou, God's darling! heed thy private dream: thou wilt not be missed in the scorning and skepticism: there are enough of

---

13. **Poussin . . . St. Jerome:** Nicolas Poussin (1594-1665) was a French painter of historical scenes and events. Salvatore Rosa (1615-1673) was an Italian painter who specialized in landscapes. *The Transfiguration* by Raphael, *The Last Judgment* by Michelangelo, and *The Communion of St. Jerome* by Il Domenichino are paintings in major art museums in Rome, Florence, and Paris.

14. **Gentoos and Grahamites:** Gentoos was an early term for Hindus, who are vegetarians; Grahamites were followers of Sylvester Graham (1794-1851), a diet reformer who later developed the graham cracker.

them: stay there in thy closet, and toil, until the rest are agreed what to do about it. Thy sickness, they say, and thy puny habit, require that thou do this or avoid that, but know that thy life is a flitting state, a tent for a night, and do thou, sick or well, finish that stint. Thou art sick, but shalt not be worse, and the universe, which holds thee dear, shall be the better.

Human life is made up of the two elements, power and form, and the proportion must be invariably kept, if we would have it sweet and sound. Each of these elements in excess makes a mischief as hurtful as its defect. Everything runs to excess: every good quality is noxious, if unmixed, and, to carry the danger to the edge of ruin, nature causes each man's peculiarity to superabound. Here, among the farms, we adduce the scholars as examples of this treachery. They are nature's victims of expression. You who see the artist, the orator, the poet, too near, and find their life no more excellent than that of mechanics or farmers, and themselves victims of partiality, very hollow and haggard, and pronounce them failures, – not heroes, but quacks, – conclude very reasonably, that these arts are not for man, but are disease. Yet nature will not bear you out. Irresistible nature made men such, and makes legions more of such, every day. You love the boy reading in a book, gazing at a drawing, or a cast: yet what are these millions who read and behold, but incipient writers and sculptors? Add a little more of that quality which now reads and sees, and they will seize the pen and chisel. And if one remembers how innocently he began to be an artist, he perceives that nature joined with his enemy. A man is a golden impossibility. The line he must walk is a hair's breadth. The wise through excess of wisdom is made a fool.

How easily, if fate would suffer it, we might keep forever these beautiful limits, and adjust ourselves, once for all, to the perfect calculation of the kingdom of known cause and effect. In the street and in the newspapers, life appears so plain a business, that manly resolution and adherence to the multiplication-table through all weathers, will insure success. But ah! presently comes a day, or is it only a a half-hour, with its angel-whispering, – which discomfits the conclusions of nations and of years! Tomorrow again, everything looks real and angular, the habitual standards are reinstated, common sense is as rare as genius, – is the basis of genius, and experience is hands and feet to every enterprise; – and yet, he who should do his business on this understanding, would be quickly bankrupt. Power keeps quite another road than the turnpikes of choice and will, namely, the subterranean and invisible tunnels and channels of life. It is ridiculous that we are diplomatists, and doctors, and considerate people: there are no dupes like these. Life is a series of surprises, and would not be worth taking or keeping, if it were not. God delights to isolate us every day, and hide from us the past and the future. We would look about us, but with grand politeness he draws down before us an impenetrable screen of purest sky, and another behind us of purest sky. 'You will not remember,' he seems to say, 'and you will not expect.' All good conversation, manners, and action, come from a spontaneity which forgets usages, and makes the moment great. Nature hates calculators; her methods are saltatory and impulsive. Man lives by pulses; our organic movements are such; and the chemical and ethereal agents are undulatory and alternate; and the mind goes antagonizing on, and never prospers but by fits. We thrive by casualties. Our chief experiences have been casual. The most attractive class of people are those who are powerful obliquely, and not by the direct stroke: men of genius, but not yet accredited: one gets the cheer of their light, without paying too great a tax. Theirs is the beauty of the bird or the morning light, and not of art. In the thought of genius there is always a surprise; and the moral sentiment is well called "the newness," for it is never other; as new to the oldest intelligence as to the young child, – "the kingdom that cometh without observation."[15] In like manner, for practical success, there must not be too much design. A man will not be observed in doing that which he can do best. There is a certain magic about his properest action, which stupefies your powers of observation, so that though it is done before you, you wist not of it. The art of life has a pudency, and will not be exposed. Every man is an impossibility, until he is born; every thing impossible, until we see a success. The ardors of piety agree at last with the coldest skepticism, – that nothing is of us or our works, – that all is of God. Nature will not spare us the smallest leaf of laurel. All writing comes by the grace of God, and all doing and having. I would gladly be moral, and keep due metes and bounds, which I dearly love, and allow the most to the will of man, but I have set my heart on honesty in this chapter, and I can see nothing at last, in success or failure, than more or less of vital force supplied from the Eternal. The results of life are uncalculated and uncalculable. The years teach much which the days never know. The persons who compose our company, converse, and come and go, and design and execute many things, and somewhat comes of it all, but an unlooked for result. The individual is always mistaken. He designed many things, and drew in other persons as coadjutors, quarrelled with some or all, blundered much, and something is done; all are a little advanced, but the individual is always mistaken. It turns out somewhat new, and very unlike what he promised himself.

The ancients, struck with this irreducibleness of the elements of human life to calculation, exalted Chance into a divinity, but that is to stay too long at the spark, – which glitters truly at one point, – but the universe is warm with the latency of the same fire. The miracle of life which will not be expounded, but will remain a miracle, introduces a new element. In the growth of the embryo, Sir Everard Home,[16] I think, noticed that the evolution was not from one central point, but co-active from three or more points. Life has no memory. That which proceeds in succession might be remembered, but that which is coexistent, or ejaculated from a deeper cause, as yet far from being conscious, knows not its own tendency. So is it with us, now skeptical, or without unity, because immersed in forms and effects all seeming to be of equal yet hostile value, and now religious, whilst in the reception of spiritual law. Bear with these distractions, with this coetaneous growth of the parts: they will one day be *members*, and obey one will. On that one will, on that secret cause, they nail our attention and hope. Life is hereby melted into an expectation or a religion. Underneath the inharmonious and trivial particulars, is a musical perfection, the Ideal journeying always with us, the heaven without rent or seam. Do but observe the mode of our illumination. When I converse with a profound

15. **"the . . . observation":** Luke 17:20.
16. **Sir Everard Home:** (1756–1832) Scottish surgeon.

mind, or if at any time being alone I have good thoughts, I do not at once arrive at satisfactions, as when, being thirsty, I drink water, or go to the fire, being cold: no! but I am at first apprised of my vicinity to a new and excellent region of life. By persisting to read or to think, this region gives further sign of itself, as it were in flashes of light, in sudden discoveries of its profound beauty and repose, as if the clouds that covered it parted at intervals, and showed the approaching traveller the inland mountains, with the tranquil eternal meadows spread at their base, whereon flocks graze, and shepherds pipe and dance. But every insight from this realm of thought is felt as initial, and promises a sequel. I do not make it; I arrive there, and behold what was there already. I make! O no! I clap my hands in infantine joy and amazement, before the first opening to me of this august magnificence, old with the love and homage of innumerable ages, young with the life of life, the sunbright Mecca of the desert. And what a future it opens! I feel a new heart beating with the love of the new beauty. I am ready to die out of nature, and be born again into this new yet unapproachable America I have found in the West.

> "Since neither now nor yesterday began
> These thoughts, which have been ever, nor yet can
> A man be found who their first entrance knew."[17]

If I have described life as a flux of moods, I must now add, that there is that in us which changes not, and which ranks all sensations and states of mind. The consciousness in each man is a sliding scale, which identifies him now with the First Cause, and now with the flesh of his body; life above life, in infinite degrees. The sentiment from which it sprung determines the dignity of any deed, and the question ever is, not, what you have done or forborne, but, at whose command you have done or forborne it.

Fortune, Minerva,[18] Muse, Holy Ghost, – these are quaint names, too narrow to cover this unbounded substance. The baffled intellect must still kneel before this cause, which refuses to be named, – ineffable cause, which every fine genius has essayed to represent by some emphatic symbol, as, Thales by water, Anaximenes by air, Anaxagoras[19] by (Νοῦς) thought, Zoroaster[20] by fire, Jesus and the moderns by love: and the metaphor of each has become a national religion. The Chinese Mencius[21] has not been the least successful in his generalization. "I fully understand language," he said, "and nourish well my vast-flowing vigor." – "I beg to ask what you call vast-flowing vigor?" – said his companion. "The explanation," replied Mencius, "is difficult. This vigor is supremely great, and in the highest degree unbending. Nourish it correctly, and do it no injury, and it will fill up the vacancy between heaven and earth. This vigor accords with and assists justice and reason, and leaves no hunger." – In our more correct writing, we give to this generalization the name of Being, and thereby confess that we have arrived as far as we can go. Suffice it for the joy of the universe, that we have not arrived at a

17. **"Since . . . knew":** From *Antigone* by the ancient Greek dramatist Sophocles.
18. **Minerva:** Roman goddess of wisdom.
19. **Thales . . . Anaximenes . . . Anaxagoras:** Ancient Greek philosophers.
20. **Zoroaster:** Sixth-century BCE Persian prophet.
21. **Mencius:** Third-century Confucian philosopher Meng-Tse.

wall, but at interminable oceans. Our life seems not present, so much as prospective; not for the affairs on which it is wasted, but as a hint of this vast-flowing vigor. Most of life seems to be mere advertisement of faculty: information is given us not to sell ourselves cheap; that we are very great. So, in particulars, our greatness is always in a tendency or direction, not in an action. It is for us to believe in the rule, not in the exception. The noble are thus known from the ignoble. So in accepting the leading of the sentiments, it is not what we believe concerning the immortality of the soul, or the like, but *the universal impulse to believe*, that is the material circumstance, and is the principal fact in the history of the globe. Shall we describe this cause as that which works directly? The spirit is not helpless or needful of mediate organs. It has plentiful powers and direct effects. I am explained without explaining, I am felt without acting, and where I am not. Therefore all just persons are satisfied with their own praise. They refuse to explain themselves, and are content that new actions should do them that office. They believe that we communicate without speech, and above speech, and that no right action of ours is quite unaffecting to our friends, at whatever distance; for the influence of action is not to be measured by miles. Why should I fret myself, because a circumstance has occurred, which hinders my presence where I was expected? If I am not at the meeting, my presence where I am, should be as useful to the commonwealth of friendship and wisdom, as would be my presence in that place. I exert the same quality of power in all places. Thus journeys the mighty Ideal before us; it never was known to fall into the rear. No man ever came to an experience which was satiating, but his good is tidings of a better. Onward and onward! In liberated moments, we know that a new picture of life and duty is already possible; the elements already exist in many minds around you, of a doctrine of life which shall transcend any written record we have. The new statement will comprise the skepticisms, as well as the faiths of society, and out of unbeliefs a creed shall be formed. For, skepticisms are not gratuitous or lawless, but are limitations of the affirmative statement, and the new philosophy must take them in, and make affirmations outside of them, just as much as it must include the oldest beliefs.

It is very unhappy, but too late to be helped, the discovery we have made, that we exist. That discovery is called the Fall of Man. Ever afterwards, we suspect our instruments. We have learned that we do not see directly, but mediately, and that we have no means of correcting these colored and distorting lenses which we are, or of computing the amount of their errors. Perhaps these subject-lenses have a creative power; perhaps there are no objects. Once we lived in what we saw; now, the rapaciousness of this new power, which threatens to absorb all things, engages us. Nature, art, persons, letters, religions, – objects, successively tumble in, and God is but one of its ideas. Nature and literature are subjective phenomena; every evil and every good thing is a shadow which we cast. The street is full of humiliations to the proud. As the fop contrived to dress his bailiffs in his livery, and make them wait on his guests at table, so the chagrins which the bad heart gives off as bubbles, at once take form as ladies and gentlemen in the street, shopmen or bar-keepers in hotels, and threaten or insult whatever is threatenable and unsuitable in us. 'Tis the same with our idolatries. People forget that it is the eye which makes the horizon, and the rounding mind's eye which makes this or that man a type or representative of humanity with the name of hero or saint. Jesus the "providential man," is a good man on whom many people are agreed that these optical laws shall take effect. By love on one part, and by forbearance to press objection on the other part, it is for a time settled, that we will look at him in the centre of the horizon, and ascribe to him the properties that will attach to any man so seen. But the longest love or aversion has a speedy term. The great and crescive self, rooted in absolute nature, supplants all relative existence, and ruins the kingdom of mortal friendship and love. Marriage (in what is called the spiritual world) is impossible, because of the inequality between every subject and every object. The subject is the receiver of Godhead, and at every comparison must feel his being enhanced by that cryptic might. Though not in energy, yet by presence, this magazine of substance cannot be otherwise than felt: nor can any force of intellect attribute to the object the proper deity which sleeps or wakes forever in every subject. Never can love make consciousness and ascription equal in force. There will be the same gulf between every me and thee, as between the original and the picture. The universe is the bride of the soul. All private sympathy is partial. Two human beings are like globes, which can touch only in a point, and, whilst they remain in contact, all other points of each of the spheres are inert; their turn must also come, and the longer a particular union lasts, the more energy of appetency the parts not in union acquire.

Life will be imaged, but cannot be divided nor doubled. Any invasion of its unity would be chaos. The soul is not twin-born, but the only begotten, and though revealing itself as child in time, child in appearance, is of a fatal and universal power, admitting no co-life. Every day, every act betrays the ill-concealed deity. We believe in ourselves, as we do not believe in others. We permit all things to ourselves, and that which we call sin in others, is experiment for us. It is an instance of our faith in ourselves, that men never speak of crime as lightly as they think: or, every man thinks a latitude safe for himself, which is nowise to be indulged to another. The act looks very differently on the inside, and on the outside; in its quality, and in its consequences. Murder in the murderer is no such ruinous thought as poets and romancers will have it; it does not unsettle him, or fright him from his ordinary notice of trifles: it is an act quite easy to be contemplated, but in its sequel, it turns out to be a horrible jangle and confounding of all relations. Especially the crimes that spring from love, seem right and fair from the actor's point of view, but, when acted, are found destructive of society. No man at last believes that he can be lost, nor that the crime in him is as black as in the felon. Because the intellect qualifies in our own case the moral judgments. For there is no crime to the intellect. That is antinomian or hypernomian,[22] and judges law as well as fact. "It is worse than a crime, it is a blunder," said Napoleon, speaking the language of the intellect. To it, the world is a problem in mathematics or the science of quantity, and it leaves out praise and blame, and all weak emotions. All stealing is comparative. If you come to absolutes,

22. **antinomian or hypernomian:** Opposed to or beyond the control of law.

pray who does not steal? Saints are sad, because they behold sin, (even when they speculate,) from the point of view of the conscience, and not of the intellect; a confusion of thought. Sin seen from the thought, is a diminution or *less*: seen from the conscience or will, it is pravity or *bad*. The intellect names it shade, absence of light, and no essence. The conscience must feel it as essence, essential evil. This it is not: it has an objective existence, but no subjective.

Thus inevitably does the universe wear our color, and every object fall successively into the subject itself. The subject exists, the subject enlarges; all things sooner or later fall into place. As I am, so I see; use what language we will, we can never say anything but what we are; Hermes, Cadmus, Columbus, Newton, Buonaparte,[23] are the mind's ministers. Instead of feeling a poverty when we encounter a great man, let us treat the newcomer like a travelling geologist, who passes through our estate, and shows us good slate, or limestone, or anthracite, in our brush pasture. The partial action of each strong mind in one direction, is a telescope for the objects on which it is pointed. But every other part of knowledge is to be pushed to the same extravagance, ere the soul attains her due sphericity. Do you see that kitten chasing so prettily her own tail? If you could look with her eyes, you might see her surrounded with hundreds of figures performing complex dramas, with tragic and comic issues, long conversations, many characters, many ups and downs of fate, – and meantime it is only puss and her tail. How long before our masquerade will end its noise of tamborines, laughter, and shouting, and we shall find it was a solitary performance? – A subject and an object, – it takes so much to make the galvanic circuit complete, but magnitude adds nothing. What imports it whether it is Kepler[24] and the sphere; Columbus and America; a reader and his book; or puss with her tail?

It is true that all the muses and love and religion hate these developments, and will find a way to punish the chemist, who publishes in the parlor the secrets of the laboratory. And we cannot say too little of our constitutional necessity of seeing things under private aspects, or saturated with our humors. And yet is the God the native of these bleak rocks. That need makes in morals the capital virtue of self-trust. We must hold hard to this poverty, however scandalous, and by more vigorous self-recoveries, after the sallies of action, possess our axis more firmly. The life of truth is cold, and so far mournful; but it is not the slave of tears, contritions, and perturbations. It does not attempt another's work, nor adopt another's facts. It is a main lesson of wisdom to know your own from another's. I have learned that I cannot dispose of other people's facts; but I possess such a key to my own, as persuades me against all their denials, that they also have a key to theirs. A sympathetic person is placed in the dilemma of a

---

23. **Hermes . . . Buonaparte:** Hermes, multitalented Greek god of wealth, trade, and invention; Cadmus, an ancient Greek military genius and mythical inventor of the alphabet; Christopher Columbus, Italian navigator and explorer; Isaac Newton, discoverer of the laws of gravity; and Napoleon Bonaparte, French military general who conquered much of Europe and became emperor of France.

24. **Kepler:** Johannes Kepler (1571–1630), German astronomer.

swimmer among drowning men, who all catch at him, and if he give so much as a leg or a finger, they will drown him. They wish to be saved from the mischiefs of their vices, but not from their vices. Charity would be wasted on this poor waiting on the symptoms. A wise and hardy physician will say, *Come out of that,* as the first condition of advice.

In this our talking America, we are ruined by our good nature and listening on all sides. This compliance takes away the power of being greatly useful. A man should not be able to look other than directly and forthright. A preoccupied attention is the only answer to the importunate frivolity of other people: an attention, and to an aim which makes their wants frivolous. This is a divine answer, and leaves no appeal, and no hard thoughts. In Flaxman's drawing of the Eumenides of Aeschylus, Orestes supplicates Apollo, whilst the Furies sleep on the threshold. The face of the god expresses a shade of regret and compassion, but calm with the conviction of the irreconcilableness of the two spheres. He is born into other politics, into the eternal and beautiful. The man at his feet asks for his interest in turmoils of the earth, into which his nature cannot enter. And the Eumenides there lying express pictorially this disparity. The god is surcharged with his divine destiny.

Illusion, Temperament, Succession, Surface, Surprise, Reality, Subjectiveness, – these are threads on the loom of time, these are the lords of life. I dare not assume to give their order, but I name them as I find them in my way. I know better than to claim any completeness for my picture. I am a fragment, and this is a fragment of me. I can very confidently announce one or another law, which throws itself into relief and form, but I am too young yet by some ages to compile a code. I gossip for my hour concerning the eternal politics. I have seen many fair pictures not in vain. A wonderful time I have lived in. I am not the novice I was fourteen, nor yet seven years ago. Let who will ask, where is the fruit? I find a private fruit sufficient. This is a fruit, – that I should not ask for a rash effect from meditations, counsels, and the hiving of truths. I should feel it pitiful to demand a result on this town and county, an overt effect on the instant month and year. The effect is deep and secular as the cause. It works on periods in which mortal lifetime is lost. All I know is reception; I am and I have: but I do not get, and when I have fancied I had gotten anything, I found I did not. I worship with wonder the great Fortune. My reception has been so large, that I am not annoyed by receiving this or that superabundantly. I say to the Genius, if he will pardon the proverb, *In for a mill, in for a million.* When I receive a new gift, I do not macerate my body to make the account square, for, if I should die, I could not make the account square. The benefit overran the merit the first day, and has overran the merit ever since. The merit itself, so-called, I reckon part of the receiving.

Also, that hankering after an overt or practical effect seems to me an apostasy. In good earnest, I am willing to spare this most unnecessary deal of doing. Life wears to me a visionary face. Hardest, roughest action is visionary also. It is but a choice between soft and turbulent dreams. People disparage knowing and the intellectual life, and urge doing. I am very content with knowing, if only I could know. That is an august entertainment, and would suffice me a great while. To know a little, would be worth the expense of this world. I hear always the law of Adrastia,[25] "that every soul which had acquired any truth, should be safe from harm until another period."

I know that the world I converse with in the city and in the farms, is not the world I *think*. I observe that difference, and shall observe it. One day, I shall know the value and law of this discrepance. But I have not found that much was gained by manipular attempts to realize the world of thought. Many eager persons successively make an experiment in this way, and make themselves ridiculous. They acquire democratic manners, they foam at the mouth, they hate and deny. Worse, I observe, that, in the history of mankind, there is never a solitary example of success, – taking their own tests of success. I say this polemically, or in reply to the inquiry, why not realize your world? But far be from me the despair which prejudges the law by a paltry empiricism,– since there never was a right endeavor, but it succeeded. Patience and patience, we shall win at the last. We must be very suspicious of the deceptions of the element of time. It takes a good deal of time to eat or to sleep, or to earn a hundred dollars, and a very little time to entertain a hope and an insight which becomes the light of our life. We dress our garden, eat our dinners, discuss the household with our wives, and these things make no impression, are forgotten next week; but in the solitude to which every man is always returning, he has a sanity and revelations, which in his passage into new worlds he will carry with him. Never mind the ridicule, never mind the defeat: up again, old heart! – it seems to say, – there is victory yet for all justice; and the true romance which the world exists to realize, will be the transformation of genius into practical power.

[1844]

25. **Adrastia:** Another name for Nemesis, the Greek goddess of fate or destiny.

Margaret Fuller

[1810-1850]

Margaret Fuller was born in Cambridgeport, Massachusetts, on May 23, 1810. Although her mother, Margarett Crane Fuller, had been a teacher in her local school in Canton, Massachusetts, Fuller was largely educated by her father, Timothy, a politician who was elected to the House of Representatives in 1818. Determined that his daughter would have a first-class education, Timothy Fuller began teaching her English and Latin grammar at the age of six. Greek soon followed, as well as studies in French and Italian. The precocious Margaret consequently had an introduction to language and cultural study that rivaled that of almost any young man being prepared for a college education in the nineteenth century. At the age of fourteen, Fuller was sent to a school for women, but she had difficulty acclimating herself to the less rigorous standards of the school and found her classmates cliquish and dull. Returning home, she continued to study with her father, who encouraged her to become a writer. Her first publication was "In Defense of Brutus," an article on the often-maligned leader of the plot to assassinate Julius Caesar, which appeared in the *Boston Daily Advertiser & Patriot* in 1834.

Conviction dwells upon her lips.
-Ralph Waldo Emerson

When Timothy Fuller died suddenly in 1835, Fuller was forced to find a way of earning a living and supporting her nearly destitute family. She first opened a school for girls and young women in Boston. Fuller proved to be a popular teacher, but she found the work frustrating and decided to try to make a living as a writer. In 1838, she began an innovative series of "Conversations" for women, organizing them as discussion classes for which the participants would pay tuition. Fuller also became close friends with Ralph Waldo Emerson and other transcendentalists. Like them, she was deeply interested in German literature and philosophy. In fact, her first two books were translations of German books: *Eckermann's Conversations with Goethe* (1839) and *Correspondence of Fraulein Günderode with Bettine von Arnim* (1842). In 1840, Fuller also became the first editor of the *Dial*, the unofficial journal of the transcendentalists. Since the position did not pay a salary, however, Fuller gave it up in favor of conducting more "conversations" and devoting herself to writing. After an ambitious trip to the Great Lakes, then the edge of the frontier in the United States, Fuller published an account of her travels, *Summer on the Lakes, in 1843* (1844).

Margaret Fuller
This portrait, the only surviving photograph of Fuller, is a copy of a lost daguerreotype made in July 1846, shortly before she sailed to Europe on assignment for the *New-York Tribune.*

During the following few years, Fuller moved outward from Boston to the national and then the international scene, becoming one of the most famous and influential women of her generation. In the fall of 1844, she wrote *Woman in the Nineteenth Century* (1845), a central text in the history of American feminism. After she completed the book, Fuller assumed the position of literary editor for the *New-York Tribune*, through which she reached a broad national audience for the first time. Fuller wrote over 250 articles and reviews for the newspaper, covering a wide range of topics that included art, music, literature, and increasingly social reform. By the fall of 1846, when she accepted an invitation to travel to Europe with friends and to become the *Tribune*'s first woman foreign correspondent, Fuller was well prepared to cover the social upheaval that would soon begin to shake the Continent. After touring England and France, where she was entertained by some of the notable literary and cultural figures of the period, Fuller arrived in Italy at a moment when revolutionary activity was spreading across Europe. She quickly became engaged in Italian politics and wrote vivid articles for the *Tribune*, providing American readers with a fascinating, personal account of the Italian revolutions of 1848. Her personal life was as dramatic as the political events unfolding around her. When the Roman Republic was overthrown in 1849, she fled to Florence with her lover, Giovanni Angelo, Marchese d'Ossoli, and their son. Fuller decided to return with them to the United States, which was then being convulsed by the bitter controversy over the Compromise of 1850. But the possibility that she might help shape the course of events in her native country abruptly ended with her death on July 17, 1850, when the ship that was returning Fuller and her family home to New York City sank in a storm off Long Island.

Fuller's *Woman in the Nineteenth Century.* In the July 1843 issue of the *Dial*, the literary journal that she had edited from 1840-1842, Fuller published an essay about the relationship between the sexes, "The Great Lawsuit: Man *versus* Men, Woman *versus* Women." With the encouragement of her friends, Fuller in 1844 decided to expand the essay into a book, *Woman in the Nineteenth Century* (1845). It was among the first books published in the United States to take up the question of the ways in which society restricts the role of women. Seeking to liberate both men and women from conventional attitudes and assumptions about gender roles, Fuller argued that women were responsible for developing their full potential. She also asserted that men, traditionally in positions of power, must rethink social and political boundaries in order to facilitate the full development of members of both sexes. *Woman in the Nineteenth Century* defies an easy description or brief summary, since it includes Fuller's accounts of famous women in history and myth, quasi-autobiographical passages, meditations on the importance of self-development, and extended arguments in favor of liberated, independent lives for men and women. In fact, the book's challenge to conventional literary standards mirrors Fuller's challenge to conventional thinking about the proper boundaries or roles of men and women. The text of the following selection is taken from the first American edition of *Woman in the Nineteenth Century* (1845).

bedfordstmartins.com/ americanlit *for research links on Fuller*

From WOMAN IN THE NINETEENTH CENTURY

Here, as elsewhere, the gain of creation consists always in the growth of individual minds, which live and aspire, as flowers bloom and birds sing, in the midst of morasses; and in the continual development of that thought, the thought of human destiny, which is given to eternity adequately to express, and which ages of failure only seemingly impede. Only seemingly, and whatever seems to the contrary, this country is as surely destined to elucidate a great moral law, as Europe was to promote the mental culture of man.

Though the national independence be blurred by the servility of individuals, though freedom and equality have been proclaimed only to leave room for a monstrous display of slave-dealing and slave-keeping; though the free American so often feels himself free, like the Roman, only to pamper his appetites and his indolence through the misery of his fellow beings, still it is not in vain, that the verbal statement has been made, "All men are born free and equal." There it stands, a golden certainty wherewith to encourage the good, to shame the bad. The new world may be called clearly to perceive that it incurs the utmost penalty, if it reject or oppress the sorrowful brother. And, if men are deaf, the angels hear. But men cannot be deaf. It is inevitable that an external freedom, an independence of the encroachments of other men, such as has been achieved for the nation, should be so also for every member of it. That which has once been clearly conceived in the intelligence cannot fail sooner or later to be acted out. It has become a law as irrevocable as that of the Medes[1] in their ancient dominion; men will privately sin against it, but the law, as expressed by a leading mind of the age,

"Tutti fatti a sembianza d'un Solo,
Figli tutti d'un solo riscatto,
In qual'ora, in qual parte del suolo
Trascorriamo quest' aura vital,
Siam fratelli, siam stretti ad un patto:
Maladetto colui che lo infrange,
Che s'innalza sul fiacco che piange
Che contrista uno spirto immortal."[2]

"All made in the likeness of the One,
All children of one ransom,
In whatever hour, in whatever part of the soil,
We draw this vital air,
We are brothers; we must be bound by one compact,
Accursed he who infringes it,
Who raises himself upon the weak who weep,
Who saddens an immortal spirit."

This law cannot fail of universal recognition. Accursed be he who willingly saddens an immortal spirit, doomed to infamy in later, wiser ages, doomed in future stages of his own being to deadly penance, only short of death. Accursed be he who sins in ignorance, if that ignorance be caused by sloth.

We sicken no less at the pomp than the strife of words. We feel that never were lungs so puffed with the wind of declamation, on moral and religious subjects, as now. We are tempted to implore these "word-heroes," these word-Catos,[3] word-Christs, to beware of cant[4] above all things; to remember that hypocrisy is the most hopeless as well as the meanest of crimes, and that those must surely be polluted by it, who do not reserve a part of their morality and religion for private use. Landor[5] says that he cannot have a great deal of mind who cannot afford to let the larger part of it lie fallow, and what is true of genius is not less so of virtue. The tongue is a valuable member, but should appropriate but a small part of the vital juices that are needful all over the body. We feel that the mind may "grow black and rancid in the smoke" even "of altars." We start up

---

1. **Medes:** By the sixth century BCE, the Medes, a people who originally lived in present-day Iran, had established a vast empire that covered the area from present-day Azerbaijan to Central Asia and Afghanistan.
2. ***Tutti . . . immortal:*** Manzoni. [Fuller's note.] Alessandro Manzoni (1785–1873), Italian poet and novelist.
3. **word-Catos:** Marcus Porcius Cato (Cato the Elder) (234–149 BCE) was a Roman statesman and orator, known for his opposition to the spread of Greek culture in Rome.
4. **beware of cant:** Dr. Johnson's one piece of advice should be written on every door; "Clear your mind of cant." But Byron, to whom it was so acceptable, in clearing away the noxious vine, shook down the building. Sterling's emendation is worthy of honor: "Realize your cant, not cast it off." [Fuller's note.] She refers to Samuel Johnson (1709–1784), English essayist and critic; George Gordon, Lord Byron (1788–1824), English poet notorious for his rejection of religious and social conventions; and John Sterling (1806–1844), English novelist and poet.
5. **Landor:** Walter Savage Landor (1775–1864), English poet.

from the harangue to go into our closet and shut the door. There inquires the spirit, "Is this rhetoric the bloom of healthy blood or a false pigment artfully laid on?" And yet again we know where is so much smoke, must be some fire; with so much talk about virtue and freedom, must be mingled some desire for them; that it cannot be in vain that such have become the common topics of conversation among men, rather than schemes for tyranny and plunder, that the very newspapers see it best to proclaim themselves Pilgrims, Puritans, Heralds of Holiness. The king that maintains so costly a retinue cannot be a mere boast, or Carabbas fiction.[6] We have waited here long in the dust; we are tired and hungry, but the triumphal procession must appear at last.

Of all its banners, none has been more steadily upheld, and under none have more valor and willingness for real sacrifices been shown, than that of the champions of the enslaved African. And this band it is, which, partly from a natural following out of principles, partly because many women have been prominent in that cause, makes, just now, the warmest appeal in behalf of woman.

Though there has been a growing liberality on this subject, yet society at large is not so prepared for the demands of this party, but that they are and will be for some time, coldly regarded as the Jacobins[7] of their day.

"Is it not enough," cries the irritated trader, "that you have done all you could to break up the national union, and thus destroy the prosperity of our country, but now you must be trying to break up family union, to take my wife away from the cradle and the kitchen hearth to vote at polls, and preach from a pulpit? Of course, if she does such things, she cannot attend to those of her own sphere. She is happy enough as she is. She has more leisure than I have, every means of improvement, every indulgence."

"Have you asked her whether she was satisfied with these *indulgences*?"

"No, but I know she is. She is too amiable to wish what would make me unhappy, and too judicious to wish to step beyond the sphere of her sex. I will never consent to have our peace disturbed by any such discussions."

"'Consent – you?' it is not consent from you that is in question, it is assent from your wife."

"Am not I the head of my house?"

"You are not the head of your wife. God has given her a mind of her own."

"I am the head and she the heart."

"God grant you play true to one another then. I suppose I am to be grateful that you did not say she was only the hand. If the head represses no natural pulse of the heart, there can be no question as to your giving your consent. Both will be of one accord, and there needs but to present any question to get a full and true answer. There is no need of precaution, of indulgence, or consent. But our doubt is whether the heart does consent with the head, or only obeys its decrees with a passiveness that precludes the exercise of its natural powers, or a repugnance that turns sweet qualities to bitter, or a doubt that

6. **Carabbas fiction:** The Marquess of Carabbas was the name the cat gave his master in the popular French story "Le Chat Botté ("Puss in Boots") by Charles Perrault (1628–1703).

7. **Jacobins:** The political club that became a radical republican organization during the French Revolution.

lays waste the fair occasions of life. It is to ascertain the truth, that we propose some liberating measures."

Thus vaguely are these questions proposed and discussed at present. But their being proposed at all implies much thought and suggests more. Many women are considering within themselves, what they need that they have not, and what they can have, if they find they need it. Many men are considering whether women are capable of being and having more than they are and have, *and*, whether, if so, it will be best to consent to improvement in their condition.

This morning, I open the Boston "*Daily Mail*," and find in its "poet's corner," a translation of Schiller's[8] "Dignity of Woman." In the advertisement of a book on America, I see in the table of contents this sequence, "Republican Institutions. American Slavery. American Ladies."

I open the "*Deutsche Schnellpost*," published in New-York, and find at the head of a column, *Juden- und Frauen-emancipation in Ungarn.* Emancipation of Jews and Women in Hungary.

The past year has seen action in the Rhode-Island legislature, to secure married women rights over their own property, where men showed that a very little examination of the subject could teach them much; an article in the Democratic Review[9] on the same subject more largely considered, written by a woman, impelled, it is said, by glaring wrong to a distinguished friend having shown the defects in the existing laws, and the state of opinion from which they spring; and an answer from the revered old man, J. Q. Adams, in some respects the Phocion[10] of his time, to an address made him by some ladies. To this last I shall again advert in another place.

These symptoms of the times have come under my view quite accidentally: one who seeks, may, each month or week, collect more.

The numerous party, whose opinions are already labelled and adjusted too much to their mind to admit of any new light, strive, by lectures on some model-woman of bride-like beauty and gentleness, by writing and lending little treatises, intended to mark out with precision the limits of woman's sphere, and woman's mission, to prevent other than the rightful shepherd from climbing the wall, or the flock from using any chance to go astray.

Without enrolling ourselves at once on either side, let us look upon the subject from the best point of view which to-day offers. No better, it is to be feared, than a high house-top. A high hill-top or at least a cathedral spire, would be desirable.

It may well be an Anti-Slavery party that pleads for woman, if we consider merely that she does not hold property on equal terms with men; so that, if a husband dies without making a will, the wife, instead of taking at once his place as head of the family,

---

8. **Schiller's:** Friedrich von Schiller (1759–1805), German philosopher.
9. **Democratic Review:** The *United States Magazine and Democratic Review*, an influential literary and political journal.
10. **J. Q. Adams . . . Phocion:** John Quincy Adams (1767–1848), well regarded for his eloquent speeches, was the sixth president of the United States; Phocion (402–318 BCE), Athenian ruler known for his integrity and powerful speeches.

inherits only a part of his fortune, often brought him by herself, as if she were a child, or ward only, not an equal partner.

We will not speak of the innumerable instances in which profligate and idle men live upon the earnings of industrious wives; or if the wives leave them, and take with them the children, to perform the double duty of mother and father, follow from place to place, and threaten to rob them of the children, if deprived of the rights of a husband, as they call them, planting themselves in their poor lodgings, frightening them into paying tribute by taking from them the children, running into debt at the expense of these otherwise so overtasked helots. Such instances count up by scores within my own memory. I have seen the husband who had stained himself by a long course of low vice, till his wife was wearied from her heroic forgiveness, by finding that his treachery made it useless, and that if she would provide bread for herself and her children, she must be separate from his ill fame. I have known this man come to instal himself in the chamber of a woman who loathed him and say she should never take food without his company. I have known these men steal their children whom they knew they had no means to maintain, take them into dissolute company, expose them to bodily danger, to frighten the poor woman, to whom, it seems, the fact that she alone had borne the pangs of their birth, and nourished their infancy, does not give an equal right to them. I do believe that this mode of kidnapping, and it is frequent enough in all classes of society, will be by the next age viewed as it is by Heaven now, and that the man who avails himself of the shelter of men's laws to steal from a mother her own children, or arrogate any superior right in them, save that of superior virtue, will bear the stigma he deserves, in common with him who steals grown men from their mother land, their hopes, and their homes.

I said, we will not speak of this now, yet I have spoken, for the subject makes me feel too much. I could give instances that would startle the most vulgar and callous, but I will not, for the public opinion of their own sex is already against such men, and where cases of extreme tyranny are made known, there is private action in the wife's favor. But she ought not to need this, nor, I think, can she long. Men must soon see that, on their own ground, that woman is the weaker party, she ought to have legal protection, which would make such oppression impossible. But I would not deal with "atrocious instances" except in the way of illustration, neither demand from men a partial redress in some one matter, but go to the root of the whole. If principles could be established, particulars would adjust themselves aright. Ascertain the true destiny of woman, give her legitimate hopes, and a standard within herself; marriage and all other relations would by degrees be harmonized with these.

But to return to the historical progress of this matter. Knowing that there exists in the minds of men a tone of feeling towards women as towards slaves, such as is expressed in the common phrase, "Tell that to women and children," that the infinite soul can only work through them in already ascertained limits; that the gift of reason, man's highest prerogative, is allotted to them in much lower degree; that they must be kept from mischief and melancholy by being constantly engaged in active labor, which is to be furnished and directed by those better able to think, &c., &c.; we need not multiply instances, for who can review the experience of last week without recalling words which imply, whether in jest or earnest, these views or views like these; knowing this, can we wonder that many reformers think that measures are not likely to be taken in behalf of women, unless their wishes could be publicly represented by women?

That can never be necessary, cry the other side. All men are privately influenced by women; each has his wife, sister, or female friends, and is too much biased by these relations to fail of representing their interests, and, if this is not enough, let them propose and enforce their wishes with the pen. The beauty of home would be destroyed, the delicacy of the sex be violated, the dignity of halls of legislation degraded by an attempt to introduce them there. Such duties are inconsistent with those of a mother; and then we have ludicrous pictures of ladies in hysterics at the polls, and senate chambers filled with cradles.

But if, in reply, we admit as truth that woman seems destined by nature rather for the inner circle, we must add that the arrangements of civilized life have not been, as yet, such as to secure it to her. Her circle, if the duller, is not the quieter. If kept from "excitement," she is not from drudgery. Not only the Indian squaw carries the burdens of the camp, but the favorites of Louis the Fourteenth accompany him in his journeys, and the washerwoman stands at her tub and carries home her work at all seasons, and in all states of health. Those who think the physical circumstances of woman would make a part in the affairs of national government unsuitable, are by no means those who think it impossible for the negresses to endure field work, even during pregnancy, or the sempstresses to go through their killing labors.

As to the use of the pen, there was quite as much opposition to woman's possessing herself of that help to free agency, as there is now to her seizing on the rostrum or the desk; and she is likely to draw, from a permission to plead her cause that way, opposite inferences to what might be wished by those who now grant it.

As to the possibility of her filling with grace and dignity, any such position, we should think those who had seen the great actresses, and heard the Quaker preachers of modern times, would not doubt, that woman can express publicly the fulness of thought and creation, without losing any of the peculiar beauty of her sex. What can pollute and tarnish is to act thus from any motive except that something needs to be said or done. Women could take part in the processions, the songs, the dances of old religion; no one fancied their delicacy was impaired by appearing in public for such a cause.

As to her home, she is not likely to leave it more than she now does for balls, theatres, meetings for promoting missions, revival meetings, and others to which she flies, in hope of an animation for her existence, commensurate with what she sees enjoyed by men. Governors of ladies' fairs are no less engrossed by such a change, than the Governor of the state by his; presidents of Washingtonian societies no less away from home than presidents of conventions. If men look straitly to it, they will find that, unless their lives are domestic, those of the women will not be. A house is no home unless it contain food and fire for the mind as well as for the body. The female Greek, of our day, is as much in the street as the male to cry, What news? We doubt not it was the same in Athens of old. The women, shut out from the market place, made up for it at the religious festivals. For human beings are not so constituted that they can live without expansion. If they do not get it one way, they must another, or perish.

As to men's representing women fairly at present, while we hear from men who owe to their wives not only all that is comfortable or graceful, but all that is wise in the arrangement of their lives, the frequent remark, "You cannot reason with a woman," when from those of delicacy, nobleness, and poetic culture, the contemptuous phrase "women and children," and that in no light sally of the hour, but in works intended to give a permanent statement of the best experiences, when not one man, in the million, shall I say? no, not in the hundred million, can rise above the belief that woman was made *for man*, when such traits as these are daily forced upon the attention, can we feel that man will always do justice to the interests of woman? Can we think that he takes a sufficiently discerning and religious view of her office and destiny, *ever* to do her justice, except when prompted by sentiment, accidentally or transiently, that is, for the sentiment will vary according to the relations in which he is placed. The lover, the poet, the artist, are likely to view her nobly. The father and the philosopher have some chance of liberality; the man of the world, the legislator for expediency, none.

Under these circumstances, without attaching importance, in themselves, to the changes demanded by the champions of woman, we hail them as signs of the times. We would have every arbitrary barrier thrown down. We would have every path laid open to woman as freely as to man. Were this done and a slight temporary fermentation allowed to subside, we should see crystallizations more pure and of more various beauty. We believe the divine energy would pervade nature to a degree unknown in the history of former ages, and that no discordant collision, but a ravishing harmony of the spheres would ensue.

Yet, then and only then, will mankind be ripe for this, when inward and outward freedom for woman as much as for man shall be acknowledged as a right, not yielded as a concession. As the friend of the negro assumes that one man cannot by right, hold another in bondage, so should the friend of woman assume that man cannot, by right, lay even well-meant restrictions on women. If the negro be a soul, if the woman be a soul, appareled in flesh, to one Master only are they accountable. There is but one law for souls, and if there is to be an interpreter of it, he must come not as man, or son of man, but as son of God.

[1845]

Fuller's Early Journalism. As the literary editor for the *New-York Daily Tribune* from December 1, 1844, until August 1, 1846, Fuller was responsible for writing and editing a wide variety of articles and reviews on literature and culture. The newspaper was edited by Horace Greeley, who was committed to social reforms of many kinds, and who gave Fuller wide latitude in expressing her views. In less than two years, she wrote over 250 articles and reviews on many topics, from current musical performances to recently published books to issues of social reform. Fuller's articles for the *Tribune* were published anonymously, but she signed virtually all of them with a star or an asterisk (*) at the end. Many of the articles were subsequently reprinted in the *New-York Weekly Tribune*, which reached an even larger national audience. The texts of the articles are taken from the *New-York Weekly Tribune* of December 28, 1844, and March 22, 1845.

New Year's Day

It was a beautiful custom among some of the Indian tribes, once a year, to extinguish all the fires, and, by a day of fasting and profound devotion, to propitiate the Great Spirit for the coming year. They then produced sparks by friction, and lit up afresh the altar and the hearth with the new fire.

And this was considered as the most precious and sacred gift from one person to another, binding them in bonds of inviolate friendship for that year, certainly; with a hope that the same might endure through life. From the young to the old it was a token of the highest respect; from the old to the young, of a great expectation.

To us might it be granted to solemnize the new year by the mental renovation of which this ceremony was the eloquent symbol! Might we extinguish, if only for a day, those fires where an uninformed religious ardor has led to human sacrifices; which have warmed the household, but, also, prepared pernicious, more than wholesome, viands for their use.

The Indian produced the new spark by friction. It would be a still more beautiful emblem, and expressive of the more extended powers of civilized men, if we should draw the spark from the centre of our system and the source of light by means of the burning glass.

Where, then, is to be found the new knowledge, the new thought, the new hope, that shall begin a new year in a spirit not discordant with 'the acceptable year of the Lord?' Surely, there must be such existing, if latent – some sparks of new fire, pure from ashes and from smoke, worthy to be offered as a new-year's gift? Let us look at the signs of the times, to see in what spot this fire shall be sought – on what fuel it may be fed. The ancients poured out libations of the choicest juices of Earth, to express their gratitude to the Power that had enabled them to be sustained from her bosom. They enfranchised slaves, to show that devotion to the Gods induced a sympathy with men.

Let us look about us to see with what rites, what acts of devotion, this modern Christian nation greets the approach of the New Year; by what signs she denotes the clear morning of a better day, such as may be expected when the eagle has entered into covenant with the dove.

This last week brings tidings that a portion of the inhabitants of Illinois, the rich and blooming region on which every gift of nature has been lavished to encourage the industry and brighten the hopes of man, not only refuses a libation to the Power that has so blessed their fields, but declares that the dew is theirs, and the sunlight is theirs, that they live from and for themselves, acknowledging no obligation and no duty to God or to man.

One man has freed a slave, – but a great part of the nation is now busy in contriving measures that may best rivet the fetters on those now chained, and forge them strongest for millions yet unborn.

Selfishness and tyranny no longer wear the mask; they walk haughtily abroad, affronting with their hard-hearted boasts and brazen resolves the patience of the sweet heavens. National Honor is trodden under foot for a National bribe, and neither sex nor age defends the redresser of injuries from the rage of the injurer.

Yet, amid these reports which come flying on the paper wings of every day, the scornful laugh of the gnomes, who begin to believe they can buy all souls with their gold, was checked a moment when the aged knight of the better cause answered the challenge – truly in keeping with the "chivalry" of the time, – "You are in the wrong, and I will kick you," by holding the hands of the chevalier till those around secured him. We think the man of old must have held him with his eye, as physicians of moral power can insane patients; – great as are his exploits for his age, he cannot have much bodily strength, unless by miracle.

The treatment of Mr. Adams and Mr. Hoar[1] seems to show that we are not fitted to emulate the savages in preparation for the new fire. The Indians knew how to reverence the old and the wise.

Among the manifestos of the day it is impossible not to respect that of the Mexican Minister[2] for the manly indignation with which he has uttered truths, however deep our mortification at hearing them. It has been observed for the last fifty years that the tone of diplomatic correspondence was much improved as to simplicity and directness. Once, diplomacy was another name for intrigue, and a paper of this sort was expected to be a mesh of artful phrases, through which the true meaning might be detected, but never actually grasped. Now here is one where an occasion being afforded by the unutterable folly of the corresponding party, a Minister speaks the truth as it lies in his mind, directly and plainly, as man speaks to man. His statement will command the sympathy of the civilized world.

As to the State papers that have followed, they are of a nature to make the Austrian despot sneer, as he counts in his oratory the woolen stockings he has got knit by imprisoning all the free geniuses in his dominions. He, at least, only appeals to the legitimacy of blood; these dare appeal to legitimacy, as seen from a moral point of view. History will class them with the brags of sharpers, who bully their victims about their honor, while they stretch forth their hands for the gold they have won with loaded dice. – "Do you dare to say the dice are loaded? Prove it; *and* I will shoot you for injuring my honor."

The Mexican makes his gloss on the page of American Honor. The girl in the Kentucky prison on that of her Freedom.[3] The delegate of Massachusetts on that of her Union. Ye stars! whose image she has placed upon her banner, answer us! Are not your Unions of a different sort? Do they not work to other results?

Yet we cannot lightly be discouraged or alarmed as to the destiny of our Country. The

---

1. **Mr. Adams and Mr. Hoar:** After his election to the House of Representatives in 1830, former president John Quincy Adams (1767–1848) fought for the repeal of a congressional rule that automatically tabled petitions against slavery. He was finally successful in 1844. Samuel Hoar (1778–1856), an emissary sent by the Massachusetts government to Charleston, South Carolina, in late 1844, failed in his efforts to lobby the South Carolina legislature to stop the practice of imprisoning free black sailors aboard ships from Massachusetts and then selling them into slavery. The legislature had him expelled from the city.
2. **the Mexican Minister:** Manuel C. Rejon, diplomat who argued against the American annexation of Mexican lands in "The Mexican Manifesto Against the Annexation of Texas," as reported in the *New-York Tribune* on December 13, 1844.
3. **The girl . . . Freedom:** Delia Webster, an abolitionist, was jailed in Lexington, Kentucky, for helping three fugitive slaves, as reported in the *New-York Tribune* on December 20, 1844.

whole history of its discovery and early progress indicates too clearly the purposes of Heaven with regard to it. Could we relinquish the thought that it was destined for the scene of a new and illustrious act in the great drama, the Past would be inexplicable, no less than the Future without hope.

Last week, which brought us so many unpleasant notices of home affairs, brought also an account of the magnificent telescope lately perfected by the Earl of Rosse. With means of observation, now almost divine, we perceive that some of the brightest stars, of which Sirius is one, have dark companions, whose presence is, by earthly spectators, only to be detected from the inequalities they cause in the motions of their radiant companions.

It was a new and most imposing illustration how, in carrying out the Divine scheme, of which we have as yet only spelt out the few first lines, the dark is made to wait upon and, in the full result, harmonize with, the bright. The sense of such pervasive analogies should enlarge patience and animate hope.

Yet, if offences must come, wo be to those by whom they come, and that of men, who sin against a heritage like ours, is as that of the backsliders among the Chosen People of the elder day. We too have been chosen, and plain indications been given, by a wonderful conjunction of auspicious influences, that the ark of human hopes has been placed for the present in our charge. Wo be to those who betray this trust! On their heads are to be heaped the curses of unnumbered ages!

Can he sleep, who in this past year has wickedly or lightly committed acts calculated to injure the few or many – who has poisoned the ears and the hearts he might have rightly informed – who has steeped in tears the cup of thousands – who has put back, as far as in him lay, the accomplishment of general good and happiness for the sake of his selfish aggrandizement or selfish luxury – who has sold to a party what is meant for mankind? If such sleep, dreadful shall be the waking.

Deliver us from evil. In public or in private it is easy to give pain – hard to give pure pleasure; easy to do evil – hard to do good. God does His good in the whole, despite of bad men; but only from a very pure mind will He permit original good to proceed in the day. Happy those who can feel that during the past year, they have, to the best of their knowledge, refrained from evil. Happy those who determine to proceed in this by the light of Conscience. It is but a spark; yet from that spark may be drawn fire-light enough for worlds and systems of worlds, and that light is ever new.

And with this thought rises again the memory of the fair lines that light has brought to view in the histories of some men. If the nation tends to wrong, there are yet present the ten just men. The hands and lips of this great form may be impure, but pure blood flows yet within her veins – the blood of the noble bands who first sought these shores from the British isles and France for conscience sake. Too many have come since for bread alone. We cannot blame – we must not reject them, but let us teach them in giving them bread, to prize that salt, too, without which all on earth must lose its savor. Yes! let us teach them, not rail at their inevitable ignorance and unenlightened action, but teach them and their children as our own; if we do so, their children and ours may yet act as one body obedient to one soul, and if we should act rightly now, that soul a pure soul.

And ye, sable bands, forced hither against your will, kept down here now by a force hateful to Nature, a will alien from God; it does sometimes seem as if the Avenging

Angel wore your hue and would place in your hands the sword to punish the cruel injustice of our fathers, the selfish perversity of the sons. Yet, are there no means of atonement? Must the innocent suffer with the guilty? Teach us, oh All-Wise! the clue out of this labyrinth, and if we faithfully encounter its darkness and dread, and emerge into clear light, wilt Thou not bid us 'go and sin no more?'[4]

Meanwhile, let us proceed as we can, *picking our steps* along the slippery road. If we keep the right direction, what matters it that we must pass through so much mud? The promise is sure:

Angels shall free the feet from stain, to their own hue of snow,
If, undismayed, we reach the hills where the true olives grow.
  The olive groves, which we must seek in cold and damp,
  Alone can yield us oil for a perpetual lamp.
Then sound again the golden horn with promise ever new;
The princely deer will ne'er be caught by those that slack pursue;
Let the 'White Doe' of angel hopes be always kept in view.

  Yes! sound again the horn – of Hope the golden horn!
  Answer it, flutes and pipes, from valleys still and lorn;
  Warders, from your high towers, with trumps of silver scorn,
  And harps in maidens' bowers, with strings from deep hearts torn,
  All answer to the horn – of Hope the golden horn!

There is still hope, there is still an America, while private lives are ruled by the Puritan, by the Huguenot conscientiousness, and while there are some who can repudiate, not their debts, but the supposition that they will not strive to pay their debts to their age, and to Heaven who gave them a share in its great promise.

[1844]

4. 'go and sin no more': Christ's final words to the woman taken in adultery (John 8:11).

OUR CITY CHARITIES

VISIT TO BELLEVUE ALMS HOUSE, TO THE FARM SCHOOL, THE ASYLUM FOR THE INSANE, AND PENITENTIARY ON BLACKWELL'S ISLAND

The aspect of Nature was sad; what is worse, it was dull and dubious, when we set forth on these visits. The sky was leaden and lowering, the air unkind and piercing, the little birds sat mute and astonished at the departure of the beautiful days which had lured them to premature song. It was a suitable day for such visits. The pauper establishments that belong to a great city take the place of the skeleton at the banquets of old. They admonish us of stern realities, which must bear the same explanation as the frequent blight of Nature's bloom. They should be looked at by all, if only for their own sakes, that they may not sink listlessly into selfish ease, in a world so full of disease. They should be looked at by all who wish to enlighten themselves as to the means of aiding their fellow-creatures in any way, public or private. For nothing can really be done till the right principles are discovered, and it would seem they still need to be discovered or elucidated, so little is done, with a great deal of desire in the heart of the community to do what is right. Such visits are not yet calculated to encourage and exhilarate, as does the story of the Prodigal Son; they wear a grave aspect and suit the grave mood of a *cold* Spring day.

At the Alms House there is every appearance of kindness in the guardians of the poor, and there was a greater degree of cleanliness and comfort than we had expected. But the want of suitable and sufficient employment is a great evil. The persons who find here either a permanent or temporary refuge have scarcely any occupation provided except to raise vegetables for the establishment, and prepare clothing for themselves. The men especially have the most vagrant, degraded air, and so much indolence must tend to confirm them in every bad habit. We were told that, as they are under no strict discipline, their labor at the various trades could not be made profitable; yet surely the means of such should be provided, even at some expense. Employments of various kinds must be absolutely needed, if only to counteract the bad effects of such a position. Every establishment in aid of the poor should be planned with a view to their education. There should be instruction, both practical and in the use of books, openings to a better intercourse than they can obtain from their miserable homes, correct notions as to cleanliness, diet, and fresh air. A great deal of pains would be lost in their case, as with all other arrangements for the good of the many, but here and there the seed would fall into the right places, and some members of the downtrodden million, rising a little from the mud, would raise the whole body with them.

As we saw old women enjoying their dish of gossip and their dish of tea, and mothers able for a while to take care in peace of their poor little children, we longed and hoped for that genius, who shall teach how to make, of these establishments, places of rest and instruction, not of degradation.

The causes which make the acceptance of public charity so much more injurious to the receiver than that of private are obvious, but surely not such that the human mind which has just invented the magnetic telegraph and Anastatic printing,[1] may not obviate them. A deeper religion at the heart of Society would devise such means. Why should it be that the poor may still feel themselves men; paupers not? The poor man does not feel himself injured but benefitted by the charity of the doctor who gives him back the bill he is unable to pay, because the doctor is acting from intelligent sympathy – from love. Let Society do the same. She might raise the man, who is accepting her bounty, instead of degrading him.

Indeed, it requires great nobleness and faith in human nature, and God's will concerning it, for the officials not to take the tone toward those under their care, which their vices and bad habits prompt, but which must confirm them in the same. Men

---

1. **magnetic telegraph and Anastatic printing:** Recent innovations in communication and printing were the telegraph (1844) invented by Samuel Morse and the development of lithographic reproduction of illustrations for periodicals and books.

treated with respect are reminded of self-respect, and if there is a sound spot left in the character, the healthy influence spreads.

We were sorry to see mothers with their newborn infants exposed to the careless scrutiny of male visitors. In the hospital, those who had children scarce a day old were not secure from the gaze of the stranger. This cannot be pleasant to them, and, if they have not refinement to dislike it, those who have should teach it to them. But we suppose there is no woman who has so entirely lost sight of the feelings of girlhood as not to dislike the scrutiny of strangers at a time which is sacred, if any in life is. Women they may like to see, even strangers, if they can approach them with delicacy.

In the yard of the hospital, we saw a little Dutch girl, a dwarf, who would have suggested a thousand poetical images and fictions to the mind of Victor Hugo or Sir Walter Scott.[2] She had been brought here to New-York, as we understood, by some showman and then deserted, so that this place was her only refuge. No one could communicate with her or know her feelings, but she showed what they were, by running to the gate whenever it was opened, though treated with familiar kindness and seeming pleased by it. She had a large head, ragged dark hair, a glowering wizard eye, an uncouth yet pleasant smile, like an old child; – she wore a gold ring, and her complexion was as yellow as gold, if not as bright; altogether she looked like a gnome, more than any attempt we have ever known to embody in Art that fabled inhabitant of the mines and secret caves of earth.

From the Alms House we passed in an open boat to the Farm School. We were unprepared to find this, as we did, only a school upon a small farm, instead of one in which study is associated with labor. The children are simply taken care of and taught the common English branches till they are twelve years old, when they are bound out to various kinds of work. We think this plan very injudicious. It is bad enough for the children of rich parents, not likely in after life to bear a hard burden, and who are, at any rate, supplied with those various excitements required to develope the character in the earliest years; it is bad enough, we say, for these to have no kind of useful labor mingled with their plays and studies. Even these children would expand more, and be more variously called forth, and better prepared for common life, if another course were pursued. But, in schools like this at the farm, where the children, on leaving it, will be at once called on for adroitness and readiness of mind and body, and where the absence of natural ties and the various excitements that rise from them inevitably give to life a mechanical routine calculated to cramp and chill the character, it would be peculiarly desirable to provide various occupations, and such as are calculated to prepare for common life. As to economy of time, there is never time lost, by mingling other pursuits with the studies of children; they have vital energy enough for many things at once, and learn more from books when their attention is quickened by other kinds of culture.

---

2. **Victor Hugo or Sir Walter Scott:** Victor Hugo (1802–1885), French poet and novelist; Sir Walter Scott (1771–1832), Scottish novelist whose works were very popular in the United States.

Some of these children were pretty, and they were healthy and well-grown, considering the general poverty or vice of the class from which they were taken. That terrible scourge, opthalmia,[3] disfigured many among them. This disease, from some cause not yet detected, has been prevalent here for many years. We trust it may yield to the change of location next summer. There is not water enough here to give the children decent advantages as to bathing. This, too, will be remedied by the change. The Principal, who has been almost all his life connected with this establishment and that at Bellevue, seemed to feel a lively interest in his charge. He has arranged the dormitories with excellent judgment, both as to ventilation and neatness. This, alone, is a great advantage these children have over those of poor families living at home. They may pass the night in healthy sleep, and have thereby a chance for innocent and active days.

We saw with pleasure the little children engaged in the kind of drill they so much enjoy, of gesticulation regulated by singing. It was also pretty to see the babies sitting in a circle and the nurses in the midst feeding them, alternately, with a spoon. It seemed like a nest full of little birds, each opening its bill as the parent returns from her flight.

Hence we passed to the Asylum for the Insane. Only a part of this building is completed, and it is well known that the space is insufficient. Twice as many are inmates here as can be properly accommodated. A tolerable degree, however, of order and cleanliness is preserved. We could not but observe the vast difference between the appearance of the insane here and at Bloomingdale, or other Institutions where the number of attendants and nature of the arrangements permit them to be the objects of individual treatment; that is, where the wants and difficulties of each patient can be distinctly and carefully attended to. At Bloomingdale, the shades of character and feeling were nicely kept up, decorum of manners preserved, and the insane showed in every way that they felt no violent separation betwixt them and the rest of the world, and might easily return to it. The eye, though bewildered, seemed lively, and the tongue prompt. But *here*, insanity appeared in its more stupid, wild, or despairing forms. They crouched in corners; they had no eye for the stranger, no heart for hope, no habitual expectation of light. Just as at the Farm School, where the children show by their unformed features and mechanical movements that they are treated by wholesale, so do these poor sufferers. It is an evil incident to public establishments, and which only a more intelligent public attention can obviate.

One figure we saw, here also, of high poetical interest. It was a woman seated on the floor, in the corner of her cell, with a shawl wrapped gracefully around her head and chest, like a Nun's veil. Her hair was grey, her face attenuated and very pallid, her eyes large, open, fixed and bright with a still fire. She never moved them nor ceased chanting the service of the Church. She was a Catholic, who became insane while preparing to be a Nun. She is surely a Nun now in her heart; and a figure from which a painter might study for some of the most consecrated subjects.

Passing to the Penitentiary, we entered on one of the gloomiest scenes that deforms this great metropolis. Here are the twelve hundred, who receive the punishment due to

3. **opthalmia:** Common disease of the eyes in the nineteenth century.

the vices of so large a portion of the rest. And under what circumstances! Never was punishment treated more simply as a social convenience, without regard to pure right, or a hope of reformation.

Public attention is now so far awake to the state of the Penitentiary that it cannot be long, we trust, before proper means of classification are devised, a temporary asylum provided for those who leave this purgatory, even now, unwilling to return to the inferno from which it has for a time kept them, and means presented likely to lead some, at least, among the many, who seem hardened, to better views and hopes. It must be that the more righteous feeling which has shown itself in regard to the prisons at Sing Sing[4] and elsewhere, must take some effect as to the Penitentiary also. The present Superintendent enters into the necessity of such improvements, and, should he remain there, will do what he can to carry them into effect.

The want of proper matrons, or any matrons, to take the care so necessary for the bodily or mental improvement or even decent condition of the seven hundred women assembled here, is an offence that cries aloud. It is impossible to take the most cursory survey of this assembly of women; especially it is impossible to see them in the Hospital, where the circumstances are a little more favorable, without seeing how many there are in whom the feelings of innocent childhood are not dead, who need only good influences and steady aid to raise them from the pit of infamy and wo into which they have fallen. And, if there was not one that could be helped, at least Society owes them the insurance of a decent condition while here. We trust that interest on this subject will not slumber.

The recognized principles of all such institutions which have any higher object than the punishment of fault, (and we believe few among us are so ignorant as to avow that as the only object, though they may, from want of thought, act as if it were,) are – Classification as the first step, that the bad may not impede those who wish to do well; 2d. Instruction, practical, oral, and by furnishing books which may open entirely new hopes and thoughts to minds oftener darkened than corrupted; 3d. A good Sanitary system, which promotes self-respect, and, through health and purity of body, the same in mind.

In visiting the Tombs[5] the other day, we found the air in the upper galleries unendurable, and felt great regret that those confined there should be constantly subjected to it. Give the free breath of Heaven to all who are still permitted to breathe. – We cannot, however, wonder at finding this barbarity in a prison, having been subjected to it at the most fashionable places of public resort. Dr. Griscom[6] has sent us his excellent lecture on the health of New-York, which we recommend to all who take a vital interest in the city where they live, and have intellect to discern that a cancer on the body must in time affect the head and heart also. We thought, while reading, that it was not surprising

---

4. **Sing Sing:** Prison established near New York City in 1825; female prisoners were placed in a separate wing in 1837.
5. **the Tombs:** Informal name for the Halls of Justice and House of Detention, a prison built in New York City in 1840. The massive structure was designed to look like an ancient Egyptian tomb.
6. **Dr. Griscom:** John Hoskins Griscom (1809-1874), physician and author of *The Sanitary Condition of the Laboring Population of New York* (1845).

typhus fever and opthalmia should be bred in the cellars, while the families of those who live in palaces breathe such infected air at public places, and receive their visitors on New Year's day by candlelight. (That was a sad omen for the New Year – did they mean to class themselves among those who love darkness rather than light?)

We hope to see the two thousand poor people, and the poor children, better situated in their new abode, when we visit them again. The Insane Asylum will gain at once by enlargement of accommodations; but more attendance is also necessary, and, for that purpose, the best persons should be selected. We saw, with pleasure, tame pigeons walking about among the most violent of the insane, but we also saw two attendants with faces brutal and stolid. Such a charge is too delicate to be intrusted to any but excellent persons. Of the Penitentiary we shall write again. All criticism, however imperfect, should be welcome. There is no reason why New-York should not become a model for other States in these things. There is wealth enough, intelligence, and good desire enough, and *surely, need enough.* If she be not the best cared for city in the world, she threatens to surpass in corruption London and Paris. Such bane is as constantly poured into her veins demands powerful antidotes.

But nothing effectual can be achieved while both measures and men are made the sport of political changes. It is a most crying and shameful evil, which does not belong to our institutions, but is a careless distortion of them, that the men and measures are changed in these institutions with changes from Whig to Democrat, from Democrat to Whig. Churches, Schools, Colleges, the care of the Insane, and suffering Poor, should be preserved from the uneasy tossings of this delirium. The Country, the State, should look to it that only those fit for such officers should be chosen for such, apart from all considerations of political party. Let this be thought of; for without an absolute change in this respect no permanent good whatever can be effected; and farther, let not economy but utility be the rule of expenditure, for, here, parsimony is the worst prodigality.

[1845]

Fuller's "Things and Thoughts in Europe." From 1846 until the fall of the Roman Republic in 1849, Fuller sent thirty-seven dispatches from Europe to be published in the *New-York Tribune.* The first several dispatches were sent from England and France, where Fuller wrote about cultural matters: writers and other notables she met, musical performances she attended, and tourist sites she visited. When she arrived in Italy, however, Fuller was almost immediately swept up in the political turmoil of the revolutions that swept across Europe during 1848. As an observer of the Italian revolutions for an American audience, Fuller was well qualified. Already fluent in several languages, she mastered Italian quickly. Since she lived very simply among mostly poor people throughout her stay in the country, Fuller was also well aware of the privations of most Italians, living under the control of despotic rulers. Finally, her increasing interest in reform movements helped Fuller understand and sympathize with the aspirations of the revolutionaries in Italy. In this dispatch, published on January 1, 1848, she took the occasion of the new year to provide lessons to Americans about how their squandering of democratic opportunities appeared to the rest of the world. The text of the dispatch, originally published under the heading "Things and Thoughts in Europe, Number 18," is taken from the *New-York Daily Tribune*, January 1, 1848.

THINGS AND THOUGHTS IN EUROPE, NUMBER 18

This letter will reach the United States about the 1st of January; and it may not be impertinent to offer a few New Year's reflections. Every new year, indeed, confirms the old thoughts, but also presents them under some new aspects.

The American in Europe, if a thinking mind, can only become more American. In some respects it is a great pleasure to be here. Although we have an independent political existence, our position toward Europe, as to Literature and the Arts, is still that of a colony, and one feels the same joy here that is experienced by the colonist in returning to the parent home. What was but picture to us becomes reality; remote allusions and derivations trouble no more: we see the pattern of the stuff, and understand the whole tapestry. There is a gradual clearing up on many points, and many baseless notions and crude fancies are dropped. Even the post haste passage of the business American through the great cities, escorted by cheating couriers and ignorant *valets de place*, unable to hold intercourse with the natives of the country, and passing all his leisure hours with his countrymen, who know no more than himself, clears his mind of some mistakes – lifts some mists from his horizon.

There are three species: first, the servile American – a being utterly shallow, thoughtless, worthless. He comes abroad to spend his money and indulge his tastes. His object in Europe is to have fashionable clothes, good foreign cookery, to know some titled persons, and furnish himself with coffee house gossip, which he wins importance at home by retailing among those less traveled and as uninformed as himself.

I look with unspeakable contempt on this class – a class which has all the thoughtlessness and partiality of the exclusive classes in Europe, without any of their refinement, or the chivalric feeling which still sparkles among them here and there. However, though these willing serfs in a free age do some little hurt, and cause some annoyance at present, it cannot last: our country is fated to a grand, independent existence, and, as its laws develop, these parasites of a by-gone period must wither and drop away.

Then there is the conceited American, instinctively bristling and proud of – he knows not what. – He does not see, not he, that the history of Humanity for many centuries is likely to have produced results it requires some training, some devotion, to appreciate and profit by. With his great clumsy hands, only fitted to work on a steam-engine, he seizes the old Cremona violin, makes it shriek with anguish in his grasp, and then declares he thought it was all humbug before he came, and now he knows it; that there is not really any music in these old things; that the frogs in one of our swamps make much finer, for *they* are young and alive. To him the etiquettes of courts and camps, the ritual of the Church, seem simply silly – and, no wonder, profoundly ignorant as he is of their origin and meaning. Just so the legends which are the subjects of pictures, the profound myths which are represented in the antique marbles, amaze and revolt him; as, indeed, such things need to be judged of by another standard from that of the Connecticut Blue Laws. He criticises severely pictures, feeling quite sure that his natural senses are better means of judgment than the rules of connoisseurs – not feeling that to see such objects mental vision as well as fleshly eyes are needed, and that something is aimed at in Art beyond the imitation of the commonest forms of Nature.

This is Jonathan in the sprawling state, the booby truant not yet aspiring enough to be a good school-boy. Yet in his folly there is meaning; add thought and culture to his independence and he will be a man of might; he is not a creature without hope, like the thick-skinned dandy of the class first specified.

The Artistes form a class by themselves. Yet among them, though seeking special aims by special means, may also be found the lineaments of these two classes, as well as of the third of which I am to speak.

3d. The thinking American – a man who, recognizing the immense advantage of being born to a new world and on a virgin soil, yet does not wish one seed from the Past to be lost. He is anxious to gather and carry back with him all that will bear a new climate and new culture. Some will dwindle; others will attain a bloom and stature unknown before. He wishes to gather them clean, free from noxious insects. He wishes to give them a fair trial in his new world. And that he may know the conditions under which he may best place them in that new world, he does not neglect to study their history in this.

The history of our planet in some moments seems so painfully mean and little, such terrible bafflings and failures to compensate some brilliant successes – such a crashing of the mass of men beneath the feet of a few, and these, too, often the least worthy – such a small drop of honey to each cup of gall, and, in many cases, so mingled, that it is never one moment in life purely tasted, – above all, so little achieved for Humanity as a whole, such tides of war and pestilence intervening to blot out the traces of each triumph, that no wonder if the strongest soul sometimes pauses aghast! No wonder if the many indolently console themselves with gross joys and frivolous prizes. Yes! those men *are* worthy of admiration who can carry this cross faithfully through fifty years; it is a great while for all the agonies that beset a lover of good, a lover of men; it makes a soul worthy of a speedier ascent, a more productive ministry in the next sphere. Blessed are they who ever keep that portion of pure, generous love with which they began life! How blessed those who have deepened the fountains, and have enough to spare for the thirst of others! Some such there are; and, feeling that, with all the excuses for failure, still only the sight of those who triumph gives a meaning to life or makes its pangs endurable, we must arise and follow.

Eighteen hundred years of this Christian culture in these European Kingdoms, a great theme never lost sight of, a mighty idea, an adorable history to which the hearts of men invariably cling, yet are genuine results rare as grains of gold in the river's sandy bed! Where is the genuine Democracy to which the rights of all men are holy? where the child-like wisdom learning all through life more and more of the will of God? where the aversion to falsehood in all its myriad disguises of cant, vanity, covetousness, so clear to be read in all the history of Jesus of Nazareth? Modern Europe is the sequel to that history, and see this hollow England, with its monstrous wealth and cruel poverty, its conventional life, and low, practical aims; see this poor France, so full of talent, so adroit, yet so shallow and glossy still, which could not escape from a false position with all its baptism of blood! see that lost Poland and this Italy bound down by treacherous hands in all the force of genius! see Russia with its brutal Czar and innumerable slaves! see Austria and its royalty that represents nothing, and its people who, as people, are and have nothing! If we consider the amount of truth that has really been spoken out in the world, and the love that has bent in private hearts – how Genius has decked each spring time with such splendid flowers, conveying each one enough of instruction in its life of harmonious energy, and how continually, unquenchably the spark of faith has striven to burst into flame and light up the Universe – the public failure seems amazing, seems monstrous.

Still Europe toils and struggles with her idea, and, at this moment, all things bode and declare a new outbreak of the fire, to destroy old palaces of crime! May it fertilize also many vineyards! – Here at this moment a successor of St. Peter, after the lapse of near two thousand years, is called "Utopian" by a part of this Europe because he strives to get some food to the mouths of the *leaner* of his flock. A wonderful state of things, and which leaves, as the best argument against despair, that men do not, *cannot* despair amid such dark experiences, and thou, my country! will thou not be more true? does no greater success await thee? All things have so conspired to teach, to aid! A new world, a new chance, with oceans to wall in the new thought against interference from the old! – Treasures of all kinds, gold, silver, corn, marble, to provide for every physical need! A noble, constant, starlike soul, an Italian he led the way to its shores, and, in the first days, the strong, the pure, those too brave, too sincere for the life of the Old World hastened to people them. A generous struggle then shook off what was foreign and gave the nation a glorious start for a worthy goal. Men rocked the cradle of its hopes, great, firm, disinterested, men who saw, who wrote, as the basis of all that was to be done, a statement of the rights, the inborn rights of men, which, if fully interpreted and acted upon, leaves nothing to be desired.

Yet, Oh Eagle, whose early flight showed this clear sight of the Sun, how often dost thou near the ground, how show the vulture in these later days! Thou wert to be the advance guard of Humanity, the herald of all progress; how often hast thou betrayed this high commission! Fain would the tongue in clear triumphant accents draw example from thy story, to encourage the hearts of those who almost faint and die beneath the old oppressions. But we must stammer and blush when we speak of many things. I take pride here that I may really say the Liberty of the Press works well, and that checks and balances naturally evolve from it which suffice to its government. I may say the minds of our people are alert, and that talent has a free chance to rise. It is much. But dare I say that political ambition is not as darkly sullied as in other countries? Dare I say that men of most influence in political life are those who represent most virtue or even intellectual power? Is it easy to find names in that career of which I can speak with enthusiasm? Must I not confess in my country to a boundless lust of gain? Must I not confess to the weakest vanity, which bristles and blusters at each foolish taunt of the foreign press; and must I not admit that the men who make these undignified rejoinders seek and find popularity so? Must I not confess that there is as yet no antidote cordially adopted that will defend even that great, rich country against the evils that have grown out of the commercial system in the old world? Can I say our social laws are generally better, or show a nobler insight to the wants of man and woman? I do, indeed, say what I believe, that voluntary association for improvement in these particulars will be the grand means for my nation to grow and give a nobler harmony to the coming age. But it is only of a small minority that I can say they as yet seriously take to heart these things; that they earnestly meditate on what is wanted for their country, – for mankind, – for our cause is, indeed, the cause of all mankind at present. Could we succeed, really succeed, combine a deep religious love with practical development, the achievements of genius with the happiness of the multitude, we might believe Man had now reached a commanding point in his ascent, and would stumble and faint no more. Then there is this horrible cancer of Slavery, and this wicked War,[1] that has grown out of it. How dare I speak of these things here? I listen to the same arguments against the emancipation of Italy, that are used against the emancipation of our blacks; the same arguments in favor of the spoliation of Poland as for the conquest of Mexico. I find the cause of tyranny and wrong everywhere the same – and lo! my country! The darkest offender, because with the least excuse, forsworn to the high calling with which she was called, – no champion of the rights of men, but a robber and a jailer; the scourge hid behind her banner; her eyes fixed, not on the stars, but on the possessions of other men.

How it pleases me here to think of the Abolitionists! I could never endure to be with them at home, they were so tedious, often so narrow, always so rabid and exaggerated in their tone. But, after all, they had a high motive, something eternal in their desire and life; and, if it was not the only thing worth thinking of it was really something worth living and dying for to free a great nation from such a terrible blot, such a threatening plague. God strengthen them and make them wise to achieve their purpose!

I please myself, too, with remembering some ardent souls among the American youth who, I trust, will yet expand and help to give soul to the huge, over fed, too hastily grown-up body. May they be constant. "Were Man but constant he were perfect!" it has been said; and it is true that he who could be constant to those moments in which he has been truly human – not brutal, not mechanical – is on the sure path to his perfection and to effectual service of the Universe.

It is to the youth that Hope addresses itself, to those who yet burn with aspiration, who are not hardened in their sins. But I dare not expect too much of them. I am not very old, yet of those who, in life's morning, I saw touched by the light of a high hope, many have seceded. Some have become voluptuaries; some mere family men, who think it is quite life enough to win bread for half a dozen people and treat them decently; others are lost through indolence and vacillation. Yet some remain constant,

"I have witnessed many a shipwreck, yet still beat noble hearts."

I have found many among the youth of England, of France – of Italy also – full of high desire, but will they have courage and purity to fight the battle through in the

1. **wicked War:** The Mexican War (1846–1848), which was viewed by many Americans as an unjustified invasion of Mexico and an effort to extend the slave territories.

sacred, the immortal band? Of some of them I believe it and await the proof. If a few succeed amid the trial, we have not lived and loved in vain.

To these, the heart of my country, a Happy New Year! I do not know what I have written, I have merely yielded to my feelings in thinking of America: but something of true love must be in these lines – receive them kindly, my friends; it is, by itself, some merit for printed words to be sincere.

[1848]

Harriet Beecher Stowe

[1811-1896]

Harriet Beecher Stowe was born in Litchfield, Connecticut, in 1811. The daughter, sister, and eventually wife and mother of Protestant clergymen, she was raised in a family in which religion was an integral part of life. Education was also regarded as vital for everyone, and the young Harriet attended her sister Catherine Beecher's Hartford Female Seminary, one of the first schools that provided a serious education for girls. At the seminary, she met women who either were or would become famous writers, including Lydia Sigourney and Sara Willis, later widely known by her pen name, Fanny Fern. In 1832, Stowe's father, the ardent Presbyterian minister Lyman Beecher, accepted the presidency of Lane Theological Seminary and moved his family to Cincinnati, just across the Ohio River from the slaveholding state of Kentucky. There, Stowe observed fugitive slaves and became involved in antislavery activities. As a member of a local literary group, Stowe began to write short articles and stories, though her first publication was a highly successful textbook, *Primary Geography for Children* (1833). In 1836, she married Calvin Stowe, a young widower and professor at Lane Seminary. For the next fourteen years, Stowe balanced the responsibilities of caring for their young children and managing a household on a small academic salary. When she could claim some time to herself, she wrote articles and sketches for various periodicals, including *Godey's Lady's Book*, the popular magazine for women, and the *New-York Evangelist*, a religious newspaper devoted to reforms such as antislavery and temperance. Stowe also published a collection of domestic sketches and fiction, *The Mayflower, or Sketches of*

Harriet Beecher Stowe

The Boston firm of Southworth and Hawes, which specialized in portraits of celebrities, made this daguerreotype of Stowe in 1843. By then a rising literary star, Stowe would later gain even greater fame as the author of *Uncle Tom's Cabin.*

Scenes and Characters among the Descendents of the Pilgrims (1843). Although it did not sell well, Stowe was gradually making a name for herself as a writer, and her steady work was supplementing the household income.

In 1850, Calvin Stowe accepted a new position as a professor at Bowdoin College in Brunswick, Maine, where the family moved from Ohio. Stowe soon agreed to become a contributor to the *National Era*, a new antislavery newspaper edited by Gamaliel Bailey. In the prospectus for the newspaper – published in Washington, DC, where slavery was legal – Bailey explained that his purpose was "to lay before the Southern men . . . such facts and arguments as may serve to throw further light upon the question of slavery, and its disposition." Determined to use literature as well as political articles to illustrate the evils of slavery, Bailey invited a number of popular women writers to participate in this purpose, including E.D.E.N. Southworth, Grace Greenwood, Alice and Phoebe Cary, and Stowe. After she wrote several brief sketches for the *Era*, Bailey invited Stowe to write a new story, one that might be serialized over a few weeks. Like many northerners, Stowe and her family were reeling from the enactment in 1850 of the Fugitive Slave Act, which she decided to fight by writing a story about slavery. The first installment of *Uncle Tom's Cabin; or, Life among the Lowly* appeared in the *Era* on June 5, 1851. Initially planned as a three- or four-part serial, the story continued through forty-one installments, finally ending on April 1, 1852. During that period, the subscription list of the *National Era* grew from 8,000 to 28,000. The two-volume novel published shortly after the serialization concluded was even more successful. In fact, *Uncle Tom's Cabin* was the publication phenomenon of the century, selling 10,000 copies in the first week and 300,000 copies by the end of the year. It was the first blockbuster novel published in the United States, and Stowe was among the earliest of American celebrity writers.

__bedfordstmartins.com/ americanlit__ for research links on Stowe

Although nothing else she produced would or probably could have matched the success of *Uncle Tom's Cabin*, Stowe continued to write and publish. In order to counter Southern criticism that she had no firsthand knowledge of slavery, and that her novel was full of falsehoods, Stowe published a collection of articles, stories, and accounts of slavery called *The Key to Uncle Tom's Cabin* (1853). Her second antislavery novel, *Dred: A Tale of the Great Dismal Swamp*, appeared in 1856. The following year she assisted in the founding of an important new literary monthly, the *Atlantic Monthly*, one of the numerous magazines to which she contributed essays, sketches, stories, and serialized fiction during the following two decades. Although she maintained her interest in abolition, Stowe increasingly returned to the domestic subjects of her early work, especially in a series of novels set in New England: *The Minister's Wooing* (1859), *The Pearl of Orr's Island* (1862), *Oldtown Folks* (1869), and *Poganuc People* (1878), which was closely based upon her childhood in Connecticut. Although she lived for eighteen more years, until 1896, that elegiac novel effectively marked the end of her long and prolific literary career, which had made Stowe internationally famous as a writer and a revered cultural figure in the United States.

Stowe's "Trials of a Housekeeper." This sketch appeared in the popular *Godey's Lady's Book* in January 1839. Famous for its colored illustrations of fashions, recipes, and advice on a range of domestic matters, *Godey's* also published a wide variety of literary works by both men and women. Writers such as Nathaniel Hawthorne and Edgar Allan Poe were eager to have their work accepted by Sarah Josepha Hale, who edited the magazine from 1837 to 1877. "Trials of a Housekeeper" is a lighthearted account of the difficulties of finding and keeping good domestic help, a frequent topic in the pages of *Godey's*. Most middle-class households in the North employed a servant or two, frequently a woman who served as an all-purpose housekeeper. Having a domestic servant was not necessarily an indication of affluence but rather a sign of class consciousness and social status. While "ladies" were expected to know how to do fine sewing and manage a household, they were not expected to cook, clean, and take care of menial chores. The text is taken from the original printing in *Godey's Lady's Book* (January 1839).

TRIALS OF A HOUSEKEEPER

I have a detail of very homely grievances to present, but such as they are, many a heart will feel them to be heavy – *the trials of a housekeeper.*

"Poh!" says one of the lords of creation, taking his cigar out of his mouth, and twirling it between his two first fingers, "what a fuss these women do make of this simple matter of *managing a family*! I can't see for my life, as there is any thing so extraordinary to be done, in this matter of housekeeping – only three meals a day to be got and cleared off, and it really seems to take up the whole of their mind from morning till night. *I* could keep house without so much of a flurry, I know."

Now prithee, good brother, listen to my story, and see how much you know about it. I came to this enlightened west about a year since, and was duly established in a comfortable country residence within a mile and a half of the city, and there commenced the enjoyment of domestic felicity. I had been married about three months, and had been previously *in love* in the most approved romantic way with all the proprieties of moon light walks, serenades sentimental, billet-doux, and everlasting attachment.

After having been allowed, as I said, about three months to get over this sort of thing, and to prepare for realities, I was located for life, as aforesaid. My family consisted of myself and husband, a female friend as a visiter, and two brothers of my good man, who were engaged with him in business.

I pass over the two or three first days spent in that process of hammering boxes, breaking crockery, knocking things down and picking them up again, which is commonly called getting to housekeeping; as usual, carpets were sewed and stretched, laid down and taken up to be sewed over – things were *re*formed, *trans*formed, and *con*formed, till at last a settled order began to appear. But now came up the great point of all. During our confusion, we had cooked and eaten our meals in a very miscellaneous and pastoral manner; eating now from the top of a barrel, and now from a fireboard, laid on two chairs, and drinking some from tea cups and some from saucers, and some from tumblers, and some from a pitcher big enough to be drowned in, and sleeping, some on sofas, and some on straggling beds and mattrasses, thrown down here and there, wherever there was room. All these pleasant barbarities were now at an end – the house was in order – the dishes put up in their places – three regular meals were to be administered in one day, all in an orderly civilized form – beds were to be made – rooms swept and dusted – dishes washed – knives scoured, and all the et cetera to be attended to. Now for getting "*help*," as Mrs. Trollope[1] says, and where and how were we to get it; we knew very few persons in the city, and how were we to accomplish the matter. At length the "house of *employment*" was mentioned, and my husband was despatched thither regularly every day for a week, while I, in the mean time, was very nearly *despatched*, by the abundance of work at home. At length one evening as I was sitting completely exhausted, thinking of resorting to the last feminine expedient for supporting life, viz. a *good fit of crying*, my husband made his appearance with a most triumphant air at the door – "There! Margaret! I have got you a couple at last – cook and chamber-maid!" – so saying he flourished open the door, and gave to my view the picture of a little, dry, snuffy looking old woman, and a great staring Dutch girl in a green bonnet with red ribbons – mouth wide open, and hands and feet that would have made a Greek sculptor open *his* mouth too. I addressed forthwith a few words of encouragement to each of this cultivated looking couple, and proceeded to ask their names, and forthwith the old woman began to snuffle and to wipe her face with what was left of an old silk pocket-handkerchief, preparatory to speaking, while the young lady opened her mouth wider, and looked around with a frightened air, as if meditating an escape. After some preliminaries, however, I found out that my old woman was Mrs. Tibbins, and my Hebe's name was *Kotterin*; also, that she knew much more Dutch than English, and not any too much of either. The old lady was the cook – I ventured a few inquiries – "Had she ever cooked?"

"Yes, ma'am, sartin; she had lived at two or three places in the city."

"I expect, my dear;" said my husband, confidently, "that she is an experienced cook, and so your troubles are over," and he went to reading his newspaper. I said no more, but determined to wait till morning. The breakfast, to be sure did not do much honour to the talents of my official, but it was the first time, and the place was new to her. After breakfast was cleared away, I proceeded to give directions for dinner; it was merely a plain joint of meat, I said, to be roasted in the tin oven.[2] The *experienced cook* looked at me, with a stare of entire vacuity – "the tin oven," I repeated, "stands there," pointing to it.

She walked up to it and touched it with as much appearance of suspicion as if it had been an electrical battery, and then looked round at me with a look of such helpless ignorance that my soul was moved – "I never see one of them things before," said she.

1. **Mrs. Trollope:** Frances Trollope (1780–1863), an English writer, wrote a critical commentary on the United States in her two-volume *Domestic Manners of the Americans* (1832). Her book, unpopular with many Americans, prompted a series of defensive comments, books, and articles.
2. **tin oven:** A common kitchen utensil was a vertical tin reflecting oven in which meat for roasting was suspended over a drip pan. The tin sides and top reflected the heat of the fire and roasted the meat evenly and efficiently.

"Never saw a tin oven!" I exclaimed. "I thought you said you had cooked in two or three families."

"They does not have such things as them, though," rejoined my old lady. Nothing was to be done of course, but to instruct her into the philosophy of the case, and having spitted the joint, and given numberless directions, I walked off to my room to superintend the operations of Kotterin, to whom I had committed the making of my bed, and the sweeping of my room; it never having come into my head that there *could be* a wrong way of making a bed, and to this day it is a marvel to me how any one could arrange pillows and quilts to make such a non-descript appearance as mine now presented. One glance showed me that Kotterin, also, was "*just caught*," and that I had as much to do in her department as that of my old lady.

Just then the door bell rang – "Oh, there is the door bell!" I exclaimed – "run Kotterin, and show them into the parlour."

Kotterin started to run, as directed, and then stopped, and stood looking round on all the doors, and on me with a wofully puzzled air – "The street door," said I, pointing towards the entry. Kotterin blundered into the entry, and stood gazing up with a look of stupid wonder at the bell ringing without any hands, while I went to the door and let in the company, before she could fairly be made to understand the connection between the ringing and the phenomena of admission.

As dinner time approached, I sent word into my kitchen to have it sent on, but recollecting the state of the heads of department there, I soon followed my own orders. I found the tin oven standing out in the middle of the kitchen, and my cook seated a la-Turk in front of it, contemplating the roast meat, with full as puzzled an air as in the morning. I once more explained the mystery of taking it off, and assisted her to get it on to the platter, though somewhat cooled by having been so long set out for inspection. I was standing holding the spit in my hands, when Kotterin, who had heard the door bell ringing, and was determined this time to be in season, ran into the hall, and soon returning opened the kitchen door, and politely ushered in three or four fashionable looking ladies, exclaiming, "here she is!" As these were strangers from the city who had come to make their first call, this introduction was far from proving an eligible one – the look of thunderstruck astonishment with which I greeted their first appearance, as I stood brandishing the spit, and the terrified snuffling and staring of poor Mrs. Tibbins, who had again recourse to her old pocket handkerchief, almost entirely vanquished their gravity, and it was evident that they were on the point of a broad laugh; so recovering my self-possession, I apologised, and led the way to the parlour.

Let these few incidents be a specimen of the four eventful weeks that I spent with these "*helps*," during which time I did almost as much work, with twice as much anxiety, as when there was nobody there, and yet every thing went wrong besides. The young gentlemen complained of the patches of starch grimmed to their collars, and the streaks of black coal ironed into their dickies; while one week every pocket handkerchief in the house was starched so stiff that you might as well have carried an earthen plate in your pocket – the tumblers looked muddy – the plates were never washed clean or wiped dry, unless I attended to each one; and as to eating and drinking, we experienced a variety that we had not before considered possible.

At length the old woman vanished from the stage, and was succeeded by a knowing, active, capable damsel, with a temper like a steel trap, who remained with me just one week, and then went off in a fit of spite. To her succeeded a rosy, good-natured, merry lass, who broke the crockery, burnt the dinner, tore the clothes in ironing, and knocked down every thing that stood in her way about the house, without at all discomposing herself about the matter. One night she took the stopper from a barrel of molasses and came singing off up stairs, while the molasses ran soberly out into the cellar bottom all night, till by morning it was in a state of *universal emancipation*. Having done this, and also despatched an entire set of tea things, by letting the waiter fall, she one day made her disappearance.

Then for a wonder, there fell to my lot a tidy efficient trained English girl – pretty, and genteel and neat, and knowing how to do every thing, and with the sweetest temper in the world. "Now," said I to myself, "I shall *rest* from my labours." Every thing about the house began to go right, and looked as clean and genteel as Mary's own pretty self. But alas, this period of repose was interrupted by the vision of a clever, trim looking young man, who for some weeks could be heard scraping his boots at the kitchen door every Sunday night – and at last Miss Mary, with some smiling and blushing, gave me to understand that she must leave in two weeks.

"Why, Mary," said I, feeling a little mischievous, "don't you like the place?"

"Oh, yes, ma'am."

"Then why do you look for another?"

"I am not going to another place."

"What, Mary, are you going to learn a trade?"

"No, ma'am."

"Why, then, what do you mean to do?"

"I expect to keep house *myself* ma'am," said she, laughing and blushing.

"Oh, ho," said I, "that is it" – and so in two weeks I lost the best little girl in the world – peace to her memory.

After this came an interregnum, which put me in mind of the chapter in Chronicles that I used to read with great delight when a child, where Basha and Elah, and Tihni, and Zimri, and Omri, one after the other came on to the throne of Israel,[3] all in the compass of half-a-dozen verses. We had one old woman who staid a week and went away with the misery in her tooth – one *young* woman who ran away and got married – one cook, who came at night and went off before light in the morning – one very clever girl, who staid a month and then went away because her mother was sick – another who staid six weeks, and was taken with the fever herself, and during all this time who can speak the damage and destruction wrought in the domestic paraphernalia, by passing through these multiplied hands?

What shall we do? Shall we go for slavery, or shall we give up houses, have no furniture to take care of – keep merely a bag of meal, a porridge pot, and a pudding stick, and sit in our tent door in real patriarchial independence? What shall we do?

[1839]

3. **Basha . . . throne of Israel:** Stowe refers to the brief genealogies of several kings of Israel, as described in 1 Chronicles.

Stowe's "The Seamstress." This sketch was published in Stowe's second book, *The Mayflower, or Sketches of Scenes and Characters among the Descendents of the Pilgrims* (1843). As the title indicates, the collection primarily concerned life in New England, but Stowe wrote the stories and sketches while she was a member of a Cincinnati literary group, the Semi-Colon Club. In a preface to the book, her sister Catherine Beecher commented on the proliferation of sketches and tales that were being published in the 1830s, observing that "The worst stands about an equal chance with the best." To Beecher, her sister's work was among the best, and *The Mayflower* certainly established Stowe as a serious writer. In this early story advocating social reform, Stowe reveals the plight of widowed women left without the resources to make livings for themselves. The text is taken from the second edition, published as *The May Flower and Miscellaneous Writings* (1855).

THE SEAMSTRESS

"Few, save the poor, feel for the poor;
    The rich know not how hard
It is to be of needful food
    And needful rest debarred.

Their paths are paths of plenteousness;
    They sleep on silk and down;
They never think how wearily
    The weary head lies down.

They never by the window sit,
    And see the gay pass by,
Yet take their weary work again,
    And with a mournful eye."

– L. E. L.[1]

However fine and elevated, in a sentimental point of view, may have been the poetry of this gifted writer, we think we have never seen any thing from this source that *ought* to give a better opinion of her than the little ballad from which the above verses are taken.

They show that the accomplished authoress possessed, not merely a knowledge of the dreamy ideal wants of human beings, but the more pressing and homely ones, which the fastidious and poetical are often the last to appreciate. The sufferings of poverty are not confined to those of the common, squalid, every day inured to hardships, and ready, with open hand, to receive charity, let it come to them as it will. There is another class on whom it presses with still heavier power – the generous, the decent, the self-respecting, who have struggled with their lot in silence, "bearing all things, hoping all things,"

1. **Few . . . a mournful eye:** The epigraph was written by Letitia Elizabeth Landon (1802-1838), an English poet who signed her work L. E. L.

and willing to endure all things, rather than breathe a word of complaint, or to acknowledge, even to themselves, that their own efforts will not be sufficient for their own necessities.

Pause with me a while at the door of yonder room, whose small window overlooks a little court below. It is inhabited by a widow and her daughter, dependent entirely on the labors of the needle, and those other slight and precarious resources, which are all that remain to woman when left to struggle her way through the world alone. It contains all their small earthly store, and there is scarce an article of its little stock of furniture that has not been thought of, and toiled for, and its price calculated over and over again, before every thing could be made right for its purchase. Every article is arranged with the utmost neatness and care; nor is the most costly furniture of a fashionable parlor more sedulously guarded from a scratch or a rub, than is that brightly-varnished bureau, and that neat cherry tea table and bedstead. The floor, too, boasted once a carpet; but old Time has been busy with it, picking a hole here, and making a thin place there; and though the old fellow has been followed up by the most indefatigable zeal in darning, the marks of his mischievous fingers are too plain to be mistaken. It is true, a kindly neighbor has given a bit of faded baize, which has been neatly clipped and bound, and spread down over an entirely unmanageable hole in front of the fireplace; and other places have been repaired with pieces of different colors; and yet, after all, it is evident that the poor carpet is not long for this world.

But the best face is put upon every thing. The little cupboard in the corner, that contains a few china cups, and one or two antiquated silver spoons, relics of better days, is arranged with jealous neatness, and the white muslin window curtain, albeit the muslin be old, has been carefully whitened and starched, and smoothly ironed, and put up with exact precision; and on the bureau, covered by a snowy cloth, are arranged a few books and other memorials of former times, and a faded miniature, which, though it have little about it to interest a stranger, is more precious to the poor widow than every thing besides.

Mrs. Ames is seated in her rocking chair, supported by a pillow, and busy cutting out work, while her daughter, a slender, sickly-looking girl, is sitting by the window, intent on some fine stitching.

Mrs. Ames, in former days, was the wife of a respectable merchant, and the mother of an affectionate family. But evil fortune had followed her with a steadiness that seemed like the stern decree of some adverse fate rather than the ordinary dealings of a merciful Providence. First came a heavy run of losses in business; then long and expensive sickness in the family, and the death of children. Then there was the selling of the large house and elegant furniture, to retire to a humbler style of living; and finally, the sale of all the property, with the view of quitting the shores of a native land, and commencing life again in a new one. But scarcely had the exiled family found themselves in the port of a foreign land, when the father was suddenly smitten down by the hand of death, and his lonely grave made in a land of strangers. The widow, broken-hearted and discouraged, had still a wearisome journey before her ere she could reach any whom she could consider as her friends. With her two daughters, entirely unattended, and with her finances impoverished by detention and sickness, she performed the tedious journey.

Arrived at the place of her destination, she found herself not only without immediate resources, but considerably in debt to one who had advanced money for her travelling expenses. With silent endurance she met the necessities of her situation. Her daughters, delicately reared, and hitherto carefully educated, were placed out to service, and Mrs. Ames sought for employment as a nurse. The younger child fell sick, and the hard earnings of the mother were all exhausted in the care of her; and though she recovered in part, she was declared by her physician to be the victim of a disease which would never leave her till it terminated her life.

As soon, however, as her daughter was so far restored as not to need her immediate care, Mrs. Ames resumed her laborious employment. Scarcely had she been able, in this way, to discharge the debts for her journey and to furnish the small room we have described, when the hand of disease was laid heavily on herself. Too resolute and persevering to give way to the first attacks of pain and weakness, she still continued her fatiguing employment till her system was entirely prostrated. Thus all possibility of pursuing her business was cut off, and nothing remained but what could be accomplished by her own and her daughter's dexterity at the needle. It is at this time we ask you to look in upon the mother and daughter.

Mrs. Ames is sitting up, the first time for a week, and even to-day she is scarcely fit to do so; but she remembers that the month is coming round, and her rent will soon be due; and in her feebleness she will stretch every nerve to meet her engagements with punctilious exactness.

Wearied at length with cutting out, and measuring, and drawing threads, she leans back in her chair, and her eye rests on the pale face of her daughter, who has been sitting for two hours intent on her stitching.

"Ellen, my child, your head aches; don't work so steadily."

"O, no, it don't ache *much*," said she, too conscious of looking very much tired. Poor girl! had she remained in the situation in which she was born, she would now have been skipping about, and enjoying life as other young girls of fifteen do; but now there is no choice of employments for her – no youthful companions – no visiting – no pleasant walks in the fresh air. Evening and morning, it is all the same; headache or sideache, it is all one. She must hold on the same unvarying task – a wearisome thing for a girl of fifteen.

But see! the door opens, and Mrs. Ames's face brightens as her other daughter enters. Mary has become a domestic in a neighboring family, where her faithfulness and kindness of heart have caused her to be regarded more as a daughter and a sister than as a servant. "Here, mother, is your rent money," she exclaimed; "so do put up your work and rest a while. I can get enough to pay it next time before the month comes around again."

"Dear child, I do wish you would ever think to get any thing for yourself," said Mrs. Ames. "I cannot consent to use up all your earnings, as I have done lately, and all Ellen's too; you must have a new dress this spring, and that bonnet of yours is not decent any longer."

"O, no, mother! I have made over my blue calico, and you would be surprised to see how well it looks; and my best frock, when it is washed and darned, will answer some time longer. And then Mrs. Grant has given me a ribbon, and when my bonnet is whitened and trimmed it will look very well. And so," she added, "I brought you some wine this afternoon; you know the doctor says you need wine."

"Dear child, I want to see you take some comfort of your money yourself."

"Well, I do take comfort of it, mother. It is more comfort to be able to help you than to wear all the finest dresses in the world."

Two months from this dialogue found our little family still more straitened and perplexed. Mrs. Ames had been confined all the time with sickness, and the greater part of Ellen's time and strength was occupied with attending to her.

Very little sewing could the poor girl now do, in the broken intervals that remained to her; and the wages of Mary were not only used as fast as earned, but she anticipated two months in advance.

Mrs. Ames had been better for a day or two, and had been sitting up, exerting all her strength to finish a set of shirts which had been sent in to make. "The money for them will just pay our rent," sighed she; "and if we can do a little more this week —"

"Dear mother, you are so tired," said Ellen; "do lie down, and not worry any more till I come back."

Ellen went out, and passed on till she came to the door of an elegant house, whose damask and muslin window curtains indicated a fashionable residence.

Mrs. Elmore was sitting in her splendidly-furnished parlor, and around her lay various fancy articles which two young girls were busily unrolling. "What a lovely pink scarf!" said one, throwing it over her shoulders and skipping before a mirror; while the other exclaimed, "Do look at these pocket handkerchiefs, mother! what elegant lace!"

"Well, girls," said Mrs. Elmore, "these handkerchiefs are a shameful piece of extravagance. I wonder you will insist on having such things."

"La, mamma, every body has such now; Laura Seymour has half a dozen that cost more than these, and her father is no richer than ours."

"Well," said Mrs. Elmore, "rich or not rich, it seems to make very little odds; we do not seem to have half as much money to spare as we did when we lived in the little house in Spring Street. What with new furnishing the house, and getting every thing you boys and girls say you must have, we are poorer, if any thing, than we were then."

"Ma'am, here is Mrs. Ames's girl come with some sewing," said the servant.

"Show her in," said Mrs. Elmore.

Ellen entered timidly, and handed her bundle of work to Mrs. Elmore, who forthwith proceeded to a minute scrutiny of the articles; for she prided herself on being very particular as to her sewing. But, though the work had been executed by feeble hands and aching eyes, even Mrs. Elmore could detect no fault in it.

"Well, it is very prettily done," said she. "What does your mother charge?"

Ellen handed a neatly-folded bill which she had drawn for her mother. "I must say, I think your mother's prices are very high," said Mrs. Elmore, examining her nearly empty purse; "every thing is getting so dear that one hardly knows how to live." Ellen looked at the fancy articles, and glanced around the room with an air of innocent astonishment. "Ah," said Mrs. Elmore, "I dare say it seems to you as if persons in our situation had no need of economy; but, for my part, I feel the need of it more and more every day." As she spoke she handed Ellen the three dollars, which, though it was not a quarter the price of one of the handkerchiefs, was all that she and her sick mother could claim in the world.

"There," said she; "tell your mother I like her work very much, but I do not think I can afford to employ her, if I can find any one to work cheaper."

Now, Mrs. Elmore was not a hard-hearted woman, and if Ellen had come as a beggar to solicit help for her sick mother, Mrs. Elmore would have fitted out a basket of provisions, and sent a bottle of wine, and a bundle of old clothes, and all the *et cetera* of such occasions; but the sight of *a bill* always aroused all the instinctive sharpness of her business-like education. She never had the dawning of an idea that it was her duty to pay any body any more than she could possibly help; nay, she had an indistinct notion that it was her *duty* as an economist to make every body take as little as possible. When she and her daughters lived in Spring Street, to which she had alluded, they used to spend the greater part of their time at home, and the family sewing was commonly done among themselves. But since they had moved into a large house, and set up a carriage, and addressed themselves to being genteel, the girls found that they had altogether too much to do to attend to their own sewing, much less to perform any for their father and brothers. And their mother found her hands abundantly full in overlooking her large house, in taking care of expensive furniture, and in superintending her increased train of servants. The sewing, therefore, was put out; and Mrs. Elmore *felt it a duty* to get it done the cheapest way she could. Nevertheless, Mrs. Elmore was too notable a lady, and her sons and daughters were altogether too fastidious as to the make and quality of their clothing, to admit the idea of its being done in any but the most complete and perfect manner.

Mrs. Elmore never accused herself of want of charity for the poor; but she had never considered that the best class of the poor are those who never ask charity. She did not consider that, by paying liberally those who were honestly and independently struggling for themselves; she was really doing a greater charity than by giving indiscriminately to a dozen applicants.

"Don't you think, mother, she says we charge too high for this work!" said Ellen, when she returned. "I am sure she did not know how much work we put in those shirts. She says she cannot give us any more work; she must look out for some body that will do it cheaper. I do not see how it is that people who live in such houses, and have so many beautiful things, can feel that they cannot afford to pay for what costs us so much."

"Well, child, they are more apt to feel so than people who live plainer."

"Well, I am sure," said Ellen, "we cannot afford to spend so much time as we have over these shirts for less money."

"Never mind, my dear," said the mother, soothingly; "here is a bundle of work that another lady has sent in, and if we get it done, we shall have enough for our rent, and something over to buy bread with."

It is needless to carry our readers over all the process of cutting, and fitting, and gathering, and stitching, necessary in making up six fine shirts. Suffice it to say that on

Saturday evening all but one were finished, and Ellen proceeded to carry them home, promising to bring the remaining one on Tuesday morning. The lady examined the work, and gave Ellen the money; but on Tuesday, when the child came with the remaining work, she found her in great ill humor. Upon reexamining the shirts, she had discovered that in some important respects they differed from directions she meant to have given, and supposed she had given; and, accordingly, she vented her displeasure on Ellen.

"Why didn't you make these shirts as I told you?" said she, sharply.

"We did," said Ellen, mildly; "mother measured by the pattern every part, and cut them herself."

"Your mother must be a fool, then, to make such a piece of work. I wish you would just take them back and alter them over;" and the lady proceeded with the directions, of which neither Ellen nor her mother till then had had any intimation. Unused to such language, the frightened Ellen took up her work and slowly walked homeward.

"O, dear, how my head does ache!" thought she to herself; "and poor mother! she said this morning she was afraid another of her sick turns was coming on, and we have all this work to pull out and do over."

"See here, mother," said she, with a disconsolate air, as she entered the room; "Mrs. Rudd says, take out all the bosoms, and rip off all the collars, and fix them quite another way. She says they are not like the pattern she sent; but she must have forgotten, for here it is. Look, mother; it is exactly as we made them."

"Well, my child, carry back the pattern, and show her that it is so."

"Indeed, mother, she spoke so cross to me, and looked at me so, that I do not feel as if I could go back."

"I will go for you, then," said the kind Maria Stephens, who had been sitting with Mrs. Ames while Ellen was out. "I will take the pattern and shirts, and tell her the exact truth about it. I am not afraid of her." Maria Stephens was a tailoress, who rented a room on the same floor with Mrs. Ames, a cheerful, resolute, go-forward little body, and ready always to give a helping hand to a neighbor in trouble. So she took the pattern and shirts, and set out on her mission.

But poor Mrs. Ames, though she professed to take a right view of the matter, and was very earnest in showing Ellen why she ought not to distress herself about it, still felt a shivering sense of the hardness and unkindness of the world coming over her. The bitter tears would spring to her eyes, in spite of every effort to suppress them, as she sat mournfully gazing on the little faded miniature before mentioned. "When *he* was alive, I never knew what poverty or trouble was," was the thought that often passed through her mind. And how many a poor forlorn one has thought the same!

Poor Mrs. Ames was confined to her bed for most of that week. The doctor gave absolute directions that she should do nothing, and keep entirely quiet – a direction very sensible indeed in the chamber of ease and competence, but hard to be observed in poverty and want.

What pains the kind and dutiful Ellen took that week to make her mother feel easy! How often she replied to her anxious questions, "that she was quite well," or "that her head did not ache *much!*" and by various other evasive expedients the child tried to persuade herself that she was speaking the truth. And during the times her mother slept, in the day or evening, she accomplished one or two pieces of plain work, with the price of which she expected to surprise her mother.

It was towards evening when Ellen took her finished work to the elegant dwelling of Mrs. Page. "I shall get a dollar for this," said she; "enough to pay for mother's wine and medicine."

"This work is done very neatly," said Mrs. Page, "and here is some more I should like to have finished in the same way."

Ellen looked up wistfully, hoping Mrs. Page was going to pay her for the last work. But Mrs. Page was only searching a drawer for a pattern, which she put into Ellen's hands, and after explaining how she wanted her work done, dismissed her without saying a word about the expected dollar.

Poor Ellen tried two or three times, as she was going out, to turn round and ask for it; but before she could decide what to say, she found herself in the street.

Mrs. Page was an amiable, kind-hearted woman, but one who was so used to large sums of money that she did not realize how great an affair a single dollar might seem to other persons. For this reason, when Ellen had worked incessantly at the new work put into her hands, that she might get the money for all together, she again disappointed her in the payment.

"I'll send the money round to-morrow," said she, when Ellen at last found courage to ask for it. But to-morrow came, and Ellen was forgotten; and it was not till after one or two applications more that the small sum was paid.

But these sketches are already long enough, and let us hasten to close them. Mrs. Ames found liberal friends, who could appreciate and honor her integrity of principle and loveliness of character, and by their assistance she was raised to see more prosperous days; and she, and the delicate Ellen, and warm-hearted Mary were enabled to have a home and fireside of their own, and to enjoy something like the return of their former prosperity.

We have given these sketches, drawn from real life, because we think there is in general too little consideration on the part of those who give employment to those in situations like the widow here described. The giving of employment is a very important branch of charity, inasmuch as it assists that class of the poor who are the most deserving. It should be looked on in this light, and the arrangements of a family be so made that a suitable compensation can be given, and prompt and cheerful payment be made, without the dread of transgressing the rules of economy.

It is better to teach our daughters to do without expensive ornaments or fashionable elegances; better even to deny ourselves the pleasure of large donations or direct subscriptions to public charities, rather than to curtail the small stipend of her whose "candle goeth not out by night," and who labors with her needle for herself and the helpless dear ones dependent on her exertions.

[1843, 1855]

Stowe's "The Freeman's Dream: A Parable." This brief sketch was Stowe's first significant expression of her antislavery sentiments. A "parable" designed to reveal the inhumanity of slavery, the sketch appeared in the *National Era* on August 1, 1850, at the height of the controversy over the Compromise of 1850. A key provision of the Compromise, the Fugitive Slave Act, had by then already generated months of contentious debate in the Senate, the greatest debate in congressional history. By contributing the sketch to the *Era*, which was published in Washington, D.C., Stowe perhaps sought both to shape public opinion and to fuel congressional opposition to the bill. Nonetheless, the bill passed the Senate on August 12 and the House on September 12, after which it was signed into law by President Fillmore on September 18, 1850, roughly six weeks after Stowe's sketch was published. The text is taken from the *National Era*, August 1, 1850.

THE FREEMAN'S DREAM: A PARABLE

It seemed to him that it was a fair summer evening, and he was walking calmly up and down his estate, watching the ripening grain and listening to the distant voices of his children, as they played by his door, and the song of his wife as she rocked her babe to rest, and the soul of the man grew soft within him, and he gave God thanks with a full heart.

But now there came towards him in the twilight a poor black man, worn and wasted, his clothes rent and travel-soiled, and his step crouching and fearful. He was one that had dwelt in darkness, and as one that had been long dead; and behind him stood, fearfully, a thin and trembling woman, with a wailing babe at her bosom, and a frightened child clinging to her skirts; and the man held out his hand wistfully, and begged for food and shelter, if only for one night, for the pursuer was behind him, and his soul failed him for fear.

The man was not hard, and his heart misgave him when he looked on the failing eye and toil-worn face – when he saw the worn and trembling hands stretched forth; but then he bethought him of human laws, and he feared to befriend him, and he hardened his heart, and set his face as a flint, and bade him pass on, and trouble him not.

And it was so that after he passed on, he saw that the pursuers came up with him, and the man and the woman could not escape, because they were weary and footsore, and there was no more strength in them. And the man heard their screams, and saw them bound and taken by them that would not show mercy.

And after these things the man dreamed, and it seemed to him that the sky grew dark, and the earth rocked to and fro, and the heavens flashed with strange light, and a distant rush, as of wings, was heard, and suddenly, in mid heavens, appeared the sign of the Son of Man, with his mighty angels. Upward, with countless myriads, dizzied and astounded, he seemed to be borne from the earth towards the great white throne and Him that sat thereon, before whose face the heavens and the earth fled away.

Onward, a resistless impulse impelled him towards the bar of the mighty Judge, and before him, as if written in fire, rose in a moment all the thoughts and words and deeds of his past life; and as if he had been the only son of earth to be judged, he felt himself standing alone and trembling before that all-searching Presence. Then an awful voice pierced his soul, saying – "Depart from me ye accursed! for I was an hungered, and ye gave me no meat; I was thirsty, and ye gave me no drink; I was a stranger, and ye took me not in."[1] And, terrified and subdued, the man made answer, "Lord, where?" And immediately rose before him these poor fugitive slaves, whom he had spurned from his door; and the Judge made answer – "Inasmuch as ye did it not to one of the least of these my brethren, ye did it not to me."[2] And with that, terrified and affrighted, the man awoke.

Of late, there have seemed to be many in this nation, who seem to think that there is no standard of right and wrong higher than an act of Congress, or an interpretation of the United States Constitution. It is humiliating to think that there should be in the church of Christ men and ministers who should need to be reminded that the laws of their Master are above human laws which come in conflict with them; and that though heaven and earth pass away, His word shall not pass away.

Are not the hungry, the thirsty, the stranger, the naked, the prisoner, and every form of bleeding, suffering humanity, as much under the protection of Christ in the person of the black as the white – of the bond as the free? Has he not solemnly told us, and once for all, that every needy human being is His brother, and that neglect of his wants is neglect of Himself?

Shall any doubt if he *may* help the toil-worn, escaping fugitive, sick in heart, weary in limb, hungry and heartsore – let him rather ask, shall he dare refuse him help? To him, too, shall come a dread hour, when a lonely fugitive from life's shore, in unknown lands, he must beg for shelter and help. The only Saviour in that hour is Him who has said, "Inasmuch as ye did it not to the least of these my brethren, ye did it not to *me*!"

[1850]

1. "Depart from me . . . ye took me not in": Matthew 25:43.
2. "Inasmuch . . . ye did it not to me": Matthew 25:45.

Stowe's Preface to *Uncle Tom's Cabin*. In March 1852, as *Uncle Tom's Cabin* was nearing the end of its serialization in the *National Era*, Stowe signed a contract for its publication in book form by John P. Jewett. According to Jewett, his wife had closely followed the serialization and had frequently urged him to publish the book, which became the best-selling novel in the United States. Already well aware of the impact that her story had made on readers of the *Era*, Stowe wrote for the book edition the following preface, in which she explained her purpose in writing the novel and her hopes for its impact on the American public. The text is taken from the first edition of *Uncle Tom's Cabin; or, Life among the Lowly* (1852).

PREFACE TO *UNCLE TOM'S CABIN*

The scenes of this story, as its title indicates, lie among a race hitherto ignored by the associations of polite and refined society; an exotic race, whose ancestors, born beneath a tropic sun, brought with them, and perpetuated to their descendants, a character so essentially unlike the hard and dominant Anglo-Saxon race,[1] as for many years to have won from it only misunderstanding and contempt.

But another and better day is dawning; every influence of literature, of poetry, and of art, in our times, is becoming more and more in unison with the great master chord of Christianity, "good-will to man." The poet, the painter, and the artist now seek out and embellish the common and gentler humanities of life, and, under the allurements of fiction, breathe a humanizing and subduing influence, favorable to the development of the great principles of Christian brotherhood.

The hand of benevolence is everywhere stretched out, searching into abuses, righting wrongs, alleviating distresses, and bringing to the knowledge and sympathies of the world the lowly, the oppressed, and the forgotten. In this general movement, unhappy Africa is at last remembered; Africa, who began the race of civilization and human progress in the dim, gray dawn of early time, but who, for centuries, has lain bound and bleeding at the foot of civilized and Christianized humanity, imploring compassion in vain.

But the heart of the dominant race, who have been her conquerors, her hard masters, has at length been turned towards her in mercy; and it has been seen how far nobler it is in nations to protect the feeble than to oppress them. Thanks be to God, the world has at length outlived the slave-trade!

The object of these sketches is to awaken sympathy and feeling for the African race, as they exist among us; to show their wrongs and sorrows, under a system so necessarily cruel and unjust as to defeat and do away the good effects of all that can be attempted for them, by their best friends, under it. In doing this, the author can sincerely disclaim any invidious feeling towards those individuals who, often without any fault of their own, are involved in the trials and embarrassments of the legal relations of slavery. Experience has shown her that some of the noblest of minds and hearts are often thus involved; and no one knows better than they do, that what may be gathered of the evils of slavery from sketches like these is not the half that could be told of the unspeakable whole.

In the Northern States, these representations may, perhaps, be thought caricatures; in their Southern States are witnesses who know their fidelity. What personal knowledge the author has had, of the truth of incidents such as are here related, will appear in its time. It is a comfort to hope, as so many of the world's sorrows and wrongs have, from age to age, been lived down, so a time shall come when sketches similar to these shall be valuable only as memorials of what has long ceased to be. When an enlightened and

1. **Anglo-Saxon race:** Stowe refers to a common notion in the nineteenth century that the descendents of the Anglo-Saxons in England were a superior race.

Christianized community shall have, on the shores of Africa,[2] laws, language, and literature, drawn from among us, may then, the scenes from the house of bondage be to them like the remembrance of Egypt to the Israelite, – a motive of thankfulness to Him who hath redeemed them! For, while politicians contend, and men are swerved this way and that by conflicting tides of interest and passion, the great cause of human liberty is in the hands of One, of whom it is said: –

"He shall not fail nor be discouraged
Till he have set judgment in the earth."

"He shall deliver the needy when he crieth,
The poor, and him that hath no helper."

"He shall redeem their soul from deceit and violence,
And precious shall their blood be in his sight."[3]

[1852]

---

2. **on the shores of Africa:** Some of those involved in the antislavery movement supported colonization, a plan to establish colonies for freed slaves in Africa.
3. **He . . . in his sight:** Isaiah 42:4 and Psalms 72:12-14.

Harriet Jacobs

[1813-1897]

Harriet Ann Jacobs was born into slavery in Edenton, North Carolina, in 1813. Following the death of her mother in 1819, Jacobs was sold to Margaret Horniblow, who taught her to read and sew. After Horniblow's death in 1825, Jacobs became the property of Horniblow's three-year-old niece, Mary Matilda Norcom, the daughter of James Norcom, a physician. As a teenager, Jacobs was constantly subject to sexual harassment by Norcom and blamed by his wife for his unwelcome attention to her. While embroiled in that impossible situation, Jacobs fell in love with Samuel Tredwell Sawyer, a white attorney and later U.S. congressman (1837-39). With Sawyer, Jacobs had two children: a son, Joseph, born in 1829, and a daughter, Louisa Matilda, born in 1833. Jacobs's consensual relationship with Sawyer infuriated Norcom, who sent Jacobs to a nearby plantation where she endured brutal treatment. Jacobs escaped from the plantation and, with the help of her family and friends, hid first in a swamp and then in the attic of her free grandmother, Molly Horniblow. Norcom, who never gave up trying to capture the elusive Jacobs, issued a $100 reward for her return, noting in an advertisement published on July 4, 1835, that "She speaks easily and fluently." (See p. 783.) Soon after her flight, Sawyer bought Jacobs's children from Norcom but did not free them. In 1842, after

bedfordstmartins.com/americanlit *for research links on Jacobs* seven years of hiding in her grandmother's attic, Jacobs escaped to New York City and worked as a domestic servant for Nathaniel P. Willis, a successful journalist and writer. She later lived for a time in Rochester, New York, where she became friendly with Frederick Douglass and two Quaker abolitionists, Isaac and Amy Post. Fearing capture as a result of the passage of the fugitive slave law, Jacobs returned to New York City in 1852 to work again as a domestic for Willis. In that year, Willis's wife, Cornelia Grinnell Willis, purchased Jacobs and her children and arranged for their emancipation.

Throughout her years of flight and hiding, Jacobs read and developed her skills as a writer. While she was living in Rochester, she worked in the antislavery reading room of Douglass's newspaper, the *North Star*. Jacobs's first publication was an anonymous "Letter from a Fugitive Slave," published in 1853. She subsequently published other letters and began to write the narrative of her experiences in and escape from slavery, *Incidents in the Life of a Slave Girl*, which was published with the assistance of Lydia Maria Child in 1861. Although the book received favorable reviews and was warmly welcomed by the abolitionists, the outbreak of the Civil War blunted the force of Jacobs's story and sales were disappointing. Between 1862 and 1868, Jacobs worked with the Quakers to organize schools and other institutions for newly freed slaves, first in Washington, D.C., and after the Union victory in Virginia and Georgia. While in the

Emblem of American Abolitionists

The figure of a chained and kneeling male slave became famous as the emblem of Britain's Society for the Abolition of Slavery. American abolitionists adopted the image, later adding a second figure that revealed their growing awareness of the plight of female slaves as well as their support of women's rights. Many antislavery activists, both male and female, were also deeply involved in the early feminist movement in the United States.

South, she briefly returned to her birthplace and scenes of her traumatic early experiences in North Carolina, a visit she described in a letter to Ednah Dow Cheney, secretary of the New England Freedmen's Aid Society. "I am sitting under a tree not twelve feet from where I suffered all the crushing weight of slavery," Jacobs observed; "thank God the bitter cup is drained of its last dreg." At the end of the letter, Jacobs noted that she had sent Cheney's daughter some jasmine blossoms, adding, "tell her they bear the fragrance of freedom." After returning to the North, Jacobs lived with her daughter in Cambridge, Massachusetts, and later in Washington, D.C., where she died in 1897.

Jacobs's "Letter from a Fugitive Slave." This letter, subtitled "Slaves Sold under Peculiar Circumstances," was published anonymously on June 21, 1853, in the *New-York Tribune*, an influential newspaper edited by Horace Greeley. As Jacobs indicates, the letter was prompted by the controversy over an article written by "Mrs. Tyler," that is, Julia Gardiner Tyler, wife of former president John Tyler (1841-45). Although she was born and raised in New York, after her marriage Julia Tyler had ardently embraced the views of her husband, a plantation owner from Virginia. In "To the Duchess of Sutherland and the Ladies of England," published in the *Southern Literary Messenger* in February 1853, she consequently rejected pleas by English women to women in the South to help end slavery, affirming that it was a civilizing influence and arguing that slaves lived better than the poor of London. The text of Jacobs's vigorous reply is taken from the first printing of the letter in the *New-York Tribune*, June 21, 1853.

LETTER FROM A FUGITIVE SLAVE

Slaves Sold under Peculiar Circumstances.

[We publish the subjoined communication exactly as written by the author, with the exception of corrections in punctuation and spelling, and the omission of one or two passages. – Ed.]

To the Editor of the *N.Y. Tribune*.

SIR: Having carefully read your paper for some months I became very much interested in some of the articles and comments written on Mrs. Tyler's Reply to the Ladies of England. Being a slave myself, I could not have felt otherwise. Would that I could write an article worthy of notice in your columns. As I never enjoyed the advantages of an education, therefore I could not study the arts of reading and writing, yet poor as it may be, I had rather give it from my own hand, than have it said that I employed others to do it for me. The truth can never be told so well through the second and third person as from yourself. But I am straying from the question. In that Reply to the Ladies of England,

Mrs. Tyler said that slaves were never sold only under very peculiar circumstances. As Mrs. Tyler and her friend Bhains were so far used up, that he could not explain what those peculiar circumstances were, let one whose peculiar sufferings justifies her in explaining it for Mrs. Tyler.

I was born a slave, reared in the Southern hot-bed until I was the mother of two children, sold at the early age of two and four years old. I have been hunted through all of the Northern States, but no, I will not tell you of my own suffering – no, it would harrow up my soul, and defeat the object that I wish to pursue. Enough – the dregs of that bitter cup have been my bounty for many years.

And as this is the first time that I ever took my pen in hand to make such an attempt, you will not say that it is fiction, for had I the inclination I have neither the brain or talent to write it. But to this very peculiar circumstance under which slaves are sold.

My mother was held as property by a maiden lady; when she married, my younger sister was in her fourteenth year, whom they took into the family. She was as gentle as she was beautiful. Innocent and guileless child, the light of our desolate hearth! But oh, my heart bleeds to tell you of the misery and degradation she was forced to suffer in slavery. The monster who owned her had no humanity in his soul. The most sincere affection that his heart was capable of, could not make him faithful to his beautiful and wealthy bride the short time of three months, but every stratagem was used to seduce my sister. Mortified and tormented beyond endurance, this child came and threw herself on her mother's bosom, the only place where she could seek refuge from her persecutor; and yet she could not protect her child that she bore into the world. On that bosom with *bitter tears* she told her troubles, and entreated her mother to save her. And oh, Christian mothers! you that have daughters of your own, can you think of your sable sisters without offering a prayer to that God who created all in their behalf! My poor mother, naturally high-spirited, smarting under what she considered as the wrongs and outrages which her child had to bear, sought her master, entreating him to spare her child. Nothing could exceed his rage at this what he called impertinence. My mother was dragged to jail, there remained twenty-five days, with negro traders to come in as they liked to examine her, as she was offered for sale. My sister was told that she must yield, or never expect to see her mother again. There were three younger children; on no other condition could she be restored to them, without the sacrifice of one. That child gave herself up to her master's bidding, to save one that was dearer to her than life itself. And can you, Christian, find it in your heart to despise her? Ah, no! not even Mrs. Tyler; for though we believe that the vanity of a name would lead her to bestow her hand where her heart could never go with it, yet, with all her faults and follows, she is nothing more than a *woman*. For if her domestic hearth is surrounded with slaves, ere long before this she has opened her eyes to the evils of slavery, and that the mistress as well as the slave must submit to the indignities and vices imposed on them by their lords of body and soul. But to one of those peculiar circumstances.

At fifteen, my sister held to her bosom an innocent offspring of her guilt and misery. In this way she dragged a miserable existence of two years, between the fires of her mistress's jealousy and her master's brutal passion. At seventeen, she gave birth to another helpless infant, heir to all the evils of slavery. Thus life and its sufferings was meted out to her until her twenty-first year. Sorrow and suffering had made its ravages upon her – she was less the object to be desired by the fiend who had crushed her to the earth; and as her children grew, they bore too strong a resemblance to him who desired to give them no other inheritance save Chains and Handcuffs, and in the dead hour of the night, when this young, deserted mother lay with her little ones clinging around her, little dreaming of the dark and inhuman plot that would be carried into execution before another dawn, and when the sun rose on God's beautiful earth, that broken-hearted mother was far on her way to the capitol of Virginia. That day should have refused her light to so disgraceful and inhuman an act in your boasted country of Liberty. Yet, reader, it is true, those two helpless children were the *sons* of one of your sainted Members in Congress; that agonized mother, his victim and slave. And where she now is God only knows, who has kept a record on high of all that she has suffered on earth.

And, you would exclaim, Could not the master have been more merciful to his children? God is merciful to all of his children, but it is seldom that a slaveholder has any mercy for his slave child. And you will believe it when I tell you that mother and her children were sold to make room for another sister, who was now the age of that mother when she entered the family. And this selling appeased the mistress's wrath, and satisfied her desire for *revenge* and made the path more smooth for her young rival at first. For there is a strong rivalry between a handsome mulatto girl and a jealous and *faded* mistress, and her liege lord sadly neglects those little attentions for a while that once made her happy. For the master will either neglect his wife or double his attentions, to save him from being suspected by his wife. Would you not think that Southern Women had cause to despise that Slavery which forces them to bear so much deception practiced by their *husbands*? Yet all this is true, for a slaveholder seldom takes a white mistress, for she is an expensive commodity, not submissive as he would like to have her, but more apt to be tyrannical; and when his passion seeks another object, he must leave her in quiet possession of all the gewgaws that she has sold herself for. But not so with his poor *slave victim*, that he has robbed of everything that can make life desirable; she must be torn from the little that is left to bind her to life, and sold by her *seducer* and *master*, caring not where, so that it puts him in possession of enough to purchase another victim. And such are the peculiar circumstances of American Slavery – of all the evils in God's sight the most to be abhorred.

Perhaps while I am writing this you too, dear Emily, may be on your way to the Mississippi River, for those peculiar circumstances occur every day in the midst of my poor oppressed fellow-creatures in bondage. And oh ye Christians, while your arms are extended to receive the oppressed of all nations, while you exert every power of your soul to assist them to raise funds, put weapons in their hands, tell them to return to their own country to slay every foe until they break the accursed yoke from off their necks, not buying and selling; this they never do under any circumstances. But while Americans do all this, they forget the millions of slaves they have at home, bought and sold under very peculiar circumstances.

And because one friend of the slave has dared to tell of their wrongs you would annihilate her. But in *Uncle Tom's Cabin* she has not told the half. Would that I had one spark from her store house of genius and talent I would tell you of my own sufferings – I would tell you of wrongs that Hungary has never endured, nor England ever dreamed of in this free country where all nations fly for liberty, equal rights and protection under your stripes and stars. It should be stripes and scars, for they go along with Mrs. Tyler's peculiar circumstances, of which I have told you only one.

A FUGITIVE SLAVE

[1853]

Jacobs's *Incidents in the Life of a Slave Girl.* Encouraged by her friend Amy Post, a Quaker abolitionist, as well as by the phenomenal success of Harriet Beecher Stowe's *Uncle Tom's Cabin* (1852), Jacobs apparently, as early as 1853, began to write an account of her experiences in slavery and as a fugitive. Although she completed it by 1858, Jacobs could not find a publisher for the work. After first asking Stowe for help, Jacobs turned to Lydia Maria Child. Child's correspondence indicates that she worked over the manuscript fairly heavily, dividing it into chapters and making other alterations designed to make Jacobs's story "more clear and entertaining." In her introduction to the book, however, Child emphasized that she had strictly provided editorial assistance to Jacobs, having had "no reason for changing her lively and dramatic way of telling her own story." She also emphasized the importance of *Incidents in the Life of a Slave Girl*, which was among the first slave narratives written by a woman and the first to deal frankly with what Child called the "monstrous features" of slavery for women – their sexual harassment by white masters.

Reluctant to use her real name and in order to protect herself and her children, Jacobs published the book under the pseudonym "Linda Brent." In a letter to the *Liberator*, Jacobs's friend William C. Nell wrote that the narrative

> presents features more attractive than many of its predecessors purporting to be histories of slave life in America, because, in contrast with their mingling of fiction with fact, this record of complicated experience in the life of a young woman, a doomed victim to America's peculiar institution . . . surely needs not the charms that any pen of fiction, however gifted and graceful, could lend.

Ironically, the account later came to be viewed as a fictional slave narrative, partly because so little was known about its author and partly because portions of the story seemed so unlikely. Through the work of the scholar Jean Fagin Yellin, we now know much more about Harriet Jacobs; we also know that the details of her story are supported by strong historical evidence.

The text is taken from the first edition of *Incidents in the Life of a Slave Girl, Written by Herself*, edited by L. Maria Child (1861). The title page included two epigraphs. The first, identified as the statement of "A Woman of North Carolina," reads: "Northerners know nothing at all about Slavery. They think it is perpetual bondage only. They have no conception of the depth of *degradation* involved in that word, Slavery; if they had, they would never cease their efforts until so horrible a system was overthrown." The second epigraph was a verse from Isaiah 32:9: "Rise up, ye women that are at ease! Hear my voice, ye careless daughters! Give ear unto my speech."

From INCIDENTS IN THE LIFE OF A SLAVE GIRL

Preface by the Author

READER, be assured this narrative is no fiction. I am aware that some of my adventures may seem incredible; but they are, nevertheless, strictly true. I have not exaggerated the wrongs inflicted by Slavery; on the contrary, my descriptions fall far short of the facts. I have concealed the names of places, and given persons fictitious names. I had no motive for secrecy on my own account, but I deemed it kind and considerate towards others to pursue this course.

I wish I were more competent to the task I have undertaken. But I trust my readers will excuse deficiencies in consideration of circumstances. I was born and reared in Slavery; and I remained in a Slave State twenty-seven years. Since I have been at the North, it has been necessary for me to work diligently for my own support, and the education of my children. This has not left me much leisure to make up for the loss of early opportunities to improve myself; and it has compelled me to write these pages at irregular intervals, whenever I could snatch an hour from household duties.

When I first arrived in Philadelphia, Bishop Paine[1] advised me to publish a sketch of my life, but I told him I was altogether incompetent to such an undertaking. Though I have improved my mind somewhat since that time, I still remain of the same opinion; but I trust my motives will excuse what might otherwise seem presumptuous. I have not written my experiences in order to attract attention to myself; on the contrary, it would have been more pleasant to me to have been silent about my own history. Neither do I care to excite sympathy for my own sufferings. But I do earnestly desire to arouse the women of the North to a realizing sense of the condition of two millions of women at the South, still in bondage, suffering what I suffered, and most of them far worse. I want to add my testimony to that of abler pens to convince the people of the Free States what Slavery really is. Only by experience can any one realize how deep, and dark, and foul is that pit of abominations. May the blessing of God rest on this imperfect effort in behalf of my persecuted people!

LINDA BRENT

I. Childhood

I was born a slave; but I never knew it till six years of happy childhood had passed away. My father was a carpenter, and considered so intelligent and skilful in his trade, that,

1. **Bishop Paine:** Daniel A. Payne (1811–1893), bishop of the African Methodist Episcopal Church.

when buildings out of the common line were to be erected, he was sent for from long distances, to be head workman. On condition of paying his mistress two hundred dollars a year, and supporting himself, he was allowed to work at his trade, and manage his own affairs. His strongest wish was to purchase his children; but, though he several times offered his hard earnings for that purpose, he never succeeded. In complexion my parents were a light shade of brownish yellow, and were termed mulattoes. They lived together in a comfortable home; and, though we were all slaves, I was so fondly shielded that I never dreamed I was a piece of merchandise, trusted to them for safe keeping, and liable to be demanded of them at any moment. I had one brother, William, who was two years younger than myself – a bright, affectionate child. I had also a great treasure in my maternal grandmother, who was a remarkable woman in many respects. She was the daughter of a planter in South Carolina, who, at his death, left her mother and his three children free, with money to go to St. Augustine, where they had relatives. It was during the Revolutionary War; and they were captured on their passage, carried back, and sold to different purchasers. Such was the story my grandmother used to tell me; but I do not remember all the particulars. She was a little girl when she was captured and sold to the keeper of a large hotel. I have often heard her tell how hard she fared during childhood. But as she grew older she evinced so much intelligence, and was so faithful, that her master and mistress could not help seeing it was for their interest to take care of such a valuable piece of property. She became an indispensable personage in the household, officiating in all capacities, from cook and wet nurse to seamstress. She was much praised for her cooking; and her nice crackers became so famous in the neighborhood that many people were desirous of obtaining them. In consequence of numerous requests of this kind, she asked permission of her mistress to bake crackers at night, after all the household work was done; and she obtained leave to do it, provided she would clothe herself and her children from the profits. Upon these terms, after working hard all day for her mistress, she began her midnight bakings, assisted by her two oldest children. The business proved profitable; and each year she laid by a little, which was saved for a fund to purchase her children. Her master died, and the property was divided among his heirs. The widow had her dower in the hotel, which she continued to keep open. My grandmother remained in her service as a slave; but her children were divided among her master's children. As she had five, Benjamin, the youngest one, was sold, in order that each heir might have an equal portion of dollars and cents. There was so little difference in our ages that he seemed more like my brother than my uncle. He was a bright, handsome lad, nearly white; for he inherited the complexion my grandmother had derived from Anglo-Saxon ancestors. Though only ten years old, seven hundred and twenty dollars were paid for him. His sale was a terrible blow to my grandmother; but she was naturally hopeful, and she went to work with renewed energy, trusting in time to be able to purchase some of her children. She had laid up three hundred dollars, which her mistress one day begged as a loan, promising to pay her soon. The reader probably knows that no promise or writing given to a slave is legally binding; for, according to Southern laws, a slave, *being* property, can *hold* no property. When my grandmother lent her hard earnings to her mistress, she trusted solely to her honor. The honor of a slaveholder to a slave!

To this good grandmother I was indebted for many comforts. My brother Willie and I often received portions of the crackers, cakes, and preserves, she made to sell; and after we ceased to be children we were indebted to her for many more important services.

Such were the unusually fortunate circumstances of my early childhood. When I was six years old, my mother died; and then, for the first time, I learned, by the talk around me, that I was a slave. My mother's mistress was the daughter of my grandmother's mistress. She was the foster sister of my mother; they were both nourished at my grandmother's breast. In fact, my mother had been weaned at three months old, that the babe of the mistress might obtain sufficient food. They played together as children; and, when they became women, my mother was a most faithful servant to her whiter foster sister. On her death-bed her mistress promised that her children should never suffer for any thing; and during her lifetime she kept her word. They all spoke kindly of my dead mother, who had been a slave merely in name, but in nature was noble and womanly. I grieved for her, and my young mind was troubled with the thought who would now take care of me and my little brother. I was told that my home was now to be with her mistress; and I found it a happy one. No toilsome or disagreeable duties were imposed upon me. My mistress was so kind to me that I was always glad to do her bidding, and proud to labor for her as much as my young years would permit. I would sit by her side for hours, sewing diligently, with a heart as free from care as that of any free-born white child. When she thought I was tired, she would send me out to run and jump; and away I bounded, to gather berries or flowers to decorate her room. Those were happy days – too happy to last. The slave child had no thought for the morrow; but there came that blight, which too surely waits on every human being born to be a chattel.

When I was nearly twelve years old, my kind mistress sickened and died. As I saw the cheek grow paler, and the eye more glassy, how earnestly I prayed in my heart that she might live! I loved her; for she had been almost like a mother to me. My prayers were not answered. She died, and they buried her in the little churchyard, where, day after day, my tears fell upon her grave.

I was sent to spend a week with my grandmother. I was now old enough to begin to think of the future; and again and again I asked myself what they would do with me. I felt sure I should never find another mistress so kind as the one who was gone. She had promised my dying mother that her children should never suffer for any thing; and when I remembered that, and recalled her many proofs of attachment to me, I could not help having some hopes that she had left me free. My friends were almost certain it would be so. They thought she would be sure to do it, on account of my mother's love and faithful service. But, alas! we all know that the memory of a faithful slave does not avail much to save her children from the auction block.

After a brief period of suspense, the will of my mistress was read, and we learned that she had bequeathed me to her sister's daughter, a child of five years old. So vanished our hopes. My mistress had taught me the precepts of God's Word: "Thou shalt love thy neighbor as thyself."[1] "Whatsoever ye would that men should do unto you, do ye even so

1. **"Thou . . . as thyself"**: Mark 12:31.

unto them."[2] But I was her slave, and I suppose she did not recognize me as her neighbor. I would give much to blot out from my memory that one great wrong. As a child, I loved my mistress; and, looking back on the happy days I spent with her, I try to think with less bitterness of this act of injustice. While I was with her, she taught me to read and spell; and for this privilege, which so rarely falls to the lot of a slave, I bless her memory.

She possessed but few slaves; and at her death those were all distributed among her relatives. Five of them were my grandmother's children, and had shared the same milk that nourished her mother's children. Notwithstanding my grandmother's long and faithful service to her owners, not one of her children escaped the auction block. These God-breathing machines are no more, in the sight of their masters, than the cotton they plant, or the horses they tend.

VII. The Lover

Why does the slave ever love? Why allow the tendrils of the heart to twine around objects which may at any moment be wrenched away by the hand of violence? When separations come by the hand of death, the pious soul can bow in resignation, and say, "Not my will, but thine be done, O Lord!" But when the ruthless hand of man strikes the blow, regardless of the misery he causes, it is hard to be submissive. I did not reason thus when I was a young girl. Youth will be youth. I loved, and I indulged the hope that the dark clouds around me would turn out a bright lining. I forgot that in the land of my birth the shadows are too dense for light to penetrate. A land

> "Where laughter is not mirth; nor thought the mind;
> Nor words a language; nor e'en men mankind.
> Where cries reply to curses, shrieks to blows,
> And each is tortured in his separate hell."[1]

There was in the neighborhood a young colored carpenter; a free born man. We had been well acquainted in childhood, and frequently met together afterwards. We became mutually attached, and he proposed to marry me. I loved him with all the ardor of a young girl's first love. But when I reflected that I was a slave, and that the laws gave no sanction to the marriage of such, my heart sank within me. My lover wanted to buy me; but I knew that Dr. Flint was too wilful and arbitrary a man to consent to that arrangement. From him, I was sure of experiencing all sorts of opposition, and I had nothing to hope from my mistress. She would have been delighted to have got rid of me, but not in that way. It would have relieved her mind of a burden if she could have seen me sold to some distant state, but if I was married near home I should be just as much in her husband's power as I had previously been, — for the husband of a slave has no power to protect her. Moreover, my mistress, like many others, seemed to think that slaves had no right to any family ties of their own; that they were created merely to wait upon the fam-

---

2. **"Whatsoever . . . unto them":** Matthew 7:12.
1. **Where . . . hell:** From "The Lament of Tasso," by the English poet George Gordon, Lord Byron (1788–1824).

ily of the mistress. I once heard her abuse a young slave girl, who told her that a colored man wanted to make her his wife. "I will have you peeled and pickled, my lady," said she, "if I ever hear you mention that subject again. Do you suppose that I will have you tending *my* children with the children of that nigger?" The girl to whom she said this had a mulatto child, of course not acknowledged by its father. The poor black man who loved her would have been proud to acknowledge his helpless offspring.

Many and anxious were the thoughts I revolved in my mind. I was at a loss what to do. Above all things, I was desirous to spare my lover the insults that had cut so deeply into my own soul. I talked with my grandmother about it, and partly told her my fears. I did not dare to tell her the worst. She had long suspected all was not right, and if I confirmed her suspicions I knew a storm would rise that would prove the overthrow of all my hopes.

This love-dream had been my support through many trials; and I could not bear to run the risk of having it suddenly dissipated. There was a lady in the neighborhood, a particular friend of Dr. Flint's, who often visited the house. I had a great respect for her, and she had always manifested a friendly interest in me. Grandmother thought she would have great influence with the doctor. I went to this lady, and told her my story. I told her I was aware that my lover's being a free-born man would prove a great objection; but he wanted to buy me; and if Dr. Flint would consent to that arrangement, I felt sure he would be willing to pay any reasonable price. She knew that Mrs. Flint disliked me; therefore, I ventured to suggest that perhaps my mistress would approve of my being sold, as that would rid her of me. The lady listened with kindly sympathy, and promised to do her utmost to promote my wishes. She had an interview with the doctor, and I believe she pleaded my cause earnestly; but it was all to no purpose.

How I dreaded my master now! Every minute I expected to be summoned to his presence; but the day passed, and I heard nothing from him. The next morning, a message was brought to me: "Master wants you in his study." I found the door ajar, and I stood a moment gazing at the hateful man who claimed a right to rule me, body and soul. I entered, and tried to appear calm. I did not want him to know how my heart was bleeding. He looked fixedly at me, with an expression which seemed to say, "I have half a mind to kill you on the spot." At last he broke the silence, and that was a relief to both of us.

"So you want to be married, do you?" said he, "and to a free nigger."

"Yes, sir."

"Well, I'll soon convince you whether I am your master, or the nigger fellow you honor so highly. If you *must* have a husband, you may take up with one of my slaves."

What a situation I should be in, as the wife of one of *his* slaves, even if my heart had been interested!

I replied, "Don't you suppose, sir, that a slave can have some preference about marrying? Do you suppose that all men are alike to her?"

"Do you love this nigger?" said he, abruptly.

"Yes, sir."

"How dare you tell me so!" he exclaimed, in great wrath. After a slight pause, he added, "I supposed you thought more of yourself; that you felt above the insults of such puppies."

I replied, "If he is a puppy I am a puppy, for we are both of the negro race. It is right and honorable for us to love each other. The man you call a puppy never insulted me, sir; and he would not love me if he did not believe me to be a virtuous woman."

He sprang upon me like a tiger, and gave me a stunning blow. It was the first time he had ever struck me; and fear did not enable me to control my anger. When I had recovered a little from the effects, I exclaimed, "You have struck me for answering you honestly. How I despise you!"

There was silence for some minutes. Perhaps he was deciding what should be my punishment; or, perhaps, he wanted to give me time to reflect on what I had said, and to whom I had said it. Finally, he asked, "Do you know what you have said?"

"Yes, sir; but your treatment drove me to it."

"Do you know that I have a right to do as I like with you, – that I can kill you, if I please?"

"You have tried to kill me, and I wish you had; but you have no right to do as you like with me."

"Silence!" he exclaimed, in a thundering voice. "By heavens, girl, you forget yourself too far! Are you mad? If you are, I will soon bring you to your senses. Do you think any other master would bear what I have borne from you this morning? Many masters would have killed you on the spot. How would you like to be sent to jail for your insolence?"

"I know I have been disrespectful, sir," I replied; "but you drove me to it; I couldn't help it. As for the jail, there would be more peace for me there than there is here."

"You deserve to go there," said he, "and to be under such treatment, that you would forget the meaning of the word *peace*. It would do you good. It would take some of your high notions out of you. But I am not ready to send you there yet, notwithstanding your ingratitude for all my kindness and forbearance. You have been the plague of my life. I have wanted to make you happy, and I have been repaid with the basest ingratitude; but though you have proved yourself incapable of appreciating my kindness, I will be lenient towards you, Linda. I will give you one more chance to redeem your character. If you behave yourself and do as I require, I will forgive you and treat you as I always have done; but if you disobey me, I will punish you as I would the meanest slave on my plantation. Never let me hear that fellow's name mentioned again. If I ever know of your speaking to him, I will cowhide you both; and if I catch him lurking about my premises, I will shoot him as soon as I would a dog. Do you hear what I say? I'll teach you a lesson about marriage and free niggers! Now go, and let this be the last time I have occasion to speak to you on this subject."

Reader, did you ever hate? I hope not. I never did but once; and I trust I never shall again. Somebody has called it "the atmosphere of hell;" and I believe it is so.

For a fortnight the doctor did not speak to me. He thought to mortify me; to make me feel that I had disgraced myself by receiving the honorable addresses of a respectable colored man, in preference to the base proposals of a white man. But though his lips disdained to address me, his eyes were very loquacious. No animal ever watched its prey more narrowly than he watched me. He knew that I could write, though he had failed to make me read his letters; and he was now troubled lest I should exchange letters with another man. After a while he became weary of silence; and I was sorry for it. One morning, as he passed through the hall, to leave the house, he contrived to thrust a note into my hand. I thought I had better read it, and spare myself the vexation of having him read it to me. It expressed regret for the blow he had given me, and reminded me that I myself was wholly to blame for it. He hoped I had become convinced of the injury I was doing myself by incurring his displeasure. He wrote that he had made up his mind to go to Louisiana; that he should take several slaves with him, and intended I should be one of the number. My mistress would remain where she was; therefore I should have nothing to fear from that quarter. If I merited kindness from him, he assured me that it would be lavishly bestowed. He begged me to think over the matter, and answer the following day.

The next morning I was called to carry a pair of scissors to his room. I laid them on the table with the letter beside them. He thought it was my answer, and did not call me back. I went as usual to attend my young mistress to and from school. He met me in the street, and ordered me to stop at his office on my way back. When I entered, he showed me his letter, and asked me why I had not answered it. I replied, "I am your daughter's property, and it is in your power to send me, or take me, wherever you please." He said he was very glad to find me so willing to go, and that we should start early in the autumn. He had a large practice in the town, and I rather thought he had made up the story merely to frighten me. However that might be, I was determined that I would never go to Louisiana with him.

Summer passed away, and early in the autumn Dr. Flint's eldest son was sent to Louisiana to examine the country, with a view to emigrating. That news did not disturb me. I knew very well that I should not be sent with *him.* That I had not been taken to the plantation before this time, was owing to the fact that his son was there. He was jealous of his son; and jealousy of the overseer had kept him from punishing me by sending me into the fields to work. Is it strange that I was not proud of these protectors? As for the overseer, he was a man for whom I had less respect than I had for a bloodhound.

Young Mr. Flint did not bring back a favorable report of Louisiana, and I heard no more of that scheme. Soon after this, my lover met me at the corner of the street, and I stopped to speak to him. Looking up, I saw my master watching us from his window. I hurried home, trembling with fear. I was sent for, immediately, to go to his room. He met me with a blow. "When is mistress to be married?" said he, in a sneering tone. A shower of oaths and imprecations followed. How thankful I was that my lover was a free man! that my tyrant had no power to flog him for speaking to me in the street!

Again and again I revolved in my mind how all this would end. There was no hope that the doctor would consent to sell me on any terms. He had an iron will, and was determined to keep me, and to conquer me. My lover was an intelligent and religious man. Even if he could have obtained permission to marry me while I was a slave, the marriage would give him no power to protect me from my master. It would have made him miserable to witness the insults I should have been subjected to. And then, if we had children, I knew they must "follow the condition of the mother."[2] What a terrible blight that would be on the heart of a free, intelligent father! For *his* sake, I felt that I ought not to link his fate with my own unhappy destiny. He was going to Savannah to see about a little property left him by an uncle; and hard as it was to bring my feelings to it, I earnestly entreated

2. **"follow the condition of the mother"**: By law, the status of the mother determined whether a child was free or a slave.

him not to come back. I advised him to go to the Free States, where his tongue would not be tied, and where his intelligence would be of more avail to him. He left me, still hoping the day would come when I could be bought. With me the lamp of hope had gone out. The dream of my girlhood was over. I felt lonely and desolate.

Still I was not stripped of all. I still had my good grandmother, and my affectionate brother. When he put his arms round my neck, and looked into my eyes, as if to read there the troubles I dared not tell, I felt that I still had something to love. But even that pleasant emotion was chilled by the reflection that he might be torn from me at any moment, by some sudden freak of my master. If he had known how we loved each other, I think he would have exulted in separating us. We often planned together how we could get to the north. But, as William remarked, such things are easier said than done. My movements were very closely watched, and we had no means of getting any money to defray our expenses. As for grandmother, she was strongly opposed to her children's undertaking any such project. She had not forgotten poor Benjamin's sufferings, and she was afraid that if another child tried to escape, he would have a similar or a worse fate. To me, nothing seemed more dreadful than my present life. I said to myself, "William *must* be free. He shall go to the north, and I will follow him." Many a slave sister has formed the same plans.

X. A Perilous Passage in the Slave Girl's Life

After my lover went away, Dr. Flint contrived a new plan. He seemed to have an idea that my fear of my mistress was his greatest obstacle. In the blandest tones, he told me that he was going to build a small house for me, in a secluded place, four miles away from the town. I shuddered; but I was constrained to listen, while he talked of his intention to give me a home of my own, and to make a lady of me. Hitherto, I had escaped my dreaded fate, by being in the midst of people. My grandmother had already had high words with my master about me. She had told him pretty plainly what she thought of his character, and there was considerable gossip in the neighborhood about our affairs, to which the open-mouthed jealousy of Mrs. Flint contributed not a little. When my master said he was going to build a house for me, and that he could do it with little trouble and expense, I was in hopes something would happen to frustrate his scheme; but I soon heard that the house was actually begun. I vowed before my Maker that I would never enter it. I had rather toil on the plantation from dawn till dark; I had rather live and die in jail, than drag on, from day to day, through such a living death. I was determined that the master, whom I so hated and loathed, who had blighted the prospects of my youth, and made my life a desert, should not, after my long struggle with him, succeed at last in trampling his victim under his feet. I would do any thing, every thing, for the sake of defeating him. What *could* I do? I thought and thought, till I became desperate, and made a plunge into the abyss.

And now, reader, I come to a period in my unhappy life, which I would gladly forget if I could. The remembrance fills me with sorrow and shame. It pains me to tell you of it; but I have promised to tell you the truth and I will do it honestly, let it cost me what it may. I will not try to screen myself behind the plea of compulsion from a master; for it was not so. Neither can I plead ignorance or thoughtlessness. For years, my master had done his utmost to pollute my mind with foul images, and to destroy the pure principles inculcated by my grandmother, and the good mistress of my childhood. The influences of slavery had had the same effect on me that they had on other young girls; they had made me prematurely knowing, concerning the evil ways of the world. I knew what I did, and I did it with deliberate calculation.

But, O, ye happy women, whose purity has been sheltered from childhood, who have been free to choose the objects of your affection, whose homes are protected by law, do not judge the poor desolate slave girl too severely! If slavery had been abolished, I, also, could have married the man of my choice; I could have had a home shielded by the laws; and I should have been spared the painful task of confessing what I am now about to relate; but all my prospects had been blighted by slavery. I wanted to keep myself pure; and, under the most adverse circumstances, I tried hard to preserve my self-respect; but I was struggling alone in the powerful grasp of the demon Slavery; and the monster proved too strong for me. I felt as if I was forsaken by God and man; as if all my efforts must be frustrated; and I became reckless in my despair.

I have told you that Dr. Flint's persecutions and his wife's jealousy had given rise to some gossip in the neighborhood. Among others, it chanced that a white unmarried gentleman had obtained some knowledge of the circumstances in which I was placed. He knew my grandmother, and often spoke to me in the street. He became interested for me, and asked questions about my master, which I answered in part. He expressed a great deal of sympathy, and a wish to aid me. He constantly sought opportunities to see me, and wrote to me frequently. I was a poor slave girl, only fifteen years old.

So much attention from a superior person was, of course, flattering; for human nature is the same in all. I also felt grateful for his sympathy, and encouraged by his kind words. It seemed to me a great thing to have such a friend. By degrees, a more tender feeling crept into my heart. He was an educated and eloquent gentleman; too eloquent, alas, for the poor slave girl who trusted in him. Of course I saw whither all this was tending. I knew the impassable gulf between us; but to be an object of interest to a man who is not married, and who is not her master, is agreeable to the pride and feelings of a slave, if her miserable situation has left her any pride or sentiment. It seems less degrading to give one's self, than to submit to compulsion. There is something akin to freedom in having a lover who has no control over you, except that which he gains by kindness and attachment. A master may treat you as rudely as he pleases, and you dare not speak; moreover, the wrong does not seem so great with an unmarried man, as with one who has a wife to be made unhappy. There may be sophistry in all this; but the condition of a slave confuses all principles of morality, and, in fact, renders the practice of them impossible.

When I found that my master had actually begun to build the lonely cottage, other feelings mixed with those I have described. Revenge, and calculations of interest, were added to flattered vanity and sincere gratitude for kindness. I knew nothing would enrage Dr. Flint so much as to know that I favored another; and it was something to triumph over my tyrant even in that small way. I thought he would revenge himself by selling me, and I was sure my friend, Mr. Sands, would buy me. He was a man of more generosity and feeling than my master, and I thought my freedom could be easily obtained from him. The crisis of my fate now came so near that I was desperate. I shuddered to think of being the mother of children that should be owned by my old tyrant. I knew that as soon as a new fancy took him, his victims were sold far off to get rid of them; especially if they had children. I had seen several women sold, with his babies at the breast. He never allowed his offspring by slaves to remain long in sight of himself and his wife. Of a man who was not my master I could ask to have my children well supported; and in this case, I felt confident I should obtain the boon. I also felt quite sure that they would be made free. With all these thoughts revolving in my mind, and seeing no other way of escaping the doom I so much dreaded, I made a headlong plunge. Pity me, and pardon me, O virtuous reader! You never knew what it is to be a slave; to be entirely unprotected by law or custom; to have the laws reduce you to the condition of a chattel, entirely subject to the will of another. You never exhausted your ingenuity in avoiding the snares, and eluding the power of a hated tyrant; you never shuddered at the sound of his footsteps, and trembled within hearing of his voice. I know I did wrong. No one can feel it more sensibly than I do. The painful and humiliating memory will haunt me to my dying day. Still, in looking back, calmly, on the events of my life, I feel that the slave woman ought not to be judged by the same standard as others.

The months passed on. I had many unhappy hours. I secretly mourned over the sorrow I was bringing on my grandmother, who had so tried to shield me from harm. I knew that I was the greatest comfort of her old age, and that it was a source of pride to her that I had not degraded myself, like most of the slaves. I wanted to confess to her that I was no longer worthy of her love; but I could not utter the dreaded words.

As for Dr. Flint, I had a feeling of satisfaction and triumph in the thought of telling *him*. From time to time he told me of his intended arrangements, and I was silent. At last, he came and told me the cottage was completed, and ordered me to go to it. I told him I would never enter it. He said, "I have heard enough of such talk as that. You shall go, if you are carried by force; and you shall remain there."

I replied, "I will never go there. In a few months I shall be a mother."

He stood and looked at me in dumb amazement, and left the house without a word. I thought I should be happy in my triumph over him. But now that the truth was out, and my relatives would hear of it, I felt wretched. Humble as were their circumstances, they had pride in my good character. Now, how could I look them in the face? My self-respect was gone! I had resolved that I would be virtuous, though I was a slave. I had said, "Let the storm beat! I will brave it till I die." And now, how humiliated I felt!

I went to my grandmother. My lips moved to make confession, but the words stuck in my throat. I sat down in the shade of a tree at her door and began to sew. I think she saw something unusual was the matter with me. The mother of slaves is very watchful. She knows there is no security for her children. After they have entered their teens she lives in daily expectation of trouble. This leads to many questions. If the girl is of a sensitive nature, timidity keeps her from answering truthfully and this well-meant course has a tendency to drive her from maternal counsels. Presently, in came my mistress, like a mad woman, and accused me concerning her husband. My grandmother, whose suspicions had been previously awakened, believed what she said. She exclaimed, "O Linda! has it come to this? I had rather see you dead than to see you as you now are. You are a disgrace to your dead mother." She tore from my fingers my mother's wedding ring and her silver thimble. "Go away!" she exclaimed, "and never come to my house, again." Her reproaches fell so hot and heavy, that they left me no chance to answer. Bitter tears, such as the eyes never shed but once, were my only answer. I rose from my seat, but fell back again, sobbing. She did not speak to me; but the tears were running down her furrowed cheeks, and they scorched me like fire. She had always been so kind to me! *So* kind! How I longed to throw myself at her feet, and tell her all the truth! But she had ordered me to go, and never to come there again. After a few minutes, I mustered strength, and started to obey her. With what feelings did I now close that little gate, which I used to open with such an eager hand in my childhood! It closed upon me with a sound I never heard before.

Where could I go? I was afraid to return to my master's. I walked on recklessly, not caring where I went, or what would become of me. When I had gone four or five miles, fatigue compelled me to stop. I sat down on the stump of an old tree. The stars were shining through the boughs above me. How they mocked me, with their bright, calm light! The hours passed by, and as I sat there alone a chilliness and deadly sickness came over me. I sank on the ground. My mind was full of horrid thoughts. I prayed to die; but the prayer was not answered. At last, with great effort I roused myself, and walked some distance further, to the house of a woman who had been a friend of my mother. When I told her why I was there, she spoke soothingly to me; but I could not be comforted. I thought I could bear my shame if I could only be reconciled to my grandmother. I longed to open my heart to her. I thought if she could know the real state of the case, and all I had been bearing for years, she would perhaps judge me less harshly. My friend advised me to send for her. I did so; but days of agonizing suspense passed before she came. Had she utterly forsaken me? No. She came at last. I knelt before her, and told her the things that had poisoned my life; how long I had been persecuted; that I saw no way of escape; and in an hour of extremity I had become desperate. She listened in silence. I told her I would bear any thing and do any thing, if in time I had hopes of obtaining her forgiveness. I begged of her to pity me, for my dead mother's sake. And she did pity me. She did not say, "I forgive you;" but she looked at me lovingly, with her eyes full of tears. She laid her old hand gently on my head, and murmured, "Poor child! Poor child!"

XIV. Another Link to Life

I had not returned to my master's house since the birth of my child. The old man raved to have me thus removed from his immediate power; but his wife vowed, by all that was good and great, she would kill me if I came back; and he did not doubt her word. Sometimes he would stay away for a season. Then he would come and renew the old threadbare discourse about his forbearance and my ingratitude. He labored, most unnecessarily, to convince me that I had lowered myself. The venomous old reprobate had no need of descanting on that theme. I felt humiliated enough. My unconscious babe was the ever-present witness of my shame. I listened with silent contempt when he talked about my having forfeited *his* good opinion; but I shed bitter tears that I was no longer worthy of being respected by the good and pure. Alas! slavery still held me in its poisonous grasp. There was no chance for me to be respectable. There was no prospect of being able to lead a better life.

Sometimes, when my master found that I still refused to accept what he called his kind offers, he would threaten to sell my child. "Perhaps that will humble you," said he.

Humble *me*! Was I not already in the dust? But his threat lacerated my heart. I knew the law gave him power to fulfil it; for slaveholders have been cunning enough to enact that "the child shall follow the condition of the *mother*," not of the *father*; thus taking care that licentiousness shall not interfere with avarice. This reflection made me clasp my innocent babe all the more firmly to my heart. Horrid visions passed through my mind when I thought of his liability to fall into the slavetrader's hands. I wept over him, and said, "O my child! perhaps they will leave you in some cold cabin to die, and then throw you into a hole, as if you were a dog."

When Dr. Flint learned that I was again to be a mother, he was exasperated beyond measure. He rushed from the house, and returned with a pair of shears. I had a fine head of hair; and he often railed about my pride of arranging it nicely. He cut every hair close to my head, storming and swearing all the time. I replied to some of his abuse, and he struck me. Some months before, he had pitched me down stairs in a fit of passion; and the injury I received was so serious that I was unable to turn myself in bed for many days. He then said, "Linda, I swear by God I will never raise my hand against you again;" but I knew that he would forget his promise.

After he discovered my situation, he was like a restless spirit from the pit. He came every day; and I was subjected to such insults as no pen can describe. I would not describe them if I could; they were too low, too revolting. I tried to keep them from my grandmother's knowledge as much as I could. I knew she had enough to sadden her life, without having my troubles to bear. When she saw the doctor treat me with violence, and heard him utter oaths terrible enough to palsy a man's tongue, she could not always hold her peace. It was natural and motherlike that she should try to defend me; but it only made matters worse.

When they told me my new-born babe was a girl, my heart was heavier than it had ever been before. Slavery is terrible for men; but it is far more terrible for women. Superadded to the burden common to all, *they* have wrongs, and sufferings, and mortifications peculiarly their own.

Dr. Flint had sworn that he would make me suffer, to my last day, for this new crime against *him*, as he called it; and as long as he had me in his power he kept his word. On the fourth day after the birth of my babe, he entered my room suddenly, and commanded me to rise and bring my baby to him. The nurse who took care of me had gone out of the room to prepare some nourishment, and I was alone. There was no alternative. I rose, took up my babe, and crossed the room to where he sat. "Now stand there," said he, "till I tell you to go back!" My child bore a strong resemblance to her father, and to the deceased Mrs. Sands, her grandmother. He noticed this; and while I stood before him, trembling; with weakness, he heaped upon me and my little one every vile epithet he could think of. Even the grandmother in her grave did not escape his curses. In the midst of his vituperations I fainted at his feet. This recalled him to his senses. He took the baby from my arms, laid it on the bed, dashed cold water in my face, took me up, and shook me violently, to restore my consciousness before any one entered the room. Just then my grandmother came in, and he hurried out of the house. I suffered in consequence of this treatment; but I begged my friends to let me die, rather than send for the doctor. There was nothing I dreaded so much as his presence. My life was spared; and I was glad for the sake of my little ones. Had it not been for these ties to life, I should have been glad to be released by death, though I had lived only nineteen years.

Always it gave me a pang that my children had no lawful claim to a name. Their father offered his; but, if I had wished to accept the offer, I dared not while my master lived. Moreover, I knew it would not be accepted at their baptism. A Christian name they were at least entitled to; and we resolved to call my boy for our dear good Benjamin, who had gone far away from us.

My grandmother belonged to the church; and she was very desirous of having the children christened. I knew Dr. Flint would forbid it, and I did not venture to attempt it. But chance favored me. He was called to visit a patient out of town, and was obliged to be absent during Sunday. "Now is the time," said my grandmother; "we will take the children to church, and have them christened."

When I entered the church, recollections of my mother came over me, and I felt subdued in spirit. There she had presented me for baptism, without any reason to feel ashamed. She had been married, and had such legal rights as slavery allows to a slave. The vows had at least been sacred to *her*, and she had never violated them. I was glad she was not alive, to know under what different circumstances her grandchildren were presented for baptism. Why had my lot been so different from my mother's? *Her* master had died when she was a child; and she remained with her mistress till she married. She was never in the power of any master; and thus she escaped one class of the evils that generally fall upon slaves.

When my baby was about to be christened, the former mistress of my father stepped up to me, and proposed to give it her Christian name. To this I added the surname of my father, who had himself no legal right to it; for my grandfather on the paternal side was a white gentleman. What tangled skeins are the genealogies of slavery! I loved my father; but it mortified me to be obliged to bestow his name on my children.

When we left the church, my father's old mistress invited me to go home with her. She clasped a gold chain round my baby's neck. I thanked her for this kindness; but I did not like the emblem. I wanted no chain to be fastened on my daughter, not even if its links were of gold. How earnestly I prayed that she might never feel the weight of slavery's chain, whose iron entereth into the soul!

XVII. The Flight

Mr. Flint was hard pushed for house servants, and rather than lose me he had restrained his malice. I did my work faithfully, though not, of course, with a willing mind. They were evidently afraid I should leave them. Mr. Flint wished that I should sleep in the great house instead of the servants' quarters. His wife agreed to the proposition, but said I mustn't bring my bed into the house, because it would scatter feathers on her carpet. I knew when I went there that they would never think of such a thing as furnishing a bed of any kind for me and my little one. I therefore carried my own bed, and now I was forbidden to use it. I did as I was ordered. But now that I was certain my children were to be put in their power, in order to give them a stronger hold on me, I resolved to leave them that night. I remembered the grief this step would bring upon my dear old grandmother; and nothing less than the freedom of my children would have induced me to disregard her advice. I went about my evening work with trembling steps. Mr. Flint twice called from his chamber door to inquire why the house was not locked up. I replied that I had not done my work. "You have had time enough to do it," said he. "Take care how you answer me!"

I shut all the windows, locked all the doors, and went up to the third story, to wait till midnight. How long those hours seemed, and how fervently I prayed that God would not forsake me in this hour of utmost need! I was about to risk every thing on the throw of a die; and if I failed, O what would become of me and my poor children? They would be made to suffer for my fault.

At half past twelve I stole softly down stairs. I stopped on the second floor, thinking I heard a noise. I felt my way down into the parlor, and looked out of the window. The night was so intensely dark that I could see nothing. I raised the window very softly and jumped out. Large drops of rain were falling, and the darkness bewildered me. I dropped on my knees, and breathed a short prayer to God for guidance and protection. I groped my way to the road, and rushed towards the town with almost lightning speed. I arrived at my grandmother's house, but dared not see her. She would say, "Linda, you are killing me;" and I knew that would unnerve me. I tapped softly at the window of a room, occupied by a woman, who had lived in the house several years. I knew she was a faithful friend, and could be trusted with my secret. I tapped several times before she heard me. At last she raised the window, and I whispered, "Sally, I have run away. Let me in, quick." She opened the door softly, and said in low tones, "For God's sake, don't. Your grandmother is trying to buy you and de chillern. Mr. Sands was here last week. He tole her he was going away on business, but he wanted her to go ahead about buying you and de chillern, and he would help her all he could. Don't run away, Linda. Your grandmother is all bowed down wid trouble now."

I replied, "Sally, they are going to carry my children to the plantation to-morrow; and they will never sell them to any body so long as they have me in their power. Now, would you advise me to go back?"

"No, chile, no," answered she. "When dey finds you is gone, dey won't want de plague ob de chillern; but where is you going to hide? Dey knows ebery inch ob dis house."

I told her I had a hiding-place, and that was all it was best for her to know. I asked her to go into my room as soon as it was light, and take all my clothes out of my trunk, and pack them in hers; for I knew Mr. Flint and the constable would be there early to search my room. I feared the sight of my children would be too much for my full heart; but I could not go out into the uncertain future without one last look. I bent over the bed where lay my little Benny and baby Ellen. Poor little ones! fatherless and motherless! Memories of their father came over me. He wanted to be kind to them; but they were not all to him, as they were to my womanly heart. I knelt and prayed for the innocent little sleepers. I kissed them lightly, and turned away.

As I was about to open the street door, Sally laid her hand on my shoulder, and said, "Linda, is you gwine all alone? Let me call your uncle."

"No, Sally," I replied, "I want no one to be brought into trouble on my account."

I went forth into the darkness and rain. I ran on till I came to the house of the friend who was to conceal me.

Early the next morning Mr. Flint was at my grandmother's inquiring for me. She told him she had not seen me, and supposed I was at the plantation. He watched her face narrowly, and said, "Don't you know any thing about her running off?" She assured him that she did not. He went on to say, "Last night she ran off without the least provocation. We had treated her very kindly. My wife liked her. She will soon be found and brought back. Are her children with you?" When told that they were, he said, "I am very glad to hear that. If they are here, she cannot be far off. If I find out that any of my niggers have had any thing to do with this damned business, I'll give 'em five hundred lashes." As he started to go to his father's, he turned round and added, persuasively, "Let her be brought back, and she shall have her children to live with her."

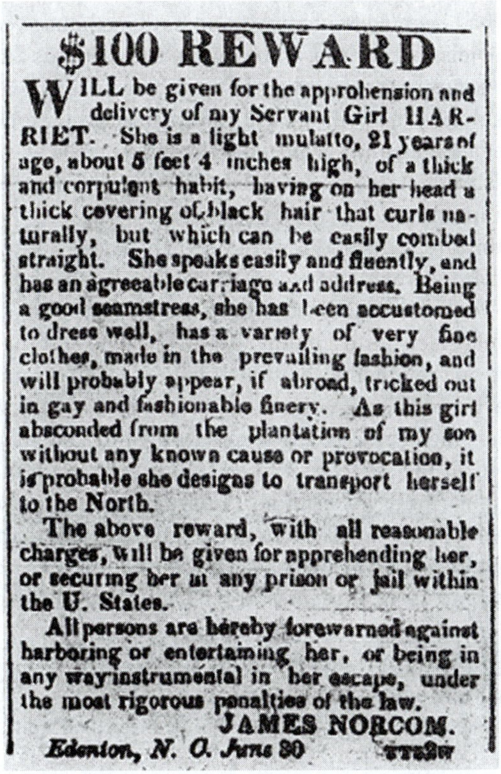

$100 REWARD

WILL be given for the apprehension and delivery of my Servant Girl HARRIET. She is a light mulatto, 21 years of age, about 5 feet 4 inches high, of a thick and corpulent habit, having on her head a thick covering of black hair that curls naturally, but which can be easily combed straight. She speaks easily and fluently, and has an agreeable carriage and address. Being a good seamstress, she has been accustomed to dress well, has a variety of very fine clothes, made in the prevailing fashion, and will probably appear, if abroad, tricked out in gay and fashionable finery. As this girl absconded from the plantation of my son without any known cause or provocation, it is probable she designs to transport herself to the North.

The above reward, with all reasonable charges, will be given for apprehending her, or securing her in any prison or jail within the U. States.

All persons are hereby forewarned against harboring or entertaining her, or being in any way instrumental in her escape, under the most rigorous penalties of the law.

JAMES NORCOM.

Edenton, N. C. June 30

$100 Reward

This is the advertisement that Dr. James Norcom, or "Dr. Flint," placed in the *American Beacon*, Norfolk, Virginia. The advertisement, which ran on Tuesdays, Thursdays, and Saturdays for two weeks beginning on June 30, 1835, differs in some significant ways from the poster Jacobs quotes in *Incidents*.

The tidings made the old doctor rave and storm at a furious rate. It was a busy day for them. My grandmother's house was searched from top to bottom. As my trunk was empty, they concluded I had taken my clothes with me. Before ten o'clock every vessel northward bound was thoroughly examined, and the law against harboring fugitives was read to all on board. At night a watch was set over the town. Knowing how distressed my grandmother would be, I wanted to send her a message; but it could not be done. Every one who went in or out of her house was closely watched. The doctor said he would take my children, unless she became responsible for them; which of course she willingly did. The next day was spent in searching. Before night, the following advertisement was posted at every corner, and in every public place for miles round: –

> "$300 REWARD! Ran away from the subscriber, an intelligent, bright, mulatto girl, named Linda, 21 years of age. Five feet four inches high. Dark eyes, and black hair inclined to curl; but it can be made straight. Has a decayed spot on a front tooth. She can read and write, and in all probability will try to get to the Free States. All persons are forbidden, under penalty of the law, to harbor or employ said slave. $150 will be given to whoever takes her in the state, and $300 if taken out of the state and delivered to me, or lodged in jail.
>
> DR. FLINT"

XXI. The Loophole of Retreat

A small shed had been added to my grandmother's house years ago. Some boards were laid across the joists at the top, and between these boards and the roof was a very small garret, never occupied by any thing but rats and mice. It was a pent roof, covered with nothing but shingles, according to the southern custom for such buildings. The garret was only nine feet long and seven wide. The highest part was three feet high, and sloped down abruptly to the loose board floor. There was no admission for either light or air. My uncle Philip, who was a carpenter, had very skil-fully made a concealed trap-door, which communicated with the storeroom. He had been doing this while I was waiting in the swamp. The storeroom opened upon a piazza. To this hole I was conveyed as soon as I entered the house. The air was stifling; the darkness total. A bed had been spread on the floor. I could sleep quite comfortably on one side; but the slope was so sudden that I could not turn on the other without hitting the roof. The rats and mice ran over my bed; but I was weary, and I slept such sleep as the wretched may, when a tempest has passed over them. Morning came. I knew it only by the noises I heard; for in my small den day and night were all the same. I suffered for air even more than for light. But I was not comfortless. I heard the voices of my children. There was joy and there was sadness in the sound. It made my tears flow. How I longed to speak to them! I was eager to look on their faces; but there was no hole, no crack, through which I could peep. This continued darkness was oppressive. It seemed horrible to sit or lie in a cramped position day after day, without one gleam of light. Yet I would have chosen this, rather than my lot as a slave, though white people considered it an easy one; and it was so compared with the fate of others. I was never cruelly over-worked; I was never lacerated with the whip from head to foot; I was never so beaten and bruised that I could not turn from one side to the other; I never had my heel-strings cut to prevent my running away; I was never chained to a log and forced to drag it about, while I toiled in the fields from morning till night; I was never branded with hot iron, or torn by bloodhounds. On the contrary, I had always been kindly treated, and tenderly cared for, until I came into the hands of Dr. Flint. I had never wished for freedom till then. But though my life in slavery was comparatively devoid of hardships, God pity the woman who is compelled to lead such a life!

My food was passed up to me through the trap-door my uncle had contrived; and my grandmother, my uncle Phillip, and aunt Nancy would seize such opportunities as they could, to mount up there and chat with me at the opening. But of course this was not safe in the daytime. It must all be done in darkness. It was impossible for me to move in an erect position, but I crawled about my den for exercise. One day I hit my head against something, and found it was a gimlet. My uncle had left it sticking there when he made the trap-door. I was as rejoiced as Robinson Crusoe could have been at finding such a treasure. It put a lucky thought into my head. I said to myself, "Now I will have some light. Now I will see my children." I did not dare to begin my work during the daytime, for fear of attracting attention. But I groped round; and having found the side next the street, where I could frequently see my children, I stuck the gimlet in and waited for evening. I bored three rows of holes, one above another; then I bored out the interstices between. I thus succeeded in making one hole about an inch long and an inch broad. I sat by it till late into the night, to enjoy the little whiff of air that floated in. In the morning I watched for my children. The first person I saw in the street was Dr. Flint. I had a shuddering, superstitious feeling that it was a bad omen. Several familiar faces passed by. At last I heard the merry laugh of children, and presently two sweet little faces were looking up at me, as though they knew I was there, and were conscious of the joy they imparted. How I longed to *tell* them I was there!

My condition was now a little improved. But for weeks I was tormented by hundreds of little red insects, fine as a needle's point, that pierced through my skin, and produced an intolerable burning. The good grandmother gave me herb teas and cooling medicines, and finally I got rid of them. The heat of my den was intense, for nothing but thin shingles protected me from the scorching summer's sun. But I had my consolations. Through my peeping-hole I could watch the children, and when they were near enough, I could hear their talk. Aunt Nancy brought me all the news she could hear at Dr. Flint's. From her I learned that the doctor had written to New York to a colored woman, who had been born and raised in our neighborhood, and had breathed his contaminating atmosphere. He offered her a reward if she could find out any thing about me. I know not what was the nature of her reply; but he soon after started for New York in haste, saying to his family that he had business of importance to transact. I peeped at him as he passed on his way to the steamboat. It was a satisfaction to have miles of land and water between us, even for a little while; and it was a still greater satisfaction to know that he believed me to be in the Free States. My little den seemed less dreary than it had done. He returned, as he did from his former journey to New York, without obtaining any satisfactory information. When he passed our house next morning, Benny was standing at the gate. He had heard them say that he had gone to find me, and he called out, "Dr. Flint, did you bring my mother home? I want to see her." The doctor stamped his foot at him in a rage, and exclaimed, "Get out of the way, you little damned rascal! If you don't, I'll cut off your head."

Benny ran terrified into the house, saying, "You can't put me in jail again. I don't belong to you now." It was well that the wind carried the words away from the doctor's ear. I told my grandmother of it, when we had our next conference at the trap-door; and begged of her not to allow the children to be impertinent to the irascible old man.

Autumn came, with a pleasant abatement of heat. My eyes had become accustomed to the dim light, and by holding my book or work in a certain position near the aperture I contrived to read and sew. That was a great relief to the tedious monotony of my life. But when winter came, the cold penetrated through the thin shingle roof, and I was dreadfully chilled. The winters there are not so long, or so severe, as in northern latitudes; but the houses are not built to shelter from cold, and my little den was peculiarly comfortless. The kind grandmother brought me bed-clothes and warm drinks. Often I was obliged to lie in bed all day to keep comfortable; but with all my precautions, my shoulders and feet were frostbitten. O, those long, gloomy days, with no object for my eye to rest upon, and no thoughts to occupy my mind, except the dreary past and the uncertain future! I was thankful when there came a day sufficiently mild for me to wrap myself up and sit at the loophole to watch the passers by. Southerners have the habit of stopping and talking in the streets, and I heard many conversations not intended to meet my ears. I heard slave-hunters planning how to catch some poor fugitive. Several times I heard allusions to Dr. Flint, myself, and the history of my children, who, perhaps, were playing near the gate. One would say, "I wouldn't move my little finger to catch her, as old Flint's property." Another would say, "I'll catch *any* nigger for the reward. A man ought to have what belongs to him, if he *is* a damned brute." The opinion was often expressed that I was in the Free States. Very rarely did any one suggest that I might be in the vicinity. Had the least suspicion rested on my grandmother's house, it would have been burned to the ground. But it was the last place they thought of. Yet there was no place, where slavery existed, that could have afforded me so good a place of concealment.

Dr. Flint and his family repeatedly tried to coax and bribe my children to tell something they had heard said about me. One day the doctor took them into a shop, and offered them some bright little silver pieces and gay handkerchiefs if they would tell where their mother was. Ellen shrank away from him, and would not speak; but Benny spoke up, and said, "Dr. Flint, I don't know where my mother is. I guess she's in New York; and when you go there again, I wish you'd ask her to come home, for I want to see her; but if you put her in jail, or tell her you'll cut her head off, I'll tell her to go right back."

XLI. Free at Last

Mrs. Bruce, and every member of her family, were exceedingly kind to me. I was thankful for the blessings of my lot, yet I could not always wear a cheerful countenance. I was doing harm to no one; on the contrary, I was doing all the good I could in my small way; yet I could never go out to breathe God's free air without trepidation at my heart. This seemed hard; and I could not think it was a right state of things in any civilized country.

From time to time I received news from my good old grandmother. She could not write; but she employed others to write for her. The following is an extract from one of her last letters :

> "Dear Daughter: I cannot hope to see you again on earth; but I pray to God to unite us above, where pain will no more rack this feeble body of mine; where sorrow and parting from my children will be no more. God has promised these things if we are faithful unto the end. My age and feeble health deprive me of going to church now; but God is with me here at home. Thank your brother for his kindness. Give much love to him, and tell him to remember the Creator in the days of his youth, and strive to meet me in the Father's kingdom. Love to Ellen and Benjamin. Don't neglect him. Tell him for me, to be a good boy. Strive, my child, to train them for God's children. May he protect and provide for you, is the prayer of your loving old mother."

These letters both cheered and saddened me. I was always glad to have tidings from the kind, faithful old friend of my unhappy youth; but her messages of love made my heart yearn to see her before she died, and I mourned over the fact that it was impossible. Some months after I returned from my flight to New England, I received a letter from her, in which she wrote, "Dr. Flint is dead. He has left a distressed family. Poor old man! I hope he made his peace with God."

I remembered how he had defrauded my grandmother of the hard earnings she had loaned; how he had tried to cheat her out of the freedom her mistress had promised her, and how he had persecuted her children; and I thought to myself that she was a better Christian than I was, if she could entirely forgive him. I cannot say, with truth, that the news of my old master's death softened my feelings towards him. There are wrongs which even the grave does not bury. The man was odious to me while he lived, and his memory is odious now.

His departure from this world did not diminish my danger. He had threatened my grandmother that his heirs should hold me in slavery after he was gone; that I never should be free so long as a child of his survived. As for Mrs. Flint, I had seen her in deeper afflictions than I supposed the loss of her husband would be, for she had buried several children; yet I never saw any signs of softening in her heart. The doctor had died in embarrassed circumstances, and had little to will to his heirs, except such property as he was unable to grasp. I was well aware what I had to expect from the family of Flints; and my fears were confirmed by a letter from the south, warning me to be on my guard, because Mrs. Flint openly declared that her daughter could not afford to lose so valuable a slave as I was.

I kept close watch of the newspapers for arrivals; out one Saturday night, being much occupied, I forgot to examine the Evening Express as usual. I went down into the parlor for it, early in the morning, and found the boy about to kindle a fire with it. I took it from him and examined the list of arrivals. Reader, if you have never been a slave, you cannot imagine the acute sensation of suffering at my heart, when I read the names of Mr. and Mrs. Dodge, at a hotel in Courtland Street. It was a third-rate hotel, and that circumstance convinced me of the truth of what I had heard, that they were short of funds and had need of my value, as *they* valued me; and that was by dollars and cents. I hastened with the paper to Mrs. Bruce. Her heart and hand were always open to every one in distress, and she always warmly sympathized with mine. It was impossible to tell how near the enemy was. He might have passed and repassed the house while we were sleeping. He might at that moment be waiting to pounce upon me if I ventured out of doors. I had never seen the husband of my young mistress, and therefore I could not distinguish him from any other stranger. A carriage was hastily ordered; and, closely veiled, I followed Mrs. Bruce, taking the baby again with me into exile. After various turnings and crossings, and returnings, the carriage stopped at the house of one of Mrs. Bruce's friends, where I was kindly received. Mrs. Bruce returned immediately, to instruct the domestics what to say if any one came to inquire for me.

It was lucky for me that the evening paper was not burned up before I had a chance to examine the list of arrivals. It was not long after Mrs. Bruce's return to her house, before several people came to inquire for me. One inquired for me, another asked for my daughter Ellen, and another said he had a letter from my grandmother, which he was requested to deliver in person.

They were told, "She *has* lived here, but she has left."

"How long ago?"

"I don't know, sir."

"Do you know where she went?"

"I do not, sir." And the door was closed.

This Mr. Dodge, who claimed me as his property, was originally a Yankee pedler in the south; then he became a merchant, and finally a slaveholder. He managed to get introduced into what was called the first society, and married Miss Emily Flint. A quarrel arose between him and her brother, and the brother cowhided him. This led to a family feud, and he proposed to remove to Virginia. Dr. Flint left him no property, and his own means had become circumscribed, while a wife and children depended upon him for support. Under these circumstances, it was very natural that he should make an effort to put me into his pocket.

I had a colored friend, a man from my native place, in whom I had the most implicit confidence. I sent for him, and told him that Mr. and Mrs. Dodge had arrived in New York. I proposed that he should call upon them to make inquiries about his friends at the south, with whom Dr. Flint's family were well acquainted. He thought there was no impropriety in his doing so, and he consented. He went to the hotel, and knocked at the door of Mr. Dodge's room, which was opened by the gentleman himself, who gruffly inquired, "What brought you here? How came you to know I was in the city?"

"Your arrival was published in the evening papers, sir; and I called to ask Mrs. Dodge about my friends at home. I didn't suppose it would give any offence."

"Where's that negro girl, that belongs to my wife?"

"What girl, sir?"

"You know well enough. I mean Linda, that ran away from Dr. Flint's plantation, some years ago. I dare say you've seen her, and know where she is."

"Yes, sir, I've seen her, and know where she is. She is out of your reach, sir."

"Tell me where she is, or bring her to me, and I will give her a chance to buy her freedom."

"I don't think it would be of any use, sir. I have heard her say she would go to the ends of the earth, rather than pay any man or woman for her freedom, because she thinks she has a right to it. Besides, she couldn't do it, if she would, for she has spent her earnings to educate her children."

This made Mr. Dodge very angry, and some high words passed between them. My friend was afraid to come where I was; but in the course of the day I received a note from him. I supposed they had not come from the south, in the winter, for a pleasure excursion; and now the nature of their business was very plain.

Mrs. Bruce came to me and entreated me to leave the city the next morning. She said her house was watched, and it was possible that some clew to me might be obtained. I refused to take her advice. She pleaded with an earnest tenderness, that ought to have moved me; but I was in a bitter, disheartened mood. I was weary of flying from pillar to post. I had been chased during half my life, and it seemed as if the chase was never to end. There I sat, in that great city, guiltless of crime, yet not daring to worship God in any of the churches. I heard the bells ringing for afternoon service, and, with contemptuous sarcasm, I said, "Will the preachers take for their text, 'Proclaim liberty to the captive, and the opening of prison doors to them that are bound'? or will they preach from the text, 'Do unto others as ye would they should do unto you'?"[1] Oppressed Poles and Hungarians could find a safe refuge in that city; John Mitchell[2] was free to proclaim in the City Hall his desire for "a plantation well stocked with slaves;" but there I sat, an oppressed American, not daring to show my face. God forgive the black and bitter thoughts I indulged on that Sabbath day! The scripture says, "Oppression makes even a wise man mad;"[3] and I was not wise.

I had been told that Mr. Dodge said his wife had never signed away her right to my children, and if he could not get me, he would take them. This it was, more than any thing else, that roused such a tempest in my soul. Benjamin was with his uncle William in California, but my innocent young daughter had come to spend a vacation with me. I thought of what I had suffered in slavery at her age, and my heart was like a tiger's when a hunter tries to seize her young.

Dear Mrs. Bruce! I seem to see the expression of her face, as she turned away discouraged by my obstinate mood. Finding her expostulations unavailing, she sent Ellen to entreat me. When ten o'clock in the evening arrived and Ellen had not returned, this watchful and unwearied friend became anxious. She came to us in a carriage, bringing a

1. **"Proclaim . . . unto you":** Isaiah 61:1; Matthew 7:12.
2. **John Mitchell:** (1815-1875) proslavery Irish American immigrant and editor of the *Citizen*, published in New York City.
3. **"Oppression . . . mad":** Ecclesiastes 7:7.

well-filled trunk for my journey – trusting that by this time I would listen to reason. I yielded to her, as I ought to have done before.

The next day, baby and I set out in a heavy snow storm, bound for New England again. I received letters from the City of Iniquity, addressed to me under an assumed name. In a few days one came from Mrs. Bruce, informing me that my new master was still searching for me, and that she intended to put an end to this persecution by buying my freedom. I felt grateful for the kindness that prompted this offer, but the idea was not so pleasant to me as might have been expected. The more my mind had become enlightened, the more difficult it was for me to consider myself an article of property; and to pay money to those who had so grievously oppressed me seemed like taking from my sufferings the glory of triumph. I wrote to Mrs. Bruce, thanking her, but saying that being sold from one owner to another seemed too much like slavery; that such a great obligation could not be easily cancelled; and that I preferred to go to my brother in California.

Without my knowledge. Mrs. Bruce employed a gentleman in New York to enter into negotiations with Mr. Dodge. He proposed to pay three hundred dollars down, if Mr. Dodge would sell me, and enter into obligations to relinquish all claim to me or my children forever after. He who called himself my master said he scorned so small an offer for such a valuable servant. The gentleman replied, "You can do as you choose, sir. If you reject this offer you will never get any thing; for the woman has friends who will convey her and her children out of the country."

Mr. Dodge concluded that "half a loaf was better than no bread," and he agreed to the proffered terms. By the next mail I received this brief letter from Mrs. Bruce: "I am rejoiced to tell you that the money for your freedom has been paid to Mr. Dodge. Come home to-morrow. I long to see you and my sweet babe."

My brain reeled as I read these lines. A gentleman near me said, "It's true; I have seen the bill of sale." "The bill of sale!" Those words struck me like a blow. So I was *sold* at last! A human being *sold* in the free city of New York! The bill of sale is on record, and future generations will learn from it that women were articles of traffic in New York, late in the nineteenth century of the Christian religion. It may hereafter prove a useful document to antiquaries, who are seeking to measure the progress of civilization in the United States. I well know the value of that bit of paper; but much as I love freedom, I do not like to look upon it. I am deeply grateful to the generous friend who procured it, but I despise the miscreant who demanded payment for what never rightfully belonged to him or his.

I had objected to having my freedom bought, yet I must confess that when it was done I felt as if a heavy load had been lifted from my weary shoulders. When I rode home in the cars I was no longer afraid to unveil my face and look at people as they passed. I should have been glad to have met Daniel Dodge himself; to have had him seen me and known me, that he might have mourned over the untoward circumstances which compelled him to sell me for three hundred dollars.

When I reached home, the arms of my benefactress were thrown round me, and our tears mingled. As soon as she could speak, she said, "O Linda, I'm *so* glad it's all over! You wrote to me as if you thought you were going to be transferred from one owner to another. But I did not buy you for your services. I should have done just the same, if you had been going to sail for California to-morrow. I should, at least, have the satisfaction of knowing that you left me a free woman."

My heart was exceedingly full. I remembered how my poor father had tried to buy me, when I was a small child, and how he had been disappointed. I hoped his spirit was rejoicing over me now. I remembered how my good old grandmother had laid up her earnings to purchase me in later years, and how often her plans had been frustrated. How that faithful, loving old heart would leap for joy, if she could look on me and my children now that we were free! My relatives had been foiled in all their efforts, but God had raised me up a friend among strangers, who had bestowed on me the precious, long-desired boon. Friend! It is a common word often lightly used. Like other good and beautiful things, it may be tarnished by careless handling; but when I speak of Mrs. Bruce as my friend, the word is sacred.

My grandmother lived to rejoice in my freedom; but not long after, a letter came with a black seal. She had gone "where the wicked cease from troubling, and the weary are at rest."[4]

Time passed on, and a paper came to me from the south, containing an obituary notice of my uncle Phillip. It was the only case I ever knew of such an honor conferred upon a colored person. It was written by one of his friends, and contained these words: "Now that death has laid him low, they call him a good man and a useful citizen; but what are eulogies to the black man, when the world has faded from his vision? It does not require man's praise to obtain rest in God's kingdom." So they called a colored man a *citizen*! Strange words to be uttered in that region!

Reader, my story ends with freedom; not in the usual way, with marriage. I and my children are now free! We are as free from the power of slaveholders as are the white people of the north; and though that, according to my ideas, is not saying a great deal, it is a vast improvement in *my* condition. The dream of my life is not yet realized. I do not sit with my children in a home of my own. I still long for a hearthstone of my own, however humble. I wish it for my children's sake far more than for my own. But God so orders circumstances as to keep me with my friend Mrs. Bruce. Love, duty, gratitude, also bind me to her side. It is a privilege to serve her who pities my oppressed people, and who has bestowed the inestimable boon of freedom on me and my children.

It has been painful to me, in many ways, to recall the dreary years I passed in bondage. I would gladly forget them if I could. Yet the retrospection is not altogether without solace; for with those gloomy recollections come tender memories of my good old grandmother, like light, fleecy clouds floating over a dark and troubled sea.

[1861]

4. "where . . . at rest": Job 3:17.

Henry David Thoreau

[1817–1862]

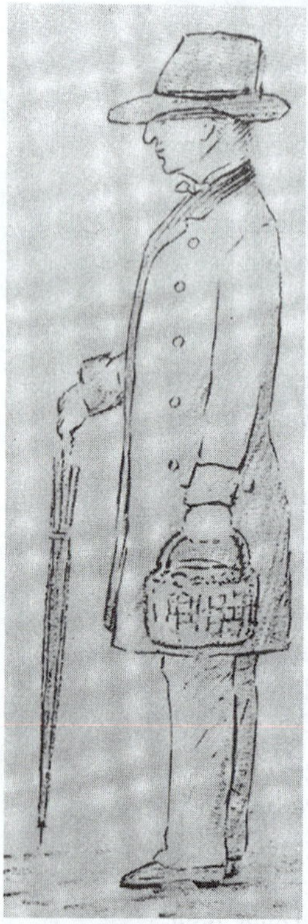

Henry David Thoreau

This pencil sketch shows Thoreau in his traveling outfit, as he presented himself at the door of Daniel Ricketson's house in New Bedford, Massachusetts, in December 1854.

bedfordstmartins.com/ americanlit *for research links on Thoreau*

Henry David Thoreau was born on July 12, 1817, in Concord, Massachusetts. He was educated at the Concord Academy and Harvard College, from which he graduated in 1837. Returning to Concord, Thoreau confronted a problem he would grapple with throughout his life: how to earn a living without sacrificing his own freedom and autonomy. As a college graduate, Thoreau would have been expected to embark on a successful career in business, law, or one of the other professions. Instead, he accepted a teaching position in a public school in Concord. When the school committee told him that he was expected to use corporal punishment to discipline the students, Thoreau resigned. He and his older brother, John, then opened a private school in Concord.

Teaching allowed Thoreau ample time for study and, increasingly, for writing. His literary aspirations were strongly encouraged by Ralph Waldo Emerson, whose successful career as a writer and lecturer offered a powerful model to Thoreau. Partly in an effort to support such aspiring young writers, Emerson helped establish the *Dial*, a periodical in which Thoreau's earliest essays and reviews appeared. After his brother's failing health obliged them to close their school in 1841, Thoreau joined the Emerson household, where he did odd jobs and helped to edit the *Dial*. With the assistance of Nathaniel Hawthorne, who moved to Concord in 1842, Thoreau also published several pieces in periodicals in Boston and New York City. But his efforts to gain a foothold in the larger literary marketplace were unsuccessful. Consequently, after the *Dial* ceased publication in 1844, he lost the last ready outlet for his writings. When Emerson bought some land on the shore of Walden Pond, Thoreau received his permission to build a cabin on the property, where he moved on July 4, 1845.

The two years, two months, and two days that Thoreau lived at Walden Pond constituted the most productive and satisfying period of his often-frustrating literary career. During that period, he wrote the bulk of his first book, *A Week on the Concord and Merrimack Rivers*, and the first draft of his masterpiece, *Walden*. Unable to find a publisher for *A Week* in 1847, when he left the pond, Thoreau continued to revise the book until 1849, when he published it at his own expense. Although it received some admiring reviews, the book was a commercial flop: Of an edition of one thousand, it sold fewer than three hundred copies by 1853, when its publisher returned the unsold copies to Thoreau. "I have now a library of more than nine hundred volumes, over seven hundred of which I wrote myself," Thoreau ruefully recorded in his journal. Living with his family, he supported himself and paid off his debt to the publisher by working as a surveyor and lending a hand in his father's pencil business.

The failure of his first book did not deter Thoreau from pursuing other literary projects, especially *Walden*, which he revised and expanded before it was published in 1854. He was thereafter frequently called "the hermit of Walden Pond," which he had in fact left seven years earlier, and despite the fact that during the 1850s he lectured and published essays on a range of other subjects, including his trips to Canada, Cape Cod, and the wilderness of Maine. Thoreau also delivered two celebrated antislavery addresses: "Slavery in Massachusetts" (1854), a protest against the enforcement of the Fugitive Slave Act, and "A Plea for John Brown," an eloquent defense of the leader of the 1859 raid on the federal arsenal at Harpers Ferry, Virginia. For the most part, however, Thoreau sought to remain aloof from the heated social and political controversies of the period. He primarily devoted himself to the study of natural history, the focus of lectures like "Autumnal Tints," "The Succession of Forest Trees," and "Wild Apples," all of which he delivered in 1859-60, on the eve of the Civil War. Those lectures were small fragments of far more ambitious projects, *The Dispersion of Seeds* and *Wild Fruits*, massive manuscripts that Thoreau was not able to complete before he died from tuberculosis on May 6, 1862.

Mr. Thoreau is a keen and delicate observer of nature . . . and Nature, in return for his love, seems to adopt him as her especial child, and shows him secrets which few others are allowed to witness.
-Nathaniel Hawthorne

Thoreau's "Resistance to Civil Government." Now better known as "Civil Disobedience," the title of a revised version first published in 1866, this is Thoreau's most well-known essay. Indeed, it was an inspiration to leaders of social movements around the world during the twentieth century, notably Mohandas Gandhi and Martin Luther King Jr. But the essay was written in response to local events and to the immediate concerns of the 1840s. As early as 1842, Thoreau began to withhold his poll tax – a tax levied on all adult males in Massachusetts – first as a protest against slavery and later in opposition to the Mexican War, which broke out in the spring of 1846. That July, he was arrested and jailed for one night until one of his friends or relatives paid the tax for him. In response to those who were critical of his stand, including many of his fellow townspeople, Thoreau in January 1848 delivered a lecture on "The Rights and Duties of the Individual in Relation to the State" at the Concord Lyceum. The following year the lecture was published as "Resistance to Civil Government" in the first and only issue of *Aesthetic Papers*, a periodical edited by the reformer Elizabeth Peabody. It probably would have languished in obscurity if the revised version had not been included in a posthumously published collection, *A Yankee in Canada, with Anti-Slavery and Reform Papers* (1866). Thereafter, the essay was later reprinted and translated countless times, often together with Thoreau's other most-famous work, *Walden*. The text is taken from the original printing of "Resistance to Civil Government" in *Aesthetic Papers* (1849).

Resistance to Civil Government

I heartily accept the motto, – "That government is best which governs least;"[1] and I should like to see it acted up to more rapidly and systematically. Carried out, it finally amounts to this, which also I believe, – "That government is best which governs not at all;" and when men are prepared for it, that will be the kind of government which they will have. Government is at best but an expedient; but most governments are usually, and all governments are sometimes, inexpedient. The objections which have been brought against a standing army, and they are many and weighty, and deserve to prevail, may also at last be brought against a standing government. The standing army is only an arm of the standing government. The government itself, which is only the mode which the people have chosen to execute their will, is equally liable to be abused and perverted before the people can act through it. Witness the present Mexican War, the work of comparatively a few individuals using the standing government as their tool; for, in the outset, the people would not have consented to this measure.

This American government, – what is it but a tradition, though a recent one, endeavoring to transmit itself unimpaired to posterity, but each instant losing some of its integrity? It has not the vitality and force of a single living man; for a single man can bend it to his will. It is a sort of wooden gun to the people themselves; and, if ever they should use it in earnest as a real one against each other, it will surely split. But it is not the less necessary for this; for the people must have some complicated machinery or other and hear its din, to satisfy that idea of government which they have. Governments show thus how successfully men can be imposed on, even impose on themselves, for their own advantage. It is excellent, we must all allow; yet this government never of itself furthered any enterprise, but by the alacrity with which it got out of its way. *It* does not keep the country free. *It* does not settle the West. *It* does not educate. The character inherent in the American people has done all that has been accomplished; and it would have done somewhat more, if the government had not sometimes got in its way. For government is an expedient by which men would fain succeed in letting one another alone; and, as has been said, when it is most expedient, the governed are most let alone by it. Trade and commerce, if they were not made of India rubber, would never manage to bounce over the obstacles which legislators are continually putting in their way; and, if one were to judge these men wholly by the effects of their actions, and not partly by their intentions, they would deserve to be classed and punished with those mischievous persons who put obstructions on the railroads.

But, to speak practically and as a citizen, unlike those who call themselves no-government men,[2] I ask for, not at once no government, but *at once* a better government. Let every man make known what kind of government would command his respect, and that will be one step toward obtaining it.

---

1. **"That . . . least":** This motto was used on the masthead of the *Democratic Review*, an influential literary and political journal to which Thoreau had contributed several articles.
2. **no-government men:** Common name for the nonresistants, Christian anarchists and pacifists who called for the dissolution of what they called *human governments* which were to be replaced by the government of God.

After all, the practical reason why, when the power is once in the hands of the people, a majority are permitted, and for a long period continue, to rule, is not because they are most likely to be in the right, nor because this seems fairest to the minority, but because they are physically the strongest. But a government in which the majority rule in all cases cannot be based on justice, even as far as men understand it. Can there not be a government in which majorities do not virtually decide right and wrong, but conscience? – in which majorities decide only those questions to which the rule of expediency is applicable? Must the citizen ever for a moment, or in the least degree, resign his conscience to the legislator? Why has every man a conscience, then? I think that we should be men first, and subjects afterward. It is not desirable to cultivate a respect for the law, so much as for the right. The only obligation which I have a right to assume, is to do at any time what I think right. It is truly enough said, that a corporation has no conscience; but a corporation of conscientious men is a corporation *with* a conscience. Law never made men a whit more just; and, by means of their respect for it, even the well-disposed are daily made the agents of injustice. A common and natural result of an undue respect for law is, that you may see a file of soldiers, colonel, captain, corporal, privates, powder-monkeys[3] and all, marching in admirable order over hill and dale to the wars, against their wills, aye, against their common sense and consciences, which makes it very steep marching indeed, and produces a palpitation of the heart. They have no doubt that it is a damnable business in which they are concerned; they are all peaceably inclined. Now, what are they? Men at all? or small moveable forts and magazines, at the service of some unscrupulous man in power? Visit the Navy Yard, and behold a marine, such a man as an American government can make, or such as it can make a man with its black arts, a mere shadow and reminiscence of humanity, a man laid out alive and standing, and already, as one may say, buried under arms with funeral accompaniments, though it may be

"Not a drum was heard, nor a funeral note,
As his corse to the ramparts we hurried;
Not a soldier discharged his farewell shot
O'er the grave where our hero we buried."[4]

The mass of men serve the State thus, not as men mainly, but as machines, with their bodies. They are the standing army, and the militia, jailers, constables, *posse comitatus*,[5] etc. In most cases there is no free exercise whatever of the judgment or of the moral sense; but they put themselves on a level with wood and earth and stones; and wooden men can perhaps be manufactured that will serve the purpose as well. Such command no more respect than men of straw, or a lump of dirt. They have the same sort of worth only as horses and dogs. Yet such as these even are commonly esteemed good citizens. Others, as most legislators, politicians, lawyers, ministers, and office-holders, serve the

---

3. **powder-monkeys**: Young boys in the military whose job it was to carry gunpowder from a storehouse to the cannons.
4. **"Not . . . buried."**: Thoreau is loosely quoting the first stanza of "The Burial of Sir John Moore at Corunna" by Charles Wolfe (1791–1823).
5. ***posse comitatus***: A body of citizens summoned by a sheriff to help keep the peace.

State chiefly with their heads; and, as they rarely make any moral distinctions, they are as likely to serve the devil, without intending it, as God. A very few, as heroes, patriots, martyrs, reformers in the great sense, and *men*, serve the State with their consciences also, and so necessarily resist it for the most part; and they are commonly treated by it as enemies. A wise man will only be useful as a man, and will not submit to be "clay," and "stop a hole to keep the wind away,"[6] but leave that office to his dust at least: –

> "I am too high-born to be propertied,
> To be a secondary at control,
> Or useful serving-man and instrument
> To any sovereign state throughout the world."[7]

He who gives himself entirely to his fellow-men appears to them useless and selfish; but he who gives himself partially to them is pronounced a benefactor and philanthropist.

How does it become a man to behave toward this American government to-day? I answer that he cannot without disgrace be associated with it. I cannot for an instant recognize that political organization as *my* government which is the *slave's* government also.

All men recognize the right of revolution; that is, the right to refuse allegiance to and to resist the government, when its tyranny or its inefficiency are great and unendurable. But almost all say that such is not the case now. But such was the case, they think, in the Revolution of '75.[8] If one were to tell me that this was a bad government because it taxed certain foreign commodities brought to it ports, it is most probable that I should not make an ado about it, for I can do without them: all machines have their friction; and possibly this does enough good to counterbalance the evil. At any rate, it is a great evil to make a stir about it. But when the friction comes to have its machine, and oppression and robbery are organized, I say, let us not have such a machine any longer. In other words, when a sixth of the population of a nation which has undertaken to be the refuge of liberty are slaves, and a whole country is unjustly overrun and conquered by a foreign army, and subjected to military law, I think that it is not too soon for honest men to rebel and revolutionize. What makes this duty the more urgent is the fact, that the country so overrun is not our own, but ours is the invading army.

Paley,[9] a common authority with many on moral questions, in his chapter on the "Duty of Submission to Civil Government," resolves all civil obligation into expediency; and he proceeds to say, "that so long as the interest of the whole society requires it, that is, so long as the established government cannot be resisted or changed without public inconveniency, it is the will of God that the established government be obeyed, and no

---

6. **"clay . . . away":** See Shakespeare, *Hamlet*, 5.1.236-37: "Imperious Caesar, dead and turn'd to clay, / Might stop a hole to keep the wind away."

7. **I . . . world:** Shakespeare, *King John*, 5.2.79-82.

8. **Revolution of '75:** The American Revolution, which began with the battles of Lexington and Concord in 1775.

9. **Paley:** William Paley (1743-1805), author of several influential books on Christianity and ethics; from his *Principles of Moral and Political Philosophy* (1785).

longer." – "This principle being admitted, the justice of every particular case of resistance is reduced to a computation of the quantity of the danger and grievance on the one side, and of the probability and expense of redressing it on the other." Of this, he says, every man shall judge for himself. But Paley appears never to have contemplated those cases to which the rule of expediency does not apply, in which a people, as well as an individual, must do justice, cost what it may. If I have unjustly wrested a plank from a drowning man, I must restore it to him though I drown myself. This, according to Paley, would be inconvenient. But he that would save his life, in such a case, shall lose it.[10] This people must cease to hold slaves, and to make war on Mexico, though it cost them their existence as a people.

In their practice, nations agree with Paley; but does any one think that Massachusetts does exactly what is right at the present crisis?

> "A drab of state, a cloth-o'-silver slut,
> To have her train borne up, and her soul trail in the dirt."[11]

Practically speaking, the opponents to a reform in Massachusetts are not a hundred thousand politicians at the South, but a hundred thousand merchants and farmers here, who are more interested in commerce and agriculture than they are in humanity, and are not prepared to do justice to the slave and to Mexico, *cost what it may.* I quarrel not with far-off foes, but with those who, near at home, co-operate with, and do the bidding of those far away, and without whom the latter would be harmless. We are accustomed to say, that the mass of men are unprepared; but improvement is slow, because the few are not materially wiser or better than the many. It is not so important that many should be as good as you, as that there be some absolute goodness somewhere; for that will leaven the whole lump. There are thousands who are *in opinion* opposed to slavery and to the war, who yet in effect do nothing to put an end to them; who, esteeming themselves children of Washington and Franklin, sit down with their hands in their pockets, and say that they know not what to do, and do nothing; who even postpone the question of freedom to the question of free-trade, and quietly read the prices-current along with the latest advices from Mexico, after dinner, and, it may be, fall asleep over them both. What is the price-current of an honest man and patriot to-day? They hesitate, and they regret, and sometimes they petition; but they do nothing in earnest and with effect. They will wait, well disposed, for others to remedy the evil, that they may no longer have it to regret. At most, they give only a cheap vote, and a feeble countenance and Godspeed, to the right, as it goes by them. There are nine hundred and ninety-nine patrons of virtue to one virtuous man; but it is easier to deal with the real possessor of a thing than with the temporary guardian of it.

All voting is a sort of gaming, like chequers or backgammon, with a slight moral tinge to it, a playing with right and wrong, with moral questions; and betting naturally

---

10. **But . . . lose it:** Compare Christ's words to his disciples, "He that findeth his life shall lose it: And he that loseth his life for my sake shall find it" (Matthew 10:38).
11. **A . . . dirt:** Cyril Tourneur (1575?-1626), *The Revenger's Tragedy*, 4.4.72-73.

accompanies it. The character of the voters is not staked. I cast my vote, perchance, as I think right; but I am not vitally concerned that that right should prevail. I am willing to leave it to the majority. Its obligation, therefore, never exceeds that of expediency. Even voting *for the right* is *doing* nothing for it. It is only expressing to men feebly your desire that it should prevail. A wise man will not leave the right to the mercy of chance, nor wish it to prevail through the power of the majority. There is but little virtue in the action of masses of men. When the majority shall at length vote for the abolition of slavery, it will be because they are indifferent to slavery, or because there is but little slavery left to be abolished by their vote. *They* will then be the only slaves. Only *his* vote can hasten the abolition of slavery who asserts his own freedom by his vote.

I hear of a convention to be held at Baltimore, or elsewhere, for the selection of a candidate for the Presidency, made up chiefly of editors, and men who are politicians by profession; but I think, what is it to any independent, intelligent, and respectable man what decision they may come to, shall we not have the advantage of his wisdom and honesty, nevertheless? Can we not count upon some independent votes? Are there not many individuals in the country who do not attend conventions? But no: I find that the respectable man, so called, has immediately drifted from his position, and despairs of his country, when his country has more reason to despair of him. He forthwith adopts one of the candidates thus selected as the only *available* one, thus proving that he is himself *available* for any purposes of the demagogue. His vote is of no more worth than that of any unprincipled foreigner or hireling native, who may have been bought. Oh for a man who is a *man*, and, as my neighbor says, has a bone in his back which you cannot pass your hand through! Our statistics are at fault: the population has been returned too large. How many *men* are there to a square thousand miles in this country? Hardly one. Does not America offer any inducement for men to settle here? The American has dwindled into an Odd Fellow,[12] – one who may be known by the development of his organ of gregariousness, and a manifest lack of intellect and cheerful self-reliance; whose first and chief concern, on coming into the world, is to see that the alms-houses are in good repair; and, before yet he has lawfully donned the virile garb,[13] to collect a fund for the support of the widows and orphans that may be; who, in short, ventures to live only by the aid of the mutual insurance company, which has promised to bury him decently.

It is not a man's duty, as a matter of course, to devote himself to the eradication of any, even the most enormous wrong; he may still properly have other concerns to engage him; but it is his duty, at least, to wash his hands of it, and, if he gives it no thought longer, not to give it practically his support. If I devote myself to other pursuits and contemplations, I must first see, at least, that I do not pursue them sitting upon another man's shoulders. I must get off him first, that he may pursue his contemplations too. See what gross inconsistency is tolerated. I have heard some of my townsmen say, "I should like to have them order me out to help put down an insurrection of the

---

12. **Odd Fellow:** A member of the Independent Order of Odd Fellows, a secret fraternal organization.
13. **virile garb:** The *toga virilis*, clothing a Roman boy was allowed to wear when he reached the age of fourteen.

slaves, or to march to Mexico, – see if I would go;" and yet these very men have each, directly by their allegiance, and so indirectly, at least, by their money, furnished a substitute. The soldier is applauded who refuses to serve in an unjust war by those who do not refuse to sustain the unjust government which makes the war; is applauded by those who own act and authority he disregards and sets at nought; as if the State were penitent to that degree that it hired one to scourge it while it sinned, but not to that degree that it left off sinning for a moment. Thus, under the name of order and civil government, we are all made at last to pay homage to and support our own meanness. After the first blush of sin, comes its indifference; and from immoral it becomes, as it were, *un*moral, and not quite unnecessary to that life which we have made.

The broadest and most prevalent error requires the most disinterested virtue to sustain it. The slight reproach to which the virtue of patriotism is commonly liable, the noble are most likely to incur. Those who, while they disapprove of the character and measures of a government, yield to it their allegiance and support, are undoubtedly its most conscientious supporters, and so frequently the most serious obstacles to reform. Some are petitioning the State to dissolve the Union,[14] to disregard the requisitions of the President. Why do they not dissolve it themselves, – the union between themselves and the State, – and refuse to pay their quota into its treasury? Do not they stand in the same relation to the State, that the State does to the Union? And have not the same reasons prevented the State from resisting the Union, which have prevented them from resisting the State?

How can a man be satisfied to entertain an opinion merely, and enjoy *it*? Is there any enjoyment in it, if his opinion is that he is aggrieved? If you are cheated out of a single dollar by your neighbor, you do not rest satisfied with knowing that you are cheated, or with saying that you are cheated, or even with petitioning him to pay you your due; but you take effectual steps at once to obtain the full amount, and see that you are never cheated again. Action from principle, – the perception and the performance of right, – changes things and relations; it is essentially revolutionary, and does not consist wholly with any thing which was. It not only divides states and churches, it divides families; aye, it divides the *individual*, separating the diabolical in him from the divine.

Unjust laws exist: shall we be content to obey them, or shall we endeavor to amend them, and obey them until we have succeeded, or shall we transgress them at once? Men generally, under such a government as this, think that they ought to wait until they have persuaded the majority to alter them. They think that, if they should resist, the remedy would be worse than the evil. But it is the fault of the government itself that the remedy *is* worse than the evil. *It* makes it worse. Why is it not more apt to anticipate and provide for reform? Why does it not cherish its wise minority? Why does it cry and resist before it is hurt? Why does it not encourage its citizens to be on the alert to point out its faults, and *do* better than it would have them? Why does it always crucify Christ, and excommunicate Copernicus and Luther, and pronounce Washington and Franklin rebels?

---

14. **Some . . . dissolve the Union:** Radical abolitionists, whose motto and official policy was "No Union with Slaveholders."

One would think, that a deliberate and practical denial of its authority was the only offence never contemplated by government; else, why has it not assigned its definite, its suitable and proportionate penalty? If a man who has no property refuses but once to earn nine shillings[15] for the State, he is put in prison for a period unlimited by any law that I know, and determined only by the discretion of those who placed him there; but if he should steal ninety times nine shillings from the State, he is soon permitted to go at large again.

If the injustice is part of the necessary friction of the machine of government, let it go, let it go: perchance it will wear smooth, – certainly the machine will wear out. If the injustice has a spring, or a pulley, or a rope, or a crank, exclusively for itself, then perhaps you may consider whether the remedy will not be worse than the evil; but if it is of such a nature that it requires you to be the agent of injustice to another, then, I say, break the law. Let your life be a counter friction to stop the machine. What I have to do is to see, at any rate, that I do not lend myself to the wrong which I condemn.

As for adopting the ways which the State has provided for remedying the evil, I know not of such ways. They take too much time, and a man's life will be gone. I have other affairs to attend to. I came into this world, not chiefly to make this a good place to live in, but to live in it, be it good or bad. A man has not every thing to do, but something; and because he cannot do *every thing*, it is not necessary that he should do *something* wrong. It is not my business to be petitioning the governor or the legislature any more than it is theirs to petition me; and, if they should not hear my petition, what should I do then? But in this case the State has provided no way: its very Constitution is the evil. This may seem to be harsh and stubborn and unconciliatory; but it is to treat with the utmost kindness and consideration the only spirit that can appreciate or deserves it. So is all change for the better, like birth and death which convulse the body.

I do not hesitate to say, that those who call themselves abolitionists should at once effectually withdraw their support, both in person and property, from the government of Massachusetts, and not wait till they constitute a majority of one, before they suffer the right to prevail through them. I think that it is enough if they have God on their side, without waiting for that other one. Moreover, any man more right than his neighbors, constitutes a majority of one already.

I meet this American government, or its representative the State government, directly, and face to face, once a year, no more, in the person of its tax-gatherer; this is the only mode in which a man situated as I am necessarily meets it; and it then says distinctly, Recognize me; and the simplest, the most effectual, and, in the present posture of affairs, the indispensablest mode of treating with it on this head, of expressing your little satisfaction with and love for it, is to deny it then. My civil neighbor, the tax-gatherer, is the very man I have to deal with, – for it is, after all, with men and not with parchment that I quarrel, – and he has voluntarily chosen to be an agent of the government. How shall he ever know well what he is and does as an officer of the government, or as a man, until he is obliged to consider whether he shall treat me, his neighbor, for whom he has respect, as a neighbor and well-disposed man, or as a maniac and dis-

15. **nine shillings:** The amount of the poll tax Thoreau refused to pay, about $2.25.

turber of the peace, and see if he can get over this obstruction to his neighborliness without a ruder and more impetuous thought or speech corresponding with his action? I know this well, that if one thousand, if one hundred, if ten men whom I could name, – if ten *honest* men only, – aye, if *one* HONEST man, in this State of Massachusetts, *ceasing to hold slaves*, were actually to withdraw from this copartnership, and be locked up in the county jail therefor, it would be the abolition of slavery in America. For it matters not how small the beginning may seem to be: what is once well done is done for ever. But we love better to talk about it: that we say is our mission. Reform keeps many scores of newspapers in its service, but not one man. If my esteemed neighbor, the State's ambassador,[16] who will devote his days to the settlement of the question of human rights in the Council Chamber, instead of being threatened with the prisons of Carolina, were to sit down the prisoner of Massachusetts, that State which is so anxious to foist the sin of slavery upon her sister, – though at present she can discover only an act of inhospitality to be the ground of a quarrel with her, – the Legislature would not wholly waive the subject the following winter.

Under a government which imprisons any unjustly, the true place for a just man is also a prison. The proper place to-day, the only place which Massachusetts has provided for her freer and less desponding spirits, is in her prisons, to be put out and locked out of the State by her own act, as they have already put themselves out by their principles. It is there that the fugitive slave, and the Mexican prisoner on parole, and the Indian come to plead the wrongs of his race, should find them; on that separate, but more free and honorable ground, where the State places those who are not *with* her but *against* her, – the only house in a slave-state in which a free man can abide with honor. If any think that their influence would be lost there, and their voices no longer afflict the ear of the State, that they would not be as an enemy within its walls, they do not know by how much truth is stronger than error, nor how much more eloquently and effectively he can combat injustice who has experienced a little in his own person. Cast your whole vote, not a strip of paper merely, but your whole influence. A minority is powerless while it conforms to the majority; it is not even a minority then; but it is irresistible when it clogs by its whole weight. If the alternative is to keep all just men in prison, or give up war and slavery, the State will not hesitate which to choose. If a thousand men were not to pay their tax-bills this year, that would not be a violent and bloody measure, as it would be to pay them, and enable the State to commit violence and shed innocent blood. This is, in fact, the definition of a peaceable revolution, if any such is possible. If the tax-gatherer, or any other public officer, asks me, as one has done, "But what shall I do?" my answer is, "If you really wish to do any thing, resign your office." When the subject has refused allegiance, and the officer has resigned his office, then the revolution is accomplished. But even suppose blood should flow. Is there not a sort of blood shed when the conscience is wounded? Through this wound a man's real manhood and immortality flow out, and he bleeds to an everlasting death. I see this blood flowing now.

---

16. **the State's ambassador:** Samuel Hoar (1778-1856), a lawyer and congressman from Concord. In 1844, he had been sent to Charleston, South Carolina, to protest the seizure of black seamen on ships from Massachusetts. He was forcibly expelled by order of the legislature of South Carolina.

I have contemplated the imprisonment of the offender, rather than the seizure of his goods, – though both will serve the same purpose, – because they who assert the purest right, and consequently are most dangerous to a corrupt State, commonly have not spent much time in accumulating property. To such the State renders comparatively small service, and a slight tax is wont to appear exorbitant, particularly if they are obliged to earn it by special labor with their hands. If there were one who lived wholly without the use of money, the State itself would hesitate to demand it of him. But the rich man – not to make any invidious comparison – is always sold to the institution which makes him rich. Absolutely speaking, the more money, the less virtue; for money comes between a man and his objects, and obtains them for him; and it was certainly no great virtue to obtain it. It puts to rest many questions which he would otherwise be taxed to answer; while the only new question which it puts is the hard but superfluous one, how to spend it. Thus his moral ground is taken from under his feet. The opportunities of living are diminished in proportion as what are called the "means" are increased. The best thing a man can do for his culture when he is rich is to endeavour to carry out those schemes which he entertained when he was poor. Christ answered the Herodians according to their condition. "Show me the tribute-money," said he; – and one took a penny out of his pocket; – If you use money which has the image of Caesar on it, and which he has made current and valuable, that is, *if you are men of the State*, and gladly enjoy the advantages of Caesar's government, then pay him back some of his own when he demands it; "Render therefore to Caesar that which is Caesar's, and to God those things which are God's,"[17] – leaving them no wiser than before as to which was which; for they did not wish to know.

When I converse with the freest of my neighbors, I perceive that, whatever they may say about the magnitude and seriousness of the question, and their regard for the public tranquillity, the long and the short of the matter is, that they cannot spare the protection of the existing government, and they dread the consequences of disobedience to it to their property and families. For my own part, I should not like to think that I ever rely on the protection of the State. But, if I deny the authority of the State when it presents its tax-bill, it will soon take and waste all my property, and so harass me and my children without end. This is hard. This makes it impossible for a man to live honestly and at the same time comfortably in outward respects. It will not be worth the while to accumulate property; that would be sure to go again. You must hire or squat somewhere, and raise but a small crop, and eat that soon. You must live within yourself, and depend upon yourself, always tucked up and ready for a start, and not have many affairs. A man may grow rich in Turkey even, if he will be in all respects a good subject of the Turkish government. Confucius said, – "If a State is governed by the principles of reason, poverty and mercy are subjects of shame; if a State is not governed by the principles of reason, riches and honors are the subjects of shame." No: until I want the protection of Massachusetts to be extended to me in some distant southern port, where my liberty is endan-

---

17. **"Show . . . God's":** The account of Christ speaking to the Herodians, a political party in support of the Roman government, is in Mark 12:13–17.

gered, or until I am bent solely on building up an estate at home by peaceful enterprise, I can afford to refuse allegiance to Massachusetts, and her right to my property and life. It costs me less in every sense to incur the penalty of disobedience to the State, than it would to obey. I should feel as if I were worth less in that case.

Some years ago, the State met me in behalf of the church,[18] and commanded me to pay a certain sum toward the support of a clergyman whose preaching my father attended, but never I myself. "Pay it," it said, "or be locked up in the jail." I declined to pay. But, unfortunately, another man saw fit to pay it. I did not see why the schoolmaster should be taxed to support the priest, and not the priest the schoolmaster; for I was not the State's schoolmaster, but I supported myself by voluntary subscription. I did not see why the lyceum should not present its tax-bill, and have the State to back its demand, as well as the church. However, at the request of the selectmen, I condescended to make some such statement as this in writing: – "Know all men by these presents, that I, Henry Thoreau, do not wish to be regarded as a member of any incorporated society which I have not joined." This I gave to the town-clerk; and he has it. The State, having thus learned that I did not wish to be regarded as a member of that church, has never made a like demand on me since; though it said that it must adhere to its original presumption that time. If I had known how to name them, I should then have signed off in detail from all the societies which I never signed on to; but I did not know where to find a complete list.

I have paid no poll-tax for six years. I was put into a jail once on this account, for one night; and, as I stood considering the walls of solid stone, two or three feet thick, the door of wood and iron, a foot thick, and the iron grating which strained the light, I could not help being struck with the foolishness of that institution which treated me as if I were mere flesh and blood and bones, to be locked up. I wondered that it should have concluded at length that this was the best use it could put me to, and had never thought to avail itself of my services in some way. I saw that, if there was a wall of stone between me and my townsmen, there was a still more difficult one to climb or break through, before they could get to be as free as I was. I did not for a moment feel confined, and the walls seemed a great waste of stone and mortar. I felt as if I alone of all my townsmen had paid my tax. They plainly did not know how to treat me, but behaved like persons who are underbred. In every threat and in every compliment there was a blunder; for they thought that my chief desire was to stand the other side of that stone wall. I could not but smile to see how industriously they locked the door on my meditations, which followed them out again without let or hinderance, and *they* were really all that was dangerous. As they could not reach me, they had resolved to punish my body; just as boys, if they cannot come at some person against whom they have a spite, will abuse his dog. I saw that the State was half-witted, that it was timid as a lone woman with her silver spoons, and that it did not know its friends from its foes, and I lost all my remaining respect for it, and pitied it.

18. **in behalf of the church:** At the time, members of a congregation were taxed by their church, and the money was collected by town officials. Since Thoreau's parents attended the First Parish Church (Unitarian), the church had assumed that he, too, wished to be considered a member.

Thus the State never intentionally confronts a man's sense, intellectual or moral, but only his body, his senses. It is not armed with superior wit or honesty, but with superior physical strength. I was not born to be forced. I will breathe after my own fashion. Let us see who is the strongest. What force has a multitude? They only can force me who obey a higher law than I. They force me to become like themselves. I do not hear of *men* being *forced* to live this way or that by masses of men. What sort of life were that to live? When I meet a government which says to me, "Your money or your life," why should I be in haste to give it my money? It may be in a great strait, and not know what to do: I cannot help that. It must help itself; do as I do. It is not worth the while to snivel about it. I am not responsible for the successful working of the machinery of society. I am not the son of the engineer. I perceive that, when an acorn and a chestnut fall side by side, the one does not remain inert to make way for the other, but both obey their own laws, and spring and grow and flourish as best they can, till one, perchance, overshadows and destroys the other. If a plant cannot live according to its nature, it dies; and so a man.

The night in prison was novel and interesting enough. The prisoners in their shirt-sleeves were enjoying a chat and the evening air in the door-way, when I entered. But the jailer said, "Come, boys, it is time to lock up"; and so they dispersed, and I heard the sound of their steps returning into the hollow apartments. My room-mate was introduced to me by the jailer, as "a first-rate fellow and a clever man." When the door was locked, he showed me where to hang my hat, and how he managed matters there. The rooms were whitewashed once a month; and this one, at least, was the whitest, most simply furnished, and probably the neatest apartment in the town. He naturally wanted to know where I came from, and what brought me there; and, when I had told him, I asked him in my turn how he came there, presuming him to be an honest man, of course; and, as the world goes, I believe he was. "Why," said he, "they accuse me of burning a barn; but I never did it." As near as I could discover, he had probably gone to bed in a barn when drunk, and smoked his pipe there; and so a barn was burnt. He had the reputation of being a clever man, had been there some three months waiting for his trial to come on, and would have to wait as much longer; but he was quite domesticated and contented, since he got his board for nothing, and thought that he was well treated.

He occupied one window, and I the other; and I saw, that, if one stayed there long, his principal business would be to look out the window. I had soon read all the tracts that were left there, and examined where former prisoners had broken out, and where a grate had been sawed off, and heard the history of the various occupants of that room; for I found that even here there was a history and a gossip which never circulated beyond the walls of the jail. Probably this is the only house in the town where verses are composed, which are afterward printed in a circular form, but not published. I was shown quite a long list of verses which were composed by some young men who had been detected in an attempt to escape, who avenged themselves by singing them.

I pumped my fellow-prisoner as dry as I could, for fear I should never see him again; but at length he showed me which was my bed, and left me to blow out the lamp.

It was like travelling into a far country, such as I had never expected to behold, to lie there for one night. It seemed to me that I never had heard the town-clock strike before, nor the evening sounds of the village; for we slept with the windows open, which were inside the grating. It was to see my native village in the light of the middle ages, and our Concord was turned into a Rhine stream, and visions of knights and castles passed before me.

They were the voices of old burghers that I heard in the streets. I was an involuntary spectator and auditor of whatever was done and said in the kitchen of the adjacent village-inn, – a wholly new and rare experience to me. It was a closer view of my native town. I was fairly inside of it. I never had seen its institutions before. This is one of its peculiar institutions; for it is a shire town.[19] I began to comprehend what its inhabitants were about.

In the morning, our breakfasts were put through the hole in the door, in small oblong-square tin pans, made to fit, and holding a pint of chocolate, with brown bread, and an iron spoon. When they called for the vessels again, I was green enough to return what bread I had left; but my comrade seized it, and said that I should lay that up for lunch or dinner. Soon after, he was let out to work at haying in a neighboring field, whither he went every day, and would not be back till noon; so he bade me good-day, saying that he doubted if he should see me again.

When I came out of prison, – for some one interfered, and paid the tax, – I did not perceive that great changes had taken place on the common, such as he observed who went in a youth, and emerged a tottering and gray-headed man; and yet a change had to my eyes come over the scene, – the town, and State, and country, – greater than any that mere time could effect. I saw yet more distinctly the State in which I lived. I saw to what extent the people among whom I lived could be trusted as good neighbors and friends; that their friendship was for summer weather only; that they did not greatly purpose to do right; that they were a distinct race from me by their prejudices and superstitions, as the Chinamen and Malays are; that, in their sacrifices to humanity, they ran no risks, not even to their property; that, after all, they were not so noble but they treated the thief as he had treated them, and hoped, by a certain outward observance and a few prayers, and by walking in a particular straight though useless path from time to time, to save their souls. This may be to judge my neighbors harshly; for I believe that most of them are not aware that they have such an institution as the jail in their village.

It was formerly the custom in our village, when a poor debtor came out of jail, for his acquaintances to salute him, looking through their fingers, which were crossed to represent the grating of a jail window, "How do ye do?" My neighbors did not thus salute me, but first looked at me, and then at one another, as if I had returned from a long journey. I was put into jail as I was going to the shoemaker's to get a shoe which was mended. When I was let out the next morning, I proceeded to finish my errand, and, having put on my mended shoe, joined a huckleberry party, who were impatient to put themselves under my conduct; and in half an hour, – for the horse was soon tackled, – was in the midst of a huckleberry field, on one of our highest hills, two miles off; and then the State was nowhere to be seen.

This is the whole history of "My Prisons."[20]

I have never declined paying the highway tax, because I am as desirous of being a good neighbor as I am of being a bad subject; and, as for supporting schools, I am doing my part to educate my fellow-countrymen now. It is for no particular item in the tax-bill that I refuse to pay it. I simply wish to refuse allegiance to the State, to withdraw and stand aloof from it effectually. I do not care to trace the course of my dollar, if I could, till it buys a man, or a musket to shoot one with, – the dollar is innocent, – but I am concerned

---

19. **shire town:** County seat; Concord was therefore the home of the Middlesex County Jail.
20. **"My Prisons":** A reference to a popular prison memoir of that title, *Le Mie Prigioni* (1832), by the Italian poet Silvio Pellico (1788–1854).

to trace the effects of my allegiance. In fact, I quietly declare war with the State, after my fashion, though I will still make what use and get what advantage of her I can, as is usual in such cases.

If others pay the tax which is demanded of me, from a sympathy with the State, they do but what they have already done in their own case, or rather they abet injustice to a greater extent than the State requires. If they pay the tax from a mistaken interest in the individual taxed, to save his property or prevent his going to jail, it is because they have not considered wisely how far they let their private feelings interfere with the public good.

This, then, is my position at present. But one cannot be too much on his guard in such a case, lest his action be biased by obstinacy, or an undue regard for the opinions of men. Let him see that he does only what belongs to himself and to the hour.

I think sometimes, Why, this people mean well; they are only ignorant; they would do better if they knew how: why give your neighbors this pain to treat you as they are not inclined to? But I think, again, this is no reason why I should do as they do, or permit others to suffer much greater pain of a different kind. Again, I sometimes say to myself, When many millions of men, without heat, without ill-will, without personal feeling of any kind, demand of you a few shillings only, without the possibility, such is their constitution, of retracting or altering their present demand, and without the possibility, on your side, of appeal to any other millions, why expose yourself to this overwhelming brute force? You do not resist cold and hunger, the winds and the waves, thus obstinately; you quietly submit to a thousand similar necessities. You do not put your head into the fire. But just in proportion as I regard this as not wholly a brute force, but partly a human force, and consider that I have relations to those millions as to so many millions of men, and not of mere brute or inanimate things, I see that appeal is possible, first and instantaneously, from them to the Maker of them, and, secondly, from them to themselves. But, if I put my head deliberately into the fire, there is no appeal to fire or to the Maker of fire, and I have only myself to blame. If I could convince myself that I have any right to be satisfied with men as they are, and to treat them accordingly, and not according, in some respects, to my requisitions and expectations of what they and I ought to be, then, like a good Mussulman[21] and fatalist, I should endeavor to be satisfied with things as they are, and say it is the will of God. And, above all, there is this difference between resisting this and a purely brute or natural force, that I can resist this with some effect; but I cannot expect, like Orpheus,[22] to change the nature of the rocks and trees and beasts.

I do not wish to quarrel with any man or nation. I do not wish to split hairs, to make fine distinctions, or set myself up as better than my neighbors. I seek rather, I may say, even an excuse for conforming to the laws of the land. I am but too ready to conform to them. Indeed I have reason to suspect myself on this head; and each year, as the tax-gatherer comes round, I find myself disposed to review the acts and position of the general and state governments, and the spirit of the people, to discover a pretext for

---

21. **Mussulman:** A Mohammedan, or Muslim.
22. **Orpheus:** Figure in Greek mythology whose music had magical powers over the natural world.

conformity. I believe that the State will soon be able to take all my work of this sort out of my hands, and then I shall be no better a patriot than my fellow-countrymen. Seen from a lower point of view, the Constitution, with all its faults, is very good; the law and the courts are very respectable; even this State and this American government are, in many respects, very admirable and rare things, to be thankful for, such as a great many have described them; but seen from a point of view a little higher, they are what I have described them; seen from a higher still, and the highest, who shall say what they are, or that they are worth looking at or thinking of at all?

However, the government does not concern me much, and I shall bestow the fewest possible thoughts on it. It is not many moments that I live under a government, even in this world. If a man is thought-free, fancy-free, imagination-free, that which *is not* never for a long time appearing *to be* to him, unwise rulers or reformers cannot fatally interrupt him.

I know that most men think differently from myself; but those whose lives are by profession devoted to the study of these or kindred subjects, content me as little as any. Statesmen and legislators, standing so completely within the institution, never distinctly and nakedly behold it. They speak of moving society, but have no resting-place without it. They may be men of a certain experience and discrimination, and have no doubt invented ingenious and even useful systems, for which we sincerely thank them; but all their wit and usefulness lie within certain not very wide limits. They are wont to forget that the world is not governed by policy and expediency. Webster[23] never goes behind government, and so cannot speak with authority about it. His words are wisdom to those legislators who contemplate no essential reform in the existing government; but for thinkers, and those who legislate for all time, he never once glances at the subject. I know of those whose serene and wise speculations on this theme would soon reveal the limits of his mind's range and hospitality. Yet, compared with the cheap professions of most reformers, and the still cheaper wisdom and eloquence of politicians in general, his are almost the only sensible and valuable words, and we thank Heaven for him. Comparatively, he is always strong, original, and, above all, practical. Still his quality is not wisdom, but prudence. The lawyer's truth is not Truth, but consistency, or a consistent expediency. Truth is always in harmony with herself, and is not concerned chiefly to reveal the justice that may consist with wrong-doing. He well deserves to be called, as he has been called, the Defender of the Constitution. There are really no blows to be given by him but defensive ones. He is not a leader, but a follower. His leaders are the men of '87.[24] "I have never made an effort," he says, "and never propose to make an effort; I have never countenanced an effort, and never mean to countenance an effort, to disturb the arrangement as originally made, by which the various States came into the Union." Still thinking of the sanction which the Constitution gives to slavery, he says, "Because it was a part of the original compact, – let it stand." Notwithstanding his special acuteness and ability, he is unable to take a fact out of its merely political relations,

23. **Webster:** Daniel Webster (1782–1852), the famed senator from Massachusetts.
24. **men of '87:** Members of the Federal Constitutional Convention, held in 1787.

and behold it as it lies absolutely to be disposed of by the intellect, – what, for instance, it behoves a man to do here in America to-day with regard to slavery, but ventures, or is driven, to make some such desperate answer as the following, while professing to speak absolutely, and as a private man, – from which what new and singular code of social duties might be inferred? – "The manner," says he, "in which the governments of those States where slavery exists are to regulate it, is for their own consideration, under their responsibility to their constituents, to the general laws of propriety, humanity, and justice, and to God. Associations formed elsewhere, springing from a feeling of humanity, or any other cause, have nothing whatever to do with it. They have never received any encouragement from me, and they never will."[25]

They who know of no purer sources of truth, who have traced up its stream no higher, stand, and wisely stand, by the Bible and the Constitution, and drink at it there with reverence and humility; but they who behold where it comes trickling into this lake or that pool, gird up their loins once more, and continue their pilgrimage toward its fountainhead.

No man with a genius for legislation has appeared in America. They are rare in the history of the world. There are orators, politicians, and eloquent men, by the thousand; but the speaker has not yet opened his mouth to speak, who is capable of settling the much-vexed questions of the day. We love eloquence for its own sake, and not for any truth which it may utter, or any heroism it may inspire. Our legislators have not yet learned the comparative value of free-trade and of freedom, of union, and of rectitude, to a nation. They have no genius or talent for comparatively humble questions of taxation and finance, commerce and manufactures and agriculture. If we were left solely to the wordy wit of legislators in Congress for our guidance, uncorrected by the seasonable experience and the effectual complaints of the people, America would not long retain her rank among the nations. For eighteen hundred years, though perchance I have no right to say it, the New Testament has been written; yet where is the legislator who has wisdom and practical talent enough to avail himself of the light which it sheds on the science of legislation?

The authority of government, even such as I am willing to submit to, – for I will cheerfully obey those who know and can do better than I, and in many things even those who neither know nor can do so well, – is still an impure one: to be strictly just, it must have the sanction and consent of the governed. It can have no pure right over my person and property but what I concede to it. The progress from an absolute to a limited monarchy, from a limited monarchy to a democracy, is a progress toward a true respect for the individual. Is a democracy, such as we know it, the last improvement possible in government? Is it not possible to take a step further towards recognizing and organizing the rights of man? There will never be a really free and enlightened State, until the State comes to recognize the individual as a higher and independent power, from which all its own power and authority are derived, and treats him accordingly. I please myself with

25. "I . . . will": These extracts have been inserted since the Lecture was read. [Thoreau's note] The extracts include quotations from two of Webster's speeches in the Senate: "The Admission of Texas," delivered December 22, 1845; and "Exclusion of Slavery from the Territories," delivered August 12, 1848, more than six months after Thoreau delivered his lecture at the Concord Lyceum.

imagining a State at last which can afford to be just to all men, and to treat the individual with respect as a neighbor; which even would not think it inconsistent with its own repose, if a few were to live aloof from it, not meddling with it, nor embraced by it, who fulfilled all the duties of neighbors and fellow-men. A State which bore this kind of fruit, and suffered it to drop off as fast as it ripened, would prepare the way for a still more perfect and glorious State, which also I have imagined, but not yet anywhere seen.

[1849]

Thoreau's *Walden*. Thoreau built his cabin at Walden Pond in the spring of 1845, and he evidently began to plan an account of his life there soon after he settled into that ten-by-fifteen-foot dwelling that July. In February 1847, he delivered a lecture, "A History of Myself" – apparently a portion of which became the opening chapter, "Economy" – at the Concord Lyceum. By the time he left the pond in September 1847, Thoreau had completed the first draft of *Walden*, which he soon prepared for publication. When his first book, *A Week on the Concord and Merrimack Rivers*, was published in 1849, it included an announcement that *Walden* would soon be published. But the commercial failure of *A Week* delayed the publication of Thoreau's second book, which he heavily revised and greatly expanded before it was finally published as *Walden; or, Life in the Woods* in 1854. In a letter written shortly before his death in 1862, Thoreau asked his publisher to omit the subtitle in all future editions, so his most famous book is now simply and widely known as *Walden*.

Thoreau's book has been read and appreciated in a wide variety of ways. On one level, it may be read as an inspirational manual of individual self-reform, a challenge to the organized social reformers who were so active in the decades before the Civil War. Like many other works of the period, *Walden* also represented a sweeping challenge to American materialism and ideas of progress. As the reformer and writer Lydia Maria Child admiringly observed in a contemporary review, "The life exhibited in [Thoreau's books] teaches us that this Western activity of which we are so proud, these material improvements, this commercial enterprise, this rapid accumulation of wealth, even our external associated philanthropic action, are very easily overrated." Readers have been drawn to *Walden* by Thoreau's eloquent advocacy of the simple life, with its emphasis on spiritual ends over material gains. Others have celebrated the literary artistry of *Walden*, as displayed by Thoreau's dense and allusive prose style, as well as by the symbolic patterns and the seasonal structure of the book, in which he compressed the events of his more than two years at the pond into a narrative of a single year. Still others have been drawn to the book by Thoreau's descriptions of the natural world and emphasis on our vital connections to nature. Indeed, the book has assumed a central place in the tradition of American nature writing, even as it has served as an ongoing inspiration for the environmental movement in the United States. Certainly for many readers, Thoreau's messages are even more urgent today than they were when the book was first published in 1854. The text of the following selections is taken from that first edition of *Walden; or, Life in the Woods.*

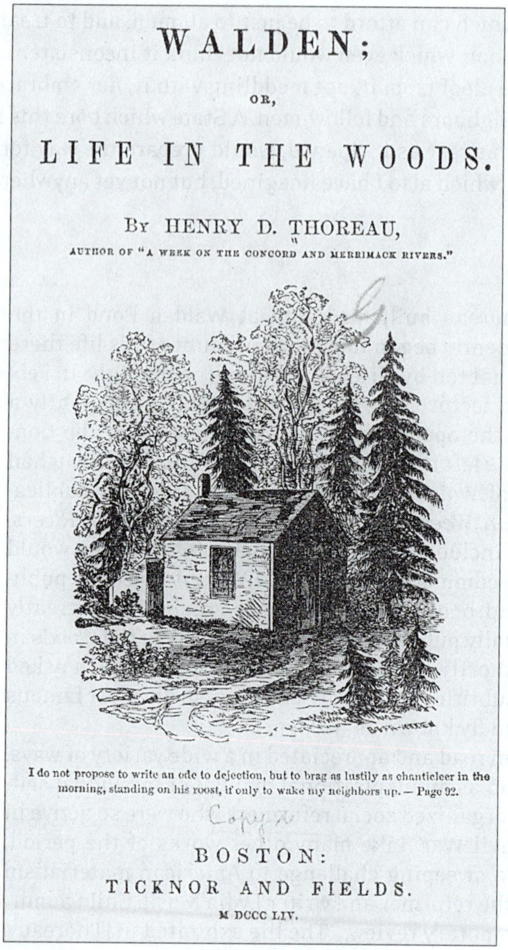
WALDEN;

OR,

LIFE IN THE WOODS.

BY HENRY D. THOREAU,

AUTHOR OF "A WEEK ON THE CONCORD AND MERRIMACK RIVERS."

I do not propose to write an ode to dejection, but to brag as lustily as chanticleer in the morning, standing on his roost, if only to wake my neighbors up. — Page 92.

BOSTON:

TICKNOR AND FIELDS.

M DCCC LIV.

Title Page of the First Edition of *Walden* (1854)

The etching of Thoreau's cabin at Walden Pond was based on a sketch by his sister Sophia Thoreau. The epigraph is a sentence from the second chapter, "Where I Lived, and What I Lived For," where Thoreau announces: "I do not propose to write an ode to dejection, but to brag as lustily as chanticleer in the morning, standing on his roost, if only to wake my neighbors up."

From WALDEN

From Economy

When I wrote the following pages, or rather the bulk of them, I lived alone, in the woods, a mile from any neighbor, in a house which I had built myself, on the shore of Walden Pond, in Concord, Massachusetts, and earned my living by the labor of my hands only. I lived there two years and two months. At present I am a sojourner in civilized life again.

I should not obtrude my affairs so much on the notice of my readers if very particular inquiries had not been made by my townsmen concerning my mode of life, which some would call impertinent, though they do not appear to me at all impertinent, but, considering the circumstances, very natural and pertinent. Some have asked what I got to eat; if I did not feel lonesome; if I was not afraid; and the like. Others have been curious to learn what portion of my income I devoted to charitable purposes; and some, who have large families, how many poor children I maintained. I will therefore ask those of my readers who feel no particular interest in me to pardon me if I undertake to answer some of these questions in this book. In most books, the *I*, or first person, is omitted; in this it will be retained; that, in respect to egotism, is the main difference. We commonly do not remember that it is, after all, always the first person that is speaking. I should not talk so much about myself if there were any body else whom I knew as well. Unfortunately, I am confined to this theme by the narrowness of my experience. Moreover, I, on my side, require of every writer, first or last, a simple and sincere account of his own life, and not merely what he has heard of other men's lives; some such account as he would send to his kindred from a distant land; for if he has lived sincerely, it must have been in a distant land to me. Perhaps these pages are more particularly addressed to poor students. As for the rest of my readers, they will accept such portions as apply to them. I trust that none will stretch the seams in putting on the coat, for it may do good service to him whom it fits.

I would fain say something, not so much concerning the Chinese and Sandwich Islanders[1] as you who read these pages, who are said to live in New England; something about your condition, especially your outward condition or circumstances in this world, in this town, what it is, whether it is necessary that it be as bad as it is, whether it cannot be improved as well as not. I have travelled a good deal in Concord; and every where, in shops, and offices, and fields, the inhabitants have appeared to me to be doing penance in a thousand remarkable ways. What I have heard of Bramins[2] sitting exposed to four fires and looking in the face of the sun; or hanging suspended, with their heads downward, over flames; or looking at the heavens over their shoulders "until it becomes impossible for them to resume their natural position, while from the twist of the neck nothing but liquids can pass into the stomach"; or dwelling, chained for life, at the foot of a tree; or measuring with their bodies, like caterpillars, the breadth of vast empires; or standing on one leg on the tops of pillars, – even these forms of conscious penance are hardly more incredible and astonishing than the scenes which I daily witness. The twelve labors of Hercules were trifling in comparison with those which my neighbors have undertaken; for they were only twelve, and had an end; but I could never see that these men slew or captured any monster or finished any labor. They have no friend Iolas to burn with a hot iron the root of the hydra's head, but as soon as one head is crushed, two spring up.[3]

I see young men, my townsmen, whose misfortune it is to have inherited farms, houses, barns, cattle, and farming tools; for these are more easily acquired than got rid of. Better if they had been born in the open pasture and suckled by a wolf,[4] that they

---

1. **Sandwich Islanders:** Hawaiians; travel lectures were popular staples at lyceums, where Thoreau originally delivered portions of *Walden*.

2. **Bramins:** Usually spelled *Brahmins* or *Brahmans*, members of the highest or priestly caste of Hindus.

3. **The twelve labors . . . spring up:** The son of the Greek god Zeus and a mortal, Hercules was commanded to undertake twelve seemingly impossible tasks. His servant Iolas helped him slay the Hydra, a monster with nine heads.

4. **suckled by a wolf:** Romulus and Remus, the legendary founders of Rome, were said to have been abandoned as infants and mothered by a she-wolf.

might have seen with clearer eyes what field they were called to labor in. Who made them serfs of the soil? Why should they eat their sixty acres, when man is condemned to eat only his peck of dirt? Why should they begin digging their graves as soon as they are born? They have got to live a man's life, pushing all these things before them, and get on as well as they can. How many a poor immortal soul have I met well nigh crushed and smothered under its load, creeping down the road of life, pushing before it a barn seventy-five feet by forty, its Augean stables[5] never cleansed, and one hundred acres of land, tillage, mowing, pasture, and wood-lot! The portionless, who struggle with no such unnecessary inherited encumbrances, find it labor enough to subdue and cultivate a few cubic feet of flesh.

But men labor under a mistake. The better part of the man is soon ploughed into the soil for compost. By a seeming fate, commonly called necessity, they are employed, as it says in an old book, laying up treasures which moth and rust will corrupt and thieves break through and steal.[6] It is a fool's life, as they will find when they get to the end of it, if not before. It is said that Deucalion and Pyrrha[7] created men by throwing stones over their heads behind them: –

Inde genus durum sumus, experiensque laborum,
Et documenta damus quâ simus origine nati.

Or, as Raleigh rhymes it in his sonorous way, –

"From thence our kind hard-hearted is, enduring pain and care,
Approving that our bodies of a stony nature are."

So much for a blind obedience to a blundering oracle, throwing the stones over their heads behind them, and not seeing where they fell.

Most men, even in this comparatively free country, through mere ignorance and mistake, are so occupied with the factitious cares and superfluously coarse labors of life that its finer fruits cannot be plucked by them. Their fingers, from excessive toil, are too clumsy and tremble too much for that. Actually, the laboring man has not leisure for a true integrity day by day; he cannot afford to sustain the manliest relations to men; his labor would be depreciated in the market. He has no time to be any thing but a machine. How can he remember well his ignorance – which has growth requires – who has so often to use his knowledge? We should feed and clothe him gratuitously sometimes, and recruit him with our cordials, before we judge of him. The finest qualities of our nature, like the bloom on fruits, can be preserved only by the most delicate handling. Yet we do not treat ourselves nor one another thus tenderly.

Some of you, we all know, are poor, find it hard to live, are sometimes, as it were,

---

5. **Augean stables:** One of the twelve labors of Hercules was to clean in one day the stables of Augeas, where several thousand oxen were housed and which had not been cleaned for thirty years.
6. **old book . . . steal:** The Bible; see Matthew 6:19.
7. **Deucalion and Pyrrha:** Deucalion, the son of Prometheus, and his wife, Pyrrha, were the only survivors of the flood Zeus sent to destroy the degenerate race of mortals. Realizing that the earth was his mother, whose bones were rocks and stones, Deucalion and Pyrrha threw these over their heads to repopulate the world. The quotation that follows is from Ovid's *Metamorphoses*, 1.414–15; the translation is from Sir Walter Raleigh's *History of the World* (1614).

gasping for breath. I have no doubt that some of you who read this book are unable to pay for all the dinners which you have actually eaten, or for the coats and shoes which are fast wearing or are already worn out, and have come to this page to spend borrowed or stolen time, robbing your creditors of an hour. It is very evident what mean and sneaking lives many of you live, for my sight has been whetted by experience; always on the limits, trying to get into business and trying to get out of debt, a very ancient slough, called by the Latins *aes alienum*, another's brass, for some of their coins were made of brass; still living, and dying, and buried by this other's brass; always promising to pay, promising to pay, to-morrow, and dying to-day, insolvent; seeking to curry favor, to get custom, by how many modes, only not state-prison offences; lying, flattering, voting, contracting yourselves into a nutshell of civility, or dilating into an atmosphere of thin and vaporous generosity, that you may persuade your neighbor to let you make his shoes, or his hat, or his coat, or his carriage, or import his groceries for him; making yourselves sick, that you may lay up something against a sick day, something to be tucked away in an old chest, or in a stocking behind the plastering, or, more safely, in the brick bank; no matter where, no matter how much or how little.

I sometimes wonder that we can be so frivolous, I may almost say, as to attend to the gross but somewhat foreign form of servitude called Negro Slavery, there are so many keen and subtle masters that enslave both north and south. It is hard to have a southern overseer; it is worse to have a northern one; but worst of all when you are the slave-driver of yourself. Talk of a divinity in man! Look at the teamster on the highway, wending to market by day or night; does any divinity stir within him? His highest duty to fodder and water his horses! What is his destiny to him compared with the shipping interests? Does not he drive for Squire Make-a-stir? How godlike, how immortal, is he? See how he cowers and sneaks, how vaguely all the day he fears, not being immortal nor divine, but the slave and prisoner of his own opinion of himself, a fame won by his own deeds. Public opinion is a weak tyrant compared with our own private opinion. What a man thinks of himself, that it is which determines, or rather indicates, his fate. Self-emancipation even in the West Indian provinces of the fancy and imagination, – what Wilberforce[8] is there to bring that about? Think, also, of the ladies of the land weaving toilet cushions against the last day, not to betray too green an interest in their fates! As if you could kill time without injuring eternity.

The mass of men lead lives of quiet desperation. What is called resignation is confirmed desperation. From the desperate city you go into the desperate country, and have to console yourself with the bravery of minks and muskrats. A stereotyped but unconscious despair is concealed even under what are called the games and amusements of mankind. There is no play in them, for this comes after work. But it is a characteristic of wisdom not to do desperate things.

When we consider what, to use the words of the catechism, is the chief end of man,[9] and what are the true necessaries and means of life, it appears as if men had deliberately

---

8. **Wilberforce:** William Wilberforce (1759–1833), English abolitionist who led the parliamentary battle to end slavery in the British West Indies.

9. **the chief end of man:** In the words of the Shorter Catechism from the *New England Primer*, "the chief end of man . . . is to glorify God and to enjoy him forever."

chosen the common mode of living because they preferred it to any other. Yet they honestly think there is no choice left. But alert and healthy natures remember that the sun rose clear. It is never too late to give up our prejudices. No way of thinking or doing, however ancient, can be trusted without proof. What every body echoes or in silence passes by as true to-day may turn out to be falsehood to-morrow, mere smoke of opinion, which some had trusted for a cloud that would sprinkle fertilizing rain on their fields. What old people say you cannot do you try and find that you can. Old deeds for old people, and new deeds for new. Old people did not know enough once, perchance, to fetch fresh fuel to keep the fire a-going; new people put a little dry wood under a pot, and are whirled round the globe with the speed of birds, in a way to kill old people, as the phrase is. Age is no better, hardly so well, qualified for an instructor as youth, for it has not profited so much as it has lost. One may almost doubt if the wisest man has learned any thing of absolute value by living. Practically, the old have no very important advice to give the young, their own experience has been so partial, and their lives have been such miserable failures, for private reasons, as they must believe; and it may be that they have some faith left which belies that experience, and they are only less young than they were. I have lived some thirty years on this planet, and I have yet to hear the first syllable of valuable or even earnest advice from my seniors. They have told me nothing, and probably cannot tell me any thing, to the purpose. Here is life, an experiment to a great extent untried by me; but it does not avail me that they have tried it. If I have any experience which I think valuable, I am sure to reflect that this my Mentors said nothing about.

One farmer says to me, "You cannot live on vegetable food solely, for it furnishes nothing to make bones with;" and so he religiously devotes a part of his day to supplying his system with the raw material of bones; walking all the while he talks behind his oxen, which, with vegetable-made bones, jerk him and his lumbering plough along in spite of every obstacle. Some things are really necessaries of life in some circles, the most helpless and diseased, which in others are luxuries merely, and in others still are entirely unknown.

The whole ground of human life seems to some to have been gone over by their predecessors, both the heights and the valleys, and all things to have been cared for. According to Evelyn,[10] "the wise Solomon prescribed ordinances for the very distances of trees; and the Roman praetors have decided how often you may go into your neighbor's land to gather the acorns which fall on it without trespass, and what share belongs to that neighbor." Hippocrates[11] has even left directions how we should cut our nails; that is, even with the ends of the fingers, neither shorter nor longer. Undoubtedly the very tedium and ennui which presume to have exhausted the variety and the joys of life are as old as Adam. But man's capacities have never been measured; nor are we to judge of what he can do by any precedents, so little has been tried. Whatever have been thy failures hitherto, "be not afflicted, my child, for who shall assign to thee what thou hast left undone?"[12]

---

10. **According to Evelyn:** John Evelyn (1620–1706), English author and naturalist; the following quotation is from his *Sylva; or, a Discourse of Forest-Trees* (1664). "Roman praetors" were elected officials.
11. **Hippocrates:** Ancient Greek physician known as the "Father of Medicine."
12. **"be . . . undone?":** From the ancient Hindu scripture *Vishnu Purana.*

We might try our lives by a thousand simple tests; as, for instance, that the same sun which ripens my beans illumines at once a system of earths like ours. If I had remembered this it would have prevented some mistakes. This was not the light in which I hoed them. The stars are the apexes of what wonderful triangles! What distant and different beings in the various mansions of the universe are contemplating the same one at the same moment! Nature and human life are as various as our several constitutions. Who shall say what prospect life offers to another? Could a greater miracle take place than for us to look through each other's eyes for an instant? We should live in all the ages of the world in an hour; ay, in all the worlds of the ages. History, Poetry, Mythology! – I know of no reading of another's experience so startling and informing as this would be.

The greater part of what my neighbors call good I believe in my soul to be bad, and if I repent of any thing, it is very likely to be my good behavior. What demon possessed me that I behaved so well? You may say the wisest thing you can old man, – you who have lived seventy years, not without honor of a kind, – I hear an irresistible voice which invites me away from all that. One generation abandons the enterprises of another like stranded vessels.

I think that we may safely trust a good deal more than we do. We may waive just so much care of ourselves as we honestly bestow elsewhere. Nature is as well adapted to our weakness as to our strength. The incessant anxiety and strain of some is a well nigh incurable form of disease. We are made to exaggerate the importance of what work we do; and yet how much is not done by us! or, what if we had been taken sick? How vigilant we are! determined not to live by faith if we can avoid it; all the day long on the alert, at night we unwillingly say our prayers and commit ourselves to uncertainties. So thoroughly and sincerely are we compelled to live, reverencing our life, and denying the possibility of change. This is the only way, we say; but there are as many ways as there can be drawn radii from one centre. All change is a miracle to contemplate; but it is a miracle which is taking place every instant. Confucius said, "To know that we know what we know, and that we do not know what we do not know, that is true knowledge." When one man has reduced a fact of the imagination to be a fact to his understanding, I foresee that all men will at length establish their lives on that basis.

• • •

Where I Lived, and What I Lived For

At a certain season of our life we are accustomed to consider every spot as the possible site of a house. I have thus surveyed the country on every side within a dozen miles of where I live. In imagination I have bought all the farms in succession, for all were to be bought, and I knew their price. I walked over each farmer's premises, tasted his wild apples, discoursed on husbandry with him, took his farm at his price, at any price, mortgaging it to him in my mind; even put a higher price on it, – took every thing but a deed of it, – took his word for his deed, for I dearly love to talk, – cultivated it, and him too to some extent, I trust, and withdrew when I had enjoyed it long enough, leaving him to carry it on. This experience entitled me to be regarded as a sort of real-estate broker by my friends. Wherever I sat, there I might live, and the landscape radiated from me accordingly. What is a house but a *sedes*, a seat? – better if a country seat. I discovered many a site for a house not likely to be soon improved, which some might have thought too far from the village, but to my eyes the village was too far from it. Well, there I might live, I said; and there I did live, for an hour, a summer and a winter life; saw how I could let the years run off, buffet the winter through, and see the spring come in. The future inhabitants of this region, wherever they may place their houses, may be sure that they have been anticipated. An afternoon sufficed to lay out the land into orchard, woodlot, and pasture, and to decide what fine oaks or pines should be left to stand before the door, and whence each blasted tree could be seen to the best advantage; and then I let it lie, fallow perchance, for a man is rich in proportion to the number of things which he can afford to let alone.

My imagination carried me so far that I even had the refusal of several farms, – the refusal was all I wanted, – but I never got my fingers burned by actual possession. The nearest that I came to actual possession was when I bought the Hollowell place, and had begun to sort my seeds, and collected materials with which to make a wheelbarrow to carry it on or off with; but before the owner gave me a deed of it, his wife – every man has such a wife – changed her mind and wished to keep it, and he offered me ten dollars to release him. Now, to speak the truth, I had but ten cents in the world, and it surpassed my arithmetic to tell, if I was that man who had ten cents, or who had a farm, or ten dollars, or all together. However, I let him keep the ten dollars and the farm too, for I had carried it far enough; or rather, to be generous, I sold him the farm for just what I gave for it, and, as he was not a rich man, made him a present of ten dollars, and still had my ten cents, and seeds, and materials for a wheelbarrow left. I found thus that I had been a rich man without any damage to my poverty. But I retained the landscape, and I have since annually carried off what it yielded without a wheelbarrow. With respect to landscapes, –

> "I am monarch of all I *survey*,
> My right there is none to dispute."[1]

I have frequently seen a poet withdraw, having enjoyed the most valuable part of a farm, while the crusty farmer supposed that he had got a few wild apples only. Why, the owner does not know it for many years when a poet has put his farm in rhyme, the most admirable kind of invisible fence, has fairly impounded it, milked it, skimmed it, and got all the cream, and left the farmer only the skimmed milk.

The real attractions of the Hollowell farm, to me, were; its complete retirement, being about two miles from the village, half a mile from the nearest neighbor, and separated from the highway by a broad field; its bounding on the river, which the owner said protected it by its fogs from frosts in the spring, though that was nothing to me; the gray color and ruinous state of the house and barn, and the dilapidated fences, which put such an interval between me and the last occupant; the hollow and lichen-covered apple trees, gnawed by rabbits, showing what kind of neighbors I should have; but above all, the recollection I had of it from my earliest voyages up the river, when the house was

---

1. **I . . . dispute:** From "Verses Supposed to Be Written by Alexander Selkirk," by the English poet William Cowper (1731-1800). Thoreau italicized the word *survey* to call attention to his pun.

concealed behind a dense grove of red maples, through which I heard the house-dog bark. I was in haste to buy it, before the proprietor finished getting out some rocks, cutting down the hollow apple trees, and grubbing up some young birches which had sprung up in the pasture, or, in short, had made any more of his improvements. To enjoy these advantages I was ready to carry it on; like Atlas, to take the world on my shoulders, – I never heard what compensation he received for that, – and do all those things which had no other motive or excuse but that I might pay for it and be unmolested in my possession of it; for I knew all the while that it would yield the most abundant crop of the kind I wanted if I could only afford to let it alone. But it turned out as I have said.

All that I could say, then, with respect to farming on a large scale, (I have always cultivated a garden,) was, that I had had my seeds ready. Many think that seeds improve with age. I have no doubt that time discriminates between the good and the bad; and when at last I shall plant, I shall be less likely to be disappointed. But I would say to my fellows, once for all, As long as possible live free and uncommitted. It makes but little difference whether you are committed to a farm or the county jail.

Old Cato,[2] whose "De Re Rusticâ" is my "Cultivator," says, and the only translation I have seen makes sheer nonsense of the passage, "When you think of getting a farm, turn it thus in your mind, not to buy greedily; nor spare your pains to look at it, and do not think it enough to go round it once. The oftener you go there the more it will please you, if it is good." I think I shall not buy greedily, but go round and round it as long as I live, and be buried in it first, that it may please me the more at last.

The present was my next experiment of this kind, which I purpose to describe more at length; for convenience, putting the experience of two years into one. As I have said, I do not propose to write an ode to dejection, but to brag as lustily as chanticleer in the morning, standing on his roost, if only to wake my neighbors up.

When first I took up my abode in the woods, that is, began to spend my nights as well as days there, which, by accident, was on Independence day, or the fourth of July, 1845, my house was not finished for winter, but was merely a defence against the rain, without plastering or chimney, the walls being of rough weather-stained boards, with wide chinks, which made it cool at night. The upright white hewn studs and freshly planed door and window casings gave it a clean and airy look, especially in the morning, when its timbers were saturated with dew, so that I fancied that by noon some sweet gum would exude from them. To my imagination it retained throughout the day more or less of this auroral character, reminding me of a certain house on a mountain which I had visited the year before. This was an airy and unplastered cabin, fit to entertain a travelling god, and where a goddess might trail her garments. The winds which passed over my dwelling were such as sweep over the ridges of mountains, bearing the broken strains, or celestial parts only, of terrestrial music. The morning wind forever blows, the poem of creation is uninterrupted; but few are the ears that hear it. Olympus is but the outside of the earth every where.

---

2. **Old Cato:** Marcus Porcius Cato, the Elder (234–149 BCE), Roman statesman; the following quotation is from his *De agri cultura*, 1.1, as translated by Thoreau.

The only house I had been the owner of before, if I except a boat, was a tent, which I used occasionally when making excursions in the summer, and this is still rolled up in my garret; but the boat, after passing from hand to hand, has gone down the stream of time. With this more substantial shelter about me, I had made some progress toward settling in the world. This frame, so slightly clad, was a sort of crystallization around me, and reacted on the builder. It was suggestive somewhat as a picture in outlines. I did not need to go out doors to take the air, for the atmosphere within had lost none of its freshness. It was not so much within doors as behind a door where I sat, even in the rainiest weather. The Harivansa[3] says, "An abode without birds is like a meat without seasoning." Such was not my abode, for I found myself suddenly neighbor to the birds; not by having imprisoned one, but having caged myself near them. I was not only nearer to some of those which commonly frequent the garden and the orchard, but to those wilder and more thrilling songsters of the forest which never, or rarely, serenade a villager, – the wood-thrush, the veery, the scarlet tanager, the field-sparrow, the whippoorwill, and many others.

I was seated by the shore of a small pond, about a mile and a half south of the village of Concord and somewhat higher than it, in the midst of an extensive wood between that town and Lincoln, and about two miles south of that our only field known to fame, Concord Battle Ground;[4] but I was so low in the woods that the opposite shore, half a mile off, like the rest, covered with wood, was my most distant horizon. For the first week, whenever I looked out on the pond it impressed me like a tarn high up on the side of a mountain, its bottom far above the surface of other lakes, and, as the sun arose, I saw it throwing off its nightly clothing of mist, and here and there, by degrees, its soft ripples or its smooth reflecting surface was revealed, while the mists, like ghosts, were stealthily withdrawing in every direction into the woods, as at the breaking up of some nocturnal conventicle. The very dew seemed to hang upon the trees later into the day than usual, as on the sides of mountains.

This small lake was of most value as a neighbor in the intervals of a gentle rain storm in August, when, both air and water being perfectly still, but the sky overcast, mid-afternoon had all the serenity of evening, and the wood-thrush sang around, and was heard from shore to shore. A lake like this is never smoother than at such a time; and the clear portion of the air above it being shallow and darkened by clouds, the water, full of light and reflections, becomes a lower heaven itself so much the more important. From a hill top near by, where the wood had been recently cut off, there was a pleasing vista southward across the pond, through a wide indentation in the hills which form the shore there, where their opposite sides sloping toward each other suggested a stream flowing out in that direction through a wooded valley, but stream there was none. That way I looked between and over the near green hills to some distant and higher ones in the horizon, tinged with blue. Indeed, by standing on tiptoe I could catch a glimpse of some of the peaks of the still bluer and more distant mountain ranges in the north-west,

3. **Harivansa:** An ancient Hindu epic.
4. **Concord Battle Ground:** Site of the second battle of the American Revolution, in April 1775.

those true-blue coins from heaven's own mint, and also of some portion of the village. But in other directions, even from this point, I could not see over or beyond the woods which surrounded me. It is well to have some water in your neighborhood, to give buoyancy to and float the earth. One value even of the smallest well is, that when you look into it you see that earth is not continent but insular. This is as important as that it keeps butter cool. When I looked across the pond from this peak toward the Sudbury meadows, which in time of flood I distinguished elevated perhaps by a mirage in their seething valley, like a coin in a basin, all the earth beyond the pond appeared like a thin crust insulated and floated even by this small sheet of intervening water, and I was reminded that this on which I dwelt was but *dry land*.

Though the view from my door was still more contracted, I did not feel crowded or confined in the least. There was pasture enough for my imagination. The low shrub-oak plateau to which the opposite shore arose, stretched away toward the prairies of the West and the steppes of Tartary, affording ample room for all the roving families of men. "There are none happy in the world but beings who enjoy freely a vast horizon," – said Damodara,[5] when his herds required new and larger pastures.

Both place and time were changed, and I dwelt nearer to those parts of the universe and to those eras in history which had most attracted me. Where I lived was as far off as many a region viewed nightly by astronomers. We are wont to imagine rare and delectable places in some remote and more celestial corner of the system, behind the constellation of Cassiopeia's Chair,[6] far from noise and disturbance. I discovered that my house actually had its site in such a withdrawn, but forever new and unprofaned, part of the universe. If it were worth the while to settle in those parts near to the Pleiades or the Hyades, to Aldebaran or Altair,[7] then I was really there, or at an equal remoteness from the life which I had left behind, dwindled and twinkling with as fine a ray to my nearest neighbor, and to be seen only in moonless nights by him. Such was that part of creation where I had squatted; –

> "There was a shepherd that did live,
> And held his thoughts as high
> As were the mounts whereon his flocks
> Did hourly feed him by."[8]

What should we think of the shepherd's life if his flocks always wandered to higher pastures than his thoughts?

Every morning was a cheerful invitation to make my life of equal simplicity, and I may say innocence, with Nature herself. I have been as sincere a worshipper of Aurora[9] as the Greeks. I got up early and bathed in the pond; that was a religious exercise, and

5. **Damodara:** A name for Krishna, an incarnation of Vishnu, second god of the Hindu trinity; the following quotation is from the *Harivansa*.
6. **Cassiopeia's Chair:** The five brightest stars in the constellation Cassiopeia.
7. **Pleiades . . . Altair:** Names of various stars and constellations.
8. **There . . . by:** From an anonymous Renaissance poem reprinted in *Old Ballads* (1810).
9. **Aurora:** The Roman Goddess of the dawn.

one of the best things which I did. They say that characters were engraven on the bathing tub of king Tching-thang[10] to this effect: "Renew thyself completely each day; do it again, and again, and forever again." I can understand that. Morning brings back the heroic ages. I was as much affected by the faint hum of a mosquito making its invisible and unimaginable tour through my apartment at earliest dawn, when I was sitting with door and windows open, as I could be by any trumpet that ever sang of fame. It was Homer's requiem; itself an Iliad and Odyssey in the air, singing its own wrath and wanderings. There was something cosmical about it; a standing advertisement, till forbidden,[11] of the everlasting vigor and fertility of the world. The morning, which is the most memorable season of the day, is the awakening hour. Then there is least somnolence in us; and for an hour, at least, some part of us awakes which slumbers all the rest of the day and night. Little is to be expected of that day, if it can be called a day, to which we are not awakened by our Genius, but by the mechanical nudgings of some servitor, are not awakened by our own newly-acquired force and aspirations from within, accompanied by the undulations of celestial music, instead of factory bells, and a fragrance filling the air – to a higher life than we fell asleep from; and thus the darkness bear its fruit, and prove itself to be good, no less than the light. That man who does not believe that each day contains an earlier, more sacred, and auroral hour than he has yet profaned, has despaired of life, and is pursuing a descending and darkening way. After a partial cessation of his sensuous life, the soul of man, or its organs rather, are reinvigorated each day, and his Genius tries again what noble life it can make. All memorable events, I should say, transpire in morning time and in a morning atmosphere. The Vedas[12] say, "All intelligences awake with the morning." Poetry and art, and the fairest and most memorable of the actions of men, date from such an hour. All poets and heroes, like Memnon,[13] are the children of Aurora, and emit their music at sunrise. To him whose elastic and vigorous thought keeps pace with the sun, the day is a perpetual morning. It matters not what the clocks say or the attitudes and labors of men. Morning is when I am awake and there is a dawn in me. Moral reform is the effort to throw off sleep. Why is it that men give so poor an account of their day if they have not been slumbering? They are not such poor calculators. If they had not been overcome with drowsiness they would have performed something. The millions are awake enough for physical labor; but only one in a million is awake enough for effective intellectual exertion, only one in a hundred millions to a poetic or divine life. To be awake is to be alive. I have never yet met a man who was quite awake. How could I have looked him in the face?

We must learn to reawaken and keep ourselves awake, not by mechanical aids, but by an infinite expectation of the dawn, which does not forsake us in our soundest sleep. I know of no more encouraging fact than the unquestionable ability of man to elevate his

---

10. **Tching-thang:** Confucius (c. 551–c. 479 BCE), Chinese philosopher and teacher; the quotation is from *The Great Learning*, chapter 1.

11. **till forbidden:** The abbreviation "t f," or "till forbidden," was a printer's sign for standing advertisements in newspapers.

12. **Vedas:** Hindu scriptures; the specific source of the quotation is unknown.

13. **Memnon:** In Greek mythology, Memnon was an Ethiopian king who was killed by Achilles in the Trojan War.

life by a conscious endeavor. It is something to be able to paint a particular picture, or to carve a statue, and so to make a few objects beautiful; but it is far more glorious to carve and paint the very atmosphere and medium through which we look, which morally we can do. To affect the quality of the day, that is the highest of arts. Every man is tasked to make his life, even in its details, worthy of the contemplation of his most elevated and critical hour. If we refused, or rather used up, such paltry information as we get, the oracles would distinctly inform us how this might be done.

I went to the woods because I wished to live deliberately, to front only the essential facts of life, and see if I could not learn what it had to teach, and not, when I came to die, discover that I had not lived. I did not wish to live what was not life, living is so dear; nor did I wish to practise resignation, unless it was quite necessary. I wanted to live deep and suck out all the marrow of life, to live so sturdily and Spartan-like as to put to rout all that was not life, to cut a broad swath and shave close, to drive life into a corner, and reduce it to its lowest terms, and, if it proved to be mean, why then to get the whole and genuine meanness of it, and publish its meanness to the world; or if it were sublime, to know it by experience, and be able to give a true account of it in my next excursion. For most men, it appears to me, are in a strange uncertainty about it, whether it is of the devil or of God, and have *somewhat hastily* concluded that it is the chief end of man here to "glorify God and enjoy him forever."[14]

Still we live meanly, like ants; though the fable tells us that we were long ago changed into men;[15] like pygmies we fight with cranes; it is error upon error, and clout upon clout, and our best virtue has for its occasion a superfluous and evitable wretchedness. Our life is frittered away by detail. An honest man has hardly need to count more than his ten fingers, or in extreme cases he may add his ten toes, and lump the rest. Simplicity, simplicity, simplicity! I say, let your affairs be as two or three, and not a hundred or a thousand; instead of a million count half a dozen, and keep your accounts on your thumb nail. In the midst of this chopping sea of civilized life, such are the clouds and storms and quicksands and thousand-and-one items to be allowed for, that a man has to live, if he would not founder and go to the bottom and not make his port at all, by dead reckoning, and he must be a great calculator indeed who succeeds. Simplify, simplify. Instead of three meals a day, if it be necessary eat but one; instead of a hundred dishes, five; and reduce other things in proportion. Our life is like a German Confederacy, made up of petty states, with its boundary forever fluctuating, so that even a German cannot tell you how it is bounded at any moment. The nation itself, with all its so called internal improvements, which, by the way, are all external and superficial, is just such an unwieldy and overgrown establishment, cluttered with furniture and tripped up by its own traps, ruined by luxury and heedless expense, by want of calculation and a worthy aim, as the million households in the land; and the only cure for it as for them is in a rigid economy, a stern and more than Spartan simplicity of life and elevation of purpose. It lives too fast. Men think that it is essential that the *Nation* have commerce, and

14. **"glorify . . . forever"**: See "Economy," note 9.
15. **ants . . . men**: The Greek god Zeus turned ants into men to repopulate the earth; in the opening lines of book 3 of the *Iliad*, Homer compares the Trojans to cranes fighting with pygmies.

export ice, and talk through a telegraph, and ride thirty miles an hour, without a doubt, whether *they* do or not; but whether we should live like baboons or like men, is a little uncertain. If we do not get out sleepers, and forge rails, and devote days and nights to the work, but go to tinkering upon our *lives* to improve *them*, who will build railroads? And if railroads are not built, how shall we get to heaven in season? But if we stay at home and mind our business, who will want railroads? We do not ride on the railroad; it rides upon us. Did you ever think what those sleepers[16] are that underlie the railroad? Each one is a man, an Irishman, or a Yankee man. The rails are laid on them, and they are covered with sand, and the cars run smoothly over them. They are sound sleepers, I assure you. And every few years a new lot is laid down and run over; so that, if some have the pleasure of riding on a rail, others have the misfortune to be ridden upon. And when they run over a man that is walking in his sleep, a supernumerary sleeper in the wrong position, and wake him up, they suddenly stop the cars, and make a hue and cry about it, as if this were an exception. I am glad to know that it takes a gang of men for every five miles to keep the sleepers down and level in their beds as it is, for this is a sign that they may sometime get up again.

Why should we live with such hurry and waste of life? We are determined to be starved before we are hungry. Men say that a stitch in time saves nine, and so they take a thousand stitches to-day to save nine to-morrow. As for *work*, we haven't any of any consequence. We have the Saint Vitus' dance,[17] and cannot possibly keep our heads still. If I should only give a few pulls at the parish bell-rope, as for a fire, that is, without setting the bell, there is hardly a man on his farm in the outskirts of Concord, notwithstanding that press of engagements which was his excuse so many times this morning, nor a boy, nor a woman, I might almost say, but would forsake all and follow that sound, not mainly to save property from the flames, but, if we will confess the truth, much more to see it burn, since burn it must, and we, be it known, did not set it on fire, – or to see it put out, and have a hand in it, if that is done as handsomely; yes, even if it were the parish church itself. Hardly a man takes a half hour's nap after dinner, but when he wakes he holds up his head and asks, "What's the news?" as if the rest of mankind had stood his sentinels. Some give directions to be waked every half hour, doubtless for no other purpose; and then, to pay for it, they tell what they have dreamed. After a night's sleep the news is as indispensable as the breakfast. "Pray tell me any thing new that has happened to a man any where on this globe," – and he reads it over his coffee and rolls, that a man has had his eyes gouged out this morning on the Wachito River;[18] never dreaming the while that he lives in the dark unfathomed mammoth cave of this world, and has but the rudiment of an eye himself.

For my part, I could easily do without the post-office. I think that there are very few important communications made through it. To speak critically, I never received more than one or two letters in my life – I wrote this some years ago – that were worth the

---

16. **sleepers:** Wooden ties upon which rails were laid.
17. **Saint Vitus' dance:** St. Vitus was the patron saint of those afflicted with chorea, a nervous disorder characterized by jerky, spasmodic movements.
18. **Wachito River:** The Ouachito River in southern Arkansas, then a notoriously rough part of the country.

postage. The penny-post is, commonly, an institution through which you seriously offer a man that penny for his thoughts which is so often safely offered in jest. And I am sure that I never read any memorable news in a newspaper. If we read of one man robbed, or murdered, or killed by accident, or one house burned, or one vessel wrecked, or one steamboat blown up, or one cow run over on the Western Railroad, or one mad dog killed, or one lot of grasshoppers in the winter, – we never need read of another. One is enough. If you are acquainted with the principle, what do you care for a myriad instances and applications? To a philosopher all *news*, as it is called, is gossip, and they who edit and read it are old women over their tea. Yet not a few are greedy after this gossip. There was such a rush, as I hear, the other day at one of the offices to learn the foreign news by the last arrival, that several large squares of plate glass belonging to the establishment were broken by the pressure, – news which I seriously think a ready wit might write a twelvemonth or twelve years beforehand with sufficient accuracy. As for Spain, for instance, if you know how to throw in Don Carlos and the Infanta, and Don Pedro and Seville and Granada, from time to time in the right proportions, – they may have changed the names a little since I saw the papers, – and serve up a bull-fight when other entertainments fail, it will be true to the letter, and give us as good an idea of the exact state or ruin of things in Spain as the most succinct and lucid reports under this head in the newspapers: and as for England, almost the last significant scrap of news from that quarter was the revolution of 1649;[19] and if you have learned the history of her crops for an average year, you never need attend to that thing again, unless your speculations are of a merely pecuniary character. If one may judge who rarely looks into the newspapers, nothing new does ever happen in foreign parts, a French revolution[20] not excepted.

What news! how much more important to know what that is which was never old! "Kieou-he-yu (great dignitary of the state of Wei) sent a man to Khoung-tseu to know his news. Khoung-tseu caused the messenger to be seated near him, and questioned him in these terms: What is your master doing? The messenger answered with respect: My master desires to diminish the number of his faults, but he cannot come to the end of them. The messenger being gone, the philosopher remarked: What a worthy messenger! What a worthy messenger!" The preacher, instead of vexing the ears of drowsy farmers on their day of rest at the end of the week, – for Sunday is the fit conclusion of an ill-spent week, and not the fresh and brave beginning of a new one, – with this one other draggle-tail of a sermon, should shout with thundering voice, – "Pause! Avast! Why so seeming fast, but deadly slow?"

Shams and delusions are esteemed for soundest truths, while reality is fabulous. If men would steadily observe realities only, and not allow themselves to be deluded, life, to compare it with such things as we know, would be like a fairy tale and the Arabian

19. **revolution of 1649:** When forces led by Oliver Cromwell overthrew the English monarchy and established the Puritan Commonwealth, which lasted until 1660.
20. **French revolution:** The Revolution of 1848, which had been widely reported in American newspapers. The revolution was swiftly quelled, leading to the establishment in 1852 of an authoritarian regime under Napoleon III.

Nights' Entertainments. If we respected only what is inevitable and has a right to be, music and poetry would resound along the streets. When we are unhurried and wise, we perceive that only great and worthy things have any permanent and absolute existence, – that petty fears and petty pleasures are but the shadow of the reality. This is always exhilarating and sublime. By closing the eyes and slumbering, and consenting to be deceived by shows, men establish and confirm their daily life of routine and habit every where, which still is built on purely illusory foundations. Children, who play life, discern its true law and relations more clearly than men, who fail to live it worthily, but who think that they are wiser by experience, that is, by failure. I have read in a Hindoo book, that "there was a king's son, who, being expelled in infancy from his native city, was brought up by a forester, and, growing up to maturity in that state, imagined himself to belong to the barbarous race with which he lived. One of his father's ministers having discovered him, revealed to him what he was, and the misconception of his character was removed, and he knew himself to be a prince. So soul," continues the Hindoo philosopher, "from the circumstances in which it is placed, mistakes its own character, until the truth is revealed to it by some holy teacher, and then it knows itself to be *Brahme*."[21] I perceive that we inhabitants of New England live this mean life that we do because our vision does not penetrate the surface of things. We think that that *is* which *appears* to be. If a man should walk through this town and see only the reality, where, think you, would the "Mill-dam"[22] go to? If he should give us an account of the realities he beheld there, we should not recognize the place in his description. Look at a meeting-house, or a court-house, or a jail, or a shop, or a dwelling-house, and say what that thing really is before a true gaze, and they would all go to pieces in your account of them. Men esteem truth remote, in the outskirts of the system, behind the farthest star, before Adam and after the last man. In eternity there is indeed something true and sublime. But all these times and places and occasions are now and here. God himself culminates in the present moment, and will never be more divine in the lapse of all the ages. And we are enabled to apprehend at all what is sublime and noble only by the perpetual instilling and drenching of the reality that surrounds us. The universe constantly and obediently answers to our conceptions; whether we travel fast or slow, the track is laid for us. Let us spend our lives in conceiving then. The poet or the artist never yet had so fair and noble a design but some of his posterity at least could accomplish it.

Let us spend one day as deliberately as Nature, and not be thrown off the track by every nutshell and mosquito's wing that falls on the rails. Let us rise early and fast, or break fast, gently and without perturbation; let company come and let company go, let the bells ring and the children cry, – determined to make a day of it. Why should we knock under and go with the stream? Let us not be upset and overwhelmed in that terrible rapid and whirlpool called a dinner, situated in the meridian shallows. Weather this danger and you are safe, for the rest of the way is down hill. With unrelaxed nerves, with

---

21. **a Hindoo book . . . *Brahme*"**: The source of this quotation has not been identified; in Hindu thought, Brahma is the supreme essence or spirit of the universe.
22. **"Mill-dam"**: The business and shopping center of Concord.

morning vigor, sail by it, looking another way, tied to the mast like Ulysses.[23] If the engine whistles, let it whistle till it is hoarse for its pains. If the bell rings, why should we run? We will consider what kind of music they are like. Let us settle ourselves, and work and wedge our feet downward through the mud and slush of opinion, and prejudice, and tradition, and delusion, and appearance, that alluvion which covers the globe, through Paris and London, through New York and Boston and Concord, through church and state, through poetry and philosophy and religion, till we come to a hard bottom and rocks in place, which we can call *reality*, and say, This is, and no mistake; and then begin, having a *point d'appui*,[24] below freshet and frost and fire, a place where you might found a wall or a state, or set a lamp-post safely, or perhaps a gauge, not a Nilometer,[25] but a Realometer, that future ages might know how deep a freshet of shams and appearances had gathered from time to time. If you stand right fronting and face to face to a fact, you will see the sun glimmer on both its surfaces, as if it were a cimeter, and feel its sweet edge dividing you through the heart and marrow, and so you will happily conclude your mortal career. Be it life or death, we crave only reality. If we are really dying, let us hear the rattle in our throats and feel cold in the extremities; if we are alive, let us go about our business.

Time is but the stream I go a-fishing in. I drink at it; but while I drink I see the sandy bottom and detect how shallow it is. Its thin current slides away, but eternity remains. I would drink deeper; fish in the sky, whose bottom is pebbly with stars. I cannot count one. I know not the first letter of the alphabet. I have always been regretting that I was not as wise as the day I was born. The intellect is a cleaver; it discerns and rifts its way into the secret of things. I do not wish to be any more busy with my hands than is necessary. My head is hands and feet. I feel all my best faculties concentrated in it. My instinct tells me that my head is an organ for burrowing, as some creatures use their snout and fore-paws, and with it I would mine and burrow my way through these hills. I think that the richest vein is somewhere hereabouts; so by the divining rod and thin rising vapors I judge; and here I will begin to mine.

The Bean-Field

Meanwhile my beans, the length of whose rows, added together, was seven miles already planted, were impatient to be hoed, for the earliest had grown considerably before the latest were in the ground; indeed they were not easily to be put off. What was the meaning of this so steady and self-respecting, this small Herculean labor, I knew not. I came to love my rows, my beans, though so many more than I wanted. They attached me to the earth, and so I got strength like Antaeus.[1] But why should I raise them? Only Heaven

23. **Ulysses:** The Roman name for Odysseus, who in Homer's *Odyssey* has himself tied to a mast so that he may hear but not succumb to the song of the Sirens.
24. ***point d'appui:*** Point of leverage or support; a solid footing.
25. **Nilometer:** Gauge used in ancient times to measure the rise and fall of the Nile.
1. **Antaeus:** Giant in Greek mythology who drew his strength from contact with his mother, the earth. He was killed in a fight with Hercules, who lifted him from the ground.

knows. This was my curious labor all summer, – to make this portion of the earth's surface, which had yielded only cinquefoil, blackberries, johnswort, and the like, before, sweet wild fruits and pleasant flowers, produce instead this pulse. What shall I learn of beans or beans of me? I cherish them, I hoe them, early and late I have an eye to them; and this is my day's work. It is a fine broad leaf to look on. My auxiliaries are the dews and rains which water this dry soil, and what fertility is in the soil itself, which for the most part is lean and effete. My enemies are worms, cool days, and most of all woodchucks. The last have nibbled for me a quarter of an acre clean. But what right had I to oust johnswort and the rest, and break up their ancient herb garden? Soon, however, the remaining beans will be too tough for them, and go forward to meet new foes.

When I was four years old, as I well remember, I was brought from Boston to this my native town, through these very woods and this field, to the pond. It is one of the oldest scenes stamped on my memory. And now to-night my flute has waked the echoes over that very water. The pines still stand here older than I; or, if some have fallen, I have cooked my supper with their stumps, and a new growth is rising all around, preparing another aspect for new infant eyes. Almost the same johnswort springs from the same perennial root in this pasture, and even I have at length helped to clothe that fabulous landscape of my infant dreams, and one of the results of my presence and influence is seen in these bean leaves, corn blades, and potato vines.

I planted about two acres and a half of upland; and as it was only about fifteen years since the land was cleared, and I myself had got out two or three cords of stumps, I did not give it any manure; but in the course of the summer it appeared by the arrow-heads which I turned up in hoeing, that an extinct nation had anciently dwelt here and planted corn and beans ere white men came to clear the land, and so, to some extent, had exhausted the soil for this very crop.

Before yet any woodchuck or squirrel had run across the road, or the sun had got above the shrub-oaks, while all the dew was on, though the farmers warned me against it, – I would advise you to do all your work if possible while the dew is on, – I began to level the ranks of haughty weeds in my bean-field and throw dust upon their heads. Early in the morning I worked barefooted, dabbling like a plastic artist in the dewy and crumbling sand, but later in the day the sun blistered my feet. There the sun lighted me to hoe beans, pacing slowly backward and forward over that yellow gravelly upland, between the long green rows, fifteen rods, the one end terminating in a shrub oak copse where I could rest in the shade, the other in a blackberry field where the green berries deepened their tints by the time I had made another bout. Removing the weeds, putting fresh soil about the bean stems, and encouraging this weed which I had sown, making the yellow soil express its summer thought in bean leaves and blossoms rather than in wormwood and piper and millet grass, making the earth say beans instead of grass, – this was my daily work. As I had little aid from horses or cattle, or hired men or boys, or improved implements of husbandry, I was much slower, and became much more intimate with my beans than usual. But labor of the hands, even when pursued to the verge of drudgery, is perhaps never the worst form of idleness. It has a constant and imperishable moral, and to the scholar it yields a classic result. A very *agricola laboriosus*[2] was I to travellers bound westward through Lincoln and Wayland to nobody knows where; they sitting at their ease in gigs, with elbows on knees, and reins loosely hanging in festoons; I the home-staying, laborious native of the soil. But soon my homestead was out of their sight and thought. It was the only open and cultivated field for a great distance on either side of the road; so they made the most of it; and sometimes the man in the field heard more of travellers' gossip and comment than was meant for his ear: "Beans so late! peas so late!" – for I continued to plant when others had began to hoe, – the ministerial husbandman[3] had not suspected it. "Corn, my boy, for fodder; corn for fodder." "Does he *live* there?" asks the black bonnet of the gray coat; and the hard-featured farmer reins up his grateful dobbin to inquire what you are doing where he sees no manure in the furrow, and recommends a little chip dirt, or any little waste stuff, or it may be ashes or plaster. But here were two acres and a half of furrows, and only a hoe for cart and two hands to draw it, – there being an aversion to other carts and horses, – and chip dirt far away. Fellow-travellers as they rattled by compared it aloud with the fields which they had passed, so that I came to know how I stood in the agricultural world. This was one field not in Mr. Coleman's report. And, by the way, who estimates the value of the crop which Nature yields in the still wilder fields unimproved by man? The crop of *English* hay is carefully weighed, the moisture calculated, the silicates and the potash; but in all dells and pond holes in the woods and pastures and swamps grows a rich and various crop only unreaped by man. Mine was, as it were, the connecting link between wild and cultivated fields; as some states are civilized, and others half-civilized, and others savage or barbarous, so my field was, though not in a bad sense, a half-cultivated field. They were beans cheerfully returning to their wild and primitive state that I cultivated, and my hoe played the *Rans de Vaches*[4] for them.

Near at hand, upon the topmost spray of a birch, sings the brown-thrasher – or red mavis, as some love to call him – all the morning, glad of your society, that would find out another farmer's field if yours were not here. While you are planting the seed, he cries, – "Drop it, drop it, – cover it up, cover it up, – pull it up, pull it up, pull it up." But this was not corn, and so it was safe from such enemies as he. You may wonder what his rigmarole, his amateur Paganini[5] performances on one string or on twenty, have to do with your planting, and yet prefer it to leached ashes or plaster. It was a cheap sort of top dressing in which I had entire faith.

As I drew a still fresher soil about the rows with my hoe, I disturbed the ashes of unchronicled nations who in primeval years lived under these heavens, and their small

---

2. ***agricola laboriosus***: Latin for "hard-working farmer"; the road past Walden Pond leads from Concord to the neighboring town of Lincoln and from there westward to Wayland, Massachusetts.

3. **ministerial husbandman**: The Reverend Henry Coleman (1785-1849), author of several surveys of agriculture in Massachusetts, which Thoreau refers to later in this paragraph.

4. ***Rans des Vaches***: A song sung or played by Swiss herdsmen to call their cattle. The vogue of such mountain songs in the 1840s led to the publication of several collections, notably William Bradbury's *The Alpine Glee Singer* (1850).

5. **Paganini**: Nicolo Paganini (1782-1840), Italian composer and violin virtuoso acclaimed for his ability to play on one string.

implements of war and hunting were brought to the light of this modern day. They lay mingled with other natural stones, some of which bore the marks of having been burned by Indian fires, and some by the sun, and also bits of pottery and glass brought hither by the recent cultivators of the soil. When my hoe tinkled against the stones, that music echoed to the woods and the sky, and was an accompaniment to my labor which yielded an instant and immeasurable crop. It was no longer beans that I hoed, nor I that hoed beans; and I remembered with as much pity as pride, if I remembered at all, my acquaintances who had gone to the city to attend the oratorios. The night-hawk circled overhead in the sunny afternoons – for I sometimes made a day of it – like a mote in the eye, or in heaven's eye, falling from time to time with a swoop and a sound as if the heavens were rent, torn at last to very rags and tatters, and yet a seamless cope remained; small imps that fill the air and lay their eggs on the ground on bare sand or rocks on the tops of hills, where few have found them; graceful and slender like ripples caught up from the pond, as leaves are raised by the wind to float in the heavens; such kindredship is in Nature. The hawk is aerial brother of the wave which he sails over and surveys, those his perfect air-inflated wings answering to the elemental unfledged pinions of the sea. Or sometimes I watched a pair of hen-hawks circling high in the sky, alternately soaring and descending, approaching and leaving one another, as if they were the imbodiment of my own thoughts. Or I was attracted by the passage of wild pigeons from this wood to that, with a slight quivering winnowing sound and carrier haste; or from under a rotten stump my hoe turned up a sluggish portentous and outlandish spotted salamander, a trace of Egypt and the Nile, yet our contemporary. When I paused to lean on my hoe, these sounds and sights I heard and saw any where in the row, a part of the inexhaustible entertainment which the country offers.

On gala days the town fires its great guns, which echo like popguns to these woods, and some waifs of martial music occasionally penetrate thus far. To me, away there in my bean-field at the other end of the town, the big guns sounded as if a puff ball had burst; and when there was a military turnout of which I was ignorant, I have sometimes had a vague sense all the day of some sort of itching and disease in the horizon, as if some eruption would break out there soon, either scarlatina or canker-rash, until at length some more favorable puff of wind, making haste over the fields and up the Wayland road, brought me information of the "trainers."[6] It seemed by the distant hum as if somebody's bees had swarmed, and that the neighbors, according to Virgil's advice,[7] by a faint *tintinnabulum* upon the most sonorous of their domestic utensils, were endeavoring to call them down into the hive again. And when the sound died quite away, and the hum had ceased, and the most favorable breezes told no tale, I knew that they had got the last drone of them all safely into the Middlesex hive, and that now their minds were bent on the honey with which it was smeared.

---

6. **On gala days . . . "trainers"**: Concord was the home of the Concord Artillery, a state militia unit known as the "trainers," who fired their guns on the gala days of April 19, the anniversary of the Concord fight of 1775, and July 4. They evidently also fired them to celebrate news of victories in the Mexican War, which Thoreau alludes to in the following paragraphs.
7. **Virgil's advice**: In book 4 of the *Georgics*.

I felt proud to know that the liberties of Massachusetts and of our fatherland were in such safe keeping; and as I turned to my hoeing again I was filled with an inexpressible confidence, and pursued my labor cheerfully with a calm trust in the future.

When there were several bands of musicians, it sounded as if all the village was a vast bellows, and all the buildings expanded and collapsed alternately with a din. But sometimes it was a really noble and inspiring strain that reached these woods, and the trumpet that sings of fame, and I felt as if I could spit a Mexican with a good relish, – for why should we always stand for trifles? – and looked round for a woodchuck or a skunk to exercise my chivalry upon. These martial strains seemed as far away as Palestine, and reminded me of a march of crusaders in the horizon, with a slight tantivy and tremulous motion of the elm-tree tops which overhang the village. This was one of the *great* days; though the sky had from my clearing only the same everlastingly great look that it wears daily, and I saw no difference in it.

It was a singular experience that long acquaintance which I cultivated with beans, what with planting, and hoeing, and harvesting, and threshing, and picking over, and selling them, – the last was the hardest of all, – I might add eating, for I did taste. I was determined to know beans. When they were growing, I used to hoe from five o'clock in the morning till noon, and commonly spent the rest of the day about other affairs. Consider the intimate and curious acquaintance one makes with various kinds of weeds, – it will bear some iteration in the account, for there was no little iteration in the labor, – disturbing their delicate organizations so ruthlessly, and making such invidious distinctions with his hoe, levelling whole ranks of one species, and sedulously cultivating another. That's Roman wormwood, – that's pigweed, – that's sorrel, – that's piper-grass, – have at him, chop him up, turn his roots upward to the sun, don't let him have a fibre in the shade, if you do he'll turn himself t'other side up and be as green as a leek in two days. A long war, not with cranes, but with weeds, those Trojans who had sun and rain and dews on their side. Daily the beans saw me come to their rescue armed with a hoe, and thin the ranks of their enemies, filling up the trenches with weedy dead. Many a lusty crest-waving Hector,[8] that towered a whole foot above his crowding comrades, fell before my weapon and rolled in the dust.

Those summer days which some of my contemporaries devoted to the fine arts in Boston or Rome, and others to contemplation in India, and others to trade in London or New York, I thus, with the other farmers of New England, devoted to husbandry. Not that I wanted beans to eat, for I am by nature a Pythagorean, so far as beans are concerned, whether they mean porridge or voting,[9] and exchanged them for rice; but, perchance, as some must work in fields if only for the sake of tropes and expression, to serve a parable-maker one day. It was on the whole a rare amusement, which, continued too long, might have become a dissipation. Though I gave them no manure, and did not hoe them all once, I hoed them unusually well as far as I went, and was paid for it in the end,

---

8. **Hector:** The bravest of the Trojan warriors in Homer's *Iliad.*

9. **Pythagorean . . . voting:** The Greek philosopher Pythagoras (582-507? BCE) refused to eat beans, which in ancient times were also often used to tally votes.

"there being in truth," as Evelyn[10] says, "no compost or laetation whatsoever comparable to this continual motion, repastination, and turning of the mould with the spade." "The earth," he adds elsewhere, "especially if fresh, has a certain magnetism in it, by which it attracts the salt, power, or virtue (call it either) which gives it life, and is the logic of all the labor and stir we keep about it, to sustain us; all dungings and other sordid temperings being but the vicars succedaneous to this improvement." Moreover, this being one of those "worn-out and exhausted lay fields which enjoy their sabbath," had perchance, as Sir Kenelm Digby[11] thinks likely, attracted "vital spirits" from the air. I harvested twelve bushels of beans.

But to be more particular, for it is complained that Mr. Coleman has reported chiefly the expensive experiments of gentlemen farmers, my outgoes were, –

For a hoe,	$ 0 54
Ploughing, harrowing, and furrowing,	7 50, Too much.
Beans for seed,	3 12½
Potatoes "	1 33
Peas "	0 40
Turnip seed,	0 06
White line for crow fence,	0 02
Horse cultivator and boy three hours,	1 00
Horse and cart to get crop,	0 75
In all,	$14 72½

My income was, (*patrem familias vendacem, non emacem esse oportet*,[12]) from

Nine bushels and twelve quarts of beans sold,	$16 94
Five " large potatoes,	2 50
Nine " small,	2 25
Grass,	1 00
Stalks,	0 75
In all,	$23 44

Leaving a pecuniary profit, as I have elsewhere said, of $ 8 71½.

This is the result of my experience in raising beans. Plant the common small white bush bean about the first of June, in rows three feet by eighteen inches apart, being careful to select fresh round and unmixed seed. First look out for worms, and supply vacancies by planting anew. Then look out for woodchucks, if it is an exposed place, for they will nibble off the earliest tender leaves almost clean as they go; and again, when the young tendrils make their appearance, they have notice of it, and will shear them off

10. **Evelyn:** John Evelyn (1620-1706), English diarist and writer; from his *Terra, a Philosophical Discourse of Earth* (1729).

11. **Sir Kenelm Digby:** English scientist (1603-1665); quoted in Evelyn's *Sylva, or a Discourse of Forest-Trees* (1679).

12. ***patrem . . . oportet*:** Cato, *De agri cultura*, 2.7: "The father of the family should have the habit of selling, not buying" (Latin).

with both buds and young pods, sitting erect like a squirrel. But above all harvest as early as possible, if you would escape frosts and have a fair and salable crop; you may save much loss by this means.

This further experience also I gained. I said to myself, I will not plant beans and corn with so much industry another summer, but such seeds, if the seed is not lost, as sincerity, truth, simplicity, faith, innocence, and the like, and see if they will not grow in this soil, even with less toil and manurance, and sustain me, for surely it has not been exhausted for these crops. Alas! I said this to myself; but now another summer is gone, and another, and another, and I am obliged to say to you, Reader, that the seeds which I planted, if indeed they *were* the seeds of those virtues, were wormeaten or had lost their vitality, and so did not come up. Commonly men will only be brave as their fathers were brave, or timid. This generation is very sure to plant corn and beans each new year precisely as the Indians did centuries ago and taught the first settlers to do, as if there were a fate in it. I saw an old man the other day, to my astonishment, making the holes with a hoe for the seventieth time at least, and not for himself to lie down in! But why should not the New Englander try new adventures, and not lay so much stress on his grain, his potato and grass crop, and his orchards, – raise other crops than these? Why concern ourselves so much about our beans for seed, and not be concerned at all about a new generation of men? We should really be fed and cheered if when we met a man we were sure to see that some of the qualities which I have named, which we all prize more than those other productions, but which are for the most part broadcast and floating in the air, had taken root and grown in him. Here comes such a subtile and ineffable quality, for instance, as truth or justice, though the slightest amount or new variety of it, along the road. Our ambassadors should be instructed to send home such seeds as these, and Congress help to distribute them over all the land.[13] We should never stand upon ceremony with sincerity. We should never cheat and insult and banish one another by our meanness, if there were present the kernel of worth and friendliness. We should not meet thus in haste. Most men I do not meet at all, for they seem not to have time; they are busy about their beans. We would not deal with a man thus plodding ever, leaning on a hoe or a spade as a staff between his work, not as a mushroom, but partially risen out of the earth, something more than erect, like swallows alighted and walking on the ground: –

> "And as he spake, his wings would now and then
> Spread, as he meant to fly, then close again,"[14]

so that we should suspect that we might be conversing with an angel. Bread may not always nourish us; but it always does us good, it even takes stiffness out of our joints, and makes us supple and buoyant, when we knew not what ailed us, to recognize any generosity in man or Nature, to share any unmixed and heroic joy.

---

13. **Congress . . . land:** It was then a popular custom for members of Congress to send free seeds to constituents who requested them.
14. **And . . . again:** From *The Shepherd's Oracles*, by the English poet Frances Quarles (1592–1644).

Ancient poetry and mythology suggest, at least, that husbandry was once a sacred art; but it is pursued with irreverent haste and heedlessness by us, our object being to have large farms and large crops merely. We have no festival, nor procession, nor ceremony, not excepting our Cattle-shows and so called Thanksgivings, by which the farmer expresses a sense of the sacredness of his calling, or is reminded of its sacred origin. It is the premium and the feast which tempt him. He sacrifices not to Ceres and the Terrestrial Jove, but to the infernal Plutus[15] rather. By avarice and selfishness, and a grovelling habit, from which none of us is free, of regarding the soil as property, or the means of acquiring property chiefly, the landscape is deformed, husbandry is degraded with us, and the farmer leads the meanest of lives. He knows Nature but as a robber. Cato says that the profits of agriculture are particularly pious or just, (*maximeque pius quoestus,*) and according to Varro the old Romans "called the same earth Mother and Ceres, and thought that they who cultivated it led a pious and useful life, and that they alone were left of the race of King Saturn."[16]

We are wont to forget that the sun looks on our cultivated fields and on the prairies and forests without distinction. They all reflect and absorb his rays alike, and the former make but a small part of the glorious picture which he beholds in his daily course. In his view the earth is all equally cultivated like a garden. Therefore we should receive the benefit of his light and heat with a corresponding trust and magnanimity. What though I value the seed of these beans, and harvest that in the fall of the year? This broad field which I have looked at so long looks not to me as the principal cultivator, but away from me to influences more genial to it, which water and make it green. These beans have results which are not harvested by me. Do they not grow for woodchucks partly? The ear of wheat, (in Latin *spica,* obsoletely *speca,* from *spe,* hope,) should not be the only hope of the husbandman; its kernel or grain (*granum,* from *gerendo,* bearing,) is not all that it bears. How, then, can our harvest fail? Shall I not rejoice also at the abundance of the weeds whose seeds are the granary of the birds? It matters little comparatively whether the fields fill the farmer's barns. The true husbandman will cease from anxiety, as the squirrels manifest no concern whether the woods will bear chestnuts this year or not, and finish his labor with every day, relinquishing all claim to the produce of his fields, and sacrificing in his mind not only his first but his last fruits also.

The Village

After hoeing, or perhaps reading and writing, in the forenoon, I usually bathed again in the pond, swimming across one of its coves for a stint, and washed the dust of labor from my person, or smoothed out the last wrinkle which study had made, and for the afternoon was absolutely free. Every day or two I strolled to the village to hear some of the gossip which is incessantly going on there, circulating either from mouth to mouth,

15. **Ceres . . . Jove . . . Plutus:** In Roman mythology, Ceres was the goddess of the harvest; Jove, or Jupiter, was the ruler of heaven and earth; and Plutus was the god of wealth.
16. **"called . . . Saturn":** From the *Rerum Rusticarum* by Marcus Terentius Varro (116–27 BCE); Saturn was the Roman god of agriculture.

or from newspaper, to newspaper, and which, taken in homoeopathic doses,[1] was really as refreshing in its way as the rustle of leaves and the peeping of frogs. As I walked in the woods to see the birds and squirrels, so I walked in the village to see the men and boys; instead of the wind among the pines I heard the carts rattle. In one direction from my house there was a colony of muskrats in the river meadows; under the grove of elms and buttonwoods in the other horizon was a village of busy men, as curious to me as if they had been prairie dogs, each sitting at the mouth of its burrow, or running over to a neighbor's to gossip. I went there frequently to observe their habits. The village appeared to me a great news room; and on one side, to support it, as once at Redding & Company's on State Street, they kept nuts and raisins, or salt and meal and other groceries. Some have such a vast appetite for the former commodity, that is, the news, and such sound digestive organs, that they can sit forever in public avenues without stirring, and let it simmer and whisper through them like the Etesian winds,[2] or as if inhaling ether, it only producing numbness and insensibility to pain, – otherwise it would often be painful to hear, – without affecting the consciousness. I hardly ever failed, when I rambled through the village, to see a row of such worthies, either sitting on a ladder sunning themselves, with their bodies inclined forward and their eyes glancing along the line this way and that, from time to time, with a voluptuous expression, or else leaning against a barn with their hands in their pockets, like caryatides, as if to prop it up. They, being commonly out of doors, heard whatever was in the wind. These are the coarsest mills, in which all gossip is first rudely digested or cracked up before it is emptied into finer and more delicate hoppers within doors. I observed that the vitals of the village were the grocery, the bar-room, the post-office, and the bank; and, as a necessary part of the machinery, they kept a bell, a big gun, and a fire-engine, at convenient places; and the houses were so arranged as to make the most of mankind, in lanes and fronting one another, so that every traveller had to run the gantlet, and every man, woman, and child might get a lick at him. Of course, those who were stationed nearest to the head of the line, where they could most see and be seen, and have the first blow at him, paid the highest prices for their places; and the few straggling inhabitants in the outskirts, where long gaps in the line began to occur, and the traveller could get over walls or turn aside into cow paths, and so escape, paid a very slight ground or window tax. Signs were hung out on all sides to allure him; some to catch him by the appetite, as the tavern and victualling cellar; some by the fancy, as the dry goods store and the jeweller's; and others by the hair or the feet or the skirts, as the barber, the shoemaker, or the tailor. Besides, there was a still more terrible standing invitation to call at every one of these houses, and company expected about these times. For the most part I escaped wonderfully from these dangers, either by proceeding at once boldly and without deliberation to the goal, as is recommended to those who run the gantlet, or by keeping my thoughts on high things, like Orpheus, who, "loudly singing the praises of the gods to his lyre,

1. **homoeopathic doses:** In homeopathic medicine, doctors sought to cure diseases by giving patients small doses of drugs that in healthy people produced symptoms similar to those of the disease.
2. **Etesian winds:** Winds in the Mediterranean that blow from the north every summer.

drowned the voices of the Sirens, and kept out of danger."[3] Sometimes I bolted suddenly, and nobody could tell my whereabouts, for I did not stand much about gracefulness, and never hesitated at a gap in a fence. I was even accustomed to make an irruption into some houses, where I was well entertained, and after learning the kernels and very last sieve-ful of news, what had subsided, the prospects of war and peace, and whether the world was likely to hold together much longer, I was let out through the rear avenues, and so escaped to the woods again.

It was very pleasant, when I staid late in town, to launch myself into the night, especially if it was dark and tempestuous, and set sail from some bright village parlor or lecture room, with a bag of rye or Indian meal upon my shoulder, for my snug harbor in the woods, having made all tight without and withdrawn under hatches with a merry crew of thoughts, leaving only my outer man at the helm, or even tying up the helm when it was plain sailing. I had many a genial thought by the cabin fire "as I sailed." I was never cast away nor distressed in any weather, though I encountered some severe storms. It is darker in the woods, even in common nights, than most suppose. I frequently had to look up at the opening between the trees above the path in order to learn my route, and, where there was no cart-path, to feel with my feet the faint track which I had worn, or steer by the known relation of particular trees which I felt with my hands, passing between two pines for instance, not more than eighteen inches apart, in the midst of the woods, invariably in the darkest night. Sometimes, after coming home thus late in a dark and muggy night, when my feet felt the path which my eyes could not see, dreaming and absent-minded all the way, until I was aroused by having to raise my hand to lift the latch, I have not been able to recall a single step of my walk, and I have thought that perhaps my body would find its way home if its master should forsake it, as the hand finds its way to the mouth without assistance. Several times, when a visitor chanced to stay into evening, and it proved a dark night, I was obliged to conduct him to the cart-path in the rear of the house, and then point out to him the direction he was to pursue, and in keeping which he was to be guided rather by his feet than his eyes. One very dark night I directed thus on their way two young men who had been fishing in the pond. They lived about a mile off through the woods, and were quite used to the route. A day or two after one of them told me that they wandered about the greater part of the night, close by their own premises, and did not get home till toward morning, by which time, as there had been several heavy showers in the mean while, and the leaves were very wet, they were drenched to their skins. I have heard of many going astray even in the village streets, when the darkness was so thick that you could cut it with a knife, as the saying is. Some who live in the outskirts, having come to town a-shopping in their wagons, have been obliged to put up for the night; and gentlemen and ladies making a call have gone half a mile out of their way, feeling the sidewalk only with their feet, and not knowing when they turned. It is a surprising and memorable, as well as valuable experience, to be lost in the woods any time. Often in a snow storm, even by day, one will come out upon a well-known road and yet find it impossible to tell which way leads to the village. Though

3. **"loudly . . . danger":** This is apparently Thoreau's translation or close paraphrase of a passage from the *Argonautica*, written in ancient Greek by the Alexandrian poet Apollonius Rhodius.

he knows that he has travelled it a thousand times, he cannot recognize a feature in it, but it is as strange to him as if it were a road in Siberia. By night, of course, the perplexity is infinitely greater. In our most trivial walks, we are constantly, though unconsciously, steering like pilots by certain well-known beacons and headlands, and if we go beyond our usual course we still carry in our minds the bearing of some neighboring cape; and not till we are completely lost, or turned round, – for a man needs only to be turned round once with his eyes shut in this world to be lost, – do we appreciate the vastness and strangeness of Nature. Every man has to learn the points of compass again as often as he awakes, whether from sleep or any abstraction. Not till we are lost, in other words, not till we have lost the world, do we begin to find ourselves, and realize where we are and the infinite extent of our relations.

One afternoon, near the end of the first summer, when I went to the village to get a shoe from the cobbler's, I was seized and put into jail, because, as I have elsewhere related,[4] I did not pay a tax to, or recognize the authority of, the state which buys and sells men, women, and children, like cattle at the door of its senate-house. I had gone down to the woods for other purposes. But, wherever a man goes, men will pursue and paw him with their dirty institutions, and, if they can, constrain him to belong to their desperate odd-fellow society. It is true, I might have resisted forcibly with more or less effect, might have run "amok" against society; but I preferred that society should run "amok" against me, it being the desperate party. However, I was released the next day, obtained my mended shoe, and returned to the woods in season to get my dinner of huckleberries on Fair-Haven Hill. I was never molested by any person but those who represented the state. I had no lock nor bolt but for the desk which held my papers, not even a nail to put over my latch or windows. I never fastened my door night or day, though I was to be absent several days; not even when the next fall I spent a fortnight in the woods of Maine. And yet my house was more respected than if it had been surrounded by a file of soldiers. The tired rambler could rest and warm himself by my fire, the literary amuse himself with the few books on my table, or the curious, by opening my closet door, see what was left of my dinner, and what prospect I had of a supper. Yet, though many people of every class came this way to the pond, I suffered no serious inconvenience from these sources, and I never missed any thing but one small book, a volume of Homer, which perhaps was improperly gilded, and this I trust a soldier of our camp has found by this time. I am convinced, that if all men were to live as simply as I then did, thieving and robbery would be unknown. These take place only in communities where some have got more than is sufficient while others have not enough. The Pope's Homers[5] would soon get properly distributed. –

"Nec bella fuerunt,
Faginus astabat dum scyphus ante dapes."[6]
"Nor wars did men molest,
When only beechen bowls were in request."

---

4. **as I have elsewhere related:** In "Resistance to Civil Government."
5. **Pope's Homers:** The English poet Alexander Pope (1688–1744) translated both the *Iliad* and the *Odyssey*.
6. ***Nec . . . dapes*:** From the *Elegies* of the Roman poet Albius Tibullus (55?–19? BCE).

"You who govern public affairs, what need have you to employ punishments? Love virtue, and the people will be virtuous. The virtues of a superior man are like the wind; the virtues of a common man are like the grass; the grass, when the wind passes over it, bends."[7]

Spring

The opening of large tracts by the ice-cutters[1] commonly causes a pond to break up earlier; for the water, agitated by the wind, even in cold weather, wears away the surrounding ice. But such was not the effect on Walden that year, for she had soon got a thick new garment to take the place of the old. This pond never breaks up so soon as the others in this neighborhood, on account both of its greater depth and its having no stream passing through it to melt or wear away the ice. I never knew it to open in the course of a winter, not excepting that of '52-3, which gave the ponds so severe a trial. It commonly opens about the first of April, a week or ten days later than Flints' Pond and Fair-Haven, beginning to melt on the north side and in the shallower parts where it began to freeze. It indicates better than any water hereabouts the absolute progress of the season, being least affected by transient changes of temperature. A severe cold of a few days' duration in March may very much retard the opening of the former ponds, while the temperature of Walden increases almost uninterruptedly. A thermometer thrust into the middle of Walden on the 6th of March, 1847, stood at 32°, or freezing point; near the shore at 33°; in the middle of Flints' Pond, the same day, at 32½°; at a dozen rods from the shore, in shallow water under ice a foot thick, at 36°. This difference of three and a half degrees between the temperature of the deep water and the shallow in the latter pond, and the fact that a great proportion of it is comparatively shallow, show why it should break up so much sooner than Walden. The ice in the shallowest part was at this time several inches thinner than in the middle. In mid-winter the middle had been the warmest and the ice thinnest there. So, also, every one who has waded about the shores of a pond in summer must have perceived how much warmer the water is close to the shore, where only three or four inches deep, than a little distance out, and on the surface where it is deep, than near the bottom. In spring the sun not only exerts an influence through the increased temperature of the air and earth, but its heat passes through ice a foot or more thick, and is reflected from the bottom in shallow water, and so also warms the water and melts the under side of the ice, at the same time that it is melting it more directly above, making it uneven, and causing the air bubbles which it contains to extend themselves upward and downward until it is completely honey-combed, and at last disappears suddenly in a single spring rain. Ice has its grain as well as wood, and when a cake begins to rot or "comb," that is, assume the appearance of honey-comb, whatever may be its position, the air cells are at right angles with what was the water

7. **"You . . . bends"**: Confucius, *Analects*, 12.19.

1. **ice-cutters:** As described in the preceding chapter, "The Pond in Winter," ice from ponds in New England was harvested for export all over the world.

surface. Where there is a rock or a log rising near to the surface the ice over it is much thinner, and is frequently quite dissolved by this reflected heat; and I have been told that in the experiment at Cambridge to freeze water in a shallow wooden pond, though the cold air circulated underneath, and so had access to both sides, the reflection of the sun from the bottom more than counterbalanced this advantage. When a warm rain in the middle of the winter melts off the snow-ice from Walden, and leaves a hard dark or transparent ice on the middle, there will be a strip of rotten though thicker white ice, a rod or more wide, about the shores, created by this reflected heat. Also, as I have said, the bubbles themselves within the ice operate as burning glasses to melt the ice beneath.

The phenomena of the year take place every day in a pond on a small scale. Every morning, generally speaking, the shallow water is being warmed more rapidly than the deep, though it may not be made so warm after all, and every evening it is being cooled more rapidly until the morning. The day is an epitome of the year. The night is the winter, the morning and evening are the spring and fall, and the noon is the summer. The cracking and booming of the ice indicate a change of temperature. One pleasant morning after a cold night, February 24th, 1850, having gone to Flints' Pond to spend the day, I noticed with surprise, that when I struck the ice with the head of my axe, it resounded like a gong for many rods around, or as if I had struck on a tight drum-head. The pond began to boom about an hour after sunrise, when it felt the influence of the sun's rays slanted upon it from over the hills; it stretched itself and yawned like a waking man with a gradually increasing tumult, which was kept up three or four hours. It took a short siesta at noon, and boomed once more toward night, as the sun was withdrawing his influence. In the right stage of the weather a pond fires its evening gun with great regularity. But in the middle of the day, being full of cracks, and the air also being less elastic, it had completely lost its resonance, and probably fishes and muskrats could not then have been stunned by a blow on it. The fishermen say that the "thundering of the pond" scares the fishes and prevents their biting. The pond does not thunder every evening, and I cannot tell surely when to expect its thundering; but though I may perceive no difference in the weather, it does. Who would have suspected so large and cold and thick-skinned a thing to be so sensitive? Yet it has its law to which it thunders obedience when it should as surely as the buds expand in the spring. The earth is all alive and covered with papillae. The largest pond is as sensitive to atmospheric changes as the globule of mercury in its tube.

One attraction in coming to the woods to live was that I should have leisure and opportunity to see the spring come in. The ice in the pond at length begins to be honeycombed, and I can set my heel in it as I walk. Fogs and rains and warmer suns are gradually melting the snow; the days have grown sensibly longer; and I see how I shall get through the winter without adding to my wood-pile, for large fires are no longer necessary. I am on the alert for the first signs of spring, to hear the chance note of some arriving bird, or the striped squirrel's chirp, for his stores must be now nearly exhausted, or see the woodchuck venture out of his winter quarters. On the 13th of March, after I had heard the bluebird, song-sparrow, and red-wing, the ice was still nearly a foot thick. As the weather grew warmer, it was not sensibly worn away by the water, nor broken up and floated off as in rivers, but, though it was completely melted for half a rod in width about the shore, the middle was merely honey-combed and saturated with water, so that you could put your foot through it when six inches thick; but by the next day evening, perhaps, after a warm rain followed by fog, it would have wholly disappeared, all gone off with the fog, spirited away. One year I went across the middle only five days before it disappeared entirely. In 1845 Walden was first completely open on the 1st of April; in '46, the 25th of March; in '47, the 8th of April; in '51, the 28th of March; in '52, the 18th of April; in '53, the 23d of March; in '54, about the 7th of April.

Every incident connected with the breaking up of the rivers and ponds and the settling of the weather is particularly interesting to us who live in a climate of so great extremes. When the warmer days come, they who dwell near the river hear the ice crack at night with a startling whoop as loud as artillery, as if its icy fetters were rent from end to end, and within a few days see it rapidly going out. So the alligator comes out of the mud with quakings of the earth. One old man, who has been a close observer of Nature, and seems as thoroughly wise in regard to all her operations as if she had been put upon the stocks when he was a boy, and he had helped to lay her keel, – who has come to his growth, and can hardly acquire more of natural lore if he should live to the age of Methuselah,[2] – told me, and I was surprised to hear him express wonder at any of Nature's operations, for I thought that there were no secrets between them, that one spring day he took his gun and boat, and thought that he would have a little sport with the ducks. There was ice still on the meadows, but it was all gone out of the river, and he dropped down without obstruction from Sudbury, where he lived, to Fair-Haven Pond, which he found, unexpectedly, covered for the most part with a firm field of ice. It was a warm day, and he was surprised to see so great a body of ice remaining. Not seeing any ducks, he hid his boat on the north or back side of an island in the pond, and then concealed himself in the bushes on the south side, to await them. The ice was melted for three or four rods from the shore, and there was a smooth and warm sheet of water, with a muddy bottom, such as the ducks love, within, and he thought it likely that some would be along pretty soon. After he had lain still there about an hour he heard a low and seemingly very distant sound, but singularly grand and impressive, unlike any thing he had ever heard, gradually swelling and increasing as if it would have a universal and memorable ending, a sullen rush and roar, which seemed to him all at once like the sound of a vast body of fowl coming in to settle there, and, seizing his gun, he started up in haste and excited; but he found, to his surprise, that the whole body of the ice had started while he lay there, and drifted in to the shore, and the sound he had heard was made by its edge grating on the shore, – at first gently nibbled and crumbled off, but at length heaving up and scattering its wrecks along the island to a considerable height before it came to a stand still.

At length the sun's rays have attained the right angle, and warm winds blow up mist and rain and melt the snow banks, and the sun dispersing the mist smiles on a check-

2. **age of Methuselah:** Said to have lived 969 years (Genesis 5:27).

ered landscape of russet and white smoking with incense, through which the traveller picks his way from islet to islet, cheered by the music of a thousand tinkling rills and rivulets whose veins are filled with the blood of winter which they are bearing off.

Few phenomena gave me more delight than to observe the forms which thawing sand and clay assume in flowing down the sides of a deep cut on the railroad through which I passed on my way to the village, a phenomenon not very common on so large a scale, though the number of freshly exposed banks of the right material must have been greatly multiplied since railroads were invented. The material was sand of every degree of fineness and of various rich colors, commonly mixed with a little clay. When the frost comes out in the spring, and even in a thawing day in the winter, the sand begins to flow down the slopes like lava, sometimes bursting out through the snow and overflowing it where no sand was to be seen before. Innumerable little streams overlap and interlace one with another, exhibiting a sort of hybrid product, which obeys half way the law of currents, and half way that of vegetation. As it flows it takes the forms of sappy leaves or vines, making heaps of pulpy sprays a foot or more in depth, and resembling, as you look down on them, the laciniated lobed and imbricated thalluses of some lichens; or you are reminded of coral, of leopards' paws or birds' feet, of brains or lungs or bowels, and excrements of all kinds. It is a truly *grotesque* vegetation, whose forms and color we see imitated in bronze, a sort of architectural foliage more ancient and typical than acanthus, chiccory, ivy, vine, or any vegetable leaves; destined perhaps, under some circumstances, to become a puzzle to future geologists. The whole cut impressed me as if it were a cave with it stalactites laid open to the light. The various shades of the sand are singularly rich and agreeable, embracing the different iron colors, brown, gray, yellowish, and reddish. When the flowing mass reaches the drain at the foot of the bank it spreads out flatter into *strands*, the separate streams losing their semi-cylindrical form and gradually becoming more flat and broad, running together as they are more moist, till they form an almost flat *sand*, still variously and beautifully shaded, but in which you can trace the original forms of vegetation; till at length, in the water itself, they are converted into *banks*, like those formed off the mouths of rivers, and the forms of vegetation are lost in the ripple marks on the bottom.

The whole bank, which is from twenty to forty feet high, is sometimes overlaid with a mass of this kind of foliage, or sandy rupture, for a quarter of a mile on one or both sides, the produce of one spring day. What makes this sand foliage remarkable is its springing into existence thus suddenly. When I see on the one side the inert bank, – for the sun acts on one side first, – and on the other this luxuriant foliage, the creation of an hour, I am affected as if in a peculiar sense I stood in the laboratory of the Artist who made the world and me, – had come to where he was still at work, sporting on this bank, and with excess of energy strewing his fresh designs about. I feel as if I were nearer to the vitals of the globe, for this sandy overflow is something such a foliaceous mass as the vitals of the animal body. You find thus in the very sands an anticipation of the vegetable leaf. No wonder that the earth expresses itself outwardly in leaves, it so labors with the idea inwardly. The atoms have already learned this law, and are pregnant by it. The overhanging leaf sees here its prototype. *Internally*, whether in the globe or animal body, it is a moist thick *lobe*, a word especially applicable to the liver and lungs and the *leaves* of fat, (*λείβω, labor, lapsus,* to flow or slip downward, a lapsing; *λοβος, globus,* lobe, globe; also lap, flap, and many other words,) *externally* a dry thin *leaf,* even as the *f* and *v* are a pressed and dried *b.* The radicals of lobe are *lb,* the soft mass of the *b* (single lobed, or B, double lobed,) with a liquid *l* behind it pressing it forward. In globe, *glb,* the guttural *g* adds to the meaning the capacity of the throat. The feathers and wings of birds are still drier and thinner leaves. Thus, also, you pass from the lumpish grub in the earth to the airy and fluttering butterfly. The very globe continually transcends and translates itself, and becomes winged in its orbit. Even ice begins with delicate crystal leaves, as if it had flowed into moulds which the fronds of water plants have impressed on the watery mirror. The whole tree itself is but one leaf, and rivers are still vaster leaves whose pulp is intervening earth, and towns and cities are the ova of insects in their axils.

When the sun withdraws the sand ceases to flow, but in the morning the streams will start once more and branch and branch again into a myriad of others. You here see perchance how blood vessels are formed. If you look closely you observe that first there pushes forward from the thawing mass a stream of softened sand with a drop-like point, like the ball of the finger, feeling its way slowly and blindly downward, until at last with more heat and moisture, as the sun gets higher, the most fluid portion, in its effort to obey the law to which the most inert also yields, separates from the latter and forms for itself a meandering channel or artery within that, in which is seen a little silvery stream glancing like lightning from one stage of pulpy leaves or branches to another, and ever and anon swallowed up in the sand. It is wonderful how rapidly yet perfectly the sand organizes itself as it flows, using the best material its mass affords to form the sharp edges of its channel. Such are the sources of rivers. In the silicious matter which the water deposits is perhaps the bony system, and in the still finer soil and organic matter the fleshy fibre or cellular tissue. What is man but a mass of thawing clay? The ball of the human finger is but a drop congealed. The fingers and toes flow to their extent from the thawing mass of the body. Who knows what the human body would expand and flow out to under a more genial heaven? Is not the hand a spreading *palm* leaf with its lobes and veins? The ear may be regarded, fancifully, as a lichen, *umbilicaria,* on the side of the head, with its lobe or drop. The lip – *labium,* from *labor* (?) – laps or lapses from the sides of the cavernous mouth. The nose is a manifest congealed drop or stalactite. The chin is a still larger drop, the confluent dripping of the face. The cheeks are a slide from the brows into the alley of the face, opposed and diffused by the cheek bones. Each rounded lobe of the vegetable leaf, too, is a thick and now loitering drop, larger or smaller; the lobes are the fingers of the leaf; and as many lobes as it has, in so many directions it tends to flow, and more heat or other genial influences would have caused it to flow yet farther.

Thus it seemed that this one hillside illustrated the principle of all the operations of Nature. The Maker of this earth but patented a leaf. What Champollion[3] will decipher this hieroglyphic for us, that we may turn over a new leaf at last? This phenomenon is

3. **Champollion:** Jean Francois Champollion (1790–1832), French scholar who deciphered the hieroglyphic characters inscribed on the Rosetta stone, the tablet that provided the key to ancient Egyptian writing.

more exhilarating to me than the luxuriance and fertility of vineyards. True, it is somewhat excrementitious in its character, and there is no end to the heaps of liver lights and bowels, as if the globe were turned wrong side outward; but this suggests at least that Nature has some bowels, and there again is mother of humanity. This is the frost coming out of the ground; this is Spring. It precedes the green and flowery spring, as mythology precedes regular poetry. I know of nothing more purgative of winter fumes and indigestions. It convinces me that Earth is still in her swaddling clothes, and stretches forth baby fingers on every side. Fresh curls spring from the baldest brow. There is nothing inorganic. These foliaceous heaps lie along the bank like the slag of a furnace, showing that Nature is "in full blast" within. The earth is not a mere fragment of dead history, stratum upon stratum like the leaves of a book, to be studied by geologists and antiquaries chiefly, but living poetry like the leaves of a tree, which precede flowers and fruit, – not a fossil earth, but a living earth; compared with whose great central life all animal and vegetable life is merely parasitic. Its throes will heave our exuviae from their graves. You may melt your metals and cast them into the most beautiful moulds you can; they will never excite me like the forms which this molten earth flows out into. And not only it, but the institutions upon it, are plastic like clay in the hands of the potter.

Ere long, not only on these banks, but on every hill and plain and in every hollow, the frost comes out of the ground like a dormant quadruped from its burrow, and seeks the sea with music, or migrates to other climes in clouds. Thaw with his gentle persuasion is more powerful than Thor[4] with his hammer. The one melts, the other but breaks in pieces.

When the ground was partially bare of snow, and a few warm days had dried its surface somewhat, it was pleasant to compare the first tender signs of the infant year just peeping forth with the stately beauty of the withered vegetation which had withstood the winter, – life-everlasting, golden-rods, pinweeds, and graceful wild grasses, more obvious and interesting frequently than in summer even, as if their beauty was not ripe till then; even cotton-grass, cat-tails, mulleins, johnswort, hard-hack, meadow-sweet, and other strong stemmed plants, those unexhausted granaries which entertain the earliest birds, – decent weeds, at least, which widowed Nature wears. I am particularly attracted by the arching and sheaf-like top of the wool-grass; it brings back the summer to our winter memories, and is among the forms which art loves to copy, and which, in the vegetable kingdom, have the same relation to types already in the mind of man that astronomy has. It is an antique style older than Greek or Egyptian. Many of the phenomena of Winter are suggestive of an inexpressible tenderness and fragile delicacy. We are accustomed to hear this king described as a rude and boisterous tyrant; but with the gentleness of a lover he adorns the tresses of Summer.

At the approach of spring the red-squirrels got under my house, two at a time, directly under my feet as I sat reading or writing, and kept up the queerest chuckling and chirruping and vocal pirouetting and gurgling sounds that ever were heard; and

4. **Thor:** The god of thunder in Norse mythology.

when I stamped they only chirruped the louder, as if past all fear and respect in their mad pranks, defying humanity to stop them. No you don't – chickaree – chickaree. They were wholly deaf to my arguments, or failed to perceive their force, and fell into a strain of invective that was irresistible.

The first sparrow of spring! The year beginning with younger hope than ever! The faint silvery warblings heard over the partially bare and moist fields from the blue-bird, the song-sparrow, and the red-wing, as if the last flakes of winter tinkled as they fell! What at such a time are histories, chronologies, traditions, and all written revelations? The brooks sing carols and glees to the spring. The marsh-hawk sailing low over the meadow is already seeking the first slimy life that awakes. The sinking sound of melting snow is heard in all dells, and the ice dissolves apace in the ponds. The grass flames up on the hillsides like a spring fire, – *"et primitus oritur herba imbribus primoribus evocata,"*[5] – as if the earth sent forth an inward heat to greet the returning sun; not yellow but green is the color of its flame; – the symbol of perpetual youth, the grass-blade, like a long green ribbon, streams from the sod into the summer, checked indeed by the frost, but anon pushing on again, lifting its spear of last year's hay with the fresh life below. It grows as steadily as the rill oozes out of the ground. It is almost identical with that, for in the growing days of June, when the rills are dry, the grass blades are their channels, and from year to year the herds drink at this perennial green stream, and the mower draws from it betimes their winter supply. So our human life but dies down to its root, and still puts forth its green blade to eternity.

Walden is melting apace. There is a canal two rods wide along the northerly and westerly sides, and wider still at the east end. A great field of ice has cracked off from the main body. I hear a song-sparrow singing from the bushes on the shore, – *olit, olit, olit,* – *chip, chip, chip, che char,* – *che wiss, wiss, wiss.* He too is helping to crack it. How handsome the great sweeping curves in the edge of the ice, answering somewhat to those of the shore, but more regular! It is unusually hard, owing to the recent severe but transient cold, and all watered or waved like a palace floor. But the wind slides eastward over its opaque surface in vain, till it reaches the living surface beyond. It is glorious to behold this ribbon of water sparkling in the sun, the bare face of the pond full of glee and youth, as if it spoke the joy of the fishes within it, and of the sands on its shore, – a silvery sheen as from the scales of a *leuciscus*, as it were all one active fish. Such is the contrast between winter and spring. Walden was dead and is alive again. But this spring it broke up more steadily, as I have said.

The change from storm and winter to serene and mild weather, from dark and sluggish hours to bright and elastic ones, is a memorable crisis which all things proclaim. It is seemingly instantaneous at last. Suddenly an influx of light filled my house, though the evening was at hand, and the clouds of winter still overhung it, and the eaves were dripping with sleety rain. I looked out the window, and lo! where yesterday was cold gray ice there lay the transparent pond already calm and full of hope as in a summer evening, reflecting a summer evening sky in its bosom, though none was visible overhead, as if it

---

5. ***"et . . . evocata"***: From Varro's *Rerum Rusticarum:* "and for the first time, the grass rises up, called forth by the first rains" (Latin).

had intelligence with some remote horizon. I heard a robin in the distance, the first I had heard for many a thousand years, methought, whose note I shall not forget for many a thousand more, – the same sweet and powerful song as of yore. O the evening robin, at the end of a New England summer day! If I could ever find the twig he sits upon! I mean *he*; I mean *the twig*. This at least is not the *Turdus migratorius*.[6] The pitch-pines and shrub-oaks about my house, which had so long drooped, suddenly resumed their several characters, looked brighter, greener, and more erect and alive, as if effectually cleansed and restored by the rain. I knew that it would not rain any more. You may tell by looking at any twig of the forest, ay, at your very wood-pile, whether its winter is past or not. As it grew darker, I was startled by the *honking* of geese flying low over the woods, like weary travellers getting in late from southern lakes, and indulging at last in unrestrained complaint and mutual consolation. Standing at my door, I could hear the rush of their wings; when, driving toward my house, they suddenly spied my light, and with hushed clamor wheeled and settled in the pond. So I came in, and shut the door, and passed my first spring night in the woods.

In the morning I watched the geese from the door through the mist, sailing in the middle of the pond, fifty rods off, so large and tumultuous that Walden appeared like an artificial pond for their amusement. But when I stood on the shore they at once rose up with a great flapping of wings at the signal of their commander, and when they had got into rank circled about over my head, twenty-nine of them, and then steered straight to Canada, with a regular *honk* from the leader at intervals, trusting to break their fast in muddier pools. A "plump" of ducks rose at the same time and took the route to the north in the wake of their noisier cousins.

For a week I heard the circling groping clangor of some solitary goose in the foggy mornings, seeking its companion, and still peopling the woods with the sound of a larger life than they could sustain. In April the pigeons were seen again flying express in small flocks, and in due time I heard the martins twittering over my clearing, though it had not seemed that the township contained so many that it could afford me any, and I fancied that they were peculiarly of the ancient race that dwelt in hollow trees ere white men came. In almost all climes the tortoise and the frog are among the precursors and heralds of this season, and birds fly with song and glancing plumage, and plants spring and bloom, and winds blow, to correct this slight oscillation of the poles and preserve the equilibrium of Nature.

As every season seems best to us in its turn, so the coming in of spring is like the creation of Cosmos out of Chaos and the realization of the Golden Age.[7] –

> *"Eurus ad Auroram, Nabathacaque regna recessit,*
> *Persidaque, et radiis juga subdita matutinis."*
>
> "The East-Wind withdrew to Aurora and the Nabathaean kingdom,
> And the Persian, and the ridges placed under the morning rays.

---

6. ***Turdus migratorius***: Ornithologists then listed the robin under this name.

7. **Cosmos . . . Golden Age**: In Greek mythology, the Golden Age of innocence and happiness was ushered in soon after the creation of the Cosmos, or the universe, out of Chaos. The lines that follow are from Ovid's *Metamorphoses*, 1.61-62, 78-81.

* * * *

> Man was born. Whether that Artificer of things,
> The origin of a better world, made him from the divine seed;
> Or the earth being recent and lately sundered from the high
> Ether, retained some seeds of cognate heaven."

A single gentle rain makes the grass many shades greener. So our prospects brighten on the influx of better thoughts. We should be blessed if we lived in the present always, and took advantage of every accident that befell us, like the grass which confesses the influence of the slightest dew that falls on it; and did not spend our time in atoning for the neglect of past opportunities, which we call doing our duty. We loiter in winter while it is already spring. In a pleasant spring morning all men's sins are forgiven. Such a day is a truce to vice. While such a sun holds out to burn, the vilest sinner may return. Through our own recovered innocence we discern the innocence of our neighbors. You may have known your neighbor yesterday for a thief, a drunkard, or a sensualist, and merely pitied or despised him, and despaired of the world; but the sun shines bright and warm this first spring morning, recreating the world, and you meet him at some serene work, and see how his exhausted and debauched veins expand with still joy and bless the new day, feel the spring influence with the innocence of infancy, and all his faults are forgotten. There is not only an atmosphere of good will about him, but even a savor of holiness groping for expression, blindly and ineffectually perhaps, like a new-born instinct, and for a short hour the south hill-side echoes to no vulgar jest. You see some innocent fair shoots preparing to burst from his gnarled rind and try another year's life, tender and fresh as the youngest plant. Even he has entered into the joy of his Lord. Why the jailer does not leave open his prison doors, – why the judge does not dismiss his case, – why the preacher does not dismiss his congregation! It is because they do not obey the hint which God gives them, nor accept the pardon which he freely offers to all.

"A return to goodness produced each day in the tranquil and beneficent breath of the morning, causes that in respect to the love of virtue and the hatred of vice, one approaches a little the primitive nature of man, as the sprouts of the forest which has been felled. In like manner the evil which one does in the interval of a day prevents the germs of virtues which began to spring up again from developing themselves and destroys them.

"After the germs of virtue have thus been prevented many times from developing themselves, then the beneficent breath of evening does not suffice to preserve them. As soon as the breath of evening does not suffice longer to preserve them, then the nature of man does not differ much from that of the brute. Men seeing the nature of this man like that of the brute, think that he has never possessed the innate faculty of reason. Are those the true and natural sentiments of man?"[8]

> "The Golden Age was first created, which without any avenger
> Spontaneously without law cherished fidelity and rectitude.
> Punishment and fear were not; nor were threatening words read

8. "A return . . . man?": From the *Works of Mencius* (6.1), by the Chinese philosopher Meng-tse.

On suspended brass; nor did the suppliant crowd fear
The words of their judge; but were safe without an avenger.
Not yet the pine felled on its mountains had descended
To the liquid waves that it might see a foreign world,
And mortals knew no shores but their own.

* * * *

There was eternal spring, and placid zephyrs with warm
Blasts soothed the flowers born without seed."[9]

On the 29th of April, as I was fishing from the bank of the river near the Nine-Acre-Corner bridge, standing on the quaking grass and willow roots, where the muskrats lurk, I heard a singular rattling sound, somewhat like that of the sticks which boys play with their fingers, when, looking up, I observed a very slight and graceful hawk, like a night-hawk, alternately soaring like a ripple and tumbling a rod or two over and over, showing the underside of its wings, which gleamed like a satin ribbon in the sun, or like the pearly inside of a shell. This sight reminded me of falconry and what nobleness and poetry are associated with that sport. The Merlin it seemed to me it might be called: But I care not for its name. It was the most ethereal flight I had ever witnessed. It did not simply flutter like a butterfly, nor soar like the larger hawks, but it sported with proud reliance in the fields of air; mounting again and again with its strange chuckle, it repeated its free and beautiful fall, turning over and over like a kite, and then recovering from its lofty tumbling, as if it had never set its foot on *terra firma*. It appeared to have no companion in the universe, – sporting there alone, – and to need none but the morning and the ether with which it played. It was not lonely, but made all the earth lonely beneath it. Where was the parent which hatched it, its kindred, and its father in the heavens? The tenant of the air, it seemed related to the earth but by an egg hatched some time in the crevice of a crag; – or was its native nest made in the angle of a cloud, woven of the rainbow's trimmings and the sunset sky, and lined with some soft midsummer haze caught up from earth? Its eyry now some cliffy cloud.

Beside this I got a rare mess of golden and silver and bright cupreous fishes, which looked like a string of jewels. Ah! I have penetrated to those meadows on the morning of many a first spring day, jumping from hummock to hummock, from willow root to willow root, when the wild river valley and the woods were bathed in so pure and bright a light as would have waked the dead, if they had been slumbering in their graves, as some suppose. There needs no stronger proof of immortality. All things must live in such a light. O Death, where was thy sting? O Grave, where was thy victory, then?[10]

Our village life would stagnate if it were not for the unexplored forests and meadows which surround it. We need the tonic of wildness, – to wade sometimes in marshes where the bittern and the meadow-hen lurk, and hear the booming of the snipe; to smell the whispering sedge where only some wilder and more solitary fowl builds her nest, and the mink crawls with its belly close to the ground. At the same time that we are

9. **The Golden Age . . . seed:** Ovid's *Metamorphoses*, 1.89–96, 107–8.
10. **O Death . . . then?:** See I Corinthians 15:55: "O Death, where is thy sting? O Grave, where is thy victory?"

earnest to explore and learn all things, we require that all things be mysterious and unexplorable, that land and sea be infinitely wild, unsurveyed and unfathomed by us because unfathomable. We can never have enough of Nature. We must be refreshed by the sight of inexhaustible vigor, vast and Titanic features, the sea-coast with its wrecks, the wilderness with its living and its decaying trees, the thunder cloud, and the rain which lasts three weeks and produces freshets. We need to witness our own limits transgressed, and some life pasturing freely where we never wander. We are cheered when we observe the vulture feeding on the carrion which disgusts and disheartens us and deriving health and strength from the repast. There was a dead horse in the hollow by the path to my house, which compelled me sometimes to go out of my way, especially in the night when the air was heavy, but the assurance it gave me of the strong appetite and inviolable health of Nature was my compensation for this. I love to see that Nature is so rife with life that myriads can be afforded to be sacrificed and suffered to prey on one another; that tender organizations can be so serenely squashed out of existence like pulp, – tadpoles which herons gobble up, and tortoises and toads run over in the road; and that sometimes it has rained flesh and blood! With the liability to accident, we must see how little account is to be made of it. The impression made on a wise man is that of universal innocence. Poison is not poisonous after all, nor are any wounds fatal. Compassion is a very untenable ground. It must be expeditious. Its pleadings will not bear to be stereotyped.

Early in May, the oaks, hickories, maples, and other trees, just putting out amidst the pine woods around the pond, imparted a brightness like sunshine to the landscape, especially in cloudy days, as if the sun were breaking through mists and shining faintly on the hill-sides here and there. On the third or fourth of May I saw a loon in the pond, and during the first week of the month I heard the whippoorwill, the brown-thrasher, the veery, the wood-pewee, the chewink, and other birds. I had heard the wood-thrush long before. The phoebe had already come once more and looked in at my door and window, to see if my house was cavern-like enough for her, sustaining herself on humming wings with clinched talons, as if she held by the air, while she surveyed the premises. The sulphur-like pollen of the pitch-pine soon covered the pond and the stones and rotten wood along the shore, so that you could have collected a barrel-ful. This is the "sulphur showers" we hear of. Even in Calidas' drama of Sacontala, we read of "rills dyed yellow with the golden dust of the lotus." And so the seasons went rolling on into summer, as one rambles into higher and higher grass.

Thus was my first year's life in the woods completed; and the second year was similar to it. I finally left Walden September 6th, 1847.

Conclusion

To the sick the doctors wisely recommend a change of air and scenery. Thank Heaven, here is not all the world. The buck-eye does not grow in New England, and the mocking-bird is rarely heard here. The wild-goose is more of a cosmopolite than we; he breaks his fast in Canada, takes a luncheon in the Ohio, and plumes himself for the night in a southern bayou. Even the bison, to some extent, keeps pace with the seasons, cropping the pastures of the Colorado only till a greener and sweeter grass awaits him by the Yellowstone. Yet we think that if rail-fences are pulled down, and stone-walls piled up on our farms, bounds are henceforth set to our lives and our fates decided. If you are chosen town-clerk, forsooth, you cannot go to Tierra del Fuego this summer: but you may go to the land of infernal fire nevertheless. The universe is wider than our views of it.

Yet we should oftener look over the tafferel of our craft, like curious passengers, and not make the voyage like stupid sailors picking oakum.[1] The other side of the globe is but the home of our correspondent. Our voyaging is only great-circle sailing, and the doctors prescribe for diseases of the skin merely. One hastens to Southern Africa to chase the giraffe; but surely that is not the game he would be after. How long, pray, would a man hunt giraffes if he could? Snipes and woodcocks also may afford rare sport; but I trust it would be nobler game to shoot one's self. –

> "Direct your eye right inward, and you'll find
> A thousand regions in your mind
> Yet undiscovered. Travel them, and be
> Expert in home-cosmography."[2]

What does Africa, – what does the West stand for? Is not our own interior white on the chart? black though it may prove, like the coast, when discovered. Is it the source of the Nile, or the Niger, or the Mississippi, or a North-West Passage around this continent, that we would find? Are these the problems which most concern mankind? Is Franklin the only man who is lost, that his wife should be so earnest to find him? Does Mr. Grinnell[3] know where he himself is? Be rather the Mungo Park, the Lewis and Clarke and Frobisher,[4] of your own streams and oceans; explore your own higher latitudes, – with shiploads of preserved meats to support you, if they be necessary; and pile the empty cans sky-high for a sign. Were preserved meats invented to preserve meat merely? Nay, be a Columbus to whole new continents and worlds within you, opening new channels, not of trade, but of thought. Every man is the lord of a realm beside which the earthly empire of the Czar is but a petty state, a hummock left by the ice. Yet some can be patriotic who have no *self*-respect, and sacrifice the greater to the less. They love the soil which makes their graves, but have no sympathy with the spirit which may still animate their clay. Patriotism is a maggot in their heads. What was the meaning of that South-Sea Exploring Expedition,[5] with all its parade and expense, but an indirect recognition

---

1. **picking oakum:** Used for caulking seams in a ship, oakum was obtained by the tedious process of untwisting and picking out strands of old rope.
2. **Direct . . . home-cosmography:** From "To My Honored Friend Sir Ed. P. Knight" by the English poet William Habbington (1605-1664). The first line in the original version of the poem read "eye sight," not "eye right," though it is not clear whether that alteration was intentional or simply a printer's error.
3. **Franklin . . . Grinnell:** John Franklin (1786-1847), English explorer lost in the Arctic while trying to find the Northwest Passage; several expeditions were sent to find him, including one funded by Henry Grinnell (1799-1874), a wealthy merchant from New York.
4. **Mungo Park . . . Frobisher:** Mungo Park (1771-1806), Scottish explorer of Africa; Martin Frobisher (1535?-1594), English explorer and navigator who attempted to find the Northwest Passage.
5. **South-Sea Exploring Expedition:** Charles Wilkes (1798-1877) led a U.S. exploring expedition to the Antarctic and Pacific in 1838-1842.

of the fact, that there are continents and seas in the moral world, to which every man is an isthmus or an inlet, yet unexplored by him, but that it is easier to sail many thousand miles through cold and storm and cannibals, in a government ship with five hundred men and boys to assist one, than it is to explore the private sea, the Atlantic and Pacific Ocean of one's being alone. –

> *"Erret, et extremos alter scrutetur Iberos.*
> *Plus habet hic vitae, plus habet ille viae."* [6]
>
> Let them wander and scrutinize the outlandish Australians.
> I have more of God, they more of the road.

It is not worth the while to go round the world to count the cats in Zanzibar.[7] Yet do this even till you can do better, and you may perhaps find some "Symmes' Hole"[8] by which to get at the inside at last. England and France, Spain and Portugal, Gold Coast and Slave Coast, all front on this private sea; but no bark from them has ventured out of sight of land, though it is without doubt the direct way to India. If you would learn to speak all tongues and conform to the customs of all nations, if you would travel farther than all travellers, be naturalized in all climes, and cause the Sphinx[9] to dash her head against a stone, even obey the precept of the old philosopher, and Explore thyself. Herein are demanded the eye and the nerve. Only the defeated and deserters go to the wars, cowards that run away and enlist. Start now on that farthest western way, which does not pause at the Mississippi or the Pacific, nor conduct toward a worn-out China or Japan, but leads on direct a tangent to this sphere, summer and winter, day and night, sun down, moon down, and at last earth down too.

It is said that Mirabeau[10] took to highway robbery "to ascertain what degree of resolution was necessary in order to place one's self in formal opposition to the most sacred laws of society." He declared that "a soldier who fights in the ranks does not require half so much courage as a foot-pad," – "that honor and religion have never stood in the way of a well-considered and a firm resolve." This was manly, as the world goes; and yet it was idle, if not desperate. A saner man would have found himself often enough "in formal opposition" to what are deemed "the most sacred laws of society," through obedience to yet more sacred laws, and so have tested his resolution without going out of his way. It is not for a man to put himself in such an attitude to society, but to maintain himself in whatever attitude he find himself through obedience to the laws of his being, which will never be one of opposition to a just government, if he should chance to meet with such.

---

6. ***Erret . . . viae***: From "The Old Man of Verona" by the fourth-century Latin poet Claudian.
7. **cats in Zanzibar:** One of the many subjects discussed in Charles Pickering's *The Races of Man* (1851). Zanzibar is an island off the east coast of Africa.
8. **"Symmes' Hole":** In 1818, John Symmes published a pamphlet in which he argued that "the earth is hollow and habitable within."
9. **Sphinx:** In Greek mythology, a winged monster with a woman's head and a lion's body who killed passersby who could not solve her riddle. When Oedipus did so, she destroyed herself by dashing her head against a rock.
10. **Mirabeau:** Honoré-Gabriel Riqueti, Comte de Mirabeau (1749-1791), statesman of the French Revolution.

I left the woods for as good a reason as I went there. Perhaps it seemed to me that I had several more lives to live, and could not spare any more time for that one. It is remarkable how easily and insensibly we fall into a particular route, and make a beaten track for ourselves. I had not lived there a week before my feet wore a path from my door to the pond-side; and though it is five or six years since I trod it, it is still quite distinct. It is true, I fear that others may have fallen into it, and so helped to keep it open. The surface of the earth is soft and impressible by the feet of men; and so with the paths which the mind travels. How worn and dusty, then, must be the highways of the world, how deep the ruts of tradition and conformity! I did not wish to take a cabin passage, but rather to go before the mast and on the deck of the world, for there I could best see the moonlight amid the mountains. I do not wish to go below now.

I learned this, at least, by my experiment; that if one advances confidently in the direction of his dreams, and endeavors to live the life which he has imagined, he will meet with success unexpected in common hours. He will put some things behind, will pass an invisible boundary; new, universal, and more liberal laws will begin to establish themselves around and within him; or the old laws be expanded, and interpreted in his favor in a more liberal sense, and he will live with the license of a higher order of beings. In proportion as he simplifies his life, the laws of the universe will appear less complex, and solitude will not be solitude, nor poverty poverty, nor weakness weakness. If you have built castles in the air, your work need not be lost; that is where they should be. Now put the foundations under them.

It is a ridiculous demand which England and America make, that you shall speak so that they can understand you. Neither men nor toad-stools grow so. As if that were important, and there were not enough to understand you without them. As if Nature could support but one order of understandings, could not sustain birds as well as quadrupeds, flying as well as creeping things, and *hush* and *who*, which Bright[11] can understand, were the best English. As if there were safety in stupidity alone. I fear chiefly lest my expression may not be *extra-vagant* enough, may not wander far enough beyond the narrow limits of my daily experience, so as to be adequate to the truth of which I have been convinced. *Extra vagance!* it depends on how you are yarded. The migrating buffalo, which seeks new pastures in another latitude, is not extravagant like the cow which kicks over the pail, leaps the cow-yard fence, and runs after her calf, in milking time. I desire to speak somewhere *without* bounds; like a man in a waking moment, to men in their waking moments; for I am convinced that I cannot exaggerate enough even to lay the foundation of a true expression. Who that has heard a strain of music feared then lest he should speak extravagantly any more forever? In view of the future or possible, we should live quite laxly and undefined in front, our outlines dim and misty on that side; as our shadows reveal an insensible perspiration toward the sun. The volatile truth of our words should continually betray the inadequacy of the residual statement. Their truth is instantly *translated*; its literal monument alone remains. The words which express our faith and piety are not definite; yet they are significant and fragrant like frankincense to superior natures.

---

11. **Bright:** Common name for an ox.

Why level downward to our dullest perception always, and praise that as common sense? The commonest sense is the sense of men asleep, which they express by snoring. Sometimes we are inclined to class those who are once-and-a-half witted with the half-witted, because we appreciate only a third part of their wit. Some would find fault with the morning-red, if they ever got up early enough. "They pretend," as I hear, "that the verses of Kabir have four different senses; illusion, spirit, intellect, and the exoteric doctrine of the Vedas";[12] but in this part of the world it is considered a ground for complaint if a man's writings admit of more than one interpretation. While England endeavors to cure the potato-rot, will not any endeavor to cure the brain-rot, which prevails so much more widely and fatally?

I do not suppose that I have attained to obscurity, but I should be proud if no more fatal fault were found with my pages on this score than was found with the Walden ice. Southern customers objected to its blue color, which is the evidence of its purity, as if it were muddy, and preferred the Cambridge ice, which is white, but tastes of weeds. The purity men love is like the mists which envelop the earth, and not like the azure ether beyond.

Some are dinning in our ears that we Americans, and moderns generally, are intellectual dwarfs compared with the ancients, or even the Elizabethan men. But what is that to the purpose? A living dog is better than a dead lion. Shall a man go and hang himself because he belongs to the race of pygmies, and not be the biggest pygmy that he can? Let every one mind his own business, and endeavor to be what he was made.

Why should we be in such desperate haste to succeed, and in such desperate enterprises? If a man does not keep pace with his companions, perhaps it is because he hears a different drummer. Let him step to the music which he hears, however measured or far away. It is not important that he should mature as soon as an apple-tree or an oak. Shall he turn his spring into summer? If the condition of things which we were made for is not yet, what were any reality which we can substitute? We will not be shipwrecked on a vain reality. Shall we with pains erect a heaven of blue glass over ourselves, though when it is done we shall be sure to gaze still at the true ethereal heaven far above, as if the former were not?

There was an artist in the city of Kouroo who was disposed to strive after perfection. One day it came into his mind to make a staff. Having considered that in an imperfect work time is an ingredient, but into a perfect work time does not enter, he said to himself, It shall be perfect in all respects, though I should do nothing else in my life. He proceeded instantly to the forest for wood, being resolved that it should not be made of unsuitable material; and as he searched for and rejected stick after stick, his friends gradually deserted him, for they grew old in their works and died, but he grew not older by a moment. His singleness of purpose and resolution, and his elevated piety, endowed him, without his knowledge, with perennial youth. As he made no compromise with Time, Time kept out of his way, and only sighed at a distance because he could not over-

12. **"They . . . Vedas":** From Garcin de Tassy, *Histoire de la Littérature Hindoui* (1839); Kabir was a fifteenth-century poet and mystic who attracted both Hindu and Moslem followers.

come him. Before he had found a stock in all respects suitable the city of Kouroo was a hoary ruin, and he sat on one of its mounds to peel the stick. Before he had given it the proper shape the dynasty of the Candahars was at an end, and with the point of the stick he wrote the name of the last of that race in the sand, and then resumed his work. By the time he had smoothed and polished the staff Kalpa was no longer the pole-star; and ere he had put on the ferule and the head adorned with precious stone, Brahma had awoke and slumbered many times. But why do I stay to mention these things? When the finishing stroke was put to his work, it suddenly expanded before the eyes of the astonished artist into the fairest of all the creations of Brahma. He had made a new system in making a staff, a world with full and fair proportions; in which, though the old cities and dynasties had passed away, fairer and more glorious ones had taken their places. And now he saw by the heap of shavings still fresh at his feet, that, for him and his work, the former lapse of time had been an illusion, and that no more time had elapsed than is required for a single scintillation from the brain of Brahma to fall on and inflame the tinder of a mortal brain. The material was pure, and his art was pure; how could the result be other than wonderful?[13]

No face which we can give to a matter will stead us so well at last as the truth. This alone wears well. For the most part, we are not where we are, but in a false position. Through an infirmity of our natures, we suppose a case, and put ourselves into it, and hence are in two cases at the same time, and it is doubly difficult to get out. In sane moments we regard only the facts, the case that is. Say what you have to say, not what you ought. Any truth is better than make-believe. Tom Hyde, the tinker, standing on the gallows, was asked if he had any thing to say. "Tell the tailors," said he, "to remember to make a knot in their thread before they take the first stitch." His companion's prayer is forgotten.

However mean your life is, meet it and live it; do not shun it and call it hard names. It is not so bad as you are. It looks poorest when you are richest. The fault-finder will find faults even in paradise. Love your life, poor as it is. You may perhaps have some pleasant, thrilling, glorious hours, even in a poor-house. The setting sun is reflected from the windows of the alms-house as brightly as from the rich man's abode; the snow melts before its door as early in the spring. I do not see but a quiet mind may live as contentedly there, and have as cheering thoughts, as in a palace. The town's poor seem to me often to live the most independent lives of any. May be they are simply great enough to receive without misgiving. Most think that they are above being supported by the town; but it oftener happens that they are not above supporting themselves by dishonest means, which should be more disreputable. Cultivate poverty like a garden herb, like sage. Do not trouble yourself much to get new things, whether clothes or friends. Turn the old; return to them. Things do not change; we change. Sell your clothes and keep your thoughts. God will see that you do not want society. If I were confined to a corner of

---

13. **There . . . wonderful?:** Although it sounds like a version of a story from one of the ancient Hindu texts that were so important to Thoreau, he almost certainly composed this parable. In Hindu literature, Kalpa is not "the pole-star," as he indicates, but the long period of time between the creation and destruction of the world, at the end of which it is absorbed into Brahma and then re-created.

a garret all my days, like a spider, the world would be just as large to me while I had my thoughts about me. The philosopher said: "From an army of three divisions one can take away its general, and put it in disorder; from the man the most abject and vulgar one cannot take away his thought."[14] Do not seek so anxiously to be developed, to subject yourself to many influences to be played on; it is all dissipation. Humility like darkness reveals the heavenly lights. The shadows of poverty and meanness gather around us, "and lo! creation widens to our view."[15] We are often reminded that if there were bestowed on us the wealth of Croesus,[16] our aims must still be the same, and our means essentially the same. Moreover, if you are restricted in your range by poverty, if you cannot buy books and newspapers, for instance, you are but confined to the most significant and vital experiences; you are compelled to deal with the material which yields the most sugar and the most starch. It is life near the bone where it is sweetest. You are defended from being a trifler. No man loses ever on a lower level by magnanimity on a higher. Superfluous wealth can buy superfluities only. Money is not required to buy one necessary of the soul.

I live in the angle of a leaden wall, into whose composition was poured a little alloy of bell metal. Often, in the repose of my mid-day, there reaches my ears a confused *tintinnabulum* from without. It is the noise of my contemporaries. My neighbors tell me of their adventures with famous gentlemen and ladies, what notabilities they met at the dinner-table; but I am no more interested in such things than in the contents of the Daily Times. The interest and the conversation are about costume and manners chiefly; but a goose is a goose still, dress it as you will. They tell me of California and Texas, of England and the Indies, of the Hon. Mr. — of Georgia or of Massachusetts, all transient and fleeting phenomena, till I am ready to leap from their court-yard like the Mameluke bey.[17] I delight to come to my bearings, – not walk in procession with pomp and parade, in a conspicuous place, but to walk even with the Builder of the universe, if I may, – not to live in this restless, nervous, bustling, trivial Nineteenth Century, but stand or sit thoughtfully while it goes by. What are men celebrating? They are all on a committee of arrangements, and hourly expect a speech from somebody. God is only the president of the day, and Webster is his orator.[18] I love to weigh, to settle, to gravitate toward that which most strongly and rightfully attracts me; – not hang by the beam of the scale and try to weigh less, – not suppose a case, but take the case that is; to travel the only path I can, and that on which no power can resist me. It affords me no satisfaction to commence to spring an arch before I have got a solid foundation. Let us not play at kittly-

---

14. **"From . . . thought":** Confucius, *Analects*, 9.25.
15. **"and lo! . . . view":** From "Night and Death" by the ecclesiastical poet Joseph White (1775–1841).
16. **wealth of Croesus:** Croesus, ruler of the ancient Greek kingdom Lydia from 560–546 BCE, was renowned for his legendary wealth.
17. **like the Mameluke bey:** The Mamelukes were an Egyptian military caste massacred in 1811, all except one officer, or "bey," who reportedly escaped their citadel by leaping from a wall onto a horse.
18. **Webster is his orator:** Daniel Webster (1782–1852), senator from Massachusetts and one of the most famous orators of the period, who abolitionists like Thoreau believed had betrayed the antislavery cause by supporting the Compromise of 1850.

benders.[19] There is a solid bottom every where. We read that the traveller asked the boy if the swamp before him had a hard bottom. The boy replied that it had. But presently the traveller's horse sank in up to the girths, and he observed to the boy, "I thought you said that this bog had a hard bottom." "So it has," answered the latter, "but you have not got half way to it yet." So it is with the bogs and quicksands of society; but he is an old boy that knows it. Only what is thought said or done at a certain rare coincidence is good. I would not be one of those who will foolishly drive a nail into mere lath and plastering; such a deed would keep me awake nights. Give me a hammer, and let me feel for the furrowing. Do not depend on the putty. Drive a nail home and clinch it so faithfully that you can wake up in the night and think of your work with satisfaction, – a work at which you would not be ashamed to invoke the Muse. So will help you God, and so only. Every nail driven should be as another rivet in the machine of the universe, you carrying on the work.

Rather than love, than money, than fame, give me truth. I sat at a table where were rich food and wine in abundance, and obsequious attendance, but sincerity and truth were not; and I went away hungry from the inhospitable board. The hospitality was as cold as the ices. I thought that there was no need of ice to freeze them. They talked to me of the age of the wine and the fame of the vintage; but I thought of an older, a newer, and purer wine, of a more glorious vintage, which they had not got, and could not buy. The style, the house and grounds and "entertainment" pass for nothing with me. I called on the king, but he made me wait in his hall, and conducted like a man incapacitated for hospitality. There was a man in my neighborhood who lived in a hollow tree. His manners were truly regal. I should have done better had I called on him.

How long shall we sit in our porticoes practising idle and musty virtues, which any work would make impertinent? As if one were to begin the day with long-suffering, and hire a man to hoe his potatoes; and in the afternoon go forth to practise Christian meekness and charity with goodness aforethought! Consider the China pride[20] and stagnant self-complacency of mankind. This generation reclines a little to congratulate itself on being the last of an illustrious line; and in Boston and London and Paris and Rome, thinking of its long descent, it speaks of its progress in art and science and literature with satisfaction. There are the Records of the Philosophical Societies, and the public Eulogies of *Great Men*! It is the good Adam contemplating his own virtue. "Yes, we have done great deeds, and sung divine songs, which shall never die," – that is, as long as *we* can remember them. The learned societies and great men of Assyria, – where are they? What youthful philosophers and experimentalists we are! There is not one of my readers who has yet lived a whole human life. These may be but the spring months in the life of the race. If we have had the seven-years' itch, we have not seen the seventeen-year locust yet in Concord. We are acquainted with a mere pellicle of the globe on which we live. Most have not delved six feet beneath the surface, nor leaped as many above it. We know

19. **kittlybenders:** A game in which children sought to run over thin ice without breaking through it.
20. **China pride:** In Thoreau's time, the Chinese were commonly viewed as smug and arrogant.

not where we are. Beside, we are sound asleep nearly half our time. Yet we esteem ourselves wise, and have an established order on the surface. Truly, we are deep thinkers, we are ambitious spirits! As I stand over the insect crawling amid the pine needles on the forest floor, and endeavoring to conceal itself from my sight, and ask myself why it will cherish those humble thoughts, and hide its head from me who might, perhaps, be its benefactor, and impart to its race some cheering information, I am reminded of the greater Benefactor and Intelligence that stands over me the human insect.

There is an incessant influx of novelty into the world, and yet we tolerate incredible dulness. I need only suggest what kind of sermons are still listened to in the most enlightened countries. There are such words as joy and sorrow, but they are only the burden of a psalm, sung with a nasal twang, while we believe in the ordinary and mean. We think that we can change our clothes only. It is said that the British Empire is very large and respectable, and that the United States are a first-rate power. We do not believe that a tide rises and falls behind every man which can float the British Empire like a chip, if he should ever harbor it in his mind. Who knows what sort of seventeen-year locust will next come out of the ground? The government of the world I live in was not framed, like that of Britain, in after-dinner conversations over the wine.

The life in us is like the water in the river. It may rise this year higher than man has ever known it, and flood the parched uplands; even this may be the eventful year, which will drown out all our muskrats. It was not always dry land where we dwell. I see far inland the banks which the stream anciently washed, before science began to record its freshets. Every one has heard the story which has gone the rounds of New England, of a strong and beautiful bug which came out of the dry leaf of an old table of apple-tree wood, which had stood in a farmer's kitchen for sixty years, first in Connecticut, and afterward in Massachusetts, – from an egg deposited in the living tree many years earlier still, as appeared by counting the annual layers beyond it, which was heard gnawing out for several weeks, hatched perchance by the heat of an urn. Who does not feel his faith in a resurrection and immortality strengthened by hearing of this? Who knows what beautiful and winged life, whose egg has been buried for ages under many concentric layers of woodenness in the dead dry life of society, deposited at first in the alburnum of the green and living tree, which has been gradually converted into the semblance of its well-seasoned tomb, – heard perchance gnawing out now for years by the astonished family of man, as they sat round the festive board, – may unexpectedly come forth from amidst society's most trivial and handselled furniture, to enjoy its perfect summer life at last!

I do not say that John or Jonathan[21] will realize all this; but such is the character of that morrow which mere lapse of time can never make to dawn. The light which puts out our eyes is darkness to us. Only that day dawns to which we are awake. There is more day to dawn. The sun is but a morning star.

[1854]

---

21. **John or Jonathan:** Common names for John Bull, the Englishman, and Brother Jonathan, the American.

Frederick Douglass

[1818–1895]

Frederick Douglass, who would become internationally known as the most distinguished African American of his generation, did not know when he was born, who his white father was, or even much about the ancestry of his mother, a slave named Harriet Bailey. Douglass would have been proud to know that he had deep roots in the national heritage, which he so passionately proclaimed to be the shared heritage of black and white Americans. In fact, we now know that he was descended on his mother's side from a family whose history in America went back at least five generations, to the earliest settlement of the eastern shore of Maryland, where Douglass was born Frederick Bailey in February 1818.

We wish that everyone may read his book and see what a mind might have been stifled in bondage.
–Margaret Fuller

The story of Douglass's life, which he told and retold, is a classic American success story, though it illustrates not only a triumph over poverty and obscurity but also over slavery and racism. Raised on a plantation

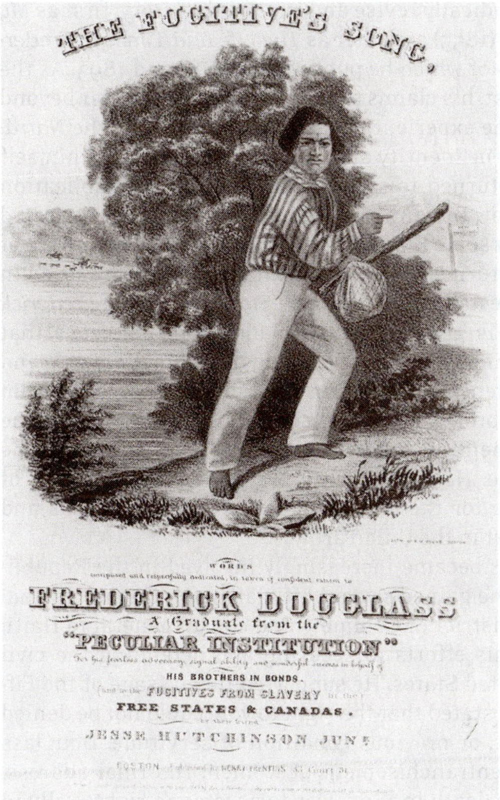

"The Fugitive's Song"

This sheet music was copyrighted in July 1845, shortly after the publication of Douglass's *Narrative*. It was dedicated to him by Jesse Hutchinson Jr., a member of The Hutchinson's, a popular singing group that often performed at antislavery meetings. Douglass did not describe his means of escape in the *Narrative*, so the designer of this cover depicted him as the stereotypical fugitive slave, fleeing barefoot from two mounted pursuers and their pack of dogs, shown across the river on the left. Douglass points down the road to the right, where a sign reads "New England."

***bedfordstmartins.com/ americanlit** for research links on Douglass*

until he was ten years old, he was then sent to work for his master's brother and sister-in-law in Baltimore, where Douglass lived for the next five years. There, the precocious boy taught himself to read, discovering books like *The Columbian Orator*, a collection of patriotic and revolutionary speeches that fueled his growing desire for freedom. After being returned to the plantation in 1833, Douglass first sought to escape in 1836, but the plan was discovered and he was returned to Baltimore. Two years later, posing as a free black sailor, he took a train to New York, where he changed his name from Bailey to Douglass and began to make a new life for himself. After he married Anna Murray, a free black woman who had aided his escape, the couple moved to New Bedford, Massachusetts. Precluded by his race from working in the shipyard as a caulker, for which he had been trained in Baltimore, Douglass took on various menial jobs until a speech he delivered at an antislavery meeting in 1839 brought him to the attention of William Lloyd Garrison, editor of the *Liberator* and president of the New England Anti-Slavery Society. As an agent of the society, Douglass traveled throughout the North for the next six years, rehearsing on the lecture platform the story he finally published in 1845 as *Narrative of the Life of Frederick Douglass, an American Slave, Written by Himself.*

Douglass would later radically revise and expand that story, first as *My Bondage and My Freedom* (1855) and later as *The Life and Times of Frederick Douglass*, two versions of which he published in 1881 and 1893. As the titles of those texts suggest, his claims to fame ultimately went far beyond the powerful account of the experience of slavery contained in the *Narrative.* Having revealed his true identity and consequently exposing himself to the danger of being returned to slavery, shortly after its publication Douglass sailed for Great Britain, where his lecture tour generated tremendous acclaim. After some English friends arranged the purchase of his freedom in 1846, he returned to the United States, where he settled in Rochester, New York, and established the *North Star*, later called *Frederick Douglass's Newspaper.* His growing independence and insistence that blacks must assume a primary role in the struggle against slavery and racism led to increasing tensions with Garrison and his followers, from whom Douglass formally broke in 1851. During the following decade, he joined with political opponents of slavery; he also began to emphasize the need for armed resistance. He consequently welcomed the outbreak of the Civil War, first calling for the arming of slaves and free blacks and later urging blacks to enlist in the Union army.

After the war, Douglass became increasingly involved in the Republican Party, through which he gained several official appointments, including U.S. marshal for the District of Columbia and consul general to Haiti. But he devoted most of his efforts to securing and defending the civil rights of blacks in the United States. He supported the passage of the Fifteenth Amendment, which stated that the right to vote could not be denied on the basis of race, color, or previous condition of servitude. Douglass also campaigned for the enfranchisement of women. His final address, delivered on the day of his death in 1895, was to a women's rights rally in Washington, D.C. When she learned of his death the following day, his old friend Elizabeth Cady Stanton recalled the first time she had seen Douglass, at an antislavery rally in Boston. There, Stanton wrote, he had been surrounded by "the great antislavery orators of the day." But, she declared, "all the other speakers seemed tame after Frederick Douglass," who "stood there like an African prince, majestic in his wrath." Ironically, however, when that princely figure was buried, the inscription on his simple tombstone read "To the memory of Frederick Douglass, 1817-1895," perpetuating his own mistaken guess about the year of his birth, which to the end of his life Douglass never knew.

Douglass's *Narrative of the Life of Frederick Douglass.* Douglass wrote and published his famous narrative in 1845. In part, the account was a response to doubts about the authenticity of the story he had been telling during his years on the antislavery lecture circuit, where Douglass had been obliged to conceal key details that would have revealed his true identity. He later stated, "I was induced to write out the leading facts connected with my experience in slavery, giving names of persons, places, and dates – thus putting it in the power of any who doubted, to ascertain the truth or falsehood of my story of being a fugitive slave." As early portraits of him vividly illustrate, Douglass certainly did not fit the conventional image of a fugitive slave. To many, the mastery of language and rhetoric Douglass displayed on the lecture platform also seemed at odds with his story of laboriously teaching himself to read and write. In fact, the *Narrative* itself struck some skeptical readers as too well written to have been solely the product of his pen. Anticipating such doubts, and as was customary in slave narratives, Douglass included testimonials by two white abolitionists: a preface by William Lloyd Garrison, editor of the antislavery newspaper the *Liberator*, and a letter from Wendell Phillips, a distinguished Bostonian who had joined the antislavery crusade nearly a decade earlier. For most readers, however, their contributions were overshadowed by the compelling story Douglass told in the *Narrative*, which was both a critical and commercial success. Published in Boston in May 1845, it sold 4,500 copies by the time Douglass sailed for England in September and continued to sell briskly in both the United States and Great Britain. The text is taken from the first edition of *Narrative of the Life of Frederick Douglass, an American Slave, Written by Himself* (1845).

NARRATIVE OF THE LIFE OF FREDERICK DOUGLASS, AN AMERICAN SLAVE, WRITTEN BY HIMSELF

Preface

In the month of August, 1841, I attended an anti-slavery convention in Nantucket, at which it was my happiness to become acquainted with Frederick Douglass, the writer of the following Narrative. He was a stranger to nearly every member of that body; but, having recently made his escape from the southern prison-house of bondage, and feeling his curiosity excited to ascertain the principles and measures of the abolitionists, – of whom he had heard a somewhat vague description while he was a slave, – he was induced to give his attendance, on the occasion alluded to, though at that time a resident in New Bedford.[1]

Fortunate, most fortunate occurrence! – fortunate for the millions of his manacled brethren, yet panting for deliverance from their awful thraldom! – fortunate for the cause of negro emancipation, and of universal liberty! – fortunate for the land of his birth, which he has already done so much to save and bless! – fortunate for a large circle of friends and acquaintances whose sympathy and affection he has strongly secured by the many sufferings he has endured by his virtuous traits of character, by his ever-abiding remembrance of those who are in bonds, as being bound with them! – fortunate for the multitudes in various parts of our republic, whose minds he has enlightened on the subject of slavery, and who have been melted to tears by his pathos, or roused to virtuous indignation by his stirring eloquence against the enslavers of men! – fortunate for himself, as it at once brought him into the field of public usefulness, "gave the world assurance of a MAN,"[2] quickened the slumbering energies of his soul, and consecrated him to the great work of breaking the rod of the oppressor, and letting the oppressed go free!

I shall never forget his first speech at the convention – the extraordinary emotion it excited in my own mind – the powerful impression it created upon a crowded auditory, completely taken by surprise – the applause which followed from the beginning to the end of his felicitous remarks. I think I never hated slavery so intensely as at that moment; certainly, my perception of the enormous outrage which is inflicted by it, on the godlike nature of its victims, was rendered far more clear than ever. There stood one, in physical proportion and stature commanding and exact – in intellect richly endowed – in natural eloquence a prodigy – in soul manifestly "created but a little lower than the angels"[3] – yet a slave, ay, a fugitive slave, – trembling for his safety, hardly daring to believe that on the American soil, a single white person could be found who would befriend him at all hazards, for the love of God and humanity! Capable of high attainments as an intellectual and moral being – needing nothing but a comparatively small amount of cultivation to make him an ornament to society and a blessing to his race – by the law of the land, by the voice of the people, by the terms of the slave code, he was only a piece of property, a beast of burden, a chattel personal, nevertheless!

A beloved friend from New Bedford prevailed on Mr. Douglass to address the convention. He came forward to the platform with a hesitancy and embarrassment, necessarily the attendants of a sensitive mind in such a novel position. After apologizing for his ignorance, and reminding the audience that slavery was a poor school for the human intellect and heart, he proceeded to narrate some of the facts in his own history as a

1. **New Bedford:** In September 1838, Douglass had escaped from slavery in Maryland and eventually settled in New Bedford, Massachusetts.
2. **"gave . . . MAN":** Shakespeare, *Hamlet*, 3.4.62.
3. **"created . . . angels":** Psalms 8:5 and Hebrews 2:7, 9.

slave, and in the course of his speech gave utterance to many noble thoughts and thrilling reflections. As soon as he had taken his seat, filled with hope and admiration, I rose, and declared that Patrick Henry, of revolutionary fame, never made a speech more eloquent in the cause of liberty, than the one we had just listened to from the lips of that hunted fugitive. So I believed at that time – such is my belief now. I reminded the audience of the peril which surrounded this self-emancipated young man at the North, – even in Massachusetts, on the soil of the Pilgrim Fathers, among the descendants of revolutionary sires; and I appealed to them, whether they would ever allow him to be carried back into slavery, – law or no law, constitution or no constitution. The response was unanimous and in thunder-tones – "NO!" "Will you succor and protect him as a brother-man – a resident of the old Bay State?"[4] "YES!" shouted the whole mass, with an energy so startling, that the ruthless tyrants south of Mason and Dixon's line might almost have heard the mighty burst of feeling, and recognized it as the pledge of an invincible determination, on the part of those who gave it, never to betray him that wanders but to hide the outcast, and firmly to abide the consequences.

It was at once deeply impressed upon my mind, that, if Mr. Douglass could be persuaded to consecrate his time and talents to the promotion of the anti-slavery enterprise, a powerful impetus would be given to it, and a stunning blow at the same time inflicted on northern prejudice against a colored complexion. I therefore endeavored to instil hope and courage into his mind, in order that he might dare to engage in a vocation so anomalous and responsible for a person in his situation; and I was seconded in this effort by warm-hearted friends especially by the late General Agent of the Massachusetts Anti-Slavery Society, Mr. John A. Collins, whose judgment in this instance entirely coincided with my own. At first, he could give no encouragement; with unfeigned diffidence, he expressed his conviction that he was not adequate to the performance of so great a task; the path marked out was wholly an untrodden one; he was sincerely apprehensive that he should do more harm than good. After much deliberation, however, he consented to make a trial; and ever since that period, he has acted as a lecturing agent, under the auspices either of the American or the Massachusetts Anti-Slavery Society. In labors he has been most abundant; and his success in combating prejudice, in gaining proselytes, in agitating the public mind, has far surpassed the most sanguine expectations that were raised at the commencement of his brilliant career. He has borne himself with gentleness and meekness, yet with true manliness of character. As a public speaker, he excels in pathos, wit, comparison, imitation, strength of reasoning, and fluency of language. There is in him that union of head and heart, which is indispensable to an enlightenment of the heads and a winning of the hearts of others. May his strength continue to be equal to his day! May he continue to "grow in grace, and in the knowledge of God," that he may be increasingly serviceable in the cause of bleeding humanity, whether at home or abroad!

It is certainly a very remarkable fact, that one of the most efficient advocates of the slave population, now before the public, is a fugitive slave, in the person of Frederick

---

4. **Bay State:** Nickname for Massachusetts.

Douglass; and that the free colored population of the United States are as ably represented by one of their own number, in the person of Charles Lenox Remond,[5] whose eloquent appeals have extorted the highest applause of multitudes on both sides of the Atlantic. Let the calumniators of the colored race despise themselves for their baseness and illiberality of spirit and henceforth cease to talk of the natural inferiority of those who require nothing but time and opportunity to attain to the highest point of human excellence.

It may, perhaps, be fairly questioned, whether any other portion of the population of the earth could have endured the privations, sufferings and horrors of slavery, without having become more degraded in the scale of humanity than the slaves of African descent. Nothing has been left undone to cripple their intellects, darken their minds, debase their moral nature, obliterate all traces of their relationship to mankind; and yet how wonderfully they have sustained the mighty load of a most frightful bondage, under which they have been groaning for centuries! To illustrate the effect of slavery on the white man, – to show that he has no powers of endurance, in such a condition, superior to those of his black brothers, – Daniel O'Connell,[6] the distinguished advocate of universal emancipation, and the mightiest champion of prostrate but not conquered Ireland, relates the following anecdote in a speech delivered by him in the Conciliation Hall, Dublin, before the Loyal National Repeal Association, March 31, 1845. "No matter," said Mr. O'Connell, "under what specious term it may disguise itself, slavery is still hideous. *It has a natural, an inevitable tendency to brutalize every noble faculty of man.* An American sailor, who was cast away on the shore of Africa, where he was kept in slavery for three years, was, at the expiration of that period, found to be imbruted and stultified – he had lost all reasoning power; and having forgotten his native language, could only utter some savage gibberish between Arabic and English, which nobody could understand, and which even he himself found difficulty in pronouncing. So much for the humanizing influence of THE DOMESTIC INSTITUTION!" Admitting this to have been an extraordinary case of mental deterioration, it proves at least that the white slave can sink as low in the scale of humanity as the black one.

Mr. Douglass has very properly chosen to write his own Narrative, in his own style, and according to the best of his ability, rather than to employ some one else. It is, therefore, entirely his own production; and, considering how long and dark was the career he had to run as a slave, – how few have been his opportunities to improve his mind since he broke his iron fetters, – it is, in my judgment, highly creditable to his head and heart. He who can peruse it without a tearful eye, a heaving breast, an afflicted spirit, – without being filled with an unutterable abhorrence of slavery and all its abettors, and animated with a determination to seek the immediate overthrow of that execrable system, – without trembling for the fate of this country in the hands of a righteous God, who is ever on the side of the oppressed, and whose arm is not shortened that it cannot

---

5. **Charles Lenox Remond:** Remond (1810-1873), born to free parents, was the first African American employed as a lecturer by the Massachusetts Anti-Slavery Society.
6. **Daniel O'Connell:** O'Connell (1775-1847) was an Irish politician who fought for Catholic emancipation and Irish independence from England.

save, – must have a flinty heart, and be qualified to act the part of a trafficker "in slaves and the souls of men." I am confident that it is essentially true in all its statements; that nothing has been set down in malice, nothing exaggerated, nothing drawn from the imagination; that it comes short of the reality, rather than overstates a single fact in regard to SLAVERY AS IT IS.[7] The experience of Frederick Douglass, as a slave, was not a peculiar one; his lot was not especially a hard one; his case may be regarded as a very fair specimen of the treatment of slaves in Maryland, in which State it is conceded that they are better fed and less cruelly treated than in Georgia, Alabama, or Louisiana. Many have suffered incomparably more, while very few on the plantations have suffered less, than himself. Yet how deplorable was his situation! what terrible chastisements were inflicted upon his person! what still more shocking outrages were perpetrated upon his mind! with all his noble powers and sublime aspirations, how like a brute was he treated, even by those professing to have the same mind in them that was in Christ Jesus! to what dreadful liabilities was he continually subjected! how destitute of friendly counsel and aid, even in his greatest extremities! how heavy was the midnight of woe which shrouded in blackness the last ray of hope, and filled the future with terror and gloom! what longings after freedom took possession of his breast, and how his misery augmented, in proportion as he grew reflective and intelligent, – thus demonstrating that a happy slave is an extinct man! how he thought, reasoned, felt, under the lash of the driver, with the chains upon his limbs! what perils he encountered in his endeavors to escape from his horrible doom! and how signal have been his deliverance and preservation in the midst of a nation of pitiless enemies!

This Narrative contains many affecting incidents, many passages of great eloquence and power; but I think the most thrilling one of them all is the description Douglass gives of his feelings, as he stood soliloquizing respecting his fate, and the chances of his one day being a freeman, on the banks of the Chesapeake Bay – viewing the receding vessels as they flew with their white wings before the breeze, and apostrophizing them as animated by the living spirit of freedom. Who can read that passage, and be insensible to its pathos and sublimity? Compressed into it is a whole Alexandrian library of thought, feeling, and sentiment – all that can, all that need be urged, in the form of expostulation, entreaty, rebuke, against that crime of crimes, – making man the property of his fellow-man! O, how accursed is that system, which entombs the godlike mind of man, defaces the divine image, reduces those who by creation were crowned with glory and honor to a level with four-footed beasts, and exalts the dealer in human flesh above all that is called God! Why should its existence be prolonged one hour? Is it not evil, only evil, and that continually? What does its presence imply but the absence of all fear of God, all regard for man, on the part of the people of the United States? Heaven speed its eternal overthrow!

So profoundly ignorant of the nature of slavery are many persons, that they are stubbornly incredulous whenever they read or listen to any recital of the cruelties which are

7. SLAVERY AS IT IS: Probably a reference to Theodore Dwight Weld's *American Slavery As It Is* (1839), a collection of reports on the brutality of slavery gathered from southern newspapers.

daily inflicted on its victims. They do not deny that the slaves are held as property; but that terrible fact seems to convey to their minds no idea of injustice, exposure to outrage, or savage barbarity. Tell them of cruel scourgings, of mutilations and brandings, of scenes of pollution and blood, of the banishment of all light and knowledge, and they affect to be greatly indignant at such enormous exaggerations, such wholesale misstatements, such abominable libels on the character of the southern planters! As if all these direful outrages were not the natural results of slavery! As if it were less cruel to reduce a human being to the condition of a thing, than to give him a severe flagellation, or to deprive him of necessary food and clothing! As if whips, chains, thumb-screws, paddles, bloodhounds, overseers, drivers, patrols, were not all indispensable to keep the slaves down, and to give protection to their ruthless oppressors! As if, when the marriage institution is abolished, concubinage, adultery, and incest, must not necessarily abound; when all the rights of humanity are annihilated, any barrier remains to protect the victim from the fury of the spoiler; when absolute power is assumed over life and liberty, it will not be wielded with destructive sway! Skeptics of this character abound in society. In some few instances, their incredulity arises from a want of reflection; but, generally, it indicates a hatred of the light, a desire to shield slavery from the assaults of its foes, a contempt of the colored race, whether bond or free. Such will try to discredit the shocking tales of slaveholding cruelty which are recorded in this truthful Narrative; but they will labor in vain. Mr. Douglass has frankly disclosed the place of his birth, the names of those who claimed ownership in his body and soul, and the names also of those who committed the crimes which he has alleged against them. His statements, therefore, may easily be disproved, if they are untrue.

In the course of his Narrative, he relates two instances of murderous cruelty, – in one of which a planter deliberately shot a slave belonging to a neighboring plantation, who had unintentionally gotten within his lordly domain in quest of fish; and in the other, an overseer blew out the brains of a slave who had fled to a stream of water to escape a bloody scourging. Mr. Douglass states that in neither of these instances was any thing done by way of legal arrest or judicial investigation. The Baltimore American, of March 17, 1845, relates a similar case of atrocity, perpetrated with similar impunity – as follows: – "*Shooting a Slave.* – We learn, upon the authority of a letter from Charles county, Maryland, received by a gentleman of this city, that a young man named Matthews, a nephew of General Matthews, and whose father, it is believed, holds an office at Washington, killed one of the slaves upon his father's farm by shooting him. The letter states that young Matthews had been left in charge of the farm; that he gave an order to the servant, which was disobeyed, when he proceeded to the house, *obtained a gun, and, returning, shot the servant.* He immediately, the letter continues, fled to his father's residence, where he still remains unmolested." – Let it never be forgotten, that no slaveholder or overseer can be convicted of any outrage perpetrated on the person of a slave, however diabolical it may be, on the testimony of colored witnesses, whether bond or free. By the slave code, they are adjudged to be as incompetent to testify against a white man, as though they were indeed a part of the brute creation. Hence, there is no legal protection in fact, whatever there may be in form, for the slave population; and any amount of cruelty may be inflicted on them with impunity. Is it possible for the human mind to conceive of a more horrible state of society?

The effect of a religious profession on the conduct of southern masters is vividly described in the following Narrative, and shown to be any thing but salutary. In the nature of the case, it must be in the highest degree pernicious. The testimony of Mr. Douglass, on this point, is sustained by a cloud of witnesses, whose veracity is unimpeachable. "A slaveholder's profession of Christianity is a palpable imposture. He is a felon of the highest grade. He is a man-stealer. It is of no importance what you put in the other scale."

Reader! are you with the man-stealers in sympathy and purpose, or on the side of their down-trodden victims? If with the former, then are you the foe of God and man. If with the latter, what are you prepared to do and dare in their behalf? Be faithful, be vigilant, be untiring in your efforts to break every yoke, and let the oppressed go free. Come what may – cost what it may – inscribe on the banner which you unfurl to the breeze, as your religious and political motto – "NO COMPROMISE WITH SLAVERY! NO UNION WITH SLAVEHOLDERS!"

Wm. Lloyd Garrison

Boston, May 1, 1845

Letter from Wendell Phillips, Esq.

Boston, April 22, 1845

My Dear Friend:

You remember the old fable of "The Man and the Lion," where the lion complained that he should not be so misrepresented "when the lions wrote history."

I am glad the time has come when the "lions write history." We have been left long enough to gather the character of slavery from the involuntary evidence of the masters. One might, indeed, rest sufficiently satisfied with what, it is evident, must be, in general, the results of such a relation, without seeking farther to find whether they have followed in every instance. Indeed, those who stare at the half-peck of corn a week, and love to count the lashes on the slave's back, are seldom the "stuff" out of which reformers and abolitionists are to be made. I remember that, in 1838, many were waiting for the results of the West India experiment,[8] before they could come into our ranks. Those "results" have come long ago; but, alas! few of that number have come with them, as converts. A man must be disposed to judge of emancipation by other tests than whether it has increased the produce of sugar, – and to hate slavery for other reasons than because it starves men and whips women, – before he is ready to lay the first stone of his anti-slavery life.

I was glad to learn, in your story, how early the most neglected of God's children waken to a sense of their rights, and of the injustice done them. Experience is a keen

8. **West India experiment:** Slavery was abolished in the British West Indies in 1833, leading many to ask how emancipation would affect the government and economy of the colonies.

teacher; and long before you had mastered your A B C, or knew where the "white sails" of the Chesapeake were bound, you began, I see, to gauge the wretchedness of the slave, not by his hunger and want, not by his lashes and toil, but by the cruel and blighting death which gathers over his soul.

In connection with this, there is one circumstance which makes your recollections peculiarly valuable, and renders your early insight the more remarkable. You come from that part of the country where we are told slavery appears with its fairest features. Let us hear, then, what it is at its best estate – gaze on its bright side, if it has one; and then imagination may task her powers to add dark lines to the picture, as she travels southward to that (for the colored man) Valley of the Shadow of Death, where the Mississippi sweeps along.

Again, we have known you long, and can put the most entire confidence in your truth, candor, and sincerity. Every one who has heard you speak has felt, and, I am confident, every one who reads your book will feel, persuaded that you give them a fair specimen of the whole truth. No one-sided portrait, – no wholesale complaints, – but strict justice done, whenever individual kindliness has neutralized, for a moment the deadly system with which it was strangely allied. You have been with us, too, some years, and can fairly compare the twilight of rights, which your race enjoy at the North, with that "noon of night" under which they labor south of Mason and Dixon's line. Tell us whether, after all, the half-free colored man of Massachusetts is worse off than the pampered slave of the rice swamps!

In reading your life, no one can say that we have unfairly picked out some rare specimens of cruelty. We know that the bitter drops, which even you have drained from the cup, are no incidental aggravations, no individual ills, but such as must mingle always and necessarily in the lot of every slave. They are the essential ingredients, not the occasional results, of the system.

After all, I shall read your book with trembling for you. Some years ago, when you were beginning to tell me your real name and birthplace, you may remember I stopped you, and preferred to remain ignorant of all. With the exception of a vague description, so I continued, till the other day, when you read me your memoirs. I hardly knew, at the time, whether to thank you or not for the sight of them, when I reflected that it was still dangerous, in Massachusetts, for honest men to tell their names! They say the fathers, in 1776, signed the Declaration of Independence with the halter about their necks. You, too, publish your declaration of freedom with danger compassing you around. In all the broad lands which the Constitution of the United States overshadows, there is no single spot, – however narrow or desolate, – where a fugitive slave can plant himself and say, "I am safe." The whole armory of Northern Law has no shield for you. I am free to say that, in your place, I should throw the MS. into the fire.

You, perhaps, may tell your story in safety, endeared as you are to so many warm hearts by rare gifts, and a still rarer devotion of them to the service of others. But it will be owing only to your labors, and the fearless efforts of those who, trampling the laws and Constitution of the country under their feet, are determined that they will "hide the outcast," and that their hearths shall be, spite of the law, an asylum for the oppressed, if, some time or other, the humblest may stand in our streets, and bear witness in safety against the cruelties of which he has been the victim.

Yet it is sad to think, that these very throbbing hearts which welcome your story, and form your best safeguard in telling it, are all beating contrary to the "statute in such case made and provided." Go on, my dear friend, till you, and those who, like you, have been saved, so as by fire, from the dark prison-house, shall stereotype these free, illegal pulses into statutes; and New England, cutting loose from a blood-stained Union, shall glory in being the house of refuge for the oppressed; – till we no longer merely "*hide* the outcast," or make a merit of standing idly by while he is hunted in our midst; but, consecrating anew the soil of the Pilgrims as an asylum for the oppressed, proclaim our *welcome* to the slave so loudly, that the tones shall reach every hut in the Carolinas, and make the broken-hearted bondman leap up at the thought of old Massachusetts.

God speed the day!
Till then, and ever,
Yours truly,
Wendell Phillips

Chapter I

I was born in Tuckahoe, near Hillsborough, and about twelve miles from Easton, in Talbot county, Maryland. I have no accurate knowledge of my age, never having seen any authentic record containing it. By far the larger part of the slaves know as little of their age as horses know of theirs, and it is the wish of most masters within my knowledge to keep their slaves thus ignorant. I do not remember to have ever met a slave who could tell of his birthday. They seldom come nearer to it than planting-time, harvest-time, cherry-time, spring-time, or fall-time. A want of information concerning my own was a source of unhappiness to me even during childhood. The white children could tell their ages. I could not tell why I ought to be deprived of the same privilege. I was not allowed to make any inquiries of my master concerning it. He deemed all such inquiries on the part of a slave improper and impertinent, and evidence of a restless spirit. The nearest estimate I can give makes me now between twenty-seven and twenty-eight years of age. I come to this, from hearing my master say, some time during 1835, I was about seventeen years old.

My mother was named Harriet Bailey. She was the daughter of Isaac and Betsey Bailey, both colored, and quite dark. My mother was of a darker complexion than either my grandmother or grandfather.

My father was a white man. He was admitted to be such by all I ever heard speak of my parentage. The opinion was also whispered that my master was my father; but of the correctness of this opinion, I know nothing; the means of knowing was withheld from me. My mother and I were separated when I was but an infant – before I knew her as my mother. It is a common custom, in the part of Maryland from which I ran away, to part children from their mothers at a very early age. Frequently, before the child has reached its twelfth month, its mother is taken from it, and hired out on some farm a considerable distance off, and the child is placed under the care of an old woman, too old for field labor. For what this separation is done, I do not know, unless it be to hinder the development of the child's affection toward its mother, and to blunt and destroy the natural affection of the mother for the child. This is the inevitable result.

I never saw my mother, to know her as such, more than four or five times in my life; and each of these times was very short in duration, and at night. She was hired by a Mr. Stewart, who lived about twelve miles from my home. She made her journeys to see me in the night, travelling the whole distance on foot, after the performance of her day's work. She was a field hand, and a whipping is the penalty of not being in the field at sunrise, unless a slave has special permission from his or her master to the contrary – a permission which they seldom get, and one that gives to him that gives it the proud name of being a kind master. I do not recollect of ever seeing my mother by the light of day. She was with me in the night. She would lie down with me, and get me to sleep, but long before I waked she was gone. Very little communication ever took place between us. Death soon ended what little we could have while she lived, and with it her hardships and suffering. She died when I was about seven years old, on one of my master's farms, near Lee's Mill. I was not allowed to be present during her illness, at her death, or burial. She was gone long before I knew any thing about it. Never having enjoyed, to any considerable extent, her soothing presence, her tender and watchful care, I received the tidings of her death with much the same emotions I should have probably felt at the death of a stranger.

Called thus suddenly away, she left me without the slightest intimation of who my father was. The whisper that my master was my father, may or may not be true; and, true or false, it is of but little consequence to my purpose whilst the fact remains, in all its glaring odiousness, that slaveholders have ordained, and by law established, that the children of slave women shall in all cases follow the condition of their mothers; and this is done too obviously to administer to their own lusts, and make a gratification of their wicked desires profitable as well as pleasurable; for by this cunning arrangement, the slaveholder, in cases not a few, sustains to his slaves the double relation of master and father.

I know of such cases; and it is worthy of remark that such slaves invariably suffer greater hardships, and have more to contend with, than others. They are, in the first place, a constant offence to their mistress. She is ever disposed to find fault with them; they can seldom do any thing to please her; she is never better pleased than when she sees them under the lash, especially when she suspects her husband of showing to his mulatto children favors which he withholds from his black slaves. The master is frequently compelled to sell this class of his slaves, out of deference to the feelings of his white wife; and, cruel as the deed may strike any one to be, for a man to sell his own children to human flesh-mongers, it is often the dictate of humanity for him to do so; for, unless he does this, he must not only whip them himself, but must stand by and see one white son tie up his brother, of but few shades darker complexion than himself, and ply the gory lash to his naked back; and if he lisp one word of disapproval, it is set down to his parental partiality, and only makes a bad matter worse, both for himself and the slave whom he would protect and defend.

Every year brings with it multitudes of this class of slaves. It was doubtless in consequence of a knowledge of this fact, that one great statesman of the south predicted the downfall of slavery by the inevitable laws of population. Whether this prophecy is ever fulfilled or not, it is nevertheless plain that a very different-looking class of people are springing up at the south, and are now held in slavery, from those originally brought to this country from Africa; and if their increase will do no other good, it will do away the force of the argument, that God cursed Ham,[1] and therefore American slavery is right. If the lineal descendants of Ham are alone to be scripturally enslaved, it is certain that slavery at the south must soon become unscriptural; for thousands are ushered into the world, annually, who, like myself, owe their existence to white fathers, and those fathers most frequently their own masters.

I have had two masters. My first master's name was Anthony. I do not remember his first name. He was generally called Captain Anthony – a title which, I presume, he acquired by sailing a craft on the Chesapeake Bay. He was not considered a rich slave-holder. He owned two or three farms, and about thirty slaves. His farms and slaves were under the care of an overseer. The overseer's name was Plummer. Mr. Plummer was a miserable drunkard, a profane swearer, and a savage monster. He always went armed with a cowskin and a heavy cudgel. I have known him to cut and slash the women's heads so horribly, that even master would be enraged at his cruelty, and would threaten to whip him if he did not mind himself. Master, however, was not a humane slaveholder. It required extraordinary barbarity on the part of an overseer to affect him. He was a cruel man, hardened by a long life of slaveholding. He would at times seem to take great pleasure in whipping a slave. I have often been awakened at the dawn of day by the most heart-rending shrieks of an own aunt of mine, whom he used to tie up to a joist, and whip upon her naked back till she was literally covered with blood. No words, no tears, no prayers, from his gory victim, seemed to move his iron heart from its bloody purpose. The louder she screamed, the harder he whipped; and where the blood ran fastest, there he whipped longest. He would whip her to make her scream, and whip her to make her hush; and not until overcome by fatigue, would he cease to swing the blood-clotted cowskin. I remember the first time I ever witnessed this horrible exhibition. I was quite a child, but I well remember it. I never shall forget it whilst I remember any thing. It was the first of a long series of such outrages, of which I was doomed to be a witness and a participant. It struck me with awful force. It was the blood-stained gate, the entrance to the hell of slavery, through which I was about to pass. It was a most terrible spectacle. I wish I could commit to paper the feelings with which I beheld it.

This occurrence took place very soon after I went to live with my old master, and under the following circumstances. Aunt Hester went out one night, – where or for what I do not know, – and happened to be absent when my master desired her presence. He had ordered her not to go out evenings, and warned her that she must never let him catch her in company with a young man, who was paying attention to her belonging to Colonel Lloyd. The young man's name was Ned Roberts, generally called Lloyd's Ned.

1. **God cursed Ham**: In chapter 9 of Genesis, Noah curses his youngest son, Ham, declaring that Ham's son Canaan shall be "a servant of servants . . . unto his brethren." Many proslavery apologists read the story as a biblical defense of slavery.

Why master was so careful of her, may be safely left to conjecture. She was a woman of noble form, and of graceful proportions, having very few equals, and fewer superiors, in personal appearance, among the colored or white women of our neighborhood.

Aunt Hester had not only disobeyed his orders in going out, but had been found in company with Lloyd's Ned; which circumstance, I found, from what he said while whipping her, was the chief offence. Had he been a man of pure morals himself, he might have been thought interested in protecting the innocence of my aunt; but those who knew him will not suspect him of any such virtue. Before he commenced whipping Aunt Hester, he took her into the kitchen, and stripped her from neck to waist, leaving her neck, shoulders, and back, entirely naked. He then told her to cross her hands, calling her at the same time a d—d b—h. After crossing her hands, he tied them with a strong rope, and led her to a stool under a large hook in the joist, put in for the purpose. He made her get upon the stool, and tied her hands to the hook. She now stood fair for his infernal purpose. Her arms were stretched up at their full length, so that she stood upon the ends of her toes. He then said to her, "Now, you d—d b—h, I'll learn you how to disobey my orders!" and after rolling up his sleeves, he commenced to lay on the heavy cowskin, and soon the warm, red blood (amid heart-rending shrieks from her, and horrid oaths from him) came dripping to the floor. I was so terrified and horror-stricken at the sight, that I hid myself in a closet, and dared not venture out till long after the bloody transaction was over. I expected it would be my turn next. It was all new to me. I had never seen any thing like it before. I had always lived with my grandmother on the outskirts of the plantation, where she was put to raise the children of the younger women. I had therefore been, until now, out of the way of the bloody scenes that often occurred on the plantation.

Chapter II

My master's family consisted of two sons, Andrew and Richard; one daughter, Lucretia, and her husband, Captain Thomas Auld. They lived in one house, upon the home plantation of Colonel Edward Lloyd. My master was Colonel Lloyd's clerk and superintendent. He was what might be called the overseer of the overseers. I spent two years of childhood on this plantation in my old master's family. It was here that I witnessed the bloody transaction recorded in the first chapter; and as I received my first impressions of slavery on this plantation, I will give some description of it, and of slavery as it there existed. The plantation is about twelve miles north of Easton, in Talbot county, and is situated on the border of Miles River. The principal products raised upon it were tobacco, corn, and wheat. These were raised in great abundance; so that, with the products of this and the other farms belonging to him, he was able to keep in almost constant employment a large sloop, in carrying them to market at Baltimore. This sloop was named Sally Lloyd, in honor of one of the colonel's daughters. My master's son-in-law, Captain Auld, was master of the vessel; she was otherwise manned by the colonel's own slaves. Their names were Peter, Isaac, Rich, and Jake. These were esteemed very highly by the other slaves, and looked upon as the privileged ones of the plantation; for it was no small affair, in the eyes of the slaves, to be allowed to see Baltimore.

Colonel Lloyd kept from three to four hundred slaves on his home plantation, and owned a large number more on the neighboring farms belonging to him. The names of the farms nearest to the home plantation were Wye Town and New Design. "Wye Town" was under the overseership of a man named Noah Willis. New Design was under the overseership of a Mr. Townsend. The overseers of these, and all the rest of the farms, numbering over twenty, received advice and direction from the managers of the home plantation. This was the great business place. It was the seat of government for the whole twenty farms. All disputes among the overseers were settled here. If a slave was convicted of any high misdemeanor, became unmanageable, or evinced a determination to run away, he was brought immediately here, severely whipped, put on board the sloop, carried to Baltimore, and sold to Austin Woolfolk, or some other slave-trader, as a warning to the slaves remaining.

Here, too, the slaves of all the other farms received their monthly allowance of food, and their yearly clothing. The men and women slaves received, as their monthly allowance of food, eight pounds of pork, or its equivalent in fish, and one bushel of corn meal. Their yearly clothing consisted of two coarse linen shirts, one pair of linen trousers, like the shirts, one jacket, one pair of trousers for winter, made of coarse negro cloth, one pair of stockings, and one pair of shoes; the whole of which could not have cost more than seven dollars. The allowance of the slave children was given to their mothers, or the old women having the care of them. The children unable to work in the field had neither shoes, stockings, jackets, nor trousers, given to them; their clothing consisted of two coarse linen shirts per year. When these failed them, they went naked until the next allowance-day. Children from seven to ten years old, of both sexes, almost naked, might be seen at all seasons of the year.

There were no beds given the slaves, unless one coarse blanket be considered such, and none but the men and women had these. This, however, is not considered a very great privation. They find less difficulty from the want of beds, than from the want of time to sleep; for when their day's work in the field is done, the most of them having their washing, mending, and cooking to do, and having few or none of the ordinary facilities for doing either of these, very many of their sleeping hours are consumed in preparing for the field the coming day; and when this is done, old and young, male and female, married and single, drop down side by side, on one common bed, – the cold, damp floor, – each covering himself or herself with their miserable blankets; and here they sleep till they are summoned to the field by the driver's horn. At the sound of this, all must rise, and be off to the field. There must be no halting; every one must be at his or her post; and woe betides them who hear not this morning summons to the field; for if they are not awakened by the sense of hearing, they are by the sense of feeling: no age nor sex finds any favor. Mr. Severe, the overseer, used to stand by the door of the quarter, armed with a large hickory stick and heavy cowskin, ready to whip any one who was so unfortunate as not to hear, or, from any other cause, was prevented from being ready to start for the field at the sound of the horn.

Mr. Severe was rightly named: he was a cruel man. I have seen him whip a woman, causing the blood to run half an hour at the time; and this, too, in the midst of her crying children, pleading for their mother's release. He seemed to take pleasure in manifesting his fiendish barbarity. Added to his cruelty, he was a profane swearer. It was enough to chill the blood and stiffen the hair of an ordinary man to hear him talk. Scarce a sentence escaped him but that was commenced or concluded by some horrid oath. The field was the place to witness his cruelty and profanity. His presence made it both the field of blood and of blasphemy. From the rising till the going down of the sun, he was cursing, raving, cutting, and slashing among the slaves of the field, in the most frightful manner. His career was short. He died very soon after I went to Colonel Lloyd's; and he died as he lived, uttering, with his dying groans, bitter curses and horrid oaths. His death was regarded by the slaves as the result of a merciful providence.

Mr. Severe's place was filled by a Mr. Hopkins. He was a very different man. He was less cruel, less profane, and made less noise, than Mr. Severe. His course was characterized by no extraordinary demonstrations of cruelty. He whipped, but seemed to take no pleasure in it. He was called by the slaves a good overseer.

The home plantation of Colonel Lloyd wore the appearance of a country village. All the mechanical operations for all the farms were performed here. The shoemaking and mending, the blacksmithing, cartwrighting, coopering, weaving, and grain-grinding, were all performed by the slaves on the home plantation. The whole place wore a business-like aspect very unlike the neighboring farms. The number of houses, too, conspired to give it advantage over the neighboring farms. It was called by the slaves the *Great House Farm.* Few privileges were esteemed higher, by the slaves of the out-farms, than that of being selected to do errands at the Great House Farm. It was associated in their minds with greatness. A representative could not be prouder of his election to a seat in the American Congress, than a slave on one of the out-farms would be of his election to do errands at the Great House Farm. They regarded it as evidence of great confidence reposed in them by their overseers; and it was on this account, as well as a constant desire to be out of the field from under the driver's lash, that they esteemed it a high privilege, one worth careful living for. He was called the smartest and most trusty fellow, who had this honor conferred upon him the most frequently. The competitors for this office sought as diligently to please their overseers, as the office-seekers in the political parties seek to please and deceive the people. The same traits of character might be seen in Colonel Lloyd's slaves, as are seen in the slaves of the political parties.

The slaves selected to go to the Great House Farm, for the monthly allowance for themselves and their fellow-slaves, were peculiarly enthusiastic. While on their way, they would make the dense old woods, for miles around, reverberate with their wild songs, revealing at once the highest joy and the deepest sadness. They would compose and sing as they went along, consulting neither time nor tune. The thought that came up, came out; – if not in the word, in the sound; – and as frequently in the one as in the other. They would sometimes sing the most pathetic sentiment in the most rapturous tone, and the most rapturous sentiment in the most pathetic tone. Into all of their songs they would manage to weave something of the Great House Farm. Especially would they do this, when leaving home. They would then sing most exultingly the following words: –

> I am going away to the Great House Farm!
> O, yea! O, yea! O!

This they would sing, as a chorus, to words which to many would seem unmeaning jargon, but which, nevertheless, were full of meaning to themselves. I have sometimes thought that the mere hearing of those songs would do more to impress some minds with the horrible character of slavery, than the reading of whole volumes of philosophy on the subject could do.

I did not, when a slave, understand the deep meaning of those rude and apparently incoherent songs. I was myself within the circle; so that I neither saw nor heard as those without might see and hear. They told a tale of woe which was then altogether beyond my feeble comprehension; they were tones loud, long, and deep; they breathed the prayer and complaint of souls boiling over with the bitterest anguish. Every tone was a testimony against slavery, and a prayer to God for deliverance from chains. The hearing of those wild notes always depressed my spirit, and filled me with ineffable sadness, I have frequently found myself in tears while hearing them. The mere recurrence to those songs, even now, afflicts me; and while I am writing these lines, an expression of feeling has already found its way down my cheek. To those songs I trace my first glimmering conception of the dehumanizing character of slavery. I can never get rid of that conception. Those songs still follow me, to deepen my hatred of slavery, and quicken my sympathies for my brethren in bonds. If any one wishes to be impressed with the soul-killing effects of slavery, let him go to Colonel Lloyd's plantation, and, on allowance-day, place himself in the deep pine woods, and there let him, in silence, analyze the sounds that shall pass through the chambers of his soul, – and if he is not thus impressed, it will only be because "there is no flesh in his obdurate heart."[1]

I have often been utterly astonished, since I came to the north, to find persons who could speak of the singing, among slaves, as evidence of their contentment and happiness. It is impossible to conceive of a greater mistake. Slaves sing most when they are most unhappy. The songs of the slave represent the sorrows of his heart; and he is relieved by them, only as an aching heart is relieved by its tears. At least, such is my experience. I have often sung to drown my sorrow, but seldom to express my happiness. Crying for joy, and singing for joy, were alike uncommon to me while in the jaws of slavery. The singing of a man cast away upon a desolate island might be as appropriately considered as evidence of contentment and happiness, as the singing of a slave; the songs of the one and of the other are prompted by the same emotion.

Chapter III

Colonel Lloyd kept a large and finely cultivated garden, which afforded almost constant employment for four men, besides the chief gardener, (Mr. M'Durmond.) This garden was probably the greatest attraction of the place. During the summer months, people came from far and near – from Baltimore, Easton, and Annapolis – to see it. It abounded in fruits of almost every description, from the hardy apple of the north to the

1. **"there . . . obdurate heart"**: From book 2, line 8 of *The Task* (1785), a popular poem by the English poet William Cowper (1731–1800).

delicate orange of the south. This garden was not the least source of trouble on the plantation. Its excellent fruit was quite a temptation to the hungry swarms of boys, as well as the older slaves, belonging to the colonel, few of whom had the virtue or the vice to resist it. Scarcely a day passed, during the summer, but that some slave had to take the lash for stealing fruit. The colonel had to resort to all kinds of stratagems to keep his slaves out of the garden. The last and most successful one was that of tarring his fence all around; after which, if a slave was caught with any tar upon his person, it was deemed sufficient proof that he had either been into the garden, or had tried to get in. In either case, he was severely whipped by the chief gardener. This plan worked well; the slaves became as fearful of tar as of the lash. They seemed to realize the impossibility of touching *tar* without being defiled.

The colonel also kept a splendid riding equipage. His stable and carriage-house presented the appearance of some of our large city livery establishments. His horses were of the finest form and noblest blood. His carriage-house contained three splendid coaches, three or four gigs, besides dearborns and barouches of the most fashionable style.

This establishment was under the care of two slaves – old Barney and young Barney – father and son. To attend to this establishment was their sole work. But it was by no means an easy employment; for in nothing was Colonel Lloyd more particular than in the management of his horses. The slightest inattention to these was unpardonable, and was visited upon those, under whose care they were placed, with the severest punishment; no excuse could shield them, if the colonel only suspected any want of attention to his horses – a supposition which he frequently indulged, and one which, of course, made the office of old and young Barney a very trying one. They never knew when they were safe from punishment. They were frequently whipped when least deserving, and escaped whipping when most deserving it. Every thing depended upon the looks of the horses, and the state of Colonel Lloyd's own mind when his horses were brought to him for use. If a horse did not move fast enough, or hold his head high enough, it was owing to some fault of his keepers. It was painful to stand near the stable-door, and hear the various complaints against the keepers when a horse was taken out for use. "This horse has not had proper attention. He has not been sufficiently rubbed and curried, or he has not been properly fed; his food was too wet or too dry; he got it too soon or too late; he was too hot or too cold; he had too much hay, and not enough of grain; or he had too much grain, and not enough of hay; instead of old Barney's attending to the horse, he had very improperly left it to his son." To all these complaints, no matter how unjust, the slave must answer never a word. Colonel Lloyd could not brook any contradiction from a slave. When he spoke, a slave must stand, listen, and tremble; and such was literally the case. I have seen Colonel Lloyd make old Barney, a man between fifty and sixty years of age, uncover his bald head, kneel down upon the cold, damp ground, and receive upon his naked and toil-worn shoulders more than thirty lashes at the time. Colonel Lloyd had three sons – Edward, Murray, and Daniel, – and three sons-in-law, Mr. Winder, Mr. Nicholson, and Mr. Lowndes. All of these lived at the Great House Farm, and enjoyed the luxury of whipping the servants when they pleased, from old Barney down to William Wilkes, the coach-driver. I have seen Winder make one of the house-servants stand off from him a suitable distance to be touched with the end of his whip, and at every stroke raise great ridges upon his back.

To describe the wealth of Colonel Lloyd would be almost equal to describing the riches of Job.[1] He kept from ten to fifteen house-servants. He was said to own a thousand slaves, and I think this estimate quite within the truth. Colonel Lloyd owned so many that he did not know them when he saw them; nor did all the slaves of the out-farms know him. It is reported of him, that, while riding along the road one day, he met a colored man, and addressed him in the usual manner of speaking to colored people on the public highways of the south: "Well, boy, whom do you belong to?" "To Colonel Lloyd," replied the slave. "Well, does the colonel treat you well?" "No, sir," was the ready reply. "What, does he work you too hard?" "Yes, sir." "Well, don't he give you enough to eat?" "Yes, sir, he gives me enough, such as it is."

The colonel, after ascertaining where the slave belonged, rode on; the man also went on about his business, not dreaming that he had been conversing with his master. He thought, said, and heard nothing more of the matter, until two or three weeks afterwards. The poor man was then informed by his overseer that, for having found fault with his master, he was now to be sold to a Georgia trader. He was immediately chained and handcuffed; and thus, without a moment's warning, he was snatched away, and forever sundered, from his family and friends, by a hand more unrelenting than death. This is the penalty of telling the truth, of telling the simple truth, in answer to a series of plain questions.

It is partly in consequence of such facts, that slaves, when inquired of as to their condition and the character of their masters, almost universally say they are contented, and that their masters are kind. The slaveholders have been known to send in spies among their slaves, to ascertain their views and feelings in regard to their condition. The frequency of this has had the effect to establish among the slaves the maxim, that a still tongue makes a wise head. They suppress the truth rather than take the consequences of telling it, and in so doing prove themselves a part of the human family. If they have any thing to say of their masters, it is generally in their masters' favor, especially when speaking to an untried man. I have been frequently asked, when a slave, if I had a kind master, and do not remember ever to have given a negative answer; nor did I, in pursuing this course, consider myself as uttering what was absolutely false; for I always measured the kindness of my master by the standard of kindness set up among slaveholders around us. Moreover, slaves are like other people, and imbibe prejudices quite common to others. They think their own better than that of others. Many, under the influence of this prejudice, think their own masters are better than the masters of other slaves; and this, too, in some cases, when the very reverse is true. Indeed, it is not uncommon for slaves even to fall out and quarrel among themselves about the relative goodness of their masters, each contending for the superior goodness of his own over that of the others. At the very same time, they mutually execrate their masters when viewed separately. It was so on our plantation. When Colonel Lloyd's slaves met the slaves of Jacob Jepson, they seldom parted without a quarrel about their masters;

1. **riches of Job:** See the description of his herds and "great household" in Job 1:3.

Colonel Lloyd's slaves contending that he was the richest, and Mr. Jepson's slaves that he was the smartest, and most of a man. Colonel Lloyd's slaves would boast his ability to buy and sell Jacob Jepson. Mr. Jepson's slaves would boast his ability to whip Colonel Lloyd. These quarrels would almost always end in a fight between the parties, and those that whipped were supposed to have gained the point at issue. They seemed to think that the greatness of their masters was transferable to themselves. It was considered as being bad enough to be a slave; but to be a poor man's slave was deemed a disgrace indeed!

Chapter IV

Mr. Hopkins remained but a short time in the office of overseer. Why his career was so short, I do not know, but suppose he lacked the necessary severity to suit Colonel Lloyd. Mr. Hopkins was succeeded by Mr. Austin Gore, a man possessing, in an eminent degree, all those traits of character indispensable to what is called a first-rate overseer. Mr. Gore had served Colonel Lloyd, in the capacity of overseer, upon one of the out-farms, and had shown himself worthy of the high station of overseer upon the home or Great House Farm.

Mr. Gore was proud, ambitious, and persevering. He was artful, cruel, and obdurate. He was just the man for such a place, and it was just the place for such a man. It afforded scope for the full exercise of all his powers, and he seemed to be perfectly at home in it. He was one of those who could torture the slightest look, word, or gesture, on the part of the slave, into impudence, and would treat it accordingly. There must be no answering back to him; no explanation was allowed a slave, showing himself to have been wrongfully accused. Mr. Gore acted fully up to the maxim laid down by slaveholders, – "It is better that a dozen slaves suffer under the lash, than that the overseer should be convicted, in the presence of the slaves, of having been at fault." No matter how innocent a slave might be – it availed him nothing, when accused by Mr. Gore of any misdemeanor. To be accused was to be convicted, and to be convicted was to be punished; the one always following the other with immutable certainty. To escape punishment was to escape accusation; and few slaves had the fortune to do either, under the overseership of Mr. Gore. He was just proud enough to demand the most debasing homage of the slave, and quite servile enough to crouch, himself, at the feet of the master. He was ambitious enough to be contented with nothing short of the highest rank of overseers, and persevering enough to reach the height of his ambition. He was cruel enough to inflict the severest punishment, artful enough to descend to the lowest trickery, and obdurate enough to be insensible to the voice of a reproving conscience. He was, of all the overseers, the most dreaded by the slaves. His presence was painful; his eye flashed confusion; and seldom was his sharp, shrill voice heard, without producing horror and trembling in their ranks.

Mr. Gore was a grave man, and, though a young man, he indulged in no jokes, said no funny words, seldom smiled. His words were in perfect keeping with his looks, and his looks were in perfect keeping with his words. Overseers will sometimes indulge in a witty word, even with the slaves; not so with Mr. Gore. He spoke but to command, and commanded but to be obeyed; he dealt sparingly with his words, and bountifully with his whip, never using the former where the latter would answer as well. When he whipped, he seemed to do so from a sense of duty, and feared no consequences. He did nothing reluctantly, no matter how disagreeable; always at his post, never inconsistent. He never promised but to fulfill. He was, in a word, a man of the most inflexible firmness and stone-like coolness.

His savage barbarity was equalled only by the consummate coolness with which he committed the grossest and most savage deeds upon the slaves under his charge. Mr. Gore once undertook to whip one of Colonel Lloyd's slaves, by the name of Demby. He had given Demby but few stripes, when, to get rid of the scourging, he ran and plunged himself into a creek, and stood there at the depth of his shoulders, refusing to come out. Mr. Gore told him that he would give him three calls, and that, if he did not come out at the third call, he would shoot him. The first call was given. Demby made no response, but stood his ground. The second and third calls were given with the same result. Mr. Gore then, without consultation or deliberation with any one, not even giving Demby an additional call, raised his musket to his face, taking deadly aim at his standing victim, and in an instant poor Demby was no more. His mangled body sank out of sight, and blood and brains marked the water where he had stood.

A thrill of horror flashed through every soul upon the plantation, excepting Mr. Gore. He alone seemed cool and collected. He was asked by Colonel Lloyd and my old master, why he resorted to this extraordinary expedient. His reply was, (as well as I can remember,) that Demby had become unmanageable. He was setting a dangerous example to the other slaves, – one which, if suffered to pass without some such demonstration on his part, would finally lead to the total subversion of all rule and order upon the plantation. He argued that if one slave refused to be corrected, and escaped with his life, the other slaves would soon copy the example; the result of which would be, the freedom of the slaves, and the enslavement of the whites. Mr. Gore's defence was satisfactory. He was continued in his station as overseer upon the home plantation. His fame as an overseer went abroad. His horrid crime was not even submitted to judicial investigation. It was committed in the presence of slaves, and they of course could neither institute a suit, nor testify against him; and thus the guilty perpetrator of one of the bloodiest and most foul murders goes unwhipped of justice, and uncensured by the community in which he lives. Mr. Gore lived in St. Michael's, Talbot county, Maryland, when I left there; and if he is still alive, he very probably lives there now; and if so, he is now, as he was then, as highly esteemed and as much respected as though his guilty soul had not been stained with his brother's blood.

I speak advisedly when I say this, – that killing a slave, or any colored person, in Talbot county, Maryland, is not treated as a crime, either by the courts or the community. Mr. Thomas Lanman, of St. Michael's, killed two slaves, one of whom he killed with a hatchet, by knocking his brains out. He used to boast of the commission of the awful and bloody deed. I have heard him do so laughingly, saying, among other things, that he was the only benefactor of his country in the company, and that when others would do as much as he had done, we should be relieved of "the d—d niggers."

The wife of Mr. Giles Hick, living but a short distance from where I used to live, murdered my wife's cousin, a young girl between fifteen and sixteen years of age, mangling her person in the most horrible manner, breaking her nose and breastbone with a stick, so that the poor girl expired in a few hours afterward. She was immediately buried, but had not been in her untimely grave but a few hours before she was taken up and examined by the coroner, who decided that she had come to her death by severe beating. The offence for which this girl was thus murdered was this: – She had been set that night to mind Mrs. Hick's baby and during the night she fell asleep, and the baby cried. She, having lost her rest for several nights previous, did not hear the crying. They were both in the room with Mrs. Hicks. Mrs. Hicks, finding the girl slow to move, jumped from her bed, seized an oak stick of wood by the fireplace, and with it broke the girl's nose and breastbone, and thus ended her life. I will not say that this most horrid murder produced no sensation in the community. It did produce sensation, but not enough to bring the murderess to punishment. There was a warrant issued for her arrest, but it was never served. Thus she escaped not only punishment, but even the pain of being arraigned before a court for her horrid crime.

Whilst I am detailing bloody deeds which took place during my stay on Colonel Lloyd's plantation, I will briefly narrate another, which occurred about the same time as the murder of Demby by Mr. Gore.

Colonel Lloyd's slaves were in the habit of spending a part of their nights and Sundays in fishing for oysters, and in this way made up the deficiency of their scanty allowance. An old man belonging to Colonel Lloyd, while thus engaged, happened to get beyond the limits of Colonel Lloyd's, and on the premises of Mr. Beal Bondly. At this trespass, Mr. Bondly took offence, and with his musket came down to the shore, and blew its deadly contents into the poor old man.

Mr. Bondly came over to see Colonel Lloyd the next day, whether to pay him for his property, or to justify himself in what he had done, I know not. At any rate, this whole fiendish transaction was soon hushed up. There was very little said about it at all, and nothing done. It was a common saying, even among little white boys, that it was worth a half-cent to kill a "nigger," and a half-cent to bury one.

Chapter V

As to my own treatment while I lived on Colonel Lloyd's plantation, it was very similar to that of the other slave children. I was not old enough to work in the field, and there being little else than field work to do, I had a great deal of leisure time. The most I had to do was to drive up the cows at evening, keep the fowls out of the garden, keep the front yard clean, and run of errands for my old master's daughter, Mrs. Lucretia Auld. The most of my leisure time I spent in helping Master Daniel Lloyd in finding his birds, after he had shot them. My connection with Master Daniel was of some advantage to me. He became quite attached to me, and was a sort of protector of me. He would not allow the older boys to impose upon me, and would divide his cakes with me.

I was seldom whipped by my old master, and suffered little from any thing else than hunger and cold. I suffered much from hunger, but much more from cold. In hottest summer and coldest winter, I was kept almost naked – no shoes, no stockings, no jacket, no trousers, nothing on but a coarse tow linen shirt, reaching only to my knees. I had no bed. I must have perished with cold, but that, the coldest nights, I used to steal a bag which was used for carrying corn to the mill. I would crawl into this bag, and there sleep on the cold, damp, clay floor, with my head in and feet out. My feet have been so cracked with the frost, that the pen with which I am writing might be laid in the gashes.

We were not regularly allowanced. Our food was coarse corn meal boiled. This was called *mush*. It was put into a large wooden tray or trough, and set down upon the ground. The children were then called, like so many pigs, and like so many pigs they would come and devour the mush; some with oyster-shells, others with pieces of shingle, some with naked hands, and none with spoons. He that ate fastest got most; he that was strongest secured the best place; and few left the trough satisfied.

I was probably between seven and eight years old when I left Colonel Lloyd's plantation. I left it with joy. I shall never forget the ecstasy with which I received the intelligence that my old master (Anthony) had determined to let me go to Baltimore, to live with Mr. Hugh Auld, brother to my old master's son-in-law, Captain Thomas Auld. I received this information about three days before my departure. They were three of the happiest days I ever enjoyed. I spent the most part of all these three days in the creek, washing off the plantation scurf, and preparing myself for my departure.

The pride of appearance which this would indicate was not my own. I spent the time in washing, not so much because I wished to, but because Mrs. Lucretia had told me I must get all the dead skin off my feet and knees before I could go to Baltimore; for the people in Baltimore were very cleanly, and would laugh at me if I looked dirty. Besides, she was going to give me a pair of trousers, which I should not put on unless I got all the dirt off me. The thought of owning a pair of trousers was great indeed! It was almost a sufficient motive, not only to make me take off what would be called by pig-drovers the mange, but the skin itself. I went at it in good earnest, working for the first time with the hope of reward.

The ties that ordinarily bind children to their homes were all suspended in my case. I found no severe trial in my departure. My home was charmless; it was not home to me; on parting from it, I could not feel that I was leaving any thing which I could have enjoyed by staying. My mother was dead, my grandmother lived far off, so that I seldom saw her. I had two sisters and one brother, that lived in the same house with me; but the early separation of us from our mother had well nigh blotted the fact of our relationship from our memories. I looked for home elsewhere, and was confident of finding none which I should relish less than the one which I was leaving. If, however, I found in my new home hardship, hunger, whipping, and nakedness, I had the consolation that I should not have escaped any one of them by staying. Having already had more than a taste of them in the house of my old master, and having endured them there, I very naturally inferred my ability to endure them elsewhere, and especially at Baltimore; for I had something of the feeling about Baltimore that is expressed in the proverb, that "being hanged in England is preferable to dying a natural death in Ireland." I had the strongest desire to see Baltimore. Cousin Tom, though not fluent in speech, had inspired me with that desire by his eloquent description of the place. I could never point out any thing at the Great House, no matter how beautiful or powerful, but that he had seen something at Baltimore far exceeding, both in beauty and strength, the object which I pointed out to him. Even the Great House itself, with all its pictures, was far inferior to many buildings in Baltimore. So strong was my desire, that I thought a gratification of it would fully compensate for whatever loss of comforts I should sustain by the exchange. I left without a regret, and with the highest hopes of future happiness.

We sailed out of Miles River for Baltimore on a Saturday morning. I remember only the day of the week, for at that time I had no knowledge of the days of the month, nor the months of the year. On setting sail, I walked aft, and gave to Colonel Lloyd's plantation what I hoped would be the last look. I then placed myself in the bows of the sloop, and there spent the remainder of the day in looking ahead, interesting myself in what was in the distance rather than in things near by or behind.

In the afternoon of that day, we reached Annapolis, the capital of the State. We stopped but a few moments, so that I had no time to go on shore. It was the first large town that I had ever seen, and though it would look small compared with some of our New England factory villages, I thought it a wonderful place for its size – more imposing even than the Great House Farm!

We arrived at Baltimore early on Sunday morning, landing at Smith's Wharf, not far from Bowley's Wharf. We had on board the sloop a large flock of sheep; and after aiding in driving them to the slaughter-house of Mr. Curtis on Louden Slater's Hill, I was conducted by Rich, one of the hands belonging on board of the sloop, to my new home in Alliciana Street, near Mr. Gardner's ship-yard, on Fells Point.

Mr. and Mrs. Auld were both at home, and met me at the door with their little son Thomas, to take care of whom I had been given. And here I saw what I had never seen before; it was a white face beaming with the most kindly emotions; it was the face of my new mistress, Sophia Auld. I wish I could describe the rapture that flashed through my soul as I beheld it. It was a new and strange sight to me, brightening up my pathway with the light of happiness. Little Thomas was told, there was his Freddy, – and I was told to take care of little Thomas; and thus I entered upon the duties of my new home with the most cheering prospect ahead.

I look upon my departure from Colonel Lloyd's plantation as one of the most interesting events of my life. It is possible, and even quite probable, that but for the mere circumstance of being removed from that plantation to Baltimore, I should have to-day, instead of being here seated by my own table, in the enjoyment of freedom and the happiness of home, writing this Narrative, been confined in the galling chains of slavery. Going to live at Baltimore laid the foundation, and opened the gateway, to all my subsequent prosperity. I have ever regarded it as the first plain manifestation of that kind providence which has ever since attended me, and marked my life with so many favors. I regarded the selection of myself as being somewhat remarkable. There were a number of slave children that might have been sent from the plantation to Baltimore. There were those younger, those older, and those of the same age. I was chosen from among them all, and was the first, last, and only choice.

I may be deemed superstitious, and even egotistical, in regarding this event as a special interposition of divine Providence in my favor. But I should be false to the earliest sentiments of my soul, if I suppressed the opinion. I prefer to be true to myself, even at the hazard of incurring the ridicule of others, rather than to be false, and incur my own abhorrence. From my earliest recollection, I date the entertainment of a deep conviction that slavery would not always be able to hold me within its foul embrace; and in the darkest hours of my career in slavery, this living word of faith and spirit of hope departed not from me, but remained like ministering angels to cheer me through the gloom.[1] This good spirit was from God, and to him I offer thanksgiving and praise.

Chapter VI

My new mistress proved to be all she appeared when I first met her at the door, – a woman of the kindest heart and finest feelings. She had never had a slave under her control previously to myself, and prior to her marriage she had been dependent upon her own industry for a living. She was by trade a weaver; and by constant application to her business, she had been in a good degree preserved from the blighting and dehumanizing effects of slavery. I was utterly astonished at her goodness. I scarcely knew how to behave towards her. She was entirely unlike any other white woman I had ever seen. I could not approach her as I was accustomed to approach other white ladies. My early instruction was all out of place. The crouching servility, usually so acceptable a quality in a slave, did not answer when manifested toward her. Her favor was not gained by it; she seemed to be disturbed by it. She did not deem it impudent or unmannerly for a slave to look her in the face. The meanest slave was put fully at ease in her presence, and none left without feeling better for having seen her. Her face was made of heavenly smiles, and her voice of tranquil music.

But, alas! this kind heart had but a short time to remain such. The fatal poison of irresponsible power was already in her hands, and soon commenced its infernal work. That cheerful eye, under the influence of slavery, soon became red with rage; that voice, made all of sweet accord, changed to one of harsh and horrid discord; and that angelic face gave place to that of a demon.

Very soon after I went to live with Mr. and Mrs. Auld, she very kindly commenced to teach me the A, B, C. After I had learned this, she assisted me in learning to spell words of three or four letters. Just at this point of my progress, Mr. Auld found out what was going on, and at once forbade Mrs. Auld to instruct me further, telling her, among other things, that it was unlawful, as well as unsafe, to teach a slave to read. To use his own words, further, he said, "If you give a nigger an inch, he will take an ell. A nigger should know nothing but to obey his master – to do as he is told to do. Learning would *spoil* the best nigger in the world. Now," said he, "if you teach that nigger (speaking of myself) how to read, there would be no keeping him. It would forever unfit him to be a slave. He would at once become unmanageable, and of no value to his master. As to himself, it could do him no good, but a great deal of harm. It would make him discontented and unhappy." These words sank deep into my heart, stirred up sentiments within that lay slumbering, and called into existence an entirely new train of thought. It was a new and

1. **ministering angels . . . gloom:** Compare the description of Christ's temptation in the wilderness in Matthew 4:11: "Then the devil leaveth him, and, behold, angels came and ministered unto him."

special revelation, explaining dark and mysterious things, with which my youthful understanding had struggled, but struggled in vain. I now understood what had been to me a most perplexing difficulty – to wit, the white man's power to enslave the black man. It was a grand achievement, and I prized it highly. From that moment, I understood the pathway from slavery to freedom. It was just what I wanted, and I got it at a time when I the least expected it. Whilst I was saddened by the thought of losing the aid of my kind mistress, I was gladdened by the invaluable instruction which, by the merest accident, I had gained from my master. Though conscious of the difficulty of learning without a teacher, I set out with high hope, and a fixed purpose, at whatever cost of trouble, to learn how to read. The very decided manner with which he spoke, and strove to impress his wife with the evil consequences of giving me instruction, served to convince me that he was deeply sensible of the truths he was uttering. It gave me the best assurance that I might rely with the utmost confidence on the results which, he said, would flow from teaching me to read. What he most dreaded, that I most desired. What he most loved, that I most hated. That which to him was a great evil, to be carefully shunned, was to me a great good, to be diligently sought; and the argument which he so warmly urged, against my learning to read, only served to inspire me with a desire and determination to learn. In learning to read, I owe almost as much to the bitter opposition of my master, as to the kindly aid of my mistress. I acknowledge the benefit of both.

I had resided but a short time in Baltimore before I observed a marked difference, in the treatment of slaves, from that which I had witnessed in the country. A city slave is almost a freeman, compared with a slave on the plantation. He is much better fed and clothed, and enjoys privileges altogether unknown to the slave on the plantation. There is a vestige of decency, a sense of shame, that does much to curb and check those outbreaks of atrocious cruelty so commonly enacted upon the plantation. He is a desperate slaveholder, who will shock the humanity of his nonslaveholding neighbors with the cries of his lacerated slave. Few are willing to incur the odium attaching to the reputation of being a cruel master; and above all things, they would not be known as not giving a slave enough to eat. Every city slaveholder is anxious to have it known of him, that he feeds his slaves well; and it is due to them to say, that most of them do give their slaves enough to eat. There are, however, some painful exceptions to this rule. Directly opposite to us, on Philpot Street, lived Mr. Thomas Hamilton. He owned two slaves. Their names were Henrietta and Mary. Henrietta was about twenty-two years of age, Mary was about fourteen; and of all the mangled and emaciated creatures I ever looked upon, these two were the most so. His heart must be harder than stone, that could look upon these unmoved. The head, neck, and shoulders of Mary were literally cut to pieces. I have frequently felt her head and found it nearly covered with festering sores, caused by the lash of her cruel mistress. I do not know that her master ever whipped her, but I have been an eye-witness to the cruelty of Mrs. Hamilton. I used to be in Mr. Hamilton's house nearly every day. Mrs. Hamilton used to sit in a large chair in the middle of the room, with a heavy cowskin always by her side, and scarce an hour passed during the day but was marked by the blood of one of these slaves. The girls seldom passed her without her saying, "Move faster, you *black gip*!" at the same time giving them a blow with the cowskin over the head or shoulders, often drawing the blood. She would then say, "Take that, you *black gip*!" – continuing, "If you don't move faster, I'll move you!" Added to the cruel lashings to which these slaves were subjected, they were kept nearly half-starved. They seldom knew what it was to eat a full meal. I have seen Mary contending with the pigs for the offal thrown into the street. So much was Mary kicked and cut to pieces, that she was oftener called "*pecked*" than by her name.

Chapter VII

I lived in Master Hugh's family about seven years. During this time, I succeeded in learning to read and write. In accomplishing this, I was compelled to resort to various stratagems. I had no regular teacher. My mistress, who had kindly commenced to instruct me, had, in compliance with the advice and direction of her husband, not only ceased to instruct, but had set her face against my being instructed by any one else. It is due, however, to my mistress to say of her, that she did not adopt this course of treatment immediately. She at first lacked the depravity indispensable to shutting me up in mental darkness. It was at least necessary for her to have some training in the exercise of irresponsible power, to make her equal to the task of treating me as though I were a brute.

My mistress was, as I have said, a kind and tender-hearted woman; and in the simplicity of her soul she commenced, when I first went to live with her, to treat me as she supposed one human being ought to treat another. In entering upon the duties of a slaveholder, she did not seem to perceive that I sustained to her the relation of a mere chattel, and that for her to treat me as a human being was not only wrong, but dangerously so. Slavery proved as injurious to her as it did to me. When I went there, she was a pious, warm, and tender-hearted woman. There was no sorrow or suffering for which she had not a tear. She had bread for the hungry, clothes for the naked, and comfort for every mourner that came within her reach. Slavery soon proved its ability to divest her of these heavenly qualities. Under its influence, the tender heart became stone, and the lamblike disposition gave way to one of tiger-like fierceness. The first step in her downward course was in her ceasing to instruct me. She now commenced to practise her husband's precepts. She finally became even more violent in her opposition than her husband himself. She was not satisfied with simply doing as well as he had commanded; she seemed anxious to do better. Nothing seemed to make her more angry than to see me with a newspaper. She seemed to think that here lay the danger. I have had her rush at me with a face made all up of fury, and snatch from me a newspaper, in a manner that fully revealed her apprehension. She was an apt woman; and a little experience soon demonstrated, to her satisfaction, that education and slavery were incompatible with each other.

From this time I was most narrowly watched. If I was in a separate room any considerable length of time, I was sure to be suspected of having a book, and was at once called to give an account of myself. All this, however, was too late. The first step had been taken. Mistress, in teaching me the alphabet, had given me the *inch*, and no precaution could prevent me from taking the *ell*.

The plan which I adopted, and the one by which I was most successful, was that of making friends of all the little white boys whom I met in the street. As many of these as I could, I converted into teachers. With their kindly aid, obtained at different times and in different places, I finally succeeded in learning to read. When I was sent to errands, I always took my book with me, and by going one part of my errand quickly, I found time to get a lesson before my return. I used also to carry bread with me, enough of which was always in the house, and to which I was always welcome; for I was much better off in this regard than many of the poor white children in our neighborhood. This bread I used to bestow upon the hungry little urchins, who, in return, would give me that more valuable bread of knowledge. I am strongly tempted to give the names of two or three of those little boys, as a testimonial of the gratitude and affection I bear them; but prudence forbids; – not that it would injure me, but it might embarrass them; for it is almost an unpardonable offence to teach slaves to read in this Christian country. It is enough to say of the dear little fellows, that they lived on Philpot Street, very near Durgin and Bailey's ship-yard. I used to talk this matter of slavery over with them. I would sometimes say to them, I wished I could be as free as they would be when they got to be men. "You will be free as soon as you are twenty-one, *but I am a slave for life*! Have not I as good a right to be free as you have?" These words used to trouble them; they would express for me the liveliest sympathy, and console me with the hope that something would occur by which I might be free.

I was now about twelve years old, and the thought of being *a slave for life* began to bear heavily upon my heart. Just about this time, I got hold of a book entitled "The Columbian Orator."[1] Every opportunity I got, I used to read this book. Among much of other interesting matter, I found in it a dialogue between a master and his slave. The slave was represented as having run away from his master three times. The dialogue represented the conversation which took place between them, when the slave was retaken the third time. In this dialogue, the whole argument in behalf of slavery was brought forward by the master, all of which was disposed of by the slave. The slave was made to say some very smart as well as impressive things in reply to his master – things which had the desired though unexpected effect; for the conversation resulted in the voluntary emancipation of the slave on the part of the master.

In the same book, I met with one of Sheridan's mighty speeches on and in behalf of Catholic emancipation.[2] These were choice documents to me. I read them over and over again with unabated interest. They gave tongue to interesting thoughts of my own soul, which had frequently flashed through my mind, and died away for want of utterance. The moral which I gained from the dialogue was the power of truth over the conscience of even a slaveholder. What I got from Sheridan was a bold denunciation of slavery, and a powerful vindication of human rights. The reading of these documents enabled me to utter my thoughts, and to meet the arguments brought forward to sustain slavery; but

---

1. **"The Columbian Orator":** Caleb Bingham, *The Columbian Orator: Containing a Variety of Original and Selected Pieces Together with Rules Calculated to Improve Youth and Others in the Ornamental and Useful Art of Eloquence* (1797). A popular schoolbook, the collection included speeches from ancient and modern times on subjects like democracy, freedom, liberty, and virtue.

2. **Sheridan's mighty speeches . . . emancipation:** Richard Brinsley Sheridan (1751–1816) was an Irish political leader and playwright, but Douglass was actually recalling Daniel O'Connor's "Speech in the House of Commons, in Favour of the Bill for Emancipating the Roman Catholics" (1795).

while they relieved me of one difficulty, they brought on another even more painful than the one of which I was relieved. The more I read, the more I was led to abhor and detest my enslavers. I could regard them in no other light than a band of successful robbers, who had left their homes, and gone to Africa, and stolen us from our homes, and in a strange land reduced us to slavery. I loathed them as being the meanest as well as the most wicked of men. As I read and contemplated the subject, behold! that very discontentment which Master Hugh had predicted would follow my learning to read had already come, to torment and sting my soul to unutterable anguish. As I writhed under it, I would at times feel that learning to read had been a curse rather than a blessing. It had given me a view of my wretched condition, without the remedy. It opened my eyes to the horrible pit, but to no ladder upon which to get out. In moments of agony, I envied my fellow-slaves for their stupidity. I have often wished myself a beast. I preferred the condition of the meanest reptile to my own. Any thing, no matter what, to get rid of thinking! It was this everlasting thinking of my condition that tormented me. There was no getting rid of it. It was pressed upon me by every object within sight or hearing, animate or inanimate. The silver trump of freedom had roused my soul to eternal wakefulness. Freedom now appeared, to disappear no more forever. It was heard in every sound, and seen in every thing. It was ever present to torment me with a sense of my wretched condition. I saw nothing without seeing it, I heard nothing without hearing it, and felt nothing without feeling it. It looked from every star, it smiled in every calm, breathed in every wind, and moved in every storm.

I often found myself regretting my own existence, and wishing myself dead; and but for the hope of being free, I have no doubt but that I should have killed myself, or done something for which I should have been killed. While in this state of mind, I was eager to hear any one speak of slavery. I was a ready listener. Every little while, I could hear something about the abolitionists. It was some time before I found what the word meant. It was always used in such connections as to make it an interesting word to me. If a slave ran away and succeeded in getting clear, or if a slave killed his master, set fire to a barn, or did any thing very wrong in the mind of a slaveholder, it was spoken of as the fruit of *abolition.* Hearing the word in this connection very often, I set about learning what it meant. The dictionary afforded me little or no help. I found it was "the act of abolishing;" but then I did not know what was to be abolished. Here I was perplexed. I did not dare to ask any one about its meaning, for I was satisfied that it was something they wanted me to know very little about. After a patient waiting, I got one of our city papers, containing an account of the number of petitions from the north, praying for the abolition of slavery in the District of Columbia, and of the slave trade between the States. From this time I understood the words *abolition* and *abolitionist,* and always drew near when that word was spoken, expecting to hear something of importance to myself and fellow slaves. The light broke in upon me by degrees. I went one day down on the wharf of Mr. Waters; and seeing two Irishmen unloading a scow of stone, I went, unasked, and helped them. When we had finished, one of them came to me and asked me if I were a slave. I told him I was. He asked, "Are ye a slave for life?" I told him that I was. The good Irishman seemed to be deeply affected by the statement. He said to the other that it was a pity so fine a little fellow as myself should be a slave for life. He said it was a shame to hold me. They both advised me to run away to the north; that I should find friends there, and that I should be free. I pretended not to be interested in what they said, and treated them as if I did not understand them; for I feared they might be treacherous. White men have been known to encourage slaves to escape, and then, to get the reward, catch them and return them to their masters. I was afraid that these seemingly good men might use me so; but I nevertheless remembered their advice, and from that time I resolved to run away. I looked forward to a time at which it would be safe for me to escape. I was too young to think of doing so immediately; besides, I wished to learn how to write, as I might have occasion to write my own pass. I consoled myself with the hope that I should one day find a good chance. Meanwhile, I would learn to write.

The idea as to how I might learn to write was suggested to me by being in Durgin and Bailey's ship-yard, and frequently seeing the ship carpenters, after hewing, and getting a piece of timber ready for use, write on the timber the name of that part of the ship for which it was intended. When a piece of timber was intended for the larboard side, it would be marked thus – "L." When a piece was for the starboard side, it would be marked thus – "S." A piece for the larboard side forward, would be marked thus – "L.F." When a piece was for starboard side forward, it would be marked thus – "S.F." For larboard aft, it would be marked thus – "L.A." For starboard aft, it would be marked thus – "S.A." I soon learned the names of these letters, and for what they were intended when placed upon a piece of timber in the ship-yard. I immediately commenced copying them, and in a short time was able to make the four letters named. After that, when I met with any boy who I knew could write, I would tell him I could write as well as he. The next word would be, "I don't believe you. Let me see you try it." I would then make the letters which I had been so fortunate as to learn, and ask him to beat that. In this way I got a good many lessons in writing, which it is quite possible I should never have gotten in any other way. During this time, my copy-book was the board fence, brick wall, and pavement; my pen and ink was a lump of chalk. With these, I learned mainly how to write. I then commenced and continued copying the Italics in Webster's Spelling Book, until I could make them all without looking on the book. By this time, my little Master Thomas had gone to school, and learned how to write, and had written over a number of copy-books. These had been brought home, and shown to some of our near neighbors, and then laid aside. My mistress used to go to class meeting at the Wilk Street meeting-house every Monday afternoon, and leave me to take care of the house. When left thus, I used to spend the time in writing in the spaces left in Master Thomas's copy-book, copying what he had written. I continued to do this until I could write a hand very similar to that of Master Thomas. Thus, after a long, tedious effort for years, I finally succeeded in learning how to write.

Chapter VIII

In a very short time after I went to live at Baltimore, my old master's youngest son Richard died; and in about three years and six months after his death, my old master, Captain Anthony, died, leaving only his son, Andrew, and daughter, Lucretia, to share his estate. He died while on a visit to see his daughter at Hillsborough. Cut off thus unexpectedly, he left no will as to the disposal of his property. It was therefore necessary to have a valuation of the property, that it might be equally divided between Mrs. Lucretia and Master Andrew. I was immediately sent for, to be valued with the other property. Here again my feelings rose up in detestation of slavery. I had now a new conception of my degraded condition. Prior to this, I had become, if not insensible to my lot, at least partly so. I left Baltimore with a young heart overborne with sadness, and a soul full of apprehension. I took passage with Captain Rowe, in the schooner Wild Cat, and, after a sail of about twenty-four hours, I found myself near the place of my birth. I had now been absent from it almost, if not quite, five years. I, however, remembered the place very well. I was only about five years old when I left it, to go and live with my old master on Colonel Lloyd's plantation; so that I was now between ten and eleven years old.

We were all ranked together at the valuation. Men and women, old and young, married and single, were ranked with horses, sheep, and swine. There were horses and men, cattle and women, pigs and children, all holding the same rank in the scale of being, and were all subjected to the same narrow examination. Silvery-headed age and sprightly youth, maids and matrons, had to undergo the same indelicate inspection. At this moment, I saw more clearly than ever the brutalizing effects of slavery upon both slave and slaveholder.

After the valuation, then came the division. I have no language to express the high excitement and deep anxiety which were felt among us poor slaves during this time. Our fate for life was now to be decided. We had no more voice in that decision than the brutes among whom we were ranked. A single word from the white men was enough – against all our wishes, prayers, and entreaties – to sunder forever the dearest friends, dearest kindred, and strongest ties known to human beings. In addition to the pain of separation, there was the horrid dread of falling into the hands of Master Andrew. He was known to us all as being a most cruel wretch, – a common drunkard, who had, by his reckless mismanagement and profligate dissipation, already wasted a large portion of his father's property. We all felt that we might as well be sold at once to the Georgia traders, as to pass into his hands; for we knew that that would be our inevitable condition, – a condition held by us all in the utmost horror and dread.

I suffered more anxiety than most of my fellow-slaves. I had known what it was to be kindly treated; they had known nothing of the kind. They had seen little or nothing of the world. They were in very deed men and women of sorrow, and acquainted with grief. Their backs had been made familiar with the bloody lash, so that they had become callous; mine was yet tender; for while at Baltimore I got few whippings, and few slaves could boast of a kinder master and mistress than myself, and the thought of passing out of their hands into those of Master Andrew – a man who, but a few days before, to give me a sample of his bloody disposition, took my little brother by the throat, threw him on the ground, and with the heel of his boot stamped upon his head till the blood gushed from his nose and ears – was well calculated to make me anxious as to my fate. After he had committed this savage outrage upon my brother, he turned to me, and said that was the way he meant to serve me one of these days, – meaning, I suppose, when I came into his possession.

Thanks to a kind Providence, I fell to the portion of Mrs. Lucretia, and was sent immediately back to Baltimore, to live again in the family of Master Hugh. Their joy at my return equalled their sorrow at my departure. It was a glad day to me. I had escaped a worse than lion's jaws. I was absent from Baltimore, for the purpose of valuation and division, just about one month, and it seemed to have been six.

Very soon after my return to Baltimore, my mistress, Lucretia, died, leaving her husband and one child, Amanda; and in a very short time after her death, Master Andrew died. Now all the property of my old master, slaves included, was in the hands of strangers, – strangers who had had nothing to do with accumulating it. Not a slave was left free. All remained slaves, from the youngest to the oldest. If any one thing in my experience, more than another, served to deepen my conviction of the infernal character of slavery, and to fill me with unutterable loathing of slaveholders, it was their base ingratitude to my poor old grandmother. She had served my old master faithfully from youth to old age. She had been the source of all his wealth; she had peopled his plantation with slaves; she had become a great grandmother in his service. She had rocked him in infancy, attended him in childhood, served him through life, and at his death wiped from his icy brow the cold death-sweat, and closed his eyes forever. She was nevertheless left a slave – a slave for life – a slave in the hands of strangers; and in their hands she saw her children, her grandchildren, and her great-grandchildren, divided, like so many sheep, without being gratified with the small privilege of a single word, as to their or her own destiny. And, to cap the climax of their base ingratitude and fiendish barbarity, my grandmother, who was now very old, having outlived my old master and all his children, having seen the beginning and end of all of them, and her present owners finding she was of but little value, her frame already racked with the pains of old age, and complete helplessness fast stealing over her once active limbs, they took her to the woods, built her a little hut, put up a little mud-chimney, and then made her welcome to the privilege of supporting herself there in perfect loneliness; thus virtually turning her out to die! If my poor old grandmother now lives, she lives to suffer in utter loneliness; she lives to remember and mourn over the loss of children, the loss of grandchildren, and the loss of great-grandchildren. They are, in the language of the slave's poet, Whittier, –

Gone, gone, sold and gone
To the rice swamp dank and lone
Where the slave-whip ceaseless swings,
Where the noisome insect stings,
Where the fever-demon strews
Poison with the falling dews,
Where the sickly sunbeams glare
Through the hot and misty air: –
  Gone, gone, sold and gone
  To the rice swamp dank and lone,
  From Virginia hills and waters –
  Woe is me, my stolen daughters![1]

1. **Gone . . . daughters!:** From "The Farewell: Of a Virginia Slave Mother to Her Daughter Sold into Southern Bondage" (1835), by the poet and abolitionist John Greenleaf Whittier (1807–1882). See page 1220.

The hearth is desolate. The children, the unconscious children, who once sang and danced in her presence, are gone. She gropes her way, in the darkness of age, for a drink of water. Instead of the voices of her children she hears by day the moans of the dove, and by night the screams of the hideous owl. All is gloom. The grave is at the door. And now, when weighed down by the pains and aches of old age, when the head inclines to the feet, when the beginning and ending of human existence meet, and helpless infancy and painful old age combine together – at this time, this most needful time, the time for the exercise of that tenderness and affection which children only can exercise towards a declining parent – my poor old grandmother, the devoted mother of twelve children, is left all alone, in yonder little hut, before a few dim embers. She stands – she sits – she staggers – she falls – she groans – she dies – and there are none of her children or grandchildren present, to wipe from her wrinkled brow the cold sweat of death, or to place beneath the sod her fallen remains. Will not a righteous God visit for these things?[2]

In about two years after the death of Mrs. Lucretia, Master Thomas married his second wife. Her name was Rowena Hamilton. She was the eldest daughter of Mr. William Hamilton. Master now lived in St. Michael's. Not long after his marriage, a misunderstanding took place between himself and Master Hugh; and as a means of punishing his brother, he took me from him to live with himself at St. Michael's. Here I underwent another most painful separation. It, however, was not so severe as the one I dreaded at the division of property; for, during this interval, a great change had taken place in Master Hugh and his once kind and affectionate wife. The influence of brandy upon him, and of slavery upon her, had effected a disastrous change in the characters of both; so that, as far as they were concerned, I thought I had little to lose by the change. But it was not to them that I was attached. It was to those little Baltimore boys that I felt the strongest attachment. I had received many good lessons from them, and was still receiving them, and the thought of leaving them was painful indeed. I was leaving, too, without the hope of ever being allowed to return. Master Thomas had said he would never let me return again. The barrier betwixt himself and brother he considered impassable.

I then had to regret that I did not at least make the attempt to carry out my resolution to run away; for the chances of success are tenfold greater from the city than from the country.

I sailed from Baltimore for St. Michael's in the sloop Amanda, Captain Edward Dodson. On my passage, I paid particular attention to the direction which the steamboats took to go to Philadelphia. I found, instead of going down, on reaching North Point they went up the bay, in a north-easterly direction. I deemed this knowledge of the utmost importance. My determination to run away was again revived. I resolved to wait only so long as the offering of a favorable opportunity. When that came, I was determined to be off.

---

2. **Will not . . . these things?:** See Jeremiah 5:29: "Shall I not visit for these *things*? saith the Lord: shall not my soul be avenged on such a nation as this?"

Chapter IX

I have now reached a period of my life when I can give dates. I left Baltimore, and went to live with Master Thomas Auld, at St. Michael's, in March, 1832. It was now more than seven years since I lived with him in the family of my old master, on Colonel Lloyd's plantation. We of course were now almost entire strangers to each other. He was to me a new master, and I to him a new slave. I was ignorant of his temper and disposition; he was equally so of mine. A very short time, however, brought us into full acquaintance with each other. I was made acquainted with his wife not less than with himself. They were well matched, being equally mean and cruel. I was now, for the first time during a space of more than seven years, made to feel the painful gnawings of hunger – a something which I had not experienced before since I left Colonel Lloyd's plantation. It went hard enough with me then, when I could look back to no period at which I had enjoyed a sufficiency. It was tenfold harder after living in Master Hugh's family, where I had always had enough to eat, and of that which was good. I have said Master Thomas was a mean man. He was so. Not to give a slave enough to eat, is regarded as the most aggravated development of meanness even among slaveholders. The rule is, no matter how coarse the food, only let there be enough of it. This is the theory; and in the part of Maryland from which I came, it is the general practice, – though there are many exceptions. Master Thomas gave us enough of neither coarse nor fine food. There were four slaves of us in the kitchen – my sister Eliza, my aunt Priscilla, Henny, and myself; and we were allowed less than a half of a bushel of corn-meal per week, and very little else, either in the shape of meat or vegetables. It was not enough for us to subsist upon. We were therefore reduced to the wretched necessity of living at the expense of our neighbors. This we did by begging and stealing, whichever came handy in the time of need, the one being considered as legitimate as the other. A great many times have we poor creatures been nearly perishing with hunger, when food in abundance lay mouldering in the safe and smoke-house, and our pious mistress was aware of the fact; and yet that mistress and her husband would kneel every morning, and pray that God would bless them in basket and store!

Bad as all slaveholders are, we seldom meet one destitute of every element of character commanding respect. My master was one of this rare sort. I do not know of one single noble act ever performed by him. The leading trait in his character was meanness; and if there were any other element in his nature, it was made subject to this. He was mean; and, like most other mean men, he lacked the ability to conceal his meanness. Captain Auld was not born a slaveholder. He had been a poor man, master only of a Bay craft. He came into possession of all his slaves by marriage; and of all men, adopted slaveholders are the worst. He was cruel, but cowardly. He commanded without firmness. In the enforcement of his rules, he was at times rigid, and at times lax. At times, he spoke to his slaves with the firmness of Napoleon and the fury of a demon; at other times, he might well be mistaken for an inquirer who had lost his way. He did nothing of himself. He might have passed for a lion, but for his ears. In all things noble which he attempted, his own meanness shone most conspicuous. His airs, words, and actions, were the airs, words, and actions of born slaveholders, and, being assumed, were awkward enough. He was not even a good imitator. He possessed all the disposition to deceive, but wanted the power. Having no resources within himself, he was compelled to be the copyist of many, and being such, he was forever the victim of inconsistency; and of consequence he was an object of contempt, and was held as such even by his slaves. The luxury of having slaves of his own to wait upon him was something new and unprepared for. He was a slaveholder without the ability to hold slaves. He found himself incapable of managing his slaves either by force, fear, or fraud. We seldom called him "master;" we generally called him "Captain Auld," and were hardly disposed to title him at all. I doubt not that our conduct had much to do with making him appear awkward, and of consequence fretful. Our want of reverence for him must have perplexed him greatly. He wished to have us call him master, but lacked the firmness necessary to command us to do so. His wife used to insist upon our calling him so, but to no purpose. In August, 1832, my master attended a Methodist camp-meeting held in the Bay-side, Talbot county, and there experienced religion. I indulged a faint hope that his conversion would lead him to emancipate his slaves, and that, if he did not do this, it would, at any rate, make him more kind and humane. I was disappointed in both these respects. It neither made him to be humane to his slaves, nor to emancipate them. If it had any effect on his character, it made him more cruel and hateful in all his ways; for I believe him to have been a much worse man after his conversion than before. Prior to his conversion, he relied upon his own depravity to shield and sustain him in his savage barbarity; but after his conversion, he found religious sanction and support for his slaveholding cruelty. He made the greatest pretensions to piety. His house was the house of prayer. He prayed morning, noon, and night. He very soon distinguished himself among his brethren, and was soon made a class-leader and exhorter. His activity in revivals was great, and he proved himself an instrument in the hands of the church in converting many souls. His house was the preacher's home. They used to take great pleasure in coming there to put up; for while he starved us, he stuffed them. We have had three or four preachers there at a time. The names of those who used to come most frequently while I lived there, were Mr. Storks, Mr. Ewery, Mr. Humphry, and Mr. Hickey. I have also seen Mr. George Cookman at our house. We slaves loved Mr. Cookman. We believed him to be a good man. We thought him instrumental in getting Mr. Samuel Harrison, a very rich slaveholder, to emancipate his slaves; and by some means got the impression that he was laboring to effect the emancipation of all the slaves. When he was at our house, we were sure to be called in to prayers. When the others were there, we were sometimes called in and sometimes not. Mr. Cookman took more notice of us than either of the other ministers. He could not come among us without betraying his sympathy for us, and, stupid as we were, we had the sagacity to see it.

While I lived with my master in St. Michael's, there was a white young man, a Mr. Wilson, who proposed to keep a Sabbath school for the instruction of such slaves as might be disposed to learn to read the New Testament. We met but three times, when Mr. West and Mr. Fairbanks, both class-leaders, with many others, came upon us with sticks and other missiles, drove us off, and forbade us to meet again. Thus ended our little Sabbath school in the pious town of St. Michael's.

I have said my master found religious sanction for his cruelty. As an example, I will state one of many facts going to prove the charge. I have seen him tie up a lame young woman, and whip her with a heavy cowskin upon her naked shoulders, causing the warm red blood to drip; and, in justification of the bloody deed, he would quote this passage of Scripture – "He that knoweth his master's will, and doeth it not, shall be beaten with many stripes."[1]

Master would keep his lacerated young woman tied up in this horrid situation four or five hours at a time. I have known him to tie her up early in the morning, and whip her before breakfast; leave her, go to his store, return at dinner, and whip her again, cutting her in the places already made raw with his cruel lash. The secret of master's cruelty toward "Henny" is found in the fact of her being almost helpless. When quite a child, she fell into the fire, and burned herself horribly. Her hands were so burnt that she never got the use of them. She could do very little but bear heavy burdens. She was to master a bill of expense; and as he was a mean man, she was a constant offence to him. He seemed desirous of getting the poor girl out of existence. He gave her away once to his sister; but, being a poor gift, she was not disposed to keep her. Finally, my benevolent master, to use his own words, "set her adrift to take care of herself." Here was a recently-converted man, holding on upon the mother, and at the same time turning out her helpless child, to starve and die! Master Thomas was one of the many pious slaveholders who hold slaves for the very charitable purpose of taking care of them.

My master and myself had quite a number of differences. He found me unsuitable to his purpose. My city life, he said, had had a very pernicious effect upon me. It had almost ruined me for every good purpose, and fitted me for every thing which was bad. One of my greatest faults was that of letting his horse run away, and go down to his father-in-law's farm, which was about five miles from St. Michael's. I would then have to go after it. My reason for this kind of carelessness, or carefulness, was, that I could always get something to eat when I went there. Master William Hamilton, my master's father-in-law, always gave his slaves enough to eat. I never left there hungry, no matter how great the need of my speedy return. Master Thomas at length said he would stand it no longer. I had lived with him nine months, during which time he had given me a number of severe whippings, all to no good purpose. He resolved to put me out, as he said, to be broken; and, for this purpose, he let me for one year to a man named Edward Covey. Mr. Covey was a poor man, a farm-renter. He rented the place upon which he lived, as also the hands with which he tilled it. Mr. Covey had acquired a very high reputation for breaking young slaves, and this reputation was of immense value to him. It enabled him to get his farm tilled with much less expense to himself than he could have had it done without such a reputation. Some slaveholders thought it not much loss to allow Mr. Covey to have their slaves one year, for the sake of the training to which they were subjected, without any other compensation. He could hire young help with great ease, in consequence of this reputation. Added to the natural good qualities of Mr. Covey, he was a professor of religion – a pious soul – a member and a class-leader in the Methodist church. All of this added weight to his reputation as a "nigger-breaker." I was aware of all the facts, having been made acquainted with them by a young man who had lived

1. **"He . . . many stripes"**: Luke 12:47.

there. I nevertheless made the change gladly; for I was sure of getting enough to eat, which is not the smallest consideration to a hungry man.

Chapter X

I left Master Thomas's house, and went to live with Mr. Covey, on the 1st of January, 1833. I was now, for the first time in my life, a field hand. In my new employment, I found myself even more awkward than a country boy appeared to be in a large city. I had been at my new home but one week before Mr. Covey gave me a very severe whipping, cutting my back causing the blood to run, and raising ridges on my flesh as large as my little finger. The details of this affair are as follows: Mr. Covey sent me, very early in the morning of one of our coldest days in the month of January, to the woods, to get a load of wood. He gave me a team of unbroken oxen. He told me which was the in-hand ox, and which the off-hand one. He then tied the end of a large rope around the horns of the in-hand ox, and gave me the other end of it, and told me, if the oxen started to run, that I must hold on upon the rope. I had never driven oxen before, and of course I was very awkward. I, however, succeeded in getting to the edge of the woods with little difficulty; but I had got a very few rods into the woods, when the oxen took fright, and started full tilt, carrying the cart against trees, and over stumps, in the most frightful manner. I expected every moment that my brains would be dashed out against the trees. After running thus for a considerable distance, they finally upset the cart, dashing it with great force against a tree, and threw themselves into a dense thicket. How I escaped death, I do not know. There I was, entirely alone, in a thick wood, in a place new to me. My cart was upset and shattered, my oxen were entangled among the young trees, and there was none to help me. After a long spell of effort, I succeeded in getting my cart righted, my oxen disentangled, and again yoked to the cart. I now proceeded with my team to the place where I had, the day before, been chopping wood, and loaded my cart pretty heavily, thinking in this way to tame my oxen. I then proceeded on my way home. I had now consumed one half of the day. I got out of the woods safely, and now felt out of danger. I stopped my oxen to open the woods gate; and just as I did so, before I could get hold of my ox-rope, the oxen again started, rushed through the gate, catching it between the wheel and the body of the cart, tearing it to pieces, and coming within a few inches of crushing me against the gate-post. Thus twice, in one short day, I escaped death by the merest chance. On my return, I told Mr. Covey what had happened and how it happened. He ordered me to return to the woods again immediately. I did so, and he followed on after me. Just as I got into the woods, he came up and told me to stop my cart, and that he would teach me how to trifle away my time, and break gates. He then went to a large gum tree, and with his axe cut three large switches, and, after trimming them up neatly with his pocket-knife, he ordered me to take off my clothes. I made him no answer, but stood with my clothes on. He repeated his order. I still made him no answer, nor did I move to strip myself. Upon this he rushed at me with the fierceness of a tiger, tore off my clothes, and lashed me till he had worn out his switches, cutting me so savagely as to leave the marks visible for a long time after. This whipping was the first of a number just like it, and for similar offences.

I lived with Mr. Covey one year. During the first six months, of that year, scarce a week passed without his whipping me. I was seldom free from a sore back. My awkwardness was almost always his excuse for whipping me. We were worked fully up to the point of endurance. Long before day we were up, our horses fed, and by the first approach of day we were off to the field with our hoes and ploughing teams. Mr. Covey gave us enough to eat, but scarce time to eat it. We were often less than five minutes taking our meals. We were often in the field from the first approach of day till its last lingering ray had left us; and at saving-fodder time, midnight often caught us in the field binding blades.

Covey would be out with us. The way he used to stand it, was this. He would spend the most of his afternoons in bed. He would then come out fresh in the evening, ready to urge us on with his words, example, and frequently with the whip. Mr. Covey was one of the few slaveholders who could and did work with his hands. He was a hard-working man. He knew by himself just what a man or a boy could do. There was no deceiving him. His work went on in his absence almost as well as in his presence; and he had the faculty of making us feel that he was ever present with us. This he did by surprising us. He seldom approached the spot where we were at work openly, if he could do it secretly. He always aimed at taking us by surprise. Such was his cunning, that we used to call him, among ourselves, "the snake." When we were at work in the cornfield, he would sometimes crawl on his hands and knees to avoid detection, and all at once he would rise nearly in our midst, and scream out, "Ha, ha! Come, come! Dash on, dash on!" This being his mode of attack, it was never safe to stop a single minute. His comings were like a thief in the night. He appeared to us as being ever at hand. He was under every tree, behind every stump, in every bush, and at every window, on the plantation. He would sometimes mount his horse, as if bound to St. Michael's, a distance of seven miles, and in half an hour afterwards you would see him coiled up in the corner of the wood-fence, watching every motion of the slaves. He would, for this purpose, leave his horse tied up in the woods. Again, he would sometimes walk up to us, and give us orders as though he was upon the point of starting on a long journey, turn his back upon us, and make as though he was going to the house to get ready; and, before he would get half way thither, he would turn short and crawl into a fence-corner, or behind some tree, and there watch us till the going down of the sun.

Mr. Covey's *forte* consisted in his power to deceive. His life was devoted to planning and perpetrating the grossest deceptions. Every thing he possessed in the shape of learning or religion, he made conform to his disposition to deceive. He seemed to think himself equal to deceiving the Almighty. He would make a short prayer in the morning, and a long prayer at night; and, strange as it may seem, few men would at times appear more devotional than he. The exercises of his family devotions were always commenced with singing; and, as he was a very poor singer himself, the duty of raising the hymn generally came upon me. He would read his hymn, and nod at me to commence. I would at times do so; at others, I would not. My non-compliance would almost always produce much confusion. To show himself independent of me, he would start and stagger through with his hymn in the most discordant manner. In this state of mind, he prayed with more than ordinary spirit. Poor man! such was his disposition, and success at deceiving, I do verily believe that he sometimes deceived himself into the solemn belief, that he was a sincere worshipper of the most high God; and this, too, at a time when he may be said to have been guilty of compelling his woman slave to commit the sin of adultery. The facts in the case are these: Mr. Covey was a poor man; he was just commencing in life; he was only able to buy one slave; and, shocking as is the fact, he bought her, as he said, for a *breeder*. This woman was named Caroline. Mr. Covey bought her from Mr. Thomas Lowe, about six miles from St. Michael's. She was a large, able-bodied woman, about twenty years old. She had already given birth to one child, which proved her to be just what he wanted. After buying her, he hired a married man of Mr. Samuel Harrison, to live with him one year; and him he used to fasten up with her every night! The result was, that, at the end of the year, the miserable woman gave birth to twins. At this result Mr. Covey seemed to be highly pleased, both with the man and the wretched woman. Such was his joy, and that of his wife, that nothing they could do for Caroline during her confinement was too good, or too hard, to be done. The children were regarded as being quite an addition to his wealth.

If at any one time of my life more than another, I was made to drink the bitterest dregs of slavery, that time was during the first six months of my stay with Mr. Covey. We were worked in all weathers. It was never too hot or too cold; it could never rain, blow, hail, or snow, too hard for us to work in the field. Work, work, work, was scarcely more the order of the day than of the night. The longest days were too short for him, and the shortest nights too long for him. I was somewhat unmanageable when I first went there, but a few months of this discipline tamed me. Mr. Covey succeeded in breaking me. I was broken in body, soul, and spirit. My natural elasticity was crushed, my intellect languished, the disposition to read departed, the cheerful spark that lingered about my eye died; the dark night of slavery closed in upon me; and behold a man transformed into a brute!

Sunday was my only leisure time. I spent this in a sort of beast-like stupor, between sleep and wake, under some large tree. At times I would rise up, a flash of energetic freedom would dart through my soul, accompanied with a faint beam of hope, that flickered for a moment, and then vanished. I sank down again, mourning over my wretched condition. I was sometimes prompted to take my life, and that of Covey, but was prevented by a combination of hope and fear. My sufferings on this plantation seem now like a dream rather than a stern reality.

Our house stood within a few rods of the Chesapeake Bay, whose broad bosom was ever white with sails from every quarter of the habitable globe. Those beautiful vessels, robed in purest white, so delightful to the eye of freemen, were to me so many shrouded ghosts, to terrify and torment me with thoughts of my wretched condition. I have often, in the deep stillness of a summer's Sabbath, stood all alone upon the lofty banks of that noble bay, and traced, with saddened heart and tearful eye, the countless number of sails moving off to the mighty ocean. The sight of these always affected me powerfully. My thoughts would compel utterance; and there, with no audience but the Almighty, I would pour out my soul's complaint, in my rude way, with an apostrophe to the moving multitude of ships: –

"You are loosed from your moorings, and are free; I am fast in my chains, and am a slave! You move merrily before the gentle gale, and I sadly before the bloody whip! You are freedom's swift-winged angels, that fly round the world; I am confined in bands of iron! O that I were free! O, that I were on one of your gallant decks, and under your protecting wing! Alas! betwixt me and you, the turbid waters roll. Go on, go on. O that I could also go! Could I but swim! If I could fly! O, why was I born a man, of whom to make a brute! The glad ship is gone; she hides in the dim distance. I am left in the hottest hell of unending slavery. O God, save me! God, deliver me! Let me be free! Is there any God? Why am I a slave? I will run away. I will not stand it. Get caught, or get clear! I'll try it. I had as well die with ague as the fever. I have only one life to lose. I had as well be killed running as die standing. Only think of it; one hundred miles straight north, and I am free! Try it? Yes! God helping me, I will. It cannot be that I shall live and die a slave. I will take to the water. This very bay shall yet bear me into freedom. The steamboats steered in a north-east course from North Point. I will do the same; and when I get to the head of the bay, I will turn my canoe adrift, and walk straight through Delaware into Pennsylvania. When I get there, I shall not be required to have a pass; I can travel without being disturbed. Let but the first opportunity offer, and, come what will, I am off. Meanwhile, I will try to bear up under the yoke. I am not the only slave in the world. Why should I fret? I can bear as much as any of them. Besides, I am but a boy, and all boys are bound to some one. It may be that my misery in slavery will only increase my happiness when I get free. There is a better day coming."

Thus I used to think, and thus I used to speak to myself; goaded almost to madness at one moment, and at the next reconciling myself to my wretched lot.

I have already intimated that my condition was much worse, during the first six months of my stay at Mr. Covey's, than in the last six. The circumstances leading to the change in Mr. Covey's course toward me form an epoch in my humble history. You have seen how a man was made a slave; you shall see how a slave was made a man. On one of the hottest days of the month of August, 1833, Bill Smith, William Hughes, a slave named Eli, and myself, were engaged in fanning wheat. Hughes was clearing the fanned wheat from before the fan, Eli was turning, Smith was feeding, and I was carrying wheat to the fan. The work was simple, requiring strength rather than intellect; yet, to one entirely unused to such work, it came very hard. About three o'clock of that day, I broke down; my strength failed me; I was seized with a violent aching of the head, attended with extreme dizziness; I trembled in every limb. Finding what was coming, I nerved myself up, feeling it would never do to stop work. I stood as long as I could stagger to the hopper with grain. When I could stand no longer, I fell, and felt as if held down by an immense weight. The fan of course stopped; every one had his own work to do; and no one could do the work of the other, and have his own go on at the same time.

Mr. Covey was at the house, about one hundred yards from the treading-yard where we were fanning. On hearing the fan stop, he left immediately, and came to the spot where we were. He hastily inquired what the matter was. Bill answered that I was sick, and there was no one to bring wheat to the fan. I had by this time crawled away under the side of the post and rail-fence by which the yard was enclosed, hoping to find relief by getting out of the sun. He then asked where I was. He was told by one of the hands. He came to the spot, and, after looking at me awhile, asked me what was the matter. I told him as well as I could, for I scarce had strength to speak. He then gave me a savage kick in the side, and told me to get up. I tried to do so, but fell back in the attempt. He gave me another kick, and again told me to rise. I again tried, and succeeded in gaining my feet; but, stooping to get the tub with which I was feeding the fan, I again staggered and fell. While down in this situation, Mr. Covey took up the hickory slat with which Hughes had been striking off the half-bushel measure, and with it gave me a heavy blow upon the head, making a large wound, and the blood ran freely; and with this again told me to get up. I made no effort to comply, having now made up my mind to let him do his worst. In a short time after receiving this blow, my head grew better. Mr. Covey had now left me to my fate. At this moment I resolved, for the first time, to go to my master, enter a complaint, and ask his protection. In order to [do] this, I must that afternoon walk seven miles; and this, under the circumstances, was truly a severe undertaking. I was exceedingly feeble; made so as much by the kicks and blows which I received, as by the severe fit of sickness to which I had been subjected. I, however, watched my chance, while Covey was looking in an opposite direction, and started for St. Michael's. I succeeded in getting a considerable distance on my way to the woods, when Covey discovered me, and called after me to come back, threatening what he would do if I did not come. I disregarded both his calls and his threats, and made my way to the woods as fast as my feeble state would allow; and thinking I might be overhauled by him if I kept the road, I walked through the woods, keeping far enough from the road to avoid detection, and near enough to prevent losing my way. I had not gone far before my little strength again failed me. I could go no farther. I fell down, and lay for a considerable time. The blood was yet oozing from the wound on my head. For a time I thought I should bleed to death; and think now that I should have done so, but that the blood so matted my hair as to stop the wound. After lying there about three quarters of an hour, I nerved myself up again, and started on my way, through bogs and briers, barefooted and bareheaded, tearing my feet sometimes at nearly every step; and after a journey of about seven miles, occupying some five hours to perform it, I arrived at master's store. I then presented an appearance enough to affect any but a heart of iron. From the crown of my head to my feet, I was covered with blood. My hair was all clotted with dust and blood; my shirt was stiff with blood. My legs and feet were torn in sundry places with briers and thorns, and were also covered with blood. I suppose I looked like a man who had escaped a den of wild beasts, and barely escaped them. In this state I appeared before my master, humbly entreating him to interpose his authority for my protection. I told him all the circumstances as well as I could, and it seemed, as I spoke, at times to affect him. He would then walk the floor, and seek to justify Covey by saying he expected I deserved it. He asked me what I wanted. I told him, to let me get a new home; that as sure as I lived with Mr. Covey again, I should live with but to die with him; that Covey would surely kill me; he was in a fair way for it. Master Thomas ridiculed the idea that there was any danger of Mr. Covey's killing me, and said that he knew Mr. Covey; that he was a good man, and that he could not think of taking me from him; that, should he do so, he would lose the whole year's wages; that I belonged to Mr. Covey for one year, and that I must go back to him, come what might; and that I must not trouble him with any more stories, or that he would himself *get hold of me*. After threatening me thus, he gave me a very large dose of salts, telling me that I might remain in St. Michael's that night, (it being quite late,) but that I must be off back to Mr. Covey's early in the morning; and that if I did not, he would *get hold of me*, which meant that he would whip me. I remained all night, and, according to his orders, I started off to Covey's in the morning, (Saturday morning,) wearied in body and broken in spirit. I got no supper that night, or breakfast that morning. I reached Covey's about nine o'clock; and just as I was getting over the fence that divided Mrs. Kemp's fields from ours, out ran Covey with his cowskin, to give me another whipping. Before he could reach me, I succeeded in getting to the cornfield; and as the corn was very high, it afforded me the means of hiding. He seemed very angry, and searched for me a long time. My behavior was altogether unaccountable. He finally gave up the chase, thinking, I suppose, that I must come home for something to eat; he would give himself no further trouble in looking for me. I spent that day mostly in the woods, having the alternative before me, – to go home and be whipped to death, or stay in the woods and be starved to death. That night, I fell in with Sandy Jenkins, a slave with whom I was somewhat acquainted. Sandy had a free wife who lived about four miles from Mr. Covey's; and it being Saturday, he was on his way to see her. I told him my circumstances, and he very kindly invited me to go home with him. I went home with him, and talked this whole matter over, and got his advice as to what course it was best for me to pursue. I found Sandy an old adviser. He told me, with great solemnity, I must go back to Covey; but that before I went, I must go with him into another part of the woods, where there was a certain *root*, which, if I would take some of it with me, carrying it *always on my right side*, would render it impossible for Mr. Covey, or any other white man, to whip me. He said he had carried it for years; and since he had done so, he had never received a blow, and never expected to while he carried it. I at first rejected the idea, that the simple carrying of a root in my pocket would have any such effect as he had said, and was not disposed to take it; but Sandy impressed the necessity with much earnestness, telling me it could do no harm, if it did no good. To please him, I at length took the root, and, according to his direction, carried it upon my right side. This was Sunday morning. I immediately started for home; and upon entering the yard gate, out came Mr. Covey on his way to meeting. He spoke to me very kindly, made me drive the pigs from a lot near by, and passed on towards the church. Now, this singular conduct of Mr. Covey really made me begin to think that there was something in the *root* which Sandy had given me; and had it been on any other day than Sunday, I could have attributed the conduct to no other cause than the influence of that root; and as it was, I was half inclined to think the *root* to be something more than I at first had taken it to be. All went well till Monday morning. On this morning, the virtue of the *root* was fully tested. Long before daylight, I was called to go and rub, curry, and feed, the horses. I obeyed, and was glad to obey. But whilst thus engaged, whilst in the act of throwing down some blades from the loft, Mr. Covey entered the stable with a long rope; and just as I was half out of the loft, he caught hold of my legs, and was about tying me. As soon as I found what he was up to, I gave a sudden spring, and as I did so, he holding to my legs, I was brought sprawling on the stable floor. Mr. Covey seemed now to think he had me, and could do what he pleased; but at this moment – from whence came the spirit I don't know – I resolved to fight; and, suiting my action to the resolution, I seized Covey hard by the throat; and as I did so, I rose. He held on to me, and I to him. My resistance was so entirely unexpected, that

Covey seemed taken all aback. He trembled like a leaf. This gave me assurance, and I held him uneasy, causing the blood to run where I touched him with the ends of my fingers. Mr. Covey soon called out to Hughes for help. Hughes came, and, while Covey held me, attempted to tie my right hand. While he was in the act of doing so, I watched my chance, and gave him a heavy kick close under the ribs. This kick fairly sickened Hughes, so that he left me in the hands of Mr. Covey. This kick had the effect of not only weakening Hughes, but Covey also. When he saw Hughes bending over with pain, his courage quailed. He asked me if I meant to persist in my resistance. I told him I did, come what might; that he had used me like a brute for six months, and that I was determined to be used so no longer. With that, he strove to drag me to a stick that was lying just out of the stable door. He meant to knock me down. But just as he was leaning over to get the stick, I seized him with both hands by his collar, and brought him by a sudden snatch to the ground. By this time, Bill came. Covey called upon him for assistance. Bill wanted to know what he could do. Covey said, "Take hold of him, take hold of him!" Bill said his master hired him out to work, and not to help to whip me; so he left Covey and myself to fight our own battle out. We were at it for nearly two hours. Covey at length let me go, puffing and blowing at a great rate, saying that if I had not resisted, he would not have whipped me half so much. The truth was, that he had not whipped me at all. I considered him as getting entirely the worst end of the bargain; for he had drawn no blood from me, but I had from him. The whole six months afterwards, that I spent with Mr. Covey, he never laid the weight of his finger upon me in anger. He would occasionally say, he didn't want to get hold of me again. "No," thought I, "you need not; for you will come off worse than you did before."

This battle with Mr. Covey was the turning-point in my career as a slave. It rekindled the few expiring embers of freedom, and revived within me a sense of my own manhood. It recalled the departed self-confidence, and inspired me again with a determination to be free. The gratification afforded by the triumph was a full compensation for whatever else might follow, even death itself. He only can understand the deep satisfaction which I experienced, who has himself repelled by force the bloody arm of slavery. I felt as I never felt before. It was a glorious resurrection, from the tomb of slavery, to the heaven of freedom. My long-crushed spirit rose, cowardice departed, bold defiance took its place; and I now resolved that, however long I might remain a slave in form, the day had passed forever when I could be a slave in fact. I did not hesitate to let it be known of me, that the white man who expected to succeed in whipping, must also succeed in killing me.

From this time I was never again what might be called fairly whipped, though I remained a slave four years afterwards. I had several fights, but was never whipped.

It was for a long time a matter of surprise to me why Mr. Covey did not immediately have me taken by the constable to the whipping-post, and there regularly whipped for the crime of raising my hand against a white man in defence of myself. And the only explanation I can now think of does not entirely satisfy me; but such as it is, I will give it. Mr. Covey enjoyed the most unbounded reputation for being a first-rate overseer and negro-breaker. It was of considerable importance to him. That reputation was at stake; and had he sent me – a boy about sixteen years old – to the public whipping-post, his reputation would have been lost; so, to save his reputation, he suffered me to go unpunished.

My term of actual service to Mr. Edward Covey ended on Christmas day, 1833. The days between Christmas and New Year's day are allowed as holidays; and, accordingly, we were not required to perform any labor, more than to feed and take care of the stock. This time we regarded as our own, by the grace of our masters; and we therefore used or abused it nearly as we pleased. Those of us who had families at a distance, were generally allowed to spend the whole six days in their society. This time, however, was spent in various ways. The staid, sober, thinking and industrious ones of our number would employ themselves in making corn-brooms, mats, horse-collars, and baskets; and another class of us would spend the time in hunting opossums, hares, and coons. But by far the larger part engaged in such sports and merriments as playing ball, wrestling, running footraces, fiddling, dancing, and drinking whisky; and this latter mode of spending the time was by far the most agreeable to the feelings of our masters. A slave who would work during the holidays was considered by our masters as scarcely deserving them. He was regarded as one who rejected the favor of his master. It was deemed a disgrace not to get drunk at Christmas; and he was regarded as lazy indeed, who had not provided himself with the necessary means, during the year, to get whisky enough to last him through Christmas.

From what I know of the effect of these holidays upon the slave, I believe them to be among the most effective means in the hands of the slaveholder in keeping down the spirit of insurrection. Were the slaveholders at once to abandon this practice, I have not the slightest doubt it would lead to an immediate insurrection among the slaves. These holidays serve as conductors, or safety-valves, to carry off the rebellious spirit of enslaved humanity. But for these, the slave would be forced up to the wildest desperation; and woe betide the slaveholder, the day he ventures to remove or hinder the operation of those conductors! I warn him that, in such an event, a spirit will go forth in their midst, more to be dreaded than the most appalling earthquake.

The holidays are part and parcel of the gross fraud, wrong, and inhumanity of slavery. They are professedly a custom established by the benevolence of the slaveholders; but I undertake to say, it is the result of selfishness, and one of the grossest frauds committed upon the downtrodden slave. They do not give the slaves this time because they would not like to have their work during its continuance, but because they know it would be unsafe to deprive them of it. This will be seen by the fact, that the slaveholders like to have their slaves spend those days just in such a manner as to make them as glad of their ending as of their beginning. Their object seems to be, to disgust their slaves with freedom, by plunging them into the lowest depths of dissipation. For instance, the slaveholders not only like to see the slave drink of his own accord, but will adopt various plans to make him drunk. One plan is, to make bets on their slaves, as to who can drink the most whisky without getting drunk; and in this way they succeed in getting whole multitudes to drink to excess. Thus, when the slave asks for virtuous freedom, the cunning slaveholder, knowing his ignorance, cheats him with a dose of vicious dissipation, artfully labelled with the name of liberty. The most of us used to drink it down, and the result was just what might be supposed: many of us were led to think that there was little to choose between liberty and slavery. We felt, and very properly too, that we had almost as well be slaves to man as to rum. So, when the holidays ended, we staggered up from the filth of our wallowing, took a long breath, and marched to the field, – feeling, upon the whole, rather glad to go, from what our master had deceived us into a belief was freedom, back to the arms of slavery.

I have said that this mode of treatment is a part of the whole system of fraud and inhumanity of slavery. It is so. The mode here adopted to disgust the slave with freedom, by allowing him to see only the abuse of it, is carried out in other things. For instance, a slave loves molasses; he steals some. His master, in many cases, goes off to town, and buys a large quantity; he returns, takes his whip, and commands the slave to eat the molasses, until the poor fellow is made sick at the very mention of it. The same mode is sometimes adopted to make the slaves refrain from asking for more food than their regular allowance. A slave runs through his allowance, and applies for more. His master is enraged at him; but, not willing to send him off without food, gives him more than is necessary, and compels him to eat it within a given time. Then, if he complains that he cannot eat it, he is said to be satisfied neither full or fasting, and is whipped for being hard to please! I have an abundance of such illustrations of the same principle, drawn from my own observation, but think the cases I have cited sufficient. The practice is a very common one.

On the first of January, 1834, I left Mr. Covey, and went to live with Mr. William Freeland, who lived about three miles from St. Michael's. I soon found Mr. Freeland a very different man from Mr. Covey. Though not rich, he was what would be called an educated southern gentleman. Mr. Covey, as I have shown, was a well-trained negro-breaker and slavedriver. The former (slaveholder though he was) seemed to possess some regard for honor, some reverence for justice, and some respect for humanity. The latter seemed totally insensible to all such sentiments. Mr. Freeland had many of the faults peculiar to slaveholders, such as being very passionate and fretful; but I must do him the justice to say, that he was exceedingly free from those degrading vices to which Mr. Covey was constantly addicted. The one was open and frank, and we always knew where to find him. The other was a most artful deceiver, and could be understood only by such as were skilful enough to detect his cunningly-devised frauds. Another advantage I gained in my new master was, he made no pretensions to, or profession of, religion; and this, in my opinion, was truly a great advantage. I assert most unhesitatingly, that the religion of the south is a mere covering for the most horrid crimes, – a justifier of the most appalling barbarity, – a sanctifier of the most hateful frauds, – and a dark shelter under which the darkest, foulest, grossest, and most infernal deeds of slaveholders find the strongest protection. Were I to be again reduced to the chains of slavery, next to that enslavement, I should regard being the slave of a religious master the greatest calamity that could befall me. For of all slaveholders with whom I have ever met, religious slaveholders are the worst. I have ever found them the meanest and basest, the most cruel and cowardly, of all others. It was my unhappy lot not only to belong to a religious slaveholder, but to live in a community of such religionists. Very near Mr. Freeland lived the

Rev. Daniel Weeden, and in the same neighborhood lived the Rev. Rigby Hopkins. These were members and ministers in the Reformed Methodist Church. Mr. Weeden owned, among others, a woman slave, whose name I have forgotten. This woman's back, for weeks, was kept literally raw, made so by the lash of this merciless, *religious* wretch. He used to hire hands. His maxim was, Behave well or behave ill, it is the duty of a master occasionally to whip a slave, to remind him of his master's authority. Such was his theory, and such his practice.

Mr. Hopkins was even worse than Mr. Weeden. His chief boast was his ability to manage slaves. The peculiar feature of his government was that of whipping slaves in advance of deserving it. He always managed to have one or more of his slaves to whip every Monday morning. He did this to alarm their fears, and strike terror into those who escaped. His plan was to whip for the smallest offences, to prevent the commission of large ones. Mr. Hopkins could always find some excuse for whipping a slave. It would astonish one, unaccustomed to a slaveholding life, to see with what wonderful ease a slaveholder can find things, of which to make occasion to whip a slave. A mere look, word, or motion, – a mistake, accident, or want of power, – are all matters for which a slave may be whipped at any time. Does a slave look dissatisfied? It is said, he has the devil in him, and it must be whipped out. Does he speak loudly when spoken to by his master? Then he is getting high-minded, and should be taken down a buttonhole lower. Does he forget to pull off his hat at the approach of a white person? Then he is wanting in reverence, and should be whipped for it. Does he ever venture to vindicate his conduct, when censured for it? Then he is guilty of impudence, – one of the greatest crimes of which a slave can be guilty. Does he ever venture to suggest a different mode of doing things from that pointed out by his master? He is indeed presumptuous, and getting above himself; and nothing less than a flogging will do for him. Does he, while ploughing, break a plough, – or, while hoeing, break a hoe? It is owing to his carelessness, and for it a slave must always be whipped. Mr. Hopkins could always find something of this sort to justify the use of the lash, and he seldom failed to embrace such opportunities. There was not a man in the whole county, with whom the slaves who had the getting their own home, would not prefer to live, rather than with this Rev. Mr. Hopkins. And yet there was not a man any where round, who made higher professions of religion, or was more active in revivals, – more attentive to the class, love-feast, prayer and preaching meetings, or more devotional in his family, – that prayed earlier, later, louder, and longer, – than this same reverend slave-driver, Rigby Hopkins.

But to return to Mr. Freeland, and to my experience while in his employment. He, like Mr. Covey, gave us enough to eat; but, unlike Mr. Covey, he also gave us sufficient time to take our meals. He worked us hard, but always between sunrise and sunset. He required a good deal of work to be done, but gave us good tools with which to work. His farm was large, but he employed hands enough to work it, and with ease, compared with many of his neighbors. My treatment, while in his employment, was heavenly, compared with what I experienced at the hands of Mr. Edward Covey.

Mr. Freeland was himself the owner of but two slaves. Their names were Henry Harris and John Harris. The rest of his hands he hired. These consisted of myself,

Sandy Jenkins,[1] and Handy Caldwell. Henry and John were quite intelligent, and in a very little while after I went there, I succeeded in creating in them a strong desire to learn how to read. This desire soon sprang up in the others also. They very soon mustered up some old spelling-books, and nothing would do but that I must keep a Sabbath school. I agreed to do so, and accordingly devoted my Sundays to teaching these my loved fellow-slaves how to read. Neither of them knew his letters when I went there. Some of the slaves of the neighboring farms found what was going on, and also availed themselves of this little opportunity to learn to read. It was understood, among all who came, that there must be as little display about it as possible. It was necessary to keep our religious masters at St. Michael's unacquainted with the fact, that, instead of spending the Sabbath in wrestling, boxing, and drinking whisky, we were trying to learn how to read the will of God; for they had much rather see us engaged in those degrading sports, than to see us behaving like intellectual, moral, and accountable beings. My blood boils as I think of the bloody manner in which Messrs. Wright Fairbanks and Garrison West, both class-leaders, in connection with many others, rushed in upon us with sticks and stones, and broke up our virtuous little Sabbath school, at St. Michael's – all calling themselves Christians! humble followers of the Lord Jesus Christ! But I am again digressing.

I held my Sabbath school at the house of a free colored man, whose name I deem it imprudent to mention; for should it be known, it might embarrass him greatly, though the crime of holding the school was committed ten years ago. I had at one time over forty scholars, and those of the right sort, ardently desiring to learn. They were of all ages, though mostly men and women. I look back to those Sundays with an amount of pleasure not to be expressed. They were great days to my soul. The work of instructing my dear fellow-slaves was the sweetest engagement with which I was ever blessed. We loved each other, and to leave them at the close of the Sabbath was a severe cross indeed. When I think that these precious souls are to-day shut up in the prison-house of slavery, my feelings overcome me, and I am almost ready to ask, "Does a righteous God govern the universe? and for what does he hold the thunders in his right hand, if not to smite the oppressor, and deliver the spoiled out of the hand of the spoiler?"[2] These dear souls came not to Sabbath school because it was popular to do so, nor did I teach them because it was reputable to be thus engaged. Every moment they spent in that school, they were liable to be taken up, and given thirty-nine lashes. They came because they wished to learn. Their minds had been starved by their cruel masters. They had been shut up in mental darkness. I taught them, because it was the delight of my soul to be

---

1. **Sandy Jenkins:** This is the same man who gave me the roots to prevent my being whipped by Mr. Covey. He was a "clever soul." We used frequently to talk about the fight with Covey, and as often as we did so, he would claim my success as the result of the roots which he gave me. This superstition is very common among the more ignorant slaves. A slave seldom dies but that his death is attributed to trickery. [Douglass's note.]

2. **"Does a righteous God . . . spoiler?":** Douglass echoes several biblical passages, including Exodus 15:6-17 and Isaiah 33:1: "Woe to thee that spoilest . . . when thou shalt cease to spoil, thou shalt be spoiled."

doing something that looked like bettering the condition of my race. I kept up my school nearly the whole year I lived with Mr. Freeland; and, beside my Sabbath school, I devoted three evenings in the week, during the winter, to teaching the slaves at home. And I have the happiness to know, that several of those who came to Sabbath school learned how to read; and that one, at least, is now free through my agency.

The year passed off smoothly. It seemed only about half as long as the year which preceded it. I went through it without receiving a single blow. I will give Mr. Freeland the credit of being the best master I ever had, *till I became my own master*. For the ease with which I passed the year, I was, however, somewhat indebted to the society of my fellow-slaves. They were noble souls; they not only possessed loving hearts, but brave ones. We were linked and interlinked with each other. I loved them with a love stronger than any thing I have experienced since. It is sometimes said that we slaves do not love and confide in each other. In answer to this assertion, I can say, I never loved any or confided in any people more than my fellow-slaves, and especially those with whom I lived at Mr. Freeland's. I believe we would have died for each other. We never undertook to do any thing, of any importance, without a mutual consultation. We never moved separately. We were one; and as much so by our tempers and dispositions, as by the mutual hardships to which we were necessarily subjected by our condition as slaves.

At the close of the year 1834, Mr. Freeland again hired me of my master, for the year 1835. But, by this time, I began to want to live *upon free land* as well as *with Freeland*; and I was no longer content, therefore, to live with him or any other slaveholder. I began, with the commencement of the year, to prepare myself for a final struggle, which should decide my fate one way or the other. My tendency was upward. I was fast approaching manhood, and year after year had passed, and I was still a slave. These thoughts roused me – I must do something. I therefore resolved that 1835 should not pass without witnessing an attempt, on my part, to secure my liberty. But I was not willing to cherish this determination alone. My fellow-slaves were dear to me. I was anxious to have them participate with me in this, my life-giving determination. I therefore, though with great prudence, commenced early to ascertain their views and feelings in regard to their condition, and to imbue their minds with thoughts of freedom. I bent myself to devising ways and means for our escape, and meanwhile strove, on all fitting occasions, to impress them with the gross fraud and inhumanity of slavery. I went first to Henry, next to John, then to the others. I found, in them all, warm hearts and noble spirits. They were ready to hear, and ready to act when a feasible plan should be proposed. This was what I wanted. I talked to them of our want of manhood, if we submitted to our enslavement without at least one noble effort to be free. We met often, and consulted frequently, and told our hopes and fears, recounted the difficulties, real and imagined, which we should be called on to meet. At times we were almost disposed to give up, and try to content ourselves with our wretched lot; at others, we were firm and unbending in our determination to go. Whenever we suggested any plan, there was shrinking – the odds were fearful. Our path was beset with the greatest obstacles; and if we succeeded in gaining the end of it, our right to be free was yet questionable – we were yet liable to be returned to bondage. We could see no spot this side of the ocean, where we could be free. We knew nothing about Canada. Our knowledge of the north did not extend farther than New

York; and to go there, and be forever harassed with the frightful liability of being returned to slavery – with the certainty of being treated tenfold worse than before – the thought was truly a horrible one, and one which it was not easy to overcome. The case sometimes stood thus: At every gate through which we were to pass, we saw a watchman – at every ferry a guard – on every bridge a sentinel – and in every wood a patrol. We were hemmed in upon every side. Here were the difficulties, real or imagined – the good to be sought, and the evil to be shunned. On the one hand, there stood slavery, a stern reality, glaring frightfully upon us, – its robes already crimsoned with the blood of millions, and even now feasting itself greedily upon our own flesh. On the other hand, away back in the dim distance, under the flickering light of the north star, behind some craggy hill or snow-covered mountain, stood a doubtful freedom – half frozen – beckoning us to come and share its hospitality. This in itself was sometimes enough to stagger us; but when we permitted ourselves to survey the road, we were frequently appalled. Upon either side we saw grim death, assuming the most horrid shapes. Now it was starvation, causing us to eat our own flesh; – now we were contending with the waves, and were drowned; – now we were overtaken, and torn to pieces by the fangs of the terrible bloodhound. We were stung by scorpions, chased by wild beasts, bitten by snakes, and finally, after having nearly reached the desired spot, – after swimming rivers, encountering wild beasts, sleeping in the woods suffering hunger and nakedness, – we were overtaken by our pursuers, and, in our resistance, we were shot dead upon the spot! I say, this picture sometimes appalled us, and made us

> rather bear those ills we had,
> Than fly to others, that we knew not of.[3]

In coming to a fixed determination to run away, we did more than Patrick Henry, when he resolved upon liberty or death. With us it was a doubtful liberty at most, and almost certain death if we failed. For my part, I should prefer death to hopeless bondage.

Sandy, one of our number, gave up the notion, but still encouraged us. Our company then consisted of Henry Harris, John Harris, Henry Bailey, Charles Roberts, and myself. Henry Bailey was my uncle, and belonged to my master. Charles married my aunt: he belonged to my master's father-in-law, Mr. William Hamilton.

The plan we finally concluded upon was, to get a large canoe belonging to Mr. Hamilton, and upon the Saturday night previous to Easter holidays, paddle directly up the Chesapeake Bay. On our arrival at the head of the bay, a distance of seventy or eighty miles from where we lived, it was our purpose to turn our canoe adrift, and follow the guidance of the north star till we got beyond the limits of Maryland. Our reason for taking the water route was, that we were less liable to be suspected as runaways; we hoped to be regarded as fishermen; whereas, if we should take the land route, we should be subjected to interruptions of almost every kind. Any one having a white face, and being so disposed, could stop us, and subject us to examination.

---

3. **rather . . . knew not of:** Shakespeare, *Hamlet*, 3.1.81–82.

The week before our intended start, I wrote several protections, one for each of us. As well as I can remember, they were in the following words, to wit: –

> This is to certify that I, the undersigned, have given the bearer, my servant, full liberty to go to Baltimore, and spend the Easter holidays. Written with mine own hand, &c., 1835.
>
> *William Hamilton*
>
> Near St. Michael's, in Talbot county, Maryland

We were not going to Baltimore; but, in going up the bay, we went toward Baltimore, and these protections were only intended to protect us while on the bay.

As the time drew near for our departure, our anxiety became more and more intense. It was truly a matter of life and death with us. The strength of our determination was about to be fully tested. At this time, I was very active in explaining every difficulty, removing every doubt, dispelling every fear, and inspiring all with the firmness indispensable to success in our undertaking; assuring them that half was gained the instant we made the move; we had talked long enough; we were now ready to move; if not now, we never should be; and if we did not intend to move now, we had as well fold our arms, sit down, and acknowledge ourselves fit only to be slaves. This, none of us were prepared to acknowledge. Every man stood firm; and at our last meeting, we pledged ourselves afresh, in the most solemn manner, that, at the time appointed, we would certainly start in pursuit of freedom. This was in the middle of the week, at the end of which we were to be off. We went, as usual, to our several fields of labor, but with bosoms highly agitated with thoughts of our truly hazardous undertaking. We tried to conceal our feelings as much as possible; and I think we succeeded very well.

After a painful waiting, the Saturday morning, whose night was to witness our departure, came. I hailed it with joy, bring what of sadness it might. Friday night was a sleepless one for me. I probably felt more anxious than the rest, because I was, by common consent, at the head of the whole affair. The responsibility of success or failure lay heavily upon me. The glory of the one, and the confusion of the other, were alike mine. The first two hours of that morning were such as I never experienced before, and hope never to again. Early in the morning, we went, as usual, to the field. We were spreading manure: and all at once, while thus engaged, I was overwhelmed with an indescribable feeling, in the fulness of which I turned to Sandy, who was near by, and said, "We are betrayed!" "Well," said he, "that thought has this moment struck me." We said no more. I was never more certain of any thing.

The horn was blown as usual, and we went up from the field to the house for breakfast. I went for the form, more than for want of any thing to eat that morning. Just as I got to the house, in looking out at the lane gate, I saw four white men, with two colored men. The white men were on horseback, and the colored ones were walking behind, as if tied. I watched them a few moments till they got up to our lane gate. Here they halted, and tied the colored men to the gate-post. I was not yet certain as to what the matter was. In a few moments, in rode Mr. Hamilton, with a speed betokening great excitement. He came to the door, and inquired if Master William was in. He was told he was at the barn. Mr. Hamilton, without dismounting, rode up to the barn with extraordinary speed. In a few moments, he and Mr. Freeland returned to the house. By this time, the three constables rode up, and in great haste dismounted, tied their horses, and met Master William and Mr. Hamilton returning from the barn; and after talking awhile, they all walked up to the kitchen door. There was no one in the kitchen but myself and John. Henry and Sandy were up at the barn. Mr. Freeland put his head in at the door, and called me by name, saying, there were some gentlemen at the door who wished to see me. I stepped to the door, and inquired what they wanted. They at once seized me, and, without giving me any satisfaction, tied me – lashing my hands closely together. I insisted upon knowing what the matter was. They at length said, that they had learned I had been in a "scrape," and that I was to be examined before my master; and if their information proved false, I should not be hurt.

In a few moments, they succeeded in tying John. They then turned to Henry, who had by this time returned, and commanded him to cross his hands. "I won't!" said Henry, in a firm tone, indicating his readiness to meet the consequences of his refusal. "Won't you?" said Tom Graham, the constable. "No. I won't!" said Henry, in a still stronger tone. With this, two of the constables pulled out their shining pistols, and swore, by their Creator, that they would make him cross his hands or kill him. Each cocked his pistol, and, with fingers on the trigger, walked up to Henry, saying, at the same time, if he did not cross his hands, they would blow his damned heart out. "Shoot me! shoot me!" said Henry; "you can't kill me but once. Shoot, shoot, – and be damned! *I won't be tied*!" This he said in a tone of loud defiance; and at the same time, with a motion as quick as lightning, he with one single stroke dashed the pistols from the hand of each constable. As he did this, all hands fell upon him, and, after beating him some time, they finally overpowered him, and got him tied.

During the scuffle, I managed, I know not how, to get my pass out, and, without being discovered, put it into the fire. We were all now tied; and just as we were to leave for Easton jail, Betsy Freeland, mother of William Freeland, came to the door with her hands full of biscuits, and divided them between Henry and John. She then delivered herself of a speech, to the following effect: – addressing herself to me, she said, "*You devil! You yellow devil!* it was you that put it into the heads of Henry and John to run away. But for you, you long-legged mulatto devil! Henry nor John would never have thought of such a thing." I made no reply, and was immediately hurried off towards St. Michael's. Just a moment previous to the scuffle with Henry, Mr. Hamilton suggested the propriety of making a search for the protections which he had understood Frederick had written for himself and the rest. But, just at the moment he was about carrying his proposal into effect, his aid was needed in helping to tie Henry; and the excitement attending the scuffle caused them either to forget, or to deem it unsafe, under the circumstances, to search. So we were not yet convicted of the intention to run away.

When we got about half way to St. Michael's, while the constables having us in charge were looking ahead, Henry inquired of me what he should do with his pass. I told him to eat it with his biscuit, and own nothing; and we passed the word around, "*Own nothing*;" and "*Own nothing!*" said we all. Our confidence in each other was unshaken. We were resolved to succeed or fail together, after the calamity had befallen us as much as before. We were now prepared for any thing. We were to be dragged that morning fifteen miles behind horses, and then to be placed in the Easton jail. When we reached

St. Michael's, we underwent a sort of examination. We all denied that we ever intended to run away. We did this more to bring out the evidence against us, than from any hope of getting clear of being sold; for, as I have said, we were ready for that. The fact was, we cared but little where we went, so we went together. Our greatest concern was about separation. We dreaded that more than any thing this side of death. We found the evidence against us to be the testimony of one person; our master would not tell who it was; but we came to a unanimous decision among ourselves as to who their informant was. We were sent off to the jail at Easton. When we got there, we were delivered up to the sheriff, Mr. Joseph Graham, and by him placed in jail. Henry, John, and myself, were placed in one room together – Charles, and Henry Bailey, in another. Their object in separating us was to hinder concert.

We had been in jail scarcely twenty minutes, when a swarm of slave traders, and agents for slave traders, flocked into jail to look at us, and to ascertain if we were for sale. Such a set of beings I never saw before! I felt myself surrounded by so many fiends from perdition. A band of pirates never looked more like their father, the devil. They laughed and grinned over us, saying, "Ah, my boys! we have got you, haven't we." And after taunting us in various ways, they one by one went into an examination of us, with intent to ascertain our value. They would impudently ask us if we would not like to have them for our masters. We would make them no answer, and leave them to find out as best they could. Then they would curse and swear at us, telling us that they could take the devil out of us in a very little while, if we were only in their hands.

While in jail, we found ourselves in much more comfortable quarters than we expected when we went there. We did not get much to eat, nor that which was very good; but we had a good clean room, from the windows of which we could see what was going on in the street, which was very much better than though we had been placed in one of the dark, damp cells. Upon the whole, we got along very well, so far as the jail and its keeper were concerned. Immediately after the holidays were over, contrary to all our expectations, Mr. Hamilton and Mr. Freeland came up to Easton, and took Charles, the two Henrys, and John, out of jail, and carried them home, leaving me alone. I regarded this separation as a final one. It caused me more pain than any thing else in the whole transaction. I was ready for any thing rather than separation. I supposed that they had consulted together, and had decided that, as I was the whole cause of the intention of the others to run away, it was hard to make the innocent suffer with the guilty; and that they had, therefore, concluded to take the others home, and sell me, as a warning to the others that remained. It is due to the noble Henry to say, he seemed almost as reluctant at leaving the prison as at leaving home to come to the prison. But we knew we should, in all probability, be separated, if we were sold; and since he was in their hands, he concluded to go peaceably home.

I was now left to my fate. I was all alone, and within the walls of a stone prison. But a few days before, and I was full of hope. I expected to have been safe in a land of freedom; but now I was covered with gloom, sunk down to the utmost despair. I thought the possibility of freedom was gone. I was kept in this way about one week, at the end of which, Captain Auld, my master, to my surprise and utter astonishment, came up, and took me out, with the intention of sending me, with a gentleman of his acquaintance, into

Alabama. But, from some cause or other, he did not send me to Alabama, but concluded to send me back to Baltimore, to live again with his brother Hugh, and to learn a trade.

Thus, after an absence of three years and one month, I was once more permitted to return to my old home at Baltimore. My master sent me away, because there existed against me a very great prejudice in the community, and he feared I might be killed.

In a few weeks after I went to Baltimore, Master Hugh hired me to Mr. William Gardner, an extensive ship-builder, on Fell's Point. I was put there to learn how to calk. It, however, proved a very unfavorable place for the accomplishment of this object. Mr. Gardner was engaged that spring in building two large man-of-war brigs, professedly for the Mexican government. The vessels were to be launched in the July of that year, and in failure thereof, Mr. Gardner was to lose a considerable sum; so that when I entered, all was hurry. There was no time to learn any thing. Every man had to do that which he knew how to do. In entering the ship-yard, my orders from Mr. Gardner were, to do whatever the carpenters commanded me to do. This was placing me at the beck and call of about seventy-five men. I was to regard all these as masters. Their word was to be my law. My situation was a most trying one. At times I needed a dozen pair of hands. I was called a dozen ways in the space of a single minute. Three or four voices would strike my ear at the same moment. It was – "Fred., come help me to cant this timber here." – "Fred., come carry this timber yonder." – "Fred., bring that roller here." – "Fred., go get a fresh can of water." – "Fred., come help saw off the end of this timber." – "Fred., go quick, and get the crowbar." – "Fred., hold on the end of this fall." – "Fred., go to the blacksmith's shop, and get a new punch." – "Hurra, Fred.! run and bring me a cold chisel." – "I say, Fred., bear a hand, and get up a fire as quick as lightning under that steam-box." – "Halloo, nigger! come, turn this grindstone." – "Come, come! move, move! and *bowse*[4] this timber forward." – "I say, darky, blast your eyes, why don't you heat up some pitch?" – "Halloo! halloo! halloo!" (Three voices at the same time.) "Come here! – Go there! – Hold on where you are! Damn you, if you move, I'll knock your brains out!"

This was my school for eight months; and I might have remained there longer, but for a most horrid fight I had with four of the white apprentices, in which my left eye was nearly knocked out, and I was horribly mangled in other respects. The facts in the case were these: Until a very little while after I went there, white and black ship-carpenters worked side by side, and no one seemed to see any impropriety in it. All hands seemed to be very well satisfied. Many of the black carpenters were freemen. Things seemed to be going on very well. All at once, the white carpenters knocked off, and said they would not work with free colored workmen. Their reason for this, as alleged, was, that if free colored carpenters were encouraged, they would soon take the trade into their own hands, and poor white men would be thrown out of employment. They therefore felt called upon at once to put a stop to it. And, taking advantage of Mr. Gardner's necessities, they broke off, swearing they would work no longer, unless he would discharge his black carpenters. Now, though this did not extend to me in form, it did reach me in fact. My fellow-apprentices very soon began to feel it degrading to them to work with me.

4. ***bowse***: To pull or haul, as on a tackle or other hoisting device.

They began to put on airs, and talk about the "niggers" taking the country, saying we all ought to be killed; and, being encouraged by the journeymen, they commenced making my condition as hard as they could, by hectoring me around, and sometimes striking me. I, of course, kept the vow I made after the fight with Mr. Covey, and struck back again, regardless of consequences; and while I kept them from combining, I succeeded very well; for I could whip the whole of them, taking them separately. They, however, at length combined, and came upon me, armed with sticks, stones, and heavy handspikes. One came in front with a half brick. There was one at each side of me, and one behind me. While I was attending to those in front, and on either side, the one behind ran up with the handspike, and struck me a heavy blow upon the head. It stunned me. I fell, and with this they all ran upon me, and fell to beating me with their fists. I let them lay on for a while, gathering strength. In an instant, I gave a sudden surge, and rose to my hands and knees. Just as I did that, one of their number gave me, with his heavy boot, a powerful kick in the left eye. My eyeball seemed to have burst. When they saw my eye closed, and badly swollen, they left me. With this I seized the handspike, and for a time pursued them. But here the carpenters interfered, and I thought I might as well give it up. It was impossible to stand my hand against so many. All this took place in sight of not less than fifty white ship-carpenters, and not one interposed a friendly word; but some cried, "Kill the damned nigger! Kill him! kill him! He struck a white person." I found my only chance for life was in flight. I succeeded in getting away without an additional blow, and barely so; for to strike a white man is death by Lynch law,[5] – and that was the law in Mr. Gardner's ship-yard; nor is there much of any other out of Mr. Gardner's ship-yard.

I went directly home, and told the story of my wrongs to Master Hugh; and I am happy to say of him, irreligious as he was, his conduct was heavenly, compared with that of his brother Thomas under similar circumstances. He listened attentively to my narration of the circumstances leading to the savage outrage, and gave many proofs of his strong indignation at it. The heart of my once overkind mistress was again melted into pity. My puffed-out eye and blood-covered face moved her to tears. She took a chair by me, washed the blood from my face, and, with a mother's tenderness, bound up my head, covering the wounded eye with a lean piece of fresh beef. It was almost compensation for my suffering to witness, once more, a manifestation of kindness from this, my once affectionate old mistress. Master Hugh was very much enraged. He gave expression to his feelings by pouring out curses upon the heads of those who did the deed. As soon as I got a little the better of my bruises, he took me with him to Esquire Watson's, on Bond Street, to see what could be done about the matter. Mr. Watson inquired who saw the assault committed. Master Hugh told him it was done in Mr. Gardner's ship-yard, at midday, where there were a large company of men at work. "As to that," he said, "the deed was done, and there was no question as to who did it." His answer was, he could do nothing in the case, unless some white man would come forward and testify. He could issue no warrant on my word. If I had been killed in the presence of a thousand colored people, their testimony combined would have been insufficient to have arrested one of the murderers. Master Hugh, for once, was compelled to say this state of things was too

5. **Lynch law:** The practice of executing an individual by mob action without due process of law.

bad. Of course, it was impossible to get any white man to volunteer his testimony in my behalf, and against the white young men. Even those who may have sympathized with me were not prepared to do this. It required a degree of courage unknown to them to do so; for just at that time, the slightest manifestation of humanity toward a colored person was denounced as abolitionism, and that name subjected its bearer to frightful liabilities. The watchwords of the bloody-minded in that region, and in those days, were, "Damn the abolitionists!" and "Damn the niggers!" There was nothing done, and probably nothing would have been done if I had been killed. Such was, and such remains, the state of things in the Christian city of Baltimore.

Master Hugh, finding he could get no redress, refused to let me go back again to Mr. Gardner. He kept me himself, and his wife dressed my wound till I was again restored to health. He then took me into the ship-yard of which he was foreman, in the employment of Mr. Walter Price. There I was immediately set to calking, and very soon learned the art of using my mallet and irons. In the course of one year from the time I left Mr. Gardner's, I was able to command the highest wages given to the most experienced calkers. I was now of some importance to my master. I was bringing him from six to seven dollars per week. I sometimes brought him nine dollars per week: my wages were a dollar and a half a day. After learning how to calk, I sought my own employment, made my own contracts, and collected the money which I earned. My pathway became much more smooth than before; my condition was now much more comfortable. When I could get no calking to do, I did nothing. During these leisure times, those old notions about freedom would steal over me again. When in Mr. Gardner's employment, I was kept in such a perpetual whirl of excitement, I could think of nothing, scarcely, but my life; and in thinking of my life, I almost forgot my liberty. I have observed this in my experience of slavery, – that whenever my condition was improved, instead of its increasing my contentment, it only increased my desire to be free, and set me to thinking of plans to gain my freedom. I have found that, to make a contented slave, it is necessary to make a thoughtless one. It is necessary to darken his moral and mental vision, and, as far as possible, to annihilate the power of reason. He must be able to detect no inconsistencies in slavery; he must be made to feel that slavery is right; and he can be brought to that only when he ceases to be a man.

I was now getting, as I have said, one dollar and fifty cents per day. I contracted for it; I earned it; it was paid to me; it was rightfully my own; yet, upon each returning Saturday night, I was compelled to deliver every cent of that money to Master Hugh. And why? Not because he earned it, – not because he had any hand in earning it, – not because I owed it to him, – not because he possessed the slightest shadow of a right to it; but solely because he had the power to compel me to give it up. The right of the grim-visaged pirate upon the high seas is exactly the same.

Chapter XI

I now come to that part of my life during which I planned, and finally succeeded in making, my escape from slavery. But before narrating any of the peculiar circumstances, I deem it proper to make known my intention not to state all the facts connected with the transaction. My reasons for pursuing this course may be understood from the following: First, were I to give a minute statement of all the facts, it is not only possible, but quite probable, that others would thereby be involved in the most embarrassing difficulties. Secondly, such a statement would most undoubtedly induce greater vigilance on the part of slaveholders than has existed heretofore among them; which would, of course be the means of guarding a door whereby some dear brother bondman might escape his galling chains. I deeply regret the necessity that impels me to suppress any thing of importance connected with my experience in slavery. It would afford me great pleasure indeed, as well as materially add to the interest of my narrative, were I at liberty to gratify a curiosity, which I know exists in the minds of many, by an accurate statement of all the facts pertaining to my most fortunate escape. But I must deprive myself of this pleasure, and the curious of the gratification which such a statement would afford. I would allow myself to suffer under the greatest imputations which evil-minded men might suggest, rather than exculpate myself, and thereby run the hazard of closing the slightest avenue by which a brother slave might clear himself of the chains and fetters of slavery.

I have never approved of the very public manner in which some of our western friends have conducted what they call the *underground railroad*, but which, I think, by their open declarations, has been made most emphatically the *upper-ground railroad*. I honor those good men and women for their noble daring, and applaud them for willingly subjecting themselves to bloody persecution, by openly avowing their participation in the escape of slaves. I, however, can see very little good resulting from such a course, either to themselves or the slaves escaping; while, upon the other hand, I see and feel assured that those open declarations are a positive evil to the slaves remaining, who are seeking to escape. They do nothing towards enlightening the slave, whilst they do much towards enlightening the master. They stimulate him to greater watchfulness, and enhance his power to capture his slave. We owe something to the slaves south of the line as well as to those north of it; and in aiding the latter on their way to freedom, we should be careful to do nothing which would be likely to hinder the former from escaping from slavery. I would keep the merciless slaveholder profoundly ignorant of the means of flight adopted by the slave. I would leave him to imagine himself surrounded by myriads of invisible tormentors, ever ready to snatch from his infernal grasp his trembling prey. Let him be left to feel his way in the dark; let darkness commensurate with his crime hover over him; and let him feel that at every step he takes, in pursuit of the flying bondman, he is running the frightful risk of having his hot brains dashed out by an invisible agency. Let us render the tyrant no aid; let us not hold the light by which he can trace the footprints of our flying brother. But enough of this. I will now proceed to the statement of those facts, connected with my escape, for which I am alone responsible and for which no one can be made to suffer but myself.

In the early part of the year 1838, I became quite restless. I could see no reason why I should, at the end of each week, pour the reward of my toil into the purse of my master. When I carried to him my weekly wages, he would, after counting the money, look me in the face with a robber-like fierceness, and ask, "Is this all?" He was satisfied with nothing less than the last cent. He would, however, when I made him six dollars, sometimes give me six cents, to encourage me. It had the opposite effect. I regarded it as a sort of admission of my right to the whole. The fact that he gave me any part of my wages was proof, to my mind, that he believed me entitled to the whole of them. I always felt worse for having received any thing; for I feared that the giving me a few cents would ease his conscience, and make him feel himself to be a pretty honorable sort of robber. My discontent grew upon me. I was ever on the look-out for means of escape; and, finding no direct means, I determined to try to hire my time, with a view of getting money with which to make my escape. In the spring of 1838, when Master Thomas came to Baltimore to purchase his spring goods, I got an opportunity, and applied to him to allow me to hire my time. He unhesitatingly refused my request, and told me this was another stratagem by which to escape. He told me I could go nowhere but that he could get me; and that, in the event of my running away, he should spare no pains in his efforts to catch me. He exhorted me to content myself, and be obedient. He told me, if I would be happy, I must lay out no plans for the future. He said, if I behaved myself properly, he would take care of me. Indeed, he advised me to complete thoughtlessness of the future, and taught me to depend solely upon him for happiness. He seemed to see fully the pressing necessity of setting aside my intellectual nature, in order to find contentment in slavery. But in spite of him, and even in spite of myself, I continued to think, and to think about the injustice of my enslavement, and the means of escape.

About two months after this, I applied to Master Hugh for the privilege of hiring my time. He was not acquainted with the fact that I had applied to Master Thomas, and had been refused. He too, at first, seemed disposed to refuse; but, after some reflection, he granted me the privilege, and proposed the following term: I was to be allowed all my time, make all contracts with those for whom I worked, and find my own employment; and, in return for this liberty, I was to pay him three dollars at the end of each week; find myself in calking tools, and in board and clothing. My board was two dollars and a half per week. This, with the wear and tear of clothing and calking tools, made my regular expenses about six dollars per week. This amount I was compelled to make up, or relinquish the privilege of hiring my time. Rain or shine, work or no work, at the end of each week the money must be forthcoming, or I must give up my privilege. This arrangement, it will be perceived, was decidedly in my master's favor. It relieved him of all need of looking after me. His money was sure. He received all the benefits of slaveholding without its evils; while I endured all the evils of a slave, and suffered all the care and anxiety of a freeman. I found it a hard bargain. But, hard as it was, I thought it better than the old mode of getting along. It was a step towards freedom to be allowed to bear the responsibilities of a freeman, and I was determined to hold on upon it. I bent myself to the work of making money. I was ready to work at night as well as day, and by the most untiring perseverance and industry, I made enough to meet my expenses, and lay up a little money every week. I went on thus from May till August. Master Hugh then refused to allow me to hire my time longer. The ground for his refusal was a failure on my part, one Saturday night, to pay him for my week's time. This failure was occasioned by my attending a camp meeting about ten miles from Baltimore. During the week, I had entered into an engagement with a number of young friends to start from Baltimore to the camp ground early Saturday evening; and being detained by my employer, I was unable to get down to Master Hugh's without disappointing the company. I knew that

Master Hugh was in no special need of the money that night. I therefore decided to go to camp meeting, and upon my return pay him the three dollars. I staid at the camp meeting one day longer than I intended when I left. But as soon as I returned, I called upon him to pay him what he considered his due. I found him very angry; he could scarce restrain his wrath. He said he had a great mind to give me a severe whipping. He wished to know how I dared go out of the city without asking his permission. I told him I hired my time, and while I paid him the price which he asked for it, I did not know that I was bound to ask him when and where I should go. This reply troubled him; and, after reflecting a few moments, he turned to me, and said I should hire my time no longer; that the next thing he should know of, I would be running away. Upon the same plea, he told me to bring my tools and clothing home forthwith. I did so; but instead of seeking work, as I had been accustomed to do previously to hiring my time, I spent the whole week without the performance of a single stroke of work. I did this in retaliation. Saturday night, he called upon me as usual for my week's wages. I told him I had no wages; I had done no work that week. Here we were upon the point of coming to blows. He raved, and swore his determination to get hold of me. I did not allow myself a single word; but was resolved, if he laid the weight of his hand upon me, it should be blow for blow. He did not strike me, but told me that he would find me in constant employment in future. I thought the matter over during the next day, Sunday, and finally resolved upon the third day of September, as the day upon which I would make a second attempt to secure my freedom. I now had three weeks during which to prepare for my journey. Early on Monday morning, before Master Hugh had time to make any engagement for me, I went out and got employment of Mr. Butler, at his ship-yard near the drawbridge, upon what is called the City Block, thus making it unnecessary for him to seek employment for me. At the end of the week, I brought him between eight and nine dollars. He seemed very well pleased, and asked me why I did not do the same the week before. He little knew what my plans were. My object in working steadily was to remove any suspicion he might entertain of my intent to run away; and in this I succeeded admirably. I suppose he thought I was never better satisfied with my condition than at the very time during which I was planning my escape. The second week passed, and again I carried him my full wages; and so well pleased was he, that he gave me twenty-five cents, (quite a large sum for a slaveholder to give a slave,) and bade me to make a good use of it. I told him I would.

Things went on without very smoothly indeed, but within there was trouble. It is impossible for me to describe my feelings as the time of my contemplated start drew near. I had a number of warm-hearted friends in Baltimore, – friends that I loved almost as I did my life, – and the thought of being separated from them forever was painful beyond expression. It is my opinion that thousands would escape from slavery, who now remain, but for the strong cords of affection that bind them to their friends. The thought of leaving my friends was decidedly the most painful thought with which I had to contend. The love of them was my tender point, and shook my decision more than all things else. Besides the pain of separation, the dread and apprehension of a failure exceeded what I had experienced at my first attempt. The appalling defeat I then sustained returned to torment me. I felt assured that, if I failed in this attempt, my case would be a hopeless one – it would seal my fate as a slave forever. I could not hope to get off with anything less than the severest punishment, and being placed beyond the means of escape. It required no very vivid imagination to depict the most frightful scenes through which I should have to pass, in case I failed. The wretchedness of slavery, and the blessedness of freedom, were perpetually before me. It was life and death with me. But I remained firm, and, according to my resolution, on the third day of September, 1838, I left my chains, and succeeded in reaching New York without the slightest interruption of any kind. How I did so, – what means I adopted, – what direction I travelled, and by what mode of conveyance, – I must leave unexplained, for the reasons before mentioned.

I have been frequently asked how I felt when I found myself in a free State. I have never been able to answer the question with any satisfaction to myself. It was a moment of the highest excitement I ever experienced. I suppose I felt as one may imagine the unarmed mariner to feel when he is rescued by a friendly man-of-war from the pursuit of a pirate. In writing to a dear friend, immediately after my arrival at New York, I said I felt like one who had escaped a den of hungry lions. This state of mind, however, very soon subsided; and I was again seized with a feeling of great insecurity and loneliness. I was yet liable to be taken back, and subjected to all the tortures of slavery. This in itself was enough to damp the ardor of my enthusiasm. But the loneliness overcame me. There I was in the midst of thousands, and yet a perfect stranger; without home and without friends, in the midst of thousands of my own brethren – children of a common Father, and yet I dared not to unfold to any one of them my sad condition. I was afraid to speak to any one for fear of speaking to the wrong one, and thereby falling into the hands of money-loving kidnappers, whose business it was to lie in wait for the panting fugitive, as the ferocious beasts of the forest lie in wait for their prey. The motto which I adopted when I started from slavery was this – "Trust no man!" I saw in every white man an enemy, and in almost every colored man cause for distrust. It was a most painful situation; and, to understand it, one must needs experience it, or imagine himself in similar circumstances. Let him be a fugitive slave in a strange land – a land given up to be the hunting-ground for slaveholders – whose inhabitants are legalized kidnappers – where he is every moment subjected to the terrible liability of being seized upon by his fellowmen, as the hideous crocodile seizes upon his prey! – I say, let him place himself in my situation – without home or friends – without money or credit – wanting shelter, and no one to give it – wanting bread, and no money to buy it, – and at the same time let him feel that he is pursued by merciless men-hunters, and in total darkness as to what to do, where to go, or where to stay, – perfectly helpless both as to the means of defence and means of escape, – in the midst of plenty, yet suffering the terrible gnawings of hunger, – in the midst of houses, yet having no home, – among fellow-men, yet feeling as if in the midst of wild beasts, whose greediness to swallow up the trembling and half-famished fugitive is only equalled by that with which the monsters of the deep swallow up the helpless fish upon which they subsist, – I say, let him be placed in this most trying situation, – the situation in which I was placed, – then, and not till then, will he fully appreciate the hardships of, and know how to sympathize with, the toil worn and whip-scarred fugitive slave.

Thank Heaven, I remained but a short time in this distressed situation. I was relieved from it by the humane hand of Mr. David Ruggles,[1] whose vigilance, kindness, and perseverance, I shall never forget. I am glad of an opportunity to express, as far as words can, the love and gratitude I bear him. Mr. Ruggles is now afflicted with blindness, and is himself in need of the same kind offices which he was once so forward in the performance of toward others. I had been in New York but a few days, when Mr. Ruggles sought me out, and very kindly took me to his boarding-house at the corner of Church and Lespenard Streets. Mr. Ruggles was then very deeply engaged in the memorable *Darg* case, as well as attending to a number of other fugitive slaves, devising ways and means for their successful escape; and, though watched and hemmed in on almost every side, he seemed to be more than a match for his enemies.

Very soon after I went to Mr. Ruggles, he wished to know of me where I wanted to go; as he deemed it unsafe for me to remain in New York. I told him I was a calker, and should like to go where I could get work. I thought of going to Canada; but he decided against it, and in favor of my going to New Bedford, thinking I should be able to get work there at my trade. At this time, Anna,[2] my intended wife, came on; for I wrote to her immediately after my arrival at New York, (notwithstanding my homeless, houseless, and helpless condition,) informing her of my successful flight, and wishing her to come on forthwith. In a few days after her arrival, Mr. Ruggles called in the Rev. J. W. C. Pennington, who, in the presence of Mr. Ruggles, Mrs. Michaels, and two or three others, performed the marriage ceremony, and gave us a certificate, of which the following is an exact copy: –

> This may certify, that I joined together in holy matrimony Frederick Johnson[3] and Anna Murray, as man and wife, in the presence of Mr. David Ruggles and Mrs. Michaels.
>
> *James W. C. Pennington*[4]
>
> New York, Sept. 15, 1838

Upon receiving this certificate, and a five-dollar bill from Mr. Ruggles, I shouldered one part of our baggage, and Anna took up the other, and we set out forthwith to take passage on board of the steamboat John W. Richmond for Newport, on our way to New Bedford. Mr. Ruggles gave me a letter to a Mr. Shaw in Newport, and told me, in case my money did not serve me to New Bedford, to stop in Newport and obtain further assistance; but upon our arrival at Newport, we were so anxious to get to a place of safety, that, notwithstanding we lacked the necessary money to pay our fare, we decided to take seats in the stage, and promise to pay when we got to New Bedford. We were encouraged to do this by two excellent gentlemen, residents of New Bedford, whose names I afterward ascertained to be Joseph Ricketson and William C. Taber. They seemed at once to understand our circumstances, and gave us such assurance of their friendliness as put

1. **Mr. David Ruggles:** Ruggles (1810–1849), a free black abolitionist, was the founder of the New York Vigilance Committee, an organization established to aid fugitive slaves.
2. **Anna:** She was free. [Douglass's note.]
3. **Frederick Johnson:** I had changed my name from Frederick *Bailey* to that of *Johnson*. [Douglass's note.]
4. ***James W. C. Pennington*:** Pennington (1807–1870), who escaped from slavery in Maryland in 1827, later became a Presbyterian minister.

us fully at ease in their presence. It was good indeed to meet with such friends, at such a time. Upon reaching New Bedford, we were directed to the house of Mr. Nathan Johnson, by whom we were kindly received, and hospitably provided for. Both Mr. and Mrs. Johnson took a deep and lively interest in our welfare. They proved themselves quite worthy of the name of abolitionists. When the stage-driver found us unable to pay our fare, he held on upon our baggage as security for the debt. I had but to mention the fact to Mr. Johnson, and he forthwith advanced the money.

We now began to feel a degree of safety, and to prepare ourselves for the duties and responsibilities of a life of freedom. On the morning after our arrival at New Bedford, while at the breakfast-table, the question arose as to what name I should be called by. The name given me by my mother was, "Frederick Augustus Washington Bailey." I, however, had dispensed with the two middle names long before I left Maryland so that I was generally known by the name of "Frederick Bailey." I started from Baltimore bearing the name of "Stanley." When I got to New York, I again changed my name to "Frederick Johnson," and thought that would be the last change. But when I got to New Bedford, I found it necessary again to change my name. The reason of this necessity was, that there were so many Johnsons in New Bedford, it was already quite difficult to distinguish between them. I gave Mr. Johnson the privilege of choosing me a name, but told him he must not take from me the name of "Frederick." I must hold on to that, to preserve a sense of my identity. Mr. Johnson had just been reading the "Lady of the Lake," and at once suggested that my name be "Douglass."[5] From that time until now I have been called "Frederick Douglass"; and as I am more widely known by that name than by either of the others, I shall continue to use it as my own.

I was quite disappointed at the general appearance of things in New Bedford. The impression which I had received respecting the character and condition of the people of the north, I found to be singularly erroneous. I had very strangely supposed, while in slavery, that few of the comforts, and scarcely any of the luxuries, of life were enjoyed at the north, compared with what were enjoyed by the slaveholders of the south. I probably came to this conclusion from the fact that northern people owned no slaves. I supposed that they were about upon a level with the non-slaveholding population of the south. I knew *they* were exceedingly poor, and I had been accustomed to regard their poverty as the necessary consequence of their being non-slaveholders. I had somehow imbibed the opinion that, in the absence of slaves, there could be no wealth, and very little refinement. And upon coming to the north, I expected to meet with a rough, hard-handed, and uncultivated population, living in the most Spartan-like simplicity, knowing nothing of the ease, luxury, pomp, and grandeur of southern slaveholders. Such being my conjectures, any one acquainted with the appearance of New Bedford may very readily infer how palpably I must have seen my mistake.

In the afternoon of the day when I reached New Bedford, I visited the wharves, to take a view of the shipping. Here I found myself surrounded with the strongest proofs of wealth. Lying at the wharves, and riding in the stream, I saw many ships of the finest

5. **"Douglass":** James of Douglas, the Earl of Bothwell, was the hero of *The Lady of the Lake*, a popular Romantic poem by Sir Walter Scott (1771–1832).

model, in the best order, and of the largest size. Upon the right and left, I was walled in by granite warehouses of the widest dimensions, stowed to their utmost capacity with the necessaries and comforts of life. Added to this, almost every body seemed to be at work, but noiselessly so, compared with what I had been accustomed to in Baltimore. There were no loud songs heard from those engaged in loading and unloading ships. I heard no deep oaths or horrid curses on the laborer. I saw no whipping of men; but all seemed to go smoothly on. Every man appeared to understand his work, and went at it with a sober, yet cheerful earnestness, which betokened the deep interest which he felt in what he was doing, as well as a sense of his own dignity as a man. To me this looked exceedingly strange. From the wharves I strolled around and over the town, gazing with wonder and admiration at the splendid churches, beautiful dwellings, and finely-cultivated gardens; evincing an amount of wealth, comfort, taste, and refinement, such as I had never seen in any part of slaveholding Maryland.

Every thing looked clean, new and beautiful. I saw few or no dilapidated houses, with poverty-stricken inmates; no half-naked children and barefooted women, such as I had been accustomed to see in Hillsborough, Easton, St. Michael's, and Baltimore. The people looked more able, stronger, healthier, and happier, than those of Maryland. I was for once made glad by a view of extreme wealth, without being saddened by seeing extreme poverty. But the most astonishing as well as the most interesting thing to me was the condition of the colored people, a great many of whom, like myself, had escaped thither as a refuge from the hunters of men. I found many, who had not been seven years out of their chains, living in finer houses, and evidently enjoying more of the comforts of life, than the average of slaveholders in Maryland. I will venture to assert that my friend Mr. Nathan Johnson (of whom I can say with a grateful heart, "I was hungry, and he gave me meat; I was, thirsty, and he gave me drink; I was a stranger, and he took me in")[6] lived in a neater house; dined at a better table; took, paid for, and read, more newspapers; better understood the moral, religious, and political character of the nation, – than nine tenths of the slaveholders in Talbot county, Maryland. Yet Mr. Johnson was a working man. His hands were hardened by toil, and not his alone, but those also of Mrs. Johnson. I found the colored people much more spirited than I had supposed they would be. I found among them a determination to protect each other from the blood-thirsty kidnapper, at all hazards. Soon after my arrival, I was told of a circumstance which illustrated their spirit. A colored man and a fugitive slave were on unfriendly terms. The former was heard to threaten the latter with informing his master of his whereabouts. Straightway a meeting was called among the colored people, under the stereotyped notice, "Business of importance!" The betrayer was invited to attend. The people came at the appointed hour, and organized the meeting by appointing a very religious old gentleman as president, who, I believe, made a prayer, after which he addressed the meeting as follows: *"Friends, we have got him here, and I would recommend that you young men just take him outside the door, and kill him!"* With this, a number of them bolted at him; but they were intercepted by some more timid than themselves, and the betrayer escaped their vengeance, and has not been seen in New Bedford since. I believe there

6. **"I was hungry . . . he took me in"**: Matthew 25:35.

have been no more such threats, and should there be hereafter, I doubt not that death would be the consequence.

I found employment, the third day after my arrival, in stowing a sloop with a load of oil. It was new, dirty, and hard work for me; but I went at it with a glad heart and a willing hand. I was now my own master. It was a happy moment, the rapture of which can be understood only by those who have been slaves. It was the first work, the reward of which was to be entirely my own. There was no Master Hugh standing ready, the moment I earned the money, to rob me of it. I worked that day with a pleasure I had never before experienced. I was at work for myself and newly-married wife. It was to me the starting-point of a new existence. When I got through with that job, I went in pursuit of a job of calking; but such was the strength of prejudice against color, among the white calkers, that they refused to work with me, and of course I could get no employment.[7] Finding my trade of no immediate benefit, I threw off my calking habiliments, and prepared myself to do any kind of work I could get to do. Mr. Johnson kindly let me have his wood-horse and saw, and I very soon found myself a plenty of work. There was no work too hard – none too dirty. I was ready to saw wood, shovel coal, carry the hod, sweep the chimney, or roll oil casks, – all of which I did for nearly three years in New Bedford, before I became known to the antislavery world.

In about four months after I went to New Bedford, there came a young man to me, and inquired if I did not wish to take the "Liberator."[8] I told him I did; but, just having made my escape from slavery, I remarked that I was unable to pay for it then. I, however, finally became a subscriber to it. The paper came, and I read it from week to week with such feelings as it would be quite idle for me to attempt to describe. The paper became my meat and my drink. My soul was set all on fire. Its sympathy for my brethren in bonds – its scathing denunciations of slaveholders – its faithful exposures of slavery – and its powerful attacks upon the upholders of the institution – sent a thrill of joy through my soul, such as I had never felt before!

I had not long been a reader of the "Liberator," before I got a pretty correct idea of the principles, measures and spirit of the anti-slavery reform. I took right hold of the cause. I could do but little; but what I could, I did with a joyful heart, and never felt happier than when in an anti-slavery meeting. I seldom had much to say at the meetings, because what I wanted to say was said so much better by others. But, while attending an anti-slavery convention at Nantucket, on the 11th of August, 1841, I felt strongly moved to speak, and was at the same time much urged to do so by Mr. William C. Coffin, a gentleman who had heard me speak in the colored people's meeting at New Bedford. It was a severe cross, and I took it up reluctantly. The truth was, I felt myself a slave, and the idea of speaking to white people weighed me down. I spoke but a few moments, when I felt a degree of freedom, and said what I desired with considerable ease. From that time until now, I have been engaged in pleading the cause of my brethren – with what success, and with what devotion, I leave those acquainted with my labors to decide.

---

7. **employment:** I am told that colored persons can now get employment at calking in New Bedford – a result of anti-slavery effort. [Douglass's note.]

8. **"Liberator":** Antislavery newspaper edited by William Lloyd Garrison.

Appendix

I find, since reading over the foregoing Narrative that I have, in several instances, spoken in such a tone and manner, respecting religion, as may possibly lead those unacquainted with my religious views to suppose me an opponent of all religion. To remove the liability of such misapprehension, I deem it proper to append the following brief explanation. What I have said respecting and against religion, I mean strictly to apply to the *slaveholding religion* of this land, and with no possible reference to Christianity proper; for, between the Christianity of this land, and the Christianity of Christ, I recognize the widest possible difference – so wide, that to receive the one as good, pure, and holy, is of necessity to reject the other as bad, corrupt, and wicked. To be the friend of the one, is of necessity to be the enemy of the other. I love the pure, peaceable, and impartial Christianity of Christ: I therefore hate the corrupt, slaveholding, women-whipping, cradle-plundering, partial and hypocritical Christianity of this land. Indeed, I can see no reason, but the most deceitful one, for calling the religion of this land Christianity. I look upon it as the climax of all misnomers, the boldest of all frauds, and the grossest of all libels. Never was there a clearer case of "stealing the livery of the court of heaven to serve the devil in." I am filled with unutterable loathing when I contemplate the religious pomp and show, together with the horrible inconsistencies, which every where surround me. We have men-stealers for ministers, women-whippers for missionaries, and cradle-plunderers for church members. The man who wields the blood-clotted cowskin during the week fills the pulpit on Sunday, and claims to be a minister of the meek and lowly Jesus. The man who robs me of my earnings at the end of each week meets me as a class-leader on Sunday morning, to show me the way of life, and the path of salvation. He who sells my sister, for purposes of prostitution, stands forth as the pious advocate of purity. He who proclaims it a religious duty to read the Bible denies me the right of learning to read the name of the God who made me. He who is the religious advocate of marriage robs whole millions of its sacred influence, and leaves them to the ravages of wholesale pollution. The warm defender of the sacredness of the family relation is the same that scatters whole families, – sundering husbands and wives, parents and children, sisters and brothers, – leaving the hut vacant, and the hearth desolate. We see the thief preaching against theft, and the adulterer against adultery. We have men sold to build churches, women sold to support the gospel, and babes sold to purchase Bibles for the *poor heathen! all for the glory of God and the good of souls!* The slave auctioneer's bell and the church-going bell chime in with each other, and the bitter cries of the heart-broken slave are drowned in the religious shouts of his pious master. Revivals of religion and revivals in the slave-trade go hand in hand together. The slave prison and the church stand near each other. The clanking of fetters and the rattling of chains in the prison, and the pious psalm and solemn prayer in the church, may be heard at the same time. The dealers in the bodies and souls of men erect their stand in the presence of the pulpit, and they mutually help each other. The dealer gives his blood-stained gold to support the pulpit, and the pulpit, in return, covers his infernal business with the garb of Christianity. Here we have religion and robbery the allies of each other – devils dressed in angels' robes, and hell presenting the semblance of paradise.

Just God! and these are they,
Who minister at thine altar, God of right!
Men who their hands, with prayer and blessing, lay
On Israel's ark of light.

What! preach, and kidnap men?
Give thanks, and rob thy own afflicted poor?
Talk of thy glorious liberty, and then
Bolt hard the captive's door?

What! servants of thy own
Merciful Son, who came to seek and save
The homeless and the outcast, fettering down
The tasked and plundered slave!

Pilate and Herod friends!
Chief priests and rulers, as of old, combine!
Just God and holy! is that church which lends
Strength to the spoiler thine?[1]

The Christianity of America is a Christianity, of whose votaries it may be as truly said, as it was of the ancient scribes and Pharisees,[2] "They bind heavy burdens, and grievous to be borne, and lay them on men's shoulders, but they themselves will not move them with one of their fingers. All their works they do for to be seen of men. — They love the uppermost rooms at feasts, and the chief seats in the synagogues, ... and to be called of men, Rabbi, Rabbi. — But woe unto you, scribes and Pharisees, hypocrites! for ye shut up the kingdom of heaven against men; for ye neither go in yourselves, neither suffer ye them that are entering to go in. Ye devour widows' houses, and for a pretence make long prayers; therefore ye shall receive the greater damnation. Ye compass sea and land to make one proselyte, and when he is made, ye make him twofold more the child of hell than yourselves. — Woe unto you, scribes and Pharisees, hypocrites! for ye pay tithe of mint, and anise, and cumin, and have omitted the weightier matters of the law, judgment, mercy, and faith; these ought ye to have done, and not to leave the other undone. Ye blind guides! which strain at a gnat, and swallow a camel. Woe unto you, scribes and Pharisees, hypocrites! for ye make clean the outside of the cup and of the platter, but within, they are full of extortion and excess. — Woe unto you, scribes and Pharisees, hypocrites! for ye are like unto whited sepulchres, which indeed appear beautiful outward, but are within full of dead men's bones, and of all uncleanness. Even so ye also outwardly appear righteous unto men, but within ye are full of hypocrisy and iniquity."

Dark and terrible as is this picture, I hold it to be strictly true of the overwhelming mass of professed Christians in America. They strain at a gnat, and swallow a camel. Could any thing be more true of our churches? They would be shocked at the proposition

---

1. **Just God! . . . thine?:** From "Clerical Oppressors," by the poet and abolitionist John Greenleaf Whittier (1807–1882).
2. **ancient scribes and Pharisees:** See Christ's denunciation of the scribes and Pharisees in Matthew 23.

of fellowshipping a *sheep*-stealer; and at the same time they hug to their communion a *man*-stealer, and brand me with being an infidel, if I find fault with them for it. They attend with Pharisaical strictness to the outward forms of religion, and at the same time neglect the weightier matters of the law, judgment, mercy, and faith. They are always ready to sacrifice, but seldom to show mercy. They are they who are represented as professing to love God whom they have not seen, whilst they hate their brother whom they have seen. They love the heathen on the other side of the globe. They can pray for him, pay money to have the Bible put into his hand, and missionaries to instruct him; while they despise and totally neglect the heathen at their own doors.

Such is, very briefly, my view of the religion of this land; and to avoid any misunderstanding, growing out of the use of general terms, I mean, by the religion of this land, that which is revealed in the words, deeds, and actions, of those bodies, north and south, calling themselves Christian churches, and yet in union with slaveholders. It is against religion, as presented by these bodies, that I have felt it my duty to testify.

I conclude these remarks by copying the following portrait of the religion of the south, (which is, by communion and fellowship, the religion of the north,) which I soberly affirm is "true to the life," and without caricature or the slightest exaggeration. It is said to have been drawn, several years before the present anti-slavery agitation began, by a northern Methodist preacher, who, while residing at the south, had an opportunity to see slaveholding morals, manners, and piety, with his own eyes. "Shall I not visit for these things? saith the Lord. Shall not my soul be avenged on such a nation as this?"[3]

A PARODY[4]

Come, saints and sinners, hear me tell
How pious priests whip Jack and Nell,
And women buy and children sell,
And preach all sinners down to hell,
    And sing of heavenly union.

They'll bleat and baa, [go on] like goats,
Gorge down black sheep, and strain at motes,
Array their backs in fine black coats,
Then seize their negroes by their throats,
    And choke, for heavenly union.

They'll church you if you sip a dram,
And damn you if you steal a lamb;
Yet rob old Tony, Doll, and Sam,
Of human rights, and bread and ham;
    Kidnapper's heavenly union.

3. **"Shall . . . a nation as this?":** Jeremiah 5:9.
4. **A Parody:** This parody of the popular southern hymn "Heavenly Union" was apparently written by Douglass, who was famous for his ability to mimic southern clergy.

They'll loudly talk of Christ's reward,
And bind his image with a cord,
And scold, and swing the lash abhorred,
And sell their brother in the Lord
 To handcuffed heavenly union.

They'll read and sing a sacred song,
And make a prayer both loud and long,
And teach the right and do the wrong,
Hailing the brother, sister throng,
 With words of heavenly union.

We wonder how such saints can sing,
Or praise the Lord upon the wing,
Who roar, and scold, and whip, and sting,
And to their slaves and mammon cling,
 In guilty conscience union.

They'll raise tobacco, corn, and rye,
And drive, and thieve, and cheat, and lie,
And lay up treasures in the sky,
By making switch and cowskin fly,
 In hope of heavenly union.

They'll crack old Tony on the skull,
And preach and roar like Bashan bull,
Or braying ass, of mischief full,
Then seize old Jacob by the wool,
 And pull for heavenly union.

A roaring, ranting, sleek man-thief,
Who lived on mutton, veal, and beef,
Yet never would afford relief
To needy, sable sons of grief,
 Was big with heavenly union.

"Love not the world," the preacher said,
And winked his eye, and shook his head;
He seized on Tom, and Dick, and Ned,
Cut short their meat, and clothes, and bread,
 Yet still loved heavenly union.

Another preacher whining spoke
Of One whose heart for sinners broke:
He tied old Nanny to an oak,
And drew the blood at every stroke,
 And prayed for heavenly union.

Two others oped their iron jaws,
And waved their children-stealing paws;
There sat their children in gewgaws;

By stinting negroes' backs and maws,
  They kept up heavenly union.

All good from Jack another takes,
And entertains their flirts and rakes
Who dress as sleek as glossy snakes,
And cram their mouths with sweetened cakes;
  And this goes down for union.

Sincerely and earnestly hoping that this little book may do something toward throwing light on the American slave system, and hastening the glad day of deliverance to the millions of my brethren in bonds – faithfully relying upon the power of truth, love, and justice, for success in my humble efforts – and solemnly pledging myself anew to the sacred cause, – I subscribe myself,

Frederick Douglass

Lynn, Mass., April 28, 1845

[1845]

Douglass through a Modern Lens

FREDERICK DOUGLASS was the most respected African American writer of the nineteenth century, and during the last forty years his *Narrative* has come to be viewed as one of the central texts of the American Renaissance. Nonetheless, his importance was not then and is not now simply or even primarily literary. In an introduction to Douglass's second autobiography, *My Bondage and My Freedom* (1855), the distinguished African American doctor James M'Cune Smith hailed him as "a representative American man – a type of his countrymen." Few then could have accepted a man of mixed African American and Caucasian heritage as a representative American, but Smith recognized that in his life and writings Douglass embodied the fundamental social and political values of the country. "I shall place this book in the hands of the only child spared me, bidding him to strive to emulate its noble example," Smith continued. "You may do likewise. It is an American book, for Americans, in the fullest sense of the idea." That "idea" was an ideal of freedom and equality, not simply for slaves in the South or colored people in the North, but for all Americans. When he died in 1895, Douglass himself no doubt recognized the deep divide between his dream of a truly egalitarian and fully integrated society and the harsh realities of life in the United States. But his life and writings have remained an inspiration to those who have shared that dream, including the African American poet Robert Hayden (1913-1980). Appropriately, Hayden published the following poem in 1962, at the height of a renewed struggle to fulfill Douglass's dream, and just two years before the passage of what was in its own way another tribute to him, the Civil Rights Act of 1964.

Frederick Douglass

A daguerreotype of Douglass taken when he was in his twenties, about the time he published his *Narrative*.

The text is taken from Hayden's *Collected Poems*, edited by Frederick Glaysher (1985).

Robert Hayden

[1913-1980]

Frederick Douglass

When it is finally ours, this freedom, this liberty, this beautiful
and terrible thing, needful to man as air,
usable as earth; when it belongs at last to all,
when it is truly instinct, brain matter, diastole, systole,
reflex action; when it is finally won; when it is more
than the gaudy mumbo jumbo of politicians:
this man, this Douglass, this former slave, this Negro
beaten to his knees, exiled, visioning a world
where none is lonely, none hunted, alien,
this man, superb in love and logic, this man
shall be remembered. Oh, not with statues' rhetoric,
not with legends and poems and wreaths of bronze alone,
but with the lives grown out of his life, the lives
fleshing his dream of the beautiful, needful thing.

[1962, 1985]

African American Slave Songs

[1800-1865]

Recalling the slave songs he heard as a boy, early in his *Narrative* Frederick Douglass observes: "Every tone was a testimony against slavery, and a prayer to God for deliverance from chains." In part, Douglass was responding to proslavery arguments and accounts of some visitors to the South, who pointed to such songs as evidence of the slaves' contentment with their lot. But the passage also serves as a reminder that those who remained in bondage had no voice, apart from the songs they composed and sang.

Those songs, however, gave powerful expression to feelings and thoughts that slaves could not otherwise express. Although some of the songs were secular, most of them were deeply religious. In an early collection of what he called "Negro Spirituals," published in the *Atlantic Monthly* in 1867, Thomas Wentworth Higginson described the songs of the slaves as "the vocal expression of the simplicity of their faith and the sublimity of their long resignation." But many of the songs were less resigned than resistant to slavery. Certainly that was true of "Go Down, Moses," with its militant appeal to the prophet who led the children of Israel out of bondage in Egypt. In fact, its lyrics were so explicit that some slaveholders apparently banned the singing of the song. Faced with such proscriptions, slaves developed a coded form of communication in which the spiritual topography of the Bible and Protestant hymn books came to mirror the landscape of slavery and freedom in the United States. *Home*, for example, was at once the Christian's spiritual "home" in heaven and an oblique reference to that "home" of freedom north of the Ohio River, frequently figured as the "river Jordan." "Steal Away to Jesus" might well signal another form of stealing away, and the flight to freedom was sometimes aided by the underground railroad, evoked in songs like "Swing Low, Sweet Chariot." As the prospect for freedom for all slaves grew nearer, their songs grew bolder. "Many Thousand Go," for example, was composed and sung in secret by slaves who had been forced to build Confederate fortifications in South Carolina in 1863, shortly after President Lincoln issued the Emancipation Proclamation.

The first major collection of spirituals was *Slave Songs of the United States*, edited by William Francis Allen, Charles Pickard White, and Lucy McKim Garrison (1867). The lyrics for the first three songs in this section are from that text. The lyrics of the other songs are from two other important collections: *The Book of American Negro Spirituals* and *The Second Book of American Negro Spirituals*, both edited by James Weldon Johnson and J. Rosamond Johnson (1927). The editors of all those collections sought to give the words of the songs in their original dialect, and those spellings are retained in the following texts.

Roll, Jordan, Roll

These are the opening bars from one of the most famous African American spirituals, as it was printed in *Slave Songs of the United States* (1867).
(Documenting the American South [http://docsouth.unc.edu], The University of North Carolina at Chapel Hill Libraries Rare Book Collection.)

ROLL, JORDAN, ROLL

My brudder sittin' on de tree of life,
An' he yearde[1] when Jordan roll;
Roll, Jordan, Roll, Jordan, Roll, Jordan, roll!
O march de angel march,
O march de angel march;
O my soul arise in Heaven, Lord,
For to yearde when Jordan roll.

Little chil'en, learn to fear de Lord,
And let your days be long;
O march de angel march,
O march de angel march;
O my soul arise in Heaven, Lord,
For to yearde when Jordan roll.

---

1. yearde: Hear.

O, let no false nor spiteful word
Be found upon your tongue;
O march de angel march,
O march de angel march;
O my soul arise in Heaven, Lord,
For to yearde when Jordan roll.

Nobody Knows the Trouble I've Had

Nobody knows de trouble I've had,[2]
Nobody knows but Jesus,
Nobody knows de trouble I've had,
(Sing) Glory hallelu!

One morning I was a-walking down, O yes, Lord!
I saw some berries a-hanging down, O yes, Lord!

I pick de berry and I suck de juice, O yes, Lord!
Just as sweet as the honey in de comb, O yes, Lord!

Sometimes I'm up, sometimes I'm down,
Sometimes I'm almost on de groun'.

What make ole Satan hate me so?
Because he got me once and he let me go.

Many Thousand Go

No more peck o' corn for me,
No more, no more;
No more peck o' corn for me,
Many tousand go.

No more driver's lash for me,
No more, no more;
No more driver's lash for me,
Many tousand go.

No more pint o' salt[3] for me,
No more, no more;

2. **I've had:** I see.
3. **peck o' corn . . . pint o' salt:** A slave's rations.

No more pint o' salt for me,
Many tousand go.

No more hundred lash for me,
No more, no more;
No more hundred lash for me,
Many tousand go.

No more mistress' call for me,
No more, no more;
No more mistress' call for me,
Many tousand go.

Go Down, Moses

Go down, Moses,
'Way down in Egypt land,
Tell ole Pharaoh,
To let my people go.

When Israel was in Egypt's land;
Let my people go,
Oppressed so hard they could not stand,
Let my people go.

"Thus spoke the Lord," bold Moses said;
Let my people go,
If not I'll smite your first born dead,
Let my people go.

Go down, Moses,
'Way down in Egypt land,
Tell ole Pharaoh,
To let my people go,
O let my people go.

Swing Low Sweet Chariot

Swing low sweet chariot,
Comin' for to carry me home,
Swing low sweet chariot,
Comin' for to carry me home.

I look'd over Jordan, an' what did I see,
Comin' for to carry me home,

A band of angels comin' after me,
Comin' for to carry me home.

If you get-a dere befo' I do,
Comin' for to carry me home,
Tell all my friends I'm comin' too,
Comin' for to carry me home.

O, Swing low sweet chariot,
Comin' for to carry me home,
Swing low sweet chariot,
Comin' for to carry me home,
Comin' for to carry me home.

Steal Away to Jesus

Steal away, steal away, steal away to Jesus!
Steal away, steal away home,
I ain't got long to stay here.

My Lord, He calls me,
He calls me by the thunder,
The trumpet sounds within a my soul,
I ain't got long to stay here.

Steal away, steal away, steal away to Jesus!
Steal away, steal away home,
I ain't got long to stay here.

Green trees a-bending, po' sinner stand a-trembling,
The trumpet sounds within a my soul,
I ain't got long to stay here,
Oh, Lord I ain't got long to stay here.

I Thank God I'm Free at Las'

Free at las' free at las'
I thank God I'm free at las'
Free at las' free at las'
I thank God I'm free at las'.

Way down yonder in de graveyard walk,
I thank God I'm free at las'
Me an' my Jesus gwineter meet an' talk,
I thank God I'm free at las'.

On a my knees when de light pass by,
I thank God I'm free at las'
Tho't my soul would-a rise an' fly,
I thank God I'm free at las'.

Some o'dese mornin's bright an' fair,
I thank God I'm free at las'
Gwineter meet my Jesus in de middle of de air,
I thank God I'm free at las'.

Free at las' free at las',
I thank God I'm free at las'
Free at las' free at las'
I thank God I'm free at las'.

Slave Songs through a Modern Lens

FOLLOWING THE CIVIL WAR, some feared that the end of slavery would lead to the decay and ultimate extinction of the rich tradition of slave songs. A century later, however, Dr. Martin Luther King Jr. demonstrated the deep resonance and ongoing vitality of such songs in a speech delivered at a civil-rights rally at the Lincoln Memorial on August 28, 1963. Responding to the growing enthusiasm of the crowd, estimated at a quarter of a million people, King put aside his prepared text and spoke extemporaneously of his dream of a future in which the nation would finally live out the true meaning of its creed "that all men are created equal." When that finally happens, King eloquently concluded, people of all races and religions "will be able to join hands and sing in the words of the old Negro spiritual, 'Free at last, free at last. Thank God Almighty, we are free at last.'"

The Fisk Jubilee Singers

This group, formed to raise money for one of the first African American colleges, was largely responsible for popularizing "Negro spirituals" after the Civil War. In "The Jubilee Singers" (1880), a poem inspired by their concerts in northern cities, John Greenleaf Whittier emphasized the role the group and their songs might play in the ongoing struggle for freedom and equality in the United States: "Voice of a ransomed race, sing on / Till Freedom's every right is won, / And slavery's every wrong undone!"

Many groups and individuals helped promote the emergence of spirituals from the obscurity of slave culture into an appreciation of their vital role in American culture. Although the earliest collection of the songs was published in 1801, and other collections appeared shortly after the Civil War, the songs did not gain a large audience until they were performed by the Fisk Jubilee Singers. Formed in 1871 to raise money for Fisk University, a liberal-arts institution established in 1866 for the education of newly freed slaves, the singers gained acclaim and fame during their extensive tours of the United States and Europe. The meaning of the songs was later sensitively explored by a graduate of Fisk, the African American scholar and writer W. E. B. Du Bois, who in *The Souls of Black Folk* (1903) affirmed that they stood "not simply as the sole American music, but as the most beautiful expression of human experience born this side the seas." What DuBois called "the sorrow-songs" were also a deep source of inspiration for African American writers whose work was rooted in the folk traditions of black America, notably James Weldon Johnson, a poet and the coeditor of *The Book of American Negro Spirituals* (1927). Fittingly, Johnson began his introduction to that volume with the following poem, a tribute he had first published almost twenty years earlier in the *Century Magazine.*

James Weldon Johnson

[1871-1938]

O Black and Unknown Bards

O black and unknown bards of long ago,
How came your lips to touch the sacred fire?
How, in your darkness, did you come to know
The power and beauty of the minstrel's lyre?
Who first from midst his bonds lifted his eyes?
Who first from out the still watch, lone and long,
Feeling the ancient faith of prophets rise
Within his dark-kept soul, burst into song?

Heart of what slave poured out such melody
As "Steal away to Jesus"? On its strains
His spirit must have nightly floated free,
Though still about his hands he felt his chains.
Who heard great "Jordan roll"? Whose starward eye
Saw chariot "swing low"? And who was he

That breathed that comforting, melodic sigh,
"Nobody knows de trouble I see"?

What merely living clod, what captive thing,
Could up toward God through all its darkness grope,
And find within its deadened heart to sing
These songs of sorrow, love and faith, and hope?
How did it catch that subtle undertone,
That note in music heard not with the ears?
How sound the elusive reed so seldom blown,
Which stirs the soul or melts the heart to tears?

Not that great German master[1] in his dream
Of harmonies that thundered amongst the stars
At the creation, ever heard a theme
Nobler than "Go down, Moses." Mark its bars,
How like a mighty trumpet call they stir
The blood. Such are the notes that men have sung
Going to valorous deeds; such tones there were
That helped make history when time was young.

There is a wide, wide wonder in it all,
That from degraded rest and servile toil
The fiery spirit of the seer should call
These simple children of the sun and soil.
O black slave singers, gone forgot, unfamed,
You – you alone, of all the long, long line
Of those who've sung untaught, unknown, unnamed,
Have stretched out upward, seeking the divine.

You sang not deeds of heroes or of kings;
No chant of bloody war, no exulting paean
Of arms-won triumphs; but your humble strings
You touched in chord with music empyrean.
You sang far better than you knew; the songs
That for your listeners' hungry hearts sufficed
Still live, – but more than this to you belongs:
You sang a race from wood and stone to Christ.

[1908, 1927]

1. **German master:** Gottfried Wilhelm Leibnitz (1646–1716), mathematician and philosopher who believed that God's goodness led him to create the best and most harmonious of possible universes.

BALM OF

American Facts and American Fiction

In 1837, Julia A. Parker, a schoolteacher from Vermont, wrote to a friend, "I have spent the winter very, very pleasantly, – with my books has the time been mostly passed; what very kind friends they are; my reading has been both entertaining and instructive." By then, reading "entertaining and instructive" material was becoming an important pastime that was made possible in ways it had never been before. More efficient methods for producing printed materials, rising literacy rates, the lower cost of books, increased leisure time, especially for middle-class women, and the growing number of circulating libraries all contributed to the rapid growth of

◀ **Fetridge and Company's Periodical Arcade**

By the 1850s, there was growing demand for books and periodicals, both of which became important commodities in the emerging consumer society of the United States. This engraving from an 1852 issue of *Gleason's Pictorial Drawing Room Companion* shows the bustling interior of Fetridge and Company's Periodical Arcade in Boston, where men, women, and children could find newspapers and magazines designed for every age and interest, as well as general-interest periodicals like *Gleason's*.

reading in the United States. For fiction writers, however, finding readers remained a challenge. With its emphasis on the imaginary as opposed to the real, fiction was viewed with suspicion by many Americans, especially those imbued with the persistent Puritan attitudes of colonial America. For fiction and fiction writers, however, the period from 1830 through the Civil War was marked by significant developments that would forever alter the literary marketplace in the United States.

Although it had been an independent nation for over fifty years in 1830, the development of a national literature, especially fiction, still faced many obstacles. One of the most formidable was the serious competition of celebrated British writers. In the absence of an international copyright law, American publishers could obtain copies of British books, print, and sell them without paying any royalties to the authors. The Harper Brothers, for example, built their successful firm primarily by publishing cheap reprints of mostly British novels, rather than publishing works by untried American writers. By far the most celebrated fiction writer in the United States during the first half of the nineteenth century was Sir Walter Scott, the Scottish poet and author of historical romances that were entertaining and instructive by almost any reader's standards. Scott's twenty-seven novels, beginning with *Waverly* (1814) and ending with *Castle Dangerous* (1831), were all reprinted in the United States immediately after their publication in Great Britain. Magazines and newspapers lavishly praised his novels in lengthy reviews. American writers, even successful ones, faced constant comparisons with the British; James Fenimore Cooper was dubbed the "American Scott." When the greatly mourned Scott died in 1832, another British fiction writer was already emerging to take his place. By the mid-1830s, Charles Dickens's short fiction, *Sketches by Boz*, began to appear in American magazines. When Dickens began to write novels, beginning with *The Pickwick Papers* (1836-37), American readers demanded more. Soon Dickens's novels were taking America by storm – appearing as serials in periodicals, listed with booksellers, and widely available in circulating libraries. As other British fiction writers emerged in the 1840s and 1850s – such as Charles Reade, Charlotte and Emily Brontë, Wilkie Collins, and William Makepeace Thackeray – their works were also widely reprinted and avidly read in the United States.

In the view of many writers and intellectuals, the popularity of the British writers made the need for an American literature all the more pressing. Calls for the development of a national literature were amplified by Ralph Waldo Emerson, Margaret Fuller, and other transcendentalists in and around Boston. But few of them displayed much interest in fiction. The establishment of a powerful tradition of American fiction depended not only on ideas but also on the actions of a group of editors and writers who could make their cultural commitments work in the marketplace. A nationalistic group of editors and writers in New York City, who described their movement as "Young America," took the lead in promoting American writers. The group included Evert and George Duyckinck, editors of the *Literary World*, and emerging prose writers of similar literary interests and with strongly Democratic sympathies, such as Herman Melville and a southern writer, William Gilmore Simms. Other writers trying to claim a place in the literary marketplace were also involved in the movement, including Edgar Allan Poe, though he did not share the Democratic politics and principles of some of the leaders of Young America.

Periodicals were viewed by many as an important means of developing a national literature, and several magazines founded in the 1830s were expressly designed to support new works and help American writers become established. In the first issue of the *Knickerbocker*, founded in New York City in 1833, a reviewer called on writers to focus on the "natural beauty of our delightful country" instead of the "exhausted fields of Europe." The editors of the magazine thus solicited the work of popular fiction writers like Washington Irving and James Kirke Paulding, as well as that of the young Nathaniel Hawthorne.

A reviewer called on writers to focus on the "natural beauty of our delightful country" instead of the "exhausted fields of Europe."

If there was a leader of the Young America movement, it was probably Hawthorne's friend John L. O'Sullivan. In 1837, he helped establish the *United States Magazine and Democratic Review* in order to advance the interests of the Democratic Party and combat what O'Sullivan referred to as the "literary toryism" (in other words, the conservative British emphasis) of other American magazines. A variety of emerging fiction writers appeared in the pages of the magazine, including the young Walt Whitman, who was not then writing much poetry but who published eight stories in the magazine during 1841-42. Hawthorne published nearly twenty-five essays and stories in the *Democratic Review* (as it was usually called), which also featured the regional work of writers like Henry William Herbert, who wrote as "Frank Forester."

Much of the fiction published in both the *Knickerbocker* and the *Democratic Review* tended to be based on history, which underscored the nationalistic dimension of such works even as it made them seem closer to reality. Indeed, many pieces published in magazines were called "tales" or "sketches," blurring the boundaries between fiction and reality in such works and consequently making them all the more appealing to readers who had lingering concerns about the value of imaginative literature.

Despite such resistance, writers of fiction began to explore a range of subject matter and played a major role in the development of the short story. The popularity of European writers who wrote novels and stories about magic, mystery, and psychological terror prompted many American writers to adopt what was described as "gothic" elements in their work. Hawthorne blended such elements into his historical fictions, while Poe wrote stories with sensational plots and horrific details, designed to startle and captivate readers.

Nicolino Calyo, *Reading Room of the Astor House*

This satirical watercolor, painted around 1840, shows three men absorbed in their newspapers in the reading room of the Astor House, which opened in New York City in 1836 and which for many years was considered the finest hotel in the United States.

Domestic fiction was also becoming an increasingly popular staple of periodical literature during the 1830s and 1840s. In 1830, Louis A. Godey began the publication of *Godey's Lady's Book*, a periodical that became the most popular magazine for women before the Civil War. The magazine was intended to be a "mirror of woman's mind," and its editor for forty years, Sarah Josepha Hale, filled *Godey's* with fashion illustrations, sheet music, recipes, reviews, and advice as well as articles on travel and the arts. But the magazine also published a wide range of American writers. Alongside the works of Hawthorne and Poe, and the young Harriet Beecher Stowe were stories by now-forgotten writers who adhered to a standard plot line: A peaceful domestic household is threatened by an errant husband, relative, or child – rarely a wife – and eventually order is restored by the actions of Christian characters. Although such stories were deeply rooted in the day-to-day realities of domestic life, for women readers they were anything but dull. On the contrary, domestic fiction provided many middle-class women with solace and companionship during long hours spent within the confines of "woman's sphere," especially as men began to spend a growing number of hours away from the home. Women, who achieved the same literacy rates as men by midcentury, were becoming important consumers and increasingly vital producers of reading material. Smart publishers and editors studied and catered to the tastes and interests of this influential group of readers.

A Reading Party

"The young ladies are no longer dependent upon the other sex for literary information, but converse with as much facility upon the merits of modern writers as the male portion of the community," a writer for the *Philadelphia Album and Ladies Literary Portfolio* observed in 1827. During the following decades, reading became an even more important form of recreation and self-improvement for middle-class women, both individually and socially, as indicated by this illustration from an 1846 issue of *Godey's Lady's Book*.

At the same time, some very different trends were also emerging in American fiction. Just as literacy rates for women were increasing, so were the numbers of working-class Americans who could read. One of the best-selling books of the 1840s was the journalist George Lippard's *The Monks of Monk Hall* (later called *The Quaker City*), a sensational account of life and crime in Philadelphia. Forerunners of the "true crime" genre so popular today, stories about urban depravity became a staple in some periodicals. Temperance fiction, designed to demonstrate the evils of drink, was equally vivid in its representation of urban squalor. Walt Whitman published a temperance novel, *Franklin Evans* (1842), which was printed in an extra edition of the *New World*. Many other writers, such as Stowe, published stories with similar themes. In contrast, another respected woman author Louisa May Alcott wrote dozens of melodramatic thrillers (always under a pen name) during her long career. Sensational fiction was aimed mainly at lower-class audiences. It was cheap, it sold well, and it was consequently regarded with deep suspicion by editors and writers who wanted something more substantial for American literature.

Periodicals designed for a more educated and cultured audience exerted a powerful force on the shaping of American fiction. Making a bid for the audience that *Godey's* was attracting (but also pointedly including men in the title), *Graham's Lady's and Gentleman's Magazine* was established in 1841 for the purpose of publishing American writers. For nine years, *Graham's* was the best and the most popular literary magazine in the country. It published not only domestic fiction by women writers but also stories by Poe (who briefly edited the magazine) and Hawthorne. In 1844, Robert Bonner, an Irish immigrant, founded the *New York Ledger* as a family story-paper designed to provide weekly entertainment within the home. Determined to devote the *Ledger* to "choice literature, romance, the news, and commerce," Bonner sought out lively and informative works by the best writers he could afford. When Fanny Fern was becoming a household name for her witty columns in other periodicals, Bonner recruited her by publishing her novella, *Fanny Ford* (1855). He also employed a number of the increasingly popular women writers who were making a name for themselves in periodicals, including Alcott, Grace Greenwood, and E.D.E.N. Southworth.

Several of the literary magazines established in the 1850s had an even more lasting effect on American fiction. *Harper's New Monthly Magazine* (1850), *Putnam's Monthly* (1853), and the *Atlantic Monthly* (1857) were considered the most important venues for writers of American fiction, but they differed in some fundamental ways. Although it published some shorter works by American writers, including Melville and Elizabeth Barstow Stoddard, *Harper's* heavily relied on serializations of British novels. In contrast, *Putnam's* strongly promoted American writers. It also tended to publish shorter works, rather than offer an alternative to books by publishing lengthy serializations. Wishing to engage a broad national audience, the editors of *Putnam's* invited Charles Dudley Warner to write about California and John Pendleton Kennedy to write about the South.

By the beginning of the Civil War, American fiction was firmly established as a significant part of American culture, in large part due to the influence of periodicals.

The *Atlantic Monthly* ultimately provided an even more distinguished and enduring home for the new American literature. The inspiration of writers such as Ralph Waldo Emerson, Oliver Wendell Holmes, and James Russell Lowell, established the magazine as a monthly journal whose cultural mission was to guide the age in literature, politics, science, and the arts. Originally, however, it focused narrowly on New England, publishing writers like Hawthorne and Stowe. After the *Atlantic* was purchased in 1859 by the publishing company of Ticknor and Fields, the magazine sought to break out of the Northeast by including writers from other geographic locations, especially women like Rebecca Harding Davis of West Virginia, whose *Life in the Iron-Mills* appeared in 1861. One other literary magazine established in the 1850s was the *Anglo-*

HARPER'S
NEW MONTHLY MAGAZINE.
No. LXXIX.—DECEMBER, 1856.—VOL. XIV.

THE quaint historian, Diedrich Knickerbocker, says it was traditionary in his family, that when the worthy Master Hendrick Hudson first laid eyes upon the marvelous beauties of the great waters which now bear his honored name, astonishment and admiration wrung from his taciturn lips the remarkable exclamation, "See there!" That the susceptible navigator really did give expression to his unwonted emotions in these supreme terms, or at least "in words to that

Entered according to Act of Congress, in the year 1856, by Harper and Brothers, in the Clerk's Office of the District Court for the Southern District of New York.

VOL. XIV.—No. 79.—A

Sunnyside

A mass-circulation magazine targeted at a national audience, *Harper's* often included lavish illustrations, especially for its numerous travel essays and articles on famous places like "Sunnyside," the house on the Hudson River where Washington Irving lived until his death in 1859. Despite its tribute to that most revered and successful of earlier American writers, most of the fiction published in *Harper's* consisted of reprints of works by popular British novelists, especially Charles Dickens, who offered formidable competition to his counterparts in the United States.

African Magazine (1859). The first magazine devoted exclusively to publishing the works of African American writers like Martin Delany and Frances E. W. Harper, it was specifically intended to compete with magazines devoted to white writers.

By the beginning of the Civil War, American fiction was firmly established as a significant part of American culture, in large part due to the influence of periodicals. For young, unknown writers, publishing in magazines and newspapers offered a way to achieve a literary reputation. In fact, of all the writers represented in this section, only Melville started off by writing a series of novels. He turned to writing periodical fiction only when his career as a novelist faltered. But most novelists began by writing primarily for periodicals. Although he published an immature novel in 1828, the dozens of sketches and stories Hawthorne wrote for magazines during the 1830s and 1840s paved the way for the major novels he published in the 1850s, including *The Scarlet Letter* (1850), *The House of the Seven Gables* (1851), and *The Blithedale Romance* (1852). The enthusiastic reception of a sketch Donald Grant Mitchell ("Ik Marvel") published in the *Southern Literary Messenger* prompted him to expand it into *Reveries of a Bachelor* (1850), one of the most enduringly popular books of the nineteenth century. Because of Stowe's success as a regular writer of short sketches for magazines and newspapers, the editor of the *National Era* invited her to submit installments of the story that would eventually become the best-selling novel of the 1850s, *Uncle Tom's Cabin.* A temperance novel by Timony Shay Arthur, *Ten Nights in a Bar Room* (1854), was another bestseller and came close to rivaling the sales of Stowe's hugely successful novel. *Uncle Tom's Cabin* radically altered the literary landscape, establishing the novel as the most popular of all kinds of writing in the United States. Stowe's novel also gained a wide audience in England, where Queen Victoria was among the many enthusiastic readers of an edition published in London in 1852.

Novels by American women dominated fiction in the United States during the 1850s, when the best-selling novelists included Susan Warner,

America's First Blockbuster

Stowe's best-selling novel sold 300,000 copies during its first year of book publication in 1852. As this bookseller's advertisement indicates, the novel was available in different languages and various editions, priced from 37½¢ to $5.

author of *The Wide, Wide World* (1852), and Maria Susanna Cummins, author of *The Lamplighter* (1854). Their popularity led a rather bitter Hawthorne to complain to his editor about the success of such "scribbling women." At the same time, periodicals continued to be the preferred place of publication for prominent writers like Fanny Fern, even as literary magazines offered a crucial outlet for the work of young writers like Alcott, Davis, and Elizabeth Barstow Stoddard in the years before and during the Civil War. In whatever form, whether in novels or stories published in periodicals, American fiction had finally become a powerful presence in the literary marketplace.

American Contexts

"Countless Phenomena of the Times": The Role of the Periodical Press

THE DEVELOPMENT OF PERIODICALS in the United States during the first half of the nineteenth century is a story of increasing numbers. Innovations in technology, especially the development of mechanical power-presses, and improvements in the transportation system made possible the swift publication and wide distribution of periodicals. In 1800, there were about 300 magazines and newspapers in the United States. By 1840, there were approximately 1,500. With good reason, the editors of the *New-York Mirror* proclaimed it the "golden age of the periodical." Periodicals had become an integral part of print culture in the United States.

Periodicals varied widely. Many of the earliest magazines were little more than imitators of British journals, and British writers were a fixture in most literary publications. Newspapers, often established along partisan political lines or founded to promote a specific cause such as antislavery, printed poetry and fiction alongside news features. Most newspapers were originally published weekly, but by the 1830s daily "penny papers" offered local and national news. As the population grew and business interests expanded, the demand for news increased and major daily newspapers were established, such as the *New York Times*, which was founded in 1851. At the same time, magazines were also developing quickly. There was no standard size, format, or frequency of publication

William Morris Hunt, *Girl Reading* (1853)

This painting of a young working-class woman absorbed in reading, probably a work of fiction in a magazine, suggests the broad appeal of the stories and serialized novels that became staples of periodical literature by the 1850s. (Photograph © 2006 Museum of Fine Arts, Boston.)

rate for magazines. Many of them were indistinguishable from newspapers, with narrow rows of vertical columns, while others looked like unbound books, with chapters of small print. Initially, only a few magazines offered illustrations, or "embellishments," as they were then called. But as the techniques for reproducing engravings improved, the public increasingly demanded illustrations, which most magazines had in abundance by the 1840s.

Periodicals appealed to widely different audiences. Many were designed for a general audience, and reading stories aloud from magazines and newspapers was a staple of evening entertainment for the whole family. Enterprising publishers also began to develop periodicals for special interests and audiences. There were religious newspapers and magazines for children, as well as periodicals designed to reach a geographic audience, including the South and the West. Many editors targeted particular audiences with publications about medicine, agriculture, and increasingly the interests of middle-class women. As many as 110 periodicals for women appeared between 1800 and the beginning of the Civil War. Other editors and publishers responded to the call for a national literature, seeking to create high-quality literary magazines that would feature American

bedfordstmartins.com/ americanlit *for research links on the authors in this section*

writers and American topics, even as the lack of an international copyright law made it possible to print the work of popular British writers without the payment of royalties. Literary magazines became an important vehicle for American writers – to get their works published, establish an audience, and create interest and demand for more work. In fact, periodicals played a crucial role in the professionalization of authorship in the United States.

As Charles F. Briggs suggested in his introduction to *Putnam's Monthly Magazine* (reprinted on p. 958), periodicals provided "a running commentary on the countless phenomena of the times." One of the signal developments of the first half of the nineteenth century was the proliferation of periodicals and their increasing role in entertainment and the communication of ideas. In 1845, a reviewer in *Godey's Lady's Book* observed that periodicals were rapidly becoming the dominant reading material of the day: "A large percentage of books published scarce find a publisher; a number of those purchased are never read and many that *are* read, are read by one or two persons, while with periodicals the *un*-read are the exception. One has but to look into circulating libraries, reading-rooms, and the like places to see that an extensive class of readers finds time or inclination for little else." The following essays suggest the variety of ways in which editors and writers were actively promoting American writers through the new medium of periodical literature.

James Ewell Heath

[1792-1862]

James Ewell Heath was a Virginia-born author of a book on banking as well as a novel, *Edge Hill* (1828). He was a close friend of Thomas Willis White (1788-1843), a Virginia printer who founded the *Southern Literary Messenger* in August 1834. Weary of the dominance of northeastern writers and periodicals in the United States, White wanted to establish a magazine that would compete with the successful literary magazines of the North and create a vehicle for southern writers. For thirty years, the *Southern Literary Messenger* accomplished White's mission by publishing articles, stories, poems, travelogues, and reviews by a wide variety of writers, including Donald Grant Mitchell ("Ik Marvel") and Edgar Allan Poe, who was the assistant editor of the magazine from 1835 to 1837. Although White was the major force behind the magazine, Heath was its first editor, working long hours to collect articles and correspond with potential contributors. The following introductory article appeared in the first issue of the *Southern Literary Messenger*, August 1834.

SOUTHERN LITERATURE

It is understood that the first number of the "Messenger," will be sent forth by its Publisher, as a kind of pioneer, to spy out the land of literary promise, and to report whether the same be fruitful or barren, before he resolves upon future action. It would be a mortifying discovery, if instead of kindness and good will, he should be repulsed by the coldness and neglect of a Virginia public. Hundreds of similar publications thrive and prosper north of the Potomac, sustained as they are by the liberal hand of patronage. *Shall not one be supported in the whole south?* This is a question of great importance; – and one which ought to be answered with sober earnestness by all who set any value upon public character, or who are in the least degree jealous of that individual honor and dignity which is in some measure connected with the honor and dignity of the state. Are we to be doomed forever to a kind of vassalage[1] to our northern neighbors – a dependence for our literary food upon our brethren, whose superiority in all the great points of character, – in valor – eloquence and patriotism, we are no wise disposed to admit? Is it not altogether extraordinary that in this extensive commonwealth, containing a white population of upwards of six hundred thousand souls – a vast deal of agricultural wealth, and innumerable persons of both sexes, who enjoy both leisure and affluence – there is not one solitary periodical exclusively literary? What is the cause? We are not willing to borrow our political, – religious, or even our agricultural notions from the other side of Mason and Dixon's line,[2] and we generously patronize various domestic journals devoted to those several subjects. Why should we consider the worthy descendants of the pilgrims – of the Hollanders of Manhattan, or the German adventurers of Pennsylvania, as exclusively entitled to cater for us in our choicest intellectual aliment?[3] Shall it be said that the empire of literature has no geographical boundaries, and that local jealousies ought not to disturb its harmony? To this there is an obvious answer. If we continue to be *consumers* of northern productions, we shall never ourselves become *producers*. We may take from them the fabrics of their looms, and give in exchange without loss our agricultural products – but if we depend exclusively upon their *literary* supplies, it is certain that the spirit of invention among our own sons, will be damped, if not entirely extinguished. The value of a *domestic* publication of the kind, consists in its being at once accessible to all who choose to venture into the arena as rivals for renown. It imparts the same energy, and exercises the same influence upon mental improvement, that a rail road does upon agricultural labor, when passing by our doors and through our estates. The literary spirit which pervades some portions of New

---

1. **vassalage:** Condition of servitude, as on a feudal estate where servants or vassals performed services for an overlord in exchange for protection.
2. **Mason and Dixon's line:** Originally established by two surveyors in the middle of the eighteenth century to settle a property dispute, the boundary line eventually separated Pennsylvania from Virginia and Maryland (and Maryland from Delaware). According to the Missouri Compromise of 1820, the states north of the line were designated free and the states south of the line were designated as slaveholding. The exception was Delaware, to the east of the line, which remained a part of the Union during the Civil War although it was a slaveholding state.
3. **aliment:** Food or nourishment.

England and the northern cities, would never have existed, at least in the same degree, if the journals and repositories designed to cherish and promote it, had been derived exclusively from London and Edinburgh. In like manner, if we look entirely to Boston, New York or Philadelphia, for that delightful mental enjoyment and recreation, which such publications afford, we must content ourselves with being the readers and admirers of other men's thoughts, and lose all opportunity for stirring up our own minds, and breathing forth our own meditations. In other words, we must be satisfied to partake of the feast, as it is set before us by our more industrious and enterprising countrymen, and if peradventure, the cookery should not be altogether to our taste, we must, nevertheless, with our characteristic courtesy, be thankful, – and like honest Sancho,[4] "bid God bless the giver."

It is not intended to be intimated that the aristarchy of the north and east, cherish any unkind feelings towards the literary claims of the south. Oh no! In truth, they have no cause whatsoever, either for unkindness or jealousy. If we only continue to patronize their multitudinous magazines, they will pocket our money and praise us as a very generous and chivalrous race; or if, perchance, some juvenile drama, or poem, or some graver duodecimo[5] of southern manufacture, should find its way to the seats of learning and criticism beyond the Susquehanna,[6] it is an even chance, that in order to preserve the monopoly of the southern market, they will dole out to us a modicum of praise, and render some faint tribute to rising merit. Without therefore intending any thing invidious, or without cherishing any unkind or unmanly sentiment towards our political confederates, we ought forthwith to buckle on our armour, and assert our mental independence. All their own lofty and generous spirits will approve the resolution, and be among the first to welcome the dawn of a brighter era in a region of comparative twilight. Their Irvings and Pauldings, their Everetts and Neals, their Coopers and Verplancks, their Kennedys and Flints, their Hallecks and Bryants, their Sedgwicks and Sigourneys,[7] will rejoice in the emancipation of the south, from the shackles which either indolence, indifference, or the love of pleasure, have imposed upon us. We are too old, and ought to be too proud to lag behind even some of our younger sisters, in the cultivation of one of the most attractive departments of human knowledge. It is folly to boast of political ascendancy, of moral influence, of professional eminence, or unri-

---

4. **Sancho:** Sancho Panza was the loyal, realistic companion of the visionary hero and the title character of the novel *Don Quixote*, by Miguel de Cervantes (1547–1616).

5. **duodecimo:** A page size – about 5 x 7.5 inches, or one-twelfth the size of the large sheets of paper – used in printing. In this context, a duodecimo refers to a book of this size, which was a common format in the nineteenth century.

6. **Susquehanna:** The Susquehanna River flows from central New York through Pennsylvania and Maryland and into the Chesapeake Bay.

7. **Irvings . . . Sigourneys:** A list of well-known northern writers: Washington Irving (1783–1859), James Kirke Paulding (1778–1860), Edward Everett (1794–1865), John Neal (1793–1870), James Fenimore Cooper (1789–1851), Gulian Crommelin Verplanck (1786–1870), John Pendleton Kennedy (1795–1870), Timothy Flint (1780–1840), Fitz-Greene Halleck (1795–1867), William Cullen Bryant (1794–1878), Catharine Maria Sedgwick (1789–1867), and Lydia Sigourney (1791–1865).

valled oratory, when, in all the Corinthian graces[8] which adorn the structure of mind, we are lamentably deficient. It is worse than folly to talk of this "ancient and unterrified commonwealth" – if we suffer ourselves to be *terrified* at the idea of supporting one poor periodical, devoted to letters and mental improvement. It would be an indelible reproach to us, that whilst we waste so many thousands annually in luxury – whilst we squander our means in expensive tours of recreation and pleasure, – and even impoverish our resources in indulgences too gross to be mentioned – we should be unwilling to contribute a single mite towards building up a character of our own, and providing the means of imbodying and concentrating the neglected genius of our country. Let the hundreds of our gifted sons, therefore, who have talents and acquirements, come forth to this work of patriotism, with a firm resolution to persevere until victory is achieved. Let them dismiss their apprehensions, – that because as yet they are unpractised in composition – and the highway to literary eminence is already thronged with competitors – that, therefore, the most vigorous effort will be vanquished in the contest. In the race for political or professional distinction, who is influenced by such timid suggestions? In that noble strife, which animates southern bosoms to control by the magic of oratory the passions of the multitude, or in a more learned arena "the applause of listening senates to command" – who ever heard of discouragements and difficulties sufficient to chill their ardor, or restrain their aspirations? And yet is it less difficult to attain the prize of eloquence – to rival the fame of a Henry, or a Wirt,[9] than to achieve the task of vigorous and graceful composition?

To our lovely and accomplished countrywomen, may not a successful appeal be also addressed, to lend their aid in this meritorious task. Their influence upon the happiness and destiny of society, is so extensively felt and acknowledged, that to dwell upon its various bearings and relations, would be altogether superfluous. It is to the watchful care of a mother's love, that those first principles of moral wisdom are implanted in childhood, which ripen into the blossoms and fruit of maturer years; and it is to the reproving virtues and refining tenderness of the sex, through all its mutations, from blooming sixteen to the matronly grace of forty – that man is indebted for all that is soft, and for much that is noble and wise, in his own character. It is true that there is another side to this picture. If a woman's education has itself been neglected; if she has been trained up in the paths of folly and vanity – and been taught to ornament the casket in preference to the celestial jewel which it contains, – she will neither be a fit companion for the sterner sex, nor be qualified to assume the divine responsibility of maternal instruction. To diffuse therefore not only the benefits of moral but intellectual culture, among those whom heaven has given to restore in part the blessings of a lost Eden – to withdraw their minds from vain and unprofitable pursuits – to teach them to emulate the distinguished names of their own sex, who have given lustre to literature,

---

8. **Corinthian graces:** In ancient Greece, the Corinthians were considered to have elaborate cultural and aesthetic tastes.

9. **Henry, or a Wirt:** The colonial orators Patrick Henry (1736–1799), a Virginia-born lawyer and statesman, and William Wirt (1772–1834), a Maryland-born lawyer who acted as prosecutor in the trial of Aaron Burr (1807).

and scattered sweets in the paths of science – is a duty not only of paramount importance on our part, but claims the united and cordial support of the fair and interesting objects of our care.

Let no one therefore presume to disparage this humble effort to redeem our country's escutcheon[10] from the reproach which has been cast upon it. Let the miser open his purse – the prodigal save a pittance from his health-wasting and mind-destroying expenditures – the lawyer and physician, spare a little from their fees – the merchant and mechanic, from their speculations and labor – and the man of fortune, devote a part, a very small part of his abundance, towards the creation of a new era in the annals of this blessed Old Dominion.[11] It may possibly be the means of effecting a salutary reform in public taste and individual habits; of overcoming that tendency to mental repose and luxurious indulgence supposed to be peculiar to southern latitudes; and of awakening a spirit of inquiry and a zeal for improvement, which cannot fail ultimately to exalt and adorn society.

[1834]

---

10. **escutcheon:** A shield upon which is displayed a coat of arms.
11. **Old Dominion:** The nickname for the state of Virginia.

John L. O'Sullivan

[1813-1895]

John L. O'Sullivan and his partner, Samuel D. Langtree, founded the *United States Magazine and Democratic Review* in 1837. Originally published in Washington, D.C., and later in New York City, the magazine was a national publication designed to advance the interests of the Democratic Party. It also offered a nationalistic alternative to the British orientation of many other literary and political magazines of the period. Indeed, the *Democratic Review* (as it was later called), published dozens of American writers, including William Ellery Channing, Elizabeth Ellet, Nathaniel Hawthorne, James Russell Lowell, William Gilmore Simms, Henry David Thoreau, and John Greenleaf Whittier. In 1858, seven years after the magazine folded, Walt Whitman recalled that the *Democratic Review* under O'Sullivan's editorship was a "monthly magazine of profounder quality of talent than any since."

In the first issue of the magazine, O'Sullivan explained that the main goal of the periodical was to advance the principles of American democracy. Affirming the "virtue, intelligence, and full capacity of self-government, of the great mass our people," O'Sullivan also emphasized that "Democracy is the cause of Humanity." Why then, he asked, was "the young mind of our country so deeply tainted with anti-democratic sentiment"? O'Sullivan enumerated various reasons, including the fact that "the anti-democratic cause possesses at least two-thirds of the press of the country," and – as he asserted in the following passage, at the end of his introductory essay – that the nation lacked a truly democratic national literature. The text is taken from *United States Magazine and Democratic Review*, October 1837.

From INTRODUCTION

But a more potent influence than any yet noticed, is that of our national literature. Or rather we have no national literature. We depend almost wholly on Europe, and particularly England, to think and write for us, or at least to furnish materials and models after which we shall mould our own humble attempts. We have a considerable number of writers; but not in that consists a national literature. The vital principle of an American national literature must be democracy. Our mind is enslaved to the past and present literature of England. Rich and glorious as is that vast collection of intellectual treasure, it would have been far better for us had we been separated from it by the ocean of a difference of language, as we are from the country itself by our sublime Atlantic. Our mind would then have been compelled to think for itself and to express itself, and its animating spirit would have been our democracy. As it now is, we are cowed by the mind of England. We follow feebly and afar in the splendid track of a literature moulded on the whole (notwithstanding a number of noble exceptions) by the ideas and feelings of an utterly anti-democratic social system. We give back but a dim reflection – a faint echo of the expression of the English mind. No one will misunderstand us as disparaging the literature of our mother language – far from it. We appreciate it with a profound veneration and gratitude, and would use it, without abusing it by utterly submitting our own minds to it; but we look upon it, as we do upon the political system of the country, as a something magnificent, venerable, splendid, and powerful, and containing a considerable infusion of the true principle; yet the one no more suitable to be adopted as our own, or as a model for slavish imitation, than the other. In the spirit of her literature we can never hope to rival England. She is immeasurably in advance of us, and is rich with ever active energies, and resources of literary habits and capital (so to speak) which mock our humble attempts at imitation. But we should not follow in her wake; a radiant path invites us forward in another direction. We have a principle – an informing soul – of our own, our democracy, though we allow it to languish uncultivated; this must be the animating spirit of our literature, if, indeed, we would have a national American literature. There is an immense field open to us, if we would but enter it boldly and cultivate it as our own. All history has to be re-written; political science and the whole scope of all moral truth have to be considered and illustrated in the light of the democratic principle. All old subjects of thought and all new questions arising, connected more or less directly with human existence, have to be taken up again and re-examined in this point of view. We *ought* to exert a powerful moral influence on Europe, and yet we are entirely unfelt; and as it is only by its literature that one nation can utter itself and make itself known to the rest of the world, we are really entirely unknown. In the present general fermentation of popular ideas in Europe, turning the public thoughts naturally to the great democracy across the Atlantic, the voice of America might be made to produce a powerful and beneficial effect on the development of truth; but as it is, American writings are never translated, because they almost always prove to be a diluted and tardy second edition of English thought.

The anti-democratic character of our literature, then, is a main cause of the evil of which we complain; and this is both a mutual cause and effect, constantly acting and re-acting. Our 'better educated classes' drink in an anti-democratic habit of feeling and thinking from the copious, and it must be confessed delicious, fountain of the literature of England; they give the same spirit to our own, in which we have little or nothing that is truly democratic and American. Hence this tone of sentiment of our literary institutions and of our learned professions, poisoning at the spring the young mind of our people.

If the "United States Magazine and Democratic Review" shall be able, by the influence of example and *the most liberal* encouragement, to contribute in any degree towards the remedy of this evil, (as of the other evils in our institutions which may need reform,) by vindicating the true glory and greatness of the democratic principle, by infusing it into our literature, and by rallying the mind of the nation from the state of torpor and even of demoralization in which so large a proportion of it is sunk, one of the main objects of its establishment will have been achieved.

[1837]

Sarah Josepha Hale

[1788–1879]

Sarah Josepha Hale was the editor of the popular women's magazine *Godey's Lady's Book* from 1837 to 1877. Although she often shared editorial responsibilities with the magazine's founder, Louis Godey, Hale was the undisputed power behind the highly successful publication. Combining literature by a stellar cast of American writers – including Nathaniel Hawthorne, Edgar Allan Poe, Henry Wadsworth Longfellow, and a young Harriet Beecher (later Stowe) – with articles on fashion, hairstyles, domestic management, and childcare, the magazine reached a circulation of 150,000 just before the Civil War. Conservative and cautious in tone, the magazine scrupulously avoided political controversies – the word *slavery*, for example, was never mentioned in *Godey's*. Although she was opposed to women's suffrage, she supported property rights for married women and constantly encouraged women to educate themselves and provide spiritual leadership in the home. Hale urged women to take active roles in the cultivation of moral and religious values. Beginning in 1847, Hale also used her editorial column to promote a national holiday of Thanksgiving on the fourth Thursday of every November. She envisioned

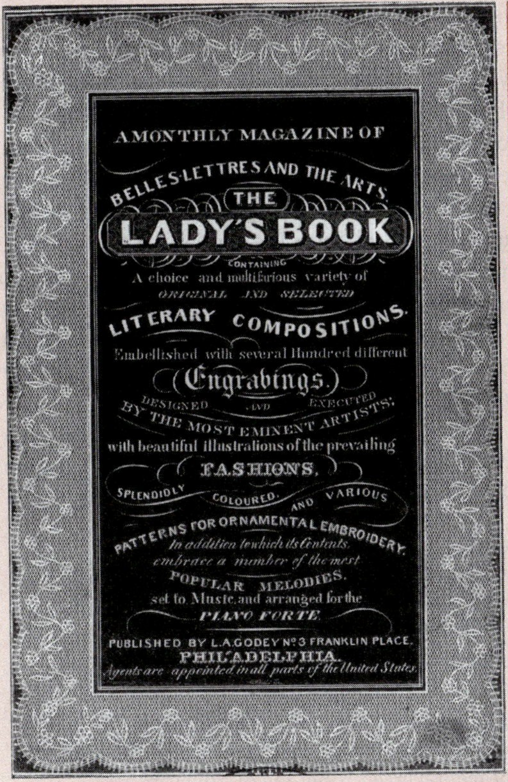

Godey's Lady's Book

This elaborate cover of an 1834 issue of *Godey's*, the most widely read women's magazine of the period, indicates the range of its contents, from fashion plates and patterns for embroidery to "literary compositions." In fact, the magazine published the work of some of the most popular and respected American writers of the period, including Nathaniel Hawthorne, Edgar Allan Poe, and Harriet Beecher Stowe.

the holiday as a way to inspire "gratitude and patriotism," as she frequently wrote, in every citizen. Hale's successful campaign culminated on October 3, 1863, when President Abraham Lincoln issued the Thanksgiving Day Proclamation, establishing the national holiday. Committed also to what she called "women's intellectual progress," Hale advanced the careers of many women writers by promoting them in the pages of *Godey's*, where the following piece appeared in January 1850.

EDITORS' TABLE[1]

The beginning of a new volume and a new year naturally excites the inquiry – What have we to do? To answer this question rightly, we must well understand, not only what we have done, but also what we have intended to accomplish. What has been our aim? The Lady's Book has had, from the first, but one grand design – to subserve the best interests of WOMAN.

1. **Editors' Table:** Virtually all nineteenth-century magazines included space for the editor to comment on the contents of the magazine and provide miscellaneous items of interest to readers.

What a wonderful change in public opinion concerning the powers of the female mind has been effected since our journal was first published! Then – that is, twenty years ago – very little interest was taken in female education. The subject of "woman's rights"[2] had been foolishly and clamorously urged by a few, who, with a "zeal without knowledge" or discretion, would have broken down the barriers of true modesty, and destroyed the retiring graces of woman's nature, in which her most beneficial influence is concealed, like the flower in its calyx.[3]

Gently to unfold this flower, as the sun's rays in the spring warm and expand the rose till its beauty is seen and its sweet incense induces the admirer to preserve it for its virtues as well as its loveliness, has been the work of the Lady's Book.

And now, who questions the beneficial influence of woman's cultivated intellect? or doubts the great effect it is to exercise on the improvement and happiness of the world?

We are intending, in this Table, to serve up a few of the recent opinions of English and American writers on these interesting subjects – Woman, and her intellectual and moral influence, selected from works not, probably, yet seen by the greater portion of our readers. And first from a *true poet*: –

Woman is not undeveloped man,
But diverse: could we make her as the man,
Sweet love were slain, whose dearest bond is this,
Not like to like, but like in difference:
Yet in the long years liker must they grow;
The man be more of woman, she of man;
He gain in sweetness and in moral height,
Nor lose the wrestling thews that throw the world;
She mental breadth, nor fail in childward care:
More as the double-natured poet each;
Till, at the last, she set herself to man
Like perfect music unto noble words;
And so these twain, upon the skirts of Time,
Sit side by side, full-summed in all their powers,
Dispensing harvest, sowing the To-be,
Self-reverent each, and reverencing each,
Distinct in individualities,
But like each other, even as those who love.
Then comes the statelier Eden back to men;
Then reigns the world's great bridals chaste and calm;
Then springs the crowning race of humankind.
May these things be! – *Tennyson's Princess*[4]

---

2. **woman's rights:** Hale refers to increasing activism among women for expanded rights, including the right to vote, especially following the Seneca Falls Woman's Rights Convention in 1848.
3. **calyx:** Outer covering that protects a flower before it blooms.
4. ***Tennyson's Princess***: The lines are from *The Princess* (1847), a long narrative poem, by the popular English poet Alfred, Lord Tennyson (1809–1892).

We come to men for philosophy, to women for consolation. And the thousand weaknesses and regrets; the sharp sands of the minutiae that make up *sorrow* – all these, which I would have betrayed to no *man* – not even to him the dearest and tenderest of all men – I showed without shame to thee, my mother! – *Bulwer.*[5]

The difference between the mental qualities of the sexes is owing, we apprehend, far more to education than to nature. At all events, there is no such natural difference as warrants the distinction we make in the mental discipline we provide for them. There are certain professional studies with which no one thinks of vexing the mind of any one, man or woman, but those who intend to practice the professions; but why, in a good English library, there should be one-half of it, and that the better half, which a young woman is not expected to read – this we never could understand, and never reflect on with common patience. Why may not a Locke, or a Paley, or a Dugald Stewart,[6] train the mind of the future mother of a family? Or why may not an intelligent young woman be a companion for her brother or her husband in his more serious moods of thought, as well as in his gayer and more trifling? Would the world lose anything of social happiness or moral refinement by this intellectual equality of the two sexes? You vex the memory of a young girl with dictionaries and vocabularies without end; you tax her memory in every conceivable manner; and, at an after age, you give the literature of sentiment freely to her pillage; but that which should step between the two – the culture of the reason – this is entirely forbidden. If she learns a dozen modern languages, she does not read a single book in any one of them that would make her think. Even in her religious library, the same distinction is preserved. Books of sentimental piety – some of them maudlin enough – are thrust, with kindest anxiety and most liberal profusion, upon her; any work of theology, any work that discusses and examines, is as carefully excluded. – *Blackwood's Magazine*[7]

But matters are mending, and will continue to mend. There are so many women of richly cultivated minds who have distinguished themselves in letters or in society, and made it highly feminine to be intelligent as well as good, and to have elevated as well as amiable feelings, that, by and by, the whole sex must adopt a new standard of education. It must, we presume, be by leaders of their own, starting out of their own body, that the rest of the soft and timid flock must be led. – *Ibid.*[8]

The mothers of this generation must form the men and women of the next. No degree of masculine cultivation can make up for a lack of mental and physical development in women. It is the mother who gives the elements of greatness. Every day's observation teaches us this lesson; and no society, no nation can advance where the culture, and all that goes to form the character of woman, are neglected; and no nation can fail of greatness where women are held in genuine respect.

---

5. ***Bulwer***: Edward George Earl Bulwer-Lytton (1803–1873), a popular English novelist whose books were widely read in nineteenth-century America.
6. **Locke . . . Stewart**: John Locke (1632–1704) and William Paley (1743–1805) were English philosophers; Dugald Stewart (1753–1828) was a Scottish philosopher.
7. ***Blackwood's Magazine***: Established in 1817 by William Blackwood, a Scottish publisher, *Blackwood's* was among the best and most prominent of the British literary magazines.
8. ***Ibid***: In the same place (Latin), meaning that the quotation is from another article in *Blackwood's Magazine.*

We have said little of the "Rights of Woman." Her first right is to education, in its widest sense – to such education as will give her the full development of all her personal, mental, and moral qualities. Having that, there will be no longer any question about her rights; and rights are liable to be perverted to wrongs when we are incapable of rightly exercising them. Give woman health, beauty, high intelligence, and that purity of soul and benevolence of heart which belong to her nature, and she would have no difficulty in making her proper place in society; for she would have the forming of the thought, and taste, and moral sentiment of the world. It seems hard to regenerate the world; but the work would be easy, if we could but see the means which God has appointed. We have only to give full play and free development to the love principle, which finds its form and expression in the pure nature of woman, in order to reform the world.

There is no danger that we shall ever esteem too highly, honor too much, or treat with a too tender consideration, the mothers of our race. No chivalry was ever extravagant; it was only misguided. The impulse was holy, but mis-directed. That impulse gave us civilization; the same chivalric feeling, with more enlightenment, will give us that state of society that glows in beauty in our radiant dreams of the future. Physically and morally, God has made woman worthy to be the mother of mankind. Her nature is as exalted as her function. Love, and truth, and purity are the instincts of her being. Religion is the grand impulse of her soul. Even in her present imperfect state, after ages of neglect and suffering, she commands our admiration, and receives our love and worship. All that is truly good and beautiful in society, we owe to woman. The regeneration of the race, and the opening of a higher and happier existence to mankind, are sufficient motives to influence us in using all our exertions to improve the condition of woman; while her elevation and happiness will be the most gratifying feature of a new order of society.

Woman must be the motive power of all human progress. Man may be, to whatever extent we please to contend, the head and hands of any true movement; but woman must be its warm heart. Hers is the empire of the affections; and her attractions are sufficient to elevate the world, if she be only elevated to the vantage-ground that belongs to her. If woman, for the past century, had not been shut out from her rightful share of the advantages of education and opportunities for culture, the world would have made more rapid advances. The great mistake of men has been, to leave her behind, and to endeavor to get along without her. Such a one-sided advance is impossible. Woman must advance step by step with man; in some things, she must even lead and guide him, or there can be no advancement. For man to endeavor to move on alone, leaving his "better half" to lag behind him, can only produce discord, mischief, and misery. Humanity becomes a divided body, without a living soul.

If any difference be allowed in the means of education and the facilities for improvement, it should be in favor of the female sex; for, in the period of our youth, it is the highest ambition of every man to make himself agreeable, acceptable to, and worthy of the other sex. The intelligence and refinement of woman, therefore, would secure the education and elevation of man, in the present generation, by the law of sexual attraction, while it would still more secure the improvement of both sexes of the coming generations, by the laws of hereditary descent.

As philosophers, recognizing the laws of the material and moral universe; as philanthropists, seeking the elevation and happiness of our species; as Christians, having faith in the goodness and wisdom of God, and in the temporal and eternal salvation of his children – we should work earnestly to undo the wrongs of ages, and give to woman that place in society for which God designed her; and that opportunity for the development of her gifts and graces which would secure her own happiness, fulfill the promise of the future,

> and make her the glory of the race, in that condition of social order and moral harmony to which all the attractions of humanity tend, and in which the highest earthly destiny of the human race shall be accomplished. – *Thomas L. Nichols*[9]

Our selections are from masculine writers; and from hundreds of others, of the highest genius and most eminent fame, similar sentiments might be quoted. We are encouraged and guided by this popular opinion. THE LADY'S BOOK (including the Boston Lady's Magazine)[10] was the first avowed advocate of the holy cause of woman's intellectual progress; it has been the pioneer in the wonderful change of public sentiment respecting female education, and the employment of female talent in the work of educating the young.

We intend to go on, sustained and accelerated by this universal encouragement, till our grand aim is accomplished, till *female education* shall receive the same careful attention and liberal support from public legislation as are bestowed on that of the other sex.

Such is the mission of the *Lady's Book* for 1850.

Does not every *Lady* in America wish success to her own BOOK? We are sure its readers do; and, in return, this number is charged with the greetings of its editors to all their friends. May each and all enjoy a happy New Year!

[1850]

9. ***Thomas L. Nichols***: (1815–1901) American physician and author of *The Lady in Black: A Study of New York Life, Morals, and Manners* (1844) and *Woman in All Ages and Nations* (1849).
10. **Boston Lady's Magazine**: Hale first edited this magazine in 1828; it later became the *American Ladies' Magazine* and, at the end of 1836, merged with *Godey's Lady's Book*.

Charles F. Briggs

[1804–1877]

Charles F. Briggs was the author of a novel, *The Adventures of Henry Franco* (1839), and an experienced editor by the time he became the first editor-in-chief of *Putnam's Monthly Magazine*, established in 1853 and published by George Palmer Putnam. From the beginning, *Putnam's* was designed to showcase the work of American writers, and Briggs and his assistant editors consequently solicited contributions from major figures like Horace Greeley, Caroline Kirkland, Henry Wadsworth Longfellow, Herman Melville, and Henry David Thoreau. *Putnam's* also tried to be inclusive by publishing works by western writers, such as Charles Dudley Warner, and southerners like William Swinton and Mrs. R. B. Hicks (as she was known). For a few years, *Putnam's* was regarded as an outstanding literary magazine, but after Putnam sold it to another company the magazine faltered and finally failed in 1857. The following introductory essay appeared in the first issue of *Putnam's*, January 1853.

INTRODUCTORY[1]

Astronomers assert that the nebulous mist with which the ether is charged is perpetually taking form – that the regions of space are but a celestial dairy, in which the milky way is for ever churned into stars. Nor do the new stars extinguish the old; for, as the thirteenth man in the omnibus always says – there is room for one more. It will not, therefore, surprise the public to see a new Magazine. The reader, like the astronomer cognizant of infinite star-dust, knows very well that in the rapid life of this country there is a constant scintillation of talent, which needs only a nucleus to be combined into beams of light and heat.

Taking the reader, therefore, by the hand, or rather by the eye, here at the portal, we invite a moment's conversation before he passes within.

A man buys a Magazine to be amused – to be instructed, if you please, but the lesson must be made amusing. He buys it to read in the cars, in his leisure hours at home – in the hotel, at all chance moments. It makes very little difference to him whether the article date from Greece or Guinea, if it only interest him. He does not read upon principle, and troubles himself little about copyright and justice to authors. If a man goes to Timbuctoo and describes his visit picturesequely and well, the reader devours the story, and is not at all concerned because the publisher may have broken the author's head or heart, to obtain the manuscript. A popular Magazine must amuse, interest and instruct, or the public will pass by upon the other side. Nor will it be persuaded to "come over and help us" by any consideration of abstract right. It says, very justly, "if you had no legs, why did you try to walk?"

It is because we are confident that neither Greece nor Guinea can offer the American reader a richer variety of instruction and amusement in every kind, than the country whose pulses throb with his, and whose every interest is his own, that this Magazine presents itself to-day. The genius of the old world is affluent; we owe much to it, and we hope to owe more. But we have no less faith in the opulence of our own resources. Not alone in the discussion of those graver contemporary interests of every kind, which is the peculiar province of the foreign Quarterly Review, but in the treatment of minor matters of daily experience, which makes so much of the distinctive charm of a Magazine, we hold to the conviction that our genius is as good as it is in practical affairs. To an American eye, life in New-York, for instance, offers more, and more interesting, aspects, than life in London or Paris. Or, again, life in London and Paris is more interesting and intelligible to an American when reported by an American, than by the man of any other country. America practically goes to Europe with every American. We do not mean, of course, with every man whose birth chanced to fall in America, and to whom Europe is Paris, and Paris a *Jardin Mabille*, or a *Magasin des Modes*,[2] but with every man who sees through "American spectacles," as a late anonymous author expresses it. We all understand his impressions and estimates, because they are made by a standard

1. **Introductory:** Although unsigned, the article was clearly written by the editor, Charles F. Briggs.
2. ***Jardin Mabille*, or a *Magasin des Modes*:** Infamous outdoor dance hall in Paris, or a fashionable shop (French).

common to ourselves. And if we add to this, the essential freshness of feeling and true poetic sense of the American, we find some reason for the opinion that not only does an American know how to travel, but he knows how to tell his travels well. Hence, in a popular Magazine, which is a running commentary upon the countless phenomena of the times as they rise – not, as in a newspaper, in the form of direct criticism, but in the more permanently interesting shapes of story, essay, poem and sketch – this local reality is a point of the utmost importance. If there are as sharp-eyed and cunning-handed men in New-York or Cincinnati, or New Orleans, for instance, who can walk into the markets, and search all the mysteries of characteristic life in those cities, and then with emphasis and skill, make all of us see as they saw, why is it not as interesting as the same thing done in London?

This is true in other spheres – of thought, as well as life. We trust to show not only the various aspects of life, but to hint at their significance. In what paper or periodical do you now look to find the criticism of American thought upon the times? We hope to answer that question, too, by heaping upon our pages the results of the acutest observations, and the most trenchant thought, illustrated by whatever wealth of erudition, of imagination and of experience, they may chance to possess.

A Magazine, like a poet, we know must be born and not made. That is, it must be founded upon fact. No theory of what a good Magazine should be, will make a Magazine good, if it be not genuine in itself and genuinely related to the time. And it has been already announced in our prospectus, that we have no desire to try an experiment.

Are we then so sure? Has not the long and dreary history of Magazines opened our eyes? Is there some siren seduction in theatres and periodicals that for ever woos managers and publishers to a certain destruction? Why do we propose another twelve-month voyage in pea-green covers,[3] toward obscurity and the chaos of failures?

These are fair and friendly questions, while we stand chatting at the portal. With the obstinacy of Columbus, – if you please – we incredulously hear you, and still believe in the West. No alchemist, after long centuries of labor, ever discovered the philosopher's stone, nor found that any thing but genius and thrift would turn plaster and paper into gold. But, if even he had withstood his consuming desire, he would have perished at first of despair, as he did, at last, of disappointment.

So our Magazine is a foregone conclusion. Columbus believed in his Cathay of the West[4] – and discovered it.

We pray the reader to enter, and pardon this delay at the door. Within he will find poets, wits, philosophers, critics, artists, travellers, men of erudition and science, all strictly masked, as becomes worshippers of that invisible Truth which all our efforts and aims will seek to serve. And as he turns from us to accost those masks we remind the reader of the young worshipper of Isis.[5] For in her temple at Saïs, upon the Nile,

3. **pea-green covers:** The covers of *Putnam's Monthly Magazine* were green with illustrations of stalks of corn and sugarcane.
4. **Cathay of the West:** Cathay was the ancient name for China; Christopher Columbus set out to discover new trade routes to Asia and instead arrived in the Bahamas and Cuba on his first voyage in 1492.
5. **Isis:** Egyptian goddess of fertility, whose home was the ancient city of Saïs in the delta of the Nile River.

stood her image, for ever veiled. And when an ardent neophyte passionately besought that he might see her, and would take no refusal, his prayer was granted. The veil was lifted, and the exceeding splendor of that beauty dazzled him to death. Let it content you, ardent reader, to know that behind these masks are those whom you much delight to honor – those whose names, like the fame of Isis, have gone into other lands.

Finally, our Magazine shall say for itself what was said in the person of a young enthusiast born into the world and determined to reform it: "Now, though I am very peaceable, and on my private account could well enough die, since it appears there was some mistake in my creation, and that I have been missent to this earth, where all the seats were already taken, – yet I feel called upon in behalf of rational nature, which I represent, to declare to you my opinion, that, if the earth is yours, so also is it mine. My genius leads me to build a different manner of life from any of yours."[6]

This, says Putnam's Monthly, to its contemporaries who have already taken front seats in this prosperous world.

[1853]

---

6. **"Now . . . yours":** The lines are from "The Conservative" (1841), by Ralph Waldo Emerson.

Thomas Hamilton

[1822–1865]

Thomas Hamilton was the editor of the short-lived *Anglo-African Magazine* (1859–60). Frustrated by the lack of opportunities for his fellow African-American writers to publish in periodicals other than those sponsored by abolitionists and antislavery societies, Hamilton in his "Apology," or defense, explained that the central mission of the *Anglo-African Magazine* was to promote "the products of the pens of colored men and women" and to establish "an independent voice in the 'fourth estate.'" He consequently published poetry and essays by Frances E. W. Harper and a partial serialization of Martin R. Delany's *Blake; or, The Huts of America.* The magazine also published articles on education, the history of African Americans in America, and notices of books, such as James Redpath's *The Roving Editor; or, Talks with Slaves in the Southern States* (1859). When Hamilton found that he could not sustain the magazine, he published a newspaper, the *Weekly Anglo-African*, which continued until 1865. The text is taken from the first issue of the *Anglo-African Magazine*, January 1859.

Apology[1]

(Introductory)

The publisher of this Magazine was "brought up" among Newspapers, Magazines, &c. The training of his boyhood and the employment of his manhood have been in the arts and mysteries which pertain to the neighborhood of Spruce and Nassau streets[2] in the city of New York. Of course the top of the strata, the upper-crust of the laminae[3] in his geologic region is – the Publisher. . . . To become a Publisher, was the dream of his youth (not altogether a dream, for, while yet a boy he published, for several months, the People's Press, a not unnoticed weekly paper,) and the aim of his manhood. He understands the business thoroughly, and intends, if the requisite editorial matter can be furnished, to make this Magazine "one of the institutions of the country."

He would seem to be the right man in the right place; for the class of whom he is the representative in Printing House Square, sorely need an independent voice in the *"fourth estate."*[4] Frederick Douglass[5] has said that "the twelve millions of blacks in the United States and its environs must occupy the notice and the care of the Almighty": these millions, in order to assert and maintain their rank as men among men, must speak for themselves; no outside tongue, however gifted with eloquence, can tell their story; no outside eye, however penetrating, can see their wants; no outside organization, however benevolently intended, nor however cunningly contrived, can develope the energies and aspirations which make up their mission.

The wealth, the intellect, the Legislation, (Sate and Federal,) the pulpit, and the science of America, have concentrated on no one point so heartily as in the endeavor to write down the negro as something less than a man: yet at the very moment of the triumph of this effort, there runs through the marrow of those who make it, an unaccountable consciousness, an aching dread, that this *noir faineant*,[6] this great black slaggard, is somehow endowed with forces which are felt rather than seen, and which may in "some grim revel,"

> "Shake the pillars of the commonweal!"[7]

And there is indeed reason for this "aching dread." The negro is something more than mere endurance; he is a force. And when the energies which now imbrute him

1. **Apology:** A reasoned argument in defense of a position or doctrine.
2. **Spruce and Nassau streets:** The center of "Printing House Row," a five-block area in lower Manhattan near city hall, where the majority of newspaper offices were located.
3. **laminae:** Thin piece of wood (Latin).
4. ***"fourth estate"*:** The press.
5. **Frederick Douglass:** In addition to writing his *Narrative of the Life of Frederick Douglass* (1845), Douglass was a successful journalist who published a weekly newspaper, first called the *North Star* (1847-1851) and then *Frederick Douglass' Paper* (1851-1860).
6. ***noir faineant*:** Black idler (French).
7. **"Shake . . . commonweal!":** From the last stanza of "The Warning," a poem that equated the blind Samson of the Bible with the condition of African Americans in the United States, by Henry Wadsworth Longfellow (1807-1882).

exhaust themselves – as they inevitably must – the force which he now expends in resistance will cause him to rise: his force can hardly be measured to-day; the opinions regarding him are excessive; his foes estimate him too low – his friends, perhaps, too high: besides, there is not a-wanting among these latter, in spite of their own good feelings, that "tribe idolatry" which regards him as "not quite us." Twenty-five years ago, in the heat of the conflict which terminated in the Emancipation Act of Great Britain, there was held an anti-slavery meeting in the city of Glasgow,[8] at which a young black made a speech of such fashion, that it "brought down the house." He was followed by the eccentric but earnest and eloquent William Anderson, a minister of the Relief denomination: Dr. Wardlaw, with silver tongue, had spoken, and George Thompson had revelled in his impetuous eloquence. Rev. Mr. Anderson's subject was a minor one in the programme, a sort of side dish; yet he began, continued, and ended in one of the most extraordinary bursts of eloquence, wit and sarcasm ever heard in Dr. Wardlaw's chapel; people were carried away: at the end of the meeting a friend congratulated Mr. Anderson, and casually asked how it was that he had got off such a grand speech? "Hech mon!" said Mr. Anderson, "d'ye think I was gaen to be beaten by a black?"

But although we cannot fairly estimate the forces of the negro, we may approximate them. A handful of English subdued Ireland, and English rule rather than English arms have so impenetrated the Celtic mind with oppression, that the only resistance to this oppression in the middle of the nineteenth century culminated in Smith O'Brien, Thomas F. Meagher, and JOHN MITCHEL![9] Compare these with Sam Ward, Frederick Douglass, or those who fought in Christiana, or the man who suffered himself to be scourged to death in Tennessee rather than betray his associate insurrectionists.

The negro under the yoke of slavery has increased, without additions made by immigration, as rapidly during the last forty years, as have the whites in the whole country, aided by an immense immigration and the increase of the immigrants; and this increase of the negro in America, unlike that of the Irish in Ireland, is of a strong, healthy, durable stock. Now let the European immigration diminish, and the African slave trade revive – both which events are in *esse*[10] – and the next forty years will present us with the slave States containing ten millions of whites, and nearly fifteen millions of slaves: and the proportion of the blacks to the whites in the United States, which

---

8. **Emancipation Act . . . Glasgow:** The Emancipation Act of 1833 outlawed slavery in the British colonies of the West Indies, as of August 1, 1834. Located in one of the major cities of Great Britain in the nineteenth century, the Glasgow Emancipation Society was an important and large abolitionist organization. In the following passage, Hamilton refers to George Thompson (1804–1878), an English abolitionist; Ralph Wardlaw (1779–1853), a prominent Congregationalist theologian and minister who was active in the abolitionist movement; and William Anderson (1799–1872), the minister of John Street Relief Church in Glasgow, who was a staunch champion of many reform movements, including abolition.

9. **O'Brien . . . Mitchel:** Militant leaders of various groups for Catholic emancipation and relief for the famine in nineteenth-century Ireland included William Smith O'Brien (1803–1864), Thomas F. Meagher (1823–1867), and John Mitchel (1815–1874).

10. ***esse*:** Essential nature or essence (Latin).

is now one-seventh, will be nearly one-half. In that event, it requires no prophet to foresee that the Underground Railroad,[11] and the Christian Religion – the two great safety-valves for the restless and energetic among the slaves – will be utterly incompetent to put off that event which was brought about by bloodshed in Hayti, and by timely legislation in the British West Indies.[12]

In 1850, a black man insulted by a white boy in the streets of Sacramento, mildly resented by pushing the boy away: a white man passing by with a saw in his hand, caught the black by the wrist and sawed his hand off. The black went before a magistrate to complain, when the minister of justice declined receiving the complaint, on the ground that no redress could be obtained. In 1858, we find a magistrate in California, in defiance of statute law, admitting testimony of black men, and in the same year a bill to prevent further immigration of blacks, was defeated in the legislature of that State. In the debate on the subject, a member stated that "the six thousand free blacks in California were an industrious people, with six millions of dollars in personal and real estate." This is about one thousand dollars per individual – a sum three times as great as the census of 1850 gives to the individuals composing the farming population of Vermont.

In a school exhibition in the city of New York, in December 1858, there were productions from twenty white, and one colored, Ward Schools; of the thirty prizes awarded, three were gained by the colored school; which may be thus formularized for the use of that distinguished archaeologist, craniologist and ethnologist, Dr. Nott,[13] of Alabama: – $^3/_{10} : ^1/_{20}$ :: black children's intellect : white children's intellect.

In the *Concours* of the colleges of France in 1858, the laurels once worn by Abelard, fell upon the brows of a black youth from Hayti, M. Faubert, who won the highest prize, two other young Haytiens winning other prizes. It is well-known that not a few white Americans are among the students of the French colleges; as none of these have yet won this distinguished honor, we must again formularize for Dr. Nott – $^0/_0 : 1$ :: white American students in Paris : black Haytien students in Paris.

Here, then, we have the vital force, the physical force, and some slight inklings of the yet undeveloped mental power of the negro. The negro is a constant quantity; other races may be, and are, variables; he is positive and reliable, and seems fixed so. The panic of 1857 was arrested by the cotton crop, and even at this moment, when the West is bankrupt, with its "enchanted" free laborers, and "enchanted" stores of grain, the vitality of trade is maintained by the products of black labor, which it is the ambition of the so-called republican party to sweep from the land. What a glorious destiny awaits the

11. **Underground Railroad:** A secret, cooperative network of people who helped slaves escape to Canada before the Civil War.

12. **Hayti . . . British West Indies:** In 1791, Toussaint L'Ouverture led a successful slave rebellion against the French colonial rule in Haiti, which paved the way to the establishment of Haiti in 1804 as the first independent black nation in the Western world. With the passage of the Emancipation Act of 1833, the British ended slavery in their territories and the West Indies.

13. **Dr. Nott:** Josiah Clark Nott (1804–1873), Alabama physician and self-proclaimed enthnologist who published a later discredited theory of black inferiority.

negro when soil now fertilized by his agony and bloody sweat, shall teem under his energies, renewed and developed by freedom! for

> "Freedom hand in hand with labor,
> Walketh strong and brave,
> On the forehead of his neighbor
> No man writeth slave!"[14]

The negro is the "coming man," heralded by Dr. Arnold.[15] The European race would seem to have reached its destined development – of Arts in Greece, of Jurisprudence in Rome, and of Industrial Economies in England and the United States. To advance still further, the tide of civilization requires what the great commoner of England prescribed for Ireland – new blood. And whence can this be procured, unless from a race hitherto unmixed in the current of civilization?

In addition to an exposé of the condition of the blacks, this Magazine will have the aim to uphold and encourage the now depressed hopes of thinking black men, in the United States – the men who, for twenty years and more have been active in conventions, in public meetings, in societies, in the pulpit, and through the press, cheering on and laboring on to promote emancipation, affranchisement and education; some of them in, and some of them past the prime of life, yet see, as the apparent result of their work and their sacrifices, only Fugitive Slave laws and Compromise bills, and the denial of citizenship on the part of the Federal and State Governments, and saddest of all, such men as Seward and Preston King[16] insulting the rights of their black constituents by voting to admit Oregon as a state with a constitution denying to black men even an entrance within its borders.

It is not astonishing that the faith of such should grow weak, or that they should set up a breast-work in distant regions; yet it is clear that they are wrong to despond, wrong to change the scene of the contest. The sterner and fiercer the conflict, the sterner and steadier should be the soldiers engaged in it,

> "Be sure, no earnest work
> Of any honest creature, howbeit weak,
> Imperfect, ill-adapted, fails so much
> It is not gathered as a grain of sand
> For carrying out God's end. No creature works
> So ill observed, that there he's cashiered.
> The honest, earnest man must stand and work."[17]

---

14. **"Freedom . . . slave!"**: From "Songs of Labor: The Lumberman," a poem by John Greenleaf Whittier (1807–1892).
15. **Dr. Arnold**: Matthew Arnold (1822–1888), English critic, essayist, and poet.
16. **Seward and Preston King**: Both Republican senators from New York, William H. Seward (1801–1872) and Preston King (1806–1865) voted in favor of Oregon's admittance as the thirty-third state in 1859. The state's constitution included an "exclusion law," which severely limited the rights of blacks to settle in the state.
17. **"Be . . . work"**: From book 8 of *Aurora Leigh*, by the English poet Elizabeth Barrett Browning (1806–1861).

Neither can it aid our cause to found an empire in Yoruba;[18] they might as well have built a battery at Gibraltar to destroy Sevastopol.[19] The guns won't reach. Our cause is something higher, something holier than the founding of states. Any five hundred men with thews and sinews, and a moderate share of prudence, can found a state; it is nothing new or wonderful to do. And after we had founded such a state, our work in the United States would remain to be done by other hands. Our work here, is, to purify the State, and purify Christianity from the foul blot which here rests upon them.

All articles in the Magazine, not otherwise designated, will be the products of the pens of colored men and women, from whom we earnestly solicit contributions, which, when used, will be paid for, according to the means of the Publisher.

We hope from these sources, articles grave and gay, things serious, and as the Rev. Mr. Hudson quaintly says, "things juicy." "The Tales of the Fugitives," to be initiated in our next number, will leave the heart and the imagination not untouched. This one is "got up" in rather a hurry, and we beg pardon for its many deficiencies.

[1859]

18. **Yoruba:** Region of southwestern Nigeria, where the American Colonization Society wanted to relocate blacks in a colony.
19. **Gibraltar . . . Sevastopol:** Gibraltar, on the southern tip of Spain facing the Mediterranean Sea, is approximately 2,000 miles from Sevastopol (or Sebastopol), on the Black Sea in southern Ukraine.

Nathaniel Hawthorne

[1804–1864]

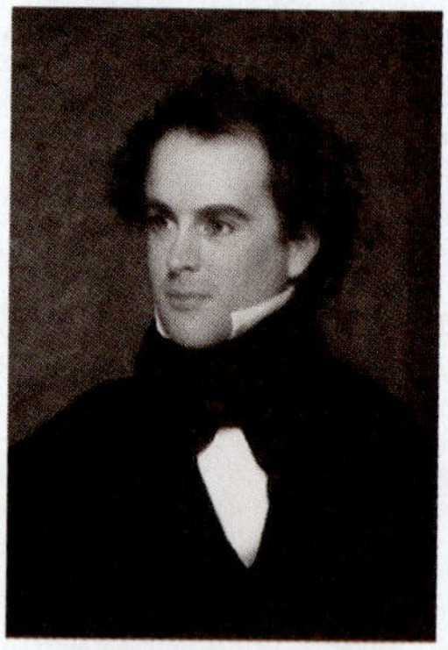

Nathaniel Hawthorne

Charles Osgood painted this portrait in 1840, when Hawthorne was thirty-six and working in the Boston Custom House. Hawthorne had the portrait sent to his family in Salem, joking that since they had the likeness they might "very well dispense with the original."

In the field of letters, Hawthorne is the most valuable example of the American genius.

–Henry James

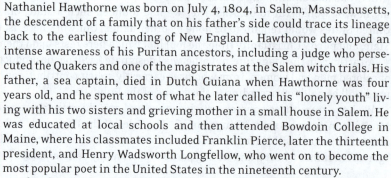

Nathaniel Hawthorne was born on July 4, 1804, in Salem, Massachusetts, the descendent of a family that on his father's side could trace its lineage back to the earliest founding of New England. Hawthorne developed an intense awareness of his Puritan ancestors, including a judge who persecuted the Quakers and one of the magistrates at the Salem witch trials. His father, a sea captain, died in Dutch Guiana when Hawthorne was four years old, and he spent most of what he later called his "lonely youth" living with his two sisters and grieving mother in a small house in Salem. He was educated at local schools and then attended Bowdoin College in Maine, where his classmates included Franklin Pierce, later the thirteenth president, and Henry Wadsworth Longfellow, who went on to become the most popular poet in the United States in the nineteenth century.

After his graduation from Bowdoin in 1825, Hawthorne also set out to become a professional writer. He returned to Salem and lived with his mother and sisters for the next twelve years, during which time Hawthorne wrote constantly. In 1828, he anonymously published his first novel, *Fanshawe*, a melodramatic tale of sexual intrigue and undergraduate life set in an isolated college in New England around the middle of the eighteenth century. The reviews were mixed, and Hawthorne himself was deeply dissatisfied with the novel, so much so that he later tried to conceal his authorship. But the novel gained him some attention, and Hawthorne was far more successful in the historical sketches and stories he soon began to publish in periodicals like the *American Monthly Magazine* and the *New-England Magazine*. He hoped to publish a sequence of historical stories to be called *Provincial Tales* but reluctantly allowed them to be published individually in *The Token: Christmas and New Year's Present*, a finely bound and lavishly illustrated annual edited by Samuel G. Goodrich. Goodrich paid Hawthorne less than a dollar a page for the twenty-seven sketches and tales he contributed to *The Token* between 1831 and 1837. Nonetheless, it was a respectable place to publish, especially for a young, unknown writer. Although all of his contributions to *The Token* appeared anonymously, Hawthorne gradually made a name for himself in the world of periodicals, then an important step in the careers of most writers. In 1837, this time under his own name, Hawthorne published *Twice-Told Tales*, a collection of his early sketches and stories. The positive reception of the book – "It comes from the hand of a man of genius," Longfellow exclaimed in the *North American Review* – generated renewed demand for Hawthorne's work, which he began to publish in prominent magazines like the *Knickerbocker* and the *Democratic Review*. Nonetheless, having already met his future wife, Sophia Peabody, Hawthorne worried that his income from writing would not allow him to marry and begin a family. Consequently, in 1839, he took a minor position in the Boston Custom House, the first of three government jobs he would hold.

bedfordstmartins.com/ americanlit *for research links on Hawthorne*

Hawthorne produced serious literary work only during periods when he was not employed in those jobs. In his two years of work at the Boston Custom House, he managed to publish a few sketches and three children's books: *Grandfather's Chair, Famous Old People,* and *Liberty Tree.* After resigning his position in 1841, Hawthorne invested his meager savings in Brook Farm, an experimental utopian community outside Boston. Finding communal life unsatisfying, Hawthorne once again determined to make a living as a full-time writer. In 1842, he published an expanded edition of *Twice-Told Tales.* In a lengthy review, Edgar Allan Poe emphasized what few others fully recognized, the innovative quality of the tales, observing that "Mr. Hawthorne's distinctive trait is invention, creation, imagination, originality." Although sales of the volume were disappointing, Hawthorne felt confident and financially secure enough to marry Sophia in July 1842. The couple moved to Concord, Massachusetts, where they rented a house, the "Old Manse," owned by the Ralph Waldo Emerson family. Through Emerson, Hawthorne met many members of the transcendental circle, including Margaret Fuller and Henry David Thoreau. During four years in Concord, Hawthorne published numerous sketches and stories, many of which he gathered in another highly regarded collection, *Mosses from an Old Manse,* published in 1846. Still struggling to earn enough from writing to support his growing family, however, he accepted the well-paid and undemanding position of surveyor in the Salem Custom House. The position was a choice piece of political patronage; Hawthorne, who was active in local Democratic politics, was dismissed after a Whig, Zachary Taylor, became president in 1849.

Having written almost nothing during the previous few years, Hawthorne worked at a furious pace during the following three. He immediately began a long tale that developed into the most famous of all novels about the Puritans, *The Scarlet Letter,* which created a sensation when it appeared in 1850. Widely acclaimed as the most important author of prose fiction in the country, Hawthorne moved his family to Lenox, Massachusetts, where he met a young writer who also aspired to literary greatness, Herman Melville. The two writers became close friends, and Melville dedicated his novel *Moby-Dick* (1851) to Hawthorne, "In Token of My Admiration for His Genius." Following up on the success of *The Scarlet Letter,* Hawthorne in 1851 published two collections of his early stories – a new edition of *Twice-Told Tales* and *The Snow-Image, and Other Twice-Told Tales* – as well as *The House of the Seven Gables,* a novel set in New England during the 1840s. He then wrote a sequence of stories for children, *A Wonder-Book for Girls and Boys,* and a novel loosely based on his experiences at Brook Farm, *The Blithedale Romance,* both of which Hawthorne published in 1852.

But his remarkable period of productivity was short lived. In 1852, Hawthorne agreed to write a campaign biography of his old college friend, Franklin Pierce, the Democratic nominee for president. After Pierce was elected, he assigned Hawthorne to the lucrative position of American consul in Liverpool, England. Hawthorne and his family lived in Europe for the rest of the decade, first in England and then, after his consular term ended in 1857, in Italy. Drawing upon his experiences there, he wrote *The Marble Faun,* a novel published shortly before Hawthorne returned with his family to the United States in June 1860. Settling in Concord, he wrote articles for the *Atlantic Monthly* and a collection of sketches based on his years in England, *Our Old Home* (1863). Hawthorne also began several novels, but his failing health and declining creative powers prevented him from completing them before his death on May 19, 1864.

Hawthorne's "The Wives of the Dead." This poignant tale is one of a sequence of early stories Hawthorne initially hoped to publish in a collection called *Provincial Tales* but instead allowed Samuel G. Goodrich to print individually in his popular annual, *The Token: Christmas and New Year's Present.* Like the other stories in the projected sequence, "The Wives of the Dead" is set in colonial New England. But in contrast to most of those stories, which focus on the experiences and psyche of men, "The Wives of the Dead" concerns two women who married brothers and who on consecutive days learn of their husbands' deaths, one in a military skirmish in Canada and the other in a shipwreck in the Atlantic. Hawthorne, who was only four when his father died during a voyage to the South Seas, sensitively explores the nature of grief and the power of dreams, a central theme in many of his early stories. Hawthorne did not include the story in his first collections, *Twice-Told Tales* (1837, 1842). In 1843, however, he published "The Wives of the Dead" again in the *Democratic Review*; he also included it in *The Snow-Image and Other Twice-Told Tales* (1851). The text is taken from its first printing in *The Token,* where it was published anonymously along with three other stories by Hawthorne in 1832.

The Wives of the Dead

The following story, the simple and domestic incidents of which may be deemed scarcely worth relating, after such a lapse of time, awakened some degree of interest, a hundred years ago, in a principal seaport of the Bay Province.[1] The rainy twilight of an autumn day; a parlor on the second floor of a small house, plainly furnished, as beseemed the middling circumstances of its inhabitants, yet decorated with little curiosities from beyond the sea, and a few delicate specimens of Indian manufacture, – these are the only particulars to be premised in regard to scene and season. Two young and comely women sat together by the fireside, nursing their mutual and peculiar sor-

1. **principal seaport of the Bay Province:** The province of Massachusetts Bay, a British colony organized in 1691, originally included much of present-day Massachusetts, Maine, and Nova Scotia. At the time this story takes place, about 1730, the city of Salem was developing into a major fishing, shipbuilding, and maritime trading center for the colonies.

rows. They were the recent brides of two brothers, a sailor and a landsman, and two successive days had brought tidings of the death of each, by the chances of Canadian warfare,[2] and the tempestuous Atlantic. The universal sympathy excited by this bereavement, drew numerous condoling guests to the habitation of the widowed sisters. Several, among whom was the minister, had remained till the verge of evening; when one by one, whispering many comfortable passages of Scripture, that were answered by more abundant tears, they took their leave and departed to their own happier homes. The mourners, though not insensible to the kindness of their friends, had yearned to be left alone. United, as they had been, by the relationship of the living, and now more closely so by that of the dead, each felt as if whatever consolation her grief admitted, were to be found in the bosom of the other. They joined their hearts, and wept together silently. But after an hour of such indulgence, one of the sisters, all of whose emotions were influenced by her mild, quiet, yet not feeble character, began to recollect the precepts of resignation and endurance, which piety had taught her, when she did not think to need them. Her misfortune, besides, as earliest known, should earliest cease to interfere with her regular course of duties; accordingly, having placed the table before the fire, and arranged a frugal meal, she took the hand of her companion.

"Come, dearest sister; you have eaten not a morsel to day," she said, "Arise, I pray you, and let us ask a blessing on that which is provided for us."

Her sister-in-law was of a lively and irritable temperament, and the first pangs of her sorrow had been expressed by shrieks and passionate lamentation. She now shrunk from Mary's words, like a wounded sufferer from a hand that revives the throb.

"There is no blessing left for me, neither will I ask it," cried Margaret, with a fresh burst of tears. "Would it were His will that I might never taste food more."

Yet she trembled at these rebellious expressions, almost as soon as they were uttered, and, by degrees, Mary succeeded in bringing her sister's mind nearer to the situation of her own. Time went on, and their usual hour of repose arrived. The brothers and their brides, entering the married state with no more than the slender means which then sanctioned such a step, had confederated themselves in one household, with equal rights to the parlor, and claiming exclusive privileges in two sleeping rooms contiguous to it. Thither the widowed ones retired, after heaping ashes upon the dying embers of their fire, and placing a lighted lamp upon the hearth. The doors of both chambers were left open, so that a part of the interior of each, and the beds with their unclosed curtains, were reciprocally visible. Sleep did not steal upon the sisters at one and the same time. Mary experienced the effect often consequent upon grief quietly borne, and soon sunk into temporary forgetfulness, while Margaret became more disturbed and feverish, in proportion as the night advanced with its deepest and stillest hours. She lay listening to the drops of rain, that came down in monotonous succession, unswayed by a breath of wind; and a nervous impulse continually caused her to lift her head from the pillow, and gaze into Mary's chamber and the intermediate apartment. The cold light of

2. **Canadian warfare:** The eighteenth century was punctuated by wars between Great Britain and France over the control of Canada.

the lamp threw the shadows of the furniture up against the wall, stamping them immoveably there, except when they were shaken by a sudden flicker of the flame. Two vacant arm-chairs were in their old positions on opposite sides of the hearth, where the brothers had been wont to sit in young and laughing dignity, as heads of families; two humbler seats were near them, the true thrones of that little empire, where Mary and herself had exercised in love, a power that love had won. The cheerful radiance of the fire had shone upon the happy circle, and the dead glimmer of the lamp might have befitted their reunion now. While Margaret groaned in bitterness, she heard a knock at the street-door.

"How would my heart have leapt at that sound but yesterday!" thought she, remembering the anxiety with which she had long awaited tidings from her husband. "I care not for it now; let them begone, for I will not arise."

But even while a sort of childish fretfulness made her thus resolve, she was breathing hurriedly, and straining her ears to catch a repetition of the summons. It is difficult to be convinced of the death of one whom we have deemed another self. The knocking was now renewed in slow and regular strokes, apparently given with the soft end of a doubled fist, and was accompanied by words, faintly heard through several thicknesses of wall. Margaret looked to her sister's chamber, and beheld her still lying in the depths of sleep. She arose, placed her foot upon the floor, and slightly arrayed herself, trembling between fear and eagerness as she did so.

"Heaven help me!" sighed she. "I have nothing left to fear, and methinks I am ten times more a coward than ever."

Seizing the lamp from the hearth, she hastened to the window that overlooked the street-door. It was a lattice, turning upon hinges; and having thrown it back, she stretched her head a little way into the moist atmosphere. A lantern was reddening the front of the house, and melting its light in the neighboring puddles, while a deluge of darkness overwhelmed every other object. As the window grated on its hinges, a man in a broad brimmed hat and blanket-coat,[3] stepped from under the shelter of the projecting story, and looked upward to discover whom his application had aroused. Margaret knew him as a friendly innkeeper of the town.

"What would you have, goodman Parker?" cried the widow.

"Lack-a-day, is it you, mistress Margaret?" replied the innkeeper. "I was afraid it might be your sister Mary; for I hate to see a young woman in trouble, when I haven't a word of comfort to whisper her."

"For Heaven's sake, what news do you bring?" screamed Margaret.

"Why, there has been an express through the town within this half hour," said goodman Parker, "travelling from the eastern jurisdiction with letters from the governor and council. He tarried at my house to refresh himself with a drop and a morsel, and I asked him what tidings on the frontiers. He tells me we had the better in the skirmish you wot of, and that thirteen men reported slain, are well and sound, and your husband among

3. **blanket-coat:** A winter garment pieced together from thick blankets, worn by Indians, hunters, and traders.

them. Besides, he is appointed of the escort to bring the captivated Frenchers and Indians home to the province jail. I judged you wouldn't mind being broke of your rest, and so I stept over to tell you. Good night."

So saying, the honest man departed; and his lantern gleamed along the street, bringing to view indistinct shapes of things, and the fragments of a world, like order glimmering through chaos, or memory roaming over the past. But Margaret staid not to watch these picturesque effects. Joy flashed into her heart, and lighted it up at once, and breathless, and with winged steps, she flew to the bedside of her sister. She paused, however, at the door of the chamber, while a thought of pain broke in upon her.

"Poor Mary!" said she to herself. "Shall I waken her, to feel her sorrow sharpened by my happiness? No; I will keep it within my own bosom till the morrow."

She approached the bed to discover if Mary's sleep were peaceful. Her face was turned partly inward to the pillow, and had been hidden there to weep; but a look of motionless contentment was now visible upon it, as if her heart, like a deep lake, had grown calm because its dead had sunk down so far within. Happy is it, and strange, that the lighter sorrows are those from which dreams are chiefly fabricated. Margaret shrunk from disturbing her sister-in-law, and felt as if her own better fortune, had rendered her involuntarily unfaithful, and as if altered and diminished affection must be the consequence of the disclosure she had to make. With a sudden step, she turned away. But joy could not long be repressed, even by circumstances that would have excited heavy grief at another moment. Her mind was thronged with delightful thoughts, till sleep stole on and transformed them to visions, more delightful and more wild, like the breath of winter, (but what a cold comparison!) working fantastic tracery upon a window.

When the night was far advanced, Mary awoke with a sudden start. A vivid dream had latterly involved her in its unreal life, of which, however, she could only remember that it had been broken in upon at the most interesting point. For a little time, slumber hung about her like a morning mist, hindering her from perceiving the distinct outline of her situation. She listened with imperfect consciousness to two or three volleys of a rapid and eager knocking; and first she deemed the noise a matter of course, like the breath she drew; next, it appeared a thing in which she had no concern; and lastly, she became aware that it was a summons necessary to be obeyed. At the same moment, the pang of recollection darted into her mind; the pall of sleep was thrown back from the face of grief; the dim light of the chamber, and the objects therein revealed, had retained all her suspended ideas, and restored them as soon as she unclosed her eyes. Again, there was a quick peal upon the street-door. Fearing that her sister would also be disturbed, Mary wrapped herself in a cloak and hood, took the lamp from the hearth, and hastened to the window. By some accident, it had been left unhasped, and yielded easily to her hand.

"Who's there?" asked Mary, trembling as she looked forth.

The storm was over, and the moon was up; it shone upon broken clouds above, and below upon houses black with moisture, and upon little lakes of the fallen rain, curling into silver beneath the quick enchantment of a breeze. A young man in a sailor's dress, wet as if he had come out of the depths of the sea, stood alone under the window. Mary recognised him as one whose livelihood was gained by short voyages along the coast;

nor did she forget, that, previous to her marriage, he had been an unsuccessful wooer of her own.

"What do you seek here, Stephen?" said she.

"Cheer up, Mary, for I seek to comfort you," answered the rejected lover. "You must know I got home not ten minutes ago, and the first thing my good mother told me was the news about your husband. So, without saying a word to the old woman, I clapt on my hat, and ran out of the house. I couldn't have slept a wink before speaking to you, Mary, for the sake of old times."

"Stephen, I thought better of you!" exclaimed the widow, with gushing tears, and preparing to close the lattice; for she was no whit inclined to imitate the first wife of Zadig.[4]

"But stop, and hear my story out," cried the young sailor. "I tell you we spoke a brig yesterday afternoon, bound in from Old England. And who do you think I saw standing on deck, well and hearty, only a bit thinner than he was five months ago?"

Mary leaned from the window, but could not speak.

"Why, it was your husband himself," continued the generous seaman. "He and three others saved themselves on a spar, when the Blessing turned bottom upwards. The brig will beat into the bay by daylight, with this wind, and you'll see him here tomorrow. There's the comfort I bring you, Mary, and so good night."

He hurried away, while Mary watched him with a doubt of waking reality, that seemed stronger or weaker as he alternately entered the shade of the houses, or emerged into the broad streaks of moonlight. Gradually, however, a blessed flood of conviction swelled into her heart, in strength enough to overwhelm her, had its increase been more abrupt. Her first impulse was to rouse her sister-in-law, and communicate the new-born gladness. She opened the chamber-door, which had been closed in the course of the night, though not latched, advanced to the bedside, and was about to lay her hand upon the slumberer's shoulder. But then she remembered that Margaret would awake to thoughts of death and woe, rendered not the less bitter by their contrast with her own felicity. She suffered the rays of the lamp to fall upon the unconscious form of the bereaved one. Margaret lay in unquiet sleep, and the drapery was displaced around her; her young cheek was rosy-tinted, and her lips half opened in a vivid smile; an expression of joy, debarred its passage by her sealed eyelids, struggled forth like incense from the whole countenance.

"My poor sister! you will waken too soon from that happy dream," thought Mary.

Before retiring, she set down the lamp and endeavored to arrange the bed-clothes, so that the chill air might not do harm to the feverish slumberer. But her hand trembled against Margaret's neck, a tear also fell upon her cheek, and she suddenly awoke.

[1832]

---

4. **wife of Zadig**: In *Zadig; or, The Book of Fate* by François Marie Arouet Voltaire (1694–1778), the main character, Zadig, is appalled to witness an Arabian widow commit suicide by throwing herself on top of her dead husband's funeral pyre.

Hawthorne's "My Kinsman, Major Molineux." This is probably the most celebrated of the sequence of early stories Hawthorne initially hoped to publish in a collection called *Provincial Tales* but instead allowed Samuel G. Goodrich to print individually in his popular annual, *The Token: Christmas and New Year's Present.* Set in the turbulent period before the American Revolution, "My Kinsman, Major Molineux" is in part an ironic coming-of-age story, for both its protagonist, Robin, and the country he may be understood to represent. As Robin confronts the darker sides of colonial life in his search for his relative, Hawthorne explores some of the key themes of his early fiction, especially the nature of innocence and of experience and the relation between appearance and reality in the dream-like and moon-drenched setting of the story. Hawthorne did not include this challenging story in his earliest collections, *Twice-Told Tales* (1837, 1842), but he later included it in *The Snow-Image and Other Twice-Told Tales* (1851). The text is taken from the first printing in *The Token* (1832), where it appeared along with three of Hawthorne's other stories, and where it was ascribed to "the author of 'Sights from a Steeple,'" a sketch he had published in the annual the previous year.

MY KINSMAN, MAJOR MOLINEUX

After the kings of Great Britain had assumed the right of appointing the colonial governors, the measures of the latter seldom met with the ready and general approbation, which had been paid to those of their predecessors, under the original charters.[1] The people looked with most jealous scrutiny to the exercise of power, which did not emanate from themselves, and they usually rewarded the rulers with slender gratitude, for the compliances, by which, in softening their instructions from beyond the sea, they had incurred the reprehension of those who gave them. The annals of Massachusetts Bay will inform us, that of six governors, in the space of about forty years from the surrender of the old charter, under James II., two were imprisoned by a popular insurrection; a third, as Hutchinson[2] inclines to believe, was driven from the province by the whizzing of a musket ball; a fourth, in the opinion of the same historian, was hastened to his grave by continual bickerings with the house of representatives; and the remaining two, as well as their successors, till the Revolution,[3] were favored with few and brief intervals of peaceful sway. The inferior members of the court party,[4] in times of high

1. **original charters:** In 1684, the charter of the Massachusetts Bay Colony, which had allowed it to function as a self-governing commonwealth, was annulled by the Court of Chancery in England. The royal charter issued in 1691 incorporated Plymouth and Maine into the province of Massachusetts Bay and provided for a governor to be appointed by the crown.

2. **Hutchinson:** Thomas Hutchinson (1711–1780), the last royal governor of Massachusetts Bay; he wrote *The History of the Colony and Province of Massachusetts-Bay* (1764, 1767).

3. **Revolution:** The American Revolution, which began with the battles of Lexington and Concord in April 1775.

4. **court party:** Supporters of the British royal government.

political excitement, led scarcely a more desirable life. These remarks may serve as preface to the following adventures, which chanced upon a summer night, not far from a hundred years ago.[5] The reader, in order to avoid a long and dry detail of colonial affairs, is requested to dispense with an account of the train of circumstances, that had caused much temporary inflammation of the popular mind.

It was near nine o'clock of a moonlight evening, when a boat crossed the ferry with a single passenger, who had obtained his conveyance, at that unusual hour, by the promise of an extra fare. While he stood on the landing-place, searching in either pocket for the means of fulfilling his agreement, the ferryman lifted a lantern, by the aid of which, and the newly risen moon, he took a very accurate survey of the stranger's figure. He was a youth of barely eighteen years, evidently country-bred, and now, as it should seem, upon his first visit to town. He was clad in a coarse grey coat, well worn, but in excellent repair; his under garments were durably constructed of leather, and sat tight to a pair of serviceable and well-shaped limbs; his stockings of blue yarn, were the incontrovertible handiwork of a mother or a sister; and on his head was a three-cornered hat, which in its better days had perhaps sheltered the graver brow of the lad's father. Under his left arm was a heavy cudgel, formed of an oak sapling, and retaining a part of the hardened root; and his equipment was completed by a wallet,[6] not so abundantly stocked as to incommode the vigorous shoulders on which it hung. Brown curly hair, well-shaped features, and bright, cheerful eyes, were nature's gifts, and worth all that art could have done for his adornment.

The youth, one of whose names was Robin, finally drew from his pocket the half of a little province-bill[7] of five shillings, which, in the depreciation of that sort of currency, did but satisfy the ferryman's demand, with the surplus of a sexangular piece of parchment valued at three pence. He then walked forward into the town, with as light a step, as if his day's journey had not already exceeded thirty miles, and with as eager an eye, as if he were entering London city, instead of the little metropolis of a New England colony. Before Robin had proceeded far, however, it occurred to him, that he knew not whither to direct his steps; so he paused, and looked up and down the narrow street, scrutinizing the small and mean wooden buildings, that were scattered on either side.

"This low hovel cannot be my kinsman's dwelling," thought he, "nor yonder old house, where the moonlight enters at the broken casement; and truly I see none hereabouts that might be worthy of him. It would have been wise to inquire my way of the ferryman, and doubtless he would have gone with me, and earned a shilling from the Major for his pains. But the next man I meet will do as well."

He resumed his walk, and was glad to perceive that the street now became wider, and the houses more respectable in their appearance. He soon discerned a figure moving on moderately in advance, and hastened his steps to overtake it. As Robin drew nigh, he saw that the passenger was a man in years, with a full periwig of grey hair, a wide-

5. **a hundred years ago:** The story is set in the early 1730s.
6. **wallet:** Backpack.
7. **province-bill:** Paper money issued in colonies.

skirted coat of dark cloth, and silk stockings rolled about his knees. He carried a long and polished cane, which he struck down perpendicularly before him, at every step; and at regular intervals he uttered two successive hems, of a peculiarly solemn and sepulchral intonation. Having made these observations, Robin laid hold of the skirt of the old man's coat, just when the light from the open door and windows of a barber's shop, fell upon both their figures.

"Good evening to you, honored Sir," said he, making a low bow, and still retaining his hold of the skirt. "I pray you to tell me whereabouts is the dwelling of my kinsman, Major Molineux?"

The youth's question was uttered very loudly; and one of the barbers, whose razor was descending on a well-soaped chin, and another who was dressing a Ramillies wig,[8] left their occupations, and came to the door. The citizen, in the meantime, turned a long favored countenance upon Robin, and answered him in a tone of excessive anger and annoyance. His two sepulchral hems, however, broke into the very centre of his rebuke, with most singular effect, like a thought of the cold grave obtruding among wrathful passions.

"Let go my garment, fellow! I tell you. I know not the man you speak of. What! I have authority, I have – hem, hem – authority; and if this be the respect you show your betters, your feet shall be brought acquainted with the stocks,[9] by daylight, tomorrow morning!"

Robin released the old man's skirt, and hastened away, pursued by an ill-mannered roar of laughter from the barber's shop. He was at first considerably surprised by the result of his question, but, being a shrewd youth, soon thought himself able to account for the mystery.

"This is some country representative," was his conclusion, "who has never seen the inside of my kinsman's door, and lacks the breeding to answer a stranger civilly. The man is old, or verily – I might be tempted to turn back and smite him on the nose. Ah, Robin, Robin! even the barber's boys laugh at you, for choosing such a guide! You will be wiser in time, friend Robin."

He now became entangled in a succession of crooked and narrow streets, which crossed each other, and meandered at no great distance from the water-side. The smell of tar was obvious to his nostrils, the masts of vessels pierced the moonlight above the tops of the buildings, and the numerous signs, which Robin paused to read, informed him that he was near the centre of business. But the streets were empty, the shops were closed, and lights were visible only in the second stories of a few dwelling-houses. At length, on the corner of a narrow lane, through which he was passing, he beheld the broad countenance of a British hero swinging before the door of an inn,[10] whence proceeded the voices of many guests. The casement of one of the lower windows was thrown

---

8. **Ramillies wig:** An elaborate wig with a braid, named in honor of a decisive British victory over the French in Ramillies, Belgium, during the War of Spanish Succession, May 23, 1706.
9. **stocks:** A wooden frame with holes for securing a person's ankles and wrists, in which criminals were exposed to public punishment and ridicule.
10. **door of an inn:** Hanging signboards with images were used to designate the nature of a business.

back, and a very thin curtain permitted Robin to distinguish a party at supper, round a well-furnished table. The fragrance of the good cheer steamed forth into the outer air, and the youth could not fail to recollect, that the last remnant of his travelling stock of provision had yielded to his morning appetite, and that noon had found, and left him, dinnerless.

"Oh, that a parchment three-penny might give me a right to sit down at yonder table," said Robin, with a sigh. "But the Major will make me welcome to the best of his victuals; so I will even step boldly in, and inquire my way to his dwelling."

He entered the tavern, and was guided by the murmur of voices, and fumes of tobacco, to the public room. It was a long and low apartment, with oaken walls, grown dark in the continual smoke, and a floor, which was thickly sanded, but of no immaculate purity. A number of persons, the larger part of whom appeared to be mariners, or in some way connected with the sea, occupied the wooden benches, or leather-bottomed chairs, conversing on various matters, and occasionally lending their attention to some topic of general interest. Three or four little groups were draining as many bowls of punch, which the great West India trade had long since made a familiar drink in the colony. Others, who had the aspect of men who lived by regular and laborious handicraft, preferred the insulated bliss of an unshared potation, and became more taciturn under its influence. Nearly all, in short, evinced a predilection for the Good Creature[11] in some of its various shapes, for this is a vice, to which, as the Fast-day sermons[12] of a hundred years ago will testify, we have a long hereditary claim. The only guests to whom Robin's sympathies inclined him, were two or three sheepish countrymen, who were using the inn somewhat after the fashion of a Turkish Caravansary;[13] they had gotten themselves into the darkest corner of the room, and, heedless of the Nicotian atmosphere,[14] were supping on the bread of their own ovens, and the bacon cured in their own chimney-smoke. But though Robin felt a sort of brotherhood with these strangers, his eyes were attracted from them, to a person who stood near the door, holding whispered conversation with a group of ill-dressed associates. His features were separately striking almost to grotesqueness, and the whole face left a deep impression in the memory. The forehead bulged out into a double prominence, with a vale between; the nose came boldly forth in an irregular curve, and its bridge was of more than a finger's breadth; the eyebrows were deep and shaggy, and the eyes glowed beneath them like fire in a cave.

While Robin deliberated of whom to inquire respecting his kinsman's dwelling, he was accosted by the innkeeper, a little man in a stained white apron, who had come to pay his professional welcome to the stranger. Being in the second generation from a French protestant, he seemed to have inherited the courtesy of his parent nation; but no

---

11. **Good Creature:** A reference to rum, which was consumed at the rate of 12 million gallons per year in colonial America.
12. **Fast-day sermons:** Sermons given on days set aside for public penitence.
13. **Turkish Caravansary:** An inn built around a large courtyard to accommodate a group of travelers journeying together.
14. **Nicotian atmosphere:** Smoky with tobacco fumes; Jean Nicot (c. sixteenth century) introduced tobacco into France in 1559.

variety of circumstance was ever known to change his voice from the one shrill note in which he now addressed Robin.

"From the country, I presume, Sir?" said he, with a profound bow. "Beg to congratulate you on your arrival, and trust you intend a long stay with us. Fine town here, Sir, beautiful buildings, and much that may interest a stranger. May I hope for the honor of your commands in respect to supper?"

"The man sees a family likeness! the rogue has guessed that I am related to the Major!" thought Robin, who had hitherto experienced little superfluous civility.

All eyes were now turned on the country lad, standing at the door, in his worn three-cornered hat, grey coat, leather breeches, and blue yarn stockings, leaning on an oaken cudgel, and bearing a wallet on his back. Robin replied to the courteous innkeeper, with such an assumption of consequence, as befitted the Major's relative.

"My honest friend," he said, "I shall make it a point to patronise your house on some occasion, when –" here he could not help lowering his voice – "I may have more than a parchment three-pence in my pocket. My present business," continued he, speaking with lofty confidence, "is merely to inquire the way to the dwelling of my kinsman, Major Molineux."

There was a sudden and general movement in the room, which Robin interpreted as expressing the eagerness of each individual to become his guide. But the innkeeper turned his eyes to a written paper on the wall, which he read, or seemed to read, with occasional recurrences to the young man's figure.

"What have we here?" said he, breaking his speech into little dry fragments. "'Left the house of the subscriber, bounden servant,[15] Hezekiah Mudge – had on when he went away, grey coat, leather breeches, master's third best hat. One pound currency reward to whoever shall lodge him in any jail in the province.' Better trudge, boy, better trudge."

Robin had began to draw his hand towards the lighter end of the oak cudgel, but a strange hostility in every countenance, induced him to relinquish his purpose of breaking the courteous innkeeper's head. As he turned to leave the room, he encountered a sneering glance from the bold-featured personage whom he had before noticed; and no sooner was he beyond the door, than he heard a general laugh, in which the innkeeper's voice might be distinguished, like the dropping of small stones into a kettle.

"Now is it not strange," thought Robin, with his usual shrewdness, "is it not strange, that the confession of an empty pocket, should outweigh the name of my kinsman, Major Molineux? Oh, if I had one of these grinning rascals in the woods, where I and my oak sapling grew up together, I would teach him that my arm is heavy, though my purse be light!"

On turning the corner of the narrow lane, Robin found himself in a spacious street, with an unbroken line of lofty houses on each side, and a steepled building at the upper end, whence the ringing of a bell announced the hour of nine. The light of the moon, and

15. **bounden servant:** An indentured servant, bound by a contract to serve for a period of years in repayment for transportation to the colonies.

the lamps from numerous shop windows, discovered people promenading on the pavement, and amongst them, Robin hoped to recognise his hitherto inscrutable relative. The result of his former inquiries made him unwilling to hazard another, in a scene of such publicity, and he determined to walk slowly and silently up the street, thrusting his face close to that of every elderly gentleman, in search of the Major's lineaments. In his progress, Robin encountered many gay and gallant figures. Embroidered garments, of showy colors, enormous periwigs, gold-laced hats, and silver hilted swords, glided past him and dazzled his optics. Travelled youths, imitators of the European fine gentlemen of the period, trod jauntily along, half-dancing to the fashionable tunes which they hummed, and making poor Robin ashamed of his quiet and natural gait. At length, after many pauses to examine the gorgeous display of goods in the shop windows, and after suffering some rebukes for the impertinence of his scrutiny into people's faces, the Major's kinsman found himself near the steepled building, still unsuccessful in his search. As yet, however, he had seen only one side of the thronged street; so Robin crossed, and continued the same sort of inquisition down the opposite pavement, with stronger hopes than the philosopher seeking an honest man,[16] but with no better fortune. He had arrived about midway towards the lower end, from which his course began, when he overheard the approach of some one, who struck down a cane on the flag-stones at every step, uttering, at regular intervals, two sepulchral hems.

"Mercy on us!" quoth Robin, recognising the sound.

Turning a corner, which chanced to be close at his right hand, he hastened to pursue his researches, in some other part of the town. His patience was now wearing low, and he seemed to feel more fatigue from his rambles since he crossed the ferry, than from his journey of several days on the other side. Hunger also pleaded loudly within him, and Robin began to balance the propriety of demanding, violently and with lifted cudgel, the necessary guidance from the first solitary passenger, whom he should meet. While a resolution to this effect was gaining strength, he entered a street of mean appearance, on either side of which, a row of ill-built houses was straggling towards the harbor. The moonlight fell upon no passenger along the whole extent, but in the third domicile which Robin passed, there was a half-opened door, and his keen glance detected a woman's garment within.

"My luck may be better here," said he to himself.

Accordingly, he approached the door, and beheld it shut closer as he did so; yet an open space remained, sufficing for the fair occupant to observe the stranger, without a corresponding display on her part. All that Robin could discern was a strip of scarlet petticoat,[17] and the occasional sparkle of an eye, as if the moonbeams were trembling on some bright thing.

"Pretty mistress," – for I may call her so with a good conscience, thought the shrewd youth, since I know nothing to the contrary – "my sweet pretty mistress, will you be

---

16. **honest man:** Diogenes (412?–323 BCE) was a Greek philosopher who carried a lantern with him in his futile search to find an honest man.

17. **scarlet petticoat:** Red underskirts were often worn by prostitutes.

kind enough to tell me whereabouts I must seek the dwelling of my kinsman, Major Molineux?"

Robin's voice was plaintive and winning, and the female, seeing nothing to be shunned in the handsome country youth, thrust open the door, and came forth into the moonlight. She was a dainty little figure, with a white neck, round arms, and a slender waist, at the extremity of which her scarlet petticoat jutted out over a hoop, as if she were standing in a balloon. Moreover, her face was oval and pretty, her hair dark beneath the little cap, and her bright eyes possessed a sly freedom, which triumphed over those of Robin.

"Major Molineux dwells here," said this fair woman.

Now her voice was the sweetest Robin had heard that night, the airy counterpart of a stream of melted silver; yet he could not help doubting whether that sweet voice spoke gospel truth. He looked up and down the mean street, and then surveyed the house before which they stood. It was a small, dark edifice of two stories, the second of which projected over the lower floor; and the front apartment had the aspect of a shop for petty commodities.

"Now truly I am in luck," replied Robin, cunningly, "and so indeed is my kinsman, the Major, in having so pretty a housekeeper. But I prithee trouble him to step to the door; I will deliver him a message from his friends in the country, and then go back to my lodgings at the inn."

"Nay, the Major has been a-bed this hour or more," said the lady of the scarlet petticoat; "and it would be to little purpose to disturb him to night, seeing his evening draught was of the strongest. But he is a kind-hearted man, and it would be as much as my life's worth, to let a kinsman of his turn away from the door. You are the good old gentleman's very picture, and I could swear that was his rainy-weather hat. Also, he has garments very much resembling those leather — But come in, I pray, for I bid you hearty welcome in his name."

So saying, the fair and hospitable dame took our hero by the hand; and though the touch was light, and the force was gentleness, and though Robin read in her eyes what he did not hear in her words, yet the slender waisted woman, in the scarlet petticoat, proved stronger than the athletic country youth. She had drawn his half-willing footsteps nearly to the threshold, when the opening of a door in the neighborhood, startled the Major's housekeeper, and, leaving the Major's kinsman, she vanished speedily into her own domicile. A heavy yawn preceded the appearance of a man, who, like the Moonshine of Pyramus and Thisbe,[18] carried a lantern, needlessly aiding his sister luminary in the heavens. As he walked sleepily up the street, he turned his broad, dull face on Robin, and displayed a long staff, spiked at the end.

"Home, vagabond, home!" said the watchman, in accents that seemed to fall asleep as soon as they were uttered. "Home, or we'll set you in the stocks by peep of day!"

---

18. **Moonshine of Pyramus and Thisbe:** In act 5 of Shakespeare's *A Midsummer Night's Dream*, amateurs produce a hilarious version of the tragic tale of Pyramus and Thisbe in which one character dresses as the moon and carries a lantern in order to represent the moonshine under which the lovers meet.

"This is the second hint of the kind," thought Robin. "I wish they would end my difficulties, by setting me there to-night."

Nevertheless, the youth felt an instinctive antipathy towards the guardian of midnight order, which at first prevented him from asking his usual question. But just when the man was about to vanish behind the corner, Robin resolved not to lose the opportunity, and shouted lustily after him—

"I say, friend! will you guide me to the house of my kinsman, Major Molineux?"

The watchman made no reply, but turned the corner and was gone; yet Robin seemed to hear the sound of drowsy laughter stealing along the solitary street. At that moment, also, a pleasant titter saluted him from the open window above his head; he looked up, and caught the sparkle of a saucy eye; a round arm beckoned to him, and next he heard light footsteps descending the staircase within. But Robin, being of the household of a New England clergyman, was a good youth, as well as a shrewd one; so he resisted temptation, and fled away.

He now roamed desperately, and at random, through the town, almost ready to believe that a spell was on him, like that, by which a wizard of his country, had once kept three pursuers wandering, a whole winter night, within twenty paces of the cottage which they sought. The streets lay before him, strange and desolate, and the lights were extinguished in almost every house. Twice, however, little parties of men, among whom Robin distinguished individuals in outlandish attire, came hurrying along, but though on both occasions they paused to address him, such intercourse did not at all enlighten his perplexity. They did but utter a few words in some language of which Robin knew nothing, and perceiving his inability to answer, bestowed a curse upon him in plain English, and hastened away. Finally, the lad determined to knock at the door of every mansion that might appear worthy to be occupied by his kinsman, trusting that perseverance would overcome the fatality which had hitherto thwarted him. Firm in this resolve, he was passing beneath the walls of a church, which formed the corner of two streets, when, as he turned into the shade of its steeple, he encountered a bulky stranger, muffled in a cloak. The man was proceeding with the speed of earnest business, but Robin planted himself full before him, holding the oak cudgel with both hands across his body, as a bar to further passage.

"Halt, honest man, and answer me a question," said he, very resolutely. "Tell me, this instant, whereabouts is the dwelling of my kinsman, Major Molineux?"

"Keep your tongue between your teeth, fool, and let me pass," said a deep, gruff voice, which Robin partly remembered. "Let me pass, I say, or I'll strike you to the earth!"

"No, no, neighbor!" cried Robin, flourishing his cudgel, and then thrusting its larger end close to the man's muffled face. "No, no, I'm not the fool you take me for, nor do you pass, till I have an answer to my question. Whereabouts is the dwelling of my kinsman, Major Molineux?"

The stranger, instead of attempting to force his passage, stept back into the moonlight, unmuffled his own face and stared full into that of Robin.

"Watch here an hour and Major Molineux will pass by," said he.

Robin gazed with dismay and astonishment, on the unprecedented physiognomy of the speaker. The forehead with its double prominence, the broad-hooked nose, the shaggy eyebrows, and fiery eyes, were those which he had noticed at the inn, but the man's complexion had undergone a singular, or more properly, a two-fold change. One side of the face blazed of an intense red, while the other was black as midnight, the division line being in the broad bridge of the nose; and a mouth, which seemed to extend from ear to ear, was black or red, in contrast to the color of the cheek. The effect was as if two individual devils, a fiend of fire and a fiend of darkness, had united themselves to form this infernal visage. The stranger grinned in Robin's face, muffled his party-colored features, and was out of sight in a moment.

"Strange things we travellers see!" ejaculated Robin.

He seated himself, however, upon the steps of the church-door, resolving to wait the appointed time for his kinsman's appearance. A few moments were consumed in philosophical speculations, upon the species of the *genus homo*,[19] who had just left him, but having settled this point shrewdly, rationally, and satisfactorily, he was compelled to look elsewhere for amusement. And first he threw his eyes along the street; it was of more respectable appearance than most of those into which he had wandered, and the moon, "creating, like the imaginative power, a beautiful strangeness in familiar objects," gave something of romance to a scene, that might not have possessed it in the light of day. The irregular, and often quaint architecture of the houses, some of whose roofs were broken into numerous little peaks; while others ascended, steep and narrow, into a single point; and others again were square; the pure milk-white of some of their complexions, the aged darkness of others, and the thousand sparklings, reflected from bright substances in the plastered walls of many; these matters engaged Robin's attention for awhile, and then began to grow wearisome. Next he endeavored to define the forms of distant objects, starting away with almost ghostly indistinctness, just as his eye appeared to grasp them; and finally he took a minute survey of an edifice, which stood on the opposite side of the street, directly in front of the church-door, where he was stationed. It was a large square mansion, distinguished from its neighbors by a balcony, which rested on tall pillars, and by an elaborate gothic window, communicating therewith.

"Perhaps this is the very house I have been seeking," thought Robin.

Then he strove to speed away the time, by listening to a murmur, which swept continually along the street, yet was scarcely audible, except to an unaccustomed ear like his; it was a low, dull, dreamy sound, compounded of many noises, each of which was at too great a distance to be separately heard. Robin marvelled at this snore of a sleeping town, and marvelled more, whenever its continuity was broken, by now and then a distant shout, apparently loud where it originated. But altogether it was a sleep-inspiring sound, and to shake off its drowsy influence, Robin arose, and climbed a window-frame, that he might view the interior of the church. There the moonbeams came trembling in, and fell down upon the deserted pews, and extended along the quiet aisles. A fainter, yet more awful radiance, was hovering round the pulpit, and one solitary ray had dared to rest upon the opened page of the great bible. Had Nature, in that deep hour, become a

19. ***genus homo***: Human being (Latin).

worshipper in the house, which man had builded? Or was that heavenly light the visible sanctity of the place, visible because no earthly and impure feet were within the walls? The scene made Robin's heart shiver with a sensation of loneliness, stronger than he had ever felt in the remotest depths of his native woods; so he turned away, and sat down again before the door. There were graves around the church, and now an uneasy thought obtruded into Robin's breast. What if the object of his search, which had been so often and so strangely thwarted, were all the time mouldering in his shroud? What if his kinsman should glide through yonder gate, and nod and smile to him in passing dimly by?

"Oh, that any breathing thing were here with me!" said Robin.

Recalling his thoughts from this uncomfortable track, he sent them over forest, hill, and stream, and attempted to imagine how that evening of ambiguity and weariness, had been spent by his father's household. He pictured them assembled at the door, beneath the tree, the great old tree, which had been spared for its huge twisted trunk, and venerable shade, when a thousand leafy brethren fell. There, at the going down of the summer sun, it was his father's custom to perform domestic worship, that the neighbors might come and join with him like brothers of the family, and that the wayfaring man might pause to drink at that fountain, and keep his heart pure by freshening the memory of home. Robin distinguished the seat of every individual of the little audience; he saw the good man in the midst, holding the scriptures in the golden light that shone from the western clouds; he beheld him close the book, and all rise up to pray. He heard the old thanksgiving for daily mercies, the old supplications for their continuance, to which he had so often listened in weariness, but which were now among his dear remembrances. He perceived the slight inequality of his father's voice when he came to speak of the Absent One; he noted how his mother turned her face to the broad and knotted trunk, how his elder brother scorned, because the beard was rough upon his upper lip, to permit his features to be moved; how his younger sister drew down a low hanging branch before her eyes; and how the little one of all, whose sports had hitherto broken the decorum of the scene, understood the prayer for her playmate, and burst into clamorous grief. Then he saw them go in at the door; and when Robin would have entered also, the latch tinkled into its place, and he was excluded from his home.

"Am I here, or there?" cried Robin, starting; for all at once, when his thoughts had become visible and audible in a dream, the long, wide, solitary street shone out before him.

He aroused himself, and endeavored to fix his attention steadily upon the large edifice which he had surveyed before. But still his mind kept vibrating between fancy and reality; by turns, the pillars of the balcony lengthened into the tall, bare stems of pines, dwindled down to human figures, settled again in their true shape and size, and then commenced a new succession of changes. For a single moment, when he deemed himself awake, he could have sworn that a visage, one which he seemed to remember, yet could not absolutely name as his kinsman's, was looking towards him from the Gothic window. A deeper sleep wrestled with, and nearly overcame him, but fled at the sound of footsteps along the opposite pavement. Robin rubbed his eyes, discerned a man passing at the foot of the balcony, and addressed him in a loud, peevish, and lamentable cry.

"Halloo, friend! must I wait here all night for my kinsman, Major Molineux?"

The sleeping echoes awoke, and answered the voice; and the passenger, barely able to discern a figure sitting in the oblique shade of the steeple, traversed the street to obtain a nearer view. He was himself a gentleman in his prime, of open, intelligent, cheerful, and altogether prepossessing countenance. Perceiving a country youth, apparently homeless and without friends, he accosted him in a tone of real kindness, which had become strange to Robin's ears.

"Well, my good lad, why are you sitting here?" inquired he. "Can I be of service to you in any way?"

"I am afraid not, Sir," replied Robin, despondingly; "yet I shall take it kindly, if you'll answer me a single question. I've been searching half the night for one Major Molineux; now, Sir, is there really such a person in these parts, or am I dreaming?"

"Major Molineux! The name is not altogether strange to me," said the gentleman, smiling. "Have you any objection to telling me the nature of your business with him?"

Then Robin briefly related that his father was a clergyman, settled on a small salary, at a long distance back in the country, and that he and Major Molineux were brothers' children. The Major, having inherited riches, and acquired civil and military rank, had visited his cousin in great pomp a year or two before; had manifested much interest in Robin and an elder brother, and, being childless himself, had thrown out hints respecting the future establishment of one of them in life. The elder brother was destined to succeed to the farm, which his father cultivated, in the interval of sacred duties; it was therefore determined that Robin should profit by his kinsman's generous intentions, especially as he had seemed to be rather the favorite, and was thought to possess other necessary endowments.

"For I have the name of being a shrewd youth," observed Robin, in this part of his story.

"I doubt not you deserve it," replied his new friend, good naturedly; "but pray proceed."

"Well, Sir, being nearly eighteen years old, and well grown, as you see," continued Robin, raising himself to his full height, "I thought it high time to begin the world. So my mother and sister put me in handsome trim, and my father gave me half the remnant of his last year's salary, and five days ago I started for this place, to pay the Major a visit. But would you believe it, Sir? I crossed the ferry a little after dusk, and have yet found nobody that would show me the way to his dwelling; only an hour or two since, I was told to wait here, and Major Molineux would pass by."

"Can you describe the man who told you this?" inquired the gentleman.

"Oh, he was a very ill-favored fellow, Sir," replied Robin, "with two great bumps on his forehead, a hook nose, fiery eyes, and, what struck me as the strangest, his face was of two different colors. Do you happen to know such a man, Sir?"

"Not intimately," answered the stranger, "but I chanced to meet him a little time previous to your stopping me. I believe you may trust his word, and that the Major will very shortly pass through this street. In the mean time, as I have a singular curiosity to witness your meeting, I will sit down here upon the steps, and bear you company."

He seated himself accordingly, and soon engaged his companion in animated discourse. It was but of brief continuance, however, for a noise of shouting, which had long been remotely audible, drew so much nearer, that Robin inquired its cause.

"What may be the meaning of this uproar?" asked he. "Truly, if your town be always as noisy, I shall find little sleep, while I am an inhabitant."

"Why, indeed, friend Robin, there do appear to be three or four riotous fellows abroad to-night," replied the gentleman. "You must not expect all the stillness of your native woods, here in our streets. But the watch will shortly be at the heels of these lads, and —"

"Aye, and set them in the stocks by peep of day," interrupted Robin, recollecting his own encounter with the drowsy lantern-bearer. "But, dear Sir, if I may trust my ears, an army of watchmen would never make head against such a multitude of rioters. There were at least a thousand voices went to make up that one shout."

"May not one man have several voices, Robin, as well as two complexions?" said his friend.

"Perhaps a man may; but heaven forbid that a woman should!" responded the shrewd youth, thinking of the seductive tones of the Major's housekeeper.

The sounds of a trumpet in some neighboring street, now became so evident and continual, that Robin's curiosity was strongly excited. In addition to the shouts, he heard frequent bursts from many instruments of discord, and a wild and confused laughter filled up the intervals. Robin rose from the steps, and looked wistfully towards a point, whither several people seemed to be hastening.

"Surely some prodigious merrymaking is going on," exclaimed he. "I have laughed very little since I left home, Sir, and should be sorry to lose an opportunity. Shall we just step round the corner by that darkish house, and take our share of the fun?"

"Sit down again, sit down, good Robin," replied the gentleman, laying his hand on the skirt of the grey coat. "You forget that we must wait here for your kinsman; and there is reason to believe that he will pass by, in the course of a very few moments."

The near approach of the uproar had now disturbed the neighborhood; windows flew open on all sides; and many heads, in the attire of the pillow, and confused by sleep suddenly broken, were protruded to the gaze of whoever had leisure to observe them. Eager voices hailed each other from house to house, all demanding the explanation, which not a soul could give. Half-dressed men hurried towards the unknown commotion, stumbling as they went over the stone steps, that thrust themselves into the narrow footwalk. The shouts, the laughter, and the tuneless bray, the antipodes of music, came onward with increasing din, till scattered individuals, and then denser bodies, began to appear round a corner, at the distance of a hundred yards.

"Will you recognise your kinsman, Robin, if he passes in this crowd?" inquired the gentleman.

"Indeed, I can't warrant it, Sir; but I'll take my stand here, and keep a bright look out," answered Robin, descending to the outer edge of the pavement.

A mighty stream of people now emptied into the street, and came rolling slowly towards the church. A single horseman wheeled the corner in the midst of them, and close behind him came a band of fearful wind-instruments, sending forth a fresher discord, now that no intervening buildings keep it from the ear. Then a redder light disturbed the moonbeams, and a dense multitude of torches shone along the street, concealing by their glare whatever object they illuminated. The single horseman, clad in a military dress, and bearing a drawn sword, rode onward as the leader, and, by his fierce and variegated countenance, appeared like war personified; the red of one cheek was an emblem of fire and sword; the blackness of the other betokened the mourning which attends them. In his train, were wild figures in the Indian dress, and many fantastic shapes without a model, giving the whole march a visionary air, as if a dream had broken forth from some feverish brain, and were sweeping visibly through the midnight streets. A mass of people, inactive, except as applauding spectators, hemmed the procession in, and several women ran along the sidewalks, piercing the confusion of heavier sounds, with their shrill voices of mirth or terror.

"The double-faced fellow has his eye upon me," muttered Robin, with an indefinite but uncomfortable idea, that he was himself to bear a part in the pageantry.

The leader turned himself in the saddle, and fixed his glance full upon the country youth, as the steed went slowly by. When Robin had freed his eyes from those fiery ones, the musicians were passing before him, and the torches were close at hand; but the unsteady brightness of the latter formed a veil which he could not penetrate. The rattling of wheels over the stones sometimes found its way to his ear, and confused traces of a human form appeared at intervals, and then melted into the vivid light. A moment more, and the leader thundered a command to halt; the trumpets vomited a horrid breath, and held their peace; the shouts and laughter of the people died away, and there remained only an universal hum, nearly allied to silence. Right before Robin's eyes was an uncovered cart. There the torches blazed the brightest, there the moon shone out like day, and there, in tar-and-feathery dignity, sate his kinsman, Major Molineux!

He was an elderly man, of large and majestic person, and strong, square features, betokening a steady soul; but steady as it was, his enemies had found the means to shake it. His face was pale as death, and far more ghastly; the broad forehead was contracted in his agony, so that the eyebrows formed one dark grey line; his eyes were red and wild, and the foam hung white upon his quivering lip. His whole frame was agitated by a quick, and continual tremor, which his pride strove to quell, even in those circumstances of overwhelming humiliation. But perhaps the bitterest pang of all was when his eyes met those of Robin; for he evidently knew him on the instant, as the youth stood witnessing the foul disgrace of a head that had grown grey in honor. They stared at each other in silence, and Robin's knees shook, and his hair bristled, with a mixture of pity and terror. Soon, however, a bewildering excitement began to seize upon his mind; the preceding adventures of the night, the unexpected appearance of the crowd, the torches, the confused din, and the hush that followed, the spectre of his kinsman reviled by that great multitude, all this, and more than all, a perception of tremendous ridicule in the whole scene, affected him with a sort of mental inebriety. At that moment a voice of sluggish merriment saluted Robin's ears; he turned instinctively, and just behind the corner of the church stood the lantern-bearer, rubbing his eyes, and drowsily enjoying the lad's amazement. Then he heard a peal of laughter like the ringing of silvery bells; a woman twitched his arm, a saucy eye met his, and he saw the lady of the scarlet petticoat. A sharp, dry cachinnation appealed to his memory, and, standing on tiptoe in the crowd, with his white apron over his head, he beheld the courteous little innkeeper. And lastly, there sailed over the heads of the multitude a great, broad laugh, broken in the midst by two deep sepulchral hems; thus –

"Haw, haw, haw – hem, hem – haw, haw, haw, haw!"

The sound proceeded from the balcony of the opposite edifice, and thither Robin turned his eyes. In front of the Gothic window stood the old citizen, wrapped in a wide gown, his grey periwig exchanged for a nightcap, which was thrust back from his forehead, and his silk stockings hanging down about his legs. He supported himself on his polished cane in a fit of convulsive merriment, which manifested itself on his solemn old features, like a funny inscription on a tomb-stone. Then Robin seemed to hear the voices of the barbers; of the guests of the inn; and of all who had made sport of him that night. The contagion was spreading among the multitude, when, all at once, it seized upon Robin, and he sent forth a shout of laughter that echoed through the street; every man shook his sides, every man emptied his lungs, but Robin's shout was the loudest there. The cloud-spirits peeped from their silvery islands, as the congregated mirth went roaring up the sky! The Man in the Moon heard the far bellow; "Oho," quoth he, "the old Earth is frolicsome to-night!"

When there was a momentary calm in that tempestuous sea of sound, the leader gave the sign, and the procession resumed its march. On they went, like fiends that throng in mockery round some dead potentate, mighty no more, but majestic still in his agony. On they went, in counterfeited pomp, in senseless uproar, in frenzied merriment, trampling all on an old man's heart. On swept the tumult, and left a silent street behind.

"Well, Robin, are you dreaming?" inquired the gentleman, laying his hand on the youth's shoulder.

Robin started, and withdrew his arm from the stone post, to which he had instinctively clung, while the living stream rolled by him. His cheek was somewhat pale, and his eye not quite so lively as in the earlier part of the evening.

"Will you be kind enough to show me the way to the Ferry?" said he, after a moment's pause.

"You have then adopted a new subject of inquiry?" observed his companion, with a smile.

"Why, yes, Sir," replied Robin, rather dryly. "Thanks to you, and to my other friends, I have at last met my kinsman, and he will scarce desire to see my face again. I begin to grow weary of a town life, Sir. Will you show me the way to the Ferry?"

"No, my good friend Robin, not to-night, at least," said the gentleman. "Some few days hence, if you continue to wish it, I will speed you on your journey. Or, if you prefer to remain with us, perhaps, as you are a shrewd youth, you may rise in the world, without the help of your kinsman, Major Molineux."

[1832]

Hawthorne's "Young Goodman Brown." Probably the most famous of Hawthorne's early stories of the Puritans, "Young Goodman Brown" was one of seventeen sketches and stories he published anonymously in the *New-England Magazine.* Established in 1831 as a vehicle for New England writers, the magazine enjoyed early success but failed as a result of declining sales in 1835. The editors attracted a variety of well-known writers, including Oliver Wendell Holmes, Henry Wadsworth Longfellow, and Lydia Sigourney, as well as virtual unknowns like Hawthorne. Although it paid only $1 per page for his contributions, publishing in the magazine was a boon to Hawthorne, who was seeking to establish himself as a writer. Like many of his other pieces in the magazine, "Young Goodman Brown" is set in colonial New England and refers to actual events, including the most infamous episode in the history of Hawthorne's native town, the Salem witch trials of 1692. Indeed, the story may be read, not only as a powerful exploration of the corrosive effects of the Puritan conscience, but also as a probing analysis of the moral psychology of a Puritan community in which people could believe their neighbors were witches in league with the devil. Hawthorne did not include the sobering story in his earliest collections, *Twice-Told Tales* (1837, 1842), but he later included it in *Mosses from an Old Manse* (1846). The text is taken from the first printing in the *New-England Magazine* (April 1835), where it was ascribed to "the author of 'The Gray Champion,'" a story Hawthorne had published in the magazine three months earlier.

YOUNG GOODMAN BROWN

Young goodman[1] Brown came forth, at sunset, into the street of Salem village, but put his head back, after crossing the threshold, to exchange a parting kiss with his young wife. And Faith, as the wife was aptly named, thrust her own pretty head into the street, letting the wind play with the pink ribbons of her cap, while she called to goodman Brown.

"Dearest heart," whispered she, softly and rather sadly, when her lips were close to his ear, "pr'y thee, put off your journey until sunrise, and sleep in your own bed to-night. A lone woman is troubled with such dreams and such thoughts, that she's afeard of herself, sometimes. Pray, tarry with me this night, dear husband, of all nights in the year!"

"My love and my Faith," replied young goodman Brown, "of all nights in the year, this one night must I tarry away from thee. My journey, as thou callest it, forth and back again, must needs be done 'twixt now and sunrise. What, my sweet, pretty wife, dost thou doubt me already, and we but three months married!"

1. **goodman:** A courteous title for a man of humble birth.

"Then, God bless you!" said Faith, with the pink ribbons, "and may you find all well, when you come back."

"Amen!" cried goodman Brown. "Say thy prayers, dear Faith, and go to bed at dusk, and no harm will come to thee."

So they parted; and the young man pursued his way, until, being about to turn the corner by the meeting-house, he looked back, and saw the head of Faith still peeping after him, with a melancholy air, in spite of her pink ribbons.

"Poor little Faith!" thought be, for his heart smote him. "What a wretch am I, to leave her on such an errand! She talks of dreams, too. Methought, as she spoke, there was trouble in her face, as if a dream had warned her what work is to be done to-night. But, no, no! 'twould kill her to think it. Well; she's a blessed angel on earth; and after this one night, I'll cling to her skirts and follow her to Heaven."

With this excellent resolve for the future, goodman Brown felt himself justified in making more haste on his present evil purpose. He had taken a dreary road, darkened by all the gloomiest trees of the forest, which barely stood aside to let the narrow path creep through, and closed immediately behind. It was all as lonely as could be; and there is this peculiarity in such a solitude, that the traveler knows not who may be concealed by the innumerable trunks and the thick boughs overhead; so that, with lonely footsteps, he may yet be passing through an unseen multitude.

"There may be a devilish Indian behind every tree," said goodman Brown, to himself; and he glanced fearfully behind him, as he added, "What if the devil himself should be at my very elbow!"

His head being turned back, he passed a crook of the road, and looking forward again, beheld the figure of a man, in grave and decent attire, seated at the foot of an old tree. He arose, at goodman Brown's approach, and walked onward, side by side with him.

"You are late, goodman Brown," said he. "The clock of the Old South[2] was striking as I came through Boston; and that is full fifteen minutes agone."

"Faith kept me back awhile," replied the young man, with a tremor in his voice, caused by the sudden appearance of his companion, though not wholly unexpected.

It was now deep dusk in the forest, and deepest in that part of it where these two were journeying. As nearly as could be discerned, the second traveler was about fifty years old, apparently in the same rank of life as goodman Brown, and bearing a considerable resemblance to him, though perhaps more in expression than features. Still, they might have been taken for father and son. And yet, though the elder person was as simply clad as the younger, and as simple in manner too, he had an indescribable air of one who knew the world, and would not have felt abashed at the governor's dinner-table, or in king William's court,[3] were it possible that his affairs should call him thither. But the only thing about him, that could be fixed upon as remarkable, was his staff, which bore

2. **Old South:** The Old South Church in Boston; since one not could travel from Boston to Salem in fifteen minutes, the speed suggests a supernatural force.

3. **king William's court:** King William II and Queen Mary II were the joint rulers of England from 1689-1702.

the likeness of a great black snake, so curiously wrought, that it might almost be seen to twist and wriggle itself, like a living serpent. This, of course, must have been an ocular deception, assisted by the uncertain light.

"Come, goodman Brown!" cried his fellow-traveler, "this is a dull pace for the beginning of a journey. Take my staff, if you are so soon weary."

"Friend," said the other, exchanging his slow pace for a full stop, "having kept covenant by meeting thee here, it is my purpose now to return whence I came. I have scruples, touching the matter thou wot'st of."

"Sayest thou so?" replied he of the serpent, smiling apart. "Let us walk on, nevertheless, reasoning as we go, and if I convince thee not, thou shalt turn back. We are but a little way in the forest, yet."

"Too far, too far!" exclaimed the goodman, unconsciously resuming his walk. "My father never went into the woods on such an errand, nor his father before him. We have been a race of honest men and good Christians, since the days of the martyrs.[4] And shall I be the first of the name of Brown, that ever took this path, and kept" –

"Such company, thou wouldst say," observed the elder person, interpreting his pause. "Good, goodman Brown! I have been as well acquainted with your family as with ever a one among the Puritans; and that's no trifle to say. I helped your grandfather, the constable, when he lashed the Quaker woman so smartly through the streets of Salem. And it was I that brought your father a pitch-pine knot, kindled at my own hearth, to set fire to an Indian village, in king Philip's war.[5] They were my good friends, both; and many a pleasant walk have we had along this path, and returned merrily after midnight. I would fain be friends with you, for their sake."

"If it be as thou sayest," replied goodman Brown, "I marvel they never spoke of these matters. Or, verily, I marvel not, seeing that the least rumor of the sort would have driven them from New-England. We are a people of prayer, and good works, to boot, and abide no such wickedness."

"Wickedness or not," said the traveler with the twisted staff, "I have a very general acquaintance here in New-England. The deacons of many a church have drunk the communion wine with me; the selectmen, of divers towns, make me their chairman; and a majority of the Great and General Court[6] are firm supporters of my interest. The governor and I, too – but these are state-secrets."

"Can this be so!" cried goodman Brown, with a stare of amazement at his undisturbed companion. "Howbeit, I have nothing to do with the governor and council; they have their own ways, and are no rule for a simple husbandman,[7] like me. But, were I to go on with thee, how should I meet the eye of that good old man, our minister,

---

4. **days of the martyrs:** Protestant martyrs executed in England during the reign of the Catholic queen Mary Tudor (1553–1558).
5. **king Philip's war:** The chief of the Wampanoag Indians, called "King Philip" by the colonists, led uprisings against them from 1675–1676.
6. **Great and General Court:** The colonial legislature.
7. **husbandman:** Farmer.

at Salem village? Oh, his voice would make me tremble, both Sabbath-day and lecture-day!"[8]

Thus far, the elder traveler had listened with due gravity, but now burst into a fit of irrepressible mirth, shaking himself so violently, that his snake-like staff actually seemed to wriggle in sympathy.

"Ha! ha! ha!" shouted he, again and again; then composing himself, "Well, go on, goodman Brown, go on; but, pr'y thee, don't kill me with laughing!"

"Well, then, to end the matter at once," said goodman Brown, considerably nettled, "there is my wife, Faith. It would break her dear little heart; and I'd rather break my own!"

"Nay, if that be the case," answered the other, "e'en go thy ways, goodman Brown. I would not, for twenty old women like the one hobbling before us, that Faith should come to any harm."

As he spoke, he pointed his staff at a female figure on the path, in whom goodman Brown recognized a very pious and exemplary dame, who had taught him his catechism, in youth, and was still his moral and spiritual adviser, jointly with the minister and deacon Gookin.

"A marvel, truly, that goody Cloyse[9] should be so far in the wilderness, at night-fall!" said he. "But, with your leave, friend, I shall take a cut through the woods, until we have left this Christian woman behind. Being a stranger to you, she might ask whom I was consorting with, and whither I was going."

"Be it so," said his fellow-traveler. "Betake you to the woods, and let me keep the path."

Accordingly, the young man turned aside, but took care to watch his companion, who advanced softly along the road, until he had come within a staff's length of the old dame. She, meanwhile, was making the best of her way, with singular speed for so aged a woman, and mumbling some indistinct words, a prayer, doubtless, as she went. The traveler put forth his staff, and touched her withered neck with what seemed the serpent's tail.

"The devil!" screamed the pious old lady.

"Then goody Cloyse knows her old friend?" observed the traveler, confronting her, and leaning on his writhing stick.

"Ah, forsooth, and is it your worship, indeed?" cried the good dame. "Yea, truly is it, and in the very image of my old gossip, goodman Brown, the grandfather of the silly fellow that now is. But, would your worship believe it? my broomstick hath strangely disappeared, stolen, as I suspect, by that unhanged witch, goody Cory, and that, too, when I was all anointed with the juice of smallage and cinque-foil and wolf's-bane" — [10]

---

8. **lecture-day:** Sermon delivered on a weekday.

9. **goody Cloyse:** *Goody* was a shortened form of "goodwife," a courteous form of address for a married woman of humble status. Cloyse and "goody Cory," referred to later in this passage, were the names of women sentenced to death during the Salem witch trials of 1692.

10. **smallage . . . wolf's-bane:** Wild plants, some of them poisonous, associated with witchcraft.

"Mingled with fine wheat and the fat of a new-born babe," said the shape of old goodman Brown.

"Ah, your worship knows the receipt," cried the old lady, cackling aloud. "So, as I was saying, being all ready for the meeting, and no horse to ride on, I made up my mind to foot it; for they tell me, there is a nice young man to be taken into communion to-night. But now your good worship will lend me your arm, and we shall be there in a twinkling."

"That can hardly be," answered her friend. "I may not spare you my arm, goody Cloyse, but here is my staff, if you will."

So saying, he threw it down at her feet, where, perhaps, it assumed life, being one of the rods which its owner had formerly lent to the Egyptian Magi.[11] Of this fact, however, goodman Brown could not take cognizance. He had cast up his eyes in astonishment, and looking down again, beheld neither goody Cloyse nor the serpentine staff, but his fellow-traveler alone, who waited for him as calmly as if nothing had happened.

"That old woman taught me my catechism!" said the young man; and there was a world of meaning in this simple comment.

They continued to walk onward, while the elder traveler exhorted his companion to make good speed and persevere in the path, discoursing so aptly, that his arguments seemed rather to spring up in the bosom of his auditor, than to be suggested by himself. As they went, he plucked a branch of maple, to serve for a walking-stick, and began to strip it of the twigs and little boughs, which were wet with evening dew. The moment his fingers touched them, they became strangely withered and dried up, as with a week's sunshine. Thus the pair proceeded, at a good free pace, until suddenly, in a gloomy hollow of the road, goodman Brown sat himself down on the stump of a tree, and refused to go any farther.

"Friend," said he, stubbornly, "my mind is made up. Not another step will I budge on this errand. What if a wretched old woman do choose to go to the devil, when I thought she was going to Heaven! Is that any reason why I should quit my dear Faith, and go after her?"

"You will think better of this, by-and-by," said his acquaintance, composedly. "Sit here and rest yourself awhile; and when you feel like moving again, there is my staff to help you along."

Without more words, he threw his companion the maple stick, and was as speedily out of sight, as if he had vanished into the deepening gloom. The young man sat a few moments, by the road-side, applauding himself greatly, and thinking with how clear a conscience he should meet the minister, in his morning-walk, nor shrink from the eye of good old deacon Gookin. And what calm sleep would be his, that very night, which was to have been spent so wickedly, but purely and sweetly now, in the arms of Faith! Amidst these pleasant and praiseworthy meditations, goodman Brown heard the tramp of horses along the road, and deemed it advisable to conceal himself within the verge of

11. **Egyptian Magi:** In the Old Testament, Aaron demonstrates the power of God to the Pharaoh by turning his staff into a serpent. When the Pharaoh's magicians replicate the feat, Aaron's staff swallows theirs (Exodus 7:8-13).

the forest, conscious of the guilty purpose that had brought him thither, though now so happily turned from it.

On came the hoof-tramps and the voices of the riders, two grave old voices, conversing soberly as they drew near. These mingled sounds appeared to pass along the road, within a few yards of the young man's hiding-place; but owing, doubtless, to the depth of the gloom, at that particular spot, neither the travelers nor their steeds were visible. Though their figures brushed the small boughs by the way-side, it could not be seen that they intercepted, even for a moment, the faint gleam from the strip of bright sky, athwart which they must have passed. Goodman Brown alternately crouched and stood on tip-toe, pulling aside the branches, and thrusting forth his head as far as he durst, without discerning so much as a shadow. It vexed him the more, because he could have sworn, were such a thing possible, that he recognized the voices of the minister and deacon Gookin, jogging along quietly, as they were wont to do, when bound to some ordination or ecclesiastical council. While yet within hearing, one of the riders stopped to pluck a switch.

"Of the two, reverend Sir," said the voice like the deacon's, "I had rather miss an ordination-dinner than to-night's meeting. They tell me that some of our community are to be here from Falmouth[12] and beyond, and others from Connecticut and Rhode-Island; besides several of the Indian powows,[13] who, after their fashion, know almost as much deviltry as the best of us. Moreover, there is a goodly young woman to be taken into communion."

"Mighty well, deacon Gookin!" replied the solemn old tones of the minister. "Spur up, or we shall be late. Nothing can be done, you know, until I get on the ground."

The hoofs clattered again, and the voices, talking so strangely in the empty air, passed on through the forest, where no church had ever been gathered, nor solitary Christian prayed. Whither, then, could these holy men be journeying, so deep into the heathen wilderness? Young goodman Brown caught hold of a tree, for support, being ready to sink down on the ground, faint and overburthened with the heavy sickness of his heart. He looked up to the sky, doubting whether there really was a Heaven above him. Yet, there was the blue arch, and the stars brightening in it.

"With Heaven above, and Faith below, I will yet stand firm against the devil!" cried goodman Brown.

While he still gazed upward, into the deep arch of the firmament, and had lifted his hands to pray, a cloud, though no wind was stirring, hurried across the zenith, and hid the brightening stars. The blue sky was still visible, except directly overhead, where this black mass of cloud was sweeping swiftly northward. Aloft in the air, as if from the depths of the cloud, came a confused and doubtful sound of voices. Once, the listener fancied that he could distinguish the accents of town's-people of his own, men and women, both pious and ungodly, many of whom he had met at the communion-table, and had seen others rioting at the tavern. The next moment, so indistinct were the sounds,

12. **Falmouth:** A town on Cape Cod in Massachusetts.
13. **Indian powows:** Medicine men. A powwow is a conference or gathering.

he doubted whether he had heard aught but the murmur of the old forest, whispering without a wind. Then came a stronger swell of those familiar tones, heard daily in the sunshine, at Salem village, but never, until now, from a cloud of night. There was one voice, of a young woman, uttering lamentations, yet with an uncertain sorrow, and entreating for some favor, which, perhaps, it would grieve her to obtain. And all the unseen multitude, both saints and sinners, seemed to encourage her onward.

"Faith!" shouted goodman Brown, in a voice of agony and desperation; and the echoes of the forest mocked him, crying – "Faith! Faith!" as if bewildered wretches were seeking her, all through the wilderness.

The cry of grief, rage, and terror, was yet piercing the night, when the unhappy husband held his breath for a response. There was a scream, drowned immediately in a louder murmur of voices, fading into far-off laughter, as the dark cloud swept away, leaving the clear and silent sky above goodman Brown. But something fluttered lightly down through the air, and caught on the branch of a tree. The young man seized it, and beheld a pink ribbon.

"My Faith is gone!" cried he, after one stupefied moment. "There is no good on earth; and sin is but a name. Come, devil! for to thee is this world given."

And maddened with despair, so that he laughed loud and long, did goodman Brown grasp his staff and set forth again, at such a rate, that he seemed to fly along the forest-path, rather than to walk or run. The road grew wilder and drearier, and more faintly traced, and vanished at length, leaving him in the heart of the dark wilderness, still rushing onward, with the instinct that guides mortal man to evil. The whole forest was peopled with frightful sounds; the creaking of the trees, the howling of wild beasts, and the yell of Indians; while, sometimes, the wind tolled like a distant church-bell, and sometimes gave a broad roar around the traveler, as if all Nature were laughing him to scorn. But he was himself the chief horror of the scene, and shrank not from its other horrors.

"Ha! ha! ha!" roared goodman Brown, when the wind laughed at him. "Let us hear which will laugh loudest! Think not to frighten me with your deviltry! Come witch, come wizard, come Indian powow, come devil himself! and here comes goodman Brown. You may as well fear him as he fear you!"

In truth, all through the haunted forest, there could be nothing more frightful than the figure of goodman Brown. On he flew, among the black pines, brandishing his staff with frenzied gestures, now giving vent to an inspiration of horrid blasphemy, and now shouting forth such laughter, as set all the echoes of the forest laughing like demons around him. The fiend in his own shape is less hideous, than when he rages in the breast of man. Thus sped the demoniac on his course, until, quivering among the trees, he saw a red light before him, as when the felled trunks and branches of a clearing have been set on fire, and throw up their lurid blaze against the sky, at the hour of midnight. He paused, in a lull of the tempest that had driven him onward, and heard the swell of what seemed a hymn, rolling solemnly from a distance, with the weight of many voices. He knew the tune; it was a familiar one in the choir of the village meeting-house. The verse died heavily away, and was lengthened by a chorus, not of human voices, but of all the sounds of the benighted wilderness, pealing in awful harmony together. Goodman

Brown cried out; and his cry was lost to his own ear, by its unison with the cry of the desert.

In the interval of silence, he stole forward, until the light glared full upon his eyes. At one extremity of an open space, hemmed in by the dark wall of the forest, arose a rock, bearing some rude, natural resemblance either to an altar or a pulpit, and surrounded by four blazing pines, their tops a flame, their stems untouched, like candles at an evening meeting. The mass of foliage, that had overgrown the summit of the rock, was all on fire, blazing high into the night, and fitfully illuminating the whole field. Each pendent twig and leafy festoon was in a blaze. As the red light arose and fell, a numerous congregation alternately shone forth, then disappeared in shadow, and again grew, as it were, out of the darkness, peopling the heart of the solitary woods at once.

"A grave and dark-clad company!" quoth goodman Brown.

In truth, they were such. Among them, quivering to-and-fro, between gloom and splendor, appeared faces that would be seen, next day, at the council-board of the province, and others which, Sabbath after Sabbath, looked devoutly heavenward, and benignantly over the crowded pews, from the holiest pulpits in the land. Some affirm, that the lady of the governor was there. At least, there were high dames well known to her, and wives of honored husbands, and widows, a great multitude, and ancient maidens, all of excellent repute, and fair young girls, who trembled, lest their mothers should espy them. Either the sudden gleams of light, flashing over the obscure field, bedazzled goodman Brown, or he recognized a score of the church-members of Salem village, famous for their especial sanctity. Good old deacon Gookin had arrived, and waited at the skirts of that venerable saint, his revered pastor. But, irreverently consorting with these grave, reputable, and pious people, these elders of the church, these chaste dames and dewy virgins, there were men of dissolute lives and women of spotted fame, wretches given over to all mean and filthy vice, and suspected even of horrid crimes. It was strange to see, that the good shrank not from the wicked, nor were the sinners abashed by the saints. Scattered, also, among their pale-faced enemies, were the Indian priests, or powows, who had often scared their native forest with more hideous incantations than any known to English witchcraft.

"But, where is Faith?" thought goodman Brown; and, as hope came into his heart, he trembled.

Another verse of the hymn arose, a slow and solemn strain, such as the pious love, but joined to words which expressed all that our nature can conceive of sin, and darkly hinted at far more. Unfathomable to mere mortals is the lore of fiends. Verse after verse was sung, and still the chorus of the desert swelled between, like the deepest tone of a mighty organ. And, with the final peal of that dreadful anthem, there came a sound, as if the roaring wind, the rushing streams, the howling beasts, and every other voice of the unconverted wilderness, were mingling and according with the voice of guilty man, in homage to the prince of all. The four blazing pines threw up a loftier flame, and obscurely discovered shapes and visages of horror on the smoke-wreaths, above the impious assembly. At the same moment, the fire on the rock shot redly forth, and formed a glowing arch above its base, where now appeared a figure. With reverence be it spoken, the apparition bore no slight similitude, both in garb and manner, to some grave divine of the New-England churches.

"Bring forth the converts!" cried a voice, that echoed through the field and rolled into the forest.

At the word, goodman Brown stept forth from the shadow of the trees, and approached the congregation, with whom he felt a loathful brotherhood, by the sympathy of all that was wicked in his heart. He could have well nigh sworn, that the shape of his own dead father beckoned him to advance, looking downward from a smoke-wreath, while a woman, with dim features of despair, threw out her hand to warn him back. Was it his mother? But he had no power to retreat one step, nor to resist, even in thought, when the minister and good old deacon Gookin, seized his arms, and led him to the blazing rock. Thither came also the slender form of a veiled female, led between Goody Cloyse, that pious teacher of the catechism, and Martha Carrier,[14] who had received the devil's promise to be queen of hell. A rampant hag was she! And there stood the proselytes, beneath the canopy of fire.

"Welcome, my children," said the dark figure, "to the communion of your race! Ye have found, thus young, your nature and your destiny. My children, look behind you!"

They turned; and flashing forth, as it were, in a sheet of flame, the fiend-worshippers were seen; the smile of welcome gleamed darkly on every visage.

"There," resumed the sable form, "are all whom ye have reverenced from youth. Ye deemed them holier than yourselves, and shrank from your own sin, contrasting it with their lives of righteousness, and prayerful aspirations heavenward. Yet, here are they all, in my worshipping assembly! This night it shall be granted you to know their secret deeds; how hoary-bearded elders of the church have whispered wanton words to the young maids of their households; how many a woman, eager for widow's weeds, has given her husband a drink at bed-time, and let him sleep his last sleep in her bosom; how beardless youths have made haste to inherit their fathers' wealth; and how fair damsels – blush not, sweet ones! – have dug little graves in the garden, and bidden me, the sole guest, to an infant's funeral. By the sympathy of your human hearts for sin, ye shall scent out all the places – whether in church, bed-chamber, street, field, or forest – where crime has been committed, and shall exult to behold the whole earth one stain of guilt, one mighty blood-spot. Far more than this! It shall be yours to penetrate, in every bosom, the deep mystery of sin, the fountain of all wicked arts, and which, inexhaustibly supplies more evil impulses than human power – than my power, at its utmost! – can make manifest in deeds. And now, my children, look upon each other."

They did so; and, by the blaze of the hell-kindled torches, the wretched man beheld his Faith, and the wife her husband, trembling before that unhallowed altar.

"Lo! there ye stand, my children," said the figure, in a deep and solemn tone, almost sad, with its despairing awfulness, as if his once angelic nature could yet mourn for our miserable race. "Depending upon one another's hearts, ye had still hoped, that virtue were not all a dream. Now are ye undeceived! Evil is the nature of mankind. Evil must be your only happiness. Welcome, again, my children, to the communion of your race!"

"Welcome!" repeated the fiend-worshippers, in one cry of despair and triumph.

And there they stood, the only pair, as it seemed, who were yet hesitating on the verge

14. **Martha Carrier:** At the Salem witch trials, Martha Carrier was tried and convicted of being a witch. She was condemned to death and hung on August 19, 1692.

of wickedness, in this dark world. A basin was hollowed, naturally, in the rock. Did it contain water, reddened by the lurid light? or was it blood? or, perchance, a liquid flame? Herein did the Shape of Evil dip his hand, and prepare to lay the mark of baptism upon their foreheads, that they might be partakers of the mystery of sin, more conscious of the secret guilt of others, both in deed and thought, than they could now be of their own. The husband cast one look at his pale wife, and Faith at him. What polluted wretches would the next glance shew them to each other, shuddering alike at what they disclosed and what they saw!

"Faith! Faith!" cried the husband. "Look up to Heaven, and resist the Wicked One!"

Whether Faith obeyed, he knew not. Hardly had he spoken, when he found himself amid calm night and solitude, listening to a roar of wind, which died heavily away through the forest. He staggered against the rock and felt it chill and damp, while a hanging twig, that had been all on fire, besprinkled his cheek with the coldest dew.

The next morning, young goodman Brown came slowly into the street of Salem village, staring around him like a bewildered man. The good old minister was taking a walk along the graveyard, to get an appetite for breakfast and meditate his sermon, and bestowed a blessing, as he passed, on goodman Brown. He shrank from the venerable saint, as if to avoid an anathema. Old deacon Gookin was at domestic worship, and the holy words of his prayer were heard through the open window. "What God doth the wizard pray to?" quoth goodman Brown. Goody Cloyse, that excellent old Christian, stood in the early sunshine, at her own lattice, catechising a little girl, who had brought her a pint of morning's milk. Goodman Brown snatched away the child, as from the grasp of the fiend himself. Turning the corner by the meeting-house, he spied the head of Faith, with the pink ribbons, gazing anxiously forth, and bursting into such joy at sight of him, that she skipt along the street, and almost kissed her husband before the whole village. But, goodman Brown looked sternly and sadly into her face, and passed on without a greeting.

Had goodman Brown fallen asleep in the forest, and only dreamed a wild dream of a witch-meeting?

Be it so, if you will. But, alas! it was a dream of evil omen for young goodman Brown. A stern, a sad, a darkly meditative, a distrustful, if not a desperate man, did he become, from the night of that fearful dream. On the Sabbath-day, when the congregation were singing a holy psalm, he could not listen, because an anthem of sin rushed loudly upon his ear, and drowned all the blessed strain. When the minister spoke from the pulpit, with power and fervid eloquence, and, with his hand on the open bible, of the sacred truths of our religion, and of saint-like lives and triumphant deaths, and of future bliss or misery unutterable, then did goodman Brown turn pale, dreading, lest the roof should thunder down upon the gray blasphemer and his hearers. Often, awaking suddenly at midnight, he shrank from the bosom of Faith, and at morning or eventide, when the family knelt down at prayer, he scowled, and muttered to himself, and gazed sternly at his wife, and turned away. And when he had lived long, and was borne to his grave, a hoary corpse, followed by Faith, an aged woman, and children and grand-children, a goodly procession, besides neighbors, not a few, they carved no hopeful verse upon his tomb-stone; for his dying hour was gloom.

[1835]

Hawthorne's "The Minister's Black Veil." This story is among Hawthorne's most provocative explorations of the Puritan mind and its psychology, a frequent focus of his fiction. "The Minister's Black Veil: A Parable" has strong symbolic overtones, recalling the parables Christ used to instruct his disciples and a long tradition of Christian allegory. But the meaning of Hawthorne's haunting parable remains as elusive as the reason its main character dons a black veil that covers half of his face, shrouding him (and the world he sees) in gloom. The dark tale, one of twenty-seven sketches and stories Hawthorne published anonymously in *The Token: Christmas and New Year's Present* between 1831 and 1837, was included in his earliest collection, *Twice-Told Tales* (1837). The text is taken from the first printing in *The Token* (1836), where it appeared along with two of Hawthorne's other stories, and where it was ascribed to "the author of 'Sights from a Steeple,'" a sketch he had published in the annual five years earlier.

THE MINISTER'S BLACK VEIL

A Parable[1]

The sexton stood in the porch of Milford meeting-house, pulling lustily at the bell-rope. The old people of the village came stooping along the street. Children, with bright faces, tript merrily beside their parents, or mimicked a graver gait, in the conscious dignity of their sunday clothes. Spruce bachelors looked sidelong at the pretty maidens, and fancied that the sabbath sunshine made them prettier than on week-days. When the throng had mostly streamed into the porch, the sexton began to toll the bell, keeping his eye on the Reverend Mr. Hooper's door. The first glimpse of the clergyman's figure was the signal for the bell to cease its summons.

"But what has good Parson Hooper got upon his face?" cried the sexton in astonishment.

All within hearing immediately turned about, and beheld the semblance of Mr. Hooper, pacing slowly his meditative way towards the meeting-house. With one accord they started, expressing more wonder than if some strange minister were coming to dust the cushions of Mr. Hooper's pulpit.

"Are you sure it is our parson?" inquired Goodman Gray of the sexton.

"Of a certainty it is good Mr. Hooper," replied the sexton. "He was to have exchanged pulpits with Parson Shute of Westbury; but Parson Shute sent to excuse himself yesterday, being to preach a funeral sermon."

---

1. **The Minister's Black Veil: A Parable:** Another clergyman in New-England, Mr. Joseph Moody, of York, Maine, who died about eighty years since, made himself remarkable by the same eccentricity that is here related of the Reverend Mr. Hooper. In this case, however, the symbol had a different import. In early life he had accidentally killed a beloved friend; and from that day till the hour of his own death, he hid his face from men. [Hawthorne's note.]

The cause of so much amazement may appear sufficiently slight. Mr. Hooper, a gentlemanly person of about thirty, though still a bachelor, was dressed with due clerical neatness, as if a careful wife had starched his band, and brushed the weekly dust from his Sunday's garb. There was but one thing remarkable in his appearance. Swathed about his forehead, and hanging down over his face, so low as to be shaken by his breath, Mr. Hooper had on a black veil. On a nearer view, it seemed to consist of two folds of crape, which entirely concealed his features, except the mouth and chin, but probably did not intercept his sight, farther than to give a darkened aspect to all living and inanimate things. With this gloomy shade before him, good Mr. Hooper walked onward, at a slow and quiet pace, stooping somewhat and looking on the ground, as is customary with abstracted men, yet nodding kindly to those of his parishioners who still waited on the meeting-house steps. But so wonder-struck were they, that his greeting hardly met with a return.

"I can't really feel as if good Mr. Hooper's face was behind that piece of crape," said the sexton.

"I don't like it," muttered an old woman, as she hobbled into the meeting-house. "He has changed himself into something awful, only by hiding his face."

"Our parson has gone mad!" cried Goodman Gray, following him across the threshold.

A rumor of some unaccountable phenomenon had preceded Mr. Hooper into the meeting-house, and set all the congregation astir. Few could refrain from twisting their heads towards the door; many stood upright, and turned directly about; while several little boys clambered upon the seats, and came down again with a terrible racket. There was a general bustle, a rustling of the women's gowns and shuffling of the men's feet, greatly at variance with that hushed repose which should attend the entrance of the minister. But Mr. Hooper appeared not to notice the perturbation of his people. He entered with an almost noiseless step, bent his head mildly to the pews on each side, and bowed as he passed his oldest parishioner, a white-haired great-grandsire, who occupied an arm-chair in the centre of the aisle. It was strange to observe, how slowly this venerable man became conscious of something singular in the appearance of his pastor. He seemed not fully to partake of the prevailing wonder, till Mr. Hooper had ascended the stairs, and showed himself in the pulpit, face to face with his congregation, except for the black veil. That mysterious emblem was never once withdrawn. It shook with his measured breath as he gave out the psalm; it threw its obscurity between him and the holy page, as he read the Scriptures; and while he prayed, the veil lay heavily on his uplifted countenance. Did he seek to hide it from the dread Being whom he was addressing?

Such was the effect of this simple piece of crape, that more than one woman of delicate nerves was forced to leave the meeting-house. Yet perhaps the pale-faced congregation was almost as fearful a sight to the minister, as his black veil to them.

Mr. Hooper had the reputation of a good preacher, but not an energetic one: he strove to win his people heaven-ward, by mild persuasive influences, rather than to drive them thither, by the thunders of the Word. The sermon which he now delivered, was marked by the same characteristics of style and manner, as the general series of his pulpit oratory. But there was something, either in the sentiment of the discourse itself, or in the imagination of the auditors, which made it greatly the most powerful effort that they had ever heard from their pastor's lips. It was tinged, rather more darkly than usual, with the gentle gloom of Mr. Hooper's temperament. The subject had reference to secret sin, and those sad mysteries which we hide from our nearest and dearest, and would fain conceal from our own consciousness, even forgetting that the Omniscient can detect them. A subtle power was breathed into his words. Each member of the congregation, the most innocent girl, and the man of hardened breast, felt as if the preacher had crept upon them, behind his awful veil, and discovered their hoarded iniquity of deed or thought. Many spread their clasped hands on their bosoms. There was nothing terrible in what Mr. Hooper said; at least, no violence; and yet, with every tremor of his melancholy voice, the hearers quaked. An unsought pathos came hand in hand with awe. So sensible were the audience of some unwonted attribute in their minister, that they longed for a breath of wind to blow aside the veil, almost believing that a stranger's visage would be discovered, though the form, gesture, and voice were those of Mr. Hooper.

At the close of the services, the people hurried out with indecorous confusion, eager to communicate their pent-up amazement, and conscious of lighter spirits, the moment they lost sight of the black veil. Some gathered in little circles, huddled closely together, with their mouths all whispering in the centre; some went homeward alone, wrapt in silent meditation; some talked loudly, and profaned the Sabbath-day with ostentatious laughter. A few shook their sagacious heads, intimating that they could penetrate the mystery; while one or two affirmed that there was no mystery at all, but only that Mr. Hooper's eyes were so weakened by the midnight lamp, as to require a shade. After a brief interval, forth came good Mr. Hooper also, in the rear of his flock. Turning his veiled face from one group to another, he paid due reverence to the hoary heads, saluted the middle-aged with kind dignity, as their friend and spiritual guide, greeted the young with mingled authority and love, and laid his hands on the little children's heads to bless them. Such was always his custom on the Sabbath-day. Strange and bewildered looks repaid him for his courtesy. None, as on former occasions, aspired to the honor of walking by their pastor's side. Old Squire Saunders, doubtless by an accidental lapse of memory, neglected to invite Mr. Hooper to his table, where the good clergyman had been wont to bless the food, almost every Sunday since his settlement. He returned, therefore, to the parsonage, and, at the moment of closing the door, was observed to look back upon the people, all of whom had their eyes fixed upon the minister. A sad smile gleamed faintly from beneath the black veil, and flickered about his mouth, glimmering as he disappeared.

"How strange," said a lady, "that a simple black veil, such as any woman might wear on her bonnet, should become such a terrible thing on Mr. Hooper's face!"

"Something must surely be amiss with Mr. Hooper's intellects," observed her husband, the physician of the village. "But the strangest part of the affair is the effect of this vagary, even on a sober-minded man like myself. The black veil, though it covers only our pastor's face, throws its influence over his whole person, and makes him ghostlike from head to foot. Do you not feel it so?"

"Truly do I," replied the lady; "and I would not be alone with him for the world. I wonder he is not afraid to be alone with himself!"

"Men sometimes are so," said her husband.

The afternoon service was attended with similar circumstances. At its conclusion, the bell tolled for the funeral of a young lady. The relatives and friends were assembled in the house, and the more distant acquaintances stood about the door, speaking of the good qualities of the deceased, when their talk was interrupted by the appearance of Mr. Hooper, still covered with his black veil. It was now an appropriate emblem. The clergyman stepped into the room where the corpse was laid, and bent over the coffin, to take a last farewell of his deceased parishioner. As he stooped, the veil hung straight down from his forehead, so that, if her eye-lids had not been closed for ever, the dead maiden might have seen his face. Could Mr. Hooper be fearful of her glance, that he so hastily caught back the black veil? A person, who watched the interview between the dead and living, scrupled not to affirm, that, at the instant when the clergyman's features were disclosed, the corpse had slightly shuddered, rustling the shroud and muslin cap, though the countenance retained the composure of death. A superstitious old woman was the only witness of this prodigy. From the coffin, Mr. Hooper passed into the chamber of the mourners, and thence to the head of the staircase, to make the funeral prayer. It was a tender and heart-dissolving prayer, full of sorrow, yet so imbued with celestial hopes, that the music of a heavenly harp, swept by the fingers of the dead, seemed faintly to be heard among the saddest accents of the minister. The people trembled, though they but darkly understood him, when he prayed that they, and himself, and all of mortal race, might be ready, as he trusted this young maiden had been, for the dreadful hour that should snatch the veil from their faces. The bearers went heavily forth, and the mourners followed, saddening all the street, with the dead before them, and Mr. Hooper in his black veil behind.

"Why do you look back?" said one in the procession to his partner.

"I had a fancy," replied she, "that the minister and the maiden's spirit were walking hand in hand."

"And so had I, at the same moment," said the other.

That night, the handsomest couple in Milford village were to be joined in wedlock. Though reckoned a melancholy man, Mr. Hooper had a placid cheerfulness for such occasions, which often excited a sympathetic smile, where livelier merriment would have been thrown away. There was no quality of his disposition which made him more beloved than this. The company at the wedding awaited his arrival with impatience, trusting that the strange awe, which had gathered over him throughout the day, would now be dispelled. But such was not the result. When Mr. Hooper came, the first thing that their eyes rested on was the same horrible black veil, which had added deeper gloom to the funeral, and could portend nothing but evil to the wedding. Such was its immediate effect on the guests, that a cloud seemed to have rolled duskily from beneath the black crape, and dimmed the light of the candles. The bridal pair stood up before the minister. But the bride's cold fingers quivered in the tremulous hand of the bridegroom, and her death-like paleness caused a whisper, that the maiden who had been buried a few hours before, was come from her grave to be married. If ever another wedding were so dismal, it was that famous one, where they tolled the wedding-knell.[2] After performing the ceremony, Mr. Hooper raised a glass of wine to his lips, wishing happiness to the new-married couple, in a strain of mild pleasantry that ought to have brightened the features of the guests, like a cheerful gleam from the hearth. At that instant, catching a glimpse of his figure in the looking-glass, the black veil involved his own spirit in the horror with which it overwhelmed all others. His frame shuddered – his lips grew white – he spilt the untasted wine upon the carpet – and rushed forth into the darkness. For the Earth, too, had on her Black Veil.

The next day, the whole village of Milford talked of little else than Parson Hooper's black veil. That, and the mystery concealed behind it, supplied a topic for discussion between acquaintances meeting in the street, and good women gossiping at their open windows. It was the first item of news that the tavern-keeper told to his guests. The children babbled of it on their way to school. One imitative little imp covered his face with an old black handkerchief, thereby so affrighting his playmate, that the panic seized himself, and he well nigh lost his wits by his own waggery.

It was remarkable, that, of all the busy-bodies and impertinent people in the parish, not one ventured to put the plain question to Mr. Hooper, wherefore he did this thing. Hitherto, whenever there appeared the slightest call for such interference, he had never lacked advisers, nor shown himself averse to be guided by their judgment. If he erred at all, it was by so painful a degree of self-distrust, that even the mildest censure would lead him to consider an indifferent action as a crime. Yet, though so well acquainted with this amiable weakness, no individual among his parishioners chose to make the black veil a subject of friendly remonstrance. There was a feeling of dread, neither plainly confessed nor carefully concealed, which caused each to shift the responsibility upon another, till at length it was found expedient to send a deputation of the church, in order to deal with Mr. Hooper about the mystery, before it should grow into a scandal. Never did an embassy so ill discharge its duties. The minister received them with friendly courtesy, but became silent, after they were seated, leaving to his visiters the whole burthen[3] of introducing their important business. The topic, it might be supposed, was obvious enough. There was the black veil, swathed round Mr. Hooper's forehead, and concealing every feature above his placid mouth, on which, at times, they could perceive the glimmering of a melancholy smile. But that piece of crape, to their imagination, seemed to hang down before his heart, the symbol of a fearful secret between him and them. Were the veil but cast aside, they might speak freely of it, but not till then. Thus they sat a considerable time, speechless, confused, and shrinking uneasily from Mr. Hooper's eye, which they felt to be fixed upon them with an invisible glance. Finally, the deputies returned abashed to their constituents, pronouncing the

---

2. **wedding-knell:** A reference to Hawthorne's "The Wedding Knell," in which the elderly groom enters the church in his funeral shroud and tells his elderly bride that they should wed and then go to their graves. She agrees, they marry, and the organ plays the wedding anthem even as the funeral bell tolls. The story appeared along with "The Minister's Black Veil" in the 1836 volume of *The Token*.

3. **burthen:** Early form of *burden*.

matter too weighty to be handled, except by a council of the churches, if, indeed, it might not require a general synod.

But there was one person in the village, unappalled by the awe with which the black veil had impressed all beside herself. When the deputies returned without an explanation, or even venturing to demand one, she, with the calm energy of her character, determined to chase away the strange cloud that appeared to be settling round Mr. Hooper, every moment more darkly than before. As his plighted wife, it should be her privilege to know what the black veil concealed. At the minister's first visit, therefore, she entered upon the subject, with a direct simplicity, which made the task easier both for him and her. After he had seated himself, she fixed her eyes steadfastly upon the veil, but could discern nothing of the dreadful gloom that had so overawed the multitude: it was but a double fold of crape, hanging down from his forehead to his mouth, and slightly stirring with his breath.

"No," said she aloud, and smiling, "there is nothing terrible in this piece of crape, except that it hides a face which I am always glad to look upon. Come, good sir, let the sun shine from behind the cloud. First lay aside your black veil: then tell me why you put it on."

Mr. Hooper's smile glimmered faintly.

"There is an hour to come," said he, "when all of us shall cast aside our veils. Take it not amiss, beloved friend, if I wear this piece of crape, till then."

"Your words are a mystery too," returned the young lady. "Take away the veil from them, at least."

"Elizabeth, I will," said he, "so far as my vow may suffer me. Know, then, this veil is a type[4] and a symbol, and I am bound to wear it ever, both in light and darkness, in solitude and before the gaze of multitudes, and as with strangers, so with my familiar friends. No mortal eye will see it withdrawn. This dismal shade must separate me from the world: even you, Elizabeth, can never come behind it!"

"What grievous affliction hath befallen you," she earnestly inquired, "that you should thus darken your eyes for ever?"

"If it be a sign of mourning," replied Mr. Hooper, "I, perhaps, like most other mortals, have sorrows dark enough to be typified by a black veil."

"But what if the world will not believe that it is the type of an innocent sorrow?" urged Elizabeth. "Beloved and respected as you are, there may be whispers, that you hide your face under the consciousness of secret sin. For the sake of your holy office, do away this scandal!"

The color rose into her cheeks, as she intimated the nature of the rumors that were already abroad in the village. But Mr. Hooper's mildness did not forsake him. He even smiled again – that same sad smile, which always appeared like a faint glimmering of light, proceeding from the obscurity beneath the veil.

"If I hide my face for sorrow, there is cause enough," he merely replied; "and if I cover it for secret sin, what mortal might not do the same?"

---

4. **type**: Here used in the sense of a symbol or foreshadowing.

And with this gentle, but unconquerable obstinacy, did he resist all her entreaties. At length Elizabeth sat silent. For a few moments she appeared lost in thought, considering, probably, what new methods might be tried, to withdraw her lover from so dark a fantasy, which, if it had no other meaning, was perhaps a symptom of mental disease. Though of a firmer character than his own, the tears rolled down her cheeks. But, in an instant, as it were, a new feeling took the place of sorrow: her eyes were fixed insensibly on the black veil, when, like a sudden twilight in the air, its terrors fell around her. She arose, and stood trembling before him.

"And do you feel it then at last?" said he mournfully.

She made no reply, but covered her eyes with her hand, and turned to leave the room. He rushed forward and caught her arm.

"Have patience with me, Elizabeth!" cried he passionately. "Do not desert me, though this veil must be between us here on earth. Be mine, and hereafter there shall be no veil over my face, no darkness between our souls! It is but a mortal veil – it is not for eternity! Oh! you know not how lonely I am, and how frightened to be alone behind my black veil. Do not leave me in this miserable obscurity for ever!"

"Lift the veil but once, and look me in the face," said she.

"Never! It cannot be!" replied Mr. Hooper.

"Then, farewell!" said Elizabeth.

She withdrew her arm from his grasp, and slowly departed, pausing at the door, to give one long, shuddering gaze, that seemed almost to penetrate the mystery of the black veil. But, even amid his grief, Mr. Hooper smiled to think that only a material emblem had separated him from happiness, though the horrors which it shadowed forth, must be drawn darkly between the fondest of lovers.

From that time no attempts were made to remove Mr. Hooper's black veil, or, by a direct appeal, to discover the secret which it was supposed to hide. By persons who claimed a superiority to popular prejudice, it was reckoned merely an eccentric whim, such as often mingles with the sober actions of men otherwise rational, and tinges them all with its own semblance of insanity. But with the multitude, good Mr. Hooper was irreparably a bug-bear.[5] He could not walk the street with any peace of mind, so conscious was he that the gentle and timid would turn aside to avoid him, and that others would make it a point of hardihood to throw themselves in his way. The impertinence of the latter class compelled him to give up his customary walk, at sunset, to the burial ground; for when he leaned pensively over the gate, there would always be faces behind the grave-stones, peeping at his black veil. A fable went the rounds, that the stare of the dead people drove him thence. It grieved him, to the very depth of his kind heart, to observe how the children fled from his approach, breaking up their merriest sports, while his melancholy figure was yet afar off. Their instinctive dread caused him to feel, more strongly than aught else, that a preternatural horror was interwoven with the threads of the black crape. In truth, his own antipathy to the veil was known to be so great, that he never willingly passed before a mirror, nor stooped to drink at a still

5. **bug-bear:** An early term for an imaginary being who frightened children.

fountain, lest, in its peaceful bosom, he should be affrighted by himself. This was what gave plausibility to the whispers, that Mr. Hooper's conscience tortured him for some great crime, too horrible to be entirely concealed, or otherwise than so obscurely intimated. Thus, from beneath the black veil, there rolled a cloud into the sunshine, an ambiguity of sin or sorrow, which enveloped the poor minister, so that love or sympathy could never reach him. It was said, that ghost and fiend consorted with him there. With self-shudderings and outward terrors, he walked continually in its shadow, groping darkly within his own soul, or gazing through a medium that saddened the whole world. Even the lawless wind, it was believed, respected his dreadful secret, and never blew aside the veil. But still good Mr. Hooper sadly smiled, at the pale visages of the worldly throng as he passed by.

Among all its bad influences, the black veil had the one desirable effect, of making its wearer a very efficient clergyman. By the aid of his mysterious emblem – for there was no other apparent cause – he became a man of artful power, over souls that were in agony for sin. His converts always regarded him with a dread peculiar to themselves, affirming, though but figuratively, that, before he brought them to celestial light, they had been with him behind the black veil. Its gloom, indeed, enabled him to sympathize with all dark affections. Dying sinners cried aloud for Mr. Hooper, and would not yield their breath till he appeared; though ever, as he stooped to whisper consolation, they shuddered at the veiled face so near their own. Such were the terrors of the black veil, even when death had bared his visage! Strangers came long distances to attend service at his church, with the mere idle purpose of gazing at his figure, because it was forbidden them to behold his face. But many were made to quake ere they departed! Once, during Governor Belcher's administration, Mr. Hooper was appointed to preach the election sermon.[6] Covered with his black veil, he stood before the chief magistrate, the council, and the representatives, and wrought so deep an impression, that the legislative measures of that year, were characterized by all the gloom and piety of our earliest ancestral sway.

In this manner Mr. Hooper spent a long life, irreproachable in outward act, yet shrouded in dismal suspicions; kind and loving, though unloved, and dimly feared; a man apart from men, shunned in their health and joy, but ever summoned to their aid in mortal anguish. As years wore on, shedding their snows above his sable veil, he acquired a name throughout the New-England churches, and they called him Father Hooper. Nearly all his parishioners, who were of mature age when he was settled, had been borne away by many a funeral: he had one congregation in the church, and a more crowded one in the church-yard; and having wrought so late into the evening, and done his work so well, it was now good Father Hooper's turn to rest.

Several persons were visible by the shaded candle-light, in the death-chamber of the old clergyman. Natural connections he had none. But there was the decorously grave, though unmoved physician, seeking only to mitigate the last pangs of the patient whom he could not save. There were the deacons, and other eminently pious members of his

---

6. **election sermon:** A major sermon preached by an honored minister at the inauguration of each new colonial governor of the Massachusetts Bay Colony.

church. There, also, was the Reverend Mr. Clark, of Westbury, a young and zealous divine, who had ridden in haste to pray by the bed-side of the expiring minister. There was the nurse, no hired handmaiden of death, but one whose calm affection had endured thus long, in secrecy, in solitude, amid the chill of age, and would not perish, even at the dying hour. Who, but Elizabeth! And there lay the hoary head of good Father Hooper upon the death-pillow, with the black veil still swathed about his brow and reaching down over his face, so that each more difficult gasp of his faint breath caused it to stir. All through life that piece of crape had hung between him and the world: it had separated him from cheerful brotherhood and woman's love, and kept him in that saddest of all prisons, his own heart; and still it lay upon his face, as if to deepen the gloom of his darksome chamber, and shade him from the sunshine of eternity.

For some time previous, his mind had been confused, wavering doubtfully between the past and the present, and hovering forward, as it were, at intervals, into the indistinctness of the world to come. There had been feverish turns, which tossed him from side to side, and wore away what little strength he had. But in his most convulsive struggles, and in the wildest vagaries of his intellect, when no other thought retained its sober influence, he still showed an awful solicitude lest the black veil should slip aside. Even if his bewildered soul could have forgotten, there was a faithful woman at his pillow, who, with averted eyes, would have covered that aged face, which she had last beheld in the comeliness of manhood. At length the death-stricken old man lay quietly in the torpor of mental and bodily exhaustion, with an imperceptible pulse, and breath that grew fainter and fainter, except when a long, deep, and irregular inspiration seemed to prelude the flight of his spirit.

The minister of Westbury approached the bedside.

"Venerable Father Hooper," said he, "the moment of your release is at hand. Are you ready for the lifting of the veil, that shuts in time from eternity?"

Father Hooper at first replied merely by a feeble motion of his head; then, apprehensive, perhaps, that his meaning might be doubtful, he exerted himself to speak.

"Yes," said he, in faint accents, "my soul hath a patient weariness until that veil be lifted."

"And is it fitting," resumed the Reverend Mr. Clark, "that a man so given to prayer, of such a blameless example, holy in deed and thought, so far as mortal judgment may pronounce; is it fitting that a father in the church should leave a shadow on his memory, that may seem to blacken a life so pure? I pray you, my venerable brother, let not this thing be! Suffer us to be gladdened by your triumphant aspect, as you go to your reward. Before the veil of eternity be lifted, let me cast aside this black veil from your face!"

And thus speaking, the Reverend Mr. Clark bent forward to reveal the mystery of so many years. But, exerting a sudden energy, that made all the beholders stand aghast, Father Hooper snatched both his hands from beneath the bed-clothes, and pressed them strongly on the black veil, resolute to struggle, if the minister of Westbury would contend with a dying man.

"Never!" cried the veiled clergyman. "On earth, never!"

"Dark old man!" exclaimed the affrighted minister, "with what horrible crime upon your soul are you now passing to the judgment?"

Father Hooper's breath heaved; it rattled in his throat; but, with a mighty effort, grasping forward with his hands, he caught hold of life, and held it back till he should speak. He even raised himself in bed; and there he sat, shivering with the arms of death around him, while the black veil hung down, awful, at that last moment, in the gathered terrors of a life-time. And yet the faint, sad smile, so often there, now seemed to glimmer from its obscurity, and linger on Father Hooper's lips.

"Why do you tremble at me alone?" cried he, turning his veiled face round the circle of pale spectators. "Tremble also at each other! Have men avoided me, and women shown no pity, and children screamed and fled, only for my black veil? What, but the mystery which it obscurely typifies, has made this piece of crape so awful? When the friend shows his inmost heart to his friend; the lover to his best-beloved; when man does not vainly shrink from the eye of his Creator, loathsomely treasuring up the secret of his sin; then deem me a monster, for the symbol beneath which I have lived, and die! I look around me, and, lo! on every visage a black veil!"

While his auditors shrank from one another, in mutual affright, Father Hooper fell back upon his pillow, a veiled corpse, with a faint smile lingering on the lips. Still veiled, they laid him in his coffin, and a veiled corpse they bore him to the grave. The grass of many years has sprung up and withered on that grave, the burial-stone is moss-grown, and good Mr. Hooper's face is dust; but awful is the thought, that it mouldered beneath the black veil!

[1836]

Hawthorne's "The Birth-Mark." This cautionary tale was first published in the *Pioneer*, a monthly magazine established by the poet James Russell Lowell in January 1843. Among his lofty aims for the magazine was a commitment to publish only original works by "American writers of the highest reputation," and Lowell did just that. Although the underfinanced magazine lasted for only three issues, its contributors included Edgar Allan Poe, John Greenleaf Whittier, and Hawthorne, who had earned a substantial reputation as an author of sketches and stories. By 1843, however, the focus of those works had increasingly shifted from the past and its relation to the present – the primary concern of much of Hawthorne's early short fiction – to contemporary social developments. Among the developments that Hawthorne observed most closely was the emergence of a wide array of reforms, idealistic efforts to perfect the individual and society, as well as a host of pseudosciences like homeopathy, mesmerism, and phrenology. For Hawthorne, those and a myriad of other early forms of "human engineering" raised troubling questions about the exercise of power over others and the consequent threats to personal autonomy and the integrity of the self. Certainly the extraordinary enthusiasm such pseudosciences generated in the United States forms a significant backdrop to "The Birth-Mark," one of the "mad scientist" stories Hawthorne wrote during the early 1840s and included in his collection *Mosses from an Old Manse* (1846). The text of the story is taken from its first printing in the *Pioneer*, March 1843.

THE BIRTH-MARK

In the latter part of the last century, there lived a man of science – an eminent proficient in every branch of natural philosophy – who, not long before our story opens, had made experience of a spiritual affinity, more attractive than any chemical one. He had left his laboratory to the care of an assistant, cleared his fine countenance from the furnace-smoke, washed the stain of acids from his fingers, and persuaded a beautiful woman to become his wife. In those days, when the comparatively recent discovery of electricity, and other kindred mysteries of nature, seemed to open paths into the region of miracle, it was not unusual for the love of science to rival the love of woman, in its depth and absorbing energy. The higher intellect, the imagination, the spirit, and even the heart, might all find their congenial aliment in pursuits which, as some of their ardent votaries[1] believed, would ascend from one step of powerful intelligence to another, until the philosopher should lay his hand on the secret of creative force, and perhaps make new worlds for himself. We know not whether Aylmer possessed this degree of faith in man's ultimate control over nature. He had devoted himself, however, too unreservedly to scientific studies, ever to be weaned from them by any second passion. His love for his young wife might prove the stronger of the two; but it could only be by intertwining itself with his love of science, and uniting the strength of the latter to its own.

Such an union accordingly took place, and was attended with truly remarkable consequences, and a deeply impressive moral. One day, very soon after their marriage, Aylmer sat gazing at his wife, with a trouble in his countenance that grew stronger, until he spoke.

"Georgiana," said he, "has it never occurred to you that the mark upon your cheek might be removed?"

"No, indeed," said she, smiling; but perceiving the seriousness of his manner, she blushed deeply. "To tell you the truth, it has been so often called a charm, that I was simple enough to imagine it might be so."

"Ah, upon another face, perhaps it might," replied her husband. "But never on yours! No, dearest Georgiana, you came so nearly perfect from the hand of Nature, that this slightest possible defect – which we hesitate whether to term a defect or a beauty – shocks me, as being the visible mark of earthly imperfection."

"Shocks you, my husband!" cried Georgiana, deeply hurt; at first reddening with momentary anger, but then bursting into tears. "Then why did you take me from my mother's side? You cannot love what shocks you!"

To explain this conversation, it must be mentioned, that, in the centre of Georgiana's left cheek, there was a singular mark, deeply interwoven, as it were, with the texture and substance of her face. In the usual state of her complexion, – a healthy, though delicate bloom, – the mark wore a tint of deeper crimson, which imperfectly defined its shape amid the surrounding rosiness. When she blushed, it gradually became more indistinct, and finally vanished amid the triumphant rush of blood, that bathed the whole cheek

---

1. **votaries:** Devoted followers.

with its brilliant glow. But, if any shifting emotion caused her to turn pale, there was the mark again, a crimson stain upon the snow, in what Aylmer sometimes deemed an almost fearful distinctness. Its shape bore not a little similarity to the human hand, though of the smallest pigmy size. Georgiana's lovers were wont to say, that some fairy, at her birth-hour, had laid her tiny hand upon the infant's cheek, and left this impress there, in token of the magic endowments that were to give her such sway over all hearts. Many a desperate swain would have risked life for the privilege of pressing his lips to the mysterious hand. It must not be concealed, however, that the impression wrought by this fairy sign-manual varied exceedingly, according to the difference of temperament in the beholders. Some fastidious persons – but they were exclusively of her own sex – affirmed that the Bloody Hand, as they chose to call it, quite destroyed the effect of Georgiana's beauty, and rendered her countenance even hideous. But it would be as reasonable to say, that one of those small blue stains, which sometimes occur in the purest statuary marble, would convert the Eve of Powers[2] to a monster. Masculine observers, if the birth-mark did not heighten their admiration, contented themselves with wishing it away, that the world might possess one living specimen of ideal loveliness, without the semblance of a flaw. After his marriage – for he thought little or nothing of the matter before – Aylmer discovered that this was the case with himself.

Had she been less beautiful – if Envy's self could have found aught else to sneer at – he might have felt his affection heightened by the prettiness of this mimic hand, now vaguely portrayed, now lost, now stealing forth again, and glimmering to-and-fro with every pulse of emotion that throbbed within her heart. But seeing her otherwise so perfect, he found this one defect grow more and more intolerable, with every moment of their united lives. It was the fatal flaw of humanity, which Nature, in one shape or another, stamps ineffaceably on all her productions, either to imply that they are temporary and finite, or that their perfection must be wrought by toil and pain. The Crimson Hand expressed the ineludible gripe, in which mortality clutches the highest and purest of earthly mould, degrading them into kindred with the lowest, and even with the very brutes, like whom their visible frames return to dust. In this manner, selecting it as the symbol of his wife's liability to sin, sorrow, decay, and death, Aylmer's sombre imagination was not long in rendering the birth-mark a frightful object, causing him more trouble and horror than ever Georgiana's beauty, whether of soul or sense, had given him delight.

At all the seasons which should have been their happiest, he invariably, and without intending it – nay, in spite of a purpose to the contrary – reverted to this one disastrous topic. Trifling as it at first appeared, it so connected itself with innumerable trains of thought, and modes of feeling, that it became the central point of all. With the morning twilight, Aylmer opened his eyes upon his wife's face, and recognised the symbol of imperfection; and when they sat together at the evening hearth, his eyes wan-

---

2. Eve of Powers: Hiram Powers (1805–1873), American sculptor whose nude statues, *Eve Tempted* (1842) and *The Greek Slave* (1843), caused a sensation when they toured the United States. *Eve Tempted* is a pure white marble statue of an idealized, naked woman turning an apple over in her hand.

dered stealthily to her cheek, and beheld, flickering with the blaze of the wood fire, the spectral Hand that wrote mortality, where he would fain have worshipped. Georgiana soon learned to shudder at his gaze. It needed but a glance, with the peculiar expression that his face often wore, to change the roses of her cheek into a deathlike paleness, amid which the Crimson Hand was brought strongly out, like a bas-relief of ruby on the whitest marble.

Late, one night, when the lights were growing dim, so as hardly to betray the stain on the poor wife's cheek, she herself, for the first time, voluntarily took up the subject.

"Do you remember, my dear Aylmer," said she, with a feeble attempt at a smile – "have you any recollection of a dream, last night, about this odious Hand?"

"None! – none whatever!" replied Aylmer, starting; but then he added in a dry, cold tone, affected for the sake of concealing the real depth of his emotion: – "I might well dream of it; for, before I fell asleep, it had taken a pretty firm hold of my fancy."

"And you did dream of it," continued Georgiana, hastily; for she dreaded lest a gush of tears should interrupt what she had to say – "A terrible dream! I wonder that you can forget it. Is it possible to forget this one expression? – 'It is in her heart now – we must have it out!' – Reflect, my husband; for by all means I would have you recall that dream."

The mind is in a sad state, when Sleep, the all-involving, cannot confine her spectres within the dim region of her sway, but suffers them to break forth, affrighting this actual life with secrets that perchance belong to a deeper one. Aylmer now remembered his dream. He had fancied himself, with his servant Aminidab, attempting an operation for the removal of the birth-mark. But the deeper went the knife, the deeper sank the Hand, until at length its tiny grasp appeared to have caught hold of Georgiana's heart; whence, however, her husband was inexorably resolved to cut or wrench it away.

When the dream had shaped itself perfectly in his memory, Aylmer sat in his wife's presence with a guilty feeling. Truth often finds its way to the mind close-muffled in robes of sleep, and then speaks with uncompromising directness of matters in regard to which we practise an unconscious self-deception, during our waking moments. Until now, he had not been aware of the tyrannizing influence acquired by one idea over his mind, and of the lengths which he might find in his heart to go, for the sake of giving himself peace.

"Aylmer," resumed Georgiana, solemnly, "I know not what may be the cost to both of us, to rid me of this fatal birth-mark. Perhaps its removal may cause cureless deformity. Or, it may be, the stain goes as deep as life itself. Again, do we know that there is a possibility, on any terms, of unclasping the firm gripe of this little Hand, which was laid upon me before I came into the world?"

"Dearest Georgiana, I have spent much thought upon the subject," hastily interrupted Aylmer – "I am convinced of the perfect practicability of its removal."

"If there be the remotest possibility of it," continued Georgiana, "let the attempt be made, at whatever risk. Danger is nothing to me; for life – while this hateful mark makes me the object of your horror and disgust – life is a burthen which I would fling down with joy. Either remove this dreadful Hand, or take my wretched life! You have deep science! All the world bears witness of it. You have achieved great wonders! Cannot you remove this little, little mark, which I cover with the tips of two small fingers? Is this beyond your power, for the sake of your own peace, and to save your poor wife from madness?"

"Noblest – dearest – tenderest wife!" cried Aylmer, rapturously. "Doubt not my power. I have already given this matter the deepest thought – thought which might almost have enlightened me to create a being less perfect than yourself. Georgiana, you have led me deeper than ever into the heart of science. I feel myself fully competent to render this dear cheek as faultless as its fellow; and then, most beloved, what will be my triumph, when I shall have corrected what Nature left imperfect, in her fairest work! Even Pygmalion,[3] when his sculptured woman assumed life, felt not greater ecstasy than mine will be."

"It is resolved, then," said Georgiana, faintly smiling, – "And, Aylmer, spare me not, though you should find the birth-mark take refuge in my heart at last."

Her husband tenderly kissed her cheek – her right cheek – not that which bore the impress of the Crimson Hand.

The next day, Aylmer apprized his wife of a plan that he had formed, whereby he might have opportunity for the intense thought and constant watchfulness, which the proposed operation would require; while Georgiana, likewise, would enjoy the perfect repose essential to its success. They were to seclude themselves in the extensive apartments occupied by Aylmer as a laboratory, and where, during his toilsome youth, he had made discoveries in the elemental powers of nature, that had roused the admiration of all the learned societies in Europe. Seated calmly in this laboratory, the pale philosopher had investigated the secrets of the highest cloud-region, and of the profoundest mines; he had satisfied himself of the causes that kindled and kept alive the fires of the volcano; and had explained the mystery of fountains, and how it is that they gush forth, some so bright and pure, and others with such rich medicinal virtues, from the dark bosom of the earth. Here, too, at an earlier period, he had studied the wonders of the human frame, and attempted to fathom the very process by which Nature assimilates all her precious influences from earth and air, and from the spiritual world, to create and foster Man, her masterpiece. The latter pursuit, however, Aylmer had long laid aside, in unwilling recognition of the truth, against which all seekers sooner or later stumble, that our great creative Mother, while she amuses us with apparently working in the broadest sunshine, is yet severely careful to keep her own secrets, and, in spite of her pretended openness, shows us nothing but results. She permits us, indeed, to mar, but seldom to mend, and, like a jealous patentee, on no account to make. Now, however, Aylmer resumed these half-forgotten investigations; not, of course, with such hopes or wishes as first suggested them; but because they involved much physiological truth, and lay in the path of his proposed scheme for the treatment of Georgiana.

As he led her over the threshold of the laboratory, Georgiana was cold and tremulous. Aylmer looked cheerfully into her face, with intent to reassure her, but was so startled with the intense glow of the birth-mark upon the whiteness of her cheek, that he could not restrain a strong convulsive shudder. His wife fainted.

---

3. **Pygmalion:** According to a Greek myth, Pygmalion fell in love with the statue of a woman he created; Aphrodite granted his wish to bring it to life.

"Aminidab! Aminidab!" shouted Aylmer, stamping violently on the floor.

Forthwith, there issued from an inner apartment a man of low stature, but bulky frame, with shaggy hair hanging about his visage, which was grimed with the vapor of the furnace. This personage had been Aylmer's under-worker during his whole scientific career, and was admirably fitted for that office by his great mechanical readiness, and the skill with which, while incapable of comprehending a single principle, he executed all the practical details of his master's experiments. With his vast strength, his shaggy hair, his smoky aspect, and the indescribable earthiness that incrusted him, he seemed to represent man's physical nature; while Aylmer's slender figure, and pale, intellectual face, were no less apt a type of the spiritual element.

"Throw open the door of the boudoir, Aminidab," said Aylmer, "and burn a pastille."[4]

"Yes, master," answered Aminidab, looking intently at the lifeless form of Georgiana; and then he muttered to himself; – "If she were my wife, I'd never part with that birth-mark."

When Georgiana recovered consciousness, she found herself breathing an atmosphere of penetrating fragrance, the gentle potency of which had recalled her from her deathlike faintness. The scene around her looked like enchantment. Aylmer had converted those smoky, dingy, sombre rooms, where he had spent his brightest years in recondite pursuits, into a series of beautiful apartments, not unfit to be the secluded abode of a lovely woman. The walls were hung with gorgeous curtains, which imparted the combination of grandeur and grace, that no other species of adornment can achieve; and as they fell from the ceiling to the floor, their rich and ponderous folds, concealing all angles and straight lines, appeared to shut in the scene from infinite space. For aught Georgiana knew, it might be a pavilion among the clouds. And Aylmer, excluding the sunshine, which would have interfered with his chemical processes, had supplied its place with perfumed lamps, emitting flames of various hue, but all uniting in a soft, empurpled radiance. He now knelt by his wife's side, watching her earnestly, but without alarm; for he was confident in his science, and felt that he could draw a magic circle round her, within which no evil might intrude.

"Where am I? – Ah, I remember!" said Georgiana, faintly; and she placed her hand over her cheek, to hide the terrible mark from her husband's eyes.

"Fear not, dearest!" exclaimed he, "Do not shrink from me! Believe me, Georgiana, I even rejoice in this single imperfection, since it will be such rapture to remove it."

"Oh, spare me!" sadly replied his wife – "Pray do not look at it again. I never can forget that convulsive shudder."

In order to soothe Georgiana, and, as it were, to release her mind from the burthen of actual things, Aylmer now put in practice some of the light and playful secrets, which science had taught him among its profounder lore. Airy figures, absolutely bodiless ideas, and forms of unsubstantial beauty, came and danced before her, imprinting their momentary footsteps on beams of light. Though she had some indistinct idea of the method of these optical phenomena, still the illusion was almost perfect enough to

---

4. **pastille:** A tablet that is burned in order to deodorize or fumigate the air.

warrant the belief, that her husband possessed sway over the spiritual world. Then again, when she felt a wish to look forth from her seclusion, immediately, as if her thoughts were answered, the procession of external existence flitted across a screen. The scenery and the figures of actual life were perfectly represented, but with that bewitching, yet indescribable difference, which always makes a picture, an image, or a shadow, so much more attractive than the original. When wearied of this, Aylmer bade her cast her eyes upon a vessel, containing a quantity of earth. She did so, with little interest at first, but was soon startled, to perceive the germ of a plant, shooting upward from the soil. Then came the slender stalk – the leaves gradually unfolded themselves – and amid them was a perfect and lovely flower.

"It is magical!" cried Georgiana, "I dare not touch it."

"Nay, pluck it," answered Aylmer, "pluck it, and inhale its brief perfume while you may. The flower will wither in a few moments, and leave nothing save its brown seed-vessels – but thence may be perpetuated a race as ephemeral as itself."

But Georgiana had no sooner touched the flower than the whole plant suffered a blight, its leaves turning coal-black, as if by the agency of fire.

"There was too powerful a stimulus," said Aylmer thoughtfully.

To make up for this abortive experiment, he proposed to take her portrait by a scientific process of his own invention. It was to be effected by rays of light striking upon a polished plate of metal. Georgiana assented – but, on looking at the result, was affrighted to find the features of the portrait blurred and indefinable; while the minute figure of a hand appeared where the cheek should have been. Aylmer snatched the metallic plate, and threw it into a jar of corrosive acid.

Soon, however, he forgot these mortifying failures. In the intervals of study and chemical experiment, he came to her, flushed and exhausted, but seemed invigorated by her presence, and spoke in glowing language of the resources of his art. He gave a history of the long dynasty of the Alchemists, who spent so many ages in quest of the universal solvent, by which the Golden Principle might be elicited from all things vile and base.[5] Aylmer appeared to believe, that, by the plainest scientific logic, it was altogether within the limits of possibility to discover this long-sought medium; but, he added, a philosopher who should go deep enough to acquire the power, would attain too lofty a wisdom to stoop to the exercise of it. Not less singular were his opinions in regard to the Elixir Vitae.[6] He more than intimated, that it was at his option to concoct a liquid that should prolong life for years – perhaps interminably – but that it would produce a discord in nature, which all the world, and chiefly the quaffer of the immortal nostrum, would find cause to curse.

"Aylmer, are you in earnest?" asked Georgiana, looking at him with amazement and fear; "it is terrible to possess such power, or even to dream of possessing it!"

---

5. **vile and base:** The object of alchemy, a medieval science, was to find a process to turn base metals into gold.
6. **Elixir Vitae:** A potion that could prolong life (Latin).

"Oh, do not tremble, my love!" said her husband, "I would not wrong either you or myself, by working such inharmonious effects upon our lives. But I would have you consider how trifling, in comparison, is the skill requisite to remove this little Hand."

At the mention of the birth-mark, Georgiana, as usual, shrank, as if a red-hot iron had touched her cheek.

Again Aylmer applied himself to his labors. She could hear his voice in the distant furnace-room, giving directions to Aminidab, whose harsh, uncouth, misshapen tones were audible in response, more like the grunt or growl of a brute than human speech. After hours of absence, Aylmer re-appeared, and proposed that she should now examine his cabinet of chemical products and natural treasures of the earth. Among the former he showed her a small vial, in which, he remarked, was contained a gentle, yet most powerful fragrance, capable of impregnating all the breezes that blow across a kingdom. They were of inestimable value, the contents of that little vial; and, as he said so, he threw some of the perfume into the air, and filled the room with piercing and invigorating delight.

"And what is this?" asked Georgiana, pointing to a small crystal globe, containing a gold-colored liquid. "It is so beautiful to the eye, that I could imagine it the Elixir of Life."

"In one sense it is," replied Aylmer, "or rather the Elixir of Immortality. It is the most precious poison that ever was concocted in this world. By its aid, I could apportion the lifetime of any mortal at whom you might point your finger. The strength of the dose would determine whether he were to linger out years, or drop dead in the midst of a breath. No king, on his guarded throne, could keep his life, if I, in my private station, should deem that the welfare of millions justified me in depriving him of it."

"Why do you keep such a terrific drug?" inquired Georgiana in horror.

"Do not mistrust me, dearest!" said her husband, smiling; "its virtuous potency is yet greater than its harmful one. But, see! here is a powerful cosmetic. With a few drops of this, in a vase of water, freckles may be washed away as easily as the hands are cleansed. A stronger infusion would take the blood out of the cheek, and leave the rosiest beauty a pale ghost."

"Is it with this lotion that you intend to bathe my cheek?" asked Georgiana anxiously.

"Oh, no!" hastily replied her husband – "this is merely superficial. Your case demands a remedy that shall go deeper."

In his interviews with Georgiana, Aylmer generally made minute inquiries as to her sensations, and whether the confinement of the rooms, and the temperature of the atmosphere, agreed with her. These questions had such a particular drift, that Georgiana began to conjecture that she was already subjected to certain physical influences, either breathed in with the fragrant air, or taken with her food. She fancied, likewise – but it might be altogether fancy – that there was a stirring up of her system, – a strange, indefinite sensation creeping through her veins, and tingling, half painfully, half pleasurably, at her heart. Still, whenever she dared to look into the mirror, there she beheld herself, pale as a white rose, and with the crimson birth-mark stamped upon her cheek. Not even Aylmer now hated it so much as she.

To dispel the tedium of the hours which her husband found it necessary to devote to the processes of combination and analysis, Georgiana turned over the volumes of his scientific library. In many dark old tomes, she met with chapters full of romance and poetry. They were the works of the philosophers of the middle ages, such as Albertus Magnus, Cornelius Agrippa, Paracelsus, and the famous friar who created the prophetic Brazen Head.[7] All these antique naturalists stood in advance of their centuries, yet were imbued with some of is credulity, and therefore were believed, and perhaps imagined themselves, to have acquired from the investigation of nature a power above nature, and from physics a sway over the spiritual world. Hardly less curious and imaginative were the early volumes of the Transactions of the Royal Society,[8] in which the members, knowing little of the limits of natural possibility, were continually recording wonders, or proposing methods whereby wonders might be wrought.

But, to Georgiana, the most engrossing volume was a large folio from her husband's own hand, in which he had recorded every experiment of his scientific career, with its original aim, the methods adopted for its development, and its final success or failure, with the circumstances to which either event was attributable. The book, in truth, was both the history and emblem of his ardent, ambitious, imaginative, yet practical and laborious, life. He handled physical details, as if there were nothing beyond them; yet spiritualized them all, and redeemed himself from materialism, by his strong and eager aspiration towards the infinite. In his grasp, the veriest clod of earth assumed a soul. Georgiana, as she read, reverenced Aylmer, and loved him more profoundly than ever, but with a less entire dependence on his judgment than heretofore. Much as he had accomplished, she could not but observe that his most splendid successes were almost invariably failures, if compared with the ideal at which he aimed. His brightest diamonds were the merest pebbles, and felt to be so by himself, in comparison with the inestimable gems which lay hidden beyond his reach. The volume, rich with achievements that had won renown for its author, was yet as melancholy a record as ever mortal hand had penned. It was the sad confession, and continual exemplification, of the short-comings of the composite man – the spirit burthened with clay and working in matter – and of the despair that assails the higher nature, at finding itself so miserably thwarted by the earthly part. Perhaps every man of genius, in whatever sphere, might recognise the image of his own experience in Aylmer's journal.

So deeply did these reflections affect Georgiana, that she laid her face upon the open volume, and burst into tears. In this situation she was found by her husband.

"It is dangerous to read in a sorcerer's books," said he, with a smile, though his countenance was uneasy and displeased. "Georgiana, there are pages in that volume, which I can scarcely glance over and keep my senses. Take heed lest it prove as detrimental to you!"

---

7. **Brazen Head:** Roger Bacon (1214?-1294), an English monk and early scientist, constructed a bronze head for predicting the weather. Albertus Magnus (1206?-1280) and Cornelius Agrippa (1486-1535) were German theologians and writers. Philippus Aureolus Paracelsus (1493-1541) was a Swiss physician and alchemist.
8. **Royal Society:** An organization chartered in London in 1662 for the advancement of science.

"It has made me worship you more than ever," said she.

"Ah! wait for this one success," rejoined he, "then worship me if you will. I shall deem myself hardly unworthy of it. But, come! I have sought you for the luxury of your voice. Sing to me, dearest!"

So she poured out the liquid music of her voice to quench the thirst of his spirit. He then took his leave, with a boyish exuberance of gaiety, assuring her that her seclusion would endure but a little longer, and that the result was already certain. Scarcely had he departed, when Georgiana felt irresistibly impelled to follow him. She had forgotten to inform Aylmer of a symptom, which, for two or three hours past, had begun to excite her attention. It was a sensation in the fatal birth-mark, not painful, but which induced a restlessness throughout her system. Hastening after her husband, she intruded, for the first time, into the laboratory.

The first thing that struck her eye was the furnace, that hot and feverish worker, with the intense glow of its fire, which, by the quantities of soot clustered above it, seemed to have been burning for ages. There was a distilling apparatus in full operation. Around the room were retorts, tubes, cylinders, crucibles, and other apparatus of chemical research. An electrical machine stood ready for immediate use. The atmosphere felt oppressively close, and was tainted with gaseous odors, which had been tormented forth by the processes of science. The severe and homely simplicity of the apartment, with its naked walls and brick pavement, looked strange, accustomed as Georgiana had become to the fantastic elegance of her boudoir. But what chiefly, indeed almost solely, drew her attention, was the aspect of Aylmer himself.

He was pale as death, anxious, and absorbed, and hung over the furnace as if it depended upon his utmost watchfulness whether the liquid, which it was distilling, should be the draught of immortal happiness or misery. How different from the sanguine and joyous mien that he had assumed for Georgiana's encouragement!

"Carefully now, Aminidab! Carefully, thou human machine! Carefully, thou man of clay!" muttered Aylmer, more to himself than his assistant. "Now, if there be a thought too much or too little, it is all over!"

"Hoh! hoh!" mumbled Aminidab – "look, master, look!"

Aylmer raised his eyes hastily, and at first reddened, then grew paler than ever, on beholding Georgiana. He rushed towards her, and seized her arm with a gripe that left the print of his finger upon it.

"Why do you come hither? Have you no trust in your husband?" cried he impetuously. "Would you throw the blight of that fatal birth-mark over my labors? It is not well done. Go, prying woman, go!"

"Nay, Aylmer," said Georgiana, with the firmness of which she possessed no stinted endowment, "it is not you that have a right to complain. You mistrust your wife! You have concealed the anxiety with which you watch the development of this experiment. Think not so unworthily of me, my husband! Tell me all the risk we run; and fear not that I shall shrink, for my share in it is far less than your own!"

"No, no, Georgiana!" said Aylmer impatiently, "it must not be."

"I submit," replied she, calmly. "And, Aylmer, I shall quaff whatever draught you bring me; but it will be on the same principle that would induce me to take a dose of poison, if offered by your hand."

"My noble wife," said Aylmer, deeply moved, "I knew not the height and depth of your nature, until now. Nothing shall be concealed. Know, then, that this Crimson Hand, superficial as it seems, has clutched its grasp into your being, with a strength of which I had no previous conception. I have already administered agents powerful enough to do aught except to change your entire physical system. Only one thing remains to be tried. If that fail us, we are ruined!"

"Why did you hesitate to tell me this?" asked she.

"Because, Georgiana," said Aylmer, in a low voice, "there is danger!"

"Danger? There is but one danger – that this horrible stigma shall be left upon my cheek!" cried Georgiana. "Remove it! remove it! – whatever be the cost – or we shall both go mad!"

"Heaven knows, your words are too true," said Aylmer, sadly. "And now, dearest, return to your boudoir. In a little while, all will be tested."

He conducted her back, and took leave of her with a solemn tenderness, which spoke far more than his words how much was now at stake. After his departure, Georgiana became wrapt in musings. She considered the character of Aylmer, and did it completer justice than at any previous moment. Her heart exulted, while it trembled, at his honorable love, so pure and lofty that it would accept nothing less than perfection, nor miserably make itself contented with an earthlier nature than he had dreamed of. She felt how much more precious was such a sentiment, than that meaner kind which would have borne with the imperfection for her sake, and have been guilty of treason to holy love, by degrading its perfect idea to the level of the actual. And, with her whole spirit, she prayed, that, for a single moment, she might satisfy his highest and deepest conception. Longer than one moment, she well knew, it could not be; for his spirit was ever on the march – ever ascending – and each instant required something that was beyond the scope of the instant before.

The sound of her husband's footsteps aroused her. He bore a crystal goblet, containing a liquor colorless as water, but bright enough to be the draught of immortality. Aylmer was pale; but it seemed rather the consequence of a highly wrought state of mind, and tension of spirit, than of fear or doubt.

"The concoction of the draught has been perfect," said he, in answer to Georgiana's look. "Unless all my science have deceived me, it cannot fail."

"Save on your account, my dearest Aylmer," observed his wife, "I might wish to put off this birth-mark of mortality by relinquishing mortality itself, in preference to any other mode. Life is but a sad possession to those who have attained precisely the degree of moral advancement at which I stand. Were I weaker and blinder, it might be happiness. Were I stronger, it might be endured hopefully. But, being what I find myself, methinks I am of all mortals the most fit to die."

"You are fit for heaven without tasting death!" replied her husband. "But why do we speak of dying? The draught cannot fail. Behold its effect upon this plant!"

On the window-seat there stood a geranium, diseased with yellow blotches, which had over-spread all its leaves. Aylmer poured a small quantity of the liquid upon the soil in which it grew. In a little time, when the roots of the plant had taken up the moisture, the unsightly blotches began to be extinguished in a living verdure.

"There needed no proof," said Georgiana, quietly. "Give me the goblet. I joyfully stake all upon your word."

"Drink, then, thou lofty creature!" exclaimed Aylmer, with fervid admiration. "There is no taint of imperfection on thy spirit. Thy sensible frame, too, shall soon be all perfect!"

She quaffed the liquid, and returned the goblet to his hand.

"It is grateful," said she, with a placid smile. "Methinks it is like water from a heavenly fountain; for it contains I know not what of unobtrusive fragrance and deliciousness. It allays a feverish thirst, that had parched me for many days. Now, dearest, let me sleep. My earthly senses are closing over my spirit, like the leaves round the heart of a rose, at sunset."

She spoke the last words with a gentle reluctance, as if it required almost more energy than she could command to pronounce the faint and lingering syllables. Scarcely had they loitered through her lips, ere she was lost in slumber. Aylmer sat by her side, watching her aspect with the emotions proper to a man, the whole value of whose existence was involved in the process now to be tested. Mingled with this mood, however, was the philosophic investigation, characteristic of the man of science. Not the minutest symptom escaped him. A heightened flush of the cheek – a slight irregularity of breath – a quiver of the eye-lid – a hardly perceptible tremor through the frame – such were the details which, as the moments passed, he wrote down in his folio volume. Intense thought had set its stamp upon every previous page of that volume; but the thoughts of years were all concentrated upon the last.

While thus employed, he failed not to gaze often at the fatal Hand, and not without a shudder. Yet once, by a strange and unaccountable impulse, he pressed it with his lips. His spirit recoiled, however, in the very act, and Georgiana, out of the midst of her deep sleep, moved uneasily and murmured, as if in remonstrance. Again, Aylmer resumed his watch. Nor was it without avail. The Crimson Hand, which at first had been strongly visible upon the marble paleness of Georgiana's cheek, now grew more faintly outlined. She remained not less pale than ever; but the birth-mark, with every breath that came and went, lost somewhat of its former distinctness. Its presence had been awful; its departure was more awful still. Watch the stain of the rainbow fading out of the sky; and you will know how that mysterious symbol passed away.

"By Heaven, it is well nigh gone!" said Aylmer to himself, in almost irrepressible ecstasy. "I can scarcely trace it now. Success! Success! And now it is like the faintest rose-color. The slightest flush of blood across her cheek would overcome it. But she is so pale!"

He drew aside the window-curtain, and suffered the light of natural day to fall into the room, and rest upon her cheek. At the same time, he heard a gross, hoarse chuckle, which he had long known as his servant Aminidab's expression of delight.

"Ah, clod! Ah, earthly mass!" cried Aylmer, laughing in a sort of frenzy. "You have served me well! Matter and Spirit – Earth and Heaven – have both done their part in this! Laugh, thing of the senses! You have earned the right to laugh."

These exclamations broke Georgiana's sleep. She slowly unclosed her eyes, and gazed into the mirror, which her husband had arranged for that purpose. A faint smile flitted over her lips, when she recognised how barely perceptible was now that Crimson Hand, which had once blazed forth with such disastrous brilliance as to scare away all their happiness. But then her eyes sought Aylmer's face, with a trouble and anxiety that he could by no means account for.

"My poor Aylmer!" murmured she.

"Poor? Nay, richest! Happiest! Most favored!" exclaimed he. "My peerless bride, it is successful! You are perfect!"

"My poor Aylmer!" she repeated, with a more than human tenderness. "You have aimed loftily! – you have done nobly! Do not repent, that, with so high and pure a feeling, you have rejected the best that earth could offer. Aylmer – dearest Aylmer – I am dying!"

Alas, it was too true! The fatal Hand had grappled with the mystery of life, and was the bond by which an angelic spirit kept itself in union with a mortal frame. As the last crimson tint of the birth-mark – that sole token of human imperfection – faded from her cheek, the parting breath of the now perfect woman passed into the atmosphere, and her soul, lingering a moment near her husband, took its heavenward flight. Then a hoarse, chuckling laugh was heard again! Thus ever does the gross Fatality of Earth exult in its invariable triumph over the immortal essence, which, in this dim sphere of half-development, demands the completeness of a higher state. Yet, had Aylmer reached a profounder wisdom, he need not thus have flung away the happiness, which would have woven his mortal life of the selfsame texture with the celestial. The momentary circumstance was too strong for him; he failed to look beyond the shadowy scope of Time, and living once for all in Eternity, to find the perfect Future in the present.

[1843]

Edgar Allan Poe

[1809–1849]

His greatness is that he turned his back and faced inland, to originality, with the identical gesture of a [Daniel] Boone.
–William Carlos Williams

Edgar Allan Poe was born on January 19, 1809, in Boston, Massachusetts, the second of three children of David and Elizabeth Arnold Poe, actors in a theatrical company. Shortly after the birth of their third child, the alcoholic David Poe abandoned the family and disappeared. Elizabeth Poe, a well-known leading lady, supported the family until her own death in December 1811 in Richmond, Virginia. The penniless children were sent to live with different foster parents. Although Poe was not legally adopted by John Allan, a prosperous merchant, and his wife Frances, they raised him as their son. In 1815, the Allans went to live in England, and Poe was sent to school in London. Five years later, the family returned to Richmond, where Poe continued his education until he entered the University of Virginia in February 1826.

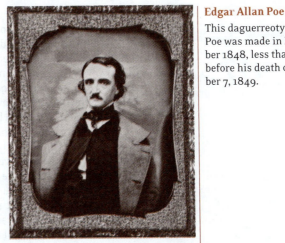

Edgar Allan Poe
This daguerreotype of Poe was made in November 1848, less than a year before his death on October 7, 1849.

The following years were marked by growing conflicts between John Allan and Poe, over both his behavior and his choice of career. During his first year at the University of Virginia, Poe was a good student, especially in Latin and French. Believing that the allowance he received from Allan was not adequate, however, he soon began to gamble and lost $2,000. An angry Allan refused to honor the debt or to send Poe back to the university for the spring semester of 1827. Bitter, humiliated, and increasingly estranged from his foster father, Poe left home shortly after his eighteenth birthday. By then, he had already written a good deal of poetry, and Poe immediately arranged for the publication of his book *Tamerlane and Other Poems* (1827), which he later revised and expanded as *Al Aaraaf, Tamerlane, and Minor Poems* (1829). But he had no prospect of earning a living as a poet, so in 1827 he enlisted in the army as "Edgar A. Perry." Poe enjoyed some advancement in the military, reaching the rank of sergeant major. He was also partially reconciled with John Allan, who refused to support Poe's literary aspirations but who helped him obtain an appointment to the United States Military Academy at West Point in 1830. Although he had no real interest in a military career, Poe hoped that success there would prompt Allan to make him his heir. But Poe's sympathetic foster mother was now dead, and Allan was out of patience with his foster son. After he dashed Poe's hopes for an inheritance once more, Poe deliberately disobeyed rules, received a court-martial, and was expelled from West Point in 1831.

bedfordstmartins.com/americanlit *for research links on Poe*

The break with his foster father was now irreparable, and Poe determined to make his way as a professional writer. His friends at West Point helped him pay for the publication of a third book, *Poems: Second Edition* (1831). He then moved to Baltimore, where he lived in poverty with his aunt, Maria Clemm, and her daughter Virginia, whom Poe secretly married in 1835, when she was thirteen, and publicly remarried in 1836. Meanwhile, he had become a regular contributor to the Philadelphia *Saturday Courier*, where Poe's first story was published anonymously in 1832. Three years later, he moved back to Richmond, where he became the assistant editor of a new journal, the *Southern Literary Messenger*. Poe contributed reviews and stories to the *Messenger*. Before he was fired early in 1837, the journal also ran the first two installments of his novel, *The Narrative of Arthur Gordon Pym*, which was published as a book in 1838. By then, Poe had moved with his wife and aunt, first to New York City and then to Philadelphia, where he continued to eke out a precarious living by writing criticism and stories for periodicals like the *American Museum of Literature and the Arts* and, as its coeditor, for *Burton's Gentleman's Magazine.* In 1839, a two-volume collection of his early stories was published as *Tales of the Grotesque and Arabesque.* Although it sold poorly, Poe was becoming a significant literary figure, known for both his stories and his reviews of poetry and fiction. After a brief stint as editor of *Graham's Magazine*, a distinguished literary monthly, Poe in 1844 moved his family back to New York City. There, he earned a living by writing journalism and doing editorial work. But he achieved his greatest literary success with the publication early in 1845 of "The Raven," a poem that caused a sensation in the United States and Europe.

The astonishing success of that poem made Poe a literary celebrity. Within a few months of its appearance, two collections of his writings were published: *Tales*, a collection of eighteen stories, and *The Raven and Other Poems.* Poe embarked on a lecture tour, offering a series of talks on "Poets and Poetry of America." He also became the editor and then owner of the *Broadway Journal.* But his reviews, often quite negative and even vindictive, alienated many members of the literary establishment, including Nathaniel Hawthorne and Henry Wadsworth Longfellow, whom Poe accused of plagiarism in an extended series of combative articles in the *Broadway Journal.* After the journal failed in 1846, Poe's financial difficulties were compounded by personal problems, especially the serious illness of his wife, Virginia, who died in 1847. Poe himself was often ill and depressed, and he drank frequently. Nonetheless, he wrote constantly, publishing criticism, poetry, and stories, as well as a book-length prose poem, *Eureka* (1848). He also continued to lecture, partly in an ongoing effort to gain backing for a new journal he had long planned to call the *Stylus.* Returning in the fall of 1849 from a visit to Richmond, where he lectured and was received as a literary lion, Poe stopped off in Baltimore. What happened to him there remains a mystery. Within a week, he was found lying on the street, barely conscious and extremely disoriented. Poe died a few days later, on October 7, 1849.

Poe's "Ligeia." This hallucinatory tale was first published in the *American Museum of Literature and the Arts.* One of many short-lived literary periodicals that appeared during the first half of the nineteenth century, the magazine was established in 1838 in Baltimore by Nathan C. Brooks, a schoolteacher, as a replacement for his first failed magazine, the *North American Quarterly.* Even with gripping stories like "Ligeia," one of Poe's masterpieces of gothic terror, the *American Museum* attracted only a small readership and survived for less than a year. "Ligeia" was included in Poe's first collection of short stories, *Tales of the Grotesque and Arabesque* (1839). The text is taken from its first printing in the *American Museum*, September 1838.

Ligeia

> And the will therein lieth, which dieth not. Who knoweth the mysteries of the will, with its vigour? For God is but a great will pervading all things by nature of its intentness. Man doth not yield himself to the angels, nor unto death utterly, save only through the weakness of his feeble will.
>
> -Joseph Glanvill[1]

I cannot, for my soul, remember how, when, or even precisely where I first became acquainted with the lady Ligeia. Long years have since elapsed, and my memory is feeble through much suffering: or, perhaps, I cannot *now* bring these points to mind, because, in truth, the character of my beloved, her rare learning, her singular yet placid cast of beauty, and the thrilling and enthralling eloquence of her low, musical language, made their way into my heart by paces, so steadily and stealthily progressive, that they have been unnoticed and unknown. Yet I know that I met her most frequently in some large, old, decaying city near the Rhine. Of her family – I have surely heard her speak – that they are of a remotely ancient date cannot be doubted. Ligeia! Buried in studies of a nature, more than all else, adapted to deaden impressions of the outward world, it is by that sweet word alone – by Ligeia, that I bring before mine eyes in fancy the image of her who is no more. And now, while I write, a recollection flashes upon me that I have *never known* the paternal name of her who was my friend and my betrothed, and who became the partner of my studies, and eventually the wife of my bosom. Was it a playful charge on the part of my Ligeia? or was it a test of my strength of affection that I should institute no inquiries upon this point? or was it rather a caprice of my own – a wildly romantic offering on the shrine of the most passionate devotion? I but indistinctly recall the fact itself – what wonder that I have utterly forgotten the circumstances which originated or attended it? And indeed, if ever that spirit which is entitled *Romance* – if ever she, the wan, and the misty-winged *Ashtophet*[2] of idolatrous Egypt, presided, as they tell, over marriages ill-omened; then most surely she presided over mine.

There is one dear topic, however, on which my memory faileth me not. It is the person of Ligeia. In stature she was tall, somewhat slender, and in her latter days even emaciated. I would in vain attempt to pourtray the majesty, the quiet ease of her demeanour, or the incomprehensible lightness and elasticity of her footfall. She came and departed like a shadow. I was never made aware of her entrance into my closed study save by the dear music of her low sweet voice, as she placed her delicate hand upon my shoulder. In beauty of face no maiden ever equalled her. It was the radiance of an opium dream – an airy and spirit-lifting vision more wildly divine than the phantasies which hovered about the slumbering souls of the daughters of Delos.[3] Yet her features were not of that regular mould which we have been falsely taught to worship in the classical labors of the Heathen. "There is no exquisite beauty," saith Verülam, Lord Bacon, speaking truly of

---

1. **Joseph Glanvill:** (1636-1680) English philosopher who defended witchcraft and is sometimes cited as the originator of psychic research. The epigraph was probably written by Poe and simply credited to Glanvill.
2. ***Ashtophet*:** Another name for Ashtoreth, the Phoenician goddess of fertility and sexual love.
3. **Delos:** The Aegean island where the Greek gods Apollo and Artemis were born and protected by maidens.

all the forms and *genera* of beauty, "without some *strangeness* in the proportions."[4] Yet, although I saw that the features of Ligeia were not of classic regularity, although I perceived that her loveliness was indeed "exquisite," and felt that there was much of "strangeness" pervading it, yet I have tried in vain to detect the irregularity, and to trace home my own perception of "the strange." I examined the contour of the lofty and pale forehead – it was faultless – how cold indeed that word when applied to a majesty so divine! The skin rivaling the purest ivory, the commanding breadth and repose, the gentle prominence of the regions above the temples, and then the raven-black, the glossy, the luxuriant and naturally-curling tresses, setting forth the full force of the Homeric epithet, "hyacinthine;" I looked at the delicate outlines of the nose – and nowhere but in the graceful medallions of the Hebrews had I beheld a similar perfection. There was the same luxurious smoothness of surface, the same scarcely perceptible tendency to the aquiline, the same harmoniously curved nostril speaking the free spirit. I regarded the sweet mouth. Here was indeed the triumph of all things heavenly – the magnificent turn of the short upper lip – the soft, voluptuous repose of the under – the dimples which sported, and the colour which spoke – the teeth glancing back, with a brilliancy almost startling, every ray of the holy light which fell upon them in her serene, and placid, yet most exultingly radiant of all smiles. I scrutinized the formation of the chin – and here, too, I found the gentleness of breadth, the softness and the majesty, the fulness and the spirituality, of the Greek, the contour which the God Apollo revealed but in a dream to Cleomenes,[5] the son of the Athenian. And then I peered into the large eyes of Ligeia.

For eyes we have no models in the remotely antique. It might have been, too, that in these eyes of my beloved lay the secret to which Lord Verülam alludes. They were, I must believe, far larger than the ordinary eyes of our race. They were even far fuller than the fullest of the Gazelle eyes of the tribe of the valley of Nourjabad.[6] Yet it was only at intervals – in moments of intense excitement – that this peculiarity became more than slightly noticeable in Ligeia. And at such moments was her beauty – in my heated fancy thus it appeared perhaps – the beauty of beings either above or apart from the earth – the beauty of the fabulous Houri[7] of the Turk. The colour of the orbs was the most brilliant of black, and far over them hung jetty lashes of great length. The brows, slightly irregular in outline, had the same hue. The "strangeness," however, which I have found in the eyes of my Ligeia was of a nature distinct from the formation, or the colour, or the brilliancy of the feature, and must, after all, be referred to the *expression*. Ah, word of no meaning! behind whose vast latitude of mere sound we intrench our ignorance of so much of the spiritual. The expression of the eyes of Ligeia! How, for long hours have I

---

4. **"There is no . . . proportions"**: The exact quotation is "There is no excellent beauty, that hath not some strangeness in the proportion," from the essay "Of Beauty" by Francis Bacon, Baron Verulam (1561–1626).
5. **Cleomenes**: Greek sculptor (c. 200 BCE) whose name is inscribed on the base of an ancient statue, the *Venus de' Medici*, thought to be the epitome of female beauty.
6. **Nourjabad**: *The History of Nourjahad* (1767), a romantic tale written in an orientalist style popular in the late eighteenth century, by the English writer Frances Sheridan (1724–1766).
7. **Houri**: From *hawra'* (Arabic), a term for a beautiful virgin who awaits a devout Muslim in the afterlife.

pondered upon it! How have I, through the whole of a mid-summer night, struggled to fathom it! What was it – that something more profound than the well of Democritus[8] – which lay far within the pupils of my beloved? What *was* it? I was possessed with a passion to discover. Those eyes! those large, those shining, those divine orbs! they became to me twin stars of Leda,[9] and I to them devoutest of astrologers. Not for a moment was the unfathomable meaning of their glance, by day or by night, absent from my soul.

There is no point, among the many incomprehensible anomalies of the science of mind, more thrillingly exciting than the fact – never, I believe noticed in the schools – that in our endeavours to recall to memory something long forgotten we often find ourselves *upon the very verge* of remembrance without being able, in the end, to remember. And thus, how frequently, in my intense scrutiny of Ligeia's eyes, have I felt approaching the full knowledge of the secret of their expression – felt it approaching – yet not quite be mine – and so at length utterly depart. And (strange, oh strangest mystery of all!) I found, in the commonest objects of the universe, a circle of analogies to that expression. I mean to say that, subsequently to the period when Ligeia's beauty passed into my spirit, there dwelling as in a shrine, I derived from many existences in the material world, a sentiment, such as I felt always aroused within me by her large and luminous orbs. Yet not the more could I define that sentiment, or analyze, or even steadily view it. I recognized it, let me repeat, sometimes in the commonest objects of the universe. It has flashed upon me in the survey of a rapidly-growing vine – in the contemplation of a moth, a butterfly, a chrysalis, a stream of running water. I have felt it in the ocean, in the falling of a meteor. I have felt it in the glances of unusually aged people. And there are one or two stars in heaven – (one especially, a star of the sixth magnitude, double and changeable, to be found near the large star in Lyra[10]) in a telescopic scrutiny of which I have been made aware of the feeling. I have been filled with it by certain sounds from stringed instruments, and not unfrequently by passages from books. Among innumerable other instances, I well remember something in a volume of Joseph Glanvill, which, perhaps merely from its quaintness – who shall say? never failed to inspire me with the sentiment. – "And the will therein lieth, which dieth not. Who knoweth the mysteries of the will, with its vigor? For God is but a great will pervading all things by nature of its intentness. Man doth not yield himself to the angels, nor unto death utterly, but only through the weakness of his feeble will."

Length of years, and subsequent reflection, have enabled me to trace, indeed, some remote connexion between this passage in the old English moralist and a portion of the character of Ligeia. An *intensity* in thought, action, or speech was possibly, in her, a result, or at least an index, of that gigantic volition which, during our long intercourse, failed to give other and more immediate evidence of its existence. Of all women whom I

---

8. **well of Democritus:** Democritus (460–370 BCE), ancient Greek scientist and philosopher whose saying was, "In reality we know nothing, for truth lies at the deep bottom of the well."
9. **twin stars of Leda:** Raped by the Greek god Zeus, who assumed the form of a swan to commit the act, Leda was the mother of the twins Castor and Pollux, also the names of two bright stars in the constellation Gemini.
10. **Lyra:** A constellation of stars, roughly forming the shape of a lyre.

have ever known, she, the outwardly calm, the ever placid Ligeia, was the most violently a prey to the tumultuous vultures of stern passion. And of such passion I could form no estimate, save by the miraculous expansion of those eyes which at once so delighted and appalled me, by the almost magical melody, modulation, distinctness and placidity of her very low voice, and by the fierce energy, (rendered doubly effective by contrast with her manner of utterance) of the words which she uttered.

I have spoken of the learning of Ligeia: it was immense – such as I have never known in woman. In all the classical tongues was she deeply proficient, and as far as my own acquaintance extended in regard to the modern dialects of Europe, I have never known her at fault. Indeed upon any theme of the most admired, because simply the most abstruse, of the boasted erudition of the academy, have I *ever* found Ligeia at fault? How singularly, how thrillingly, this one point in the nature of my wife has forced itself, at this late period, only, upon my attention! I said her knowledge was such as I had never known in woman. Where breathes the man who, like her, has traversed, and successfully, *all* the wide areas of moral, natural, and mathematical science? I saw not then what I now clearly perceive, that the acquisitions of Ligeia were gigantic, were astounding – yet I was sufficiently aware of her infinite supremacy to resign myself, with a childlike confidence, to her guidance through the chaotic world of metaphysical investigation at which I was most busily occupied during the earlier years of our marriage. With how vast a triumph – with how vivid a delight – with how much of all that is ethereal in hope – did I *feel*, as she bent over me, in studies but little sought for – but less known that delicious vista by slow but very perceptible degrees expanding before me, down whose long, gorgeous, and all untrodden path I might at length pass onward to the goal of a wisdom too divinely precious not to be forbidden!

How poignant, then, must have been the grief with which, after some years, I beheld my well-grounded expectations take wings to themselves and flee away! Without Ligeia I was but as a child groping benighted. Her presence, her readings alone, rendered vividly luminous the many mysteries of the transcendentalism in which we were immersed. Letters, lambent and golden, grew duller than Saturnian lead[11] wanting the radiant lustre of her eyes. And now those eyes shone less and less frequently upon the pages over which I poured. Ligeia grew ill. The wild eye blazed with a too – too glorious effulgence; the pale fingers became of the transparent waxen hue of the grave – and the blue veins upon the lofty forehead swelled and sunk impetuously with the tides of the most gentle emotion. I saw that she must die – and I struggled desperately in spirit with the grim Azrael.[12] And the struggles of the passionate Ligeia were, to my astonishment, even more energetic than my own. There had been much in her stern nature to impress me with the belief that, to her, death would have come without its terrors – but not so. Words are impotent to convey any just idea of the fierceness of resistance with which Ligeia wrestled with the dark shadow. I groaned in anguish at the pitiable spec-

11. **Saturnian lead:** An archaic term for lead.
12. **Azrael:** In the Islamic and Jewish religions, the angel Azrael separates the soul from the body at the moment of death.

tacle. I would have soothed – I would have reasoned; but in the intensity of her wild desire for life – for life – *but* for life, solace and reason were alike the uttermost of folly. Yet not for an instant, amid the most convulsive writhings of her fierce spirit, was shaken the external placidity of her demeanor. Her voice grew more gentle – grew more low – yet I would not wish to dwell upon the wild meaning of the quietly-uttered words. My brain reeled as I hearkened, entranced, to a melody more than mortal – to assumptions and aspirations which mortality had never before known.

That Ligeia loved me, I should not have doubted; and I might have been easily aware that, in a bosom such as hers, love would have reigned no ordinary passion. But in death only, was I fully impressed with the intensity of her affection. For long hours, detaining my hand, would she pour out before me the overflowings of a heart whose more than passionate devotion amounted to idolatry. How had I deserved to be so blessed by such confessions. – How had I deserved to be so cursed with the removal of my beloved in the hour of her making them? But upon this subject I cannot bear to dilate. Let me say only, that in Ligeia's more than womanly abandonment to love, alas, all unmerited, all unworthily bestowed; I at length recognised the principle of her longing, with so wildly earnest a desire for the life which was now fleeing so rapidly away. It is this wild longing – it is this eager intensity of desire for life – *but* for life – that I have no power to pourtray – no utterance capable to express. Methinks I again behold the terrific struggles of her lofty, her nearly idealized nature, with the might and the terror, and the majesty of the great Shadow. But she perished. The giant *will* succumbed to a power more stern. And I thought, as I gazed upon the corpse, of the wild passage in Joseph Glanvill. "The will therein lieth, which dieth not. Who knoweth the mysteries of the will, with its vigor? For God is but a great will pervading all things by nature of its intentness. Man doth not yield himself to the angels, *nor unto death utterly*, save only through the weakness of his feeble will."

She died – and I, crushed into the very dust with sorrow, could no longer endure the lonely desolation of my dwelling in the dim and decaying city by the Rhine. I had no lack of what the world terms wealth – Ligeia had brought me far more, very far more, than falls ordinarily to the lot of mortals. After a few months, therefore, of weary and aimless wandering, I purchased, and put in some repair, an abbey, which I shall not name, in one of the wildest and least frequented portions of fair England. The gloomy and dreary grandeur of the building, the almost savage aspect of the domain, the many melancholy and time-honored memories connected with both, had much in unison with the feelings of utter abandonment which had driven me into that remote and musical region of the country. Yet, although the external abbey, with its verdant decay hanging about it, suffered but little alteration, I gave way with a child-like perversity, and perchance with a faint hope of alleviating my sorrows, to a display of more than regal magnificence within. For such follies even in childhood I had imbibed a taste, and now they came back to me as if in the dotage of grief. Alas, I now feel how much even of incipient madness might have been discovered in the gorgeous and fantastic draperies, in the solemn carvings of Egypt, in the wild cornices and furniture of Arabesque, in the bedlam patterns of the carpets of tufted gold! I had become a bounden slave in the trammels of opium, and my labors and my orders had taken a colouring from my dreams. But these absurdities I must not pause to detail. Let me speak only of that one chamber, ever accursed, whither, in a moment of mental alienation, I led from the altar as my bride – as the successor of the unforgotten Ligeia – the fair-haired and blue-eyed lady Rowena Trevanion, of Tremaine.

There is not any individual portion of the architecture and decoration of that bridal chamber which is not now visibly before me. Where were the souls of the haughty family of the bride, when, through thirst of gold, they permitted to pass the threshold of an apartment *so* bedecked, a maiden and a daughter so beloved? I have said that I minutely remember the details of the chamber – yet I am sadly forgetful on topics of deep moment – and here there was no system, no keeping, in the fantastic display, to take hold upon the memory. The room lay in a high turret of the castellated abbey, was pentagonal in shape, and of capacious size. Occupying the whole southern face of the pentagon was the sole window – an immense sheet of unbroken glass from Venice – a single pane, and tinted of a leaden hue, so that the rays of either the sun or moon, passing through it, fell with a ghastly lustre upon the objects within. Over the upper portion of this huge window extended the open trellice-work of an aged vine which clambered up the massy walls of the turret. The ceiling, of gloomy-looking oak, was excessively lofty, vaulted, and elaborately fretted with the wildest and most grotesque specimens of a semi-Gothic, semi-druidical device. From out the most central recess of this melancholy vaulting, depended, by a single chain of gold, with long links, a huge censer of the same metal, Arabesque in pattern, and with many perforations so contrived that there writhed in and out of them, as if endued with a serpent vitality, a continual succession of parti-coloured fires. Some few ottomans and golden candelabras of Eastern figure were in various stations about – and there was the couch, too, the bridal couch, of an Indian model, and low, and sculptured, of solid ebony, with a canopy above. In each of the angles of the chamber, stood on end a gigantic sarcophagus of black granite, from the tombs of the kings over against Luxor,[13] with their aged lids full of immemorial sculpture. But in the draping of the apartment lay, alas! the chief phantasy of all. The lofty walls – gigantic in height – even unproportionally so, were hung from summit to foot, in vast folds with a heavy and massy looking tapestry – tapestry of a material which was found alike as a carpet on the floor, as a covering for the ottomans, and the ebony bed, as a canopy for the bed, and as the gorgeous volutes of the curtains which partially shaded the window. This material was the richest cloth of gold. It was spotted all over, at irregular intervals, with Arabesque figures, of about a foot in diameter, and wrought upon the cloth in patterns of the most jetty black. But these figures partook of the true character of the Arabesque only when regarded from a single point of view. By a contrivance now common, and indeed traceable to a very remote period of antiquity, they were made changeable in aspect. To one entering the room they bore the appearance of ideal monstrosities; but, upon a farther advance, this appearance suddenly departed; and, step by step, as the visiter moved his station in the chamber, he saw him-

---

13. **Luxor:** City on the Nile River in central Egypt; the site of the ancient city of Thebes, it contains ruins of a temple and monuments erected by the Pharaohs.

self surrounded by an endless succession of the ghastly forms which belong to the superstition of the Northman, or arise in the guilty slumbers of the monk. The phantasmagoric effect was vastly heightened by the artificial introduction of a strong continual current of wind behind the draperies – giving a hidious and uneasy vitality to the whole.

In halls such as these – in a bridal chamber such as this, I passed, with the lady of Tremaine, the unhallowed hours of the first month of our marriage – passed them with but little disquietude. That my wife dreaded the fierce moodiness of my temper – that she shunned me, and loved me but little, I could not help perceiving – but it gave me rather pleasure than otherwise. I loathed her with a hatred belonging more to demon than to man. My memory flew back, (oh with what intensity of regret!) to Ligeia, the beloved, the beautiful, the entombed. I revelled in recollections of her purity, of her wisdom, of her lofty, her ethereal nature, of her passionate, her idolatrous love. Now, then, did my spirit fully and freely burn with more than all the fires of her own. In the excitement of my opium dreams for I was habitually fettered in the iron shackles of the drug I would call aloud upon her name, during the silence of the night, or among the sheltered recesses of the glens by day, as if, by the wild eagerness, the solemn passion, the consuming intensity of my longing for the departed Ligeia, I could restore the departed Ligeia to the pathways she had abandoned upon earth.

About the commencement of the second month of the marriage, the lady Rowena was attacked with sudden illness from which her recovery was slow. The fever which consumed her, rendered her nights uneasy, and, in her perturbed state of half-slumber, she spoke of sounds, and of motions, in and about the chamber of the turret which had no origin save in the distemper of her fancy, or, perhaps, in the phantasmagoric influences of the chamber itself. She became at length convalescent – finally well. Yet but a brief period elapsed, ere a second more violent disorder again threw her upon a bed of suffering – and from this attack her frame, at all times feeble, never altogether recovered. Her illnesses were, after this period, of alarming character, and of more alarming recurrence, defying alike the knowledge and the great exertions of her medical men. With the increase of the chronic disease which had thus, apparently, taken too sure hold upon her constitution to be eradicated by human means, I could not fail to observe a similar increase in the nervous irritability of her temperament, and in her excitability by trivial causes of fear. Indeed reason seemed fast tottering from her throne. She spoke again, and now more frequently and pertinaciously, of the sounds, of the slight sounds, and of the unusual motions among the tapestries, to which she had formerly alluded. It was one night near the closing in of September, when she pressed this distressing subject with more than usual emphasis upon my attention. She had just awakened from a perturbed slumber, and I had been watching, with feelings half of anxiety, half of a vague terror, the workings of her emaciated countenance. I sat by the side of her ebony bed, upon one of the ottomans of India. She partly arose, and spoke, in an earnest low whisper, of sounds which she *then* heard, but which I could not hear, of motions which she *then* saw, but which I could not perceive. The wind was rushing hurriedly behind the tapestries, and I wished to show her (what, let me confess it, I could not *all* believe) that those faint, almost articulate, breathings, and the very gentle variations of the figures upon the wall, were but the natural effects of that customary rushing of the wind. But a deadly pallor overspreading her face, had proved to me that my exertions to re-assure her would be fruitless. She appeared to be fainting, and no attendants were within call. I remembered where was deposited a decanter of some light wine which had been ordered by her physicians, and hastened across the chamber to procure it. But, as I stepped beneath the light of the censer, two circumstances of a startling nature attracted my attention. I had felt that some palpable object had passed lightly by my person; and I saw that there lay a faint, indefinite shadow upon the golden carpet in the very middle of the rich lustre thrown from the censer. But I was wild with the excitement of an immoderate dose of opium, and heeded these things but little, nor spoke of them to Rowena. Finding the wine, I re-crossed the chamber, and poured out a goblet-ful, which I held to the lips of the fainting lady. But she had now partially recovered, and took, herself, the vessel, while I sank upon the ottoman near me, with my eyes rivetted upon her person. It was then that I became distinctly aware of a gentle foot-fall upon the carpet, and near the couch; and, in a second thereafter, as Rowena was in the act of raising the wine to her lips, I saw, or may have dreamed that I saw, fall within the goblet, as if from some invisible spring in the atmosphere of the room, three or four large drops of a brilliant and ruby colored fluid. If this I saw – not so Rowena. She swallowed the wine unhesitatingly, and I forbore to speak to her of a circumstance which must, after all, I considered, have been but the suggestion of a vivid imagination, rendered morbidly active by the terror of the lady, by the opium, and by the hour.

Yet I cannot conceal it from myself, after this period, a rapid change for the worse took place in the disorder of my wife, so that, on the third subsequent night, the hands of her menials prepared her for the tomb, and on the fourth, I sat alone, with her shrouded body, in that fantastical chamber which had received her as my bride. Wild visions, opium engendered, flitted, shadow-like, before me. I gazed with unquiet eye upon the sarcophagi in the angles of the room, upon the varying figures of the drapery, and upon the writhing of the parti-colored fires in the censer overhead. My eyes then fell, as I called to mind the circumstances of a former night, to the spot beneath the glare of the censer where I had beheld the faint traces of the shadow. It was there, however, no longer, and, breathing with greater freedom, I turned my glances to the pallid and rigid figure upon the bed. Then rushed upon me a thousand memories of Ligeia – and then came back upon my heart, with the turbulent violence of a flood, the whole of that unutterable woe with which I had regarded *her* thus enshrouded. The night waned; and still, with a bosom full of bitter thoughts of the one only and supremely beloved, I remained with mine eyes rivetted upon the body of Rowena.

It might have been midnight, or perhaps earlier, or later, for I had taken no note of time, when a sob, low, gentle, but very distinct, startled me from my revery. I *felt* that it came from the bed of ebony – the bed of death. I listened in an agony of superstitious terror – but there was no repetition of the sound; I strained my vision to detect any motion in the corpse, but there was not the slightest perceptible. Yet I could not have been deceived. I had heard the noise, however faint, and my whole soul was awakened within me, as I resolutely and perseveringly kept my attention rivetted upon the body. Many minutes elapsed before any circumstance occurred tending to throw light upon the mystery. At length it became evident that a slight, a very faint, and barely noticeable tinge of colour had flushed up within the cheeks, and along the sunken small veins of the eyelids. Through a species of unutterable horror and awe, for which the language of mortality has no sufficiently energetic expression, I felt my brain reel, my heart cease to beat, my limbs grow rigid where I sat. Yet a sense of duty finally operated to restore my self-possession. I could no longer doubt that we had been precipitate in our preparations for interment – that Rowena still lived. It was necessary that some immediate exertion be made; yet the turret was altogether apart from the portion of the Abbey tenanted by the servants – there were none within call, and I had no means of summoning them to my aid without leaving the room for many minutes – and this I could not venture to do. I therefore struggled alone in my endeavors to call back the spirit still hovering. In a short period it became evident however, that a relapse had taken place; the color utterly disappeared from both eyelid and cheek, leaving a wanness even more than that of marble; the lips became doubly shrivelled and pinched up in the ghastly expression of death; a coldness surpassing that of ice, overspread rapidly the surface of the body, and all the usual rigorous stiffness immediately supervened. I fell back with a shudder upon the ottoman from which I had been so startlingly aroused, and again gave myself up to passionate waking visions of Ligeia.

An hour thus elapsed when, (could it be possible?) I was a second time aware of some vague sound issuing from the region of the bed. I listened – in extremity of horror. The sound came again – it was a sigh. Rushing to the corpse, I saw – distinctly saw – a tremor upon the lips. In a minute after they slightly relaxed, disclosing a bright line of the pearly teeth. Amazement now struggled in my bosom with the profound awe which had hitherto reigned therein alone. I felt that my vision grew dim, that my brain wandered, and it was only by a convulsive effort that I at length succeeded in nerving myself to the task which duty thus, once more, had pointed out. There was now a partial glow upon the forehead, upon the cheek and throat – a perceptible warmth pervaded the whole frame – there was even a slight pulsation at the heart. The lady lived; and with redoubled ardour I betook myself to the task of restoration. I chafed, and bathed the temples, and the hands, and used every exertion which experience, and no little medical reading, could suggest. But in vain. Suddenly, the colour fled, the pulsation ceased, the lips resumed the expression of the dead, and, in an instant afterwards, the whole body took upon itself the icy chillness, the livid hue, the intense rigidity, the sunken outline, and each and all of the loathsome peculiarities of that which has been, for many days, a tenant of the tomb.

And again I sunk into visions of Ligeia – and again (what marvel that I shudder while I write?) *again* there reached my ears a low sob from the region of the ebony bed. But why shall I minutely detail the unspeakable horrors of that night? Why shall I pause to relate how, time after time, until near the period of the grey dawn, this hideous drama of revivification was repeated, and how each terrific relapse was only into a sterner and apparently more irredeemable death? Let me hurry to a conclusion.

The greater part of the fearful night had worn away, and the corpse of Rowena once again stirred – and now more vigorously than hitherto, although arousing from a dissolution more appalling in its utter hopelessness than any. I had long ceased to struggle or to move, and remained sitting rigidly upon the ottoman, a helpless prey to a whirl of violent emotions, of which extreme awe was perhaps the least terrible, the least consuming. The corpse, I repeat, stirred, and now more vigorously than before. The hues of life flushed up with unwonted energy into the countenance – the limbs relaxed – and, save that the eyelids were yet pressed heavily together, and that the bandages and draperies of the grave still imparted their charnal character to the figure, I might have dreamed that Rowena had indeed shaken off, utterly, the fetters of Death. But if this idea was not, even then, altogether adopted, I could, at least, doubt no longer, when, arising from the bed, tottering, with feeble steps, with closed eyes, and with the air of one bewildered in a dream, the lady of Tremaine stood bodily and palpably before me.

I trembled not – I stirred not – for a crowd of unutterable fancies connected with the air, the demeanour of the figure, rushing hurriedly through my brain, sent the purple blood ebbing in torrents from the temples to the heart. I stirred not – but gazed upon her who was before me. There was a mad disorder in my thoughts – a tumult unappeasable. Could it, indeed, be the *living* Rowena who confronted me? Why, *why* should I doubt it? The bandage lay heavily about the mouth – but then it was the mouth of the breathing lady of Tremaine. And the cheeks – there were the roses as in her noon of health – yes, these were indeed the fair cheeks of the living lady of Tremaine. And the chin, with its dimples, as in health, was it not hers? – but – but *had she then grown taller since her malady*? What inexpressible madness seized me with that thought? One bound, and I had reached her feet! Shrinking from my touch, she let fall from her head, unloosened, the ghastly cerements which had confined it, and there streamed forth, into the rushing atmosphere of the chamber, huge masses of long and dishevelled hair. *It was blacker than the raven wings of the midnight!* And now the eyes opened of the figure which stood before me. "Here then at least," I shrieked aloud, "can I never – can I never be mistaken – these are the full, and the black, and the wild eyes of the lady – of the lady Ligeia!"

[1838]

Poe's "The Fall of the House of Usher." Perhaps the most familiar of Poe's celebrated tales of psychological terror, "The Fall of the House of Usher" first appeared in *Burton's Gentleman's Magazine and American Monthly Review.* Founded by Williams Evans Burton (1804-1860) and published under several titles between July 1837 and November 1840, the magazine was designed specifically for "gentlemen" readers, and its tone and subject matter were distinctly male. Outdoor recreations for men, such as archery and hunting, were frequent topics, as were articles on travel and brief biographies of important men in American history. Poe became the coeditor of the magazine in July 1839. Under his direction, the magazine became more diverse and published poetry and tales of a much higher quality, including several of Poe's own stories. Unhappy with the direction that the magazine was taking, however, Burton reassumed full editorship in June 1840. "The Fall of the House of Usher" was included in both *Tales of the Grotesque and Arabesque* (1839) and *Tales* (1845). The text is taken from its first printing in *Burton's Gentleman's Magazine*, September 1839.

The Fall of the House of Usher

During the whole of a dull, dark, and soundless day in the autumn of the year, when the clouds hung oppressively low in the heavens, I had been passing alone, on horseback, through a singularly dreary tract of country; and at length found myself, as the shades of the evening drew on, within view of the melancholy House of Usher. I know not how it was – but, with the first glimpse of the building, a sense of insufferable gloom pervaded my spirit. I say insufferable; for the feeling was unrelieved by any of that half-pleasurable, because poetic, sentiment, with which the mind usually receives even the sternest natural images of the desolate or terrible. I looked upon the scene before me – upon the mere house, and the simple landscape features of the domain – upon the bleak walls – upon the vacant eye-like windows – upon a few rank sedges – and upon a few white trunks of decayed trees – with an utter depression of soul which I can compare to no earthly sensation more properly than to the after-dream of the reveller upon opium – the bitter lapse into common life – the hideous dropping off of the veil. There was an iciness, a sinking, a sickening of the heart – an unredeemed dreariness of thought which no goading of the imagination could torture into aught of the sublime. What was it – I paused to think – what was it that so unnerved me in the contemplation of the House of Usher? It was a mystery all insoluble; nor could I grapple with the shadowy fancies that crowded upon me as I pondered. I was forced to fall back upon the unsatisfactory conclusion, that while, beyond doubt, there *are* combinations of very simple natural objects which have the power of thus affecting us, still the reason, and the analysis, of this power, lie among considerations beyond our depth. It was possible, I reflected, that a mere different arrangement of the particulars of the scene, of the details of the picture, would be sufficient to modify, or perhaps to annihilate its capacity for sorrowful impression; and, acting upon this idea, I reined my horse to the precipitous brink of a black and lurid tarn[1] that lay in unruffled lustre by the dwelling, and gazed down – but with a shudder even more thrilling than before – upon the re-modelled and inverted images of the gray sedge, and the ghastly tree-stems, and the vacant and eye-like windows.

Nevertheless, in this mansion of gloom I now proposed to myself a sojourn of some weeks. Its proprietor, Roderick Usher, had been one of my boon companions in boyhood; but many years had elapsed since our last meeting. A letter, however, had lately reached me in a distant part of the country – a letter from him – which, in its wildly importunate nature, had admitted of no other than a personal reply. The MS.[2] gave evidence of nervous agitation. The writer spoke of acute bodily illness – of a pitiable mental idiosyncrasy which oppressed him – and of an earnest desire to see me, as his best, and indeed, his only personal friend, with a view of attempting, by the cheerfulness of my society, some alleviation of his malady. It was the manner in which all this, and much more, was said – it was the apparent *heart* that went with his request – which allowed

1. **tarn:** Small mountain lake.
2. **MS.:** Standard editorial abbreviation for "manuscript."

me no room for hesitation – and I accordingly obeyed, what I still considered a very singular summons, forthwith.

Although, as boys, we had been even intimate associates, yet I really knew little of my friend. His reserve had been always excessive and habitual. I was aware, however, that his very ancient family had been noted, time out of mind, for a peculiar sensibility of temperament, displaying itself, through long ages, in many works of exalted art, and manifested, of late, in repeated deeds of munificent yet unobtrusive charity, as well as in a passionate devotion to the intricacies, perhaps even more than to the orthodox and easily recognizable beauties, of musical science. I had learned, too, the very remarkable fact, that the stem of the Usher race, all time-honored as it was, had put forth, at no period, any enduring branch; in other words, that the entire family lay in the direct line of descent, and had always, with very trifling and very temporary variation, so lain. It was this deficiency, I considered, while running over in thought the perfect keeping of the character of the premises with the accredited character of the people, and while speculating upon the possible influence which the one, in the long lapse of centuries, might have exercised upon the other – it was this deficiency, perhaps, of collateral issue, and the consequent undeviating transmission, from sire to son, of the patrimony with the name, which had, at length, so identified the two as to merge the original title of the estate in the quaint and equivocal appellation of the "House of Usher" – an appellation which seemed to include, in the minds of the peasantry who used it, both the family and the family mansion.

I have said that the sole effect of my somewhat childish experiment, of looking down within the tarn, had been to deepen the first singular impression. There can be no doubt that the consciousness of the rapid increase of my superstition – for why should I not so term it? – served mainly to accelerate the increase itself. Such, I have long known, is the paradoxical law of all sentiments having terror as a basis. And it might have been for this reason only, that, when I again uplifted my eyes to the house itself, from its image in the pool, there grew in my mind a strange fancy – a fancy so ridiculous, indeed, that I but mention it to show the vivid force of the sensations which oppressed me. I had so worked upon my imagination as really to believe that around about the whole mansion and domain there hung an atmosphere peculiar to themselves and their immediate vicinity – an atmosphere which had no affinity with the air of heaven, but which had reeked up from the decayed trees, and the gray walls, and the silent tarn, in the form of an inelastic vapor or gas – dull, sluggish, faintly discernible, and leaden-hued. Shaking off from my spirit what *must* have been a dream, I scanned more narrowly the real aspect of the building. Its principal feature seemed to be that of an excessive antiquity. The discoloration of ages had been great. Minute fungi overspread the whole exterior, hanging in a fine tangled web-work from the eaves. Yet all this was apart from any extraordinary dilapidation. No portion of the masonry had fallen; and there appeared to be a wild inconsistency between its still perfect adaptation of parts, and the utterly porous, and evidently decayed condition of the individual stones. In this there was much that reminded me of the specious totality of old wood-work which has rotted for long years in some neglected vault, with no disturbance from the breath of the external air. Beyond this indication of extensive decay, however, the fabric gave little token of instability. Perhaps the eye of a scrutinizing observer might have discovered a barely perceptible fissure, which, extending from the roof of the building in front, made its way down the wall in a zig-zag direction, until it became lost in the sullen waters of the tarn.

Noticing these things, I rode over a short causeway to the house. A servant in waiting took my horse, and I entered the Gothic archway of the hall. A valet, of stealthy step, thence conducted me, in silence, through many dark and intricate passages in my progress to the studio of his master. Much that I encountered on the way contributed, I know not how, to heighten the vague sentiments of which I have already spoken. While the objects around me – while the carvings of the ceilings, the sombre tapestries of the walls, the ebon blackness of the floors, and the phantasmagoric armorial trophies which rattled as I strode, were but matters to which, or to such as which, I had been accustomed from my infancy – while I hesitated not to acknowledge how familiar was all this – I still wondered to find how unfamiliar were the fancies which ordinary images were stirring up. On one of the staircases, I met the physician of the family. His countenance, I thought, wore a mingled expression of low cunning and perplexity. He accosted me with trepidation and passed on. The valet now threw open a door and ushered me into the presence of his master.

The room in which I found myself was very large and excessively lofty. The windows were long, narrow, and pointed, and at so vast a distance from the black oaken floor as to be altogether inaccessible from within. Feeble gleams of encrimsoned light made their way through the trelliced panes, and served to render sufficiently distinct the more prominent objects around; the eye, however, struggled in vain to reach the remoter angles of the chamber, or the recesses of the vaulted and fretted ceiling. Dark draperies hung upon the walls. The general furniture was profuse, comfortless, antique, and tattered. Many books and musical instruments lay scattered about, but failed to give any vitality to the scene. I felt that I breathed an atmosphere of sorrow. An air of stern, deep, and irredeemable gloom hung over and pervaded all.

Upon my entrance, Usher arose from a sofa upon which he had been lying at full length, and greeted me with a vivacious warmth which had much in it, I at first thought of an overdone cordiality – of the constrained effort of the ennuyé[3] man of the world. A glance, however, at his countenance convinced me of his perfect sincerity. We sat down; and for some moments, while he spoke not, I gazed upon him with a feeling half of pity, half of awe. Surely, man had never before so terribly altered, in so brief a period, as had Roderick Usher! It was with difficulty that I could bring myself to admit the identity of the wan being before me with the companion of my early boyhood. Yet the character of his face had been at all times remarkable. A cadaverousness of complexion; an eye large, liquid, and luminous beyond comparison; lips somewhat thin and very pallid, but of a surpassingly beautiful curve; a nose of a delicate Hebrew model, but with a

3. **ennuyé:** Bored (French).

breadth of nostril unusual in similar formations; a finely moulded chin, speaking, in its want of prominence, of a want of moral energy; hair of a more than web-like softness and tenuity; these features, with an inordinate expansion above the regions of the temple, made up altogether a countenance not easily to be forgotten. And now in the mere exaggeration of the prevailing character of these features, and of the expression they were wont to convey, lay so much of change that I doubted to whom I spoke. The now ghastly pallor of the skin, and the now miraculous lustre of the eye, above all things startled and even awed me. The silken hair, too, had been suffered to grow all unheeded, and as, in its wild gossamer texture, it floated rather than fell about the face, I could not, even with effort, connect its arabesque expression with any idea of simple humanity.

In the manner of my friend I was at once struck with an incoherence – an inconsistency; and I soon found this to arise from a series of feeble and futile struggles to overcome an habitual trepidancy, an excessive nervous agitation. For something of this nature I had indeed been prepared, no less by his letter, than by reminiscences of certain boyish traits and by conclusions deduced from his peculiar physical conformation and temperament. His action was alternately vivacious and sullen. His voice varied rapidly from a tremulous indecision (when the animal spirits seemed utterly in abeyance) to that species of energetic concision – that abrupt, weighty, unhurried, and hollow-sounding enunciation – that leaden, self-balanced and perfectly modulated guttural utterance, which may be observed in the moments of the intensest excitement of the lost drunkard, or the irreclaimable eater of opium.

It was thus that he spoke of the object of my visit, of his earnest desire to see me, and of the solace he expected me to afford him. He entered, at some length, into what he conceived to be the nature of his malady. It was, he said, a constitutional and a family evil, and one for which he despaired to find a remedy – a mere nervous affection, he immediately added, which would undoubtedly soon pass off. It displayed itself in a host of unnatural sensations. Some of these, as he detailed them, interested and bewildered me – although, perhaps, the terms, and the general manner of the narration had their weight. He suffered much from a morbid acuteness of the senses; the most insipid food was alone endurable; he could wear only garments of certain texture; the odors of all flowers were oppressive; his eyes were tortured by even a faint light; and there were but peculiar sounds, and those from stringed instruments, which did not inspire him with horror.

To an anomalous species of terror I found him a bounden slave. "I shall perish," said he, "I *must* perish in this deplorable folly. Thus, thus, and not otherwise, shall I be lost. I dread the events of the future, not in themselves, but in their results. I shudder at the thought of any, even the most trivial, incident, which may operate upon this intolerable agitation of soul. I have, indeed, no abhorrence of danger, except in its absolute effect – in terror. In this unnerved – in this pitiable condition – I feel that I must inevitably abandon life and reason together in my struggles with some fatal demon of fear."

I learned, moreover, at intervals, and through broken and equivocal hints, another singular feature of his mental condition. He was enchained by certain superstitious impressions in regard to the dwelling which he tenanted, and from which, for many years, he had never ventured forth – in regard to an influence whose supposititious force was conveyed in terms too shadowy here to be restated – an influence which some peculiarities in the mere form and substance of his family mansion, had, by dint of long sufferance, he said, obtained over his spirit – an effect which the *physique* of the gray walls and turrets, and of the dim tarn into which they all looked down, had, at length, brought about upon the *morale* of his existence.

He admitted, however, although with hesitation, that much of the peculiar gloom which thus afflicted him could be traced to a more natural and far more palpable origin – to the severe and long-continued illness – indeed to the evidently approaching dissolution – of a tenderly beloved sister; his sole companion for long years – his last and only relative on earth. "Her decease," he said, with a bitterness which I can never forget, "would leave him (him the hopeless and the frail) the last of the ancient race of the Ushers." As he spoke, the lady Madeline (for so was she called) passed slowly through a remote portion of the apartment, and, without having noticed my presence, disappeared. I regarded her with an utter astonishment not unmingled with dread. Her figure, her air, her features – all, in their very minutest development were those – were identically (I can use no other sufficient term) were identically those of the Roderick Usher who sat beside me. A feeling of stupor oppressed me, as my eyes followed her retreating steps. As a door, at length, closed upon her exit, my glance sought instinctively and eagerly the countenance of the brother – but he had buried his face in his hands, and I could only perceive that a far more than ordinary wanness had overspread the emaciated fingers through which trickled many passionate tears.

The disease of the lady Madeline had long baffled the skill of her physicians. A settled apathy, a gradual wasting away of the person, and frequent although transient affections of a partially cataleptical character, were the unusual diagnosis. Hitherto she had steadily borne up against the pressure of her malady, and had not betaken herself finally to bed; but, on the closing in of the evening of my arrival at the house, she succumbed, as her brother told me at night with inexpressible agitation, to the prostrating power of the destroyer – and I learned that the glimpse I had obtained of her person would thus probably be the last I should obtain – that the lady, at least while living, would be seen by me no more.

For several days ensuing, her name was unmentioned by either Usher or myself; and, during this period, I was buried in earnest endeavors to alleviate the melancholy of my friend. We painted and read together – or I listened, as if in a dream, to the wild improvisations of his speaking guitar. And thus, as a closer and still closer intimacy admitted me more unreservedly into the recesses of his spirit, the more bitterly did I perceive the futility of all attempt at cheering a mind from which darkness, as if an inherent positive quality, poured forth upon all objects of the moral and physical universe, in one unceasing radiation of gloom.

I shall ever bear about me, as Moslems in their shrouds at Mecca, a memory of the many solemn hours I thus spent alone with the master of the House of Usher. Yet I should fail in any attempt to convey an idea of the exact character of the studies, or of the occupations, in which he involved me, or led me the way. An excited and highly distempered ideality threw a sulphurous lustre over all. His long improvised dirges will ring for ever in my ears. Among other things, I bear painfully in mind a certain singular perversion and amplification of the wild air of the last waltz of Von Weber.[4] From the paintings over which his elaborate fancy brooded, and which grew, touch by touch, into vaguenesses at which I shuddered the more thrillingly, because I shuddered knowing not why, from these paintings (vivid as their images now are before me) I would in vain endeavor to educe more than a small portion which should lie within the compass of merely written words. By the utter simplicity, by the nakedness, of his designs, he arrested and over-awed attention. If ever mortal painted an idea, that mortal was Roderick Usher. For me at least – in the circumstances then surrounding me – there arose out of the pure abstractions which the hypochondriac contrived to throw upon his canvas, an intensity of intolerable awe, no shadow of which felt I ever yet in the contemplation of the certainly glowing yet too concrete reveries of Fuseli.[5]

One of the phantasmagoric conceptions of my friend, partaking not so rigidly of the spirit of abstraction, may be shadowed forth, although feebly, in words. A small picture presented the interior of an immensely long and rectangular vault or tunnel, with low walls, smooth, white, and without interruption or device. Certain accessory points of the design served well to convey the idea that this excavation lay at an exceeding depth below the surface of the earth. No outlet was observed in any portion of its vast extent, and no torch, or other artificial source of light was discernible – yet a flood of intense rays rolled throughout, and bathed the whole in a ghastly and inappropriate splendor.

I have just spoken of that morbid condition of the auditory nerve which rendered all music intolerable to the sufferer, with the exception of certain effects of stringed instruments. It was, perhaps, the narrow limits to which he thus confined himself upon the guitar, which gave birth, in great measure, to the fantastic character of his performances. But the fervid *facility* of his impromptus could not be so accounted for. They must have been, and were, in the notes, as well as in the words of his wild fantasias, (for he not unfrequently accompanied himself with rhymed verbal improvisations,) the result of that intense mental collectedness and concentration to which I have previously alluded as observable only in particular moments of the highest artificial excitement. The words of one of these rhapsodies I have easily borne away in memory. I was, perhaps, the more forcibly impressed with it, as he gave it, because, in the under or mystic current of its meaning, I fancied that I perceived, and for the first time, a full consciousness on the part of Usher, of the tottering of his lofty reason upon her throne. The verses, which were entitled "The Haunted Palace," ran very nearly, if not accurately, thus:

I

In the greenest of our valleys,
By good angels tenanted,
Once a fair and stately palace –
Snow-white palace – reared its head.

4. **Von Weber:** Carl Maria von Weber (1786–1826), German composer of Romantic operas.
5. **Fuseli:** Henry Fuseli (1741–1825), Swiss painter of fantastic, Gothic subjects and themes.

In the monarch Thought's dominion –
    It stood there!
Never seraph spread a pinion
    Over fabric half so fair.

II

Banners yellow, glorious, golden,
    On its roof did float and flow;
(This – all this – was in the olden
    Time long ago)
And every gentle air that dallied,
    In that sweet day,
Along the ramparts plumed and pallid,
    A winged odor went away.

III

Wanderers in that happy valley
    Through two luminous windows saw
Spirits moving musically
    To a lute's well-tunéd law,
Round about a throne, where sitting
    (Porphyrogene!)[6]
In state his glory well befitting,
    The sovereign of the realm was seen.

IV

And all with pearl and ruby glowing
    Was the fair palace door,
Through which came flowing, flowing, flowing,
    And sparkling evermore,
A troop of Echoes whose sole duty
    Was but to sing,
In voices of surpassing beauty,
    The wit and wisdom of their king.

V

But evil things, in robes of sorrow,
    Assailed the monarch's high estate;
(Ah, let us mourn, for never morrow
    Shall dawn upon him, desolate!)

---

6. **Porphyrogene:** Born in the purple, of royalty.

And, round about his home, the glory
That blushed and bloomed
Is but a dim-remembered story
Of the old time entombed.

VI

And travellers now within that valley,
Through the red-litten windows, see
Vast forms that move fantastically
To a discordant melody;
While, like a rapid ghastly river,
Through the pale door,
A hideous throng rush out forever,
And laugh – but smile no more.[7]

I well remember that suggestions arising from this ballad led us into a train of thought wherein there became manifest an opinion of Usher's which I mention not so much on account of its novelty, (for other men have thought thus,) as on account of the pertinacity with which he maintained it. This opinion, in its general form, was that of the sentience of all vegetable things. But, in his disordered fancy, the idea had assumed a more daring character, and trespassed, under certain conditions, upon the kingdom of inorganization. I lack words to express the full extent, or the earnest *abandon* of his persuasion. The belief, however, was connected (as I have previously hinted) with the gray stones of the home of his forefathers. The condition of the sentience had been here, he imagined, fulfilled in the method of collocation of these stones – in the order of their arrangement, as well as in that of the many fungi which overspread them, and of the decayed trees which stood around – above all, in the long undisturbed endurance of this arrangement, and in its reduplication in the still waters of the tarn. Its evidence – the evidence of the sentience – was to be seen, he said, (and I here started as he spoke,) in *the gradual yet certain condensation of an atmosphere of their own about the waters and the walls.* The result was discoverable, he added, in that silent, yet importunate and terrible influence which for centuries had moulded the destinies of his family, and which made *him* what I now saw him – what he was. Such opinions need no comment, and I will make none.

Our books[8] – the books which, for years, had formed no small portion of the mental existence of the invalid – were, as might be supposed, in strict keeping with this character of phantasm. We pored together over such works as the Ververt et Chartreuse of

---

7. **In the greenest . . . but smile no more:** The poem is by Poe; in the first printing of "The Fall of the House of Usher," the story was followed by an editorial note: "The ballad of 'The Haunted Palace,' introduced in this tale, was published separately, some months ago, in the Baltimore 'Museum.'" That magazine was the *American Museum*, published in Baltimore, Maryland.

8. **Our books:** All the titles listed here are real books dealing with demonism, the occult, and other aspects of pseudoscience.

Gresset; the Belphegor of Machiavelli; the Selenography of Brewster; the Heaven and Hell of Swedenborg; the Subterranean Voyage of Nicholas Klimm de Holberg; the Chiromancy of Robert Flud, of Jean d'Indaginé, and of De la Chambre; the Journey into the Blue Distance of Tieck; and the City of the Sun of Campanella. One favorite volume was a small octavo edition of the Directorium Inquisitorium, by the Dominican Eymeric de Gironne; and there were passages in Pomponius Mela, about the old African Satyrs and Oegipans, over which Usher would sit dreaming for hours. His chief delight, however, was found in the earnest and repeated perusal of an exceedingly rare and curious book in quarto Gothic – the manual of a forgotten church – the *Vigilae Mortuorum secundum Chorum Ecclesiae Maguntinae.*

I could not help thinking of the wild ritual of this work, and of its probable influence upon the hypochondriac, when, one evening, having informed me abruptly that the lady Madeline was no more, he stated his intention of preserving her corpse for a fortnight, previously to its final interment, in one of the numerous vaults within the main walls of the building. The wordly reason, however, assigned for this singular proceeding, was one which I did not feel at liberty to dispute. The brother had been led to his resolution (so he told me) by considerations of the unusual character of the malady of the deceased, of certain obtrusive and eager inquiries on the part of her medical men, and of the remote and exposed situation of the burial ground of the family. I will not deny that when I called to mind the sinister countenance of the person whom I met upon the staircase, on the day of my arrival at the house, I had no desire to oppose what I regarded as at best but a harmless, and not by any means an unnatural precaution.

At the request of Usher, I personally aided him in the arrangements for the temporary entombment. The body having been encoffined, we two alone bore it to its rest. The vault in which we placed it (and which had been so long unopened that our torches, half smothered in its oppressive atmosphere, gave us little opportunity for investigation) was small, damp, and utterly without means of admission for light; lying, at great depth, immediately beneath that portion of the building in which was my own sleeping apartment. It had been used, apparently, in remote feudal times, for the worst purposes of a donjon-keep, and, in later days, as a place of deposit for powder, or other highly combustible substance, as a portion of its floor, and the whole interior of a long archway through which we reached it, were carefully sheathed with copper. The door, of massive iron, had been, also, similarly protected. Its immense weight caused an unusually sharp grating sound, as it moved upon its hinges.

Having deposited our mournful burden upon tressels within the region of horror, we partially turned aside the yet unscrewed lid of the coffin, and looked upon the face of the tenant. The exact similitude between the brother and sister even here again startled and confounded me. Usher, divining, perhaps, my thoughts, murmured out some few words from which I learned that the deceased and himself had been twins, and that sympathies of a scarcely intelligible nature had always existed between them. Our glances, however, rested not long upon the dead – for we could not regard her unawed. The disease which had thus entombed the lady in the maturity of youth, had left, as usual in all maladies of a strictly cataleptical character, the mockery of a faint blush upon the bosom and the face, and that suspiciously lingering smile upon the lip which is so terrible in death. We replaced and screwed down the lid, and, having secured the door of iron, made our way, with toil, into the scarcely less gloomy apartments of the upper portion of the house.

And now, some days of bitter grief having elapsed, an observable change came over the features of the mental disorder of my friend. His ordinary manner had vanished. His ordinary occupations were neglected or forgotten. He roamed from chamber to chamber with hurried, unequal, and objectless step. The pallor of his countenance had assumed, if possible, a more ghastly hue – but the luminousness of his eye had utterly gone out. The once occasional huskiness of his tone was heard no more; and a tremulous quaver, as if of extreme terror, habitually characterized his utterance. – There were times, indeed, when I thought his unceasingly agitated mind was laboring with an oppressive secret, to divulge which he struggled for the necessary courage. At times, again, I was obliged to resolve all into the mere inexplicable vagaries of madness, as I beheld him gazing upon vacancy for long hours, in an attitude of the profoundest attention, as if listening to some imaginary sound. It was no wonder that his condition terrified – that it infected me. I felt creeping upon me, by slow yet certain degrees, the wild influences of his own fantastic yet impressive superstitions.

It was, most especially, upon retiring to bed late in the night of the seventh or eighth day after the entombment of the lady Madeline, that I experienced the full power of such feelings. Sleep came not near my couch – while the hours waned and waned away. I struggled to reason off the nervousness which had dominion over me. I endeavored to believe that much, if not all of what I felt, was due to the phantasmagoric influence of the gloomy furniture of the room – of the dark and tattered draperies, which, tortured into motion by the breath of a rising tempest, swayed fitfully to and fro upon the walls, and rustled uneasily about the decorations of the bed. But my efforts were fruitless. An irrepressible tremor gradually pervaded my frame; and, at length, there sat upon my very heart an incubus of utterly causeless alarm. Shaking this off with a gasp and a struggle, I uplifted myself upon the pillows, and, peering earnestly within the intense darkness of the chamber, harkened – I know not why, except that an instinctive spirit prompted me – to certain low and indefinite sounds which came, through the pauses of the storm, at long intervals, I knew not whence. Overpowered by an intense sentiment of horror unaccountable yet unendurable, I threw on my clothes with haste, for I felt that I should sleep no more during the night, and endeavored to arouse myself from the pitiable condition into which I had fallen, by pacing rapidly to and fro through the apartment.

I had taken but few turns in this manner, when a light step on an adjoining staircase arrested my attention. I presently recognized it as that of Usher. In an instant afterwards he rapped, with a gentle touch, at my door, and entered, bearing a lamp. His countenance was, as usual, cadaverously wan – but there was a species of mad hilarity in his eyes – an evidently restrained hysteria in his whole demeanor. His air appalled me – but any thing was preferable to the solitude which I had so long endured, and I even welcomed his presence as a relief.

"And you have not seen it!" he said abruptly, after having stared about him for some moments in silence – "you have not then seen it? – but, stay! you shall." Thus speaking, and having carefully shaded his lamp, he hurried to one of the gigantic casements, and threw it freely open to the storm.

The impetuous fury of the entering gust nearly lifted us from our feet. It was, indeed, a tempestuous yet sternly beautiful night, and one wildly singular in its terror and its beauty. A whirlwind had apparently collected its force in our vicinity; for here were frequent and violent alterations in the direction of the wind; and the exceeding density of the clouds (which hung so low as to press upon the turrets of the house) did not prevent our perceiving the life-like velocity with which they flew careering from all points against each other, without passing away into the distance. I say that even their exceeding density did not prevent our perceiving this – yet we had no glimpse of the moon or stars – nor was there any flashing forth of the lightning. But the under surfaces of the huge masses of agitated vapor, as well as all terrestrial objects immediately around us, were glowing in the unnatural light of a faintly luminous and distinctly visible gaseous exhalation which hung about and enshrouded the mansion.

"You must not – you shall not behold this!" said I, shudderingly, to Usher, as I led him, with a gentle violence, from the window to a seat. "These appearances, which bewilder you, are merely electrical phenomena not uncommon – or it may be that they have their ghastly origin in the rank miasma of the tarn. Let us close this casement – the air is chilling and dangerous to your frame. Here is one of your favorite romances. I will read, and you shall listen – and so we will pass away this terrible night together."

The antique volume which I had taken up was the "Mad Trist" of Sir Launcelot Canning[9] – but I had called it a favorite of Usher's more in sad jest than in earnest; for, in truth, there is little in its uncouth and unimaginative prolixity which could have had interest for the lofty and spiritual ideality of my friend. It was, however, the only book immediately at hand; and I indulged a vague hope that the excitement which now agitated the hypochondriac might find relief (for the history of mental disorder is full of similar anomalies) even in the extremeness of the folly which I should read. Could I have judged, indeed, by the wild, overstrained air of vivacity with which he harkened, or apparently harkened, to the words of the tale, I might have well congratulated myself upon the success of my design.

I had arrived at that well-known portion of the story where Ethelred, the hero of the Trist, having sought in vain for peaceable admission into the dwelling of the hermit, proceeds to make good an entrance by force. Here, it will be remembered, the words of the narrative run thus –

"And Ethelred, who was by nature of a doughty heart, and who was now mighty withal, on account of the powerfulness of the wine which he had drunken, waited no longer to hold parley with the hermit, who, in sooth, was of an obstinate and maliceful turn, but, feeling the rain upon his shoulders, and fearing the rising of the tempest, uplifted his mace outright, and, with blows, made quickly room in the plankings of the

9. **Canning:** The author and title of the tale are apparently fictitious, though its hero bears the name of an early English king, Ethelred (968?-1016).

door for his gauntleted hand, and now pulling therewith sturdily, he so cracked, and ripped, and tore all asunder, that the noise of the dry and hollow-sounding wood alarummed and reverberated throughout the forest."

At the termination of this sentence I started, and, for a moment, paused; for it appeared to me (although I at once concluded that my excited fancy had deceived me) – it appeared to me that, from some very remote portion of the mansion or of its vicinity, there came, indistinctly, to my ears, what might have been, in its exact similarity of character, the echo (but a stifled and dull one certainly) of the very cracking and ripping sound which Sir Launcelot had so particularly described. It was, beyond doubt, the coincidence alone which had arrested my attention; for, amid the rattling of the sashes of the casements, and the ordinary commingled noises of the still increasing storm, the sound; in itself, had nothing, surely, which should have interested or disturbed me. I continued the story.

"But the good champion Ethelred, now entering within the door, was sore enraged and amazed to perceive no signal of the maliceful hermit; but, in the stead thereof, a dragon of a scaly and prodigious demeanor, and of a fiery tongue, which sate in guard before a palace of gold, with a floor of silver; and upon the wall there hung a shield of shining brass with this legend enwritten –

> Who entereth herein, a conqueror hath bin,
> Who slayeth the dragon, the shield he shall win.

And Ethelred uplifted his mace, and struck upon the head of the dragon, which fell before him, and gave up his pesty breath, with a shriek so horrid and harsh, and withal so piercing, that Ethelred had fain to close his ears with his hands against the dreadful noise of it, the like whereof was never before heard."

Here again I paused abruptly, and now with a feeling of wild amazement – for there could be no doubt whatever that, in this instance, I did actually hear (although from what direction it proceeded I found it impossible to say) a low and apparently distant, but harsh, protracted, and most unusual screaming or grating sound – the exact counterpart of what my fancy had already conjured up as the sound of the dragon's unnatural shriek as described by the romancer.

Oppressed, as I certainly was, upon the occurrence of this second and most extraordinary coincidence, by a thousand conflicting sensations, in which wonder and extreme terror were predominant, I still retained sufficient presence of mind to avoid exciting, by any observation, the sensitive nervousness of my companion. I was by no means certain that he had noticed the sounds in question; although, assuredly, a strange alteration had, during the last few minutes, taken place in his demeanor. From a position fronting my own, he had gradually brought round his chair, so as to sit with his face to the door of the chamber, and thus I could but partially perceive his features, although I saw that his lips trembled as if he were murmuring inaudibly. His head had dropped upon his breast – yet I knew that he was not asleep, from the wide and rigid opening of the eye, as I caught a glance of it in profile. The motion of his body, too, was at variance with this idea – for he rocked from side to side with a gentle yet constant and uniform sway. Having rapidly taken notice of all this, I resumed the narrative of Sir Launcelot, which thus proceeded: –

"And now, the champion, having escaped from the terrible fury of the dragon, bethinking himself of the brazen shield, and of the breaking up of the enchantment which was upon it, removed the carcass from out of the way before him, and approached valorously over the silver pavement of the castle to where the shield was upon the wall; which in sooth tarried not for his full coming, but fell down at his feet upon the silver floor, with a mighty great and terrible ringing sound."

No sooner had these syllables passed my lips, than – as if a shield of brass had indeed, at the moment, fallen heavily upon a floor of silver – I became aware of a distinct, hollow, metallic, and clangorous, yet apparently muffled reverberation. Completely unnerved, I started convulsively to my feet, but the measured rocking movement of Usher was undisturbed. I rushed to the chair in which he sat. His eyes were bent fixedly before him, and throughout his whole countenance there reigned a more than stony rigidity. But, as I laid my hand upon his shoulder, there came a strong shudder over his frame; a sickly smile quivered about his lips; and I saw that he spoke in a low, hurried, and gibbering murmur, as if unconscious of my presence. Bending closely over his person, I at length drank in the hideous import of his words.

"Not hear it? – yes, I hear it, and *have* heard it. Long – long – long – many minutes, many hours, many days, have I heard it – yet I dared not – oh, pity me, miserable wretch that I am! – I dared not – *I dared* not speak! *We have put her living in the tomb!* Said I not that my senses were acute? – I *now* tell you that I heard her first feeble movements in the hollow coffin. I heard them – many, many days ago – yet I dared not – *I dared not speak!* And now – to-night – Ethelred – ha! ha! – the breaking of the hermit's door, and the death-cry of the dragon, and the clangor of the shield – say, rather, the rending of the coffin, and the grating of the iron hinges, and her struggles within the coppered archway of the vault! Oh whither shall I fly? Will she not be here anon? Is she not hurrying to upbraid me for my haste? Have I not heard her footsteps on the stair? Do I not distinguish that heavy and horrible beating of her heart? Madman!" – here he sprung violently to his feet, and shrieked out his syllables, as if in the effort he were giving up his soul – "Madman! *I tell you that she now stands without the door!*"

As if in the superhuman energy of his utterance there had been found the potency of a spell – the huge antique pannels to which the speaker pointed, threw slowly back, upon the instant, their ponderous and ebony jaws. It was the work of the rushing gust – but then without those doors there *did* stand the lofty and enshrouded figure of the lady Madeline of Usher. There was blood upon her white robes, and the evidence of some bitter struggle upon every portion of her emaciated frame. For a moment she remained trembling and reeling to and fro upon the threshold – then, with a low moaning cry, fell heavily inward upon the person of her brother, and in her horrible and now final death-agonies, bore him to the floor a corpse, and a victim to the terrors he had dreaded.

From that chamber, and from that mansion, I fled aghast. The storm was still abroad in all its wrath as I found myself crossing the old causeway. Suddenly there shot along the path a wild light, and I turned to see whence a gleam so unusual could have issued –

for the vast house and its shadows were alone behind me. The radiance was that of the full, setting, and blood-red moon, which now shone vividly through that once barely-discernible fissure, of which I have before spoken, as extending from the roof of the building, in a zig-zag direction, to the base. While I gazed, this fissure rapidly widened – there came a fierce breath of the whirlwind – the entire orb of the satellite burst at once upon my sight – my brain reeled as I saw the mighty walls rushing asunder – there was a long tumultuous shouting sound like the voice of a thousand waters – and the deep and dank tarn at my feet closed sullenly and silently over the fragments of the "*House of Usher.*"

[1839]

Poe's "The Tell-Tale Heart." This powerfully compressed tale, one of the shortest Poe wrote, was first published in the *Pioneer: A Literary and Critical Magazine*, a monthly established by the poet James Russell Lowell. Lowell's lofty ambitions for the magazine included the idea that it should "take as high an aim in art as may be" and that the contributors would have the freedom to publish what they pleased, free of any editorial meddling or restrictions. In a letter inviting Poe to contribute, Lowell promised him "*carte blanche* for prose or verse as may best please you" and offered $10 for each contribution – a reasonable sum at a time when many magazines paid contributors very little, or nothing at all. Poe's macabre tale of guilt and obsession, essentially a monologue in which an accused murderer protests his sanity, appeared alongside poems by Lowell and articles on Beethoven and the Boston Athenaeum, one of the oldest libraries and art galleries in the United States. Poe published one more story as well as an essay during the short run of the magazine, which ended in March 1843 – barely four months after it was established – when Lowell had insufficient funds to pay the printers and authors with whom he had contracts. The text of "The Tell-Tale Heart" is taken from its first printing in the *Pioneer*, January 1843.

The Tell-Tale Heart

Art is long and Time is fleeting,
And our hearts, though stout and brave,
Still, like muffled drums, are beating
Funeral marches to the grave.
-*Longfellow*[1]

True! – nervous – very, very dreadfully nervous I had been, and am; but why *will* you say that I am mad? The disease had sharpened my senses – not destroyed – not dulled

1. **Longfellow:** The epigraph is from "A Psalm of Life" by Henry Wadsworth Longfellow (1807-1882).

them. Above all was the sense of hearing acute. I heard all things in the heaven and in the earth. I heard many things in hell. How, then, am I mad? Harken! and observe how healthily – how calmly I can tell you the whole story.

It is impossible to say how first the idea entered my brain; but, once conceived, it haunted me day and night. Object there was none. Passion there was none. I loved the old man. He had never wronged me. He had never given me insult. For his gold I had no desire. I think it was his eye! – yes, it was this! He had the eye of a vulture – a pale blue eye, with a film over it. Whenever it fell upon me, my blood ran cold; and so, by degrees – very gradually – I made up my mind to take the life of the old man, and thus rid myself of the eye forever.

Now this is the point. You fancy me mad. Madmen know nothing. But you should have seen *me*. You should have seen how wisely I proceeded – with what caution – with what foresight – with what dissimulation I went to work! I was never kinder to the old man than during the whole week before I killed him. And every night, about midnight, I turned the latch of his door and opened it – oh so gently! And then, when I had made an opening sufficient for my head, I first put in a dark lantern, all closed, closed, so that no light shone out, and then I thrust in my head. Oh, you would have laughed to see how cunningly I thrust it in! I moved it slowly – very, very slowly, so that I might not disturb the old man's sleep. It took me an hour to place my whole head within the opening so far that I could see the old man as he lay upon his bed. Ha! – would a madman have been so wise as this? And then, when my head was well in the room, I undid the lantern cautiously – oh, so cautiously (for the hinges creaked) – I undid it just so much that a single thin ray fell upon the vulture eye. And this I did for seven long nights – every night just at midnight – but I found the eye always closed; and so it was impossible to do the work; for it was not the old man who vexed me, but his Evil Eye. And every morning, when the day broke, I went boldly into his chamber, and spoke courageously to him, calling him by name in a hearty tone, and inquiring how he had passed the night. So you see he would have been a very profound old man, indeed, to suspect that every night, just at twelve, I looked in upon him while he slept.

Upon the eighth night I was more than usually cautious in opening the door. A watch's minute-hand moves more quickly than did mine. Never, before that night, had I *felt* the extent of my own powers – of my sagacity. I could scarcely contain my feelings of triumph. To think that there I was, opening the door, little by little, and the old man not even to dream of my secret deeds or thoughts. I fairly chuckled at the idea. And perhaps the old man heard me; for he moved in the bed suddenly, as if startled. Now you may think that I drew back – but no. His room was as black as pitch with the thick darkness, (for the shutters were close fastened, through fear of robbers,) and so I knew that he could not see the opening of the door, and I kept on pushing it steadily, steadily.

I had got my head in, and was about to open the lantern, when my thumb slipped upon the tin fastening, and the old man sprang up in the bed, crying out – "Who's there?"

I kept quite still and said nothing. For another hour I did not move a muscle, and in the meantime I did not hear the old man lie down. He was still sitting up in the bed, listening; – just as I have done, night after night, hearkening to the death-watches in the wall.[2]

Presently I heard a slight groan, and I knew that it was the groan of mortal terror. It was not a groan of pain, or of grief – oh, no! – it was the low, stifled sound that arises from the bottom of the soul when overcharged with *awe*. I knew the sound well. Many a night, just at midnight, when all the world slept, it has welled up from my own bosom, deepening, with its dreadful echo, the terrors that distracted me. I say I knew it well. I knew what the old man felt, and pitied him, although I chuckled at heart. I knew that he had been lying awake ever since the first slight noise, when he had turned in the bed. His fears had been, ever since, growing upon him. He had been trying to fancy them causeless, but could not. He had been saying to himself – "It is nothing but the wind in the chimney – it is only a mouse crossing the floor," or "it is merely a cricket which has made a single chirp." Yes, he had been trying to comfort himself with these suppositions; but he had found all in vain. *All in vain*: because death, in approaching the old man, had stalked with his black shadow before him, and the shadow had now reached and enveloped the victim. And it was the mournful influence of the unperceived shadow that caused him to feel – although he neither saw nor heard me – to *feel* the presence of my head within the room.

When I had waited a long time, very patiently, without hearing the old man lie down, I resolved to open a little – a very, very little crevice in the lantern. So I opened it – you cannot imagine how stealthily, stealthily – until, at length, a single dim ray, like the thread of the spider, shot from out the crevice and fell full upon the vulture eye.

It was open – wide, wide open – and I grew furious as I gazed upon it. I saw it with perfect distinctness – all a dull blue, with a hideous veil over it that chilled the very marrow in my bones; but I could see nothing else of the old man's face or person; for I had directed the ray, as if by instinct, precisely upon the damned spot.

And now – have I not told you that what you mistake for madness is but over acuteness of the senses? – now, I say, there came to my ears *a low dull, quick sound — much such a sound as a watch makes when enveloped in cotton*. I knew *that* sound well, too. It was the beating of the old man's heart. It increased my fury, as the beating of a drum stimulates the soldier into courage.

But even yet I refrained and kept still. I scarcely breathed. I held the lantern motionless. I tried how steadily I could maintain the ray upon the eye. Meantime the hellish tattoo of the heart increased. It grew quicker, and louder and louder every instant. The old man's terror *must* have been extreme! It grew louder, I say, louder every moment: – do you mark me well? I have told you that I am nervous: – so I am. And now, at the dead hour of night, and amid the dreadful silence of that old house, so strange a noise as this excited me to uncontrollable wrath. Yet, for some minutes longer, I refrained and kept still. But the beating grew louder, *louder*! I thought the heart must burst! And now a new anxiety seized me – the sound would be heard by a neighbor! The old man's hour had

---

2. **death-watches in the wall:** Several kinds of beetles make a clicking sound by striking their heads against wood, which was sometimes thought to be predictive of death.

come! With a loud yell, I threw open the lantern and leaped into the room. He shrieked once – once only. In an instant I dragged him to the floor, and pulled the heavy bed[3] over him. I then sat upon the bed and smiled gaily, to find the deed so far done. But, for many minutes, the heart beat on, with a muffled sound. This, however, did not vex me; it would not be heard through the walls. At length it ceased. The old man was dead. I removed the bed and examined the corpse. Yes, he was stone, stone dead. I placed my hand upon the heart and held it there many minutes. There was no pulsation. The old man was stone dead. His eye would trouble *me* no more.

If, still, you think me mad, you will think so no longer when I describe the wise precautions I took for the concealment of the body. The night waned, and I worked hastily, but in silence. First of all I dismembered the corpse. I cut off the head and the arms and the legs. I then took up three planks from the flooring of the chamber, and deposited all between the scantlings.[4] I then replaced the boards so cleverly, so cunningly, that no human eye – not even *his* – could have detected anything wrong. There was nothing to wash out – no stain of any kind – no blood-spot whatever. I had been too wary for that. A tub had caught all – ha! ha!

When I had made an end of these labors, it was four o'clock – still dark as midnight. As the bell sounded the hour, there came a knocking at the street door. I went down to open it with a light heart, – for what had I *now* to fear? There entered three men, who introduced themselves, with perfect suavity, as officers of the police. A shriek had been heard by a neighbor during the night; suspicion of foul play had been aroused; information had been lodged at the police-office, and they (the officers) had been deputed to search the premises.

I smiled, – for *what* had I to fear? I bade the gentlemen welcome. The shriek, I said, was my own in a dream. The old man, I mentioned, was absent in the country. I took my visiters all over the house. I bade them search – search *well*. I led them, at length, to *his* chamber. I showed them his treasures, secure, undisturbed. In the enthusiasm of my confidence, I brought chairs into the room, and desired them *here* to rest from their fatigues; while I myself, in the wild audacity of my perfect triumph, placed my own seat upon the very spot beneath which reposed the corpse of the victim.

The officers were satisfied. My *manner* had convinced them. I was singularly at ease. They sat, and, while I answered cheerily, they chatted of familiar things. But, ere long, I felt myself getting pale and wished them gone. My head ached, and I fancied a ringing in my ears: but still they sat and still chatted. The ringing became more distinct: I talked more freely, to get rid of the feeling; but it continued and gained definitiveness – until, at length, I found that the noise was *not* within my ears.

No doubt I now grew *very* pale; – but I talked more fluently, and with a heightened voice. Yet the sound increased – and what could I do? It was *a low, dull, quick sound – much such a sound as a watch makes when enveloped in cotton*. I gasped for breath – and yet the officers heard it not. I talked more quickly – more vehemently; – but the

3. **heavy bed:** A heavy comforter often used as a mattress.
4. **scantlings:** Upright planks supporting the walls of a house.

noise steadily increased. I arose, and argued about trifles, in a high key and with violent gesticulations; – but the noise steadily increased. Why *would* they not be gone? I paced the floor to and fro, with heavy strides, as if excited to fury by the observations of the men; – but the noise steadily increased. Oh God! what *could* I do? I foamed – I raved – I swore! I swung the chair upon which I had sat, and grated it upon the boards; – but the noise arose over all and continually increased. It grew louder – louder – *louder*! And still the men chatted pleasantly, and smiled. Was it possible they heard not? Almighty God! – no, no! They heard! – they suspected! – they *knew*! – they were making a mockery of my horror! – this I thought, and this I think. But anything better than this agony! Anything was more tolerable than this derision! I could bear those hypocritical smiles no longer! I felt that I must scream or die! – and now – again! – hark! louder! louder! louder! *louder*! – "Villains!" I shrieked, "dissemble no more! I admit the deed! – tear up the planks! – here, here! – it is the beating of his hideous heart!"

[1843]

Poe's "The Purloined Letter." This story is among the more famous of Poe's "tales of ratiocination," stories based on logical and methodical reasoning. Poe is considered by many to be the first writer of American detective stories, and his amateur detective, C. Auguste Dupin, is the forerunner of Sherlock Holmes, the enormously popular detective later created by the English writer Arthur Conan Doyle. In fact, Holmes mentions reading Poe and admiring his work in Doyle's story "The Cardboard Box" (1893). "The Purloined Letter," the third story to feature Dupin, first appeared in *The Gift*, one of the series of popular gift books published from the mid-1820s through the Civil War. Such literary annuals were beautifully bound and illustrated volumes that usually appeared late in the year (with the following year's publication date), just in time to be given as Christmas presents. By the mid-1840s, about sixty such gift books were being published each year. *The Gift* for 1845 included poetry by Henry Wadsworth Longfellow, Lydia Sigourney, and Ralph Waldo Emerson, as well as stories by Caroline Kirkland, Nathaniel P. Willis, and Poe. "The Purloined Letter" was included in Poe's second collection of stories, *Tales* (1845). The text is taken from its first printing in *The Gift* (1845).

THE PURLOINED LETTER

At Paris, just after dark one gusty evening in the autumn of 18–, I was enjoying the twofold luxury of meditation and a meerschaum, in company with my friend C. Auguste Dupin, in his little back library, or book-closet, *au troisième*,[1] *No.* 33, *Rue Dunôt, Faubourg St. Germain.* For one hour at least we had maintained a profound silence;

1. ***au troisième***: On the third floor; since the French do not number the ground floor, an American would locate Dupin's apartment on the fourth floor.

while each, to any casual observer, might have seemed intently and exclusively occupied with the curling eddies of smoke that oppressed the atmosphere of the chamber. For myself, however, I was mentally discussing certain topics which had formed matter for conversation between us at an earlier period of the evening; I mean the affair of the Rue Morgue, and the mystery attending the murder of Marie Roget. I looked upon it, therefore, as something of a coincidence, when the door of our apartment was thrown open and admitted our old acquaintance, Monsieur G—, the Prefect of the Parisian police.

We gave him a hearty welcome; for there was nearly half as much of the entertaining as of the contemptible about the man, and we had not seen him for several years. We had been sitting in the dark, and Dupin now arose for the purpose of lighting a lamp, but sat down again, without doing so, upon G.'s saying that he had called to consult us, or rather to ask the opinion of my friend, about some official business which had occasioned a great deal of trouble.

"If it is any point requiring reflection," observed Dupin, as he forbore to enkindle the wick, "we shall examine it to better purpose in the dark."

"That is another of your odd notions," said the Prefect, who had a fashion of calling every thing "odd" that was beyond his comprehension, and thus lived amid an absolute legion of "oddities."

"Very true," said Dupin, as he supplied his visiter with a pipe, and rolled towards him a very comfortable chair.

"And what is the difficulty now?" I asked. "Nothing more in the assassination way, I hope?"

"Oh no; nothing of that nature. The fact is, the business is *very* simple indeed, and I make no doubt that we can manage it sufficiently well ourselves; but then I thought Dupin would like to hear the details of it, because it is so excessively *odd*."

"Simple and odd," said Dupin.

"Why, yes; and not exactly that, either. The fact is, we have all been a good deal puzzled because the affair *is* so simple, and yet baffles us altogether."

"Perhaps it is the very simplicity of the thing which puts you at fault," said my friend.

"What nonsense you *do* talk!" replied the Prefect, laughing heartily.

"Perhaps the mystery is a little *too* plain," said Dupin.

"Oh, good heavens! who ever heard of such an idea?"

"A little *too* self-evident."

"Ha! ha! ha! – ha! ha! ha! – ho! ho! ho!" roared out our visiter, profoundly amused, "oh, Dupin, you will be the death of me yet!"

"And what, after all, *is* the matter on hand?" I asked.

"Why, I will tell you," replied the Prefect, as he gave a long, steady, and contemplative puff, and settled himself in his chair. "I will tell you in a few words; but, before I begin, let me caution you that this is an affair demanding the greatest secrecy, and that I should most probably lose the position I now hold, were it known that I confided it to any one."

"Proceed," said I.

"Or not," said Dupin.

"Well, then; I have received personal information, from a very high quarter, that a certain document of the last importance, has been purloined from the royal apartments.

The individual who purloined it is known; this beyond a doubt; he was seen to take it. It is known, also, that it still remains in his possession."

"How is this known?" asked Dupin.

"It is clearly inferred," replied the Prefect, "from the nature of the document, and from the non-appearance of certain results which would at once arise from its passing *out* of the robber's possession; – that is to say, from his employing it as he must design in the end to employ it."

"Be a little more explicit," I said.

"Well, I may venture so far as to say that the paper gives its holder a certain power in a certain quarter where such power is immensely valuable." The Prefect was fond of the cant of diplomacy.

"Still I do not quite understand," said Dupin.

"No? Well; the disclosure of the document to a third person, who shall be nameless, would bring in question the honour of a personage of most exalted station; and this fact gives the holder of the document an ascendancy over the illustrious personage whose honour and peace are so jeopardized."

"But this ascendancy," I interposed, "would depend upon the robber's knowledge of the loser's knowledge of the robber. Who would dare –"

"The thief," said G, "is the – Minister D—, who dares all things, those unbecoming as well as those becoming a man. The method of the theft was not less ingenious than bold. The document in question – a letter, to be frank – had been received by the personage robbed while alone in the royal *boudoir*. During its perusal she was suddenly interrupted by the entrance of the other exalted personage from whom especially it was her wish to conceal it. After a hurried and vain endeavour to thrust it in a drawer, she was forced to place it, open as it was, upon a table. The address, however, was uppermost, and the contents thus unexposed, the letter escaped notice. At this juncture enters the Minister D—. His lynx eye immediately perceives the paper, recognises the handwriting of the address, observes the confusion of the personage addressed, and fathoms her secret. After some business transactions, hurried through in his ordinary manner, he produces a letter somewhat similar to the one in question, opens it, pretends to read it, and then places it in close juxtaposition to the other. Again he converses, for some fifteen minutes, upon the public affairs. At length, in taking leave, he takes also from the table the letter to which he had no claim. Its rightful owner saw, but, of course, dared not call attention to the act, in the presence of the third personage who stood at her elbow. The minister decamped; leaving his own letter – one of no importance – upon the table."

"Here, then," said Dupin to me, "you have precisely what you demand to make the ascendancy complete – the robber's knowledge of the loser's knowledge of the robber."

"Yes," replied the Prefect; "and the power thus attained has, for some months past, been wielded, for political purposes, to a very dangerous extent. The personage robbed is more thoroughly convinced, every day, of the necessity of reclaiming her letter. But this, of course, cannot be done openly. In fine, driven to despair, she has committed the matter to me."

"Than whom," said Dupin, amid a perfect whirlwind of smoke, "no more sagacious agent could, I suppose, be desired, or even imagined."

"You flatter me," replied the Prefect; "but it is possible that some such opinion may have been entertained."

"It is clear," said I, "as you observe, that the letter is still in possession of the minister; since it is this possession, and not any employment, of the letter, which bestows the power. With the employment the power departs."

"True," said G—; "and upon this conviction I proceeded. My first care was to make thorough search of the minister's hotel; and here my chief embarrassment lay in the necessity of searching without his knowledge. Beyond all things, I have been warned of the danger which would result from giving him reason to suspect our design."

"But," said I, "you are quite *au fait*[2] in these investigations. The Parisian police have done this thing often before."

"O yes; and for this reason I did not despair. The habits of the minister gave me, too, a great advantage. He is frequently absent from home all night. His servants are by no means numerous. They sleep at a distance from their master's apartments, and, being chiefly Neapolitans, are readily made drunk. I have keys, as you know, with which I can open any chamber or cabinet in Paris. For three months a night has not passed, during the greater part of which I have not been engaged, personally, in ransacking the D— Hotel. My honour is interested, and, to mention a great secret, the reward is enormous. So I did not abandon the search until I had become fully satisfied that the thief is a more astute man than myself. I fancy that I have investigated every nook and corner of the premises in which it is possible that the paper can be concealed."

"But is it not possible," I suggested, "that although the letter may be in possession of the minister, as it unquestionably is, he may have concealed it elsewhere than upon his own premises?"

"This is barely possible," said Dupin. "The present peculiar condition of affairs at court, and especially of those intrigues in which D— is known to be involved, would render the instant availability of the document – its susceptibility of being produced at a moment's notice – a point of nearly equal importance with its possession."

"Its susceptibility of being produced?" said I.

"That is to say, of being *destroyed*," said Dupin.

"True," I observed; "the paper is clearly then upon the premises. As for its being upon the person of the minister, we may consider that as out of the question."

"Entirely," sad the Prefect. "He has been twice waylaid, as if by footpads[3] and his person rigorously searched under my own inspection."

"You might have spared yourself this trouble," said Dupin. "D—, I presume, is not altogether a fool, and, if not, must have anticipated these waylayings, as a matter of course."

"Not *altogether* a fool," said G—, "but then he's a poet, which I take to be only one remove from a fool."

"True;" said Dupin, after a long and thoughtful whiff from his meerschaum, "although I have been guilty of certain doggerel myself."

"Suppose you detail," said I, "the particulars of your search."

---

2. ***au fait***: Informed (French).
3. **footpads**: Early term for street robbers on foot.

"Why the fact is, we took our time, and we searched *every where*. I have had long experience in these affairs. I took the entire building, room by room; devoting the nights of a whole week to each. We examined, first, the furniture of each apartment. We opened every possible drawer; and I presume you know that, to a properly trained police agent, such a thing as a *secret* drawer is impossible. Any man is a dolt who permits a 'secret' drawer to escape him in a search of this kind. The thing is *so* plain. There is a certain amount of bulk – of space – to be accounted for in every cabinet. Then we have accurate rules. The fiftieth part of a line could not escape us. After the cabinets we took the chairs. The cushions we probed with the fine long needles you have seen me employ. From the tables we removed the tops."

"Why so?"

"Sometimes the top of a table, or other similarly arranged piece of furniture, is removed by the person wishing to conceal an article; then the leg is excavated, the article deposited within the cavity, and the top replaced. The bottoms and tops of bed-posts are employed in the same way."

"But could not the cavity be detected by sounding?" I asked.

"By no means, if, when the article is deposited, a sufficient wadding of cotton be placed around it. Besides, in our case, we were obliged to proceed without noise."

"But you could not have removed – you could not have taken to pieces *all* articles of furniture in which it would have been possible to make a deposit in the manner you mention. A letter may be compressed into a thin spiral roll, not differing much in shape or bulk from a large knitting-needle, and in this form it might be inserted into the rung of a chair, for example. You did not take to pieces all the chairs?"

"Certainly not; but we did better – we examined the rungs of every chair in the hotel, and, indeed, the jointings of every description of furniture, by the aid of a most powerful microscope. Had there been any traces of recent disturbance we should not have failed to detect it *instanter*.[4] A single grain of gimlet-dust, or saw-dust, for example, would have been as obvious as an apple. Any disorder in the glueing – any unusual gaping in the joints – would have sufficed to insure detection."

"Of course you looked to the mirrors, between the boards and the plates, and you probed the beds and the bed-clothes, as well as the curtains and carpets."

"That of course; and when we had absolutely completed every particle of the furniture in this way, then we examined the house itself. We divided its entire surface into compartments, which we numbered, so that none might be missed; then we scrutinized each individual square inch throughout the premises, including the two houses immediately adjoining, with the microscope, as before."

"The two houses adjoining!" I exclaimed; "you must have had a great deal of trouble."

"We had; but the reward offered is prodigious."

"You include the *grounds* about the houses?"

"All the grounds are paved with brick. They gave us comparatively little trouble. We examined the moss between the bricks, and found it undisturbed."

4. ***instanter***: At the instant; instantly (French).

"And the roofs?"

"We surveyed every inch of the external surface, and probed carefully beneath every tile."

"You looked among D—'s papers, of course, and into the books of the library?"

"Certainly; we opened every package and parcel; we not only opened every book, but we turned over every leaf in each volume, not contenting ourselves with a mere shake, according to the fashion of some of our police officers. We also measured the thickness of every book-*cover*, with the most accurate admeasurement, and applied to them the most jealous scrutiny of the microscope. Had any of the bindings been recently meddled with, it would have been utterly impossible that the fact should have escaped observation. Some five or six volumes, just from the hands of the binder, we carefully probed, longitudinally, with the needles."

"You explored the floors beneath the carpets?"

"Beyond doubt. We removed every carpet, and examined the boards with the microscope."

"And the paper on the walls?"

"Yes."

"You looked into the cellars?"

"We did; and, as time and labour were no objects, we dug up every one of them to the depth of four feet."

"Then," I said, "you have been making a miscalculation, and the letter is *not* upon the premises, as you suppose."

"I fear you are right there," said the Prefect. "And now, Dupin, what would you advise me to do?"

"To make a thorough re-search of the premises."

"That is absolutely needless," replied G—. "I am not more sure that I breathe than I am that the letter is not at the Hotel."

"I have no better advice to give you," said Dupin. "You have, of course, an accurate description of the letter?"

"Oh yes!" – And here the Prefect, producing a memorandum-book, proceeded to read aloud a minute account of the internal, and especially of the external, appearance of the missing document. Soon after finishing the perusal of this description, he took his departure, more entirely depressed in spirits than I had ever known the good gentleman before.

In about a month afterwards he paid us another visit, and found us occupied very nearly as before. He took a pipe and a chair, and entered into some ordinary conversation. At length I said, –

"Well, but G—, what of the purloined letter? I presume you have at last made up your mind that there is no such thing as overreaching the Minister?"

"Confound him, say I – yes; I made the re-examination, however, as Dupin suggested – but it was all labour lost, as I knew it would be."

"How much was the reward offered, did you say?" asked Dupin.

"Why, a very great deal – a *very* liberal reward – I don't like to say how much, precisely; but one thing I *will* say, that I wouldn't mind giving my individual check for fifty thousand francs to any one who could obtain me that letter. The fact is, it is becoming of more and more importance every day; and the reward has been lately doubled. If it were trebled, however, I could do no more than I have done."

"Why, yes," said Dupin, drawlingly, between the whiffs of his meerschaum, "I really – think, G—, you have not exerted yourself – to the utmost in this matter. You might – do a little more, I think, eh?"

"How? – in what way?"

"Why – puff, puff – you might – puff, puff – employ counsel in the matter, eh? – puff, puff, puff. Do you remember the story they tell of Abernethy?"

"No; hang Abernethy!"

"To be sure! hang him and welcome. But, once upon a time, a certain rich miser conceived the design of spunging upon this Abernethy for a medical opinion. Getting up, for this purpose, an ordinary conversation in a private company, he insinuated his case to the physician, as that of an imaginary individual.

"'We will suppose,' said the miser, 'that his symptoms are such and such; now, doctor, what would *you* have directed him to take?'

"'Take!' said Abernethy, 'why, take *advice*, to be sure.'"

"But," said the Prefect, a little discomposed, "*I* am *perfectly* willing to take advice, and to pay for it. I would *really* give fifty thousand francs, every *centime* of it, to any one who would aid me in the matter!"

"In that case," replied Dupin, opening a drawer, and producing a check-book, "you may as well fill me up a check for the amount mentioned. When you have signed it, I will hand you the letter."

I was astounded. The Prefect appeared absolutely thunder-stricken. For some minutes he remained speechless and motionless, looking incredulously at my friend with open mouth, and eyes that seemed starting from their sockets; then, apparently recovering himself in some measure, he seized a pen, and after several pauses and vacant stares, finally filled up and signed a check for fifty thousand francs, and handed it across the table to Dupin. The latter examined it carefully and deposited it in his pocket-book; then, unlocking an *escritoire*,[5] took thence a letter and gave it to the Prefect. This functionary grasped it in a perfect agony of joy, opened it with a trembling hand, cast a rapid glance at its contents, and then, scrambling and struggling to the door, rushed at length unceremoniously from the room and from the house, without having uttered a solitary syllable since Dupin had requested him to fill up the check.

When he had gone, my friend entered into some explanation.

"The Parisian police," he said, "are exceedingly able in their way. They are persevering, ingenious, cunning, and thoroughly versed in the knowledge which their duties seem chiefly to demand. Thus, when G— detailed to us his mode of searching the premises at the Hotel D—, I felt entire confidence in his having made a satisfactory investigation – so far as his labours extended."

"So far as his labours extended?" said I.

5. ***escritoire***: Writing desk (French).

"Yes," said Dupin. "The measures adopted were not only the best of their kind, but carried out to absolute perfection. Had the letter been deposited within the range of their search, these fellows would, beyond a question, have found it."

I merely laughed – but he seemed quite serious in all that he said.

"The measures, then," he continued, "were good in their kind, and well executed; their defect lay in their being inapplicable to the case, and to the man. A certain set of highly ingenious resources are, with the Prefect, a sort of Procrustean bed,[6] to which he forcibly adapts his designs. But he perpetually errs by being too deep or too shallow, for the matter in hand; and many a schoolboy is a better reasoner than he. I knew one about eight years of age, whose success at guessing in the game of 'even and odd' attracted universal admiration. This game is simple, and is played with marbles. One player holds in his hand a number of these toys, and demands of another whether that number is even or odd. If the guess is right, the guesser wins one; if wrong, he loses one. The boy to whom I allude won all the marbles of the school. Of course he had some principle of guessing; and this lay in mere observation and admeasurement of the astuteness of his opponents. For example, an arrant simpleton is his opponent, and, holding up his closed hand, asks, 'are they even or odd?' Our schoolboy replies, 'odd,' and loses; but upon the second trial he wins, for he then says to himself, 'the simpleton had them even upon the first trial, and his amount of cunning is just sufficient to make him have them odd upon the second; I will therefore guess odd;' – he guesses odd, and wins. Now, with a simpleton a degree above the first, he would have reasoned thus: 'this fellow finds that in the first instance I guessed odd, and, in the second, he will propose to himself, upon the first impulse, a simple variation from even to odd, as did the first simpleton; but then a second thought will suggest that this is too simple a variation, and finally he will decide upon putting it even as before. I will therefore guess even;' – he guesses even, and wins. Now this mode of reasoning in the schoolboy, whom his fellows termed 'lucky,' – what, in its last analysis, is it?"

"It is merely," I said, "an identification of the reasoner's intellect with that of his opponent."

"It is," said Dupin; "and, upon inquiring of the boy by what means he effected the *thorough* identification in which his success consisted, I received answer as follows: 'When I wish to find out how wise, or how stupid, or how good, or how wicked is any one, or what are his thoughts at the moment, I fashion the expression of my face, as accurately as possible, in accordance with the expression of his, and then wait to see what thoughts or sentiments arise in my mind or heart, as if to match or correspond with the expression.' This response of the schoolboy lies at the bottom of all the spurious profundity which has been attributed to Rochefoucault, to La Bougive, to Machiavelli, and to Campanella."[7]

---

6. **Procrustean bed:** In Greek mythology, Procrustes was a robber who forced travelers to lie on a bed and either cut off parts of their limbs or stretched them to fit; *procrustean* means the enforcement of conformity by arbitrary means and without regard for natural variation.

7. **Rochefoucault . . . Campanella:** Printer's errors in this passage may account for some misspelling. François La Rochefoucauld (1613-1680) was a French writer known for his epigrams and pithy sayings. La Bougive is probably Jean La Bruyére (1645-1696), a French writer of maxims and character sketches. Niccolò Machiavelli (1469-1527) was an Italian political writer, best known for *The Prince*, a treatise on the uses of power and the art of ruling. Tommaso Campanella (1568-1639) was an Italian philosopher.

"And the identification," I said, "of the reasoner's intellect with that of his opponent, depends, if I understand you aright, upon the accuracy with which the opponent's intellect is admeasured."

"For its practical value it depends upon this," replied Dupin; "and the Prefect and his cohort fail so frequently, first, by default of this identification, and, secondly, by ill-admeasurement, or rather through non-admeasurement, of the intellect with which they are engaged. They consider only their *own* ideas of ingenuity; and, in searching for any thing hidden, advert only to the modes in which *they* would have hidden it. They are right in this much – that their own ingenuity is a faithful representative of that of *the mass*; but when the cunning of the individual felon is diverse in character from their own, the felon foils them, of course. This always happens when it is above their own, and very usually when it is below. They have no variation of principle in their investigations; at best, when urged by some unusual emergency – by some extraordinary reward – they extend or exaggerate their old modes of *practice*, without touching their principles. What, for example, in this case of D—, has been done to vary the principle of action? What is all this boring, and probing, and sounding, and scrutinizing with the microscope, and dividing the surface of the building into registered square inches – what is it all but an exaggeration *of the application* of the one principle or set of principles of search, which are based upon the one set of notions regarding human ingenuity, to which the Prefect, in the long routine of his duty, has been accustomed? Do you not see he has taken it for granted that *all* men proceed to conceal a letter, – not exactly in a gimlet-hole bored in a chair-leg – but, at least, in *some* out-or-the-way hole or corner suggested by the same tenor of thought which would urge a man to secrete a letter in a gimlet-hole bored in a chair-leg? And do you not see also, that such *recherches*[8] nooks for concealment are adapted only for ordinary occasions, and would be adopted only by ordinary intellects; for, in all cases of concealment, a disposal of the article concealed – a disposal of it in this *recherché* manner, – is, in the very first instance, presumed and presumable; and thus its discovery depends, not at all upon the acumen, but altogether upon the mere care, patience, and determination of the seekers; and where the case is of importance – or, what amounts to the same thing in the policial eyes, when the reward is of magnitude, the qualities in question have *never* been known to fail. You will now understand what I meant in suggesting that, had the purloined letter been hidden any where within the limits of the Prefect's examination – in other words, had the principle of its concealment been comprehended within the principles of the Prefect – its discovery would have been a matter altogether beyond question. This functionary, however, has been thoroughly mystified; and the remote source of his defeat lies in the supposition that the Minister is a fool, because he has acquired renown as a poet. All fools are poets; this the Prefect *feels*; and he is merely guilty of a *non distributio medii*[9] in thence inferring that all poets are fools."

---

8. ***recherches***: Sought after (French).

9. ***non distributio medii***: The undistributed middle (Latin) refers to a fallacy in formal logic in which the two premises of a syllogism do not justify the conclusion.

"But is this really the poet?" I asked. "There are two brothers, I know; and both have attained reputation in letters. The Minister I believe has written learnedly on the Differential Calculus. He is a mathematician, and no poet."

"You are mistaken; I know him well; he is both. As poet *and* mathematician, he would reason well; as poet, profoundly; as mere mathematician, he could not have reasoned at all, and thus would have been at the mercy of the Prefect."

"You surprise me," I said, "by these opinions, which have been contradicted by the voice of the world. You do not mean to set at naught the well-digested idea of centuries. The mathematical reason has been long regarded as *the* reason *par excellence*."

"'Il y a à parièr,' replied Dupin, quoting from Chamfort, 'que toute idée publique, toute convention reçue, est une sottise, car elle a convenue au plus grand nombre.'[10] The mathematicians, I grant you, have done their best to promulgate the popular error to which you allude, and which is none the less an error for its promulgation as truth. With an art worthy a better cause, for example, they have insinuated the term 'analysis' into application to algebra. The French are the originators of this particular deception; but if a term is of any importance – if words derive any value from applicability – then 'analysis' conveys 'algebra' about as much as, in Latin '*ambitus*' implies 'ambition,' '*religio*' 'religion,' or '*homines honesti*,' a set of *honourable* men."

"You have a quarrel on hand, I see," said I, "with some of the algebraists of Paris; but proceed."

"I dispute the availability, and thus the value, of that reason which is cultivated in any especial form other than the abstractly logical. I dispute, in particular, the reason educed by mathematical study. The mathematics are the science of form and quantity; mathematical reasoning is merely logic applied to observation upon form and quantity. The great error lies in supposing that even the truths of what is called *pure* algebra, are abstract or general truths. And this error is so egregious that I am confounded at the universality with which it has been received. Mathematical axioms are *not* axioms of general truth. What is true of *relation* – of form and quantity – is often grossly false in regard to morals, for example. In this latter science it is very usually *un*true that the aggregated parts are equal to the whole. In chemistry also the axiom fails. In the consideration of motive it fails; for two motives, each of a given value, have not, necessarily, a value when united, equal to the sum of their values apart. There are numerous other mathematical truths which are only truths within the limits of *relation*. But the mathematician argues, from his *finite truths*, through habit, as if they were of an absolutely general applicability – as the world indeed imagines them to be. Bryant,[11] in his very learned 'Mythology,' mentions an analogous source of error, when he says that 'although the Pagan fables are not believed, yet we forget ourselves continually, and make

---

10. **'Il y a . . . nombre'**: From a maxim of the French writer Sébastien Roch Nicolas Chamfort (1741-1794): "The odds are that every common notion, every accepted convention, is nonsense, precisely because it has suited itself to the majority."

11. **Bryant**: Jacob Bryant (1715-1804), English author of *A New System; or, An Analysis of Ancient Mythology* (1774).

inferences from them as existing realities.' With the algebraist, however, who are Pagans themselves, the 'Pagan fables' *are* believed, and the inferences are made, not so much through lapse of memory, as through an unaccountable addling of the brains. In short, I never yet encountered the mere mathematician who could be trusted out of equal roots, or one who did not clandestinely hold it as a point of his faith that $x^2 + px$ was absolutely and unconditionally equal to q. Say to one of these gentlemen, by way of experiment, if you please, that you believe occasions may occur where $x^2 + px$ is *not* altogether equal to q, and, having made him understand what you mean, get out of his reach as speedily as convenient, for, beyond doubt, he will endeavour to knock you down.

"I mean to say," continued Dupin, while I merely laughed at his last observations, "that if the Minister had been no more than a mathematician, the Prefect would have been under no necessity of giving me this check. Had he been no more than a poet, I think it probable that he would have foiled us all. I knew him, however, as both mathematician and poet, and my measures were adapted to his capacity, with reference to the circumstances by which he was surrounded. I knew him as a courtier, too, and as a bold *intriguant.* Such a man, I considered, could not fail to be aware of the ordinary policial modes of action. He could not have failed to anticipate – and events have proved that he did not fail to anticipate – the waylayings to which he was subjected. He must have foreseen, I reflected, the secret investigations of his premises. His frequent absences from home at night, which were hailed by the Prefect as certain aids to his success, I regarded only as *ruses*, to afford opportunity for thorough search to the police, and thus the sooner to impress them with the conviction to which G—, in fact, did finally arrive – the conviction that the letter was not upon the premises. I felt, also, that the whole train of thought, which I was at some pains in detailing to you just now, concerning the invariable principle of policial action in searches for articles concealed – I felt that this whole train of thought would necessarily pass through the mind of the Minister. It would imperatively lead him to despise all the ordinary *nooks* of concealment. *He* could not, I reflected, be so weak as not to see that the most intricate and remote recess of his hotel would be as open as his commonest closets to the eyes, to the probes, to the gimlets, and to the microscopes of the Prefect. I saw, in fine, that he would be driven, as a matter of course, to *simplicity*, if not deliberately induced to it as a matter of choice. You will remember, perhaps, how desperately the Prefect laughed when I suggested, upon our first interview, that it was just possible this mystery troubled him so much on account of its being so *very* self-evident."

"Yes," said I, "I remember his merriment well. I really thought he would have fallen into convulsions."

"The material world," continued Dupin, "abounds with very strict analogies to the immaterial; and thus some colour of truth has been given to the rhetorical dogma, that metaphor, or simile, may be made to strengthen an argument, as well as to embellish a description. The principle of the *vis inertiae*,[12] for example, with the amount of *momentum* proportionate with it and consequent upon it, seems to be identical in physics and

12. ***vis inertiae***: The power of inertia (Latin).

metaphysics. It is not more true in the former, that a large body is with more difficulty set in motion than a smaller one, and that its subsequent *impetus* is commensurate with this difficulty, than it is, in the latter, that intellects of the vaster capacity, while more forcible, more constant, and more eventful in their movements than those of inferior grade, are yet the less readily moved, and more embarrassed and full of hesitation in the first few steps of their progress. Again: have you ever noticed which of the street signs, over the shop-doors, are the most attractive of attention?"

"I have never given the matter a thought," I said.

"There is a game of puzzles," he resumed, which is played upon a map. One party playing requires another to find a given word – the name of town, river, state, or empire – any word, in short, upon the motley and perplexed surface of the chart. A novice in the game generally seeks to embarrass his opponents by giving them the most minutely lettered names; but the adept selects such words as stretch, in large characters, from one end of the chart to the other. These, like the over-largely lettered signs and placards of the street, escape observation by dint of being excessively obvious; and here the physical oversight is precisely analogous with the moral inapprehension by which the intellect suffers to pass unnoticed those considerations which are too obtrusively and too palpably self-evident. But this is a point, it appears, somewhat above or beneath the understanding of the Prefect. He never once thought it probable, or possible, that the Minister had deposited the letter immediately beneath the nose of the whole world, by way of best preventing any portion of that world from perceiving it.

"But the more I reflected upon the daring, dashing, and discriminating ingenuity of D—; upon the fact that the document must always have been *at hand*, if he intended to use it to good purpose; and upon the decisive evidence, obtained by the Prefect, that it was not hidden within the limits of that dignitary's ordinary search – the more satisfied I became that, to conceal this letter, the Minister had resorted to the comprehensive and sagacious expedient of not attempting to conceal it at all.

"Full of these ideas, I prepared myself with a pair of green spectacles, and called one fine morning, quite by accident, at the ministerial hotel. I found D— at home, yawning, lounging, and dawdling as usual, and pretending to be in the last extremity of *ennui*.[13] He is, perhaps, the most really energetic human being now alive – but that is only when nobody sees him.

"To be even with him, I complained of my weak eyes, and lamented the necessity of the spectacles, under cover of which I cautiously and thoroughly surveyed the whole apartment, while seemingly intent only upon the conversation of my host.

"I paid especial attention to a large writing-table near which he sat, and upon which lay confusedly, some miscellaneous letters and other papers, with one or two musical instruments and a few books. Here, however, after a long and very deliberate scrutiny, I saw nothing to excite particular suspicion.

"At length my eyes, in going the circuit of the room, fell upon a trumpery fillagree card-rack of pasteboard, that hung dangling by a dirty blue riband, from a little brass

13. ***ennui***: Boredom (French).

knob just beneath the middle of the mantel-piece. In this rack, which had three or four compartments, were five or six visiting-cards, and a solitary letter. This last was much soiled and crumpled. It was torn nearly in two, across the middle – as if a design, in the first instance, to tear it entirely up as worthless, had been altered, or stayed, in the second. It had a large black seal, bearing the D— cipher *very* conspicuously, and was addressed, in a diminutive female hand, to D—, the minister, himself. It was thrust carelessly, and even, as it seemed, contemptuously, into one of the uppermost divisions of the rack.

"No sooner had I glanced at this letter, than I concluded it to be that of which I was in search. To be sure, it was, to all appearance, radically different from the one of which the Prefect had read us so minute a description. Here the seal was large and black, with the D— cipher; there, it was small and red, with the ducal arms of the S— family. Here, the address, to the minister, was diminutive and feminine; there, the superscription, to a certain royal personage, was markedly bold and decided; the size alone formed a point of correspondence. But, then, the *radicalness* of these differences, which was excessive; the dirt, the soiled and torn condition of the paper, so inconsistent with the *true* methodical habits of D—, and so suggestive of a design to delude the beholder into an idea of the worthlessness of the document; these things, together with the hyperobtrusive situation of this document, full in the view of every visiter, and thus exactly in accordance with the conclusions to which I had previously arrived; these things, I say, were strongly corroborative of suspicion, in one who came with the intention to suspect.

"I protracted my visit as long as possible, and, while I maintained a most animated discussion with the minister, upon a topic which I knew well had never failed to interest and excite him, I kept my attention really riveted upon the letter. In this examination, I committed to memory its external appearance and arrangement in the rack; and also fell, at length, upon a discovery which set at rest whatever trivial doubt I might have entertained. In scrutinizing the edges of the paper, I observed them to be more *chafed* than seemed necessary. They presented the *broken* appearance which is manifested when a stiff paper, having been once folded and pressed with a folder, is refolded in a reversed direction, in the same creases or edges which had formed the original fold. This discovery was sufficient. It was clear to me that the letter had been turned, as a glove, inside out, re-directed, and re-sealed. I bade the minister good morning, and took my departure at once, leaving a gold snuff-box upon the table.

"The next morning I called for the snuff-box, when we resumed, quite eagerly, the conversation of the preceding day. While thus engaged, however, a loud report, as if of a pistol, was heard immediately beneath the windows of the hotel, and was succeeded by a series of fearful screams, and the shoutings of a terrified mob. D— rushed to a casement, threw it open, and looked out. In the meantime, I stepped to the card-rack, took the letter, put it in my pocket, and replaced it by a *fac-simile*, which I had carefully prepared at my lodgings – imitating the D— cipher, very readily, by means of a seal formed of bread.

"The disturbance in the street had been occasioned by the frantic behaviour of a man with a musket. He had fired it among a crowd of women and children. It proved, however, to have been without ball, and the fellow was suffered to go his way as a lunatic or a drunkard. When he had gone, D— came from the window, whither I had followed him immediately upon securing the object in view. Soon afterwards I bade him farewell. The pretended lunatic was a man in my own pay."

"But what purpose had you," I asked, "in replacing the letter by a *fac-simile*? Would it not have been better, at the first visit, to have seized it openly, and departed?"

"D—," replied Dupin, "is a desperate man, and a man of nerve. His hotel, too, is not without attendants devoted to his interests. Had I made the wild attempt you suggest, I should never have left the ministerial presence alive. The good people of Paris would have heard of me no more. But I had an object apart from these considerations. You know my political prepossessions. In this matter, I act as a partisan of the lady concerned. For eighteen months the minister has had her in his power. She has now him in hers – since, being unaware that the letter is not in his possession, he will proceed with his exactions as if it was. Thus will he inevitably commit himself, at once, to his political destruction. His downfall, too, will not be more precipitate than awkward. It is all very well to talk about the *facilis descensus Averni*;[14] but in all kinds of climbing, as Catalini[15] said of singing, it is far more easy to get up than to come down. In the present instance I have no sympathy – at least no pity – for him who descends. He is that *monstrum horrendum*,[16] an unprincipled man of genius. I confess, however, that I should like very well to know the precise character of his thoughts, when, being defied by her whom the Prefect terms 'a certain personage,' he is reduced to opening the letter which I left for him in the card-rack."

"How? did you put any thing particular in it?"

"Why – it did not seem altogether right to leave the interior blank – that would have been insulting. To be sure, D—, at Vienna once, did me an evil turn, which I told him, quite good-humouredly, that I should remember. So, as I knew he would feel some curiosity in regard to the identity of the person who had outwitted him, I thought it a pity not to give him a clue. He is well acquainted with my MS., and I just copied into the middle of the blank sheet the words,

"'—Un dessein si funeste,
S'il n'est digne d'Atrée, est digne de Thyeste.'

They are to be found in Crébillon's 'Atrée.'"[17]

[1845]

---

14. ***facilis descensus Averni***: From the *Aeneid* by the Roman poet Virgil (70-19 BCE), meaning the descent to hell is easy.
15. **Catalini**: Probably a printer's error for Angelica Catalani (1780-1849), an Italian singer.
16. ***monstrum horrendum***: Frightful monster. Virgil's name for Polyphemus, a one-eyed, man-eating giant.
17. **"Un dessein . . . Atrée"**: "A design so deadly, if not worthy of Atreus is worthy of Thyestes," from *Atrée et Thyeste* by Prosper Jolyot de Crébillon (1674-1762). In the tragedy, Thyestes seduces Atreus's wife and, in revenge, Atreus kills Thyestes' sons and serves them to him at a dinner.

Fanny Fern
(Sara Payson Willis Parton)

[1811–1872]

Fanny Fern was born Sara Payson Willis on July 9, 1811, in Portland, Maine, the daughter of Nathaniel and Hannah Parker Willis. Fern's family was deeply involved in periodical publication. Her father founded the *Boston Recorder,* the first religious newspaper in the United States, and the *Youth's Companion,* the first children's newspaper. Fern's older brother, the popular poet and writer Nathaniel P. Willis, was the influential editor of the *New York Mirror* and later the *Home Journal.* Educated at Catharine Beecher's Female Seminary in Hartford, Connecticut, Fern also proved to be adept at writing and occasionally published articles in the *Hartford Courant.* In 1837, she married Charles Harrington Eldredge, a cashier at a Boston bank. When Eldredge died of typhoid fever in 1846, Fern and her two young daughters were left nearly penniless. Receiving only limited support from her father and father-in-law, Fern tried unsuccessfully to find work as a teacher and then as a seamstress. In 1849, under pressure from her father, she married Samuel P. Farrington, a cruel and jealous man, whom Fern left after two years. Farrington obtained a divorce on the grounds of desertion in 1852, a drastic measure in the mid-nineteenth century.

bedfordstmartins.com/ americanlit *for research links on Fern*

Facing the censure of her relatives and determined to make a living for herself and her children, Fern decided to follow in the family tradition of

Sketch of Fanny Fern

This sketch of Fanny Fern reading was drawn by her daughter Ellen around 1860. The text at the base of the sketch reads: "*Sarah Willis Parton* – copied from a 'picture that little Nellie drew' of her mother; described by her sister Grace as 'a very bad likeness – yet funnily like, too, in some respects.'" (Sophia Smith Collection, Smith College.)

journalism. After months of effort, she sold her first article to a popular family newspaper, the *Olive Branch*, where "The Model Husband" appeared on June 28, 1851. She was soon writing reviews and articles on a variety of domestic and social topics for both the *Olive Branch* and another family newspaper, the *True Flag*. By the fall of 1851, her work was appearing under the name of "Fanny Fern," which she took as her legal name. In September 1852, when she entered into an agreement to write a weekly article for the *Musical World and Times*, she became the first weekly newspaper columnist in the United States. Her first collection of articles, *Fern Leaves from Fanny's Port-Folio*, was published in June 1853 and sold an astonishing 70,000 copies in the first year. *Little Ferns for Fanny's Little Friends*, a collection of essays for children, appeared later that year; and *Fern Leaves from Fanny's Port-Folio*, Second Series, appeared in 1854. Now a highly successful journalist, Fern moved to New York City. There, she wrote for a variety of prominent periodicals. Taking advantage of her growing fame, she also published a novel, *Ruth Hall* (1854), a thinly veiled account of her difficult early life. After reading the novel, Nathaniel Hawthorne declared, "The woman writes as if the devil was in her," an admiring reference to Fern's rejection of the social and stylistic conventions governing many works written by women during the period. Two other works of fiction followed: *Fanny Ford* (1855), a serialized novella, and *Rose Clarke* (1856).

Everybody buys Fern Leaves, big Ferns and little Ferns, and everybody reads, and everybody laughs and cries over it.
–Frederick Douglass

By then, Fern was the best-paid writer, male or female, in the United States. On January 5, 1856, she married James Parton, a writer and biographer. In an act that was almost unheard of at the time, when a married woman had no legal right to her own earnings, the couple signed a prenuptial agreement stipulating that the income Fern made from her writing was her own. Fern had just signed a contract to write exclusively for the *New York Ledger*, where her first weekly column appeared on her wedding day. Some of her enormously popular columns, devoted to witty cultural commentary and sharp social criticism, were subsequently collected in *Fresh Leaves* (1857), *Folly as It Flies* (1868), *Ginger Snaps* (1870), and *Caper-Sauce* (1872). During almost seventeen years, Fern never missed a deadline for the *Ledger*, where her final weekly column appeared two days after her death from cancer on October 10, 1872.

Fern's Early Journalism. The following two articles first appeared in the *Olive Branch*, a popular family newspaper published in Boston. Short articles and stories printed in the newspaper were frequently read aloud by families gathered for evening amusement, and Fern developed a breezy, colloquial style designed to engage a broad audience. Her columns were often witty commentaries on marriage and the domestic lives of women. She also took up social issues such as the growing consumerism and materialism of life in the United States. Fern was paid $2 for each of her articles, which were often reprinted without her knowledge or permission in other periodicals, since copyright laws did not prevent such "copying" of periodical writings. The text of "The Tear of a Wife," which appeared in the *Olive Branch* on August 28, 1852, is taken from *Fern Leaves from Fanny's Port-Folio* (1853); the text of "Dollars and Dimes," which appeared in the *Olive Branch* on June 18, 1853, is taken from *Fern Leaves from Fanny's Port-Folio,* Second Series (1854).

THE TEAR OF A WIFE

"The tear of a loving girl is like a dew-drop on a rose; but on the cheek of a wife, is a drop of poison to her husband."[1]

It is "an ill wind that blows nobody any good." Papas will be happy to hear that twenty-five dollar pocket-handkerchiefs can be dispensed with now, in the bridal *trousseau.*[2] Their "occupation's gone"! Matrimonial tears "are poison." There is no knowing what you will do, girls, with that escape-valve shut off; but that is no more to the point, than – whether you have anything to smile at or not; one thing is settled – you must not cry! Never mind back-aches, and side-aches, and head-aches, and dropsical complaints, and smoky chimneys, and old coats, and young babies! Smile! It flatters your husband. He wants to be considered the source of your happiness, whether he was baptized Nero or Moses! Your mind never being supposed to be occupied with any other subject than himself, of course a tear is a tacit reproach. Besides, you miserable little whimperer! what have you to cry for? A-i-n-t y-o-u m-a-r-r-i-e-d? Is n't that the *summum bonum,*[3] – the height of feminine ambition? You can't get beyond that! It is the jumping-off place! You've arriv! – got to the end of your journey! Stage puts up there! You have nothing to do but retire on your laurels, and spend the rest of your life endeavoring to be thankful that you are Mrs. John Smith! "Smile!" you simpleton!

[1852, 1853]

1. **"The tear . . . husband":** The quotation is unidentified, but the sentiment was a common one in the nineteenth century.
2. ***trousseau*:** Clothing for a bride (French).
3. ***summum bonum*:** The greatest or supreme good (Latin).

DOLLARS AND DIMES

"Dollars and dimes, dollars and dimes,
An empty pocket is the worst of crimes."[1]

Yes; and don't you presume to show yourself anywhere, until you get it filled. "Not among good people?" No, my dear Simplicity, not among "good people." They will receive

1. **"Dollars . . . crimes":** The epigraph is from "The Popular Creed" (c. 1852), a song written by Charles P. Shiras (1824–1854). Stephen Foster (1826–1864) may have composed the music for the song, which was frequently performed by the Hutchinson Family, a popular group that sang songs about abolition, labor, women's rights, and temperance.

you with a galvanic ghost of a smile, scared up by an indistinct recollection of the "ten commandments," but it will be as short-lived as their stay with you. You are not welcome – that's the amount of it. They are all in a perspiration lest you should be delivered of a request for their assistance, before they can get rid of you. They are "very busy," and what's more, they always will be busy when you call, until you get to the top of fortune's ladder.

Climb, man! climb! Get to the top of the ladder, though adverse circumstances and false friends break every round in it! and see what a glorious and extensive prospect of human nature you'll get when you arrive at the summit! Your gloves will be worn out shaking hands with the very people who did n't recognize your existence two months ago. "You must come and make me a long visit;" "you must stop in at any time;" "*you'll* always be welcome;" it is such a *long* time since they had the pleasure of a visit from you, that they begin to fear you never intended to come; and they'll cap the climax by inquiring with an injured air, "if you are nearsighted, or why you have so often passed them in the street without speaking."

Of course, you will feel very much like laughing in their faces, and so you can. You can't do anything wrong, now that your "pocket is full." At the most, it will only be "an eccentricity." You can use anybody's neck for a footstool, bridle anybody's mouth with a silver bit, and have as many "golden opinions" as you like. You won't see a frown again between this and your tombstone!

[1853, 1854]

Fern's Writings for the *New York Ledger*. Beginning with her first column on January 5, 1856, Fern wrote exclusively for the *New York Ledger*, a weekly edited by Robert Bonner. Although the family story-paper was designed to provide entertainment within the home, Bonner had no interest in dull, conventional material. Determined to make the *Ledger* a first-rate literary periodical, he set about hiring the best writers he could sign, including Lydia Sigourney, John Greenleaf Whittier, Henry Wadsworth Longfellow, and Louisa May Alcott. Unlike many other editors of the day, who paid little or nothing for irregular contributions from both known and unknown writers, Bonner also developed a system of exclusive contracts for regular contributors, who earned fixed and generous salaries. When "Fanny Fern" was becoming a household name for her articles in several competing periodicals, Bonner secured such a contract with her. At the end of 1855, when Bonner proudly announced that Fern would become an exclusive writer for the *Ledger*, its circulation stood at 100,000; during the following year, it grew to 180,000. By 1860, circulation topped 400,000, in large part as a result of the powerful appeal of Fern's weekly columns. The following articles indicate some of her characteristic concerns, including the social criticism of "Blackwell's Island," which appeared in three consecutive installments in August 1858, and, as always, the condition of women, addressed in "The 'Coming' Woman," which appeared on February 12, 1859. The texts are taken from the first printings of the columns in the *New York Ledger*.

BLACKWELL'S ISLAND[1]

Number I

Prior to visiting Blackwell's Island last week, my ideas of that place were very forlorn and small-pox-y. It makes very little difference, to be sure, to a man, or a woman, shut up in a cell eight feet by four, how lovely are the out-door surroundings; how blue the river that plashes against the garden wall below, flecked with white sails, and alive with gay pleasure-seekers, whose merry laugh has no monotone of sadness, that the convict wears the badge of degradation; and yet after all, one involuntarily says to oneself, so instinctively do we turn to the cheerful side, I am glad they are located on this lovely island. Do you shrug your shoulders, Sir Cynic, and number over the crimes they have committed? Are *your* crimes against society less, that they are written down only in God's book of remembrance? Are *you* less guilty that you have been politic enough to commit only those that a short-sighted, unequal, human law sanctions? Shall I pity these poor wrecks of humanity less, because they are so recklessly self-wrecked? because they turn away from my pity? Before I come to this, I must know, as their Maker knows, what evil influences have encircled their cradles. How many times when their stomachs have been empty, some full-fed, whining disciple, has presented them with a Bible or a Tract, saying, Be ye warmed and filled. I must know how often when their feet have tried to climb the narrow, up-hill path of right, the eyes that have watched, have watched only for their halting; never noting, as God notes, the steps that did *not* slip – never holding out the strong right hand of help when the devil with a full larder was tugging furiously at their skirts to pull them backward; – but only saying – "I told you so," when he, laughing at your pharasaical stupidity, succeeded.

I must go a great way back of those hard, defiant faces, where hate of their kind seems indelibly burnt in; – back – back – to the soft blue sky of infancy, overclouded before the little one had strength to contend with the flashing lightning and pealing thunder of misfortune and poverty which stunned and blinded his moral perceptions. I cannot see that mournful procession of men, filing off into those dark cells, none too dark, none too narrow, alas! to admit troops of devils, without wishing that some white-winged angel might enter too; and when their shining eye-balls peer at my retreating figure through the gratings, my heart shrieks out in its pain – oh! believe that there is pity here – only pity; – and I hate the bolts and bars, and I say this is *not* the way to make bad men good; or, at least if it be, these convicts should not, when discharged, be thrust out loose into the world with empty pockets, and a bad name, to earn a speedy "through-ticket" back again. I say, if this *be* the way, let humanity not stop here, but take one noble step forward, and when she knocks off the convict's fetters, and lands him on

1. **Blackwell's Island:** In the mid-nineteenth century, Blackwell's Island was the site of a complex of buildings that included a penitentiary, a workhouse, an almshouse, and a lunatic asylum. One of the three islands located in the East River in New York City, Blackwell's (now Roosevelt's Island) earned a reputation as a dangerous, frightening place. Conditions for both men and especially women were harsh, and many women reformers of the period, including Margaret Fuller, visited and wrote about Blackwell's in order to call attention to the need for institutional and social change.

the opposite shore, let her not turn her back and leave him there as if her duty were done; but let her *there* erect a noble institution where he can find a *kind* welcome and *instant* employment; before temptation joining hands with his necessities, plunge him again headlong into the gulf of sin.

And here seems to me to be the loose screw in all these institutions; admirably managed as many of them are, according to the prevalent ideas on the subject. You may tell me that I am a woman, and know nothing about it; and I tell you that I *want* to know. I tell you, that I don't believe the way to restore a man's lost self-respect, is to degrade him before his fellow-creatures; to brand him, and chain him, and poke him up to show his points, like a hyena in a menagerie. No wonder that he growls at you, and grows vicious; no wonder that he eats the food you thrust between the bars of his cage with gnashing teeth, and a vow to take it out of the world somehow, when he gets out; no wonder that he thinks the Bible you place in his cell a humbug, and God a myth. I would have you startle up his self-respect by placing him in a position to show that you trusted him; I would have you give him something to hold in charge, for which he is in honor responsible; appeal to his *better* feelings, or if they smolder almost to extinction, fan them into a flame for him out of that remnant of God's image which the vilest can never wholly destroy. *Anything but shutting a man up with hell in his heart to make him good.* The devils may well chuckle at it. And above all – tear down that taunting inscription over the prison-hall door at Blackwell's Island – "The way of transgressors is hard" – and place instead of it, "Neither do I condemn thee; go and sin no more."[2]

Number II

It is a great blessing when they who are about the sick in any department, are themselves of robust physique, cheerful countenance, and winning speech. The invalid is insensibly magnetized by such a healthful atmosphere, catching the inspiration of the bright eye and springing step. Certain it is that I never look upon such without feeling my chest expand and my breath come freer; what then must be the effect upon the feeble and dispirited? Mark the introduction of a merry traveling party at some dull way-station, into a car full of jaded, hungry, cross travelers. See one after another shake himself up from his ungraceful posture; mark the brow unknit, and the compressed lips relax into smiles. He who, a moment ago, was at swords-points with all the world, is now bursting off his waistband buttons in the attempt to raise or shut a window for a person he never set eyes on before, and may never see again after that day's travel. Thank God, then, I say, for every man or woman with a smiling face and *cheery* voice; and thank Him doubly when such have the desire, as well as the power, to unweave the tangled web which insanity has spun over the delicate brain. For these and other reasons, Dr. Ranney

2. **"The way of transgressors is hard . . . sin no more":** The inscription over the main door of the prison was taken from Proverbs 13:5: "Good understanding giveth favor: but the way of the transgressors is hard." Fern suggests that the inscription should be replaced by Christ's words to the woman taken in adultery: "Neither do I condemn thee: go, and sin no more" (John 8:11).

seems to me admirably well calculated to fill the responsible office of physician to the lunatic department[3] on Blackwell's Island; and as I saw his patients walking up and down the long halls, out of which their neatly appointed rooms opened, the window of each commanding a view of sea, sky and woodland, as diverse as beautiful, I could not but thankfully contrast it with the stupid past-time tyranny which placed such unfortunate sufferers on a par with criminals, lashing and goading their unsettled intellects far beyond the faintest hope of recall.

It is curious how each lunatic inevitably hugs to his deluded breast the idea that he is the only sane person in the establishment. (I have known many people *out* of a lunatic asylum give the same convincing proof of their qualifications to be in it!) One gentleman, whose appearance interested me, and with whom I conversed as we walked up and down the lawn, thought the Island a fine place for "these people," as he patronizingly termed his fellow sufferers. Doctor Ranney, finding his patients disinclined to exercise, hit upon the ingenious expedient of organizing a military company, who, with caps and drum, were parading under the trees after their own fashion, with a ludicrously solemn earnestness that would have quite *doubled up* the "seventh regiment."[4] "Do you like us, your friends, to come from the city to see you?" I asked of a quiet-looking woman, who was pacing up and down the hall. "When you don't stay too long, and talk too much," was her sharp reply. I amused myself imagining the diplomatic world we had left, "speaking out in meetin'," after this fashion. I am not at all sure that the wheels of society need be greased with so much fibbing and flattery to keep them from creaking. A young girl, into the half-opened door of whose room I glanced as I passed, started to her indignant feet with such a tragic "How *dare* you?" that I was forced to believe that the proverb, "Every man's house should be his castle," held as true of the lunatic as of any body else. The more violent of Dr. Ranney's patients are in a secure building by themselves, and much as I wished to see them, I could not urge it, when I learned that such visits were to their injury; but in my dreams that night their pale hands, as I saw them extended through the gratings when I passed, seemed to beckon me back, and my sleep was broken and unrefreshing.

Not the least interesting portion of the inmates were the paupers, especially the long halls appropriated to the mothers with their new-born babies – bright, lovely little things they were, too, fated, perhaps, who knows? to come back to that very spot with *their* babies, as their mothers had before them. One pretty little creature lay nestled on a bed alone by itself, with its little fat arms tossed gracefully above its rosy face, as if some sculptor had laid it there. And so He had! and I questioned not His goodness, or wisdom, or mercy; though its sleeping hours may be all it ever knows of Heaven this side

3. **lunatic department**: One of the areas of Blackwell's Island was devoted to an asylum for "lunatics," or those suffering from various kinds of mental disease. Since diagnosis of these illnesses was in its infancy, the asylum was a complex place, difficult to organize and administer. Dr. Ranney, mentioned occasionally in newspapers and journals of the time as a specialist in mental diseases, was probably Lafayette Ranney, MD (1819–1883).

4. **"seventh regiment"**: The Seventh Regiment of Manhattan, dubbed the "Silk Stocking Regiment" because of its socially prominent members.

the grave; though I know not why He should have lain it on that pauper bed, instead of the downy one which plenty delights to deck for its own.

Oh, the soft blue, and bright black eyes in those baby heads! the flitting smile on the waxen features; the little gleeful, dancing hands; the pride of motherhood, so touching then and there to see, and which, beaming forth from the coarsest face, makes it for the time angelic.

The mystery of life! who can solve it? Eternity were none too long to turn its blotted pages. Faith can trust and wait.

Number III

You can step aside, Mrs. Grundy;[5] what I am about to write is not for your over-fastidious ear. *You*, who take by the hand the polished roue, and welcome him with a sweet smile to the parlor where sit your young, trusting daughters; you, who "have no business with his private life, so long as his manners are gentlemanly;" you who, while saying this, turn away with bitter, unwomanly words from his penitent, writhing victim. I ask no leave of *you* to speak of the wretched girls picked out of the gutters of New York streets, to inhabit those cells at Blackwell's Island. I speak not to *you* of what was tugging at my heartstrings as I saw them, that beautiful summer afternoon, file in, two by two, to their meals, followed by a man carrying a cowhide in his hand, by way of reminder; all this would not interest you; but when you tell me that these women are not to be named to ears polite, that our sons and our daughters should grow up ignorant of their existence, I stop my ears. As if they could, or did! As if they can take a step in the public streets without being jostled or addressed by them, or pained by their passing ribaldry; as if they could return from a party or concert at night, without meeting droves of them; as if they could, even in broad daylight, sit down to an ice-cream without having one for a vis-à-vis. As if they could ride in a car or omnibus, or cross in a ferry-boat, or go to a watering-place, without being unmistakably confronted by them. No, Mrs. Grundy; you know all this as well as I do. You would push them "anywhere out of the world," as unfit to live, as unfit to die; *they*, the weaker party, while their partners in sin, for whom you claim greater mental superiority, and who, by your own finding, should be much better able to learn and *to teach* the lesson of self-control – to them you extend perfect absolution. Most consistent Mrs. Grundy, get out of my way while I say what I was going to, without fear or favor of yours.

If I believed, as legislators, and others with whom I have talked on this subject, pretend to believe, they best know why, that God ever made one of those girls for the life they lead, for this in plain Saxon is what their talk amounts to, I should curse Him. If I could temporise as they do about it, as "a necessary evil," and "always has been, and always will be," and (then add this beautiful tribute to manhood) "that pure women would not be safe were it not so" – and all the other budget of excuses which this sin makes to cover its deformity – I would forswear my manhood.

5. **Mrs. Grundy:** A nineteenth-century term for a person who is overly concerned with conventional standards of propriety.

You say their intellects are small, they are mere animals, naturally coarse and groveling. Answer me this – are they, or are they not *immortal*? Decide the question whether *this* life is to be *all* to them. Decide before you shoulder the responsibility of such a girl's future. Granted she has only *this* life. God knows how much misery may be crowded into that. But you say, "Bless your soul, why do you talk to *me*? I have nothing to do with it; I am as virtuous as St. Paul." St. Paul was a bachelor, and of course is not my favorite apostle; but waiving that, I answer, you *have* something to do with it when you talk thus, and throw your influence on the wrong side. No matter how outwardly correct your past life may have been, if you *really believe* what you say, I would not give a fig for your virtue if temptation and opportunity favored; and if you talk so for talk's sake, and do not believe it, you had better "tarry at Jericho till your beard be grown."[6]

But you say to me, "Oh, you don't know anything about it; men are differently constituted from women; woman's sphere is home." That don't suspend the laws of her being. That don't make it that she don't need sympathy and appreciation. That don't make it that she is never weary and needs amusement to restore her. Fudge. I believe in no difference that makes this distinction. Women lead, most of them, lives of unbroken monotony, and have much more need of exhilarating influences than men, whose life is out of doors in the breathing, active world.[7] Don't tell me of shoemakers at their lasts, and tailors at their needles. Do either ever have to lay down their customers' coats and shoes fifty times a day, and wonder when the day is over why their work is *not* done, though they have struggled through fire and water to finish it? Do not both tailor and shoemaker have at least the variation of a walk to or from the shop to their meals? Do not their customers talk their beloved politics to them while they stitch, and do not their "confreres" run for a bottle of ale and crack merry joke with them as their work progresses? Sirs! if monotony is to be avoided in man's life as injurious; if "variety" and exhilaration must always be the spice to his pursuits, how much more must it be necessary to a sensitively organized woman? If home is not sufficient, (and I will persist that any *industrious, virtuous, unambitious* man, may have a home if he chooses); if home is not sufficient for him, why should it suffice for her? whose work is never done – who can have literally *no* such thing as system, (and here's where a mother's discouragement comes in), while her babes are in their infancy; who often says to herself at night, though she would not for worlds part with one of them – "I can't tell what I have accomplished to-day, and yet I have not been idle a minute;" and day after day passes on in this way, and perhaps for weeks she does not pass the threshold for a breath of air, and yet men talk of "monotony!" and being "differently constituted," and needing amusement and exhilaration; and "business" is the broad mantle which it is not always safe for a

6. **"tarry . . . grown"**: See 2 Samuel 10: "When they told it unto David, he sent to meet them, because the men were greatly ashamed: and the king said, Tarry at Jericho until your beards be grown, and then return."
7. **Women . . . world**: Fern is paraphrasing Charlotte Brontë's *Jane Eyre* (1847), a popular British novel that was widely read in the United States. In chapter 12, Jane meditates: "Women are supposed to be very calm generally: but women feel just as men feel; they need exercise for their faculties and a field for their efforts as much as their brothers do."

wife to lift. I have no faith in putting women in a pound, that men may trample down the clover in a forty-acre lot. But enough for that transparent excuse.

The great Law-giver made no distinction of sex, as far as I can find out, when he promulgated the seventh commandment, nor should we. You tell me "society makes a difference;" more shame to it – more shame to the women who help to perpetuate it. You tell me that infidelity on the wife's part involves an unjust claim upon the husband and provider; and I ask you, on the other hand, if a good and virtuous wife has not a right to expect *healthy* children?

Let both be equally pure; let every man look upon every woman, whatsoever her rank or condition, as a sister whom his manhood is bound to protect, even, if need be, against herself, and let every woman turn the cold shoulder to any man of her acquaintance, how polished soever he may be, who would degrade her sex. Then this vexed question would be settled; there would be no such libels upon womanhood as I saw at Blackwell's Island, driven in droves to their cells. No more human traffic in those gilded palaces, which our children must not hear mentioned, forsooth! though their very fathers may help to support them, and which our tender-hearted legislators "can't see their way clear about." Then our beautiful rivers would no longer toss upon our island shores the "dead bodies of unfortunate young females."

[1858]

THE "COMING" WOMAN

Men often say, "When *I* marry, my wife must be this, that and the other," enumerating all physical, mental, and moral perfections. One cannot but smile to look at the men who say these things; smile to think of the equivalent they will bring for all the amiability, beauty, health, intellectuality, domesticity and faithfulness they so modestly require; smile to think of the perforated hearts, damaged morals, broken-down constitutions, and irritable temper, which this bright, pure, innocent girl is to receive with her wedding ring. If one-half the girls knew the previous life of the men they marry, the list of old maids would be wonderfully increased.

Doubted? Well, if there is room for a doubt now, thank God the "coming" woman's Alpha and Omega[1] will not be matrimony. *She* will not of necessity sour into a pink-nosed old maid, or throw herself at any rickety old shell of humanity, whose clothes are as much out of repair as his morals. No, the future man has got to "step lively;" *this* wife is not to be had for the whistling. He will have a long canter round the pasture for her, and then she will leap the fence and leave him limping on the ground. Thick-soled boots and skating are coming in, and "nerves," novels and sentiment (by consequence) are going out. The coming woman, as I see her, is not to throw aside her needle; neither is

1. **Alpha and Omega:** The first and last letters of the Greek alphabet frequently used to mean "the beginning and the end."

she to sit embroidering worsted dogs and cats, or singing doubtful love ditties, and rolling up her eyes to "the chaste moon."

Heaven forbid she should stamp round with a cigar in her mouth, elbowing her *fellows*, and puffing smoke in their faces; or stand on the free-love platform, *public or private — call it by what specious name you will* – wooing men who, low as they may have sunk in their own self-respect, would die before they would introduce her to the unsullied sister who shared their cradle.

Heaven forbid the coming woman should not have warm blood in her veins, quick to rush to her cheek, or tingle at her fingers' ends when her heart is astir. No, the coming woman shall be no cold, angular, flat-chested, narrow-shouldered, *skimpy*, sharp-visaged Betsey, but she shall be a bright-eyed, full-chested, broad-shouldered, large-souled, intellectual being; able to walk, able to eat, able to fulfill her maternal destiny, and able – if it so please God – to go to her grave happy, self-poised and serene, though unwedded; for this world, though it may do for men, is, after all, but a narrow place for a woman's heart to beat in. That many die and make no sign, is no proof that martyrdom died out with John Rogers.[2]

[1859]

2. **John Rogers:** During the reign of the Roman Catholic queen Mary I of England, the Protestant martyr John Rogers (c. 1500-1555), a former Catholic priest who converted to Protestantism, was burned at the stake for his faith.

Herman Melville

[1819-1891]

Herman Melville was born on August 1, 1819, in New York City to Allan and Maria Gansevoort Melvill, the spelling of which the family later altered to Melville. He attended the New-York Male High School until 1830, when his father's business as an importer and wholesale merchant collapsed. The family then moved to Albany, New York, where their fortunes improved enough for Melville to enroll in the Albany Academy. By late 1831, the family business failed again; in January 1832, an ill and exhausted Allan Melvill died. As the older sons tried to recoup the family finances, the thirteen-year-old Melville was taken out of school and apprenticed as a clerk in an Albany bank. For the next five years, he worked in the bank, as a helper on his uncle's farm in Pittsfield, Massachusetts, and then as an assistant in his brother's store. After briefly returning to school in Albany, where he joined a reading and debating club, Melville taught for a single term in 1837 in a school near Pittsfield. Still vainly searching for a career, however, he decided to study surveying and engineering at the Lansingburgh Academy, near Albany, in order to prepare for a job working on the Erie Canal.

He can neither believe, nor be comfortable in his unbelief; and he is too honest and courageous not to try to do one or the other.

–Nathaniel Hawthorne

In fact, he would spend most of the following five years, not on that canal between Albany and Buffalo, New York, but on the high seas, gaining experiences that would finally lead him to become a writer. Unable to find a job in 1839, Melville agreed to his brother's proposal that they join the crew of the *St. Lawrence*, which maintained regular service between New York and Liverpool, England. The voyage was fairly horrifying to the youthful Melville, who was shocked by the sometimes brutal behavior of the sailors. Nonetheless, after returning to New York and another brief stint as a teacher, in January 1839 Melville signed up for a four-year voyage aboard the *Acushnet*, a whaling ship bound from New Bedford, Massachusetts, to the South Seas. The lack of success in finding whales and the captain's low spirits made morale on board very bad. In company with another crewman, Melville deserted his ship on the Marquesas Islands, where they stayed for a month, fearful of cannibalism. Melville joined the crew of another whaler, the *Lucy Ann*; was briefly held in Tahiti as a mutineer; and finally sailed to Hawaii, where he spent several months before shipping home as a common seaman aboard the navy frigate *United States*.

By October 1844, Melville was back in Lansingburgh, New York, his career as a sailor now over and his work as a writer about to begin. Within a couple of months, Melville began his first book, published in 1846 as *Typee; or, A Peep at Polynesian Life*. That Romantic and highly colored account of the brief period he had spent among the "cannibals" in the Marquesas was an immediate commercial and critical success. An influential reviewer and later one of Melville's closest friends, Evert Duyckinck, observed that the book was "a happy hit whichever way you look at it, whether as travels, romance, poetry, or humor." Swiftly following up on his success, Melville immediately wrote a sequel, *Omoo* (1847), which proved to be yet another hit. Increasingly ambitious, however, he followed that with *Mardi* (1849), a long, complex, allegorical work that sold poorly and generated considerable critical resistance. Chastened by the response, Melville – now married to Elizabeth Shaw and a new father – swiftly produced two books in his earlier mode, *Redburn* (1849) and *White-Jacket* (1850), both of which proved to be enormously popular with readers and reviewers alike.

But Melville's popularity did not last and his finances remained precarious. In 1850, he moved his family to a farm, Arrowhead, near Pittsfield, Massachusetts. There, he became friendly with Nathaniel Hawthorne, who had just published *The Scarlet Letter*. Melville himself was beginning work on yet another autobiographical narrative, this one based on his early experiences aboard the whaling ship *Acushnet*. Partly inspired by the presence of Hawthorne, to whom he later dedicated *Moby-Dick*, Melville began to transform the novel into something far different, even as he recognized the risks he was running by doing so. "Dollars damn me," he wrote to Hawthorne in 1851. "What I most feel moved to write, that is banned, – it will not sell. Yet, altogether, write the *other* way I cannot. So the product is a final hash, and all my books are botches." Although his powerful novel was anything but a hash, Melville was all too prophetic about what would

Herman Melville

This portrait of the successful young author was painted by Asa W. Twitchell in 1847, when Melville was twenty-eight. Friends nicknamed him "Typee," a reference to his first and most popular book, published in 1846.

bedfordstmartins.com/ americanlit *for research links on Melville*

result if he indulged his taste for metaphysical speculation and his hunger for literary greatness, as he did in *Moby-Dick* (1851). Despite a few admiring reviews, most critics were deeply hostile, and they were even more outraged by what many of them viewed as the immorality and sacrilege of his next novel, *Pierre* (1852). The reviewer for the *New York Herald* spoke for many when he flatly stated that "Mr. Melville has written himself out."

In an effort to revive his flagging literary career, Melville began to publish stories and sketches in two recently established literary journals, *Putnam's Monthly Magazine* and *Harper's New Monthly Magazine.* Those efforts resulted in his next two books: *Israel Potter* (1855), a satirical historical novel first serialized in *Putnam's*, and a collection of shorter pieces Melville had also published there, *The Piazza Tales* (1856). That collection included his novella *Benito Cereno*, an enigmatic meditation on slavery based on an American sea captain's earlier account of a slave insurrection aboard a Spanish ship. Emboldened by the modest success of such works, Melville then wrote *The Confidence-Man* (1857), a biting satire of American values and life in the United States. The book was a commercial and critical disaster that effectively marked the end of Melville's career as a novelist. During the remaining twenty-four years of his life, he published only two more major works: *Battle-Pieces and Aspects of the War* (1866), a collection of Civil War poems, and *Clarel* (1876), a long narrative poem about the quest for religious faith. He also privately published two small collections of poems, in 1888 and 1891. Melville spent most of those years working as a deputy inspector of customs in New York City, where he died in obscurity and relative poverty on September 28, 1891. His final work of fiction, *Billy Budd, Sailor*, was not published until 1924, when Melville finally began to gain the recognition and, at last, the literary reputation that had eluded him during his lifetime.

Melville's "Bartleby, the Scrivener." Following the poor reception of *Moby-Dick* (1851) and *Pierre* (1852), Melville decided to enter the periodical marketplace in an effort to boost his sagging reputation and make a living for his family. The first story he published in a periodical was "Bartleby, the Scrivener: A Story of Wall-Street," which appeared in *Putnam's Monthly Magazine.* When George Palmer Putnam decided that his publishing company would start a magazine, Melville was one of the writers to whom he appealed to help him establish *Putnam's*, which began in January 1853. Putnam and the first editor, Charles Briggs, wanted to publish a magazine of American literature rather than rely on British and other European writings, as many of the other periodicals did. The magazine published fiction, poetry, reviews of literature and the arts, social criticism, and travel writing by authors like William Cullen Bryant, Caroline Kirkland, Henry Wadsworth Longfellow, and Henry David Thoreau. Among the many social concerns addressed in *Putnam's* were urbanization and the changing world of work in the United States, concerns that

Wall Street

By 1850, when this photograph was taken, Wall Street had become the financial capital of the United States. The view is west toward Trinity Church, the fashionable Episcopalian church at the head of Wall Street at Broadway.

were also reflected in Melville's story of Wall Street. Although it was published anonymously, the story attracted a great deal of attention, and it was soon well known that Melville was the author. He later included it in *The Piazza Tales*, a collection of his periodical fiction Melville published in 1856. "Bartleby, the Scrivener" has remained one of Melville's most widely read and frequently debated stories. A central source of critical controversy over the story is its haunting principal character, who has been variously interpreted as a veiled portrait of the author, an example of passive resistance to unjust authority, and a representative of alienated workers in modern commercial society. The text is taken from its first printing as a two-part story in *Putnam's Monthly Magazine*, November and December 1853.

BARTLEBY, THE SCRIVENER[1]

A Story of Wall-Street

I am a rather elderly man. The nature of my avocations for the last thirty years has brought me into more than ordinary contact with what would seem an interesting and somewhat singular set of men, of whom as yet nothing that I know of has ever been written: – I mean the law-copyists or scriveners. I have known very many of them, professionally and privately, and if I pleased, could relate divers histories, at which good-natured

1. Scrivener: An early term for a scribe, or someone who copies documents.

gentlemen might smile, and sentimental souls might weep. But I waive the biographies of all other scriveners for a few passages in the life of Bartleby, who was a scrivener the strangest I ever saw or heard of. While of other law-copyists I might write the complete life, of Bartleby nothing of that sort can be done. I believe that no materials exist for a full and satisfactory biography of this man. It is an irreparable loss to literature. Bartleby was one of those beings of whom nothing is ascertainable, except from the original sources, and in his case those are very small. What my own astonished eyes saw of Bartleby, *that* is all I know of him, except, indeed, one vague report which will appear in the sequel.

Ere introducing the scrivener, as he first appeared to me, it is fit I make some mention of myself, my *employés*, my business, my chambers, and general surroundings; because some such description is indispensable to an adequate understanding of the chief character about to be presented.

Imprimis:[2] I am a man who, from his youth upwards, has been filled with a profound conviction that the easiest way of life is the best. Hence, though I belong to a profession proverbially energetic and nervous, even to turbulence, at times, yet nothing of that sort have I ever suffered to invade my peace. I am one of those unambitious lawyers who never addresses a jury, or in any way draws down public applause; but in the cool tranquillity of a snug retreat, do a snug business among rich men's bonds and mortgages and title-deeds. All who know me, consider me an eminently *safe* man. The late John Jacob Astor,[3] a personage little given to poetic enthusiasm, had no hesitation in pronouncing my first grand point to be prudence; my next, method. I do not speak it in vanity, but simply record the fact, that I was not unemployed in my profession by the late John Jacob Astor; a name which, I admit, I love to repeat, for it hath a rounded and orbicular sound to it, and rings like unto bullion. I will freely add, that I was not insensible to the late John Jacob Astor's good opinion.

Some time prior to the period at which this little history begins, my avocations had been largely increased. The good old office, now extinct in the State of New-York, of a Master in Chancery,[4] had been conferred upon me. It was not a very arduous office, but very pleasantly remunerative. I seldom lose my temper; much more seldom indulge in dangerous indignation at wrongs and outrages; but I must be permitted to be rash here and declare, that I consider the sudden and violent abrogation of the office of Master in Chancery, by the new Constitution, as a — premature act; inasmuch as I had counted upon a life-lease of the profits, whereas I only received those of a few short years. But this is by the way.

My chambers were up stairs at No. – Wall-street. At one end they looked upon the

---

2. **Imprimis:** First of all (Latin).
3. **John Jacob Astor:** (1763–1848) German-born fur trader who amassed a fortune through his business and real-estate dealings. In his will, he provided for $350,000 toward the founding of the New York Public Library.
4. **Master in Chancery:** A position in the Court of Chancery, or equity, in which the officeholder often received lucrative fees while cases over property rights were needlessly prolonged. The position was abolished when the New York State constitution was revised in 1846.

white wall of the interior of a spacious sky-light shaft, penetrating the building from top to bottom. This view might have been considered rather tame than otherwise, deficient in what landscape painters call "life." But if so, the view from the other end of my chambers offered, at least, a contrast, if nothing more. In that direction my windows commanded an unobstructed view of a lofty brick wall, black by age and everlasting shade; which wall required no spy-glass to bring out its lurking beauties, but for the benefit of all near-sighted spectators, was pushed up to within ten feet of my window panes. Owing to the great height of the surrounding buildings, and my chambers being on the second floor, the interval between this wall and mine not a little resembled a huge square cistern.

At the period just preceding the advent of Bartleby, I had two persons as copyists in my employment, and a promising lad as an office-boy. First, Turkey; second, Nippers; third, Ginger Nut. These may seem names, the like of which are not usually found in the Directory. In truth they were nicknames, mutually conferred upon each other by my three clerks, and were deemed expressive of their respective persons or characters. Turkey was a short, pursy[5] Englishman of about my own age, that is, somewhere not far from sixty. In the morning, one might say, his face was of a fine florid hue, but after twelve o'clock, meridian – his dinner hour – it blazed like a grate full of Christmas coals; and continued blazing – but, as it were, with a gradual wane – till 6 o'clock, P.M. or thereabouts, after which I saw no more of the proprietor of the face, which gaining its meridian with the sun, seemed to set with it, to rise, culminate, and decline the following day, with the like regularity and undiminished glory. There are many singular coincidences I have known in the course of my life, not the least among which was the fact, that exactly when Turkey displayed his fullest beams from his red and radiant countenance, just then, too, at that critical moment, began the daily period when I considered his business capacities as seriously disturbed for the remainder of the twenty-four hours. Not that he was absolutely idle, or averse to business then; far from it. The difficulty was, he was apt to be altogether too energetic. There was a strange, inflamed, flurried, flighty recklessness of activity about him. He would be incautious in dipping his pen into his inkstand. All his blots upon my documents, were dropped there after twelve o'clock, meridian. Indeed, not only would he be reckless and sadly given to making blots in the afternoon, but some days he went further, and was rather noisy. At such times, too, his face flamed with augmented blazonry, as if cannel coal had been heaped on anthracite.[6] He made an unpleasant racket with his chair; spilled his sand-box; in mending his pens, impatiently split them all to pieces, and threw them on the floor in a sudden passion; stood up and leaned over his table, boxing his papers about in a most indecorous manner, very sad to behold in an elderly man like him. Nevertheless, as he was in many ways a most valuable person to me, and all the time before twelve o'clock, meridian, was the quickest, steadiest creature too, accomplishing a great deal of work

5. **pursy**: Short-winded because of obesity.
6. **cannel coal . . . anthracite**: Cannel coal is highly volatile; when it is heaped on anthracite, a hard coal with little volatility, both burn with a bright flame.

in a style not easy to be matched – for these reasons, I was willing to overlook his eccentricities, though indeed, occasionally, I remonstrated with him. I did this very gently, however, because, though the civilest, nay, the blandest and most reverential of men in the morning, yet in the afternoon he was disposed, upon provocation, to be slightly rash with his tongue, in fact, insolent. Now, valuing his morning services as I did, and resolved not to lose them; yet, at the same time made uncomfortable by his inflamed ways after twelve o'clock; and being a man of peace, unwilling by my admonitions to call forth unseemly retorts from him; I took upon me, one Saturday noon (he was always worse on Saturdays), to hint to him, very kindly, that perhaps now that he was growing old, it might be well to abridge his labors; in short, he need not come to my chambers after twelve o'clock, but, dinner over, had best go home to his lodgings and rest himself till tea-time. But no; he insisted upon his afternoon devotions. His countenance became intolerably fervid, as he oratorically assured me – gesticulating with a long ruler at the other end of the room – that if his services in the morning were useful, how indispensable, then, in the afternoon?

"With submission, sir," said Turkey on this occasion, "I consider myself your right-hand man. In the morning I but marshal and deploy my columns; but in the afternoon I put myself at their head, and gallantly charge the foe, thus!" – and he made a violent thrust with the ruler.

"But the blots, Turkey," intimated I.

"True, – but, with submission, sir, behold these hairs! I am getting old. Surely, sir, a blot or two of a warm afternoon is not to be severely urged against gray hairs. Old age – even if it blot the page – is honorable. With submission, sir, we *both* are getting old."

This appeal to my fellow-feeling was hardly to be resisted. At all events, I saw that go he would not. So I made up my mind to let him stay, resolving, nevertheless, to see to it, that during the afternoon he had to do with my less important papers.

Nippers, the second on my list, was a whiskered, sallow, and, upon the whole, rather piratical-looking young man of about five and twenty. I always deemed him the victim of two evil powers – ambition and indigestion. The ambition was evinced by a certain impatience of the duties of a mere copyist, an unwarrantable usurpation of strictly professional affairs, such as the original drawing up of legal documents. The indigestion seemed betokened in an occasional nervous testiness and grinning irritability, causing the teeth to audibly grind together over mistakes committed in copying; unnecessary maledictions, hissed, rather than spoken, in the heat of business; and especially by a continual discontent with the height of the table where he worked. Though of a very ingenious mechanical turn, Nippers could never get this table to suit him. He put chips under it, blocks of various sorts, bits of pasteboard, and at last went so far as to attempt an exquisite adjustment by final pieces of folded blotting-paper. But no invention would answer. If, for the sake of easing his back, he brought the table lid at a sharp angle well up towards his chin, and wrote there like a man using the steep roof of a Dutch house for his desk: – then he declared that it stopped the circulation in his arms. If now he lowered the table to his waistbands, and stooped over it in writing, then there was a sore aching in his back. In short, the truth of the matter was, Nippers knew not what he wanted. Or, if he wanted any thing, it was to be rid of a scrivener's table altogether.

Among the manifestations of his diseased ambition was a fondness he had for receiving visits from certain ambiguous-looking fellows in seedy coats, whom he called his clients. Indeed I was aware that not only was he, at times, considerable of a ward-politician, but he occasionally did a little business at the Justices' courts, and was not unknown on the steps of the Tombs.[7] I have good reason to believe, however that one individual who called upon him at my chambers, and who, with a grand air, he insisted was his client, was no other than a dun,[8] and the alleged title-deed, a bill. But with all his failings, and the annoyances he caused me, Nippers, like his compatriot Turkey, was a very useful man to me; wrote a neat, swift hand; and, when he chose, was not deficient in a gentlemanly sort of deportment. Added to this, he always dressed in a gentlemanly sort of way; and so, incidentally, reflected credit upon my chambers. Whereas with respect to Turkey, I had much ado to keep him from being a reproach to me. His clothes were apt to look oily and smell of eating-houses. He wore his pantaloons very loose and baggy in summer. His coats were execrable; his hat not to be handled. But while the hat was a thing of indifference to me, inasmuch as his natural civility and deference, as a dependent Englishman, always led him to doff it the moment he entered the room, yet his coat was another matter. Concerning his coats, I reasoned with him; but with no effect. The truth was, I suppose, that a man with so small an income, could not afford to sport such a lustrous face and a lustrous coat at one and the same time. As Nippers once observed, Turkey's money went chiefly for red ink. One winter day I presented Turkey with a highly-respectable looking coat of my own, a padded gray coat, of a most comfortable warmth, and which buttoned straight up from the knee to the neck. I thought Turkey would appreciate the favor, and abate his rashness and obstreperousness of afternoons. But no. I verily believe that buttoning himself up in so downy and blanket-like a coat had a pernicious effect upon him; upon the same principle that too much oats are bad for horses. In fact, precisely as a rash, restive horse is said to feel his oats, so Turkey felt his coat. It made him insolent. He was a man whom prosperity harmed.

Though concerning the self-indulgent habits of Turkey I had my own private surmises, yet touching Nippers I was well persuaded that whatever might be his faults in other respects, he was, at least, a temperate young man. But indeed, nature herself seemed to have been his vintner, and at his birth charged him so thoroughly with an irritable, brandy-like disposition, that all subsequent potations were needless. When I consider how, amid the stillness of my chambers, Nippers would sometimes impatiently rise from his seat, and stooping over his table, spread his arms wide apart, seize the whole desk, and move it, and jerk it, with a grim, grinding motion on the floor, as if the table were a perverse voluntary agent, intent on thwarting and vexing him; I plainly perceive that for Nippers, brandy and water were altogether superfluous.

It was fortunate for me that, owing to its peculiar cause – indigestion – the irritability and consequent nervousness of Nippers, were mainly observable in the morning,

---

7. **the Tombs:** Informal name for the Halls of Justice and House of Detention, a prison built in New York City in 1840. The massive structure was designed to look like an ancient Egyptian tomb.
8. **dun:** Slang name for a bill collector.

while in the afternoon he was comparatively mild. So that Turkey's paroxysms only coming on about twelve o'clock, I never had to do with their eccentricities at one time. Their fits relieved each other like guards. When Nippers' was on, Turkey's was off; and *vice versa.* This was a good natural arrangement under the circumstances.

Ginger Nut, the third on my list, was a lad some twelve years old. His father was a carman,[9] ambitious of seeing his son on the bench instead of a cart, before he died. So he sent him to my office as student at law, errand boy, and cleaner and sweeper, at the rate of one dollar a week. He had a little desk to himself, but he did not use it much. Upon inspection, the drawer exhibited a great array of the shells of various sorts of nuts. Indeed, to this quick-witted youth the whole noble science of the law was contained in a nut-shell. Not the least among the employments of Ginger Nut, as well as one which he discharged with the most alacrity, was his duty as cake and apple purveyor for Turkey and Nippers. Copying law papers being proverbially a dry, husky sort of business, my two scriveners were fain to moisten their mouths very often with Spitzenbergs[10] to be had at the numerous stalls nigh the Custom House and Post Office. Also, they sent Ginger Nut very frequently for that peculiar cake – small, flat, round, and very spicy – after which he had been named by them. Of a cold morning when business was but dull, Turkey would gobble up scores of these cakes, as if they were mere wafers – indeed they sell them at the rate of six or eight for a penny – the scrape of his pen blending with the crunching of the crisp particles in his mouth. Of all the fiery afternoon blunders and flurried rashnesses of Turkey, was his once moistening a ginger-cake between his lips, and clapping it on to a mortgage for a seal. I came within an ace of dismissing him then. But he mollified me by making an oriental bow, and saying – "With submission, sir, it was generous of me to find you in stationery on my own account."

Now my original business – that of a conveyancer and title hunter,[11] and drawer-up of recondite documents of all sorts – was considerably increased by receiving the master's office. There was now great work for scriveners. Not only must I push the clerks already with me, but I must have additional help. In answer to my advertisement, a motionless young man one morning, stood upon my office threshold, the door being open, for it was summer. I can see that figure now – pallidly neat, pitiably respectable, incurably forlorn! It was Bartleby.

After a few words touching his qualifications, I engaged him, glad to have among my corps of copyists a man of so singularly sedate an aspect, which I thought might operate beneficially upon the flighty temper of Turkey, and the fiery one of Nippers.

I should have stated before that ground glass folding-doors divided my premises into two parts, one of which was occupied by my scriveners, the other by myself. According to my humor I threw open these doors, or closed them. I resolved to assign Bartleby a corner by the folding-doors, but on my side of them, so as to have this quiet man within easy call, in case any trifling thing was to be done. I placed his desk close up to a small side-

9. **carman:** A streetcar driver or conductor.
10. **Spitzenbergs:** A variety of apple grown in New York State.
11. **conveyancer and title hunter:** A lawyer who arranges documents for the transfer of property, ensuring that the title is free of any encumbrances.

window in that part of the room, a window which originally had afforded a lateral view of certain grimy back-yards and bricks, but which, owing to subsequent erections, commanded at present no view at all, though it gave some light. Within three feet of the panes was a wall, and the light came down from far above, between two lofty buildings, as from a very small opening in a dome. Still further to a satisfactory arrangement, I procured a high green folding screen, which might entirely isolate Bartleby from my sight, though not remove him from my voice. And thus, in a manner, privacy and society were conjoined.

At first Bartleby did an extraordinary quantity of writing. As if long famishing for something to copy, he seemed to gorge himself on my documents. There was no pause for digestion. He ran a day and night line, copying by sun-light and by candle-light. I should have been quite delighted with his application, had he been cheerfully industrious. But he wrote on silently, palely, mechanically.

It is, of course, an indispensable part of a scrivener's business to verify the accuracy of his copy, word by word. Where there are two or more scriveners in an office, they assist each other in this examination, one reading from the copy, the other holding the original. It is a very dull, wearisome, and lethargic affair. I can readily imagine that to some sanguine temperaments it would be altogether intolerable. For example, I cannot credit that the mettlesome poet Byron would have contentedly sat down with Bartleby to examine a law document of, say five hundred pages, closely written in a crimpy hand.

Now and then, in the haste of business, it had been my habit to assist in comparing some brief document myself, calling Turkey or Nippers for this purpose. One object I had in placing Bartleby so handy to me behind the screen, was to avail myself of his services on such trivial occasions. It was on the third day, I think, of his being with me, and before any necessity had arisen for having his own writing examined that, being much hurried to complete a small affair I had in hand, I abruptly called to Bartleby. In my haste and natural expectancy of instant compliance, I sat with my head bent over the original on my desk, and my right hand sideways, and somewhat nervously extended with the copy, so that immediately upon emerging from his retreat, Bartleby might snatch it and proceed to business without the least delay.

In this very attitude did I sit when I called to him, rapidly stating what it was I wanted him to do – namely, to examine a small paper with me. Imagine my surprise, nay, my consternation, when without moving from his privacy, Bartleby in a singularly mild, firm voice, replied, "I would prefer not to."

I sat awhile in perfect silence, rallying my stunned faculties. Immediately it occurred to me that my ears had deceived me, or Bartleby had entirely misunderstood my meaning. I repeated my request in the clearest tone I could assume. But in quite as clear a one came the previous reply, "I would prefer not to."

"Prefer not to," echoed I, rising in high excitement, and crossing the room with a stride. "What do you mean? Are you moon-struck? I want you to help me compare this sheet here – take it," and I thrust it towards him.

"I would prefer not to," said he.

I looked at him steadfastly. His face was leanly composed; his gray eye dimly calm. Not a wrinkle of agitation rippled him. Had there been the least uneasiness, anger, impatience or impertinence in his manner; in other words, had there been any thing ordinarily human about him, doubtless I should have violently dismissed him from the premises. But as it was, I should have as soon thought of turning my pale plaster-of-paris bust of Cicero[12] out of doors. I stood gazing at him awhile, as he went on with his own writing, and then reseated myself at my desk. This is very strange, thought I. What had one best do? But my business hurried me. I concluded to forget the matter for the present, reserving it for my future leisure. So calling Nippers from the other room, the paper was speedily examined.

A few days after this, Bartleby concluded four lengthy documents, being quadruplicates of a week's testimony taken before me in my High Court of Chancery. It became necessary to examine them. It was an important suit, and great accuracy was imperative. Having all things arranged I called Turkey, Nippers and Ginger Nut from the next room, meaning to place the four copies in the hands of my four clerks, while I should read from the original. Accordingly Turkey Nippers and Ginger Nut had taken their seats in a row, each with his document in hand, when I called to Bartleby to join this interesting group.

"Bartleby! quick, I am waiting."

I heard a slow scrape of his chair legs on the uncarpeted floor, and soon he appeared standing at the entrance of his hermitage.

"What is wanted?" said he mildly.

"The copies, the copies," said I hurriedly. "We are going to examine them. There" – and I held towards him the fourth quadruplicate.

"I would prefer not to," he said, and gently disappeared behind the screen.

For a few moments I was turned into a pillar of salt,[13] standing at the head of my seated column of clerks. Recovering myself, I advanced towards the screen and demanded the reason for such extraordinary conduct.

"*Why* do you refuse?"

"I would prefer not to."

With any other man I should have flown outright into a dreadful passion, scorned all further words, and thrust him ignominiously from my presence. But there was something about Bartleby that not only strangely disarmed me, but in a wonderful manner touched and disconcerted me. I began to reason with him.

"These are your own copies we are about to examine. It is labor saving to you, because one examination will answer for your four papers. It is common usage. Every copyist is bound to help examine his copy. Is it not so? Will you not speak? Answer!"

"I prefer not to," he replied in a flute-like tone. It seemed to me that while I had been addressing him, he carefully revolved every statement that I made; fully comprehended the meaning; could not gainsay the irresistible conclusion; but, at the same time, some paramount consideration prevailed with him to reply as he did.

---

12. **Cicero:** (106–42 BCE) Roman orator and politician.
13. **pillar of salt:** In the Old Testament story, Lot's wife is turned into a pillar of salt when she disobeys a command from God not to turn and look back upon the destruction of the cities of Sodom and Gomorrah (Genesis 19:26).

"You are decided, then, not to comply with my request – a request made according to common usage and common sense?"

He briefly gave me to understand that on that point my judgment was sound. Yes: his decision was irreversible.

It is not seldom the case that when a man is browbeaten in some unprecedented and violently unreasonable way, he begins to stagger in his own plainest faith. He begins, as it were, vaguely to surmise that, wonderful as it may be, all the justice and all the reason is on the other side. Accordingly, if any disinterested persons are present, he turns to them for some reinforcement for his own faltering mind.

"Turkey," said I, "what do you think of this? Am I not right?"

"With submission, sir," said Turkey, with his blandest tone, "I think that you are."

"Nippers," said I, "what do *you* think of it?"

"I think I should kick him out of the office."

(The reader of nice perceptions will here perceive that, it being morning, Turkey's answer is couched in polite and tranquil terms, but Nippers replies in ill-tempered ones. Or, to repeat a previous sentence, Nippers's ugly mood was on duty, and Turkey's off.)

"Ginger Nut," said I, willing to enlist the smallest suffrage in my behalf, "what do *you* think of it?"

"I think, sir, he's a little *luny*," replied Ginger Nut, with a grin.

"You hear what they say," said I, turning towards the screen, "come forth and do your duty."

But he vouchsafed no reply. I pondered a moment in sore perplexity. But once more business hurried me. I determined again to postpone the consideration of this dilemma to my future leisure. With a little trouble we made out to examine the papers without Bartleby, though at every page or two, Turkey deferentially dropped his opinion that this proceeding was quite out of the common; while Nippers, twitching in his chair with a dyspeptic nervousness, ground out between his set teeth occasional hissing maledictions against the stubborn oaf behind the screen. And for his (Nippers's) part, this was the first and the last time he would do another man's business without pay.

Meanwhile Bartleby sat in his hermitage, oblivious to every thing but his own peculiar business there.

Some days passed, the scrivener being employed upon another lengthy work. His late remarkable conduct led me to regard his ways narrowly. I observed that he never went to dinner; indeed that he never went any where. As yet I had never of my personal knowledge known him to be outside of my office. He was a perpetual sentry in the corner. At about eleven o'clock though, in the morning, I noticed that Ginger Nut would advance toward the opening in Bartleby's screen, as if silently beckoned thither by a gesture invisible to me where I sat. The boy would then leave the office jingling a few pence, and reappear with a handful of ginger-nuts which he delivered in the hermitage, receiving two of the cakes for his trouble.

He lives, then, on ginger-nuts, thought I; never eats a dinner, properly speaking; he must be a vegetarian then; but no; he never eats even vegetables, he eats nothing but ginger-nuts. My mind then ran on in reveries concerning the probable effects upon the human constitution of living entirely on ginger-nuts. Ginger-nuts are so called because they contain ginger as one of their peculiar constituents, and the final flavoring one. Now what was ginger? A hot, spicy thing. Was Bartleby hot and spicy? Not at all. Ginger, then, had no effect upon Bartleby. Probably he preferred it should have none.

Nothing so aggravates an earnest person as a passive resistance. If the individual so resisted be of a not inhumane temper, and the resisting one perfectly harmless in his passivity; then, in the better moods of the former, he will endeavor charitably to construe to his imagination what proves impossible to be solved by his judgment. Even so, for the most part, I regarded Bartleby and his ways. Poor fellow! thought I, he means no mischief; it is plain he intends no insolence; his aspect sufficiently evinces that his eccentricities are involuntary. He is useful to me. I can get along with him. If I turn him away, the chances are he will fall in with some less indulgent employer, and then he will be rudely treated, and perhaps driven forth miserably to starve. Yes. Here I can cheaply purchase a delicious self-approval. To befriend Bartleby; to humor him in his strange wilfulness, will cost me little or nothing, while I lay up in my soul what will eventually prove a sweet morsel for my conscience. But this mood was not invariable with me. The passiveness of Bartleby sometimes irritated me. I felt strangely goaded on to encounter him in new opposition, to elicit some angry spark from him answerable to my own. But indeed I might as well have essayed to strike fire with my knuckles against a bit of Windsor soap. But one afternoon the evil impulse in me mastered me, and the following little scene ensued:

"Bartleby," said I, "when those papers are all copied, I will compare them with you."

"I would prefer not to."

"How? Surely you do not mean to persist in that mulish vagary?"

No answer.

I threw open the folding-doors near by, and turning upon Turkey and Nippers, exclaimed in an excited manner –

"He says, a second time, he won't examine his papers. What do you think of it, Turkey?"

It was afternoon, be it remembered. Turkey sat glowing like a brass boiler, his bald head steaming, his hands reeling among his blotted papers.

"Think of it?" roared Turkey; "I think I'll just step behind his screen, and black his eyes for him!"

So saying, Turkey rose to his feet and threw his arms into a pugilistic position. He was hurrying away to make good his promise, when I detained him, alarmed at the effect of incautiously rousing Turkey's combativeness after dinner.

"Sit down, Turkey," said I, "and hear what Nippers has to say. What do you think of it, Nippers? Would I not be justified in immediately dismissing Bartleby?"

"Excuse me, that is for you to decide, sir. I think his conduct quite unusual, and indeed unjust, as regards Turkey and myself. But it may only be a passing whim."

"Ah," exclaimed I, "you have strangely changed your mind then – you speak very gently of him now."

"All beer," cried Turkey; "gentleness is effects of beer – Nippers and I dined together to-day. You see how gentle *I* am, sir. Shall I go and black his eyes?"

"You refer to Bartleby, I suppose. No, not to-day, Turkey," I replied; "pray, put up your fists."

I closed the doors, and again advanced towards Bartleby. I felt additional incentives tempting me to my fate. I burned to be rebelled against again. I remembered that Bartleby never left the office.

"Bartleby," said I, "Ginger Nut is away; just step round to the Post Office, won't you? (it was but a three minutes walk,) and see if there is any thing for me."

"I would prefer not to."

"You *will* not?"

"I *prefer* not."

I staggered to my desk, and sat there in a deep study. My blind inveteracy returned. Was there any other thing in which I could procure myself to be ignominiously repulsed by this lean, penniless wight? – my hired clerk? What added thing is there, perfectly reasonable, that he will be sure to refuse to do?

"Bartleby!"

No answer.

"Bartleby," in a louder tone.

No answer.

"Bartleby," I roared.

Like a very ghost, agreeably to the laws of magical invocation, at the third summons, he appeared at the entrance of his hermitage.

"Go to the next room, and tell Nippers to come to me."

"I prefer not to," he respectfully and slowly said, and mildly disappeared.

"Very good, Bartleby," said I, in a quiet sort of serenely severe self-possessed tone, intimating the unalterable purpose of some terrible retribution very close at hand. At the moment I half intended something of the kind. But upon the whole, as it was drawing towards my dinner-hour, I thought it best to put on my hat and walk home for the day, suffering much from perplexity and distress of mind.

Shall I acknowledge it? The conclusion of this whole business was, that it soon became a fixed fact of my chambers, that a pale young scrivener, by the name of Bartleby, had a desk there; that he copied for me at the usual rate of four cents a folio (one hundred words); but he was permanently exempt from examining the work done by him, that duty being transferred to Turkey and Nippers, out of compliment doubtless to their superior acuteness; moreover, said Bartleby was never on any account to be dispatched on the most trivial errand of any sort; and that even if entreated to take upon him such a matter, it was generally understood that he would prefer not to – in other words, that he would refuse point-blank.

As days passed on, I became considerably reconciled to Bartleby. His steadiness, his freedom from all dissipation, his incessant industry (except when he chose to throw himself into a standing revery behind his screen), his great stillness, his unalterableness of demeanor under all circumstances, made him a valuable acquisition. One prime thing was this, – *he was always there*; – first in the morning, continually through the day, and the last at night. I had a singular confidence in his honesty. I felt my most precious papers perfectly safe in his hands. Sometimes to be sure I could not, for the very soul of me, avoid falling into sudden spasmodic passions with him. For it was exceeding difficult to bear in mind all the time those strange peculiarities, privileges, and unheard of exemptions, forming the tacit stipulations on Bartleby's part under which he remained in my office. Now and then, in the eagerness of dispatching pressing business, I would inadvertently summon Bartleby, in a short, rapid tone, to put his finger, say, on the incipient tie of a bit of red tape with which I was about compressing some papers. Of course, from behind the screen the usual answer, "I prefer not to," was sure to come; and then, how could a human creature with the common infirmities of our nature, refrain from bitterly exclaiming upon such perverseness – such unreasonableness. However, every added repulse of this sort which I received only tended to lessen the probability of my repeating the inadvertence.

Here it must be said, that according to the custom of most legal gentlemen occupying chambers in densely-populated law buildings, there were several keys to my door. One was kept by woman residing in the attic, which person weekly scrubbed and daily swept and dusted my apartments. Another was kept by Turkey for convenience sake. The third I sometimes carried in my own pocket. The fourth I knew not who had.

Now, one Sunday morning I happened to go to Trinity Church, to hear a celebrated preacher, and finding myself rather early on the ground, I thought I would walk round to my chambers for a while. Luckily I had my key with me; but upon applying it to the lock, I found it resisted by something inserted from the inside. Quite surprised, I called out; when to my consternation a key was turned from within; and thrusting his lean visage at me, and holding the door ajar, the apparition of Bartleby appeared, in his shirt sleeves, and otherwise in a strangely tattered dishabille, saying quietly that he was sorry, but he was deeply engaged just then, and – preferred not admitting me at present. In a brief word or two, he moreover added, that perhaps I had better walk round the block two or three times, and by that time he would probably have concluded his affairs.

Now, the utterly unsurmised appearance of Bartleby, tenanting my law-chambers of a Sunday morning, with his cadaverously gentlemanly *nonchalance*, yet withal firm and self-possessed, had such a strange effect upon me, that incontinently I slunk away from my own door, and did as desired. But not without sundry twinges of impotent rebellion against the mild effrontery of this unaccountable scrivener. Indeed, it was his wonderful mildness chiefly, which not only disarmed me, but unmanned me, as it were. For I consider that one, for the time, is a sort of unmanned when he tranquilly permits his hired clerk to dictate to him and order him away from his own premises. Furthermore, I was full of uneasiness as to what Bartleby could possibly be doing in my office in his shirt sleeves, and in an otherwise dismantled condition of a Sunday morning. Was any thing amiss going on? Nay, that was out of the question. It was not to be thought of for a moment that Bartleby was an immoral person. But what could he be doing there? – copying? Nay again, whatever might be his eccentricities, Bartleby was an eminently decorous person. He would be the last man to sit down to his desk in any state approaching to nudity. Besides, it was Sunday; and there was something about Bartleby that forbade the supposition that he would by any secular occupation violate the proprieties of the day.

Nevertheless, my mind was not pacified; and full of a restless curiosity, at last I returned to the door. Without hindrance I inserted my key, opened it, and entered. Bartleby was not to be seen. I looked round anxiously, peeped behind his screen; but it was very plain that he was gone. Upon more closely examining the place, I surmised that for an indefinite period Bartleby must have ate, dressed, and slept in my office, and that too without plate, mirror, or bed. The cushioned seat of a ricketty old sofa in one corner bore the faint impress of a lean, reclining form. Rolled away under his desk, I found a blanket; under the empty grate, a blacking box and brush; on a chair, a tin basin, with soap and a ragged towel; in a newspaper a few crumbs of ginger-nuts and a morsel of cheese. Yes, thought I, it is evident enough that Bartleby has been making his home here, keeping bachelor's hall all by himself. Immediately then the thought came sweeping across me, What miserable friendlessness and loneliness are here revealed! His poverty is great; but his solitude, how horrible! Think of it. Of a Sunday, Wall-street is deserted as Petra;[14] and every night of every day it is an emptiness. This building too, which of week-days hums with industry and life, at nightfall echoes with sheer vacancy, and all through Sunday is forlorn. And here Bartleby makes his home; sole spectator of a solitude which he has seen all populous – a sort of innocent and transformed Marius[15] brooding among the ruins of Carthage!

For the first time in my life a feeling of overpowering stinging melancholy seized me. Before, I had never experienced aught but a not-unpleasing sadness. The bond of a common humanity now drew me irresistibly to gloom. A fraternal melancholy! For both I and Bartleby were sons of Adam. I remembered the bright silks and sparkling faces I had seen that day, in gala trim, swan-like sailing down the Mississippi of Broadway; and I contrasted them with the pallid copyist, and thought to myself, Ah, happiness courts the light, so we deem the world is gay; but misery hides aloof, so we deem that misery there is none. These sad fancyings – chimeras, doubtless, of a sick and silly brain – led on to other and more special thoughts, concerning the eccentricities of Bartleby. Presentiments of strange discoveries hovered round me. The scrivener's pale form appeared to me laid out, among uncaring strangers, in its shivering winding sheet.

Suddenly I was attracted by Bartleby's closed desk, the key in open sight left in the lock.

I mean no mischief, seek the gratification of no heartless curiosity, thought I; besides, the desk is mine, and its contents too, so I will make bold to look within. Every thing was methodically arranged, the papers smoothly placed. The pigeon holes were deep, and removing the files of documents, I groped into their recesses. Presently I felt something there, and dragged it out. It was an old bandanna handkerchief, heavy and knotted. I opened it, and saw it was a savings' bank.

I now recalled all the quiet mysteries which I had noted in the man. I remembered that he never spoke but to answer; that though at intervals he had considerable time to

14. **Petra:** The ruins of an ancient city, located in present-day Jordan, discovered by European explorers in 1812.

15. **Marius:** Gaius Marius (157–86 BCE), powerful Roman general and politician who lost favor and was sent into exile.

himself, yet I had never seen him reading – no, not even a newspaper; that for long periods he would stand looking out, at his pale window behind the screen, upon the dead brick wall; I was quite sure he never visited any refectory or eating house; while his pale face clearly indicated that he never drank beer like Turkey, or tea and coffee even, like other men; that he never went any where in particular that I could learn; never went out for a walk, unless indeed that was the case at present; that he had declined telling who he was, or whence he came, or whether he had any relatives in the world; that though so thin and pale, he never complained of ill health. And more than all, I remembered a certain unconscious air of pallid – how shall I call it? – of pallid haughtiness, say, or rather an austere reserve about him, which had positively awed me into my tame compliance with his eccentricities, when I had feared to ask him to do the slightest incidental thing for me, even though I might know, from his long-continued motionlessness, that behind his screen he must be standing in one of those dead-wall reveries of his.

Revolving all these things, and coupling them with the recently discovered fact that he made my office his constant abiding place and home, and not forgetful of his morbid moodiness; revolving all these things, a prudential feeling began to steal over me. My first emotions had been those of pure melancholy and sincerest pity; but just in proportion as the forlornness of Bartleby grew and grew to my imagination, did that same melancholy merge into fear, that pity into repulsion. So true it is, and so terrible too, that up to a certain point the thought or sight of misery enlists our best affections; but, in certain special cases, beyond that point it does not. They err who would assert that invariably this is owing to the inherent selfishness of the human heart. It rather proceeds from a certain hopelessness of remedying excessive and organic ill. To a sensitive being, pity is not seldom pain. And when it last it is perceived that such pity cannot lead to effectual succor, common sense bids the soul be rid of it. What I saw that morning persuaded me that the scrivener was the victim of innate and incurable disorder. I might give alms to his body; but his body did not pain him; it was his soul that suffered, and his soul I could not reach.

I did not accomplish the purpose of going to Trinity Church that morning. Somehow, the things I had seen disqualified me for the time from church-going. I walked homeward, thinking what I would do with Bartleby. Finally, I resolved upon this; – I would put certain calm questions to him the next morning, touching his history, &c., and if he declined to answer them openly and unreservedly (and I supposed he would prefer not), then to give him a twenty dollar bill over and above whatever I might owe him, and tell him his services were no longer required; but that if in any other way I could assist him, I would be happy to do so, especially if he desired to return to his native place, wherever that might be, I would willingly help to defray the expenses. Moreover, if, after reaching home, he found himself at any time in want of aid, a letter from him would be sure of a reply.

The next morning came.

"Bartleby," said I, gently calling to him behind his screen.

No reply.

"Bartleby," said I, in a still gentler tone, "come here; I am not going to ask you to do any thing you would prefer not to do – I simply wish to speak to you."

Upon this he noiselessly slid into view.

"Will you tell me, Bartleby, where you were born?"

"I would prefer not to."

"Will you tell me *any thing* about yourself?"

"I would prefer not to."

"But what reasonable objection can you have to speak to me? I feel friendly towards you."

He did not look at me while I spoke, but kept his glance fixed upon my bust of Cicero, which as I then sat, was directly behind me, some six inches above my head.

"What is your answer, Bartleby?" said I, after waiting a considerable time for a reply, during which his countenance remained immovable, only there was the faintest conceivable tremor of the white attenuated mouth.

"At present I prefer to give no answer," he said, and retired into his hermitage.

It was rather weak in me I confess, but his manner on this occasion nettled me. Not only did there seem to lurk in it a certain calm disdain, but his perverseness seemed ungrateful, considering the undeniable good usage and indulgence he had received from me.

Again I sat ruminating what I should do. Mortified as I was at his behavior, and resolved as I had been to dismiss him when I entered my office, nevertheless I strangely felt something superstitious knocking at my heart, and forbidding me to carry out my purpose, and denouncing me for a villain if I dared to breathe one bitter word against this forlornest of mankind. At last, familiarly drawing my chair behind his screen, I sat down and said: "Bartleby, never mind then about revealing your history; but let me entreat you, as a friend, to comply as far as may be with the usages of this office. Say now you will help to examine papers to-morrow or next day: in short, say now that in a day or two you will begin to be a little reasonable: – say so, Bartleby."

"At present I would prefer not to be a little reasonable," was his mildly cadaverous reply.

Just then the folding-doors opened, and Nippers approached. He seemed suffering from an unusually bad night's rest, induced by severer indigestion than common. He overheard those final words of Bartleby.

"*Prefer not*, eh?" gritted Nippers – "I'd *prefer* him, if I were you, sir," addressing me – "I'd *prefer* him; I'd give him preferences, the stubborn mule! What is it, sir, pray, that he *prefers* not to do now?"

Bartleby moved not a limb.

"Mr. Nippers," said I, "I'd prefer that you would withdraw for the present."

Somehow, of late I had got into the way of involuntarily using this word "prefer" upon all sorts of not exactly suitable occasions. And I trembled to think that my contact with the scrivener had already and seriously affected me in a mental way. And what further and deeper aberration might it not yet produce? This apprehension had not been without efficacy in determining me to summary means.

As Nippers, looking very sour and sulky, was departing, Turkey blandly and deferentially approached.

"With submission, sir," said he, "yesterday I was thinking about Bartleby here, and I think that if he would but prefer to take a quart of good ale every day, it would do much towards mending him, and enabling him to assist in examining his papers."

"So you have got the word too," said I, slightly excited.

"With submission, what word, sir," asked Turkey, respectfully crowding himself into the contracted space behind the screen, and by so doing, making me jostle the scrivener. "What word, sir?"

"I would prefer to be left alone here," said Bartleby, as if offended at being mobbed in his privacy.

"*That's* the word, Turkey," said I – "*that's* it."

"Oh, *prefer*? oh yes – queer word. I never use it myself. But, sir, as I was saying, if he would but prefer –"

"Turkey," interrupted I, "you will please withdraw."

"Oh certainly, sir, if you prefer that I should."

As he opened the folding-door to retire, Nippers at his desk caught a glimpse of me, and asked whether I would prefer to have a certain paper copied on blue paper or white. He did not in the least roguishly accent the word prefer. It was plain that it involuntarily rolled from his tongue. I thought to myself, surely I must get rid of a demented man, who already has in some degree turned the tongues, if not the heads of myself and clerks. But I thought it prudent not to break the dismission at once.

The next day I noticed that Bartleby did nothing but stand at his window in his dead-wall revery. Upon asking him why he did not write, he said that he had decided upon doing no more writing.

"Why, how now? what next?" exclaimed I, "do no more writing?"

"No more."

"And what is the reason?"

"Do you not see the reason for yourself," he indifferently replied.

I looked steadfastly at him, and perceived that his eyes looked dull and glazed. Instantly it occurred to me, that his unexampled diligence in copying by his dim window for the first few weeks of his stay with me might have temporarily impaired his vision.

I was touched. I said something in condolence with him. I hinted that of course he did wisely in abstaining from writing for a while; and urged him to embrace that opportunity of taking wholesome exercise in the open air. This, however, he did not do. A few days after this, my other clerks being absent, and being in a great hurry to dispatch certain letters by the mail, I thought that, having nothing else earthly to do, Bartleby would surely be less inflexible than usual, and carry these letters to the post-office. But he blankly declined. So, much to my inconvenience, I went myself.

Still added days went by. Whether Bartleby's eyes improved or not, I could not say. To all appearance, I thought they did. But when I asked him if they did, he vouchsafed no answer. At all events, he would do no copying. At last, in reply to my urgings, he informed me that he had permanently given up copying.

"What!" exclaimed I; "suppose your eyes should get entirely well – better than ever before – would you not copy then?"

"I have given up copying," he answered, and slid aside.

He remained as ever, a fixture in my chamber. Nay – if that were possible – he became still more of a fixture than before. What was to be done? He would do nothing in the office: why should he stay there? In plain fact, he had now become a millstone to me, not only useless as a necklace, but afflictive to bear. Yet I was sorry for him. I speak less than truth when I say that, on his own account, he occasioned me uneasiness. If he would but have named a single relative or friend, I would instantly have written, and urged their taking the poor fellow away to some convenient retreat. But he seemed alone, absolutely alone in the universe. A bit of wreck in the mid Atlantic. At length, necessities connected with my business tyrannized over all other considerations. Decently as I could I told Bartleby that in six days' time he must unconditionally leave the office. I warned him to take measures, in the interval, for procuring some other abode. I offered to assist him in this endeavor, if he himself would but take the first step towards a removal. "And when you finally quit me, Bartleby," added I, "I shall see that you go not away entirely unprovided. Six days from this hour, remember."

At the expiration of that period, I peeped behind the screen, and lo! Bartleby was there.

I buttoned up my coat, balanced myself; advanced slowly towards him, touched his shoulder, and said, "The time has come; you must quit this place; I am sorry for you; here is money; but you must go."

"I would prefer not," he replied, with his back still towards me.

"You *must*."

He remained silent.

Now I had an unbounded confidence in this man's common honesty. He had frequently restored to me sixpences and shillings carelessly dropped upon the floor, for I am apt to be very reckless in such shirt-button affairs. The proceeding then which followed will not be deemed extraordinary.

"Bartleby," said I, "I owe you twelve dollars on account; here are thirty-two; the odd twenty are yours. – Will you take it?" and handed the bills towards him.

But he made no motion.

"I will leave them here then," putting them under a weight on the table. Then taking my hat and cane and going to the door I tranquilly turned and added – "After you have removed your things from these offices, Bartleby, you will of course lock the door – since every one is now gone for the day but you – and if you please, slip your key underneath the mat, so that I may have it in the morning. I shall not see you again; so good-bye to you. If hereafter in your new place of abode I can be of any service to you, do not fail to advise me by letter. Good-bye, Bartleby, and fare you well."

But he answered not a word; like the last column of some ruined temple, he remained standing mute and solitary in the middle of the otherwise deserted room.

As I walked home in a pensive mood, my vanity got the better of my pity. I could not but highly plume myself on my masterly management in getting rid of Bartleby. Masterly I call it, and such it must appear to any dispassionate thinker. The beauty of my procedure seemed to consist in its perfect quietness. There was no vulgar bullying, no bravado of any sort, no choleric hectoring, and striding to and fro across the apartment, jerking out vehement commands for Bartleby to bundle himself off with his beggarly traps. Nothing of the kind. Without loudly bidding Bartleby depart – as an inferior genius might have done – I *assumed* the ground that depart he must; and upon that assumption built all I had to say. The more I thought over my procedure, the more I was charmed with it. Nevertheless, next morning, upon awakening, I had my doubts, – I had somehow slept off the fumes of vanity. One of the coolest and wisest hours a man has, is just after he awakes in the morning. My procedure seemed as sagacious ever, – but only in theory. How it would prove in practice – there was the rub. It was truly a beautiful thought to have assumed Bartleby's departure; but, after all, that assumption was simply my own, and none of Bartleby's. The great point was, not whether I had assumed that he would quit me, but whether he would prefer so to do. He was more a man of preferences than assumptions.[16]

After breakfast, I walked down town, arguing the probabilities *pro* and *con*. One moment I thought it would prove a miserable failure, and Bartleby would be found all alive at my office as usual; the next moment it seemed certain that I should see his chair empty. And so I kept veering about. At the corner of Broadway and Canal-street, I saw quite an excited group of people standing in earnest conversation.

"I'll take odds he doesn't," said a voice as I passed.

"Doesn't go? – done!" said I, "put up your money."

I was instinctively putting my hand in my pocket to produce my own, when I remembered that this was an election day. The words I had overheard bore no reference to Bartleby, but to the success or non-success of some candidate for the mayoralty. In my intent frame of mind, I had, as it were, imagined that all Broadway shared in my excitement, and were debating the same question with me. I passed on, very thankful that the uproar of the street screened my momentary absent-mindedness.

As I had intended, I was earlier than usual at my office door. I stood listening for a moment. All was still. He must he gone. I tried the knob. The door was locked. Yes, my procedure had worked to a charm; he indeed must be vanished. Yet a certain melancholy mixed with this: I was almost sorry for my brilliant success. I was fumbling under the door mat for the key, which Bartleby was to have left there for me, when accidentally my knee knocked against a panel, producing a summoning sound, and in response a voice came to me from within – "Not yet; I am occupied."

It was Bartleby.

I was thunderstruck. For an instant I stood like the man who, pipe in mouth, was killed one cloudless afternoon long ago in Virginia, by summer lightning; at his own warm open window he was killed, and remained leaning out there upon the dreamy afternoon, till some one touched him, when he fell.

"Not gone!" I murmured at last. But again obeying that wondrous ascendancy which the inscrutable scrivener had over me, and from which ascendancy, for all my chafing, I could not completely escape, I slowly went down stairs and out into the street, and while

16. **assumptions:** In the original printing in *Putnam's*, the first part of the story ended at this point. The story continued in the next month's issue.

walking round the block, considered what I should next do in this unheard-of perplexity. Turn the man out by an actual thrusting I could not; to drive him away by calling him hard names would not do; calling in the police was an unpleasant idea; and yet, permit him to enjoy his cadaverous triumph over me, – this too I could not think of. What was to be done? or, if nothing could be done, was there any thing further that I could *assume* in the matter? Yes, as before I had prospectively assumed that Bartleby would depart, so now I might retrospectively assume that departed he was. In the legitimate carrying out of this assumption, I might enter my office in a great hurry, and pretending not to see Bartleby at all, walk straight against him as if he were air. Such a proceeding would in a singular degree have the appearance of a home-thrust. It was hardly possible that Bartleby could withstand such an application of the doctrine of assumptions. But upon second thoughts the success of the plan seemed rather dubious. I resolved to argue the matter over with him again.

"Bartleby," said I, entering the office, with a quietly severe expression, "I am seriously displeased. I am pained, Bartleby. I had thought better of you. I had imagined you of such a gentlemanly organization, that in any delicate dilemma a slight hint would suffice – in short, an assumption. But it appears I am deceived. Why," I added, unaffectedly starting, "you have not even touched that money yet," pointing to it, just where I had left it the evening previous.

He answered nothing.

"Will you, or will you not, quit me?" I now demanded in a sudden passion, advancing close to him.

"I would prefer *not* to quit you," he replied, gently emphasizing the *not*.

"What earthly right have you to stay here? Do you pay any rent? Do you pay my taxes? Or is this property yours?"

He answered nothing.

"Are you ready to go on and write now? Are your eyes recovered? Could you copy a small paper for me this morning? or help examine a few lines? or step round to the post-office? In a word, will you do any thing at all, to give a coloring to your refusal to depart the premises?"

He silently retired into his hermitage.

I was now in such a state of nervous resentment that I thought it but prudent to check myself at present from further demonstrations. Bartleby and I were alone. I remembered the tragedy of the unfortunate Adams and the still more unfortunate Colt[17] in the solitary office of the latter; and how poor Colt, being dreadfully incensed by Adams, and imprudently permitting himself to get wildly excited, was at unawares hurried into his fatal act – an act which certainly no man could possibly deplore more than the actor himself. Often it had occurred to me in my ponderings upon the subject, that

17. **Adams . . . Colt:** John C. Colt was a wealthy New York businessman who murdered a printer, Samuel Adams, in 1841. Adams had visited Colt in his lower Manhattan office to collect a debt, and Colt killed Adams with a hatchet. To cover up the crime, Colt crated the body for shipment to New Orleans, but it was discovered and Colt was arrested and sentenced for the murder. Claiming that the crime was an act of self-defense, Colt stabbed himself to death in the Tombs before he was to be hanged on November 18, 1842.

had that altercation taken place in the public street, or at a private residence, it would not have terminated as it did. It was the circumstance of being alone in a solitary office, up stairs, of a building entirely unhallowed by humanizing domestic associations – an uncarpeted office, doubtless, of a dusty, haggard sort of appearance; – this it must have been, which greatly helped to enhance the irritable desperation of the hapless Colt.

But when this old Adam of resentment rose in me and tempted me concerning Bartleby, I grappled him and threw him. How? Why, simply by recalling the divine injunction: "A new commandment give I unto you, that ye love one another." Yes, this it was that saved me. Aside from higher considerations, charity often operates as a vastly wise and prudent principle – a great safeguard to its possessor. Men have committed murder for jealousy's sake, and anger's sake, and hatred's sake, and selfishness' sake, and spiritual pride's sake; but no man that ever I heard of, ever committed a diabolical murder for sweet charity's sake. Mere self-interest, then, if no better motive can be enlisted, should, especially with high-tempered men, prompt all beings to charity and philanthropy. At any rate, upon the occasion in question, I strove to drown my exasperated feelings towards the scrivener by benevolently construing his conduct. Poor fellow, poor fellow! thought I, he don't mean any thing; and besides, he has seen hard times, and ought to be indulged.

I endeavored also immediately to occupy myself, and at the same time to comfort my despondency. I tried to fancy that in the course of the morning, at such time as might prove agreeable to him, Bartleby, of his own free accord, would emerge from his hermitage, and take up some decided line of march in the direction of the door. But no. Half-past twelve o'clock came; Turkey began to glow in the face, overturn his inkstand, and become generally obstreperous; Nippers abated down into quietude and courtesy; Ginger Nut munched his noon apple; and Bartleby remained standing at his window in one of his profoundest dead-wall reveries. Will it be credited? Ought I to acknowledge it? That afternoon I left the office without saying one further word to him.

Some days now passed, during which, at leisure intervals I looked a little into "Edwards on the Will," and "Priestley on Necessity."[18] Under the circumstances, those books induced a salutary feeling. Gradually I slid into the persuasion that these troubles of mine touching the scrivener, had been all predestinated from eternity, and Bartleby was billeted upon me for some mysterious purpose of an all-wise Providence, which it was not for a mere mortal like me to fathom. Yes, Bartleby, stay there behind your screen, thought I; I shall persecute you no more; you are harmless and noiseless as any of these old chairs; in short, I never feel so private as when I know you are here. At last I see it, I feel it; I penetrate to the predestinated purpose of my life. I am content. Others may have loftier parts to enact; but my mission in this world, Bartleby, is to furnish you with office-room for such period as you may see fit to remain.

---

18. **"Edwards on the Will" and "Priestley on Necessity":** Jonathan Edwards (1703–1758), a colonial American clergyman and theologian, was the author of *Freedom of the Will* (1754); Joseph Priestley (1733–1804), a British scientist and clergyman, wrote *Doctrine of Philosophical Necessity Illustrated* (1777). Both writers argued that events were predestined and that humans have no free will.

I believe that this wise and blessed frame of mind would have continued with me, had it not been for the unsolicited and uncharitable remarks obtruded upon me by my professional friends who visited the rooms. But thus it often is, that the constant friction of illiberal minds wears out at last the best resolves of the more generous. Though to be sure, when I reflected upon it, it was not strange that people entering my office should be struck by the peculiar aspect of the unaccountable Bartleby, and so be tempted to throw out some sinister observations concerning him. Sometimes an attorney having business with me, and calling at my office, and finding no one but the scrivener there, would undertake to obtain some sort of precise information from him touching my whereabouts; but without heeding his idle talk, Bartleby would remain standing immovable in the middle of the room. So after contemplating him in that position for a time, the attorney would depart, no wiser than he came.

Also, when a Reference[19] was going on, and the room full of lawyers and witnesses and business was driving fast; some deeply occupied legal gentleman present, seeing Bartleby wholly unemployed, would request him to run round to his (the legal gentleman's) office and fetch some papers for him. Thereupon, Bartleby would tranquilly decline, and yet remain idle as before. Then the lawyer would give a great stare, and turn to me. And what could I say? At last I was made aware that all through the circle of my professional acquaintance, a whisper of wonder was running round, having reference to the strange creature I kept at my office. This worried me very much. And as the idea came upon me of his possibly turning out a long-lived man, and keep occupying my chambers, and denying my authority; and perplexing my visitors; and scandalizing my professional reputation; and casting a general gloom over the premises; keeping soul and body together to the last upon his saving (for doubtless he spent but half a dime a day), and in the end perhaps outlive me, and claim possession of my office by right of his perpetual occupancy: as all these dark anticipations crowded upon me more and more, and my friends continually intruded their relentless remarks upon the apparition in my room; a great change was wrought in me. I resolved to gather all my faculties together, and for ever rid me of this intolerable incubus.

Ere revolving any complicated project, however, adapted to this end, I first simply suggested to Bartleby the propriety of his permanent departure. In a calm and serious tone, I commended the idea to his careful and mature consideration. But having taken three days to meditate upon it, he apprised me that his original determination remained the same; in short, that he still preferred to abide with me.

What shall I do? I now said to myself, buttoning up my coat to the last button. What shall I do? what ought I to do? what does conscience say I *should* do with this man, or rather ghost. Rid myself of him, I must; go, he shall. But how? You will not thrust him, the poor, pale, passive mortal, – you will not thrust such a helpless creature out of your door? you will not dishonor yourself by such cruelty? No, I will not, I cannot do that. Rather would I let him live and die here, and then mason up his remains in the wall. What then will you do? For all your coaxing, he will not budge. Bribes he leaves under

---

19. **Reference:** A legal proceeding in which a dispute is argued before a referee.

your own paperweight on your table; in short, it is quite plain that he prefers to cling to you.

Then something severe, something unusual must be done. What! surely you will not have him collared by a constable, and commit his innocent pallor to the common jail? And upon what ground could you procure such a thing to be done? – a vagrant, is he? What! he a vagrant, a wanderer, who refuses to budge? It is because he will *not* be a vagrant, then, that you seek to count him *as* a vagrant. That is too absurd. No visible means of support: there I have him. Wrong again: for indubitably he *does* support himself, and that is the only unanswerable proof that any man can show of his possessing the means so to do. No more then. Since he will not quit me, I must quit him. I will change my offices; I will move elsewhere; and give him fair notice that if I find him on my new premises I will then proceed against him as a common trespasser.

Acting accordingly, next day I thus addressed him: "I find these chambers too far from the City Hall; the air is unwholesome. In a word, I propose to remove my offices next week, and shall no longer require your services. I tell you this now, in order that you may seek another place."

He made no reply, and nothing more was said.

On the appointed day I engaged carts and men, proceeded to my chambers, and having but little furniture, every thing was removed in a few hours. Throughout, the scrivener remained standing behind the screen, which I directed to be removed the last thing. It was withdrawn; and being folded up like a huge folio, left him the motionless occupant of a naked room. I stood in the entry watching him a moment, while something from within me upbraided me.

I re-entered, with my hand in my pocket – and – and my heart in my mouth.

"Good-bye, Bartleby; I am going – good-bye, and God some way bless you; and take that," slipping something in his hand. But it dropped upon the floor, and then, – strange to say – I tore myself from him whom I had so longed to be rid of.

Established in my new quarters, for a day or two I kept the door locked, and started at every footfall in the passages. When I returned to my rooms after any little absence, I would pause at the threshold for an instant, and attentively listen, ere applying my key. But these fears were needless. Bartleby never came nigh me.

I thought all was going well, when a perturbed looking stranger visited me, inquiring whether I was the person who had recently occupied rooms at No. – Wall-street.

Full of forebodings, I replied that I was.

"Then sir," said the stranger, who proved a lawyer, "you are responsible for the man you left there. He refuses to do any copying; he refuses to do any thing; he says he prefers not to; and he refuses to quit the premises."

"I am very sorry, sir," said I, with assumed tranquillity, but an inward tremor, "but, really, the man you allude to is nothing to me – he is no relation or apprentice of mine, that you should hold me responsible for him."

"In mercy's name, who is he?"

"I certainly cannot inform you. I know nothing about him. Formerly I employed him as a copyist; but he has done nothing for me now for some time past."

"I shall settle him then, – good morning, sir."

Several days passed, and I heard nothing more; and though I often felt a charitable prompting to call at the place and see poor Bartleby, yet a certain squeamishness of I know not what withheld me.

All is over with him, by this time, thought I at last, when through another week no further intelligence reached me. But coming to my room the day after, I found several persons waiting at my door in a high state of nervous excitement.

"That's the man – here he comes," cried the foremost one, whom I recognized as the lawyer who had previously called upon me alone.

"You must take him away, sir, at once," cried a portly person among them, advancing upon me, and whom I knew to be the landlord of No. – Wall-street. "These gentlemen, my tenants, cannot stand it any longer; Mr. B—" pointing to the lawyer, "has turned him out of his room, and he now persists in haunting the building generally, sitting upon the banisters of the stairs by day, and sleeping in the entry by night. Every body is concerned; clients are leaving the offices; some fears are entertained of a mob; something you must do, and that without delay."

Aghast at this torrent, I fell back before it, and would fain have locked myself in my new quarters. In vain I persisted that Bartleby was nothing to me – no more than to any-one else. In vain: – I was the last person known to have any thing to do with him, and they held me to the terrible account. Fearful then of being exposed in the papers (as one person present obscurely threatened) I considered the matter, and at length said, that if the lawyer could give me a confidential interview with the scrivener, in his (the lawyer's) own room, I would that afternoon strive my best to rid them of the nuisance they complained of.

Going up stairs to my old haunt, there was Bartleby silently sitting upon the banister at the landing.

"What are you doing here, Bartleby?"

"Sitting upon the banister," he mildly replied.

I motioned him into the lawyer's room, who then left us.

"Bartleby," said I, "are you aware that you are the cause of great tribulation to me, by persisting in occupying the entry after being dismissed from the office?"

No answer.

"Now one of two things must take place. Either you must do something, or something must be done to you. Now what sort of business would you like to engage in? Would you like to re-engage in copying for some one?"

"No; I would prefer not to make any change."

"Would you like a clerkship in a dry-goods store?"

"There is too much confinement about that. No, I would not like a clerkship; but I am not particular."

"Too much confinement," I cried, "why you keep yourself confined all the time!"

"I would prefer not to take a clerkship," he rejoined, as if to settle that little item at once.

"How would a bar-tender's business suit you? There is no trying of the eyesight in that."

"I would not like it at all; though, as I said before, I am not particular."

His unwonted wordiness inspirited me. I returned to the charge.

"Well then, would you like to travel through the country collecting bills for the merchants? That would improve your health."

"No, I would prefer to be doing something else."

"How then would going as a companion to Europe, to entertain some young gentleman with your conversation, – how would that suit you?"

"Not at all. It does not strike me that there is any thing definite about that. I like to be stationary. But I am not particular."

"Stationery you shall be then," I cried, now losing all patience, and for the first time in all my exasperating connection with him fairly flying into a passion. "If you do not go away from these premises before night, I shall feel bound – indeed I *am* bound – to – to – to quit the premises myself!" I rather absurdly concluded, knowing not with what possible threat to try to frighten his immobility into compliance. Despairing of all further efforts, I was precipitately leaving him, when a final thought occurred to me – one which had not been wholly unindulged before.

"Bartleby," said I, in the kindest tone I could assume under such exciting circumstances, "will you go home with me now – not to my office, but my dwelling – and remain there till we can conclude upon some convenient arrangement for you at our leisure? Come, let us start now, right away."

"No: at present I would prefer not to make any change at all."

I answered nothing; but effectually dodging every one by the suddenness and rapidity of my flight, rushed from the building, ran up Wall-street towards Broadway, and jumping into the first omnibus was soon removed from pursuit. As soon as tranquillity returned I distinctly perceived that I had now done all that I possibly could, both in respect to the demands of the landlord and his tenants, and with regard to my own desire and sense of duty, to benefit Bartleby, and shield him from rude persecution. I now strove to be entirely care-free and quiescent; and my conscience justified me in the attempt; though indeed it was not so successful as I could have wished. So fearful was I of being again hunted out by the incensed landlord and his exasperated tenants, that, surrendering my business to Nippers, for a few days I drove about the upper part of the town and through the suburbs, in my rockaway;[20] crossed over to Jersey City and Hoboken, and paid fugitive visits to Manhattanville and Astoria. In fact I almost lived in my rockaway for the time.

When again I entered my office, lo, a note from the landlord lay upon the desk. I opened it with trembling hands. It informed me that the writer had sent to the police, and had Bartleby removed to the Tombs as a vagrant. Moreover, since I knew more about him than any one else, he wished me to appear at that place, and make a suitable statement of the facts. These tidings had a conflicting effect upon me. At first I was indignant; but at last almost approved. The landlord's energetic, summary disposition had led him to adopt a procedure which I do not think I would have decided upon myself; and yet as a last resort, under such peculiar circumstances, it seemed the only plan.

---

20. **rockaway:** A four-wheeled, enclosed carriage with two seats inside.

As I afterwards learned, the poor scrivener, when told that he must be conducted to the Tombs, offered not the slightest obstacle, but in his pale unmoving way, silently acquiesced.

Some of the compassionate and curious bystanders joined the party; and headed by one of the constables arm in arm with Bartleby, the silent procession filed its way through all the noise, and heat, and joy of the roaring thoroughfares at noon.

The same day I received the note I went to the Tombs, or to speak more properly, the Halls of Justice. Seeking the right officer, I stated the purpose of my call, and was informed that the individual I described was indeed within. I then assured the functionary that Bartleby was a perfectly honest man, and greatly to be compassionated, however unaccountably eccentric. I narrated all I knew, and closed by suggesting the idea of letting him remain in as indulgent confinement as possible till something less harsh might be done – though indeed I hardly knew what. At all events, if nothing else could be decided upon, the alms-house must receive him. I then begged to have an interview.

Being under no disgraceful charge, and quite serene and harmless in all his ways, they had permitted him freely to wander about the prison, and especially in the inclosed grass-platted yards thereof. And so I found him there, standing all alone in the quietest of the yards, his face towards a high wall, while all around, from the narrow slits of the jail windows, I thought I saw peering out upon him the eyes of murderers and thieves.

"Bartleby!"

"I know you," he said, without looking round, – "and I want nothing to say to you."

"It was not I that brought you here, Bartleby," said I, keenly pained at his implied suspicion. "And to you, this should not be so vile a place. Nothing reproachful attaches to you by being here. And see, it is not so sad a place as one might think. Look, there is the sky, and here is the grass."

"I know where I am," he replied, but would say nothing more, and so I left him.

As I entered the corridor again, a broad meat-like man, in an apron, accosted me, and jerking his thumb over his shoulder said – "Is that your friend?"

"Yes."

"Does he want to starve? If he does, let him live on the prison fare, that's all."

"Who are you?" asked I, not knowing what to make of such an unofficially speaking person in such a place.

"I am the grub-man. Such gentlemen as have friends here, hire me to provide them with something good to eat."

"Is this so?" said I, turning to the turnkey.

He said it was.

"Well then," said I, slipping some silver into the grub-man's hands (for so they called him). "I want you to give particular attention to my friend there; let him have the best dinner you can get. And you must be as polite to him as possible."

"Introduce me, will you?" said the grub-man, looking at me with an expression which seem to say he was all impatience for an opportunity to give a specimen of his breeding.

Thinking it would prove of benefit to the scrivener, I acquiesced; and asking the grub-man his name, went up with him to Bartleby.

"Bartleby, this is Mr. Cutlets; you will find him very useful to you."

"Your sarvant, sir, your sarvant," said the grub-man, making a low salutation behind his apron. "Hope you find it pleasant here, sir; – spacious grounds – cool apartments, sir – hope you'll stay with us some time – try to make it agreeable. May Mrs. Cutlets and I have the pleasure of your company to dinner, sir, in Mrs. Cutlets' private room?"

"I prefer not to dine to-day," said Bartleby, turning away. "It would disagree with me; I am unused to dinners." So saying he slowly moved to the other side of the inclosure, and took up a position fronting the dead-wall.

"How's this?" said the grub-man, addressing me with a stare of astonishment. "He's odd, aint he?"

"I think he is a little deranged," said I, sadly.

"Deranged? deranged is it? Well now, upon my word, I thought that friend of yourn was a gentleman forger; they are always pale and genteel-like, them forgers. I can't help pity 'em – can't help it, sir. Did you know Monroe Edwards?"[21] he added touchingly, and paused. Then, laying his hand pityingly on my shoulder, sighed, "he died of consumption at Sing-Sing. So you weren't acquainted with Monroe?"

"No. I was never socially acquainted with any forgers. But I cannot stop longer. Look to my friend yonder. You will not lose by it. I will see you again."

Some few days after this, I again obtained admission to the Tombs, and went through the corridors in quest of Bartleby; but without finding him.

"I saw him coming from his cell not long ago," said a turnkey, "may be he's gone to loiter in the yards."

So I went in that direction.

"Are you looking for the silent man?" said another turnkey passing me. "Yonder he lies – sleeping in the yard there. 'Tis not twenty minutes since I saw him lie down."

The yard was entirely quiet. It was not accessible to the common prisoners. The surrounding walls, of amazing thickness, kept off all sounds behind them. The Egyptian character of the masonry weighed upon me with its gloom. But a soft imprisoned turf grew under foot. The heart of the eternal pyramids, it seemed, wherein, by some strange magic, through the clefts, grass-seed, dropped by birds, had sprung.

Strangely huddled at the base of the wall, his knees drawn up, and lying on his side, his head touching the cold stones, I saw the wasted Bartleby. But nothing stirred. I paused; then went close up to him; stooped over, and saw that his dim eyes were open; otherwise he seemed profoundly sleeping. Something prompted me to touch him. I felt his hand, when a tingling shiver ran up my arm and down my spine to my feet.

The round face of the grub-man peered upon me now. "His dinner is ready. Won't he dine to-day, either? Or does he live without dining?"

"Lives without dining," said I, and closed the eyes.

---

21. **Monroe Edwards:** Edwards (1803?–1847) was a swindler and forger who notoriously defrauded several New York banks with bogus letters of credit. In 1842, he was arrested, convicted, and sentenced to ten years at Sing Sing, a brutal, "no-frills" prison on the banks of the Hudson River north of New York City – thus the expression "sent up the river." After an unsuccessful attempt to commit suicide and then to escape, Edwards died in the prison.

"Eh! – He's asleep, aint he?"

"With kings and counsellors,"[22] murmured I.

There would seem little need for proceeding further in this history. Imagination will readily supply the meagre recital of poor Bartleby's interment. But ere parting with the reader, let me say, that if this little narrative has sufficiently interested him, to awaken curiosity as to who Bartleby was, and what manner of life he led prior to the present narrator's making his acquaintance, I can only reply, that in such curiosity I fully share, but am wholly unable to gratify it. Yet here I hardly know whether I should divulge one little item of rumor, which came to my ear a few months after the scrivener's decease. Upon what basis it rested, I could never ascertain; and hence, how true it is I cannot now tell. But inasmuch as this vague report has not been without a certain strange suggestive interest to me, however sad, it may prove the same with some others; and so I will briefly mention it. The report was this: that Bartleby had been a subordinate clerk in the Dead Letter Office[23] at Washington, from which he had been suddenly removed by a change in the administration. When I think over this rumor, I cannot adequately express the emotions which seize me. Dead letters! does it not sound like dead men? Conceive a man by nature and misfortune prone to a pallid hopelessness, can any business seem more fitted to heighten it than that of continually handling these dead letters, and sorting them for the flames? For by the cart-load they are annually burned. Sometimes from out the folded paper the pale clerk takes a ring: – the finger it was meant for, perhaps, moulders in the grave; a bank-note sent in swiftest charity: – he whom it would relieve, nor eats nor hungers any more; pardon for those who died despairing; hope for those who died unhoping; good tidings for those who died stifled by unrelieved calamities. On errands of life, these letters speed to death.

Ah Bartleby! Ah humanity!

[1853]

---

22. **kings and counselors:** In the Old Testament, the afflicted Job curses the day he was born and asks: "Why died I not from the womb? Why did I not give up the ghost when I came out of the belly? Why did the knees prevent me? or why the breasts that I should suck? For now should I have lain still and been quiet, I should have slept: then had I been at rest, With kings and counsellors of the earth, which build desolate places for themselves" (Job 3:11-14).

23. **Dead Letter Office:** A room or department in the post office for letters that are undeliverable and unreturnable because of partial or incorrect addresses.

Melville's "The Paradise of Bachelors and the Tartarus of Maids."

These paired stories were based on two of Melville's travel experiences. In 1849, while he was in London arranging for the publication of *White-Jacket*, he visited the Temple and the Inns of Court, where he dined with his friend Robert Francis Cooke. In 1851, Melville journeyed to a paper mill in Dalton, Massachusetts, to buy paper for himself. But those experiences simply form the factual background to his densely symbolic stories, which are rich in cultural, historical, and religious allusions. Melville first submitted the stories to *Putnam's Monthly Magazine*, but the editor turned them down, fearing that the pieces might be offensive to the religious sentiments of some readers. Melville then sent them to *Harper's New Monthly Magazine*, founded in 1850. *Harper's* was initially designed to publish mostly British literature, since the lack of an international copyright law allowed the magazine to reprint the works of popular British writers, such as Charles Dickens and William Makepeace Thackeray, without paying royalties to the authors. But the editor of *Harper's*, Henry J. Raymond, eagerly accepted Melville's paired stories, then a popular form of magazine fiction. At the same time, the English setting of the first of the paired stories and the social criticism of the second would have appealed to many readers of *Harper's*. The text is taken from its first printing there, in April 1855.

THE PARADISE OF BACHELORS AND THE TARTARUS OF MAIDS

I. The Paradise of Bachelors

It lies not far from Temple-Bar.[1]

Going to it, by the usual way, is like stealing from a heated plain into some cool, deep glen, shady among harboring hills.

Slick with the din and soiled with the mud of Fleet Street – where the Benedick[2] tradesmen are hurrying by, with ledger-lines ruled along their brows, thinking upon rise of bread and fall of babies – you adroitly turn a mystic corner – not a street – glide down a dim, monastic way, flanked by dark, sedate, and solemn piles, and still wending on, give the whole care-worn world the slip, and, disentangled, stand beneath the quiet cloisters of the Paradise of Bachelors.[3]

Sweet are the oases in Sahara; charming the isle-groves of August prairies; delectable pure faith amidst a thousand perfidies: but sweeter, still more charming, most delectable, the dreamy Paradise of Bachelors, found in the stony heart of stunning London.

---

1. **Temple-Bar:** In medieval London, gates separated the City of London from surrounding districts. As a replacement to the old gate, the architect Christopher Wren (1631-1723) designed the Temple-Bar, an elaborate arched gate that separated one street into two: Fleet Street, the location of many bookstores and publishing offices, and, on the other side of the gate, the Strand, a thoroughfare of hotels, shops, and restaurants. In the nineteenth century, the name "Fleet Street" was synonymous with writers and publishing.
2. **Benedick:** A form of *benedict*, a newly married man who was previously considered a confirmed bachelor; the name is taken from Benedick, a character in Shakespeare's *Much Ado about Nothing*.
3. **Paradise of Bachelors:** Melville echoes the opening of "London Antiques," from *The Sketch Book* by Washington Irving (1783-1859), which describes the parklike setting of the four Inns of Court, just off Fleet Street, a campus of offices and living quarters for lawyers and law students.

In mild meditation pace the cloisters; take your pleasure, sip your leisure, in the garden waterward; go linger in the ancient library; go worship in the sculptured chapel: but little have you seen, just nothing do you know, not the sweet kernel have you tasted, till you dine among the banded Bachelors, and see their convivial eyes and glasses sparkle. Not dine in bustling commons, during term-time, in the hall; but tranquilly, by private hint, at a private table; some fine Templar's[4] hospitably invited guest.

Templar? That's a romantic name. Let me see. Brian de Bois Gilbert[5] was a Templar, I believe. Do we understand you to insinuate that those famous Templars still survive in modern London? May the ring of their armed heels be heard, and the rattle of their shields, as in mailed prayer the monk-knights kneel before the consecrated Host? Surely a monk-knight were a curious sight picking his way along the Strand, his gleaming corselet and snowy surcoat spattered by an omnibus. Long-bearded, too, according to his order's rule; his face fuzzy as a pard's;[6] how would the grim ghost look among the crop-haired, close-shaven citizens? We know indeed – sad history recounts it – that a moral blight tainted at last this sacred Brotherhood. Though no sworded foe might outskill them in the fence, yet the worm of luxury crawled beneath their guard, gnawing the core of knightly troth, nibbling the monastic vow, till at last the monk's austerity relaxed to wassailing, and the sworn knights-bachelors grew to be but hypocrites and rakes.

But for all this, quite unprepared were we to learn that Knights-Templars (if at all in being) were so entirely secularized as to be reduced from carving out immortal fame in glorious battling for the Holy Land, to the carving of roast-mutton at a dinner-board. Like Anacreon,[7] do these degenerate Templars now think it sweeter far to fall in banquet than in war? Or, indeed, how can there be any survival of that famous order? Templars in modern London! Templars in their red-cross mantles smoking cigars at the Divan![8] Templars crowded in a railway train, till, stacked with steel helmet, spear, and shield, the whole train looks like one elongated locomotive!

No. The genuine Templar is long since departed. Go view the wondrous tombs in the Temple Church;[9] see there the rigidly-haughty forms stretched out, with crossed arms upon their stilly hearts, in everlasting and undreaming rest. Like the years before the flood, the bold Knights-Templars are no more. Nevertheless, the name remains, and the nominal society, and the ancient grounds, and some of the ancient edifices. But the iron heel is changed to a boot of patent-leather; the long two-handed sword to a one-handed

---

4. **Templar's:** A Templar was a knight in a religious military order founded in Jerusalem during the Crusades in the twelfth century. *Templar* is also British usage for a lawyer or law student with rooms in one of the Inns of Court, called the Inner Temple and the Middle Temple.
5. **Brian de Bois Gilbert:** Sir Brian de Bois Guilbert was an evil Knight Templar in the popular historical romance *Ivanhoe* (1819), by Sir Walter Scott (1771–1832).
6. **pard's:** Leopard's.
7. **Anacreon:** Ancient Greek lyric poet who lived in the sixth century BCE.
8. **Divan:** Two meanings of *divan* are invoked here: a public audience or counsel room in Muslim countries or a public smoking room or coffeehouse furnished with sofas.
9. **Temple Church:** Constructed in 1185 and part of two of the Inns of Courts, the Inner Temple and the Middle Temple.

quill; the monk-giver of gratuitous ghostly counsel now counsels for a fee; the defender of the sarcophagus (if in good practice with his weapon) now has more than one case to defend; the vowed opener and clearer of all highways leading to the Holy Sepulchre,[10] now has it in particular charge to check, to clog, to hinder, and embarrass all the courts and avenues of Law; the knight-combatant of the Saracen, breasting spear-points at Acre, now fights law-points in Westminster Hall.[11] The helmet is a wig. Struck by Time's enchanter's wand, the Templar is to-day a Lawyer.

But, like many others tumbled from proud glory's height – like the apple, hard on the bough but mellow on the ground – the Templar's fall has but made him all the finer fellow.

I dare say those old warrior-priests were but gruff and grouty at the best; cased in Birmingham hardware,[12] how could their crimped arms give yours or mine a hearty shake? Their proud, ambitious, monkish souls clasped shut, like horn-book missals;[13] their very faces clapped in bomb-shells; what sort of genial men were these? But best of comrades, most affable of hosts, capital diner is the modern Templar. His wit and wine are both of sparkling brands.

The church and cloisters, courts and vaults, lanes and passages, banquet-halls, refectories, libraries, terraces, gardens, broad walks, domicils, and dessert-rooms, covering a very large space of ground, and all grouped in central neighborhood, and quite sequestered from the old city's surrounding din; and every thing about the place being kept in most bachelor-like particularity, no part of London offers to a quiet wight so agreeable a refuge.

The Temple is, indeed, a city by itself. A city with all the best appurtenances, as the above enumeration shows. A city with a park to it, and flower-beds, and a river-side – the Thames flowing by as openly, in one part, as by Eden's primal garden flowed the mild Euphrates. In what is now the Temple Garden the old Crusaders used to exercise their steeds and lances; the modern Templars now lounge on the benches beneath the trees, and, switching their patent-leather boots, in gay discourse exercise at repartee.

Long lines of stately portraits in the banquet-halls, show what great men of mark – famous nobles, judges, and Lord Chancellors – have in their time been Templars. But all Templars are not known to universal fame; though, if the having warm hearts and warmer welcomes, full minds and fuller cellars, and giving good advice and glorious dinners, spiced with rare divertisements of fun and fancy, merit immortal mention, set down, ye muses, the names of R. F. C.[14] and his imperial brother.

---

10. **Holy Sepulchre:** The Church of the Holy Sepulchre in Jerusalem is the site of the supposed tomb of Jesus Christ.

11. **Saracen . . . Westminster Hall:** A Saracen was an Arab or Muslim at the time of the Crusades; Acre was an important Mediterranean seaport in what is now Israel; and Westminster Hall, built in 1097–99, was later used for a time as a law court.

12. **Birmingham hardware:** The manufacturing of various metals for a variety of domestic and industrial uses was a major industry in this west-central English city.

13. **missals:** Devotional books.

14. **R. F. C.:** The initials of Robert Francis Cooke, who entertained Melville at a dinner in Elm Court on December 19, 1849.

Though to be a Templar, in the one true sense, you must needs be a lawyer, or a student at the law, and be ceremoniously enrolled as member of the order, yet as many such, though Templars, do not reside within the Temple's precincts, though they may have their offices there, just so, on the other hand, there are many residents of the hoary old domicils who are not admitted Templars. If being, say, a lounging gentleman and bachelor, or a quiet, unmarried, literary man, charmed with the soft seclusion of the spot, you much desire to pitch your shady tent among the rest in this serene encampment, then you must make some special friend among the order, and procure him to rent, in his name but at your charge, whatever vacant chamber you may find to suit.

Thus, I suppose, did Dr. Johnson,[15] that nominal Benedick and widower but virtual bachelor, when for a space he resided here. So, too, did that undoubted bachelor and rare good soul, Charles Lamb.[16] And hundreds more, of sterling spirits, Brethren of the Order of Celibacy, from time to time have dined, and slept, and tabernacled here. Indeed, the place is all a honeycomb of offices and domicils. Like any cheese, it is quite perforated through and through in all directions with the snug cells of bachelors. Dear, delightful spot! Ah! when I bethink me of the sweet hours there passed, enjoying such genial hospitalities beneath those time-honored roofs, my heart only finds due utterance through poetry; and, with a sigh, I softly sing, "Carry me back to old Virginny!"

Such then, at large, is the Paradise of Bachelors. And such I found it one pleasant afternoon in the smiling month of May, when, sallying from my hotel in Trafalgar Square, I went to keep my dinner-appointment with that fine Barrister, Bachelor, and Bencher,[17] R. F. C. (he *is* the first and second, and *should be* the third; I hereby nominate him), whose card I kept fast pinched between my gloved forefinger and thumb, and every now and then snatched still another look at the pleasant address inscribed beneath the name, "No. – , Elm Court, Temple."

At the core he was a right bluff, care-free, right comfortable, and most companionable Englishman. If on a first acquaintance he seemed reserved, quite icy in his air – patience; this Champagne will thaw. And if it never do, better frozen Champagne than liquid vinegar.

There were nine gentlemen, all bachelors, at the dinner. One was from "No. – , King's Bench Walk, Temple;" a second, third, and fourth, and fifth, from various courts or passages christened with some similarly rich resounding syllables. It was indeed a sort of Senate of the Bachelors, sent to this dinner from widely-scattered districts, to represent the general celibacy of the Temple. Nay it was, by representation, a Grand Parliament of the best Bachelors in universal London; several of those present being from distant quarters of the town, noted immemorial seats of lawyers and unmarried men – Lincoln's Inn, Furnival's Inn; and one gentleman, upon whom I looked with a sort of collateral awe, hailed from the spot where Lord Verulam[18] once abode a bachelor – Gray's Inn.

---

15. **Dr. Johnson:** Samuel Johnson (1775-1834), English writer and lexicographer who lived near Fleet Street.
16. **Charles Lamb:** (1775-1834) English essayist who also lived in various lodgings near Fleet Street.
17. **Bencher:** A judge.
18. **Lord Verulam:** Francis Bacon (1561-1626), English philosopher.

The apartment was well up toward heaven. I know not how many strange old stairs I climbed to get to it. But a good dinner, with famous company, should be well earned. No doubt our host had his dining-room so high with a view to secure the prior exercise necessary to the due relishing and digesting of it.

The furniture was wonderfully unpretending, old, and snug. No new shining mahogany, sticky with undried varnish; no uncomfortably luxurious ottomans, and sofas too fine to use, vexed you in this sedate apartment. It is a thing which every sensible American should learn from every sensible Englishman, that glare and glitter, gimcracks and gewgaws, are not indispensable to domestic solacement. The American Benedick snatches, down-town, a tough chop in a gilded show-box; the English bachelor leisurely dines at home on that incomparable South Down[19] of his, off a plain deal board.

The ceiling of the room was low. Who wants to dine under the dome of St. Peter's?[20] High ceilings! If that is your demand, and the higher the better, and you be so very tall, then go dine out with the topping giraffe in the open air.

In good time the nine gentlemen sat down to nine covers, and soon were fairly under way.

If I remember right, ox-tail soup inaugurated the affair. Of a rich russet hue, its agreeable flavor dissipated my first confounding of its main ingredient with teamster's gads and the raw-hides of ushers.[21] (By way of interlude, we here drank a little claret.) Neptune's was the next tribute rendered – turbot coming second; snow-white, flaky, and just gelatinous enough, not too turtleish in its unctuousness.

(At this point we refreshed ourselves with a glass of sherry.) After these light skirmishers had vanished, the heavy artillery of the feast marched in, led by that well-known English generalissimo, roast beef. For aids-de-camp we had a saddle of mutton, a fat turkey, a chicken-pie, and endless other savory things; while for avant-couriers came nine silver flagons of humming ale. This heavy ordnance having departed on the track of the light skirmishers, a picked brigade of game-fowl encamped upon the board, their camp-fires lit by the ruddiest of decanters.

Tarts and puddings followed, with innumerable niceties; then cheese and crackers. (By way of ceremony, simply, only to keep up good old fashions, we here each drank a glass of good old port.)

The cloth was now removed; and like Blucher's army coming in at the death on the field of Waterloo,[22] in marched a fresh detachment of bottles, dusty with their hurried march.

All these manoeuvrings of the forces were superintended by a surprising old field-marshal (I can not school myself to call him by the inglorious name of waiter), with

---

19. **South Down:** Meat taken from an English breed of sheep; also referred to as "mutton," it was served on a wooden plate.

20. **St. Peter's:** St. Peter's Basilica in Rome.

21. **gads . . . ushers:** Drivers used goads or gads made from oxtails; an usher was an assistant schoolteacher who often used oxtails as whips.

22. **Waterloo:** Napoleon was defeated at Waterloo in 1815, in part by Gebhard von Blucher (1742–1819), leader of the Prussian troops.

snowy hair and napkin, and a head like Socrates. Amidst all the hilarity of the feast, intent on important business, he disdained to smile. Venerable man!

I have above endeavored to give some slight schedule of the general plan of operations. But any one knows that a good, genial dinner is a sort of pell-mell, indiscriminate affair, quite baffling to detail in all particulars. Thus, I spoke of taking a glass of claret, and a glass of sherry, and a glass of port, and a mug of ale – all at certain specific periods and times. But those were merely the state bumpers,[23] so to speak. Innumerable impromptu glasses were drained between the periods of those grand imposing ones.

The nine bachelors seemed to have the most tender concern for each other's health. All the time, in flowing wine, they most earnestly expressed their sincerest wishes for the entire well-being and lasting hygiene of the gentlemen on the right and on the left. I noticed that when one of these kind bachelors desired a little more wine (just for his stomach's sake, like Timothy),[24] he would not help himself to it unless some other bachelor would join him. It seemed held something indelicate, selfish, and unfraternal, to be seen taking a lonely, unparticipated glass. Meantime, as the wine ran apace, the spirits of the company grew more and more to perfect genialness and unconstraint. They related all sorts of pleasant stories. Choice experiences in their private lives were now brought out, like choice brands of Moselle or Rhenish, only kept for particular company. One told us how mellowly he lived when a student at Oxford; with various spicy anecdotes of most frank-hearted noble lords, his liberal companions. Another bachelor, a gray-headed man, with a sunny face, who, by his own account, embraced every opportunity of leisure to cross over into the Low Countries,[25] on sudden tours of inspection of the fine old Flemish architecture there – this learned, white-haired, sunny-faced old bachelor, excelled in his descriptions of the elaborate splendors of those old guild-halls, town-halls, and stadthold-houses, to be seen in the land of the ancient Flemings. A third was a great frequenter of the British Museum, and knew all about scores of wonderful antiquities, of Oriental manuscripts, and costly books without a duplicate. A fourth had lately returned from a trip to Old Granada, and, of course, was full of Saracenic scenery. A fifth had a funny case in law to tell. A sixth was erudite in wines. A seventh had a strange characteristic anecdote of the private life of the Iron Duke,[26] never printed, and never before announced in any public or private company. An eighth had lately been amusing his evenings, now and then, with translating a comic poem of Pulci's.[27] He quoted for us the more amusing passages.

And so the evening slipped along, the hours told, not by a water-clock, like King Alfred's, but a wine-chronometer. Meantime the table seemed a sort of Epsom Heath;[28] a

23. **bumpers:** Large glasses used for ceremonial toasts.
24. **Timothy:** In the New Testament, Paul advised Timothy to "Drink no longer water, but use a little wine for thy stomach's sake and thine often infirmities" (1 Timothy 5:23).
25. **Low Countries:** The regional name given to the Netherlands, Belgium, and Luxembourg.
26. **Iron Duke:** The name given to the Duke of Wellington (1769-1852), leader of the English army that defeated Napoleon at Waterloo in 1815.
27. **Pulci's:** Luigi Pulci (1432-1484) was an Italian poet.
28. **Epsom Heath:** Racetrack where the famous Derby horse race is run.

regular ring, where the decanters galloped round. For fear one decanter should not with sufficient speed reach his destination, another was sent express after him to hurry him; and then a third to hurry the second; and so on with a fourth and fifth. And throughout all this nothing loud, nothing unmannerly, nothing turbulent. I am quite sure, from the scrupulous gravity and austerity of his air, that had Socrates, the field-marshal, perceived aught of indecorum in the company he served, he would have forthwith departed without giving warning. I afterward learned that, during the repast, an invalid bachelor in an adjoining chamber enjoyed his first sound refreshing slumber in three long, weary weeks.

It was the very perfection of quiet absorption of good living, good drinking, good feeling, and good talk. We were a band of brothers. Comfort – fraternal, household comfort, was the grand trait of the affair. Also, you could plainly see that these easy-hearted men had no wives or children to give an anxious thought. Almost all of them were travelers, too; for bachelors alone can travel freely, and without any twinges of their consciences touching desertion of the fireside.

The thing called pain, the bugbear styled trouble – those two legends seemed preposterous to their bachelor imaginations. How could men of liberal sense, ripe scholarship in the world, and capacious philosophical and convivial understandings – how could they suffer themselves to be imposed upon by such monkish fables? Pain! Trouble! As well talk of Catholic miracles. No such thing – Pass the sherry, Sir – Pooh, pooh! Can't be! – The port, Sir, if you please. Nonsense; don't tell me so. – The decanter stops with you, Sir, I believe.

And so it went.

Not long after the cloth was drawn our host glanced significantly upon Socrates, who, solemnly stepping to a stand, returned with an immense convolved horn, a regular Jericho horn,[29] mounted with polished silver, and otherwise chased and curiously enriched; not omitting two life-like goat's heads, with four more horns of solid silver, projecting from opposite sides of the mouth of the noble main horn.

Not having heard that our host was a performer on the bugle, I was surprised to see him lift this horn from the table, as if he were about to blow an inspiring blast. But I was relieved from this, and set quite right as touching the purposes of the horn, by his now inserting his thumb and forefinger into its mouth; whereupon a slight aroma was stirred up, and my nostrils were greeted with the smell of some choice Rappee.[30] It was a mull of snuff. It went the rounds. Capital idea this, thought I, of taking snuff about this juncture. This goodly fashion must be introduced among my countrymen at home, further ruminated I.

The remarkable decorum of the nine bachelors – a decorum not to be affected by any quantity of wine – a decorum unassailable by any degree of mirthfulness – this was again set in a forcible light to me, by now observing that, though they took snuff very

29. **Jericho horn:** In the Old Testament, the city of Jericho was captured by the Israelites after seven of their priests blew loud blasts on their horns for seven days. On the final day, the walls of the city fell and Joshua took the city (Joshua 6:1-20).

30. **Rappee:** A strong snuff made from pulverized tobacco.

freely, yet not a man so far violated the proprieties, or so far molested the invalid bachelor in the adjoining room as to indulge himself in a sneeze. The snuff was snuffed silently, as if it had been some fine innoxious powder brushed off the wings of butterflies.

But fine though they be, bachelors' dinners, like bachelors' lives, can not endure forever. The time came for breaking up. One by one the bachelors took their hats, and two by two, and arm-in-arm they descended, still conversing, to the flagging of the court; some going to their neighboring chambers to turn over the Decameron[31] ere retiring for the night; some to smoke a cigar, promenading in the garden on the cool river-side; some to make for the street, call a hack, and be driven snugly to their distant lodgings.

I was the last lingerer.

"Well," said my smiling host, "what do you think of the Temple here, and the sort of life we bachelors make out to live in it?"

"Sir," said I, with a burst of admiring candor – "Sir, this is the very Paradise of Bachelors!"

II. The Tartarus[32] of Maids

It lies not far from Woedolor Mountain in New England. Turning to the east, right out from among bright farms and sunny meadows, nodding in early June with odorous grasses, you enter ascendingly among bleak hills. These gradually close in upon a dusky pass, which, from the violent Gulf Stream of air unceasingly driving between its cloven walls of haggard rock, as well as from the tradition of a crazy spinster's hut having long ago stood somewhere hereabouts, is called the Mad Maid's Bellows'-pipe.

Winding along at the bottom of the gorge is a dangerously narrow wheel-road, occupying the bed of a former torrent. Following this road to its highest point, you stand as within a Dantean gateway.[33] From the steepness of the walls here, their strangely ebon hue, and the sudden contraction of the gorge, this particular point is called the Black Notch. The ravine now expandingly descends into a great, purple, hopper-shaped hollow, far sunk among many Plutonian, shaggy-wooded mountains. By the country people this hollow is called the Devil's Dungeon. Sounds of torrents fall on all sides upon the ear. These rapid waters unite at last in one turbid brick-colored stream, boiling through a flume among enormous boulders. They call this strange-colored torrent Blood River. Gaining a dark precipice it wheels suddenly to the west, and makes one maniac spring of sixty feet into the arms of a stunted wood of gray-haired pines, between which it thence eddies on its further way down to the invisible lowlands.

Conspicuously crowning a rocky bluff high to one side, at the cataract's verge, is the ruin of an old saw-mill, built in those primitive times when vast pines and hemlocks superabounded throughout the neighboring region. The black-mossed bulk of those

31. **Decameron:** A collection of bawdy tales by the Italian writer Giovanni Boccaccio (1313-1375).
32. **Tartarus:** The lower region of hell in Greek mythology.
33. **Dantean gateway:** In *Inferno*, Dante Alighieri (1265-1321) describes the ugly gates of hell, with their inscription, "Abandon hope, all ye who enter here."

immense, rough-hewn, and spike-knotted logs, here and there tumbled all together, in long abandonment and decay, or left in solitary, perilous projection over the cataract's gloomy brink, impart to this rude wooden ruin not only much of the aspect of one of rough-quarried stone, but also a sort of feudal, Rhineland, and Thurmberg[34] look, derived from the pinnacled wildness of the neighboring scenery.

Not far from the bottom of the Dungeon stands a large white-washed building, relieved, like some great white sepulchre,[35] against the sullen background of mountain-side firs, and other hardy evergreens, inaccessibly rising in grim terraces for some two thousand feet.

The building is a paper-mill.

Having embarked on a large scale in the seedsman's business (so extensively and broadcast, indeed, that at length my seeds were distributed through all the Eastern and Northern States, and even fell into the far soil of Missouri and the Carolinas), the demand for paper at my place became so great, that the expenditure soon amounted to a most important item in the general account. It need hardly be hinted how paper comes into use with seedsmen, as envelopes. These are mostly made of yellowish paper, folded square; and when filled, are all but flat, and being stamped, and superscribed with the nature of the seeds contained, assume not a little the appearance of business-letters ready for the mail. Of these small envelopes I used an incredible quantity – several hundreds of thousands in a year. For a time I had purchased my paper from the wholesale dealers in a neighboring town. For economy's sake, and partly for the adventure of the trip, I now resolved to cross the mountains, some sixty miles, and order my future paper at the Devil's Dungeon paper-mill.

The sleighing being uncommonly fine toward the end of January, and promising to hold so for no small period, in spite of the bitter cold I started one gray Friday noon in my pung,[36] well fitted with buffalo and wolf robes; and, spending one night on the road, next noon came in sight of Woedolor Mountain.

The far summit fairly smoked with frost; white vapors curled up from its white-wooded top, as from a chimney. The intense congelation made the whole country look like one petrifaction. The steel shoes of my pung craunched and gritted over the vitreous, chippy snow, as if it had been broken glass. The forests here and there skirting the route, feeling the same all-stiffening influence, their inmost fibres penetrated with the cold, strangely groaned – not in the swaying branches merely, but likewise in the vertical trunk – as the fitful gusts remorselessly swept through them. Brittle with excessive frost, many colossal tough-grained maples, snapped in twain like pipe-stems, cumbered the unfeeling earth.

Flaked all over with frozen sweat, white as a milky ram, his nostrils at each breath

---

34. **Thurmberg:** A castle on the Rhine River in Germany that Melville visited in 1849.
35. **whited sepulchre:** See Christ's sermon in Matthew 23:27: "Woe unto you, scribes and Pharisees, hypocrites! for ye are like unto whited sepulchres, which indeed appear beautiful outward, but are within full of dead men's bones, and of all uncleanness."
36. **pung:** A one-horse sleigh.

sending forth two horn-shaped shoots of heated respiration, Black, my good horse, but six years old, started at a sudden turn, where, right across the track – not ten minutes fallen – an old distorted hemlock lay, darkly undulatory as an anaconda.

Gaining the Bellows'-pipe, the violent blast, dead from behind, all but shoved my high-backed pung up-hill. The gust shrieked through the shivered pass, as if laden with lost spirits bound to the unhappy world. Ere gaining the summit, Black, my horse, as if exasperated by the cutting wind, slung out with his strong hind legs, tore the light pung straight up-hill, and sweeping grazingly through the narrow notch, sped downward madly past the ruined saw-mill. Into the Devil's Dungeon horse and cataract rushed together.

With might and main, quitting my seat and robes, and standing backward, with one foot braced against the dash-board, I rasped and churned the bit, and stopped him just in time to avoid collision, at a turn, with the bleak nozzle of a rock, couchant like a lion in the way – a road-side rock.

At first I could not discover the paper-mill.

The whole hollow gleamed with the white, except, here and there, where a pinnacle of granite showed one wind-swept angle bare. The mountains stood pinned in shrouds – a pass of Alpine corpses. Where stands the mill? Suddenly a whirling, humming sound broke upon my ear. I looked, and there, like an arrested avalanche, lay the large white-washed factory. It was subordinately surrounded by a cluster of other and smaller buildings, some of which, from their cheap, blank air, great length, gregarious windows, and comfortless expression, no doubt were boarding-houses of the operatives.[37] A snow-white hamlet amidst the snows. Various rude, irregular squares and courts resulted from the somewhat picturesque clusterings of these buildings, owing to the broken, rocky nature of the ground, which forbade all method in their relative arrangement. Several narrow lanes and alleys, too, partly blocked with snow fallen from the roof, cut up the hamlet in all directions.

When, turning from the traveled highway, jingling with bells of numerous farmers – who, availing themselves of the fine sleighing, were dragging their wood to market – and frequently diversified with swift cutters dashing from inn to inn of the scattered villages – when, I say, turning from that bustling main-road, I by degrees wound into the Mad Maid's Bellows'-pipe, and saw the grim Black Notch beyond, then something latent, as well as something obvious in the time and scene, strangely brought back to my mind my first sight of dark and grimy Temple-Bar. And when Black, my horse, went darting through the Notch, perilously grazing its rocky wall, I remembered being in a runaway London omnibus, which in much the same sort of style, though by no means at an equal rate, dashed through the ancient arch of Wren. Though the two objects did by no means completely correspond, yet this partial inadequacy but served to tinge the similitude not less with the vividness than the disorder of a dream. So that, when upon reining up at the protruding rock I at last caught sight of the quaint groupings of the factory-buildings, and with the traveled highway and the Notch behind, found myself all alone,

37. **operatives:** Factory workers.

silently and privily stealing through deep-cloven passages into this sequestered spot, and saw the long, high-gabled main factory edifice, with a rude tower – for hoisting heavy boxes – at one end, standing among its crowded outbuildings and boarding-houses, as the Temple Church amidst the surrounding offices and dormitories, and when the marvelous retirement of this mysterious mountain nook fastened its whole spell upon me, then, what memory lacked, all tributary imagination furnished, and I said to myself, "This is the very counterpart of the Paradise of Bachelors, but snowed upon, and frost-painted to a sepulchre."

Dismounting, and warily picking my way down the dangerous declivity – horse and man both sliding now and then upon the icy ledges – at length I drove, or the blast drove me, into the largest square, before one side of the main edifice. Piercingly and shrilly the shotted blast blew by the corner; and redly and demoniacally boiled Blood River at one side. A long woodpile, of many scores of cords, all glittering in mail of crusted ice, stood crosswise in the square. A row of horse-posts, their north sides plastered with adhesive snow, flanked the factory wall. The bleak frost packed and paved the square as with some ringing metal.

The inverted similitude recurred – "The sweet, tranquil Temple garden, with the Thames bordering its green beds," strangely meditated I.

But where are the gay bachelors?

Then, as I and my horse stood shivering in the wind-spray, a girl ran from a neighboring dormitory door, and throwing her thin apron over her bare head, made for the opposite building.

"One moment, my girl; is there no shed hereabouts which I may drive into?"

Pausing, she turned upon me a face pale with work, and blue with cold; an eye supernatural with unrelated misery.

"Nay," faltered I, "I mistook you. Go on; I want nothing."

Leading my horse close to the door from which she had come, I knocked. Another pale, blue girl appeared, shivering in the doorway as, to prevent the blast, she jealously held the door ajar.

"Nay, I mistake again. In God's name shut the door. But hold, is there no man about?"

That moment a dark-complexioned well-wrapped personage passed, making for the factory door, and spying him coming, the girl rapidly closed the other one.

"Is there no horse-shed here, Sir?"

"Yonder, to the wood-shed," he replied, and disappeared inside the factory.

With much ado I managed to wedge in horse and pung between the scattered piles of wood all sawn and split. Then, blanketing my horse, and piling my buffalo on the blanket's top, and tucking in its edges well around the breast-band and breeching, so that the wind might not strip him bare, I tied him fast, and ran lamely for the factory door, stiff with frost, and cumbered with my driver's dread-naught.[38]

Immediately I found myself standing in a spacious place, intolerably lighted by long rows of windows, focusing inward the snowy scene without.

---

38. **dread-naught:** A thick, heavy coat.

At rows of blank-looking counters sat rows of blank-looking girls, with blank, white folders in their blank hands, all blankly folding blank paper.

In one corner stood some huge frame of ponderous iron, with a vertical thing like a piston periodically rising and falling upon a heavy wooden block. Before it – its tame minister – stood a tall girl, feeding the iron animal with half-quires of rose-hued note paper, which, at every downward dab of the piston-like machine, received in the corner the impress of a wreath of roses. I looked from the rosy paper to the pallid cheek, but said nothing.

Seated before a long apparatus, strung with long, slender strings like any harp, another girl was feeding it with foolscap sheets,[39] which, so soon as they curiously traveled from her on the cords, were withdrawn at the opposite end of the machine by a second girl. They came to the first girl blank; they went to the second girl ruled.

I looked upon the first girl's brow, and saw it was young and fair; I looked upon the second girl's brow, and saw it was ruled and wrinkled. Then, as I still looked, the two – for some small variety to the monotony – changed places; and where had stood the young, fair brow, now stood the ruled and wrinkled one.

Perched high upon a narrow platform, and still higher upon a high stool crowning it, sat another figure serving some other iron animal; while below the platform sat her mate in some sort of reciprocal attendance.

Not a syllable was breathed. Nothing was heard but the low, steady, overruling hum of the iron animals. The human voice was banished from the spot. Machinery – that vaunted slave of humanity – here stood menially served by human beings, who served mutely and cringingly as the slave serves the Sultan. The girls did not so much seem accessory wheels to the general machinery as mere cogs to the wheels.

All this scene around me was instantaneously taken in at one sweeping glance – even before I had proceeded to unwind the heavy fur tippet from around my neck. But as soon as this fell from me the dark-complexioned man, standing close by, raised a sudden cry, and seizing my arm, dragged me out into the open air, and without pausing for a word instantly caught up some congealed snow and began rubbing both my cheeks.

"Two white spots like the whites of your eyes," he said; "man, your cheeks are frozen."

"That may well be," muttered I; " 'tis some wonder the frost of the Devil's Dungeon strikes in no deeper. Rub away."

Soon a horrible, tearing pain caught at my reviving cheeks. Two gaunt blood-hounds, one on each side, seemed mumbling them. I seemed Actaeon.[40]

Presently, when all was over, I re-entered the factory, made known my business, concluded it satisfactory, and then begged to be conducted throughout the place to view it.

"Cupid is the boy for that," said the dark-complexioned man. "Cupid!" and by this odd fancy-name calling a dimpled, red-cheeked, spirited-looking, forward little fellow, who was rather impudently, I thought, gliding about among the passive-looking girls – like

---

39. **foolscap sheets:** Plain, 13 x 16 inch sheets of writing paper.
40. **Actaeon:** In Greek mythology, Actaeon was a hunter who angered the goddess Artemis when he watched her bathe naked in a river. She changed him into a deer, and he was torn apart by his own dogs.

a gold fish through hueless waves – yet doing nothing in particular that I could see, the man bade him lead the stranger through the edifice.

"Come first and see the water-wheel," said this lively lad, with the air of boyishly-brisk importance.

Quitting the folding-room, we crossed some damp, cold boards, and stood beneath a great wet shed, incessantly showering with foam, like the green barnacled bow of some East India-man in a gale. Round and round here went the enormous revolutions of the dark colossal water-wheel, grim with its one immutable purpose.

"This sets our whole machinery a-going, Sir; in every part of all these buildings; where the girls work and all."

I looked, and saw that the turbid waters of Blood River had not changed their hue by coming under the use of man.

"You make only blank paper; no printing of any sort, I suppose? All blank paper, don't you?"

"Certainly; what else should a paper-factory make?"

The lad here looked at me as if suspicious of my common-sense.

"Oh, to be sure!" said I, confused and stammering; "it only struck me as so strange that red waters should turn out pale chee – paper, I mean."

He took me up a wet and rickety stair to a great light room, furnished with no visible thing but rude, manger-like receptacles running all round its sides; and up to these mangers, like so many mares haltered to the rack, stood rows of girls. Before each was vertically thrust up a long, glittering scythe, immovably fixed at bottom to the manger-edge. The curve of the scythe, and its having no snath to it, made it look exactly like a sword. To and fro, across the sharp edge, the girls forever dragged long strips of rags, washed white, picked from baskets at one side; thus ripping asunder every seam, and converting the tatters almost into lint. The air swam with the fine, poisonous particles, which from all sides darted, subtilely, as motes in sunbeams, into the lungs.

"This is the rag-room," coughed the boy.

"You find it rather stifling here," coughed I, in answer; "but the girls don't cough."

"Oh, they are used to it."

"Where do you get such hosts of rags?" picking up a handful from a basket.

"Some from the country round about; some from far over sea – Leghorn and London."

"'Tis not unlikely, then," murmured I, "that among these heaps of rags there may be some old shirts, gathered from the dormitories of the Paradise of Bachelors. But the buttons are all dropped off. Pray, my lad, do you ever find any bachelor's buttons hereabouts?"

"None grow in this part of the country. The Devil's Dungeon is no place for flowers."

"Oh! you mean the *flowers* so called – the Bachelor's Buttons?"

"And was not that what you asked about? Or did you mean the gold bosom-buttons of our boss, Old Bach, as our whispering girls all call him?"

"The man, then, I saw below is a bachelor, is he?"

"Oh, yes, he's a Bach."

"The edges of those swords, they are turned outward from the girls, if I see right; but their rags and fingers fly so, I can not distinctly see."

"Turned outward."

Yes, murmured I to myself; I see it now; turned outward; and each erected sword is so borne, edge-outward, before each girl. If my reading fails me not, just so, of old, condemned state-prisoners went from the hall of judgment to their doom: an officer before, bearing a sword, its edge turned outward, in significance of their fatal sentence. So, through consumptive pallors of this blank, raggy life, go these white girls to death.

"Those scythes look very sharp," again turning toward the boy.

"Yes; they have to keep them so. Look!"

That moment two of the girls, dropping their rags, plied each a whet-stone up and down the sword-blade. My unaccustomed blood curdled at the sharp shriek of the tormented steel.

Their own executioners; themselves whetting the very swords that slay them; meditated I.

"What makes those girls so sheet-white, my lad?"

"Why" – with a roguish twinkle, pure ignorant drollery, not knowing heartlessness – "I suppose the handling of such white bits of sheets all the time makes them so sheety."

"Let us leave the rag-room now, my lad."

More tragical and more inscrutably mysterious than any mystic sight, human or machine, throughout the factory, was the strange innocences of cruel-heartedness in this usage-hardened boy.

"And now," said he, cheerily, "I suppose you want to see our great machine, which cost us twelve thousand dollars only last autumn. That's the machine that makes the paper, too. This way, Sir."

Following him, I crossed a large, bespattered place, with two great round vats in it, full of a white, wet, woolly-looking stuff, not unlike the albuminous part of an egg, soft-boiled.

"There," said Cupid, tapping the vats carelessly, "these are the first beginnings of the paper; this white pulp you see. Look how it swims bubbling round and round, moved by the paddle here. From hence it pours from both vats into that one common channel yonder; and so goes, mixed up and leisurely, to the great machine. And now for that."

He led me into a room, stifling with a strange, blood-like, abdominal heat, as if here, true enough, were being finally developed the germinous particles lately seen.

Before me, rolled out like some long Eastern manuscript, lay stretched one continuous length of iron frame-work – multitudinous and mystical, with all sorts of rollers, wheels, and cylinders, in slowly-measured and unceasing motion.

"Here first comes the pulp now," said Cupid, pointing to the nighest end of the machine. "See; first it pours out and spreads itself upon this wide, sloping board; and then – look – slides, thin and quivering, beneath the first roller there. Follow on now, and see it as it slides from under that to the next cylinder. There; see how it has become just a very little less pulpy now. One step more, and it grows still more to some slight consistence. Still another cylinder, and it is so knitted – though as yet mere dragon-fly wing – that it forms an air-bridge here, like a suspended cobweb, between two more separated rollers; and flowing over the last one, and under again, and doubling about there out of sight for a minute among all those mixed cylinders you indistinctly see, it reappears here, looking now at last a little less like pulp and more like paper, but still quite delicate and defective yet awhile. But – a little further onward, Sir, if you please – here now, at this further point, it puts on something of a real look, as if it might turn out to be something you might possibly handle in the end. But it's not yet done, Sir. Good way to travel yet, and plenty more of cylinders must roll it."

"Bless my soul!" said I, amazed at the elongation, interminable convolutions, and deliberate slowness of the machine; "it must take a long time for the pulp to pass from end to end, and come out paper."

"Oh! not so long," smiled the precocious lad, with a superior and patronizing air; "only nine minutes. But look; you may try it for yourself. Have you a bit of paper? Ah! here's a bit on the floor. Now mark that with any word you please, and let me dab it on here, and we'll see how long before it comes out at the other end."

"Well, let me see," said I, taking out my pencil; "come, I'll mark it with your name."

Bidding me take out my watch, Cupid adroitly dropped the inscribed slip on an exposed part of the incipient mass.

Instantly my eye marked the second-hand on my dial-plate.

Slowly I followed the slip, inch by inch; sometimes pausing for full half a minute as it disappeared beneath inscrutable groups of the lower cylinders, but only gradually to emerge again; and so, on, and on, and on – inch by inch; now in open sight, sliding along like a freckle on the quivering sheet; and then again wholly vanished; and so, on, and on, and on – inch by inch; all the time the main sheet growing more and more to final firmness – when, suddenly, I saw a sort of paper-fall, not wholly unlike a waterfall; a scissory sound smote my ear, as of some cord being snapped; and down dropped an unfolded sheet of perfect foolscap, with my "Cupid" half faded out of it, and still moist and warm.

My travels were at an end, for here was the end of the machine.

"Well, how long was it?" said Cupid.

"Nine minutes to a second," replied I, watch in hand.

"I told you so."

For a moment a curious emotion filled me, not wholly unlike that which one might experience at the fulfillment of some mysterious prophecy. But how absurd, thought I again; the thing is a mere machine, the essence of which is unvarying punctuality and precision.

Previously absorbed by the wheels and cylinders, my attention was now directed to a sad-looking woman standing by.

"That is rather an elderly person so silently tending the machine-end here. She would not seem wholly used to it either."

"Oh," knowingly whispered Cupid, through the din, "she only came last week. She was a nurse formerly. But the business is poor in these parts, and she's left it. But look at the paper she is piling there."

"Ay, foolscap," handling the piles of moist, warm sheets, which continually were being delivered into the woman's waiting hands. "Don't you turn out any thing but foolscap at this machine?"

"Oh, sometimes, but not often, we turn out finer work – cream-laid and royal sheets, we call them. But foolscap being in chief demand, we turn out foolscap most."

It was very curious. Looking at that blank paper continually dropping, dropping, dropping, my mind ran on in wonderings of those strange uses to which those thousand sheets eventually would be put. All sorts of writings would be writ on those now vacant things – sermons, lawyers' briefs, physicians' prescriptions, love-letters, marriage certificates, bills of divorce, registers of births, death-warrants, and so on, without end. Then, recurring back to them as they here lay all blank, I could not but bethink me of that celebrated comparison of John Locke,[41] who, in demonstration of his theory that man had no innate ideas, compared the human mind at birth to a sheet of blank paper; something destined to be scribbled on, but what sort of characters no soul might tell.

Pacing slowly to and fro along the involved machine, still humming with its play, I was struck as well by the inevitability as the evolvement-power in all its motions.

"Does that thin cobweb there," said I, pointing to the sheet in its more imperfect stage, "does that never tear or break? It is marvelous fragile, and yet this machine it passes through is so mighty."

"It never is known to tear a hair's point."

"Does it never stop – get clogged?"

"No. It *must* go. The machinery makes it go just *so*; just that very way, and at that very pace you there plainly *see* it go. The pulp can't help going."

Something of awe now stole over me, as I gazed upon this inflexible iron animal. Always, more or less, machinery of this ponderous, elaborate sort strikes, in some moods, strange dread into the human heart, as some living, panting Behemoth might. But what made the thing I saw so specially terrible to me was the metallic necessity, the unbudging fatality which governed it. Though, here and there, I could not follow the thin, gauzy veil of pulp in the course of its more mysterious or entirely invisible advance, yet it was indubitable that, at those points where it eluded me, it still marched on in unvarying docility to the autocratic cunning of the machine. A fascination fastened on me. I stood spell-bound and wandering in my soul. Before my eyes – there, passing in slow procession along the wheeling cylinders, I seemed to see, glued to the pallid incipience of the pulp, the yet more pallid faces of all the pallid girls I had eyed that heavy day. Slowly, mournfully, beseechingly, yet unresistingly, they gleamed along, their agony dimly outlined on the imperfect paper, like the print of the tormented face on the handkerchief of Saint Veronica.[42]

"Halloa! the heat of the room is too much for you," cried Cupid, staring at me.

"No – I am rather chill, if any thing."

---

41. **John Locke:** (1632-1704) English philosopher.

42. **Saint Veronica:** According to a story in several medieval texts, a woman named Veronica wiped the face of Jesus Christ with a cloth as he struggled to carry the cross to Golgotha. Thereafter, the cloth retained the imprint of his face.

"Come out, Sir – out – out," and, with the protecting air of a careful father, the precocious lad hurried me outside.

In a few moments, feeling revived a little, I went into the folding-room – the first room I had entered, and where the desk for transacting business stood, surrounded by the blank counters and blank girls engaged at them.

"Cupid here has led me a strange tour," said I to the dark-complexioned man before mentioned, whom I had ere this discovered not only to be an old bachelor, but also the principal proprietor. "Yours is a most wonderful factory. Your great machine is a miracle of inscrutable intricacy."

"Yes, all our visitors think it so. But we don't have many. We are in a very out-of-the-way corner here. Few inhabitants, too. Most of our girls come from far-off villages."

"The girls," echoed I, glancing round at their silent forms. "Why is it, Sir, that in most factories, female operatives, of whatever age, are indiscriminately called girls, never women?"

"Oh! as to that – why, I suppose, the fact of their being generally unmarried – that's the reason, I should think. But it never struck me before. For our factory here, we will not have married women; they are apt to be off-and-on too much. We want none but steady workers: twelve hours to the day, day after day, through the three hundred and sixty-five days, excepting Sundays, Thanksgiving, and Fast-days. That's our rule. And so, having no married women, what females we have are rightly enough called girls."

"Then these are all maids," said I, while some pained homage to their pale virginity made me involuntarily bow.

"All maids."

Again the strange emotion filled me.

"Your cheeks look whitish yet, Sir," said the man, gazing at me narrowly. "You must be careful going home. Do they pain you at all now? It's a bad sign, if they do."

"No doubt, Sir," answered I, "when once I have got out of the Devil's Dungeon, I shall feel them mending."

"Ah, yes; the winter air in valleys, or gorges, or any sunken place, is far colder and more bitter than elsewhere. You would hardly believe it now, but it is colder here than at the top of Woedolor Mountain."

"I dare say it is, Sir. But time presses me; I must depart."

With that, remuffling myself in dread-naught and tippet, thrusting my hands into my huge seal-skin mittens, I sallied out into the nipping air, and found poor Black, my horse, all cringing and doubled up with the cold.

Soon, wrapped in furs and meditations, I ascended from the Devil's Dungeon.

At the Black Notch I paused, and once more bethought me of Temple-Bar. Then, shooting through the pass, all alone with inscrutable nature, I exclaimed – Oh! Paradise of Bachelors! and oh! Tartarus of Maids!

[1855]

Donald Grant Mitchell (Ik Marvel)

[1822–1908]

Donald Grant Mitchell was born on April 12, 1822, in Norwich, Connecticut. His father, the Reverend Alfred Mitchell, was a Congregational minister deeply dedicated to his church and family. His mother, Lucretia Woodbridge Mitchell, was an avid reader who encouraged a variety of reading in the family home, especially in the evenings. Mitchell's happy early childhood was short-lived. At the age of eight, he was sent to a boarding school in Ellington, Connecticut. His father died the following year, in 1831. By 1839, his mother and two of Mitchell's eight siblings were also dead. Throughout his school years, Mitchell distinguished himself in a difficult curriculum, including the study of Latin and Greek. In 1837, he was admitted to Yale College, where Mitchell lived mostly on his own – working hard at his studies, constantly reading, and writing for the *Yale Literary Magazine.* Elected valedictorian of his class, he graduated in 1841. Three years later, Mitchell was appointed to a job as a secretary in the United States consular office in Liverpool, England, where he lived for two years.

When he returned to the United States, Mitchell set out on what proved to be a long and highly successful literary career. Commissioned to write a series of sketches on a newcomer's experiences in Washington, D.C., for the New York newspaper the *Courier and Enquirer,* Mitchell decided to publish them under a pseudonym, "J. K. Marvel." On the first of his "Capitol Sketches," a printer's error turned that into "Ik Marvel," which Mitchell decided to retain as his pen name. His earlier experiences in England were the subject of the travel sketches that formed his first book, *Fresh Gleanings* (1847). The following year, Mitchell returned to Europe as a foreign correspondent for the *Courier and Enquirer.* His dispatches on the revolutions of 1848 formed the basis of a second book, *The Battle Summer,* published when he returned to the United States in 1849. At about the same time he became engaged to be married, Mitchell wrote a short sketch, "A Bachelor's Reverie," which was published in the *Southern Literary Messenger* in October 1849. The sketch proved to be such a success that Mitchell immediately began to develop it into a longer work, *Reveries of a Bachelor; or, A Book of the Heart* (1850).

bedfordstmartins.com/ americanlit *for research links on Mitchell*

That best-selling book and its sequel, *Dream-Life* (1851), made Ik Marvel a household name and Mitchell a financially secure writer. From that point on, he published essays and stories in all the major literary magazines, including *Harper's, Knickerbocker Magazine,* and the *Atlantic Monthly.* In 1855, Mitchell bought Edgewood, a large farm near New Haven, Connecticut, which became his permanent residence. There, he wrote countless articles, sketches, and stories, as well as nearly two dozen books – novels, collections of essays, and books on farming, landscape design, and American history. But he remained best known as the author of *Reveries of a Bachelor* and its sequel. Looking back on the authors whose works he had read as a young man, the noted critic and novelist William Dean

Howells recalled in 1895: "I am rather glad that among them was the gentle and kindly Ik Marvel, whose *Reveries of a Bachelor* and whose *Dream-Life* the young people of that day were reading with a tender rapture which would not be altogether surprising, I dare say, to the young people of this." Indeed, the two books went through innumerable editions, and *Reveries of a Bachelor* alone sold more than a million copies by the time Mitchell died on December 15, 1908.

Ik Marvel's "A Bachelor's Reverie." This sketch was published in the *Southern Literary Messenger*, established in 1834 in Richmond, Virginia. Determined to broaden the scope of literature beyond New England, the founding editor of the *Messenger*, Thomas Willis White, sought to make it into a magazine that would at once offer a southern perspective and appeal to a national audience. Several other southern magazines had failed by the early 1830s, but the *Messenger* lasted for thirty years, finally succumbing during the Civil War. White gained a reputation for publishing high-quality literature by securing the services of a broad range of writers, including the popular poet Lydia Sigourney; Edgar Allan Poe, who edited the magazine for a year; and Donald Grant Mitchell, who published "A Bachelor's Reverie" under his pen name, Ik Marvel. A meditation on the nature of love and marriage from a bachelor's perspective, the humorous and touching sketch powerfully appealed to a large audience of men and women who themselves affirmed the value of domesticity and the key role of marriage in American society. The text is taken from the first printing of the sketch in the October 1849 issue of the *Southern Literary Messenger.*

A Bachelor's Reverie

in Three Parts

I. Smoke – Signifying Doubt. II. Blaze – Signifying Cheer.
III. Ashes – Signifying Desolation.

I have got a quiet farmhouse in the country, a very humble place to be sure, tenanted by a worthy enough man, of the old New-England stamp, where I sometimes go for a day or two in the winter, to look over the farm-accounts, and to see how the stock is thriving on the winter's keep.

One side the door, as you enter from the porch, is a little parlor, scarce twelve feet by ten, with a cozy looking fire place – a heavy oak floor – a couple of arm chairs – a brown table with carved lions' feet. Out of this room opens a little cabinet, only big enough for a broad bachelor bedstead, where I sleep upon feathers, and wake in the morning, with my eye upon a saucy colored, lithographic print of some fancy "Bessy."

It happens to be the only house in the world, of which I am *bona-fide* owner; and I take a vast deal of comfort in treating it just as I choose. I manage to break some article of furniture, almost every time I pay it a visit; and if I cannot open the window readily of a morning, to breathe the fresh air, I knock out a pane or two of glass with my boot. I lean against the wall in a very old arm-chair there is on the premises, and scarce ever fail to worry such a hole in the plastering, as would set me down for a round charge for damages in town, or make a prim housewife fret herself into a raging fever. I laugh out loud with myself, in my big arm-chair, when I think that I am neither afraid of one, nor the other.

As for the fire, I keep the little hearth so hot, as to warm half the cellar below, and the whole space between the jams, roars for hours together, with white flame. To be sure, the windows are not very tight, between broken panes, and bad joints, so that the fire, large as it is, is by no means an extravagant comfort.

As night approaches, I have a huge pile of oak and hickory, placed beside the hearth; I put out the tallow candle on the mantel, (using the family snuffers, with one leg broke,) – then, drawing my chair directly in front of the blazing wood, and setting one foot on each of the old iron fire-dogs, (until they grow too warm,) I dispose myself for an evening of such sober, and thoughtful quietude, as I believe, on my soul, that very few of my fellow-men have the good fortune to enjoy.

My tenant meantime, in the other room, I can hear now and then, though there is a thick stone chimney, and broad entry between, multiplying contrivances with his wife, to put two babies to sleep. This occupies them, I should say, usually an hour; though my only measure of time, (for I never carry a watch into the country,) is the blaze of my fire. By ten, or thereabouts, my stock of wood is nearly exhausted; I pile upon the hot coals what remains, and sit watching how it kindles, and blazes, and goes out – even like our joys! – and then, slip by the light of the embers into my bed, where I luxuriate in such sound, and healthful slumber, as only such rattling window frames, and country air, can supply.

But to return: the other evening – it happened to be on my last visit to my farm-house – when I had exhausted all the ordinary rural topics of thought, had formed all sorts of conjectures as to the income of the year, had planned a new wall around one lot, and the clearing up of another, now covered with patriarchal wood; and wondered if the little ricketty house would not be after all, a snug enough box, to live and to die in – I fell on a sudden, into such an unprecedented line of thought, which took such deep hold of my sympathies – sometimes even starting tears – that I determined, the next day, to set as much of it as I could recal, on paper.

Something – it may have been the home-looking blaze, (I am a bachelor, of – say, six and twenty,) or possibly a plaintive cry of the baby in my tenant's room, had suggested to me the thought of – marriage.

I piled upon the heated fire-dogs, the last arm-full of my wood; and now, said I, bracing myself courageously between the arms of my chair, – "I'll not flinch; – I'll pursue the thought wherever it leads, though it lead me to the — (I am apt to be hasty,) at least," continued I, softening, "until my fire is out."

The wood was green, and at first showed no disposition to blaze. It smoked furiously. Smoke, thought I, always goes before blaze; and so does doubt go before decision: and my Reverie, from that very starting point, slipped into this shape: –

I. Smoke – Signifying Doubt

– Hum, – a wife! A wife? – hum!

Why? And pray, my dear sir, why not – why? Why not doubt? Why not hesitate? Why not tremble?

Does a man buy a ticket in a lottery – a poor man, whose whole earnings go in to secure the ticket, – without trembling, hesitating, doubting?

Can a man stake his bachelor respectability, independence, comfort, upon the die of absorbing, unchanging, relentless marriage, without trembling at the venture?

Shall a man who has been free to chase his fancies over the wide-world, without let or hindrance, shut himself up to marriage-ship, within four walls called Home, that are to claim him, his time, his trouble, his tears, thenceforward forevermore, without doubts thick, and thick-coming as Smoke?

Shall he who has been hitherto a mere observer of other men's cares, and business – moving off where they made him sick of heart, approaching whenever and wherever they made him gleeful – shall he now undertake administration of just such cares and business, without qualms? Shall he, whose whole life has been but a nimble succession of escapes from trifling difficulties, now broach without doubtings – that matrimony, where if difficulty beset him, there is no escape? Shall this brain of mine, careless-working, never tired with idleness, feeding on long vagaries, and high, gigantic castles, dreaming out beatitudes hour by hour – turn itself at length to such dull task-work as thinking out a livelihood for wife and children?

Where thenceforward, will be those sunny dreams, in which I have warmed my fancies, and my heart, and lighted my eye with crystal? This very marriage, which a brilliant working imagination has invested time and again with brightness, and delight, can serve no longer as a mine for teeming fancy: all, alas, will be gone – reduced to the dull standard of the actual! No more room for intrepid forays of imagination – no more gorgeous realm-making – all is over!

Why not, I thought, go on dreaming? Can any wife be prettier than an after dinner fancy, idle and yet vivid, can paint for you? Can any children make less noise, than the little rosy-cheeked ones who have no existence, except in the *omnium gatherum*[1] of your own brain? Can any housewife be more unexceptionable, than she who goes sweeping daintily the cobwebs that gather in your dreams? Can any domestic larder be better stocked, than the private larder of your head dozing on a cushioned chair-back at Delmonico's?[2] Can any family purse be better filled than the exceeding plump one, you dream of, after reading such pleasant books as Munchausen, or Typee?[3]

---

1. ***omnium gatherum***: A miscellaneous gathering, a hodgepodge (Latin).
2. **Delmonico's**: Opened in 1837 near Wall Street, this restaurant immediately became popular with the professional elite of New York City.
3. **Munchausen, or Typee**: *The Adventures of Baron Munchausen*, a popular collection of fantastic adventure and hunting stories, was first published anonymously by a German librarian, Rudolf Erich Raspe (1737-1794), in 1787; it was later expanded and republished by other authors. *Typee: A Peep at Polynesian Life* (1846), the first novel published by Herman Melville (1819-1891), was a Romantic tale based on his adventures in the South Seas.

But if, after all, it must be – duty, or what-not, making provocation – what then? And I clapped my feet hard against the fire-dogs, and leaned back, and turned my face to the ceiling, as much as to say; – And where on earth, then, shall a poor devil look for a wife?

Somebody says, Lyttleton or Shaftesbury[4] I think, that "marriages would be happier if they were all arranged by the Lord Chancellor." Unfortunately, we have no Lord Chancellor to make this commutation of our misery.

Shall a man then scour the country on a mule's back, like Honest Gil Blas of Santillane;[5] or shall he make application to some such intervening providence as Madame St. Marc, who, as I see by the Presse,[6] manages these matters to one's hand, for some 5 per cent on the fortunes of the parties?

I have trouted, when the brook was so low, and the sky so hot, that I might as well have thrown my fly upon the turnpike; and I have hunted hare at noon, and wood-cock in snow-time, never despairing, scarce doubting; but, for a poor hunter of his kind, without traps or snares, or any aid of police or constabulary, to traverse the world, where are swarming, on a moderate computation, some three hundred and odd millions of unmarried women, for a single capture – irremediable, unchangeable – and yet a capture which by strange metonomy, not laid down in the books, is very apt to turn captor into captive, and make game of hunter – all this, surely, surely may make a man shrug in doubt!

Then – again, – there are the plaguey wife's relations. Who knows how many third, fourth, or fifth cousins, will appear at careless complimentary intervals long after you had settled into the placid belief that all congratulatory visits were at end? How many twisted headed brothers will be putting in their advice, as a friend to Peggy?

How many maiden aunts will come to spend a month or two with their "dear Peggy," and want to know every tea-time, "if she isn't a dear love of a wife?" Then, dear father-in-law, will beg, (taking dear Peggy's hand in his,) to give a little wholesome counsel, and will be very sure to advise just the contrary of what you had determined to undertake. And dear mamma-in-law, must set her nose into Peggy's cupboard, and insist upon having the key to your own private locker in the wainscot.

Then, perhaps, there is a little bevy of dirty-nosed nephews who come to spend the holy-days, and eat up your East India sweetmeats, and who are forever tramping over your head, or raising the Old Harry[7] below, while you are busy with your clients. Last, and worst, is some fidgety old uncle, forever too cold or too hot, who vexes you with his patronizing airs, and impudently kisses his little Peggy!

---

4. **Lyttleton or Shaftesbury:** The English writers Thomas Lyttleton (1422–1481) and Anthony Ashley Cooper Shaftesbury (1671–1713) wrote, respectively, about the law and philosophy. The quotation is not identifiable as the words of either writer, but Samuel Johnson (1709–1784), the English lexicographer, is quoted as saying, "I believe marriages would in general be as happy, often more so, if they were all made by the Lord Chancellor, upon a due consideration of characters and circumstances, without the parties having any choice in the matter" (James Boswell, *Life of Samuel Johnson*, part VI).
5. **Honest Gil Blas of Santillane:** *Gil Blas de Santillane*, a picaresque romance first published in 1715 by the French writer Alain-René Lesage (1668–1747), tells the story of the ups and downs of the life of Gil Blas.
6. **Madame St. Marc . . . the Presse:** A French marriage broker; *La Presse*, founded in Paris in 1836, was a highly regarded newspaper with a large circulation.
7. **raising the Old Harry:** Making mischief; "Old Harry" was a common name for the devil.

– That could be borne, however; for perhaps he has promised his fortune to Peggy. Peggy, then, will be rich: – (and the thought made me rub my shins, which were now getting comfortably warm upon the fire-dogs.) Then, she will be forever talking of *her* fortune; and pleasantly reminding you on occasion of a favorite purchase,– how lucky *she* had the means; and dropping hints about economy, and buying very extravagant Paisleys.[8]

She will annoy you by looking over the stock-list at breakfast time; and mention quite carelessly to your clients, that she is interested in *such* or such a speculation.

She will be provokingly silent when you hint to a tradesman that you have not the money by you, for his small bill; – in short, she will tear the life out of you, making you pay in righteous retribution of annoyance, grief, vexation, shame, and sickness of heart, for the superlative folly of "marrying rich."

– But if not rich, then poor. Bah! the thought made me stir the coals, but there was still no blaze. The paltry earnings you are able to wring out of clients by the sweat of your brow, will now be all *our* income; you will be pestered for pin-money, and pestered with poor wife's relations. Ten to one she will stickle about taste – "Sir Visto's"[9] – and want to make this so pretty, and that so charming, if she *only* had the means, and is sure Paul (a kiss) can't deny his little Peggy such a trifling sum, and all for the common benefit!

Then she, for one, means that *her* children shan't go a begging for clothes, – and another pull at the purse. Trust a poor mother to dress her children in finery!

Perhaps she is ugly; – not noticeable at first; but growing on her, and (what is worse) growing faster on you. You wonder why you didn't see that vulgar nose long ago: and that lip – it is very strange, you think, that you ever thought it pretty. And, then, to come to breakfast, with her hair looking as it does, and you, not so much as daring to say – "Peggy, *do* brush your hair!" Her foot too – not very bad when decently *chaussée*[10] – but now since she's married, she does wear such infernal slippers! And yet for all this, to be prigging up for an hour, when any of my old chums come to dine with me!

"Bless your kind hearts! my dear fellows," said I, thrusting the tongs into the coals, and speaking out loud, as if my voice could reach from Virginia to Paris – "not married yet!"

Perhaps Peggy is pretty enough – only shrewish.

No matter for cold coffee; – you should have been up before.

What sad, thin, poorly cooked chops, to eat with your rolls!

– She thinks they are very good and wonders how you can set such an example to your children.

The butter is nauseating.

– She has no other, and hopes you'll not raise a storm about butter a little turned. I think I see myself – ruminated I – sitting meekly at table, scarce daring to lift up my eyes, utterly fagged out with some quarrel of yesterday, choking down detestably sour

8. **Paisleys:** Shawls made of soft wool with intricate, curved and swirling designs.
9. **"Sir Visto's":** An allusion to "Epistle IV: To Richard Boyle, Earl of Burlington" by the English poet Alexander Pope (1688–1744): "What brought Sir Visto's ill got wealth to waste? / Some daemon whisper'd, 'Visto! have a taste.'"
10. ***chausée*:** Adorned in footwear or shoes (French).

muffins, that my wife thinks are "delicious" – slipping in dried mouthfuls of burnt ham off the side of my fork tines, – slipping off my chair side-ways at the end, and slipping out with my hat between my knees, to business, and never feeling myself a competent, sound-minded man, till the oak door is between me, and Peggy!

– "Ha, ha, – not yet!" said I; and in so earnest a tone, that my dog started to his feet – cocked his eye to have a good look into my face – met my smile of triumph with an amiable wag of the tail, and curled up again in the corner.

Again, Peggy is rich enough, well enough, mild enough, only she doesn't care a fig for you. She has married you because father, or grandfather thought the match eligible, and because she didn't wish to disoblige them. Besides, she didn't positively hate you, and thought you were a respectable enough person – she has told you so repeatedly at dinner. She wonders you like to read poetry; she wishes you would buy her a good cookbook; and insists upon your making your will at the birth of the first baby.

She thinks Captain So and So a splendid looking fellow, and wishes you would trim up a little were it only for appearance' sake.

You need not hurry up from the office so early at night; – she, bless her dear heart! – does not feel lonely. You read to her a love tale; she interrupts the pathetic parts with directions to her seamstress. You read of marriages; she sighs, and asks if Captain So and So has left town? She hates to be mewed up in a cottage, or between brick walls; she does *so* love the Springs!

But, again, Peggy loves you; – at least she swears it, with her hand on the Sorrows of Werther.[11] She has pin-money which she spends for the Literary World and the Friends in Council.[12] She is not bad-looking, saving a bit too much of forehead; nor is she sluttish, unless a *negligé* till 3 o'clock, and an ink stain on the fore finger be sluttish; – but then she is such a sad blue!

You never fancied when you saw her buried in a three volume novel, that it was anything more than a girlish vagary; and when she quoted Latin, you thought innocently, that she had a capital memory for her samplers.

But to be bored eternally about Divine Danté and funny Goldoni,[13] is too bad. Your copy of Tasso, a treasure print of 1680,[14] is all bethumbed and dog's-eared, and spotted with baby gruel. Even your Seneca – an Elzevir[15] – is all sweaty with handling. She adores La Fontaine, reads Balzac[16] with a kind of artist-scowl, and will not let Greek alone.

11. **Sorrows of Werther:** *The Sorrows of Young Werther*, a novel about unrequited love by the German writer Johann von Goethe (1792-1854).
12. **Literary World and the Friends in Council:** *The Literary World*, established in 1847, was a weekly New York periodical which included book reviews, essays, and news about publishing. *Friends in Council* (1847), a series of conversations about moral and social problems, was published by Sir Arthur Helps (1813-1875).
13. **Divine Danté and funny Goldoni:** The Italian poet and writer, Dante Alighieri (1265-1321), author of the *Divine Comedy*; Carlo Goldoni (1707-1793), Italian writer of comic dramas.
14. **Tasso:** Torquato Tasso (1544-1595), Italian poet whose popular epic about the First Crusade, *Jerusalem Liberated* (1575), was published in many editions, including one in Venice in 1680.
15. **Seneca – an Elzevir:** Lucius Anneaeus Seneca (4 BCE-65 CE), Roman philosopher and statesman; the Elzevirs, a Dutch family of printers, publishers, and booksellers. From 1622-1680, they were the most influential names in European publishing, producing many editions of Greek and Roman works.
16. **La Fontaine . . . Balzac:** Jean de La Fountaine (1621-1695), French poet, and Honoré de Balzac (1799-1850), highly regarded French novelist.

You hint at broken rest and an aching head at breakfast, and she will fling you a scrap of Anthology – in lieu of camphor bottle – or chant the *αἰαῖ! αἰαῖ!* of tragic chorus.[17]

– The nurse is getting dinner; you are holding the baby; Peggy is reading Bruyère.[18]

The fire smoked thick as pitch, and puffed out little clouds over the chimney piece. I gave the fore-stick a kick, at thought of Peggy, baby, and Bruyère.

– Suddenly the flame flickered bluely athwart the smoke – caught at a twig below – rolled round the mossy oak-stick – twined among the crackling tree-limbs – mounted – lit up the whole body of smoke, and blazed out cheerily and bright. Doubt vanished with Smoke, and Hope began with Flame.

II. Blaze – Signifying Cheer

I pushed my chair back; drew up another; stretched out my feet cozily upon it, rested my elbows on the chair arms, leaned my head on one hand, and looked straight into the leaping, and dancing flame.

– Love is a flame – ruminated I; and (glancing round the room) how a flame brightens up a man's habitation.

"Carlo," said I, calling up my dog into the light, "good fellow, Carlo:" and I patted him kindly, and he wagged his tail, and laid his nose across my knee, and looked wistfully up in my face, then strode away, – turned to look again, and lay down to sleep.

"Pho, the brute!" said I, "it is not enough after all to like a dog."

– If now in that chair yonder, not the one your feet lie upon, but the other, beside you – closer yet – were seated a sweet-faced girl, with a pretty little foot lying out upon the hearth – a bit of lace running round the swelling throat – the hair parted to a charm over a forehead fair as any of your dreams, – and if you could reach an arm around that chair back, without fear of giving offence, and suffer your fingers to play idly with those curls that escape down the neck, and if you could clasp with your other hand those little white, taper fingers of hers, which lie so temptingly within reach, – and so, talk softly and low in presence of the blaze, while the hours slip without knowledge, and the winter winds whistle uncared for; – if, in short, you were no bachelor, but the husband of some such sweet image – (dream, call it, rather,) would it not be far pleasanter than this cold single night-sitting – counting the sticks – reckoning the length of the blaze, and the height of the falling snow?

And if, some or all of those wild vagaries that grow on your fancy at such an hour, you could whisper into listening, because loving ears – ears not tired with listening, because it is you who whisper – ears ever indulgent because eager to praise; – and if your darkest fancies were lit up, not merely with bright wood fire, but with ringing laugh of that sweet face turned up in fond rebuke – how far better, than to be waxing black, and sour, over pestilential humours – alone – your very dog asleep!

---

17. **αἰαῖ! αἰαῖ! of tragic chorus:** A common expression of lament by the chorus in an ancient Greek tragedy.
18. **Bruyère:** Jean de La Bruyère (1645–1696), French satirist.

And if when a glowing thought comes into your brain, quick and sudden, you could tell it over as to a second self, to that sweet creature, who is not away, because she loves to be there; and if you could watch the thought catching that girlish mind, illuming that fair brow, sparkling in those pleasantest of eyes – how far better than to feel it slumbering, and going out, heavy, lifeless, and dead, in your own selfish fancy. And if a generous emotion steals over you – coming, you know not whither, would there not be a richer charm in lavishing it in caress, or endearing word, upon that fondest, and most dear one, than in patting your glossy coated dog, or sinking lonely to smiling slumbers?

How would not benevolence ripen with such monitor to task it! How would not selfishness grow faint and dull, leaning ever to that second self, which is the loved one! How would not guile shiver, and grow weak, before that girl-brow, and eye of innocence! How would not all that boyhood prized of enthusiasm, and quick blood, and life, renew itself in such presence!

The fire was getting hotter, and I moved into the middle of the room. The shadows the flames made, were playing like fairy forms over floor, and wall, and ceiling.

My fancy would surely quicken, thought I, if such being were in attendance. Surely imagination would be stronger, and purer, if it could have the playful fancies of dawning womanhood to delight it. All toil would be torn from mind-labor, if but another heart grew into this present soul, quickening it, warming it, cheering it, bidding it ever, God speed!

Her face would make a halo, rich as rainbow, atop of all such noisome things, as we lonely souls, call trouble. Her smile would illumine the blackest of crowding cares; and darkness that now seats you despondent, in your solitary chair for days together, weaving bitter fancies, dreaming bitter dreams, would grow light and thin, and spread, and float away, – chased by that beloved smile.

Your friend – poor fellow! – dies: – never mind, that gentle clasp of *her* fingers, as she steals behind you, telling you not to weep – it is worth all friends!

Your sister, sweet one, is dead – buried. The worms are busy with all her fairness. How it makes you think earth nothing but a spot to dig graves upon!

– It is more: *she*, she says, will be a sister; and the waving curls as she leans upon your shoulder, touch your cheek, and your wet eye turns to meet those other eyes – God has sent his angel, surely!

Your mother, alas for it, she is gone! Is there any bitterness to a youth, alone, and homeless, like this?

But you are not homeless; you are not alone: *she* is there; – her tears softening yours, her smile lighting yours, her grief killing yours; and you live again, to assuage that kind sorrow of hers.

Then – those children, rosy, fair-haired; no, they do not disturb you with prattle now – they are yours. Toss away there on the greensward – never mind the hyacinths, the snowdrops, the violets, if so be any are there; the perfume of their healthful lips is worth all the flowers of the world. No need now to gather wild bouquets to love, and cherish: – flower, tree, sunlight, are all dead things; things livelier hold your soul.

And she, the mother, sweetest and fairest of all, watching, tending, caressing, loving, till your own heart grows pained with tenderest jealousy, and cures itself with loving.

You have no need now of cold lecture to teach thankfulness: your heart is full of it. No need now, as once, of bursting blossoms, of trees taking leaf, and greenness, to turn thought kindly, and thankfully; for ever, beside you, there is bloom, and ever beside you there is fruit, for which eye, heart, and soul are full of unknown, and unspoken, because unspeakable, thank-offering.

And if sickness catches you, binds you, lays you down – no lonely moanings, and wicked curses at careless stepping nurses. *The* step is noiseless, and yet distinct beside you. The white curtains are drawn, or withdrawn by the magic of that other presence; and the soft, cool hand is upon your brow.

No cold comfortings of friend-watchers, merely come in to steal a word away from that outer world which is pulling at their skirts, but, ever, the sad, shaded brow of her, whose lightest sorrow for your sake is your greatest grief, – if it were not a greater joy.

The blaze was leaping light and high, and the wood falling under the growing heat. – So, continued I, this heart would be at length itself; – striving with every thing gross, even now as it clings to grossness. Love would make its strength native and progressive. Earth's cares would fly. Joys would double. Susceptibilities be quickened; Love master self; and having made the mastery, stretch onward, and upward toward Infinitude.

And, if the end came, and sickness brought that follower – Great Follower – which sooner or later is sure to come after, then the heart, and the hand of Love, ever near, are giving to your tired soul, daily and hourly, lessons of that love which consoles, which triumphs, which circleth all, and centereth in all – Love Infinite, and Divine!

Kind hands – none but *hers* – will smooth the hair upon your brow as the chill grows damp, and heavy on it; and her fingers – none but hers – will lie in yours as the wasted flesh stiffens, and hardens for the ground. *Her* tears, – you could feel no others, if oceans fell – will warm your drooping features once more to life; – once more your eye lighted in joyous triumph, kindle in her smile, and then –

The fire fell upon the hearth; the blaze gave a last leap – a flicker – then another – caught a little remaining twig – blazed up – wavered – went out.

There was nothing but a bed of glowing embers, over which the white ashes gathered fast. I was alone, with only my dog for company.

III. Ashes – Signifying Desolation

After all, thought I, ashes follow blaze, inevitably as Death follows Life. Misery treads on the heels of Joy; Anguish rides swift after Pleasure.

"Come to me again, Carlo," said I, to my dog; and I patted him fondly now only by the light of the dying embers.

It is but little pleasure one takes in fondling brute favorites, but it is a pleasure that when it passes, leaves no void. It is only a little alleviating redundance in your solitary heart-life, which if lost, another can be supplied.

But if your heart, not solitary – not quieting its humors with mere love of chase, or dog – not repressing year after year, its earnest yearnings after something better, more spiritual, – has fairly linked itself by bonds strong as life to another heart – is the casting off easy, then?

Is it then only a little heart redundancy cut off, which the next bright sunset will fill up?

And my fancy, as it had painted doubt under the smoke, and cheer under warmth of the blaze, so now it began under faint light of smouldering embers to picture heart-desolation.

– What kind congratulatory letters, hosts of them, coming from old and half-forgotten friends, now that your happiness is a year, or two years old!

"Beautiful."

– Aye, to be sure beautiful!

"Rich."

– Pho, the dawdler! how little he knows of heart-treasure, who speaks of wealth to a man who loves his wife, as a wife should only be loved!

"Young."

– Young indeed; guileless as infancy; charming as the morning.

Ah, these letters bear a sting: they bring to mind, with new, and newer freshness, if it be possible, the value of that, which you tremble lest you lose.

How anxiously you watch that step – if it lose not its buoyancy; How you study the colour on that cheek, if it grow not fainter; How you tremble at the lustre in those eyes, if it be not the lustre of Death; How you totter under the weight of that muslin sleeve – a phantom weight! How you fear to do it, and yet press forward, to note if that breathing be quickened, as you ascend the home-heights, to look off on sunset lighting the plain.

Is your sleep, quiet sleep, after that she has whispered to you her fears, and in the same breath – soft as a sigh, sharp as an arrow – bid you bear it bravely?

But then, – the embers were now glowing fresher, a little kindling, before the ashes – she triumphs over disease.

But Poverty, the world's almoner, has come to you with ready, spare hand. Alone, with your dog living on bones, and you, on hope – kindling each morning, dying slowly each night, – this could be borne. Philosophy would bring home its stores to the lone-man. Money is not in his hand, but Knowledge is in his brain! and from that brain he draws out faster, as he draws slower from his pocket. He remembers; and on remembrance he can live for days, and weeks. The garret, if garret covers him, is rich in fancies. The rain if it pelts, pelts only him used to rain-peltings. And his dog crouches not in dread, but in companionship. His crust he divides with him, and laughs. He crowns himself with glorious memories of Cervantes, though he begs: if he nights it under the stars, he dreams heaven-sent dreams of prisoned, and homeless Gallileo.[19]

He hums old sonnets, and snatches of poor Jonson's plays. He chants Dryden's odes, and dwells on Otway's rhyme.[20] He reasons with Bolingbroke or Diogenes,[21] as the

---

19. **Cervantes . . . Gallileo:** Miguel de Cervantes Saavedra (1547–1616), Spanish novelist and author of *Don Quixote*; Galileo Galilei (1564–1642), Italian astronomer and physicist imprisoned by the Inquisition for his belief that the earth revolves around the sun.

20. **Jonson's plays . . . Otway's rhyme:** Ben Jonson (1572–1637), English dramatist; John Dryden (1631–1700) and Thomas Otway (1652–1685) were English poets.

21. **Bolingbroke or Diogenes:** Henry St. John Bolingbroke (1678–1751), English statesman and philosopher; Diogenes (412?–323 BCE), Greek philosopher famous for his rejection of luxury and contempt for riches.

humour takes him; and laughs at the world: for the world, thank Heaven, has left him alone!

Keep your money, old misers, and your palaces, old princes, – the world is mine!

> I care not Fortune what you me deny, –
> You cannot rob me of free nature's grace,
> You cannot shut the windows of the sky;
> You cannot bar my constant feet to trace
> The woods and lawns, by living streams, at eve.
> Let health, my nerves and finer fibres brace,
> And I, their toys, to the great children, leave,
> Of Fancy, Reason, Virtue, naught can me bereave![22]

But – if not alone?

If *she* is clinging to you for support, for consolation, for home, for life – she reared in luxury perhaps, is faint for bread?

Then, the iron enters the soul; then the nights darken under any sky light. Then the days grow long, even in solstice of winter.

She may not complain; what then?

Will your heart grow strong, if the strength of her love can dam up the fountains of tears, and the tied tongue not tell of bereavement? Will it solace you to find her parting the poor treasure of food you have stolen for her, with begging, foodless children?

But this ill, strong hands, and Heaven's help, will put down. Wealth again; Flowers again; Patrimonial acres again; Brightness again. But your little Bessy, your favorite child is pining.

Would to God! you say in agony, that wealth could bring fulness again into that blanched cheek, or round those little thin lips once more; but it cannot. Thinner and thinner they grow; plaintive and more plaintive her sweet voice.

"Dear Bessy" – and your tones tremble; you feel she is on the edge of the grave. Can you pluck her back? Can endearments stay her? Business is heavy, away from the loved child; home, you go, to fondle while yet time is left – but *this* time you are too late.

She is gone.

She cannot hear you; she cannot thank you for the violets you put within her stiff white hand.

And then – the grassy mound – the cold shadow of head-stone!

The wind, growing with the night, is rattling at the window panes, and whistles dismally. I wipe a tear, and in the interval of my Reverie, thank God, that I am no such mourner.

But gaiety, snail-footed, creeps back to the house-hold. All is bright again.

> The violet's bed 's not sweeter, than the delicious breath
> Marriage sends forth.[23]

---

22. **I care not Fortune . . . can me bereave!:** From *The Castle of Indolence*, canto 2, stanza 3, by the English poet James Thomson (1700–1748).
23. **The violet's . . . forth:** This passage has not been identified.

Her lip is rich and full; her cheek delicate as a flower. Her frailty doubles your love.

And the little one she clasps – frail too – too frail; – the boy you had set your hopes and heart on. You have watched him growing, ever prettier, ever winning more and more upon your soul. The love you bore to him when he first lisped names – your name and hers – has doubled in strength now that he asks innocently to be taught of this, or that, and promises you by that lively curiosity that flashes in his eye, a mind full of intelligence.

And some hair-breadth escape by sea, or flood, that he perhaps may have had – which unstrung your soul to such tears as you pray God, may be spared you again – has endeared the little fellow to your heart a thousand fold.

And now, with his pale sister in the grave, all *that* love has come away from the mound, where worms feast, and centers on the boy.

How you watch the storms lest they harm him! How often you steal to his bed late at night and lay your hand lightly upon the brow, where the curls cluster thick, rising and falling with the throbbing temples, and watch, for minutes together, the little lips half parted, and listen – your ear close to them – if the breathing be regular and sweet!

But the day comes – the night rather – when you can catch no breathing.

Aye, put your hair away, – compose yourself – listen again.

No, there is nothing.

Put your hand now to his brow, – damp indeed – but not with healthful night-sleep; it is not your hand, no, do not deceive yourself – it is your loved boy's forehead that is so cold; and your loved boy will never speak to you again – never play again – he is dead!

Oh, the tears – the tears; – what blessed things are tears! Never fear now to let them fall on his forehead, or his lip, lest you waken him! Clasp him – clasp him harder – you cannot hurt, you cannot waken him! Lay him down, gently or not, it is the same; he is stiff; he is stark and cold.

But courage is elastic; it is our pride. It recovers itself easier, thought I, than these embers will get into blaze again.

But courage, and patience, and faith, and hope have their limit. Blessed be the man who escapes such trial as will determine limit!

To a lone-man it comes not near; for how can trial take hold where there is nothing by which to try?

A funeral? You reason with philosophy. A grave-yard? You read Hervey[24] and muse upon the wall. A friend dies? You sigh, you pat your dog, – it is over. Losses? You retrench – you light your pipe – it is forgotten. Calumny? You laugh – you sleep.

But with that childless wife clinging to you in love and sorrow – what then?

Can you take down Seneca[25] now and coolly blow the dust from the leaf-tops? Can you crimp your lip with Voltaire?[26] Can you smoke idly, your feet dangling with the ivies,

---

24. **Hervey:** James Hervey (1714–1758), English clergyman and author of *Meditations among the Tombs* (1746).
25. **Seneca:** See note 15.
26. **Voltaire:** The pen name of François-Marie Arouet (1694–1778), French writer and philosopher.

your thoughts all waving fancies, upon a church-yard wall – a wall that borders the grave of your boy?

Can you amuse yourself with turning stinging Martial[27] into rhyme? Can you pat your dog, and seeing him wakeful and kind, say, "it is enough?" Can you sneer at calumny and sit by your fire dozing?

Blessed, thought I again, is the man who escapes such trial as will measure limit of patience and limit of courage!

But the trial comes: colder and colder were growing the embers.

That wife, over whom your love broods, is fading. Not beauty fading; – that now that your heart is wrapped in her being would be nothing.

She sees with quick eye your dawning apprehension, and she tries hard to make that step of hers elastic.

Your trials and your loves together have centered your affections. They are not now as when you were a lone man, wide-spread and superficial. They have caught from domestic attachments a finer tone and touch. They cannot shoot out tendrils into barren world-soil and suck up thence strengthening nutriment. They have grown under the forcing glass of home-roof, they will not now bear exposure.

You do not now look men in the face as if a heart-bond was linking you – as if a community of feeling lay between. There is a heart-bond that absorbs all others; there is a community that monopolizes your feeling. When the heart lay wide open, before it had grown upon, and closed around particular objects, it could take strength and cheer from a hundred connections that now seem colder than ice.

And now those particular objects – alas for you! – are failing.

What anxiety pursues you! How you struggle to fancy – there is no danger; how she struggles to pursuade you – there is no danger!

How it grates now on your ear – the toil and turmoil of the city! It was music when you were alone; it was pleasant even, when from the din, you were elaborating comforts for the cherished objects – when you had such sweet escape as evening drew on.

Now it maddens you to see the world careless while you are steeped in care. They hustle you in the street; they smile at you across the table; they bow carelessly over the way; they do not know what canker is at your heart.

The undertaker comes with his bill for the dead boy's funeral. He knows your grief; he is respectful. You bless him in your soul. You wish the laughing street-goers were all undertakers.

Your eye follows the physician as he leaves your house: is he wise, you ask yourself; is he prudent? is he the best? Did he never fail – is he never forgetful?

And now the hand that touches yours, is it no thinner – no whiter than yesterday? Sunny days come when she revives; colour comes back; she breathes freer; she picks flowers; she meets you with a smile: hope lives again.

But the next day of storm she is fallen. She cannot talk even; she presses your hand.

---

27. **Martial:** Marcus Valerius Martialis (38-103), Spanish-born Latin poet known for the wit of his fourteen books entitled *Epigrams.*

You hurry away from business before your time. What matter for clients – who is to reap the rewards? What matter for fame – whose eye will it brighten? What matter for riches – whose is the inheritance?

You find her propped with pillows; she is looking over a little picture book bethumbed by the dear boy she has lost. She hides it in her chair; she has pity on you.

Another day of revival, when the spring sun shines, and flowers open out of doors; she leans on your arm, and strolls into the garden where the first birds are singing. Listen to them with her; – what memories are in bird-songs! You need not shudder at her tears – they are tears of Thanksgiving! Press the hand that lies light upon your arm, and you too, thank God, while yet you may!

You are early home – mid-afternoon. Your step is not light; it is heavy, terrible. They have sent for you.

She is lying down; her eyes half closed; her breathing long and interrupted.

She hears you; her eye opens; you put your hand in hers; yours trembles, her does not. Her lips move; it is your name.

"Be strong," she says, "God will help you!"

She presses harder your hand: – "Adieu!" A long breath – another; you are alone again! No tears now; poor man! You cannot find them!

Again home early. There is a smell of varnish in your house. A coffin is there; they have clothed the body in decent grave clothes, and the undertaker is screwing down the lid, slipping round on tip-toe. Does he fear to waken her?

He asks you a simple question about the inscription upon the plate, rubbing it with his coat cuff. You look him straight in the eye; you motion to the door; you dare not speak.

He takes up his hat and glides out stealthful as a cat.

The man has done his work well, for all. It is a nice coffin – a very nice coffin! Pass your hand over it – how smooth!

Some sprigs of mignionette[28] are lying carelessly in a little gilt edged saucer. She loved mignionette.

It is a good staunch table the coffin rests on; – it is your table; you are a housekeeper – a man of family!

Aye, of family! – keep down outcry, or the nurse will be in. Look over at the pinched features; is this all that is left of her! And where is your heart now! No, don't thrust your nails into your hands, nor mangle your lip, nor grate your teeth together. If you could only weep!

– Another day. The coffin is gone out. The stupid mourners have wept – what idle tears! She, with your crushed heart, is gone out!

Will you have pleasant evenings at your home now?

Go into your parlor that your prim house-keeper has made comfortable with clean hearth and blaze of sticks.

---

28. **mignionette:** A plant with small, fragrant, light green flowers; in the symbolism of flowers, it signified "I live for thee."

Sit down in your chair; there is another velvet cushioned one, over against yours, empty. You press your fingers on your eye-balls, as if you would press out something that hurt the brain; but you cannot. Your head leans upon your hand; your eyes rest upon the flashing blaze.

Ashes always come after blaze.

Go now into the room where she was sick – softly, lest the prim house-keeper hear you and come after.

They have put new dimity upon her chair; they have hung new curtains over the bed. They have removed from the stand its phials and silver bell; they have put a little vase of flowers in their place; the perfume will not offend the sick nurse now. They have half opened the window, that the room, so long closed, may have air. It will not be too cold. She is not there.

Oh, God! thou who dost temper the wind to the Shorn Lamb[29] – be kind!

The embers were dark; I stirred them; there was no sign of life. My dog was asleep. The clock in my tenant's chamber had struck one.

I dashed a tear or two from my eyes – how they came I know not. I half ejaculated a prayer of thanks that such desolation had not yet come nigh me; and a prayer of hope that it might never come.

In a half hour more, I was sleeping soundly. My revery was ended.

[1849]

---

29. **temper . . . Shorn Lamb:** An idiom meaning to ease or alleviate pain and suffering.

Elizabeth Barstow Stoddard

[1823–1902]

Elizabeth Barstow Stoddard was born on May 6, 1823, the second of nine children of Betsy Drew and William Barstow, a prosperous shipbuilder in Mattapoisett, Massachusetts. Raised in that small coastal community, Stoddard developed considerable personal and intellectual independence. An avid reader, she attended Wheaton Female Seminary in nearby Norton, Massachusetts, but Stoddard left without taking a certificate of completion. In 1852, she married Richard Henry Stoddard, a poet, and moved to New York City. Richard Stoddard was friendly with Nathaniel Hawthorne and later with Herman Melville, but most of the couple's friends were lesser-known writers like Bayard Taylor, Thomas Bailey Aldrich, and Edmund Clarence Stedman. From the beginning of their marriage, the Stoddards struggled financially. With the help of Hawthorne, Richard Stoddard eventually got a job at the New York Custom House. The income from that position was insufficient for the growing family, however, and he constantly sought to supplement it by writing and doing literary hack work.

Richard Stoddard also encouraged his wife to pursue a literary career. Her first published work, a brief sketch on the importance of nature to human beings, appeared in the *Literary World* in 1852. In 1854, Stoddard became "Our Lady Correspondent" for the *Daily Alta California*, the first daily newspaper in San Francisco, where transplanted northeasterners seeking their fortunes were hungry for news of the literature, politics, and society of New York City. In the course of writing those successful columns, she refined her informal style and developed a technique of ironic understatement, as well as a keen eye for small but telling details. Those characteristics also distinguished her fiction, especially the stories Stoddard wrote after her work for the *Alta California* ended in 1858. Four years later, she published what is now generally viewed as her most important work, *The Moregesons*, a strongly autobiographical and unconventional novel about a young woman determined to live life on her own terms. George Ripley, the reviewer for the *New York Tribune*, observed that the novel "will be read as a development of powerful, erratic, individual passion, – a somewhat bitter, but perhaps not unwholesome commentary on life and society." The novel was read by very few, however, partly because it appeared at the moment attention in the North was focused on the disastrous defeat of the Union forces at the Second Battle of Bull Run in August 1862. Stoddard's next novels – *Two Men* (1865) and *Temple House* (1867) – gained some critical acclaim but did not sell well. She consequently turned to writing stories targeted at a more popular audience, as well as ephemeral works like *Lolly Dinks's Doings*, a children's book published in 1874. In the 1880s, her old friend Edmund Stedman arranged for new editions of her three novels. Although that generated a small renewal of interest in her work, sales were once again disappointing. "The failure of my novels to sell is always the 'black drop,' when they are praised, and it chokes me into silence," she bitterly wrote to Stedman in 1891. Stoddard's final book, a volume of poems, appeared in 1895. She died of pneumonia on August 1, 1902.

bedfordstmartins.com/ americanlit *for research links on Stoddard*

Stoddard's "Lemorne *versus* Huell." During the 1860s, when she published her three novels, Stoddard also published numerous stories, most of them in *Harper's New Monthly Magazine*, where "Lemorne *versus* Huell" appeared in 1863. *Harper's* was a well-regarded, illustrated literary journal with a large readership – its circulation stood at 200,000 in 1860, though that declined during the Civil War, when it and other northern journals lost subscribers in the South. Unlike more prestigious journals like the *Atlantic Monthly* and *Putnam's Monthly Magazine*, where some of Stoddard's work also appeared, *Harper's* was not committed to publishing mainly American literature. During the year that "Lemorne *versus* Huell" appeared, *Harper's* also published serializations of works by two prominent English novelists, Anthony Trollope's *The Small House at Allingham* and George Eliot's *Romola.* In contrast, many of Stoddard's stories were distinctly regional in character, taking as their primary subject the landscape and character types of New England. Others, like "Lemorne *versus* Huell," were complex variations on the kind of courtship or Cinderella stories so popular with the editors and readers of middlebrow journals like *Harper's.* The text is taken from its first printing in the magazine, in March 1863.

LEMORNE *VERSUS* HUELL

The two months I spent at Newport[1] with Aunt Eliza Huell, who had been ordered to the sea-side for the benefit of her health, were the months that created all that is dramatic in my destiny. My aunt was troublesome, for she was not only out of health, but in a lawsuit. She wrote to me, for we lived apart, asking me to accompany her – not because she was fond of me, or wished to give me pleasure, but because I was useful in various ways. Mother insisted upon my accepting her invitation, not because she loved her late husband's sister, but because she thought it wise to cotton to her in every particular, for Aunt Eliza was rich, and we – two lone women – were poor.

I gave my music-pupils a longer and earlier vacation than usual, took a week to arrange my wardrobe – for I made my own dresses – and then started for New York, with the five dollars which Aunt Eliza had sent for my fare thither. I arrived at her house in Bond Street at 7 A.M., and found her man James in conversation with the milkman. He informed me that Miss Huell was very bad, and that the housekeeper was still in bed. I supposed that Aunt Eliza was in bed also, but I had hardly entered the house when I heard her bell ring as she only could ring it – with an impatient jerk.

"She wants hot milk," said James, "and the man has just come."

I laid my bonnet down, and went to the kitchen. Saluting the cook, who was an old acquaintance, and who told me that the "divil" had been in the range that morning, I took a pan, into which I poured some milk, and held it over the gaslight till it was hot; then I carried it up to Aunt Eliza.

"Here is your milk, Aunt Eliza. You have sent for me to help you, and I begin with the earliest opportunity."

"I looked for you an hour ago. Ring the bell."

I rang it.

"Your mother is well, I suppose. She would have sent you, though, had she been sick in bed."

"She has done so. She thinks better of my coming than I do."

The housekeeper, Mrs. Roll, came in, and Aunt Eliza politely requested her to have breakfast for her niece as soon as possible.

---

1. **Newport:** A fashionable resort town on the coast of Rhode Island.

"I do not go down of mornings yet," said Aunt Eliza, "but Mrs. Roll presides. See that the coffee is good, Roll."

"It is good generally, Miss Huell."

"You see that Margaret brought me my milk."

"Ahem!" said Mrs. Roll, marching out.

At the beginning of each visit to Aunt Eliza, I was in the habit of dwelling on the contrast between her way of living and ours. We lived from "hand to mouth." Every thing about her wore a hereditary air; for she lived in my grandfather's house, and it was the same as in his day. If I was at home when these contrasts occurred to me I should have felt angry; as it was, I felt them as in a dream – the china, the silver, the old furniture, and the excellent fare soothed me.

In the middle of the day Aunt Eliza came down stairs, and after she had received a visit from her doctor, decided to go to Newport on Saturday. It was Wednesday; and I could, if I chose, make any addition to my wardrobe. I had none to make, I informed her. What were my dresses? – had I a black silk? she asked. I had no black silk, and thought one would be unnecessary for hot weather.

"Who ever heard of a girl of twenty-four having no black silk! You have slimsy muslins, I dare say?"

"Yes."

"And you like them?"

"For present wear."

That afternoon she sent Mrs. Roll out, who returned with a splendid heavy silk for me, which Aunt Eliza said should be made before Saturday, and it was. I went to a fashionable dress-maker of her recommending, and on Friday it came home, beautifully made and trimmed with real lace.

"Even the Pushers could find no fault with this," said Aunt Eliza, turning over the sleeves and smoothing the lace. Somehow she smuggled into the house a white straw-bonnet, with white roses; also a handsome mantilla. She held the bonnet before me with a nod, and deposited it again in the box, which made a part of the luggage for Newport.

On Sunday morning we arrived in Newport, and went to a quiet hotel in the town. James was with us, but Mrs. Roll was left in Bond Street, in charge of the household. Monday was spent in an endeavor to make an arrangement regarding the hire of a coach and coachman. Several livery-stable keepers were in attendance, but nothing was settled, till I suggested that Aunt Eliza should send for her own carriage. James was sent back the next day, and returned on Thursday with coach, horses, and William her coachman. That matter being finished, and the trunks being unpacked, she decided to take her first bath in the sea, expecting me to support her through the trying ordeal of the surf. As we were returning from the beach we met a carriage containing a number of persons with a family resemblance.

When Aunt Eliza saw them she angrily exclaimed, "Am I to see those Uxbridges every day?"

Of the Uxbridges this much I knew – that the two brothers Uxbridge were the lawyers of her opponents in the lawsuit which had existed three or four years. I had never felt any interest in it, though I knew that it was concerning a tract of ground in the city which had belonged to my grandfather, and which had, since his day, become very valuable. Litigation was a habit of the Huell family. So the sight of the Uxbridge family did not agitate me as it did Aunt Eliza.

"The sly, methodical dogs! but I shall beat Lemorne yet!"

"How will you amuse yourself then, aunt?"

"I'll adopt some boys to inherit what I shall save from his clutches."

The bath fatigued her so she remained in her room for the rest of the day; but she kept me busy with a hundred trifles. I wrote for her, computed interest, studied out bills of fare, till four o'clock came, and with it a fog. Nevertheless I must ride on the Avenue, and the carriage was ordered.

"Wear your silk, Margaret; it will just about last your visit through – the fog will use it up."

"I am glad of it," I answered.

"You will ride every day. Wear the bonnet I bought for you also."

"Certainly; but won't that go quicker in the fog than the dress?"

"Maybe; but wear it."

I rode every day afterward, from four to six, in the black silk, the mantilla, and the white straw. When Aunt Eliza went she was so on the alert for the Uxbridge family carriage that she could have had little enjoyment of the ride. Rocks never were a passion with her, she said, nor promontories, chasms, or sand. She came to Newport to be washed with salt-water; when she had washed up to the doctor's prescription she should leave, as ignorant of the peculiar pleasures of Newport as when she arrived. She had no fancy for its conglomerate societies, its literary cottages, its parvenue suits of rooms, its saloon habits, and its bathing herds.

I considered the rides a part of the contract of what was expected in my two months' performance. I did not dream that I was enjoying them, any more than I supposed myself to be enjoying a sea-bath while pulling Aunt Eliza to and fro in the surf. Nothing in the life around me stirred me, nothing in nature attracted me. I liked the fog; somehow it seemed to emanate from me instead of rolling up from the ocean, and to represent me. Whether I went alone or not, the coachman was ordered to drive a certain round; after that I could extend the ride in whatever direction I pleased, but I always said, "Any where, William." One afternoon, which happened to be a bright one, I was riding on the road which led to the glen, when I heard the screaming of a flock of geese which were waddling across the path in front of the horses. I started, for I was asleep probably, and, looking forward, saw the Uxbridge carriage, filled with ladies and children, coming toward me; and by it rode a gentleman on horseback. His horse was rearing among the hissing geese, but neither horse nor geese appeared to engage him; his eyes were fixed upon me. The horse swerved so near that its long mane almost brushed against me. By an irresistible impulse I laid my ungloved hand upon it, but did not look at the rider. Carriage and horseman passed on, and William resumed his pace. A vague idea took possession of me that I had seen the horseman before on my various drives. I had a vision of a man galloping on a black horse out of the fog, and into it again. I was very sure, however, that I had never seen him on so pleasant a day as this! William did not bring his horses to time; it was after six when I went into Aunt Eliza's parlor, and found her impatient for her tea and toast. She was crosser than the occasion warranted; but I understood it when she gave me the outlines of a letter she desired me to write to her lawyer in New York. Something had turned up, he had written her; the Uxbridges believed that they had ferreted out what would go against her. I told her that I had met the Uxbridge carriage.

"One of them is in New York; how else could they be giving me trouble just now?"

"There was a gentleman on horseback beside the carriage."

"Did he look mean and cunning?"

"He did not wear his legal beaver up, I think; but he rode a fine horse and sat it well."

"A lawyer on horseback should, like the beggar of the adage, ride to the devil."[2]

"Your business now is the 'Lemorne?'"

"You know it is."

"I did not know but that you had found something besides to litigate."

"It must have been Edward Uxbridge that you saw. He is the brain of the firm."

"You expect Mr. Van Horn?"

"Oh, he must come; I can not be writing letters."

We had been in Newport two weeks when Mr. Van Horn, Aunt Eliza's lawyer, came. He said that he would see Mr. Edward Uxbridge. Between them they might delay a term, which he thought would be best. "Would Miss Huell ever be ready for a compromise?" he jestingly asked.

"Are you suspicious?" she inquired.

"No; but the Uxbridge chaps are clever."

He dined with us; and at four o'clock Aunt Eliza graciously asked him to take a seat in the carriage with me, making some excuse for not going herself.

"Hullo!" said Mr. Van Horn when we had reached the country road, "there's Uxbridge now." And he waved his hand to him.

It was indeed the black horse and the same rider that I had met. He reined up beside us, and shook hands with Mr. Van Horn.

"We are required to answer this new complaint?" said Mr. Van Horn.

Mr. Uxbridge nodded.

"And after that the judgment?"

Mr. Uxbridge laughed.

"I wish that certain gore of land had been sunk instead of being mapped in 1835."

"The surveyor did his business well enough, I am sure."

They talked together in a low voice for a few minutes, and then Mr. Van Horn leaned back in his seat again. "Allow me," he said, "to introduce you, Uxbridge, to Miss Margaret Huell, Miss Huell's niece. Huell *vs.* Brown, you know," he added, in an explanatory tone; for I was Huell *vs.* Brown's daughter.

"Oh!" said Mr. Uxbridge, bowing, and looking at me gravely. I looked at him also; he was a pale, stern-looking man, and forty years old certainly. I derived the impression at

2. **"A lawyer . . . devil"**: Set a beggar on horseback and he'll ride to the devil (German proverb).

once that he had a domineering disposition, perhaps from the way in which he controlled his horse.

"Nice beast that," said Mr. Van Horn.

"Yes," he answered, laying his hand on its mane, so that the action brought immediately to my mind the recollection that I had done so too. I would not meet his eye again, however.

"How long shall you remain, Uxbridge?"

"I don't know. You are not interested in the lawsuit, Miss Huell?" he said, putting on his hat.

"Not in the least; nothing of mine is involved."

"We'll gain it for your portion yet, Miss Margaret," said Mr. Van Horn, nodding to Mr. Uxbridge, and bidding William drive on. He returned the next day, and we settled into the routine of hotel life. A few mornings after, she sent me to a matinée, which was given by some of the Opera people, who were in Newport strengthening the larynx with applications of brine. When the concert was half over, and the audience were making the usual hum and stir, I saw Mr. Uxbridge against a pillar, with his hands incased in pearl-colored gloves, and holding a shiny hat. He turned half away when he caught my eye, and then darted toward me.

"You have not been much more interested in the music than you are in the lawsuit," he said, seating himself beside me.

"The *tutoyer*[3] of the Italian voice is agreeable, however."

"It makes one dreamy."

"A child."

"Yes, a child; not a man nor a woman."

"I teach music. I can not dream over 'one, two, three.'"

"*You* – a music teacher!"

"For six years."

I was aware that he looked at me from head to foot, and I picked at the lace on my invariable black silk; but what did it matter whether I owned that I was a genteel pauper, representing my aunt's position for two months, or not?

"Where?"

"In Waterbury."

"Waterbury differs from Newport."

"I suppose so."

"You suppose!"

A young gentleman sauntered by us, and Mr. Uxbridge called to him to look up the Misses Uxbridge, his nieces, on the other side of the hall.

"Paterfamilias Uxbridge has left his brood in my charge," he said. "I try to do my duty," and he held out a twisted pearl-colored glove, which he had pulled off while talking. What white nervous fingers he had! I thought they might pinch like steel.

3. ***tutoyer***: To address familiarly (French); here suggesting that the singer's tone has a familiar, intimate quality.

"You suppose," he repeated.

"I do not look at Newport."

"Have you observed Waterbury?"

"I observe what is in my sphere."

"Oh!"

He was silent then. The second part of the concert began; but I could not compose myself to appreciation. Either the music or I grew chaotic. So many tumultuous sounds I heard – of hope, doubt, inquiry, melancholy, and desire; or did I feel the emotions which these words express? Or was there magnetism stealing into me from the quiet man beside me? He left me with a bow before the concert was over, and I saw him making his way out of the hall when it was finished.

I had been sent in the carriage, of course; but several carriages were in advance of it before the walk, and I waited there for William to drive up. When he did so, I saw by the oscillatory motion of his head, though his arms and whip-hand were perfectly correct, that he was inebriated. It was his first occasion of meeting fellow-coachmen in full dress, and the occasion had proved too much for him. My hand, however, was on the coach door, when I heard Mr. Uxbridge say, at my elbow,

"It is not safe for you."

"Oh, Sir, it is in the programme that I ride home from the concert." And I prepared to step in.

"I shall sit on the box, then."

"But your nieces?"

"They are walking home, squired by a younger knight."

Aunt Eliza would say, I thought, "Needs must when a lawyer drives;" and I concluded to allow him to have his way, telling him that he was taking a great deal of trouble. He thought it would be less if he were allowed to sit inside; both ways were unsafe.

Nothing happened. William drove well from habit; but James was obliged to assist him to dismount. Mr. Uxbridge waited a moment at the door, and so there was quite a little sensation, which spread its ripples till Aunt Eliza was reached. She sent for William, whose only excuse was "dampness."

"Uxbridge knew my carriage, of course," she said, with a complacent voice.

"He knew me," I replied.

"You do not look like the Huells."

"I look precisely like the young woman to whom he was introduced by Mr. Van Horn."

"Oh ho!"

"He thought it unsafe for me to come alone under William's charge."

"Ah ha!"

No more was said on the subject of his coming home with me. Aunt Eliza had several fits of musing in the course of the evening while I read aloud to her, which had no connection with the subject of the book. As I put it down she said that it would be well for me to go to church the next day. I acquiesced, but remarked that my piety would not require the carriage, and that I preferred to walk. Besides, it would be well for William and James to attend divine service. She could not spare James, and thought William had better clean the harness, by way of penance.

The morning proved to be warm and sunny. I donned a muslin dress of home manufacture and my own bonnet, and started for church. I had walked but a few paces when the consciousness of being *free* and *alone* struck me. I halted, looked about me, and concluded that I would not go to church, but walk into the fields. I had no knowledge of the whereabouts of the fields; but I walked straight forward, and after a while came upon some barren fields, cropping with coarse rocks, along which ran a narrow road. I turned into it, and soon saw beyond the rough coast the blue ring of the ocean – vast, silent, and splendid in the sunshine. I found a seat on the ruins of an old stone-wall, among some tangled bushes and briers. There being no Aunt Eliza to pull through the surf, and no animated bathers near, I discovered the beauty of the sea, and that I loved it.

Presently I heard the steps of a horse, and, to my astonishment, Mr. Uxbridge rode past. I was glad he did not know me. I watched him as he rode slowly down the road, deep in thought. He let drop the bridle, and the horse stopped, as if accustomed to the circumstance, and pawed the ground gently, or yawed his neck for pastime. Mr. Uxbridge folded his arms and raised his head to look seaward. It seemed to me as if he were about to address the jury. I had dropped so entirely from my observance of the landscape that I jumped when he resumed the bridle and turned his horse to come back. I slipped from my seat to look among the bushes, determined that he should not recognize me; but my attempt was a failure – he did not ride by the second time.

"Miss Huell!" And he jumped from his saddle, slipping his arm through the bridle.

"I am a runaway. What do you think of the Fugitive Slave Bill?"[4]

"I approve of returning property to its owners."

"The sea must have been God's temple first, instead of the groves."[5]

"I believe the Saurians[6] were an Orthodox tribe."

"Did you stop yonder to ponder the sea?"

"I was pondering 'Lemorne *vs.* Huell.'"

He looked at me earnestly, and then gave a tug at the bridle, for his steed was inclined to make a crude repast from the bushes.

"How was it that I did not detect you at once?" he continued.

"My apparel is Waterbury apparel."

"Ah!"

We walked up the road slowly till we came to the end of it; then I stopped for him to understand that I thought it time for him to leave me. He sprang into the saddle.

"Give us good-by!" he said, bringing his horse close to me.

"We are not on equal terms; I feel too humble afoot to salute you."

---

4. **Fugitive Slave Bill**: The most controversial provision of the Compromise of 1850, the proposed fugitive slave bill required all citizens to aid in the capture and return of runaways to their owners. The reference suggests that the story takes place in the summer of 1850, shortly before the bill was passed into law by Congress.

5. **"The sea . . . instead of the groves"**: A play on the first line – "The groves were God's first temples" – of "A Forest Hymn," a popular poem by William Cullen Bryant (1794–1878).

6. **Saurians**: Reptiles of the suborder Sauria; usually usage in the nineteenth century was in reference to dinosaurs or other extinct forms.

"Put your foot on the stirrup then."

A leaf stuck in the horse's forelock, and I pulled it off and waved it in token of farewell. A powerful light shot into his eyes when he saw my hand close on the leaf.

"May I come and see you?" he asked, abruptly. "I will."

"I shall say neither 'No' nor 'Yes.'"

He rode on at a quick pace, and I walked homeward, forgetting the sense of liberty I had started with, and proceeded straightway to Aunt Eliza.

"I have not been to church, aunt, but to walk beyond the town; it was not so nominated in the bond, but I went. The taste of freedom was so pleasant that I warn you there is danger of my 'striking.' When will you have done with Newport?"

"I am pleased with Newport now," she answered, with a curious intonation. "I like it."

"I do also."

Her keen eyes sparkled.

"Did you ever like any thing when you were with me before?"

"Never. I will tell you why I like it: because I have met, and shall probably meet, Mr. Uxbridge. I saw him to-day. He asked permission to visit me."

"Let him come."

"He will come."

But we did not see him either at the hotel or when we went abroad. Aunt Eliza rode with me each afternoon, and each morning we went to the beach. She engaged me every moment when at home, and I faithfully performed all my tasks. I clapped to the door on self-investigation – locked it against any analysis or reasoning upon any circumstance connected with Mr. Uxbridge. The only piece of treachery to my code that I was guilty of was the putting of the leaf which I brought home on Sunday between the leaves of that poem whose motto is,

> "Mariana in the moated grange."[7]

On Saturday morning, nearly a week after I saw him on my walk, Aunt Eliza proposed that we should go to Turo Street on a shopping excursion; she wanted a cap, and various articles besides. As we went into a large shop I saw Mr. Uxbridge at a counter buying gloves; her quick eye caught sight of him, and she edged away, saying she would look at some goods on the other side; I might wait where I was. As he turned to go out he saw me and stopped.

"I have been in New York since I saw you," he said. "Mr. Lemorne sent for me."

"There is my aunt," I said.

He shrugged his shoulders.

"I shall not go away soon again," he remarked. "I missed Newport greatly."

I made some foolish reply, and kept my eyes on Aunt Eliza, who dawdled unaccountably. He appeared amused, and after a little talk went away.

---

7. **"Mariana in the moated grange"**: A quotation from Shakespeare's *Measure for Measure* (3.1) used as the epigraph of "Mariana," a poem by the English poet Alfred, Lord Tennyson (1809-1892). Drawing on Shakespeare's play, Tennyson describes a woman who waits hopelessly for her lover to return.

Aunt Eliza's purchase was a rose-colored moire antique, which she said was to be made for me; for Mrs. Bliss, one of our hotel acquaintances, had offered to chaperon me to the great ball which would come off in a few days, and she had accepted the offer for me.

"There will be no chance for you to take a walk instead," she finished with.

"I can not dance, you know."

"But you will be *there*."

I was sent to a dress-maker of Mrs. Bliss's recommending; but I ordered the dress to be made after my own design, long plain sleeves, and high plain corsage, and requested that it should not be sent home till the evening of the ball. Before it came off Mr. Uxbridge called, and was graciously received by Aunt Eliza, who could be gracious to all except her relatives. I could not but perceive, however, that they watched each other in spite of their lively conversation. To me he was deferential, but went over the ground of our acquaintance as if it had been the most natural thing in the world. But for my life-long habit of never calling in question the behavior of those I came in contact with, and of never expecting any thing different from that I received, I might have wondered over his visit. Every person's individuality was sacred to me, from the fact, perhaps, that my own individuality had never been respected by any person with whom I had any relation – not even by my own mother.

After Mr. Uxbridge went, I asked Aunt Eliza if she thought he looked mean and cunning? She laughed, and replied that she was bound to think that Mr. Lemorne's lawyer could not look otherwise.

When, on the night of the ball, I presented myself in the rose-colored moire antique for her inspection, she raised her eyebrows, but said nothing about it.

"I need not be careful of it, I suppose, aunt?"

"Spill as much wine and ice-cream on it as you like."

In the dressing-room Mrs. Bliss surveyed me.

"I think I like this mass of rose-color," she said. "Your hair comes out in contrast so brilliantly. Why, you have not a single ornament on!"

"It is so easy to dress without."

This was all the conversation we had together during the evening, except when she introduced some acquaintance to fulfill her matronizing duties. As I was no dancer I was left alone most of the time, and amused myself by gliding from window to window along the wall, that it might not be observed that I was a fixed flower. Still I suffered the annoyance of being stared at by wandering squads of young gentlemen, the "curled darlings" of the ball-room. I borrowed Mrs. Bliss's fan in one of her visits for a protection. With that, and the embrasure of a remote window where I finally stationed myself, I hoped to escape further notice. The music of the celebrated band which played between the dances recalled the chorus of spirits which charmed Faust:

> "And the fluttering
> Ribbons of drapery
> Cover the plains,
> Cover the bowers,

Where lovers,
Deep in thought,
Give themselves for life."[8]

The voice of Mrs. Bliss broke its spell.

"I bring an old friend, Miss Huell, and he tells me an acquaintance of yours."

It was Mr. Uxbridge.

"I had no thought of meeting you, Miss Huell."

And he coolly took the seat beside me in the window, leaving to Mrs. Bliss the alternative of standing or of going away; she chose the latter.

"I saw you as soon as I came in," he said, "gliding from window to window, like a vessel hugging the shore in a storm."

"With colors at half-mast; I have no dancing partner."

"How many have observed you?"

"Several young gentlemen."

"Moths."

"Oh no, butterflies."

"They must keep away now."

"Are you Rhadamanthus?"

"And Charon, too.[9] I would have you row in the same boat with me."

"Now you are fishing."

"Won't you compliment me. Did I ever look better?"

His evening costume *was* becoming, but he looked pale, and weary, and disturbed. But if we were engaged for a tournament, as his behavior indicated, I must do my best at telling. So I told him that he never looked better, and asked him how I looked. He would look at me presently, he said, and decide. Mrs. Bliss skimmed by us with nods and smiles; as she vanished our eyes followed her, and we talked vaguely on various matters, sounding ourselves and each other. When a furious redowa set in which cut our conversation into rhythm he pushed up the window and said, "Look out."

I turned my face to him to do so, and saw the moon at the full, riding through the strip of sky which our vision commanded. From the moon our eyes fell on each other. After a moment's silence, during which I returned his steadfast gaze, for I could not help it, he said:

"If we understand the impression we make upon each other, what must be said?"

I made no reply, but fanned myself, neither looking at the moon, nor upon the redowa, nor upon any thing.

---

8. **"And . . . for life"**: In the first scene of *Faust*, part I, by Johann Wolfgang von Goethe (1749–1832), a group of spirits come to Faust just as the aged philosopher is about to drink a cup of poison and end his life. The passage is part of their chorus celebrating the joy of life and the beauty of nature. When their chorus ends, Faust remains despondent, only to be confronted by Mephistopheles, the devil, who offers him youth and vigor. The rest of the play concerns the price that Faust pays for agreeing to the terms of Mephistopheles.

9. **Rhadamanthus . . . Charon, too:** In Greek mythology, Rhadamanthus was the son of Zeus and Europa and one of the three judges of the dead in the underworld; Charon was the ferryman of the dead, who took them across the river Styx to the underworld.

He took the fan from me.

"Speak of yourself," he said.

"Speak you."

"I am what I seem, a man within your sphere. By all the accidents of position and circumstances suited to it. Have you not learned it?"

"I am not what I seem. I never wore so splendid a dress as this till to-night, and shall not again."

He gave the fan such a twirl that its slender sticks snapped, and it drooped like the broken wing of a bird.

"Mr. Uxbridge, that fan belongs to Mrs. Bliss."

He threw it out of the window.

"You have courage, fidelity, and patience – this character with a passionate soul. I am sure that you have such a soul?"

"I do not know."

"I have fallen in love with you. It happened on the very day when I passed you on the way to the Glen. I never got away from the remembrance of seeing your hand on the mane of my horse."

He waited for me to speak, but I could not; the balance of my mind was gone. Why should this have happened to me – a slave? As it had happened, why did I not feel exultant in the sense of power which the chance for freedom with him should give?

"What is it, Margaret? your face is as sad as death."

"How do you call me 'Margaret?'"

"As I would call my wife – Margaret."

He rose and stood before me to screen my face from observation. I supposed so, and endeavored to stifle my agitation.

"You are better," he said, presently. "Come go with me and get some refreshment." And he beckoned to Mrs. Bliss, who was down the hall with an unwieldy gentleman.

"Will you go to supper now?" she asked.

"We are only waiting for you," Mr. Uxbridge answered, offering me his arm.

When we emerged into the blaze and glitter of the supper-room I sought refuge in the shadow of Mrs. Bliss's companion, for it seemed to me that I had lost my own.

"Drink this Champagne," said Mr. Uxbridge. "Pay no attention to the Colonel on your left; he won't expect it."

"Neither must you."

"Drink."

The Champagne did not prevent me from reflecting on the fact that he had not yet asked whether I loved him.

The spirit chorus again floated through my mind:

> "Where lovers,
> Deep is thought,
> *Give* themselves for life."

I was not allowed to *give* myself – I was *taken*.

"No heel-taps," he whispered, "to the bottom quaff."

"Take me home, will you?"

"Mrs. Bliss is not ready."

"Tell her that I must go."

He went behind her chair and whispered something, and she nodded to me to go without her.

When her carriage came up, I think he gave the coachman an order to drive home in a roundabout way, for we were a long time reaching it. I kept my face to the window, and he made no effort to divert my attention. When we came to a street whose thick rows of trees shut out the moonlight my eager soul longed to leap out into the dark and demand of him his heart, soul, life, for *me*.

I struck him lightly on the shoulder; he seized my hand.

"Oh, I know you, Margaret; you are mine!"

"We are at the hotel."

He sent the carriage back, and said that he would leave me at my aunt's door. He wished that he could see her then. Was it magic that made her open the door before I reached it?

"Have you come on legal business?" she asked him.

"You have divined what I come for."

"Step in, step in; it's very late. I should have been in bed but for neuralgia. Did Mr. Uxbridge come home with you, Margaret?"

"Yes, in Mrs. Bliss's carriage; I wished to come before she was ready to leave."

"Well, Mr. Uxbridge is old enough for your protector, certainly."

"I *am* forty, ma'am."

"Do you want Margaret?"

"I do."

"You know exactly how much is involved in your client's suit?"

"Exactly."

"You know also that his claim is an unjust one."

"Do I?"

"I shall not be poor if I lose; if I gain, Margaret will be rich."

"'Margaret will be rich!'" he repeated, absently.

"What! have you changed your mind respecting the orphans, aunt?"

"She has, and is – nothing," she went on, not heeding my remark. "Her father married below his station; when he died his wife fell back to her place – for he spent his fortune – and there she and Margaret must remain, unless Lemorne is defeated."

"Aunt, for your succinct biography of my position many thanks."

"Sixty thousand dollars," she continued. "Van Horn tells me that, as yet, the firm of Uxbridge Brothers have only an income – no capital."

"It is true," he answered, musingly.

The clock on the mantle struck two.

"A thousand dollars for every year of my life," she said. "You and I, Uxbridge, know the value and beauty of money."

"Yes, there is beauty in money, and" – looking at me – "beauty without it."

"The striking of the clock," I soliloquized, "proves that this scene is not a phantasm."

"Margaret is fatigued," he said, rising. "May I come to-morrow?"

"It is my part only," replied Aunt Eliza, "to see that she is, or is not, Cinderella."

"If you have ever thought of me, aunt, as an individual, you must have seen that I am not averse to ashes."

He held my hand a moment, and then kissed me with a kiss of appropriation.

"He is in love with you," she said, after he had gone. "I think I know him. He has found beauty ignorant of itself; he will teach you to develop it."

The next morning Mr. Uxbridge had an interview with Aunt Eliza before he saw me. When we were alone I asked him how her eccentricities affected him; he could not but consider her violent, prejudiced, warped, and whimsical. I told him that I had been taught to accept all that she did on this basis. Would this explain to him my silence in regard to her?

"Can you endure to live with her in Bond Street for the present, or would you rather return to Waterbury?"

"She desires my company while she is in Newport only. I have never been with her so long before."

"I understand her. Law is a game, in her estimation, in which cheating can as easily be carried on as at cards."

"Her soul is in this case."

"Her soul is not too large for it. Will you ride this afternoon?"

I promised, of course. From that time till he left Newport we saw each other every day, and though I found little opportunity to express my own peculiar feelings, he comprehended many of my wishes, and all my tastes. I grew fond of him hourly. Had I not reason? Never was friend so considerate, never was lover more devoted.

When he had been gone a few days, Aunt Eliza declared that she was ready to depart from Newport. The rose-colored days were ended! In two days we were on the Sound, coach, horses, servants, and ourselves.

It was the 1st of September when we arrived in Bond Street. A week from that date Samuel Uxbridge, the senior partner of Uxbridge Brothers, went to Europe with his family, and I went to Waterbury, accompanied by Mr. Uxbridge. He consulted mother in regard to our marriage, and appointed it in November. In October Aunt Eliza sent for me to come back to Bond Street and spend a week. She had some fine marking to do, she wrote. While there I noticed a restlessness in her which I had never before observed, and conferred with Mrs. Roll on the matter. "She do be awake nights a deal, and that's the reason," Mrs. Roll said. Her manner was the same in other respects. She said she would not give me any thing for my wedding outfit, but she paid my fare from Waterbury and back.

She could not spare me to go out, she told Mr. Uxbridge, and in consequence I saw little of him while there.

In November we were married. Aunt Eliza was not at the wedding, which was a quiet one. Mr. Uxbridge desired me to remain in Waterbury till spring. He would not decide about taking a house in New York till then; by that time his brother might return, and if possible we would go to Europe for a few months. I acquiesced in all his plans. Indeed I was not consulted; but I was happy – happy in him, and happy in every thing.

The winter passed in waiting for him to come to Waterbury every Saturday; and in the enjoyment of the two days he passed with me. In March Aunt Eliza wrote me that Lemorne was beaten! Van Horn had taken up the whole contents of his snuff-box in her house the evening before in amazement at the turn things had taken.

That night I dreamed of the scene in the hotel at Newport. I heard Aunt Eliza saying, "If I gain, Margaret will be rich." And I heard also the clock strike two. As it struck I said, *"My husband is a scoundrel,"* and woke with a start.

[1863]

Rebecca Harding Davis

[1831–1910]

Rebecca Harding Davis was born on June 24, 1831. She was the first of five children of Richard W. Harding, a cultivated Englishman who had come to America seeking to make his fortune in business, and Rebecca Leet Harding, the well-educated daughter of a prominent family in western Pennsylvania. Davis was born in her mother's family home in Washington, a small town south of Pittsburgh, but she spent her earliest years in Alabama, where her father had first settled. In 1836, Richard Harding moved his family to Wheeling, in the northwestern and pro-Union part of Virginia that became West Virginia during the Civil War. Davis grew up there in an affluent, cultured home in which she was given an extensive education by tutors and her mother. When Davis was fourteen, she was sent to the Washington Female Seminary in Pennsylvania, where she studied a wide range of subjects, including art and music, English literature, French, philosophy, and religion. After graduating as the valedictorian of her class in 1848, Davis returned home and lived with her family for the next fourteen years, helping with the education of her younger siblings and occasionally writing for the *Wheeling Intelligencer*, the largest newspaper in western Virginia.

Rebecca Harding Davis

This photograph was taken when Davis was about thirty years old, around the same time that her first major work, *Life in the Iron-Mills*, appeared in the prestigious *Atlantic Monthly*.

Her pioneering firsts in subject matter are unequaled. She extended the realm of fiction.
–Tillie Olsen

Although she had a long and productive literary career, Davis's first significant publication is widely regarded as her best and most enduring work. When her first story, *Life in the Iron-Mills*, was published anonymously in the *Atlantic Monthly* in April 1861, it was immediately hailed as an outstanding work by a talented new writer. In accepting the story for publication, the editor of the *Atlantic*, James T. Fields, sent Davis a check for $50 and offered her $100 for another contribution. She sent him another grimly realistic story, "The Deaf and the Dumb," about a woman who is abandoned by her lover and works in the mills to support her parents. Fields thought it was too gloomy and asked her to change the title and the ending. In an example of what many critics view as a primary source of the flaws in much of her work – her willingness to tailor it to

bedfordstmartins.com/ americanlit *for research links on Davis*

suit popular taste – Davis obliged by ending the story with the promise of a happy marriage and changing its title to "A Story of To-day." The revised and expanded version was serialized in the *Atlantic* and then published as her first novel, *Margret Howth: A Story of To-day* (1862). That year, she traveled to New England and met Ralph Waldo Emerson, Louisa May Alcott, and Nathaniel Hawthorne, who had written her a congratulatory note about *Life in the Iron-Mills* and whose work Davis particularly admired. (She later observed that Hawthorne's short stories had inspired her own style of writing.) In 1863, she met one of her admiring readers, L. Clarke Davis, who had begun corresponding with her after reading her work. The couple soon married. L. Clarke Davis, a lawyer, later became the prominent editor of the *Philadelphia Inquirer* and then the *Philadelphia Public Ledger.* Throughout their long marriage and the births of three children, Davis published steadily and produced some other significant works like *Waiting for the Verdict* (1868), an ambitious novel about the Civil War. But her later writings are more distinguished by their bulk than by their quality. Scholars estimate that Davis published nearly five hundred works – including nine novels; numerous short stories and novellas; and many works of nonfiction, notably her entertaining autobiography, *Bits of Gossip* (1904), which appeared six years before her death in 1910.

Davis's *Life in the Iron-Mills*. In her autobiography, Davis described the fires of bituminous coal that burned in each room of her family home in Wheeling, Virginia. "These flames and grey ashes have always burned in my memory," Davis observed. They are also a constant motif in *Life in the Iron-Mills*, her realistic and richly symbolic depiction of a nightmarish world not very distant and yet far removed from her family's comfortable home. Davis wrote the story in 1860, an election year in which sectional divisions over slavery were leading the country toward disunion. But she focused on the sufferings of another oppressed group, the immigrant laborers in industrial centers like Wheeling, where Davis had spent most of her life and which she had frequently explored on long rambling walks around that grimy mill town on the Ohio River. An unknown writer, Davis boldly submitted the story to the most prestigious literary journal in the country, the *Atlantic Monthly*. Established in 1857 by a group of luminaries including Ralph Waldo Emerson, Oliver Wendell Holmes, and James Russell Lowell, the *Atlantic* was designed to promote American literature by publishing the work of the best writers in the country – both established figures and emerging talents, many of whom were women. Recognizing the story as a pioneering work in the emerging mode of realistic fiction, James T. Fields eagerly accepted *Life in the Iron-Mills* for publication in the *Atlantic*. It appeared there in April 1861, the month the Civil War began. After Virginia seceded from the Union, a pro-Union government was organized in Wheeling, which ultimately became the capital of the new state of West Virginia (1863). The text is taken from the first printing in the *Atlantic Monthly*.

LIFE IN THE IRON-MILLS

"Is this the end?
O Life, as futile, then, as frail!
What hope of answer or redress?"[1]

A cloudy day: do you know what that is in a town of iron-works?[2] The sky sank down before dawn, muddy, flat, immovable. The air is thick, clammy with the breath of crowded human beings. It stifles me. I open the window, and, looking out, can scarcely see through the rain the grocer's shop opposite, where a crowd of drunken Irishmen are puffing Lynchburg tobacco[3] in their pipes. I can detect the scent through all the foul smells ranging loose in the air.

The idiosyncrasy of this town is smoke. It rolls sullenly in slow folds from the great chimneys of the iron-foundries, and settles down in black, slimy pools on the muddy streets. Smoke on the wharves, smoke on the dingy boats, on the yellow river, – clinging in a coating of greasy soot to the house-front, the two faded poplars, the faces of the passers-by. The long train of mules, dragging masses of pig-iron[4] through the narrow street, have a foul vapor hanging to their reeking sides. Here, inside, is a little broken figure of an angel pointing upward from the mantel-shelf; but even its wings are covered with smoke, clotted and black. Smoke everywhere! A dirty canary chirps desolately in a cage beside me. Its dream of green fields and sunshine is a very old dream, – almost worn out, I think.

From the back-window I can see a narrow brick-yard sloping down to the river-side, strewed with rain-butts[5] and tubs. The river, dull and tawny-colored, (*la belle rivière!*)[6] drags itself sluggishly along, tired of the heavy weight of boats and coal-barges. What wonder? When I was a child, I used to fancy a look of weary, dumb appeal upon the face of the negro-like river slavishly bearing its burden day after day. Something of the same idle notion comes to me to-day, when from the street-window I look on the slow stream of human life creeping past, night and morning, to the great mills. Masses of men, with dull, besotted faces bent to the ground, sharpened here and there by pain or cunning; skin and muscle and flesh begrimed with smoke and ashes; stooping all night over boiling

1. **"Is this the end? . . . redress?":** The epigraph is taken from two sections of the popular, long elegiac poem, *In Memorian A.H.H.* (1850), by the English poet Alfred, Lord Tennyson, who wrote it to commemorate the untimely death of his friend, Arthur Henry Hallam. The first line is from section 12, lines 14–16: "'Is this the end of all my care?' / And circle moaning in the air: / 'Is this the end? Is this the end?'" The second two lines are taken from section 56, lines 25–29: "O life as futile, then, as frail! / O for thy voice to soothe and bless! / What hope of answer, or redress? / Behind the veil, behind the veil."
2. **town of iron-works?:** Although the exact location is not specified in the story, Davis portrays the pollution and economic hardships of many towns like Wheeling, Virginia (later West Virginia), where she grew up and witnessed such conditions firsthand.
3. **Lynchburg tobacco:** In the mid-1800s, Lynchburg, Virginia, had the largest market share of dark-leaf tobacco, considered inferior to lighter varieties.
4. **pig-iron:** Crude iron cast in blocks.
5. **rain-butts:** Large barrels designed to capture rainwater for domestic and industrial use.
6. ***"la belle rivière!"*:** The beautiful river (French); an ironic commentary on the polluted state of the Ohio River in the mid-nineteenth century.

caldrons of metal, laired by day in dens of drunkenness and infamy; breathing from infancy to death an air saturated with fog and grease and soot, vileness for soul and body. What do you make of a case like that, amateur psychologist? You call it an altogether serious thing to be alive: to these men it is a drunken jest, a joke, – horrible to angels perhaps, to them commonplace enough. My fancy about the river was an idle one: it is no type of such a life. What if it be stagnant and slimy here? It knows that beyond there waits for it odorous sunlight, – quaint old gardens, dusky with soft, green foliage of apple-trees, and flushing crimson with roses, – air, and fields, and mountains. The future of the Welsh puddler[7] passing just now is not so pleasant. To be stowed away, after his grimy work is done, in a hole in the muddy graveyard, and after that, — *not* air, nor green fields, nor curious roses.

Can you see how foggy the day is? As I stand here, idly tapping the window-pane, and looking out through the rain at the dirty back-yard and the coal-boats below, fragments of an old story float up before me, – a story of this old house into which I happened to come to-day. You may think it a tiresome story enough, as foggy as the day, sharpened by no sudden flashes of pain or pleasure. – I know: only the outline of a dull life, that long since, with thousands of dull lives like its own, was vainly lived and lost: thousands of them, – massed, vile, slimy lives, like those of the torpid lizards in yonder stagnant water-butt. – Lost? There is a curious point for you to settle, my friend, who study psychology in a lazy, *dilettante* way. Stop a moment. I am going to be honest. This is what I want you to do. I want you to hide your disgust, take no heed to your clean clothes, and come right down with me, – here, into the thickest of the fog and mud and foul effluvia. I want you to hear this story. There is a secret down here, in this nightmare fog, that has lain dumb for centuries: I want to make it a real thing to you. You, Egoist, or Pantheist, or Arminian,[8] busy in making straight paths for your feet on the hills, do not see it clearly, – this terrible question which men here have gone mad and died trying to answer. I dare not put this secret into words. I told you it was dumb. These men, going by with drunken faces and brains full of unawakened power, do not ask it of Society or of God. Their lives ask it; their deaths ask it. There is no reply. I will tell you plainly that I have a great hope; and I bring it to you to be tested. It is this: that this terrible dumb question is its own reply; that it is not the sentence of death we think it, but, from the very extremity of its darkness, the most solemn prophecy which the world has known of the Hope to come. I dare make my meaning no clearer, but will only tell my story. It will, perhaps, seem to you as foul and dark as this thick vapor about us, and as pregnant with death; but if your eyes are free as mine are to look deeper, no perfume-tinted dawn will be so fair with promise of the day that shall surely come.

My story is very simple, – only what I remember of the life of one of these men, – a furnace-tender in one of Kirby & John's rolling-mills, – Hugh Wolfe. You know the mills?

---

7. **puddler:** A worker who produces steel by stirring iron oxide into a molten vat of pig iron.
8. **Egoist, or Pantheist, or Arminian:** An egoist is one who is devoted to self-cultivation, which in turn leads to the improvement of all. A pantheist finds the Deity in nature; an Arminian is one who follows the teachings of Jacobus Arminius (1560–1601), a theologian who opposed the Calvinist notion of predestination.

They took the great order for the Lower Virginia railroads there last winter; run usually with about a thousand men. I cannot tell why I choose the half-forgotten story of this Wolfe more than that of myriads of these furnace-hands. Perhaps because there is a secret underlying sympathy between that story and this day with its impure fog and thwarted sunshine, – or perhaps simply for the reason that this house is the one where the Wolfes lived. There were the father and son, – both hands, as I said, in one of Kirby & John's mills for making railroad-iron, – and Deborah, their cousin, a picker[9] in some of the cotton-mills. The house was rented then to half a dozen families. The Wolfes had two of the cellar-rooms. The old man, like many of the puddlers and feeders[10] of the mills, was Welsh, – had spent half of his life in the Cornish tin-mines. You may pick the Welsh emigrants, Cornish miners, out of the throng passing the windows, any day. They are a trifle more filthy; their muscles are not so brawny; they stoop more. When they are drunk, they neither yell, nor shout, nor stagger, but skulk along like beaten hounds. A pure, unmixed blood, I fancy: shows itself in the slight angular bodies and sharply-cut facial lines. It is nearly thirty years since the Wolfes lived here. Their lives were like those of their class: incessant labor, sleeping in kennel-like rooms, eating rank pork and molasses, drinking – God and the distillers only know what; with an occasional night in jail, to atone for some drunken excess. Is that all of their lives? – of the portion given to them and these their duplicates swarming the streets to-day? – nothing beneath? – all? So many a political reformer will tell you, – and many a private reformer, too, who has gone among them with a heart tender with Christ's charity, and come out outraged, hardened.

One rainy night, about eleven o'clock, a crowd of half-clothed women stopped outside of the cellar-door. They were going home from the cotton-mill.

"Good-night, Deb," said one, a mulatto, steadying herself against the gas-post. She needed the post to steady her. So did more than one of them.

"Dah 's a ball to Miss Potts' to-night. Ye 'd best come."

"Inteet, Deb, if hur 'll[11] come, hur 'll hef fun," said a shrill Welsh voice in the crowd.

Two or three dirty hands were thrust out to catch the gown of the woman, who was groping for the latch of the door.

"No."

"No? Where 's Kit Small, then?"

"Begorra! on the spools.[12] Alleys behint, though we helped her, we dud. An wid ye! Let Deb alone! It 's ondacent frettin' a quite body. Be the powers, an' we 'll have a night of it! there 'll be lasbin's o' drink, – the Vargent[13] be blessed and praised for 't!"

They went on, the mulatto inclining for a moment to show fight, and drag the woman Wolfe off with them; but, being pacified, she staggered away.

---

9. **picker:** A worker in a cotton mill who operates a machine that separates cotton fibers.
10. **feeders:** Workers who slowly feed molten metal into the casting form in order to prevent air bubbles from forming, which would weaken the hardened iron.
11. **hur 'll:** *Hur* is a dialect pronoun used to mean she, he, her, or him.
12. **"Begorra . . . spools":** *Begorra* is an English-Irish expression meaning "by God"; spools are spindles in the cotton mill on which the cotton is stretched and then wound by the spinning machine.
13. **Vargent:** Contracted form of *Virgin Mary*.

Deborah groped her way into the cellar, and, after considerable stumbling, kindled a match, and lighted a tallow dip, that sent a yellow glimmer over the room. It was low, damp, – the earthen floor covered with a green, slimy moss, – a fetid air smothering the breath. Old Wolfe lay asleep on a heap of straw, wrapped in a torn horse-blanket. He was a pale, meek little man, with a white face and red rabbit-eyes. The woman Deborah was like him; only her face was even more ghastly, her lips bluer, her eyes more watery. She wore a faded cotton gown and a slouching bonnet. When she walked, one could see that she was deformed, almost a hunchback. She trod softly, so as not to waken him, and went through into the room beyond. There she found by the half-extinguished fire an iron saucepan filled with cold boiled potatoes, which she put upon a broken chair with a pint-cup of ale. Placing the old candlestick beside this dainty repast, she untied her bonnet, which hung limp and wet over her face, and prepared to eat her supper. It was the first food that had touched her lips since morning. There was enough of it, however: there is not always. She was hungry, – one could see that easily enough, – and not drunk, as most of her companions would have been found at this hour. She did not drink, this woman, – her face told that, too, – nothing stronger than ale. Perhaps the weak, flaccid wretch had some stimulant in her pale life to keep her up, – some love or hope, it might be, or urgent need. When that stimulant was gone, she would take to whiskey. Man cannot live by work alone. While she was skinning the potatoes, and munching them, a noise behind her made her stop.

"Janey!" she called, lifting the candle and peering into the darkness. "Janey, are you there?"

A heap of ragged coats was heaved up, and the face of a young girl emerged, staring sleepily at the woman.

"Deborah," she said, at last, "I 'm here the night."

"Yes, child. Hur 's welcome," she said, quietly eating on.

The girl's face was haggard and sickly; her eyes were heavy with sleep and hunger: real Milesian eyes[14] they were, dark, delicate blue, glooming out from black shadows with a pitiful fright.

"I was alone," she said, timidly.

"Where 's the father?" asked Deborah, holding out a potato, which the girl greedily seized.

"He 's beyant – wid Haley, – in the stone house." (Did you ever hear the word *jail* from an Irish mouth?) "I came here. Hugh told me never to stay me-lone."

"Hugh?"

"Yes."

A vexed frown crossed her face. The girl saw it, and added quickly, –

"I have not seen Hugh the day, Deb. The old man says his watch lasts till the mornin'."

The woman sprang up, and hastily began to arrange some bread and flitch[15] in a tin

14. **Milesian eyes:** Irish eyes.
15. **flitch:** Salted and cured bacon.

pail, and to pour her own measure of ale into a bottle. Tying on her bonnet, she blew out the candle.

"Lay ye down, Janey dear," she said, gently, covering her with the old rags. "Hur can eat the potatoes, if hur 's hungry."

"Where are ye goin', Deb? The rain 's sharp."

"To the mill, with Hugh's supper."

"Let him bide till th' morn. Sit ye down."

"No, no," – sharply pushing her off. "The boy 'll starve."

She hurried from the cellar, while the child wearily coiled herself up for sleep. The rain was falling heavily, as the woman, pail in hand, emerged from the mouth of the alley, and turned down the narrow street, that stretched out, long and black, miles before her. Here and there a flicker of gas lighted an uncertain space of muddy footwalk and gutter; the long rows of houses, except an occasional lager-bier shop, were closed; now and then she met a band of mill-hands skulking to or from their work.

Not many even of the inhabitants of a manufacturing town know the vast machinery of system by which the bodies of workmen are governed, that goes on unceasingly from year to year. The hands of each mill are divided into watches that relieve each other as regularly as the sentinels of an army. By night and day the work goes on, the unsleeping engines groan and shriek, the fiery pools of metal boil and surge. Only for a day in the week, in half-courtesy to public censure, the fires are partially veiled; but as soon as the clock strikes midnight, the great furnaces break forth with renewed fury, the clamor begins with fresh, breathless vigor, the engines sob and shriek like "gods in pain."

As Deborah hurried down through the heavy rain, the noise of these thousand engines sounded through the sleep and shadow of the city like far-off thunder. The mill to which she was going lay on the river, a mile below the city-limits. It was far, and she was weak, aching from standing twelve hours at the spools. Yet it was her almost nightly walk to take this man his supper, though at every square she sat down to rest, and she knew she should receive small word of thanks.

Perhaps, if she had possessed an artist's eye, the picturesque oddity of the scene might have made her step stagger less, and the path seem shorter; but to her the mills were only "summat deilish to look at by night."

The road leading to the mills had been quarried from the solid rock, which rose abrupt and bare on one side of the cinder-covered road, while the river, sluggish and black, crept past on the other. The mills for rolling iron are simply immense tent-like roofs, covering acres of ground, open on every side. Beneath these roofs Deborah looked in on a city of fires, that burned hot and fiercely in the night. Fire in every horrible form: pits of flame waving in the wind; liquid metal-flames writhing in tortuous streams through the sand; wide caldrons filled with boiling fire, over which bent ghastly wretches stirring the strange brewing; and through all, crowds of half-clad men, looking like revengeful ghosts in the red light, hurried, throwing masses of glittering fire. It was like a street in Hell. Even Deborah muttered, as she crept through, "'T looks like t' Devil's place!" It did, – in more ways than one.

She found the man she was looking for, at last, heaping coal on a furnace. He had not time to eat his supper; so she went behind the furnace, and waited. Only a few men were with him, and they noticed her only by a "Hyur comes t' hunchback, Wolfe."

Deborah was stupid with sleep; her back pained her sharply; and her teeth chattered with cold, with the rain that soaked her clothes and dripped from her at every step. She stood, however, patiently holding the pail, and waiting.

"Hout, woman! ye look like a drowned cat. Come near to the fire," – said one of the men, approaching to scrape away the ashes.

She shook her head. Wolfe had forgotten her. He turned, hearing the man, and came closer.

"I did no' think; gi' me my supper, woman."

She watched him eat with a painful eagerness. With a woman's quick instinct, she saw that he was not hungry, – was eating to please her. Her pale, watery eyes began to gather a strange light.

"Is 't good, Hugh? T' ale was a bit sour, I feared."

"No, good enough." He hesitated a moment. "Ye 're tired, poor lass! Bide here till I go. Lay down there on that heap of ash, and go to sleep."

He threw her an old coat for a pillow, and turned to his work. The heap was the refuse of the burnt iron, and was not a hard bed; the half-smothered warmth, too, penetrated her limbs, dulling their pain and cold shiver.

Miserable enough she looked, lying there on the ashes like a limp, dirty rag, – yet not an unfitting figure to crown the scene of hopeless discomfort and veiled crime: more fitting, if one looked deeper into the heart of things, – at her thwarted woman's form, her colorless life, her waking stupor that smothered pain and hunger, – even more fit to be a type of her class. Deeper yet if one could look, was there nothing worth reading in this wet, faded thing, half-covered with ashes? no story of a soul filled with groping passionate love, heroic unselfishness, fierce jealousy? of years of weary trying to please the one human being whom she loved, to gain one look of real heart-kindness from him? If anything like this were hidden beneath the pale, bleared eyes, and dull, washed-out-looking face, no one had ever taken the trouble to read its faint signs: not the half-clothed furnace-tender, Wolfe, certainly. Yet he was kind to her: it was his nature to be kind, even to the very rats that swarmed in the cellar: kind to her in just the same way. She knew that. And it might be that very knowledge had given to her face its apathy and vacancy more than her low, torpid life. One sees that dead, vacant look steal sometimes over the rarest, finest of women's faces, – in the very midst, it may be, of their warmest summer's day; and then one can guess at the secret of intolerable solitude that lies hid beneath the delicate laces and brilliant smile. There was no warmth, no brilliancy, no summer for this woman; so the stupor and vacancy had time to gnaw into her face perpetually. She was young, too, though no one guessed it; so the gnawing was the fiercer.

She lay quiet in the dark corner, listening, through the monotonous din and uncertain glare of the works, to the dull plash of the rain in the far distance, – shrinking back whenever the man Wolfe happened to look towards her. She knew, in spite of all his kindness, that there was that in her face and form which made him loathe the sight of her. She felt by instinct, although she could not comprehend it, the finer nature of the man, which made him among his fellow-workmen something unique, set apart. She knew, that, down under all the vileness and coarseness of his life, there was a groping passion for whatever was beautiful and pure, – that his soul sickened with disgust at her deformity, even when his words were kindest. Through this dull consciousness, which never left her, came, like a sting, the recollection of the dark blue eyes and lithe figure of the little Irish girl she had left in the cellar. The recollection struck through even her stupid intellect with a vivid glow of beauty and of grace. Little Janey, timid, helpless, clinging to Hugh as her only friend: that was the sharp thought, the bitter thought, that drove into the glazed eyes a fierce light of pain. You laugh at it? Are pain and jealousy less savage realities down here in this place I am taking you to than in your own house or your own heart, – your heart, which they clutch at sometimes? The note is the same, I fancy, be the octave high or low.

If you could go into this mill where Deborah lay, and drag out from the hearts of these men the terrible tragedy of their lives, taking it as a symptom of the disease of their class, no ghost Horror would terrify you more. A reality of soul-starvation, of living death, that meets you every day under the besotted faces on the street, – I can paint nothing of this, only give you the outside outlines of a night, a crisis in the life of one man: whatever muddy depth of soul-history lies beneath you can read according to the eyes God has given you.

Wolfe, while Deborah watched him as a spaniel its master, bent over the furnace with his iron pole, unconscious of her scrutiny, only stopping to receive orders. Physically, Nature had promised the man but little. He had already lost the strength and instinct vigor of a man, his muscles were thin, his nerves weak, his face (a meek, woman's face) haggard, yellow with consumption. In the mill he was known as one of the girl-men: "Molly Wolfe" was his *sobriquet*.[16] He was never seen in the cockpit,[17] did not own a terrier, drank but seldom; when he did, desperately. He fought sometimes, but was always thrashed, pommelled to a jelly. The man was game enough, when his blood was up: but he was no favorite in the mill; he had the taint of school-learning on him, – not to a dangerous extent, only a quarter or so in the free-school in fact, but enough to ruin him as a good hand in a fight.

For other reasons, too, he was not popular. Not one of themselves, they felt that, though outwardly as filthy and ash-covered; silent, with foreign thoughts and longings breaking out through his quietness in innumerable curious ways: this one, for instance. In the neighboring furnace-buildings lay great heaps of the refuse from the ore after the pig-metal is run. *Korl* we call it here: a light, porous substance, of a delicate, waxen, flesh-colored tinge. Out of the blocks of this korl, Wolfe, in his off-hours from the furnace, had a habit of chipping and moulding figures, – hideous, fantastic enough, but sometimes strangely beautiful: even the mill-men saw that, while they jeered at him. It was a curious fancy in the man, almost a passion. The few hours for rest he spent hewing and hacking with his blunt knife, never speaking, until his watch came again, –

---

16. ***sobriquet***: Nickname (French).
17. **cockpit**: The arena where fighting roosters, called cocks, are set against one another.

working at one figure for months, and, when it was finished, breaking it to pieces perhaps, in a fit of disappointment. A morbid, gloomy man, untaught, unled, left to feed his soul in grossness and crime, and hard, grinding labor.

I want you to come down and look at this Wolfe, standing there among the lowest of his kind, and see him just as he is, that you may judge him justly when you hear the story of this night. I want you to look back, as he does every day, at his birth in vice, his starved infancy; to remember the heavy years he has groped through as boy and man, – the slow, heavy years of constant, hot work. So long ago he began, that he thinks sometimes he has worked there for ages. There is no hope that it will ever end. Think that God put into this man's soul a fierce thirst for beauty, – to know it, to create it; to *be* – something, he knows not what, – other than he is. There are moments when a passing cloud, the sun glinting on the purple thistles, a kindly smile, a child's face, will rouse him to a passion of pain, – when his nature starts up with a mad cry of rage against God, man, whoever it is that has forced this vile, slimy life upon him. With all this groping, this mad desire, a great blind intellect stumbling through wrong, a loving poet's heart, the man was by habit only a coarse, vulgar laborer, familiar with sights and words you would blush to name. Be just: when I tell you about this night, see him as he is. Be just, – not like man's law, which seizes on one isolated fact, but like God's judging angel, whose clear, sad eye saw all the countless cankering days of this man's life, all the countless nights, when, sick with starving, his soul fainted in him, before it judged him for this night, the saddest of all.

I called this night the crisis of his life. If it was, it stole on him unawares. These great turning-days of life cast no shadow before, slip by unconsciously. Only a trifle, a little turn of the rudder, and the ship goes to heaven or hell.

Wolfe, while Deborah watched him, dug into the furnace of melting iron with his pole, dully thinking only how many rails the lump would yield. It was late, nearly Sunday morning; another hour, and the heavy work would be done, – only the furnaces to replenish and cover for the next day. The workmen were growing more noisy, shouting, as they had to do, to be heard over the deep clamor of the mills. Suddenly they grew less boisterous, – at the far end, entirely silent. Something unusual had happened. After a moment, the silence came nearer; the men stopped their jeers and drunken choruses. Deborah, stupidly lifting up her head, saw the cause of the quiet. A group of five or six men were slowly approaching, stopping to examine each furnace as they came. Visitors often came to see the mills after night: except by growing less noisy, the men took no notice of them. The furnace where Wolfe worked was near the bounds of the works; they halted there hot and tired: a walk over one of these great foundries is no trifling task. The woman, drawing out of sight, turned over to sleep. Wolfe, seeing them stop, suddenly roused from his indifferent stupor, and watched them keenly. He knew some of them: the overseer, Clarke, – a son of Kirby, one of the mill-owners, – and a Doctor May, one of the town-physicians. The other two were strangers. Wolfe came closer. He seized eagerly every chance that brought him into contact with this mysterious class that shone down on him perpetually with the glamour of another order of being. What made the difference between them? That was the mystery of his life. He had a vague notion that perhaps to-night he could find it out. One of the strangers sat down on a pile of bricks, and beckoned young Kirby to his side.

"This *is* hot, with a vengeance. A match, please?" – lighting his cigar. "But the walk is worth the trouble. If it were not that you must have heard it so often, Kirby, I would tell you that your works look like Dante's Inferno."[18]

Kirby laughed.

"Yes. Yonder is Farinata[19] himself in the burning tomb," – pointing to some figure in the shimmering shadows.

"Judging from some of the faces of your men," said the other, "they bid fair to try the reality of Dante's vision, some day."

Young Kirby looked curiously around, as if seeing the faces of his hands for the first time.

"They 're bad enough, that 's true. A desperate set, I fancy. Eh, Clarke?"

The overseer did not hear him. He was talking of net profits just then, – giving, in fact, a schedule of the annual business of the firm to a sharp peering little Yankee, who jotted down notes on a paper laid on the crown of his hat: a reporter for one of the city-papers, getting up a series of reviews of the leading manufactories. The other gentlemen had accompanied them merely for amusement. They were silent until the notes were finished, drying their feet at the furnaces, and sheltering their faces from the intolerable heat. At last the overseer concluded with –

"I believe that is a pretty fair estimate, Captain."

"Here, some of you men!" said Kirby, "bring up those boards. We may as well sit down, gentlemen, until the rain is over. It cannot last much longer at this rate."

"Pig-metal," – mumbled the reporter, – "um! – coal facilities, – um! – hands employed, twelve hundred, – bitumen, – um! – all right, I believe, Mr. Clarke; – sinking-fund, – what did you say was your sinking-fund?"[20]

"Twelve hundred hands?" said the stranger, the young man who had first spoken. "Do you control their votes, Kirby?"

"Control? No." The young man smiled complacently. "But my father brought seven hundred votes to the polls for his candidate last November. No force-work, you understand, – only a speech or two, a hint to form themselves into a society, and a bit of red and blue bunting to make them a flag. The Invincible Roughs, – I believe that is their name. I forget the motto: 'Our country's hope,' I think."

There was a laugh. The young man talking to Kirby sat with an amused light in his cool gray eye, surveying critically the half-clothed figures of the puddlers, and the slow swing of their brawny muscles. He was a stranger in the city, – spending a couple of months in the borders of a Slave State, to study the institutions of the South, – a brother-in-law of Kirby's, – Mitchell. He was an amateur gymnast, – hence his anatomical eye;

18. **Dante's Inferno:** The first book of *The Divine Comedy* by the Italian poet Dante Alighieri (1265–1321).
19. **Farinata:** A character in the *Inferno*; a heretic who was a leader of the Florentines.
20. **sinking-fund:** Money collected for paying corporate debts.

a patron, in a *blasé* way, of the prize-ring; a man who sucked the essence out of a science or philosophy in an indifferent, gentlemanly way; who took Kant, Novalis, Humboldt,[21] for what they were worth in his own scales; accepting all, despising nothing, in heaven, earth, or hell, but one-idead men; with a temper yielding and brilliant as summer water, until his Self was touched, when it was ice, though brilliant still. Such men are not rare in the States.

As he knocked the ashes from his cigar, Wolfe caught with a quick pleasure the contour of the white hand, the blood-glow of a red ring be wore. His voice, too, and that of Kirby's, touched him like music, – low, even, with chording cadences. About this man Mitchell hung the impalpable atmosphere belonging to the thorough-bred gentleman. Wolfe, scraping away the ashes beside him, was conscious of it, did obeisance to it with his artist sense, unconscious that he did so.

The rain did not cease. Clarke and the reporter left the mills; the others, comfortably seated near the furnace, lingered, smoking and talking in a desultory way. Greek would not have been more unintelligible to the furnace-tenders, whose presence they soon forgot entirely. Kirby drew out a newspaper from his pocket and read aloud some article, which they discussed eagerly. At every sentence, Wolfe listened more and more like a dumb, hopeless animal, with a duller, more stolid look creeping over his face, glancing now and then at Mitchell, marking acutely every smallest sign of refinement, then back to himself, seeing as in a mirror his filthy body, his more stained soul.

Never! He had no words for such a thought, but he knew now, in all the sharpness of the bitter certainty, that between them there was a great gulf never to be passed.[22] Never!

The bell of the mills rang for midnight. Sunday morning had dawned. Whatever hidden message lay in the tolling bells floated past these men unknown. Yet it was there. Veiled in the solemn music ushering the risen Saviour was a key-note to solve the darkest secrets of a world gone wrong, – even this social riddle which the brain of the grimy puddler grappled with madly to-night.

The men began to withdraw the metal from the caldrons. The mills were deserted on Sundays, except by the hands who fed the fires, and those who had no lodgings and slept usually on the ash-heaps. The three strangers sat still during the next hour, watching the men cover the furnaces, laughing now and then at some jest of Kirby's.

"Do you know," said Mitchell, "I like this view of the works better than when the glare was fiercest? These heavy shadows and the amphitheatre of smothered fires are ghostly, unreal. One could fancy these red smouldering lights to be the half-shut eyes of wild beasts, and the spectral figures their victims in the den."

---

21. **Kant, Novalis, Humboldt:** Immanuel Kant (1724–1804), German philosopher; Novalis, the pseudonym for Friedrich von Hardenberg (1772–1801), a German poet; Alexander von Humboldt (1769–1859), German naturalist and explorer.

22. **great gulf . . . passed:** In a parable Christ tells his disciples, Lazarus, a beggar, finds comfort in heaven while the rich man is tormented in hell. When the rich man appeals for mercy, Abraham, in heaven with Lazarus, replies: "between us and you there is a great gulf fixed: so that they which would pass from hence to you cannot; neither can they pass to us, that would come from thence" (Luke 16:26).

Kirby laughed. "You are fanciful. Come, let us get out of the den. The spectral figures, as you call them, are a little too real for me to fancy a close proximity in the darkness, – unarmed, too."

The others rose, buttoning their overcoats, and lighting cigars.

"Raining, still," said Doctor May, "and hard. Where did we leave the coach, Mitchell?"

"At the other side of the works. – Kirby, what's that?"

Mitchell started back, half-frightened, as, suddenly turning a corner, the white figure of a woman faced him in the darkness, – a woman, white, of giant proportions, crouching on the ground, her arms flung out in some wild gesture of warning.

"Stop! Make that fire burn there!" cried Kirby, stopping short.

The flame burst out, flashing the gaunt figure into bold relief.

Mitchell drew a long breath.

"I thought it was alive," he said, going up curiously.

The others followed.

"Not marble, eh?" asked Kirby, touching it.

One of the lower overseers stopped.

"Korl, Sir."

"Who did it?"

"Can't say. Some of the hands; chipped it out in off-hours."

"Chipped to some purpose, I should say. What a flesh-tint the stuff has! Do you see, Mitchell?"

"I see."

He had stepped aside where the light fell boldest on the figure, looking at it in silence. There was not one line of beauty or grace in it: a nude woman's form, muscular, grown coarse with labor, the powerful limbs instinct with some one poignant longing. One idea: there it was in the tense, rigid muscles, the clutching hands, the wild, eager face, like that of a starving wolf's. Kirby and Doctor May walked around it, critical, curious. Mitchell stood aloof, silent. The figure touched him strangely.

"Not badly done," said Doctor May. "Where did the fellow learn that sweep of the muscles in the arm and hand? Look at them! They are groping, – do you see? – clutching: the peculiar action of a man dying of thirst."

"They have ample facilities for studying anatomy," sneered Kirby, glancing at the half-naked figures.

"Look," continued the Doctor, "at this bony wrist, and the strained sinews of the instep! A working-woman, – the very type of her class."

"God forbid!" muttered Mitchell.

"Why?" demanded May. "What does the fellow intend by the figure? I cannot catch the meaning."

"Ask him," said the other, dryly. "There he stands," – pointing to Wolfe, who stood with a group of men, leaning on his ash-rake.

The Doctor beckoned him with the affable smile which kind-hearted men put on, when talking to these people.

"Mr. Mitchell has picked you out as the man who did this, – I'm sure I don't know why. But what did you mean by it?"

"She be hungry."

Wolfe's eyes answered Mitchell, not the Doctor.

"Oh-h! But what a mistake you have made, my fine fellow! You have given no sign of starvation to the body. It is strong, – terribly strong. It has the mad, half-despairing gesture of drowning."

Wolfe stammered, glanced appealingly at Mitchell, who saw the soul of the thing, he knew. But the cool, probing eyes were turned on himself now, – mocking, cruel, relentless.

"Not hungry for meat," the furnace-tender said at last.

"What then? Whiskey?" jeered Kirby, with a coarse laugh.

Wolfe was silent a moment, thinking.

"I dunno," he said, with a bewildered look. "It mebbe. Summat to make her live, I think, – like you. Whiskey ull do it, in a way."

The young man laughed again. Mitchell flashed a look of disgust somewhere, – not at Wolfe.

"May," he broke out impatiently, "are you blind? Look at that woman's face! It asks questions of God, and says, 'I have a right to know.' Good God, how hungry it is!"

They looked a moment; then May turned to the mill-owner: –

"Have you many such hands as this? What are you going to do with them? Keep them at puddling iron?"

Kirby shrugged his shoulders. Mitchell's look had irritated him.

"*Ce n'est pas mon affaire.*[23] I have no fancy for nursing infant geniuses. I suppose there are some stray gleams of mind and soul among these wretches. The Lord will take care of his own; or else they can work out their own salvation. I have heard you call our American system a ladder which any man can scale. Do you doubt it? Or perhaps you want to banish all social ladders, and put us all on a flat table-land, – eh, May?"

The Doctor looked vexed, puzzled. Some terrible problem lay hid in this woman's face, and troubled these men. Kirby waited for an answer, and, receiving none, went on, warming with his subject.

"I tell you, there 's something wrong that no talk of *'Liberté'* or *'Égalité'*[24] will do away. If I had the making of men, these men who do the lowest part of the world's work should be machines, – nothing more, – hands. It would be kindness. God help them! What are taste, reason, to creatures who must live such lives as that?" He pointed to Deborah, sleeping on the ash-heap. "So many nerves to sting them to pain. What if God had put your brain, with all its agony of touch, into your fingers, and bid you work and strike with that?"

"You think you could govern the world better?" laughed the Doctor.

"I do not think at all."

"That is true philosophy. Drift with the stream, because you cannot dive deep enough to find bottom, eh?"

---

23. ***Ce n'est pas mon affaire***: It's none of my business (French).

24. ***'Liberté'* or *'Égalité'***: A reference to the slogan of the French Revolution, "Liberty, Equality, Fraternity!"

"Exactly," rejoined Kirby. "I do not think. I wash my hands of all social problems, – slavery, caste, white or black. My duty to my operatives has a narrow limit, – the pay-hour on Saturday night. Outside of that, if they cut korl, or cut each other's throats, (the more popular amusement of the two,) I am not responsible."

The Doctor sighed, – a good honest sigh, from the depths of his stomach.

"God help us! Who is responsible?"

"Not I, I tell you," said Kirby, testily. "What has the man who pays them money to do with their souls' concerns, more than the grocer or butcher who takes it?"

"And yet," said Mitchell's cynical voice, "look at her! How hungry she is!"

Kirby tapped his boot with his cane. No one spoke. Only the dumb face of the rough image looking into their faces with the awful question, "What shall we do to be saved?" Only Wolfe's face, with its heavy weight of brain, its weak, uncertain mouth, its desperate eyes, out of which looked the soul of his class, – only Wolfe's face turned towards Kirby's. Mitchell laughed, – a cool, musical laugh.

"Money has spoken!" he said, seating himself lightly on a stone with the air of an amused spectator at a play. "Are you answered?" – turning to Wolfe his clear, magnetic face.

Bright and deep and cold as Arctic air, the soul of the man lay tranquil beneath. He looked at the furnace-tender as he had looked at a rare mosaic in the morning; only the man was the more amusing study of the two.

"Are you answered? Why, May, look at him! *'De profundis clamavi.'*[25] Or, to quote in English, 'Hungry and thirsty, his soul faints in him.' And so Money sends back its answer into the depths through you, Kirby! Very clear the answer, too! – I think I remember reading the same words somewhere: – washing your hands in Eau de Cologne, and saying, 'I am innocent of the blood of this man. See ye to it!' "[26]

Kirby flushed angrily.

"You quote Scripture freely."

"Do I not quote correctly? I think I remember another line, which may amend my meaning: 'Inasmuch as ye did it unto one of the least of these, ye did it unto me.'[27] Deist?[28] Bless you, man, I was raised on the milk of the Word. Now, Doctor, the pocket of the world having uttered its voice, what has the heart to say? You are a philanthropist, in a small way, – *n'est ce pas*?[29] Here, boy, this gentleman can show you how to cut korl better, – or your destiny. Go on, May!"

"I think a mocking devil possesses you to-night," rejoined the Doctor, seriously.

He went to Wolfe and put his hand kindly on his arm. Something of a vague idea possessed the Doctor's brain that much good was to be done here by a friendly word or two:

---

25. ***'De profundis clamavi'***: Latin version of the opening words of Psalm 130, "*Out of the depths have I cried* unto thee, O Lord."
26. **'I am innocent . . . to it!'**: Pontius Pilate, the Roman governor, reluctantly agreed to crucify Jesus and renounced his responsibility by washing his hands before the mob (Matthew 27:24-26).
27. **'Inasmuch . . . unto me'**: A quote of Jesus. See Matthew 25:40.
28. **Deist**: Believer in a God who created the world but exercises no control over it.
29. ***n'est ce pas?***: Isn't that so? (French)

a latent genius to be warmed into life by a waited-for sunbeam. Here it was: he had brought it. So he went on complacently: –

"Do you know, boy, you have it in you to be a great sculptor, a great man? – do you understand?" (talking down to the capacity of his hearer: it is a way people have with children, and men like Wolfe,) – "to live a better, stronger life than I, or Mr. Kirby here? A man may make himself anything he chooses. God has given you stronger powers than many men, – me, for instance."

May stopped, heated, glowing with his own magnanimity. And it was magnanimous. The puddler had drunk in every word, looking through the Doctor's flurry, and generous heat, and self-approval, into his will, with those slow, absorbing eyes of his.

"Make yourself what you will. It is your right."

"I know," quietly. "Will you help me?"

Mitchell laughed again. The Doctor turned now, in a passion, –

"You know, Mitchell, I have not the means. You know, if I had, it is in my heart to take this boy and educate him for" –

"The glory of God, and the glory of John May."

May did not speak for a moment; then, controlled, he said, –

"Why should one be raised, when myriads are left? – I have not the money, boy," to Wolfe, shortly.

"Money?" He said it over slowly, as one repeats the guessed answer to a riddle, doubtfully. "That is it? Money?"

"Yes, money, – that is it," said Mitchell, rising, and drawing his furred coat about him. "You 've found the cure for all the world's diseases. – Come, May, find your good-humor, and come home. This damp wind chills my very bones. Come and preach our Saint-Simonian doctrines[30] to-morrow to Kirby's hands. Let them have a clear idea of the rights of the soul, and I 'll venture next week they 'll strike for higher wages. That will be the end of it."

"Will you send the coach-driver to this side of the mills?" asked Kirby, turning to Wolfe.

He spoke kindly: it was his habit to do so. Deborah, seeing the puddler go, crept after him. The three men waited outside. Doctor May walked up and down, chafed. Suddenly he stopped.

"Go back, Mitchell! You say the pocket and the heart of the world speak without meaning to these people. What has its head to say? Taste, culture, refinement? Go!"

Mitchell was leaning against a brick wall. He turned his head indolently, and looked into the mills. There hung about the place a thick, unclean odor. The slightest motion of his hand marked that he perceived it, and his insufferable disgust. That was all. May said nothing, only quickened his angry tramp.

"Besides," added Mitchell, giving a corollary to his answer, "it would be of no use. I am not one of them."

---

30. **Saint-Simonian doctrines:** Claude Henry de Rouvroy, comte de Saint-Simon (1760–1825), was a French philosopher who taught that the public control of production and the principle of common property and the end of inheritances were the remedies for social ills.

"You do not mean" — said May, facing him.

"Yes, I mean just that. Reform is born of need, not pity. No vital movement of the people's has worked down, for good or evil; fermented, instead, carried up the heaving, cloggy mass. Think back through history, and you will know it. What will this lowest deep – thieves, Magdalens,[31] negroes – do with the light filtered through ponderous Church creeds, Baconian theories, Goethe schemes?[32] Some day, out of their bitter need will be thrown up their own light-bringer, – their Jean Paul, their Cromwell,[33] their Messiah."

"Bah!" was the Doctor's inward criticism. However, in practice, he adopted the theory; for, when, night and morning, afterwards, he prayed that power might be given these degraded souls to rise, he glowed at heart, recognizing an accomplished duty.

Wolfe and the woman had stood in the shadow of the works as the coach drove off. The Doctor had held out his hand in a frank, generous way, telling him to "take care of himself, and to remember it was his right to rise." Mitchell had simply touched his hat, as to an equal, with a quiet look of thorough recognition. Kirby had thrown Deborah some money, which she found, and clutched eagerly enough. They were gone now, all of them. The man sat down on the cinder-road, looking up into the murky sky.

" 'T be late, Hugh. Wunnot hur come?"

He shook his head doggedly, and the woman crouched out of his sight against the wall. Do you remember rare moments when a sudden light flashed over yourself, your world, God? when you stood on a mountain-peak, seeing your life as it might have been, as it is? one quick instant, when custom lost its force and every-day usage? when your friend, wife, brother, stood in a new light? your soul was bared, and the grave, – a foretaste of the nakedness of the Judgment-Day? So it came before him, his life, that night. The slow tides of pain he had borne gathered themselves up and surged against his soul. His squalid daily life, the brutal coarseness eating into his brain, as the ashes into his skin: before, these things had been a dull aching into his consciousness; to-night, they were reality. He griped the filthy red shirt that clung, stiff with soot, about him, and tore it savagely from his arm. The flesh beneath was muddy with grease and ashes, – and the heart beneath that! And the soul? God knows.

Then flashed before his vivid poetic sense the man who had left him, – the pure face, the delicate, sinewy limbs, in harmony with all he knew of beauty or truth. In his cloudy fancy he had pictured a Something like this. He had found it in this Mitchell, even when

---

31. **Magdalens:** Reformed prostitutes, after Mary Magdalene, a purported prostitute and a follower of Jesus.

32. **Baconian theories, Goethe schemes:** Sir Francis Bacon (1561-1626), English philosopher who stressed the importance of systematizing empirical information about the natural world; Johann Wolfgang von Goethe (1749-1832), German writer and philosopher who celebrated the power of the individual and emphasized the limitations of eighteenth-century rationalism.

33. **their Jean-Paul, their Cromwell:** Mitchell refers to two famous saviors of the people. The Swiss-born Jean-Paul Marat (1743-1793) was a revolutionary journalist who wrote *The Chains of Slavery* (1774) and edited a radical newspaper, the *Friend of the People* (1789-1793), in support of the French Revolution. Oliver Cromwell (1599-1658) was the military leader of the Puritan Revolution that led to the overthrow and execution of King Charles I and the establishment of the Puritan Commonwealth.

he idly scoffed at his pain: a Man all-knowing, all-seeing, crowned by Nature, reigning, – the keen glance of his eye falling like a sceptre on other men. And yet his instinct taught him that he too — He! He looked at himself with sudden loathing, sick, wrung his hands with a cry, and then was silent. With all the phantoms of his heated, ignorant fancy, Wolfe had not been vague in his ambitions. They were practical, slowly built up before him out of his knowledge of what he could do. Through years he had day by day made this hope a real thing to himself, – a clear, projected figure of himself, as he might become.

Able to speak, to know what was best, to raise these men and women working at his side up with him: sometimes he forgot this defined hope in the frantic anguish to escape, – only to escape, – out of the wet, the pain, the ashes, somewhere, anywhere, – only for one moment of free air on a hill-side, to lie down and let his sick soul throb itself out in the sunshine. But to-night he panted for life. The savage strength of his nature was roused; his cry was fierce to God for justice.

"Look at me!" he said to Deborah, with a low, bitter laugh, striking his puny chest savagely. "What am I worth, Deb? Is it my fault that I am no better? My fault? My fault?"

He stopped, stung with a sudden remorse, seeing her hunchback shape writhing with sobs. For Deborah was crying thankless tears, according to the fashion of women.

"God forgi' me, woman! Things go harder wi' you nor me. It 's a worse share."

He got up and helped her to rise; and they went doggedly down the muddy street, side by side.

"It 's all wrong," he muttered, slowly, – "all wrong! I dunnot understan'. But it 'll end some day."

"Come home, Hugh!" she said, coaxingly; for he had stopped, looking around bewildered.

"Home, – and back to the mill!" He went on saying this over to himself, as if he would mutter down every pain in this dull despair.

She followed him through the fog, her blue lips chattering with cold. They reached the cellar at last. Old Wolfe had been drinking since she went out, and had crept nearer the door. The girl Janey slept heavily in the corner. He went up to her, touching softly the worn white arm with his fingers. Some bitterer thought stung him, as he stood there. He wiped the drops from his forehead, and went into the room beyond, livid, trembling. A hope, trifling, perhaps, but very dear, had died just then out of the poor puddler's life, as he looked at the sleeping, innocent girl, – some plan for the future, in which she had borne a part. He gave it up that moment, then and forever. Only a trifle, perhaps, to us: his face grew a shade paler, – that was all. But, somehow, the man's soul, as God and the angels looked down on it, never was the same afterwards.

Deborah followed him into the inner room. She carried a candle, which she placed on the floor, closing the door after her. She had seen the look on his face, as he turned away: her own grew deadly. Yet, as she came up to him, her eyes glowed. He was seated on an old chest, quiet, holding his face in his hands.

"Hugh!" she said, softly.

He did not speak.

"Hugh, did hur hear what the man said, – him with the clear voice? Did hur hear? Money, money, – that it wud do all?"

He pushed her away, – gently, but he was worn out; her rasping tone fretted him.

"Hugh!"

The candle flared a pale yellow light over the cobwebbed brick walls, and the woman standing there. He looked at her. She was young, in deadly earnest; her faded eyes, and wet, ragged figure caught from their frantic eagerness a power akin to beauty.

"Hugh, it is true! Money ull do it! Oh, Hugh, boy, listen till me! He said is true! It is money!"

"I know. Go back! I do not want you here."

"Hugh, it is t' last time. I 'll never worrit hur again."

There were tears in her voice now, but she choked them back.

"Hear till me only to-night! If one of t' witch people wud come, them we heard of t' home, and gif hur all hur wants, what then? Say, Hugh!"

"What do you mean?"

"I mean money."

Her whisper shrilled through his brain.

"If one of t' witch dwarfs wud come from t' lane moors to-night, and gif hur money, to go out, – *out*, I say, – out, lad, where t' sun shines, and t' heath grows, and t' ladies walk in silken gownds, and God stays all t' time, – where t' man lives that talked to us to-night, – Hugh knows, – Hugh could walk there like a king!"

He thought the woman mad, tried to check her, but she went on, fierce in her eager haste.

"If *I* were t' witch dwarf, if I had t' money, wud hur thank me? Wud hur take me out o' this place wid hur and Janey? I wud not come into the gran' house hur wud build, to vex hur wid t' hunch, – only at night, when t' shadows were dark, stand far off to see hur."

Mad? Yes! Are many of us mad in this way?

"Poor Deb! poor Deb!" he said, soothingly.

"It is here," she said, suddenly jerking into his hand a small roll. "I took it! I did it! Me, me! – not hur! I shall be hanged, I shall be burnt in hell, if anybody knows I took it! Out of his pocket, as he leaned against t' bricks. Hur knows?"

She thrust it into his hand, and then, her errand done, began to gather chips together to make a fire, choking down hysteric sobs.

"Has it come to this?"

That was all he said. The Welsh Wolfe blood was honest. The roll was a small green pocket-book containing one or two gold pieces, and a check for an incredible amount, as it seemed to the poor puddler. He laid it down, hiding his face again in his hands.

"Hugh, don't be angry wud me! It 's only poor Deb, – hur knows?"

He took the long skinny fingers kindly in his.

"Angry? God help me, no! Let me sleep. I am tired."

He threw himself heavily down on the wooden bench, stunned with pain and weariness. She brought some old rags to cover him.

It was late on Sunday evening before he awoke. I tell God's truth, when I say he had then no thought of keeping this money. Deborah had hid it in his pocket. He found it there. She watched him eagerly, as he took it out.

"I must gif it to him," he said, reading her face.

"Hur knows," she said with a bitter sigh of disappointment. "But it is hur right to keep it."

His right! The word struck him. Doctor May had used the same. He washed himself, and went out to find this man Mitchell. His right! Why did this chance word cling to him so obstinately? Do you hear the fierce devils whisper in his ear, as he went slowly down the darkening street?

The evening came on, slow and calm. He seated himself at the end of an alley leading into one of the larger streets. His brain was clear to-night, keen, intent, mastering. It would not start back, cowardly, from any hellish temptation, but meet it face to face. Therefore the great temptation of his life came to him veiled by no sophistry, but bold, defiant, owning its own vile name, trusting to one bold blow for victory.

He did not deceive himself. Theft! That was it. At first the word sickened him; then he grappled with it. Sitting there on a broken cart-wheel, the fading day, the noisy groups, the church-bells' tolling passed before him like a panorama,[34] while the sharp struggle went on within. This money! He took it out, and looked at it. If he gave it back, what then? He was going to be cool about it.

People going by to church saw only a sickly mill-boy watching them quietly at the alley's mouth. They did not know that he was mad, or they would not have gone by so quietly: mad with hunger; stretching out his hands to the world, that had given so much to them, for leave to live the life God meant him to live. His soul within him was smothering to death; he wanted so much, thought so much, and *knew* – nothing. There was nothing of which he was certain, except the mill and things there. Of God and heaven he had heard so little, that they were to him what fairy-land is to a child: something real, but not here; very far off. His brain, greedy, dwarfed, full of thwarted energy and unused powers, questioned these men and women going by, coldly, bitterly, that night. Was it not his right to live as they, – a pure life, a good, true-hearted life, full of beauty and kind words? He only wanted to know how to use the strength within him. His heart warmed, as he thought of it. He suffered himself to think of it longer. If he took the money?

Then he saw himself as he might be, strong, helpful, kindly. The night crept on, as this one image slowly evolved itself from the crowd of other thoughts and stood triumphant. He looked at it. As he might be! What wonder, if it blinded him to delirium, – the madness that underlies all revolution, all progress, and all fall?

You laugh at the shallow temptation? You see the error underlying its argument so clearly, – that to him a true life was one of full development rather than self-restraint? that he was deaf to the higher tone in a cry of voluntary suffering for truth's sake than in

34. **panorama:** A series of large paintings attached to one another in a long roll. Popular entertainments in the nineteenth century, panoramas of natural wonders, such as Niagara Falls, would be unrolled with commentary and musical accompaniment in front of an audience.

the fullest flow of spontaneous harmony? I do not plead his cause. I only want to show you the mote in my brother's eye: then you can see clearly to take it out.[35]

The money, – there it lay on his knee, a little blotted slip of paper, nothing in itself; used to raise him out of the pit; something straight from God's hand. A thief! Well, what was it to be a thief? He met the question at last, face to face, wiping the clammy drops of sweat from his forehead. God made this money – the fresh air, too – for his children's use. He never made the difference between poor and rich. The Something who looked down on him that moment through the cool gray sky had a kindly face, he knew, – loved his children alike. Oh, he knew that!

There were times when the soft floods of color in the crimson and purple flames, or the clear depth of amber in the water below the bridge, had somehow given him a glimpse of another world than this, – of an infinite depth of beauty and of quiet somewhere, – somewhere, – a depth of quiet and rest and love. Looking up now, it became strangely real. The sun had sunk quite below the hills, but his last rays struck upward, touching the zenith. The fog had risen, and the town and river were steeped in its thick, gray damp; but overhead, the sun-touched smoke-clouds opened like a cleft ocean, – shifting, rolling seas of crimson mist, waves of billowy silver veined with blood-scarlet, inner depths unfathomable of glancing light. Wolfe's artist-eye grew drunk with color. The gates of that other world! Fading, flashing before him now! What, in that world of Beauty, Content, and Right, were the petty laws, the mine and thine, of mill-owners and mill-hands?

A consciousness of power stirred within him. He stood up. A man, – he thought, stretching out his hands, – free to work, to live, to love! Free! His right! He folded the scrap of paper in his hand. As his nervous fingers took it in, limp and blotted, so his soul took in the mean temptation, lapped it in fancied rights, in dreams of improved existences, drifting and endless as the cloud-seas of color. Clutching it, as if the tightness of his hold would strengthen his sense of possession, he went aimlessly down the street. It was his watch at the mill. He need not go, need never go again, thank God! – shaking off the thought with unbreakable loathing.

Shall I go over the history of the hours of that night? how the man wandered from one to another of his old haunts, with a half-consciousness of bidding them farewell, – lanes and alleys and backyards where the mill-hands lodged, – noting, with a new eagerness, the filth and drunkenness, the pig-pens, the ash-heaps covered with potato-skins, the bloated, pimpled women at the doors, – with a new disgust, a new sense of sudden triumph, and, under all, a new, vague dread, unknown before, smothered down, kept under, but still there? It left him but once during the night, when, for the second time in his life, he entered a church. It was a sombre Gothic pile, where the stained light lost itself in far-retreating arches; built to meet the requirements and sympathies of a

35. **show you the mote . . . take it out**: See Matthew 7:3-5: "And why beholdest thou the mote that is in thy brother's eye, but considerest not the beam that is in thine own eye? Or how wilt thou say to thy brother, Let me pull out the mote out of thine eye; and, behold, a beam is in thine own eye? Thou hypocrite, first cast out the beam out of thine own eye; and then shalt thou see clearly to cast out the mote out of thy brother's eye."

far other class than Wolfe's. Yet it touched, moved him uncontrollably. The distances, the shadows, the still, marble figures, the mass of silent kneeling worshippers, the mysterious music, thrilled, lifted his soul with a wonderful rain. Wolfe forgot himself, forgot the new life he was going to live, the mean terror gnawing underneath. The voice of the speaker strengthened the charm; it was clear, feeling, full, strong. An old man, who had lived much, suffered much; whose brain was keenly alive, dominant; whose heart was summer-warm with charity. He taught it to-night. He held up Humanity in its grand total; showed the great world-cancer to his people. Who could show it better? He was a Christian reformer; he had studied the age thoroughly; his outlook at man had been free, world-wide, over all time. His faith stood sublime upon the Rock of Ages; his fiery zeal guided vast schemes by which the gospel was to be preached to all nations. How did he preach it to-night? In burning, light-laden words he painted the incarnate Life, Love, the universal Man: words that became reality in the lives of these people, – that lived again in beautiful words and actions, trifling, but heroic. Sin, as he defied it, was a real foe to them; their trials, temptations, were his. His words passed far over the furnace-tender's grasp, toned to suit another class of culture; they sounded in his ears a very pleasant song in an unknown tongue. He meant to cure this world-cancer with a steady eye that had never glared with hunger, and a hand that neither poverty nor strychnine-whiskey[36] had taught to shake. In this morbid, distorted heart of the Welsh puddler he had failed.

Wolfe rose at last, and turned from the church down the street. He looked up; the night had come on foggy, damp; the golden mists had vanished, and the sky lay dull and ash-colored. He wandered again aimlessly down the street, idly wondering what had become of the cloud-sea of crimson and scarlet. The trial-day of this man's life was over, and he had lost the victory. What followed was mere drifting circumstance, – a quicker walking over the path, – that was all. Do you want to hear the end of it? You wish me to make a tragic story out of it? Why, in the police-reports of the morning paper you can find a dozen such tragedies: hints of shipwrecks unlike any that ever befell on the high seas; hints that here a power was lost to heaven, – that there a soul went down where no tide can ebb or flow. Commonplace enough the hints are, – jocose sometimes, done up in rhyme.

Doctor May, a month after the night I have told you of, was reading to his wife at breakfast from this fourth column of the morning-paper: an unusual thing, – these police-reports not being, in general, choice reading for ladies; but it was only one item he read.

"Oh, my dear! You remember that man I told you of, that we saw at Kirby's mill? – that was arrested for robbing Mitchell? Here he is; just listen: – 'Circuit Court. Judge Day. Hugh Wolfe, operative in Kirby & John's Loudon Mills. Charge, grand larceny. Sentence, nineteen years hard labor in penitentiary.' – Scoundrel! Serves him right! After all our kindness that night! Picking Mitchell's pocket at the very time!"

---

36. **strychnine-whiskey:** Whiskey treated with a few drops of strychnine, used in the nineteenth century to stimulate the central nervous system.

His wife said something about the ingratitude of that kind of people, and then they began to talk of something else.

Nineteen years! How easy that was to read! What a simple word for Judge Day to utter! Nineteen years! Half a lifetime!

Hugh Wolfe sat on the window-ledge of his cell, looking out. His ankles were ironed. Not usual in such cases; but he had made two desperate efforts to escape. "Well," as Haley, the jailer, said, "small blame to him! Nineteen years' imprisonment was not a pleasant thing to look forward to." Haley was very good-natured about it, though Wolfe had fought him savagely.

"When he was first caught," the jailer said afterwards, in telling the story, "before the trial, the fellow was cut down at once, – laid there on that pallet like a dead man, with his hands over his eyes. Never saw a man so cut down in my life. Time of the trial, too, came the queerest dodge of any customer I ever had. Would choose no lawyer. Judge gave him one, of course. Gibson it was. He tried to prove the fellow crazy; but it wouldn't go. Thing was plain as daylight: money found on him. 'T was a hard sentence, – all the law allows; but it was for 'xample's sake. These mill-hands are gettin' onbearable. When the sentence was read, he just looked up, and said the money was his by rights, and that all the world had gone wrong. That night, after the trial, a gentleman came to see him here, name of Mitchell, – him as he stole from. Talked to him for an hour. Thought he came for curiosity, like. After he was gone, thought Wolfe was remarkable quiet, and went into his cell. Found him very low; bed all bloody. Doctor said he had been bleeding at the lungs. He was as weak as a cat; yet, if ye 'll b'lieve me, he tried to get a-past me and get out. I just carried him like a baby, and threw him on the pallet. Three days after, he tried it again: that time reached the wall. Lord help you! he fought like a tiger, – giv' some terrible blows. Fightin' for life, you see; for he can't live long, shut up in the stone crib down yonder. Got a death-cough now. 'T took two of us to bring him down that day; so I just put the irons on his feet. There he sits, in there. Goin' to-morrow, with a batch more of 'em. That woman, hunchback, tried with him, – you remember? – she 's only got three years. 'Complice. But *she's* a woman, you know. He 's been quiet ever since I put on irons: giv' up, I suppose. Looks white, sick-lookin'. It acts different on 'em, bein' sentenced. Most of 'em gets reckless, devilish-like. Some prays awful, and sings them vile songs of the mills, all in a breath. That woman, now, she 's desper't'. Been beggin' to see Hugh, as she calls him, for three days. I 'm a-goin' to let her in. She don't go with him. Here she is in this next cell. I 'm a-goin' now to let her in."

He let her in. Wolfe did not see her. She crept into a corner of the cell, and stood watching him. He was scratching the iron bars of the window with a piece of tin which he had picked up, with an idle, uncertain, vacant stare, just as a child or idiot would do.

"Tryin' to get out, old boy?" laughed Haley. "Them irons will need a crowbar beside your tin, before you can open 'em."

Wolfe laughed, too, in a senseless way.

"I think I 'll get out," he said.

"I believe his brain's touched," said Haley, when he came out.

The puddler scraped away with the tin for half an hour. Still Deborah did not speak. At last she ventured nearer, and touched his arm.

"Blood?" she said, looking at some spots on his coat with a shudder.

He looked up at her. "Why, Deb!" he said, smiling, – such a bright, boyish smile, that it went to poor Deborah's heart directly, and she sobbed and cried out loud.

"Oh, Hugh, lad! Hugh! dunnot look at me, when it wur my fault! To think I brought hur to it! And I loved hur so! Oh, lad, I dud!"

The confession, even in this wretch, came with the woman's blush through the sharp cry.

He did not seem to hear her, – scraping away diligently at the bars with the bit of tin.

Was he going mad? She peered closely into his face. Something she saw there made her draw suddenly back, – something which Haley had not seen, that lay beneath the pinched, vacant look it had caught since the trial, or the curious gray shadow that rested on it. That gray shadow, – yes, she knew what that meant. She had often seen it creeping over women's faces for months, who died at last of slow hunger or consumption. That meant death, distant, lingering: but this — Whatever it was the woman saw, or thought she saw, used as she was to crime and misery, seemed to make her sick with a new horror. Forgetting her fear of him, she caught his shoulders, and looked keenly, steadily, into his eyes.

"Hugh!" she cried, in a desperate whisper, – "oh, boy, not that! for God's sake, not *that*!"

The vacant laugh went off his face, and he answered her in a muttered word or two that drove her away. Yet the words were kindly enough. Sitting there on his pallet, she cried silently a hopeless sort of tears, but did not speak again. The man looked up furtively at her now and then. Whatever his own trouble was, her distress vexed him with a momentary sting.

It was market-day. The narrow window of the jail looked down directly on the carts and wagons drawn up in a long line, where they had unloaded. He could see, too, and hear distinctly the clink of money as it changed hands, the busy crowd of whites and blacks shoving, pushing one another, and the chaffering and swearing at the stalls. Somehow, the sound, more than anything else had done, wakened him up, – made the whole real to him. He was done with the world and the business of it. He let the tin fall, and looked out, pressing his face close to the rusty bars. How they crowded and pushed! And he, – he should never walk that pavement again! There came Neff Sanders, one of the feeders at the mill, with a basket on his arm. Sure enough, Neff was married the other week. He whistled, hoping he would look up; but he did not. He wondered if Neff remembered he was there, if any of the boys thought of him up there, and thought that he never was to go down that old cinder-road again. Never again! He had not quite understood it before; but now he did. Not for days or years, but never! – that was it.

How clear the light fell on that stall in front of the market! and how like a picture it was, the dark-green heaps of corn, and the crimson beets, and golden melons! There was another with game: how the light flickered on that pheasant's breast, with the purplish blood dripping over the brown feathers! He could see the red shining of the drops, it was so near. In one minute he could be down there. It was just a step. So easy, as it seemed, so natural to go! Yet it could never be – not in all the thousands of years to come – that he should put his foot on that street again! He thought of himself with a sorrowful pity, as of some one else. There was a dog down in the market, walking after his master with such a stately, grave look! – only a dog, yet he could go backwards and forwards just as he pleased: he had good luck! Why, the very vilest cur, yelping there in the gutter, had not lived his life, had been free to act out whatever thought God had put into his brain; while he — No, he would not think of that! He tried to put the thought away, and to listen to a dispute between a countryman and a woman about some meat; but it would come back. He, what had he done to bear this?

Then came the sudden picture of what might have been, and now. He knew what it was to be in the penitentiary, – how it went with men there. He knew how in these long years he should slowly die, but not until soul and body had become corrupt and rotten, – how, when he came out, if he lived to come, even the lowest of the mill-hands would jeer him, – how his hands would be weak, and his brain senseless and stupid. He believed he was almost that now. He put his hand to his head, with a puzzled, weary look. It ached, his head, with thinking. He tried to quiet himself. It was only right, perhaps; he had done wrong. But was there right or wrong for such as he? What was right? And who had ever taught him? He thrust the whole matter away. A dark, cold quiet crept through his brain. It was all wrong; but let it be! It was nothing to him more than the others. Let it be!

The door grated, as Haley opened it.

"Come, my woman! Must lock up for t' night. Come, stir yerself!"

She went up and took Hugh's hand.

"Good-night, Deb," he said, carelessly.

She had not hoped he would say more; but the tired pain on her mouth just then was bitterer than death. She took his passive hand and kissed it.

"Hur 'll never see Deb again!" she ventured, her lips growing colder and more bloodless.

What did she say that for? Did he not know it? Yet he would not be impatient with poor old Deb. She had trouble of her own, as well as he.

"No, never again," he said, trying to be cheerful.

She stood just a moment, looking at him. Do you laugh at her, standing there, with her hunchback, her rags, her bleared, withered face, and the great despised love tugging at her heart?

"Come, you!" called Haley, impatiently.

She did not move.

"Hugh!" she whispered.

It was to be her last word. What was it?

"Hugh, boy, not THAT!"

He did not answer. She wrung her hands, trying to be silent, looking in his face in an agony of entreaty. He smiled again, kindly.

"It is best, Deb. I cannot bear to be hurted any more."

"Hur knows," she said, humbly.

"Tell my father good-bye; and – and kiss little Janey."

She nodded, saying nothing, looked in his face again, and went out of the door. As she went, she staggered.

"Drinkin' to-day?" broke out Haley, pushing her before him. "Where the Devil did you get it? Here, in with ye!" and he shoved her into her cell, next to Wolfe's, and shut the door.

Along the wall of her cell there was a crack low down by the floor, through which she could see the light from Wolfe's. She had discovered it days before. She hurried in now, and, kneeling down by it, listened, hoping to hear some sound. Nothing but the rasping of the tin on the bars. He was at his old amusement again. Something in the noise jarred on her ear, for she shivered as she heard it. Hugh rasped away at the bars. A dull old bit of tin, not fit to cut korl with.

He looked out of the window again. People were leaving the market now. A tall mulatto girl, following her mistress, her basket on her head, crossed the street just below, and looked up. She was laughing; but, when she caught sight of the haggard face peering out through the bars, suddenly grew grave, and hurried by. A free, firm step, a clear-cut olive face, with a scarlet turban tied on one side, dark, shining eyes, and on the head the basket poised, filled with fruit and flowers, under which the scarlet turban and bright eyes looked out half-shadowed. The picture caught his eye. It was good to see a face like that. He would try to-morrow, and cut one like it. *To-morrow!* He threw down the tin, trembling, and covered his face with his hands. When he looked up again, the daylight was gone.

Deborah, crouching near by on the other side of the wall, heard no noise. He sat on the side of the low pallet, thinking. Whatever was the mystery which the woman had seen on his face, it came out now slowly, in the dark there, and became fixed, – a something never seen on his face before. The evening was darkening fast. The market had been over for an hour; the rumbling of the carts over the pavement grew more infrequent: he listened to each, as it passed, because he thought it was to be for the last time. For the same reason, it was, I suppose, that he strained his eyes to catch a glimpse of each passer-by, wondering who they were, what kind of homes they were going to, if they had children, – listening eagerly to every chance word in the street, as if – (God be merciful to the man! what strange fancy was this?) – as if he never should hear human voices again.

It was quite dark at last. The street was a lonely one. The last passenger, he thought, was gone. No, – there was a quick step: Joe Hill, lighting the lamps. Joe was a good old chap; never passed a fellow without some joke or other. He remembered once seeing the place where he lived with his wife. "Granny Hill" the boys called her. Bedridden she was; but so kind as Joe was to her! kept the room so clean! – and the old woman, when he was there, was laughing at "some of t' lad's foolishness." The step was far down the street; but he could see him place the ladder, run up, and light the gas. A longing seized him to be spoken to once more.

"Joe!" he called, out of the grating. "Good-bye, Joe!"

The old man stopped a moment, listening uncertainly; then hurried on. The prisoner thrust his hand out of the window, and called again, louder; but Joe was too far down the street. It was a little thing; but it hurt him, – this disappointment.

"Good-bye, Joe!" he called, sorrowfully enough.

"Be quiet!" said one of the jailers, passing the door, striking on it with his club.

Oh, that was the last, was it?

There was an inexpressible bitterness on his face, as he lay down on the bed, taking the bit of tin, which he had rasped to a tolerable degree of sharpness, in his hand, – to play with, it may be. He bared his arms, looking intently at their corded veins and sinews. Deborah, listening in the next cell, heard a slight clicking sound, often repeated. She shut her lips tightly, that she might not scream; the cold drops of sweat broke over her, in her dumb agony.

"Hur knows best," she muttered at last, fiercely clutching the boards where she lay.

If she could have seen Wolfe, there was nothing about him to frighten her. He lay quite still, his arms outstretched, looking at the pearly stream of moonlight coming into the window. I think in that one hour that came then he lived back over all the years that had gone before. I think that all the low, vile life, all his wrongs, all his starved hopes, came then, and stung him with a farewell poison that made him sick unto death. He made neither moan nor cry, only turned his worn face now and then to the pure light, that seemed so far off, as one that said, "How long, O Lord? how long?"

The hour was over at last. The moon, passing over her nightly path, slowly came nearer, and threw the light across his bed on his feet. He watched it steadily, as it crept up, inch by inch, slowly. It seemed to him to carry with it a great silence. He had been so hot and tired there always in the mills! The years had been so fierce and cruel! There was coming now quiet and coolness and sleep. His tense limbs relaxed, and settled in a calm languor. The blood ran fainter and slow from his heart. He did not think now with a savage anger of what might be and was not; he was conscious only of deep stillness creeping over him. At first he saw a sea of faces: the mill-men, – women he had known, drunken and bloated, – Janeys timid and pitiful, – poor old Debs: then they floated together like a mist, and faded away, leaving only the clear, pearly moonlight.

Whether, as the pure light crept up the stretched-out figure, it brought with it calm and peace, who shall say? His dumb soul was alone with God in judgment. A Voice may have spoken for it from far-off Calvary, "Father, forgive them, for they know not what they do!"[37] Who dare say? Fainter and fainter the heart rose and fell, slower and slower the moon floated from behind a cloud, until, when at last its full tide of white splendor swept over the cell, it seemed to wrap and fold into a deeper stillness the dead figure that never should move again. Silence deeper than the Night! Nothing that moved, save the black, nauseous stream of blood dripping slowly from the pallet to the floor!

There was outcry and crowd enough in the cell the next day. The coroner and his jury, the local editors, Kirby himself, and boys with their hands thrust knowingly into their pockets and heads on one side, jammed into the corners. Coming and going all day. Only one woman. She came late, and outstayed them all. A Quaker, or Friend, as they call themselves. I think this woman was known by that name in heaven. A homely body, coarsely dressed in gray and white. Deborah (for Haley had let her in) took notice of her.

37. **"Father . . . do!"**: The words of Jesus as he is crucified (Luke 23:34).

She watched them all – sitting on the end of the pallet, holding his head in her arms – with the ferocity of a watch-dog, if any of them touched the body. There was no meekness, no sorrow, in her face; the stuff out of which murderers are made, instead. All the time Haley and the woman were laying straight the limbs and cleaning the cell, Deborah sat still, keenly watching the Quaker's face. Of all the crowd there that day, this woman alone had not spoken to her, – only once or twice had put some cordial to her lips. After they all were gone, the woman, in the same still, gentle way, brought a vase of wood-leaves and berries, and placed it by the pallet, then opened the narrow window. The fresh air blew in, and swept the woody fragrance over the dead face. Deborah looked up with a quick wonder.

"Did hur know my boy wud like it? Did hur know Hugh?"

"I know Hugh now."

The white fingers passed in a slow, pitiful way over the dead, worn face. There was a heavy shadow in the quiet eyes.

"Did hur know where they 'll bury Hugh?" said Deborah in a shrill tone, catching her arm.

This had been the question hanging on her lips all day.

"In t' town-yard? Under t' mud and ash? T' lad 'll smother, woman! He wur born on t' lane moor, where t' air is frick and strong. Take hur out, for God's sake, take hur out where t' air blows!"

The Quaker hesitated, but only for a moment. She put her strong arm around Deborah and led her to the window.

"Thee sees the hills, friend, over the river? Thee sees how the light lies warm there, and the winds of God blow all the day? I live there, – where the blue smoke is, by the trees. Look at me." She turned Deborah's face to her own, clear and earnest. "Thee will believe me? I will take Hugh and bury him there to-morrow."

Deborah did not doubt her. As the evening wore on, she leaned against the iron bars, looking at the hills that rose far off, through the thick sodden clouds, like a bright, unattainable calm. As she looked, a shadow of their solemn repose fell on her face: its fierce discontent faded into a pitiful, humble quiet. Slow, solemn tears gathered in her eyes: the poor weak eyes turned so hopelessly to the place where Hugh was to rest, the grave heights looking higher and brighter and more solemn than ever before. The Quaker watched her keenly. She came to her at last, and touched her arm.

"When thee comes back," she said, in a low, sorrowful tone, like one who speaks from a strong heart deeply moved with remorse or pity, "thee shall begin thy life again, – there on the hills. I came too late; but not for thee, – by God's help, it may be."

Not too late. Three years after, the Quaker began her work. I end my story here. At evening-time it was light. There is no need to tire you with the long years of sunshine, and fresh air, and slow, patient Christ-love, needed to make healthy and hopeful this impure body and soul. There is a homely pine house, on one of these hills, whose windows overlook broad, wooded slopes and clover-crimsoned meadows, – niched into the very place where the light is warmest, the air freest. It is the Friends' meeting-house.

Once a week they sit there, in their grave, earnest way, waiting for the Spirit of Love to speak, opening their simple hearts to receive His words. There is a woman, old, deformed, who takes a humble place among them: waiting like them: in her gray dress, her worn face, pure and meek, turned now and then to the sky. A woman much loved by these silent, restful people; more silent than they, more humble, more loving. Waiting: with her eyes turned to hills higher and purer than these on which she lives, – dim and far off now, but to be reached some day. There may be in her heart some latent hope to meet there the love denied her here, – that she shall find him whom she lost, and that then she will not be all-unworthy. Who blames her? Something is lost in the passage of every soul from one eternity to the other, – something pure and beautiful, which might have been and was not: a hope, a talent, a love, over which the soul mourns, like Esau deprived of his birthright.[38] What blame to the meek Quaker, if she took her lost hope to make the hills of heaven more fair?

Nothing remains to tell that the poor Welsh puddler once lived, but this figure of the mill-woman cut in korl. I have it here in a corner of my library. I keep it hid behind a curtain, – it is such a rough, ungainly thing. Yet there are about it touches, grand sweeps of outline, that show a master's hand. Sometimes, – to-night, for instance, – the curtain is accidentally drawn back, and I see a bare arm stretched out imploringly in the darkness, and an eager, wolfish face watching mine: a wan, woful face, through which the spirit of the dead korl-cutter looks out, with its thwarted life, its mighty hunger, its unfinished work. Its pale, vague lips seem to tremble with a terrible question. "Is this the End?" they say, – "nothing beyond? – no more?" Why, you tell me you have seen that look in the eyes of dumb brutes, – horses dying under the lash. I know.

The deep of the night is passing while I write. The gas-light wakens from the shadows here and there the objects which lie scattered through the room: only faintly, though; for they belong to the open sunlight. As I glance at them, they each recall some task or pleasure of the coming day. A half-moulded child's head; Aphrodite;[39] a bough of forest-leaves; music; work; homely fragments, in which lie the secrets of all eternal truth and beauty. Prophetic all! Only this dumb, woful face seems to belong to and end with the night. I turn to look at it. Has the power of its desperate need commanded the darkness away? While the room is yet steeped in heavy shadow, a cool, gray light suddenly touches its head like a blessing hand, and its groping arm points through the broken cloud to the far East, where, in the flickering, nebulous crimson, God has set the promise of the Dawn.

[1861]

---

38. **Esau deprived of his birthright:** Esau, the twin brother of Jacob and the son of Isaac and Rebekah, gave his birthright to his brother in exchange for food (Genesis 25:33-34).

39. **Aphrodite:** Ancient Greek goddess of love.

Louisa May Alcott

[1832–1888]

Louisa May Alcott

This photograph of Alcott was taken around 1860, when she was twenty-eight and had published her first story in the prestigious *Atlantic Monthly*.

Louisa May Alcott was born in Germantown, Pennsylvania, on November 29, 1832. She was the second of four daughters born to Bronson Alcott, a self-educated philosopher and reformer, and Abba May Alcott, the well-educated sister of Samuel May, a prominent Unitarian minister and abolitionist. Bronson Alcott was rarely able to earn a living for his family, and his wife became increasingly frustrated by both his failures and the circumscribed roles available to women. Their unhappy marriage had a profound effect on Alcott, who from an early age was determined to make her own way in the world. During her childhood, her father taught with limited success at various schools, and the family lived in Philadelphia and Boston before moving to Concord, Massachusetts. There, they enjoyed close relationships with Henry David Thoreau and Ralph Waldo Emerson, whom Alcott later described as "the man who has helped me most by his life, his books, and his society." In 1843, Bronson Alcott moved his family to a small utopian community, Fruitlands, on a farm in nearby Harvard, Massachusetts. That idealistic and impractical social experiment was a disaster; the crops failed and the winter weather was exceptionally harsh. When the small group of social reformers disbanded early in 1844, Bronson Alcott suffered a near breakdown and the family returned to Concord. Alcott, who was then only twelve, soon began to write imaginative stories, often for the entertainment of her three sisters and for Emerson's daughter, Ellen. After her family moved back to Boston in 1848, Alcott and her sisters produced a family newspaper, and she soon began to seek a larger audience for her writings.

Throughout her literary career, Alcott struggled with the conflict between her literary aspirations and the pressures of the marketplace. A story she had written in Concord, "The Rival Painters, a Tale of Rome," was published in a Boston family newspaper, the *Olive Branch*, in 1852. From that point on, Alcott wrote constantly, publishing a collection of fairy tales, *Flower Fables* (1854), and stories in various periodicals, including the prestigious *Atlantic Monthly*. As scholars have recently discovered, Alcott also wrote dozens of fantasies and sensational thrillers, often publishing them anonymously or under the pseudonym A. M. Barnard. Alcott's first major literary success was *Hospital Sketches* (1863), based on the letters she wrote to her family while serving as a volunteer nurse in an army hospital in Washington, D.C. Her first novel, *Moods* (1864), was an adult romance steeped in the transcendentalism of her friends in Concord, such as Emerson. Thomas Niles, a literary representative for the publishing company of Roberts Brothers, was eager to tap into the lucrative market for children's literature, and he suggested that Alcott write a book for children. *Little Women*, Alcott's most famous work, appeared in two volumes, the first in 1868 and the second in 1869. Based loosely on her family life, the book made Alcott a celebrity; it also gained her a steady income, vitally important since she was now her family's primary breadwinner.

She is a natural source of stories.
–Ralph Waldo Emerson

The public demand for more books like *Little Women* was tiresome to Alcott. But she wrote them for the rest of her life, publishing another dozen novels and collections of short stories, as well as numerous stories and sketches in periodicals. Although she was viewed by many as the very embodiment of New England respectability, Alcott was a member of the New England Woman Suffrage Association and a strong advocate of dress reform, physical education, and vocational opportunities for women. In fact, many of her later works contain strong messages about women's rights, notably her autobiographical novel, *Work: A Story of Experience* (1873). Alcott dedicated the novel to her mother, "whose life has been a long labor of love." Alcott's later years were troubled by ill health, the death of her mother in 1879, and the constant care of other family members, especially her ailing father, who was incapacitated by a stroke in 1882. He died six years later, at the age of eighty-eight. Alcott died two days after her father's death, on March 6, 1888.

bedfordstmartins.com/ americanlit *for research links on Alcott*

Alcott's "The Brothers." Moved by the newspaper accounts of suffering soldiers and eager for adventure, Alcott volunteered to serve as a war nurse in 1862. She was assigned to the Union Hotel Hospital in Washington, DC. The hospital had been a tavern before the war and was barely operational as a medical facility. Working conditions were extremely difficult, and there were too many patients for the largely untrained staff, who were often aided by convalescent soldiers. After only six weeks of service, Alcott contracted typhoid, a disease common in the hospitals, and was herself sent home to convalesce. Despite the short duration of her hospital work, the experience provided Alcott with a great deal of new material for her writing, including *Hospital Sketches* (1863). Her experience also inspired

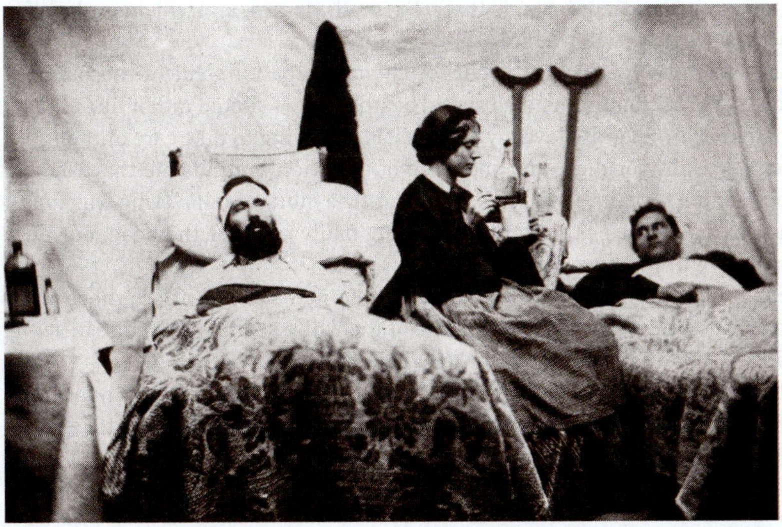

Hospital Nursing

This photograph of a nurse and her patients was taken at a Union hospital in Nashville, Tennessee. Most of the thousands of Union and Confederate women who served as nurses during the Civil War were unpaid volunteers who also spent time cleaning and cooking for their patients.

the following story, a notable example of the new realism and of the themes of death, dislocation, and loss characteristic of so much of the writing produced during the Civil War. The story was first published as "The Brothers" in the *Atlantic Monthly* and later as "My Contraband" in *Hospital Sketches and Camp and Fireside Stories* (1869), a revised and expanded version of *Hospital Sketches.* The text is taken from the first printing in the *Atlantic Monthly*, November 1863.

THE BROTHERS

Doctor Franck came in as I sat sewing up the rents in an old shirt, that Tom might go tidily to his grave. New shirts were needed for the living, and there was no wife or mother to "dress him handsome when he went to meet the Lord," as one woman said, describing the fine funeral she had pinched herself to give her son.

"Miss Dane, I'm in a quandary," began the Doctor, with that expression of countenance which says as plainly as words, "I want to ask a favor, but I wish you'd save me the trouble."

"Can I help you out of it?"

"Faith! I don't like to propose it, but you certainly can, if you please."

"Then give it a name, I beg."

"You see a Reb has just been brought in crazy with typhoid; a bad case every way; a drunken, rascally little captain somebody took the trouble to capture, but whom nobody wants to take the trouble to cure. The wards are full, the ladies worked to death, and willing to be for our own boys, but rather slow to risk their lives for a Reb. Now you've had the fever, you like queer patients, your mate will see to your ward for a while, and I will find you a good attendant. The fellow won't last long, I fancy; but he can't die without some sort of care, you know. I've put him in the fourth story of the west wing, away from the rest. It is airy, quiet, and comfortable there. I'm on that ward, and will do my best for you in every way. Now, then, will you go?"

"Of course I will, out of perversity, if not common charity; for some of these people think that because I'm an abolitionist I am also a heathen, and I should rather like to show them, that, though I cannot quite love my enemies, I am willing to take care of them."

"Very good; I thought you'd go; and speaking of abolition reminds me that you can have a contraband[1] for servant, if you like. It is that fine mulatto fellow who was found burying his Rebel master after the fight, and, being badly cut over the head, our boys brought him along. Will you have him?"

"By all means, – for I'll stand to my guns on that point, as on the other; these black boys are far more faithful and handy than some of the white scamps given me to serve, instead of being served by. But is this man well enough?"

"Yes, for that sort of work, and I think you'll like him. He must have been a handsome fellow before he got his face slashed; not much darker than myself; his master's son, I

---

1. **contraband:** Literally "against the ban" (Italian); the term was used for slaves who escaped or were brought behind Union lines during the Civil War.

dare say, and the white blood makes him rather high and haughty about some things. He was in a bad way when he came in, but vowed he'd die in the street rather than turn in with the black fellows below; so I put him up in the west wing, to be out of the way, and he's seen to the captain all the morning. When can you go up?"

"As soon as Tom is laid out, Skinner moved, Haywood washed, Marble dressed, Charley rubbed, Downs taken up, Upham laid down, and the whole forty fed."

We both laughed, though the Doctor was on his way to the dead-house and I held a shroud on my lap. But in a hospital one learns that cheerfulness is one's salvation; for, in an atmosphere of suffering and death, heaviness of heart would soon paralyze usefulness of hand, if the blessed gift of smiles had been denied us.

In an hour I took possession of my new charge, finding a dissipated-looking boy of nineteen or twenty raving in the solitary little room, with no one near him but the contraband in the room adjoining. Feeling decidedly more interest in the black man than in the white, yet remembering the Doctor's hint of his being "high and haughty," I glanced furtively at him as I scattered chloride of lime about the room to purify the air, and settled matters to suit myself. I had seen many contrabands, but never one so attractive as this. All colored men are called "boys," even if their heads are white; this boy was five-and-twenty at least, strong-limbed and manly, and had the look of one who never had been cowed by abuse or worn with oppressive labor. He sat on his bed doing nothing; no book, no pipe, no pen or paper anywhere appeared, yet anything less indolent or listless than his attitude and expression I never saw. Erect he sat, with a hand on either knee, and eyes fixed on the bare wall opposite, so rapt in some absorbing thought as to be unconscious of my presence, though the door stood wide open and my movements were by no means noiseless. His face was half averted, but I instantly approved the Doctor's taste, for the profile which I saw possessed all the attributes of comeliness belonging to his mixed race. He was more quadroon than mulatto, with Saxon features, Spanish complexion darkened by exposure, color in lips and cheek, waving hair, and an eye full of the passionate melancholy which in such men always seems to utter a mute protest against the broken law that doomed them at their birth. What could he be thinking of? The sick boy cursed and raved, I rustled to and fro, steps passed the door, bells rang, and the steady rumble of army-wagons came up from the street, still he never stirred. I had seen colored people in what they call "the black sulks," when, for days, they neither smiled nor spoke, and scarcely ate. But this was something more than that; for the man was not dully brooding over some small grievance; he seemed to see an all-absorbing fact or fancy recorded on the wall, which was a blank to me. I wondered if it were some deep wrong or sorrow, kept alive by memory and impotent regret; if he mourned for the dead master to whom he had been faithful to the end; or if the liberty now his were robbed of half its sweetness by the knowledge that some one near and dear to him still languished in the hell from which he had escaped. My heart quite warmed to him at that idea; I wanted to know and comfort him; and, following the impulse of the moment, I went in and touched him on the shoulder.

In an instant the man vanished and the slave appeared. Freedom was too new a boon to have wrought its blessed changes yet, and as he started up, with his hand at his temple and an obsequious "Yes, Ma'am," any romance that had gathered round him fled away, leaving the saddest of all sad facts in living guise before me. Not only did the manhood seem to die out of him, but the comeliness that first attracted me; for, as he turned, I saw the ghastly wound that had laid open cheek and forehead. Being partly healed, it was no longer bandaged, but held together with strips of that transparent plaster which I never see without a shiver and swift recollections of the scenes with which it is associated in my mind. Part of his black hair had been shorn away, and one eye was nearly closed; pain so distorted, and the cruel sabre-cut so marred that portion of his face, that, when I saw it, I felt as if a fine medal had been suddenly reversed, showing me a far more striking type of human suffering and wrong than Michel Angelo's bronze prisoner.[2] By one of those inexplicable processes that often teach us how little we understand ourselves, my purpose was suddenly changed, and though I went in to offer comfort as a friend, I merely gave an order as a mistress.

"Will you open these windows? this man needs more air."

He obeyed at once, and, as he slowly urged up the unruly sash, the handsome profile was again turned toward me, and again I was possessed by my first impression so strongly that I involuntarily said, –

"Thank you, Sir."

Perhaps it was fancy, but I thought that in the look of mingled surprise and something like reproach which he gave me there was also a trace of grateful pleasure. But he said, in that tone of spiritless humility these poor souls learn so soon, –

"I a'n't a white man, Ma'am, I'm a contraband."

"Yes, I know it; but a contraband is a free man, and I heartily congratulate you."

He liked that; his face shone, he squared his shoulders, lifted his head, and looked me full in the eye with a brisk –

"Thank ye, Ma'am; anything more to do fer yer?"

"Doctor Franck thought you would help me with this man, as there are many patients and few nurses or attendants. Have you had the fever?"

"No, Ma'am."

"They should have thought of that when they put him here; wounds and fevers should not be together. I'll try to get you moved."

He laughed a sudden laugh, – if he had been a white man, I should have called it scornful; as he was a few shades darker than myself, I suppose it must be considered an insolent, or at least an unmannerly one.

"It don't matter, Ma'am. I'd rather be up here with the fever than down with those niggers; and there a'n't no other place fer me."

Poor fellow! that was true. No ward in all the hospital would take him in to lie side by side with the most miserable white wreck there. Like the bat in Aesop's fable,[3] he belonged to neither race; and the pride of one, the helplessness of the other, kept him hovering alone in the twilight a great sin has brought to overshadow the whole land.

---

2. bronze prisoner: Probably a reference to a bronze casting of the celebrated sculpture of a slave struggling against his bonds, *The Rebellious Slave*, by Michelangelo Buonarroti (1475–1564).

3. the bat in Aesop's fable: In one of the fables of Aesop (c. 600 BCE), birds and mammals are at war with one another. The bat, who considers himself both bird and mammal, fights alternately on each side, depending on who is winning. In the truce that is eventually called, the birds and the mammals, outraged by his duplicitous behavior, declare that the bat is neither bird nor mammal, but an outcast with no friends.

"You shall stay, then; for I would far rather have you than my lazy Jack. But are you well and strong enough?"

"I guess I'll do, Ma'am."

He spoke with a passive sort of acquiescence, – as if it did not much matter, if he were not able, and no one would particularly rejoice, if he were.

"Yes, I think you will. By what name shall I call you?"

"Bob, Ma'am."

Every woman has her pet whim; one of mine was to teach the men self-respect by treating them respectfully. Tom, Dick, and Harry would pass, when lads rejoiced in those familiar abbreviations; but to address men often old enough to be my father in that style did not suit my old-fashioned ideas of propriety. This "Bob" would never do; I should have found it as easy to call the chaplain "Gus" as my tragical-looking contraband by a title so strongly associated with the tail of a kite.

"What is your other name?" I asked. "I like to call my attendants by their last names rather than by their first."

"I've got no other, Ma'am; we have our masters' names, or do without. Mine's dead, and I won't have anything of his about me."

"Well, I'll call you Robert, then, and you may fill this pitcher for me, if you will be so kind."

He went; but, through all the tame obedience years of servitude had taught him, I could see that the proud spirit his father gave him was not yet subdued, for the look and gesture with which he repudiated his master's name were a more effective declaration of independence than any Fourth-of-July orator could have prepared.

We spent a curious week together. Robert seldom left his room, except upon my errands; and I was a prisoner all day, often all night, by the bedside of the Rebel. The fever burned itself rapidly away, for there seemed little vitality to feed it in the feeble frame of this old young man, whose life had been none of the most righteous, judging from the revelations made by his unconscious lips; since more than once Robert authoritatively silenced him, when my gentler hushings were of no avail, and blasphemous wanderings or ribald camp-songs made my cheeks burn and Robert's face assume an aspect of disgust. The captain was a gentleman in the world's eye, but the contraband was the gentleman in mine; – I was a fanatic, and that accounts for such depravity of taste, I hope. I never asked Robert of himself, feeling that somewhere there was a spot still too sore to bear the lightest touch; but, from his language, manner, and intelligence, I inferred that his color had procured for him the few advantages within the reach of a quick-witted, kindly treated slave. Silent, grave, and thoughtful, but most serviceable, was my contraband; glad of the books I brought him, faithful in the performance of the duties I assigned to him, grateful for the friendliness I could not but feel and show toward him. Often I longed to ask what purpose was so visibly altering his aspect with such daily deepening gloom. But I never dared, and no one else had either time or desire to pry into the past of this specimen of one branch of the chivalrous "F.F.Vs."[4]

On the seventh night, Dr. Franck suggested that it would be well for some one,

4. "F.F.Vs.": Plural abbreviation for "First Family of Virginia," designating wealth and social status.

besides the general watchman of the ward, to be with the captain, as it might be his last. Although the greater part of the two preceding nights had been spent there, of course I offered to remain, – for there is a strange fascination in these scenes, which renders one careless of fatigue and unconscious of fear until the crisis is passed.

"Give him water as long as he can drink, and if he drops into a natural sleep, it may save him. I'll look in at midnight, when some change will probably take place. Nothing but sleep or a miracle will keep him now. Good night."

Away went the Doctor; and, devouring a whole mouthful of grapes, I lowered the lamp, wet the captain's head, and sat down on a hard stool to begin my watch. The captain lay with his hot, haggard face turned toward me, filling the air with his poisonous breath, and feebly muttering, with lips and tongue so parched that the sanest speech would have been difficult to understand. Robert was stretched on his bed in the inner room, the door of which stood ajar, that a fresh draught from his open window might carry the fever-fumes away through mine. I could just see a long, dark figure, with the lighter outline of a face, and, having little else to do just then, I fell to thinking of this curious contraband, who evidently prized his freedom highly, yet seemed in no haste to enjoy it. Doctor Franck had offered to send him on to safer quarters, but he had said, "No, thank yer, Sir, not yet," and then had gone away to fall into one of those black moods of his, which began to disturb me, because I had no power to lighten them. As I sat listening to the clocks from the steeples all about us, I amused myself with planning Robert's future, as I often did my own, and had dealt out to him a generous hand of trumps wherewith to play this game of life which hitherto had gone so cruelly against him, when a harsh, choked voice called, –

"Lucy!"

It was the captain, and some new terror seemed to have gifted him with momentary strength.

"Yes, here's Lucy," I answered, hoping that by following the fancy I might quiet him, – for his face was damp with the clammy moisture, and his frame shaken with the nervous tremor that so often precedes death. His dull eye fixed upon me, dilating with a bewildered look of incredulity and wrath, till he broke out fiercely, –

"That's a lie! she's dead, – and so's Bob, damn him!"

Finding speech a failure, I began to sing the quiet tune that had often soothed delirium like this; but hardly had the line,

> "See gentle patience smile on pain,"

passed my lips, when he clutched me by the wrist, whispering like one in mortal fear, –

"Hush! she used to sing that way to Bob, but she never would to me. I swore I'd whip the Devil out of her, and I did; but you know before she cut her throat she said she'd haunt me, and there she is!"

He pointed behind me with an aspect of such pale dismay, that I involuntarily glanced over my shoulder and started as if I had seen a veritable ghost; for, peering from the gloom of that inner room, I saw a shadowy face, with dark hair all about it, and a glimpse of scarlet at the throat. An instant showed me that it was only Robert leaning from his bed's-foot, wrapped in a gray army-blanket, with his red shirt just visible above it, and his long hair disordered by sleep. But what a strange expression was on his face! The unmarred side was toward me, fixed and motionless as when I first observed it, – less absorbed now, but more intent. His eye glittered, his lips were apart like one who listened with every sense, and his whole aspect reminded me of a hound to which some wind had brought the scent of unsuspected prey.

"Do you know him, Robert? Does he mean you?"

"Lord, no, Ma'am; they all own half a dozen Bobs: but hearin' my name woke me; that's all."

He spoke quite naturally, and lay down again, while I returned to my charge, thinking that this paroxysm was probably his last. But by another hour I perceived a hopeful change, for the tremor had subsided, the cold dew was gone, his breathing was more regular, and Sleep, the healer, had descended to save or take him gently away. Doctor Franck looked in at midnight, bade me keep all cool and quiet, and not fail to administer a certain draught as soon as the captain woke. Very much relieved, I laid my head on my arms, uncomfortably folded on the little table, and fancied I was about to perform one of the feats which practice readers possible, – "sleeping with one eye open," as we say: a half-and-half doze, for all senses sleep but that of hearing; the faintest murmur, sigh, or motion will break it, and give one back one's wits much brightened by the brief permission to "stand at ease." On this night, the experiment was a failure, for previous vigils, confinement, and much care had rendered naps a dangerous indulgence. Having roused half a dozen times in an hour to find all quiet, I dropped my heavy head on my arms, and, drowsily resolving to look up again in fifteen minutes, fell fast asleep.

The striking of a deep-voiced clock woke me with a start. "That is one," thought I, but, to my dismay, two more strokes followed; and in remorseful haste I sprang up to see what harm my long oblivion had done. A strong hand put me back into my seat, and held me there. It was Robert. The instant my eye met his my heart began to beat, and all along my nerves tingled with that electric flash which foretells a danger that we cannot see. He was very pale, his mouth grim, and both eyes full of sombre fire, – for even the wounded one was open now, all the more sinister for the deep scar above and below. But his touch was steady, his voice quiet, as he said, –

"Sit still, Ma'am; I won't hurt yer, nor even scare yer, if I can help it, but yer waked too soon."

"Let me go, Robert, – the captain is stirring, – I must give him something."

"No, Ma'am, yer can't stir an inch. Look here!"

Holding me with one hand, with the other he took up the glass in which I had left the draught, and showed me it was empty.

"Has he taken it?" I asked, more and more bewildered.

"I flung it out o' winder, Ma'am; he'll have to do without."

"But why, Robert? why did you do it?"

"Because I hate him!"

Impossible to doubt the truth of that; his whole face showed it, as he spoke through his set teeth, and launched a fiery glance at the unconscious captain. I could only hold my breath and stare blankly at him, wondering what mad act was coming next. I suppose I shook and turned white, as women have a foolish habit of doing when sudden danger daunts them; for Robert released my arm, sat down upon the bedside just in front of me, and said, with the ominous quietude that made me cold to see and hear, –

"Don't yer be frightened, Ma'am; don't try to run away, fer the door's locked an' the key in my pocket; don't yer cry out, fer yer'd have to scream a long while, with my hand on yer mouth, before yer was heard. Be still, an' I'll tell yer what I'm goin' to do."

"Lord help us! he has taken the fever in some sudden, violent way, and is out of his head. I must humor him till some one comes"; in pursuance of which swift determination, I tried to say, quite composedly, –

"I will be still and hear you; but open the window. Why did you shut it?"

"I'm sorry I can't do it, Ma'am; but yer'd jump out, or call, if I did, an' I'm not ready yet. I shut it to make yer sleep, an' heat would do it quicker 'n anything else I could do."

The captain moved, and feebly muttered, "Water!" Instinctively I rose to give it to him, but the heavy hand came down upon my shoulder, and in the same decided tone Robert said, –

"The water went with the physic; let him call."

"Do let me go to him! he'll die without care!"

"I mean he shall; – don't yer interfere, if yer please, Ma'am."

In spite of his quiet tone and respectful manner, I saw murder in his eyes, and turned faint with fear; yet the fear excited me, and, hardly knowing what I did, I seized the hands that had seized me, crying, –

"No, no, you shall not kill him! it is base to hurt a helpless man. Why do you hate him? He is not your master?"

"He's my brother."

I felt that answer from head to foot, and seemed to fathom what was coming, with a prescience vague, but unmistakable. One appeal was left to me, and I made it.

"Robert, tell me what it means? Do not commit a crime and make me accessory to it. There is a better way of righting wrong than by violence; – let me help you find it."

My voice trembled as I spoke, and I heard the frightened flutter of my heart; so did he, and if any little act of mine had ever won affection or respect from him, the memory of it served me then. He looked down, and seemed to put some question to himself; whatever it was, the answer was in my favor, for when his eyes rose again, they were gloomy, but not desperate.

"I *will* tell you, Ma'am; but mind, this makes no difference; the boy is mine. I'll give the Lord a chance to take him fust; if He don't, I shall."

"Oh, no! remember, he is your brother."

An unwise speech; I felt it as it passed my lips, for a black frown gathered on Robert's face, and his strong hands closed with an ugly sort of grip. But he did not touch the poor soul gasping there behind him, and seemed content to let the slow suffocation of that stifling room end his frail life.

"I'm not like to forget that, Ma'am, when I've been thinkin' of it all this week. I knew him when they fetched him in, an' would 'a' done it long 'fore this, but I wanted to ask where Lucy was; he knows, – he told to-night, – an' now he's done for."

"Who is Lucy?" I asked hurriedly, intent on keeping his mind busy with any thought but murder.

With one of the swift transitions of a mixed temperament like this, at my question Robert's deep eyes filled, the clenched hands were spread before his face, and all I heard were the broken words, –

"My wife, – he took her" —

In that instant every thought of fear was swallowed up in burning indignation for the wrong, and a perfect passion of pity for the desperate man so tempted to avenge an injury for which there seemed no redress but this. He was no longer slave or contraband, no drop of black blood marred him in my sight, but an infinite compassion yearned to save, to help, to comfort him. Words seemed so powerless I offered none, only put my hand on his poor head, wounded, homeless, bowed down with grief for which I had no cure, and softly smoothed the long neglected hair, pitifully wondering the while where was the wife who must have loved this tender-hearted man so well.

The captain moaned again, and faintly whispered, "Air!" but I never stirred. God forgive me! just then I hated him as only a woman thinking of a sister woman's wrong could hate. Robert looked up; his eyes were dry again, his mouth grim. I saw that, said, "Tell me more," and he did, – for sympathy is a gift the poorest may give, the proudest stoop to receive.

"Yer see, Ma'am, his father, – I might say ours, if I warn't ashamed of both of 'em, – his father died two years ago, an' left us all to Marster Ned, – that's him here, eighteen then. He always hated me, I looked so like old Marster: he don't, – only the light skin an' hair. Old Marster was kind to all of us, me 'specially, an' bought Lucy off the next plantation down there in South Car'lina, when he found I liked her. I married her, all I could, Ma'am; it warn't much, but we was true to one another till Marster Ned come home a year after an' made hell fer both of us. He sent my old mother to be used up in his rice-swamp in Georgy; he found me with my pretty Lucy, an' though young Miss cried, an' I prayed to him on my knees, an' Lucy run away, he wouldn't have no mercy; he brought her back, an' – took her, Ma'am."

"Oh! what did you do?" I cried, hot with helpless pain and passion.

How the man's outraged heart sent the blood flaming up into his face and deepened the tones of his impetuous voice, as he stretched his arm across the bed, saying, with a terribly expressive gesture, –

"I half murdered him, an' to-night I'll finish."

"Yes, yes, – but go on now; what came next?"

He gave me a look that showed no white man could have felt a deeper degradation in remembering and confessing these last acts of brotherly oppression.

"They whipped me till I couldn't stand, an' then they sold me further South. Yer thought I was a white man once; – look here!"

With a sudden wrench he tore the shirt from neck to waist, and on his strong brown shoulders showed me furrows deeply ploughed, wounds which, though healed, were ghastlier to me than any in that house. I could not speak to him, and, with the pathetic dignity and great grief lends the humblest sufferer, he ended his brief tragedy by simply saying, –

"That's all, Ma'am. I've never seen her since, an' now I never shall in this world, – maybe not in t' other."

"But, Robert, why think her dead? The captain was wandering when he said those sad things; perhaps he will retract them when he is sane. Don't despair; don't give up yet."

"No, Ma'am, I guess he's right; she was too proud to bear that long. It's like her to kill herself. I told her to, if there was no other way; an' she always minded me, Lucy did. My poor girl! Oh, it warn't right! No, by God, it warn't!"

As the memory of this bitter wrong, this double bereavement, burned in his sore heart, the devil that lurks in every strong man's blood leaped up; he put his hand upon his brother's throat, and, watching the white face before him, muttered low between his teeth, –

"I'm lettin' him go too easy; there's no pain in this; we a'n't even yet. I wish he knew me. Marster Ned! it's Bob; where's Lucy?"

From the captain's lips there came a long faint sigh, and nothing but a flutter of the eyelids showed that he still lived. A strange stillness filled the room as the elder brother held the younger's life suspended in his hand, while wavering between a dim hope and a deadly hate. In the whirl of thoughts that went on in my brain, only one was clear enough to act upon. I must prevent murder, if I could, – but how? What could I do up there alone, locked in with a dying man and a lunatic? – for any mind yielded utterly to any unrighteous impulse is mad while the impulse rules it. Strength I had not, nor much courage, neither time nor wit for strategem, and chance only could bring me help before it was too late. But one weapon I possessed, – a tongue, – often a woman's best defence; and sympathy, stronger than fear, gave me power to use it. What I said Heaven only knows, but surely Heaven helped me; words burned on my lips, tears streamed from my eyes, and some good angel prompted me to use the one name that had power to arrest my hearer's hand and touch his heart. For at that moment I heartily believed that Lucy lived, and this earnest faith roused in him a like belief.

He listened with the lowering look of one in whom brute instinct was sovereign for the time, – a look that makes the noblest countenance base. He was but a man, – a poor, untaught, outcast, outraged man. Life had few joys for him; the world offered him no honors, no success, no home, no love. What future would this crime mar? and why should he deny himself that sweet, yet bitter morsel called revenge? How many white men, with all New England's freedom, culture, Christianity, would not have felt as he felt then? Should I have reproached him for a human anguish, a human longing for redress, all now left him from the ruin of his few poor hopes? Who had taught him that self-control, self-sacrifice, are attributes that make men masters of the earth and lift them nearer heaven? Should I have urged the beauty of forgiveness, the duty of devout submission? He had no religion, for he was no saintly "Uncle Tom," and Slavery's black shadow seemed to darken all the world to him and shut out God. Should I have warned him of penalties, of judgments, and the potency of law? What did he know of justice, or the mercy that should temper that stern virtue, when every law, human and divine, had been broken on his hearthstone? Should I have tried to touch him by appeals to filial duty, to brotherly love? How had his appeals been answered? What memories had father and brother stored up in his heart to plead for either now? No, – all these influences, these associations, would have proved worse than useless, had I been calm enough to try them. I was not; but instinct, subtler than reason, showed me the one safe clue by which to lead this troubled soul from the labyrinth in which it groped and nearly fell. When I paused, breathless, Robert turned to me, asking, as if human assurance could strengthen his faith in Divine Omnipotence, –

"Do you believe, if I let Marster Ned live, the Lord will give me back my Lucy?"

"As surely as there is a Lord, you will find her here or in the beautiful hereafter, where there is no black or white, no master and no slave."

He took his hand from his brother's throat, lifted his eyes from my face to the wintry sky beyond, as if searching for that blessed country, happier even than the happy North. Alas, it was the darkest hour before the dawn! – there was no star above, no light below but the pale glimmer of the lamp that showed the brother who had made him desolate. Like a blind man who believes there is a sun, yet cannot see it, he shook his head, let his arms drop nervelessly upon his knees, and sat there dumbly asking that question which many a soul whose faith is firmer fixed than his has asked in hours less dark than this, – "Where is God?" I saw the tide had turned, and strenuously tried to keep this rudderless life-boat from slipping back into the whirlpool wherein it had been so nearly lost.

"I have listened to you, Robert; now hear me, and heed what I say, because my heart is full of pity for you, full of hope for your future, and a desire to help you now. I want you to go away from here, from the temptation of this place, and the sad thoughts that haunt it. You have conquered yourself once, and I honor you for it, because, the harder the battle, the more glorious the victory; but it is safer to put a greater distance between you and this man. I will write you letters, give you money, and send you to good old Massachusetts to begin your new life a freeman, – yes, and a happy man; for when the captain is himself again, I will learn where Lucy is, and move heaven and earth to find and give her back to you. Will you do this, Robert?"

Slowly, very slowly, the answer came; for the purpose of a week, perhaps a year, was hard to relinquish in an hour.

"Yes, Ma'am, I will."

"Good! Now you are the man I thought you, and I'll work for you with all my heart. You need sleep, my poor fellow; go, and try to forget. The captain is still alive, and as yet you are spared that sin. No, don't look there; I'll care for him. Come, Robert, for Lucy's sake."

Thank Heaven for the immortality of love! for when all other means of salvation failed, a spark of this vital fire softened the man's iron will until a woman's hand could bend it. He let me take from him the key, let me draw him gently away and lead him to the solitude which now was the most healing balm I could bestow. Once in his little room, he fell down on his bed and lay there as if spent with the sharpest conflict of his life. I slipped the bolt across his door, and unlocked my own, flung up the window, steadied myself with a breath of air, then rushed to Doctor Franck. He came; and till dawn we worked together, saving one brother's life, and taking earnest thought how best to secure the other's liberty. When the sun came up as blithely as if it shone only upon happy homes, the Doctor went to Robert. For an hour I heard the murmur of their voices; once I caught the sound of heavy sobs, and for a time a reverent hush, as if in the silence that good man were ministering to soul as well as sense. When he departed he took Robert with him, pausing to tell me he should get him off as soon as possible, but not before we met again.

Nothing more was seen of them all day; another surgeon came to see the captain, and another attendant came to fill the empty place. I tried to rest, but could not, with the thought of poor Lucy tugging at my heart, and was soon back at my post again, anxiously hoping that my contraband had not been too hastily spirited away. Just as night fell there came a tap, and, opening, I saw Robert literally "clothed and in his right mind." The Doctor had replaced the ragged suit with tidy garments, and no trace of that tempestuous night remained but deeper lines upon the forehead and the docile look of a repentant child. He did not cross the threshold, did not offer me his hand, – only took off his cap, saying, with a traitorous falter in his voice, –

"God bless you, Ma'am! I'm goin'."

I put out both my hands, and held his fast.

"Good bye, Robert! Keep up good heart, and when I come home to Massachusetts we'll meet in a happier place than this. Are you quite ready, quite comfortable for your journey?"

"Yes, Ma'am, yes; the Doctor's fixed everything; I'm goin' with a friend of his; my papers are all right, an' I'm as happy as I can be till I find" –

He stopped there; then went on, with a glance into the room, –

"I'm glad I didn't do it, an' I thank yer, Ma'am, for hinderin' me, – thank yer hearty; but I'm afraid I hate him jest the same."

Of course he did; and so did I; for these faulty hearts of ours cannot turn perfect in a night, but need frost and fire, wind and rain, to ripen and make them ready for the great harvest-home. Wishing to divert his mind, I put my poor mite into his hand, and, remembering the magic of a certain little book, I gave him mine, on whose dark cover whitely shone the Virgin Mother and the Child, the grand history of whose life the book contained. The money went into Robert's pocket with a grateful murmur, the book into his bosom with a long look and a tremulous –

"I never saw *my* baby, Ma'am."

I broke down then; and though my eyes were too dim to see, I felt the touch of lips upon my hands, heard the sound of departing feet, and knew my contraband was gone.

When one feels an intense dislike, the less one says about the subject of it the better; therefore I shall merely record that the captain lived, – in time was exchanged; and that, whoever the other party was, I am convinced the Government got the best of the bargain. But long before this occurred, I had fulfilled my promise to Robert; for as soon as my patient recovered strength of memory enough to make his answer trustworthy, I asked, without any circumlocution, –

"Captain Fairfax, where is Lucy?"

And too feeble to be angry, surprised, or insincere, he straightway answered, –

"Dead, Miss Dane."

"And she killed herself, when you sold Bob?"

"How the Devil did you know that?" he muttered, with an expression half-remorseful, half-amazed; but I was satisfied, and said no more.

Of course, this went to Robert, waiting far away there in a lonely home, – waiting, working, hoping for his Lucy. It almost broke my heart to do it; but delay was weak, deceit was wicked; so I sent the heavy tidings, and very soon the answer came, – only three lines; but I felt that the sustaining power of the man's life was gone.

"I thought I'd never see her any more; I'm glad to know she's out of trouble. I thank yer, Ma'am; an' if they let us, I'll fight fer yer till I'm killed, which I hope will be 'fore long."

Six months later he had his wish, and kept his word.

Every one knows the story of the attack on Fort Wagner; but we should not tire yet of recalling how our Fifty-Fourth,[5] spent with three sleepless nights, a day's fast, and a march under the July sun, stormed the fort as night fell, facing death in many shapes, following their brave leaders through a fiery rain of shot and shell, fighting valiantly for "God and Governor Andrew," – how the regiment that went into action seven hundred strong came out having had nearly half its number captured, killed, or wounded, leaving their young commander to be buried, like a chief of earlier times, with his body-guard around him, faithful to the death. Surely, the insult turns to honor, and the wide grave needs no monument but the heroism that consecrates it in our sight; surely, the hearts that held him nearest see through their tears a noble victory in the seeming sad defeat; and surely, God's benediction was bestowed, when his loyal soul answered, as Death called the roll, "Lord, here am I, with the brothers Thou hast given me!"

The future must show how well that fight was fought; for though Fort Wagner still defies us, public prejudice is down; and through the cannon-smoke of that black night the manhood of the colored race shines before many eyes that would not see, rings in many ears that would not hear, wins many hearts that would not hitherto believe.

When the news came that we were needed, there was none so glad as I to leave teaching contrabands, the new work I had taken up, and go to nurse "our boys," as my dusky flock so proudly called the wounded of the Fifty-Fourth. Feeling more satisfaction, as I assumed my big apron and turned up my cuffs, than if dressing for the President's levee, I fell to work on board the hospital-ship in Hilton-Head harbor. The scene was most familiar, and yet strange; for only dark faces looked up at me from the pallets so thickly laid along the floor, and I missed the sharp accent of my Yankee boys in the slower, softer voices calling cheerily to one another, or answering my questions with a stout, "We'll never give it up, Ma'am, till the last Reb's dead," or, "If our people's free, we can afford to die."

Passing from bed to bed, intent on making one pair of hands do the work of three, at least, I gradually washed, fed, and bandaged my way down the long line of sable heroes, and coming to the very last, found that he was my contraband. So old, so worn, so deathly weak and wan, I never should have known him but for the deep scar on his cheek. That side lay uppermost, and caught my eye at once; but even then I doubted, such an awful change had come upon him, when, turning to the ticket just above his head, I saw the name, "Robert Dane."

[1863]

---

5. **Fifty-Fourth:** The Fifty-fourth Massachusetts Infantry, formed in 1863 and led by Robert Gould Shaw, was among the first black military units organized during the Civil War.

SELECT POEMS

BY

MRS. L. H. SIGOURNEY.

Engraved by W. E. Tucker

PHILADELPHIA

CAREY AND HART.

New Poetic Voices

In the nineteenth century, educated people considered poetry the highest literary form; poetic achievement was viewed as the standard by which a national culture was measured. The desire to create a distinctly American literature consequently took on a special urgency in the realm of poetry. Nonetheless, the creation of truly indigenous poetry faced formidable obstacles in the United States. One was the dominance of the rich tradition of English poetry. Chaucer, Shakespeare, Milton, and especially the British Romantic poets – such as William Wordsworth, Lord Byron, and Percy Bysshe Shelley – exerted a powerful influence on American poets of the period. But surely, many reasoned, a nation without its own

◄ **Title page of *Select Poems* (1848) by Lydia Sigourney**

As technological developments lowered the cost of printing engravings, publishers often sought to enhance their books by adding illustrations, including portraits of the authors and elaborate title pages like this one from *Select Poems* (1848) by Lydia Sigourney. Here, a variety of flowers and plants are intertwined around a lyre, the musical instrument played by ancient poets and the Greek god Orpheus, son of Calliope, the Muse of epic poetry.

poets and poetry could not be a real nation. At the same time, some critics and writers were concerned that the democratic institutions and especially the material conditions in the United States were adverse to the development of the arts in general and poetry in particular. In response to what many perceived as the national necessity for poetry, the editor of the *Southern Quarterly Review*, Daniel Whitaker, simply announced that American poetry in fact existed. As he exclaimed in 1842: "Poetry! Why, America is *all* poetry. The pages of our Constitution, – the deeds of our patriot sires, – the deliberations of our sages and statesmen, – the civilization and progress of our people, – the wisdom of our laws, – the greatness of our name, are all covered over with the living fire of poetry."

"Poetry! Why, America is all *poetry. The pages of our Constitution, – the deeds of our patriot sires, – the deliberations of our sages and statesmen, – the civilization and progress of our people, – the wisdom of our laws, – the greatness of our name, are all covered over with the living fire of poetry."*

Just as Whitaker viewed such notable achievements as poetic acts, so did many others view the writing of poetry as a patriotic act, a necessary part of building a new and culturally independent country. In the preface to the first edition of his highly successful anthology, *The Poets and Poetry of America* (1842), Rufus Griswold stated that his intention was "to exhibit the progress and condition of Poetry in the United States." Affirming that "Literature, not less than wealth, adds to a nation's happiness and greatness," Griswold reprinted the works of dozens of poets, many of whom had become popular with readers through their frequent appearances in periodicals. Both magazines and newspapers published poetry in the nineteenth century. By mid-century, it was not uncommon for readers to find poems on the front pages of even national newspapers like the influential *New-York Tribune.* Families often read poetry aloud for evening entertainment, and in schools the memorization of poetry was an early part of training in reading. Although poetry never gained the share of the literary marketplace claimed by prose works, especially short stories and novels, the publication of books of poetry written by Americans rose steadily in the period before the Civil War. During the decade of 1830-40, some two hundred books of poetry were published in New York City alone. In the following decade, that number tripled, and the number of volumes of poetry written by Americans and published in the United States continued to climb during the 1850s.

As in the case of fiction and other prose writings, women claimed a significant share of the market for poetry. The much-admired Lydia Sigourney, who in 1830 was regularly writing for at least twenty magazines and newspapers, published more than fifty books during her lifetime. Most of those books were collections of her poems, which sold quite well. Sigourney's poems ranged from popular, sentimental accounts of the deaths of children to witty and often barbed political commentaries, including her opposition to federal policies for the removal of the Cherokee from their native lands in Georgia. Other women poets also gained a good deal of success. Elizabeth Oakes Smith published "The Sinless Child," a long narrative poem on a frequent nineteenth-century topic – the death of an innocent, young child – in the *Southern Literary Messenger* in 1842. The popularity of that poem and her other frequent contributions to periodicals prompted the publication of Smith's first book, *The Sinless Child and Other Poems*, in 1843. A complete edition of her poems followed in 1845, with a preface by the increasingly influential Rufus Griswold, who continued to publish his successful anthologies of poetry throughout the 1840s and 1850s. Like many other writers of the period, Smith published both poetry and prose; so did the popular short-story writer Rose Terry Cooke, whose *Poems* appeared in 1861, a decade after her first poem was published in the *New-York Tribune*.

Male writers also profited from the growing demand for poetry. In an earlier generation, it had not been economically feasible to make a career of writing poetry. Despite the acclaim generated by his poem "Thanatopsis" and the warm critical reception of his first collection of poetry, published in 1821, William Cullen Bryant had turned from poetry to work as a newspaper editor in order to earn a living. Like Bryant, Oliver Wendell Holmes gained early success with poems he began to publish in periodicals shortly after his graduation from Harvard in 1829. Although he published his first collection, *Poems*, in 1836, poetry remained an avocation for Holmes, who supported himself through the practice and later the teaching of medicine. When James Russell Lowell graduated from Harvard in 1839, his elders there strongly discouraged him from pursuing a career as a poet, and he dutifully went on to Harvard Law School. "Our stout Yankee nation would swap all the poems that ever were penned for a treatise on ventilation," Lowell gloomily observed in 1840. But times truly had changed during the previous few years, largely as a result of the establishment of important new literary periodicals like *Graham's Magazine* and the *Southern Literary Messenger*. In fact, the poems Lowell began to publish in such periodicals gained such immediate favor with audiences that he was soon able to publish the first of his many popular volumes of poetry, *A Year's Life* (1841). The critical success of that volume – one reviewer proclaimed that, in Lowell, the country had at last produced a poet who would write the great American poem and thus silence "the sneers of foreigners" – made his work all the more attractive to periodicals and allowed him to abandon the law for a career in literature.

The checkered career of Edgar Allan Poe illustrated the shifting position of poets and poetry in the United States. Poe was so determined to become a poet that in 1827, at the age of eighteen, he left his home in Virginia and made his way to Boston, then the center of publishing in the United States. There, he paid for the publication of his first volume of poetry, *Tamerlane and Other Poems* (1827). He published additional volumes of verse in 1829 and 1831, but the commercial failure of those collections obliged Poe to earn his living by editing magazines and writing critical articles and short stories. He continued to publish some poetry in periodicals, however, and in 1845 his poem "The Raven" caused a sensation when it was published in a New York City newspaper and then in the *American Review*. As a consequence, Poe began to lecture on American poets, became a principal reviewer for the *Broadway Journal*, and swiftly published *The Raven and Other Poems* (1845). The poems collected in that volume and a few other poems he published during the remaining four years of his life gained Poe far greater fame, both at home and abroad, than the short stories for which he is now principally known and valued as a writer.

In his critical statements on poetry, Poe insisted that its sole end was beauty, not truth. He consequently tended to dismiss forms of poetry that sought to convey ideas, teach lessons, or tell stories – that is, virtually all of the kinds of poetry that were most popular during the period. Certainly, many American poets would have challenged Poe's formulation. Much of the poetry written during the period was devoted to moral, political, or social ends. Among those who clearly recognized and early sought to exploit the growing popularity of poetry were the abolitionists, brilliant propagandists who used every form of communication at their disposal. One of the most prolific of the abolitionist poets was John Pierpont, a Harvard-educated Unitarian minister whose conservative Boston congregation accused him of wasting his time in "the making of Books," including *The Anti-Slavery Poems of John Pierpont* (1843). Pierpont was a close friend of the radical abolitionist William Lloyd Garrison – editor of the *Liberator* – and so was another notable antislavery poet John Greenleaf Whittier, the author of *Poems Written during the Progress of the Abolition Question* (1838) and *Voices of Freedom* (1846). Garrison and other abolitionists also heavily promoted the work of Frances E. W. Harper, an African American woman whose antislavery collection *Poems on Miscellaneous Subjects* sold twelve thousand copies in 1854. The most popular poet of the period, Henry Wadsworth Longfellow, contributed to the cause with his early collection *Poems on Slavery*, published in 1842. But he gained international fame through ballads, lyrics, and especially a series of long narrative poems with American settings and themes, two of which were more successful than any volumes of poetry previously published in the United States: *Hiawatha*, which sold an astonishing forty-three thousand copies within a year of its publication in 1855, and *The Courtship of Miles Standish* (1858), which on its first day of publication sold fifteen thousand copies in Boston and London.

Longfellow was but one of many poets who answered the call for "literature by native authors," as the editor of the *American Review* put it in 1845. The "Fireside Poets," as Longfellow, Bryant, Lowell, and Whittier were sometimes called, frequently invoked the comforts of hearth and home. The accessibility, didacticism, and moral seriousness of much of their poetry accounted for a later description of the group, the "Schoolroom Poets." Although readers loved the rhythms and rhymes of their poems and enjoyed the patriotic pride they inspired, some critics lamented the lack of innovation and originality in the poetry written and published in the United States. "We hear, through all the varied music, the ground-tone of conventional life," Ralph Waldo Emerson observed in "The Poet," an essay published in 1844. "Our poets are men of talents who sing, and not the children of music. The argument is secondary, the finish of the verses is primary. "For it is not metres, but a metre-making argument that makes a poem, – a thought so passionate and alive, that, like the spirit of a plant or an animal, it has an architecture of its own, and adorns nature with a new thing." In effect, Emerson suggested that American poets were content to work within narrow boundaries and established forms, rather than allowing their thoughts full freedom from both literary and social conventions. For his part, Emerson did everything he could to spur the development of a new poetry. He strongly encouraged the efforts of young writers like Henry David Thoreau, who initially aspired to be a poet before discovering his true talent for narrative and poetic prose, and William Ellery Channing, the nephew and namesake of a distinguished Unitarian minister, who had dropped out of Harvard to devote himself to poetry and later settled near Emerson in Concord, Massachusetts. Emerson published a large amount of poetry in the *Dial*, the unofficial journal of the transcendentalists. He also helped arrange for the publication of two different collections of Channing's *Poems* (1843, 1848), though they were eclipsed by Emerson's own *Poems* (1847). Like his young disciples and so many other American poets, however, Emerson discovered that it was far easier to assert the need to break with literary conventions and English poetic models than to discover compelling ways of doing so. He was consequently less important as a poet than as a prose writer whose emphasis on the need for self-cultivation and self-reliance inspired both Walt Whitman and Emily Dickinson to claim the various kinds of freedoms Emerson extolled.

"For it is not metres, but a metre-making argument that makes a poem, – a thought so passionate and alive, that, like the spirit of a plant or an animal, it has an architecture of its own, and adorns nature with a new thing."

No two poets could have been more different in background, temperament, and poetic practice than Whitman and Dickinson. The son of a farmer and laborer, Whitman quit school at the age of eleven and was largely self-educated. By the standards for women at the time, Dickinson was well educated, and the affluence of her distinguished family allowed her full time for study and writing. One of Whitman's New York friends observed that he belonged to the "crowded thoroughfare," and few writers of the period so relished the sights and sounds of urban life. The reclusive Dickinson was happiest in an upstairs room in her comfortable house in Amherst, a rural town in western Massachusetts. Although both devoted most of their lives to writing poetry, their poems were strikingly different, as were their attitudes toward publication. Dickinson preferred to "publish" her poems in letters to friends and relatives. Of the nearly 1,800 poems she wrote by the time of her death in 1886, Dickinson published only a handful in periodicals. In contrast, Whitman constantly published his poems, both in periodicals and in books and notably in the multiple editions of *Leaves of Grass* he published between 1855 and his death in 1892.

As unalike as they were, Whitman and Dickinson were united by the radical differences between their poetry and virtually all of the other poetry written during the period. Emerson warmly greeted the appearance of the first edition of *Leaves of Grass*, which he called "the most extraordinary piece of wit and wisdom that America has yet produced." Fanny Fern, the popular newspaper columnist, also praised Whitman's book for its challenge to the "forced stiff, Parnassian exotics" of other poets. But most early reviewers fiercely condemned Whitman's iconoclastic approach to form and content, especially what they described as the "coarseness" and "sensuality" of *Leaves of Grass*. One of Whitman's harshest critics was

Rufus W. Griswold

This engraving was published in 1850, by which time Griswold's popular anthologies, especially *The Poets and Poetry of America*, had made him one of the most influential literary critics in the United States.

Rufus Griswold, who in the mid-1850s was publishing anthologies of American poetry for use in schoolrooms. "It is impossible to imagine how any man's fancy could have conceived of such a mass of stupid filth," Griswold angrily exclaimed in his savage review of *Leaves of Grass.* The poems were considered particularly unsuitable for female readers. Dickinson herself later playfully said that she had never read Whitman's book "but was told that he was disgraceful." Nonetheless, as she no doubt recognized, if Dickinson had sought a wider audience for her poetry she, too, would have faced stiff resistance from critics. Although her poems would not have been viewed as violating moral laws or the laws against obscenity, Dickinson defiantly violated the metrical laws of poetry even as she subverted conventional religious values and beliefs. Indeed, if her poetry had ever been read by Griswold, the self-styled arbiter of poetic taste in the United States, he would no doubt have rejected it almost as forcefully as he rejected *Leaves of Grass.* Certainly neither the editor nor the many readers of *The Poets and Poetry of America* could then have possibly recognized that in Whitman and Dickinson the country had finally produced its first great poets, whose work would later be viewed as among the most notable achievements of nineteenth-century American literature.

American Contexts

THE AMERICAN MUSE: POETRY AT MIDCENTURY

WHITMAN AND DICKINSON have come to overshadow all other American poets of the nineteenth century, especially those of the period 1830-65. For readers at that time, however, Whitman was an obscure figure until he published the first edition of *Leaves of Grass* in 1855. After that, he was more notorious than famous. Dickinson was completely unknown until the first collection of her poems appeared in 1890, four years after her death. The following selections from the work of six poets exemplify some of the various kinds of American poetry most widely distributed and read in the United States during the decades before the Civil War. Not surprisingly, the influence of eighteenth- and early nineteenth-century British poets like William Cowper, James Thomson, and William Wordsworth can be felt strongly here, especially in the ways in which many of these poets deal with everyday subjects, the lives of ordinary people, and the details of the natural world. The topics of the poems are various, ranging from abstract philosophical issues such as immortality to topical issues like slavery, the plight of Native Americans, and the role of women in society. For the most part, however, poets of the period employed conventional forms. Emerson persistently tried to expand those forms, while Poe sought special, unconventional effects. But most of the popular poets took fairly predictable approaches to rhythm and rhyme. In fact, even at that time, some critics complained about the conventionality of much of the poetry written and published in the United States. Nonetheless, the poets represented here and many others writing during the period did important cultural work. With the aid of periodicals, in which all of them published, these writers helped develop an audience for poetry in the United States, a place which many critics at home and especially abroad viewed as inhospitable or even hostile to the arts. In fact, some of the very elements of style and subject matter that made and make such poetry seem so conventional allowed it to communicate directly and often with genuine force to large numbers of readers. Certainly, the poems gathered together in the following section indicate why Whitman's poetry never found favor with the mass audience he craved and why Dickinson mainly shared her poems with friends and relatives rather than subject her work to the pressures of a literary marketplace shaped by markedly different kinds of poetry.

bedfordstmartins.com/ americanlit *for research links on the authors in this section*

Lydia Sigourney

[1791-1865]

Lydia Sigourney

Based on a portrait by Alonzo Chappel, this engraving was printed around 1820, five years after Sigourney published the first of her many popular books, *Miscellaneous Pieces, in Prose and Verse.*

One of the most popular and prolific writers of the period, Lydia Howard Huntley Sigourney was born in Norwich, Connecticut, where she was raised in a devoutly Christian home. Deeply committed to education for women, she opened a school for young women, first in Norwich and then in Hartford, Connecticut, which would be her lifelong home. She published her first work, *Moral Pieces in Prose and Verse*, in 1815. During the remaining fifty years of her life, she published more than fifty additional books of poetry and prose, both fiction and nonfictional works, like the *History of the Condition of Women* (1837). Nonetheless, she was best known as a poet, "the sweet singer of Hartford," as she was often called in the periodicals where her works frequently appeared. Sigourney was a popular poet who used conventional forms, writing elegies to honor dead friends and lyrics about nature. But she also wrote about social and political problems in the United States. Two of her frequent topics were the status of women and the plight of Native Americans. The texts of the following poems are taken from her *Select Poems* (1848).

Indian Names

"How can the Red men be forgotten, while so many of our states and territories, bays, lakes and rivers, are indelibly stamped by names of their giving?"

Ye say, they all have passed away,[1]
  That noble race and brave,
That their light canoes have vanished
  From off the crested wave;
That 'mid the forests where they roamed
  There rings no hunter's shout;
But their name is on your waters,
  Ye may not wash it out.

'Tis where Ontario's billow
  Lake Ocean's surge is curl'd,
Where strong Niagara's thunders wake
  The echo of the world,
Where red Missouri bringeth
  Rich tributes from the west,
And Rappahannock[2] sweetly sleeps
  On green Virginia's breast.

Ye say, their cone-like cabins,
  That clustered o'er the vale,
Have fled away like withered leaves
  Before the autumn gale:
But their memory liveth on your hills
  Their baptism on your shore,

1. **passed away:** Sigourney wrote several poems about the treatment of Native Americans in the United States. She was opposed to the Removal Act of 1830, which required five tribes to give up their native lands in the southeastern United States and move to the "Indian Territory," now the state of Oklahoma. In addition to writing poems, Sigourney organized a petition on behalf of a women's association and published it in 1831 as an open letter in the *Cherokee Phoenix*, the first periodical published by Native Americans.
2. **Rappahannock:** Now spelled "Rappahanock," a river that flows through Virginia and empties into the Chesapeake Bay. Sigourney emphasizes the number of Indian names used for rivers, states, and mountains in the United States.

Your everlasting rivers speak
Their dialect of yore.

Old Massachusetts wears it
Within her lordly crown,
And broad Ohio bears it
Amid her young renown;
Connecticut hath wreathed it
Where her quiet foliage waves,
And bold Kentucky breathed it hoarse
Through all her ancient caves.

Wachuset[3] hides its lingering voice
Within his rocky heart,
And Alleghany graves its tone
Throughout his lofty chart;
Monadnock[4] on his forehead hoar
Doth seal the sacred trust,
Your mountains build their monument,
Though ye destroy their dust.

[1848]

To a Shred of Linen

Would they swept cleaner! –
Here's a littering shred
Of linen left behind – a vile reproach
To all good housewifery. Right glad am I,
That no neat lady, train'd in ancient times
Of pudding-making, and of sampler-work,
And speckless sanctity of household care,
Hath happened here, to spy thee. She, no doubt,
Keen looking through her spectacles, would say,
"*This comes of reading books*:" – or some spruce beau
Essenc'd and lily-handed, had he chanc'd
To scan thy slight superfices, 'twould be
"*This comes of writing poetry.*" – Well – well –
Come forth – offender! – hast thou aught to say?
Canst thou by merry thought, or quaint conceit,

3. **Wachuset:** Now spelled "Wachusett," a mountain in central Massachusetts.
4. **Monadnock:** A mountain in southwestern New Hampshire.

Repay this risk, that I have run for thee?
— Begin at alpha, and resolve thyself
Into thine elements. I see the stalk
And bright, blue flower of flax, which erst o'erspread
That fertile land, where mighty Moses stretch'd
His rod miraculous. I see thy bloom
Tinging, too scantly, these New England vales.
But, lo! the sturdy farmer lifts his flail,
To crush thy bones unpitying, and his wife
With 'kerchief'd head, and eyes brimful of dust,
Thy fibrous nerves, with hatchel-tooth divides.
— I hear a voice of music – and behold!
The ruddy damsel singeth at her wheel,[1]
While by her side the rustic lover sits.
Perchance, his shrewd eye secretly doth count
The mass of skeins, which, hanging on the wall,
Increaseth day by day. Perchance his thought,
(For men have deeper minds than women – sure!)
Is calculating what a thrifty wife
The maid will make; and how his dairy shelves
Shall groan beneath the weight of golden cheese,
Made by her dexterous hand, while many a keg
And pot of butter, to the market borne,
May, transmigrated, on his back appear,
In new thanksgiving coats.
Fain would I ask,
Mine own New England, for thy once loved wheel,
By sofa and piano quite displac'd.
Why dost thou banish from thy parlor-hearth
That old Hygeian harp, whose magic rul'd
Dyspepsia, as the minstrel-shepherd's skill
Exorcis'd Saul's ennui?[2] There was no need,
In those good times, of callisthenics, sure,
And there was less of gadding, and far more
Of home-born, heart-felt comfort, rooted strong
In industry, and bearing such rare fruit,
As wealth might never purchase.
But come back,

1. **wheel:** A spinning wheel, used for spinning yarn or thread.
2. **Hygeian harp . . . Saul's ennui?:** Hygeia, the Greek goddess of health, provided relief from dyspepsia or indigestion; David's playing upon the harp refreshed King Saul when "the evil spirit" was upon him (1 Samuel 16:23).

Thou shred of linen. I did let thee drop,
In my harangue, as wiser ones have lost
The thread of their discourse. What was thy lot
When the rough battery of the loom had stretch'd
And knit thy sinews, and the chemist sun
Thy brown complexion bleach'd?
Methinks I scan
Some idiosyncrasy, that marks thee out
A defunct pillow-case. – Did the trim guest,
To the best chamber usher'd, e'er admire
The snowy whiteness of thy freshen'd youth
Feeding thy vanity? or some sweet babe
Pour its pure dream of innocence on thee?
Say, hast thou listen'd to the sick one's moan,
When there was none to comfort? – or shrunk back
From the dire tossings of the proud man's brow?
Or gather'd from young beauty's restless sigh
A tale of untold love?
Still, close and mute! –
Wilt tell no secrets, ha? – Well then, go down,
With all thy churl-kept hoard of curious lore,
In majesty and mystery, go down
Into the paper-mill, and from its jaws,
Stainless and smooth, emerge. – Happy shall be
The renovation, if on thy fair page
Wisdom and truth, their hallow'd lineaments
Trace for posterity. So shall thine end
Be better than thy birth, and worthier bard
Thine apotheosis immortalise.

[1848]

Ralph Waldo Emerson

[1803–1882]

Ralph Waldo Emerson, whose life and work are described in more detail on page 653 of this volume, is best known for prose works like *Nature* (1836), *Essays* (1841), and *Essays: Second Series* (1844). Like many of the writers who called themselves transcendentalists, however, Emerson was deeply interested in poetry and gave lectures about the crucial role of the poet in American culture. In his essay "The Poet," for example, he affirmed that "the poet is representative. He stands among partial men for the complete man, and apprises us not of his wealth, but of the commonwealth." Emerson himself sought and encouraged other poets to experiment. Nonetheless, his poetry was fairly conventional in form, highly intellectual in content, and constrained in feeling. The texts of "The Rhodora," "The Snow-Storm," and "Hamatreya," are taken from his first volume of poetry, *Poems* (1847). The text of "Days" is taken from its first appearance in the inaugural issue of the *Atlantic Monthly* (November 1857). Emerson later included it in his second book of poetry, *May-Day and Other Pieces* (1867).

The Rhodora:[1] On Being Asked, Whence Is the Flower?

In May, when sea-winds pierced our solitudes,
I found the fresh Rhodora in the woods,
Spreading its leafless blooms in a damp nook,
To please the desert and the sluggish brook.
The purple petals, fallen in the pool,
Made the black water with their beauty gay;
Here might the red-bird come his plumes to cool,
And court the flower that cheapens his array.
Rhodora! if the sages ask thee why
This charm is wasted on the earth and sky,
Tell them, dear, that if eyes were made for seeing,
Then Beauty is its own excuse for being:
Why thou wert there, O rival of the rose!
I never thought to ask, I never knew;
But, in my simple ignorance, suppose
The self-same Power that brought me there brought you.

[1839, 1847]

1. **Rhodora:** A shrub that flowers in the springtime, before its leaves appear; it is common in New England.

The Snow-Storm

Announced by all the trumpets of the sky,
Arrives the snow, and, driving o'er the fields,
Seems nowhere to alight: the whited air
Hides hills and woods, the river, and the heaven,
And veils the farm-house at the garden's end.
The sled and traveller stopped, the courier's feet
Delayed, all friends shut out, the housemates sit

Around the radiant fireplace, enclosed
In a tumultuous privacy of storm.

Come see the north wind's masonry.
Out of an unseen quarry evermore
Furnished with tile, the fierce artificer
Curves his white bastions with projected roof
Round every windward stake, or tree, or door.
Speeding, the myriad-handed, his wild work
So fanciful, so savage, nought cares he
For number or proportion. Mockingly,
On coop or kennel he hangs Parian[1] wreaths;
A swan-like form invests the hidden thorn;
Fills up the farmer's lane from wall to wall,
Maugre the farmer's sighs; and, at the gate,
A tapering turret overtops the work.
And when his hours are numbered, and the world
Is all his own, retiring, as he were not,
Leaves, when the sun appears, astonished Art
To mimic in slow structures, stone by stone,
Built in an age, the mad wind's night-work,
The frolic architecture of the snow.

[1841, 1847]

1. **Parian:** White marble, often used by sculptors in the nineteenth century.

Hamatreya[1]

Minott, Lee, Willard, Hosmer, Meriam, Flint[2]
Possessed the land which rendered to their toil
Hay, corn, roots, hemp, flax, apples, wool, and wood.
Each of these landlords walked amidst his farm,
Saying, ''Tis mine, my children's, and my name's:
How sweet the west wind sounds in my own trees!
How graceful climb those shadows on my hill!

1. **Hamatreya:** In 1845, Emerson copied into his journal a passage from a Hindu sacred book *Vishnu Purana*, which includes stories of the origin of the universe. In the passage, the Earth sings to the god Maitreya, from which Emerson may have derived the name "Hamatreya."
2. **Minott . . . Flint:** Early settlers of Concord, Massachusetts. In a later version of this poem, Emerson revised this list to "Bulkeley, Hunt, Willard, Hosmer, Meriam, Flint," probably to include his own ancestor and early resident of Concord, the Reverend Peter Bulkeley (1583-1659).

I fancy these pure waters and the flags[3]
Know me, as does my dog: we sympathize;
And, I affirm, my actions smack of the soil.'
Where are these men? Asleep beneath their grounds;
And strangers, fond as they, their furrows plough.
Earth laughs in flowers, to see her boastful boys
Earth-proud, proud of the earth which is not theirs;
Who steer the plough, but cannot steer their feet
Clear of the grave.
They added ridge to valley, brook to pond,
And sighed for all that bounded their domain.
'This suits me for a pasture; that's my park;
We must have clay, lime, gravel, granite-ledge,
And misty lowland, where to go for peat.
The land is well, – lies fairly to the south.
'Tis good, when you have crossed the sea and back,
To find the sitfast acres where you left them.'
Ah! the hot owner sees not Death, who adds
Him to his land, a lump of mould the more.
Hear what the Earth says: –

EARTH-SONG

'Mine and yours;
Mine, not yours.
Earth endures;
Stars abide –
Shine down in the old sea;
Old are the shores;
But where are old men?
I who have seen much,
Such have I never seen.

'The lawyer's deed
Ran sure,
In tail,[4]
To them, and to their heirs
Who shall succeed,
Without fail,
Forevermore.

---

3. **flags:** Common name for large irises that grow by watersides.
4. **In tail:** A variant of *entail*, a legal term for the settlement of an estate over several generations of a family.

'Here is the land,
Shaggy with wood,
With its old valley,
Mound, and flood.
But the heritors?
Fled like the flood's foam, –
The lawyer, and the laws,
And the kingdom,
Clean swept herefrom.

'They called me theirs,
Who so controlled me;
Yet every one
Wished to stay, and is gone.
How am I theirs,
If they cannot hold me,
But I hold them?'

When I heard the Earth-song,
I was no longer brave;
My avarice cooled
Like lust in the chill of the grave.

[1847]

DAYS

Daughters of Time, the hypocritic Days,
Muffled and dumb, like barefoot dervishes,
And marching single in an endless file,
Bring diadems and fagots[1] in their hands.
To each they offer gifts, after his will, –
Bread, kingdoms, stars, or sky that holds them all.
I, in my pleached[2] garden, watched the pomp,
Forgot my morning wishes, hastily
Took a few herbs and apples, and the Day
Turned and departed silent. I, too late,
Under her solemn fillet saw the scorn.

[1857]

---

1. **fagots:** A bundle of sticks, used for fuel.
2. **pleached:** An arbor formed by twisting and shaping boughs of trees and shrubs.

Elizabeth Oakes Smith

[1806-1893]

Widely known in her day as both a writer and a leader of the crusade for women's rights, Elizabeth Oakes Smith was born and educated in North Yarmouth, Maine. In 1823, she married Seba Smith, the editor of the *Eastern Argus*, a weekly newspaper published in Portland, Maine. In order to help her husband, Smith wrote constantly for the *Argus*, often anonymously and occasionally over the signature *E*. After Seba Smith lost most of the family savings in speculations, the couple and their six children moved to New York City. There, Smith began to publish novels and stories under the pseudonym "Ernest Helfenstein" or as "Mrs. Seba Smith." Earning a reputation for her frequent contributions to literary magazines, she gained her greatest success with a long poem, "The Sinless Child," published serially in the *Southern Literary Messenger* in 1842. That was the title poem of a collection of poetry she published the following year; in 1845, it was followed by *The Poetical Writings of Elizabeth Oakes Smith*, which included a laudatory preface by Rufus Griswold, the successful editor of the influential anthology *The Poets and Poetry of America*. Her poems, largely conventional in style, dealt with popular themes: the deaths of innocent children, the stages of life, and the importance of the home, religious faith, and self-reliance. The following texts are taken from the second edition of her *Poetical Writings*, published in 1846.

The Unattained

And is this life? and are we born for this?
To follow phantoms that elude the grasp,
Or whatsoe'er secured, within our clasp
To withering lie, as if each earthly kiss
Were doomed death's shuddering touch alone to meet.
O Life! hast thou reserved no cup of bliss?
Must still THE UNATTAINED beguile our feet?
The UNATTAINED with yearnings fill the breast,
That rob, for aye, the spirit of its rest?
Yes, this is Life; and everywhere we meet,
Not victor crowns, but wailings of defeat;
Yet faint thou not, thou dost apply a test,
That shall incite thee onward, upward still,
The present can not sate, or e'er thy spirit fill.

[1846]

THE DROWNED MARINER

A mariner[1] sat on the shrouds one night,
The wind was piping free,
Now bright, now dimmed was the moonlight pale,
And the phosphor gleamed in the wake of the whale,
As he floundered in the sea;
The scud was flying athwart the sky,
The gathering winds went whistling by,
And the wave as it towered, then fell in spray,
Looked an emerald wall in the moonlight ray.

The mariner swayed and rocked on the mast,
But the tumult pleased him well,
Down the yawning wave his eye he cast,
And the monsters watched as they hurried past,
Or lightly rose and fell;
For their broad, damp fins were under the tide,
And they lashed as they passed the vessel's side,
And their filmy eyes, all huge and grim,
Glared fiercely up, and they glared at him.

Now freshens the gale, and the brave ship goes
Like an uncurbed steed along.
A sheet of flame is the spray she throws,
As her gallant prow the water plows –
But the ship is fleet and strong:
The topsails are reefed and the sails are furled,
And onward she sweeps o'er the watery world,
And dippeth her spars in the surging flood;
But there came no chill to the mariner's blood.

Wildly she rocks, but he swingeth at ease,
And holds him by the shroud;
And as she careens to the crowding breeze,
The gaping deep the mariner sees,
And the surging heareth loud.
Was that a face, looking up at him,
With its pallid cheek and its cold eyes dim?

1. **mariner:** A sailor. Among the nautical terms used in the poem are *shrouds*, a set of ropes that stretch from the masthead to the sides of a ship for the support of the mast, and *spars*, the poles that support the riggings on a ship.

Did it beckon him down? did it call his name?
Now rolleth the ship the way whence it came.

The mariner looked, and he saw with dread,
    A face he knew too well;
And the cold eyes glared, the eyes of the dead,
And its long hair out on the wave was spread.
    Was there a tale to tell?
The stout ship rocked with a reeling speed,
And the mariner groaned, as well he need,
For ever down, as she plunged on her side,
The dead face gleamed from the briny tide.

Bethink thee, mariner, well of the past,
    A voice calls loud for thee –
There's a stifled prayer, the first, the last,
The plunging ship on her beam is cast,
    Oh, where shall thy burial be?
Bethink thee of oaths that were lightly spoken,
Bethink thee of vows that were lightly broken,
Bethink thee of all that is dear to thee –
For thou art alone on the raging sea:

Alone in the dark, alone on the wave,
    To buffet the storm alone –
To struggle aghast at thy watery grave,
To struggle, and feel there is none to save –
    God shield thee, helpless one!
The stout limbs yield, for their strength is past,
The trembling hands on the deep are cast,
The white brow gleams a moment more,
Then slowly sinks – the struggle is o'er.

Down, down where the storm is hushed to sleep,
    Where the sea its dirge shall swell,
Where the amber drops for thee shall weep,
And the rose-lipped shell her music keep,
    There thou shalt slumber well.
The gem and the pearl lie heaped at thy side,
They fell from the neck of the beautiful bride,
From the strong man's hand, from the maiden's brow,
As they slowly sunk to the wave below.

A peopled home is the ocean bed,
    The mother and child are there –
The fervent youth and the hoary head,

The maid, with her floating locks outspread,
    The babe with its silken hair,
As the water moveth they lightly sway,
And the tranquil lights on their features play;
And there is each cherished and beautiful form,
Away from decay, and away from the storm.

[1846]

Henry Wadsworth Longfellow

[1807-1882]

The most revered poet of the period, Henry Wadsworth Longfellow was born in Portland, Maine, and educated at Bowdoin College, where he was the classmate of Nathaniel Hawthorne. Skilled at languages, Longfellow studied German, French, Italian, and Spanish during extended stays in Europe. He accepted a professorship first at Bowdoin and later at Harvard, where he taught until 1854. Adapting a wide range of European poetic techniques, Longfellow was known for his careful prosody and polished style. Always popular for his direct and graceful treatment of common themes like the importance of courage and the beauty of nature, Longfellow scored his greatest commercial successes with a series of book-length narrative poems about early American history, especially *The Song of Hiawatha* (1855) and *The Courtship of Miles Standish* (1858). His poems were popular with a wide audience, who read them aloud and memorized them for recitation in school and on public occasions. He also published shorter poems in all the major literary magazines. The texts of the following poems are taken from *Putnam's Monthly*, where they were first published in 1854 and 1855.

Henry Wadsworth Longfellow

This photograph of Longfellow was taken in Boston in 1860 or 1861, by which time he had become the most popular poet in the United States.

THE JEWISH CEMETERY AT NEWPORT[1]

How strange it seems! These Hebrews in their graves,
Close by the street of this fair sea-port town;
Silent beside the never-silent waves,
At rest in all this moving up and down!

The trees are white with dust, that o'er their sleep
Wave their broad curtains in the south-wind's breath,
While underneath such leafy tents they keep
The long, mysterious Exodus of Death.

And these sepulchral stones, so old and brown,
That pave with level flags[2] their burial-place,
Are like the tablets of the Law, thrown down
And broken by Moses at the mountain's base.

The very names recorded here are strange,
Of foreign accent, and of different climes;
Alvares and Rivera interchange
With Abraham and Jacob of old times.

"Blessed be God! for he created Death!"
The mourners said: "and Death is rest and peace."
Then added, in the certainty of faith:
"And giveth Life, that never more shall cease."

Closed are the portals of their Synagogue,
No Psalms of David now the silence break,
No rabbi reads the ancient Decalogue[3]
In the grand dialect the Prophets spake.

Gone are the living, but the dead remain,
And not neglected, for a hand unseen,
Scattering its bounty, like a summer rain,
Still keeps their graves and their remembrance green.

How came they here? What burst of Christian hate;
What persecution, merciless, and blind,
Drove o'er the sea, – that desert, desolate –
These Ishmaels and Hagars[4] of mankind?

---

1. **Newport:** In the seventeenth century, Rhode Island was the only colony that permitted Jewish immigration. The first permanent Jewish settlement was in Newport, home of the oldest synagogue in the United States.
2. **level flags:** Flagstones.
3. **Decalogue:** The Ten Commandments.
4. **Ishmaels and Hagars:** Outcasts. When Abraham's son, Isaac, was born to his wife Sarah, she had Abraham's mistress, the slave girl Hagar, and Hagar's son Ishmael driven from their home. See Genesis 21.

They lived in narrow streets and lanes obscure,
  Ghetto or Judenstrass,[5] in mirk and mire;
Taught in the school of patience to endure
  The life of anguish and the death of fire.

All their lives long, with the unleavened bread
  And bitter herbs of exile and its fears,
The wasting famine of the heart they fed,
  And slaked its thirst with marah of their tears.[6]

Anathema maranatha![7] was the cry
  That rang from town to town, from street to street;
At every gate the accursed Mordecai[8]
  Was mocked, and jeered, and spurned by Christian feet.

Pride and humiliation hand in hand
  Walked with them through the world, where'er they went;
Trampled and beaten were they as the sand,
  And yet unshaken as the continent.

For in the back-ground, figures vague and vast,
  Of patriarchs and of prophets rose sublime,
And all the great traditions of the Past
  They saw reflected in the coming time.

And thus for ever with reverted look,
  The mystic volume of the world they read,
Spelling it backward like a Hebrew book,[9]
  Till Life became a Legend of the Dead.

But ah! what once has been shall be no more!
  The groaning earth in travail and in pain
Brings forth its races, but does not restore,
  And the dead nations never rise again.

[1854]

---

5. **Ghetto or Judenstrass:** *Ghetto* (Italian) originally meant a section of a city to which Jews were restricted; *Judenstrass* is German for street of the Jews.
6. **marah of their tears:** The Hebrews wandered in the wilderness for three days without water before they arrived at a place where the water was too bitter to drink: "therefore the name of it was called Marah" (Exodus 15:23).
7. **Anathema Maranatha!:** Cursed by God. See 1 Corinthians 16:22: "If any man love not the Lord Jesus Christ, let him be Anathema Maranatha."
8. **Mordecai:** Jewish leader persecuted by the Persians. See Esther 2–8.
9. **Hebrew book:** The text of a Hebrew book is read from right to left.

My Lost Youth

Often I think of the beautiful town
That is seated by the sea;
Often in thought go up and down
The pleasant streets of that dear old town,
And my youth comes back to me.
And a verse of a Lapland song[1]
Is haunting my memory still:
A boy's will is the wind's will,
And the thoughts of youth are long, long thoughts."

I can see the shadowy lines of its trees,
And catch, in sudden gleams,
The sheen of the far-surrounding seas,
And islands that were the Hesperides[2]
Of all my boyish dreams.
And the burden of that old song,
It murmurs and whispers still:
"A boy's will is the wind's will,
And the thoughts of youth are long, long thoughts."

I remember the black wharves and the slips,
And the sea-tides tossing free;
And Spanish sailors with bearded lips,
And the beauty and mystery of the ships,
And the magic of the sea.
And the voice of that wayward song
Is singing and saying still:
"A boy's will is the wind's will,
And the thoughts of youth are long, long thoughts."

I remember the bulwarks by the shore,
And the fort upon the hill;
The sun-rise gun, with its hollow roar,
The drum-beat repeated o'er and o'er,
And the bugle wild and shrill.
And the music of that old song
Throbs in my memory still:
"A boy's will is the wind's will,
And the thoughts of youth are long, long thoughts."

---

1. **Lapland song:** Longfellow took the refrain of this poem from a song translated in John Scheffer's *The History of Lapland* (1674).
2. **Hesperides:** In Greek mythology, three nymphs, the Hesperides, maintained a beautiful garden with a tree that bore golden apples.

I remember the sea-fight far away,[3]
How it thundered o'er the tide!
And the dead captains, as they lay
In their graves, o'erlooking the tranquil bay,
Where they in battle died.
And the sound of that mournful song
Goes through me with a thrill:
"A boy's will is the wind's will,
And the thoughts of youth are long, long thoughts."

I can see the breezy dome of groves,
The shadows of Deering's Woods;
And the friendships old and the early loves
Come back with a Sabbath sound, as of doves
In quiet neighborhoods.
And the verse of that sweet old song,
It flutters and murmurs still:
"A boy's will is the wind's will,
And the thoughts of youth are long, long thoughts."

I remember the gleams and glooms that dart
Across the schoolboy's brain;
The song and the silence in the heart,
That in part are prophecies, and in part
Are longings wild and vain.
And the voice of that fitful song
Sings on, and is never still:
"A boy's will is the wind's will,
And the thoughts of youth are long, long thoughts."

There are things of which I may not speak;
There are dreams that cannot die;
There are thoughts that make the strong heart weak,
And bring a pallor into the cheek,
And a mist before the eye.
And the words of that fatal song
Come over me like a chill:
"A boy's will is the wind's will,
And the thoughts of youth are long, long thoughts."

Strange to me now are the forms I meet
When I visit the dear old town;

---

3. **sea-fight far away:** Longfellow wrote this poem about his hometown, Portland, Maine, off the shore of which the American *Enterprise* and the British *Boxer* fought a sea battle during the War of 1812.

But the native air is pure and sweet,
And the trees that o'ershadow each well-known street,
As they balance up and down,
Are singing the beautiful song,
Are sighing and whispering still:
"A boy's will is the wind's will,
And the thoughts of youth are long, long thoughts."

And Deering's Woods are fresh and fair,
And with joy that is almost pain
My heart goes back to wander there,
And among the dreams of the days that were,
I find my lost youth again.
And the strange and beautiful song,
The groves are repeating it still:
"A boy's will is the wind's will,
And the thoughts of youth are long, long thoughts."

[1855]

John Greenleaf Whittier

[1807-1892]

The son of Quakers whose values he fully embraced, John Greenleaf Whittier was born on a farm near Haverhill, Massachusetts. His first book, *Legends of New England in Prose and in Verse* (1831), reflected his deep interest in American folklore and history. But his attention was soon drawn to the injustices of his own time, especially slavery. Whittier announced himself an abolitionist in a pamphlet, *Justice and Expediency* (1833). From that year through the end of the Civil War, he devoted himself wholeheartedly to the antislavery crusade as both an editor and author – leaving "the Muses' haunt to turn the crank of an opinion mill," as Whittier himself later put it. By then, he had earned a reputation as one of the Fireside Poets and was the celebrated author of such works as *Snow-Bound* (1866), a nostalgic evocation of the rural New England of his childhood. But the subject matter for which Whittier was best known during the antebellum period is indicated by the titles of collections like *Poems Written during the Progress of the Abolition Question* (1838) and *Voices of Freedom* (1846). Many of the poems in those collections were initially published in antislavery newspapers like the *Liberator*, where the first of the following poems appeared in 1835, and the *Pennsylvania Freeman*, which Whittier edited and where the second poem appeared in 1838. The texts are taken from *The Complete Works of John Greenleaf Whittier* (1892).

THE HUNTERS OF MEN[1]

Have ye heard of our hunting, o'er mountain and glen,
Through cane-brake and forest, – the hunting of men?
The lords of our land to this hunting have gone,
As the fox-hunter follows the sound of the horn;
Hark! the cheer and the hallo! the crack of the whip,
And the yell of the hound as he fastens his grip!
All blithe are our hunters, and noble their match,
Though hundreds are caught, there are millions to catch.
So speed to their hunting, o'er mountain and glen,
Through cane-brake and forest, – the hunting of men!

Gay luck to our hunters! how nobly they ride
In the glow of their zeal, and the strength of their pride!
The priest with his cassock flung back on the wind,
Just screening the politic statesman behind;
The saint and the sinner, with cursing and prayer,
The drunk and the sober, ride merrily there.
And woman, kind woman, wife, widow, and maid,
For the good of the hunted, is lending her aid:
Her foot 's in the stirrup, her hand on the rein,
How blithely she rides to the hunting of men!

Oh, goodly and grand is our hunting to see,
In this "land of the brave and this home of the free."
Priest, warrior, and statesman, from Georgia to Maine,
All mounting the saddle, all grasping the rein;
Right merrily hunting the black man, whose sin
Is the curl of his hair and the hue of his skin!
Woe, now, to the hunted who turns him at bay!
Will our hunters be turned from their purpose and prey?
Will their hearts fail within them? their nerves tremble, when
All roughly they ride to the hunting of men?

Ho! alms for our hunters! all weary and faint,
Wax the curse of the sinner and prayer of the saint.
The horn is wound faintly, the echoes are still,
Over cane-brake and river, and forest and hill.

---

1. In a headnote to the poem, Whittier later explained: "These lines were written when the orators of the American Colonization Society were demanding that the free black should be sent to Africa, and opposing Emancipation unless expatriation followed. See the report of the proceedings of the society at its annual meeting in 1834." Like many abolitionists, Whittier favored emancipation and education for slaves and strongly opposed the idea of mandatory colonization in Africa.

Haste, alms for our hunters! the hunted once more
Have turned from their flight with their backs to the shore:
What right have they here in the home of the white,
Shadowed o'er by our banner of Freedom and Right?
Ho! alms for the hunters! or never again
Will they ride in their pomp to the hunting of men!

Alms, alms for our hunters! why will ye delay,
When their pride and their glory are melting away?
The parson has turned; for, on charge of his own,
Who goeth a warfare, or hunting, alone?
The politic statesman looks back with a sigh,
There is doubt in his heart, there is fear in his eye.
Oh, haste, lest that doubting and fear shall prevail,
And the head of his steed take the place of the tail.
Oh, haste, ere he leave us! for who will ride then,
For pleasure or gain, to the hunting of men?

[1835, 1892]

The Farewell of a Virginia Slave Mother to Her Daughters Sold into Southern Bondage

Gone, gone, – sold and gone,
To the rice-swamp dank and lone.
Where the slave-whip ceaseless swings,
Where the noisome insect stings,
Where the fever demon strews
Poison with the falling dews,
Where the sickly sunbeams glare
Through the hot and misty air;
Gone, gone, – sold and gone,
To the rice-swamp dank and lone,
From Virginia's hills and waters;
Woe is me, my stolen daughters!

Gone, gone, – sold and gone,
To the rice-swamp dank and lone.
There no mother's eye is near them,
There no mother's ear can hear them;
Never, when the torturing lash

Seams their back with many a gash,
Shall a mother's kindness bless them,
Or a mother's arms caress them.
Gone, gone, – sold and gone,
To the rice-swamp dank and lone,
From Virginia's hills and waters;
Woe is me, my stolen daughters!

Gone, gone, – sold and gone,
To the rice-swamp dank and lone.
Oh, when weary, sad, and slow,
From the fields at night they go,
Faint with toil, and racked with pain,
To their cheerless homes again,
There no brother's voice shall greet them
There no father's welcome meet them.
Gone, gone, – sold and gone,
To the rice-swamp dank and lone,
From Virginia's hills and waters;
Woe is me, my stolen daughters!

Gone, gone, – sold and gone,
To the rice-swamp dank and lone.
From the tree whose shadow lay
On their childhood's place of play;
From the cool spring where they drank;
Rock, and hill, and rivulet bank;
From the solemn house of prayer,
And the holy counsels there;
Gone, gone, – sold and gone,
To the rice-swamp dank and lone,
From Virginia's hills and waters;
Woe is me, my stolen daughters!

Gone, gone, – sold and gone,
To the rice-swamp dank and lone;
Toiling through the weary day,
And at night the spoiler's prey.
Oh, that they had earlier died,
Sleeping calmly, side by side,
Where the tyrant's power is o'er,
And the fetter galls no more!
Gone, gone, – sold and gone,

To the rice-swamp dank and lone,
From Virginia's hills and waters;
Woe is me, my stolen daughters!

Gone, gone, – sold and gone,
To the rice-swamp dank and lone.
By the holy love He beareth;
By the bruised reed He spareth;
Oh, may He, to whom alone
All their cruel wrongs are known,
Still their hope and refuge prove,
With a more than mother's love.
Gone, gone, – sold and gone,
To the rice-swamp dank and lone,
From Virginia's hills and waters;
Woe is me, my stolen daughters!

[1838, 1892]

Edgar Allan Poe

[1809-1849]

Edgar Allan Poe, whose life and work are described in more detail on page 1018 of this volume, is now best known for his short stories. But he initially set out to become a poet, publishing three collections of verse between 1827 and 1831. Finding that he could not earn a living as a poet, Poe later supported himself by editing and writing for periodicals, in which most of his prose pieces appeared. It was not until 1845, when he published "The Raven," that Poe finally gained the fame as a poet for which he had so long hungered. On the strength of that poem, which caused a sensation, Poe immediately published *The Raven and Other Poems* (1845). But he published only a few more poems before his death in 1849. Like his poetry, Poe's poetic theory was at odds with dominant conceptions of the role of poetry during the period. Poe rejected didactic poetry, insisting that poetry should appeal strictly to a sense of beauty, inducing in the reader an almost hypnotic state in which mood triumphed over thought. The texts are taken from the following sources: "[Sonnet – To Science]," from *Al Aaraaf, Tamerlane, and Minor Poems* (1829); "To Helen," from *Poems* (1831); "The Raven," from the *American Review* (1845); and "Annabel Lee," from the *Southern Literary Messenger* (1849).

[SONNET – TO SCIENCE][1]

Science! meet daughter of old Time thou art
Who alterest all things with thy peering eyes!
Why prey'st thou thus upon the poet's heart,
Vulture! whose wings are dull realities!
How should he love thee – or how deem thee wise
Who woulds't not leave him, in his wandering,
To seek for treasure in the jewell'd skies
Albeit, he soar with an undaunted wing?
Hast thou not dragg'd Diana[2] from her car,
And driv'n the Hamadryad[3] from the wood
To seek a shelter in some happier star?
The gentle Naiad[4] from her fountain-flood?
The elfin from the green grass? and from me
The summer dream beneath the shrubbery?

[1829]

---

1. The text is taken from the first printing in *Al Aaraaf* (1829), where the poem was untitled. Poe later reprinted it several times, sometimes as "Sonnet" and finally in 1845 as "Sonnet – To Science," the title by which it is widely known today.
2. **Diana:** Roman goddess of the moon, her "car."
3. **Hamadryad:** Nymphs of Roman and Greek mythology who lived in trees.
4. **Naiad:** Water nymphs of Greek mythology who lived in freshwater lakes, rivers, springs, and fountains.

TO HELEN

Helen, thy beauty is to me
Like those Nicean barks[1] of yore,
That gently, o'er a perfum'd sea,
The weary way-worn wanderer bore
To his own native shore.

On desperate seas long wont to roam,
Thy hyacinth hair,[2] thy classic face,
Thy Naiad[3] airs have brought me home
To the beauty of fair Greece,
And the grandeur of old Rome.

---

1. **Nicean barks:** Ships from the ancient Greek city of Nicea.
2. **hyacinth hair:** The Greek god Apollo created the hyacinth, a flower, after the death of a beautiful young man, Hyacinthus.
3. **Naiad:** Water nymphs of Greek mythology who lived in freshwater lakes, rivers, springs, and fountains.

Lo! in that little window-niche
How statue-like I see thee stand!
The folded scroll within thy hand –
A Psyche from the regions which
Are Holy land!

[1831]

THE RAVEN[1]

Once upon a midnight dreary, while I pondered, weak and weary,
Over many a quaint and curious volume of forgotten lore,
While I nodded, nearly napping, suddenly there came a tapping,
As of some one gently rapping, rapping at my chamber door.
" 'Tis some visiter," I muttered, "tapping at my chamber door –
Only this, and nothing more."

Ah, distinctly I remember it was in the bleak December,
And each separate dying ember wrought its ghost upon the floor.
Eagerly I wished the morrow; – vainly I had tried to borrow
From my books surcease of sorrow – sorrow for the lost Lenore –
For the rare and radiant maiden whom the angels name Lenore –
Nameless here for evermore.

And the silken sad uncertain rustling of each purple curtain
Thrilled me – filled me with fantastic terrors never felt before;
So that now, to still the beating of my heart, I stood repeating
" 'Tis some visiter entreating entrance at my chamber door –
Some late visiter entreating entrance at my chamber door; –
This it is, and nothing more."

Presently my soul grew stronger; hesitating then no longer,
"Sir," said I, "or Madam, truly your forgiveness I implore;
But the fact is I was napping, and so gently you came rapping,
And so faintly you came tapping, tapping at my chamber door,
That I scarce was sure I heard you" – here I opened wide the door; –
Darkness there, and nothing more.

Deep into that darkness peering, long I stood there wondering, fearing,
Doubting, dreaming dreams no mortal ever dared to dream before;
But the silence was unbroken, and the darkness gave no token,

1. The poem was first published anonymously in the *American Review*, where it was identified as "By — Quarles." In a long and laudatory note preceding the poem, the editor emphasized the ways in which it illustrated the alliterative, rhythmical, and metrical resources of the English language.

And the only word there spoken was the whispered word, "Lenore!"
This *I* whispered, and an echo murmured back the word, "Lenore!"
                                        Merely this, and nothing more.

Then into the chamber turning, all my soul within me burning,
Soon I heard again a tapping somewhat louder than before.
"Surely," said I, "surely that is something at my window lattice;
Let me see, then, what thereat is, and this mystery explore –
Let my heart be still a moment and this mystery explore; –
                                        'Tis the wind, and nothing more!"

Open here I flung the shutter, when, with many a flirt and flutter,
In there stepped a stately raven of the saintly days of yore;
Not the least obeisance made he; not an instant stopped or stayed he;
But, with mien of lord or lady, perched above my chamber door –
Perched upon a bust of Pallas[2] just above my chamber door –
                                        Perched, and sat, and nothing more.

Then this ebony bird beguiling my sad fancy into smiling,
By the grave and stern decorum of the countenance it wore,
"Though thy crest be shorn and shaven, thou," I said, "art sure no craven,
Ghastly grim and ancient raven wandering from the Nightly shore –
Tell me what thy lordly name is on the Night's Plutonian shore!"[3]
                                        Quoth the raven, "Nevermore."

Much I marvelled this ungainly fowl to hear discourse so plainly,
Though its answer little meaning – little relevancy bore;
For we cannot help agreeing that no sublunary being
Ever yet was blessed with seeing bird above his chamber door –
Bird or beast upon the sculptured bust above his chamber door,
                                        With such name as "Nevermore."

But the raven, sitting lonely on the placid bust, spoke only
That one word, as if his soul in that one word he did outpour.
Nothing farther then he uttered – not a feather then he fluttered –
Till I scarcely more than muttered, "Other friends have flown before –
On the morrow *he* will leave me, as my hopes have flown before."
                                        Quoth the raven, "Nevermore."

Wondering at the stillness broken by reply so aptly spoken,
"Doubtless," said I, "what it utters is its only stock and store,
Caught from some unhappy master whom unmerciful Disaster

---

2. **bust of Pallas:** Pallas Athena, the Greek goddess of wisdom and the arts.
3. **Night's Plutonian shore:** In Greek mythology, Pluto (or Hades) was the god of the underworld, his dark kingdom.

Followed fast and followed faster – so, when Hope he would adjure,
Stern Despair returned, instead of the sweet Hope he dared adjure –
That sad answer, "Nevermore!"

But the raven still beguiling all my sad soul into smiling,
Straight I wheeled a cushioned seat in front of bird, and bust, and door;
Then upon the velvet sinking, I betook myself to linking
Fancy unto fancy, thinking what this ominous bird of yore –
What this grim, ungainly, ghastly, gaunt, and ominous bird of yore
Meant in croaking "Nevermore."

This I sat engaged in guessing, but no syllable expressing
To the fowl whose fiery eyes now burned into my bosom's core;
This and more I sat divining, with my head at ease reclining
On the cushion's velvet lining that the lamplight gloated o'er,
But whose velvet violet lining with the lamplight gloating o'er,
She shall press, ah, nevermore!

Then, methought, the air grew denser, perfumed from an unseen censer
Swung by angels whose faint foot-falls tinkled on the tufted floor.
"Wretch," I cried, "thy God hath lent thee – by these angels he hath sent thee
Respite – respite and Nepenthe[4] from thy memories of Lenore!
Let me quaff this kind Nepenthe and forget this lost Lenore!"
Quoth the raven, "Nevermore."

"Prophet!" said I, "thing of evil! – prophet still, if bird or devil! –
Whether Tempter sent, or whether tempest tossed thee here ashore,
Desolate, yet all undaunted, on this desert land enchanted –
On this home by Horror haunted – tell me truly, I implore –
Is there – *is* there balm in Gilead?[5] – tell me – tell me, I implore!"
Quoth the raven, "Nevermore."

"Prophet!" said I, "thing of evil! – prophet still, if bird or devil!
By that Heaven that bends above us – by that God we both adore –
Tell this soul with sorrow laden if, within the distant Aidenn,[6]
It shall clasp a sainted maiden whom the angels name Lenore –
Clasp a rare and radiant maiden whom the angels name Lenore."
Quoth the raven, "Nevermore."

"Be that word our sign of parting, bird or fiend!" I shrieked, upstarting –
"Get thee back into the tempest and the Night's Plutonian shore!
Leave no black plume as a token of that lie thy soul hath spoken!

---

4. **Nepenthe:** Ancient drug used to ease pain or grief.
5. **Gilead:** See Jeremiah 46:11: "Is there no balm in Gilead, no physician there?" The evergreens in Gilead, a mountainous region of Jordan, were thought to have medicinal powers.
6. **Aidenn:** Probably an alternative spelling of *Eden.*

Leave my loneliness unbroken! – quit the bust above my door!
Take thy beak from out my heart, and take thy form from off my door!"
Quoth the raven, "Nevermore."

And the raven, never flitting, still is sitting, still is sitting
On the pallid bust of Pallas just above my chamber door;
And his eyes have all the seeming of a demon that is dreaming.
And the lamp-light o'er him streaming throws his shadow on the floor;
And my soul from out that shadow that lies floating on the floor
Shall be lifted – nevermore!

[1845]

ANNABEL LEE

It was many and many a year ago,
In a kingdom by the sea,
That a maiden there lived whom you may know
By the name of Annabel Lee; –
And this maiden she lived with no other thought
Than to love and be loved by me.

She was a child and *I* was a child,
In this kingdom by the sea,
But we loved with a love that was more than love –
I and my Annabel Lee –
With a love that the wingéd seraphs of Heaven
Coveted her and me.

And this was the reason that, long ago,
In this kingdom by the sea,
A wind blew out of a cloud by night
Chilling my Annabel Lee;
So that her high-born kinsmen came
And bore her away from me,
To shut her up in a sepulchre
In this kingdom by the sea.

The angels, not half so happy in Heaven,
Went envying her and me;
Yes! that was the reason (as all men know,
In this kingdom by the sea)
That the wind came out of the cloud, chilling
And killing my Annabel Lee.

But our love it was stronger by far than the love
  Of those who were older than we –
  Of many far wiser than we –
And neither the angels in Heaven above
  Nor the demons down under the sea
Can ever dissever my soul from the soul
  Of the beautiful Annabel Lee: –

For the moon never beams without bringing me dreams
  Of the beautiful Annabel Lee;
And the stars never rise but I see the bright eyes
  Of the beautiful Annabel Lee;
And so, all the night-tide, I lie down by the side
Of my darling, my darling, my life and my bride
  In her sepulchre there by the sea –
  In her tomb by the side of the sea.

[1849]

Frances E. W. Harper

[1825-1911]

Frances E. W. Harper
This undated photograph, which was later used as the frontispiece of her *Poems* (1898), is the only known portrait of Harper.

Among the first and most wide-ranging of African American women writers, Frances Ellen Watkins Harper was the only child born to free parents in Baltimore, Maryland. Forced by economic pressures to leave school at thirteen, Harper educated herself and later taught school in Ohio. Her first volume of poetry, *Forest Leaves*, appeared in 1845. With the encouragement of abolitionists, Harper later published *Poems on Miscellaneous Subjects*. Heavily promoted by William Lloyd Garrison, the editor of the abolitionist newspaper the *Liberator*, the volume sold twelve thousand copies when it was published in 1854. That same year, Harper joined the underground railroad and became a traveling lecturer for the Maine Anti-Slavery Society. She also published poems, essays, and stories in a variety of periodicals, including the new *Anglo-African Magazine*, established in 1859 to showcase the works of African American writers. After the Civil War, Harper worked for the education and enfranchisement of African Americans; she also continued to publish stories and a novel, *Iola Leroy; or, Shadows Uplifted* (1892). The texts of the following poems are taken from *Poems on Miscellaneous Subjects* (1854).

THE SLAVE MOTHER

Heard you that shriek? It rose
So wildly on the air,
It seemed as if a burden'd heart
Was breaking in despair.

Saw you those hands so sadly clasped –
The bowed and feeble head –
The shuddering of that fragile form –
That look of grief and dread?

Saw you the sad, imploring eye?
Its every glance was pain,
As if a storm of agony
Were sweeping through the brain.

She is a mother, pale with fear,
Her boy clings to her side,
And in her kirtle[1] vainly tries
His trembling form to hide.

He is not hers,[2] although she bore
For him a mother's pains;
He is not hers, although her blood
Is coursing through his veins!

He is not hers, for cruel hands
May rudely tear apart
The only wreath of household love
That binds her breaking heart.

His love has been a joyous light
That o'er her pathway smiled,
A fountain gushing ever new,
Amid life's desert wild.

1. **kirtle:** A woman's long dress or skirt.
2. **He is not hers:** By law, the status of the mother determined whether a child was free or a slave.

His lightest word has been a tone
    Of music round her heart,
Their lives a streamlet blent in one —
    Oh, Father! must they part?

They tear him from her circling arms,
    Her last and fond embrace.
Oh! never more may her sad eyes
    Gaze on his mournful face.

No marvel, then, these bitter shrieks
    Disturb the listening air:
She is a mother, and her heart
    Is breaking in despair.

[1854]

Ethiopia[1]

Yes! Ethiopia yet shall stretch
    Her bleeding hands abroad;
Her cry of agony shall reach
    The burning throne of God.

The tyrant's yoke from off her neck,
    His fetters from her soul,
The mighty hand of God shall break,
    And spurn the base control.

Redeemed from dust and freed from chains,
    Her sons shall lift their eyes;
From cloud-capt hills and verdant plains
    Shall shouts of triumph rise.

Upon her dark, despairing brow,
    Shall play a smile of peace;
For God shall bend unto her wo,
    And bid her sorrows cease.

'Neath sheltering vines and stately palms
    Shall laughing children play,
And aged sires with joyous psalms
    Shall gladden every day.

1. **Ethiopia:** A country in northeastern Africa; in the nineteenth century, *Ethiopia* was frequently synonymous with black Africa.

Secure by night, and blest by day,
Shall pass her happy hours;
Nor human tigers hunt for prey
Within her peaceful bowers.

Then, Ethiopia! stretch, oh! stretch
Thy bleeding hands abroad;
Thy cry of agony shall reach
And find redress from God.

[1854]

Rose Terry Cooke

[1827-1892]

Born in Connecticut, Rose Terry Cooke was educated at the Hartford Female Seminary and worked briefly as a teacher and a governess. When she received an inheritance in 1847, she was free to devote herself to writing. Her short stories began to appear regularly in the leading literary magazines, *Putnam's Monthly* and *Harper's Monthly*. When the *Atlantic Monthly* was established in 1857, one of her stories was the lead work of fiction in the first issue; thereafter, Cooke published frequently in the *Atlantic*. While she is now known primarily for her short stories, Cooke also wrote poetry on a variety of popular themes ranging from the changing seasons to the death of children, as well as ballads about historical events in the United States. The texts of the following poems are taken from her *Poems* (1861).

HERE

Sweet summer-night, beside the sea,
Cast all thy sweet life over me!
Thy silence and serenity,
Thy healing and content;
The rushing waves that fall and break
Unutterable music make,
And words that no man ever spake
Are to its measure lent.

The salt wind kisses into rest
Both languid eye and fevered breast,
The cool gray rock, with sea-weeds drest,

Gives shadow, still with strength;
The bitter and baptismal sea
With living water sprinkles me,
Slow patience sets her bondsman[1] free,
And blesses him at length.

There is a time in every tide
When surf and billow both subside,
And on the outward current glide
Both shark and pirate sail;
The shipwrecked sailor, cast ashore,
Perceives afar that lessening roar,
And gives one desperate struggle more.
Ah! shall that struggle fail?

[1861]

1. **bondsman:** A servant forced to work without wages; a slave.

Captive

The Summer comes, the Summer dies,
Red leaves whirl idly from the tree,
But no more cleaving of the skies,
No southward sunshine waits for me!

You shut me in a gilded cage,
You deck the bars with tropic flowers,
Nor know that freedom's living rage
Defies you through the listless hours.

What passion fierce, what service true,
Could ever such a wrong requite?
What gift, or clasp, or kiss from you
Were worth an hour of soaring flight?

I beat my wings against the wire,
I pant my trammelled heart away;
The fever of one mad desire
Burns and consumes me all the day.

What care I for your tedious love,
For tender word or fond caress?
I die for one free flight above,
One rapture of the wilderness!

[1861]

"The Harvest Is Past"[1]

Go, dead Summer, o'er the seas away;
Autumn at her vespers[2] now will kneel and pray,
Sunlit vapors on the mountains stray,
Red grows the round moon, – Summer goes away.

Go, dead Summer! the birds will care,
They will follow on the soft sea-air,
While the south-wind breathes a low prayer,
And the perfumed pine-leaves thy shroud prepare.

Go, dead Summer! go, to come again.
All things rise but madness and pain.
New green grasses flicker on the plain,
Only a lost life comes not again.

One dead Summer never shall return.
In its ashes no red embers burn.
Over it vainly the tired soul may yearn.
It is dead, wept, buried: how can it return?

[1861]

1. **"The . . . Past"**: "The harvest is past, the summer is ended, and we are not saved" (Jeremiah 8:20).
2. **vespers**: Worship services held in the late afternoon or evening.

Walt Whitman

[1819–1892]

Whitman's "I" . . . is the cosmic "I" of all peoples who seek freedom, decency, and dignity, friendship and equality between individuals and races all over the world.
– Langston Hughes

The poet familiarly known as Walt Whitman was born on May 31, 1819, on Long Island, New York, one of nine children born to a farmer, Walter Whitman Sr., and his wife, Louisa Van Velsor Whitman. In 1823 the family moved to Brooklyn, where Whitman spent his childhood, such as it was. By the age of eleven, he had left school to work as an office boy in a law firm; by fifteen, he was mostly supporting himself by working in the printing trade, perhaps initially as a compositor (a typesetter) in Manhattan. After a devastating fire destroyed much of the publishing district in 1835, Whitman rejoined his family, which had by then moved back to Long Island. Although he taught sporadically at several schools there, Whitman was clearly not suited to the classroom. In 1838 he started his own weekly newspaper, the *Long Islander*, and by the early 1840s Whitman had left teaching altogether. For the next several years, he worked as a printer in New York; edited a daily paper, the *Aurora*; and returned to Brooklyn, first to write for the *Long Island Star* and then to edit the *Brooklyn Daily Eagle*. Whitman was also writing, primarily prose pieces like the numerous literary and art reviews he printed in the *Eagle*, but also some poetry. Fired from the *Eagle* in 1848 for his free-soil politics – like a growing number of Democrats in the North, he strongly opposed the extension of slavery into territories gained during the Mexican War – Whitman was hired to be the first editor of the *Crescent*, a newspaper in New Orleans, where he headed along with his younger brother Jeff. By the end of the year, Whitman was again in New York, where he immersed himself in the pulsing life of that rising metropolis: riding the streets in horse-drawn buses or enjoying rambling walks around the city; attending the opera, which he loved, and going to museums; and spending time with his eclectic group of friends, who ranged from workingmen to artists. Whitman supported himself by working as a carpenter, but he increasingly devoted himself to reading, studying, and writing poetry, for which he finally gave up all other forms of labor.

bedfordstmartins.com/americanlit *for research links on Whitman*

In 1855, Whitman published the first edition of *Leaves of Grass*, which was thereafter the primary focus of his life and work. Whitman himself set the type for his self-published book, which he vigorously promoted by writing several anonymous reviews. He also sent a copy to Ralph Waldo Emerson, who in a congratulatory letter to Whitman exclaimed, "I greet you at the beginning of a great career, which yet must have had a long foreground somewhere, for such a start." If the Harvard-educated Emerson had then known about the unlikely foreground of *Leaves of Grass*, he would surely have been even more astonished by Whitman's remarkable poems. But few shared Emerson's appreciation of *Leaves of Grass*, which was attacked for what critics viewed as its crudeness, its vulgar language, and its scandalous subject matter. Undaunted, Whitman continued to work on the volume, adding new poems and publishing a second edition in 1856. By the beginning of the following year, he was already planning another edition,

The First Edition of *Leaves of Grass* (1855)

The portrait of Whitman was engraved from a daguerreotype made in 1854, when he was thirty-five. In contrast to the portraits of most other literary figures, who were customarily depicted in formal attire and equally formal poses, Whitman projected an image of himself as a workingman and man of the people. In an anonymous self-review of *Leaves of Grass*, Whitman described the poet portrayed in the frontispiece as "One of the roughs, his costume manly and free, his face sunburnt and bearded, his posture strong and erect."

but Whitman apparently wrote relatively few poems while he was editor of the *Brooklyn Daily Times* from March 1857 to June 1859. Freed of those editorial responsibilities, he began to expand and reconstruct *Leaves of Grass*, which a firm in Boston published in 1860. When the Civil War broke out the following year, Whitman moved to Washington, D.C., where he did volunteer work as a nurse in army hospitals and wrote the poems published as *Drum-Taps* early in 1865. Working with the wounded men made a profound impression on Whitman. In his letters to his mother and other family members, Whitman wrote frequently about the bravery of "my soldier boys," as he sometimes called them. Deeply affected by the assassination of Abraham Lincoln, whom he viewed as the representative democratic man and the martyred savior of the Union, Whitman wrote several poems on the death of the president. Those poems, along with those from *Drum-Taps*, were incorporated in the 1867 edition of *Leaves of Grass*, which was followed by yet another edition in 1871.

During those years, Whitman remained in Washington, where he worked as a clerk in the office of the attorney general. After suffering a debilitating stroke in 1873, Whitman left Washington and moved to Camden, New Jersey, where his small house at 328 Mickle Street became a kind of pilgrimage site for a growing number of admirers and disciples. Although he was often in ill health, he continued to see his many friends, to carry on an extensive international correspondence, and to put the final touches on *Leaves of Grass.* When a Boston firm published a new edition in 1881, the local district attorney threatened to sue the publisher for obscenity. By then, however, Whitman had largely won his long battle for recognition in the United States and especially in England, where some of the most influential literary figures of the period expressed lavish admiration for the poet and his *Leaves of Grass.* During the following decade, he published two shorter collections of poems, *November Boughs* (1888) and *Good-bye, My Fancy* (1891), both of which Whitman incorporated into the final edition of *Leaves of Grass*, published shortly before he died on March 26, 1892.

Whitman's *Leaves of Grass.* From the first publication of *Leaves of Grass* in 1855, Whitman worked on his book, adding new poems and sections, as well as rethinking the organization and structure. His continual revisions have made the history of the publication of *Leaves of Grass* quite complicated. From the first edition in 1855 until his death in 1892, there were five more separate American editions and at least two other reprintings of earlier editions, including what has come to be called the "Deathbed Edition" (1891-92), the last version of *Leaves of Grass* printed during his lifetime. The first edition included a preface and twelve untitled poems, one of which – later called "Song of Myself" – occupied more than half of the volume. Although Whitman's name appeared in the copyright notice, it was not announced on the title page of the volume. Instead, Whitman included a portrait of himself in a rough shirt and slouch hat. In the second edition published in 1856, Whitman added some new poems and gave titles to all of the poems in the volume, though he would later alter many of those titles. He made far more sweeping and far-reaching changes in the 1860 edition, in which Whitman first began to transform *Leaves of Grass* from a collection of miscellaneous poems into a carefully articulated and orchestrated whole. In addition to revising the poems published in the first two editions and adding a large number of new poems, Whitman grouped many of the poems in thematic clusters, including the procreation poems of "Enfans d'Adam," later "Children of Adam," and the love poems about male relationships in a group collectively entitled "Calamus."

In later editions, Whitman increasingly employed such clusters as central organizational and structural devices in *Leaves of Grass.* He achieved the final form of the volume through a long and complex process that included the continuous revision of individual poems, the omission of earlier poems and addition of new ones, and the constant rearrangement of poems within individual clusters and the volume as a whole. The 1881 edition thus began with a group of prefatory "Inscriptions" and ended with

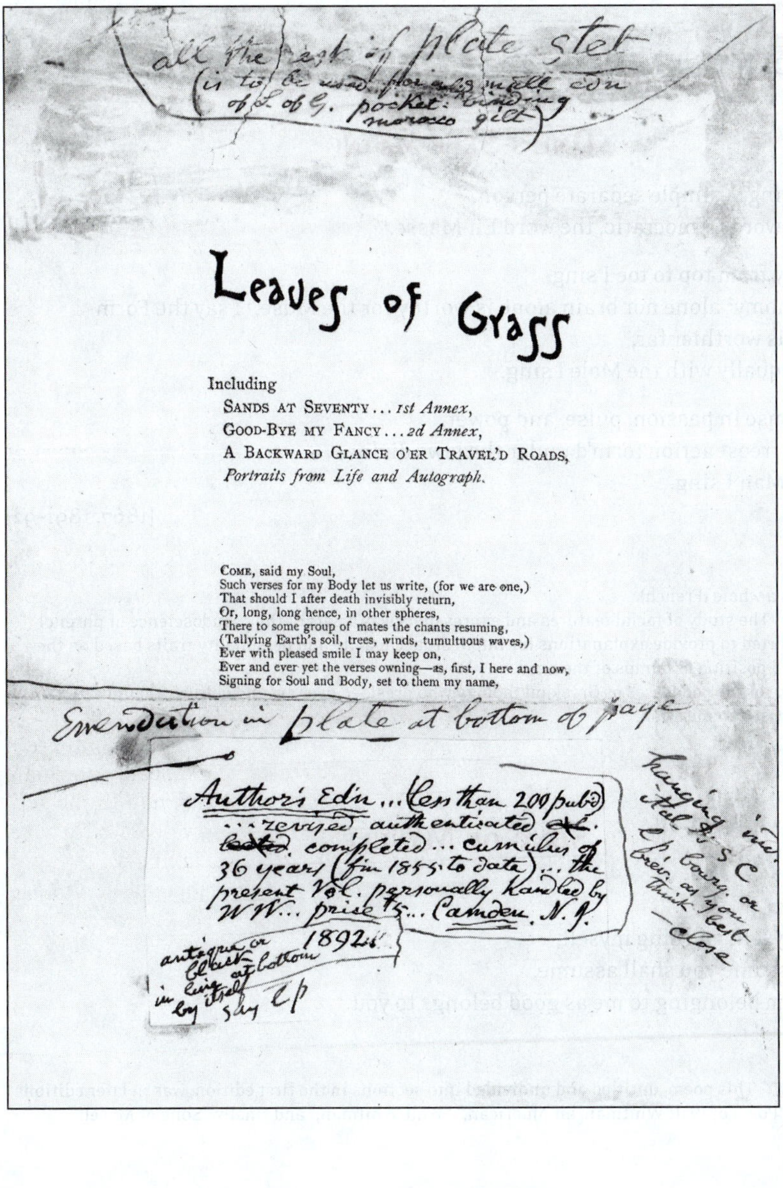

Leaves of Grass

Including

SANDS AT SEVENTY ... *1st Annex,*
GOOD-BYE MY FANCY ... *2d Annex,*
A BACKWARD GLANCE O'ER TRAVEL'D ROADS,
Portraits from Life and Autograph.

COME, said my Soul,
Such verses for my Body let us write, (for we are one,)
That should I after death invisibly return,
Or, long, long hence, in other spheres,
There to some group of mates the chants resuming,
(Tallying Earth's soil, trees, winds, tumultuous waves,)
Ever with pleased smile I may keep on,
Ever and ever yet the verses owning—as, first, I here and now,
Signing for Soul and Body, set to them my name,

The "Deathbed Edition" of *Leaves of Grass* (1891–92)

Whitman's annotations on this trial title page of the final edition he saw through to press reveal his involvement in every stage of publication, from designing to publicizing the volume. Two months before he died, Whitman announced that he "would like this new 1892 edition to absolutely supercede all previous ones."

"Songs of Parting," suggesting the overall movement from birth to death, as the poet retires from life and his lifelong work in the final poem in the volume, "So Long!" Although he later added two brief "annexes," Whitman made no other changes in the final or Deathbed Edition, where he noted: "As there are now several editions of L. of G., different texts and dates, I wish to say that I prefer this present one." The texts of the following poems are taken from – and the poems are printed here in the order they appear in – that edition of *Leaves of Grass* (1891-92).

From INSCRIPTIONS

ONE'S-SELF I SING

One's-Self I sing, a simple separate person,
Yet utter the word Democratic, the word En-Masse.[1]

Of physiology from top to toe I sing,
Not physiognomy[2] alone nor brain alone is worthy for the Muse,[3] I say the Form
complete is worthier far,
The Female equally with the Male I sing.

Of Life immense in passion, pulse, and power,
Cheerful, for freest action form'd under the laws divine,
The Modern Man I sing.

[1867, 1891-92]

1. **En-Masse:** As a whole (French).
2. **physiognomy:** The study of facial features and expressions was a part of the pseudoscience of phrenology, which purported to provide explanations for intellectual capacity and personality traits based on the overall shape and position of bumps of the head.
3. **Muse:** Any one of the goddesses of Greek mythology who presided over art and culture, thought to provide poetic or artistic inspiration.

SONG OF MYSELF[1]

1

I celebrate myself, and sing myself,
And what I assume you shall assume,
For every atom belonging to me as good belongs to you.

1. ***Song of Myself*:** This poem, untitled and undivided into sections in the first edition, was in later editions variously titled "Poem of Walt Whitman, an American," "Walt Whitman," and finally "Song of Myself."

I loafe and invite my soul,
I lean and loafe at my ease observing a spear of summer grass.

My tongue, every atom of my blood, form'd from this soil, this air,
Born here of parents born here from parents the same, and their parents the same,
I, now thirty-seven years old in perfect health begin,
Hoping to cease not till death.

Creeds and schools in abeyance,
Retiring back a while sufficed at what they are, but never forgotten,
I harbor for good or bad, I permit to speak at every hazard,
Nature without check with original energy.

2

Houses and rooms are full of perfumes, the shelves are crowded with perfumes,
I breathe the fragrance myself and know it and like it,
The distillation would intoxicate me also, but I shall not let it.

The atmosphere is not a perfume, it has no taste of the distillation, it is odorless,
It is for my mouth forever, I am in love with it,
I will go to the bank by the wood and become undisguised and naked,
I am mad for it to be in contact with me.

The smoke of my own breath,
Echoes, ripples, buzz'd whispers, love-root, silk-thread, crotch and vine,
My respiration and inspiration, the beating of my heart, the passing of blood and air through my lungs,
The sniff of green leaves and dry leaves, and of the shore and dark-color'd sea-rocks, and of hay in the barn,
The sound of the belch'd words of my voice loos'd to the eddies of the wind,
A few light kisses, a few embraces, a reaching around of arms,
The play of shine and shade on the trees as the supple boughs wag,
The delight alone or in the rush of the streets, or along the fields and hill-sides,
The feeling of health, the full-noon trill, the song of me rising from bed and meeting the sun.

Have you reckon'd a thousand acres much? have you reckon'd the earth much?
Have you practis'd so long to learn to read?
Have you felt so proud to get at the meaning of poems?

Stop this day and night with me and you shall possess the origin of all poems,
You shall possess the good of the earth and sun, (there are millions of suns left,)
You shall no longer take things at second or third hand, nor look through the eyes of the dead, nor feed on the spectres in books,
You shall not look through my eyes either, nor take things from me,
You shall listen to all sides and filter them from your self.

3

I have heard what the talkers were talking, the talk of the beginning and the end,
But I do not talk of the beginning or the end.

There was never any more inception than there is now,
Nor any more youth or age than there is now,
And will never be any more perfection than there is now,
Nor any more heaven or hell than there is now.

Urge and urge and urge,
Always the procreant urge of the world.

Out of the dimness opposite equals advance, always substance and increase, always sex,
Always a knit of identity, always distinction, always a breed of life.

To elaborate is no avail, learn'd and unlearn'd feel that it is so.

Sure as the most certain sure, plumb in the uprights, well entretied,[2] braced in the beams,
Stout as a horse, affectionate, haughty, electrical,
I and this mystery here we stand.

Clear and sweet is my soul, and clear and sweet is all that is not my soul.

Lack one lacks both, and the unseen is proved by the seen,
Till that becomes unseen and receives proof in its turn.

Showing the best and dividing it from the worst age vexes age,
Knowing the perfect fitness and equanimity of things, while they discuss I am silent, and go bathe and admire myself.

Welcome is every organ and attribute of me, and of any man hearty and clean,
Not an inch nor a particle of an inch is vile, and none shall be less familiar than the rest.

I am satisfied – I see, dance, laugh, sing;
As the hugging and loving bed-fellow sleeps at my side through the night, and withdraws at the peep of the day with stealthy tread,
Leaving me baskets cover'd with white towels swelling the house with their plenty,
Shall I postpone my acceptation and realization and scream at my eyes,
That they turn from gazing after and down the road,
And forthwith cipher and show me to a cent,
Exactly the value of one and exactly the value of two, and which is ahead?

2. entretied: A carpenter's term meaning "cross-braced."

4

Trippers and askers surround me,
People I meet, the effect upon me of my early life or the ward and city I live in, or the nation,
The latest dates, discoveries, inventions, societies, authors old and new,
My dinner, dress, associates, looks, compliments, dues,
The real or fancied indifference of some man or woman I love,
The sickness of one of my folks or of myself, or ill-doing or loss or lack of money, or depressions or exaltations,
Battles, the horrors of fratricidal war, the fever of doubtful news, the fitful events;
These come to me days and nights and go from me again,
But they are not the Me myself.

Apart from the pulling and hauling stands what I am,
Stands amused, complacent, compassionating, idle, unitary,
Looks down, is erect, or bends an arm on an impalpable certain rest,
Looking with side-curved head curious what will come next,
Both in and out of the game and watching and wondering at it.

Backward I see in my own days where I sweated through fog with linguists and contenders,
I have no mockings or arguments, I witness and wait.

5

I believe in you my soul, the other I am must not abase itself to you,
And you must not be abased to the other.

Loafe with me on the grass, loose the stop from your throat,
Not words, not music or rhyme I want, not custom or lecture, not even the best,
Only the lull I like, the hum of your valvèd voice.

I mind how once we lay such a transparent summer morning,
How you settled your head athwart my hips and gently turn'd over upon me,
And parted the shirt from my bosom-bone, and plunged your tongue to my bare-stript heart,
And reach'd till you felt my beard, and reach'd till you held my feet.

Swiftly arose and spread around me the peace and knowledge that pass all the argument of the earth,
And I know that the hand of God is the promise of my own,
And I know that the spirit of God is the brother of my own,
And that all the men ever born are also my brothers, and the women my sisters and lovers,

And that a kelson[3] of the creation is love,
And limitless are leaves stiff or drooping in the fields,
And brown ants in the little wells beneath them,
And mossy scabs of the worm fence, heap'd stones, elder, mullein and poke-weed.

6

A child said *What is the grass?* fetching it to me with full hands;
How could I answer the child? I do not know what it is any more than he.

I guess it must be the flag of my disposition, out of hopeful green stuff woven.

Or I guess it is the handkerchief of the Lord,
A scented gift and remembrancer designedly dropt,
Bearing the owner's name someway in the corners, that we may see and remark, and say *Whose?*

Or I guess the grass is itself a child, the produced babe of the vegetation.

Or I guess it is a uniform hieroglyphic,
And it means, Sprouting alike in broad zones and narrow zones,
Growing among black folks as among white,
Kanuck, Tuckahoe, Congressman, Cuff,[4] I give them the same, receive them the same.

And now it seems to me the beautiful uncut hair of graves.

Tenderly will I use you curling grass,
It may be you transpire from the breasts of young men,
It may be if I had known them I would have loved them,
It may be you are from old people, or from offspring taken soon out of their mothers' laps,
And here you are the mothers' laps.

This grass is very dark to be from the white heads of old mothers,
Darker than the colorless beards of old men,
Dark to come from under the faint red roofs of mouths.

O I perceive after all so many uttering tongues,
And I perceive they do not come from the roofs of mouths for nothing.

I wish I could translate the hints about the dead young men and women,
And the hints about old men and mothers, and the offspring taken soon out of their laps.

---

3. **kelson:** A nautical term referring to the girder that fastens to the keel of a ship for extra support.
4. **Kanuck, Tuckahoo . . . Cuff:** Nineteenth-century slang terms for a French Canadian, a Virginian, and an African American, from *cuffee.*

What do you think has become of the young and old men?
And what do you think has become of the women and children?

They are alive and well somewhere,
The smallest sprout shows there is really no death,
And if ever there was it led forward life, and does not wait at the end to arrest it,
And ceas'd the moment life appear'd.

All goes onward and outward, nothing collapses,
And to die is different from what any one supposed, and luckier.

7

Has any one supposed it lucky to be born?
I hasten to inform him or her it is just as lucky to die, and I know it.

I pass death with the dying and birth with the new-wash'd babe, and am not
contain'd between my hat and boots,
And peruse manifold objects, no two alike and every one good,
The earth good and the stars good, and their adjuncts all good.

I am not an earth nor an adjunct of an earth,
I am the mate and companion of people, all just as immortal and fathomless as
myself,
(They do not know how immortal, but I know.)

Every kind for itself and its own, for me mine male and female,
For me those that have been boys and that love women,
For me the man that is proud and feels how it stings to be slighted,
For me the sweet-heart and the old maid, for me mothers and the mothers of
mothers,
For me lips that have smiled, eyes that have shed tears,
For me children and the begetters of children.

Undrape! you are not guilty to me, nor stale nor discarded,
I see through the broadcloth and gingham whether or no,
And am around, tenacious, acquisitive, tireless, and cannot be shaken away.

8

The little one sleeps in its cradle,
I lift the gauze and look a long time, and silently brush away flies with my hand.

The youngster and the red-faced girl turn aside up the bushy hill,
I peeringly view them from the top.

The suicide sprawls on the bloody floor of the bedroom,
I witness the corpse with its dabbled hair, I note where the pistol has fallen.

The blab of the pave, tires of carts, sluff of boot-soles, talk of the promenaders,
The heavy omnibus, the driver with his interrogating thumb, the clank of the shod horses on the granite floor,
The snow-sleighs, clinking, shouted jokes, pelts of snow-balls,
The hurrahs for popular favorites, the fury of rous'd mobs,
The flap of the curtain'd litter, a sick man inside borne to the hospital,
The meeting of enemies, the sudden oath, the blows and fall,
The excited crowd, the policeman with his star quickly working his passage to the centre of the crowd,
The impassive stones that receive and return so many echoes,
What groans of over-fed or half-starv'd who fall sunstruck or in fits,
What exclamations of women taken suddenly who hurry home and give birth to babes,
What living and buried speech is always vibrating here, what howls restrain'd by decorum,
Arrests of criminals, slights, adulterous offers made, acceptances, rejections with convex lips,
I mind them or the show or resonance of them – I come and I depart.

9

The big doors of the country barn stand open and ready,
The dried grass of the harvest-time loads the slow-drawn wagon,
The clear light plays on the brown gray and green intertinged,
The armfuls are pack'd to the sagging mow.

I am there, I help, I came stretch'd atop of the load,
I felt its soft jolts, one leg reclined on the other,
I jump from the cross-beams and seize the clover and timothy,
And roll head over heels and tangle my hair full of wisps.

10

Alone far in the wilds and mountains I hunt,
Wandering amazed at my own lightness and glee,
In the late afternoon choosing a safe spot to pass the night,
Kindling a fire and broiling the fresh-kill'd game,
Falling asleep on the gather'd leaves with my dog and gun by my side.

The Yankee clipper is under her sky-sails, she cuts the sparkle and scud,
My eyes settle the land, I bend at her prow or shout joyously from the deck.

The boatmen and clam-diggers arose early and stopt for me,
I tuck'd my trowser-ends in my boots and went and had a good time;
You should have been with us that day round the chowder-kettle.

I saw the marriage of the trapper in the open air in the far west, the bride was a red girl,
Her father and his friends sat near cross-legged and dumbly smoking, they had moccasins to their feet and large thick blankets hanging from their shoulders,
On a bank lounged the trapper, he was drest mostly in skins, his luxuriant beard and curls protected his neck, he held his bride by the hand,
She had long eyelashes, her head was bare, her coarse straight locks descended upon her voluptuous limbs and reach'd to her feet.

The runaway slave came to my house and stopt outside,
I heard his motions crackling the twigs of the woodpile,
Through the swung half-door of the kitchen I saw him limpsy[5] and weak,
And went where he sat on a log and led him in and assured him,
And brought water and fill'd a tub for his sweated body and bruis'd feet,
And gave him a room that enter'd from my own, and gave him some coarse clean clothes,
And remember perfectly well his revolving eyes and his awkwardness,
And remember putting plasters on the galls of his neck and ankles;
He staid with me a week before he was recuperated and pass'd north,
I had him sit next me at table, my fire-lock lean'd in the corner.

11

Twenty-eight young men bathe by the shore,
Twenty-eight young men and all so friendly;
Twenty-eight years of womanly life and all so lonesome.

She owns the fine house by the rise of the bank,
She hides handsome and richly drest aft the blinds of the window.

Which of the young men does she like the best?
Ah the homeliest of them is beautiful to her.

Where are you off to, lady? for I see you,
You splash in the water there, yet stay stock still in your room.

Dancing and laughing along the beach came the twenty-ninth bather,
The rest did not see her, but she saw them and loved them.

The beards of the young men glisten'd with wet, it ran from their long hair,
Little streams pass'd all over their bodies.

An unseen hand also pass'd over their bodies,
It descended tremblingly from their temples and ribs.

---

5. **limpsy:** A variant of *limp*; that is, lacking energy or vigor.

The young men float on their backs, their white bellies bulge to the sun, they do
not ask who seizes fast to them,
They do not know who puffs and declines with pendant and bending arch,
They do not think whom they souse with spray.

12

The butcher-boy puts off his killing-clothes, or sharpens his knife at the stall in
the market,
I loiter enjoying his repartee and his shuffle and break-down.[6]

Blacksmiths with grimed and hairy chests environ the anvil,
Each has his main-sledge, they are all out, there is a great heat in the fire.

From the cinder-strew'd threshold I follow their movements,
The lithe sheer of their waists plays even with their massive arms,
Overhand the hammers swing, overhand so slow, overhand so sure,
They do not hasten, each man hits in his place.

13

The negro holds firmly the reins of his four horses, the block swags underneath
on its tied-over chain,
The negro that drives the long dray of the stone-yard, steady and tall he stands
pois'd on one leg on the string-piece,[7]
His blue shirt exposes his ample neck and breast and loosens over his hip-band,
His glance is calm and commanding, he tosses the slouch of his hat away from
his forehead,
The sun falls on his crispy hair and mustache, falls on the black of his polish'd
and perfect limbs.

I behold the picturesque giant and love him, and I do not stop there,
I go with the team also.

In me the caresser of life wherever moving, backward as well as forward sluing,
To niches aside and junior bending, not a person or object missing,
Absorbing all to myself and for this song.

Oxen that rattle the yoke and chain or halt in the leafy shade, what is that you
express in your eyes?
It seems to me more than all the print I have read in my life.

My tread scares the wood-drake and wood-duck on my distant and day-long ramble,
They rise together, they slowly circle around.

---

6. **shuffle and break-down:** Popular dance steps in minstrel shows.
7. **string-piece:** Heavy timber used in a wagon to keep a load in place.

I believe in those wing'd purposes,
And acknowledge red, yellow, white, playing within me,
And consider green and violet and the tufted crown intentional,
And do not call the tortoise unworthy because she is not something else,
And the jay in the woods never studied the gamut,[8] yet trills pretty well to me,
And the look of the bay mare shames silliness out of me.

14

The wild gander leads his flock through the cool night,
Ya-honk he says, and sounds it down to me like an invitation,
The pert may suppose it meaningless, but I listening close,
Find its purpose and place up there toward the wintry sky.

The sharp-hoof'd moose of the north, the cat on the house-sill, the chickadee, the prairie-dog,
The litter of the grunting sow as they tug at her teats,
The brood of the turkey-hen and she with her half-spread wings,
I see in them and myself the same old law.

The press of my foot to the earth springs a hundred affections,
They scorn the best I can do to relate them.

I am enamour'd of growing out-doors,
Of men that live among cattle or taste of the ocean or woods,
Of the builders and steerers of ships and the wielders of axes and mauls, and the drivers of horses,
I can eat and sleep with them week in and week out.

What is commonest, cheapest, nearest, easiest, is Me,
Me going in for my chances, spending for vast returns,
Adorning myself to bestow myself on the first that will take me,
Not asking the sky to come down to my good will,
Scattering it freely forever.

15

The pure contralto sings in the organ loft,
The carpenter dresses his plank, the tongue of his foreplane whistles its wild ascending lisp,
The married and unmarried children ride home to their Thanksgiving dinner,
The pilot seizes the king-pin, he heaves down with a strong arm,
The mate stands braced in the whale-boat, lance and harpoon are ready,
The duck-shooter walks by silent and cautious stretches,

8. **gamut:** The complete musical scale.

The deacons are ordain'd with cross'd hands at the altar,
The spinning-girl retreats and advances to the hum of the big wheel,
The farmer stops by the bars as he walks on a First-day[9] loafe and looks at the oats and rye,
The lunatic is carried at last to the asylum a confirm'd case,
(He will never sleep any more as he did in the cot in his mother's bed-room;)
The jour printer with gray head and gaunt jaws works at his case,[10]
He turns his quid of tobacco while his eyes blurr with the manuscript;
The malform'd limbs are tied to the surgeon's table,
What is removed drops horribly in a pail;
The quadroon girl is sold at the auction-stand, the drunkard nods by the bar-room stove,
The machinist rolls up his sleeves, the policeman travels his beat, the gate-keeper marks who pass,
The young fellow drives the express-wagon, (I love him, though I do not know him;)
The half-breed straps on his light boots to compete in the race,
The western turkey-shooting draws old and young, some lean on their rifles, some sit on logs,
Out from the crowd steps the marksman, takes his position, levels his piece;
The groups of newly-come immigrants cover the wharf or levee,
As the woolly-pates hoe in the sugarfield, the overseer views them from his saddle,
The bugle calls in the ball-room, the gentlemen run for their partners, the dancers bow to each other,
The youth lies awake in the cedar-roof'd garret and harks to the musical rain,
The Wolverine[11] sets traps on the creek that helps fill the Huron,
The squaw wrapt in her yellow-hemm'd cloth is offering moccasins and bead-bags for sale,
The connoisseur peers along the exhibition-gallery with half-shut eyes bent sideways,
As the deck-hands make fast the steamboat the plank is thrown for the shore-going passengers,
The young sister holds out the skein while the elder sister winds it off in a ball, and stops now and then for the knots,
The one-year wife is recovering and happy having a week ago borne her first child,
The clean-hair'd Yankee girl works with her sewing-machine or in the factory or mill,

9. **bars . . . First-day:** The bars are the rails of a fence; First-day is the Quaker name for Sunday.
10. **jour printer . . . case:** A journeyman printer working at his case, or tray of printing type.
11. **Wolverine:** A native of Michigan.

The paving-man leans on his two-handed rammer, the reporter's lead flies swiftly over the note-book, the sign-painter is lettering with blue and gold,
The canal boy trots on the tow-path, the book-keeper counts at his desk, the shoemaker waxes his thread,
The conductor beats time for the band and all the performers follow him,
The child is baptized, the convert is making his first professions,
The regatta is spread on the bay, the race is begun, (how the white sails sparkle!)
The drover watching his drove sings out to them that would stray,
The pedler sweats with his pack on his back, (the purchaser higgling about the odd cent;)
The bride unrumples her white dress, the minute-hand of the clock moves slowly,
The opium-eater reclines with rigid head and just-open'd lips,
The prostitute draggles her shawl, her bonnet bobs on her tipsy and pimpled neck,
The crowd laugh at her blackguard oaths, the men jeer and wink to each other,
(Miserable! I do not laugh at your oaths nor jeer you;)
The President holding a cabinet council is surrounded by the great Secretaries,
On the piazza walk three matrons stately and friendly with twined arms,
The crew of the fish-smack pack repeated layers of halibut in the hold,
The Missourian crosses the plains toting his wares and his cattle,
As the fare-collector goes through the train he gives notice by the jingling of loose change,
The floor-men are laying the floor, the tinners are tinning the roof, the masons are calling for mortar,
In single file each shouldering his hod pass onward the laborers;
Seasons pursuing each other the indescribable crowd is gather'd, it is the fourth of Seventh-month, (what salutes of cannon and small arms!)
Seasons pursuing each other the plougher ploughs, the mower mows, and the winter-grain falls in the ground;
Off on the lakes the pike-fisher watches and waits by the hole in the frozen surface,
The stumps stand thick round the clearing, the squatter strikes deep with his axe,
Flatboatmen make fast towards dusk near the cotton-wood or pecan-trees,
Coon-seekers go through the regions of the Red river or through those drain'd by the Tennessee, or through those of the Arkansas,
Torches shine in the dark that hangs on the Chattahooche or Altamahaw,[12]
Patriarchs sit at supper with sons and grandsons and great-grandsons around them,
In walls of adobie, in canvas tents, rest hunters and trappers after their day's sport,
The city sleeps and the country sleeps,
The living sleep for their time, the dead sleep for their time,

12. **Chattahooche or Altamahaw:** Rivers in Georgia.

The old husband sleeps by his wife and the young husband sleeps by his wife;
And these tend inward to me, and I tend outward to them,
And such as it is to be of these more or less I am,
And of these one and all I weave the song of myself.

16

I am of old and young, of the foolish as much as the wise,
Regardless of others, ever regardful of others,
Maternal as well as paternal, a child as well as a man,
Stuff'd with the stuff that is coarse and stuff'd with the stuff that is fine,
One of the Nation of many nations, the smallest the same and the largest the same,
A Southerner soon as a Northerner, a planter nonchalant and hospitable down by the Oconee[13] I live,
A Yankee bound my own way ready for trade, my joints the limberest joints on earth and the sternest joints on earth,
A Kentuckian walking the vale of the Elkhorn in my deer-skin leggings, a Louisianian or Georgian,
A boatman over lakes or bays or along coasts, a Hoosier, Badger, Buckeye;[14]
At home on Kanadian snow-shoes or up in the bush, or with fishermen off Newfoundland,
At home in the fleet of ice-boats, sailing with the rest and tacking,
At home on the hills of Vermont or in the woods of Maine, or the Texas ranch,
Comrade of Californians, comrade of free North-Westerners, (loving their big proportions,)
Comrade of raftsmen and coalmen, comrade of all who shake hands and welcome to drink and meat,
A learner with the simplest, a teacher of the thoughtfullest,
A novice beginning yet experient of myriads of seasons,
Of every hue and caste am I, of every rank and religion,
A farmer, mechanic, artist, gentleman, sailor, quaker,
Prisoner, fancy-man, rowdy, lawyer, physician, priest.

I resist any thing better than my own diversity,
Breathe the air but leave plenty after me,
And am not stuck up, and am in my place.

(The moth and the fish-eggs are in their place,
The bright suns I see and the dark suns I cannot see are in their place,
The palpable is in its place and the impalpable is in its place.)

---

13. **Oconee:** River in central Georgia.
14. **Hoosier, Badger, Buckeye:** Natives of Indiana, Wisconsin, and Ohio.

17

These are really the thoughts of all men in all ages and lands, they are not original with me,
If they are not yours as much as mine they are nothing, or next to nothing,
If they are not the riddle and the untying of the riddle they are nothing,
If they are not just as close as they are distant they are nothing.

This is the grass that grows wherever the land is and the water is,
This the common air that bathes the globe.

18

With music strong I come, with my cornets and my drums,
I play not marches for accepted victors only, I play marches for conquer'd and slain persons.

Have you heard that it was good to gain the day?
I also say it is good to fall, battles are lost in the same spirit in which they are won.

I beat and pound for the dead,
I blow through my embouchures my loudest and gayest for them.

Vivas to those who have fail'd!
And to those whose war-vessels sank in the sea!
And to those themselves who sank in the sea!
And to all generals that lost engagements, and all overcome heroes!
And the numberless unknown heroes equal to the greatest heroes known!

19

This is the meal equally set, this the meat for natural hunger,
It is for the wicked just the same as the righteous, I make appointments with all,
I will not have a single person slighted or left away,
The kept-woman, sponger, thief, are hereby invited,
The heavy-lipp'd slave is invited, the venerealee is invited;
There shall be no difference between them and the rest.

This is the press of a bashful hand, this the float and odor of hair,
This the touch of my lips to yours, this the murmur of yearning,
This the far-off depth and height reflecting my own face,
This the thoughtful merge of myself, and the outlet again.

Do you guess I have some intricate purpose?
Well I have, for the Fourth-month showers have, and the mica on the side of a rock has.

Do you take it I would astonish?
Does the daylight astonish? does the early redstart twittering through the woods?
Do I astonish more than they?

This hour I tell things in confidence,
I might not tell everybody, but I will tell you.

20

Who goes there? hankering, gross, mystical, nude;
How is it I extract strength from the beef I eat?

What is a man anyhow? what am I? what are you?

All I mark as my own you shall offset it with your own,
Else it were time lost listening to me.

I do not snivel that snivel the world over,
That months are vacuums and the ground but wallow and filth

Whimpering and truckling fold with powders[15] for invalids, conformity goes to the fourth-remov'd,
I wear my hat as I please indoors or out.

Why should I pray? why should I venerate and be ceremonious?

Having pried through the strata, analyzed to a hair, counsel'd with doctors and calculated close,
I find no sweeter fat than sticks to my own bones.

In all people I see myself, none more and not one a barley-corn less,
And the good or bad I say of myself I say of them.

I know I am solid and sound,
To me the converging objects of the universe perpetually flow,
All are written to me, and I must get what the writing means.

I know I am deathless,
I know this orbit of mine cannot be swept by a carpenter's compass,
I know I shall not pass like a child's carlacue[16] cut with a burnt stick at night.

I know I am august,
I do not trouble my spirit to vindicate itself or be understood,
I see that the elementary laws never apologize,
(I reckon I behave no prouder than the level I plant my house by, after all.)

---

15. **fold with powders:** Physicians then often wrapped powdered medications in twists of paper.
16. **carlacue:** A curlicue made in the air with a lighted stick.

I exist as I am, that is enough,
If no other in the world be aware I sit content,
And if each and all be aware I sit content.

One world is aware and by far the largest to me, and that is myself,
And whether I come to my own to-day or in ten thousand or ten million years,
I can cheerfully take it now, or with equal cheerfulness I can wait.

My foothold is tenon'd and mortis'd in granite,
I laugh at what you call dissolution,
And I know the amplitude of time.

21

I am the poet of the Body and I am the poet of the Soul,
The pleasures of heaven are with me and the pains of hell are with me,
The first I graft and increase upon myself, the latter I translate into a new
tongue.

I am the poet of the woman the same as the man,
And I say it is as great to be a woman as to be a man,
And I say there is nothing greater than the mother of men.

I chant the chant of dilation or pride,
We have had ducking and deprecating about enough,
I show that size is only development.

Have you outstript the rest? are you the President?
It is a trifle, they will more than arrive there every one, and still pass on.

I am he that walks with the tender and growing night,
I call to the earth and sea half-held by the night.

Press close bare-bosom'd night – press close magnetic nourishing night!
Night of south winds – night of the large few stars!
Still nodding night – mad naked summer night.

Smile O voluptuous cool-breath'd earth!
Earth of the slumbering and liquid trees!
Earth of departed sunset – earth of the mountains misty-topt!
Earth of the vitreous pour of the full moon just tinged with blue!
Earth of shine and dark mottling the tide of the river!
Earth of the limpid gray of clouds brighter and clearer for my sake!
Far-swooping elbow'd earth – rich apple-blossom'd earth!
Smile, for your lover comes.

Prodigal, you have given me love – therefore I to you give love!
O unspeakable passionate love.

22

You sea! I resign myself to you also – I guess what you mean,
I behold from the beach your crooked inviting fingers,
I believe you refuse to go back without feeling of me,
We must have a turn together, I undress, hurry me out of sight of the land,
Cushion me soft, rock me in billowy drowse,
Dash me with amorous wet, I can repay you.

Sea of stretch'd ground-swells,
Sea breathing broad and convulsive breaths,
Sea of the brine of life and of unshovell'd yet always-ready graves,
Howler and scooper of storms, capricious and dainty sea,
I am integral with you, I too am of one phase and of all phases.

Partaker of influx and efflux I, extoller of hate and conciliation,
Extoller of amies[17] and those that sleep in each others' arms.

I am he attesting sympathy,
(Shall I make my list of things in the house and skip the house that supports them?)

I am not the poet of goodness only, I do not decline to be the poet of wickedness also.

What blurt is this about virtue and about vice?
Evil propels me and reform of evil propels me, I stand indifferent,
My gait is no fault-finder's or rejecter's gait,
I moisten the roots of all that has grown.

Did you fear some scrofula out of the unflagging pregnancy?
Did you guess the celestial laws are yet to be work'd over and rectified?

I find one side a balance and the antipodal side a balance,
Soft doctrine as steady help as stable doctrine,
Thoughts and deeds of the present our rouse and early start.

This minute that comes to me over the past decillions,
There is no better than it and now.

What behaved well in the past or behaves well to-day is not such a wonder,
The wonder is always and always how there can be a mean man or an infidel.

17. amies: Friends (French).

23

Endless unfolding of words of ages!
And mine a word of the modern, the word En-Masse.

A word of the faith that never balks,
Here or henceforward it is all the same to me, I accept Time absolutely.

It alone is without flaw, it alone rounds and completes all,
That mystic baffling wonder alone completes all.

I accept Reality and dare not question it,
Materialism first and last imbuing.

Hurrah for positive science! long live exact demonstration!
Fetch stonecrop mixt with cedar and branches of lilac,
This is the lexicographer, this the chemist, this made a grammar of the old
 cartouches,[18]
These mariners put the ship through dangerous unknown seas,
This is the geologist, this works with the scalpel, and this is a mathematician.

Gentlemen, to you the first honors always!
Your facts are useful, and yet they are not my dwelling,
I but enter by them to an area of my dwelling.

Less the reminders of properties told my words,
And more the reminders they of life untold, and of freedom and extrication,
And make short account of neuters and geldings, and favor men and women fully
 equipt,
And beat the gong of revolt, and stop with fugitives and them that plot and
 conspire.

24

Walt Whitman, a kosmos, of Manhattan the son,
Turbulent, fleshy, sensual, eating, drinking and breeding,
No sentimentalist, no stander above men and women or apart from them,
No more modest than immodest.

Unscrew the locks from the doors!
Unscrew the doors themselves from their jambs!

Whoever degrades another degrades me,
And whatever is done or said returns at last to me.

18. **cartouches:** Stone tablets inscribed in ancient languages.

Through me the afflatus surging and surging, through me the current and index.

I speak the pass-word primeval, I give the sign of democracy,
By God! I will accept nothing which all cannot have their counterpart of on the same terms.

Through me many long dumb voices,
Voices of the interminable generations of prisoners and slaves,
Voices of the diseas'd and despairing and of thieves and dwarfs,
Voices of cycles of preparation and accretion,
And of the threads that connect the stars, and of wombs and of the father-stuff,
And of the rights of them the others are down upon,
Of the deform'd, trivial, fiat, foolish, despised,
Fog in the air, beetles rolling balls of dung.

Through me forbidden voices,
Voices of sexes and lusts, voices veil'd and I remove the veil,
Voices indecent by me clarified and transfigur'd.

I do not press my fingers across my mouth,
I keep as delicate around the bowels as around the head and heart,
Copulation is no more rank to me than death is.

I believe in the flesh and the appetites,
Seeing, hearing, feeling, are miracles, and each part and tag of me is a miracle.

Divine am I inside and out, and I make holy whatever I touch or am touch'd from,
The scent of these arm-pits aroma finer than prayer,
This head more than churches, bibles, and all the creeds.

If I worship one thing more than another it shall be the spread of my own body, or any part of it,
Translucent mould of me it shall be you!
Shaded ledges and rests it shall be you!
Firm masculine colter[19] it shall be you!
Whatever goes to the tilth[20] of me it shall be you!
You my rich blood! your milky stream pale strippings of my life!
Breast that presses against other breasts it shall be you!
My brain it shall be your occult convolutions!
Root of wash'd sweet-flag! timorous pond-snipe! nest of guarded duplicate eggs! it shall be you!
Mix'd tussled hay of head, beard, brawn, it shall be you!

---

19. colter: Blade of a plow.
20. tilth: Plowing or cultivation.

Trickling sap of maple, fibre of manly wheat, it shall be you!
Sun so generous it shall be you!
Vapors lighting and shading my face it shall be you!
You sweaty brooks and dews it shall be you!
Winds whose soft-tickling genitals rub against me it shall be you!
Broad muscular fields, branches of live oak, loving lounger in my winding paths,
it shall be you!
Hands I have taken, face I have kiss'd, mortal I have ever touch'd, it shall be you.

I dote on myself, there is that lot of me and all so luscious,
Each moment and whatever happens thrills me with joy,
I cannot tell how my ankles bend, nor whence the cause of my faintest wish,
Nor the cause of the friendship I emit, nor the cause of the friendship I take again.

That I walk up my stoop, I pause to consider if it really be,
A morning-glory at my window satisfies me more than the metaphysics of books.

To behold the day-break!
The little light fades the immense and diaphanous shadows,
The air tastes good to my palate.

Hefts of the moving world at innocent gambols silently rising freshly exuding,
Scooting obliquely high and low.

Something I cannot see puts upward libidinous prongs,
Seas of bright juice suffuse heaven.

The earth by the sky staid with, the daily close of their junction.
The heav'd challenge from the east that moment over my head,
The mocking taunt, See then whether you shall be master!

25

Dazzling and tremendous how quick the sun-rise would kill me,
If I could not now and always send sun-rise out of me.

We also ascend dazzling and tremendous as the sun,
We found our own O my soul in the calm and cool of the day-break.

My voice goes after what my eyes cannot reach,
With the twirl of my tongue I encompass worlds and volumes of worlds.

Speech is the twin of my vision, it is unequal to measure itself,
It provokes me forever, it says sarcastically,
Walt you contain enough, why don't you let it out then?

Come now I will not be tantalized, you conceive too much of articulation,
Do you not know O speech how the buds beneath you are folded?
Waiting in gloom, protected by frost,

The dirt receding before my prophetical screams,
I underlying causes to balance them at last,
My knowledge my live parts, it keeping tally with the meaning of all things,
Happiness, (which whoever hears me let him or her set out in search of this day.)

My final merit I refuse you, I refuse putting from me what I really am,
Encompass worlds, but never try to encompass me,
I crowd your sleekest and best by simply looking toward you.

Writing and talk do not prove me,
I carry the plenum of proof and every thing else in my face,
With the hush of my lips I wholly confound the skeptic.

26

Now I will do nothing but listen,
To accrue what I hear into this song, to let sounds contribute toward it.

I hear bravuras of birds, bustle of growing wheat, gossip of flames, clack of sticks cooking my meals,
I hear the sound I love, the sound of the human voice,
I hear all sounds running together, combined, fused or following,
Sounds of the city and sounds out of the city, sounds of the day and night,
Talkative young ones to those that like them, the loud laugh of work-people at their meals,
The angry base of disjointed friendship, the faint tones of the sick,
The judge with hands tight to the desk, his pallid lips pronouncing a death-sentence,
The heave'e'yo of stevedores unlading ships by the wharves, the refrain of the anchor-lifters,
The ring of alarm-bells, the cry of fire, the whirr of swift-streaking engines and hose-carts with premonitory tinkles and color'd lights,
The steam whistle, the solid roll of the train of approaching cars,
The slow march play'd at the head of the association marching two and two,
(They go to guard some corpse, the flag-tops are draped with black muslin.)

I hear the violoncello, ('tis the young man's heart's complaint,)
I hear the key'd cornet, it glides quickly in through my ears,
It shakes mad-sweet pangs through my belly and breast.

I hear the chorus, it is a grand opera,
Ah this indeed is music – this suits me.

A tenor large and fresh as the creation fills me,
The orbic flex of his mouth is pouring and filling me full.

I hear the train'd soprano (what work with hers is this?)
The orchestra whirls me wider than Uranus flies,
It wrenches such ardors from me I did not know I possess'd them.
It sails me. I dab with bare feet, they are lick'd by the indolent waves,
I am cut by bitter and angry hail, I lose my breath,
Steep'd amid honey'd morphine, my windpipe throttled in fakes[21] of death,
At length let up again to feel the puzzle of puzzles,
And that we call Being.

27

To be in any form, what is that?
(Round and round we go, all of us, and ever come back thither,)
If nothing lay more develop'd the quahaug[22] in its callous shell were
enough.

Mine is no callous shell,
I have instant conductors all over me whether I pass or stop,
They seize every object and lead it harmlessly through me.

I merely stir, press, feel with my fingers, and am happy,
To touch my person to some one else's is about as much as I can stand.

28

Is this then a touch? quivering me to a new identity,
Flames and ether making a rush for my veins,
Treacherous tip of me reaching and crowding to help them,
My flesh and blood playing out lightning to strike what is hardly different from
myself,
On all sides prurient provokers stiffening my limbs,
Straining the udder of my heart for its withheld drip,
Behaving licentious toward me, taking no denial,
Depriving me of my best as for a purpose,
Unbuttoning my clothes, holding me by the bare waist,
Deluding my confusion with the calm of the sunlight and pasture-fields,
Immodestly sliding the fellow-senses away,
They bribed to swap off with touch and go and graze at the edges of me,
No consideration, no regard for my draining strength or my anger,

21. **fakes:** Coils of rope.
22. **quahaug:** A clam.

Fetching the rest of the herd around to enjoy them a while,
Then all uniting to stand on a headland and worry me.

The sentries desert every other part of me,
They have left me helpless to a red marauder,
They all come to the headland to witness and assist against me.

I am given up by traitors,
I talk wildly, I have lost my wits, I and nobody else am the greatest traitor,
I went myself first to the headland, my own hands carried me there.

Your villain touch! what are you doing? my breath is tight in its throat,
Unclench your floodgates, you are too much for me.

29

Blind loving wrestling touch, sheath'd hooded sharp-tooth'd touch!
Did it make you ache so, leaving me?

Parting track'd by arriving, perpetual payment of perpetual loan,
Rich showering rain, and recompense richer afterward.

Sprouts take and accumulate, stand by the curb prolific and vital,
Landscapes projected masculine, full-sized and golden.

30

All truths wait in all things,
They neither hasten their own delivery nor resist it,
They do not need the obstetric forceps of the surgeon,
The insignificant is as big to me as any,
(What is less or more than a touch?)

Logic and sermons never convince,
The damp of the night drives deeper into my soul.

(Only what proves itself to every man and woman is so,
Only what nobody denies is so.)

A minute and a drop of me settle my brain,
I believe the soggy clods shall become lovers and lamps,
And a compend of compends is the meat of a man or woman,
And a summit and flower there is the feeling they have for each other,
And they are to branch boundlessly out of that lesson until it becomes
omnific,
And until one and all shall delight us, and we them.

31

I believe a leaf of grass is no less than the journey-work of the stars,
And the pismire[23] is equally perfect, and a grain of sand, and the egg of the wren,
And the tree-toad is a chef-d'oeuvre for the highest,
And the running blackberry would adorn the parlors of heaven,
And the narrowest hinge in my hand puts to scorn all machinery.
And the cow crunching with depress'd head surpasses any statue,
And a mouse is miracle enough to stagger sextillions of infidels.

I find I incorporate gneiss,[24] coal, long-threaded moss, fruits, grains, esculent roots,
And am stucco'd with quadrupeds and birds all over,
And have distanced what is behind me for good reasons,
But call any thing back again when I desire it.

In vain the speeding or shyness,
In vain the plutonic rocks[25] send their old heat against my approach,
In vain the mastodon retreats beneath its own powder'd bones,
In vain objects stand leagues off and assume manifold shapes,
In vain the ocean settling in hollows and the great monsters lying low,
In vain the buzzard houses herself with the sky,
In vain the snake slides through the creepers and logs,
In vain the elk takes to the inner passes of the woods,
In vain the razor-bill'd auk sails far north to Labrador,
I follow quickly, I ascend to the nest in the fissure of the cliff.

32

I think I could turn and live with animals, they are so placid and self-contain'd,
I stand and look at them long and long.

They do not sweat and whine about their condition,
They do not lie awake in the dark and weep for their sins,
They do not make me sick discussing their duty to God,
Not one is dissatisfied, not one is demented with the mania of owning things,
Not one kneels to another, nor to his kind that lived thousands of years ago,
Not one is respectable or unhappy over the whole earth.

---

23. **pismire:** An early term for ant.
24. **gneiss:** Metamorphic rock.
25. **plutonic rocks:** Igneous rocks formed by solidification well beneath the surface of the earth.

So they show their relations to me and I accept them,
They bring me tokens of myself, they evince them plainly in their possession.

I wonder where they get those tokens,
Did I pass that way huge times ago and negligently drop them?

Myself moving forward then and now and forever,
Gathering and showing more always and with velocity,
Infinite and omnigenous, and the like of these among them,
Not too exclusive toward the reachers of my remembrancers,
Picking out here one that I love, and now go with him on brotherly terms.

A gigantic beauty of a stallion, fresh and responsive to my caresses,
Head high in the forehead, wide between the ears,
Limbs glossy and supple, tail dusting the ground,
Eyes full of sparkling wickedness, ears finely cut, flexibly moving.

His nostrils dilate as my heels embrace him,
His well-built limbs tremble with pleasure as we race around and return.

I but use you a minute, then I resign you, stallion,
Why do I need your paces when I myself out-gallop them?
Even as I stand or sit passing faster than you.

33

Space and Time! now I see it is true, what I guess'd at,
What I guess'd when I loaf'd on the grass,
What I guess'd while I lay alone in my bed,
And again as I walk'd the beach under the paling stars of the morning.

My ties and ballasts leave me, my elbows rest in sea-gaps,
I skirt sierras, my palms cover continents,
I am afoot with my vision.

By the city's quadrangular houses – in log huts, camping with lumbermen,
Along the ruts of the turnpike, along the dry gulch and rivulet bed,
Weeding my onion-patch or hoeing rows of carrots and parsnips, crossing savannas, trailing in forests,
Prospecting, gold-digging, girdling the trees of a new purchase,
Scorch'd ankle-deep by the hot sand, hauling my boat down the shallow river,
Where the panther walks to and fro on a limb overhead, where the buck turns furiously at the hunter,
Where the rattlesnake suns by flabby length on a rock, where the otter is feeding on fish,
Where the alligator in his tough pimples sleeps by the bayou,

Where the black bear is searching for roots or honey, where the beaver pats the mud with his paddle-shaped tail;
Over the growing sugar, over the yellow-flower'd cotton plant, over the rice in its low moist field,
Over the sharp-peak'd farm house, with its scallop'd scum and slender shoots from the gutters,
Over the western persimmon, over the long-leav'd corn, over the delicate blue-flower flax,
Over the white and brown buckwheat, a hummer and buzzer there with the rest,
Over the dusky green of the rye as it ripples and shades in the breeze;
Scaling mountains, pulling myself cautiously up, holding on by low scragged limbs,
Walking the path worn in the grass and beat through the leaves of the brush,
Where the quail is whistling betwixt the woods and the wheat-lot,
Where the bat flies in the Seventh-month eve, where the great gold-bug drops through the dark,
Where the brook puts out of the roots of the old tree and flows to the meadow,
Where cattle stand and shake away flies with the tremulous shuddering of their hides,
Where the cheese-cloth hangs in the kitchen, where andirons straddle the hearth-slab, where cobwebs fall in festoons from the rafters;
Where trip-hammers crash, where the press is whirling its cylinders,
Wherever the human heart beats with terrible throes under its ribs,
Where the pear-shaped balloon is floating aloft, (floating in it myself and looking composedly down,)
Where the life-car[26] is drawn on the slip-noose, where the heat hatches pale-green eggs in the dented sand,
Where the she-whale swims with her calf and never forsakes it,
Where the steam-ship trails hind-ways its long pennant of smoke,
Where the fin of the shark cuts like a black chip out of the water,
Where the half-burn'd brig is riding on unknown currents,
Where shells grow to her slimy deck, where the dead are corrupting below;
Where the dense-starr'd flag is borne at the head of the regiments,
Approaching Manhattan up by the long-stretching island,
Under Niagara, the cataract falling like a veil over my countenance,
Upon a door-step, upon the horse-block of hard wood outside,
Upon the race-course, or enjoying picnics or jigs or a good game of base-ball,

26. **life-car:** Compartment suspended on a rope for transferring passengers from a ship in distress to another ship.

At he-festivals, with blackguard gibes, ironical license, bull-dances,[27] drinking, laughter,
At the cider-mill tasting the sweets of the brown mash, sucking the juice through a straw,
At apple-peelings wanting kisses for all the red fruit I find,
At musters, beach-parties, friendly bees,[28] huskings, house-raisings;
Where the mocking-bird sounds his delicious gurgles, cackles, screams, weeps,
Where the hay-rick stands in the barn-yard, where the dry-stalks are scatter'd, where the brood-cow waits in the hovel,
Where the bull advances to do his masculine work, where the stud to the mare, where the cock is treading the hen,
Where the heifers browse, where geese nip their food with short jerks,
Where sun-down shadows lengthen over the limitless and lonesome prairie,
Where herds of buffalo make a crawling spread of the square miles far and near,
Where the humming-bird shimmers, where the neck of the long-lived swan is curving and winding,
Where the laughing-gull scoots by the shore, where she laughs her near-human laugh,
Where bee-hives range on a gray bench in the garden half hid by the high weeds,
Where band-neck'd partridges roost in a ring on the ground with their heads out,
Where burial coaches enter the arch'd gates of a cemetery,
Where winter wolves bark amid wastes of snow and icicled trees,
Where the yellow-crown'd heron comes to the edge of the marsh at night and feeds upon small crabs,
Where the splash of swimmers and divers cools the warm noon,
Where the katy-did works her chromatic reed on the walnut-tree over the well,
Through patches of citrons and cucumbers with silver-wired leaves,
Through the salt-lick or orange glade, or under conical firs,
Through the gymnasium, through the curtain'd saloon, through the office or public hall;
Pleas'd with the native and pleas'd with the foreign, pleas'd with the new and old,
Pleas'd with the homely woman as well as the handsome,
Pleas'd with the quakeress as she puts off her bonnet and talks melodiously,
Pleas'd with the tune of the choir of the whitewash'd church,
Pleas'd with the earnest words of the sweating Methodist preacher, impress'd seriously at the camp-meeting;
Looking in at the shop-windows of Broadway the whole forenoon, flatting the flesh of my nose on the thick plate glass,
Wandering the same afternoon with my face turn'd up to the clouds, or down a lane or along the beach,

27. **bull-dances:** Country dances where men partner with men.
28. **friendly bees:** Occasions for work and socializing with neighbors.

My right and left arms round the sides of two friends, and I in the middle;
Coming home with the silent and dark-cheek'd bush-boy, (behind me he rides at the drape of the day,)
Far from the settlements studying the print of animals' feet, or the moccasin print,
By the cot in the hospital reaching lemonade to a feverish patient,
Nigh the coffin'd corpse when all is still, examining with a candle;
Voyaging to every port to dicker and adventure.
Hurrying with the modern crowd as eager and fickle as any,
Hot toward one I hate, ready in my madness to knife him,
Solitary at midnight in my back yard, my thoughts gone from me a long while,
Walking the old hills of Judaea with the beautiful gentle God by my side,
Speeding through space, speeding through heaven and the stars,
Speeding amid the seven satellites[29] and the broad ring, and the diameter of eighty thousand miles,
Speeding with tail'd meteors, throwing fire-balls like the rest,
Carrying the crescent child that carries its own full mother in its belly,
Storming, enjoying, planning, loving, cautioning,
Backing and filling, appearing and disappearing,
I tread day and night such roads.

I visit the orchards of spheres and look at the product,
And look at quintillions ripen'd and look at quintillions green.

I fly those flights of a fluid and swallowing soul,
My course runs below the soundings of plummets.

I help myself to material and immaterial,
No guard can shut me off, no law prevent me.

I anchor my ship for a little while only,
My messengers continually cruise away or bring their returns to me.

I go hunting polar furs and the seal, leaping chasms with a pike-pointed staff, clinging to topples of brittle and blue.

I ascend to the foretruck,
I take my place late at night in the crow's-nest,
We sail the arctic sea, it is plenty light enough,
Through the clear atmosphere I stretch around on the wonderful beauty,
The enormous masses of ice pass me and I pass them, the scenery is plain in all directions,
The white-topt mountains show in the distance, I fling out my fancies toward them,

29. **seven satellites:** Known moons of Saturn.

We are approaching some great battle-field in which we are soon to be engaged,
We pass the colossal outposts of the encampment, we pass with still feet and caution,
Or we are entering by the suburbs some vast and ruin'd city,
The blocks and fallen architecture more than all the living cities of the globe.

I am a free companion, I bivouac by invading watchfires,
I turn the bridegroom out of bed and stay with the bride myself,
I tighten her all night to my thighs and lips.

My voice is the wife's voice, the screech by the rail of the stairs,
They fetch my man's body up dripping and drown'd.

I understand the large hearts of heroes,
The courage of present times and all times,
How the skipper saw the crowded and rudderless wreck of the steam-ship, and Death chasing it up and down the storm,
How he knuckled tight and gave not back an inch, and was faithful of days and faithful of nights,
And chalk'd in large letters on a board, *Be of good cheer, we will not desert you;*
How he follow'd with them and tack'd with them three days and would not give it up,
How he saved the drifting company at last,
How the lank loose-gown'd women look'd when boated from the side of their prepared graves,
How the silent old-faced infants and the lifted sick, and the sharp-lipp'd unshaved men;
All this I swallow, it tastes good, I like it well, it becomes mine,
I am the man, I suffer'd, I was there.

The disdain and calmness of martyrs,
The mother of old, condemn'd for a witch, burnt with dry wood, her children gazing on,
The hounded slave that flags in the race, leans by the fence, blowing, cover'd with sweat,
The twinges that sting like needles his legs and neck, the murderous buckshot and the bullets,
All these I feel or am.

I am the hounded slave, I wince at the bite of the dogs,
Hell and despair are upon me, crack and again crack the marksmen,
I clutch the rails of the fence, my gore dribs, thinn'd with the ooze of my skin,
I fall on the weeds and stones,
The riders spur their unwilling horses, haul close,
Taunt my dizzy ears and beat me violently over the head with whip-stocks.

Agonies are one of my changes of garments,
I do not ask the wounded person how he feels, I myself become the wounded person,
My hurts turn livid upon me as I lean on a cane and observe.

I am the mash'd fireman with breast-bone broken,
Tumbling walls buried me in their debris,
Heat and smoke I inspired, I heard the yelling shouts of my comrades,
I heard the distant click of their picks and shovels,
They have clear'd the beams away, they tenderly lift me forth.

I lie in the night air in my red shirt, the pervading hush is for my sake,
Painless after all I lie exhausted but not so unhappy,
White and beautiful are the faces around me, the heads are bared of their fire-caps,
The kneeling crowd fades with the light of the torches.

Distant and dead resuscitate,
They show as the dial or move as the hands of me, I am the clock myself.

I am an old artillerist, I tell of my fort's bombardment,
I am there again.

Again the long roll of the drummers,
Again the attacking cannon, mortars,
Again to my listening ears the cannon responsive.

I take part, I see and hear the whole,
The cries, curses, roar, the plaudits for well-aim'd shots,
The ambulanza slowly passing trailing its red drip,
Workmen searching after damages, making indispensable repairs,
The fall of grenades through the rent roof, the fan-shaped explosion,
The whizz of limbs, heads, stone, wood, iron, high in the air.

Again gurgles the mouth of my dying general, he furiously waves with his hand,
He gasps through the clot *Mind not me — mind — the entrenchments.*

34

Now I tell what I knew in Texas in my early youth,
(I tell not the fall of Alamo,[30]

30. **I tell not the fall of Alamo:** On March 6, 1836, the Alamo, a stronghold of Anglo-American colonists revolting against Mexican rule, was stormed by an army under the command of Santa Anna, and all 187 men inside the fort died. Whitman, however, here describes a less well-known event that occurred three weeks later, when a company of Texans was massacred after their surrender to Mexican forces at Goliad.

Not one escaped to tell the fall of Alamo,
The hundred and fifty are dumb yet at Alamo,)
'Tis the tale of the murder in cold blood of four hundred and twelve young men.

Retreating they had form'd in a hollow square with their baggage for breastworks,
Nine hundred lives out of the surrounding enemy's, nine times their number, was the price they took in advance,
Their colonel was wounded and their ammunition gone,
They treated for an honorable capitulation, receiv'd writing and seal, gave up their arms and march'd back prisoners of war.

They were the glory of the race of rangers,
Matchless with horse, rifle, song, supper, courtship,
Large, turbulent, generous, handsome, proud, and affectionate,
Bearded, sunburnt, drest in the free costume of hunters,
Not a single one over thirty years of age.

The second First-day morning they were brought out in squads and massacred, it was beautiful early summer,
The work commenced about five o'clock and was over by eight.

None obey'd the command to kneel,
Some made a mad and helpless rush, some stood stark and straight,
A few fell at once, shot in the temple or heart, the living and dead lay together,
The maim'd and mangled dug in the dirt, the new-comers saw them there,
Some half-kill'd attempted to crawl away,
These were despatch'd with bayonets or batter'd with the blunts of muskets,
A youth not seventeen years old seiz'd his assassin till two more came to release him,
The three were all torn and cover'd with the boy's blood.

At eleven o'clock began the burning of the bodies;
That is the tale of the murder of the four hundred and twelve young men.

35

Would you hear of an old-time sea-fight?[31]
Would you learn who won by the light of the moon and stars?
List to the yarn, as my grandmother's father the sailor told it to me.

---

31. **old-time sea-fight:** A famous battle during the Revolutionary War between the American *Bon Homme Richard*, commanded by John Paul Jones, and the British *Serapis* in the North Sea.

Our foe was no skulk in his ship I tell you, (said he,)
His was the surly English pluck, and there is no tougher or truer, and never was, and never will be;
Along the lower'd eve he came horribly raking us.

We closed with him, the yards entangled, the cannon touch'd,
My captain lash'd fast with his own hands.

We had receiv'd some eighteen pound shots under the water,
On our lower-gun-deck two large pieces had burst at the first fire, killing all around and blowing up overhead.

Fighting at sun-down, fighting at dark,
Ten o'clock at night, the full moon well up, our leaks on the gain, and five feet of water reported,
The master-at-arms loosing the prisoners confined in the after-hold to give them a chance for themselves.

The transit to and from the magazine is now stopt by the sentinels,
They see so many strange faces they do not know whom to trust.

Our frigate takes fire,
The other asks if we demand quarter?
If our colors are struck and the fighting done?

Now I laugh content, for I hear the voice of my little captain,
We have not struck, he composedly cries, *we have just begun our part of the fighting.*

Only three guns are in use,
One is directed by the captain himself against the enemy's mainmast,
Two well serv'd with grape and canister silence his musketry and clear his decks.

The tops alone second the fire of this little battery, especially the main-top,
They hold out bravely during the whole of the action.

Not a moment's cease,
The leaks gain fast on the pumps, the fire eats toward the powder-magazine.

One of the pumps has been shot away, it is generally thought we are sinking.

Serene stands the little captain,
He is not hurried, his voice is neither high nor low,
His eyes give more light to us than our battle-lanterns.

Toward twelve there in the beams of the moon they surrender to us.

36

Stretch'd and still lies the midnight,
Two great hulls motionless on the breast of the darkness,
Our vessel riddled and slowly sinking, preparations to pass to the one we have conquer'd,
The captain on the quarter-deck coldly giving his orders through a countenance white as a sheet,
Near by the corpse of the child that serv'd in the cabin,
The dead face of an old salt with long white hair and carefully curl'd whiskers,
The flames spite of all that can be done flickering aloft and below,
The husky voices of the two or three officers yet fit for duty,
Formless stacks of bodies and bodies by themselves, dabs of flesh upon the masts and spars,
Cut of cordage, dangle of rigging, slight shock of the soothe of waves,
Black and impassive guns, litter of powder-parcels, strong scent,
A few large stars overhead, silent and mournful shining,
Delicate sniffs of sea-breeze, smells of sedgy grass and fields by the shore, death-messages given in charge to survivors,
The hiss of the surgeon's knife, the gnawing teeth of his saw,
Wheeze, cluck, swash of falling blood, short wild scream, and long, dull, tapering groan,
These so, these irretrievable.

37

You laggards there on guard! look to your arms!
In at the conquer'd doors they crowd! I am possess'd!
Embody all presences outlaw'd or suffering,
See myself in prison shaped like another man,
And feel the dull unintermitted pain.

For me the keepers of convicts shoulder their carbines and keep watch,
It is I let out in the morning and barr'd at night.

Not a mutineer walks handcuff'd to jail but I am handcuff'd to him and walk by his side,
(I am less the jolly one there, and more the silent one with sweat on my twitching lips.)

Not a youngster is taken for larceny but I go up too, and am tried and sentenced.

Not a cholera patient lies at the last gasp but I also lie at the last gasp,
My face is ash-color'd, my sinews gnarl, away from me people retreat.

Askers embody themselves in me and I am embodied in them,
I project my hat, sit shame-faced, and beg.

38

Enough! enough! enough!
Somehow I have been stunn'd. Stand back!
Give me a little time beyond my cuff'd head, slumbers, dreams, gaping,
I discover myself on the verge of a usual mistake.

That I could forget the mockers and insults!
That I could forget the trickling tears and the blows of the bludgeons and hammers!
That I could look with a separate look on my own crucifixion and bloody crowning.

I remember now,
I resume the overstaid fraction,
The grave of rock multiplies what has been confided to it, or to any graves,
Corpses rise, gashes heal, fastenings roll from me.

I troop forth replenish'd with supreme power, one of an average unending procession,
Inland and sea-coast we go, and pass all boundary lines,
Our swift ordinances on their way over the whole earth,
The blossoms we wear in our hats the growth of thousands of years.

Eleves,[32] I salute you! come forward!
Continue your annotations, continue your questionings.

39

The friendly and flowing savage, who is he?
Is he waiting for civilization, or past it and mastering it?

Is he some Southwesterner rais'd out-doors? is he Kanadian?
Is he from the Mississippi country? Iowa, Oregon, California?
The mountains? prairie-life, bush-life? or sailor from the sea?

Wherever he goes men and women accept and desire him,
They desire he should like them, touch them, speak to them, stay with them.

Behavior lawless as snow-flakes, words simple as grass, uncomb'd head, laughter, and naivetè,
Slow-stepping feet, common features, common modes and emanations,
They descend in new forms from the tips of his fingers,
They are wafted with the odor of his body or breath, they fly out of the glance of his eyes.

32. Eleves: Students (French).

40

Flaunt of the sunshine I need not your bask – lie over!
You light surfaces only, I force surfaces and depths also.

Earth! you seem to look for something at my hands,
Say, old top-knot, what do you want?

Man or woman, I might tell how I like you, but cannot,
And might tell what it is in me and what it is in you, but cannot,
And might tell that pining I have, that pulse of my nights and days.

Behold, I do not give lectures or a little charity,
When I give I give myself.

You there, impotent, loose in the knees,
Open your scarf'd chops till I blow grit within you,
Spread your palms and lift the flaps of your pockets,
I am not to be denied, I compel, I have stores plenty and to spare,
And any thing I have I bestow.

I do not ask who you are, that is not important to me,
You can do nothing and be nothing but what I will infold you.

To cotton-field drudge or cleaner of privies I lean,
On his right cheek I put the family kiss,
And in my soul I swear I never will deny him.

On women fit for conception I start bigger and nimbler babes,
(This day I am jetting the stuff of far more arrogant republics.)

To any one dying, thither I speed and twist the knob of the door,
Turn the bed-clothes toward the foot of the bed,
Let the physician and the priest go home.

I seize the descending man and raise him with resistless will,
O despairer, here is my neck,
By God, you shall not go down! hang your whole weight upon me.

I dilate you with tremendous breath, I buoy you up,
Every room of the house do I fill with an arm'd force,
Lovers of me, bafflers of graves.

Sleep – I and they keep guard all night,
Not doubt, not decease shall dare to lay finger upon you,
I have embraced you, and henceforth possess you to myself,
And when you rise in the morning you will find what I tell you is so.

41

I am he bringing help for the sick as they pant on their backs,
And for strong upright men I bring yet more needed help.

I heard what was said of the universe,
Heard it and heard it of several thousand years;
It is middling well as far as it goes – but is that all?

Magnifying and applying come I,
Outbidding at the start the old cautious hucksters,
Taking myself the exact dimensions of Jehovah,
Lithographing Kronos, Zeus his son, and Hercules his grandson,
Buying drafts of Osiris, Isis, Belus, Brahma, Buddha,
In my portfolio placing Manito loose, Allah on a leaf, the crucifix engraved,
With Odin and the hideous-faced Mexitli and every idol and image,[33]
Taking them all for what they are worth and not a cent more,
Admitting they were alive and did the work of their days,
(They bore mites as for unfledg'd birds who have now to rise and fly and sing for themselves,)
Accepting the rough deific sketches to fill out better in myself, bestowing them freely on each man and woman I see,
Discovering as much or more in a framer framing a house,
Putting higher claims for him there with his roll'd-up sleeves driving the mallet and chisel,
Not objecting to special revelations, considering a curl of smoke or a hair on the back of my hand just as curious as any revelation,
Lads ahold of fire-engines and hook-and-ladder ropes no less to me than the gods of the antique wars,
Minding their voices peal through the crash of destruction,
Their brawny limbs passing safe over charr'd laths, their white foreheads whole and unhurt out of the flames;
By the mechanic's wife with her babe at her nipple interceding for every person born,
Three scythes at harvest whizzing in a row from three lusty angels with shirts bagg'd out at their waists,
The snag-tooth'd hostler with red hair redeeming sins past and to come,
Selling all he possesses, traveling on foot to fee lawyers for his brother and sit by him while he is tried for forgery;

---

33. **every idol and image:** Whitman refers to a series of myths from several cultures. In Greek mythology, Kronos ruled the universe until he was dethroned by Zeus. Hercules won immortality by completing twelve notable acts. Osiris was the Egyptian god of nature and fertility and Isis was his wife and sister, the goddess of fertility. Belus was an Assyrian god. Brahama is the Hindu creator. Manito was the nature god of the Algonkian tribes. Allah is the supreme being in the Islam religion. Odin was the chief Norse god. Mexitli was an Aztec war god.

What was strewn in the amplest strewing the square rod about me, and not filling the square rod then,
The bull and the bug never worshipp'd half enough,
Dung and dirt more admirable than was dream'd,
The supernatural of no account, myself waiting my time to be one of the supremes,
The day getting ready for me when I shall do as much good as the best, and be as prodigious;
By my life-lumps! becoming already a creator,
Putting myself here and now to the ambush'd womb of the shadows.

42

A call in the midst of the crowd,
My own voice, orotund sweeping and final.

Come my children,
Come my boys and girls, my women, household and intimates,
Now the performer launches his nerve, he has pass'd his prelude on the reeds within.

Easily written loose-finger'd chords – I feel the thrum of your climax and close.

My head slues round on my neck,
Music rolls, but not from the organ,
Folks are around me, but they are no household of mine.

Ever the hard unsunk ground,
Ever the eaters and drinkers, ever the upward and downward sun, ever the air and the ceaseless tides,
Ever myself and my neighbors, refreshing, wicked, real,
Ever the old inexplicable query, ever that thorn'd thumb, that breath of itches and thirsts,
Ever the vexer's *hoot! hoot!* till we find where the sly one hides and bring him forth,
Ever love, ever the sobbing liquid of life,
Ever the bandage under the chin, ever the trestles of death.

Here and there with dimes on the eyes walking,
To feed the greed of the belly the brains liberally spooning,
Tickets buying, taking, selling, but in to the feast never once going,
Many sweating, ploughing, thrashing, and then the chaff for payment receiving,
A few idly owning, and they the wheat continually claiming.

This is the city and I am one of the citizens,
Whatever interests the rest interests me, politics, wars, markets, newspapers, schools,

The mayor and councils, banks, tariffs, steamships, factories, stocks, stores, real estate and personal estate.

The little plentiful manikins skipping around in collars and tail'd coats,
I am aware who they are, (they are positively not worms or fleas,)
I acknowledge the duplicates of myself, the weakest and shallowest is deathless with me,
What I do and say the same waits for them,
Every thought that flounders in me the same flounders in them.

I know perfectly well my own egotism,
Know my omnivorous lines and must not write any less,
And would fetch you whoever you are flush with myself.

Not words of routine this song of mine,
But abruptly to question, to leap beyond yet nearer bring;
This printed and bound book – but the printer and the printing-office boy?
The well-taken photographs – but your wife or friend close and solid in your arms?
The black ship mail'd with iron, her mighty guns in her turrets – but the pluck of the captain and engineers?
In the houses the dishes and fare and furniture – but the host and hostess, and the look out of their eyes?
The sky up there – yet here or next door, or across the way?
The saints and sages in history – but you yourself?
Sermons, creeds, theology – but the fathomless human brain,
And what is reason? and what is love? and what is life?

43

I do not despise you priests, all time, the world over,
My faith is the greatest of faiths and the least of faiths,
Enclosing worship ancient and modern and all between ancient and modern,
Believing I shall come again upon the earth after five thousand years,
Waiting responses from oracles, honoring the gods, saluting the sun,
Making a fetich of the first rock or stump, powowing with sticks in the circle of obis,[34]
Helping the llama or brahmin as he trims the lamps of the idols,
Dancing yet through the streets in a phallic procession, rapt and austere in the woods a gymnosophist,[35]

34. **circle of obis:** Ritual involving witchcraft in some African and West Indian religions.
35. **gymnosophist:** Member of an ancient Hindu sect.

Drinking mead from the skull-cap, to Shastas and Vedas admirant, minding the Koran,[36]
Walking the teokallis, spotted with gore from the stone and knife, beating the serpent-skin drum,
Accepting the Gospels, accepting him that was crucified, knowing assuredly that he is divine,
To the mass kneeling or the puritan's prayer rising, or sitting patiently in a pew,
Ranting and frothing in my insane crisis, or waiting dead-like till my spirit arouses me,
Looking forth on pavement and land, or outside of pavement and land,
Belonging to the winders of the circuit of circuits.

One of that centripetal and centrifugal gang I turn and talk like a man leaving charges before a journey.

Down-hearted doubters dull and excluded,
Frivolous, sullen, moping, angry, affected, dishearten'd, atheistical,
I know every one of you, I know the sea of torment, doubt, despair and unbelief.

How the flukes splash!
How they contort rapid as lightning, with spasms and spouts of blood!

Be at peace bloody flukes of doubters and sullen mopers,
I take my place among you as much as among any,
The past is the push of you, me, all, precisely the same,
And what is yet untried and afterward is for you, me, all, precisely the same.

I do not know what is untried and afterward,
But I know it will in its turn prove sufficient, and cannot fail.

Each who passes is consider'd, each who stops is consider'd, not a single one can it fail.

It cannot fail the young man who died and was buried,
Nor the young woman who died and was put by his side,
Nor the little child that peep'd in at the door, and then drew back and was never seen again,
Nor the old man who has lived without purpose, and feels it with bitterness worse than gall,
Nor him in the poor house tubercled by rum and the bad disorder,
Nor the numberless slaughter'd and wreck'd, nor the brutish koboo[37] call'd the ordure of humanity,
Nor the sacs merely floating with open mouths for food to slip in,

---

36. **Shastas . . . Koran:** Shastas and Vedas are ancient Hindu books; the Koran is the sacred text of Islam.
37. **koboo:** Native of Sumatra, an island of Indonesia.

Nor any thing in the earth, or down in the oldest graves of the earth,
Nor any thing in the myriads of spheres, nor the myriads of myriads that inhabit
them,
Nor the present, nor the least wisp that is known.

44

It is time to explain myself – let us stand up.

What is known I strip away,
I launch all men and women forward with me into the Unknown.

The clock indicates the moment – but what does eternity indicate?

We have thus far exhausted trillions of winters and summers,
There are trillions ahead, and trillions ahead of them.

Births have brought us richness and variety,
And other births will bring us richness and variety.

I do not call one greater and one smaller,
That which fills its period and place is equal to any.

Were mankind murderous or jealous upon you, my brother, my sister?
I am sorry for you, they are not murderous or jealous upon me,
All has been gentle with me, I keep no account with lamentation,
(What have I to do with lamentation?)

I am an acme of things acconplish'd, and I an encloser of things to be.

My feet strike an apex of the apices of the stairs,
On every step bunches of ages, and larger bunches between the steps,
All below duly travel'd, and still I mount and mount.

Rise after rise bow the phantoms behind me,
Afar down I see the huge first Nothing, I know I was even there,
I waited unseen and always, and slept through the lethargic mist,
And took my time, and took no hurt from the fetid carbon.

Long I was hugg'd close – long and long.

Immense have been the preparations for me,
Faithful and friendly the arms that have help'd me.

Cycles ferried my cradle, rowing and rowing like cheerful boatmen,
For room to me stars kept aside in their own rings,
They sent influences to look after what was to hold me.

Before I was born out of my mother generations guided me,
My embryo has never been torpid, nothing could overlay it.

For it the nebula cohered to an orb,
The long slow strata piled to rest it on,
Vast vegetables gave it sustenance,
Monstrous sauroids transported it in their mouths and deposited it with care.[38]

All forces have been steadily employ'd to complete and delight me,
Now on this spot I stand with my robust soul.

45

O span of youth! ever-push'd elasticity!
O manhood, balanced, florid and full.

My lovers suffocate me,
Crowding my lips, thick in the pores of my skin,
Jostling me through streets and public halls, coming naked to me at night,
Crying by day *Ahoy!* from the rocks of the river, swinging and chirping over my head,
Calling my name from flower-beds, vines, tangled underbrush,
Lighting on every moment of my life,
Bussing my body with soft balsamic busses,
Noiselessly passing handfuls out of their hearts and giving them to be mine.

Old age superbly rising! O welcome, ineffable grace of dying days!

Every condition promulges not only itself, it promulges what grows after and out of itself,
And the dark hush promulges as much as any.

I open my scuttle at night and see the far-sprinkled systems,
And all I see multiplied as high as I can cipher edge but the rim of the farther systems.

Wider and wider they spread, expanding, always expanding,
Outward and outward and forever outward.

My sun has his sun and round him obediently wheels,
He joins with his partners a group of superior circuit,
And greater sets follow, making specks of the greatest inside them.

There is no stoppage and never can be stoppage,
If I, you, and the worlds, and all beneath or upon their surfaces, were this moment reduced back to a pallid float, it would not avail in the long run.

---

38. **Monstrous sauroids . . . care:** According to legend, Sauria – prehistoric reptiles – carried their eggs in their mouths.

We should surely bring up again where we now stand,
And surely go as much farther, and then farther and farther.

A few quadrillions of eras, a few octillions of cubic leagues, do not hazard the
    span or make it impatient,
They are but parts, any thing is but a part.

See ever so far, there is limitless space outside of that,
Count ever so much, there is limitless time around that.

My rendezvous is appointed, it is certain,
The Lord will be there and wait till I come on perfect terms,
The great Camerado, the lover true for whom I pine will be there.

46

I know I have the best of time and space, and was never measured and never will
    be measured.

I tramp a perpetual journey, (come listen all!)
My signs are a rain-proof coat, good shoes, and a staff cut from the woods,
No friend of mine takes his ease in my chair,
I have no chair, no church, no philosophy,
I lead no man to a dinner-table, library, exchange,
But each man and each woman of you I lead upon a knoll,
My left hand hooking you round the waist,
My right hand pointing to landscapes of continents and the public road.

Not I, not any one else can travel that road for you,
You must travel it for yourself.

It is not far, it is within reach,
Perhaps you have been on it since you were born and did not know,
Perhaps it is everywhere on water and on land.

Shoulder your duds dear son, and I will mine, and let us hasten forth,
Wonderful cities and free nations we shall fetch as we go.

If you tire, give me both burdens, and rest the chuff of your hand on my hip,
And in due time you shall repay the same service to me,
For after we start we never lie by again.

This day before dawn I ascended a hill and look'd at the crowded heaven,
And I said to my spirit *When we become the enfolders of those orbs, and the*
    pleasure and knowledge of every thing in them, shall we be fill'd and satisfied
    then?
And my spirit said *No, we but level that lift to pass and continue beyond.*

You are also asking me questions and I hear you,
I answer that I cannot answer, you must find out for yourself.

Sit a while dear son,
Here are biscuits to eat and here is milk to drink,
But as soon as you sleep and renew yourself in sweet clothes, I kiss you with a
good-by kiss and open the gate for your egress hence.

Long enough have you dream'd contemptible dreams,
Now I wash the gum from your eyes,
You must habit yourself to the dazzle of the light and of every moment of your life.

Long have you timidly waded holding a plank by the shore,
Now I will you to be a bold swimmer,
To jump off in the midst of the sea, rise again, nod to me, shout, and laughingly
dash with your hair.

47

I am the teacher of athletes,
He that by me spreads a wider breast than my own proves the width of my own,
He most honors my style who learns under it to destroy the teacher.

The boy I love, the same becomes a man not through derived power, but in his own
right,
Wicked rather than virtuous out of conformity or fear,
Fond of his sweetheart, relishing well his steak,
Unrequited love or a slight cutting him worse than sharp steel cuts,
First-rate to ride, to fight, to hit the bull's eye, to sail a skiff, to sing a song or play
on the banjo,
Preferring scars and the beard and faces pitted with small-pox over all latherers,
And those well-tann'd to those that keep out of the sun.

I teach straying from me, yet who can stray from me?
I follow you whoever you are from the present hour,
My words itch at your ears till you understand them.

I do not say these things for a dollar or to fill up the time while I wait for a boat,
(It is you talking just as much as myself, I act as the tongue of you,
Tied in your mouth, in mine it begins to be loosen'd.)

I swear I will never again mention love or death inside a house,
And I swear I will never translate myself at all, only to him or her who privately
stays with me in the open air.

If you would understand me go to the heights or water-shore,
The nearest gnat is an explanation, and a drop or motion of waves a key,
The maul, the oar, the hand-saw, second my words.

No shutter'd room or school can commune with me,
But roughs and little children better than they.

The young mechanic is closest to me, he knows me well,
The woodman that takes his axe and jug with him shall take me with him all day,
The farm-boy ploughing in the field feels good at the sound of my voice,
In vessels that sail my words sail, I go with fishermen and seamen and love them.

The soldier camp'd or upon the march is mine,
On the night ere the pending battle many seek me, and I do not fail them,
On that solemn night (it may be their last) those that know me seek me.

My face rubs to the hunter's face when he lies down alone in his blanket,
The driver thinking of me does not mind the jolt of his wagon,
The young mother and old mother comprehend me,
The girl and the wife rest the needle a moment and forget where they are,
They and all would resume what I have told them.

48

I have said that the soul is not more than the body,
And I have said that the body is not more than the soul,
And nothing, not God, is greater to one than one's self is,
And whoever walks a furlong without sympathy walks to his own funeral drest in
  his shroud,
And I or you pocketless of a dime may purchase the pick of the earth,
And to glance with an eye or show a bean in its pod confounds the learning of all
  times,
And there is no trade or employment but the young man following it may become
  a hero,
And there is no object so soft but it makes a hub for the wheel'd universe,
And I say to any man or woman, Let your soul stand cool and composed before a
  million universes.

And I say to mankind, Be not curious about God,
For I who am curious about each am not curious about God,
(No array of terms can say how much I am at peace about God and about death.)

I hear and behold God on every object, yet understand God not in the least,
Nor do I understand who there can be more wonderful than myself.

Why should I wish to see God better than this day?
I see something of God each hour of the twenty-four, and each moment then,
In the faces of men and women I see God, and in my own face in the glass,
I find letters from God dropt in the street, and every one is sign'd by God's name,
And I leave them where they are, for I know that wheresoe'er I go,
Others will punctually come for ever and ever.

49

And as to you Death, and you bitter hug of mortality, it is idle to try to alarm me.

To his work without flinching the accoucheur[39] comes,
I see the elder-hand pressing receiving supporting,
I recline by the sills of the exquisite flexible doors,
And mark the outlet, and mark the relief and escape.

And as to you Corpse I think you are good manure, but that does not offend me,
I smell the white roses sweet-scented and growing,
I reach to the leafy lips, I reach to the polish'd breasts of melons.

And as to you Life I reckon you are the leavings of many deaths,
(No doubt I have died myself ten thousand times before.)

I hear you whispering there O stars of heaven,
O suns – O grass of graves – O perpetual transfers and promotions,
If you do not say any thing how can I say any thing?

Of the turbid pool that lies in the autumn forest,
Of the moon that descends the steeps of the soughing twilight,
Toss, sparkles of day and dusk – toss on the black stems that decay in the muck,
Toss to the moaning gibberish of the dry limbs.

I ascend from the moon, I ascend from the night,
I perceive that the ghastly glimmer is noonday sunbeams reflected,
And debouch to the steady and central from the offspring great or small.

50

There is that in me – I do not know what it is – but I know it is in me.

Wrench'd and sweaty – calm and cool then my body becomes,
I sleep – I sleep long.

I do not know it – it is without name – it is a word unsaid,
It is not in any dictionary, utterance, symbol.

Something it swings on more than the earth I swing on,
To it the creation is the friend whose embracing awakes me.

Perhaps I might tell more. Outlines! I plead for my brothers and sisters.

Do you see O my brothers and sisters?
It is not chaos or death – it is form, union, plan – it is eternal life – it is
Happiness.

---

39. **accoucheur:** Early French term for a man who works as an obstetrician or midwife.

51

The past and present wilt – I have fill'd them, emptied them,
And proceed to fill my next fold of the future.

Listener up there! what have you to confide to me?
Look in my face while I snuff the sidle of evening,
(Talk honestly, no one else hears you, and I stay only a minute longer.)

Do I contradict myself?
Very well then I contradict myself,
(I am large, I contain multitudes.)

I concentrate toward them that are nigh, I wait on the door-slab.

Who has done his day's work? who will soonest be through with his supper?
Who wishes to walk with me?

Will you speak before I am gone? will you prove already too late?

52

The spotted hawk swoops by and accuses me, he complains of my gab and my
loitering.

I too am not a bit tamed, I too am untranslatable,
I sound my barbaric yawp over the roofs of the world.

The last scud of day holds back for me,
It flings my likeness after the rest and true as any on the shadow'd wilds,
It coaxes me to the vapor and the dusk.

I depart as air, I shake my white locks at the runaway sun,
I effuse my flesh in eddies, and drift it in lacy jags,

I bequeath myself to the dirt to grow from the grass I love,
If you want me again look for me under your boot-soles.

You will hardly know who I am or what I mean,
But I shall be good health to you nevertheless,
And filter and fibre your blood.

Failing to fetch me at first keep encouraged,
Missing me one place search another,
I stop somewhere waiting for you.

[1855, 1891-92]

From CHILDREN OF ADAM

Once I Pass'd through a Populous City

Once I pass'd through a populous city imprinting my brain for future use with its
shows, architecture, customs, traditions,
Yet now of all that city I remember only a woman I casually met there who
detain'd me for love of me,
Day by day and night by night we were together – all else has long been forgotten
by me,
I remember I say only that woman who passionately clung to me,
Again we wander, we love, we separate again,
Again she holds me by the hand, I must not go,
I see her close beside me with silent lips sad and tremulous.

[1860, 1891-92]

Facing West from California's Shores

Facing west from California's shores,
Inquiring, tireless, seeking what is yet unfound,
I, a child, very old, over waves, towards the house of maternity, the land of
migrations, look afar,
Look off the shores of my Western sea, the circle almost circled;
For starting westward from Hindustan, from the vales of Kashmere,[1]
From Asia, from the north, from the God, the sage, and the hero,
From the south, from the flowery peninsulas and the spice islands,
Long having wander'd since, round the earth having wander'd,
Now I face home again, very pleas'd and joyous,
(But where is what I started for so long ago?
And why is it yet unfound?)

[1860, 1891-92]

1. vales of Kashmere: A fertile valley between what is now India and Pakistan.

As Adam Early in the Morning

As Adam early in the morning,
Walking forth from the bower refresh'd with sleep,
Behold me where I pass, hear my voice, approach,
Touch me, touch the palm of your hand to my body as I pass,
Be not afraid of my body.

[1860, 1891-92]

From CALAMUS[1]

IN PATHS UNTRODDEN

In paths untrodden,
In the growth by margins of pond-waters,
Escaped from the life that exhibits itself,
From all the standards hitherto publish'd, from the pleasures, profits,
conformities,
Which too long I was offering to feed my soul,
Clear to me now standards not yet publish'd, clear to me that my soul,
That the soul of the man I speak for rejoices in comrades,
Here by myself away from the clank of the world,
Tallying and talk'd to here by tongues aromatic,
Breast-sorrel and pinks of love, fingers that wind around tighter than vines,
Gushes from the throats of birds hid in the foliage of trees as the sun is risen,
Breezes of land and love set from living shores to you on the living sea, to you
O sailors!
Frost-mellow'd berries and Third-month twigs offer'd fresh to young persons
wandering out in the fields when the winter breaks up,
Love-buds put before you and within you whoever you are,
Buds to be unfolded on the old terms,
If you bring the warmth of the sun to them they will open and bring form, color,
perfume, to you,
If you become the aliment and the wet they will become flowers, fruits, tall
branches and trees.

[1860, 1891-92]

OF THE TERRIBLE DOUBT OF APPEARANCES

Of the terrible doubt of appearances,
Of the uncertainty after all, that we may be deluded,
That may-be reliance and hope are but speculations after all,
That may-be identity beyond the grave is a beautiful fable only,
May-be the things I perceive, the animals, plants, men, hills, shining and flowing
waters,

1. **Calamus:** Another term for sweet-flag, an aromatic grass whose erect spears sometimes grow to as much as three feet in height.

The skies of day and night, colors, densities, forms, may-be these are (as doubtless they are) only apparitions, and the real something has yet to be known,
(How often they dart out of themselves as if to confound me and mock me!
How often I think neither I know, nor any man knows, aught of them,)
May-be seeming to me what they are (as doubtless they indeed but seem) as from my present point of view, and might prove (as of course they would) nought of what they appear, or nought anyhow, from entirely changed points of view;
To me these and the like of these are curiously answer'd by my lovers, my dear friends,
When he whom I love travels with me or sits a long while holding me by the hand,
When the subtle air, the impalpable, the sense that words and reason hold not, surround us and pervade us,
Then I am charged with untold and untellable wisdom, I am silent, I require nothing further,
I cannot answer the question of appearances or that of identity beyond the grave,
But I walk or sit indifferent, I am satisfied,
He ahold of my hand has completely satisfied me.

[1860, 1891-92]

Trickle Drops

Trickle drops! my blue veins leaving!
O drops of me! trickle, slow drops,
Candid from me falling, drip, bleeding drops,
From wounds made to free you whence you were prison'd,
From my face, from my forehead and lips,
From my breast, from within where I was conceal'd, press forth red drops, confession drops,
Stain every page, stain every song I sing, every word I say, bloody drops,
Let them know your scarlet heat, let them glisten,
Saturate them with yourself all ashamed and wet,
Glow upon all I have written or shall write, bleeding drops,
Let it all be seen in your light, blushing drops.

[1860, 1891-92]

City of Orgies

City of orgies, walks and joys,
City whom that I have lived and sung in your midst will one day make you illustrious,
Not the pageants of you, not your shifting tableaus, your spectacles, repay me,
Not the interminable rows of your houses, nor the ships at the wharves,

Nor the processions in the streets, nor the bright windows with goods in them,
Nor to converse with learn'd persons, or bear my share in the soiree or feast;
Not those, but as I pass O Manhattan, your frequent and swift flash of eyes
offering me love,
Offering response to my own – these repay me,
Lovers, continual lovers, only repay me.

[1860, 1891-92]

I SAW IN LOUISIANA A LIVE-OAK GROWING

I saw in Louisiana a live-oak growing,
All alone stood it and the moss hung down from the branches,
Without any companion it grew there uttering joyous leaves of dark green,
And its look, rude, unbending, lusty, made me think of myself,
But I wonder'd how it could utter joyous leaves standing alone there without its
friend near, for I knew I could not,
And I broke off a twig with a certain number of leaves upon it, and twined around
it a little moss,
And brought it away, and I have placed it in sight in my room,
It is not needed to remind me as of my own dear friends,
(For I believe lately I think of little else than of them,)
Yet it remains to me a curious token, it makes me think of manly love;
For all that, and though the live-oak glistens there in Louisiana solitary in a wide
flat space,
Uttering joyous leaves all its life without a friend a lover near,
I know very well I could not.

[1860, 1891-92]

HERE THE FRAILEST LEAVES OF ME

Here the frailest leaves of me and yet my strongest lasting,
Here I shade and hide my thoughts, I myself do not expose them,
And yet they expose me more than all my other poems.

[1860, 1891-92]

From Sea-Drift

Out of the Cradle Endlessly Rocking[1]

Out of the cradle endlessly rocking,
Out of the mocking-bird's throat, the musical shuttle,
Out of the Ninth-month midnight,
Over the sterile sands and the fields beyond, where the child leaving his bed
    wander'd alone, bareheaded, barefoot,
Down from the shower'd halo,
Up from the mystic play of shadows twining and twisting as if they were alive,
Out from the patches of briers and blackberries,
From the memories of the bird that chanted to me,
From your memories sad brother, from the fitful risings and fallings I heard,
From under that yellow half-moon late-risen and swollen as if with tears,
From those beginning notes of yearning and love there in the mist,
From the thousand responses of my heart never to cease,
From the myriad thence-arous'd words,
From the word stronger and more delicious than any,
From such as now they start the scene revisiting,
As a flock, twittering, rising, or overhead passing,
Borne hither, ere all eludes me, hurriedly,
A man, yet by these tears a little boy again,
Throwing myself on the sand, confronting the waves,
I, chanter of pains and joys, uniter of here and hereafter,
Taking all hints to use them, but swiftly leaping beyond them,
A reminiscence sing.

Once Paumanok,[2]
When the lilac-scent was in the air and Fifth-month grass was growing,
Up this seashore in some briers,
Two feather'd guests from Alabama, two together,
And their nest, and four light-green eggs spotted with brown,
And every day the he-bird to and fro near at hand,
And every day the she-bird crouch'd on her nest, silent, with bright eyes,
And every day I, a curious boy, never too close, never disturbing them,
Cautiously peering, absorbing, translating.

---

1. **"Out of the Cradle Endlessly Rocking":** This poem was first published as "A Child's Reminiscence" in the *New York Saturday Press* on December 24, 1859. An editorial notice in the weekly newspaper noted that "Our readers may, if they choose, consider as our Christmas or New Year's present to them [this] curious warble, by Walt Whitman." The poem was titled "A Word Out of the Sea" in the 1860 and 1867 editions and "Out of the Cradle Endlessly Rocking" in all later editions of *Leaves of Grass*.
2. **Paumanok:** Indian name for Long Island.

Shine! shine! shine!
Pour down your warmth, great sun!
While we bask, we two together.

Two together!
Winds blow south, or winds blow north,
Day come white, or night come black,
Home, or rivers and mountains from home,
Singing all time, minding no time,
While we two keep together.

Till of a sudden,
May-be kill'd, unknown to her mate,
One forenoon the she-bird crouch'd not on the nest,
Nor return'd that afternoon, nor the next,
Nor ever appear'd again.

And thenceforward all summer in the sound of the sea,
And at night under the full of the moon in calmer weather,
Over the hoarse surging of the sea,
Or flitting from brier to brier by day,
I saw, I heard at intervals the remaining one, the he-bird,
The solitary guest from Alabama.

Blow! blow! blow!
Blow up sea-winds along Paumanok's shore;
I wait and I wait till you blow my mate to me.

Yes, when the stars glisten'd,
All night long on the prong of a moss-scallop'd stake,
Down almost amid the slapping waves,
Sat the lone singer wonderful causing tears.

He call'd on his mate,
He pour'd forth the meanings which I of all men know.

Yes my brother I know,
The rest might not, but I have treasur'd every note,
For more than once dimly down to the beach gliding,
Silent, avoiding the moonbeams, blending myself with the shadows,
Recalling now the obscure shapes, the echoes, the sounds and sights after their
sorts,
The white arms out in the breakers tirelessly tossing,
I, with bare feet, a child, the wind wafting my hair,
Listen'd long and long.

Listen'd to keep, to sing, now translating the notes,
Following you my brother.

Soothe! soothe! soothe!
Close on its wave soothes the wave behind,
And again another behind embracing and lapping, every one close,
But my love soothes not me, not me.

Low hangs the moon, it rose late,
It is lagging — O I think it is heavy with love, with love.

O madly the sea pushes upon the land,
With love, with love.

O night! do I not see my love fluttering out among the breakers?
What is that little black thing I see there in the white?

Loud! loud! loud!
Loud I call to you, my love!

High and clear I shoot my voice over the waves,
Surely you must know who is here, is here,
You must know who I am, my love.

Low-hanging moon!
What is that dusky spot in your brown yellow?
O it is the shape, the shape of my mate!
O moon do not keep her from me any longer.

Land! land! O land!
Whichever way I turn, O I think you could give me my mate back again if you only would,
For I am almost sure I see her dimly whichever way I look.

O rising stars!
Perhaps the one I want so much will rise, will rise with some of you.

O throat! O trembling throat!
Sound clearer through the atmosphere!
Pierce the woods, the earth,
Somewhere listening to catch you must be the one I want.

Shake out carols!
Solitary here, the night's carols!
Carols of lonesome love! death's carols!
Carols under that lagging, yellow, waning moon!
O under that moon where she droops almost down into the sea!
O reckless despairing carols.

But soft! sink low!
Soft! let me just murmur,
And do you wait a moment you husky-nois'd sea,
For somewhere I believe I heard my mate responding to me,

So faint, I must be still, be still to listen,
But not altogether still, for then she might not come immediately to me.

Hither my love!
Here I am! here!
With this just-sustain'd note I announce myself to you,
This gentle call is for you my love, for you.

Do not be decoy'd elsewhere,
That is the whistle of the wind, it is not my voice,
That is the fluttering, the fluttering of the spray,
Those are the shadows of leaves.

O darkness! O in vain!
O I am very sick and sorrowful.

O brown halo in the sky near the moon, drooping upon the sea!
O troubled reflection in the sea!
O throat! O throbbing heart!
And I singing uselessly, uselessly all the night.

O past! O happy life! O songs of joy!
In the air, in the woods, over fields,
Loved! loved! loved! loved! loved!
But my mate no more, no more with me!
We two together no more.

The aria sinking,
All else continuing, the stars shining,
The winds blowing, the notes of the bird continuous echoing,
With angry moans the fierce old mother incessantly moaning,
On the sands of Paumanok's shore gray and rustling,
The yellow half-moon enlarged, sagging down, drooping, the face of the sea
    almost touching,
The boy ecstatic, with his bare feet the waves, with his hair the atmosphere
    dallying,
The love in the heart long pent, now loose, now at last tumultuously bursting,
The aria's meaning, the ears, the soul, swiftly depositing,
The strange tears down the cheeks coursing,
The colloquy there, the trio, each uttering,
The undertone, the savage old mother incessantly crying,
To the boy's soul's questions sullenly timing, some drown'd secret hissing,
To the outsetting bard.

Demon or bird! (said the boy's soul,)
Is it indeed toward your mate you sing? or is it really to me?
For I, that was a child, my tongue's use sleeping, now I have heard you,
Now in a moment I know what I am for, I awake,

And already a thousand singers, a thousand songs, clearer, louder and more sorrowful than yours,
A thousand warbling echoes have started to life within me, never to die.

O you singer solitary, singing by yourself, projecting me,
O solitary me listening, never more shall I cease perpetuating you,
Never more shall I escape, never more the reverberations,
Never more the cries of unsatisfied love be absent from me,
Never again leave me to be the peaceful child I was before what there in the night,
By the sea under the yellow and sagging moon,
The messenger there arous'd, the fire, the sweet hell within,
The unknown want, the destiny of me.

O give me the clew! (it lurks in the night here somewhere,)
O if I am to have so much, let me have more!

A word then, (for I will conquer it,)
The word final, superior to all,
Subtle, sent up – what is it? – I listen;
Are you whispering it, and have been all the time, you sea-waves?
Is that it from your liquid rims and wet sands?

Whereto answering, the sea,
Delaying not, hurrying not,
Whisper'd me through the night, and very plainly before day-break.
Lisp'd to me the low and delicious word death,
And again death, death, death, death,
Hissing melodious, neither like the bird nor like my arous'd child's heart,
But edging near as privately for me rustling at my feet,
Creeping thence steadily up to my ears and laving me softly all over,
Death, death, death, death, death.

Which I do not forget,
But fuse the song of my dusky demon and brother,
That he sang to me in the moonlight on Paumanok's gray beach,
With the thousand responsive songs at random,
My own songs awaked from that hour,
And with them the key, the word up from the waves,
The word of the sweetest song and all songs,
That strong and delicious word which, creeping to my feet,
(Or like some old crone rocking the cradle, swathed in sweet garments, bending aside,)
The sea whisper'd me.

[1860, 1891-92]

From BY THE ROADSIDE

WHEN I HEARD THE LEARN'D ASTRONOMER

When I heard the learn'd astronomer,
When the proofs, the figures, were ranged in columns before me,
When I was shown the charts and diagrams, to add, divide, and measure them,
When I sitting heard the astronomer where he lectured with much applause in the lecture-room,
How soon unaccountable I became tired and sick,
Till rising and gliding out I wander'd off by myself,
In the mystical moist night-air, and from time to time,
Look'd up in perfect silence at the stars.

[1865, 1891-92]

I SIT AND LOOK OUT

I sit and look out upon all the sorrows of the world, and upon all oppression and shame,
I hear secret convulsive sobs from young men at anguish with themselves, remorseful after deeds done,
I see in low life the mother misused by her children, dying, neglected, gaunt, desperate,
I see the wife misused by her husband, I see the treacherous seducer of young women,
I mark the ranklings of jealousy and unrequited love attempted to be hid, I see these sights on the earth,
I see the workings of battle, pestilence, tyranny, I see martyrs and prisoners,
I observe a famine at sea, I observe the sailors casting lots who shall be kill'd to preserve the lives of the rest,
I observe the slights and degradations cast by arrogant persons upon laborers, the poor, and upon negroes, and the like;
All these – all the meanness and agony without end I sitting look out upon,
See, hear, and am silent.

[1860, 1891-92]

THE DALLIANCE OF THE EAGLES

Skirting the river road, (my forenoon walk, my rest,)
Skyward in air a sudden muffled sound, the dalliance of the eagles,
The rushing amorous contact high in space together,
The clinching interlocking claws, a living, fierce, gyrating wheel,

Four beating wings, two beaks, a swirling mass tight grappling,
In tumbling turning clustering loops, straight downward falling,
Till o'er the river pois'd, the twain yet one, a moment's lull,
A motionless still balance in the air, then parting, talons loosing,
Upward again on slow-firm pinions slanting, their separate diverse flight,
She hers, he his, pursuing.

[1880, 1891-92]

From DRUM-TAPS

Beat! Beat! Drums!

Beat! beat! drums! – blow! bugles! blow!
Through the windows – through doors – burst like a ruthless force,
Into the solemn church, and scatter the congregation,
Into the school where the scholar is studying;
Leave not the bridegroom quiet – no happiness must he have now with his bride,
Nor the peaceful farmer any peace, ploughing his field or gathering his grain,
So fierce you whirr and pound you drums – so shrill you bugles blow.

Beat! beat! drums! – blow! bugles! blow!
Over the traffic of cities – over the rumble of wheels in the streets;
Are beds prepared for sleepers at night in the houses? no sleepers must sleep in those beds,
No bargainers' bargains by day – no brokers or speculators – would they continue?
Would the talkers be talking? would the singer attempt to sing?
Would the lawyer rise in the court to state his case before the judge?
Then rattle quicker, heavier drums – you bugles wilder blow.

Beat! beat! drums! – blow! bugles! blow!
Make no parley – stop for no expostulation,
Mind not the timid – mind not the weeper or prayer,
Mind not the old man beseeching the young man,
Let not the child's voice be heard, nor the mother's entreaties,
Make even the trestles to shake the dead where they lie awaiting the hearses,
So strong you thump O terrible drums – so loud you bugles blow.

[1865, 1891-92]

CAVALRY CROSSING A FORD

A line in long array here they wind betwixt green islands,
They take a serpentine course, their arms flash in the sun – hark to the musical clank,
Behold the silvery river, in it the splashing horses loitering stop to drink,
Behold the brown-faced men, each group, each person a picture, the negligent rest on the saddles,
Some emerge on the opposite bank, others are just entering the ford – while,
Scarlet and blue and snowy white,
The guidon flags flutter gayly in the wind.

[1865, 1891–92]

VIGIL STRANGE I KEPT ON THE FIELD ONE NIGHT

Vigil strange I kept on the field one night;
When you my son and my comrade dropt at my side that day,
One look I but gave which your dear eyes return'd with a look I shall never forget,
One touch of your hand to mine O boy, reach'd up as you lay on the ground,
Then onward I sped in the battle, the even-contested battle,
Till late in the night reliev'd to the place at last again I made my way,
Found you in death so cold dear comrade, found your body son of responding kisses, (never again on earth responding,)
Bared your face in the starlight, curious the scene, cool blew the moderate night-wind,
Long there and then in vigil I stood, dimly around me the battle-field spreading,
Vigil wondrous and vigil sweet there in the fragrant silent night,
But not a tear fell, not even a long-drawn sigh, long, long I gazed,
Then on the earth partially reclining sat by your side leaning my chin in my hands,
Passing sweet hours, immortal and mystic hours with you dearest comrade – not a tear, not a word,
Vigil of silence, love and death, vigil for you my son and my soldier,
As onward silently stars aloft, eastward new ones upward stole,
Vigil final for you brave boy, (I could not save you, swift was your death,
I faithfully loved you and cared for you living, I think we shall surely meet again,)
Till at latest lingering of the night, indeed just as the dawn appear'd,
My comrade I wrapt in his blanket, envelop'd well his form,
Folded the blanket well, tucking it carefully over head and carefully under feet,
And there and then and bathed by the rising sun, my son in his grave, in his rude-dug grave I deposited,

Ending my vigil strange with that, vigil of night and battle-field dim,
Vigil for boy of responding kisses, (never again on earth responding,)
Vigil for comrade swiftly slain, vigil I never forget, how as day brighten'd,
I rose from the chill ground and folded my soldier well in his blanket,
And buried him where he fell.

[1865, 1891-92]

A SIGHT IN CAMP IN THE DAYBREAK GRAY AND DIM

A sight in camp in the daybreak gray and dim,
As from my tent I emerge so early sleepless,
As slow I walk in the cool fresh air the path near by the hospital tent,
Three forms I see on stretchers lying, brought out there untended lying,
Over each the blanket spread, ample brownish woolen blanket,
Gray and heavy blanket, folding, covering all.

Curious I halt and silent stand,
Then with light fingers I from the face of the nearest the first just lift the blanket;
Who are you elderly man so gaunt and grim, with well-gray'd hair, and flesh all sunken about the eyes?
Who are you my dear comrade?

Then to the second I step – and who are you my child and darling?
Who are you sweet boy with cheeks yet blooming?

Then to the third – a face nor child nor old, very calm, as of beautiful yellow-white ivory;
Young man I think I know you – I think this face is the face of the Christ himself,
Dead and divine and brother of all, and here again he lies.

[1865, 1891-92]

THE WOUND-DRESSER

1

An old man bending I come among new faces,
Years looking backward resuming in answer to children,
Come tell us old man, as from young men and maidens that love me,
(Arous'd and angry, I'd thought to beat the alarum, and urge relentless war,
But soon my fingers fail'd me, my face droop'd and I resign'd myself,
To sit by the wounded and soothe them, or silently watch the dead;)
Years hence of these scenes, of these furious passions, these chances,
Of unsurpass'd heroes, (was one side so brave? the other was equally brave;)

Now be witness again, paint the mightiest armies of earth,
Of those armies so rapid so wondrous what saw you to tell us?
What stays with you latest and deepest? of curious panics,
Of hard-fought engagements or sieges tremendous what deepest remains?

2

O maidens and young men I love and that love me,
What you ask of my days those the strangest and sudden your talking recalls,
Soldier alert I arrive after a long march cover'd with sweat and dust,
In the nick of time I come, plunge in the fight, loudly shout in the rush of
successful charge,
Enter the captur'd works – yet lo, like a swift-running river they fade,
Pass and are gone they fade – I dwell not on soldiers' perils or soldiers' joys,
(Both I remember well – many the hardships, few the joys, yet I was content.)

But in silence, in dreams' projections,
While the world of gain and appearance and mirth goes on,
So soon what is over forgotten, and waves wash the imprints off, the sand,
With hinged knees returning I enter the doors, (while for you up there,
Whoever you are, follow without noise and be of strong heart.)

Bearing the bandages, water and sponge,
Straight and swift to my wounded I go,
Where they lie on the ground after the battle brought in,
Where their priceless blood reddens the grass the ground,
Or to the rows of the hospital tent, or under the roof'd hospital,
To the long rows of cots up and down each side I return,
To each and all one after another I draw near, not one do I miss,
An attendant follows holding a tray, he carries a refuse pail,
Soon to be fill'd with clotted rags and blood, emptied, and fill'd again.

I onward go, I stop,
With hinged knees and steady hand to dress wounds,
I am firm with each, the pangs are sharp yet unavoidable,
One turns to me his appealing eyes – poor boy! I never knew you,
Yet I think I could not refuse this moment to die for you, if that would save you.

3

On, on I go, (open doors of time! open hospital doors!)
The crush'd head I dress, (poor crazed hand tear not the bandage away,)
The neck of the cavalry-man with the bullet through and through I examine,
Hard the breathing rattles, quite glazed already the eye, yet life struggles hard,

(Come sweet death! be persuaded O beautiful death!
In mercy come quickly.)

From the stump of the arm, the amputated hand,
I undo the clotted lint, remove the slough, wash off the matter and blood,
Back on his pillow the soldier bends with curv'd neck and side-falling head,
His eyes are closed, his face is pale, he dares not look on the bloody stump,
And has not yet look'd on it.

I dress a wound in the side, deep, deep,
But a day or two more, for see the frame all wasted and sinking,
And the yellow-blue countenance see.

I dress the perforated shoulder, the foot with the bullet-wound,
Cleanse the one with a gnawing and putrid gangrene, so sickening, so offensive,
While the attendant stands behind aside me holding the tray and pail.

I am faithful, I do not give out,
The fractur'd thigh, the knee, the wound in the abdomen,
These and more I dress with impassive hand, (yet deep in my breast a fire, a burning flame.)

4

Thus in silence in dreams' projections,
Returning, resuming, I thread my way through the hospitals,
The hurt and wounded I pacify with soothing hand,
I sit by the restless all the dark night, some are so young,
Some suffer so much, I recall the experience sweet and sad,
(Many a soldier's loving arms about this neck have cross'd and rested,
Many a soldier's kiss dwells on these bearded lips.)

[1865, 1891-92]

Reconciliation

Word over all, beautiful as the sky,
Beautiful that war and all its deeds of carnage must in time be utterly lost,
That the hands of the sisters Death and Night incessantly softly wash again, and ever again, this soil'd world;
For my enemy is dead, a man divine as myself is dead,
I look where he lies white-faced and still in the coffin – I draw near,
Bend down and touch lightly with my lips the white face in the coffin.

[1865-66, 1891-92]

From MEMORIES OF PRESIDENT LINCOLN

WHEN LILACS LAST IN THE DOORYARD BLOOM'D[1]

1

When lilacs last in the dooryard bloom'd,
And the great star[2] early droop'd in the western sky in the night,
I mourn'd, and yet shall mourn with ever-returning spring.

Ever-returning spring, trinity sure to me you bring,
Lilac blooming perennial and drooping star in the west,
And thought of him I love.

2

O powerful western fallen star!
O shades of night – O moody, tearful night!
O great star disappear'd – O the black murk that hides the star!
O cruel hands that hold me powerless – O helpless soul of me!
O harsh surrounding cloud that will not free my soul.

3

In the dooryard fronting an old farm-house near the white-wash'd palings,
Stands the lilac-bush tall-growing with heart-shaped leaves of rich green,
With many a pointed blossom rising delicate, with the perfume strong I love,
With every leaf a miracle – and from this bush in the dooryard,
With delicate-color'd blossoms and heart-shaped leaves of rich green,
A sprig with its flower I break.

4

In the swamp in secluded recesses,
A shy and hidden bird is warbling a song.

---

1. **"When Lilacs Last in the Dooryard Bloom'd":** Whitman wrote his elegy to Abraham Lincoln in the weeks following the president's assassination on April 14, 1865. The poem was first published in a "Sequel" to *Drum-Taps* (1865), his collection of poetry on the Civil War. He later incorporated it into *Leaves of Grass*, initially in a cluster headed "President Lincoln's Burial Hymn" and later titled "Memories of President Lincoln."
2. **great star:** Venus.

Solitary the thrush,
The hermit withdrawn to himself, avoiding the settlements,
Sings by himself a song.

Song of the bleeding throat,
Death's outlet song of life, (for well dear brother I know,
If thou wast not granted to sing thou would'st surely die.)

5

Over the breast of the spring, the land, amid cities,
Amid lanes and through old woods, where lately the violets peep'd from the ground, spotting the gray debris,
Amid the grass in the fields each side of the lanes, passing the endless grass,
Passing the yellow-spear'd wheat, every grain from its shroud in the dark-brown fields uprisen,
Passing the apple-tree blows[3] of white and pink in the orchards,
Carrying a corpse to where it shall rest in the grave,
Night and day journeys a coffin.

6

Coffin that passes through lanes and streets,
Through day and night with the great cloud darkening the land,
With the pomp of the inloop'd flags with the cities draped in black,
With the show of the States themselves as of crape-veil'd women standing,
With processions long and winding and the flambeaus of the night,
With the countless torches lit, with the silent sea of faces and the unbared heads,
With the waiting depot, the arriving coffin, and the sombre faces,
With dirges through the night, with the thousand voices rising strong and solemn,
With all the mournful voices of the dirges pour'd around the coffin,
The dim-lit churches and the shuddering organs – where amid these you journey,
With the tolling tolling bells' perpetual clang,
Here, coffin that slowly passes,
I give you my sprig of lilac.

7

(Nor for you, for one alone,
Blossoms and branches green to coffins all I bring,

---

3. **blows:** Blossoms.

For fresh as the morning, thus would I chant a song for you O sane and sacred death.

All over bouquets of roses,
O death, I cover you over with roses and early lilies,
But mostly and now the lilac that blooms the first,
Copious I break, I break the sprigs from the bushes,
With loaded arms I come, pouring for you,
For you and the coffins all of you O death.)

8

O western orb sailing the heaven,
Now I know what you must have meant as a month since I walk'd,
As I walk'd in silence the transparent shadowy night,
As I saw you had something to tell as you bent to me night after night,
As you droop'd from the sky low down as if to my side, (while the other stars all look'd on,)
As we wander'd together the solemn night, (for something I know not what kept me from sleep,)
As the night advanced, and I saw on the rim of the west how full you were of woe,
As I stood on the rising ground in the breeze in the cool transparent night,
As I watch'd where you pass'd and was lost in the netherward black of the night,
As my soul in its trouble dissatisfied sank, as where you sad orb,
Concluded, dropt in the night, and was gone.

9

Sing on there in the swamp,
O singer bashful and tender, I hear your notes, I hear your call,
I hear, I come presently, I understand you,
But a moment I linger, for the lustrous star has detain'd me,
The star my departing comrade holds and detains me.

10

O how shall I warble myself for the dead one there I loved?
And how shall I deck my song for the large sweet soul that has gone?
And what shall my perfume be for the grave of him I love?

Sea-winds blown from east and west,
Blown from the Eastern sea and blown from the Western sea, till there on the prairies meeting,
These and with these and the breath of my chant,
I'll perfume the grave of him I love.

11

O what shall I hang on the chamber walls?
And what shall the pictures be that I hang on the walls,
To adorn the burial-house of him I love?

Pictures of growing spring and farms and homes,
With the Fourth-month eve at sundown, and the gray smoke lucid and bright,
With floods of the yellow gold of the gorgeous, indolent, sinking sun, burning, expanding the air,
With the fresh sweet herbage under foot, and the pale green leaves of the trees prolific,
In the distance the flowing glaze, the breast of the river, with a wind-dapple here and there,
With ranging hills on the banks, with many a line against the sky, and shadows,
And the city at hand with dwellings so dense, and stacks of chimneys,
And all the scenes of life and the workshops, and the workmen homeward returning.

12

Lo, body and soul – this land,
My own Manhattan with spires, and the sparkling and hurrying tides, and the ships,
The varied and ample land, the South and the North in the light, Ohio's shores and flashing Missouri,
And ever the far-spreading prairies cover'd with grass and corn.

Lo, the most excellent sun so calm and haughty,
The violet and purple morn with just-felt breezes,
The gentle soft-born measureless light,
The miracle spreading bathing all, the fulfill'd noon,
The coming eve delicious, the welcome night and the stars,
Over my cities shining all, enveloping man and land.

13

Sing on, sing on you gray-brown bird,
Sing from the swamps, the recesses, pour your chant from the bushes,
Limitless out of the dusk, out of the cedars and pines.

Sing on dearest brother, warble your reedy song,
Loud human song, with voice of uttermost woe.

O liquid and free and tender!
O wild and loose to my soul – O wondrous singer!

You only I hear – yet the star holds me, (but will soon depart,)
Yet the lilac with mastering odor holds me.

14

Now while I sat in the day and look'd forth,
In the close of the day with its light and the fields of spring, and the farmers preparing their crops,
In the large unconscious scenery of my land with its lakes and forests,
In the heavenly aerial beauty, (after the perturb'd winds and the storms,)
Under the arching heavens of the afternoon swift passing, and the voices of children and women,
The many-moving sea-tides, and I saw the ships how they sail'd,
And the summer approaching with richness, and the fields all busy with labor,
And the infinite separate houses, how they all went on, each with its meals and minutia of daily usages,
And the streets how their throbbings throbb'd, and the cities pent – lo, then and there,
Falling upon them all and among them all, enveloping me with the rest,
Appear'd the cloud, appear'd the long black trail,
And I knew death, its thought, and the sacred knowledge of death.

Then with the knowledge of death as walking one side of me,
And the thought of death close-walking the other side of me,
And I in the middle as with companions, and as holding the hands of companions,
I fled forth to the hiding receiving night that talks not,
Down to the shores of the water, the path by the swamp in the dimness,
To the solemn shadowy cedars and ghostly pines so still.

And the singer so shy to the rest receiv'd me,
The gray-brown bird I know receiv'd us comrades three,
And he sang the carol of death, and a verse for him I love.

From deep secluded recesses,
From the fragrant cedars and the ghostly pines so still,
Came the carol of the bird.

And the charm of the carol rapt me,
As I held as if by their hands my comrades in the night,
And the voice of my spirit tallied the song of the bird.

Come lovely and soothing death,
Undulate round the world, serenely arriving, arriving,
In the day, in the night, to all, to each,
Sooner or later delicate death.

Prais'd be the fathomless universe,
For life and joy, and for objects and knowledge curious,
And for love, sweet love — but praise! praise! praise!
For the sure-enwinding arms of cool-enfolding death.

Dark mother always gliding near with soft feet,
Have none chanted for thee a chant of fullest welcome?
Then I chant it for thee, I glorify thee above all,
I bring thee a song that when thou must indeed come, come unfalteringly.

Approach strong deliveress,
When it is so, when thou hast taken them I joyously sing the dead,
Lost in the loving floating ocean of thee,
Laved in the flood of thy bliss O death.

From me to thee glad serenades,
Dances for thee I propose saluting thee, adornments and feastings for thee,
And the sights of the open landscape and the high-spread sky are fitting,
And life and the fields, and the huge and thoughtful night.

The night in silence under many a star,
The ocean shore and the husky whispering wave whose voice I know,
And the soul turning to thee O vast and well-veil'd death,
And the body gratefully nestling close to thee.

Over the tree-tops I float thee a song,
Over the rising and sinking waves, over the myriad fields and the prairies wide,
Over the dense-pack'd cities all and the teeming wharves and ways,
I float this carol with joy, with joy to thee O death.

15

To the tally of my soul,
Loud and strong kept up the gray-brown bird,
With pure deliberate notes spreading filling the night.

Loud in the pines and cedars dim,
Clear in the freshness moist and the swamp-perfume,
And I with my comrades there in the night.

While my sight that was bound in my eyes unclosed,
As to long panoramas of visions.

And I saw askant[4] the armies,
I saw as in noiseless dreams hundreds of battle-flags,

4. **askant:** Early term meaning sideways or obliquely.

Borne through the smoke of the battles and pierc'd with missiles I saw them,
And carried hither and yon through the smoke, and torn and bloody,
And at last but a few shreds left on the staffs, (and all in silence,)
And the staffs all splinter'd and broken.

I saw battle-corpses, myriads of them,
And the white skeletons of young men, I saw them,
I saw the debris and debris of all the slain soldiers of the war,
But I saw they were not as was thought,
They themselves were fully at rest, they suffer'd not,
The living remain'd and suffer'd, the mother suffer'd,
And the wife and the child and the musing comrade suffer'd,
And the armies that remain'd suffer'd.

16

Passing the visions, passing the night,
Passing, unloosing the hold of my comrades' hands,
Passing the song of the hermit bird and the tallying song of my soul,
Victorious song, death's outlet song, yet varying ever-altering song,
As low and wailing, yet clear the notes, rising and falling, flooding the night,
Sadly sinking and fainting, as warning and warning, and yet again bursting with joy,
Covering the earth and filling the spread of the heaven,
As that powerful psalm in the night I heard from recesses,
Passing, I leave thee lilac with heart-shaped leaves,
I leave thee there in the door-yard, blooming, returning with spring.

I cease from my song for thee,
From my gaze on thee in the west, fronting the west, communing with thee,
O comrade lustrous with silver face in the night.

Yet each to keep and all, retrievements out of the night,
The song, the wondrous chant of the gray-brown bird,
And the tallying chant, the echo arous'd in my soul,
With the lustrous and drooping star with the countenance full of woe,
With the holders holding my hand nearing the call of the bird,
Comrades mine and I in the midst, and their memory ever to keep, for the dead I loved so well,
For the sweetest, wisest soul of all my days and lands – and this for his dear sake,
Lilac and star and bird twined with the chant of my soul,
There in the fragrant pines and the cedars dusk and dim.

[1865-66, 1891-92]

From WHISPERS OF HEAVENLY DEATH

A NOISELESS PATIENT SPIDER

A noiseless patient spider,
I mark'd where on a little promontory it stood isolated,
Mark'd how to explore the vacant vast surrounding,
It launch'd forth filament, filament, filament, out of itself,
Ever unreeling them, ever tirelessly speeding them.

And you O my soul where you stand,
Surrounded, detached, in measureless oceans of space,
Ceaselessly musing, venturing, throwing, seeking the spheres to connect them,
Till the bridge you will need be form'd, till the ductile anchor hold,
Till the gossamer thread you fling catch somewhere, O my soul.

[1868, 1891-92]

From SONGS OF PARTING

SO LONG!

To conclude, I announce what comes after me.

I remember I said before my leaves sprang at all,
I would raise my voice jocund and strong with reference to consummations.

When America does what was promis'd,
When through these States walk a hundred millions of superb persons,
When the rest part away for superb persons and contribute to them,
When breeds of the most perfect mothers denote America,
Then to me and mine our due fruition.

I have press'd through in my own right,
I have sung the body and the soul, war and peace have I sung, and the songs of life and death,
And the songs of birth, and shown that there are many births.

I have offer'd my style to every one, I have journey'd with confident step;
While my pleasure is yet at the full I whisper *So long!*
And take the young woman's hand and the young man's hand for the last time.

I announce natural persons to arise,
I announce justice triumphant,
I announce uncompromising liberty and equality,
I announce the justification of candor and the justification of pride.

I announce that the identity of these States is a single identity only,
I announce the Union more and more compact, indissoluble,
I announce splendors and majesties to make all the previous politics of the earth insignificant.

I announce adhesiveness,[1] I say it shall be limitless, unloosen'd,
I say you shall yet find the friend you were looking for.

I announce a man or woman coming, perhaps you are the one, (*So long!*)
I announce the great individual, fluid as Nature, chaste, affectionate, compassionate, fully arm'd.

I announce a life that shall be copious, vehement, spiritual, bold,
I announce an end that shall lightly and joyfully meet its translation.

I announce myriads of youths, beautiful, gigantic, sweet-blooded,
I announce a race of splendid and savage old men.

O thicker and faster – (*So long!*)
O crowding too close upon me,
I foresee too much, it means more than I thought,
It appears to me I am dying.

Hasten throat and sound your last,
Salute me – salute the days once more. Peal the old cry once more.

Screaming electric, the atmosphere using,
At random glancing, each as I notice absorbing,
Swiftly on, but a little while alighting,
Curious envelop'd messages delivering,
Sparkles hot, seed ethereal down in the dirt dropping,
Myself unknowing, my commission obeying, to question it never daring,
To ages and ages yet the growth of the seed leaving,
To troops out of the war arising, they the tasks I have set promulging,
To women certain whispers of myself bequeathing, their affection me more clearly explaining,
To young men my problems offering – no dallier I – I the muscle of their brains trying,
So I pass, a little time vocal, visible, contrary,
Afterward a melodious echo, passionately bent for, (death making me really undying,)
The best of me then when no longer visible, for toward that I have been incessantly preparing.

1. **adhesiveness:** The instinct for friendship, located in a particular area of the brain. This term was used in phrenology, the popular pseudoscience that suggested the overall shape and bumps of the head provided clues to the intellectual capacities and personality traits of an individual.

What is there more, that I lag and pause and crouch extended with unshut mouth?
Is there a single final farewell?

My songs cease, I abandon them,
From behind the screen where I hid I advance personally solely to you.

Camerado,[2] this is no book,
Who touches this touches a man,
(Is it night? are we here together alone?)
It is I you hold and who holds you,
I spring from the pages into your arms – decease calls me forth.

O how your fingers drowse me,
Your breath falls around me like dew, your pulse lulls the tympans of my ears,
I feel immerged from head to foot,
Delicious, enough.

Enough O deed impromptu and secret,
Enough O gliding present – enough O summ'd-up past.

Dear friend whoever you are take this kiss,
I give it especially to you, do not forget me,
I feel like one who has done work for the day to retire awhile,
I receive now again of my many translations, from my avataras[3] ascending, while others doubtless await me,
An unknown sphere more real than I dream'd, more direct, darts awakening rays about me, *So long!*
Remember my words, I may again return,
I love you, I depart from materials,
I am as one disembodied, triumphant, dead.

[1860, 1891-92]

---

2. **Camerado:** From either *camarada* (Spanish) or *camarade* (French), meaning a male or female friend.
3. **avataras:** Hindu term for the incarnation of a god; more generally, as in the English *avatar*, the incarnation or embodiment of the essence of a concept or a person.

Whitman through a Modern Lens

THROUGHOUT HIS LONG LIFE, Walt Whitman sought a wide audience for his writings, especially for *Leaves of Grass*, numerous editions of which he published between 1855 and his death in 1892. But, as a writer for the *Critic* observed in 1881:

> One great anomaly of Whitman's case has been that while he is an aggressive champion of democracy and of the working-man, in a broad sense of the term working-man, his admirers have been almost exclusively of a class the furthest possibly removed from that which labors for daily bread by manual work. Whitman has always been truly caviare to the multitude. It was only those that knew much of poetry and loved it greatly who penetrated the singular shell of his verses and rejoiced in the rich, pulpy kernel.

Certainly his work has had a powerful and profound impact on other American poets, for whom Whitman has been a steady source of inspiration and stimulation. In a poem commemorating Whitman's death in 1892, Edwin Arlington Robinson wrote:

> His piercing and eternal cadence rings
> Too pure for us – too powerfully pure,
> Too lovingly triumphant, and too large;
> But there are some that hear him, and
> they know
> That he shall sing to-morrow for all
> men,
> And that all time shall listen.

Thomas Eakins, *Walt Whitman*

A friend and admirer of Whitman, Eakins in 1887 made an unannounced visit to the poet's house to paint this portrait. Whitman, in turn, admired the painting for its realistic depiction of him in old age. As he observed, Eakins was the only artist Whitman knew "who could resist the temptation to see what they ought to be rather than what is."

Some of the diverse notes twentieth-century poets have heard in Whitman's verse are recorded in the following two poems, written at the time of centennial celebrations of the publication of the first edition of *Leaves of Grass* in 1855. The first poem is by Langston Hughes (1902-1967), perhaps the most admired of all African American poets. The text is taken from *Poems: 1951-1967* (2001), in the *Collected Works of Langston Hughes.* The second poem is by Allen Ginsberg (1926-1997), the iconoclastic poet of the Beat generation. The text is taken from his *Collected Poems 1947-1980* (1984).

Langston Hughes

[1902-1967]

Old Walt

Old Walt Whitman
Went finding and seeking,
Finding less than sought
Seeking more than found,
Every detail minding
Of the seeking or the finding.

Pleasured equally
In seeking as in finding,
Each detail minding,
Old Walt went seeking
And finding.

[1954, 2001]

Allen Ginsberg

[1926-1997]

A Supermarket in California

What thoughts I have of you tonight, Walt Whitman, for I walked down the sidestreets under the trees with a headache self-conscious looking at the full moon.

In my hungry fatigue, and shopping for images, I went into the neon fruit supermarket, dreaming of your enumerations!

What peaches and what penumbras! Whole families shopping at night! Aisles full of husbands! Wives in the avocados, babies in the tomatoes! – and you, García Lorca,[1] what were you doing down by the watermelons?

I saw you, Walt Whitman, childless, lonely old grubber, poking among the meats in the refrigerator and eyeing the grocery boys.

I heard you asking questions of each: Who killed the pork chops? What price bananas? Are you my Angel?

I wandered in and out of the brilliant stacks of cans following you, and followed in my imagination by the store detective.

We strode down the open corridors together in our solitary fancy tasting artichokes, possessing every frozen delicacy, and never passing the cashier.

Where are we going, Walt Whitman? The doors close in an hour. Which way does your beard point tonight?

(I touch your book and dream of our odyssey in the supermarket and feel absurd.)

Will we walk all night through solitary streets? The trees add shade to shade, lights out in the houses, we'll both be lonely.

Will we stroll dreaming of the lost America of love past blue automobiles in driveways, home to our silent cottage?

Ah, dear father, graybeard, lonely old courage-teacher, what America did you have when Charon quit poling his ferry and you got out on a smoking bank and stood watching the boat disappear on the black waters of Lethe?[2]

Berkeley, 1955

[1955, 1984]

1. **García Lorca:** Frederico García Lorca (1898-1936), Spanish poet and dramatist.

2. **Charon . . . Lethe?:** In Greek mythology, Charon ferried the dead across the Lethe, the river of forgetfulness that flows through the underworld.

Emily Dickinson

[1830-1886]

Emily Dickinson wrote about the kinds of experience few poets have the daring to explore or the genius to sing.
–Galway Kinnell

Emily Dickinson was born on December 10, 1830, in Amherst, Massachusetts. At a time when the country was becoming increasingly urban, Dickinson cherished the rural, small-town atmosphere of Amherst. She left her home there only occasionally: for a year at Mount Holyoke Female Seminary in 1847-48; for trips to Washington, D.C., and Philadelphia with her family; and for short visits to Boston for treatment of ongoing problems with her eyesight. As she grew older, Dickinson was increasingly reluctant to leave her house, called "The Homestead," a large and imposing mansion which had been built by her grandfather in 1813. Dickinson was in her element in her comfortable room on the second floor of the Homestead, where she wrote approximately 1,789 poems and thousands of letters.

Dickinson's world was thoroughly domestic, at least to all outward appearances. Although neither she nor her sister, Lavinia, ever married, they lived together in the midst of family and friends, taking pride in light housekeeping, caring for relatives, and spending time in the substantial gardens surrounding the Homestead. The period of Dickinson's adolescence and young adulthood was a time of religious revivalism in Amherst and throughout New England, but she remained skeptical of conventional religion. She was especially suspicious of the puritanical doctrines of the

The Homestead

Dickinson was born and lived most of her life in this house, her family home in Amherst, Massachusetts.

First Church of Christ, which her mother joined in 1832 and her father and sister joined in 1850. Although she persistently explored religious issues in her poetry, Dickinson resolutely refused to join or attend church, preferring to establish a community for herself in other ways. That community was formed by a wide circle of family members and friends, with whom she enjoyed a lively, extensive correspondence throughout her life. Dickinson's father and her brother, Austin, both attorneys, were deeply involved with Amherst College, which had been founded by her grandfather and others in 1821. The Homestead was consequently a social center in Amherst. When Austin married Dickinson's dearest friend, Susan Gilbert, in 1856, the couple moved into "The Evergreens," the house next door, which had been built by Dickinson's father in order to keep the family close together. During the Civil War, Dickinson was at her most prolific, writing hundreds of poems and corresponding with dozens of new friends, including prominent writers and reformers like Thomas Wentworth Higginson and Helen Hunt Jackson.

bedfordstmartins.com/ americanlit *for research links on Dickinson*

After the war, Dickinson's life was saddened by the death of those closest to her. Her father died in 1874 and her mother in 1882. In addition, Austin began a long affair with Mabel Loomis Todd. Dickinson, who had continued to have an intensely intimate relationship with Austin's wife, "Sue" – as Dickinson called her – found that relationship strained by the inevitable tensions brought about by the increasingly well-known affair. One of the most traumatic events of Dickinson's later years was the death of her beloved eight-year-old nephew, Gilbert, in 1883. Dickinson herself was increasingly ill in these last years and died from kidney disease on May 15, 1886.

Dickinson's Poems. Although the larger reading public did not have access to Dickinson's poems during her lifetime, she was to become the most widely read American woman poet. At least eleven of Dickinson's poems were published in newspapers and magazines during her lifetime, but her attitude toward publication was complex. "Publication – is the Auction / Of the Mind," she declared in one of her poems (see p. 1336). Yet, as many scholars have pointed out, she "published" her poems by sending them to friends and family members, often enclosed with or incorporated into letters, such as those to Thomas Wentworth Higginson. Of the approximately 1,789 poems we have today, Dickinson sent about one-third of them in letters to friends and relatives, and the number was probably much higher since only a small percentage of her letters have survived.

After Dickinson's death, her sister, Lavinia, found over a thousand poems in her desk, most of them bound into small packets called "fascicles," collections of the manuscripts of the poems. Many of them were first published through the efforts of Mabel Loomis Todd, who began to transcribe the poems at Lavinia's request and who then enlisted the aid of Higginson in editing the first collection of Dickinson's *Poems* (1890). That was followed by a second series of *Poems* (1891), edited by Higginson and Todd, and a third series of *Poems* (1896), edited by Todd, who was largely responsible for bringing Dickinson's work to the attention of critics and the public. That effort was continued by Dickinson's niece, Martha Dickinson Bianchi, who published eight more volumes of poems between 1914 and 1937. In 1945, more than six hundred new poems were published as *Bolts of Melody*, edited by Bianchi and Millicent Todd Bingham, who had inherited the manuscripts from her mother, Mabel Loomis Todd. Ten years later, Thomas H. Johnson published a three-volume "variorum" edition of all Dickinson's poems, identifying them by numbers in what he viewed as their chronological order. More recently, R. W. Franklin published a new edition of the poems, establishing a different chronological arrangement and correcting some editorial errors in the earlier edition. The texts of the poems included here are taken from Thomas H. Johnson's one-volume edition of *The Complete Poems of Emily Dickinson* (1960). With the exception of the first poem, the poems appear here in the order established by Johnson, with his number followed in square brackets by the number of the poem in *The Poems of Emily Dickinson* (1999), edited by R. W. Franklin.

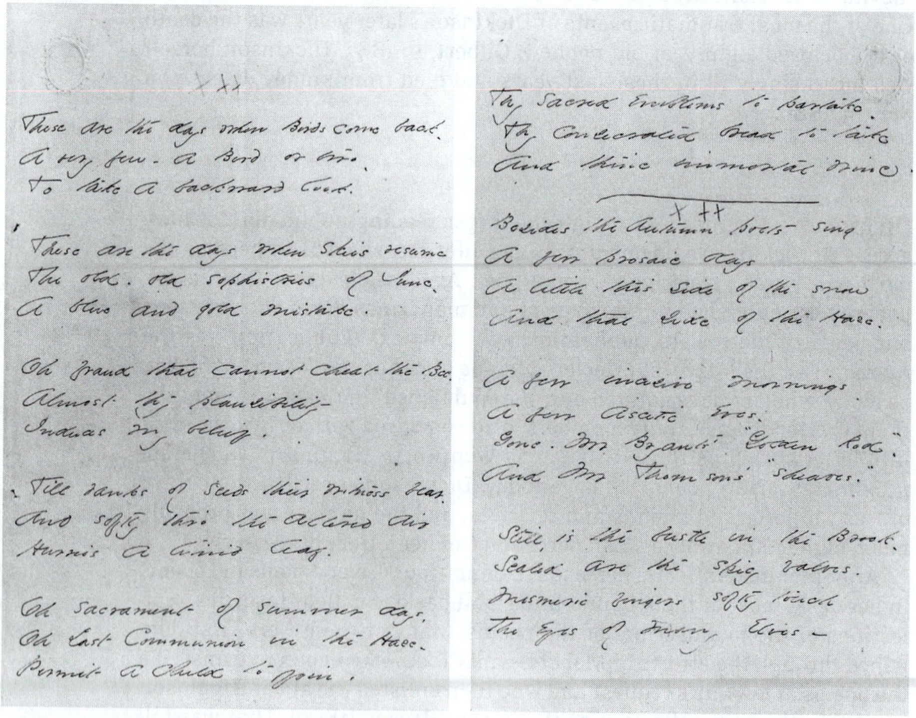

These are the days when Birds come back.
A very few - a Bird or two.
To take a backward look.

These are the days when Skies resume
The old - old sophistries of June.
A blue and gold mistake.

Oh fraud that cannot cheat the Bee.
Almost thy plausibility
Induces my belief.

Till ranks of Seeds their witness bear
And softly thro' the altered air
Hurries a timid leaf.

Oh Sacrament of summer days,
Oh Last Communion in the Haze.
Permit a child to join.

Thy sacred emblems to partake.
Thy consecrated bread to take
And thine immortal wine.

Besides the Autumn poets sing
A few prosaic days
A little this side of the snow
And that side of the Haze.

A few incisive mornings.
A few Ascetic eves.
Gone - Mr Bryant's "Golden Rod."
And Mr Thomson's "Sheaves."

Still, is the bustle in the Brook.
Sealed are the spicy valves.
Mesmeric fingers softly touch
The Eyes of many Elves -

Manuscript version of "These are the days when Birds come back –"

Since Dickinson did not prepare her poems for print publication, all editors have confronted the task of deciphering her difficult handwriting and interpreting other features of her manuscripts. Some of those editorial complications are illustrated by the first poem reprinted here: "These are the days when Birds come back –" (130; Fr 122). There were several manuscript versions of this poem; the manuscript reproduced here is the copy found by Lavinia. Dickinson had sent another manuscript of the poem to Susan Dickinson, probably in 1859; yet another copy was clearly sent to the editor of the newspaper *Drum Beat*, where the poem was published as "October" on March 11, 1864. It is not known, however, who sent the poem to the newspaper. The manuscript of the poem is reproduced here along with two published versions, one from the first collection of *Poems by Emily Dickinson* (1890) and the other from Johnson's 1960 edition. Comparing the various versions of the poem demonstrates some of the liberties the early editors took, adding a title and altering some words of the manuscript. Such a comparison also illustrates the ways in which different editors have handled Dickinson's idiosyncratic capitalization and punctuation, two of the most striking features of her poems.

Indian Summer

These are the days when birds come
back,
A very few, a bird or two,
To take a backward look.

These are the days when skies put on
The old, old sophistries of June, –
A blue and gold mistake.

Oh, fraud that cannot cheat the bee,
Almost thy plausibility
Induces my belief,

Till ranks of seeds their witness bear,
And softly through the altered air
Hurries a timid leaf!

Oh, sacrament of summer days,
Oh, last communion in the haze,
Permit a child to join,

Thy sacred emblems to partake,
Thy consecrated bread to break,
Taste thine immortal wine!

[c. 1859, 1890]

130 [Fr 122]

These are the days when Birds come
back –
A very few – a Bird or two –
To take a backward look.

These are the days when skies resume
The old – old sophistries of June –
A blue and gold mistake.

Oh fraud that cannot cheat the Bee –
Almost thy plausibility
Induces my belief.

Till ranks of seeds their witness bear –
And softly thro' the altered air
Hurries a timid leaf.

Oh Sacrament of summer days,
Oh Last Communion in the Haze –
Permit a child to join.

Thy sacred emblems to partake –
Thy consecrated bread to take
And thine immortal wine!

[c. 1859, 1960]

49 [Fr 39]

I never lost as much but twice,
And that was in the sod.
Twice have I stood a beggar
Before the door of God!

Angels – twice descending
Reimbursed my store –
Burglar! Banker – Father!
I am poor once more!

[c. 1858, 1960]

67 [Fr 112]

Success is counted sweetest
By those who ne'er succeed.
To comprehend a nectar
Requires sorest need.

Not one of all the purple Host
Who took the Flag today
Can tell the definition
So clear of Victory

As he defeated – dying –
On whose forbidden ear
The distant strains of triumph
Burst agonized and clear!

[c. 1859, 1960]

84 [Fr 121]

Her breast is fit for pearls,
But I was not a "Diver" –
Her brow is fit for thrones
But I have not a crest.
Her heart is fit for *home* –
I – a Sparrow – build there
Sweet of twigs and twine
My perennial nest.

[c. 1859, 1960]

185 [FR 202]

"Faith" is a fine invention
When Gentlemen can *see* –
But *Microscopes* are prudent
In an Emergency.

[c. 1860, 1960]

199 [FR 225]

I'm "wife" – I've finished that –
That other state –
I'm Czar – I'm "Woman" now –
It's safer so –

How odd the Girl's life looks
Behind this soft Eclipse –
I think that Earth feels so
To folks in Heaven – now –

This being comfort – then
That other kind – was pain –
But why compare?
I'm "Wife"! Stop there!

[c. 1860, 1960]

211 [FR 205]

Come slowly – Eden!
Lips unused to Thee –
Bashful – sip thy Jessamines[1] –
As the fainting Bee –

Reaching late his flower,
Round her chamber hums –
Counts his nectars –
Enters – and is lost in Balms.

[c. 1860, 1960]

1. **Jessamines:** A variant of jasmine, a vine or shrub bearing fragrant white flowers.

214 [Fr 207]

I taste a liquor never brewed –
From Tankards scooped in Pearl –
Not all the Vats upon the Rhine[2]
Yield such an Alcohol!

Inebriate of Air – am I –
And Debauchee of Dew –
Reeling – thro endless summer days –
From inns of Molten Blue –

When "Landlords" turn the drunken Bee
Out of the Foxglove's door –
When Butterflies – renounce their "drams" –
I shall but drink the more!

Till Seraphs[3] swing their snowy Hats –
And Saints – to windows run –
To see the little Tippler
Leaning against the – Sun –

[c. 1860, 1960]

216 [Fr 124]

Safe in their Alabaster Chambers[4] –
Untouched by Morning
And untouched by Noon –
Sleep the meek members of the Resurrection –
Rafter of satin,
And Roof of stone.

Light laughs the breeze
In her Castle above them –
Babbles the Bee in a stolid Ear,
Pipe the Sweet Birds in ignorant cadence –
Ah, what sagacity perished here!

[version of 1859, 1960]

---

2. **Rhine:** The Rhine River flows through major wine-producing areas in Germany.
3. **Seraphs:** Angels guarding God's throne.
4. **Alabaster Chambers:** Crypts made of translucent, white marble.

Safe in their Alabaster Chambers –
Untouched by Morning –
And untouched by Noon –
Lie the meek members of the Resurrection –
Rafter of Satin – and Roof of Stone!

Grand go the Years – in the Crescent – above them –
Worlds scoop their Arcs –
And Firmaments – row –
Diadems – drop – and Doges[5] – surrender –
Soundless as dots – on a Disc of Snow –

[version of 1861, 1960]

241 [FR 339]

I like a look of Agony,
Because I know it's true –
Men do not sham Convulsion,
Nor simulate, a Throe –

The Eyes glaze once – and that is Death –
Impossible to feign
The Beads upon the Forehead
By homely Anguish strung.

[c. 1861, 1960]

249 [FR 269]

Wild Nights – Wild Nights!
Were I with thee
Wild Nights should be
Our luxury!

Futile – the Winds –
To a Heart in port –
Done with the Compass –
Done with the Chart![6]

5. **Doges:** Powerful magistrates serving in the Italian republics of Venice and Genoa from the eleventh through the sixteenth centuries.
6. **Chart:** A navigational map used by sailors.

Rowing in Eden –
Ah, the Sea!
Might I but moor – Tonight –
In Thee!

[c. 1861, 1960]

252 [Fr 312]

I can wade Grief –
Whole Pools of it –
I'm used to that –
But the least push of Joy
Breaks up my feet –
And I tip – drunken –
Let no Pebble – smile –
'Twas the New Liquor –
That was all!

Power is only Pain –
Stranded, thro' Discipline,
Till Weights – will hang –
Give Balm – to Giants –
And they'll wit, like Men –
Give Himmaleh[7] –
They'll Carry – Him!

[c. 1861, 1960]

258 [Fr 320]

There's a certain Slant of light,
Winter Afternoons –
That oppresses, like the Heft
Of Cathedral Tunes –

Heavenly Hurt, it gives us –
We can find no scar,
But internal difference,
Where the Meanings, are –

7. **Himmaleh:** The Himalayas, a vast mountain range in Asia that includes some of the highest peaks in the world.

None may teach it – Any –
'Tis the Seal Despair –
An imperial affliction
Sent us of the Air –

When it comes, the Landscape listens –
Shadows – hold their breath –
When it goes, 'tis like the Distance
On the look of Death –

[c. 1861, 1960]

271 [Fr 307]

A solemn thing – it was – I said –
A woman – white – to be –
And wear – if God should count me fit –
Her blameless mystery –

A hallowed thing – to drop a life
Into the purple well –
Too plummetless – that it return –
Eternity – until –

I pondered how the bliss would look –
And would it feel as big –
When I could take it in my hand –
As hovering – seen – through fog –

And then – the size of this "small" life –
The Sages[8] – call it small –
Swelled – like Horizons – in my vest –
And I sneered – softly – "small"!

[c. 1861, 1960]

280 [Fr 340]

I felt a Funeral, in my Brain,
And Mourners to and fro
Kept treading – treading – till it seemed
That Sense was breaking through –

8. Sages: Persons celebrated for their wisdom.

And when they all were seated,
A Service, like a Drum –
Kept beating – beating – till I thought
My Mind was going numb –

And then I heard them lift a Box
And creak across my Soul
With those same Boots of Lead, again,
Then Space – began to toll,

As all the Heavens were a Bell,
And Being, but an Ear,
And I, and Silence, some strange Race
Wrecked, solitary, here –

And then a Plank in Reason, broke,
And I dropped down, and down –
And hit a World, at every plunge,
And Finished knowing – then –

[c. 1861, 1960]

288 [Fr 260]

I'm Nobody! Who are you?
Are you – Nobody – Too?
Then there's a pair of us?
Don't tell! they'd advertise – you know!

How dreary – to be – Somebody!
How public – like a Frog –
To tell one's name – the livelong June –
To an admiring Bog!

[c. 1861, 1960]

303 [Fr 409]

The Soul selects her own Society –
Then – shuts the Door –
To her divine Majority –
Present no more –

Unmoved – she notes the Chariots – pausing –
At her low Gate –
Unmoved – an Emperor be kneeling
Upon her Mat –

I've known her – from an ample nation –
Choose One –
Then – close the Valves of her attention –
Like Stone –

[c. 1862, 1960]

324 [FR 236]

Some keep the Sabbath going to Church –
I keep it, staying at Home –
With a Bobolink for a Chorister –
And an Orchard, for a Dome –

Some keep the Sabbath in Surplice[9] –
I just wear my Wings –
And instead of tolling the Bell, for Church,
Our little Sexton[10] – sings.

God preaches, a noted Clergyman –
And the sermon is never long,
So instead of getting to Heaven, at last –
I'm going, all along.

[c. 1860, 1960]

327 [FR 336]

Before I got my eye put out
I liked as well to see –
As other Creatures, that have Eyes
And know no other way –

But were it told to me – Today –
That I might have the sky
For mine – I tell you that my Heart
Would split, for size of me –

The Meadows – mine –
The Mountains – mine –
All Forests – Stintless Stars –

9. **Surplice:** A loose-fitting white gown worn by clergymen, acolytes, and choristers during Christian church services.
10. **Sexton:** An employee of a church responsible for ringing the bells to call the congregation to church services.

As much of Noon as I could take
Between my finite eyes –

The Motions of the Dipping Birds –
The Morning's Amber Road –
For mine – to look at when I liked –
The News would strike me dead –

So safer – guess – with just my soul
Upon the Window pane –
Where other Creatures put their eyes –
Incautious – of the Sun –

[c. 1862, 1960]

328 [Fr 359]

A Bird came down the Walk –
He did not know I saw –
He bit an Angleworm in halves
And ate the fellow, raw,

And then he drank a Dew
From a convenient Grass –
And then hopped sidewise to the Wall
To let a Beetle pass –

He glanced with rapid eyes
That hurried all around –
They looked like frightened Beads, I thought –
He stirred his Velvet Head

Like one in danger, Cautious,
I offered him a Crumb
And he unrolled his feathers
And rowed him softer home –

Than Oars divide the Ocean,
Too silver for a seam –
Or Butterflies, off Banks of Noon
Leap, plashless[11] as they swim.

[c. 1862, 1960]

11. **plashless:** Without making the sound of a light splash.

338 [Fr 365]

I know that He exists.
Somewhere – in Silence –
He has hid his rare life
From our gross eyes.

'Tis an instant's play.
'Tis a fond Ambush –
Just to make Bliss
Earn her own surprise!

But – should the play
Prove piercing earnest –
Should the glee – glaze –
In Death's – stiff – stare –

Would not the fun
Look too expensive!
Would not the jest –
Have crawled too far!

[c. 1862, 1960]

341 [Fr 372]

After great pain, a formal feeling comes –
The Nerves sit ceremonious, like Tombs –
The stiff Heart questions was it He, that bore,
And Yesterday, or Centuries before?

The Feet, mechanical, go round –
Of Ground, or Air, or Ought –
A Wooden way
Regardless grown,
A Quartz contentment, like a stone –

This is the Hour of Lead –
Remembered, if outlived,
As Freezing persons, recollect the Snow –
First – Chill – then Stupor – then the letting go –

[c. 1862, 1960]

357 [Fr 615]

God is a distant – stately Lover –
Woos, as He states us – by His Son –
Verily, a Vicarious Courtship –
"Miles", and "Priscilla",[12] were such an One –

But, lest the Soul – like fair "Priscilla"
Choose the Envoy – and spurn the Groom –
Vouches, with hyperbolic archness –
"Miles", and "John Alden" were Synonym –

[c. 1862, 1960]

401 [Fr 675]

What Soft – Cherubic Creatures –
These Gentlewomen are –
One would as soon assault a Plush –
Or violate a Star –

Such Dimity Convictions[13] –
A Horror so refined
Of freckled Human Nature –
Of Deity – ashamed –

It's such a common – Glory –
A Fisherman's – Degree –
Redemption – Brittle Lady –
Be so – ashamed of Thee –

[c. 1862, 1960]

409 [Fr 545]

They dropped like Flakes –
They dropped like Stars –
Like Petals from a Rose –
When suddenly across the June
A wind with fingers – goes –

---

12. **"Miles" and "Priscilla":** A reference to Henry Wadsworth Longfellow's popular narrative poem about the Pilgrims, *The Courtship of Miles Standish* (1858), in which Miles Standish asks John Alden to propose for him to Priscilla Mullens, who famously asks John to speak for himself.
13. **Dimity Convictions:** Dimity, a cotton cloth woven with raised stripes or fancy figures, was then often used to make bedcovers, curtains, and dresses. Dickinson's ironic phrase seems to suggest self-consciously dainty or genteel convictions.

They perished in the Seamless Grass –
No eye could find the place –
But God can summon every face
On his Repealless – List.

[c. 1862, 1960]

435 [Fr 620]

Much Madness is divinest Sense
To a discerning Eye –
Much Sense – the starkest Madness –
'Tis the Majority
In this, as All, prevail –
Assent – and you are sane –
Demur – you're straightway dangerous –
And handled with a Chain –

[c. 1862, 1960]

441 [Fr 519]

This is my letter to the World
That never wrote to Me –
The simple News that Nature told –
With tender Majesty

Her Message is committed
To Hands I cannot see –
For love of Her – Sweet – countrymen –
Judge tenderly – of Me

[c. 1862, 1960]

444 [Fr 524]

It feels a shame to be Alive –
When Men so brave – are dead –
One envies the Distinguished Dust –
Permitted – such a Head –

The Stone – that tells defending Whom
This Spartan put away
What little of Him we – possessed
In Pawn for Liberty –

The price is great – Sublimely paid –
Do we deserve – a Thing –
That lives – like Dollars – must be piled
Before we may obtain?

Are we that wait – sufficient worth –
That such Enormous Pearl
As life – dissolved be – for Us –
In Battle's – horrid Bowl?

It may be – a Renown to live –
I think the Man who die –
Those unsustained – Saviors –
Present Divinity –

[c. 1862, 1960]

448 [Fr 446]

This was a Poet – It is That
Distills amazing sense
From ordinary Meanings –
And Attar[14] so immense

From the familiar species
That perished by the Door –
We wonder it was not Ourselves
Arrested it – before –

Of Pictures, the Discloser –
The Poet – it is He –
Entitles Us – by Contrast –
To ceaseless Poverty –

Of Portion – so unconscious –
The Robbing – could not harm –
Himself – to Him – a Fortune –
Exterior – to Time –

[c. 1862, 1960]

14. Attar: Oil extracted from flowers and used to make perfume.

449 [Fr 448]

I died for Beauty – but was scarce
Adjusted in the Tomb
When One who died for Truth, was lain
In an adjoining Room –

He questioned softly "Why I failed"?
"For Beauty", I replied
"And I – for Truth – Themself are One –
We Brethren, are", He said –

And so, as Kinsmen, met a Night –
We talked between the Rooms –
Until the Moss had reached our lips –
And covered up – our names –

[c. 1862, 1960]

465 [Fr 591]

I heard a Fly buzz – when I died –
The Stillness in the Room
Was like the Stillness in the Air –
Between the Heaves of Storm –

The Eyes around – had wrung them dry –
And Breaths were gathering firm
For that last Onset – when the King
Be witnessed – in the Room –

I willed my Keepsakes – Signed away
What portion of me be
Assignable – and then it was
There interposed a Fly –

With Blue – uncertain stumbling Buzz –
Between the light – and me –
And then the Windows failed – and then
I could not see to see –

[c. 1862, 1960]

501 [Fr 373]

This World is not Conclusion.
A Species stands beyond –
Invisible, as Music –

But positive, as Sound –
It beckons, and it baffles –
Philosophy – don't know –
And through a Riddle, at the last –
Sagacity, must go –
To guess it, puzzles scholars –
To gain it, Men have borne
Contempt of Generations
And Crucifixion, shown –
Faith slips – and laughs, and rallies –
Blushes, if any see –
Plucks at a twig of Evidence –
And asks a Vane,[15] the way –
Much Gesture, from the Pulpit –
Strong Hallelujahs roll –
Narcotics cannot still the Tooth
That nibbles at the soul –

[c. 1862, 1960]

502 [Fr 377]

At least – to pray – is left – is left –
Oh Jesus – in the Air –
I know not which thy chamber is –
I'm knocking – everywhere –

Thou settest Earthquake in the South –
And Maelstrom, in the Sea –
Say, Jesus Christ of Nazareth –
Hast thou no Arm for Me?

[c. 1862, 1960]

508 [Fr 353]

I'm ceded – I've stopped being Theirs –
The name They dropped upon my face
With water, in the country church
Is finished using, now,

15. **Vane:** A weathervane, a revolving device mounted on buildings that shows the direction of the wind.

And They can put it with my Dolls,
My childhood, and the string of spools,
I've finished threading – too –

Baptized, before, without the choice,
But this time, consciously, of Grace –
Unto supremest name –
Called to my Full – The Crescent dropped –
Existence's whole Arc, filled up,
With one small Diadem.

My second Rank – too small the first –
Crowned – Crowing – on my Father's breast –
A half unconscious Queen –
But this time – Adequate – Erect,
With Will to choose, or to reject,
And I choose, just a Crown –

[c. 1862, 1960]

510 [FR 355]

It was not Death, for I stood up,
And all the Dead, lie down –
It was not Night, for all the Bells
Put out their Tongues, for Noon.

It was not Frost, for on my Flesh
I felt Siroccos[16] – crawl –
Nor Fire – for just my Marble feet
Could keep a Chancel, cool –

And yet, it tasted, like them all,
The Figures I have seen
Set orderly, for Burial,
Reminded me, of mine –

As if my life were shaven,
And fitted to a frame,
And could not breathe without a key,
And 'twas like Midnight, some –

16. Siroccos: Hot desert winds that blow from North Africa across the Mediterranean to southern Europe.

When everything that ticked – has stopped –
And Space stares all around –
Or Grisly frosts – first Autumn morns,
Repeal the Beating Ground –

But, most, like Chaos – Stopless – cool –
Without a Chance, or Spar –
Or even a Report of Land –
To justify – Despair.

[c. 1862, 1960]

512 [Fr 360]

The Soul has Bandaged moments –
When too appalled to stir –
She feels some ghastly Fright come up
And stop to look at her –

Salute her – with long fingers –
Caress her freezing hair –
Sip, Goblin, from the very lips
The Lover – hovered – o'er –
Unworthy, that a thought so mean
Accost a Theme – so – fair –

The soul has moments of Escape –
When bursting all the doors –
She dances like a Bomb, abroad,
And swings upon the Hours,

As do the Bee – delirious borne –
Long Dungeoned from his Rose –
Touch Liberty – then know no more,
But Noon, and Paradise –

The Soul's retaken moments –
When, Felon led along,
With shackles on the plumed feet,
And staples, in the Song,

The Horror welcomes her, again,
These, are not brayed of Tongue –

[c. 1862, 1960]

605 [Fr 513]

The Spider holds a Silver Ball
In unperceived Hands –
And dancing softly to Himself
His Yarn of Pearl – unwinds –

He plies from Nought to Nought –
In unsubstantial Trade –
Supplants our Tapestries with His –
In half the period –

An Hour to rear supreme
His Continents of Light –
Then dangle from the Housewife's Broom –
His Boundaries – forgot –

[c. 1862, 1960]

632 [Fr 598]

The Brain – is wider than the Sky –
For – put them side by side –
The one the other will contain
With ease – and You – beside –

The Brain is deeper than the sea –
For – hold them – Blue to Blue –
The one the other will absorb –
As Sponges – Buckets – do –

The Brain is just the weight of God –
For – Heft them – Pound for Pound –
Nor We so much as check our speech –
Nor stop to cross Ourselves –

[c. 1862, 1960]

640 [Fr 706]

I cannot live with You –
It would be Life –
And Life is over there –
Behind the Shelf

The Sexton keeps the Key to –
Putting up.
Our Life – His Porcelain –
Like a Cup –

Discarded of the Housewife –
Quaint – or Broke –
A newer Sevres[17] pleases –
Old Ones crack –

I could not die – with You –
For One must wait
To shut the Other's Gaze down –
You – could not –

And I – Could I stand by
And see You – freeze –
Without my Right of Frost –
Death's privilege?

Nor could I rise – with You –
Because Your Face
Would put out Jesus' –
That New Grace

Glow plain – and foreign
On my homesick Eye –
Except that You than He
Shone closer by –

They'd judge Us – How –
For You – served Heaven – You know,
Or sought to –
I could not –

Because You saturated Sight –
And I had no more Eyes
For sordid excellence
As Paradise

And were You lost, I would be –
Though My Name
Rang loudest
On the Heavenly fame –

17. Sevres: Fine porcelain made in France.

And were You – saved –
And I – condemned to be
Where You were not –
That self – were Hell to Me –

So We must meet apart –
You there – I – here –
With just the Door ajar
That Oceans are – and Prayer –
And that White Sustenance –
Despair –

[c. 1862, 1960]

650 [Fr 760]

Pain – has an Element of Blank –
It cannot recollect
When it begun – or if there were
A time when it was not –

It has no Future – but itself –
Its Infinite contain
Its Past – enlightened to perceive
New Periods – of Pain.

[c. 1862, 1960]

657 [Fr 466]

I dwell in Possibility –
A fairer House than Prose –
More numerous of Windows –
Superior – for Doors –

Of Chambers as the Cedars –
Impregnable of Eye –
And for an Everlasting Roof
The Gambrels[18] of the Sky –

Of Visitors – the fairest –
For Occupation – This –
The spreading wide my narrow Hands
To gather Paradise –

[c. 1862, 1960]

18. **Gambrels:** A ridged roof with two sloping sides, one with a higher pitch.

675 [FR 772]

Essential Oils – are wrung –
The Attar from the Rose
Be not expressed by Suns – alone –
It is the gift of Screws –

The General Rose – decay –
But this – in Lady's Drawer
Make Summer – When the Lady lie
In Ceaseless Rosemary –

[c. 1863, 1960]

709 [FR 788]

Publication – is the Auction
Of the Mind of Man –
Poverty – be justifying
For so foul a thing

Possibly – but We – would rather
From Our Garret go
White – Unto the White Creator –
Than invest – Our Snow –

Thought belong to Him who gave it –
Then – to Him Who bear
Its Corporeal illustration – Sell
The Royal Air –

In the Parcel – Be the Merchant
Of the Heavenly Grace –
But reduce no Human Spirit
To Disgrace of Price –

[c. 1863, 1960]

712 [FR 479]

Because I could not stop for Death –
He kindly stopped for me –
The Carriage held but just Ourselves –
And Immortality.

We slowly drove – He knew no haste
And I had put away
My labor and my leisure too,
For His Civility –

We passed the School, where Children strove
At Recess – in the Ring –
We passed the Fields of Gazing Grain –
We passed the Setting Sun –

Or rather – He passed Us –
The Dews drew quivering and chill –
For only Gossamer, my Gown –
My Tippet – only Tulle[19] –

We paused before a House that seemed
A Swelling of the Ground –
The Roof was scarcely visible –
The Cornice – in the Ground –

Since then – 'tis Centuries – and yet
Feels shorter than the Day
I first surmised the Horses' Heads
Were toward Eternity –

[c. 1863, 1960]

754 [FR 764]

My Life had stood – a Loaded Gun –
In Corners – till a Day
The Owner passed – identified –
And carried Me away –

And now We roam in Sovereign Woods –
And now We hunt the Doe –
And every time I speak for Him –
The Mountains straight reply –

And do I smile, such cordial light
Upon the Valley glow –
It is as a Vesuvian face
Had let its pleasure through –

And when at Night – Our good Day done –
I guard My Master's Head –
'Tis better than the Eider-Duck's
Deep Pillow – to have shared –

19. **Gossamer . . . Tulle:** Light clothing, including a dress made of fine, gauzy fabric and a shawl made of stiffly netted silk.

To foe of His – I'm deadly foe –
None stir the second time –
On whom I lay a Yellow Eye –
Or an emphatic Thumb –

Though I than He – may longer live
He longer must – than I –
For I have but the power to kill,
Without – the power to die –

[c. 1863, 1960]

883 [Fr 930]

The Poets light but Lamps –
Themselves – go out –
The Wicks they stimulate –
If vital Light

Inhere as do the Suns –
Each Age a Lens
Disseminating their
Circumference –

[c. 1864, 1960]

986 [Fr 1096]

A narrow Fellow in the Grass
Occasionally rides –
You may have met Him – did you not
His notice sudden is –

The Grass divides as with a Comb –
A spotted shaft is seen –
And then it closes at your feet
And opens further on –

He likes a Boggy Acre
A Floor too cool for Corn –
Yet when a Boy, and Barefoot –
I more than once at Noon
Have passed, I thought, a Whip lash
Unbraiding in the Sun
When stooping to secure it
It wrinkled, and was gone –

Several of Nature's People
I know, and they know me –
I feel for them a transport
Of cordiality –

But never met this Fellow
Attended, or alone
Without a tighter breathing
And Zero at the Bone –

[c. 1865, 1960]

1052 [Fr 800]

I never saw a Moor[20] –
I never saw the Sea –
Yet know I how the Heather looks
And what a Billow be.

I never spoke with God
Nor visited in Heaven –
Yet certain am I of the spot
As if the Checks were given –

[c. 1865, 1960]

1072 [Fr 194]

Title divine – is mine!
The Wife – without the Sign!
Acute Degree – conferred on me –
Empress of Calvary![21]
Royal – all but the Crown!
Betrothed – without the swoon
God sends us Women –
When you – hold – Garnet to Garnet –
Gold – to Gold –
Born – Bridalled – Shrouded –
In a Day –
Tri Victory

20. **Moor:** A tract of open wasteland sometimes covered with heather, a small flowering shrub.
21. **Calvary:** The hill outside Jerusalem where Christ was crucified.

"My Husband" – women say –
Stroking the Melody –
Is *this* – the way?

[c. 1862, 1960]

1078 [Fr 1108]

The Bustle in a House
The Morning after Death
Is solemnest of industries
Enacted upon Earth –

The Sweeping up the Heart
And putting Love away
We shall not want to use again
Until Eternity.

[c. 1866, 1960]

1082 [Fr 1044]

Revolution is the Pod
Systems rattle from
When the Winds of Will are stirred
Excellent is Bloom

But except its Russet Base
Every Summer be
The Entomber of itself,
So of Liberty –

Left inactive on the Stalk
All its Purple fled
Revolution shakes it for
Test if it be dead.

[c. 1866, 1960]

1129 [Fr 1263]

Tell all the Truth but tell it slant –
Success in Circuit lies
Too bright for our infirm Delight
The Truth's superb surprise

As Lightning to the Children eased
With explanation kind
The Truth must dazzle gradually
Or every man be blind –

[c. 1868, 1960]

1463 [FR 1489]

A Route of Evanescence
With a revolving Wheel –
A Resonance of Emerald –
A Rush of Cochineal[22] –
And every Blossom on the Bush
Adjusts its tumbled Head –
The mail from Tunis,[23] probably,
An easy Morning's Ride –

[c. 1879, 1960]

1545 [FR 1577]

The Bible is an antique Volume –
Written by faded Men
At the suggestion of Holy Spectres –
Subjects – Bethlehem –
Eden – the ancient Homestead –
Satan – the Brigadier –
Judas – the Great Defaulter –
David – the Troubadour –
Sin – a distinguished Precipice
Others must resist –
Boys that "believe" are very lonesome –
Other Boys are "lost" –
Had but the Tale a warbling Teller –
All the Boys would come –
Orpheus' Sermon captivated[24] –
It did not condemn –

[c. 1882, 1960]

---

22. **Cochineal:** A brilliant red dye made from the bodies of insects.
23. **Tunis:** The capital city of the North African country of Tunisia.
24. **Orpheus' Sermon captivated:** In Greek mythology, Orpheus was the greatest of all musicians, whose singing and playing upon the lyre could captivate both animate and inanimate nature.

1624 [Fr 1668]

Apparently with no surprise
To any happy Flower
The Frost beheads it at its play –
In accidental power –
The blonde Assassin passes on –
The Sun proceeds unmoved
To measure off another Day
For an Approving God.

[c. 1884, 1960]

1651 [Fr 1715]

A Word made Flesh[25] is seldom
And tremblingly partook
Nor then perhaps reported
But have I not mistook
Each one of us has tasted
With ecstasies of stealth
The very food debated
To our specific strength –

A Word that breathes distinctly
Has not the power to die
Cohesive as the Spirit
It may expire if He –
"Made Flesh and dwelt among us"
Could condescension be
Like this consent of Language
This loved Philology.

[?, 1960]

1732 [Fr 1773]

My life closed twice before its close –
It yet remains to see
If Immortality unveil
A third event to me

So huge, so hopeless to conceive
As these that twice befell.

25. **A Word made Flesh:** See John 1:14: "And the Word was made flesh, and dwelt among us, (and we beheld his glory, the glory as of the only begotten of the Father,) full of grace and truth."

Parting is all we know of heaven,
And all we need of hell.

[?, 1960]

1737 [FR 267]

Rearrange a "Wife's" affection!
When they dislocate my Brain!
Amputate my freckled Bosom!
Make me bearded like a man!

Blush, my spirit, in thy Fastness –
Blush, my unacknowledged clay –
Seven years of troth have taught thee
More than Wifehood ever may!

Love that never leaped its socket –
Trust entrenched in narrow pain –
Constancy thro' fire – awarded –
Anguish – bare of anodyne![26]

Burden – borne so far triumphant –
None suspect me of the crown,
For I wear the "Thorns" till *Sunset* –
Then – my Diadem put on.

Big my Secret but it's *bandaged* –
It will never get away
Till the Day its Weary Keeper
Leads it through the Grave to thee.

[?, 1960]

1739 [FR 586]

Some say goodnight – at night –
I say goodnight by day –
Good-bye – the Going utter me –
Goodnight, I still reply –

For parting, that is night,
And presence, simply dawn –
Itself, the purple on the height
Denominated morn.

[?, 1960]

26. **anodyne:** Something that soothes or relieves.

1760 [Fr 1590]

Elysium[27] is as far as to
The very nearest Room
If in that Room a Friend await
Felicity or Doom –

What fortitude the Soul contains,
That it can so endure
The accent of a coming Foot –
The opening of a Door –

[c. 1882, 1960]

Dickinson's Letters. Dickinson wrote thousands of letters to a series of correspondents. Her most frequent correspondent was her sister-in-law, Susan Gilbert Dickinson, with whom Dickinson had a close, intense relationship for much of her adult life. The exchange between Dickinson and her sister-in-law reprinted here demonstrates the way in which Dickinson revised one of her poems in light of Susan's suggestions. Another of Dickinson's most important correspondents was writer and reformer Thomas Wentworth Higginson. Dickinson first wrote to him in response to his "Letter to a Young Contributor," an article published in the *Atlantic Monthly* in April 1862 in which Higginson offered practical advice to potential contributors to the magazine. In her first letter to him, Dickinson included four of her poems and asked Higginson, "Are you too deeply occupied to say if my Verse is alive?" In her second letter, Dickinson thanked him for his "surgery" – that is, Higginson's comments on the poems – and sent along some others, as he had requested. In response to his comments on that second group of poems, Dickinson wrote the letter printed here. As it suggests, Dickinson frequently adopted an ironic or playful tone in her letters to Higginson, who became one of her closest friends and, after her death, the coeditor of the first collections of her poems. The texts of the two letters are taken from *The Letters of Emily Dickinson*, edited by Thomas H. Johnson (1958).

Exchange with Susan Gilbert Dickinson

[To Susan Gilbert Dickinson *summer 1861]*

Safe in their Alabaster Chambers,
Untouched by morning

27. **Elysium:** In Greek mythology, the home of the blessed in the afterlife; also called the Elysium of Elysian Fields.

And untouched by noon,
Sleep the meek members of the Resurrection,
Rafter of satin
And Roof of stone.

Light laughs the breeze
In her Castle above them,
Babbles the Bee in a stolid Ear,
Pipe the Sweet Birds in ignorant cadence, –
Ah, what sagacity perished here!

[The earlier version, above, ED sent to Sue during the summer of 1861. Sue appears to have objected to the second stanza, for ED sent her the following:]

Safe in their Alabaster Chambers,
Untouched by Morning –
And untouched by Noon –
Lie the meek members of the Resurrection –
Rafter of Satin – and Roof of Stone –

Grand go the Years – in the Crescent – about them –
Worlds scoop their Arcs –
And Firmaments – row –
Diadems – drop – and Doges – surrender –
Soundless as dots – on a Disc of Snow –

Perhaps this verse would please you better – Sue –

Emily –

[The new version elicited an immediate response:]

I am not suited dear Emily with the second verse – It is remarkable as the chain lightening that blinds us hot nights in the Southern sky but it does not go with the ghostly shimmer of the first verse as well as the other one – It just occurs to me that the first verse is complete in itself it needs no other, and can't be coupled – Strange things always go alone – as there is only one Gabriel and one Sun – You never made a peer for that verse, and I *guess* you[r] kingdom does'nt hold one – I always go to the fire and get warm after thinking of it, but I never *can* again – The flowers are sweet and bright and look as if they would kiss one – ah, they expect a humming-bird – Thanks for them of course – and not thanks only recognition either – Did it ever occur to you that is all there is here after all – "Lord that I may receive my sight" –

Susan is tired making *bibs* for her bird – her ring-dove – he will paint my cheeks when I am old to pay me –

Sue –
Pony Express

[ED answered thus:]

Is *this frostier?*

Springs – shake the sills –
But – the Echoes – stiffen –
Hoar – is the Window –
And numb – the Door –
Tribes of Eclipse – in Tents of Marble –
Staples of Ages – have buckled – there –

Dear Sue –

Your praise is good – to me – because I *know* it *knows* – and *suppose* – it *means* –

Could I make you and Austin[28] – proud – sometime – a great way off – 'twould give me taller feet –

Here is a crumb – for the "Ring dove" – and a spray for *his Nest*, a little while ago – *just – "Sue."*

Emily.

TO THOMAS WENTWORTH HIGGINSON

[To T. W. Higginson *7 June 1862]*

Dear friend.

Your letter gave no Drunkenness, because I tasted Rum before – Domingo[29] comes but once – yet I have had few pleasures so deep as your opinion, and if I tried to thank you, my tears would block my tongue –

My dying Tutor[30] told me that he would like to live till I had been a poet, but Death was much of Mob as I could master – then – And when far afterward – a sudden light on Orchards, or a new fashion in the wind troubled my attention – I felt a palsy, here – the Verses just relieve –

Your second letter surprised me, and for a moment, swung – I had not supposed it. Your first – gave no dishonor, because the True – are not ashamed – I thanked you for your justice – but could not drop the Bells whose jingling cooled my Tramp – Perhaps the Balm, seemed better, because you bled me, first.

---

28. **Austin:** Austin Dickinson (1829–1895), Susan's husband and Emily Dickinson's brother.
29. **Rum . . . Domingo:** Rum, alcoholic liquor manufactured in the Caribbean, is here used synonymously with *Domingo*, which in the nineteenth century referred to San Domingo, or Haiti.
30. **My dying Tutor:** Benjamin Franklin Newton (1821–1853), a law student in Edward Dickinson's office from 1847 to 1849, encouraged Dickinson's interest in poetry and later sent her a copy of Ralph Waldo Emerson's *Poems* (1847). His death at age thirty-two was a blow to Dickinson.

I smile when you suggest that I delay "to publish" – that being foreign to my thought, as Firmament to Fin –

If fame belonged to me, I could not escape her – if she did not, the longest day would pass me on the chase – and the approbation of my Dog, would forsake me – then – My Barefoot-Rank is better –

You think my gait "spasmodic" – I am in danger – Sir –

You think me "uncontrolled" – I have no Tribunal.[31]

Would you have time to be the "friend" you should think I need? I have a little shape – it would not crowd your Desk – nor make much Racket as the Mouse, that dents your Galleries –

If I might bring you what I do – not so frequent to trouble you – and ask you if I told it clear – 'twould be control, to me –

The Sailor cannot see the North – but knows the Needle can –

The "hand you stretch me in the Dark," I put mine in, and turn away – I have no Saxon,[32] now –

As if I asked a common Alms,
And in my wondering hand
A Stranger pressed a Kingdom,
And I, bewildered, stand –
As if I asked the Orient
Had it for me a Morn –
And it should lift it's purple Dikes,
And shatter me with Dawn!

But, will you be my Preceptor,[33] Mr Higginson?

Your friend
E Dickinson –

---

31. **Tribunal:** A panel of judges.
32. **I have no Saxon:** The editor of the letters, Thomas H. Johnson, points out that this phrase means "language fails me."
33. **Preceptor:** A teacher or an instructor.

Dickinson through a Modern Lens

IN AN EPIGRAPH to a collection of poems inspired by the life and work of Emily Dickinson, the poet Robert Francis observes, "In Amherst when someone leans out of a car window and asks the way to Emily's grave, one does not ask, 'Emily who?'" Indeed, Dickinson is so frequently read and taught that her name, along with those of Walt Whitman and Robert Frost, is surely among the most familiar of all American poets. Frost, who as a teenager read Dickinson's posthumously published *Poems* shortly after the volume appeared in 1890, was drawn to the formal qualities of her verse and fascinated by the fact that she, too, was "troubled by many things" about death. Her poetry has been admired by modernist poets as different as Hart Crane and Marianne Moore. Moore, who was sometimes compared to Dickinson, told a friend in 1924 that "to be associated with Emily Dickinson's rigorous splendor is rare and trembling praise." Crane paid tribute to her lifelong poetic quest in his posthumously published poem "To Emily Dickinson" (1933). A variety of more recent poets have also written poems about her, including Galway Kinnell, Maxine Kumin, Joyce Carol Oates, and Billy Collins, the poet laureate of the United States from 2001-03. The following two poems reveal Dickinson's far-flung influence on women poets of different generations and diverse backgrounds. The first, by the feminist poet and social critic Adrienne Rich (b. 1929), is from her *Collected Early Poems, 1950-1977* (1993). The second is from *The Land of Bliss* (2001), the fourth collection of poems by the Hawaii-born Cathy Song (b. 1955).

Emily Dickinson

This daguerreotype was taken in 1847, when Dickinson was seventeen and a student at the Mount Holyoke Female Seminary.
(Amherst College Archives and Special Collections.)

Adrienne Rich

[b. 1929]

"I Am in Danger – Sir –"[1]

"Half-cracked" to Higginson, living,
afterward famous in garbled versions,[2]
your hoard of dazzling scraps a battlefield,
now your old snood

mothballed at Harvard[3]
and you in your variorum monument
equivocal to the end –
who are you?

Gardening the day-lily,
wiping the wine-glass stems,
your thought pulsed on behind
a forehead battered paper-thin,

you, woman, masculine
in single-mindedness,
for whom the word was more
than a symptom –

a condition of being.
Till the air buzzing with spoiled language
sang in your ears
of Perjury

---

1. **"I . . . Sir –":** A sentence from Dickinson's letter to Thomas Wentworth Higginson (1823-1911), a well-known writer who had critiqued some poems she had sent him in 1862 (see p. 1346). In the first line of the poem, Rich alludes to a letter in which Higginson described Dickinson as "my partially cracked Poetess at Amherst."

2. **garbled versions:** The editors of the early collections of Dickinson's poems frequently took liberties with the manuscripts, adding titles and altering her punctuation and frequently her wording. The "variorum monument" referred to in the following stanza is a reference to the three-volume *Poems of Emily Dickinson*, a scholarly edition edited by Thomas H. Johnson (1955).

3. **your old snood . . . Harvard:** A snood is an ornamental hairnet worn over the back of a woman's head; many of Dickinson's manuscripts, letters, and personal belongings are at the Houghton Library, Harvard University.

and in your half-cracked way you chose
silence for entertainment,
chose to have it out at last
on your own premises.

[1964, 1993]

Cathy Song

[b. 1955]

A Poet in the House

Emily's job was to think.
She was the only one of us
who had that to do.
- Lavinia Dickinson[4]

Seemingly small her work,
minute to the point of invisibility –
she vanished daily into paper, famished,
hungry for her next encounter –
but she opened with a string of humble
words necessity,
necessary as the humble work
of bringing well to water, roast to knife, cake to frost,
the coarse, loud, grunting labor of the rest of us
who complained not at all
for the noises she heard
we deemed divine, if
claustrophobic and esoteric –
and contented ourselves to the apparent,
the menial, set our heads
to the task of daily maintenance,
the simple order at the kitchen table,

4. **Lavinia Dickinson:** Dickinson's sister, who lived with her and conducted most of the domestic affairs in their family house in Amherst, Massachusetts.

while she struggled with a different thing –
the pressure seized upon her mind –
we could ourselves not bear such strain
and, in gratitude, heaved the bucket,
squeezed the rag, breathed the sweet,
homely odor of soap.
Lifting dirt from the floor
I swear
we could hear her thinking.

[2001]

American Contexts

"Mine Eyes Have Seen the Glory": The Meanings of the Civil War

The Civil War was a seismic event in American history, the reverberations of which are still widely felt in the United States. One consequence of the war was to transform the *United States*, which had previously always been used in the plural, into a singular noun, a grammatical shift signaling that it was "one nation, indivisible," in the words of the Pledge of Allegiance. As the following documents illustrate, however, the meaning of the conflict between the North and the South was deeply contested – before, during, and after the Civil War. The war was the culmination of decades of growing sectional divisions. Those divisions were deepened by the strife between proslavery and antislavery settlers in Kansas in 1855-57, as well as by the attack led by John Brown at Harpers Ferry in 1859. By then, many radical abolitionists had concluded that violent means were justified in the struggle to end slavery – that, as Brown puts it in a note written before his execution, "the crimes of this guilty land will never be purged away but with blood." Brown's final speech is reprinted here, as are important speeches by the political leaders of the opposing sides in the Civil War. In his inaugural address, the president of the Confederacy, Jefferson Davis, appeals to the political ideals outlined in the Declaration of Independence. In fact, southern secessionists frequently compared their struggle to the American Revolution. Abraham Lincoln, whose election as president in

1860 led to the secession of the southern states, initially insisted that his sole purpose in going to war was not to end slavery but to preserve the Union established by the Founding Fathers. Even the Emancipation Proclamation, which Lincoln issued in 1862, freed slaves only in areas that were not then under the control of the federal government. But in his Gettysburg Address, Lincoln affirms that the war was being fought to bring about "a new birth of freedom," a fulfillment of the promise of the Declaration of Independence. In his second inaugural address, delivered near the end of the war, Lincoln thus suggests that the carnage was the price exacted for 250 years of slavery in America.

Although Lincoln's famous speeches are among the most memorable efforts to explicate the meaning of the war, the conflict generated a wide range of expression, from poems and songs to diaries, editorials, and sermons. The other documents included here also reveal some of the complexities and contradictions generated by the war. The most popular

John Steuart Curry, *Tragic Prelude*

Curry, whose ancestors were abolitionists, painted this allegorical mural at the State Capitol Building in Topeka, Kansas, between 1937 and 1942. The mural is dominated by the larger-than-life image of John Brown, a Moses-like figure with his arms outstretched, holding a rifle in one hand and a Bible in the other. He is flanked by contending antislavery and proslavery settlers, whose violent clashes in Kansas are represented as the "tragic prelude" to the Civil War. The tornado and prairie fire in the background suggest the destructive forces unleashed by the struggle over slavery, while the two prone figures in the foreground symbolize the million dead and wounded of the Civil War.

southern song was "Dixie's Land," a blackface minstrel song composed and originally performed in "Negro" dialect by a Northerner, Daniel Emmett. Meanwhile, northern soldiers marched to "John Brown's Body" and the "Battle Hymn of the Republic," both of which were written to the tune of a popular southern camp-meeting song, "Say, Brothers, Will You Meet Us?" At the very time Frederick Douglass and other African American leaders were urging black men to enlist in the Union army, Herman Melville meditated on the brutal antidraft and antiblack riots that broke out in New York City in 1863. Near the end of the war, the influential African American minister Henry Highland Garnet hoped that the end of slavery would be the first step toward full equality between the races. Meanwhile, the Southerner Mary Chesnut mourned the loss of a way of life that depended on slavery. For Chesnut, the assassination of Lincoln was "a warning to tyrants." For the poet William Cullen Bryant and most Northerners, the fallen president was a martyr for the cause of freedom and the Union. Following the war, poets gave expression to similarly conflicting attitudes and emotions. Sarah Piatt bitterly placed much of the responsibility for the carnage on Confederate general Robert E. Lee. In the South, Lee emerged as the noble symbol of "The Lost Cause," commemorated in works like Henry Timrod's famous "Ode." In sharp contrast, Frances E. W. Harper expressed the aspirations of the former slaves, freed at last from the control of the bitter and defeated "Rebs." Indeed, the only things that all Americans held in common after the war were rituals of mourning and an understanding of the terrible toll it had taken in human lives. In the final document in this section, Walt Whitman thus suggests that the shared grief for those who had died fighting in the war might serve as a powerful bond among all Americans, finally helping to reunite the North and the South.

bedfordstmartins.com/ americanlit *for research links on the authors in this section*

John Brown

[1800-1859]

Born in Connecticut and raised in Ohio, John Brown was unsuccessful at farming and business before he found his true vocation in the antislavery crusade, work for which he believed he had been called upon by God. He was active in the underground railroad and in groups organized to protect fugitive slaves. But he first gained national attention during 1855-57, when Brown emerged as a militant leader of free-soil settlers in their struggle with proslavery militia for control of the Kansas Territory. Returning east, where he met and gained the sympathetic support of writers

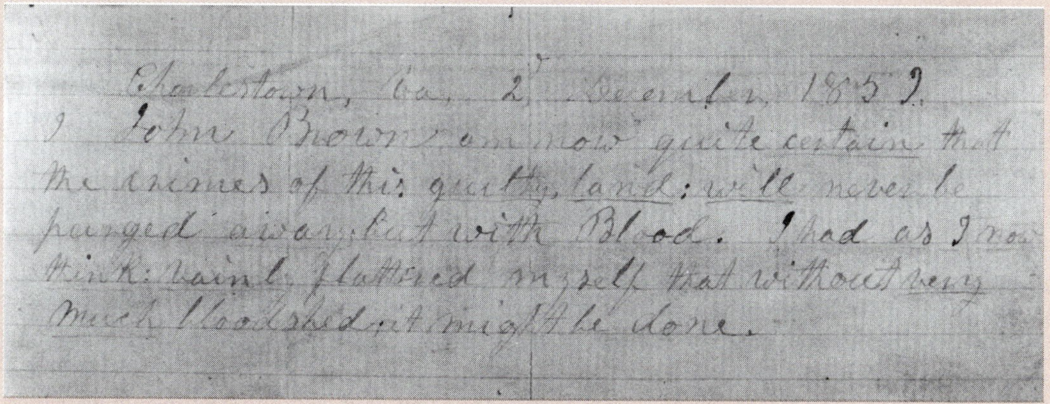
Charlestown, Va, 2nd December, 1859.
I John Brown am now quite certain that the crimes of this guilty, land: will never be purged away; but with Blood. I had as I now think: vainly flattered myself that without very much bloodshed it might be done.

John Brown's Last Note

On December 2, 1859, the day of his execution, Brown wrote this prophetic note: "I John Brown am now quite certain that the crimes of this guilty land will never be purged away but with Blood. I had as I now think vainly flattered myself that without very much bloodshed it might be done."
(Chicago Historical Society [AHD-142].)

like Emerson and Thoreau, Brown began to plan a direct attack on slavery in the South. Despite the warnings of Frederick Douglass – who argued that the plan was suicidal – on October 16, 1859, Brown and eighteen followers, including three of his sons, seized the federal arsenal at Harpers Ferry, Virginia (now West Virginia). Brown hoped to start an insurrection that would attract large numbers of slaves to his small band. Within two days, however, his men were either killed or captured, as Brown was, by federal troops under the command of Brevet Colonel Robert E. Lee. Accused of treason, murder, and conspiring with slaves to rebel, Brown was swiftly tried, convicted, and sentenced to hang. Before his sentence was read, Brown delivered the following speech, which – along with the numerous letters he wrote from prison in the month between his sentencing and execution on December 2, 1859 – gained him tremendous sympathy in the North, where he was widely hailed as a Christlike martyr of the antislavery cause. The text of the speech is taken from Robert M. Dewitt, *The Life, Trial and Conviction of Capt. John Brown* (1860).

John Brown's Last Speech

I have, may it please the Court, a few words to say. In the first place, I deny everything but what I have all along admitted, of a design on my part to free slaves. I intended certainly to have made a clean thing of that matter, as I did last winter when I went into Missouri, and there took slaves without the snapping of a gun on either side, moving them through the country, and finally leaving them in Canada.[1] I designed to have done the same thing again on a larger scale. That was all I intended to do. I never did intend murder or treason, or the destruction of property, or to excite or incite the slaves to rebellion, or to make insurrection. I have another objection, and that is that it is unjust that I should suffer such a penalty. Had I interfered in the manner which I admit, and which I admit has been fairly proved – for I admire the truthfulness and candor of the greater portion of the witnesses who have testified in this case – had I so interfered in behalf of the rich, the powerful, the intelligent, the so-called great, or in behalf of any of their friends, either father, mother, brother, sister, wife, or children, or any of that class, and suffered and sacrificed what I have in this interference, it would have been all right, and every man in this Court would have deemed it an act worthy of reward rather than punishment. This Court acknowledges, too, as I suppose, the validity of the law of God. I see a book kissed, which I suppose to be the Bible, or at least the New Testament, which teaches me that all things whatsoever I would that men should do to me, I should do even so to them.[2] It teaches me further to remember them that are in bonds as bound with them. I endeavored to act up to that instruction. I say I am yet too young to understand that God is any respecter of persons. I believe that to have interfered as I have done, as I have always freely admitted I have done in behalf of His despised poor, is no wrong, but right. Now, if it is deemed necessary that I should forfeit my life for the furtherance of the ends of justice, and mingle my blood further with the blood of my children and with the blood of millions in this slave country whose rights are disregarded by wicked, cruel, and unjust enactments, I say let it be done. Let me say one word further. I feel entirely satisfied with the treatment I have received on my trial. Considering all the circumstances, it has been more generous than I expected. But I feel no consciousness of guilt. I have stated from the first what was my intention, and what was not. I never had any design against the liberty of any person, nor any disposition to commit treason or excite slaves to rebel or make any general insurrection. I never encouraged any man to do so, but always discouraged any idea of that kind. Let me say also in regard to the statements made by some of those who were connected with me, I fear it has been stated by some of them that I have induced them to join me, but the contrary is true. I do not say this to injure them, but as regretting their weakness. Not one but joined me of his own accord, and the greater part at their own expense. A number of them I never saw, and never had a word of conversation with till the day they came to me, and that was for the purpose I have stated. Now, I am done.

[1859, 1860]

---

1. **I went into Missouri . . . leaving them in Canada:** In December 1858, Brown led a group of men on a raid into Missouri. There, they attacked two homesteads, confiscating property and liberating eleven slaves, whom Brown conducted to freedom in Canada.

2. **whatsoever . . . to them:** See Matthew 7:12: "Therefore all things whatsoever ye would that men should do to you, do ye even so to them: for this is the law and the prophets."

Jefferson Davis

[1808-1889]

Jefferson Davis

This photograph was apparently taken in 1861, around the time Davis became president of the Confederate States of America.

Born in Kentucky, Jefferson Davis initially seemed destined for a distinguished career in the military. His father and uncles had been soldiers in the Revolutionary War, and his three older brothers served in the War of 1812. After his graduation from the military academy at West Point, Davis himself served at various wilderness outposts in the Northwest before he resigned from the army in 1835. He then became a successful cotton planter in Mississippi, where he entered politics in 1845. Elected to the House of Representatives, he left to serve as an officer in the Mexican War (1846-48). He was later appointed secretary of war (1853-57) by Franklin Pierce and elected for two terms in the Senate (1847-51, 1857-61), from which he resigned when Mississippi seceded from the Union. After being named the head of the provisional government by the Congress of the Confederate States, he was elected to a six-year term as president of the Confederate States of America. At the end of the war, he was captured, charged with war crimes, and imprisoned for two years in Virginia. But he was never tried, which he had demanded. After his release from prison, Davis retired to Biloxi, Mississippi, where he wrote *The Rise and Fall of the Confederacy* (1878-81). Davis delivered his inaugural address on February 18, 1861, in Montgomery, Alabama, the first capital of the Confederacy. The text is taken from *Southern Historical Society Papers*, Vol. 1, No. 1 (January 1876).

Jefferson Davis's Inaugural Address

Gentlemen of the Congress of the Confederate States of America:

Called to the difficult and responsible station of Executive Chief of the Provisional Government which you have instituted, I approach the discharge of the duties assigned me with an humble distrust of my abilities, but with a sustaining confidence in the wisdom of those who are to aid and guide me in the administration of public affairs, and an abiding faith in the patriotism and virtue of the people. Looking forward to the speedy establishment of a provisional government to take the place of the present one, and which, by its great moral and physical powers, will be better able to contend with the difficulties which arise from the conflicting incidents of separate nations, I enter upon the duties of the office for which I have been chosen with the hope that the beginning of our career as a Confederacy may not be obstructed by hostile opposition to the enjoyment of that separate and independent existence which we have asserted, and which, with the blessing of Providence, we intend to maintain.

Our present position has been achieved in a manner unprecedented in the history of nations. It illustrates the American idea that government rests upon the consent of the governed, and that it is the right of the people to alter or abolish a government whenever it becomes destructive of the ends for which it was established.[1] The declared purposes of the compact of Union from which we have withdrawn were to establish justice, insure domestic tranquillity, to provide for the common defence, to promote the general welfare, and to secure the blessings of liberty for ourselves and our posterity; and when in the judgment of the sovereign States now comprising this Confederacy it had been perverted from the purposes for which it was ordained, and had ceased to answer the ends for which it was established, an appeal to the ballot box declared that so far as they were concerned the government created by that compact should cease to exist. In this they merely asserted a right which the Declaration of Independence of 1776 defined to be inalienable. Of the time and occasion for its exercise, they, as sovereign, were the final judges each for itself. The impartial and enlightened verdict of mankind will vindicate the rectitude of our conduct, and He who knows the hearts of men will judge the sincerity with which we have labored to preserve the government of our fathers, in its spirit and in those rights inherent in it, which were solemnly proclaimed at the birth of the States, and which have been affirmed and reaffirmed in the Bills of Rights of the several States. When they entered into the Union of 1789, it was with the undeniable recognition of the power of the people to resume the authority delegated for the purposes of that government whenever, in their opinion, its functions were perverted and its ends defeated. By virtue of this authority, the time and occasion requiring them to exercise it having arrived, the sovereign States here represented have seceded from that Union, and it is a gross abuse of language to denominate the act rebellion or revolution. They have formed a new alliance, but in each State its government has remained as before. The rights of person and property have not been disturbed. The agency through which they have communicated with foreign powers has been changed, but this does not necessarily interrupt their international relations.

Sustained by a consciousness that our transition from the former Union to the present Confederacy has not proceeded from any disregard on our part of our just obligations, or any failure to perform every constitutional duty – moved by no intention or design to invade the rights of others – anxious to cultivate peace and commerce with all nations – if we may not hope to avoid war, we may at least expect that posterity will acquit us of having needlessly engaged in it. We are doubly justified by the absence of wrong on our part, and by wanton aggression on the part of others. There can be no cause to doubt that the courage and patriotism of the people of the Confederate States will be

---

1. **government . . . for which it was established:** Here, as elsewhere in his speech, Davis paraphrases the Declaration of Independence: "That to secure these rights, Governments are instituted among Men, deriving their just powers from the consent of the governed, – That whenever any Form of Government becomes destructive of these ends, it is the Right of the People to alter or to abolish it, and to institute new Government, laying its foundation on such principles and organizing its powers in such form, as to them shall seem most likely to effect their Safety and Happiness." The full text of the Declaration of Independence is printed on pages 448-52.

found equal to any measure of defence which may be required for their security. Devoted to agricultural pursuits, their chief interest is the export of a commodity required in every manufacturing country.[2] Our policy is peace, and the freest trade our necessities will permit. It is alike our interest, and that of all those to whom we would sell and from whom we would buy, that there should be the fewest practicable restrictions upon interchange of commodities. There can be but little rivalry between us and any manufacturing or navigating community, such as the Northwestern States of the American Union.

It must follow, therefore, that mutual interest would invite good will and kindness between them and us. If, however, passion or lust of dominion should cloud the judgment and inflame the ambition of these States, we must prepare to meet the emergency, and maintain, by the final arbitrament of the sword, the position we have assumed among the nations of the earth. We have now entered upon our career of independence, and it must be inflexibly pursued.

Through many years of controversy with our late associates, the Northern States, we have vainly endeavored to secure tranquillity and obtain respect for the rights to which we were entitled. As a necessity, not a choice we have resorted to separation, and henceforth our energies must be devoted to the conducting of our own affairs, and perpetuating the Confederacy we have formed. If a just perception of mutual interest shall permit us peaceably to pursue our separate political career, my most earnest desire will have been fulfilled. But if this be denied us, and the integrity and jurisdiction of our territory be assailed, it will but remain for us with a firm resolve to appeal to arms and invoke the blessings of Providence upon a just cause.

As a consequence of our new constitution, and with a view to meet our anticipated wants, it will be necessary to provide a speedy and efficient organization of the several branches of the executive departments having special charge of our foreign intercourse, financial and military affairs, and postal service. For purposes of defence, the Confederate States may, under ordinary circumstances rely mainly upon their militia; but it is deemed advisable, in the present condition of affairs, that there should be a well instructed, disciplined army, more numerous than would be usually required for a peace establishment.

I also suggest that for the protection of our harbors and commerce on the high seas, a navy adapted to those objects be built up. These necessities have doubtless engaged the attention of Congress.

With a constitution differing only in form from that of our forefathers, in so far as it is explanatory of their well known intents, freed from sectional conflicts which have so much interfered with the pursuits of the general welfare, it is not unreasonable to expect that the States from which we have parted may seek to unite their fortunes with ours under the government we have instituted. For this your constitution has made adequate provision, but beyond this, if I mistake not the judgment and will of the people, our reunion with the States from which we have separated is neither practicable nor desirable. To increase power, develop the resources, and promote the happiness of this

---

2. **a commodity . . . country:** Cotton, the major product of the South, was an important element in the emerging global economy of the period. By 1860, the southern states exported two-thirds of the world's supply of cotton and three-fourths of the cotton used in the lucrative textile industries of France and Great Britain.

Confederacy, it is necessary that there should be so much homogeneity as that the welfare of every portion be the aim of the whole. When this homogeneity does not exist, antagonisms are engendered which must and should result in separation.

Actuated solely by a desire to protect and preserve our own rights and promote our own welfare, the secession of the Confederate States has been marked by no aggression upon others, and followed by no domestic convulsion. Our industrial pursuits have received no check; the cultivation of our fields has progressed as heretofore; and even should we be involved in war, there would be no considerable diminution in the production of the great staple which constitutes our exports, and in which the commercial world has an interest scarcely less than our own. This common interest of producer and consumer can only be interrupted by external force, which would obstruct shipments to foreign markets – a course of conduct which would be detrimental to manufacturing and commercial interests abroad. Should reason guide the action of the government from which we have separated, a policy so injurious to the civilized world, the Northern States included, could not be dictated even by the strongest desire to inflict injury upon us; but if otherwise, a terrible responsibility will rest upon it, and the suffering of millions will bear testimony to the folly and wickedness of our aggressors. In the meantime there will remain to us, besides the ordinary remedies before suggested, the well known resources for retaliation upon the commerce of our enemy.

Experience in public stations of subordinate grade to this which your kindness has conferred on me, has taught me that care and toil and disappointments are the price of official elevation. You will have many errors to forgive, many deficiencies to tolerate, but you will not find in me either a want of zeal or fidelity to a cause that has my highest hopes and most enduring affection. Your generosity has bestowed upon me an undeserved distinction, one which neither sought nor desired. Upon the continuance of that sentiment, and upon your wisdom and patriotism, I rely to direct and support me in the performance of the duties required at my hands. We have changed the constituent parts, not the system of our government. The constitution formed by our fathers is the constitution of the "Confederate States." In *their* exposition of it, and in the judicial constructions it has received, it has a light that reveals its true meaning. Thus instructed as to the just interpretations of that instrument, and ever remembering that all public offices are but trusts, held for the benefit of the people, and that delegated powers are to be strictly construed, I will hope that by due diligence in the discharge of my duties, though I may disappoint your expectations, yet to retain, when retiring, something of the good will and confidence which welcome my entrance into office. It is joyous in perilous times to look around upon a people united in heart, who are animated and actuated by one and the same purpose and high resolve, with whom the sacrifices to be made are not weighed in the balance against honor, right, liberty and equality. Obstacles may retard, but cannot prevent their progressive movements. Sanctified by justice and sustained by a virtuous people, let me reverently invoke the God of our fathers to guide and protect us in our efforts to perpetuate the principles which by HIS blessing they were able to vindicate, establish and transmit to their posterity, and with the continuance of HIS favor, ever to be gratefully acknowledged, let us look hopefully forward to success, to peace, and to prosperity.

[1861, 1876]

Civil War Songs

Dozens of songs were composed during the Civil War, ranging from marching songs to inspirational songs sung in both army camps and on the home fronts. One of the most familiar of the Southern songs, "Dixie" or "Dixie's Land," was composed by a Northerner, Daniel Emmett (1815-1904). A member of several popular minstrel bands, groups of white musicians who performed in blackface and sang in heavy "Negro" dialect, Emmett composed the song in 1859 for Bryant's Minstrels in New York City. Although it was also popular in the North, after the outbreak of the Civil War (and to the dismay of Emmett) the song became almost exclusively associated with the South. By the time the war began, Union soldiers were already singing "John Brown's Body," whose anonymous author apparently wrote the lyrics to the tune of a popular camp-meeting song composed in 1856 by William Steffe of South Carolina. The most famous of all Union songs was written later to the same tune. During a visit to a Union army camp in 1861, Julia Ward Howe and her friend James Freeman Clarke heard the troops sing "John Brown's Body." In response to Clarke's challenge that she compose more dignified and noble lyrics for the song, Howe wrote "Battle Hymn of the Republic," a poem that appeared on the first page of the February 1862 issue of the *Atlantic Monthly.* The lyrics swiftly supplanted those of "John Brown's Body," though the chorus of that song was adapted for the "Battle Hymn of the Republic." None of the five stanzas of Howe's poem was followed by a chorus. But the song is traditionally sung and is here printed with the stirring chorus beginning "Glory, Glory Hallelujah," a phrase that in itself conveys the passion and religious fervor that ran through so many of the songs sung in both the North and the South during the Civil War.

Dixie's Land

I wish I was in the land of cotton,
Old times there are not forgotten;
    Look away! Look away! Look away, Dixie's Land!
In Dixie's Land where I was born in,
Early on one frosty morning,
    Look away! Look away! Look away, Dixie's Land!

(Chorus)
Then I wish I was in Dixie! Hooray! Hooray!
In Dixie's Land I'll take my stand, to live and die in Dixie!
Away! Away! Away down South in Dixie!
Away! Away! Away down South in Dixie!

Old Missus married "Will the Weaver";
William was a gay deceiver!
    Look away! Look away! Look away, Dixie's Land!

But when he put his arm around her,
Smiled as fierce as a forty-pounder![1]
    Look away! Look away! Look away, Dixie's Land!
(Chorus)

His face was sharp as a butcher's cleaver;
But that did not seem to grieve her!
    Look away! Look away! Look away, Dixie's Land!
Old Missus acted the foolish part
And died for a man that broke her heart!
    Look away! Look away! Look away, Dixie's Land!
(Chorus)

Now here's a health to the next old missus
And all the gals that want to kiss us!
    Look away! Look away! Look away, Dixie's Land!
But if you want to drive away sorrow,
Come and hear this song tomorrow!
    Look away! Look away! Look away, Dixie's Land!
(Chorus)

There's buckwheat cakes and Injin batter,[2]
Makes you fat or a little fatter!
    Look away! Look away! Look away, Dixie's Land!
Then hoe it down and scratch your gravel,
To Dixie's Land I'm bound to travel!
    Look away! Look away! Look away, Dixie's Land!
(Chorus)

[1859]

1. **forty-pounder:** Nickname for a large cannon.
2. **Injin batter:** Mixture of corn meal, molasses, and yeast, used to make small cakes.

John Brown's Body

John Brown's body lies a-mouldering in the grave,
John Brown's body lies a-mouldering in the grave,
John Brown's body lies a-mouldering in the grave,
But his soul goes marching on.

(Chorus)
Glory, glory, hallelujah,
Glory, glory, hallelujah,
Glory, glory, hallelujah,
His soul goes marching on.

He's gone to be a soldier in the Army of the Lord,
He's gone to be a soldier in the Army of the Lord,
He's gone to be a soldier in the Army of the Lord,
His soul goes marching on.
(Chorus)

John Brown's knapsack is strapped upon his back,
John Brown's knapsack is strapped upon his back,
John Brown's knapsack is strapped upon his back,
His soul goes marching on.
(Chorus)

John Brown died that the slaves might be free,
John Brown died that the slaves might be free,
John Brown died that the slaves might be free,
But his soul goes marching on.
(Chorus)

The stars above in Heaven now are looking kindly down,
The stars above in Heaven now are looking kindly down,
The stars above in Heaven now are looking kindly down,
On the grave of old John Brown.
(Chorus)

[1860-61]

Battle Hymn of the Republic

Mine eyes have seen the glory of the coming of the Lord;
He is trampling out the vintage where the grapes of wrath are stored;
He hath loosed the fateful lightning of his terrible swift sword,
His truth is marching on.

(Chorus)
Glory, Glory Hallelujah,
Glory, Glory Hallelujah,
Glory, Glory Hallelujah,
His truth is marching on.

I have seen Him in the watch fires of a hundred circling camps;
They have builded Him an altar in the evening dews and damps;
I can read his righteous sentence by the dim and flaring lamps,
His day is marching on.
(Chorus)

I have read a fiery gospel write in burnished rows of steel:
"As ye deal with My contemners, so with you My Grace shall deal;

Let the Hero, born of woman, crush the serpent with his heel,
Since God is marching on."
(Chorus)

He has sounded forth the trumpet that shall never call retreat;
He is sifting out the hearts of men before His Judgement Seat;
Oh! be swift, my soul, to answer Him, be jubilant, my feet!
Our God is marching on.
(Chorus)

In the beauty of the lilies Christ was born across the sea,
With a glory in his bosom that transfigures you and me;
As He died to make men holy, let us die to make men free,
While God is marching on.
(Chorus)

[1862]

Frederick Douglass

[1818–1895]

Frederick Douglass, whose life and work are described in more detail on page 855 of this volume, was a tireless champion of the Union cause during the Civil War. After the outbreak of the conflict, he devoted much of the space in his magazine *Douglass's Monthly* to news of the battles, as well as to articles on the importance of putting down the "slave-holding rebellion" of the South, as the war was often characterized in the abolitionist press. Because of prejudice and racial stereotyping, the Union was initially reluctant to enlist black soldiers, despite the fact that many free blacks and former slaves were eager to serve. On July 17, 1862, Congress passed two acts which allowed the enlistment of African Americans, but enrollment did not officially begin until after the Emancipation Proclamation was issued in September 1862. The next month, the First Kansas Colored Volunteers defeated Confederate soldiers at Island Mound, Missouri. In the spring of 1863, the first full regiment of black troops was organized in Massachusetts. In the following editorial in *Douglass's Monthly* – published in Rochester, New York, a state that had not yet established a company for black men – Douglass urges men of his state to enlist in Massachusetts. Two months later, on May 13, 1863, black volunteers were mustered into service as the Fifty-fourth Regiment of the Massachusetts Volunteer Infantry, under the command of Robert Gould Shaw. Eventually about 180,000 African Americans served in the Union army during the Civil War. The text of Douglass's signed editorial is taken from the March 1863 issue of *Douglass's Monthly.*

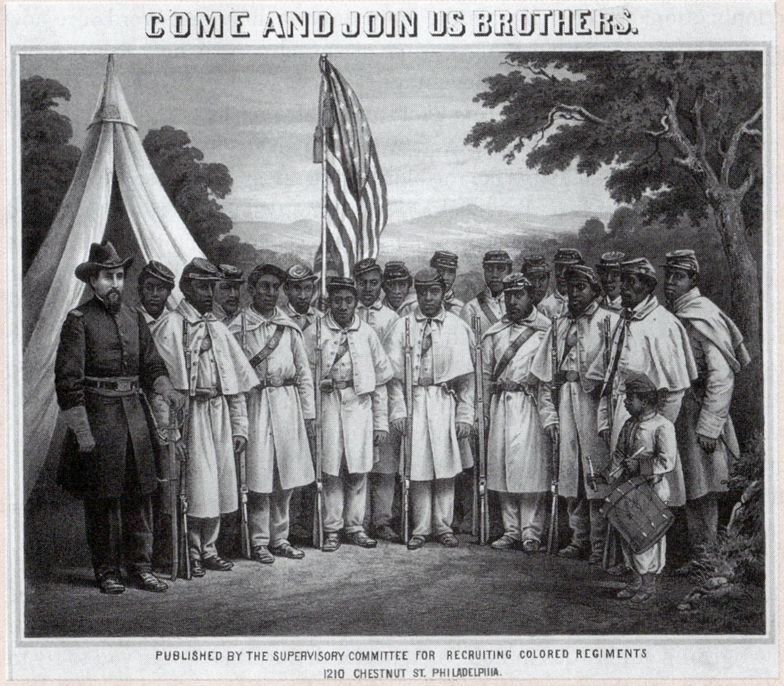

Come and Join Us Brothers

This lithograph, published in 1863, was part of a campaign to enlist African Americans in the Union army during the Civil War.
(Chicago Historical Society [ICHi-22051].)

MEN OF COLOR, TO ARMS!

When first the rebel cannon shattered the walls of Sumter,[1] and drove away its starving garrison, I predicted that the war, then and there inaugurated would not be fought out entirely by white men. Every month's experience during these two dreary years, has confirmed that opinion. A war undertaken and brazenly carried on for the perpetual enslavement of colored men, calls logically and loudly upon colored men to help to suppress it. Only a moderate share of sagacity was needed to see that the arm of the slave was the best defence against the arm of the slaveholder. Hence with every reverse to the National arms, with every exulting shout of victory raised by the slaveholding rebels, I have implored the imperrilled nation to unchain against her foes her powerful black hand. Slowly and reluctantly that appeal is beginning to be heeded. Stop not now to complain that it was not heeded sooner. It may, or it may not have been best that it should not. This is not the time to discuss that question. Leave it to the future. When the war is over, the country is saved, peace is established, and the black man's rights are secured, as they will be, history with an impartial hand, will dispose of that and sundry other

1. **Sumter:** The first shots of the Civil War were fired at Fort Sumter, a Union outpost in the harbor of Charleston, South Carolina, which was shelled by Confederate artillery in April 1861.

questions. Action! action! not criticism, is the plain duty of this hour. Words are now useful only as they stimulate to blows. The office of speech now is only to point out when, here and how, to strike to the best advantage. There is no time for delay. The tide is at its flood that leads on to fortune.[2] From East to West, from North to South, the sky is written all over "NOW OR NEVER." Liberty won by white men would lose half its lustre. Who would be free themselves must strike the blow. Better even to die free, than to live slaves. This is the sentiment of every brave colored man amongst us. There are weak and cowardly men in all nations. We have them amongst us. They tell you that this is the "white man's war"; – that you will be no "better off after, than before the war"; that the getting of you into the army is to "sacrifice you on the first opportunity." Believe them not – cowards themselves, they do not wish to have their cowardice shamed by your brave example. Leave them to their timidity, or to whatever motive may hold them back.

I have not thought lightly of the words I am now addressing to you. The counsel I give comes of close observations of the great struggle now in progress – and of the deep conviction that this is your hour, and mine.

In good earnest then, and after the best deliberation, I now for the first time during this war feel at liberty to call and counsel you to arms. By every consideration which binds you to your enslaved fellow country-men, and the peace and welfare of your country; by every aspiration which you cherish for the freedom and equality of yourselves and your children; by all the ties of blood and identity which make us one with the brave black men, now fighting our battles in Louisana, in South Carolina, I urge you to fly to arms, and smite with death the power that would bury the Government and your Liberty in the same hopeless grave. I wish I could tell you that the State of New York calls you to this high honor. For the moment her constituted authorities are silent on the subject. They will speak by and by, and doubtless on the right side; but we are not compelled to wait for her. We can get at the throat of treason and slavery, through the State of Massachusetts.

She was first in the war of Independence; first to break the chains of her slaves; first to make the black man equal before the law; first to admit colored children to her common schools, and she was first to answer with her blood the alarm cry of the nation – when its capital was menaced by rebels. You know her patriotic Governor, and you know Charles Sumner[3] – I need not add more.

Massachusetts now welcomes you to arms as her soldiers. She has but a small colored population from which to recruit. She has full leave of the General Government to send one regiment to the war, and she has undertaken to do it. Go quickly and help fill up this first colored regiment from the north. I am authorized to assure you that you will receive the same wages, the same rations, the same equipments, the same protec-

---

2. **The tide . . . fortune:** A paraphrase of Shakespeare's *Julius Caesar*: "There is a tide in the affairs of men, / Which, taken at the flood, leads on to fortune" (4.3.217-18).

3. **her patriotic Governor . . . Charles Sumner:** Both John Albion Andrew (1818-1867), the Republican governor of Massachusetts from 1861-66, and Charles Sumner (1811-1874), a senator from Massachusetts from 1851-74, were strong opponents of slavery who urged emancipation at the outbreak of the Civil War.

tion, the same treatment and the same bounty secured to white soldiers. You will be led by able and skillful officers – men who will take especial pride in your efficiency and success. They will be quick to accord to you all the honor you shall merit by your valor – and see that your rights and feelings are respected by other soldiers. I have assured myself on these points – and can speak with authority. More than twenty years unswerving devotion to our common cause, may give me some humble claim to be trusted at this momentous crisis.

I will not argue. To do so implies hesitation and doubt, and you do not hesitate. You do not doubt. The day dawns – the morning star is bright upon the horizon! The Iron gate of our prison stands half open. One gallant rush from the North will fling it wide open, while four millions of our brothers and sisters, shall march out into Liberty! The chance is now given you to end in a day the bondage of centuries; and to rise in one bound from social degredation to the plane of common equality with all other varieties of men. Remember Denmark Vesey of Charleston. – Remember Nathaniel Turner of South Hampton, remember Shields Green, and Copeland who followed noble John Brown, and fell as glorious martyrs for the cause of the slave.[4] – Remember that in a contest with oppression the Almighty has no attribute which can take sides with oppressors. The case is before you. This is our golden opportunity – let us accept it – and forever wipe out the dark reproaches unsparingly hurled against us by our enemies. Win for ourselves the gratitude of our Country – and the best blessings of our posterity through all time. The nucleus of this first regiment is now in camp at Readville, a short distance from Boston. I will undertake to forward to Boson all persons adjudged fit to be mustered into the regiment, who shall apply to me at any time within the next two weeks.

[1863]

---

4. **Remember . . . martyrs for the cause of the slave:** Douglass lists several men who died in the abolitionist cause. Denmark Vesey (1767-1822), a former slave who had bought his freedom in 1800, was executed in June 1822 for organizing a slave rebellion in Charleston, South Carolina. Nathaniel Turner (1800-1831), a slave who organized a rebellion that killed fifty-five white people in Virginia, was captured and then hanged and skinned in November 1831. Shields Green was the assumed name of a fugitive slave, and Copeland was John Anthony Copeland Jr., a free black; both men were with John Brown during the raid on Harpers Ferry in 1859.

Herman Melville

[1819-1891]

Herman Melville, whose life and work are described in more detail on page 1072 of this volume, increasingly turned from fiction to poetry after his literary career began to falter during the 1850s. Ten years after the appearance of his final novel, he published a collection of poems about the Civil War, *Battle-Pieces and Aspects of the War* (1866). Melville dedicated it "to

Draft Riots in New York City

This engraving depicts the antidraft and antiblack riots that erupted in New York City in July 1863. After a mob looted and burned the Colored Orphan Asylum, where two hundred children were left homeless, the fire spread to other buildings, forcing the inhabitants to flee with whatever possessions they could salvage.

the memory of the three hundred thousand who in the war for the maintenance of the Union fell devotedly under the flag of their fathers," and most of the poems in the volume commemorated the battles and campaigns in which so many of those devoted men had died. In the following poem, however, Melville recalls an aspect of the war that many would have liked to forget, the brutal riots that erupted in New York City in July 1863. Early in the month, the North gained a major victory at the Battle of Gettysburg, but the number of Union casualties was high: more than 23,000 were killed, wounded, or missing in action. Newspapers were reporting those grim statistics just as the first draft law, the Conscription Act of March 1863, was being enforced in New York City. (The Confederacy had adopted a conscription act a year earlier, in April 1862.) In the North, the brunt of the draft was borne by immigrant laborers, especially the Irish, who could not afford to hire a substitute or pay the $300 fee that exempted wealthy young men from service. When the names of new draftees began to be published in the papers, a riot broke out on July 13. Most of the violence was directed at African Americans, who were blamed for the war, and many of whom were lynched or beaten to death on the streets. Mobs also burned a black orphanage and destroyed homes and businesses of people who supported abolition or hired black workers. Damage was extensive, and as many as one thousand people died in the four-day riots, which ended only when President Lincoln sent in Union troops to restore order in the city. As Melville powerfully suggests in "The House-top," the riots remained one of the darkest and most troubling memories of the Civil War. The text of the poem is taken from the first edition of *Battle-Pieces and Aspects of the War* (1866).

THE HOUSE-TOP

A Night Piece

(JULY, 1863)

No sleep. The sultriness pervades the air
And binds the brain – a dense oppression, such
As tawny tigers feel in matted shades,
Vexing their blood and making apt for ravage.
Beneath the stars the roofy desert spreads
Vacant as Libya.[1] All is hushed near by.
Yet fitfully from far breaks a mixed surf
Of muffled sound, the Atheist roar of riot.
Yonder, where parching Sirius[2] set in drought,
Balefully glares red Arson – there – and there.
The Town is taken by its rats – ship-rats
And rats of the wharves. All civil charms
And priestly spells which late held hearts in awe –
Fear-bound, subjected to a better sway
Than sway of self; these like a dream dissolve,
And man rebounds whole aeons[3] back in nature.
Hail to the low dull rumble, dull and dead,
And ponderous drag that shakes the wall.
Wise Draco comes,[4] deep in the midnight roll
Of black artillery; he comes, though late;
In code corroborating Calvin's creed[5]
And cynic tyrannies of honest kings;
He comes, nor parlies; and the Town, redeemed,
Gives thanks devout; nor, being thankful, heeds
The grimy slur on the Republic's faith implied,
Which holds that Man is naturally good,
And – more – is Nature's Roman, never to be scourged.

[1866]

---

1. **Vacant as Libya:** Much of Libya, a country in North Africa, is covered by the Sahara Desert.
2. **parching Sirius:** The brightest star in the sky, Sirius is sometimes called the "scorching star."
3. **aeons:** Variant spelling of *eons*, indefinite and very long periods of time.
4. **Wise Draco comes:** Draco was an ancient Athenian legislator notorious for the severity of his laws; the reference here is to the arrival of Union troops and the declaration of martial law in the city.
5. **Calvin's creed:** John Calvin (1509-1564), influential Protestant theologian popularly associated with the doctrines of original sin, human depravity, and predestination.

Abraham Lincoln

[1809-1865]

Abraham Lincoln

This photograph of Lincoln was taken in 1864 by the renowned photographer Mathew Brady.

Abraham Lincoln, the sixteenth president of the United States, was born on a farm in Kentucky in 1809. His family moved first to Indiana and then to Illinois. Largely self-educated, Lincoln worked on farms and in stores and studied law as an apprentice. He served in the Illinois legislature and then in the U.S. House of Representatives, slowly gaining a national reputation that finally earned him the Republican nomination for president in 1860. Lincoln carried all eighteen free states but failed to gain a single electoral vote in any of the fourteen slave states, eleven of which seceded within three months of his election. The Civil War began a month after his inauguration in March 1861 and ended only a few days before his assassination in April 1865. Major sources of Lincoln's success as a politician and as a wartime leader were his abilities as a writer and the power of his rhetoric, as illustrated by the following two addresses. Both are among the most famous speeches in American history. The addresses are also among the most eloquent expositions of what the war ultimately meant to Lincoln and many others in the North, as the initial effort to preserve the Union also became a mission to end slavery in the United States.

Lincoln's Gettysburg Address. From July 1-3, 1863, one of the bloodiest and most decisive battles of the Civil War was fought at Gettysburg, Pennsylvania, where roughly ninety thousand Union troops repulsed an invading army of more than seventy thousand led by General Robert E. Lee. The thousands of Union dead were buried in the Soldiers National Cemetery, established on the grounds of the battlefield and dedicated in November 1863. The major speaker was the acclaimed orator Everett Emerson of Massachusetts, who delivered a two-hour address. Lincoln was invited to offer what the program simply described as "Remarks," but he made the most of the occasion. Speaking for only two or three minutes, Lincoln movingly dedicated the cemetery at Gettysburg. He also dedicated the nation to the principle that "all men are created equal," the phrase from the Declaration of Independence quoted in the first sentence of the Gettysburg Address. The text of the speech, which was widely reprinted in newspapers, is that of the "final text" printed in volume 7 of *The Collected Works of Abraham Lincoln*, edited by Roy P. Basler (1953).

The Battle of Gettysburg

A photograph of Union dead on the battleground at Gettysburg, where over three thousand Union troops and nearly four thousand Confederate troops were killed in three days of fighting in July 1863.

THE GETTYSBURG ADDRESS

Address Delivered at the Dedication of the Cemetery at Gettysburg, November 19, 1863

Four score and seven years ago our fathers brought forth on this continent, a new nation, conceived in Liberty, and dedicated to the proposition that all men are created equal.

Now we are engaged in a great civil war, testing whether that nation, or any nation so conceived and so dedicated, can long endure. We are met on a great battle-field of that war. We have come to dedicate a portion of that field, as a final resting place for those who here gave their lives that that nation might live. It is altogether fitting and proper that we should do this.

But, in a larger sense, we can not dedicate – we can not consecrate – we can not hallow – this ground. The brave men, living and dead, who struggled here, have consecrated it, far above our poor power to add or detract. The world will little note, nor long remember what we say here, but it can never forget what they did here. It is for us the living, rather, to be dedicated here to the unfinished work which they who fought here have thus far so nobly advanced. It is rather for us to be here dedicated to the great task remaining before us – that from these honored dead we take increased devotion to that cause for which they gave the last full measure of devotion – that we here highly resolve that these dead shall not have died in vain – that this nation, under God, shall have a new birth of freedom – and that government of the people, by the people, for the people, shall not perish from the earth.

[1863, 1953]

Lincoln's Second Inaugural Address. After winning election to a second term in 1864, Lincoln delivered his second inaugural address on March 4, 1865. By then, a series of military victories by Union forces clearly indicated that the Civil War was drawing to a close. It was equally clear by then just how costly the war had been: together, the number of dead on both sides of the conflict exceeded 600,000, more than in all the other wars in American history combined. Mindful of that terrible toll, Lincoln at once sought to articulate the meaning of the war and to lay the groundwork for peace, reconstruction, and reunification. The text of the address is taken from volume 8 of *The Collected Works of Abraham Lincoln*, edited by Roy P. Basler (1953).

SECOND INAUGURAL ADDRESS, MARCH 4, 1865

At this second appearing to take the oath of the presidential office, there is less occasion for an extended address than there was at the first.[1] Then a statement, somewhat in detail, of a course to be pursued, seemed fitting and proper. Now, at the expiration of four years, during which public declarations have been constantly called forth on every point and phase of the great contest which still absorbs the attention, and engrosses the energies of the nation, little that is new could be presented. The progress of our arms, upon which all else chiefly depends, is as well known to the public as to myself; and it is, I trust, reasonably satisfactory and encouraging to all. With high hope for the future, no prediction in regard to it is ventured.

On the occasion corresponding to this four years ago, all thoughts were anxiously directed to an impending civil-war. All dreaded it – all sought to avert it. While the inaugeral address was being delivered from this place, devoted altogether to *saving* the Union without war, insurgent agents were in the city seeking to *destroy* it without war – seeking to dissolve the Union, and divide effects, by negotiation. Both parties deprecated war; but one of them would *make* war rather than let the nation survive; and the other would *accept* war rather than let it perish. And the war came.

One eighth of the whole population were colored slaves, not distributed generally over the Union, but localized in the Southern part of it. These slaves constituted a peculiar and powerful interest. All knew that this interest was, somehow, the cause of the war. To strengthen, perpetuate, and extend this interest was the object for which the insurgents would rend the Union, even by war; while the government claimed no right to do more than to restrict the territorial enlargement of it. Neither party expected for the war, the magnitude, or the duration, which it has already attained. Neither anticipated that the *cause* of the conflict might cease with, or even before, the conflict itself should cease. Each looked for an easier triumph, and a result less fundamental and astounding. Both read the same Bible, and pray to the same God; and each invokes His aid against the other. It may seem strange that any men should dare to ask a just God's

1. **at the first:** Lincoln's first and much-longer inaugural address was delivered on March 4, 1861.

assistance in wringing their bread from the sweat of other men's faces; but let us judge not that we be not judged.[2] The prayers of both could not be answered; that of neither has been answered fully. The Almighty has His own purposes. "Woe unto the world because of offences! for it must needs be that offences come; but woe to that man by whom the offence cometh!"[3] If we shall suppose that American Slavery is one of those offences which, in the providence of God, must needs come, but which, having continued through His appointed time, He now wills to remove, and that He gives to both North and South, this terrible war, as the woe due to those by whom the offence came, shall we discern therein any departure from those divine attributes which the believers in a Living God always ascribe to Him? Fondly do we hope – fervently do we pray – that this mighty scourge of war may speedily pass away. Yet, if God wills that it continue, until all the wealth piled by the bond-man's two hundred and fifty years of unrequited toil shall be sunk, and until every drop of blood drawn with the lash, shall be paid by another drawn with the sword, as was said three thousand years ago, so still it must be said "the judgments of the Lord, are true and righteous altogether."[4]

With malice toward none; with charity for all; with firmness in the right, as God gives us to see the right, let us strive on to finish the work we are in; to bind up the nation's wounds; to care for him who shall have borne the battle, and for his widow, and his orphan – to do all which may achieve and cherish a just, and a lasting peace, among ourselves, and with all nations.

[1865, 1953]

---

2. **judge not . . . judged:** See Christ's words in the Sermon on the Mount: "Judge not, that ye be not judged" (Matthew 7:1).
3. **"Woe . . . cometh!":** Matthew 18:7. In that chapter of Matthew, Christ teaches his disciples humility, forgiveness, and compassion for others.
4. **"the judgments . . . altogether":** See Psalms 19:9: "The fear of the LORD is clean, enduring forever: the judgments of the Lord are true and righteous altogether."

Henry Highland Garnet

[1815-1882]

Henry Highland Garnet was born a slave in Maryland. When he was nine years old, Garnet's entire family escaped to New York City. He received an excellent education there, and Garnet continued his studies at a school in New Hampshire and then at the Oneida Institute in central New York, where he prepared for the ministry. Garnet became the minister of a predominantly white Presbyterian church in Troy, New York, in 1842. The following year he delivered "An Address to the Slaves of the United States," in which Garnet exhorted his enslaved brethren to rise and strike for "their lives and liberties." During the following two decades, his militant position was endorsed by a growing number of abolitionists, and Garnet was

Henry Highland Garnet

This photograph was taken in 1865, when Garnet became the first African American to deliver a sermon (or any other address) to the assembled members of Congress.
(Courtesy of Picture History.)

among the first to press the government to enlist African American troops to fight in the Civil War. In 1864, Garnet became the pastor of the influential Fifteenth Street Presbyterian Church in Washington, D.C. Following the passage of the Thirteenth Amendment to the Constitution, which ended slavery in the United States, President Lincoln invited Garnet to deliver a sermon at the House of Representatives, the first time an African American had ever done so. In his "Memorial Discourse," Garnet reviewed the history of slavery and praised the assembled members of Congress for their passage of the Thirteenth Amendment. In his final exhortation, printed below, he urges the legislators to go even further, erasing all distinctions based on race from the laws and Constitution of the United States. The text of the selection is taken from *A Memorial Discourse; by Rev. Henry Highland Garnet, Delivered in the Hall of the House of Representatives, Washington, D.C. on Sabbath, February 12, 1865* (1865).

From A MEMORIAL DISCOURSE

It is often asked when and where will the demands of the reformers of this and coming ages end? It is a fair question, and I will answer.

When all unjust and heavy burdens shall be removed from every man in the land. When all invidious and proscriptive distinctions shall be blotted out from our laws, whether they be constitutional, statute, or municipal laws. When emancipation shall be followed by enfranchisement, and all men holding allegiance to the government shall enjoy every right of American citizenship.[1] When our brave and gallant soldiers shall have justice done unto them. When the men who endure the sufferings and perils of the battle-field in the defence of their country, and in order to keep our rulers in their places, shall enjoy the well-earned privilege of voting for them. When in the army and navy, and in every legitimate and honorable occupation, promotion shall smile upon merit without the slightest regard to the complexion of a man's face. When there shall be no more class-legislation, and no more trouble concerning the black man and his rights, than there is in regard to other American citizens. When, in every respect, he shall be equal before the law, and shall be left to make his own way in the social walks of life.

---

1. **When emancipation . . . citizenship:** All those born or naturalized in the United States were later declared to be citizens by the Fourteenth Amendment (1868); "enfranchisement," or the right to vote, was finally guaranteed to black men by the Fifteenth Amendment (1870).

We ask, and only ask, that when our poor frail barks are launched on life's ocean –

> "Bound on a voyage of awful length
> And dangers little know,"[2]

that, in common with others, we may be furnished with rudder, helm, and sails, and charts, and compass. Give us good pilots to conduct us to the open seas; lift no false lights along the dangerous coasts, and if it shall please God to send us propitious winds, or fearful gales, we shall survive or perish as our energies or neglect shall determine. We ask no special favors, but we plead for justice. While we scorn unmanly dependence; in the name of God, the universal Father, we demand the right to live, and labor, and to enjoy the fruits of our toil. The good work which God has assigned for the ages to come, will be finished, when our national literature shall be so purified as to reflect a faithful and a just light upon the character and social habits of our race, and the brush, and pencil, and chisel, and Lyre of Art, shall refuse to lend their aid to scoff at the afflictions of the poor, or to caricature, or ridicule a long-suffering people. When caste and prejudice in Christian churches shall be utterly destroyed, and shall be regarded as totally unworthy of Christians, and at variance with the principles of the gospel. When the blessings of the Christian religion, and of sound, religious education, shall be freely offered to all, then, and not till then, shall the effectual labors of God's people and God's instruments cease.

If slavery has been destroyed merely from *necessity*, let every class be enfranchised at the dictation of *justice*. Then we shall have a Constitution that shall be reverenced by all: rulers who shall be honored, and revered, and a Union that shall be sincerely loved by a brave and patriotic people, and which can never be severed.

Great sacrifices have been made by the people; yet, greater still are demanded ere atonement can be made for our national sins. Eternal justice holds heavy mortgages against us, and will require the payment of the last farthing.[3] We have involved ourselves in the sin of unrighteous gain, stimulated by luxury, and pride, and the love of power and oppression; and prosperity and peace can be purchased only by blood, and with tears of repentance. We have paid some of the fearful installments, but there are other heavy obligations to be met.

The great day of the nation's judgment has come, and who shall be able to stand? Even we, whose ancestors have suffered the afflictions which are inseparable from a condition of slavery, for the period of two centuries and a half, now pity our land and weep with those who weep.

Upon the total and complete destruction of this accursed sin depends the safety and perpetuity of our Republic and its excellent institutions.

---

2. **"Bound . . . known"**: The lines are from "Human Frailty," by the English poet William Cowper (1731-1800): "Bound on a voyage of awful length / And dangers little known, / A stranger to superior strength, / Man vainly trusts his own."
3. **farthing**: Formerly a coin in Great Britain, equal to a quarter of a penny.

Let slavery die. It has had a long and fair trial. God himself has pleaded against it. The enlightened nations of the earth have condemned it. Its death warrant is signed by God and man. Do not commute its sentence. Give it no respite, but let it be ignominiously executed.

Honorable Senators and Representatives! illustrious rulers of this great nation! I cannot refrain this day from invoking upon you, in God's name, the blessings of millions who were ready to perish, but to whom a new and better life has been opened by your humanity, justice, and patriotism. You have said, "Let the Constitution of the country be so amended that slavery and involuntary servitude shall no longer exist in the United States, except in punishment for crime."[4] Surely, an act so sublime could not escape Divine notice; and doubtless the deed has been recorded in the archives of heaven. Volumes may be appropriated to your praise and renown in the history of the world. Genius and art may perpetuate the glorious act on canvass and in marble, but certain and more lasting monuments in commemoration of your decision are already erected in the hearts and memories of a grateful people.

The nation has begun its exodus from worse than Egyptian bondage;[5] and I beseech you that you say to the people, "*that they go forward.*" With the assurance of God's favor in all things done in obedience to his righteous will, and guided by day and by night by the pillars of cloud and fire, let us not pause until we have reached the other and safe side of the stormy and crimson sea. Let freemen and patriots mete out complete and equal justice to all men, and thus prove to mankind the superiority of our Democratic, Republican Government.

Favored men, and honored of God as his instruments, speedily finish the work which he has given you to do. *Emancipate, Enfranchise, Educate, and give the blessings of the gospel to every American citizen.* . . .

Then before us a path of prosperity will open, and upon us will descend the mercies and favors of God. Then shall the people of other countries, who are standing tip-toe on the shores of every ocean, earnestly looking to see the end of this amazing conflict, behold a Republic that is sufficiently strong to outlive the ruin and desolations of civil war, having the magnanimity to do justice to the poorest and weakest of her citizens. Thus shall we give to the world the form of a model Republic, founded on the principles of justice, and humanity, and Christianity, in which the burdens of war and the blessings of peace are equally borne and enjoyed by all.

[1865]

---

4. **"Let . . . crime":** A close paraphrase of the Thirteenth Amendment, which had been adopted two months earlier, in December 1864.

5. **Egyptian bondage:** The ancient Israelites were led by Moses out of bondage and slavery in Egypt to the Promised Land, as told in the book of Exodus in the Old Testament.

Mary Boykin Miller Chesnut

[1823-1886]

Mary Boykin Miller, the daughter of Southern planters, married James Chesnut Jr., a lawyer, in 1840. They lived in comfort at Mulberry, a plantation owned by James Chesnut's parents near the small town of Camden, South Carolina. Even before the state seceded from the Union, James Chesnut resigned his U.S. Senate seat in order to support the Confederacy, soon becoming an aide to President Jefferson Davis. On November 8, 1860, Mary Chesnut began a diary that she kept throughout the war, writing her final entry on August 2, 1865. Although she was devoted to the Southern cause, Chesnut clearly had mixed feelings about slavery. At Mulberry, she had taught some of the slaves to read and write; in her diary, she speculated about the fate of female slaves sold at auction. At the same time, she viewed slavery as crucial to the Southern way of life, to which Chesnut was deeply committed. "Slavery has to go, of course, and joy go with it," she asserts in an entry in her diary. "These Yankees may kill us and lay waste our land for a while, but conquer us – never!" Late in her life, Chesnut decided to edit the diary for publication, but she died before completing her work on it. The text of the following selections is taken from *A Diary from Dixie, as written by Mary Boykin Chesnut, wife of James Chesnut, Jr., United States Senator from South Carolina, 1859-1861, and afterward an Aide to Jefferson Davis and a Brigadier-General in the Confederate Army*, edited by Isabella D. Martin and Myrta Lockett Avary (1905).

Lee's Surrender

The headline from a special edition of the Philadelphia *Evening Dispatch* announcing the surrender of General Robert E. Lee and his Confederate army in April 1865.
(Chicago Historical Society [ICHi-22119].)

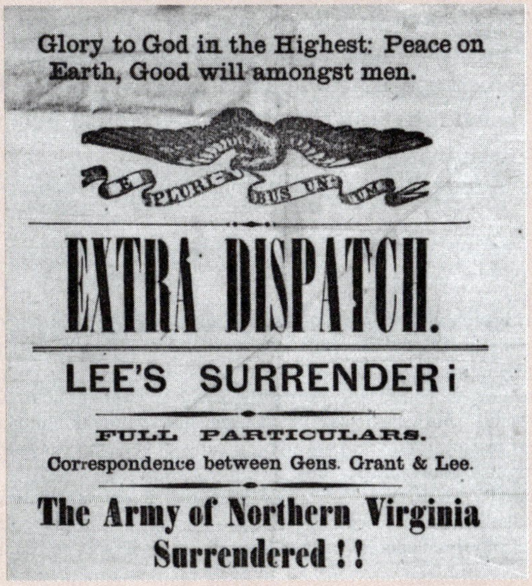
Glory to God in the Highest: Peace on Earth, Good will amongst men.
E PLURIBUS UNUM
EXTRA DISPATCH.
LEE'S SURRENDER!
FULL PARTICULARS.
Correspondence between Gens. Grant & Lee.
The Army of Northern Virginia Surrendered!!

A DIARY FROM DIXIE, APRIL 19–22, 1865

April 19th [1865]. Just now, when Mr. Clay dashed up-stairs, pale as a sheet, saying, "General Lee has capitulated," I saw it reflected in Mary Darby's face before I heard him speak. She staggered to the table, sat down, and wept aloud. Mr. Clay's eyes were not dry. Quite beside herself Mary shrieked, "Now we belong to negroes and Yankees!" Buck said, "I do not believe it."

How different from ours of them is their estimate of us. How contradictory is their attitude toward us. To keep the despised and iniquitous South within their borders, as part of their country, they are willing to enlist millions of men at home and abroad, and to spend billions, and we know they do not love fighting *per se*, nor spending money. They are perfectly willing to have three killed for our one. We hear they have all grown rich, through "shoddy,"[1] whatever that is. Genuine Yankees can make a fortune trading jack-knives.

"Somehow it is borne in on me that we will have to pay the piper," was remarked to-day. "No; blood can not be squeezed from a turnip. You can not pour anything out of an empty cup. We have no money even for taxes or to be confiscated."

While the Preston girls are here, my dining-room is given up to them, and we camp on the landing, with our one table and six chairs. Beds are made on the dining-room floor. Otherwise there is no furniture, except buckets of water and bath-tubs in their improvised chamber. Night and day this landing and these steps are crowded with the *élite* of the Confederacy, going and coming, and when night comes, or rather, bedtime, more beds are made on the floor of the landing-place for the war-worn soldiers to rest upon. The whole house is a bivouac. As Pickens[2] said of South Carolina in 1861, we are "an armed camp."

My husband is rarely at home. I sleep with the girls, and my room is given up to soldiers. General Lee's few, but undismayed, his remnant of an army, or the part from the South and West, sad and crestfallen, pass through Chester.[3] Many discomfited heroes find their way up these stairs. They say Johnston will not be caught as Lee was. He can retreat; that is his trade. If he would not fight Sherman in the hill country of Georgia, what will he do but retreat in the plains of North Carolina with Grant, Sherman, and Thomas all to the fore?[4]

We are to stay here. Running is useless now; so we mean to bide a Yankee raid, which

---

1. **"shoddy":** During the Civil War, fortunes were made by those who produced poor-quality supplies for the armies. Such supplies were generally called "shoddy," originally a term for an inferior-quality fabric made from waste woolen cloth.
2. **Pickens:** Francis Wilkinson Pickens (1805–1869), the governor of South Carolina from 1860–62.
3. **Chester:** A town just south of Richmond, Virginia, and a major shipping point on the Petersburg Railroad until Union forces destroyed the tracks in 1864. During most of the war, the Chesnuts lived in a hotel in Richmond, the capital of the Confederacy.
4. **They say Johnston . . . to the fore?:** Chesnut refers to a number of key military leaders in the final stages of the war: Confederate general Joseph Eggleston Johnston (1807–1891); Union general William Tecumsah Sherman (1820–1891); Union general Ulysses S. Grant (1822–1885); and Union general Edward Lloyd Thomas (1825–1898).

they say is imminent. Why fly? They are everywhere, these Yankees, like red ants, like the locusts and frogs which were the plagues of Egypt.[5]

The plucky way in which our men keep up is beyond praise. There is no howling, and our poverty is made a matter of laughing. We deride our own penury. Of the country we try not to speak at all.

April 22d. This yellow Confederate quire of paper,[6] my journal, blotted by entries, has been buried three days with the silver sugar-dish, teapot, milk-jug, and a few spoons and forks that follow my fortunes as I wander. With these valuables was Hood's silver cup, which was partly crushed when he was wounded at Chickamauga.[7]

It has been a wild three days, with aides galloping around with messages, Yankees hanging over us like a sword of Damocles.[8] We have been in queer straits. We sat up at Mrs. Bedon's dressed, without once going to bed for forty-eight hours, and we were aweary.

Colonel Cadwallader Jones came with a despatch, a sealed secret despatch. It was for General Chesnut. I opened it. Lincoln, old Abe Lincoln, has been killed, murdered, and Seward wounded![9] Why? By whom? It is simply maddening, all this.

I sent off messenger after messenger for General Chesnut. I have not the faintest idea where he is, but I know this foul murder will bring upon us worse miseries. Mary Darby says, "But they murdered him themselves. No Confederates are in Washington." "But if they see fit to accuse us of instigating it?" "Who murdered him? Who knows?" "See if they don't take vengeance on us, now that we are ruined and can not repel them any longer."

The death of Lincoln I call a warning to tyrants.[10] He will not be the last President put to death in the capital, though he is the first.

[1865, 1905]

---

5. **plagues of Egypt:** The calamities visited on the Egyptians by God in order to force the Pharaoh to allow the Israelites to leave and seek the Promised Land, as described in Exodus 7-10.
6. **quire of paper:** Four sheets of paper folded in half to form eight pages.
7. **Hood's silver cup . . . Chickamauga:** Confederate general John Bell Hood (1831-1879) was severely wounded and lost his right leg in the battle of Chickamauga, in September 1863.
8. **sword of Damocles:** In order to teach his talkative official a lesson, the ancient Greek tyrant Dionysius had a sword suspended by a thread over Damocles's seat at a banquet. The sword of Damocles came to refer to the constant possibility of disaster or doom.
9. **Lincoln . . . and Seward wounded!:** Lincoln was shot by John Wilkes Booth on April 14, 1865, while the president and his wife attended a play at Ford's Theatre in Washington, D.C. The assassination was part of a conspiracy to avenge the defeat of the Confederacy by assassinating Lincoln, Vice President Andrew Johnson, and William Seward, the secretary of state. Lincoln died early in the morning of April 15. Seward suffered stab wounds at the hands of one of the coconspirators, but he was not seriously hurt. Johnson was not attacked.
10. **warning to tyrants:** Chesnut expressed a sentiment common among Southerners and sympathizers with their cause. After he shot President Lincoln and leaped to the stage of Ford's Theatre, many in the audience thought they heard John Wilkes Booth proclaim "*sic semper tyrannis*" – Latin for "as always to tyrants" and the motto of the state of Virginia.

William Cullen Bryant

[1794-1878]

William Cullen Bryant, whose life and works are described in more detail elsewhere in this volume (p. 567), was a staunch abolitionist throughout his career as a poet and an editor of the influential New York *Evening Post.* He was also a great admirer of President Lincoln, whose assassination in April 1865 – only five days after Robert E. Lee surrendered his Confederate army to Ulysses S. Grant at Appomattox Court House, Virginia – generated profound shock and an outpouring of grief in the North. Lincoln was shot by John Wilkes Booth on April 14, Good Friday. His death early the following morning transformed him in the eyes of many into a Christlike figure, a martyr who had sacrificed his life to free the slaves and to preserve the Union. The first of many funeral services was conducted on April 19 at the White House, after which a horse-drawn hearse carrying Lincoln's remains was accompanied by a procession to the Capitol, where he lay in state in the rotunda. Two days later, his coffin was placed aboard a special train that stopped for funeral services in ten cities on its twelve-day journey to Springfield, Illinois, where Lincoln was buried on May 4. Many poets wrote tributes to the slain president, among the most famous of which are Walt Whitman's "When Lilacs Last in the Dooryard Bloom'd," printed on page 1299, and Bryant's more public elegy, "The Death of Lincoln." The text is taken from *Poems, by William Cullen Bryant. Collected and arranged by the author* (1876).

Lincoln's Funeral Procession

In this photograph of the funeral procession in Washington, D.C., a horse-drawn hearse carries Lincoln's coffin from the White House to the Capitol, where he lay in state in the rotunda.

THE DEATH OF LINCOLN

Oh, slow to smite and swift to spare,
Gentle and merciful and just!
Who, in the fear of God, didst bear
The sword of power, a nation's trust!

In sorrow by thy bier[1] we stand,
Amid the awe that hushes all,
And speak the anguish of a land
That shook with horror at thy fall.

Thy task is done; the bond[2] are free:
We bear thee to an honored grave.
Whose proudest monument shall be
The broken fetters of the slave.

Pure was thy life: its bloody close
Hath placed thee with the sons of light,
Among the noble host of those
Who perished in the cause of Right.

[1865, 1876]

1. **bier:** A movable frame on which a coffin is placed for movement to a burial ground.
2. **bond:** An alternate term for *bondsmen*, or slaves.

Sarah Morgan Bryan Piatt

[1836-1919]

Sarah Morgan Bryan was born into a distinguished slaveholding family in Lexington, Kentucky. After her graduation from Henry Female College in 1855, she began to publish poems in both local newspapers in Kentucky and national periodicals like the *New York Ledger*. In June 1861, two months after the opening of the Civil War, she married John James Piatt, a poet from Ohio. The couple lived in Washington, D.C., for the next six years, during which Piatt broke completely with the southern way of life in which she had been raised. That breach is apparent in the following poem, "Arlington Heights." The title refers to Arlington National Cemetery, established in 1864 on the grounds of the former estate of Robert E. Lee in Arlington, Virginia. Ironically, the first monument erected there was a burial vault containing the remains of 1,800 Union soldiers killed at the battle of Bull Run, where Lee's Confederate forces had earned a decisive victory in 1861. Piatt clearly blames Lee, the spectral figure who appears in the final stanza of the poem, for those deaths and the carnage of the Civil War. The text of the poem, which Piatt later collected as "Army of Occupation," is taken from its first printing in *Harper's Weekly* (August 25, 1866).

ARLINGTON HEIGHTS

The summer blew its little drifts of sound –
Tangled with wet leaf-shadows and the light
Small breath of scattered morning buds – around
The yellow path through which our footsteps wound.
Below, the Capitol rose glittering white.[1]

There stretch'd a sleeping army. One by one,
They took their places until thousands met;
No leader's stars flash'd on before, and none
Lean'd on his sword or stagger'd with his gun.
I wonder if their feet have rested yet.

They saw the dust, they join'd the moving mass,
They answer'd the fierce music's cry for blood,
Then straggled there and lay down in the grass:
Wear flowers for such, shores whence their tents did pass;
Sing tenderly, O river's haunted flood![2]

They had been sick, and worn, and weary, when
They stopp'd on this calm hill beneath the trees;
Yet, if in some red-clouded dawn again
The country should be calling to her men,
Shall the réveillé not remember these?

Beside them underneath the mid-day skies
The dreadful phantoms of the living walk,
And by low moons and darkness, with their cries –
The mothers, sisters, wives with faded eyes
That call still names among their broken talk.

1. **the Capitol . . . white:** In 1863, the early wooden dome of the U.S. Capitol Building was replaced by a larger, cast-iron dome that dominated the view of the city from Arlington Heights.
2. **Sing tenderly, . . . flood!:** Arlington National Cemetery is across the Potomac River from Washington, D.C. The line echoes "Sweet Thames, run softly till I end my song," the famous refrain from the "Prothalamion," or wedding song, by the English poet Edmund Spenser (1552-1599).

And there is one who comes alone and stands
At his dim fireless hearth – chill'd and opprest
By Something he has summon'd to his lands,
While the weird pallor of its many hands
Points at his rusted sword in his own breast!

[1866]

Henry Timrod

[1828–1867]

Born in Charleston, South Carolina, Henry Timrod was educated at Franklin College, now the University of Georgia. The only volume of poetry Timrod published during his life appeared in 1860, shortly before the outbreak of the Civil War. But he gained his enduring reputation as the unofficial poet laureate of the Confederacy. Made unfit for military duty by tuberculosis, he spent the war years writing poetry and editing the *South Carolinian.* Shortly before his death in 1867, Timrod wrote his most famous poem, the following "Ode." As its subtitle indicates, the "Ode" was sung on the day set aside for "decorating," or placing flowers upon, the

The Lost Cause

After the Civil War, it was frequently memorialized as "The Lost Cause," both in the South and later in the North, where this lithograph was produced by Currier & Ives in 1871. The scene illustrates the loss of loved ones and the passing of a way of life, symbolized by the sun setting behind a fading Confederate flag in the evening sky.

graves of the more than 1,700 Confederate soldiers buried at Magnolia Cemetery in Charleston, South Carolina. Decoration Day, as it was originally called, was observed in various localities in both the North and the South before Congress in 1868 proclaimed May 30 as a day for decorating the graves of those who had died in the Civil War. Since the day was initially designed to commemorate the Union dead, northern and southern states recognized different days as Decoration Day. After World War I, Decoration Day became Memorial Day, a national holiday set aside to honor all of those who had died in American wars. Nonetheless, several southern states still designate a separate and additional day for honoring the Confederate dead, those "martyrs of a fallen cause" Timrod memorializes in his "Ode." The text of the poem is taken from *The Poems of Henry Timrod* (1872).

The Charleston Ode

Sung on the Occasion of Decorating the Graves of the Confederate Dead, at Magnolia Cemetery, Charleston, S.C., 1867

I

Sleep sweetly in your humble graves,
Sleep, martyrs of a fallen cause;
Though yet no marble column craves
The pilgrim here to pause.

II

In seeds of laurel[1] in the earth
The blossom of your fame is blown,
And somewhere, waiting for its birth,
The shaft is in the stone!

III

Meanwhile, behalf the tardy years
Which keep in trust your storied tombs,
Behold! your sisters bring their tears,
And these memorial blooms.

1. **laurel:** In classical times, the foliage of the laurel or bay tree was woven into crowns or wreaths worn as emblems of victory or marks of honor.

IV

Small tributes! but your shades will smile
More proudly on these wreaths to-day,
Than when some cannon-moulded pile
Shall overlook this bay.

V

Stoop, angels, hither from the skies!
There is no holier spot of ground
Than where defeated valor lies,
By mourning beauty crowned!

[1867, 1872]

Frances E. W. Harper

[1825-1911]

Frances E. W. Harper, whose life and work are described in more detail on page 1228 of this volume, was both an antislavery activist and one of the most important African American writers of the nineteenth century. But she began her career as a teacher, and she remained deeply concerned with education, especially in the aftermath of the Civil War. In many of the southern states, slaves had been prohibited by law from being taught to read and write, and it was also illegal to provide them with any reading materials, including Bibles. Education was consequently one of the highest priorities after emancipation. Even before the end of the war, many white Northerners went into areas occupied by Union troops and began to teach the newly freed slaves to read and write. During Reconstruction, northern benevolent societies sent teachers to help organize "freedman's schools" throughout the South. Despite white resistance to such efforts, by 1868 most of the southern state governments were also providing some funding for black education and colleges were established for the training of teachers. As Harper reminds us in the following poem, however, long before emancipation many slaves had struggled to teach themselves and other slaves how to read. In one of a number of poems in which she adopted the persona and vernacular language of a former slave, Aunt Chloe, Harper thus associates true freedom and happiness with the liberating process of "Learning to Read." The text of the poem is taken from her collection *Sketches of Southern Life* (1872).

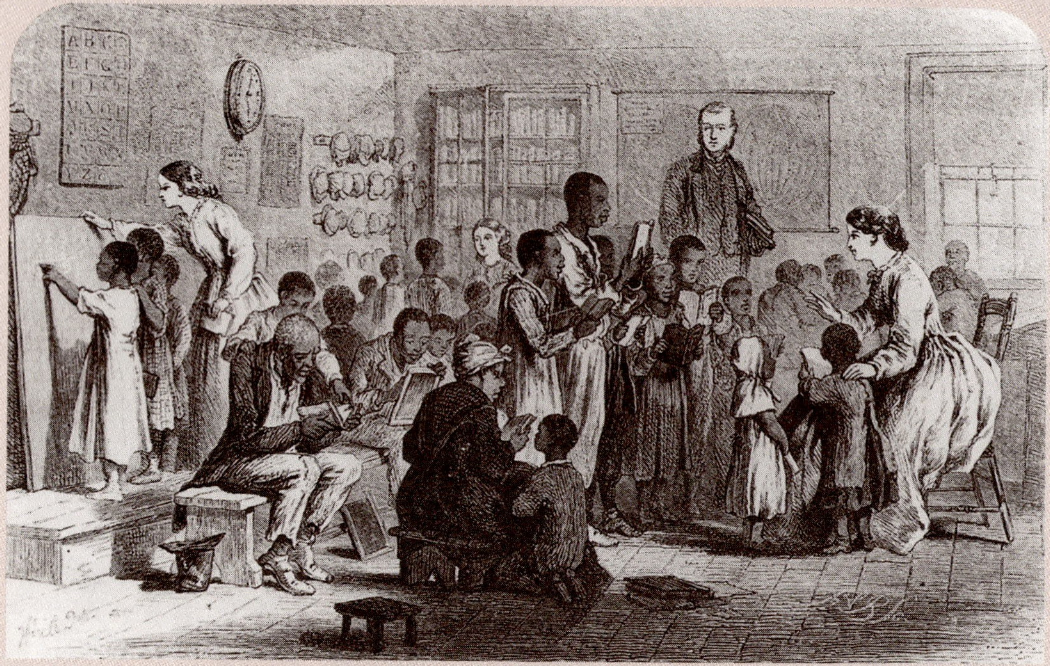

Teaching the Freedmen

Published in 1868, this engraving shows the interior of one of more than three thousand Freedmen's Schools established after the war to educate the newly freed slaves. This picture of white teachers with their black pupils tells only part of the story, since some slaves had surreptitiously taught themselves and others to read and write, and many African Americans became teachers in the Freedmen's Schools.

LEARNING TO READ

Very soon the Yankee teachers
  Came down and set up school;
But, oh! how the Rebs did hate it, –
  It was agin' their rule.

Our masters always tried to hide
  Book learning from our eyes;
Knowledge didn't agree with slavery –
  'Twould make us all too wise.

But some of us would try to steal
A little from the book,
And put the words together,
And learn by hook or crook.

I remember Uncle Caldwell,
Who took pot liquor fat
And greased the pages of his book,
And hid it in his hat.

And had his master ever seen
The leaves upon his head,
He'd have thought them greasy papers,
But nothing to be read.

And there was Mr. Turner's Ben,
Who heard the children spell,
And picked the words right up by heart,
And learned to read 'em well.

Well, the Northern folks kept sending
The Yankee teachers down;
And they stood right up and helped us,
Though Rebs did sneer and frown.

And, I longed to read my Bible,
For precious words it said;
But when I begun to learn it,
Folks just shook their heads,

And said there is no use trying,
Oh! Chloe, you're too late;
But as I was rising sixty,
I had no time to wait.

So I got a pair of glasses,
And straight to work I went,
And never stopped till I could read
The hymns and Testament.

Then I got a little cabin
A place to call my own –
And I felt as independent
As the queen upon her throne.

[1872]

Walt Whitman

[1819-1892]

Walt Whitman, whose life and work are described in more detail on page 1234 of this volume, is the American writer most closely associated with the Civil War. His *Drum-Taps* (1865) is the most famous collection of poetry to emerge from the war, and Whitman wrote a series of celebrated elegies on the death of his hero President Lincoln. During the war, Whitman also kept notebooks in which he jotted down the impressions he gathered as a volunteer nurse in army hospitals in and around Washington, D.C. A decade after the end of the war, Whitman gathered together and published those jottings as *Memoranda during the War.* As he noted in an introduction to the small book, most of it consisted of verbatim transcripts of the notes he had made between 1862 and 1865. At the end of the book, however, Whitman sought to summarize the experience of the war, both his own and that of his country. As the nation approached its centennial, Whitman was deeply concerned with the continuing bitterness and divisions between the North and the South. Memories of the war were a major source of those divisions, but Whitman suggested that the shared sense of grief and the ongoing mourning for all those who had died in the conflict might serve as a means of reuniting the nation. Appealing to the restorative powers of nature, he thus concludes his book with images of healing and on a note of reconciliation between the North and the South. The text of the following selections is taken from the first edition of *Memoranda during the War* (1875-76).

From Memoranda during the War

Three Years Summ'd Up

During my past three years in Hospital, camp or field, I made over 600 visits or tours, and went, as I estimate, among from 80,000 to 100,000 of the wounded and sick, as sustainer of spirit and body in some degree, in time of need. These visits varied from an hour or two, to all day or night; for with dear or critical cases I always watch'd all night. Sometimes I took up my quarters in the Hospital, and slept or watch'd there several nights in succession. Those three years I consider the greatest privilege and satisfaction, (with all their feverish excitements and physical deprivations and lamentable sights,) and, of course, the most profound lesson and reminiscence, of my life. I can say that in my ministerings I comprehended all, whoever came in my way, Northern or Southern, and slighted none. It afforded me, too, the perusal of those subtlest, rarest, divinest volumes of Humanity, laid bare in its inmost recesses, and of actual life and death, better than the finest, most labor'd narratives, histories, poems in the libraries. It arous'd and brought out and decided undream'd-of depths of emotion. It has given me my plainest and most fervent views of the true *ensemble* and extent of The States. While I was with wounded and sick in thousands of cases from the New England States, and from New York, New

Jersey, and Pennsylvania, and from Michigan, Wisconsin, Ohio, Indiana, Illinois, and all the Western States, was with more or less from all the States, North and South, without exception. I was with many from the Border States, especially from Maryland and Virginia; and found, during those lurid years 1862-65, far more Union Southerners, especially Tennesseans, than is supposed. I was with many rebel officers and men among our wounded, and gave them always what I had, and tried to cheer them the same as any. I was among the army teamsters considerably, and, indeed, always found myself drawn to them. Among the black soldiers, wounded or sick, and in the contraband camps, I also took my way whenever in their neighborhood, and did what I could for them.

The Million Dead, Too, Summ'd Up – the Unknown

The Dead in this War – there they lie, strewing the fields and woods and valleys and battle-fields of the South – Virginia, the Peninsula – Malvern Hill and Fair Oaks – the banks of the Chickahominy – the terraces of Fredericksburgh – Antietam bridge – the grisly ravines of Manassas – the bloody promenade of the Wilderness – the varieties of the *strayed* dead, (the estimate of the War Department is 25,000 National soldiers kill'd in battle and never buried at all, 5,000 drown'd – 15,000 inhumed strangers or on the march in haste, in hitherto unfound localities – 2,000 graves cover'd by sand and mud, by Mississippi freshets, 3,000 carried away by caving-in of banks, &c.,) – Gettysburgh, the West, Southwest – Vicksburg – Chattanooga – the trenches of Petersburgh – the numberless battles, camps, Hospitals everywhere pass'd away since that War, and its wholesale deaths, burials, graves. (*They* make indeed the true Memoranda of the War – mute, subtle, immortal.) From ten years' rain and snow, in their seasons – grass, clover, pine trees, orchards, forests – from all the noiseless miracles of soil and sun and running streams – how peaceful and how beautiful appear to-day even the Battle-Trenches, and the many hundred thousand Cemetery mounds! Even at Andersonville,[1] to-day, innocence and a smile. (A late account says, "The stockade has fallen to decay, is grown upon, and a season more will efface it entirely, except from our hearts and memories. The *dead line*, over which so many brave soldiers pass'd to the freedom of eternity rather than endure the misery of life, can only be traced here and there, for most of the old marks the last ten years have obliterated. The thirty-five wells, which the prisoners dug with cups and spoons, remain just as they were left. And the wonderful spring which was discover'd one morning, after a thunder storm, flowing down the hillside, still yields its sweet, pure water as freely now as then. The Cemetery, with its thirteen thousand graves, is on the slope of a beautiful hill. Over the quiet spot already trees give the cool shade which would have been so gratefully sought by the poor fellows whose lives were ended under the scorching sun.")

And now, to thought of these – on these graves of the dead of the War, as on an altar – to memory of these, or North or South, I close and dedicate my book.

[1875-76]

---

1. **Andersonville:** Built in Georgia in 1864, Andersonville was one of the largest and the most infamous of the Confederate military prisons. Of the forty-five thousand Union prisoners confined there during the fourteen months the prison existed, thirteen thousand died of disease, exposure, or malnutrition.

Acknowledgments (continued from p. vi)

John and Abigail Adams, letters reprinted by permission of the publisher from *The Adams Papers: Adams Family Correspondence, Volumes I–II*, edited by L. H. Butterfield (Cambridge, MA: The Belknap Press of Harvard University Press). Copyright © 1963 by The Massachusetts Historical Society. Also in *The Book of Abigail and John: Selected Letters of the Adams Family 1762-1784*, edited with an introduction by L. H. Butterfield, Marc Friedlander, and Mary-Jo Kline.

Paula Gunn Allen, "Pocahontas to Her English Husband, John Rolfe" from *Life Is a Fatal Disease: Collected Poems 1962-1995*. Copyright © 1997 by Paula Gunn Allen. Reprinted with the permission of West End Press, Albuquerque, NM.

Elizabeth Ashbridge, from *Some Accounts of the Fore Part of the Life of Elizabeth Ashbridge*, edited by Daniel B. Shea in *Journeys in New Worlds: Early American Women's Narratives*, edited by William L. Andrews. Copyright © 1990. Reprinted by permission of the University of Wisconsin Press.

Anne Bradstreet, "The Prologue," "In Honour of that High and Mighty Princess Queen Elizabeth of Happy Memory," "An Epitaph on My Dear and Ever-Honoured Mother Mrs. Dorothy Dudley . . . ," "To Her Father with Some Verses," "The Flesh and the Spirit," "The Author to Her Book," "Before the Birth of One of Her Children," "To My Dear and Loving Husband," "A Letter to Her Husband, Absent upon Public Employment," "Here Follows Some Verses upon the Burning of Our House . . . ," and "As Weary Pilgrim" from *The Works of Anne Bradstreet*, edited by Jeannine Hensley (Cambridge, MA: The Belknap Press of Harvard University Press).

Christopher Columbus, "Letter of Columbus, Describing the Results of His First Voyage" ("Letter to Luis de Santangel Regarding the First Voyage, February 15, 1393") from *Select Documents Illustrating the Four Voyages of Columbus*, translated by Cecil Jane. Reprinted by permission of The Hakluyt Society.

Emily Dickinson, "These are the days when Birds come back –" "I never lost as much but twice," "Success is counted Sweetest" "Her breast is fit for pearls," "'Faith' is a fine invention" "I'm 'wife' – I've finished that –" "Come slowly – Eden!" "I taste a liquor never brewed –" "Safe in their Alabaster Chambers –" "I like a look of Agony," "Wild Nights – Wild Nights!" "I can wade Grief –" "There's a certain Slant of light," "A solemn thing – it was – I said –" "I felt a funeral, in my Brain," "I'm Nobody! Who are You?" "The Soul selects her own Society –" "Some keep the Sabbath going to Church –" "Before I got my eye put out" "A Bird came down the Walk –" "I know that He exists." "After great pain, a formal feeling comes –" "God is a distant – stately Lover –" "What Soft – Cherubic Creatures –" "They dropped like Flakes –" "Much Madness is divinest Sense" "This is my letter to the World" "It feels a shame to be Alive –" "This was a Poet – It is That" "I died for Beauty – but was scarce" "I heard a Fly buzz – when I died –" "This World is not Conclusion." "At least – to pray – is left – is left –" "I'm ceded – I've stopped being Theirs –" "It was not Death, for I stood up," "The Soul has Bandaged moments –" "The Spider holds a Silver Ball" "The Brain – is wider than the Sky –" "I cannot live with You –" "Pain – has an Element of Blank –" "I dwell in Possibility –" "Essential Oils – are wrung –" "Publication – is the Auction" "Because I could not stop for Death –" "My Life had stood – a Loaded Gun –" "The Poets light but Lamps –" "A narrow Fellow in the Grass" "I never saw a Moor –" "Title divine – is mine!" "The Bustle in a House" "Revolution is the Pod" "Tell all the Truth but tell it slant –" "A Route of Evanescence" "The Bible is an antique Volume –" "Apparently with no surprise" "A Word made Flesh is seldom" "My life closed twice before its close –" "Rearrange a 'Wife's' affection!" "Some say goodnight – at night –" and "Elysium is as far as to" reprinted by permission of the publishers and the Trustees of Amherst College from *The Poems of Emily Dickinson*, edited by Thomas H. Johnson (Cambridge, MA: The Belknap Press of Harvard University Press). Copyright © 1951, 1955, 1979, 1983 by the President and Fellows of Harvard College."Exchange with Susan Gilbert Dickinson, summer 1861" and "To Thomas Wentworth Higginson, 7 June 1862" reprinted with permission of the publishers from *The Letters of Emily Dickinson*, edited by Thomas H.

Johnson (Cambridge, MA: The Belknap Press of Harvard University Press). Copyright © 1958, 1986 by the President and Fellows of Harvard College; 1914, 1924, 1932, 1942 by Martha Dickinson Bianchi; 1952 by Alfred Leete Hampson; 1960 by Mary L. Hampson.

Jonathan Edwards, "Images or Shadows of Divine Things" excerpted from *The Works of Jonathan Edwards: Typological Writings*, Volume 11, by Jonathan Edwards, edited by Wallace Anderson, Mason Lowance, and David Watters. Copyright © 1993. "On Sarah Pierpont" and "Personal Narrative" from *The Works of Jonathan Edwards: Letters and Personal Writings*, Volume 16, by Jonathan Edwards, edited by George S. Claghorn. Copyright © 1998. "Sinners in the Hands of an Angry God" from *The Works of Jonathan Edwards: Sermons and Discourses 1739-1743*, by Jonathan Edwards, edited by Harry Stout, Nathan Hatch, and Kyle Farley. Copyright © 2003. Reprinted by permission of Yale University Press.

Benjamin Franklin, "The Autobiography, Parts I and II" excerpted from *The Autobiography of Benjamin Franklin: A Genetic Text*, edited by J. A. Leo LeMay and P. M. Zall. Reprinted by permission of Dr. J. A. Leo LeMay.

Allen Ginsberg, "A Supermarket in California" from *Collected Poems 1947-1980* by Allen Ginsberg. Copyright © 1955 by Allen Ginsberg. Reprinted by permission of HarperCollins Publishers.

Robert Hayden, "Frederick Douglass" © 1966 by Robert Hayden from *Collected Poems of Robert Hayden*, edited by Frederick Glaysher. Used by permission of Liveright Publishing Corporation.

Langston Hughes, "Old Walt" from *The Collected Poems of Langston Hughes*, by Langston Hughes, copyright © 1994 by The Estate of Langston Hughes. Used by permission of Alfred A. Knopf, a division of Random House, Inc.

Hupa, "The Boy Who Grew Up at Ta'k'imiłding" translated by Victor Golla from *Surviving through the Days: Translations of Native California Stories and Songs*, edited by Herbert W. Luthin. Reprinted by permission of the University of California Press.

Thomas Jefferson, selections reprinted from *Thomas Jefferson: Writings*, edited by Merrill D. Peterson (The Library of America, 1984).

Lakota, "*Wohpe* and the Gift of the Pipe" reprinted from *Lakota Belief and Ritual* by James R. Walker, edited by Raymond J. DeMallie and Elaine A. Jahner, by permission of the University of Nebraska Press. Copyright © 1980, 1991 by the University of Nebraska Press.

Abraham Lincoln, "The Gettysburg Address" and "Second Inaugural Address" are reprinted by permission of the Abraham Lincoln Association.

Robert Lowell, "Mr. Edwards and the Spider" from *Lord Weary's Castle*, copyright 1946, and renewed 1974 by Robert Lowell. Reprinted by permission of Harcourt, Inc.

N. Scott Momaday, "The Becoming of the Native: Man in America before Columbus" from *America in 1492* by Alvin Josephy Jr., copyright © 1992 by Alvin M. Josephy Jr. Used by permission of Alfred A. Knopf, a division of Random House, Inc.

Rose Murray, "Puritan Woman" from *The Best Fiction and Poetry from California State University, Northridge: 1962-1988*, edited by Warren Wedin, is reprinted by permission of the editor.

Samson Occom, "A Short Narrative of My Life" from the Raunder Special Collections, Dartmouth College Library. Reprinted courtesy of Dartmouth College Library.

James Ottery, "The Diary of Samson Occum" appeared in "Samson Occom's Diary and D'Arcy McNicle's 'Train Time': The Real Imperative of 'Native' Education in American Indian Literature" by James Ottery in *SAIL: Studies in American Indian Literatures*, ser. 2, vol. 13, no. 4: Winter 2001, and is reprinted by permission of the author.

Adrienne Rich, "I Am in Danger – Sir –" Copyright © 2002 by Adrienne Rich. Copyright © 1966 by W. W. Norton & Company, Inc., from *The Fact of a Doorframe: Selected Poems, 1950-2001* by Adrienne Rich. Used by permission of the author and W. W. Norton & Company, Inc.

Jane Johnston Schoolcraft, "Mishosha, or the Magician and His Daughters: A Chippewa Tale or Legend" from *The Literary Voyager or Muzzeniegun*, edited by Philip P. Mason. Reprinted by permission of Michigan State University Press.

Samuel Sewall, excerpts from *The Diary of Samuel Sewall 1674-1729*, edited by M. Halsey Thomas. Copyright © 1973 by Farrar, Straus & Giroux, Inc. Reprinted by permission of Farrar, Straus and Giroux, LLC.

Captain John Smith, excerpts from *The Complete Works of Captain John Smith, 1580-1631*, edited by Philip L. Barbour, with a foreword by Thad W. Tate. Published for the Omohundro Institute of Early American History and Culture. Copyright © 1986 by the University of North Carolina Press. Used by permission of the publisher.

Cathy Song, "A Poet in the House" from *The Land of the Bliss* by Cathy Song, © 2001. Reprinted by permission of the University of Pittsburgh Press.

Edward Taylor, "The Prologue," "Meditation 8," and "Meditation 38" (from *Preparatory Meditations*); "The Preface" and "The Joy of Church Fellowship Rightly Attended" (from *God's Determinations*); "Upon Wedlock, and Death of Children," "Upon a Spider Catching a Fly," "Huswifery," and "A Fig for Thee Oh! Death" (from *Miscellaneous Poems*) from *The Poems of Edward Taylor*, edited by Donald E. Stanford. Copyright © 1960, 1963, and 1989 by Donald E. Stanford. Reprinted by permission of the University of North Carolina Press.

Wamsutta (Frank B.) James, "Suppressed Speech on the 350th Anniversary of the Pilgrims' Landing at Plymouth Rock, September 10, 1970" reprinted by permission of Moonanum (Roland) James, United American Indians of New England.

George Washington, "Letter to the Touro Synagogue, Newport, Rhode Island, 1790." Courtesy of B'nai B'rith Klutznick National Jewish Museum, on long-term loan from the Morganstern Foundation.

Phillis Wheatley, "On Being Brought from Africa to America," "To the University of Cambridge, in New England," "To the Right Honorable William, Earl of Dartmouth . . . ," "To S. M., a Young *African* Painter, on Seeing His Works," "A Farewell to America. To Mrs. S.W.," "To His Excellency General Washington," "Liberty and Peace, A Poem," and "Letter to Samsom Occom, February 11, 1774" from *The Poems of Phillis Wheatley*, edited and with an introduction by Julian D. Mason Jr. Copyright © 1966 by the University of North Carolina Press. Used by permission of the publisher.

John Woolman, excerpts from *The Journal and Major Essays of John Woolman*, edited by P. P. Moulton, Friends United Press. Used by permission.

Kevin Young, "Homage to Phillis Wheatley" from *Giant Steps: The New Generation of African American Writers*, edited by Kevin Young. Copyright © 2000 by Kevin Young. Reprinted by permission of the author.

"Go Down, Moses," "Swing Low Sweet Chariot," "Steal Away to Jesus," and "I Thank God I'm Free at Las'" from *The Books of American Negro Spirituals* by James Weldon Johnson and J. Rosamond Johnson, copyright 1925, 1926 by The Viking Press, renewed 1953 by Lawrence Brown, 1953, © 1954 by Grace Nail Johnson and J. Rosamond Johnson. Used by permission of Viking Penguin, a division of Penguin Group (USA) Inc.

Image Credits

LITERATURE TO 1750

Pages xii–1: Courtesy of the John Carter Brown Library at Brown University

Page 11: Laboratory of Anthropology / Museum of Indian Arts and Culture, Santa Fe, NM, 70.1/365

Page 12: Hulton Archive / Getty Images

Pages 4 (detail) and 15: Courtesy of the John Carter Brown Library at Brown University

Page 17: Courtesy of the John Carter Brown Library at Brown University

Page 20: Library of Congress Rare Book and Special Collections Division

Page 22: Courtesy of the State Library of Massachusetts

Page 23: Library of Congress Rare Book and Special Collections Division

Pages 7 (detail) and 26: Courtesy of the John Carter Brown Library at Brown University

Page 28: Manuscripts Division, Department of Rare Books and Special Collections, Princeton University Library

Page 30: New York State Museum, Albany, NY

Page 32: Courtesy of the John Carter Brown Library at Brown University

Pages 3 (detail) and 38: Rosenbach Museum & Library, Philadelphia
Page 40: Smithsonian American Art Museum, Washington, DC / Art Resource, NY
Page 44: An illustration by J. Ross Browne from his *Adventures in the Apache Country; A Tour through Arizona and Sonora, with Notes on the Silver Regions of Nevada,* Harper & Brothers, NY, 1869.
Page 47: Library of Congress
Page 51: Indian Jump Dance, Pecwan, Klamath River; Ericson Collection, Humboldt State University Library
Page 54: Gilcrease Museum, Tulsa, OK
Page 60: Courtesy of the John Carter Brown Library at Brown University
Page 62: Library of Congress Rare Book and Special Collections Division
Page 64: Robert Dechert Collection, Rare Book and Manuscript Library, University of Pennsylvania
Pages 3 (detail) and 67: Library of Congress Rare Book and Special Collections Division
Pages 4 (detail) and 74: Library of Congress Rare Book and Special Collections Division
Pages 4 (detail) and 86: Robert Dechert Collection, Rare Book and Manuscript Library, University of Pennsylvania
Pages 5 (detail) and 92: Architect of the Capitol
Pages 4 (detail) and 94: Courtesy of the John Carter Brown Library at Brown University
Page 96: Ashmolean Museum, University of Oxford, UK / Bridgeman Art Library
Pages 8 (detail) and 99: Beinecke Rare Book and Manuscript Library, Yale University
Page 101: Courtesy of the Museum of Art, Rhode Island School of Design, Providence, RI. Gift of Mr. Robert Winthrop. Photograph by Del Bogart.
Page 103: Rare Book and Manuscript Library, University of Pennsylvania
Pages 9 (detail) and 105: Private Collection / Bridgeman Art Library
Pages 5 (detail) and 107: Private Collection / Bridgeman Art Library
Page 109: Library of Congress Rare Book and Special Collections Division
Pages 5 (detail) and 120: Virginia Historical Society, Richmond, VA
Page 124: Don Teague Photography
Page 127: Courtesy of the State Library of Massachusetts
Page 147: Courtesy of the John Carter Brown Library at Brown University
Pages 6 (detail) and 153: Courtesy American Antiquarian Society
Page 168: Beinecke Rare Book and Manuscript Library, Yale University
Pages 6 (detail) and 187: LaDonna Gulley Warrick
Pages 8 (detail) and 191: Courtesy of the Trustees of the Boston Public Library
Page 229: Robert Posson, The Association for Gravestone Studies
Page 254: John Smibert, American (born in Scotland), 1688-1751. *Judge Samuel Sewall,* 1729. Oil on canvas, 76.2 x 63.5 cm (30 x 25 in.). Museum of Fine Arts, Boston. Bequest of William L. Barnard (by exchange), and Emily L. Ainsley Fund 58.358.
Pages 8 (detail) and 260: Library of Congress
Page 265: Special Collections, Connecticut College Library, New London
Page 271: Colonial Williamsburg Foundation
Page 276: Joseph Badger, *Jonathan Edwards,* 1720. Yale University Art Gallery. Bequest of Eugene Philips Edwards.
Page 291: Rare Books Division, The New York Public Library, Astor, Lenox and Tilden Foundations
Page 306: Detail from John Ferguson Weir, *Reverend Jonathan Edwards* (after an unknown artist). Yale University Art Gallery. Gift of Arthur Reed Kimball, B.A. 1877.

AMERICAN LITERATURE, 1750–1830

Pages 310–11: I. N. Phelps Stokes Collection, Miriam and Ira D. Wallach Division of Art, Prints and Photographs, The New York Public Library, Astor, Lenox and Tilden Foundations
Pages 314 (detail) and 320: Library of Congress
Page 322: The Library Company of Philadelphia
Page 323: Library of Congress
Page 324: Boston Athenaeum
Pages 317 (detail) and 325: Library of Congress Rare Book and Special Collections Division
Pages 316 (detail) and 328: Library of Congress Rare Book and Special Collections Division
Page 332: Print Collection, Miriam and Ira D. Wallach Division of Art, Prints and Photographs, The New York Public Library, Astor, Lenox and Tilden Foundations
Pages 313 (detail) and 334: George Dunlop Leslie,

Benjamin Franklin (after Mason Chamberlain), a detail. Yale University Art Gallery. Gift of Avery Rockefeller for the University Library. Acc. 2 June 1948.
Page 337: Beinecke Rare Book and Manuscript Library, Yale University
Page 339: Newport Historical Society
Page 343: The Library Company of Philadelphia
Page 372: Alan Schein Photography / Corbis
Page 376: Courtesy of the Yale University Library
Page 390: Haverford College Library, Haverford, PA: Quaker Collection
Pages 314 (detail) and 402: Bowdoin College Museum of Art, Brunswick, ME. Bequest of the Honorable James Bowdoin III.
Page 410: Hood Museum of Art, Dartmouth College, Hanover, NH. Gift of Mrs. Robert W. Birch.
Pages 315 (detail) and 414: Courtesy American Antiquarian Society
Page 415: Courtesy American Antiquarian Society
Page 428: Library of Congress Rare Book and Special Collections Division
Page 430: After a portrait by Joseph Vallière, 1786. From the 1925 Yale University Press reprint of St. John de Crèvecoeur, *Sketches of Eighteenth-Century America: More "Letters from an American Farmer."*
Pages 316 (detail) and 442 (right): Massachusetts Historical Society, Boston / Bridgeman Art Library
Page 442 (left): Massachusetts Historical Society, Boston / Bridgeman Art Library
Pages 317 (detail) and 447: National Archives
Page 447: Library of Congress
Page 459: Library of Congress
Page 461: Delaware Art Museum, Gift of Absalom Jones School, 1971, DAM#1971-8
Page 464: Library of Congress
Page 466: Bettmann / Corbis
Page 469: Library of Congress Rare Book and Special Collections Division
Page 471: Beinecke Rare Book and Manuscript Library, Yale University
Page 473: Gift of John D. Rockefeller Jr., Historic Hudson Valley, Tarrytown, NY.
Pages 315 (detail) and 479: Brown University Library
Page 481: Terra Foundation for American Art, Chicago / Art Resource, NY
Page 484: Library of Congress
Pages 319 (detail) and 493: Fenimore Art Museum, Cooperstown, NY. Photo by Richard Walker.
Page 496: Bettmann / Corbis
Page 504: Corbis
Page 517 (detail): Library of Congress Rare Book and Special Collections Division
Page 520: Henry W. and Albert A. Berg Collection of English and American Literature, The New York Public Library, Astor, Lenox and Tilden Foundations
Page 522: John Quidor, *The Return of Rip Van Winkle.* Andrew W. Mellon Collection. Image © Board of Trustees, National Gallery of Art, Washington, DC.
Pages 318 (detail) and 543: Library of Congress
Page 557: Documenting the American South (http://docsouth.unc.edu), The University of North Carolina at Chapel Hill Libraries
Page 567: Samuel F. B. Morse, *William Cullen Bryant.* Oil on canvas, 29½ x 34¾ in. National Academy Museum, New York (892-P).
Page 578: Johnston Family Papers, Bentley Historical Library, University of Michigan

AMERICAN LITERATURE, 1830–1865
Pages 586–87: The Saint Louis Art Museum. Gift of Bank of America.
Pages 590 (detail) and 595: Courtesy, American Antiquarian Society
Page 596: Gift of Edgar William and Bernice Chrysler Garbisch. © 2004 Board of Trustees, National Gallery of Art, Washington, DC.
Page 598: Corbis
Page 599: Courtesy American Antiquarian Society
Page 600: Geoffrey Clements / Corbis
Page 601: Corbis
Page 606: Madison County Historical Society, Oneida, NY
Page 609: Woolaroc Museum, Bartlesville, OK
Page 611: By permission of The Houghton Library, Harvard University. © The President and Fellows of Harvard College.
Page 613: The Gilder Lehrman Collection, on Deposit at the New York Historical Society, New York (GLC 5826)
Page 615: Chicago Historical Society (ICHi-22003)
Page 622: Boston Athenaeum
Pages 591 (detail) and 624: Courtesy George Eastman House
Page 630: Library of Congress
Pages 592 (detail) and 637: Library of Congress Manuscript Division

Page 639: Rosenbach Museum & Library, Philadelphia
Pages 590 (detail) and 653: Courtesy Concord Free Public Library
Page 726: The Granger Collection, New York
Page 747: Southworth & Hawes, *Harriet Beecher Stowe*, c. 1843–48. Hallmark Photographic Collection, Hallmark Cards, Inc., Kansas City, MO. © Hallmark Cards, Inc.
Page 764: Boston Athenaeum
Page 783: Courtesy of The North Carolina State Archives
Page 792: Brown University Library
Page 810: Library of Congress Rare Book and Special Collections Division
Pages 592 (detail) and 855: Library of Congress
Page 923 (detail): National Portrait Gallery, Smithsonian Institution / Art Resource, NY
Page 926: William Francis Allen et al., *Slave Songs of the United States*, New York: A. Simpson & Co., 1867. Documenting the American South (http://docsouth.unc.edu), The University of North Carolina at Chapel Hill Libraries Rare Book Collection.
Page 931: Culver Pictures
Page 934: Courtesy Ablah Library, Wichita State University, Wichita, KS
Page 938: Nicolino Calyo, *Astor House Reading Room*, c. 1840, Museum of the City of New York
Page 939: Boston Athenaeum
Page 941: Courtesy of the Boston Public Library
Page 942: New-York Historical Society / Bridgeman Art Library
Page 945: William Morris Hunt, American, 1824–1879. *Girl Reading*, 1853. Oil on canvas, 54.61 x 40.64 cm (21½ x 16 in.). Museum of Fine Arts, Boston. Gift of Mrs. Charles W. Dabney, 93.1455. Photograph © 2006 Museum of Fine Arts, Boston.
Pages 589 (detail) and 953: Boston Athenaeum
Page 966: Charles Osgood, *Nathaniel Hawthorne*. Photograph courtesy Peabody Essex Museum.
Pages 589 (detail) and 1019: Bettmann / Corbis
Page 1062: Sophia Smith Collection, Smith College
Pages 593 (detail) and 1073: Asa W. Twitchell, *Herman Melville*. Berkshire Athenaeum, Pittsfield, MA.
Page 1075: Bettmann / Corbis
Page 1149: From *The Richard Harding Davis Years* by Gerald Langford, © 1981 by Gerald Langford. Photograph from the collection of Mrs. Hope Davis Kehrig. Reprinted by permission of Henry Holt and Company, LLC.
Page 1178: Bettmann / Corbis
Page 1179: U.S. Army Military History Institute
Page 1192: Courtesy of the University of Nebraska, Lincoln
Page 1198: Hulton Archive / Getty Images
Page 1202: Hulton Archive / Getty Images
Page 1213: Library of Congress
Page 1228: Library of Congress
Page 1235: Library of Congress Rare Book and Special Collections Division
Page 1237: Library of Congress Manuscript Division
Page 1309: Courtesy of the Pennsylvania Academy of the Fine Arts, Philadelphia. General Fund.
Page 1312: Beinecke Rare Book and Manuscript Library, Yale University
Page 1314: By permission of The Houghton Library, Harvard University, MS Am 1118.3 (11a). © The President and Fellows of Harvard College.
Page 1348: Amherst College Archives and Special Collections
Page 1353: Kansas State Historical Society
Page 1355: Chicago Historical Society (AHD-142)
Page 1357: Library of Congress
Page 1365: Chicago Historical Society (ICHi-22051)
Page 1368: Library of Congress
Pages 593 (detail) and 1370: National Archives
Page 1371: Library of Congress
Page 1374: Courtesy of Picture History
Page 1377: Chicago Historical Society (ICHi-22119)
Page 1380: Library of Congress
Page 1383: Library of Congress
Page 1386: Courtesy American Antiquarian Society

Index of Authors and Titles